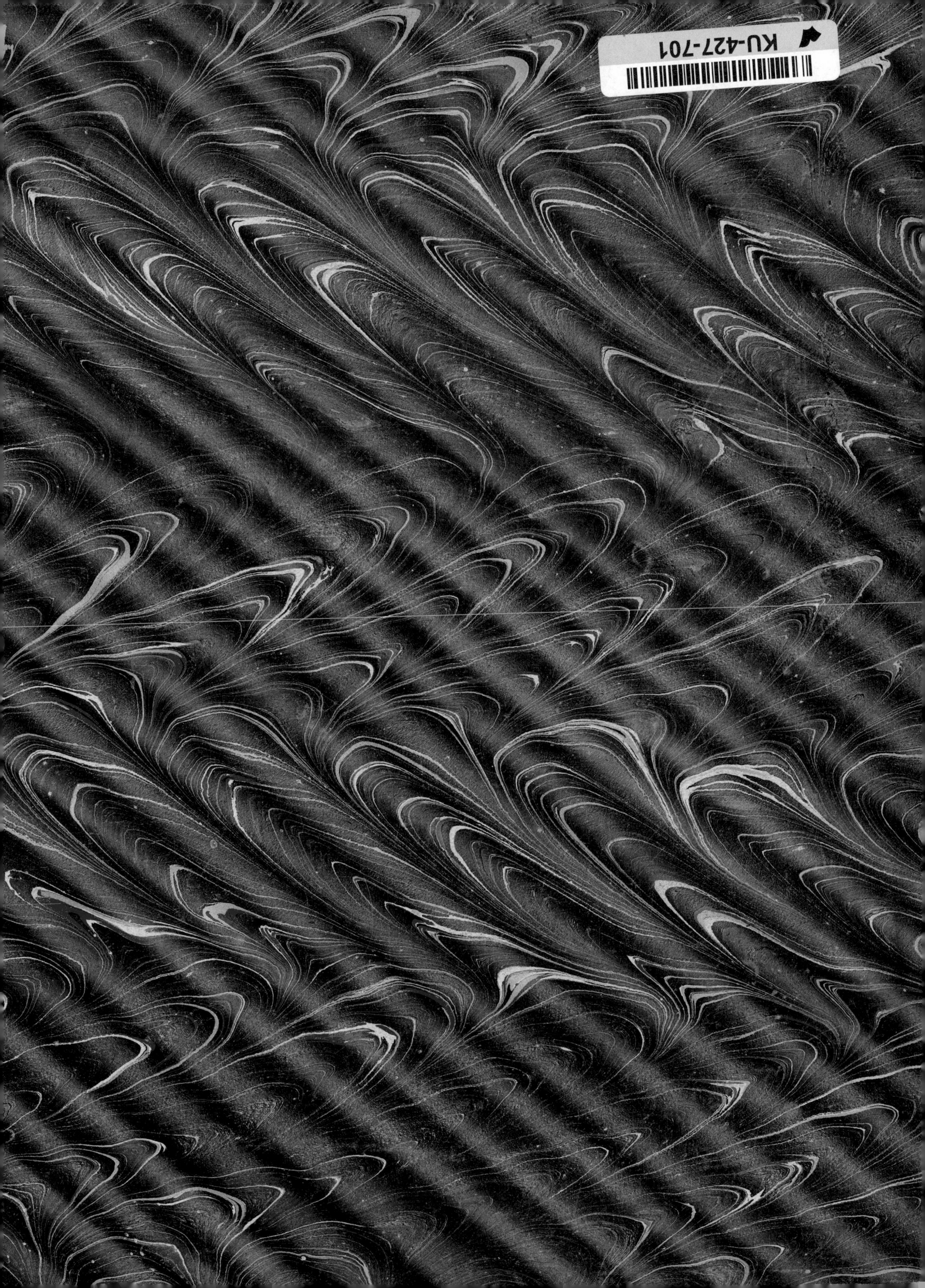

ENCYCLOPÆDIA BRITANNICA

NINTH EDITION

THE

ENCYCLOPÆDIA BRITANNICA

A

DICTIONARY

OF

ARTS, SCIENCES, AND GENERAL LITERATURE

NINTH EDITION

VOLUME XXIV

EDINBURGH: ADAM AND CHARLES BLACK

MDCCCLXXXVIII

ENCYCLOPÆDIA BRITANNICA.

URAL-ALTAIC LANGUAGES

URAL-ALTAIC LANGUAGES. The Ural-Altaic, Finno-Tatar, or "Turanian" languages constitute one of the primary linguistic families (see PHILOLOGY, vol. xviii. p. 779) of the eastern hemisphere, occupying a vast domain, which extends with few interruptions from the Balkan Peninsula, Hungary, and Lapland eastwards to the Pacific Ocean, and from the Arctic Ocean southwards to China proper, Tibet, and the Mediterranean. It thus comprises nearly the whole of Asiatic and a considerable section of European Russia, the northern half of the Chinese empire, a large part of north Persia, by far the greater part of Asia Minor, and extensive tracts in European Turkey, Austria, and Scandinavia, with an area of not less than 10,000,000 square miles and a total population of over 40,000,000. Philologists recognize six well-marked branches, which, with their main subdivisions and four outlying doubtful or extinct members of the family, may be tabulated as under:—

I. SAMOYEDIC.	*Yurak* and *Yenisei*, White Sea to the Yenisei. *Tavghi*, between lower Yenisei and Khatanga rivers. *Kamasin*, upper Yenisei.
II. FINNIC.	*Finnish*, Finland, parts of Norway, Lakes Onega and Ladoga. *Lapp*, Russian and Scandinavian Lapland. *Esthonian* and *Livonian*, south side of Gulf of Finland. *Mordvinian* and *Tcheremissian*, middle Volga. *Permian*, *Votyak*, and *Siryenian*, between the Vyatka and Petchora rivers.
III. UGRIC.	*Ostiak*, middle and upper Obi and its eastern affluents. *Vogul*, east slopes of the Ural Mountains. *Magyar*, central and south-eastern Hungary.
IV. TURKIC.	*Uigur* or *East Turki*, including *Uigur proper* of Kashgar, Kulja, and Yarkand; *Jagatai* of Bokhara, Ferghana, Khiva; *Kara-Kalpak*, south-eastern side of Aral Sea; *Turkoman* (*Turkmenian*), west Turkestan, north Persia, and Asia Minor. *Seljuk* or *West Turki* or *Osmanli*, Asia Minor and the Balkan Peninsula; *Tchuvash*, south-west of Kazan and about Simbirsk. *Kipchak* (*Kapchak*): *Coman*, extinct, formerly current throughout the Kipchak empire from the Altai Mountains to the Black Sea; *Kazan Tatar*, middle Volga; *Kirghiz*, West Siberian steppes, lower Volga, the Pamir, and west slopes of the Altai, Thian-Shan, and Kuen-Lun Mountains; *Nogai* with *Kumuk*, Bessarabia, Crimea, Volga delta, Daghestan, Terek valley. *Yakut*, middle and lower Lena and northern slopes of the Sayan Mountains.
IV. TURKIC—*continued.*	*Siberian Tatar: Teleut, Koibal, Soyot, Kotta, Bashkir, Mescheryak*, and other corrupt Turki dialects spoken by Tatarized Finn populations from the Altai to the Urals.
V. MONGOLIC.	*Sharra* or *East Mongolian*, Mongolia; *Kalmuck*, Dzungaria and lower Volga, thence to lower Don; *Buriat* or *Siberian Mongolian*, east and west of Lake Baikal.
VI. TUNGUSIC.	*Tungus proper*, from the middle Yenisei to the Pacific; *Lamut*, western coast of the sea of Okhotsk; *Manchu*, Manchuria.
VII.	JAPANESE, Japan and Riu-Kiu (Lew-Chew) Islands; doubtful.
VIII.	COREAN, Corea; doubtful.
IX. and X.	ACCAD and ETRUSCAN; both doubtful and extinct.

In its morphology Ural-Altaic belongs to the agglutinating order of speech, differing from other languages of this order chiefly in the exclusive use of suffixes attached to the unmodified root, and partly blended with it by the principle of progressive vowel harmony, in virtue of which the vowels of all the suffixes are assimilated to that of the root. Thus the typical formula is R + R + R + R, &c., where R is the root, always placed first, and R, R, R . . . the successive postfixed relational elements, whose vowels conform by certain subtle laws of euphony to that of the root, which never changes. These suffixes differ also from the case and verbal endings of true inflecting languages (Aryan, Semitic) in their slighter fusion with the root, with which they are rather mechanically united (agglutinated) than chemically fused into a term in which root and relational element are no longer separable. Hence it is that the roots, which in Aryan are generally obscured, blurred, often even changed past the possibility of identification, in Ural-Altaic are always in evidence, unaffected by the addition of any number of formative particles, and controlling the whole formation of the word. For instance, the infinitive element *mak* of the Osmanli *yaz-mak* = to write becomes *mek* in *sev-mek* = to love (vowel harmony), and shifts its place in *sev-il-mek* = to be loved (imperfect fusion with the root), while the root itself remains unchanged as to form and position in *sev-ish-il-mek* = to be impelled to love, or in any other possible combination with suffixed elements. The facility with which particles are in this way tacked on produces an exuberance, especially of verbal forms, which in Osmanli, Finnish, Magyar, Tungus, and Mordvinian may be said to run riot. This is particularly the case when the numerous modal forms become further complicated by incorporating the direct pronominal object, as in the Magyar *varjak* = they await him, and the Mordvinian *palasa* = I embrace him. Thus arise endless verbal combinations, reckoned in Turki at nearly 30,000, and past counting in the Ugrian group.

Another marked peculiarity of the Ural-Altaic, at least as compared with the inflecting orders of speech, is weak subjectivity, the subject or agent being slightly, the object of the action strongly accentuated, so that "it was done by him" becomes "it was done with him, through him, or in his place" (*apud eum*). From this feature, which seems to be characteristic of all the branches, there follow some important consequences, such as a great preponderance of locative forms in the declension,—the nominative, and often even the possessive, being expressed by no special suffix. Hence also the object normally precedes the subject, while the idea of possession (to have) is almost everywhere replaced by that of being (to be), so that, even in the highly developed Osmanli, "I have no money" becomes "money-to-me not-is" (*Akchehim yokdür*). In fact the verb is not clearly differentiated from the noun, so that the conjugation is mainly participial, being effected by agglutinating pronominal, modal, temporal, negative, passive, causative, reciprocal, reflexive, and other suffixes to nominal roots or gerunds: I write = writing-to-me-is. Owing to this confusion of noun and verb, the same suffixes are readily attached indifferently to both, as in the Osmanli *ján* = soul, *ján-ler* = souls, and *yăzăr* = he will write, *yăzăr-ler* = they will write. So also, by assimilation, the Yakut *kötördör kötöllör* = the birds fly (from root *köt* = flying), where *kötöl* stands for *kötör*, and *dör* for *lör*, the Osmanli *ler*, or suffix of plurality.

But, notwithstanding this wealth of nominal or verbal forms, there is a great dearth of general relational elements, such as the relative pronoun, grammatical gender, degrees of comparison, conjunctions, and even postpositions. Byrne's remark, made in reference to Tungus, that "there is a great scarcity of elements of relation, very few conjunctions, and no true postpositions, except those which are given in the declension of the noun,"[1] is mainly true of the whole family, in which nouns constantly do duty for formative suffixes. Thus nearly all the Ostiak postpositions are nouns which take the possessive suffix and govern other nouns in the genitive, precisely as in the Hindi: *ădmī-kī-ṭărăf* (*meṇ*) *găyā* = man-of-direction (in) I went = I went towards the man, where the so-called postposition *ṭărăf*, being a feminine noun = direction, requires the preceding possessive particle to be also feminine (*kī* for *kē*).

As there are thus only two classes of words,—the roots, which always remain roots, and the suffixes, which always remain suffixes,—it follows that there can be no true composition or word-building, but only derivation. Even the numerous Magyar nominal and adjectival compounds are not true compounds, but merely two words in juxtaposition, unconnected by vowel harmony and liable to be separated in construction by intervening particles. Thus in *aran-sinü* = gold-colour = golden, the first part *aran* receives the particle of comparison, the second remaining unchanged, as if we were to say "gold-er-colour" for "more golden"; and *ata-fi* = relative becomes *ata m-fi-a* = my relative, with intrusion of the pronominal *m* = my.

But, while these salient features are common, or nearly common, to all, it is not to be supposed that the various groups otherwise present any very close uniformity of structure or vocabulary. Excluding the doubtful members, the relationship between the several branches is far less intimate than between the various divisions of the Semitic and even of the Aryan family, so that, great as is, for instance, the gap between English and Sanskrit, that between Lapp and Manchu is still greater.

After the labours of Castrén, Csink, Gabelentz, Schmidt, Böhtlingk, Zenker, Almqvist, Radloff, Munkacsi-Berat, and especially Winkler, their genetic affinity can no longer be seriously doubted. But the order of their genetic descent from a presumed common organic Ural-Altaic language is a question presenting even greater difficulties than the analogous Aryan problem. The reason is, not only because these groups are spread over a far wider range, but because the dispersion from a common centre took place at a time when the organic speech was still in a very low state of development. Hence the various groups, starting with little more than a common first germ, sufficient, however, to give a uniform direction to their subsequent evolution, have largely diverged from each other during their independent development since the remotest prehistoric times. Hence also, while the Aryan as now known to us represents a descending line of evolution from the synthetic to the analytic state, the Ural-Altaic represents on the contrary an upward growth, ranging from the crudest syntactical arrangements in Manchu to a highly agglutinating but not true inflecting state in Finnish.[2] No doubt Manchu also, like its congeners, had formerly possessive affixes and personal elements, lost probably through Chinese influences; but it can never have possessed the surprisingly rich and even superabundant relational forms so characteristic of Magyar, Finn, Osmanli, and other western branches. As regards the mutual relations of all the groups, little more can now be said than that they fall naturally into two main divisions—Mongolo-Turkic and Finno-Ugro-Samoyedo-Tungusic—according to the several methods of employing the auxiliary elements. Certainly Turkic lies much closer to Mongolic than it does to Samoyedic and Tungusic, while Finno-Ugric seems to occupy an intermediate position between Turkic and Samoyedic, agreeing chiefly in its roots with the former, in its suffixes with the latter. Finno-Ugric must have separated much earlier, Mongolic much later, from the common connexion, and the latter, which has still more than half its roots and numerous forms in common with Turkic, appears on the whole to be the most typical member of the family. Hence many Turkic forms and words can be explained only by reference to Mongolic, which has at the same time numerous relations to Finno-Ugric and Samoyedic that have been lost in Turkic and Tungusic. It may therefore be concluded that the Finno-Ugric migrations to the north and west and the Tungusic to the east had been completed while the Turkic and Mongolic tribes were still dwelling side by side on the Altai steppes, the probable cradle of the Ural-Altaic peoples.

How profoundly the several groups differ one from the other even in their structure is evident from the fact that such assumed universal features as unchangeable roots and vowel harmony are subject to numerous exceptions, often spread over wide areas. Not only is assimilation of final consonants very common, as in the Osmanli *bulun-mak* for the Uigur *bulul-mak*, but the root vowel itself is frequently subject to *umlaut* through the influence of suffixed vowels, as in the Aryan family. Thus in the Surgut dialect of Ostiak the long vowels of nominal stems become modified before the possessive suffix, *ā* and *ē* to *ī* and *ō* to *ū* (Castrén). It is still more remarkable to find that the eastern (Yenisei) Ostiak has even developed verbal forms analogous to the Teutonic strong conjugation, the presents *tabāq'*, *abbatag'an*, and *datpaq'* becoming in the past *tobāq'*, *abbatog'an*, and *datpiyaq'* respectively; so also *taig*, *tōrg*, and *tārg*, present, past, and imperative, are highly suggestive of Teutonic inflexion, but more probably are due to Tibetan influences. In the same dialects many nouns form their plurals either by modifying the root vowel, in combination with a suffixed element, or by modification alone, the suffix having disappeared, as in the English *fōot—feet*, *goose—geese*. So also vowel harmony, highly developed in Finnish, Magyar, and Osmanli, and of which two distinct forms occur in Yakutic, scarcely exists at all in Tcheremissian, Votyak, and the Revel dialect of Esthonian, while in Mordvinian and Siryenian, not the whole word, but the final vowels alone are harmonized. The unassimilated Uiguric *kilur-im* answers to the Osmanli *kilur-um*, while in Manchu the concordance is neglected, especially when two consonants intervene between the root and the suffixed vowels. But too much weight should not be attached to the phenomenon of vowel harmony, which is of comparatively recent origin, as shown in the oldest Magyar texts of the 12th century, which abound in such discordances as *halál-nek*,

[1] *Gen. Prin. of Struct. of Lang.*, i. p. 391, London, 1885.

[2] "Meine Ansichten werden sich im Fortgange ergeben, so namentlich dass ich nicht entfernt die finnischen Sprachen für flexivische halten kann" (H. Winkler, *Uralaltaische Völker*, i. p. 54). Yet even true inflexion can scarcely be denied at least to some of the so-called Yenisei Ostiak dialects, such as Kotta and others still surviving about the middle Yenisei and on its affluents, the Agul and Kan (Castrén, *Yen., Ostjak., und Kott. Sprachlehre*, 1858, Preface, pp. v-viii). These, however, may be regarded as aberrant members of the family, and on the whole it is true that the Ural-Altaic system nowhere quite reaches the stage of true inflexion.

tiszta-seg, for the modern *halál-nak*, *tiszta-sag*. It clearly did not exist in the organic Ural-Altaic speech, but was independently developed by the different branches on different lines after the dispersion, its origin being due to the natural tendency to merge root and suffix in one harmonious whole. The principle being thus of a purely psychological character, and necessarily an after-growth, it is not surprising to find no traces of it in the oldest and even in the later Accad texts, as seen by comparing the old *idi bar-mun-sib* with the more recent *igi mun-sib-bar*.

This progressive vocalic harmony has been compared to a sort of progressive *umlaut*, in which the suffixed vowels are brought by assimilation into harmony with those of the root. All vowels are broadly divided into two categories, the guttural or hard and the palatal or weak, the principle requiring that, if the root vowel be hard, the suffixed must also be hard, and *vice versa*. But in some of the groups there is an intermediate class of "neutral" vowels, which do not require to be harmonized, being indifferent to either category. In accordance with these general principles the vowels in some of the leading members of the Altaic family are thus classified by L. Adam—[1]

	Gutturals.	Palatals.	Neutrals.
Finnish	u, o, a	ü, ö, ä	e, i
Magyar	u, o, a	ü, ö	e, i
Mordvinian	u, o, a	ä, i	..
Siryenian	ô, a	ä, i, e	..
Osmanli	u, o, a, e	ü, ö, e, i	..
Mongolian	u, o, a	ü, ö, ä	i
Buriat	u, o, a	ü, ö, ä	e, i
Manchu	ô, o, a	e	u, i

A close analogy to this law is presented by the Irish rule of "broad to broad" and "slender to slender," according to which under certain conditions a broad (*a*, *o*, *u*) must be followed in the next syllable by a broad, and a slender (*e*, *i*) by a slender. Obvious parallelisms are also such forms in Latin as *annus*, *perennis*, *ars*, *iners*, *lego*, *diligo*, where, however, the root vowel is modified by the affix, not the affix by the root. But such instances suffice to show that the harmonic principle is not peculiar to the Ural-Altaic, but only more systematically developed in that than in most other linguistic families.

This is not the place to discuss the vexed question of the relation of the Babylonian Accad and Sumirian, or of the Etruscan, with the Ural-Altaic linguistic stock. It must therefore suffice to state in a general way that, according to the latest views, both of those long extinct languages were really branches either of the Finno-Ugric or of the Turko-Mongolic division of that family. In reply to the objection that Sumirian was a prefix language, it is pointed out that Neo-Sumirian, extinct some 1600 years before the Christian era, had already become postfixing, so that the *nin-gar* of the oldest answers to the *garra-bi* of the later texts, from root *gar*=to make. Nevertheless the point is far from settled, as may be judged from the fact that such specialists as Dr Zimmern and Dr Hommel are still at issue on the fundamental question of the Ural-Altaic affinities of Accad and Sumirian. The position of Etruscan is much the same, the main outcome of recent controversy being that this primitive Italian language can scarcely have been a member of the Aryan, whatever its relationship to the Finno-Tataric family.

Regarding the Japanese and Corean languages, it may be remarked that Winkler agrees with Boller in unhesitatingly including the former, while doubtfully excluding the latter from this connexion. On the other hand, W. G. Aston (*Journ. Roy. Asiat. Soc.*, August 1879) considers that both are as nearly related to one another as English and Sanskrit. The probability therefore is that Japanese and Corean are aberrant branches of the Ural-Altaic family, and that they separated at long intervals from the parent stock and at such remote periods that their affinities can no longer be clearly traced.

Bibliography.—Besides the references given above, the chief general treatises on Ural-Altaic philology are—Kellgren, *Die Grundzüge der finnischen Sprachen mit Rücksicht auf die Ural-Altaischen Sprachstämme*, Berlin, 1847; Castrén, *Ueber die Ursitze des finnischen Volkes*, Helsingfors, 1849; Id., *Syrjaen. Gram.*, *Samojed. Gram.*, and numerous other comparative grammars, dictionaries, and general treatises, chiefly on the Finno-Ugric and Samoyedic groups; W. Thomsen, *Ueber den Einfluss der germanischen Sprachen auf die Finnisch-Lappischen* (Germ. trans. by Sievers, Halle, 1870—a classical work); Abel Rémusat, *Recherches sur les Langues Tartares*, Paris, 1820; L. Adam, *Gram. de la Langue Mandchoue*, Paris, 1872, and *Gram. de la L. Tongouse*, Paris, 1874; Böhtlingk, *Die Sprache der Jakuten*, St Petersburg, 1851; Radloff, *Volksliteratur der türkischen Stämme Sud-Sibiriens*, St Petersburg, 1872, and "Remarks on the Codex Comanicus," *Bull. St Petersb. Acad. Sc.*, xxxi., No. 1; Zenker, *Gram. der türkischen-tatarischen Sprachen*; Schmidt, *Mongol. Gram.*; Gabelentz, *Gram. Mandchoue*, Altenburg, 1833; Csink, *Hung. Gram.*, London, 1853; and Vambéry, *Das Türkenvolk*, Leipsic, 1885, and *Uïgurische Sprach-Monumente u. das Kudatkü Bilik*, Innsbruck, 1870. For further particulars relating to the affinities and characteristics of the various branches, and of their associated members, see the articles FINLAND (vol. ix. p. 219), HUNGARY (vol. xii. p. 374), RUSSIA (vol. xxi. p. 79), TURKS (vol. xxiii. p. 661), MONGOLS (vol. xvi. p. 750), and SIBERIA (vol. xxii. p. 8).
(A. H. K.)

[1] *De l'Harmonie des Voyelles dans les Langues Ouralo-Altaïques*, Paris, 1874.

URAL MOUNTAINS. The girdle of mountains which extends from the Arctic Ocean southwards nearly to the Caspian Sea, and is now regarded as separating Europe from Asia, was anciently the subject of various myths. Even the Slavonians, who in the 11th century frequently visited the region of the Urals for trade with the Ugrians (which people at that time lived there), described them as mountains reaching to the sky, intersected by terrible precipices, and as being inhabited by a population of cave-dwellers. Although crossed by a continuous stream of Russian colonizers from the 16th century onwards, the Ural Mountains still retained something of their mythical character in Western literature, and in the 18th century they received from geographers the high-sounding designation of *montes dicti angulus terræ*. The Russians describe them either as Kameñ (stone) merely or by the appropriate name of Poyas (girdle), while the name of Urals (*Uraty*)—derived either from the Ostiak *urr* (chain of mountains) or from the Turkish *aral-tau* or *ural-tau*—has with them become a generic name for extensive mountain chains. (See plate II. vol. xxi. and plate I. vol. xxii.).

Notwithstanding numerous scientific expeditions by which the exploration of various parts of the range began to be undertaken from the earlier portion of the 19th century, and notwithstanding partial accurate surveys and levellings and numerous geological researches made within the last thirty years, the real structure of the Urals, both orographical and geological, remains still imperfectly known. Even on maps otherwise good they are still very often represented as an unbroken chain, at least 1200 miles in length, running north and south from the Arctic Ocean to the sources of the river Ural. But every fresh addition to our knowledge has made it increasingly apparent that their real structure is much more complicated; and in view of recent explorations it becomes plain that the Urals consist of a series of several separate upheavals, some having a north-western direction and some a north-eastern, which reach their maximum heights along a zone which lies nearly north and south. They have thus some resemblance to the mountain-chains of Central Asia and Siberia,—which also have north-eastern and north-western directions, but are grouped in zones which, roughly speaking, lie west and east,—although in both cases chains running either along meridians or along parallels are, wherever they exist at all, only rare exceptions.

The composite nature of the Urals is best seen at the northern and southern extremities of the system, where the upheavals assume the character of distinct chains of mountains. The Pai-hoi Mountains are a ridge which, beginning at the head of Kara Bay, runs north-west, and is continued in the Island of Vaigatch and the southern island of Nova Zembla; and the Northern Urals, which join the Pai-hoi chain at the head of Kara Bay, run north-east and south-west as far south as 64° N. lat. In their middle portion the architecture of the Urals is complicated by the plateaus of middle Russia. The southern parts do not consist, as Humboldt supposed, of ramifications from main meridional chain, but of a series of parallel ranges running distinctly from north-east to south-west, as is plainly seen in the excellent maps recently published by the Russian Geological Committee.[2] The structure of the separate parts of the Ural complexus is explained in some detail below.

I. The Pai-hoi or coast ridge (Samoyedic "stony ridge") is quite independent of the Urals proper, from which it is separated by a marshy *tundra*, some 30 miles wide. It has a distinct north-north-westerly and north-westerly trend along the shores of the Kara Sea; and, although it is cut by the Ugrian Strait, there is no doubt

[2] *Carte Géologique Générale de la Russie d'Europe*, sheet 139; and "Description Orographique," by A. Karpinsky and Th. Tchernycheff, in *Mémoires du Comité Géologique*, vol. iii. No. 2, 1886.

that it is continued in Vaigatch Island and NOVA ZEMBLA (*q.v.*). Its dome-shaped summits, which attain a height of about 1000 feet above the *tundra* (Vozaipai, 1312 feet), are completely bare of trees, and its stony crags are separated by broad marshy tundras. It is uninhabited.

II. The Obdorsk or Northern Urals, which begin within a few miles of the head of Kara Bay (Konstantinoff Kameñ, in 68° 30′ N. lat., 1490 feet), and extend in a south-western direction as far as the 64th parallel, form a distinct ridge of mountains, stony and craggy, sloping steeply towards the south-east and gently towards the marshes of Russia. Its highest elevations are on the 66th and 67th parallels (3600 to 4370 feet). Sometimes the main chain has on the west two or three secondary ones, formed by the upheaval of sedimentary rocks, and it is towards the southern extremity of one of those that the highest peaks of the Urals occur (Sablya, 5407 feet, in 64° 47′ N. lat., and Teplos-iz, 5540 feet, in 63° 55′). Dense coniferous forests, consisting chiefly of fir, pine, and larch, cover the slopes of the mountains and the narrow valleys; but, as the less hospitable latitudes are approached, every species except the larch gradually disappears and the upper limit of vegetation (2400 feet in the south) rapidly descends till it reaches the very base of the mountains towards the Arctic Circle, and forest vegetation disappears altogether about 65° lat. (67° in the plains of Russia and Siberia). These inhospitable hill-tracts, rising from the wide tundras which stretch for hundreds of miles to the west and east of the Urals, are quite uninhabited, save for a few hunters, who visit them in the summer in pursuit of the reindeer which here seek refuge from the mosquitoes of the lowlands.

III. Although usually reckoned to the Northern Urals, the section between the 64th and 61st parallels has again a wholly distinct character. It is represented on the maps as a girdle of chains, 20 to 35 miles in width, running north and south, and separated by long valleys. From the broad plateaus, or *parmas*, which stretch towards the north-west, it might be conjectured, however, that the structure is more complicated; and the recent researches by MM. Fedoroff and Ivanoff have, in fact, shown that what is described as the main chain (or, more correctly, the main water-parting) of the Urals is a succession of plateaus stretching in a north-westerly direction,[1] with broad, flat, marshy valleys, and rising here and there into isolated dome-shaped flat summits, mostly under 3000 feet (Yang-tuny, 62° 43′ N. lat., 4166 feet). The whole region, except the mountain summits, is densely clothed with coniferous forests, birch appearing only occasionally in the south, and even the Scotch pine only in a few valleys. This part of the range is also uninhabited.

IV. The Middle Urals, between 61° and 55° 30′ N. lat., and about 80 miles in breadth, are the best known, as they contain the richest iron, copper, and gold mines (Bogosłovsk, Gorobłagodatsk, and Ekaterinburg Urals). The Deneshkin Kameñ in the north (4238 feet) and the Tara-tash in the south (2800 feet) may be considered as marking the limits of this section. Here the orographical structure is still more complicated, and the necessity of distinguishing the separate upheavals becomes still more apparent. In the north (61st to 60th parallel) there is a succession of chains with a distinct north-eastern trend; and it still remains an open question whether, for two degrees farther south, the whole of the Bogosłovsk Urals (5135 feet in the Konjakoff Kameñ, and from 3000 to 4000 feet in several other summits) do not consist of chains having the same direction. Farther south a broad swelling, which crosses northern Russia from the Kanin peninsula in the north to the sources of the river Petchora in the south-east, joins the Urals, and is continued into Asia by the plateau of the Tura and Isset rivers. To the south of the Katchkanar (2891 feet), *i.e.*, from the 58th to the 56th parallel, therefore, the Urals assume the appearance of broad swellings from 1000 to 2000 feet in height, deeply ravined and with gentle slopes. These low and ravine-broken plateaus, the higher parts of which can be reached from Russia on a very gentle gradient, have been utilized for centuries as the chief highway to Siberia. They have none of the aspects of an alpine tract; and the traveller to Siberia cannot but experience a feeling of disappointment as his horses, still running at full speed, reach the marble column, inscribed "Europe" on one side and "Asia" on the other, which marks the water-parting (1180 feet) between the Russian and Siberian rivers. The eastern slope is steeper, but even there Ekaterinburg is only 350 feet below the water-parting. The valleys have a decidedly south-eastern direction, and such is also the course of the railway from Perm to Tyumeñ, as soon as it reaches the Siberian slope. The plateau-like swellings of this division terminate farther south in a depression, about 70 miles broad, stretching from north-west to south-east, where the water-parting has a height of only a few hundred feet. The Middle Urals are still densely forested, notwithstanding the immense quantities of timber and fuel which are constantly being taken from them. The vegetation is much more varied than in the north (birch, oak, lime, and maple), a rich undergrowth of bushes growing together with the conifers, and the banks of the rivers being adorned with the wild cherry (*Prunus padus*), poplar, willow, and alder. The valleys and lower slopes are covered with a thick sheet of rich humus and have become the site of large and wealthy villages. The mines also have given rise to a considerable population. The southern parts of the Middle Urals may be estimated to have a total agricultural and mining population of nearly 1,500,000.

[1] See map in the *Izvestia* of the Russ. Geogr. Soc., vol. xxii., 1886.

V. The Southern Urals (from 55° 30′ to 51° N. lat.) are now well known both orographically and geologically;[2] and it appears that, instead of consisting of three chains of mountains radiating from Mount Yurma, as was formerly supposed, they consist of a series of three parallel chains running north-east and south-west, and therefore constitute a quite independent part of the Ural complexus. The Ural-tau proper is a low sinuous chain extending due south-west and hardly exceeding 2200 to 2800 feet in height. It slopes gently towards the north-west and abruptly towards the south-east, where several short and low chains (Ilmeñ, Irenty, &c.) rise in the basins of the Mias and the Ui. In the west a chain separated from the Ural-tau by a longitudinal valley accompanies it throughout its entire length. This, although pierced by the rivers which rise in the longitudinal valley just mentioned (Ai, upper Byełaya), nevertheless rises to a much greater height than the Ural-tau. Its wild stony ridge has an altitude of 3375 feet in the Yurma, and 3950 feet in the Taganai; while the Urenga and Iremel Mountains exceed 3500 feet, and the peaks bearing these names reach 4013 and 5040 feet respectively. Farther west, another series of chains, parallel to the above, is described under various names (Zurat-kul, Zigałga, Nary); they reach nearly the same altitudes (Zigałga and Yaman-tau, 4880 and 5400 feet respectively). A number of other chains, also parallel and ranging from 2000 to 3000 feet, accompany them in the west. The whole system has thus the character of a swelling nearly 65 miles wide, intersected by a series of parallel chains, the results of as many foldings of the sedimentary rocks, which have undergone extensive denudation. Some of the chains are exceedingly craggy, and most of them are covered with masses of angular *débris*, sometimes concealed under thick sheets of marshy mosses. The gorges by which the rivers pierce the Devonian limestones on their way towards the lower terraces are most picturesque in the west, where the Urals assume an alpine character. The forests are no longer continuous; the gentle slopes of the hilly tracts are dotted with woods, mostly of deciduous trees, while the hollows contain rich pasture grounds. The thick layers of sedimentary rock which are lifted *en masse* on the western slope cover a wide area farther to the west in the shape of a plateau which already assumes the features of a steppe (see UFA). The whole region, formerly the abode of Bashkirs, is rapidly being colonized by Russians.

Farther south, between the 53d and 51st parallels, the Ural-tau, still composed of crystalline rocks (diorite, serpentine, granite), continues in the same direction, but is covered as we advance by horizontal Cretaceous deposits and, except when deeply trenched by rivers, assumes the appearance of a plateau which hardly reaches 1500 feet. It is continued farther south-west (towards the Volga) under the name of Obschiy Syrt. A narrow longitudinal valley watered by the Sakmara (right-hand tributary of the Ural) separates the Ural-tau and the Guberlinsk Mountains (as the preceding tract is called) from the Irendyk chain, about 20 miles in width, which reaches 2300 feet in its higher parts. It is cut by the Ural river at Orsk and extends farther south-west towards the sources of the Ilek; while in the east a wide granitic plateau, with only a few remainders of its former Devonian and Carboniferous covering, some 130 miles broad and nearly 1000 feet high, lies about the sources of the Siberian rivers, and is known by such local names as Kara-Edyr-tau, Djabik-Karagai, and the like.

VI. As a rule the Urals are not shown on maps to the south of the great bend of the Ural river, where quite independent ranges of hills, or flat swellings, are represented (Jaman-tau, Mugojar Hills). It appears, however, from recent exploration[3] that the Mugojar Hills may safely be regarded as a farther continuation of the upheavals which constitute the Urals. The Cretaceous plateau north of the Ural river is continued to the south of it; it again assumes a mountainous character in the Jaman-tau (50° N. lat.) and joins the Mugojar Hills, which consist of diorites and crystalline slates and reach their maximum in the Airuk Mountain (about 1000 feet). A range of heights connects the Mugojar Hills with the Ust-Urt plateau (see TRANSCASPIAN REGION). It is hardly necessary to say that these plateaus and flat hills to the south of the river Ural have all the characters of the Ciscaspian and Transcaspian steppes.

Geology.—Whatever the variety of the orographically independent systems of mountains and plateaus embodied under the general name of Urals, a certain "geotectonic" similarity may be observed in all of them. Denudation has been active on so grand a scale that entire strata of sedimentary deposits have been removed from their original positions and scattered in the form of *débris* to distances of more than 100 miles on both sides of the Urals, so as

[2] *Carte Géologique*, sheet 139, *ut sup.*

[3] P. Nazaroff, in *Bull. de la Soc. des Naturalistes de Moscou*, 1886, No. 4.

considerably to reduce their former height. But, if this agency be taken into account, the Urals seem to come under the category of what the Germans call asymmetric *Faltengebirge*, and thus exhibit a great resemblance to the western Alps. A broad strip of granites, syenites, diorites, and porphyries, with their subordinate gneisses and crystalline slates, belonging to the Laurentian and Huronian systems, constitutes the main axis of upheaval, and this axis is invariably situated in the eastern part of the mountain region. The asymmetry thus resulting is the more pronounced as the Azoic rocks are mostly covered directly by Tertiary and Quaternary deposits on their Siberian slope; while towards the west they are covered with vast layers of Silurian, Devonian, Carboniferous, Permian, and Triassic rocks, which are manifoldly folded so as to constitute a series of chains parallel to the main axis and mostly lifted to much greater heights than the older Azoic rocks.

The crystalline rocks which must have constituted the primary ridges mostly appear in the shape of plateaus, water- and glacier-worn, with undulating surfaces; and the hills which rise above the plateaus are mostly dome-shaped and are seldom marked by the craggy characters which are met with in the limestone and sandstone mountains of the subsequent formations. Masses of angular *débris* and great blocks cover both the plateaus and the mountains; and only a very few traces of the sediments which may have partially covered the Azoic crystalline rocks are sporadically met with. But, as a rule, they have remained a continent since the Huronian epoch. As for the Primary and Secondary deposits of the western slope, they are represented by Silurian, Devonian, Carboniferous, Permio-Carboniferous, Permian, and Triassic deposits, attaining great thicknesses and following one another in succession so as to appear on the surface as strips lying parallel to the Urals. The strip occupied by the Silurian quartzites, limestones, and slates is narrow, even in its northern portion. Farther south it disappears, and the deposits which formerly were assigned to the Silurian period are now considered to be mostly Devonian. These latter, mostly littoral in character and much resembling those of the Eifel and Belgium, occupy wide areas to the west of the main axis of the Urals. Their lower parts are much metamorphosed. The Carboniferous deposits,—coal-bearing in the Middle and Southern Urals,—although appearing at the surface only as a narrow strip in the west Urals, occupy an extensive area, but are concealed by the largely developed Permian deposits, and that series of sediments which must be considered as intermediate between the Carboniferous and the Permian. These latter, described as "Permo-Carbon" by Russian and German geologists, are largely developed in the west Urals. Their fossils belong to a fauna intermediate between the Carboniferous and the Permian, which was formerly known as that of Artinsk; but since two more series of the same intermediate character have been described the whole has been brought under the general name of Permio-Carboniferous deposits. The Permian deposits cover a wide zone all along the western slope of the Urals from north to south, and are most important on account of their copper ores, salt-beds, and salt-springs. They are also covered with variegated marls which are almost quite destitute of fossil organisms, so that their age is not yet quite settled. Some Russian geologists continue to consider them as Permian, while the majority of recent explorers assign them to the Triassic age.

The glaciation of the Urals is still a debated question. Even those geologists who now acknowledge that the Scandinavian ice-sheet covered middle Russia hesitate to admit the existence of an ice-cap covering the Middle and Southern Urals,—the want of polished and striated rocks being the chief argument for the negative. But, if the disintegrated state of the rocks which are best fitted to maintain glacial polishing and striation, their thick coverings of *débris*, and the action of lichens and mosses in obliterating the traces of glaciation be taken into account, as also the prevalence of erratic blocks, and the character of the deposits filling up the valleys, it must be regarded as most probable that the Urals, too, must soon be included within the limits of former glaciation (as has been already done by a few explorers, such as Polyakoff). The Lacustrine (Post-Glacial) deposits are widely spread all over the slopes of the Urals. Immense marshes, which have recently emerged, in the north, and numberless lakes in the south, which are but small in comparison with their size at a recent period, as also Lacustrine deposits in the valleys, all go to show that during the Lacustrine period the Urals were as much dotted with lakes as Finland is at the present time.

Climatic, Geo-Botanical, and Geo-Zoological Importance.—The importance of the Urals as a climatic and geo-botanical boundary can no longer be regarded as very great. Most European species of plants freely cross the Urals into Siberia, and several Siberian species travel across them into northern Russia. But, being a zone of hilly tracts extending from north to south in a meridional direction, the Ural Mountains necessarily exercise a powerful influence in driving a colder northern climate, as well as a northern flora and fauna, farther towards the south along their axis. The harshness of the climate at the meteorological stations of Bogoslovsk, Zlatoust, and Ekaterinburg is not owing merely to their elevation a few hundred feet above sea-level. Even if reduced to sea-level, the average temperatures of the Ural meteorological stations are such as to produce a local deflexion of the isotherms towards the south. The same is true with regard to the limits of distribution of vegetable and animal species. It has been already stated that the northern limits of tree-vegetation descend towards more southern latitudes on the Northern Urals and in the vicinity of the chain. The same is true with regard to many other species of plants. In like manner several Arctic species of animals come much farther south than they might otherwise have done: the reindeer, for instance, is met with as far south as the 52d parallel. The Southern Urals introduce amidst the Ciscaspian steppes the forest vegetation, flora, and fauna of middle Russia.

In the distribution of the races of mankind the Urals have also played an important part. To the present day the Northern Urals are the abodes of Finnish stems (Samoyedes, Zyrians, Voguls, and Permians) who have been driven from their former homes by Slavonian colonization, while the steppes on the slopes of the Southern Urals have continued to be inhabited by the Turkish stems of the Bashkirs. The Middle Urals were also in the 9th century the abode of the Ugrians, and their land, Biarmia (now Perm), was well known to the Byzantine historians for its mineral wealth,—there being at that time a lively intercourse between the Ugrians and the Greeks. Compelled to abandon their abodes, they moved south on the Ural slopes towards the land of the Khazars, and through the prairies of south-eastern and southern Russia (the Λεβεδία of Constantine Porphyrogenitus) towards the Danube and to their present seat—Hungary,—leaving but a very few memorials in the Northern and Middle Urals.[1] At present the Urals, especially the Middle and the Southern, are being more and more colonized by Great Russian immigrants, while the Finnish stems are rapidly melting away.

Metallurgy and Mining.—The mineral wealth of the Urals was known to the Greeks in the 9th century, and afterwards to the Novgorodians, who penetrated there in the 11th century for trade with the Ugrians. When the colonies of Novgorod (Vyatka, Perm) fell under the rule of Moscow, the Russian czars soon understood the importance of the Ural mines, and Ivan III. sent out German engineers to explore that region. In 1558 the whole of the present government of Perm was given by the rulers of Moscow to the brothers Strogonoff, who began to establish salt-works and mines for iron and copper. Peter I. gave a new impulse to the mining industry by founding several iron-works, and from 1745, when gold was first discovered, the Russian colonization of the Urals took a new departure. The colonization was, however, of a double character, being partly free—chiefly by Nonconformists in search of religious freedom in the wildernesses of the Urals—and partly compulsory,—the Government sending peasant settlers who became serfs to the iron and copper works, and were bound to supply them with ores and wood for fuel. Until 1861 all work at the mines was done by serfs belonging either to private persons (the Strogonoffs, Demidoffs, and others) or to the crown. At present (1888) only a few works, maintained for supplying the army, belong to the crown.

Gold is found both in veins and in alluvial or diluvial deposits, and is extracted from both; but the former yield only a moderate quantity annually (2180 to 2780 ℔ in 1882-84). The gold from the Ural mines constitutes nearly one-fifth of the total amount obtained throughout the Russian empire. Platinum is found either in connexion with gold dust or separately, the platinum mines of the Urals being the only ones worked in Russia. Osmium, iridium, and nickel are found at several places, but their industrial importance is small. Silver is also met with at several places, but only 2383 ℔ were extracted during the years 1875 to 1884. The copper mines, chiefly in Perm, but partly also in Ufa, are very important, nearly two-thirds of the total amount of the metal mined in Russia being obtained from eight works in the Urals. The average amount of gold, platinum, and copper annually yielded by the Ural mines is given in the following table:—

	Gold.	Platinum.	Copper.		Gold.	Platinum.	Copper.
	℔	℔	cwts.		℔	℔	cwts.
1860-64	11,296	..	78,500	1875-79	16,114	4048	30,508
1865-69	13,997	3666	60,880	1880-84	18,042	6949	48,004
1870-74	13,845	3890	45,310				

Iron is widely diffused and is extracted in the governments of Perm, Ufa, and Orenburg, the chief works being in Perm. Of the 198 blast furnaces in the Russian empire 103 are in the Urals, and they supply nearly two-thirds of all the pig-iron produced in Russia. One-half of the iron and one-sixth of the steel obtained both from home and foreign pig-iron in the empire are prepared in the Urals; and, while the St Petersburg and Polish steel works, which prepare steel (chiefly for rails) from imported iron, show great fluctuations in their production, the Ural works have a steady

[1] Comp. *Moravia and the Madiars*, by K. J. Groth; Zabyelin's *History of Russian Life* and the polemics on the subject in *Izvestia* of the Russ. Geogr. Soc., xix., 1883.

increase. The average yearly production of iron in the Urals is best seen from the following:—

	Pig-Iron.	Iron.	Steel.
	cwts.	cwts.	cwts.
1875-80	6,623,000	3,406,000	259,600
1881-83	6,378,000	3,517,000	612,800
1884	6,740,000	3,874,000	763,340

Owing to the immense extent of forest, the coal mining industry is but of recent origin in the Urals. Only six pits were at work in Perm in 1884; and of recent years from 3,000,000 to 4,000,000 cwts. have been annually extracted (about 5 per cent. of the coal raised in the Russian empire). Finally, salt was raised in Perm, Orenburg, and Uralsk to the amount of 9,422,000 cwts. in 1884.

The precious (amethyst, topaz, emerald, tourmaline, &c.) and ornamental (malachite, carsovite, &c.) stones of the Urals are familiar in all European museums, and are found in most beautiful varieties. The crown works at Ekaterinburg supply admirable works of art, while a numerous population at Ekaterinburg and in the neighbouring villages support themselves by searching for precious and ornamental stones and preparing them for export. Of the 330,750 workmen engaged in 1884 in mining and metallurgical industries throughout the Russian empire 183,914 were employed in the Urals, as well as nearly one-half of the motive power (steam-engines and water-wheels) used at the mining and metallurgical works of Russia, Poland, and Finland. The exports from the Urals are made chiefly by means of the rivers, which are navigable in their upper parts only during the spring. There is not as yet any railway connecting the Urals with Russia. The line of Siberian railway which now connects the iron-works of the eastern slope with the Kama at Perm has certainly increased the exports; but they are still so small in comparison with the expense of the line that the railway is worked at a loss, the deficiency being made good from the imperial budget, and the whole mining and metallurgical industry of the Urals is still maintained by means of high protective duties imposed on foreign metals and metallic wares.

Several wealthy towns have grown up in the Ural valleys in connexion with mining industry and administration. EKATERINBURG (*q.v.*) and NIJNE-TAGHILSK (*q.v.*) both had more than 30,000 inhabitants in 1885, while ZLATOUST (*q.v.*), Neviansk, Neivinsk, and Kyshtym in Perm, Votkinsk and Izhevsk in Vyatka, had from 21,000 to 12,500 inhabitants. The Revdinsk, Bogoslovsk, Turinsk, Shaitanovsk, Gorobiagodat, Artinsk, Nijne-Saldinsk, Usolie, and Sysertsk mining towns in Perm, Katav-Ivanovsk, Kusinsk, and Satkinsk in Ufa, Byeloryetsk, Tirlansk, and Avzyano-Petrovsk have populations from 5000 to 10,000.

Bibliography.—1. The following general works may be mentioned as of chief importance:—Hermann, *Versuch einer miner. Beschr. des Ural Erzgebirges*, 1789; Humboldt, *Fragments*, 1831; Hofmann and Helmersen, *Geogn. Unters. des Süd-Uralgebirges*, 1831; Kupffer, *Voyage*, 1833; L. von Buch, *Beitr. zur Bestimm. der Gebirgsform. in Russland*, 1840; Eversmann, *Orenburg Region* (Russian), 1840; Schurowsky, *Urals* (Russian), 1841; Helmersen, *Reise*, 1841; Rose, *Reise*, 1842; Murchison, *Geol. of Russia*, 1845 (with Ozerskiy's Appendix to Russ. translation); Keyserling and Krusenstern, *Wiss. Beobachtungen*, 1846; Leonhardt, *Geologie des Eur. Russland*, 1848; Hofmann, *Nördl. Ural*, 1853-56; Meglitzky and Antipoff, *Bergbau im Ural*, 1861; Ludwig, *Ueberblick und Beobacht. in Russland*, 1862; Möller, *Geological Map of the Urals*, 1869; Ruprecht, *Verbr. der Pflanzen in nördl. Ural*; Panaeff, *Climatology of the Urals* (Russian), 1882; *Carte Géologique de la Russie d'Europe* (139), 1886. For further bibliographical information see "Ural," "Perm," "Orenburg," &c., in the *Geographical Dictionary* (Russian) by P. Semenoff. 2. Monographs dealing with separate parts of the Urals occur in great numbers in the *Gornyi Journal*, the *Verhandl. der Russ. Miner. Ges.*, the publications of the Russ. Geogr. Soc., the Ural, Kazan, and Moscow Societies of Naturalists, and in the *Izvestia* and *Memoirs* of the Russ. Geological Committee. See also the yearly *Indexes* by M. Mezhoff and those of the Kieff Society of Naturalists. (P. A. K.)

URALSK, a province of south-eastern Russia, lying to the north of the Caspian Sea, with an area of 141,174 square miles. It is bounded by Astrakhan on the west, Samara and Orenburg on the north, Turgai and the Sea of Aral on the east, and the Transcaspian Region on the south. It is geographically situated mostly within the boundaries of Asia, *i.e.*, to the east of the Ural river, and both its physical features and its inhabitants are, to a very large extent, Asiatic. Administratively, it belongs to the "Kirghiz provinces," or governor-generalship of the steppes. Apart from a narrow strip of land in the north, where the slopes of the Obschiy Syrt, covered with a fertile black earth and stretches of forest, descend towards the Ural river, and the gentle slopes of the Mugojar Hills in the north-east, Uralsk consists of dry steppes and deserts, which fall with an imperceptible gradient towards the Caspian. Most of the province is below sea-level, the zero-altitude line running from Kamyshin on the Volga to the south of the town of Uralsk. The steppe-land consists for the most part of sandy clay, sands containing shells of molluscs now living in the Caspian, salt clay, and shifting sands. It is also dotted with numerous salt lakes, partly remains of old lagoons of the Caspian. To the south-east Uralsk extends over the northern part of the Ust-Urt plateau. Red sandstones (Permian?) and chalk are met with only in the north, the remainder of the province being covered with Post-Pliocene Caspian deposits, which conceal the underlying rocks.

Uralsk is watered by the Ural, which rises in Orenburg at a height of 2100 feet above sea-level, but soon descends to the lowlands, where it flows south, west, and south, entering the Caspian after a course of 800 miles. Its chief tributaries, the Sakmara, the Or, and the Ilek, are in the north; along its lower course the Great and Little Uzeñs and many small streams on the left bank fail to join the main river, being lost in lakes before reaching it. The Emba, which has its course in the north of the Ust-Urt plateau, reaches the Caspian by a series of shallow lagoons, which were navigable in the 18th century.

The climate is influenced by the Central Asian steppes. A cold and dry winter is succeeded by a hot and still drier summer, during which the grass, and sometimes all the crops, are destroyed by the burning heat. Uralsk, although lying wholly to the south of 51° 30′ N. lat., has the same average yearly temperature as Moscow and south Finland (39°·5); its January is colder than that of north Finland (3°), while July averages 73°

The character of the vegetation can be easily inferred from the above. The prairies and forest tracts of the north soon disappear, their place being taken by the vegetation of the south Russian steppes. This has, however, to struggle with the much poorer vegetation, Central Asian in character, of the sandy regions to the west of the lower Ural, and the saliniferous vegetation of the clayey deserts of the Emba. The Ust-Urt has herbaceous steppes, where the want of irrigation and rain destroys all vegetation by the end of summer. Wide belts of rushes grow along the banks of the rivers and on the shores of the Caspian.

The population of the province, 525,330 in 1883, is made up of three different elements,—Ural Cossacks, who constitute about one-fifth, and numbered nearly 90,000 in 1879, some 15,000 Russian peasants, and Kirghiz. Of these 405,000 are still nomads. The Kirghiz are almost entirely dependent on cattle-breeding, and before the outbreak of the murrain of 1879 were reckoned to have 429,500 horses, 221,800 head of cattle, 1,411,000 sheep, and 175,000 camels. From that epidemic the Russians lost two-thirds of their horses and one-third of their other stock, whilst the Khirgiz lost more than three-fourths of both horses and cattle. The Ural Cossacks, descendants of those independent communities of free settlers and Raskolniks who are so often mentioned in Russian history under the name of Yaik Cossacks, owing to their unwillingness to submit to the rule of the czars, are fine representatives of the Great Russian race, though not without some admixture of Tartar and Kalmuck blood. Their chief occupations are cattle-breeding and fishing, the latter a most important source of income. The rich fisheries in the Ural and the Caspian are the property of the community as a whole (the *voisko*), and are subdivided according to the needs and working powers of the separate villages.[1] They give employment to about 7000 Cossacks and 2000 hired labourers. There are also fisheries in the Emba. Walrus-hunting is also engaged in. Agriculture was first introduced between 1830 and 1840; but now more than 300,000 cwts. of wheat are exported annually. Nearly 130,000 cwts. of salt are obtained from the lakes every year. The manufactures of the province, which possesses a few steam flour-mills and a number of tanneries and tallow-melting works, are unimportant. Trade by barter is extensively carried on with the Kirghiz. Fish, corn, cattle, hides, tallow, and the like are exported, while manufactured wares are imported to the value of about £1,500,000 per annum.

Uralsk is divided into four districts, the chief towns of which are—Uralsk (20,680 inhabitants in 1879), Kalmykoff (1510), Gurieff at the mouth of the Ural (4380), and Temirsk, a small port, now the administrative centre of the district of Embinsk. Several villages have populations of from 2000 to 5000 each.

History.—In the first half of the 16th century Uralsk was occupied by the Nogai horde, a remnant of the Golden Horde, which retired there after the fall of Astrakhan and Kazan; the khans resided at Saraitchik on the Ural. At the same time the lower parts of the Ural were occupied by Russian runaway serfs and free Cossacks who did not recognize the authority of Moscow. They took Saraitchik in 1560 and formed an independent community, like the *sitch* of the Zaporog Cossacks. The Moscow princes, recognizing the importance of these military settlements,

[1] See Haxthausen's *Russia* for a description of the Cossack community; comp. also the more recent works of Ryabinin and Khoroshkhin and many separate monographs in Russian periodicals; also Baer's *Kaspische Studien* and Danilevsky on the fishing.

tried to win their allegiance by the grant of various privileges. But, when they attempted to bring them under the centralized rule of the empire and prosecuted them for nonconformity, the Cossacks revolted, first under Razin, and afterwards under Pugatcheff. After the latter rising, the name of Ural was officially given to the Yaik river and the Yaik Cossacks. The disbanding of their artillery, the planting of Russian garrisons within the domains of the *voisko*, and the interference of Russian officials in their interior organization during the 19th century occasioned a series of smaller outbreaks, the latest of which, in 1874, against the new law of military service, resulted in the deportation of 2500 Cossacks, with their families, to Turkestan.

URALSK, capital of the above province, is situated on the upper Ural, at its confluence with the Tchagan, 1095 miles south-east from Moscow. The town is well built, with regular streets; among its prominent buildings are the theatre, the club, and two gymnasiums; and it is beautified by numerous gardens. The scientific society issues publications of great value. There is a very brisk trade in fish, cattle, hides, tallow, grain (exported), and in manufactured goods (imported). The population in 1879 was 20,680.

URANIUM, the name of a rather rare metallic element, already briefly referred to under CHEMISTRY (vol. v. p. 542). The credit of its discovery as an element must be assigned to Klaproth, who in 1789 isolated from pitch-blende a yellow oxide which, while obviously metallic, was foreign to all the known metals. He accordingly viewed it as the oxide of a new metal, which he named uranium, after the newly discovered planet of Herschel. From the yellow oxide he obtained, by reduction with charcoal at a high temperature, what he took to be metallic uranium. Berzelius about 1823 found that the yellow oxide, when treated with excess of sulphuric acid, united with it into a sulphate, not unlike the ferric salt $Fe_2O_3.3SO_3$ in its character. Hence he concluded that the uranium salt is $Ur_2O_3.3SO_3$, where Ur_2O_3, according to his analysis, represents 864 parts of yellow oxide, if $Fe_2O_3=160$ or $O=16$. Like Fe_2O_3, the yellow oxide lost 48 parts of oxygen per $Ur_2O_3=864$ parts as water, while $Ur_2=816$ parts of metal remained.[1] These results were universally adopted until Péligot in 1840 discovered that Berzelius's (and Klaproth's) metal contains oxygen, and that his $(Ur_2)O_3$ really is $(U_6O_6).O_3=3U_2O_3$, where $U=120$ is one atomic weight of real uranium. Péligot's results, though called in question by Berzelius, have been amply confirmed by all subsequent investigators; only now, on theoretical grounds, first set forth by Mendeljeff, we have come to double Péligot's atomic weight, so that throughout this article U signifies 240 parts of uranium, while UO_3 stands as the formula of the yellow oxide, and UO_2 as that of Berzelius's metal.

The only practically available raw material for the extraction of uranium is pitch-blende (Germ. and Fr. *Uranpecherz*), which occurs associated with lead and silver ores, chiefly in Joachimsthal and at Przibram in Bohemia, at Schneeberg in Saxony, and at Redruth in Cornwall, forming greenish or brownish black masses clustering together like grapes. Its hardness is 5·5. The specific gravity varies from 6·4 to 8, the mineral almost invariably presenting itself in intimate intermixture with a host of foreign metallic compounds, such as sulphides, arsenides, &c. Pure pitch-blende is U_3O_8, which in relatively good specimens forms some 80 per cent. or more of the whole.

In the chemical treatment of the ore, it is expedient to begin by removing at least part of the arsenic and sulphur of the admixtures by roasting, and then to wash away the light oxides with water or dissolve them away with hydrochloric acid. In one of the many processes proposed the purified ore is disintegrated with hot nitric acid, to produce nitrates, which are then converted into sulphates by evaporation with oil of vitriol. The sulphates are treated with water, which dissolves the uranium and other soluble salts, while silica, sulphate of lead, &c., remain; these are removed by filtration. From the solution the arsenic, copper, &c., are precipitated by sulphuretted hydrogen as sulphides, which are filtered off. The filtrate contains the uranium as uranous and the iron as ferrous salt. These are oxidized by means of chlorine or some other oxidizing agent, and precipitated conjointly by excess of ammonia. The precipitate, after having been collected and washed, is digested with a warm concentrated solution of carbonate of ammonia, which dissolves the uranium as a yellow solution of uranate of ammonia, while the hydrated oxide of iron, the alumina, &c., remain. These are filtered off hot, and the filtrate is allowed to cool, when crystals of the uranate separate out. The mother liquor includes generally more or less of nickel, cobalt, zinc, and other heavy metals, which, as Wöhler showed, can be removed as insoluble sulphides by the addition of sulphide of ammonium; uranium, under the circumstances, is not precipitated by sulphide of ammonium. The filtrate, on being boiled down, yields a second crop of uranate of ammonia. This uranate when ignited in a platinum crucible leaves a green oxide of the composition U_3O_8, *i.e.*, artificial pitch-blende, which serves as a starting point for the preparation of uranium compounds. The green oxide, as a rule, requires to be further purified. One method for this purpose is to convert it into a solution of the nitrate $UO_2(NO_3)_2$, and from it to precipitate the metal as oxalate by the addition of oxalic acid (Péligot). The latter $(UO_2.C_2O_4)$ yields a purer oxide, UO_2, or, in the presence of air, U_3O_8, on ignition.

Metallic uranium, as shown by Péligot, can be obtained by the reduction of a mixture of dry chloride of potassium and dry uranous chloride, UCl_4, with sodium at a red heat (for details see handbooks of chemistry). The metal, which is easily separated from the slag by treatment with water, remains as a dark heavy powder or in white compact globules, according to the temperature at which it was produced. According to Zimmermann, to whom we owe a recent investigation on the matter, pure compact uranium is a white malleable metal, which is pretty hard, though "softer than steel." Its specific gravity has the high value 18·7; its specific heat is 0·02765, corresponding to $U=240$. The fusing point, from Zimmermann's statements on its preparation, seems to lie at bright redness. The compact metal when exposed to the air tarnishes only very slowly. The powdery metal when heated in air to 150° or 170° C. catches fire and burns brilliantly into U_3O_8. Dilute sulphuric acid attacks it but slowly; hydrochloric acid, especially if strong, dissolves it readily, with the formation, more immediately, of a hyacinth-coloured solution of U_2Cl_6, which, however, readily absorbs oxygen from the air, with the formation of a green solution of UCl_4, which in its turn gradually passes into one of yellow uranyl salt, $UO_2.Cl_2$.

Uranous Compounds.—The oxide UO_2 (Berzelius's metal) is prepared by heating the green oxide U_3O_8 in hydrogen. It dissolves in hot oil of vitriol; the mass, when treated with water, dissolves; from the solution green crystals, $U(SO_4)_2+8H_2O$, are obtainable. The anhydrous chloride UCl_4 was prepared for the first time by Péligot by heating an intimate mixture of the green oxide and charcoal to redness in a current of dry chlorine; it is obtained as sublimate of black-green metallic-looking octahedra. The chloride is very hygroscopic. Uranous salts pass into uranic (uranyl) compounds under the same circumstances under which ferrous salts become ferric, only they do so far more readily.

Uranic Compounds.—By keeping the nitrate $UO_2(NO_3)_2$ at a temperature of 250° for a sufficient time the oxide UO_3 is obtained as a chamois-yellow solid, insoluble in water, but soluble in acids, with the formation of uranyl salts, $UO_2.Cl_2$, &c. The oxide, in other words, behaves to acids as if it were the monoxide of a radical (UO_2) uranyl. The sulphate $(UO_2)SO_4+3$ or $3·5H_2O$ is deposited from a syrupy solution in yellow crystals. The nitrate $(UO_2)(NO_3)_2+6H_2O$ forms large yellow crystals easily soluble in water. This salt is used in photography, also in analysis as a characteristic precipitant for phosphoric acid. If a solution of a uranyl salt is mixed with one of ammonia, or potash, or soda, the uranium is precipitated in the form of a uranate, $U_2O_6R_2O$, of the respective alkali. Uranate of soda, forming yellow crystals of the composition $Na_2U_2O_7+6H_2O$, is made industrially, being used for the production of yellow uranium glass in porcelain painting. The Joachimsthal works in 1875 produced 70 cwts. of this "oxide," representing a value of £8500.

Analysis.—A borax bead dissolves uranium oxides in the reducing flame with a green, in the oxidizing flame with a yellow, colour. Solutions of uranyl salts (nitrate, &c.) behave to reagents as follows: sulphuretted hydrogen produces green uranous salt with precipitation of sulphur; sulphide of ammonium in neutral solutions gives a black precipitate of UO_2S, which settles slowly and, while being washed in the filter, breaks up partially into hydrated UO_2 and sulphur; ammonia gives a yellow precipitate of uranate of ammonia, characteristically soluble in hot carbonate of ammonia solution; prussiate of potash gives a brown precipitate which in appearance is not unlike the precipitate produced by the same reagent in cupric salts. (W. D.)

URANUS (*i.e.*, Heaven) is in Greek mythology the husband of Gæa (Earth) and father of Cronus (Saturn) and other deities. See MYTHOLOGY, vol. xvii. p. 155, and SATURN.

[1] We substitute for Berzelius's actual numbers the corresponding values calculated from our present constants.

URBAN, St, first pope of that name, was bishop of Rome from 222 to 230. He had been preceded by Calixtus and was followed by Pontianus. He is mentioned by Eusebius (*H. E.*, vi. 23), and is named in an inscription in the cœmeterium Callisti, but of his life nothing is known. The Roman *Breviary* (25th May) speaks of his numerous converts, among whom were Valerianus, husband of St Cecilia, and his brother Tiburtius, and states that he suffered martyrdom, and was buried in the cœmeterium Prætextati.

URBAN II. (Eudes or Odo), pope from 1088 to 1099, was born of knightly rank, at Lagery (near Châtillon-sur-Marne), and was educated for the church. He had already become archdeacon of Rheims when, under the influence of St Bruno, his teacher, he resigned his preferment and entered the cloister at Cluny, where he rose to be prior. In 1078 Gregory VII. summoned him to Italy, and made him cardinal-bishop of Ostia. He was one of the most prominent and energetic supporters of Hildebrandism, especially as legate in Germany in 1084, and was among the few whom Gregory nominated as possible successors. Desiderius of Monte Casino (Victor III.) was chosen in the first instance to the difficult post, but at the next vacancy Odo was elected by acclamation (March 1088) at a small meeting of cardinals and other prelates held in Terracina. He frankly took up the policy of his great predecessor, but while pursuing it with equal determination showed greater flexibility and diplomatic finesse. At the outset he had to reckon with the presence of the powerful antipope Clement III. in Rome; but a series of well-attended synods held in Rome, Amalfi, Benevento, and Troia supported him in renewed declarations against simony, lay investiture, and clerical marriages, and a continued policy of opposition to Henry IV. In accordance with this last policy, the marriage of the countess Matilda with Guelph of Bavaria was promoted, Prince Conrad was helped in his rebellion against his father and crowned king of the Romans at Milan in 1093, and the empress (Adelaide or Praxedes) encouraged in her disgraceful charges against her husband. In a protracted struggle also with Philip I. of France, whom he had excommunicated, Urban II. finally proved victorious. But the most prominent feature in his pontificate, a feature indeed which marks an epoch in the history of Latin Christianity, is his connexion with the first crusade (see CRUSADES, vol. vi. pp. 623-624), which united Christendom under the headship of the pope into one vast warlike confederacy (comp. POPEDOM, vol. xix. p. 499). The crusading movement first took shape at Piacenza, where in March 1095 Urban received an embassy from the emperor Alexius I., asking help against the infidel, and where a great council met, attended by numerous Italian, Burgundian, and French bishops and by so vast a concourse of monks and laymen that the public meetings had to be held in the open air outside the city. The still more enthusiastic council of Clermont was held in November of the same year. Urban II. died on 29th July 1099, fourteen days after the fall of Jerusalem, but before the tidings of that great event had reached Italy; his successor was Paschal II.

URBAN III. (Uberto Crivelli), pope from 1185 to 1187, was by birth a Milanese, and was made cardinal and archbishop of Milan by Lucius III., whom he succeeded (25th November 1185). He vigorously took up his predecessor's quarrels with the emperor Frederick I., including the standing dispute about the succession to the territories of the countess Matilda. Even after his elevation to the popedom he continued to hold the archbishopric of Milan, and in this capacity refused to crown as king of Italy Frederick's son Henry, who had married Constantia, the heiress of the kingdom of Sicily. While Henry in the south co-operated with the rebel senate of Rome, Frederick in the north blocked the passes of the Alps and cut off all communication between the pope, then living in Verona, and his German adherents. Urban now resolved on excommunicating Frederick, but the Veronese protested against such a proceeding being resorted to within their walls; he accordingly withdrew to Ferrara, but died (19th October) before he could give effect to his intention. His successor was Gregory VIII.

URBAN IV. (Jacques Pantaléon), pope from 1261 to 1264, was the son of a cobbler in Troyes, studied theology and common law in Paris, became bishop of Verdun, was employed in various missions by Innocent IV., and was made patriarch of Jerusalem by Alexander IV. He was at Viterbo seeking help for the oppressed Christians in the East when the last-named pope died, and after a three months' vacancy he was chosen to succeed him (29th August 1261). As pope he endeavoured, but without success, to stir up a new crusade on behalf of his former diocese of Jerusalem. In domestic matters the chief problems of his pontificate arose out of the competing claims for the crown of the Two Sicilies. Before the arrival of Charles of Anjou, the candidate whom he favoured, Urban died at Perugia on 2nd October 1264. His successor was Clement IV. The festival of Corpus Christi was instituted by Urban IV. in 1264.

URBAN V. (Guillaume de Grimoald), pope from 1362 to 1370, was a native of Grisac in Languedoc. He became a Benedictine and a doctor in canon law, teaching at Montpellier and Avignon. He held the office of abbot of St Victor in Marseilles; and at Avignon, on his way back from Naples, whither he had been sent as papal legate, he was elected pope (28th October 1362) in succession to Innocent VI. As pope he was a severe disciplinarian, discountenanced the pomp and luxury of the cardinals, introduced considerable reforms in the administration of justice, and liberally patronized learning. His pontificate witnessed one of the last flickers of crusading zeal in the expedition of Peter of Lusignan, king of Cyprus, who took Alexandria (11th October 1365), but soon afterwards abandoned it. The great feature of Urban V.'s reign was the effort to restore the papacy to Italy, and to suppress its powerful rivals for the temporal sovereignty there. In 1363 he excommunicated Bernabo Visconti, and ordered a crusade to be preached throughout Italy against him and his kindred, the robbers of the church's estate; but in the following year he found it necessary to purchase peace by removing his ban and making other humiliating concessions. Continued troubles in Italy caused him to set out for Rome, which he reached on 16th October 1367; but, though he was greeted by the clergy and people with joy, and had the satisfaction of being attended by the emperor in St Peter's and of placing the crown upon the head of the empress, it soon became clear that by changing the seat of his government he had not increased its power. Unable any longer to resist the urgency of the French cardinals, he took ship again at Corneto on 5th September 1370, and, arriving at Avignon on the 24th of the same month, died on 19th December. He was succeeded by Gregory XI.

URBAN VI. (Bartolommeo Prignani), pope from 1378 to 1389, was a native of Naples, born in 1318. A devout monk and learned casuist, he became archbishop of Bari in 1377, and, on the death of Gregory XI., the Roman populace clamorously demanding an Italian pope, was unanimously chosen (8th April 1378) by the French cardinals under this pressure to be his successor. The arrogant and imperious temper of the new pope, intoxicated by his unexpected fortune, showed itself in ways so intolerable that five months afterwards the majority of the cardinals met at Fondi, and, repudiating their previous action, proceeded to elect Robert of Geneva (20th September), who assumed the title of Clement VII. Thus began the great schism which divided Christendom for nearly forty years (see POPEDOM, vol. xix. p. 502). The measures of Urban were not without vigour, but at the same time were characterized by such a want of prudence and self-control as has given rise to the not improbable assertion that he actually was, at times at least, a lunatic. Clement VII. was, of course, excommunicated, and designated the Antichrist; twenty-six new cardinals were created in a single day, and, by an arbitrary alienation of the estates and property of the church, funds were raised for open war. The castle of St Angelo was besieged and taken, and the antipope put to flight, while Charles of Durazzo was invested in the sovereignty of Naples, forfeited by Queen Joanna. In 1384, however, Charles began to resist the papal pretensions, and Urban was shut up in Nocera, from the walls of which he daily fulminated his anathemas against his besiegers; he afterwards succeeded in making his escape to Genoa, and, on the death of Charles, set himself at the head of his troops, apparently with the intention of seizing Naples for his nephew if not for himself. To raise funds he proclaimed a jubilee, though only thirty-three years had elapsed since that celebrated under Clement VI., but before the celebration he died at Rome of injuries caused by a fall from his mule, on 15th October 1389. His successor was Boniface IX.

URBAN VII. (Giovanni Battista Castagna), pope for twelve days in September 1590, was of Genoese origin, and was born in Rome in 1521. He was chosen successor of Sixtus V. on 15th September 1590, but died (27th September) before consecration. He was succeeded by Gregory XIV.

URBAN VIII. (Maffeo Barberini), pope from 1623 to 1644, belonged to a Florentine family which had been greatly enriched by commerce, and was born in 1568. Through the influence of an uncle, who had become apostolic protonotary, he, while still a young man, received various promotions from Sixtus V. and Gregory XIV. By Clement VIII. he was himself made protonotary and nuncio to the French court; Paul V. also employed him in a similar capacity, afterwards raising him to the cardinalate, and giving him the legation of Bologna. On 6th August 1623 he was chosen successor to Gregory XV. The period of his pontificate, covering as it did twenty-one years of the Thirty Years' War, was an eventful one, and the ultimate result of that great struggle was largely determined by Urban's policy, which was aimed less at the restoration of Catholicism in Europe than at such an adjustment of the balance of parties as might best favour his own independence and strength as a temporal power in Italy (see POPEDOM, vol. xix. p. 506). In 1626 the duchy of Urbino was incorporated into the papal dominions, and in 1627, when the direct male line of the Gonzagas in Mantua became extinct, he favoured the succession of the duke of Nevers against the claims of the Hapsburgs, whose preponderance he dreaded. He was the last pope to extend the papal territory, and Castelfranco on the Mantuan frontier was fortified by him. In Rome he greatly strengthened the castle of St Angelo, removing, for the purpose of making cannons, the massive tubular girders of bronze from the portico of the Pantheon ("quod non fecerunt barbari, fecerunt Barberini"), establishing also an arsenal in the Vatican, as well as a manufactory of arms at Tivoli, and fortifying the harbour of Civita Vecchia. It was during the pontificate of Urban that Galileo was summoned to Rome to make his great recantation in 1633; on the other hand, the Poussins and Claude Lorraine were patronized by him, and it was he who brought Athanasius Kircher to Rome, and who employed Bernini to build the Palazzo Barberini, the college of the Propaganda, the Fontana del Tritone, and other prominent structures in the city. He was the last to practise nepotism on a grand scale: various members of his house were enormously enriched by him, so that it seemed to contemporaries as if he aimed at establishing a Barberini dynasty. He canonized many saints, among whom the most conspicuous are Ignatius Loyola, Francis Xavier, Al. Gonzaga, and Filippo Neri. Urban VIII. was a clever writer of Latin verse, and a collection of Scriptural paraphrases as well as original hymns of his composition has been frequently reprinted. His death (29th July 1644) is said to have been hastened by chagrin at the result of a war he had undertaken against the duke of Parma. He was succeeded by Innocent X.

URBANA, a city of the United States, the county seat of Champaign county, Ohio. It lies 95 miles nearly due north of Cincinnati, in the midst of a rich agricultural region. It has railroad communication by means of three lines, the New York, Lake Erie, and Western, the Pittsburgh, Cincinnati, and St Louis, and the Indiana, Bloomington, and Western. It has some manufactures, particularly of agricultural tools, machines, and railway rolling stock, and is the site of a Swedenborgian or New Church college. The population in 1880 was 6252, an increase of 46 per cent. since 1870. Urbana was laid out in 1805, when the county was organized.

URBINO, a mediæval walled city of Italy, on the site of the Roman *Urbinum Hortense*, in the Marches of Ancona, stands in a commanding position on a spur of the Tuscan Apennines, near the valley of the Metaurus, about 20 miles from the Adriatic. It grew up, chiefly in the 14th century, around the stronghold of the Montefeltro family. Federigo da Montefeltro, lord of Urbino from 1444 to 1482, was one of the most successful condottieri chiefs of his time, and not only a man of great military and political ability, but also an enthusiastic patron of art and literature, on which he lavished immense sums of money. Federigo much strengthened his position, first by his own marriage with Battista, one of the powerful Sforza family, and secondly by marrying his daughter to Giovanni della Rovere, the favourite nephew of Pope Sixtus IV., who in return conferred upon Federigo the title of duke. Federigo's only son Guidubaldo, who succeeded his father, married in 1489 a very gifted lady, Elizabeth Gonzaga, of the ruling family in Mantua. In 1497 he was expelled from Urbino by Cæsar Borgia, son of Alexander VI., but regained his dukedom in 1503, after Cæsar's death. Guidubaldo was the last duke of the Montefeltro line; at his death in 1508 he bequeathed his coronet to Francesco Maria della Rovere, nephew of Julius II., and for about a century Urbino was ruled by its second dynasty of the Della Rovere family. In 1626 the last descendant of Francesco, called Francesco Maria II., when old and childless abdicated in favour of Pope Urban VIII., after which time Urbino, with its subject towns of Pesaro, Fano, Fossombrone, Gubbio, Castel Durante, Cagli, and about 300 small villages, became part of the Papal States until the suppression of the temporal power in 1870.

During the reigns of Federigo and Guidubaldo, Urbino was one of the foremost centres of activity in art and literature in Italy, and was known as the Italian Athens. In 1468 Federigo gave orders to a Dalmatian architect, Luciano da Laurana, to build him a magnificent fortified palace; it was finished and enlarged by the Florentine Baccio Pintelli during Guidubaldo's reign. Rich friezes, sculptured architraves of doors and windows, and other decorations in marble, painting, and wood-work were executed by the sculptor Ambrogino di Milano, and by Francesco di Giorgio Martini of Siena (1439-1506), whom Vasari wrongly states to have been the principal architect of the palace. Federigo adorned his palace with fine series of paintings by Piero della Francesca, Melozzo da Forli, Paolo Uccello, and Raphael's father, Giovanni Santi; and, in addition to the crowd of able Italian artists whom he invited to his court, Flemish painters, such as Justus of Ghent, visited and worked in this hospitable city.[1] The rich wood-work in the palace, decorated with *tarsia*, or wood mosaic, was executed by Gondolo Tedesco; the rooms were filled with magnificent furniture, costly gold and silver plate, and works of art of all kinds. Literature was no less encouraged under the patronage of Federigo: it was at his court that Piero della Francesca wrote his celebrated work on the science of perspective, Francesco di Giorgio his *Trattato d'Architettura* (published by Saluzzo, Turin, 1841), and Giovanni Santi his poetical account of the chief artists of his time, among whom, probably from jealousy, he has omitted to mention either Justus of Ghent or Francesco di Giorgio, the latter a man of extraordinarily versatile talents, who was much employed by the duke to design fortifications and military engines, to paint wall decorations, and to carve sculptured ornaments.[2] Though stripped of its art treasures and dismantled of its decorations, the ducal palace still exists in a good state of preservation: it is a very picturesque, massive building of irregular plan, suited to its uneven site, and stands up very nobly on the hill, dominating all the rest of the city.[3] The refined magnificence of Guidubaldo's court is eloquently described by Baldassare CASTIGLIONE (*q.v.*) in his *Cortegiano*. When Henry VII. of England conferred the order of the Garter on Guidubaldo, Count Castiglione was sent to England with a letter of thanks and with the small picture, now in the Louvre, of St George and the Dragon, painted by Raphael[4] in 1504, as a present to the English king. This painting was among Charles I.'s collection which was sold by order of the Commonwealth in 1649.

Throughout the whole of the 16th century the state of Urbino was one of the chief centres for the production of majolica (see POTTERY, vol. xix. p. 625 *sq.*), especially the towns of Gubbio and Castel Durante. Most of the finest pieces of Urbino ware were made specially for the dukes, who covered their sideboards with the rich storied *piatti di pompa*, of which fine specimens have recently sold for from £2000 to £3000.[5] Among the distinguished names which have been associated with Urbino are those of the Ferrarese painter and friend of Raphael, Timoteo della Vite, who spent most of his life there, and Bramante, the greatest architect of his age.[6] The Milanese sculptor, Ambrogino, who worked so much for Federigo, married a lady of Urbino, and was the progenitor of the Baroccio family, among whom were many able mathematicians and painters. Federigo Baroccio, Ambrogino's grandson, was a very popular painter, some of whose works still exist in the cathedral and elsewhere in Urbino. This city was also the birthplace of Pope Clement XI., of several cardinals of the Albano family, and of Bernardino Baldi, Fabretti, and other able scholars.

The modern city of Urbino, with a population of 5087 in 1880, is the seat of an archbishop, and still possesses a small university, but is not a thriving place. The cathedral, a building of no special interest, stands in the great piazza opposite the ducal palace, which is now used for municipal purposes and contains the city archives. In the sacristy there is a very beautiful miniature-like painting of the Scourging of Christ, by Piero della Francesca. One of the finest paintings by this artist is a large altar-piece of the Madonna enthroned between angels and saints, now in the Brera at Milan; it contains a very noble kneeling figure of Federigo in full armour, showing his strange profile disfigured by a bullet, which carried away part of the bridge of his nose. It was originally a votive retable given by the duke to the monastic church of San Bernardino, about a mile outside the walls of Urbino, where Federigo and Guidubaldo were buried. The modest house where Raphael was born and spent his boyhood is still preserved. It is now the property of a society of artists, and so is safe from destruction. Its rooms form a sort of museum of engravings and other records of Raphael's works, together with a picture of the Madonna by his father, Giovanni Santi, formerly thought to be by Raphael himself. The Institute of the Fine Arts in the Marches contains a small but interesting collection of pictures, including works by Giovanni Santi, Justus of Ghent, Timoteo della Vite, and other 15th-century artists. The picture of the Holy Communion by Justus is specially valuable from its containing fine portraits of the Montefeltro family and members of the ducal court. On the walls of the chapel of the guild or confraternity of San Giovanni are some valuable early frescos, painted by Lorenzo da San Severino and his brother, of the Florentine school, about 1416. An interesting collection of Roman inscriptions, arranged by the palæographer Fabretti, is still preserved on the upper walls of a court in the ducal palace. In the church of S. Spirito are two paintings by Luca Signorelli, the Crucifixion and the Day of Pentecost, originally intended for a processional banner. The theatre, decorated by Girolamo Genga, is one of the earliest in Italy; in it was performed the first Italian comedy, the *Calandria* of Cardinal Bibbiena, the friend of Leo X. and Raphael. The magnificent library formed by the Montefeltro and Della Rovere dukes has been removed to Rome.

In addition to works quoted above, see Dennistoun, *Memoirs of the Dukes of Urbino*, London, 1851; Card. di San Clemente, *Memorie concernenti la Città di Urbino*, Rome, 1724; and Sismondi, *Histoire des Républiques Italiennes*, Paris, 1807-8. An interesting view of Urbino, in the first half of the 16th century, occurs among the pen drawings in the MSS. *Arte del Vasajo*, by the potter Piccolpasso, now in the South Kensington Museum. (J. H. M.)

UREA is known chiefly as a component of urine. Referring to the article NUTRITION (vol. xvii. pp. 682-685) for its physiological relations, we consider it here only as a chemical substance. Urea, $CO(NH_2)_2$, was discovered by H. M. Rouelle in 1773; Fourcroy and Vauquelin in 1799 published the first exact investigation on it. In 1828 Wöhler showed that it can be obtained by the union in aqueous solutions of cyanic acid with ammonia, and thus for the first time effected what was then considered an impossibility, namely, the artificial preparation of an organic compound from mineral matter. For the extraction of urea from urine the latter is concentrated by evaporation (more or less, according to its original strength), and then, after cooling, mixed with a large excess of pure[7] nitric acid of 1·4 specific gravity. On standing in the cold most of the urea separates out as a crystalline nitrate, $CO.N_2H_4.HNO_3$, which is collected over glass wool and washed with nitric acid. To convert it into urea, it is treated with water and carbonate of baryta, which acts upon the HNO_3 as if it were present as such, the urea being liberated. The mixed solution of urea and the nitrate is evaporated to a small volume and allowed to stand, when the bulk of the barytic nitrate crystallizes out. The rest is removed by evaporating the mother liquor to dryness over a water-bath and extracting the urea with strong alcohol. To obtain fine crystals, the filtered alcoholic solution is evaporated to dryness, the residual urea dissolved in a very little hot water, and the solution allowed to cool

[1] The works of art from the palace of Urbino were scattered in the 17th century. Two paintings of the Sciences, part of a series executed for Federigo, are now in the National Gallery, London, where they are doubtfully attributed to Melozzo da Forli. Another by Justus of Ghent is in the royal collection at Windsor.

[2] The very high esteem felt for Francesco's personal character and genius by the duke is shown in a letter which Federigo wrote to the commune of Siena; see Ricci, *Storia d' Architettura*, vol. ii. p. 538. His life is given by Vasari, part i.

[3] See Arnold, *Der herzogliche Palast von Urbino*, Leipsic, 1857; and Baldi, *Descrizione del Palazzo Ducale di Urbino*, Rome, 1724.

[4] For Raphael's birth in Urbino, and his subsequent connexion with that town, see RAPHAEL.

[5] The Bargello at Florence and the South Kensington Museum possess the finest collections of Urbino ware.

[6] Much information about Urbino and its crowd of artists is given by Pungileoni, *Elogio Storico di Giov. Santi*, Urbino, 1822.

[7] This word points chiefly to the absence of nitrous acid, which, if present, decomposes its equivalent of urea into nitrogen, water, and carbonic acid, thus:—

$$\underset{\text{Urea}}{CO(NH_2)_2} + \underset{\text{Nitrous acid.}}{2HO.NO} = \underset{\text{Carbonic acid.}}{CO(OH)_2} + \underset{\text{Nitrogen.}}{2N_2} + \underset{\text{Water.}}{2H_2O}.$$

slowly, when part of the urea crystallizes out in long colourless columns, not unlike those of nitrate of potash.

Wöhler's synthetical method for preparative purposes usually assumes the following form. Powdered prussiate of potash (see PRUSSIC ACID) is dehydrated by heating, the anhydrous salt mixed with half its weight of anhydrous binoxide of manganese, and the mixture heated in a flat iron pan until the deflagration, which soon sets in, is completed. The residue now consists of oxides of iron and manganese and of cyanate of potash, NCO.K, formed from the cyanide of potassium of the prussiate by oxidation. The cyanate of potash is extracted by means of the least sufficient quantity of cold water (hot water decomposes the salt, with the formation of ammonia and carbonate of potash), and the solution is mixed at once with the calculated weight of sulphate of ammonia, $1(NH_4)_2SO_4$ for 2NCO.K. The two salts decompose each other into sulphate of potash and cyanate of ammonia; the latter, however, passes spontaneously and almost instantaneously into urea:—

$$\underset{\text{Cyanate of ammonia.}}{NCO.NH_4} = \underset{\text{Urea.}}{CO(NH_2)_2}.$$

The sulphate of potash is eliminated exactly as the nitrate of baryta is in the urine method. That urea is not cyanate of ammonia itself is proved, first by the fact that real cyanate of ammonia (preparable by the union of anhydrous cyanic acid with ammonia gas) is a different substance, and secondly by its not yielding any ammonia when dissolved in cold caustic potash ley. Urea behaves to certain strong acids like a feeble basis, uniting (CON_2H_4 parts) with HNO_3 parts of nitric, $\frac{1}{2}H_2SO_4$ of sulphuric, and $\frac{1}{2}C_2O_4H_2$ of oxalic acid into crystalline salts. As shown by its formula, urea is the amide of carbonic acid: *i.e.*, it is $CO(OH)_2 - 2OH + 2NH_2$, and consequently an anhydride of carbonate of ammonia, $CO(O.NH_4)_2$. An aqueous solution of urea, when heated to 200° in a sealed-up tube, breaks up into carbonic acid and ammonia; and dry carbonate of ammonia, when kept at a certain temperature, suffers partial conversion into urea and water.

Of the many methods for the quantitative determination of the urea in urine, the simplest is to treat a measured volume with excess of solution of hypobromite of soda (a solution of bromine in caustic soda ley) and to measure the volume of nitrogen evolved. By theory $CON_2H_4 + 3NaBrO = 3NaBr + CO_2 + 2H_2O$ (the CO_2 is absorbed by the excess of alkali); but in practice, according to Dupré, through unknown causes only 91 per cent. of the nitrogen is actually evolved, which must be remembered in the calculation of the result.

URGA, a city of Mongolia and the administrative centre of the Northern and Eastern Khalkha tribes, is situated in 48° 20′ N. lat. and 107° 30′ E. long., on the Tola river. The Chinese and Mongolian towns which make up Huræ, as the Mongols call Urga, stand on the high road from Peking to Kiachta (Kiakhta), about 700 miles from the Chinese capital and 165 from Kiachta, and are separated from each other by an interval of 2 or 3 miles. The Chinese town is the great trading quarter, and there the wealth of the district is collected. The houses in this part are more substantially built than in the Mongol town, and the streets have a well-to-do appearance. The population is estimated at about 5000, and the law which prohibits Chinamen from bringing their wives and families into the place tends to check increase. The population of the Mongol quarter is reckoned at about 10,000, though on the occasions of the religious festivals the numbers are much larger. Although trade is not altogether excluded, the *raison d'être* of the town is that it is the residence of the metropolitan of the Khalkha tribes, who ranks third in degree of veneration among the dignitaries of the Lamaist Church. This "resplendently divine lama" resides in a sacred quarter on the western side of the town, and acts as the spiritual colleague of the Chinese lieutenant-general, who controls all mundane matters at Urga itself, and who is also especially charged with the control of the frontier town of Kiachta and the trade conducted there with the Russians. Until quite lately bricks of tea formed the only circulating medium for the retail trade at Urga, but Chinese brass cash are now beginning to pass current in the markets. The temples in the Mongol quarter are numerous and imposing in appearance, and in one is a gilt image of Maitreya Bodhisattva, 33 feet in height and weighing 125 tons. By the Chinese Urga is called K'ulun.

URI,[1] one of the Forest Cantons of Switzerland, ranks as fourth in the Confederation. It comprises the upper basin of the Reuss from its source to the Lake of Lucerne, the southern arm of which is also within the canton. Its total area is 415·4 square miles; of these 184·4 are classed as productive, 40·3 are covered with forests, 44·3 consist of glaciers, and 7·7 of the lake. The highest point in the canton is the Galenstock (11,802 feet). The population in 1880 amounted to 23,694 (men having a majority of 3000 over women), showing an increase of 7649, or 39·4 per cent., since 1870, owing to the St Gotthard Railway. German is the native tongue of 18,024 persons, Italian of 5313. The canton has always been very strongly Roman Catholic (23,149 in 1880). It was included up to 1814 in the diocese of Constance (except the valley of Urseren, which was in that of Chur), and since then has formed part of no diocese, but is provisionally administered by the bishop of Chur. In Uri the limits of the ecclesiastical parishes are the same as those of the civil communes. The capital is Altdorf (2901 inhabitants). Göschenen (2990) and Wasen (2744) have increased since the opening of the St Gotthard Railway (1880), which runs through the greater part of the canton. The inhabitants are occupied in agricultural and pastoral pursuits, and are very saving and industrious. The main valley is fertile, but the side glens are very wild. Education is still very backward and largely in the hands of the priests; but an improvement was made in 1885. The main characteristics of the people are extreme conservatism and a passionate attachment to their religion.

Uri is first mentioned in history in 732 as the place to which Eto, abbot of Reichenau, was banished. For the early history of the canton, see SWITZERLAND, vol. xxii. pp. 783-787. In 1410 a perpetual alliance was made with the upper valley of Urseren or Val Orsera, the latter being allowed its own headman and assembly, and courts under those of Uri, with which it was not fully incorporated till 1803. In 1440 Uri alone won the Val Leventina for good, the title being confirmed by a treaty of 1466 with the duke of Milan and by the bloody fight of Giornico (1478). At the Reformation, Uri clung to the old faith (see SWITZERLAND, vol. xxii. pp. 790-791). In 1798 on the formation of the Helvetic republic Uri lost all its Italian possessions. In September 1799 Suwaroff and the Russian army, having crossed the St Gotthard to Altdorf, were forced by the French to pass over into Schwyz, instead of sailing down the lake to Lucerne. In 1803 Uri became an independent canton again, with Urseren, but without the Val Leventina. It tried hard to bring back the old state of things in 1814-15, and opposed all attempts at reform, joining the League of Sarnen in 1832 to maintain the pact of 1815, opposing the proposed revision of the pact, and being one of the members of the Sonderbund in 1843. Despite defeat in the war of 1847, Uri voted against the federal constitution of 1848, and by a crushing majority against that of 1874. The existing constitution of Uri is that framed in 1850 and amended in 1851, 1872, 1879, and 1881. The "landesgemeinde," composed of all male citizens of twenty years of age, meets annually on 1st May, and is the supreme legislative assembly. There is a subordinate legislative assembly (landrath), consisting of the landammann or headman and his deputy, 4 of the members of the executive, and 70 elected members (1 for every 300 of the population), which drafts bills and passes laws provisionally in case of necessity. The executive consists of 9 members—the landammann, his deputy, and the treasurer, with 6 elected members. By an immemorial custom 7 men of 7 different families, bearing different names, can cause an extraordinary meeting of the assembly of their "gemeinde" to be summoned, or call on the landrath to do the same in the case of the "landesgemeinde."

See K. F. Lusser's *Gesch. des Kantons Uri* (1862).

URIC ACID, as explained fully in the article NUTRITION (vol. xvii. p. 683), is one of the penultimate products of the tissue waste in the human body. While the bulk of the nitrogen of the albuminoids passes off through the bladder as UREA (*q.v.*), a small portion of it stops at the uric acid stage. Human urine contains only a fraction of a per cent. of the acid, chiefly as soda salt; abundance of

[1] The name is probably connected with the same obscure root as Urseren and Reuss, and is popularly derived from *Urochs*, "wild bull," a bull's head having been for ages borne on the cantonal shield.

uric acid is met with in the excrement of serpents and birds, with whom it is the principal nitrogenous product of tissue waste. For the preparation of uric acid ($C_5H_4N_4O_3$), GUANO (*q.v.*) is boiled repeatedly with a solution of borax in 120 parts of water. The filtered solution is acidified with hydrochloric acid, when impure uric acid separates out as a brown precipitate, which is washed with cold water. For its purification it is dissolved in hot dilute caustic potash or soda ley, the solution filtered, and the filtrate saturated with carbonic acid. An almost insoluble acid urate of alkali separates out, which is collected on a filter, washed, and decomposed by adding it in instalments to hot dilute hydrochloric acid. Uric acid separates out as a white precipitate, which is filtered off, washed, and dried, to be re-purified by a repetition of the alkali process or otherwise. Pure uric acid forms a snow-white micro-crystalline powder, devoid of smell or taste, soluble in 1800 parts of boiling and in 14,000 parts of cold water, but insoluble in alcohol and in ether. When heated it suffers complete decomposition.

For its detection in urine, the urine is mixed with excess of hydrochloric acid, and allowed to stand, when the uric acid separates out, generally coloured reddish by impurities. To identify the precipitate, it is dissolved in a few drops of nitric acid on a watch-glass, and the solution cautiously evaporated to dryness. The residue, if exposed to ammonia gas as it comes off from the stopper of a liquor ammoniæ bottle, assumes the intense purple colour of "murexide."

Urates.—Uric acid dissolves in excess of caustic potash ley as dipotassic salt, $C_5H_2K_2N_4O_3$, soluble in 44 parts of cold water, with the formation of a strongly alkaline solution. On the saturation of the solution with carbonic acid one-half of the potash is eliminated as bicarbonate, and a neutral salt, $C_5H_3KN_4O_3$, comes down as a precipitate, soluble in 800 parts of cold water. Soda and the alkaline earths behave similarly. But more interesting than its salts are the numerous derivatives obtainable from it, chiefly by the action of oxidizing agents. Most of these were discovered and investigated by Liebig and Wöhler in a classical research published in 1838. From 1861 to 1863 Adolf Bäyer supplemented their work by important new discoveries. He showed that all those metamorphoses of uric acid fall in naturally with the assumption that the molecule of uric acid consists of two urea rests—(NH)(CO)(NH)—united each by its two nitrogen affinities with a tricarbon group, (C_3O), by carbon affinities of the latter. To give an example of the practical meaning of the theory,—if uric acid is oxidized cautiously with nitric acid, one of the urea rests by uniting with the 2H of an H_2O is split off as urea, while the rest unites with the oxygen of the H_2O and other $O + H_2O$ into alloxan,—

$$\underbrace{(HN) - (CO \cdot C(OH)_2 \cdot CO) - (NH)}_{CO},$$

the ureid of mesoxalic acid, $HO - (CO \cdot C(OH)_2 \cdot CO) - OH$. On the application of more energetic oxidizing agents, that one urea rest still survives, but the tricarbon nucleus burns down into C_2O_2, the radical of oxalic acid, with formation of parabanic acid,

$$\underbrace{(HN) - (C_2O_2) - (NH)}_{CO},$$

the ureid of oxalic acid, $HO(C_2O_2)OH$.

URINE. See UREA and URIC ACID; also NUTRITION, vol. xvii. pp. 682-684.

URMIA, or URUMIAH, a town of Persia, in the province of Azerbijan (Adarbaijan), lies 112 miles south-west of Tabriz and 10 from the west side of Lake Urmia, in the midst of an extremely fertile, highly cultivated, and densely peopled plain. Within the enclosures, consisting of a wall and deep ditch that can be flooded, there is a mixed Mohammedan and Christian population of from 25,000 to 30,000, while the surrounding district is studded with over 300 populous villages. Some of the streets are broader than is usual in Oriental towns and several are traversed by running water; but, beyond a busy bazaar and two or three old mosques, there is nothing of any interest. The chief industries are weaving, dyeing, and especially tillage, abundant crops of rice, melons, cotton, and excellent tobacco being raised in the neighbourhood. Urmia has for many years been the centre of an American mission, which has had considerable success, especially amongst the so-called "Chaldean" or Nestorian Christians. According to an old tradition, Urmia was the birthplace of Zoroaster.

The lake, which takes its name from the town, and which is also known as the Daria-cha, or "Little Sea," is a completely landlocked basin, filling a shallow depression at the east foot of the Kurdish Highlands, but still about 5000 feet above sea-level. It is 90 miles long north and south, 30 miles broad, and 250 round, with a total area of 1600 square miles, but a mean depth of not more than 10 or 12 feet (45 in the deepest part sounded by Monteith), so that the whole volume is at least six times less than that of the much smaller lake of Geneva. There are as many as fifty-six islands, grouped chiefly towards the south, the largest 5 miles by 2, the smallest mere rocks, and none permanently inhabited, although they are tilled or used for grazing horses and sheep in winter. Although fed by numerous streams, the lake is intensely saline, more so even than the Dead Sea, and is consequently inhabited by no fish or other aquatic fauna, except a peculiar species of small crustacean, which affords abundant food to numerous swans and other wild-fowl. The salt, which forms extensive incrustations some inches thick round about the shelving north-eastern and southern shores, appears to be derived from Tertiary beds (Dr E. Tietze), and the geological formation appears to resemble that of Lake Niris in southern Persia (Blanford). The whole lacustrine basin, including the farthest sources of its influents, has an area of about 20,000 square miles, and the flooded part stood formerly at a much higher level than at present, as is shown by the watermarks on the encircling heights, and by the Shahi peninsula in the north-east, which at one time was certainly an island. In recent years the evaporation has on the whole balanced the inflow, although the lake is now said to be slightly rising, owing to the larger discharge from the Jaghatu and Tatau, which were formerly to a great extent absorbed in irrigating the southern Miandab plain. Near the Selmas river and at the village of Dihkergan in the south-east occur the famous "marble springs," yielding the pink, yellow, and white "marble of Tabriz," used for ornamenting many public buildings throughout western Asia.

URQUHART, or URCHARD,[1] SIR THOMAS (*c.* 1605-1660), one of the most original and raciest translators from any foreign language into English, was the son of Sir Thomas Urquhart of Cromarty, the representative of a very ancient family, and of Christian, daughter of the fourth Lord Elphinstone. His birth-year is uncertain, but it is guessed at 1605, and his birthplace was the old mansion-house of Cromarty. Not much is known of his youth, or indeed of any part of his life; but he was certainly well educated, travelled over Europe, succeeded to a considerable, though much embarrassed inheritance, and got together a remarkable library, which, however, fell into the hands of his creditors. All his later life was disturbed by pecuniary and political difficulties. He was an enthusiastic Royalist; and, so far as religious matters went, his principles may be judged from his favourite signature, "C. P.," for Christianus Presbyteromastix. He took part in the "Trot of Turriff" in 1639, and was rewarded by being knighted on 7th April 1641 by the king's own hand at Whitehall. He took occasion by this visit to London to see through the press his first work, a collection of *Epigrams* of no great merit. Four years later, in 1645, he produced a tract called *Trissotetras*, a treatise on logarithms, adjusted to a kind of memoria technica, like that of the scholastic logic. In 1649 he was proclaimed a rebei and traitor at the Cross of Edinburgh; but this does not seem to have done him much harm, and, though he took part in the march to Worcester, and was there wounded and taken prisoner, his always embarrassed affairs do not seem to have been much worsened thereby. He published in rapid succession during 1652 and 1653 a series of tracts with quaint titles and quainter contents. *Pantochronochanon* (sic) is an almost unbelievable genealogy of the house of Urquhart up to Adam, with the names extemporized for the earlier ages in a kind of gibberish, which seems to be after the pattern of the giants and heathens in the *Amadis*. *Ecskubalauron*, supposed to be a treatise on the virtues of a jewel found in the streets of Worcester, is in reality a rather elaborate treatise on the virtues of the Scottish character, as shown in the Admirable Crichton

[1] So spelt on the title page of his first work.

and others. Finally, *Logopandecteision* handles the subject of a universal language. These original works of Urquhart's, as far as intrinsic literary merits go, are not of much account; but they show perhaps better than anything else that singular mixture of patriotism, generosity, shrewdness, humour, with prejudice, almost insane family pride, crotchet, pedantry, and apparent insensibility to some kinds of the ridiculous which was the dominant characteristic of a certain part of the Scottish nation, and which has furnished Sir Walter Scott with some of his most matchless studies and touches. The *Translation of Rabelais*, which Urquhart produced in 1653, is a very different work from the literary point of view, entering into and reproducing the author's spirit with wonderful success, and, though by no means technically faithful, far excelling in value all merely faithful versions. Next to nothing is known of Urquhart after its date; it is said that he sought a refuge, like other cavaliers, on the Continent, and died (1660) of a fit of laughing, brought on by joy at hearing of the Restoration.

His original *Works*, with such scanty particulars of his life as are known, and with reproductions of two original and curious frontispieces, which represent him as a handsome and dandified wearer of full cavalier costume, were published in a stately quarto volume by the Maitland Club (Edinburgh, 1834). The Rabelais has been repeatedly reprinted, and with Motteux's additions forms the substance of *Gargantua and Pantagruel* in Bohn's Extra Series.

URSINUS, ZACHARIAS (1534-1583), German theologian, and one of the authors of the *Heidelberg Catechism* (see vol. v. p. 219), was a native of Breslau, and became a disciple of Melanchthon at Wittenberg. He afterwards studied divinity at Geneva under Calvin and Hebrew at Paris under Mercier. In 1561 he was appointed professor in the Collegium Sapientiæ at Heidelberg, where in 1563 at the instance of the elector-palatine, Frederick III., he drew up the *Catechism* in cooperation with Kaspar Olevian. The death of the elector in 1577 led to the removal of Ursinus, who from 1578 till his death in 1583 occupied a professorial chair at Neustadt-an-der-Haardt. His *Works* were published in 1587-89, and a more complete edition by his son and two of his pupils, Pareus and Reuterus, in 1612.

URSULA, ST, and her companions, virgins and martyrs, are commemorated by the Roman Church on 21st October. The *Breviary* gives no legend; but in current works, such as Butler's *Lives of the Saints*, it is to the effect that "these holy martyrs seem . . . to have met a glorious death in defence of their virginity from the army of the Huns. . . . They came originally from Britain, and Ursula was the conductor and encourager of the holy troop." The scene of the martyrdom is placed near the lower Rhine.

The date has been assigned by different writers to 238, *c.* 283, and *c.* 451. The story, however, is unknown both to Jerome and to Gregory of Tours—and this though the latter gives a somewhat detailed description of the Cologne church dedicated to that Theban legion with which the tradition of the martyred virgins was very early associated. The story of their fate is not entered under 21st October in the martyrology of Bede (*ob. c.* 735), of Ado (*c.* 858), of Usuard (*ante* 877), Notker Balbulus (896), or Hrabanus Maurus (845); but a 9th-century life of St Cunibert (*ob.* 663) associates a prominent incident in the life of this saint with the basilica of the sacred virgins at Cologne (Surius, vi. 275, ed. 1575). Not only does Archbishop Wichfrid attest a grant to the church of the sacred virgins outside the walls of Cologne (in 927), but he was a large donor in his own person. Still earlier a Cologne martyrology, written, as Binterim plausibly urges, between 889 and 891, has the following entry under 21st October: "xi. virg. Ursule Sencie Gregorie Pinose Marthe Saule Britule Satnine Rabacie Saturie Paladie." Much shorter entries are found in two of the old martyrologies printed in Migne (cxxxviii. 1207, 1275). A more definite allusion to the legend may be found (*c.* 847) in Wandelbert's metrical martyrology (21st October):

"Tunc numerosa simul Rheni per littora fulgent
Christi virgineis erecta tropæa maniplis
Agrippinæ urbi, quarum furor impius olim
Millia mactavit ductricibus inclyta sanctis."

The full legend first makes its appearance in a festival discourse (*sermo*) for 21st October, written, as internal evidence seems to show, between 731 and 839. This *sermo* does not mention St Ursula, but makes Pinnosa or Vinnosa the leader of these spiritual "amazons," who, to avoid Maximian's persecution, left their island home of Britain, following their bridegroom Christ towards that East whence their faith had come a hundred years before. The concurrent traditions of Britain, Batavia (where many chapels still preserved their memory), and Cologne are called in evidence to prove the same origin. The legend was already very old and the festival "nobis omni tempore celeberrima"; but, as all written documents had disappeared since the burning of the early church erected over the sacred bones, the preacher could only appeal to the continuous and careful memory of the society to which he belonged (*nostrates*). Even in his time there were sceptics who pointed dubiously to the full-grown bones of "widows" and of men among the so-called virgin relics. But to *a priori* reasoners who mocked at the notion of gathering so large a band of virgins in one place there was a triumphant answer ready: if Christ, while yet a man on earth, could summon "twelve legions of angels" to his aid, surely we could allow that a meagre band of "less than 12,000 virgins might follow the stainless lamb" in heaven. The author of the *sermo* pointedly rejects the two theories that connected the holy virgins with the Theban band and brought them as pilgrims from the East to the West; but he adds that even in his days there still existed an inscription in the church, showing how it had been restored from its foundations by a certain "Clematius, vir consularis, ex partibus Orientis."

Two or three centuries later the *Passio XI. MM. SS. Virginum*, based apparently on the revelations made to Helentrude, a nun of Heerse near Paderborn, gives a wonderful increase of detail. The narrative in its present form may date somewhere between 900 and 1100, while Helentrude apparently flourished before 1050. According to her account, the son of a powerful pagan king demands in marriage Ursula, the beautiful daughter of Deonotus, a king "in partibus Britanniæ." Ursula is warned by a dream to demand a respite of three years, during which time her companions are to be 11,000 virgins collected from both kingdoms. After vigorous exercise in all kinds of manly sports to the admiration of the populace, they are carried off by a sudden breeze in eleven triremes to Thiel in Guelderland on the Waal. Thence they sail up the Rhine by way of Cologne to Basel, at which place they make fast their vessels and proceed on foot to Rome. Returning, they re-enter their ships at Basel, but are slaughtered by the Huns when they reach Cologne. Their relics are then collected and buried "sicut hodie illic est cernere," in a spot where "to this day" no meaner sepulture is permitted. Then follows the usual allusion to Clematius; the date is expressly fixed at 238; and the whole revelation is seemingly ascribed to St Cordula, one of the eleven thousand, who, after escaping death on the first day by hiding in one of the vessels, on the morrow gave herself up to death of her own accord. Towards the beginning of the 12th century Sigebert of Gembloux (*ob.* 1112) gives a brief *résumé* of the same story. He is the first to introduce the name of Attila, and dates the occurrence 453.

Passing over the visions and exhumations of the first half of the 12th century, we come to the singular revelations of St Elizabeth of Schönau. These revelations, delivered in Latin, German, or a mixed jargon of both languages, were turned into simple Latin by Elizabeth's brother Egbert, from whose words it would seem that in 1156 an old burial ground had lately been laid open near Cologne. The cemetery was naturally associated with the legend of St Ursula; and, this identification once accepted, it is not unlikely that, when more careful investigation revealed male skeletons and tombstones bearing the names of men, other and more definite epitaphs were invented to reconcile the old traditions with the facts of such a damaging discovery. Hence perhaps the barefaced imposture: "Cyriacus, papa Romanus, qui cum gaudio suscepit sanctas virgines et cum eis Coloniam reversus martyrium suscepit." One or two circumstantial forgeries of this kind would form the basis of a scheme for explaining not a few other problems of the case, such as the plain inscription "Jacobus," whom St Elizabeth promptly transformed into a supposititious British archbishop of Antioch, brother to the equally imaginary British Pope Cyriacus. For these epitaphs, with others of a humbler kind, were brought before St Elizabeth to be identified in her ecstatic converse with St Verena, her cousin St Ursula, and others. Elizabeth herself at times distrusted her own revelations: there was no Cyriac in the list of the popes; Antherus, who was said to be his successor (235-236), died more than two centuries before Attila, to whom common report assigned the massacre; and it was hardly credible that James of Antioch could cut eleven thousand epitaphs in less than three days. Every doubt, however, was met by the invention of a new and still more improbable detail. According to St Verena, the virgins suffered when Maximus and "Africanus" were *principes* at Rome (? 387-388).

In 1183 the mantle of St Elizabeth fell upon Hermann Joseph, a Præmonstratensian canon at Steinfeld. He had to solve a more difficult problem than St Elizabeth's; for the skeletons of little children, ranging in age from two months to seven years, had now been found buried with the sacred virgins. But even such a difficulty Hermann explains away as readily as he does the fact of his having changed St Elizabeth's name for the royal bridegroom from Ætherius to Holofernes: the prince in question had two names, and the little children were brothers, sisters, or more distant relatives of the eleven thousand. Hermann's revelations are mainly taken up with an attempt to show the mutual relationship of nearly all the characters he introduces. The names are a most extraordinary mixture. Among British bishops we have Michael William, James, and Columbanus. Sovereign princes,—an Oliver, a Clovis, and a Pippin,—start out in every page, till the writer finds it necessary to apologize for the number of his kings and his own blunders. But, for all this, Hermann exposes his own doubts when he tells that often, as he was preparing to write, he heard a voice bidding him lay down the pen, "for whatever you write will be an unmixed lie." Hermann makes St Ursula a native of Brittany, and so approximates to the version of the story given by Geoffrey of Monmouth (*Historia Britonum*), according to whom Maximian, after fleeing from Rome, and acquiring Britain by marriage, proceeds to conquer Brittany and settle it with men from the island opposite. For these settlers he has to find British wives, and to this end collects 11,000 noble and 60,000 plebeian virgins, who are wrecked on their passage across. Certain of the vessels being driven upon "barbarous islands," their passengers are slain by Guanius and Melga, "kings of the Huns and Picts," whom Gratian had called in to his aid against Maximian. In this version St Ursula is a daughter of Dionotus, king of Cornwall. Hermann alludes more than once to the *Historia Britonum*, and even to King Arthur.

The legend of St Ursula is perhaps the most curious instance of the development of an ecclesiastical myth. We know, however, too little about its earlier stages to justify any serious attempt at estimating what amount of historic truth underlies it, and it is doubtful whether many of the efforts in this direction do not make a larger demand on human credulity than the legend itself. Even in the earliest form known to us this legend is probably the complex growth of centuries, and any claim to the discovery of the first germ can hardly approve itself to the historic sense. These remarks apply especially to that venerable rationalization which evolves the whole legend from a misreading of *Undecimilla* into *undecim millia*. A more modern theory makes St Ursula the Christianized representative of the old Teutonic goddess Freya, who, in Thuringia, under the name of Hörsel, welcomed the souls of dead maidens. Not a few singular coincidences seem to point in the same direction, especially the two virgins, "Martha and Saula," whom Usuard states to have suffered "cum aliis pluribus" on 20th October, whence they were probably transferred to 21st October. It is curious to note that Jerome and many of the earliest martyrologies extant have on 21st October the entry "Dasius Zoticus, Gaius *cum duodecim militibus*." Even in copies of Jerome this is transformed into *millibus*; and it is perhaps not impossible that to this misreading we may indirectly owe the "thousands" in the Ursula legend. So far as is known to the present writer, the two entries are mutually exclusive in all the early martyrologies mentioned in this article, and in those printed in Migne, cxxxvii. The earlier "Dasius" entry seems to disappear steadily, though slowly, as the Ursula legend works its way into current martyrologies.

See Crombach, *Vita et Martyrium S. Ursulæ*, Cologne, 1647, and the Bollandist *Acta Sanctorum*, 21st October. The rationalization of the story is to be found in Oscar Schade's *Die Sage von der heiligen Ursula*, Hanover, 1854, of which there is a short *résumé* in Baring-Gould's *Lives of the Saints*. Schade's results seem to be now generally accepted. (T. A. A.)

URSULINES, a religious order founded at Brescia by Angela de Merici[1] in 1537, primarily for the education of girls. It was approved in 1544 by Paul III., and in 1572 Gregory XIII., at the instance of Charles Borromeo, made enclosure obligatory and declared it a religious order under the rule of St Augustine. In the following century it was powerfully encouraged and supported by St Francis de Sales; and towards the beginning of the 18th century, the period of its greatest prosperity, the order embraced some 20 congregations, with 350 convents and from 15,000 to 20,000 nuns. It still has some importance and possesses about 36 convents in Germany and Austria alone.

Plate I.

URUGUAY. The republic of Uruguay, officially known as the Oriental Republic of the Uruguay, and long locally called the Banda Oriental (meaning the land on the eastern side of the large river from which the country takes its modern name), is the smallest independent state in South America. It runs conterminous with the southern border o. the empire of Brazil and lies between 30° and 35° S. lat. and 53° 25′ and 57° 42′ W. long.; its area is 73,185 square miles. The country is in some sense a peninsula, having a seaboard on the Atlantic Ocean of 120 miles, a shore line to the south on the river Plate of 235 miles, and another of 270 miles along the Uruguay on the west. The boundaries separating it from Rio Grande do Sul, a province of Brazil, are Lake Mirim, the rivers Chuy, Yaguaron, and Cuareim, and a *cuchilla* or low range of hills called Santa Ana. The extent of the northern frontier from the Cuareim to the bar of the Chuy on the coast of the Atlantic is 450 miles.

Boundaries.

Rivers.

Uruguay is intersected nearly from west to north-east by the river Negro and its affluent the Yi. The Uruguay (see Plate River, vol. xix. p. 187) is navigable all the year by steamers from the island of Martin Garcia at the mouth to Salto (200 miles). Above this place the navigation is interrupted by rapids. The ordinary volume of water in the Uruguay averages 11 millions of cubic feet per minute. The Negro, of which the principal port is the city of Mercedes, is the only important and to any practical extent navigable inland river. Others are navigable for short distances and by steamers of light draught. Besides the rivers mentioned, the chief streams are the Santa Lucia, which falls into the Plate a little west of Montevideo; the Queguay in Paysandú; and the Cebollati, rising in the sierras in Minas and flowing into Lake Mirim. These rivers as well as the Uruguay are fed by innumerable smaller streams or "arroyos," many of which have the importance and sometimes the names of rivers, such as the Arapey in Salto, the Dayman in Paysandú, the Yaguary (an affluent of the Negro) in Tacuarembó, the Arroyo Grande between the departments of Soriano and San José, and the San José (an affluent of the Santa Lucia).

Mountains.

None of the sierras or mountains in Uruguay exceed (or perhaps even attain) a height of 2000 feet; but, contrasting in their tawny colour with the grassy undulating plains, they loom up high and are often picturesque. They are ramifications of a range which, breaking away from the Andes in about 20° S. lat., reaches the frontier of Uruguay in 32°. Here the chain divides, forming the Cuchilla de Haedo on the north and west and the Cuchilla Grande on the south and east. In the departments of Minas and Maldonado the second range takes the name of the Ghost Mountains. No accurate geological survey has yet been made, but it is known that the hills in the north are chiefly gneiss and granite and in other parts porphyry and sandstone. The hilly districts in the north and east contain minerals of many kinds, including gold, lead, copper, agate, amethyst, alabaster, and marble. The limestone, granite, and marble quarries have some commercial value; but so far little progress has been made in the working of metallic veins. For the gold mines, see below.

The seat of government is the city of Montevideo (*q.v.*) at the entrance of the river Plate. The harbour and roadstead of that port form the only good natural refuge for shipping for hundreds of miles south of Rio de Janeiro.

Climate.

Uruguay has a healthy climate. Endemic diseases are unknown and epidemics are rare. According to the tables of mortality for 1882, out of a total of 9640 deaths 45 were of persons over 100 years of age. In the interior, away from the sea and the shores of the great rivers, the temperature frequently rises in summer as high as 86° Fahr. and in winter falls as low as 35°·6 Fahr. In the districts bordering on the coast the thermometer seldom falls below 37°; and only for a few moments and at long intervals has it been known to rise as high as 105°. The annual rainfall is stated to be more than twice that of Paris (19·68 inches). This arises not from the frequency of rain but from the greater quantity which falls in a given time. Observations made during the years 1842 to 1852 inclusive showed that there were in Montevideo in the summer season—November, December, and January—70·1 fine days, 14·1 cloudy, and 6·1 wet; in winter—May, June, and July—there were 54·3 fine, 27·1 cloudy, and 10·6 wet days.

[1] Born 1470, died 1540, canonized 1807.

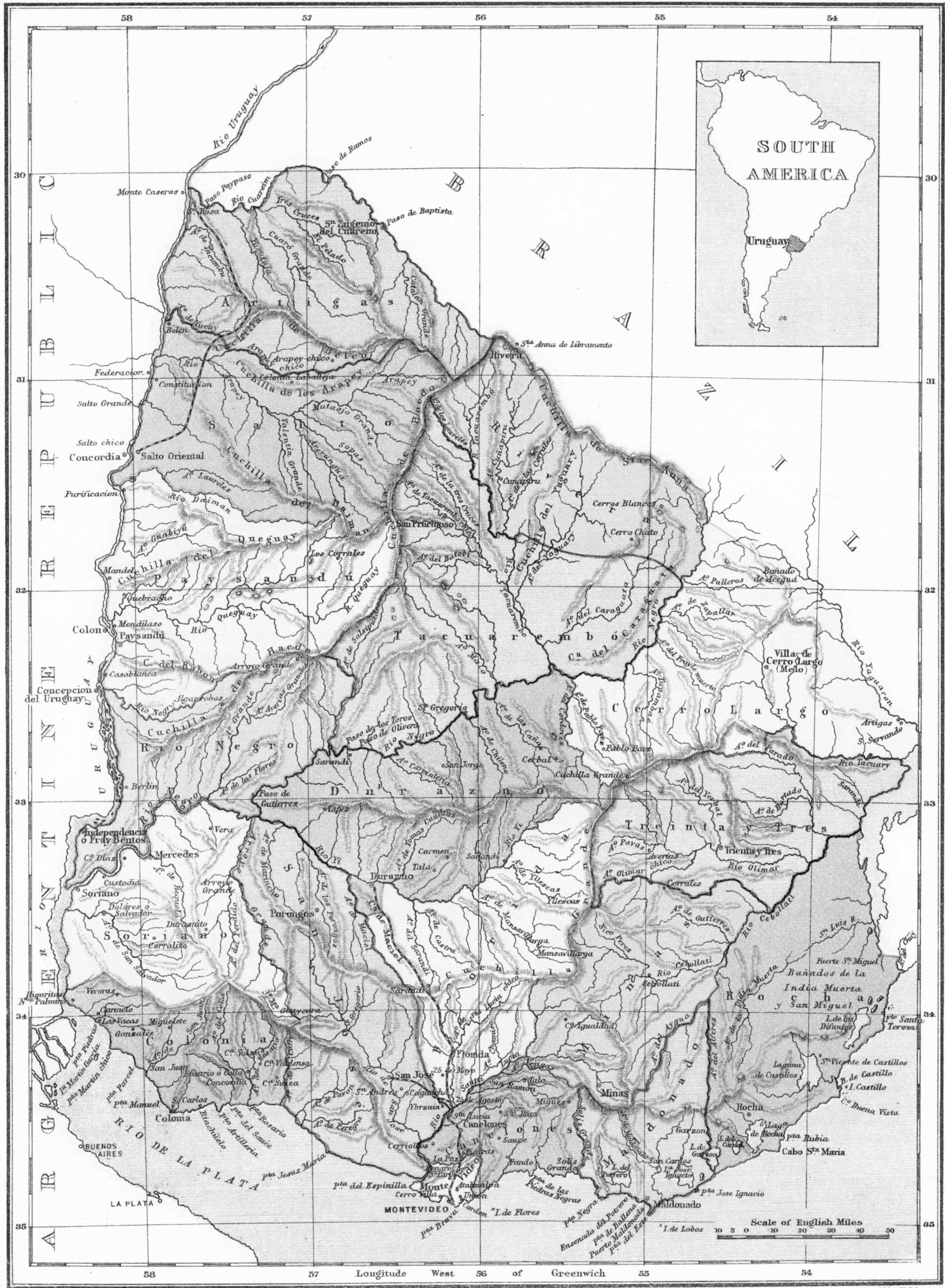

W. & A. K. Johnston.

Flora.

The pastoral wealth of Uruguay as of the neighbouring Argentine Republic is due to the fertilizing constituents of "pampa mud," geologically associated with gigantic antediluvian animals, whose fossil remains are found abundantly in those regions. The country is rich in hard woods, suitable for cabinet work and certain building purposes. The principal trees are the alder, aloe, palm, poplar, acacia, willow, and eucalyptus (recently introduced). The "montes," by which are understood plantations as well as native thickets, produce amongst other woods the algarrobo, a poor imitation of oak; the guayabo, a substitute for boxwood; the quebracho, of which the red kind is compared to sandalwood; and the urunday, black and white, not unlike rosewood. Indigenous palms grow in the valleys of the Sierra José Ignacio, also to some extent in the departments of Minas, Maldonado, and Paysandú. The myrtle, rosemary, mimosa, and the scarlet-flowered ceibo are amongst the plants commonly seen. The valleys within the hill ranges are fragrant with aromatic shrubs. In the plains below the swards are gay with the scarlet and white verbena and other wild flowers of brilliant hues. The country abounds in medicinal plants. The sarsaparilla even colours the water of the Rio Negro and gives to it its name—the "black river."

Fauna.

Amongst the wild animals the tiger or ounce—called in the Guaraní language the "ja-guá" or "big dog"—and the puma are found on the frontier of Brazil and on the wooded islets and banks of the larger rivers. The tapir, fox, deer, wild cat, wild dog, carpincho or water hog, and a few small rodents nearly complete the list of quadrupeds. A little armadillo, the mulita, must be mentioned as the living representative of the antediluvian giants, the mylodon, mastodon, megatherium, &c. The ostrich—*Rhea americana*—roams everywhere in the plains; and there are a few specimens of the vulture tribe, a native crow (lean, tall, and ruffed), partridges, and quails. Parakeets are plentiful in the "montes," and the lagoons swarm with waterfowl of all descriptions. The most esteemed is the "pato real," a large duck. Of the birds of bright plumage the humming bird and the cardinal—the scarlet, the yellow, and the white—are the most attractive. The fish of the lagoons and streams are coarse, and some of them primitive in type; but two or three kinds, found generally in the large rivers, are much prized. The varieties of fish on the sea coast are many and excellent; 130 species are known. More than 2000 species of insects have been classified. The scorpion is rarely seen; but large and venomous spiders are common. The principal reptiles are a lizard, a tortoise, the "vivora de la cruz," a dangerous viper, so called from marks like a cross on its head, and the rattlesnake, this last in Maldonado and the stony lands of Las Minas.

Population.

At the commencement of the 19th century the population of Montevideo and the surrounding territory was estimated by Azara at 30,000, one-half of these being given to the city of Montevideo. This total seems not to have included what remained of the indigenous inhabitants in the north and west, though the Indian population of the Jesuit missions before these were destroyed, about the year 1767, was known to be very numerous. But the aborigines have now completely disappeared. They have been supplanted by half-breeds, from whom the class known as gauchos are mostly recruited. The gauchos are now being supplanted by European immigrants and their progeny. In 1829, the epoch of the declaration of independence, the population is stated to have numbered 74,000, and in 1852, after the great war, 131,969. In 1860 the number had risen to 221,300 and in 1873 to 450,000. Comparatively recent estimates place it between 450,000 and 700,000, the latest official estimate being 551,768; but no formal census has yet been taken. In the eighteen departments of the state the proportion of foreigners is 25·41 per cent. of the population (in the department of Montevideo 42·29 per cent. and in the others 24·66 per cent.), consisting of 39,780 Spaniards, 36,303 Italians, 20,178 Brazilians, 15,546 Argentinians, 14,375 French (principally Basques), 2772 English, 2125 Germans, and 9143 of other nations. The density of the population in the metropolitan department is 365 inhabitants per square mile; in the whole republic it is 4·83, in the agricultural department of Canelones 27·37, and in the remote departments of Tacuarembó and Rivera about 1·6. In respect of numbers the males have a slight preponderance over the females. Of the children 20·23 per cent. are illegitimate, in the metropolitan department 7·73 and in the rural departments 23·24. Illegitimate births have recently decreased, a fact which may be explained by the institution of civil marriage and by the appointment of registrars in the remote country districts. Marriages take place at the rate of 6·8 per 1000. The death-rate is only 16·5 per 1000.

Administrative divisions.

The country is divided into eighteen departments, of which that of Montevideo is the smallest, although it contains one-fourth of the total population. Adjoining this is Canelones; and in a northerly direction are those of Florida, Durazno, Tacuarembó, and Rivera, the last-named bordering on Brazil. To the eastward on the Atlantic are Maldonado and Rocha, and north and west of these Minas, Treinta y Tres, and Cerro Largo. To the west, along the Plate and Uruguay, are San José, Colonia, Soriano, Rio Negro, and Paysandú; and farther north towards the Brazilian frontier are Salto and Artigas. The principal inland town is San José. The chief ports, besides Montevideo, are Salto, Paysandú, Fray Bentos, Mercedes, Colonia, and Maldonado.

Agriculture and industry.

More than two centuries ago the Banda Oriental was looked upon by the Spanish colonies on the opposite banks of the Plate and Uruguay as a station for the breeding of live stock and the cutting of timber and firewood. And at this day, in spite of the thriving foreign trade of Montevideo, it still partakes largely of this character. It boasts of 20,000,000 sheep—perhaps 14,000,000 would be nearer the mark—and 8,000,000 head of cattle. The country being in general pastoral, sheep and cattle grazing is the main occupation of the people; the sheep flourish best in the southern and western departments, whilst the principal cattle districts are towards the north and east. More than two-thirds of the public wealth, estimated variously between £80,000,000 and £120,000,000, consist of land, live stock, and rural properties. Ninety-six per cent. of the exports of the country consists of live stock and their produce—wool, hides, horns, hair, sheepskins, tallow, grease, bones, bone-ash, and jerked beef. More than half the fixed property and commercial capital is in the hands of foreigners. At Fray Bentos, in the department of Rio Negro, is the Liebig factory of extract of meat; at Colonia there is a branch of the River Plate Frozen Meat Company. But, apart from these, and some breweries, flour-mills, tanneries, establishments in Montevideo for the making of boots and shoes and clothing, and a few local industries, unnaturally fostered by high import duties, there are no manufactures to speak of. Agriculture is still in a promising infancy. Latterly it has made great strides; yet the export of agricultural produce appears to be relatively insignificant. At intervals during the last twenty years agricultural settlements (colonies) have been established with great success in different departments, but principally in Colonia, where the settlers are mostly Italians and Swiss. These prosperous colonies have already in Colonia outgrown the space originally allotted; but owing to the irregular and illegal appropriation of the public lands there is no more land to bestow on settlers, native or foreign, except at the exorbitant rates demanded by private owners and speculators.

Minerals.

At Cuñapirú in Tacuarembó gold was accidentally discovered in 1842. The mines have been worked at intervals since 1867, but, partly owing to difficulties of communication, with indifferent success. But gold-mining seems to have lately assumed a more hopeful aspect, owing to the employment of improved and economical machinery introduced by a French company. The metals of Uruguay are found in two quite distinct systems of hills. The Cuñapirú mines are in the Santa Ana range, the auriferous quartz being found in thin layers embedded in rocks of red porphyry. The formation of the system in general resembles that of the gold-producing regions in Brazil, California, and Australia. The Pan de Azucar (Sugar-Loaf Mountain), near the south coast of Maldonado, forms the extremity of a second system, which has its origin as far north as Pernambuco in Brazil; as developed in Uruguay it is Huronian, limestone and slate being superposed on the gneiss and granite. The metals of this system are principally silver, lead, copper, and an argentiferous lead, which in earlier times the Spaniards mistook for silver. Two copper mines at the foot of the Pan de Azucar are now in active operation.

Commerce.

Since the beginning of the 19th century the value of the exports and imports has increased twenty-fold, and with some relapses has more than doubled in the last twenty years. In 1881 the total value was £8,116,680, and in 1885 £10,750,747. The value of the exports is always a little in excess of that of the imports. Within the last ten years the number of vessels entering the port of Montevideo has increased only about 10 per cent., whereas the total tonnage has increased 100 per cent., owing to the large ocean steamers which trade with the port or make it a place of call. A few years ago the imports from Great Britain amounted to about a third of the whole, and the exports to the same country to about one-fourth of the whole. But much of the produce from the river Plate countries in general which formerly was shipped to England or to Antwerp now goes direct to France or to Hamburg and Bremen.

Communication.

Telegraph lines, with a total length of 661 miles, exist in most of the departments. Submarine cables communicate with Buenos Ayres and the ports of Brazil, and thence with Europe. The railways are comprehended in three main systems, the central, northwestern, and eastern; their combined length barely reaches 300 miles. There are no public roads in the country; but communication in the more inhabited parts is easily effected over the nearly level grassy plains.

Education.

The system of national education is gratuitous and compulsory. The number of school children is over 30,000, about 5·4 per cent. of the total population. The teaching at the national schools is irrespective of religious creed or denomination. In higher education much has yet to be accomplished. There is a school of arts and trades in the capital. The university of Montevideo, founded in 1838, numbers about 1300 students. The state religion is Roman Catholic; but all sects enjoy complete toleration, unless a decided non-toleration of the Jesuits be regarded as an exception to the rule.

Government. The legislative power of the state rests with the general assembly, consisting of two chambers, one of senators (18) and one of representatives (51). The deputies of the lower house are elected annually and directly by the people, one deputy for every 3000 of the population, or any fraction not less than 2000. One senator is named for each department. The executive power is exercised by the president of the republic, who is elected by the general assembly. The judicial power is vested in a superior court, composed of two courts of appeal, which temporarily supply the place of a supreme court of justice, not yet created.

Army and navy. The permanent army on a peace footing consists of 3260 men. The national guard numbers about 20,000. On an emergency the Government could put into the field 30,000 men. The regular troops are well armed and accoutred after the European fashion. The navy consists of a few small steamers and gunboats.

Finance. The estimated revenue for 1886-87 was £2,775,362 (about two-thirds from custom dues, the rest from taxes on property and from stamps, trade licences, &c.). Of the estimated expenditure about two-fifths are devoted to the payment of the interest on the public debt, which in 1883 amounted to £11,127,000. On 1st July 1886 the debt was officially stated to be £14,718,089.

History. The history of Uruguay dates from 1512, when Juan Diaz de Solis entered the Paraná-guazú or "sealike" estuary of the Plate and landed about 70 miles east of the present city of Montevideo. Uruguay at that time was inhabited by Indians, of whom the dominant tribe was called Charrúas, a people described as physically strong and well-formed, and endowed with a natural nobility of character. Their habits were simple, and they were disfigured neither by the worst crimes nor by the primitive superstitions of savages. They are said to have revealed no vestiges of religion. The Charrúas are generally classified as a yellow-skinned race, of the same family as the Pampa Indians; but they are also represented as tanned almost black by the sun and air, without any admixture of red or yellow in their complexions. Almost beardless, and with thin eyebrows, they had on their heads thick, black, lustrous hair, which neither fell off nor turned grey until the possessors reached the age of eighty. They lived principally upon fish, venison, and honey. In the Guarani language "Charrúa" means turbulent, and by their enemies the Charrúas were accounted as such, and even ferocious, although admitted to be generous to their captives. They were a curiously taciturn and reticent race. Their weapons were the bow and arrow and stones.

Solis, on his second visit, 1515-16, was slain by the Charrúas in Colonia. Eleven years later Ramon, the lieutenant of Sebastian Cabot, was defeated by the same tribe. In 1603 they destroyed in a pitched battle a veteran force of Spaniards under Saavedra. During the next fifty years three unsuccessful attempts were made by the Spaniards to subdue this courageous people. The real conquest of Uruguay was commenced under Philip III. by the Jesuit missions. It was gradually consummated by the military and commercial settlements of the Portuguese, and subsequently by the Spaniards, who established themselves formally in Montevideo under General Zavala in 1729, and finally demolished the rival Portuguese settlement in Colonia in 1777. From 1750 Montevideo enjoyed a provincial government independent of that of Buenos Ayres. The American rebellion, the French Revolution, and the British invasions of Montevideo and Buenos Ayres (1806-7) under Generals Auchmuty and Whitelock all contributed to the final extinction of the Spanish power on the river Plate. During the war of independence Montevideo was taken in 1814 by the Buenos-Ayrean general Alvear. A long struggle for dominion in Uruguay between Brazil and the revolutionary Government of Buenos Ayres was concluded in 1828, through the mediation of Great Britain, Uruguay being declared a free and independent state. The republic was formally constituted in 1830. Subsequently Juan Manuel Rosas, dictator of Buenos Ayres, interfered in the intestine quarrels of Uruguay; and Montevideo was besieged by his forces, allied with the native partizans of General Oribe, for nine years (1842-51). From the era of its independence to about 1870 the history of Uruguay is a long record of foreign invasions and intrigues, financial ruin, and political folly and crime.

See *Album de la Republica Oriental del Uruguay*, by F. A. Berro, A. de Vedia, and M. de Pena (Montevideo, 1882); *Anuario Estadistico* for 1885 and preceding years, official documents and reports published by the Government of Uruguay; Bauza, *La Dominacion Española en el Uruguay* (Montevideo, 1880); G. E. Bordoni, *La Repubblica dell' Uruguay* (Milan, 1885); M. G. and E. T. Mulhall, *Handbook of the River Plate* (London, 1885); *The Republic of Uruguay* (London, 1883); an official and statistical pamphlet by Lomba; *Reports* by W. Gifford Palgrave (1885 and 1887). (J. GR.)

URUMIAH. See URMIA.

USBEGS. See BOKHARA, KHIVA, MONGOLS, TURKESTAN, and TURKS.

USHANT (Fr. *Ouessant*), the most westerly of the islands off the coast of France, 26 miles west-north-west from Brest, belongs administratively to the department of Finistère. It is about 4½ miles in length, and almost entirely granitic, with steep and rugged coasts, accessible only at a few points. The island affords pasturage to a few sheep and horses, and contains some small villages, the chief being St Michel. The inhabitants are principally pilots and fishermen. The total population in 1886 was 2307.

USHER, JAMES (1580-1656), prelate and scholar, was born in the parish of St Nicholas, Dublin, on 4th January 1580. He was the eldest son of Arnold Usher, one of the six clerks in Chancery, and descended from the house of Nevill, one of whose scions, accompanying John Plantagenet to Ireland in the capacity of usher in 1185, adopted his official title as a surname. James Usher was sent to a school in Dublin opened by two political agents of James VI. of Scotland, who adopted this manner of averting the suspicions of Elizabeth's Government from their real object, which was to secure a party for James in Ireland in the event of the queen's death. In 1593 Usher matriculated as one of the first students at the newly-founded university of Dublin, whose charter had been obtained in 1592 by his uncle Henry Usher, archbishop of Armagh. He proved a diligent student, devoting much attention to controversial theology, graduated as M.A. in 1600, and became a fellow of Trinity College. On the death of his father in 1598 he resigned the family estate to his younger brother, reserving only a small rent-charge upon it for his own maintenance, and prepared to enter into holy orders. When he was but nineteen he accepted a challenge put forth by Henry Fitzsimons, a learned Jesuit, then a prisoner in Dublin, inviting discussion of Bellarmine's arguments in defence of Roman Catholicism, and acquitted himself with much distinction. In 1600 he was appointed proctor of his college and catechetical lecturer in the university, though still a layman, and was ordained deacon and priest on the same day, in 1601, while still under the canonical age, by his uncle the primate. In 1606 he became regius professor of divinity and also chancellor of St Patrick's cathedral, Dublin. He was a frequent visiter to England to purchase books for his college library, and upon similar errands, making on these occasions the acquaintance of the most eminent scholars in London, Oxford, and Cambridge, such as Camden, Selden, Sir Thomas Bodley, and Sir Robert Cotton. He took his degree of D.D. in 1612, and in the following year published his first printed work, though not his first literary composition,—*Gravissimæ Quæstionis de Christianarum Ecclesiarum, in Occidentis præsertim partibus, ab Apostolicis temporibus ad nostram usque ætatem, continua successione et statu, Historica Explicatio*, wherein he took up the history of the Western Church from the point where Jewel had left off in his *Apology for the Church of England*, and carried it on from the 6th till past the middle of the 13th century, but never completed it. In this same year he married Phœbe, daughter of Dr Luke Chaloner, a wealthy heiress. In 1615 he took part in an attempt of the Irish clergy to impose a Calvinistic confession, embodying the Lambeth Articles of 1595, upon the Irish Church, and was delated to King James in consequence. But on his next visit to England in 1619 he brought with him an attestation to his orthodoxy and high professional standing, signed by the lord deputy and the members of the privy council, which, together with his own demeanour in a private conference with the king, so influenced the latter that he nominated Usher to the vacant see of Meath, of which he was consecrated bishop in 1620. In 1622 he published a controversial *Discourse of the Religion anciently Professed by the Irish and British*, designed to show that they were in agreement with the Church of England and opposed to the Church of Rome on the points in debate between those churches. In 1623 he was made a privy councillor for Ireland, and in the same year was summoned to England by the king that he might more readily carry on a work he had already begun upon the antiquity of the British churches. While he was detained on this business the archbishop of Armagh died in January 1624, and the king at once nominated Usher to the vacant primacy; but severe illness and other causes impeded his return to Ireland until August 1626.

For many years Archbishop Usher was actively employed both in the government of his diocese and in the publication of several learned works, amongst which may be specified *Emmanuel* (a treatise upon the Incarnation), published in 1638, and *Britannicarum Ecclesiarum Antiquitates*, in 1639. In 1634 he took part in the convocation which drafted the code of canons that formed the basis of Irish ecclesiastical law till the disestablishment of the Irish Church in 1869, and defeated the attempt of Bramhall, then bishop of Derry and later his own successor in Armagh, to conform the Irish Church exactly to the doctrinal standards of the English. He put the matter on the ground of preserving the independence of the Irish Church, but the real motive at work was to maintain the Calvinistic element introduced in 1615. In 1640 he paid another visit to England on one of his usual scholarly errands, meaning to return when it was accomplished. But the rebellion of 1641 broke out while he was still at Oxford, and he never saw his native country again. He published a collection of tracts at Oxford in that year, inclusive of a defence of Episcopacy and of the doctrine of non-resistance. One blot on his memory is that, being one of the five prelates whom Charles I. consulted whether he could conscientiously assent to the Act of attainder against the earl of Strafford after having pledged his word to him for his safety, Usher joined in the casuistical advice given by all except Juxon, who alone told the king that his pledged word could not be lawfully broken. All Usher's property in Ireland was lost to him through the rebellion, except his books and some plate and furniture, but he was assigned the temporalities of the vacant see of Carlisle for his support. In 1643 he was offered a seat in the Assembly of Divines at Westminster, but declined it publicly in terms which drew upon him the anger of the House of Commons, and an order for the confiscation of his library was averted only by the interposition of Selden. He quitted Oxford in 1645 and went into Wales, where he remained till 1646, when he returned to London, and was in 1647 elected preacher to the Society of Lincoln's Inn, an office he continued to hold till a little before his death. During his residence in Wales a hyper-Calvinistic work entitled *A Body of Divinity; or the Sum and Substance of the Christian Religion*, was published under his name by Downham; and, though he repudiated the authorship in a letter to the editor, stating that the manuscript from which it was printed was merely a commonplace-book into which he had transcribed the opinions of Cartwright and other English divines, often disapproving of them and finding them dissonant from his own judgment, yet it has been persistently cited ever since as Usher's genuine work, and as lending his authority to positions which he had long abandoned, if he ever maintained them. In 1648 he had a conference with Charles I. in the Isle of Wight, assisting him in the abortive negotiations with Parliament on the question of Episcopacy. In 1650-54 he published the work which at the time and for more than a century afterwards was accounted his most important production, the *Annales Veteris et Novi Testamenti*, in which he propounded a scheme of Biblical chronology which held its ground until disproved by very recent advances in scholarship, and whose dates were inserted by some unknown authority in the margin of reference editions of the authorized version. He was to some extent favoured by Cromwell after he became lord protector, who seems to have promised Usher a pension and a grant for twenty-one years of the lands belonging to the see of Armagh; but there is no proof that either was actually carried out. In 1655 Usher published his last work, *De Græca LXX. Interpretum Versione Syntagma*. He died on 20th March 1656, in Lady Peterborough's house at Reigate in Surrey. His body was buried in Westminster abbey, in the chapel of St Erasmus. To one daughter who survived him he left his library, and she sold it to the officers and soldiers of Cromwell's army in Ireland, who deposited it in Dublin castle, whence it was removed at the Restoration and given, according to Usher's original purpose, by direction of Charles II. to the library of Trinity College, of which it still forms a part.

Usher's works are very numerous, and were first collected by Elrington and Todd, Dublin, 1847, in 17 vols. (R. F. L.)

USKUP, Uskub, or Skoplie, a town of European Turkey, capital of the sanjak of the same name and of the vilayet of Kossova, on the upper Vardar river, about 160 miles north-west of Saloniki. It occupies a picturesque and important strategic position near the southern foot of the Skhar-dagh (Scodrus), which connects the Balkan range in the east with the Bosnian and Albanian highlands in the west, and forms the water-parting between the streams flowing north to the Danube and those going south to the Ægean. Here also converge the ethnological domains of the Albanians and Slavs (Servians, Bosnians, and Bulgarians), so that the population, estimated at 28,000, is of a somewhat mixed character. Uskup has some flourishing industries, such as leather and metal-work, weaving and dyeing, and is the centre of a rich agricultural district growing large quantities of fruits and cereals. It is the residence of the provincial governor, the seat of a Greek archbishop, and one of the chief stations on the main line of railway which runs from Saloniki up the Vardar valley to Bosnia. It communicates with the Simnitza valley and with Prisren by practicable roads running north and north-west over the encircling ranges.

Uskup retains in a slightly modified form the ancient name of Skupi (Skopi), a city of Pæonia (north Macedonia), forming a northern outpost of Greek and Roman culture towards Dardania and Dacia Aureliani.

USURY. An ancient legal conception, it has been said, corresponds not to one but to several modern conceptions; and the proposition is equally true when economic is substituted for legal. Until quite recent times the term "usury" covered a number of essentially different social phenomena. "Thou shalt not lend upon usury to thy brother, usury of money, usury of victuals, usury of anything that is lent upon usury. Unto a stranger thou mayest lend upon usury; but unto thy brother thou shalt not lend upon usury, that the Lord thy God may bless thee" (Deut. xxiii. 19, 20). In this sentence we find interest of all kinds blended together, and the natural economic tendencies directly counteracted by the moral and religious law. At the present day, "usury," if used in the old sense of the term, would embrace a multitude of modes of receiving interest upon capital to which not the slightest moral taint is attached. The man who does not in some shape or other lend his capital upon "usury" is, in the modern world, generally considered as lacking in his duty to himself or his family. The change in the moral attitude towards usury is perhaps best expressed by saying that in ancient times so much of the lending at interest was associated with cruelty and hardship that all lending was branded as immoral (or all interest was usury in the moral sense), whilst at present so little lending takes place, comparatively, except on commercial principles, that all lending is regarded as free from an immoral taint. This change in the attitude of common-sense morality in respect to "anything that is lent upon usury" is one of the most peculiar and instructive features in the economic progress of society.

"It is worthy of remark," says Grote (*History of Greece*, vol. iii. p. 144), "that the first borrowers must have been for the most part men driven to this necessity by the pressure of want and contracting debt as a desperate resource without any fair prospect of ability to pay; debt and famine run together in the mind of the poet Hesiod. The borrower is in this unhappy state rather a distressed man soliciting aid than a solvent man capable of making and fulfilling a contract; and if he cannot find a friend to make a free gift to him in the former character he would not under the latter character obtain a loan from a stranger except by the promise of exorbitant interest and by the fullest eventual power over his person which he is in a position to grant." This remark, though suggested by the state of society in ancient Greece, is largely applicable throughout the world until the close of the early Middle Ages. Borrowers were not induced to borrow as a rule with the view of employing the capital so obtained at a greater profit, but they were compelled of necessity to borrow as a last resort. The conditions of ancient usury find a graphic illustration in the account of the building of the second temple at Jerusalem (Neh. v. 1-12). The reasons for borrowing are famine and tribute. Some said, "We have mortgaged our lands, vineyards, and houses, that we might buy corn, because of the dearth;" others said, "We have borrowed money for the king's tribute, and that upon our lands and vineyards . . . and, lo, we bring into bondage our sons and our daughters to be servants, . . . neither is it in our power to redeem them, for other men have our lands and vineyards." In ancient Greece we find similar examples of the evil effects of usury, and a law of bankruptcy resting on slavery. In Athens about the time of Solon's legislation (594 B.C.) the bulk of the population, who had originally been small proprietors or metayers, became gradually indebted to the rich to such an extent that they were practically slaves. Those who still kept their property nominally were in the position of Irish cottiers: they owed more than they could pay, and stone pillars erected on their land showed the amount of the debts and the names of the lenders. Usury had given all the power of the state to a small plutocracy. The remedy which Solon adopted was of a kind that we are accustomed to consider as purely modern. In the first place, it is true that according to ancient practice he proclaimed a general *seisachtheia*, or shaking off of burdens: he cancelled all the debts made on the security of the land or the person of the debtor. This measure alone would, however, have been of little service, had he not at the same time enacted that henceforth no loans could be made on the bodily security of the debtor, and the creditor was confined to a share of the property. The consequence of this simple but effective reform was that Athens was never again disturbed by the agitation of insolvent debtors. Solon left the rate of interest to be determined by free contract, and sometimes the rate was exceedingly high, but none of the evils so generally prevalent in antiquity were experienced.

When we turn to Rome, we find exactly the same difficulties arising, but they were never successfully met. As in Athens in early times, the mass of the people were yeomen, living on their own small estates, and in time they became hopelessly in debt. Accordingly the legislation of the XII. Tables, about 500 B.C., was intended to strike at the evil by providing a maximum rate of interest. Unfortunately, however, no alteration was made in the law of debt, and the attempt to regulate the rate of interest utterly failed. In the course of two or three centuries the small free farmers were utterly destroyed. By the pressure of war and taxes they were all driven into debt, and debt ended practically, if not technically, in slavery. It would be difficult to over-estimate the importance of the influence of usury on the social and economic history of the Roman republic. In the provinces the evils of the system reached a much greater height. In 84 B.C. the war tax imposed by Sulla on the province of Asia was at first advanced by Roman capitalists, and rose within fourteen years to six times its original amount. It is interesting to observe that the old law of debt was not really abolished until the dictatorship of Julius Cæsar, who practically adopted the legislation of Solon more than five centuries before; but it was too late then to save the middle class. About this time the rate of interest on first-class security in the city of Rome was only about 4 per cent., whilst in the provinces from 25 to 50 per cent. were rates often exacted. Justinian made the accumulation of arrears (*anatocismus*) illegal and fixed the rate at 6 per cent., except for mercantile loans, in which the rate received was 8 per cent. On the whole it was truly said of usury during the republic and early years of the empire: "Sed vetus urbi fenebre malum et seditionum discordiarumque creberrima causa." Even when it came to be authorized by Roman law under certain restrictions, it was still looked upon as a pernicious crime. "Cicero mentions that Cato, being asked what he thought of usury, made no other answer to the question than by asking the person who spoke to him what he thought of murder."

It was only natural, considering the evils produced by usury in ancient Greece and Rome, that philosophers should have tried to give an *a priori* explanation of these abuses. The opinion of Aristotle on the barrenness of money became proverbial, and was quoted with approval throughout the Middle Ages. This condemnation by the moralists was enforced by the fathers of the church on the conversion of the empire to Christianity. They held usury up to detestation, and practically made no distinction between interest on equitable moderate terms and what we now term usurious exactions.[1] The consequence of the condemnation of usury by the church was to throw all the dealing in money in the early Middle Ages into the hands of the Jews. A full account of the mode in which this traffic was conducted in England is given by Madox in chapter vii. of his *History of the Exchequer* (London, 1711). The Jews were considered as deriving all their privileges from the hand of the king, and every privilege was dearly bought. There can be no doubt that they were subjected to most arbitrary exactions. At the same time, however, their dealings were nominally under the supervision of the Jews' exchequer, and a number of regulations were enforced, partly with the view of protecting borrowers and partly that the king might know how much his Jews could afford to pay. It was probably mainly on account of this money-lending that the Jews were so heartily detested and liable to such gross ill-treatment by the people. A curious illustration of this popular animosity is found in the insertion of a clause in the charters granted by Henry III. to Newcastle and Derby, forbidding any Jew to reside in either place. Ultimately in 1290 the Jews were expelled in a body from the kingdom under circumstances of great barbarity, and were not allowed to return until the time of Cromwell. Before the expulsion of the Jews, however, in spite of canonical opposition, Christians had begun to take interest openly; and one of the most interesting examples of the adaptation of the dogmas of the Church of

[1] For a popular account of the reasons given in support of the canonical objections to usury, and of the modifications and exceptions admitted in some quarters, see W. Cunningham's *Usury*.

Rome to the social and economic environment is found in the growth of the recognized exceptions to usury. In this respect the canonical writers derived much assistance from the later Roman law. Without entering into technicalities, it may be said generally that an attempt was made to distinguish between usury, in the modern sense of unjust exaction, and interest on capital. Unfortunately, however, the modifications which were really admitted were not openly and avowedly made by a direct change in the statutes, but for the most part they were effected (as so many early reforms) under the cover of ingenious legal fictions. One of the most curious and instructive results of this treatment has been well brought out by Walter Ross in the introduction to his *Lectures on the Law of Scotland* (1793). He shows, in a very remarkable manner and at considerable length, that "to the devices fallen upon to defeat those laws (*i.e.*, against usury) the greatest part of the deeds now in use both in England and Scotland owe their original forms" (vol. i. p. 4). One of the consequences of this indirect method of reforming the law was that in some cases the evil was much exaggerated. "The judges," says Ross, "could not award interest for the money; that would have been contrary to law, a moral evil, and an oppression of the debtor; but, upon the idea of damages and the failure of the debtor in performance, they unmercifully decreed for double the sum borrowed." He may well remark that imagination itself is incapable of conceiving a higher degree of inconsistency in the affairs of men (compare Blackstone, vol. iii. pp. 434, 435).

In the limits assigned to this article it is impossible to enter further into the history of the question, but an attempt may be made to summarize the principal results so far as they bear upon the old controversy, which has again been revived in some quarters, as to the proper relation of law to usury and interest. (1) The opinion of Bentham that the attempt directly to suppress usury (in the modern sense) will only increase the evil is abundantly verified. Mere prohibition under penalties will practically lead to an additional charge as security against risk. The evils must be partly met by the general principles applicable to all contracts (the fitness of the contracting parties, &c.) and partly by provisions for bankruptcy. Peculiar forms of the evil, such as mortgaging to excessive amounts in countries largely occupied by peasant proprietors, may be met by particular measures, as, for example, by forbidding the accumulation of arrears. (2) The attempt to control interest in the commercial sense is both useless and harmful. It is certain to be met by fictitious devices which at the best will cause needless inconvenience to the contracting parties; restraints will be placed on the natural flow of capital, and industry will suffer. (3) In the progress of society borrowing for commercial purposes has gradually become of overwhelming importance compared with borrowing for purposes of necessity, as in earlier times. By far the greater part of the interest now paid in the civilized world is, in the language of the English economists, only a fair reward for risk of loss and for management of capital, and a necessary stimulus to saving.

For information upon the modern legislation affecting the subject, see INTEREST and PLEDGE.

On the increasing share of the products of industry given to labour compared with capital, compare Leroy-Beaulieu's *Répartition des Richesses* (1880), and E. Atkinson's *Distribution of Products* (1885) and *Margin of Profits*. (J. S. N†.)

Plate II.

UTAH, a Territory of the United States, bounded on the N. by Idaho and Wyoming, on the E. by Colorado, on the S. by Arizona, and on the W. by Nevada. The eastern boundary coincides with 109° and the western with 114° W. long. The southern boundary is the 37th parallel of latitude; the northern is on the 42d parallel between the meridians of 114° and 111°, while east of the latter meridian it follows the 41st parallel. The area of Utah is 84,970 square miles.

Physical features.

The surface is greatly diversified, containing high mountains, broad arid valleys, and desert plateaus. Near the middle of the northern boundary the Wahsatch Mountains enter the Territory, and they extend southward along its middle line, finally degenerating into plateaus whose elevation diminishes southward. This is the principal mountain range of the Territory, and its position marks the highest land, from which, as a watershed, the streams flow off eastward and westward, the former to the Colorado of the West, the latter to sink in the Great Basin. Eastward from the Wahsatch, along the northern boundary of Utah, stretches a broad, massive range, known as the Uintah. These mountains are exceptional in that their trend is east and west, *i.e.*, nearly at right angles to the other uplifts of the Rocky Mountain system. South of this range and east of the Wahsatch is a region of plateaus, horizontal or but slightly inclined, and receding step by step from the high mountains. In this region all the streams flow in cañons carved in the nearly horizontal sandstones and limestones, to depths ranging from a few hundreds to several thousands of feet. West of the Wahsatch stretches the Great Basin, a region having no outlet to the sea. Its surface presents an alternation of broad desert valleys and narrow abrupt mountain ranges, rising sharply from the valleys. The mean elevation of the Territory is 6100 feet. The lowest portion is near the southern border, where it is less than 3000 feet above the sea; but, on the other hand, many mountain summits exceed 13,000 feet in height. Of the principal peaks may be mentioned Mount Nebo (11,680 feet) in the Wahsatch Range, and Gilberts Peak (13,987), La Motte (12,892), and Burro (12,834) in the Uintah Range. The principal stream of eastern Utah is the Colorado of the West. This is formed by the junction of Green river, which rises in the Wind River Mountains of Wyoming, and the Grand, whose sources are in the snow-fields upon Long's Peak in Colorado. The Green and the Colorado receive numerous branches from the Uintah and Wahsatch Ranges, among them the Uintah, Price, Fremont, San Rafael, and Virgin. With the exception of the first-named, all these streams have their courses far below the general surface, in the characteristic cañons of this strange region. In western Utah the climate is very arid, and, consequently, there are few living streams. The Great Basin, of which this region forms a part, consists of a large number of basins, differing greatly in magnitude. In each of these the waters from the surrounding mountains sink or collect in a lake, which, having no outlet, rises or falls with the excess of supply or evaporation. The largest of these basins is that of Great Salt Lake, which stretches along the western base of the Wahsatch Range. The lowest part of this valley is occupied by the lake, into which drain the rivers from the western slope of the mountains, the chief being the Bear, Weber, and Ogden, while the Provo, Spanish Fork, and American Fork contribute to it through Utah Lake and the river Jordan. In former geologic times Great Salt Lake had an extent vastly greater than at present, as is evidenced by the well-marked shore-lines upon the mountains around and within its basin. These shore lines have an altitude nearly 1000 feet higher than the present level of the lake. This higher stage, which has been named Lake Bonneville, was reduced to its present stage primarily by the formation of an outlet at the northern end of Cache valley, by which its waters flowed off through Snake and Columbia rivers to the Pacific, and secondarily by the excess of evaporation over supply. Since the settlement of the country, the surface of the lake rose, so that from an area of 1700 square miles in 1849 it had expanded in 1870 to about 2360. But in more recent years it has been slowly receding. Together with these general movements, slight oscillations with the changes of season are constantly going on. As Great Salt Lake has no outlet save evaporation, its water contains a large amount of saline matter in solution. The proportion varies inversely with the varying height of the water in the lake, ranging from 14·8 to 22·4 per cent. by weight. The only other bodies of water of considerable magnitude are Bear and Utah Lakes, both fresh and both tributary to Great Salt Lake. Besides the tributaries to Great Salt Lake, the only other stream of importance west of the Wahsatch is the Sevier, which, rising in the plateaus south of the Wahsatch, passes by a circuitous route into the deserts to the west, where it sinks. Formerly it flowed into Sevier Lake, whence its waters were evaporated, but the extensive use of the river for irrigation has caused the lake to disappear.

Geology. The Wahsatch Range is in general terms a great monoclinal uplift, although in detail it is a complicated system of uplifts and faults. The general dip of the beds is towards the east, while the fractured edges face the Great Basin. The core of the range is composed of Archæan rocks, while sedimentary beds, as high as the Jurassic, are found upon its eastern flank. The Uintah Range is a broad anticlinal, surmounted by rocks of the Carboniferous age, with more recent formations lying upon its north and south flanks. The rocks of the plateau region are almost entirely sedimentary and lie horizontally, or nearly so. The ranges of the Great Basin are of diversified character, a large proportion of them being monoclinal uplifts, exposing the Archæan rocks, with sedimentaries tilted upon their slopes. The valleys have in all cases a floor of Quaternary deposits, which effectually cover the rock formations that underlie them.

Fauna and flora. The animal and vegetable life presents variety corresponding with that of the topography. Upon the mountains and high plateaus are forests of *Coniferæ*, with groves of aspen skirting them at their lower limit. Here are found bears of different species, the mule deer, and occasionally the elk (wapiti) and the antelope. Upon the lower plateaus and in the desert valleys of the Great Basin life is not abundant. Piñon pine and cedar, *Artemisia*, cacti, and yucca characterize the vegetation; while of animals there are few except the coyote, prairie dog, rattlesnake, and scorpion.

Population. The settled portion of Utah lies mainly along the western base of the Wahsatch and in the valleys of that range, particularly in the northern part of the Territory. There are also considerable settlements near the southern boundary, in the valleys of the Virgin river. The population numbered 143,963 in 1880, showing an increase of 65·8 per cent. since 1870. The population is at present (1888) probably not far from 175,000. In 1850 the total was only 11,380; in 1860 it had risen to 40,273, and in 1870 to 86,786. Probably four-fifths of the population are adherents of the "Church of Jesus Christ of Latter Day Saints" or Mormons, as they are popularly designated (see MORMONISM). This proportion is steadily diminishing as the mining industries, the manufactures, and transportation increase, thus bringing in a constantly-increasing "Gentile" element. Of the aggregate population males are decidedly in excess of females: in 1880 there were 100 of the former to 93 of the latter, showing that polygamy was not generally practised. The proportion of foreign-born inhabitants is exceptionally large: in 1880 there were 44 foreign-born to 100 natives, *i.e.*, nearly one-third of the population were immigrants. Of this foreign element there came from England, 19,654; Denmark, 7791; Sweden, 3750; Scotland, 3201; Wales, 2390; Ireland, 1321; Norway, 1214; Switzerland, 1040; Germany, 885. Thus England supplies nearly one-half and Denmark nearly one-fifth, while Germany and Ireland, which furnish the great bulk of the immigrants to the United States at large, are but feebly represented among the Mormons.

Utah is divided into twenty-four counties, enumerated, with their population in 1880, in the subjoined table.

County.	Pop.	County.	Pop.	County.	Pop.
Beaver	3,918	Kane	3,085	Sevier	4,457
Box Elder	6,761	Millard	3,727	Summit	4,921
Cache	12,562	Morgan	1,783	Tooele	4,497
Davis	5,279	Pi Ute	1,651	Uintah	799
Emery	556	Rich	1,263	Utah	17,973
Garfield[1]	..	Salt Lake	31,977	Wahsatch	2,927
Iron	4,013	San Juan	204	Washington	4,235
Juab	3,474	San Pete	11,557	Weber	12,344

The principal cities, with their populations in 1880, are,—Salt Lake City, the capital of the Territory, 20,768; Ogden, in the Salt Lake valley, at the confluence of the Ogden and Weber rivers, 6069; Provo, in the valley of Utah Lake, 3432; and Logan, in Cache valley, 3396. There are numerous other smaller places, making a large aggregate of city and village population. This is a result of the policy of the Mormon Church, which has favoured the grouping of the farming population in villages.

Climate. As everywhere throughout the western United States, with the altitude above the sea there is a gradation of climate with respect to aridity. Upon the higher mountains there is sufficient rainfall for the needs of vegetation. But upon the low country the precipitation is slight, so that irrigation is almost universally practised by the agriculturist. The annual rainfall at Salt Lake City, which is very favourably situated, being south-east of Great Salt Lake and at the immediate base of the Wahsatch Mountains, is about 30 inches. In all other habitable parts of the Territory it is less, being not greater than 10 inches in the southern and western portions. Temperature, also, has a wide range in different parts of the Territory. The mean annual temperature at Salt Lake City, which may serve as an average of the habitable parts of Utah, is about 45°. The range of temperature between summer and winter and between day and night is very great, and the changes of temperature are often startling in their magnitude and abruptness.

Industry. The principal industries of Utah are agriculture and mining. At Salt Lake City and Ogden some manufacturing is done, and in the remote parts of the Territory cattle and sheep raising is carried on to a limited extent. Agriculture is confined mainly to the Mormons, while mining enterprise is carried on almost exclusively by Gentiles. In 1880 the area of land in farms was 655,524 acres, or 1·2 per cent. of the total area of the Territory. A little over two-thirds of this was classed as improved, and nearly all the available water in the Territory was used to cultivate it. The average size of the farms was 69 acres, which was less than in any other State or Territory. The total value of the annual agricultural produce was valued at $3,337,410. The number of manufacturing establishments was 640 and the value of the product $4,324,992. The principal mineral products are silver and lead, which are found associated in the same ores. The mines are situated almost entirely in the Wahsatch Range, east and south-east of Salt Lake City. During 1885 silver to the value of $6,750,000 and 23,000 tons of lead were mined. Of the latter metal Utah, next to Colorado, produces the largest quantity of any State or Territory of the Union.

Communication. Utah is well supplied with railroads. The Union and Central Pacific Railroads cross it near the northern boundary, the junction of these two lines being at Ogden. From this place a branch of the Union Pacific runs northward to Montana and another southward to Salt Lake City and thence to the southern part of the Territory. The Denver and Rio Grande Western connects Salt Lake City with Pueblo, in Colorado. In addition to these, there are

[1] Formed since the census of 1880 was taken.

numerous short branches in the mountains, making a total length of 876 miles in operation at the close of 1885.

Administration. The executive is administered by a governor and a secretary, appointed by the president of the United States, and by a treasurer, nominated by the governor. There is a legislature, the members of which are chosen by the people. The judiciary consists of a chief justice and two associate justices, together with a United States district attorney and a marshal, all appointed by the president of the United States. The Territory has no debt. The taxable property was assessed in 1885 at $34,821,957. The rate of taxation was $1·20 per $100. One-fourth of the sum raised is for the support of common schools.

Recent legislation. While in some respects the influence of the Mormon Church upon its communicants is for good, in promoting industry, economy, and sobriety, there are other features of it which are not only objectionable but dangerous. Polygamy is but an incident of the system, and the only objectionable one which can be successfully combated. The all-powerful influence of the church in things temporal as well as in things spiritual is a dangerous feature, and one which can only be corrected by slow-moving social influences. For many years Congress has been trying to frame legislation which would destroy polygamy in Utah, but until recently the action of the courts was frustrated and the laws nullified by the power of the Mormon Church. All elective offices were filled by Mormons. Juries were necessarily made up mainly of Mormons, whose obligations to the church were superior to any Gentile oath. The Edmunds Bill, passed in 1882, was the first efficient piece of legislation. This measure declared all elective offices vacant, and constituted a commission to oversee elections and appoint the judges and other officers of election. It disfranchised all polygamists. It annulled the action of the Territorial legislature in extending the ballot to women. It disqualified from service on juries all who accepted the dogmas of the Mormon Church regarding polygamy. Under the operation of this Act the leading polygamists have either been sent to jail or have gone into hiding. A bill of a still more drastic nature was passed by Congress in 1887. It annulled all Acts of the Territorial legislature designed in the remotest degree for the protection of polygamy. It provided that in trials for polygamy the wife may be a competent witness, that every marriage ceremony shall be made a matter of public record, and that all illegitimate children shall be disinherited. It annulled all Acts of the legislature incorporating and continuing the charters of the Mormon Church and of the Perpetual Emigration Fund Co., and confiscated their property, with the exception of the church buildings and parsonages, devoting it to the support of common schools in the Territory.

History. The area of Utah was acquired by the United States from Mexico in 1848, under the provisions of the treaty of Guadelupe Hidalgo. It was organized as a Territory in 1850, and at that time it comprised all the country lying between the eastern boundary of California and the western border of the Great Plains. The subsequent creation of Nevada, Colorado, and Wyoming reduced it to its present limits. In 1847 the Mormons, under the leadership of Brigham Young, had commenced to make settlements in Salt Lake valley, and they rapidly extended themselves over the fertile valleys of the Territory. Prior to the advent of railroads very few Gentiles settled in Utah; but in recent years, as this once remote region has become easily accessible, the Gentile element has greatly increased. For further details of the history of the Territory, see MORMONS. (H. G*.)

UTICA (Ἰτύκη), an ancient Phœnician colony in Africa near the mouth of the Bagradas (Majerda), about 20 miles north-west of Carthage. The site, which is still covered with ruins, including those of a vast amphitheatre, lies on a hill which is now 8 or 10 miles from the coast, but in ancient times a bay ran close up to the city, and the remains of quays can still be traced. Founded 1101 B.C. (see vol. xviii. p. 806), Utica was nearly three centuries older than Carthage. The two cities were generally allies; but Utica, jealous of its neighbour, sometimes acted independently, and in the Third Punic War it made a separate peace with Rome, and reaped the fruits of the destruction of the greater Punic city, becoming the emporium of Roman trade and the capital of the province, till Carthage was rebuilt by Cæsar in 44 B.C. It was here that the younger Cato killed himself. Utica received the Roman *civitas* from Augustus, was made a colony by Hadrian, and received the *jus Italicum* from Septimius Severus. The city was finally destroyed by the Arabs.

The name of Utica is probably Phœnician, and is generally taken to stand for עתיקה, the "old" city, perhaps as distinguished from Carthage, the "new city." Olshausen, however, suggests the form עִתּוּק ("colony"). The ruins at Bú Shátir were identified with Utica by Shaw. For plans and a reconstruction, see Daux, *Emporia Phéniciens*, and atlas to Tissot, *Géog. Prov. Rom. d'Afrique* (1888).

UTICA, a city of Oneida county, New York, United States, about 180 miles north-north-west from New York City, is situated on the south bank of the Mohawk, about 400 feet above sea-level. The site of the city has a gentle slope towards the river. The surrounding country is thickly settled, the principal industries being the manufacture of cotton, woollen, and iron goods, the production of butter and cheese, and the raising of hops. Utica is the chief market for cheese in the United States. The city is touched by five railroads, the New York Central and Hudson River; New York, Ontario, and Western; Rome, Watertown, and Ogdensburg; Delaware, Lackawanna, and Western; and New York, West Shore, and Buffalo; and by the Erie Canal. The city is irregularly built. Of the manufacturing industries, which are varied, the most important is that of clothing, and next to it is that of boots and shoes. One of the State lunatic asylums is in Utica. The population of the city in 1880 was 33,914, an increase in ten years of less than 12 per cent., and in 1887 it was estimated at 40,000.

The first settlement at Utica was made near the middle of the 18th century. In 1798 the village was incorporated, and it received a city charter in 1832.

UTILITARIANISM. See ETHICS, vol. viii. pp. 605-7.

UTRECHT, a province of Holland, bounded north by North Holland and the Zuyder Zee, east by Guelderland, south by Guelderland and South Holland, and west by South Holland, has an area of 534 square miles and a population (1886) of 212,454. It belongs chiefly to the basin of the Rhine: the Neder Rijn, which skirts its southern border, after sending off the Kromme Rijn at Wijk, becomes the Lek, and the Kromme Rijn, in its turn, after sending off the Vecht at Utrecht to the Zuyder Zee, assumes the name of the Oude Rijn. The north-eastern portion of the province is drained by the Eem, which falls into the Zuyder Zee. In the west the province is flat and in many places below sea-level; towards the east, where the Veluwe begins, it is more undulating, and at Zeist reaches a height of 164 feet. The more productive region is in the west; towards the east the soil becomes sandy and heath-clad. Nearly half (46·5 per cent.) of the total area is under grass; the chief agricultural products are corn (buckwheat) and tobacco; bee-keeping is extensively carried on in the east, and there is a bee market at Veenendaal. The province is traversed by railways to Amsterdam, Rotterdam, Leyden, and The Hague, Bois-le-duc, Arnheim, Zutphen, and Zwolle, all converging in Utrecht; it is also amply provided with navigable water-ways. Of the total population 62 per cent. are returned as Protestant, 37 per cent. as Roman Catholic, and 1 as Jewish. Besides UTRECHT (see below), the capital, only one other town, Amersfoort, has a population exceeding 5000 (15,178 in 1887); but in density of population Utrecht ranks third among the provinces of Holland.

UTRECHT, capital of the above province, 22 miles by rail south-south-east from Amsterdam, 38 north-east from Rotterdam, and 35 nearly west from Arnheim, is situated at the point where the Kromme Rijn bifurcates into the Vecht and the Oude Rijn. The town is traversed by two canals or arms of the river, which are crossed by numerous bridges; it is surrounded by strong forts and strategically covers Amsterdam, though its old ramparts were demolished in 1830 and have given place to shady promenades. The streets are more regular, the squares more spacious, and the canals fewer than in most Dutch towns. Of its twenty churches the most important is the old cathedral of St Martin, a large Gothic building erected in 1254-67, on the site of the original structure founded by

St Willibrord about 720 and completed by Bishop Adelbold about 1015. Only the choir, transept, and western tower (338 feet) now remain, the nave having been blown down by a violent hurricane (1st August 1674); the interior (30 feet

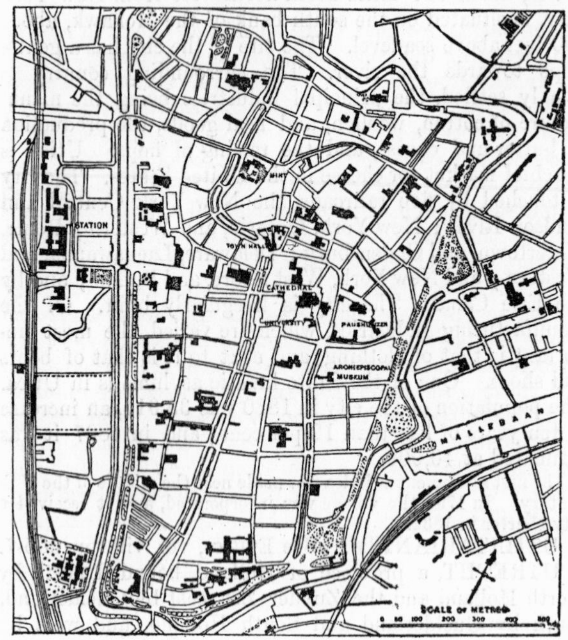

Plan of Utrecht.

wide and 115 feet in height) has been clumsily fitted up with pews and galleries for Protestant worship, so that the effect of its eighteen slender columns is almost entirely lost. On the south side are fine Gothic cloisters, adjoining which are the plain buildings of the university, founded in 1634 (with 41 professors and nearly 600 students); connected with the university are a valuable library (150,000 volumes), a museum of natural history, physical and chemical laboratories, a botanic garden, and an observatory. The town-hall (built in 1830) and the Museum Kunstliefde have small collections of pictures and other objects of art, and the archiepiscopal museum, opened in 1872, also contains excellent examples of the sacred art of the Netherlands. Among other buildings of interest may be mentioned the royal mint, and the Paushuizen ("pope's house"), built by Adrian Floriszoon Boeyens, afterwards Pope Adrian VI., a native of Utrecht, in 1517. Utrecht has excellent schools and several literary and scientific societies, besides barracks, a large military hospital, and a veterinary school. The most important industrial establishments are cigar-factories, manufactories of chemicals and earthenware, and brass-foundries. There is an active trade in the produce of the manufactures, and also in corn, cattle, butter, and cheese. To the east of the town is the Maliebaan or Mall, a triple avenue of trees about half a mile in length. The population of Utrecht in 1876 was 66,106, and in 1887 it was 79,166.

Utrecht ("Oude Trecht" or "old ford"), the Trajectum ad Rhenum of the *Itinerary* of Antoninus, was known as Wiltaburg by the Frisians and Franks. Dagobert, king of the East Franks, built a chapel here in 630, and under St Willibrord Utrecht in 696 became an episcopal see. The bishops rose to great power during the Middle Ages, and the city was frequently an imperial residence. Conrad II. (1039) and Henry V. (1125) both died at Utrecht, and their hearts were buried in the crypt of the cathedral. The city was handed over to Charles V. by Bishop Henry in 1527. The first confederation of the Dutch provinces was formed in Utrecht in 1579. The celebrated peace of Utrecht between France and Great Britain, Savoy, Portugal, Prussia, and the states of Holland was concluded here on 11th April 1713. Utrecht has since 1723 been the headquarters of the JANSENISTS (*q.v.*).

UTRERA, a town of Spain, in the province of Seville, 18 miles to the south-south-east of that city, on the railway to Jerez and Cadiz, at the junction for Moron and Osuna, lies about 8 miles from the left bank of the Guadalquivir, in a pleasant valley between two gentle undulations of the foot-hills of the southern sierra. It has no buildings of special interest; the principal church, which is large and prominent, is Gothic in style and dates chiefly from the 15th century, but some of its most conspicuous features belong to the 17th. The place enjoys considerable prosperity, due mainly to the fertility of the surrounding district, which produces large quantities of corn, and also fruit of various sorts, oil, and wine. The uncultivated "dehesas" skirting the Guadalquivir support large numbers of sheep and brood mares, and are famous throughout Spain for the bulls they send to the bull-ring. Many of the inhabitants are enterprising landowners or large farmers, and pursue highly enlightened methods of agriculture. An important fair is held at Utrera in September. The population within the municipal limits in 1877 was 15,093.

Utrera was of some importance during the Mohammedan period and has the remains of a Moorish castle. It was taken by St Ferdinand, but did not finally become subject to the sovereigns of Castile until the reign of Alphonso XI. (1340).

UXBRIDGE, an ancient borough and market town of Middlesex, England, is pleasantly situated on the Colne and Frayswater, on the Grand Junction Canal, and on a branch of the Great Western Railway, $15\frac{1}{2}$ miles west of London. The principal street is spacious and contains a number of good shops, but the streets leading off it are narrow and tortuous. The suburbs have of late greatly increased. The Colne is crossed by a brick bridge of five arches. The principal public buildings are the church of St Margaret in the Perpendicular style, consisting of nave, aisles, and low embattled tower, the town-hall (1836), and the cottage hospital. There are a large number of charities. On the banks of the Colne are several flour-mills. The town possesses several breweries and an iron-foundry. By the Grand Junction Canal, near which there are several saw-mills, a considerable trade is carried on in timber, slates, and coal. The town is governed by a local board of eighteen members. The population of the urban sanitary district (area 496 acres) was 7497 in 1871 and 7669 in 1881.

Uxbridge was one of the small boroughs originated by Alfred the Great. It is not mentioned in Domesday. For a long period it was of considerable importance as a frontier town, and latterly possessed a regular garrison. At Uxbridge negotiations were begun, on 30th January 1645, between the commissioners of Charles I. and the Parliament, but were broken off on 22d February. In 1647 the Parliamentary forces had for some time their headquarters in the town. It remained a garrison town until 1689. It obtained the grant of a market from Henry II. Until the close of the 17th century it was governed by bailiffs.

UZ. The "land of Uz" (ארץ עוץ) is best known as the scene of the story of Job. Job seems to be represented as living in the country east of Palestine and not far from Edom, to which his friend Eliphaz the Temanite belonged. In Lam. iv. 21 the Edomites appear as in possession of the land of Uz, while in Gen. xxxvi. 28 Uz is one of the pre-Edomite inhabitants of Seir. On the other hand, in Gen. x. 23 and xxii. 21 Uz (or Huz) is Aramæan. Finally in Jer. xxv. 20 "the kings of the land of Uz" appear in a clause, absent from the LXX., which seems to be a gloss on the preceding clause, and so to refer to Arabs. Mediæval tradition places the home of Job in the Hauran (see Wetzstein in Delitzsch, *Iob*), but it is doubtful whether all the Biblical references can apply to one district. The Septuagint forms from Uz the adjective Αὐσῖτις, which points to a pronunciation Auṣ = Arabic Aud, the name of a god whose worship was widely spread and might therefore be readily borne by tribes or attached to districts in several regions.

V

V is our twenty-second letter; it represents the voiced labio-dental to which F corresponds as the voiceless sound. It has been shown under U that these two symbols were originally one, and that their differentiation took place for convenience of writing only. But it was afterwards put to a good use, although not quite the natural one. It would have been better, while retaining *u* for the vowel, to have used *v* for the corresponding labial consonant, which is actually denoted by *w*. The difference of *u* and *w* is simply that of vowel and consonant: for *u* there is a sufficient opening of the lips to allow the voice to pass through without friction; but for *w* the aperture is so much closed, by bringing together either the inner edges of the lips (as in England) or the outer edges (as in some parts of Germany), that there is an audible amount of friction as the voice passes. The organs employed are the lips only in each case, whereas for *v* the upper teeth and the lower lip are the factors of the sound.

The symbol *v* does not occur in the oldest of our texts; it is represented by *f*, as in "heofon," "ofer," "hlaford" (lord). The *f* generally is voiced when medial, but voiceless when initial. This absence of two symbols for the corresponding pairs of fricative consonants has been noted already in the use of đ (or þ) for both *th* and *dh* (see under T); *s* also did duty, as it often does still, for both *s* and *z*. In Middle English *u* appears commonly for *v*. The introduction of *v* into English writing is due to French scribes; as a matter of fact almost all the words which begin with *v* are of French origin.

It is tolerably certain that in Latin *v* represented the labial and not the labio-dental consonant. The arguments in favour of this view are singly not very important, but they are fairly numerous. The interchange of the *u* and *v* sounds, as in "genua" and "genva," "solvo" and "soluo," &c., is most easily explained on the hypothesis that $v = w$; so are the loss of *v*, as in "audi(v)i," "ama(ve)ram," &c., and the retention of *o* after *v* in words like "cervos" (whereas in other combinations *o* sank to *u*), because "cerwoos" would have been a more inconvenient combination than "cervoos." Again, the name of the letter should have been "ev," not "ve," like all other fricative sounds, "ef," "el," "es," &c.; but in explosives "be," "de," "pe," "te," with the vowel *following*. There is no reason why this should not have been the case if *v* were really our *v*, a labio-dental; but if it was *w* the name "ew" was practically impossible, because the *w* would have been inaudible; therefore it went over to the other class of names. To these arguments may be added others drawn from transliteration. Mr A. J. Ellis (*E. E. P.*, ii. p. 513) agrees that Latin *v* cannot have been our labio-dental, but he thinks it probable that it was the South-German *w*, which differs from the North-German *w* (our *v*, labio-dental) in the manner described above, with some other points of difference. His chief ground is that it is hard to imagine *w* producing *v* except through an intermediate labial of the North-German kind. There is something in this argument. In any case the difference between these two *w*-sounds is slight compared with the difference between either of them and the labio-dental *v*. At what time the labial passed into the labio-dental of the Romance languages is uncertain. We can fix limits of time before which the change must have taken place: *e.g.*, it must have been before the time when the Romanized Gauls, trying to pronounce the Teutonic *w* in "werra," "ward," &c., produced "guerra," "guard," &c. If their *v* had then had the *w*-sound there would have been no difficulty in producing the same sound in Teutonic words.

In the Roman system of numerals V stands for five. The reason is uncertain. The old view that it represents half ten (X), as D (500) represents half a thousand (M, originally ↀ), has no very high degree of probability. It is perhaps as likely that I., II., III., IIII., denoted the uplifted fingers used in counting, and that V denoted the whole hand with the thumb on one side and the four fingers together on the other.

VACCINATION (from Lat. *vacca*, a cow), the name given in France to the Jennerian practice of cowpoxing, shortly after the practice began in England (1799). The procedure was based almost exactly on the earlier practice of inoculating the smallpox, the matter being inserted under the skin of the arm by a lancet point; also the continuance of the same stock from arm to arm through a series of cases was an idea taken from some of the more adroit variolators. To replace smallpox inoculation by cowpox inoculation under certain specified circumstances was Jenner's tentative project. The history of the introduction of cowpoxing, given in the article JENNER (vol. xiii. p. 623), is here supplemented from the point of view of historical criticism.

Relations of smallpox, cowpox, and grease of horse.

It is right to say that the views expressed in the present article diverge in many points from the opinions generally received among medical men, and must be regarded not as the exposition of established and undisputed doctrine, but as the outcome of an independent and laborious research.

Jenner.

Jenner's originality consisted in boldly designating cowpox as *variolæ vaccinæ* or smallpox of the cow, and in tracing cowpox itself back to the grease of the horse's hocks. The latter contention was at length set aside by practical men as a crude fancy; the former designation is just as arbitrary and untenable. It was elaborately shown by Pearson in 1802, and has often been confirmed by subsequent writers, that the vesicle of inoculated cowpox, even while it remains a vesicle, is quite unlike a single pustule of smallpox. But it is only for the vesicular stage of cowpox that there is even an allegation of likeness to variola; the vesicle of natural or unmodified cowpox is only the stage of the disease before it becomes an ulcer, either inflammatory or indurated. Inoculated horse grease has the same vesicular stage; and so also has the venereal pox when it is inoculated experimentally on the skin.[1] These three very different infections have the same kind of vesicle, in every case unlike a smallpox pustule, and the same natural termination in a phagedenic or indurated sore.

Jenner's originality in starting vaccination in practice is for the most part misunderstood. When he published his *Inquiry* in June 1798, he had twice succeeded in raising vaccine vesicles by experiment,—the first time in 1796 with matter from a milker's accidental sore, and the second time in March 1798 with matter direct from the cow. The first experiment was not carried beyond one remove from the cow; the second was carried to the fifth remove, when the succession failed. A third experiment, in the summer of 1798, failed from the outset; and his fourth and last experiment, in November-December 1798, led to nothing but extensive phagedenic ulceration in two cases out of six vaccinated.

[1] See Ricord, *Traité Complet*, 1851, plate i. figs. 6 and 7 and ii. 7, 8, and 9; also H. Lee, *Med. Chir. Trans.*, xliv. p. 238, 2d plate, fig. 2.

Historical sources of vaccine lymph. In this posture of affairs Woodville of the inoculation hospital, London, succeeded in January 1799 in starting a succession of arm-to-arm vaccinations from a London cow, which were exceptionally free from the ulcerative termination. From that source Jenner himself was supplied with lymph in February, while more than two hundred practitioners both at home and abroad were supplied some three weeks later. There was a quarrel with Woodville in due course, and an attempt to set up an authentic Jennerian lymph independent of the London stock. But the merits of this claim (which otherwise rests on the vague evidence of Marshall) may be judged of by the fact that Ring's application to Jenner in September 1799 for genuine lymph was answered by the latter with a supply of matter which was none other than Woodville's own stock, after six months' use in the country. Woodville's stock was used all over the world down to 1836. By that time there were numerous complaints that the lymph was degenerating, and a widespread feeling that it was necessary to "go back to the cow." Apart from the numerous original cases of cowpox alleged to have been found in Würtemberg, the first new authentic source was the Passy cow of 1836. From the accidental vesicles on the milker's hand Bousquet, the director of vaccination in Paris, started a new stock, which partly superseded Woodville's lymph hitherto in use in France. In 1838 Estlin of Bristol, after several years' vain endeavours, heard of original cowpox in Jenner's own parish of Berkeley (Gloucestershire), where the disease was so far forgotten that the milkers were for several days unaware that the vesicles on their hands had been contracted from cows. Estlin's new geniture is one of the most fully recorded in the history of vaccination. In the same year, and the two following years (1838-41), Ceely of Aylesbury found some half-dozen distinct occurrences of cowpox in the dairy-farms of his district, and cultivated lymph from them. His account of the natural history of cowpox in the cow, and of the effects of primary lymph when inoculated on the human arm, is by far the most comprehensive and candid that has ever been given; without it we should hardly have understood the real nature of cowpox. Bousquet, Estlin, and Ceely are the chief writers who have authentically described the establishment of new stocks of cowpox lymph since Woodville's original report of 1799. There are numerous other references, less detailed, to original cowpox in the cow, and to vaccinations therefrom, in England, on the Continent, and in the United States; some of these came to light in the inquiry of the Epidemiological Society in 1852. One of the best-known cases of comparatively recent times is the Beaugency cow of 1866, which has been the source of much of the calf-lymph of the Dutch, Belgian, and other vaccine "farms." Another French case occurred in the Gironde in November 1881, and is described in the *Bulletin* of the Academy of Medicine (p. 17, 1882). In England the editors of the *Veterinarian* inserted a notice in the number for August 1879, making a request to their readers for lymph "from vesicles on the teats of cows in cases of so-called natural cowpox." The only answer to it hitherto has been an intimation in June 1880 that there was a case of cowpox at Halstead in Essex, which was visited by Ceely and others and pronounced by the former to be of the nature of eczema. In 1876 the disease was found at a farm near Reykjavik in Iceland, where it had never been seen before; it was of the old type, producing sores on the milkers' hands, and causing much alarm by its unfamiliar character.[1]

Calf lymph. The so-called calf lymph is as remote from the cow as ordinary humanized lymph; it differs from the latter merely in the circumstance that the calf (on its shaven belly) becomes the vaccinifer, instead of the child, and that the cycle of the disease is very much abbreviated or contracted in the calf: the vesicles are distended with lymph about the fourth or fifth day, instead of the seventh or eighth, and are almost unattended by areolar redness and constitutional disturbance, the animal being able to support fifty to a hundred or more vesicles without the smallest inconvenience. On the child's arm the vesicles after calf-lymph are slower in development than in the calf, and are attended by areola, &c.

Anomalous sources of vaccine. Under the influence of theory, "vaccine" lymph has been got from two sources that have absolutely nothing to do with cowpox; and, oddly enough, the matter from these sources has been so managed as to produce correct vesicles on the child's arm. One source is the grease of the horse's hocks and the other is smallpox itself.

Grease of the horse. The grease of the horse was known to produce vesicles and subsequent ulcers on the hands almost indistinguishable from those of accidental cowpox. There was also the tradition (which breaks down when tested by facts) that accidental infection with the grease protected from smallpox. Jenner held that all "genuine" cowpox came from horse-grease; and, after he had raised vaccine vesicles on the arms of children by matter from the cow's teats, he proceeded to try whether he could not raise the same kind of vesicle experimentally by matter once removed from the horse's hocks. The experiment succeeded, just as the accident had done. The vesicle (represented in plate 2 of the *Inquiry*) ulcerated, and the boy died of what is vaguely termed a "fever" in one place and a "contagious fever" in another. The same kind of inconsequent logic suggested the experiment of inoculating the matter of horse-grease upon the skin of the cow's teats, the object being to prove the identity of cowpox with the grease. That too succeeded in the hands of Loy of Whitby. Loy also inoculated children with the same matter, and raised vesicles on their arms, which were, of course, the same as the accidental vesicles (compared to the blister raised by a burn). Sacco of Milan actually used the equine matter on a large scale, instead of cowpox matter; and De Carro of Vienna "equinated" many persons in that city with lymph sent him by Sacco. Baron prints a memorandum of Jenner, dated 23d July 1813, relating to "equine virus which I have been using from arm to arm for these two months past, without observing the smallest deviation in the progress and appearance of the pustules from those produced by vaccine," and a second note, dated 17th May 1817, in which Jenner says he "took matter from Jane King (equine direct) for the National Vaccine Establishment. The pustules beautifully correct." This is not the place to enter upon the pathology of horse-grease; and, as a matter of fact, equination has not been much practised on the whole. According to Jenner's own data, it was an occasional constitutional disease of the horse's hocks in wet seasons, which was communicable to the hands of men in the form of large whitish vesicles, ending in corroding and painful open sores (see the case reported to him by Fewster, *op. cit.*, ed. 1800, p. 96).

Human smallpox. The other anomalous source of "vaccine" is human smallpox. Jenner having succeeded in passing off his doctrine that cowpox is smallpox of the cow, it occurred to some persons about forty years after to prove the doctrine by experiment, the proof being to variolate the cow on the udder. This was accomplished in 1838, after much trouble, by Thiele in Kazan (Russia), who inoculated several thousands of persons with the variolous matter "passed through the system of the cow." Within a few months of that experiment, the same thing was attempted by Ceely of Aylesbury, who succeeded, after many failures, in raising a large variolous pock, not on the udder of the cow, but on the mucous membrane of the vulva. The first experiment with the matter of this pock was undesigned; his assistant pricked his hand with the lancet which had just been dipped into the large pustule, and in due course had an attack of smallpox. Ceely persevered with his experiments (having meanwhile variolated another heifer at five places on the vulva), and in due time so "managed" his matter as to produce vesicles on the human arm (without general eruption on the skin), which were regarded at Cheltenham and other places as

[1] Cowpox of the original ulcerating type still occurs, but is now hardly recognized as such. The inquiry into an outbreak of scarlet fever in December 1885, traced to a dairy at Hendon (Middlesex), elicited the fact that the inculpated cows, as well as seventy or eighty at two other farms, were affected with what the dairymen called "cowpox" (see Cameron, *Trans. Epid. Soc.*, April 1886). A similar outbreak in November 1887, involving 160 cows and 7 milkers at four farms in Wiltshire, was clearly proved by Crookshank to be the historical cowpox of Jenner and Ceely, by the evidence of identity in the sores on the cows' teats and in the sores or vesicles on the milkers' hands or faces, and by the production of correct vaccine vesicles in calves inoculated with lymph from a vesicle on the face of a milker (*Brit. Med. Journ.*, 17th December 1887 and 21st January 1888).

on the whole better than the cowpox vesicle of the period. But the real practical application of this idea was reserved for Badcock, a dispensing chemist at Brighton. It does not appear that any authentic or fully detailed account of Badcock's experiments has been published;[1] but he thus summarized the results some forty years later (*Pall Mall Gazette*, Jan. 23, 1880):—"By careful and repeated experiments I produced, by the inoculation of the cow with smallpox, a benign lymph of a non-infectious and highly protective character. My lymph has now been in use at Brighton for forty years, and is at the present time the principal stock of lymph employed there, being that exclusively used by the public vaccinators." At Boston, U.S., the same kind of lymph was raised and put in use in 1852. But at Attleborough, Mass., the same experiment had in 1836 led to disaster. Smallpox was inoculated on a cow's udder, and the product used to vaccinate about fifty persons. The result was an epidemic of smallpox, a panic, and the suspension of business.[2] On the face of it this method was simply variolating the cow (on a mucous membrane if the hairless or shaven skin failed) and inoculating the human subject with that curiously disguised smallpox matter. However, it was thought necessary to hold an experimental inquiry upon it, and in 1865 a commission of the Lyons Society of Medicine reported that, "in vaccinating according to the method of Thiele and Ceely, we are merely practising the old inoculation, rendered uniformly benign, it may be, by the care taken to inoculate only the first product (*l'accident primitif*), but preserving for certain all its risks in respect to contagion."[3] A negative result was come to by Klein in 1879, in an inquiry for the Local Government Board, wherein he had Ceely's cooperation. In 1879 the Irish Local Government Board prevented the use of similar variolous lymph by threatening to prosecute under the Act making the inoculation of smallpox penal. Notwithstanding the common sense of the case, and these experimental proofs, the official view taken by the medical department in 1857, that Thiele, Ceely, and Badcock had established the correctness of Jenner's doctrine of variolæ vaccinæ, is still held very tenaciously by the profession. It is too simple and attractive to be soon given up; but perhaps the best way to get rid of it is to state in plain terms what cowpox itself really is.

Natural history of cowpox. Although there is no difficulty in drawing up a complete natural history of cowpox, thanks to the laborious and exact studies of Ceely, yet the attention has been so much diverted to side issues that the facts to be stated in this section will come before most readers with the aspect of novelty. The other original authorities besides Ceely are Jenner himself, Pearson (who collected information by circular in the months following Jenner's *Inquiry*), Bousquet (1836), Estlin (1838), and Crookshank (1888). The Würtemberg inquiry, published by Hering (Stuttgart, 1839), is made up of very indifferently authenticated or incomplete statements, which have not the same value as the rest, and are at variance with them on the most essential points.

Its origination. Cowpox as an infective disease arises in cow-houses here and there, and at wide intervals of time, out of a common physiological or constitutional eruption of some particular cow, usually a heifer in her first milk, very often in the spring season or at some other crisis of the year or of the animal's life-history. It never arises except in milch cows; it occurs nowhere in the cow but on the teats, or, by infection, on adjoining parts of the udder. All the characters by which we know it distinctively as cowpox are associated with the fact of milking, or with the inevitable traction on teats that are the subject of an otherwise unimportant eruption. The primary disorder, as Ceely describes it, is an eruption of a few pimples, the size of a vetch or larger, hard and solid at first, but at length slightly vesiculated on the summit. It is only rarely that a series of events ensues on this basis which constitute cowpox as we know it; they ensue in some one animal out of many in the same byre, and years may elapse before the event happens again. The pimples on the teats are made to bleed by what Ceely calls "the merciless manipulations of the milkers"; the blood forms crusts, which are dislodged every six hours; and indurated ulcers form on the sites of the original pimples.

Its infective properties. The process being thus made inveterate owing to the incessant interference of the milker's hands, it becomes communicable to the other cows. The milkers can usually point out some one cow in which the disease began; and it spreads slowly through a byre, taking sometimes as long as three months to go the round of all the animals. An animal already infected at one or more places on its teats may become infected at other places on the teats and body of the udder, either by the traction of milking or by the contact of parts when the cow is lying down.

The ulcers heal sometimes slowly, sometimes more quickly; they may heal under crusts, or as open sores; induration and rounding of the edges are distinctive, along with much thickening of the base. The scars are also indurated, rounded and elevated at the edges, and smooth or puckered on the surface; they are often as large as a walnut. It is not easy to see a vesicular stage of the disease even in the cows infected from the initial spontaneous case; and Ceely had for the most part to be content with the coagulated matter of crusts to vaccinate with. The process is, in fact, bound up from first to last in the most intimate and essential manner with the operation of milking. Cowpox "undisturbed by the milker's hands" has no existence in the originating cow; it is the persistent irritation that makes it a pox. It is communicable, also, to the hands of the milkers themselves, and by their filthy hands to their faces. Jenner mentions a good many such cases; Pearson has collected several; and Ceely gives three in very full detail.

Progress of the disease. As in the inoculated venereal pox, the infection proceeds for a time under the skin, making a bluish-white vesicle; it eats away the tissues round the margin, where the fluid makes the skin bulge out into the characteristic tumid ring. After the fourteenth day the vesicle will have become an eschar, the average size of a sixpenny piece, which comes away and leaves a sore. The open sore is a regular part of the infection in the milker's hand. Various regions of the face get infected by contact from the hands: Jenner mentions the case of "a poor girl who produced an ulceration on her lip by frequently holding her finger to her mouth to cool the raging of a cowpox sore by blowing upon it"; another of Jenner's cases had the sore on the wing of the nose; one of Ceely's cases had an ulcer on the temple three-quarters of an inch long; in a case observed by Crookshank there was a very large vesicle and subsequent sore over the left cheek-bone. The local infection is accompanied by constitutional disturbance, more or less severe, including headache, pains in the loins, vomiting, and sometimes delirium. The axillary glands become painful, usually about the fourth day, and remain hard for some time. Eruptions occurred, but there is very little said about them.

Humanized cowpox. As might have been expected, the effects of experimental infection with cowpox matter were the same as the accidental. They are spoken of as the effects of "primary lymph," that is to say, lymph direct from the cow's teats or from the milker's sore hand, or in the earlier removes from these sources. Jenner's experience of primary lymph was very much the same as Bousquet's, Estlin's, and Ceely's forty years later. Woodville's, on the other hand, was exceptionally reassuring;[4] had it not been so, it is not likely that cowpoxing on the large scale would ever have survived the initial discouragements entailed by the use of primary lymph. The process on the child's arm was on the whole the same as on the milker's hand, allowing for the more deliberate mode of inoculation and for different texture of the skin. The vesicle grew to a great size up to the four-

[1] See Hodgson, *Brit. Med. Journ.*, 26th November 1881.

[2] *Bost. Med. and Surg. Journ.*, 1860, p. 77.

[3] *Vaccine et Variole*, Paris, 1865, p. 101.

[4] But Addington (*On the Inoculation of the Cowpox*, Birmingham, 1801), who got his lymph from Woodville, was not equally fortunate: of eleven cases at the beginning of his series five ended in ulceration; after that the cases all ended in a "dry scab."

teenth day, and often became an ulcer, either excavated under the crust or absolutely open. Estlin did not entirely get rid of ulceration until after the twenty-ninth remove from the cow. The constitutional disturbance was often severe in infants: axillary tenderness and swelling were somewhat constant, and eruptions were especially frequent about the second to the fourth week, including macular roseola, lichen, and pemphigoid bullæ. At each successive remove from the cow the cycle of the process became more contracted, and the constitutional disturbance, *cæteris paribus*, became less. Bousquet gives a plate which shows by parallel series of figures the differences between the vesicles of the old lymph (Woodville's, nearly forty years old) and the lymph from the Passy cow. The new lymph induced a process more protracted at every stage: the vesicle continued to enlarge at the periphery for several days after the common vaccine vesicle of the period would have ceased to extend. It was not at its maximum until about the end of the second week, and it then became an eschar and a sore. Bousquet confesses that he first understood "les frayeurs de Jenner" when he saw the ulcerative and other effects of primary lymph. After a certain number of removes from the cow the cycle became so contracted that the vesicle was full at the eighth or ninth day; the abbreviation of its life-history enabled it to heal without ulcerating. It thus becomes the ordinary vaccine vesicle as we know it, which heals under a scab, and leaves the peculiar punctated scar of subcrustaceous repair. The abbreviation or mitigation is effected by taking lymph from each successive vaccinifer at as early a period as it can be got, until the golden mean of safe vaccination, namely, maturity at the eighth day, is reached. That corresponds to Jenner's rule of taking the matter for vaccination before the areola appears; if the vesicle be emptied after that period, the lymph from it is apt to cause ulceration, or, as Ceely puts it, we have "all the inconveniences of primary lymph." It is thus clear that humanized cowpox might be easily cultivated back to its original type; and, as a matter of fact, it has sometimes been so cultivated back by misadventure, with serious consequences to the vaccinated.

Risks of vaccination.

The risks of vaccination may be divided into the risks inherent in the cowpox infection and the risks contingent to the puncture of the skin. Of the latter nothing special requires to be said; the former will be discussed under the five heads of (1) erysipelas, (2) jaundice, (3) skin eruptions, (4) vaccinal ulcers, and (5) so-called vaccinal syphilis.

Erysipelas.

(1) A slight degree of erysipelas was recognized by Jenner himself, and even postulated by him, as part of the natural history of cowpox in man; and it is so recognized by the more unbiased writers of recent date.[1] The usual time for it corresponds to the appearance of the areola (eighth or ninth day), that efflorescence round the pock being normally a slight erysipelas. It may start, however, from the puncture or scratch in the skin, after a day or two's interval; but that form of it (the "early erysipelas" of German writers) is much rarer than the erysipelas of the areola, or "late erysipelas." Primary lymph, or lymph in the first removes, is most apt to excite an extensive and spreading areolar redness. In the ordinary course of vaccination remote from the cow the intensity of the superficial redness and deep infiltration would seem to depend mostly on the child's constitution, or on whatever concurrence of circumstances serves to recall the "inconveniences of primary lymph." The registrar-general's tables of mortality for England and Wales have contained an entry of "erysipelas after vaccination" from 1855 down to 1881, when the entry was changed to "cowpox and other effects of vaccination," the numbers at the same time nearly doubling. The fatal cases of erysipelas in infants under one year referred to vaccination are but a small fraction of the whole mortality from erysipelas at that age, a mortality which is far greater than at any other period of life. It is quite certain that in foundling hospitals, such as that of St Petersburg, the erysipelas of vaccination has been the starting-point of disastrous epidemics of erysipelas affecting the inmates generally. There is no means of knowing whether the same has been the case among the population at large. In Table I. the column of deaths from erysipelas in general, among infants of the first year in England and Wales, is given side by side with the column of deaths from erysipelas after vaccination.

	Erysipelas after Vaccination.	Erysipelas.		Erysipelas after Vaccination.	Erysipelas.
1855	0	583	1870	20	685
1856	5	610	1871	22	716
1857	0	421	1872	16	617
1858	0	599	1873	19	675
1859	5	569	1874	27	867
1860	2	514	1875	36	796
1861	2	492	1876	21	700
1862	3	458	1877	26	667
1863	7	612	1878	35	582
1864	11	618	1879	31	561
1865	10	579	1880	32	618
1866	9	527	1881	56[2]	644
1867	3	467	1882	65[2]	696
1868	8	647	1883	51[2]	641
1869	19	589	1884	49[2]	618

The post-vaccinal inflammation sometimes takes the form of phlegmon; but there is no separate entry for that as a special sequel of vaccination. Many of the alleged deaths from erysipelas after vaccination have been the subject of coroner's inquests; the verdict is often an open one, and even such cases as those near Gainsborough in 1876 and at Norwich in 1882 were found to have been returned (all but one) by the certifying medical practitioners as due to erysipelas merely. It may be assumed that "after vaccination" is not certified unless the case has left no doubt in the minds of the jury or of the certifying medical attendant. The increase in the first column from 0 in 1855 to 32 in 1880 is probably in appearance only, and due to more correct diagnosis.

Jaundice

(2) It is only within the last few years that jaundice has been recognized as a post-vaccinal effect; and at present there is only one accepted instance of it on the large scale. This was the epidemic among re-vaccinated adults in a large shipyard at Bremen from October 1883 to April 1884. Owing to an alarm of smallpox, 1289 workmen were re-vaccinated between the 13th August and 1st September with the same humanized lymph preserved in glycerin; of these 191 had jaundice at various intervals down to the month of April following. Circumstantial evidence (agreement and difference) clearly traced the epidemic to the vaccination.[3] In future an outlook will be kept for this effect of vaccination; at present it has no intelligible theory. It may be noted that the lymph which caused the Bremen epidemic was mixed with glycerin.

Skin eruptions

(3) The eruptions that follow vaccination are proper to cowpox infection. Although little is said about them in the accidental infection of milkers, they were very common in the practice of Estlin, Ceely, and others with primary lymph. The eruption is a kind of exanthem, or "secondary" of the local infection, and does not ordinarily appear before the second week. One of its commonest forms is a patchy rose-rash, or macular roseola, not easily distinguishable from the macular roseola of syphilis.[4] Another form is lichen or dry papules, apt to scale; it may also occur as a vesicular eruption, and in the form of pemphigoid bullæ or blebs. In one of Ceely's cases the eruption extended to the whole mucous membrane of the mouth and throat. A peculiarity of the exanthem is that it may come and go several times before it finally disappears; and, like other skin eruptions, specific or non-specific, it may become inveterate. The widespread belief that much of the eczema of childhood dates from vaccination is not by any means to be dismissed as a mere fancy. The skin-disorders that followed vaccination in the first years of the practice were declared by Birch and others to be new in type. At present the vaccinal eruption, especially on the scalp, is sometimes distinguished by the size and form of the crusts, and by scars remaining for a time.

Vaccinal ulcers.

(4) Ulceration of the vaccine vesicle, or of the site of it, is one of the commoner forms of "bad arm." It is a return to the native or untamed characters of cowpox on the cow's teats, or on the milker's hands or face, or in the child's arm after experimental inoculation with primary lymph. It crops out not unfrequently in everyday practice, and is probably dependent for the most part on the lateness at which the lymph was taken for vaccination, or on retardation of the process in the vaccinifer, or on emptying the latter's vesicles too much; however, it may result from picking the scab or otherwise dislodging it. The ulceration usually proceeds to some depth in the form of a crater under the crust, and is attended with induration and rounding of the edges and induration of the base. According to Bohn (*op. cit.*, p. 166), it may alarm practitioners by its resemblance to syphilis. In other cases the crust is wanting and the ulceration has the distinct type of phagedena. The de-

[1] Bohn, *Handbuch der Vaccination*, Leipsic, 1875, p. 174.

[2] Cowpox and other effects of vaccination.

[3] See Lürman, *Berl. klin. Wochenschrift*, 1885, p. 20

[4] Parrot, *La Syphilis Héréditaire*, 1886, p. 33.

struction of tissue in either case may be very extensive, going "down to the bone" and having as much as an inch or more of superficial area. Healing is frequently an affair of weeks, and may be aided by mercurial treatment. There are no statistics of this sequel of vaccination; but the frequency or infrequency of it may be learned in conversation with any intelligent chemist whose shop is resorted to by the poor, or with a medical practitioner of average experience.

Vaccinal syphilis.

(5) It has been proved by many experiments, undesigned or otherwise, in Paris (1831 and 1839), Vienna (1854), and elsewhere, that an infant with congenital syphilis develops correct vaccinal vesicles, provided its skin be clear of eruption and the lymph have been taken at the usual time; also that the lymph taken from the correct vesicles of a syphilitic child produces correct vesicles in its turn, but does not produce syphilis in the vaccinated child. The congenital taint is, in fact, irrelevant to the course of cowpox infection. So far as experiment and casual experience can prove anything, that has been proved; the recent attempt to disprove it by an officer of the Local Government Board (*Report* for 1882, p. 46) is vitiated by fallacies, and has no value against the overwhelming testimony collected thirty or forty years ago. What, then, is the meaning of the numerous outbreaks of syphilis in groups of children or adults vaccinated or re-vaccinated with lymph from one source?

A careful examination of these cases shows that syphilis at the source of the vaccine matter was in all cases an after-thought, that in most of the cases there was no evidence for it, and that in the remaining cases the evidence was so far-fetched as to be unlikely (apart from the known *a priori* improbability), or that the traces of constitutional infection found in the vaccinifer were subsequent to vaccination, and therefore capable of being explained as an effect concurrent with the more obvious symptoms in those vaccinated therefrom. The effects, however, were very much the same as in the venereal pox. The vaccine vesicle either became an indurated or phagedenic sore, as described in the foregoing section on vaccinal ulcers, or the scar opened into an indurated sore after the usual subcrustaceous healing was complete, or became indurated without opening. The axillary and cervical glands were often indurated. In most of the epidemics there were a certain number of cases in which the effects were purely local, or confined to one only of the seats of puncture; if these had not occurred along with others in a group, they would have been counted as ordinary vaccinal ulcers. But there were often secondary symptoms as well, including the roseolar, lichenous, or (rarely) pemphigoid eruption, and not unfrequently condylomata *circa anum et genitalia*. In some epidemics (but not in all) there were, in a small minority of the cases, mucous patches on the tonsils, tongue, or lips, tending to ulcerate; and in some of the Italian outbreaks the infection spread among the mothers and other members of the households in the form of specific sores of the nipples, with or without constitutional symptoms. Affections of the bones and viscera do not seem to have followed; fatalities were not very common.

It will be hard to persuade medical authorities that these secondary effects are not the result exclusively of the venereal pox. The evidence, however, does not allow us to assume any other specific infection than that of cowpox, which, as we know, has its proper secondary exanthem in the form of macular roseola, lichen, or pemphigus; the eruption has even been known to affect the mouth and throat. The evidence from epidemics of vaccinal sore arms teaches us that condylomata, mucous patches of the tonsils, tongue, and lips, and even iritis, are also possible, although far from invariable, among the "secondaries" of the primary vaccinal ulcer. The most general fact that comes out in these epidemics is that the lymph was taken late from the vaccinifer, or that the vesicles of the vaccinifer were drained dry to vaccinate a large number, or that the same vaccinifer was used for arm-to-arm inoculation on two successive days. It is not difficult to see how, in those circumstances, the abbreviated cycle of humanized cowpox may be departed from and the native or untamed characters of cowpox infection reverted to. Cowpox, indeed, is parallel with the venereal pox, both in the circumstances of its becoming an infective ulceration (indurated or suppurating) and in its secondary or constitutional manifestations as an infection in man. But the "bad" lymph has hardly ever been used beyond the second remove; and there the parallel fails.

The following is a list of the so-called syphilitic epidemics after vaccination, including those that have been considered spurious, because they were either anomalous in type from the point of view of syphilitic infection or had no obvious causal connexion with that disease.

Udine, 1814 (see Viennois, in *Syph. Vaccinale*, p. 221). Cremona, 1821 (see Depaul, "Projet de Rapport," in *Syph. Vacc.*). Grumello, 1841 (*ibid.*). Coblenz, 1849 (Wegeler, in *Preuss. Vereins-Ztg.*, 1850, No. 14; abstract in *Schmidt's Jahrb.*, vol. lxvii., 1852, p. 62). Upper Franconia (the Hübner case), 1852 (*Intelligenzbl. der Bayr. Aerzte*, 1854; Bohn, *loc. cit.*). Lupara (Italian prov. Molise), 1856 (see Depaul, *loc. cit.*). Dispon near Pesth, 1855-57 (*Oester. Zeitschr. für prakt. Heilk.*, 1862; Bohn, *loc. cit.*, p. 322). Rivalta (Piedmont), 1861 (Pacchiotti, *Sifilide Trasmessa per Mezzo della Vaccinazione in Rivalta presso Acqui*, Turin, 1862). Torre de' Busi near Bergamo, 1862 (see Depaul, *loc. cit.*). United States (troops on both sides in the Civil War), 1861-65 (Jones, *Circular II.*, *Louisiana Board of Health*, Baton Rouge, 1884). Argenta near Ferrara, 1866 (Gamberini, in *Gaz. des Hôpitaux*, 1870, p. 505). Morbihan (neighbourhood of Vannes and Auray), 1866 (Depaul, *Bull. de l'Acad. de Méd.*, xxxii., 1866-67, p. 201; Bodelio, *ibid.*, p. 1033). Cardaillac (Lot), 1866 (*Bull. de l'Acad. de Méd.*, 28th February 1867). Schleinitz (Styria), 1870 (Kochevar, *Allgem. Wiener Med. Ztg.*, 1870, Nos. 21 and 24; abstract in *Arch. für Dermatologie und Syph.*, 1870). London (two series), 1871 (Hutchinson, *Med. Chir. Trans.*, liv., 1871). Switzerland, 1878 (*Bull. de la Soc. de la Suisse Romande*). Algiers, 1880-81 (*Journ. d'Hygiène*, 25th August 1881). Lyck (East Prussia), June 1878 (Pincus, *Vierteljhschr. f. gericht. Med.*, 1879, p. 193). Asprières (Aveyron), March 1885 (P. Brouardel, *Rapport*, Paris, 1886).

Attention was drawn to these cases because they occurred in groups varying in number from 10 to 100 or more, which made considerable stir, especially in country districts. It is unlikely that all cases have been reported. In the third *Report* of the clinical hospital of Manchester, Whitehead states the results of his inquiries on post-vaccinal illness in children. Setting aside most of the cases of illness vaguely alleged by the mothers to have been the consequence of vaccination, he admits as truly post-vaccinal 34 cases of syphilis or pseudo-syphilis; of these he enumerates only 14 in his table of 63 cases of children's syphilis of all kinds, the other 20 cases being omitted, it would appear, not because there was any doubt of their being post-vaccinal, but because they were not of the perfect type of infantine syphilis. Such was the experience of a competent observer at a single hospital during a period of 20 months. Whitehead's *Report* was published in 1859; but, when Hutchinson published his first series of London cases in 1871, the subject was considered to be quite new. Here again it was the concurrence of some ten cases in a group that helped the reluctant assent of the profession. The first group of London cases had hardly begun to be talked of when one of Hutchinson's colleagues was led by two cases of skin disease at a hospital to follow up the traces of another group, the very existence of which was unsuspected by the public vaccinator or general practitioners in whose district the eleven patients with vaccinal ulcers and occasional secondaries resided.

In the registrar-general's tables of mortality for England and Wales about one-half of the deaths from "cowpox and other effects of vaccination," or nearly thirty per annum, may be put down to effects of vaccination other than erysipelas; but there is nothing to show that these were fatal cases of vaccinal ulcers with constitutional symptoms or marasmus. On the other hand, the table of deaths from syphilis shows an enormous and steady increase in the number of deaths of infants under the age of one. In the first year of compulsory vaccination (1854) the deaths suddenly increased by one-half, and the increase has gone on steadily since then (see Table II.) The interpretation of the fact is by no means easy or free

Infantine Deaths from Syphilis (England and Wales).

	Infants under One Year.	All Other Ages.		Infants under One Year.	All Other Ages.
1847	255	310	1868	1364	522
[1]1852	380	243	1869	1361	498
[1]1853	380	242	1870	1422	436
[1]1854	591	373	1871	1317	425
1855	579	368	1872	1410	421
1856	579	300	1873	1376	467
1857	656	301	1874	1484	513
1858	684	322	1875	1554	580
1859	778	311	1876	1580	554
1860	767	300	1877	1550	524
1861	798	379	1878	1647	535
1862	867	378	1879	1493	536
1863	983	403	1880	1588	571
1864	1089	461	1881	1540	557
1865	1155	492	1882	1666	561
1866	1180	482	1883	1813	500
1867	1241	457	1884	1733	547

from fallacies. There are doubtless other and better reasons for the increase besides vaccination; and it is significant that the tables for Scotland show the mortality to be chiefly in the first three months of life, whereas the statutory limit for vaccination in that country is six months.

Other alleged effects of vaccination.

In the polemical writings of anti-vaccinists, such diseases as scrofula, tubercle, hooping-cough, diarrhœa, and other common causes of infantine mortality are alleged to have increased owing to vaccination. There is little or no reason, in theory or in experience, to suspect that tuberculous or scrofulous infection is ever communicated by vaccine lymph. As regards the above and other infantine maladies, vaccination may predispose the child to fall into them, in so far as it produces, or ought in theory to produce, a considerable constitutional disturbance and presumably a loss, for a brief period, of the natural power to

[1] The proportion assigned to the first year of life is calculated from the specimen table for 1852 (females only) and from the tables of London mortality.

resist the various noxious influences by which the age of infancy, especially among the poor, is beset.

The value of cowpox as a protection against smallpox may now be judged of apart from the fanciful doctrine of variolæ vaccinæ by which it was originally recommended. It has been put to a test extending over eighty years; and in some circumstances it has been possible to apply the logical methods of agreement and difference with a good deal of cogency. The besetting fallacy of all vaccination logic is that of *post hoc ergo propter hoc*; and the only way to escape it is to hold intelligent views of the history, the natural history, and the epidemiology of smallpox. This will necessitate a brief excursus.

Smallpox.

Smallpox, which is really a tropical skin disease of the nature of lichen turned pustular, or of ecthyma, must be judged according to what we know of foreign pestilences in general. Perhaps we are safest to take a line through the behaviour of the plague. Plague in western Europe had the start of smallpox by a good many years, if we speak only of prevalence on the large scale. "Throughout the 16th century," says Hirsch, "the plague was a permanent form of disease on the continent of Europe. . . . During the first two-thirds of the 17th century we still meet with it over an equally wide area and equally often. But in the last thirty years of that century the plague was observed to be retreating gradually from the soil of Europe." It was not only in London after the fire of 1666 but also in Denmark and Sweden, in Italy, in Holland and Belgium, in Switzerland, in France, in western Germany, and in Spain that the years 1660-1680 saw the last of plague; it lingered only in the Levant, in Poland, and in other parts of north-eastern Europe, with occasional epidemic visits, such as those of Messina and Marseilles. Now it has left the Levant and Egypt, has abandoned even Mesopotamia and Arabia, and retreated to a few poor villages on the Perso-Armenian frontier. Or, take the example of leprosy, which owed its existence rather to the widespread or national concurrence of the same causes in various countries than to the travelling of an infection: Italy had it first and lost it first, and nearly every other country in Europe saw its rise, its general prevalence, its decline, and its extinction, the northern countries keeping it longest. Again, typhus fever was a standing disease so long as Europe was the theatre of protracted wars and all their consequences; but, like other infections, typhus gradually declined and has almost disappeared since the conditions on which it depended ceased.

Leaving these parallels and coming to the facts of smallpox itself, it rose to prominence in western Europe in the 16th century, and in England in the 17th.[1] From the early part of the 18th century a remission was noted; but the latter half of that century saw a considerable extension of the area of the disease, for which the practice of inoculation has been blamed. It is a mistake to suppose that smallpox has shown a tendency towards a universal infection; for all its chances it has kept within moderate limits of age and place, and extended only by repeated provocation. Thus, Hirsch says of the western hemisphere, "A still more terrible source for America was the importation of Negro slaves, so much so that in after years, particularly in South America and the West Indies, not only the first appearances of smallpox, but every fresh outbreak of it, could be traced to importation from Africa,"—the African continent being then, as now and always, one of its principal native seats. In Europe it has been peculiarly a disease of infancy and of the most crowded parts of cities. It has had victims among the upper classes, just as cholera has had; but, like that disease, its habitat is among the crowded poor; and it would have touched the well-to-do-classes less in former times if there had always been spacious west-end quarters in cities or the modern "passion for clean linen," personal ablutions, and fresh air. Tenement houses and ill-ventilated courts or alleys have been the natural harbourage of smallpox; in proportion as these have been demolished the disease has disappeared or been circumscribed in its area. It is fallacious to estimate its prevalence now in ratio of the whole population; for a just comparison of one period with another, we have to take into account, not the death-rate per million living, but the death-rate per million still living under the old-world conditions. From the earliest period of its history in Europe, the disease has had its seasons of quickening or revival, with long intervals of quiescence; only in the most crowded parts of Western cities has it ever been endemic from year to year. These epidemic outbursts have varied much in intensity and in area, the conditions of variation being mostly unknown. In that respect, it need hardly be said, smallpox is like other epidemic diseases.

Influence of vaccination upon smallpox.

During the early years of the 19th century there was a marked remission of the epidemic outbursts of the disease in most parts of Europe. The amount of vaccination during those years was inconsiderable; in particular it hardly touched the poor. Thus, at the time of the Norwich epidemic of 1819, it was estimated (by Cross) that only one-fourth of the inhabitants were vaccinated, and these almost exclusively the well-to-do. At the same time the practice of inoculating smallpox, which was with good reason blamed for keeping the contagion generally diffused and active among the non-inoculated, began to be discontinued and soon ceased altogether. Undoubtedly there was a marked decline in smallpox during the first fifteen years of the century, but the associated circumstances are as complex as the fact itself is simple. We have to bear in mind the old law of periodic exacerbation and dormancy, the cessation of a practice (inoculation) which almost certainly interfered with the natural tendency of smallpox as a foreign pestilence to die out, and the unusual prevalence of typhus fever (on the Continent), and other displacing or substitutive factors in the death-rate. To what extent vaccination was a factor will have to be decided by the experience of a period when the practice was much more generally in vogue. For that purpose we may here restrict the inquiry to England and Wales, premising that the experience of other European countries where vaccination has been equally practised is not different.

The following table (III.) begins with the year 1847; the registration reports go back to 1838, but there is a break in the tables for five years near the beginning.

Deaths from Smallpox from 1847 to 1884, with the numbers among Children under five.

Year.	Total of All Ages.	Children under Five.	All Other Ages.	Year.	Total of All Ages.	Children under Five.	All Other Ages.
1847	4227	3114	1113	1866	3029	1662	1367
1848	6903	4782	2121	1867	2513	1370	1143
1849	4644	3146	1498	1868	2052	1234	818
1850	4665	3265	1400	1869	1565	892	673
1851	6997	4869	2128	1870	2620	1245	1375
[2]*1852*	*7320*	*5076*	*2244*	*1871*	*23126*	*7770*	*15356*
1853	3151	2164	987	1872	19094	5758	13336
1854	2808	1659	1149	1873	2364	587	1777
1855	2525	1323	1202	1874	2162	543	1619
1856	2277	1299	978	1875	849	176	673
1857	3936	2335	1601	1876	2408	612	1796
1858	*6460*	*3585*	*2875*	*1877*	*4278*	*1056*	*3222*
1859	3848	2247	1601	1878	1856	472	1384
1860	2749	1544	1205	1879	536	130	406
1861	1320	723	597	1880	648	170	478
1862	1628	931	697	*1881*	*3098*	*740*	*2358*
1863	5964	3267	2697	1882	1317	275	1042
1864	*7684*	*4294*	*3390*	1883	957	226	731
1865	6411	3262	3149	1884	2234	503	1731

In the first years of the table the deaths from smallpox of children under five were to those of all other ages in the ratio of 3 to 1 or of 5 to 2 (at Norwich in 1819 there were 530 deaths, of which half were in infants under two, and all the rest save ten were in children under ten years); the disproportion lessened gradually, until about 1864 it was nearly 4 to 3; in 1870 the proportion was nearly equal; and from that time onward the preponderance leaves the age of infancy and childhood, so that in 1884 the deaths under five were three times fewer than those at all other ages. The great epidemic of 1871-72 brought out that remarkable change of incidence most decidedly. Taking the mortality of 1871 as an instance, the significance of the changed incidence on the periods of life is that the 7770 deaths under the age of five would, in pre-compulsion times, have had a complement of no more than 2500 deaths in the later periods of life, or that the actual mortality of 15,356 above the age of five would have had a complement of some 40,000 or 45,000 deaths below that age. (In British India in 1884 of 333,000 deaths 72 per cent. were of children under 12 in Bengal, and 64 per cent. in Madras.) Apart from the changed incidence of smallpox, Table III. shows merely the caprices of the disease as an epidemic. After every epidemic outburst the disease declines and sometimes looks as if it were about to die out altogether. The alarm attending each severe epidemic has induced the legislature to make the vaccination law more stringent and vaccinators to insert more of the virus, so that the periodic subsidence has corresponded to, and has seemed to be owing to, the better enforcement of the practice; but there have always been alternating periods of quiescence and exacerbation, irrespective of any prophylactic. Moreover, smallpox being a foreign contagious skin disease lurking in congenial haunts, it would be quite according to precedent that it should one day cease absolutely in a community where sanitary progress had advanced so far as to take the ground from under the feet of the pestilence; such absolute cessation would have no more necessary connexion with almost universal vaccination than the alternating quiescence and recrudescence of epidemics have been connected with each new Act of Parliament. The epidemic of 1871-72 was one of the worst in the whole history of European smallpox; and it may be that it was one of the last flickers of a slowly expiring flame. The universal practice of cowpoxing, however, is based upon the

[1] The first known use of the term "small pocks" is in Holinshed's *Chronicle* (1577), an epidemic of *pestis* in 1365 being so rendered, although it was probably the ordinary bubo-plague of the period. The pox of Elizabethan writers was the French pox or great pox (syphilis), which overran Europe as an epidemic in 1494. Its prominent character at its first appearance was the loathsome affection of the skin (especially the face); hence when variola came on the scene it was called the lesser pox, or smallpox.

[2] The Italic numerals indicate the periodic maxima.

assumption that this contagious skin disease imported from the tropics is a thing that Europe must reckon with for an indefinite time. On the other hand, the teaching of epidemiology is that a foreign pestilence never stays unless it finds quarters suited to its existence, and that it may even take its departure capriciously, as in the case of the plague, after it has had a certain career, or on being displaced by some congener such as typhus. Vaccination is considered to have turned smallpox in great part aside from the early years of life and thrown it more than ever upon the later ages, while measles and other maladies proper to childhood have at the same time increased.[1]

Its utility to the individual.

Thus far as regards the utility of vaccination to the state; we have now to consider its utility to the individual. Do the vaccinated escape in an epidemic? or, if they do not escape an attack of smallpox, do they escape death from it? In answer to the first question, apart from the familiar negative experience of everyone, we have the statistics of smallpox hospitals, which relate to the poorer class and probably do full justice to the fact of non-vaccination, inasmuch as the unvaccinated residue is mostly to be found in those slums and tenements of the poor where smallpox (now as always) is apt to linger. At the Eastern Metropolitan Hospital (Homerton) from its opening early in 1871 to the end of 1878 there were 6533 admissions for smallpox, of which 4283 had vaccination marks, 793 had no marks although vaccinated, and 1477 were unvaccinated, giving a proportion of 0·29 unvaccinated. In the epidemic hospitals of Liverpool, Glasgow, and Dublin the proportion was 0·25 during the same period. For some of the German states the proportion of unvaccinated cases comes out a good deal less than one-fourth; thus, in Bavaria in 1871 of 30,742 cases 29,429 were in vaccinated persons, or 95·7 per cent., and 1313 in the unvaccinated, or 4·3 per cent.[2] In some of the small local outbreaks of recent years the victims have been nearly all vaccinated (*e.g.*, at Bromley in 1881, a total of 43 cases, including sixteen confluent, all vaccinated).[3] In the army and navy, where vaccination and re-vaccination are absolutely without exception, the proportion is accordingly 0. It would thus appear that the rather excessive proportion of cases among the small residue of unvaccinated in the civil population must have other associated circumstances besides non-vaccination; and these are not far to seek.

Death-rates among vaccinated and unvaccinated.

The next question is the death-rate among the vaccinated and unvaccinated respectively. The total death-rate from smallpox in modern times is almost the same as it was in the 18th century; large aggregates collected by Jurin and others in pre-vaccination times show a mortality of 18·8 per cent., and corresponding aggregates in English and American hospitals, mostly since 1870, show a mortality of 18·5 per cent. It has, however, to be borne in mind that the division into discrete, confluent, and malignant smallpox is an old one; that a mild type was quite common in the 17th and 18th centuries, and was now and then characteristic of whole epidemics, just as in the case of scarlatina; and that the vaccinated are at present liable to be attacked by the confluent and malignant disease as well as by the discrete. But are the vaccinated liable to the fatal forms of smallpox in the same proportion as the unvaccinated? It is only since 1879 that the registrar-general's tables for England and Wales have attempted to supply data bearing on this; and it will be seen from the following abstracts (Tables IV.-VII.) that the data are still far from being sufficient:—

Table IV.—Deaths from Smallpox, showing the Numbers of the Unvaccinated.

Year.	Total Deaths.	Unvaccinated.	Vaccinated.	Not stated.	Year.	Total Deaths.	Unvaccinated.	Vaccinated.	Not stated.
1879	536	231	117	188	1882	1317	325	176	816
1880	648	282	121	245	1883	957	162	78	717
1881	3098	1068	652	1378	1884	2234	595	493	1146

Table (V.),—Same for the Provinces (Metropolitan Deaths deducted).

Year.	Total Deaths in Provinces.	Unvaccinated.	Vaccinated.	Not stated.	Year.	Total Deaths in Provinces.	Unvaccinated.	Vaccinated.	Not stated.
1879	86	20	9	57	1882	887	143	66	678
1880	171	43	14	114	1883	821	111	35	675
1881	731	133	90	508	1884	1336	282	239	815

Table VI.—Deaths from Smallpox in Infants under One Year.

Year.	Total Deaths.	Unvaccinated.	Vaccinated.	Not stated.	Year.	Total Deaths.	Unvaccinated.	Vaccinated.	Not stated.
1881	319	144	14	161	1883	126	32	1	93
1882	129	43	2	84	1884	254	118	7	129

Table (VII.),—Same for the Provinces (Metropolitan Deaths deducted).

Year.	Total Deaths in Provinces.	Unvaccinated.	Vaccinated.	Not stated.	Year.	Total Deaths in Provinces.	Unvaccinated.	Vaccinated.	Not stated.
1881	66	13	1	52	1883	108	21	1	86
1882	90	20	1	69	1884	146	56	5	85

These figures may be made to prove anything, according to the bias of the individual; the column of "not stated" commands the situation. The official figures[4] for Bavaria in 1871 are more precise: among the 29,429 cases of smallpox in vaccinated persons there were 3994 deaths, while among the 1313 unvaccinated cases there were 790 deaths; of the latter no fewer than 743 deaths were of infants in their first year. The mortality among both the vaccinated and the unvaccinated is always excessive for infancy. Feeble health, as well as non-vaccination, is a factor in the very excessive smallpox mortality at that tender age.

The returns from special smallpox hospitals make out a very small death-rate (6 per cent.) among the vaccinated and a very large death-rate (40 to 60 per cent.) among the unvaccinated. The result is doubtful *qua* vaccination, for the reason that in pre-vaccination times the death-rate (18·8 per cent.) was almost the same as it is now in the vaccinated and unvaccinated together (18·5). At the Homerton Hospital from 1871 to 1878 there were admitted 793 cases in which "vaccination is stated to have been performed, but without any evidence of its performance"; the deaths in that important contingent were 216, or 27·2 per cent., but they are not permitted to swell the mortality among the "'vaccinated."[5] Again, the explanatory remarks of the medical officer for Birkenhead in 1877 reveal to us the rather surprising fact that his column of "unvaccinated" contained, not only cases that were admittedly not vaccinated, but also those that were "without the faintest mark"; of the 72 cases in that column no fewer than 53 died. His column of "unknown" contained 80 per cent. of patients who protested that they had been vaccinated (28 deaths in 220 cases or 12·7 per cent.). Those who passed muster as veritably vaccinated were 233, of whom 12 died (5·1 per cent.). With reference to this question of the marks, it has to be said that cowpox scars may be temporary, that their "goodness" or "badness" depends chiefly on the texture of the individual's skin and the thickness or thinness of the original crust, and that the aspect of the scar, or even its total absence some years or even months after, may be altogether misleading as to the size and correctness in other respects of the vaccine vesicle, and of the degree of constitutional disturbance that attended it. This was candidly recognized by Ceely,[6] and will not be seriously disputed by anyone who knows something of cowpox and of how it has been mitigated, and of the various ways in which the tissues of individuals may react to an inoculated infection. In confluent cases the marks on the arm would be less easily seen.

The following statistical table (VIII.) shows death from smallpox to be comparatively rare where the marks are many and "good."

Table VIII., showing the Number and Kind of Arm Marks in 379 Fatal Cases of Smallpox at Homerton Hospital, 1871-80 (Gayton).

Vaccinal Marks.	Admissions.		Deaths.		Mortality per cent.	
	Under 10 Years.	Over 10 Years.	Under 10 Years.	Over 10 Years.	Under 10 Years.	Over 10 Years.
4 good	56	247	0	4	0·0	2·5
3 good	44	388	0	12		
2 good	41	528	1	19	2·4	4·1
1 good	43	422	1	20		
4 imperfect	91	317	3	17	3·0	6·9
3 imperfect	107	545	3	43		
2 imperfect	142	930	17	92	12·5	12·6
1 imperfect	138	820	18	129		

Re-vaccination.

The practice of re-vaccination was first recommended in England by G. Gregory, and in Germany for the army by Heim (1829). It has been more or less the law in Prussia since 1835:[7] "re-vaccination of school pupils at the age of twelve is an integral part of the vaccination law." Notwithstanding the fact that Prussia was the best re-vaccinated country in Europe, its mortality from smallpox in the epidemic of 1871 was higher (59,839) than in any other northern state. The efficacy of re-vaccination is sometimes sought to be proved by the immunity of nurses in smallpox hospitals. The experiment of not re-vaccinating the nurses was tried at the smallpox hospital of the South Dublin Union in 1871-72; 29 out of the 36 attendants had not been re-vaccinated, and these all escaped smallpox as well as the other seven.[8] But nurses are not rarely chosen from among those who have had smallpox, and cases of smallpox in re-vaccinated nurses are not unknown.[9] The evidence as to re-vaccination on a large scale comes from the army. According to a competent statistician (A. Vogt), the death-rate from small-

[1] See Farr, *Reg. Gen. Report* for 1867, p. 213: "To operate on mortality, protection against every one of the fatal zymotic diseases is required; otherwise the suppression of one disease-element opens the way to another" (p. 219). He quotes Watt (1813) to show that the decrease of smallpox mortality among infants in Glasgow from 1783 to 1812 was balanced by a great increase in the infantine deaths from measles. See also Guy, *Journ. Statist. Soc.*, 1882, p. 430.

[2] Majer, *Vierteljahrschrift für gericht. Med.*, xxii. 355.

[3] Nicolson, *Lancet*, 27th August 1881.

[4] Majer, *op. cit.*

[5] *Parliamentary Return*, 24th February 1880.

[6] *Trans. Prov. Med. and Surg. Assoc.*, viii., 1840.

[7] Hern's *Medicinal-Wesen in Preussen*, ed. Eulenberg, Berlin, 1873-74, pp. 160 and 215.

[8] *Med. Press and Circ.*, 27th March 1872.

[9] Sweeting, *Rep. Fulham Hosp.*, 1881.

pox in the German army, in which all recruits are re-vaccinated, was 60 per cent. more than among the civil population of the same age; it was ten times greater among the infantry than among the cavalry, and sixty times more among the Hessians than among the Würtembergers. The Bavarian contingent, which was re-vaccinated without exception, had five times the death-rate from smallpox in the epidemic of 1870-71 that the Bavarian civil population of the same ages had, although re-vaccination is not obligatory among the latter.

The susceptibility to cowpox infection diminishes with age; among the pupils of twelve years in Prussian schools it fails in about one-fourth of the attempts, and at later periods of life the proportion of failures is still greater.

It is often alleged that the unvaccinated are so much inflammable material in the midst of the community, and that smallpox begins among them and gathers force so that it sweeps even the vaccinated before it. Inquiry into the facts has shown that at Cologne in 1870 the first unvaccinated person attacked by smallpox was the 174th in order of time, at Bonn the same year the 42d, and at Liegnitz in 1871 the 225th.

Legislation.

State-supported facilities for vaccination began in England in 1808 with the National Vaccine Establishment. In 1840 vaccination fees were made payable out of the rates. The first compulsory Act was passed in 1853, the guardians of the poor being intrusted with the carrying out of the law; in 1854 the public vaccinations under one year of age were 408,824, as against an average of 180,960 for several years before. In 1867 a new Act was passed, rather to remove some technical difficulties than to enlarge the scope of the former Act; and in 1871 the Act was passed which compelled the boards of guardians to appoint vaccination officers. The guardians also appoint a public vaccinator, who must be duly qualified to practise medicine, and whose duty it is to vaccinate (for a fee of not less than eighteenpence) any child resident within his district brought to him for that purpose, to examine the same a week after, to give a certificate, and to certify to the vaccination officer the fact of vaccination or of insusceptibility. The Local Government Board awards a considerable sum in premiums for totals of successful vaccination, at a higher scale of one shilling for each case, and a lower scale of sixpence. The vaccination officer sees that all infants are vaccinated, either publicly or privately, before they are three months old (in Scotland six months), unless there is reason for postponing the operation. He acts also as registrar of vaccinations. Parents refusing to obey the summons taken out by the vaccination officer are liable to a penalty of twenty shillings for each offence. In 1880 the president of the Local Government Board brought in a bill to repeal the part of the Act relating to cumulative penalties; but the bill was withdrawn owing to protests from the medical profession. In a number of populous unions of England a majority of the guardians are decided not to prosecute under the Vaccination Act; in other unions prosecutions are not unfrequent, the convictions having amounted in 1885 to upwards of two thousand, and having usually led to distraint of goods (rarely to imprisonment) in default of paying the fine. In England about two-thirds of all infants are vaccinated at the public expense.

Vaccination was made compulsory in Bavaria in 1807, and subsequently in the following countries:—Denmark (1810), Sweden (1814), Würtemberg, Hesse, and other German states (1818), Prussia (1835), Roumania (1874), Hungary (1876), and Servia (1881). It is compulsory by cantonal law in ten out of the twenty-two Swiss cantons; an attempt to pass a federal compulsory law was defeated by a plebiscite in 1881.

In the following countries there is no compulsory law, but Governmental facilities and compulsion on various classes more or less directly under Governmental control, such as soldiers, state employés, apprentices, school pupils, &c.:—France, Italy, Spain, Portugal, Belgium, Norway, Austria, Turkey.

In a few States or cities of the American Union there is a vaccination statute. In Lower Canada there is no compulsion; but vaccination has been compulsory in South Australia since 1872, in Victoria since 1874, and in Western Australia since 1878. In Tasmania a compulsory Act was passed in 1882. In New South Wales there is no compulsion, but free facilities for vaccination. Compulsion was adopted at Calcutta in 1880 and since then at eighty other towns of Bengal, at Madras in 1884, and at Bombay and elsewhere in the presidency a few years earlier.

Re-vaccination was made compulsory in Denmark in 1871 and in Roumania in 1874; in Holland it was enacted for all school pupils in 1872. The various laws and administrative orders which had been for many years in force as to vaccination and re-vaccination in the several German states were consolidated in an imperial statute of 1874.

Authorities.—Jenner, *Inquiry*, London, 1798, and *Further Observations*, 1799; G. Pearson, *Inquiry concerning the History of Cowpox*, London, 1798; Woodville, *Reports of a Series of Inoculations for the Variolæ Vaccinæ or Cowpox*, London, 1799; Baron, *Life of Edward Jenner, M.D.*, 2 vols., London, 1838; Bousquet, *Sur le Cow-pox, découvert à Passy*, Paris, 1836; Estlin, in *Lond. Med. Gazette*, 1838-39; Ceely, *Trans. Prov. Med. and Surg. Assoc.*, viii. (1840) and x. (1842); Hering, *Ueber Kuhpocken an Kühen*, Stuttgart, 1839; Viennois and others, in *Syphilis Vaccinale*, Paris, 1865; Bohn, *Handbuch der Vaccination*, Leipsic, 1875; E. C. Seaton, *Handbook of Vaccination*, London, 1868; *Reports on Sanitary Measures in India, 1884-85*; W. White, *Story of a Great Delusion*, London, 1885; M'Vail, *Vaccination Vindicated*, London, 1887; Lotz, *Pocken und Vaccination*, 2d ed., Basel, 1880; G. Fr. Kolb, *Der heutige Stand der Impffrage*, Leipsic, 1879; A. Vogt, *Der alte u. d. neue Impfglaube*, Bern, 1881; and Creighton, *Natural History of Cowpox and Vaccinal Syphilis*, London, 1887. (C. C.)

VÁCZ (Germ. *Waitzen*), a market town in Hungary, on the left bank of the Danube, 20 miles north of Buda-Pesth. It gives its name to a Roman Catholic bishopric (established by Stephen, first king of Hungary, in 1000) and various schools, convents, and charities connected therewith, and has a state deaf and dumb institute and a central Government prison. The cathedral, a magnificent structure, is an imitation of St Peter's at Rome, with mediæval relics and pictures. The majority of the inhabitants are engaged in agriculture and cattle-breeding; but exportation of grapes from the neighbouring hilly district is also largely carried on. Vácz is a station on the Austrian-Hungarian railway system. The population, mostly Magyars by nationality, was 13,199 in 1880, and in 1887 was estimated to number nearly 17,000.

VAGA, PERINO DEL (1500-1547), a painter of the Roman school, whose true name was PERINO (or PIERO) BUONACCORSI. He was born in Florence on 28th June 1500. His father ruined himself by gambling, and became a soldier in the invading army of Charles VIII. His mother dying when he was but two months old, he was suckled by a she-goat; but shortly afterwards he was taken up by his father's second wife. Perino was first apprenticed to a druggist, but soon passed into the hands of a mediocre painter, Andrea da Ceri, and, when eleven years of age, of Ridolfo Ghirlandajo. Perino rapidly surpassed his fellow-pupils, applying himself especially to the study of Michelangelo's great cartoon. Another mediocre painter, Vaga from Toscanella, undertook to settle the boy in Rome, but first set him to work in Toscanella. Perino, when he at last reached Rome, was utterly poor, and with no clear prospect beyond journey-work for trading decorators. He, however, studied with great severity and spirit from Michelangelo and the antique, and was eventually entrusted with some of the subordinate work undertaken by Raphael in the Vatican. He assisted Giovanni da Udine in the stucco and arabesque decorations of the loggie of the Vatican, and executed some of those small but finely composed Scriptural subjects which go by the name of "Raphael's Bible"—Raphael himself furnishing the designs. Perino's examples are Abraham about to Sacrifice Isaac, Jacob Wrestling with the Angel, Joseph and his Brethren, the Hebrews Crossing the Jordan, the Fall and Capture of Jericho, Joshua Commanding the Sun to Stand Still, the Birth of Christ, His Baptism, and the Last Supper. Some of these are in bronze-tint, while others are in full colour. He also painted, after Raphael's drawings, the figures of the planets in the great hall of the Appartamenti Borgia. Perino exhibited very uncommon faculty in these works and was soon regarded as second only to Giulio Romano among the great painter's assistants. To Raphael himself he was always exceedingly respectful and attentive, and the master loved him almost as a son. He executed many other works about Rome, always displaying a certain mixture of the Florentine with the Roman style.

After Raphael's death in 1520 a troublous period ensued for Perino, with a plague which ravaged Rome in 1523, and again with the sack of that city in 1527. Then he accepted an invitation to Genoa, where he was employed in decorating the Doria palace, and rapidly founded a quasi-Roman school of art in the Ligurian city. He ornamented the palace in a style similar to that of Giulio Romano in the Mantuan Palazzo del Tè, and frescoed historical and mythological subjects in the apartments, fanciful and graceful arabesque-work, sculptural and architectural details—in short, whatever came to hand. Among the principal works are the War between the Gods and Giants, Horatius Cocles Defending the Bridge, and the Fortitude of Mutius Scævola. The most important work of all, the Shipwreck of Æneas, is no longer extant. Perino was particularly good in the technique and colouring of fresco, and his stucco-work was no less highly prized than his pictures; his Genoese paintings are, however, very inferior to those of Raphael in finish, as in other higher qualities, and his style in the nude tends rather towards Michelangelo. The Doria work is moreover extremely unequal. From Genoa Perino twice visited Pisa, and began some painting in the cathedral. Finally he returned to Rome, where Paul III. allowed him a regular salary till the painter's death. He retouched many of the works of Raphael, and laboured hard on his own account, undertaking all sorts of jobs, important or trivial. Working for any price, he made large gains, but fell into mechanical negligence. Perino was engaged in the general decoration of the Sala Reale, begun by Paul III., when his health, undermined by constant work and as constant irregularities, gave way, and he fell down dead on 19th October 1547. He is buried in the Pantheon.

Perino, though his character and habits of life were not such as to inspire respect, seems to have been generally liked in a certain way; he was, however, jealous of rivals, particularly of Titian when in Rome, and grudging in the instruction of his pupils. He produced some excellent portraits, and his smaller oil pictures combine with the manner of Raphael something of that of Andrea del Sarto. Many of his works were engraved, even in his own lifetime. Daniele da Volterra, Girolamo Siciolante da Sermoneta, Luzio Romano, and Marcello Venusti (Mantovano) were among his principal assistants.

VAIR, GUILLAUME DU (1556-1621), one of the fathers of French prose, and at the same time one of the most brilliant ornaments of the great school of French lawyers in the 16th and 17th centuries, was born at Paris on 7th March 1556. Du Vair was in orders, and, though during the greater part of his life he exercised only legal functions, he in 1617 accepted the see of Lisieux and died bishop thereof. His reputation, however, is that of a lawyer, a statesman, and a man of letters. He was for a considerable time a member (councillor) of the parlement of Paris, and it was in this capacity that he pronounced his most famous politico-legal discourse, an argument nominally for the Salic Law, but in reality directed against the alienation of the crown of France to the Spanish infanta, which was advocated by the extreme Leaguers. It was also during his tenure of the same post that he published (in 1595) a *Traité de l'Éloquence Française*, which both advocates and exhibits a great improvement on the ordinary prose style of the day. In 1599 he became first president of the parlement of Provence (Aix), and in order not to give up this position he refused the see of Marseilles. In 1616 he received the highest promotion open to a French lawyer and became keeper of the seals. His death took place at Tonneins (Lot-et-Garonne) on 3d August 1621. Both as speaker and writer he holds a very high rank, and his character was equal to his abilities. Like other political lawyers of the time, Du Vair busied himself not a little in the study of philosophy (of a Christian stoical cast) and in that of classical antiquity, translating Cicero, Demosthenes, and Epictetus, and writing various treatises, on which Charron, a general plagiarist, is held to have drawn freely. Du Vair's works were published in folio at Paris in 1641.

VALAIS (Germ., *Wallis*), one of the Swiss cantons, ranking as twentieth in the Confederation. Its name has been explained to mean the "Welsh land," as the Teutons called all non-Teutonic lands; but it is far more probably derived from "vallis," for Valais is simply the "Vallis Pœnina," or valley of the Rhone, from its source to the gorge of St Maurice, together with some villages south of the Simplon Pass, and Monthey, Val d'Illiez, and Bouveret beyond St Maurice, on the left bank of the river. The total area of the canton is 2026·3 square miles, which is exceeded only by that of Grisons (Graubünden) and of Bern. Of this 930·4 square miles are classed as productive, forests covering 243·2 and vineyards 9; of the remainder 375·1 square miles consist of snow and ice. The highest point of the canton is Monte Rosa (15,217 feet), and within its borders rises the Dom (14,942 feet), the loftiest peak entirely in Swiss territory. The population in 1880 was 100,216 (males predominating), an increase of 3329 since 1870. French is the native tongue of 67,214 and German of 31,962, the former dwelling (roughly speaking) west and the latter east of a line drawn north and south across the valley of the Rhone between Sierre and Leuk. The bulk (99,316) of the inhabitants are staunch Roman Catholics. The canton forms the diocese of Sion (founded in 4th century), which before 1513 was in the ecclesiastical province of Moutiers-en-Tarentaise (Savoy), and since then has been immediately dependent on the pope. In the canton there are three famous houses of Austin canons regular—St Maurice (founded as a Benedictine monastery, as distinct from the see, in 515 by Sigismund of Burgundy), the hospice on the Great St Bernard (first mentioned in 1125), and that on the Simplon Pass (first mentioned in 1235). Ecclesiastical affairs are managed without any control or interference on the part of the state, though the cantonal legislative assembly selects as bishop one of four candidates nominated by the chapter of Sion. The only town of any size is the capital, Sion or Sitten (4871 inhabitants in 1880). The population are mainly engaged in agricultural pursuits, and great efforts have been made to improve matters lately, while the Rhone has been embanked to prevent disastrous floods. Much wine (*e.g.*, Muscat and Vin du Glacier) and a vast quantity of grapes are exported. Education is compulsory and free, but very backward. A railway runs from Brieg to Bouveret. The mineral waters of Leukerbad and Saxon are well known, and in summer the canton is a favourite haunt of tourists.

The Vallis Pœnina was won by the Romans after a great fight at Octodurus (Martigny) in 57 B.C., and was so thoroughly Romanized that the Celtic aboriginal inhabitants and the Teutonic Burgundian invaders (5th cent.) became Romance-speaking peoples. According to a tradition which can be traced back to the middle of the 8th century, the "Theban legion" was martyred at St Maurice about 285. Valais formed part of the kingdom of Transjurane Burgundy (888), which fell to the empire in 1032, and later of the duchy of Burgundia Minor, which was held from the emperors by the house of Zäringen (extinct 1218). In 999 Rudolph III. of Burgundy gave all temporal rights and privileges to the bishop of Sion, who was later styled "præfect and count of the Valais," and is still a prince of the Holy Roman empire; the pretended donation of Charlemagne is not genuine. The bishops had much to do in keeping back the Zäringen, and later the counts of Savoy. The latter, however, succeeded in winning most of the land west of Sion, while in the upper part of the valley there were many feudal lords (such as the lords of Raron and the counts of Visp). About the middle of the 13th century we find independent communities or "tithings" ("dizains" or "zehnten") growing up. In the same century the upper part of the valley was colonized by Germans from Hasli (Bern), who thoroughly Teutonized it, though many Romance local names still remain. In 1354 the liberties of the seven "tithings" (Sion, Sierre, Leuk, Raron, Visp, Brieg, and Conches) were confirmed by the emperor Charles IV. A little later the influence of Savoy became predominant, and the count secured to his family the bishopric of Sion, of which he was already the suzerain. His progress was resisted by the tithings, which in 1388 utterly defeated the forces of the bishop, the count, and the nobles at Visp, this being a victory of the Teutonic over the Romance element in the land. From 1384 the Morge stream (a little below Sion) was recognized as the boundary between Savoyard or Lower Valais and episcopal or Upper Valais. For the connexion of the latter with the Val d'Ossola, see SWITZERLAND, vol. xxii. p. 785. By the election of Walther von Supersax of Conches as bishop in 1457 the Teutonic element finally won the supremacy. On the outbreak of the Burgundian War the bishop of Sion and the tithings made a treaty with Bern. In November of the same year (1475) they seized all Lower Valais up to Martigny, and in 1476 (March), after the victory of Granson, won St Maurice, Evian, Thonon, and Monthey. The last three districts were given up in 1477, but won again in 1536, though finally by the treaty of 1569 Monthey, Val d'Illiez, and Bouveret alone were permanently annexed to Valais. These conquered districts (or Lower Valais) were always ruled as subject lands by the bishop and tithings of Upper Valais. In 1533 a close alliance was made with the Catholic cantons; but by 1551 the Protestants had won so much ground that toleration was proclaimed by the local assembly. In 1586 Upper Valais became a member of the Golden League, and finally in 1603-4 the four tithings of Conches, Brieg, Visp, and Raron carried the day in favour of the old faith against those of Leuk, Sierre, and Sion. In 1790-91 Lower Valais rose in revolt; but it was not finally freed till 1798, when the whole of Valais became part of the Rhodanic, and then one of the cantons of the Helvetic, Republic. Such prolonged and fierce resistance was, however, offered to French rule by the inhabitants that in 1802 Bonaparte declared Valais an independent republic, yet in 1810, for strategic reasons, he incorporated it with France as the "department of the Simplon," and it was not freed till the Austrians came in 1813. In 1815 a local assembly was created, in which each of the seven tithings of Upper and each of the six of Lower Valais (though the latter had nearly double the population of the former) elected four members, the bishop being given four votes. In 1832 Valais joined the League of Sarnen to maintain the Federal Pact of 1815. In 1838-40 it was convulsed by a struggle between the Conservative and Radical parties, the split into two half cantons being only prevented by the arrival of Federal troops. The constitution was revised in 1839 and 1844; the local assembly was to be elected according to population, and the bishop was given a seat instead of his four votes. In 1843 Valais was one of the Sonderbund, and in 1844 civil war raged, many Liberals being slain at the bridge of Trient (May 1844). The introduction of the Jesuits embittered matters, and Valais was the last canton to submit in the Sonderbund War (1847); it contented itself, however, with voting steadily against the acceptance of the Federal constitutions of 1848 and 1874. By the constitution of 1847 all ecclesiastical immunities were swept away, and the bishop lost his seat in the assembly. That constitution was revised in 1852, and the present one is dated 1875. There is now a legislative assembly of 101 members, elected for four years by all male citizens of twenty years, in the proportion of one member to 1000 inhabitants, and an executive council of five members, holding office for four years, and chosen by the legislative assembly, though in a certain proportion to the different districts of the canton (two for the upper part, one for Sion, two for the lower part). The "financial referendum" exists, by which when a capital expenditure of £2400, or an annual one of £800 for three years, is to be incurred, or it is proposed to raise the property tax higher than 1½ per cent., the proposal must be submitted to and approved by a popular vote.

See Furrer, *Gesch. von Wallis* (3 vols., 1852-54); Gingins La Sarra, *Développement de l'Indépendance du Haut Valais et Conquête du Bas Valais* (1844); and J. Gremaud, *Documents Relatifs à l'Histoire du Valais* (1875 sq.). (W. A. B. C.)

VALDEPEÑAS, a town of Spain, in the province of Ciudad Real, on the railway line from Madrid to Cordova, is situated in the midst of a district thickly clothed with vineyards at the foot of the northern slope of the Sierra Morena. It is a straggling place and its only industry is that of wine-making (see WINE). The population within the municipal boundaries in 1877 was 13,876.

VALDES, JUAN DE (*c.* 1500-1541), Spanish religious writer, born about 1500 at Cuenca in Castile, was the younger of twin sons of Fernando de Valdes, hereditary regidor of Cuenca. Juan has often been confounded with his twin-brother Alphonso, who was in the suite of Charles V. in 1520, acted as his Latin secretary from 1524, and died in 1532 at Vienna. It has been conjectured that Juan studied at the university of Alcala. We first meet him as the anonymous author of a politico-religious *Diálogo de Mercurio y Caron*, apparently written in 1528 and published then or soon after. As this *Diálogo* reflected strongly on the corruptions of the Roman Church, Valdes got into difficulties with the Spanish Inquisition, and left Spain for Naples in 1530. He removed in 1531 to Rome. On 12th January 1533 he writes from Bologna, where he was in attendance upon the pope, Clement VII.; his criticisms of papal policy had been condoned, inasmuch as in his *Diálogo* he had defended the validity of the marriage of Catherine of Aragon to Henry VIII. But in the autumn of 1533 he returned to Naples, and seems never to have left it again. His name has been Italianized into Valdesso and Val d'Esso. It has frequently been asserted that he was appointed by Charles V. as secretary to the viceroy at Naples, Don Pedro de Toledo; but of this there is no evidence, and it seems a "harmonizing" conjecture, based on the confusion between Alphonso and Juan. Curione (writing in 1544) calls him "cavalliere di Cesare," but there is no proof of his having ever held an official appointment. At his house on the Chiaja he was the centre of a very distinguished circle, literary and religious, and the influence of his conversations and his writings, chiefly circulated in manuscript, stimulated the desire for a spiritual reformation of the church. The first-fruit of his cultured leisure at Naples was a philological treatise, *Diálogo de la Lengua* (written 1533); but, though his friends urged him to seek distinction by his humanistic studies, his bent was towards the spiritual problems of Biblical interpretation and the deep things of the devout life. Vermigli (Peter Martyr) and Marcantonio Flaminio were leading spirits in the coterie of Valdes, which included Vittoria Colonna and her sister-in-law Giulia Gonzaga. On Ochino, whom he furnished with themes for sermons, his influence was very great. Carnesecchi, who had known Valdes at Rome as "a modest and wellbred courtier," found him at Naples in 1540 "wholly intent upon the study of Holy Scripture," portions of which he translated from the Hebrew and Greek into Spanish, with comments and suggestive prefaces. To his teaching Carnesecchi ascribes his own complete adoption of the Evangelical doctrine of justification by faith, and at the same time his estrangement from the policy of the Lutheran schism. Valdes died at Naples in May 1541.

The death of Valdes scattered his band of associates. Ochino and Vermigli abandoned the hope of a regenerated Catholicism, and left Italy. By degrees some of Valdes's writings were translated into Italian and published. They exhibit great originality and penetration, combined with a delicate vein of semi-mystical spirituality, and retain a large measure of that personal charm which is attributed to their author in all contemporary notices. Llorente finds traces in Valdes of the influence of Tauler's writings; any such influence must have been at second hand. Valdes was in relations with Fra Benedetto of Mantua, the anonymous author of *Del Benefizio di Gesù Cristo Crocefisso*, which was revised by Flaminio (reprinted by Dr Babington, Cambridge, 1855). The suggestion that Valdes was unsound on the doctrine of the Trinity was first made in 1567 by the Transylvanian bishop, Francis Dávid (see SOCINUS, vol. xxii. p. 230); it has been adopted by Sand (1684), Wallace (1850), and other anti-Trinitarian writers, and is countenanced by Bayle. Some colour has been given to this view by isolated expressions in his writings, and by the subsequent course of Ochino, whose orthodoxy seems, however, to have been unjustly suspected, from the speculative insight with which he presented objections. But Valdes, though he never treats of the Trinity, even when commenting upon Matt. xxviii. 19, reserving it in his *Latte Spirituale* as a topic for advanced Christians, explicitly affirms the consubstantiality of the Son, whom he unites in doxologies with the Father and the Holy Spirit (*Opusc.*, p. 145). His interest centred in matters of practical rather than of speculative theology: his great aim was the promotion of a healthy and personal piety.

The following is a list of his writings.

(1) *Diálogo de Mercurio y Caron*, 8vo (no date or place of printing; 1528 ?). An Italian translation, by Nicolo Franco, was printed at Venice without date, and reprinted at the same place in 1545. Both with the original and the translation is generally found a *Diálogo* on the sack of Rome in 1527, by Alphonso de Valdes, printed at the same time. Both are ascribed to Juan in the reprint *Dos Diálogos* of 1850. (2) *Diálogo de la Lengua*, written in 1533, first printed at Madrid, 1737, reprinted 1860 and 1873. (3) *Qual Maniera si devrebbe tenere a informare . . . gli Figliuoli de Christiani delle Cose della Religione* (no date or place of printing; before 1545, as it was made use of by the Italian translator of Calvin's catechism, 1545). No Spanish original is known. It was reproduced as *Latte Spirituale*, Basel, 1549, and Paris, 1550. A Latin version, by Pierpaolo Vergerio, was published in 1554 and again in 1557; it has been translated into German twice, into Polish, into English by J. T. Betts, 1882, and into Spanish by Ed. Boehmer, in *Revista Cristiana*, Madrid, February 1882 (also separately published). (4) *Trataditos*, first published at Bonn, 1881, from a manuscript in the Palatine Library

at Vienna. An Italian translation, *I Cinque Tratatelli Evangelici*, was published at Rome, 1545, reprinted 1869. An English translation, by J. T. Betts, is in *XVII. Opuscules*, 1882. (5) *Alfabeto Christiano*, Venice, 1545, an Italian translation of an unpublished and lost Spanish original. An English version, by B. B. Wiffen, was published in 1861. (6) *Çiento i Diez Conçideraçiones*; the original is said to have been published, and all copies suppressed by the Spanish Inquisition; thirty-nine of the *Conçideraçiones* were published with the *Trataditos* from a Vienna manuscript. An Italian translation, by Celio Secondo Curione, *Le Cento et Dieci Divine Considerationi*, was published at Basel, 1550, 8vo. A French translation, by Claude de Kerquifinen, was published at Lyons, 1563, 8vo, and Paris, 1565, 8vo. The English translation by Nicholas Ferrar was published at Oxford, 1638, 4to, at the instance of George Herbert; it was reprinted at Cambridge, 1646; a new translation, by J. T. Betts, was issued in 1865. A translation into Spanish from the Italian, by Luis Usóz i Rio, was published in 1855. (7) *Seven Doctrinal Letters*, printed with the *Trataditos*, from a Vienna manuscript, and translated by J. T. Betts in the *XVII. Opuscules*. (8) *Comentario Breve . . . sobre la Epistola de San Pablo a los Romanos*, Venice, 1556; translation and commentary, edited by Juan Perez de Pineda, reprinted 1856; English version, by J. T. Betts, 1883. (9) *Comentario Breve . . . sobre la Primera Epistola de San Pablo a los Corintios*, Venice, 1557; translation and commentary, edited, reprinted, and translated as No. 8. (10) *El Evangelio de San Mateo*, translation and commentary, first published in 1881, from a Vienna manuscript; English version, by J. T. Betts, 1883. (11) *El Salterio*, translation of the Psalms from Hebrew into Spanish, published with the *Trataditos*, from a Vienna manuscript. (12) At Vienna is an unpublished commentary in Spanish on Psalms i.-xli. (13) Sand mentions a commentary on St John's Gospel, which is not known to exist.

The notices of Valdes in Sand (*Biblioth. Antitrinitar.*, 1684, p. 2), Bayle, and Wallace (*Antitrin. Biog.*, 1850, ii. 8) are very inadequate. The revival of interest in him is due to M'Crie, *Hist. Ref. in Italy*, 1827, and *Hist. Ref. in Spain*, 1829. But the full knowledge of his life and teachings was first opened up by Benjamin B. Wiffen, whose *Life* of Valdes was prefixed in 1865 to the new translation of the *Considerations*. Since then important discoveries have been made in the Aulic Library, Vienna, by Dr Edward Boehmer; compare his *Span. Reformers of Two Centuries*, 1874, and *Lives of the Twin Brothers, J. and A. de Valdes*, prefixed to *Biblioth. Wiffeniana*, 1882, also separately, with introd. by J. T. Betts. For an interesting sketch of Valdes, see Benrath's *Bernardino Ochino*, 1875. Respecting his theological standpoint, compare Bonet-Maury, *Early Sources of Eng. Unit. Christianity*, trans. by Hall, 1884. (A. GO.)

VALDO. See WALDO.

VALENCE, a town of France, chef-lieu of the department of Drôme and an episcopal see, is situated on the left bank of the Rhone, 65 miles south of Lyons on the railway to Marseilles. The river is here crossed by a fine suspension bridge. The cathedral of St Apollinaris (originally of St Stephen) was rebuilt in the 11th century in the Auvergnesque variety of the Romanesque style, and consecrated in 1095 by Urban II. It was greatly injured in the Wars of Religion, but restored in 1604. The porch was rebuilt in 1861; above it rises a stone tower (187 feet). The church contains the monument of Pius VI. (bust by Canova), who died at Valence in 1799. A curious house (Les Têtes) of the 16th century has a sculptured front with heads of Homer, Hippocrates, Aristotle, Pythagoras, &c. The antique "little seminary" is occupied by a gallery of pictures, a museum of natural history, a library (25,000 volumes), and a collection of antiquities. Valence possesses a botanic garden, a champ de Mars, artillery barracks, and a departmental prison, worked on the solitary system. The chief industries are the spinning and weaving of silk, oil-pressing, distilling, metal-founding, and the manufacture of macaroni. A considerable trade is carried on in the product of this industry and in wine and agricultural produce. The population in 1881 was 21,941 (commune 25,402) and in 1886 22,453 (commune 24,761).

Valentia colonia Julia, Valentia Segalaunorum urbs, or *civitas Valentinorum*, was the capital of the Segalauni, and the seat of a celebrated school prior to the Roman conquest, a colony under Augustus, and an important town of *Viennensis Prima* under Valentinian. It was ravaged by the Alani and other barbarians, and fell successively under the power of the Burgundians, the Franks, the sovereigns of Arles, the emperors of Germany, the dukes of Valentinois, the counts of Toulouse, and its own bishops. The inhabitants rose unsuccessfully against these last in 1229, but obtained protection with the help of the dauphin in 1345. In 1450 they had their rights and privileges confirmed by Louis XI. and put on an equal footing with those of the rest of Dauphiné. In the 16th century Protestantism spread freely under Bishop Jean de Montluc, and Valence became the capital of the Protestants of the province in 1563. The town was fortified by Francis I. It had become the seat of a celebrated university in 1454; but the revocation of the Edict of Nantes struck a fatal blow at its industry, commerce, and population. Valence was the birthplace of General Championnet and of President Bonjean (shot by the Commune of Paris in 1871); the family of Montalivet had its origin here.

VALENCIA, a province of Spain, one of the three into which the former "kingdom" of Valencia is now divided, has an area of 4352 square miles and a population (1877) of 679,030, being thus, next to Barcelona, the most populous province in the kingdom. It is bounded on the N. by Teruel and Castellon de la Plana, on the E. by the Mediterranean, on the S. by Alicante, and on the W. by Albacete and Cuenca. The surface is very much diversified; along the coast it is for the most part low and level, the fertile "vegas" of Valencia, Játiva, and Gandia in many places rising very little above sea-level; to the west of these is a series of tablelands of a mean elevation of about 1000 feet, which in turn rise into the mountains that form the eastern boundary of the tableland of New Castile, and attain within the province a maximum elevation of nearly 4000 feet. The principal rivers are the Guadalaviar or Turia and the Jucar. The former enters the province in the extreme north-west, flows south-east, and falls into the sea below the town of Valencia; it receives numerous tributaries of little importance, and it dispenses fertility by numerous "acequias," mostly of Moorish origin, throughout the whole of the lower part of its course. The Jucar is joined on the left at Cofrentes ("Confluentes") by the Cabriel, a stream nearly as considerable as itself, and lower down by the Magro; its chief right-hand tributary is the Albayda. Both the Jucar and the Albayda, like the Turia, supply an extensive irrigation. Almost every kind of geological formation from the Silurian to the Quaternary is represented in Valencia: the vegas are Quaternary; nearly three-fourths of the entire province belong to the Cretaceous; large areas, especially to the west, in the district of Requena and Utiel, are of the Tertiary period; in the north the Jurassic is prominent; and Triassic is found along many of the river-valleys. The coast is skirted by considerable stretches of sand dune, and by a series of these the lagoon of Albufera (21,000 acres) is separated from the Mediterranean. The vegas enjoy an exceptionally fine, almost sub-tropical climate. In their low-lying portions rice is the favourite crop; elsewhere wheat, maize, and all kinds of fruit are abundantly grown; the mulberry is cultivated for silk; and wine and oil are produced. Esparto grass is grown in the less fertile areas. The tablelands produce according to their elevation and exposure figs, almonds, olives, and vines. The pastures of the higher grounds sustain numerous sheep and goats; but cattle and horses are relatively few in Valencia. The hillsides are somewhat bare of timber. The mineral resources of the province are little developed. The fishing industry on the coast is considerable. The manufactures include those of silk, glass, pottery, and leather; there are also iron foundries, distilleries, and soap manufactories. The coast railway from Tarragona to Encina passes through Valencia, whence another line has been carried along the Cuenca road as far as to Utiel ($54\frac{1}{2}$ miles). The province is divided into twenty-one partidos judiciales and has 275 ayuntamientos. There are six "cities"—Valencia (see below), Gandia (7604 inhabitants in 1877), Játiva (14,534), Requena (13,527), Sagunto (6287), and Alcira (16,146).

VALENCIA, capital of the above province, is situated in the beautiful "huerta" of Valencia, on the right bank of the Guadalaviar or Turia, 3 miles above its mouth, and 304 miles by rail east-south-east from Madrid. Until 1871 it was enclosed by a wall, built in 1356 by Pedro IV.; two picturesque gateways with machicolated towers still remain. The river, reduced, except in time of flood, to a scanty stream by the demands made upon it for purposes of irrigation, is crossed by five bridges, of which the longest has thirteen arches. The streets are for the most part narrow, crooked, and somewhat gloomy, but in the more modern quarters there are some broad and handsome thoroughfares. The cathedral (La Seo), begun in 1262, was afterwards (1459) lengthened in its original Gothic style, but in such a way as to spoil its proportions, and in the 18th century it was further injured by Pseudo-Classic additions. It possesses some fine examples of the sculpture and metal-work of the 15th century, as well as of the Valencian school of painting. The campanile (El Miguelete), an isolated octagonal Gothic tower, 162 feet in height, commands an extensive view of the town and surrounding country. Near the cathedral is the episcopal palace; its large and valuable library, rich in medals and other antiquities, suffered greatly during the French occupation in 1812. Besides the cathedral, Valencia has fourteen parish churches and numerous other ecclesiastical buildings, none of them of great architectural beauty or interest; the church of St Nicholas (of Moorish origin) has, however, good specimens of Juanes as well as frescos by Dinis Vidal; and Ribalta can be studied in the chapel of the Colegio de Corpus or del Patriarcha. The university buildings, dating from the 16th century, are large but uninteresting; the library (about 42,000 volumes) suffered severely in 1812, and, like the other appointments of the university, falls considerably short of modern requirements. There is a collection of pictures (about 1000) in the city gallery, but only a few,—almost entirely of the local school,—are of any importance. Among other public buildings may be mentioned the court-house, a Doric edifice, dating from the time of Ferdinand the Catholic, and having curious frescos (1592) in its "chamber of deputies"; the custom-house (1758), now a cigar manufactory, employing some 3500 women; and the silk exchange, a large and elegant Gothic hall (1482). The citadel, on the north-east of the town, was built by Charles V. as a protection against Barbarossa, the sea-rover; in the south-west of the town is the former College of Saint Augustine, now used as a model prison, adjoining which is a large hospital. Outside the walls are a botanic garden, a large bull-ring, and various shady promenades, including the beautiful "Glorieta," and, on the north side of the river, the alameda, leading to the port of El Grao. The principal manufacture is silk, and the town is also celebrated for its coloured tiles or "azulejos." Linen and woollen fabrics, hats, leather, paper, cigars, glass, and pottery are also manufactured, and there are foundries and printing-works. Corn, rice, silk, saffron, oranges, raisins, almonds, figs, and other fruits are extensively exported, and iron, hardware, timber, and colonial produce are imported. The port is at El Grao (Villanueva del Grao; population 4433 in 1877), 3 miles distant, where a commodious harbour with a minimum depth of 20 feet has been constructed. The works were begun in 1792. The population of Valencia in 1877 was 143,856, and in 1888 about 170,000 (estimated).

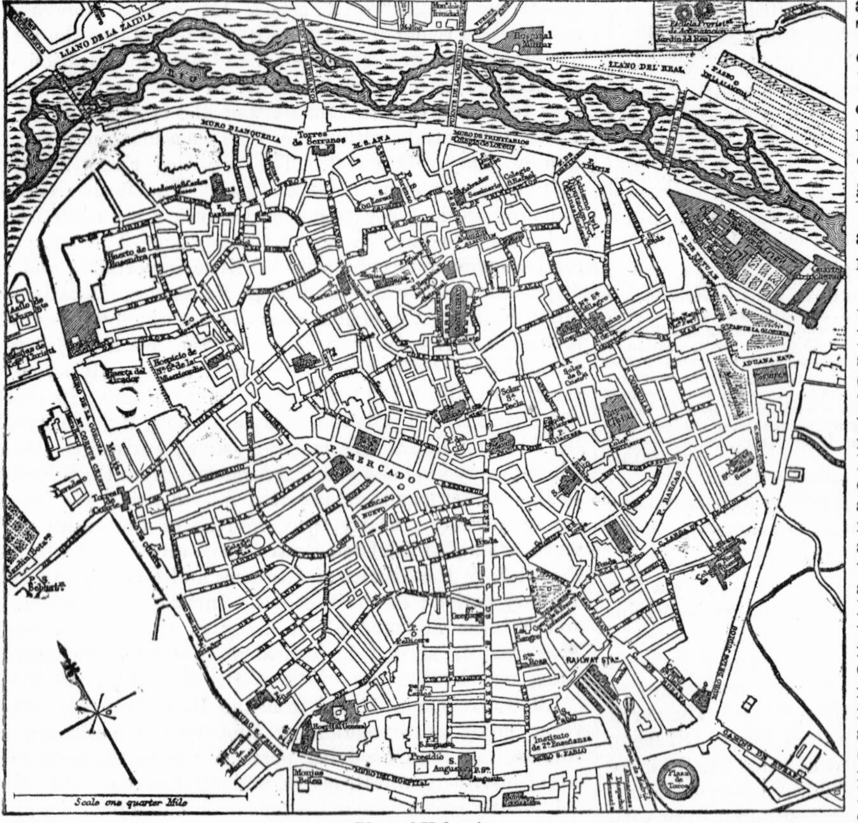

Plan of Valencia.

The earliest historical mention of Valencia (*Valentia*) is by Livy (*Epit.*, lv.), according to whom Junius Brutus settled the soldiers of Viriathus here (136 B.C.). It sided with Sertorius (*c.* 77 B.C.), and was accordingly severely punished by Pompey, but must have recovered speedily, being mentioned by Pliny (iii. 4) as a colony in the region of the Edetani, and spoken of by Mela as an important place. It was taken from the Goths by the Moors in 714, and from the Moors by the Cid (see vol. v. p. 774) in 1094, from whom it is sometimes called Valencia del Cid. The Moors recovered possession in 1101, but were compelled finally to relinquish it in 1238, when Jayme I. of Aragon ("El Conquistador") added it to his dominions. In the 16th and 17th centuries it became the seat of a considerable school of painting, of which Juanes (1506-79) may be regarded as the founder, and to which belonged also Francisco de Ribalta (1550-1628), Juan de Ribalta (1597-1628), José Ribera (1588-1656), Pedro Orrente (1560-1644), and J. G. Espinosa (1600-1680). In the beginning of the 17th century Valencia and its surrounding district suffered greatly from the expulsion of the Moors, its most industrious and enterprising cultivators. In the War of Succession Valencia sided emphatically with the house of Austria, for which it was punished by being deprived of many of its ancient privileges. In 1808 an abortive attempt to capture it was made by the French; they succeeded, however, in 1812, and held it till June 1813.

VALENCIA, a town in the United States of Venezuela, capital of the state of Carabobo, situated amidst savannas and tropical plantations, 1800 feet above sea-level, in the valley between the two chains of the Maritime Andes. It is about 3 or 4 miles distant from the Lagoon of Tacarigua or Lake of Valencia (about 45 miles in length and from 10 to 13 in width). The town is connected by cart-roads with Carácas and other places in the interior, as well as with its port, Puerto Cabello. A railway across the northern chain of the Maritime Andes, with a total length of $33\frac{1}{2}$ miles, was nearly completed between Valencia and its seaport in the end of 1887. The town is well built, with straight streets cutting one another at right angles. The *plaza* or chief square, which is adorned with an early Spanish church, commands a magnificent view of the

Maritime Andes. There are several manufactories, among them a weaving factory and one for the making of machinery and agricultural implements. An iron aqueduct supplies the town with drinking water. Among the educational institutions are a college of science and a normal school. The climate is said to be healthy. The highest temperature is equal to 85° Fahr., the lowest 68°, the mean 76°·5. The population in 1883 was 36,145.

VALENCIENNES, a town of France and a first-class fortress, in the department of Nord, is 157 miles north-north-east of Paris on the railway to Brussels, at the point where the river Rhonelle joins the Scheldt. The latter here divides into two branches, one of which flows through the town, while the other, canalized, fills the trenches of the citadel and skirts the fortifications. Valenciennes is the centre of a rich coal-field, which has called into existence numerous foundries, forges, rolling-mills, wire-works, and machine shops. There is also an extensive beetroot cultivation, with attendant sugar-works and distilleries. Cambrics and lawns are manufactured and calico-printing is carried on, though little of the famous lace is now made. There are a court of first instance, a chamber of commerce, a conseil de prud'hommes, a chamber of agriculture, and a sugar exchange. The town-hall, rebuilt after the old plan in 1867-68, and surmounted by a square campanile, contains examples of the three Watteaus, Van Dyck, Velazquez, Rubens (the Stoning of St Stephen), as well as numerous productions of the native school of fine arts (founded in 1782). There are also collections of medals and seals and a fine specimen of old Valenciennes tapestry. The library, formed at the Revolution from the libraries of the religious houses of Valenciennes, St Amand, and the neighbourhood, contains 25,000 printed volumes and 980 MSS., the latter including valuable works in early Romance. Valenciennes also contains several interesting private collections, and has associations for the promotion of agriculture, science, art, music, &c. The church of Notre Dame du Cordon, of the 13th-century style, was consecrated in 1864. The church of St Géry has a graceful modern tower; but only a few pillars remain of the old building of 1225. The crooked and ill-paved streets contain some houses of the 15th and 16th centuries. Statues of Watteau and Froissart adorn the town. Of the six gates three have some architectural pretensions. The population in 1881 was 23,291 (commune 27,607) and in 1886 22,919 (commune 27,575).

Valenciennes, so named because founded or restored by the emperor Valentinian I., was a residence of Clovis, and it was hither that Charlemagne summoned his first assembly of states in 771. The Normans were repulsed from its fortifications in 881. Valenciennes by turns belonged to Hainault and was independent, till taken by Baldwin of Flanders in 1003. It espoused the cause of Jean d'Avesnes in 1353, and was unsuccessfully besieged by the Flemings. In the 16th century Valenciennes became the stronghold of Protestantism in Hainault, but was conquered by the Spaniards, who committed all sorts of excesses. In 1656 the Spaniards under Condé made a successful defence against the French under Turenne; but in 1677 Louis XIV. took the town after an eight days' siege, and Vauban constructed the citadel. Valenciennes has since always belonged to France. In 1793, after forty-three days' bombardment, the garrison, reduced to 3000 men, surrendered to the allied forces numbering some 140,000 or 150,000 men, with 400 cannon. In 1815 it defended itself successfully. Among the natives of Valenciennes may be mentioned Isabella of Hainault, wife of Philip Augustus of France, Baldwin IX. of Flanders (emperor of Constantinople), Jeanne of Flanders, Henry VII. of Luxemburg (emperor of Germany), Froissart, the painters Watteau (3), Pater, and Abel de Pujol, the sculptors De Crauck, Durez, Saly, Carpeaux, and Lemaire, the soldiers Jacques de Lalaing and Charles de Lannoy (viceroy of Naples), and the navigator Lemaire.

VALENS, emperor of the East from 364 to 378, owed his elevation in the thirty-sixth year of his age to his brother Valentinian, who chose him to be his associate in the empire, of which a formal division into East and West was now once for all definitively arranged (see VALENTINIAN I.). Valens had been attached to Julian's bodyguard, but he was not much of a soldier, though his father, Gratian of Pannonia, had risen from the ranks to a high position. A revolt headed by Procopius in the second year of his reign, and backed up by the public opinion of Constantinople and the sympathy of the Gothic princes and chiefs on the Danube, seemed so alarming that he thought of negotiation; but in the following year the revolt collapsed at the prompt action of a loyal and able veteran officer. In the year 366 Valens at one stroke reduced the taxes of the empire by one-fourth, a very popular measure, though one of questionable policy in the face of the threatening attitude of the Goths on the lower Danube. Before venturing on a campaign against them, Valens received baptism from Eudoxus, the bishop of Constantinople and the leader of the Arian party. After some small successes over the Goths, won by his generals, Valens concluded a peace with them, which lasted six years, on a general understanding that the Danube was to be the boundary between Goths and Romans. On his return to Constantinople in 369-370 Valens began to persecute his orthodox and Catholic subjects. Yet he can hardly have been a hearty and willing persecutor, or he would not have suffered the orthodox Basil to remain bishop of Cæsarea in Cappadocia, nor can he have been a thoroughgoing religious fanatic, or he would not have restrained many of his subjects from burying themselves in monasteries to escape the duties of citizens. Indeed he had not the strength of will or force of character to have been either the one or the other.

In the years 371 to 377 Valens was in Asia Minor, most of the time at the Syrian Antioch. The late war with Persia under the emperors Julian and Jovian had not been satisfactorily concluded: the question as to the possession or the protectorate of Armenia was still in suspense. Valens, though anxious to avoid an Eastern war, because of danger nearer home from the restlessness of the Goths, was compelled to take the field against Sapor, who had invaded and occupied Armenia. It seems that Valens[1] crossed the Euphrates in 373, and in Mesopotamia his troops drove back the king of Persia to the farther bank of the Tigris. But the Roman success was by no means decisive, and no definite understanding as to boundaries was come to with Persia. Valens returned to Antioch, where in the winter of 373 a young man of high rank, Theodorus by name, was made to believe by a pack of fortune-tellers and magicians that the emperor's successor would be a man whose name began with "Theod." Theodorus was put to death, with many others whose name began with the same fatal letters; and this led to a vindictive persecution throughout the province of Asia of all who professed or practised magic and necromancy. The age was a very superstitious and inquisitive one, and Valens certainly shared its weakness. Between 374 and 377 we read of grievous complaints of injustice and extortion perpetrated under legal forms, the result probably of the recent panic, and pointing to an increasing weakness and timidity at headquarters. Although preparations were made for following up the war with Persia and securing the frontier, a truce was patched up, rather to the disadvantage of the empire, Armenia and the adjacent country being half conquered and annexed by Sapor. The armies of Rome, in fact, were wanted in another quarter. The Huns, of whom we now hear for the first time, were beginning in 376 to press the Goths from the north, and the latter asked leave of the emperor to cross the Danube into Roman territory. This they were allowed to do, on the condition that they came unarmed, and their children were

[1] Amm. Marc., xxix. 1; the narrative is brief and not very clear.

transported to Asia as hostages. The conditions, however, were not strictly enforced, and the whole affair was treacherously mismanaged by the imperial generals, who for their own profit forced the new settlers to buy food at famine prices. Accordingly the enraged Goths, under their chief Frithigern, streamed across the Balkans into Thrace and the country round Adrianople, plundering, burning, and slaughtering as they went. They were driven back for a time, but returned in the spring of 378 in greater force, with Huns and Alans to fight with them against the empire; and again, after one or two repulses, they penetrated to the neighbourhood of Adrianople. Valens, who had now returned to Constantinople, left the capital in May 378 with a strong and well-officered army. Without awaiting the arrival of his nephew Gratian, emperor of the West, who had just won a great victory over one of the barbarous tribes of Germany in Alsace, Valens attacked the enemy at once, although his troops had to go into action heated and fatigued by a long march on a sultry August day. The battle was decided mainly by the cavalry of the Alans and Sarmatians, the Roman infantry being outnumbered, outmanœuvred, and finally so hemmed in that the men could scarcely draw their swords. The slaughter went on for hours, till the imperial army was destroyed. Valens either perished on the field or, as some said, in a cottage fired by the enemy. From the battle of Adrianople the Goths permanently established themselves south of the Danube.

Ammianus Marcellinus, a contemporary writer, is our chief authority for the reigns of Valens and Valentinian. See also Gibbon's sketch of the period in the 26th and 27th chapters of his *Decline and Fall* and Hodgkin's *Italy and her Invaders*.

VALENTINE, or VALENTINUS, the name of a considerable number of saints,[1] three of whom may be particularized. 1. VALENTINUS, presbyter and martyr, according to the authorized Roman legend (see lesson for second nocturn, 14th February, in the diocese of Tortosa), was arrested and thrown into chains at the instance of the emperor Claudius (Gothicus), and handed over to Calphurnius, who employed one Asterius to try to win him back to idolatry. Valentine miraculously healed the blind daughter of Asterius, who accordingly believed and was baptized, with all his house. The saint after long imprisonment was beaten with clubs and finally beheaded on the Flaminian Way (14th February). 2. VALENTINUS of Interamna (Terni), bishop and martyr, miraculously healed Chæremon, the deformed son of Craton, a Greek rhetorician living in Rome, who along with various other prominent persons was accordingly converted. This Valentine, who also is commemorated on 14th February, is invoked, especially in Italy and Germany (St Velten), in cases of epilepsy and cognate disorders. 3. VALENTINUS, who is spoken of as the apostle of Rhætia, and venerated in Passau as its first bishop, flourished during the first half of the fifth century.

For the peculiar observances that used to be connected with St Valentine's Eve and Day in England, Scotland, and also (it is said) in some parts of France, and to which allusion is so frequently made by English writers from Shakespeare onwards, such works as Brand's *Popular Antiquities*, Hone's *Every-Day Book*, or Chambers's *Book of Days* may be consulted. Their appropriateness to the spring season is, in a general way, perhaps, obvious enough; and, as for the name, it has been suggested that there is at least a similarity in sound between Valentine and *galentin* (Fr. dim. from *galant*).

VALENTINIAN I., emperor of the West from 364 to 375. He had been an officer of the guard under Julian and Jovian, and had risen high in the imperial service. With a fine robust frame, he possessed great courage and great military capacity. He was chosen emperor in his forty-third year by the officers of the army at Nicæa in Bithynia early in 364, and shortly afterwards named his brother VALENS (*q.v.*) colleague with him in the empire. The two brothers, after passing through the chief cities of the neighbouring district, arranged the partition of the empire at Naissus (Nissa) in Upper Mœsia. As emperor of the West, Valentinian took Italy, Illyricum, Spain, the Gauls, Britain, and Africa, leaving to Valens the eastern half of the Balkan Peninsula, Greece, Egypt, Syria, and Asia Minor as far as Persia. During the short reign of Valentinian there were wars in Africa, in Germany, and in Britain, and Rome came into collision with barbarian peoples of whom we now hear for the first time,—Burgundians, Saxons, Alemanni. The emperor's chief work was guarding the frontiers and establishing military positions. Milan was at first his headquarters for settling the affairs of northern Italy; next year (365) he was at Paris, and then at Rheims, to direct the operations of his generals against the Alemanni. This people were driven back to the German bank of the Rhine, and checked for a while by a chain of military posts and fortresses, though at the close of 367 they swooped down on Moguntiacum (Mainz) and plundered the city. In that same year Valentinian was at Amiens, and there, before his assembled troops, he gave the title of Augustus to his son Gratian, eight years of age. The next three years he spent at Treves, organizing the defence of the Rhine frontier against the Alemanni and Saxons, and personally superintending the construction of numerous forts. Treves was, in fact, his headquarters during most of his reign. His general administration seems to have been thoroughly honest and able, in some respects beneficent. If he was hard and exacting in the matter of taxes, he spent them in the defence and improvement of his dominions, not in idle show or luxury. Though himself a plain and almost illiterate soldier, he was a founder of schools, and he also provided medical attendance for the poor of Rome, by appointing a physician for each of the fourteen districts of the city. He was a Christian, an orthodox Catholic, and in his life perfectly pure; but he permitted absolute religious freedom to all his subjects. Against all abuses, both civil and ecclesiastical, he steadily set his face, even against the increasing wealth and worldliness of the clergy. Valentinian was in many ways a good and able ruler at a particularly difficult time. The great blot on his memory is his cruelty, which at times was frightful, and showed itself in its full fierceness in the punishment of persons accused of witchcraft, soothsaying, or magical practices. In 374 the Quadi, a German tribe in what is now Moravia and Hungary, resenting the erection of Roman forts to the north of the Danube in what they considered to be their own territory, crossed the river and laid waste the province of Pannonia, Valentinian's native land. The emperor in the April of the following year entered Illyricum with a powerful army, and gave audience to an embassy from the Quadi at Bregetio on the Danube, somewhere near Pressburg. Their defence threw him into a paroxysm of rage, in which he suddenly fell down, apparently in a fit of apoplexy, and died in a few hours. His two sons, Gratian and Valentinian II., were jointly his successors.

VALENTINIAN II., an infant of four years of age, with his half-brother Gratian, a lad of about seventeen, became the emperors of the West on the death of their father, Valentinian I., in 375. They made Milan their home; and the empire was nominally divided between them, Gratian taking the trans-Alpine provinces, whilst Italy, Illyricum in part, and Africa were to be under the rule of Valentinian II., or rather of his mother, Justina. Justina was an Arian, and the imperial court at Milan pitted itself against the Catholics, under the famous Ambrose, bishop of that city. But so great was his popularity that the court was decidedly worsted in the contest, and the emperor's authority materially shaken. In 387 Maximus,

[1] The *Heiligenlexicon* of Stadler-Ginal enumerates fifty-two.

who had commanded a Roman army in Britain, and had in 383 (the year of Gratian's death) made himself master of the northern provinces, crossed the Alps into the valley of the Po and threatened Milan. The emperor and his mother fled to Thessalonica, to Theodosius, the emperor of the East and husband of Galla, Valentinian's sister. At their entreaty he marched into Italy with an army, decisively defeated Maximus, and set Valentinian once more on the throne (388). He also converted the lad to orthodox Catholicism. Four years later Valentinian was dead. A barbarian warrior, a Frank named Arbogast, who had fought for Gratian and Theodosius, so presumed on his services that Valentinian was provoked into giving him a letter of dismissal. But Arbogast tore the letter up before the emperor's face and openly defied him. Soon afterwards Valentinian was slain, no doubt by Arbogast's order, at Vienne in Gaul, while taking part in some athletic sports. Eugenius, a humble dependent of the barbarian, succeeded to the empire of the West, a disgrace noted by the poet Claudian (*De Tertio Consulatu Honorii*, lxvi.).

VALENTINIAN III., emperor of the West from 425 to 455, the son of Constantius and Placidia, daughter of the great Theodosius, was declared Cæsar at Thessalonica under the auspices of Theodosius II., and again the following year at Rome, in the seventh year of his age. His reign of thirty years was a period of great and terrible events associated with the names of Attila, Genseric, and Aetius, the "last of the Romans." This period is marked by the dismemberment of the Western empire, the conquest of the province of Africa by the Vandals in 439, the final abandonment of Britain in 446, the loss of great portions of Spain and Gaul, in which the barbarians had established themselves, and the ravaging of Sicily and of the western coasts of the Mediterranean by the fleets of Genseric. As a set-off against these calamities there was the great victory of Aetius over Attila in 451 in the neighbourhood of Châlons. (See ROME, vol. xx. p. 781.) The burden of taxation became more and more intolerable as the power of Rome decreased, although there were a partial remission of taxes in 450 and a cancelling of arrears in consequence of the general impoverishment of Rome's subjects. Ravenna was Valentinian's usual residence; but he fled to Rome in 452 on the approach of Attila, who, after ravaging the north of Italy, died in the following year. In 454 Aetius, between whose son and a daughter of the emperor a marriage had been arranged, was treacherously murdered by Valentinian. Next year, however, the crime was avenged by the assassination of the emperor as he was looking on at some games in the Campus Martius. He was a contemptible creature, cowardly, self-indulgent, without spirit, and without ability. With Valentinian III. the family of Theodosius became extinct.

Our chief original sources for the reign of Valentinian III. are Jordanes, Prosper's *Chronicles*, written in the 6th century and ending with the year 455, and the poet Sidonius Apollinaris. See also Gibbon's history of the period (*Decline and Fall*, c. xxxiii.-xxxv.) and Hodgkin's *Italy and her Invaders* (1880).

VALENTINUS AND VALENTINIANS. Valentinus was the most important Christian theologian before Origen. Clement and Origen both were his pupils. In his school all those problems were started which afterwards engrossed the Greek fathers, and a large proportion of the solutions given by him and his followers subsequently became, though in a modified form, accepted doctrines. The dogmatic of Origen lies at the foundation of the orthodox dogmatic of the church, and it in its turn had its prototype in that of the Valentinian school. Valentinus was the first man in Christendom who for other than merely apologetic purposes sought to fuse together the results of Greek philosophy with the substance of the Gospel, combined the exalted ethic of the Platonic and Neopythagorean schools with the preaching of the evangelical pulpit, and treated the manifestation of Jesus as the keystone in the great structure of thought which Greek science had reared. His theology is, so to speak, the central pier of the bridge connecting the Jewish with the Christian Alexandrians. He may perhaps be regarded as superior to Philo in sobermindedness and in acuteness, and as having excelled Origen at once in delicacy of religious and moral perception and in vigour of language, though he was far behind him in learning and in extent of knowledge.[1] His success as a teacher was brilliant. Tertullian tells us that among all the Christian "collegia" that of Valentinus was the most crowded,[2] and the numerous branches into which his scholars soon divided are evidence of the wealth of his influence. Even his enemies have praised his "ingenium et eloquium" (*Adv. Valent.*, 4). Tertullian, Clement, Origen, Jerome, and Adamantius agree in testifying that he was a man of singular gifts. The few extant fragments of his writings fully confirm this: there is not one of them that is not marked by originality and depth. And his disciples, although they have partly deteriorated his teachings by undisciplined fancies and inappropriate mythologizing, have, every one of them, something particular and valuable to say. Their influence did not cease until in the catechetical school of Alexandria the church found teachers of her own who were at once scientific theologians and defenders of the church of orthodoxy.

Valentinus.—Of Valentinus himself almost nothing is known. That he was an Egyptian by birth and received his education in Alexandria is probable but not certain.[3] He came to Rome under Hyginus about 138, flourished under Pius (140-155), and was still there in the time of Anicetus (*c.* 155-166). This we learn from Irenæus (iii. 4, 3), who lets us see that his main activity was in Rome. He further tells us that Polycarp during his sojourn in that city was the means of converting some Valentinians. Tertullian supplements (*De Præscr.*, 30) Irenæus with the information that Valentinus originally attached himself in Rome to the main body of the church, but "ob inquietam semper curiositatem qua fratres quoque vitiabat," after having been twice temporarily suspended from communion, he was ultimately cut off. This statement shows that the Roman Church did not, to begin with, possess the standards by which to try Valentinus. The sections of the *Shepherd* of Hermas which treat of the Gnostics represent them as still continuing to exist within the church, although their dangerous character was already known. It was not, then, until the bishopric of Anicetus that the Roman Church succeeded in ridding itself of the Valentinian collegia. It seems very doubtful whether there is any good foundation for Tertullian's further allegation (*Adv. Valent.*, 4) that Valentinus was ambitious of obtaining the episcopate of Rome and that his failure in this caused him to break with the church. Hippolytus will have it (see Epiphanius and Philaster) that Valentinus afterwards went to Cyprus as a declared heretic. We are not in a position to control this statement; but the words of Irenæus would almost lead to the conclusion that he died in Rome. At any rate there is no reason to suppose that he was alive much later than 160. Tertullian, in spite of a disposition to bring him down to as recent a period as possible, does not seem to think of him as living in the time of Marcus Aurelius. But in the school of Valentinus it was asserted that their master had been a pupil of Theodas, a γνώριμος Παύλου;[4] in that case he must have been a very old man in 160.

[1] Jerome nevertheless calls him "doctissimus" (*Comm. in Osee*, ii. 10).

[2] Tert., *Adv. Valent.*; *cf.* Origen, *Hom.*, ii. 5, and *Comm.*, xiv. p. 40, "robustissima secta."

[3] Epiph., *Hær.*, 31; *Mur. Fragm.*, *fin.*

[4] Clem., *Strom.*, vii. 17, 106.

Valentinus was the author of several epistles, three fragments of which have been preserved by Clement;[1] one of these was addressed to a certain Agathopus. He also composed homilies (one entitled *On Friends*), of which we possess four fragments.[2] An expression of Tertullian's (*Adv. Valent.*, 2) seems to imply that Valentinus was also the author of a treatise entitled *Sophia*. Perhaps this is the source from which Irenæus's systematic account of the Valentinian doctrine (i. 11, 1) was indirectly taken. Tertullian speaks of *Psalms* of Valentinus (*De Car.*, xvii. 20); the author of the *Muratorian Fragment* seems also to refer to these; and in the *Philosophumena* of Hippolytus (vi. 37) a considerable fragment from them is given. The "gospel" of Valentinus is spoken of below.

Sources.—All that we possess of Valentinus and his disciples are the fragments preserved by their opponents, the fathers of the church. We cannot therefore put implicit confidence in all that they tell us, or accept as of primary importance in the doctrine of the Valentinians all that they represent as such. The extant fragments of the writings of Valentinus himself, as well as of those of his scholars (Ptolemæus, Heracleon, Theodotus, and others), fortunately enable us to set their theology in a more worthy light than does the fantastic "system" which Irenæus has given. Of the four ancient treatises against the Valentinians known to Tertullian we possess but one, that of Irenæus, those of Justin, Miltiades, and Proculus being lost. The loss of Justin is most to be regretted, for he was a contemporary, and wrote his *Syntagma* probably in Rome at the time when Valentinus was actually labouring there. In Rome some sixty years later the author of the *Muratorian Fragment* also took notice of him. Proculus wrote a special polemic against him, while Miltiades wrote in the same sense in Asia Minor and Irenæus in Gaul about 180. Tertullian's *Adversus Valentinianos* was composed in Carthage some twenty years later, and Clement engaged in a work of a similar nature almost simultaneously at Alexandria. Against the Marcionite Church the fathers were equally energetic, Marcion and Valentinus during the period between 150 and 230 passing for the most dangerous heretics. Our oldest and at the same time fullest source is the work of Irenæus, which rests upon a tract of Ptolemæus and probably makes use of the *Syntagma*[3] of Justin. In all probability he had read nothing of Valentinus himself. Tertullian's *Adversus Valentinianos* is largely taken from Irenæus, but contains some things that are original and of very great value: he had either himself read some Valentinian works, or had at least obtained authentic information as to their contents. Our best sources for Valentinus himself are the *Stromata* and *Eclogues* of Clement of Alexandria, who had read much of Valentinus and something of Heracleon, and gives extracts from both. His *Excerpta ex Theodoto* are also invaluable. Hippolytus in both his works against heretics has transcribed Irenæus; yet in his *Philosophumena* he has followed a new source in describing the Valentinian system. Origen made a careful study of Heracleon's *Commentary on John's Gospel*, and in his own *Commentary* he frequently refers to it both approvingly and otherwise. The numerous fragments he has preserved have very great value for the historian. Lastly, Irenæus and Hippolytus have been transcribed by Epiphanius, who also has preserved various matters of importance, particularly the letter of Ptolemæus to Flora.

Valentinians.—The school of Valentinus soon divided into two main branches, that of Italy and that of Asia Minor.[4] Both in turn subdivided into various sections; but the Asiatic branch on the whole preserved most faithfully the teaching of the master. His influence spread even beyond the limits of the schools. Tatian, for example, in his later period indubitably derived much from Valentinus, and the fathers of the Alexandrian school were very largely indebted to him. Even in the time of Epiphanius Valentinians still existed in some districts of Egypt. The Italian branch had as heads of its schools Secundus, another master of uncertain name (Colarbasus? Epiphanius? see Iren., i. 11, 3), Ptolemæus, Heracleon, Theotimus, and Alexander. Secundus modified the master's doctrine of the æons and introduced a dualism into it. The anonymous scholar shows tokens of Pythagorean influence. But the most important, exceeding in the extent of their influence even the master himself, were Ptolemæus and Heracleon. The former made into hypostases the æons which Valentinus himself had regarded as impersonal powers of the one Godhead. He is the systematic and Biblical theologian *par excellence* of the Valentinian school, conspicuous for a powerful if also undisciplined phantasy; and in his letter to Flora he shows how thorough has been his study of the Old Testament, and how penetrating, how carefully considered, and how pointed his criticism of it. Heracleon, mentioned also by Irenæus, earned distinction by his *Commentary* (ὑπομνήματα) *on the Gospel according to John*, for it is probably the first scientific commentary that Christendom produced. Clement (*Strom.*, iv. 9, 73) calls him the most eminent teacher of the Valentinian school. He appears to have shown much greater sobriety than Ptolemæus, whose speculations recall those of the later Neoplatonists in a most striking manner, just as we find Valentinianism generally to have anticipated, not only the later scientific theology of the Catholic Church, but also Neoplatonism. Of Theotimus all that we know is Tertullian's remark (*Adv. Valent.*, 4): "multum circa imagines legis operatus est." Tertullian is also our sole informant about Alexander (*De Carne*, 17-20). He seems to have busied himself specially with the Christological problem, and to have written under the title of *Syllogismi* a treatise into which quotations from Valentinus's *Psalms* were introduced as authorities.

The names mentioned as those of leaders of the Asiatic school are Axionicus, Theodotus, and above all Bardesanes; we also have some fragments of Valentinian writings belonging to the East, but of which the origin is otherwise unknown.[5] Axionicus at Antioch[6] was the master's most faithful disciple. Clement of Alexandria has preserved excerpts of a very inconsecutive character and in a very corrupt text from a systematic work, and some commentaries of Theodotus (Ἐκ τῶν Θεοδότου καὶ τῆς ἀνατολικῆς καλουμένης διδασκαλίας κατὰ τοὺς Οὐαλεντίνου χρόνους ἐπιτομαί). These excerpts, which constitute one of the most important sources for Gnosticism generally, have not hitherto received the attention they deserve. Zahn (*Forschungen*, iii. p. 123 *sq.*) has tried to make out that Theodotus is identical with Theodas, Valentinus's master. But from the excerpts it seems hardly probable that they should be the work of a man who must have written at latest under the emperor Trajan. Bardesanes, though originally influenced by Valentinus, ultimately took up peculiar and independent ground of his own, and through him Valentinus exercised a great influence upon the Syrian Church, which continued until the 4th century (see SYRIAC LITERATURE, vol. xxii. p. 827). In Asia Minor the Valentinian collegia continued until past the middle of the 4th century (see *Epp. Juliani*). The church fathers bring into connexion with Valentinus the Magian Marcus, as to whose doctrine we are very adequately informed by Irenæus, but it is questionable whether he can really be reckoned as one of the disciples of that master.

Teaching of Valentinus.—Valentinus made his appearance at a time when the Christian communities were still destitute of any fixed doctrinal system: they were still associations pledged to a holy life on the ground of their faith in the one spiritual God and in His Son Jesus Christ, closely held together by the bonds of brotherly love, and strictly separated from the world and from them that are without by the consciousness of having received the Holy Ghost. But an enormous volume of facts, of sayings, and of thoughts had by this time become current within the church, material drawn from the Old Testament, from the Gospel history, from the Pauline epistles, from other early Christian writings, and from the Hellenistic and apocalyptic literature of the Jews. How this material was to be arranged, how it was to be kept within bounds, and with what degree of authority it was to be invested were questions still unsettled. But one thing was certain—Paul had declared it, and every Christian apostle, prophet, and teacher had repeated it—that the Christian faith guaranteed knowledge supreme and complete, and led on from truth to truth. Another thing was sure—that all human wisdom was but folly in presence of this new "divine" wisdom, which was inclusive of all human knowledge. The means, moreover, by which every saying, every fact was to be turned into a profound thought had for long been known and in use in the Christian communities,—that of allegory. But as yet there was no settled principle fixing the manner in which the allegorical method was to be applied, or determining what were the ruling thoughts of Scripture. The attitude of Christian teachers towards the Jewish wisdom was as indeterminate as it was towards Greek philosophy. The Pauline theology was intelligible only to a very few, and the Old Testament was as it were a veritable sphinx. It was understood to be a superhuman book, but it was also understood that much of its contents, if taken literally, was valueless. In what sense was it to be understood? How much of it was to be taken literally and how much spiritually? Was everything to be taken spiritually? According to what principle was it on this assumption to be interpreted? Was the whole of it the revealed word of the Most High, or were various authors to be recognized? Might it possibly be that part of it was divine, part heroical, part genial, part natural, part false, and part devilish? Or was it perhaps true that no part of the book proceeded from the Most High God, that nothing was pneumatic, but all psychical or carnal? And, if the Old Testament was

[1] *Strom.*, ii. 8, 36; ii. 20, 114; iii. 7, 59.

[2] *Strom.*, iv. 13, 91; iv., 13, 92; vi. 6, 52; Hippol., *Philos.*, vi. 42.

[3] His use of this work, however, is not beyond all question, and it is impossible to tell the nature and amount of his indebtedness.

[4] See Hippol., *Philos.*, vi. 35; Tert., *Adv. Valent.*, 4.

[5] See Epiph., *Hær.*, iii. 5, 6; Method., Περὶ αὐτεξουσίου; Adamant., *De recta in Deum fide.*

[6] Hippol., *Philos.*, iv. 35; *Adv. Valent.*, 4.

to be allegorized, must not the narratives and the sayings of the Gospels be also treated in the same way? Was not allegory here also the pathway to the thought? If the opening chapters of Genesis and the histories of the patriarchs and of the people of Israel were a profound philosophical poem, why should not also the life of Jesus Christ be only the veil of a cosmic mystery? All these questions had within the period from 60 to 130 exercised, not indeed the great mass of believers, for these were uneducated, but thinking Christians; and the more the Christian preaching enlarged its scope, the more Christians came into contact with Syrian, Samaritan, Egyptian, and Greek wisdom, and the more they found themselves called upon to make comparisons and to bring into clearness that which is peculiar to and distinctive of Christianity, it was inevitable that these questions should stir the minds of educated Christians all the more intensely. Upon the one basis of faith in Jesus Christ accordingly there were about the year 130 a great variety of groups, differing from one another in doctrine, worship, organization, and the like,[1] but differing also in their attitude to Christianity at large, some keeping themselves aloof from it because they regarded it as wholly perverted, others being driven out from it, others again, while remaining within the main body, yet forming special schools, or "mystery" unions, and so on. In Syria, as also in other portions of the Roman empire, the gospel was associated with Semitic "cultus wisdom" and with the abstruse speculations of a physical science still in its childhood; the entire Old Testament was rejected and an attitude of opposition assumed towards fellow-members in the great Christian union.

These developments, however, could reckon on only a relatively small degree of encouragement within the Græco-Roman world. The barbaric elements they contained were too conspicuous, and on the other hand they were too far removed from Jewish-Christian tradition and from Christian common sense. But the attractiveness must have been very great when, on the basis of Christian tradition and the mysterious traditions of Oriental peoples, a system was set up with the aids of Greek philosophical science for a school of "knowing ones" or "Gnostics," and a cultus organized for a community of the "initiated." This was what Basilides and Valentinus achieved. The importance of Valentinus lies in the facts, firstly, that he recognized the relationship (for such a relationship really existed) between the theogonic-cosmogonic myth-wisdom of western Asia and the Neopythagorean, Platonic, and Philonic philosophy; secondly, that he touched all this rich and varied material which he had appropriated with the magic wand of the Platonic conception of the universe, and thus transmuted the whole into entities of a purely spiritual character; and thirdly, that he gave a decisive part to the appearance of Jesus Christ in that great drama which the history of the higher and the lower cosmos presented to his mind. In all this he had no design of setting up a new "confession," and still less any notion (as Marcion had) of utterly remodelling Christianity. He was prevented from cherishing any such ideas by his conviction that men were divided by the inalterable constitution of their natures into three classes,—the "pneumatic," men of the spirit, genial natures, in whom sparks of the divinity are found; the "psychical," moral men, who can if they choose be ethically good; and "hylic" or carnal, hopelessly chained to that which is perceived by the senses. The ordinary members of Christendom at large he held to be "psychical," and esteemed them as such. But he did not regard their Christianity as *the* Christianity, rather only as its exoteric form. Alongside of the exoteric there had all along, according to him, existed an esoteric. The apostles did not say out everything to everybody, but on the contrary communicated to the "spiritual ones" a secret doctrine into which only select persons might be initiated, and that not until after long and careful probation. This secret teaching included a special dogmatic, a special ethic, and a special worship. But it was not out of all connexion with the Christianity that was publicly taught. We can observe in the history of the Valentinian schools the zeal with which they strove to adapt themselves to the Christianity publicly professed, and to follow it in all its developments. The Valentinians always, so far as they possibly could, accepted such things as the development of the canon (agitated for by themselves) within the church at large, the building up of a tradition, the symbols framed, and the like; to this Irenæus, Tertullian, and the Alexandrians all bear witness. In this they present the strongest possible contrast to Marcion and his church, who from the outset took up an attitude of the utmost hostility to the main body of Christians. Hence they expressly even controverted Marcionitism, as the letter of Ptolemæus to Flora and the polemic of Bardesanes against the Marcionite Prepon show. If such was the unvarying attitude of Valentinus's scholars, it is fair to attribute it also to Valentinus himself. In his day indeed the dogmatic, ethical, and legal advances of Christendom at large were still in their most rudimentary stage, but what there was of them must have been valued by him even then as the exoteric form of Christianity, to which he superadded his own Gnostic esoteric form. In this respect he was the forerunner of Clement and Origen, who likewise distinguish Gnostic from common Christianity, and very probably learned the distinction from Valentinus and his scholars. But his connexion with both was of a still more intimate character. They are related not only by virtue of the fact that they all regarded the gospel as the religion of the perfect Hellenically-cultured spiritual man, but also by the large-hearted disposition they cherished, and the settled purpose they manifested, to appropriate everything noble and great in the history of humanity, to rank it according to its proper value, and to find a place for it in the edifice of Christian philosophy. And it is very interesting to notice that they completely set aside the Greek and Roman mythologies, regarding them as worthless and devilish. The formal peculiarity of the Valentinian Gnosis is that it places all moral and intellectual ideas, possessions, and entities in a descending scheme of genetic development. With Valentinus himself they figure as "motus et affectus" of the Godhead, the ultimate cause of all things, the alone Good; by his scholars they are hypostatized. This descending development (self-revelation) of the Godhead takes place with a holy rhythm. At this point the Pythagorean speculations about numbers on the one hand and the ancient Semitic astrological wisdom on the other seemed important to Valentinus; but everything is made spiritual: even the old Semitic antithesis of "male" and "female" is adopted, but with an altered meaning.[2] The whole inner development of the primal cause (*βύθος*) into the pleroma, the cosmos of perfection, is designed to explain how it was that this world of appearance, of mixture, and of sin arose. Valentinus was a strict monotheist, but at the same time he discerned in the present world the mingling of irreconcilable elements. The problem then was how, while acknowledging the absolute perfection, goodness, and causality of God, to reconcile with this the existence of the actual pneumatico-psychico-hylic world, and at the same time to show the possibility of redemption in the case of those who are capable of it. Valentinus solved this problem by assuming that the self-unfolding of the Godhead is at the same time to be thought of as a dissipation of energy. God alone is *ἀγέννητος*. The powers emanating from Him (*νοῦς, ἀλήθεια, λόγος, ζωή, ἄνθρωπος* =ideal man, *ἐκκλησία*, and so on) are *γεννητά*. Hence, although *ὁμοούσια* with the Godhead, they have nevertheless a limitation attaching to them. They are copies of the Godhead in a descending line; but the copy is never of equal value with the pattern. The thirtieth and last æon, Sophia,[3] has the element of imperfection in the strongest degree. This belongs to it in the form of "passion" (*πάθος*), the passionate desire after full knowledge of and fusion with the primal God. This passion for the pleroma, having seduced the æon into overstepping its proper bounds, is accordingly separated from it and removed out of oneness with it; it thus falls into nothingness, the *κένωμα*, but gives the impulse to the making of this world. This world is the outward shaping of nothingness, of appearance, through connexion with the fallen wisdom. It is a feeble copy of the pleroma without any abiding hold, but it includes pneumatic portions, though these have fallen very low. It was fashioned by the demiurge, an intermediate being brought forth by the fallen wisdom. The demiurge is psychical, and thus has no feeling and no understanding for the pneumatic which adhered to the elements of the world he framed. But over against the sensuous powers included in this world, so far as it is derived from nothingness, the demiurge is the representative of order, righteousness, freedom for better things, and the men who have received something of his spirit are those earnest moral natures who strive against their passions and aim at *justitia civilis*. Far above these stand the pneumatic ones, who, like their mother, have the strong passion of genius towards that which is highest, and in this possession, in knowledge and in the desire for knowledge, are raised far above the antithesis of the hylic (the devil) and the psychic (the demiurge). They carry within them an indestructible and divine element which is unintelligible to their very maker, but they are placed in a world which is foreign to them; they are as men imprisoned and fettered. Here it is that the Christian idea of redemption comes in. Jesus Christ appears. The declarations about Him in the Valentinian school were exceedingly various. We can find traces in them of all the contemporary and later Christologies of the Christian Church, even of the Adoptian. What they all had in common was (1) the idea that Jesus Christ made manifest was an exceedingly complex Being, in whom two or three natures, or even a greater number, had to be distinguished (compare Origen's Christology); (2) the conviction that the highest element in the Redeemer was not one of the æons which had somehow parted with some of its potential energy, but was the perfect self-manifestation of the Good, the Supreme God Himself; (3) the conception that

[1] See Harnack, *Dogmengesch.*, i. p. 171 *sq.*

[2] The earliest opponents of the Valentinians distinguished them sharply from the "Gnostics." They rightly perceived that the Semitic and mythological element was for the Valentinians merely the material, which they filled with the spirit of Hellenism. Some of the heads of schools, however, dealt with this material in a highly fantastic fashion, and accordingly the church fathers say with justice that "inolescentes doctrinæ Valentinianorum in silvas jam exoleverunt Gnosticorum" (Tert., *Adv. Valent.*, 39).

[3] The number 30 comes from astronomy: at bottom the æons of Valentinus are 29½, the number of days in the lunar month.

the physical nature of Jesus Christ was no actual corporeity, but either something psychical or something pneumatical. This Jesus Christ then delivers all who are pneumatic in the world by communicating knowledge. By full knowledge of God, of the world, and of themselves they are raised above the world, enter upon their undying divine life, and finally are brought by Christ into the pleroma. But psychical persons also are redeemed by Him. They who hitherto have been brought up according to the laws of the Old Testament, that is, of the demiurge, now receive the perfect law; Jesus moreover by His death procured for them the forgiveness of sins. They are now therefore in a position to lead a perfect moral life, and after death, if they have made a right use of their freedom, shall be brought to an abode of bliss. The Valentinian ethic shows a fine combination of spiritual freedom with the element of asceticism. Their thesis, that primarily it is not the outward act but the intention that is important, was misunderstood by the fathers of the church as if they had given permission to pneumatic persons to live in licence, to deny the faith under persecution, and the like. But there is no foundation for this. The fragments we possess from writings of Valentinus and his school show rather that they were second to no Christian body in moral earnestness. The Valentinians appear to have joined in the religious worship of the main body of the church so long as they were tolerated within it. But along with this they celebrated their own mysteries, in which only the initiated might take part.

In the foregoing sketch only the broad general outlines of the Valentinian theology have been indicated. In all the schools, and even with Valentinus himself, it was much richer and more complicated than has been indicated. But all was strictly wrought out, and even the apparently abstruse served always for the expression of a weighty thought. Very manifold and various were in particular the doctrines about the fallen wisdom (Sophia) and about its relations to the world and the demiurge; very various also were the views of Jesus and of Christ and of their relation to the pleroma of the æons. Finally their representations about "Horos" differed widely. "As a harlot daily changes her attire," says Tertullian in his malicious way, "so do the Valentinians change their opinions." But none of these differences affected the oneness of the general view. That the history of redemption constitutes along with the history of nature and of the world one grand drama, that it is for scientific cosmology to explain how it is that the "mixtures" have come to pass, and that it is for scientific soteriology to show how the "separations" have been brought about, as to these matters all were at one. Equally were they at one in their view of Christ as the absolute revelation of God, and in the persuasion that the creator of the world is identical with the God of the Old Testament, and is an "intermediate" Being. But the various Valentinian schools were above all united in their attitude towards the Scriptures. They were Biblical theologians: that is to say, they started from the conviction that complete wisdom lay only in the words of Jesus Christ, or, in other words, in the Gospels. They accordingly sought to base their systems throughout on the words of the Lord, applying to these the allegorical method. In a secondary degree they availed themselves also of the writings of the apostles. Their dogmatic claimed—as afterwards did that of Origen—to be evangelical and apostolic; but, since they interpreted the New Testament after the same method as that which Philo applied to the Old, it was as a rule Platonic thought that they introduced into the plain and simple words of Jesus, and thus the fathers of the church were not without justification in calling them "sectatores Platonis" (Tert., *De Præscr.*, 30). As their method of exegesis supplied them with the means of everywhere finding the sense that suited them, it is highly improbable that they were at the trouble to prepare any new scriptures. The fathers do not as a rule charge them with either fabrication or falsification, but only with perversion of the Word through wrong interpretations. Nor did they dispute or reject the Roman creed; they simply, by a peculiar interpretation, put their own meaning upon it; yet at the same time they had alongside of it their own "regula fidei." It is hardly probable that they possessed an "evangelium veritatis" of their own, but it is not impossible. They subjected the Old Testament to an admirable religious criticism. Ptolemæus distinguished in the law (1) what the demiurge had said, (2) what came from Moses, (3) what the later teachers of the law had added. Amongst those portions which were regarded as having proceeded from the demiurge himself, he again distinguished three groups:—(*a*) the Decalogue, which is of perpetual obligation, and which only required to be completed by Christ (in the sermon on the mount); (*b*) those commands which were given only for a season on account of the shortcomings of the people, and which were abolished by Christ; (*c*) the ceremonial law, which had a typical meaning that was fulfilled by Christ. They denied that anything in the Old Testament came from the supreme God, the God of goodness and love.

From the fragments of Valentinus and of Heracleon and Theodotus the student can learn how these Valentinians anticipated the ecclesiastical speculations of subsequent centuries. The following points may be mentioned in this connexion:—(1) the speculation as to *ὁμοούσιος*, *ὅμοιος*, *ἑτερούσιος*, *ἀγέννητος*, and *γεννητός*, by which they prepared the way for the Unitarian problem in its scientific shape; (2) their speculation about "Jesus" and "Christ" and about His various natures, by which they opened the way for later Christology; (3) their scientific allegorical treatment of the New Testament Scriptures and their undertaking to found their whole system upon the sacred writings of Christianity, thus anticipating Origen's dogmatic; (4) their distinction of the perficienda, abroganda, and implenda in the Old Testament, which paved the way for the doctrine of Irenæus and Tertullian in reference to the law; (5) their doctrine of baptism; (6) their doctrine of the Lord's Supper; (7) their doctrine of purification after death, in which they anticipated the later dogma of purgatory (Origen, Augustine, Gregory I.); (8) their twofold ethic (for psychical and for pneumatic persons; see Clement and Origen, as also the monachism of the Catholic Church); (9) and finally the view destined later to play so large a part within the church, that the soul of the Christian Gnostic is the bride of Christ.

Literature.—The fragments have been collected by Grabe (*Spicilegium*, ii. 430 *sq.*) and Hilgenfeld (*Ztschr. f. wiss. Theol.*, 1880, p. 280; 1881, p. 214; 1883, p. 356). The system is set forth more or less in the works on Gnosticism by Neander, Matter, Baur, Lipsius, Hilgenfeld, Mansel, and Möller. See also Heinrici, *Die Valent. Gnosis u. d. heil. Schrift* (1871), and Rossel, *Ges. Schriften* (1847).

(A. HA.)

VALENTINUS, pope for thirty or forty days in 827, in succession to Eugenius II. (824-827), was a Roman by birth, and, according to the *Liber Pontificalis*, was first made a deacon by Paschal I. (817-824). Nothing further is known of his history. His successor was Gregory IV. (827-844).

VALERIAN, a genus of herbaceous perennial plants of the natural order *Valerianaceæ*. Two species—*Valeriana officinalis*, L. (see vol. iv. pl. VIII.), and *V. dioica*, L., —are indigenous in England, while a third, *V. pyrenaica*, L., is naturalized in some parts of Scotland and the west of England. The valerians have opposite leaves and small flowers, usually of a white or reddish tint, and arranged in terminal cymes. The limb of the calyx is remarkable for being at first inrolled and afterwards expanding in the form of pappus. The genus comprises about 150 species. In medicine the root of *V. officinalis* is intended when valerian is mentioned. The plant grows throughout Europe from Spain to the Crimea, and from Iceland through northern Europe and Asia to the coasts of Manchuria. Several varieties of the plant are known, those growing in hilly situations being considered the most valuable for medicinal purposes. Valerian is cultivated in England (in several villages near Chesterfield in Derbyshire), but to a much greater extent in Prussian Saxony (in the neighbourhood of Cölleda, north of Weimar), in Holland, and in the United States (Vermont, New Hampshire, and New York).

The dried root or rhizome consists of a short central erect portion, about the thickness of the little finger, surrounded by numerous rootlets about $\frac{1}{10}$ of an inch in diameter, the whole being of a dull brown colour. When first taken from the ground it has no distinctive smell; but on drying it acquires a powerful odour of valerianic acid. This odour, now regarded as intolerable, was in the 16th century considered to be fragrant, the root being placed among clothes as a perfume (Turner, *Herbal*, part iii., 1568, p. 76), just as *V. celtica* and some Himalayan species of the genus are still used in the East (see SPIKENARD). By the poorer classes in the north of England it was esteemed of such medicinal value that "no broth, pottage, or physical meat" was considered of any value without it (Gerard, *Herball*, 1636, p. 1078).

Valerian owes its medicinal properties to a volatile oil, which is contained in the dried root to the extent of one or, more rarely, two per cent., plants growing on dry or stony soil yielding the largest quantity. The oil is a complex body, consisting of a terpene, $C_{10}H_{16}$; an alcohol, $C_{10}H_{18}O$, isomeric with borneol, and compounds of the alcohol with formic, acetic, and valerianic acids; and an ether having the formula $C_{10}H_{17}O$. The valerianic acid occurring in the oil is not the normal acid, but iso-valerianic acid. The other constituents of the root are malic acid, resin, sugar, &c. Valerian is employed in medicine as a stimulant and antispasmodic in various forms of hysteria, and in chorea and hooping-cough; it is also stated to possess anthelmintic properties. The red valerian of cottage gardens is *Centranthus ruber*, also belonging to the *Valerianaceæ*; but Greek valerian is *Polemonium cæruleum*, belonging to the natural order *Polemoniaceæ*. Cats are nearly as fond of the smell of this plant as of the true valerian, and will frequently roll on the plant and injure it.

VALERIANUS, PUBLIUS LICINIUS, Roman emperor from 253 to 260, was a man of ancient family and is first mentioned in the year 238 as *princeps senatus.* Some thirteen years later, when Decius restored the censorship and added to the office legislative and executive powers so extensive that it embraced the best part of the civil authority of the emperor, Valerian was chosen censor by the senate, to whom the appointment was committed. The death of Decius cut short this novel experiment in government, but Valerian retained the confidence of Gallus, who sent him to fetch troops to quell the rebellion of Æmilianus. The soldiers in Rhætia, however, proclaimed Valerian emperor; and marching slowly towards Rome he found both his rivals dead. Valerian was already an elderly man—he is said to have been seventy years old at his death—and had scarcely the vigour to confront with success the enemies that threatened every frontier of the empire, but he applied himself to his heavy task with diligence and goodwill. Taking his son Gallienus as colleague, and leaving the wars in Europe to his direction, under which matters went from bad to worse and the whole West fell into disorder, Valerian chose for his own part the war in the East, where Antioch had fallen into the hands of a Persian vassal and Armenia was occupied by Shápúr, while in 258 the Goths ravaged Asia Minor. Valerian recovered Antioch, fought in Mesopotamia with mixed success, and finally was taken captive (see PERSIA, vol. xviii. p. 608). His ultimate fate is unknown.

VALERIUS, PUBLIUS, surnamed PUBLICOLA, the colleague of Brutus in the consulship in the first year of the Roman republic. According to the legend represented by Livy and Plutarch (see ROME), he was a member of one of the noblest Roman families, being son of Volusus, a descendant of a Sabine of that name who had settled in Rome along with King Tatius. He was one of those who witnessed the death of Lucretia, and joined in the oath to avenge her wrongs. He took a prominent part in the expulsion of the Tarquins, and though not originally chosen as the colleague of Brutus he soon afterwards took the place of Tarquinius Collatinus. On the death of Brutus, which left him alone in the consulship, the people began to fear that he was aiming at kingly power. To calm their apprehensions, he discontinued the building of a house which he had begun on the top of the Velian Hill, overlooking the Forum, and also gave orders that the fasces should henceforward be lowered whenever he appeared before the people. He introduced various laws further to protect the liberties of the citizens, one of these enacting that whosoever should attempt to make himself a king might be slain by any man at any time, and another providing an appeal to the people on behalf of any citizen condemned by a magistrate. For these services the surname of Publicola or Poplicola was conferred on himself and on his descendants for ever. He was thrice re-elected to the consulship, and during his fourth term of office he received the honour of a triumph for his victory over the Sabines. He died in the following year (503 B.C.), and was buried at the public expense, the matrons mourning him for ten months.

VALERIUS FLACCUS. See FLACCUS.

VALERIUS MAXIMUS, Latin writer, author of a collection of historical anecdotes, published his work in the reign of Tiberius. Prefixed to many MSS. of the collection is a life of the author, but it is a late and worthless compilation, and the only trustworthy information concerning his career is drawn from a few passing allusions in the book itself. The family of Valerius was poor and undistinguished; for the great Valerii Maximi who are conspicuous in the annals of the early Roman republic cannot be traced lower than the Punic Wars. Valerius himself professes to have owed everything to Sextus Pompeius, who was descended from a paternal uncle of the great Pompey. This Pompeius was a kind of minor Mæcenas, and the centre of a literary circle to which Ovid belonged; he was also the intimate of the most literary prince of the imperial family, Germanicus. He took Valerius with him when he went to Asia as proconsul. Although Valerius does not state that his profession was that of a teacher of rhetoric, the fact is betrayed by every page of his writings. In his prooemium he plainly intimates that he is putting forth a kind of commonplace book of historical anecdotes for use in the schools of rhetoric, where the pupils were severely trained in the art of embellishing speeches by references to history. The title for the work in the MSS. is "Books of Memorable Deeds and Utterances." No ancient reader would have expected accuracy in such a book, and the indignation expressed by many modern scholars at its glaring historical errors has been much misplaced. The stories are very loosely and irregularly arranged in nine books, each book being divided into sections, and each section bearing as its title the topic, most commonly some virtue or vice, or some merit or demerit, which the stories in the section are intended to illustrate. Most of the tales are from Roman history, but each section has an appendix consisting of extracts from the annals of other peoples, principally the Greeks. The exposition exhibits strongly the two currents of feeling which are intermingled by almost every Roman writer of the empire,—the feeling that the Romans of the writer's own day are degenerate creatures when confronted with their own republican predecessors, and the feeling that, however degenerate, the latter-day Romans still tower above the other peoples of the world, and in particular may take much comfort to themselves from their moral superiority to the Greeks.

The range of authorities from whom the collection is drawn is undoubtedly narrow. It has even been maintained that Valerius used four authors only,—Cicero, Livy, Sallust, and Pompeius Trogus; there are, however, clear traces of others, as of Varro, Asinius Pollio, and Herodotus. By far the largest part of the material comes from Cicero and Livy, though each is only mentioned once by name. Valerius was neither a well-read nor an able man. His treatment of his material was careless and unintelligent in the extreme; but for all that he did not miss his aim. Even though in one tale Tanaquil be made the wife of Ancus Martius, and in another Æschylus be mistaken for Pericles, though the Scipios and the Catos be mingled in confusion, though conflicting versions of the same occurrence be given, and the most startling anachronisms presented, yet the excerpts are none the less apt illustrations, from the rhetorician's point of view, of the circumstance or quality they were meant to illustrate. Scholars have long since ceased to corrupt the text of Valerius, as Pighius did, to save his character for historical accuracy, nor do they now, with Perizonius, distort his meaning for the pleasure of adding to the list of his sins. What, then, are his claims to the attention of modern students? In the first place, the existing literary remains of the time in which he wrote are extremely scanty, and mere scarcity confers value on many articles which are in themselves poor. And even on the historical side we owe something to Valerius. He often used sources now lost to us, and where he touches on his own time he affords us some glimpses of the much debated and very imperfectly recorded reign of Tiberius. His attitude towards the imperial household has often been misunderstood, and he has been represented as a mean flatterer of the same type with Martial. But, if the references to the imperial administration be carefully scanned, they will be seen to be extravagant neither in kind nor in number. Few will now grudge to Tiberius, when his whole action as a ruler is taken into account, such a title as "salutaris princeps," which seemed to a former generation a specimen of shameless adulation. The few allusions to Cæsar's murderers and to Augustus hardly pass beyond the conventional style of the writer's day. The only passage which can fairly be called fulsome is a rhetorical pæan over the death of Sejanus. But it is as a chapter in the history of the Latin language that the work of Valerius chiefly deserves study. Without it our view of the transition of classical into silver Latin would be much more imperfect than it is. Erasmus declared that Valerius is no more like

Cicero than a mule is like a man, which is only another way of saying that he had in excess the faults of his age. The entire life, thought, and literature of the first century and a half of the empire were steeped in the influences of rhetoric, enthroned in the seat of education. In Valerius are presented to us, in a rude and palpable form, all the rhetorical tendencies of the age, unsobered by the sanity of Quintilian and unrefined by the taste and subtlety of Tacitus. Here we have the loathing for direct and simple statement and the pursuit of novelty at any price. Every device which can put a gloss of newness on the language is eagerly adopted. The barrier between the diction of poetry and that of prose is broken down; the uses of words are strained; monstrous metaphors are invented; there are startling contrasts, dark innuendoes, and highly coloured epithets; the most unnatural variations are played upon the artificial scale of grammatical and rhetorical figures of speech. It is a most instructive lesson in the history of Latin to set side by side and compare minutely with each other a passage of Valerius and its counterpart in Cicero or Livy.

In the MSS. of Valerius a tenth book is given, which consists of the so-called "liber de prænominibus," the work of some grammarian of a much later date. The collection of Valerius was much used for school purposes, and its popularity in the Middle Ages is attested by the large number of MSS. in which it has been preserved. Like other school books it was epitomated. One complete epitome, probably of the 4th or 5th century, bearing the name of Julius Paris, has come down to us; also a portion of another by Januarius Nepotianus. The best edition of Valerius with explanatory matter is that by C. Kempf (Berlin, 1854); the best text is that by C. Halm (Leipsic, 1865).

VALETTA, or VALLETTA. See MALTA, vol. xv. pp. 340-341. The population was 24,854 in 1881, and was estimated at 26,700 in 1888.

VALLA, LORENZO (*c.* 1406-1457), one of the most salient personalities of the earlier Italian Renaissance, was born at Rome, of parents derived from Piacenza, possibly in the year 1406-07, or perhaps somewhat earlier. He was educated in the humanistic schools of Rome, according to the customs of that age, learning grammar from some humble dominie and afterwards attending the classes of eminent professors. Valla mentions Leonardo of Arezzo as his chief master in Latin and Giovanni Aurispa in Greek. He wished to establish himself as apostolic secretary in the Eternal City. But for some reason or other this office was refused him. At the age of twenty-four he went to Piacenza on family affairs, and from this city proceeded to Pavia, where he obtained a professorship of eloquence. Like all the scholars of that time, Valla wandered from university to university, accepting short engagements and airing his talents as a lecturer in many cities. It appears that he professed the New Learning in Milan and Genoa as well as Pavia. Somewhere, and at some uncertain date during this period, he came into relations with Alphonso of Aragon, who conquered the kingdom of Naples. Valla did not, however, follow this prince's fortunes in the early days of their acquaintance. We find him once more in Rome in 1443 during the pontificate of Eugenius IV. At this period of his career Valla won the highest reputation by his dialogue *De Voluptate* and his treatise on the *Elegances of the Latin Language.* In the former work he contrasted the principles of the Stoics with the tenets of Epicurus, openly proclaiming his sympathy with those who claimed the right of free indulgence for man's natural and sensuous appetites. It was a remarkable utterance, since the paganism of the Renaissance here found, for the first time, deliberate expression in a work of scholarly and philosophical value. The *Elegantiæ* was no less original, though in a different sphere of thought. This work subjected the forms of Latin grammar, the rules of Latin style and rhetoric, to critical investigation. It placed the practice of composition upon a foundation of analysis and inductive reasoning. But there was a third essay composed by Valla during the pontificate of Eugenius which displayed the same originality and a like critical acumen. This bore the title of a *Treatise on the Donation of Constantine*; and in it Valla proved that the claims founded by the Roman see upon that supposed grant reposed on forged documents and legendary fables. It was not published until 1440, when Valla had been already three years resident at Alphonso's court in Naples.

There was every reason why the king of Naples should be interested in a man of Valla's stamp. He wished to attract scholars of the highest ability to his capital, and he was always on bad terms with the papacy. Valla combined the qualities of an elegant humanist, an acute critic, a freethinker, and a venomous pamphleteer who had committed himself to a destructive polemic against the temporalities of Rome. Accordingly the king made him his private secretary, encouraged him to open a school of rhetoric in Naples, and defended him against the attacks of friars and inquisitors. From Naples Valla continued his war of pamphlets against the church. He proved that the letter of Christ to Abgarus was a forgery, ridiculed the Latinity of the Vulgate, questioned the authenticity of the Apostles' Creed, and accused St Augustine of heresy. It is a singular note of that period in Italy that, on the death of Eugenius IV., his successor, Nicholas V., invited Valla to Rome, not to arraign him before the bar of the Inquisition, not to punish him for his insolent criticism, but in order to confer upon him the post of apostolic secretary, with substantial pecuniary appointments. This entrance of Valla into the Roman curia has been justly called "the triumph of humanism over orthodoxy and tradition." Nicholas had no other object than that of fixing one of the chief scholars of the age near his own person. He allowed Valla to open a school of eloquence in Rome, and he paid him munificently for translating Thucydides into Latin. Thus, for the sake of his erudition and stylistic talents, the supreme pontiff rewarded a man whose chief titles to fame are the stringent criticism with which he assailed the temporalities of the church, and the frank candour with which he defended a pagan theory of human conduct.

All the biographical notices of Valla are loaded with long accounts of his literary quarrels. Intolerant of rivalry, inordinately vain, and greedily self-seeking as the scholars of that epoch were, they indulged in the fiercest internecine warfare among themselves. The bulky folios of their works contain hundreds of invectives which may be ranked among the most obscene, the most wearisome, and the most disgraceful products of the human intellect. Valla won a regrettable celebrity by the number and the virulence of his enmities. Bartolomeo Fazio, Georgios Trapezuntios, and Poggio felt the stabbing sharpness of his pen. It must, however, be admitted that these antagonists gave back quite as good as they got. It is almost impossible to form a just estimate of Valla's private life and character through the dust-clouds of abuse and dirt which these controversies stirred up around his memory. He died at Naples in the year 1457. Posterity honours in him not so much the stylist and the scholar as the initiator of a bold critical method, applied to language, historical documents, and ethical opinions.

The collected edition of Valla's *Works* is that of Basel, 1465. For detailed accounts of his life and work, consult Tiraboschi; Voigt's *Wiederbelebung des Alterthums*; and Symonds's *Renaissance in Italy* (vols. ii. and v.).

VALLADOLID, a province of Spain, one of the eight into which Old Castile is now divided, is bounded on the N. by Leon and Palencia, on the E. by Burgos, on the S. by Segovia, Avila, and Salamanca, and on the W. by Zamora. The area is 3043 square miles and the population in 1877 was 247,458. The province belongs entirely to the basin of the Douro, which traverses it from east to west, and within its limits receives the Pisuerga (with the Esgueva) on the right, and the Duraton, Adaja (with the Eresma), and Zapardiel on the left. The country watered by these rivers is for the most part flat and exceedingly fertile, the only part that can be called in any sense hilly being in the north-west, where the low Montes de Torozos occur. For the excellence and abundance of its grain crops Valladolid shares with La Mancha the title of granary of the peninsula. Besides the ordinary cereals and pulses, the province produces hemp, flax, various fruits, red and white wine, oil, and madder. The Montes de Torozos are well clad with oak and other timber. The pastures are extensive and large numbers of horses, mules, and sheep, as well as some cattle, are reared, while honey, wax, and silk are also produced. The woollen fabrics of Valladolid were once highly esteemed, but this industry has now greatly declined. Some trade is carried on, facilitated by the Canal of Castile, which connects Valladolid, on the Pisuerga, with Alar del Rey, in Palencia, also on that river. The province is traversed by the national highways from Madrid to Santander, Leon, and Coruña, and the Calatayud and Salamanca roads may also be regarded as trunk lines. It is also traversed from north to south by the northern railway, which has a branch from Valladolid to Rioseco. There are 11 partidos judiciales and 237 ayuntamientos. The most important places besides Valladolid, the capital (see below), are Medina de Rioseco (4776 inhabitants in 1877) and Medina del Campo (5296).

VALLADOLID, capital of the above province, on the left bank of the Pisuerga, at its confluence with the Esgueva, which traverses the town by two channels, is situated (about 2250 feet above sea-level) 150 miles by rail to the north-west of Madrid. The site is in a small valley enclosed by steep and broken, though not very high, ground. The town, which was formerly surrounded by walls and entered by four principal gates, contains some fine streets and squares, especially the so-called Plaza Mayor, but on the whole it has a dull and deserted aspect, though of late years its industrial and commercial activity has somewhat revived. The granite cathedral, begun in 1585, would, if carried out according to the original design of Herrera, be a magnificent specimen of the Græco-Roman style of that architect; only the nave, however, was ever completed, and the tower (one of four in the plan) fell in 1841. The interior is well proportioned, but bare. The tower and nave of the church of Sta Maria la Antigua date from about 1200. The church of San Pablo is later (1286); its chief feature of interest is a beautiful flamboyant portal, and formerly it had exquisite cloisters. Adjoining is San Gregorio (15th century) with a fine Plateresque façade. San Benito, dating from the end of the 14th century, is an elegant Gothic building with a lofty roof finely groined. The college of Santa Cruz, a Classical building founded in 1479, now houses a collection of pictures and sculptures of little value, except for some examples of Rubens and of the work of Berruguete. The university was founded in 1346; but the present Rococo building dates from the decadence of architecture in Spain. Among other public buildings of Valladolid may be mentioned the royal palace, built in the beginning of the 17th century, and the court-house and town-hall; several ex-convents are now used as barracks. Along the banks of the rivers are several public walks adorned with trees and fountains. The principal industries are the manufacture of linen, silk, and woollen fabrics, pottery, gold and silver work, leather, and paper. There is a considerable trade in the abundant agricultural produce of the vicinity. The population in 1877 was 52,206.

Valladolid is usually identified with the ancient Pintia of Ptolemy, described in the *Itinerary* as a town of the Vaccæi on the road from Asturica to Cæsaraugusta. The present name is usually, but rather obscurely, explained as equivalent to Beled Walid, "the land of Walid." The town was recovered from the Moors in the 10th century, but is first named in a public document by Sancho II. of Leon in 1072. The cortes of Castile frequently met here in the following centuries, and in the beginning of the 15th century John II. made it his principal residence. After the removal of the capital to Madrid by Philip II. in 1560 it began rapidly to decay. In December 1808 it was taken and sacked by the French, and in the January following Bonaparte resided here for some days, and caused the destruction of many fine buildings and works of art. Columbus died (1506) and Philip II. was born (1527) at Valladolid.

VALLADOLID, a city of the state of Michoacan de Ocampo, in Mexico. See Morelia.

VALLADOLID, a town in the state of Yucatan, Mexico, lying towards the centre of the northern plateau, on the river Bolina, about 90 miles south-east of Merida, with which it is about to be connected by a railway. Valladolid, which with the suburban district has a population (1885) of 18,470, mostly Indians and half-castes, is situated in the healthiest and best cultivated part of Yucatan, and is accordingly much frequented by invalids. The town is well built, with regular streets, and low but substantial houses, generally fronted by a garden plot and shady trees. Amongst its buildings are seven fine churches, a large Jesuit college, a town-hall, a hospital, and a well-constructed aqueduct. But like everything else in Yucatan the place presents a general appearance of decay, although there is a considerable local cotton industry. Some miles to the east lie the remarkable ruins of Chichen-Itza, covering a space of nearly two miles in circumference. Amongst these remains are several sonatos, or tanks, from 65 to 200 feet in diameter and 50 to 110 feet deep, with steep rocky sides, in which water is still stored.

Valladolid is one of the oldest Spanish settlements in Yucatan, having been originally founded by Francesco de Montejo at a place called Chauachaa in 1543. But it was removed the next year to Zaqui, about 15 miles from the sea, with easy access to the port of El Cuyo, and soon after to its present position.

VALLE, Pietro della (1586-1652), to whom we owe one of the best books of Eastern travel, came of a noble Roman family which had produced two cardinals, and was born, on 11th April 1586, in the family palace built by Cardinal Andrea. His early life was divided between the pursuits of literature and arms. He saw active service against the Moors of Barbary, but also became a member of the Roman Academy of the *Umoristi*, and acquired some reputation as a versifier and rhetorician. To the latter quality we owe some tedious passages in his *Travels*; but that book gives also sufficient evidence of solid and useful learning in the classical authors, which served him well, particularly in the first part of his wanderings. The idea of travelling in the East was suggested by a disappointment in love, as an alternative to suicide, and was ripened to a fixed purpose by a visit to the learned Mario Schipano, professor of medicine in Naples, to whom the record of Pietro's travels was addressed in the form of very elaborate letters, based on a full diary. Before leaving Naples he took a vow of pilgrimage to the Holy Land, and, sailing from Venice on 8th June 1614, reached Constantinople, where he remained for more than a year, and acquired a good knowledge of Turkish and a little Arabic. On 25th September 1615 he sailed for Alexandria with a suite of nine persons, for he travelled always as a nobleman of distinction, and with every advantage due to his rank. From Alexandria he went on to Cairo, and, after an excursion to Mount Sinai, left Cairo for the Holy Land on 8th March 1616, in time to assist at the Easter celebrations at Jerusalem. Having sedulously visited the holy sites, he journeyed by Damascus to Aleppo, and thence to Baghdad, where he married a Syrian Christian named Maani, a native of Mardin. He now desired to visit Persia; but, as that country was then at war with Turkey, he had to leave Baghdad by stealth (4th January 1617). Accompanied by his wife, who was the courageous and constant companion of his Persian journeys until her death in consequence of a miscarriage (30th December 1621), he proceeded by Hamadan to Ispahan, and joined Shah Abbas in a campaign in northern Persia, in the summer of 1618.

Here he was well received at court and treated as the shah's guest. On his return to Ispahan he was occupied with political schemes hostile to the Turk, the alliance of Persia with the Cossacks and the king of Poland, and also with a project for the foundation of a Catholic colony in Persia; at the same time he diligently continued his Oriental studies and observations. He now began to think of returning by India rather than adventure himself again in Turkey; but the state of his health, and the war between Persia and the Portuguese at Ormuz, created difficulties. In October 1621 he started from Ispahan, and, visiting Persepolis and Shiraz, made his way to the coast; but, after long delay and many troubles—his wife dying at Mina—he was forced to return to Shiraz, after the capture of Ormuz, and it was not till January 1623 that he found passage for Surat on the English ship "Whale." In India he remained till November 1624, his headquarters being Surat and Goa. He was at Muscat in January 1625, and at Bussorah in March. In May he started by the desert route for Aleppo, and, after a short stay there and a visit to Antioch, took ship at Alexandretta on a French vessel. Touching at Cyprus and doing quarantine at Malta, he reached Rome on 28th March 1626, and he was received with much honour, not only by literary circles, but by Pope Urban VIII., who appointed him a gentleman of his bedchamber. The rest of his life was uneventful; he married as second wife a Georgian orphan of noble family, Mariuccia (Tinatin de Ziba), whom his first wife had adopted as a child, and who had accompanied him in all his journeys. By her he had fourteen sons. He died at Rome on 21st April 1652.

In Pietro della Valle's lifetime there were printed (1) a *Funeral Oration on his Wife Maani*, whose remains he brought with him to Rome and buried there (1627); (2) an *Account of Shah Abbas*, printed at Venice in 1628, but not published; (3) the first part of the letters describing his *Travels* (Turkey, 1650). The *Travels* in Persia (2 parts) were published by his sons in 1658, and the third part (India) in 1663. An English translation appeared in 1665 (fol.). Of the Italian text the edition of Brighton, 1843 (2 vols. 8vo), is more esteemed than the other reprints. It contains a sketch of the author's life by Gio. P. Bellori (1622). Della Valle's story is often prolix, with a tendency to the rhetorical. He has no turn for incident, an absolute want of humour, and little real literary faculty of any kind; but he is clear and exact, well informed, and very instructive, so that his work still possesses high value.

VALLEJO, a city of Solano county, California, United States, is situated on the shore of San Pablo Bay, near the western end of the Straits of Carquinez. It has an excellent harbour, and railroad communication by a branch of the Central Pacific Railroad. The city contains large flour-mills; the population in 1880 was 5987. Vallejo, which takes its name from the Mexican general M. G. Vallejo, who took the country from the Indians in 1835, was in 1854 the capital of the State of California.

VALLOMBROSA, ORDER OF. See MONACHISM, vol. xvi. p. 708.

VALLS, a town of Spain, in the province of Tarragona, 11 miles to the north of that town, on a height near the Francoli. It is an old town and its walls and towers still remain. The usual Catalonian industries of wool and cotton spinning and weaving, as well as dyeing, distilling, paper-making, and tanning are carried on with considerable activity. The population within the municipal boundaries in 1877 was 13,250.

VALPARAISO, a city of Chili, the chief town of the province of the same name, and one of the principal commercial ports on the west coast of South America, is situated on a fine bay of the South Pacific Ocean, in 33° 0′ 2″ S. lat. and 71° 41′ 15″ W. long., 70 miles north-west of Santiago, with which there is communication by a circuitous railway of 115 miles. The city lies at the south part of the bay, which is 2½ miles wide, semicircular in form, and well sheltered, except towards the north. There is good anchorage in the roadstead. There are two floating docks, capable of accommodating vessels of from 1400 to 3000 tons. The city is situated at the base of a range of barren hills, varying from 1000 to 1400 feet in height, which have a narrow strip of low land between them and the sea; on this and on sites formed by cutting away the cliffs most of the houses are built. Further space is afforded by the deep dells or water-courses between the hills. These open towards the sea, and are on both sides covered with houses. Much of the foreshore has been raised by earthquakes. The erection of an extensive embankment was begun in 1885. The older portion (Puerto) of the city, in which are the principal public and commercial buildings, is separated from the newer portion, called the Almendral, by a projecting point. The city is defended by a chain of forts, begun in 1866. The principal public buildings are the Government palace, the custom house, the large bonded Government warehouses, the hospital, the city hall, and two theatres. The educational institutions include a theological seminary, a naval academy, and a lyceum; the last-named had 415 students in 1884 and 481 in 1885. The commercial enterprise of the city is largely dependent on the foreign merchants, especially Englishmen, Americans, and Germans. It is the commercial capital of Chili, and the principal residence of the foreign consuls. The principal industrial establishments are the Government railway shops, a large foundry and machine shops, coach-building and wheel-wright works, and a very large sugar refinery, the raw material for which is obtained from Peru. The population (97,737 in 1875) was 95,000 in 1885, of whom about a tenth were foreigners.

Plan of Valparaiso.

The number of vessels in the foreign trade that entered the port in 1885 was 587 of 582,066 tons, the number that cleared 348 of 373,551 tons. More than half of the tonnage was British,—Chilian, German, and French following in the order named. In the coasting trade the number of vessels that entered in 1885 was 781 of 434,486 tons, the number that cleared 1050 of 640,138 tons. About nine-tenths of the tonnage was British and Chilian, the latter having a slight advantage. The following table shows the value of the import and export trade during five years, 1881 to 1885:—

Year.	Imports.			Exports.			Total.		
	£	s.	d.	£	s.	d.	£	s.	d.
1881	7,437,545	8	2	7,891,783	0	0	15,329,328	8	2
1882	8,563,650	17	4	10,713,669	6	8	19,277,320	4	0
1883	9,673,618	13	6	11,441,571	7	4	21,115,190	0	10
1884	9,414,841	1	0	9,441,757	1	8	18,856,598	2	8
1885	6,620,326	18	2	8,324,446	17	8	14,944,773	15	10

The foreign trade is chiefly with Great Britain, France, Germany, and the United States, the value of the exports to these countries in 1885 being £1,356,583, £110,312, £262,065, and £15,424 respectively, and of the imports £1,787,310, £911,080, £900,066, and £318,629 respectively. The principal exports are metals (nitrate, bar copper, silver produce, copper and silver regulus, and gold and silver specie), wheat, barley, flour, wool, nuts, hay, beans, honey, iodine, coal, hides, and guano; and the imports include iron, steel, wire, nails, machines and tools, sugar, rice, cashmeres, prints, shawls, wines, and beer.

Valparaiso was founded in 1536 by the Spanish officer Juan de Saavedra, who named it after his birthplace near Cuenca in Spain. In 1578 the city was captured by Drake, the exact date of his appearance before it being 5th December; and it was again taken by Hawkins's expedition in 1596. In 1600 it was sacked by the Dutch corsair, Van Noort. It was visited by severe earthquakes in 1730 and 1822, and by earthquake shocks in 1839 and 1873. It suffered from fire in November 1858; and on 31st March 1866 it was bombarded by the Spanish fleet under Admiral Nunez, when a large part of the town was laid in ruins.

VALS, or VALS-LÈS-BAINS, a village of France, in the department of Ardèche, with a population of 2186 in 1886, is noted chiefly for its alkaline waters, which are similar to those of Vichy (see vol. xvi. p. 435). Within the commune, which in 1886 had a population of 3911, paper is manufactured to a small extent, and some silk is spun.

VALTELLINA, or VALTELLINE, the upper valley of the Adda, in the extreme north of Italy (province of Sondrio), derives its name from Teglio, the former capital, not far from Tirano (Val di Teglio, Val Teglina; Germ., Veltlin), and has a length, from Bormio to the Lake of Como, of about 68 miles. The chief town is Sondrio (4014 inhabitants in 1881), other important places being Tirano (3119) and Morbegno (3240). Near Bormio (Germ., Worms) there are some frequented mineral springs (sulphur and lime), known in Pliny's time, and efficacious in diseases of the skin. There are several other baths in the side valleys, such as Santa Caterina (chalybeate), Masino, and Le Prese (sulphur). The highest points in the ranges enclosing the valley are the Piz Zupo (13,121 feet) in the Bernina group and the Königsspitze (12,645 feet) in the Ortler district; the Monte della Disgrazia (12,074 feet) is the highest peak comprised entirely within the water-basin of the valley. Three well-marked Alpine passes are traversed by good carriage-roads—the Stelvio Pass or Stilfserjoch (9046 feet, the highest carriage-road in Europe) from Bormio to Meran in the Adige valley, the Bernina Pass (7628 feet) from Tirano to Samaden in the Upper Engadine, and the Aprica Pass (4049 feet) from Tirano to the Val Camonica and the Lake of Iseo. The main valley is traversed from end to end by a magnificent carriage-road constructed by the Austrian Government in 1820-25. A railway from Colico, on the Lake of Como, to Sondrio (27 miles) was opened in 1884, and is being pushed on towards Tirano. The population is wholly Italian-speaking and Roman Catholic, the valley being in the diocese of Como. The shrine of the Madonna of Tirano (founded 1520) annually attracts a large number of pilgrims. The valley, particularly in its lower portion, is extremely fertile; and of late years vigorous measures have been taken to prevent the damage caused by the frequent inundations of the Adda. Chestnuts, vines, mulberry trees, and fig trees abound; and there are many picturesquely-situated churches, castles, and villages. The chief articles exported are wine and honey. The wine is largely consumed in north Italy and Switzerland, the best varieties being Grumello, Sassella, and Montagna. About 20,000 lb weight of honey is annually sent abroad. Politically the whole valley belongs to the kingdom of Italy, except the side valley of Poschiavo (Puschlav), which belongs to the Swiss canton of the Grisons (Graubünden).

The political history of Valtellina is made up of the histories of three districts,—(1) the "free community" of Poschiavo (first mentioned as such in 1200-01); (2) the county of Bormio (first mentioned as a county in 1347); and (3) Valtellina proper, extending from the defile of the Serra di Morignone on the east to the Lake of Como on the west. After the defeat of the Lombards (774) these three districts were given by Charlemagne to the abbey of St Denis near Paris, which never seems to have exercised its rights. In 824 Lothair I., confirming an earlier donation made by Charlemagne, gave the churches of Poschiavo and Bormio to the bishop of Como. Bormio was in 1205 won by the men of Como, who in 1006 had received one-half of Valtellina from the emperor, and by 1114 they were masters of the entire valley. They retained Bormio till 1300, when it freed itself; but in 1336 it belonged to the bishop of Chur. In 1335 the Visconti, lords (later dukes) of Milan, became lords of Como, and therefore of Valtellina. In 1350 they seized on Bormio and Poschiavo, the latter being won back by the bishop of Chur in 1394, and again lost to the Visconti in 1435. As early as 1360 the men of Rhætia made incursions into Valtellina under the pretext that it had formed part of ancient Rhætia. This idea was confirmed in 1404, when, in return for kind treatment received during his exile, Mastino Visconti (son of Barnabo) gave to the bishop of Chur his share of the Milanese, including Poschiavo, Bormio, and Valtellina. Relying on this donation, the men of the Three Leagues of Rhætia (best known by the name of one, Graubünden) invaded the valley in 1486-87, Poschiavo becoming in 1486 permanently a member (not a subject land) of the *Gotteshausbund*. This donation served too as the excuse for seizing, in 1512, on Bormio and Valtellina, which were harshly ruled as "subject bailiwicks." Under the governor at Sondrio there were four "podestas" for the three divisions of Valtellina (Morbegno and Traona, Sondrio, and Tirano), besides one at Teglio and one at Bormio. Mastino Visconti's donation was solemnly confirmed in 1516 by the emperor Maximilian I. In 1530 the bishop of Chur was forced to sell to the Three Leagues for a small sum his title to these two districts. At the time of the Reformation Poschiavo became Protestant. The other two districts clung to the old faith and came under the influence of Carlo Borromeo, who, when founding in 1579 his "Collegium Helveticum" at Milan for Swiss students for the priesthood, reserved for Valtellina six out of the forty-two places. Valtellina was extremely important to the Hapsburgs as affording the direct route between their possessions of the Milanese and Tyrol. Hence a great struggle, into which religious questions and bribery largely entered, took place between Austria and Spain on one side and France and Venice on the other. In 1603 Fuentes, the Spanish governor of the Milanese, built a fortress (of which traces still remain) close to the Lake of Como and at the entrance to the valley, in order to overawe it. The religious conflicts in Graubünden led to reprisals in the "subject land" of Valtellina. In 1620 (19th July–4th August) the Spanish and Romanist faction (headed by the Planta family) massacred a great number of Protestants in the valley, 350 to 600 according to different accounts (*Veltliner Mord*). For the next twenty years the valley was the scene of great strife, being held by the Spaniards (1620, 1621-23, 1629-31, 1637-39), by the French (1624-26, 1635-37), and by the pope (1623, 1627). At length George Jenatsch, a former pastor, who had been the active and unscrupulous leader of the Protestant party, became a Romanist (1635) in order to free the land from the French by aid of the Spaniards (1637), who finally (1639) gave it back to its old masters on condition that the Protestants were excluded from the valley. In this way the local struggles of Valtellina came to be mixed up with the Thirty Years' War. In 1797 Bormio and Valtellina were annexed to the Cisalpine republic, in 1805 to the kingdom of Italy (of which Napoleon was king), and in 1815 (despite the remonstrances of the Rhætian leagues) to the kingdom of Lombardo-Venetia, held by the emperor of Austria. In 1859 they became, like the rest of Lombardy, part of the kingdom of united Italy. Poschiavo followed the fortunes of the "Gotteshausbund." It became (after 1798) part of the canton Rhætia of the Helvetic republic, and in 1803 of the canton of the Graubünden or Grisons, which was then first received a full member of the Swiss Confederation.

See G. Leonhardi, *Das Veltlin* and *Das Poschiavinothal* (1859); Romegialli, *Storia della Valtellina* (1834-39, 5 vols.); C. von Moor, *Geschichte von Currätien* (1870-74); P. C. von Planta, *Die currätischen Herrschaften in der Feudalzeit* (1881); Coxe, *Travels in Switzerland*, &c. (4th ed., 1801; Letters 74-78); Henne-Am Rhyn, *Geschichte des Schweizervolkes* (1865); L. von Ranke, *History of the Popes*, bk. vii.; and H. Reinhardt, "Das Veltliner Mord," in *Geschichtsfreund* (vol. xl., 1885).

VALUE. In most departments of economic theory it is convenient to use as the basis of the exposition the opinions of J. S. Mill, not only because he has embodied in his treatise in a remarkable manner nearly everything of importance from the theoretical standpoint in the work of his predecessors, but also because most of the recent advances in economic science have been made by way of criticism or development of his views. This observation is especially true of the theory of value. In this subject Mill had digested the mass of previous learning with such effect that he commences his treatment with the remark: "Happily there is nothing in the laws of value which remains for the present or any future writer to clear up; the theory of the subject is complete. The only difficulty to be overcome is that of so stating it as to solve by anticipation the chief perplexities which occur in applying it." Curiously enough this part of economic theory was the first to receive at the hands of Jevons and others serious modification, the nature and need for which can, however, only be properly understood after a preliminary examination of the old orthodox position.

Value in use and in exchange.

As regards the question of definition, Mill starts with the distinction somewhat loosely drawn by Adam Smith between value in use and value in exchange. When we say that a thing possesses a certain value in use, we say in more words than are necessary that it is useful: that is to say, value in use is an awkward phrase for utility. The conception of utility (see WEALTH) is the most fundamental in economics. It is held by Mill to mean the capacity to satisfy a desire or serve a purpose, and thus "useful," the corresponding adjective, is as fitly applied to ices as to steam-engines. But utility is obviously much wider than value, and Mill proceeds to say that by value in political economy we should always understand exchange value. This language seems familiar and definite, but on analysis it is clear that exchange implies two terms at least. If we say that a thing can be exchanged, we imply that it can be exchanged for something else, and when we speak of the exchange value of a thing we must directly or indirectly refer to the value of some other thing or things. In practice in modern societies this other thing is standard money: an Englishman who talks of the exchange value of anything means the number of pounds sterling (or parts thereof) which it will fetch in the market or be appraised at by a fair arbitrator. On this view then the value of a thing is its price; but a very little experience in the theory or history of economics will show that it is often desirable, and sometimes necessary, to contrast value with price. "At the same time and place," says Adam Smith, "money is the exact measure of the real exchangeable value of all commodities. It is so, however, at the same time and place only." If, however, the exchange value of a thing is not its price, what is it? According to Mill, "The value of a thing is its general power of purchasing, the command which its possession gives over purchasable commodities in general." But what, we may well ask with Mill, is meant by command over commodities in general? Are we to understand the complete national inventory of wealth, or the total of things consumed in a given time by a nation? Obviously such conceptions are extremely vague and possibly unworkable. If, however, we make a selection on any representative principle, this selection will be more or less arbitrary. Mill is to some extent aware of these difficulties, although he never subjected them to a rigorous analysis; and he points to the obvious fact that a coat, for example, may exchange for less bread this year than last, but for more glass or iron, and so on through the whole range of commodities it may obtain more of some and less of others. But in this case are we to say that the value of the coat has risen or fallen? On what principles are we to strike an average? The attempt to answer these questions in a satisfactory manner is at present engaging the attention of economists more than any other problem in the pure theory. Mill, however, instead of attempting to solve the problem, frankly assumed that it is impossible to say except in one simple case. If, owing to some improvement in manufacture, the coat exchanges for less of all other things, we should certainly say that its value had fallen. This line of argument leads to the position: "The idea of general exchange value originates in the fact that there really are causes which tend to alter the value of a thing in exchange for things generally, that is, for all things that are not themselves acted upon by causes of similar tendency." There can be no doubt as to the truth of the latter part of this statement, especially if we substitute for one commodity groups of commodities. But it is doubtful if the idea of general exchange value arises from a consideration of the causes of value; and recent writers have constantly emphasized the distinction between any change and the causes of the change. Following out the idea in the last sentence quoted, Mill goes on to say that any change in the value of one thing compared with things in general may be due either to causes affecting the one thing or the large group of all other things, and that in order to investigate the former it is convenient to assume that all commodities but the one in question remain invariable in their relative values. On this assumption any one of them may be taken as representing all the rest, and thus the money value of the thing will represent its general purchasing power. That is to say, if for the sake of simplicity we assume that the prices of all other things remain constant, but that one thing falls or rises in price, the fall or rise in price in this thing will indicate the extent of the change in its value compared with things in general. There can be no doubt that, in discussing any practical problem as to the changes in the relative value of any particular thing, it is desirable to take the changes in price as the basis, and much confusion and cumbrousness of expression would have been avoided in the theory of the subject if, to adapt a phrase of Cournot's, money had by Mill and others been used to oil the wheels of thought, just as in practice it is used to oil the wheels of trade.

Price.

Requisites for value.

By this method of abstraction the treatment of the theory of value becomes essentially an examination of the causes which determine the values of particular commodities relatively to a standard which is assumed to be fixed. Now in order that anything may possess value in this sense, that it may exchange for any portion of standard money or its representatives, it is evident on the first analysis that two conditions must be satisfied. First, the thing must have some utility; and secondly, there must be some difficulty in its attainment. As regards utility, Mill apparently regards it simply as a kind of entrance examination which every commodity must pass to enter the list of valuables, whilst the place in the list is determined by variations in the degree of the difficulty of attainment. Later writers, however (more particularly Jevons), have given much more prominence to utility, and have drawn a careful distinction between final and total utility. This distinction is useful in throwing light on the advantages of, and motives for, exchanging commodities. Suppose that on a desert island A possesses all the food, so many measures—(say) pecks—of corn, and B all the drinking water, so many measures—(say) pints. Then A, taking into account present and future needs, might ascribe to the possession of each portion of his stock so much utility. The utility of the first few pecks of corn might be regarded as practically infinite; but, if his stock were abundant, and a speedy rescue probable, the utility ascribed to successive portions would be less and less. In the same way B might make an estimate of the utility of successive measures of the drinking water. Now, if we regard only *total* utilities from the point of view of each, both are infinite. If an exchange were made of the total stocks of both men, the position of neither would be improved. But, if A sets aside (say) half his stock, then it may well happen that he could advantageously exchange the rest against part of B's drinking water. In precisely the same way B might set aside so much of his stock for his own consumption, and then the utility of the remaining portion would be much less than the utility he would gain if he obtained in exchange A's surplus. Thus, if the two men exchange their remainders, both will gain in utility; in the case supposed they will make an enormous gain. For simplicity we have supposed each stock to be divided into two portions, but nothing has been said of the principles of the division. It is, however, clear that A can advantageously go on exchanging a measure of corn for a measure of water so long as by doing so he makes a gain of utility. Conversely B can advantageously offer water so long as he gains greater utility from the corn received in exchange. The utility of the last portion of corn retained by A (or of water by B) is the *final* utility of the stock retained, and similarly the utility of the last

Final and total utility.

measure obtained in exchange may be called the final utility of the stock purchased. A will have done his best if these utilities are just equal. For at this point, if he were to offer (at the same rate of exchange) more corn, it is clear that he would lose more utility than he would gain. *Mutatis mutandis*, the same reasoning applies to B; and thus the rate of exchange will be so adjusted as to bring about this equality of final utilities on both sides.[1] It follows that, if A gains on the last portion received just as much utility as he loses on the portion parted with, on all the other portions received he will have gained more than he lost. The total of these gains over successive portions has been called by Prof. Marshall *consumer's rent.*

Difficulty of attainment.

However useful this theory of final utility may be in throwing light on the fundamental nature of value, and on the advantages of exchange, it is obviously too abstract to be applied to the explanation of the relative values of the endless series of commodities and services which constitute a nation's stock of valuables at any time. For this purpose we must resort to the law of supply and demand, which requires a very careful statement owing to the ambiguities of popular language. Mill has succeeded in getting rid of most of these ambiguities, but he has hardly given due emphasis to the fundamental character of the law. He argues, after the brief consideration allotted to the element of utility, that the other preliminary condition necessary for value—difficulty of attainment—is not always the same kind of difficulty, and he arrives at three distinct laws of value, according to three forms or degrees of this difficulty.

Three laws of value.

(1) In the first place the difficulty may consist in an absolute limitation of the supply, and in this case the corresponding law is said to be the law of supply and demand. Even on Mill's view the class of commodities which comes under this heading is both large and important, for it includes not only the favourite examples of old pictures, china, &c., but also land, and especially building sites in large cities. Again, it is pointed out that, although comparatively few commodities may be absolutely limited, almost all commodities may be so locally and temporarily, which is really only another way of saying that the law of supply and demand governs all market values; for it is obvious that the supply actually forthcoming or obtainable in a specified time in any market is limited,—a point which may be well illustrated by the extreme case of a "corner." Again, under certain circumstances the supply may be artificially limited, as in the case of monopolies, a typical example being the destruction by the Dutch of some of their spice, in order that the limited quantity might sell for a total higher price. Besides all these important instances of the operation of the law of supply and demand, Mill is compelled also to bring under the same law the wages of labour, the values of the staples of international trade, and some other peculiar cases of value. In fact, step by step he is almost forced to the conclusion, now generally accepted, that the law of supply and demand is the fundamental law of value, of which the other laws are only particular cases. At the outset, however, he appears to consider the two others as of co-ordinate importance. (2) When the difficulty of attainment consists not in the absolute limitation but simply in the fact that the article requires labour and capital to produce it, the normal or natural value is said to be determined by the cost of production. (3) In the last case taken by Mill it is supposed that an article can be increased in quantity, but only at an increasing cost, and in this case the corresponding law of value is the cost of production of that portion which is obtained under the most unfavourable circumstances. These three laws of value may now be examined critically and their mutual relations discussed, for the last two, if not properly of co-ordinate importance with the first, are at any rate wide generalizations.

Law of supply and demand.

In order to understand the law of supply and demand, it is best to take separately the general law of demand and the general law of supply, and then effect a combination. Demand must be defined as the quantity of any article demanded at some particular price, it being assumed of course that the bidder of the price can meet his engagements, or, as is sometimes said, that the demand is an effectual demand. It is quite clear that by demand we cannot simply mean desire to possess, because in a sense every one desires everything, and the less the means of payment so much greater in general is the desire. Again, it is obviously necessary to insert the qualifying clause "at some particular price," because, as a rule, with a change in price a different quantity will be demanded. It is, indeed, this variation of quantity demanded, according to variation in price, which gives rise to the statement of the general law of demand, namely:

Law of demand.

As the price of any article falls, other things remaining the same, the quantity demanded increases, and, conversely, as the price rises the quantity demanded decreases. A very good example of this law is found in the effects of the remission of taxes. The repeal of a tax leads to a fall in price and the fall in price is accompanied by increased consumption. Conversely, it has often been found that to increase the amount of a tax does not increase the revenue from it, because the demand for the article falls off. The precise connexion between the price and the quantity demanded differs in different cases, and, strictly speaking, is probably never the same for any two commodities. At the same time, however, commodities may be placed in large classes according to the general character of the variation. The variation of quantity demanded according to price will ultimately rest on the principle of *final utility* explained above. A person with a limited amount of money to spend will hit the economic mark in the centre if the final utilities of his several purchases are equal. This is a rather technical way of saying that a prudent man will not spend a penny more on any particular thing if the penny spent upon some new object would give him a little greater satisfaction. Reverting to the variations of demand according to price, a contrast will at once be observed between necessaries and luxuries. However much the price rises, so long as people have the means they must consume a certain amount of necessaries, but, however much the price falls, the limit of consumption of bread, for example, must soon be reached. On the other hand, a great fall in price of many luxuries may cause an enormous increase in the demand, whilst a great rise may almost destroy the demand. A great deal of light might be thrown on many interesting problems in the progress of a nation and of its various component classes, if the laws of demand, or the statistics of consumption according to price, were obtainable.

Law of supply.

Turning to the element of supply, this term in a similar way may be defined as the quantity offered for sale at some particular price, and the general law of supply may be stated thus: As the price rises, other things remaining the same, the quantity offered tends to increase, and, conversely, as the price falls the quantity offered tends to diminish. Expressed in this manner, supply appears to be exactly analogous to demand, and the analogy seems to hold good even when we push the analysis up to the utility to the seller as compared with the utility to the buyer. For, as the price rises, the seller will obtain greater utility, and will thus retain less for his own use or will be induced to produce more. On closer inspection, however, the law of supply is found to be not so simple as the law

[1] For a full account of the theory of which only the principles are here indicated, see Jevons, *Theory of Pol. Econ.*, London 1871.

of demand. It would only be so if the seller had simply to compare the relative advantages of exchanging his commodity and of retaining it for his own use, without any further reference to the conditions of, or the motives for, production. In most commodities, however, the determining influence is not the comparative utility of consumption by the owner on the one hand or of the consumption of something else obtained by exchange on the other, but it is rather a comparison of the trouble of producing with the advantage of selling the article when produced. Of course, if we are considering finished products in any market the case is more simple; but even here the question of the relative advantages of present sale and reservation for a future market or distant place must be determined, and then the element of cost of production will again be brought back.

Before considering the relation of cost of production to supply, it will be convenient to combine the laws of supply and demand, taking the former in its simplest aspect, and to state the general law of supply and demand as governing value. Excluding the simple case of the barter of two commodities of which the rate of exchange will be determined as explained above in reference to final utility, and meaning by demand the quantity demanded in a market at a certain price, and by supply the quantity there and then offered at a certain price, the general law may be stated thus: In any market the price of any article will be so adjusted that the quantity demanded will exactly equal the quantity offered at that price. The force by which the adjustment is made is, in general, competition. Thus, if the price were above the point indicated by the law, there would be a lessened demand and the competition of sellers would tend to lower the price. Conversely, if the price were lower the competition caused by the increased demand would tend to raise it. The law as thus stated corresponds to what Mill calls the equation between demand and supply. He was induced to adopt this phrase in place of the more popular expression, the ratio of demand to supply, on the ground of its greater accuracy. And, if the term ratio is to be taken strictly, no doubt Mill's criticism is perfectly just. At the same time the equation must be stated very carefully to avoid falling into the truism suggested by Cairnes, namely, that in any market the quantity bought at any price is equal to the quantity sold at that price. The point is that in accordance with the general principles of supply and demand the quantities offered and demanded vary with the price. And, however inaccurate the literal use of the term ratio may be, it has the advantage of suggesting a change of price according to changes in demand and supply.

Equation between demand and supply.

Monopoly values.

It may be useful at this point to consider the principles by which monopoly values are regulated. The simplest case is when one individual possesses the whole stock and the cost of production is so small that it may be neglected. Take the case, for example, of some natural well having a unique character for the mineral waters it supplies. The monopolist will, in the first place, have to discover the law of demand for his article. If he fixes a very high price, he may only occasionally sell a pint to a king or a millionaire, whilst, if he fixes a very low price, he may sell to every peasant and yet get a very poor return. He will, in fact, have to work out a problem in mathematics, and must so adjust his price that the quantity sold multiplied by the price per unit will be a maximum. The same kind of difficulty is found in the case in which the expenses of production, although considerable, are practically fixed or only increase slightly in proportion to the quantity furnished. The minimum price will be given by the expenses of production, whilst the actual price will tend to be such as to yield the maximum profit. Take, for example, the case of a steamer which has a practical monopoly and is not controlled by Government. The owner will not send out the steamer at all unless the passengers and cargo pay the expenses; but, if there is a great demand, he will raise the price so as to secure a maximum profit. In general, however, any increase in the quantity of the article produced (or the service rendered) will be accompanied by an increase in the necessary outlays, and this increase may be greater or less per unit. In these cases the calculation of the maximum profit is a matter of great difficulty. Take, for example, the case of a railway which has a monopoly in a certain tract of country. The manager may aim at keeping down expenses and charging high rates, being contented with a moderate traffic; or he may lower his charges and incur additional expense to increase the gross income. It is worthy of remark that in many cases the monopolist has a choice of two methods which give practically equally good results, one starting with low and the other with high prices. But it is clear that the mass of the general public or the great body of consumers have an interest in low prices being adopted, whilst, on the other hand, the tendency is usually for the monopolist to charge higher prices than are really profitable in a maximum degree. The simplicity of the method of high prices is always attractive and often deceptive. Accordingly, even on these very general grounds, the interference of Government with monopolies may be defended as being in the interests of the public and not against the interests of the monopolists. The case of the parliamentary third-class tickets furnishes an instructive example. At first the railways made their parliamentary trains as slow and inconvenient as possible, whereas now there is hardly a train which does not carry passengers at parliamentary rates without compulsion. In a similar way many cases of Governmental interference with landowners may be justified, for very often there is a tacit combination on the part of a few great landowners to act on certain customs.[1] As a rule, however, in modern commercial countries monopolies are an exception. Any one, for example, can prosecute any trade or manufacture if he can provide the requisite skill, labour, and capital, and even as regards land,—at any rate in the greater part of England and Scotland,—there is from the point of view of cultivation no real monopoly. But, when competition arises, exceptional profit ceases, and thus a new principle for determining values comes into play. If the producer of any article is obtaining more than the usual rate of profit, he at once provokes competition, and thus even the dread of this possible competition may keep down prices. This is often expressed by saying that the potential supply affects prices almost as much as the actual supply. It thus becomes obvious that, as regards freely produced commodities the production of which may be extended indefinitely at the same or at a decreasing cost, the value tends to conform to the minimum cost of production, and that any other value is consequently unstable. It will be observed, however, that cost of production only determines values by operating through the actual or potential supply, and thus that the law of demand and supply is fundamental. Once a thing is made, the actual cost of production has no influence on its value, except as indicating the conditions of future possible supply.

Competition values.

Cost of production.

At this point it becomes necessary to analyse and explain the nature of cost of production. In the last resort it will be found that nothing can be produced without labour, and in a modern society capital must be added. Thus the component elements of production are labour and capital

[1] The general theory of monopolies is admirably treated by the French mathematician and economist Cournot, *Revue Sommaire des Doctrines Économiques*, Paris, 1877.

acting by natural forces upon raw material. But, since both the forces and the produce of nature require labour and capital for their exploitation, the elements that must be considered primary and fundamental in the case of commodities that can be indefinitely increased are labour and capital. Capital, again, is itself a product of labour, and it is also wealth set aside by the owner for future use instead of for present consumption. Accordingly, in order that a thing may be continuously produced, labour must obtain a sufficient reward for toil and capital a sufficient reward for "abstinence," or for preservation and accumulation of wealth. Thus the ultimate elements in the real cost of production are the toil and trouble and irksomeness of labour and of saving. But this toil and trouble will not be submitted to unless in any particular case the fair reward of industrial competition is forthcoming. However much pleasure a good workman may take in his work or a prudent man in his savings, in the industrial world as at present constituted both labour and capital will be attracted towards the point of highest reward (compare WAGES); and, accordingly, it is a necessary condition of the production of any article that the price obtained will yield the average rate of wages and profit obtainable for that species of work. Now these rates of wages and profit can be expressed in terms of money, and may be designated, following Prof. Marshall, the *expenses of production* as distinguished from the *real cost*. The real cost of production would on analysis consist of a confused unworkable mass of "efforts and abstinences," and the relation of these mental strains to their material rewards is the problem of wages and profits. But for the purpose of relative values it is not necessary to push the analysis so far, and thus, if we regard the capitalist as the producer, we may look on the elements of production as consisting of wages and profits. And this is quite in accordance with customary thought and language: every one who asks for the details of the cost of a thing expects to have a statement of the wages and profits directly involved, and of the material, which again directly involves wages and profits. So far, then, as freely produced commodities are concerned, the general law is that they tend to sell at such a price as will yield on the average the ordinary rate of wages and profits which by industrial competition the occupation can command. It is at this point that the difficulty emerges as to the precise nature of the connexion between the prices of commodities and the money wages and profits of producers. Are we to consider that the former are determined by the latter, or the latter by the former? If, for example, commodity A sells for twice as much as commodity B, are we to say that this is because wages are higher in the former case, or are the wages higher because the price is higher? The answer to this question is given in the theory of WAGES (*q.v.*). It is sufficient to state here that, in discussing relative values, we may assume that industrial competition has established certain relative rates of wages and profits in various employments, and that any prices of articles which yielded more than these rates, whilst in other cases no corresponding rise took place, would be unstable. Thus, in discussing the normal values of freely produced commodities, we have to consider the quantity of labour and the rates of wages and the quantity of capital and the rate of profits, the *normal* rates of these wages and profits being given.

Expenses of production.

Wages and values.

Normal value.

The use of the term "normal" requires some explanation. The word *norma* properly refers to the square used by masons and carpenters, &c., and thus a thing may be said to be in its normal position when no change will be made: that is to say, the normal position is the stable position, or it is the position to which the workman will try to adjust his work. And, similarly, by the use of normal as applied to wages and profits, we mean the stable rate or the rate towards which they are attracted. It is thus quite possible that the normal rate may differ from the average rate or the rate obtained over a term of years. For it may easily happen that as regards wages, for example, a high rate for a short period may lead to such an increase in that kind of production that for a much longer period the rate will fall below the normal. The normal rate seems to refer to the actual conditions of industry, the rate which can be obtained for a given amount of exertion, taking the average of employments at the time, rather than to the particular rate obtained for some class of work over a period of years.

With these explanations the proposition holds good that the normal values of freely produced commodities tend to be equal to their cost, or rather expenses, of production, and any price which yields a greater or less return to labour and capital is unstable.

Elements of expenses of production.

If all commodities were produced directly by the expenditure of labour, and in such a way that capital need not be considered, as in the simple natural state of society taken by Ricardo, then the only element to consider in value would be the quantity of labour. And in a society of a more developed character, in which wages are paid, if we consider that the rate of wages is uniform, and that profits may be disregarded in comparison with wages, the quantity of labour is the most important consideration, and a fall in the relative value of any article can only take place through some economy of labour. But, as we approach more nearly to the actual constitution of modern industrial societies, we find serious differences in the rates of wages in different employments, the use of fixed capital becomes of greater importance, and in some cases the lapse of time necessary for the completion of the commodity is considerable. Thus interest and profits, as well as the differential rates of wages, have to be taken into account just as much as the quantity of labour, and it is generally convenient to consider also the established differences in various returns to capital under different conditions (risk, irregularity, &c.). Indirectly, of course, since all capital in the ordinary sense is the result of labour, the quantity of labour is always of primary importance; but, in considering the proximate causes of relative values, it is best to consider capital and labour as independent factors. It follows, then, that, in order to compare the relative values of two commodities, A and B, freely produced in a modern industrial society, we must take into account, first of all, the relative wages and relative profits, and the relative amounts of labour and capital employed. If the producers of A are skilled workmen, and if the return to the capital is uncertain, whilst in the case of B the labour is unskilled and profit steady, then the value of A will be higher than that of B, supposing each produced by the same amount of capital and the same quantity of labour. Obviously, too, any change in the relative wages and profits will affect the relative values. If the commodities considered are not capable of division into similar parts (such as yards of cloth or silk), but must be considered in their entirety (*e.g.*, ships and houses), then we must take into account also the different quantities of labour and capital required for their completion, as well as the relative rates of wages and profits. As regards changes of value in this case, it will be observed that, if the proportions are different in which labour and capital are employed in the production of two commodities, then any change in the *general* rates of wages and profits will affect relative values. By making various suppositions as to changes in the different elements of the expenses of production, a great many cases may be obtained, as is done, for example, by Mill (*Pol. Econ.*, bk. iii. ch. iv.). All the

General formula for expenses of production.

cases enumerated and others may, however, be deduced from a general formula. Let E_1 represent the total expenses of production of commodity A. Let Q_1 be the quantity of fixed capital employed, and let r_1 be the rate of wear and tear per annum, so that the loss is Q_1/r_1. Let P_1 be the rate of profits per cent per annum which must be obtained on the whole capital. Let Q_2 be the number of labourers, and w_2 the rate of wages per annum. Let t_1 represent the time taken for production reckoned in years (t_1 may be less than unity, thus t_1/Q_2 would be weeks). Then the total expenses of production are

$$E_1 = \left\{ Q_1\left(\frac{P_1}{100} + \frac{1}{r}\right) + Q_2 . w_2\left(1 + \frac{P_1}{100}\right) \right\} t_1 .$$

This simply means that the commodity must return in the normal case profits on the fixed capital with repair of waste, and also the wages expended (the amount depending on the number of labourers and the rate of wages), with profit on the circulating capital over all the time necessary to complete production. In some cases, it may be observed, it would be necessary to take t differently for the fixed capital and the labour or circulating capital. Then, in a similar way E_2, the expenses of production of B, may be expressed:

$$E_2 = \left\{ Q_3\left(\frac{P_3}{100} + \frac{1}{r_3}\right) + Q_4 . w_4\left(1 + \frac{P_3}{100}\right) \right\} t_2 .$$

Changes in relative values.

Thus the relative values of A and B will be found by comparing the aggregate of these several elements expressed on the right hand sides of the equations. It will now be evident on what a number of variable elements relative values must depend, even when we consider that the commodities can be indefinitely increased by the proper expenditure of capital and employment of labour. With the progress of invention and the development of industrial competition, constant changes are taking place in the various elements, and in the somewhat complicated formula given certain practical elements have been eliminated. Even if we suppose, for the sake of simplicity, that P_1 and P_3 are equal, as also w_2 and w_4 and t_1 and t_2,—that is, if we suppose a uniform rate of wages and profits, and the same amount of time required,—still any change in these *general* rates will affect relative values, owing to the different proportions in which fixed and circulating capital may be employed in the two cases. Thus, for example, we arrive at Mill's statement: "All commodities in the production of which machinery bears a large part, especially if the machinery is very durable, are lowered in their relative value when profits fall." And it will be found on trial that by making various suppositions as to the identity of certain of the elements, or as to their disappearance, many other causes of changes in relative values may be deduced. Two important practical conclusions of a general character may be drawn from this analysis. (1) Relative values are liable to constant disturbances, and accordingly, since relative prices tend to be adjusted to relative values, relative prices must be constantly changing. (2) It is extremely difficult to measure changes in the value of the monetary standard, or movements in the general level of prices, or variations in the purchasing power of money incomes.

Value and rent.

These difficulties are further increased by the importance of the group of commodities which can only be increased (the arts of production remaining the same) at an increasing cost, and which are placed by Mill under a third law of value. The most important examples of this law are agricultural and mining produce. In order to make the principles on which this law depends clear and intelligible, it is necessary to proceed at first by the abstract method so well described by Cairnes (*Logical Method of Pol. Econ.*, 2d ed., London, 1885). Assume then that there is an isolated country and that its agricultural produce consists of corn. Then at any given stage of the growth of wealth and population the amount of corn may be increased (the art of agriculture remaining stationary) either by taking into cultivation inferior lands or else by cultivating with greater care and expense the lands already in cultivation. But in either case what is known as the law of diminishing return would come into play, and the additional supply could only be obtained at an additional cost. It may be assumed that at any stage of development the cultivation would be carried to such a point as to give just the ordinary return to capital on the last "dose" of capital expended. Further it cannot be carried, for no farmer will work at a continuous loss; and competition will insure that it is carried so far, for, if this last application of capital yields ordinary profit, the former "doses" must yield more, that is to say, rent as well as profit. It thus becomes manifest that, under the conditions supposed, the extent to which "the margin of cultivation" will extend depends upon the price of the produce, and in the normal case—The price must be equal to the expenses of production of that part which is produced under the most unfavourable circumstances. This then is the third law of value, from which the economic theory of rent is an immediate deduction. For, if the last dose obtains just a sufficient return, the former doses must yield more, and the sum of these extra profits is rent. It thus appears, also, that rent depends upon price and not price upon rent.[1]

Qualifications of pure theory of rent.

The pure theory of rent is arrived at by making certain hypotheses and abstractions, and accordingly it must not be applied to particular practical cases without further consideration. The theory certainly indicates the effect of very important causes, but requires in practice a certain amount of qualification. (1) The essence of the theory is that the return to each dose of capital applied can be separated, and that the application of capital will cease when the last dose yields only ordinary profits; and no doubt it is roughly true to say that a farmer will discover on trial at what point he should cease applying capital, and that this will depend upon the price of the produce. At the same time, however, it is quite possible that a farmer who owns the land which he tills may find it advantageous to carry cultivation to a further pitch than if he only rented his land. For he will apply his own labour and capital at a less return on his own land. There can be little doubt that very many important improvements made by landowners have yielded less than the ordinary rate of profit, just as peasant proprietors obtain a poor return by way of wages for their own labour. A landowner cultivating his own land has the whole margin of economic rent to fall back upon, but a farmer has to pay his rent as a first charge. Thus it is possible, provided always that the land is cultivated in both cases with the same skill, that food would be cheaper if all the land were cultivated by the owner and not by tenants farming for a profit, and thus the fact that the American farmers pay no rent may account partially for the lower prices at which they sell their corn. (2) Again, the pure theory takes no account of the size of the portions into which the land is divided, nor of the kind of crops which are grown. But, when most of the land of a country is rented, both of these factors have to be considered, and it may be more convenient to the landowner to let the land with certain restrictions, which again indirectly operate on the price. (3) It has been well observed by Passy[2] that the principal

[1] An excellent account of the economic theory of rent, in which recent criticisms from different points of view (*e.g.*, by P. Leroy-Beaulieu, Henry George, &c.) are examined, is *Land and its Rent*, by Francis A. Walker, London, 1884.

[2] *Systèmes de Culture en France.*

effect of various land laws is to increase or diminish the amount of the gross produce, which in Ricardian phraseology would mean to extend or contract the margin of cultivation. It thus appears that it is not always true to say that the payment of rent makes no real difference to the general public, and that it is simply a necessary method of equalizing farmers' profits. At the same time, however, with the necessary qualifications, there is no doubt that price determines rent and not rent price, especially when prices are affected by foreign competition. Recently in Great Britain a striking example has been afforded both of the abandonment of inferior lands (the contraction of the margin) and of a heavy fall in rent under the influence of falling prices.

Progress and rent. The hypothetical history implied in Ricardo's theory as to the effects of the progress of society upon the value of agricultural produce also requires some criticism, such as that given by the historian of agriculture and prices, Thorold Rogers. The theory assumes that in the first place population increases, and thus there is a greater demand for food, and that therefore the margin of cultivation extends and the price rises, and rent rises also. But, as Rogers observes, history shows that agricultural improvements of all kinds have first of all increased the amount of food, and thus allowed of an increase in population. It is worth noticing that in our own times an increasing population in rural districts (*e.g.*, the Highlands of Scotland and the west of Ireland) may indirectly tend to lower or destroy rents through minute subdivision. Ricardo's theory, however, accounts very well for the rise in the ground-rents of towns and cities, and it is there far more than in the rural districts that the unearned increment is to be found.

Value of mining produce. The value of mining produce is determined generally in the same way as that of agricultural produce; but similar qualifications must be introduced. The theory is that both extensively and intensively the produce of mines is subject to the law of diminishing return, that the margin recedes as the price falls and extends as it rises, and that thus the price is determined by the most costly portion which it just pays to bring to market. And no doubt the main facts of the theory are correct; and recently the mines of Great Britain no less than its lands have illustrated the retrogression of the margin and the fall in rents. The principal point to observe is that mines are gradually quite exhausted.[1] In general the produce of mines is, like that of land, consumed in a comparatively short time, and thus the value is subject to fluctuations according to the conditions of the annual demand and supply.

Precious metals. The peculiar durability of the precious metals, however, makes them in this respect differ widely from most mining produce. It is of course undeniable that (supposing coinage free) the value of standard coins will be equal to the value of the same amount of bullion, and, conversely, that the bullion will be equal in value to the same amount of coins. The older economists argued that the precious metals had their value determined by their cost of production under the most unfavourable circumstances, and then argued that in consequence the value of money (or coins) tended to be governed by the cost of production of bullion. If, however, it is remembered that the annual production does not probably amount to two per cent. of the quantity in the hands of man, that cost of production can only operate through actual or potential supply, and that in the case of money the increase must be real to affect prices, it will be readily seen that the value of bullion is determined by the general level of prices (or the value of money), and not that the value of money depends upon the value of the bullion. At the same time, however, it is true that, if prices become very high,—in other words, if the value of money, and thus of bullion, becomes very low,—then a check is placed upon production from the mines, and, conversely, with falling prices or a rise in the value of the precious metals mining for them is extended and encouraged. But the difference in the annual supply due to this influence will be small under present or similar conditions. On the whole, this case of the precious metals furnishes perhaps the best example of the way in which the cost of production can only act through the law of supply and demand.

Law governing value of joint products. There is one other part of the general theory of value which requires some notice. Some articles can only be produced in conjunction with others (*e.g.*, hides and beef, wool and mutton), and some modification of the theory is needed to suit this case. The law deduced is that—The sum of the values must be equal to the joint expenses of production, and the relative values *inter se* are determined by demand and supply. Thus the Australian sheep-farmers will extend their sheep-farms so long as for wool and mutton together they obtain a fair profit, but the amount contributed by each portion will be determined by the relative demand. It is interesting to observe that in the progress of society the value of the meat has risen as compared with that of the hides and the wool. The same principle determines the kind of produce which will be raised from land, though the application is rather more difficult owing to rotation of crops, &c.

Theory of international values. Much discussion has taken place recently on the question whether a distinct theory of international values is required. In the limits assigned to this article it is only possible to indicate the principal points in dispute. The "orthodox" theory, as held by Ricardo, Mill, and Cairnes, has been attacked by Cournot, Prof. Sidgwick, and others, and has been re-stated with admirable clearness and much original power by Prof. Bastable.[2] The best way to answer the question seems to be to make clear the assumptions on which the values of commodities produced within any "nation" are determined, and then to consider whether any change must be made when we bring in other nations. We are at once met with the difficulty, What is a "nation"? The orthodox answer appears to be that within any nation (for which the term "economic area" might perhaps be advantageously substituted) there is effective industrial and commercial competition. This appears to imply no more than is contained in the principle noticed above, that relative values tend to be equal to the normal expenses of production (*commercial* competition), and that the expenses tend to be proportioned to the real cost (*industrial* competition). The question then arises, Do these conditions not exist in international trade? **Comparative cost.** The answer appears to be, first, that commercial competition certainly holds good; for as soon as a trade is established the commodities will sell at the same prices in both countries (allowance being made for cost of carriage). It would plainly be absurd to say that the value of Manchester goods is determined by their expenses of production if they are consumed in England, but by something else if they are sent to India. If then there is any difference between domestic and international values, it must arise owing to the absence of effective industrial competition; that is to say, in the same country (or economic area) the real cost determines the expenses of production on account of the supposed perfect mobility of labour and capital, but between different economic areas these agents of production do not pass with sufficient readiness to secure a similar correspondence. It thus follows that a country may import articles which it could produce at less real

[1] Cp. Marshall's *Economics of Industry*, London, 1879, bk. ii. chap. iii. § 5.

[2] *Theory of International Trade.*

cost, provided that it pays for these imports with exports which cost even less. A very striking example of this doctrine of *comparative cost*, as it is termed, is furnished by Victoria after the great gold discoveries. All kinds of produce were imported and paid for with gold, because there was less real cost involved in obtaining the gold to pay for imports than in making the articles. According to this theory every country will devote its labour and capital to its most productive uses; and, if by some new imports a domestic industry is checked or abolished, it is argued that the labour and capital will be devoted to increasing the exports so as to pay for the new imports. It must clearly be assumed as axiomatic that in the absence of loans, tributes, &c., imports can in the long run only be paid for by exports, and also that those articles will be exported which can be produced at the least comparative real cost. This theory then may be held to explain in a satisfactory manner the origin and development of international *trade*; but the question of *values* is still undetermined.

Reciprocal demand.

Consistently with exports paying for imports many different rates of exchange are possible, and the particular rate actually adopted is said to depend entirely on reciprocal demand. And in an extreme case, in which new countries trade solely in articles of which each has a monopoly, this answer would seem to be correct; but, when we consider that under present conditions trading countries have many articles in common, and that a slight margin of profit suffices to expand or diminish an export trade, this answer seems too vague and unreal. The most probable solution seems to be that the rates of exchange will be so adjusted as to give to the exporters the ordinary rate of profits current in their respective countries.

Foreign exchanges.

In general it is clear that the rate will be determined independently of the foreign trade, or at least that the foreign trade is only one factor to be considered. It is said, for example, that the annual value of the agricultural produce of the United Kingdom exceeds the total amount of the exports. If the rate of profit falls, a trade which before was impossible becomes possible. The opinion may be hazarded that the best way of explaining the general theory of international values would be to start with the foreign exchanges; but such an investigation is too technical and difficult for this place. (J. S. N.)

VAMPIRE, a term, apparently of Servian origin (*wampir*), originally applied in eastern Europe to blood-sucking ghosts, but in modern usage transferred to one or more species of blood-sucking bats inhabiting South America.

In the first-mentioned meaning a vampire is usually supposed to be the soul of a dead man which quits the buried body by night to suck the blood of living persons. Hence, when the vampire's grave is opened, his corpse is found to be fresh and rosy from the blood which he has thus absorbed. To put a stop to his ravages, a stake is driven through the corpse, or the head cut off, or the heart torn out and the body burned, or boiling water and vinegar are poured on the grave. The persons who turn vampires are generally wizards, witches, suicides, and persons who have come to a violent end or have been cursed by their parents or by the church. But any one may become a vampire if an animal (especially a cat) leaps over his corpse or a bird flies over it. Sometimes the vampire is thought to be the soul of a living man which leaves his body in sleep, to go in the form of a straw or fluff of down and suck the blood of other sleepers. The belief in vampires chiefly prevails in Slavonic lands, as in Russia (especially White Russia and the Ukraine), Poland, and Servia, and among the Czechs of Bohemia and the other Slavonic races of Austria. It became specially prevalent in Hungary between the years 1730 and 1735, whence all Europe was filled with reports of the exploits of vampires. Several treatises were written on the subject, among which may be mentioned Ranft's *De Masticatione Mortuorum in Tumulis* (1734) and Calmet's *Dissertation on the Vampires of Hungary*, translated into English in 1750. It is probable that this superstition gained much ground from the reports of those who had examined the bodies of persons who had been buried alive though believed to be dead, and was based on the twisted position of the corpse, the marks of blood on the shroud and on the face and hands,—results of the frenzied struggle in the coffin before life became extinct. The belief in vampirism has also taken root among the Albanians and modern Greeks, but here it may be due to Slavonic influence.

Two species of blood-sucking bats (the only species known)—*Desmodus rufus* and *Diphylla ecaudata*—representing two genera (see MAMMALIA, vol. xv. p. 415), inhabit the tropical and part of the subtropical regions of the New World, and are restricted to South and Central America. They appear to be confined chiefly to the forest-clad parts, and their attacks on men and other warm-blooded animals were noticed by some of the earliest writers. Thus Peter Martyr (Anghiera), who wrote soon after the conquest of South America, says that in the Isthmus of Darien there were bats which sucked the blood of men and cattle when asleep to such a degree as to even kill them. Condamine, a writer of the 18th century, remarks that at Borja (Ecuador) and in other places they had entirely destroyed the cattle introduced by the missionaries. Sir Robert Schomburgk relates that at Wicki, on the river Berbice, no fowls could be kept on account of the ravages of these creatures, which attacked their combs, causing them to appear white from loss of blood. The present writer, when in South and Central America, had many accounts given him as to the attacks of the vampires, and it was agreed upon by most of his informants that these bats when attacking horses showed a decided preference for those of a grey colour. It is interesting to speculate how far the vampire bats may have been instrumental—when they were, perhaps, more abundant—in causing the destruction of the horse, which had disappeared from America previous to the discovery of that continent.

Although these bats were known thus early to Europeans, the species to which they belonged were not determined until about fifty years ago, several of the large frugivorous species having been wrongly set down as blood-suckers, and named accordingly. Thus the name *Vampyrus* was suggested to Geoffroy and adopted by Spix, who also considered that the long-tongued bats of the group *Glossophagæ* were addicted to blood, and accordingly described *Glossophaga soricina* as a very cruel blood-sucker (*sanguisuga crudelissima*), believing that the long brush-tipped tongue was used to increase the flow of blood. *Vampyrus spectrum*, L., a large bat inhabiting Brazil, of sufficiently forbidding aspect, which was long considered by naturalists to be thoroughly sanguivorous in its habits, and named accordingly by Geoffroy, has been shown by the observations of modern travellers to be mainly frugivorous, and is considered by the inhabitants of the countries in which it is found to be perfectly harmless. Waterton believed *Artibeus planirostris*, a common bat in British Guiana, usually found in the roofs of houses, and now known to be frugivorous, to be the veritable vampire; but neither he nor any of the naturalists that preceded him had succeeded in detecting any bat in the act of drawing blood. It fell to the lot of Charles Darwin to determine one of the blood-sucking species at least, and the following is his account of the circumstances under which the discovery of the sanguivorous habits of *Desmodus rufus* was made:—"The vampire bat is often the cause of much trouble by biting the horses on their withers. The injury is generally not so much owing to the loss of blood as to the inflammation which the pressure of the saddle afterwards produces. The whole circumstance has lately been doubted in England; I was therefore fortunate in being present when one was actually caught on a horse's back. We were bivouacking late one evening near Coquimbo, in Chili, when my servant, noticing that one of the horses was very restive, went to see what was the matter, and, fancying he could detect something, suddenly put his hand on the beast's withers, and secured the vampire" (*Naturalist's Voyage Round the World*, p. 22).

Desmodus rufus, Weid, the common blood-sucking bat, is widely spread over the tropical and subtropical parts of Central and South America from Oaxaca to southern Brazil and Chili. It is a comparatively small bat, a little larger than the common noctule, the head and body about 3 inches in length, the forearm 2½, with a remarkably long and strong thumb; it is destitute of a tail, and has a very peculiar physiognomy, well represented in fig. 1. The body is covered with rather short fur of a reddish brown colour but varying in shade, the extremities of the hairs sometimes ashy. The teeth are peculiar and characteristic, admirably adapted for the purposes for which they are employed. The upper front teeth (incisors), of which there are only two, are enormously enlarged (see fig. 2), and in shape obliquely triangular like small guillotines. The canines, though smaller than the incisors, are large and sharp; but the back teeth, so well developed in all other bats, are very small and reduced in number to two above and three below, on each side, with laterally compressed crowns rising but slightly above the level of the gum, their longitudinally disposed cutting edges (in the upper jaw) being continuous with the base of the canine and with each other. The lower front teeth (incisors) are small, bifid, in pairs, and are separated from the canines, with a space in front. The lower back teeth are narrow, like those in the upper jaw, but the anterior tooth is slightly larger than the others, and separated by a small space from the canines. Behind the lower incisors the jaw is deeply hollowed out to receive the extremities of the large upper incisors.

Fig. 1.—Head of *Desmodus rufus*, Weid.

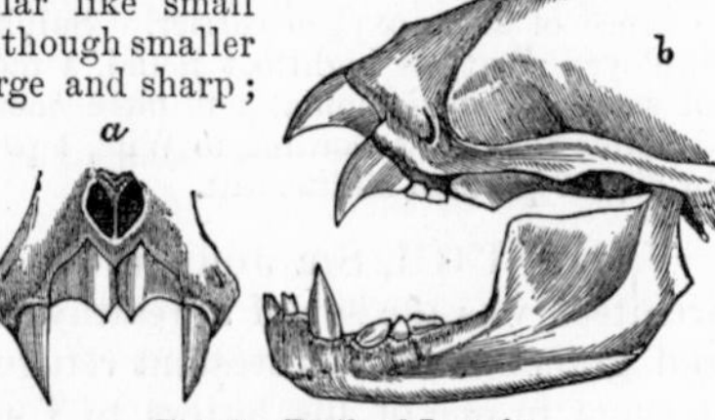

Fig. 2.—Teeth of *D. rufus*.

With this peculiar dentition there is associated as remarkable a departure from the general type in the form of the digestive apparatus. The exceedingly narrow œsophagus opens at right angles into a narrow, intestine-like stomach, which almost immediately terminates on the right, without a distinct pylorus, in the duodenum, but on the left forms a greatly elongated cæcum, bent and folded upon itself, which appears at first sight like part of the intestines. This, the cardiac extremity of the stomach, is, for a short distance to the left of the entrance of the œsophagus, still very narrow, but soon increases in size, till near its termination it attains a diameter quite three times that of the short pyloric portion. The length of this cardiac diverticulum of the stomach appears to vary from 2 to 6 inches, the size in each specimen probably depending on the amount of food obtained by the animal before it was captured.

The only other known species of blood-sucking bat, *Diphylla ecaudata*, Spix, inhabits Brazil, and appears to be much less abundant than *Desmodus rufus*, from which it is distinguished by its slightly smaller size, by the absence of a groove in the front of the lower lip, by the non-development of the interfemoral membrane in the centre, and by the presence of a short calcaneum (absent in *D. rufus*), but more particularly by the presence of an additional rudimentary back tooth (? molar) above and below, and by the very peculiar form of the lower incisors, which are much expanded in the direction of the jaws and pectinated, forming a semicircular row touching each other, the outer incisors being wider than the inner ones, with six notches, the inner incisors with three each.

Thus constituted, these bats present, in this extraordinary differentiation of the manducatory and digestive apparatus, a departure from the type of other species of the family (*Phyllostomidæ*) to which they belong unparalleled in any of the other orders of *Mammalia*, standing apart from all other mammals as being fitted only for a diet of blood, and capable of sustaining life upon that alone. Travellers describe the wounds inflicted by the large sharp-edged incisors as being similar to those caused by a razor when shaving: a portion of the skin is shaved off and, a large number of severed capillary vessels being thus exposed, a constant flow of blood is maintained. From this source the blood is drawn through the exceedingly narrow gullet—too narrow for anything solid to pass—into the intestine-like stomach, whence it is, probably, gradually drawn off during the slow process of digestion, while the animal, sated with food, is hanging in a state of torpidity from the roof of its cave or from the inner sides of a hollow tree. (G. E. D.)

VAN, a city of Asiatic Turkey, capital of a vilayet, is situated two miles to the east of the lake to which it gives its name, in 38° 30′ N. lat. and 43° 18′ E. long. It lies on the ill-defined borderland between Armenia and Kurdistan, in an extremely fertile plain some 40 miles in circuit, which is described as one of the gardens of the East, whence the local saying: "Van in this world, heaven in the next." Its low flat-roofed houses are grouped irregularly at the southern base of a nummulitic limestone eminence, somewhat resembling a camel's back, which rises 100 feet sheer above the plain and is crowned by the so-called citadel, the fortifications of which are mostly in a dilapidated state. But it is naturally a position of great strength and of considerable strategic importance, standing at the junction of two military routes, which here diverge westwards through Músh and Kharpút to Asia Minor and southwards to Mosul and Mesopotamia, besides commanding the approaches to the Persian frontier at Kotúr and Bayezid. The town itself, which contains four mosques, two large churches, an Armenian bazaar, baths, and caravanserais, is enclosed within a double line of crenellated walls and ditches on the three sides not protected by the rock; and beyond these enclosures lies the suburban district of Baghlar, or the "Gardens." The population, estimated at from 30,000 to 35,000, are Turks, except about 2000 Armenians and a few hundred Mohammedan and Nestorian Kurds. Besides trade and agriculture, the inhabitants are engaged in a few industries, such as the making of coarse cotton chintzes, a highly prized goat-hair waterproof moire antique, a thick woollen cloth called *shayak*, and an excellent soap, prepared from the saline efflorescences of Lakes Van and Erchek, which consist in about equal proportions of the carbonate and sulphate of soda.

Armenian tradition derives the name of Van from an Armenian king who reigned a little before Alexander the Great, and speaks of an older city founded by Semiramis (Shemiramagerd). This is of course fable; but the Vannic inscriptions (vol. xiii. p. 116) show that the region was the seat of an Armenian kingdom, whose native name was Biaina, as early as the 9th century B.C. In the isolated rock towering above the plain there are numerous galleries, flights of steps, crypts, and cuneiform rock inscriptions, one of which is trilingual, like that of Behistún, and like it relates the deeds of Xerxes, son of Darius. Others are in the Haikan or Old Armenian language; while for others scattered over the district a solution has been sought by Prof. Sayce with doubtful success in the present language of Georgia.

The vilayet of Van, one of the finest but also one of the least developed regions of Asiatic Turkey, lies on the Persian frontier between Erzerum (north) and Baghdad (south). It has an area of 15,000 square miles, with a population of over 1,000,000.

Lake Van.

Lake Van, called *Arsissa Palus* by the ancients, and also *Thospitis*, from its Armenian name Tosp, is 80 miles long and 30 broad, with a total area of 1500 square miles. Although of smaller extent than Lake Urmia, it contains a much larger volume of water owing to its much greater depth, which is at least 80 feet near Van and still more along the south side. The lake stands about 5400 feet above sea-level on the south Armenian plateau, which is encircled by the lofty ranges that bifurcate west and south from Ararat and culminate in the Sipan-Dagh (12,000 feet) on the north side of the lake. These mountains are clad with dense forests of beech, chestnut, ash, and walnut, while the broad fertile belt between their base and the lake is planted with melon gardens and orchards of plums, peaches, apricots, figs, and pomegranates, festooned with a vine which yields a palatable wine.

Lake Van, which is too brackish to be drinkable for man or beast, is inhabited by a species of blay or bleak, which abound especially about the mouths of the influents, and come to the surface when the spring floods spread over the heavier saline layers. This lake is a completely land-locked basin, or at least has no visible outlet. But the natives speak of underground channels through which it communicates south-westwards with the head-waters of the Tigris, attributing to the occasional obstruction of these channels the great oscillations of level that have undoubtedly occurred in past and recent times. In the 17th century and again about 1840 the water rose from 10 to 12 feet, and is even now (1888) rising. Lake Erchek perhaps marks its extreme eastern limit in former times. Lake Van is also indirectly connected with the Euphrates through the little Lake of Nazik, which lies west of the Sipan-Dagh, on the water-parting between the lacustrian and fluvial basins, and which by a rare phenomenon sends emissaries to both. The narrow part of Lake Van, which runs for nearly 40 miles towards the north-east, and gives the lake somewhat the appearance of a frying-pan, is very shallow, and was once, according to tradition, a fertile plain. The lake is not regularly navigated. Scattered along the south-east shore are a few picturesque islets, one of which, Aktamar, is the seat of an Armenian patriarch.

VANADIUM, a rare element discovered in 1830 by Sefström, when analysing a kind of iron obtained from the ores of Taberg in Sweden. Berzelius, in the course of an extensive investigation on vanadium, came to the conclusion that it is analogous to chromium, forming like it an acid trioxide, $VanO_3$, in which "Van" signifies 134·4[1] parts of a radical analogous to the Cr = 52 parts of chromium in chromic acid, CrO_3. He succeeded in isolating this radical, and, as it exhibited semi-metallic properties, he had no doubt that it was the element vanadium itself. His results were universally adopted as correct until Roscoe (in 1867) found that Berzelius's vanadium is an oxide containing $O_2 = 32$ parts of oxygen per Van, whence it followed that the presumed trioxide, $VanO_3$, is really a pentoxide, V_2O_5, where $V_2 = 2 \times 51{\cdot}2 = 2$ atoms of the real element. Our present knowledge of vanadium is based chiefly upon his investigations. Of vanadium minerals, which are all very rare, we name two only,—mottramite, $(Pb,Cu)_3(VO_4)_2 + 2(Pb,Cu)(OH)_2$, and vanadinite, $3Pb_3(VO_4)_2 + PbCl_2$. This last is amorphous with apatite, which previous to Roscoe's discovery was difficult to explain. See CHEMISTRY, vol. v. p. 539.

Traces of vanadium are found in certain iron ores and in many other minerals. Roscoe utilized a kind of sandstone from Alderley Edge and Mottram in Cheshire which contains a small admixture of mottramite. Another suitable material is the "Bohnerz" of Steinlade and Haverloh, essentially a hydrated ferric oxide. For the extraction of vanadium from this latter mineral Wöhler recommends the following method. The finely powdered mineral is mixed with one-third of its weight of nitre and the mixture kept at a dull red heat for an hour. The ignited mass is powdered and lixiviated with water, which extracts the potash salts of the oxides $V_2O_5, CrO_3, MoO_3, As_2O_5, P_2O_5$, and SiO_2. The filtered solution is almost neutralized with nitric acid, but not completely, or else some of the V_2O_5 would be reduced by the nitrous acid to lower oxides; and the vanadic and most of the other acids named are precipitated as baryta salts by addition of chloride of barium. From the washed precipitate the acids are liberated by boiling dilute sulphuric acid, and the sulphate of baryta is filtered off. The solution is neutralized with ammonia, concentrated by evaporation, and, after cooling, kept in contact with a solid piece of sal-ammoniac more than sufficient to saturate the solution with this salt. Meta-vanadate of ammonia, $V_2O_5(NH_4)_2O$, being characteristically insoluble in sal-ammoniac solution, separates out as a yellowish crystalline precipitate. This is collected, washed with sal-ammoniac solution and after that with alcohol, and purified by re-crystallization or otherwise. The pure salt when heated to dull redness leaves the pentoxide, V_2O_5 (vanadic acid), as a red liquid, which freezes into a red-brown crystalline mass of sp. gr. 3·35 (J. J. Watts). It dissolves in about 1000 parts of water, forming a yellow solution which reddens litmus. The pentoxide, though capable of uniting with strong acids, *e.g.*, with sulphuric into a salt, $V_2O_2(SO_4)_3$, behaves on the whole as an acid oxide analogous in its combining habits to phosphoric (see PHOSPHORUS, vol. xviii. p. 818, and CHEMISTRY, vol. v. p. 540). Solutions of vanadates are easily recognized: on addition of mineral acid they assume the yellow colour characteristic of the pentoxide, and if the mixture is then kept in contact with zinc it passes through all shades of (intense) green till it ultimately assumes a lavender colour. The solution then contains a chloride corresponding to the oxide V_2O_2 (Berzelius's metal). It absorbs atmospheric oxygen with an extraordinary degree of avidity, assuming, in the absence of free acid, a dark brown colour. An acidified vanadate solution, if shaken with peroxide of hydrogen and ether, furnishes a dark red reduction product, which passes into the ethereal layer. One part of vanadic acid in 40,000 parts of water can thus be rendered distinctly visible (Werther). If a mixture of the pentoxide and charcoal is heated in dry chlorine, it is converted into an oxychloride, $VOCl_3$ (trichloride of Berzelius), which distils over and may be purified by re-distillation over sodium. It is a canary-yellow mobile liquid, freezing below −15° C. and boiling at 126°·7 C., and its sp. gr. at 14° C. is 1·841. Water decomposes it with formation of hydrochloric acid and pentoxide V_2O_5. If the vapour of this chloride is passed over red-hot charcoal in a current of chlorine, the tetrachloride VCl_4 is produced as a dark brown liquid, boiling at about 154° C. A mixture of the vapour of this chloride with hydrogen, when passed through a dull-red-hot tube, yields (more or less of "sesqui-" chloride, V_2Cl_6, and) the dichloride VCl_2, which, if pure, forms apple-green, mica-like, hexagonal plates. From this dichloride Roscoe for the first time prepared the true metal by heating it to redness in hydrogen gas, a simple enough method in theory, but in practice one of the most difficult of operations, because the dichloride is very difficult to prepare and highly hygroscopic, and because the metal is extremely prone to take up oxygen. Even the purest product which Roscoe succeeded in obtaining contained an appreciable admixture of oxide. Vanadium is a light grey powder, which under the microscope appears crystalline and exhibits a silvery lustre, sp. gr. = 5·5. Of its chemical properties the most remarkable is that it combines directly with nitrogen gas, N_2, into a bronze-coloured nitride, VN.

Rare and expensive as vanadium is, it has found a practical application in the production of aniline black. The black is produced from aniline by the action of chloric acid, aided by the presence of some oxygen carrier. Sulphide of copper is usually employed; but, as Lightfoot found, a mere trace of vanadic acid (or vanadate of ammonia) acts more energetically than any other available agent. According to Witz, 1 part of vanadic acid suffices for 67,000 parts of aniline salt.

[1] Calculated from our present constants.

VANBRUGH, SIR JOHN (1666?-1726), dramatist and architect, was the son of a wealthy sugar-baker in Cheshire and grandson of a Protestant refugee of Ghent. From a passage in one of his letters to Tonson it might be supposed that he was born in the Bastille, though in what year is uncertain, probably in 1666. He was educated in France, but what he learnt there, whether architecture or merely that art of good-fellowship which he found to be the true Aladdin's lamp of social life, is a question that will be variously answered by those who, like Sir Joshua Reynolds, admire Blenheim and Castle Howard, and those who, like the wits of Vanbrugh's time, scoff at them. This, however, is certain, that after his return from the Continent to England what he did was, not to pursue architecture, but to work, with a gusto and a success that are humorous and exhilarating, the "Aladdin's lamp" above mentioned. His first step towards becoming a power in society was, of course, to enter the army. Perhaps, however, had he begun life in any other way his advance would have been just as rapid. For, strong as are social conditions, character is stronger still, and Vanbrugh's equipment—wit, tempered by good humour, a genuine feeling of comradeship, an exceedingly fine presence (according to Noble's description), and a winsome face (according to Kneller's portrait)—would, under any circumstances, have been irresistible. One of the points of difference between the dialogue in Vanbrugh's comedies and the dialogue in the comedies of Congreve is this: we feel that the characters in the *Relapse* and the *Confederacy* talk as Vanbrugh must have talked; we feel that the characters in the *Old Bachelor* and the *Way of the World* talk, not as Congreve talked, but as Congreve wrote. We feel that, while such dazzling sword-play as Congreve's would in society have chilled, even as it illumined the air, talk so hearty, good-humoured, frank, and daring as that we get in Vanbrugh's plays would have made the fortune of any man of fashion, made it as certainly at a Roman supper party in the time of Augustus as at a London drinking-bout in the days of

Queen Anne. It is no wonder then that he was a favourite, no wonder that the two best haters of the time, Swift and Pope, tried in vain to hate the "man of wit and honour," Vanbrugh. During the martial period of his life, Vanbrugh wrote the first sketches of the *Relapse* and the *Provoked Wife.* These he showed to Sir Thomas Skipworth, one of the shareholders of Drury Lane, and with fortunate results.

In 1695 he was offered—whether through the court interest which he had secured or whether because he really had acquired a knowledge of architecture in France is not known—the post of secretary to the commission for endowing Greenwich Hospital. He accepted the post, and by way of fulfilling his functions as an architect turned his attention to the amours of "Lord Foppington." His *Relapse or Virtue in Danger*, a sequel to Colley Cibber's *Love's Last Shift*, was produced at Drury Lane in 1697. When a comic dramatist of the school of Wycherley confesses that the fine gentleman of his play, "drinking his mistresses' health in Nantes brandy from six in the morning to the time he waddled on upon the stage in the evening, had toasted himself up to such a pitch of vigour" that something too outrageous even for such an audience seemed imminent, we may assume that he has enjoyed a satisfactory first night. The success was so triumphant that Montague, afterwards Lord Halifax, asked at once for the *Provoked Wife* for the theatre in Lincoln's Inn Fields, and—Skipworth waiving, for the advantage of Vanbrugh, his own claim upon the play—it was produced at that theatre in the following year. All that could be said in answer to those who condemned it on account of its unblushing libertinism was that Sir John Brute is sufficiently brutal to drive any woman into rebellion, and that since the glorious days of the Restoration a wife's rebellion and a wife's adultery were synonymous terms. The play was a complete triumph.

And now, having succeeded as a man of fashion, as an architectural commissioner, and as a comic dramatist of the school of Wycherley, Vanbrugh turned his attention to morals. Though *Æsop*—produced at Drury Lane in the same year as the *Provoked Wife*—was an adaptation of Boursault's dramatic sermon on the same subject, it was an improvement on the French play. As usual with Vanbrugh, who never did things by halves, he surpassed the Frenchman on that very point where the Frenchman had been pronounced unsurpassable. Just as in the *Relapse*, when he aspired to be merry, his merriment had entirely surpassed that of Cibber's play, of which his own was meant to be a sequel, and just as afterwards, when in Castle Howard and Blenheim he aspired to rival in massiveness the "thick rotundity of the earth," he laid on her a structure only a "few tons lighter than herself," so now, when he aspired to surpass the Frenchman in gravity, he achieved a kind of dulness compared with which the owl-like dulness of Boursault was as the wit of Voltaire. In a word, the humour of the piece lies in the fact that it was written by the author of the *Relapse* and the *Provoked Wife.* The play ran during a week only. Vanbrugh, accepting the failure with his usual good-temper, seems then to have turned his attention completely to architecture; for the adaptation in 1700 of the *Pilgrim* of Beaumont and Fletcher, and the production in 1702 of *A False Friend*, could hardly have engaged his serious efforts at all, so perfunctory are they and so inferior to all that he had done before.

Castle Howard in Yorkshire, which he had built for the earl of Carlisle, was a great success so far as pleasing his patron went, who as a reward gave him yet another opening in life by presenting him,—the most ignorant man perhaps in England of heraldry, judging from the fun he made of the appointment,—with the tabard of Clarencieux king-at-arms. But, if the dangerous moment in every man's life is when he has just scored a brilliant success, it is especially so with genial glowing natures like Vanbrugh's. It seems to have been the success of Castle Howard that caused him to entertain the rash project of building a theatre, from his own design, for the acting of his own plays. The joyous courage with which, having persuaded thirty people in the fashionable world to aid him in finding the money, and Congreve to aid him in finding the plays, he began to build in perfect unconsciousness of the danger before him is the only passage in his life which may be called pathetic, save of course his struggle with the "wicked woman of Marlborough." No doubt any architect who builds a theatre is always in danger of letting his ideas run riot in the wide field of experiment, but he who builds a theatre for his own plays seems doomed by the malice aforethought of fate. The magnitude of Vanbrugh's architectural ideas grew as the work went on, and with the ideas the structure grew till a theatre meant for the delicate *bijouterie* work of polite comedy seemed growing to the proportions of the Roman Colosseum. Whether Congreve endeavoured to put a check upon his friend's architectural and authorial fervour does not appear. But it must be remembered that not only Vanbrugh's plays but his own were to be acted there, and that, although Congreve was a man of great sagacity, no man, not even he who pretended to set his gentility above his genius, is sagacious when confronted by the surpassing excellence of his own poems and plays.

When at length the time came to test the acoustics of the pile, it was found to be sadly defective. What changes were made to rectify the errors of structure does not appear. The theatre was opened to the public with an Italian opera, which was followed by three of Molière's comedies, and these by the *Confederacy*, Vanbrugh's masterpiece on the whole, though perhaps its finest scenes are not equal to the finest scenes in the *Relapse.*

Vanbrugh at last withdrew from the disastrous speculation; Congreve had already withdrawn. But a man to whom fortune had been so kind as she had been to Vanbrugh could hardly be depressed by any of her passing frowns. Queen Anne at once sent him abroad on an important state errand, and afterwards he was commissioned to build Blenheim. Upon the merits and demerits of this famous "hollowed quarry" there has been much conflict of opinion. As to the sarcasms by Swift, Walpole, Evans, and the rest, they are as nothing when set against Sir Joshua Reynolds's defence of Vanbrugh and his style. For in England the general sense for architecture seems to be even rarer than the general sense for poetry and painting. The truth is that Vanbrugh imported largely into architecture what in all the plastic arts should be allowed to fructify but sparsely, namely, literary ideas, and even these literary ideas of his seem to lack that fusion which we see in the works of the great masters. Hence, impressive as are the parts, they do not form an impressive whole. Blenheim, however, was a source of great sorrow to the kindly dramatist. Though Parliament had voted for the building of it, no provision had been made for the supplies. The queen while she lived paid them, and then Vanbrugh was left to the meanness of the duke of Marlborough and afterwards to the insolence of the "wicked woman," who did her best to embitter his life. Besides Castle Howard and Blenheim, he built many other country mansions, such as Grimsthorpe and Duncombe Hall in Yorkshire, Eastbury in Dorsetshire, Seaton-Delaval in Northumberland, King's Weston near Bristol, Oulton Hall in Cheshire, &c.

About the end of 1710 Vanbrugh married Henrietta

Maria, daughter of Colonel Yarborough of Haslington, and four years afterwards, at the accession of George I., he was knighted. He afterwards wrote again for the stage, and the unfinished fragment left at his death, which took place on 26th March 1726 at his house in Scotland Yard, London, shows that his powers remained to the last as fine as ever.

In order to find and fix Vanbrugh's place among English comic dramatists, an examination of the very basis of the comedy of repartee inaugurated by Etheredge would be necessary, and, of course, such an examination would be impossible here. It is chiefly as a humorist, however, that he demands attention.

Given the humorous temperament—the temperament which impels a man to get his enjoyment by watching the harlequinade of life, and contrasting it with his own ideal standard of good sense, which the harlequinade seems to him to mock and challenge—given this temperament, then the quality of its humorous growths depends of course on the quality of the intellectual forces by means of which the temperament gains expression. Hence it is very likely that in original endowment of humour, as distinguished from wit, Vanbrugh was superior to Congreve. And this is saying a great deal: for, while Congreve's wit has always been made much of, it has, since Macaulay's time, been the fashion among critics to do less than justice to his humour,—a humour which, in such scenes as that in *Love for Love* where Sir Sampson Legend discourses upon the human appetites and functions, moves beyond the humour of convention and passes into natural humour. It is, however, in spontaneity, in a kind of lawless merriment, almost Aristophanic in its *verve*, that Vanbrugh's humour seems so deep and so fine, seems indeed to spring from a fountain deeper and finer and rarer than Congreve's. A comedy of wit, like every other drama, is a story told by action and dialogue, but to tell a story lucidly and rapidly by means of repartee is exceedingly difficult, not but that it is easy enough to produce repartee. But in comic dialogue the difficulty is to move rapidly and yet keep up the brilliant ball-throwing demanded in this form, and without lucidity and rapidity no drama, whether of repartee or of character, can live. Etheredge, the father of the comedy of repartee, has at length had justice done to him by Mr Gosse. Not only could Etheredge tell a story by means of repartee alone: he could produce a tableau too; so could Congreve, and so also could Vanbrugh, but often—far too often—Vanbrugh's tableau is reached, not by fair means, as in the tableau of Congreve, but by a surrendering of probability, by a sacrifice of artistic fusion, by an inartistic mingling of comedy and farce, such as Congreve never indulges in. Jeremy Collier was perfectly right therefore in his strictures upon the farcical improbabilities of the *Relapse*. So farcical indeed are the tableaux in that play that the broader portions of it were (as Mr Swinburne discovered) adapted by Voltaire and acted at Sceaux as a farce. Had we space here to contrast the *Relapse* with the *Way of the World*, we should very likely come upon a distinction between comedy and farce such as has never yet been drawn. We should find that farce is not comedy with a broadened grin—Thalia with her girdle loose and run wild—as the critics seem to assume. We should find that the difference between the two is not one of degree at all, but rather one of kind, and that mere breadth of fun has nothing to do with the question. No doubt the fun of comedy may be as broad as that of farce, as is shown indeed by the celebrated Dogberry scenes in *Much Ado about Nothing* and by the scene in *Love for Love* between Sir Sampson Legend and his son, alluded to above; but here, as in every other department of art, all depends upon the quality of the imaginative belief that the artist seeks to arrest and secure. Of comedy the breath of life is dramatic illusion. Of farce the breath of life is mock illusion. Comedy, whether broad or genteel, pretends that its mimicry is real. Farce, whether broad or genteel, makes no such pretence, but by a thousand tricks, which it keeps up between itself and the audience, says, "My acting is all sham, and you know it." Now, while Vanbrugh was apt too often to forget this the fundamental difference between comedy and farce, Congreve never forgot it, Wycherley rarely. Not that there should be in any literary form any arbitrary laws. There is no arbitrary law declaring that comedy shall not be mingled with farce, and yet the fact is that in vital drama they cannot be so mingled. The very laws of their existence are in conflict with each other, so much so that where one lives the other must die, as we see in the drama of our own day. The fact seems to be that probability of incident, logical sequence of cause and effect, are as necessary to comedy as they are to tragedy, while farce would stifle in such an air. Rather it would be poisoned by it, just as comedy is poisoned by what farce flourishes on, that is to say, inconsequence of reasoning—topsy-turvy logic. Born in the fairy country of topsy-turvy, the logic of farce would be illogical if it were not upside-down. So with coincidence, with improbable accumulation of convenient events,—farce can no more exist without these than comedy can exist with them. Hence we affirm that Jeremy Collier's strictures on the farcical adulterations of the *Relapse* pierce more deeply into Vanbrugh's art than do the criticisms of Leigh Hunt and Hazlitt. In other words, perhaps the same lack of fusion which mars Vanbrugh's architectural ideas mars also his comedy. (T. W.)

VAN BUREN, Martin (1782-1862), eighth president of the United States, was the son of a small farmer, and was born 5th December 1782 at Kinderhook, Columbia, New York State, on the banks of the Hudson. He was educated at the village school, and, entering on the study of law at the age of fourteen, was called to the bar in 1803. Possessing in addition to his other abilities a peculiar power of winning personal trust and influence, his rise both in his profession and political reputation was rapid. In 1808 he was chosen surrogate of Columbia county, and in 1812 a member of the State legislature. From 1815 to 1819 he was attorney-general of the State, and during this period came to be recognized as the ruling spirit of the new Democratic school known as the Albany regency. In 1821 he was chosen to the United States senate and the same year was elected a member of the convention for revising the State constitution, in which, though advocating an extension of the franchise, he opposed universal suffrage. In 1828 he was appointed governor of New York State. From March 1829 to April 1831 he was secretary of state in the administration of President Jackson, of whom he was the chief political adviser. During the recess he was appointed minister to England; but, on the ground that he had previously shown a too submissive attitude towards that country, and also a tendency to be influenced in his foreign predilections by home politics, the senate refused to ratify the appointment. In the following year he was, however, chosen vice-president of the United States, and in 1837 he succeeded Jackson as president. He entered upon office at the time of a severe commercial crisis (see United States), and, although the methods he adopted to deal with it were in themselves admirable, the financial strain which existed during his term of office weakened for a time the influence of his party. Besides the establishment of the independent treasury system, Van Buren's name is associated with the pre-emption law giving settlers on public lands the preference in their purchase. On the expiry of his term of office he was again, in 1840, nominated for the presidency, but lost by a large majority. In 1844 a majority of the delegates to the Democratic convention were pledged to support him, but on account of his opposition to the annexation of Texas they allowed a motion to be introduced making a two-thirds vote necessary for nomination. This he failed to obtain and his name was withdrawn. In 1848 he was nominated by the anti-slavery section of his party, but the split caused the defeat of both Democratic candidates. The remainder of his life was spent chiefly in retirement on his estate at Kinderhook. In 1853-55 he went on a European tour. He died at Kinderhook, 24th July 1862. His *Inquiry into the Origin and Course of Political Parties in the United States* was published by his sons in 1867.

See W. Allen Butler, *Martin Van Buren, Lawyer, Statesman, and Man*, New York, 1862.

VANCOUVER, George (*c.* 1758-1798), English navigator, was born about 1758. He entered the navy at the age of thirteen, and accompanied Cook in his second (1772-74) and third (1776-79) voyages of discovery. After serving for several years on the Jamaica station, Vancouver was appointed to command an expedition to the north-west coast of America, the object being to take over from the Spaniards their territory in that region, and to explore the coast from 30° N. lat. round to Cook's Inlet (or river as it was then called), with a view to the discovery of an eastward passage to the great lakes in the British dominions. The special point which he had to

VANCOUVER ISLAND

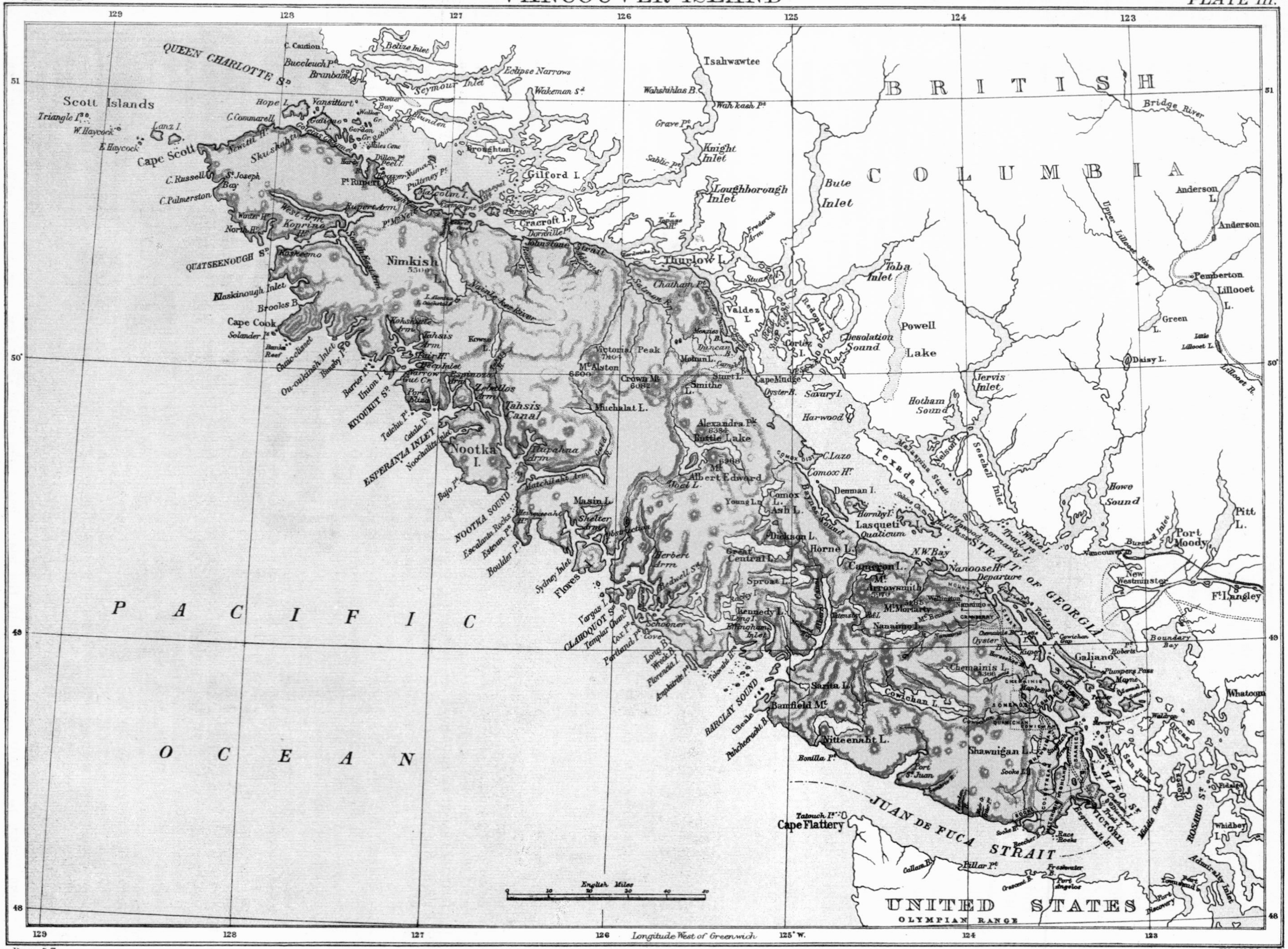
BRITISH COLUMBIA
PACIFIC OCEAN
UNITED STATES
OLYMPIAN RANGE
QUEEN CHARLOTTE S^D
Scott Islands
Cape Scott
C. Russell
C. Palmerston
Nimkish L.
QUATSEENOUGH S^D
Klaskinough Inlet
Brooks B.
Cape Cook
Solander I^d
KYOQUOT S^D
ESPERANZA INLET
Nootka I.
NOOTKA SOUND
Tahsis Canal
Muchalat L.
Crown M^t 6082
Victoria Peak
Alexandra P^k 6384
Buttle Lake
Mt Albert Edward
Comox L.
Ash L.
Great Central L.
Sproat L.
Flores I.
CLAYOQUOT S^D
BARCLAY SOUND
Nitteenaht L.
Bonilla P^t
Port St Juan
Shawnigan L.
Cowichan L.
Chemainis L.
Nanaimo L.
Cameron L.
Mt Arrowsmith
STRAIT OF GEORGIA
JUAN DE FUCA STRAIT
HARO S^T
ROSARIO S^T
VICTORIA
Esquimalt H^r
Cape Flattery
Tatouch I^d
Texada I.
Lasqueti I.
Denman I.
Hornby I.
Galiano I.
C. Lazo
Comox H^r
Harwood
Savary I.
Cortez I.
Valdez I.
Thurlow I.
Gilford I.
Broughton I.
Malcolm I.
Cracroft I.
Johnstone Strait
Salmon R.
Chatham P^t
Bute Inlet
Toba Inlet
Desolation Sound
Powell Lake
Jervis Inlet
Hotham Sound
Seschell Inlet
Howe Sound
Burrard Inlet
Vancouver
Port Moody
New Westminster
F^t Langley
Pitt L.
Boundary Bay
Whatcom
Whidbey I.
Admiralty Inlet
Port Townsend
Port Angeles
Pillar P^t
Anderson L.
Anderson
Pemberton
Lillooet L.
Little Lillooet L.
Green L.
Daisy L.
Lillooet R.
Upper Lillooet River
Bridge River
Isahwawtee
Knight Inlet
Loughborough Inlet
Wakeman S^d
Seymour Inlet
Belize Inlet
Eclipse Narrows
Buccleuch P^t
C. Caution
Hope I.
English Miles
0 10 20 30 40 50
129 128 127 126 125 124 123
51 50° 49 48
Longitude West of Greenwich
W. & A. K. Johnston.

ENCYCLOPÆDIA BRITANNICA, NINTH EDITION.

ascertain was whether the Strait of Juan de Fuca really was a strait. Vancouver, accompanied by Lieutenant Broughton, left Falmouth on 1st April 1791, and, after spending some weeks at the Cape, made for the coast of Australia, where a very careful survey of the south-west coast was made, especially of King George's Sound, the value of which as a harbour Vancouver pointed out. He next made for Dusky Bay, New Zealand. After a short stay, he proceeded north-east, discovered the little island of Oparo (27° 36′ S. lat. and 144° 12′ W. long.) by the way, and on 30th December reached Tahiti, where he was again joined by Lieutenant Broughton, who meanwhile had discovered Chatham Island. After staying about three weeks at Tahiti and several weeks at the Sandwich Islands, Vancouver on 18th April 1792 sighted the west coast of North America (California, then known as New Albion) in 39° 27′ N. lat. Here he proceeded to examine the coast up to 52° 18′ N. lat. with minute care, surveying all inlets and navigating the passage through Juan de Fuca which separates the Island of Vancouver from the mainland. Most of February and March 1793 was spent again at the Sandwich Islands, with the natives of which Vancouver had much intercourse, and in the affairs of which he took much interest. In April he resumed his exploration of the coast, which he examined and surveyed as far north as 56° N. lat. Part of the autumn was spent in visiting the Spanish settlements in New California, and surveying the coast and coast region as far south as 35° N. lat. From January to the beginning of March Vancouver's headquarters were again at the Sandwich Islands, the cession of which to Great Britain he accepted, though the cession seems never to have been officially ratified. Quitting the Sandwich Islands again about the middle of March 1784, Vancouver made direct for Cook's Inlet by Tchernigoff Island and Kodiak Island. Cook's Inlet was carefully explored and the fact established that it was not a river. The coast eastwards and southwards was surveyed as far as the limit of the former voyages. After spending some time about Nootka and visiting some parts of the coast, Vancouver set out homewards in the middle of October 1794. Several points were examined and surveyed on the west coast of America on the way southwards, including Cape St Lucas, the southern point of Lower California. After touching at Cocos Island and making a somewhat careful examination of the Galapagos Islands, Vancouver continued his voyage by way of Cape Horn, finally entering the mouth of the Shannon on 13th September 1795. He immediately set about the preparation of the narrative of his voyage, but died at Petersham in Surrey, 10th May 1798, before he had quite completed his task. Under the care of his brother the narrative was published in 1798 (3 vols. 4to), with a folio volume of magnificent maps and plates.

Vancouver's work on the west and north-west coast of America was of the highest character, and has formed the basis of all subsequent surveys. His zeal led him to take an active share in all operations, and the hardships he thus suffered tended no doubt to shorten his life. He was a man of great tact, humanity, generosity, and uprightness of character.

Plate III. VANCOUVER ISLAND, which is included in the territory of British Columbia, lies in a north-west and south-east direction parallel with the coast. From Washington Territory (U.S.) on the south it is separated by Juan de Fuca Strait, which leads into the Gulf of Georgia and Johnstone's Strait on the east of the island, Queen Charlotte Sound entering this last from the north-west. These channels vary from 5 to 80 miles in width. The island extends from 48° 20′ to 51° N. lat. and from 123° to 128° 30′ W. long. Its length is about 250 miles and its breadth varies from 10 to 70. The area is estimated at from 12,000 to 16,000 square miles; but the island has never been completely surveyed. The coast-line generally is precipitous. The west coast is much broken by bays and fringed with numerous reefs and islands, which render navigation somewhat dangerous. Barclay Sound on the south-west, Nootka Sound behind Nootka Island on the west, and Quatseenough Sound on the north-west send branches into the heart of the island. The east coast is much less broken, though the channel separating it from the mainland is studded with islands. Vancouver generally is mountainous, with peaks rising from 6000 to 9000 feet. There are some level areas on the south-east coast, while in the interior a few narrow well-watered valleys are suitable for agriculture. Short streams run down both coasts, and the island is dotted with lakes,—Buttle and Dickson in the centre, Cowichan in the south, and Niinkish in the north. The mountains, much broken, run generally along the length of the island, the highest peaks (estimated at 9000 feet) being south-east of Nootka Sound, while farther to the north are Victoria Peak (7484 feet) and Mount Alston (6500 feet). To the south of Buttle Lake, Mount Albert Edward rises to 6968 feet. The mountains in the south of the island are generally lower.

The island is essentially a mountain range composed of metamorphic and trappean rocks, fringed by a belt of Carboniferous limestones and other sedimentary deposits. Among the metamorphic and erupted rocks are gneiss and killas or clayslate, permeated by quartz veins, quartz and hornblende rocks, compact bituminous slate, highly crystalline felspathic traps, and semi-crystalline concretionary limestone. Among the sedimentary rocks are sandstones and stratified limestones, fine and coarse grits, conglomerates, and fossiliferous limestones, shales, &c., associated with seams of coal. The country is strewn with erratic boulders and other marks of Glacial action. So far as is known at present the chief mineral resource is coal, which is worked in large quantities at Nanaimo on the east coast, and in quality is reputed the best on the whole Pacific coast. While limited areas in the south-east of the island and in the inland valleys are well adapted to agriculture (about 300,000 acres in all), and while farming is carried on to some extent, the country is too mountainous ever to develop agriculture on any large scale. The mountains are, however, covered with forests, mainly the Douglas pine, yielding splendid supplies of timber. These forests, with its coal and its fisheries, may be regarded as the chief resources of the island. The climate of Vancouver, especially in the south, is wonderfully mild for the latitude, as mild as that of Great Britain, with drier summers. The mean temperature of December at Victoria, in the south of the island, is about 38° Fahr., while that of July is 53°. A rainfall of 35·87 inches in the year has been recorded at Esquimault. In the northern parts and in the west the climate gets much more severe, and there the rainfall is greater than on the south and east coasts. Cereals of all kinds, all fruits of the temperate zone, pulse, and vegetables flourish on the patches suited to agriculture, while cattle and sheep can be easily reared in small numbers. The population of the island in 1881 was 9991, of whom 5925 lived in the city of Victoria. In 1887 the population was estimated at 25,000 (19,000 whites and Chinese, and 6000 Indians).

The capital of the island is VICTORIA (*q.v.*). Three and a half miles to the west of Victoria is the town of Esquimault at the head of Parry Bay. There has been a British Admiralty station here for many years, the harbour having an average depth of from 6 to 8 fathoms. There are Government offices, two churches, a public school, and various other buildings. The Canadian Government has constructed a dry dock, 450 feet long, 26 feet deep, and 65 feet wide at the entrance. The completion of the Canadian Pacific Railway renders Esquimault of increasing importance. Seventy-three miles north of Victoria and connected with it by railway is the town of Nanaimo, the centre of the coal mining industry; the average output of coal in the five years ending 1887 was 250,000 tons per annum. The mines employ about 1100 men. There are a good harbour and wharves. The population in 1887 was estimated at 4000. There are smaller communities in the island, mainly in the south corner. Sixty miles north-west of Nanaimo is Comox, the chief centre of the lumber industry. On the mainland, opposite Nanaimo, on a peninsula to the south of Burrard's Inlet, a city named Vancouver has recently been formed (incorporated 1886) at the terminus of the Canadian Pacific Railway.

History.—Vancouver Island was discovered by Juan de Fuca in 1592. In 1778 Captain Cook roughly surveyed the coast, this work being extended by Captain Vancouver, who surveyed the Strait of Juan de Fuca and the Gulf of Georgia. The first settlement on the island was made by the Hudson's Bay Company on the site of Victoria in 1843. Six years later Vancouver Island was constituted a colony. Its union with British Columbia was effected in 1866.

VANDALS. The Vandals, one of the leading Teutonic nations that overthrew the Roman empire, were of the Low German stock and closely allied to the Goths. We first hear of them in the time of Pliny and Tacitus as occupying a district nearly corresponding to Brandenburg and Pomerania. From thence, in the 2d century, they pressed southwards to the confines of Bohemia, where they gave their name to the mountains now called the Riesengebirge. After a century of hostile and desultory operations against the Roman empire, having been signally defeated by Aurelian (271), they made peace with Rome, one of the conditions being that they should supply 2000 *fœderati* to the imperial army. Sixty years later they sustained a great defeat from the Goths under their king Geberich, after which they humbly sought and obtained permission from Constantine to settle as Roman subjects within the province of Pannonia. Here they remained seventy years, and during this period they probably made some advances in civilization and became Christians of the Arian type. In 406, when the empire under Honorius was falling into ruin, they crossed the Rhine and entered Gaul. Stilicho, the chief adviser of Honorius, who was a man of Vandal extraction, was accused by his enemies of having invited them into the empire, but this is probably a groundless calumny. In Gaul they fought a great battle with the Franks, in which they were defeated with the loss of 2000 men, and their king Godigisclus was slain. In 409 his son Gunderic led them across the Pyrenees. They appear to have settled in Spain in two detachments. One, the Asdingian Vandals, occupied Galicia, the other, the Silingian, Andalusia. Twenty years of bloody and purposeless warfare with the armies of the empire and with their fellow-barbarians, the Goths and the Suevi, followed. The Silingian Vandals were well-nigh exterminated, but their Asdingian brethren (with whom were now associated the remains of a Turanian people, the Alans, who had been utterly defeated by the Goths) marched across Spain and took possession of Andalusia.

In 428 or 429 the whole nation set sail for Africa, upon an invitation received by their king from Bonifacius, count of Africa, who had fallen into disgrace with the court of Ravenna. Gunderic was now dead and supreme power was in the hands of his bastard brother, who is generally known in history as Genseric, though the more correct form of his name is Gaiseric. This man, short of stature and with limping gait, but with a great natural capacity for war and dominion, reckless of human life and unrestrained by conscience or pity, was for fifty years the hero of the Vandal race and the terror of Constantinople and Rome. In the month of May 428 (?) he assembled all his people on the shore of Andalusia, and numbering the males among them from the graybeard down to the newborn infant found them to amount to 80,000 souls. The passage was effected in the ships of Bonifacius, who, however, soon returning to his old loyalty, besought his new allies to depart from Africa. They, of course, refused, and Bonifacius turned against them, too late, however, to repair the mischief which he had caused. Notwithstanding his opposition the progress of the Vandals was rapid, and by May 430 only three cities of Roman Africa—Carthage, Hippo, and Cirta—remained untaken. The long siege of Hippo (May 430 to July 431), memorable for the last illness and death of St Augustine, which occurred during its progress, ended unsuccessfully for the Vandals. At length (30th January 435) peace was made between the emperor Valentinian III. and Genseric. The emperor was to retain Carthage and the small but rich proconsular province in which it was situated, while Hippo and the other six provinces of Africa were abandoned to the Vandal. Genseric observed this treaty no longer than suited his purpose. On the 19th of October 439, without any declaration of war, he suddenly attacked Carthage and took it. The Vandal occupation of this great city, the third among the cities of the Roman empire, lasted for ninety-four years. Genseric seems to have counted the years of his sovereignty from the date of its capture. Though most of the remaining years of Genseric's life were passed in war, plunder rather than territorial conquest seems to have been the object of his expeditions. He made, in fact, of Carthage a pirate's stronghold, from whence he issued forth, like the Barbary pirates of a later day, to attack, as he himself said, "the dwellings of the men with whom God is angry," leaving the question who those men might be to the decision of the elements. Almost alone among the Teutonic invaders of the empire he set himself to form a powerful fleet, and was probably for thirty years the leading maritime power in the Mediterranean. Genseric's celebrated expedition against Rome (455), undertaken in response to the call of Eudoxia, widow of Valentinian, was only the greatest of his marauding exploits. He took the city without difficulty, and for fourteen days, in a calm and business-like manner, emptied it of all its movable wealth. The sacred vessels of the Jewish temple, brought to Rome by Titus, are said to have been among the spoils carried to Carthage by the conqueror. Eudoxia and her two daughters were also carried into captivity. One of the princesses, Eudocia, was married to Huneric, eldest son of Genseric; her mother and sister, after long and tedious negotiations, were sent to Constantinople.

There does not seem to be in the story of the capture of Rome by the Vandals any justification for the charge of wilful and objectless destruction of public buildings which is implied in the word "vandalism." It is probable that this charge grew out of the fierce persecution which was carried on by Genseric and his son against the Catholic Christians, and which is the darkest stain on their characters. This persecution is described with great vividness, and no doubt with some exaggeration, by the nearly contemporary Victor Vitensis. Churches were burned; bishops and priests were forced by cruel and revolting tortures to reveal the hiding-places of the sacred vessels; the rich provincials who were employed about the court, and who still adhered to the Catholic faith, were racked and beaten, and put to death. The bishops were almost universally banished, and the congregations were forbidden to elect their successors, so that the greater part of the churches of Africa remained "widowed" for a whole generation. In 475, at the very close of Genseric's life, by a treaty concluded with the Eastern emperor, the bishops were permitted to return. There was then a short lull in the persecution; but on the death of Genseric (477) and the accession of Huneric (a bitter Arian, made more rancorous by the orthodoxy of his wife Eudocia) it broke out again with greater violence than ever, the ferocity of Huneric being more thoroughly stupid and brutal than the calculating cruelty of his father.

On the death of Huneric (484) he was succeeded by his cousin Gunthamund, Genseric having established seniority among his own descendants as the law of succession to his throne. Gunthamund (484-496) and his brother Thrasamund (496-523), though Arians, abated some of the rigour of the persecution, and maintained the external credit of the monarchy. Internally, however, it was rapidly declining, the once chaste and hardy Vandals being demoralized by the fervid climate of Africa and the sinful delights of their new capital, and falling ever lower into sloth, effeminacy, and vice. On the death of Thrasamund, Hilderic (523-531), the son of Huneric and Eudocia, at length succeeded to the throne. He adhered to the creed of his mother rather than to that of his father; and, in spite of a solemn oath sworn to his predecessor that he would not restore the Catholic churches to their owners, he at once proceeded to do so and to recall the bishops. Hilderic, elderly, Catholic, and timid, was very unpopular with his subjects, and after a reign of eight years he was thrust into prison by his warlike cousin Gelimer (531-534).

The wrongs of Hilderic, a Catholic, and with the blood of Theodosius in his veins, afforded to Justinian a long-coveted pretext for overthrowing the Vandal dominion, the latent weakness of which was probably known to the statesmen of Constantinople. A great expedition under the command of Belisarius (in whose train was the historian Procopius) sailed from the Bosphorus in June 533, and after touching at Catana in Sicily finally reached Africa in the beginning of September. Gelimer, who was strangely ignorant of the plans of Justinian, had sent his brother Tzazo with some of his best troops to quell a rebellion in Sardinia (that island as well as the Balearic Isles forming part of the Vandal dominions), and the landing of Belisarius was entirely unopposed. He marched rapidly towards Carthage and on the 13th of September was confronted by Gelimer at Ad Decimum, 10 miles from Carthage. The battle did not reflect any great credit either on Byzantine or Vandal generalship. It was in fact a series of blunders on both sides, but Belisarius made the fewest and victory remained with him. On the 14th of September 533 the imperial general entered Carthage and ate the feast prepared in Gelimer's palace for its lord. Belisarius, however, was too late to save the life of Hilderic, who had been slain by his rival's orders as soon as the news came of the landing of the imperial army. Still Gelimer with many of the Vandal warriors was at liberty. On the return of Tzazo from Sardinia a force was collected considerably larger than the imperial army, and Gelimer met Belisarius in battle at a place about twenty miles from Carthage, called Tricamarum (December 533). This battle was far more stubbornly contested than that of Ad Decimum, but it ended in the utter rout of the Vandals and the flight of Gelimer. He took refuge in a mountain fortress called Pappua on the Numidian frontier, and there, after enduring great hardships in the squalid dwellings of the Moors, surrendered to his pursuers in March 534. The well-known stories of his laughter when he was introduced to Belisarius, and his chant, "Vanitas vanitatum," when he walked before the triumphal car of his conqueror through the streets of Constantinople, probably point to an intellect disordered by his reverses and hardships. The Vandals who were carried captive to Constantinople were enlisted in five squadrons of cavalry and sent to serve against the Parthians under the title "Justiniani Vandali." Four hundred escaped to Africa and took part in a mutiny of the imperial troops which was with difficulty quelled by Belisarius (536). After this the Vandals disappear from history. The overthrow of their kingdom undoubtedly rendered easier the spread of Saracen conquest along the northern shore of Africa in the following century. In this as in many other fields Justinian sowed that Mohammed might reap.

Authorities.—Procopius, *De Bello Vandalico*, a first-rate authority for contemporary events, must be used with caution for those which happened two or three generations before him. Consult especially i. 5 for the land settlement of Genseric, and also Victor Vitensis and Possidius (*Vita Augustini*) for the persecution of the Catholics. The chroniclers Idatius, Prosper, Victor Tunnunensis supply some facts. The *Chronicon* of Isidore adds little to our knowledge and is absurdly wrong in its chronology. Of modern treatises that of Papencordt (*Gesch. d. Vandal. Herrschaft in Afrika*) is the most complete. Consult also Dahn (*Könige der Germanen*, part I.), Gibbon (chaps. xxxiii. and xli.), and Hodgkin (*Italy and her Invaders*, vols. ii. and iii.). (T. H.)

VAN DER HELST. See Helst.

VANDEVELDE, Adrian (1639-1672), animal and landscape painter, a brother of William Vandevelde (see below), the marine painter, was born at Amsterdam in 1639. He was trained in the studio of Jan Wynants, the landscape painter, where he made the acquaintance of Philip Wouwerman, who is believed to have aided him in his studies of animals, and to have exercised a powerful and beneficial influence upon his art. Having made exceptionally rapid progress, he was soon employed by his master to introduce figures into his landscape compositions, and he rendered a similar service to Hobbema, Ruysdael, Verboom, and other contemporary artists. His favourite subjects are scenes of open pasture land, with sheep, cattle, and goats, which he executed with admirable dexterity, with much precision of touch and truth of draughtsmanship, and with clear silvery colouring. He painted a few small but excellent winter scenes with skaters, and several religious subjects, such as the Descent from the Cross, for the Roman Catholic church in Amsterdam. In addition to his paintings, of which nearly two hundred have been catalogued, he executed about twenty etchings, several of which appear from their dates to have been done in his fourteenth year. They are simple but pleasing in tonality, and are distinguished by great directness of method, and by delicacy and certainty of touch. Adrian Vandevelde died at Amsterdam in January 1672.

VANDEVELDE, William (1633-1707), the younger, marine painter, a son of William Vandevelde, the elder, also a painter of sea-pieces, was born at Amsterdam in 1633. He was instructed by his father, and afterwards by Simon de Vlieger, a marine painter of repute at the time, and had achieved great celebrity by his art before he came to London. In 1674 he was engaged by Charles II., at a salary of £100, to aid his father in "taking and making draughts of sea-fights," his part of the work being to reproduce in colour the drawings of the elder Vandevelde. He was also patronized by the duke of York and by various members of the nobility. He died in London on 6th April 1707.

It seems probable that most of Vandevelde's finest works were executed before his residence in England, for they represent views off the coast of Holland, with Dutch shipping. His best productions are delicate, spirited, and finished in handling, and correct in the drawing of the vessels and their rigging. The numerous figures are tellingly introduced, and the artist is successful in his renderings of sea, whether in calm or storm. His later productions are less carefully finished, and less pure and transparent in colour. Vandevelde was a most prolific artist: in addition to his paintings, of which Smith catalogues about three hundred and thirty, he executed an immense number of drawings, sketches, and studies, which are prized by collectors.

VAN DIEMEN'S LAND. See Tasmania.

VAN DYCK, Sir Anthony (1599-1641), painter, was born in Antwerp on 22d March 1599. Though the name of Van Dyck is frequently met with in the list of Antwerp painters, Anthony's pedigree cannot be traced beyond his grandparents, who were silk mercers of some standing. He was the seventh of twelve children of Francis Van Dyck, an Antwerp tradesman in good circumstances, and not, as has been asserted, a painter on glass at Bois-le-Duc. His mother, Maria Cupers, who died when he was scarcely eight years of age, seems to have attained a certain degree of excellence in art needlework. Of the boy's early education nothing is known. He was little over ten when he was apprenticed to Henry Van Balen, the painter of many delicate little pictures, also an occasional collaborator of Rubens, and the master of Snyders. From a document discovered some twenty years ago in the state paper office at Brussels, relating to a lawsuit between a picture dealer and an Antwerp churchman, which arose out of the sale, in 1660, of a series of Apostles' heads ascribed to Van Dyck, it appears that, as far back as 1615, Van Dyck had worked independently, with pupils of his own, and that his pictures were greatly valued by artists and amateurs.[1] Before he was nineteen (February 1618) Van Dyck became a full member of the Antwerp guild of painters; and some idea of his ability at the time may be gained from the excellent portraits of an old lady and gentleman, ascribed till quite recently to Rubens, in the Dresden gallery (Nos. 854 and 855). Dated 1618, they were originally entered as works of Van Dyck, and, as Prof. Woermann observes, are undoubtedly the same as those spoken of by Mols in his MS. annotations on Walpole's *Anecdotes*, now in the library at Brussels. But the same admiration cannot be accorded to the earliest religious composition known to have been painted by him—Christ Falling under the Cross, in St Paul's at Antwerp. This picture, of some ten life-size figures, still preserved in the place for which it was originally destined, distinctly proves that from the outset of his career Van Dyck's power of conception was vastly inferior to his refined taste as a portrait painter. At first sight it would seem also that with him, as with most other Flemish painters of the period, every conception, whether sacred or profane, needed to be cast in the mould of Rubens. It would be too much, however, to assert that Van Dyck at this time stood under the guidance of that master; their association indeed does not seem to have begun until 1619, and Bellori (1672), who got his information from Sir Kenelm Digby, Van Dyck's bosom friend, tells us that he was first employed in making drawings (probably also chiaroscuros) for the use of the great master's engravers, and that among works of the kind one of the first was the Battle of the Amazons (1619).

In 1620 we know that Van Dyck was working with Rubens, for on 20th March, in making arrangements with the Antwerp Jesuits for the decoration of their church, the great master is allowed to avail himself of his pupil's assistance, and obtains for him the promise of a picture. This proof of Van Dyck's personal reputation is fully confirmed (17th July) by a correspondent of the earl of Arundel, who speaks of Van Dyck as a young man of one and twenty whose works are scarcely less esteemed than those of his master, and adds that, his relations being people of considerable wealth, he could hardly be expected to leave his home. Van Dyck was, however, thus persuaded, for on 28th November Sir Toby Mathew mentions the artist's departure to Sir Dudley Carleton, adding that he is in receipt of an annual pension of £100 from the king. There is evidence of Van Dyck's presence in London till the end of February 1621. He is first mentioned in the order-books of the Exchequer on the 17th of that month as receiving a reward of £100 "for special service by him performed for His Majesty," and on the 28th, "Antonio van Dyck, gent., *His Majesties servant*, is allowed to travaile 8 months, he havinge obtayneid his Maties leave in that behalf, as was signified by the E. of Arundell." What Van Dyck did in London is not known. Among his numerous paintings still preserved in English houses one only is admitted as belonging to the period of this first visit, a full-length portrait of James I. in the royal collection. That he was at the time a portrait painter of the rarest merit may easily be seen from his own likeness of himself when still quite young and beardless, in the National Gallery (London), in the Pinakothek at Munich, and in the private collections of the duke of Grafton and Sir Richard Wallace. In this last admirable specimen the young painter has represented himself in the character of Paris. Early paintings by Van Dyck are certainly not scarce in British galleries; and at Dulwich there is his admirable Samson and Delilah, wrongly ascribed to Rubens.

Van Dyck is supposed to have profited by his leave of absence to visit Paris and The Hague; but it is much more probable that the eight months were spent in Antwerp, where Rubens was greatly in need of his assistance for the church of the Jesuits. After this Van Dyck most probably returned to London and remained there till the end of 1622, when his father died. The precise date of his departure for Italy—perhaps at the beginning and certainly in the course of 1623—has not been ascertained. But he is known to have left with Rubens a considerable number of paintings, most of which have been identified in Madrid, Berlin, Dresden, &c., and show that study, as well as advice, had long since made the painter acquainted, through Rubens, with those principles of picturesque expression which he was now about to see exemplified so splendidly in the works of the Venetian and Genoese schools. His previous acquaintance with many excellent examples of Titian, Tintoretto, and others in Rubens's own collection can alone account for the remarkably glowing tints of Van Dyck's earliest paintings. In fact, such works as the Martyrdom of St Peter (Brussels), the Crowning with Thorns (Berlin), the Betrayal of Christ (Madrid and Lord Methuen), St Martin Dividing his Cloak (Windsor Castle),—a magnificent production, generally ascribed to Rubens, but easily identified through Van Dyck's admirable sketch at Dorchester House,—incontestably prove that, in point of colouring, Venice at this moment stood higher in his predilection than Antwerp.

It is unnecessary to dwell on a number of tales connected with Van Dyck's early life, all of which have on closer examination proved to be apocryphal; but one story has been too frequently told to be altogether ignored. At the very outset of his Italian journey the inflammable youth was captivated by the beauty of a country girl, and for the love of her painted the altar-piece still to be seen in the church at Saventhem near Brussels, in which he himself is supposed to be represented on a grey horse, given by Rubens to his pupil. It is now known, however, that the picture was commissioned by a gentleman living at Saventhem (to the charms of whose daughter Van Dyck in reality seems not to have been altogether insensible), and a closer study makes it almost certain that it was executed after, not before, his Italian journey. On a reduced scale, and with the omission of two or three figures, the St Martin at Saventhem is a reproduction of the picture at Windsor Castle.

No master from beyond the Alps ever took up a higher position than Van Dyck among the most celebrated representatives of Italian art. Study, as a matter of course, had been one of his principal objects. No doubt can be entertained as to the great influence exerted by the works of Titian and Paul Veronese in the development of his genius; still the individuality of the painter remains a striking feature of what may be termed his Italian works, especially portraits. Their peculiar character seems to originate even more in the stateliness of the personages

[1] Prof. Woermann has identified several of the Apostles' heads here spoken of with some paintings in the gallery at Dresden.

he was fortunate enough to have as sitters than in any desire to follow individual predilection or prevailing fashion. As in later years Van Dyck gives us a striking picture of the higher classes in England, so at this stage he makes us acquainted with Italian beauty and style; and at no other period is his talent more advantageously shown than in some of the glorious portraits he painted at Rome, at Florence, and above all at Genoa. At Rome he resided with Cardinal Guido Bentivoglio, who had been papal nuncio in Flanders from 1607 to 1617. For this patron were painted several works of very great importance, the most renowned being the prelate's own portrait, now in the Pitti Palace at Florence. Another work was a Crucifixion, representing Christ dying on the cross with uplifted eyes. Most probably the picture spoken of by Bellori ought to be identified with the admirable edition now in the gallery at Naples, catalogued as "Scuola di Van Dyck," unsurpassed by any of those at Antwerp, Paris, Vienna, Rome, or elsewhere. Besides these he painted religious subjects and portraits, several of which are reckoned among his finest examples, such as the portrait of Francis Duquesnoy, the famous sculptor, belonging to the king of the Belgians, and those of Sir Robert Shirley and his wife, in Persian attire, now at Petworth.

Bellori tells us of Van Dyck's prepossessing appearance, of his elegance and distinction, altogether so different from the habits of his compatriots in Rome, who formed a jovial "gang," as they termed their association. Van Dyck seems to have kept out of their way, and incurred in consequence such annoyance as made his stay in Rome much shorter than it would otherwise have been. In the company of Lady Arundel, who tried to persuade him to return to England, he travelled to Turin, and perhaps produced some of the paintings now in the royal gallery there, such as the spirited portrait of Thomas of Savoy on his splendid black charger. But he was eager to reach Genoa, where Rubens had worked with great success some twenty years before, and where his Antwerp friends, Luke and Cornelis de Wael, for many years resident in Italy, now were. Van Dyck remained their guest for several months, and their portraits, now in the Pinacoteca Capitolina at Rome (engraved by W. Hollar from the monochrome at Cassel), may be supposed to have been one of his first Genoese productions. Though several of the palaces of the "superb" city no longer retain their treasures, and among the specimens of Van Dyck's genius still left too many have been greatly injured by cleaning and retouching, Genoa can still boast of a good number of his most attractive productions, portraits of the beautiful ladies and haughty cavaliers of the noble houses of Doria, Brignole Sale, Pallavicini, Balbi, Cattaneo, Spinola, Lommelini, and Grimaldi. It would scarcely be possible to speak too highly of such works as the portrait of the lady in white satin and the Durazzo children at the Durazzo Palace, the Balbi children at Panshanger, the Marchesa Balbi at Dorchester House, the equally beautiful portraits of the Lommelini and of the knight in black armour, buff jacket, and boots in the national gallery at Edinburgh, or the Marchesa Brignole Sala at Warwick Castle. Van Dyck's "Genoese manner" is a current expression, and indeed his Genoese portraits are remarkable for their richness of tonality and what might be called royal splendour, perhaps never before attained in works of the kind. This we may suppose to have had its origin, not only in his recent study of Titian (Van Dyck having, it is said, first spent some time at Venice), but also in decorative necessities,—the size of the palatial galleries and the rich hues of the Genoese velvets, on which these portraits were to find their place, obliging the painter to find a most uncommon strength of contrast. It must also be acknowledged that the beauty and distinction of Van Dyck's models are greatly enhanced by a splendour of costume entirely different from the dulness then prevalent almost everywhere else. In Italy, moreover, he found the reality of those gorgeous backgrounds,—flowing draperies, beautiful gardens, ornamental pillars, marble terraces and balustrades,—which elsewhere must be regarded as fictions merely. Here, finally, he was for the first time called upon to paint some of his grandest equestrian portraits, and the often-recurring grey steed with flowing mane (an admirable study of which belongs to Lord Brownlow) was first employed for the portrait of Antonio Giulio Brignole (still at Genoa) and for another picture which we may suppose to represent the same personage at Stafford House. As with Rubens, Titian seems to have been paramount in Van Dyck's regard. Copies in great number we know he possessed of the master's best works, and several little sketches in the British Museum bear proof of his devout study of the great Venetian. Some of Van Dyck's earlier paintings, religious and mythological,—the Tribute Money (Brignole Palace), Holy Family (Turin), Virgin and Saints (Louvre), Virgin (Grosvenor House), Martyrdom of St Lawrence (S. Maria dell' Orto, Venice), Bacchanal (Lord Belper), engraved at Genoa as early as 1628, St Sebastian (Edinburgh),—are certainly Titianesque in the extreme. Still the master's individuality is not obliterated, and the gallery at Parma has a Virgin with the Infant Asleep which may be termed a marvel of realistic simplicity.

Van Dyck is said to have sailed from Genoa to Palermo and there to have painted several persons of rank, including the viceroy, Emmanuel Philibert of Savoy. While in Sicily he became acquainted with the painter Sofonisba Anguisciola (or Angussola), who was then over ninety years of age and blind; and he was wont to say he had received more valuable information from a blind woman than from many a seeing man. No important works of Van Dyck are now to be found in Sicily. Bellori tells us that a plague broke out and compelled him to leave abruptly, taking with him an unfinished picture of St Rosalia, destined for a confraternity of that name, and which was completed in Genoa. The composition was repeated in Antwerp for the Bachelors' Brotherhood, a picture now in Vienna. Van Dyck most probably remained in Genoa till 1627, and here in all likelihood he met and painted the sculptor George Petel, whose portrait is now in Munich, and who was frequently employed by Rubens; the De Jodes, father and son, the celebrated engravers, who are represented together in a masterly portrait in the Capitol at Rome, the companion picture to the brothers De Wael; and Nicholas Laniere, musician-in-chief to Charles I., a painting spoken of in Van der Dort's catalogue as "done beyond the seas." Laniere was in Italy precisely at this time and it was through his portrait (now at Windsor Castle), Walpole assures us, that Van Dyck attracted the notice of Charles I.

Embarking for Marseilles, Van Dyck is said to have stopped at Aix with Peiresc, the famous scholar and friend of Rubens, and thence to have gone to Paris, where most probably he painted the beautiful portrait of Langlois the print-seller (belonging to Mr W. Garnett), a work still influenced by Italian reminiscences, and had the opportunity of meeting Callot, Simon Vouet, and Dupuy, the king's librarian,—all of whose portraits were engraved from his drawings in Antwerp. According to some authors, he also worked in Holland before returning to his native town; but the supposition rests entirely on two portraits in the museum at The Hague, dated 1627 and 1628, and representing a lady and gentleman, with the Sheffield arms. The lady is easily identified by a well-known print by Clouwet as Anne Wake. The Wake family resided in

Antwerp, and both portraits may have been painted there. There is no recorded proof of Van Dyck's return to Antwerp before 6th March 1628. One of his sisters had died in a convent the year before, and he now made a will in favour of Susan and Isabella, two other sisters, also nuns. That Van Dyck was in Antwerp on 18th May is proved by a letter from Lord Carlisle to Buckingham (Sainsbury, CIII.), but it is stated in Bullart's *Académie*, published in 1682, that he returned again to London in 1629, without, however, attracting the king's attention. It is very likely that Lady Arundel's endeavours to get him back to England were now successful, and that the beautiful portrait of Lord Thomas, at Stafford House, belongs to this period.

Great as may have been the strength of Italian reminiscence, from the moment Van Dyck again trod Flemish soil the influence of Rubens became predominant, and we can scarcely doubt that a competition speedily arose between master and pupil. At this period churches and convents were numerous and richly endowed; and the number of pictures, stained glass windows, and elaborate carvings in Belgian churches before the French conquest was enormous. Hardly fifty years had elapsed since these buildings had been stripped of their artistic treasures, and the devout were now eager once more to adorn them with productions of the greatest painters. Hence Van Dyck's share could be very copious without in any degree interfering with the vast undertakings assigned to Rubens. The latter was also absent for many months in 1629 and 1630, so that Van Dyck was for a time the first master in the Netherlands. Among the earliest works after his return to Antwerp we find the Crucifixion, given to the Dominican nuns, in accordance with the wish expressed by the painter's dying father, and now in the Antwerp museum. The figures are life-size, and at the foot of the cross, besides a weeping angel, are St Catherine of Siena and St Dominic. Neither in type nor in general effect does it suggest the master's immediately preceding works. As a new feature we observe a kind of elegance, not entirely free from mannerism, which is often conspicuous with Van Dyck even when the technical excellence commands our warmest admiration. Inspiration, as Waagen observes, was far more limited with Van Dyck than with Rubens. His truly delicate nature led him to restrain his conceptions within the bounds of an academic evenness, generally more pleasing to the uninitiated than the strength of expression which sometimes imparts a sort of violence to the works of Rubens. To Van Dyck's second—more justly speaking third—manner belong some of his best religious works. The Crucifixion in the cathedral at Mechlin is termed by Sir Joshua Reynolds one of the finest pictures in the world. Other Crucifixions are in St Michael's at Ghent (sketches in Lord Brownlow's collection and the Brussels museum) and in the church at Termonde. Still finer are the two works painted for the Antwerp Jesuits and now at Vienna,—the Blessed Herman Joseph Kneeling before the Virgin and St Rosalia Crowned by the Infant Saviour. To this period likewise belong the celebrated Elevation of the Cross at Courtrai and the St Augustine in Ecstasy, in the church of the Jesuits at Antwerp; the general effect of this last, it must be acknowledged with Reynolds, is inferior to the beautiful engraving by De Jode, and also to the earl of Northbrook's magnificent sketch. At Dulwich we find the first idea of the composition, with many interesting differences. It may be a matter of individual preference to pronounce Van Dyck's Flemish portraits superior to those of an earlier period; but nobody can fail to admit that, technically speaking, they indicate a further step towards perfection. The darkness of the Genoese portraits has vanished; broad daylight now freely illuminates the model, and such works as the portraits of Cornelius Van der Geest (National Gallery, London) and Ambrogio Spinola (Rev. W. H. Wayne) are perhaps as close to material excellence as any painting could be. The full-length likenesses of Philip Le Roy (1630) and his wife (1631) (at Manchester House) and of Mary Louisa of Tassis (Prince Liechtenstein, Vienna) are not only the finest examples of the master's talent, but deserve to rank among the most beautiful portraits ever painted. The Snyders at Castle Howard is regarded by Waagen as not inferior to the most celebrated Raphaels, Titians, or Holbeins; and of almost equal excellence are the Wife of Colin de Nole in the Munich gallery, the Lady and her Daughter at the Louvre, and the Lady in Black at Cassel.

Rapidly rising to honour and wealth, Van Dyck shared with Rubens the official title of court painter, and his numerous portraits of the Infanta in her monastic garb (Paris, Vienna, Turin, Parma, &c.) bear testimony to the great favour in which he stood with her. When Mary de' Medici, after her flight from France, took up her residence in Brussels (1631), she honoured Van Dyck, as well as Rubens, with repeated visits, and several times called upon him to paint her likeness, as well as those of Gaston of Orleans and his wife Margaret of Lorraine, and several of the personages of their court. From Gerbier's letters we learn that Van Dyck at this time was contemplating another journey to England, and was very anxious to be commissioned by the infanta and the queen of France to take over their portraits as presents for the king and royal family. He soon travelled to The Hague to paint the prince and princess of Orange and their son. Quite at the beginning of 1632 Constantine Huygens, who was then living at The Hague, inscribes in his diary, "Pingor a Van Dyckio." When, towards the end of March, Van Dyck sailed for England, he took all these portraits with him, as we learn from an account of the 8th of August 1632 (Carpenter's *Pictorial Notices*). Dutch authors speak of a visit paid by Van Dyck to Frans Hals at Haarlem, and of a portrait of the latter through which the Antwerp master was at once recognized by his Dutch colleague. An engraving of a portrait of Hals after Van Dyck seems to confirm the story.

In undertaking this new journey to London, Van Dyck was assured of success, for Gerbier's letters show that the king had personally desired his presence. As early as March 1629 Endymion Porter, one of the gentlemen of the king's bedchamber, had been commissioned to order a picture from Van Dyck, Rinaldo and Armida. The composition is well known through De Balliu's first-rate engraving, and the canvas, now belonging to the duke of Newcastle, may be looked upon as one of the master's finest creations. Rubens was in London at the time the picture arrived, and to him we may in a great measure attribute the realization of Van Dyck's plans and the exceptional favours bestowed upon him almost from the day of his arrival in London. Besides the title of painter in ordinary, and the grant of an annual pension of £200, he received the honour of knighthood after a residence of less than three months at court (5th July 1632). Van Dyck rapidly achieved popularity among the higher classes, and, as Walpole says, his works are so frequent in England that to most Englishmen it is difficult to avoid thinking of him as their countryman.

His refined nature is strikingly illustrated in his admirable interpretation of English beauty and style. And, if Van Dyck be compared to Mytens and Cornelius Janssen, the most distinguished painters employed by the English court immediately before him, few artists, whether in England or elsewhere, have more richly endowed their models with distinction of feature and elegance in bearing. To him may be applied what Opie says of Titian, "that he combines resemblance with dignity, costume with taste, and art with simplicity." We are particularly struck with the thorough and immediate identification of his talent with local tastes and exigencies. Charles I. and Henrietta Maria, although pictured by several other painters, are known to posterity exclusively through Van Dyck, not from a greater closeness of resemblance to the original, but from a particular power of expression and bearing, which, once seen, it is impossible to forget. Lodged at the expense of the crown, with a summer residence at Eltham Palace, Van Dyck was frequently honoured with the visits of the king at his studio at Blackfriars. Portraits now followed each other with a rapidity scarcely credible to those unacquainted with the artist's method. In fact, his mode of living and his love of pleasure sufficiently explain his great need of money. During the first year of his presence in England he painted the king and queen a dozen times. The first of these noble portraits is the admirable full length of Charles I., with the queen and their two eldest children, at Windsor Castle. The style he adopted in England is generally termed his third manner; we might better say his fourth, as he already had a very particular style before he set out on his Italian journey. De Piles gives us some account of Van Dyck's methods at this period of his career. He began with a small sketch on grey paper with black and white chalks, or a monochrome in oils. This study was passed on to assistants in order to be copied on the required scale. When the clothes were sufficiently advanced by the pupils from those sent by the model, as well as the background and accessories, the master was enabled in a few sittings of an hour each to complete the work. Van Dyck excelled in painting the hands; he is said to have kept special models for this part of his work. It need hardly be said that a system of this kind, although employed by Rubens for his larger creations, was exceedingly ill adapted to portrait painting. In Van Dyck's later productions we too often detect marks of haste, as if the pencil were becoming a mere implement of trade.

Nearly the whole of 1634 and 1635 were spent by Van Dyck in the Netherlands.[1] The archduchess died on 1st December 1633, and Van Dyck naturally wished to get his official title renewed by her successor, Ferdinand of Austria, brother of Philip IV. That Van Dyck's residence in Antwerp was only to be temporary is shown by the power given to his sister Susan for the administration of his affairs in Belgium (14th April 1634). On the arrival of the new governor Van Dyck was immediately called upon to paint his likeness, a picture now in the Madrid gallery, where the same personage is also represented by Rubens and Velazquez. Several other portraits of Ferdinand, either in his cardinal's robes or in military dress, by Van Dyck, occur elsewhere. One on horseback was exhibited at the Grosvenor Gallery, London, in 1887 as the duke of Alva (the property of Mr S. Kynaston Mainwaring). Van Dyck was greatly in demand at this time, and his prices were correspondingly high, as the Antwerp municipality found when they asked for a portrait of the late infanta to decorate one of the triumphal arches for the reception of the new governor. The most important of Van Dyck's works, at any rate as a portrait painter, belong to this period. The picture representing in life size the members of the Brussels corporation, which was destroyed by fire during the siege of 1695, is spoken of with intense admiration by several writers. Bullart, for instance, is very enthusiastic about its fine colour and lifelike qualities. Among the religious paintings of undisputed excellence belonging to the same period are the Adoration of the Shepherds in the church at Termonde, and the Deposition, where the body of Christ rests upon the lap of the Virgin, in the Antwerp museum. Among the portraits are the admirable full length of Scaglia, the king's frequent agent in the Netherlands (at Dorchester House; a replica in the museum at Antwerp), the equestrian portrait of Albert of Arenberg (Arenberg Palace at Brussels), and a portrait of the same nobleman on foot, in the black velvet Spanish dress with golden chamberlain's key (long said to be Rubens) at Althorpe, the full length of Helena Fourment, Rubens's second wife (at St Petersburg), the beautiful duchess of Havre, Mary Clara de Croy, signed and dated 1634 (Mr Ayscough Fawkes), and other members of the same family (at Munich), Thomas of Savoy (at Berlin), an admirable half length of a lady in black (in the Belvedere at Vienna), and above all the grandiose picture in which John of Nassau is represented at full length, with his wife and children (at Panshanger). Several portraits of Brussels and Antwerp magistrates must also be mentioned, the most important being John Van Merstraeten, a Brussels lawyer (at Cassel).

[1] It is not generally known that his brother, an Antwerp priest, had been called over by the queen to act as her chaplain.

After being chosen honorary president of the Antwerp guild of St Luke, Van Dyck returned to London before the end of 1635. In spite of the vast number of his later portraits, some of them deserve to be ranked among the most celebrated of his productions. The royal children in the gallery at Turin (1635), the portraits of Charles I. in the Louvre and in the National Gallery, London, the picture of the Pembroke family at Wilton House, Sir George and Sir Francis Villiers, and the earls of Bristol and Bedford, at Althorpe, as well as those of Francis Russell, fourth earl of Bedford, and Anne Carr, his consort, at Woburn Abbey (1636), all belong to the years immediately following the master's return from the Netherlands.

He now married Lady Mary Ruthven, daughter of Sir Patrick Ruthven and grand-daughter of the earl of Gowrie. There are several portraits of her by her husband, the most important being in the Munich gallery, in which she is represented in white satin, playing on the violoncello. She is also said to figure as the Virgin in a picture belonging to Lord Lyttelton. There is a capital engraving of her by Bolswert. In another picture, said to be Mary Ruthven (belonging to Mr J. C. Herford), an exceedingly handsome lady is represented as Herminia Putting on Clarinda's Armour. There can be no doubt as to the model having been Margaret Lemon, a celebrated beauty, whose portrait was engraved by W. Hollar and J. Morin and painted by Van Dyck at Hampton Court. "She was," says M. Law, in his excellent catalogue of this gallery, "the most beautiful and celebrated, though far from being the only mistress of Van Dyck. The great artist, in fact, loved beauty in every form, and found the seduction of female charms altogether irresistible. She lived with him at his house at Blackfriars." The precise date of Van Dyck's marriage has not been ascertained. It was probably towards the end of 1639. The union is said to have been promoted by the artist's friends in order to save him from the consequence of his pernicious way of living. Margaret Lemon resented the event most cruelly, and tried to maim Van Dyck's right hand.

Van Dyck found few occasions in England to paint anything but portraits. He seems to have been decidedly underrated by the king and queen as an imaginative painter. At the very time of his employment on the beautiful portraits of Henrietta Maria, destined to serve as models for Bernini's bust, Gerbier was secretly negotiating with Jordaens, by order of Charles, for the decoration of the queen's apartments at Greenwich (1639). There exists at Belvoir Castle a sketch by Van Dyck representing a procession of the knights of the Garter, a really grandiose composition, engraved by Cooper. We know from Bellori that Van Dyck had suggested through his friend Sir Kenelm Digby, for the banqueting room at Whitehall, a series of decorations illustrating the history of the order of the Garter, and that the king had been much pleased with the idea. The plan, however, failed through the excessively high price asked by the painter, and perhaps also because the king had thought of having the work done in tapestry. Van Dyck's pension was five years in arrear, and, instead of £560, he received finally, besides his pension, only £200.

When the news of Rubens's death reached London (June 1640) Van Dyck contemplated a return to his native country, and a letter from Ferdinand of Austria to Philip IV. speaks of his intended journey to Antwerp on St Luke's Day (18th October). Rubens had left unfinished a series of paintings commanded by the king of Spain, and from correspondence published by Professor Justi we learn that Van Dyck had been thought of to give them the finishing touch. But he absolutely refused to finish them. It was then agreed that he should paint an independent canvas destined to complete the series. Van Dyck was delighted with this order, and Ferdinand tells his brother that he returned to London in great haste "to make preparations for his change of residence; possibly," adds the letter, "he may still change his mind, for he is stark mad." Whether Van Dyck found it possible to work during his short stay in the Netherlands is a matter of doubt. In the museum at The Hague are six medallion portraits of Constantine Huygens and his children, dated 1640. They have till lately been ascribed to Van Dyck, but are now said to be by Adrian Hannemann, a Dutchman, and one of his ablest assistants. In any case they are of small importance. Most authors suppose that Van Dyck's principal object in travelling to the Continent was to be entrusted with the decoration of one of the galleries of the Louvre. There may be some truth in this, for Mariette speaks of a letter he saw, written by Claude Vignon, the French painter, in January 1641, asking Langlois for an introduction to Van Dyck, who was then in Paris. Unfortunately the great painter was thwarted in his aspirations. His health was beginning to fail. After his return to London he was frequently obliged to interrupt his work; and a letter written (13th August) from Richmond by Lady Anne Roxburgh to Baron W. van Brederode at The Hague states that the portraits of the Princess Mary had been greatly delayed through Van Dyck's illness, and that the prince's (William II. of Orange) would be ready in eight days. "As Van Dyck intends leaving England in the course of ten or twelve days at latest," she adds, "he will take the paintings himself to the princess of Orange." These portraits, now in the museum at Amsterdam, are the last Van Dyck painted in England. They are considered to be inferior; and the last edition of the catalogue terms them copies. But of works dated 1639 the portrait of Lady Pembroke, in the gallery at Darmstadt, is a really fine specimen; and to the same year belongs a full-length portrait of Arthur Goodwin at Chatsworth. The twin portrait of Thomas Carew and Thomas Killigrew, in the royal collection, dated 1638, is certainly most delicate, but very weak in tone and slight in handling. Van Dyck sailed in September, and probably spent some time with his Antwerp friends. In October he reached Paris, and succeeded in obtaining some important work, when, on 16th November, he was compelled to resign his commissions on account of the state of his health. Scarcely three weeks later (9th December 1641) he died at his residence at Blackfriars. Van Dyck was buried in old St Paul's, where a Latin inscription was placed on his tomb by Charles I.

An elegy in Cowley's *Miscellanies* speaks, not only of the painter's talent, but of his amiable disposition. We may perhaps point to the coincidence that a Mrs Cowley is in Van Dyck's will (of 1st December) named guardian of his child, Justiniana Anna, born only eight days before her father's death. The painter had in the Netherlands an illegitimate daughter, Maria Theresia, who was entrusted to his sister, and to whom he bequeathed £4000. The name of her mother is not known. Not long after her husband's death Lady Van Dyck became the second wife of Sir Richard Pryse of Gogerddan in Cardiganshire. She was dead in 1645. Justiniana Van Dyck, who was married when scarcely twelve years old to Sir John Stepney of Prendergast, was also something of an artist: she painted a Crucifixion, with four angels receiving Christ's blood in chalices. A similar subject had been painted by Van Dyck, as Bellori tells us, for the duke of Northumberland. After the Restoration a pension of £200 for life was granted to Justiniana Van Dyck, who died before 1690.

Van Dyck is one of the most brilliant figures in the history of art. That he should, in the same subjects chosen by Rubens, have attained the same degree of expression was scarcely possible. Rubens was exceptional precisely through the sweep and power of his imagination; but Van Dyck, applying the same principles to portrait painting, was no less exceptional. Titian, Raphael, Rembrandt, Velazquez, and Frans Hals are not, on the whole, superior to him in this branch. They often delight us with their technical excellence or penetrating study of individuality, but their conception remains entirely different from that of Van Dyck. With him as with Rubens physiognomical interpretation is so intimately connected with picturesque necessity that his portraits scarcely ever fail to leave an indelible impression on the mind. Burnet observes that with Van Dyck the union of the figure and the background seems to have been a principle, not only in respect of light and shade, but also of colour. Thus the shapes of his lights are extended or doubled by means of a curtain in the background, &c. Hence Van Dyck, quite unlike the Dutch, is not what may be termed an intimate portraitist. In his eyes a prince, a warrior, a statesman, an artist belong to the world and to posterity, and in the realization of this idea he attains a degree of excellence seldom if ever attained before him. His works may be found lacking in solidity or displaying an unnecessary amount of motion in attitude, but these defects are easily compensated by a sense of proportion, an elegance in outline, a variety of conception united in his best works to the most able technic.

Properly speaking, Van Dyck cannot be said to have formed a school. He was followed to London by some of his earlier collaborators, and there soon met a considerable number of others. Jan van Reyn, David Beek, Adrian Hannemann, Mathew Merian, John Bockhorst (Lang Jan), Remy van Leemput, and Peter Thys were foremost among foreigners, Henry Stone and William Dobson among Englishmen. To their assistance the master owed much; but they are also responsible for the vast number of constantly-recurring copies which go by his name. It often requires a very discriminating eye to distinguish some of these copies from the original paintings. Nevertheless after Van Dyck's death many of his coadjutors produced works of undeniable merit. No school more strikingly reflects the influence of Van Dyck than the British school. Stone and Dobson were, properly speaking, the most fortunate of his continuators; and there is little doubt that such masters as Reynolds, Gainsborough, Lawrence, and Raeburn owe a large measure of their superiority to their study of his works.

Though Van Dyck's reputation greatly suffered through the numerous copies he allowed his pupils to take from his works, the case is otherwise with engraving: Vorsterman, Pontius, Peter de Jode, P. Balliu, and S. Bolswert were seldom more fortunate than when under his guidance. De Jode's St Augustine, Bolswert's Ecce Homo and Crucifixion, Vorsterman's Deposition, and especially Pontius's Herman Joseph rank among the masterpieces of the art of engraving. Van Dyck was himself an incomparable etcher, and with the needle arrived at a degree of excellence scarcely inferior to that exhibited in his paintings. Such prints as the portraits of Vorsterman, John de Wael, Snyders, Josse de Momper, Adam van Noort, and above all his own effigy, bear witness to his prodigious knowledge of design. Print collectors pay extravagant prices for a first proof taken from the plates engraved by Van Dyck himself. Mr Sackville Bale's copy of the portrait of Wawerius fetched £600. Van Dyck also employed some of the best engravers of his time for the production of a gallery of illustrious heads, men and women, of different countries. Whether all were taken from life is questionable. Gustavus Adolphus and Wallenstein he can hardly have met. Du Breucq, the architect, he never knew. But all the sketches and drawings were done by himself, and are often met with in public and private galleries. The engravings are sometimes very beautiful and in their first states very rare. Published successively by Martin van der Enden, Giles Hendrickx, and John Meyssens, the collection originally consisted of sixteen warriors and statesmen, twelve scholars, and fifty-two artists. Hendrickx raised the number to ninety-nine, and used as a frontispiece the portrait of Van Dyck, with the following inscription:—*Icones principum, virorum doctorum, etc., etc., numero centum ab Antonio Van Dyck pictore ad vivum expressæ eiusq. sumtibus æri incisæ*, 1645. Seventeen editions were published, the last in 1759, with 124 plates. Many of the plates are now the property of the French Government, and belong to the Chalcographie Nationale in Paris.

Literature.—See W. Hookham Carpenter, *Pictorial Notices, consisting of a Memoir of Sir Anthony Van Dyck, with a descriptive catalogue of the etchings executed by him* (London, 1844); John Smith, *A Catalogue Raisonné of the Works of the most Eminent Dutch, Flemish, and French Painters*, part iii. (London, 1841); J. Guiffrey, *Antoine Van Dyck, sa Vie et son Œuvre* (Paris, 1882); A. Michiels, *Ant. Van Dyck et ses Élèves* (Paris, 1881); Ign. von Szwykowski, *A. Van Dyck's Bildnisse bekannter Personen* (Leipsic, 1858); Fr. Wibiral, *L'Iconographie d'A. Van Dyck d'après les Recherches d. H. Weber* (Leipsic, 1877); Carl Lemcke, *A. Van Dyck* (in Robert Dohme's *Kunst und Künstler*, vol. i., Leipsic, 1877); Alfr. Woltmann and K. Woermann, *Gesch. der Malerei*, vol. iii. (Leipsic, 1886); Max Rooses, *Geschiedenis der Antwerpsche Schilderschool* (Ghent, 1879); F. J. Van den Branden, *Gesch. der Antw. Schilderschool* (Antwerp, 1883); Percy Rendall Head, *Van Dyck* (London, 1887); F. G. Stephens, *Catalogue of the Exhibition of the Works of Sir A. Van Dyck* (London, 1887). (H. H.)

VANE, Sir Henry (1612-1662), the younger, was the son of Sir Henry Vane and Frances Darcy. His father, of an ancient family in Durham, was secretary of state and comptroller of the household under Charles I. Henry was born in 1612 at Hadlow in Kent; and after an education at Westminster, where he was noted for his high and reckless spirits, and at Magdalen, Oxford, where he neither matriculated nor took his degree, he was sent to France and Geneva. Here he no doubt acquired the strongly Puritan views for which he had been prepared by a remarkable change of mind when quite a boy. In spite of the personal efforts of Laud, who made the attempt at the king's request, he refused to give them up, and fell especially under the influence of Pym. In 1635 he emigrated to Massachusetts, where he was elected governor in 1636, though only twenty-four years of age. After two years of office, during which he showed striking administrative ability, he was defeated by Winthrop, the former governor, chiefly on account of the protection he had given to Mrs Hutchinson in the religious controversies which she raised.

Vane returned to England in August 1637. Being elected to the Short Parliament for Kingston-upon-Hull, he speedily became a leader of the Independents and a marked man. In order to secure him for the court he was made joint-treasurer of the navy with Sir W. Russell, and was knighted. In November 1640 he was again elected for Hull to the Long Parliament. Accidentally finding among his father's papers some notes of Strafford's advice to the king after the dissolution of the Short Parliament, in which Strafford justified the use of force, he handed them to Pym, and on 10th April 1641 was examined upon them by the House; this disclosure was largely instrumental in bringing about Strafford's downfall. He carried up the impeachment of Laud from the Commons, was a strong supporter, when on the committee of religion, of the "Root and Branch" bill, and in June 1641 put forward a scheme of church government by which commissioners, half lay and half cleric, were to assume ecclesiastical jurisdiction in each diocese. He was, in fact, foremost in all the doings of the Long Parliament. When war broke out he surrendered his office of treasurer of the navy, but was replaced in it by the Parliament. Hereupon he gave a rare example of disinterestedness by relinquishing all the profits of the office, stated at £30,000 a year, stipulating only that £1000 should be paid to a deputy. In August 1642 he was on the committee of defence. In 1643 he was the leading man among the commissioners sent to treat for a league with the Scots. Vane, who was bitterly opposed to the tyranny of the Presbyterian system, was successful in two important points. The aim of the Scots was chiefly the propagation of their discipline in England and Wales, and for this they wanted only a "covenant." The English desired a political "league." Vane succeeded in getting the bond termed the Solemn League and Covenant, and further in substituting the expression "*according to the word of God* and the example of the best Reformed churches" for the latter phrase alone. In the Westminster Assembly, too, he joined Cromwell in insisting upon full religious liberty, and in opposing the view that the taking of the Covenant should be necessary for ordination. In 1644 he was charged by Essex with holding communication with the court, but explained that he had done so in order to acquire information of the Royalist plans, and was fully acquitted by the House of Lords. He was on the committee of two kingdoms, and was engaged in the negotiations with Charles at Uxbridge in 1645. He was, with Cromwell, a prime mover in the Self-Denying Ordinance and the New Model, and it was he who suggested the filling up of the vacant seats in parliament. His views of government at this time and throughout his life may be best studied in an important paper, the *People's Case Stated*, written shortly before his death. "The power which is directive, and states and ascertains the morality of the rule of obedience, is in the hand of God; but the original, from whence all just power arises, which is magistratical and coercitive, is from the will or free gift of the people, who may either keep the power in themselves or give up their subjection and will in the hand of another." The king, then, having transgressed the condition, and having been conquered, the people were free to change their form of government and, if they pleased, resort to a republic. In 1646 Vane was one of the English commissioners for the preservation of peace with Scotland, and in 1648 was appointed with others to negotiate with Charles at the Isle of Wight. Radical as were his views, he refused all participation in Pride's "purge"—the point where he first broke with Cromwell—and remained in privacy at Raby Castle in Durham until after the king's death, a measure in which he took no part. In 1649, however, he returned to London and was placed on the council of state, though he refused to take the oath which expressed approbation of the king's execution. He was chairman of the committee appointed to consider the mode of election of future parliaments, and his proposals were brought forward in January 1650. He acknowledged the Commonwealth only so far as he found it "consonant to the principles which have given rise to the law and the monarchy itself in England," and he recognized in a parliament, conforming in other respects to the ancient laws, the supreme authority of the state, whether there were a king at the head of it or not. He wished to reform the franchise on the property basis, to disfranchise some of the existing boroughs, and to give increased representation to the large towns; the sitting members, however, were to retain their seats. In this he was opposed by Cromwell, who desired an entirely new parliament and the supremacy of the army representation; and Vane stands henceforward as the champion of the doctrine of pure parliamentary government. His most useful qualities were exhibited, however, when in March 1653 he became the head of the commission for managing the army and navy. It was by his exertions in organization that Blake was fitted out with the fleet with which Van Tromp was defeated and the supremacy of England at sea assured. It was at this time that Milton's sonnet was addressed to him. On 20th April Cromwell forcibly dissolved the Long Parliament, when Vane especially received from the Protector studied insult. He was, however, almost at once invited to rejoin the Government. "He answered the invitation by a letter extracted from the Apocalypse wherein the reign of the saints is mentioned, which faith he believes will now begin." In his retirement at Raby he now wrote the *Retired Man's Meditations*. In 1656 he proposed in *A Healing Question* a new form of government, insisting as before upon a Puritan parliament supreme over the army. This he sent to Cromwell, and so alarmed was the Protector at the interest it excited that Vane was summoned on 12th August to the council in consequence. Refusing to give security not to disturb the public peace, he was on 9th September sent prisoner to Carisbrooke Castle, and there remained until 31st December. He had previously, according to his opponents, excited the jealousy of the Government by "going up and down among the Quakers, and endeavouring to withdraw them from their submission to the Government." After the death of Cromwell he stood for Kingston and Bristol successively, and was elected, but the court managers gave the certificate of election to the defeated candidates; finally, however, he was chosen for Whitchurch and took his seat on 27th January 1659, at the head of the small body of forty republicans. He was at once urgent in pressing that, before Richard Cromwell, for whom he had a great contempt, was acknowledged protector, the limitations of his power, and the full security of parliament and subjects, should be settled. Upon Richard's abdication he joined the army leaders in reviving the Rump; and, when the breach occurred between it and the army, he adhered to the latter, accepting a commission from them. He was one of the committee of safety and also of the council of state appointed in May; he was, too, chairman of the army and navy commission, and soon afterwards of another special commission for the navy. In September he was made president of the council. He had, morever, in May, been appointed with Lambert and others to treat with the Dutch ambassador for freeing the commerce of the Baltic. When Monk arrived in London Vane was ordered to his seat in Lincolnshire, having been discharged from the parliament for espousing the cause of the army.

At the Restoration Vane was imprisoned in the Tower by the king's order. After several conferences between the Houses of Parliament it was agreed that he should be excepted from the indemnity bill, but that a petition should be sent to Charles asking that his life might be spared. The petition was granted. During the conferences he had been moved from prison to prison, and was finally placed in a castle in the Scilly Isles. In his captivity he wrote the *People's Case Stated*, with many other political and religious works of the highest eloquence and beauty. On 7th March 1662, the Convention Parliament being no longer in existence, he was taken to London, and on 2d June put upon his trial, which was conducted with a shameless absence of equity. He was refused the assistance of counsel and was not allowed to see the indictment before it was read. In his own behalf he spoke courageously and well, pleading the authority of the Long Parliament for his acts, and maintaining that the House of Commons, "representing the whole body of the people in case of a difference between the authority, royal and politic, possessed a just power to defend the right of the people, and to authorize the people of England and every one of them to defend them." Charles, however, was determined that he should die, and, in spite of his answer to the petition mentioned above, wrote himself to Clarendon declaring that Vane was "too dangerous a man to let live, if we can honestly put him out of the way." He was therefore sentenced on 11th June to death. On the 14th he was taken out to execution, and died with the serenity and courage which had marked his life. (O. A.)

VANILLA, a flavouring agent largely used in the manufacture of chocolate, in confectionery, and in perfumery. It consists of the fermented and dried pods of several species of orchids belonging to the genus *Vanilla*.[1] The great bulk of the commercial article is the produce of *V. planifolia*, Andrews, a native of eastern Mexico, but now largely cultivated in several tropical countries, especially in Réunion, the Seychelles, and Java. The plant has a long fleshy stem and attaches itself by its aerial rootlets to trees, and appears to be little dependent on the soil for nourishment. The leaves are alternate, oval-lanceolate, and fleshy; and the greenish white flowers form axillary

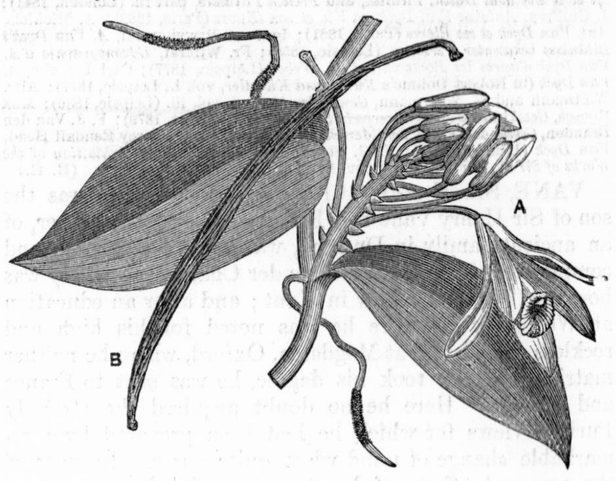

Vanilla plant. A. Flower, leaf, and aerial rootlets. B. Pod or fruit.

spikes. The fruit is a pod from 6 to 12 inches long, and when mature about half an inch in diameter. The wild plant yields a smaller and less aromatic fruit, distinguished in Mexico as *Baynilla cimarona*, the cultivated vanilla being known as *B. corriente*. Mexican vanilla is regarded as the best. It is principally consumed in the United States, which import about 100,000 ℔ of it annually. Réunion produces about the same quantity, which is sent to Bordeaux, the chief centre of the trade in France. Its odour is said to differ from the Mexican variety in having a suggestion of tonqua bean. Guadaloupe produces about 5000 ℔ per annum, which is likewise shipped to Bordeaux. Mauritius exported 20,481 ℔ in 1877. The Seychelles have lately produced large quantities of exceedingly fine quality; the produce of these islands goes chiefly to the London market. The Java vanilla, grown chiefly in Krawang and the Preanger Regencies, is shipped to Holland. The amount exported from the East Indian Archipelago to Holland in 1876 amounted to about 5000 ℔. The best varieties of vanilla pods are of a dark chocolate brown or nearly black colour, and are covered with a crystalline efflorescence technically known as *givre*, the presence of which is taken as a criterion of quality. The peculiar fragrance of vanilla is due to vanillin, $C_8H_8O_3$, which forms this efflorescence. Chemically speaking, it is the aldehyde of methyl-protocatechuic acid. It is not naturally present in the fleshy exterior of the pod, but is secreted by hair-like papillæ lining its three internal angles, and ultimately becomes diffused through the viscid oily liquid surrounding the seeds. The amount of vanillin varies according to the kind: Mexican vanilla yields 1·69, Bourbon or Réunion 1·9 to 2·48, and Java 2·75 per cent. Besides vanillin, the pods contain vanillic acid (which is odourless), about 11 per cent. of fixed oil, 2·3 per cent. of soft resin, sugar, gum, and oxalate of lime.

Vanillin forms crystalline needles, fusible at 81° C., and soluble in alcohol and ether, hardly soluble in cold, but more so in boiling water. Like other aldehydes, it forms a compound with the alkaline bisulphites, and can by this means be extracted from bodies containing it. Vanillin has been found in Siam benzoin and in raw sugar, and has been prepared artificially from coniferin, a substance found in the sapwood of fir-trees, from asafœtida, and from a constituent of oil of cloves named eugenol. It is from the last-named that vanillin is now prepared on a commercial scale, chiefly in Germany. Vanillin does not appear to have any physiological

[1] Span. *vainilla*, dim. of *vaina*, a pod.

action on human beings when taken in small doses, as much as 10 to 15 grains having been administered without noxious results. On small animals, however, such as frogs, it appears to act as a convulsive. It has been suggested as a stimulant of an excito-motor character in atonic dyspepsia. The poisonous effects that have on several occasions followed from eating ices flavoured with vanilla are not to be attributed to the vanilla, but probably to the presence of *tyrotoxicon* (*Pharm. Journ.* [3], xvii. p. 150), a poison found in milk which has undergone certain putrefactive changes, and producing choleraic effects, or perhaps to the presence of microscopic fungi in the vanilla, the plantations being liable to the attack of *Bacterium putredinis.* Workmen handling the beans in the Bordeaux factories are subject to itching of the hands and face; but this is caused by an *Acarus* which occupies the end of the pod. In some cases, however, symptoms of dizziness, weariness, and malaise, with muscular pains, have been felt, due probably to the absorption of the oily juice by the hands of the workmen. These symptoms have been attributed to the variety of vanilla known as vanillon, but it seems equally probable that they are due to idiosyncrasy.

The method of cultivation and preparation of vanilla for the market varies somewhat in different countries. In Mexico a clearing is made in the forest, where a few young trees, 12 or 15 feet apart, are left to serve as a support for the climbing stems of the vanilla plant. Close to each tree two cuttings, 3 to 5 feet in length, are inserted in the soil to the depth of about a foot, the upper part being tied to the tree. The cuttings become rooted in about a month, but do not bear fruit until the third year. They continue to bear for about thirty years. In Réunion, Mauritius, and the Seychelles the young plants are supported by a rude trellis made between the trunks of trees. Although the plants are probably fertilized by insects in their native country, in Réunion and elsewhere fertilization has to be promoted by hand. Only the finest flowers of each spike are fertilized, or the plants would die of exhaustion. The pods are cut off separately as they ripen, since, if over-ripe, they are apt to split in drying, and if unripe the product will be of inferior colour and fragrance. The pods take a month to arrive at full size and six months longer to ripen. The exact time for collecting is judged by the crackling of the pod when pinched between the fingers. The aroma of vanilla is developed by fermentation, and is said not to pre-exist in the ripe fruit.

In Mexico the pods, after they are gathered, are placed in heaps under a shed until they begin to shrivel, and are then submitted to a sweating process. They are next wrapped in a woollen cloth and exposed to the sun during the day, or heated in an oven to 140° Fahr. if the weather is cloudy, and then enclosed in air-tight boxes at night to sweat. In twenty-four to thirty-six hours, according to size, the pods have acquired a fine chestnut-brown colour. They are then spread in the sun for about two months to dry, and are subsequently tied up into small packets of uniform length. In Réunion the pods are sorted into lengths and scalded in boiling water, the long pods being immersed ten seconds, those of a medium size fifteen seconds, and the short ones for fully one minute. They are next exposed to the sun between woollen blankets for about a week, until they assume the characteristic brown colour. They are then spread out under zinc-roofed sheds and turned frequently to ensure equal drying. When the beans can be twisted round the finger without cracking, the "smoothing process" is commenced. This consists in passing the beans between the fingers frequently, apparently to distribute equally the unctuous liquid which exudes as the fermentation proceeds, and to which the lustre and suppleness of the bean are due. When dry they are tied up in bundles of uniform length. These are divided into three commercial sorts,—(1) those which are nearly black and glossy and which soon become frosted; (2) those which are lighter in colour, more or less spotted with grey, and not so glossy; (3) those which are gathered in an unripe condition and become little, if at all, frosted over with crystals. In Guiana, where an inferior quality is prepared, the beans are placed on ashes and left until they begin to shrivel; they are then wiped, rubbed over with oil, and, the lower end of the pod having been tied, are hung up in the air to dry.

Other Varieties.—In Brazil, Peru, and other parts of South America a broad and fleshy vanilla is prepared, which has an inferior odour. It is believed to be obtained from *V. pompona*, Schiede, which has been found to contain, besides from ·4 to ·7 per cent. of vanillin, another ingredient, benzaldehyde, by which the odour of vanilla is modified. This variety is often distinguished as vanillon in commerce. It is destitute of *givre.* Rio vanilla is collected on the banks of the Parahyba river in the province of Rio de Janeiro, Brazil, and is obtained from *V. palmarum*, Lindl. It has been found to yield 1·03 per cent. of vanillin. It is of inferior quality, but might be improved if more attention were paid to the curing process. Guiana vanilla is a coarse variety obtained from *V. guianensis*, Splitberger. The pods are short, thick, and frequently split open, and of inferior fragrance. None of the South-American vanillas appear to be used in Great Britain for flavouring purposes, but solely for perfumery. (E. M. H.)

VANINI, LUCILIO (1585-1619), philosopher, was born at Taurisano, near Naples, in 1585. He studied philosophy and theology at Rome, and after his return to Naples applied himself to the physical studies which had come into vogue with the Renaissance. Though unmethodically cultivated and destitute of definite results, physical science powerfully affected men's imaginations in this transition period between the break-up of scholasticism and the rise of modern thought, and exercised an important influence upon philosophy. Giordano Bruno is perhaps the most striking instance of this, and Vanini in some respects resembles Bruno, though much his inferior both intellectually and morally. Both represent the spirit of revolt against the old, the ferment and unrest of the 16th century. Vanini resembles Bruno, not only in his wandering life, but also in his anti-Christian bias, and in the tragic death which he suffered at the hands of the constituted authorities. From Naples Vanini proceeded to Padua, where he came under the influence of Pomponatius, whom he styles his divine master. Pomponatius belonged to the Alexandrist school of Aristotelians, and denied the immortality of the soul. Vanini speaks of Aristotle as "the god of philosophers, the dictator of human nature, and the sovereign pontiff of the sages," but gives the same naturalistic turn to the Aristotelian doctrine. At Padua, where he appears to have remained for several years, Vanini added law to his other acquirements, and he is at pains to print himself in his books as *doctor utriusque juris.* He was also ordained priest; but, on leaving Padua, he led a roving life in France, Switzerland, and the Low Countries, supporting himself by giving lessons and using the opportunity, it would seem, for the dissemination of anti-religious views. He was obliged to flee from Lyons to England in 1614, but was imprisoned in London for some reason for forty-nine days. Being set at liberty, he returned to Italy and made an attempt to teach in Genoa, but the same complaints being made against him drove him once more to France. Here he made a valiant effort to clear himself of suspicion by publishing a book against atheists,—*Amphitheatrum Æternæ Providentiæ Divino-Magicum, necnon Astrologo-Catholicum, adversus Veteres Philosophos, Atheos, Epicureos, Peripateticos, et Stoicos* (1615). It has been said that by the weakness of his answers he designedly gives his opponents the victory under pretence of refuting them; but, though the definitions of God are somewhat pantheistic, the book is sufficiently orthodox. Yet it cannot be taken as expounding his own views. Vanini expressly tells us so in his second (and only other published) work, and the tone of that work would be sufficient proof without this assurance. Though certified by two doctors of the Sorbonne, the second book undoubtedly preaches a pantheism nearly akin to atheism, and a sensualistic ethics strongly tinged with immorality. The title (*De Admirandis Naturæ Reginæ Deæque Mortalium Arcanis*) correctly indicates its general tenor. It was published at Paris in 1616, and was soon afterwards re-examined by the Sorbonne and condemned to the flames. This was the occasion of Vanini's leaving Paris, where he had been staying as chaplain to Marshal de Bassompierre, to whom the book is dedicated. He began to teach in Toulouse, but soon roused the clergy and magistrates against him. He was arrested in November 1618, and after a prolonged trial was condemned, as an atheist, to have his tongue cut out, and to be strangled at the stake, his body to be afterwards burned to ashes. This savage sentence was executed on 9th February 1619. During his imprisonment, it is said, he professed the most orthodox Catholicism, but as soon as all hope was gone gave vent to his true feelings in ribald impieties. He appears to have met his fate with courage, mingled perhaps with bravado. His moral character was loose and vicious, and his writings show him to have been a man of inordinate vanity. Though he possessed unquestionable gifts, neither originality nor profundity can be claimed for him as a thinker. His fate, however, has given him a species of fame.

The best modern account of Vanini is to be found in Cousin's *Fragments de Philosophie Cartésienne*. His works have been republished by Rousselot.

VANLOO, CHARLES ANDREW (1705-1765), subject painter, a younger brother of John Baptist Vanloo (see below), was born at Nice on 15th February 1705. He received some instruction from his brother, and like him studied in Rome under Luti. Leaving Italy in 1723, he worked in Paris, where he gained the first prize for historical painting. After again visiting Italy in 1727, he was employed by the king of Sardinia, for whom he painted a series of subjects illustrative of Tasso. In 1734 he settled in Paris, and in 1735 became a member of the French Academy; and he was decorated with the order of St Michael and appointed principal painter to the king. By his simplicity of style and correctness of design, the result of his study of the great Italian masters, he did much to purify the modern French school; but the contemporary praise that was lavished upon his productions now appears undue and excessive. His Marriage of the Virgin is preserved in the Louvre. He died at Paris on 15th July 1765.

VANLOO, JOHN BAPTIST (1684-1745), subject and portrait painter, was born at Aix in Provence on 14th January 1684. He was instructed in art by his father. Having at an early age executed several pictures for the decoration of the church and public buildings at Aix, he was employed on similar work at Toulon, which he was obliged to leave during the siege of 1707. He was patronized by the prince of Carignan, who sent him to Rome, where he studied under Benedetto Luti. Here he was much employed on church pictures, and in particular executed a greatly praised Scourging of Christ for St Maria in Monticelli. At Turin he painted the duke of Savoy and several members of his court. Then, removing to Paris, where he was elected a member of the French Academy, he executed various altar-pieces and restored the works of Primaticcio at Fontainebleau. In 1737 he came to England, where he attracted attention by his portrait of Colley Cibber and of Owen McSwiny, the theatrical manager; the latter, like many other of Vanloo's works, was engraved in mezzotint by the younger Faber. He also painted Sir Robert Walpole, whose portrait by Vanloo in his robes as chancellor of the exchequer is in the National Portrait Gallery (London), and the Prince and Princess of Wales. He did not, however, practise long in England, for his health failing he retired to Paris in 1742, and afterwards to Aix, where he died on 19th December 1745. His likenesses were striking and faithful, but seldom flattering, and his heads are forcible in colouring. The draperies and accessories in his pictures were usually painted by Van Achen, Eccardt, and Root.

VANNES (Breton *Gwened*), a town of France, chef-lieu of the department of Morbihan and an episcopal see, is situated on a little stream, 10 miles from the Gulf of Morbihan and 84 north-west of Nantes on the railway to Brest. The narrow, steep, and crooked streets of the old town, which lie on a hill facing the south, are surrounded by fortifications of the 14th, 15th, and 17th centuries, pierced by four gates and flanked by nine towers and five bastions, connected by battlements. Some of the remains are Roman, and in the Constable's Tower Olivier de Clisson was confined in 1387. The modern suburbs, with public buildings, barracks, convents, squares, walks, and the port surround the old town. The archæological museum contains one of the richest collections of prehistoric remains in Europe. There are also a museum of natural history and a library (10,000 volumes). The cathedral of St Peter overlooks the old town; burnt by the Normans in the 10th century, it was rebuilt in the 13th, 15th, and 18th centuries. It has no architectural interest, but contains the relics and tomb of St VINCENT FERRER (*q.v.*). The curious round Chapelle du Pardon was built in 1557 in the Italian style. Some interesting old houses, including that of St Vincent Ferrer and that of the parlement of Brittany, the rich private collections of M. de Limur, the huge barracks, and three large hospitals should also be mentioned. In 1882 thirty-five vessels (3480 tons) entered and seventy-four (7225 tons) left the port of Vannes, which is accessible to vessels of 150 tons; those of 800 tons can come to within 2 miles. The population in 1881 was 16,667 (commune 19,284), and had increased by 1886 to 18,127 (commune 20,036).

Vannes (*Dariorigum*), the capital of the Veneti, was at the head of the Armorican league against Julius Cæsar, who in 56 B.C. overcame their fleet and opened up their country by six roads. St Paternus, the first bishop, was consecrated in 465. In the 5th century Vannes was ruled for a time by independent counts, but soon came under the yoke of the Franks. Nominoe, the lieutenant of Louis the Pious in Brittany, assumed the title of king in 843, and one of his brothers was the founder of a line of counts who distinguished themselves against the Normans in the 9th and 10th centuries. Vannes became part of the duchy of Brittany under Geoffrey, who died in 1008, and the estates of Brittany met there for the first time after the death of Arthur of Brittany. In the course of the War of Succession the town was besieged four times in 1342. Duke John IV. built here the castle of L'Hermine and made it his habitual residence. In 1487 the town was for a year in the hands of Charles VIII. of France. In 1532 Brittany was definitively united to France. The estates met at Vannes several times in the 17th and 18th centuries. During the Revolution this town was the scene of highly dramatic episodes, including the execution of some of the prisoners of Quiberon.

VANNUCCI. See PERUGINO.

VAPOUR. See EVAPORATION.

VAR, a department of France, formed in 1790 of part of Provence, but reduced in 1860 by the formation of the department of Alpes-Maritimes, so that the Var no longer flows through the department to which it gives its name. Situated between 42° 58′ and 43° 55′ N. lat. and 5° 39′ and 6° 57′ E. long., Var is bounded by the Mediterranean on the S., by Alpes-Maritimes on the E., by Basses-Alpes on the N., and by Bouches-du-Rhône on the W. In the N.W. it touches the department of Vaucluse. The river Verdon on the N. and the Siagne on the N.E. are natural boundaries. The surface of the department is one of the most broken in France; the highest point is in the north-east, where a peak of the Alps rises to 5620 feet and is surrounded by others ranging from 4500 to 5000 feet. These calcareous hills are much fissured and very dry on the higher plateaus, but are rich in springs, which occasion a very beautiful verdure in the valleys. Towards the west rises the St Baume (3700 to 3800 feet), which is connected on the south with the hills above Toulon (2300 feet). The Maures (2550 feet), which extend between the coast from Hyères to Fréjus, and the valley of the Argens form, geologically speaking, a sort of island in Provence, being composed of granite, gneiss, and schists. To the north of the Argens rises the independent Estérel Range (2020 feet), mostly composed of igneous rocks, with some schists and porphyry. The principal river is the Argens (71 miles), which drains the larger portion of the department, traversing it from west to east, and falling into the sea a little south of Fréjus. Its minimum volume is 72,000 cubic feet, even in the driest weather and when most lavishly drawn on for irrigation. Nominally it is navigable for 11 miles, but in point of fact it is used only for floating timber. Draguignan, the chef-lieu of Var, is situated on the Nartuby, the principal tributary of the Argens. Other streams are, in the north the Verdon, a tributary of the Durance, in the west the Huvaune and Arc, in the south the Gapeau, and in the east the Siagne. The coast-line, which is one of the most beautiful and picturesquely varied in France, runs from west to east between the Gulf of La Ciotat and Cape Comarat, then from south-west to north-east between the Gulfs of St Tropez and La Napoule. The shore is dotted from west to east with the sand-covered remains of the Phocæan city of Tauroentum; the little ports of Bandol and St Nazaire; the peninsula of Cape Sicié, 1180 feet high, with its projection Cape Cépet (see TOULON); the roads of Toulon; the roads of Giens, the site of the Gallo-Roman town of Pomponiana; the peninsula of Giens, formerly an island attached to the mainland by two long spits of sand, between which lies the lagoon of Les Pesquiers with its "salines"; the great anchorage of Hyères, shut off from the Mediterranean on the south by the hilly and wooded islands of Porquerolles, Port-Cros, and Le Levant; the bold promontories of the Maures Mountains, dividing the coast into lovely bays; Cape Comarat (430 feet), with a lighthouse; the deep Gulf of St Tropez, with perhaps the best anchorage in all Provence; the Gulf of Fréjus, where owing to the accumulated alluvial deposits of the Argens the site of the Roman port of Forum Julii is now occupied by the inland town of St Raphael; the porphyry headlands of the Estérel Range, with the roads of Agay between them; and Cape Roux (1486 feet). The climate is remarkably fine and mild on the coast, where there is complete shelter from the north wind, but is more severe in the mountains. Hyères and St Raphael are favourite invalid resorts. The average temperature is 58° Fahr. at Toulon, 59° at Hyères. The annual rainfall is 19 inches at Toulon and 24 in the valley of the Argens.

Of the total area of 1,489,488 acres 379,021 are arable, 529,660 under wood, 185,333 under vineyards, 14,857 are meadows and orchards, 49,606 pasture, and 142,466 uncultivated. The live stock includes 8460 horses (many of Arab blood), 13,230 mules, 5420 asses, 3015 cattle, 105,840 sheep (wool-clip in 1879, 234 tons 4 cwts., valued at £10,000), 19,900 pigs, and 14,815 goats. There were 14,380 beehives (42 tons 10 cwts. of honey and 28 tons 7 cwts. of wax in 1879). In 1884 366 tons 15 cwts. of silk cocoons were produced. The crops in 1884 were 1,485,000 bushels of wheat, 13,200 of meslin, 11,000 of rye, 30,250 of barley, 7150 of maize, 2640 of millet, 125,400 of oats, 4,840,000 of potatoes, 2512 tons of beetroot, and 103,000 tons of different kinds of fodder. The vines, reduced by 60 per cent. since 1875 by the phylloxera, yielded in 1884 over 7,000,000 gallons of wine (average of previous 10 years over 29,000,000 gallons). In 1879 olives occupied 77,777 acres and yielded 1,384,856 bushels; four-fifths of the crop was pressed for oil and yielded 5256 tons. Mulberries, strawberries, pears, peaches, plums, figs, almonds, oranges, pomegranates, lemons, jujubes, guavas, and Japanese medlars are grown; and the laurel, palm tree, date tree, eucalyptus, cactus, and sugar cane flourish. An export trade is carried on in flowers, and also in truffles, capers, and onions. The forests are planted with white and evergreen oaks, cork trees, maritime pines, and chestnuts. In the dense, and almost virgin, forest of St Baume are beeches, maples, limes, oaks, elms, yews, and pines, and the flora of the district is botanically most interesting. Var possesses mines of iron, lead, aluminium, and coal (2846 tons of coal, 2075 tons of lignite in 1885). From 300 to 400 workmen are employed in the production of salt and chemicals. Hyères (population 13,170 in 1886) produces annually from 20,000 to 25,000 tons of salt. Marble, plaster, stone, chalk, clay, sandstone, and sand for glass are quarried or dug. There are 200 manufactories of pottery, earthenware, and tiles. Toulon (57,635), La Seyne (12,186), St Tropez (3622), and Bandol, where ships are built, are the chief industrial centres. There are silk, woollen (250 spindles, 6 looms), and cotton (350 spindles, 9 looms) mills, hat, cloth, and cork manufactories (1000 workmen), tan-yards, paper-mills (670 tons in 1879), printing establishments, tinned food manufactories, soap-works (172 tons), breweries, glass-works, oil-mills—in all 173 establishments. There are tunny, anchovy, and sardine fisheries. The department has 140 miles of railway, 164 of national roads, and 2448 of other roads. About half the population of 288,577 (1881) were agricultural, 46,691 manufacturing, and 30,228 marine. In 1886 the total population of the department numbered 283,689. Var is divided into 3 arrondissements (Draguignan, the chef-lieu, with 8562 inhabitants in 1886; Brignoles, with 4393 inhabitants; and TOULON (*q.v.*), 28 cantons, and 145 communes; it forms the diocese of Fréjus, and belongs to the jurisdiction of the Aix court of appeal and to the district of the Marseilles army corps.

VARASD (Germ. *Warasdin*), a royal free city of Hungary, in the county of Varasd, in Croatia, lies about 40 miles north-north-east of Zágráb (Agram), on the river Drave. It was once used as a stronghold, but now only the castle remains fortified. Varasd possesses several churches of interest, a fine new county hall, two gymnasia, and a real school. It has also tobacco and liqueur factories, and enjoys a brisk trade in wood and fruits, especially plums. The inhabitants numbered 13,701 in 1880.

VARENIUS, BERNHARDUS, or BERNHARD VAREN (1622-1670), geographer, was born at Hitzacker on the Elbe, in the Lüneburg district of Hanover. His early years were spent at Uelzen, where his father was court preacher to the duke of Brunswick. Varenius studied at the gymnasium of Hanover and at Königsberg and Leyden universities, where he devoted himself to medicine, taking his degree in 1649. He then settled at Amsterdam, intending to practise medicine. But the recent discoveries of Tasman, Schouten, and other Dutch navigators, and his friendship for Blauw and other geographers, roused in Varenius an interest in geography, and it was in this study that the principal achievements of his life were gained. He died in 1670.

In 1649 he published, through Elzevir, his *Descriptio Regni Japoniæ*, an excellent compilation, which may still be read with profit. In this was included a translation into Latin of Schouten's account of Siam and chapters on the religions of various peoples. Next year appeared the work by which he is best known, his *Geographia Generalis*, in which he endeavoured to lay down the general principles of the subject on a wide scientific basis, according to the knowledge of his day. The work is divided into (1) absolute geography, (2) relative geography, and (3) comparative geography. The first investigates mathematical facts relating to the earth as a whole, its figure, dimensions, motions, their measurement, &c. The second part considers the earth as affected by the sun and stars, climates, seasons, the difference of apparent time at different places, variations in the length of the day, &c. The third part treats briefly of the actual divisions of the surface of the earth, their relative positions, globe and map construction, longitude, navigation, &c. Though the subject as treated by Varenius is crude and ill-defined, still, with the materials at his command, he dealt with it on the whole in a really philosophic and scientific spirit; and it long held its position as the best treatise on scientific geography in existence. The work went through many editions. Sir Isaac Newton introduced several important improvements into the Cambridge edition of 1672; in 1712 Dr Jurin issued an edition with a valuable appendix; in 1733 the whole work was translated into English by Dugdale; and in 1736 Dugdale's second edition was revised by Shaw. In 1755 a French translation of Shaw's edition appeared in Paris. There was also an Italian edition printed at Naples in 1716.

See a paper on Varenius by H. Blink in *Tijdschr. van het Nederl. Aardrijks. Genootschap*, ser. ii. pt. iii., 1887.

VARIABLE, COMPLEX. 1. The solution of a quadratic equation involves the extraction of the square root of a quantity which may be negative. In that case the solution is of the form $a+\sqrt{-b^2}$, which may be written $a+b\sqrt{-1}$, or $a+ib$, putting, with Gauss, for brevity, $\sqrt{-1}=i$. Analysis was, therefore, at a very early stage compelled to contemplate the possibility that symbols of magnitude may represent combinations of dissimilar constituents; but it is only within the 19th century, mainly owing to the initiative of Cauchy and of Gauss, that the whole domain of analysis has been explored from this point of view. A quantity, $a+ib$, consisting of a real part containing a units and an imaginary part containing b units, was called by Gauss a complex number, and the conception of it includes those of each kind, the real and the purely imaginary as they are found from it by making in succession $b=0$ and $a=0$. Quantities thus expressed are subject to all the ordinary algebraic rules applicable to real quantities, and in addition to the relation $i^2=-1$. The occurrence of this symbol i in an identity thus singles out two distinct identities: for instance, if the product of $a+ib$ and $a'+ib'$ be $A+iB$, we have $A=aa'-bb'$ and $B=ab'+ba'$; and in this sense Cauchy, as lately as 1844, still maintained that every imaginary equation was only the symbolic representation of two equations between real quantities. If either or both of the real quantities be variable, the quantity is called a complex variable; adopting the usual notation, it is then written $x+iy=z$. In order that z may vanish, both x and y must do so, as it is not possible for the real part to cancel the imaginary. But either part becoming infinite renders z infinite, and a breach of continuity in the change of the variable z arises when either x or y is discontinuous; but, as long as both change continuously, z is also a continuous complex variable.

2. As long as a variable is conceived to admit of real values only, the distances from a fixed point, measured along a right line, are sufficient to represent it. These may be taken positively or negatively, and in both directions, through all magnitudes, from a vanishing amount to values large beyond conception, *i.e.*, infinite. But, inasmuch as a complex variable $z=x+iy$ depends on two perfectly independent real variables, x and y, its geometrical realization demands a field of two dimensions. When this is assumed to be a plane, to each value $z=x+iy$ corresponds a point P of the plane whose rectangular coordinates referred to an arbitrarily assumed pair of axes in the plane have the real values x and y. Thus to all real quantities in the old sense correspond the points of the axis of abscissæ and to pure imaginaries those of the axis of ordinates. The coordinates of the point P may change quite independently, just as the variables x and y do. If the point P be given, the corresponding value of z is known, and also for a given value of z the corresponding point P is known. The continuous variation of z is exhibited by the motion of P on a curve. The complex number may also be written in the following form, which is found as early as Euler. Joining the point P to the origin O, the line $OP=\rho$ is called the *modulus*, and the angle $XOP=\theta$ which this line forms with the positive axis of x, or the prime axis, is called the *argument* (or *amplitude*) of the complex $x+iy$.

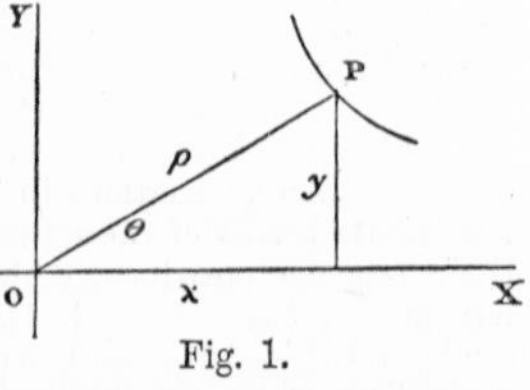

Fig. 1.

Thus $\rho=+\sqrt{x^2+y^2}$, $\cos\theta=x/\rho$, $\sin\theta=y/\rho$, and $z=x+iy=\rho(\cos\theta+i\sin\theta)=\rho e^{i\theta}$. This, again, shows that the variable vanishes only when $x=0$ and $y=0$, *i.e.*, when $\rho=0$, since no real angle makes $\cos\theta+i\sin\theta=0$. In this way the quantity is represented by rotating through the angle θ from the prime axis a line whose length is ρ. The value of the radical $\sqrt{x^2+y^2}$ is always taken positively; the difference of sign arises from a reversal of direction and is indicated by the angle in the factor $e^{i\theta}$. When P is given, ρ is unique and θ is determined by $\cos\theta$ and $\sin\theta$: that is to say, it admits only of a certain value or of those which differ from it by integer multiples of 2π. Thus two quantities are equal whose moduli are equal and their directions parallel. The modulus varies continuously with z, and so does the argument, except when z vanishes: that is, when the curve passes through the origin, the argument then undergoes generally a sudden change by π.

3. Complex numbers form a system complete in themselves, and any process of calculation on complex numbers always reproduces a complex number. Thus, as any such quantity is represented by a point approached from a given point, the result of calculation also has a point or points to represent it. This is illustrated as follows.

The addition of the quantity $z=x+iy$ to $z'=x'+iy'$ produces $z_1=x+x'+i(y+y')$; the point z_1 has the coordinates $x+x'$, $y+y'$: that is, it is the extremity of the diagonal of the parallelogram included by the lines Oz and Oz'. If a third quantity $z''=x''+iy''$ were added on, the result would be represented by the diagonal of the parallelogram included by Oz_1 and Oz''; and so on. Subtraction is the addition of a line with opposite sign. The modulus of the sum or difference of two quantities is found by assuming $\rho_1\cos\theta_1=\rho\cos\theta\pm\rho'\cos\theta'$ and $\rho_1\sin\theta_1=\rho\sin\theta\pm\rho'\sin\theta'$, whence $\rho_1^2=\rho^2+\rho'^2\pm2\rho\rho'\cos(\theta-\theta')$. Thus the modulus of the sum is never greater than the sum of the moduli and the modulus of the difference never less than their difference. The line zz_1 in fig. 2 is found by subtracting z from z_1, and is thus seen to be equal to the parallel line Oz'. The multiplication of $z=\rho e^{i\theta}$ by $z'=\rho' e^{i\theta'}$ gives $Z=zz'=\rho\rho' e^{i(\theta+\theta')}$: that is, we have to measure along a line inclined to the prime axis at an angle equal to the sum of the arguments a length representing the product of the moduli; in order to determine this, the unit of length must be introduced. If this be OU measured along the prime axis, Z is constructed by placing on Oz' a triangle $z'OZ$ similar and similarly placed to UOz. From this we can proceed at once to division; as an example, when $\dfrac{z''_1-z'_1}{z'_1-z_1}=\dfrac{z''-z'}{z'-z}$, the triangle formed by the three points representing z_1, z'_1, z''_1 is homothetic with that formed by z, z', z''.

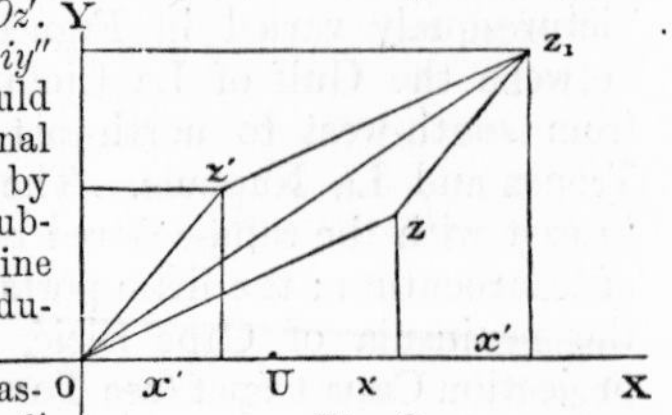

Fig. 2.

In like manner we might proceed to powers of complex quantities with real exponents: *e.g.*, every complex number has n distinct nth roots included in the form $\sqrt[n]{z}=\sqrt[n]{\rho}\,.\,e^{i(\theta+2k\pi)/n}$; then to powers with complex exponents; to logarithms of complex numbers: for example, every number has infinitely many logarithms to the base e, which differ by multiples of $2i\pi$, in accordance with the formula $\log z=\log\rho+i(\theta\pm2k\pi)$; and, finally, to powers with complex base and complex exponent. All these in turn lead again to complex numbers, and to such only.

4. In dealing with real numbers any definite range of values is represented by the points of a finite right line; but to realize a definite range of complex numbers we must have recourse in general to a "region" of two dimensions of the plane bounded by some curve. For instance, all complex numbers whose modulus is less than ρ and greater than ρ' occupy a region bounded by two concentric circles with radii ρ and ρ' round the origin. All those whose moduli are equal to ρ form a linear region, namely, the circumference of the circle round the origin with that radius. A region of two dimensions is called *connected* when we can pass from any point within it to any other point within it without crossing the boundary curve. A quantity is said to be *unrestrictedly variable* in a region when it can assume all numerical values in this region. It is said to be *continuously variable* when all values which it assumes always belong to a finite connected region. Thus a variable is said to be unrestrictedly continuous for a certain value when it can take all the values which belong to a finite region, however small, which includes this value. The variable is restrictedly continuous for this value when the values it takes near this one form a region on whose boundary the value itself occurs, or it may be a region of one dimension. It is discontinuous for this value when the point is isolated, and does not belong to any region. When we know two definite values of a real variable, we know all the intermediate values which it must assume in passing from one to the other; but in the case of the complex variable there is an essential difference: it can pass continuously from one given value to another by infinitely numerous series of continuously consecutive values. In geometric terms, with the real variable we can only travel along the axis

of x, with the complex we can travel along any path whatever leading from one point to the other.

5. When the values of one complex variable $w=u+iv$ are determined by the values of another $z=x+iy$, in such a way that for each value of z within a definite region one or more values can be assigned to w by performing a definite set of mathematical operations on z, then w is said to be a function of the complex variable z. Functions are distinguished as *one-valued* and *many-valued* according to the number of values of w which belong to one value of z, as *algebraic* and *transcendental* according to the form in which the variables appear, and as *implicit* and *explicit* according as the relation is solved for w or not. The course of the function w will accordingly be illustrated by points in another plane or planes having the rectangular coordinates u and v, and its dependence on z will be geometrically a transformation from one plane to the other. A very simple instance is when $w=1/z$, where the transformation is equivalent to geometric inversion. If the explicit function $w=f(z)$ is to be unrestrictedly continuous in the region for which it has definite values, there must be a finite connected area, however small, around any admissible value of z, to which corresponds a connected region of w: that is, u and v must vary continuously when x and y do so. Let z be increased by $\Delta z=\Delta x+i\Delta y$ and put $w+\Delta w=(u+\Delta u)+i(v+\Delta v)=f(z+\Delta z)$; then in whatever way Δx and Δy may converge to zero we must have $\lim \Delta u=0$ and $\lim \Delta v=0$: in other words, w is continuous for a value z when this value can be included in a region such that for every value $z+\Delta z$ within it the modulus of the difference $\text{mod}(\Delta w)=\text{mod}[f(z+\Delta z)-f(z)]=\sqrt{\Delta u^2+\Delta v^2}$ is less than any assignable small number.

6. We proceed to give some elementary examples of functions.

Ex. 1. *The power with positive integer exponent.* $w=z^m$ is a one-valued (*monotrope*) function which is continuous for the entire plane, since $u=\rho^m\cos m\theta$, $v=\rho^m\sin m\theta$ are continuous functions of ρ and θ which do not alter when the argument θ is increased by multiples of 2π. When z becomes infinite so does w, and thus this value z is a *singular* one (*pole*) for the function, as contrasted with a *regular* one, which is such that a function has a finite value continuously changing with z.

Ex. 2. *Any rational integer function of the nth degree in z.* $f(z)=a_0+a_1z+a_2z^2+\ldots+a_nz^n$ is one-valued and continuous for the entire plane and has no singularity, except for $z=\infty$, for which it becomes infinite (pole).

Ex. 3. *The power with a rational fractional index.*

$$w=z^{p/q}=\rho^{p/q}\left(\cos\frac{p}{q}(\theta+2k\pi)+i\sin\frac{p}{q}(\theta+2k\pi)\right),$$

where k takes all integer values from 0 to $q-1$. Each value of k determines at each spot the value of a *branch* of the function, which is therefore a many-valued (*polytrope*) one. At the points $z=0$ and $z=\infty$ all branches have the same value. Thus, if $p/q>0$, at $z=0$ the value of w is 0; at $z=\infty$ its value is ∞. These two points are called *branch* (*critical*) *points* of the function. If we wish to contemplate the values of the function which belong to one branch, so as to have each branch by itself in general a continuous function, we employ the method of Cauchy: that is, we draw from the origin to the point infinity a curve which does not enclose any space, for instance, the positive part of the axis of x. Suppose we let $p=1$, $q=2$, then $w=\rho^{\frac{1}{2}}e^{\frac{1}{2}(\theta+2k\pi)i}$, where $k=0$ or 1. Taking $k=0$, the values of the independent variable and of the function along the prime axis for $\theta=0$ are $z=\rho$ and $w=\rho^{\frac{1}{2}}$; along the axis of y when $\theta=\pi/2$ they are $z=\rho i$ and $w=\rho^{\frac{1}{2}}e^{\frac{1}{4}\pi i}$; along the negative axis of x when $\theta=\pi$ they are $z=-\rho$ and $w=\rho^{\frac{1}{2}}e^{\frac{1}{2}\pi i}$; along the negative axis of y, when $\theta=3\pi/2$, $z=-\rho i$ and $w=\rho^{\frac{1}{2}}e^{\frac{3}{4}\pi i}$; and along the prime axis, on completing a rotation, when $\theta=2\pi$, $z=\rho$ and $w=-\rho^{\frac{1}{2}}$. Hence, for any value of ρ, w is continuous all round the circle, but its ultimate value is different from its initial value.

Thus, as will happen in general with many-valued functions along their branching sections, the values belonging to points alongside of the prime axis having positive ordinates, however small, differ by finite amounts from those for the corresponding points, however near that line, having negative ordinates. The branch of the function so constructed is therefore discontinuous along the prime axis. Accordingly we conceive the plane cut through along this prime axis, and the branch of the function is easily seen to be continuous in the connected surface, which consists of the infinite plane so cut through. Riemann perfected this method of Cauchy and enabled us to keep all the branches simultaneously in view, and thus regard the function as unique and continuous upon all admissible paths without restriction. His process is in the case of a q-valued function to let the variable z move upon q different plane leaves.

Thus, as above, when $p=1$, $q=2$, taking the case $k=1$, let us suppose z to move in a second plane; proceeding as before for the points of the prime axis, we have now $\theta=0$, $z=\rho$, $w=\rho^{\frac{1}{2}}e^{\pi i}=-\rho^{\frac{1}{2}}$; and, when $\theta=2\pi$, $z=\rho$ and $w=\rho^{\frac{1}{2}}e^{2\pi i}=\rho^{\frac{1}{2}}$. Thus, though the rotation has brought w round continuously from the values for small positive ordinates to those for small negative ones, these last differ finitely from the first. Now these final values in the second plane are the same as the initial ones in the first plane; moreover, the final values in the first leaf are the same as the initial ones in the second; hence, if the second leaf be cut through all along the prime axis, as the first was, and if we conceive the leaves to cross one another (as indicated in profile in fig. 3) all along the cut, we have a connected two-leaved surface, called by Riemann a *winding surface of the first order*, to each point of which corresponds a definite value of the function $w=z^{\frac{1}{2}}$, and to each continuous curve in it, whether in the same leaf or passing through both, correspond values of the function which vary continuously; every closed curve which crosses the branching section either an even number of times or not at all leads finally back to the initial value. This conception can evidently be extended to surfaces with a greater number of leaves corresponding to functions admitting of a greater number of values.

Fig. 3.

7. In considering infinite series we must explain the conception of absolute convergence introduced by Cauchy: an infinite series of real quantities is *absolutely convergent* when the sum of its positive terms taken apart, and likewise that of its negative terms taken by themselves, are each finite. When these are not separately finite, a series which converges for some value of the variable is *semi-convergent*. A complex series $\Sigma(u+iv)$ converges absolutely when the u series and the v series are both absolutely convergent. Hence it can be shown that the necessary and sufficient condition that a complex series may converge absolutely is that the series of the moduli of its terms converges. Such a series presents the same value if the sequence of its terms is rearranged according to any law whatever. Thus an infinite series of ascending powers of z the complex variable, $a_0+a_1z+a_2z^2+\ldots+a_nz^n+\ldots=f(z)$, with complex coefficients, is absolutely convergent for any value of z for which the series $A_0+A_1\rho+A_2\rho^2+\ldots+A_n\rho^n+\ldots$ formed by the moduli of its terms is convergent; and *vice versa*. In geometric language, if such a series be absolutely convergent for the point corresponding to any value of z, it is absolutely convergent for all other points equally distant from the origin of coordinates; these are therefore situated on a circle. It is also absolutely convergent at all points within this circle, and therefore the region of convergence of this series is always a circle round the origin. The radius of the circle of convergence of a series is the greatest value of ρ for which the series of moduli converges. It is found by the condition that as n increases indefinitely we must have $\frac{A_{n+1}\rho}{A_n}<1$ or $\rho<\frac{A_n}{A_{n+1}}$. As the terms of an infinite series of powers are one-valued, the series itself, so long as it converges, is a one-valued function of the complex variable, which does not become infinite anywhere. It can also be proved that this function is continuous: that is, if z and $z\pm\delta$ be values of z for which it converges, then $\lim[f(z\pm\delta)-f(z)]=0$, when $\delta=0$.

8. When a variable quantity depends upon two others in such a wav that, if their values are given, its value is

known, it is of course a function of them; but, inasmuch as for real values of x and y, when $z(=x+iy)$ is given, we know both x and y, Cauchy considered any function $F(x, y)$ to be a function of z. On the other hand, Riemann considered a function $F(x, y)$ to be one of z when it contains x and y only in the combination $x+iy$. In fact, if we have $dF=\frac{\delta F}{\delta x}dx+\frac{\delta F}{\delta y}dy$ for any indefinitely small increments dx and dy, inasmuch as this may be written $dF=\frac{1}{2}\left(\frac{\delta F}{\delta x}+i\frac{\delta F}{\delta y}\right)(dx-idy)+\frac{1}{2}\left(\frac{\delta F}{\delta x}-i\frac{\delta F}{\delta y}\right)(dx+idy)$, and if dF must always be zero as long as $d(x+iy)$ vanishes, then we must have $\frac{\delta F}{\delta x}+i\frac{\delta F}{\delta y}=0$. This, which is the condition that, when x and y are perfectly unrestricted (and so may each be complex), they may enter only in the combination $x+iy$, must also hold when they can both admit only real values, in order that F may be in Riemann's sense a function of z. Cauchy called the function *monogène* when it satisfies this relation. The further significance of this relation is seen if we put $dx=\rho\cos\theta$ and $dy=\rho\sin\theta$, whence $dz=\rho e^{i\theta}$ and $dx-idy=\rho e^{-i\theta}$; for then in general $\frac{dF}{dz}=\frac{1}{2}\left(\frac{\delta F}{\delta x}+i\frac{\delta F}{\delta y}\right)e^{-2i\theta}+\frac{1}{2}\left(\frac{\delta F}{\delta x}-i\frac{\delta F}{\delta y}\right)$ depends not only on the value of z but also on the direction θ of the adjacent point. When $\frac{\delta F}{\delta x}+i\frac{\delta F}{\delta y}=0$ we have $\frac{dF}{dz}=\frac{\delta F}{\delta x}=\frac{1}{i}\frac{\delta F}{\delta y}$: that is, for each point z, in case the function is *monogeneous*, there is a derived function with regard to the complex variable, independent of the direction in which this variable is supposed to change. If the relation do not hold, there is a different derived for each such direction. When we separate F into its real and imaginary parts, we may write $F=u+iv$, and the preceding relation becomes $\frac{\delta u}{\delta x}-\frac{\delta v}{\delta y}+i\left(\frac{\delta v}{\delta x}+\frac{\delta u}{\delta y}\right)=0$, whence $\frac{\delta u}{\delta x}-\frac{\delta v}{\delta y}=0$ and $\frac{\delta u}{\delta y}+\frac{\delta v}{\delta x}=0$. Hence further $\frac{\delta^2 u}{\delta x^2}+\frac{\delta^2 u}{\delta y^2}=0$ and $\frac{\delta^2 v}{\delta x^2}+\frac{\delta^2 v}{\delta y^2}=0$.

9. A function of a complex variable which is continuous, one-valued, and has a derived function when the variable moves in a certain region of the plane is called by Cauchy *synectic* in this region, and by Briot and Bouquet[1] *holomorphe*, to indicate that it is like an integer function, for which this property holds throughout the entire plane. Weierstrass styles it an *analytic* function. The property that dw/dz is independent of dy/dx furnishes a geometrical relation between the figure which w describes in its plane and that which z describes. In fact, let values w_1, w_2, w_3 correspond to the values z_1, z_2, z_3, then, if $\frac{w_3-w_1}{w_2-w_1}=\frac{z_3-z_1}{z_2-z_1}$, as already observed, the triangle for the values w is similar and similarly placed to that for the values z; in that case $\frac{w_3-w_1}{z_3-z_1}=\frac{w_2-w_1}{z_2-z_1}$. But, if we suppose z_3 to close up to z_1, then w_3 closes up to w_1, and, if z_2 close up to z_1, w_2 closes up to w_1. In the limit the equality of these quotients for all directions of variation of z shows that the figure which w describes in its plane is in its infinitely small parts similar to that described by z, and two intersecting curves in the plane of w cut at the same angle as the corresponding curves in the plane of z, provided always that dw/dz is neither zero nor infinity.

10. Let $z+h$ be a complex value within the circle of convergence of the series $f(z)=a_0+a_1z+a_2z^2+\ldots+a_nz^n+\ldots$, then we have

$$f(z+h)=a_0+a_1(z+h)+a_2(z+h)^2+\ldots+a_n(z+h)^n+\ldots$$

Now, if we arrange this absolutely convergent series by powers of h, the coefficients are infinite series which can be proved to be the successive derived functions of $f(z)$; thus, when a one-valued function $f(z)$ can be expanded in a series of powers of z, the expansion can be made only in a single manner. We have therefore

$$f(z+h)=f(z)+\frac{h}{1}f'(z)+\frac{h^2}{\underline{|2}}f''(z)+\ \ldots\ +\frac{h^n}{\underline{|n}}f^{(n)}(z)+\ \ldots,$$

which is Taylor's theorem for a function given by an infinite series of powers of a complex variable.

11. We proceed to examine at how many points within a circle of convergence of radius R the function $f(z)$ vanishes, *i.e.*, has a root. In the first place it can be shown that, if R be finite, the function cannot vanish at infinitely many points in the circle without vanishing identically, that is, being zero everywhere in the circle. Hence we can only have a finite number of roots in any finite portion of the plane, and we may suppose none of these to lie upon the boundary circle. If the function vanish at any point z_1, then, when we take the expansion

$$f(z)=f(z_1+\overline{z-z_1})=f(z_1)+\frac{z-z_1}{1}f'(z_1)+\frac{(z-z_1)^2}{1.2}f''(z_1)+\text{\&c.},$$

we have $f(z_1)=0$. We may also have $f'(z_1)=0$, $f''(z_1)=0$, &c. Suppose that the first of these which does not vanish is $f^{(a)}(z_1)$, or that the function $f(z)$ vanishes for $z=z_1$ to the order a, then $\frac{f(z)}{(z-z_1)^a}=\frac{1}{\underline{|a}}f^{(a)}(z_1)+\frac{z-z_1}{\underline{|a+1}}f^{(a+1)}(z_1)+$ &c. Now let this quotient be rearranged according to powers of z, and suppose the function to vanish at z_2 to the order β, we can expand by powers of $z-z_2$, whence we get $\frac{f(z)}{(z-z_1)^a(z-z_2)^\beta\ldots}$, ultimately $=\phi(z)$,—a series not vanishing anywhere within the region. If $f(z)$ were a rational integer algebraic function, we should find $\phi(z)$ a constant, and we see that $a+\beta+\ldots$ &c. $=n$: that is, such a function cannot have more than n roots in the region of convergence, *i.e.*, in the entire plane. Taking logarithms, we have $\log f(z)=a\log(z-z_1)+\beta\log(z-z_2)+\ldots+\log\phi(z)$. Hence, taking for each logarithm on the right one of its innumerable values, let z move from any point A round the circumference of the boundary circle, keeping its interior on the left. Since $z-z_1$ vanishes only once within the circle, namely, for $z=z_1$, $\log(z-z_1)=\log\rho+i\theta$ will become $\log\rho+i(\theta+2\pi)$ when z returns to A. Similarly $\log(z-z_2)$ will differ from its initial value by $2i\pi$; and so for the others. But, as $\phi(z)$ does not vanish anywhere in the circle, $\log\phi(z)$ will return to its original value at A. Hence, if there be ν vanishing points or roots within the circle of convergence, the value of $\log f(z)$ changes by $2i\pi\nu$, when z travels all round the circumference. Conversely, if the logarithm alter by $2i\pi\nu$ as z travels round the circle of convergence, the number of roots within the circle is ν.

12. This theorem of Cauchy's at once leads to the fundamental theorem of algebra, that every equation of the nth degree $f(z)=a_0+a_1z+a_2z^2+\ \ldots\ +a_nz^n=0$ has n complex roots. For we can take the radius of the circle so great that the value of a_nz^n far exceeds that of the other terms; and, writing $f(z)=a_nz^n(1+P)$, the modulus of P can be made as small as we please. Hence $\log f(z)=\log(a_nz^n)+\log(1+P)$. Now as we go round the circle $\log(1+P)$ differs as little as we please from $\log(1)=\pm 2ki\pi$, and so, whatever value we begin with, as the corresponding

[1] The word *monodrome* is used by Cauchy and *monotrope* by Briot and Bouquet to indicate the case in which, supposing z has to move in a certain region, all the paths that lead from an initial point z_0 to any point z within the region lead to one and the same value of w; in other cases w will be *polytrope*. When w is *holomorphe* in a region except at a point z_1, where it becomes infinite without $1/w$ ceasing to be *holomorphe* near this, this point is called a *pole* or an *infinity* of w. A rational fraction has the roots of its denominator as poles; and a function otherwise *holomorphe* having poles is called by these writers *méromorphe*. Some writers prefer the terms *integer* and *fractional* functions.

logarithm varies continuously, the value of $\log(1+P)$ will not have changed by a multiple of $2\pi i$ when we return to the point we set out from. But, since the point $z=0$ is within the circle, $\log(a_n z^n) = n\log(a_n^{\frac{1}{n}} z)$ changes its argument by $n.2\pi i$ in consequence of the circuit. Hence $\log f(z)$ changes by $2\pi i n$: that is, in the circle of convergence whose radius is as large as may be required there are always n values for which the rational function $a_0 + a_1 z + a_2 z^2 + \ldots + a_n z^n$ vanishes. Some of these may be coincident; but in all cases the total number of the orders of the different vanishings is n.

13. If two given points z_0 and Z be joined by any curve of finite length, and if we take as many intermediate points as we please $z_1, z_2, \ldots z_{n-1}$ upon the curve and form the sum $f(z_0)(z_1-z_0)+f(z_1)(z_2-z_1)+f(z_2)(z_3-z_2)+\ldots+f(z_{n-1})(Z-z_{n-1})$, then the complex limiting value to which this sum tends as n is increased indefinitely is called the *definite integral* of the function $f(z)$, formed from z_0 to Z *along the path* prescribed by the equation of the curve. Having first examined, after the manner of the theorems regarding real integrals, under what conditions this sum has a determinate limiting value, we have next to take into account that a definite complex integral differs essentially from a real one in that the path along which the variable z may travel from one limit to the other is perfectly arbitrary. We have therefore to investigate this problem: When is the integral of a complex function a unique function of its superior limit independent of the path of integration? In order to answer this we must recall an important theorem concerning the reduction of a double integral of a function to simple integrals along the boundary curve, which is in fact a case of Green's theorem (see INFINITESIMAL CALCULUS, vol. xiii. p. 58) when confined to two variables.

14. Suppose P and Q are two real functions of x and y which are everywhere within a certain boundary finite and continuous, the theorem is then that the double integral $\iint\left(\frac{\delta Q}{\delta x} - \frac{\delta P}{\delta y}\right)dxdy$ taken over the entire region is equal to the simple integral $\int(Pdx+Qdy)$ taken along the entire boundary of the region.

Taking the positive directions of the axes as usual, we define the positive direction along the boundary to be that for which the bounded surface is on the left hand; then, if we have to exclude any portion, *e.g.*, a circular space altogether within the external boundary, so that the points within it are to be regarded as not included in the region, the positive direction of the boundary is that indicated by the arrows in fig. 4. In all the simple integrals the integration must be effected in the positive direction thus explained.

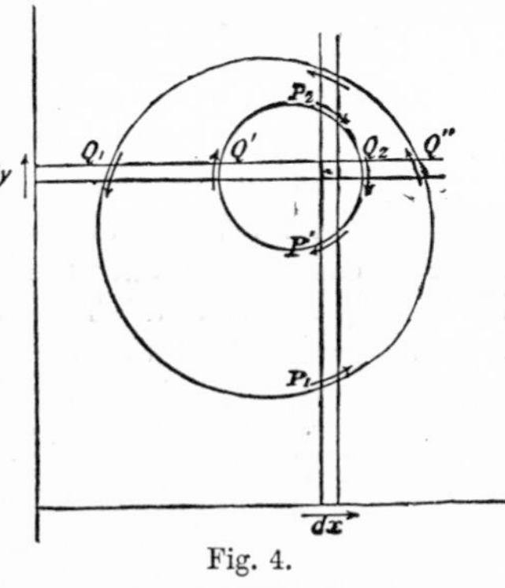

Fig. 4.

To integrate $\iint\frac{\delta Q}{\delta x}dxdy$ with respect to x, let us split up the region into elements by parallels to the axis of x. Select any one and, reading from left to right, denote the values of Q where the element crosses the boundary at the entrances by Q_1, Q_2, &c., and at the exits by Q', Q'', &c.; then $\int\frac{\delta Q}{\delta x}dx = -Q_1 + Q' - Q_2 + Q'' - \text{\&c.}$, and thus $\iint\frac{\delta Q}{\delta x}dxdy = \int -Q_1 dy + \int Q'dy + \int -Q_2 dy + \int Q''dy - \text{\&c.}$ Now in each of these integrals y goes through all its values from the least to the greatest, therefore dy is always to be taken positively. But, denoting by dy_1, dy_2, &c., and by dy', dy'', &c., the projections on the axis of y of the arcs of the boundary cut by the element as above, when we take the positive direction of the boundary into account, we have $dy = -dy_1 = -dy_2 = \text{\&c.} \quad = +dy' = +dy'' = \text{\&c.}$; thus $\iint\frac{\delta Q}{\delta x}dxdy = \int Q_1 dy_1 + \int Q'dy' + \int Q_2 dy_2 + \text{\&c.} = \int Qdy$, where this is taken along the entire boundary in the positive direction. In like manner, dividing the region into elements parallel to the axis of y, and denoting the values of P at the entrances, proceeding from below upwards, by P_1, P_2, &c., and at the exits by P', P'', &c., we have $\iint\frac{\delta P}{\delta y}dxdy = -\int P_1 dx + \int P'dx - \int P_2 dx + \text{\&c.}$, where dx is positive. Hence, as before, taking account of the positive direction of the boundary, $dx = +dx_1 = +dx_2 = \text{\&c.} = -dx' = -dx'' = \text{\&c.}$, and consequently $\iint\frac{\delta P}{\delta y}dxdy = -\int P_1 dx_1 - \int P'dx' - \int P_2 dx_2 - \text{\&c.} = -\int Pdx$, taking the integral in the positive direction along the entire boundary. Accordingly, putting these both together, we have the surface integral $\iint\left(\frac{\delta Q}{\delta x} - \frac{\delta P}{\delta y}\right)dxdy = \int(Pdx+Qdy)$, taken positively along the entire boundary. This proposition may be extended to complex values: when $P = P' + iP''$ and $Q = Q' + iQ''$, as the proposition is already proved for real values, we can put $\iint\left(\frac{\delta Q}{\delta x} - \frac{\delta P}{\delta y}\right)dxdy = \iint\left(\frac{\delta Q'}{\delta x} - \frac{\delta P'}{\delta y}\right)dxdy + i\iint\left(\frac{\delta Q''}{\delta x} - \frac{\delta P''}{\delta y}\right)dxdy$; then, applying it to each of these, $\iint\left(\frac{\delta Q}{\delta x} - \frac{\delta P}{\delta y}\right)dxdy = \int(P'dx + Q'dy) + i\int(P''dx + Q''dy) = \int(Pdx+Qdy)$. We assumed that there were no branch-points within the region, or other points at which P or Q are discontinuous. If there were such, we should have to surround them with actual closed lines, as small as we please, and thus exclude them, introducing these lines as parts of the boundary of the region.

15. We can now let $P=f(z)$, $Q=if(z)$. We see that, if $f(z)$ be an analytic function of z without exception in any simply connected region, $\int f(z)dz = 0$ when taken all round the boundary of that region. If we take any two paths from z_0 to Z in this region, since these paths from z_0 through A to Z and back through B to z_0 include such a region, we have $I(z_0AZBz_0) = 0$ or $I(z_0AZ) + I(ZBz_0) = 0$. But, as the value of the integral $I(ZBz_0) = -I(z_0BZ)$ along the same path, the last equation becomes $I(z_0AZ) = I(z_0BZ)$, or the value with which the integral starting from z_0 arrives at Z is independent of the path travelled under the conditions supposed: it is a function of the upper limit only. The path z_0BZ is said to be *reconcilable* with the path z_0AZ. If the region within which $f(z)$ is an analytic function be multiply connected, $\int f(z)dz$ vanishes when taken positively all round the boundary. The integral has a definite value along each separate boundary curve. For instance, if within the region we take a closed curve which includes a simply connected region, as α in fig. 5, the integral along this curve vanishes. But for a curve which includes a region along with a boundary curve, as β in fig. 5, the integral has the same value as it has for this boundary curve. Whence, if a function $f(z)$ which has to be integrated lose the character of an analytic function in isolated places,

these must be excluded by surrounding them by curves as near them as we please and taking these curves as part of the boundary; it can then be integrated in the multiply connected region so found. The integral for the boundary of such a place may vanish or not. If not, the integral function is many-valued and branches at this place. If it vanish, the integral remains one-valued, but the point may still be a singular one for the integral: that is, the integral may at it cease to be finite or to be an analytic function.

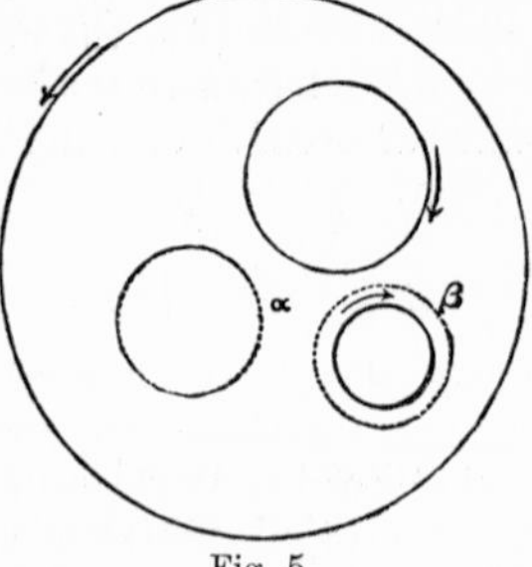

Fig. 5.

16. If we know the value of any function and those of all its derived functions at any one point, and if we know that it is an analytic function within a finite connected region,—that is, that it is unique, continuous, and has a determinate first derived,—then Taylor's series for it converges throughout a circle round this point, which is included within the region; and for each point within the region the function can be developed in a similar series. In other words, every function which is analytic without exception in a connected region can be expanded around each point of the region in a series of ascending positive integer powers. The method in which we show this is due to Cauchy. Let $f(z)$ be an analytic function without any exception in a simply connected region (including the boundary); then, if $t=u+iv$ be any point within the region, the quotient $\frac{f(z)}{z-t}$ is likewise an analytic function within the region, only the point $z=t$ is a singular one. Surrounding t by a circle whose radius ρ is as small as we please, we obtain a region bounded by two curves in which the quotient is analytic without exception. Hence, integrating the quotient along both boundaries, the sum of both integrals vanishes. In regard to the small circle put $z-t=\rho e^{i\theta}$; therefore we get $dz=i\rho e^{i\theta}d\theta$, and for it $\int\frac{f(z)}{z-t}dz=-i\int_0^{2\pi}f(t+\rho e^{i\theta})d\theta$. Now f is continuous near $z=t$. Hence ρ can be taken so small that for all values of θ the difference of $f(t)$ and $f(t+\rho e^{i\theta})$ may be less than δ, where the modulus of δ is as small as we please. Hence $i\int_0^{2\pi}f(t+\rho e^{i\theta})d\theta$ and $i\int_0^{2\pi}f(t)d\theta=2i\pi f(t)$ differ by a quantity whose modulus is less than that of $2\pi\delta$: thus, whatever be the value of ρ, we have $i\int_0^{2\pi}f(t+\rho e^{i\theta})d\theta=2i\pi f(t)$. Hence we have $\int\frac{f(z)}{z-t}dz-2i\pi f(t)=0$, or $f(t)=\frac{1}{2i\pi}\int\frac{f(z)}{z-t}dz$, when the integral is taken positively along the outer boundary, and so along any curve which includes the point t. This is what Cauchy called the *residue* of the quotient function relative to its infinite t. We thus see that, when the values of a function $f(z)$ are given along a closed curve, and the function is analytic without exception within this curve, the value of $f(z)$ can be found for each internal point by means of a definite integral.

It was assumed that $f(z)$ has throughout a derived. This can be exhibited as a definite integral. In fact $\frac{f(t+\Delta t)-f(t)}{\Delta t}=\frac{1}{2i\pi}\int f(z)\frac{dz}{(z-t-\Delta t)(z-t)}$; whence, letting Δt converge to zero, $f'(t)=\frac{1}{2i\pi}\int\frac{f(z)dz}{(z-t)^2}$, where the integral may be taken along any path round t, provided it remain within the original region. But it follows that throughout this $f'(t)$ also is an analytic function, for, as before, $f''(t)=\frac{2.1}{2i\pi}\int\frac{f(z)dz}{(z-t)^3}$. In like manner $f^{(n)}(t)=\frac{\lfloor n}{2i\pi}\int\frac{f(z)dz}{(z-t)^{n+1}}$. Thus for all points in the region the function has higher deriveds of all orders, and they are all analytic functions.

17. We can now develop the function $f(t)$ in a series of powers. Let us select a point a, otherwise arbitrary, such that the largest possible circle which can be drawn round it without going outside the region may include the point t, for which the function is to be expanded. For every point on the circumference of this circle we have $\text{mod}(t-a)<\text{mod}(z-a)$; and therefore $\frac{1}{z-t}=\frac{1}{z-a}\frac{1}{1-\frac{t-a}{z-a}}$ $=\frac{1}{z-a}\left\{1+\frac{t-a}{z-a}+\frac{(t-a)^2}{(z-a)^2}+\frac{(t-a)^3}{(z-a)^3}+\ldots\right\}$ is a convergent series. Now, substituting this in the equation $f(t)=\frac{1}{2i\pi}\int\frac{f(z)}{z-t}dz$ and taking the circle as curve of integration, we find $f(t)=\frac{1}{2i\pi}\left\{\int\frac{f(z)}{z-a}dz+(t-a)\int\frac{f(z)}{(z-a)^2}dz+(t-a)^2\int\frac{f(z)}{(z-a)^3}dz+\&c.\right\}$, which by the equations already established may also be written $f(t)=f(a)+(t-a)f'(a)+\frac{(t-a)^2}{1.2}f''(a)+\frac{(t-a)^3}{1.2.3}f'''(a)+\ldots$. This expansion converges unconditionally for all values of t within the circle round a which does not go outside the original region. This is Taylor's series for a complex function, and this deduction of it shows definitely how far its convergence extends, namely, to all points t which are less distant from a than the nearest point of discontinuity or of ramification. Thus a function whose value, as well as those of all its derived functions, is known for a point is analytic in the neighbourhood of this point only when a finite circle, however small, can be assigned within which this series converges. The series arrived at will, in general, not converge for all values of t within the original region in which $f(z)$ was assumed to be analytic. But we can vary the centre a so as to arrive at a circle, and thereby at a development, which embraces any such required point. If t be at a finite distance, however small, from the circle, draw any curve from a to t which shall be always at a finite distance from the boundaries. Let the circle round a meet this curve in the point a' between a and t: then by means of the series we can calculate the function f and its deriveds for a point on the curve and within the circle as near as we please to a', and thus take this as the centre of a new development all whose coefficients are known. The new circle of convergence cuts the curve in a point a'', which is certainly nearer to t. The continuation of this process must ultimately lead to a circle which includes the point t, since the radii cannot diminish below a finite assignable quantity, the path $a\,a'\,a''\ldots t$ being always at finite distance from the boundaries. By this process we can also carry on an analytic function that is defined by a series of powers beyond its circle of convergence into a region which does not contain any singular point. Each such series of powers defines the function for a determinate circular region of convergence, and is said to be an *element* of the function. Different elements of the function are got according to the centre chosen for the expansion, and even the same value of the argument belongs to different elements of the function; but for a unique function the different elements must lead to the same value for the same argument. Two or more analytic functions, however defined within given regions, are to be regarded as belonging to the same function only when the elements of one function can be derived from those of the others.

18. We conclude with illustrating by a few applica-

tions to elliptic functions of a complex variable. Calling $R(z)=(z-a)(z-b)(z-c)(z-d)$, then $\sqrt{R(z)}$ will be expressed as a unique function by means of a two-leaved Riemann's surface. Its branches take the same values at each of the points a, b, c, d. Let the leaves be pierced through and joined transversely along the lines a to b and c to d (fig. 6). Assume that in the upper leaf $\sqrt{R(z)}$ at the origin is $+R$ and in the under leaf is $-R$. Every path which, when projected on the upper leaf, goes an odd number of times round an odd number of branch-points leads from one leaf into the other; on the other hand, a path which goes an even number of times round an odd number of branch-points, or which goes round an even number of branch-points, ends in the leaf in which it originally began. Now let us investigate what changes in value accrue to $\int \frac{dz}{\sqrt{R(z)}}$ and to $\int \sqrt{R(z)}dz$ when z describes part of a vanishing circle round the branch-point a. First, let $z=a+\rho e^{i\theta}$, then $dz=i\rho e^{i\theta}d\theta$, $R(z)=\rho e^{i\theta}(a-b+\rho e^{i\theta})(a-c+\rho e^{i\theta})(a-d+\rho e^{i\theta})=\rho e^{i\theta}S$. Hence $\frac{dz}{\sqrt{R(z)}}=i\rho^{\frac{1}{2}}e^{i\theta/2}\frac{d\theta}{\sqrt{S}}$ and $\sqrt{R(z)}\,.\,dz=i\rho^{\frac{3}{2}}e^{\frac{3}{2}i\theta}d\theta\sqrt{S}$. But, when ρ is evanescent, $\lim\sqrt{S}=\sqrt{[(a-b)(a-c)(a-d)]}=T$, and is therefore neither infinitely great nor evanescent; integrating therefore between θ_0 and θ_1, we find $\lim\sqrt{\rho}\,.\,\frac{i}{T}\int_{\theta_0}^{\theta_1}e^{i\theta/2}d\theta$ and $\lim\sqrt{\rho^3}\frac{i}{T}\int_{\theta_0}^{\theta_1}e^{\frac{3}{2}i\theta}d\theta$. Since these vanish when ρ does, and the other factors are not infinite, we see that, when $\int\frac{dz}{\sqrt{R(z)}}$ and $\int\sqrt{R(z)}dz$ are taken along paths surrounding indefinitely closely a single branch-point, both these integrals vanish.

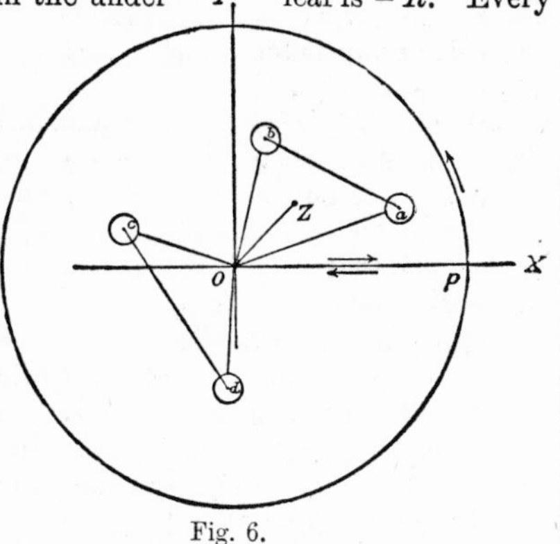

Fig. 6.

If now we confine our attention to the integral of the first kind, let z go from the origin in the upper leaf along a straight line to near the point a; then the integral $\int\frac{dz}{\sqrt{R(z)}}$, putting $y=mx$ in $z=x+iy=(1+im)x$, may be calculated as for a real variable, and it increases by $\int_0^a\frac{dz}{\sqrt{R(z)}}$. Next let z go round a in a vanishing circle, the integral gains nothing; then let z return to the origin along the same line, it proceeds now in the lower leaf; thus both $\sqrt{R(z)}$ and dz have signs opposite, but values equal to, what they had on the outward path. Thus on the whole by travelling this elementary contour (*lacet*, *Schleife*) from O to near a, round a, and back to O, the value of the integral is increased by $A=2\int_0^a\frac{dz}{\sqrt{R(z)}}$. In like manner we have for the elementary contours or loops round b, c, d the three increments $B=2\int_0^b\frac{dz}{\sqrt{R(z)}}$, $C=2\int_0^c\frac{dz}{\sqrt{R(z)}}$, and $D=2\int_0^d\frac{dz}{\sqrt{R(z)}}$.

19. Now, if the loop round a be described twice in succession, the integral changes by $A-A=0$ and so on. But if, after a is once described, b is described once, the change is $A-B$. If then z go straight to any arbitrary point for which the value of the rectilinear integral is w, the value along the entire path, or along any path reconcilable with it, is $A-B+w$. The two loops round a and b may be taken as often as we please before going by the straight course from O to z; thus $A-B$ is a *period* of the integral, which is accordingly an infinitely many-valued function of z. As there are three independent differences of any four quantities, it would seem as if there should be three periods; but we can show that $A-D$ arises from a combination of $A-B$ and $A-C$. In fact, describe round the origin a circle to include all the four points; then let z go straight from the origin to a point p on this circle, travel round it positively, and return from p to the origin. The integral has along this path the same value as along the four loops in succession, since between the two paths there is not any singular point and both have the same origin and goal. Thus the value of the integral along this path is $A-B+C-D$. But, when z goes round the circle from p, the radical changes sign four times. If loops be described from p round a, b, c, d, they are reconcilable with the circumference of the circle. Hence the radical has the same sign when it returns to p as that it set out with; accordingly, since along Op and pO the radical has the same sign, the integrals $I(\mathrm{O}p)$ and $I(p\mathrm{O})$ cancel, and the integral along the four loops in succession has the same value as along the circle alone. To find this value, put $z=\rho e^{i\theta}$ and it becomes

$$\frac{i}{\rho}\int_{\theta_0}^{\theta_0+2\pi}\frac{e^{i\theta}d\theta}{\sqrt{\left(e^{i\theta}-\frac{a}{\rho}\right)\left(e^{i\theta}-\frac{b}{\rho}\right)\left(e^{i\theta}-\frac{c}{\rho}\right)\left(e^{i\theta}-\frac{d}{\rho}\right)}}.$$

But, as the radical is unique along the circumference of the circle, the value of this integral is the same whatever be the value of ρ, provided it be large enough to include all the singular points. Hence we can let ρ increase indefinitely and then this has the limiting value zero. Consequently $A-B+C-D=0$, or $A-D=A-C-(A-B)$; thus the third period is composed from the other two. Hence the periods reduce to $A-B$ and $A-C$. It can thus be shown that all values of the integral for all possible paths of integration between O and z are included in the two formulæ $m(A-B)+n(A-C)+w$ and $m(A-B)+n(A-C)+A-w$.

20. If a new variable z' be introduced, homographically related to z by the equation $\alpha+\beta z'+\gamma z+\delta zz'=0$, it transforms the integral $\int\frac{dz}{\sqrt{R(z)}}$ into $(\alpha\delta-\beta\gamma)\int\frac{dz'}{\sqrt{R_1(z')}}$. The coefficients of $R_1(z')$ can be determined so that it may differ only by a constant multiplier from $(1-z'^2)(1-k^2z'^2)$. As k is given by a reciprocal quadratic equation, it is always possible to choose such a value that its modulus may be less than 1. In other words, it is possible by a homographic transformation to convert the quadrilateral a, b, c, d into a parallelogram, the new origin being at the intersection of its diagonals (fig. 7). This leads to Jacobi's form of the integral when k is supposed real. The integrals along the loops are here $A=2\int_0^1\frac{dz}{\sqrt{(1-z^2)(1-k^2z^2)}}$, $B=2\int_0^{1/k}\frac{dz}{\sqrt{(1-z^2)(1-k^2z^2)}}$, $C=2\int_0^{-1}\frac{dz}{\sqrt{(1-z^2)(1-k^2z^2)}}$, $D=2\int_0^{-(1/k)}\frac{dz}{\sqrt{(1-z^2)(1-k^2z^2)}}$. Hence $A-C=2A$.

$A-B$ is the integral taken consecutively along the loops of a, b; but for these paths we may substitute the following: proceed straight from O to α near a, then round a back to α, then straight from α to β near b, next round b back to β, then again straight to α, and straight back to O. The integral takes the same value by this path as by the other, since there is no singular point between them and both paths have the same origin and goal. Now the radical changes sign as z goes round a, and again as it goes round b; hence it returns to a with the same sign. Thus Oa is travelled in the two directions with the root having the same sign; hence $I(Oa)$ and $I(aO)$ cancel. By decreasing indefinitely the radii of the circles, the circular integrals vanish; and, as the root is negative along $a\beta$ and positive along βa, the value of $A-B$ reduces to the negative double value of the integral from a to β, that is, from a to b for vanishing radii; thus

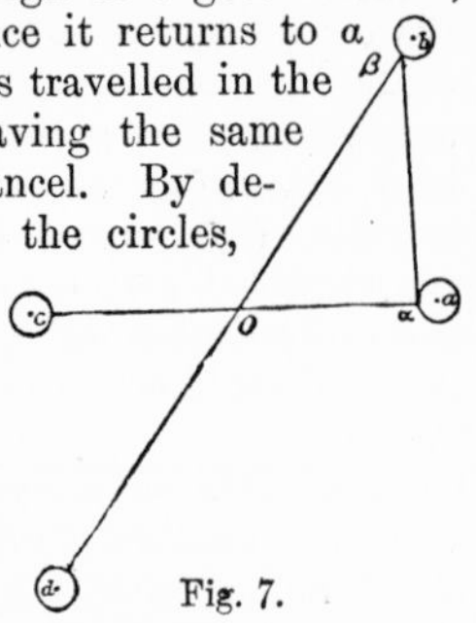

Fig. 7.

$A-B=-2\int_1^{1/k}\frac{dz}{\sqrt{(1-z^2)(1-k^2z^2)}}$. The rectilinear integrals required are now only between the limits 0, 1, and $1/k$, so that they do not cross any singular point. In case k is a positive proper fraction we have in Jacobi's notation $A=2K$, $A-C=4K$, $A-B=2iK'$; therefore all values of the elliptic integral $\int_0^z\frac{dz}{\sqrt{(1-z^2)(1-k^2z^2)}}$, whatever be the path taken between the limits 0 and z, are included in the two formulæ $4nK+2miK'+w$ and $4nK+2miK'+2K-w$. Hence the inverse function $z=\sin am w$ is doubly periodic for $4K$ and $2iK'$, thus—

$$\sin am(4nK+2miK'+w)=\sin am w$$
$$\sin am(2(2n+1)K+2miK'-w)=\sin am w.$$

This last shows that $\sin am\, w$ takes the same value for two different values of w within the same period. In fact, in the plane of w measure a series of parallels (see fig. 8) to the axis of ordinates at distances $4K$, and to the prime axis at distances $2K'$, then the plane will be divided into rectangles such that in each $\sin am w$ goes through all its values

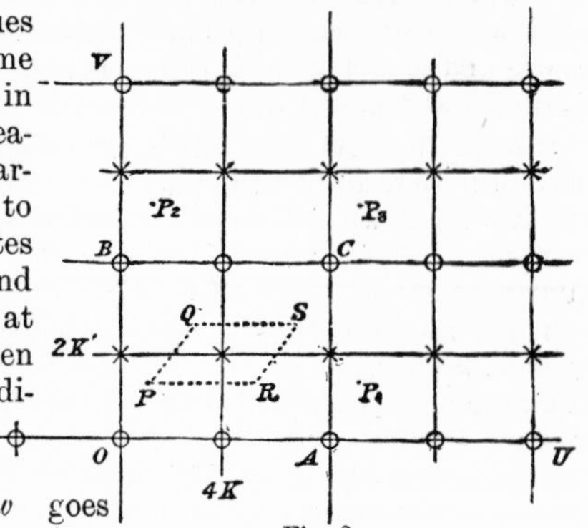

Fig. 8.

and has equal values at corresponding points of different rectangles: thus, whatever it is at P for $w=u+iv$, it is the same again at P_1, P_2, and P_3; at Q, where $w=2K-u+i(2K'-v)$, it has the same value; at R, where $w=2K+u+iv$, and at S, where $w=4K-u+i(2K'-v)$, it has the equal and opposite negative value. The value of $\sin am\, w$ vanishes at the points marked in fig. 8 by circles and is infinite at those denoted by crosses. (B. W.)

VARIATION AND SELECTION

It is not proposed in the present article to trace the successive steps by which the general doctrine of the origin of species by descent with modification has come to gain acceptance among naturalists (see Evolution). The present problem is concerned solely with the determinant factors of evolution, with searching out the mechanism of the evolutionary process, and of discerning if possible such order as may lie under the apparent flux of change. Yet a brief retrospect of the essential views of successive evolutionists is still necessary, but only in so far as these have been concerned, not simply with the empirical evidence for descent with modification, but with the deeper attempt to explain the rationale of this process, to show how it is that modifications come to arise, persist, and increase at all. In other words, just as there are these two essential aspects of the doctrine of evolution, which must on pain of immediate confusion be clearly kept apart, so it is necessary to distinguish between the corresponding sides of its historical development, and, passing beyond the simple hypothesis and evidences of descent, consider the attempts to explain the actual process of modification.

Theories of Variation.

If we pass over the speculations of the earliest evolutionists—De Maillet, Maupertuis, Robinet, Bonnet, &c.—as too vague for rapid summary, and note that Linnæus was not quite a consistent creationist, since he admitted that many species may be simply fertile hybrids, the history of definite speculation as to the factors of variation may be fairly said to begin with Buffon, whose distinct though covert suggestion of the doctrine of descent with modification was supported by emphatic insistence upon the importance of external conditions. He endeavoured to show how "natures, instincts, and most inward qualities" are modified through bodily habits, how new functions seem to arise in response to new conditions, and how changes in climate, food, and other conditions of life bring about direct modifications in organisms exposed to them. Kant, on the other hand, viewed the evolution of species as related essentially to the mechanical laws of the organism itself, although in his latest writings he allowed for the influence of geographical distribution, food, &c., noted the importance of selection in artificial breeding, and even hinted at the notion of struggle for existence, which was soon afterwards more clearly emphasized by Herder (*Ideen z. Phil. d. Geschichte*, 1790) in a striking passage, which may be briefly quoted in free translation: "All is in struggle, each one for himself. . . . Space is too small for the number. . . . Each genus looks after itself as if it were the only one. . . . In this way the whole was preserved. . . . Thus were forces cradled, and limbs counted, and tendencies determined, and the earth came to bear what it could."

Buffon. Kant. Herder.

Erasmus Darwin (*Zoonomia*, 1794) believed that the organism has the faculty of improving by its own inherent activity, that it has the power of attaining new parts attended with new propensities. Yet the strongest and most active animals are those which propagate and hand on improvements. Transformations, too, may be produced in part by the exertions of the organism in consequence of its desires for food, security, and reproduction. Changed conditions, such as climate, have an indirect influence in changing desires, and thus actions, and so finally structure; and they may also operate directly. Treviranus (1802-1831) assumed an indefinite variability of the organism, with considerable power of adaptation to surroundings, and even anticipated much recent speculation in his suggestion of a possible factor of modification in the union of sexual elements. The well-known theory of Lamarck (1801-1809) laid special emphasis on function and environment; for, though the sense of need in association with suitable environment calls out a succession of efforts, and so originates incipient structural modifications, it is to increased functioning that the increase of these modifications must be ascribed, while similarly disuse explains degeneration. Changed conditions produce new wants, nutritive and reproductive; hence changes in climate, or the like, change the organism by changing its habits. Rapid increase is checked by other organisms: the strongest and best-armed for attack devour the weaker, and the less

Erasmus Darwin. Treviranus. Lamarck.

perfect genera are kept down by the more perfect. The less definite view of Goethe included, besides recognition of the conservative or centripetal force of heredity, that of a progressive or centrifugal tendency to adaptation to environment. Oken (1809) similarly regarded all progress from his primeval "Urschleim" as having been in terms of its interaction with the external conditions of life. In 1813 Wells made his now well-known suggestion of the importance of natural selection in determining the varieties of the human species; and in 1831 Patrick Matthew published his much more developed, yet equally disregarded, statement of the same doctrine in its more general applications. In 1828-30 Geoffroy St-Hilaire, afterwards ably succeeded by his son Isidore, denied indefinite variation, regarding function as of secondary importance, and laying special stress on the direct influence of the environment: for instance, it was not so much the effort to fly as the (supposed) diminished proportion of carbonic acid in the atmosphere which determined the evolution of birds from saurians. The veteran geographer Von Buch naturally inclined to emphasize the influence of geographical isolation (locality, climate, soil, food, &c.), and laid stress on the restriction of the area of possible sexual union as bearing upon the origin of varieties. The embryologist Von Baer (1834) dwelt especially upon the organismal nature of variation, on the unfolding, as it were, of new structures; and Schleiden (1838) and other naturalists more or less distinctly advanced similar opinions. In 1844 appeared the *Vestiges of Creation*, which in its later editions (1853) formulated an hypothesis of progress (1) by rhythmic impulse through grades of organization, (2) by another impulse tending to modify organic structures in accordance with external circumstances. In 1852 Naudin argued for the formation of new species in nature in a similar way to that of varieties under cultivation, further attaching great importance to an assumed "principle of finality," apparently a kind of organismal fate. Herbert Spencer, whose weighty arguments for evolution date from 1852, laid special stress upon the modifying influences of environment, this involving changes of function, and so ultimately of structure. Finally, in 1853 Victor Carus argued for a progressive adaptation to changing external conditions. An undefined hypothesis of internal modifiability appears also to have floated before the mind of Owen.

Goethe. Oken. Wells and Matthew. The St-Hilaires. Von Buch. Von Baer. Schleiden. Naudin. Herbert Spencer. Carus.

Summary of these views.

In this succession of variational theories we recognize the repeated general insistence upon every separate factor in the problem,—organism, function, and environment,—the successive authors, in fact, almost falling into as many schools. Yet these are singularly unprogressive: the same hypothesis is stated again and again, but always fails to carry conviction; many employ the merest abstractional explanations, in terms of what is simply the old pre-physiological "vital force" (see BIOLOGY), or attempt to cut the knot by the more or less open introduction of a *deus ex machina*. Even the more definite and scientific theories of Erasmus Darwin, Lamarck, Geoffroy, and Spencer fail adequately to establish in a sufficient number of concrete cases the supposed potency of environment or function, much less of internal or volitional moods, in determining extensive changes; moreover, they are constantly confronted by cases in which any one set of changes seems to take place independently of the other. Hence, despite the deep and unanimous conviction of so many biological thinkers as to the origin of species by evolution, the essential problem remained unsolved. For, until some explanation, rational and concrete, detailed yet universal, of the origin of species should be reached, the cautious naturalist could not feel justified in accepting as a scientific certainty a doctrine which rested so largely upon undemonstrable grounds. Any really new attempt at establishing the doctrine of evolution had thus, not simply to reorganize and strengthen the empirical evidence, by marshalling beside the generalizations of morphological unity of type the facts of more strictly historic bearing,—distributional, palæontological, and embryological,—but also to meet this deeper theoretic want by showing not only that evolution has taken place but how. Hence the importance and rapid acceptance of the *Origin of Species* (1859), for which the time was fully ripe. For it is evident from the preceding historical outline that the view still frequently promulgated of the exclusive and, as it were, catastrophic importance of this work in the establishment of the doctrine of evolution must be replaced by a more uniformitarian and, so to speak, less creationist view. It should not seriously be supposed that the theory of descent which had been held in one form or another by the leading biological thinkers of that and the two preceding generations, with almost the individual exception of Cuvier, had been decisively abandoned by men of science, or that the public which had purchased ten editions of the *Vestiges of Creation* in as many years, and which took up the first edition of the *Origin of Species* on the day of publication, could be quite unprepared for the acceptance of the major thesis of both works. Yet that a lull had taken place is also unquestionable, for the failure of wave after wave of speculative effort had produced a widespread feeling of discouragement, and a tendency to concentration upon more concrete and smaller (for the most part Linnæan or Cuvierean) problems alone, since of these the solution was comparatively sure. The dramatic coincidence between Darwin's and Wallace's conclusions[1] soon helped to gain immediate attention to the new theory; and this was thoroughly developed and retained by the prompt appearance of the first and second editions of the *Origin of Species*. Without entering upon a review of this classic treatise, much less a retrospect of the controversy it provoked, it is evident that it was upon almost all sides so much stronger than preceding attempts, its central doctrine so lucid and obvious a statement of the everyday facts of life, its mode of presentation so temperate yet so forcible, its self-criticism so frank and unconcealed, that its marvellous success was owing far more to intrinsic merit than favourable circumstances. The required re-statement of the evidence for the historic fact of evolution was at last learnedly and forcibly done, and the salient difficulties in its way, like that of the imperfection of the geological record, admirably met; yet this portion of the work sinks into comparative ineffectiveness beside the long-sought *modal* explanation of the process proffered in the theory of natural selection, which was soon seen to throw a new and searching light upon the smallest details of structure, function, and distribution,—in fact, to afford the instrument of a new and systematic interpretation of organic nature. Of this doctrine, then, a brief account is needed, and this may be best given by following as closely as possible upon the lines of the *magnum opus* itself, although the full title of this—*The Origin of Species by means of Natural Selection, or the Preservation of Favoured Races in the Struggle for Life*—is its own best and briefest summary.

Charles Darwin.

THEORY OF NATURAL SELECTION.

Analysis of *Origin of Species.*

After mentioning that his first light upon the origin of species was derived from his early distributional studies, Darwin points out that "a naturalist, reflecting on the mutual affinities of organic beings, on their embryological relations, their geographical distribution, geological succession, and such other facts, might come to the conclusion that species had not been independently created, but had

[1] *Journ. and Proc. Linn. Soc.*, 1858.

descended like varieties from other species. Nevertheless, such a conclusion, even if well founded, would be unsatisfactory until it could be shown how the innumerable species inhabiting this world have been modified so as to acquire that perfection of structure and co-adaptation which justly excites our admiration." Again, "It is therefore of the highest importance to gain a clear insight into the means of modification and co-adaptation. At the commencement of my observations it seemed to me probable that a careful study of domesticated animals and cultivated plants would offer the best chance of making out this obscure problem. Nor have I been disappointed: in this and all other perplexing cases I have invariably found that our knowledge, imperfect though it be, of variation under domestication affords the best and safest clue." Hence the first chapter is devoted to an account of those extensive studies of variation under domestication which later formed the subject of a separate work.

Variation under domestication. A comparison between individuals of the same variety of cultivated plants or animals shows a greater degree of variation than between individuals of any one species or variety in nature. This higher variability of domestic productions is to be ascribed to the less uniform conditions of their upbringing, perhaps in part also to excess of food. Exposure to new conditions must be continued for generations to set up any great variation; but this, once set up, continues indefinitely. Changed conditions may directly influence the whole organization or certain parts alone, or act indirectly through the reproductive system. With respect to the direct action, the nature of the organization seems more important than that of the conditions. The effect on offspring may be definite: *e.g.*, size may depend upon the amount of food, colour upon quality of food, thickness of skin and hair upon climate, &c. But indefinite variability is a much commoner result of changed conditions, and has probably played a much more important part in the formation of our domestic races. The reproductive system is peculiarly sensitive to very slight external changes. Many plants and animals will not reproduce in domestication, even though individually vigorous; others, though weak and sickly, breed freely. Hence we need not be surprised at the reproductive system acting irregularly and producing variations. But that variation is not exclusively associated with sexual reproduction is demonstrated by the case of plants "sporting" through bud-variations. Such cases, moreover, prove the nature of the organism to be of more importance than the conditions.

Changed habits and use and disuse produce an inherited effect; witness the lighter wing- and heavier leg-bones of the domestic duck, the enlarged udders of milch-cows, or the drooping (unpricked) ears of domestic mammals. Variations are often definitely correlated: short-beaked pigeons have small feet; hairless dogs have imperfect teeth; and blue-eyed white tom-cats are deaf. Hence selection of any one character will probably modify others indirectly. Although the laws governing inheritance are mostly unknown, probably most, if not all, characters tend to be inherited. The popular statement that domestic varieties, when they run wild, revert to the primitive stock is unsupported by satisfactory evidence; and, although reversions occasionally occur in domestication, there is no sign of any general tendency to the loss of acquired characters. Except in being less uniform than natural species, in often differing more widely in some single part, and in being fertile when crossed, there are no well-marked distinctions between our domestic races and the so-called true species of a genus. The many breeds of dogs and cattle may arise from more than one species; but probably those of horses and fowls, and clearly those of rabbits, ducks, and pigeons, are each descended from a single species. In this respect the breeds of pigeons are of peculiar importance, since not only carrier and tumbler, runt and barb, pouter and fantail, but at least a score of varieties might be chosen which differ so thoroughly, internally as well as externally, that an ornithologist, treating them as wild birds, would be compelled to grant them specific, and even distinct generic rank. Yet, since all these have indisputably arisen from the wild rock-dove (*Columba livia*), it is clear that naturalists who admit a unity to such domestic races, which professed breeders have often laughed to scorn, should in turn be cautious before deriding the unity of wild ones.

How then have domestic races been produced? By external conditions or habits alone? One of their most remarkable features is in exhibiting adaptation, not to their own good, but to man's use or fancy. We know that all the breeds were not produced as perfect as we now see them, and the key is man's power of accumulative selection: nature gives successive variations; man adds them up, making for himself useful breeds. Skilful breeders speak of the organization as plastic and under control, and have effected extensive modifications within our own generation. Unconscious selection, which results from every one trying to possess and breed the best individuals, is even more important. This accumulated change explains why we so often cannot recognize the wild parent stocks of our cultivated plants, while its absence in countries inhabited by uncivilized man explains why these never yield plants worth immediate culture. Man's power of selection is facilitated by keeping large numbers, in which variations are more likely to occur. Facility in preventing crosses is also of importance, as of pigeons as contrasted with cats; some species are, however, less variable than others, *e.g.*, the goose.

Variation under nature. Individual differences arise even in the offspring of the same parents and tend to be inherited; hence they afford material for natural selection to act on and accumulate, precisely as they would for human selection. (Polymorphic genera—*e.g.*, *Rosa*, *Rubus*, *Hieracium*, &c.—may perhaps owe their protean character to their variations being of no service or disservice, and consequently not being acted on by natural selection.) In determining whether a form should be ranked as species or variety, the opinion of naturalists of sound judgment and wide experience is the only guide, yet this lacks unanimity (see SPECIES): for example, of the polymorphic genera of the British flora alone Bentham reckons 112 species but Babington 251. Wallace has shown that no certain criterion can possibly be given by which to define his convenient working categories of Malayan *Lepidoptera*, &c., viz., variable forms, local forms, sub-species, and representative species. As De Candolle concluded from his monograph on oaks (in which he shows at least two-thirds of his 300 species to be provisional), "so long as a genus is imperfectly known and its species founded upon a few specimens" they seem clearly limited; but, "just as we come to know them better, intermediate forms flow in and doubts as to specific limits augment." The terms variety and species are thus arbitrarily applied to indefinable groups of more or less closely similar individuals. Common species that range wide and are much diffused are those which vary most. The species of the larger genera in each country vary more frequently than the species of the smaller genera. The species of large genera present strong analogies with varieties, which we can only understand if they originated as such.

Struggle for existence. The term "struggle for existence" is used in a wide sense, including dependence of one being upon another, and embracing (which is more important), not only the life of the individual, but success in leaving progeny. From the high (geometrical) rate of increase of all organic beings (slow breeders only requiring a few more years to people a whole district) struggle inevitably follows, either one individual with another of the same species, or with the individuals of a distinct species, or with the physical conditions of life. It is the doctrine of Malthus applied with manifold force to the entire animal and vegetable kingdoms, for in this case there can be no artificial increase of food and no prudential restraints from marriage. The checks to increase are most obscure. Eggs or young animals generally suffer most, and plants, mostly as seedlings, both from germinating on ground already occupied and from animals. The amount of food, of course, gives the extreme limit of numbers, very frequently, however, the attacks of enemies, as of game by vermin. Climate plays an important part, and periodical seasons of extreme cold have destroyed as many as four-fifths of the birds of an observed area. Epidemics, too, may occur. In many a species a large stock of individuals is often essential to its preservation. Complex and unexpected checks and relations exist between organic beings which have to struggle together; witness the profound alteration of the flora and fauna of a heath when planted with Scotch fir, these again being wholly dependent upon the exclusion of cattle. But in several parts of the world insects determine the existence of cattle. Again, red clover depends for fertilization upon the humble-bees, these upon immunity from the attacks of field-mice, and thus indirectly upon the numbers of cats; hence no bees, no clover, and the more cats, the more clover! The struggle will almost invariably be most severe between the individuals of the same species, for they frequent the same districts, require the same food, and are exposed to the same dangers. In the case of varieties of the same species the struggle will generally be almost equally severe, and we sometimes see the contest soon decided (as in the case of varieties of wheat or sweet pea, of the mountain-sheep or medicinal leech). Similarly, the struggle between species of the same genus will generally be more severe than between the species of distinct genera, *e.g.*, the replacement of the black rat by the brown or of the large cockroach by the small. The structure of every being is related to that of all the others with which it competes, from which it escapes, or on which it preys; witness alike the teeth and talons of the tiger, or the legs and claws of the parasite clinging to his hair. The albumen of a seedling favours its struggle with plants already growing around it.

Natural selection. How will this struggle for existence act in regard to variation? Can the principle of selection, so potent in the hands of man, apply under nature? Most efficiently; for, when we bear in mind the constant occurrence of variation, with the strength of the hereditary tendency, also how infinitely close and complex are the mutual relations of organic beings to each other and to their physical conditions of life, and consequently what infinitely varied diversities of structure might be of use to each being under changing conditions of life, can it be thought improbable, seeing that variations useful to man have undoubtedly occurred, that other variations, useful in some way to each being in the great and complex battle of life, should occur in the course of many generations? And, if such do occur, can we doubt (remembering that many more individuals are born than can possibly survive) that individuals having any advantage, however slight, over others would have the best chance of surviving and procreating their kind? On the other hand, we may feel sure that any variation in the least degree injurious would be inevitably destroyed. This preservation of favourable and this destruction of injurious variations are called natural selection, or, less metaphorically, the survival of the fittest. The probable course of natural selection may be understood from the case of a country undergoing change of climate. The proportional numbers of its species will be changed; some will probably become extinct; and these changes would seriously affect the others. Immigration of new forms might occur, with further serious disturbance, or, where this is impossible, we should have places in the economy of nature which might be better filled up. In such cases slight modifications which in any way favoured the individuals of any species, by adapting them better to their altered conditions, would tend to be preserved, and natural selection would have free scope for the work of improvement. Moreover, changed conditions increase variability. As man produces a great result, what may not natural selection effect? The former acts only for his own good, nature for that of the being itself; man on mere external characters, nature on the whole machinery of life; man irregularly and imperfectly for a short time, nature by accumulation during whole geological periods. Natural selection is daily and hourly scrutinizing, throughout the world, the slightest variations, rejecting those that are bad, preserving and adding up all that are good, silently and insensibly working, *whenever and wherever opportunity offers*, at the improvement of each organic being in relation to its organic and inorganic conditions of life. It may operate on characters which we are apt to consider of very trifling importance, and its accumulation of small variations may set up unexpected correlative changes. It may modify the egg, seed, or young as easily as the adult, the structure of young to parent and of parent to young, and in social animals it will adapt the structure of each for the benefit of all.[1] The theory of natural selection is next illustrated (1) by supposing the formation of swift varieties of wolves, much as greyhounds have been developed by man; (2) by reference to the excretion of nectar by flowers, its use to insects, the action of these in carrying pollen, its advantage in intercrossing, and the resultant modification and adaptation of flower and insect to each other through the preservation of their advantageous variations. Circumstances favourable for the production of new forms through natural selection are great variability, large numbers of individuals, the complex effects of intercrossing, isolation in confined areas (yet probably still more extension over continental ones, especially if oscillating in level), and considerable lapse of time, although this by itself must not be supposed to do anything (as if the forms of life were undergoing change by some innate law), but merely to afford increased opportunity for variation and environmental change. Extinction, to which rare species are on the way, is caused by natural selection.

Divergence of character.

The divergence of character brought about by artificial selection in domestic breeds is efficiently paralleled in nature, since the more diversified the offspring of each species, the more they will seize on diverse places in the economy of nature, and so increase in numbers. The greatest amount of life can be supported by great diversification of structure. This divergence of character, with extinction of intermediate forms, explains the difficulties of taxonomy, which are then discussed in detail with the aid of a diagram. This, of course, takes the form of a genealogical tree, and suggests that of "the great tree of life, which fills with its dead and broken branches the crust of the earth and covers the surface with its ever-branching and beautiful ramifications."

Natural selection controversy.

The preceding summary of the classical statement of the doctrine of natural selection should be supplemented by reference not only to the original work, to the corroborative labours of its author, and to the able independent treatise (*Natural Selection*) of Wallace, but to the enormous mass of exposition, argument, and illustration accumulated by subsequent writers, commencing with Hooker and Asa Gray, Huxley and Haeckel, but soon becoming too numerous even for mention. At the same time the history of the controversy which has arisen out of that statement should also be treated, in so far as it has kept within scientific bounds. The leading objections which have been brought against natural selection, together with the replies to them, should all be summarized, as, for instance, Fleeming Jenkin's important criticism as to the swamping of individual variations by crossing,[2] Mivart's vigorous and detailed polemic against natural selection as capable of accounting for the incipient stages of useful structures, &c.,[3] and so on. But this could not be done to the satisfaction of either party without far exceeding the present limits; happily, however, two chapters of the *Origin of Species* (v. and vi.) are generally admitted to have at least made the attempt up to 1872, the date of the final edition, with great candour and fairness. The various constructive efforts to supplement the hypothesis of natural selection by introducing additional factors of evolutionary change should also be mentioned, headed of course by Darwin's own accessory hypothesis of sexual selection.

Huxley's advocacy.

We must not, however, leave natural selection without a fuller statement of its services and claims, and this may most appropriately be taken from the recent and, as it were, judicial deliverance of their veteran advocate, Prof. Huxley.[4] He first points out the grounds of his agnostic position (up to 1858) with respect to evolution as promulgated by Lamarck, Chambers, and even Spencer: "Firstly, that up to that time the evidence in favour of transmutation was wholly insufficient; and, secondly, no suggestion respecting the causes of the transmutation assumed, which had been made, was in any way adequate to explain the phenomena." He then goes on to say—

"The suggestion that new species may result from the selective action of external conditions upon the variations from their specific type which individuals present—and which we call "spontaneous" because we are ignorant of their causation—is as wholly unknown to the historian of scientific ideas as it was to biological specialists before 1858. But that suggestion is the central idea of the *Origin of Species*, and contains the quintessence of Darwinism. . . . That which we were looking for, and could not find, was an hypothesis respecting the origin of known organic forms which assumed the operation of no causes but such as could be proved to be actually at work. We wanted, not to pin our faith to that or any other speculation, but to get hold of clear and definite conceptions which could be brought face to face with facts and have their validity tested. The *Origin* provided us with the working hypothesis we sought. . . . The facts of variability, of struggle for existence, of adaptation to conditions were notorious enough, but none of us had suspected that the road to the heart of the species problem lay through them till Darwin and Wallace dispelled the darkness, and the beacon-fire of the *Origin* guided the benighted. . . . The only rational course for those who had no other object than the attainment of truth was to accept "Darwinism" as a working hypothesis and see what could be made of it. Either it would prove its capacity to elucidate the facts of organic life or it would break down under the strain. . . . Whatever may be the ultimate fate of the particular theory put forward by Darwin, I venture to affirm that, so far as my knowledge goes, all the ingenuity and all the learning of hostile critics have not enabled them to adduce a solitary fact of which it can be said, this is irreconcilable with the Darwinian theory."[5]

Darwin's reasons.

Darwin's own case for natural selection has also been tersely put.[6] "The belief in natural selection must at present be grounded entirely on general considerations,—(1) on its being a *vera causa*, from the struggle for existence and the certain geological fact that species do somehow change; (2) from the analogy of change under domestication by man's selection; (3) and chiefly from this view connecting under an intelligible point of view a host of facts."

Applying to natural selection the accepted tests of a good theory—(1) power of explaining all phenomena and meeting all objections, (2) power of meeting new facts as they occur, (3) applicability as an instrument of research,

[1] In the later editions of the *Origin* a brief account of sexual selection is given at this point, *vide infra*, p. 82.

[2] *North British Review*, 1867.

[3] *Genesis of Species*, 1871.

[4] *Life of Darwin*, vol. ii., "On the Reception of the *Origin of Species*."

[5] *Cf.*, however, *op. cit.*, p. 129, note 4.

[6] Letter to Bentham, 1863, in *Life of Darwin*, iii. p. 25.

and (4) power of prediction,—it seems difficult for the most sceptical of critics to avoid ranking it very high, while to those who regard it as triumphantly surviving this assay the "law of parsimony" appears to preclude the necessity of seeking any further explanation of evolution.[1]

Survival of fittest a *vera causa*.

As no serious critic wholly denies the fact of a struggle for existence, nor even a certain preponderance among the survivors in any given area of those best fitted for the struggle, however much he may consider the importance of these facts to have been overstrained in certain directions, we are fairly entitled at the outset to regard natural selection, not only as provisionally superseding earlier attempts at solving the problems of geological and geographical distribution, but as adequately,—it might almost seem finally,—explaining them (see BIOLOGY, DISTRIBUTION). This claim at any rate must be allowed even by those who deny the importance of natural selection as a substantial factor in evolution in the other sub-sciences of physiology and morphology, and this not simply because it was as experts in distribution that Darwin and Wallace themselves arrived at their hypothesis, nor because all subsequent workers in that field of science have adopted it, but because no valid objection, or even supplementary hypothesis, has ever, as regards this important department of science, been so much as proposed. The survival of the fittest, then, is unquestionably a *vera causa*, and one of no small importance in the study of nature (in fact, in undisputed possession of at least one entire field), as also in the study of social life, from which both Darwin and Wallace were directly inspired.[2] The importance of breeding and artificial selection is also undisputed; nor can some small scope for natural selection in the formation of varieties of wild races be denied even by the most grudging of critics who may be versed in the facts of natural history at all. But this amounts to admitting that natural selection, already the undisputed explanation of distributional changes, is at any rate a partial cause in structural and functional ones; while older explanations of these facts, even if not melting into merely abstractional ones, have not succeeded in gaining acceptance.

Uniformitarianism in natural change.

At this point comes in with ponderous weight the conception by which Lyell had for nearly thirty years been preparing the way for Darwin, that of uniformitarianism in natural change. For, although it was perhaps almost as much owing to the unfavourable opinion of Lyell as to the hostility of Cuvier that the doctrine of Lamarck had fallen into such disesteem, and although Lyell himself was accustomed "to keep the name of creation for a natural process which he imagined to be incomprehensible," he was, notwithstanding, as he claimed and as Huxley frankly allows, "strongly disposed to account for the origination of all past and present species of living things by natural causes," and his influence was, therefore, for Huxley, as no doubt for others, "perhaps more potent than any other in keeping alive a sort of pious conviction that evolution after all would turn out true." For, given the principle of Lyell's work,—"the principle that the past must be explained by the present, unless good cause be shown to the contrary, and the fact that, so far as our knowledge of the past history of life on our globe goes, no other cause can be shown,"—it is evident that "consistent uniformitarianism postulates evolution as much in the organic as in the inorganic world. The origin of a new species by other than ordinary agencies would be a vastly greater 'catastrophe' than any of those which Lyell successfully eliminated from geological speculation."

Bearing in mind, then, the lesson of Lyell, that any efficient cause, even though slow or at first sight trifling, can be shown, if acting steadily for vast periods of time, to effect enormous results, the apparent difficulty of adding up varietal differences to specific ones, these to generic, and these again to still larger distinctions, becomes only the inevitable continuation of that summation of individual into varietal differences which no one can deny to be happening around us. Thus the *onus probandi* that species have not arisen in this way comes fairly to be thrown by the advocates of natural selection upon its adversaries. And, as these come individually to realize, through those concrete studies which necessarily underlie all active conviction on one side or the other, the importance of the masses of concrete evidence which have been steadily accumulating, it is little wonder that their majority should not only have so rapidly dwindled, but actually have changed sides so generally as has been the case. Thus, to cite only a single case,—(1) we are now in actual possession of an unbroken and geologically successive series of fossil horses, perfectly gradated through some forty-five "species" back to a five-toed ancestor; (2) we can trace the continued evolution of the existing species in the bones, teeth, and finest peculiarities of the specimens around us, as well as the increasing differentiation of well-marked varieties through artificial selection; (3) we can see that such continuous improvement of skeleton, teeth, &c., as is now and has all along been in progress, must have been profitable to the animals possessing them in the wild state, just as they now are in the tame (since implying better locomotion, digestion, &c.). Hence we soon come to feel a real difficulty in understanding (1) how the continuous summation of small individual advantages through varietal characters into specific, and even generic ones, can be doubted, much less denied, and consequently (2) how the general applicability of the theory of natural selection to interpret the gradual process of historic change can any longer be called in question.

Variation along definite lines.

At this point it is right to notice that several evolutionists have suggested or argued for the progress of variation along definite lines; but this return upon pre-Darwinian standpoints has been energetically and, it must be admitted, on the whole as yet successfully combated. Thus Asa Gray (1861-76) has argued for variation along definite and useful lines. Nägeli (1865) regarded the acquisition of certain characters which appear to be of no service to plants as offering a difficulty to natural selection, and as affording a proof of some innate tendency in plants towards perfection, corresponding to what Kölliker entitles the "law of creation." Mivart (1871) has maintained that variations are definite, and frequently sudden and considerable. With such positions must also be noticed the continuous and increasing insistence of Spencer (1852-86) upon environmental action and functional change, although spontaneous variation is not excluded nor considerable importance to natural selection denied. Butler in England, and Cope, Hyatt, and other "Neo-Lamarckians" in America, have more fully developed this reaction, for which experimental evidence has been especially sought in Germany by Semper. And, while Darwin himself long continued an uncompromising opponent of all such heresies, a distinct, though partial, change of opinion was admitted by himself in later years, and has been fully insisted upon both by Mivart and Spencer. While in the *Origin of Species* up to 1869 variations are spoken of as "accidental" (no doubt only in that sense in which a scientific man may fairly use the word), and there is ample proof of Darwin's origin-

[1] Romanes, *Scientific Evidence of Organic Evolution*, 1886.

[2] Through reading Malthus, *On Population* (see *Origin*, p. 3 *sq.*). It is worthy of notice also that Herder's early suggestion (*vide supra*) was made in his *Philosophy of History*, Wells's early statement with respect to the races of man, and Patrick Matthew's in a treatise for practical purposes, while an early statement of the doctrine, hitherto apparently overlooked, was made with respect to machines by James Watt (*cf. Catalogue of Industrial Exhibition*, 1851).

ally even contemptuous attitude towards Lamarck, and of his substantial rejection of the comparative importance of function or environment in determining variations, these views are unquestionably modified in the well-known peroration to the *Origin of Species.* The further diminishing importance of natural selection is admitted in subsequent editions, as Spencer has pointed out, in the preface to the *Descent of Man*, and indeed elsewhere; while a recent pungent criticism [1] cites evidence of a certain measure of apparently contradictory and indefinite fluctuation of opinion between increased insistence upon use and disuse on the one hand and upon spontaneous variability on the other.

Pleas for indefinite variation.

Since, however, Darwin never developed the grounds of this diminishing reliance upon natural selection, which still remains the central theme of his works, and that upon which their originality, as well as their importance to the theory of evolution, essentially depends (of course as distinguished from their services in summing up the concrete evidence for the fact of evolution and their vast utility in diffusing it), too much weight must not be attached to such isolated expressions of opinion as those referred to above, the more so as these are nowhere borne out by any general change in the tenor of his works. In the absence of any theory of definite and progressive change, and in the presence of multitudinous variations under domestication and in nature which we can neither analyse, rationalize, nor hardly even classify, we are not only justified but logically compelled to regard variation as spontaneous or indefinite, *i.e.*, practically indeterminate in direction, and "therefore unimportant, except as the groundwork for selection to act on." Conversely, variation must be indefinite, else the paramount importance of natural selection must be proportionally impaired as this becomes definite (*cf.* EVOLUTION, vol. viii. p. 751); for we cannot speak of selecting a course from one line of variation, nor even for that matter in the old sense of "variation" at all. Thus, "if it should hereafter be shown that variability is definite and determined in certain directions rather than others" (in short "fated" rather than "spontaneous"), "the importance of natural selection would not be impaired," since it would still have to be regarded as a *vera causa* in the history of species, yet the function ascribed to it would be practically reversed. It would exchange its former supremacy as the supposed determinant among the indefinite possibilities of structure and function for that of simply accelerating, retarding, or terminating the process of otherwise determined change. It would furnish the brake rather than the steam or rails upon the journey of life; or, in other words, instead of guiding the ramifications of the tree of life, it would, in Mivart's phrase, do little more than apply the pruning knife to them.[2] In fact, its functions would be restricted to those of the third Fate, and would no longer, as at present, be supposed to include those of the second. Under these circumstances it is unnecessary to appeal at length to the unanimity with which the later generation of Darwin's exponents (*e.g.*, Lankester, Romanes, Allen, &c.) concur with all preceding ones in the necessary proposition, that "natural selection trusts to the chapter of accidents in the matter of variation." The thesis thus summarized by Lankester thoroughly permeates the *Variation of Animals and Plants under Domestication*, as may be seen from the brief summary of it given below (p. 82).[3] Special reference must, however, be made to the important researches of Weismann,[4] since these were devised with the deliberate intention of testing "whether, besides natural selection and the direct action of external conditions, together with the correlative results of these two factors, there might not lie concealed in the organism some other transforming power," such as the "perfecting principle" of Nägeli or the like. The results of these investigations have tended entirely to confirm the theory of natural selection in its classic form; moreover, the same naturalist has since adduced weighty arguments against the transmissibility of individual variations,[5] whether acquired by habit or impressed by environment, and thus proportionally weakened the arguments of Spencer and others in favour of the revival of the Lamarckian factors of change. Variation seems therefore to be driven in more and more upon the reproductive function, and thus an ultra-Darwinian insistence upon the obscure and as yet wholly indefinite factor of variation is strongly forced upon us, and natural selection seems more than ever to be our only possible clue.

Darwin's biological works.

Armed, however, with this, we have a consistent means of re-investigation of the whole organic world, in the course of which, not only our existing accumulations, as of taxonomy and of comparative anatomy, acquire a new interest, and all existing lines of research receive a potent stimulus, but the marvellous variety of adaptation comes into intelligibility and order,—a new teleology thus replacing the old. Of this profound change in the standpoint and interest of modern biology we can form an idea most simply, yet most representatively, by glancing at Darwin's own biological works. Before the *Origin of Species* we have the slow and laborious production of the substantial, yet conventional and comparatively arid, *Zoology of the Beagle* and *Manual of the Cirripedia*, while afterwards the well-known and fascinating new series of zoological and botanical discoveries and generalizations were poured out with remarkable rapidity. The many bold and ingenious applications of the theory of natural selection which we owe to Darwin and his school should here be reviewed seriatim; but it is impossible to do more than mention some of them, *e.g.*, the renascence and development of Sprengel's discovery of the relations of flowers to insects, the elaborate studies on *Fertilization in Orchids*, the *Forms of Flowers*, *Insectivorous Plants*, *Climbing Plants*, *Movement in Plants*, &c. Again, the interpretation of the problems presented by bee and ant society led him to grapple with the problems of mind and language, in the *Descent of Man* and the *Expression of the Emotions*; and the systematic application of the conceptions of biological science to those of psychology, sociology, and ethics, which had been commenced by Comte and continued by Spencer, rapidly passed from its comparative philosophic isolation into wide diffusion through the movement of literature and science.[6]

Application of natural selection to biological science;

This passage from the inductive verification of the theory of natural selection to its deductive application as an engine of research is conspicuously associated with the labours of Haeckel, whose *Generelle Morphologie* (1866) and other minor works have a central historic place amid the first fruit and seed of the new movement in German biology, which was henceforward almost completely Darwinian; and they have equally strong claims to be considered as the starting-point of those logical and unflinching attempts to view all problems in the light of natural selection which have since become more common. By transcending the limits of ordinary biological specialism independently of Darwin, and dispensing with his initial

[1] Butler, *Luck or Cunning*, London, 1887, chap. xii.; see also his *Evolution, Old and New*, London, 1879.

[2] "On the Theory of Individuality," in *Proc. Roy. Soc.*, 1886.

[3] See, however, chapter xxi. of *Variation*, &c., conclusion.

[4] *Studies in the Theory of Descent*, Eng. ed., London, 1882.

[5] The reservations with respect to mind and language made by evolutionists so contrasted in many respects as Wallace and Mivart should here be mentioned; see Mivart's *Lessons from Nature*, also his "Limit to Evolution," in *Nineteenth Century*, 1884.

[6] *Die Continuität d. Keimplasmas*, Jena, 1885, and *Die Bedeutung d. sexuellen Fortpflanzung*, Jena, 1886.

reservation as to the possible creation of primeval forms and with Wallace's final *caveat* as to the origin of man, a thoroughly "monistic" view of biology and its kindred sciences is obtained. The systematic exclusion of the traditional teleology and of that operation of the consciousness of the organism assumed by Lamarck (since indefinite structural variations cannot be associated with, much less developed by, definite psychical ones, and still less by any permanent psychical bias or character) also necessarily follows; and along with this goes the conception of the operation of an extra-organismal mind. The struggle for existence is the sole condition of human progress; and the conception of prevalent or predominant altruism, as systematized by past philosophy and tradition, is thus an alloy of sentimental illusion with baser elements. The doctrine of natural selection is in this way fully developed into a substantially Neo-Lucretian philosophy, and, in justice to the logical clearness of the author to whom we especially owe this systematization, it must be admitted that those who grant his postulates, without endorsing his conclusions, have in all cases either refrained from continuing their development or fallen back upon the insertion of some *caveat* or *deus ex machina* at an arbitrary point.

To organic structure and function.

In the same way we have this view of all things in struggle applied to the explanation of the internal structure and function of the organism itself. Once more to quote Huxley,[1] "It is a probable hypothesis that what the world is to organisms in general each organism is to the molecules of which it is composed. Multitudes of these, having diverse tendencies, are competing with one another for opportunity to exist and multiply, and the organism as a whole is as much the product of the molecules which are victorious as the fauna or flora of a country is the product of the victorious organic beings in it." This view has more recently been considerably developed by Roux,[2] and from its logical continuity with the major theory of which it is a corollary is gaining widened acceptance.

With regard to the destructive criticism of the old teleology, which has been led by Haeckel, and aided or acquiesced in by other natural selectionists, it is important to note that the obvious proposition has also repeatedly been urged (*e.g.*, by Huxley and Weismann no less than by their critics, such as Von Hartmann and Lotze), that, just in proportion as our explanation of the origin of organic structures, functions, and adaptations becomes increasingly mechanical, so does an increasingly rigorous teleological view of this mechanism reappear. At most, therefore, we should have exchanged an external and mechanical view of teleology for an (at least relatively) internal and dynamical one.

Sexual selection.

The later hypotheses accessory to natural selection can here be only very briefly outlined. Partly in course of his inquiries into the descent of man, partly also to account for many remarkable phenomena of sexual differentiation in animals (see SEX), Darwin was led to develop the hypothesis of sexual selection which he had already suggested in the *Origin of Species*. Not merely do individuals struggle for existence, but the males struggle for the females; thus the more vigorous tend to obtain mates, and so leave most progeny to repeat the struggle. Special weapons are used in the struggle, both offensive, like the cock's spurs or the stag's horns, and defensive, like the lion's mane; and advantageous variations of these tend to be accumulated. But, as the more beautiful or melodious males appear often to obtain the preference of the females, there is also ground for the conception that the æsthetic advantages frequent in the male sex have similarly been acquired, the more so as we have common experience of how rapidly artificial selection can accumulate superiorities of plumage or song. After the operation of sexual selection has been traced as far as possible through the animal kingdom, the doctrine is applied to man, with the conclusion "that of all the causes which have led to the differences in external appearance between the races of man, and to a certain extent between man and the lower animals, sexual selection had been the most efficient." Acceptance of this hypothesis has been much less general than of natural selection. Criticism has been busy, and this ranges from the serious yet partial dissent of Wallace to fundamental contrast, such as is involved in the theory of the nature and origin of sex suggested in the article SEX, which views the degree of development of the external characters of sex as essentially the outward expression of a proportional stage of the evolution of constitutional "maleness" or "femaleness" (*i.e.*, katabolic and anabolic diathesis respectively).

Physiological selection

Under the title of "physiological selection" G. J. Romanes has lately proposed "an additional suggestion as to the origin of species," of which the more critical than constructive essence may be briefly given in the author's own words: "As a theory of origin of species natural selection has in its way three cardinal difficulties,—(1) the difference between species and varieties in respect of mutual fertility, (2) the swamping effects of free intercrossing upon an individual variation, (3) the inutility to species of so large a proportion of specific distinctions. . . . Natural selection is not, properly speaking, a theory of the origin of *species*: it is a theory of the origin—or rather of the cumulative development—of *adaptations*. Whenever any variation in the highly variable reproductive system occurs, tending to sterility with the parent form, without entailing fertility with the varietal form, a physiological barrier must interpose, dividing the species into two parts, free to develop distinct histories, without mutual intercrossing, or by independent variation. By regarding mutually sterile species as records of variation in reproductive systems, we are at work, so to speak, on the foundation of the matter."[3]

LAWS OF VARIATION.

Origin of variations.

Even those who attach most importance to the doctrine of natural selection as affording a rationale of the process of organic evolution will not seriously dispute that, even were this explanation completely extended to all the details of plant and animal life, another and deeper explanation would still be necessary. That is, the theory of natural selection, being from the external standpoint only—that of the adaptation of the organism to survive the pressures of the environment—would all the more urgently stand in need of a complementary internal explanation, which should elucidate the physiological process of change through which the organism has actually been enabled to adapt itself. As a recent writer tersely expresses it, "The survival of variations is a matter secondary to their origin, and it is becoming realized more and more that this is the point to be explained." How, in short, do we get the variations without which natural selection would have nothing on which to operate? Here we can no longer remain satisfied with the merely general conception of variation as essentially indefinite, with which we have become familiar as the postulate (p. 81) of the theory of natural selection,[4] but must add to it a retrospect of the theories of earlier authors such as has been already outlined,—(*a*) a summary and discussion of the extensive labours of Darwin upon the problems of variation from which this conception of indefiniteness was generalized, followed by (*b*) an account of subsequent progress. Unfortunately the voluminousness of this literature makes such a task practically impossible: instead of the enormous wealth of concrete details accumulated with respect to the *Variation of Animals and Plants under Domestication*, a reference to the volumes under that title must almost suffice. Some acquaintance with this work is, of course, necessary adequately to appreciate the force of its author's general conclusions; these may, however, be briefly outlined from the chapter of the *Origin of Species* (chap. v.) devoted to the laws of variation, and from those (xxii.-xxvi.) of the larger work which contain an ample yet similar discussion.

Darwin's theory.

Environment.

"Our ignorance of the laws of variation is profound. Not in one case out of a hundred can we pretend to assign any reason why this or that part has varied." Changed conditions generally induce mere fluctuating variability in individuals, yet sometimes

[1] A frank and uncompromising application of this doctrine to the interpretation of nature and society will also be found in Huxley's "Struggle for Existence," in *Nineteenth Century*, February 1888.

[2] *Der Kampf d. Theile im Organismus*, Leipsic, 1876.

[3] *Journ. Linn. Soc.*, xix., 1886. For the criticisms of Wallace, Argyll, Meldola, Catchpool, and others, see *Nature*, vol. xxxiv.

[4] Comp. *Variation under Domestication*, chap. xxi., conclusion.

direct and definite effects upon the mass. The facts and considerations for and against the belief that the conditions of existence act in a potent manner in causing definite modifications of structure are confronted in detail. In some few instances a marked effect has been rapidly produced, *e.g.*, on European men in the United States, European dogs in India, horses in the Falkland Islands, oysters in the Mediterranean, &c. The chemical compounds of some plants and the state of their tissues are readily affected by changed conditions. The production of galls, &c., shows how great changes in structure and colour may result from chemical changes. We almost certainly know that organic beings in a state of nature may be modified in various definite ways by the conditions to which they have been long exposed; but it is difficult to distinguish between the definite result of changed conditions and the accumulation through natural selection of indefinite variations which have proved serviceable. But, even granting the utmost weight to conditions, we can rarely see the precise relation between cause and effect. Moreover, many animals and plants of wide range and great diversity of experience yet remain uniform in character. Again, the degree to which domesticated birds, &c., have varied does not stand in any close relation to the amount of change to which they have been subjected. In fact, we may have similar modifications under different conditions, different modifications under similar change of conditions, or no modifications at all. Closely parallel varieties are often produced from distinct races or even species without ascertainable unity of conditions. Bird-variations, too, seem conspicuously independent of circumstances. All these considerations tend to force on our minds the conviction that what we call the external conditions of life are in many cases quite insignificant in comparison with the organization or constitution of the being which varies. No doubt each variation may have its efficient cause, but it is as hopeless to search for the cause of each as to say why a chill or a poison affects one man differently from another. With respect to acclimatization, although habit does something towards the success of the process, yet the appearance of constitutionally different individuals is a far more effective agent.

Use and disuse.

Increased use adds to the size of muscles, together with the blood-vessels, nerves, bony crests of origin, and even the whole bones; it also increases glands and strengthens sense-organs. Increased and intermittent pressure thickens the epidermis; change of food modifies the coats of the stomach and alters the length of the intestine. Disuse weakens and diminishes all parts of the organization,—lungs and chest, wings and their associated bones, &c. Although in domesticated animals this never goes so far that a mere rudiment is left, it seems often to have occurred in nature, the effects of disuse being aided by economy of growth with intercrossing. Changed habits may lead to use or disuse of organs, and consequently to their modification; yet the effects of habit, use, and disuse have often been largely combined with the natural selection of innate variations and sometimes overmastered by it.

Correlated variation.

Correlated variation means that the whole organization is so tied together during its growth and development that, when slight variations in any part occur, and are accumulated through natural selection, other parts become modified, apparently irrespective of advantage in the change. Variations of structure in the young often affect those of the mature animal; the influence of hard parts, mechanical pressure, the relative position of parts, and the size of the whole body all have important influences. Homologous tissues may exhibit associated variations, *e.g.*, hoofs, hair, and teeth. In most cases the correlation is, however, quite obscure, and may seem to be of no utility to the species, as with various monstrosities and diseases. Colour may be associated with other constitutional peculiarities. Although correlation is of much importance, we may also falsely attribute to it structures which are simply due to inheritance or natural selection, or its effects may be inextricably commingled with those of increased use and of accumulation by natural selection, *e.g.*, the gigantic horns of the Irish elk with the changes necessarily associated with the acquirement of them.

Variability of homologous parts.

Homologous and multiple parts are peculiarly variable, and often tend to cohere. Rudimentary and lowly organized structures are variable. The law of compensation of Goethe and Geoffroy, "that in order to spend on one side nature is forced to economize on the other," holds true to a certain extent with domestic production, but more doubtfully in nature.

Mechanical pressure, &c.

Mechanical pressure and relative position of parts seem to be of some importance in determining variations; but such changes are often due to reversion to long-lost characters, which may frequently occur. A part extraordinarily developed in any species tends to be highly variable. Specific characters are more variable than generic characters. Distinct species present analogous variations; but this may arise either from analogous constitution or from reversion. Secondary sexual characters are highly variable. "Whatever the cause may be of each slight difference between the offspring and their parents—and a cause for each must exist—we have reason to believe that it is the steady accumulation of beneficial differences which has given rise to all the more important modifications of structure in relation to the habits of each species."

Results of recent research and opinion.

The preceding outline of Darwin's main positions (which are in harmony with his essential doctrine of indefinite variability) prepares us for the discussion of more recent research and opinion. But for our present concrete knowledge of the influence of environment, use and disuse, including all such researches as those of Semper,[1] or the peculiarly brilliant and luminous investigations of Poulton,[2] the recent valuable summary of Arthur Thomson[3] may conveniently be referred to. The corresponding theoretic argument for the definite causation of most variations by these agencies has been recently re-stated by Spencer,[4] along with his proposed limitation of natural selection. This should be taken along with the testimony of the American Neo-Lamarckian school, among which the learned and suggestive, though too undigested, essays of Cope[5] are especially prominent. The views of Nägeli, Mivart, and other advocates of internal variation here present themselves anew, along with the criticisms and replies to them, as also Weismann's doctrine of variability as being ultimately germinal. But space precludes the survey of this voluminous and unfinished controversy, which, moreover, would not at present yield any general result, since neither the various inductive and deductive arguments, nor the organismal, functional, &c., and environmental explanations which these variously favour, have been as yet exhaustively stated, still less properly confronted, and least of all reconciled, by any author.

Proposed fresh theory of variational laws.

It may be more profitable to attempt, though necessarily in barest outline, a fresh re-examination of the entire field. This may be most appropriately introduced, and the initial conception of the present part of the discussion re-stated, by a passage from Weismann, whose substantial acceptance of the doctrine of natural selection has already been noticed (p. 81). "We certainly cannot remain at the purely empirical conception of variability and heredity as laid down by Darwin in his admirable work. If the theory of selection is to furnish a method of mechanical explanation, it is essential that its factors should be formulated in a precise mechanical sense. But, as soon as we attempt to do this, it is seen that, in the first enthusiasm over the newly discovered principle of selection, the one factor of transformation contained in this principle has been unduly pushed into the background to make way for the other more apparent and better known factors. The first indispensable factor, and perhaps the most important in any case, in every transformation is the physical nature of the organism itself." Let us briefly summarize, therefore, the main results of a fresh survey of the leading variations presented by plants and animals, *i.e.*, no longer commencing with the analogy of human selection upon the smallest varietal and specific distinctions, and arguing on Lyell's principle for the cumulative origin of the characters of larger groups, but considering these larger differences from the standpoint of general physiology, without any hypothesis at all.

Preponderance of species maintaining ends over individual struggle and development.

The physiological principle invoked is simply that antithesis between reproductive functions and individual ones which has been familiar since the dawn of physiology, and which, when reduced to its physical terms, is obviously deducible from the principle of conservation of energy. Instead of the generally received doctrine, summarized above, that of indefinite variation, with progress by means of struggle for existence among individuals, its systematic application furnishes a detailed re-interpretation of the forms presented by plants and animals comparable to that afforded by the received hypothesis, but with an essentially altered view of the process and factors of organic evolution as a whole. Briefly stated,

[1] *Animal Life*, Int. Sci. Series, 1881.

[2] *Proc. Roy. Soc.*, 1884-88.

[3] "A Synthetic Summary of the Influence of Environment," in *Trans. Roy. Phys. Soc. Edin.*, 1887-88.

[4] *Factors of Organic Evolution*, London, 1886 (reprinted from *Nineteenth Century*).

[5] *The Origin of the Fittest*, London and New York, 1887.

the view of evolution thus reached is that of definite variation, with progress essentially through the subordination of individual struggle and development to species-maintaining ends.

Arrest of vegetation by reproduction.

Let us commence with the origin of the flower, which all botanists agree in regarding as a shortened branch. The apparent explanation of natural selection (from two other alternatives, one lengthened, the other unshortened), although morphologically reasonable, is at once excluded by the physiological one of *inevitable* shortening, since the expense of the reproductive functions necessarily checks the vegetative ones, and since we cannot speak of *selection* where the imaginable alternatives are physically impossible. Similarly, the shortening of the inflorescence from raceme to spike or flower-head, or its hollowing into a fig, with the corresponding reduction in the size of the flowers, receives the same explanation—growth of axis and of appendages checked by reproduction—superseding that current, viz., by mere convenient adaptation to fertilization by insects. The internal structure of the flower is similarly modified, as may be shown in detail in the passage from hypogyny through perigyny to epigyny (these being simply stages of the progressive arrest of the growth of the axis), in the reduction of the floral envelopes and stamens and the number of carpels and ovules, and even in the transition from perispermic to endospermic and finally exalbuminous seeds. But these are the most important of floral variations, and furnish the essentially distinguishing characters of the natural orders; hence, when these are seen, instead of being indefinite, to be parallel and definite (*i.e.*, determined through the continuous checking of vegetation by reproduction along what is thus a single and definite groove of progressive change), the importance of natural selection changes wholly from that of selecting and accumulating supposed indefinite variations to that of retarding definite ones after the stage of maximum utility has been independently reached. The same simple conception unlocks innumerable problems of floral morphology, large and small alike: *e.g.*, it interprets with equal ease the inevitable development of gymnosperm into angiosperm (by continuous subordination of the reproductive carpellary leaf) and the origin of refined minor adaptations, like the splitting fruit of the geranium or the cupped stigma of the pansy, not as achievements of natural selection from among fortuitous variations, but as naturally traceable to the checked vegetation of their respective types of leaf organ, just as in the familiar case of the pinnately-lobed outer sepals of the rose bud. The origin of floral colour as primarily an inevitable consequence of the same principle of vegetative subordination through reproductive preponderance was long ago pointed out by Spencer, who unfortunately, however, also accepted without scrutiny the orthodox hypothesis that this incipient floral colour would revert to the ordinary green vegetation but for the accident of its attractiveness to insects, and consequently must have owed its accumulation simply to the repeated preservation of the offspring of the accidentally brightest coloured; whereas we now see that the arrest of vegetative greenness in the flower and the exclusive appearance of those colouring matters associated with the imperfect vegetation of spring and autumn are a continuous process of its subordination as a vegetative, and its development as a reproductive, apparatus. Adaptation to insects thus takes a quite secondary place; similarly with the leafy arrest and floral coloration of bracts; while a detailed examination of thorny plants practically excludes the hypothesis of mammalian selection altogether, and shows spines to arise as an expression of the diminishing vegetativeness—in fact the ebbing vitality—of a shoot or even of an entire species. Evergreens tend to arise in all orders among the forms of more vegetative habit, and in such forms the amount of flowering is usually diminished relatively to the deciduous members of the same group, whilst such constitutional vegetativeness checks the progress of floral evolution. Hence it is that evergreens, and even orders in which they largely occur, are usually less differentiated than their deciduous congeners. The apparently indefinite variations presented by domesticated plants, *e.g.*, the cabbage tribe, are at once classified and interpreted as so many stages along the same course (from leafy kale, through Brussels sprouts with many leaf buds, to cabbage with apical flower bud, and finally to cauliflower). The importance of this line of evidence for the Darwinian view of variation and selection becomes still further reduced, although also broadly settled, when we note that, since the subordination of vegetative to reproductive preponderance gave us the origin of ordinal characters, the converse improvement of individual characters at the expense of reproductive ones (on which domestication usually insists and artificial selection depends) can only give us minor ones, for the most part varietal or specific, if so much. The Lyellian analogy for the ultimate accumulation of varietal differences into ordinal characters has thus been misleading. The preceding transition of both organography and physiology from empirical to rational carries with it a similar transition from empirical to rational taxonomy as well: the antagonism of vegetative and reproductive habit is seen to be also general and constitutional. Just as the liliaceous type ranges on one side towards the characteristically vegetative grass or reproductive orchid, so is it with the main variations of every natural alliance, be this order, genus, or even species. Thus the *Ranunculaceæ* have their grassy and their orchid-like types in meadow-rue and larkspur, yet the species of these very genera show examples of the opposite swing of variation; again, the two species or varieties of British oak (*Q. pedunculata* and *Q. sessiliflora*) are thus, so to speak, the incipient grass and orchid forms of their common ancestor (*Q. Robur*). What we call higher or lower species or orders are thus the leaders or the laggards along one or other of these two lines of variation, the representatives of some stage of the predominance on one side or other of that oscillating balance between vegetative and reproductive processes which have long been known as the essential functions of organic life.

Working of the law in animal world.

The results of a similar survey of the animal world, despite the greater intricacy of the problem, are scarcely less definite or comprehensive, and at once lead to a deeper interpretation of the whole. Commencing with an ascending survey, we recognize such essential animal types of *Protozoa* as the rhizopods, gregarines, and infusors, not as the empirically selected products of spontaneous variation among indefinite possibilities, but simply as the predominatingly amœboid, encysted, and motile phases of the primeval cell-cycle (see MORPHOLOGY), these three forms of which are fixed by the properties of protoplasm itself (see SEX, vol. xxi. pp. 720-724), each particular phase being fixed by the constitutional bias (diathesis) of its type towards anabolism or katabolism (see PHYSIOLOGY, PROTOPLASM). This rationale of variation in ultimate terms, *i.e.*, both cellular and protoplasmic, both morphological and physiological, may be continued through all fields, *e.g.*, embryological or pathological, for some diseases are coming to be interpreted as the progressive variation of some function and organ which only disturbs the general balance in its progress towards a new and higher equilibrium.[1] This conception of physiological as well as merely structural life-history rationalizes both animal and vegetable taxonomy. Thus the greatest of all steps in morphological progress, that from the *Protozoa* to the *Metazoa*, is not due to the selection of the more individuated and highly adapted forms, but to the union of relatively unindividuated cells into an aggregate in which each becomes diminishingly competitive and increasingly subordinated to the social whole. Passing to trifling variations, such as the internal deposition of spicules, we interpret these neither as mere accidents, nor as pure advantages for support or defence, but as arising like plant-crystals or gouty deposits as unremoved waste products, accumulating with local or constitutional passivity. How the inevitable constitutional preponderance of anabolism or katabolism excludes spontaneous variation and subordinates external selection in the formation of types would become clear could we pass in review the animal kingdom, and note how its various alliances all range from passive to more active forms. We should compare the coral or sponge at one end of the scale with the similarly passive (and consequently also skeletal) tortoise and glyptodon at the other. We should read in their anabolic diathesis the secret of accumulating size and of inevitable extinction (nay, even unravel the apparent contradictions with respect to the influence of the environment, as being specially strong upon the passive types, which hence are far richer in species than the corresponding less readily influenced active forms).

Finally, the preponderating importance of the species-maintaining over the individual functions should again be noted in animals as in plants, since the conviction thus becomes inevitable that, in stating the process of evolution essentially in terms of the survival of the fittest in competition, the centre of gravity of the subject has been misplaced. The constant primary insistence upon individual competition for food, and the very subordinate recognition of the importance of sexual and social co-operation for well-being, which are characteristic of the prevalent theory (witness their proportion in the preceding summary), are traceable at once to the confusion of putting the nutritive factors "in the first place" because they precede the reproductive in time; whereas the organism inevitably enters upon reproduction and so cedes the preponderance—"the first place"—to the other-regarding functions. That increase of reproductive sacrifice which at once makes the mammal and marks its essential stages of further progress (monotreme, marsupial, placental), that increase of parental care, that frequent appearance of sociality and co-operation which even in its rudest forms so surely secures the success of the species attaining it, be it mammal or bird, insect or even worm,—all these phenomena of survival of the truly fittest, through love, sacrifice, and co-operation—need far other prominence than they could possibly receive on the hypothesis of the essential progress of the species through internecine struggle of its individuals at the margin of subsistence. Yet these cases are only the supreme outcomes of that continuous and definite process of variation through individual subordination and species-maintaining preponderance which we have seen modelling even the vegetable world.

In short, while no more denying the existence of competition in nature than the fact of organic progress, we deny the assumed relation of these as cause and effect,

[1] *Cf.* Sutton, *General Pathology*, London, 1886.

and propose an interpretation in essential respects directly converse, without denying the minor agency of use and disuse, environment, &c. Each of the greater steps of progress is definitely associated with an increased measure of subordination of individual competition to reproductive or social ends, and of interspecific competition to co-operative adaptation. The ideal of evolution is thus an Eden; and, although competition can never be wholly eliminated, and progress must thus be asymptotic, it is much for our pure natural history to see no longer struggle, but love, as "creation's final law." While ceasing to speak of indefinite variation, we may of course still conveniently retain the rest of the established phraseology, and continue to speak of "natural selection" and of "survival of the fittest," always provided that, in passing from the explanation of the *distributional* survival of individuals or species in contest within a given area to the interpretation of the main line of their morphological and physiological progress, we make the transition from the self-regarding to the other-regarding (in ethical language, from the egoistic to the altruistic) sense of these terms which has above been outlined.[1]

It would be premature to enter upon the extended or deductive application of these considerations, since, pending their acceptance, the preceding statement of the received doctrine of natural selection from spontaneous variations, with all its logical consequences (pp. 81-82), remains valid. Conversely, it is of course obvious that their adoption would involve the extensive modification of the received doctrine, as well as the complementing of new constructive attempts by a re-examination of earlier views of both the process and the philosophy of evolution.[2] (P. GE.)

VARIATIONS, CALCULUS OF. 1. It has been observed (MAXIMA AND MINIMA, vol. xv. p. 643) that the origin of the calculus of variations may be traced to John Bernoulli's celebrated problem, published in 1696 in the *Acta Eruditorum* of Leipsic, under the following form, *Datis in plano verticali duobus punctis A et B, assignare mobili M viam AMB per quam gravitate sua descendens, et moveri incipiens a puncto A, brevissimo tempore perveniat ad punctum B.* This problem introduced considerations entirely different from those hitherto involved in the discussion of curves, for in its treatment it is necessary to conceive a curve as changing its form in a continuous manner, that is, as undergoing what is styled *deformation.* This change of form can be treated analytically as follows.

Suppose $y=f(x)$ to represent the equation of a curve, and let us write $y=f(x)+\alpha\psi(x)$ ....(1), where α is an infinitesimal quantity, and $\psi(x)$ any function of x subject only to the condition of being finite for all values of x within the limits of the problem. Then equation (1) represents a new curve indefinitely close to the curve $y=f(x)$; and by varying the form of $\psi(x)$ we may regard (1) as representative of any continuous curve indefinitely near to the original curve.

2. Again $\alpha\psi(x)$ is the difference of the y ordinates of the two curves for the same value of x; this indefinitely small difference is called the *variation* of y, and is denoted by δy. It may be regarded as the change in y arising solely from a change in the relation connecting y with x, while x itself remains unaltered. In general, if y be a function of any number of independent variables $x_1, x_2, \dots x_n$, then δy represents any indefinitely small change in y arising solely from a change in the form of the function, while x_1, x_2, &c., are unchanged. Thus the variable y may receive two essentially distinct kinds of increment,—one arising from a change in one or more of the variables, the other arising solely from a change in the relation which connects y with these variables. The former increments are those contemplated and treated of in the ordinary calculus; the latter are those principally considered in the calculus of variations.

We shall follow Strauch, Jellett, Moigno, and the principal modern writers on the subject, by restricting, in general, the symbol δ to the latter species of increment. In many problems both kinds of increment have place simultaneously. Thus, if $y=f(x_1, x_2, x_3)$, and if Δy denote the total increment of y, we have

$$\Delta y=\delta y+\frac{df}{dx_1}dx_1+\frac{df}{dx_2}dx_2+\frac{df}{dx_3}dx_3 \text{..............(2)};$$

and so on in all cases.

3. It is readily seen that $\delta\frac{dy}{dx}=\frac{d}{dx}\delta y$, and in general that $\delta\frac{d^ny}{dx^n}=\frac{d^n}{dx^n}\delta y$. The last equation may be written

$$\delta D^n y=D^n\delta y \text{ ....(3)},$$

where D stands for the symbol of differentiation, $\frac{d}{dx}$.

4. We shall adopt Newton's notation and write $\dot{y}$ for $\frac{dy}{dx}$, $\ddot{y}$ for $\frac{d^2y}{dx^2}$, $y^{(n)}$ for $\frac{d^ny}{dx^n}$, and proceed to consider the variation of the general expression $V=f(x, y, \dot{y}, \ddot{y}, \dots y^{(n)})$, in which the form of the function f is given, while that of y in terms of x is indeterminate. Here, considering x as unchanged, we have

$$\delta V=\frac{dV}{dy}\delta y+\frac{dV}{d\dot{y}}\delta\dot{y}+\dots+\frac{dV}{dy^{(n)}}\delta y^{(n)}.$$

Now let $\frac{dV}{dy}=P,\ \frac{dV}{d\dot{y}}=P_1, \dots \frac{dV}{dy^{(n)}}=P_n$,

then we have

$$\delta V=P\delta y+P_1D\delta y+P_2D^2\delta y+\dots+P_nD^n\delta y \text{...........(4)}.$$

5. Next let us consider the variation of the definite integral $U=\int_{x_0}^{x_1}Vdx$, where V does not contain either of the limits x_0 and x_1. Here, when the limits are unchanged, we have $\delta U=\int_{x_0}^{x_1}\delta Vdx$, and, when the limits undergo change,

$$\delta U=\delta\int_{x_0}^{x_1}Vdx=\int_{x_0}^{x_1}\delta Vdx+V_1dx_1-V_0dx_0 \text{ ....(5)}.$$

6. We shall here bring in a new symbol, called the *sign of substitution*, which was introduced by Sarrus.[3] Thus, if F be any function of x, y, &c., the result of substituting x_1 for x in F—the other variables being unchanged—is represented by $\Big/^{x_1}F$ in the form of notation adopted by Moigno and Lindelöf.[4] The difference between $\Big/^{x_1}F$ and $\Big/^{x_0}F$ is represented by $\Big/^{x_1}_{x_0}F$. Employing this notation, (5) is written

$$\delta U=\int_{x_0}^{x_1}\delta Vdx+\Big/^{x_1}_{x_0}Vdx \text{.....................(6)}.$$

7. We now proceed to transform the last equation, commencing with the case in which V is a function of x, y, and $\dot{y}$ solely.

Here
$$\delta U=\int_{x_0}^{x_1}(P\delta y+P_1D\delta y)dx+\Big/^{x_1}_{x_0}Vdx,$$
$$=\int_{x_0}^{x_1}\left(P-\frac{dP_1}{dx}\right)\delta ydx+\Big/^{x_1}_{x_0}P_1\delta y+\Big/^{x_1}_{x_0}Vdx \text{ ....(7)}.$$

Next let V be a function of x, y, $\dot{y}$, and $\ddot{y}$, then

$$\delta U=\int_{x_0}^{x_1}(P\delta y+P_1D\delta y+P_2D^2\delta y)dx+\Big/^{x_1}_{x_0}Vdx.$$

---

[1] Geddes, "On Variation in Plants," "On the Origin of Thorns and Prickles," and "On the Origin of Evergreens," in *Trans. Bot. Soc. Edin.*, 1886, 1887, 1888.

[2] Geddes, "A Restatement of the Theory of Organic Evolution," *Roy. Soc. Edin.*, 1888.

[3] *Recherches sur le Calcul des Variations*, 1848.

[4] *Calc. des Var.*, 1861.

Hence, observing that

$$\frac{d}{dx}\left(\frac{dP_2}{dx}\delta y - P_2\frac{d\delta y}{dx}\right) = \frac{d^2P_2}{dx^2}\delta y - P_2\frac{d^2\delta y}{dx^2},$$

we get
$$\delta U = \int_{x_0}^{x_1}\left(P - \frac{dP_1}{dx} + \frac{d^2P_2}{dx^2}\right)\delta y dx + \Big/_{x_0}^{x_1} V dx$$
$$+ \Big/_{x_0}^{x_1}\left(P_1 - \frac{dP_2}{dx}\right)\delta y + \Big/_{x_0}^{x_1} P_2\delta\dot{y} \quad \text{.......................(8).}$$

In general, if V be a function of x, y, $\dot{y}$, $\ddot{y}$, ... $y^{(n)}$, we have

$$\delta U = \int_{x_0}^{x_1}(P\delta y + P_1 D\delta y + \ldots + P_n D^n \delta y)dx + \Big/_{x_0}^{x_1} V dx.$$

Now let D_1 denote the differentiation of δy, and D_2 the differentiation of P_1, P_2, &c.; we may write

$$P_m D^m \delta y - (-1)^m \delta y D^m P_m = ({D_1}^m - (-1)^m {D_2}^m)P_m\delta y$$
$$= (D_1 + D_2)({D_1}^{m-1} - {D_1}^{m-2}D_2 + \ldots \pm {D_2}^{m-1})P_m\delta y$$
$$= \frac{d}{dx}\left(P_m D^{m-1}\delta y - \frac{dP_m}{dx}D^{m-2}\delta y + \ldots + (-1)^{m-1}\delta y\frac{d^{m-1}P_m}{dx^{m-1}}\right).$$

Hence
$$\int_{x_0}^{x_1} P_m D^m \delta y dx = (-1)^m \int_{x_0}^{x_1}\frac{d^m P_m}{dx^m}\delta y dx$$
$$+ \Big/_{x_0}^{x_1}\left(P_m D^{m-1}\delta y - \frac{dP_m}{dx}D^{m-2}\delta y + \ldots + (-1)^{m-1}\delta y\frac{d^{m-1}P_m}{dx^{m-1}}\right).$$

Applying this to the different terms in the value of δU given above, we get

$$\delta U = \int_{x_0}^{x_1}\left(P - \frac{dP_1}{dx} + \frac{d^2P_2}{dx^2} - \ldots + (-1)^n\frac{d^nP_n}{dx^n}\right)\delta y dx$$
$$+ \Big/_{x_0}^{x_1}\left(P_1 - \frac{dP_2}{dx} + \ldots + (-1)^{n-1}\frac{d^{n-1}P_n}{dx^{n-1}}\right)\delta y$$
$$+ \Big/_{x_0}^{x_1}\left(P_2 - \frac{dP_3}{dx} + \ldots + (-1)^{n-2}\frac{d^{n-2}P_n}{dx^{n-2}}\right)\frac{d\delta y}{dx}$$
$$\cdot \quad \cdot \quad \cdot \quad \cdot \quad \cdot \quad \cdot \quad \cdot \quad \cdot$$
$$+ \Big/_{x_0}^{x_1} P_n\frac{d^{n-1}\delta y}{dx^{n-1}} + \Big/_{x_0}^{x_1} V dx \quad \text{..................(9).}$$

This result may be written

$$\delta U = \int_{x_0}^{x_1}(P)\delta y dx + \Big/_{x_0}^{x_1} V dx$$
$$+ \Big/_{x_0}^{x_1}\{(P_1)\delta y + (P_2)\delta\dot{y} + \ldots + (P_n)\delta y^{(n-1)}\} \text{......(10).}$$

where $(P) = P - \frac{dP_1}{dx} + \frac{d^2P_2}{dx^2} - \ldots$, $(P_1) = P_1 - \frac{dP_2}{dx} + \frac{d^2P_3}{dx^2} - \ldots$, and so on.

8. This expression consists of three parts,—(1) the definite integral $\int_{x_0}^{x_1}(P)\delta y dx$, which depends on δy, the change in the form of the function y; (2) the expression $\Big/_{x_0}^{x_1} V dx$, which depends solely on the change in the limiting values of x; and (3) the quantity $\Big/_{x_0}^{x_1}\{(P_1)\delta y + (P_2)\delta\dot{y} + \ldots\}$, which depends on the variations of y, $\dot{y}$, &c., at the limits. It is often convenient to write (10) in the abbreviated form

$$\delta U = L + \int_{x_0}^{x_1} M\delta y dx \quad \text{.....................(11).}$$

9. The principal applications of the calculus of variations have reference to the determination of the form of one or more unknown functions contained in a definite integral, in such a manner that the integral shall have a maximum or minimum value. For instance, to determine the form of the function y which renders $U = \int_{x_0}^{x_1} V dx$ a maximum or a minimum, we have as above $\delta U = L + \int_{x_0}^{x_1} M\delta y dx$. Here, as in the differential calculus (see INFINITESIMAL CALCULUS, § 64), for a maximum or minimum value of U it is readily seen that we must have $\delta U = 0$; this leads to $L = 0$ and $\int_{x_0}^{x_1} M\delta y dx = 0$. Now the latter integral cannot be zero for all indefinitely small values of δy unless $M = 0$ for all values within the limits of integration. Hence we get the differential equation in y,

$$P - \frac{dP_1}{dx} + \frac{d^2P_2}{dx^2} - \ldots + (-1)^n\frac{d^nP_n}{dx^n} = 0 \quad \text{.........(12).}$$

10. We here suppose that there is no restriction on δy, so that for any value of x the increments $+\delta y$ and $-\delta y$ are equally compatible with the conditions of the problem. The reasoning consequently will not apply if the conditions render this impossible. For instance, if a curve be restricted to lie within a given boundary, then for all points on the boundary the displacements must be inwards, and the opposite displacements are impossible. In this case [1] the curve satisfying a required maximum or minimum condition consists partly of portions of the boundary and partly of portions of a curve satisfying the equation $M = 0$.

11. The equation $M = 0$ is in general a differential equation of the degree $2n$; accordingly its solution usually contains $2n$ arbitrary constants. The values of these constants are to be determined by aid of the equations deduced from $L = 0$ in combination with the given conditions at the limits. For example, if V be a function of x, y, and $\dot{y}$ solely, the solution of $P - \frac{dP_1}{dx} = 0$ is in general of the form $y = f(x, c_1, c_2)$. Now, suppose that the limiting points are restricted to the curves $y_0 = f_0(x_0)$ and $y_1 = f_1(x_1)$, then we get at the limits $\delta y_0 + \dot{y}_0 dx_0 = f_0'(x_0)dx_0$ and $\delta y_1 + \dot{y}_1 dx_1 = f_1'(x_1)dx_1$. Hence, substituting in $L = 0$ the values of δy_0 and δy_1 derived from these equations, we get, since dx_0 and dx_1 are arbitrary,

$$\left.\begin{array}{l} V_0 + (P_1)_0(f_0'(x_0) - \dot{y}_0) = 0 \\ V_1 + (P_1)_1(f_1'(x_1) - \dot{y}_1) = 0 \end{array}\right\} \text{..................(13).}$$

We have therefore six equations for the determination of the six quantities x_0, y_0, x_1, y_1, c_1, and c_2.

The integration of the equation $M = 0$ is much simplified in particular cases.

(1) Let V be a function of x and $\dot{y}$ solely, then we have $\frac{dP_1}{dx} = 0$, therefore

$$P_1 = c \quad \text{.............................(14).}$$

(2) If V be a function of y and $\dot{y}$ solely, $P = \frac{dP_1}{dx}$, also $\frac{d}{dx}(V) = P\dot{y} + P_1\ddot{y} = \frac{dP_1}{dx}\dot{y} + P_1\ddot{y}$. Hence, integrating, we get

$$V = P_1\dot{y} + c \quad \text{...........................(15),}$$

where c is an arbitrary constant.

12. For example, let us consider Bernoulli's problem of the curve of quickest descent under the action of gravity. Take the axis of x vertical and that of y horizontal, and suppose the particle to start from the point x_0, y_0, with the velocity due to the height h; then, if v be the velocity at any point, we have $v^2 = 2g(x + h - x_0)$, also $dt = \frac{ds}{v} = \frac{\sqrt{1+\dot{y}^2}dx}{\sqrt{2g}\sqrt{x+h-x_0}}$. Here, neglecting a constant factor, we may write $U = \int_{x_0}^{x_1}\frac{\sqrt{1+\dot{y}^2}dx}{\sqrt{x+h-x_0}}$; and by (14) we get $\frac{\dot{y}}{\sqrt{1+\dot{y}^2}} = c\sqrt{x+h-x_0}$. Now, writing a for $1/c^2$ and assuming $x + h - x_0 = a\sin^2\theta$, we find $dy = \tan\theta dx = a(1 - \cos 2\theta)d\theta$; therefore $y = a(\theta - \sin\theta\cos\theta) + K$, and we infer that the curve is a cycloid.

(α) If we suppose the upper limit to be fixed and the lower restricted to the curve $y_1 = f_1(x_1)$, we get from (13)

$$1 + \tan\theta_1 f_1'(x_1) = 0 \quad \text{....................(16);}$$

accordingly the curve intersects the bounding curve orthogonally.

(β) Next let the upper limit be restricted to the curve $y_0 = f_0(x_0)$; then since V contains x_0, we have an additional term in δU arising from the change in x_0, viz., $dx_0\int_{x_0}^{x_1}\frac{dV}{dx_0}dx$; consequently the coefficient of dx_0 in δU is

$$\int_{x_0}^{x_1}\frac{dV}{dx_0}dx - \{V_0 + (P_1)_0(f_1'(x_0) - \dot{y}_0)\},$$

and we have
$$\int_{x_0}^{x_1}\frac{dV}{dx_0}dx = V_0 + (P_1)_0(f_0'(x_0) - \dot{y}_0) \text{..............(17).}$$

If we substitute for V its value, we get without difficulty from this equation $1 + \tan\theta_1 f_0'(x_0) = 0$. Comparing this with (16), we see that the tangents to the bounding curves at the extremities of the trajectory are parallel (Moigno, *op. cit.*, p. 230).

13. More generally, consider the curve for which $U = \int_{x_0}^{x_1}\mu ds = \int_{x_0}^{x_1}\mu\sqrt{1+\dot{y}^2}dx$ is a maximum or a minimum, where μ is a given function of x and y. Here $P = \frac{d\mu}{dy}\sqrt{1+\dot{y}^2}$, $P_1 = \frac{\mu\dot{y}}{\sqrt{1+\dot{y}^2}}$, and we get $\frac{d\mu}{dy}\sqrt{1+\dot{y}^2} = \frac{\dot{y}}{\sqrt{1+\dot{y}^2}}\left(\frac{d\mu}{dx} + \dot{y}\frac{d\mu}{dy}\right) + \mu\frac{d}{dx}\left(\frac{\dot{y}}{\sqrt{1+\dot{y}^2}}\right)$; hence, if ρ be the radius of curvature, we have

$$\frac{1}{\rho} = -\frac{1}{\mu}\left(\cos\alpha\frac{d\mu}{dx} + \cos\beta\frac{d\mu}{dy}\right) \text{..................(18),}$$

where α, β are the angles which the normal makes with the co-

[1] For a full discussion of such cases, see Todhunter, *On the Calculus of Variations*, 1871 (Adams prize essay), Cambridge.

ordinate axes respectively. Jellett remarks[1] that, if the proposed integral had been $\int \frac{ds}{\mu}$, we should then have arrived at the equation $\frac{1}{\rho}=\frac{1}{\mu}\left(\cos\alpha\frac{d\mu}{dx}+\cos\beta\frac{d\mu}{dy}\right)$, and consequently have seen that the two curves contained under the equation $\rho^2=f(x,y,\dot{y})$ are such that, if one renders $\int \mu ds$ a maximum or a minimum, the other possesses the same property with regard to $\int \frac{ds}{\mu}$.

14. Next, to find the curve such that the surface generated by its revolution round a given line shall be a minimum. Here, neglecting a constant multiplier, we may write $U=\int_{x_0}^{x_1} y\sqrt{1+\dot{y}^2}dx$; accordingly by (15) we have $y=c\sqrt{1+\dot{y}^2}$. This gives $\frac{dy}{\sqrt{y^2-c^2}}=\frac{dx}{c}$; and hence $\frac{x+b}{c}=\log\left(y+\frac{\sqrt{y^2-c^2}}{c}\right)$,

or
$$y=\frac{c}{2}\left(e^{(x+b)/c}+e^{-(x+b)/c}\right) \qquad \text{(19)},$$
which represents the common catenary.

15. We now proceed to generalize the results in § 11. If V be a function of $x, \dot{y}, \ddot{y}, \ldots y^{(n)}$, not containing y explicitly, we have by integration
$$P_1-\frac{dP_2}{dx}+\frac{d^2P_3}{dx^2}-\ldots+(-1)^{n-1}\frac{d^{n-1}P_n}{dx^{n-1}}=c \qquad \text{(20)},$$
where c is an arbitrary constant. Again, if V does not contain x explicitly, $\frac{d}{dx}(V)=\dot{y}P+\ddot{y}P_1+\ldots+y^{(n+1)}P_n$. Also, from the equation $M=0$ we see that $P=\frac{dP_1}{dx}-\frac{d^2P_2}{dx^2}+\ldots-(-1)^n\frac{d^nP_n}{dx^n}$; hence
$$\frac{d}{dx}(V)=\ddot{y}P_1+\dot{y}\frac{dP_1}{dx}+\dddot{y}P_2-\dot{y}\frac{d^2P_2}{dx^2}+\ldots+y^{(n+1)}P_n-(-1)^n\dot{y}\frac{d^nP_n}{dx^n}$$
$$=(D_1+D_2)(\dot{y}P_1)+(D_1^{\,2}-D_2^{\,2})(\dot{y}P_2)+\ldots+(D_1^{\,n}-(-1)^nD_2^{\,n})(\dot{y}P_n),$$
where D_1 represents the differentiation of $\dot{y}, \ddot{y}$, &c., and D_2 that of P_1, P_2, &c. Consequently, by integration
$$V=c+\dot{y}(P_1)+\ddot{y}(P_2)+\ldots+y^{(n)}P_n \qquad \text{(21)},$$
a differential equation of the order $2n-2$ at the highest. Again, if V contains neither x nor y explicitly, we may substitute c' for (P_1), and consequently we have
$$V=c+c'\dot{y}+\ddot{y}(P_2)+\ldots+y^{(n)}P_n \qquad \text{(22)}.$$

16. As an example, let us investigate the curve for which the area between the curve, its evolute, and the extreme radii of curvature shall be a minimum. Here $U=\int_{s_0}^{s_1}\rho ds=\int_{x_0}^{x_1}\frac{(1+\dot{y}^2)^2}{\ddot{y}}dx$. Hence by (22), since $\ddot{y}P_2=-V$, we have $V=c_1+c_2\dot{y}$, or $\rho=\frac{c_1}{\sqrt{1+\dot{y}^2}}+\frac{c_2\dot{y}}{\sqrt{1+\dot{y}^2}}$; therefore $\frac{ds}{d\phi}=c_1\cos\phi+c_2\sin\phi$, where ϕ is the angle made by the tangent with the axis of x. This leads to
$$s=-c_1\sin\phi+c_2\cos\phi+c_3 \qquad \text{(23)},$$
which shows that the curve is a cycloid. Again, (1) if the extreme points be fixed, the equations at the limits are $(P_2)_0=0$, $(P_2)_1=0$. This shows that the radius of curvature vanishes at both limits and the curve must be a complete cycloid. (2) If the extremities lie on the curves $y_0=f_0(x_0)$, $y_1=f_1(x_1)$; then the equations furnished by $L=0$ are
$$\left.\begin{array}{ll} V_0+(P_1)_0\{f_0{}'(x_0)-\dot{y}_0\}=0, & (P_2)_0=0 \\ V_1+(P_1)_1\{f_1{}'(x_1)-\dot{y}_1\}=0, & (P_2)_1=0 \end{array}\right\} \qquad \text{(24)}.$$
Hence the extreme points are cusps on the cycloid; moreover, since in this case $V_0=0$ and $V_1=0$, we have $\dot{y}_0-f_0{}'(x_0)=0$, $\dot{y}_1-f_1{}'(x_1)=0$, which show that the cycloid at each of its extremities touches these curves, and that the line joining the extreme points is normal to each of the bounding curves.

It is easily seen that the minimum area is four times that of the circle which generates the cycloid.

17. Next let us consider the variation of $U=\int_{x_0}^{x_1} Vdx$, where V is a given function of $x, y, z, \dot{y}, \dot{z}, \ddot{y}, \ddot{z}, \ldots y^{(n)}, z^{(m)}$, and y, z are undetermined functions of x.

Let
$$Q=\frac{dV}{dz},\ Q_1=\frac{dV}{d\dot{z}},\ \text{\&c.},$$
then
$$\delta U=\Big/_{x_0}^{x_1} Vdx+\int_{x_0}^{x_1}(P\delta y+P_1D\delta y+\ldots+P_nD^n\delta y)dx$$
$$+\int_{x^0}^{x_1}(Q\delta z+Q_1D\delta z+\ldots+Q_mD^m\delta z)dx.$$

Proceeding as in § 7, we find
$$\delta U=\int_{x_0}^{x_1}(P)\delta ydx+\int_{x_0}^{x_1}(Q)\delta zdx+\Big/_{x_0}^{x_1} Vdx$$
$$+\Big/_{x_0}^{x_1}\{(P_1)\delta y+(P_2)\delta\dot{y}+\ldots+P_n\delta y^{(n-1)}\}$$
$$+\Big/_{x_0}^{x_1}\{(Q_1)\delta z+(Q_2)\delta\dot{z}+\ldots+Q_m\delta z^{(m-1)}\} \qquad \text{(25)},$$
where (P), (P_1), ... have the same meaning as in § 7, and (Q), (Q_1), ... are the corresponding functions for the variable z.

18. The determination of y and z where $\int_{x_0}^{x_1} Vdx$ is a maximum or a minimum leads, as in § 8, to the equations $(P)=0$, $(Q)=0$, along with the equation at the limits
$$\Big/_{x_0}^{x_1} Vdx+\Big/_{x_0}^{x_1}\{(P_1)\delta y+\ldots P_n\delta y^{(n-1)}\}+\Big/_{x_0}^{x_1}\{(Q_1)\delta z+\ldots Q_m\delta z^{(m-1)}\}=0.$$
The mode of treatment is similar to that for a single dependent variable.

19. In the discussion of a curve which possesses a maximum or minimum property, if we limit the investigation to all curves of a given length or which satisfy some other condition, we have a distinct class of problems, which originated in the isoperimetrical problems of James Bernoulli. They were originally styled *isoperimetrical*, but are now called problems of *relative maxima and minima*. Thus, let it be proposed to determine the form of y which renders $U=\int_{x_0}^{x_1} Vdx$ a maximum or a minimum, and which also satisfies the condition $U'=\int_{x_0}^{x_1} V'dx=$ constant, where V and V' are given functions of $x, y, \dot{y}$, &c. It is obvious that, if U is a maximum or a minimum, so also is $U+aU'$, where a is any arbitrary constant. Accordingly the problem reduces to the determination of the maximum or minimum value of the integral $\int_{x_0}^{x_1}(V+aV')dx$, regarding a as a constant, whose value is to be determined by aid of the given value of U'.

20. Another class of problems closely allied to the preceding is that in which the variables are connected by one or more equations of condition: for instance, when $y, \dot{y}, \ddot{y}$, &c., $z, \dot{z}$, &c., are connected by a relation $W=0$, we investigate the maximum or minimum values of
$$U=\int_{x_0}^{x_1}(V+\lambda W)dx \qquad \text{(26)},$$
where λ is an indeterminate function of x. We will illustrate these principles by examples.

21. To find the curve connecting two fixed points such that the surface generated by its revolution round a fixed line shall be given, and the volume of the generated solid shall be a maximum. Taking the fixed line as the axis of x, we may write $U=\int_{x^0}^{x_1}(y^2+ay\sqrt{1+\dot{y}^2})dx$.

Hence by (15) we have $y^2+ay\sqrt{1+\dot{y}^2}=c+\frac{ay\dot{y}^2}{\sqrt{1+\dot{y}^2}}$,

or
$$y^2+\frac{ay}{\sqrt{1+\dot{y}^2}}=c \qquad \text{(27)}.$$
If the curve meets the fixed axis we have $c=0$, and the curve is a circle whose centre lies on the axis.

The further integration of (27) depends on elliptic functions; it can, however, be shown without difficulty, as was proved by Delauney, that the curve is that generated by the focus of an ellipse or hyperbola which rolls on a fixed right line.

22. As an illustration of the method of § 20 we shall consider again the problem of § 13, taking the arc for independent variable. Let $\dot{x}=\frac{dx}{ds}$, $\dot{y}=\frac{dy}{ds}$, then we have the relation $\dot{x}^2+\dot{y}^2-1=0$; and we write

$U=\int_{s_0}^{s_1}\{\mu+\frac{1}{2}\lambda(\dot{x}^2+\dot{y}^2-1)\}ds=\int_{s_0}^{s_1}Vds$, where $V=\mu+\frac{1}{2}\lambda(\dot{x}^2+\dot{y}^2-1)$.

Hence for a maximum or minimum we have
$$\frac{d\mu}{dx}=\frac{d}{ds}(\lambda\dot{x}),\quad \frac{d\mu}{dy}=\frac{d}{ds}(\lambda\dot{y}) \qquad \text{(28)};$$
therefore
$$\frac{d\mu}{ds}=\dot{x}\frac{d\mu}{dx}+\dot{y}\frac{d\mu}{dy}=\frac{d\lambda}{ds},$$
or
$$\mu=\lambda+c \qquad \text{(29)}.$$

[1] *Calculus of Variations*, p. 140.

Again, the equation at the limits is

$$\int_{s_0}^{s_1}\mu ds+\int_{s_0}^{s_1}\lambda(\dot{x}\delta x+\dot{y}\delta y)=0 \quad\text{.........(30)};$$

also at each limit we have $dx=\delta x+\dot{x}ds$, $dy=\delta y+\dot{y}ds$; hence (30) transforms into $\int_{s_0}^{s_1}(\mu-\lambda)ds+\int_{s_0}^{s_1}\lambda(\dot{x}dx+\dot{y}dy)=0$,

or
$$cd(s_1-s_0)+\int_{s_0}^{s_1}\lambda(\dot{x}dx+\dot{y}dy)=0 \quad\text{.........(31)}.$$

Now if the length of the curve be given, the first term in (31) vanishes; whereas, if the length be not given, we must have $c=0$. Consequently in the isoperimetrical problem we have $\mu=\lambda+c$, and in the general case $\lambda=\mu$. If we substitute μ for λ in (28) we can readily deduce the results already given in § 13.

23. More generally, let μ be a function of x, y, $\dot{x}$, and $\dot{y}$, then we have $V=\mu+\frac{1}{2}\lambda(\dot{x}^2+\dot{y}^2-1)$. Here we readily deduce

$$V=c+\dot{x}\frac{dV}{d\dot{x}}+\dot{y}\frac{dV}{d\dot{y}} \quad\text{.........(32)};$$

and the equation at the limits becomes

$$cd(s_1-s_0)+\int_{s_0}^{s_1}\left(\frac{dV}{d\dot{x}}dx+\frac{dV}{d\dot{y}}dy\right)=0.$$

This shows, as before, that when the length of the curve is not given we have $c=0$.

24. The criterion for distinguishing between maximum and minimum solutions was investigated by Legendre, Lagrange, and other eminent mathematicians, for whose contributions to the solution of this problem, see Todhunter's *History of the Calculus of Variations.* The full analytical investigation was, however, first given by Jacobi, of whose results we here give a brief discussion.

In this investigation, as in ordinary problems of maxima and minima, it is necessary to take into consideration the squares and the higher powers of our indefinitely small variations. Thus, if $U=\int_{x_0}^{x_1}Vdx$, the complete variation of U may be written $\delta U+\frac{1}{2}\delta^2 U+$ &c., where δU depends on the first powers of δy, $\delta\dot{y}$, &c., and $\delta^2 U$ on their second powers, &c. Again, we will suppose that the limiting values of y and of its first $n-1$ differential coefficients are fixed, then $\delta U=\int_{x_0}^{x_1}\delta Vdx=\int_{x_0}^{x_1}M\delta ydx$, and $\delta^2 U=\int_{x_0}^{x_1}\delta M\delta ydx$. The solutions of the problem, as already observed (§ 8), are given by the equation $M=0$. Also for a true maximum it is necessary that $\delta^2 U$ should be constantly negative, and for a minimum that it should be positive. If $\delta^2 U=0$, or if it change its sign between the limits of integration, the result is in general neither a maximum nor a minimum. As before, we suppose V a function of x, y, $\dot{y}\ldots y^{(n)}$, and

$$M=P-\frac{dP_1}{dx}+\frac{d^2P_2}{dx^2}-\ldots+(-1)^n\frac{d^nP_n}{dx^n}$$
$$=\left(\frac{d}{dy}-D\frac{d}{d\dot{y}}+D^2\frac{d}{d\ddot{y}}-\ldots\right)V;$$

therefore
$$\delta M=\left(\frac{d}{dy}-D\frac{d}{d\dot{y}}+D^2\frac{d}{d\ddot{y}}-\ldots\right)\delta V$$
$$=\left(\frac{d}{dy}-D\frac{d}{d\dot{y}}+D^2\frac{d}{d\ddot{y}}-\ldots\right)\left(\frac{dV}{dy}+\frac{dV}{d\dot{y}}D+\ldots+\frac{dV}{dy^{(n)}}D^n\right)\delta y \quad (33).$$

When this is developed, we see that every term, disregarding sign, is of the form $D^l\dfrac{d^2V}{dy^{(l)}\,dy^{(m)}}D^m\delta y$. Also, if we combine this with the corresponding term, and make $l=m+r$, we readily see that

$$\delta M=\Sigma(-1^l)D^m\left\{D^r\frac{d^2V}{dy^{(l)}\,dy^{(m)}}+(-1)^r\frac{d^2V}{dy^{(l)}\,dy^{(m)}}D^r\right\}D^m\delta y \;(34).$$

Hence δM is reducible to the form

$$\delta M=(A_0+DA_1D+D^2A_2D^2+\ldots+D^nA_nD^n)\delta y \;\ldots(35),$$

provided it can be shown that $D^ru+(-1)^r uD^r$ is reducible to an operation of such a form. Now this is readily seen, for $Du-uD\equiv\dot{u}$, therefore $D^2u-DuD\equiv D\dot{u}$ and $DuD-uD^2\equiv\dot{u}D$; consequently $D^2u+uD^2\equiv 2DuD+\ddot{u}$. In like manner $D^3u-uD^3\equiv 2D\dot{u}D+\dddot{u}$, and the proposed result can be readily shown by induction. Hence we infer that we may write δM in the form (35).

25. We have in the next place to show that the *symbolic operator* $u(A_0+DA_1D+\ldots+D^nA_nD^n)u$ may be written in the form $B_0+DB_1D+\ldots+D^nB_nD^n$. To establish this, it is sufficient to show that $uD^rA_rD^ru$ can be transformed into the shape in question. By Leibnitz's theorem we have

$$D^ru\equiv uD^r+r\dot{u}D^{r-1}+\frac{r(r-1)}{1.2}\ddot{u}D^{r-2}+\ldots$$

and
$$uD^r\equiv D^ru-rD^{r-1}\dot{u}+\frac{r(r-1)}{1.2}D^{r-2}\ddot{u}-\ldots$$

But these may be written

$$D^ru\equiv uD^r+L_1D^{r-1}+L_2D^{r-2}+\ldots+L_r,$$
$$uD^r\equiv D^ru-D^{r-1}L_1+D^{r-2}L_2-\ldots,$$

therefore $uD^rA_rD^ru\equiv(D^ru-D^{r-1}L_1+\ldots)A_r(uD^r+L_1D^{r-1}+\ldots)$. Hence by § 24 we readily see that $uD^rA_rD^ru$ is of the required form. Accordingly we may write
$u(A_0+DA_1D+\ldots+D^nA_nD^n)uv=(B_0+DB_1D+\ldots+D^nB_nD^n)v$(36).
If $uv=\delta y$, we get from (35)

$$u\delta M=(B_0+DB_1D+\ldots+D^nB_nD^n)\frac{\delta y}{u} \quad\text{.......(37)};$$

again, if $v=1$ in (36), we have

$$u(A_0+DA_1D+\ldots+D^nA_nD^n)u=B_0 \quad\text{........(38)}.$$

Hence, if u_1 be a solution of $(A_0+DA_1D+\ldots+D^nA_nD^n)u=0$, that is, if it be a solution of $\delta M=0$, the corresponding value of B_0 is 0. Consequently we have from (36)

$$u_1\delta M=D(B_1+DB_2D+\ldots+D^{n-1}B_nD^{n-1})D\frac{\delta y}{u_1}.$$

If $u_1=\dfrac{1}{z_1}$, this becomes

$$\delta M=z_1D(B_1+DB_2D+\ldots D^{n-1}B_nD^{n-1})Dz_1\delta y \quad\text{......(39)}.$$

Again, the symbolic operator $B_1+DB_2D+\ldots+D^{n-1}B_{n-1}D^{n-1}$ can be transformed into $z_2D(C_1+DC_2D+\ldots+D^{n-2}C_{n-1}D^{n-2})Dz_2$, and so on. Finally we get

$$\delta M=z_1Dz_2D\ldots z_{n-1}Dz_nDz_{n-1}\ldots Dz_2Dz_1\delta y \quad\text{........(40)}.$$

Thus we obtain

$$\delta^2U=\int_{x_0}^{x_1}\delta yz_1Dz_2D\ldots Dz_nD\ldots Dz_2Dz_1\delta ydx \quad\text{........(41)}.$$

If we integrate by parts, then, since the limiting values of y, $\dot{y}\ldots$ are fixed, we get $\delta^2U=-\int_{x_0}^{x_1}(Dz_1\delta y)(z_2Dz_3\ldots z_2Dz_1\delta y)dx$, and after n successive integrations

$$\delta^nU=(-1)^n\int_{x_0}^{x_1}z_n(Dz_{n-1}Dz_{n-2}\ldots D_1z\delta y)^2dx \quad\text{........(42)}.$$

Again, from (33) we see that $A_n=(-1)^n\dfrac{d^2V}{dy^{(n)2}}$; also from (40) we find without difficulty

$$A_n=z_n(z_1z_2\ldots z_{n-1})^2 \quad\text{..................(43)}.$$

Hence we get finally

$$\delta^2U=\int_{x_0}^{x_1}Q_n\left(\frac{Dz_{n-1}Dz_{n-2}\ldots Dz_1\delta y}{z_{n-1}z_{n-2}\ldots z_1}\right)^2dx\ldots \quad\text{........(44)},$$

where $Q_n=\dfrac{d^2V}{dy^{(n)2}}$. From this it follows that the sign of δ^2U depends in general on that of Q_n or $\dfrac{d^2V}{dy^{(n)2}}$. Accordingly for a maximum or minimum solution it is necessary that Q_n should have the same sign for all values of x between the limits of integration, dx being supposed always positive. The reader will find no difficulty in applying this criterion to any of the examples which we have hitherto given.

26. A new and complete discussion of the criteria for the discrimination of maximum and minimum solutions has been given by Mr Culverwell in *Trans. Roy. Soc.*, vol. clxxviii. (1887). Owing to want of space we can only make an allusion to this remarkable memoir, which contains an elementary investigation of the criteria for maxima and minima not only in the case of one but for any number of dependent variables, as also for multiple integrals.

27. We now proceed to the application of the calculus of variations to multiple integrals, commencing with the double integral $U=\int_{x_0}^{x_1}\int_{y_0}^{y_1}Vdxdy$, where V is a function of x, y, z, p, q, r, s, and t, in which $p=\dfrac{dz}{dx}$, $q=\dfrac{dz}{dy}$, $r=\dfrac{d^2z}{dx^2}$, $s=\dfrac{d^2z}{dxdy}$, $t=\dfrac{d^2z}{dy^2}$, in accordance with the ordinary notation.

Let $V_1=\int_{y_0}^{y_1}Vdy$, then $U=\int_{x_0}^{x_1}V_1dx$; therefore by (6) we have

$$\delta U=\int_{x_0}^{x_1}\delta V_1dx+\int_{x_0}^{x_1}V_1dx$$
$$=\int_{x_0}^{x_1}\int_{y_0}^{y_1}\delta Vdxdy+\int_{x_0}^{x_1}\int_{y_0}^{y_1}V\delta ydx+\int_{x_0}^{x_1}dx\int_{y_0}^{y_1}V_1dy.$$

Again $\delta V=N\delta z+P\delta p+Q\delta q+R\delta r+S\delta s+T\delta t$, where $N=\dfrac{dV}{dz}$,

$P=\frac{dV}{dp}$, $Q=\frac{dV}{dq}$, $R=\frac{dV}{dr}$, $S=\frac{dV}{ds}$, $T=\frac{dV}{dt}$. Hence $\int_{x_0}^{x_1}\int_{y_0}^{y_1}\delta V dxdy$

$$=\int_{x_0}^{x_1}\int_{y_0}^{y_1}(N\delta z+P\delta p+Q\delta q+R\delta r+S\delta s+T\delta t)dxdy \text{.........(45).}$$

In the transformation of this expression we shall employ the following formulæ, which are easily established,

$$\int_{x_0}^{x_1}\int_{y_0}^{y_1}\frac{du}{dx}dxdy=\Big/_{x_0}^{x_1}dx\int_{y_0}^{y_1}udy-\int_{x_0}^{x_1}\Big/_{y_0}^{y_1}u\frac{dy}{dx}dx \text{......(46),}$$

and $$\int_{x_0}^{x_1}\int_{y_0}^{y_1}\frac{du}{dy}dxdy=\int_{x_0}^{x_1}\Big/_{y_0}^{y_1}udx \text{ ....(47).}$$

Hence we get $$\int_{x_0}^{x_1}\int_{y_0}^{y_1}P\frac{d\delta z}{dx}dxdy$$

$$=-\int_{x_0}^{x_1}\int_{y_0}^{y_1}\frac{dP}{dx}\delta zdxdy+\Big/_{x_0}^{x_1}dx\int_{y_0}^{y_1}P\delta zdy-\int_{x_0}^{x_1}\Big/_{y_0}^{y_1}P\frac{dy}{dx}\delta zdy,$$

also $$\int_{x_0}^{x_1}\int_{y_0}^{y_1}Q\frac{d\delta z}{dy}dxdy=-\int_{x_0}^{x_1}\int_{y_0}^{y_1}\frac{dQ}{dy}\delta zdxdy+\int_{x_0}^{x_1}\Big/_{y_0}^{y_1}Q\delta zdx.$$

Next, to transform $\int_{x_0}^{x_1}\int_{y_0}^{y_1}R\frac{d^2\delta z}{dx^2}dxdy$, we have

$$\int_{x_0}^{x_1}\int_{y_0}^{y_1}\left(R\frac{d^2\delta z}{dx^2}+\frac{dR}{dx}\frac{d\delta z}{dx}\right)dxdy=\int_{x_0}^{x_1}\int_{y_0}^{y_1}\frac{d}{dx}\left(R\frac{d\delta z}{dx}\right)dxdy$$
$$=\Big/_{x_0}^{x_1}dx\int_{y_0}^{y_1}R\frac{d\delta z}{dx}dy-\int_{x_0}^{x_1}\Big/_{y_0}^{y_1}R\frac{d\delta z}{dx}\frac{dy}{dx}dx,$$

also $$\int_{x_0}^{x_1}\int_{y_0}^{y_1}\left(\frac{dR}{dx}\frac{d\delta z}{dx}+\frac{d^2R}{dx^2}\delta z\right)dxdy=\int_{x_0}^{x_1}\int_{y_0}^{y_1}\frac{d}{dx}\left(\frac{dR}{dx}\delta z\right)dxdy$$
$$=\Big/_{x_0}^{x_1}dx\int_{y_0}^{y_1}\frac{dR}{dx}\delta zdy-\int_{x_0}^{x_1}\Big/_{y_0}^{y_1}\frac{dR}{dx}\frac{dy}{dx}\delta zdy.$$

Consequently, by subtraction, $\int_{x_0}^{x_1}\int_{y_0}^{y_1}\left(R\frac{d^2\delta z}{dx^2}-\frac{d^2R}{dx^2}\delta z\right)dxdy$

$$=\Big/_{x_0}^{x_1}dx\int_{x_0}^{y_1}\left(R\frac{d\delta z}{dx}-\frac{dR}{dx}\delta z\right)dy+\int_{x_0}^{x_1}\Big/_{y_0}^{y_1}\left(\frac{dR}{dx}\delta z-R\frac{d\delta z}{dx}\right)\frac{dy}{dx}dx.$$

Again, in transforming the latter integral it is necessary to observe that y_1 and y_0 are functions of x, and accordingly that in that integral we have $\frac{d\delta z}{dx}=\frac{d}{dx}(\delta z)-\frac{dy}{dx}\frac{d\delta z}{dy}$; hence

$$-\int_{x_0}^{x_1}\Big/_{y_0}^{y_1}R\frac{d\delta z}{dx}\frac{dy}{dx}dx=\int_{x_0}^{x_1}\Big/_{y_0}^{y_1}R\left(\frac{dy}{dx}\right)^2\frac{d\delta z}{dy}dx-\int_{x_0}^{x_1}\Big/_{y_0}^{y_1}R\frac{dy}{dx}\frac{d}{dx}(\delta z)dx,$$

also $$\int_{x_0}^{x_1}\Big/_{y_0}^{y_1}R\frac{dy}{dx}\frac{d}{dx}(\delta z)dy=\int_{x_0}^{x_1}\Big/_{y_0}^{y_1}\frac{d}{dx}(R\frac{dy}{dx}\delta z)dy$$
$$-\int_{x_0}^{x_1}\Big/_{y_0}^{y_1}\delta z\frac{d}{dx}\left(R\frac{dy}{dx}\right)dx.$$

But $$\frac{d}{dx}\left(R\frac{dy}{dx}\right)=R\frac{d^2y}{dx^2}+\frac{dy}{dx}\left(\frac{dR}{dx}+\frac{dy}{dx}\frac{dR}{dy}\right);$$ hence we get

$$\int_{x_0}^{x_1}\int_{y_0}^{y_1}R\frac{d^2\delta z}{dx^2}dxdy=\int_{x_0}^{x_1}\int_{y_0}^{y_1}\frac{d^2R}{dx^2}\delta zdxdy+\Big/_{x_0}^{x_1}\int_{y_0}^{y_1}\left(R\frac{d\delta z}{dx}-\frac{dR}{dx}\delta z\right)dy$$
$$+\int_{x_0}^{x_1}\Big/_{y_0}^{y_1}\left\{R\frac{d^2y}{dx^2}+2\frac{dR}{dx}\frac{dy}{dx}+\frac{dR}{dy}\left(\frac{dy}{dx}\right)^2\right\}\delta zdx$$
$$+\int_{x_0}^{x_1}\Big/_{y^0}^{y_1}R\left(\frac{dy}{dx}\right)^2\frac{d\delta z}{dy}dx+\Big/_{x_0}^{x_1}\Big/_{y_0}^{y_1}R\frac{dy}{dx}\delta z \text{..................(48).}$$

Next, to transform $\int_{x_0}^{x_1}\int_{y_0}^{y_1}S\frac{d^2\delta z}{dxdy}dxdy$. Here

$$\int_{x_0}^{x_1}\int_{y_0}^{y_1}\left(S\frac{d^2\delta z}{dxdy}+\frac{dS}{dx}\frac{d\delta z}{dy}\right)dxdy=\int_{x_0}^{x_1}\int_{y_0}^{y_1}\frac{d}{dx}\left(S\frac{d\delta z}{dy}\right)dxdy$$
$$=\Big/_{x_0}^{x_1}\int_{y_0}^{y_1}S\frac{d\delta z}{dy}dy-\int_{x_0}^{x_1}\Big/_{y_0}^{y_1}S\frac{d\delta z}{dy}\frac{dy}{dx}dx,$$

also $$\int_{x_0}^{x_1}\int_{y_0}^{y_1}\left(\frac{dS}{dx}\frac{d\delta z}{dy}+\delta z\frac{d^2S}{dxdy}\right)dxdy=\int_{x_0}^{x_1}\Big/_{y_0}^{y_1}\frac{dS}{dx}\delta zdx;$$

hence by subtraction $\int_{x_0}^{x_1}\int_{y_0}^{y_1}\left(S\frac{d^2\delta z}{dxdy}-\delta z\frac{d^2S}{dxdy}\right)dxdy$

$$=\Big/_{x_0}^{x_1}\int_{y_0}^{y_1}S\frac{d\delta z}{dy}dy-\int_{x_0}^{x_1}\Big/_{y_0}^{y_1}\left(\frac{dS}{dx}\delta z+S\frac{d\delta z}{dy}\frac{dy}{dx}\right)dx \text{.........(49).}$$

Finally, to transform $\int_{x_0}^{x_1}\int_{y_0}^{y_1}T\frac{d^2\delta z}{dy^2}dxdy$, we have

$$\int_{x_0}^{x_1}\int_{y_0}^{y_1}\left(T\frac{d^2\delta z}{dy^2}+\frac{dT}{dy}\frac{d\delta z}{dy}\right)=\int_{x_0}^{x_1}\int_{y_0}^{y_1}\frac{d}{dy}\left(T\frac{d\delta z}{dy}\right)dxdy=\int_{x_0}^{x_1}\Big/_{y_0}^{y_1}T\frac{d\delta z}{dy}dx,$$

and $\int_{x_0}^{x_1}\int_{y_0}^{y_1}\left(\frac{dT}{dy}\frac{d\delta z}{dy}+\frac{d^2T}{dy^2}\delta z\right)dxdy=\int_{x_0}^{x_1}\Big/_{y_0}^{y_1}\frac{dT}{dy}\delta zdx$, consequently

$$\int_{x_0}^{x_1}\int_{y_0}^{y_1}\left(T\frac{d^2\delta z}{dy^2}-\frac{d^2T}{dy^2}\delta z\right)dxdy=\int_{x_0}^{x_1}\Big/_{y_0}^{y_1}\left(T\frac{d\delta z}{dy}-\frac{dT}{dy}\delta z\right)dx. \text{(50).}$$

Combining the preceding results, we get $\delta U=\delta\int_{x_0}^{x_1}\int_{y_0}^{y_1}Vdxdy$

$$=\int_{x_0}^{x_1}\int_{y_0}^{y_1}\left(N-\frac{dP}{dx}-\frac{dQ}{dy}+\frac{d^2R}{dx^2}+\frac{d^2S}{dxdy}+\frac{d^2T}{dy^2}\right)\delta zdxdy$$
$$+\int_{x_0}^{x_1}\Big/_{y_0}^{y_1}\left(Q-P\frac{dy}{dx}+R\frac{d^2y}{dx^2}+2\frac{dR}{dx}\frac{dy}{dx}+\frac{dR}{dy}\left(\frac{dy}{dx}\right)^2-\frac{dS}{dx}-\frac{dT}{dy}\right)\delta zdx$$
$$+\int_{x_0}^{x_1}\Big/_{y_0}^{y_1}\left(R\left(\frac{dy}{dx}\right)^2-S\frac{dy}{dx}+T\right)\frac{d\delta z}{dy}dx$$
$$+\int_{x_0}^{x_1}\Big/_{y_0}^{y_1}V\delta ydx+\Big/_{x_0}^{x_1}\int_{y_0}^{y_1}Vdxdy+\Big/_{x_0}^{x_1}\int_{y_0}^{y_1}\left(P-\frac{dR}{dx}-\frac{dS}{dy}\right)\delta zdy$$
$$+\Big/_{x_0}^{x_1}\int_{y_0}^{y_1}R\frac{d\delta z}{dx}dy+\Big/_{x_0}^{x_1}\Big/_{y_0}^{y_1}\left(S-R\frac{dy}{dx}\right)\delta z \text{ ....(51).}$$

28. In many applications the limits of x and y are determined from a single equation. Thus, suppose the integral $U=\iint Vdxdy$ to express the sum of the elements $Vdxdy$ for all values of x and y which satisfy either $\phi(x, y) > 0$ or $\phi(x, y) < 0$, then the limits are given by the equation $\phi(x, y)=0$. In this case the preceding value of δU becomes much simplified, for y_0, y_1 are determined from the equation[1] $\phi=0$; and the extreme values of x are found by eliminating y between the equations $\phi=0$ and $d\phi/dy=0$. But these are the conditions that $\phi=0$ should have equal roots in y; we consequently infer that, when either $x=x_0$ or $x=x_1$, we have $y_0=y_1$. Hence we observe that $\Big/^{x_0}\int_{y_0}^{y_1}udy=0$ and $\Big/^{x_1}\int_{y_0}^{y_1}udy=0$ for all values of u, so that the last four terms in the expression for δU in (51) disappear in this case.

The methods and results of this and the preceding section can without difficulty be extended to triple and higher multiple integrals.

29. The method of application of the calculus of variations to the determination of maximum or minimum values of multiple definite integrals proceeds on the same principles as those already considered in § 9 for single integrals.

We shall limit the discussion to a brief consideration of the double integral $U=\iint Vdxdy$, in which V is a function of x, y, z, p, and q solely, and the limits are determined, as in § 28, by an equation of the form $\phi(x, y)=0$. Such problems readily admit of geometrical interpretation.

Here (51) reduces to

$$\delta U=\int_{x_0}^{x_1}\int_{y_0}^{y_1}\left(N-\frac{dP}{dx}-\frac{dQ}{dy}\right)\delta zdxdy$$
$$+\int_{x_0}^{x_1}\Big/_{y_0}^{y_1}\left\{\left(Q-P\frac{dy}{dx}\right)\delta z+V\delta y\right\}dx \text{...........(52).}$$

Consequently, as in the case of single integrals, for a maximum or minimum value of U we must have

$$N-\frac{dP}{dx}-\frac{dQ}{dy}=0 \text{ ....(53),}$$

and $$\Big/_{y_0}^{y_1}\left\{\left(Q-P\frac{dy}{dx}\right)\delta z+V\delta y\right\}=0 \text{ ....(54).}$$

The former is in this case a partial differential equation of the second order, whose solution, whenever it can be obtained, consists of an equation between x, y, z having two arbitrary functions. The form of these functions in each case is to be determined by aid of (54) combined with the given limiting conditions of the problem. Thus, let us suppose the upper limit restricted to points in the surface $z=f_1(x, y)$, and let $p'=\frac{df_1}{dx}$, $q'=\frac{df_1}{dy}$; then $\delta\Big/^{y_1}z=\Big/^{y_1}q'\delta y$; and $\Big/^{y_1}(\delta z+q\delta y)=\Big/^{y_1}q'\delta y$. This gives

$$\Big/^{y_1}\{\delta z+(q-q')\delta y\}=0 \text{..................(55).}$$

Substituting in (54), we get

$$\Big/^{y_1}\left\{V+\left(Q-P\frac{dy}{dx}\right)(q'-q)\right\}=0 \text{ ....(56).}$$

Again, along the limiting curve we have $dz=pdx+qdy$ and $dz=p'dx+q'dy$; hence we get $\frac{dy}{dx}=-\frac{p'-p}{q'-q}$. Substituting in (56), we have along the limiting curve

$$V+P(p'-p)+Q(q'-q)=0 \text{ ....(57).}$$

[1] If the equation $\phi=0$ gives for y several values, y_0, y_1, y_2, y_3, y_4, ... then we substitute $\int Vdy=\int_{y_0}^{y_1}Vdy+\int_{y_2}^{y_3}Vdy+\ldots$, and each integral is to be treated as above.

A similar equation holds if the lower limit be restricted by another surface.

By aid of these equations the arbitrary functions involved in the solution of (53) are determinable. For example, to find the surface such that $\iint \mu dS$ shall be a minimum, dS being an element of the surface and μ a given function of the co-ordinates x, y, z. Here $V=\mu\sqrt{1+p^2+q^2}, P=\frac{\mu p}{\sqrt{1+p^2+q^2}}, Q=\frac{\mu q}{\sqrt{1+p^2+q^2}}$. Hence the equation $N-\frac{dP}{dx}-\frac{dQ}{dy}=0$ leads to $\frac{d}{dx}\left(\frac{p}{\sqrt{1+p^2+q^2}}\right)+\frac{d}{dy}\left(\frac{q}{\sqrt{1+p^2+q^2}}\right)$

$$=\frac{1}{\mu\sqrt{1+p^2+q^2}}\left\{\frac{d\mu}{dz}-p\frac{d\mu}{dx}-q\frac{d\mu}{dy}\right\},$$

or

$$\frac{1}{R}+\frac{1}{R'}=-\frac{1}{\mu}\left(\cos\alpha\frac{d\mu}{dx}+\cos\beta\frac{d\mu}{dy}+\cos\gamma\frac{d\mu}{dz}\right) \quad \ldots\ldots(58),$$

where R and R' are the principal radii of curvature of the surface at the point, and α, β, γ the angles which the normal to the surface makes with the co-ordinate axes. Again, if we suppose the surface limited by two fixed surfaces, the equation $V+P(p'-p)+Q(q'-q)=0$ reduces to

$$1+pp'+qq'=0 \quad \ldots\ldots\ldots\ldots\ldots\ldots\ldots(59).$$

This shows that the surface intersects each of its bounding surfaces orthogonally. As a particular case of (58) we infer that the surface of minimum area is in general such that its principal radii of curvature at every point are equal and of opposite signs. A remarkable investigation of the equation of this surface was given by Bonnet in *Liouville's Journal*, 1860. Again, in the surface of given area and of maximum volume we have $V=z-a\sqrt{1+p^2+q^2}$. The equation $N-\frac{dP}{dx}-\frac{dQ}{dy}=0$ readily leads in this case to $\frac{1}{R}+\frac{1}{R'}=a$.

30. The principles and method of the calculus of variations are largely employed in all branches of mathematics, both pure and applied. Want of space prevents our entering into any account of such application. The reader will find the history of this calculus fully detailed in Todhunter's treatise, already mentioned. The most important recent work in English is Mr Carll's *Calculus of Variations*, New York and London, 1885. (B. W.)

VARICOSE VEINS. See SURGERY, vol. xxii. p. 684.

VARLEY, CORNELIUS (1781-1873), water-colour painter, a younger brother of John Varley (see below), was born at Hackney, London, on 21st November 1781. He was educated by his uncle, a philosophical instrument maker, and under him acquired a knowledge of the natural sciences; but about 1800 he joined his brother in a tour through Wales, and began the study of art. He was soon engaged in teaching drawing. From 1803 till 1859 he was an occasional exhibitor in the Royal Academy; and he also contributed regularly to the displays of the Water-Colour Society, of which, in 1803, he was one of the founders, and of which he continued a member till 1821. His works, which are not numerous, consist mainly of carefully finished classical subjects, with architecture and figures. He published a series of etchings of Boats and other Craft on the River Thames, and during his life as an artist he continued deeply interested in scientific pursuits. For his improvements in the camera lucida, the camera obscura, and the microscope he received the Isis gold medal of the Society of Arts; and at the International Exhibition of 1851 he gained a medal for his invention of the graphic telescope. He died at Hampstead on 2nd October 1873.

VARLEY, JOHN (1778-1842), water-colour painter, was born at Hackney, London, on 17th August 1778. His father, a man of scientific attainments and tutor in the family of Lord Stanhope, discouraged his leanings towards art, and placed him under a silversmith. But on his parent's death Varley escaped from this uncongenial employment, and, after working with a portrait painter, engaged himself at the age of sixteen to an architectural draughtsman, who took him on a provincial tour to sketch the principal buildings in the towns they visited. His spare hours were employed in sketching from nature, and in the evenings he was permitted, like Turner and Girtin, to study in the house of Dr Munro. In 1798 he exhibited his first work, a View of Peterborough Cathedral, in the Royal Academy. In 1799 he visited North Wales, and in its wild mountain scenery found the subjects best suited to his brush. He returned to the same district in 1800, and again in 1802, and the impressions then received powerfully influenced the whole course of his art. In 1804 he became a foundation member of the Water-Colour Society, and contributed over forty works to its first exhibition. He had married in the previous year; and, in order to provide for the wants of an increasing family, he was obliged to produce for the dealers much work of a slight and commonplace character. He also taught drawing, and some of his pupils, such as John Linnell and William Hunt, afterwards became celebrated. He was a firm believer in astrology, skilful in casting horoscopes; and some curious instances were related of the truth of his predictions. It was at his house that his friend William Blake sketched his celebrated Visionary Heads. Varley died at London on 17th November 1842.

Varley's landscapes are graceful and solemn in feeling, and simple and broad in treatment, being worked with a full brush and pure fresh transparent tints, usually without any admixture of body-colour. Though his works are rather mannered and conventional, they are well considered and excellent in composition. Some of his earlier water-colours, including his Views of the Thames, were painted upon the spot, and possess greater individuality than his later productions, which are mainly compositions of mountain and lake scenery, produced without direct reference to nature. Among his literary works are *Zodiacal Physiology*, 1828; *Observations on Colour and Sketching from Nature*, 1830; *A Practical Treatise on Perspective, and Principles of Landscape Design for Young Artists.*

VARNA, a fortified town and seaport of Bulgaria, in 43° 12′ N. lat. and 27° 56′ E. long., about midway between the Danube delta and the Bosphorus, lies on the north side of the Bay of Varna, at the opening of the Pravadi valley, 5 miles wide and skirted by hills on both sides. The town, which covers the slope of one of these hills, facing seawards, comprises Greek, Bulgarian, Turkish, Jewish, and Gipsy quarters, with a total population (1888) of 25,256 (8449 Bulgarians, 7569 Turks, 5423 Greeks). It has many finely built houses and shops. Its principal buildings are the gymnasium, a hospital, the barracks, and several churches and mosques. Amongst the industrial establishments are soap factories, breweries, distilleries, and tanneries. More than 3,740,000 gallons of wine are made annually within the department of Varna. The town is well supplied with good water, and is not unhealthy. Although open to the south and south-east, the bay affords safe anchorage, being sheltered from the north and north-east winds. Through the Pravadi it communicates with Lake Devno, which, if connected, as has been proposed, by a navigable canal with the bay, would form one of the best harbours in the Euxine. Varna is the chief outlet for the grain and agricultural produce of Bulgaria for Constantinople and the west of Europe, the export of grain in 1887 amounting in value to £244,210 (total exports, £349,030) and the total imports to £580,300. It lies 48 miles east of Shumla (Shumna), with which it is connected by the main Bulgarian railway, running thence to the Danube at Rustchuk,—these three fortresses forming with Silistria (on the Danube) the Bulgarian "quadrilateral." The old stone walls of Varna have been destroyed to make room for earth-fortifications.

Varna has been identified with the ancient Milesian colony of *Odessus* on the coast of Mœsia Inferior. It figures largely in the history of more recent times, and close by was fought in 1444 the battle in which Amurath (Murad) II. slew the Hungarian King Ladislaus, and routed his forces commanded by the renowned John Hunyady. Varna was occupied in 1828 by the Russians, in 1854 by the allies, who here organized the invasion of the Crimea, and in 1877 by the Egyptian troops summoned to the defence of Turkey against the Russians. The following year it was ceded to the principality of Bulgaria. It has long been the seat of a Greek metropolitan and since 1870 of a Bulgarian bishop.

VARNHAGEN VON ENSE, Karl August (1785-1858), German biographer, was born at Düsseldorf on 21st February 1785. He went to Berlin to study medicine, but devoted his attention chiefly to philosophy and literature, which he afterwards studied more thoroughly at Hamburg, Halle, and Tübingen. He began his literary career in 1804 as joint-editor with A. von Chamisso of a *Musen-almanach*. In 1809 he joined the Austrian army, and was wounded at the battle of Wagram. Soon afterwards he accompanied his superior officer, Prince Bentheim, to Paris, where he carried on his studies. In 1812 he joined the Prussian civil service at Berlin, but in the following year resumed his military career, this time as a captain in the Russian army. He accompanied Tettenborn to Hamburg and Paris, and his experiences were recorded in his *Geschichte der Hamburger Ereignisse* (1813) and his *Geschichte der Kriegszüge Tettenborn's* (1814). At Paris he entered the diplomatic service of Prussia, and in 1814 acted under Hardenberg at the congress of Vienna. He also accompanied Hardenberg to Paris in 1815. He was resident minister for some time at Carlsruhe, but was recalled in 1819, after which he lived chiefly at Berlin as a privy councillor of legation (*Geheimer Legationsrath*). He had no fixed official appointment, but was often employed in important political business.

In 1814 he married Rahel Antonie Friederike, originally called Levin, afterwards Robert. She was born in 1771 at Berlin, where she died in 1833. By birth she was a Jewess; but before her marriage she made profession of Christianity. Although she never wrote anything for publication, she was a woman of remarkable intellectual qualities, and exercised a powerful influence on many men of high ability. Her husband, who was devotedly attached to her, found in her sympathy and encouragement one of the chief sources of his inspiration as a writer. After her death he published a selection from her papers, and afterwards much of her correspondence was printed. Varnhagen von Ense never fully recovered from the shock caused by her death. He himself died suddenly in Berlin on 10th October 1858.

He made some reputation as an imaginative and critical writer, but he is famous chiefly as a biographer. He possessed a remarkable power of grouping facts so as to bring out their essential significance, and his style is distinguished for its strength, grace, and purity. Among his principal works are *Goethe in den Zeugnissen der Mitlebenden* (1824); *Biographische Denkmale* (five vols., 1824-30); and "Lives" of General von Seydlitz (1834), Sophia Charlotte, queen of Prussia (1837), Field-Marshal Schwerin (1841), Field-Marshal Keith (1844), and General Bülow von Dennewitz (1853). His *Denkwürdigkeiten und vermischte Schriften* appeared in seven volumes in 1837-46. After his death were published two additional volumes of *Denkwürdigkeiten*, some volumes of his correspondence with eminent men, his *Tagebücher* (14 vols.), *Blätter aus der preussischen Geschichte* (5 vols.), and *Biographische Porträts*. His selected writings appeared in nineteen volumes in 1871-76.

VARNISH. A varnish is a fluid preparation which, when spread out in thin layers, dries either by evaporation or by chemical action into a hard, transparent, and glossy film. Varnishes are used to communicate lustre and brilliance to many different kinds of dressed surfaces,—metal-work, wood, paint, paper, leather, &c.,—and to protect such surfaces from the influence of air and damp. The chief requisites of a good varnish are that it forms a firmly-adherent layer on the surface over which it is spread, that it dries hard, yet with sufficient elasticity and tenacity not to crack with changes of temperature, that it forms a glossy durable surface, and that it dries quickly. The materials which almost exclusively form the permanent body of varnishes are the drying oils and resinous substances, the chief of which are the copals, lac, dammar, elemi, amber, sandarac, mastic, and rosin. For certain forms of varnish the drying oils themselves act as the solvent for the resins, but in other cases volatile solvents are employed. The solvents chiefly used are methylated spirit, wood spirit, ether, benzin, and turpentine and other essential oils. Soluble colouring ingredients are also, in some cases, used in varnishes and lacquers, those principally available being gamboge, dragon's blood. aloes, cochineal, turmeric, and coal-tar dyes.

According to the solvents employed, the ordinary kinds of varnish are divided into three classes,—(1) spirit, (2) turpentine, and (3) oil varnishes. Spirit varnishes dry with great rapidity owing to the volatilization of the solvent spirit, leaving a coating of pure resin of great hardness and brilliance, but the film is deficient in tenacity, cracking and scaling readily on exposure. The resin lac, either as grain, shell, or bleached lac, is the basis of most spirit varnishes; but sandarac is also largely used, and to these are added in varying proportions the softer resins,—elemi, Venice turpentine, Canada balsam, mastic, &c.,—which give elasticity and tenacity to the varnish. The solvent is almost exclusively methylated spirit. The resins are ground and mixed with powdered glass, which prevents the resinous particles from agglutinating, and thus facilitates the solvent action of the spirit. The solution is effected by agitation in closed vessels with the aid of heat, and the varnish when strained off must be kept tightly closed from the air. Spirit varnishes are used principally for cabinet-work and turnery, stationery, gilding, and metal-work. Coloured spirit varnishes and lacquers are largely employed for metal-work, for imitation gilding and bronzing, for toys, &c. Turpentine is the solvent principally used for making dammar varnish, the solution being effected by powdering the resin and boiling it with a proportion of spirit of turpentine, after which more turpentine is added in the cold state to bring the preparation to a proper consistency. To increase the tenacity of such dammar varnish some proportion of boiled linseed oil or of oil copal varnish may be added. In place of oil of turpentine other essential oils may be used as solvents, and in practice oil of spike is largely utilized in preparing fine varnishes for oil paintings. Turpentine varnishes are also made in which the principal resinous bodies are sandarac and common rosin; and, moreover, turpentine is largely employed to reduce the consistency and to improve the drying properties of copal varnishes. The basis or solvent of oil or fatty varnishes consists principally of linseed oil; but the other drying oils—poppy and walnut, &c.—may also be used. These oils, without the addition of resins, themselves form varnishes which on exposure in thin layers dry by a process of oxidation into tough glossy films; but the drying proceeds very slowly unless the oils are previously boiled with the red oxide of lead or otherwise treated to increase their power of absorbing oxygen (see Linseed Oil, vol. xiv. p. 677). It is in the form of boiled oil or of oil prepared with driers that these oils are used in varnish-making. Oil varnishes thus differ from the other classes in the circumstance that the principal solvent is not volatile and dissipated on exposure, but in itself forms an essential and permanent ingredient in the preparation. The resin principally used in oil varnishes is copal, and its varieties differ very much in hardness, that is, in the temperature at which they melt and distil. Hard and semi-hard copals can only be made to mix with and dissolve in oils at the temperature at which they distil, which ranges from 230° to 360° C. The copal in varnish-making is melted and brought to the requisite temperature in a copper vessel. Simultaneously the oil is heated to the boiling-point in a separate copper vessel, and at the proper moment a measured quantity of the boiling oil is added to the liquefied resin. They are then boiled together till the mixture becomes perfectly clear, and by a series of alternate additions of oil and resin at proper temperatures the solution is brought to the desired consistency. After the mixture of oil and resin has sufficiently cooled, oil of turpentine in certain proportion is added. The making of copal varnish is attended with great risk of burning, and special precautions have to be observed for the extinction of the fire that frequently bursts out in these highly-heated and most inflammable bodies. Copal varnish is also made by boiling together the requisite proportions of resin and oil under pressure in a closed vessel, and subsequently adding turpentine, or by dissolving the resin and turpentine at the high heat and adding the oil afterwards. Amber varnish is prepared by the same methods as those followed in preparing copal, but, the resin being still more refractory and insoluble, a higher heat is required. A peculiar varnish forms the basis of the celebrated Japanese lacquer. The substance is a resinous exudation, which is obtained by making incisions in the bark of the Japanese urushi or lacquer-tree, *Rhus vernicifera.* The resinous juice on settling in vats separates into two layers, the upper and thinner of which, on mixture with a drying oil, forms a transparent varnish, having a rich yellow colour, which dries into coatings of remarkable tenacity, durability, and lustre (see JAPANNING, vol. xiii. p. 592).

VARRO, MARCUS TERENTIUS, Roman polymath and man of letters, lived from 116 to 27 B.C. When he was born, the Gracchan agitation had only just been laid to rest, and the year of his death saw the final and formal establishment of the empire. Into the changing life of that stirring time Varro entered deeply, and there was no current in thought, culture, literature, and even politics, with which he was not closely in contact. Few have ever so thoroughly combined the pursuit of scholarship and literature with experience of practical affairs. Dionysius of Halicarnassus well described him as the man of widest experience during his age. Nothing is known of Varro's ancestors but that they were natives of the Sabine country, where Varro himself was born in the town of Reate. Here he imbibed in his earlier years a good measure of the hardy simplicity and strong seriousness which the later Romans attributed to the men of the early republic,—characteristics which were supposed to linger in the Sabine land after they had fled from the rest of Italy. The chief teacher of Varro was L. Ælius Stilo, the first systematic student, critic, and teacher of Latin philology and literature, and of the antiquities of Rome and Italy. We know from Cicero that Varro also studied at Athens, especially under the philosopher Antiochus of Ascalon. It was the aim of this teacher to lead back the Academic school from the scepticism of Arcesilaus and Carneades to the tenets of the early Platonists, as he understood them. His opponents, however, declared that he identified Platonism with Stoic dogmatism, and that a very slight change in his views would have converted him into a Stoic of the Stoics. When Cicero wrote his *Posterior Academics*, he introduced Varro as an interlocutor, and made him expound the views of Antiochus. The influence of Antiochus is most plainly to be traced in the extant remains of Varro's writings, and indirectly in works like the *De Civitate Dei* of Augustine, which owe much to Varro. In spite of controversial statements to the contrary, the differences between Antiocheanism and Stoicism were great and marked, and it is a serious, though a common, error to treat Varro as an adherent of the Stoic school. The political career of Varro seems to have been late and slow; but he arrived at the prætorship, after having been tribune of the people, quæstor, and curule ædile. In politics and war he followed Pompey's lead; but it is probable that he was discontented with the course on which his leader entered when the first triumvirate was formed, and he may thus have lost his chance of rising to the consulate. He actually ridiculed the coalition in a work entitled the *Three-Headed Monster* (Τρικάρανον in the Greek of Appian). He did not, however, refuse to join the commission of twenty by whom the great agrarian scheme of Cæsar for the resettlement of Capua and Campania was carried into execution (59 B.C.). Despite the difference between them in politics, Varro and Cæsar had literary tastes in common, and were friends in private life. Under Pompey Varro saw much active service: he was attached to Pompey as pro-quæstor, probably during the war against Sertorius in Spain. We next find him, as legate, in command of a fleet which kept the seas between Delos and Sicily, while Pompey was suppressing the pirates, and he even won the "naval crown," a coveted reward of personal prowess. A little later he was legate during the last Mithradatic war. In the conflict between Cæsar and the Pompeian party Varro was more than once actively engaged. In his *Civil War* (ii. 17-20) Cæsar tells how Varro, when legate in Spain along with Afranius and Petreius, lost his two legions without striking a blow, because the whole region where he was quartered joined the enemy. Cæsar curiously intimates that, though Varro did his best for Pompey from a sense of duty, his heart was really with the other leader. Nevertheless he proceeded to Epirus before the battle of Pharsalia, and awaited the result at Dyrrachium in the company of Cicero and Cato. Like Cicero, Varro received harsh treatment from Mark Antony after the Pompeian defeat. Some of his property was actually plundered, but restored at the bidding of Cæsar, to whom Varro in gratitude immediately dedicated one of his most important writings. The dictator employed the scholar in aiding him to collect and arrange great stores of Greek and Latin literature for the vast public library which he intended to found. We have glimpses of Varro at this time in the *Letters* of Cicero. The two, though alike in political inclinations and in their love for literature, were antipathetic in their natures,—the one soft in fibre, and vain, richly abundant in expression, and subtly sensitive, the other somewhat harsh, severe, and retiring, solid in learning, and no master of literary form. The impression of Varro's personality which Cicero gives is unattractive enough, but probably on the whole true. The formation of the second triumvirate again plunged Varro into danger. Antony took possession anew of the property he had been compelled to surrender, and inserted Varro's name on the list of the proscribed. His friends, however, afforded him protection. He was able to make peace with the triumvirs, but sacrificed his property and much of his beloved library. He was permitted to spend in quiet study and in writing the last fifteen years of his life. He is said to have died (27 B.C.) almost pen in hand.

Varro was not surpassed in the compass of his writings by any ancient, not even by any one of the later Greek philosophers, to some of whom tradition ascribes a fabulous number of separate works. In a passage quoted by Gellius, Varro himself, when over seventy years of age, estimated the number of "books" he had written at 490; but "book" here means, not merely such a work as was not subdivided into portions, but also a portion of a subdivided work. For example, the *Menippean Satires* numbered 150, and are all counted separately in Varro's estimate. Jerome made or copied a catalogue of Varro's works which has come down to us in a mutilated form. From this and from other extant materials Ritschl has set down the number of the distinct literary works at 74 and the number of separate "books" at about 620. The later years of the author's life were therefore even more fruitful than the earlier. The complete catalogue may be roughly arranged under three heads,—(1) belles lettres, (2) history and antiquities, (3) technical treatises on philosophy, law, grammar, mathematics, philology, and other subjects.

The first of these three classes no doubt mainly belonged to Varro's earlier life. In poetry he seems to have attempted nothing that was very elaborate, and little of a serious character. His genius tended naturally in the direction of burlesque and satire.

In belles lettres he showed himself throughout, both in matter and form, the pupil and admirer of Lucilius. He wrote satires in the style of his master, and he may be one of those to whom Horace alludes (*Sat.*, i. 10, 47) as having "tried satire in vain." One poetical work probably consisted of short pieces in the style of the more satirical poems of Catullus. It is doubtful whether, as has often been supposed, Varro wrote a philosophical poem somewhat in the style of Lucretius; if so, it should rather be classed with the prose technical treatises. One curious production was an essay in popular illustrated literature, which was almost unique in ancient times. Its title was *Imagines*, and it consisted of 700 prose biographies of Greek and Roman celebrities, with a metrical *elogium* for each, accompanied in each case by a portrait. But the lighter works of Varro have perished almost to the last line, with the exception of numerous fragments of the *Menippean Satires.* The Menippus whom Varro imitated lived in the first half of the third century B.C., and was born a Phœnician slave. He became a Cynic philosopher, and is a figure familiar to readers of Lucian. He flouted life and all philosophies but the Cynic in light compositions, partly in prose and partly in verse. The fragments of Varro's imitations have been frequently collected and edited, most recently by Riese and by Bücheler. The glowing and picturesque account of these fragments given by Mommsen in his *History of Rome* is known to all students of Roman literature, but few readers could pass from Mommsen's picture to a careful study of the passages themselves without severe disappointment. That the remains exhibit variety and fertility, that there are in them numerous happy strokes of humour and satire, and many felicitous phrases and descriptions, is true, but the art is on the whole heavy, awkward, and forced, and the style rudely archaic and untasteful. The Latin is frequently as rough and uncouth as that of Lucilius. No doubt Varro contemned the Hellenizing innovations by which the hard and rude Latin of his youth was transformed into the polished literary language of the late republican and the Augustan age. The titles of the *Menippean Satires* are very diverse. Sometimes personal names are chosen, and they range from the gods and demigods to the slaves, from Hercules to Marcipor. Frequently a popular proverb or catchword in Greek or Latin supplies the designation: thus we have as titles "I've got You" (Ἔχω σε); "You don't Know what Evening is to Bring" (*Nescis quid vesper serus vehat*); "Know Thyself" (Γνῶθι σεαυτόν). Occasionally the heading indicates that the writer is flying at some social folly, as in "Old Men are Children for the Second Time" (Δὶς παῖδες οἱ γέροντες) and in the "Bachelor" (*Cælebs*). In many satires the philosophers were pounded, as in the "Burial of Menippus" and "Concerning the Sects" (Περὶ αἱρεσέων). Each composition seems to have been a genuine medley or "lanx satura": any topic might be introduced which struck the author's fancy at the moment. There are many allusions to persons and events of the day, but political bitterness seems to have been commonly avoided. The whole tone of the writer is that of a "laudator temporis acti," who can but scoff at all that has come into fashion in his own day. From the numerous citations in later authors it is clear that the *Menippean Satires* were the most popular of Varro's writings. Not very unlike the *Menippean Satires* were the *Libri Logistorici*, or satirical and practical expositions, possibly in dialogue form, of some theme most commonly taken from philosophy on its ethical side. A few fragments in this style have come down to us and a number of titles. These are twofold: that is to say, a personal name is followed by words indicating the subject-matter, as *Marius, de Fortuna*, from which the contents may easily be guessed, and *Sisenna, de Historia*, most likely a dialogue in which the old annalist of the name was the chief speaker, and discoursed of the principles on which history should be written. Among the lighter and more popular works may be mentioned twenty-two books of *Orations* (probably never spoken), some funeral eulogies (*Laudationes*), some "exhortations" (*Suasiones*), conceivably of a political character, and an account of the author's own life.

The second section of Varro's works, those on history and antiquities, form to the present day the basis on which a large part of our knowledge of the earlier Roman history, and in particular of Roman constitutional history, ultimately rests. These writings were used as a quarry by the compilers and dilettanti of later times, such as Pliny, Plutarch, Gellius, Festus, Macrobius, and by Christian champions like Tertullian, Arnobius, and Augustine, who did not disdain to seek in heathen literature the means of defending their faith. These men have saved for us a few remains from the great wreck made by time. Judging from what has been casually preserved, if any considerable portion of Varro's labours as antiquarian and historian were to be now discovered, scholars might find themselves compelled to reconstruct the earlier history of the Roman republic from its very foundations. Varro's greatest predecessor in this field of inquiry, the man who turned over the virgin soil, was Cato the Censor. His example, however, seems to have remained unfruitful till the time of Varro's master, Lucius Ælius Stilo Præconinus. From his age to the decay of Roman civilization there were never altogether wanting men devoted to the study of their nation's past; but none ever pursued the task with the advantages of Varro's comprehensive learning, his indefatigable industry, and his reverent, yet discriminating regard for the men and the institutions of the earlier ages. The greatest work of this class was that on *Antiquities*, divided into forty-one books. Of these the first twenty-five were entitled the *Antiquities of Human Things* (*Antiquitates Rerum Humanarum*), while the remaining sixteen were designated the *Antiquities of Things Divine* (*Antiquitates Rerum Divinarum*). The book was the fruit of Varro's later years, in which he gathered together the material laboriously amassed through the period of an ordinary lifetime. The second division of the work was dedicated to Cæsar as supreme pontiff. The design was as far-reaching as that of the *Natural History* of Pliny. The general heads of the exposition in the secular portion of the book were four,—(1) "who the men are who act (*qui agant*), (2) the places in which they act (*ubi*), (3) the times at which they act (*quando*), (4) the results of their action (*quid agant*)." In the portion relating to divine affairs there were divisions parallel to these four, with a fifth, which dealt with the gods in whose honour action in divine affairs is taken. Our knowledge of this great book is to a large extent derived from the works of the early Christian writers, and especially from Augustine's *De Civitate Dei.* These lights of the church, as was natural, directed their attention mainly to the portion which treated of the religion of Rome. A glance at the authorities quoted in such a book as Preller's *Römische Mythologie* will suffice to show how largely the imperfect indeed, but nevertheless invaluable, information now attainable concerning the older and un-Hellenized forms of Roman and Italian religious rites depends on the citations by Christian authorities from the *Antiquitates Rerum Divinarum.* It is a great misfortune that no similar series of citations from the secular part of the *Antiquitates* has come down to us. Most of the other historical and antiquarian writings of Varro were special elaborations of topics which he could not treat with sufficient fulness and minuteness in the larger book. The treatise on the *Genealogy of the Roman People* dealt mainly with the relation of Roman chronology to the chronology of Greece and the East. Dates were assigned even to mythological occurrences, because Varro believed in the theory of Euhemerus, that all the beings worshipped as gods had once lived as men. To Varro's researches are due the traditional dates assigned to the era of the kings and to that of the early republic. Minor writings of the same class were the *De Vita Populi Romani*, apparently a kind of history of Roman civilization; the *De Familiis Trojanis*, an account of the families who "came over" with Æneas; the *Ætia* (Αἴτια), an explanation of the origin of Roman customs, on which Plutarch drew largely in his *Quæstiones Romanæ*; a *Tribuum Liber*, used by Festus; and the constitutional handbook written for the instruction of Pompey when he became consul. Nor must the labour expended by Varro in the study of literary history be forgotten. His activity in this direction, as in others, took a wide range. One of his greatest achievements was to fix the canon of the genuine plays of Plautus. The "Varronian plays" were the twenty which have come down to us, along with one which has been lost.

The third class of treatises, which we have called technical, was also numerous and very varied. Philosophy, grammar, the history and theory of language, rhetoric, law, arithmetic, astronomy, geometry, mensuration, agriculture, naval tactics, were all represented. The only works of this kind which have come down to our days are the *De Lingua Latina* (in part) and the *De Re Rustica.* The former originally comprised twenty-five books, three of which (the three succeeding the first) are dedicated to a P. Septimius who had served with the author in Spain and the last twenty-one to Cicero. The whole work was divided into three main sections, the first dealing with the origin of Latin words, the second with their inflexions and other modifications, the third with syntax. The books still preserved (somewhat imperfectly) are those from the fifth to the tenth inclusive. The Latin style is harsh, rugged, and far from lucid. As Mommsen remarks, the clauses of the sentences are often arranged on the thread of the relative pronoun like thrushes on a string. The arrangement of the subject-matter, while pretending to much precision, is often far from logical. The fifth, sixth, and seventh books give Varro's views on the etymology of Latin words. The principles he applies are those which he had learned from the philosophers of the Stoic school,—Chrysippus, Antipater, and others. The study of language as it existed in Varro's day was thoroughly dominated by Stoic influences. Varro's etymologies could be only *a priori* guesses, but he was well aware of their character, and very clearly states at the outset of the fifth book the hindrances that barred the way to sound knowledge. He was thoroughly alive to the importance of not arguing merely from the forms and meanings of words as they existed in his day, and was fully conscious that language and its mechanism should be studied historically. The books from the eighth to the tenth inclusive are devoted to the inflexions of words and their other modifications. These Varro classes all under the head of "declinatio," which implies a swerving aside from a type. Thus *Herculi* from *Hercules* and *manubria* from *manus* are equally regarded as examples of *declinatio*. Varro adopts a compromise between the two opposing schools of grammarians, those who held that nature intended the *declinationes* of all words of the same class to proceed uniformly (which uniformity was called *analogia*) and those who deemed that nature aimed at irregularity (*anomalia*). The matter is treated with considerable confusion of thought. But the *facts* incidentally cited concerning old Latin, and the statements of what had been written and thought about language by Varro's predecessors, are of extreme value to the student of Latin. The other extant prose work, the *De Re Rustica*, is in three books, each of which is in the form of a dialogue, the circumstances and in the main the interlocutors being different for each. The dramatic introductions and a few of the interludes are bright and interesting, and the Latin style, though still awkward and unpolished, is far superior to that of the *De Lingua Latina*.

A complete collection of the remains of Varro is still a desideratum. The fragments of the different treatises have been partially collected in many separate publications of recent date. The best editions of the *De Lingua Latina* are those by C. O. Müller and by L. Spengel (re-edited by his son in 1885). The most recent and best recension of the *De Re Rustica* is that of Keil (Leipsic, 1884). Of modern scholars Ritschl has deserved best of Varro. Several papers in his *Opuscula* treat of the nature of Varro's works which have not come down to us. (J. S. R.)

VARRO, PUBLIUS TERENTIUS, with the cognomen ATACINUS, a Roman poet whose life extended from 82 to about 37 B.C. The name Atacinus, given to distinguish him from the more famous Varro of Reate, is drawn from Atax, the name of a small district or river in Narbonensian Gaul, near to which he was born. He was perhaps the first Roman born beyond the Alps who reached to eminence in literature. He seems to have taken at first Ennius and Lucilius as his models, and wrote an epic, entitled *Bellum Sequanicum*, eulogizing the exploits of Cæsar in Gaul and Britain, and also *Satires*, of which Horace speaks slightingly. Jerome has preserved a statement that Varro began to study Greek literature with great avidity in his thirty-fifth year. The last ten years of his life were given up to the imitation of Greek poets of the Alexandrian school. Quintilian (indirectly confirming the judgment of Horace concerning the *Satires*) says that Varro made his name as an *interpres operis alieni*—"a translator of other men's works," for such is the force of the word *interpres*. Even in this capacity Quintilian bestows on him restricted praise as "by no means to be despised." But Quintilian probably much undervalued the Roman imitators of the Alexandrians, Catullus included. From other evidence we may conclude that, though he had not sufficient power to excel in the historical epic or in the serious work of the Roman *satira*, Varro yet possessed in considerable measure the lighter gifts which we admire in Catullus. His chief poem of the later period was the *Argonautica*, modelled, somewhat closely it would seem, on the epic of Apollonius Rhodius. The age was prolific of epics, both historical and mythological, and that of Varro seems to have held a high rank among them. Ovid asks what age will ever be unacquainted with the story of the first ship as told by Varro. In one of Ovid's lists of Roman poets Varro stands between Ennius and Lucretius, while in another he is linked with Virgil. Statius, in his poem on the birthday of Lucan, gives to the epic of Varro an equally distinguished place. Later he published erotic poems, probably in the elegiac metre. These Propertius seems to have valued highly, for in a well-known passage he ranks the Leucadia celebrated by Varro along with the Lesbia of Catullus, the Quintilia of Calvus, the Lycoris of Gallus, and his own Cynthia. The other titles which have been preserved are the *Cosmographia*, or *Chorographia*, a poem on geography, imitated from the Greek of Alexander, an Ephesian, described by Cicero (*Att.*, ii. 22) as a careless man and no good poet; and the *Ephemeris*, a poem on weather-signs, in hexameters, after Aratus. The Varro whom Quintilian (i. 4, 4) mentions in company with Lucretius as author of a poem on philosophy can hardly have been either Varro of Atax or Varro of Reate. The fragments of Varro Atacinus which remain, about fifty lines in all, are put together by Riese at the end of his edition of the fragments of the greater Varro's *Menippean Satires*; but there is not enough of them to enable us to form a judgment on his style.

VASA, GUSTAVUS. See GUSTAVUS I.

VÁSÁRHELY. See HÓDMEZÖ-VASARHELY and MAROS-VÁSÁRHELY.

VASARI, GIORGIO (1513-1574), a painter and architect, whose main distinction rests on his valuable history of Italian art,[1] was born at Arezzo in 1513. At a very early age he became a pupil of Guglielmo da Marsiglia, a very skilful painter of stained glass. At the age of sixteen he went to Florence, where he studied under Michelangelo and Andrea del Sarto, aided by the patronage of the Medici princes. In 1529 he visited Rome and studied the works of Raphael and others of his school. The paintings of Vasari were much admired by the rapidly degenerating taste of the 16th century; but they possess the smallest amount of merit, being in the main feeble parodies of the powerful works of Michelangelo. Vasari was largely employed in Florence, Rome, Naples, Arezzo, and other places. Many of his pictures still exist, the most important being the wall and ceiling paintings in the great hall of the Palazzo Vecchio in Florence, and his frescos on the cupola of the cathedral, which, however, were not completed at the time of his death. As an architect he was perhaps more successful: the loggia of the Uffizi by the Arno, and the long passage connecting it with the Pitti Palace, are his chief works. Unhappily he did much to injure the fine mediæval churches of S. Maria Novella and Santa Croce, from both of which he removed the original rood-screen and loft, and remodelled the retro-choir in the degraded taste of his time. Vasari enjoyed a very high repute during his lifetime and amassed a considerable fortune. He built himself in 1547 a fine house in Arezzo, and spent much labour in decorating its walls and vaults with paintings. He was elected one of the municipal council or priori of his native town, and finally rose to the supreme office of gonfaloniere. He died at Florence on 27th June 1574.

Personally Vasari was a man of upright character, free from vanity, and always ready to appreciate the works of others: in spite of the narrow and meretricious taste of his time, he expresses a warm admiration of the works of such men as Cimabue and Giotto, which is very remarkable. As an art historian of his country he must always occupy the highest rank. His great work was first published in 1550, and afterwards partly rewritten and enlarged in 1568, bearing the title *Delle Vite de' piu Eccellenti Pittori, Scultori, ed Architettori*. It was dedicated to Cosimo de' Medici, and was printed at Florence by the Giunti; it is a small quarto illustrated with many good woodcut portraits. This *editio princeps* of the complete work is usually bound in three volumes, and also contains a very valuable treatise on the technical methods employed in all branches of the arts, entitled *Le Tre Arti del Disegno, cioè Architettura, Pittura, e Scoltura*.

The best edition of Vasari's works is that published at Florence by Milanesi, 1878-82, which embodies the valuable notes in the earlier edition by Le Monnier. The *Lives* has been translated into French, German, and English (by Mrs Foster, London, 1850). They are written in a very pleasant style, interspersed with amusing stories, and are in the main trustworthy, except some of the biographies of early artists.[2] With a few exceptions Vasari's judgment is acute and unbiassed.

VASCO DA GAMA. See GAMA, VASCO DA.

[1] Vasari gives a sketch of his own biography at the end of his *Vite*, and adds further details about himself and his family in his lives of Lazzaro Vasari and Francesco Salviati. He was related to the painter Luca Signorelli.

[2] As in most other kindred subjects the tendency of modern criticism is to underestimate the historical accuracy of Vasari's work.

VASCULAR SYSTEM

THE term *vascular system* designates all the arrangements in the body connected with the circulation of the blood. A description of the anatomy of the various organs as found in man is given under ANATOMY (vol. i. p. 899 *sq.*), and an account of various modifications of the circulatory apparatus under the headings designating the great groups of the animal kingdom, such as MOLLUSCA, CRUSTACEA, ICHTHYOLOGY, AMPHIBIA, REPTILES, BIRDS; and reference may be made to the articles NUTRITION and RESPIRATION for details as to the formation, physical and chemical properties, and functions of the blood. The present article is devoted to a consideration of the mechanism by which the circulation is carried on in the *Mammalia* and in man, a branch of physiology which has been more successfully investigated than any other department of the science.

HISTORICAL SKETCH.

Galen.

Galen, following Erasistratus and Aristotle, clearly distinguished arteries from veins, and was the first to overthrow the old theory of Erasistratus that the arteries contained air. According to him, the vein arose from the liver in two great trunks, the *vena porta* and *vena cava*. The first was formed by the union of all the abdominal veins, which absorbed the chyle prepared in the stomach and intestines, and carried it to the liver, where it was converted into blood. The vena cava arose in the liver, divided into two branches, one ascending through the diaphragm to the heart, furnishing the proper veins of this organ; there it received the *vena azygos*, and entered the right ventricle, along with a large trunk from the lungs, evidently the pulmonary artery. The vena azygos was the *superior vena cava*, the great vein which carries the venous blood from the head and upper extremities into the right auricle. The descending branch of the great trunk supposed to originate in the liver was the *inferior vena cava*, below the junction of the hepatic vein. The arteries arose from the left side of the heart by two trunks, one having thin walls, the pulmonary veins, the other having thick walls, the aorta. The first was supposed to carry blood to the lungs, and the second to carry blood to the body. The heart consisted of two ventricles, communicating by pores in the septum; the lungs were parenchymatous organs communicating with the heart by the pulmonary veins. The blood-making organ, the liver, separates from the blood subtle vapours, the *natural spirits*, which, carried to the heart, mix with the air introduced by respiration, and thus form the *vital spirits*; these, in turn carried to the brain, are elaborated into *animal spirits*, which are distributed to all parts of the body by the nerves.[1] Such were the views of Galen, taught until early in the 16th century.

Vesalius.

Jacobus Berengarius of Carpi (*ob.* 1527) investigated the structure of the valves of the heart. Andreas Vesale or Vesalius (1514-1564) contributed largely to anatomical knowledge, especially to the anatomy of the circulatory organs. He determined the position of the heart in the chest; he studied its structure, pointing out the fibrous rings at the bases of the ventricles; he showed that its wall consists of layers of fibres connected with the fibrous rings; and he described these layers as being of three kinds,—straight or vertical, oblique, and circular or transverse. From the disposition of the fibres he reasoned as to the mechanism of the contraction and relaxation of the heart. He supposed that the relaxation, or diastole, was accounted for principally by the longitudinal fibres contracting so as to draw the apex towards the base, and thus cause the sides to bulge out; whilst the contraction, or systole, was due to contraction of the transverse or oblique fibres. He showed that the pores of Galen, in the septum between the ventricles, did not exist, so that there could be no communication between the right and left sides of the heart, except by the pulmonary circulation. He also investigated minutely the internal structure of the heart, describing the valves, the *columnæ carneæ*, and the *musculi papillares*. He described the mechanism of the valves with much accuracy. He had, however, no conception either of a systemic or of a pulmonary circulation. To him the heart was a reservoir from which the blood ebbed and flowed, and there were two kinds of blood, arterial and venous, having different circulations and serving different purposes in the body. Vesalius was not only a great anatomist: he was a great teacher; and his pupils carried on the work in the spirit of their master. Prominent among them was Gabriel Fallopius (1523-1562), who studied the anastomoses of the blood-vessels, without the art of injection, which was invented by Frederick Ruysch (1638-1731) more than a century later. Another pupil was Columbus (Matthieu Reald Columbo, *ob.* 1559), first a prosector in the anatomical rooms of Vesalius and afterwards his successor in the chair of anatomy in Padua; his name has been mentioned as that of one who anticipated Harvey in the discovery of the circulation of the blood. A study of his writings clearly shows that he had no true knowledge of the circulation, but only a glimpse of how the blood passed from the right to the left side of the heart. In his work there is evidently a sketch of the pulmonary circulation, although it is clear that he did not understand the mechanism of the valves, as Vesalius did. As regards the systemic circulation, there is the notion simply of an oscillation of the blood from the heart to the body and from the body to the heart. Further, he upholds the view of Galen, that all the veins originate in the liver; and he even denies the muscular structure of the heart.[2] In 1553 Michael Servetus (1511-1553), a pupil or junior fellow-student of Vesalius, in his *Christianismi Restitutio*, described accurately the pulmonary circulation.[3] Servetus perceived the course of the circulation from the right to the left side of the heart through the lungs, and he also recognized that the change from venous into arterial blood took place in the lungs and not in the left ventricle. Not so much the recognition of the pulmonary circulation, as that had been made previously by Columbus, but the discovery of the respiratory changes in the lungs constitutes Servetus's claim to be a pioneer in physiological science.

Columbus.

Servetus.

Cesalpino.

Andrea Cesalpino (1519-1603), a great naturalist of this period, also made important contributions towards the discovery of the circulation, and in Italy he is regarded as the real discoverer.[4] Cesalpinus knew the pulmonary circulation. Further, he was the first to use the term

[1] See Burggraeve's *Histoire de l'Anatomie*, Paris, 1880, in which he refers to many of the older authors, also to the articles GALEN and ANATOMY.

[2] An interesting account of the views of the precursors of Harvey will be found in Willis's edition of the *Works* of Harvey, published by the Sydenham Society. Comp. also P. Flourens, *Histoire de la Découverte de la Circulation du Sang* (Paris, 1854), and Prof. R. Owen, *Experimental Physiology, its Benefits to Mankind, with an Address on Unveiling the Statue of W. Harvey, at Folkestone, 6th August 1881.*

[3] The passage is quoted under ANATOMY, vol. i. p. 810 n.; comp. also HARVEY. See Willis, *Servetus and Calvin*, London, 1877.

[4] A learned and critical series of articles by Sampson Gamgee in the *Lancet*, in 1876, gives an excellent account of the controversy as to whether Cesalpinus or Harvey was the true discoverer of the circulation; see also the Harveian oration for 1882 by George Johnston (*Lancet*, July 1882), and Prof. G. M. Humphry, *Journ. Anat. and Phys.*, October 1882.

"circulation," and he went far to demonstrate the systemic circulation. He experimentally proved that, when a vein is tied, it fills below and not above the ligature. The following passage from his *Quæstiones Medicæ* (lib. v., cap. 4, fol. 125), quoted by Gamgee, shows his views:—

"The lungs, therefore, drawing the warm blood from the right ventricle of the heart through a vein like an artery, and returning it by anastomosis to the venal artery (pulmonary vein), which tends towards the left ventricle of the heart, and air, being in the meantime transmitted through the channels of the aspera arteria (trachea and bronchial tubes), which are extended near the venal artery, yet not communicating with the aperture as Galen thought, tempers with a touch only. This circulation of the blood (*huic sanguinis circulationi*) from the right ventricle of the heart through the lungs into the left ventricle of the same exactly agrees with what appears from dissection. For there are two receptacles ending in the right ventricle and two in the left. But of the two only one intromits; the other lets out, the membranes (valves) being constituted accordingly."

Still Cesalpinus clung to the old idea of there being an efflux and reflux of blood to and from the heart, and he had confused notions as to the veins conveying nutritive matter, whilst the arteries carried the vital spirits to the tissues. He does not even appear to have thought of the heart as a contractive and propulsive organ, and attributed the dilatation to "an effervescence of the spirit," whilst the contraction,—or, as he termed it, the "collapse,"—was due to the appropriation by the heart of nutritive matter. Whilst he imagined a communication between the termination of the arteries and the commencement of the veins, he does not appear to have thought of a direct flow of blood from the one to the other. Thus he cannot be regarded as the true discoverer of the circulation of the blood. More recently Ercolani has put forward claims on behalf of Carlo Ruini as being the true discoverer. Ruini published the first edition of his anatomical writings in 1598, the year William Harvey entered at Padua as a medical student. This claim has been carefully investigated by Gamgee, who has come to the conclusion that it cannot be maintained.[1]

Discovery of circulation of blood.

The anatomy of the heart was examined, described, and figured by Bartolomeo Eustacheo (*c.* 1500-1574) and by Julius Cæsar Aranzi or Arantius (*c.* 1530-1589), whose name is associated with the fibro-cartilaginous thickenings on the free edge of the semilunar valves (*corpora Arantii*). Hieronymus Fabricius of Acquapendente (1537-1619), the immediate predecessor and teacher of Harvey, made the important step of describing the valves in the veins; but he thought they had a subsidiary office in connexion with the collateral circulation, supposing that they diverted the blood into branches near the valves; thus he missed seeing the importance of the anatomical and experimental facts gathered by himself. At the time when Harvey arose the general notions as to the circulation may be briefly summed up as follows: the blood ebbed and flowed to and from the heart in the arteries and veins; from the right side at least a portion of it passed to the left side through the vessels in the lungs, where it was mixed with air; and, lastly, there were two kinds of blood,—the venous, formed originally in the liver, and thence passing to the heart, from which it went out to the periphery by the veins and returned by those to the heart, and the arterial,—containing "spirits" produced by the mixing of the blood and the air in the lungs—sent out from the heart to the body and returning to the heart by the same vessels. The pulmonary circulation was understood so far, but its relation to the systemic circulation was unknown. The action of the heart, also, as a propulsive organ was not recognized. It was not until 1628 that Harvey announced his views to the world by publishing his treatise *De Motu Cordis et Sanguinis* (see vol. xi. pp. 503-504). His conclusions are given in the following celebrated passage:—

Harvey.

"And now I may be allowed to give in brief my view of the circulation of the blood, and to propose it for general adoption. Since all things, both argument and ocular demonstration, show that the blood passes through the lungs and heart by the auricles and ventricles, and is sent for distribution to all parts of the body, where it makes its way into the veins and pores of the flesh, and then flows by the veins from the circumference on every side to the centre, from lesser to the greater veins, and is by them finally discharged into the vena cava and right auricle of the heart, and this in such a quantity, or in such a flux and reflux, thither by the arteries, hither by the veins, as cannot possibly be supplied by the ingestor, and is much greater than can be required for mere purposes of nutrition, it is absolutely necessary to conclude that the blood in the animal body is impelled in a *circle*, and is in a state of ceaseless motion, that this is the act or function which the heart performs by means of its pulse, and that it is the sole and only end of the motion and contraction of the heart" (bk. x. ch. xiv. p. 68).

Opposed by Caspar Hofmann of Nuremberg, Veslingius of Padua, and J. Riolanus the younger, this new theory was supported by Roger Drake, a young Englishman, who chose it for the subject of a graduation thesis at Leyden in 1637, by Rolfink of Jena, and especially by Descartes, and quickly gained the ascendant; and its author had the satisfaction of seeing it confirmed by the discovery of the capillary circulation, and universally adopted. The circulation in the capillaries between the arteries and the veins was discovered by Marcellus Malpighi (1628-1694) of Bologna in 1661. He saw it first in the lungs and the mesentery of a frog, and the discovery was announced in the second of two letters, *Epistola de Pulmonibus*, addressed to Borelli, and dated 1661.[2] Malpighi actually showed the capillary circulation to the astonished eyes of Harvey. Anthony van Leeuwenhoek (1632-1723) in 1673 repeated Malpighi's observations, and studied the capillary circulation in a bat's wing, the tail of a tadpole, and the tail of a fish. William Molyneux studied the circulation in the lungs of a water newt in 1683.[3]

Capillary circulation.

The idea that the same blood was propelled through the body in a circuit suggested that life might be sustained by renewing the blood in the event of some of it being lost. About 1660 Lower, a London physician (died 1691), succeeded in transferring the blood of one animal directly from its blood-vessels into those of another animal. This was first done by passing a "quill" or a "small crooked pipe of silver or brass" from the carotid artery of one dog to the jugular vein of another.[4] This experiment was repeated and modified by Sir Edmund King, Coxe, Gayant, and Denys with such success as to warrant the operation being performed on man, and accordingly it was carried out by Lower and King on 23d November 1667, when blood from the arteries of a sheep was directly introduced into the veins of a man.[5] It would appear that the operation had previously been performed with success in Paris.

Transfer of blood.

The doctrine of the circulation being accepted, physiologists next directed their attention to the force of the heart, the pressure of the blood in the vessels, its velocity, and the phenomena of the pulse wave. Giovanni Alphonso Borelli (1608-1679) investigated the circulation during the lifetime of Harvey. He early conceived the design of applying mathematical principles to the explanation of animal functions; and, although he fell into many errors, he must be regarded as the founder of animal mechanics. In his *De Motu Animalium* (1680-85) he stated his theory of the circulation in eighty propositions, and in prop. lxxiii., founding on a supposed relation between the bulk and the strength of muscular fibre as found in the ventricles, erroneously concluded that the force of the heart was equal to the pressure of a weight of 180,000 ℔. He also

Force of heart and velocity of blood.

Borelli.

[1] Gamgee, "Third Historical Fragment," in *Lancet*, 1876.

[2] See his *Opera Omnia*, vol. i. p. 328.

[3] Lowthorp, *Abridgement of Trans. Roy. Soc.*, 5th ed., vol. iii. p. 230.

[4] *Ibid.*, p. 231.

[5] *Ibid.*, p. 226.

recognized and figured the spiral arrangement of fibres in the ventricles. The question was further investigated by James Keill, a Scottish physician (1673-1719), who in his *Account of Animal Secretion, the Quantity of Blood in the Human Body, and Muscular Motion* (1708) attempted to estimate the velocity of blood in the aorta, and gave it at 52 feet per minute. Then, allowing for the resistance of the vessels, he showed that the velocity diminishes towards the smaller vessels, and arrived at the amazing conclusion that in the smallest vessels it travels at the rate of $\frac{1}{4}$ inch in 278 days,—a good example of the extravagant errors made by the mathematical physiologists of the period. Keill further described the hydraulic phenomena of the circulation in papers communicated to the Royal Society and collected in his *Essays on Several Parts of the Animal Œconomy* (1717). In these essays, by estimating the quantity of blood thrown out of the heart by each contraction, and the diameter of the aortic orifice, he calculated the velocity of the blood. He stated (pp. 84, 87) that the blood sent into the aorta with each contraction would form a cylinder 8 inches (2 ounces) in length and be driven along with a velocity of 156 feet per minute. Estimating then the resistances to be overcome in the vessels, he found the force of the heart to be "little above 16 ounces,"—a remarkable difference from the computation of Borelli. Keill's method was ingenious, and is of historical interest as being the first attempt to obtain quantitative results; but it failed to obtain true results, because the data on which he based his calculations were inaccurate. These calculations attracted the attention not only of the anatomico-physiologists, such as Haller, but also of some of the physicists of the time, notably of Jurin and D. Bernoulli. Jurin (died 1750) gave the force of the left ventricle at 9 ℔ 1 oz. and that of the right ventricle at 6 ℔ 3 oz. He also stated with remarkable clearness, considering that he reasoned on the subject as a physicist, without depending on experimental data gathered by himself, the influence on the pulse induced by variations in the power of the heart or in the resistance to be overcome.[1] The experimental investigation of the problem was supplied by Stephen Hales (1677-1761), rector of Teddington in Middlesex, who in 1708 devised the method of estimating the force of the heart by inserting a tube into a large artery and observing the height to which the blood was impelled into it. Hales is the true founder of the modern experimental method in physiology. He observed in a horse that the blood rose in the vertical tube, which he had connected with the crural artery, to the height of 8 feet 3 inches perpendicular above the level of the left ventricle of the heart. But it did not attain its full height at once: it rushed up about half way in an instant, and afterwards gradually at each pulse 12, 8, 6, 4, 2, and sometimes 1 inch. When it was at its full height, it would rise and fall at and after each pulse 2, 3, or 4 inches; and sometimes it would fall 12 or 14 inches, and have there for a time the same vibrations up and down at and after each pulse as it had when it was at its full height, to which it would rise again after forty or fifty pulses.[2] He then estimated the capacity of the left ventricle by a method of employing waxen casts, and, after many such experiments and measurements in the horse, ox, sheep, fallow deer, and dog, he calculated that the force of the left ventricle in man is about equal to that of a column of blood $7\frac{1}{2}$ feet high, weighing $51\frac{1}{2}$ ℔, or, in other words, that the pressure the left ventricle has to overcome is equal to the pressure of that weight. When we contrast the enormous estimate of Borelli (180,000 ℔) with the underestimate of Keill (16 oz.), and when we know that the estimate of Hales, as corroborated by recent investigations by means of elaborate scientific appliances, is very near the truth, we recognize the far higher service rendered to science by careful and judicious experiment than by speculations, however ingenious. With the exception of some calculations by Dan Bernoulli in 1748, there was no great contribution to hæmadynamics till 1808, when two remarkable papers appeared from Thomas Young (1773-1829). In the first, entitled "Hydraulic Investigations," which appeared in the *Phil. Trans.*, he investigated the friction and discharge of fluids running in pipes and the velocity of rivers, the resistance occasioned by flexures in pipes and rivers, the propagation of an impulse through an elastic tube, and some of the phenomena of pulsations. This paper was preparatory to the second, "On the Functions of the Heart and Arteries,"—the Croonian lecture for 1808—in which he showed more clearly than had hitherto been done (1) that the blood-pressure gradually diminishes from the heart to the periphery; (2) that the velocity of the blood becomes less as it passes from the greater to the smaller vessels; (3) that the resistance is chiefly in the smaller vessels, and that the elasticity of the coats of the great arteries comes into play in overcoming this resistance in the interval between systoles; and (4) that the contractile coats do not act as propulsive agents, but assist in regulating the distribution of blood.[3]

Keill. Hales. Thomas Young.

The next epoch of physiological investigation is characterized by the introduction of instruments for accurate measurement, and the graphic method of registering phenomena, now so largely used in science.[4] In 1825 appeared E. and W. Weber's *Wellenlehre*, and in 1838 E. Weber's *Ad Notat. Anatom. et Physiolog.*, i., both of which contain an exposition of E. H. Weber's *schema* of the circulation, a scheme which presents a true and consistent theory. In 1826 Poiseuille invented the hæmadynamometer.[5] This was adapted with a marker to a recording cylinder by Ludwig in 1847, so as to form the instrument named by Volkmann the kymograph. Volkmann devised the hæmadromometer for measuring the velocity of the blood in 1850; for the same purpose Vierordt constructed the hæmatachometer in 1858; Chauveau and Lortet first used their hæmadromograph in 1860; and lastly, Ludwig and Dogiel obtained the best results as regards velocity by the "stream-clock" in 1867. As regards the pulse, the first sphygmograph was constructed by Vierordt in 1856; and Marey's form, of which there are now many modifications, appeared in 1860. In 1861 Chauveau and Marey obtained tracings of the variations of pressure in the heart cavities (see p. 99 below) by an experiment which is of great historical importance. During the past twenty-five years vast accumulations of facts have been made through the instruments of precision above alluded to, so that the conditions of the circulation, as a problem in hydrodynamics, have been thoroughly investigated. Since 1845, when the brothers Weber discovered the inhibitory action of the vagus, and 1858, when Claude Bernard formulated his researches showing the existence of a vaso-motor system of nerves, much knowledge has been acquired as to the relations of the nervous to the circulatory system. The Webers, John Reid, Claude Bernard, and Carl Ludwig may be regarded as masters in physiology equal in standing to those whose researches have been more especially alluded to in this historical sketch. The Webers took the first step towards recognizing the great principle of

Use of instruments.

[1] Jones, *Abridgement of Phil. Trans.*, 3d ed. 1749, vol. v. p. 223. See also for an account of the criticisms of D. Bernoulli the elder and others, Haller's *Elementa Physiologiæ*, vol. i. p. 448.

[2] Hales, *Statical Essays, containing Hæmastatics*, &c., 1733, vol. ii. p. 1.

[3] See *Miscellaneous Works*, ed. Peacock, 2 vols., London, 1855.

[4] See Marey, *La Méthode Graph. dans les Sc. Expér.*, Paris, 1878.

[5] Magendie's *Journal*, vol. viii. p. 272.

inhibitory action; John Reid showed how to investigate the functions of nerves by his classical research on the eighth pair of cranial nerves; Claude Bernard developed the fundamental conception of vaso-motor nerves; and Ludwig showed how this conception, whilst it certainly made the hydraulic problems of the circulation infinitely more complicated than they were even to the scientific imagination of Thomas Young, accounted for some of the phenomena and indicated at all events the solidarity of the arrangements in the living being. Further, Ludwig and his pupils used the evidence supplied by some of the phenomena of the circulation to explain even more obscure phenomena of the nervous system, and they taught pharmacologists how to study in a scientific manner the physiological action of drugs.

PHYSIOLOGY, &c., OF CIRCULATION.

Vessels and course of circulation.

The blood is contained during life in a continuous system of more or less elastic and contractile vessels. These are (1) the *arteries*, terminating in (2) the *capillaries*, from which originate (3) the *veins*, whilst a special contractile organ, (4) the *heart*, is placed at the commencement of the arteries and the termination of the veins (see fig. 1). The heart may be regarded as a double organ, each half consisting of an auricle and a ventricle, the right half containing blood which has been returned from the body to be sent to the lungs, and the left half containing blood which has been returned from the lungs to be distributed to the body. There are thus, in a sense, two circulations,—the one pulmonary, from the right side of the heart, by the pulmonary artery to the lungs, through the capillaries of the lungs, and back to the left side of the heart by the pulmonary veins, and the other systemic, from the left side of the heart, by the aorta, and the arteries which ramify from it, to the capillaries throughout the tissues, and from thence by the veins to the right side of the heart. Thus the course of the circulation may be traced (1) from right auricle to right ventricle, through the right auriculo-ventricular opening, guarded by the tricuspid valve; (2) from right ventricle by the pulmonary artery, through the capillaries of the lungs, to the pulmonary veins, which open into the left auricle; (3) from left auricle to left ventricle, through the left auriculo-ventricular opening, guarded by the mitral valve; (4) from the left ventricle through the greater arteries, the medium-sized arteries, and the arterioles into the capillaries of the tissues and organs; and (5) from thence by the veins, opening into larger and larger trunks, so as ultimately to constitute the superior and inferior venæ cavæ, which open into the right auricle, the point from which we started. Remembering that the walls of these tubes are all more or less elastic, imagine them to be distended with blood; there would then be a condition of permanent tension, which would be varied if pressure were applied to any part of the system. Such a variation of pressure would produce a movement of the fluid in the direction of less pressure, and, as the fluid cannot escape, there would be a circulation, which would be carried in the same direction by mechanical arrangements of valves. In the living body the contractions of the heart force blood into the arterial system and increase the pressure in that part of the circulation; the arteries empty part of their contents into the capillaries, which carry the blood to the veins, so as to tend to an equalization of pressure between the venous and arterial systems. If the pressure in both systems became equal, there would be no circulation; but, as the veins pour a portion of the blood back again into the heart, this organ on being refilled again contracts, forcing more blood into the arterial system and again raising the pressure there; thus the possibility during life of an equalization of arterial and venous pressure is prevented. In describing more fully the mechanism by which this circulation is maintained we shall consider (1) the action of the heart, and (2) the action of the blood-vessels, arteries, capillaries, and veins.

FIG. 1.—General course of circulation and some of principal vessels. H′, right ventricle; H, left ventricle; A, A, A, aorta; *k*, part of left auricle; P, pulmonary artery, going to lungs; P′, pulmonary veins; *v*, ascending or lower vena cava; *e*, trachea or wind-pipe; *p*, *p*′, bronchial tubes; *a*′, *a*, right and left carotid arteries; *v*, *v*′, veins from root of neck (internal jugular and subclavian), joining to form descending or upper vena cava; *i*, hepatic artery; *l*, hepatic vein; I, superior mesenteric artery, going to mesentery and bowels; L, portal vein, going to liver; *k*′, renal artery; *k*, renal vein; V, inferior vena cava, splitting into the two iliac veins, *v*, *v*. (After Allen Thomson.)

The Action of the Heart.

Physiological anatomy.

The form, position, and general arrangements of the heart are described under ANATOMY (vol. i. pp. 899-908), and it is only necessary here to allude to certain points of physiological importance.

Muscular structure.

The substance of the heart is composed of a special variety of muscular tissue, along with connective tissue, blood-vessels, lymphatics, nerves, and ganglia. The muscular fibres are of an irregularly cubical form, faintly striated transversely, from $\frac{1}{500}$ to $\frac{1}{350}$ inch in length by $\frac{1}{1600}$ to $\frac{1}{1000}$ inch in breadth, destitute of sarcolemma, frequently having bands at the broad ends by which they anastomose, and showing an oval nucleus. A large mass of fibrous tissue and fibro-cartilage (which in some animals, as the ox, is bony) is found at the base of the heart, in the angle between the aortic and two auriculo-ventricular openings; from it processes pass in various directions, and form the bases of the fibrous or tendinous rings of the auriculo-ventricular and arterial openings, and to these many if not all of the bands of muscular fibre are attached. These bands are arranged in layers. According to Pettigrew (1864), there are seven layers of fibres forming the wall of each ventricle,—three external, one central, and three internal,—and they are so arranged that the first or outer external layer is continuous with the seventh or inner internal layer, the second with the sixth, and the third with the fifth. Ludwig (1849) gives a simpler arrangement,—(1) an outer longitudinal layer extending from the base, where the fibres are attached to the tendinous structures around the orifices, and passing obliquely towards the apex to enter by a twist into the interior of the ventricle; (2) an inner longitudinal layer composed of the same fibres of the outer layer,—some of these becoming continuous with the papillary muscles (fig. 2) and others forming an irregular stratum of fibres, which terminate in the fibrous rings at the base of the ventricle (fig. 3); and (3) an intermediate or transverse layer, the thickest of the three, formed of fibres passing with less and less obliquity until they are transverse. These arrangements are shown in figs. 4 and 5, and they account for the following physiological phenomena. (1) The auricles contract independently of the ventricles. So long as the rhythmic movement is normal, the auricular contractions are equal in number to the ventricular; but, as the heart dies, there may be several beats of the auricle for one of the ventricle, and at last only the auricles contract. The auricular portion of the right auricle is the last to cease beating; hence it is termed the *ultimum moriens*. Sometimes also contractions of the vena cava and pulmonary veins may be noticed after the heart beats have ceased. (2) The contraction of the circular fibres around the orifices of the veins empties these vessels into the auricles; and no doubt these fibres have also a sphincter-like action during the contraction of the cavities, preventing the regurgitation of blood, and thus doing away with the necessity for valves at these orifices. (3) The double arrangement of fibres around the auricles produces, when the fibres contract, a uniform diminution of the auricular cavity. (4) The spiral arrangement of the fibres in the ventricular walls expels the blood with great force, as if it were propelled by wringing or twisting the walls of the cavity.

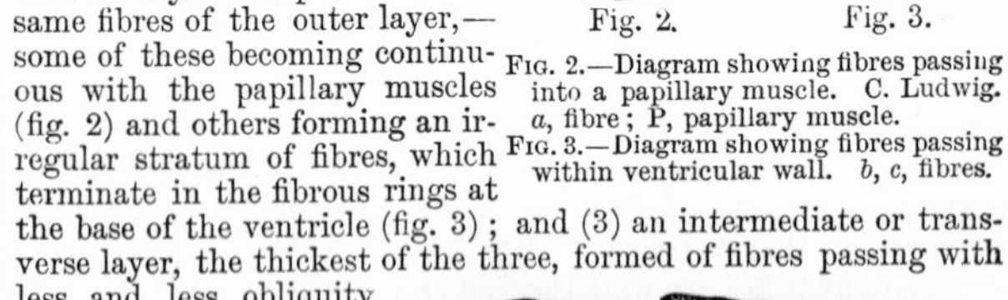

Fig. 2. Fig. 3.

FIG. 2.—Diagram showing fibres passing into a papillary muscle. C. Ludwig. *a*, fibre; P, papillary muscle.
FIG. 3.—Diagram showing fibres passing within ventricular wall. *b*, *c*, fibres.

FIG. 4.—View of fibres of sheep's heart dissected at apex to show the "vortex." *a*, *a*, fibres entering apex posteriorly at *b*; *c*, *c*, fibres entering apex anteriorly at *d*. (Pettigrew, Quain's *Anatomy*.)

Valves of heart.

The valves of the heart are as follows (see ANATOMY, vol. i. p. 900, fig. 89). (1) The tricuspid guards the right auriculo-ventricular opening, and consists of three flaps, formed of fibrous tissue (containing many elastic fibres) covered with endocardium. These flaps are continuous at their base, forming an annular membrane surrounding the auricular opening, and they are kept in position by the *chordæ tendineæ*, which are attached to their ventricular surfaces and free margins. (2) The bicuspid or mitral valve, at the left auriculo-ventricular orifice, consists of two pointed segments or cusps, having the same structure as those of the tricuspid valve. The auriculo-ventricular valves contain striated muscular fibres, radiating from the auricles into the segments of the valve. These probably shorten the valves towards their base and make a larger opening for the passage of the blood into the ventricles. A concentric layer of fibres, found near the base of the segments, has a sphincter-like action, approximating the base of the valves (Paladino). Some of the larger chordæ tendineæ contain striated muscle (Oehl), whilst a delicate muscular network exists in the valvulæ Thebesii (guarding the openings of small veins from the substance of the heart into the right auricle) and in the Eustachian valve (a crescentic fold of membrane in front of the opening of the inferior vena cava) (Landois). The aortic and pulmonary openings are guarded by the sigmoid or semilunar valves, each of which consists of three semicircular flaps, each flap being attached by its convex border to the wall of the artery, whilst its free border projects into the interior of the vessel. The segments consist of fibrous tissue covered with endocardium. At the middle of the free border there is a fibro-cartilaginous thickening called the nodulus or corpus Arantii. From this nodulus numerous tendinous fibres radiate to the attached border of the valve, but along the margin of the valve the membrane is thin and destitute of such fibres. These thin parts are called the *lunulæ*. Opposite each semilunar flap there is a bulging of the wall of the vessel, the *sinuses of Valsalva*. In the aorta these are situated one anteriorly and two posteriorly (right and left). From the anterior arises the right coronary artery, and from the left posterior the left coronary artery,—these vessels being for the supply of blood to the substance of the heart (Quain).

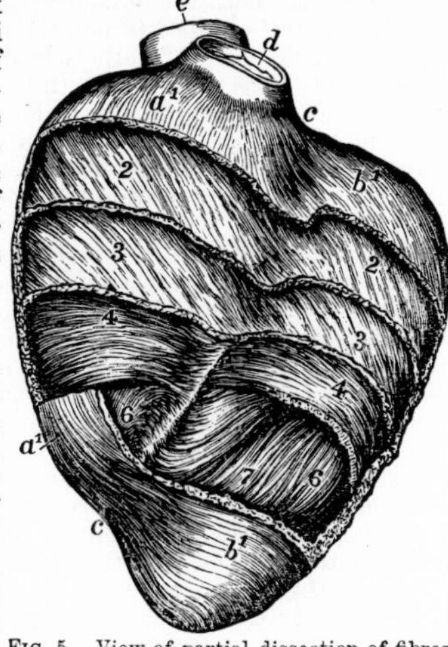

Fig. 5.—View of partial dissection of fibres in anterior wall of ventricles in a sheep's heart, showing different degrees of obliquity of fibres. At the base and apex the superficial fibres are displayed in the intervening space; more and more of the fibres have been removed from above downwards, reaching to a greater depth on the left than on the right side. a^1, a^1, superficial fibres of right ventricle; b^1, b^1, superficial fibres of left ventricle; 2, superficial fibres removed so as to expose those underneath, which have the same direction as the superficial ones over the left ventricle, but a different direction from those over the right ventricle; at 3 some of these have been removed, but the direction is only slightly different; 4, transverse or annular fibres occupying middle of thickness of ventricular walls; 6, 7, internal fibres passing downwards towards apex to emerge at the whorl; *c*, *c*, anterior coronary or interventricular groove, over which the superficial fibres cross; in the remaining part of the groove some of the deep fibres turn backwards into the septum; *d*, pulmonary artery; *e*, aorta. (Allen Thomson, Quain's *Anatomy*.)

Dimensions and weight.

According to Laennec, the size of the heart is about equal to the closed fist of the individual. Its mean weight is about 9 to 10 oz. John Reid's tables give the average weight in the adult male as 11 oz. and in the female as 9 oz. The proportion of the weight of the heart to that of the body is from 1 to 150 to 1 to 170 (Quain). W. Müller gives the ratio of heart weight to body weight in the child, and until the body weighs 88 ℔, as ·176 oz. to 2·2 ℔; when the body weight is from 110 to 200 ℔ the ratio is ·141 oz. to 2·2 ℔; and when the weight of the body reaches 220 ℔ the ratio is as ·123 oz. to 2·2 ℔. The volume of the heart, according to Beneke, is as follows:—new-born infant, 1·34 cubic inches; 15 years of age, 9·15 to 9·76; at 20 years, 15·25; up to the 50th year, 17·08 cubic inches; after that there is a slight diminution. There is scarcely any difference between the capacities of the two ventricles, although in the ordinary modes of death the right is always found more capacious than the left, probably because it is distended with blood; the left ventricle after death is usually empty and more contracted. The wall of the left ventricle is much thicker than that of the right. The specific gravity of heart muscle is 1·069. The thickness of the left ventricle in the middle is in man ·44 inch and in woman ·43; that of the right is ·16 and ·14 inch respectively. The circumference of the tricuspid orifice in man is 4·62 inches and in woman 4·33; of the mitral, 4·13 and 3·78 respectively. The circumference of the pulmonary artery is 2·94 inches; of the aorta 2·77; of the superior vena cava ·702 to 1·05 inch; of the inferior vena cava 1·05 to 1·4; and the diameter of the pulmonary veins, ·53 to ·62.

Modes of examining living heart.

When the hand is applied to the side, a little to the left of the left nipple, and in the interval between the fifth and sixth ribs, a shock or impulse is felt. If the whole hand be placed flat over the region of the heart, one may notice the presence or absence of the heart-beat, also its situation and extent, and any alterations in its character. In some rare cases, where there is a congenital fissure of the sternum, the finger can be applied to various parts of the heart's surface, with the integuments and pericardium intervening. This mode of examination may be termed *palpation*. Again, when the ear is applied, either directly, or indirectly by means of the stethoscope, over the position of the heart, sounds are heard the duration and rhythm of which are of physiological significance. This mode is known as *auscultation*. By *percussing* over the region of the heart the anatomical limits of the organ may be exactly defined, and information obtained as to its actual size, as to any alterations in the relation of the lungs to the heart, and as to the presence or absence of fluid in the pericardium. The direct registration of the movements of the heart has been accomplished by the aid of various recording instruments.[1]

Movements of heart.

The movements of the heart consist of a series of contractions which succeed each other with a certain rhythm. The period of contraction is called the *systole*, and that of relaxation the *diastole*. The two auricles contract and relax synchronously, and these movements are followed by a simultaneous contraction and relaxation of the ventricles. Thus there is a systole and diastole of the auricles and a systole and diastole of the ventricles. But in each half of the heart the contractions and relaxations of the auricle and the contractions and relaxations of the ventricle are successive. Finally, there is a very short period in which the heart is entirely in diastole. The whole series of movements, from the commencement of one auricular systole to the commencement of the one immediately following, is known as the *cardiac cycle* or *period of revolution* of the heart. In fig. 6 the systole is represented by the curve above the horizontal lines and the diastole by the curve below them. The auricular changes are traced on the upper line *au* and those of the ventricle on the lower line *vent*. The length of the lines represents the total duration of a cardiac revolution. The diagram shows that the auricular systole occupies one-fifth of the total time of a revolution of the heart and the ventricular systole two-fifths, that the auricular systole immediately precedes the ventricular systole, that the commencement of the ventricular systole coincides with the commencement of the auricular diastole, and that during two-fifths of the total period both auricles and ventricles are in a state of diastole. There are thus three periods,—(1) one of auricular systole, one-fifth; (2) one of ventricular systole, two-fifths; and (3) one of repose, two-fifths. The impulse of the apex against the wall of the chest, the moment of which is indicated by ×, occurs at the middle of the time occupied by the ventricular systole.

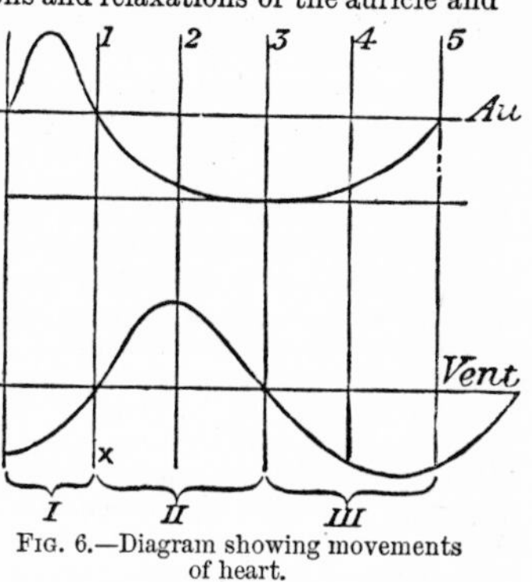

Fig. 6.—Diagram showing movements of heart.

In 1861 Chauveau and Marey obtained a direct record of the movements of the heart of a horse, determined the duration of the events happening in the heart, and measured the endocardiac pressure by an instrument termed a cardiac sound. When the sound was introduced into the right auricle and right ventricle,—the animal being anæsthetized,—the tracings shown in fig. 7 were

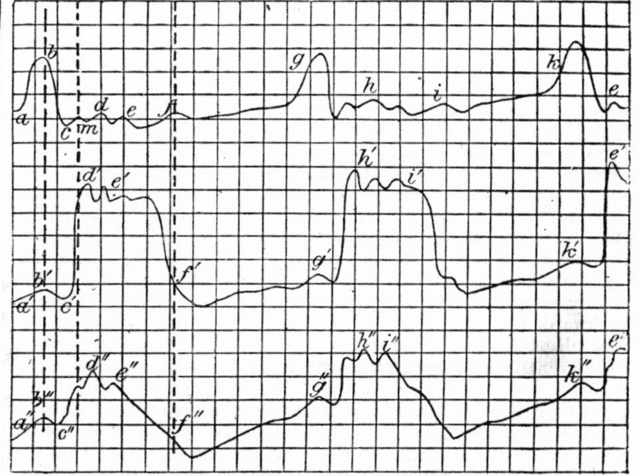

Fig. 7.—Tracings from the heart of a horse, by Chauveau and Marey. The upper tracing is from the right auricle, the middle from the right ventricle, and the lowest from the apex of the heart. The horizontal lines represent time, and the vertical amount of pressure. The vertical dotted lines mark coincident points in the three movements. The breadth of one of the small squares represents one-tenth of a second.

obtained. From this diagram we learn the following facts. (1) The auricular contraction is less sudden than the ventricular, as is indicated by the line *ab* being more oblique than the line *c′ d′*. (2) The auricular contraction lasts only for a very short time, as the curve almost immediately begins to descend, whereas the ventricle remains contracted for a considerable time, and then

[1] See Marey, *La Méthode Graphique, ut supra.*

slowly relaxes. (3) The time of the contraction of the auricle and that of its relaxation are about equal, but the time of the relaxation of the ventricle is nearly twice as long as that of its contraction; the movements of the auricle are thus uniform and wave-like, whilst those of the ventricle have more of a spasmodic character. (4) The auricular movement (*ab*, *a'b'*, *a''b''*, *g*, *g'*, *g''*) precedes the ventricular, and the latter coincides with the impulse of the apex against the wall of the chest, as is seen from the second vertical dotted line. (5) The contraction of the auricle, by forcing blood onwards, affects the pressure for an instant in the ventricle, as is indicated by the little elevation immediately before the ventricular contraction. (6) During the period of contraction of the ventricle there are oscillations of pressure affecting both the auricle and the ventricle; these are indicated by the little waves *d*, *e*, *f*, *d'*, *e'*, *f'*, *d''*, *e''*, and *f''*; similar waves are seen at *h*, *i*, *h'*, *i'*, *h''*, and *i''*. The letters *k*, *e*, *k'*, *e'*, and *k''*, *e''* represent a third set of waves.

Sketch of cardiac revolution.

With these facts in view, we may now describe the phenomena which happen in a complete cardiac revolution. Suppose the blood to be pouring from the venæ cavæ and the pulmonary veins into the two auricles. At that moment the auricles are passing into a state of complete diastole, and their cavity is increased by the funnel-shaped aperture at the auriculo-ventricular openings formed by the segments of the valves guarding these orifices. The distension of the auricles is due partly to the pressure in the venæ cavæ and pulmonary veins being less than in the interior of the auricles and partly to the aspirating action of the thorax during inspiration, sucking, as it were, the blood from the veins outside the chest to those inside the chest, and thus favouring the flow of blood to the heart. During this time both ventricles are filling with blood, the auriculo-ventricular orifices being open. When the distension of the auricles is complete (which happens before the distension of the ventricles, because the capacity of the auricles is much smaller than that of the ventricles), the auricular systole commences by the contraction and emptying of the auricular appendix towards the general cavity of the auricle, and by the mouths of the veins becoming narrowed by contraction of the circular fibres in their coats. These rhythmic movements are propagated quickly over the auricular walls, causing them to contract simultaneously towards the auriculo-ventricular orifices. The contracting wall forces the blood chiefly in the direction of least resistance, that is, into the ventricle, which at the same time is only partially full of blood, and is passing into a state of complete relaxation. The pressure in the veins, aided by their rhythmic contraction at the commencement of the auricular systole, is sufficient to prevent the blood from passing backwards, except to a very slight extent; but there is a momentary arrest of the flow in the large venous trunks. Thus the auricles act, not only as passive reservoirs for the blood in its passage from the veins to the auricles, but as rhythmic cavities tending to keep up a mean pressure in the veins, in diminishing by their extensibility the pressure which tends to increase during the ventricular systole, and in increasing the pressure by their contraction at a time when the venous pressure would diminish, that is, towards the close of the ventricular diastole. Both auricles and ventricles exercise, during their diastole, a certain aspirating or sucking action, like that seen during the relaxation of a compressed india-rubber bag; but this force is very feeble in the case of the heart.

The amount of blood discharged into the ventricles (already partially filled during the relaxation of the auricles) by the auricular systole is sufficient to fill their cavities, and consequently the ventricular systole immediately follows the contraction of the auricles. During the inflow of blood from auricles to ventricles the auriculo-ventricular valves are floated upwards into a more or less horizontal position, and the assumption of this position is further aided by the contraction of the longitudinal muscular fibres that pass from the auricles into the cusps of the valves. When the ventricular walls contract, the margins of the auriculo-ventricular valves are closely pressed together, and the cusps are kept from being folded backwards into the auricle by the simultaneous contraction of the musculi papillares pulling on the chordæ tendineæ which are affixed to the ventricular aspect of the valves. The close apposition of the cusps is also increased, even along their margins, by the arrangement that the chordæ tendineæ of one papillary muscle always pass to the adjoining edges of two cusps. Thus the valves, tricuspid on the right side and mitral on the left, are tightly closed and the blood cannot regurgitate into the auricles. The blood, thus compressed, can only pass into the pulmonary artery from the right ventricle and into the aorta from the left. The positive pressure in the ventricles is at its maximum at the beginning of their contraction; during the contraction it diminishes; and at the close of the systole (Marey), or in the diastole immediately thereafter (Goltz and Gaule), or even, according to Moens, shortly before the systole has reached its height, the pressure may even become negative. Moens "explains this aspiration as being due to the formation of an empty space in the ventricle caused by the energetic expulsion of the blood through the aorta and pulmonary artery" (Landois and Stirling). As the blood passes from the ventricles into the pulmonary artery and aorta, the segments of the sigmoid valves are forced open and stretched across the dilatations or sinuses behind each cusp, without being actually pressed against the walls of the vessels; and, as both the pulmonary artery and the aorta contained a certain amount of blood before, the pressure in these vessels is increased, and the walls of both yield to a considerable extent. As already stated, the ventricle continues in the contracted state for a brief space of time, and then it relaxes. Simultaneously with the commencement of relaxation, the auriculo-ventricular orifices open, thus permitting the passage of blood from the auricles; and at the same time the elastic walls of the aorta and pulmonary arteries recoil and force a portion of the blood backwards towards the cavities of the ventricles, in which, as they are passing into diastole, the pressure is much less than in the vessels. This blood, however, by filling the sinuses of Valsalva and the crescentic pouches of the sigmoid valves, closes these latter, and thus prevents any blood from passing into the ventricles. From the end of the ventricular contraction to the moment when the auricles are again full, all the cavities of the heart are in a condition of dilatation and the cavities are filling with blood. This is the period of the pause, during which the heart may be supposed to be in a state of rest.

Change in shape of heart.

When one watches an actively beating heart exposed in an anæsthetized animal, the movements are so tumultuous and rapid that the eye cannot follow them so as to convey to the mind a correct conception of the rapid changes in form. Owing to this our notions of such changes have been derived chiefly from an inspection of the heart after death. Recent ingenious investigations by Ludwig and Hesse have shown that the post-mortem form is not the natural shape of the living heart either in diastole or in systole, but such as is shown, for example, in fig. 8.

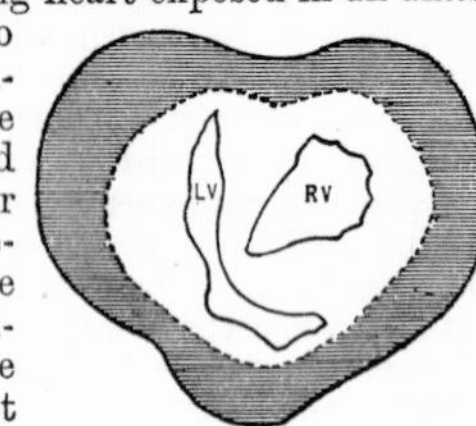

FIG. 8.—Projection of the base in systole and diastole; *RV*, right ventricle; *LV*, left ventricle.

Apex beat.

The apex beat or shock of the heart is synchronous with the systole, and is caused normally by the apex of the ventricle pressing more firmly against the chest wall, from which it is separated when the heart is at rest by the thin margin of the lung. At the time of ventricular systole, as already seen, the heart, instead of being an oblique cone having an elliptical base, as in rest, becomes more like a regular cone, having a circular base. When contraction occurs, the apex is carried from below and behind, upwards and forwards, and is forced into the intercostal space, and at the same time the ventricular portion twists on its long axis from left to right, so as to expose partially the left ventricle. It is the twisting motion that gives the shock or impulse, and it is caused chiefly by the contraction of the oblique fibres in the ventricles which lift up the apex; it is also assisted by the slightly spiral arrangement of the aorta and pulmonary artery. Some have supposed that the movement is partly due to the recoil of the ventricles after discharging their blood (like that of an exploded gun), causing the apex to go in the opposite direction, downwards and outwards; others have held that the discharge of blood into the pulmonary artery and aorta causes an elongation of these vessels, whereby the apex is pushed downwards and forwards. Both of these mechanisms, however, must have only a slight effect, as the cardiac impulse occurs even when from hæmorrhage the pulsating heart is practically empty.

Cardiographic tracings.

To obtain a tracing of the apex beat an instrument termed the cardiograph is employed, various forms of which are figured in Landois and Stirling's *Human Physiology*, vol. i. p. 89 *sq*. Figs. 9 and 10 are examples of tracings obtained by this instrument.

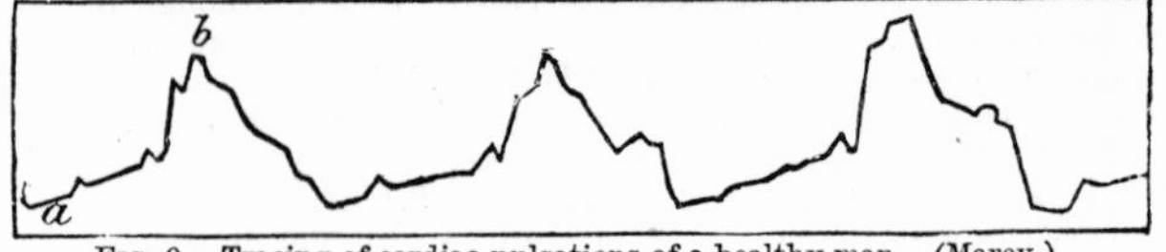

FIG. 9.—Tracing of cardiac pulsations of a healthy man. (Marey.)

From the latter figure we learn the subjoined information. The time of the pause and the contraction of the auricle are represented by *ab*, and it is evident that the latter phenomenon causes the apex of the heart to move towards the intercostal space. The portion *bc* corresponds to the contraction of the ventricles and is synchronous with the first sound. The curve then rapidly falls as the ventricles relax, and during the descent there are two elevations, *d* and *e*, synchronous with the second sound. As already stated, when the ventricles relax, the blood in the aorta and pulmonary artery, driven backwards by the elastic recoil of the walls of these vessels, closes the semilunar valves.

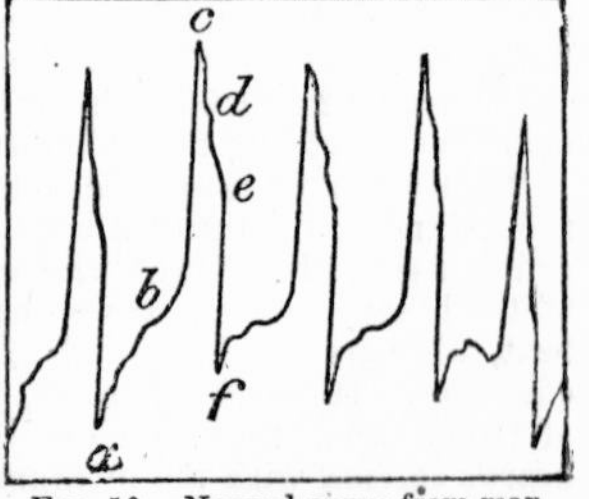

FIG. 10.—Normal curve from man. (Landois.)

This shock is propagated to the apex of the ventricles and thus causes a vibration of the intercostal space. The elevation *d* is synchronous with the closure of the aortic valves and *e* with that of the pulmonary valves; it is also apparent that these valves are not closed at the same moment, but are separated in time by ·05 to ·09 of a second,—an effect due, as already explained, to the greater blood pressure in the aorta than in the pulmonary artery. Finally, *ef* corresponds to the remaining part of the ventricular diastole.

Nature of heart's contraction.

Much discussion has taken place as to whether the contraction of the heart is to be regarded as a simple contraction, like the "twitch" of a muscle obtained by a single stimulation, or as a tetanic contraction, like cramp, such as is caused by the application of a number of stimuli in rapid succession. It is true that many of the phenomena of a cardiac contraction resemble those of a skeletal muscle: thus, fatigue diminishes the amplitude and increases the duration of the contraction; and the effects of changes of temperature are similar. The period of latent stimulation of a cardiac muscle (one-third of a second) is much longer than that of skeletal muscle (one-hundredth of a second). The systolic contraction, as regards duration, is more like a tetanic spasm than a twitch, being from eight to ten times longer. The electrical phenomena, on the other hand, resemble those of a twitch more than those of tetanus. Thus, when the heart is examined with a sensitive galvanometer, and with the aid of the appliances described under PHYSIOLOGY (vol. xix. p. 24 *sq.*), there is a "negative variation" with each beat. The fact appears to be that, just as the heart muscle shows histological characters intermediate between voluntary striated muscle and involuntary non-striated muscle, so it likewise shows physiological properties partaking of both.

Time of cardiac movements.

The time occupied by cardiac movements has been measured by various observers by a study of tracings obtained from the impulse of the apex of the heart against the wall of the chest, as recorded by the cardiograph. If the velocity of the surface on which the tracing is obtained be known, and if a correct interpretation is given of the causes of the various parts of the curve, it is not difficult to determine approximately the time occupied by the phases of a cardiac revolution. Rollett gives the following results in fractions of a second as determined by Landois (Hermann, *Handb. d. Physiol.*, vol. iv. p. 157).

Events in the Heart.	Rate of Heart-Beat per Minute.				
	55	55	74·2	109·7	113·1
	Duration of Phases.				
1. From beginning of pause to end of auricular contraction	·563	·584	·494	·213	·247
2. Contraction of ventricle	·243	·274	·079	·066	·057
3. Relaxation of ventricle to closure of semilunar valves	·066	·072	·144	·194	·133
4. From close of pulmonary valves to beginning of pause	·259	·200	·092	·090	·103
5. Between 1st and 2d sounds	·309	·346	·223	·244	·190
6. Between 2d sound and next 1st sound	·822	·784	·586	·303	·394
7. Time from 1 to 4 inclusive (complete cardiac revolution)	1·133	1·133	·809	·547	·539
8. From closure of aortic valves to closure of pulmonary valves	..	..	·078	·100	·057

Frequency of cardiac pulsations.

In the adult man cardiac pulsations occur at the rate of 65 to 75 per minute. There is a certain relation between the amount of blood in the circulation and the frequency of heart-beats. Thus, in the animal series, as the beats of the heart increase in frequency the quantity of blood which passes per minute in one kilogramme (2·2 lb) of body weight also increases, as is shown in the following table by Vierordt:—

	Quantity of Blood per Minute and per Kilogramme of Body Weight.	Number of Pulsations per Minute.
Horse	152 grammes	55
Man	207 ,,	72
Dog	272 ,,	96
Rabbit	620 ,,	220
Guinea-pig	892 ,,	320

Quantity of blood in heart.

It has been determined, both by direct measurement and by calculation based on the velocity of the blood in the aorta and the transverse section of the orifice of that vessel, that from a heart of average size each left ventricular systole ejects about 180 grammes (6·35 oz.). This is the figure usually given, but it must be regarded merely as approximative. The amount may vary even in the same individual according to the state of vigour of the muscular walls of the organ.

Sounds of heart.

When the ear is applied over the cardiac region of the chest of a healthy man two sounds are heard, the one with greatest intensity over the apex and the other over the base of the heart. The dull long sound heard over the apex has received several names, such as the first, the long, the inferior, and the systolic sound, whilst that over the base,—clearer, sharper, shorter, higher,—has been called the second, the short, the superior, the diastolic sound. Suppose the heart sounds to be expressed by the syllables *lupp dupp*; then the accent is on lupp (the first sound) when the stethoscope is over the apex—thus, lúpp dupp, lúpp dupp—and on dupp (the second sound) when over the base—thus, lupp dúpp, lupp dúpp. There is a pause between the second sound and the next succeeding first sound, and a much shorter pause (almost inappreciable) between the first and second sounds: thus—

At apex—lúpp dupp (pause), lúpp dupp (pause), lúpp dupp.
At base—lupp dúpp (pause), lupp dúpp (pause), lupp dúpp.

These relations are well seen in fig. 11. Dr Walshe states that, if the cardiac cycle be divided into tenths, the first sound will last four-tenths, the short pause one-tenth, the second sound two-tenths, and the long pause three-tenths. There has been considerable difference of opinion as to the cause of the first sound. Some have supposed it to be due to vibrations of the auriculo-ventricular valves; others believe that it is muscular, and due to the contraction of the ventricles; not a few have attributed it to movements of the blood through the aortic and pulmonary orifices; whilst yet others have thought that it might be the result of a fusion of these effects. It is certainly not due to the shock

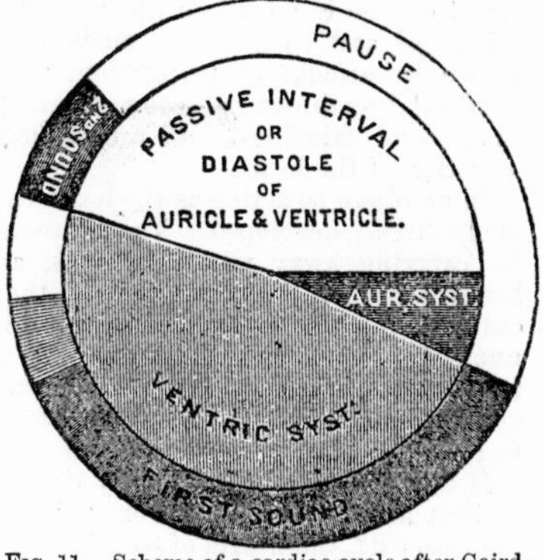

FIG. 11.—Scheme of a cardiac cycle after Gairdner and Sharpey. The inner circle shows what events occur in the heart, and the outer the relation of the sounds and silences to these events.

of the heart against the chest wall, as it has been heard after removal of the heart from the chest. The most likely view is that it is a muscular sound, varying in quality from the ordinary sound of a contracting muscle in accordance with the peculiar arrangement of the cardiac fibres, and that this sound is modified by the vibrations of the tense auriculo-ventricular valves. The fact that the sound has been heard from an excised heart still pulsating but empty of blood strongly supports this view; and there is further the pathological evidence that in cases where the muscular walls have been much weakened by fatty changes (as in the advanced stages of typhus, fatty degeneration, &c.) the first sound may disappear. No doubt exists as to the cause of the second sound: it is produced by the sudden sharp closure of the sigmoid valves. As already mentioned, the aortic and pulmonary valves do not close absolutely simultaneously.

For practical purposes it is important to bear in mind what is happening in the heart whilst one listens to its sounds. With the first sound we have (1) contraction of the ventricles, (2) closure of the auriculo-ventricular valves, (3) rushing of the blood into the aortic and pulmonary artery, (4) impulse of the apex against the chest, and (5) filling of the auricles. With the second sound we have (1) closure of the semilunar valves from the elastic recoil of the aorta and pulmonary artery, (2) relaxation of the ventricular walls, (3) opening of the auriculo-ventricular valves so as to allow the passage of blood from auricle to ventricle, and (4) diminished pressure of apex against chest wall. With the long pause there are (1) gradual refilling of the ventricle from the auricle and (2) contraction of the auricle so as to entirely fill the ventricle. The sound of the tricuspid valve is loudest at the junction of the lower right costal cartilage with the sternum, of the mitral at the apex beat, of the semilunar valves at the aortic orifice in the direction of the aorta, where it is nearest to the surface, at the second right costal cartilage, and of the valves at the pulmonary orifice over the third left costal cartilage, to the left and external to the margin of the sternum.

For an account of the mechanical work performed by the heart, see NUTRITION, vol. xvii. pp. 685-686.

Nutrition of heart.

The heart is directly nourished by the blood flowing through its cavities in some of the lower Vertebrates, as the frog; but in the hearts of larger animals, in which nutritional changes must be actively carried on, there is a special arrangement of vessels or cardiac circulation. The coronary arteries originate at the aortic orifice in the region of the sinus of Valsalva, rather above the upper border of the semilunar valves, so that when the ventricle contracts the mouths of these arteries are not covered by the segments of the valves. The branches of the coronary arteries, after dividing and again dividing, penetrate the muscular substance and end in a rich plexus of capillaries, which carry arterial blood to the structure of the heart. From these the radicles of the cardiac veins originate, and these veins carry the blood, now rendered venous, into the right auricle by the larger anterior cardiac veins and by numerous small veins constituting the foramina of Thebesius or the *venæ minimæ cordis*. The coronary vein is dilated before entering the auricle, forming the coronary sinus, and at the junction of the vein with the dilated portion there is a valve consisting of one or two segments. Other veins enter the coronary sinus, each having a valve. These valves serve two purposes: (1) they interrupt the flow of blood during the contraction of the right auricle, preventing regurgitation and venous congestion of the wall of the heart, and (2), as the valves open towards the right auricle, they prevent the backward flow of blood during contraction of the ventricles and favour its onward flow, and thus the stream of blood is accelerated, as in the veins of a contracting muscle. The blood is sent through the cardiac circulation by the systole of the ventricle, and not, as was advocated by Brücke, during its diastole. Heart disease in advanced life, when the coronary arteries are often thickened and their calibre much diminished by sclerosis, may be shown by attacks of palpitation, weakness of the heart, altered rhythm, breathlessness, congestions, pulmonary œdema, hæmorrhage, and faintings,—all due to interference with the normal nutrition of the heart.

Lymphatics of heart.

In an organ so active as the heart the lymphatic system is necessarily largely developed. These vessels, acting like drainage-tubes for carrying away waste products, are found in great numbers beneath both the pericardium and the endocardium, and throughout the muscular tissue. Amongst the muscular fibres there are numerous lacunæ or spaces lined by endothelial cells, which are the origins of the lymphatics. The lymph is carried into lymphatic glands between the aorta and the trachea, and ultimately finds its way into the right innominate vein and the thoracic duct.

Persistence of cardiac movement.

It has been known from early times that the heart will continue to beat after its removal from the body. This is more especially the case with the hearts of cold-blooded animals. The frog's heart may continue to pulsate for two and a half days, whilst that of a rabbit will do so only for a period of from three to thirty minutes. The average duration of the beats of the warm-blooded heart is said to be eleven minutes. The right auricular appendix, which beats longest, has been observed to pulsate in the rabbit fifteen hours after death, in the mouse forty-six, and in the dog ninety-six hours. After the heart has ceased beating, it may again be caused to contract by direct stimulation or by heat. The injection of arterial blood into the coronary vessels will restore excitability in the Mammalian heart after it has ceased to beat (Ludwig).

Cardio-pneumatic movement.

If a wide glass tube filled with smoke be inserted into one nostril, while the other nostril and the mouth are closed, the smoke will be seen to move with each pulsation of the heart (Stirling). This phenomenon has been studied by Ceradini and Landois. It is explained by the fact that when the heart contracts it occupies less space in the chest, and consequently, if the glottis be open, air will be drawn into the lungs. The reverse will happen during the diastole.

The heart and lungs being contained in an air-tight cavity, the chest or thorax, it is evident that the increase and decrease in the size of the chest during inspiration and expiration must affect the amount of pressure on the outer surface of the heart, and consequently its movements. When an inspiration is made by the descent of the diaphragm and the elevation of the ribs, the lungs expand; there is then less pressure on the outer surface of the heart and the heart is in a state of distension in diastole. In consequence also of the removal of pressure during inspiration from the great veins entering the chest and reaching the right side of the heart, the flow of venous blood towards the heart is favoured. These effects are more marked if after a deep expiration the glottis be closed, so as to prevent air entering the lungs, and if then the chest be dilated by a powerful inspiratory effort (J. Müller). This causes a dilatation of the heart, and venous blood flows freely into the right side; this sends it on to the lungs, causing them to become engorged, whilst at the same time the dilated left side of the heart is unable to send out a sufficient amount of blood into the arterial system. The pulse in such conditions may disappear, and there is an intense feeling of distress. On the other hand, expiration increases the pressure on the outer surface of the heart and of the great veins; only a small amount of blood flows into the right side; the heart is contracted; the systole is small; and the pulse is reduced in volume. This condition is intensified in what is termed Valsalva's experiment, in which after a deep inspiration the glottis is closed and a powerful expiratory effort is made. When this is done, the flow of venous blood into the heart is interrupted, the veins in the face and neck swell, and the blood is forced out of the compressed lungs into the left side of the heart, which throws it into the arterial circulation. The pulse and heart sounds disappear and there is the risk of syncope or fainting. Both these experiments, Müller's and Valsalva's, are dangerous and should not be often repeated. They are extreme conditions of the normal state of things, in which inspiration favours the flow of blood into the heart and the dilatation of the heart, whilst expiration has the opposite effect; and they also explain the mechanism by which air may be sucked into the veins from wounds in the neck or armpit. This is most likely to occur during inspiration, and when it does occur speedy death is the result.

Innervation of heart.

In treating of the innervation of the heart we have to consider (1) the influence of the great nerves connecting the heart with the central nervous organs, or what may be termed the *extrinsic nervous mechanism*, and (2) the nervous arrangements in the heart itself, or the *intrinsic nervous mechanism*. (1) The extrinsic arrangements, consisting of the nerves given off by the cardiac plexuses derived partly from the cerebro-spinal and partly from the sympathetic system, have been investigated chiefly in the larger animals, such as the tortoise, rabbit, and dog, and the general results have been described under PHYSIOLOGY (vol. xix. p. 29 *sq.*). They may be briefly summarized as follows: (α) there are fibres in the vagus nerve exercising a controlling or inhibitory action on the heart, and these fibres originate in the medulla oblongata; (β) the sympathetic nerve supplies accelerating fibres to the heart, and these fibres originate in the cerebro-spinal system. (2) The intrinsic arrangements have been investigated more especially in the heart of the frog, a view of which is given in figs. 12 and 13. It will be seen

Extrinsic.

Intrinsic.

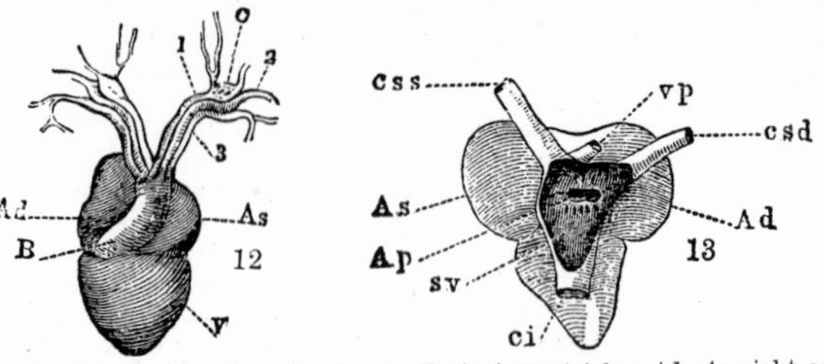

FIG. 12.—Heart of frog from the front. *V*, single ventricle; *Ad*, *As*, right and left auricles; *B*, bulbus arteriosus; 1, carotid, 2, aorta, and 3, pulmonary artery; *C*, carotid gland. (Ecker.)

FIG. 13.—Heart of frog from behind. *sv*, sinus venosus opened; *ci*, inferior vena cava; *csd*, *css*, right and left superior venæ cavæ; *vp*, pulmonary vein; *Ad* and *As*, right and left auricles; *Ap*, communication between right and left auricle. (Ecker.)

that the frog's heart possesses two auricles, communicating by a foramen in the septum, and a single ventricle. The venous blood from the body is poured in the first instance, not into the right auricle, but into a cavity called the *sinus venosus*, which communicates with the right auricle. The left auricle receives the arterial blood from the lungs by the pulmonary veins. Both auricles empty into the common ventricle, which contains therefore a mixture of arterial and venous blood, and when the ventricle contracts some of this blood is again sent to the lungs, whilst the remainder passes into a dilatation at the commencement of the arterial system, called the *bulbus arteriosus*, and thence into the aorta.

Results of excision experiment.

After the heart of a decapitated frog has been removed from its body, and so from the influence of the great nervous centres, rhythmical movements may continue for some time independently of those centres. If the apex of the heart be then cut off, it will remain motionless, whilst the larger part will still beat rhythmically. Successive slices may be removed from the larger portion without affecting rhythmical contraction, until a section is made through the auriculo-ventricular groove, when the ventricular portion of the heart ceases to beat. If the motionless apex, or the separate portions rendered motionless by the above procedure, be mechanically irritated, a single contraction, not a series of rhythmic contractions, follows. When the ventricle is separated from the rest of the heart by a ligature, or by concision at the level of the auriculo-ventricular groove, the ventricle stops, but the auricles and the sinus go on beating. To continue the rhythmic movement of the ventricle, it is necessary to have attached to it a small portion of the auricular part of the heart, especially the lower margin of the septum. It would, therefore, appear that impulses pass from this auricular portion into the ventricular and cause the latter to pulsate. If the sinus venosus be separated from the auricles by incision or ligature, the veins and the sinus continue to beat, whilst the auricles and ventricles are arrested in diastole. Suppose another incision be made through the auriculo-ventricular groove, the ventricle frequently begins to beat, but the auricles remain in diastole. It is also observed in these circumstances that the ventricle beats more slowly than under normal conditions. Although the rhythmical contractions of the heart are influenced by the nervous arrangements, it cannot be said that ganglionic nerve cells and nerve fibres are a necessary part of the mechanism. It has been shown by Engelmann that, if the ventricle of a frog's heart be cut into two or more strips in a zigzag manner, so that the parts still remain connected with each other by muscular tissue, the strips still beat in a regular progressive manner, provided one strip is caused to contract.

Experiment of Descartes.

Experiment of Stannius.

The Action of the Blood-Vessels.

Flow of fluids through tubes.

It is evident that a general study of the flow of fluids through tubes ought to precede that of the flow of the blood through the complicated system of tubes constituting the arteries, capillaries, and veins. In this place, however, it is necessary to allude only to those facts in hydraulics which have a special bearing on the phenomena of the circulation (comp. HYDROMECHANICS, vol. xii. pp. 440 *sq.* and 459 *sq.*). When a stream of water is transmitted intermittently by the strokes of a pump through a long elastic tube, formed, say, of india-rubber, the fluid does not issue from the other end in a series of jets, which would be the case if the tube were rigid, but it flows continuously, because during the pause between the successive strokes the outflow still continues. Consequently a continuous flow is kept up in elastic tubes when the time between two strokes is shorter than the duration of the outflow after the first stroke. If the finger be placed on any part of such a tube, and more especially near the pump, an expansion and relaxation will be felt with each stroke. Further, if the right fore-finger be placed over the tube near the pump, and the left fore-finger over a more distant portion, a stronger impulse will be felt with the right than with the left finger. Thus a wave is transmitted along the tube, diminishing in amplitude as the distance from the pump increases. We must distinguish between the transmission of this wave (an oscillatory movement or change of form in the column of fluid) and the transmission of the current, that is, the translation of a mass of fluid along the tube. In elastic tubes the current is much slower than the transmission of the wave. The progress of the wave of oscillation may be traced graphically by an apparatus devised by Marey.[1] E. H. Weber gives the velocity of waves in elastic tubes at 36·76 feet per second, and Donders states it at 36 to 42½ feet. Increase of pressure in the tube appears to lessen the velocity of the wave. The specific gravity of the liquid also affects the velocity: thus the wave is propagated four times more slowly in mercury than in water.

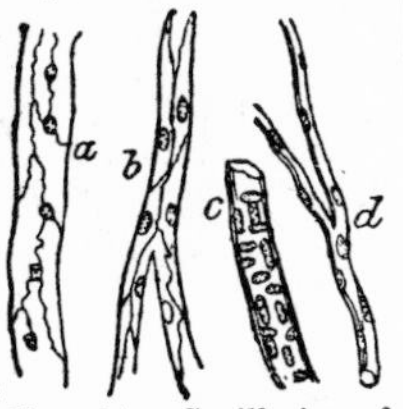

Fig. 14.—Capillaries of various size. *a*, capillary much magnified and acted on by nitrate of silver, to show that it is composed of flattened cells; *b*, a smaller vessel showing the same; *c*, a small artery or vein showing transverse or longitudinal nuclei; *d*, ultimate capillary from *pia mater* of sheep's brain.

General structure of blood-vessels. The blood-vessels consist, as already stated, of the arteries, the capillaries, and the veins. (*a*) The ultimate or most minute capillaries have the simplest type of structure (fig. 14), consisting of tubes formed of a single layer of transparent, thin, nucleated, endothelial cells, joined at their margins. A perfectly fresh capillary does not show the edges of the cells, owing to the uniform refractive property of the wall of the tube. The nuclei show an internuclear plexus of fibrils. The cement substance uniting the cells is stained black by a ¼ per cent. solution of nitrate of silver. Here and there minute dots or slits may be seen, which have been supposed by some to be openings (stomata or stigmata). In the transparent parts of animals, such as the web of the frog's foot, the mesentery and the lung of the frog, and the tail of a fish, the blood may be seen (fig. 15) flowing through the capillary network from the arteries into the veins. The current is rapid in the small arteries, less rapid in the veins, and slow in the capillaries. It is also fastest in the centre of the vessel and slowest near the wall. The colourless corpuscles of the blood may be seen to pass from the centre of the stream to the margins, to adhere to the inner surface of the blood-vessel, and occasionally to pass through the coats of the more minute vessels, appearing in the surrounding tissues as migratory cells. Capillaries form networks (fig. 15), which vary much in the size and closeness of the meshes, according to the degree of activity of the tissue elements.

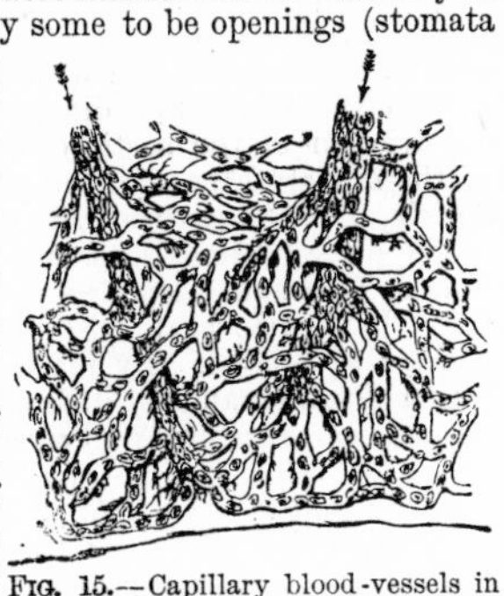

Fig. 15.—Capillary blood-vessels in web of a frog's foot, as seen with the microscope. The arrows indicate the course of the blood. (Schäfer.)

(*b*) An artery has three coats,—an inner or elastic, a middle or muscular, and an external or areolar (fig. 16). The inner coat is formed of two layers,—one of pavement epithelium, sometimes called endothelium, and the other composed of fine elastic fibres interlacing, or of a fine membrane perforated with holes of various sizes (fenestrated membrane of Henle). In some vessels there is a thin layer of connective tissue between the epithelium and the elastic layer. The middle coat is formed of a layer of non-striated muscular fibres circularly disposed around the vessel, mixed with numerous elastic fibres connected with the perforated membrane of the inner coat. The outer coat consists of connective tissue, mixed also with elastic fibres. In the aorta there is a considerable amount of sub-epithelial connective tissue (Schäfer), and the elastic coat attains great thickness and strength. As a general rule, the smaller arteries show a considerable development of the muscular coat, whilst in the larger it is the elastic coat that attains the preponderance. In many of the larger arteries there are longitudinal muscular fibres at the boundary of the middle and inner coats. Whilst the circular fibres, on contracting, must narrow the calibre of the artery, the longitudinal may tend to keep the vessel open. In the external coat of the larger arteries minute vessels, *vasa vasorum*, exist for the nourishment of the tissue elements of the arterial wall.

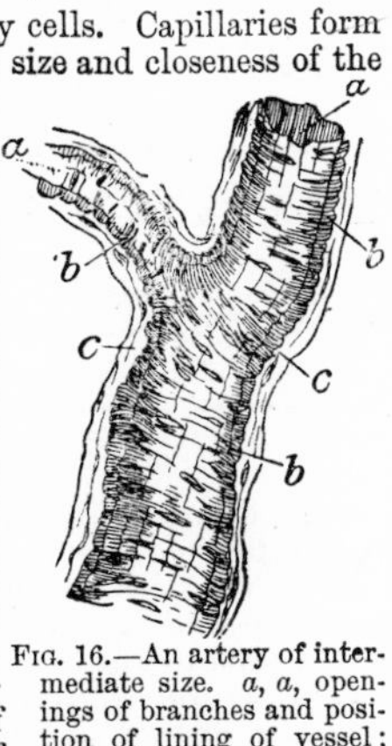

Fig. 16.—An artery of intermediate size. *a*, *a*, openings of branches and position of lining of vessel; *b*, *b*, *b*, muscular coat showing transverse nuclei; *c*, *c*, coat of areolar tissue.

[1] Figured in M'Kendrick's *Outlines of Physiology*, pp. 338-339.

(*c*) The veins have similar coats to those of an artery, with differences in detail. The elastic layer is less developed in the internal coat; the middle coat is much thinner and has less elastic tissue, but more connective tissue. Many veins have semilunar folds of the internal coat strengthened with fibrous tissue, forming valves. In some veins (iliac, femoral, umbilical) longitudinal muscular fibres are found in the inner part of the middle coat; in the inferior vena cava, hepatic veins, and portal veins these longitudinal fibres are external to the circular coat; in the superior vena cava and upper part of the inferior vena cava the circular coat is wanting; and the veins of the pia mater, brain and spinal cord, retina, bones, and the venous sinuses of the dura mater and placenta have no muscular tissue (Schäfer). Valves exist in the larger veins only, especially in those of the limbs; they are not found in the veins of the viscera, of the cranium and vertebral canal, or of the bones, nor in the umbilical vein.

(*d*) The arterioles and venules are the small vessels, simpler in structure than the larger above described, but containing the same elements. In the smallest veins the elastic layer has disappeared, and the muscular layer is also very thin. Sometimes the muscular layer is represented only by a single layer of contractile cells, and in such minute vessels the outer coat and elastic layer have also disappeared, so that the vessel is merely a tube composed of pavement cells with a few elongated fusiform muscular cells twisted around it. Even in the smallest vessels the following differences may be observed between arterioles and venules: "The veins are larger than the corresponding arteries; they branch at less acute angles; their muscular cells are fewer, and their epithelium cells less elongated; the elastic layer of the inner coat is always less marked, and sooner disappears" (Schäfer).

(*e*) The cavernous spaces, as existing in erectile tissues (*corpus cavernosum* of the penis), consist of the anastomosis of large veins of unequal calibre. The walls and partitions have numerous perforations; threads of delicate tissue, covered with epithelium, pass through the cavities; and the walls are strengthened by connective tissue. Similar structures connected with arteries form the carotid gland of the frog and the coccygeal gland of man.

Properties of blood-vessels. The physical properties of blood-vessels are cohesion and elasticity. The cohesion is great and the elasticity is small and perfect. The walls of blood-vessels have the property of contractility, by which alterations take place in the calibre of the vessel, and consequently in the amount of blood supplied to a part.

Arterial circulation. *Arterial Circulation.*—The arterial walls are both muscular and elastic, the muscular coat predominating in the smaller, whilst the elastic coat is strong in the greater arteries. The chief function of the elasticity of the greater vessels is to transmute the unequal movement of the blood in the large arteries, caused by the intermittent action of the ventricle, into a uniform flow in the capillaries. Thus, when the ventricle contracts, it propels a certain amount of blood into the elastic aorta, which expands in all directions. On the commencement of the diastole of the ventricle the *vis a tergo* is removed; the aorta owing to its elasticity recoils, so as to close, on the one hand, the semilunar valves and, on the other, to force part of its contents into the vessels farther onwards. These, in turn, as they already contain a quantity of blood, expand, recover by an elastic recoil, and transmit the movements with diminished intensity. Thus the blood is driven along the vessels by the action (1) of the ventricular systole, and (2) of the elastic recoil of the walls of the vessels occurring during the intervals between the ventricular systole (see p. 104 below). By these actions a series of movements, consisting of expansions and contractions, gradually diminishing in amplitude, pass along the arterial system from the greater to the smaller vessels, the latter becoming, as already pointed out, less and less elastic. These expansions and relaxations of the arterial wall, passing along like a wave, constitute the pulse. **Pulse.** The pulse therefore represents merely the transmission of an undulating movement of the blood, not its progression in the vessels. The undulations of the pulse travel at the rate of 354⅓ inches per second, about 30 times faster than the movement of the blood, which in the carotid artery of the horse has been estimated to travel 11·8 inches per second.

Sphygmograph. The pulse can be registered graphically by means of a SPHYGMOGRAPH (*q.v.*). Vierordt constructed the first sphygmograph in 1855, substituting for a column of fluid a lever placed on the pulse, which communicated with a system of levers and thus amplified the movement. Of those subsequently devised the best form is that of Marey, invented in 1861. It consists essentially of a long lever, which is moved near the fulcrum by a screw acting on a small horizontal wheel, from whose axis there projects a long, light, wooden lever. The point of the screw rests on a flat disk of steel or ivory, at the end of an elastic spring, which presses the ivory disk or pad on the artery. The lever inscribes the movements on a blackened surface, usually a strip of paper smoked in the flame of a lamp burning turpentine, carried in front of the point of the lever by clock-work. In the instrument as modified by Mahomed, Byrom Bramwell, and others there is an arrangement for adjusting the amount of pressure made on the artery by the ivory pad, so that tracings may be taken at different times from the same artery with different or with the same pressures. The tracings are "fixed" by passing them through shellac or photographic varnish.

Sphygmograph or pulse tracing. The following changes take place in an artery when it pulsates:—(1) it dilates and at the same time lengthens to a small extent; (2) the pressure of the blood increases in the artery, and a feeling of hardness and resistance is experienced when the artery is compressed with the finger. These facts are illustrated in the sphygmographic curve shown diagrammatically in fig. 17. The ascending line *ab* (line of ascent, up-stroke, or percussion stroke) corresponds to the distension of the artery produced by the systole of the left ventricle, and the descending line *bcd* to its elastic recoil; the length of the line *ad* represents the total duration of the movement, which is divided into two portions by the perpendicular line *be*. The distance *ae* measures the duration of the distension of the artery and *ed* the time of its elastic recoil. In a continuous tracing the durations of the individual pulsations are equal, and in inverse ratio to the number of pulsations in a unit of time. In a normal pulse the distension and the elastic recoil of the vessel succeed each other without interruption, so that there is no period of repose in the artery. When, however, the pressure of blood in the artery falls below a certain point, these characters disappear or are modified. Fig. 17 shows that the duration of the distension of the artery is only about one-third of that of its contraction. The rapidity and slowness of the pulse depend on the ratio of these periods. The pulse is quick when the duration of the arterial distension diminishes, and slow when it increases. The line *ab* becomes less oblique and more nearly vertical, in proportion as the time of the distension is short, quick, and nearly instantaneous. The rapidity of the pulse is increased by quick action of the heart, considerable power of yielding in the arterial walls, easy afflux of blood owing to dilatation of smaller vessels, and nearness to the heart. The term *quickness* has reference to a single pulse-beat, and *frequency* to the number of beats in a given time, say, one minute. The line *bcd* is always more oblique than *ab*, and in careful tracings it presents several elevations or notches (see fig. 18). If we refer the different portions of the curve to their origin the result is as follows:—(1) the up-stroke corresponds to the systole of the left ventricle, opening the aortic valves, pouring the blood into the arteries, and distending them; (2) the downstroke represents the time during which the blood is flowing out of the arteries at their periphery into the capillaries; (3) the larger wave in the descent, *i.e.*, the dicrotic, recoil, or aortic systolic wave, represents the time of the closure of the aortic valves; (4) the predicrotic, first tidal, or second ventricular systolic wave occurs after the first systolic wave and during the ventricular contraction (Byrom Bramwell). In many pulse-tracings there are still smaller secondary waves, due to elastic vibrations of the wall of the vessel. The three factors causing an arterial pulsation are (1) the more or less energetic contraction of the ventricle, (2) the quantity and pressure of the blood, and (3) the elastic and contractile properties of the arterial wall. If these factors be in any way modified there will be a corresponding modification in the physical characters of the pulse. The character of a pulse-tracing is affected by the amount of pressure applied to the artery. With a light pressure the dicrotic wave is relatively less; with a moderate pressure ($3\frac{1}{2}$ to 7 oz.) it is well marked, whilst the curve is lower; and with greater pressure it is again reduced. With $7\frac{3}{4}$ to $10\frac{1}{2}$ oz. pressure small secondary waves appear before the dicrotic.

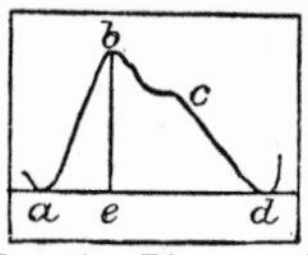

FIG. 17.—Diagram of a sphygmographic tracing.

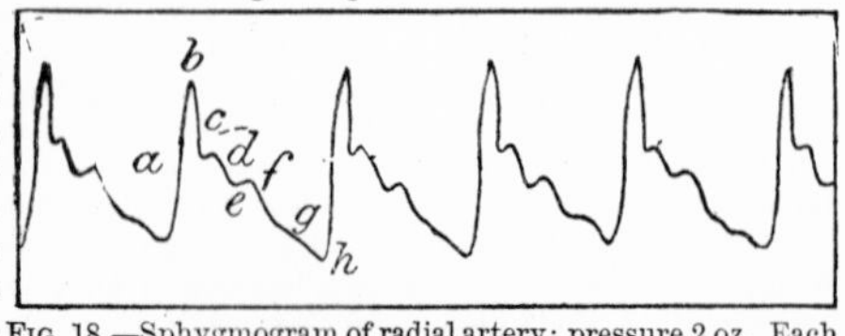

FIG. 18.—Sphygmogram of radial artery; pressure 2 oz. Each part of the curve between the base of one up-stroke and the base of the next corresponds to a beat of the heart, so that this figure shows five heart-beats and part of a sixth; *ab*, the ascent; *b*, apex of up-stroke; *b* to *h*, the descent, with an elevation *d*, the first tidal or predicrotic wave; *e*, aortic notch; *f*, a second elevation, the dicrotic wave; *g*, a slight curve, sometimes called the second tidal wave. (Landois and Stirling.)

Physiological characters of pulse. The normal pulse-rate in man is about 72 per minute, in woman about 80 per minute; but in some individuals a state of health is consistent with a pulse-rate as rapid as 100 or as slow as 50 beats per minute. The pulse-rate is influenced by the undermentioned factors. (1) *Age*: a newly-born child, 130 to 140 beats per minute; 1 year, 120 to 130; 2 years, 105; 3 years, 100; 4 years, 97; 5 years, 94 to 90; 10 years, about 90; 10 to 15 years, 78; 15 to 50 years, 70; 60 years, 74; 80 years, 79; 80 to 90 years, over 80. (2) *Length of body*: Czarnecki, Volkmann, and Rameaux have shown that as the height increases the pulse slows. (3) *Bodily states*: active muscular exercise, increased blood-pressure, active digestion, pain, nervous excitement, extreme debility quicken the pulse. (4) *Temperature*: increase of temperature quickens the pulse. An increase of 1° above 98° Fahr. is associated with an increase of 10 beats per minute: thus, at 98° Fahr. the pulse-rate will be 60 per minute; at 99°, 70; at 100°, 80; at 101°, 90; at 102°, 100; at 103°, 110; at 104°, 120; at 105°, 130; and at 106°, 140 (Aitken). (5) *Posture*: the pulse is more frequent when one stands than when one sits, and still slower when one lies down. (6) *Sensory impressions*: music is said by Dogiel to quicken the pulse. (7) *Pressure*: increased barometric pressure slows the pulse. (8) *Diurnal rhythm*: 3 to 6 A.M., 61 beats; 8 to 11.30 A.M., 74; towards 2 P.M., a decrease; towards 3 (at dinner-time) another rise, which goes on until 6 to 8 P.M., when it may be 70; towards midnight, 54; a rise again towards 2 A.M., when it soon falls again, and afterwards rises, as before, towards 3 A.M. (Landois and Stirling).

Colin gives the following pulse-rates in various animals:—elephant, 25 to 28 beats per minute; camel, 28 to 32; giraffe, 66; horse, 36 to 40; ox, 45 to 50; tapir, 44; ass, 46 to 50; pig, 70 to 80; lion, 40; lioness, 68; tiger, 74; sheep, 70 to 80; goat, 70 to 80; leopard, 60; wolf (female), 96; hyæna, 55; dog, 90 to 100; cat, 120 to 140; rabbit, 120 to 150; mouse, 120; goose, 110; pigeon, 136; hen, 140; snake, 24; carp, 20; frog, 80; salamander, 77.

Strength of pulse. A pulse is said to be strong or weak according to the weight it is able to raise. The strength is usually estimated by pressing the finger on the artery until the pulse-beat beyond the point of pressure disappears. **Tension.** The pulse is said to be hard or soft according to the degree of resistance experienced. In feeling the pulse it is important to notice whether the tension is great during the distension of the vessel, or whether it is hard during the intervals between the pulse-beats as well as during the beats themselves. On the other hand, it may be soft in these intervals in consequence of the semilunar valves at the aorta not closing perfectly (aortic incompetence), thus allowing the blood partially to flow back into the ventricle. This softness and the feeling of sudden collapse of the arterial wall are the pulse characteristics of unfilled arteries. **Volume.** A pulse may be large in volume, as where a large amount of blood is thrown into the aorta, owing to hypertrophy of the left ventricle, or it may be small and thready when a small quantity of blood passes into the aorta, either owing to a diminished total amount of blood, or from constriction of the aortic orifice (aortic stenosis), or from disease of the mitral valve allowing the blood to regurgitate into the left auricle, or when the ventricle contracts feebly.

Velocity of pulse-wave. The pulse becomes later and later in time as we recede from the heart. Czermak estimated the delay as follows:—carotid pulse, after the cardiac beat, ·087 second; radial, ·159 second; posterior tibial, ·193 second. By placing delicate tambours or electromagnetic sphygmographs at different points of the circulation and recording the movements on a rapidly moving surface, E. H. Weber found the velocity of the pulse-wave to be 30·31 feet per second; Garrod found it to be from 29·52 to 35·43 feet per second; Crashey determined it at 27·89 feet per second; and Moens at 27·23. In the arteries of the upper limb it is stated to be 30·84 and in those of the lower limb 31·82 feet per second. The wave-length is obtained "by multiplying the duration of the inflow of blood into the aorta = ·08 to ·09 second by the velocity of the pulse-wave." This would give the wave-length at 2·46 feet.

Influence of respiration on pulse. As already pointed out, inspiration favours the flow of blood into the veins and retards the flow in the arteries, whilst expiration has the reverse effect. The tension of the arteries during inspiration is therefore less than in expiration, and this affects the form of the pulse-curve, as is seen in fig. 19. (1) "The greater distension of the arteries during expiration causes all the parts of the curve occurring during this phase to be higher; (2) the line of ascent is heightened during expiration, because the expiratory thoracic movement helps to increase the force of the expiratory wave; (3) owing to increase of the pressure the dicrotic wave must be less during expiration; and (4) for the same reason the elastic elevations (secondary waves) are more distinct and occur higher in the curve near its apex" (Landois and Stirling, *op. cit.*). See also p. 102 above.

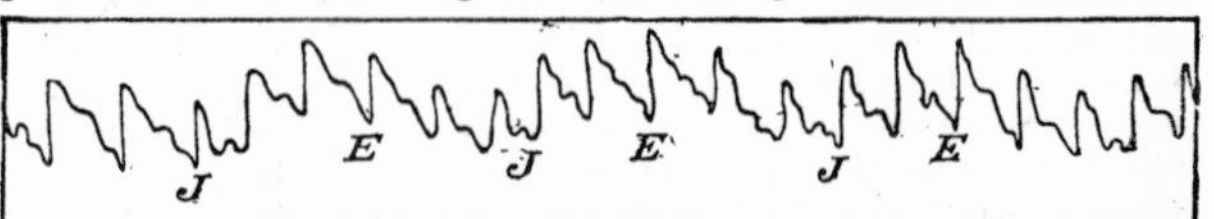

FIG. 19.—Sphygmographic tracing showing influence of respiration on pulse. J, during inspiration; E, during expiration. (Riegel.)

Contractility of arteries. Non-striated muscle, as has been already stated, exists to a considerable amount in the walls of the smaller arteries, and the calibre of these vessels may consequently be changed by the activity of the contractile coat. The contractility of vessels may appear under two forms:—(1) as rhythmical contractions, such as have been seen in the vessels of a rabbit's ear or in a bat's wing, which are independent both of the pulse and of respiratory movements; and (2) as persistent contractions, under the influence of the nervous system, which play an important part in the distribution of the blood. The amount of contraction of an artery will affect the pressure of the blood in its interior: it will accelerate or retard the rapidity of the blood current; and it will regulate the supply of blood to the capillary area to which the vessel is distributed. By such arrangements, also, the distribution of blood to various organs is regulated, thus establishing what has been termed a *balance of local circulations*. For example, if the vessels in one organ remain permanently contracted, whilst those in a neighbouring organ are dilated, more blood will pass to the latter than to the former, and some end of physiological importance may be served. Thus physiological correlations may be established between the cerebral and thyroid circulations, the gastro-hepatic and the splenic circulations, and the distribution of blood in the lower extremities as related to the abdominal organs.

Arterial sounds

If a stethoscope be placed over a large artery, a murmur, sound, or bruit will be heard, caused by the blood rushing through the vessel narrowed by the pressure of the instrument. The fluid escapes into a wider portion of the vessel beyond the point of pressure, and the sound is caused by the particles of fluid there being thrown into rapid vibration, not by vibrations of the wall of the vessel. Such sounds are favoured by a certain degree of elasticity in the walls of the vessel, by diminished peripheral resistance allowing the blood to flow away freely, and by a considerable difference of the pressure in the narrow and wide parts of the tube. They are always heard over an aneurism, when the arterial tube is dilated, and when pressure is applied to a large vessel. The placental souffle or bruit heard during pregnancy is a sound of this kind, arising from pressure on the widely dilated uterine arteries. In cases of insufficient aortic valves a double blowing murmur may be heard, the first being due to the rush of blood into the vessel caused by the ventricular contraction, and the second by the flowing back of the blood into the heart during diastole. Comp. p. 106 below.

Capillary circulation.

Capillary Circulation.—The circulation in the capillaries may be readily studied by placing under the microscope any transparent membrane containing vessels, such as the web of a frog's foot, the mesentery, lung, or tongue of a frog, the tail of a fish or a tadpole, the wing of a bat, the third eyelid of the pigeon or fowl, the liver of a frog or a newt, the mucous membrane of the inner surface of the human lip, or the conjunctiva of the eyeballs and eyelids. Under favourable conditions the following phenomena may clearly be noticed. (1) The diameter of the finest capillaries is such as to permit the passage of corpuscles in single file only, and it may vary from $\frac{1}{5000}$ to $\frac{1}{12,500}$ of an inch. (2) The average length is about $\frac{1}{50}$ of an inch. (3) The number varies according to the degree of activity of the tissue, being numerous where nutritive processes are active, as in the liver and muscles. (4) They form networks or anastomoses, the form and arrangement of which are determined by the tissue elements. (5) In the smaller arterioles and venules, and in the capillaries, the current is continuous and there is no pulse. Owing to the elasticity of the larger vessels the intermittent movement of the blood caused by each ventricular contraction is in the capillaries transformed into a continuous flow. (6) In some of the larger vessels the current is more rapid than in others of equal calibre: that is to say, it is more rapid in small arteries than in small veins. (7) The current appears to have a uniform velocity in all ultimate capillaries of the same size. (8) Sometimes a slight acceleration of the rapidity, even in the smallest vessels, may be observed to follow each cardiac beat. (9) In a vessel larger than an ultimate capillary, so large as to permit the passage of several coloured corpuscles abreast, these may be seen travelling with great apparent velocity in the centre of the stream, whilst the colourless corpuscles move more slowly and with a rolling motion next the walls of the tube, in a layer of plasma called Poiseuille's space. The coloured corpuscles also remain separate from each other, and do not exhibit any tendency to adhere together or stick to the walls of the vessels, whereas the colourless corpuscles do both, more especially after the membrane has been exposed for some time to the air, so as to excite the early stages of inflammation. Prof. D. J. Hamilton has shown that the nearer a suspended body approaches the specific gravity of the liquid in which it is immersed the more it tends to keep in the centre of the stream, and he states that the reason why the coloured corpuscles keep the centre and the colourless the sides of the stream is that the specific gravity of the former is the same or slightly greater than the blood plasm, whilst that of the colourless corpuscles is less. (10) If the calibre of an ultimate capillary be marked at the beginning of an observation, and again some time afterwards, it will frequently be noticed that it has become narrower or wider, indicating that contractility is one of the properties of capillaries. (11) The velocity is greater in the pulmonary than in the systemic capillaries. (12) The phenomenon known as *diapedesis*, or migration of the white blood corpuscles, first described by Waller in 1846, is readily seen in the mesentery of the frog after inflammation has been excited by exposure to the air for one or two hours (see fig. 20). It consists of the adhesion to the wall of the vessel of the colourless corpuscles and their protrusion through the wall into the surrounding tissues. Hering is of opinion that it is due partly to the filtration of the colloidal matter of the cell under blood-pressure. Diapedesis is of importance as constituting a part of the inflammatory process. The colourless cells become pus corpuscles (Cohenheim); see PATHOLOGY, vol. xviii. p. 365. (13) If a vascular membrane be gently irritated whilst under the microscope, the capillaries become first slightly narrowed and then dilated, crowded with corpuscles, whilst the blood-stream becomes slower. By and by the stream oscillates and then altogether stops. This constitutes *stastis*, a part of the inflammatory process, and is followed by exudation of the plasma of the blood, along with colourless corpuscles, and more rarely coloured corpuscles.

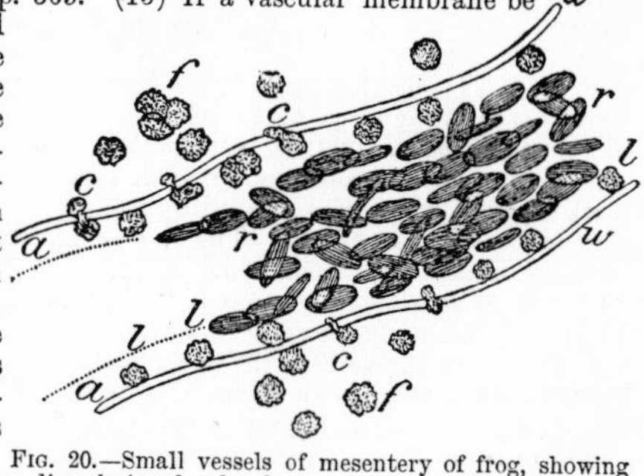

FIG. 20.—Small vessels of mesentery of frog, showing diapedesis of colourless corpuscles. *w*, *w*, vascular walls; *aa*, Poiseuille's space; *r*, *r*, red corpuscles; *l*, *l*, colourless corpuscles adhering to wall; *c*, *c*, colourless corpuscles in various stages of extrusion; *f*, *f*, extruded corpuscles. (Landois and Stirling.)

Vital properties of capillaries.

The most important vital property of capillaries is, as already mentioned, contractility, by which their calibre may be modified. The protoplasm forming their walls contracts when stimulated. Some investigators have supposed the nuclei to be active agents in contraction; but more probably the cell substance is the seat of change. Oxygen causes the nuclei to swell, whilst carbonic acid has the opposite effect. Roy and Graham Brown attach much importance to the active contractility of the capillaries as regulating the distribution of blood, now contracting, now relaxing, according to the needs of the tissues in their vicinity. Elasticity is also a characteristic of the capillary walls.

Arrangement of capillaries.

The arrangement of the capillaries in an organ or tissue is adapted to its functional activity. Where there is great functional activity there is a rich plexus of capillaries, and in the converse case the converse is also true. Contrast, for example, the capillary supply in cartilage with that of muscle, or that of the grey matter of the nerve centres with that of the white matter (see PHYSIOLOGY, vol. xix. p. 23 *sq.*). But, in addition, the distribution of capillaries always corresponds to the intimate structural arrangements of the tissue or organ. So precisely is this the case that a good histologist is able to identify the organ from an injected preparation showing the vessels, although none of the ultimate histological elements of the organ or tissue are to be seen. In muscle, for example, the capillaries exist in the form of elongated meshes; in connective tissue, such as is found beneath the skin, in an irregular network; in the papillæ of the skin, in loops; and to form the glomeruli of the kidney in close reticulations (see NUTRITION, vol. xvii. p. 673, fig. 5).

Attractive influence of tissues.

The movement in the capillaries is due to the force of the heart, as modified by the vessels (*vis a tergo*). Some have supposed that it is supplemented by an attractive influence exerted by the tissues (*vis a fronte*); and the statement is supported by the observation that, when there is an increased demand for blood owing to active nutritional changes, there is an increase in the amount of blood flowing to the part, such as occurs, for example, in the mammary gland during lactation, and in the growth of the stag's horn. Such an attractive influence on the part of the tissues is quite conceivable as a force assisting in the inward flow of blood, acting along with capillarity; but its amount is infinitesimally small in comparison with the force exerted by the heart. The force of the heart is sufficient to drive the blood through the capillaries into the veins.

Capillary pulse

When capillaries are examined in a transparent membrane of a living animal no pulse-like movement is visible. Owing to the elasticity of the vessels the pulse-wave has been almost, if not quite, extinguished, and what might have remained of it is destroyed by the great resistance offered by the numerous capillaries. If these and the arterioles be widely dilated, a pulse may appear in the veins, as occurs when the vaso-dilator fibres of the chorda tympani nerve are stimulated, causing a pulse-like movement in the veins of the sub-maxillary gland (see PHYSIOLOGY, vol. xix. p. 30). By increasing the extra-vascular pressure pulsations may occur in the capillaries (Roy and Graham Brown). The well-known throbbing in the finger when constricted by an india-rubber band and the throbbing of inflammatory swellings are examples of pulsation in capillaries.

Venous circulation.

Venous Circulation.—The walls of the veins are thinner, less elastic, and more distensible than the walls of the arteries. They contain both elastic and contractile tissue, though to a smaller extent than the arteries. Numerous anastomoses exist between veins and even between superficial and deep veins, so that if the flow of blood be obstructed in one direction it readily finds a passage in another. The circulation in the veins depends (1) on inequality of blood-pressure, the pressure being much less in the veins than in the arteries; (2) on muscular action compressing the veins, and thus, in consequence of the valves found in many veins opening towards the heart, forcing on the blood in the direction of that organ; (3) on the movements of respiration,—inspiration, as already seen, favouring the flow of blood in the great veins towards the heart; and (4) on the suction-like action of the right auricle, and in the case of the lungs that of the left auricle, drawing the blood towards the heart. During venesection, muscular action increases the flow of blood from the divided vein; hence the use of the barber's pole, which was grasped by the patient during bleeding by the barber-surgeon of old. The flow of blood in veins is continuous, or nearly so; when, therefore, a vein is cut, it does not "spurt" as an artery does, but it "wells out" in a stream.

Occasional pulse in veins.

There is normally no pulse in veins; but sometimes a pulse may be observed in the veins of the neck, isochronous with the auricular systole, when there is an obstruction to the passage of blood from the right auricle into the right ventricle. Pulse-tracings (fig. 21) taken in these circumstances are very similar to those of the cardiac impulse. In this tracing the part *ab* represents the right auricular contraction. During the systole of the right ventricle the tricuspid valve closes, and, if it be insufficient,—that is, if it does not close properly,—a positive wave is transmitted along the superior vena cava to the jugular (*bc* in the pulse-tracing). The closure of the pulmonary is indicated at *e*. During the diastole of the right auricle and ventricle the blood flows to the heart and the curve descends, *f*. It has also been pointed out by Friedreich that a pulse in the jugular vein does not necessarily mean insufficiency of the tricuspid valve but a weakened condition of the valve in the jugular vein itself, as the pulse will not be propagated into the jugular, even in cases of insufficiency of the tricuspid valve, if the jugular valve be perfect. If there is great obstruction at the mitral orifice, a venous pulse may also be observed, which is associated with engorgement of the right auricle. Sometimes a pulse in the veins occurs when there is such rigidity from atheroma in the walls of the great vessels as to destroy the elastic influence of these parts, and at the same time such a degree of dilatation of the arterioles and capillaries as to admit of the onward propulsion of the movement caused by the heart's contraction. Lastly, a pulse may occur when the blood-pressure rises and falls suddenly, as in insufficiency of the aortic valves, and when the arterioles are much dilated. Towards the close of life, when the heart is feeble and effusion may be taking place into the pericardium, a venous pulse may be observed.

FIG. 21.—Tracing of venous pulse from insufficiency of the tricuspid valve. (Friedreich.)

Venous sounds.

If a stethoscope be placed at the root of the neck above the collar bones, and on the right side in particular, a whistling, rushing, or blowing sound will be heard. This is the *bruit de diable*, familiar to physicians. If heard without pressure being made by the stethoscope it is abnormal, as it occurs in conditions of anæmia from almost any cause; but it may be heard in a healthy person when pressure is applied and when the head is turned to the opposite side. It is held to be due to the vibration of the blood in rushing from the contracted portion of the common jugular vein into the more dilated part of this vessel. During the auricular diastole and during inspiration it is more marked, as the blood then flows more rapidly in the veins towards the heart.

Phenomena of General Circulation.

Prime factors influencing circulation.

Having described the structure and functions of the organs concerned in the circulation,—namely, heart, arteries, capillaries, and veins,—we are in a position to consider the phenomena of the circulation as a whole. Consider the organs of the circulation as a closed system of tubes, over-filled with blood; when the tubes are in a state of rest, it is evident that, if the blood be uniformly diffused and under the same pressure, it will remain motionless and in equilibrium. When the pressure is changed at any point, as occurs when the left ventricle contracts and throws blood into the arterial system, the blood will move from the part where the pressure is higher to where it is lower; in other words, there will be circulation as a consequence of the difference of pressure. When the heart stops beating, the blood continues to flow more and more slowly until the difference of pressure is equalized, and then there is no circulation. Each stroke of the heart throws as much blood into the arteries as flows into the heart from the veins; the orifices of the veins at the heart are more distensible than the beginnings of the arteries, and consequently the arterial pressure rises more rapidly than the venous pressure diminishes, and thus the beating of the heart raises the mean pressure throughout the arterial system. The circulation is therefore influenced by two factors,—(1) the heart, as regards number, strength, and volume of beats; and (2) the amount of resistance in the arterioles. Modifications of these influences are the pressure and the velocity of the blood.

Blood-pressure in vessels

As the blood is circulating through the vessels under the influence of the action of the heart, it exerts a certain pressure or tension, the existence of which is shown by the jet of blood which spurts out on the puncture of an artery, and the amount of which is indicated by the height to which the jet is propelled. An instrument for measuring this pressure, termed a kymograph, has been devised by Ludwig. But this apparatus, owing to the inertia of the mass of mercury,—the medium used,—can only register mean blood-pressure, and the more delicate variations escape notice. Fick in 1864 attempted to register these smaller fluctuations by means of a curved spring-kymograph, consisting of a hollow spring, which is made to oscillate by variations of pressure communicated to the interior. Small portions of a tracing taken with the mercurial manometric kymograph of Ludwig are shown in fig. 22. From this

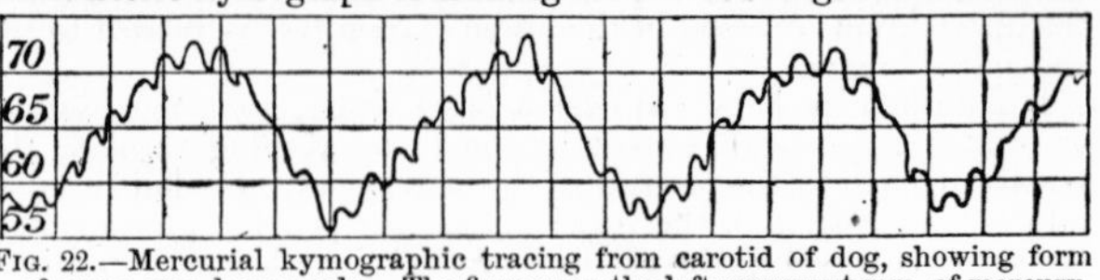

FIG. 22.—Mercurial kymographic tracing from carotid of dog, showing form of curve on a large scale. The figures on the left represent mm. of mercury. (Marey.)

it will be observed that there is (1) an increase and diminution of blood-pressure with each cardiac beat, as is shown in the smaller curves, and (2) an increase and diminution produced by respiratory movements, the increase occurring chiefly during inspiration and the decrease chiefly during expiration, as is indicated by the larger waves. It is evident also that all the smaller curves have the same general character, and that they reveal nothing as to variation in pressure during individual beats. To show such variations, Fick's kymograph must be used, when a tracing will be obtained in which slight oscillations of pressure in the down-stroke of each separate beat may be observed. By employing the different forms of kymograph the following conclusions have been arrived at.

Arterial pressure.

(*a*) *Arterial Pressure.*—(1) The pressure diminishes from the heart to the capillaries. (2) It attains its maximum in the ventricle at the moment of systole, and its minimum in the auricle at the moment of diastole, at which time also the pressure in the auricles and in the great veins may be negative, that is, below atmospheric pressure. (3) The mean blood-pressure in the large arteries of large mammals and of man is equal to that of a mercurial column 5·5 to 6·3 inches in height. (4) The blood-pressure in various animals has been ascertained to be as follows, the results being expressed in terms of a column of mercury of the indicated number of inches in height. Carotid of horse, 6·34; carotid of dog, 5·89 (Poiseuille). Carotid of horse, 4·8 to 8·42; carotid of dog, 5·89; carotid of goat, 4·64 to 5·31; carotid of rabbit, 3·54; carotid of fowl, 3·46 to 6·73; aorta of frog, ·86 to 1·14; gill artery of pike, 1·38 to 3·3 (Volkmann). Carotid of dog, 5·12 to 7·48 (Ludwig). Carotid of calf, 6·97; carotid of sheep, 6·65; carotid of goose, 6·38; carotid of stork, 6·34; brachial artery of pigeon, 6·57; carotid of cat, 5·9; brachial artery of man during operation, 4·33 to 4·72 (Faivre). Anterior tibial artery of boy, 3·93 to 6·3 (E. Albert). It no doubt varies even in animals of the same species. (5) The arterial pressure at any given point undergoes periodic variations, increasing at the instant of ventricular systole and diminishing during diastole; they are most marked in the arteries near the heart. (6) These periodic variations may be observed in the intermittent spurting of an artery when it is punctured. (7) It is necessary to distinguish between the mean arterial pressure at any point of an artery and the mean pressure of the blood in the whole arterial system, which can only be obtained by taking the mean of the pressures in many different arteries at various distances from the heart. (8) The mean arterial pressure depends directly on the quantity of blood in the arterial system, and consequently on the total calibre of the system, so that any diminution of calibre, produced mechanically or by nervous influences, will increase the mean arterial pressure. (9) The mean arterial pressure increases with the energy of the beats of the heart. (10) The blood-pressure becomes greater with increased and accelerated action of the heart, sometimes with plethora, and after an increase in the amount of blood, such as occurs after a full meal or after transfusion of blood, whilst it becomes smaller during diminished or enfeebled action of the heart, in anæmia, and after hæmorrhage or excretions from the blood by the skin, kidneys, or bowels (Landois). (11) The pressure is affected by the degree of contraction or of dilatation of the blood-vessels, according as they are influenced by the nervous system. (12) The pressure is increased in cases of sclerosis or hardening of the arterial walls, in lead poisoning, after injection of ergotin (which contracts the small arterioles) or of digitalis (which acts on the heart), where there is granular or contracted kidney, and in cardiac hypertrophy with dilatation. And (13) the pressure is diminished in fever, in chlorotic anæmia, in phthisis, and by severe hæmorrhage.

Venous pressure.

(*b*) *Venous Pressure.*—(1) In the veins near the heart the pressure is only one twentieth to one-tenth of that of the corresponding arteries. (2) During auricular diastole the pressure in the veins near the heart may become negative (= – ·0039 inch of mercury). (3) There are no periodic variations of pressure in the veins as in the arteries, except in the great venous trunks in the neck and near the heart, where there is a diminution of pressure during auricular diastole and an increase during auricular systole. (4) Great activity of the heart diminishes venous, while it increases arterial pressure. (5) The pressure increases in the veins according to their distance from the heart: thus, in the external facial vein of the sheep it is equal to a column of mercury ·12 inch in height; in the trachial to a column ·16 inch high; in branches of the trachial, ·35 inch; in the crural vein, ·45 (H. Jacobson). (6) Plethora increases venous pressure, whilst anæmia diminishes it. (7) Inspiration causes in the great veins near the heart an increase in pressure, whilst expiration diminishes it; but the respiratory movements "do not affect the venous stream in peripheral veins" (Stirling). (7) Changes in the position of the limbs affect venous pressure hydrostatically: thus, elevation of the extremities favours the flow of blood towards the heart; but, if the heart hangs downwards, the face becomes turgid, as the outflow by the veins is retarded. (8) Gravity favours the emptying of descending and hinders the emptying of ascending veins, so that the pressure becomes less in the former and greater in the latter. (9) As already stated, muscular movement by compressing the veins, aided by the mechanism of the valves, favours the flow of blood towards the heart, and thus increases the pressure in these vessels.

Capillary pressure.

(*c*) *Capillary Pressure.*—For obvious reasons capillary pressure has not been directly measured. Von Kries has measured the amount of pressure necessary to occlude the capillaries in an area abounding in these vessels, such as the skin at the root of the nail on the terminal phalanx or on the ear in man, and on the mucous membrane of the gum in rabbits. He found the pressure in the capillaries of the hand, when the hand is raised, to be equal to ·95 inch of mercury, when it hangs down, 2·13, in the ear ·79, and in the gum 1·26. Roy and Graham Brown also measured the pressure necessary to close the capillaries in the web of the frog's foot, in the tongue and mesentery of the frog, and in the tail of newts and small fishes. It is evident that any condition favouring the afflux of blood to a capillary area will increase the pressure in the capillaries, such as the dilatation of the small arterioles conveying blood to an area of capillaries, contraction of the venules carrying off the blood from it, or any increase of pressure in the arterioles or in the venules. The arrangement and position of the capillary network must affect the pressure: the pressure in the capillaries of the glomeruli of the kidney must, for instance, be greater than in those of the skin, as in the former position there is increased resistance owing to the double set of capillaries (see NUTRITION, vol. xvii. p. 684). Finally, any change in the degree of contraction of the wall of the capillary itself will affect the pressure.

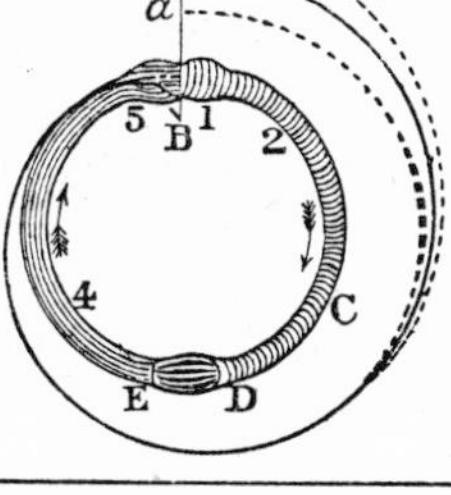

Fig. 23.—Diagram showing pressure in vascular system. 1, Ventricle; 2, arteries; E, D, capillaries; 4, veins; 5, auricle; A to C, line of pressure in great arteries; C to D, in small arteries; D to E, in capillaries; E to B in veins. The dotted lines indicate pressure during ventricular systole (*a*C) and diastole (*a′*C). Beyond C the blood-pressure is uniform as far as the auricle B, where it is negative during auricular diastole. (Beaunis.)

The general facts regarding pressure in arteries, capillaries, and veins are illustrated by fig. 23.

Velocity of blood.

Various attempts have been made by Volkmann, Vierordt, Ludwig and Dogiel, Hering, and Chauveau and Lortet to measure the velocity of the circulation, and special instruments have been invented for that purpose. In 1850 Volkmann constructed the hæmadromometer; this was followed by the hæmatachometer of Vierordt in 1858 and by the hæmadromograph of Chauveau and Lortet in 1867. These instruments are not now much used, having been superseded by the *stromuhr* (current-clock) or rheometer of Ludwig and Dogiel, which was invented in 1867. This instrument measures the amount of blood which passes through an artery in a given time. It consists of two glass bulbs of equal capacity communicating by a tube. One of the bulbs is filled with oil, which is expelled by the blood into the second (empty) bulb. The instrument is then reversed on its socket so that the bulb containing the blood is farthest from the heart, and the former process is repeated. From the time occupied in filling and refilling the velocity of the blood in the artery of supply can be calculated.

Results of experiment as to velocity.

The following figures give, in inches per second, the velocities of the blood in different vessels. Carotid of dog, 8·07 to 14·06; carotid of horse, 12·05; maxillary of horse, 9·13; metatarsal of horse, 2·2 (Volkmann). Mean velocity in carotid of dog, 10·28; in carotid of dog at end of diastole, 8·46; at end of systole, 11·69; in crural artery of dog at end of diastole, 5·51; at end of systole, 9·41 (Vierordt). During systole in carotid of horse, 9·84; at time of dicrotic wave, 8·66; at end of diastole, 5·9 (Chauveau, Bertolus, Laroyenne). In carotid of rabbits, from 3·7 to 8·9; in carotid of dog, weighing 51·2 lb, poisoned with morphia, from 13·74 to 28·86; in carotid of another dog, weighing 26·69 lb, from 9·57 to 20·47; in carotid of dog, weighing 7·85 lb, in which the sympathetic nerve had been cut, from 8·03 to 13·35; and in carotid of another dog, weighing 6·97 lb, poisoned with morphia, from 13·35 to 18·03 (Dogiel). The velocity in the capillaries cannot be directly measured. E. H. Weber gives it at ·032 inch per second in capillaries of mammals and ·021 in those of the frog. Vierordt gives the velocity in man as ·024 to ·035 inch per second. Volkmann states that the flow of blood in mammalian capillaries is five hundred times slower than in the aorta. Donders asserts that the velocity of the current in the smaller arterioles is ten times faster than in the capillaries. When the current reaches the veins it is accelerated in consequence of diminished resistance, but even in the larger venous trunks it is ·5 to ·75 times less than in the corresponding arteries. The following general conclusions may be drawn. (1) The velocity of the blood is in inverse ratio to the total calibre of the vessels: rapid in the aorta, it diminishes as we recede from it. (2) Each systole is followed by an increase in the velocity of the blood in the larger vessels. (3) In the smaller arteries, capillaries, and smaller veins the velocity is uniform and constant. (4) The velocity increases in the venous system as we approach the heart. (5) In the large arteries the movements of inspiration retard the velocity, whilst those of expiration increase it. (6) In the large veins the movement of respiration, and also the suction action of the auricle during diastole, cause a rhythmic increase and diminution of the velocity. The explanation of these variations in velocity is obvious. As the arteries pass outwards they give off branches, the united calibre of which is, with rare exceptions, greater than that of the parent vessel. Thus, as Küss expresses it, the arterial system may be regarded as a cone, the base of which ends in the capillaries, whilst the summit is at the aorta; and the venous system is a second cone, the base being also at the capillaries and the apex at the right auricle. Vierordt states that the sectional area of the capillaries is to that of the aorta as 800 to 1; but, as the sectional area of the venous orifices at the heart is greater than that of the arterial orifices, the ratio of the sectional area of the capillaries to that of the veins at the heart has been stated as 400 to 1. The increased sectional area retards the velocity, and the velocity of the blood-current in sections of the vessels at various points is inversely as their calibre. The velocity of the blood does not depend on the mean blood-pressure, and, as was pointed out by Ludwig and Dogiel, the velocity in any section of a vessel depends on (1) the *vis a tergo* (*i.e.*, action of the heart) and (2) the amount of resistance at the periphery.

Duration of circulation.

It is important to distinguish between the rapidity of the blood current and the time occupied by a blood corpuscle in making a complete circuit through the heart and vessels, say, from the left ventricle to the left ventricle again. Attempts have been made to measure the time, starting from the jugular vein. Hering injected into that vein a few drops of a 2 per cent. solution of ferro-cyanide of potassium, and then examined the blood of the opposite jugular every five seconds by testing with perchloride of iron,—the formation of Prussian blue indicating the moment when the ferro-cyanide made its appearance in the blood of the jugular after having made a tour of the circulation. Vierordt modified the method by examining the blood received from the jugular each half second. The duration of the circulation as thus determined for various animals is as follows,—horse, 31·5 seconds; dog, 16·7; rabbit, 7·79; hedgehog, 7·61; cat, 6·69; goose, 10·86; duck, 10·64; buzzard, 6·73; and common fowl, 5·17 seconds. Vierordt also made the discovery that in most animals the duration of the circulation is equal to the time in which the heart makes about twenty-seven beats. These facts are illustrated in the following table:—

Animal.	Weight of body.	Pulse Beats per Minute.	Number of Pulsations in the Circulation.
Guinea-pig	7·83 oz.	320	23·7
Cat	46·28 ,,	240	26·8
Hedgehog	32·13 ,,	189	23·8
Rabbit	50·59 ,,	220	28·5
Dog	20·28 lb	96	26·7
Horse	83·78 ,,	55	28·8
Fowl	46·98 oz.	354	30·5
Buzzard	24·44 ,,	282	31·6
Duck	46·7 ,,	163	28·9
Goose	99·54 ,,	144	26·0

It may also be shown by another method that a volume of blood equal to that in the whole body passes through the heart in about thirty pulsations. Taking the quantity of blood in the body as one-twelfth of the total weight, a man weighing 140 lb contains 11⅔ lb, or 5292 grammes, of blood, which represent in capacity 5302 cubic centimetres. Each beat of the heart throws 172 cubic centimetres into the aorta; therefore the equivalent of the total quantity of blood in the body passes through the heart in about 30 pulsations. Taking the pulse beat at 72 per minute, it follows that the duration of the circulation is about 26 seconds.

Volume of organs. It has been satisfactorily proved by Mosso, Von Basch, Dogiel, and François Franck that there is a slight change in the volume of any distensible organ with each beat of the heart. Mosso devised the plethysmograph,[1] an instrument by which the following results have been obtained. (1) The volume of an organ is not fixed, but varies according to the amount of blood contained in it. (2) Its volume changes with each cardiac pulsation, increasing when blood is forced into it and diminishing by the emptying of the capillaries into the veins. (3) Variations in the volume of one or more organs, say, by compression, or by the application of cold, or by the internal administration of substances which affect the calibre of blood-vessels, such as ergot, cause corresponding variations in the volume of other organs. (4) The pulsatile variations are very similar to the pulse-curve, and there are respiratory undulations corresponding to similar variations in blood-pressure tracings. (5) Movements of the limb cause diminution in volume, as was shown by Glisson in 1677, in consequence of acceleration of the venous current. (6) Mental exercise and sleep cause a diminution in the volume of the limb (Mosso). (7) So delicately attuned is the organism that music has been observed to cause a rise and fall in the tracings (Dogiel).

Distribution of blood. The blood is distributed throughout the body in varying proportions, according to the requirement of any set of organs at a particular time. When any tissue or organ is active, there is a determination of blood towards it, the amount being increased from 30 to 50 per cent.: thus, during digestion the mucous membrane of the stomach and intestinal organs is richly supplied with blood. Increased muscular velocity is always accompanied by increased vascularity; but, whilst this is the rule, there are organs, such as the heart, the muscles of respiration, and nervous centres like those in the medulla oblongata, in which there is a condition of continuous activity, and in which there is a uniform vascularity. Seeing that the activity of certain organs varies at different times, it follows that, whilst some organs are congested, others are at rest. In the child there appears to be a different distribution of blood from what obtains in the adult. The heart of a child is relatively small up to puberty, while the vessels are relatively large; after puberty the reverse is the case. Arterial pressure is less in the child than in the adult, whilst the pressure in the pulmonary circulation is larger in the child than in the adult (Beneke). Attempts have been made to estimate the distribution of blood after death. Ranke states that one-fourth of the total blood is in the muscles, one-fourth in the liver, one-fourth in the heart and vessels, and the remaining fourth in the rest of the organs.

Special Forms of Circulation.

Cranial. The cranial circulation has been already described under PHYSIOLOGY, vol. xix. pp. 42-43.

Hepatic. The peculiarity of the portal circulation is that the blood passes through two sets of capillaries. Arterial blood is conveyed to the stomach, spleen, pancreas, and intestines by branches of the abdominal aorta. These branches divide and subdivide, terminating in a capillary plexus in the various organs above enumerated. From this plexus the radicles of the various veins spring, and they unite with each other into larger and larger trunks, until by the confluence of the mesenteric veins with the splenic vein the portal vein is formed. The portal vein conveys the blood to the liver, where it divides into smaller and smaller branches constituting a plexus in the lobules of the liver. From this plexus spring the roots of the hepatic vein, which conveys the blood from the liver to the inferior vena cava (see NUTRITION, vol. xvii. p. 678). There are thus in the portal circulation two sets of capillaries,—one in the abdominal viscera and the other in the liver. Ligature of the portal vein causes distension of all the abdominal vessels and a highly congested state of the abdominal viscera, whilst the blood-pressure quickly falls, and the animal dies. So distensible are the abdominal vessels that they can contain nearly all the blood in the body. Blood from such congested vessels has toxic properties (Schiff and Lautenbach). The ventricular systole may send a pulse down the valveless inferior vena cava and cause a pulse in the liver. The liver swells with each systole and relaxes with each diastole of the heart.

Pulmonary. The pulmonary artery, carrying venous blood, divides and subdivides, and the smallest branches end in a plexus of capillaries on the walls of the air-cells of the lung. From this plexus the radicles of the pulmonary veins originate; and finally the four portal veins, two from each lung, carry the arterialized blood to the left auricle. Considering the apparently small extent of the pulmonary as compared with the systemic circulation, and the fact that the two ventricles, of about equal capacity, empty themselves simultaneously, it is clear that the pulmonary circulation presents many points of interest. In the first place, the pressure in the pulmonary artery is considerably less than that of the aorta. In 1850 it was determined by Ludwig and Beutner to be in the dog equal to a mercurial column of 1·17 inches, in the cat to one of ·69 inch, and in the rabbit ·47 inch, or about three times less in the dog, four times less in the rabbit, and five times less in the cat than the pressure in the aorta. Hering passed simultaneously a tube through the muscular walls of each ventricle of a calf, and the blood rose in the tube in the right ventricle 21 inches and in the left 33·4 inches (quoted by Landois and Stirling). Fick and Badoud found a pressure of 3·54 in the pulmonary artery of the dog, whilst the carotid pressure at the same time was 4·17 inches. The ratio of pulmonary to aortic pressure has been stated as 1 to 3 (Beutner and Marey) and as 2 to 5 (Goltz and Gaule).

Influence of respiration in pulmonary circulation. Next, it is important to note the peculiar physical conditions in the chest during respiration. As already shown (p. 102), the lungs are distended in consequence of the positive pressure on their inner surfaces being greater than the negative pressure on their outer pleural surfaces. But when the lungs are distended by a full inspiration they exert an elastic force (termed elastic recoil or "elastic traction") amounting to about 1·18 inches of mercury. Outside the lungs, in the cavity of the chest, the surface of the heart and vessels is subjected to a pressure which is the difference between atmospheric pressure (29·92 inches) and the "elastic traction" (1·18 inches) or 28·74 inches. It is clear that the more the lungs are distended the greater is the elastic traction, and consequently the less the pressure on the outer surface of the vessels. The thin-walled pulmonary veins yield more during a deep inspiration, thus diminishing pressure, than the thicker-walled pulmonary artery, whereby the flow of blood from the capillaries of the lung by the pulmonary veins to the left auricle is favoured. On the other hand, expiration by increasing the pressure tends to retard the flow of blood. Further, the velocity of the stream of blood is accelerated in the pulmonary vessels by inspiration and retarded by expiration. As regards the influence of the movements of the lung on the calibre of the pulmonary capillaries and smaller vessels, experiment has shown that the blood-vessels of the lungs containing air and distended are wider than those of collapsed lungs. Suppose an elastic bag having minute tubes in its walls to be dilated in a free space, the lumen of these tubes will be diminished; but, if it be placed in a closed space, as in a wide glass bottle, and if the pressure on its outer surface be diminished by removing air from the space between the bag and the side of the bottle, the bag will distend and the lumen of the tubes will be increased. Thus it is evident that inspiration, by increasing the calibre of the pulmonary vessels, draws blood towards the lungs, and the movements of the lungs become an effective force in carrying on the pulmonary circulation. The velocity of the blood is greater in the pulmonary than in the systemic capillaries, and greater in the pulmonary veins than in the pulmonary arteries. The great degree of distensibility of the pulmonary vessels allows of frequent adjustments being made, so that, within limits, as much blood in a given time will pass through the pulmonary as through the systemic circulation. This adjustment, however, may be readily disturbed. For example, violent muscular exertion hurries the blood along the veins to the right side of the heart, and by the right ventricle the blood is discharged into the pulmonary circulation. If more arrives than can be transmitted to the left auricle by the pulmonary veins in a given time, the pulmonary capillaries become engorged, breathing becomes quick and possibly irregular, the right side of the heart becomes engorged, signs of venous congestion appear in the flushed face and turgid veins, and perhaps the pulmonary capillaries may rupture, causing hæmorrhage from the lung. The weaker the muscular structure of the heart the more likely is this to occur. Hence the breathlessness in many cardiac affections, aggravated by muscular exertion, more especially in ascending a stair or hill.

Fœtal. In the mature fœtus the fluid brought from the placenta by the umbilical vein is partly conveyed at once to the vena cava ascendens by means of the *ductus venosus* and partly flows through two trunks that unite with the portal vein, returning the blood from the intestines into the substance of the liver, thence to be carried back to the vena cava by the hepatic vein. Having thus been transmitted through the placenta and the liver, the blood that enters the vena cava is purely arterial in character; but, being mixed in the vessels with the venous blood returned from the trunk and lower extremities, it loses this character in some degree by the time that it reaches the heart. In the right auricle, which it then enters, it would also be mixed with the venous blood brought down from the head and upper extremities by the descending vena cava were it not that a provision exists to impede (if it does not entirely prevent) any further admixture. This consists in the arrangement of the Eustachian valve, which directs the arterial current (that flows upwards through the ascending vena cava) into the left side of the heart, through the foramen ovale,—an opening in the septum between the auricles,—whilst it directs the venous current (that is being returned by the superior vena cava) into the right ventricle. When the ventricles contract, the arterial blood contained in the left is propelled into the ascending aorta, and supplies the branches that proceed to the head and upper extremities before it undergoes any further admixture, whilst the venous blood contained in the right

[1] Figured in M'Kendrick's *Physiology*, p. 365, fig. 99.

ventricle is forced into the pulmonary artery, and thence through the *ductus arteriosus*—branching off from the pulmonary artery before it passes to the two lungs—into the descending aorta, mingling with the arterial currents which that vessel previously conveyed, and thus supplying the trunk and lower extremities with a mixed fluid. A portion of this is conveyed by the umbilical arteries to the placenta, in which it undergoes the renovating influence of the maternal blood, and from which it is returned in a state of purity. In consequence of this arrangement the head and upper extremities are supplied with pure blood returning from the placenta, whilst the rest of the body receives blood which is partly venous. This is probably the explanation of the fact that the head and upper extremities are most developed, and from their weight occupy the inferior position in the uterus. At birth the course of the circulation undergoes changes. As soon as the lungs are distended by the first inspiration, a portion of the blood of the pulmonary artery is diverted into them and undergoes aeration; and, as this portion increases with the full activity of the lungs, the ductus arteriosus gradually shrinks, and its cavity finally becomes obliterated. At the same time the foramen ovale is closed by a valvular fold, and thus the direct communication between the two auricles is cut off. When these changes have been accomplished, the circulation, which was before carried on upon the plan of that of the higher reptiles, becomes that of the complete warm-blooded animal, all the blood which has been returned in a venous state to the right side of the heart being transmitted through the lungs before it can reach the left side or be propelled from its arterial trunks (Allen Thomson). After birth the umbilical arteries shrink and close up and become the lateral ligaments of the bladder, while their upper parts remain as the superior vesical arteries. The umbilical vein becomes the ligamentum teres. The ductus venosus also shrinks and finally is closed. The foramen ovale is also closed, and the ductus arteriosus shrivels and becomes the ligamentum arteriosum.

The Innervation of Blood-Vessels.

Effects upon circulation of stimulating various nerves.

This has already been described under PHYSIOLOGY (vol. xix. p. 30); but there are several points of interest that can only be thoroughly understood after studying the general conditions affecting, and the mode of measuring, the pressure of the blood. Stimulation of the pneumogastric nerve in the neck slows the rate of the heart-beat, and, if the stimulation be strong, arrests the heart in a state of diastole. Suppose a kymograph to be connected with the carotid in the neck of a rabbit deeply under the influence of chloral so as to be quite unconscious of pain; if then one of the vagi in the neck be stimulated, the blood-pressure curve at once falls; and on removing the stimulation it rises to its former height by a few leaps and bounds. Whilst this occurs in the arteries, the venous pressure rises in consequence of the flow of blood into them from the arteries. But the pressure may be influenced by another method. As was pointed out by Ludwig and Owsjannikow, a centre exists in the medulla oblongata (vaso-motor centre) whence influences emanate that tend to keep the vessels in a more or less contracted condition. If this centre be injured, the smaller blood-vessels throughout the body dilate,—in short, they are paralysed,—and receive more blood, and consequently the pressure in the larger vessels at once falls. This vaso-motor centre in turn can be influenced by impressions reaching it from the periphery. This was clearly proved by Cyon in 1866, when he discovered the function of the depressor nerve, a small nerve (the superior cardiac) originating in the rabbit from the superior laryngeal and from the pneumogastric nerve, but in many animals blended with the pneumogastric nerve. Stimulation of the distal end of this nerve produces no effect; but stimulation of the cephalic end causes a great fall of blood pressure and a diminution in the frequency of the pulse (see PHYSIOLOGY, vol. xix. p. 29 and fig. 11). Similar depressor filaments exist in the trunk of the vagus below the origin of the superior cardiac nerve (depressor of Cyon), in the nerves coming from the lungs, in the great auricular nerve, in the tibial, and in all probability in all sensory nerves. Further, it may be influenced by nerve fibres the stimulation of which excites the centre, causing a rise in pressure (pressor nerves). Such filaments have been experimentally demonstrated to exist in the superior and inferior laryngeal nerves, in the trigeminus, and in the cervical sympathetic. The vaso-motor centre is therefore under the influence of two antagonistic sets of impulses,—one stimulating it, causing constriction of the smaller vessels and a rise of arterial pressure, the other inhibiting it, causing dilatation of the smaller vessels together with a fall of pressure.

Connexion of respiratory undulations with vaso-motor centre.

But this is not all. On examining a blood-pressure tracing it is seen that the arterial pressure is influenced by the movements of respiration, the larger waves corresponding to these movements. To ascertain precisely how much of the wave corresponds to inspiration and how much to expiration, suppose a blood pressure taken from the carotid artery, whilst at the same time arrangements are made for recording simultaneously the variations of intra-thoracic pressure. It is then easily seen that, when expiration begins and the expiratory pressure rises the blood pressure rises, while when inspiration begins both fall. Inspiration removes pressure from the outer surface of the vessels and thus allows the walls both of the great veins and of the aorta to distend; but the thin-walled veins yield to a greater extent than the thick-walled aorta. Consequently during inspiration the blood tends to accumulate in the great veins and in the right side of the heart and less escapes by the aorta, and the blood pressure in the aorta falls. On the other hand, during expiration the blood pressure rises, owing to the opposite set of conditions. Roughly speaking therefore, during inspiration blood pressure falls, whilst during expiration it rises. But a careful examination of the curves shows that they do not exactly coincide as to their maxima and minima. Thus the blood pressure rises before the rise of expiratory pressure; or, in other words, during the first part of inspiration there is a fall of pressure and during the second part a rise. This cannot be explained by the mechanical movements of the chest wall, but is caused, partially at all events, by the action of the vaso-motor centre. During the latter portion of the inspiratory period impulses pass from this centre, causing constriction of the smaller vessels, and consequently the rise of arterial pressure observed during this time. Again, an examination of a blood-pressure tracing shows that during the fall of the respiratory curve the smaller curves are larger and fewer in number than during the rise of the curve. After section of the vagi this difference disappears, and it can only therefore be explained by stating that during the first portion of the time of inspiration, and during the fall of arterial pressure, the cardio-inhibitory centre also acts, slowing the beat of the heart. Another important fact showing that the respiratory undulations cannot be accounted for by the mechanical movements of the chest wall is that they appear in a blood-pressure tracing taken during artificial respiration. When a canula is inserted into the trachea and air is forced into the chest by a bellows, it is evident that the mechanical conditions are not those of ordinary respiration. When air is forced in, inflating the lungs to correspond to inspiration, the intra-thoracic pressure is increased instead of diminished as in ordinary respiration, and when the air is sucked out to correspond to expiration the intra-thoracic pressure is diminished instead of being increased as in ordinary expiration; and still the respiratory curves remain. If artificial respiration be suddenly stopped, the blood pressure quickly rises; but this does not occur to nearly the same extent if the spinal cord be divided. In other words, the rise of blood pressure when artificial respiration is arrested is due to stimulation of the vaso-motor centre in the medulla by the circulation through it of blood too highly venous owing to stoppage of the circulation, as is proved by the fact that, if the influence of the vaso-motor centre be removed, the rise of blood pressure does not take place. Finally, if during artificial respiration both vagi be cut so as to remove the influence of the cardio-inhibitory centre, and respiration be stopped, the pressure will rise as already described, and in a short time a series of undulations will appear in the blood-pressure tracing known as the Traube-Hering curves,—a rising and falling of blood pressure not due to the action of the heart, as they continue even when a pump is substituted for that organ, nor to the movements of respiration, but to a "waxing and waning" of the activity of the vaso-motor centre itself, contracting and dilating the blood-vessels and thus influencing the peripheral resistance. To sum up, the circulation is affected by the nervous system—(1) by the inhibitory action of the vagi in restraining the activity of the heart; (2) by the accelerating action of fibres in the sympathetic, stimulating the activity of the heart; (3) by the action of the intrinsic cardiac ganglia affecting the heart directly; (4) by the action of the vaso-motor centre (vaso-constrictor nerves) in the medulla, tending to keep up a greater or less degree of constriction of the vessels; (5) by the action of vaso-dilator nerves inhibiting the vessels, allowing them to dilate in a manner similar to the cardio-inhibitory action of fibres in the vagi; (6) by the influence on the vaso-motor centre of impulses coming from the periphery,—pressor fibres stimulating it, depressor fibres inhibiting it; (7) by the diffusion of impulses in the medulla from the respiratory centres; (8) by the interaction of the vaso-motor, respiratory, and cardio-inhibitory centres in the medulla; and (9) by rhythmic changes in the vaso-motor centre itself. See PHYSIOLOGY, vol. xix. p. 28 *sq*.

Bibliography.—A copious list of works relating to the anatomy of the organs of the circulation will be found in Quain's *Anatomy*, edited by Allen Thomson, E. A. Schäfer, and George D. Thane, 9th ed., vol. ii. p. 916; and on the physiology of the circulation in Beaunis's *Physiologie Humaine*, 2d ed., 1885, and in Landois and Stirling's *Text-Book of Human Physiology*, 2d ed., vol. i. p. 557. To this last able work, to A. Rollett's elaborate essay, "Physiologie der Blutbewegung," in Hermann's *Handbuch der Physiologie*, and to Prof. Michael Foster's *Text-Book of Physiology*, 4th ed., the author is specially indebted in the preparation of this article. As to the action of drugs and poisons on the circulation, reference is made to Lauder Brunton's *Text-Book of Pharmacology*, &c., 2d ed., 1886. For a brief account of the historical development of our knowledge of the circulation, see abstracts of lectures by the present writer, delivered before the Royal Institution, in *British Medical Journal* for 1883.

(J. G. M.)

VASILKOFF, a district town of Russia, in the government of Kieff, is situated 22 miles by rail to the south-west of that city. Its 16,600 inhabitants support themselves chiefly by agriculture and the transport of merchandise; there is also some manufacture of tobacco and soap.

Vasilkoff was founded in the 10th century, but laid waste during the Mongolian invasion. In 1320 it was taken by the Lithuanians, and later on by the Poles, under whom it remained until 1686, when it was annexed to Russia.

VASTO, a fortified town of Italy, in the province of Chieti, stands high on an olive-clad slope, about a mile from the Adriatic and 131 miles south-east from Ancona. It is still surrounded by its mediæval walls, and commands fine views extending to the Tremiti Islands and Monte Gargano. The cathedral, with a Gothic façade, has no special interest; the municipal buildings contain a collection of Roman antiquities and inscriptions. There are manufactures of earthenware, woollen cloth, and silk; but the inhabitants are chiefly employed in the culture of the olive and in fishing. The population in 1881 was 9761 (commune 13,883).

Vasto, the *Histonium* of the ancient geographers, was a flourishing municipal town under the Roman empire, as is shown by the numerous remains of theatres, baths, and other public edifices. It was, and still is, subject to severe earth tremors.

VATICAN COUNCIL. The Vatican Council is the first and only plenary council of the Latin Church held since the close of the Council of Trent in 1563. But it bears very slight resemblance to that assembly in the circumstances of its origin, objects, and proceedings. The Council of Trent was all but forced upon the Papacy by the demands of the principal Catholic states of Europe, and by the religious and political necessities of the time. It was convened for the purposes of endeavouring to secure the return of the Lutherans, Calvinists, and other revolted bodies to the Roman Church, and of applying stringent measures of reform to amend the numerous practical abuses and scandals which had mainly caused the revolt. And, while it failed conspicuously in the former of these objects, it did achieve a certain degree of success in the latter, by a variety of disciplinary enactments covering a large range of subjects, and was followed, in point of fact, by a marked improvement in clerical morals and diligence. The Vatican Council, contrariwise, originated with the Papacy alone, and was neither demanded nor desired by Roman Catholic Christendom. Its object was confined to securing the triumph of the hyper-Ultramontane school within the Roman obedience by establishing papal autocracy as divine and infallible; and it made no attempt whatever beyond a sterile discussion, not published in its Acts, to deal with any of the abuses and scandals which had either survived the Tridentine reforms or had sprung up since. While the Council of Trent did much to repair the damage done to the personal authority of the popes by the incidents of the "great schism" and the character of the pontiffs who sat during the close of the 15th and the beginning of the 16th century, it left several questions concerning the source and extent of papal authority undecided, which proved a fruitful cause of debate between the Gallican and Ultramontane schools of theology, the former minimizing the papal claims as far as is compatible with acceptance of the tenet of the Petrine privilege, and viewing the Papacy as a constitutional monarchy under strict limitations, the latter holding it to be an autocracy resting on a divine charter, and incapable of restraint on the part of its subjects. But the French Revolution, by breaking up the old Gallican Church, led to the substitution of a largely Ultramontane episcopate in France under the concordat between Pius VII. and Napoleon I., and thereby to the permanent declension of the moderate school, while, on the other hand, a variety of causes brought the Jesuits, recalled into corporate existence by the same Pius VII. in 1814, after forty years' suppression, again into the same position of chief influence in the Latin Church which they had occupied in the heyday of the counter-Reformation. They have always held steadily to the military ideas of their founder, and have therefore unceasingly striven to centralize and concentrate ecclesiastical authority, to remove constitutional limitations upon its exercise, and to make it prompt, unfaltering, and trenchant in action. Clearly, if the Papacy could be converted into an absolute monarchy, this end would be attained at a single stroke, because the mere fiat of the supreme pontiff would thenceforward suffice as warrant for all ecclesiastical action, thus dispensing with cumbrous and dilatory machinery of every kind; and his delegated authority would enable any person wielding it to act with similar efficacy and despatch.

With the accession of Pius IX. to the papal chair in 1846 a favourable opportunity for carrying out this programme presented itself, for, weak in character and wholly unversed in theological learning, while strongly holding the very highest views of his own prerogatives and eagerly receptive of everything which tended to exalt them further, he was exactly the instrument suited for its execution. Two experiments, to test at once how far he was prepared to go, and how far Latin Christendom was prepared to submit in the matter of decrees on faith and morals issuing from himself singly, with no previous conciliar examination or decision, were tried in 1854 by the promulgation of the tenet of the Immaculate Conception and in 1864 by that of the Syllabus of Errors. The former of these met with little resistance, the latter with none, and it was therefore judged safe to proceed with the bolder and more far-reaching scheme which they but foreshadowed. Its success appeared to be almost a foregone conclusion; for, not only could a compact and docile Italian majority be as surely reckoned on as it was at Trent, but the far larger number of Roman Catholic bishops all over the world had been virtually appointed by Pius IX. during his long pontificate, and that exclusively from the Ultramontane school. Nevertheless there was still a minority important enough to make some caution desirable in the earlier stages of the preliminaries, and the proposal to hold an œcumenical council was first laid privately before the congregation of rites by the pope himself in December 1864, contemporaneously with the issue of the Syllabus, and immediately afterwards before all the cardinals then at Rome, who were desired to give their opinions as to the opportuneness of convoking the council at all and as to the subjects it should discuss if convoked. Nineteen cardinals approved the proposal; two opposed it; and one remained neutral. In March 1865 a congregation of direction was formed to take further steps towards the desired end, and private communications were made to various bishops and to the nuncios at the different courts, who were asked to send competent theologians to take part in the preliminary congregations. Some communications were also made privately in 1866 to bishops of the Oriental rite. The first directly public intimation of the approaching council was made in June 1867, through a circular letter of Cardinal Caterini to the 500 bishops present in Rome at the 18th centenary festival of the martyrdom of St Peter and St Paul, inviting their reply to a schedule of inquiries. In September 1868 an invitation to attend was despatched to the Oriental bishops not in communion with Rome, and also to "Protestants and non-Catholics." But, as it was intended that no Oriental prelate should be admitted to a seat in the council till he had first made profession of the Roman Catholic system in its entirety, and as Protestants were merely to be referred to "experienced men" to convince them of their errors, the insincere invitation met with no acceptance whatever. The bull of convocation was promulged on 29th June 1869, appointing 8th December 1869 as the day of meeting. A few days before this latter date, 27th November, Pius IX. issued the brief *Multiplices inter*, prescribing the mode of conciliar procedure and effectually fettering the council from the outset, so that it had never even the shadow of freedom which ostensibly was allowed to the Tridentine synod. This brief consists of a preamble and ten chapters, containing, amongst much else, the following provisions. Any member desiring to bring forward a proposal had to deliver it privately in writing to a special committee named by the pope (of which there were six for various departments), and it should contain nothing foreign to the traditions of the Roman Church. Unless the committee passed it, no further action could be taken upon it. Strict secrecy as to the proceedings of the council, and even as to the opinions of particular members, was to be observed towards all outsiders. All new decrees and canons were to be discussed in preliminary congregations before the public sessions, drafts being supplied some days previously, and those who desired to speak to the questions were obliged to give notice at least a day beforehand. Priority of speech was secured for these; if others desired to speak afterwards they had to obtain the permission of the presidents, all of whom were cardinals of the court party. If little or no debate arose, the draft decrees were to be officially formulated; if there were division of opinion, the question should be referred to the sub-committee (*deputatio*) corresponding to each congregation's subject of discussion, which should decide the matter if no further difficulty were raised. All the officers of the council were named directly by the pope, and in no case elected by the council itself, which was thus deprived of several conciliar rights held previously to be inherent and indefeasible, and which had been exercised even at Trent.

The assemblage of the council was looked on with little favour by a large part of the Roman Catholic world, and in particular two German documents attested the alarm it aroused. In April 1869 Prince Hohenlohe, Bavarian foreign minister, sent a circular letter to the European courts, warning them of the political dangers likely to ensue; and most of the German bishops, assembled at Fulda in September of that year, sent an address to the pope, anxiously deprecating the definition of papal infallibility which had been recommended in the *Civiltà Cattolica* of 6th February 1869, to be made by the summary process of acclamation. This proposal drew forth two able books in opposition to the dogma,—one which appeared anonymously (Janus) in Germany, and *Du Concile Général et de la Paix Religieuse*, by Maret, bishop of Sura and dean of theology at the Sorbonne, published in France; but they did not delay the measures being taken for its declaration.

The council assembled punctually on the appointed day, 8th December 1869, and owing to the modern facilities of intercommunication it was by far the largest gathering of the kind in history, no fewer than 749 bishops, cardinals, abbots, and generals of orders being present,—a number afterwards increased to 764,—and including nearly three-fourths of the whole Roman Catholic episcopate. Of these it has been estimated that the minority opposed to the infallibility dogma amounted to at least 160, while in the majority were reckoned 53 bishops *in partibus*, who, as having no real dioceses, and being thus unable to attest the historical belief of their flocks, had properly no right of suffrage upon dogmatic questions in a council, such attestation being the one function dischargeable by bishops assembled in synod when considering articles of belief. To these are to be added about 125 bishops of sees too modern to have any ancient tradition to attest, such as those in North and South America, Australasia, and Oceania, who were thus for conciliar purposes on the same footing of incompetence to speak for any one save themselves. And, besides these two large groups, there was a third, consisting of about 90 missionary bishops entirely under the control of the Propaganda, and thus not free agents, while their sees were in most cases of very recent origin, so that they also could allege only their personal opinion, having no ancient records to attest. By far the larger number in these groups were on the side of the court majority. The Italian bishops, numbering about 170, and the Spanish, 40 in number, were also infallibilists almost to a man, but included scarcely one theologian in their ranks. And no fewer than 300 of this majority were the personal guests of Pius IX., lodged, boarded, and maintained at his cost, and thus openly retained to do his bidding. The minority consisted chiefly of the German and Austrian bishops, a considerable section of Hungarian, French, and North-American prelates, and many of those Orientals of the Latin Church who occupied dioceses other than mere titular and paper ones. But this minority, though composed mainly of natives of the most highly educated and intellectual countries, and containing almost every bishop of note for ability and theological learning, was by no means so compact and united as were the bishops of the majority; and there was not even full agreement amongst its members as to the grounds for opposing the new dogma, many going no further than its inopportuneness, but not entertaining deeper objections to it. Thus, even apart from its numerical inferiority, the opposition was at a disadvantage in face of the curialists, and lost not a few members to them during the progress of the council. Not only were the efforts to obtain freedom from the fetters of the brief *Multiplices inter* vain, but no member of the opposition could secure a place on any of the commissions or sub-committees, which consisted exclusively of infallibilists.

The matter of most importance in the first congregation, which was held on 10th December 1869, was the publication of a bull, decreeing that, if the pope should die during the council, it should at once be prorogued and take no part in the election of a pontiff, which was to be restricted to the college of cardinals. The session which followed was little more than formal; but two steps towards bringing about the intended result were taken before the next time of assembling. The "theologians" were forbidden to attend any meetings of the bishops, or even to meet among themselves to discuss any conciliar matters, being restricted each to private conference with the particular bishop to whose person he was attached; and various petitions for the definition of the new dogma were drawn up and signed, one being the result of a letter to the bishops of the council, issued by Archbishop Manning and the conductors of the *Civiltà Cattolica*, and signed by some hundreds, another from the Italian prelates, a third from those of the Franciscan order, and a fourth from the Uniat Armenians, besides several of less note. The opposition issued a counter-memorial with 135 signatures; but, as it is therein admitted that papal decrees *ex cathedra* on faith and morals are irreversible, even without the consent of the church being known in any way, and that true obedience to every decree of the see of Rome is due by all Christians, no weight could attach to it as a serious plea for rejecting, or even delaying, the definition. The second session (6th January 1870) was also formal only, so far as the direct transaction of business was concerned; but by the adoption of a measure causing all the members present to recite the creed of Pius IV., containing a clause professing obedience to the pope (this clause being omitted by the pope himself), and then to renew the episcopal oath of feudal submission to the Papacy, powerful pressure was brought to bear upon the weaker of the opposition, who were thus reminded how far they had pledged themselves already, and how unreasonable it therefore was to haggle about taking but one step in advance on the self-same road. The time between the second and third sessions was mainly occupied in preparing the drafts (*schemata*) of constitutions on the faith and on the church, and also with discussions of sundry disciplinary measures (notably as regards clerical immorality) and the preparation of a new catechism; but none of these last were proceeded with. By the pope's direct command the cardinal-presidents of the congregations issued, on 20th February 1870, rules to check long debates, which drew yet tighter than before the cords that deprived the council of all freedom. Speakers were confined to touching upon such clauses only of any amendment as they had given previous notice of meaning to discuss, and were not allowed to take part otherwise in a debate, while the closure could be applied by the presidents at the demand of any ten members. This latter drastic measure drew out a protest from more than one hundred bishops, who urged that it was destructive of conciliar liberty (already much hampered by the noisy attempts of the infallibilists to stifle free discussion), and that the steps being taken disregarded the note of moral unanimity which should mark the decisions of a general council, thereby exposing the council itself to hostile criticism and even rejection. They pointed out several other serious faults in the new rules, but could obtain no modification of them. The constitution on the faith (usually cited now as *Dei Filius*), however,—a long and far from clearly worded document,—directed chiefly against modern rationalism, and enforced by 18 canons of anathema, was completed; it passed the congregation without difficulty, was signed by all the 667 members present, and was published in the third session, 24th April 1870, with papal confirmation, or rather in the unprecedented form of a proclamation by the pope singly, "the sacred council approving,"—an innovation which was intended to mark it as solely his act, and to settle in this summary manner the long-standing controversy as to the relative superiority of popes and councils. There were few, however, even of the opposition, who cared to contest such a point, and there was nothing of a contentious nature, as regards the two parties in the council, in the constitution itself, so that no debate was raised upon it.

The real struggle was yet to come, namely, over the constitution on the church, into which the new dogma was to be introduced. This constitution (now usually cited as *Pastor Æternus*) asserted the following propositions:—(1) that a proper primacy of jurisdiction over the whole church was conferred upon St Peter directly and singly, and not mediately through any delegation to him, as chief minister in the church, of a primacy held by the church corporately; (2) that this Petrine primacy vests by divine institution and right in the line of Roman pontiffs; (3) that the pope's jurisdiction is immediate in all churches—*i.e.*, he is the universal ordinary, the actual bishop of every see (all other bishops being merely his curates and deputies), and is not a remote or merely appellate authority—so that in questions not of faith and morals alone, but of discipline and government also, all the faithful, of whatever rite or dignity, both pastors and laity, are bound, individually and collectively, to submit themselves thereto; (4) that it is unlawful to appeal from the judgments of the Roman pontiffs to an œcumenical council, as though to a higher authority; and (5) that the Roman pontiff, when he speaks *ex cathedra*, and defines a doctrine of faith or morals to be held by the universal church, is infallible, and such definitions are accordingly irreformable of themselves, and not from the consent of the church. This document was voted upon in the congregation of 13th July 1870, consisting of 671 members. Of these 451 voted in the affirmative; 88 voted against it; 62 voted *placet juxta modum*, meaning that they would accept it if it were seriously modified; and 70 did not vote at all. By the canonical theory of councils such a division of opinion as this voided the decision of the majority, and made it null. For, while a bare majority in a council suffices to pass a mere disciplinary canon, being a variable matter, contrariwise, to enact a dogmatic decree requires practical unanimity, since nothing can be imposed as of faith for which the two attesting notes of universal prevalence and historical continuity cannot be adduced. And, as the dissent of any appreciable number of members denotes that they do not know it as the local tradition of their several dioceses, it thereby destroys the claim to these notes. Not only so; but in view of the character in which bishops appear at councils, as representing their laity, it is clear that the size and population of their several dioceses have to be taken into account when estimating the weight attaching to their individual testimony as to the reception of any dogma within their jurisdictions. Tried by this standard, the opposition was very much more important than its muster-roll seems to indicate, for it included the bishops from many of the most populous Roman Catholic dioceses, such as the archbishops of Paris, with 2,000,000 Catholics, Breslau with 1,700,000, Cologne with 1,400,000, Vienna with about the same number, and Cambrai with 1,300,000; whereas 62 bishops of the Papal States, for example, represented no more than 700,000 altogether, apart from the hundred and more titulars, who had no flocks at all. This matter may be summed up thus: every vote cast for the new dogma stood for 142,570 lay folks; but every vote cast against it stood for 492,520. Nor is this all: a council claiming to be œcumenical must speak with the consent of both East and West. But, even if the very large concession be made that the Uniat churches in communion with Rome are in truth the lawful representatives of the ancient Oriental Church, the fact remains that the number and rank of the Orientals in the minority was such as to make the vote at best only a Latin one. The Melchite and Syrian patriarchs of Antioch, the Chaldee patriarch of Babylon, the Melchite archbishop of Tyre, the Maronite archbishops of Tyre and Sidon, of Beyrout, and of Aleppo, with several others, were in one or other of the three groups of dissentients, and thus nullified the Eastern suffrages in the majority. Immediately after this preliminary voting nearly all the bishops of the minority abruptly quitted Rome, after previously lodging a protest against the proceedings. Their flight was prompted by fears for their personal safety. They were given to understand that each of them would have two papers tendered to him for his signature in the ensuing session, one being a profession of adhesion to the infallibility dogma, the other a resignation of his diocese in case he refused such adhesion. And they had good reason to think that the pope, who had declared that he meant to be proclaimed infallible "without limitation" (*senza condizione*), and had shown open enmity to more than one of their number, would employ direct coercion in the event of continued resistance, bringing his temporal power as sovereign of Rome to bear on the rebels within his territory. Accordingly, when the public session was held on 18th July 1870, while 535 bishops voted for the constitution *Pastor Æternus*, only two, those of Ajaccio and of Little Rock, remained to utter their "non-placet." The pope thereupon confirmed the decree, and the proceedings virtually ended.

By one of the most singular of historical coincidences,

on that very day Napoleon III. proclaimed war against Prussia, and entered on that great conflict amongst the immediate results of which were the overthrow of the temporal power of the Papacy and the occupation of Rome by the troops of the king of Italy in two months' time from the last meeting of the council. It was formally prorogued by Pius IX. on 20th October, and is thus technically still in existence; but the prorogation is a virtual dissolution.

The opposition collapsed everywhere after the promulgation of the decree, as even the German bishops, who had been the mainstay of the minority, consented to publish it in their dioceses. This led to the genesis of the Old Catholic communion (see Old Catholics) as a refuge for such as were conscientiously unable to accept the new dogma, but equally unwilling to join any of the Protestant societies. But submission to the dogma is not identical with belief in it, at any rate in the sense wherein Pius IX. understood it and meant it to be received. The majority had, indeed, achieved their "triumph over history": they had done what warning voices had declared beforehand to be their purpose—annihilated the independence of the episcopate, abrogated the teaching and attesting functions of the dispersive church, and contracted the Roman Catholic creed into the single article of belief in the pope. But they had failed in three matters essential to the ultimate success of their plans. They had not even seemed to make any reply, save that of their superior voting strength in the council, to the destructive criticism which had established the falsehood and novelty of the infallibility dogma; they were not able to pass it so as to be canonically or theologically binding; and they could not secure its unqualified acceptance in its original form. Instead of terminating all controversy, the new dogma (as might have been anticipated by any one familiar either with the laws of the human intellect or the facts of ecclesiastical history) at once became itself a topic of debate, receiving contradictory interpretations, partly due to its vague and clumsy wording, and partly the expression of competing opinions, ranging from the widest to the narrowest view of its scope and force. The "senza condizione" of Pius IX. proved hopelessly unworkable, and it was soon found necessary to modify the decree so as to make it a not intolerable burden for intelligent consciences. Accordingly, Bishop Fessler of St Pölten, secretary-general of the council, published in 1871, with a brief of approbation from the pope, his treatise *Die wahre und falsche Unfehlbarkeit der Päpste*, soon reproduced in French and English, which provides that "juxta modum" limitation vainly sought from the tyrannical majority in the council itself. Ostensibly a reply to an anti-infallibilist work by the learned canonist Von Schulte, it is in fact a studious minimizing of the incidence of the dogma, arguing that the occasions when the attribute of papal infallibility has been actually exercised and formulated in *ex cathedra* decrees have been, and must continue to be, of extremely rare occurrence, and further attenuating the dogma itself, so as to approach in some measure the old Gallican view of the pope's constitutional and limited authority as official spokesman of the church. In England, where the evidence collected by Pitt in the 18th century, and by the earl of Liverpool in the 19th, when aiming at the abolition of the penal laws, on the opinions held by Roman Catholic theologians as to the prerogatives and attributes of the popes, made their general repudiation of papal infallibility familiarly known, the question was even more trenchantly dealt with. For Dr Newman, who had anxiously deprecated the coming definition, speaking of it in a letter to Bishop Ullathorne as a "great calamity," wantonly forced on by "an aggressive, insolent faction," explained the manner of his own belief and acceptance of it in a letter to the duke of Norfolk, and that in terms which to less subtle (and, it may be, more practical) intellects are indistinguishable from disbelief and rejection. Not only does he limit the attribute itself, and the occasions of its exercise, within much straiter bounds than those set by Fessler, but he specifies a number of cases wherein he would disobey a papal mandate, and, after saying that each such mandate must be decided on its own merits, adds: "I should look to see what theologians could do for me, what the bishops and clergy around me, what my confessor, what friends whom I revered; and if, after all, I could not take their view of the matter, then I must rule myself by my own judgment and my own conscience." That this deliverance is in effect a complete evacuation of the dogma will appear at once by supposing cognate language to be used in the civil sphere by the subject of an absolute temporal sovereign when defining the limits of his allegiance. But the subsequent elevation of its author to the cardinalate proves that his view is regarded as fairly tenable in the Roman Church, and the infallibility dogma is thus, for the present at least, dismissed from the domain of practical action to that of speculative theory.

The bibliography of the Vatican Council is very copious, but the following works will suffice for most students to consult:—Cecconi, *Storia del Concilio Vaticano*, Rome, 1873; J. Friedrich, *Geschichte des vatikanischen Konzils*, Bonn, 1877-87; Id., *Tagebuch, während des vaticanischen Concils geführt*, Nördlingen, 1873; Id., *Documenta ad Illustrandum Concilium Vaticanum*, Nördlingen, 1873; Quirinus, *Römische Briefe vom Concil 1870* (also an English version); Pomponio Leto, *Otto Mesi a Roma durante il Concilio Vaticano*, Florence, 1873 (also an English version); Michelis, *Kurze Geschichte des vaticanischen Concils*, Constance, 1875; Friedberg, *Sammlung der Aktenstücke zum ersten vaticanischen Concil*, Tübingen, 1872; Frommann, *Geschichte und Kritik des vaticanischen Concils*, Gotha, 1872; Pius IX., *Discorsi del Sommo Pontefice Pio IX. pronunziati in Vaticano*, Rome, 1872-73; Frond, *Actes et Histoire du Concile Œcuménique de Rome*, Paris, 1870-73, 8 vols. folio; Arthur, *The Pope, the Kings, and the People*, Belfast, 1877. (R. F. L.)

VATTEL, Emer de (1714-1767), an eminent jurist, was the son of a Protestant minister, and was born at Couvet, in the principality of Neuchâtel, on 25th August 1714. He studied at Basel and Geneva. During his early years his favourite pursuit was philosophy; and, having carefully examined the works of Leibnitz and Wolf, he published in 1741 a defence of Leibnitz's system against Crousaz. In the same year Vattel, who was born a subject of the king of Prussia, repaired to Berlin in the hope of obtaining some public employment from Frederick II., but was disappointed in his expectation. Two years later he proceeded to Dresden, where he experienced a very favourable reception from Count Brühl, the minister of Saxony. In 1746 he obtained from the elector, Augustus III., the title of councillor of embassy, accompanied with a pension, and was sent to Bern in the capacity of the elector's minister. His diplomatic functions did not occupy his whole time and much of his leisure was devoted to literature and jurisprudence. Among other works he published *Loisirs Philosophiques* (1747) and *Mélanges de Littérature, de Morale, et de Politique* (1757). But his reputation chiefly rests on his *Droit des Gens, ou Principes de la Loi Naturelle appliqués à la Conduite et aux Affaires des Nations et des Souverains* (Neuchâtel, 1758). During the same year he was recalled from Switzerland, to be employed in the cabinet of Dresden, and was soon afterwards honoured with the title of privy councillor. His labours now became so intense as to exhaust his strength, and his health broke down. After a period of rest he returned to Dresden in 1766; but his renewed exertions soon produced a relapse, and he made another excursion to Neuchâtel, where he died on 20th December 1767. His last work was entitled *Questions de Droit Naturel, ou Observations sur le Traité du Droit de la Nature, par Wolf* (Bern, 1762).

Vattel's *Droit des Gens*, which is founded on the works of Wolf, had in its day a great success, in truth, greater than it deserved. His principal and only merit consists in his having rendered the ideas of that author accessible to the political and diplomatic world. The *Droit des Gens* passed through many editions, and was translated into various languages (English in 1760).

VAUBAN, Sebastien le Prestre de (1633-1707), marshal of France, was born in the neighbourhood of Saulieu in Burgundy (now in the department of Côte-d'Or) on 15th May 1633. At an early age he was left an orphan in very poor circumstances, and his boyhood and youth were spent among the peasantry of his native place, thus enabling him to gain that sympathetic insight into the condition of the agricultural classes which he afterwards showed in his economic writings. He owed his early education and his first instruction in the rudiments of mathematics and surveying to a friendly curé, who had taken an interest in him and discerned his abilities. At the age of seventeen he joined the Spanish troops under the prince of Condé, but after about a year's campaigning was taken prisoner by the French. He then became known to Mazarin, who treated him with kindness and enlisted him in the service of the king. In 1653 he first earned repute as an engineer by the share he had in the capture of Sainte-Menehould, and after further distinction at Stenay and Clermont he was given a lieutenancy and received in 1655 his commission as an "ingénieur du roi." Between that year and the peace of 1659 he took part in numerous successful sieges—especially those of Gravelines, Ypres, and Oudenarde. After the cession of Dunkirk, Fort

Louis, and Mardyke in 1662 he had charge of the work of fortifying them as frontier towns. On the renewal of war in 1667 he saw much service in Flanders, and gained special distinction in the siege of Lille, of which town he ultimately became governor, the king making him a lieutenant in the guards and bestowing on him a pension. The originality and success of his methods were now fully recognized, and in 1669 he drew up, at the instance of Louvois, his first exposition of the theory of fortification (*Mémoire pour Servir d' Instruction dans la Conduite des Siéges*), which was afterwards published at Leyden (1740). In 1673 Vauban accompanied Louis XIV. on his Dutch campaign, and directed the more important sieges, afterwards superintending the demolition or reconstruction of the captured places. In the following year his principal achievement was the capture of Maestricht, and in 1677 he had the chief credit for the fall of Valenciennes and Cambrai. In the latter year he was appointed commissary-general of fortifications in succession to Clerville, and thus gained an opportunity, which in the following year he diligently used, for practically reconstructing the entire land-defences of France. In the short war of 1683-84 he gained further distinction by the fall of Luxembourg, and during the campaign of 1691-92 the names of Mons and Namur were added to the long list of his successes. In 1686 Vauban had the courage to make a representation to the king in favour of the republication of the Edict of Nantes; and about 1697 he wrote his almost equally bold *Projet d'une Dixme Royale*, which, however, was not published until 1707 (see POLITICAL ECONOMY, vol. xix. p. 359). In 1693 he was made a grand cross of the order of St Louis, and in 1703 marshal of France. The close of his life, which was saddened by the consciousness of waning influence and failing health, he devoted largely to the arrangement of the voluminous manuscripts (*Mes Oisivetés*) which contained his reflexions on such subjects as the art of war, administration and finance, agriculture, commerce, and the like. He died at Paris on 30th March 1707.

For Vauban's work as a military engineer, see FORTIFICATION (vol. ix. pp. 441-446). The *Oisivetés* long remained unpublished, and of the twelve manuscript volumes containing them several seem to have been hopelessly lost; the fragmentary remains were published in three volumes at Paris in 1841-43. The *Traité de l'Attaque des Places*, written in 1703, and that *De la Défense des Places*, written a few months before his death, were published together in 1737. Among the subjects in which Vauban took a lively interest, and on which he wrote memoirs, may be mentioned the fortification of Paris, the inland navigation of France, its army organization, especially in the artillery service, and the limits of ecclesiastical power in temporal matters. The introduction of the socket-bayonet into the French army is usually ascribed to Vauban.

VAUCLUSE, a department of France, formed in 1793 out of the county of Venaissin (695 square miles), the principality of Orange (62½ square miles), and a part of Provence (515½ square miles), lies between 43° 39′ and 44° 26′ N. lat. and 4° 38′ and 5° 45′ E. long., is bounded by Drôme on the N., Basses-Alpes on the E., Bouches-du-Rhône (from which it is separated by the Durance) on the S., and Gard and Ardèche (from which it is separated by the Rhone) on the W. It has also an enclave, the canton of Valréas, in the department of Drôme. The western third of Vaucluse belongs to the Rhone valley, and consists of the rich and fertile plains of Orange, Carpentras, and Cavaillon. To the east, with a general west-south-west direction and parallel to one another, are the steep barren ranges of Ventoux, Vaucluse, and Lubéron, consisting of limestones and sandstones. The first-mentioned, which is the most northerly, has a maximum elevation of 6273 feet; the culminating peak, on which is a meteorological observatory, is isolated and majestic. The Vaucluse chain does not rise above 4075 feet. The most southerly range, that of Lubéron (3691 feet), is rich in palæontological remains of extant mammals (the lion, gazelle, wild boar, &c.). The Rhone is joined on the left by the Aygues, the Sorgue (rising in Petrarch's celebrated fountain of Vaucluse, which has given its name to the department), and the impetuous Durance. The Sorgue has an important tributary in the Ouvèze and the Durance in the Coulon (or Calavon). These and other streams feed numerous irrigation canals; their channels are sometimes quite dry in summer. The climate is that of the Mediterranean region. The valley of the Rhone suffers from the mistral (see vol. ix. p. 507); but the other valleys are sheltered by the mountains, and produce the oleander, pomegranate, olive, jujube, fig, and other southern trees and shrubs. The mean annual temperature is 55° Fahr. at Orange and 58° at Avignon; the extremes of temperature are 5° and 105° Fahr. Snow is rare. The south wind, which is frequent in summer, brings rain. The average annual rainfall is 29 inches in the hill region and 22 in the plains.

Of the total area of 881,610 acres 679,737 are cultivated,—cereals occupying 232,250 acres, market and other gardens 41,085, meadows, pastures, and orchards 89,950, industrial vegetable products 18,993, summer fallows 58,489, vines 24,699, and woods and forests 197,049. The live stock in 1880 included 11,412 horses, 16,602 mules, 4410 asses, 2079 head of cattle, 46,406 pigs, 11,660 goats, and 165,040 sheep of native and 6983 of improved breed. There were 11,701 beehives (104 tons of honey and 23 tons of wax). Amongst wild animals the otter and beaver occur along the bank of the Rhone. The crops in 1884 were returned as follows—2,151,385 bushels of wheat, 7309 of meslin, 39,476 of rye, 60,208 of barley, 1677 of buckwheat, 17,162 of maize, 240,850 of millet, 445,920 of oats, 4,247,600 of potatoes, 21,680 tons of beetroot, and 197 tons of tobacco. In 1880 early vegetables were produced to the value of £384,940, and stone fruit to the value of £13,341. The olive crop amounted to 233,928 bushels (622 tons 17 cwts. of oil). In 1884 4,779,236 gallons of wine were obtained (average for preceding ten years 2,562,384 gallons). In the same year 766 tons of silk cocoons were produced. The phylloxera has reduced the area of the vineyards from 79,000 to 13,000 or 14,000 acres; American vines are now being introduced. The culture of madder and the mulberry is diminishing, while the Chinese grass-cloth plant, beetroot, sorghum, and millet are grown in increasing quantities. The truffle markets of Carpentras and Apt are important. Lignite and coal (11,382 tons in 1882), iron, and sulphur are mined; rich deposits of plaster, stone, clay, and ochre are worked; and there is a large variety of mineral springs. The chief industrial establishments are manufactories of madder dye, silk-mills (4295 workmen), silk-spinning factories (3365 spindles and 411 workmen), oil-mills, flour-mills, paper-mills (1047 workmen and 2700 tons of paper in 1880), wool-spinning factories (2645 spindles and 369 workmen), confectionery establishments, manufactories of pottery, earthenware, bricks, mosaics, tinned provisions, chemicals, candles, soap (2500 tons in 1880), and hats, breweries, puddling works, iron and copper foundries, cabinet workshops, blast furnaces, saw-mills, edge-tool workshops, and nursery gardens. Coarse cloth, carpets, blankets, and ready-made clothes are also produced. Vaucluse has 135 miles of railway, 97 of national roads, and 2380 of other roads. The population increased by 74,670 between 1801 and 1865, but from that date to 1886 it diminished by 24,304, owing to the decay of the madder and wine industries. In 1881 the department had 244,149 inhabitants, and in 1886 241,787. Vaucluse forms the archiepiscopal diocese of Avignon, has its court of appeal at Nîmes, and belongs to the Marseilles army corps. It is divided into 4 arrondissements (Avignon, chef-lieu of the department, with 35,355 inhabitants in 1886; Apt, 4293; Carpentras, 8563; and Orange, 6904), 22 cantons, and 150 communes. Cavaillon (5164 inhabitants) is famous for its early vegetables and its fruit. Vaison (1988 inhabitants) is rich in Roman remains, and possesses an interesting cathedral and a ruined castle of the counts of Toulouse.

VAUD (Germ. *Waadt*), a canton of Switzerland, ranking as nineteenth in the Confederation, takes its name either from the German *Wald* (a wood) or, more probably, from *Wälsch*, the term applied by Teutonic to non-Teutonic tribes. It is of very irregular shape, as it owes its existence solely to historical causes. Roughly speaking, it includes the whole north shore of the Lake of Geneva. It stretches on the south-east as far as St Maurice and takes in Château d'Oex, while to the north-west the Jura and the Lake of Neuchâtel are its boundaries. The district of Avenches (entirely surrounded by the canton of

Freiburg) and a long narrow tongue running up to Payerne are also within its boundaries. The total area is 1244·3 square miles, larger than that of any other Swiss canton except Graubünden (Grisons), Bern, and Valais. Of this total 1053·6 square miles are classed as productive, forests occupying 282 and vines 24·8 square miles. This is a larger extent under vines than in any other canton save Tessin (Ticino), and more than one-fifth of the total wine-growing districts in the whole Confederation. Of the unproductive portion lakes occupy 164·1 and glaciers 4·3 square miles, while towns and buildings cover 5·7. The highest point is the Diablerets (10,667 feet) in the south-east corner. The population in 1880 amounted to 238,730 (an increase of 7030 since 1870), a larger number than in any other canton except Bern and Zurich. Of these 212,164 are French-speaking, 21,692 German-speaking (many persons from the German-speaking cantons coming thither to learn French), and 2518 Italian-speaking. In religion 219,427 are Protestants (Calvinists), divided between the "national church" (19·20) and the "free church" (1·20). The capital is Lausanne (30,179 inhabitants, or with the surrounding districts 37,427), which since 1874 has been the seat of the federal tribunal. It is the largest town in the Confederation after Zurich, Basel, Geneva, and Bern. Other important places are Vevay (7820 inhabitants) and Yverdon (5968).

Agriculture is the main occupation of the people; the land is much subdivided and very highly cultivated. The vineyards employ 20,000 persons. About one-third of the wine produced is exported, the best-known varieties being Yvorne (white) and Cortaillod (red). There is not much industry, except that of the watch-makers in the Jura; and the commerce is comparatively unimportant. Many foreigners reside in the canton, particularly on the shores of the Lake of Geneva, from Lausanne to Villeneuve (as formerly Gibbon, Voltaire, and Rousseau). Montreux is a favourite winter residence, and its growth may be judged of from the fact that its inhabitants increased from 3211 in 1849 to 4379 in 1860, 6659 in 1870, and 8017 in 1880, the increase being specially marked since the opening of the railway in 1861. The railways are 168 miles in length, besides a "ligne régionale" on the high road from Lausanne to Échallens, and the cable railways from Lausanne to Ouchy and from Territet to Glion. In educational matters the canton holds a high place. The academy of Lausanne dates from 1537; and there are a very large number of schools and educational establishments at Morges, Lausanne, Vevay, and elsewhere. Pestalozzi's celebrated institution flourished at Yverdon from 1805 to 1825. Among the remarkable historical spots in the canton are Avenches (the chief Roman settlement in Helvetia), Granson (scene of the famous battle in 1476 against Charles the Bold), and the castle of Chillon (where Bonnivard, the prior of St Victor at Geneva, was imprisoned from 1531 to 1536 for defending the freedom of Geneva against the duke of Savoy).

History.—The early history of the main part of the territories comprised in the present canton is identical with that of south-west Switzerland generally. The Romans conquered (58 B.C.) the Celtic Helvetii, and so thoroughly colonized the land that it has remained a Romance-speaking district, despite conquests by the Burgundians (5th century) and Franks (532) and the incursions of the Saracens (10th century). It formed part of the empire of Charlemagne, and of the kingdom of Transjurane Burgundy (888-1032), the memory of "good queen Bertha," wife of King Rudolph II., being still held in high honour. On the extinction of the house of Zäringen (1218) the counts of Savoy gradually won the larger part of it, especially in the days of Peter II., "le petit Charlemagne" (died 1268). The bishop of Lausanne (to which place the see had been transferred from Aventicum by Marius the Chronicler at the end of the 6th century), however, still maintained the temporal power given to him in 1011 by the king of Burgundy, and in 1270 became a prince of the empire. (We must be careful to distinguish between the present canton of Vaud and the old mediæval Pays de Vaud: the districts forming the present canton very nearly correspond to the Pays Romand.) In the 15th century Bern began to acquire lands to the south from the dukes of Savoy, and it was out of those conquests that the canton was formed in 1798. In 1475 she seized Aigle, in 1475-76 (in concert with Freiburg) Échallens and Granson as well as Orbe (the latter held of the duchy of Burgundy). Vaud had been occupied by Bern for a time (1475-76), but the final conquest did not take place till 1536, when both Savoyard Vaud and the bishopric of Lausanne were overrun and annexed by Bern (formally ceded in 1564), who added to them (1555) Château d'Oex, as her share of the domains of the debt-laden count of Gruyères in the division of the spoil she made with Freiburg. In 1565 the liberties of Vaud were, by a special treaty, placed under the guarantee of France. Bern in 1526 sent Farel, a preacher from Dauphiné, to carry out the Reformation at Aigle, and after 1536 the new religion was imposed by force of arms and the bishop's residence moved to Freiburg (permanently from 1663). Thus the whole land became Protestant, save the district of Échallens. Vaud was ruled very harshly by bailiffs from Bern. In 1588 a plot of some nobles to hand it over to Savoy was crushed, and in 1723 the enthusiastic idealist Davel lost his life in an attempt to raise it to the rank of a canton. Political feeling was therefore much excited by the outbreak of the French Revolution, and a Vaudois, F. C. de la Harpe, an exile and a patriot, persuaded the Directory in Paris to march on Vaud in virtue of the rights conferred by the treaty of 1565. The French troops were received enthusiastically, and the "Lemanic republic" was proclaimed (January 1798), succeeded by the short-lived Rhodanic republic, till in March 1798 the canton of Leman was formed as a district of the Helvetic republic. This corresponded precisely with the present canton minus Avenches and Payerne, which were restored to it in 1803. The new canton was thus made up of the Bernese conquests of 1475, 1475-76, 1536, and 1555. The constitutions of 1803 and 1815 favoured the towns and wealthy men, so that an agitation went on for a radical change, which was effected in the constitution of 1831. Originally acting as a mediator, Vaud finally joined the anti-Jesuit movement (especially after the Radicals came into power in 1845), opposed the Sonderbund, and accepted the new federal constitution of 1848, of which Druey of Vaud was one of the two drafters. From 1839 to 1846 the canton was distracted by religious struggles, owing to the attempt of the Radicals to turn the church into a simple department of state, a struggle which ended in the splitting off of the "free church." The cantonal feeling in Vaud is very strong, and was the main cause of the failure of the project of revising the federal constitution in 1872, though that of 1874 was accepted. In 1879 Vaud was one of the three cantons which voted (though in vain) against a grant in aid of the St Gotthard Railway. In 1882 the Radicals obtained a great majority, and in 1885 the constitution of 1861 was revised. The Government consists of a great council (one member to every 300 electors) for legislative and a council of state of 7 members (chosen by the great council) for executive purposes. 6000 citizens can compel consideration of any project by the legislature ("initiative," first in 1845), and the *referendum* exists in its "facultative" form, if demanded by 6000 citizens, and also in case of expenditure of over a million francs. Capital punishment was abolished in 1874. The canton has lately been passing through serious financial difficulties. In 1862 the south-west frontier was slightly altered in consequence of a dispute with France as to the valley of Dappes.

See A. Verdeil, *Histoire du Canton de Vaud* (2d ed., 4 vols.), and L. Vulliemin, *Le Canton du Vaud* (3d ed., 1885).

VAUDOIS. See WALDENSES.

VAUGHAN, HENRY (1621-1693), called "the Silurist," poet and mystic, was born into an ancient Welsh family settled at Skethiog-on-Usk, in the parish of Llansaintfraed, Brecknockshire, in 1621. From 1632 to 1638 he and his twin brother Thomas were privately educated by the rector of Llangattock, and then they proceeded to Jesus College, Oxford. At what time Henry left the university is not known; but it was evidently after he had studied for some time in London and had been introduced into the society of men of letters that he printed his first volume, *Poems, with the Tenth Satire of Juvenal Englished* (1646). Of this publication he was afterwards, very needlessly, ashamed. Vaughan presently became a physician and returned to his native country, first for a while practising in the town of Brecon, and then settling down for the remainder of his life in Skethiog. From this place he sent forth his collection of sacred poems, *Silex Scintillans*, in 1650, of which a second part appeared in 1655, and the secular poems of his *Olor Iscanus*, prepared for the press in 1647, and published without his consent by his brother Thomas in 1651. A mystical treatise in prose, *The Mount of Olives*, followed in 1652, and then two prose translations, *Flores Solitudinis*, 1654, and *Hermetical Physick*, 1655. The world took little notice of these performances. In 1678 an Oxford friend collected the miscellaneous verses of Vaughan's middle life in a volume entitled *Thalia Rediviva.* Henry Vaughan died at Skethiog on 23d April 1693, and lies buried in the churchyard of Llansaintfraed.

As a poet Vaughan comes latest in the so-called "metaphysical" school of the 17th century. He is the most remote of the disciples of Donne, and follows him mainly as he saw him reflected in George Herbert. He analyses his experiences, amatory and sacred, with excessive ingenuity, striking out, every now and then, through his extreme intensity of feeling and his close though limited observation of nature, lines and phrases of marvellous felicity. He is of imagination all compact, and is happiest when he abandons himself most completely to his vision. His verse is apt to seem crabbed and untunable in comparison with that of Crashaw, and even of Herbert at his best. "The Retreat," with its Wordsworthian intimations, "The World," mainly because of the magnificence of its opening lines, and "Beyond the Veil" are by far the most popular of Vaughan's poems and represent him at his best. His passion for the Usk, and his desire to immortalize that pastoral river, are pathetically prominent in his writings. His metrical ear was not fine, and he affected, almost more than Herbert himself, tortured and tuneless forms of self-invented stanza.

The earlier works of Henry Vaughan, in prose and verse, were collected in a very limited private edition in four volumes, in 1871, by Dr A. B. Grosart. The Rev. H. F. Lyte edited the sacred poems alone in 1847, up to which time Vaughan was practically unknown as a poet.

VAUGHAN, THOMAS (1621-1665), "the Rosicrucian," was the twin brother of Henry VAUGHAN (see above). When Thomas left Oxford he went into the church and became rector of his native parish Llansaintfraed until his ejectment, when he settled at Oxford as an alchemist. He died at Albury on 27th February 1665, poisoned by the fumes of a cauldron. Under the pseudonym of Eugenius Philalethes, Thomas Vaughan produced eleven volumes defending and describing the tenets of the Rosicrucians. The titles of these—among which are *The Man-Mouse*, 1650; *The Second Wash*, 1651; *The Fame and Confession of the Fraternity of the Rosy Cross*, 1652; *Aula Lucis*, 1652; and *Euphrates*, 1653—are not more extraordinary than their style. Henry More the Platonist engaged in controversy with Thomas Vaughan, deep calling unto deep in pamphlets.

VAUQUELIN, LOUIS NICOLAS (1763-1829), French analytical chemist, was born at Saint-André-d'Hébertot in Normandy on 16th May 1763. His parents, although very poor, sent him to school to fit him for the coveted post of a gentleman's servant at the château. At the age of thirteen or fourteen Vauquelin went to Rouen as laboratory boy with an apothecary. He did not remain long there; but his interest in chemistry was fairly aroused, and he began to make experiments and take notes. His master, finding him so engaged on one occasion, tore up his note-book and ordered him to keep to his menial work for the future. Vauquelin had spirit enough to resent this treatment: he borrowed six francs from a friend and walked to Paris to seek his fortune. For a time his prospects were very dark: after getting and losing two situations he became ill, was sent to the public hospital, and when convalescent found himself once more without money or friends. At length, however, he met a humane apothecary, Cheradame, who took him in and treated him with kindness. Vauquelin at once resumed his studies, and devoted every spare minute to learning. Cheradame introduced him to Fourcroy, who had himself worked his way up from poverty, and from this time Vauquelin's fortune was made. Henceforward he devoted his attention to chemical analysis without intermission or variety until his death, which occurred at his birthplace on 14th November 1829. At first his work appeared as that of his friend and patron, then in their joint names; but in 1790 he commenced to publish on his own authority, and wrote perhaps more papers than any other chemist has ever done. Either together or successively Vauquelin held the offices of inspector of mines, professor at the School of Mines and at the Polytechnic School, assayer of gold and silver goods, professor of chemistry in the College of France, member of the Council of Industry and Commerce, commissioner on the pharmacy laws, examiner to the Polytechnic School, and, finally, was successor to Fourcroy himself; at this last step all the other candidates retired in his favour.

Vauquelin's life was uneventful; his nature was quiet and retiring; he never desired to mix with the world; and even in the turmoil of the Revolution his interest centred in the laboratory. He was emphatically one who lived for his work alone. He never married. He does not appear to have communicated with his parents after he became wealthy. The one bright feature in the somewhat colourless character of his later life was the fact that he supported Fourcroy's aged sisters after his old friend died.

As an analyst Vauquelin came at the right time. The theory of chemistry was being built afresh on a basis of experiment; all substances, natural and artificial, were being classified by their composition; and it would be hard to mention any mineral or any plant or animal or product of life that Vauquelin did not examine. With Fourcroy he drove the piles on which the first theories in pure chemistry were founded; with Haüy he put mineralogy on a satisfactory footing; but he himself was neither chemist nor mineralogist. Vauquelin's name is associated with 376 papers published between 1790 and 1833, and, with the exception of one or two criticisms and claims for priority, these were all simple records of patient and laborious analytical operations. He propounded no theories, was guided by no generalizations, and was troubled by no problems save those of his methods. Given a substance, he did his best to find its composition, devising new processes where these seemed necessary, but this was all. Considering the amount of work he did, one is surprised that only two new elements are associated with his name. He detected glucina in beryl when analysing that mineral for Haüy, and in a red lead ore from Siberia he discovered chromium, although, strange to say, eight years elapsed between his first examination of the ore and his separation of chromic acid. It is even more extraordinary that he never suspected the existence of alkaloids in the vegetable and animal juices he was continually analysing. Cuvier in his *éloge* argues from this that without the concurrence of a happy chance the greatest perseverance and the most admirable patience often miss the mark; a more legitimate inference might be that work carried on "for work's ignoble sake" is fruitless in higher results, and that perseverance apart from a definite aim can accomplish little.

VAUVENARGUES, LUC DE CLAPIERS, MARQUIS DE (1715-1747), a moralist and miscellaneous writer of considerable originality and power, was born at Aix in Provence on 6th August 1715. His family was poor though noble; he was very badly educated; and his health was weak. He, however, entered the army early and served for more than ten years, taking part in the Italian campaign of 1736, and in the disastrous expedition to Bohemia six years later in support of Frederick the Great's designs on Silesia, in which the French were abandoned by their ally. Vauvenargues suffered greatly from the hardships of Belle-Isle's winter retreat, and indeed never recovered from them. He was also much troubled by his poverty, and in a private letter written to a very intimate friend he discusses the possibility of obtaining a loan from a certain rich acquaintance by undertaking, first to get his son into his own regiment, or secondly to marry one of his daughters within a short time and with only a reasonable dowry. Nevertheless Vauvenargues was, according to the standard of that time, a most honourable man. Indeed he seems to have pushed honour to the point of naivety, if it be true that, weary of waiting for promotion, he addressed himself, not to any minister, or, more wisely still, to some favourite, but to the king himself. This unsophisticated proceeding had of course no result, and Vauvenargues threw up his commission, hoping—but unsuccessfully—to obtain a post in the diplomatic service. His ill-luck pursued him: for, having joined his family in Provence, he fell ill with a bad form of smallpox, which still further weakened him. This was in 1744. He had, besides the correspondence above referred to with a certain M. de Saint Vincens, maintained one, still more interesting and likewise only recently known, with the celebrated and eccentric Marquis de Mirabeau, the author of *L'Ami des Hommes*, the father of the great Mirabeau. He had also, when in garrison at Nancy, begun an exchange of letters with Voltaire, who had a very high opinion of him, and this, with his natural inclinations, determined him to literature. He published in 1746 an *Introduction à la Connaissance de l'Esprit Humain*, with certain *Réflexions* and *Maximes* appended. He died of lung disease at Paris on 28th May 1747.

The bulk of Vauvenargues's work is very small, but its interest is very considerable. In the *Introduction*, in the *Réflexions*, and in the minor fragments it consists, in fact, of detached and somewhat desultory thoughts, in the style wherein the 18th century so much delighted, on questions of moral philosophy and of literary criticism. Sainte-Beuve has mildly said that as a literary critic Vauvenargues "shows inexperience." It would be truer to say that this part of his work has no value or interest beyond that of curiosity. He had no knowledge of any language but his own, and his literary criticism is limited to a repetition in crude form of the stock ideas of his time. Thus he exaggerates immensely the value of Racine and Boileau, but depreciates Corneille and even Molière. It is almost sufficient to say that he blames Molière for choosing "des sujets si bas," and shows an entire ignorance of all French literature before the 17th century, and of all other literature whatsoever, except a certain second-hand acquaintance with the classics. As a writer he stands far higher. His style is indeed, according to strict Academic judgment, somewhat incorrect, and when he attempts rhetorical flourishes (which is not often) they have usually the artificial and affected character—stilted or namby-pamby—which mars so much 18th-century work. His strength, however, is not really in any way that of a man of letters, but that of a moralist. Even here he is not superior to the weaknesses of his time. In his day the anti-religious or anti-Christian movement of thought was not fully declared, and he did not adopt the complete *philosophe* attitude; in his letters, at any rate, he poses somewhat ostentatiously as "neutral" between the religious and the anti-religious school. In some of his maxims about politics there is also traceable the hollow and confused jargon about tyrants and liberty which did so much to bring about, and to embitter when brought about, the struggles of the Revolution. It is in morals proper, in the discussion and application of general principles of conduct, that Vauvenargues shines. No century has ever excelled the 18th in moral theory, whatever may have been its deserts in respect of moral practice, and no 18th-century moralist has excelled Vauvenargues. He is not an exact psychologist, much less a rigorous metaphysician. He has no worked-out or workable theory of moral obligation or of the moral sense. His terminology is merely popular and loose, and he hardly attempts the co-ordination of his ideas into any system. His real strength is in a department which the French have always cultivated with greater success than any other modern people,—the expression in more or less epigrammatic language of the results of acute observation of human conduct and motives. The chief distinction between Vauvenargues and his great predecessor La Rochefoucauld is that Vauvenargues, unlike La Rochefoucauld, thinks nobly of man, and is altogether inclined rather to the Stoic than to the Epicurean theory. He has indeed been called a modern Stoic, and, allowing for the vagueness of all such phrases, there is much to be said for the description.

An edition of the *Works* of Vauvenargues, slightly enlarged, appeared in the year of his death, and in part or in whole has been frequently reprinted, all editions, however, being superseded by that of M. Gilbert (2 vols., Paris, 1857), which contains the previously unpublished correspondences above referred to and all other attainable matter, including some *Dialogues of the Dead*, some "characters" in imitation of Theophrastus and La Bruyère, and numerous short pieces of criticism and moralizing. Vauvenargues has been frequently written about, the comments best worth reading, besides those contained in Gilbert's edition, being four essays by Sainte-Beuve in *Causeries du Lundi*, vols. iii. and xiv.

VECELLIO. See TITIAN.

VEDANTA. The Vedānta is the first and most impressive structure of Indian philosophy, the creed of intellectual Hindus, and the basis of the popular Hindu religions. Its earliest germs lie in the Mantra portion of the Veda. The Nāsadīyasūkta (*Rigveda*, x. 129) propounds the genesis of the world from an inscrutable principle, darkness, neither existent nor non-existent, and from "one that breathed without afflation, other than which there was nothing, beyond it nothing." The genesis of things from a universal soul is taught in the Purushasūkta (*Rigveda*, x. 90). The unreality of the internal and external orders of things, and the sole reality of a supreme spirit, or impersonal self, are set forth in the Upanishads or later portions of the Veda. The teaching of these Upanishads explicated and systematized, with little or no addition, constitutes the Vedānta. It has innumerable expositors among the Indian schoolmen, of whom the most illustrious is Śankarāchārya (see SANSKRIT LITERATURE, vol. xxi. p. 290), a philosopher of Kerala or Malabar, who lived, it is supposed, between 650 and 740.

The term "vedānta," end of the Veda, is a synonym of "upanishad." Upanishad is said by the Indian scholiasts to denote, in the first place, the knowledge of the impersonal self, the science of absolute being, *paramātmajñāna*, *brahmavidyā*, in the second place, any treatise imparting that knowledge. The doctrines of the Upanishads constitute the *jñānakāṇḍa*, or gnostic portion of the Veda, as distinguished from the *karmakāṇḍa*, or ritual portion, comprised in the Saṃhitās and Brāhmaṇas. They constitute also the *parāvidyā*, or superior science, dealing with cessation from volition and action, and leading to extrication from metempsychosis, as distinguished from the *aparāvidyā*, or inferior science, of the Saṃhitās, Brāhmaṇas, and Vedāngas, which deals with action, and prolongs metempsychosis, leading only to higher embodiments in this world or in the paradises of the deities. The Vedānta philosophy is also called Aupanishadī Mīmāṇsā, Brāhmī Mīmāṇsā, Śārīrakī Mīmāṇsā. The Sūtras or mnemonic formulas in which the system is developed are the Vedāntasūtra, Brahmasūtra, and Śārīrakasūtra. They are ascribed to Vyāsa or Bādarāyaṇa. The system is further styled the Uttaramīmāṇsā, as an investigation of the later portion of the Veda, as distinguished from the Pūrvamīmāṇsā of Jaimini, which is an investigation of the earlier portion of the Veda. The purport of the Pūrvamīmāṇsā is *dharmajijñāsā*, inquiry into sacred prescription; the purport of the Uttaramīmāṇsā, or Vedānta, is *brahmajijñāsā*, inquiry into the real nature of the soul.

There is, according to the Vedānta, but one substance or reality, ingenerable, immutable, incorruptible, eternal, and this is the supreme spirit, the impersonal self, the spiritual absolute, *ātman*, *paramātman*, *brahman*. The series of bodies and of environments through which the soul appears to pass in its μετενσωμάτωσις are illusive, unreal, the figments of a fictitious illusion, *māyā*, *prakriti*, *avyakta*, *avyākrita*. The individual soul, *jīvātman*, *vijñānātman*, is personal only in fictitious semblance, only so long as it is implicated in the series of transmigratory states, and is in truth impersonal, one with the undifferenced self or Brahman. Its apparent and fictitious individuality, and its apparent action and suffering, are the individuality, the action, and the suffering of its illusory adjuncts, the organism and the faculties. The unity of all souls in the one soul is the highest truth, or, properly speaking, the only truth. On reaching and realizing this truth the individual soul returns to its isolation or state of pure indetermination. The duality of experience is fictitious and is surmounted by the true intuition, *samyagjñāna*. On the side of this intuition there abides only "the existent, the intelligence, the beatitude."

Indian philosophy, and in particular its earliest form, the philosophy of the Upanishads, or Vedānta, is governed throughout by two needs. First, there is the need to give consistency and coherence to existing imagery, physical and hyperphysical, to work out a conception of the totality of things. Secondly, there is the need to put a stop to the miseries of metempsychosis. The idea of transmigration, foreign to the Indo-Aryans of the Vedic hymns, appears to have been taken up by their successors from the lower races with which they intermingled, while retaining their supremacy among them. The Indo-Aryans of the Vedic hymns found life pleasurable and exciting. They prayed to the gods for their hundred years of it, and for an after-life with the whole body. This view of life was replaced by one of horror and aversion, pervading everything Indian with its gloom,—the expectation of care, bereavement, sickness, pain, and death, in body after body, and through æon after æon.

The effort to work out a coherent and complete idea by means of some principle of unity appears in the following passages.

In the Muṇḍaka Upanishad: "Saunaka, the householder, approached Angiras and said, 'Holy sir, by knowing what may all this universe be known?' Angiras replied, 'Two sciences are to be known which they that transmit the Veda propound, a superior and an inferior science. Of these the inferior is the *Rigveda*, &c. The superior is that by which that undecaying being is attained. That which none can see, none can handle, which is without kindred, without colour, which has neither eyes nor ears, neither hands nor feet, which is imperishable, infinitely diversified, everywhere present, wholly imperceptible,—that is the immutable, that it is that sages behold as the source of all.'" In reference to this text the scholiast Ānandagiri says, "If we know the *principium*, the *upādāna*, of things, we shall know all things, inasmuch as all things have pre-existed in and are identical with their causes." Śaṅkarāchārya says: "In daily life things are known to ordinary people, if the unities are known under which those things are contained. For example, individual pieces of gold are known under the nature of gold. Thus the question of the text is, what is the one cause or emanatory principle of the diversity of the universe, which known everything else is known?"

In the Chhāndogya Upanishad: "His father said to him, 'Śvetaketu, thou art high-minded, wise in thy own conceit, and proud. Tell me, hast thou asked for that instruction by which the unheard is heard, the unthought thought, the unknown known?' He answered, 'How is that instruction given, sir?' His father said, 'Dear son, as by one lump of clay all that is made of clay becomes known, being a modification of speech only, a change, a name, and the clay being the only reality; as by one piece of iron all that is made of iron becomes known, being a modification of speech only, a change, a name, and the iron being the only reality; as by a pair of scissors all that is made of steel becomes known, being a modification of speech only, a change, a name, and the steel being the only reality:—such is the method of that instruction.' Śvetaketu said, 'Sir, doubtless my teacher knew not that, for, had he known it, how could he have failed to tell me of it? Do thou therefore tell me of it.' His father said, 'Be it so, my dear son. Existent only, fair youth, was this in the beginning, one only, without duality. Some indeed have said, non-existent only was this in the beginning, one only, without duality. From that non-existent the existent proceeded. But how could this be so? how could entity proceed out of non-entity?'"

In the Śvetāśvatara Upanishad: "Those that proclaim Brahman say, What is the *principium*? Is it the impersonal self? From what have we proceeded into life? into what do we return? By what are we upheld as we pass through pleasures and pains? Is time the *principium*? Is the inherent property of things their *principium*? Is chance? Are the elements? Or is the individual soul the origin of all things? Or is the sum of these the *principium*? Neither is any one of these, nor are all of these, the *principium*, for it is the impersonal self. It is not the individual self, for that is not independent, being subject to pleasures and to pains."

The most powerful incentive to speculation was the yearning to escape the miseries of transmigration. The soul has to pass through hunger and thirst, sorrow, bereavement, decrepitude, death, in body after body, through age after age. The individual soul has to look forward to continual suffering through a countless series of embodiments. The series is without beginning, and, until the individual learns his impersonal nature, without end. The series of transmigratory spheres is projected and retracted, projected and retracted, from before all time. Periods of evolution and of dissolution follow each other from and to eternity. Any intervals of pleasure in the series of states through which the soul passes are fugitive and unsatisfying. Even the pleasures of the paradises of the deities are tainted with the fear of their expiry, and with the inequalities amongst the participants. They also are part of the darkness in which everything appears to be involved.

The transmigratory series, or *saṃsāra*, is said to consist of agents, actions, and fruits of action. The fruits of action are the bodies and the environments allotted according to good or evil works. It is described as an unbroken succession of evils,—birth, death, bereavement, and other sorrows,—arising from transition from body to body. The individual soul floats down the stream, "like a gourd upon the waters," through embodiment after embodiment, "from a patch of grass to the first of the divinities," through forms, inorganic and organic, vegetable, animal, human, ultra-human, infernal, and celestial. Each later stage is determined by the good or evil actions of the individual in his earlier embodiments, by a blindly, a fatally operating law of retribution, *adrishṭa*. It is in conformity to this principle that the *opifex ædificatorque mundi deus*, the Demiurgus, Īśvara, puts together and rules the transmigratory series through the successive æons. It is this principle that clears the Demiurgus of the charge of cruelty and injustice on account of the miseries and inequalities of life. In all that it does and suffers the soul is reaping the fruits of its own actions. Its actions proceed from preferences and aversions; its preferences and aversions proceed from illusion, from its identifying itself with its *per se* unconscious senses, faculties, and organism. Merit, no less than demerit, prolongs the series, and must be shunned as sin by the aspirant to extrication.

The world, then, was pictured by the Indian sages as a series, beginningless and endless, of bodies and environments, through which personal souls—that is, the one soul illusively viewing itself as many—pass. They pass through it for the fruition of their works, *bhoga*. The material of which it is built up at each period of evolution is the cosmical illusion, *ajnāna*, *avidyā*, *māyā*, *prakriti*. This is the principle by which soul mistakes itself for not-self, identifies itself with fictitious adjuncts, *upādhi*, with the organs, the faculties, the organism. It is this illusion that gives rise to the unreal world of duality, generable, mutable, corruptible, *avidyāparikalpitaṃ dvaitam*. It is illusion that projects the manifold of experience, *nānātvapratyupasthāpikā māyā*. As the flow of transmigratory experiences is a succession of pleasures, pains, and neutral states, the world-projecting illusion is defined to be pleasure, pain, and indolence in equilibrium, *guṇatrayasāmya*. Pleasure, pain, indifference, are the three *primordia rerum*, the factors of experience, the three strands of the rope that holds the soul in bondage. The world-projecting illusion is further spoken of as the power of the Demiurgus, his all-creative power, "the power of the divine spirit latent in its constituent *primordia*." Thus Śaṅkarāchārya in his Bhāshya on the Vedāntasūtra says: "Name and form (*i.e.*, all that is heard and seen), the fictitious products of illusion, and the body of the omniscient Demiurgus,—name and form, inexplicable as entity and as nonentity, the germs of the transmigratory series,—are called the illusion, the power, the productiveness (*prakṛiti*) of the Demiurgus." This illusion is "neither existent nor non-existent, nor both in one, neither to be explained as entity or as nonentity, fictitiously proceeding from and to all eternity." It is the illusory adjunct, *upādhi*, of Brahman. The internal and the external order of things are illusorily superposed (*adhyasta, adhyāropita*) upon the one and only real, the impersonal self, by an illusion that has imagined itself from all eternity.

To illustrate this in the figures of the Vedānta:—"As a spider extends and retracts his threads, as plants grow up upon the earth, as the hairs of the head and body spring from the living man, so the world arises from the imperishable." "As from the blazing fire its kindred sparks proceed in thousands, so the diverse creatures proceed from that imperishable principle and into it return." All that presents itself to the soul in life after life, in sphere after sphere, lies in fictitious semblance above the real, like the blueness seen in the sky, though in the sky it has no existence; like the waters of a mirage; like the bubbles on the surface of a river; like the airy fabric of a day-dream; like the visions of a dream; like the silver seen, or seeming to be seen, on the shell of the pearl-oyster; like the snake seen by the belated traveller in a piece of rope; like the gloom that surrounds the owl amidst the noontide glare. The soul is confined to the body as within a prison. Its doings and sufferings are as unreal as the apparent motion of the trees upon the bank to one sailing down the river. The experience of life after life is the phantasmagory of a waking dream. The unreality, the fictitious nature, of the things of experience is implied everywhere in the Upanishads, and explicated with a profusion of imagery, by the Indian schoolmen.

The contents of this transmigratory series are supplied from the popular religion, the earlier imagery being built up into the new conception. A place is found in it for the deities and their paradises; only these deities and their paradises, up to the Demiurgus himself, the Īśvara, and the *brahmaloka*, the sphere of Brahmā, are *per se* fictitious, unreal, illusory. A sojourn in these paradises is promised to the religionist; assimilation to these deities is promised to those that worship them with knowledge as well as with rites. Every man, the Indian schoolmen say, shall be assimilated to the deity he worships. The highest reward of obedience to sacred prescription and of worship of the deities is continuance in the *brahmaloka* till the end of an æon, "relative immortality," *āpekshikaṃ nityatvam*. The only real immortality is extrication from metempsychosis, reunion with the impersonal self, to be reached not by works but by knowledge. They that delight in works, in rites, and the spheres won by works, wander in darkness, are like the blind led by the blind. Works and worship are, however, necessary to purify the intellect of the aspirant to extrication. The process of purification may go on through several successive lives. Good works performed without a view to recompense, and as an offering to the Demiurgus, produce that purity of the internal faculties which is requisite to the knowledge that terminates in liberation from metempsychosis. They are thus instrumental to emancipation. Good works are necessary, says Śaṅkarāchārya, to the rise of the spiritual intuition; they are unnecessary when it has once arisen. The qualified aspirant to liberation, the *adhikārin*, must renounce all works, the good as well as the evil, for they serve only to prolong the series of his embodiments. It is thus that the popular religion is taken up and fitted into the Vedānta philosophy. *Karmavidyā* is preliminary to *brahmavidyā*.

Māyā, the inexplicable illusion, self-imagined, has been the unreal adjunct, *upādhi*, illusorily overspread upon Brahman from all eternity. Brahman in its first connexion with ignorance or illusion is the Demiurgus, Īśvara, Parameśvara, the constructive and superintending deity of the Vedāntins. Before describing the process of things at a period of evolution, the conception of Brahman, the impersonal self, must be unfolded in the terms of the Vedānta.

Brahman is the one and real that underlies the many and apparent. It is ingenerable, immutable, incorruptible. It is the ultimate residuum of abstraction, to be spoken of only under negative predicates, *sarvanishedhāvadhi.* It transcends duality, the world of subject and object, *jnātrijñeyabhāvātirikta.* It is one only without internal and external differences. "There is nothing before it, nor after it, nor within it, nor without it." It is everlasting, objectless cognition, *nityam nirvishayam jñānam.* "Of the sight of the seer there is no intermission, for it is imperishable." It is no object of the understanding, and it cannot be expounded in language. "From it words turn back, with the thinking faculty, not reaching it." And this Brahman, this impersonal self, is I, *aham brahmāsmi.*

The impersonal self, Brahman, is "existent, intelligence, beatitude," *sachchidānanda*:—existent, as imparting existence and manifestations to everything that is known and seems to be, *sattāsphūrtipradatayā*; intelligence, as being self-luminous, as giving light to all things, making to appear all things that do appear, *svaprakāśaka, sarvāvabhāsaka*; beatitude, as exempt from all the miseries of metempsychosis, from evil, pain, and sorrow, a beatitude in which there is no distinction between the bliss and the blissful subject, *ānanda* and *ānandin*, a beatitude like the repose of dreamless sleep. It is "ever pure, intelligent, and free," *nityaśuddhabuddhamukta*:—pure, as free from desire and aversion, and passionless, and as unaffected by illusory limitations, *nirupādhika*; intelligent, as irradiating all things, illuminating the otherwise dark or unconscious modifications of the sensories and intellects of personal spirits, and as illuminating the objects of those modifications; free, as unaffected by the experiences of those spirits, exempt from implication in the unreal. It is unmodifiable, and therefore neither knows, nor acts, nor suffers. All cognition, action, and passion belong to the unreal world of duality, and are the modifications of the sensory and intellect of personal souls. These modifications would be dark, that is unconscious, but for the light of the underlying real self, in which they shine forth. In the absence of that real self the whole transmigratory order would be involved in blindness, *tadabhāve jagadāndhyam prasajyeta.* It is the witness,—that is, the inner light—of the cognitions of the intellects of all personal souls, *sarvabuddhipratyayasākshin.* It is "the light of lights beyond the darkness." "To it the sun gives no light, nor the moon and the stars, nor the lightning,—how then this fire? That, as it shines, all the world shines after. By the light of that all this world shines forth."

Brahman is said to abide especially within the heart, for it is there that the internal faculties are lodged, and it is by the light of Brahman that they are illumined. It is "the one spirit internal to all sentiencies," *ekaḥ sarvabhūtāntarātmā.* It is present to them all, as the one sun is mirrored upon many watery surfaces, as the ether one and indivisible in many water-jars. The personal self, the *jīvātman*, is said to be resolved into the impersonal Brahman in three states,—in dreamless sleep, in a period of dissolution between two æons, and in emancipation. Dreamless sleep is called a "daily dissolution," *dainandinaḥ pralayaḥ.*

To Brahman alone belongs existence in the strict sense of the term, *pāramārthikī sattā.* It is; everything else appears to be. The things of daily life have a conventional existence, sufficient for acting upon, insufficient to the reason, *vyāvahārikī sattā.* The silver seen upon the shell, the snake seen in the piece of rope, have an apparent existence, *prātibhāsikī sattā.* For the sage conventional existence is only apparent existence. At the foot of the scale of being stand things impossible or absurd, *tuchcha*, as the flowers of the sky, the horns of the hare.

Brahman is both the real and the operative cause of the world, the *upādāna* and the *nimitta.* It is the real cause, inasmuch as the transmigratory series fictitiously overlies it. "Over this the sky, the earth, the welkin, are woven." "Illusion," says Śankarāchārya, "the aggregate of the powers of all causes and effects, reposes upon Brahman, woven across and across it, as the potentiality of the banyan-tree reposes in the seed of the tree." "A fictitious object," says Ānandagiri, "such as the snake seen in a piece of rope, has a relatively real substratum in the piece of rope; the transmigratory series, unreal because phenomenal, has a real substance beneath it." Brahman is the operative cause of the world, inasmuch as the world-projecting illusion, inert of itself, becomes active by proximity to Brahman, as iron is set in motion by the loadstone, the iron being inert of itself, and the loadstone unmoved and unchanged.

A process of evolution is called a "differentiation under name and form," *nāmarūpavyākarana.* Processes of evolution and of dissolution follow one another from eternity to eternity. Embodiments have proceeded from works, and works from embodiments, in a series without beginning, as plants proceed from seeds and seeds from plants. The series must proceed for each individual until he learns his real nature, and becomes re-immersed in the fontal unity. The one, the ultimate spiritual reality, is knowledge. The many is ignorance, the semblance of knowledge, fictitious cognition, illusion. Ignorance is not mere privation of knowledge: it has a kind of being; it is a false identification of self with not-self, *bhāvarūpam ajñānam, viparītajñānam ajñānam.*

A process of evolution is as follows:—

(1) Brahman overspread with illusion manifests itself as Īśvara, the Demiurgus. The illusion of Īśvara is one with the illusion of each and every sentiency, and of all sentiencies, or *jīvas.* It is at once one and many. As one it is the causal body of the Demiurgus; as many it is the beatific *involucra* of sentiencies, their *ānandamayakosha.* The Demiurgus and the sentiencies are one. Their state is a state of dreamless sleep, a state of beatitude. Īśvara, the Demiurgus, is the first figment of the cosmical illusion. The Demiurgus allots to transmigrating spirits their several bodies and spheres of fruition, in accordance with the law of retribution, and retracts them into himself at the dissolution of the æon. Knowledge of the real nature of his soul frees a man from all fear of Īśvara.

(2) Brahman overspread with illusion next manifests itself as Hiranyagarbha. As one it manifests itself as Hiranyagarbha; as many it is the sentiencies or *jīvas* in the state of dreaming sleep, *taijasa.* Illusion has two powers,—that with which it envelops the soul, hiding from it its proper nature, the *āvaraṇaśakti*, and that with which it projects the seeming bodies and their seeming spheres, the *vikshepaśakti.* The elements, as yet imperceptible, come into being. Out of these the tenuous *involucra*, the vestures of the spirit in its passage from body to body, are evolved. Out of the imperceptible elements the perceptible are afterwards evolved. The soul clothed upon with a tenuous *involucrum*, and passing with it from body to body, from sphere to sphere, is the individual soul, the *jīvātman.* Hiranyagarbha is spirit identifying itself with the as yet imperceptible elements, and with the tenuous *involucra.* It passes through them as a thread passes through the beads of a necklace, and is called the thread-soul, Sūtrātman.

(3) Brahman overspread with illusion finally manifests itself as Vaiśvānara or Virāt. As one it is Vaiśvānara, as many it is the sentiencies or *jīvas* in the waking state, *viśva.* Vaiśvānara is the Purusha of the Purushasūkta: "A thousand heads has Purusha, a thousand eyes, a thousand feet." Purusha is Brahman, illusorily identifying itself with the perceptible elements, and with the bodies of all transmigrating spirits. Every sentiency, every man, in the waking state, is Brahman illusively identified with this or that visible and tangible organism. The perceptible are evolved out of the imperceptible elements by the process of quintuplication, *pañchīkarana.* Each of the later of the five elements has the property of the earlier elements in addition to its own. Ether has the property of sound; air the properties of sound and tangibility; fire the properties of sound, tangibility, and colour; water the properties of sound, tangibility, colour, and taste; earth the properties of sound, tangibility, colour, taste, and smell. Of these elements the bodies of transmigrating spirits, and their several spheres of fruition, are composed.

Such is the order of evolution. An evolution is conceived by the Vedāntins as an instantaneous process, rapid as a flash of light.

There are, then, three orders of intelligence in three states of experience—(1) the Demiurgus, and the individual soul in the state of dreamless sleep; (2) Hiranyagarbha, and the individual soul in the state of dreaming sleep; (3) Vaiśvānara, and the individual soul in the waking state.

There are for these three orders of bodies—(1) the causal body of the Demiurgus, and the wrapper of bliss; (2) the tenuous *involucra* of transmigrating spirits—(these are made up of three wrappers, laid above the wrapper of bliss, viz., the cognitional wrapper, or the intellect and the organs of sense; the sensorial wrapper, or the common sensory and the organs of action; the respiratory wrapper, or the five vital airs, and the organs of action);—(3) the gross *involucra*, the visible and tangible bodies of transmigrating spirits, or nutrimentitious wrapper. Invested in these five successive wrappers, one above the other, the impersonal self manifests itself in the shape of innumerable sentiencies, as beast, as man, as god. It is present in all, as the one sun reflects itself upon many pools, as the one ether spreads itself through many water-jars. It is at the same time, apart from these illusory adjuncts, untouched with mundane sorrows, as the sun looks down upon the impurities of the earth without defilement.

Out of these successive *involucra* the individual soul, to extricate itself from metempsychosis, has to extract itself "like the pith out of a reed." It extracts itself by returning to its proper nature. And to learn and recover his proper nature, his real self, a man must purify his intellect, perhaps through several lives, and must put himself under a spiritual preceptor to whom the Vedantic doctrine has descended through an unbroken line of authorized exponents. Brahman is to be known by traditional exponents, not by the mere exercise of the intellect. "Not he that has not ceased from evil, not he that rests not from sensations, not he that is not concentrated, not he whose faculties are not quiescent, can reach that self by the intuition." "This spiritual reality is not to be reached by learning, by memory, by much spiritual study. But if he choose this reality it may be reached by him; to him the self unfolds its own essence."

The aspirant to extrication, the *mumukshu*, must renounce every.

thing in this and in future spheres of fruition. He must become a *sannyāsin.* In the words of the Bṛihadāraṇyaka Upanishad: "'They that know the breath of the breath, the eye of the eye, the ear of the ear, the thought of the thought, they have seen this fontal spirit, primeval, existing from before all time. It is to be seen with the intellect only. In it there is nought that is manifold. From death to death he goes that looks on this as manifold. It is to be seen in one way only. It is unthinkable, imperishable, unsullied, beyond illusion. Unborn, infinite, imperishable, is Self. Let the patient Brāhman know that and learn wisdom. Let him not learn many words, for that is a weariness of the voice. This indeed is the great, Unborn Self. This it is that holy mendicants yearn after in setting out upon their wandering life. Yearning after this it was that the ancient sages desired no offspring, saying, 'What have we to do with children, we to whom this spiritual reality belongs in the real sphere? They arose, and forsook the desire of children, of wealth, and of worldly existence, and set out as holy mendicants.'" The tardy aspirant, *mandādhikārin*, who seeks for gradual emancipation, *kramamukti*, is enjoined to mutter and to ponder incessantly upon the mystic syllable Om. This is said to be the nearest image of Brahman, to be identical with all words, and with all things.

"They make mistake who leave me out,
Me, when they fly, I am the wings;
I am the doubter and the doubt,
And I the hymn the Brahman sings."

The spiritual preceptor proceeds by the way of "illusory superposition, and the sublation of that superposition," *adhyāropāpavādanyāyena.* Illusory superposition is the viewing of the unreal, the fictitious series of souls and their environments, upon the one and only real. The sublation of this superposition is the position of the impersonal self, Brahman, as the sole reality, and the recognition of the falsity of the fictitious illusion and of all its figments. The doctrine of sublation is expounded as follows in Nrisiṇhasarasvatī's Subodhinī: "Sublation is the annulment of the series proceeding from illusion. The states in this series are illusory emanations, *vivartta*, of Brahman, and to annul them is to abide as pure, undifferenced spirit. The apparent snake of the familiar example, seen by the belated wayfarer, illusorily proceeds from, or is fictitiously produced upon, the piece of rope, without any change of nature taking place in the rope itself. It is sublated when the piece of rope resumes its proper shape. A thing may retain its own nature, and become otherwise than it was, in two manners, viz., by modification, *pariṇāma*, and by illusory emanation, *vivartta.* Modification is when a thing really quits its proper form and takes another shape. Milk, for example, quits its proper form to take the form of curds and whey. Illusory emanation is where a thing, without quitting its proper form, takes another and a fictitious shape. The piece of rope takes the fictitious appearance of a snake without quitting its proper form: it remains a piece of rope. The transmigratory series is not allowed in the Vedānta to be a modification of Brahman. Brahman, if modified as the milk is modified, would be mutable, and therefore perishable. The doctrine of illusory emanation is not exposed to this difficulty. The series superposed on Brahman being fictitious, Brahman remains unchanged. A fictitious thing, then, is said to be sublated when only the real thing abides upon which it was imposed. The transmigratory series is sublated when only the pure intelligence remains upon which it was fictitiously outspread."

By continuous contemplation the aspirant refunds each entity into the entity from which it emanated, till he passes beyond illusion to the fontal unity of undifferenced spiritual existence. He follows the order of dissolution, the inverse of the order of evolution, till he arrives at Brahman. He thus realizes the import of the great text, the *mahāvākya*, "that art thou," *tat tvam asi* (Chhāndogya Upanishad, sixth Prapāṭhaka). Particular souls are one with the universal soul, the Demiurgus, and the universal soul is one with Brahman. This knowledge is the last and highest of cognitions, the final modification of the aspirant's intellect as it melts away into the fontal unity. This is the *phalitam brahma*, "the resultant impersonal self." The *phalitam brahma* is a modification of the aspirant's sensorium, his *antaḥkaraṇa*, and passes away, that the impersonal self, the supreme spirit, may alone remain. He to whose inner faculties this vision is present has the spiritual intuition, *samyagdarśana.* He is extricated but alive, *jīvanmukta*, and remains in the body till those merits are exhausted which have led to his present life. Disengaged from metempsychosis, and still in the body, the perfected sage is said to be untouched by merit and demerit, unsoiled by sin, uninjured by anything he does or leaves undone. No evil, the scholiasts say, arises from this freedom, as the purificatory virtues of the aspirant cling to the accomplished seer,—his humility, his sincerity, his tenderness to all, remaining upon him like ornaments even after the rise of the spiritual intuition. Finally his body falls away, and his spirit is freed for ever. It abides in itself. It is undifferenced existence, undifferenced intelligence, undifferenced beatitude. This is the consummation of *brahmavidyā.*

The soul has found itself, has loosed itself, not that in verity it is ever loosed or bound. From the highest point of view bondage and liberation, implication and extrication, are unreal. The Vedāntins compare the individual spirit seeking to regain its impersonal nature to one searching for that which he unwittingly carries about with him, to a man trembling at his own shadow. The soul of the finished sage knows itself, and therefore is itself. In the words of the Muṇḍaka Upanishad: "Burst are his heart's ties, broken his doubts, his merits spent, when he has seen the principle supreme at once and not supreme. In the golden, perfect *involucrum* is the unsullied Self, without parts, luminous, which they know that know the soul." "As all rivers flowing onwards disappear in the sea, quitting name and form, so the sage extricated from name and form enters into the self-luminous spirit beyond the last of things, beyond illusion." In the words of the Brihadāraṇyaka: "He that knows it is no longer sullied by evil deeds. Repressing his senses, quiescent, free from all desires, ready to suffer all things, his thoughts fixed, he sees within himself the Self, the universal soul. Imperfection reaches him no more; he passes beyond imperfection. He burns up all his imperfection. He that knows Brahman becomes free from imperfection, free from uncertainty, insphered in Brahman. This same great, unborn, Self is undecaying, undying, imperishable, beyond all fear. Brahman is beyond all fear. He that knows this becomes the spiritual reality beyond all fear." (A. E. G.)

VEDAS. See BRAHMANISM and SANSKRIT LITERATURE.

VEDDAHS, or WEDDAHS, that is, "Hunters," a primitive people of Ceylon, probably representing the Yakkos of Sanskrit writers, who appear to have been the true aborigines and the sole inhabitants of the island prior to the Hindu conquest. During the Dutch occupation (1644-1796) they were met in scattered groups as far north as Jaffna, but are now confined to the south-eastern district, about the wooded Bintenne, Badulla, and Nilgala Hills, and thence to the coast near Batticaloa. They constitute three distinct social groups—the *coast people*, who are settled and partly civilized, freely intermingling with their Singhalese neighbours; the *wild* or *rock people*, who keep entirely aloof, living exclusively on the produce of the chase; and the *village people*, semi-nomad agriculturists, intermediate in every respect between the other two. The Veddahs are thus in a state of transition from the lowest to a relatively high degree of culture; and their physical appearance gives evidence of their intermediate position between the aboriginal and the intruding races of Ceylon. Virchow[1] finds (1) that the Veddahs and Singhalese have much in common, which is probably due to the intermingling of the aborigines with the Hindu immigrants, as is also suggested by historic and anthropological considerations; (2) that both differ very decidedly from the Tamils of north Ceylon and south India; (3) that the Veddahs show certain analogies with the small dark pre-Dravidian element in this region, which De Quatrefages calls "Negrito," and which Huxley groups with his "Australoid" division of mankind. The true Veddahs of Bintenne are almost a dwarfish race, averaging about 5 feet (men, 5 feet 2 inches; women, 4 feet 10 inches), with correspondingly low cranial capacity, narrow high skull like the Papuan (index 70), mesognathous jaw, slightly prominent cheekbones, straight, but shaggy rather than lank, black hair, and features altogether more Hindu than Negroid, although of somewhat darker complexion than the ordinary olive-brown Singhalese. They wander about in small family groups, which have not reached the tribal state, being absolutely destitute of any political or communal organization whatsoever. Their dwellings are the caves of the rocks or the forest trees; they clothe themselves with foliage; and they devour uncooked vermin, reptiles, and whatever other quarry they are able to capture with their rude weapons. It is stated that they can neither count, mark the succession of time, nor distinguish colours; but what is more certain is that they never laugh, in this respect differing from nearly all other races. They also

[1] *Ueber die Weddas von Ceylon und ihre Beziehungen zu den Nachbarstämmen*, Berlin, 1882.

appear to be the only savage people who speak an Aryan language, for their present speech at least seems to be a degraded form of Singhalese, consisting mainly of Sanskrit intermingled with Dravidian elements. This circumstance has given rise to the theory that the Veddahs are a degraded group of Hindu outcastes, whereas they call themselves the "sons of kings," and claim to belong to a superior caste, a claim which, strange to say, appears to be admitted by their neighbours. Their religion has been described as a kind of demon-worship, consisting of rude dances and shouts raised to scare away the evil spirits, whom they confound with their ancestors. But these "demons" and "spirits" are purely anthropomorphic beings; of a supernatural order as understood by more cultured peoples they have no idea. Owing to an increasingly low birth-rate, the Veddahs are disappearing as a distinct ethnical group; even including the Rhodiyas of the western uplands they numbered only 2284 in 1886 (Ferguson's *Directory*). But they should not be confounded with these Rhodiyas, who, although true outcastes, are nevertheless a much finer race, tall, well-proportioned, with regular features, and speak a language said to be radically distinct from all the Aryan and Dravidian dialects current in Ceylon. There is, however, in Travancore, on the mainland, a low-caste "Veda" tribe, nearly black, with wavy or frizzly hair, and now speaking a Malayâlim (Dravidian) dialect (Jagor), who probably approach nearer than the insular Veddahs to the aboriginal pre-Dravidian "Negrito" element of southern India and Malaysia.

VEGA CARPIO, LOPE FELIX DE (1562-1635), Spanish dramatist and poet, was born on 25th November 1562 at Madrid, in a house in the Platerias or jewellers' quarter adjoining the Puerta de Guadalajara. His father and mother, Felix de Vega and Francisca Hernandez, belonged to the lesser provincial nobility, and originally came from the valley of Carriedo in Asturias, where the hamlet of Vega still exists. How they came by the illustrious name of Carpio is not very clear; the family tradition which made them descendants of the famous Bernardo seems insufficiently supported. Lope himself frankly ridiculed the aristocratic pretensions of his parents; but this did not prevent him from invariably signing his comedies at full length as Lope de Vega Carpio. Lope began his studies in the imperial college, the principal establishment of the Jesuits in Madrid, where he was instructed in grammar and rhetoric. His precocity was extraordinary and his memory astounding. At five he read not only Spanish but Latin, and already showed such a passion for poetry that he would give up part of his meals to the older boys in exchange for their services in writing out verses to his dictation. It was not the way of the Jesuits to turn out pedants; educators of the nobility, their single aim was to make their pupils accomplished men of the world, and accordingly Lope learned with them, besides the ordinary book-lessons, the accomplishments of singing and dancing and fencing. On leaving college—where he had been guilty of an escapade of some sort along with one of his companions—he was placed by his parents, who were far from wealthy, in the service of Don Gerónimo Manrique, bishop of Avila. Such an arrangement did not at that time involve any sacrifice of dignity: it was almost the only resource open to a multitude of needy gentlemen, *hidalgos*, who, to avoid entering a trade, which would have compromised their position, found in the palaces of the higher aristocracy, first as pages and afterwards as secretaries, the wherewithal to *pasar la vida*, as the phrase ran. In the service of Don Gerónimo, Lope appears to have begun the composition of his earlier dramas. But after a while he quitted the bishop's service to enter the university of Alcalá, where for four years he devoted himself to what was then honoured with the name of philosophy, crammed his brain with names and citations from ancient writers, and acquired the habit of disputing in accordance with the formulæ of the schools. It was then that he accumulated the materials for the pedantic dissertations with which the prefaces to his various works are encumbered, in which he so complacently displays everything that he has remembered of his university days. Leaving Alcalá with the degree of bachelor in arts, Lope became secretary to the duke of Alva. Some time afterwards, about 1584, he married Isabel de Urbina, daughter of a herald-at-arms of Philip II. An incident such as he often afterwards reproduced in his plays soon arose to disturb the union. Some one who had spoken ill of Lope, and had in turn been severely lampooned by the poet, challenged him. In the encounter Lope wounded his opponent; but he was unable to put himself right with the law and was compelled to take to flight. Perhaps he may have had upon his conscience some other peccadilloes which prejudiced him in the eyes of his judges, as seems to be hinted in Montalban's words, "This vexatious affair, and certain other bad turns of fortune, . . . compelled him to leave his home, his country, and his wife." He retired to Valencia, where he met with an enthusiastic reception from a group of young poets, who were destined afterwards to range themselves under the banner of the creator of the new comedy. After the lapse of two years Lope returned to Madrid; but in 1588 his wife died after giving birth to a daughter, who did not long survive her mother. The death of his wife and daughter were doubtless what now led him to join the Invincible Armada, in which expedition he had one of his brothers shot dead by his side. Once more at Madrid, he again entered service, becoming secretary, first to the marquis of Malpica and afterwards to the duke of Lemos. Meanwhile he married a second wife, Juana de Guardio, a Madrileña, by whom he had two children (Carlos, who died in infancy, and Feliciana Felix); but she died, shortly after giving birth to the latter, in 1612. During this wife's lifetime the poet had by a mistress, Maria de Luxan, two other children,—Marcela del Carpio, who became a nun, and Lope Felix del Carpio y Luxan, who chose the profession of arms and perished at sea at the age of fifteen. Widowed a second time, Lope, like many other men of letters of the period, sought a refuge in the church. After a period of initiation, and after having been for some time affiliated to a tertiary order, he took priest's orders. At this juncture, that is to say, about 1614, he was in the very zenith of his glory. A veritable dictator and pope in the Spanish world of letters, he wielded over all the authors of his nation a sort of magisterial power similar to that which was exercised in France at a later period by Voltaire. At this distance of time we fail to see in Lope anything more than a great dramatic poet, the founder of the Spanish theatre; but to his contemporaries he was a great deal more. His epics, his pastorals, his odes, his sonnets, buried though they now are in oblivion, all placed him in the front rank of authorship. Such was his prestige that he dealt with his noble patrons almost on a footing of equality. The duke of Sesa in particular, his last Mæcenas, was also his personal friend, and the tone of the letters addressed to him by the poet is that of a frank familiarity, modified only by some forms of deference,—a fact sufficiently striking to be worthy of notice at a time when talent, however great, in no way diminished differences of rank, and when the man of letters under the protection of a patron was neither more nor less than a kind of domestic in the house of a *grand seigneur*. Lope's fame, too, had travelled abroad: foreigners of distinction passing through Madrid made a point of visiting him; papal legates brought him the compliments of their master; in 1627 Urban VIII., a Barberini, sent him the diploma of doctor of theology in the Collegium Sapientiæ and the cross of the order of St John of Jerusalem (whence the poet's titles of *Doctor* and *Frey*). Since Lope's correspondence with the duke of Sesa has made us acquainted with the closing period of his life, we may well ask whether his retirement within the church was the result of any genuine vocation, and up to what point his devotion was sincere. It is difficult to avoid inquiring whether it may not have been due to a mere selfish desire for tranquillity, a desire to protect himself against any further reverse of fortune. This feeling may very well have had something to do with his decision; still it would be unjust to regard Lope as nothing better than a mere hypocrite. Certainly he was far from being an ideal priest; we now know something of the nature of the services which he often rendered to the duke of Sesa, and we know how lightly he held one of his most sacred vows, maintaining for a long period illicit relations with Marta de Nevares Santoyo, a married woman, by whom he even had a daughter, who was baptized very publicly at San Sebastian in Madrid (26th August 1617), the son of the duke of Sesa acting as godfather. But, on the other hand, we must not forget his penitence, frequently expressed in touching terms, the sincerity of which ought to be above suspicion: "Mal haya amor que se quiere oponer al cielo!" He has a claim also to our pity for having been at an advanced age the victim of foolish passion which his extreme mobility of character and his utter want of balance made him unable to resist: "Yo nací en dos extremos que son amar y aborrecer; no he tenido medio jamás." His last years were years of severe penance: Montalban tells us that every Friday the poet scourged himself so severely that the walls of his room were sprinkled with his blood. His death, on 27th August 1635, was followed by national mourning. The duke of Sesa, his executor, was chief mourner; the nobility and the church were represented by high dignitaries; the populace crowded the streets. After the funeral came a multitude of funeral orations and of panegyrics in prose and verse. Montalban has collected into a volume the tributes of posthumous admiration thus paid by Spanish authors; another collection was printed in Italy under the auspices of Marini.

In the intercourse of everyday life, in his relations with his contemporaries, Lope was affable and kindly. He sometimes defended himself when attacked, especially on the subject of his dramatic writings, but always in measured terms and without any pretence that his high position exempted him from criticism by his less successful rivals. Some severe and unjust criticisms on other writers, notably on Cervantes, are quoted against him; but it is only fair to remember that they occur in letters to his intimates and that it is not necessary to regard them as deliberate. It would be just as fair to set him down as an enemy of the secular clergy because in writing to the duke of Sesa he on one occasion expressed himself thus freely about the monks: "Los frailes son los hombres mas discretos del mundo: no van a la guerra, ni pagan millones, gozan lo mejor, y danles dineros, . . . ellos hacen hijos y otros los crian, perdone lo descalzo." It would indeed be more just to reproach him with his universal and uniform indulgence, which he extends to all, great and small, good and bad, and with his mania for praising in hyperbolical and extravagant terms. He loved all the arts, particularly painting; his little house in the Calle de Francos was full of pictures. He himself writes to a friend in 1619: "With some garden flowers, half-a-dozen pictures, and a few books, I live without envy, without desire, without fear, and without hope" (dedication of *El Alcalde Mayor*). But his most marked taste was for flowers. He had a small garden, which he himself tended with jealous care; he sought out rare species and tried to acclimatize in Spain varieties of plants sent by his friends from abroad. In particular he was a tulip-fancier; hence his dedication of *Lucinda Perseguida* to Manuel Sueiro, a Spaniard resident in Flanders who had supplied him with fine specimens. Tending this garden became the great occupation of his old age; he watered it with his own hands, and, according to Montalban, the chill which led to his death was caught while he was thus engaged.

One can easily detect in his writings the traces of this taste. It is not that he had in a higher degree than his contemporaries the feeling for nature, but the form, the colour, the perfume of flowers largely supply him with his figures and metaphors—his flowers of rhetoric, in short. It is to be regretted that this delicate taste of his, a taste very rare in Spain, where flowers and trees have never been greatly cared for, should have contributed rather to augment than to lessen the elaborateness, pomposity, and affectation of his style. But these faults were shared by all the writers of that age. In his comedies, for example, where he does not pique himself on a fine style and does not attempt to take the Latins or the Italians for his models, his language is, if not nervous and self-restrained, at least limpid and flowing, in this respect contrasting very favourably with the florid and laboured style of his epics and prose pastorals. Viewed broadly, and leaving out of account certain theories which in the long run greatly influenced his manner of writing, Lope belonged in literature to what may be called the school of good sense; he made it his boast that he was a Spaniard *pur sang*, and steadfastly maintained that a writer's business is to write so as to make himself understood. When brought face to face with the coterie of the *précieux* and *quintessenciés*, the "cultos," and "críticos," and "conceptistas," Lope takes the position of a defender of the language of ordinary life, the good old Castilian tongue. In the dispute which arose between the partisans of the two schools of "cultos" or "culteranos" and "llanos," the dramatist ranged himself on the side of the latter. In the matter of versification he refuses to admit that the long Italian verse has the advantage of the Castilian octosyllabic: "No pienso que el verso largo Italiano haga ventaja al nuestro, que si en España lo dizen es porque, no sabiendo hazer el suyo, se passan al estrangero como mas largo y licencioso. . . . Qué cosa iguala á una redondilla de Garci Sanchez ó Don Diego de Mendoza?" (Preface to *Isidro*). Unfortunately the books that he read, his literary connexions, his fear of being unfavourably judged by the Italians, all exercised an influence upon his naturally robust spirit, and, like so many others, he caught the prevalent contagion of mannerism and of empty and pompous phraseology. In his studies at the imperial college and at Alcalá Lope had never found his way up to the truest and highest sources of the beautiful; he had never attempted Greek, but had contented himself with Latin, which he chose to regard as the only ancient tongue which a man of letters needed to learn. To his natural son, Lope Felix del Carpio, when entering upon his Latin studies, he wrote, "So you have begun to grapple with the rudiments? It is one of the things which cannot possibly be avoided; but, for all that, if I could find some one to teach you your own language well, I should be quite satisfied, for I have seen too many of those who, having learned Latin, are ignorant of their native tongue and affect to despise everything written in the vulgar idiom. What presumption to forget that the Greeks did not write in Latin or the Latins in Greek! I confess I laugh whenever I see men giving themselves out for Latin poets who write in their own language like mere barbarians; and I conclude that they cannot possibly have been born poets, for the true poet (there is not more than one, they say, in a generation) writes in his own language, and it is therein that he shows his excellence,—witness Petrarch in Italy, Ronsard in France, and Garcilaso in Spain. Nevertheless I do not wish to discourage you from learning that queen of languages (Latin), the third in the world in point of antiquity. Try to know it as well as you can, my son, but by no means learn Greek, for I would not have you like those who strut and give themselves airs because they have acquired a smattering of it. Greek tends too much to vanity, and what is the use of learning a language which is known to so few?" After thus warning his son against the dangers of Greek, Lope adds other counsels which reveal to us his feelings towards his own bygone days. "Have but few books, and those choose with care; diligently observe the thoughts they contain, and do not let anything noteworthy pass without a mark on the margin. Should it be your misfortune to become a maker of verses (which God forbid!) try at least not to make that your chief occupation, nor let it divert you from more important matters, for therein you will spend your time to no profit. The less of verse you make the more you will be esteemed and appreciated. You need only take an example from me. Certainly you will never be able to render more services than I have done to so many patrons, and see to what my diligence has brought me,—to the smallest of houses, a narrow bed, a poor table, and a patch of garden, the flowers of which dispel my cares and supply me with ideas." Lope knew only Latin, but this he knew well. Yet, instead of filling himself with the spirit of antiquity, and purifying his taste by contact with its literary masters, he regarded their writings as nothing more than repertories of beautiful and out-of-the-way expressions. After the Latins Lope turned by preference to the Italians. Like every other Spanish man of letters of his time, he had been reared on Italian literature: he knew intimately the works of its great poets of the Renaissance, especially Ariosto and Tasso, as well as Sannazaro, the last-named of whom he imitated on several occasions;

he kept a steady watch upon all that was published in Italy, cultivated carefully the connexions he had established with Italian writers of repute, and was always flattered by the eulogies which reached him from that quarter. His principal friend and correspondent in Italy was the Neapolitan poet, G. B. Marini, one of the worst corrupters of Italian literature (see vol. xiii. p. 511). He puts himself at Marini's feet, calls him *antistes Musarum* and *Italiæ decos*, sends him his portrait, and humbly begs his indulgence for a drama which he has been so bold as to dedicate to him (see dedication to *Virtud, Pobreza, y Muger*). Lope knew French also, and his works give evidence of an acquaintance with French poetry of the 16th and 17th centuries such as is rare in Spain; he occasionally quotes Ronsard and Malherbe, and shows solicitude as to French opinion about his dramatic writings. In a word, his literary culture was chiefly Latin-Italian; and, if he defends the tradition of the nation, and the pure simplicity of the old Castilian against "los de la nueva poesía," that is to say, the innovators of the school of Gongora, and against the jargon of the "cultos," still he does not wish to be taken for an uninformed person, for a mere casual litterateur devoid of classical training: he especially emphasizes the fact that he has passed through the university, and is continually accentuating the difference between the "ingenios científicos" (those who know Latin) and "legos ignorantes" (ignorant laymen). With what a sense of superiority, for example, does he mention that Cervantes was not to his mind sufficiently "científico" (preface to *Las Fortunas de Diana*), the fact being that Cervantes had been neither at Alcalá nor at Salamanca!

For a rapid survey of the works of Lope, it is convenient to begin with those which the Spaniards include under the name of *Obras Sueltas*, the title of the large collection of the poet's non-dramatic works (Madrid, 21 vols. 4to, 1776-79). We shall enumerate the most important of these, as far as possible in the order of publication. The *Arcadia* (1598), a pastoral romance, composed at the instance of the duke of Alva, and inspired by Sannazaro, Montemayor, and Cervantes, is one of the poet's feeblest and most wearisome productions. *Isidro* (1599), a narrative of the life of Isidore, patron of Madrid, is called a Castilian poem on account of the rhythm in which it is composed,—*quintillas* of octosyllabic verse. The *Hermosura de Angélica* (1602), in three books, is a sort of continuation of the *Orlando Furioso*, in octaves after the fashion of the original poem. Similar in form is *La Dragontea*, a fantastic history of the last expedition and the death of Sir Francis Drake, who was such a terror to the fleets and the coast of Spain that his name had become a synonym for that of the evil one. Finally the *Rimas* are a miscellany of short pieces. In 1604 was published the *Peregrino en su Patria*, a romance in prose and verse, similar in kind to the *Æthiopica* of Heliodorus; it is a mediocre work, but of great bibliographical interest, on account of its authentic list of the comedies which Lope recognized as having been written by him up to that date, a list which he augmented by 114 new titles in the 1618 edition of the novel. The more Lope composed poetry the more he went to the Italian poets for inspiration, labouring to show that the mechanism of the Italian octave was as familiar to him as that of the national redondilla. Having imitated Ariosto, he proceeded to imitate Tasso; but his *Jerusalem Conquistada* (1609) has preserved nothing of the art shown in its model, and is a dull and insipid performance. Little need be said about the *Pastores de Belen* (1612), a sort of pious pastoral, dedicated to his son Carlos, which forms a pendant to his secular *Arcadia*, or about the incidental pieces which he published in connexion with the solemnities of the beatification and canonization of St Isidore in 1620 and 1622. And it is enough simply to mention *La Filomena* (1621), *La Circe* (1624), and other poems published about the same date, as also the four prose novels, *Las Fortunas de Diana, El Desdichado por la Honra, La Mas Prudente Venganza*, and *Guzman el Bravo*. The great success of the *Novelas Egemplares* of Cervantes (1613) had stimulated Lope, who wished to measure himself with the author of *Don Quixote* on the field of the novel; and, as this literary form had been borrowed from the Italians, he expected to achieve a success as great as that which he supposed to be already his in the fields of pastoral romance and epic poetry. But in this instance at least the "científico" was completely defeated by the "lego": Lope's novels have none of the grace, naturalness, or interest which characterize those of his rival. The last important work which has to be mentioned before we leave the narrative poetry of Lope is the *Laurel de Apolo* (1630). This piece describes the coronation of the poets of Spain on Helicon by Apollo. All of them—good, middling, and bad—share in the ceremonial, and among the poets properly so called appear some other men of letters, certain important personages to whom Lope felt under obligations, which could not be more satisfactorily paid than in the current coin of verse which he had so readily at his command. This work is more meritorious as a bibliographical manual of Spanish poetry at that time than as genuine poetry. One other "obra suelta," closely akin to Lope's dramatic works, though not properly speaking a drama, is *La Dorotea* (1632). Lope describes it as an "action in prose," but it is rather a "romance in dialogue"; for, although divided into acts, the narrative has nothing dramatic about it except its outward form; and on account of its size and the digressions with which it is encumbered it has never succeeded in finding its way to the stage. It belongs to the class of which *Celestina* is the type, in so far as one of the principal characters, La Gerarda, is a go-between; but Lope has amplified his model, idealized it, and purged away much of the grossness belonging to the mean surroundings of the character of the original *Celestina* and common to the numerous works of the 16th and 17th centuries to which it gave rise. Of all Lope's productions *Dorotea* is undoubtedly that which shows most observation and study; the style also is unusually simple and easy. The attempt has sometimes been made to discover in the adventures of Fernando, one of its heroes, allusions to Lope's early youth; but there is nothing conclusive in any of the supposed coincidences between fact and fiction which Fauriel and others after him have sought to establish. Of all this mass of *Obras Sueltas*, filling more than twenty volumes, very little (leaving *Dorotea* out of account) holds its own in the impartial judgment of posterity. The long epic or narrative poems are quite unreadable, and almost the same must be said of the pastorals and novels. The lyrical element alone retains some vitality. From the *Rimas* and other collections of detached pieces one could compile a pleasing anthology of sonnets, epistles, elegies, and romances, to which it would be proper to add the *Gatomaquia*, a burlesque poem published along with other metrical pieces in 1634 by Lope under the pseudonym of Tomé de Burguillos. But here the list would have to stop.

It is, however, to his dramatic writings that Lope owes his very considerable place in literary history. It is very curious to notice how he himself seizes every available occasion for depreciating the work of the drama, treats the art of comedy-writing as one of the humblest of trades (*de pane lucrando*), and protests against the supposition that in writing for the stage his aim is glory and not money.[1] The reason is not far to seek. The Spanish drama, which, if not literally the creation of Lope, at least owes to him its definitive form—the three-act comedy—was totally regardless of the precepts of the school, the pseudo-Aristotelianism of the doctors of the period. Lope accordingly, who stood in awe of the criticism of the "científicos," felt bound to let them see that, from the point of view of literary art, he attached no value to the "rustic fruits of his humble *vega*." In his *Arte Nuevo de Hacer Comedias en Este Tiempo*, which was published in 1609 and is the *Ars Poetica* of the new school, Lope begins by showing that he knows as well as any one the established rules of poetry, and then excuses himself for his inability to follow them on the ground that the "vulgar" Spaniard cares nothing about them. "Let us then speak to him in the language of fools, since it is he who pays us." Under such conditions all that the dramatic poet can do is to plan ingenious plots, so as adroitly to sustain the interest and retard as long as possible the denouement, for nothing is more displeasing to the ordinary public than to be able to divine too soon the solution of the problem set before them on the boards of the theatre. Such, with a few pieces of advice as to the choice of metres and the costume of the actors, is the recipe for the new or free comedy, a barbarous kind of literature, according to Lope, and outside the region of art, yet the only drama possible in Spain.[2] Another reason, more serious still, which made it necessary for him to speak deprecatingly of his dramatic works is the circumstance that the vast majority of them were written in haste and to order, precisely like so many feuilleton romances of Alexandre Dumas; they are for the most part *comedias de repente*, hurriedly conceived at the request of some grandee or of some impresario or manager. The poet does not hesitate to confess that "more than a hundred of my comedies have taken only twenty-four hours to pass from my brain to the boards of the theatre." Perez de Montalban, who has a great admiration for this kind of cleverness, tells how, at Toledo, on a certain occasion, Lope composed fifteen acts in fifteen days—that is to say, five entire comedies, which he read to his friends step by step with the process of their composition. On another occasion, when pressed by a manager who wanted something for the carnival, Lope took Montalban as a collaborateur; the two friends parcelled out the comedy between them, Lope undertaking the first act, Montalban the second, and the third, to save time, was divided between them. In two days they had finished the first two acts, and on the third Montalban rose at two in the morning and at eleven he had finished. Then he went in search of Lope, who, when questioned as to his progress, replied: "I got up at five, finished the act, breakfasted, wrote an epistle of fifty tercets, and have now finished watering the garden, and a rather tough business it has been." This is not art; it is handicraft, and one understands why Lope sometimes found it prudent to lay stress on the fact that his comedies had been written for the ears of spectators, not for readers in

[1] Algunos que piensan que las escribo por opinion; desengañeles V. M. y digales que por dinero.

[2] Las comedias de España no guardan el arte . . . porque con aquel rigor de ninguna manera fueran oidas de los Españoles.

their studies.[1] Nevertheless, he did write some dramas in which the plan is more fully matured and the execution more carefully carried out; still, hurried composition and reckless production are after all among the most distinctive marks of his theatrical works. Towards the close of his career Lope somewhat modified the severe and disdainful judgments he had formerly passed upon his dramatic performances; he seems to have had a presentiment that posterity, in spite of the grave defects of his work in that department, would nevertheless place it much higher than the *Jerusalem Conquistada*, *La Dragontea*, and other works of which he himself thought so much. In his *Egloga á Claudio*, which is, so to say, his literary last will and testament, he claims to have been a creator: "It is to me that the art (of comedy) owes its beginnings, although I have departed from the strictness of Terence, and do not for a moment pretend to deny the part which belongs to the three or four great geniuses who have watched over the infancy of the drama. To whom are we indebted, Claudio, for so many delineations of love and jealousy, so many moving pieces of eloquence, such a copious supply of all the figures which rhetoric has ever been able to invent? All that is produced to-day is nothing but imitation of what art created yesterday. The path,—it is I who have opened it up and made it practicable, and everybody now traverses it with ease. It was I who gave the example which is followed and copied on all hands." We may certainly credit Lope with creative power, with the instinct which enabled him to reproduce the facts of history or those supplied by the imagination in a multitude of dramatic situations with an astonishing cleverness and flexibility of expression; but unfortunately, instead of concentrating his talent upon the production of a limited number of works which he might have brought to perfection, he dissipated it, so to say, and scattered it to the winds.

The catalogue of Lope's comedies has been drawn up by himself; and, in spite of some discrepancies in his figures, it is established that up to 1604 he had composed, in round numbers, as many as 230. In 1609 the figure had risen to 500, in 1618 to 800, in 1620 to 900, in 1625 to 1070, and in 1632 to 1500. Ultimately Montalban in his general survey published in 1636 (*Fama Posthuma*) set down the total of Lope's dramatic productions at 1800 comedies and 400 *autos sacramentales.* Of this number there are nearly 608 comedies of which the text is extant, or which are at least known to us by their titles (from the lists of the *Peregrino*); but the printed or MS. text of only 439 is actually accessible, besides some 40 *autos* and a few *entremeses.* Very many of these pieces were printed during Lope's lifetime, either in collections of *varios autores* or as separate issues by booksellers who bought from the actors in an underhand way the manuscripts of their *rôles* or else caused the unpublished comedy to be written down from memory by persons whom they sent to attend the first representation. Such pieces therefore as do not figure in the collection published under Lope's own direction or under that of his friends cannot be regarded as perfectly authentic, and it would be unfair to hold their author responsible for all the faults and defects they exhibit. On the other hand, there exist in various libraries entire comedies in Lope's own handwriting which have never been printed.

The classification of this enormous mass of dramatic literature is a task of great difficulty, inasmuch as the terms usually employed, such as comedy, tragedy, and the like, do not apply here. There is not explicitness enough in the division current in Spain, which recognizes three categories:—(1) *comedias de capa y espada*, the subjects of which are drawn from everyday life and in which the persons appear as simple *caballeros*; (2) *comedias de ruido* or *de teatro*, in which kings and princes are the leading characters and the action is accompanied with a greater display of dramatic machinery; (3) *comedias divinas* or *de santos.* Some other arrangement must be attempted. In the first place Lope's work belongs essentially to the drama of intrigue; be the subject what it may, it is always the plot that determines everything else, not the delineation of manners or of character. Lope in the whole range of his dramatic works has not a single piece comparable to *La Verdad Sospechosa* of Alarcon, the most finished example in Spanish literature of the comedy of character; and what is called the comedy of manners is no better represented: only *El Rufian Castrucho*, *El Anzuelo de Fenisa*, and one or two others can be named. It is from history, and particularly Spanish history, that he has borrowed more than from any other source. It would in fact be difficult to say what national and patriotic subjects, from the reign of the half fabulous King Pelayo down to the history of his own age, he has not put upon the stage. Sometimes he contents himself with serving up old chronicles afresh or stringing together fragments of old popular songs, as in *El Bastardo Mudarra*, with inventing here and there a few secondary characters when the original material is not sufficiently rich and complicated, as in *Las Doncellas de Simancas*, *Los Benavides*, *El Casamiento en la Muerte*, and many others, or sometimes even with clothing with complete dramatic action one single fact of history, as in one of his most famous plays, *La Estrella de Sevilla*, in *Porfiar hasta Morir*, in *El Mejor Alcalde el Rey*, and others. Even current events as they took place under his eyes furnished him with motives. In an age when people read but little, the theatre was a channel of information and a means of rousing patriotic sentiment. A victory of the Spanish arms in Flanders or the success of hardy adventurers in planting the royal banner of Castile in some virgin land in the West,—events like these promptly gave rise to a comedy. On the basis of any sort of report of battle or conquest Lope improvises a dramatic action, or at least a narrative in dialogue. Thus under the title of *La Mayor Victoria de Alemania* he describes a victory won in the Palatinate by Don Gonzalo de Córdoba, brother of the duke of Sesa, his patron. Such are the principal varieties of historical or heroic comedy. But it is to the class of *capa y espada*—also called *novelesco*, because the subjects are almost always love intrigues complicated with affairs of honour—that Lope's most celebrated plays belong. In these he has most fully displayed his powers of imagination (the subjects being all invented) and his skill in elaborating a plot. Among the plays of this class which are those best known in Europe, and most frequently imitated and translated, may be specially mentioned *Los Ramilletes de Madrid*, *La Boba para los Otros y Discreta para sí*, *El Perro del Hortelano*, *La Viuda de Valencia*, and *El Maestro de Danzar.* In some of them Lope has sought to set forth some moral maxim, and illustrate its abuse by a living example. Thus, on the theme that "poverty is no crime," we have the play entitled *Las Flores de Don Juan*, in which he shows in the history of two brothers the triumph of virtuous poverty over opulent vice; at the same time he attacks indirectly the institution of primogeniture, which often places in the hands of an unworthy person the honour and substance of a family when the younger members would be much better qualified for the trust. Such pieces are, however, rare in Lope's repertory; in common with all other writers of his order in Spain, with the occasional exception of Alarcon, his sole aim is to amuse and stir his public, not troubling himself about its instruction. The strong point of such writers is and always will be their management of the plot. As has been said by Le Sage, a good judge: "The Spaniards are our masters in the art of planning and skilfully working out a plot; they know how to set forth their subject with infinite art and in the most advantageous light." It is not necessary to dwell here upon the other varieties of comedy represented in Lope's works, that is, the *comedias divinas*, *fiestas* (mythological dramas for the most part), *entremeses*, and *autos.* In none of them has he produced anything of the highest order, or even comparable to the better performances of his contemporaries and successors.

To sum up, Lope found a poorly organized drama, plays being composed sometimes in four acts, sometimes in three; and, though they were written in verse, the structure of the versification was left far too much to the caprice of the individual writer. The style of drama then in vogue he adopted, because the Spanish public liked it. The narrow framework it afforded he enlarged to an extraordinary degree, introducing everything that could possibly furnish material for dramatic situations,—the Bible, ancient mythology, the lives of the saints, ancient history, Spanish history, the legends of the Middle Ages, the writings of the Italian novelists, current events, Spanish life in the 17th century. Before him manners and the conditions of persons and characters had been barely sketched; with fuller observation and more careful description he created real types, and gave to each social order the language and drapery appropriate to it. The old comedy was awkward and poor in its versification; he introduced order into the use of all the forms of national poetry, from the old romance couplets to the rarest lyrical combinations borrowed from Italy. Hence he was justified in saying that those who should come after him had only to go on along the path which he had opened up. Calderon notably, whose merit has been much exaggerated, especially since the Germans took him under their protection, is merely a pupil and inferior to his master; at all events, his indebtedness to the latter is enormous and has not as yet been adequately recognized.

Bibliography.—For the life of Lope, see Juan Perez de Montalban's *Fama Posthuma* (4to, Madrid, 1636; reprinted in *Bibl. Rivadeneyra*); La Barrera, *Catálogo del Teatro Antiguo Español*; Von Schack, *Geschichte der dramatischen Literatur und Kunst in Spanien*, vol. ii.; and *Ultimos Amores de Lope de Vega Carpio* (8vo, Madrid, 1876), an extract by Francisco Asenjo Barbieri from an unpublished biography written by La Barrera in connexion with the poet's correspondence with the duke of Sesa. For Lope's literary theories and doctrine of dramatic art, reference may be made to Menéndez-Pelayo, *Historia de las Ideas Estéticas en España*, and to A. Morel-Fatio, *La Comédie Espagnole du XVIIme Siècle* (8vo, Paris, 1885). The *Obras Sueltas* were published by Francisco Cerdá y Rico (21 vols. 4to, Madrid, 1776-79). For the bibliography of the comedies, see La Barrera. The selection of comedies published by Hartzenbusch in four volumes in the *Biblioteca Rivadeneyra* is fairly good; but the same cannot be said of its choice of *Obras Sueltas*. (A. M.-F.)

VEGA, GARCILASO DE LA. See GARCILASO.

VEGETABLE KINGDOM.[2] There is one peculiar factor which enters into the problem of the classification

[1] No las escriví . . . para que de los oydos del teatro se trasladáran á la censura de los aposentos.

[2] The problem of classification being essentially the same in the animal and vegetable kingdoms, the reader is referred to the general discussion of it in the article ANIMAL KINGDOM.

of plants and materially adds to its complexity. It is the polymorphism of the individual: that is, the life-history is usually complex, the individual assuming different forms in various stages of its life-history. Thus, in the great majority of plants there is a well-marked alternation of generations,—an alternation, that is, of a sexual form, the *gametophyte*, with an asexual form, the *sporophyte* (see REPRODUCTION, vol. xx. p. 423). And not only so, but in many cases one or other of these generations presents a number of different forms. Hence the true affinities of any individual cannot be regarded as satisfactorily ascertained unless its life-history is fully known; and, since in most cases the various forms are perfectly separate, and often quite dissimilar, there is difficulty in obtaining all the information necessary for determining the true systematic position of a plant,—a difficulty which has not yet been overcome in very many cases.

Comparatively little light is thrown on the affinities of existing plants by the information which has been accumulated with regard to the extinct fossil forms. In no case can the genealogy of an existing plant be traced as in the case of the horse among animals (see ANIMAL KINGDOM).

The vegetable kingdom is usually divided into the four following sub-kingdoms:—I. THALLOPHYTA; II. BRYOPHYTA; III. PTERIDOPHYTA; IV. PHANEROGAMIA (SPERMAPHYTA).

All of these, except some *Thallophyta*, present a more or less clearly marked alternation of generations. In all cases the more conspicuous form is considered to be "the plant." Thus, in the *Thallophyta* generally the plant is the gametophyte, the sporophyte being comparatively inconspicuous and in many cases merely an appendage on the gametophyte; in the *Bryophyta* likewise the gametophyte is the plant, the sporophyte being an appendage on the gametophyte. In the *Pteridophyta* and in the *Phanerogamia* the plant is the sporophyte, the gametophyte being comparatively inconspicuous. In the *Pteridophyta* the gametophyte is still an independent organism; but in ascending from the lower to the higher forms it becomes more and more reduced. In the *Phanerogamia* the gametophyte is still further reduced and becomes a mere appendage on the sporophyte.

SUB-KINGDOM I. THALLOPHYTA.

This sub-kingdom includes the most lowly organized of plants. They are characterized by the total absence, or the imperfection, of that differentiation of the body into root, stem, and leaf which is so marked a feature in the higher plants, and by the simplicity of their internal structure, especially by the absence of woody vascular tissue. In those *Thallophyta* which present an alternation of generations the gametophyte is generally the more conspicuous, constituting the plant. The gametophyte is commonly capable of producing spores, not only sexually, but also asexually.

The sub-kingdom is naturally divided into two main classes, the ALGÆ or SEA-WEEDS and the FUNGI, to which may be added, as a subsidiary group, the LICHENS. It is becoming usual to regard the *Algæ* and *Fungi* as distinct sub-kingdoms; but it is preferable, as they have so much in common, to continue to regard them as classes of the sub-kingdom *Thallophyta*.

CLASS I. ALGÆ.—There is so much variety in the form and structure of the *Algæ* (see article ALGÆ) that no more precise definition of them can be given than that they are Thallophytes which contain chlorophyll (see PHYSIOLOGY, vol. xix. p. 52). Though they characteristically live in water, this is by no means universally the case, for the natural habitat of many of them is damp soil. All *Algæ* contain chlorophyll, but many of them contain other colouring-matters in addition,—a feature which forms a convenient basis for classification. On this basis the *Algæ* are classified into the four following sub-classes:—

I. **Cyanophyceæ**, containing a bluish colouring-matter, *phycocyanin*, and having a blue-green colour.
II. **Chlorophyceæ**, green *Algæ*, containing no colouring-matter, except chlorophyll and its derivatives.
III. **Phæophyceæ**, containing a yellow or brown colouring-matter, *phycophæin*, and having a brown colour.
IV. **Rhodophyceæ**, containing a red colouring-matter, *phycoerythrin*, and having a red or purple colour.

These four sub-classes are by no means co-extensive. The *Cyanophyceæ* include only very simple forms; the *Chlorophyceæ* and the *Phæophyceæ* include a series of forms from the simplest to the most complex; the *Rhodophyceæ* include only forms which, though their vegetative structure is frequently very simple, are comparatively highly developed as regards their reproductive organs.

Sub-Class I. **Cyanophyceæ**, or Blue-Green *Algæ*.—The body may consist of a single, more or less nearly spherical cell, as in most of the *Chroococcaceæ* (*e.g.*, *Glœocapsa*), or it may be a multicellular layer one cell thick (*e.g.*, *Merismopedia*), or it may be filamentous, consisting of a single row of cells, as in *Rivularia*, *Nostoc*, *Oscillaria*. When the body is filamentous, it sometimes presents a distinction of base and apex, as in *Rivularia*; and it is frequently branched, the branching being either spurious (*e.g.*, *Scytonema*) or true (*e.g.*, *Sirosiphon*). In most cases growth and cell-division go on in all the cells of the body, but in the *Scytonemeæ* and *Sirosiphoneæ* only at the apices. A characteristic feature of the sub-class is the more or less bulky mucilaginous cell-wall which invests the cells and filaments.

Reproduction is mainly effected in a purely vegetative manner. In the unicellular forms each cell-division necessarily leads to the formation of new individuals. In the flattened forms (*e.g.*, *Merismopedia*), when the body reaches a certain limit of size, it simply breaks up into a number of separate portions. In the filamentous forms the body is marked out into segments by inert cells, termed *heterocysts*, which are quite different in appearance from the living cells of the filament. Eventually these segments, termed *hormogonia*, separate, and, escaping from the mucilaginous matrix, develop by growth and cell-division into new individuals. In many cases special reproductive cells, *spores*, are developed. Each spore is formed from a single cell of the body, which surrounds itself with a thick firm wall of its own. It is probable that ciliated spores, *zoospores*, are produced, but the existing observations on this point are inconclusive. There is no evidence of the existence of any form of sexual reproduction in this group.

The *Cyanophyceæ* are divided into a number of orders:—

Order 1. *Chroococcaceæ*.	Order 4. *Rivulariaceæ*.
,, 2. *Nostocaceæ*.	,, 5. *Scytonemeæ*.
,, 3. *Oscillariaceæ*.	,, 6. *Sirosiphoneæ* (*Stigonemeæ*).

It is doubtful to what extent these orders really represent distinct forms; for there is some evidence that certain *Cyanophyceæ* assume the different forms characteristic of several of these orders at various stages of their development and under various external conditions: in other words, some, at least, of the *Cyanophyceæ* are polymorphic, and this necessarily renders their classification difficult.

The *Cyanophyceæ* resemble the *Schizomycetes* (*Fungi*) in many respects, as, for instance, in their general structure, in their simple vegetative reproduction and in their spore formation, in the production of a bulky mucilaginous matrix, and in their polymorphism. On these grounds they are frequently placed along with the *Schizomycetes* in a distinct class under the name *Schizophyta*. But this arrangement does not seem to secure any special advantage. It is simpler to regard the *Cyanophyceæ* and the *Schizomycetes* as parallel groups, the one belonging to the *Algæ*, the other to the *Fungi*.

Sub-Class II. **Chlorophyceæ**.—The body may consist of a single cell (*e.g.*, *Protococcoideæ*), or it may be multinucleate and unseptate (*e.g.*, *Siphoneæ*), or septate and therefore multicellular (*e.g.*, *Characeæ*). It presents all degrees of morphological differentiation: thus, it may be spherical (as in *Hæmatococcus* and in *Volvox*), or flattened (as in *Ulva*), or filamentous (as in *Spirogyra*, *Ulothrix*, &c.), with a differentiation of root and shoot (as in *Œdogonium*); or it may even present rudimentary differentiation into stem, leaf, and root, as in the *Siphoneæ* (*e.g.*, *Caulerpa*) and *Characeæ*. The structure of the body is peculiar in the *Hydrodictyeæ*, being composed of a number of originally separate cells; such a body is termed a *cœnobium*.

Vegetative multiplication, though not universal, is not uncommon in this sub-class. Reproduction by means of asexually-produced spores is very general, and the spores are commonly ciliated zoospores. A sexual process has been observed in members of every order of this sub-class. It consists either in the fusion of similar sexual cells, when it is said to be *isogamous*; or a large non-motile female cell (oosphere) is fertilized by a small motile male cell (antherozoid), when it is said to be *oogamous*. The isogamous process usually takes place between free-swimming ciliated cells (*planogametes*); but in the group of the *Conjugatæ* it takes place between gametes which are not set free into the water and are not ciliated (see REPRODUCTION). In those *Chlorophyceæ* in which both sexual and asexual spore-formation occurs, there is generally a distinction of sexual and asexual forms, so that the life-history presents an alternation of generations. Thus, in *Acetabularia* the plant is the sporophyte, producing asexually non-motile spores, which on germination give rise to sexual reproductive cells or gametes. Each of these spores represents a sexual form or gametophyte. Again, in *Coleochæte* the plant is the gametophyte, producing the sexual organs, the sporophyte being represented by a small flattened plate of cells, developed from the fertilized female cell or oospore, which never produces any sexual organs, but only spores.

The *Chlorophyceæ* may be classified as follows:—

Order 1. Protococcoideæ.—Unicellular plants; the body frequently spherical and unattached, but presenting in some forms a distinction of base and apex, and then it is attached by the base. Reproduction by vegetative division, or by zoospores, or by a sexual process, the sexual cells being similar planogametes. This order may be divided into two families,—the *Protococcaceæ* and the *Palmellaceæ*, the distinction being that in the latter the cell-walls are swollen and mucilaginous, so that the cells are held together, whereas in the former the cells are free. Vegetative multiplication by division is universal in the *Palmellaceæ*, but is commonly wanting in the *Protococcaceæ*.

Order 2. Volvocineæ.—Unicellular or multicellular plants; body free-swimming by means of cilia, either spherical or a flat plate.

a. Isogamous forms: *Pandorina*, *Stephanosphæra* (spherical), *Gonium* (flattened).
b. Oogamous forms: *Volvox*, *Eudorina*, *Chlamydomonas* (unicellular).

Order 3. Hydrodictyeæ.—Multicellular plants; body unattached, a net (*Hydrodictyon*) or a flat plate (*Pediastrum*), formed by the combination of originally separate cells (a *cœnobium*). The sexual process is isogamous.

Order 4. Siphoneæ.—Unseptate multinucleate plants; body vesicular and unbranched, or filamentous and branched, assuming most various forms, presenting distinction of base and apex, attached by base; sometimes (*Caulerpa*) presenting differentiation into root, stem, and leaf. The sexual process is isogamous or oogamous.

a. Isogamous forms: *Codieæ*, *Dasycladeæ*, *Caulerpeæ*, *Botrydieæ*.
b. Oogamous forms: *Vaucheriaceæ*.

Order 5. Confervoideæ.—Septate multicellular plants (body unicellular in some Desmids); cells uni- or multi-nucleate; body filamentous, branched or unbranched, sometimes presenting distinction of root and shoot, and then attached by the root, or a flat plate or hollow tube of cells. The sexual process is isogamous or oogamous.

a. Isogamous forms—
- α. Gametes not free-swimming or ciliated: *Conjugatæ* (including *Desmidieæ*, *Mesocarpeæ*, *Zygnemeæ*).
- β. Gametes free-swimming and ciliated.
  - Body filamentous, unbranched: *Ulothricaceæ*.
  - Body filamentous, branched: *Cladophoreæ*, *Chætophoreæ*.
  - Body a flat or tubular layer of cells: *Ulvaceæ*.

b. Oogamous forms: body filamentous—
- α. Sexual organs undifferentiated: *Sphæropleæ*.
- β. Sexual organs differentiated.
  - *Œdogonieæ*; body unbranched (except *Bulbochæte*); oogonium without trichogyne; sporophyte, a single cell (oospore).
  - *Coleochæteæ*; body branched; oogonium with trichogyne; sporophyte multicellular.

Order 6. Characeæ.—Multicellular plants; body presenting differentiation into leaf, stem, and root. There is no asexual production of spores; the sexual process is oogamous, the sexual organs being highly differentiated.

The distinction of the genera, and to some extent also that of the orders, is rendered difficult in many cases by polymorphism. For instance, it has been ascertained that many plants which have been referred to the *Protococcoideæ* are simply forms of some of the *Confervoideæ*, *Siphoneæ*, &c.; and similarly some of the *Ulvaceæ* have Ulothricoid forms. Still, there can be no doubt that each of the above orders includes some autonomous forms.

With regard to the affinities and phylogeny of the orders of *Chlorophyceæ*, the *Protoccoideæ* must be taken as the starting-point from which the other orders have sprung, their evolution having taken place in various directions. Beginning with the simple spherical *Protococcaceæ*, the origin of the *Volvocineæ* from these by cell-division can be readily traced through *Chlamydomonas*, the higher forms being simply motile multicellular *Protococcaceæ*. Closely allied to the *Volvocineæ* are the *Hydrodictyeæ*. The *Siphoneæ* can be readily traced back to the simplest *Protococcaceæ* through the attached *Protococcaceæ*, such as *Characium*. The *Confervoideæ* are probably also derived from the *Protococcaceæ*; and a certain relationship between some members of this order—the *Cladophoreæ*—and the *Siphoneæ* is indicated by the multinucleate cells of the former. Thus, *Valonia*, which is septate, and therefore really belongs to the *Confervoideæ*, closely resembles some of the *Siphoneæ* in its general habit. The phylogeny of the *Characeæ* is obscure, but it is probable that they have sprung from the *Confervoideæ*, possibly from the *Cladophoreæ*. It is of interest to note that the large cells of the *Characeæ* become multinucleate.

Sub-Class III. **Phæophyceæ.**—The form of the body is very various; it may consist of a single cell; when multicellular it may be filamentous and branched, or a flattened expansion, or cylindrical or vesicular, hollow or solid. It presents also various degrees of morphological differentiation: in some forms it is quite undifferentiated; in others it presents a differentiation of base and apex, and is then attached by the base; in others it presents indications of differentiation into root, stem, and leaf. Vegetative multiplication is common only in the lowest forms; in the higher it occurs in some cases, and is effected by the abstriction of modified members of the parent, termed *gemmæ*. The existence of a sexual process has been ascertained in several forms; but in many others further investigation is required to determine its presence or absence. In those forms in which it occurs it may be either isogamous or oogamous; the isogamous process may take place between free-swimming gametes, or between gametes which are not free-swimming or ciliated. The life-history of the plants of this group is imperfectly known; but it has been ascertained that in some there is, and in others there is not, an alternation of generations.

The *Phæophyceæ* may be classified as follows:—

Order 1. Diatomaceæ.—Unicellular plants, either free, or connected into filaments or masses by mucilage. Reproduction, vegetative by division or by means of asexually-produced spores (*auxospores*); or sexual isogamous by the fusion of non-ciliated gametes. The cell-wall is impregnated with silica.

Order 2. Syngeneticæ.—Body unicellular, the cells being held together by mucilage. Reproduction by division and by asexually-produced spores. The order includes the two forms, *Chromophyton* and *Hydrurus*. The former is distinguished by being unattached and by the motility of its spores, which have a single long cilium. *Hydrurus* grows attached, and the spores are not motile.

Order 3. Phæosporeæ.—Multicellular plants; the body is filamentous and branched or flattened, always presenting differentiation of base and apex, and in some cases more or less well-marked differentiation into root, stem, and leaf, usually attached by the base. Reproduction, vegetative by gemmæ or by means of asexually-produced zoospores, or by a sexual process which is essentially isogamous, the gametes being ciliated, but in the higher forms tending to become oogamous. The principal families of the *Phæosporeæ* are *Ectocarpeæ*, *Sphacelarieæ*, *Mesoglœaceæ*, *Desmarestieæ*, *Scytosiphoneæ*, *Cutleriaceæ*, and *Laminarieæ*. The filamentous type of structure obtains in the *Ectocarpeæ*, *Sphacelarieæ*, *Mesoglœaceæ*, and *Desmarestieæ*. The filaments may consist of single rows of cells (*monosiphonous*), as in most *Ectocarpeæ*, or of several rows of cells (*polysiphonous*), as in the *Mesoglœaceæ*; or they may be polysiphonous with a more or less well-developed cortical layer, as in the *Sphacelarieæ*, in which case there is also a large apical cell. The structure of the *Desmarestieæ* (*e.g.*, *Desmarestia* and *Arthrocladia*) is similar to that of the *Sphacelarieæ*, but the growing point is not apical, as in the *Sphacelarieæ*, but intercalary, as in the *Ectocarpeæ*. In some of these forms (*e.g.*, *Cladostephus* among the *Sphacelarieæ*) there is an indication of the differentiation of the shoot into stem and leaf. The type of structure obtaining in the *Scytosiphoneæ*, *Cutleriaceæ*, and *Laminarieæ* is that of a flattened expansion of parenchymatous tissue, though in the *Laminarieæ* there is a certain degree of histological differentiation, as is indicated by the presence of elongated cells forming structures resembling the sieve-tubes of the vascular plants. In some of the *Scytosiphoneæ* there is a large internal cavity, so that the body presents a cylindrical or vesicular form. Vegetative reproduction by gemmæ is only known in the *Sphacelarieæ*. Reproduction by means of asexually-produced spores (zoospores) is known to occur in the majority of the *Phæosporeæ*, but it has not yet been detected in some forms (*e.g.*, *Arthrocladia*, *Scytosiphon*, *Phyllitis*, *Colpomenia*). The asexual organs are unilocular sporangia. The sexual organs (*gametangia*) are multilocular. They have been found in all the families except the *Laminarieæ*, but not yet in all the genera (*e.g.*, *Asperococcus*). The gametangia are all quite similar, except in the *Cutleriaceæ* and in *Tilopteris* (a genus allied to *Desmarestia*), in which also the gametes differ in appearance. A sexual process has only been observed in a few species of *Ectocarpeæ* and *Scytosiphoneæ* (*Ectocarpus siliculosus* and *E. pusillus*, *Giraudia sphacelarioides*, *Scytosiphon lomentarius*), and in the *Cutleriaceæ*. A full account of the sexual process in these forms is given in the article REPRODUCTION, vol. xx. p. 425.

Order 4. Dictyotaceæ.—Body multicellular, thalloid, flattened, ribbon-like, as in *Dictyota, Phycopteris, Dictyopteris*, or broader and fan-shaped, as in *Taonia, Padina, Zonaria*; usually attached by the base, but by root-hairs developed on the under surface in *Zonaria*. Asexual reproduction by spores, formed four (*tetraspores*) in each unilocular sporangium; spores not motile. Though a sexual process has not been observed, there are apparently male and female organs,—antheridia and oogonia. The supposed male cells are set free and are not motile; the supposed female cells are not set free. The sporangia and the sexual organs are borne on distinct individuals, and in some genera (*e.g.*, *Dictyota, Taonia*) the male and female organs are borne on distinct individuals.

Order 5. Fucaceæ.—Body multicellular; generally differentiated into root and shoot; shoot usually thalloid, cylindrical, or flattened, but differentiated into stem and leaves in *Sargassum*. No asexual production of spores. Sexual organs antheridia or oogonia. Male cells numerous, set free, ciliated; female cells (oospheres) either one (*Pycnophycus, Himanthalia, Cystoseira, Sargassum*), two (*Pelvetia*), four (*Ozothallia*), or eight (*Fucus*) in an oogonium, set free, not motile.

The life-history of the *Phæophyceæ* is in most cases imperfectly known. In the *Fucaceæ*, since there is no asexual formation of spores, there is no alternation of generations, and there is no indication of any other kind of polymorphism. In those forms in which the sexual and asexual organs are restricted to separate individuals, as in *Cladostephus* (*Sphacelarieæ*), in the *Cutleriaceæ*, and in the *Dictyotaceæ*, there may be an alternation of generations. In the *Cutleriaceæ* it is, in fact, highly probable. In the one genus, *Zanardinia*, the two generations are similar, differing only in the nature of their reproductive organs. In *Cutleria*, the other genus, the two generations are dissimilar, the form known as *Cutleria* being the gametophyte, whereas the sporophyte appears to be a form which has been regarded as a distinct genus, under the name of *Aglaozonia*. In some genera of *Dictyotaceæ* (*Taonia, Padina, Dictyopteris*) there is a further indication of polymorphism, in that the spore (whether tetraspore or oospore) produces on germination a spherical or cylindrical protonematoid body, from which spring the shoots of the characteristic form.

Since the life-history of the *Phæophyceæ* is so imperfectly known, the relations of the various orders cannot be accurately determined. The *Diatomaceæ* and the *Syngeneticæ* are apparently isolated groups. The families of the *Phæosporeæ* form a series leading from the simple isogamous *Ectocarpeæ* through the *Cutleriaceæ* to the oogamous *Fucaceæ*. There are also points of resemblance in the vegetative parts between some of the *Scytosiphoneæ* and the *Laminarieæ*.

Sub-Class IV. **Rhodophyceæ.**—This sub-class includes the single order *Florideæ*.

Order Florideæ.—Multicellular plants; body flattened or filamentous; when filamentous, either monosiphonous or polysiphonous, with or without a cortex; thalloid, or with indications of differentiation into stem and leaf. Asexual reproduction, by means of unciliated naked spores, which are usually tetraspores (wanting in *Lemanea*), produced in unilocular sporangia. Sexual reproduction by means of male and female organs, termed antheridia and procarpia; the procarpium is generally multicellular, but sometimes unicellular (*Bangiaceæ, Nemalieæ*), is always closed, and generally consists of two parts, the *carpogonium* or sporogenous portion and the *trichogyne* or receptive portion. The male cells are non-motile and have a cell-wall (*spermatia*); there is no differentiated female cell in the procarpium. After fertilization the carpogenous cell (or cells) divides to form the mother-cells of spores, and each mother-cell gives rise to a single naked spore (*carpospore*), which is not ciliated and is usually non-motile; in the *Bangiaceæ* the carpospores exhibit amœboid movements for a time. The group of sporogenous cells formed from the fertilized carpogenous cell (or cells) is termed a *cystocarp*; in many cases these cells become surrounded by an investment developed from the adjacent vegetative tissue. The structure of the cystocarp is very simple in the *Bangiaceæ*, consisting only of eight spore mother-cells. The principal orders of the *Florideæ* are *Bangiaceæ, Lemaneaceæ, Nemalieæ, Ceramiaceæ, Corallineæ, Rhodomelaceæ, Cryptonemiaceæ, Rhodymeniaceæ, Wrangeliaceæ, Squamariaceæ, Sphærococcaceæ*.

With regard to the life-history of the *Florideæ*, it is generally considered to present a well-marked alternation of generations, the plant being the gametophyte, the fructification (cystocarp) formed in consequence of fertilization being the sporophyte. Further polymorphism has been detected in the genera *Lemanea* and *Batrachospermum*. Here the carpospore does not at once give rise to the plant, but to a filamentous or flattened body, which in *Batrachospermum* reproduces itself by spores, and from which the parent form springs as lateral branches. This filamentous form appears to be identical with species of the genus *Chantransia*; it is therefore known as the *Chantransia*-form.

Mutual Affinities and Phylogeny of Sub-Classes of Algæ.

Comparison of the four sub-classes shows that, whereas the *Chlorophyceæ* and the *Phæophyceæ* present two fairly complete series of parallel forms, ranging from unicellular undifferentiated to multicellular more or less highly differentiated organisms, the *Cyanophyceæ* consist only of comparatively simple forms in which sexual reproduction is unknown, and the *Rhodophyceæ* of comparatively complex forms in all of which a sexual process obtains. It has been suggested by Cohn, Berthold, and others that there is a close relation between the lowest *Rhodophyceæ* (*Bangia*) and the higher filamentous *Cyanophyceæ* (*Scytonemeæ, Sirosiphoneæ*), and that possibly the latter may have been derived from the former. On this view the *Cyanophyceæ* and the *Rhodophyceæ*, taken together, constitute a series which is on a level with those of the *Chlorophyceæ* and of the *Phæophyceæ*. On comparing these three series together, it will be observed that they present a general correspondence, in that the main types of form are to be found in all. Thus, the *Chroococcaceæ* among the *Cyanophyceæ*, the *Palmellaceæ* among the *Chlorophyceæ*, and the *Syngeneticæ* among the *Phæophyceæ* are corresponding groups; similarly, the *Confervoideæ* among the *Chlorophyceæ* correspond to the *Ectocarpeæ* and other filamentous *Phæophyceæ*, and to various forms of *Rhodophyceæ*, such as *Bangia, Porphyra, Griffithsia*, and *Callithamnion*; and *Chara* (*Chlorophyceæ*) resembles, at least in its vegetative structure, such forms as *Cladostephus* (*Phæophyceæ*) and *Polysiphonia* (*Rhodophyceæ*). There are, however, forms belonging to some of the sub-classes which have no representatives in others. Thus the orders *Siphoneæ, Volvocineæ, Hydrodictyeæ*, belonging to the *Chlorophyceæ*, are unrepresented in the other sub-classes, and this is true also of the *Fucaceæ* and the *Laminarieæ* among the *Phæophyceæ*. The Conjugate *Chlorophyceæ* also form a peculiar group, the only corresponding forms being the *Diatomaceæ* (*Phæophyceæ*), which present many points of resemblance to the *Desmidieæ*.

With regard to the phylogeny of the *Algæ*, the possible derivation of the *Rhodophyceæ* from the *Cyanophyceæ* has already been pointed out. Assuming this, there are three series of *Algæ* closely allied in their origin, in each of which evolution has proceeded on more or less divergent lines, thus leading to the development of a number of corresponding forms in the three series. It is not impossible that the *Chlorophyceæ* and the *Phæophyceæ* may also have sprung from the *Cyanophyceæ*, not, like the *Rhodophyceæ*, from the higher forms, but from the lower. But, if the *Cyanophyceæ* be regarded, not as primitive, but as degenerate, forms—and for this view there are good grounds—then the simpler *Chlorophyceæ* are probably to be regarded as the forms from which the others have been derived.

Literature of Algæ.—Special papers referred to:—Cohn, *Beiträge zur Physiologie der Phycochromaceen*, 1867; Berthold, "Die Bangiaceen," in *Fauna und Flora des Golfes von Neapel*, 1882; Zopf, *Zur Morphologie der Spaltpflanzen*, Leipsic, 1882; Hansgirg, *Physiologische und Algologische Studien*, Prague, 1887. Of general works consult—Harvey, *Phycologia Britannica*; Cooke, *British Fresh water Algæ*, London, 1882; Thuret and Bornet, *Notes Algologiques*, i., ii., 1882-86, and *Études Phycologiques*, 1878; Falkenberg, "Algen," in Schenk's *Handbuch der Botanik*, ii., Breslau, 1881-84; Hauck, "Die Meeresalgen," in Rabenhorst's *Kryptogamen-Flora*, 2d ed., Leipsic, 1885; Goebel, *Outlines of Classification and Special Morphology*, Oxford, 1886. These works contain references to all the more important isolated papers on the *Algæ*.

CLASS II. FUNGI.—In view of the description of these plants given in the article FUNGUS (*q.v.*), it is unnecessary to define them here further than as Thallophytes which are devoid of chlorophyll.

The classification followed here differs in detail from that given in the previous article. It is as follows:—

Sub-Class I. **Myxomycetes.**
,, II. **Schizomycetes.**
,, III. **Phycomycetes.**
a. Zygomycetes. — Order 1. *Chytridiaceæ.* ,, 2. *Mucorini.* ,, 3. *Entomophthoreæ.* ,, 4. *Ustilagineæ.*
b. Oomycetes. — Order 1. *Ancylisteæ.* ,, 2. *Peronosporeæ.* ,, 3. *Saprolegnieæ.*
,, IV. **Ascomycetes.**
Order 1. *Gymnoasceæ.* Order 2. *Pyrenomycetes.* Order 3. *Discomycetes.*
,, V. **Æcidiomycetes.**
Order 1. *Uredineæ.*
,, VI. **Basidiomycetes.**
Order 1. *Tremellini.* Order 2. *Hymenomycetes.* Order 3. *Gasteromycetes.*

The chief points of difference between this classification and that given in the article FUNGUS, besides the introduction of some additional orders, are the division of the *Phycomycetes* into *Zygomycetes* and *Oomycetes*, the removal of the *Ustilagineæ* from the *Uredineæ* to the *Phycomycetes*, and the inclusion of the *Erysipheæ* and *Tuberaceæ* in the *Pyrenomycetes*, this order being considered as containing all the *Ascomycetes* which have well-developed, but more or less completely closed, apothecia (perithecia),—in a word, all *Ascomycetes* which are neither *Gymnoasceæ* nor *Discomycetes*. The division of the *Phycomycetes* into *Zygomycetes* and *Oomycetes* is necessary in order to distinguish those forms which are isogamous, and in which the sexual process is one of conjugation (see REPRODUCTION), from those which are oogamous, and in which the sexual process is one of fertilization, the former constituting the group *Zygomycetes*, the latter the group *Oomycetes*. The change in position of the *Ustil-*

agineæ is made in accordance with the views of recent writers, such as De Bary and Brefeld, the *Ustilagineæ* being regarded as sexually degenerate *Zygomycetes*.

A brief description of the newly introduced orders, namely, the *Chytridiaceæ*, the *Entomophthoreæ*, the *Ancylisteæ*, and the *Gymnoasceæ*, may be given. The *Chytridiaceæ* are extremely simple *Fungi*, consisting in some forms of a single spherical cell and in others of a small mycelium. The *Entomophthoreæ* have a well-developed mycelium, which, unlike that of most *Phycomycetes*, is septate. The *Ancylisteæ* are merely the simplest forms of the *Oomycetes*. The *Gymnoasceæ* are characterized by the simple structure of their fructification, the asci (or, in some cases, the single ascus) not being surrounded by an investment of sterile tissue. This group includes typical forms, such as *Gymnoascus* and *Eremascus*, as well as aberrant forms, such as *Exoascus*, *Saccharomyces*, &c.

Mutual Affinities and Phylogeny of Sub-Classes of Fungi.

The *Myxomycetes* and the *Schizomycetes* are so peculiar that they cannot be connected in any way with the other sub-classes of *Fungi*. Beginning, then, with the *Zygomycetes*, there can be no doubt that the *Chytridiaceæ* are closely connected with the *Mucorini* by such forms as *Polyphagus* and *Zygochytrium*, and with the *Ancylisteæ* among the *Oomycetes*. On the other hand, they are connected with the *Ustilagineæ* (especially *Protomyces*) by *Cladochytrium*. The *Entomophthoreæ* seem to be most nearly related to the *Mucorini*. The *Ancylisteæ* are closely related to the *Peronosporeæ* (especially *Pythium*), and these again to the *Saprolegnieæ*. Coming now to the *Ascomycetes*, there is an obvious similarity between the simpler *Gymnoasceæ* and the *Mucorini*. Thus in *Eremascus* the sexual organs are quite similar, and the sexual process is one of conjugation, as in the *Mucorini*; but there is this difference, that the product of the sexual process in *Eremascus* is an ascus, whereas in the *Mucorini* it is a zygospore (see REPRODUCTION). Those *Ascomycetes* which, like *Pyronema*, have differentiated sexual organs, show some resemblance to the *Oomycetes*. The *Uredineæ* appear to be closely connected with the *Ascomycetes* on the one hand, the æcidium being homologous with the apothecium, and on the other hand with the *Tremellini* among the *Basidiomycetes*, through the Tremelloid *Uredineæ* (*Leptopuccinieæ*), which have lost their æcidia, possessing only asexually-produced spores (teleutospores). The *Hymenomycetes* and the *Gasteromycetes* appear to form two parallel series starting from the *Tremellini*.

In attempting to express these relations in terms of phylogeny, the first question which arises is as to whether or not the *Chytridiaceæ* are to be taken as the primitive forms. It is possible to regard them, not as primitive forms, but as degraded *Mucorini*, their degradation being due to their aquatic habit; but there are no conclusive grounds for this assumption. Then there is the question as to the origin of the *Ascomycetes*. De Bary inclines to the opinion that they are derived from the *Oomycetes* (especially *Peronospora*), on account of the similarity of the sexual organs of such *Ascomycetes* as *Podosphæra* to those of the *Peronosporeæ*. But how, on this view, is the development of *Ascomycetes* with similar sexual organs to be accounted for? It seems more reasonable to trace the *Ascomycetes* back through *Eremascus* to the *Mucorini*, and to assume that the differentiation of the sexual organs arose in the Ascomycetous series. The following scheme expresses the phylogeny of the *Fungi* as suggested in the foregoing remarks.

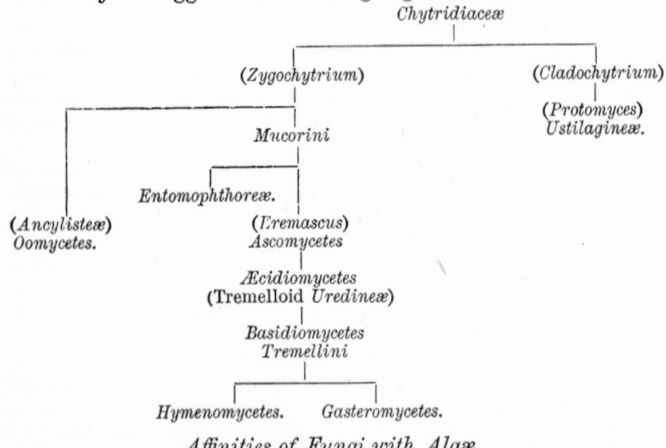

Affinities of Fungi with Algæ.

With the exception of the *Basidiomycetes*, the sub-classes of *Fungi* present resemblances to various forms of *Algæ*, as might be expected, for the *Fungi* must have sprung from the *Algæ*. The *Myxomycetes* resemble the *Hydrodictyeæ*, in that the body (plasmodium) is a cœnobium, formed by the aggregation of originally separate cells. The similarity of the *Schizomycetes* to the *Cyanophyceæ* has been already mentioned (p. 125). The *Phycomycetes* resemble the *Siphoneæ* in their typically unseptate multinucleate structure; but the *Mucorini* approach the Conjugate *Algæ*, and the *Oomycetes* the oogamous *Siphoneæ*, in the sexual process. The simpler *Chytridiaceæ* closely resemble the *Protococcaceæ* in their general form, as also in the production of ciliated zoospores. The *Ascomycetes*, especially those in which male cells (spermatia) are formed, and probably also the *Æcidiomycetes*, resemble the *Rhodophyceæ* in many important features. In both groups the female organ contains no distinctly differentiated female cell (oosphere); and the effect of fertilization is to cause the female organ to grow into a sporogenous fructification (apothecium, cystocarp), which constitutes the asexual generation or sporophyte in the life-history.

With regard to the derivation of the *Fungi* from the *Algæ*, it appears that there are at least two distinct origins. The *Schizomycetes* doubtless arose from the *Cyanophyceæ*; but, as pointed out above, the *Schizomycetes* cannot be regarded as having given rise to higher forms of *Fungi*. These sprang independently from the *Algæ*; and probably the *Chytridiaceæ* were derived from the *Protococcaceæ*; and from the *Chytridiaceæ* the higher forms were developed as indicated in the above sketch of the phylogeny of the *Fungi*, the evolution of the *Fungi* proceeding along much the same lines as that of the *Algæ*, and thus giving rise to forms which have their representatives in the *Algæ*, and terminating in the *Basidiomycetes*, which are altogether and peculiarly Fungal. The origin of the *Chytridiaceæ* from the *Protococcaceæ* is suggested by the fact that many of the latter are "endophytic": that is, they inhabit the tissues of higher plants; and the *Chytridiaceæ* may be regarded as *Protococcaceæ* which have become truly parasitic, and have consequently lost their chlorophyll.

Additional Literature to Fungi.—De Bary and Woronin, *Beiträge zur Morphologie und Physiologie der Pilze*, 4th and 5th series, 1881-82; Brefeld, *Untersuchungen*, parts v.-vii., 1883-88; De Bary, *Comparative Morphology and Biology of the Fungi*, Oxford, 1887.

SUBSIDIARY GROUP, LICHENES.—As pointed out in the article FUNGUS, a Lichen is a compound organism consisting of a *Fungus* and an *Alga* living symbiotically. In that article only those Lichens are considered in which the *Fungus* belongs to the *Ascomycetes*; but Lichens are now known in which the *Fungus* belongs to the *Basidiomycetes*.

The Lichens may be classified as follows:—

Ascolichenes (Ascomycetous Lichens).
1. *Discolichenes* (Discomycetous Lichens).
2. *Pyrenolichenes* (Pyrenomycetous Lichens).

Basidiolichenes (Basidiomycetous Lichens).
1. *Hymenolichenes* (Hymenomycetous Lichens).
2. *Gasterolichenes* (Gasteromycetous Lichens).

Literature.—Massee, "On Gasterolichenes," in *Phil. Trans.*, vol. clxxviii., 1887.

SUB-KINGDOM II. BRYOPHYTA (*Muscineæ*).

The *Bryophyta* may be characterized as plants which present a definite alternation of generations, the plant being the gametophyte and the fructification or sporogonium the sporophyte. The sporophyte is not independent, but remains permanently attached to the gametophyte. The shoot of the gametophyte is sometimes thalloid; but more frequently it is differentiated into stem and leaf. The shoot of the sporophyte is not differentiated into stem and leaf, though there is in some cases an indication of such differentiation. The gametophyte commonly reproduces its like by means of gemmæ; the female organ is an archegonium. The *Bryophyta* are divided into two classes—the HEPATICÆ or LIVERWORTS and the MUSCI or MOSSES. (For details see MUSCINEÆ.)

Mutual Affinities and Phylogeny of Mosses and Liverworts.

In consequence of the well-marked alternation of generations in these classes, it is essential to trace their resemblances in both generations.

a. Gametophyte (plant).—The higher Liverworts (foliose *Jungermannieæ*) resemble the Mosses in that the shoot is differentiated into stem and leaf; but there is this general difference, that the shoot of these Liverworts has dorsi-ventral symmetry, whereas that of the Mosses has radial symmetry. The connecting form is afforded by *Haplomitrium*, which alone among the foliose Liverworts has radial symmetry.

b. Sporophyte (sporogonium).—The main differences between the sporogonium of the Liverworts and that of the Mosses are these: the structure of the sporogonium is simpler in the Liverworts than it is in the Mosses; in the former it usually has no columella and produces elaters, whereas in the latter a columella is always present, and there are no elaters. In the Liverworts the sporogonium remains enclosed in the enlarged venter of the archegonium (calyptra) until the spores are ripe, but in most Mosses the developing sporogonium bursts the calyptra at an early stage. A connecting form is afforded by the sporogonium of *Anthoceros* (Liverwort), which has a columella and bears stomata like the sporogonia of the Mosses, and in which the elaters are rudimentary. *Sphagnum* and *Archidium* among Mosses resemble the Liverworts in that the sporogonium is enclosed in the calyptra until near maturity.

Although there are so many points of resemblance between them, there is no evidence to show that the Mosses and Liverworts form one continuous series. This might perhaps be assumed if the gametophyte alone were considered; but it cannot when the sporophyte is taken into account as well. The more important features in the comparative morphology of the sporophyte are as follows. Taking first the Liverworts, in the *Ricciew* proper (*Riccia, Oxymitra*) both the epibasal and hypobasal halves of the oospore (fertilized female cell) form sporogenous tissue. In the allied *Corsinieæ*, the *Marchantieæ*, and the *Anthoceroteæ* the epibasal half alone gives rise to sporogenous tissue, the hypobasal half forming an organ of absorption and attachment which is the *true foot*. In the *Jungermannieæ*, likewise, the sporogenous tissue is developed entirely from the epibasal half of the oospore, which also gives rise to the seta or stalk of the sporogonium; but the hypobasal half is aborted and gives rise to only a rudimentary foot; in some foliose forms a *false foot* is formed by a dilatation of the base of the seta. In the Mosses there is not in any family such a simple sporophyte as that of the *Ricciew* among the Liverworts; but there are forms which present the same morphological difference as that which in the Liverworts distinguishes the *Marchantieæ* and the *Anthoceroteæ*, on the one hand, from these *Jungermannieæ*, on the other. Thus, among Mosses the *Sphagnaceæ*, *Andreæaceæ*, and *Phascaceæ* have a true foot, whereas in the *Bryineæ* there is a spurious foot at the base of the seta, as in some *Jungermannieæ*. Taking all the foregoing facts into account, it is clear that the *Ricciew* are the most primitive of existing *Muscineæ*, and it is probably from them that the true Mosses, as well as the other Liverworts, have been derived.

The following phylogeny may be suggested. As regards the Liverworts, there can be no doubt that the *Marchantieæ* are to be traced back through the *Corsinieæ* to the *Ricciew*, and it is probable that, as Leitgeb points out, the frondose *Jungermannieæ* were derived from the *Corsinieæ* through the *Riellew*. With regard to the *Anthoceroteæ*, Leitgeb seems to suggest that they may have been derived through *Notothylas* from the *Jungermannieæ*; but in opposition to this must be set the difference between the two groups as regards the morphology of the foot. Probably the *Anthoceroteæ* arose independently from the *Corsinieæ*. The Mosses are to be traced back to the *Anthoceroteæ*, on account of the general similarity in the structure of the sporogonium. The genus *Anthoceros* shows its special relation to the *Sphagnaceæ* in the development of the sporogenous cells from the amphithecium, whereas the genus *Notothylas* resembles the other Mosses in that the sporogenous cells are developed from the endothecium. The following scheme will serve to illustrate these remarks.

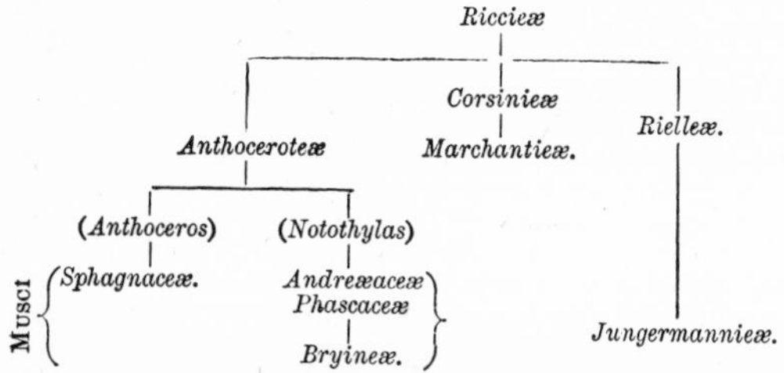

The phylogeny of the *Muscineæ* can be traced with exceptional clearness in both generations. With regard to the gametophyte, it must be remembered (see MUSCINEÆ) that at its first development from the spore it is a *protonema*, which is either filamentous, as usually in Mosses, or a flattened expansion, as generally in Liverworts, the shoot which bears the sexual organs being a secondary development on the protonema. Both these forms of protonema bear a striking resemblance to various Confervoid *Chlorophyceæ*, and there can be little doubt that it is from this group that the *Muscineæ* have arisen. This view is supported by the close resemblance of the simple sporophyte of *Riccia* among the *Muscineæ* to that of *Coleochæte* among the Confervoid *Chlorophyceæ*. There is, however, this difference, that in *Riccia* the cells resulting from the division of the oospore are differentiated into an external sterile layer, forming the wall of the capsule, and an internal mass of sporogenous cells, whereas in *Coleochæte* all the cells are sporogenous.

SUB-KINGDOM III. PTERIDOPHYTA (VASCULAR CRYPTOGAMS).

In these plants the gametophyte is a filamentous or tuberous, or more commonly a membranous, flattened *prothallium*, exhibiting no differentiation into stem and leaf. The sexual organs are antheridia and archegonia, as in the *Muscineæ*. The sporophyte becomes quite independent of the gametophyte, constituting the plant. The shoot is always differentiated into stem and leaf, and the tissues are highly differentiated.

The sub-kingdom is divided into three classes,—FILICINÆ, EQUISETINÆ, LYCOPODINÆ.

Each of these classes includes two series of forms,—the *homosporous*, in which all the spores are alike, and the *heterosporous*, in which the spores are of two kinds, namely, large spores (*macrospores*) and small spores (*microspores*). On germination the spore of the homosporous forms gives rise to a well-developed prothallium, which becomes quite free from the spore, and usually bears both antheridia (male) and archegonia (female). The spores of the heterosporous forms give rise on germination to comparatively inconspicuous prothallia, which remain connected with the spores, and bear either exclusively male or exclusively female organs. Thus, in the heterosporous forms the gametophyte is represented by a male and a female organism, the former being much the smaller. The male prothallium is always developed from a microspore, the female prothallium from a macrospore (see REPRODUCTION).

CLASS 1. FILICINÆ.—The *Filicinæ* are characterized by having relatively large and few leaves. The spore-bearing or fertile leaves (*sporophylls*) are generally similar to the foliage leaves, and are not aggregated on special shoots, so as to form flowers. The embryo sporophyte has no suspensor; but it has generally (except in *Salvinia*) a primary root.

Series A. **Homosporous Filicinæ.**—This series consists of the sub-class *Filices*, which includes the Ferns. It seems to be certain that all existing Ferns are homosporous, and apparently all the known fossil forms are homosporous also, though it is not impossible that there may have been heterosporous *Filices*. The orders of existing Ferns are arranged in two categories, according to the mode of development of the sporangia.

Leptosporangiate Filices: the sporangium is developed from a single epidermal cell:—

Order 1. *Hymenophyllaceæ*.	Order 4. *Gleicheniceæ*.
,, 2. *Cyatheaceæ*.	,, 5. *Schizæaceæ*.
,, 3. *Polypodiaceæ*.	,, 6. *Osmundaceæ*.

Eusporangiate Filices: the sporangium is developed from a group of epidermal cells:—

Order 1. *Ophioglossaceæ*.	Order 2. *Marattiaceæ*.

Series B. **Heterosporous Filicinæ.**—As far as is known at present, this series contains the sub-class *Hydropterideæ* or *Rhizocarpæ*. In addition to the various peculiarities connected with their heterospory, its members are characterized by the development of an investment round the clusters of sporangia (*sori*), the whole forming a *sporocarp*. They are all Leptosporangiate.

The *Hydropterideæ* are arranged in two orders, according to the structure of the sporocarp.

Order 1. *Salviniaceæ*: wall of sporocarp formed as a superficial outgrowth of the sporophyll; each sporocarp contains a single sorus either of macrosporangia or of microsporangia (*Salvinia, Azolla*).

Order 2. *Marsileaceæ*: the wall of the sporocarp is formed by a portion of the sporophyll; each sporocarp contains several sori; and each sorus includes both macrosporangia and microsporangia (*Marsilea, Pilularia*).

It is possible that *Isoetes* represents the heterosporous eusporangiate *Filices* (see *infra*).

CLASS 2. EQUISETINÆ.—These plants are characterized by their rudimentary foliage leaves arranged in whorls at the nodes, and by their highly modified sporophylls, which are aggregated together at the ends of shoots, so as to form cone-like flowers. The embryo sporophyte has no suspensor, but a primary root.

Series A. **Homosporous Equisetinæ.**—All the existing forms belong to this series and constitute the order *Equisetaceæ*; they all belong to the genus *Equisetum*. The gametophyte is a green flattened prothallium, like that most commonly found in the *Filices*; but it is much branched, and generally diœcious.

Series B. **Heterosporous Equisetinæ.**—There are no existing heterosporous *Equisetinæ*; it is probable that some fossil plants, such as *Annularia* and *Asterophyllites*, represent the extinct heterosporous forms.

CLASS 3. LYCOPODINÆ.—The *Lycopodinæ* are generally characterized by their small and numerous foliage leaves, which are not arranged in whorls, though they are almost entirely wanting in *Psilotum*. The sporophylls are not highly modified, but they are frequently aggregated at the ends of shoots, so as to form cone-like flowers. So far as the embryology of this class is known at present, the embryo sporophyte has a suspensor, but no primary root.

Series A. **Homosporous Lycopodinæ.**

Order 1. *Lycopodiaceæ*: the sporangia are borne on sporophylls (*Lycopodium, Phylloglossum*).

Order 2. *Psilotaceæ*: the sporangia are borne on the stem (*Psilotum, Tmesipteris*).

Series B. **Heterosporous Lycopodinæ.**

Order 1. *Selaginellaceæ* (*Selaginella*).

The existing heterosporous *Lycopodinæ* are usually considered to consist of a family, termed the *Ligulatæ*, which includes the two genera *Selaginella* and *Isoetes*. This arrangement is not accepted here, for the reason that *Selaginella* and *Isoetes* have nothing in common beyond the ligule, and the fact that they are both heterosporous vascular cryptogams. It is in fact a question whether or not *Isoetes* should be included in the *Lycopodinæ* at all; for it has few and large leaves, and the embryo sporophyte has no suspensor, but it has a primary root. This being the case, it is impossible to frame any definition of the group *Lycopodinæ* which would apply to all the members, if *Isoetes* be included in it. In many features *Isoetes* resembles the *Filicinæ*, and especially the *Hydropterideæ*. It may be suggested here that *Isoetes* is a representative of the heterosporous eusporangiate *Filicinæ*. The only member of the *Lycopodinæ* which *Isoetes* at all resembles is *Phylloglossum*.

Mutual Affinities and Phylogeny of Pteridophyta.

Beyond the characteristics which they possess in common, and which have caused them to be collected into one class, there are no special points of contact between the three sub-classes of the *Pteridophyta*. The classes have each its own well-marked habit; and it therefore appears probable that they are to be regarded as equivalent branches of the *Pteridophyta*, springing from a common origin, in each of which a differentiation of homosporous and heterosporous forms has taken place. The relation of the homosporous to the heterosporous forms in each class is a point of interest. There is little or nothing to be said on this subject as regards the *Equisetinæ*. But in the *Filicinæ* it appears probable that the simpler heterosporous forms have sprung from the simpler homosporous forms, that is, the *Salviniaceæ* from the *Hymenophyllaceæ*; and in the *Lycopodinæ* that *Selaginella* has sprung from *Lycopodium*. Assuming that *Isoetes* belongs to the *Lycopodinæ*, its nearest ally would appear to be *Phylloglossum*; but this point must remain undecided until the whole life-history, especially the embryogeny, of *Phylloglossum* is known, and its true systematic position thereby fixed.

Various attempts have been made to trace back the sporophyte of the *Pteridophyta* to that of the *Muscineæ*, the points of contact being the *Hymenophyllaceæ* on the one hand and *Anthoceros* on the other; but these attempts cannot be considered to have been successful. The differences between the known forms of sporophyte in the two classes are too great to be explained away on any hypothesis. The case is different with regard to the gametophyte; there are, in fact, many points of resemblance between the prothallium of the *Pteridophyta* and the gametophyte of the *Muscineæ*. As Goebel and Bower have pointed out, the prothallium of some species of *Trichomanes* is a branched filamentous structure, closely resembling Moss protonema; and in most ferns, as also in *Equisetum* and *Lycopodium*, the prothallium is at first filamentous. The filamentous prothallium gives rise to one or more flattened expansions, on which the sexual organs, or at least the archegonia, are developed (*archegoniophores*). Thus there are indications in the gametophyte of many *Pteridophyta* of that distinction of protonema and sexual shoot which is so characteristic of the gametophyte of the *Muscineæ*. But this remarkable correspondence in the gametophyte does not warrant the conclusion that the *Pteridophyta* have sprung from the *Muscineæ*. It rather indicates that they are groups having a common origin in the Confervoid *Chlorophyceæ*, but diverging from the first in the relation of the sporophyte to the gametophyte, so that, whereas in the *Muscineæ* the sporophyte remains attached to the gametophyte throughout its whole existence, in the *Pteridophyta* the sporophyte develops as an independent organism. There can be little doubt that in the primitive *Pteridophyta* the two generations resembled each other, and that, as evolution proceeded, they became more and more widely dissimilar, the gametophyte losing, the sporophyte gaining, in both morphological and histological differentiation. An indication of this is still afforded by the general resemblance of the sporophyte of *Phylloglossum* to the gametophyte of *Lycopodium cernuum* as described by Treub, and of the sporophyte of *Lycopodium Phlegmaria* to its gametophyte (Treub). It will probably be found, when material is obtained for investigating it, that the sporophyte and the gametophyte of *Phylloglossum* are very similar.

The phylogeny of the *Pteridophyta*, as suggested in the foregoing remarks, is indicated in the following table:—

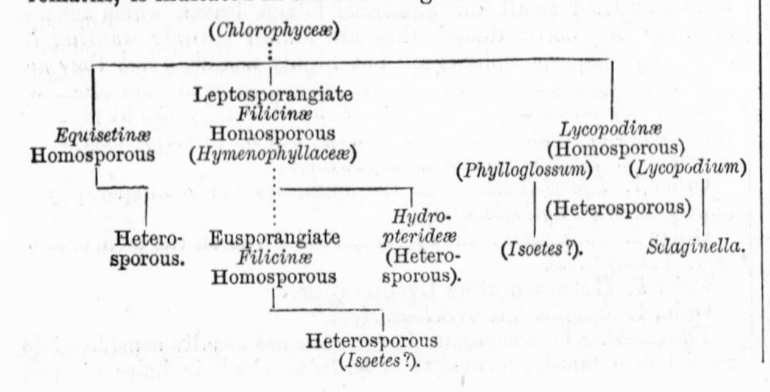

Literature of Pteridophyta.—Affinities and phylogeny:—Prantl, *Untersuchungen zur Morphologie der Gefässkryptogamen*, i.-ii., Leipsic, 1875-81; Goebel, *Annales du Jardin Botanique de Buitenzorg*, vii., 1887; Bower, "On some Normal and Abnormal Developments of the Oophyte of *Trichomanes*," in *Annals of Botany*, vol. i., 1888; Id., On the Morphology of *Phylloglossum Drummondii*, in *Phil. Trans.*, part II., 1885; Treub, "Recherches sur les Lycopodiacées," in *Ann. du Jardin Botanique de Buitenzorg*, iii.-iv., 1884-86; Id., *Annals of Botany*, i., 1888; Kny, "Die Entwickelung der Parkeriaceen," in *Nova Acta d. k. Leop. Akad.*, xxxvii., 1875. For general works, see Goebel, *Outlines of Classification and Special Morphology*, Oxford, 1887; Sadebeck, "Die Gefässkryptogamen," in Schenk's *Handbuch der Botanik*, i., 1879.

SUB-KINGDOM IV. PHANEROGAMIA.

These plants are commonly known as "flowering plants"; but they are more correctly designated "seed-bearing plants," or *Spermaphyta*, for the production of a seed is the one feature which distinguishes the members of this sub-kingdom from those of the other sub-kingdoms.

There is a definite alternation of generations in the life-history of these plants, but it is obscured by the extreme reduction which the gametophyte has undergone (see REPRODUCTION). The sporophyte is the plant; a suspensor is formed in its embryogeny; and it is heterosporous. The sporophylls are aggregated on special shoots, frequently with other floral leaves (bracteoles, perianth leaves), to form flowers. The two kinds of sporangia are in all cases borne on distinct sporophylls. In the microsporangium there are numerous fertile sporogenous cells, each of which produces four microspores; in the macrosporangium there are generally but few sporogenous cells, of which only one is usually fertile, and this one produces a single macrospore without division. The microspores are set free from the sporangium producing them, whereas the macrospore is not. It is this last peculiarity which determines the formation of the seed.

In the above account of the asexual reproductive organs of the *Phanerogamia*, the terms employed are those which are applied in the case of the heterosporous *Pteridophyta*; the advantage gained by the use of these terms is that the true homologies of the reproductive organs in the two sub-kingdoms are kept in view. The relation between these terms and those more commonly in use is as follows:—stamen = leaf bearing microsporangia (microsporophyll); carpel = leaf bearing macrosporangia (macrosporophyll); pollen-sac = microsporangium; anther = sorus of microsporangia; ovule (nucellus) = macrosporangium; pollen-grain = microspore; embryo sac = macrospore. Stamens and carpels are commonly borne by the same individual and in the same flower; but in many cases they are confined to distinct individuals (*diœcious*) or to distinct flowers (*diclinous*) on the same individual.

Inasmuch as these plants are heterosporous, the sexual generation is represented by male and female gametophytes. The male gametophyte, formed by the germination of the microspore (pollen-grain), consists of two or sometimes three or four cells, one of which becomes the male organ (pollen tube = antheridium of other sub-kingdoms), while the rest have nothing to do with reproduction, but constitute the rudimentary vegetative portion of the prothallium. The female gametophyte, commonly known as the *endosperm* (= female prothallium), is formed in the interior of the macrospore or embryo sac, and usually does not come at all into relation with the exterior. From certain cells of this endosperm one or more female organs are formed, which are equivalent to, and in some Phanerogams closely resemble, the archegonia of the *Pteridophyta*; each of these female organs possesses, as its essential constituent, the female cell (oosphere, ovum).

The process of fertilization (see REPRODUCTION) depends upon the pollen-grains being brought near to the ovules, so that, when the pollen-grains germinate, the pollen tubes may be able, in the course of their growth, to come into close relation with the female cells which the ovules contain. In many cases the transference of the pollen-grains is effected by the wind; the plants in which this is the case are characterized by their inconspicuous flowers, and are termed *anemophilous*. In other cases the transference is effected by means of insects; the plants in which this is the case are termed *entomophilous*, and are characterized by their conspicuous flowers, in which the perianth leaves are highly developed and brightly coloured, to attract the visits of insects,—an end which is further attained by the secretion of scented volatile oils and of sugary liquid (nectar). It is the conspicuous flowers of these entomophilous *Phanerogamia* which have earned for the whole group the designation of "flowering plants," which, however, is by no means generally applicable.

The *Phanerogamia* are divided into two classes,—the GYMNOSPERMÆ and the ANGIOSPERMÆ.

CLASS I. GYMNOSPERMÆ.—The carpels are sometimes absent, and, when present, they do not form an ovary; hence the ovules are naked. There is no stigma, consequently the pollen-grain comes into direct contact with the ovule. The whole of the female prothallium is formed in the embryo sac before fertilization. The female organ is in most cases a fully developed archegonium. The embryo is developed from a portion only of the fertilized female cell or oospore (*meroblastic embryogeny*); frequently several embryos are developed from one oospore (*polyembryony*). The flowers are diœcious or diclinous.

This class consists of the following orders:—

Order 1. Cycadaceæ: characterized generally by the unbranched stem and by the large branched leaves. The order includes nine genera:—*Cycas, Dioon, Ceratozamia, Zamia, Macrozamia, Encephalartos, Stangeria, Bowenia*, and *Microcycas*. The genus *Cycas* is peculiar, in that the carpels are not borne on special shoots, so as to form flowers, but on the main shoot, in the same way as the foliage leaves. The stamens of *Cycas*, as also both the stamens and carpels in the other genera, are highly modified sporophylls which are borne on special shoots forming cone-like flowers.

Order 2. Coniferæ: characterized by the much-branched stem and by the very numerous, small, unbranched leaves. The staminal flowers are generally cone-like. This order includes the Pines, Firs, Larches, Yews, Cypresses, &c., arranged in the following families:—

Series A. **Pinoideæ**: the carpellary flowers are cones:—

Fam. 1. *Abietineæ*. Fam. 3. *Cupressineæ*.
,, 2. *Araucarieæ*. ,, 4. *Taxodineæ*.

Series B. **Taxoideæ**: the carpellary flowers are not cones:—

Fam. 1. *Taxineæ*. Fam. 2. *Podocarpeæ*.

Order 3. Gnetaceæ: habit various; the flowers are not cones, and have a perianth. This order includes the three genera *Ephedra, Gnetum*, and *Welwitschia*. In *Gnetum* and *Welwitschia* the female organ (archegonium) is reduced to a single cell, the oosphere.

Mutual Affinities and Phylogeny of Gymnospermæ.

There is but little resemblance between the *Cycadaceæ* and the other two orders. *Gingko* or *Salisburia*, a remarkable genus which is usually placed in the *Taxineæ*, though it is in many respects peculiar, resembles the *Cycadaceæ* in the structure of the archegonium, in the fleshy character assumed by the outer portion of the seed-coat, and in the fact that the development of the embryo does not begin until after the seed has been shed. Probably the fossil plants known as the *Cordaitaceæ* may be regarded as a group intermediate between the *Cycadaceæ* and the *Coniferæ*. The *Coniferæ* and the *Gnetaceæ* are more closely allied, so much so in fact that the latter have been regarded by various writers as a family of the *Coniferæ*. The structure of the flowers in *Ephedra* is very similar to that in *Taxus*.

The connexion of the Gymnosperms with the *Pteridophyta* is undoubted. The development of the microsporangium in the Gymnosperms is the same as that of the sporangium of *Lycopodium*. The development of the macrosporangium presents in most cases the characteristic Phanerogamic features; but in certain cases (*Ceratozamia longifolia, Cupressus sempervirens, Callitris quadrivalvis*) there is a mass of sporogenous cells, as in the sporangia of the *Pteridophyta*, though only one of these cells is fertile, and it produces a single macrospore without division. In fact, there is a marked general resemblance in the development of the macrosporangium between these species and *Isoetes*. Another point of importance is the fact that, although the female prothallium (endosperm) is under ordinary conditions entirely and permanently enclosed in the macrospore (embryo sac)—a feature which is characteristic of the *Phanerogamia*—yet in the *Cycadaceæ*, if the first-formed archegonia are not fertilized, the prothallium resumes its growth and bursts the macrospore, coming to the surface of the ovule and turning green in consequence of exposure to light. Taking into consideration their general habit and the peculiarities in the development of their sporangia, it appears that the *Cycadaceæ* find in the Eusporangiate *Filices* their nearest allies among the *Pteridophyta*. This suggestion presupposes the existence of heterosporous *Eusporangiata*, although all the known forms are homosporous. But this difficulty will be met, if, as suggested above, it turns out that *Isoetes* really belongs to the Eusporangiate *Filices*. The *Coniferæ* resemble more nearly the *Lycopodinæ*, such as *Lycopodium* and *Selaginella*, in their general habit and in the cone-like form of their flowers. However, the position of the pollen-sacs on the under surface of the peltate sporophyll is a feature which connects them with the *Equisetinæ*; but, on the other hand, the ligular outgrowth on the upper surface of the macrosporophyll in *Araucaria*, which in the *Abietineæ* becomes the large ovuliferous scale, is another point of resemblance to *Selaginella* and *Isoetes*. In view of these resemblances to the *Lycopodinæ* and the *Equisetinæ*, it is hardly possible to trace back the *Coniferæ* to either of these groups: it is more probable that they sprang from forms of *Pteridophyta* intermediate in character between the *Lycopodinæ* and the *Equisetinæ*. The mutual relations and the phylogeny of the three genera of *Gnetaceæ* cannot at present be determined with any degree of probability. The one point which affords any clue is the resemblance in general structure between the flowers of *Gnetum* and those of the *Taxineæ*. The flower of *Welwitschia*, more than that of any other Gymnosperm, resembles that of an Angiosperm, especially in the fact that the staminal flower contains a rudimentary ovule.

CLASS II. ANGIOSPERMÆ.—The carpel or carpels form an ovary, in which the ovules are enclosed. A portion of the carpel forms a stigma, which receives the pollen-grains. The pollen-grains germinate on the stigma, and therefore do not come into direct relation with the ovules. A part only of the female prothallium (*primary endosperm*) is formed before fertilization, the remainder (*secondary endosperm*) after fertilization. The female organ is a reduced archegonium, consisting merely of the female cell (oosphere). The general occurrence of both macrosporophylls and microsporophylls in the same flower is a characteristic feature of this group, as is also the whorled arrangement of the floral leaves.

The *Angiospermæ* are divided into two sub-classes,—the *Monocotyledons* and the *Dicotyledons*, according to the number of the primary leaves or cotyledons of the embryo; hence, in the former sub-class the first leaves are alternate, in the latter opposite. In the Monocotyledons, with few exceptions, the growing-point of the embryonic stem is lateral; in the Dicotyledons it is always terminal. There are other distinguishing features, such as the parallel venation of the leaves of Monocotyledons and the reticulate venation in Dicotyledons; but they are not sufficiently constant to be of much taxonomic value.

The **Monocotyledons** may be conveniently arranged in the following series:—

Series 1. *Nudifloræ*: usually diclinous or diœcious; perianth wanting or rudimentary. This series includes the *Spadicifloræ* (Aroids, Palms, *Naiadeæ*) and the *Glumifloræ* (Grasses, Sedges).

Series 2. *Petaloideæ*: usually monoclinous; perianth present, and usually well-developed and coloured. This series includes the Lilies, Orchids, Irises, &c.

The **Dicotyledons** are usually classified as follows:—

Series 1. *Monochlamydeæ*: usually diclinous or diœcious; perianth absent or simple.

Series 2. *Polypetalæ*: usually monoclinous; perianth usually consists of calyx and coloured corolla, the petals being free.

Series 3. *Gamopetalæ*: usually monoclinous; perianth usually consists of calyx and coloured corolla, the petals being coherent.

Phylogeny of the Angiospermæ.

There can be no doubt that the *Angiospermæ* have been derived from the *Pteridophyta*; but it is a question whether they have had an independent origin from that group or whether they are to be traced back to it through the Gymnosperms. In view of the wide gulf which separates the Angiosperms from even the highest *Pteridophyta*, and of the affinities of the Gymnosperms to the *Pteridophyta* on the one hand and to the Angiosperms on the other, the latter suggestion would appear to be the more probable.

Although the Monocotyledons and the Dicotyledons have so many features in common, it is probable that they have not had the same origin. The Gymnospermous forms to which the Dicotyledons are most nearly allied are the *Coniferæ*, and *Gnetum* among the *Gnetaceæ*. The marked Angiospermous characters of *Gnetum*, and its general similarity in habit to a Dicotyledonous plant, afford some ground for regarding this genus as the starting-point of the Dicotyledons. But more probably the Dicotyledons are to be traced back to the *Coniferæ*, and the *Gnetaceæ* to be regarded as a lateral offshoot of the *Coniferæ*, with an Angiospermous tendency, but not leading on to higher forms. The Gymnosperms which most resemble the Monocotyledons are the *Cycadaceæ*; and, if it be assumed that the Angiosperms have sprung from the Gymnosperms, it is to this order of the latter class that the Monocotyledons are to be traced. The Monocotyledons in which this resemblance is most conspicuous are those, such as the Aroids and Palms, which belong to the series *Nudifloræ*.

Literature.—On the *Phanerogamia*, see Goebel, *Outlines of Classification and Special Morphology*, Oxford, 1887; Le Maout and Decaisne, *Traité de Botanique* (English ed. by Hooker, 1868); and Engler and Prantl, *Die Pflanzenfamilien*, Leipsic (in course of publication).

On the phylogeny of plants, see Nägeli, *Theorie d. Abstammungslehre*, Munich, 1884; and Saporta and Marion, *L'Évolution du Règne Végétal* (Int. Sci. Series, vols. xxxix. and lii.), Paris, 1881-85. Descriptions of the numerous natural orders will be found in the various text-books which treat of systematic botany, as well as in the above.

(S. H. V.)

VEGETABLE MARROW. See GOURD and HORTICULTURE, vol. xii. p. 283.

VEGETIUS, FLAVIUS RENATUS, the compiler of a treatise on the art of war, dedicated to Valentinian II. (375-392). Nothing is known of his life save that in MSS. he is called *vir illustris* and also *comes.* His sources, according to his own statement, were Cato, Cornelius Celsus, Frontinus, Paternus, and the imperial constitutions of Augustus, Trajan, and Hadrian. The book, which is a poor compilation, has to be used with great caution. The first edition appeared at Utrecht in 1473; the latest is that of Lang (Leipsic, 1869). The book has been often translated; an English version through the French was published by Caxton in 1489.

VEGLIA (Slavonic, *Krk*), an island in the Gulf of Quarnero, Adriatic Sea, belonging to the Austrian district of Istria, is separated from the mainland by the narrow channel of Morlacca or Maltempo and from the island of Cherso on the south-west by that of Mezzo. It is 24 miles long and about 14 miles across at its widest part. The surface is mostly rugged and mountainous; but the central, southern, and western districts are fertile, producing wine, grain, oil, timber, and various kinds of fruit, besides pasturage for numerous live-stock. Silk, marble, and salt are also produced; and fishing is carried on along the coast. In 1880 the island contained 18,089 inhabitants; the capital is Veglia, a town on the south-west side, with 1580 inhabitants and a good harbour.

VEHMIC COURTS. See FEHMIC COURTS.

VEII. See ETRURIA, vol. viii. p. 634.

VELAZQUEZ, DIEGO DE SILVA (1599-1660), the head of the Spanish school of painting and one of the mightiest painters the world has known, was born in Seville early in June 1599, the year in which Van Dyck also first saw the light at Antwerp. His European fame is of comparatively recent origin, dating from the first quarter of the 19th century. Till then his pictures had lain immured in the palaces and museum of Madrid; and from want of popular appreciation they had to a large extent escaped the rapacity of the French marshals during the Peninsular War. In 1828 Sir David Wilkie[1] wrote from Madrid that he felt himself in the presence of a new power in art as he looked at the works of Velazquez, and at the same time found a wonderful affinity between this master and the English school of portrait painters, being specially reminded of the firm square touch of Raeburn. He was struck by the sense of modernness of impression, of direct contact with nature, and of vital force which pervaded all the work of Velazquez, in landscape as well as in portraiture. Time and criticism have now fully established his reputation as one of the most consummate of painters, and accordingly Mr Ruskin says of him that "everything Velazquez does may be taken as absolutely right by the student." At the present day his marvellous technique and strong individuality have given him a power in European art such as is exercised by no other of the old masters. Acquainted with all the Italian schools, the friend of the foremost painters of his day, he was strong enough to withstand every external influence and to work out for himself the development of his own nature and his own principles of art. A realist of the realists, he painted only what he saw; consequently his imagination seems limited. His religious conceptions are of the earth earthy, although some of his works, such as the Crucifixion and the Scourging, are characterized by an intensity of pathos in which he ranks second to no painter. His men and women seem to breathe; his horses are full of action and his dogs of life; so quick and close is his grasp of his subject. England was the first nation to recognize his extraordinary merit, and it owns by far the largest share of his works outside of Spain.[2] But Velazquez can only be seen in all his power in the gallery of the Prado at Madrid, where over sixty of his works are preserved, including historical, mythological, and religious subjects, as well as landscapes and portraits. It is hardly creditable to the patriotism of Seville, his native town, that no example of his work is to be seen in the gallery of that city. Seville was then in the height of its prosperity, "the pearl of Spain," carrying on a great trade with the New World, and was also a vigorous centre of literature and art. For more than a hundred years it had fostered a native school of painting which ranked high in the Peninsula, and it reckoned among its citizens many whose names are prominent in Spanish literature.

Velazquez was the son of Rodriguez de Silva, a lawyer in Seville, descended from a noble Portuguese family, and was baptized on 6th June 1599. Following a common Spanish usage, he is known by his mother's name Velazquez. There has been considerable diversity of opinion as to his full name, but he was known to his contemporaries as Diego de Silva Velazquez, and signed his name thus. He was educated, says Palomino, by his parents in the fear of God, and was intended for a learned profession, for which he received a good training in languages and philosophy. But the bent of the boy was towards art, and he was placed under the elder Herrera, a vigorous painter who disregarded the Italian influence of the early Seville school. From his works in Seville we can see that Herrera was a bold and effective painter; but he was at the same time a man of unruly temper and his pupils could seldom stay long with him. Velazquez remained but one year, long enough, however, to influence his life. It was from Herrera that he learned to use long brushes, or, as Mr J. E. Hodgson, R.A., suggests, brushes with long bristles, by means of which his colours seem to be floated on the canvas by a light fluent touch, the envy and despair of his successors. From Herrera's studio Velazquez betook himself to a very different master, the learned and pedantic Pacheco, the author of a heavy book on painting, and, as we see by his works at Madrid, a dull commonplace painter. In this school he remained for five years, studying proportion and perspective, and seeing all that was best in the literary and artistic circles of Seville. Here also—and this may explain much—he fell in love with his master's daughter Juana, whom he married in 1618 with the hearty approval of Pacheco, who praises his hand and heart, claiming at the same time all the credit of having been his master. He must, however, have found Velazquez a wayward pupil; for, instead of looking to Raphael, according to orders, the young painter set himself to copy the commonest things about him,—earthenware jars of the country people, birds, fish, fruit, and flowers of the market-place. To paint well and thoroughly what he saw, to model with his brush, and to colour under the influence of light and shade were for him the vital purpose, the first lesson, in his art. It was with deliberate purpose that Velazquez painted these *bodegones* (tavern-pieces), as they were called; for we are told that he said he would rather be the first painter of common things than the second in higher art. Carrying out this idea still further, Velazquez felt that to master the subtlety of the human face he must make this a special study, and he accordingly engaged a peasant lad to be his servant and model, making innumerable studies in charcoal and chalk, and catching his every expression. We see this model in the laughing Peasant Boy of the

[1] See Cunningham's *Life*, vol. ii.

[2] Of the 274 works attributed to Velazquez by Mr Curtis 121 are in the United Kingdom, while France has but 13, Austria-Hungary 12, Russia 7, and Germany about the same number.

Belvedere Gallery at Vienna. In such work as this, and in his studies by the wayside, Velazquez laid the foundation of his subsequent mastery of expression, of penetration into character, and of rendering the life of his sitter to the quick. He saw the world around him teeming with life and objects of interest to the painter, and he set himself to render these. His manner is as national as that of Cervantes. He lived and died racy of the soil. The position and reputation of Velazquez were now assured at Seville. There his wife bore him two daughters,—all his family so far as is known. The younger died in infancy, while the elder, Francisca, in due time married Bautista del Mazo, a painter, whose large family is probably that which is represented in the important picture of later years in Vienna, the so-called Family of Velazquez. Mr Curtis, however, is inclined to believe that this picture is by Mazo. In the gallery at Madrid there is at least one portrait of this daughter, painted in these early days at Seville, as also a portrait of Juana his wife, holding a drawing-tablet on her knee. There was formerly in the possession of Lord Dudley another portrait of his wife by Velazquez, painted, perhaps, in the first year of their happy marriage. Of this early Seville manner we have an excellent example in El Aguador (the Water-Carrier) at Apsley House (London). Firm almost to hardness, it displays close study of nature. One can see in it the youthful struggle to portray the effects of light stealing here and there over the prominent features of the face, groping after the effects which the painter was to master later on. The brushwork is bold and broad, and the outlines firmly marked. As is usual with Velazquez at this time, the harmony of colours is red, brown, and yellow, reminding one of Ribera. For sacred subjects we may turn to the Adoration of the Magi at Madrid, dated 1619, and the Adoration of the Shepherds in the London National Gallery, in both of which we have excellent examples of his realism. The peasants offering their gifts of poultry are the hard-featured women of the market-place of Seville, pre-Raphaelite in their uncompromising truthfulness. Thus also in the St John in the Desert we find his peasant boy transformed into the saint.

But Velazquez was now eager to see more of the world. Madrid, with its fine Titians, held out strong inducements. Accordingly in 1622, fortified with letters of introduction to Fonseca, who held a good position at court, he spent some months there, accompanied only by his servant. Here he painted the portrait of the poet Gongora, a commission from Pacheco, which now hangs in the gallery at Madrid. The impression which Velazquez made in the capital must have been very strong, for in the following year he was summoned to return by Olivares, the all-powerful minister of Philip IV., fifty ducats being allowed to defray his expenses. On this occasion he was accompanied by his father-in-law. Next year (1624) he received from the king three hundred ducats to pay the cost of the removal of his family to Madrid, which became his home for the remainder of his life. Weak and worthless as a king, Philip had inherited the art-loving propensities of his race, and was proud to be considered a poet and a painter. It is one of the best features of his character that he remained for a period of thirty-six years the faithful and attached friend of Velazquez, whose merit he soon recognized, declaring that no other painter should ever paint his portrait. By his equestrian portrait of the king, painted in 1623, Velazquez secured admission to the royal service with a salary of twenty ducats per month, besides medical attendance, lodgings, and payment for the pictures he might paint. The portrait was exhibited on the steps of San Felipe, and was received with enthusiasm, being vaunted by poets, among them Pacheco. It has unfortunately disappeared, having probably perished in one of the numerous fires which occurred in the royal palaces. The Prado, however, has two portraits (Nos. 1070 and 1071) which are most probably studies for this picture. In them the harshness of the Seville period has disappeared and the tones are more delicate. The modelling is firm, recalling that of Antonio Moro, the Dutch portrait-painter of Philip II., who exercised a considerable influence on the Spanish school. In the same year the prince of Wales (afterwards Charles I.) arrived at the court of Spain. We are told that he sat to Velazquez, but the picture has disappeared.[1] It was during this period also that he painted the hunting-scenes of which examples are to be found in the collections of Sir Richard Wallace, Lord Clarendon, and others, and which served him in the production of the great Boar Hunt of the London National Gallery, painted, however, in the later years of his life,—a magnificent work in spite of some restorations. It was then too that he painted the groups of Court Gallants in their gay costumes, accompanied, as in the Boar Hunt, by their servants and dogs. The splendid Meeting of Artists (as it is absurdly named) in the Louvre was doubtless executed at a later time from studies taken in these early years, for it displays all the qualities of his finer work, space and air being thrown round the figures, which are touched with great mastery and ease.

In 1628 Rubens visited Madrid on a diplomatic mission for nine months, and Velazquez was appointed by the king to be his guide among the art treasures of Spain. Rubens was then at the height of his fame, and had undertaken as a commission from Olivares the large pictures which now adorn the great hall in Grosvenor House (London). These months might have been a new turning-point in the career of a weaker man than Velazquez, for Rubens added to his brilliant style as a painter the manner of a fascinating courtier. Rubens had a high opinion of the talent of Velazquez, as is attested by Fuensalida, but he effected no change in the style of the strong Spaniard. He impressed him, however, with the desire to see Italy and the works of her mighty painters. In 1627 the king had given for competition among the painters of Spain the subject of the Expulsion of the Moors. Velazquez bore off the palm; but his picture was destroyed in a fire at the palace in 1734. Palomino, however, describes it. Philip III. points with his baton to a crowd of men and women driven off under charge of soldiers, while Spain, a majestic female, sits looking calmly on. The triumph of Velazquez was rewarded by his being appointed gentleman usher. To this was shortly afterwards added a daily allowance of twelve reals, the same amount as was allowed to the court barbers, and ninety ducats a year for dress, which was also paid to the dwarfs, buffoons, and players about the king's person—truly a curious estimate of talent at the court of Spain. As an extra payment he received (though it was not paid for five years) one hundred ducats for the picture of Bacchus, painted in 1629 (No. 485 of the Madrid gallery). The spirit and aim of this work are better understood from its Spanish name, Los Borrachos or Los Bebedores (the Topers), who are paying mock homage to a half-naked ivy-crowned young man seated on a wine barrel. It is like a story by Cervantes, and is brimful of jovial humour. One can easily see in this picture of national manners how Velazquez had reaped the benefit of his close study of peasant life. The painting is firm and solid, and the light and shade are more deftly handled than in former works. Altogether, this production

[1] In 1847 Mr John Snare of Reading exhibited a picture which had come from the sale of Lord Fife in 1809, and which he maintained to be the long lost work. This led to much controversy; but the claim was rejected by experts and the picture is said to be now in America.

may be taken as the most advanced example of the first style of Velazquez. It is usual to divide his artistic career by his two visits to Italy, his second style following the first visit and his third the second. Roughly speaking, this somewhat arbitrary division may be accepted, though it will not always apply, for, as is usual in the case of many great painters, his styles at times overlap each other. Velazquez rarely signed his pictures, and the royal archives only give the dates of his more important works. Internal evidence and history, as regards his portraits, supply to a certain extent the rest.

In 1629 Philip gave Velazquez permission to carry out his desire of visiting Italy, without loss of salary, making him besides a present of 400 ducats, to which Olivares added 200. He sailed from Barcelona in August in the company of the marquis De Spinola, the conqueror of Breda, then on his way to take command of the Spanish troops at Milan. It was during this voyage that Velazquez must have heard the details of the surrender of Breda from the lips of the victor, and he must have sketched his fine head, known to us also by the portrait by Van Dyck. But the great picture was not painted till many years later, for Spinola had fallen into disfavour at court. In Venice Velazquez made copies of the Crucifixion and the Last Supper of Tintoretto, which he sent to the king, and in Rome he copied Michelangelo and Raphael, lodging in the Villa Medici till fever compelled him to remove into the city. Here he painted the Forge of Vulcan (No. 1059 of the Madrid gallery), in which Apollo narrates to the astonished Vulcan, a village blacksmith, the news of the infidelity of Venus, while four Cyclops listen to the scandal. The mythological treatment is similar to that of the Bacchus: it is realistic and Spanish to the last degree, giving a picture of the interior of an Andalusian smithy, with Apollo thrown in to make the story tell. The conception is commonplace, yet the impression it produces is undoubted from the vividness of the representation and the power of expression. The modelling of the half-naked figures is excellent. Altogether this picture is much superior to the other work painted at the same time, Joseph's Coat, which now hangs in the Escorial. This work has been much praised—overpraised in the opinion of the present writer—and this opinion is shared by Don Federico de Madrazo, the director of the Madrid museum, who looks on it as one of the weakest of the productions of Velazquez. Both these works are evidently painted from the same models. In looking at these two pictures what strikes one especially is that they betray no trace of the influence of the Italians. Velazquez remained true to himself. At Rome he also painted the two beautiful landscapes of the Gardens of the Medici, now in the Madrid museum, full of sparkle and charm. Landscape as a form of art never had attraction for the Spaniards; but Velazquez here, and in the silvery landscapes painted some years later at Aranjuez, shows how great a master he was in this branch of art. After a visit to Naples in 1631, where he worked with his countryman Ribera, and painted a charming portrait of the infanta Maria, sister of Philip, he returned early in the year to Madrid.

He then painted the first of many portraits of the young prince Don Baltasar Carlos, the heir to the throne, dignified and lordly even in his childhood, caracolling in the dress of a field-marshal on his prancing steed. Sir Richard Wallace owns a fine example; but the finest in the United Kingdom is the well-known picture at Grosvenor House, a masterly example of the second manner of Velazquez. The colour is warm and bright, the workmanship solid and fused like enamel, while light and air pervade every corner. The scene is in the riding-school of the palace, the king and queen looking on from a balcony, while Olivares is in attendance as master of the horse to the prince. Don Baltasar died in 1646 at the age of seventeen, so that judging by his age this picture must have been painted about 1641, two years before the fall of Olivares. This powerful minister was the early and constant patron of the painter. His impassive saturnine face is familiar to us from the many portraits painted by Velazquez, a face which, like his royal master's, seems never to have known a smile, and in which are written pride and disdain. Two must be named of surpassing excellence,—the full length belonging to Mr. Holford (exhibited at Burlington House in 1887), stately and dignified, in which he wears the green cross of Alcantara and holds a wand, the badge of his office as master of the horse; the other the great equestrian portrait of the Madrid gallery (No. 487), in which he is flatteringly represented as a field-marshal in all his pomp during an action. It is difficult to overpraise the excellence of this work, either as regards its dramatic power or its masterly execution. In these portraits Velazquez has well repaid the debt of gratitude which he owed to his first patron, whom he stood by in his fall, thus exposing himself to the risk—and it was not a light one—of incurring the anger of the jealous Philip. The king, however, showed no sign of malice towards his favoured painter. Faithful in few things, Philip kept true to Velazquez, whom he visited daily in his studio in the palace, and to whom he stood in many attitudes and costumes, as a huntsman with his dogs, as a warrior in command of his troops, and even on his knees at prayer, wearing ever the same dull uninterested look. His pale face and lack-lustre eye, his fair flowing hair and moustaches curled up to his eyes, and his heavy projecting Austrian lip are known in many a portrait and nowhere more supremely than in the wonderful canvas of the London National Gallery (No. 745), where he seems to live and breathe. Few portraits in the whole range of art will compare with this work, in which the consummate handling of Velazquez is seen at its best, for it is in his late and most perfect manner.[1] From one of the equestrian portraits of the king, painted in 1638, the sculptor Montañas modelled a statue which was cast in bronze by the Florentine sculptor Tacca, and which now stands in the Plaza del Oriente at Madrid, "a solid Velazquez," as it has been well named by Ford. This portrait exists no more; but there is no lack of others, for Velazquez was in constant and close attendance on Philip, accompanying him in his journeys to Aragon in 1642 and 1644, and was doubtless present with him when he entered Lerida as a conqueror. It was then that he painted the great equestrian portrait (No. 1066 of the Madrid gallery) in which the king is represented as a great commander leading his troops,—a rôle which Philip never played except in a theatrical pageant. All is full of animation except the stolid face of the king. It hangs as a pendant to the great Olivares portrait,—fit rivals of the neighbouring Charles V. by Titian, which doubtless fired Velazquez to excel himself, and both remarkable for their silvery tone, and their feeling of open air and harmony combined with brilliancy. The light plays on the armour and scarf thrown to the wind, showing how completely Velazquez had mastered the effects he strove to reach in his early days. Of these two great works Sir Richard Wallace possesses small but excellent replicas.

[1] In this and in all his portraits Philip wears the *golilla*, a stiff linen collar projecting at right angles from the neck. It was invented by the king, who was so proud of it that he celebrated it by a festival, followed by a procession to church to thank God for the blessing (Madame D'Aulnoy, *Voyage d'Espagne*). The *golilla* was thus the height of fashion and appears in most of the male portraits of the period. In regard to the wonderful structure of Philip's moustaches, it is said that, to preserve their form, they were encased during the night in perfumed leather covers called *bigoteras*.

But, besides the forty portraits of Philip which are known, we have portraits of other members of the royal family, of Philip's first wife, Isabella of Bourbon, and her children, especially of her eldest son, Don Baltasar Carlos, of whom, besides those already mentioned, there is a beautiful full length in a private room at Buckingham Palace. Cavaliers, soldiers, churchmen, and poets of the court, as for example the Quevedo at Apsley House (Burlington House, 1887), sat to the painter and, even if forgotten by history, will live on his canvas. The admirable Pareja of Lord Radnor's collection (Burlington House, 1873) is said to have been taken by Philip for the living man. It has been remarked that the Spaniards have always been chary of committing to canvas the portraits of their beautiful women. Queens and infantas may be painted and exhibited, but ladies rarely. One wonders who the beautiful woman can be that adorns the gallery of Sir Richard Wallace, the splendid brunette so unlike the usual fair-haired female sitters to Velazquez. She belongs to this period of his work, to the ripeness of his middle period. Instinct with life, her bosom seems to heave and the blood to pulsate through her veins. The touch is firm but free, showing the easy strength of the great master. Rarely has flesh been painted with such a glow, yet with such reserve. This picture was one of the ornaments of the Bethnal Green collection. But, if we have few ladies of the court of Philip, we have in great plenty his buffoons and dwarfs. Even these deformed creatures attract our sympathy as we look at their portraits by Velazquez, who, true to his nature, treats them gently and kindly, as in El Primo (the Favourite), whose intelligent face and huge folio with ink bottle and pen by his side show him to be a wiser and better-educated man than many of the gallants of the court. El Bobo de Coria, El Niño de Vallecas, and Pablillos, a buffoon evidently acting a part, all belong to this middle period. From these commissioned portraits of the menials of the court it is pleasant to turn to one of the greatest of historical works, the Surrender of Breda, often known as Las Lanzas, from the serried rank of lances breaking the sky, which is believed to have been painted about 1647. It represents the moment when the vanquished Justin of Nassau in front of his Dutch troops is submissively bending as he offers to his conqueror Spinola the keys of the town, which, with courteous grace, the victor refuses to accept, as he lays his hand gently on the shoulder of his defeated foe.[1] Behind Spinola stand the Spanish troops bearing their lances aloft, while beyond is a long stretch of the Low Country, dotted with fortifications and giving the impression of vast space and distance. The picture is full of light and air and is perhaps the finest example of the silvery bluish style of Velazquez. In conception it is as fine as in execution, and one looks in vain for a trace of "the malicious pencil" which Sir William Stirling-Maxwell discerned in the treatment of Justin and his gallant Dutchmen.

The greatest of the religious paintings by Velazquez belongs also to this middle period, the Christ on the Cross (Madrid gallery, No. 1055). Palomino says it was painted in 1638 for the convent of San Placido. It is a work of tremendous power and of great originality, the moment chosen being that immediately after death. The Saviour's head hangs on his breast and a mass of dark tangled hair conceals part of the face. The beautiful form is projected against a black and hopeless sky from which light has been blotted out. The figure stands absolutely alone without any accessory. The skull and serpent described by Sir William Stirling-Maxwell were added by some pious bungler at a much later date. The picture was lengthened to suit its place in an oratory; but this addition has since been removed.

Velazquez's son-in-law Mazo had succeeded him as usher in 1634, and he himself had received steady promotion in the royal household, receiving a pension of 500 ducats in 1640, increased to 700 in 1648, for portraits painted and to be painted, and being appointed inspector of works in the palace in 1647. Philip now entrusted him with the carrying out of a design on which he had long set his heart, the founding of an academy of art in Spain. Rich in pictures, Spain was weak in statuary, and Velazquez was commissioned to proceed to Italy to make purchases. Accompanied by his faithful slave Pareja, whom he taught to be a good painter, he sailed from Malaga in 1649, landing at Genoa, and proceeding thence by Milan to Venice, buying Titians, Tintorettos, and Veroneses as he went. A curious conversation which he is said to have had with Salvator Rosa is reported by Boschini,[2] in which the Spaniard with perfect frankness confesses his want of appreciation of Raphael and his admiration of Titian, "first of all Italian men." It seems a possible story, for Velazquez bought according to his likings and painted in the spirit of his own ideals. At Modena he was received with much favour by the duke, and doubtless here he painted the two splendid portraits which now adorn the Dresden gallery, for these pictures came from the Modena sale of 1746. They presage the advent of the painter's third and latest manner, a noble example of which is the great portrait of Innocent X. in the Doria palace at Rome, to which city Velazquez now proceeded. There he was received with marked favour by the pope, who presented him with a medal and gold chain. Of this portrait, thought by Sir Joshua Reynolds to be the finest picture in Rome, Palomino says that Velazquez took a copy to Spain. There exist several in different galleries, some of them possibly studies for the original or replicas painted for Philip. One of the most remarkable is that in Apsley House, exhibited in Burlington House in 1887. The modelling of the stern impassive face comes near to perfection, so delicate are the gradations in the full light; all sharpness of outline has disappeared; and the features seem moulded by the broad and masterly brushwork. When closely examined, the work seems coarse, yet at the proper distance it gives the very essence of living flesh. The handling is rapid but unerring. Velazquez had now reached the *manera abreviada*, as the Spaniards call this bolder style. This is but another way of saying that his early and laborious studies and his close observation of nature had given to him in due time, as to all great painters, the power of representing what he saw by simpler means and with more absolute truth. At Rome he painted also a portrait of his servant Pareja, probably the picture of Lord Radnor's collection, which procured his election into the Academy of St Luke. Philip was now wearying for his return; accordingly, after a visit to Naples, where he saw his old friend Ribera, he returned to Spain by Barcelona in 1651, taking with him many pictures and 300 pieces of statuary, which he afterwards arranged and catalogued for the king. Undraped sculpture was, however, abhorrent to the Spanish Church, and after Philip's death these works gradually disappeared.

Isabella of Bourbon had died in 1644, and the king had married Maria Anna of Austria, whom Velazquez now painted in many attitudes. He was specially chosen by the king to fill the high office of "aposentador major," which imposed on him the duty of looking after the quarters occupied by the court whether at home or in their journeys —a responsible function, which was no sinecure and inter

[1] This gracious attitude is also employed by Velazquez in a picture in Stafford House (representing the reception of St Francis Borgia by Loyola).

[2] See Stirling's *Velazquez and his Works*, p. 161.

fered with the exercise of his art. Yet far from indicating any decline, his works of this period are amongst the highest examples of his style. The dwarf Don Antonio el Inglés (the Englishman) with his dog, Æsop, Menippus, and the Sculptor, all in the Madrid gallery, show his surest and freest manner. To these may be added the charming portraits of the royal children in the Louvre and Vienna, among the choicest of his works. It is one of these infantas, Margarita Maria, the eldest daughter of the new queen, that is the subject of the well-known picture Las Meniñas (the Maids of Honour) in the Madrid gallery, painted in 1656, where the little lady holds court, surrounded by her ladies-in-waiting, her dwarfs, and her mastiff, while Velazquez is seen standing at his easel. This is the finest portrait we have of the great painter, and, as etched by St Raymond, it forms the frontispiece of the book by Mr Curtis. It is a face of much dignity, power, and sweetness,—like his life, equable and serene, unruffled by care. Las Meniñas was the picture of which Luca Giordano said that it was the "theology of painting," another way of expressing the opinion of Sir Thomas Lawrence, that this work is the philosophy of art, so true is it in rendering the desired effect. The result is there, one knows not by what means, as if by a first intention without labour, absolutely right. The story is told that the king painted the red cross of Santiago on the breast of the painter, as it appears to-day on the canvas. Velazquez did not, however, receive the honour till 1659, three years after the execution of this work. Even the powerful king of Spain could not make his favourite a belted knight without a commission to inquire into the purity of his lineage on both sides of the house.[1] Fortunately the pedigree could bear scrutiny, as for generations the family was found free from all taint of heresy, from all trace of Jewish or Moorish blood, and from contamination by trade or commerce. The difficulty connected with the fact that he was a painter was got over by his being painter to the king and by the declaration that he did not sell his pictures. But for this royal appointment, which enabled him to escape the censorship of the Inquisition, we should never have had his splendid Venus and Cupid, belonging to Mr Morritt of Rokeby Hall (exhibited in Manchester in 1857), painted in his latest manner and worthy of comparison with Titian. There were in truth but two patrons of art in Spain,—the church and the art-loving king and court. Murillo was the artist favoured by the church, while Velazquez was patronized by the crown. One difference, however, deserves to be noted. Murillo, who toiled for a rich and powerful church, left scarcely sufficient means to pay for his burial, while Velazquez lived and died in the enjoyment of good salaries and pensions. Yet on occasions Philip gave commissions for religious pictures to Velazquez, —among others, and belonging to this later period, the Coronation of the Virgin (Madrid), splendid in colour—a harmony of red, blue, and grey—but deficient in religious feeling and dignity. It was painted for the oratory of the queen, doubtless Maria Anna, in the palace at Madrid. Another royal commission for the hermitage of Buen Retiro was the St Anthony the Abbot and St Paul the Hermit, painted in 1659, the landscape of which excited the warm admiration of Sir David Wilkie. The last of his works which we shall name is Las Hilanderas or the Spinners (Madrid), painted about 1656, representing the interior of the royal tapestry works. The subject is nothing, the treatment everything. It is full of light, air, and movement, splendid in colour, and marvellous in handling. This picture, Raphael Mengs said, seemed to have been painted not by the hand but by the pure force of will. We see in it the full ripeness of the power of Velazquez, a concentration of all the art-knowledge he had gathered during his long artistic career of more than forty years. In no picture is he greater as a colourist. The scheme is simple,—a harmony of red, bluish green, grey, and black, which are varied and blended with consummate skill.

[1] The records of this commission have been found among the archives of the order of Santiago by M. Villaamil.

In 1660 a treaty of peace between France and Spain was to be consummated by the marriage of the infanta Maria Theresa with Louis XIV., and the ceremony was to take place in the Island of Pheasants, a small swampy island in the Bidassoa. Velazquez was charged with the decoration of the Spanish pavilion and with the whole scenic display. In the midst of the grandees of the first two courts in Christendom Velazquez attracted much attention by the nobility of his bearing and the splendour of his costume. On the 26th June he returned to Madrid, and on the 31st July he was stricken with fever. Feeling his end approaching, he signed his will, appointing as his sole executors his wife and his firm friend Fuensalida, keeper of the royal records. He died on the 6th of August 1660, passing away in the full possession of his great powers, and leaving no work behind him to show a trace of decay. He was buried in the Fuensalida vault of the church of San Juan, and within eight days his wife Juana was laid beside him. Unfortunately this church was destroyed by the French in 1811, so that his place of interment is now unknown. There was much difficulty in adjusting the tangled accounts outstanding between Velazquez and the treasury, and it was not till 1666, after the death of Philip, that they were finally settled.

Velazquez can hardly be said to have formed a school of painting. Apart from the circumstance that his occupations at court would have prevented this, his genius was too personal for transmission by teaching. Yet his influence on those immediately connected with him was considerable. In 1642 he befriended young Murillo on his arrival in Madrid, received him into his house, and directed his studies for three years. His son-in-law Mazo painted in his manner, and doubtless many pictures by Mazo are attributed to the master. Carreño, though never a pupil, was a favourite and had the good sense to appreciate him and imitate him. His faithful slave Pareja studied his methods and produced work which by the favour of Velazquez procured his manumission from Philip. But the appreciation of the fine talent of Velazquez passed away quickly in Spain, as that country began to fall to pieces.

In addition to the standard works by Palomino, Cean Bermudez, and Pacheco, see the biographical notice by Don Pedro de Madrazo in his *Catalogo del Museo del Prado* (1872); *Velazquez and his Works* (1855) and *Annals of Artists of Spain* (1848), by W. Stirling (afterwards Sir W. Stirling-Maxwell); Ford's *Handbook to Spain* (1855) and his article in the *English Cyclopædia*; *Velazquez and Murillo*, by Charles B. Curtis (1883); the works of W. Burger (T. Thoré); *Gesch. d. Malerei*, by Woltmann and Woermann; Sir Edmund Head's *Handbook of Spanish Painting* (1848); *Works of Velazquez* (prints), by G. W. Reid (1872); *Gaz. d. Beaux Arts*, art. "Velazquez", by Paul Lefort (second period 1879-82); and Justi, *Diego Velazquez u. sein Jahrhundert*, 2 vols., Bonn, 1888. (J. F. W.)

VELEIA, a town of Liguria, near the frontier of Gallia Cisalpina, on the Apennine slope, about 20 miles to the south of Placentia. The "oppidum Veleiatium" is vaguely mentioned by Pliny as belonging to Liguria, but its exact site remained unknown until 1760, when its remains began to be recovered from under a mass of debris, which showed that the city must have been overwhelmed by a landslip from the neighbouring mountain. Among the buildings that have been brought to light are a basilica, an amphitheatre, and several temples. Interesting antiquities from Veleia, including the "tabula alimentaria" of Trajan (see vol. xiii. p. 132), are deposited in the museum at Parma. None of the coins hitherto discovered on the site are later than the time of Probus (276-282).

VELEZ-MÁLAGA, a town of Spain, in the province of Malaga, and 15 miles east-north-east from that town, is finely situated in a fertile valley at the foot of steep mountains (Sierra Tejada), within a mile of the mouth of the small river Velez. Formerly it was a place of considerable commercial importance, but its prosperity has much declined in recent years, and it suffered severely in the earthquakes of 1884. It is associated with many romantic events in the history of the Moorish wars, to which period its old castle belongs. The vegetation of the neighbourhood is most luxuriant, including the aloe, palm, sugar-cane, prickly pear, orange, vine, olive, and sweet potato. The inhabitants are chiefly employed in the various industries connected with the cultivation and export of the products of these. There is also a tunny fishery. The population within the municipal boundaries in 1877 was 24,332.

VELIZH, or WELIZ, a district-town of Russia, in the government of Vitebsk, on the Dwina, 53 miles north-east of the city of Vitebsk. It has an active trade in corn and linseed, grown in the neighbouring provinces, and sent by river to Riga in exchange for fish, salt, tobacco, and groceries. The population (16,370 in 1885) has doubled since about 1860.

Velizh is supposed to have been originally founded by the Lithuanians, but it was deserted in the 16th century. In 1536 the Russians erected here a wooden fort, which, however, was soon taken by the Poles (1580), and it remained in their possession until 1772.

VELLEIUS. See PATERCULUS.

VELLETRI, a town of Italy, in the province of Rome, and 26 miles by rail to the south-east of that city, is picturesquely situated on a spur of Monte Artemisio on the southern edge of the Alban Hills and overlooking the Pontine marshes. The streets are steep, narrow, and irregular. In the highest part of the town are the municipal offices, with an important ancient inscription relating to the restoration of the amphitheatre under Valentinian and Valens. Velletri is the seat of the bishop of Ostia; the cathedral (1660) contains some good sculpture of the school of Sansovino. The neighbourhood produces a celebrated wine, a chief source of wealth to the town. The population in 1881 numbered 13,532.

At the close of the Latin War (336 B.C.) the Volscian Velitræ had its walls razed to the ground and its leading inhabitants banished beyond the Tiber, their lands being given to Roman settlers. It became a flourishing municipium, and was the native place of the Octavian family. In the neighbourhood of Velletri Don Carlos, younger son of Philip V. of Spain, in 1734 gained over the Austrians a decisive victory, which ultimately secured him as Charles III. the kingdom of the Two Sicilies.

VELLORE, a town and military cantonment of India, in North Arcot district of the Madras presidency, on the right bank of the river Palár in 12° 55′ 17″ N. lat. and 79° 10′ 17″ E. long. It has a strongly-built fortress, which was famous in the palmy days of the Carnatic, and which is overlooked by hills in the vicinity. In 1780 it withstood a siege for two years by Hyder Ali. After the fall of Seringapatam (1799) Vellore was selected as the residence of the sons of Tippoo Sahib, and to their intrigues has been attributed the revolt of the sepoys at Vellore in 1806. Besides the fortress, the town contains a handsome Vishnuvite temple with some good carving. In 1881 the population was 37,491 (males 17,605, females 19,886).

VELVET is a silken textile fabric having a short dense piled surface. It is the type of the numerous forms of piled fabric now made, the processes employed in the manufacture of which are noticed under WEAVING (*q.v.*). In all probability the art of velvet-weaving originated in the far East; and it is not till about the beginning of the 14th century that we find any mention of the textile. Fustian, however, which differs from velvet only in material, is spoken of in English ecclesiastical inventories as early as the beginning of the 13th century. The peculiar properties of velvet, the splendid yet softened depth of dye-colour it exhibited, at once marked it out as a fit material for ecclesiastical vestments, royal and state robes, and sumptuous hangings; and the most magnificent textures of mediæval times were Italian velvets. These were in many ways most effectively treated for ornamentation, such as by varying the colour of the pile, by producing pile of different lengths (pile upon pile, or double pile), and by brocading with plain silk, with uncut pile, or with a ground of gold tissue, &c. The earliest sources of European artistic velvets were Lucca, Genoa, Florence, and Venice, and to the present day Genoa continues to send out rich velvet textures. Somewhat later the art was taken up by Flemish weavers, and in the 16th century Bruges attained a reputation for velvets not inferior to that of the great Italian cities. The principal seats of the modern manufacture are Crefeld and Lyons; but, at the former centre especially, a large proportion of an inferior texture, having a silken pile on a cotton foundation and known as *velveteen*, is now made.

VENANTIUS. See FORTUNATUS.

VENDACE is the name of a British freshwater fish of the genus *Coregonus*, of which two other species are indigenous in the fresh waters of the British Islands, viz., the gwyniad and the pollan. The vendace (*C. vandesius*) is restricted to some lochs in Dumfriesshire, Scotland; it is, however, very similar to a species (*C. albula*) which inhabits some of the large and deep lakes of northern Europe. From its general resemblance to a dace the French name of the latter, *vandoise*, was transferred to it at the period when French was the language of the court and aristocracy of Scotland. So great is the local celebrity of the fish that a story has been invented ascribing to Mary Queen of Scots the merit of having introduced it into the Lochmaben lochs. It is considered a great delicacy, and on favourable days when the shoals rise to the surface, near the edges of the loch, great numbers may be taken. It spawns in November. In length it scarcely exceeds 8 inches.

Authentic accounts of the vendace have been published by Sir William Jardine, in *Edinb. Journ. of Nat. and Geog. Science*, iii. p. 4, 1830, and by Robert Knox, in *Trans. Roy. Soc. Edinb.*, xii. p. 503, 1834.

VENDÉE, a maritime department of France, formed in 1790 out of Bas-Poitou, and taking its name from an unimportant tributary of the Sèvre Niortaise, lies between 46° 16′ and 47° 5′ N. lat. and 0° 32′ and 2° 10′ W. long., and is bounded by Loire-Inférieure and Maine-et-Loire on the N., by Deux-Sèvres on the E., by Charente-Inférieure on the S., and by the Atlantic Ocean on the W. for 93 miles. The islands of Yeu (or Dieu) and Noirmoutier are included. The Sèvre Nantaise on the N.E. and the Sèvre Niortaise on the S., besides other streams of minor importance, form natural boundaries. The department falls into three divisions—woodland, plain, and marsh. The highest point (945 feet) is situated in the woodland, which occupies the greater part of Vendée, on the water-parting between the Loire and the rivers of the coast. This region, which, geologically, is composed of granite, gneiss, mica-schist, schist, and lias, abounds in springs, and is fresh and verdant; the landscape is characterized by open fields surrounded by trees, which supplied ambushes and retreats to the Vendéans in the civil war at the end of the 18th century. The plain of Vendée is bare and treeless, but fertile, though poor in springs; geologically it is composed of lias and oolite. The marshes, raised above the sea-level within historic times (four centuries ago), consist of two portions, the Breton marsh in the north and the Poitevin marsh in the south. The region includes salt marshes and cultivated areas artificially drained. Its area is constantly being increased by the alluvium of the rivers and the secular elevation of the coast. The department is drained by the Sèvre Nantaise (tributary of the Loire) and the Boulogne (a feeder of Lake Grandlieu in Loire-Inférieure), both draining into the basin of the Loire; and by the Vie, the Lay (with the Yon), and the Sèvre Niortaise (with the Autise and the Vendée), which flow into the Atlantic. The climate is that of the Girondin region, mild and damp, the temperature rarely rising above 77° or falling below 18° Fahr.; 120 to 150 days of rain give an annual rainfall of 30 inches. The woodland is colder than the plain, and the marsh is damp and unhealthy.

Out of the total area of 1,656,531 acres arable land occupies 1,023,275 acres, grass 290,503, vines 37,467, wood 65,853, and moor, pasture, and uncultivated land 136,432. In 1881 the live stock included 29,790 horses, 4500 mules, 1950 asses, 471,775 cattle, 379,950 sheep (10,000 being of superior breed; total wool-clip 395 tons), 55,000 pigs, and 1625 goats. There were 10,000 beehives (49 tons of honey and 10 tons of wax). The agricultural products in 1884 were returned as follows:—wheat 7,312,316 bushels, meslin 65,736, rye 218,720, barley 1,218,855, buckwheat 358,985, maize 33,000, millet 129,973, oats 2,815,436, potatoes 3,938,214, beetroot 324,601 tons, wine 15,569,312 gallons, colza seed 7790 tons, hemp seed 551 tons, linseed 991 tons, flax 1786 tons, and fodder 745,792 tons. The forests (oak, chestnut, pine, poplar, hornbeam, maple, ash, beech, and elm) yielded 3,180,000 cubic feet of wood, a third of which was applied to various industrial uses. Apples, pears, peaches, plums, cherries, and walnuts are the principal fruits grown. The salt marshes, 4572 acres in extent and employing 3500 workmen, yielded 2436 tons of salt in 1882. In 1884 18,409 tons of coal were mined. Iron, antimony, lead, "the Vendée diamond" (a kind of quartz), china clay, and slate are obtained; and granite, gneiss, slate schist, limestone, cement, millstones, and clay are objects of industry. The celebrated beds of sea-shells near St Michel-en-l'Herm—2300 feet long, 985 broad, and from 30 to 50 feet in depth—show to what an extent the coast has risen. The wool spinning and weaving industry occupies 12,570 spindles and 520 hand-looms; cotton, 3100 spindles and 5 looms; linen, 388 spindles and 478 looms (80 being power looms). There are potteries, paper-mills, tan-yards, dye-works, a glass-work, manufactories of hats, boots and shoes, and lampblack, flour-mills, distilleries, tile-works, and shipbuilding-yards, and sardines and tinned foods are prepared,—in all 575 industrial establishments. The sardine fishery occupies 800 boats and 2000 men, and there are extensive oyster-beds near Sables-d'Olonne. Corn, cattle, mules, fish, salt, wine, honey, wood, glass, and manure are exported; wine, wood, building material, and coal are among the imports. The shipping places are Bouin and Beauvoir in the Breton marsh, and Noirmoutier, the island of Yeu, St Gilles-sur-Vie, Sables-d'Olonne, L'Aiguillon, and Luçon in the Poitevin marsh. In 1882 a total of 391 vessels (130,688 tons) entered and cleared from all these ports. Vendée has 212 miles of railway, 335 of national and 2966 of other roads, and 82 of navigable rivers and canals. In 1881 the population was 421,642, and in 1886 434,808,—an increase of 191,382 since 1801. The department forms the diocese of Luçon, has its court of appeal and academy at Poitiers, and is included in the district of the Nantes army corps. There are three arrondissements (La Roche-sur-Yon, the chef-lieu of the department, with 10,991 inhabitants in 1886; Fontenay-le-Comte, 9282; and Sables-d'Olonne, 10,114), 30 cantons, and 300 communes. Luçon (6285 inhabitants) is connected with the sea by a canal, and has a cathedral of the 11th, 13th, 14th, 16th, and 18th centuries, with an elegant Gothic spire, a cloister of the 15th and 16th centuries, an episcopal palace, and a hospital, with portraits of the bishops of Luçon.

VENDÔME, a town of France, chief-lieu of an arrondissement in the department of Loir-et-Cher, is situated on the river Loir, 109 miles south-west of Paris by the railway to Tours, at the junction of the line from Blois to Le Mans. The abbey of the Trinity (12th to 15th century) has a fine portal in florid Gothic style. A graceful balustrade runs round the building at the spring of the roof, and two rows of flying buttresses, themselves resting on other elegant buttresses, support the nave. The high gallery of the triforium, the rich traceries of the windows, and the modern fonts are worthy of notice. Part of the building is in the Angevin style of the beginning of the 13th century. In the choir are some fine stalls and glass of the 15th and 16th centuries. The steeple, 262 feet high, which stands isolated in front of the church, belongs to the middle of the 12th century, and is one of the finest examples of Transition architecture. The lower part is rectangular and the upper octagonal, with a stone spire. It has been recently restored. The church of La Madeleine (15th century) is surmounted by a stone spire, an indifferent imitation of that of the abbey. The fine tower of St Martin (16th century) is all that remains of the church of that name. The town-hall occupies the old gate of St George; its river front is composed of two large crenellated and machicolated towers, connected by a pavilion. The ancient hospital of St James afterwards became a college of the Oratorians, in which Mascaron was a professor, but is now a lyceum; the charming chapel, dating from the 15th century, in the most florid Gothic style, is still preserved. Parts of the chateau of the counts of Vendôme are as old as the 11th century. A public promenade leads to the curious vaults under the castle. Vendôme is the seat of an archæological and scientific society, possesses a library of 15,000 volumes and 305 MSS., and a museum, mostly archæological, in front of which stands a statue of Ronsard. There are some interesting houses of the 15th and 16th centuries, and near the town are the remains of a Roman theatre. The population in 1881 was 7913 (commune 9420), the corresponding figures for 1886 being 7843 and 9325.

Vendôme (*Vindocinum*) appears originally to have been a Gallic oppidum, replaced later by a feudal castle, around which the modern town has arisen. Christianity was introduced by St Bienheuré in the 5th century, and the abbey of the Trinity was founded in 1030. About the end of the 10th century Vendôme became an independent county, and was raised to a duchy in 1515. It long belonged to a branch of the Bourbon family. During the Wars of Religion the town was sacked by the Protestants, by members of the League, and was finally taken by Henry IV. Since then its industrial and commercial importance (tanneries and manufactories of woollen stuffs and gloves) has fallen off. Marshal de Rochambeau was a native of Vendôme.

VENEERING is the art of attaching thin sheets or leaves of wood, ivory, &c., to the surface of wood or other material of a less costly or less ornamental description. It is thus in connexion with wood, ivory, &c., equivalent to plating in the working of metals. The art is largely practised in cabinet-work. Veneers are either cut or sawn from solid blocks or planks. The ordinary veneer saw is a circular instrument of large diameter, made up of segments of thin steel bolted on a strong circular iron frame, which gives the requisite stiffness and rigidity to the saw edge. The teeth of the saw are minute and finely set, so as to waste as little as possible of the valuable material as sawdust. With such a saw from 8 to 16 leaves per inch may be cut out of a block of wood and as many as 30 leaves of ivory, one-third of the solid being reduced to sawdust. Veneers are also made from certain straight-grained and pliant woods with cutting tools, either by the process of planing or of turning. For these methods of veneer-making, the wood to be operated on is first reduced to blocks of a size equal to the cutting edges by which they are to be made into veneer, and are then steamed in a closed chamber to soften the fibre. In the plane veneer-cutting machines the block of wood may be stationary and the cutter movable, or *vice versa*, and the cutting edge is applied obliquely to the block. Immediately in front of the cutter pressure is applied to the block to keep the shaving from splitting up. With the planing machine from 100 to 150 veneer leaves can be cut from each inch of thickness. By the lathe-turning method continuous strips of veneer are obtained from circular blocks the width of the cutter, and it is possible to reduce the block till a core of about only 9 inches remains. In the cutting, as opposed to the sawing, of veneers there is no waste whatever of the solid material; but cut veneers are not so serviceable, and the most valuable veneer woods, being hard, cross-fibred, and brittle, cannot be treated otherwise than by sawing. In veneering, the surfaces to be united, after roughening, so as to give grip, are coated with thin glue applied very hot, and then tightly pressed together in a veneering press, with heated cauls or plates of zinc applied to their surfaces, these cauls being contoured to the necessary outline when bent veneers are being planted. Should the veneer show any blistering after removal from the press, heat, damp, and local pressure are applied till veneer and wood are

VENEZUELA

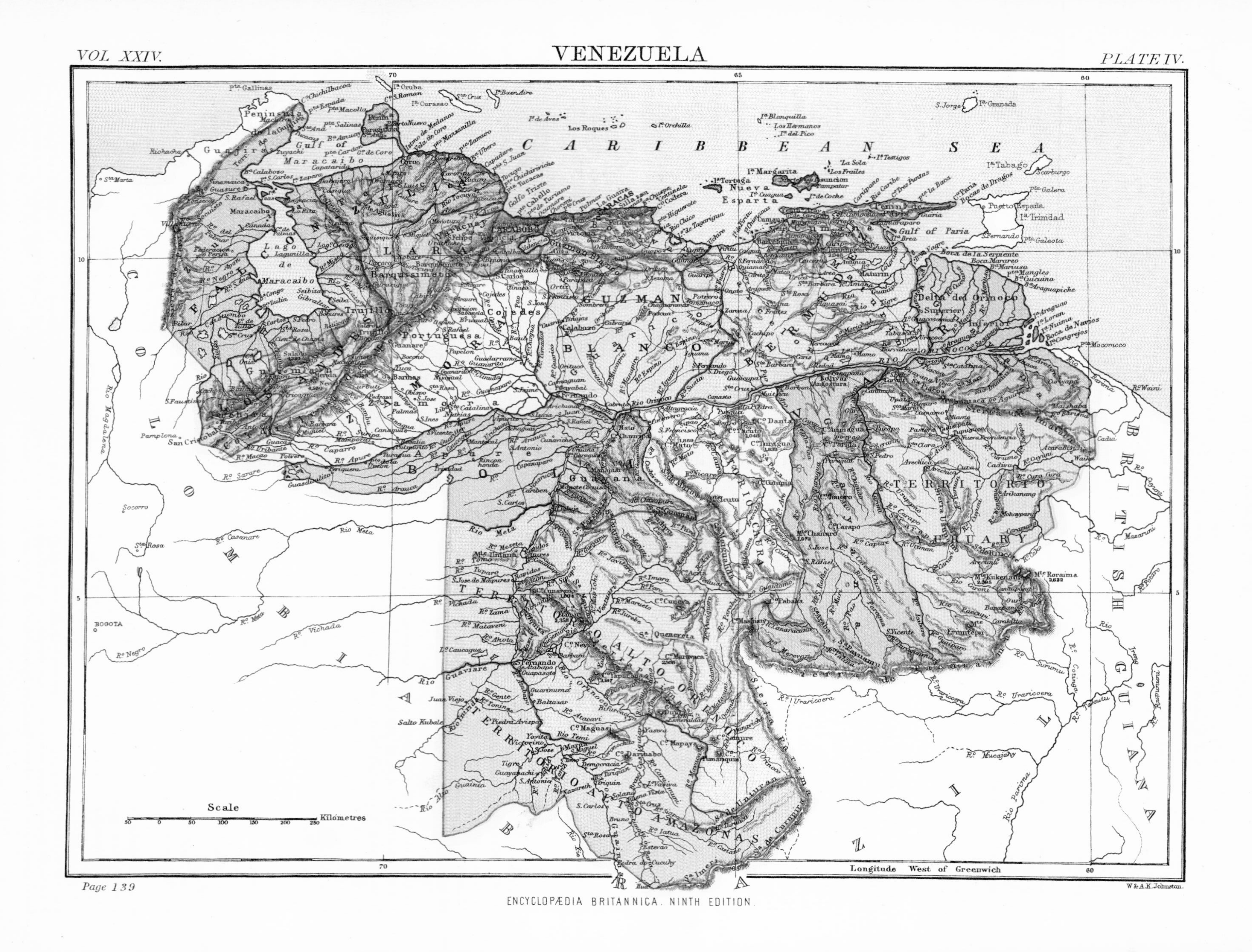
CARIBBEAN SEA
BRITISH GUIANA
COLOMBIA
BRAZIL
Gulf of Maracaibo
Lago de Maracaibo
Gulf of Paria
Delta del Orinoco
Peninsula de la Guajira
Guajira
Trujillo
Barquisimeto
Portuguesa
Cojedes
Guzman Blanco
Caracas
Carabobo
Zamora
Bermudez
Guayana
Territorio Caura
Territorio Yuruary
Territorio Alto Orinoco
Territorio Amazonas
Sierra Parima
Rio Orinoco
Rio Meta
Rio Apure
Rio Guaviare
Rio Magdalena
Maracaibo
Angostura
Maturin
Barcelona
Cumana
Nueva Esparta
I.ª Margarita
I.ª Tortuga
I.ª Orchila
Los Roques
I.ª de Aves
I.ª Curazao
I.ª Oruba
I.ª Buen Aire
I.ª Blanquilla
Los Hermanos
I.ª Trinidad
I.ª Tabago
I.ª Grenada
Puerto España
Pampatar
Asuncion
Valencia
Calabozo
Barinas
Merida
San Cristobal
Pamplona
Bogota
Socorro
S.ᵗᵃ Rosa
S.ᵗᵃ Marta
Richacha
S. Fernando
S. Carlos
Mt.ᵉ Roraima
Scale
Kilometres
50 0 50 100 150 200 250
Longitude West of Greenwich
70
65
60
10
5
W. & A. K. Johnston.

solidly cemented together. The surface is afterwards smoothed, polished, and finished as in dealing with solid cabinet woods.

VENEREAL DISEASES. See PATHOLOGY, vol. xviii. p. 404, and SURGERY, vol. xxii. p. 686.

ate IV. VENEZUELA,[1] a federal republic in South America, lying between about 57° and 73° 30′ W. long. and 1° 40′ and 12° 26′ N. lat. The republic claims that the area of its territory is 632,807 square miles; but the boundaries are not yet definitely fixed, and its area is consequently uncertain. In the south-west it claims large tracts extending to the south of the equator, which are also claimed by Colombia and Ecuador; and in the east it claims from British Guiana the upper valley of the Essequibo, together with all the territory on the left bank of that river below the influx of the Rupununi. Of the total area claimed only about 439,000 square miles are actually under Venezuelan administration.

Physical Features.—A branch of the eastern chain of the Andes enters Venezuela in the west about 7° N. lat., and under the name of the Sierra Nevada de Merida proceeds north-eastwards towards Triste Gulf. This branch consists of parallel chains enclosing elevated valleys, in one of which lies the town of Merida at the height of 5400 feet, overlooked by the highest summit of the chain (Picacho de la Sierra, 15,000 feet). The sierra contains the water-parting between the basin of the Orinoco and those of the small rivers on the north-west. Hence it may be considered to terminate where the Rio Claro, the stream on which Barquisimeto stands, after rising on its western slopes flows eastwards into the basin of the Orinoco. Beyond the Claro begin two parallel ranges known as the Maritime Andes of Venezuela, which stretch east and west along the coast. The valley between these two ranges is the most densely peopled part of Venezuela. Within it lie the town of Valencia (1800 feet), the Lake of Valencia (1400 feet), and the town of Carácas (3000 feet). Above Carácas the highest peak of the system, Pico de la Silla, rises to 8740 feet. Behind the wide bay between Cape Codera and Cumana there is an interruption in the Maritime Andes; but both ranges reappear between Cumana and the Gulf of Paria. West of the Maritime Andes low ranges (3500-5000 feet) trend northwards from the end of the Sierra de Merida towards the coast, on the east side of the Lake of Maracaibo, while the region on the west of that lake consists of lagoon-studded lowlands. East and south of the Sierra de Merida and the Maritime Andes the Venezuelan territory consists mainly of the basin of the Orinoco. This region is for the greater part of its extent thinly populated and little known. It consists of two portions,—a vast hilly or mountainous area, densely-wooded, in the south-east and south, and level plains in the north-west between the Orinoco and the Apure and the mountains. The latter is known as the llanos of the Orinoco, a region described by Humboldt as a vast "sea of grass," with islands of wood scattered here and there. Since the time of Humboldt, however, the aspect of these plains would seem to have changed very considerably. On the occasion of Appun's visit in 1850 trees seem still to have been comparatively rare; but a different aspect was presented when Dr P. Jonas visited the llanos in 1878. From the Galera, the southernmost range of hills north of the Orinoco basin, the traveller saw a vast plain thickly grown with low trees, among which the chaparro was chiefly represented. Few places were quite destitute of trees, and these of small extent. As far as Calabozo (about one-third of the distance between the hills and the Apure) it was now chaparros (evergreen oaks), now mimosas, which were the prevailing feature of the landscape, though other trees were not rare. But towards the south the open grass-covered spaces increased in number and area. To the south of Calabozo woods of considerable extent were seen. This change in the character of the landscape is due to the decline of horse and cattle rearing in the llanos, partly in consequence of political disturbances and partly of a murrain which broke out in 1843 among horses, mules, and asses, and in that and several subsequent years reduced their numbers by several thousands.

Geology.—Geologically the chief mountain ranges of Venezuela are all similar in structure. The nucleus of the Sierra Nevada de Merida is formed of plutonic or metamorphic rocks (granite, syenite, gneiss, crystalline schists, &c.), and this series is continued throughout the northern chain of the Maritime Andes. Stratified rocks belonging to the Cretaceous system are found on both sides of the plutonic nucleus of the former range, and are those chiefly seen in the southern chains of the Maritime Andes. Most of these deposits belong to the upper members of the Cretaceous system; but the lower members come to the surface in considerable patches west of the Sierra Nevada de Merida, and in the chains just referred to. Tertiary and Quaternary deposits (generally as compact marl, sand, shingle, and conglomerate) are spread over nearly all the llanos, as well as round the Gulf of Maracaibo, and in the plains drained to the north by the Unare, between the two sections of the Maritime Andes. The hills and mountains east of the Orinoco, according to Humboldt, Schomburgk, and Codazzi, seem to be mainly composed of granite, syenite, and other crystalline rocks.

Climate.—The climate and vegetation are such as might be expected from the tropical situation of the country. But Venezuela, as well as the rest of tropical South America east of the Andes, is directly exposed to the trade-winds. The temperature is thereby considerably moderated, and no such extremes of heat are to be met with as are experienced in the corresponding latitudes of northern Africa. The more populous parts of Venezuela are, however, hotter than the maritime districts of Guiana, being less directly exposed to the Atlantic breezes. At La Guaira the mean temperature of the year is 85° Fahr.; at Carácas, only 10 miles distant but 3000 feet higher, it is 71°·2 Fahr.; and the greatest extremes that have been observed at the latter station since 1868 are 83°·4 and 48° Fahr. At both stations the hottest periods are the middle of April and the end of August, when the sun is in the zenith. Everywhere there is a well-marked distinction between a dry and a rainy season, the latter occurring in the English summer months, when the sun is in the northern hemisphere and the force of the trade-wind on the north coast of South America is considerably slackened. At La Guaira the rainy season proper lasts only three months (May to August); but this season lasts longer in the mountains and in the llanos.

Fauna.—The fauna includes among the mammals the rodents and carnivores common to the rest of tropical South America. The manatee is met with nearly everywhere on the coast. In all the rivers are to be found caymans, electric eels, rays, and caribs, the last (*Pygocentrus piraya*, *P. nigricans*, *P. niger*, Müll.) consisting of several species of savage and voracious fishes armed with two rows of very sharp teeth. Among the venomous serpents are the striped rattlesnake (*Crotalus durissus*), *Lachesis mutus*, an ally of the rattlesnakes, and a rather rare species of *Cophias*. Among the non-venomous sorts the commonest are the boa constrictor, the anaconda (*Eunectes murinus*), and the *Coluber variabilis*. Among birds is a singular form known from its note as the bell-bird (*Chasmorhynchus carunculatus*). Coral banks abound on the coast; like the waters which surround the roots of the mangroves, these teem with marine life, and are peculiarly rich in beautifully coloured crustaceans. Swarms of locusts sometimes commit great ravages among the fields and plantations.

Flora.—The lower slopes of all the mountains are clad with the richest tropical vegetation. Amidst an endless variety of dicotyledonous foliage trees, interlaced by numerous twiners and climbers and adorned with epiphytic orchids, *Tillandsiæ*, aroids, and *Loranthaceæ*, grow numerous palms and tree-ferns, up to the height of about 3500 feet. From among the forest trees may be singled out for mention the silk-cotton tree (*Bombax Ceiba*), the mango (*Mangifera indica*), the saman (*Inga saman*),—remarkable, like the last-mentioned, less for its height than for the extent and density of the shade which it casts,—the cow-tree (*Brosimum Galactodendron*), and the *Attalea speciosa*,—this last being one of the finest ornaments of the palm tribe, a tree whose stem, 40 feet in height, carries erect on its crown leaves which also grow to a height of 40 feet, with a breadth of 8 feet. The mouths of the Orinoco and many parts of the coast are rendered unhealthy by mangrove swamps, which are no doubt partly to blame for the yearly recurrence of

[1] The name means "little Venice," and is a modification of the name of Venecia (Venice), originally bestowed by Alonzo de Ojeda in 1499 on an Indian village composed of pile-dwellings on the shores of the Gulf of Maracaibo, which was called by him the Gulf of Venecia.

yellow fever in many of the coast towns. From these swamps, however, La Guaira is free, and there the yellow fever is not a regular visitant.

Vegetable Products.—The two chief crops grown for food are manioc and maize, the latter being generally ground coarse and baked into a kind of cakes called *arepas*, which are eaten hot like the Mexican tortillas. Among other vegetable products which take an important place in the Venezuelan dietary are all kinds of tropical fruits, including several kinds of melons and pumpkins, the sugar-cane (the sugar in a little refined condition, known as *papelon*, being a favourite article of food), the taro, sweet potatoes, various beans (including two species of *Phaseolus*, which grow only high up in the mountains, but are highly prized everywhere), and a species of hemlock (*Conium moschatum*), which is eaten like celery. Of plantation products grown for export by far the most important are coffee and cocoa, next after which come tobacco and cotton. The following table (I.) shows (in thousands of ℔) the variations in the export of these products in several years since 1830-31 :—

Year.	Coffee.	Cocoa.	Tobacco.	Cotton.	Year.	Coffee.	Cocoa.	Tobacco.	Cotton.
1830-31	11,684	7304	103	98	1864-65	28,497	8,386	548	5405
1840-41	26,316	7770	1212	2038	1874-75	72,263	10,725	337	4601
1850-51	38,432	8259	1539	781	1885-86	86,115	11,268	156	273

This table clearly shows that coffee is rapidly taking a more and more important place as the leading staple of Venezuela. The only date at which the export of coffee shows a decline as compared with the previous date mentioned is 1864-65, when, it is clear, from a comparison of this column with that under cotton, that a considerable area must have been temporarily given up to the cultivation of cotton in consequence of the Civil War in the United States. As regards quantity, Venezuela held the fifth place among the coffee-exporting countries of the world on an average of the ten years 1872-82.[1] Both coffee and cocoa are grown under the shade of erythrinas, the scarlet racemes of which at the flowering season impart a brilliant aspect to the plantations. Besides the products above-mentioned, sugar and indigo at one time figured largely among the exports of Venezuela; but both of them have now almost disappeared from the list of exports, the former in consequence of the decline in cultivation, the latter because of the increasing consumption of papelon among the inhabitants.

The following table (II.) shows, in thousands of acres, the extent of land under the principal crops in 1875, according to Codazzi, and in 1883 according to official estimates :—

	1875.	1883.		1875.	1883.
Coffee	335·7	343·1	Manioc	42·5	67·9
Sugar-cane	86·0	97·1	Cocoa	50·9	60·8
Bananas	69·2	92·4	Tobacco	9·9	15·6
Vegetables	..	97·1	Various fruits	..	21·2
Maize	42·5	67·9	Cotton	14·8	4·9

Live-Stock.—The number of live-stock was officially returned in 1883 as follows:—cattle 2,926,733; sheep and goats 3,490,563; horses 291,603; mules 247,703; asses 658,764; pigs 976,500.

Minerals.—The principal minerals of Venezuela are gold, copper, phosphates, and coal. The rich auriferous deposits on the banks of the Yuruari lie 100 miles south-west of the principal mouth of the Orinoco. At Aroa in the north-west, about 75 miles west of Puerto Cabello, are rich deposits of copper ore. Phosphates are obtained from the islands of Orchilla and Aves, which lie to the east of the Leeward Islands of the Dutch. A large deposit of bituminous coal, said to be of very good quality, exists about 6 miles south of Barcelona, and a concession for a railway from this port to the coal-bed has been obtained from the Government. Another extensive deposit of bituminous coal has been found on the banks of the Utare, a small stream which empties itself into the sea about 40 miles east of La Guaira. Good petroleum is refined from deposits worked near Belijoque in the state of Los Andes. Both gold and copper ore are important exports, gold ranking in this respect next after coffee. The total amount of gold exported from Ciudad Bolivar from 1866 to 31st December 1886, so far as the export was controlled by the state, was 1,946,383 oz.; but it is estimated that within that time about half a million oz. were smuggled away. During the five years 1882-86 the average annual yield was about £740,000. The field from which this yield is derived is at present one of the most promising in the world, but the frontier disputes between Great Britain and Venezuela interfere with the investment of capital for the development of some portions of it to which both Governments lay claim. Silver and tin are also met with, but neither has yet attained any commercial importance.

Industry.—Manufacturing industries are in general undeveloped. Artisans from Europe and North America are now settled in all the chief towns, and cotton weaving factories have been established. The manufacturing industries most extensively pursued are the making of shoes and hats. The latter industry is chiefly in the hands of Germans. A material called jipijapa is very largely used for the making of a kind of hats in imitation of Panama straw hats.

Commerce.—The total value of the imports amounted in the year 1885-86 to £2,498,135, and that of the exports to £3,292,171. The principal exports, besides the plantation products and minerals already mentioned, are hides and skins, coir, and animals; those of minor importance are starch, indigo, sugar, tonqua beans, cinchona, caoutchouc, divi-divi, cocoa-nuts, copaiba balsam, plants, and timber. The principal imports are manufactured articles, drugs, and wine, the last from Spain. Petroleum is imported from the United States, though it is expected that the native supplies will soon meet the home demand. Foreign commerce is chiefly carried on with the United States, Germany, France, and England. There is also a coasting trade of considerable magnitude (value £2,382,719 in 1883). The chief seaports are La Guaira (14,000 inhabitants) and Puerto Cabello (10,145), which has the finest natural harbour in Venezuela, enclosed by a ring of coral reefs; the next in importance are Maracaibo (31,921), Ciudad Bolivar (10,861), Carupano (12,389), Puerto Sucre, Puerto Guzman Blanco, La Vela (the port of Coro, opposite the island of Curaçao), and Guiria (on the Gulf of Paria). Ciudad Bolivar is 236 miles up the river Orinoco, the navigation of which by any mouth has been free to all nations since the 25th of October 1886.

Communication.—The total length of railways open at the end of 1886 was 144 miles, and 263 miles were then in construction. The length of telegraph lines at the same date was 2595 miles. The railways already in existence or in construction are all short lines connecting the chief seaports with the nearest important inland towns or seats of mineral production, or lines radiating to the more important towns round Carácas. The principal inland towns, besides CARÁCAS (*q.v.*), the capital (population 70,509 in 1883), are Valencia (36,145), Barquisimeto (28,198), Merida (10,747), Calabozo, Barinas, Nutrias, and Maturin (14,743).

Population, Area, &c.—The republic is divided into eight states, eight federal territories, the federal district, and two national colonies, the names of which, with their area in square miles and their population according to an official estimate for 1st January 1886, are given below :—

	Area.	Population.		Area.	Population.
States—			Yuruari	81,123	19,852
Carabobo	2,985	167,499	Caura	22,565	..
Guzman Blanco	33,890	515,418	Goajira	3,608	36,500
Lara	9,297	245,439	Colon	166	137
Los Andes	14,720	317,195	Armisticio	7,151	..
Zamora	25,212	245,457	Delta	25,347	..
Falcon	36,213	198,260	Federal District	45	70,078
Bolivar	88,701	57,169	*Colonies—*		
Bermudez	32,243	285,377	Guzman Blanco	214	1,599
Territories—			Bolivar	9	..
Alto Orinoco, Amazonas	119,780	38,340		594,197	2,198,320

Armisticio, Alto Orinoco, Amazonas, Yuruari, and Delta include the disputed tracts of territory. The population of Caura in the preceding table is included in that of the state of Bolivar, the population of Armisticio and Delta in that of the states of Bolivar, Zamora, and Los Andes, and of the colony of Bolivar in that of the state of Guzman Blanco. The agricultural colonies are under the administration of a governor subordinated to the ministry of progress (*del fomento*). The pure white population is estimated at only 1 per cent. of the whole, the remainder of the inhabitants being Negroes (originally slaves, now all free), Indians, and mixed races (mulattos and zambos).

Religion, Education, &c.—The Roman Catholic is the religion of the state, but liberty of worship is guaranteed by law. So far as legislative enactment goes, elementary education is now well provided for; but in the year ending 30th June 1886 the total number of common, municipal, and private schools was 1957, and the number of pupils 99,466. There are also two universities (Carácas and Merida), 19 federal colleges, and various other public and private institutions for higher education. The standing army consists of about 2800 men, but every male subject between eighteen and forty-five has to be enrolled in the national militia. The monetary system of Venezuela is that of the Latin convention, the franc being represented by the *bolivar*. The French metric system of weights and measures is likewise the legal system; but the old weights, the libra = 1·014 ℔ avoir., the quintal = 101·4 ℔ avoir., and the arroba = 25·35 ℔, are also in use.

Finance.—The revenue, which is chiefly derived from customs duties, amounted in 1885-86 to £1,093,644 and the expenditure to £1,239,400. The public debt, of which the external portion alone amounted in 1878 to nearly £11,000,000, including arrears of interest, was reduced in 1881 to a total of £4,000,000 by the issue of new bonds in place of all the old ones, both external and internal. At the end of 1886 the external debt amounted to £2,680,850, bearing interest at 4 per cent.

[1] Ranking after Brazil, Java, Ceylon, and Hayti.

Constitution.—The constitution is modelled to some extent on that of the United States. At the head of the executive is a president, who is assisted by eight ministers and a federal council. The legislative authority is vested in a congress of two houses,—a senate (24 members) and a chamber of deputies (52 members). The members of the chamber of deputies (one for every 35,000 inhabitants, and one more for an excess of 15,000) are elected every four years directly by the electors of the states and the federal district, those of the senate by the legislative bodies of the different states (three for each). The congress elects the members of the federal council, in which there is one senator and one deputy for each of the political divisions of the republic, and one deputy for the federal district. The federal council elects the president. The federal council and the president remain in office for two years.

History.—The coast of Venezuela was the first part of the American mainland sighted by Columbus, who, during his third voyage in 1498, entered the Gulf of Paria and sailed along the coast of the delta of the Orinoco. In the following year a much greater extent of coast was traced out by Alonzo de Ojeda, who was accompanied by the more celebrated Amerigo Vespucci. In 1550 the territory was erected into the captain-generalcy of Carácas, and it remained under Spanish rule till the early part of the 19th century. During this period Negro slaves were introduced; but less attention was given by the Spaniards to this region than to other parts of Spanish America, which were known to be rich in the precious metals.

In 1810 Venezuela rose against the Spanish yoke, and on 14th July in the following year the independence of the territory was proclaimed. A war ensued which lasted for upwards of ten years, and the principal events of which are described under BOLIVAR (*q.v.*), a native of Carácas and the leading spirit of the revolt. It was not till 30th March 1845 that the independence of the republic was recognized by Spain in the treaty of Madrid. At the date of the battle of Carabobo (1821), by which the power of Spain in this part of the world was broken, Venezuela formed part of the federal state of Colombia, which embraced also the present Colombia and Ecuador; but a meeting of Venezuelan notables on 26th November 1829 declared for the separation of their country from the confederacy. Venezuela passed through the first years of its independent existence with more quietness than the other members of the confederacy. In 1846 there began a series of civil wars and revolutions, which continued, with but short periods of rest, down to the close of 1870. The chief rival parties in these internal dissensions were the Unionists and the Federalists; the former aimed at securing a strong central Government, while the latter, who were ultimately victorious, desired to obtain a large measure of independence for separate states. It was during these troubles that the emancipation of the slaves took place, under a law of 24th March 1854. On 28th March 1864 a federal constitution was drawn up for the republic. Three years later, however, the civil war broke out again, and matters continued in an unsettled state, till in December 1870 Don Guzman Blanco, who had taken the leading part on the side of the Federalists, was declared provisional president. From that date Blanco acted as dictator till 20th February 1873, when he was elected constitutional president for four years, and it has been chiefly owing to his energy and ability that the confederacy has since proceeded on a course of orderly development. The two flourishing agricultural colonies already mentioned were founded during his first tenure of office, in 1874. The chief event in recent years has been the re-division of the territory in 1881 into the states and territories whose names are given in the table above.

Bibliography.—See Humboldt, *Voyage aux Régions Équinoxiales*, Paris, 1804; C. F. Appun, *Unter den Tropen*, vol. i., Jena, 1871; A. Codazzi, *Resumen de la Geografia de Venezuela*, Paris, 1841; Dr R. Villavicencio, *La Republica de Venezuela bajo la Punta de Vista de la Geografia*, &c., Carácas, 1880; Dr W. Sievers, "Reiseberichte aus Venezuela," in *Mitteil. geogr. Gesellsch.*, Hamburg, 1884; Dr P. Jonas, "Nachrichten aus Venezuela," in *Petermann's Mitteilungen*, 1878 and 1879; British and U. S. *Consular Reports*, &c.; J. M. Spence, *The Land of Bolivar*, London, 2 vols., 1878. Regarding the geology, see Hermann Karsten, *Géologie de l'Ancienne Colombie Bolivarienne* (with a geological map and eight plates), Berlin, 4to, 1886; and a paper on the gold mines of Venezuela by C. Le Neve Foster, in *Quart. Journ. Geol. Sc.*, vol. xxv., 1869. Regarding the fauna and flora, see A. Ernst, *Estudios sobre la Flora y Fauna de Venezuela*, Carácas, 1877, 4to. There is a map of Venezuela by A. Codazzi in four sheets, with views and statistical tables, 1876; and a physical and political map accompanies the *Statistical Annuary* issued by the ministry of progress (Carácas, 1887). (G. G. C.)

VENICE

PART I.—HISTORY.

[Origin of the state.] ALTHOUGH the numerous marshy islands of the lagoons extending along the north-western shores of the Adriatic between Altinum and Adria are known to have been largely used from the beginning of the 5th century by the inhabitants of Venetia (compare vol. xiii. p. 447)—one of the twenty-nine provinces into which Italy was divided by Constantine—as temporary retreats from successive barbarian invasions, the first permanent settlement on the site of the present city of Venice—the Rivo Alto (Rialto) and its numerous adjacent islets—cannot with certainty be traced further back than to the beginning of the 9th century. The physical conditions with which the earliest inhabitants had to deal were such as might seem singularly unpropitious to the growth of a large and prosperous city. Their untillable and salt-encrusted soil possessed no kind of mineral wealth; the thickets which here and there diversified the surface of the barren marshes produced no serviceable timber; and even drinkable water was hardly obtainable; yet it was here that the Venetians by their inventiveness, their energy, their industry, and their genius for commerce succeeded in establishing themselves on a firm soil and maintaining their independence, in making their neighbours their tributaries, in sending their fleets to distant shores, in controlling the destiny of empires, and consolidating a naval power that is unique in the history of the world.

[Maritime tribunes.] The Venetian form of government—that of an aristocratic republic—had its first beginnings at a very early period. Originally all power had been delegated to magistrates known as *tribuni maritimi* or maritime tribunes; but in 697, in order to give greater strength to the supreme power and more unity to the popular representation, a *doge* or duke was chosen, who had his residence in the little town of Heraclea. *[Doge.]* The first to bear this title was Paulucio Anafesto; the assembly by which he was elected consisted of the entire body of the inhabitants, not only of the towns on the mainland, which were constantly under fear of renewed barbarian devastations, but also those of the islets of the lagoons. Although all had equal electoral privileges, there were gradations of social rank, the citizens being divided into three classes—the *maggiori*, the *mediocri*, and the *minori*. The new arrangement lasted only forty years, when a general assembly resolved by acclamation on the abolition of the ducal power, for which was substituted that of the *maestri della milizia*, whose term of office was to last only for a year. The inconveniences of the new system, however, soon became apparent, and five years later (742) the assembly demanded the restoration of a single popular representative with life tenure, who again bore the title of doge. On this occasion the newly elected doge transferred his residence from Heraclea to Malamocco. The practical risks involved in the new experiment are obvious. In the succession of doges some were almost sure to show themselves unfit for the supreme power, others to disregard the authority of the auxiliary magistrates associated with them for purposes of control, and some even to aim at the establishment of an hereditary tyranny. Consequently the next sixty years witnessed a succession of bloody revolts, in the course of which three doges were put to death, one deposed and exiled, and several others condemned to lose their eyes. Nor was the incapacity or the ambition of individuals the sole cause of such revolutions: new circumstances as they arose sometimes compelled the doges by the very law of their existence to seek support outside the limits of the state, at one time from the Greek empire, whose frontier extended to their very doors, at another time from the Lombards, the latest invaders of Italy, who had permanently established themselves there and were daily acquiring new influence. Foreigners who, in connexion with the interests

of commerce, had entered into close relations with the Venetians took advantage of these to stir up troubles, and sought to conciliate the doges with a view to the enlargement of their trading privileges or the concession of monopolies. Between 712 and 810 various struggles arose which called for the intervention in the lagoons of the generals of Pippin and his son Charlemagne. Doge Obelerio, a declared partisan of the Franks, allowed a war to break out between the Venetians and the Lombards, in the course of which Pippin seized Grado, the see of the patriarch, burnt Caorle, Jesolo, and Heraclea, encamped in Albiola, and, forcing his way into the lagoon, threatened Malamocco itself (see map, p. 157 below). Peace was afterwards concluded, and the danger to which the last refuge of the fugitives from the mainland had been exposed led to their increased security. For, whether from the instinct of self-preservation or from a growing consciousness of the idea of fatherland, these fishermen became drawn together more closely than ever for purposes of common defence, and found themselves possessed of a power hitherto unsuspected, so that they were able to compel their enemies to respect their independence and enter into commercial relations with them. The year 810 was one of the most important in the annals of Venice: it was then that the people finally abandoned the mainland in order to make the Rivo Alto with its surrounding islets the permanent seat of their government. The same year witnessed the beginnings of the basilica of St Mark. Angelo Partecipazio, who had proposed the migration to the Rialto, was chosen doge, and the town of Venice may be said to have been then founded.

War with Pippin.

Foundation of the city.

Early doges.

From 811 to 1026 there was a succession of eighteen doges, of whom no fewer than fifteen were selected out of three leading families, political power thus plainly tending to become hereditary. It was no uncommon thing, however, for the people again to dismiss those whom they had thus placed in power. Murder, exile, cruel punishments, closed the career of more than one of the doges who had been called to the supreme authority by a unanimous vote; whole families connected with rulers who had been deposed or put to death were compelled to quit the islands, and sought the help of the emperor Otho II. That emperor was preparing an expedition against Venice at the very moment of his death; and now once more the Venetians found safety in the very greatness of the danger which had threatened them, for the peril itself indicated to them the future at which they ought to aim if they would live and rule.

Suppression of Adriatic pirates.

From the necessities of its geographical position the new state was bound to become a maritime power and to look to the East. Towards the end of the 10th century the doge Pietro Orseolo by a vigorous effort cleared the sea of pirates, who dwelt on the eastern coast of the Adriatic and seriously harassed the Venetian commerce, and pursued them into the recesses of Quarnero and the islands of Istria. On 20th May 998, having advanced as far as Dalmatia, he came upon them in their apparently inaccessible retreats, and inflicted upon them a great slaughter. Having thus given full security to trade, he constituted himself protector of the sea from Trieste to Albania, receiving in consequence the title of duke of Dalmatia. It was to symbolize this dominion that Venice instituted the superb ceremonial of the espousals of the doge with the Adriatic, which was annually observed on Ascension Day.

Period of crusades.

The republic began henceforward to undertake the business of transporting to the East the successive armies of crusaders, to whom she lent on hire the fleets which were built in her arsenals; and these bold enterprises, at once religious, commercial, and military, procured for her in exchange important stations on the east of the Adriatic and in the islands, as well as colonies and factories advantageous for her commerce. The whole littoral from Trieste to Albania became in this way a sort of prolongation of the Venetian coast. The Byzantine emperors could hardly fail to become jealous of this great though pacific influence, and of the wealth thus created under their eyes and at their expense; and in the spring of 1171 Manuel I. ordered the sequestration of all Venetian goods and of all Venetians who had settled within the empire. Such a high-handed act at once called forth an outburst of enthusiasm, and the doge, Vitale Michieli II., sent out against Constantinople an imposing fleet to avenge the cause of the Venetian colonists. An outbreak of plague, however, on board the fleet compelled him to return to port; in so doing he brought the scourge to the town itself,—a disaster which led to his death at the hands of the infuriated populace. Even this catastrophe was not without its uses, for it led to the introduction of reforms fitted to give greater internal stability to the state.

Constitution of the state.

Under Sebastiano Ziani, Michieli's successor, the constitution underwent a further modification. The citizens, already divided into quarters (*sestieri*), nominated twelve electors, who in their turn made choice of forty picked citizens in each of the divisions of the city. The 480 thus chosen constituted the great council, a body possessing at once deliberative and executive functions. Before this period certain intimate councillors, two of them permanent, had been summoned to act as advisers of the doge in matters of importance; but now their number was increased and they were requested (hence the name *pregato*) to assist the head of the state in all circumstances. The two permanent councillors of the doge, increased to six and conjoined with the supreme magistrates on whom the administration of justice had always devolved, formed the lesser council, which afterwards came to be known as La Signoria. If we add, finally, to the powers already enumerated the council of ten, which was instituted later, and also take into account the increasing body of secretaries and the magistracies which were gradually created as need arose, we shall have an adequate conception of the perfected instrument of government by which the republic was controlled from the 13th century until its fall. While the political organization was thus rapidly developing, the change which was also passing over its democratic spirit must not be overlooked: the simple citizen gradually lost his privileges, and the increasing restrictions laid upon freedom ultimately made the government essentially aristocratic. Towards the end of the 13th century (1297) the important measure known as the "Shutting of the Great Council" (compare vol. xvii. p. 527), and subsequently the inscription in the Golden Book of the names of all branches of the noble houses, for ever shut against plebeians every avenue to power. For a long time before this the right of electing the doge had been restricted to certain carefully-selected citizens,—a constitutional change of capital importance, which had caused much discontent and raised such a ferment in the mind of the masses that the first doge who was thus chosen, realizing the danger of the situation, refused to accept the dignity. The number of the electors was consequently increased and the election made subject to a number of ballots intended to safeguard the integrity of the vote; but it remained none the less true that to the people had been left nothing more than the illusory right of approving by acclamation in the basilica of St Mark each new doge after his election. The aristocracy, as it felt its growing force, proceeded to enlarge its powers, and did not fail to guard them down to the fall of Venice by constantly increased restrictions. It was not long, it is true, before the danger attaching to so great a power separated from the living forces of the nation was perceived, and there came to be instituted special kinds of magistrates, such as the "correctors of the ducal engagement," whose function was to revise the charter to which he was to swear, and who steadily exercised it in the way of restricting his freedom in such a manner that about the 16th century his lot was little better than that of a prisoner of state. Then there were the "examiners of the deceased doge," instituted in 1501,—posthumous judges whose verdicts on each departed doge on behalf of posterity still further conspired to neutralize the dangers arising from personal power.

Period of greatest prosperity.

The history of Venice was officially written by contemporary chroniclers. The records they have left are of course exceedingly valuable; but, as they were subjected to a rigorous censorship, the element of criticism is quite absent. Modern investigators, viewing the events from the outside, have been much more successful in forming a true judgment upon them and in tracing effects to their actual causes. Those Venetians who, since the fall of their republic, have endeavoured to investigate its annals in an independent spirit have come to the conclusion that it was between the 12th and the 15th century that the state reached its highest prosperity and power. In point of fact, the republic had at the beginning of the 13th century become so powerful that the Byzantine empire fell into its hands through the conquest of Constantinople by the doge Enrico Dandolo (1204). The Venetians even sought to raise a Latin empire upon its ruins, but the attempt was frustrated by the jealousy of the rival republic of Genoa, which re-established the Greeks in 1261. The period between 1172, the date of the election of Sebastiano Ziani, and 1300, that of the election of Pietro Gradenigo, is one of the most brilliant in the history of Venice. The union that prevailed among all the citizens, the common effort of all classes, the military energy of the Government, the supple flexibility of its policy, had given them Constantinople; and the peace which they made with Palæologus on his restoration to the Byzantine throne brought them many splendid advantages. It was in virtue of these successes and in the midst of the internal peace which they had secured that Pietro Gradenigo proposed the "Shutting of the Great Council," a measure the importance of which can be traced throughout the subsequent history of the state. Its effect was to exclude from political power all who had not been members of that assembly during the previous four years; in a word, it constituted an hereditary legislature. Grave as the measure was, alternately accepted, rejected, modified, and never unopposed, it was finally carried. The new body enacted new laws and provided administrative heads for the ten departments of government,—justice, legislation, worship, finance, commerce, education, war, marine, public health, and city administration. The powerful and wealthy republic now found the honour of its alliance sought by emperors and popes; the standard of St Mark was a familiar sight all over the Mediterranean; and ultimately Venice entered the "European concert." Now, too, she began to show that devotion to architecture and the fine arts generally of which the basilica of St Mark's and the ducal palace are the most striking monuments.

Relations with the East.

Grown wealthy by commerce, and having acquired by the force of arms considerable territory on the east of the Adriatic, the Venetians now cast their eyes towards Asia. Their adventurous travellers had penetrated to the central regions of that continent, and Marco Polo on his return dazzled the populace by his wondrous tales and excited the cupidity of the merchants with visions of the riches of the East. New commercial enterprises were entered on; samples of Oriental industry with all their splendour of colour and delicacy of pattern were brought home: glass, enamels, tapestries, silks, served as models to the deft artisans, who drew from them new inspiration and, re-discovering the secrets of the smith's and potter's and glass-blower's art, reproduced the artistic triumphs of their Oriental masters. Nor were letters neglected: rich and ancient manuscripts were brought from Greece; a friendly asylum was offered to exiled men of genius and learning; and freedom of thought and intellectual independence began to be exercised.

Commercial genius of Venetians.

If Venice in the course of its history was able at one period or another to show its superiority in every field of activity, if at the same time it was able to show enduring stability in its institutions and a wealth and political power quite out of proportion to the smallness of its territory and the number of its subjects, it owed these in the first instance to its genius for commerce and to its maritime ascendency. This commercial genius led in the first place to the development of Venetian shipping, the growth of the arsenals, and large advances in the art of naval construction, and ultimately resulted in indisputable naval supremacy. The beginning of its fortune was in the salt trade, of which it had the monopoly throughout central Europe. Besides working the sources of salt which they had within their own territory, the Venetians rented those of their neighbours the Bolognese, and found access to the rock-salt deposits of Austria and Hungary; and in every instance where a treaty was made with a foreign power a clause was introduced reserving to Venice, whether as victor or as vanquished, the exclusive privilege of supplying this commodity. The arsenal of Venice, which still exists, was its palladium; the high organization of this establishment, the technical skill of its workmen, the specially selected body of the "arsenalotti," to whom the republic entrusted the duty of guarding the senate and great council, and its admirable discipline were for centuries the envy of other European powers. The enemies of the republic frequently made special efforts to destroy it by espionage and treachery. At the most critical period in its history, when it was engaged in its great struggle with the Turks towards the end of the 16th century, the arsenal regularly sent forth a fully equipped galley each morning for a hundred successive days. The power or decadence of the republic at each period may be measured by the extent of its building-yards and by the number of its workmen and seamen. Where an ambassador had once seen an imposing force of 200 galleys all fully equipped for sea, another two centuries later saw only 20 ships of war, 16 galleys, and 2 galeasses. At the acme of its prosperity the arsenal employed 16,000 workmen; but a little more than a century afterwards, even at a time of war, that number had fallen to 2000, still further diminished in peace to 500.

The arsenal.

Conspiracies of 14th century.

The 14th century is remarkable for a series of conspiracies, which the official historians have attributed to mere turbulence and malignity, but which no doubt had their main cause much deeper, in the position to which the masses had been brought by the political changes of preceding centuries. The conspiracy of Marino Bocconio in 1300, that of Bajamonte Tiepolo ten years later, a third in 1328, and finally that associated with the name of Marino Faliero (1355), without actually imperilling the existence of the state, compelled the great council to take measures against the recurrence of such movements, and resulted in the creation of the "council of the ten," that powerful and mysterious body the significance of which still continues to exercise the ingenuity of the modern historian. Of these four conspiracies the first three were certainly aimed at the restoration of popular rights; the fourth, on the other hand, arose out of an ambitious attempt to seize personal power. The legend of Marino Faliero is well known (see FALIERO). It would be difficult

Council of ten.

to describe exactly the functions of the council of the ten. Appointed merely provisionally in 1300 at the time of the conspiracy, to act as an inquisition, it was made a permanent body in 1335. Twenty years later the importance of the process against Marino Faliero led to an increase in the number of its members (*la zonta*), and thenceforward the ten, under the presidency of the doge (*il consiglio*), took cognizance of all matters, and their action extended over every department of government. It is a mistake to suppose that the council was merely an extension of the power of the aristocracy. It acted, on the contrary, as a check on the encroachments of the latter; and, if it occasionally fell into culpable excesses, if sometimes it employed what might be called "stage" machinery, allying itself with informers, rewarding traitors, surrounding its deliberations with an air of mystery only too favourable to private revenge and too threatening to public security, and in fact becoming at one time plainly the instrument of tyranny, nevertheless its constant watchfulness over the interests of the state was not without advantages and compensations.

Contest with Genoa.

As invariably happens, the threatenings of danger from without gave pause to internal sedition and served to unite more closely together the aristocracy, the people, and the middle classes. The Genoese could but ill endure the supremacy of their rivals in the Adriatic. Leaving out of account a few years of truce, from 1298, the year of the defeat of the Venetians by their rivals at Curzola, to 1379, when after various changes of fortune the complete destruction of their fleet by the Genoese at Pola allowed the latter to force a passage to the very heart of the lagoons, the struggle between the two maritime republics had gone on uninterruptedly. Never had Venice been nearer total destruction than after the disaster at Pola, but never also had the patriotism of her citizens expressed itself more clearly and unmistakably. The community of interest between all classes was fully realized: old men, women, and children flew to arms; all classes liberally contributed to the replenishment of the empty treasury; the precious things that had been brought from the East found their way into the melting pot, and even the altars were stripped. Doge Andrea Contarini, an old man of eighty, claimed the honour of leading an improvised fleet against the enemy, and Victor Pisani, a distinguished captain who had fallen under the suspicions of the ten, was brought up from his dungeon amid the acclamations of the whole people, who sacrificed every resentment to the ardour of their patriotism. Along with Carlo Zeno, just returned from the wars in the East, he gave spirit to the combatants, and drove the Genoese from Chioggia (on which they had seized). Venice was saved, and, grateful for the services rendered by certain families of the middle class who had ably assisted Pisani and Zeno, the great council added to its numbers thirty new members selected from those who had most distinguished themselves in the struggle.

Conquests on the mainland.

The large extension of its territory on the mainland in the 14th century marks an important stage in the history of Venice. From being essentially a naval power, the republic now began to be an important continental one; and henceforward down to the 17th century it threw its sword into the balance on every occasion on which Italy was made the battle-ground of Europe. The fall of the Lombard kingdom, the struggles of the Ghibellines and Guelphs, and the personal exploits of the condottieri all urged Venice to take her part in the great movement, to widen her sphere of action, while fortifying herself against the dangers of her immediate neighbourhood, and to issue from her lagoons and establish herself as a state on *terra firma*. Venice made herself mistress of Vicenza, Feltre, and Bassano in 1388; and with the help of Carmagnola, Gattamelata, and afterwards Alviano and Colleoni, Padua and Verona were added in 1405, Udine and Friuli in 1420, Brescia in 1426, Bergamo in 1427, Crema in 1449, Rovigo in 1484, and Cremona in 1499, and podestas were set over each of these provinces.

Danger from the Turks.

Meanwhile a new danger was arising to Venice out of the Turkish advance in Europe. The republic was compelled to live continually, so to speak, on the *qui vive*, perpetually on the defensive. Mohammed II. became master of Constantinople in 1453; in the following year the Venetians attempted to exorcise the plague by means of a commercial treaty; but not many years passed before hostilities broke out. The Turks were destined to become the hereditary and implacable enemies of the republic, and their attitude of hostility to cease only with the fall of the latter. And, except for one united effort towards the end of the 16th century by Spain, Venice, and the pope, which resulted in the victory of Lepanto (1571), the banner of St Mark was almost invariably unsupported in its contest with the crescent. At Negropont (1470), Smyrna, and Scutari (1474) Erizzo, Mocenigo, and Loredano valiantly maintained the honour of their flag; but after a struggle of several years the Venetian possessions in the archipelago were lost and the proud city was compelled to cede Scutari (1479), Negropont, and Modone. Nor was this all; the geographical discoveries of the Portuguese and the Spaniards were about to inflict an irreparable blow on the maritime supremacy of Venice. Although the bold feats of Columbus and Vasco da Gama deeply stirred her enthusiasm, yet times had changed. New cares and new duties called her attention elsewhere; Venice could no longer concentrate all her energies upon her navy; having now become a territorial power, she had to watch her frontiers on every side, threatened by troublesome neighbours, now by the Malatestas, now by the Estes, the Bentivoglios, and the Borgias.

Continental struggles.

Having entered into treaty relations with Florence, Milan, and the Vatican, she found herself continually involved in ceaseless struggles, which demanded the presence of her mercenaries now in the plains of Lombardy, now in the Romagna, sometimes even in the kingdom of Naples. At the close of the 15th century, after a forty years' dispute over the fragments of the Lombard kingdom, which had fallen into the hands of the condottieri, the Italians saw the Alps twice crossed by the French and their country turned into a European battlefield. The efforts of the Venetians to extend their possessions on *terra firma* along the Italian shore of the Adriatic and inwards towards Bergamo provoked the Italian captains who had founded hereditary dynasties to unite with the pope and the king of France in opposing their further progress. Thus arose the League of Cambrai, which brought the republic to the verge of extinction. Defeated at Gera D'Adda (Agnadello) in 1509, she was compelled to withdraw her armies, not only from the recently conquered territories, but also from those in which she had been established for more than a century, and she had even to release her own subjects from their oath of allegiance. She had passed through no such peril since the day of Chioggia in the struggle with Genoa, for she was now face to face with three formidable enemies, —the king of France, the emperor Maximilian, and the pope,—not to speak of numerous petty powers, her Mantuan and Ferrarese neighbours, who hoped for a share in the spoil. At this juncture the senate displayed all its adroit suppleness and all its energy; it recognized how necessary it was on such an occasion to show pliancy, to temporize, and be humble. A new league, formed against the very power which had initiated the first, proved the salvation of Venice: the king of France fell under the suspicion of his allies, who accordingly turned against him. The battle

League of Cambrai.

of Ravenna in 1512 and that of Marignano in 1515 changed the whole aspect of affairs; new combinations were formed; and the treaty of Noyon restored to the republic all the continental territory she had lost.

War with the Turks.

Nevertheless the commonwealth was not allowed to rest, but was compelled henceforth to live constantly on the defensive, on the one hand against the Turks, who were a standing menace, and on the other, watching every movement and enterprise of the Italian princes, who would not suffer her to remain neutral in their incessant conflicts. Neither under Pius V. nor under Philip II. was the combined assistance of the pope and the Catholic king of much assistance to Venice against Islam. From the peace of Noyon (1516) to the year 1571, the date of the battle of Lepanto, the republic was never able for a single moment to lay down her arms, but was constantly driven to renewed efforts, which could not fail to exhaust her more and more. One by one she lost all her colonies: at one time it was Corfu, at another the islands of the Ægean, at another Nauplia and Malvasia. Her podestas, proveditori, and ambassadors in their several departments displayed an energy and a patriotism to which there are few parallels in history: the names of Bragadin and of Marc Antonio Barbaro remain as abiding examples of disinterestedness and patriotic self-sacrifice. Born for the service of the state, her nobles were held bound to devote their energies to the republic from early manhood, and to give her the benefit of their strength and experience to their latest breath. About 1570 the Turks threatened the fleets of the Christian powers which ventured into the Adriatic; and the pirates of the Barbary coasts boarded the Christian galleys and carried their crews into captivity, where they were held at heavy ransom. The Spaniards, whose sway then extended to the African coast of the Mediterranean, were determined to put an end to these incursions; the popes for their part were always ready to do battle with the infidel and to league themselves against the enemies of Christendom; and Venice, who saw her colonial possessions falling from her one by one, could not refuse an alliance which seemed to promise the possibility of striking a grand blow by which her supremacy might be restored. On 13th May 1571 the treaty of alliance between the three powers was signed; the league against the Ottomans was to be perpetual, and its avowed object was to destroy their influence. Philip II. agreed to pay half the expenses of the expedition; the republic supplied galleys to the pope; Spain contributed her fleets and demanded in return the chief command of the expedition. The total naval force numbered no less than 300 vessels, while the troops embarked were reckoned at 50,000 foot soldiers and 5000 horse. Don John of Austria represented Spain in the command; the papal forces were entrusted to Marc Antonio Colonna; while the Venetian senate nominated Sebastian Venieri to be its admiral. The result of the battle of Lepanto, 7th October 1571 (see vol. xiii. p. 717), was apparently the complete destruction of Turkey's naval forces. But the mutual jealousies of the allied powers served to counteract the effects of the victory, and the peace which followed, instead of being advantageous to the victors, turned out much to their prejudice. The action at Lepanto had taken place in the beginning of winter; it was impossible, therefore, to undertake anything further before the spring of the following year (1572), and each of the powers believed its fleets secure in the ports where they had taken refuge, when, on the following May, the tidings reached Venice that the Turkish fleet which had been supposed annihilated was once more afloat. Don John had wintered at Messina; Colonna had returned to Civita Vecchia; while the Venetian fleet had cast anchor off Corfu. Before the scattered allies could reunite sixty Turkish galleys advanced through the archipelago and devastated the Venetian colonies. The Spaniards at Messina awaited the decision of Philip II. before they could set sail; the knights of Malta and the duke of Savoy, less hesitating, consented to join the Venetian galleys, and to go to meet the Moslems, whom they encountered at Cerigo. A battle of doubtful issue was about to be engaged in, when a message from Don John announced the co-operation of the Spanish fleet, but at Corfu, whither the Venetian admiral was requested to repair in order to concert a new plan of attack. The Venetians did not feel certain enough of success to warrant them in commencing hostilities without their ally, and, sailing for Corfu, they once more entrusted the supreme direction of affairs to Don John. But it is easy to understand how disastrous in their results such vacillation and hesitancy must necessarily be. It was not till the end of August that the allied forces, once more brought together to the number of more than 250 vessels, set sail in search of the Turkish fleet. The latter, being lighter, gave way before the enemy, and, avoiding a pitched battle, did not give opportunity even for a skirmish or the capture of a stray prize. Meanwhile the winter was approaching; navigation was becoming dangerous; the Spaniards were indisposed for action; and Don John, alleging the gravity of his responsibilities, returned to his anchorage at Messina. Thus a whole year had been lost, giving to the enemy daily opportunities of recuperation. Every day new differences and mutual recriminations arose among the allies, and at length the idea of a peace with the Turks began to be broached in the councils of the republic. Such a proposal, however unlooked for, was suggested by considerations of the most practical kind, and by a just appreciation of the resources of the Ottoman empire; and the resulting negotiations, which were secretly conducted, led to a treaty being signed on 15th March 1573. By that treaty twenty years of peace were guaranteed to the republic; but it reversed the position of parties, and the vanquished of Lepanto now figured as victors. The Turks in fact were audaciously exacting, but their negotiations were ably conducted and were completely successful. The one place which they had lost, Sopoto, was restored to them, and Venice also consented to the definitive cession of Cyprus, which had temporarily fallen into her hands before Lepanto. Nor was this all: it was not forgotten that Venice was tributary to the sultan; her dues were doubled and a war indemnity of 300,000 ducats was stipulated for. On the other hand, the commercial privileges hitherto enjoyed by the republic were confirmed, and the freedom of the seas was guaranteed.

Battle of Lepanto.

The epoch of Lepanto is, however, the most brilliant in Venetian history as regards the efflorescence of the arts and of literature; it was at this time that the artistic glory of the city was seemingly most brilliant and most developed, and exercised the greatest attraction for strangers. More closely viewed, the 15th century had attained in Venice and the subject cities of the mainland a higher degree of culture; architecture, painting, sculpture, and the minor arts were inspired by a sentiment deeper, more sincere, more elevated both in form and in idea; but the artists who arose between the middle of the 15th and the close of the 16th century had a natural disposition, with a touch of the sensual, better corresponding with the tastes of the people and with its artistic ideal, which aroused a greater enthusiasm and made their names more famous.

Arts and literature.

In literature and art Venice was the link between Italy and Greece. Its Eastern colonists learned the Greek tongue; and the fall of the Greek empire brought to them its banished men of science and letters, who taught in their university and introduced to the Venetians the works of the ancients. Guarino of Verona opened to them Xenophon, Strabo, Lucian, Orpheus, Arrian, Dio, Procopius, Diodorus of Sicily, and Plato. At the same time they made Oriental architecture their own, impressing on it the stamp of their special needs and national genius. The Arabs gave them the manufacture of gunpowder and glass, and taught them decorative art; and from Persia they learned to weave costly tissues; while their plastic arts retained a reflexion of the sunny lands which, for geographical reasons, were the source of their riches and the chief object of their preoccupation. The architecture, the painting, and the sculpture of Venice are separately treated (see below). Nor must it be forgotten that the city welcomed from the first the art of printing, and stamped it with its own individuality. Venice, more than any other town, has the credit of having rescued from oblivion, by editions and translations, the masterpieces of Greek literature. The work of the elder Aldus in this direction from 1495 to 1515 has been spoken of in the article MANUTIUS (*q.v.*). The literary talent of Venice did not shine in works of imagination; but on the utilitarian side it was really great and original. In Venice history was written to order, and so is open to suspicion. In poetry, if we may cite Pietro Bembo, Molza, Berni, Lodovico Dolce, Doni, Niccolo Franco, Rucellai, Sperone Speroni, and L. Aretino, whom his contemporaries called *Il Divino*, as all Venetians or refugees claiming the greater freedom of thought which Venice then afforded, we must yet admit the lack of a name of world-wide significance, a Dante or a Molière. But the library of St Mark's shows the respect of the republic for letters; the building that housed the MS. collections bequeathed by Petrarch and Cardinal Bessarion is, perhaps, the most perfect model of 16th-century architecture; and the librarian of the Marciana was, in virtue of his office, so high a personage that he had a title to be voted on by the senate and the great council for the ducal crown.

Condition at end of 16th century.

Such was Venice at the close of the 16th century, when some clearness of vision was still needed to foretell the approaching decay. She still had colonies, but their preservation became more difficult with the declining resources of the state. The customs were less productive, and the senate vainly sought to improve them by instituting at this period the "consuls of the merchants," the "provisors of commerce," the five "experts in exchanges." Manners, too, were degenerating into indolence and luxury, and the courtesans of Venice were more famous than those of Rome. The *proveditori alle pompe* were designed to check the dilapidations of young patricians on the wealth their ancestors had gained by trade, and the like wastefulness of plain citizens, who consoled themselves for their exclusion from public charges and honours by squandering in idle profusion the money gained by trading commissions and illicit pursuits.

If the old senators who had known austerer times were privately exercised by the perils approaching the state, they were careful in public to conceal its weakness and dazzle strangers by the splendour of their pomps and receptions, and the Oriental gorgeousness of their palaces, churches, and processions, as was seen in the magnificent fêtes given in 1574 to Henry III. on his way to assume the throne of France.[1] They desired to make the king an ally as well as a guest, and some time later favourably entertained his proposal for a loan of 100,000 crowns of gold. In 1575 the city was visited by the plague, the almost inevitable consequence of such constant communication with the East. Forty thousand Venetians fell, and the scourge passed on to the mainland, which it ravaged for four months. Next year the doge Mocenigo died, and the election fell to the old sea-lion Sebastian Venieri, the hero of Lepanto, who already reckoned three "most serene princes" in his family. He ruled but two years, and his last days were marred by the conflagration of the ducal palace. His successor was Nicolo da Ponte, a greybeard of eighty-eight years, whose age showed that in the doge the Venetians sought rather the symbol than the reality of authority. Yet he reigned for seven years, full of peace and useful public works: the ducal palace rose from its ruins; the procurazie or offices for the guardians of noble orphans were completed; Palladio fulfilled the vow of the senate on the occasion of the late plague by erecting the marble bridge of the Rialto to replace the old wooden structure, and began the church of the Redeemer; and Corfu and the Friulian frontier were fortified.

The peace of Italy had been mainly due to the religious wars of France; but the senate had wisely sought and maintained the friendship of Henry III., and after his death in 1589 had been sagacious enough to be the first of European powers to recognize Henry of Navarre, thus securing a vigorous ally against Spain, which had turned against the republic since the battle of Lepanto. The French alliance proved durable; Henry IV. mediated between Venice and the duke of Savoy, and on his marriage with Mary de' Medici his name was inscribed in the Book of Gold.

Rivalry between Venice and the pope.

The doge Pasquale Cicogna, elected in 1585, was succeeded in 1595 by Marino Grimani, whose rule was marked by grave dissensions between the senate and the Vatican. The house of Este came to an end in 1597, Pope Clement VIII. declaring Cæsar d'Este, the nephew of Alphonso II., duke of Ferrara, incapable of succeeding him. But Venice supported his claims and was ready to enforce them by war, when he ceded Ferrara to the pope, contenting himself with the dukedom of Modena and Reggio. This solution brought the Vatican into a permanent rivalry with Venice,—a grave matter, since at the beginning of the century Cæsar Borgia had seized the Romagna in the name of Alexander VI., and Julius II. had occupied Bologna, so that the Estates of the Church bordered on those of the republic. There were other causes of dissension also: Venice had never been on cordial terms with the Papacy; the recognition of Henry of Navarre had given umbrage at Rome; and, though peace was made for a time, the quarrel recommenced, and in 1606 Paul V. launched an interdict at the republic. Venice affected the greatest formal respect for the holy see; the legate sat by the side of the doge and took precedence of princes as well as ambassadors; but under all the forms of respect the extravagant pretensions of the popes were constantly repelled with inflexible firmness and energy. The ambassadors of Venice at Rome were always chosen from the most experienced and active men of affairs, and, though the pope had nearer relations with Venice than any other friendly sovereign, churchmen were constantly excluded from all political and civil posts in the republic. A man, it was held, could not serve two masters. Nay, in all discussions bearing on relations with Rome, whether in the senate or the great council, the usher's call "Fuori i Papalisti" excluded from the deliberations, not only patricians whose ties of family or interest bound them to the sacred see, but all who even held what would now be called ultramontane opinions. The Venetian clergy made no contribution to public burdens; the tithes required in time of war could be raised only by a special papal brief, and this privilege the senate claimed the right to suppress. To this Sixtus V. had consented; but his successor was less complaisant. In face of the new pretensions of the Vatican the Venetians multiplied restrictive measures against the clergy, and the conflict grew hotter on both sides, till Paul V. laid the republic under the interdict,—a step that still struck terror

[1] The commemorative inscription can still be read on the threshold of the Hall of Giants.

into nations. The hostile Spaniards were not without their share in this measure. But the supple Venetians made no appeal to temporal arms: they left the negotiation of the difficulty to theologians, and Paolo Sarpi made peace between Rome and the senate.

Scarcely was this trouble appeased when the Uskok pirates of the Adriatic coast and the Quarnero Islands recommenced their hostilities, and for ten years (1607-17) no merchant fleet could sail eastward without a convoy. The pirates were supported by Austria, which coveted Istria and Dalmatia, and the conflict was ended in 1617 by the treaty of Madrid between Venice and that power. Next year the Spanish conspiracy, originated by the Spanish ambassador, the marquis of Bedmar, broke out in the city itself, but was detected in time by the vigilance of the ten. The Spaniards meant to seize the arsenal by the help of some of the most influential senators. In 1622 Antonio Foscarini was disgraced because he was suspected of plotting with the Spanish ambassador; the Catholic king carried on his intrigues everywhere. But the republic on its part was not inactive and had stirred up against Spain a formidable enemy, the duke of Savoy, to whom in one year (1617) it lent more than a million crowns of gold. From 1627 to 1631 the two enemies were again face to face in the war of the Mantuan succession; but this time it was the duke of Savoy who made a peace to which Venice merely assented.

Conflict with Spain.

Loss of Crete to Turkey.

Peace was unbroken from 1631 to 1645. But in the latter year the Turks suddenly fell on the island of Crete; and for twenty-four years the whole forces of the republic, and every thought of the people and the nobles, were concentrated on the preservation of this colony, which had been purchased from the marquis of Montferrat at the date of the fifth crusade, and in course of time had become a place of the first importance both as a trading station and a naval port. Surprised by the suddenness of the attack, the senate appealed to Europe for aid, and the Vatican, Florence, Naples, and the knights of Malta came to their succour; but after an alliance of thirty-seven days all the helpers regained their ships and left the Venetians to confront the enemy alone. The struggle was valiantly maintained and cost Venice, between 1645 and 1669, no less than 4,392,000 ducats. The siege of Candia alone lasted twenty-two years, and for three successive years the combats were continual. At length, on 6th September 1669, the Turks were masters of the island. Europe had looked on impassively at a struggle which, disastrous as was the issue, bore the highest testimony to the valour and patriotism of the generals of the republic. Biagio Giuliani, Tommaso Morosini, Jacopo Riva, Alvisio and Lazaro Mocenigo, Giuseppe Dolfin, and Lorenzo Marcello surpassed one another in exploits worthy of the heroes of antiquity. Between May and September 1667 thirty-two assaults were delivered and repulsed before Candia, and seventeen sorties were made by the besieged. The glory of such a resistance did not compensate for the disaster, which reduced the public treasure of Venice from 6,000,000 sequins to 500,000. (See also GREECE, vol. xi. p. 121.)

The troubles excited all over Europe by the ambition of Louis XIV. gave an interval of rest and recovery to the republic, which knew how to preserve its neutrality; and the years from 1674 to 1684 were a period of profound peace. But the enmity of the Turk still counted on the visible weakness of his rival, and imposed on her humiliations which her isolation and the exhaustion of her finances compelled her to submit to. Venice was only saved by the diversion produced by the siege of Vienna and the intervention of John Sobieski; but even then their repulse in central Europe sent back the Turks more determined than ever to be done with Venice and strip her of her whole possessions. At this crisis the senate called Francesco Morosini to the command of the fleet, a post in which he covered himself with glory by his bold offensive operations in the Peloponnesus. For fourteen years the contest was bravely maintained on both sides, but the fortune of war was against the Turks. The Venetians occupied the Morea and laid siege to Athens, Morosini bombarding the Parthenon, which had been made a powder magazine. The campaigns, renewed every spring, were marked by a series of victories: Prevesa, Navarino, Modone, Argos, Lepanto, Corinth, all added glory to the name of Morosini "il Peloponesiaco." He failed, however, in his attack on Negropont, after he had been raised (1688) to the dignity of doge. Coraro, who followed him in the command of the fleet, died suddenly; and then Domenico Mocenigo, the new commander, formed the bold project of retaking Crete, and was already before the port of Canea when the news of a Turkish attack on the Morea—really no more than a feeble diversion—induced him to raise the siege and lose his opportunity. The error cost him dear: he was removed from his command, and the old doge Morosini again took the field in spite of his seventy-five years, but soon succumbed to fatigue (1694), when Sylvester Valieri succeeded to the ducal throne. The war continued under the leadership of Antonio Zeno. Scio was taken and lost again; reverses followed on victories; and the stern senate removed the captain and the proveditori. But the peace of Carlowitz (1699) between Austria and the Porte brought with it the end of the war between Venice and the sultan, and the Turks, whose humiliation dates from this epoch, were compelled, besides their concessions to Austria, Poland, and Russia, to recognize the authority of Venice in the Morea and in Dalmatia as far as the Bosnian frontier.

Morosini's Peloponnesian campaigns.

The 18th century.

The first thirteen years of the 18th century, when almost all Europe was involved in the War of the Spanish Succession, were a time of repose for Venice, which remained neutral; but hardly was the peace of Utrecht concluded when the Turks resumed the offensive against the republic, which now had no allies. One after the other the islands and colonies ceded by the peace of Carlowitz were retaken; the Morea again became Turkish; Dalmatia was saved only by the interposition of Austria, which had need of the friendship of Venice to checkmate the projects of Philip of Spain against the Italian duchies. But soon the emperor found it necessary, in view of the struggle with Spain, to come to terms with the sultan; and his allies, the Venetians, were included in the peace of Passarowitz signed between Austria and Turkey on 21st July 1718. From this moment Venice ceased to have any influence on European politics: she had no more wars, if she still had enemies, signed no more treaties, and, in a word, had abdicated her place in Europe. Not even the dispute of 1731 as to the succession to the duchy of Parma, which brought France, Austria, Spain, and Savoy into conflict at her very doors, stirred her to action; she was indeed no longer a useful ally. Her navy had fallen behind the times; her commerce had been in decadence since the way to the East by the Cape of Good Hope was opened; she could scarcely repulse the Barbary pirates from her shores; and she had to treat with Algiers, Tunis, and Morocco to put an end to their inroads, daily repeated from 1760 to 1774. Yet, the Tunisians failing in their engagements, she decided on a war with them, which was closed by a fresh treaty.

Constitutional reforms.

The government meanwhile went on in the old form. The successive doges were still tied by the restrictive laws which made them crowned prisoners; but rivalries sprang up between the great powers of the state: the senate attacked the institution of the *savii*, the ministers delegated to each branch of the administration, and in turn the magistrates known as the *quarantie* proposed to reform the senate, while, lastly, the council of ten was threatened by the great council. In the midst of these reforms, which were calculated to make a great change in the institutions of Venice, the French Revolution broke out. Ludovico Manin had just become doge (1788), but was a mere cipher in the councils of the state. No heed was paid to the information supplied by the ambassadors of Venice at the court of France; nothing was foreseen, nothing decided on, for neither senate nor council understood the vast sweep of the new movement in Europe. Soon the Venetians were called on to recognize the French republic; they refused, but did not join the coalition against it. When Bonaparte was at the gates of Mantua, they at length decided to treat with him; but it was too late. Mantua capitulated on 2d February 1797; the Venetian envoys presented themselves before Bonaparte on 25th March; and on 18th April the Austrians signed the peace of Leoben, which left Venice without an ally at the feet of the victorious invaders of Italy. On 8th May the great council decided to offer no resistance to the French; the doge abdicated on the 12th; and Napoleon entered the city on the 16th, and proclaimed the end of the republic. On 17th October following Bonaparte, by the treaty of Campo Formio, abandoned the territory of Venice to Austria. Venice was buffeted to and fro between France and Austria from 1798 to 1814, when the new coalition assigned her to Austria. Till 1866 Venice remained Austrian, save for a few hours in the insurrections of 1848-49; but her people never acknowledged the rights of those who had bought and sold them like a flock of sheep. The war between Austria and the allied Prussians and Italians in 1866 gave Venice her freedom, and the unity of Italy was at length accomplished under the sceptre of the house of Savoy (see ITALY, vol. xiii. p. 490). (C. Y.)

Napoleonic period.

PART II.—ART.

Architecture.

Early state.

For some centuries Venice must have consisted mainly of a few groups of wooden huts scattered among the many small grassy islets that lay off the coast of Venetia. At first the main occupations of the inhabitants were fishing and preparing salt by evaporation. But, as they grew richer, especially through the possession of large numbers of coasting vessels, in which they transported the merchandise or troops of foreign races at what were frequently very remunerative rates,[1] they became exposed to the inroads of Dalmatian pirates; and strongly defended castle-like houses began to be built in stone or brick, with towers at the angles and battlements all along the walls. Though no example exists of these early Venetian castles, a very interesting survival of their general form is still to be traced in the 11th and 12th century palaces, of which a considerable number are yet to be seen (see fig. 5 below). As the city increased in size and importance, great changes were made in the form of the islands on which it stands and in the network of salt-water channels which divided the smaller islands from one another. In the 13th and 14th centuries many decrees of the great council provided for the deepening of existing canals, for filling up others, for draining marshes and forming dry ground by bringing shiploads of soil from neighbouring islands, and for driving piles to form securer ground for building. The shallow salt lagoons which surround the islands of Venice form a long band, 4 to 8 miles wide, once reaching to the Roman cities of Ravenna on the south and Aquileia on the north.[2] These waters, averaging only 1 to 4 feet in depth, are separated from the deep sea by a series of long, sandy island bars. Those which form the natural breakwater to Venice are called Malamocco and Lido.

Bridges.

The early bridges of Venice were wooden structures; even that over the Rialto was of no more durable material till the present bridge was built in 1591. Many were mere planks nailed on boats. One of the earliest built in stone was that by the south-east angle of the ducal palace, called the Ponte della Paglia, which was founded in 1360. Its name ("the bridge of straw") appears to be due to the fact that it was built with money from the tax on straw,[3] large quantities of which were used to thatch the early houses of Venice. Till about the middle of the 19th century the Rialto was the only bridge across the Grand Canal.

Early churches.

According to tradition, the first church built in Venice was S. Giacomo del Rialto (founded in 432).[4] The legendary history of the founding of some other early churches is given in the *Chronicle* of Andrea Dandolo, written *c.* 1350. In the 5th century St Magnus, bishop of Altinum, who included in his see the Rialto and adjacent islands, had the following series of visions. (1) St Peter appeared and bade him found a church on that island where he should find oxen and sheep grazing; and on the little island of Olivolo, at the extreme east of Venice, he accordingly built the church of S. Pietro di Castello, which from 1091 till 1807 was the cathedral church of the Venetian patriarch. (2) The church of S. Raffaello in dorsoduro was founded in obedience to the archangel, who bade St Magnus build a church at the place where he should see a large flock of birds. (3) St Salvador was founded at the place where Christ told the bishop he would see a red cloud rest. (4) S. Maria Formosa was erected at the command of the Virgin, at the place where St Magnus saw a white cloud resting. (5) S. Giovanni in Bragola (or Bragora) and S. Zaccaria were built in obedience to the Baptist, who told the bishop to raise churches to himself and his father. (6) The twelve apostles ordered a church to be built at the place where Bishop Magnus should see a flight of twelve cranes. (7) S. Giustina, in the last vision, bade the bishop build a church in her honour at the place where he should see vines laden with grapes. Other early churches were those of S. Geminiano and St Theodore, both on the island of Rialto (see below, "St Mark's church").

Architectural styles.

Architectural Styles.—Owing to its isolated position on the verge of Italy, and its constant intercourse with the eastern shores and islands of the Mediterranean, Venetian architecture was an independent development, though with many Oriental characteristics, having a character of its own quite unlike the styles employed in other Western countries. It was a very complex growth, in which the most diverse styles were absorbed and blended together in a very beautiful way. The various strands which, woven, as it were, together, combined to form the magnificent web of Venetian architecture were chiefly these,—(1) the Byzantine, itself a most complex mixture of older styles, blended together and vivified with new life in the hands of the skilful builders and craftsmen of Justinian's time; (2) the Moslem as developed in the gorgeous mosques and palaces of Persia, Syria, and Egypt; (3) the Gothic of northern Europe, and especially of France, with a secondary strain of Florentine influence, which, however, was more marked in the sculpture than in the architecture.[5]

Byzantine.

In the 11th and 12th centuries the Byzantine style was universally employed by the Venetians. The arches of this period are semicircular, usually much stilted. The sculptured ornament is of very great beauty, and is applied freely round arches, along string-courses, and in panels, with which the external façades were often thickly studded. According to the peculiar Venetian system of decoration, the walls were built in solid brick-work and then covered with thin slabs of rich and costly marbles. The columns, with their capitals and bases, were, as a rule, the only places where solid blocks were placed. This constant method of facing with thin slabs necessitated the use of special forms of mouldings and carvings, and thus, except in the solid capitals, no deep cutting could be employed; therefore the mouldings of this period consist of small rolls, *cavettos*, or flutings contrived to enrich the surface with the least amount of cutting into the thin marble.[6] In the same way the sculptured bands are shallow in treatment, but full of the most vigorous grace, combined with the utmost spirit, in every line and curve, and rich, with an extreme delicacy, in all the details. Flowing scroll-work of semi-conventional foliage, mingled with grotesque animals, birds, or dragons, is most commonly used. As purely decorative sculpture, nothing could surpass the beauty of these early bands and panels. The round or arch-shaped or rectangular sculptured panels, used to stud the façades like rows of jewels, are of peculiar beauty and interest. Many of the designs are derived from the far East, and appear to be of Sasanian origin; favourite motives are eagles or dragons devouring hares or other animals, and peacocks treated in a conventionally decorative way, with their spreading tails forming a halo-like background to the body of the bird. Many of these panels are derived from the very ancient Assyrian subject of the sacred tree between two guardian beasts or birds; a common variety of this has two peacocks face to face drinking from a cup placed on a tall, pillar-like object, which recalls that on the lion-gate of Mycenæ. Many of these reliefs closely resemble the sculptured screens and altars of the 6th cen-

---

[1] There are many curious analogies between Venice in the early part of its career and the Phœnician city of Tyre in the 8th and 7th centuries B.C., in the position of the two cities, their mercantile habits, their custom of acting as carriers for other races, and their both being in their habits of life and in their artistic productions links between the East and West.

[2] Vitruvius (i. 4) speaks of the lagoon cities of Aquileia, Altinum, and Ravenna as being healthy sites in spite of their position. Aquileia and Altinum, which were wealthy cities, were both destroyed by Attila.

[3] In the same way old London Bridge was paid for by the wool duty.

[4] The word "Rialto" appears to have been applied, first to this deep channel of salt water, and secondly to the large adjacent island, that on which St Mark's and the ducal palace are built.

[5] See E. A. Freeman, *Subject and Neighbour Lands of Venice.*

[6] See sections of mouldings illustrated by Mr Ruskin in *Stones of Venice*, vol. iii., pls. v.-xi.

tury in Ravenna, and are probably of the same date, though used to decorate buildings not earlier than the 12th century. The church of St Mark, especially, is a rich storehouse of these examples of early sculpture. Others of exactly similar style, which exist in the churches of Thessalonica and other Eastern cities, bear witness to the unity of early Byzantine art and its wide geographical range until the downfall of the Eastern empire. One striking feature in Venetian architecture of all dates down to the 15th century is the constant use of the dentil moulding. This consists of a simple series of notchings, at once the easiest and the most effective way of enriching the thin facing-slabs when their *edges* were allowed to appear, as, for example, in those which lined the soffits of arches.

Moslem.

The influence of Moslem art is seen in the occasional use of the horse-shoe arch, in the very common ogee form which was almost universal in Venice from the 13th to the 15th century, and still more clearly in the fantastic rows of battlements, formed of thin pointed slabs of marble set on edge, which crowned the walls of nearly all the chief palaces of Venice in the 14th and the 15th century.

Gothic.

The 13th century was the time of transition from the round arched Byzantine style to the pointed arch with tracery, which in some cases was derived directly from the Gothic of northern countries. This is seen especially in the two great churches of the Dominican and Franciscan friars, SS. Giovanni e Paolo and S. Maria Gloriosa dei Frari. These two stately churches resemble those built by the friars in other places in Italy,[1] and have little of the distinctively Venetian character of the contemporary domestic buildings. In the 14th and 15th centuries one peculiarity of Venetian Gothic is the way in which tracery is used to fill rectangular and not arched openings. The result of this is that the tracery itself has to support the mass of wall above it, whereas in the Gothic of other countries the tracery is merely, as it were, a pierced screen filling in a constructional arch, which carries the whole weight of the superimposed wall and roof. Hence the Venetian tracery, of which that in the upper story of the ducal palace is a typical example, is much thicker and heavier in construction.

Early Renaissance.

In the latter part of the 15th century Venetian architecture began to lose its distinctively local character, though very beautiful examples of Early Renaissance were built by the Lombardi family and other architects, largely under the influence of Fra Giocondo (see VERONA).

Classic.

In the 16th century, under the later development of the Renaissance, the Pseudo-Classic style was paramount in Venice, and Sansovino, Palladio, and others designed many costly buildings which had nothing specially Venetian in their style. This magnificent but dull and scholastic form of architecture reached its highest development in Venice, where it was later in degenerating into tasteless decadence than was generally the case elsewhere. Even in the 17th century good models of the Revived Classic style were built, especially by Longhena (see p. 155 below). After that the degradation of architecture and sculpture took place with great rapidity.

The periods of these styles may be roughly tabulated thus:—(i.) Byzantine, 7th to end of 13th century; (ii.) Gothic, middle of 13th to *c.* 1460; (iii.) Early Renaissance, *c.* 1450-1520; (iv.) Classic, *c.* 1520-1620; (v.) Extreme Decadence, *c.* 1600 downwards.

Foundations.

Materials and Methods of Construction.—In spite of its position on a number of small sandy islands in the lagoons, Venice was built upon firm and solid foundations, so that very few houses have suffered seriously from settlement. At a depth of 10 to 16 feet there is a firm bed of very stiff clay, and below this a bed of sand and gravel, and then a thin layer of peat. Recent borings for Artesian wells to a depth of about 1500 feet have shown a regular succession of these beds—clay, gravel, and peat—repeated again and again as far down as the borings have reached. The process implied in this geological formation seems still very slowly to be going on, and the present level of the square of St Mark has been raised artificially about 20 inches above the old brick paving shown in Gentile Bellini's picture of 1496. A good example of the old method of forming foundations is shown in that of the great campanile of St Mark, *c.* 900 (see fig. 1). Here the builders dug down to the bed of stiff clay, and over the whole area of the footings of the tower drove in piles of white poplar, 10 to 11 inches in diameter, nearly touching one another. On the top of these a level platform was formed by two layers of oak trees (*Quercus robur*), each roughly squared, the upper layer being laid crosswise upon the lower one. The oak and poplar both grew along the shores close to Venice; in later times, when the Venetian territory was extended, the red larch (*Pinus Larix*) of Cadore and the Euganean Hills was largely used, as, for example, in the foundations of the ducal palace. In 1885 the foundations of the campanile were examined, and both the oak and the poplar were found to be perfectly sound.[2] On the wooden platform massive footings are laid, consisting of five courses of large blocks of trachyte and other granitic or porphyritic rocks from the Euganean Hills. Above these are six courses of similar stone arranged in step-like offsets, forming a base or plinth to the

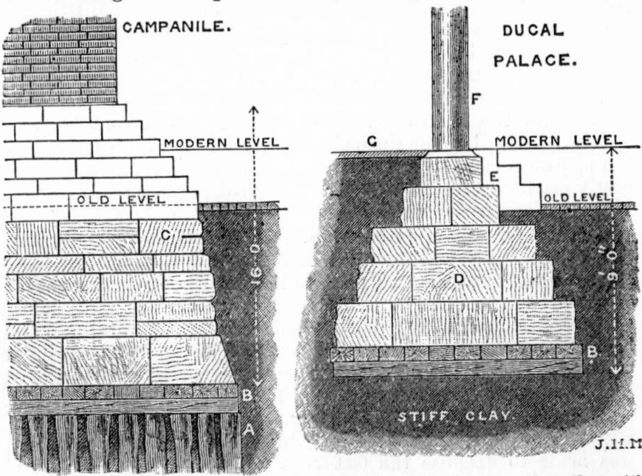

FIG. 1.—Two methods of forming foundations, one with piles, the other with wider footings and no piles, as exemplified in the campanile and the ducal palace. A. 10-inch piles of white poplar, close driven into the stiff clay. B,B. Double layers of oak planks, the same in both. C. Rough footings of campanile, made of trachyte and other volcanic stones. D. Similar footings under pillars of ducal palace. E. Stylobate of three steps, under lower loggia of palace, now hidden by raised level of modern pavement. F. One of the Istrian stone pillars of the palace. G. Paving of loggia, now flush with that outside.

tower; owing to the raising of the pavement level only two and a half of these offsets are now visible. Another way of forming foundations, which was used in rather later times, was to omit the piles altogether and build footings with a wider spread. Fig. 1, which also shows the foundations of the ducal palace, dating from the 14th century, is a typical example of this second method, in which the oak platform is laid immediately on the stiff clay. The use of trachyte for foundations was soon superseded by that of Istrian limestone, a very beautiful cream-coloured stone, extremely fine and close in texture and capable of receiving a very high polish. Though not crystalline in grain, and, technically speaking, not a true marble, this Istrian stone has for most architectural purposes all the beauty of the finest white marble, and receives from age a beautiful golden-russet patina, very much like that assumed by Pentelic marble. From the 11th century onwards it was used very largely for plinths, angle quoins, string-courses, window tracery, and other decorative purposes. It occurs, for example, in all the magnificent series of arcades in the ducal palace. Its extreme fineness of grain allows it to be worked with an ivory-like delicacy and minuteness of detail.

Main walls.

Throughout the Middle Ages the main walling of Venetian buildings was always of fine brick, usually a rich red in colour, made and fired in the kilns of Murano. In spite of its beautiful colour the brick-work was seldom left visible, the whole wall-surface being lined with thin slabs of marble in the more magnificent buildings, or else coated with stucco, on which diapers and other decorative patterns were painted.

Mortar.

Before 1405 the mortar used in Venice was made of the white lime from the Istrian limestone, which possessed no hydraulic qualities, and was consequently very perishable. But after that year, when the Venetians conquered Padua, they were able to get supplies of a strong hydraulic dark lime from Albettone, which formed a very durable cement or mortar, able to resist salt water and the destructive sea air.

Marbles.

One of the chief glories of Venice depends on its extensive use of the most beautiful and costly marbles and porphyries, which give a wealth of magnificent colour such as is to be seen in no other city in the world. In early times none of these seem to have been obtained direct from the quarries, but from older buildings, either of Roman or early Byzantine date.[3] Immense quantities of rich marbles were brought from the ruined cities of Heraclea, Ravenna, Altinum, and especially Aquileia. Under the Roman empire Aquileia contained great numbers of magnificent buildings, decorated with marbles and porphyries from Greece, Numidia, Egypt, and Arabia. The gorgeous churches and palaces of the Byzantine emperors, enriched with rare marbles stolen from Greek and Roman buildings of classic times, were in their turn stripped of their costly columns and wall-linings by the victorious Venetians. Thus Venice became a magnificent storehouse in which were heaped the rich treasures accumulated throughout many previous centuries by various peoples. The principal varieties used in the palaces of Venice are—the red porphyry of Egypt and the green

[1] Comp. S. Maria Novella and S. Croce in Florence and S. Maria sopra Minerva in Rome.

[2] An interesting account of this and other foundations in Venice is given by Giacomo Boni in the *Archivio Veneto*, ser. ii., vol. xxix., pt. ii., 1885.

[3] Early in the 15th century the Venetians began to work the rich quarries of red marble near Verona; but with this exception the decorative marbles seem to have been taken from older buildings elsewhere.

porphyry of Mount Taygetus, red and grey Egyptian granites, the beautiful lapis Atracius (verde antico), Oriental alabaster from Numidia and Arabia, the Phrygian pavonazzetto with its purple mottlings, cipollino from Carystus, and, in great quantities, the alabaster-like Proconnesian marble with bluish and amber-coloured striations.[1] Till the 14th or 15th century the white marbles used in Venice were from Greek quarries—Parian or Pentelic—being all (like the coloured marbles) stolen from older buildings, while in later times the native marble of Carrara was imported. Large quantities of red Verona marble were used to form moulded frames round panels of white sculptured marble. The greater part of these costly marbles seems to have been imported in the form of columns, immense numbers of which were sawn up lengthways into long thin slabs for use as wall-facings. Other columns, usually those of the most precious marbles, were sawn across, and thus the roundels were produced which stud like jewels the façades of many of the palaces (see fig. 6). Thin slices sawn from the same column were reversed and placed side by side, so that the natural mottlings formed a regular sort of pattern. Very rich and complicated designs were produced by placing four slabs together to form one large pattern, repeating from one centre. The whole interior of St Mark's is decorated in this magnificent way, very large areas being covered with the same pattern recurring again and again. Thus no attempt was made to disguise the fact that the marble was only a thin surface decoration of no constructional importance. The fact that many slabs had been cut from one block was frankly acknowledged by the formation of these "cut and reversed" patterns, nor is there any attempt to conceal the bronze clamps which hold the slabs in their places.

Gold and colour decoration.

The façades of the chief palaces of Venice down to the end of the 15th century were wholly covered with these magnificently coloured marbles. But that was not all; a still greater splendour of effect was given by the lavish use of gold and colour, especially the costly ultramarine blue. Very frequently the whole of the sculpture, whether on capitals, archivolts, or frieze-like bands, was thickly covered with gold leaf, the flat grounds being coloured a deep ultramarine so as to throw the reliefs into brilliant prominence. The less magnificent palaces were decorated in a simpler way. The brick surfaces between the windows and other arches were covered with fine hard stucco, made, like that of the ancient Romans, of a mixture of lime and marble dust. The whole of this was then decorated with minute diapers or other geometrical ornament in two or three earth colours, especially red, yellow, and brown ochres. Very few examples of this form of decoration still remain, owing to the corrosive action of the sea air. One notable example, dating from the 14th or 15th century, has a rich pattern formed by a series of adjacent quatrefoils, with half-figures of cherubs in the intermediate spaces, covering the whole flat surface of the wall. A few faded patches are now all that is left.

With the early years of the 16th century and the later development of the Renaissance totally different methods of architectural decoration superseded the use of precious marbles and delicate repeated ornament in colour. The Pseudo-Classic buildings of Sansovino, Palladio, and their schools were either built of white stone or marble, quite unrelieved by colour, or else stuccoed façades

Frescos.

were treated simply as a ground on which to paint large frescos with figure subjects, not designed with any sense of the true principles of architectural decoration. These frescos, which covered the otherwise unornamental façades of many of the 16th-century palaces, were often the work of the greatest painters, from Giorgione to Tintoretto; but the pictures, though no doubt beautiful in themselves, were obviously quite out of place on the façade of a house: the colossal groups dwarfed the building they were painted on, and were far inferior in decorative effect to the simpler patterns of earlier times. These, too, have mostly perished: on the *fondaco*[2] of the Germans, once covered with frescos painted jointly by Titian and Giorgione, only traces of two figures now remain. One of the best-preserved series of these exterior frescos is that inside the cloister of S. Stefano, painted by Pordenone, which has naturally suffered less than the very exposed façades on the Grand Canal.

St Mark's.

Church of St Mark.—This church stands quite alone among the buildings of the world in respect of its unequalled richness of material and decoration, and also from the fact that it has been constructed with the spoils of countless other buildings, and therefore forms a museum of sculpture of the most varied kind, nearly every century from the 4th down to the latest Renaissance being represented in some carved panel or capital, if not more largely.

[1] The splendid columns of St Mark's, which Mr Ruskin in the *Stones of Venice* speaks of as being of alabaster, really are of Proconnesian marble, and are so described by various early Byzantine writers. According to Vitruvius (ii. 8), the magnificent palaces of Crœsus of Lydia and Mausolus of Halicarnassus were chiefly adorned with Proconnesian marble.

[2] The word *fondaco*, of Arab provenance, from the Greek πανδοχεῖον, applied to several of the largest Venetian palaces, denotes the mercantile headquarters of a foreign trading nation. The *fondachi* of the Turks and of the Germans still exist, though much modernized. An analogous establishment was the *hellenium* of the trading Greeks at Naucratis in the Egyptian delta, remains of which have recently been discovered by Mr Flinders Petrie (see *Proceedings of the Egypt. Explor. Soc.*, 1886).

Site.

During the early years of Venetian history the site of the present church and square of St Mark was a large grassy field, with rows of trees, divided by a canal (which no longer exists), and containing two churches. One of these, dedicated to St Theodore, the old patron saint of Venice, stood on the site of the present church of St Mark. The other, that of S. Geminiano, was a little to the north-west of the great campanile. Fig. 3 (below) shows its position, and also the site on which it was rebuilt by Sebastiano Ziani (1173-79), when he pulled down the original church in order to extend the square westwards. In the 16th century it was again rebuilt by Cristoforo del Legname and Sansovino, and was destroyed in 1805 by Napoleon I., to make room for a new block to unite the two palaces of the procurators. The grassy *campo* where these churches stood was the property of the abbey of S. Zaccaria. At its eastern extremity a small palace was built for the doge about 810, when Venice first became the chief ducal place of residence under Angelo Partecipazio.

Original chapel.

According to the chief early chronicles, the body of St Mark was secretly brought away from Alexandria and carried to Venice in 828, the church where he was buried having been pulled down by the Moslems in order to build with its materials a palace at "Babylon," as old Cairo was then called. After the arrival of his relics, St Mark became the patron saint of Venice in place of St Theodore, and his bones were laid in the "confessio" of the small private chapel of the ducal palace.[3] This chapel, however, soon lost its private character and became the chief church of Venice, though not the cathedral church of the patriarch. The small ducal

Older church.

chapel of St Mark was burnt in 976, together with the rest of the palace, during the insurrection against Doge Candiano IV.: it was rebuilt on a larger scale by his successor, Pietro Orseolo, and the

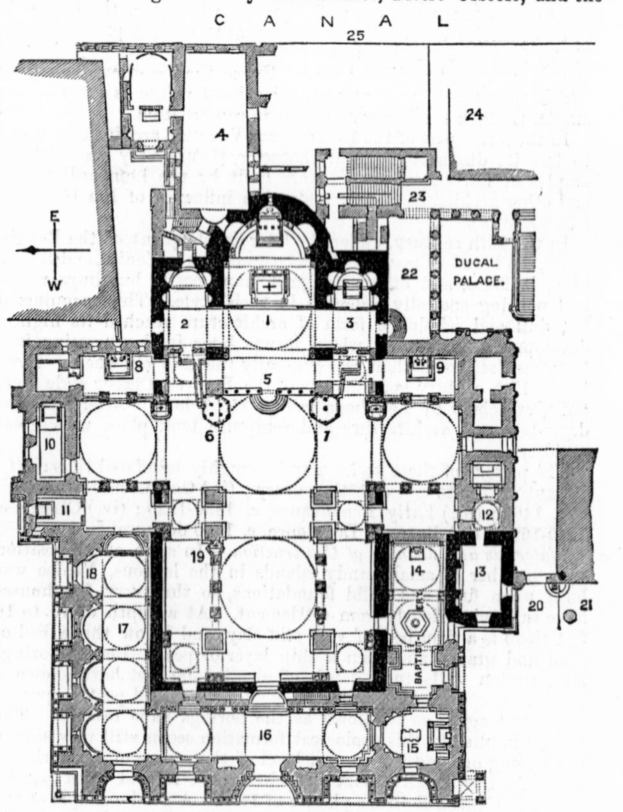

Fig. 2.—Plan of St Mark's; the black shows its older form, the shading its later development. 1. High altar, containing body of St Mark. 2. North apsidal chapel of St Peter. 3. South chapel of St Clement. 4. 15th-century sacristy. 5. Rood-screen. 6. North ambo and patriarch's throne. 7. South ambo. 8. Altar of S. Maria dei Mascoli. 9. Altar of St Leonard. 10. Chapel of S. Isidore, added in 1353-55. 11. Chapel of St John the Evangelist. 12. Ante-room to treasury. 13. Treasury, formerly a tower of ducal palace. 14. Baptistery. 15. Chapel of Cardinal Zeno. 16. Western atrium. 17. Northern atrium. 18. North door. 19. Altar against a pier of the nave. 20. Porta della Carta. 21. Loggia of ducal palace. 22. Doge's ante-room. 23. Grand staircase of palace. 24. 16th-century part of ducal palace. 25. Canal, Rio del Palazzo.

following doges, the work being carried on for about a century. An inscription now lost recorded its completion in 1071, but it was not consecrated till 1085, in the reign of Vitale Faliero (1084-1096), when it was dedicated "to God, the glorious Virgin Annun-

[3] There is much analogy between the relationship of the church of St Mark to the ducal palace and that of the abbey church to the royal palace at Westminster: both were originally built in connexion with royal palaces and both possessed special privileges as "royal peculiars."

ciate, and to the protector St Mark." The form of the church as then completed was quite different from its present aspect, both in extent of plan and in absence of rich decoration. Fig. 2 shows the size of the older church, which was originally of the simple basilica form with three eastern apses and no transepts.[1] One very interesting relic of the old ducal palace still exists, namely, the lower part of one of its towers, with walls 11 feet thick; this was made into the treasury of St Mark when the church was enlarged so as to include it in its plan, at the west corner of the south transept. Recent processes of "restoration" have shown the external design of this early church, which was of plain red brick, undecorated by marble or mosaics, and only relieved by very simple blank arcading, with round arches, not unlike those on some early Norman buildings in England.[2]

By degrees the church was enlarged: first of all transepts were added, then the baptistery on the south and the atrium extending along the west and north of the nave, about 1150-1200. Next chapels were added north and south of the two transepts: that of St Isidore was built and finished in 1354 by Andrea Dandolo. In the 15th century the sacristy at the east end was added, the altar of St Peter in the north apse being removed to make a passage to it; another way to the sacristy for the use of the clergy was cut through the massive wall of the main apse. During the long period from its dedication in 1085 till the overthrow of the Venetian republic by Napoleon every doge's reign saw some addition to the rich decorations of the church—mosaics, sculpture, wall linings, or columns of precious marbles. By degrees the whole walls inside and outside were completely faced either with glass mosaics on gold grounds or with precious coloured marbles and porphyries, plain white marble being only used for sculpture, and then thickly covered with gold. It is impossible here to give an adequate notion of the splendour of the whole effect; nothing short of the eloquence of Mr Ruskin can do justice to the subject.[3] Unfortunately the whole wall surface of the interior is so stained and caked with dirt that much of the gorgeous effect of the marbles is lost.

Decoration. The general scheme of decoration is the following. The whole of the domes and vaults, and the upper part of the walls down to the level of the floor of the triforium, are completely covered with mosaics of brilliant glass tesseræ, the ground being in most cases of gold. Below this every inch of the surface of the walls and arches is covered with richly coloured marbles, porphyries, and alabaster, relieved by pure white marble, sculptured in panels, string courses, and the like. The various marbles are arranged in broad upright bands, alternating so that one colour enhances the effect of that next to it. For example, the nave wall in the north aisle is faced thus,—(1) verde antico, (2) Proconnesian, (3) red broccatello of Verona, (4) Proconnesian, (5) magnificent Oriental alabaster, (6) Proconnesian, and (7) verde antico; below these is a narrow band of red Verona marble, and then a plinth-moulding of Athenian white marble, which rests on the seat of panelled red marble that runs all round the interior of the nave and transepts. The large columns between the brick piers, six in the nave and eight in the transepts (see fig. 2), are monoliths of fine Proconnesian marble, veined with greyish blue and amber, and the great brick piers are faced with thin slabs of the same material. This facing and most of that throughout the church are made of ancient columns sawn into slices.

Crypts. The eastern crypt or confessio extends under the whole of the choir behind the rood-screen, and has three apses like the upper church. The body of St Mark was originally placed here, but is now within the high altar of the upper church. Below the nave is an older crypt, the existence of which has only recently been discovered; it is not accessible, having been filled in with earth and rubbish at a very early period.

Choir and rood-screen. The choir, which is raised about 4 feet above the nave, is separated from it by a marble rood-screen, formed of ancient columns, bearing a straight architrave surmounted by fourteen statues, viz., St Mark, the Blessed Virgin Mary, and the twelve apostles. It extends across the aisles, forming a north apsidal chapel of St Peter and a southern one to St Clement. The rood-screen is signed as the work of the Venetians Jacobello and Pietro Paolo, sons of Antonio delle Masegne, 1394-97. The rood itself is of silver, dated 1394 and signed "Jacobus Magistri Marci Benato de Venetiis." The workmanship both of the silver crucifix and of the fourteen statues is of no great excellence. In front of the screen stand two very large ambones or pulpits, one of porphyry and the other of verde antico. In the northern ambo is a lofty patriarch's throne under a metal domed canopy, curiously like a pulpit in a Moslem mosque. There are fine marble baldacchini, supported on columns of precious marbles, over the high altar, two in the transepts, and one on the north side of the nave. No less than five hundred columns of porphyry and costly marbles are used to decorate the church, especially on the west front. Some of those inside the atrium have no constructional use, but are only set against the wall for the sake of their beauty and value.

Columns and capitals. A whole volume might be written on the sculptured capitals, panels, screens, and other features of the church. A great part of these are the spoils of other churches, especially from the East; much of the sculpture, as, *e.g.*, the parapets along the triforium gallery, dates from the 6th century or even earlier.[4] In the richly carved capitals every style from the 4th to the 12th century is represented, many of them being marvels of delicacy combined with extreme spirit of execution. Some of the larger caps are partially covered with a rich basket-work pattern completely under-cut with great technical skill; others have vine or acanthus foliage treated with vigorous realism; and a large number have the revived Byzantine treatment of the classic Corinthian or Ionic capitals, with variations showing the richest power of invention and originality. In addition to the elaborate sculpture, some of the capitals are decorated with inlaid patterns; and many of the mouldings, such as the capping of the triforium screen, are also ornamented in the same way. This use of inlay is almost peculiar to St Mark's, as is also the method of enriching sculptured reliefs with backgrounds of brilliant gold and coloured glass mosaics, producing an effect of extraordinary magnificence.[5]

Exterior. The exterior is no less magnificent than the inside, the whole façades being covered with sculpture, mosaic, or slabs of rich marble. The west façade especially is a marvel of lavish expenditure both of labour and of costly material. The design consists of two main stages, the lower one being formed by the atrium, a 12th-century addition, in front of the older façade. Each stage is divided into five great arches, decorated with richly sculptured archivolts and with tympana filled in with mosaic pictures. Only one of the original mosaics now exists on this front; all the rest have been destroyed and replaced by others of very inferior style in the 17th and 18th centuries. The one original mosaic is over the northernmost of the four doorways into the western atrium; its date is about or soon after 1220. It is of great decorative beauty, and its subject—the translation into the church of the body of St Mark—is of great interest from its careful representation of the west façade of the church as it was at the beginning of the 13th century. It shows the original form of the upper part of the façade before the addition in the 14th century of the large ogee gables with elaborate crockets, alternating with statues, and intermediate pinnacled canopies placed between the five great arches of the upper story. It also shows the marble screen-work which once filled the great central west window, the whole of which is now missing, only the columns which supported it being left.[6] Similar filling-in still exists in some of the large side windows. The lower or atrium story is enriched with a wonderful collection of columns of precious marbles and porphyries arranged in two tiers. The sculptured archivolts, with foliage mixed with figures or subjects in relief, are of great beauty and variety. They are all carved in fine white Athenian marble, and were once gilt, as appears to have been the case with nearly all the sculptured ornaments of St Mark's. This extensive use of gold is clearly shown in Gentile Bellini's picture. The top of the atrium forms a wide upper gallery communicating with the interior at the triforium level. In the centre of this gallery stand the four colossal bronze horses, from some Græco-Roman triumphal quadriga, which were brought to Venice after the conquest of Constantinople by Enrico Dandolo in 1204.[7]

Roofs. The roofs, including the five great external domes over the nave, choir, transepts, and crossing, are all covered with thick sheets of lead. The internal domes, like the rest of the vaults, are of brick, the external domes being of wood. The drums on which the outer domes rest are bound round with strong iron bands, which were

1 T. G. Jackson, in his work on *Dalmatia and Istria* (Oxford, 1887), vol. iii., gives an interesting account and valuable illustrations of the early churches at Parenzo, Grado, and Aquileia, which in their sculptured capitals, mosaics, and other details closely resembled the early portions of St Mark's. Large quantities of the sculpture and rich marbles used in Venice were brought from Grado, Aquileia, and other cities in the same district, the buildings of which were to a great extent the prototypes of those built in Venice before the 13th century. In later times the flood of influence passed in the opposite direction, and during the 14th and 15th centuries an immense number of palaces and churches were built in the Venetian style, by architects from Venice, all along the eastern shores of the Adriatic. The result is that in these Istrian cities examples are to be seen of what appears to be the architecture of Venice during its whole course of development from the 12th to the 15th century.

2 The exterior of the church of St Demetrius at Thessalonica is covered with simple brick arcading, very like that which still exists in many places behind the marble lining of St Mark's.

3 The first edition of the *Stones of Venice*, together with an unfinished series of folio plates, most of them exquisitely drawn by Mr Ruskin himself, was published in 1852; a carefully executed reprint of both was issued in 1886. This is one of the noblest monographs on any architectural subject that has ever been written.

4 The church of St Demetrius at Thessalonica contains many sculptured panels and other decorations exactly similar in style to those of St Mark's; and other churches in Thessalonica and Trebizond have mosaic paving and glass wall-mosaics closely resembling those in St Mark's. Even the plan of the Venetian basilica is Oriental in origin.

5 The most notable examples are over the doorways of the western atrium.

6 This tracery, or rather screen-work, was removed before 1496, when Gentile Bellini painted his picture of the Piazza and West Front of St Mark's. This very interesting picture shows the lost mosaics, the subjects of which appear to have been the same as those now existing.

7 These bronze horses were carried off to Paris, with many other art treasures, by Napoleon in 1797; they were restored to their place in 1815 by Francis of Austria, as is recorded in a large inscription on the arch below them.

added by Jac. Sansovino in the 16th century. The round-headed windows in the drums were once filled in with pierced screen-work of marble, some examples of which still exist in the western atrium,—an interesting relic of the method of filling windows employed at a time when glass was but little used.

Mosaics. The mosaics in the interior are among the finest and, from their variety of date, the most interesting series in the world; those dating from the 12th and 13th centuries are of special beauty. The earliest appear to be those on the five great domes, probably executed before 1150. On the nave dome the subject is the Descent of the Holy Spirit: tongues of fire radiate upon colossal figures of the apostles, and below them, on the drum of the dome, is a second series of figures representing the various nations of the world who were converted through the inspired teaching of the apostles. On the dome over the crossing is the Ascension of Christ, with bands of large figures of the Apostles, and below them the Virtues. On the choir dome are a half figure of Christ and a series of the Prophets. In the main apse is Christ in Majesty. The transept domes have series of Saints and Doctors of the Church. All have explanatory inscriptions. The whole of the rest of the vaults and the upper portion of the walls are covered with mosaic pictures, of which a mere catalogue would occupy many pages. In the atrium the subjects are taken from the Old Testament; these date from *c.* 1200-1300. In the baptistery[1] are the life of St John the Baptist and scenes from the life of Christ; on the first dome (westwards) is Christ in Majesty over a series of baptismal scenes and the Greek Doctors; on the second dome, Christ surrounded by Angels. On the barrel vault of the chapel of St Isidore is a very beautiful series of mosaics, with scenes from the saint's life and other subjects, executed in 1355, soon after the completion of the chapel. In the sacristy is a fine series of 15th-century mosaics, and in other parts of the church there are mosaics of still later date, some of them from cartoons by Tintoretto and other Venetian painters of the decadence. These later mosaics are not designed with any real sense of the special necessities of mosaic work, and are all very inferior in decorative effect to the simple Byzantine style from the 12th to the 14th century.

Most of the existing mosaics of the earlier periods have suffered very seriously from "restoration," a process which is still going on, with most fatal results to the interest and real value of the mosaics. The exterior marble facing and much of the sculpture have within recent years been completely renewed in the most tasteless way,—the fine slabs of rich Oriental marbles having been largely replaced by cheap greyish Carrara marble of the worst quality, quite devoid of the fine colours and rich veinings of the original slabs. The

Pavement. same fate now threatens the magnificent mosaic pavement of St Mark's, the surface of which has sunk into a succession of wavy hollows, owing to the settlement of the vaulting of the crypt below on which the nave paving rests.[2] The original part of the mosaic floor probably dates from about the middle of the 12th century. The nave pavement of the cathedral at Murano, which is exactly similar in style, materials, and workmanship, has an inscription dated 1140. The pavement of St Mark's consists partly of opus Alexandrinum of red and green porphyry mixed with some marble, and partly of tesselated work, made both of glass and of marble tesseræ. The two methods are obviously of the same date, as in some cases both processes are used in the same design. The opus Alexandrinum is very similar in style to that in some of the basilicas of Thessalonica, and also those in Rome, most of which are of about the same date, the 12th century. The designs executed in mosaic tesseræ are of several different styles, some being taken from the mosaics of Roman classical times, while others, with large panels of peacocks on each side of a vase, eagles or lions devouring their prey, and the like, are copied from Byzantine reliefs of much earlier date than the 12th century.[3] The originals of many of these are to be seen in the sculptured roundels which stud the façades of Byzantine palaces in Venice. A great part of the pavement of St Mark's has been repaired and renewed at various times, from the 14th century down to the present time; consequently a great variety of styles and materials occurs mixed with the original parts. The pavement in the north aisle was renewed in the most clumsy and spiritless fashion about twenty years ago, and it is much to be feared that a similar fate awaits the rest of these priceless mosaics.

Retable or Pala d'Oro. One of the great glories of St Mark's is the most magnificent gold retable in the world, most sumptuously decorated with jewels and enamels, usually known as the Pala d'Oro. It was originally (according to the Venetian chronicles) ordered in Constantinople by Doge Pietro Orseolo I. in 976; and an inscription in enamelled letters added in 1345 records that it was brought to Venice and partly renewed by Doge Ordelafo Falieri in 1105; in 1209 it was again repaired and enlarged by Doge Pietro Ziani; and finally in 1345 Andrea Dandolo reset the enamels in new framework, and added some minute gold canopies and other decoration of Gothic style. In the 19th century it was thoroughly repaired and the stolen gems replaced by new ones, easily distinguishable from the original jewels by being cut in facets, not "en cabochon" after the old fashion. This marvellous retable is made up of an immense number of microscopically minute gold cloisonné enamel pictures, of the utmost splendour in colour and detail. The enamels are partly translucent, allowing the brilliant gold backing to shine through the coloured enamel. The subjects are Christ in Majesty, figures of Archangels and Angels, and a very large number of single figures of Prophets and Saints, as well as many scenes from the life of Christ and of St Mark. No description can do justice to the splendour of effect produced by this gleaming mass of gold, jewels, and enamels; the delicacy of workmanship of the latter is only equalled by two Textus covers, also in gold cloisonné, now preserved in the treasury of St Mark, which also possesses a magnificent collection of church plate of all sorts, such as large chalices and patens in crystal and agate, reliquaries, candlesticks, altar frontals, and other kinds of church furniture, all of the most precious materials and workmanship.[4] Two silver frontals of the 14th century, now used for the high altar of St Mark, originally belonged to the cathedral of Venice, S. Pietro di Castello.

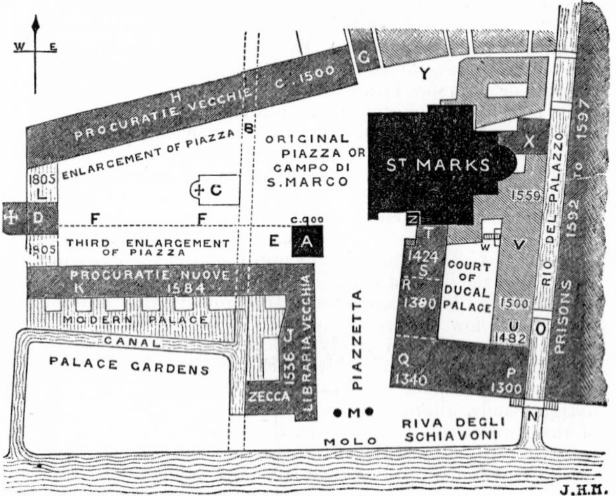

FIG. 3.—Square of St Mark and surrounding buildings. The original *campo* was bounded on the west by the canal B, with the 6th-century church of S. Geminiano, C, on its west bank. The first enlargement of the square was effected by Doge Sebastiano Ziani in 1176, when he filled up the canal and rebuilt the church on a new site at D, thus nearly doubling the size of the square. Lastly, the square was extended southwards in the 16th century, when the new palace of the procurators, K, was built by Scamozzi. Gentile Bellini's picture shows a line of houses along FF, reaching up to the great campanile, A. Napoleon I. in 1805-10 pulled down the church of S. Geminiano and built a new block at the west end of the square, L. The dates of the various parts of the existing ducal palace are indicated on the plan; the rebuilding was carried on in the following order, P, Q, R, S, T, U, V. At Z is the treasury of St Mark, which was originally one of the towers belonging to the old ducal palace; E, site of old houses; G, clock-tower; H, old palace of procurators; J, old library; M, two columns; N, Ponte della Paglia; O, Bridge of Sighs; W, Giants' Staircase; X, sacristy of St Mark; Y, Piazzetta.

Ducal palace. *The Ducal Palace.*—The original doge's palace, probably a small strongly fortified castle, was built early in the 9th century, soon after the transference of the seat of government from the island of

Early history. Malamocco to that of Rialto. In the early troublous period of Venetian history the ducal palace was frequently destroyed and rebuilt. It was burnt in 976, and again in 1106; by 1116 it had been rebuilt. At the end of the 12th century Sebastiano Ziani (1173-79) restored and enlarged it. Of his work the only fragments now in existence are some richly sculptured bands in relief, built in at intervals along the 14th-century Rio façade, by the south-east angle of the palace (see P on fig. 3). The present magnificent palace was a slow growth extending over nearly three centuries, the older building of Ziani being gradually pulled down as room was required for the new work.

Present palace. The existing palace was begun in 1300-1 by Doge Pietro Gradenigo, who built the façade (P on fig. 3) along the Rio, in which are inserted the 12th-century friezes of Ziani. About 1309 the arcaded façade along the sea front was begun at the south-east angle by the Ponte della Paglia (N on fig. 3), and the design which was then adopted was accurately followed along the whole external façade, the building of which occupied about a century and a half. Towards the end of the 14th century the façade had been carried along the Piazzetta side as far as the tenth capital (counting from the south-

[1] A complete list of the subjects of the mosaics in the baptistery is given by Mr Ruskin in his *St Mark's Rest*, 1884, p. 129 *sq.*

[2] There is no ground whatever for the notion that the wavy surface of the pavement was produced intentionally. Its lines of depression simply follow the "cells" in the crypt vaulting, the loose filling-in of which allows more settlement than the rigid crowns of the vaults.

[3] It is interesting to note that a 6th or 7th century marble relief with the vase and peacocks, which forms part of the external facing of the treasury of St Mark, has been copied exactly in one of the mosaics of the south aisle.

[4] At the end of the 18th century the rich treasures of St Mark's were sacked by the French, and much was then dispersed and lost, including many antique engraved gems and cameos from the Pala d'Oro.

west angle), which is carved with baskets of different kinds of fruit (R on fig. 3). At this point the work seems to have remained stationary for some years, and a considerable portion of Ziani's palace was still in existence; this was called the old palace to distinguish it from the 14th-century new palace. The Venetian council had decreed that a fine of 1000 gold ducats should be imposed on any of its members who proposed that the remaining part of the old palace should be rebuilt; in spite of this, in 1422, Doge Tomaso Mocenigo did propose and carried a resolution that the new palace should be extended over the site of Ziani's building. The doge paid the fine, and it was spent as a contribution towards the rebuilding, which was begun in 1424; in a few years the remainder of the external façade was completed up to the north-west angle, by the church of St Mark (S on fig. 3). The magnificent gateway which unites the palace to the church, called the Porta della Carta[1] (T on fig. 3), was added in 1439-42; it was the work of the sculptor Bartolomeo Bon and his son. Soon after the great balconied windows, which break the regularity of both fronts of the palace, were inserted in the upper story. The internal block in the great court joining the Porta della Carta to the Rio front was built by Doge Cristoforo Moro about 1462. In 1479 a fire consumed part of the 14th-century buildings along the Rio, and this part was then rebuilt, mostly between 1480 and 1550. On the southern part of this block are the arms of Doge Agostino Barbarigo, 1482 (U on fig. 3).

[F]açades. The two main façades, those towards the sea and the Piazzetta, consist of a repetition of the same design, that which was begun in the early years of the 14th century. The name of the architect who began the work and thus fixed the design of the whole is not certainly known, but it must have been a man of an earlier generation than that of Filippo Calendario, who is often stated to have been the chief architect of the older portion. Calendario was an accomplice in the conspiracy of Marino Faliero and was executed together with the doge in 1355. It appears probable that a Venetian architect and sculptor named Pietro Baseggio was the chief master-builder in the first half of the 14th century.[2] The design of these façades is very striking, and unlike that of any other building in the world. It consists of two stories with open colonnades, forming a long loggia on the ground and first floors, with seventeen arches on the sea front (see fig. 4) and eighteen on the other façade. Above this is a lofty third story, pierced with a few large windows, with pointed arches once filled with tracery, which is now lost. The columns of the middle story support heavy tracery of the characteristic Venetian form, which was copied with more or less modification in a very large number of private palaces built in Venice during the 14th and 15th centuries. The ground story has boldly moulded pointed arches, the spandrels of which were intended to be decorated with geometrical patterns in thin pieces of marble inlay. Only two of these were, however, completed. The main walls are wholly of brick; but none was left visible. The whole surface of the upper story is faced with small blocks of fine Istrian and red Verona marbles, arranged so as to make a large diaper pattern, with, in the centre of each lozenge, a cross made of verde antico and other costly marbles. The colonnades, string-courses, and other decorative features are built in solid Istrian stone. Very beautiful sculpture, executed with an ivory-like minuteness of finish, is used to decorate the whole building with wonderful profusion. At each of the three free angles is a large group immediately over the lower column. At the south-east angle is the Drunkenness of Noah, at the south-west the Fall of Man, and at the north-west the Judgment of Solomon. Over each at a much higher level is a colossal figure of an archangel,—Raphael, Michael, and Gabriel. The sculpture of all the capitals, especially of those on the thirty-six lower columns, is very beautiful and elaborate, a great variety of subjects being introduced among the decorative foliage, such as the virtues, vices, months of the year, age of man, occupations, sciences, animals, nations of the world, and the like.[3] On the whole the sculpture of the 14th-century part is finer than that of the later part near St Mark's. In many cases the 15th-century sculptors have simply copied the older capitals. A strong Florentine influence is apparent in all this sculpture, a great part of which was probably the work of Florentines.[4] Unhappily within recent years about half the old capitals have been removed and replaced by copies, which in some cases are not even accurate reproductions of the originals. A very wholesale and needless "restoration" is still in progress, not only of the sculpture, but also of the columns, arches, and traceries, which in many cases have been wholly renewed without any excuse whatever.

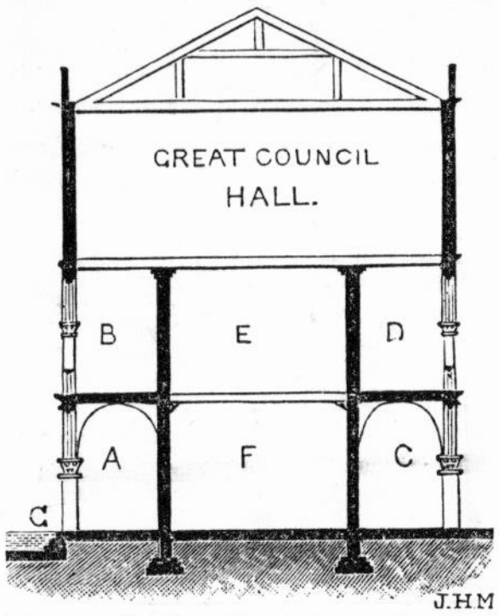

Fig. 4.—Section through sea-front of ducal palace (see P, Q in fig. 3). A. Lower loggia towards sea. B. Upper loggia towards sea. C, D. Loggie towards inner court. E. Private apartments of doge. F. Offices. G. Modern level of pavement which hides the old stylobate of three steps (see fig. 1).

Internal court. The great internal court is surrounded with arcading of very similar style; even in the 16th-century portion the same main outline has been followed, though the detail is different. From the interior of the court access is given to the upper loggia by a very beautiful staircase of early Renaissance style, built in the middle of the 15th century by the Venetian architect Antonio Ricci. Two colossal statues of Neptune and Mars at the top of these stairs were executed by Fran. Sansovino in 1554—hence the name "giants' staircase"; they are very clumsy and badly designed. Owing to a fire which gutted a great part of the palace in 1574, the internal appearance of the rooms was completely changed, and the fine series of early Paduan and Venetian paintings which decorated the walls of the chief rooms was lost.[5] At present the magnificent council chambers for the different legislative bodies of the Venetian republic and the state apartments of the doges are richly decorated with gilt carving and panelling in the style of the Later Renaissance. On the walls of the chief council chambers are a magnificent series of oil paintings by Tintoretto and other less able Venetians,—among them Tintoretto's masterpiece—Bacchus and Ariadne—and his enormous picture of Paradise, the largest oil painting in the world. All have suffered much from restoration. Some of the scenes of important Venetian naval victories are of great historical interest, though of little merit as works of art.

State prisons. In the 16th century the state prisons, which till then were on the ground floor of the ducal palace, were removed to a new building on the opposite side of the narrow canal on the east of the Rio del Palazzo (see fig. 3). A bridge, usually known as the Bridge of Sighs, was built to connect the two buildings. This bridge and the new prisons[6] were designed by a Venetian, who also built the Rialto bridge in 1588-91, and hence was nicknamed Antonio da Ponte.

Owing to the raising of the level of the Piazzetta and the Riva degli Schiavoni, the ducal palace has lost its stylobate, consisting of three steps, the level of the pavement outside being now the same as that of the lower loggia of the palace; and thus a serious injury has been done to the architectural beauty of the façades (see figs. 1 and 4). As the columns of the lower story have no bases, a stylobate is specially needed.

Piazzetta columns. By the side of the sea in the Piazzetta, on to which the west façade of the ducal palace faces, stand two ancient columns of Egyptian granite, one red and the other grey (see M, fig. 3). These great monoliths were brought as trophies to Venice by Doge Domenico Michieli in 1126, after his victories in Syria. In 1180 they were set up with their present fine capitals and bases by a Lombard engineer, Niccolo de' Barattieri. The grey column is surmounted by a fine bronze lion[7] of Byzantine style, cast in Venice for Doge Ziani about 1178; and in 1329 a marble statue of St Theodore, standing upon a crocodile, was placed on the other column.[8]

Campanile. The great campanile (see A, fig. 3) of St Mark in the square at the west of the church was founded about 900 by Doge Pietro Tribuno and finished in 1131 or soon after. It is a very massive square tower of brick, 325 feet high by 42 square, on a stone base, simply decorated with slight pilasters. The ascent to the top is made by a series of inclined planes instead of stairs. The upper part, an open lantern with a pyramidal roof, was added in the 16th century; on the apex is a fine colossal statue of an angel, formed of plates of gilt bronze on a wooden core,—a work of the end of the 15th century.

Cathedral church. *Other Churches.*—The ancient cathedral church of S. Pietro di Castello was wholly rebuilt during the latter part of the 16th century, probably from designs by Palladio. It is a well-proportioned but uninteresting structure of the usual Pseudo-Classical Palladian style; it is now seldom used.

Churches of SS. Giovanni e Paolo and the Frari. After St Mark's the two finest churches in Venice are those of the Dominican and Franciscan friars, SS. Giovanni e Paolo and S. Maria Gloriosa dei Frari. Both are built on the same plan as that of other important friars' churches, such as S. Maria Novella and S. Croce in Florence, with a large nave, aisles, transepts, and two

[1] So named because public decrees and other papers were affixed to it.

[2] The edict for further rebuilding in 1422 names Baseggio as being the original designer of the 14th-century portion of the palace.

[3] An excellent account of these sculptured capitals is given by Mr Ruskin in his *Stones of Venice*, vol. ii. A treatise on the same subject was written by Didron and Burges, *L'Iconographie du Palais Ducale*, Paris, 1857, but the authors failed to recognize the true dates of the different parts of the palace.

[4] According to Zanotti, the capital at the north-west angle was signed "Duo Soci Florentini"; but this inscription is not now visible.

[5] Considerable remains of these paintings by Altichiero and other 15th-century masters still exist, though completely hidden by the later pictures on canvas.

[6] Many distinguished prisoners have suffered from violent heat in the *piombi* or roof cells, and from damp and cold in the *pozzi* or cellars, of these prisons.

[7] This lion, carried off to Paris, together with the four bronze horses and other Venetian spoils, by Napoleon I., was sent back in a very fragmentary condition; the lion's tail, the wings, and the book under its paws were added after its return to Venice in 1816. Originally the wings were much larger, and there was no book.

[8] See Ruskin, *St Mark's Rest*, chap. ii.

or more chapels opening from the east of each transept. In the Venetian examples the choir and all the transept chapels have apsidal terminations. Both churches are built of brick, with rich marble traceried windows, and simple vaulting throughout. The details of the interior are plain, but the scale is large and the general design very noble and effective, showing a strong infusion of northern Gothic influence, which is one of the characteristics of the friars' churches throughout Italy The Dominican church of SS. Giovanni e Paolo was used as the chief burial place of the doges and other chief members of the Venetian republic;[1] it was built about the middle of the 13th century.[2] There is no foundation for Vasari's statement that Niccola Pisano was the architect of this or of any other building in Venice, although the influence of the Pisano school of sculpture was certainly very strong during the 14th century. The magnificent collection of tombs in this church, of all dates from the 13th century downwards, is one of the finest in the world. Some of the recumbent effigies of the 14th century, and the reliefs and statuettes on the sarcophagi, are works of very great beauty, distinctly Florentine in character. The later monuments of the 16th and 17th centuries are in many cases very large, costly, and pretentious, of the worst possible taste, in striking contrast to the quiet simplicity of the 14th-century tombs. A remarkable feature in the Franciscan church is its fine marble rood-screen of the 14th century, one of the very few which still exist in Italy; it is surmounted by two ambones or pulpits. The choir stalls, which extend rather more than one bay westwards of the crossing, are richly decorated with reliefs and tarsia work, executed in the later years of the 15th century. This church is the largest in Venice, even exceeding St Mark's in size; it also contains a number of fine tombs, some of them with large equestrian statues of Venetian generals. The tomb of Doge Francesco Dandolo in this church, now mutilated and removed from its place, is a very noble example of 14th-century sculpture. The sacristy, on the south of the south transept, still possesses over its altar one of Giovanni Bellini's finest pictures, signed and dated 1485, representing the Madonna Enthroned between Standing Figures of Saints, a picture of most extraordinary beauty and perfect preservation, in its original richly carved retable-frame.[3] This church, though very similar in style, was built about half a century later than that of the Dominicans, and was not completed till after 1300.

Church of S. Stefano, &c.

The influence of the chief orders of friars in the style of ecclesiastical architecture is strongly shown in many other churches, such as that of S. Stefano, especially in the frequent use of the apse as a termination both for choirs and side chapels. This church, built about 1360 by a monastery of Austin friars, has a rich west front, decorated with very delicate terra-cotta ornaments. The eastern apse extends over a small canal and is supported on a wide bridge-like arch. Of the same type are the church of S. Gregorio and that of S. Maria della Carità, both now desecrated. S. Gregorio has a very beautiful cloister, dated 1342, the columns of which support, not a series of arches, but flat wooden lintels. On the capital of each column rests a moulded wooden corbel to diminish the bearing of the lintel; this is a very characteristic Venetian mode of construction, used, not only for cloisters, but also for ground floors of houses, upper loggias, and other places, especially during the 14th and 15th centuries.[4]

S. Giacomo dall' Orio.

One of the most interesting early churches is that of S. Giacomo dall' Orio, built in the early part of the 13th century, with a complicated many-columned plan, the aisles being carried along the transepts as well as the nave. The roof is a very good example of the wooden coved type, of which the finest are at Verona (*q.v.*). One of the columns in the south transept is a monolith of the precious verde antico, of wonderful size and beauty, probably brought from some Byzantine church.

S. Maria dei Miracoli.

Venice contains some very beautiful ecclesiastical architecture of the Early Renaissance, about 1450 to 1500, with very delicate and refined detail, such as was designed by Fra Giocondo of Verona and various members of the Venetian Lombardo family. The most perfect example of this style is the little church of S. Maria dei Miracoli, so called because it was built to contain a miraculous picture of the Madonna. Very rich and varied marbles were used in its construction, and it is lavishly decorated with sculpture of wonderful refinement and beauty of detail; it was built in 1481-89 from the designs of Pietro Lombardo. The court of the guild of St John the Evangelist is another fine example of the same style.

Later Renaissance churches.

In the 16th century and even later some very stately churches of the Later Renaissance style were built in Venice by Jacopo Sansovino, Andrea Palladio, and their school. One of Sansovino's[5] best works, the church of S. Geminiano, was destroyed at the beginning of the 19th century in order to complete the west side of the square of St Mark (see fig. 3). The large church of S. Giorgio Maggiore, on an island opposite the ducal palace, was built by Palladio, and is a good example of the faults and merits of his style. S. Maria della Salute, built by Baldassare Longhena in 1632, as a thank-offering of the Venetian senate for the cessation of the great plague in 1630, is one of the most conspicuous churches in Venice owing to its magnificent site near the mouth of the Grand Canal. Though dull and heavy in detail, it has a well-designed dome, and the general mass of the building is very skilfully arranged. Most of the 17th and 18th century churches in Venice are in the worst possible taste, and extravagantly pretentious in style. A large number still possess fine campanili,—lofty square brick towers, in general form not unlike the 12th-century campanili of Rome. These in Venice range from the 11th to the 16th century, those of the 14th century being specially beautiful.

[1] Andrea Dandolo, whose tomb is in the baptistery, date 1355, was the last doge buried in St Mark's, which up to that time had been the usual ducal burying-place.

[2] It was founded about 1234, but not completed till some years later.

[3] Mr Ruskin, *Shrine of the Slaves*, p. 38, calls this one of the two finest pictures in the world, the second being another Madonna by Gian. Bellini in the church of S. Zaccaria in Venice.

[4] A fine loggia of this class exists in the ducal palace, opening on to the upper loggia of the Piazzetta façade.

[5] For others of his works in Venice, see Sansovino.

Palaces.

Palaces.—In the beauty and interest of its domestic architecture Venice ranks before any other city in the world. Fine examples of all dates from the 12th century downwards still exist, and many even of the earlier palaces are still externally in a very perfect state of preservation.

12th century Byzantine palaces.

The most notable specimens of 12th-century Byzantine palaces are those of Loredano (now municipal offices), Farsetti, and Da Mosto, all on the Grand Canal. The *fondaco* of the Turks (now the Correr Museum) was once the finest of this date, but it has been ruined first by neglect and then by wholesale restoration.[6] The general design of these Byzantine palaces appears to have been very similar in all cases; fig. 5 shows a typical example.

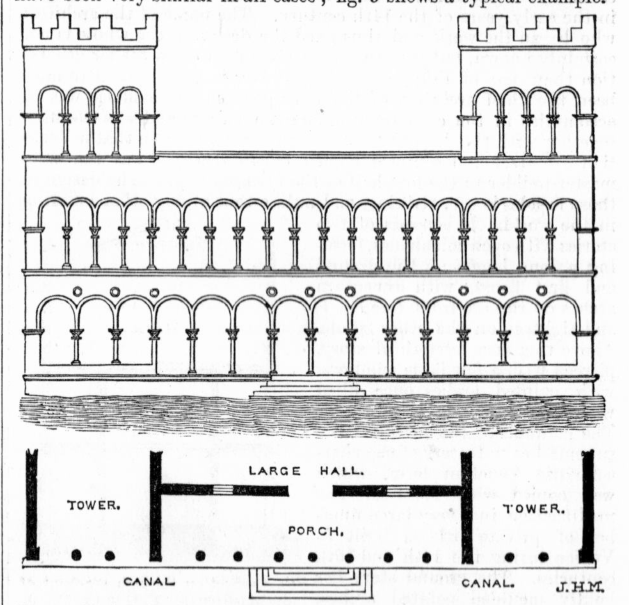

Fig. 5.—Typical façade and plan of a 12th-century Byzantine palace, with a tower at each end. No perfect example now exists, owing to the rebuilding of the upper stories with central part equal in height to the ends; but in many cases traces of this arrangement can be distinguished.[7]

The canal façade usually had a tower at each end, with a row of arches in the centre opening into a long vestibule or porch, behind which was a large hall. Along the first floor a long range of window arches extended from end to end, forming a continuous arcade; in the *fondaco* of the Turks this upper range consisted of no less than twenty-six arches. Very beautiful sculpture was used to decorate all these arches, which were of stilted semicircular form, and also the capitals on which they rested. Mr Ruskin has shown how these round arches developed into other forms, first a simple pointed ogee, and then a cusped ogee of several different varieties.

Venetian Gothic palaces.

In the 13th century the introduction of window-tracery led gradually to the development of a special form of architecture, usually called Venetian Gothic, which was unrivalled for combined magnificence of material and design. The design of about the year 1300 adopted for the façade of the ducal palace had a very extensive and prolonged influence on the private palaces of Venice. A very large number of these, built in the 14th and first half of the 15th century, still exist and are among the most beautiful and well-preserved examples of mediæval architecture which can anywhere be seen. The climax of this magnificent style was towards the end of the 14th century, to which date belongs the wonderful Ca' d'Oro or "golden house," as it is usually called, from the profusion of gilding which once covered its sculptures and mouldings.

[6] A very beautiful fragment of an early palace in the Rio Foscari has been well illustrated by Mr Ruskin in his plates to *Stones of Venice*, 1886.

[7] Mr Ruskin has shown (in *Stones of Venice*, vol. ii.) that in these Byzantine palaces there are subtle variations in the width of the arches, forming a regular gradation of sizes, hardly perceptible without actual measurement.

a' Oro.

No words can describe the magnificence of this palace on the Grand Canal, its whole façade faced with the most costly variegated Oriental marbles, once picked out with gold, vermilion, and ultramarine, the walls pierced with elaborate traceried windows and enriched with bands and panels of delicate carving,—in combined richness of form and wealth of colour giving an effect of almost dazzling splendour.[1]

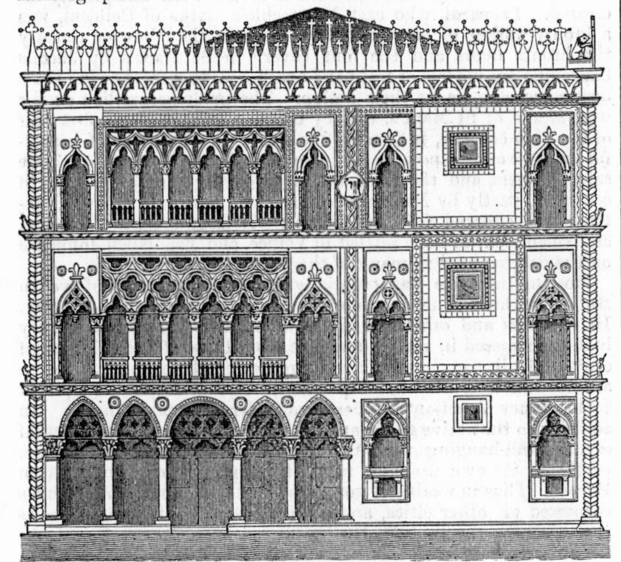

FIG. 6.—Ca' d'Oro, as originally built.

Early Renais-ance alaces.

Some of the 15th-century palaces of Early Renaissance or, as Mr Ruskin calls it, Giocondesque style are scarcely inferior in beauty to those of the Gothic period. Fra Giocondo, the Lombardi, and other architects of this era (1460-1510) still used with great skill and effect the rich Oriental marbles, which were wholly neglected by the architects of the Pseudo-Classic revival. On the Grand Canal the Corner-Spinelli, Trevisan, and Dario Palaces are specially beautiful examples of the style; the richest of all is, however, the small Guisetti Palace in the narrow Rio della Fava, faced with purple Phrygian pavonazzetto and other coloured marbles, and lavishly decorated with delicately sculptured pilasters, friezes, and corbels of the most exquisite design and workmanship. This architectural gem is now quite neglected, and used as a mere warehouse.

Among the 16th-century palaces of later style are many of great size and magnificence, though designed in a somewhat dull and scholastic fashion. The influence of these Venetian buildings on the 19th-century architecture of Europe generally has been very great.[2]

Later Renais-ance.

In most of the Venetian palaces of the Later Renaissance, such as the magnificent Grimani Palace by Sammichele, and in the library of St Mark by Sansovino, the main motive of the façade is taken from the arcading with entablature over engaged columns which was universally used for the theatres and amphitheatres of ancient Rome. In many cases the entire façade of the palace consisted of a series of columns, arches, and cornices, so that no plain wall surface was left at any part of the front, and the whole effect is too laboured and restless, and far less pleasing than the rather earlier examples of the same style, such as the Vendramini Palace on the Grand Canal and the Camerlenghi near the Rialto bridge, finished in 1525, in which some Gothic feeling still survives. One of the noblest palaces of the Later Renaissance is that of Pesaro, on the Grand Canal, built by Longhena, one of the chief Venetian architects of the 17th century, who in this case has followed the style of Sansovino or other architects of the previous century, using the Colosseum arcade for the two upper stories. In general mass and in the proportions of the parts this palace is a work of great merit, far superior to the usually degraded style of the 17th century.

Guilds.

Other Public Buildings.—Much of the splendour of Venice in her days of greatest glory was due to the wealth and religious zeal of the various trade guilds or confraternities, called *scuole* by the Venetians. The members of each guild were united for both secular and religious purposes; their meeting places and chapels were often buildings of the greatest architectural magnificence, and were decorated with sculpture and painting by the chief artists of the time. The *scuola* of St Mark, near the great Dominican church, has a magnificent façade designed in 1485 by Pietro Lombardo. A beautiful series of pictures by Vittore Carpaccio was painted for the Slavonian guild, and still exists in their chapel dedicated to St George and St Tryphonius. The *scuola* of St Rocco possesses a wonderful collection of noble pictures by Tintoretto, and the other chief guilds, such as those of St Ursula, Della Misericordia, Della Carità, and St John the Evangelist, possessed very beautiful and richly decorated buildings.

FIG. 7.—The library of St Mark's, begun in 1536.

Arsenal.

One of the most important public buildings of Venice was the arsenal,[3] including large docks and yards for building ships (see p. 143, above). The entrance gateway is an elaborate work, built in 1460 by the Lombardi; and in front of it stand four ancient marble lions, brought as trophies from the Piræus in 1687.[4] The arsenal is still an important naval depôt, and contains a museum of historically interesting objects.

Public buildings round St Mark's Square.

A stately series of public buildings surrounds the square of St Mark (see fig. 3). The north side is occupied by the old palace of the procurators, designed by Bart. Bon towards the end of the 15th century. Near it to the east stands an elaborate clock-tower built by Pietro Lombardo in 1496. On the south of the square is the newer palace of the procurators, designed in 1584 by Scamozzi, now used as part of the royal palace. The west end is occupied by an extension of the public offices built by Napoleon I. in 1805-10, partly over the site of the church of S. Geminiano. The adjoining Piazzetta is bounded on the east by the ducal palace and on the west by the magnificent library[5] of St Mark, built by Jacopo Sansovino in 1536. The mint occupies part of the same block. The façade of the library is shown in fig. 7.

In front of the west façade of St Mark's are three large flagstaffs, originally used to display the gorgeous silk and gold banners of the subject kingdoms of the Morea, Cyprus, and Candia. Their elaborate bronze sockets were cast in 1505 by the Venetian sculptor, Alessandro Leopardi, who has inserted fine medallion portraits of the reigning doge Lorenzo Loredano.

Museums and galleries.

The academy of fine arts, now in the Della Carità guild-house, contains a very large and valuable collection of pictures of the Venetian school. With one exception, Carlo Crivelli, all the chief Venetians are well represented here, and in many cases far better than in any other collection in the world. Venetian art, in fact, can only be completely studied in Venice. The academy is very rich in elaborately carved retables of the early Venetian painters, works of great decorative splendour, though not equal in drawing or composition to the work of the 14th and early 15th century painters of Florence or Siena. The Vivarini family, the Bellini, with Carpaccio and others of the Bellini school, Cima da Conegliano, Titian, Tintoretto, and Paul Veronese are all represented by a large number of their finest works. The Correr Museum, now moved from the Correr palace to the *fondaco* of the Turks, is the property of the city. It contains some fine Venetian pictures, and an interesting collection of early majolica and other mediæval works of art. The Giovanelli Palace in the Rio S. Felice possesses a fine specimen of Giorgione, the rarest of Venetian masters: it is a noble woody landscape with two figures in the foreground. The portraits by Titian and Tintoretto in the same collection are very fine.

The churches of Venice are still marvellously rich in pictures by the chief Venetian painters of all dates. Almost every church contains some notable painting; and some of them, such as S. Sebastiano, S. Giovanni in Bragora, and S. Giorgio Maggiore, possess a very great number of important works. Many private palaces contain fine collections of pictures; but great numbers of these were sold to foreign purchasers during the 19th century.

Painting.

Painting.

For an account of Venetian painting the reader is referred to the separate articles on the various painters and to SCHOOLS OF PAINTING.

[1] Signor Giacomo Boni has given, in *Proc. Inst. Brit. Arch.* for February 1887, a very interesting account of the decorations of this palace, and of the addition of its elaborate cornice (now destroyed) in 1424 by Bart. Bon, who was paid 210 gold ducats for his work.

[2] In London the façades of many of the principal public buildings have been copied with but little alteration from Venetian originals, as, *e.g.*, the Army and Navy Club in Pall Mall from Jac. Sansovino's Cornaro Palace (1532), with the omission of the middle story, and the Piccadilly School of Mines from the inner court of the doge's palace.

[3] Dante, *Infer.*, xxi. 7-15, describes the various operations in the arsenal at Venice.

[4] On the largest of these lions is cut a runic inscription recording a successful attack on the Piræus in the 11th century by a party of Norse warriors of the Varangian guard, under Harold Hardrada, who afterwards (in 1047) became king of Norway (see *Arch. Journ.*, xvi. pp. 188-192).

[5] This library contains about 65,000 volumes, with 5000 MSS., among which are some very valuable and artistically magnificent codices

Sculpture.

Sculpture. Till the 14th century Venice continued to adhere to the old Byzantine style of sculpture,[1] which, though often delicate in execution and decorative in effect, slowly lost spirit and vigour, and from continually copying older forms gradually degenerated into a dull and mechanical formalism. Early in that century the influence of Niccola Pisano and his school began to awaken a new artistic life among the archaistic sculptors of Venice; but the progress of this renaissance was very slow, and in much of the Venetian sculpture the degenerate Byzantine formalism survived till nearly the close of the 14th century. Other works of the same period were executed with much of the grace and almost realistic beauty for which the contemporary Florentines were so famous, and thus one may see in Venice, and in Venice only, two reliefs of the same date of which one is several centuries earlier in style than the other.[2] This want of originality was probably partly caused by the immense quantity of older sculptured reliefs which was imported to adorn the walls of the churches. In the early part of the 14th century Florentine influence rapidly gained ground, and many sculptors from Florence came to work on the richly carved capitals of the ducal palace and other places, and especially produced a large number of very beautiful tombs with recumbent effigies. One very graceful type, the general motive of which was first used by Arnolfo del Cambio (see ORVIETO), was frequently repeated: at the head and foot of the effigy an angel is represented drawing a curtain so as to expose the figure of the dead man.[3] The sarcophagus, on which the effigy lies, has reliefs of the Virgin and the Angel of the Annunciation, with the Crucifixion or some other sacred subject between. In later times these subjects were usually replaced by allegorical figures of the virtues,[4] and the simple curtain drawn by angels gradually became a large tent-like canopy, of rather clumsy and tasteless form. In most churches the sculptured decoration, apart from that on the tombs, was concentrated on the west façade, the tympanum of the central doorway being often filled with a very fine relief, such as that from the church of the guild Della Misericordia, now in the South Kensington Museum.

In domestic architecture sculpture was but little used after the Byzantine period, the splendour of the façades depending mostly on their rich coloured marbles, and on moulded tracery and string-courses. Nevertheless, even as late as the 15th century it was not uncommon to insert 11th or 12th century pieces of sculpture in new work; many examples of this practice are still to be seen. The sculpture of the Early Renaissance is very abundant and extremely delicate and refined, especially that of the Giocondo and Lombardi schools; S. Maria dei Miracoli contains some of the most beautiful examples.

Though not the work of a Venetian, Venice possesses what is perhaps the most magnificent equestrian statue in the world, the colossal bronze portrait of the Venetian commander-in-chief, Bartolomeo Colleoni (figured in vol. xxi. p. 568, fig. 18),[5] which stands in the square at the west end of SS. Giovanni e Paolo. It was modelled by the Florentine VERROCCHIO (*q.v.*), and was cast after his death by Alessandro Leopardi, who also designed the pedestal; the whole was completed in 1495.

With the later development of the Renaissance, sculpture rapidly declined; in domestic architecture it was but little used, except for the deep frieze under the top cornice, and with the Palladian school it became still rarer, and very mechanical in style. In the 17th century it was again used in the most lavish way as architectural decoration, but was coarse in execution and violently awkward in outline. As Venice in her best days had produced some of the finest decorative sculpture in the world, so in her extreme decadence an almost unequalled depth of degradation was reached, and this continued till the fall of the republic. The Venetian sculptor Canova was, on the whole, superior to his immediate predecessors, and was one of the leaders of the revival of classic sculpture which flourished during the first half of the 19th century.

Minor Arts.

Metal-work. During the early part of the mediæval period the Venetians had no great skill in metal-work. Some of the bronze doors in the west façade of St Mark's are importations from Byzantium. That on the right, which has rude figures of saints inlaid in silver, was brought to Venice in 1204; another with a Latin inscription appears to be native work of about the year 1112; both are very rude in design and execution. The open bronze grills of the west atrium doorways, which are signed as the work of a Venetian goldsmith, Bertuccius, in 1300, show no increase of technical skill. Nor was the silver-work any better: the large silver rood in St Mark's is a very coarse piece of work. The silver altar frontals from the old cathedral, now in St Mark's, with sacred subjects and figures of saints repoussé in each panel, made in the 14th century, are no less rude in design and feeble in execution. As in the case of marble sculpture, Venice was chiefly dependent on foreign importations for its rich stores of treasures in the precious metals. In the latter part of the 15th century Venetian skill in bronze-work had greatly increased. Leopardi, who cast Verrocchio's statue of Colleoni, was a bronze-worker of great eminence; and in the following century the bronze doors and the font cover[6] in St Mark's by Jacopo Sansovino are models of technical excellence, though showing some decadence of taste in their design. The great bronze lion on the west façade of St Mark's, cast by Gaetano Ferrari in the first half of the 19th century, is a really fine work. A great deal of beautiful metal-work, especially in copper and bronze, such as large salvers, ewers, and the like, was made during the 15th and 16th centuries, partly by Moslem workmen and partly by native Venetians who adopted Oriental designs. A large colony of Moslem craftsmen seem to have settled in Venice, and had much influence on the designs used in many of the minor arts.

Textiles. Moslem influence was especially strong in the case of woven stuffs, for which Venice became very celebrated in the 15th century. Its damasks and other silk stuffs with patterns of extraordinary beauty surpassed in variety and splendour those of the other chief centres of silk weaving, such as Florence and Genoa. Fig. 7 in the article TEXTILES (vol. xxiii. p. 209) gives a beautiful example of 15th-century Venetian silk designed under Oriental influence. In addition to the native stuffs, an immense quantity of costly Oriental carpets, wall-hangings, and other textiles was imported into Venice, partly for its own use, and partly for export throughout western Europe. Thus in wealth of gorgeous stuffs and embroideries Venice surpassed all other cities, and on occasions of festivals or pageants the balconies, the bridges, the boats, and even the façades of the houses were hung with rich Eastern carpets or patterned textiles in gold and coloured silk. **Glass-working.** The glass manufactory of MURANO (*q.v.*), a small island about 1½ miles to the north of Venice, was a great source of revenue to the republic; the glass-workers enjoyed special privileges and great pains were taken to preserve the secrets of the craft. Glass drinking cups and ornamental vessels, some decorated with enamel painting, and "silvered" mirrors were produced in great quantities from the 14th century downwards, and exported to other European countries, where they were sold for high prices. Much beautiful glass-work is still produced in Murano, but the workmen have lost all power of original design, and do little but copy the forms invented in the 15th or 16th century. Like many other arts in Venice, that of glass-making appears to have been imported from Moslem countries, and the influence of Oriental design can be traced in much of the Venetian glass. The art of making stained glass windows was not practised by the Venetians; almost the only fine glass in Venice is that in a south transept window in the Dominican church, which, though designed by able Venetian painters, is obviously the work of foreigners.

LITERATURE.—(1) *General Works.*—Sabellicus, *De Venetæ Urbis Situ*, Venice, 1492; Bembo, *Hist. Venetæ*, 1551; Sansovino, *Venezia Descritta*, Venice, 1604; Daru, *Hist. de Ven.*, Brussels, 1838; Galliciolli, *Delle Mem. Ven.*, Venice, 1795; Michieli, *Origine delle Feste Ven.*, Milan, 1829; Zendrini, *Le Isole di Ven.*, Venice, 1829; Id., *Mem. Stor. sullo Stato delle Lagune*, Venice, 1811; Fougasses, *Generall Historie of the Magnificent State of Venice* (Englished by W. Shute), London, 1612; Mutinelli, *Annali Urbani di Venezia*, Venice, 1841; Cicogna, *Inscrizioni Veneziane*, Venice, 1824; Filiasi, *Memorie Storiche dei Veneti*, Padua, 1811; Carrer, *Venezia e la sua Storia*, Venice, 1838; St Didier, *La Ville et la République de Venise*, Paris, 1858; Yriarte, *Histoire de Venise*, Paris, 1878 (Eng. ed., 1880); Anon., *Assedio di Venezia nel 1849*, Venice, 1855; Foscarini, *Letteratura Veneziana*, and its continuation by Moschini, *Lett. Ven. dal Secolo 18vo*, Venice, 1806-8; Corner, *Notizie Storiche delle Chiese di Venezia*, Padua, 1758; Hardy, *Report on the Documents in the Archives of Venice*, London, 1866; Temanza, *Antica Pianta di Venezia*, Venice, 1780. Much valuable matter has been published in the *Archivio Veneto*, which is still in progress. (2) *Architecture, Painting, and Sculpture.*—Ruskin, *Stones of Venice*, reprint 1886, and *St Mark's Rest*, 1880; Selvatico, *Architettura e Scultura in Venezia*, 1847; Cicognara, *Fabbriche di Venezia*, 1815-20; Id., *Monumenti di Venezia*, 1838-40; Cadorin, *Pareri di 15 Architetti*, Venice, 1838; Diedo and Zanotto, *Monumenti di Venezia*, Milan, 1839; Fontana, *Fabbriche di Venezia*; Temanza, *Vite degli Scultori Veneziani*, 1778; Perkins, *Italian Sculpture*, London, 1883, pp. 195-217; Ridolfi, *Maraviglie dell' Arte Ven.*, 1648; Zanetti, *Pittura Veneziana*, 1771; Boschini, *La Carta del Navegar Pittoresco*, Venice, 1660, a curious poem in the Venetian dialect about the pictures and painters of Venice. (3) *Ducal Palace.*—Sansovino, *Lettera intorno al Pal. Ducale*, printed in 1829; Bettio, *Lettera Discorsiva del Pal. Ducale*, Venice, 1837; Zanotto, *Il Palazzo Ducale*, Venice, 1853-58, a fine well-illustrated work; Ruskin, *op. cit.*; Burges and Didron, *Iconographie des Chapitaux du Palais Ducal à Venise*, Paris, 1857. (4) *St Mark's Basilica.*—Meschinello, *La Chiesa di S. Marco*, 1830; Anon., *L'Augusta Ducale Basilica*, Venice, 1761, usually called "Del Foscarini" from its dedication; Richter, "Sculpture of St Mark's," in *Macmillan's Magazine*, June 1880; Kreutz and Ongania, *La Basilica di S. Marco*, 1881-86, one of the most magnificent and costly works ever published, consisting of a large series of photographs and chromo-lithographs; *Il Tesoro di S. Marco*, 1885, a set of fine chromo-lithographs of the gold, silver, enamel, crystal, and jewelled treasures of St Mark's, also published by Ongania; and *Documenti per la Storia della Bas. di S. Marco, IX.-XVIII. Sec.*, 1885, a valuable collection of hitherto unpublished MSS. *Views of Venice.*—Thirty-eight engravings from pictures by Canaletto, entitled *Urbis Venetiarum Prospectus*, Venice, 1735-51, and its companion, Marieschi, *Pros. Urbis Ven.*, 1743; Carlevariis, *Fabriche e Vedute di Ven.*, 1703; Price, *Views of Ven.*, London, 1843. A large

---

[1] Some of the early doges are buried in sculptured sarcophagi of the 5th or 6th centuries brought from elsewhere.

[2] As, for example, the reliefs over the doorway of the cloister of the scuola Della Carità, both of the 14th century.

[3] The tomb of Andrea Dandolo in St Mark's (*c.* 1350) is one of the earliest in which this motive is used.

[4] The 14th-century tomb of the Florentine ambassador, Duccio degli Alberti, is the first in Venice which has representations of the virtues.

[5] See Vasari's *Life of Verrocchio.*

[6] This is usually attributed to Sansovino; but, according to Moschini, a document among the archives of St Mark's records that it was made by Desiderio of Florence and Tiziano of Padua.

number of 18th-century pictures by the Canaletti and by Guardi represent canal views. The fine woodcut bird's-eye view of the city in 1497, engraved by Jacobo de' Barbari, is about to be published in facsimile with descriptive text by Giacomo Boni.

Part III.—Modern City.

The modern city stands on 117 islands, separated by 150 canals (*rio*) and united by 380 bridges; all the main traffic passes along the canals. The usual range of tide-level is about 20 inches; but under exceptional circumstances there is a difference of nearly 6 feet between lowest and highest water. The name "gondola" given to the passenger boats does not occur earlier than the 14th century. As shown in Carpaccio's and Gentile Bellini's pictures (*c.* 1500), the gondola of that date was quite unlike the present boat with its heavy black cabin and absence of any colouring: the older form had an awning of rich stuffs or gold embroideries, supported on a light arched framework open at both ends.[1] The peculiar method of rowing with one oar at the stern is the same now as it was in the 15th century, and probably much earlier. Since 1880 "omnibus" steamers have been introduced on the Grand Canal, which has also

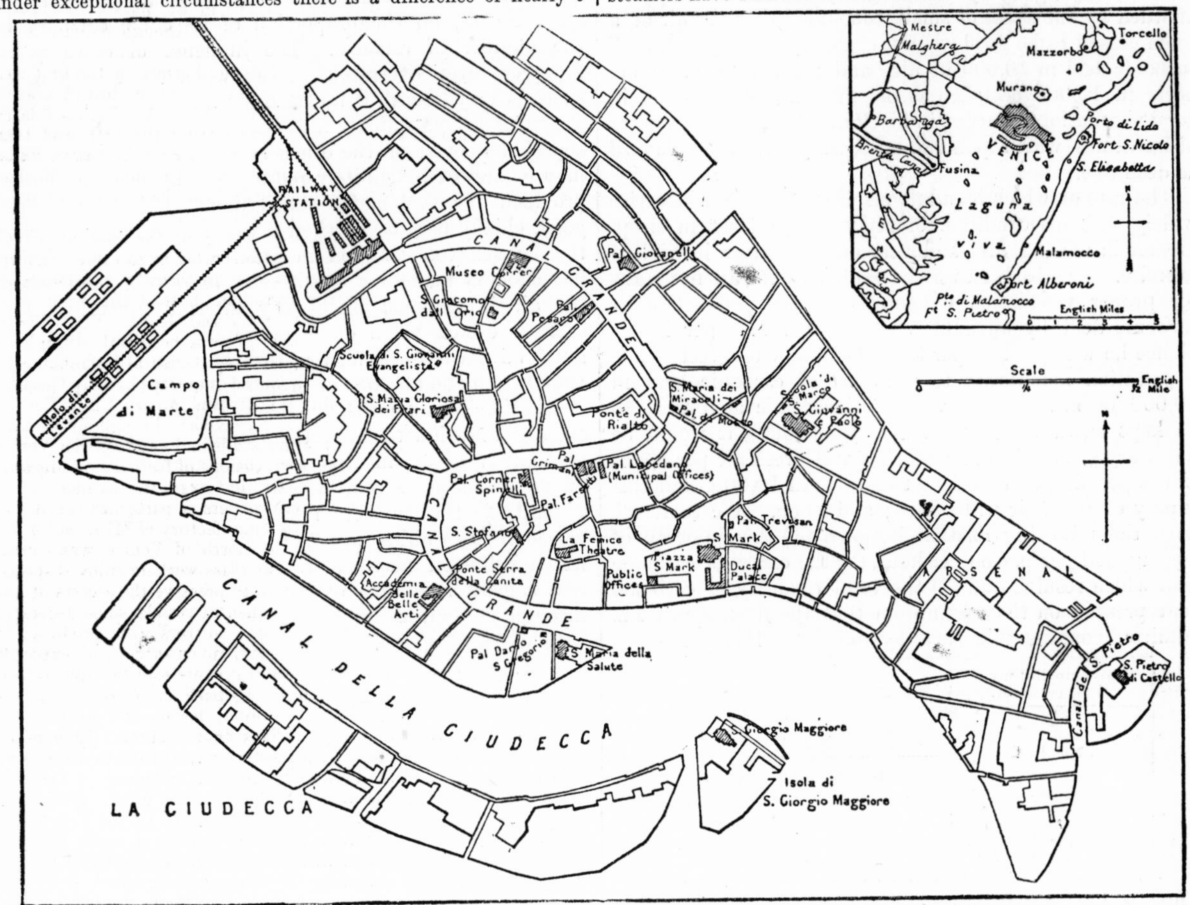

Map of the islands of Venice.

been disfigured in the 19th century by the addition of two hideous iron bridges, over one of which passes the railway that connects Venice with the mainland. Before the Venetian republic was suppressed by Napoleon I. the population amounted to nearly 200,000; in 1830 it had sunk to about 100,000; but since then it has increased, and in 1881 amounted to 132,826 (commune 145,637). The city has grown rapidly in prosperity since its restoration to the kingdom of Italy, and it is now second only to Trieste among the seaports of the Adriatic. The climate is mild but somewhat rainy, owing to the water-surrounded site. The principal manufactures of the city remain what they were in the Middle Ages, namely, gold and silver work, glass, and velvet and silk, to which must now be added cotton, in all of which, as well as in grain, oils, wine and spirits, fruits, drugs, fish, and hides and leather an active trade is carried on. In 1886 the total value of the exports from Venice to foreign countries amounted to £7,239,479 and that of the imports to £8,788,012. During the same year there entered 2595 vessels of 714,642 tons (Italian 1565 vessels of 222,217 tons) and cleared 2597 of 724,740 tons (Italian 1565 vessels of 227,021 tons). (J. H. M.)

VENLO, a frontier town of Holland, in the province of Limburg, on the right bank of the Meuse (here crossed by a bridge), is an important railway junction; Cologne lies 60 miles to the south-east and Maestricht 43 miles to the south-west. The population, which is somewhat closely packed, was 8494 in 1876 and 10,550 in 1887. None of the public buildings has any special interest attaching to it. The leading industries are distilling, brewing, tanning, spinning, needle-making, and tobacco manufacture. There is considerable trade by river with Rotterdam. Venlo was at one time a place of strength, but the fortifications were dismantled in 1868.

VENTILATION is the process of changing the air of rooms and other closed places so that a certain standard of purity may be preserved notwithstanding the vitiation which the air undergoes from the breath of inhabitants, the products of combustion of illuminating agents, and other causes. In estimating the amount of air to be supplied, account must be taken of the standard of purity which is aimed at and of the rate at which vitiation occurs.

Carbonic acid in air.

Of the various impurities that are found in the air of inhabited rooms carbonic acid forms the most ready index of the ventilation. The open air of London and other large inland towns contains about four parts by volume of this gas in 10,000 of air. In the country and in towns near the sea two or three and a half parts in 10,000 is a more usual proportion. Authorities on ventilation usually take four parts in 10,000 as the standard for pure air, and use the excess over that quantity in estimating the adequacy of the air supply. But they differ as to the proportion

[1] The use of black was made compulsory by a sumptuary edict of the great council in the 16th century.

to which the carbonic acid may be allowed to rise in good ventilation. It is generally admitted that the air in which people dwell and sleep should not under any circumstances be allowed to contain more than ten parts in 10,000. This has been accepted as the permissible proportion by Carnelley, Haldane, and Anderson, after an extensive examination of the air of middle and lower class dwellings.[1] De Chaumont, judging by the rough and unsatisfactory test afforded by the sense of smell, concluded that the air of a room ceased to be good when it contained eight volumes of carbonic acid in 10,000 of air,[2] and recommends that six parts in 10,000 be taken as the maximum permissible in good ventilation. Parkes, in his *Manual of Hygiene*, quotes observations which point to an equally exacting standard as desirable.

Standard of purity.

Rate of consumption of air.

The rate at which an adult respires carbonic acid varies widely with his condition of repose, being least in sleep, greater in waking rest, and very much greater in violent exercise. As a basis on which to calculate the air necessary for proper ventilation we may take the production of carbonic acid by an adult as 0·6 cubic feet per hour.[3] Hence he will produce per hour, in 6000 cubic feet of air, a pollution amounting to one part of carbonic acid in 10,000 of air. If the excess of carbonic acid were to be kept down to this figure (1 in 10,000), it would be necessary to supply 6000 cubic feet of fresh air per hour; if the permissible excess be two parts in 10,000, half this supply of fresh air will suffice; and so on. We therefore have the following relation between (1) the quantity of air supplied per person per hour, (2) the excess of carbonic acid which results, and (3) the total quantity of carbonic acid present, on the assumption that the fresh air that is admitted contains four parts by volume in 10,000:—

Air supplied per Adult per Hour.	Carbonic Acid (Parts by Volume in 10,000).	
Cubic Feet.	Excess due to Respiration.	Total Quantity.
1000	6	10
1200	5	9
1500	4	8
2000	3	7
3000	2	6

Thus, to preserve the lowest standard of purity tolerated by sanitarians, ventilation must go on at the rate per person of 1000 cubic feet per hour, and 3000 cubic feet per hour are required to preserve the higher standard on which some authorities insist. Parkes advises a supply of 2000 cubic feet of air per hour for persons in health and 3000 or 4000 cubic feet for sick persons. The English Barracks Improvement Commissioners[4] require that the supply be not less than 1200 cubic feet per man per hour. Pettenkofer recommends 2100 cubic feet, and Morin[5] considers that the following allowances are not too high:—

Hospitals (ordinary)	2000 to 2400 cubic feet per hour.
Do. (epidemic)	5000 ,, ,,
Workshops (ordinary)	2000 ,, ,,
Do. (unhealthy trades)	3500 ,, ,,
Prisons	1700 ,, ,,
Theatres	1400 to 1700 ,, ,,
Meeting halls	1000 to 2000 ,, ,,
Schools (per child)	400 to 500 ,, ,,
Do. (per adult)	800 to 1000 ,, ,,

[1] *Phil. Trans.*, 1887, vol. clxxviii. B, p. 61. In school-rooms well ventilated by mechanical means these authors found 13 parts of carbonic acid in 10,000 of air, which they consider a limit permissible in rooms of that class, though not in dwelling-rooms.

[2] *Proc. Roy. Soc.*, 1875, vol. xxiii. p. 187.

[3] This estimate is based on the observations of Pettenkofer, Angus Smith, and Parkes.

[4] *Report*, 1861.

[5] See *Études sur la Ventilation*, Paris, 1863; also *Proc. Inst. Mech. Eng.*, 1867, p. 63.

Vitiation by burning gas.

Gas lights add to the vitiation of the air of rooms at a rate which may be roughly estimated by treating one cubic foot of gas burnt per hour as nearly equivalent to one adult person, so far as the production of carbonic acid is concerned. Thus an ordinary burner, giving a light of about twenty candles and burning four cubic feet of gas per hour, uses the air of three or four men.

Cubic capacity of room.

The purity of the air of a room depends, of course, to some extent, on the proportion of its cubic capacity to the number of inmates. The influence of capacity is, however, often overrated. Even when the allowance of space is very liberal, if no fresh air be supplied, the atmosphere of a room quickly falls below the standard of purity specified above; on the other hand, the space per inmate may be almost indefinitely reduced if sufficient means are provided for systematic ventilation. Large rooms are good, chiefly because of their action as reservoirs of air in those cases (too common in practice) where no sufficient provision is made for continuous ventilation, and where the air is changed mainly by intermittent ventilation, such as occurs when doors or windows are opened. It must be borne in mind, too, that no room is hermetically sealed. In the absence of proper inlets and outlets casual ventilation goes on through every chink and cranny, and even by diffusion through the plaster of the walls. The ventilation given in this way is generally most inadequate; but a large room has at least the advantage over a small one that it offers more chances for the casual entrance of fresh air, as well as a larger wall-surface through which diffusion may occur. It has also the advantage that a greater volume of air may more easily be passed through it than through a small room in a given time, without causing disagreeable draughts. A general idea of the cubic capacity per inmate, allowed by law or by custom in certain cases, is given in the table below:—

Hospitals	1200 cubic feet (and upwards).
Middle class houses	1000 ,, ,,
Barracks	600 ,,
Good secondary schools	500 ,,
London board schools	130 ,,
Workhouse dormitories	300 ,,
London lodging-houses	240 ,,
One-roomed houses[6]	212 ,,

To realize the need of provision for ventilation, it is only necessary to compare these figures with those already given for the rate of consumption of air. Taking the lowest permissible degree of purity (10 parts of carbonic acid in 10,000), we see that, if no fresh air were allowed to enter, the dweller in a middle-class house would make the atmosphere of his room unfit for breathing after occupying it for 1 hour, and that the sleeping rooms of the poor would fall below the standard in 13 minutes.

Ventilation by diffusion and by currents of air.

The atmosphere of rooms is changed partly by diffusion, but chiefly by actual currents of air. The experiments of Pettenkofer have shown that air passes to a very sensible extent through the substance of brick walls. In houses built of stone the movement of air through the walls must be insignificant; but, as regards individual rooms, what is chiefly important in this connexion is the percolation through dry plaster, causing an exchange of atmosphere to occur between the inside of the room and the space within the lining of the wall, which is generally in communication with other parts of the building and with the external air. In order that the atmosphere of a room should be changed by means of air currents, three things are necessary,—(1) an inlet or inlets for the air, (2) an outlet or outlets, and (3) a motive force to produce and maintain the current. One might think it needless to

[6] Mean of 29 measurements by Carnelley, Haldane, and Anderson, *loc. cit.*

enumerate such obvious requirements were it not that, in providing appliances which are intended to act as ventilators, one or other of the three essentials is not unfrequently overlooked. In systems which are distinguished by the general name of *mechanical* or *artificial* ventilation special provision is made for driving the air, by fans, or by furnaces, or by other contrivances to be described more fully below. In what is called *natural* ventilation no special appliance is used to give motive force, but the forces are made use of which are supplied by (1) the wind, (2) the elevated temperature of the room's atmosphere, and (3) the draught of fires used for heating. A careful distinction should be drawn between cases in which these motive forces are skilfully taken advantage of, by the use of proper inlets and outlets, to give the best result attainable without special appliances for driving the air, and other cases, unfortunately too common in practice, where the ventilation is left to take care of itself. In a fair comparison of a mechanical with the natural system we should exclude examples in which the ventilation is haphazard, or in which as near an approach to no ventilation is reached as the conditions of modern architecture will permit.

Mechanical and natural ventilation.

Chimney draught.

Domestic Ventilation.—The chief agent in domestic ventilation is the chimney; when a bright fire is burning in an open grate, it rarely happens that any other outlet for foul air from a room need be provided. The column of hot air and burnt gases in the chimney is less heavy, because of its high temperature, than an equal column of air outside; the pressure at the base is therefore less than the pressure at the same level outside. This supplies a motive force compelling air to enter at the bottom through the grate and through the opening over the grate, and causing a current to ascend. The motive force which the chimney supplies has not only to do work on the column of air within the chimney, in setting it in motion and in overcoming frictional resistance to its flow: it has also to set the air entering the room in motion and to overcome frictional resistance at the inlets. In many cases the latter part of the chimney's work is the more considerable of the two. From want of proper inlets air has to be dragged in at a high velocity and against much resistance, under the doors, between the window sashes, and through a hundred other chinks and crevices for which we have to thank imperfect carpentry and half-seasoned timber. Under these conditions the air enters in small streams or narrow sheets, ill-distributed and moving so fast as to form disagreeable draughts, the pressure in the room is kept so low that an opened door or window lets in a deluge of cold air, and the current up the chimney is much reduced. If the attempt is made to stop draughts by applying sand-bags and listing to the crevices at which air streams in, matters only become worse in other respects; the true remedy of course lies in providing proper inlets.[1] The discharge of air by an ordinary open fire and chimney varies widely, depending on the rate of combustion, the height and section and form of the chimney, and the freedom with which air is entering the room. About 10,000 cubic feet per hour is probably a fair average, about enough to keep the air fresh for half-a-dozen persons.[2] Even when no fire is burning the chimney plays an important part in ventilation: the air within an inhabited room being generally warmer than the air outside, it is only necessary that an up-current should be started in order that the chimney should maintain it, and it will usually be found that a current is, in fact, passing up.[3]

Other outlets.

When a room is occupied for any considerable length of time by more than about half-a-dozen persons, the chimney outlet should be supplemented by others, which usually take the form of gratings in the ceiling or cornices in communication with flues leading to the open air. Frequently these openings are protected from down-draught by light flap valves of oiled silk or sheet mica, opening outwards. To increase the efficiency of the ventilating action of the chimney, Dr Arnott advocated (in 1849) that an opening should be made near the ceiling, into the chimney, guarded by a flap valve of this type, with the object of providing a direct exit for the foul warm air that gathers in the upper region of a room, especially when gas is burnt. To make Arnott's valve of much service it should be larger than the size usually supplied; even then it has the drawback that, notwithstanding the protection given by the valve, enough back-flow may occur to blacken the wall and ceiling with soot near the opening. If a valve near the ceiling be provided, it is probably better in most cases to lead its outlet shaft direct to the open air than to lead it into the chimney.

Inlets.

With regard to inlets, a first care must be to avoid such currents of cold air as will give the disagreeable and dangerous sensation of draught. At ordinary temperatures a current of outer air to which the body is exposed will be felt as a draught if its velocity exceeds 2, or at most 3, feet per second. The current entering a room may, however, be allowed to move with a speed much greater than this without causing discomfort, provided its direction keeps it from striking directly on the persons of the inmates. To secure this, it should enter, not horizontally nor through gratings on the floor, but vertically through openings high enough to carry the entering stream into the upper atmosphere of the room, where it will mix as completely as possible with warm air before its presence can be felt. A favourite form of inlet is Sheringham's (see fig. 1). When opened it forms a wedge-shaped projection into the room, and admits air in an upward stream through the open top. It is usually placed near the ceiling; but a lower place in the wall would be better. Other inlets are made by using hollow perforated blocks of earthenware, called air-bricks, built into the wall; these are often shaped on the inner side like an inverted louvre-board or venetian blind, with slots that slope so as to give an upward inclination to the entering stream.

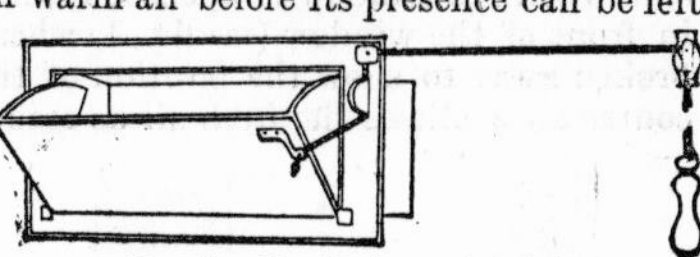
Fig. 1.—Sheringham air inlet.

Tobin tube.

In another and most valuable form of ventilator, the introduction of which is due to Mr Tobin of Leeds, the fresh air enters vertically upwards. The usual arrangement of Tobin's tube (shown in front elevation and section in fig. 2) is a short vertical shaft of metal plate or wood which leads up the wall from the floor level to a height of 5 or 6 feet. Its lower end communicates with the outer air through an air-brick or built opening in the wall; from its upper end, which is freely open, the current of fresh air rises in a smooth stream, clinging, as it were, to the wall, and scarcely changing its direction until it has passed far above the level of the opening. Various forms of section may be given to the tube: if placed in a corner it will be triangular or segmental; against a flat wall a shallow rectangular form is most usual; a lining of wood forming a dado may even be made to serve as a Tobin tube by setting it out a little way from the wall. The tube is often furnished with a regulating valve; but this is a doubtful advantage, as it tempts the inmates to stop the ventilation for no better reason than that the room is cold; in exceptional circumstances, such as the presence of an invalid, the opening may be stopped or reduced by laying a board over it. Contrivances are occasionally added for cleansing the entering air. A muslin or canvas bag hung in the tube, or a screen stretched diagonally across it, may be used to filter out dust; the same object is served in some degree by forcing the air, as it enters the tube at the bottom, to pass in close contact with the surface of water in a tray, by means of a deflecting plate. These complications have a double drawback: they require frequent attention to keep them in order and by putting resistance in the way of the stream they are apt to reduce the efficiency of the ventilation.[4] The air entering by a Tobin tube may be warmed by a coil of hot pipes within the tube or by a small gas-stove (provided of course with a flue to dis-

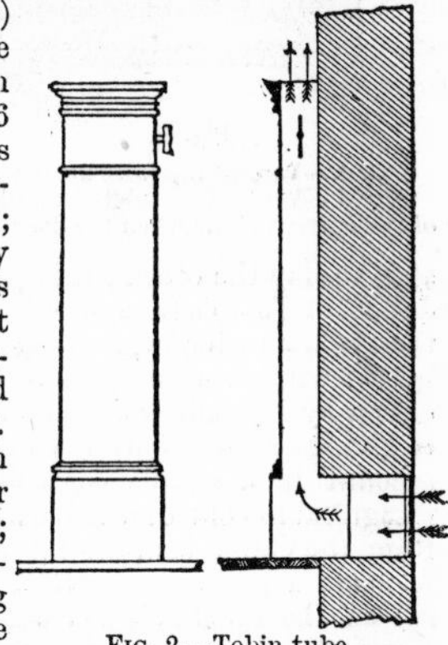
Fig. 2.—Tobin tube.

[1] The absence of proper inlets for air in a house where several fires are burning involves a danger that is much more serious than other effects of bad ventilation. When the air which is required to take the place of that discharged by the chimneys can only struggle in through small openings, the pressure within the house falls considerably below that of the outer air, the water traps under basins and closets are liable to be forced, and foul air is drawn in from every leak in soil-pipe or drain. The writer has found a house drawing what seemed to be its main supply of "fresh" air from the public sewer, through a defective joint between the soil-pipe and the (untrapped) house-drain.

[2] *Report* of the Barracks Commissioners, 1861.

[3] See observations by De Chaumont, in Parkes's *Hygiene*, 6th ed., p. 173.

[4] When the air is not filtered, and when it has been warmed before entering, the vertical direction of the stream is readily traced by dust which is deposited on the wall in a nearly upright column, spreading slightly fan-wise as it rises. With cold air the deposit of dust is comparatively slight. The difference is due to the fact noticed and explained by Mr John Aitken, that air quickly deposits any suspended particles when it is brought into contact with a surface colder than itself, but retains them in suspension if the surface be warmer than the air (*Trans. Roy. Soc. Edin.*, vol. xxxiii., 1884, p. 239). Another domestic illustration of the same fact is given by the greater dustiness of walls and furniture in a stove-heated room than in a room heated by an open fire.

charge outside the products of combustion); or the tube may draw its supply, not directly from the outer atmosphere, but from a hot-air flue or from a room or corridor where the air has been already warmed. The opening should always be about the level of a man's head, but the tube need not extend down to the floor: all that is essential is that it should have sufficient length to let the air issue in a smooth vertical current without eddies (fig. 3).

FIG. 3.—Short Tobin tube.

Ventilation by window and door.

These inlets are at once so simple and effective that no hesitation need be felt in introducing them freely in the rooms of dwelling-houses. When no special provision is made for them in the walls, the advantage of a current entering vertically may still be in some degree secured by help of certain makeshift contrivances. One of these, suggested by Dr Hinkes Bird, is to open one sash of the window a few inches and fill up the opening by a board; air then enters in a zig-zag course through the space between the sashes. Another plan is to have a permanent vertical slot between the sashes by making the top of the lower sash stand out a little from the bottom of the upper one. Still another plan is to have a light frame of wood or metal or glass made to fit in front of the lower sash when the window is opened, forming virtually a Tobin's tube in front of the window (see fig. 4, where a portion of the frame is broken away to show the position of the window sash). This last contrivance allows the fresh air as ready access as may be wished;

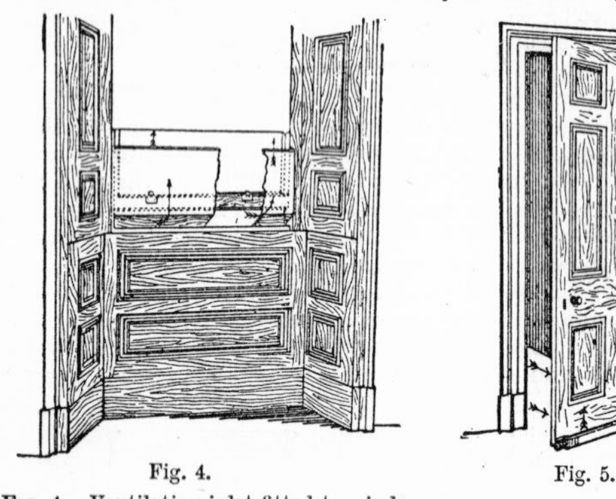

Fig. 4. Fig. 5.

FIG. 4.—Ventilating inlet fitted to window.
FIG. 5.—Ventilating inlet at foot of door. The arrows indicate the direction of the current of air when the door is closed

and, unlike the others, it is still effective when the blind is drawn down. A Tobin's tube, however, is better placed against a dead wall than below a window, for the ascending current is liable to be broken by the window recess and by the down-draught which a window causes by its cooling action on the air of the room. The principle of giving entering currents an upward direction is turned to useful account in a simple contrivance (see fig. 5) for preventing the disagreeable cold draught which comes along the floor of a room from the chink beneath the door. The clearance under the door is made a little greater than usual, and a thin piece of wood is set on the inner side as close as possible to the floor and at a distance of half an inch or so from the surface of the door; the air then enters in a vertical stream.

Arrangements in barracks;

As an example of the systematic ventilation of dwelling-rooms on a large scale, the following particulars may be quoted of arrangements that have been successfully used in English barracks for more than twenty years. One or more outlet-shafts of wood are carried from the highest part of the room, discharging some feet above the roof under a louvre; the number and size of these shafts are such as to give about 12 square inches of sectional area per head, and the chimney gives about 6 square inches more per head. About half the air enters cold through air-bricks or Sheringham valves at a height of about 9 feet from the floor, and the other half is warmed by passing through flues behind the grate. The inlets taken together give an area of about 11 square inches per head. A fairly regular circulation of some 1200 cubic feet per head per hour is found to take place, and the proportion of carbonic acid ranges from 7 to 10 parts in 10,000.[1]

In public buildings.

In the natural ventilation of churches, halls, and other large rooms we often find air admitted by gratings in the floor or near it, —an offensive plan, since it fouls the air, besides causing objectionable draughts, unless the temperature is very carefully regulated. The inlets should consist, like Tobin's tubes, of upright flues rising to a height of about 6 feet above the floor, from which the air proceeds in vertical streams. If the air is to be warmed before it enters, the supply may be drawn from a chamber warmed by hot-water or steam pipes or by a stove, and the temperature of the room may be regulated by allowing part of the air to come from a hot chamber and part from outside, the two currents mixing in the shaft from which the inlets to the room draw their supply. If a basement or story below the room to be ventilated is available, a good plan is to carry the inlet tubes vertically down through it and warm the air in them, so that the height of the warm column assists the flow. Outlets usually consist of gratings or plain openings at or near the ceiling, preferably at a considerable distance from points vertically above the inlet tubes. One of the chief difficulties in natural ventilation is to guard them against down-draught through the action of the wind. Numberless forms of cowl have been devised with this object, and often with the further intention of turning the wind to useful account by making it assist the up-current of foul air. Some of these exhaust cowls are of the revolving class: a hood or trumpet-shaped mouth, opening horizontally and supported about a vertical axis so as to be free to turn, is kept facing away from the wind by means of a large vane. To make the wind help the up-current, a horizontal conical tube is fixed within the cowl, pointing towards the wind and discharging through the trumpet-mouth of the cowl, where it exhausts by suction, on the principle of the jet-pump. Revolving cowls are liable to fail by sticking, and, apart from that, when the wind blows in shifting gusts they cannot respond quickly enough to its changes of direction to prevent it from occasionally blowing down. Fixed cowls are to be preferred; they are designed in many forms, of which Mr Buchan's may be cited as a good example. Fig. 6 shows this ventilator in horizontal section: *aa* is the vertical exhaust flue through which the foul air rises; near the top this expands into a polygonal chamber, *bbbb*, with vertical sides, consisting partly of perforated sheet-metal plates; outside of these are fixed vertical curved guide-plates, *c,c,c,c*; the wind, blowing between these and the polygonal chamber, sucks air from the centre through the perforated sides. Perhaps no form of cowl is entirely free from liability to down-draughts. The most complete safeguard is to place in the exhaust flue a set of flap-valves opening only outwards. Fig. 7 shows the arrangement of exit-valves employed by Mr Buchan; the valves *a, a, a* are flaps of oiled silk working on a wooden grid *bb*, which is inclined enough to let them hang free of it when no current is passing; beyond them is a door closing-valve *c*, worked by hand by the cord *d*; and the whole is enclosed in a box, with glass sides *ee*, through which the action of the valves may be seen. When the outlets are guarded by valves of this type they may discharge through a plain box with louvred sides; an exhaust cowl, however, may still be used with advantage to assist the ventilation under favourable conditions of the wind.[2]

Exha cowls

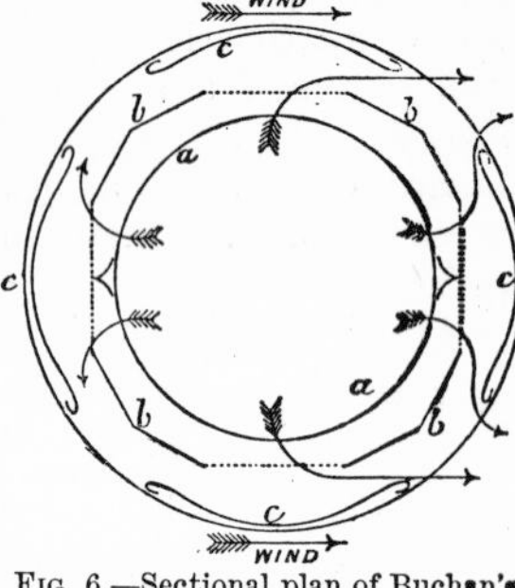

FIG. 6.—Sectional plan of Buchan's exhaust cowl.

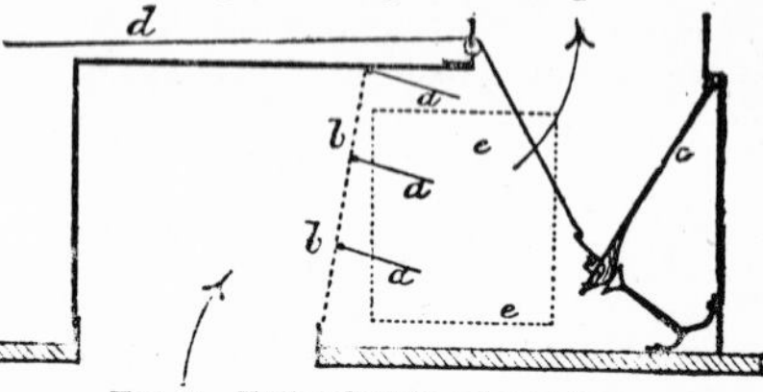

FIG. 7.—Exit valves in exhaust flue.

The two things that supply motive force in automatic ventilation—the difference of temperature between inner and outer air and the wind—are so variable that even the best arrangements of inlets and outlets give a somewhat uncertain result. To secure a strictly uniform delivery of air, unaffected by changes of season or of weather, the influence of these irregular motive forces must be as far as possible minimized, and recourse must be had to an artificial method of driving the air.

Artif venti tion.

Artificial or Mechanical Ventilation.—This finds application on the largest scale in the ventilation of collieries, by methods which are fully described under COAL (vol. vi. pp. 70-71) and MINING (vol. xvi. p. 460). Motive force is supplied to the up-cast shaft either by a furnace at the base, which heats the rising column of air, or (in more modern practice) by a centrifugal fan, such as Guibal's, exhausting air from the top. The long galleries and workings through which the air has to be driven oppose so much resistance that the pressure required to move a sufficient volume of air is immensely greater than is ever necessary or desirable in the artificial ventilation of buildings.

Vacu and plenu meth

A broad distinction may be drawn between what are sometimes called vacuum and plenum methods of artificial ventilation. In the former, as in colliery ventilation, the motive force is applied at the outlets: air is drawn from the rooms, and the pressure of their atmosphere is less than the pressure outside. In the latter the motive force is applied at the inlets: air is pushed in, and the pressure within the room is greater than outside. The plenum method has distinct advantages: it makes the air escape instead of coming

[1] De Chaumont, in Parkes's *Hygiene*, 6th ed., p. 171.

[2] For an account of tests of various forms of ventilating cowls, see S. S. Hellyer, *The Plumber and Sanitary Houses*, 4th ed., 1887.

in as a cold draught at every crevice and casual opening to the outer air; it avoids drawing foul and mouldy air from sewers and basement; and with it, more easily than with the other, one may guard against the disturbing influence of wind. In the plenum method the air is driven by pumps or by fans; in the vacuum method pumps are rarely if ever used: suction is produced by fans or by heating the column of air in a long vertical shaft through which the discharge takes place. Water jets and steam jets have also been employed to impel the air.

[Extrac-]tion by [hot-]air [shaf]t.

Extraction by a hot-air shaft is a common mode of ventilating hospitals and other public buildings.[1] Heat is applied by a furnace or stove at the bottom of the shaft, or by coils of hot-water or steam pipes, which should not extend up the shaft farther than can be helped. In the lecture theatre of the Paris art conservatory, ventilated by Morin, where this means of extraction is employed, fresh air enters through the ceiling and foul air is drawn off through the floor from under the seats; this reversal of the natural direction of the current is of course only possible when a sufficient external motive force is applied. The House of Commons furnishes another example: there the air, after being warmed and moistened, or cooled by water spray, as the state of the atmosphere may require, is admitted through large gratings in the floor, which are covered by porous matting to prevent draughts; outlets from the top of the House lead by flues to the Victoria tower, where a furnace maintains the current in an up-cast shaft.[2] In theatres and other buildings lighted by clusters of gas jets or sun-lights at the ceiling the lights may be turned to account as effective ventilating agents by letting the foul air escape through shafts placed over them, which they heat at the base.[3] What is known in America as the Ruttan or Smead system of ventilation, successfully applied in many schools there, employs a hot-air shaft to furnish motive power. In warm weather a stove at the base of the shaft is used to heat the column; in cold weather the exhaust air from the rooms is so much warmer than the atmosphere outside that the up-cast shaft acts without additional heating. This is in fact an example in which the classification of systems into natural and artificial breaks down. The supply of fresh air is warmed as it enters by passing through chambers containing tubular metal stoves; the outlets are at or near the floor level. A curious feature in the arrangements is that the foul air, in passing to the up-cast shaft, is drawn through the privies, where it desiccates all discharges.

[E]xtrac[tio]n by [fa]ns.

Extraction by fans presents no features requiring special remark. A favourite fan for the purpose is the Blackman propeller, the nearly flat form of which allows it to be readily placed in walls and partitions. One of these fans, 4 feet in diameter, when driven at a speed of about 330 revolutions per minute, is said to discharge 15,000 cubic feet of air per minute with an expenditure of one-horse-power. Though this is a good performance, it should be observed that for ventilating purposes, where air has to be driven in large volume with low velocity and under low pressure, fans, while they have the advantage of being less bulky, are less efficient than pumps, for they require that the air in passing through them should move much faster than in other parts of its course, and much of the energy of this motion is wasted in eddies. When fans are used to blow air into buildings, they should deliver into a chamber of considerable size, that the air may become nearly still before it passes into the distributing flues. Loss of power may be avoided to some extent by receiving the air in a channel which gradually enlarges as it leaves the fan.

[F]ans in [p]lenum [v]entila[t]ion.

The plenum method, with fans to drive the air, is exemplified on a large scale in the ventilation of St George's Hall, Liverpool,[4] where there are four large fans in the basement, driven by a 10-horse-power steam-engine. The building is heated by passing the air through chambers containing coils of hot-water and steam pipes; after the air is warmed it is moistened by injecting steam, and provision is made for washing it by water-spray before it reaches the fans.

When fans are used, either with suction or with pressure, the amount of the current is not strictly independent of those variable motive forces which are the sole agents in natural ventilation; the case is analogous to that of an electric circuit in which several sources of electromotive force are at work, assisting or opposing one another. The fan may be the main agent in circulating the air; but differences of temperature, and at times the action of the wind, may make large variations in the resultant effect. The case is different when pumps are used. A certain quantity of air is delivered at each stroke, and the only effect of these irregular forces is to make the power required to drive the pump sometimes greater and sometimes less. Provided there are no casual inlets and outlets, the amount of air supplied is known with certainty; the ventilation under these conditions is sometimes described as *positive*. Good recent examples of positive plenum ventilation are to be found in Dundee University College and in a number of schools in Dundee and Aberdeen, where the arrangements have been designed by Mr W. Cunningham. Some of these are ordinary double-acting reciprocating pumps, driven generally by water engines. The pumps are rectangular wooden boxes, stiffened by iron ribs, and provided at top and bottom with inlet valves, consisting of a number of short waterproof cloth flaps working against a vertical wooden grid. The piston, which is also of wood, has a vertical travel; it is held in place and worked by wire ropes above and below, which lead over pulleys to the water motor; and the piston is balanced by a counterweight on the descending branch of the upper rope. A piston 5 feet square, with a stroke of 5 feet, works at 20 strokes per minute and delivers 150,000 cubic feet per hour.

Positive plenum ventilation.

In other instances, where the volume of air is greater than could easily be dealt with by common pumps, Mr Cunningham uses revolving pumps of the Root's blower type (shown in transverse vertical section through the revolving "pistons" in fig. 8). At the Dundee College a battery of five of these blowers, each discharging over 150,000 cubic feet of air per hour, is driven easily by a gas engine of two-horse-power. The rooms are heated by having coils of Perkins's high pressure hot-water pipes in the main distributing flues. The inlets are flat upright tubes extending up the side walls to a height of nearly 6 feet, and open at the top. Ample proof of the advantage that results from giving a vertical direction to the entering current is supplied by the success of Mr Cunningham's arrangements, where this form of inlet is exclusively adopted. Alternative outlets are generally provided in the end walls, one group near the ceiling, another a few feet from the foot. They are fitted with doors which allow one or other to be closed; the high-level outlets are used in warm weather, when the fresh air that comes in is comparatively cool; the low-level ones are used in cold weather, when the fresh air, having been heated before it enters, would tend to rise and pass out too directly if the outlets near the ceiling were open. The outlet shafts communicate with a louvred tower or turrets on the roof. Each room receives a volume of air equal to its cubic capacity in about 12 minutes, so that the atmosphere is completely changed five times in an hour. The inlets are proportioned to do this without allowing the velocity with which air enters to exceed 6 feet per second.

Fig. 8.—Revolving pump for ventilation.

Water-spray ventilator.

The "Æolus" water-spray ventilator of Kind and Mestern is an example of a mechanical ventilator using a jet of water to impel the air. A nozzle at the top of a circular air-shaft delivers a conical sheet of water, which impinges on the sides of the shaft a little way below and carries down with it a considerable stream of air. This ventilator is used either to force air into rooms or to draw it out; in the former case a small gas-stove is often added to heat the supply.

For the ventilation of greenhouses and hot-houses, see vol. xi. p. 231.

Organic matter and micro-organism in air.

The advantage of ample and systematic ventilation is not to be measured only by the low proportion of carbonic acid it secures. Carbonic acid is not the only test of vitiation; it is not even the most dangerous impurity. Another criterion of the foulness of close air is the amount of oxidizable organic matter it contains; still another,—and a most valuable one,—is the number of micro-organisms, especially of bacteria. The micro-organisms may be determined by Hesse's method of slowly passing a given volume of the air to be examined through a tube coated inside with beef jelly; the germs are deposited on the nutrient jelly and each becomes in a few days the centre of a very visible colony. In outside air the number of micro-organisms, as tested in this way, varies greatly: it

[1] For examples, see Morin, *op. cit.*, or *Proc. Inst. Mech. Eng.*, 1867, p. 61.

[2] The arrangements are similar to those introduced by Dr Reid in the temporary Houses of Parliament, and described in his *Treatise on Ventilation and Warming*; see also Tomlinson's *Warming and Ventilation*, p. 265. In recent years pumps have been added, through which air may be forced into the building; but the hot shaft is generally used.

[3] See, for example, Morin's account of the ventilation of the Théâtre Lyrique, Paris.

[4] *Proc. Inst. Mech. Eng.*, 1863, p. 194.

is often less than 1 per litre (61 cubic inches); in well-ventilated rooms it ranges from 1 to 20; in close schoolrooms as many as 600 per litre have been found. The elaborate researches of Carnelley, Haldane, and Anderson[1] on the air of dwellings and schools illustrate well the value of this test. One of the uses to which they have put it has been to compare schools known to be well ventilated (by mechanical means) with schools ventilated at haphazard or not ventilated at all. A large number of trials were made in each case; in the mechanically ventilated schoolrooms the average number of micro-organisms was 17 per litre, and in the others 152. Results of great interest were obtained by the experiment of stopping the mechanical ventilators for a few hours or days. Tested by the proportion of carbonic acid, the air of course became very bad; tested by the number of micro-organisms, it remained comparatively pure, the number being, in fact, scarcely greater than when ventilation was going on, and far less than the average in "naturally ventilated" schools. This proves in a striking way the advantage of systematic ventilation. The bad effect of a foul stagnant atmosphere is cumulative. An habitually close room acts as a nursery of micro-organisms, which a casual flushing with fresh air will not remove; an habitually well-ventilated room is kept in great measure clear of these dangerous inmates, and its atmosphere may be occasionally overtaxed without causing the number of them to be seriously increased. (J. A. E.)

VENTNOR, a watering-place in the south-east of the Isle of Wight, is finely situated in the Undercliff district, at the foot of St Boniface Down (784 feet), 12 miles south-south-west of Ryde and 10 south-south-east of Newport, with both of which there is communication by coach as well as by rail. The town is finely and picturesquely built on a succession of terraces sloping towards the sea, and from its sheltered situation, equable temperature, and comparatively dry atmosphere is regarded as one of the best resorts in England for consumptive invalids. About fifty years ago it was only a small fishing hamlet; now it extends along the shore for a distance of about 2 miles, including Bonchurch to the east. It possesses assembly rooms and a literary and scientific institution. An esplanade was constructed in 1848, and a pier (645 feet in length) in 1872, which was greatly improved in 1887. There are extensive recreation grounds. The churches are all modern and without special architectural features. The church of St Boniface at Bonchurch is perhaps the oldest in the island. Among the benevolent and charitable institutions are the royal national hospital for consumptives (begun in 1869), the seaside home of the London city mission, the St Catherine's home for consumptives, and the convalescent home of the Royal Hants Hospital. An Act for establishing a market was passed in 1844. The town is governed by a board of eighteen members, established in 1858. The population of the urban sanitary district (area 215 acres) was 4841 in 1871 and 5504 in 1881; but there is a considerable population outside the district.

VENUE (from Lat. *vicenetum*) denotes in English law the place from which a jury must be brought for the trial of a case. The word occurs early in constitutional documents, for it was for a long time one of the essentials of trial by jury that the jury should belong to the neighbourhood in which the cause of action arose or the alleged crime was committed (see JURY). The phrase *duodecim legales homines de viceneto* or its equivalent is found in the Constitutions of Clarendon (1164), the Assize of the Forest (1184), and in Glanvill. In civil matters venue became after a time divided into local and transitory, the former where the cause of action could only have arisen in a particular county, such as trespass to land, the latter where it might have arisen in any county, such as debt. In the latter case the plaintiff might lay the venue where he pleased, subject to the power of the court or a judge to change it. The law on the subject is now only of antiquarian interest (unless, perhaps, in certain actions on penal statutes), for it is enacted by the Rules of the Supreme Court, 1883 (Ord. xxxvi. r. 1), that there shall be no local venue for the trial of any action, except where otherwise provided by statute. The plaintiff may name his place of trial; where no place of trial is named the place is to be the county of Middlesex. The court or a judge has discretion to alter the place of trial. In criminal practice venue is still of importance, though not as much so as formerly since the large powers of amendment of indictments given by recent legislation. The venue is named in the margin of an indictment in this form, "Middlesex to wit." By 14 and 15 Vict. c. 100 it is unnecessary to state any venue in the body of an indictment, and no indictment is to be held bad for want of a proper perfect venue.

Numerous Acts provide for, *inter alia*, the laying of the venue in the case of offences committed partly in one county and partly in another, or on the high seas, or abroad, and of special offences, such as those under the Post Office, Merchant Shipping, Slave Trade, and Foreign Enlistment Acts. The place of trial may be changed by the Queen's Bench Division, chiefly where it is rendered probable that a fair trial could not be had in the county of the venue.

In Scotch law venue is not used as a technical term; but there are statutory provisions for changing the place of trial in both civil and criminal cases.

In the United States venue may generally be changed by the courts; but in some States it is provided by their constitutions that provision for change of venue is to be made by the legislature. In other States the passing of local or special laws for change of venue is forbidden.

VENUS. See APHRODITE.

VERA, AUGUSTO (1817-1885), the chief representative of Hegelianism in Italian philosophy, was born at Amelia in the province of Perugia on 4th May 1817. He completed his education in Paris, and, after teaching classics for some years in Switzerland, was appointed professor of philosophy in connexion with the university of France. Attaching himself to Hegel's system with the enthusiasm of a disciple, Vera (who wrote fluently both in French and English as well as in Italian) became widely influential in spreading a knowledge of the Hegelian doctrine. Without any marked originality, his writings are distinguished by the lucidity of their exposition, and by their genuine philosophic spirit. Among his numerous works may be mentioned *Introduction à la Philosophie d'Hégel* (1853, 2d ed. 1864); *Problème de la Certitude* (1861); *Mélanges Philosophiques* (1862); *Essais de Philosophie Hégélienne* (1864); *Strauss, l'Ancienne et la Nouvelle Foi* (1873), an attack upon Strauss's last "confession," written from the standpoint of an orthodox Hegelian; and a comprehensive work in Italian, *Il Problema dell' Assoluto*, belonging to his later years. His English works are an *Inquiry into Speculative and Experimental Science* (1856), more recently an *Introduction to Speculative Logic and Philosophy*, and a translation of Bretschneider's *History of Religion and of the Christian Church*. Vera also translated a number of Hegel's works into French, with introductions and commentaries, including the *Logic*, the *Philosophy of Nature*, the *Philosophy of Spirit*, and the *Philosophy of Religion*. In 1860 Vera returned to Italy, where he was made professor of philosophy in the royal academy of Milan. In the following year he was transferred to Naples as professor of philosophy in the university there. His *Prolusioni alla Storia della Filosofia* and *Lezioni sulla Filosofia della Storia* connect themselves with the work of his chair, which was specially devoted to the

[1] *Phil. Trans.*, 1887, vol. clxxviii. B, p. 61.

history of philosophy and the philosophy of history. He held this post till his death, which took place at Naples in the autumn of 1885.

A *Life* of Vera, in two volumes, has been published by Signor Mariano, a friend and follower.

VERA CRUZ, a fortified town and seaport of Mexico, formerly capital of the state of Vera Cruz, is situated in 19° 11′ 50″ N. lat. and 96° 20′ W. long., at the south-west corner of the Gulf of Mexico, on a low and exposed seaboard, partly sandy partly marshy, where the true yellow fever is endemic, prevailing throughout the summer and occasionally breaking out even in winter.[1] The town, which in 1884 had a population of 16,840, is distant 263 miles by rail from Mexico and 60 from Jalapa, the summer residence of the upper classes. It has few buildings of interest, except a superb cathedral decorated in the Moorish style. Most of the streets, which are laid out at right angles, are paved with cobble-stones and have a kennel or open gutter in the middle. A characteristic feature of the place are the turkey-buzzards, who do the scavangering, and are consequently protected by law. The open roadstead, although partly protected by the neighbouring islets of Los Sacrificios and San Juan de Ulloa, is greatly exposed to the fierce "nortes" (northers), which sweep over the Gulf at intervals from October to March. A French company, which contracted with the Mexican Government to form a harbour by constructing a breakwater between the islands, has lately suspended operations. Vera Cruz is, however, the largest seaport in the republic. In 1886 over one-half of the exports of Mexico (£3,002,000 altogether) were shipped from this place (£1,625,000 to Great Britain). Of these exports £2,180,000 represented the precious metals, the other chief items being coffee (£207,000), hides and skins (£99,000), mineral ores (£84,000), tobacco (£68,000), broom root (£25,000), and sugar (£12,000). In the same year the imports amounted to £1,941,000 (£498,000 from Great Britain), and 487 vessels of 295,000 tons cleared from Vera Cruz. In 1887 the exports from Vera Cruz amounted to £1,047,000 (coffee £407,000 and minerals £208,000), and the imports to £2,159,000.

The present town of Villa Rica de Vera Cruz ("Rich City of the True Cross"), which lies several miles south of the original town founded by Cortes in 1520, was built by the viceroy Monterey at the end of the 16th century, and received the title and privileges of a city from Philip III. in 1615.

The state of Vera Cruz has a seaboard of 450 miles on the Gulf of Mexico, with a mean breadth of 55 miles. Its area is 24,700 square miles, and its total population was 640,000 in 1887, nearly all native Mexicans.

VERATRUM. The Greek physicians were acquainted with a poisonous herb which they called white hellebore, and which has been supposed to represent the existing *Veratrum*. Be this as it may, in modern times the name has been applied to a genus of herbaceous plants closely allied in their structure to *Colchicum*, but differing greatly in general appearance. *Veratrum* is a tall-growing herb, having a fibrous root-stock, an erect stem, with numerous broad, plicated leaves, placed alternately, and terminal much-branched clusters of greenish or purplish polygamous flowers. Each perfect flower consists of six regular segments, as many stamens, whose anthers open outwardly, and a three-celled superior ovary; this last ripens into a three-celled, many-seeded capsule. The genus is included in the order *Melanthaceæ*, otherwise called *Colchicaceæ*, and comprises a small number of species, natives of the temperate regions of the northern hemisphere, generally growing in pastures or woods. Some, and presumably all, contain a violently poisonous alkaloid called veratrin; but, given in small doses and under careful supervision, some of the preparations yielded by *Veratrum* are valuable medicinal agents, their effect being to lower the pulse and the heat of the body. Sabadilla seeds also furnish a drug once in more frequent use than at present. *V. album* and *V. viride* are commonly grown in gardens as ornamental perennials, but their poisonous qualities should be kept in mind, particularly as they bear a considerable resemblance in foliage to the harmless *Gentiana lutea*.

[1] "The character and extent of yellow fever at Vera Cruz has been very much exaggerated by interested parties—by those established in the port, who do not wish competition on the part of intending settlers, and by those interested in the trade from Vera Cruz to El Paso in the north of the republic" (H. Baker, *Cons. Rep.*, 1886, p. 2).

VERBENA. The vervain genus gives its name to the natural order (*Verbenaceæ*) of which it is a member. The species are herbaceous or somewhat shrubby, erect or procumbent, with opposite or whorled leaves, generally deeply cut. The sessile flowers originate in the axils of bracts, and are aggregated into close spikes. Each flower has a tubular, ribbed calyx, a more or less irregular tubular two-lipped corolla, with two or four (didynamous) stamens springing from the centre of the corolla tube. The anthers are two-celled, with or without a gland-like appendage at the apex. The ovary is entire or four-lobed, and always four-celled, with a single ovule in each cell; the two styles are free at the apex only, being elsewhere undivided. The fruit consists of four hard nuts within the persistent calyx. There are about eighty species known, mostly natives of tropical and subtropical America. *V. officinalis*, according to Bentham, is also widely dispersed in the temperate and warmer regions of the eastern hemisphere. *V. bonariensis* occurs in Africa and in Asia, while *V. supina* is indigenous only in the Mediterranean and Canarian regions. The vervein or vervain, *V. officinalis*, a common wild plant on limestone soils in England, was the object of much superstitious veneration on the part of our pagan ancestors, who attributed marvellous properties to it, provided it were gathered in a particular manner and with much complex ceremonial. The plant is now but lightly esteemed, and its medicinal virtues, if it have any, are entirely ignored. The garden verbenas, once so popular for "bedding out," are derivatives from various South-American species, such as *V. teucrioides*, a native of southern Brazil, and *V. chamædrifolia* from Uruguay. The range of colours extends from pure white to rose-coloured, carmine, violet, and purple. Striped forms also are cultivated; but of late years the cultivation of these beautiful flowers has been partially abandoned, owing to the prevalence of some ill-understood disease, probably of fungous origin, which has debilitated the plants. The lemon-scented verbena of gardens, so much valued for the fragrance of its leaves, was once referred to this genus under the name *V. triphylla*, subsequently called *Aloysia*, but now referred by Bentham to the genus *Lippia*; it differs from *Verbena* amongst other matters in having two, not four, nuts to the fruit.

VERCELLI, a town of Italy, in the province of Novara, lies 14 miles to the south-west of that town, on the river Sesia (here crossed by a bridge), at its junction with the Canterana. The walls by which Vercelli was formerly surrounded have been demolished, and their place is now occupied by boulevards, from which a fine view of the Alps (especially the Monte Rosa group) is obtained. The streets are for the most part tortuous and narrow; there is a large market-place (Piazza Cavour) with a statue of Cavour (1861). The cathedral is a large building dating from the 16th century; its library contains a number of rare ancient MSS., especially the *Codex Vercellensis*, one of the most important MSS. of the old Latin version of the Gospels, written in the 4th century by Eusebius, bishop of Vercelli. The churches of St Andrew (a Romano-Gothic building dating from 1219-24), St Paul, St Catherine, and St Christopher possess valuable examples of the work of Gaudenzio Ferrari, one of the principal ornaments of the Vercelli school of painting, which flourished in the 15th and 16th centuries, and to which belonged also Giovenoni, Defendente Ferrari, Lanini, and, one may almost add, Bazzi, who was a native of the town. Of the two hospitals of Vercelli one has a museum and botanical gardens; the town also has a lyceum, a gymnasium, a technical school, and a seminary. The leading industry is silk-spinning; and there is an active trade in the products of the surrounding district (silk, hemp, flax, and rice). The population in 1881 was 20,165 (commune, 21,169).

Vercellæ was originally the chief city of the Libici, and afterwards became a Roman municipium. In the neighbourhood (near Rotto on the Sesia) are the Raudii Campi where Hannibal won his first victory on Italian soil (218 B.C.), and where in 101 B.C. Marius and Catulus routed the Cimbri. From about 1228 till 1372 Vercelli was the seat of a university (see UNIVERSITIES).

VERD ISLANDS, CAPE. See CAPE VERD ISLANDS.

VERDUN, a town of France, chef-lieu of an arrondissement in the department of Meuse, an episcopal see, and a first-class fortress, is situated on the Meuse, 174 miles east-north-east of Paris by the railway to Metz, at the junction of the line from Lérouville to Sedan by the Meuse. The enceinte is pierced by four gates; that to the north-east consists of two crenellated towers, and is an interesting specimen of the military architecture of the 15th century. On the left bank of the river is the citadel, on the site of the old abbey of St Vannes (10th century), the remaining buildings of which are used as barracks. On all sides the approaches to the place are guarded by an important line of defensive works, including five redoubts and six forts. From afar can be seen the square towers of the cathedral, the exterior of which still recalls the original building of the 11th century. It was burnt in 1047, and reconsecrated in 1147 by Pope Eugenius III. Some interesting buttresses of the 12th century and a crypt of the 11th are worthy of notice. The three naves of the interior have Gothic vaults, separated by modern arches. The town-hall (17th century) contains a library (22,500 volumes) and a museum of art, archæology, and natural history. One of the public squares has a statue of General Chevert, a native of Verdun. The town is famous for its confectionery, sugar-plums, and liqueurs. In 1881 the population was 15,682 (commune 16,053), and in 1886 17,282 (commune 17,755).

Verdun (*Verodunum*), an important town at the time of the Roman conquest, was made a part of Belgica Prima. It was destroyed during the period of the barbarian invasions, and did not recover till towards the end of the 5th century. Clovis seized the town in 502, and it afterwards belonged to the kingdom of Austrasia. In 843 the famous treaty was signed here by the sons of Louis the Pious (see FRANCE, vol. ix. p. 534, and GERMANY, vol. x. p. 480). In the 10th century Verdun was definitively conquered by Germany and put under the temporal authority of its bishops. In the 11th century the burghers of the now free and imperial town began a struggle with their bishops, which ended in their obtaining certain rights in the 12th century. In 1553 Henry II. of France took possession of Verdun, which finally became French by the treaty of Westphalia. In 1792, after some hours of bombardment, the citizens opened their gates to the Prussians,—a weakness which the Revolutionary Government punished by the execution of some young girls who had offered flowers to the king of Prussia. In 1870 the Prussians, unable to seize the town by a *coup de main*, invested and bombarded it three different times, till it capitulated in the beginning of November.

VERGILIUS. See VIRGIL.

VERGNIAUD, PIERRE VICTURNIEN (1753-1793), French orator and Revolutionist, was born on 31st May 1753 at Limoges. He was the son of a merchant of that town, who lost the greater part of his means by speculation. The boy was early sent to the college of the Jesuits at Limoges, and soon achieved distinction. Turgot was then intendant of Limousin. In his presence young Vergniaud on one occasion recited some verses of his own composition. Turgot was struck with the talent they displayed, and by virtue of his patronage Vergniaud, having gone to Paris, was admitted to the College of Plessis. It is impossible to read the speeches of Vergniaud without being convinced of the solidity of his education, and in particular of the wide range of his knowledge of the classics, and of his acquaintance—familiar and sympathetic—with ancient philosophy and history.

Duputy, president of the parlement of Bordeaux, with whom Vergniaud became acquainted, conceived the greatest admiration and affection for him and appointed him his secretary. Vergniaud was thereafter called to the bar (1782). The influence of Duputy gained for him the beginnings of a practice; but Vergniaud, though capable of extraordinary efforts, too often relapsed into reverie, and was indisposed for study and sustained exertion, even in a cause which he approved. This weakness appears equally in his political and in his professional life: he would refuse practice if his purse were moderately well filled; he would sit for weeks in the assembly in listlessness and silence, while the policy he had shaped was being gradually undermined, and then rise, brilliant as ever, but too late to avert the calamities which he foresaw. In 1789 Vergniaud was elected a member of the general council of the department of the Gironde. Being deeply stirred by the best ideas of the Revolutionary epoch, he found a more congenial sphere for the display of his great powers in his new position. About this period he was charged with the defence of a member of the national guard of Brives, which was accused of provoking disorders in the department of La Corrèze. Abandoning all reserve, Vergniaud delivered one of the great orations of his life, depicting the misfortunes of the peasantry in language of such combined dignity, pathos, and power that his fame as an orator spread far and wide.

By the self-denying ordinance of the constituent assembly France was deprived of the whole talent and experience of its members in that new body—the legislative assembly—for which they were declared ineligible; and the election of new men was proceeded with. Vergniaud was chosen a representative of the Gironde in August 1791, and he forthwith proceeded to Paris. The legislative assembly met on 1st October. For a time, according to his habit, he refrained from speaking; but on 25th October he ascended the tribune, and he had not spoken long before the whole assembly felt that a new power had arisen which might control even the destinies of France. This judgment was re-echoed outside, and he was almost immediately elected president of the assembly for the usual brief term. Between the outbreak of the Revolution and his election to the legislative assembly the political views of Vergniaud had undergone a decided change. At first he had lauded a constitutional monarchy; but the flight of Louis filled him with distrust of the sovereign, and his views in favour of a republic were rapidly developed. The sentiments and passions which his eloquence aroused were, however, watchfully utilized by a more extreme party. It happened thus even with his first assembly speech, on the *émigrés*. His proposal was mainly that a treble annual contribution should be levied on their property; but the assembly confiscated their goods and decreed their deaths. One great blot on his reputation is that step by step he was led on to palliate violence and crime, to the excesses of which his eyes were only opened by the massacres of September, and which ultimately overwhelmed the party of Girondists which he led. The disgrace to his name is indelible that on 19th March 1792, when the perpetrators of the massacre of Avignon had been introduced to the assembly by Collot d'Herbois, Vergniaud spoke indulgently of their crimes and lent the authority of his voice to their amnesty. In language, sometimes turgid, but nearly always of pure and powerful eloquence, he worked at the theme of the *émigrés,* as it developed into that of the counter-revolution; and in his occasional appearances in the tribune, as well as in the project of an address to the French people which he presented to the assembly on 27th December 1791, he shook the heart of France, and, especially by his call to arms on 18th January, shaped the policy which culminated in the declaration of war against the king of Bohemia and Hungary on 20th April. This policy in foreign affairs, which he pursued through the winter and spring of 1791-92, he combined with another,—that of fanning the suspicions of the people against the monarchy, which he identified with the counter-revolution, and of forcing on a change of ministry. On 10th March Vergniaud delivered a powerful oration in which he denounced the intrigues of the court and uttered his famous apostrophe to the Tuileries: "In ancient times fear and terror have often issued from that famous palace, let them re-enter it to-day in the name of the law!" The speech overthrew De Lessart, whose accusation was decreed; and Roland, the nominee of the Girondists, entered the ministry. By the month of June the opposition of Vergniaud (whose voice still commanded the country) to the king rose to fever heat. On 29th May Vergniaud went so far as to support the disbanding of the king's guard. But he appears to have been unaware of the extent of the feelings of animosity which he had done much to arouse in the people, probably because he was wholly unconnected with the practices of the party of the Mountain as the instigators of actual violence. This party used Vergniaud, whose lofty and serene ideas they applauded and travestied in action. Then came the riot of the 20th of June and the invasion of the Tuileries. He rushed among the crowd, but was powerless to quell the tumult. Continuing for yet a little longer his course of feverous, almost frenzied, opposition to the throne, on 3rd July he electrified France by his bold denunciation of the king, not only as a hypocrite and a despot, but as a base traitor to the constitution. His speeches breathe the very spirit of the storm, and they were perhaps the greatest single factor in the development of the events of the time. On the 10th of August the Tuileries was stormed, and the royal family took refuge in the assembly. Vergniaud presided. To the request of the king for protection he replied in dignified and respectful language. An extraordinary commission was appointed: Vergniaud wrote and read its recommendations that a national convention be formed, the king be provisionally suspended from office, a governor appointed for his son, and the royal family be consigned to the Luxembourg. Hardly had the great orator attained the object of his aim, the overthrow of Louis as a sovereign, when he became conscious of the awful forces by which he was surrounded, and his eyes were opened to the infamy of their régime.

The terrible revelation silenced him for a time. But the massacres of September again unchained his eloquence. He denounced the massacres—their inception, their horror, and the future to which they pointed—in language so vivid and powerful that it raised for a time the spirits of the Girondists, while on the other hand it aroused the fatal opposition of Robespierre and of his followers within and without the convention.

The questions whether Louis XVI. was to be judged, and if so by whom, were the subject of protracted debate in the convention. They were of absorbing interest to Paris, to France, and to Europe; and upon them the Girondist leader at last, on 31st December 1792, broke silence, delivering one of his greatest orations, probably one of the greatest combinations of sound reasoning, sagacity, and eloquence which has ever been displayed in the annals of French politics. He pronounced in favour of an appeal to the people. He pictured the consequences of that temper of vengeance which animated the Parisian mob, and was fatally controlling the policy of the convention, and the prostration which would ensue to France after even a successful struggle with a European coalition, which would spring up after the murder of the king. The great effort failed; and four days afterwards something happened which still further endangered Vergniaud and his whole party. This was the discovery of a note signed by him along with Gaudet and Gensonné and presented to the king two or three weeks before the 10th of August. It contained nothing but sound and patriotic suggestions; but it was greedily seized upon by the enemies of the Gironde as evidence of treason. On 16th January 1793 the vote began to be taken in the convention upon the punishment of the king. Vergniaud voted early, and voted for death. The action of the great Girondist was and will always remain inscrutable; but it was followed by a similar verdict from nearly the whole party which he led. On the 17th Vergniaud presided at the convention and it fell to him, labouring under the most painful excitement, to announce the fatal result of the voting. Then for many weeks he sank, exhausted, into silence.

When the institution of a revolutionary tribunal was proposed by the Robespierrists, Vergniaud vehemently opposed the project, denouncing the tribunal as a more awful inquisition than that of Venice, and avowing that his party would all die rather than consent to it. Their death by stratagem had already been planned, and on 10th March they had to go into hiding. On the 13th Vergniaud boldly exposed the conspiracy in the convention, taking occasion to discuss the profanation by the extremists of the name of liberty, and distinguishing between a true and spurious equality, employing with reference to the latter his famous simile of the bed of Procrustes. The antagonism caused by such an attitude had reached a significant point when on 10th April Robespierre himself laid his accusation before the convention. He fastened especially upon Vergniaud's letter to the king and his support of the appeal to the people as a proof that he was a moderate in its then despised sense. Vergniaud made a brilliant extemporaneous reply, and the attack for the moment failed. But now, night after night, Vergniaud and his colleagues found themselves obliged to change their abode, to avoid assassination, a price being even put upon their heads. Still with unfaltering courage they continued their resistance to the dominant faction, till on the 2d of June 1793 things came to a head. The convention was surrounded with an armed mob, who clamoured for the "twenty-two." In the midst of this it was forced to continue its deliberations. The decree of accusation was voted, and the Girondists were proscribed.

Vergniaud was offered a safe retreat. He accepted it only for a day, and then returned to his own dwelling. He was kept under surveillance there for nearly a month, and in the early days of July was imprisoned in La Force. He carried poison with him, but never used it. His tender affection for his relatives abundantly appears from his correspondence, along with his profound attachment to the great ideas of the Revolution, and his noble love of country. On one of the walls of the Carmelite convent, to which for a short time the prisoners were removed, Vergniaud wrote in letters of blood—"Potius mori quam fœdari." Early in October the convention brought forward its indictment of the twenty-two Girondists. They were sent for trial to the Revolutionary tribunal, before which they appeared on the 27th of October. The procedure was a travesty of justice. Conscious of innocence, but certain of death, Vergniaud preserved silence, and his example was largely followed by his companions. By the end of the fourth day of trial it became evident that the demeanour of the prisoners was touching the hearts of the people and making them relent. Then suddenly came the order from the alarmed committee of safety to bring the proceedings to an end. Gensonné demanded to be heard in defence of the prisoners. This was refused; a verdict of guilty followed, and a sentence of death. Valazé stabbed himself to the heart and fell dead among his comrades. They were conducted to the conciergerie, which they entered singing the Marseillaise. Early on the following morning, 31st October 1793, they were conveyed to the scaffold, again singing on the way the national chant, and keeping up the strain till one by one they were guillotined. Vergniaud was executed last. (T. S.)

VERKHNE-URALSK, a district-town of Orenburg, Russia, at the eastern base of the Ural Mountains and on the upper Ural river, 380 miles north-east of Orenburg, is rapidly becoming an important centre of trade with the Bashkirs and Kirghiz in honey, wax, wool, hides, horses, and sheep. The population (10,354 in 1882) has doubled within the last twenty-five years.

VERMIGLI, PIETRO MARTIRE (1500-1562), commonly known as PETER MARTYR, a Reforming theologian of the 16th century, came of a good Tuscan family, and was born at Florence on 8th September 1500. In 1516 he entered the house of the Augustinian canons regular at Fiesole, and from 1519 onwards studied at Padua, where he heard lectures on the Aristotelian philosophy and taught himself some Greek. In his twenty-sixth year he was sent out as a preacher, in which capacity he visited various Italian cities,—among them Bologna, where a Jewish physician gave him lessons in Hebrew. While prior of St Peter ad Aram in Naples he was introduced to Juan de Valdes's circle, and also became intimate with Bernardino Ochino. At Lucca, whither he had gone to be prior of San Frediano, the "evangelical" tone of his preaching attracted the attention of the Inquisition, and he was compelled to quit Italy (1542). After short halts at Zurich and Basel he settled in Strasburg as professor of Old Testament exegesis, and in 1547 he removed to England, mainly at Cranmer's instance. During the next six years he taught exegesis as a professor in Oxford, conducted public disputations, took part in the adjustment of the Book of Common Prayer, and was generally active in the theological discussions of the time. The accession of Queen Mary in 1553 obliged him to leave England, and he resumed his former duties at Strasburg. From 1555 till his death in the autumn of 1562 he taught in Zurich. He took a prominent part in the abortive conference of Poissy in 1561.

His Oxford lectures on 1st Corinthians were published at Zurich in 1551 and those on the Romans in 1558. In 1559 appeared his *Defensio doctrinæ veteris et apostolicæ de S. Eucharistiæ sacramento*, and also his *Defensio ad R. Smythæi duos libellos de cœlibatu sacerdotum et votis monasticis*. The *Dialogus de utraque Christi natura* dates from 1561; and after his death a number of his commentaries on books of the Old Testament were published by his friends. In 1575 Robert Masson, a French preacher in London, published a folio volume of *loci communes* from Martyr's writings, digested according to the method of Calvin's theological system. This is a work of great value to students of the Reformation theology. A number of interesting letters by Martyr to prominent theologians are also extant.

See Schlosser's *Leben des Th. Beza u. des P. M. Vermigli* (Heidelberg, 1807) and C. Schmid's *Leben der Väter u. Begründer der reformirten Kirche*, vol. vii. (Elberfeld, 1858).

VERMILION is a brilliant scarlet pigment composed of the sulphide of mercury, HgS. To a small extent it is obtained direct from pure and bright-coloured portions of the native ore CINNABAR (*q.v.*); but it is chiefly an artificial preparation. The process of manufacture, as conducted principally in Holland, consists in making an intimate mixture of mercury with about one-sixth of its weight of sulphur, and these under the influence of a gentle heat combine to form the black sulphide of mercury called æthiop's mineral. In successive portions pieces of this compound are thrown into tall earthen pots the lower parts of which are kept at a red heat, and the mass sublimes, depositing a coating of artificial cinnabar on the iron covers and over the upper part of the pots themselves. At the end of the subliming process, the pots are broken, the deposit of cinnabar is scraped off, ground in a mill, levigated, and when dry it is ready for use as vermilion. The pigment is also prepared by the wet method (see MERCURY, vol. xvi. p. 34), and it is said that Chinese vermilion owes its superiority to being made in this way. In addition to its brilliance, vermilion is a pigment of great intensity and durability, remaining unaffected by acid fumes. Being costly, it is much subject to adulteration; but the fraudulent additions may easily be detected by volatilization, which in the case of pure vermilion leaves no residue. For antimony vermilion, see PIGMENTS, vol. xix. p. 87.

VERMONT, one of the New England States of the American Union, lies between 42° 44′ and 45° 0′ 43″ N. lat. and 71° 38′ and 73° 25′ W. long. It is bounded on the N. by the Canadian province of Quebec, on the E. by New Hampshire, from which it is separated by the Connecticut river, on the S. by Massachusetts, and on the W. by New York, from which it is separated for more than 100 miles by Lake Champlain. The Canadian boundary is 90 miles long; but from this the width of Vermont continually grows less towards the southern border, where it is 41 miles. The length is 158 miles. The boundary between Vermont and New York passes through the western side of Lake Champlain, so that three-fourths of the lake and most of its islands belong to the former. The area of the State is 10,212 square miles. Plate V.

Physical features. The surface is greatly diversified, so that the scenery is everywhere attractive and often grand. The Green Mountains, following a south-westerly trend, divide the State into nearly equal portions. Near Canada there are two ranges, the western being the larger; but near the forty-fourth parallel they unite and continue through western New England as a single range. The highest mountain is Mansfield (4430 feet), and there are five others over 4000 feet and twelve over 3500 feet. Except upon the loftiest summits, the whole range is densely covered with forests of spruce (*Abies nigra*), mingled with which are other evergreen and deciduous trees.[1] Many of the streams flowing west unite to form five rivers which enter Lake Champlain. Eleven smaller rivers flow into the Connecticut, which drains about one-third of the area of Vermont. Three streams run north and enter Lake Memphremagog, about one-fifth of which is within the State, and two flow south to join the Hudson river. Most of the larger streams pass through wide, fertile valleys. Small lakes and ponds are abundant.

Geology. The rocks of Vermont are largely metamorphic. Their age has long been disputed among geologists; it appears now, however, to be clearly established that most of them are Palæozoic, although there are a few small areas which may prove to be Archæan. Along Lake Champlain there are many outcrops of unaltered fossiliferous strata, which, from the Lower Cambrian through the Hudson River or Cincinnati formations, lie in a regular conformable series, and upon these rest Quaternary deposits. The strata have a northerly strike and a dip 5°–90° E. They form frequent headlands and cliffs upon the shore of Lake Champlain, where they can be most easily studied. The Cambrian beds, nowhere more than a few miles broad, extend from Canada southwards for about 90 miles, having a total thickness of probably not less than 10,000 feet. They consist of limestone, sandstone, shale, slate, quartzite, and conglo-

[1] Hence the old French name *Verd Mont*.

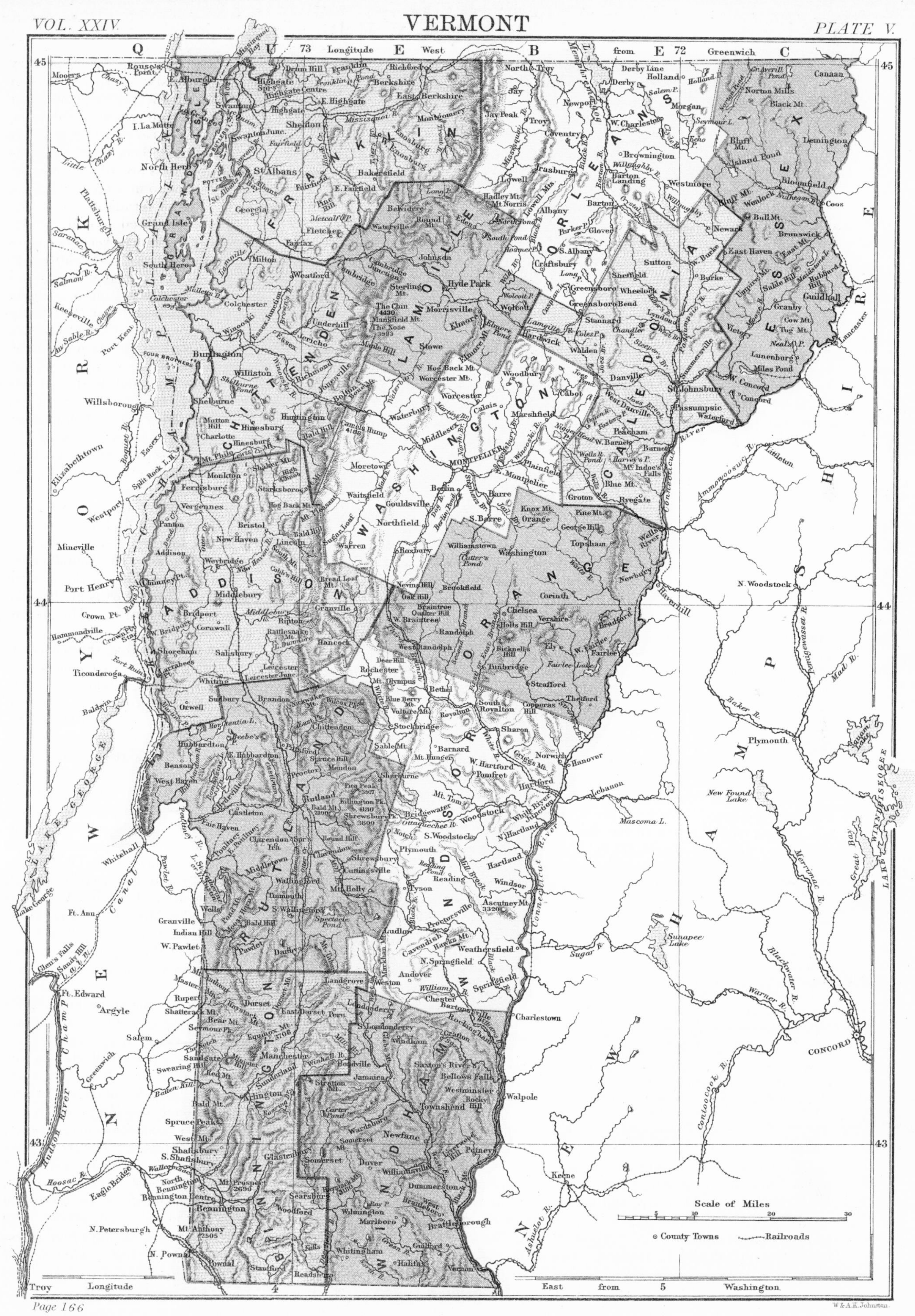

ENCYCLOPÆDIA BRITANNICA, NINTH EDITION.
W. & A.K. Johnston.

merate. The limestone is often arenaceous and dolomitic, sometimes magnesian. There are great masses of reddish, silicious limestone, the Red Sandrock of geologists, which, often destitute of fossils, contains here and there species of *Ptychoparia*, *Olenellus*, *Orthisina*, *Obolus*, *Salterella*, &c. Included in these beds are thick layers of a beautifully mottled red and white dolomite, the "Winooski marble," long used for architectural purposes. Similar fossils occur in the "Georgia shales" and elsewhere. Above the Cambrian are small patches of Calciferous and Quebec, then larger areas of Chazy, Trenton, Utica, and Hudson River. In the Chazy and Trenton there are extensive quarries upon Isle la Motte, and these formations are finely exhibited in many localities near the lake. The rocks are mostly limestones and shales of a black or dark grey colour, and frequently afford Silurian fossils in great abundance. Within a few miles of Lake Champlain the sedimentary rocks are replaced by schists, quartzites, and other metamorphic rocks, which continue beyond the mountains to Connecticut river. In the southern part of Vermont there are Lower Helderberg strata, and in the northern, about Lake Memphremagog, Upper Helderberg. These occupy but limited areas and are unconformable with the underlying rocks. Rev. A. Wing determined the age of the great marble beds of Rutland county to be mostly, if not wholly, of the Chazy epoch. He then extended his observations to the rocks of the Green Mountain mass; and by means of the results thus gained, as well as by his own long-continued independent researches, Prof. J. D. Dana seems to have substantially settled the age of the rocks which compose the mountains as Lower Silurian, and shown that the uplift ending in the range took place after the close of the Hudson River and before the Helderberg period. In the Champlain valley the rocks are traversed by dykes of trap and porphyry, which in some instances have spread over the strata. In the Utica and Hudson River shales there is most beautiful veining: innumerable seams of white calcite, from the finest line to several inches in width, cross and recross the black strata in every direction. In a narrow strip from Canada to Bennington there are Tertiary beds, which are well seen at Brandon. In this formation there are great masses of lignite, containing fossil fruits, also bog iron, manganese, kaolin, and variously and often brightly coloured clays. The entire surface of Vermont shows the effects of glaciation. Some of the Silurian ledges are striated and polished most beautifully. Drift, boulders, sands, clays occur everywhere; every stream is bordered by terraces; remains of mammoth, mastodon, beluga, are found in the drift deposits, as well as *Mya*, *Saxicava*, *Mytilus*, and other marine *Mollusca*. Sea-beaches over 2000 feet and terraces over 1000 feet above the present sea-level testify to movements of the surface. From the early Cambrian to the late Quaternary epoch Lake Champlain was an arm of the sea, and for a portion of this time it was connected with the ocean at each end, so that a current flowed from what is now New York Bay to St Lawrence Gulf, converting New England into an island.

Minerals. Ores of copper, silver, lead, gold, manganese, and iron occur; but, although numerous attempts at mining have been made, very few have continued or ever been profitable. A large amount of copper is obtained at the Ely mines, where the ore is chalco-pyrite; and gold has been found in paying quantity in river gravel, and also in veins, and is still sought in one or two places. The chief mineral wealth of the State is in its quarries. No other State in the Union produces so great a variety or quantity of marble. The annual production is nearly 2,000,000 cubic feet, and is increasing. Roofing and other slate is obtained in very large quantities and of fine quality. Most excellent granite is quarried in increasing amount, and there are large beds of soap-stone, which are worked. Besides what may be called useful minerals, the State affords a large variety of species, *e.g.*, rutile, actinolite, talc, serpentine, which are of interest to the mineralogist. The State has many mineral springs, some of which have long been places of popular resort. Most of them are sulphurous, some chalybeate, carbonate, or alkaline.

Climate. The climate of Vermont, like that of New England generally, is subject to extremes and to sudden changes. In summer the temperature varies from 65° to 75° Fahr., sometimes rising to 90°; in winter it ranges from 18° to 50°, sometimes falling to −10° or rarely −20°. At Burlington the mean annual temperature is 45°. The climate is milder in the Champlain valley than east of the Green Mountains. During the winter there is often much snow, which in the colder parts of the State covers the ground for three months. The average annual rainfall is 33 inches. The air is clear and pure. Notwithstanding the changeable climate, the death-rate is low and the people robust.

Fauna. Most of the large mammals formerly common,—the panther, wolf, lynx, beaver, otter, moose,—have either disappeared or are very rare; others, as the black bear, red deer, mink, and marten, are found only in certain localities. More common are the red fox, raccoon, skunk, porcupine, woodchuck, rabbit, squirrel, and other smaller species. Birds have changed less; but the wild turkey, golden eagle, raven, &c., have become very rare, and the white-headed eagle, large hawks, owls, herons, bitterns, and the like are far from common. The lakes are visited at certain seasons by great numbers of ducks, geese, and other water-fowl. Thrushes, blue-birds, titmice, sparrows, swallows, warblers, vireos, blackbirds, crows, and woodpeckers are common, as well as many other small birds. In Lake Champlain and the large streams which flow into it are found sturgeon, garpike, muskalonge, bass, pike, pickerel, shad, as well as many smaller species. Trout abound in the mountain streams and in some of the ponds. Reptiles and batrachians are not numerous either in species or individuals.

Flora. The flora is of great beauty and of unusual botanical interest. *Saxifraga Aizoon*, *Poa laxa*, *Arenaria grœnlandica*, and other alpine plants are found on the higher mountains. *Lathyrus maritimus*, *Hudsonia tomentosa*, and other maritime species recall the time when Lake Champlain was salt. A number of western species find their eastern limit in the Champlain valley, and a greater number of Canadian plants have ended their southward migrations in northern Vermont. Over 1300 species of phanerogams and higher cryptogams grow wild in the State. About 50 of these are found nowhere else in New England, and a few nowhere else in the United States. Ferns grow luxuriantly in many mountain forests and ravines, where 50 species may be collected, including such very rare forms as *Asplenium viride*, *Pellæa gracilis*, *Woodsia glabella* and *hyperborea*, *Aspidium Braunii*, &c. Orchids are also abundant. Of the 108 families found in the State the most numerous are the ranunculus, saxifrage, rose, composite, heath, lily, grass, and sedge. The once prevalent forests are now chiefly confined to the mountains. There are nearly 100 species of trees and large shrubs; the forests and groves consist chiefly of 11 species of oak, 6 of maple, 17 of willow, 6 of birch, 8 of poplar, 3 of elm, 17 of conifers, besides beech, ash, walnut, butternut, &c. No single species forms so characteristic a feature of the landscape as the American elm, which with great variety of form, always elegant and beautiful, grows singly or in small groups in every meadow and upon many uplands. The sugar maple is a common and conspicuous tree. (G. H. P.)

Population. The population was estimated in 1777 at 30,000. The first census taken, in 1791, gave 85,425. The different enumerations from 1800 to 1880 inclusive have been as follows:—154,465; 217,895; 235,966; 280,652; 291,948; 314,120; 315,098; 330,551; 332,286. The very slight gain in the decades succeeding 1850 is accounted for by the large emigration from Vermont to the western portions of the country. Of the total population in 1880 291,327 were natives and 40,959 foreign-born. Of the latter class British America furnished the largest contingent, 24,620; Ireland 11,657; other parts of Great Britain 3773. The number of coloured was 1057; the excess of males over females 1488. The number gathered in towns of from 4000 to 12,000 inhabitants was 37,800. The largest towns are Rutland, 12,149 (in 1886 two new towns were formed from it); Burlington, 11,365; St Albans, 7193; Bennington, 6333; Brattleboro, 5880; St Johnsbury, 5800. Montpelier, the capital, has 3219. The average density of population is 36·4 per square mile. The insane numbered 1015; idiotic, 803; blind, 486; paupers, 1564; inmates of prisons and reformatories, 261. The births in 1885 were 6592, or 22·1 per 1000 of population, and the deaths 5358 (average age as reported, 41·95 years; percentage of deaths to population, 1·61). The number of divorces in 1860 was 94, one to every 23 marriages; in 1880 the number was 129 (one to 20 marriages); and in 1885 it was 94 (one to 28·7 marriages).

Agriculture. Agriculture is the chief occupation of the State. The 35,522 farms make up a total of 4,882,588 acres, of which 3,286,461 are improved land. The western portion of the State contains the finest tracts of arable land; the climate as well as the soil of the Champlain valley is especially adapted to fruit-raising, the surface of the lake being but 90 feet above sea-level. The average size of farms in Vermont is 137 acres; the total estimated value of the farms in 1880 was $109,346,010, and of the total products in 1879 $22,082,656 Subjoined are the figures relating to the leading crops:—wheat,

337,257 bushels, averaging 16·28 bushels per acre; oats, 3,742,282 bushels, averaging 37·6 bushels per acre; Indian corn, 2,014,271; potatoes, 4,438,172 bushels; hay, 1,051,183 tons. The wool clip was 2,551,113 lb; and there were 217,033 cows, producing 25,245,826 lb of butter (12,137,980 lb in 1850) and 6,121,130 lb of cheese (8,720,834 in 1850). The value of orchard products amounted to $640,942. Of maple sugar Vermont produces more than any other State,—in 1880 11,261,077 lb, or 30·8 per cent. of the whole production of the United States, besides 128,091 gallons of molasses.

Live Stock. In 1880 the State possessed 75,215 horses, 283 mules and asses, 18,868 working oxen and 167,204 other cattle (exclusive of milch cows), 439,870 sheep, and 76,384 pigs. Much attention is given to the raising of improved stock. The rearing of fine breeds of sheep for exportation is a lucrative business.

Fisheries. Lake Champlain abounds in fish of various kinds. Great pains have been taken of late years to stock the numerous ponds and streams of the State with salmon, trout, carp, and bass. Both fish and game are protected by stringent laws, and to some extent by special police supervision.

Manufactures. In 1880 there were 2874 manufacturing and mechanical establishments, the average number of operatives 17,540, and the value produced in 1879 was $31,354,366. Eight firms manufactured cotton, 44 woollen goods, 227 flour and grist-mill products, 56 furniture, 77 leather, 95 tin-ware, copper-ware, &c., 35 agricultural tools, and 688 lumber. The State rates as nineteenth in value ($3,258,816) of lumber products, while Burlington ranks third in importance among the lumber markets of the United States. Eighteen marble quarries produced a value of $1,340,050; there are also granite and slate quarries,—61 quarries in all, with a total production in 1879 of $1,752,333.

Commerce. Burlington is the only port of entry. The State has 9 steam vessels aggregating 2380 tons, 12 sailing vessels, and 14 unrigged vessels, the total tonnage being 4594. The imports for the year ending 31st December 1887 were $5,959,813 and the exports $1,433,564; the value of the pine, spruce, and hemlock lumber imported was $1,084,599. Most of this foreign trade is carried on with Canada.

Railways. Railroad construction was begun in 1846, and by December 1849 two lines were completed from the Connecticut river to Burlington. In 1853 the working mileage had risen to 493 miles, and in 1886 it was 946 miles, mainly of trunk lines. A State board of three commissioners, appointed by the governor and senate, exercises general supervision.

Finance. Bills of credit were issued as early as 1781, and were all faithfully redeemed. The first State bank was chartered in 1806, but closed an unsuccessful career in 1814. In 1818 banks were established at Windsor and Burlington. In 1841 there were 17 incorporated banking institutions, with a capital of $1,735,000. In October 1887 there were 49 national banks, with an aggregate capital of $7,566,000, a surplus fund of $1,571,864, and $668,329 undivided profits. The circulation was $3,478,100, secured by bonds to the amount of $3,891,000. The loans and discounts amounted to $12,879,765, and the individual deposits to $6,627,090. In 1860 there were 12 institutions for savings, with deposits to the amount of $1,111,532. In June 1887 there were 28 savings banks and trust companies, with $15,587,051 to the credit of 53,810 depositors, and a surplus of $776,113. Deposits pay a state tax of $\frac{6}{10}$ per cent. The State proper has no debt.

Religion. The Congregationalists have 197 churches, 186 ministers, 20,271 members, 22,035 pupils in Sunday schools, and 13,748 families belonging to the congregations. The Baptists have 105 churches, 111 ministers, 8623 members, 8922 pupils in Sunday schools. The Methodists have 192 churches, 161 ministers, 16,067 members, 18,830 children in Sunday schools. The Episcopalians report 36 ministers in charge of 52 parishes, with 3926 communicants; number of families, 1789. The Free Baptists and Christians together have 60 churches and 4000 members; the Adventists 35 churches with 1750 members. The Roman Catholics have 39 priests in charge of 79 churches and number about 25,000.

Education. Lands were set apart for the support of schools by the proprietors of townships as early as 1761. Legislative provision for education dates from 1782. The original educational system of the State contemplated primary schools in every township, a grammar or high school in each county, and one university. Towns were authorized to subdivide into districts of convenient size, each with power to choose its own officers, levy taxes, and maintain a school. In 1870 the towns were authorized to substitute the town for the district system, but in 1886 only one in nine had made the exchange. In 1886 there were 2557 public schools of all grades, with 71,667 pupils, besides 7247 in private schools. In 1880 the number of persons above ten years unable to read was 12,993, or 4·9 per cent., the population between 5 and 20 being 99,463. The total revenue for school purposes in 1886 was $621,370. This revenue is derived partly from funds held by the State, but chiefly from town and district taxes. Facilities for advanced instruction are offered by 39 public high schools and 25 incorporated academies. The State has 3 normal schools, founded in 1866. Since 1874 State supervision is exercised through a superintendent elected by the general assembly. The State university at Burlington, chartered in 1791, was inaugurated in 1800; it provides instruction in arts, engineering, chemistry, agriculture, and medicine, with a teaching staff of 15 in the academic and 26 in the medical faculty; in 1887 there were 189 students in medicine, 148 in arts and sciences, and in all departments 487. The library contains 35,300 volumes. Middlebury College (Congregational), chartered in 1800, has a teaching staff of 9 with 63 students, and a library of 16,000 vols. Norwich university (Episcopalian) at Northfield is organized as a military school; there are 10 instructors and 56 students. The State library contains 18,600 vols., the free public library of Burlington 18,000 vols., that of St Johnsbury 12,000, and that of Lunenburg (free but not public) 14,000. In all 75 libraries were reported in 1880, 42 having over 1000 vols. each.

Administration. The governor and chief executive officers are elected by direct vote of the male citizens twenty-one years old and upwards who have resided within the State for one whole year preceding the election. The general assembly, or legislative body, is composed of a senate of 30 members apportioned among the 14 counties according to population, and a house of representatives consisting of one member from each organized township (244). The sessions of the legislature have been biennial since 1870. The State election occurs in September in the even years. The judiciary is elective throughout, the chief justice and 6 assistant justices of the supreme court being chosen by the senate and house in joint assembly. The term of service is usually a long one, by virtue of repeated re-elections. The assistant judges of county courts are chosen by the freemen of the counties, and justices of the peace by the several towns. The county courts hold two terms annually, a justice of the supreme court presiding. A general session of the supreme court is held at the capital in October or November. Probate courts are held in each county, six of the counties being divided each into two probate districts. The State is represented in the Federal Government by two senators and two representatives, and has four votes in the electoral college. Since 1852 the policy of the State in regard to intoxicating liquors has been that of prohibition.

History. *History.*—Vermont first became known to Europeans in 1609, when Champlain explored the lake since known by his name. During the next century the lake and its borders were a thoroughfare for various military expeditions in the Indian and colonial wars, and several points along the lake were occupied, mainly as military posts, by both French and English; but the first permanent settlement was made in 1724 at Fort Dummer in the limits of Brattleboro. In 1760 there were not more than 300 inhabitants, scattered along the Connecticut river within 50 miles of the southern border. Both New Hampshire and New York claimed jurisdiction over the territory under royal grants (see vol. xvii. p. 393). By 1763 New Hampshire had chartered 138 townships west of the Connecticut, and between 1765 and 1776 New York had issued grants of land, covering in all 2,418,700 acres, often embracing the same territory as the New Hampshire charters. The claims of New York were always stoutly, and sometimes forcibly, resisted by the great majority of the settlers. In 1776 the Vermonters sought admission to the provincial Congress, but through the influence of New York were refused. In January 1777 they proclaimed their independence, framed a State constitution, and again applied for a place in the confederacy. Congress hesitated as before. In 1780 British generals made overtures to the little republic, but with no result beyond a diplomatic intercourse continued until 1783, so managed by the envoys of Vermont as to gain time and save the State from invasion. In 1782 they knocked at the doors of Congress again without avail. By July 1789 New York was willing to waive its pretensions, and Vermont was admitted as the fourteenth State in March 1791. In May 1775 the "Green Mountain boys" under Ethan Allan and Seth Warner had captured Ticonderoga and Crown Point. The battle of Bennington in August 1777 was won by the combined forces of Vermont and New Hampshire. During the whole struggle the State, though unrecognized, contributed its full share of men and means. In the war of 1812-14 Vermont is credited with 5236 soldiers in regular service, exclusive of 2500 volunteers who were under arms at Plattsburgh in September 1814. In the Civil War of 1861-65 the State furnished more than its due quota of troops, 33,288 men from a total population (1860) of 315,098. The present organized force consists of but one regiment, with one battery, 565 men. The unorganized militia numbered 64,162 men in 1880.

The early history of the State may be found in Hiland Hall's and Thompson's *Histories.* Important documents are given in *Vermont State Papers* and in *Collections* of the Vermont Historical Society. Its part in the war of 1861-65 is told in Benedict's *Vermont in the Civil War.* (J. E. G.)

VERNET, the name of three eminent French painters.

I. Claude Joseph Vernet (1714-1789), who was born at Avignon on 14th August 1714, when only fourteen years of age aided his father, a skilful decorative painter, in the most important parts of his work. But the panels of sedan chairs could not satisfy his ambition and he started for Rome. The sight of the sea at Marseilles and his voyage thence to Civita Vecchia made a deep impression on him, and immediately after his arrival he entered the studio of a marine painter, Bernardino Fergioni. Slowly but surely Claude Joseph made his way and attracted notice. With a certain conventionality in design, proper to his day, he allied the results of constant and honest observation of natural effects of atmosphere, which he rendered with unusual pictorial art. Perhaps no painter of landscapes or sea-pieces has ever made the human figure so completely a part of the scene depicted or so important a factor in his design. "Others may know better," he said, with just pride, "how to paint the sky, the earth, the ocean; no one knows better than I how to paint a picture." For twenty years Vernet lived on in Rome, producing views of seaports, storms, calms, moonlights, &c., when he was recalled (1753) to Paris, and executed, by royal command, the remarkable series of the seaports of France (Louvre) by which he is best known. On his return he became a member of the academy, but he had previously contributed to the exhibitions of 1746 and following years, and he continued to exhibit, with rare exceptions, down to the date of his death, which took place in his lodgings in the Louvre on 3d December 1789. Amongst the very numerous engravers of his works may be specially cited Le Bas, Cochin, Basan, Duret, Flipart, and Le Veau in France, and in England Vivares.

II. Antoine Charles Horace Vernet (1758-1835), commonly called Carle, the youngest child of the above-named, was born at Bordeaux in 1758, where his father was painting the view from the château of La Trompette (Louvre). He showed, at the age of five, an extraordinary passion for drawing horses, but went through the regular academical course as a pupil of Lépicié. Strangely enough, on arriving in Italy after carrying off the great prize (1782) he lost all ambition and interest in his profession, so that his father had to recall him to France to prevent his entering a monastery. In Paris Carle Vernet became himself again and distinguished himself at the exhibition of 1791 by his Triumph of Paulus Æmilius, a work in which he broke with reigning traditions in classical subjects and drew the horse with the forms he had learnt from nature in stables and riding-schools. But the Revolution drew on and Carle Vernet's career for awhile seemed to end in the anguish of his sister's death on the scaffold. When he again began to produce, it was as the man of another era: his drawings of the Italian campaign brought him fresh laurels; his vast canvas, the Battle of Marengo, obtained great success; and for his Morning of Austerlitz Napoleon bestowed on him the Legion of Honour. His hunting-pieces, races, landscapes, and work as a lithographer (chiefly under the restoration) had also a great vogue. From Louis XVIII. he received the order of St Michael. In 1827 he accompanied his son Horace (see below) to Rome, and died in Paris on his return, 17th November 1835, having produced but little during the last years of his life.

III. Émile Jean Horace Vernet (1789-1863), born in Paris, 30th June 1789, was one of the most characteristic, if not one of the ablest, of the military painters of France. He was just twenty when he exhibited the Taking of an Entrenched Camp—a work which showed no depth of observation, but was distinguished by a good deal of character. His picture of his own studio (the rendezvous of the Liberals under the restoration), in which he represented himself painting tranquilly, whilst boxing, fencing, drum and horn playing, &c., were going on, in the midst of a medley of visitors, horses, dogs, and models, is one of his best works, and, together with his Defence of the Barrier at Clichy (Louvre), won for him an immense popularity. Enjoying equal favour with the court and with the opposition, he was most improperly appointed director of the school of France at Rome, from 1828 to 1835, and thither he carried the atmosphere of racket in which he habitually lived.[1] After his return the whole of the Constantine room at Versailles was decorated by him in the short space of three years. This vast work shows Vernet at his best and at his worst: as a picture it begins and ends nowhere and the composition is all to pieces; but it has good qualities of faithful and exact representation. He died at Paris on 17th January 1863. The twenty works which were exhibited after his death confirmed his reputation for extraordinary facility; he had tried every sort of subject, showing affinity for all that was anecdotic rather than dramatic, failing most wherever most was demanded of him, and never reaching either beauty of colour or dignity of line. Vernet was in short a brilliant off-hand sketcher of all he saw, as he said himself, "from his window," and even in this work there was a good deal of affectation of the impromptu.

See Lagrange, *Joseph Vernet et la Peinture au XVIII. Siècle*; C. Blanc, *Hist. de l'École Française*; and T. Sylvestre, *Peintres Contemporains*.

VERNIER, Pierre (*c.* 1580-1637), inventor of the instrument which bears his name, was born at Ornans (near Besançon) in Burgundy about 1580. He was for a considerable time commandant of the castle in his native town. In 1631 he published at Brussels a treatise entitled *Construction, usage, et propriétés du quadrant nouveau de mathématiques*, in which the instrument associated with his name is described (see Navigation, vol. xvii. p. 256, and Surveying, vol. xxii. p. 718). He died at Ornans in 1637.

The instrument invented by Vernier is frequently called a nonius; but this is incorrect, as the contrivance described by Pedro Nuñez in his work *De crepusculis* (1542) is a different one. Nuñez drew on the plane of a quadrant 44 concentric arcs divided respectively into 89,88, . . . 46 equal parts; and, if the alidade did not coincide with one of the divisions on the principal arc, it would fall more or less accurately on a division line of one of the auxiliary arcs, from which the value of the measured angle could be made out. This instrument was, however, very difficult to make, and was but little used. Vernier proposed to attach to a quadrant divided into half degrees a movable sector of a length equal to 31 half degrees, but divided into 30 equal parts, whereby single minutes could be read off by seeing which division line of the "sector" coincided with a division line of the quadrant. This movable arc was in other words divided into $\frac{n+1}{n}$ parts, and the divisions were graduated in the direction opposite to that of the graduation of the principal arc. It is now usual to divide it into $\frac{n-1}{n}$ parts, the two graduations going in the same direction. The idea had been mentioned by Christopher Clavius (1537-1612) in his *Opera mathematica*, 1612 (vol. ii. p. 5 and iii. p. 10), but he did not propose to attach permanently an arc divided in this way to the alidade; this happy application of the principle at all events belongs to Vernier.

VERNON, Edward (1684-1757), English admiral, was born in Westminster, on 12th November 1684, and is said to have been descended from the ancient family of Vernon, long resident at Hanbury in Staffordshire. His father, James Vernon, secretary of state from 1697 to 1700, is best remembered by three volumes of his letters to the duke of Shrewsbury, which were published in 1841; and his mother was Mary, daughter of Sir John Buck of Lincolnshire. Edward, their second son, was sent to Westminster school, but his heart longed for the roving life of the sea, and his stay in that "seed-plot of learning" was but brief. Outside its walls he studied, with a view to his future profession, such branches of knowledge as geometry, geography, and the construction of military weapons. He entered the navy in 1701 and from that time until 1707 took part in many expeditions in the Mediterranean and the West Indies. He served with Sir George Rooke at the taking of Gibraltar in July 1704;

[1] See a letter of Mendelssohn's cited by C. Blanc.

and on his return to England Queen Anne acknowledged his gallantry with the present of two hundred guineas. He next went to the West Indies as rear-admiral to Sir Charles Wager, a brave seaman, who afterwards rose to the highest position at the admiralty in the Whig ministry of Walpole, and was pitted against Vernon both in the House of Commons and at the polling-booth. In 1715, and again in 1726, Vernon assisted in the naval operations in the Baltic, supporting Sir John Norris in the first enterprise, and on the latter serving under his old chief, Sir Charles Wager. During the long supremacy of Walpole little opportunity arose for distinction in warfare, and Vernon's energies found relief in politics. At the general election of 1722 he was returned for both Dunwich in Suffolk and Penryn in Cornwall, but chose the latter constituency. In the succeeding parliament of 1727 he was again chosen member for Penryn; but he failed to retain his seat after the dissolution in 1734. At this period the English people regarded the Spaniards as their legitimate enemies, and the ill-feeling of the two countries was fanned both in poetry and in prose. The political antagonists of Walpole charged him with pusillanimity to Spain. With Pulteney and most of his associates this battle-ground was selected rather from expediency than from principle; but Vernon represented the natural instincts of the sea-captain, and with the sailor as with the soldier the motto was "No peace with Spain." In debate he spoke often, and frequently with effect, but his language always savoured of extravagance. He pledged himself in 1739 to capture Porto Bello with a squadron of but six ships, and the minister whom he had assailed with his invectives sent him, as vice-admiral of the blue and commander of the fleet in the West Indies, to the enterprise with the force which he had himself called sufficient. Vernon weighed anchor from Spithead on 23d July 1739 and arrived off Porto Bello on 20th November. Next day the combat began with a bombardment of an outlying fort which protected the mouth of the harbour, and on 22d November the castle and town surrendered with a loss on the English side of only seven men. The joy of the nation knew no bounds. Vernon's birthday was celebrated in 1740 in London with public illuminations, and 130 medals were struck in his honour. In February 1741 in a bye-election at Portsmouth Vernon was again sent to parliament. At the general election in the following May he was returned for Ipswich, Rochester, and Penryn, and all but succeeded in winning Westminster.[1] A larger squadron was placed under Vernon's command at the close of 1740, and with this force he resolved upon attacking Cartagena. After a fierce struggle the castle, which stood at the harbour's entrance, was gained; but in the attack upon the city the troops and sailors failed to act in concert, and, with the numbers of his forces thinned by combat and by disease, the British admiral retired to Jamaica. The incidents of this disastrous attempt are described in Smollett's *Roderick Random*, chap. xxxi., &c. A similar enterprise in July 1741 against Santiago in Cuba met with a similar reverse, and Vernon attributed the defeat to the divided command of the British forces. He landed at Bristol, 6th January 1743, and on 24th January received the freedom of the city of London. When the country dreaded the march of Prince Charles to London, the fleet in the Downs was placed under the command of Vernon; but his jealous disposition brooked no interference from the Admiralty, and on 1st January 1746 he struck his flag and handed over the command to another. His next act was to describe his grievances in a couple of angry pamphlets, revealing the communications of his official chiefs, and for this indiscretion he was struck off the list of flag officers (11th April 1746). He continued to represent the borough of Ipswich until his death, but with this proceeding his public services practically ceased. He died suddenly at Nacton in Suffolk, 30th October 1757, and was buried in the church of the village.

[1] Grego's *Parliamentary Elections*, London, 1886, pp. 95-106.

Vernon's gallantry was unquestioned; but his valour not infrequently degenerated into foolhardiness, and he dwelt more often than is usual with British seamen on the merits of his own exploits. His politics were those of the Tory party, and his differences with the Whigs and with his colleagues in the services led to his publishing several pamphlets on his political conduct. A *Memorial of Admiral Vernon from Contemporary Authorities* was printed by W. F. Vernon for private circulation in 1861.

VERONA, an important city of northern Italy, in the province of Venetia, situated (45° 26′ 8″ N. lat. and 10° 59′ 4″ E. long.) in a loop made by the winding of the Adige (ancient *Athesis*). It lies at the junction of the Adige valley railway and that from Mantua with the Milan, Vicenza, and Venice line, 25 miles north of Mantua and 30 south-south-west of Vicenza.

Church of S. Zeno.

Modern City.—The basilica of S. Zeno (an early bishop of Verona who became its patron saint), which stands outside the ancient city, is one of the most interesting churches in Italy, but has been recently much injured by "restoration." The church was remodelled in the 12th century, to which period most of the existing structure belongs, including the richly sculptured west front and the open "confessio" or crypt, which occupies the eastern half of the church, raising the choir high above the nave,—a plan adopted in S. Miniato near Florence, the cathedral of Parma, at Coire in Switzerland, and elsewhere. This arrangement was probably introduced by the northern invaders of Lombardy. The cloisters of S. Zeno, rebuilt in 1123, are an interesting example of brick and marble construction. Like many other churches in Verona, S. Zeno is mainly built of mixed brick and stone in alternate bands: four or five courses of fine red brick lie between bands of hard cream-coloured limestone or marble,[2] forming broad stripes of red and white all over the wall. A similarly variegated effect in red and white is produced by building the arches of windows and doors with alternating voussoirs in brick and marble.[3] The cathedral, consecrated in 1187 by Pope Urban III., stands at the northern extremity of the ancient city, by the bank of the Adige; it is inferior in size and importance to S. Zeno, but has a fine 12th-century west front of equal interest, richly decorated with Lombardic sculpture. The rest of the exterior is built in bands of red and white, with slightly projecting pilasters along the walls; it has a noble cloister, with two stories of arcading. Its baptistery, rebuilt early in the 12th century, is a quite separate building, with nave and apse, forming a church dedicated to S. Giovanni in Fonte. Pope Lucius III., who held a council at Verona in 1184, is buried in the cathedral, under the pavement before the high altar.

Cathedral.

Church of S. Anastasia.

The Dominican church of S. Anastasia is a mine of wealth in early examples of painting and sculpture, and one of the finest buildings in Italy of semi-Gothic style. It consists of a nave in six bays, aisles, transepts, each with two eastern chapels, and an apse, all vaulted with simple quadripartite brick groining.[4] It dates from the latter part of the 13th century, and is specially remarkable for its very beautiful and complete scheme of coloured decoration, much of which is

[2] The neighbourhood of Verona is especially rich in fine limestones and marbles of many different kinds, especially a close-grained cream-coloured marble and a rich mottled red marble, which are largely used, not only in Verona, but also in Venice and other cities of the province. The same quarry produces both kinds, and indeed the same block is sometimes half red and half white.

[3] See Street, *Brick and Marble Arch. in Italy*, London, 1855, p. 75 *sq.*

[4] This type of church was specially adopted by the Dominicans in Italy.

contemporary with the building. The vaults are very gracefully painted with floreated bands along the ribs and central patterns in each "cell," in rich soft colours on a white plastered ground. The eastern portion of the vaulting, including the choir and one bay of the nave, has the older and simpler decorations; the rest of the nave has more elaborate painted ornament,—foliage mixed with figures of Dominican saints, executed in the 15th century.

Plan of Verona.

On the walls below are many fine frescos, ranging from *c.* 1300 to the 15th century, including Pisanello's beautiful painting of St George (mentioned below). This church also contains a large number of fine sculptured tombs of the 14th and 15th centuries, with noble effigies and reliefs of saints and sacred subjects. It is mainly built of red brick, with fine nave columns of red and white marble and an elaborate marble pavement inlaid in many different patterns. Its general proportions are specially noble.

Church of S. Fermo.

The church of S. Fermo Maggiore comes next in interest. With the exception of the crypt, which is older, the existing edifice was rebuilt in the 14th century. Its plan is very unusual, consisting of a large nave without aisles, the span being between 45 and 50 feet; it also has two shallow transepts and an apsidal east end. The roof, which is especially magnificent, is the finest example of a class which as a rule is only found in Venetia:[1] the framing is concealed by coving or barrel-vaulting in wood, the surface of which is divided into small square panels, all painted and gilt, giving a very rich effect. In this case the 14th and 15th century painted decorations are well preserved. Delicate patterns cover all the framework of the panelling and fill the panels themselves; at two stages, where there is a check in the line of the coving, rows of half-figures of saints are minutely painted on blue or gold grounds, forming a scheme of indescribably splendid decoration. A simpler roof of the same class exists at S. Zeno; it is trefoil-shaped in section, with a tie-beam joining the cusps. The church of S. Maria in Organo, rebuilt by Sanmichele, contains paintings by various Veronese masters.

Other churches.

Though not built till after his death, the church of S. Giorgio in Braida, on the other side of the river, was also designed by Sanmichele, and possesses many good pictures of the Veronese school. There are several other fine churches in Verona, some of early date. One of the 14th century is dedicated to Thomas a Becket of Canterbury.

Bridges and castles.

The strongly fortified castle built by the Della Scala lords in the 14th century stands on the line of the Roman wall, close by the river. A very picturesque battlemented bridge leads from it to the other shore, sloping down over three arches of different sizes, the largest next to the castle and the smallest at the other end. There are four other bridges across the Adige; one, the graceful Ponte di Pietra, was designed by Fra Giocondo. The 16th-century lines of fortification enclose a very much larger area than the Roman city, forming a great loop to the west, and also including a considerable space on the left bank of the river. In the latter part of the city, on a steep elevation, stands the castle of St Peter, originally founded by Theodoric, mostly rebuilt by Gian Galeazzo Visconti in 1393, and dismantled by the French in 1801. This and the other fortifications of Verona were rebuilt or repaired by the Austrians, but are no longer kept up as military defences. Verona, which is the chief military centre of the Italian province of Venetia, is now being surrounded with a circle of forts far outside the obsolete city walls.

Palaces.

The early palaces of Verona, before its conquest by Venice, were of very noble and simple design, mostly built of fine red brick, with an inner court, surrounded on the ground floor by open arches like a cloister, as, for example, the Palazzo della Ragione, an assize court, begun in the 12th century. The arches, round or more often pointed in form, were decorated with moulded terra-cotta enrichments, and often with alternating voussoirs of marble. The Scaligeri Palace is a fine example, dating from the 14th century, with, in the cortile, an external staircase leading to an upper loggia, above the usual arcade on the ground floor. It has a very lofty campanile, surmounted by a graceful octagonal upper story. This palace is said to have been mainly built by Can Signorio (Della Scala) about 1370. After the conquest by Venice the domestic buildings of Verona assumed quite a different type. They became feeble copies of Venetian palaces, in which one form of window, with an ogee arch, framed by the dentil moulding is almost always used. The monotony and utter lifelessness of this form of architecture are shown in the meaningless way in which details, suited only to the Venetian methods of veneering walls with thin marble slabs, are copied in the solid marbles of Verona. From the skill of Fra Giocondo (see below), Verona was for many years one of the chief centres in which the most refined and graceful forms of the early Renaissance were developed. The town-hall, with its light open loggia of semicircular arches on the ground floor, was designed by Fra Giocondo towards the end of the 15th century; its sculptured enrichments of pilasters and friezes are very graceful, though lacking the vigorous life of the earlier mediæval sculptured ornamentation. Verona contains a number of handsome, though somewhat uninteresting, palaces designed by Sanmichele in the 16th century. The finest are those of the Bevilacqua,[2] Canossa, and Pompei families. The last of these is now the property of the city, and contains a gallery with some good pictures, especially of the Verona, Padua, and Venice schools. As in Venice, many of the 16th-century palaces in Verona had stuccoed façades, richly decorated with large fresco paintings, often by very able painters. One of these, the house of the painter Niccolo

[1] Or in churches built by Venetian architects in Istria and other subject provinces.

[2] The valuable collection of works of art once preserved in the Bevilacqua Palace has long since been dispersed.

Giolfino, still has its frescos in a good state of preservation, and gives a vivid notion of what must once have been the effect of these gorgeous pictured palaces. The episcopal palace contains the ancient and valuable chapter library, of about 12,000 volumes and over 500 MSS., among them the palimpsest of the *Institutiones* of Gaius which Niebuhr discovered. The Piazza delle Erbe (fruit market) and the Piazza dei Signori, both in the oldest part of the city, are very picturesque and beautiful, being surrounded by many fine mediæval buildings. In the former of these a copy of the lion of Venice has recently been erected.

Squares.

Population, industry, &c.

Verona had a population of 67,080 in 1871, which by 1881 had increased to 68,741. In spite of its pleasant and healthy site, Verona is in winter liable to be cold and rainy, like other places which lie along the southern spurs of the Alps. The Adige, a rapid but shallow river, shrinks to an insignificant stream during the summer. Verona possesses some silk, linen, and woollen manufactures, and carries on a considerable trade in these goods and in grain, hides, flax, hemp, marble, drugs, &c. Amongst the public institutions of the place may be mentioned the public library (1802), the agricultural academy (1768), the botanical garden, various good schools and colleges (including a theological seminary, a lyceum, and gymnasia), and numerous hospitals and charitable organizations.

Roman remains.

Roman Remains.—The most conspicuous of the existing Roman remains is the great amphitheatre, a building of the 2d or 3d century, which in general form closely resembled the Colosseum in Rome. Almost the whole of its external arcades, with three tiers of arches, have now disappeared; it was partly thrown down by an earthquake in 1184, and subsequently used as a stone-quarry to supply building materials. Many of its blocks are still visible in the walls of various mediæval buildings. The interior, with seats for about 20,000 people, has been frequently restored, till none of the old seats remain. Traces also exist of extensive baths and of a Roman theatre, the latter outside the most ancient line of walls, close to the left bank of the river. In 1885 portions of a number of fine mosaic pavements, dating from the 3d century, were discovered extending over a very large area under the cloister and other parts of the cathedral, about 5 feet below the present floor level. A large number of different patterns exist in a good state of preservation, elaborate in style, but, like all late Roman mosaics, rather coarsely executed with large *tesseræ*. The Museo Lapidario contains a fine collection of Roman and Etruscan inscriptions and sculpture, mostly collected and published by Scipione Maffei in the 18th century.

Artistic Importance.—In many respects the resemblance between Verona and Florence is very striking: in both cases we have a strongly fortified city built in a fertile valley, on the banks of a winding river, with suburbs on higher ground, rising close above the main city. In architectural magnificence and in wealth of sculpture and painting Verona almost rivalled the Tuscan city, and, like it, gave birth to a very large number of artists who distinguished themselves in all branches of the fine arts.

Painting.

Painting in Verona may be divided into four periods. (i.) The first period is characterized by wall paintings of purely native style, closely resembling the early Christian pictures in the catacombs of Rome. Examples dating from the 10th to the 11th century have been discovered hidden by whitewash on the oldest parts of the nave walls of the church of S. Zeno. They are a very interesting survival of the almost classical Roman style of painting, and appear to be quite free from the generally prevalent Byzantine influence. (ii.) The Byzantine period seems to have lasted during the 12th and 13th centuries. (iii.) The Giottesque period begins contemporaneously with Altichiero da Zevio and Giacomo degli Avanzi, whose chief works were executed during the second half of the 14th century. These two painters were among the ablest of Giotto's followers, and adorned Verona and Padua with a number of very beautiful frescos, rich in composition, delicate in colour, and remarkable for their highly finished modelling and detail. (iv.) To the fourth period belong several important painters. Pisanello or Vittore PISANO (*q.v.*), a very charming painter and the greatest medallist of Italy, was probably a pupil of Altichiero.[1] Most of his frescos in Verona have perished; but one of great beauty still exists in a very perfect state in the church of S. Anastasia, high up over the arched opening into one of the eastern chapels of the south transept. The scene represents St George and the Princess after the Conquest of the Dragon, with accessory figures, the sea, a mountainous landscape, and an elaborately painted city in the background. The only other existing fresco by Pisanello is an Annunciation in S. Fermo Maggiore. For Pisanello's pupils and other painters of subsequent date, see SCHOOLS OF PAINTING, vol. xxi. p. 443. Domenico del Riccio, usually nicknamed Brusasorci (1494-1567), was a prolific painter whose works are very numerous in Verona. Paolo Cagliari or Paul VERONESE (*q.v.*), though a native of Verona, belongs rather to the Venetian school.

Sculpture.

Verona is specially rich in early examples of decorative sculpture. (i.) The first period is that of northern or Lombardic influence, exemplified in the very interesting series of reliefs which cover the western façades of the church of S. Zeno and the cathedral, dating from the 12th century. These reliefs represent both sacred subjects and scenes of war and hunting, mixed with grotesque monsters, such as specially delighted the rude vigorous nature of the Lombards; they are all richly decorative in effect, though strange and unskilful in detail. Part of the western bronze doors[2] of S. Zeno are especially interesting as being among the earliest important examples in Italy of cast bronze reliefs. They represent scenes from the life of S. Zeno, are rudely modelled, and yet very dramatic and sculpturesque in style.[3] Many of the 12th-century reliefs and sculptured capitals in S. Zeno are signed by the sculptor, but these merely constitute lists of names about whom nothing is known. (ii.) In the 13th century the sculpture seems to have lost the Lombard vigour, without acquiring any qualities of superior grace or refinement. The font in the baptistery near the cathedral is an early example of this. Each side of the octagon is covered with a large relief of a Biblical subject, very dull in style and coarse in execution. The font itself is interesting for its early form, one common in the chief baptisteries of northern Italy: like an island in the centre of the great octagonal tank is a lobed marble receptacle, in which the officiating priest stood while he immersed the catechumens. A movable wooden bridge must have been used to enable the priest to cross the water in the surrounding tank. (iii.) The next period is that of Florentine influence. This is exemplified in the magnificently sculptured tombs of the Della Scala lords, designed with steadily growing splendour, from the simple sarcophagus of Martino I. down to the elaborate erection over the tomb of the fratricide Can Signorio, adorned with statuettes of the virtues, to the possession of which he could lay so little claim.[4] The recumbent effigies and decorative details of these tombs are very beautiful, but the smaller figures of angels, saints, and virtues are rather clumsy in proportion. The latest tomb, that of Can Signorio, erected during his lifetime (*c.* 1370), is signed "Boninus de Campigliono Mediolanensis Dioscesis." This sculptor, though of Milanese origin, belongs really to the school of the Florentine Andrea Pisano. One characteristic of the 14th and 15th centuries in Verona was the custom, also followed in other Lombardic cities, of setting large equestrian statues over the tombs of powerful military leaders, in some cases above the recumbent effigy of the dead man, as if to represent him in full vigour of life as well as in death. That which crowns the canopy over the tomb of Can Grande is a very noble, though somewhat quaint, work. (iv.) In the 15th century the influence of Venice became paramount, though this was really only a further development of the Florentine manner, Venice itself having been directly influenced in the 14th century by many able sculptors from Florence.

Architecture.

The architecture of Verona, like its sculpture, passed through Lombard, Florentine, and Venetian stages. (i.) The church of S. Zeno and the cathedral, both of which were mainly rebuilt in the 12th century, are very noble examples of the Lombardic style, with few single-light windows, and with the walls decorated externally by series of pilasters and by alternating bands of red and white, in stone or brick. The arches of this period are semicircular and rest on round columns and capitals, richly carved with grotesque figures and foliage. Most of the external ornamentation is usually concentrated on the western front, which often has a lofty arched porch on marble columns, resting on griffins or lions devouring their prey. (ii.) The Florentine period (*c.* 1250 to 1400) is represented by the church of S. Anastasia, and by many more or less mutilated palaces, with fine courts surrounded by arcades in one or more stories. The arches are mostly pointed, and in other respects the influence of northern Gothic was more direct in Verona than in Florence. Solidity of mass and simplicity of detail are among the characteristics of this period. (iii.) The Venetian period (*c.* 1400 to 1480) was one of little originality or vigour, the buildings of this date being largely rather dull copies of those at Venice. (iv.) The early Renaissance developed into very exceptional beauty in Verona, mainly through the genius of Fra Giocondo (1435-1514),

[1] There is every reason to doubt Vasari's statement that Pisanello was a pupil of Andrea del Castagno.

[2] They are frequently stated to be of beaten bronze, but they are really castings, apparently by the *cire perdue* process.

[3] Part of these doors are covered with bronze reliefs of scenes from the Bible, which are of still earlier date, and were probably brought to Verona from the Rhine provinces.

[4] See an eloquent description by Ruskin, *Stones of Venice*, iii. p. 70 *sq.*

a native of Verona, who was at first a friar in the monastery of S. Maria in Organo. He rose to great celebrity as an architect, and designed many graceful and richly sculptured buildings in Venice, Rome, and even in France; he used classical forms with great taste and skill, and with much of the freedom of the older mediæval architects, and was specially remarkable for his rich and delicate sculptured decorations. The Roman gateway of Gallienus (mentioned below) supplied a special form of window, with a circular arch on pilasters, surmounted by a cornice; this was copied by Fra Giocondo, and has been used by countless architects down to the present day without any alteration whatever,[1]—a remarkable history for a design: it was invented in the 3d century, revived in the 15th, and again copied in the 19th. Another of the leading architects of the next stage of the Renaissance was the Veronese Michele SANMICHELE (*q.v.*), a great military engineer, and designer of an immense number of magnificent palaces in Verona and other cities of Venetia. His buildings are stately and graceful in proportion, but show a tendency towards that dull scholastic classicism which in the hands of Palladio put an end to all real life in the art.

History.

History.—Nothing is certainly known of the history of Verona until it became a Roman colony with the title of *Augusta*, together with the rest of Venetia (Tac., *Hist.*, iii. 8, and Strabo, p. 213). Its fertile surroundings, its central position at the junction of several great roads, and the natural strength of its position, defended by a river along two-thirds of its circumference, all combined to make Verona one of the richest and most important cities in northern Italy, although its extent within the walls was not large. The existing remains of wall and gates are shown by inscriptions on them to date from the 3d century; the ancient *fossa* still exists as an open canal, so that the old part of the city is wholly surrounded by water. One very handsome gateway inside the Roman city, now called the Porta de' Borsari, was restored in 265 by Gallienus. There are, however, traces of a more ancient circuit wall and gates on the old line. The emperor Constantine, while advancing towards Rome from Gaul, besieged and took Verona (312); it was here, too, that Odoacer was defeated (489) by Theodoric the Goth, who built a palace at Verona and frequently resided there. Verona was the birthplace of Catullus.

In the Middle Ages Verona gradually grew in size and importance. In early times it was one of the chief residences of the Lombard kings;[2] and, though, like other cities of northern Italy, it suffered much during the Guelf and Ghibelline struggles, it rose to a foremost position both from the political and the artistic point of view under its various rulers of the Scaliger or Della Scala family. The first prominent member of this family and founder of his dynasty was Martino I. della Scala, who ruled over the city from 1260 till his death in 1277. Verona had previously fallen under the power of a less able despot, Ezzelino da Romano, who died in 1259. Alberto della Scala (died in 1301) was succeeded by his eldest son Bartolomeo, who was confirmed as ruler of Verona by the popular vote, and died in 1304. Alboino, the second son, succeeded his brother, and died in 1311, when the youngest son of Alberto, Can Grande, who since 1308 had been joint-lord of Verona with his brother, succeeded to the undivided power. Can Grande (Francesco della Scala, died in 1329) was the best and most illustrious of his line, and is specially famous as the hospitable patron of DANTE (*q.v.*). Other princes of this dynasty, which lasted for rather more than a century, were Giovanni (d. 1350), Martino II. (d. 1351), Can Grande II. (d. 1359), and Can Signorio (d. 1375). In 1389 Gian Galeazzo Visconti, duke of Milan, became by conquest lord of Verona. Soon after his death the city fell by treacherous means into the hands of Francesco II. di Carrara, lord of Padua. In 1404-5 Verona, together with Padua, was finally conquered by Venice, and remained subject to the Venetians till the overthrow of the republic by Napoleon in 1797, who in the same year, after the treaty of Campo Formio, ceded it to the Austrians with the rest of Venetia; and since that time its political history has been linked to that of Venice.

See the various works by Scipione Maffei (*Verona Illustrata*, 1728; *Museum Veronense*, 1749; and *La Antica Condizion di Verona*, 1719); also Panvinius, *Antiquitates Veronæ*, Padua, 1668; Da Pertico, *Descrizione di Verona*, 1820; and for some of the older buildings Street, *Brick and Marble Architecture*, London, 1855. (J. H. M.)

VERONESE, PAOLO (1528-1588), the name ordinarily given to PAOLO CALIARI, or CAGLIARI, the latest of the great cycle of painters of the Venetian school, was born in Verona in 1528 according to the best authorities (Zanetti and others), or in 1532 according to Ridolfi. His father, Gabriele Caliari, a sculptor, began to train Paolo to his own profession. The boy, however, showed more propensity to painting, and was therefore transferred to his uncle, the painter Antonio Badile. According to Vasari, he was the pupil of Giovanni Carotto, a painter proficient in architecture and perspective; this statement remains unconfirmed. Paolo, in his early years, applied himself to copying from the engravings of Albert Dürer and the drawings of Parmigiano; and, having in a singular degree the gifts of facility, retentiveness, and amenity, he made rapid progress. He did some work in Verona, but found there little outlet for his abilities, the field being pretty well occupied by Ligozzi, Brusasorci, Battista dal Moro, Paolo Farinato, Domenico Riccio, and other artists. Cardinal Ercole Gonzaga took him, when barely past twenty years of age, to Mantua, along with the three last-named painters, to execute in the cathedral a picture of the Temptation of St Anthony; here Caliari was considered to excel his competitors. Returning to Verona, he found himself exposed to some envy and ill-will. Hence he formed an artistic partnership with Battista Zelotti, and they painted together in the territories of Vicenza and Treviso. Finally Paolo went on to Venice. In this city his first pictures were executed in 1555 in the sacristy and church of St Sebastian, an uncle of his being prior of the monastery. The subjects on the vaulting are taken from the history of Esther; and these excited so much admiration that thenceforward Caliari, aged about twenty-eight, ranked almost on a par with Tintoretto, aged about forty-five, or with Titian in his eightieth year, and his life became a series of triumphs. Besides the Esther subjects, these buildings contain his pictures of the Baptism of Christ, the Martyrdom of St Marcus and St Marcellinus, the Martyrdom of St Sebastian, &c. As regards this last-named work, there is a vague tradition that Caliari painted it at a time when he had taken refuge in the monastery, for some reason now unknown. He entered into a competition for painting the ceiling of the library of St Mark, and not only obtained the commission but executed it with so much power that his very rivals voted him the golden chain which had been tendered as an honorary distinction. At one time he returned to Verona, and painted the Banquet in the House of Simon the Pharisee, with Jesus and Mary Magdalene, for the refectory of St Mazzaro,—a picture now in Turin. In 1560, however, he was in Venice again, working partly in the St Sebastian buildings and partly in the ducal palace. He visited Rome in 1563, in the suite of Girolamo Grimani, the Venetian ambassador, and acquired enhanced elevation of style by studying the works of Raphael and Michelangelo, and especially the antique. Returning to Venice, he was overwhelmed with commissions, almost transcending the resources even of his own marvellous assiduity, fertility, and promptitude,—qualities in which no painter perhaps has ever surpassed him. He was compelled to decline an invitation from Philip II. to go to Spain and assist in decorating the Escorial. One of his pictures of this period is the famous Venice, Queen of the Sea, in the ducal palace. He died in Venice on the 20th (or perhaps 19th) of April 1588, and was buried in the church of St Sebastian, a monument being set up to him there by his two sons, Gabriele and Carlo, and his brother, Benedetto, all of them painters.

Beyond his magnificent performances as a painter, the known incidents in the life of Paul Veronese are (as will be perceived from the above account) very few. That he was prosperous is certain, and that he was happy is an almost necessary inference from the character of his pictures, on which the joy of living is ineffaceably stamped. He was honoured and loved, being kind, amiable, generous, and an excellent father. His person is well known from the portraits left by himself and others: he was a dark man, rather good-looking than otherwise, somewhat bald in early middle age, and with nothing to mark an exceptional energy or turn of character. In his works the first quality which strikes one is the palatial splendour—grand architecture, stately vistas, personages of easy and affable dignity in sumptuous costumes, the crowded assemblies,

[1] As, for example, in Sir Gilbert Scott's Government offices, Whitehall, and many other recent buildings in London.

[2] Verona is the "Bern" of early German legendary history, and of the poems which celebrate the achievements of Charlemagne.

the luxury of environment, the air and light, the graceful and abundant poise of action and of limb, the rhythmic movement, the sweet and lordly variegation of tint. The pictorial inspiration is entirely that of the piercing and comprehensive eye and the magical hand—not of the mind; for Veronese yields none but negative results to the touchstone either of exalted and profound imagination or of searching and constructive common-sense. The human form and face are given with decorous comeliness, often with beauty. He constantly painted his figures and faces from the life, thus securing range and precision of character; but of individual apposite expression there is next to none, and of reasoned realistic contact with the professed subject matter—whether in general disposition, in costume and accessory, or in attitude and effort of mind—there is frequently no trace at all. In fact, Paolo Veronese is pre-eminently a painter working pictorially, and in no wise amenable to a literary or rationalizing standard: you can neither exhibit nor vindicate his scenic apparatus by any transcription into words. He enjoys a sight much as Ariosto enjoys a story, and displays it in form and colour with a zest like that of Ariosto for language and verse. As we have already indicated, he was supreme in representing, without huddling or confusion, numerous figures in a luminous and diffused atmosphere, while in richness of draperies and transparency of shadows he surpassed all the other Venetians or Italians. In gifts of this kind Rubens alone could be pitted against him. In the moderation of art combined with its profusion he far excelled Rubens; for, dazzling as is the first impression of a great work by Veronese, there is in it, in reality, as much of soberness and serenity as of exuberance. By variety and apposition he produces a most brilliant effect of colour; and yet his hues are seldom bright. He hoards his primary tints and his high lights, like a rich miser who knows how to play the genial host on occasion. A colossal spontaneity, to which a great result is only a small effort of faculty, is the chief and abiding impression derived from contemplating his works. He very rarely produced small pictures: the spacious was his element.

Of all Veronese's paintings the one which has obtained the greatest world-wide celebrity is the vast Marriage at Cana, now in the Louvre. It contains about a hundred and twenty figures or heads—those in the foreground being larger than life. Several of them are portraits. Among the personages specified (some of them probably without sufficient reason) are the Marquis del Vasto, Queen Eleanor of France, Francis I., Queen Mary of England, Sultan Soleyman I., Vittoria Colonna, Charles V., Tintoretto, Titian, the elder Bassano, Benedetto Caliari, and Paolo Veronese himself (the figure playing the viol). It is impossible to look at this picture without astonishment; it enlarges one's conception of what pictorial art means and can do. The only point of view from which it fails is that of the New Testament narrative; for there is no more relation between the Galilean wedding and Veronese's court-banquet than between a true portrait of Lazarus and a true portrait of Dives. This stupendous performance was executed for the refectory of the monastery of S. Giorgio Maggiore in Venice, the contract for it being signed in June 1562 and the picture completed in September 1563. Its price was 324 silver ducats (=£160), along with the artist's living-expenses and a tun of wine. There are five other great banquet-pictures by Caliari, only inferior in scale and excellence to this of Cana. One of them is also in the Louvre, a Feast in the House of Simon the Pharisee, painted towards 1570-75 for the refectory of the Servites in Venice. A different version of the same theme is in the Brera Gallery of Milan. The Feast of Simon the Leper, 1570, was done for the refectory of the monks of St Sebastian, and the Feast of Levi (St Matthew), 1573, now in the Venetian academy, for the refectory of the monks of St John and St Paul. In each instance the price barely exceeded the cost of the materials, so different were the conditions under which an artist even of the first celebrity, as Veronese then was, worked in Italy in the 16th century from the conditions prevailing at the present day. The Louvre contains ten other specimens of Veronese, notably the Susanna and the Elders, and the Supper at Emmaus. In the London National Gallery are six examples. The most beautiful is St Helena's Vision of the Cross, founded upon an engraving by Marcantonio after a drawing supposed to be the work of Raphael. Far more famous than this is the Family of Darius at the Feet of Alexander the Great after the Battle of Issus—the captives having mistaken Hephæstion for Alexander. It was bought for £13,560, and has even been termed (very unreasonably) the most celebrated of all Veronese's works. The principal figures are portraits of the Pisani family. It is said that Caliari was accidentally detained at the Pisani villa at Este, and there painted this work, and, on quitting, told the family that he had left behind him an equivalent for his courteous entertainment. Another picture in the National Gallery, Europa and the Bull, is a study for the large painting in the imperial gallery of Vienna, and resembles one in the ducal palace of Venice. The Venetian academy contains fourteen works by Veronese. One of the finest—it is indeed a singular and choice masterpiece—is a comparatively small picture of the Battle of Lepanto, with Christ in heaven pouring light upon the Christian fleet and darkness on the Turkish. In the Uffizi Gallery of Florence are two specimens of exceptional beauty—the Annunciation and Esther Presenting herself to Ahasuerus; for delicacy and charm this latter work yields to nothing that the master produced. In Verona St George and St Julian, in Brescia the Martyrdom of St Afra, and in Padua the Martyrdom of St Justina are works of leading renown. The drawings of Veronese are very fine, and he took pleasure at times in engraving on copper.

The brother and sons of Paolo already mentioned, and Battista Zelotti, were his principal assistants and followers. Benedetto Caliari, the brother, who was about ten years younger than Paolo, is reputed to have had a very large share in designing and executing the architectural backgrounds which form so conspicuous a feature in Paolo's compositions. If this is not overstated, it must be allowed that a substantial share in Paolo's fame accrues to Benedetto; for not only are the backgrounds admirably schemed and limned, but they govern to a large extent the invention and distribution of the groups. Of the two sons Carlo (or Carletto), the younger, is the better known. He was born in 1570, and was the favourite of his father, who sent him to study under Bassano. He produced various noticeable works, and died young in 1596. Gabriele, born in 1568, attended, after Carlo's death, almost entirely to commercial affairs; his works in painting are rare. All three were occupied after the death of Paolo in finishing his pictures left uncompleted.

See Ridolfi, *Le Meraviglie dell' Arte*, &c.; Dal Pozzo, *Vite de' Pittori Veronesi*, &c.; Zanetti, *Della Pittura Veneziana*, &c.; and Lanzi. (W. M. R.)

VERONICA, St. According to the Bollandists (4th Feb.), Veronica or Berenice was a pious woman of Jerusalem who, moved with pity as Jesus bore His cross to Golgotha, gave Him her kerchief that He might wipe the drops of agony from His brow. The Lord accepted the offering and after using it handed it back to her, bearing the image of His face miraculously impressed upon it. According to various forms of the legend, Veronica is identified with the niece of Herod the Great, with the woman whom Christ healed of an issue of blood (Mark v. 25 *sq.*; Matt. ix. 20 *sq.*), with a woman who afterwards, along with fifty others, young men and maidens, suffered martyrdom at Antioch, and with the beloved of one Amator, who is described as "famulus S. Virginis Mariæ et Josephi, et Domini bajulus ac nutricius," who afterwards became an ascetic and died at Roquemadore (Rupes Amatoris) near Bordeaux. Current tradition in the Roman Church has it that Veronica was able to heal Tiberius of a grievous sickness with her napkin, and that the emperor, thus convinced of the divinity of Christ, forthwith sent Pilate into exile. This napkin (*sudarium*) was in the time of Pope John VII. (705) in the church of S. Maria Maggiore in Rome, but is now in St Peter's, though possession of it is indeed claimed also by Milan and Jaen (Spain). The Bollandist form of the story cannot be traced further back than to about the second quarter of the 15th century; but in a MS. of the 8th century, now in the Vatican, Veronica is said to have painted, or caused to be painted, the portrait of Christ after she had been healed by Him. In the 13th century we find the miraculous picture itself spoken of as "figura Domini quæ Veronica dicitur," and this has suggested to archæologists the question whether the legend of the woman Veronica may not have arisen by confusion out of a totally distinct legend as to a vera icon (εἰκών), such as that which, according to Greek tradition, Jesus sent with an autograph letter to Abgarus of Edessa. St Veronica is commemorated on Shrove Tuesday, but her festival is not of obligation.

See Karl Pearson's *Die Fronica, ein Beitrag zur Geschichte des Christusbildes in Mittelalter* (Strasburg, 1887), which contains a discussion of the evolution of the story and much interesting matter relating to the hymnological, liturgical, and artistic aspects of the subject.

VERRES (*c.* 112-43 B.C.), whose name has been branded with everlasting infamy by the speeches of Cicero, was the bad son of a bad father. The elder Verres was an old hand at jobbery and bribery, and some of his son's ill-gotten gains found their way into his pocket. He had some sort of connexion with the dictator Sulla, and it was through this probably that he rose to be a senator; possibly, though this is very doubtful, he may have belonged to some branch of the Cornelian family, or have been adopted into it. The younger Verres held his first important appointment about 82 B.C. as quæstor of the consul Carbo in Cisalpine Gaul. This implies that he was then of the democratic party of Marius; but he left it the same year, after having deserted and betrayed Carbo and embezzled the public moneys of which as quæstor he had the handling. As a reward for his treachery he got out of Sulla a slice of the landed property of some of the proscribed citizens of Beneventum, and Sulla probably screened him in the following year when he was threatened with an action by the treasury officials for his peculations under Carbo. Next year, 80 B.C., he was in Asia on the staff of Dolabella, governor of Cilicia, where he again acted as quæstor. The governor and his subordinate plundered in concert, till in 78 B.C. Dolabella had to stand his trial at Rome, and was convicted, mainly on the evidence of Verres, who thus secured a pardon for himself. In 74 B.C. he was elected prætor, bribing heavily, it was said, and he had what was termed the city prætorship, which gave him all the powers of an English lord chancellor, with but inadequate checks on their abuse. Verres, as a creature of Sulla's, in several of his judicial decisions turned them to political ends for the advantage of himself and his party. After his year of prætorship Verres went as governor to Sicily, the richest and most attractive of the Roman provinces, with its treasures of Greek art, its Greek civilization, and its many noble and beautiful cities. Rome had recognized the claims of Sicily to a kindly and indulgent rule, and the people were for the most part comfortable and contented. But under Verres the island experienced more utter misery and desolation than it had felt amid the horrors of that long and fierce struggle, the First Punic War. The corn-growers, and the revenue collectors or "publicans," were ruined by exorbitant imposts or by the iniquitous cancelling of contracts; temples and private houses were robbed of their works of art, which to the Sicilian Greek were even dearer than his money; and to all this were added insult and outrage. Men who had the Roman franchise, which was now beginning to be widely diffused, were among the victims of Verres: one was scourged publicly at Messana on an unproved charge. Verres returned to Rome in 70 B.C., with plunder which he boasted would enable him to live in ease and luxury, even if he had to surrender two-thirds of it to bribe a Roman jury. The prosecution which he anticipated was commenced the same year by the provincials of Sicily, and was at their request undertaken by Cicero. Verres entrusted his defence to the most eminent of Roman advocates, Hortensius, and he had the sympathy and support of several of the leading Roman nobles. The court before which he was to be tried was composed exclusively of senators, some of whom might be his personal friends. But the presiding judge, the city prætor Acilius Glabrio, was a thoroughly honest man, and his assessors were at least not accessible to bribery. Cicero took care that the evidence should be overwhelming, and he had a host of witnesses in readiness, not only from the ill-used towns of Sicily, but from every part of the Greek world. The trial, one of the most memorable in antiquity, began early in the August of 70 B.C., after an unsuccessful attempt by the counsel for Verres to get it adjourned to the following year, when Hortensius would himself be consul and the presiding judge, Metellus, one of his political friends. Cicero opened the case with a comparatively brief speech (*Actio Prima in Verrem*), following it up with the examination of witnesses and documentary evidence, and convincing Hortensius that his client's cause was hopeless. Before the expiration of the nine days allowed for the prosecution Verres was on his way to Marseilles; there he lived in exile to the year 43 B.C., with abundant means of enjoying life in his own way. The story went (Pliny, *N. H.*, xxxiv. 2) that his name was on the proscription list of Marcus Antonius, and that in fact he owed his death to the murderer of Cicero.

Verres may not have been quite so black as he is painted by Cicero, on whose speeches we depend entirely for our knowledge of the man, but there can hardly be a doubt that he stood pre-eminent among the worst specimens of Roman provincial governors. It is cruelly unjust to the memory of Warren Hastings to suggest a comparison between him and Verres, though between the two trials, between the charges made, and the general character and circumstances of the proceedings there are points of striking resemblance. But there is a clearly marked difference. Verres cared simply for himself; Hastings thought much of the greatness and glory of his country. For one thing indeed we have to thank Verres,—for the detailed description of Sicily and its Greek art treasures which we have in Cicero's famous Verrine orations.

VERROCCHIO, ANDREA DEL (1435-1488), one of the most distinguished Florentine artists of the 15th century, equally famed as a goldsmith, sculptor, and painter, was born at Florence in 1435. He was the son of Michele di Francesco de' Cioni, and took his name from his master, the goldsmith Giuliano Verrocchi. Except through his works, little is known of his life. As a painter he occupies an important position from the fact that Leonardo da Vinci and Lorenzo di Credi worked for many years in his bottega as pupils and assistants. Only one existing painting can be attributed with absolute certainty to Verrocchio's hand, the celebrated Baptism of Christ, originally painted for the monks of Vallombrosa, and now in the academy of Florence. The figures of Christ and the Baptist are executed with great vigour and refinement of touch, but are rather hard and angular in style. As Vasari says, Verrocchio "ebbe la maniera alquanto dura e crudetta." The two angels are of a much more graceful cast; the face of one is of especial beauty, and Vasari is probably right in saying that this head was painted by the young Leonardo. Other pictures from Verrocchio's bottega probably exist, as, for example, two in the National Gallery of London wrongly attributed to Ant. Pollaiuolo—Tobias and the Angel (No. 781) and the very lovely Madonna and Angels (No. 296), both very brilliant and jewel-like in colour. One of the angel faces in the latter picture strongly recalls the expression of Leonardo's heads, while the whole scheme of pure glowing colour closely resembles that employed by Di Credi in his graceful but slightly weak pictures of the Madonna and Child. This exquisite painting, one of the gems of the National Gallery, may possibly have been painted from Verrocchio's design by Lorenzo di Credi while he was under the immediate influence of his wonderful fellow-pupil Da Vinci.[1]

In examining Verrocchio's work as a sculptor we are on surer ground. One of his earliest works was the beautiful marble medallion of the Madonna, over the tomb of Leonardo Bruni of Arezzo in the church of Santa Croce at Florence, executed some years after Bruni's death (1443). In 1472 Verrocchio completed the fine tomb of Giovanni and Piero de' Medici, between the sacristy and the lady chapel of San Lorenzo at Florence. This consists of a great porphyry sarcophagus enriched with magnificent acanthus foliage in bronze. Above it is a graceful open bronze grill, made like a network of cordage. In 1474 Verrocchio began the monument to Cardinal Forteguerra at the west end of Pistoia cathedral. The kneeling figure of the cardinal was never completed, and now lies in a room of La Sapienza, but the whole design is shown in what is probably Verrocchio's original clay sketch, now in the South Kensington Museum (see

[1] See Crowe and Cavalcaselle, *Painting in Italy*, London, 1864, ii. p. 400 *sq.*

fig.). Though this work was designed by Verrocchio, the actual execution of it was entrusted to his assistant, the Florentine Lorenzetto. In 1476 Verrocchio modelled and cast the fine but too realistic bronze statue of David, now in the Bargello (Florence); and in the following year he completed one of the reliefs of the magnificent silver altar-frontal of the Florentine baptistery, that representing the Beheading of St John. Verrocchio's other works in the precious metals are now lost, but Vasari records that he made many elaborate pieces of plate and jewellery, such as morses for copes, as well as a series of silver statues of the Apostles for the pope's chapel in the Vatican. Between 1478 and 1483 he was occupied in making the bronze group of the Unbelief of St Thomas, which still stands in one of the external niches of Or San Michele (Florence). He received 800 florins for these two figures, which are more remarkable for the excellence of their technique than for their sculpturesque beauty. The attitudes are rather rigid, and the faces hard in expression. Verrocchio's chief masterpiece was the colossal bronze equestrian statue of the Venetian general Bartolomeo Colleoni, which stands in the piazza of SS. Giovanni e Paolo at Venice. Verrocchio received the order for this statue in 1479, but had only completed the model when he died in 1488. In spite of his request that the casting should be entrusted to his pupil Lorenzo di Credi, the work was given to Alessandro Leopardi by the Venetian senate, and the statue was gilt and unveiled in 1496.[1] There appears to be no doubt that the model was completed by Verrocchio himself, and that nothing more than its reproduction in bronze should be attributed to the much feebler hand of Leopardi, who, however, has set his own name alone on the belly-band of the horse—ALEXANDER · LEOPARDVS V. F. OPUS. This is perhaps the noblest equestrian statue in the world, being in some respects superior to the antique bronze of Marcus Aurelius in Rome and to that of Gattamelata at Padua by Donatello. The horse is designed with wonderful nobility and spirit, and the easy pose of the great general, combining perfect balance with absolute ease and security in the saddle, is a marvel of sculpturesque ability.[2] Most remarkable skill is shown by the way in which Verrocchio has exaggerated the strongly marked features of the general, so that nothing of its powerful effect is lost by the lofty position of the head.[3] According to Vasari, Verrocchio was one of the first sculptors who made a practical use of casts from living and dead subjects. He is said also to have produced plastic works in terra-cotta, wood, and in wax decorated with colour. As a sculptor his chief pupil was Francesco di Simone, the son of that Simone whom Vasari wrongly calls a brother of Donatello. Another pupil was Agnolo di Polo (Paolo), who worked chiefly in terra-cotta.

Clay sketch for the monument of Cardinal Forteguerra, showing the kneeling portrait of the cardinal, which is not in the actual monument; a very poor modern figure occupies its place.

Verrocchio died in Venice in 1488, and was buried in the church of St Ambrogio in Florence. (J. H. M.)

VERSAILLES, a town of France, chef-lieu of the department of Seine-et-Oise and an episcopal see, lies 11 miles west-south-west of Paris, with which it is connected by railways on both banks of the Seine and by a tramway. The town owes its existence to the palace (460 feet above the sea) built by Louis XIV. The fresh healthy air and the nearness of the town to Paris have attracted many residents, and the interest attaching to the place draws crowds of visitors. The population in 1881 was 48,012; in 1886 it was 49,514 (commune 49,852), including about 10,000 military.

The three avenues of St Cloud, Paris, and Sceaux converge in the Place d'Armes. Between them stand the former stables of the palace, now occupied by the artillery and engineers. To the south lies the quarter of Satory, the oldest part of Versailles, with the cathedral of St Louis, and to the north the new quarter, with the church of Notre Dame. To the west a gilded iron gate and a stone balustrade shut off the great court of the palace from the Place d'Armes. On either side are allegorical groups, besides statues of the statesmen Suger, Sully, Richelieu, and Colbert, the soldiers Duguesclin, Bayard, Turenne, and Condé, the sailors Duquesne, Tourville, Duguay-Trouin, and Suffren, and the marshals Jourdan, Masséna, Lannes, and Mortier. At the highest point of the court there is an equestrian statue in bronze of Louis XIV., and to the right and left of this stretch the long wings of the palace, while behind it stand the central buildings one behind the other as far as the Marble Court. Here all the lines of construction meet, and here were the rooms of Louis XIV. To the north the Chapel Court and to the south the Princes Court, with vaulted passages leading to the gardens, separate the side from the central buildings. On the latter is the inscription "À toutes les gloires de la France," which Louis Philippe justified by forming a collection of five thousand works of art (valued at £1,000,000), commemorating the great events and persons of French history. The palace chapel (1696-1710), the roof of which can be seen from afar rising above the rest of the building, was the last work of Mansard.

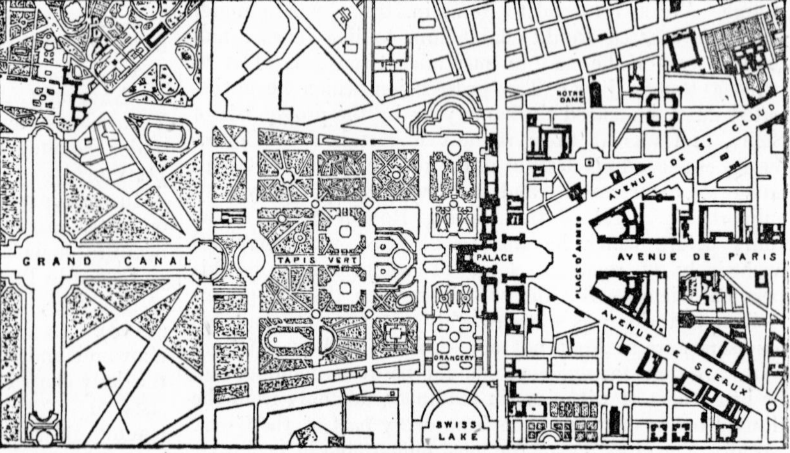

Plan of Versailles.

Opposite the altar is the king's gallery, which communicates with the rooms on the first floor of the palace. The ground-floor of the north wing on the garden side contains eleven halls of historical pictures from Clovis to Louis XIV., and on the side of the interior courts a gallery of tombs, statues, busts of kings and celebrities of France for the same period. The Halls of the Crusades open off

[1] See Gay, *Cart. Inéd.*, i. p. 367.

[2] See SCULPTURE, vol. xxi. p. 568, fig. 18.

[3] See Selvatico, *Arch. e Scult. in Venezia*, 1847; Cicognara, *Fabbriche piu Cospicue di Venezia*, 1853; and Milanesi's ed. of Vasari, iii. p. 357 *sq*.

this gallery, and are decorated with the arms of crusaders, kings, princes, lords, and knights, and with those of the grand-masters and knights of the military religious orders. On the first floor of the north wing on the garden side are ten halls of pictures commemorating historical events from 1795 to 1855; on the court side is the gallery of sculpture which contains the Joan of Arc of the Princess Marie of Orleans; and there are seven halls chiefly devoted to French campaigns and generals in Africa, Italy, the Crimea, and Mexico, with some famous war pictures by Horace Vernet. The second story has a portrait gallery. In the north wing is also the theatre built under Louis XV. by Gabriel, which was first used on the 16th of May 1770 on the marriage of the dauphin (afterwards Louis XVI.) and Marie Antoinette. Here, on 2d October 1789, the celebrated banquet was given to the Gardes du Corps, the toasts at which provoked the riots that drove the royal family from Versailles; and here the national assembly met from 10th March 1871 till the proclamation of the constitution in 1875, and the senate from 8th March 1876 till the return of the two chambers to Paris in 1879. The central buildings of the palace project into the garden. On the ground floor are the halls of celebrated warriors (once the anteroom of Madame de Pompadour), marshals, constables, and admirals. The Great Dauphin (son of Louis XIV.), the duke and duchess of Berri, the dauphin (son of Louis XV.), Madame de Montespan, Madame de Pompadour, and the daughters of Louis XV. all lived in this part of the palace. The gallery of Louis XIII., decorated with historical pictures of his and Louis XIV.'s time, leads to the halls surrounding the Marble Court. One of these contains many plans of battles, and at its door Louis XV. was wounded by Damiens in 1757. The lobbies of the ground floor are full of busts, statues, and tombs of kings and celebrated men. The famous state rooms are on the first floor. On the garden side, facing the north, are a series of seven halls,—among them that of Hercules, till 1710 the upper half of the old chapel, where the dukes of Chartres, Maine, and Burgundy were married, and Bossuet, Massillon, and Bourdaloue preached; the Hall of Mercury, where the coffin of Louis XIV. stood for eight days after his death; and the Hall of Apollo, or throne room. To the front of the palace, facing the west, are the Galleries of War and Peace, with allegorical pictures, and the Glass Gallery, built by Mansard in 1678 (240 feet long, 34 wide, and 43 high), having 34 arches, 17 of which are filled with windows looking on the gardens and 17 with large mirrors. The gallery is overloaded with ornament, and the pictures by Lebrun, the trophies and figures of children by Coysevox, and the inscriptions attributed to Boileau and Racine all glorify Louis XIV. This gallery was used by him as a throne room on state occasions. Here the king of Prussia was proclaimed emperor of Germany on 16th January 1871. Connected with the Gallery of Peace is the queen's room, occupied successively by Marie Thérèse, Marie Leczinska, and Marie Antoinette, where the duchess of Angoulême was born, the duchess of Burgundy died, and Marie Antoinette was almost assassinated on 6th October 1789. The Coronation Hall is so called from David's picture of Napoleon's coronation, which is regarded as the artist's masterpiece. This hall opens on the marble, or queen's, staircase. Behind the Glass Gallery on the side of the court are the rooms of Louis XIV. The Œil de Bœuf, named from its oval window, was the anteroom where the courtiers waited till the king rose. In it is a picture representing Louis XIV. and his family as Olympian deities; and it leads to the bedroom in which Louis XIV. died, after using it from 1701, and which Louis XV. occupied from 1722 to 1738. To the north of the Marble Court are the "petits appartements" of Louis XV. and to the south those of Marie Antoinette. Among the former is the Porcelain Gallery, where every year under Louis XVI. the best work made at Sèvres was displayed. On the second floor of the buildings surrounding the Stags Court Madame du Barry lived, and Louis XVI. afterwards worked at lockmaking. Marie Thérèse and Marie Leczinska had previously used the "petits appartements" of Marie Antoinette, one of the rooms of which is ornamented with woodwork of her time. In this part of the palace Madame de Maintenon and the duke of Burgundy had rooms, those of the latter being afterwards occupied by Cardinal de Fleury and the duke of Penthièvre. In the south wing of the palace, on the ground floor, are the Imperial Galleries (the first rooms of which were used by the duke and duchess of Bourbon under Louis XIV.) and the rooms occupied by the president of congress when the two legislative bodies meet together at Versailles. A sculpture gallery contains busts of celebrated scholars, artists, generals, and public men from the time of Louis XVI. onwards. In the south wing is also the room where the chamber of deputies met from 1876 till 1879, and where the congress has since sat to revise the constitution of 1875 and to elect the president of the republic. The first floor is almost entirely occupied by the Battle Gallery (394 feet long and 43 wide), opened in 1836 on the site of rooms used by Monsieur the brother of Louis XIV. and the duke and duchess of Chartres. It is lighted from above, and the walls are hung with pictures of French victories. In the window openings are the names of soldiers killed while fighting for France, with the names of the battles in which they fell, and there are more than eighty busts of princes, admirals, constables, marshals, and celebrated warriors who met a similar death. Another room is given up to the events of 1830 and the accession of Louis Philippe, and a gallery contains the statues and busts of kings and celebrities from Philip VI. to Louis XVI. In the rooms of the second story are portraits (mostly modern), sea-pieces, pictures of royal residences, and some historical pictures of the time of Louis Philippe.

The gardens of Versailles were planned by Le Nôtre. The best view is obtained from a balcony of the Glass Gallery. The ground falls away on every side from a terrace adorned with ornamental basins, statues, and bronze groups. Westwards from the palace extends a broad avenue, planted with large trees, and having along its centre the grass of the "Tapis Vert"; it is continued by the Grand Canal, 200 feet wide and 1 mile long. On the south two splendid staircases of 103 steps, 66 feet wide, lead past the Orangery to the Swiss Lake, 1312 feet long and 460 wide, beyond which is the wood of Satory. On the north an avenue, with twenty-two groups of three children, each group holding a marble basin, from which a jet of water rises, slopes gently down to the Basin of Neptune, remarkable for its fine sculptures and abundant water. The Orangery (built in 1685 by Mansard) is the finest piece of architecture at Versailles; the central gallery is 508 feet long and 42 wide, and each of the side galleries is 375 feet long. There are twelve hundred orange-trees, one of which is said to be 465 years old, and three hundred other kinds of trees. The alleys of the parks are ornamented with statues, vases, and regularly-cut yews, and bordered by hedges surrounding the shrubberies. Between the central terrace and the Tapis Vert is the Basin of Latona or the Frogs, with a white marble group of Latona with Apollo and Diana. Beyond the Tapis Vert is the large Basin of Apollo, who is represented in his chariot drawn by four horses; there are three jets of water, one 60, the others 50 feet in height. The Grand Canal is still used for nautical displays; under Louis XIV. it was covered with Venetian gondolas and other boats, and the evening entertainments usually ended with a display of fireworks. Around the Tapis Vert are numerous groves, the most remarkable being the Ballroom or Rockery, with a waterfall; the Queen's Shrubbery, the scene of the intrigue of the diamond necklace; that of the Colonnade, with thirty-two marble columns and a group of Pluto carrying off Proserpine, by Girardon; the King's Shrubbery, laid out in the English style by Louis Philippe; the beautiful Grove of Apollo, with a group of that god and the nymphs, by Girardon; and the Basin of Enceladus, with a jet of water 75 feet high. Among the chief attractions of Versailles are the fountains and waterworks made by Louis XIV. in imitation of those he had seen at Fouquet's chateau of Vaux. Owing to the scarcity of water at Versailles, the works at MARLY-LE-ROI (*q.v.*) were constructed in order to bring water from the Seine; but part of the supply thus obtained was diverted to the newly-erected château of Marly. Vast sums of money were spent and many lives lost in an attempt to bring water from the Eure, but the work was stopped by the war of 1688. At last the waters of the plateau between Versailles and Rambouillet were collected and led by channels (total length 98 miles) to the gardens, the soil of which covers innumerable pipes, vaults, and aqueducts. The total volume of water annually brought to Versailles is about 175,000,000 cubic feet, of which two-fifths supply the town and the rest the park.

Beyond the present park, but within that of Louis XIV., are the two Trianons. The Grand Trianon was originally erected as a retreat for Louis XIV. in 1670, but in 1687 Mansard built a new palace on its site. Louis XV., after establishing a botanic garden, made Gabriel build in 1766 the small pavilion of the Petit Trianon, where the machinery is still shown by which his supper-table came up through the floor. It was a favourite residence of Marie Antoinette, who had a garden laid out in the English style, and lived an imaginary peasant-life. The Grand Trianon is a one-storied building with two wings, and has been occupied by Monsieur (Louis XIV.'s brother), by the Great Dauphin, the duke of Burgundy, the duchess of Orleans, Napoleon I., and Louis Philippe and his court. The duke and duchess of Orleans lived in the Petit Trianon. The gardens of the Grand Trianon are in the same style as those of Versailles, and there is a museum with a curious collection of state carriages, old harness, &c.

Apart from the palace, there are no buildings of interest in Versailles, the church of Notre Dame, built by Mansard, the cathedral of St Louis, built by his grandson, the Protestant church, and the English chapel being in no way remarkable. The celebrated tennis-court is now used as a museum. The large and sumptuous palace of the prefecture was built during the second empire, and was a residence of the president of the republic from 1871 to 1879. The library consists of 60,000 volumes; and the military hospital formerly accommodated 2000 people in the service of the palace. There are a statue of General Hoche and one of Abbé de l'Épée in the town. A school of horticulture was founded in 1874, attached to an excellent garden, near the Swiss Lake.

Versailles is the seat of a school of artillery and of a school for non-commissioned officers of the artillery and engineers.

History.—Louis XIII. often hunted in the woods of Versailles, and built a small pavilion at the corner of what is now the Rue de La Pompe and the avenue of St Cloud. In 1627 he entrusted Lemercier with the plan of a château, and in 1632 bought the land from François de Gondi, first archbishop of Paris, for £2640. In 1661 Levau made some additions, and in 1682 Louis XIV. took up his residence at Versailles, and gave Mansard orders to erect the great palace in which the original buildings disappeared. Fabulous sums were spent on the palace, gardens, and works of art, the accounts for which were destroyed by the king. Till his time the town was represented by a few houses to the south of the present Place d'Armes; but land was given to the lords of the court and new houses sprang up, chiefly in the north quarter. Under Louis XV. the parish of St Louis was formed to the south for the increasing population, and new streets were built to the north on the meadows of Clagny, where in 1674 Mansard had built at Louis XIV.'s orders a château for Madame de Montespan, which was now pulled down. Under Louis XVI. the town extended to the east and received a municipality; in 1802 it gave its name to a bishopric. In 1783 the peace by which England recognized the independence of the United States was signed at Versailles. The states-general met here on 5th May 1789, and on 20th June took the solemn oath by which they bound themselves never to separate till they had given France a constitution, and which led to the riots of 5th and 6th October. Napoleon, Louis XVIII., and Charles X. merely kept up Versailles, but Louis Philippe restored its ancient splendour at the cost of £1,000,000. In 1870 and 1871 the town was the headquarters of the German army besieging Paris. After the peace Versailles was the seat of the French national assembly while the commune was triumphant in Paris, and of the two chambers till 1879, being declared the official capital of France. Versailles was the birthplace of Hoche, Abbé de l'Epée, Philip V. of Spain, Louis XV., Louis XVI., Louis XVIII., Charles X., Count de Maurepas, Prince de Polignac, Marshal Berthier (Prince of Wagram), Houdon the sculptor, Ducis the poet, Callet the mathematician, and Ferdinand de Lesseps. (G. ME.)

VERSECZ, a royal free town in the county of Temes, Hungary, 40 miles south of Temesvár. It is partly fortified and is the seat of a Greek bishop. Amongst its principal institutions are a high college for girls, a gymnasium, and a real school. Versecz is one of the principal wine-producing centres in the kingdom, its yearly export amounting to an average of five and a half million gallons. There is also a good trade in rice and silk. The population numbered 22,329 in 1880.

VERTEBRATA

VERTEBRATA, the name of a great branch or phylum of the Animal Kingdom which comprises those animals having bony "vertebræ", or pieces of bone jointed so as to form a spinal column. The first recognition of the group is due to Lamarck (1797), who united the four highest classes of Linnæus's system as "animaux à vertèbres," whilst distinguishing the rest of the animal world as "animaux sans vertèbres." The same union of the four Linnæan classes had been previously made by Batsch in 1788, who, however, proposed for the great division thus constituted the name "Knochenthiere." The significance of Lamarck's classification was materially altered, and the foundation laid of our present attempts to represent by our classifications the pedigree of the animal kingdom, when Cuvier propounded his doctrine of "types," and recognized the *Vertebrata* as one of four great types or plans of structure to be distinguished in the animal world (*1*).[1]

Lamarck's and Cuvier's classifications.

The *Vertebrata* of Lamarck and Cuvier included beasts, birds, reptiles, and fishes, and until recently the group was considered as one of the most sharply limited in the animal kingdom. The progress of anatomical studies very soon rendered it clear that all *Vertebrata* did not possess bony vertebræ; for, besides the commoner sharks and skates, with their purely cartilaginous skeletons, naturalists became acquainted with the structure of fishes, such as the sturgeons and the lampreys, which possess no vertebræ at all, but merely a continuous elastic rod (the notochord) in the place of the jointed spinal column. The muscles and their skeletal septa were seen in these fishes to be arranged in a series of segments attached to the sides of this continuous rod; and hence the structural character of bony vertebræ, as distinguishing the *Vertebrata*, gave place to the character of segmental arrangement of the muscles of the body-wall, such muscles being supported by a skeletal axis which might be itself unsegmented (notochord), or replaced by segmental cartilaginous or bony vertebræ. The studies of embryologists furnished a sound foundation for this conception by demonstrating that in the embryos of *Vertebrata* with true vertebræ these structures are preceded by an unsegmented continuous notochord. The inquiry into the structural characteristics of *Vertebrata* led further to the recognition of several additional points of structure, the combination of which was present only in the group which had been recognized by Lamarck on superficial grounds. It was found that all *Vertebrata* possess laterally-placed passages leading from the pharynx to the exterior, serving in the aquatic forms as the exits for water taken in by the mouth, and provided with vascular branchial processes, whilst in the embryos of the higher air-breathing classes they appear only as temporary structures. It was further established that the great mass of nervous tissue lying dorsally above the spinal column, and known as the cerebro-spinal nerve-centre or brain and spinal cord, is in all cases a tube, and originates as part of the dorsal surface of the embryo, which becomes depressed in the form of a long groove and finally closed in by the adhesion of its opposite edges, thus forming a tube or canal. The three structures,—notochord, gill-slits, and tubular dorsal nerve-cord,—were more than twenty years ago recognized as characterizing, together with the metameric segmentation of the musculature of the body-wall, all *Vertebrata* at some one or other period of their existence.

Essential structures of Vertebrates.

[1] These numerals refer to the bibliography at the end of the article.

The establishment by Darwin of the doctrine of organic evolution in 1859 led naturalists consciously to make the attempt to determine the genetic affinities and the probable ancestry of the various groups of animals, and enabled them to recognize in the classifications by "type", and other such conceptions of earlier systematists, the unconscious striving after genealogical representation of the relationships of organic beings. The question naturally arose in regard to the *Vertebrata*, as in regard to other great divisions of the animal kingdom, What were the characters of the earliest forms, the ancestors of those now living? Then came the further questions as to whether any surviving *Vertebrata* closely resemble the ancestral form, and whether any animals are still in existence which retain the general characters of those primeval forms which were the common ancestors at once of Vertebrates and of other large and equally well-marked phyla or branches of the animal kingdom, such as the Molluscs, the Annulates, &c. This fascinating subject of inquiry received its most important impulse from the embryological investigations of the Russian naturalist Kowalewsky, and has been for nearly a quarter of a century the fertile source of speculation and its indispensable accompaniments, new observation and research. Kowalewsky published in 1866 an account of the embryology of the lowest and simplest of then recognized Vertebrates, the lancelet (*Amphioxus lanceolatus*), in which he attempted to trace, cell for cell from the fertilized egg-cell, the origin of the characteristic

Question of Vertebrate ancestry.

Kowalewsky's labours.

Vertebrate organs of this animal (*2*). This work alone would not have acquired historic importance, although it is the starting-point of what may be called strict cellular embryology, as compared with the less severely histological works of previous students. But it was accompanied by an account (*3*) of the development of *Ascidia mamillata*, one of the so-called Tunicate Molluscs, in which it was demonstrated by Kowalewsky, not only that this supposed Mollusc possesses when first hatched from its egg-envelope a notochord, pharyngeal gill-slits, and a tubular dorsal nerve-cord and brain, but that these three characteristically Vertebrate features of organization originate from the same cell-layers of the embryo, and in essentially the same way as in *Amphioxus*, whilst the cell-layers themselves originate from the egg-cell in the two animals by precisely

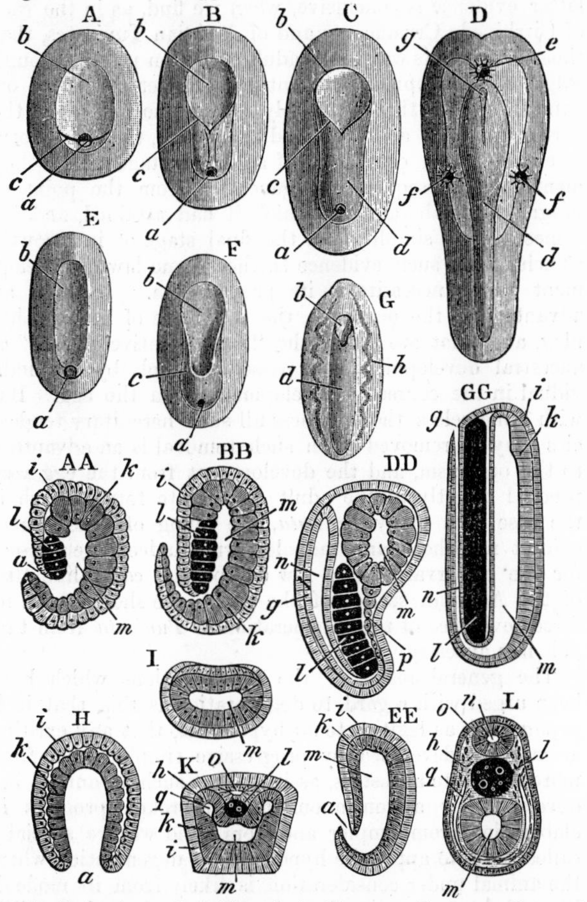

Fig. 1.—Early stages of *Ascidia* and *Amphioxus*. *a*, blastopore; *b*, neural groove; *c*, neural folds; *d*, closed portion of neural tube; *e*, commencing oral invagination (stomodæum) of Ascidian tadpole; *f*, right and left cloacal invaginations of Ascidian tadpole; *g*, anterior opening of neural tube of *Amphioxus*, coincident with the later developed olfactory pit; *h*, wall of one of the series of paired outgrowths of archenteron or cœlomic pouches of *Amphioxus*; *i*, ectoderm; *k*, endoderm (of diblastula phase); *l*, notochord, derived from endoderm; *m*, cavity of gut; *n*, cavity of nerve-tube; *o*, wall of nerve-tube, formed by upgrowth and union of neural folds; *p*, mesoblast of tail of Ascidian tadpole, derived from endoderm; *q*, lumen of cœlomic pouches of *Amphioxus*, once continuous with *m*, but nipped off in the course of development.

A, B, C, D. Four stages in development of *Ascidia*, surface views showing gradual enclosure of neural area. E, F, G. Three similar stages in development of *Amphioxus*. AA. Vertical antero-posterior median section of A. BB. Similar section of B. DD. Similar section of a stage a little earlier than D. EE. Similar section of E (*Amphioxus*). GG. Similar section of embryo represented in G. H. Transverse section of diblastula stage of *Amphioxus*, with widely open blastopore (earlier than A or E). I. Transverse (right and left) section about the middle of F, showing neural area. K. Transverse section about middle of G, showing nerve-tube, notochord, and cœlomic pouches or mesoblastic somites *q*. L. Transverse section of a much further advanced embryo of *Amphioxus*, showing nerve-tube, notochord, and gut; the walls of the cœlomic pouches are now converted into muscular tissue and the pouch cavity (*q*) compressed. (All the figures after Kowalewsky, *17*, *18*.)

similar movements of cell division and invagination (see figs. 1 and 2). Kowalewsky's discoveries established once for all that the Ascidian tadpole is identical in three very special and distinct features of structure with the frog's tadpole. No classification which pretended to set forth the genetic affinities of animals could henceforth separate

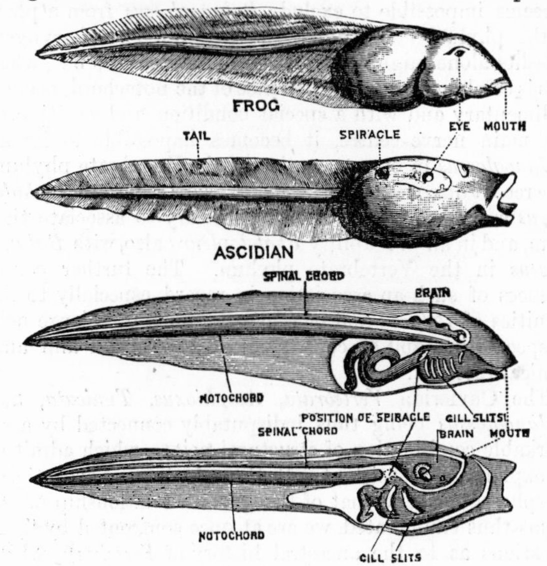

Fig. 2.—Diagram illustrating relationship of tadpoles of Frog and Ascidian. The two upper figures represent surface views of the tadpoles; the two lower ones show in place the chief Vertebrate organs, viz., notochord, gill-slits, nerve-tube, and myelonic eye. (From Lankester's *Degeneration*.)

the Ascidian from the *Vertebrata*, and with it the Ascidian brought the whole series of *Tunicata*.

Admission of *Tunicata* as Vertebrates.

The admission of *Tunicata* as a group of *Vertebrata* was proposed by the present writer as long ago as 1877 (*4*); but it required the intermediate proposition by Balfour of a group *Chordata*, to comprise the two divisions *Tunicata* and *Vertebrata*, in order to render the final admission of *Tunicata* to their proper association with the *Vertebrata* of Cuvier palatable to systematists. As an objection to the simple inclusion of *Tunicata* in the great phylum *Vertebrata* it has been urged that *Tunicata* do not possess vertebræ,—a proposition which is equally true of *Amphioxus* and of some Fishes. Shifting the objection, some writers have maintained that the vertebration of the *Vertebrata* may be understood as having reference to the segmentation of the muscles of the body-wall, which is exhibited by all Cuvier's *Vertebrata* without exception, inclusive of *Amphioxus*, though not by *Tunicata*. To this it may be replied that the Ascidian tadpole, and more clearly the free-swimming Tunicate *Appendicularia* (see fig. 9), do exhibit a segmentation of the muscles of the hinder part of the body-wall similar to and identical with that of *Amphioxus*, whilst no such strict application of a name in its original descriptive sense is desirable in systematic nomenclature. All *Gastropoda* (it has been pointed out) are not gastropodous; all *Arthropoda* are not arthropodous; and many *Echinoderma* are not echinodermous. It is, in the present writer's opinion, better to retain an historic and familiar name for the great branch of the animal pedigree to which it has become necessary to admit forms whose affinities therewith were at one time unsuspected rather than to sacrifice historical significance to a futile striving after etymological accuracy.

Inclusion of *Balanoglossus* in Vertebrate phylum.

The admission of *Tunicata* to association with Cuvier's *Vertebrata* has been followed by a further innovation. The remarkable marine worm *Balanoglossus*—originally described by Della Chiaje at the end of the 18th century—was shown in 1866 by Kowalewsky (*5*) to possess a series of pharyngeal gill-slits similar to those of *Tunicata* and *Amphioxus*. Later researches by Bateson (*6*) have demonstrated that *Balanoglossus* develops in embryonic life a short notochord, whilst its nerve-cord is, in part at least, tubular, and similar in position and relations to the median epidermal tract by the infolding of which the nerve-tube of *Tunicata* and the other *Vertebrata* is formed. Hence it seems impossible to exclude *Balanoglossus* from a place in the phylum *Vertebrata.* The possession of pharyngeal gill-slits alone might not justify the association; but, when this is combined with the presence of the notochord, though rudimentary and with a special condition and position of the main nerve-centre, it becomes impossible to ignore *Balanoglossus* in our conception of the Vertebrate phylum. The recent discoveries of Harmer (*7*) with regard to *Cephalodiscus* will hereafter render it necessary to associate that form, and in all probability *Rhabdopleura* also, with *Balanoglossus* in the Vertebrate phylum. The further consequences of such an association in regard especially to the affinities of *Polyzoa* and of *Gephyræa* open up a large field of speculation and of consequent embryological and anatomical research.

Ancestral form of Vertebrates. The Cuvierian *Vertebrata*, *Amphioxus*, *Tunicata*, and *Balanoglossus* being thus indisputably connected by a remarkable combination of structural points, which admit of no explanation consistent with the principles of evolutional morphology except that of the genetic relationship of the forms thus enumerated, we are at once confronted by those questions as to the ancestral history of *Vertebrata* which have been already mentioned above as stimulated by Kowalewsky's discoveries. Undoubtedly *Amphioxus* is lower and simpler in structure than any Fish, *Tunicata* as low as or lower than *Amphioxus*, and *Balanoglossus*, in some respects, more archaic than either *Amphioxus* or the Ascidian tadpole. The first tendency arising from the discovery of the affinities of these simpler forms with the Cuvierian *Vertebrata* was to see in them the representatives of the ancestors of all *Vertebrata.* *Amphioxus* has been pointed to by authorities in morphology as the living presentation of our common Vertebrate ancestor; a similar position corresponding to an earlier stage of development has been admitted by no less an authority than Darwin for the Ascidian. It appears, nevertheless, that all such simple solutions of the problem of Vertebrate ancestry are without warrant. They arise from a very common tendency of the mind, against which the naturalist has to guard himself,—a tendency which finds expression in the very widespread notion that the existing anthropoid apes, and more especially the gorilla, must be looked upon as the ancestors of mankind, if once the doctrine of the descent of man from ape-like forefathers is admitted. A little reflexion suffices to show that any given living form, such as the gorilla, cannot possibly be the ancestral form from which man was derived, since *ex hypothesi* that ancestral form underwent modification and development, and in so doing ceased to exist. The same considerations apply to the question of the ancestry of *Vertebrata.* Probably no existing low form of Vertebrate *closely* represents the ancestral form by the modification of which higher forms have been developed. We have no justification for assuming that such low forms do more than present to us a collateral branch of the family, and that collateral branch must, in all probability, have experienced its own special series of modifications of structure. **Arguments from simplicity of structure.** Not only this, but we have no sufficient ground for assuming that, even in respect of the simplicity of their structure, any given animal forms at present existing exhibit a mere survival of a corresponding degree of simplicity in their remote ancestors. Such an assumption was almost universally made, until a more correct view was pressed on the attention of naturalists by Dr Anton Dohrn, the founder of the zoological station of Naples (*8*). So far from its being the case that simplicity of organization necessarily implies the continuous hereditary transmission of a low stage of structural development from remote ancestors, there are numerous instances in which it is certain that the existing simplicity of structure is due to a process of degeneration, and that an existing form of simple structure is thus descended from ancestors of far higher complexity of organization than itself. Such are various parasitic worms and *Crustacea.* The evidence in favour of the occurrence of progressive simplification of structure or degeneration, in place of progressive elaboration, depends (1) upon the comparison of the adult structure of the degenerate organism with that of its nearest allies, by which it is often rendered clear that the *ensemble* of the organization of the simpler organism cannot be explained on the hypothesis that it represents an ancestral or archaic condition common to it and its more elaborate congeners, and (2) on the direct evidence of individual development or life-history. The latter evidence is conclusive, when we find, as in the case of Cirrhipede Crustaceans and of Ascidian Tunicates, that the embryo on its way to the adult condition passes through stages of development presenting a higher degree of organization than that ultimately reached, so that, as in the Cirrhipede larva and the Ascidian tadpole, the young form resembles allied organisms of a higher stage of development, and subsequently degenerates from the point of progressive elaboration to which it had attained, and becomes greatly simplified in the final stage of its growth. Conclusive as such evidence is, there is no law of development which necessitates its preservation. If it be an advantage to the organism, the full force of heredity has play, and what are called the "recapitulative phases" of ancestral development are passed through by the individual in the course of development from the egg. But with remorseless thoroughness all such hereditary tendencies may be removed when such removal is an advantage to the organism, and the development from the egg *may* proceed directly to the adult degenerate form. Such is the case with many *Tunicata*, the young of which never exhibit notochord and tadpole form; indeed, were it not for the preservation of a few exceptional cases, like that of the Ascidian section of the group, we should have no direct evidence of the degeneration of *Tunicata* from tadpole-like ancestry.

Hypothesis of degeneration. The general result of the considerations which have been urged with regard to degeneration is this, that it is *prima facie* as legitimate an hypothesis, that any existing animal has developed by progressive simplification from more elaborate ancestors, as it is that such an animal has developed by a continuous and unbroken progress in elaboration from simpler ancestors; and we are specially called upon to apply the hypothesis of degeneration where the animal under consideration is likely from its mode of life to have undergone that process. Such modes of life, tending to degeneration, are parasitism, sessile or adherent habit, burrowing in the sea-bottom, and diffuse feeding. The animal which pursues living prey, and contends with other organisms for the dominion of the regions of earth and water that are flooded with light and richly supplied with oxygen gas, is the animal which represents the outcome of a longer or shorter period of progressive elaboration. It is worth while noting in parenthesis that in all cases the "whirligig of time" has probably brought its revenges, and that the ancestry of a form evolved through a long period of progressive elaboration was at an antecedent period subject to simplification and degeneration, whilst in the past records of the present exemplars of the latter process there must certainly have been long stretches of continuous elaboration.

Genealogical tree. Applying these considerations to the construction of the genealogical tree of *Vertebrata*, we find that the task is by no means simplified. We cannot with the earliest evolutionists adopt a scale or ladder-like series, placing the simplest form on the lowest step; nor can we be satisfied with a tree-like arrangement, in which the forms at the ends of the branches are always more elaborate than those nearer the trunk. Our genealogical tree will more strictly conform to that of a parvenu human family, if we take worldly prosperity in the latter case as corresponding to elaboration of structure in the former. The strict family genealogist will include in the successive ramifications of the tree the five sons of the founder of the family, one of whom remained an agricultural labourer, whilst two became brewers and two emigrated. The cousins in the next generation will be set forth in place, the sons of one brewer becoming paupers, whilst those of the other advance to the position of Government employés, and one to the peerage. Thus in successive branchings of the family history there may be alternate progress and degeneration. And so it must be in the genealogical trees constructed by the naturalist: the fact that a branch is later in origin will not imply that it is higher in elaboration than those below it, and accordingly we must not expect to draw our tree so as to be able to trace all simpler forms to lower off-sets of the tree.

Divisions of Vertebrate phylum.

The structural features of those animals which must be admitted to the Vertebrate phylum in consequence of possessing notochord, pharyngeal gill-slits, and dorsal nerve-plate, tubular or unrolled, are such as enable us very readily to group them in four great divisions, which appear to be equally distinct from one another. As to what may be the genetic relations to one another of these four groups we will inquire subsequently; for the present we term these groups "branches." They are as follows:—

Phylum VERTEBRATA.

Branch *a*—*Craniata* (Cuvierian *Vertebrata*).
,, *b*—*Cephalochorda* (*Amphioxus*).
,, *c*—*Urochorda* (*Tunicata*).
,, *d*—*Hemichorda* (*Balanoglossus*).

The *Vertebrata* thus limited may be defined as Cœlomate *Enterozoa* (*Metazoa*) with well-developed cœlom. In all, with the exception of the more degenerate members of *Urochorda*, an elastic skeletal rod—the notochord—is developed dorsally by an outgrowth of cells forming the wall of the primitive archenteron; the notochord may or may not persist in adult life. Pharyngeal gill-slits, which may or may not persist in adult life, are developed in all Vertebrates. In all, except in certain *Urochorda*, the chief nerve-centre has the form of a dorsal, median, elongate tract, derived from the epiblast, which becomes sunk below the surface and invaginated so as to form a tube. In all there is a tendency to metameric repetition of parts, which may find its expression in a strongly-marked segmentation of the musculature of the body-wall and its skeleton, or may be recognizable only in a limited degree, as exhibited by the successive gill-slits or successive gonads.

We shall now examine the distinctive features of each of these large groups, and form an estimate of their relations to one another, and of their probable ancestry, this being the task to which we must limit ourselves in the brief space here afforded.

The Craniata.

Characters of *Craniata*.

The *Craniata* are *Vertebrata* in which the tubular cerebro-spinal nerve-mass is swollen anteriorly to form a brain, consisting primarily of three successive vesicles, in connexion with the anterior of which the special nerves of the olfactory organs and of the eyes originate. The notochord, whilst extending posteriorly to the extremity of the body, does not reach quite so far forward anteriorly as the termination of the nerve-tube. A cartilaginous cranium or brain-case develops round the anterior extremity of the nerve-cord, and rises up laterally so as to enclose and protect the brain (hence *Craniata*). Cartilage is developed in other parts of the body as a skeletal substance, though it may be subsequently replaced in the cranium, as elsewhere, by bone. The longitudinal muscles of the body-wall are divided by transverse fibrous septa into a series of segments, varying in the adult from ten to one hundred or more in number. Cartilaginous neural arches, corresponding in number and position to the fibrous septa, and resting on the notochord, are developed so as to protect the nerve-cord. Cartilaginous bars also pass outwards, with a direction at first horizontal and then ventral, from the sides of the notochord into the intermuscular fibrous septa. Very generally, but not always, a tubular cartilaginous sheath forms round the notochord; this sheath with rare exceptions becomes segmented to form a series of vertebral bodies, which lie in the planes of the fibrous intersegmental septa, and, increasing in thickness by encroaching upon the substance of the notochord, finally obliterate it almost entirely.

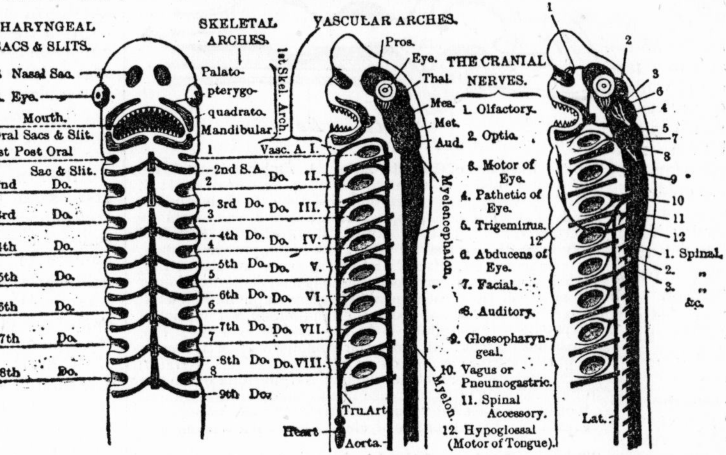

Fig. 3.—Three diagrams showing characteristic disposition of gill-slits, skeletal arches, vascular arches, and furcal nerves in a primitive ideal Craniate. The following abbreviations require explanation:—*pros.*, prosencephalon; *thal.*, thalamencephalon; *mes.*, mesencephalon; *met.*, metencephalon; *aud.*, otocyst or auditory sac; *tru. art.*, truncus arteriosus. (Original.)

The pharyngeal slits follow closely upon the mouth, and in existing *Craniata* never number more than eight pairs (see fig. 3). They are separated from one another and their apertures strengthened by a series of cartilaginous hoops, the first of which, that between the mouth and the first gill-slit, forms the primitive upper and lower jaw in all but the small and degenerate group *Cyclostoma*. The gill-slits when functional are generally protected by an opercular fold of the body-wall, which overhangs them and corresponds to the epipleural fold of *Amphioxus*, the collar of *Balanoglossus*, and doubtfully to the wall of the atrial chamber of *Urochorda*. The extension of this fold along the sides of the middle third of the body (between the pharyngeal region and the anus) acquired in ancestral *Craniata* the function of a continuous right and left lateral fin (see fig. 4). At the same time a continuous median fin, corre-

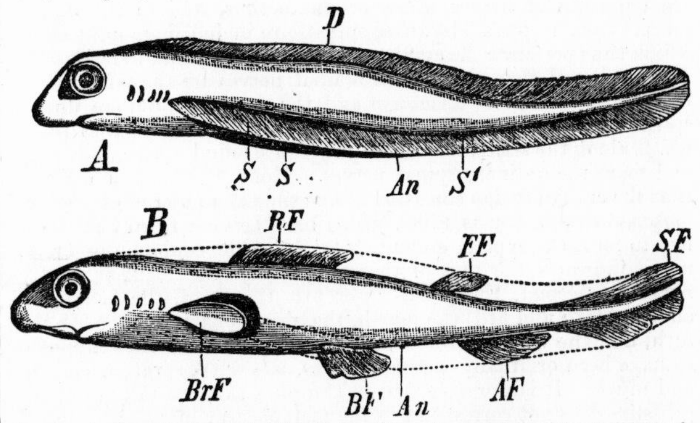

Fig. 4.—A. Hypothetical primitive Fish, with continuous lateral fins S, S (paired right and left), confluent with median azygos fin (*An*), the post-anal part of which is marked S', whilst its dorsal part is marked D. B. Actual Fish, showing relation of isolated lateral and median fins to original hypothetical fins of the upper figure. BrF, left pectoral fin (paired); BF, left pelvic fin (paired); AF, anal (post-anal) azygos fin; SF, caudal azygos fin; RF and FF, anterior and posterior azygos dorsal fins; An, anus. (From Wiedersheim.)

sponding to the dorsal, caudal, and anal fins of existing Fishes, was developed. In both lateral and median fins a cartilaginous skeleton was developed, consisting of a basal longitudinal bar, supporting a number of rods like the teeth of a comb. The primitive form of fin skeleton is retained in the median fins of some sharks; the primitive lateral fin has in all cases either entirely disappeared (*Cyclostoma*) (as has their anterior extension, the operculum, in many cases) or it has become, together with its skeletal elements, concentrated in two regions—forming the pectoral and the pelvic paired appendages or limbs, with their respective girdles.

The cerebro-spinal nerve-centre and the disposition of the nerves issuing from it present a remarkable complexity, and at the same time uniformity, of structure in all *Craniata* (see fig. 5). The foremost of the three primary cerebral vesicles gives rise to paired anterior outgrowths, the prosencephala, to a median dorsal outgrowth, the stalk of the pineal eye (rudimentary in all existing *Craniata*), and to a median ventral outgrowth, which is met by an invagination of the epidermis of the oral cavity forming the pituitary body, further, to a pair of lateral outgrowths, which become the right and left optic nerves and retinæ respectively. The modifications of the hindmost of the three primary vesicles are also extremely definite and persistent throughout the group: its anterior dorsal surface enlarges and becomes the cerebellum (the metencephalon), whilst the cavity of its hinder part (the medulla oblongata or the epencephalon) becomes comparatively wide, and is covered dorsally by a thin membrane only, in which nervous tissue does not take a part. The intermediate primary cerebral vesicle (the mesencephalon) does not give rise to outgrowths.

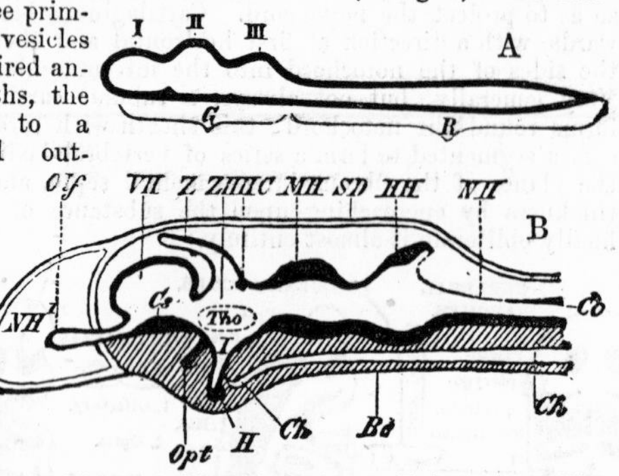

Fig. 5.—Diagrams of Craniate brain. A. Embryonic condition of neural tube. G, Cerebral portion; R, spinal cord; I, II, III, three primary cerebral vesicles. B. Longitudinal section of adult brain, applicable to any and every Craniate Vertebrate. *Bc*, Floor of skull; *Ch*, notochord; *SD*, roof of skull; NH[1], nasal cavity; VH, fore-brain, prosencephalon, or cerebrum; *Olf*, olfactory lobe; *Cs*, corpus striatum; ZH, thalamencephalon, corresponding to primary anterior vesicle, from which the prosencephalon has grown out as well as Z, the epiphysis or pineal body; I, infundibulum, with attached hypophysis or pituitary body H; *Opt*, optic nerve; *Tho*, thalamus opticus; HC, posterior commissure; MH, mesencephalon (*corpora quadrigemina* or optic lobes or mid-brain); HH, cerebellum or metencephalon; NH, medulla oblongata or epencephalon (the reference line touches the membranous roof of the so-called "fourth ventricle" of the brain); *Co*, canal of the spinal cord or myelon. (From Wiedersheim.)

In all *Craniata* nerves are given off from the cerebro-spinal cord or tube with great regularity, one right and left in each successive myomere or segment of the body-wall. Each nerve has two roots, a dorsal (sensory) and a ventral (motor). A commissure between each successive pair of deep or intestinal branches of the spinal nerves forms the so-called sympathetic nerve-cords, one on each side of the vertebral column. Nerves similar to the spinal nerves, but not identical with them, are given off from the brain, and perforate the cranial box right and left. In all *Craniata* there are ten pairs of nerves which originate thus, and in the higher forms two more pairs (elsewhere spinal) are included amongst those which thus perforate the cranium (spinal accessory and hypoglossal). The order and character of the cranial nerves are the same in all *Craniata*. The first (olfactory) and the second (optic) are unlike spinal nerves in both distribution and origin. As we pass backwards along the series, the cranial nerves are found to resemble more and more the ordinary spinal nerves. Hence it has been inferred that the cranial region consisted at one time of a number of distinct myomeres (as many as nine), which have become fused and modified to form the typical craniate "head." The oculo-motor or 3d nerve indicates the first of these segments, the trochlear or 4th nerve the second, the abducens or 6th the third, the facial and auditory (7th and 8th) the fourth, the glosso-pharyngeal or 9th the fifth, and the vagus or 10th, with certain of its branches supposed to have been originally distinct nerves, the sixth, seventh, eighth, and ninth. It is probable that in *Craniata* the metamerism of the gill-slits does not correspond to the metamerism of the body-wall. The mouth and each successive gill-slit are related to a bifurcate branch of a cranial nerve (furcal nerve) in lower *Craniata* (see fig. 3); these furcal nerves do not correspond, so far as we can at present judge, with cranial myomeres.

The lateral pair of eyes (as opposed to the rudimentary pineal or parietal eye) present a striking uniformity of origin and structure throughout *Craniata*. Not only are they uniformly developed from three elements, viz., the retinal cup which grows out from the anterior of the primary cerebral vesicles, the epidermal lens which grows inwards from the surface of the skin, and the connective tissue between these two, but we find that the muscles attached to the eyeball are identical throughout the series: that is, the superior, inferior, and internal rectus, and the inferior oblique muscles represent the first cranial myomere, the superior oblique represent the second, and the external rectus represent the third cranial myomere.

The olfactory sacs are paired in all except *Cyclostoma*, in which they are represented by a single sac which may or may not be archaic in its azygos character. The auditory sacs are paired organs which develop as invaginations from the surface,—the orifice of invagination closing up,—at the hinder part of the cranial region. They present a gradually increasing complexity of form as we pass from aquatic to terrestrial forms, but are identical in essential structure throughout.

All *Craniata*, except some Fishes, possess a muscular process on the floor of the oral cavity which may carry teeth, or act as a licking organ, or assist in suction. This is the tongue.

All *Craniata*, with degradational exceptions, possess an outgrowth, single or paired, of the post-pharyngeal region of the alimentary canal, which is filled with gas. In many Fishes this becomes shut off from the gut; in others it remains in communication with the gut by an open duct. In Fishes it functions as a hydrostatic apparatus. In terrestrial *Craniata* it is subservient to the gas-exchange of the blood and becomes the lungs.

All *Craniata* have a large and compact liver; and a pancreas is also uniformly present, except in *Cyclostoma*, some bony Fishes, and the lower *Amphibia*.

All *Craniata* have a thick-walled muscular heart, which appears first as an "atrium," receiving the great veins, attached to a "ventricle" by which the blood received from the atrium is propelled through a number of arteries, right and left, corresponding in number to the pharyngeal gill-slits between which they pass. A præatrial chamber (the sinus) and an extra-ventricular chamber (the conus) are added to the primitive chambers; but the most important modifications arise in consequence of the development of pulmonary respiration and the gradual separation of the cavities of the heart by median septa into a double series, a right and a left. The plan of the great arteries in all *Craniata* is in origin the same, and is determined by the primitive existence of a branchial circulation in the gill-slits, which is obliterated in higher forms. Similarly the plan of the great veins is identical, the primitive posterior vertebral veins of lower *Craniata*, though persistent in higher members of the group, having their function gradually usurped by the excessive development of the renal vein, and of renal-portal and ultimately of iliac veins.

All *Craniata* have a lymphatic system or series of channels by which the exudation from the capillary blood-vessels is returned to the vascular system. It includes in its space-system the cœlom and a variety of irregular and canalicular spaces in the connective tissues. Masses of spongy tissue (adenoid tissue, lymphatic glands) exist, through which the lymph filters, and there acquires corpuscular elements as well as chemical elaboration. At various points in various *Craniata* pulsating or simple communications are established between the lymphatic system and the veins. A special and characteristic communication is established in the spleen, an organ which is found in all *Craniata*, either as a single mass or as scattered masses of spongy tissue in which blood-vessels and lymphatics unite.

The renal organs of *Craniata* are primitively a series of nephridia corresponding in number to the myotomes of the mid-region of the body in which they exist. They are connected in the simplest *Craniata* by a right and a left archinephric duct, which appear to be in origin lateral grooves of the epidermal surface. This primitive renal system has been modified in some lower forms (*Cyclostoma* and Teleostean Fishes) by the atrophy of its anterior portion. But in all other *Craniata* it acquires relations to the gonads or ovary and testes, so that an anterior portion of the archinephros and a corresponding longitudinal tract of the duct become separated to serve as oviduct, a middle portion to serve as sperm-duct, while a posterior portion retains exclusively or shares with the middle portion the function of urinary excretion. The male and female gonads are, with the rarest exceptions, developed in distinct individuals, though the rudiments of the suppressed gonad may in some cases (*Amphibia*) be traceable in either sex.

Sub-divisions of *Craniata*.

The group of Craniate *Vertebrata* thus anatomically described, whilst retaining the essential unity indicated, presents an immense variety of modifications. The chief modifications are distinctly traceable to and accounted for by mechanical and physiological adaptation to a terrestrial and air-breathing life, as opposed to the earlier aquatic and branchial condition. The existing forms of *Craniata* have been arrested at several points, in the progress towards the most extreme adaptation to terrestrial conditions, which is presented by those forms that can not only breath air and live on dry ground but fly habitually in the air. The organs most obviously affected by this progressive adaptation are the skin, the skeleton, especially of the limbs, the pharyngeal gills, and the air-bladder. This fact will appear most clearly in the subjoined classification of *Craniata*; for space does not permit us to pursue further the history of these modifications.

Classification of CRANIATA.[1]

Grade A. CYCLOSTOMA.
Class I. *Myxinoidea.*
II. *Petromyzontia.*
Grade B. GNATHOSTOMA.
Grade a. **Branchiata heterodactyla.**
Class I. *Pisces.*
II. *Dipnoi.*
Grade b. **Branchiata pentadactyla.**
Class. *Amphibia.*
Grade c. **Pentadactyla lipobranchia.**
Branch a. Monocondyla. *Branch b. Amphicondyla.*
Class I. *Reptilia.* Class. *Mammalia.*
II. *Aves.*

Ancestral form of *Craniata.*

If we now briefly consider what must have been the common ancestral form from which these *Craniata* have proceeded, making use of such internal evidence as their structure affords, we find that we get no further back than such an animal as would fit the description given above, with the exception that we should be warranted in substituting in the ancestor a pair of continuous lateral fins, with comb-like cartilaginous skeleton, in place of the two pairs of fins, or their total defect, seen in living *Craniata.* We get no clear suggestion from the study of *Craniata* themselves as to the meaning of the curious shape of the brain and its outgrowths (though the pineal outgrowth has recently been explained as an eye), nor as to the original genesis of the notochord. We should, however, be justified in representing that region which now corresponds to the hinder part of the skull and brain as more fully developed and segmented, so as to give a series of separate myotomes and perhaps separate nerves corresponding to the several furcal branches of the vagus; and we may very well suppose that the number of pharyngeal gill-slits was larger in the ancestral than in any living form, though it seems improbable that in any true Craniate did each gill-slit correspond to a distinct muscular segment.

An attempt to go further than this has been made by Dr Anton Dohrn by the method of hypothesis and subsequent corroborative inquiry into facts of minute structure and embryological history. Making use of the principle of degeneration, Dohrn started with the legitimate hypothesis that the branches of *Vertebrata* other than *Craniata*—viz., *Cephalochorda*, *Urochorda*, and (though at the time he commenced his work their structure was not fully understood) *Hemichorda*—were not to be regarded as permanent records of steps in the evolution of *Craniata*, but rather as greatly degenerate offshoots from the ancestors of that group, which could throw but little light on the character of their non-degenerate ancestors. A second fundamental assumption which led Dohrn to his position was that the segmentation of the Craniates' body-wall is a primitive and essential feature in their structure, and becomes more and more fully expressed instead of less developed the further we go back in their ancestry. Dohrn, in fact, assumes that what is called metameric segmentation is a phenomenon of structure which has occurred once only in the history of animal form, and that all segmented animals are genetically related and descended from a common segmented ancestor. Assuming this, he pointed to the existing Chætopod Worms as most nearly representing at the present day the common ancestor of segmented animals. They have, as he pointed out, a high organization, little inferior to that of the lowest *Craniata*; they possess a well-developed cœlom, blood-vessels with red blood, a segmental series of nephridia (modified in some as gonaducts), segmental branchiæ, and lateral locomotive organs; not a few develop cartilage as a skeletal support; and many show a concentration and fusion of segments to form a complex head, which resembles, so far, that of *Craniata.* The ventral in place of the dorsal position of the nerve-cord led Dohrn to accept De Blainville's conception that the dorsal and ventral surfaces are reversed in *Vertebrata*, as compared with Annelids, Crustaceans, and Insects, so that the Vertebrate is compared to an Insect walking with its ventral surface upward. This led further to the notion that the mouth of the Chætopod or Annelid, which penetrates the nerve-cord, or rather passes between its two divaricated lateral constituents in those animals, has in *Craniata* disappeared, its place being taken by a new mouth derived from the modification of a pair of gill-slits. The remnant of the old mouth, which should, if the comparison instituted holds good, lie in *Craniata* somewhere on the dorsal surface of the cranial region, was sought by Dohrn in some of the peculiar and hitherto unexplained median structures of the brain: at one time the fourth ventricle with its deficient roof was suggested as thus to be explained, whilst subsequently the curious median structures,—the pineal and pituitary bodies,—were called in as possibly thus significant.

Without pursuing further the elaboration of Dohrn's views, it must be at once noted that, whilst the legitimacy of the assumption of degeneration must be admitted, the second assumption, viz., that metameric segmentation is a character bringing all forms showing it into a special genetic continuity, cannot be accepted. The property of repeating units of structure, so as to build up a complex of many similar parts united to form one individual, is a very general one in organic forms, and is exhibited in various conditions by both animals and plants. Its simplest expression is found in cell-structure and the binary division of cells. It shows itself as affecting larger masses of structure in the arborescent colonies of *Cœlentera*, in the radial or antimeric composition of Echinoderms and of Compound Ascidians, and in the linear or metameric segmentation of Worms, Arthropods, and Vertebrates. There is abundant evidence that this property is a general one, which may assert itself at any period in the history of a group of animals, and does not imply special unity of origin in forms which exhibit it. As pointed out in the article HYDROZOA, merogenesis —the name applicable to this phenomenon generally—may take an extreme and complete character, leading to the separation and independence of the units of structure produced; in that case it may be termed eumerogenesis. Or the process may be very partial, occurring only during a period of embryonic growth, and subsequently ceasing, so that later growth obscures or obliterates it altogether (dysmerogenesis). There is no ground for assuming that either one of these extremes is fundamental or original. Any mechanical or nutritional condition may lead to merogenesis in an organism in which the tissues have a certain reproductive capacity, or have not acquired final differentiation; and it will depend upon the balance of advantage, determined by natural selection, whether the segmentation (supposing the merogenesis to take the linear form) results in the separation of segment-buds, or in the formation of an annulate body, or leaves traces of its occurrence only in certain tissues and organs. The Cestoid Worms present within the range of a single group almost every grade of eumerogenesis and dysmerogenesis (*Caryophyllæus, Ligula, Tænia*). In the otherwise amerogenetic *Mollusca*, Chiton and the pearly Nautilus show dysmerogenesis in certain organs, whilst the Planarian Worms frequently exhibit eumerogenesis in their bud-segmentation (to be compared with that of the Annelid *Ctenodrilus* described by Zeppelin, *9*) and the elongated Nemertines only slight traces of dysmerogenesis.

If we deny Dohrn's assumption with reference to segmentation, we are no longer led in the direction of the Annelids (Chætopods) in our search for the ancestry of the Craniate *Vertebrata.*

The fact that the notochord is the forerunner of the segmented vertebral column, and is itself never segmental, instead of being a difficulty, acquires directive significance. The fact that the nerve tube is dorsal, and not ventral, no longer requires the large assumption that animals have reversed their habitual carriage, but suggests that the Craniates' ancestor had a dorsal median nerve, which has increased in size and importance so as to become the nerve-tube of existing forms. The explanation of the curious structure of the brain will have to be found otherwise than in the assumption of a perforating pharynx,—an assumption which the recent discovery of the true nature of the pineal body has rendered untenable in the latest form advocated by its ingenious author, whose speculations, nevertheless, deserve the fullest recognition as having stimulated inquiry and guided observation.

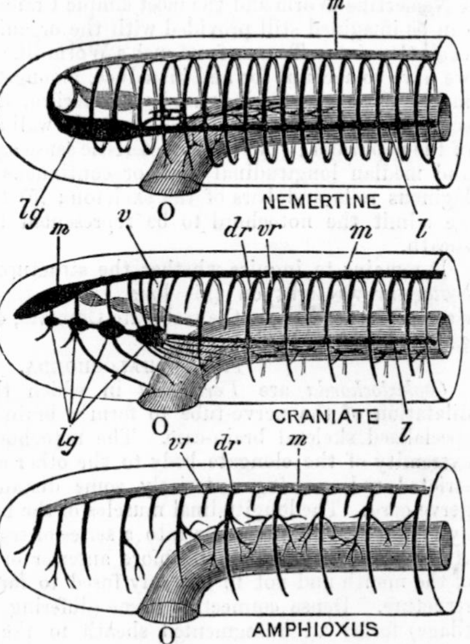

FIG. 6.—Comparison of nervous systems of a Nemertine, a primitive Craniate, and *Amphioxus*. *m*, Median dorsal nerve, which becomes the myelon in the Craniate and *Amphioxus*, acquiring an anterior enlargement in the former; *l*, lateral nerve (right and left), absent by degeneration in *Amphioxus*; *lg*, ganglia of lateral nerve, forming a single large lobe on each side in the Nemertine, and broken into a metameric series in the Craniate; *v*, roots of vagus nerve of the Craniate; *dr*, dorsal roots of nerves given off from myelon or median dorsal nerve; *vr*, ventral roots of these nerves, here represented as separate nerves; *O*, mouth. (After Hubrecht.)

Balfour (*10*) in 1878 refused to adopt Dohrn's views, and considered it probable that the dorsal position of the nerve-cord in *Vertebrata* could be accounted for, without any assumption of a substitution of a pair of gill-slits for the original mouth, by assuming that primitively the nerve-cord consisted of two lateral cords, as seen at the present time in the Nemertine Worms, and that these cords have coalesced *dorsally* in *Vertebrata*, just as it is clearly demon

[1] The classes here enumerated are described in separate articles, whilst *Cyclostoma* and *Dipnoi* are included in the article ICHTHYOLOGY.

strable that two originally lateral cords have coalesced *ventrally* to form the Annelid's ventral nerve-chain.

The comparison of the Vertebrates' nervous system with that of the Nemertines had already been made by the present writer, as cited by Hubrecht (*11*) in connexion with the latter's discovery of a complete sub-epidermal nerve-tunic in those worms. Hubrecht has more recently on two occasions (*12* and *13*) developed an interesting and important comparison of Nemertine and Vertebrate structure. He has in the first place suggested that the notochord of *Vertebrata* is nothing more than a modified survival of the proboscidean sheath of the Nemertines, whilst the oral invagination of the epidermis, in connexion with the hypophysis cerebri of the Vertebrate, may be a last remnant of the proboscis itself. More conclusively he has drawn attention to the median dorsal nerve of Nemertines as corresponding to the Vertebrate cerebro-spinal nerve-cord, whilst the great lateral nerve-cords of Nemertines, and the lateral ganglia in which they expand anteriorly, are compared to the lateral ganglia of the cephalic region of Craniate *Vertebrata* and the nerve of the lateral line (see fig. 6). The comparison is strengthened by the existence of a metameric series of transverse nerves in the Nemertine, which correspond in respect of their metamerism and their connexion with a dorsal median trunk, with the spinal nerves of *Craniata*. Hubrecht is careful to insist that he does not regard the Nemertines as representing the direct ancestry of *Vertebrata*; but he points out that from the primitive condition of an elongate animal, with a plexiform nerve-tunic, it is readily conceivable that a form was developed in which the nervous tissue was concentrated in three cords,—a median dorsal and two lateral,—and from such a form we can derive the Craniates' condition by excessive development of the median tract and relatively small development of the lateral cords, whilst the Nemertines' condition would be attained by the converse process. The tubular condition of the cerebro-spinal nerve-cord of *Vertebrata*, it may here be remarked, is now very generally regarded as being in its origin a purely developmental feature. It was primitively separated from the epidermis by delamination and in-sinking, and the mode of formation by invagination of a canal has been substituted in accordance with a general embryological law of growth, which is that bulky structures originating beneath a surface from the cells forming that surface take up their position in embryonic growth by invagination of the parent surface. The tubular form, having thus started, seems to have been utilized during one phase of Vertebrate evolution for the respiration of the nervous tissue, by the introduction through an anterior unclosed pore of a current of water, which escaped by the neuranal canal (as in larval *Amphioxus*).

There is a wide gap between any form presenting an approach to a Nemertine Worm and the most simple Craniate Vertebrate which can be imagined still provided with the organization characteristic of all *Craniata*. To pass from such a Worm-like animal to a Craniate, we have to account for and introduce, amongst other new developments, (1) a greatly increased metamerism, showing itself in the segmentation of the muscles of the body-wall and in the repetition of the nephridia; (2) the characteristic sense organs; (3) the lateral and median longitudinal folds or continuous fins; (4) the cartilaginous rods and bars of the skeleton; (5) the gill-slits, even if we admit the notochord to be represented by the proboscidean sheath.

It remains to inquire whether the structure of the other *Vertebrata* throws light on this long hypothetical passage from the simple Worm phase to the elaborate Craniate, or suggests any other ancestry.

THE CEPHALOCHORDA.

Characters of *Cephalochorda*.

Cephalochorda are *Vertebrata* in which there is no anterior dilatation of the nerve-tube to form a brain (see fig. 6) and no specialized skeletal brain-case. The notochord extends from one extremity of the elongate body to the other as a tapering unconstricted rod, passing anteriorly some distance in front of the nerve-cord. The longitudinal muscles of the body-wall are divided by transverse fibrous septa into a series of segments (sixty-two in *Amphioxus lanceolatus*), the more anterior of which are in front of the mouth and not in any way fused to form a head or cranial structure. Dense connective tissue (differing but little from cartilage) forms an unsegmented sheath to the notochord and an unbroken neural canal above it, in which the nerve-cord lies. The same tissue forms a series of metamerically repeated fin rays, which support the base of a median fin extending along the entire dorsal surface. The fin is continued ventrally from the caudal extremity as far forward as the anus, but without fin rays. Two lateral up-growths of the body-wall (the epipleura) extend one on either side from the head as far back as the anus. Each of these is divided into three regions,—(1) an anterior, which forms the præoral hood; (2) a median, which forms the wall of the great branchial chamber, the two folds meeting one another and coalescing in the ventral mid-line, excepting where they leave a posterior median aperture, the atriopore; and (3) the post-atrioporal præanal ventral fin (extending between atriopore and anus), which is formed by the complete coalescence of the two folds behind the atriopore.

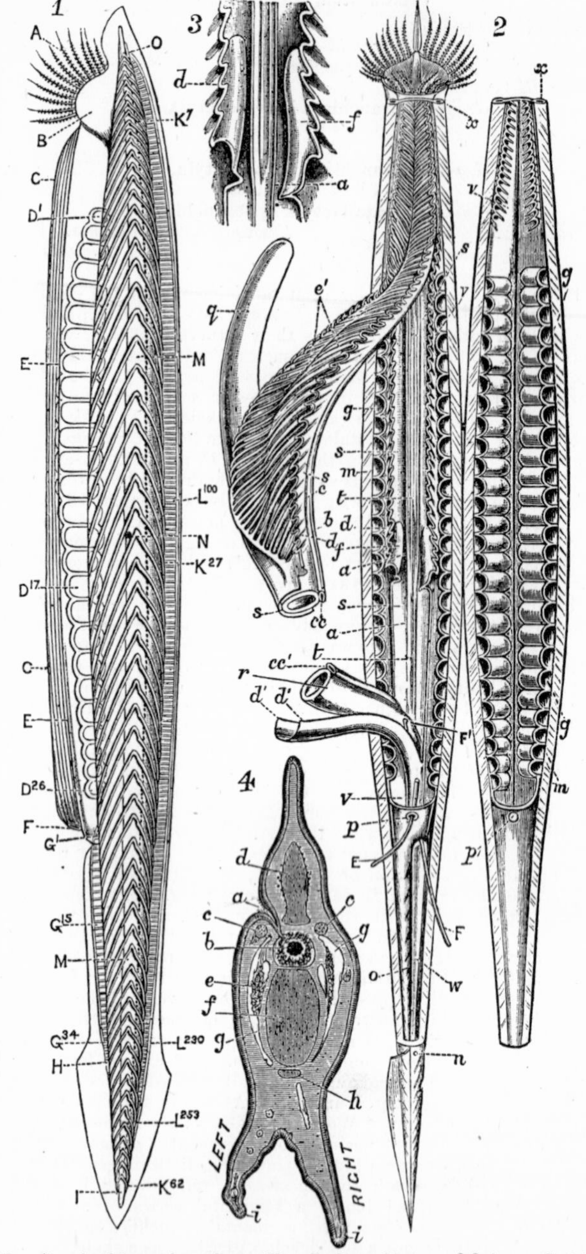

FIG. 7.—*Amphioxus lanceolatus*, Yarrell (*Branchiostoma lubricum*, Coste). (Original drawings.) (1) Lateral view of adult, to show general form, the myomeres, fin rays, and gonads. A, oral tentacles (28 to 32 in full-grown animals, 20 to 24 in half-grown specimens); B, præoral hood or præoral epipleur; C, plicated ventral surface of atrial chamber; D^1, D^{17}, D^{26}, gonads, twenty-six pairs, coincident with myotomes 10 to 36; E, metapleur or lateral ridge on atrial epipleur; F, atriopore, coincident with myotome 36; G^1, G^{15}, G^{34}, double ventral fin rays, extending from myotomes 37 to 52, but having no numerical relation to them; H, position of anus, between myotomes 51 and 52; I, notochord, projecting beyond myotomes; K^7, K^{27}, K^{62}, myotomes or muscular segments of body-wall, 62 in number; L^{100}, L^{230}, L^{253}, dorsal fin rays, about 250 in number, the hard substance of the ray being absent at the extreme ends of the body (these have no constant numerical relation to the myomeres); M, notochord as seen through the transparent myotomes, the thin double-lined spaces being the connective-tissue septa and the broader spaces the muscular tissue of the myotomes; N, position of brown funnel of left side (atrio-cœlomic canal); O, nerve-tube resting on notochord.

(2) Dissection of *Amphioxus*. By a horizontal incision on each side of the body a large ventral area has been separated and turned over, as it were on a hinge, to the animal's left side. The perforated pharyngeal region has then been detached from the adherent epipleura or opercular folds (wall of atrial or branchial chamber) by cutting the fluted pharyngo-pleural membrane *d*, and separated by a vertical cut from the intestinal region. *a*, Edge of groove formed by adhesion of median dorsal surface of alimentary canal to sheath of notochord; *b*, median dorsal surface of alimentary canal; *c*, left dorsal aorta; *cc*, single dorsal aorta, formed by union of the two anterior vessels; *cc'*, same vessel resting on intestine; *d*, cut edge of pharyngo-pleural folds of atrial tunic, really the original outer body-wall before the downgrowth of epipleura; *d'*, atrial tunic (original body-wall) at non-perforate region, cut and turned back so as to expose peri-enteric cœlom and intestine *r*; *e'*, upstanding folds of body-wall (pharyngo-pleural folds) on alternate bars of perforate region of body; *f*, atrio-cœlomic canals or brown funnels (collar-pores of *Balanoglossus*); *g*, cavity of a gonad-sac; *m*, cut musculature of body-wall; *n*, anus; *o*, post-atrioporal extension of atrial chamber in form of a

tubular cæcum; *p*, atriopore; *q*, hepatic cæcum; *r*, intestine; *s*, cœlom; *t*, area of adhesion between alimentary canal and sheath of notochord; *v*, atrial chamber or branchial cavity; *w*, post-atrioporal portion of intestine; *x*, canals of metapleura exposed by cutting; E, probe passing through atriopore into atrial or branchial chamber; FF', probe passed from cœlom, where it expands behind the atriopore, into narrower perienteric cœlom of præ-atrioporal region.

(3) Portion of (2) enlarged to show atrio-cœlomic canals ("brown funnels" of Lankester). Lettering as in (2).

(4) Section taken transversely through præoral region near termination of nerve-tube. *a*, Olfactory ciliated pit on animal's left side, its wall confluent with substance of nerve-tube; *b*, pigment spot (rudimentary eye) on anterior termination of nerve-tube; *c*, first pair of nerves in section; *d*, fin ray; *e*, myotome; *f*, notochord; *g*, space round myotome (? artifact or cœlom); *h*, subchordal canal (? blood-vessel); *i*, a symmetrical epipleura of præoral hood.

The originally double character of this part of the ventral fin is indicated by the double series of metameric fin rays which support it. It is probable that these "epipleural" folds of *Amphioxus* correspond to the opercular folds and lateral fins of *Craniata*. No cartilaginous fin rays are developed in the atrio-pleural (opercular) region of the epipleura; but a longitudinal unsegmented bar of cartilaginous consistency strengthens its side and bounds a lymph-holding canal (*x* in fig. 8).

The gill-slits in *Amphioxus* are very numerous (one hundred or more), and have no numerical relation to the metameres of the muscular body-wall, though the first few which appear in the embryo correspond at the time to successive myomeres,—a relation which they subsequently lose. The sides of the gill-slits are supported by chitinous (?) bars, and each slit is divided into two equal portions by a longitudinal tongue or bar, which grows out from the dorsal margin of the slit soon after its first formation. The number of gill-slits increases continually throughout the life of *Amphioxus* by the formation of new ones at the posterior border of the pharynx, whilst the myomeres do not increase in number after early embryonic life.

The nerves given off from the dorsal nerve-cord of *Amphioxus* are of two kinds,—dorsal and ventral. The dorsal nerves correspond in number and position to the myomeres, right and left, except in the most anterior region of the body, where two larger pairs of dorsal nerves are given off from near the extremity of the nerve-cord, and pass forward, supplying the region which lies in front of the termination of the musculature. The ventral nerves are minute, and are given off numerously, right and left, from the nerve-tube throughout its length. The dorsal and ventral nerves of a single myomere appear to correspond, respectively, to the dorsal and ventral roots of a spinal nerve of a Craniate.

There is a single olfactory pit in *Amphioxus*, which rests upon the left side of the anterior termination of the nerve-cord (see fig. 7, 4). Within the cavity of the nerve-cord at the same point a patch of brown pigment is present (eye-spot). There are no representatives of the lateral eyes of *Craniata* and no otocysts.

There is no representative of the Craniates' swim-bladder in *Amphioxus*. A single wide diverticulum of the alimentary canal represents the liver of *Craniata*; the pancreas is unrepresented.

The vascular system is singularly incomplete: large trunks exist, but few branches and no heart, whilst the blood itself is colourless, and communicates (as in *Craniata* by the lymphatic "hearts") with the cœlomic fluid at various points. A contractile ventral trunk runs along the lower face of the slit pharynx, and sends vessels right and left up the successive bars; these vessels unite above, as in *Craniata*, to form a double "dorsal aorta," which posteriorly becomes a single vessel. A portal system of veins can be traced in connexion with the hepatic cæcum.

No system of lymphatic vessels, nor lymphatic "glands," nor a spleen exist; but the cœlom, and certain other spaces in the connective tissue, contain coagulable lymph, and correspond to the lymph spaces of *Craniata*.

There is no series of nephridia, nor a renal organ formed by the coalescence of nephridia, nor are gonaducts present. The "brown funnels," a pair of funnel-shaped tubes discovered by Lankester (*14*), place the cœlomic space of the opercular (epipleural) down-growths of the body-wall in communication with the space which these folds enclose. They appear to be identical with the "collar-pores" of *Balanoglossus*, and it is doubtful whether they represent nephridia.

In the larval *Amphioxus* there is developed from the left anterior cœlomic pouch a glandular tube and a sense-organ, which are represented in the adult by the structures marked *f* in fig. 8, B. This tube is probably the same thing as the subneural gland of Ascidians and as the proboscidean gland and pore of *Balanoglossus*. Quite distinct from the foregoing is a nephridial tube lying on the left side behind the mouth of the larval *Amphioxus*. All are probably of the nature of nephridia. In the adult *Amphioxus* the nephridial tube is in an atrophied condition, though large and active in a *late* larval stage, when the olfactory pit opens into the neural canal. Hatschek (*15*) describes this condition in "*ausgebildete*" but not in *adult* examples.

The gonads are distinct ovaries and testes; they are developed in distinct male and female individuals in corresponding positions, viz., in that part of the cœlom which is carried downwards in the

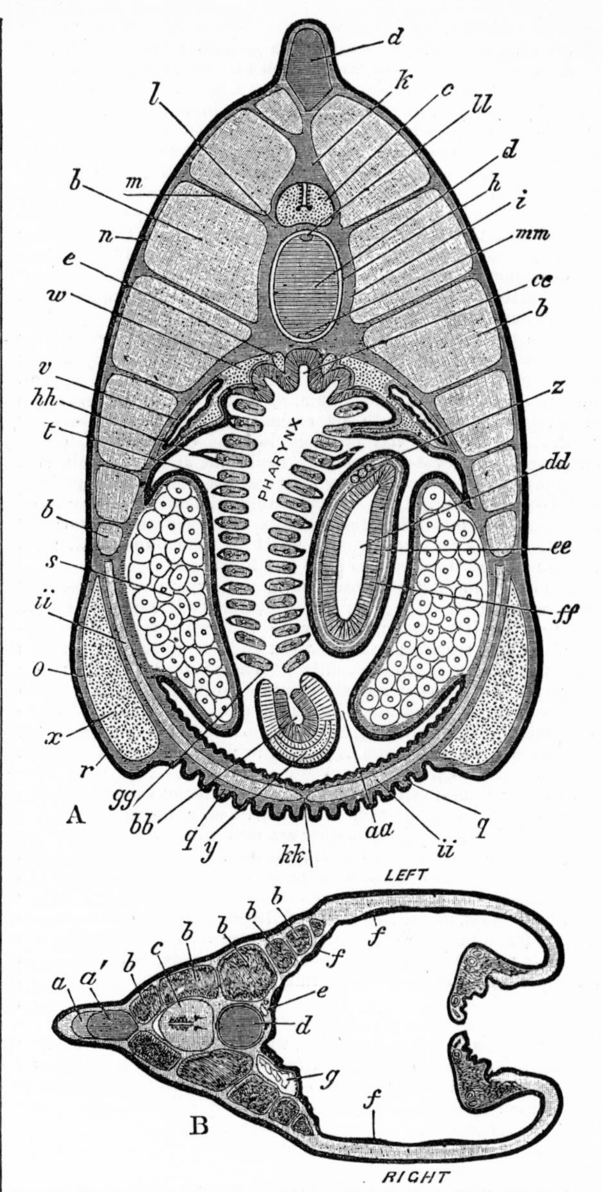

Fig. 8.—Transverse sections of *Amphioxus*. (Original.) **A. Section through region of atrio-cœlomic canals, *v*. B. Section in front of mouth; the right and** left sides are transposed. *a*, Cavity surrounding fin ray; *a'*, fin ray; *b*, muscular tissue of myotome; *c*, nerve-cord; *d*, notochord; *e*, left aorta; *f*, thickened ridges of epithelium of præoral chamber (Rader organ); *g*, coiled tube lying in a cœlomic space on *right* side of præoral hood, apparently an artery; *h*, cuticle of notochord; *i*, connective-tissue sheath of notochord; *k*, median ridge of skeletal canal of nerve-cord; *l*, skeletal canal protecting nerve-cord; *m*, inter-segmental skeletal septum of myotome; *n*, subcutaneous skeletal connective tissue; *o*, ditto of metapleur (this should be relatively thicker than it is); *q*, subcutaneous connective tissue of ventral surface of atrial wall (not a canal, as supposed by Stieda and others); *r*, epiblastic epithelium; *s*, gonad-sac containing ova; *t*, pharyngeal bar in section, one of the "tongue" bars alternating with the main bars and devoid of pharyngo-pleural fold and cœlom; *v*, atrio-cœlomic funnel; *w*, so-called "dorsal" cœlom; *x*, lymphatic space or canal of metapleur; *y*, sub-pharyngeal vascular trunk; *z*, blood-vessel (portal vein) on wall of hepatic cæcum; *aa*, space of atrial or branchial chamber; *bb*, ventral groove of pharynx (anteriorly this takes the form of a ridge); *cc*, hyperbranchial groove of pharynx; *dd*, lumen or space of hepatic cæcum; *ee*, narrow cœlomic space surrounding hepatic cæcum; *ff*, lining cell-layer of hepatic cæcum; *gg*, inner face of a pharyngeal bar clothed with hypoblast, the outer face covered with epiblast (represented black); *hh*, a main pharyngeal bar with projecting pharyngeal fold (on which the reference line rests) in section, showing cœlomic space beneath the black epiblast; *ii*, transverse ventral muscle of epipleura; *kk*, raphe or plane of fusion of two down-grown epipleura; *ll*, space and nucleated cells on dorsal face of notochord; *mm*, similar space and cells on its ventral face.

descending right and left outgrowth (epipleura, opercula) of the body-wall, which encloses the atrial or branchial chamber. The gonads are twenty-six pairs in number, corresponding to the 10-36 myomeres. They are devoid of ducts, and discharge their products by dehiscence into the atrial chamber, whence they pass to the exterior, either by the atriopore or by entering the pharynx through its slits, when they are ejected by the mouth.

In many respects *Amphioxus*, the only representative of *Cephalochorda*, bears evidence of being derived from a more highly organized

Relationship of *Cephalochorda* to *Craniata* and the Vertebrate ancestry.

ancestry. Its mode of life (burrowing in the sand in shallow water, whilst its general build is that of a swimming animal) and the nature of its food (diatoms, &c., carried into the pharynx by ciliary currents) in themselves suggest such a history. The vascular system is elaborate in plan yet incomplete in detail, suggesting an atrophy of its finer branches, which is consistent with the small size of *Amphioxus* and the general principle that a complex vascular system can only be developed in an animal which has attained to a certain bulk. The absence of well-developed sense organs and of "cephalization" in an animal which has attained to such elaboration of structure as is shown by the pharynx and atrial chamber, and which has such well-developed muscles to the body-wall, is an inconsistency best explicable by degeneration; so, too, the existence of the elaborate series of fin rays, which are out of proportion to the mechanical requirements of so small a form.

Degenerate though *Amphioxus* must be, the ancestor from which it started on its retrogressive course was probably a long way behind any living Craniate. There is no reason to suppose that this ancestor had a cranium, or that the muscular segments and segmental nerves in its cephalic region were fused and welded. *Amphioxus* has probably lost, as compared with that ancestor, lateral eyes and otocysts, nephridia, and, above all, size. The epipleural folds which now form oral hood, branchial opercula, and coalesced ventral fin were probably originally less developed lateral ridges, protecting the gill-slits anteriorly and posteriorly, serving by their undulations to assist in locomotion, whilst the median fin and its rays were large and functional.

One of the most curious features in the structure of *Amphioxus* is its asymmetry. The anus is on the animal's left side; the nasal pit upon its left; the myomeres on the two sides of the notochord do not coincide; and the right and left dorsal spinal nerves do not arise *vis-à-vis* to one another. There is no conclusive reason for regarding this as an ancestral feature, although the early larval form is as curiously asymmetrical as the adult. *Amphioxus* habitually rests upon the sand, lying upon one side of the body, and it is possible that the distortion is related to this habit, as in the case of the Pleuronectid Fishes.

However we may estimate *Amphioxus*, we are not led by it, though its muscular metamerism is so well marked, a single step in the direction of the Annelids, neither are we led directly, it is true, in the direction of *Nemertina* in connexion with those points, as to relationship of notochord with proboscis sheath and nerve-cord with median dorsal nerve, insisted on by Hubrecht. But it will be seen below that, by the agreement of *Amphioxus* with *Balanoglossus* in the structure of the perforations of the pharynx, in the possession of collar pores, and in the præoral glandular body, we do arrive at an important connexion with Nemertine-like forms.

The Urochorda.

Characters of *Urochorda*.

Urochorda are *Vertebrata* which, with the exception of the group *Larvalia* (*Appendicularia*, *Fritillaria*, *Oikopleura*), have receded very far indeed from the characteristic Vertebrate structure, showing neither notochord nor nerve-cord, and gill-slits only of the most highly modified and aberrant form; some, however (certain Ascidians), pass through a larval condition in which these structures are present in the normal form. It is necessary for the purposes of the present article to confine our attention to *Larvalia* and to the larval forms which retain ancestral characters. (For a description of the whole group, see the article Tunicata.) In *Urochorda* thus signalized the notochord never reaches forward into the anterior part of the body, but is confined to the tail (hence *Urochorda*). The longitudinal muscles of the region traversed by the notochord show traces of metameric segmentation, which are probably survivals of a more complete development of myomeres in ancestral forms (*16*). There is no trace in *Larvalia* of fin rays or other skeletal structure. Corresponding to the opercular folds and epipleura of *Craniata* and *Cephalochorda* are ridges of the body-wall, which protect the pharyngeal gill-slits, and may give rise, as in *Cephalochorda*, to an enclosed atrial chamber with atriopore. The gill-slits in these larval forms are few in number (one or two pairs), but in many of the aberrant *Urochorda* (by far the majority of the group) they become excessively numerous and complicated in structure, and are supported by a chitinous (?) framework, as in *Cephalochorda*. It has been suggested that the fenestrated structure of the pharyngeal wall in *Tunicata* does not represent a series of gill-slits, but a single pair of slits subdivided. This suggestion is worthy of further consideration.

The cerebro-spinal nerve-cord is tubular and presents itself as a dilated cerebral vesicle in front of the notochord, and as a narrower part running along the whole length of the notochord.

Sense organs are present—a single eye with pigment and lens, a single otocyst, and an olfactory pit (*Larvalia*). The mouth is dorsal in position in the Ascidian tadpole, but subterminal in *Larvalia*. The pharynx is wide, and is followed by a narrow œsophagus, stomach, and intestine, which does not open ventrally but turns upwards to the anus. The *Larvalia* have a rudimentary heart and no vascular system,—a fact connected with their diminutive size. For the same reason no vascular system develops in the Ascidian tadpole until it has ceased to be locomotive and has entered upon its later development; but in the larger adult *Urochorda* a contractile heart and a well-developed vascular system are present.

No undeniable nephridia are present in *Larvalia* nor in the larval Ascidian, and no structure comparable to the collar pores of *Balanoglossus* or the atrio-cœlomic funnels of *Amphioxus* is known in them.

The subneural gland, however, a glandular tube opening anteriorly near the mouth of the pharynx, appears to be identical with the præoral larval gland of *Amphioxus* and the proboscis pore and gland of *Balanoglossus*. It is probably to be regarded as a nephridium, and has been compared by Julin and Van Beneden to the pituitary body of *Craniata*, with which it corresponds in position and development.

The gonads of *Larvalia* are developed in irregular masses on the walls of the cœlom, ovaries and testes in the same individual.

Classification of *Urochorda*.

As above indicated, there is a small section of *Urochorda* which retain in adult life the tadpole-like form and the essential Vertebrate organs which are exhibited by the larvæ only of other *Urochorda*, and by a few only of these. This necessitates a primary division of the branch into two grades.

Grade A.—Larvalia (*Appendicularia, Fritillaria, Oikopleura*).
Grade B.—Saccata.
Class I.—*Ascidiæ* (*Simplices, Sociales, Compositæ, Pyrosomiidea*).
Class II.—*Salpiformia* (*Salpiidea, Dolioliidea*).

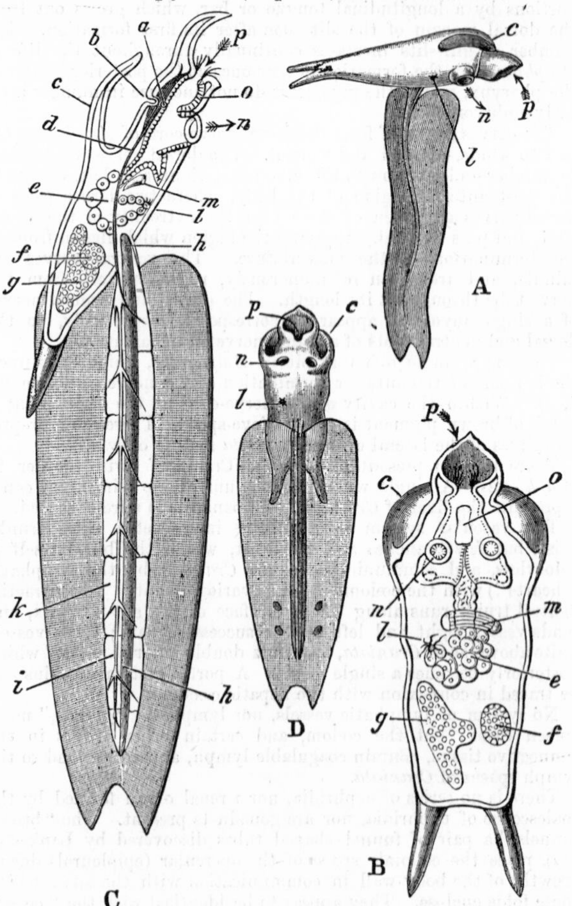

Fig. 9.—*Fritillaria* (*Appendicularia*) *furcata*, one of the *Urochorda*. (Original drawings.) A. Lateral surface view, showing habitual carriage of "body" at right angles to "tail." B. Organs of body as seen by transparency. C. Lateral view of body with tail in morphological position, showing organs by transparency. D. Surface view of animal from below to show apertures. *a*, Otocyst in connexion with brain; *b*, olfactory pit; *c*, dorsal hood; *d*, nerve-tube passing from enlarged brain to caudal region, where it forms one true ganglion and a series of minor enlargements, corresponding to the rudimentary "myotomes" or "myomeres" of the tail; *e*, stomach; *f*, ovary; *g*, testis; *h*, notochord (urochord); *i*, nerve-tube or myelon in tail; *k*, fifth myomere of tail; *l*, anus; *m*, heart; *n*, gill-slit; *o*, endostyle or hypobranchial groove; *p*, mouth.

Relations of *Urochorda* to Vertebrate ancestry.

Urochorda are so extremely aberrant, and show so little more than a transient developmental indication of the essential Vertebrate organs, that we cannot hope to get much positive information from them on the subject of Vertebrate ancestry. Only the minute *Appendicularīæ* (*Larvalia*) retain the Vertebrate structure through life, and they are obviously, on account of their minute size, extremely degenerate. It is possible to make hypotheses as to the greater or less elaboration of the ancestors of *Urochorda,* and to maintain even that their ancestry had reached as high a condition as that shown by *Craniata* ; on the other hand, it does not seem likely that their point of divergence from the main ancestral line leading to *Craniata* was lower than, or even so low as, that at which *Amphioxus* branched off. The differentiation of trunk and tail by the limitation of the notochord anteriorly is a nearer approach to Craniate structure than that shown by *Amphioxus,* whilst the definite development of a brain of considerable relative size places *Urochorda* nearer to the Craniates than is *Amphioxus.* The metameric myomeres so strongly developed in this last are not absent in *Urochorda*, as is often maintained, but exist in a rudimentary form, indicating that they had once a fuller development.

The Hemichorda.

Characters of *Hemichorda.*

Hemichorda comprise the single genus *Balanoglossus*—formerly classified by Gegenbaur as *Enteropneusta,* an independent phylum of the animal kingdom. They are *Vertebrata* of worm-like form,

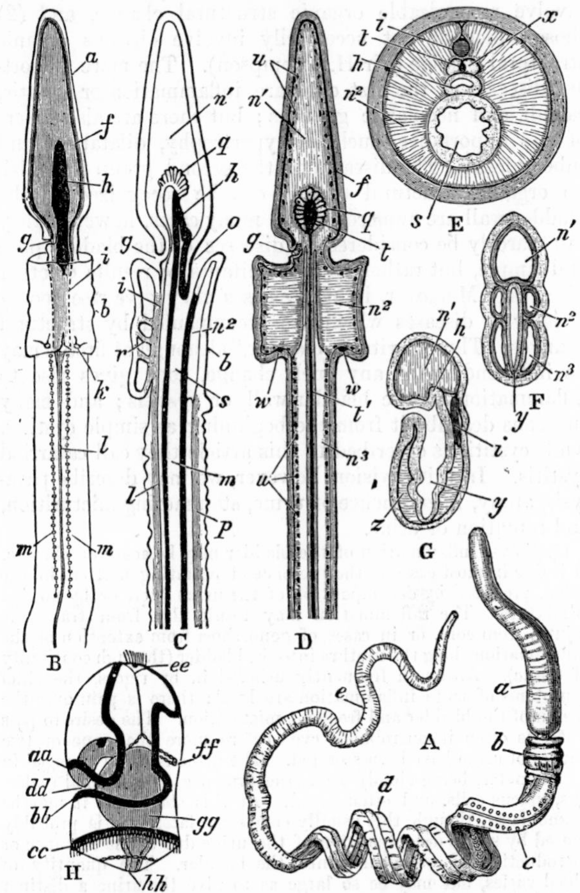

Fig. 10.—*Balanoglossus*, anatomy and development. (Modified from Bateson.) A. *Balanoglossus kowalewskii*, Bateson; from the coast of Virginia, U.S.; natural size; *a*, proboscis; *b*, collar; *c*, perforate region; *d*, flattened digestive region; *e*, cylindrical hind region. B. Diagram of dorsal view, showing certain organs as though the body-wall were transparent. C. Diagram of a vertical antero-posterior section. D. Diagram of a dorsal view to show vessels and nerves by transparency. E. Diagram of a transverse section through the collar. F. Larva of *B. kowalewskii* ; diagram of horizontal section. G. Vertical longitudinal section of an older larva of the same. Lettering B-G :—*a*, proboscis ; *b*, collar ; *f*, nerve-tunic of proboscis ; *g*, proboscis pore (ciliated orifice) ; *h*, notochord (limited to a small tract of modified tissue derived from præoral extension of alimentary canal) ; *i*, dorsal nerve-plate ; *k*, collar-pore (right and left), opening to exterior from collar cœlom just beneath the collar ; *l*, continuation of dorsal nerve-plate as a nerve-cord ; *m*, pharyngeal perforations (gill-slits) ; *n'*, cœlom of proboscis (anterior azygos primitive cœlomic pouch); *n²*, collar cœlom (right and left middle cœlomic pouches of embryo) ; *n³*, body cœlom (right and left posterior cœlomic pouches of embryo) ; *o*, mouth ; *p*, ventral nerve-tunic of body-wall ; *q*, proboscis gland ; *r*, strands connecting dorsal nerve-plate with outer wall of collar ; *s*, cavity of pharynx in front of perforate region ; *t*, dilated part (heart) of dorsal vessel within proboscis-gland ; *t'*, dorsal vessel ; *u*, blood-vessels of body-wall in section ; *w*, paired nerves of collar region in transverse section ; *x*, perihæmal cœlom, surrounding dorsal vessel in collar region ; *y*, digestive region of gut (in embryo) ; *z*, mesoblast. H. Larva of another species of *Balanoglossus*, known as the *Tornaria* larva of Johann Müller, and resembling an Echinoderm larva. *aa*, præoral ciliated band of *Tornaria* ; *bb*, post-oral ditto ; *cc*, terminal ditto ; *dd*, mouth ; *ee*, apical plate and sense organ ; *ff*, canal system and pore ; *gg*, gut ; *hh*, anus.

elongate and somewhat flattened from above downwards. In front of the mouth is a long cylindrical proboscis, and behind it a collar, the free margin of which is turned backwards, and corresponds to the opercular epipleural folds of *Cephalochorda* and *Craniata.* This agreement is supported by the existence of a pair of collar pores opening into the cœlom of the collar, as the "brown funnels" of *Amphioxus* open into the epipleural cœlom of that animal. A proboscis pore, opening on the left side into the præoral cœlom of the proboscis (paired in *B. kupfferi*), is exactly representative of the similarly placed pore which in the young *Amphioxus* (according to Hatschek, *15*) leads into the tubular organ derived from the left cœlomic chamber of the præoral lobe of that animal. The whole surface of the body is ciliated, as in Nemertines and Echinoderms, and as in no other Vertebrates. Following the collar is a perforated region of the body,—gill-slits opening from the outer surface into the pharynx. In the young form there is for a time, as in *Appendicularia* and the Ascidian tadpole, only one pair of gill-slits, but they subsequently increase in number as the animal grows in length. They resemble in form and structure those of *Amphioxus.* The notochord (*h* in fig. 10) arises at the anterior end of the hypoblast in the young, and grows forward, forming a support for the base of the proboscis. It is limited to this very small region. The cerebro-spinal nerve-cord originates by a delamination of a solid cord of epiblast in the mid-dorsal line of the middle third of the body ; then by invagination of its two ends it extends as a tube both anteriorly and posteriorly. A general network of nerve-fibres (and cells ?) exists beneath the epidermis all over the body. The blood-system is peculiar, consisting of an anterior heart and a dorsal and ventral vessel ; these are united by a plexus of subcutaneous vessels. The musculature of the body-wall is not broken into successive myomeres ; but, on the other hand, the gonads (ovaries or testes) are sac-like, and, as in *Amphioxus,* are repeated in a series throughout a great length of the body. In the pharyngeal region the gonad sacs agree in number with the gill-slits. There are no nephridia (unless proboscis pore and collar pores are to be so regarded); but the connective-tissue cells of the body-cavity are active as excreting agents, as in Echinoderms and in *Urochorda,* and a large glandular organ in the proboscis attached to the end of the notochord appears to have to do with this function. Not the least remarkable fact about *Hemichorda* is the nature of their larvæ. No other *Vertebrata* present larval forms which indicate the nature of the early ancestral history in what we may call præ-chordal times ; however interesting the Ascidian larva, or the young *Amphioxus,* and the embryo dog-fish, they do not take us out of the Vertebrate area. Some species of *Balanoglossus* (? *B. minutus*), however, pass through a banded ciliate larval condition, which was known as *Tornaria,* and was considered to be an Echinoderm larva allied to *Bipinnaria,* before its relation to *Balanoglossus* was discovered. It is not possible to view the *Tornaria* larva of *Balanoglossus* as otherwise than identical with Echinoderm larvæ, and it results that *Balanoglossus* and the Echinoderms have remote genetic affinities of a special kind.

Species of *Hemichorda.*

No classification of *Hemichorda* is possible beyond an enumeration of the species :—

1. *Balanoglossus clavigerus* (Della Chiaje), Naples.
2. *B. minutus* (Kowalewsky), „
3. *B. kowalewskii* (Al. Agassiz), east coast, United States.
4. *B. brooksii* (Bateson), „ „
5. *B. salmoneus* (Giard), Brittany.
6. *P. robinii* (Giard), „

Relations of *Hemichorda* to Vertebrate ancestry.

It seems that in *Balanoglossus* we at last find a form which, though no doubt specialized for its burrowing sand-life, and possibly to some extent degenerate, yet has not to any large extent fallen from an ancestral eminence. The ciliated epidermis, the long Worm-like form, and the complete absence of segmentation of the body-muscles lead us to forms like the Nemertines. The great proboscis of *Balanoglossus* may well be compared to the invaginable organ similarly placed in the Nemertines. The collar is the first commencement of a structure destined to assume great importance in *Cephalochorda* and *Craniata,* and perhaps protective of a single gill-slit in *Balanoglossus* before the number of those apertures had been extended. Borrowing, as we may, the nephridia from the Nemertines, and the lateral in addition to the dorsal nerve, we find that *Balanoglossus* gives the most hopeful hypothetical solution of the pedigree of Vertebrates. Space has not permitted us to go so fully into *pros* and *cons* as the speculative nature of the subject requires; but we give the final conclusion to which our consideration of the structure of the four great branches of the *Vertebrata* leads in the form of the accompanying genealogical tree.

Br. Craniata
Br. Urochorda
Br. Hemichorda
Br. Cephalochorda
Phylum Platyhelmia
Phylum Vertebrata
Phylum Echinoderma

Bibliography.—(*1*) Cuvier, "Sur un Nouveau Rapprochement," &c., in *Ann. du Musée*, 1812, vol. xix. p. 73; (*2*) Kowalewsky, "Devel. of *Amphioxus*," in *Mém. de l'Acad. Imp.*, St Petersburg, 7th series, vol. xvi., No. 12, 1866; (*3*) *Id.*, "Devel. of *Ascidia*," *ibid.*; (*4*) Lankester (E. Ray), "Notes on Embryology and Classification," in *Quart. Journ. Micr. Sci.*, vol. xvii., 1877; (*5*) Kowalewsky, "*Balanoglossus*," in *Mém. de l'Acad. Imp.*, St Petersburg, vol. x., No. 3, 1866; (*6*) Bateson, "*Balanoglossus*," in *Quart. Journ. Micr. Sci.*, April 1884; *ibid.*, supplement number 1885, *ibid.*, June 1886; (*7*) Harmer, "*Cephalodiscus*," in *Challenger Reports*, vol. xviii.; (*8*) Dohrn, *Ursprung der Wirbelthiere*, 1875; (*9*) Zeppelin, "Budding in *Ctenodrilus*," in *Zeitschr. wiss. Zoologie*, vol. xxxix.; (*10*) Balfour, *Monograph on Development of Elasmobranch Fishes*, 1878; (*11*) Hubrecht, "Nerve-Tunic of Nemertines," in *Quart. Journ. Micr. Sci.*, vol. xx., 1880; (*12*) and (*13*) Id., "Comparison of Nemertines and Vertebrates," in *Quart. Journ. Micr. Sci.*, vol. xxiii., 1883, and vol. xxvii., 1887; (*14*) Lankester (E. Ray), "Brown Funnels of *Amphioxus*," in *Quart. Journ. Micr. Sci.*, vol. xv. p. 257, 1875; (*15*) Hatschek, "Subneural Gland of *Amphioxus* and Olfactory Pit," in *Zool. Anzeiger*, p. 517, 1884; (*16*) Lankester (E. Ray), "Vertebration of the Tail of *Appendicularia*," in *Quart. Journ. Micr. Science*, vol. xxii., 1882; (*17*) Kowalewsky, "Later Researches on Ascidian Development," in *Archiv für mikroskopische Anatomie*, vol. vii., 1871; (*18*) Id., "Later Researches on *Amphioxus* Development," in *Archiv für mikroskopische Anatomie*, vol. xiii., 1876.

(E. R. L.)

VERTUE, George (1684-1756), engraver and antiquary, was born in St Martin's-in-the-Fields, London, in 1684. At the age of thirteen he was apprenticed to an heraldic engraver, a Frenchman, who failed in three or four years. Vertue then studied drawing at home, and afterwards worked for seven years as an engraver under Michael Vandergucht. He was patronized by Sir Godfrey Kneller, and was one of the first members of the Academy of Painting which that artist instituted in 1711. His plate of Archbishop Tillotson, after Kneller, commissioned by Lord Somers, established his reputation as an engraver; and he was soon in an excellent practice, engraving portraits after Dahl, Richardson, Jervas, and Gibson. In portraiture alone he executed over five hundred plates. In 1717 he was appointed engraver to the Society of Antiquaries, and his burin was employed upon many interesting statues, tombs, portraits and other subjects of an antiquarian nature. He died on the 24th of July 1756, and was buried in the cloisters of Westminster Abbey.

From the year 1713 Vertue had been indefatigable in his researches on all matters connected with the history of British art, and had accumulated about forty volumes of memoranda on the subject. These were purchased by Horace Walpole, and form the basis of that author's *Anecdotes of Painting in England*, where will be found an account of Vertue's life and a catalogue of his engravings. Vertue's own literary works include *On Holbein and Gerard's Pictures* (1740); *Medals, Coins, Great Seals, Impressions, from the Elaborate Works of Thomas Simon* (1753); *Catalogue and Description of King Charles the First's Capital Collection of Pictures, Limnings, Statues*, &c. (1757); *Catalogue of the Collection of Pictures belonging to King James II., to which is added a Catalogue of Pictures and Drawings in the Closet of Queen Caroline* (1758); *Catalogue of the Curious Collection of Pictures of George Villiers, Duke of Buckingham* (1758); *Description of the Works of that Ingenious Delineator and Engraver, W. Hollar* (1745).

VERUS, M. Aurelius. See Aurelius, vol. iii. pp. 86-87.

VERVIERS, a town of Belgium, in the province of Liége, is situated on the Vesdre, 15½ miles by rail east by south from Liége and 19 miles south-west from Aix-la-Chapelle. It is divided into an upper and a lower town, but has no striking architectural features. The staple commodity is cloth, which is manufactured here and in the immediate environs to the value of £3,200,000 annually. Other manufactures are soap, chemicals, confectionery, and machinery; dyeing, tanning, and iron and copper founding are also carried on. The town is a modern one; its manufacturing prosperity, the beginning of which dates from the 18th century, is partly attributed to the waters of the Vesdre, which are said to be peculiarly well adapted to the purposes of the dyer. The population in 1876 was 37,828.

VESALIUS, Andreas (1514-1564). See Anatomy, vol. i. pp. 807-8; also Vascular System, p. 95 above.

VESICAL DISEASES. The urinary bladder is the temporary reservoir of the renal secretion, and as such contains the urine for longer or shorter periods. In recent years diseases of the bladder have come more than formerly within the scope of operative surgery, owing especially to great advances in the methods of examining the inner wall of the bladder both by sight and touch,—by sight in virtue of the endoscope, an instrument which when introduced into the bladder enables a visual examination of the interior to be made; and by touch, as surgeons do not now hesitate to make incisions into the bladder, either from the perinæum or suprapubically, for purely diagnostic purposes. Further, more careful and improved chemical and microscopical examination of the urine enables the surgeon to judge better than formerly what the condition of the bladder is. Diseases of the bladder may be conveniently divided into two groups,—(1) those which involve recognizable organic structural change, and (2) those which do not necessarily involve obvious organic structural change (Sir H. Thompson). The more important diseases of the first class are inflammation or cystitis, calculi, and neoplastic growths; but there are also others of less importance, such as hypertrophy, dilatation, and tuberculosis. The diseases of the second group in which no organic structural change can be recognized in the bladder-wall are numerous. In many cases, however, they can scarcely be considered as diseases of the bladder pure and simple, but rather as concomitants or results of other diseases. Moreover, in many cases they give rise sooner or later to diseases which are accompanied by structural changes. Thus "irritable bladder," although at first it may be independent of any such change, soon gives rise to inflammation of the bladder-wall, or cystitis; and many surgeons describe it from the beginning as simple cystitis, while cystitis as described in this article they call catarrhal cystitis. In this division, however, we may describe paralysis, atony, incontinence of urine, stammering micturition, and retention of urine.

Acute cystitis.

Cystitis.—Inflammation of the bladder may be acute or chronic. It is due in most cases to the presence of irritating matters in the urine, produced by decomposition of the urine itself or by morbid admixture. The inflammation may result also from traumatic injury, from cold, or in cases of gonorrhœa from extension of the inflammation along the urethra into the bladder (through continuity of tissue). Although frequently ushered in by rigors, the chief symptoms of acute inflammation are local: there is pain over the region of the bladder and frequent micturition. The desire to pass water is often incontrollable, even before more than one or two ounces of urine have been secreted. The urine is much changed in its character, being cloudy from the presence of epithelial scales, pus, mucus cells, and often blood. At this stage also it may be ammoniacal, though this usually comes on later, and is probably caused by septic decomposition of the urine due to the entrance or introduction of organisms into the bladder. The quantity of blood varies, but may be so large as to give the urine a distinct reddish tinge. As a rule, the mucous membrane at the neck of the bladder is the first part to become inflamed, but the whole of the mucous membrane may be affected; resolution, however, usually takes place before more than a portion has been attacked.

Chronic cystitis.

Chronic cystitis is one of the most common affections of the bladder, and its causes are very various. It sometimes remains after an acute attack has passed off, but more commonly it results from long-continued irritation, such as may be produced by a urinary calculus in or by atony of the bladder. The symptoms are not so severe as in acute cystitis: the urine contains more mucus, but less pus and blood, and there is much less tendency to frequent micturition, the irritability of the bladder being greatly diminished. Frequently very large quantities of mucus are secreted, and the condition is then termed "catarrh of the bladder." Chronic inflammation is not in itself dangerous; but the patient, so long as it remains, is liable to an attack of acute cystitis, which, superadded to the pre-existing condition of the bladder, may be very serious. An increase in the fibrous elements of the coats of the bladder and hypertrophy of the muscular fibres are a common result of chronic cystitis.

Treatment of cystitis.

The treatment in both varieties of the disease consists in giving rest to the inflamed part and in alleviating the pain. Hot sitz-baths may be used two or three times daily for ten minutes or a quarter of an hour at a time; and, if the pain be very severe, hot fomentations with tincture of opium should be applied to the perinæum or hypogastrium, or a hot douche may be used per rectum.

Diluent drinks are given, and tincture of hyoscyamus may be prescribed, as it has a very soothing influence. It may be necessary to give morphia, but generally the pain can be allayed without its use. In chronic cystitis the treatment depends very much on the cause, which must if possible be removed. Thus, if the cystitis is due to a calculus in the bladder, the treatment is to remove the calculus (see below). Very often, however, special remedies are employed to relieve the inflammatory condition, and one of the best is washing out the bladder. This is a simple operation, based on the principle of siphon action with a head of water, and is carried out as follows. A catheter is introduced through the urethra into the bladder, and to it the stem of a T-shaped tube is fixed; to each end of the horizontal part a piece of rubber tubing is attached, one piece terminating in a vessel which contains an aseptic warm lotion and is placed at a higher level than the bladder, while the other is led into a receptacle placed lower than the bladder. Six or eight ounces of the lotion are allowed to flow into the bladder; then the flow is checked, and the fluid passes out from the bladder through the other tube. Each tube should have a stop-cock, so that the surgeon can open or close it as he desires. Occasionally bladder drainage is resorted to, and is carried out on the principle of siphon action.[1] Internal remedies have to be administered, one of the most valuable being benzoate of soda. The benzoate in its passage through the blood is changed into hippuric acid, and thus tends to render the urine less alkaline. Attention to the diet of the patient is of great importance in both acute and chronic cystitis; it should be very light, easily digested, and nutritious. Diluents are often of much value, lessening the irritability of the bladder. All wines and stimulants should be avoided.

Calculi.

Calculi.—Important information, as we have already said, is derived both by the surgeon and physician from a careful examination of the urine, whether this be done chemically or microscopically. Not infrequently on such examination crystals, varying in their chemical and physical characters, are found, and if these be in large amount distinct urinary deposits are got from the urine after it has been kept in a vessel for a time. The cause producing these crystals or their presence alone may give rise to disease, as, for instance, oxaluria, a condition in which, in addition to other symptoms, we find oxalate of lime crystals present in the urine. We have here to deal, however, with more than the mere presence of a few crystals disseminated in the urine, viz., with those conditions in which an amalgamation of crystals has occurred, giving rise to a concretion of such deposits into a mass, forming a calculus or stone. When such concretions are so small that they can be passed with the urine through the urethra they are known as *gravel*; but when they are prevented by their size from passing along the urethra they are termed *calculi*, and the patient is said to suffer from stone or calculus. Calculus of the bladder constitutes a most formidable and important disease, and its treatment, either medical or surgical, has probably attracted more attention than that of almost any other disease. Urinary calculi occur in all parts of the world and affect both sexes. They are much more common, however, in some regions than in others. Thus, in India they are very common, while in Great Britain, although many persons suffer from calculus in Norfolk and the north of Scotland, very few cases occur among people who live on the western side of the island. From the above facts many have attributed the formation of calculi to special climatic or geological influences, but it is probable that diet acts as a chief factor in their production. Calculi are much rarer in females than in males, and this may perhaps be explained by the shortness and more vertical position of the urethra, so that the contents of the bladder can be more easily evacuated, and by the fact that the habits of the female with regard to diet are more regular than those of the male. The cause of the formation of a calculus may be (*a*) a tendency in the kidneys to precipitate salts to an abnormal degree, the urine being concentrated and small in amount, or (*b*) some abnormal state of the urine in the bladder, or (*c*) the presence of a foreign body in the bladder. Probably the last is the most common cause; for very frequently, when a section of a calculus is made, it is found that some form of foreign body has acted as the nucleus round which urinary deposits have become agglutinated. Such foreign bodies may exist in the bladder or may be introduced from without. Occasionally clots of blood have been found as the nucleus; but one of the commonest is a small uric acid stone, which, having been formed in the kidney, has passed down the ureter into the bladder and there been surrounded by deposits of phosphate of lime, &c. Calculi vary much in their physical characters and chemical constitution. Most frequently only a single stone is present; but very large numbers have been removed from one bladder. The shape of the stone depends on whether it be movable or fixed, and whether there be only one or more in the bladder. A single stone is usually spherical or ovoid, but may be smooth or tuberculated or spinous, this last point being determined chiefly by the composition of the stone; when there are a number of stones present they are usually faceted or many-sided. Some stones are hard; others are soft. In size and weight they vary very much: we find them as small as a pea and as large as a child's head. The largest stone found in the bladder of a human being is in the Royal College of Surgeons' museum of England; and in the Edinburgh university surgical museum there is a stone of very large size. The weight depends not only on the size but also on the composition, and varies from a few grains to the heaviest on record, which weighed 6 ℔ 3 oz.

Varieties of calculi.

Seven different kinds of calculi are described, but only three are very common. Vesical calculi are classified according to their composition, and five different forms are very generally recognized; but layers of different salts may be found in the same calculus. (1) The first class embraces *uric acid* and *uratic* calculi. Pure uric acid stones are small and hard, and usually vary in colour from a reddish orange to a brown tint. They are frequently rough, but may be smooth. Uratic stones are seldom pure. They frequently form the nucleus of calculi the outer layers of which are phosphatic. (2) *Phosphatic* and *calcareous* calculi consist chiefly of calcium phosphate; stones formed purely of the carbonate of calcium are rare. The stones of this group are white, soft, and friable, especially those composed of phosphate of lime. They frequently attain to a large size, and most commonly occur in persons whose general health has run down to a low ebb. (3) *Oxalate of lime* calculi are excessively hard and dense, of a dark brown colour and tuberculated or spinous on their surface; hence they are often called mulberry calculi. This is a form which gives rise to great pain and irritation, so that they are generally removed before they become very large. (4) *Cystine* and (5) *xanthin* calculi are rare.

Diagnosing for calculi.

When a stone is present in the bladder, whatever its nature, it acts similarly to any other foreign body, and usually gives rise to a series of definite symptoms. The patient complains of pain in the end of the penis at the completion of micturition. Rough or jolting movements give rise to pain in the region of the bladder. Occasionally there is a sudden stoppage of the flow of urine, which is overcome by a change in position. He suffers from frequency of micturition, just as in any other irritable condition of the bladder. If, in addition to these symptoms, the patient states that at varying intervals he has passed "gravel," the surgeon is almost certain that a calculus is present; but even with all these symptoms there is only one certain diagnostic sign of the presence of a stone, and that is to feel it. This is done by "sounding" the bladder with a sound,—an instrument resembling a bougie, but made of steel and with a shorter curve. It can be easily turned from side to side within the bladder, the whole of which must be systematically examined, and not only enables the surgeon to ascertain the presence of a stone but, when judiciously used, assists him in determining the size, mobility, situation, number, and hardness of the calculi. This additional information is of the utmost importance in guiding the surgeon to the best method of treatment. In the child the stone can be occasionally felt by passing one finger into the rectum, laying the other hand above the pubes, and pressing; the stone lies between the two hands. In other cases the size can be gauged with the lithotrite, by observing the distance to which the blades are separated when the stone is grasped.

Treatment.

The treatment of calculi by other means than operative surgery has been found to be of very little value. Attempts have been made to dissolve calculi by internal remedies or by the injection of chemical agents into the bladder; but, although many such methods have been used, and have for a time in many cases been apparently successful, they have without exception been found in the long run to be practically worthless for removing calculi once actually formed. Further, the improvements in operative means for the removal of calculi have advanced to such a degree that it is probably better for a patient, in our present state of knowledge, to be treated by some one of them rather than undergo any attempt at their removal by other means. Nevertheless much can be done towards preventing the formation of calculi in those who have a tendency to their formation, by attention to diet and by the internal administration of drugs.

Removal of calculi by operation.

Urinary calculi are removed by one of three methods,—(i.) lithotomy or cutting for stone, (ii.) lithotrity or crushing the stone, and (iii.) litholapaxy, a modification of lithotrity, and the method now most commonly adopted. In about nine cases out of every ten the stone may be crushed; but occasionally there are some circumstances which render the operation of lithotomy preferable to lithotrity. Thus, where the urethra is constricted, as in organic stricture or enlarged prostate, or where the stone is very large or extremely hard, it is right to cut for the stone instead of making any attempt to crush it. Again, in children lithotomy is safer than lithotrity.

Lithotomy

Lithotomy.—Cutting for stone has been very long known and practised by surgeons; but up to the commencement of the 19th century it was performed only by a few men, who, bolder than their contemporaries, had specially worked at it and had attained celebrity as skilful lithotomists. Patients went very long distances to be operated on by them, and certain of the older surgeons, as Cheselden, performed a large number of operations with very suc-

[1] See "The Bladder Drainage," by Prof. Chiene, in *Edin. Med. Journ.*, vol. xxvi., part i., 1880-81.

cessful results. The operation is usually performed by an incision from the perinæum; but sometimes it is necessary to adopt the high or suprapubic incision. The former method is termed *perineal* lithotomy, and, as the incision most commonly made by the surgeon is a lateral one, it is ordinarily spoken of as *lateral* lithotomy. Lateral lithotomy consists of two distinct stages,—(i.) cutting into the bladder and (ii.) removing the stone. The patient is placed on a table and brought under the influence of an anæsthetic. A grooved staff is passed along the urethra into the bladder to act as a guide for the knife, and the patient is then "tied up in the lithotomy position." An assistant holds the staff in the middle line of the body and the surgeon makes an incision an inch and a half in length deeply into the perinæum, until the knife enters the groove of the staff, and then passes it along the groove, thus making an opening through the bladder-wall. The bladder having been thus cut into, a pair of lithotomy forceps is introduced by the perineal wound, and the stone is caught and removed by gently withdrawing the forceps by a rotatory movement. A lithotomy tube is now passed through the wound into the bladder and fixed in position; the patient is untied and carried back to bed. The operation of lithotomy is not a difficult one to perform, nor is it in itself dangerous; sometimes, however, there is a fatal termination, due commonly to one or other of the following causes—hæmorrhage (either primary or secondary), organic disease of the urinary organs, or blood poisoning. Hæmorrhage may be the result of unskilful operating, the incision having been incorrectly made; or one of the larger vessels in this neighbourhood may have had an abnormal distribution, so that, lying in the line of the incision, it was divided and gave rise to the bleeding which proved fatal. If the stone be a very large one, or the perinæum very narrow, it is necessary to perform the suprapubic operation.

Lithoapaxy.

Litholapaxy.—Lithotrity too can be best described if considered under two headings,—(i.) the crushing of the stone and (ii.) the removal of the detritus. The two stages are now carried out at "one sitting," instead of allowing an interval to elapse between them, as was formerly the practice, and the term *litholapaxy* is used to designate this method. The patient having been anæsthetized, the urethra is dilated by the passage of large-sized bougies. Then a few ounces of a warm neutral aseptic fluid are injected into the bladder, and the crushing instrument, the lithotrite, is passed along the urethra into the bladder. The lithotrite has two blades,—a "male" and a "female,"—the latter fenestrated, the former solid with its surface notched; these blades can be approximated both by a sliding and a screwing movement. The sliding movement is used to grasp the stone; but when the stone is fixed between the blades the screw action is used, as it enables great pressure to be applied evenly, gradually, and continuously. The lithotrite is made of very tough steel, so that even very hard stones may be crushed without any danger of the instrument breaking. It is passed into the bladder with its blades closed; they are then opened and an attempt made to grasp the stone. The stone having been fixed between the blades by the sliding movement, it is then crushed with the screw action, great care being taken not to catch the bladder-wall with the lithotrite. This danger is avoided by raising the point of the lithotrite immediately after grasping the stone and before crushing is begun. The stone breaks into two or more pieces, and these fragments must next be caught and crushed one by one, until they are all reduced to a very small size. If the stone be large and hard, half an hour or longer may be required to crush it sufficiently. When the surgeon fails to catch any more large portions of stone, the presumption is that it has been broken up into small enough pieces; the lithotrite is then withdrawn and the second stage of the operation must be begun. This consists in removing the detritus by means of an aspirator, the best form of which is that invented and used by Sir Henry Thompson. It consists of an elastic bag connected with a trap, into which fragments of stone will fall and not pass out again on the instrument being used at later periods in the operation. A large catheter, with the eye very near the distal end of the short curve, is passed into the bladder; the aspirator, full of an aseptic fluid, is attached to the catheter, and a few ounces of the fluid are expressed from the aspirator into the bladder by squeezing the india-rubber bag. When the pressure is taken off the bag, it dilates and draws by suction the fluid out of the bladder, and with it some of the detritus of the crushed stone, which falls into the trap, and is not expelled on the fluid being re-introduced into the bladder. This manœuvre is repeated again and again, until all the fragments and detritus of the stone have been removed. After the operation the patient sometimes suffers from pain and discomfort; but these are not at all severe unless some fragments have been left in the bladder. If the pain be severe, it can very generally be relieved by hot fomentations or a sitz-bath. The patient must be kept in bed for some days after the operation, and in cases where the stone has been large and the bladder irritable the surgeon should insist on him remaining in bed for at least a week. Judging by statistics, the dangers of the operation, if it be gone about with care, are not nearly so great as those of lithotomy, and certainly in those cases which go on favourably the patients are much sooner able to perform their ordinary duties. Fatal terminations, however, do now and again occur, sometimes as a result of injury to the bladder-wall setting up inflammation, which extends to the kidneys, sometimes from suppression of urine. Those cases in which there has been a fatal result most frequently have been complicated with old-standing kidney disease.

Neoplastic growths.

Neoplastic Growths.—The commonest neoplasms found in the bladder are vascular fibromata (often called villous cancers) and epitheliomata; more rarely malignant growths occur. The symptoms produced by tumours vary; but they may cause obstruction to the flow of urine and chronic cystitis, with more or less severe pain. The most important signs are the passage of blood and the presence of tumour cells in the urine. Frequently, however, microscopical examination of the urine fails to discover the presence of tumour cells. The passage of blood may be very intermittent and small in amount; but this intermittent bleeding is one of the most characteristic signs of the existence of a tumour. When the presence of a tumour is suspected, the sound is passed and an attempt made to feel it. Sometimes it can be felt, but more often doubt remains as to whether a tumour does really exist or not. In such cases the endoscope may be had recourse to; but the information derived from its use is not always satisfactory, and a diagnostic incision must then be made into the bladder to verify the diagnosis. When such a diagnostic incision is made, the surgeon must be prepared to remove the tumour, should one be present and capable of removal. Usually the diagnostic incision is perineal; but, if the bladder is capacious, or if the perinæum is deep and narrow, a more complete examination can be made by a suprapubic opening. The treatment of neoplasms is, as a rule, unsatisfactory. If the growth be pedunculated, it can be removed without great risk to the patient; more commonly, however, the tumour cannot be removed, and then only palliative measures can be adopted, such as allaying the pain and checking the hæmorrhage. Great relief is often given by washing out the bladder; but this must be done with very great care, a soft flexible catheter being used, if it can be passed into the bladder, in preference to a rigid one.

Hypertrophy and dilatation.

Hypertrophy and Dilatation.—When there is long-continued obstruction to the flow of urine, as in stricture of the urethra, enlarged prostate, &c., the bladder-wall becomes much thickened, the muscular fibres increasing both in size and number; the interstitial fibrous tissue is also increased. The wall on its inner surface becomes rugose, and the condition is technically known as *hypertrophy*. Hypertrophy may be accompanied by *dilatation* of the bladder, a condition which the bladder may assume when from any cause the evacuation of its contents is interfered with for a length of time.

Paralysis of bladder.

Paralysis of the bladder is a want of contractile power in the muscular fibres of the bladder-wall. It may result from injuries whereby the spinal cord is lacerated or pressed upon at or below the micturitory centre situated in the lumbar region. The result may be either retention or incontinence of urine: sometimes there is at first retention, which later on is followed by incontinence, while in other cases incontinence results in the first place and then retention. Paralysis is also produced in certain nervous diseases, as in locomotor ataxia, and in various cerebral lesions, as in apoplexy.

Atony of bladder.

Atony of the bladder differs from paralysis in being only a paresis or partial paralysis. It is due to a want of tone in the muscular fibres, and is most frequently the result of habitual over-distension of the bladder, such as may occur in cases of enlargement of the prostate. The patient is unable to empty the bladder, and the condition of atony gets increasingly worse.

In both paralysis and atony the indication is to carefully prevent over-distension of the bladder by the urine being retained too long, and at the same time to treat by appropriate means the cause which has produced or is keeping up the condition.

Incontinence of urine.

Incontinence of urine may occur in the adult or in the child, but is due to widely different causes in the two cases. In the child it may be simply a bad habit, the child not having been properly trained; but more frequently there seems to be a want of control in the micturitory centre, so that the child passes its water unwittingly, especially during the night. In adults it is not so much a condition of incontinence in the sense of water being passed against the will, but is rather due to a difficulty in retaining the urine in consequence generally of an over-full bladder,—the water which passes being the overflow from a too full reservoir. It is usually caused by an obstruction external to the bladder, *e.g.*, enlarged prostate or stricture of the urethra. Occasionally the presence of a calculus may produce the condition. The treatment differs in the case of the child and of the adult. In the child an attempt must be made to improve the tone of the micturitory centre by the use of belladonna or strychnia internally and of a blister or faradism externally over the lumbar region, and every effort should be made to train the child to pass its water at stated times and regular intervals. In the adult the cause which produces the over-distension must be removed if possible; but as a rule the patient has to be provided with a catheter, which he can pass into his bladder and thus thoroughly empty it before it has filled to overflowing. A soft flexible catheter should be given in preference to a rigid or semi-rigid one. The best form is the red-rubber catheter.

Stammering micturition.

The condition termed by Sir James Paget *stammering micturition* is frequently seen in young men, more rarely in children and adults. This stammering of the urinary apparatus is analogous to speech stammering, and occurs chiefly in those who are nervous and easily put out. It would seem to be due to incoordination of the sphincter and detrusor of the bladder, the former not relaxing synchronously with the contraction of the detrusor, or *vice versa*, and is sometimes caused by external irritation, such as preputial adhesions. Occasionally not a drop of urine can be passed, or a little passes and then a sudden stoppage of the flow occurs, and the more the patient strains the worse he becomes, until at last there is complete retention of urine. Very usually such errors in micturition can be cured by the removal of irritating causes, if they exist, and in these cases, as well as in those in which no such cause can be discovered, great care should be taken to avoid those difficulties which have given rise to the patient's worst failures. If at any time he should fail to perform the act of micturition, he ought not to strain, but should quietly wait for a little before making any further effort, after which he will often succeed. Regularity in the times of making water is also of much importance.

Retention of urine.

Retention of urine cannot be called a disease of the bladder, but may be the cause of, or result from, bladder disease. It may occur in paralysis of the bladder, or in conditions where the patient is suffering from an illness which blunts the nervous sensibility, *e.g.*, typhoid fever. It is, however, much more commonly due to obstruction in some part of the urinary passage anterior to the bladder, as in stricture of the urethra or enlargement of the prostate. The patient can usually tell when he last passed any urine; but, even when no such information can be obtained, there are signs which lead the surgeon to a correct diagnosis. Thus, the bladder if much distended can be felt as a rounded swelling above the pubes, and it may even have passed to the level of the umbilicus. Percussion of the hypogastrium gives a dull note. When retention of urine occurs and the bladder is over-distended, it is necessary to evacuate its contents as soon as possible. If there is no obstruction to the flow of urine, the retention being due merely to atony or paralysis of the bladder, a flexible soft catheter is passed into the bladder and the water drawn off. But, when there is an obstruction which cannot be overcome, aspiration of the bladder has to be resorted to, the needle of the aspirator being pushed through the abdominal wall into the bladder. The point of puncture in the abdominal wall is in the middle line just above the symphysis pubis. The bladder has been aspirated in this way very many times in the same person without any evil result. But in all cases strict antiseptic precautions must be adopted. (J. C.)

VESOUL, a town of France, chef-lieu of the department of Haute-Saône, is situated 147 miles south-east of Paris by the railway to Mülhausen, at the junction of branch lines to Gray and Besançon, on the river Durgeon, which here receives two tributaries. The isolated conical hill of La Motte (1483 feet), which shelters the town on the north, affords fine views of the Jura and the Vosges Mountains. On the summit is a votive chapel (1854). The chief features of Vesoul are the palace of justice, the church of St George with a fine altar, the promenade with a monument to the gardes mobiles of the department who fell at Belfort in 1870 and 1871, a library of 20,000 volumes, and an archæological museum. The population in 1881 was 9431 (commune 9553), the corresponding figures for 1886 being 9602 and 9733.

Vesoul, which is first mentioned in the 10th century, was originally a fief of the church of Besançon. It afterwards passed to the house of Burgundy, and was fortified. The castle was destroyed in the 17th century. The town suffered much during the Wars of Religion and the Thirty Years' War. Vesoul belonged temporarily to France after the death of Charles the Bold, was returned to the empire when Charles VIII. broke off his marriage with the daughter of the emperor Maximilian, and again became part of France under Louis XIV. after the peace of Nimeguen.

VESPASIAN. TITUS FLAVIUS VESPASIANUS, the tenth of the twelve Cæsars, was Roman emperor from 70 to 79 in succession to Vitellius. He was born in the year 9, in the Sabine country near Reate. His father was a tax-collector and money-lender on a small scale; his mother, however, was a lady of pretty good family, with a brother a senator. She encouraged her son to look up in the world. After having served with the army in Thrace and been a quæstor in Crete and Cyrene, Vespasian rose to be ædile and prætor, having meanwhile taken to wife the daughter of a Roman knight, Flavia Domitilla, by whom he had two sons, Titus and Domitian, both of whom succeeded him. Having already served in Germany, in the years 43 and 44, in the reign of Claudius, he had the command of a legion in Britain under Aulus Plautius, and saw much hard fighting, reducing to subjection the Isle of Wight and penetrating very possibly into Devonshire and the neighbourhood of Exeter. He proved himself a thoroughly able soldier, while in his habits he was simple and frugal; in short, says Tacitus (*Hist.*, ii. 5), "but for his avarice he was equal to the generals of old days." In 51 he was for a brief space consul; soon afterwards he went as governor to Africa, where, according to Tacitus (ii. 97), his rule was "infamous and odious," according to Suetonius (*Vesp.*, 4), "upright and highly honourable," though he admits that there was a serious local disturbance in which the governor was pelted with turnips. On leaving Africa there was a story (Suet., *Vesp.*, 4) that he got his livelihood as a dealer of some sort,[1] which, if true, shows that he did not turn his provincial governorship to profit. He went with Nero's suite to Greece, and in 67 was appointed to conduct the war in Judæa, which was threatening general commotion throughout the East, owing to a widely spread notion in those parts that from Judæa were to come the future rulers of the world. Vespasian, who had a strong vein of superstition, was made to believe that he was himself to fulfil this expectation, and all manner of omens and oracles and portents were applied to him. He also found encouragement in Mucianus, the governor of Syria; and he had a soldiery thoroughly devoted to him, although he was at the same time a strict disciplinarian and reformer of abuses. Vespasian had, however, plenty of practical good sense, and he knew well how to strike down a foe. All eyes in the East were now upon him; Mucianus and the Syrian legions were eager to back him up; and on 1st July 69, while he was at Cæsarea, he was proclaimed emperor, first by the army in Egypt, and then by his troops in Judæa. The legions of the East at once swore to him the customary oath of allegiance. Nevertheless Vitellius had on his side the veteran legions of Gaul and Germany, Rome's best troops. But the feeling in Vespasian's favour quickly gathered strength, and the armies of Mœsia, Pannonia, and Illyricum soon declared for him, and made him in fact master of half of the Roman world. They entered Italy on the north-east under the leadership of Antonius Primus, defeated the army of Vitellius at Bedriacum, sacked Cremona, and advanced on Rome, which they entered after furious fighting and a frightful confusion, in which the Capitol was destroyed by fire. The new emperor received the tidings of his rival's defeat and death at Alexandria, whence he at once forwarded supplies of corn to Rome, which were urgently needed, along with an edict or a declaration of policy, in which he gave assurance of an entire reversal of the laws of Nero, especially those relating to treason. While in Egypt he became more and more imbued with superstition, consulting astrologers and allowing himself to be flattered into a belief that he possessed a divine power which could work miracles. Leaving the war in Judæa to his son Titus, he arrived at Rome in 70, where he restored the Capitol, rebuilt a great part of the city, enforced discipline in the army, which under Vitellius had become utterly demoralized, and with the co-operation of the senate put the government and the finances on a sound footing. By his own example of simplicity of life, he put to shame the luxury and extravagance of the Roman nobles and initiated in many respects a marked improvement in the general tone of society. As censor he raised

[1] *Ad mangonicos quæstus descenderat.*

the character of the senate, removing unfit and unworthy members, and promoting good and able men, among them the excellent Julius Agricola. In 70 a formidable rising in Gaul, headed by Claudius Civilis, was suppressed; the Jewish War was brought to a close by Titus's capture of Jerusalem, and in the following year, after the joint triumph of Vespasian and Titus, memorable as the first occasion on which a father and his son were thus associated together, the temple of Janus was closed, and the Roman world had rest for the remaining nine years of Vespasian's reign. The peace of Vespasian passed into a proverbial phrase. In 78 Agricola went to Britain, and both extended and consolidated the Roman dominion in that province, pushing his arms into North Wales and the Isle of Anglesey. In the following year Vespasian died, in his 70th year.

The avarice with which both Tacitus (*Hist.*, ii. 5) and Suetonius (*Vesp.*, 16) stigmatize Vespasian seems really to have been an enlightened economy, which, in the disordered state of the Roman finances, was an absolute necessity. Vespasian could be liberal to impoverished senators and knights, to cities and towns desolated by natural calamity, and especially to men of letters and of the professor class, several of whom he pensioned with salaries of as much as £800 a year. Quintilian is said to have been the first public teacher who enjoyed this imperial favour. Vespasian may be fairly credited with doing his best to improve and elevate the tone of the age by spreading those intellectual tastes with which personally he was not much in sympathy. Pliny's great work, the *Natural History*, was written during Vespasian's reign, and dedicated to his son Titus, who almost shared the emperor's throne (see TITUS). Some of the philosophers, pedants in reality, who talked idly of the good old times of the republic, and thus indirectly encouraged conspiracy, provoked him into reviving the obsolete penal laws against this class, but only one, Helvidius Priscus, was put to death, and he had affronted the emperor by studied insults. "I will not kill a dog that barks at me" were words honestly expressing the temper of Vespasian. Much was spent on public works and the restoring and beautifying of Rome during his reign,—a new forum, the splendid temple of Peace (symbolizing the sentiment of the age), the public baths, and the vast Colosseum being begun under Vaspasian.

To the last Vespasian was a plain, blunt soldier, with decided strength of character and ability, and with a steady purpose to establish good order and secure the prosperity and welfare of his subjects. In his habits he was punctual and regular, transacting his business early in the morning, and enjoying his siesta after a drive. He had not quite the distinguished bearing looked for in an emperor. He was free in his conversation, and his humour, of which he had a good deal, was apt to take the form of rather coarse jokes. He could jest, it was said, even in his last moments. "Methinks I am becoming a god," he whispered to those around him. There is something very characteristic in the exclamation he is said to have uttered in his last illness, "An emperor ought to die standing."

The *Histories* of Tacitus and the biography of Suetonius are our chief original sources about Vespasian. Dean Merivale, in his *History of the Romans under the Empire*, gives a very complete account of him (chaps. 57, 59, 60).

VESPERS (*officium vespertinum*) in the Roman Catholic liturgy is that part of the daily office which follows none (*nona*) and precedes compline (*completorium*). In it the Pater Noster, Ave Maria, Deus in Adjutorium, &c., are followed by five psalms and five antiphons, after which come the "little chapter," the hymn and the verse, which vary according to the season, the Magnificat and its antiphon, and the appropriate collect. In its general features the use of this office can be traced back to a very early date both in the Eastern and in the Western Church. Vespers may be said or sung at any time after midday, and in some circumstances even before it.

VESPUCCI, AMERIGO (1451-1512), navigator, was born at Florence on 9th March 1451. His father, Nastugio Vespucci, was a notary, and his uncle, to whom he owed his education, was a scholarly Dominican and a friend of Savonarola. As a student Amerigo showed a preference for natural philosophy, astronomy, and geography. He was placed as a clerk in the great commercial house of the Medici, then the ruling family in Florence. About 1490 he was sent by Lorenzo de' Medici to Spain, and in January 1492 he was at Cadiz, along with an associate, Donato Nicolini, probably as an agent of the Medici. Shortly after this he seems to have entered the service of a Florentine merchant, Juonato Berardi, established at Seville, who had fitted out the second expedition of Columbus in 1493. Berardi had also undertaken to fit out twelve ships for the king of Spain, and on his death in December 1495 Vespucci was commissioned to complete the contract. There is no proof that Vespucci accompanied Columbus on either his first or his second voyage, though there can be no doubt that the two Italians were known to each other. As Ferdinand had recalled the monopoly conceded to Columbus, the new passion for exploring became widespread and adventurers of all kinds were constantly leaving Spain for the West. On the authority of Vespucci himself, he sailed, possibly as astronomer, with one of these adventurous expeditions from Cadiz, on 10th May 1497. After touching at the Canaries, the four vessels are stated to have reached after twenty-seven days "a coast which we thought to be that of a continent"; from Vespucci's account this may have been Campeachy Bay. Thence they doubled Cape Sable and may even have reached Cape Hatteras. Finally, after sailing about a hundred leagues to an archipelago, the chief island of which was called Iti, they made for Spain and reached Cadiz on 15th October 1498. Still following Vespucci's own statement, he on 16th May 1499 started on a second voyage in a fleet of three ships under Alonzo de Ojeda. They reached the coast of Brazil about Cape St Roque, sailed north to the mouth of the Amazons, round to the Gulf of Maracaibo, and on to San Domingo. The expedition returned to Cadiz on 8th September 1500. Entering the service of Dom Manuel of Portugal, Vespucci took part in a new expedition to the "Land of Parrots" (Brazil), which left Lisbon on 10th May 1501. Cape St Roque was reached on 16th August; Rio Janeiro Bay was discovered and named on New Year's Day 1502; and in April the expedition appears to have got as far as South Georgia. It reached Lisbon again on 7th September 1502. Next year, on 10th June, Vespucci started from Lisbon on his fourth expedition, with six ships under Coelho, the object being to reach Malacca by sailing west. At the island of Fernando Noronha Vespucci's ship separated from the others and sailed to Bahia and then to Cape Frio, where he built a fort. He returned to Lisbon on 18th June 1504. In 1505 he went back to Spain and re-entered the service of Ferdinand, settling in Seville. According to one account, Vespucci made two other voyages to the isthmus of Panama. In 1508 he was appointed *piloto mayor*. He died at Seville on 22d February 1512.

If his own account is trustworthy, Vespucci reached the mainland of America eighteen days before Cabot. Yet he was attached to the expedition only in a subordinate capacity, and, had it not been that his name has become attached to the New World, it is probable he would scarcely have been heard of. It seems to be credible, however, that in a letter written soon after his return from his third voyage he referred to the newly discovered lands as the "New World." Vespucci's claim to have touched the American mainland before Cabot has been hotly disputed, and the controversial literature on the subject is voluminous. The facts, as accepted by those who admit his claims, or at least his good faith, are these. After his fourth voyage, that is after 1504, he wrote a diary called *Le Quattre Giornale*. No fragment of the original exists, and it is only known by allusion. He also wrote several letters to his former schoolfellow Soderini, the gonfalier or chief magistrate of Florence. One of these only remains, and that not in the original, but in a Latin translation printed at the monastery of St Dié in the Vosges on 25th April 1507. The statement is that a French translation of Vespucci's original had been given to King René, who was patronizing the college at St Dié. Waldseemüller (Hylacomylus) made use of this letter in his *Cosmographiæ Introductio*, published at St Dié in 1507. Here it is that we have the first suggestion of a name for the New World in the words—"A fourth part of the world, which, since Amerigo found it, we may call Amerigé or America"; and again, "now a fourth part has been found by Amerigo Vespucci, and I do not see why we should be prevented from calling it

Amerigé or *America*." Since Humboldt discussed the subject in his *Examen Critique de l'Histoire de la Géographie du Nouveau Continent*, vol. iv. (1837), the general weight of opinion has been that Vespucci did not make the 1497 voyage, and that he had no share in the first discovery of the American continent, but that there is not sufficient evidence to convict him of deliberate falsification. Varnhagen, however, in his *Amerigo Vespucci* (Lima, 1845) and many other writers on the subject maintain Vespucci's right to be regarded as a member of the expedition.

The whole question is very thoroughly discussed in vol. ii. of the *Narrative and Critical History of America*, edited by Justin Winsor (1886), where will be found ample references to all the authorities on the subject. See also Major's *Prince Henry the Navigator* (1868), and a recent re-examination of the evidence for the first voyage in "Alcune Considerazioni sul Primo Viaggio," by L. Hugues, in the *Bolletino* of the Italian Geographical Society, 1885.

VESTA (Greek Ϝεστία), the goddess of fire and the domestic hearth. The cults of the Greek Hestia and the Latin Vesta, both of which involved the guardianship of an ever-burning sacred fire, are most probably derived from a very early custom, common to a great variety of races, and practised during many different ages. Among people in a primitive state of development the production of fire is a slow and very laborious process; thus it became the custom for each village to maintain a constant fire for the general use of the community, in order to avoid the troublesome necessity of obtaining a spark by friction in case of the accidental extinction at one time of all the village fires.[1] This fire, the central hearth or Ϝεστία of the village (*focus publicus*), became a sacred symbol of home and family life, and by degrees grew into a religious cult of great sanctity and importance. The form of the primitive house in which the fire was preserved, probably a round hut made of wattled osiers daubed with clay, appears to have survived both in the circular prytaneum of the Greeks and in the Ædes Vestæ in Rome. To watch this fire would naturally be the duty of women, and especially of those who were not burdened with the cares of maternity, and hence may have arisen the Roman order of virgin priestesses, whose chief duty it was to tend the sacred fire. A survival of the prehistoric method of getting a spark appears to have existed in the rule which enacted that, if ever the sacred fire of Vesta did go out, the negligent vestal was to be punished by scourging (Livy, xxviii. 11), and the fire rekindled either by friction of dry sticks[2] or, in later times, by the sun's rays brought to a focus by a concave mirror (Plut., *Numa*, 9). In the prytaneum, which existed in every Greek state, a different form of cult was developed, though the essential point, the sacred fire, was kept up, just as in the Latin worship of Vesta; and in both cases the fire was extinguished annually at the beginning of the new year, and solemnly rekindled by one of the primitive and hence sacred methods.[3] In Rome this was done on the first day of March, the Latin New Year's Day (Ovid, *Fast.*, iii. 137-145). Both among Greek and early Latin races, at the founding of a new colony fire was solemnly sent from the prytaneum or Vesta temple of the mother colony to kindle a similar sacred fire in the new settlement. Thus we find that, according to tradition, the worship of Vesta in Rome was introduced from Alba Longa (Liv., i. 20, and Ov., *Fast.*, iii. 46), which appears to have been the oldest of the Latin colonies in Latium. This intimate connexion between the Greek prytaneum fire, sacred to Hestia, and that of Vesta in Rome has been ably worked out by Mr J. G. Frazer in the paper quoted above. The most generally received Latin legend attributes the founding of the Roman temple of Vesta to Numa, who transferred the centre of the cult from Alba, together with the four vestal virgins, its priestesses (Plut., *Numa*, 10). One of the later kings, either Tarquin I. or Servius Tullius, is said to have increased the number to six (Dion. Hal., iii. 67, and Plut., *Numa*, 10), and it is not till the last years of the pagan period that we hear of a seventh vestal having been added (see Ambrose, *Epis.*, ed. Pareus, p. 477; also Plut., *Rom.* and *Cam.*).

The election (*captio*) of the vestal during the early period of Rome was in the hands of the king, and in those of the pontifex maximus under the republic and empire,[4] subject, however, to the following conditions (Aul. Gell., i. 12):—(1) the candidate was to be more than six and less than ten years of age; (2) she was to be *patrima* and *matrima*, *i.e.*, having both parents alive; (3) free from physical or mental defects; (4) daughter of a free-born resident in Italy. Certain details of the election were arranged subject to the provisions of the Lex Papia, now unknown. The selected child had her hair cut off, and was solemnly admitted by the pontifex maximus, who held her by the hand, and, addressing her by the name *amata*, pronounced an ancient formula of initiation, which is given by A. Gellius in his interesting chapter on the subject (i. 12). In early times there were certain rules by which girls could be excused from serving as vestals, but the honour soon became so eagerly sought that these provisions were practically useless. Vows were taken by the vestal for a limited period of thirty years, after which she was free to return to private life and even to marry—a thing very rarely done (Aul. Gell., vi. 7). This period of thirty years was divided into three decades: during the first the vestal learnt her duties; during the second she practised them; and during the third she instructed the young vestals. The special dignity of chief of the vestals, or *virgo vestalis maxima*, was reached in order of seniority. The inscriptions on the pedestals of statues of various *vestales maximæ* show that a number of different grades of honour were passed through before reaching the *maximatus* or highest dignity.[5] The duties of the vestals, besides the chief one of tending the holy fire (Cic., *De Leg.*, ii. 8), consisted in the daily bringing of water from the sacred spring of Egeria, near the Porta Capena, to be used for the ceremonial sweeping and sprinkling of the Ædes Vestæ.[6] They also offered sacrifices of salt cakes—*muries* and *mola salsa*—and poured on the altar of sacred fire libations of wine and oil, as is represented on the reverses of several first brasses and medallions of the empire (see fig. 1). The vestals were bound to offer daily prayers for the welfare of the Roman state, and more especially in times of danger or calamity (Cic., *Pro Font.*, 21). They were also the guardians of the seven sacred objects on which the stability of the Roman power was supposed to depend:[7] the chief of these was the Palladium, a rude archaic statue of Pallas, which was said to have been brought by Æneas from the burning

[1] Mr J. G. Frazer, in an interesting paper printed in the *Journal of Philology* (vol. xiv. pp. 145-172), on "the Worship of Vesta and its Connexion with the Greek Prytaneum," has given many examples of a similar custom still surviving among various savage races.

[2] An allusion to the earliest method of obtaining fire by rubbing two sticks together is probably contained in the myth of Prometheus, who brought fire to mortals hidden in a hollow wand.

[3] Fire obtained in this way, that is "pure elemental fire," was commonly thought to possess a special sanctity. Even throughout the Middle Ages in Catholic countries, at Easter, when the new year began, the old pagan rite still survived. On Holy Saturday all lamps in each church were extinguished, and the Paschal candlestick was lighted by the help of flint and steel. From this sacred source the other lights in the church were kindled, and the various households in the parish took a flame to relight their fires and lamps, all of which had been carefully extinguished beforehand.

[4] From the time of Augustus the emperors themselves held the office of chief pontiff, and with it the privilege of electing the vestals.

[5] These inscriptions are printed in Middleton, *Ancient Rome in 1885*, pp. 200-6, and in *Archæologia*, vol. xlix. pp. 414-422.

[6] The shrine of Vesta was not a *templum* in the strict Roman sense, as it was not consecrated by the augurs, its sanctity being far above the necessity of any such ceremony. Other natural springs might be used for the daily sprinkling, but it was forbidden to use water brought in a pipe or other artificial conduit (Tac., *Hist.*, iv. 53; see also Guhl and Koner, *Vit. Gr. et Rom.*, p. 654).

[7] See Cancellieri, *Le Sette Cose Fatali di Roma Antica*, Rome, 1812.

Troy. This sacred object was never shown to profane eyes, but it is represented on the reverse of a coin struck by Antoninus Pius in honour of his deified wife Faustina

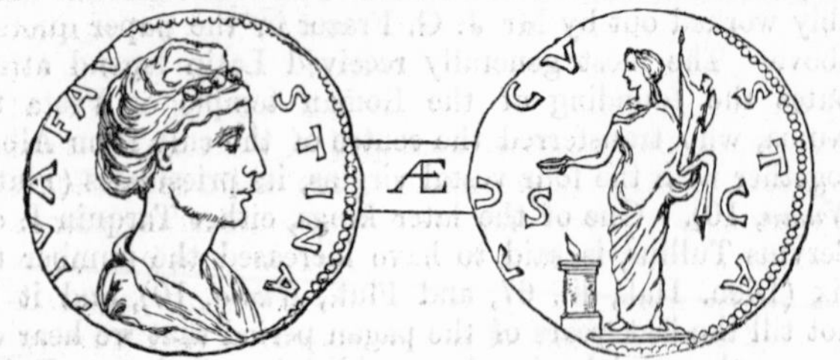

Fig. 1.—First brass struck in honour of Diva Faustina by her husband Antoninus Pius, soon after her death. On the reverse is a vestal holding the Palladium and pouring a libation on the altar of the sacred fire.

(see fig. 1). Strict observance of the vow of chastity was one of the chief obligations of the vestals, and its breach was horribly punished by burial alive at a place near the Porta Collina known as the Campus Sceleratus (see Livy, viii. 15 and 89; Plin., *Ep.*, iv. 11; and Suet., *Dom.*, 8). Cases of unchastity and its punishment were rare; and, as the evidence against the vestal was usually that of slaves, given under torture, it is probable that in many instances an innocent vestal suffered this cruel death. The case described by the younger Pliny (*sup. cit.*) is one of special pathos, as the vestal appears to have been condemned without any sufficient evidence, simply at the wish of the emperor Domitian. A fanciful reason for this fearful punishment is given by Ovid, *Fast.*, vi. 459-460.

The privileges of the vestals and their influential position were very remarkable. They were exempt from any *patria potestas*, except that of the pontifex maximus, their religious father; they could dispose by will of their property, and were in most respects not subject to the Roman laws ("legibus non tenetur," Servius, on Virg., *Æn.*, xi. 204; *cf.* Gaius, i. 130, and Dion Cass., lvi. 10). This involved freedom from taxes, and the right to drive through the streets of Rome in carriages (*plostrum* and *currus arcuatus*). Some bronze plates have been found which were once attached to the carriages of vestals; the inscription on one of them runs thus, *Flaviæ Publiciæ v.v. maximæ inmunis in jugo* (see *C. I. L.*, vi. 2146-2148; *cf.* also Pruden., *Contr. Symm.*, ii. 1088). They were preceded by a lictor when appearing on state occasions, and enjoyed other semi-royal honours (Plut., *Numa*, 10, and Dion Cass., xlvii. 19). At theatres and other places of amusement they enjoyed the best seats, except at some of the nude athletic contests, from which they were excluded; they also took an important part in all the grand religious and state ceremonies, such as when the pontifex maximus offered sacrifice on the occasion of a triumph before the temple of Capitoline Jupiter. They had power to pardon any criminal they met in the street on his way to execution, provided that the meeting were accidental. The vestals alone shared with the emperors the privilege of intramural burial (Serv., *Ad Æn.*, xi. 206). During life they were richly dowered by the state (Suet., *Aug.*, 31) and had public slaves appointed to serve them (see Tac., *Hist.*, i. 43). They were also the guardians of the emperor's will, and of other important documents of state (Suet., *J. Cæs.*, 83, and *Aug.*, 101; Tac., *Ann.*, i. 8; Plut., *Anton.*, 58; and Appian, *Civ.*, v. 73). Their influence in the appointment to many offices, both religious and secular, appears to have been very great. Many of the statues to the chief vestals which were found in the Atrium Vestæ in 1883-84 have pedestals inscribed with a dedication recording that benefits had been conferred on the donor by the vestalis maxima. Lastly, they lived in a style of very great splendour: their house,[1] the Atrium Vestæ, which stood close by the Ædes Vestæ, was very large and exceptionally magnificent both in decoration and material. The discovery already mentioned of a number of statues of vestales maximæ has thrown new light on the dress of the vestals.[2] With one or two exceptions the costume of these statues is much the same: they have a long sleeveless tunic or *stola*, girdled by the *zona* immediately below the breast. One only wears the *diploidion* over the upper part of her figure. The outer garment is an ample *pallium*, wrapped round the body in a great variety of folds, and in some cases brought over the head like a hood. All seem to have long hair, showing that the process of cutting off the hair at initiation was not repeated. One figure (see fig. 2) wears the *suffibulum*, a rectangular piece of white cloth bordered by a purple stripe, worn over the head and fastened on the breast by a *fibula*.[3]

Fig. 2.—Statue of a vestalis maxima wearing the suffibulum; time of Trajan.

According to Festus (ed. Müller, p. 348), this sacred garment was worn by the vestals only during the act of sacrificing (see also Varro, *De Ling. Lat.*, vi. 21). This is probably the only existing statue on which this rare garment is represented. In all cases the head is closely bound by *vittæ*, rope-like twists of woollen cloth, the ends of which usually fall in loops on each shoulder (see Servius, *Ad Æn.*, x. 538).

The *Regia*, or official *fanum* of the pontifex maximus, was adjacent to the vestal's house:—

> "Hic locus est Vestæ, qui Pallada servat et ignem;
> Hic fuit antiqui Regia parva Numæ."[4]

When Augustus, after his election to the office of pontifex maximus in 12 B.C., moved his place of residence from the Regia to the Palatine, he built a new Ædes Vestæ near his palace, in the magnificent Area Apollinis. This appears to have been a copy of the older temple of Vesta. No traces of it now exist; but Pirro Ligorio, in the latter part of the 16th century, made some sketches of what then existed of this second temple, to illustrate his great MS. on Roman antiquities, which is now preserved in the royal library at Turin (see Ovid, *Fast.*, iv. 949-954, and *Metam.*, xv. 864). The original course of the Sacra Via was supposed to have passed close to the temple of Vesta; but excavations made in 1886 have shown that this was not

[1] For a description of this, and also of the temple of Vesta and its vicissitudes, see Rome, vol. xix. pp. 818-819; Middleton, *Ancient Rome in 1885*, pp. 181-206; and a paper by the same author in *Archæologia*, vol. xlix. p. 391 *sq.*

[2] These statues appear to have been the work of a privileged class of sculptors, who enjoyed the title of "fictores virginum vestalium,"—an honour which is recorded in some of the dedicatory inscriptions on the pedestals.

[3] The form of the *suffibulum* as shown on this statue has a curious similarity to the amice worn by the mediæval clergy.

[4] Ov., *Tris.*, iii. 29. For the history of the Regia and its existing remains, see Rome, vol. xix. p. 819, and *Archæologia*, vol. xlix. p. 398 *sq.*

the case, the supposed line of the road being really blocked by a very early structure. There is reason to believe that this formed part of the original Regia, which was rebuilt during the reign of Augustus in a more magnificent way by Domitius Calvinus, after his Spanish triumph.

The *Vestalia*, or chief festival in honour of Vesta, was held on 9th June (Ovid, *Fast.*, vi. 249), after which the temple was closed for five days for a ceremonial cleansing.[1] In private houses the feast was celebrated by a meal of fish, bread, and herbs, eaten, not on the usual triclinium, but by the domestic hearth, in front of the effigies of the Dii Penates (Ovid, *Fast.*, vi. 309-310). The feast inaugurated by Augustus in honour of Vesta Palatina was held on 28th April, the anniversary of its consecration.

With regard to statues of the goddess, though the Greek Hestia was frequently represented in plastic art, yet among the Romans Vesta appears to have been rarely so treated. The Athenian prytaneum contained a statue of Hestia. But there was no effigy in the Roman temple of Vesta, although one is commonly shown on reverses of coins which have a representation of the temple, and it appears to have been commonly thought in Rome that a statue of Vesta did exist inside her shrine,—a mistake which Ovid corrects (*Fast.*, vi. 297-300). No Roman statue now known can be certainly considered to represent Vesta, though a very beautiful standing figure of a female with veiled head (in the Torlonia collection) has, with some probability, had this name given to it.

The worship of Vesta appears to have died out slowly in the 4th century, after the adoption of Christianity as the state religion by Constantine. Zosimus (*Hist. Nov.*, v. 38) tells an interesting story of a visit made to the Atrium Vestæ at the end of the 4th century by Serena, the wife of the Vandal Stilicho, who took a valuable necklace from one of the statues, in spite of the remonstrances of an aged woman, the last survivor of the vestal virgins. Soon after that time the building appears to have fallen into decay, its valuable marble linings and other ornaments having been stripped from its walls.

Literature.—For further information the reader is referred, in addition to the works quoted above, to Lipsius, *De Vesta et Vestalibus Syntagma*, printed in Græevius, *Thes. Ant. Rom.*, vol. v.; Cramer, *Kleine Schriften*, ed. by Ratjen, Leipsic, 1837, p. 89 *sq.*; Klausen, *Æneas und die Penaten*, ii. p. 624 *sq.*; Nardini, *Roma Antica*, ed. of 1818-20, ii. p. 185 *sq.*; Brohm, *De Jure Virginum Vestalium*, Thorn, 1835; Preuner, *Hestia-Vesta*, Tübingen, 1864; Jordan, *Vesta und die Laren*, Berlin, 1865, and more recent papers; Maes, *Vesta e Vestali*, Rome, 1883; Lanciani, *L'Atrio di Vesta*, Rome, 1884; and *C. I. L.*, vi. p. 594, No. 2131 *sq.* (J. H. M.)

VESTMENTS, in ecclesiastical law, are the garments worn during the church service by the officiating clergy. In England and Scotland before the Reformation the vestments in use were similar to those still worn by the Roman Catholic clergy,—probably modifications of the dress of Roman citizens in their origin (see COSTUME)—and were either sacrificial, as the chasuble, or non-sacrificial, as the surplice. After the Reformation the question of vestments became of comparatively small importance in the Church of Scotland; but in the Church of England it has in recent years been the cause of much controversy and litigation.

The "ornaments rubric" at the beginning of the Book of Common Prayer, dating from 1662, provides "that such ornaments of the church and of the ministers thereof at all times of their ministration shall be retained and be in use as were in this Church of England by the authority of parliament in the second year of the reign of King Edward VI." The reference in this rubric is to the vestments enjoined by the first prayer book of Edward VI. (1549). The surplice (with the addition of the hood in cathedrals and colleges, and for preaching) was the priest's dress for the service other than the communion. In the communion the bishop was to wear, besides a rochet, a surplice or alb, with a cope or vestment (also called a chasuble), and to have a pastoral staff borne by himself or his chaplain. The officiating priest was to wear a white alb, plain, with a vestment or cope, the assisting ministers albs with tunicles. The second prayer book of Edward VI. (1552) enjoined the use of the surplice only. The Act of Uniformity of Elizabeth (1 Eliz. c. 2) provided for the use of the 1549 vestments, "until other order shall be therein taken by the authority of the queen's Majesty, &c." In 1564 the Advertisements of Elizabeth were issued, under which the legal vestments were fixed to be the cope worn by the principal minister, with gospeller and epistoler agreeably, in the ministration of the communion, but at ordinary services and at prayers (other than those during the ministration of the communion) said at the communion table the surplice only. Deans and prebendaries were to wear hoods. The point which the judicial committee of the privy council has been called upon more than once to decide is whether the Advertisements of Elizabeth—coupled with the Injunctions of 1559 and subsequent visitations—were such taking of "other order" as to supersede the ornaments rubric. It has been held that they were, and the effect of the decisions has been to reduce the legal vestments to the surplice and hood for all ordinary purposes, with the addition of the cope for the administration of the communion on high feast days in cathedral and collegiate churches. The cope was also allowed by the canons of 1603-4. A bishop wears in addition a rochet. The chasuble, alb, and tunicle had, as has been said, post-Reformation authority, but the girdle, amice, stole, maniple, dalmatic, and biretta were never legally recognized since that time. The stole, however, is frequently worn, by deacons generally arranged as a scarf over the left shoulder. Much information on the subject will be found in the first *Report* of the Royal Commission on Ritual, issued in 1867.

[1] The solemn decade of the *Vestalia* began on 5th June and ended on the 15th, when the temple was closed.

VESTRY. See PARISH, vol. xviii. p. 296.

VESUVIUS, the most celebrated volcano in the world, rises from the eastern margin of the Bay of Naples in Italy, in the midst of a region which has been densely populated by a civilized community for more than twenty centuries. Hence it has served as a type for the general popular conception of a volcano, and its history has supplied a large part of the information on which geological theories of volcanic action have been based. The height of the mountain varies from time to time within limits of several hundred feet, according to the effects of successive eruptions, but averages somewhere about 4000 feet above

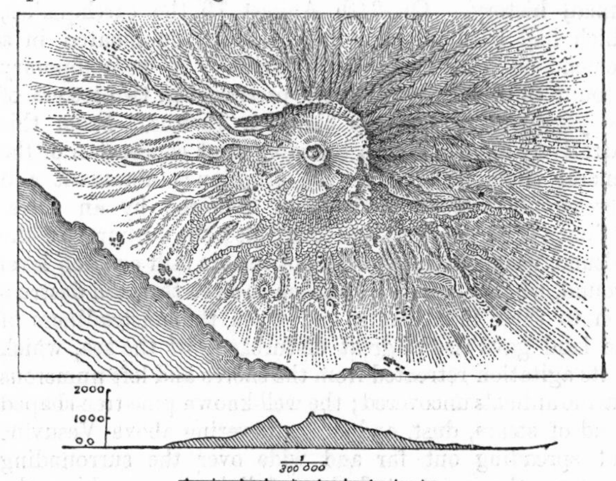

Plan of Vesuvius, together with north-and-south profile.

the sea. Vesuvius consists of two distinct portions. On the northern side a lofty semicircular cliff, reaching a height of 3747 feet, half encircles the present active cone, and descends in long slopes towards the plains below. This precipice, known as Monte Somma, forms the wall of an ancient prehistoric crater of vastly greater size than that of the present volcano. The continuation of the same wall round its southern half has been in great measure obliterated by the operations of the modern vent, which has built a younger cone upon it, and is gradually filling up the hollow of the prehistoric crater. At the time of its greatest dimensions the volcano was perhaps twice as high as it is now. By a colossal eruption, of which no historical record remains, the upper half of the cone was blown away. It was around this truncated cone that the early Greek settlers founded their little colonies.

At the beginning of the Christian era, and for many previous centuries, no eruption had been known to take place from the mountain, and the volcanic nature of the locality was perhaps not even suspected by the inhabitants who planted their vineyards along its fertile slopes, and built their numerous villages and towns around its base. The sagacious and observant geographer Strabo, however, detected the probable volcanic origin of the cone and drew attention to its cindery and evidently fire-eaten rocks. From his account and other references in classical authors we gather that in the first century of the Christian era, and probably for hundreds of years before that time, the sides of the mountain were richly cultivated, but towards the top the upward growth of vegetation had not concealed the loose ashes which still remained as evidence of the volcanic nature of the place. On this barren summit lay a wide flat depression, surrounded with rugged walls of rock, which were festooned with wild vines. The present crater-wall of Somma is doubtless a relic of that time. It was in this lofty rock-girt hollow that the gladiator Spartacus was besieged by the prætor Claudius Pulcher, and from which he escaped by twisting ropes of vine-branches and descending through an unguarded notch in the crater-rim.

After centuries of quiescence the volcanic energy began again to manifest itself in a succession of earthquakes, which spread alarm far and wide through Campania. For some sixteen years after 63 these convulsions continued, doing much damage to the surrounding towns. At Pompeii, for example, among other devastation, the temple of Isis was shaken into ruins, and, as an inscription records, it was rebuilt from the foundations by the munificence of a private citizen. This preliminary earthquake phase of volcanic excitement was succeeded by a catastrophe which stands out prominently as one of the great calamities of human history. On 24th August 79 the earthquakes, which had been growing more violent, culminated in a tremendous explosion of Vesuvius. A contemporary account of this event has been preserved in two letters of the younger Pliny to the historian Tacitus. From this narrative we can gather a tolerably clear conception of the general characteristics of the eruption:—abundant and increasingly violent earthquakes, followed by an extraordinary commotion that accompanied the outburst of the volcano, when chariots would not remain still even on level ground, when houses were shaken so as to threaten destruction to their inhabitants, and when the unsteadiness of the land gave rise to great disturbance of the sea, which in its agitation retreated from the shores and left numerous marine animals uncovered; the well-known pine-tree-shaped cloud of steam, dust, and stones towering above Vesuvius and spreading out far and wide over the surrounding country; the constant flashes of lightning marking the highly electrical condition of the column of erupted material; the showers of light cinders and ashes that fell at a distance from the mountain and the rain of hot pumice and pieces of black or glowing lava around the centre of eruption; the total darkness for three days produced by the diffusion of the finer volcanic dust through the atmosphere; the fiery glare that overspread the cloud-canopy as each explosion uncovered the glowing surface of the lava column in the chimney of the volcano; and the wide covering of ashes, which like a mantle of snow was found to have been spread over the surrounding country when the darkness cleared away and the catastrophe came to an end. This eruption was attended with great destruction of life and property. Three towns are known to have been destroyed—Herculaneum at the western base of the volcano, Pompeii on the south-east side, and Stabiæ, still farther south on the site of the modern Castellamare. The exhumation of Herculaneum and Pompeii in modern times has thrown much light upon the life of Roman citizens in the first century. There is no evidence that any lava was emitted during this eruption. But the abundant steam given off by the volcano seems to have condensed into copious rain, which, mixing with the light volcanic dust, gave rise to torrents of pasty mud, that flowed down the slopes and overwhelmed houses and villages. Herculaneum is believed to have been destroyed by these "water lavas," and there is reason to suppose that similar materials filled the cellars and lower parts of Pompeii. Comparing the statements of Pliny with the facts still observable in the district, we perceive that this first recorded eruption of Vesuvius belongs to that phase of volcanic action known as the *paroxysmal*, when, after a longer or shorter period of comparative tranquillity, a volcano rapidly resumes its energy and the partially filled-up crater is cleared out by a succession of tremendous explosions. The great eruption of Krakatoa in the Sunda Strait in 1883 is a recent example of the same stage in the history of a volcano.

For nearly fifteen hundred years after the catastrophe of 79 Vesuvius remained in a condition of feeble activity. Occasional eruptions are mentioned, but none that was of importance, and their details are given with great vagueness by the authors who allude to them. By the end of the 17th century the mountain had resumed much the same general aspect as it presented before the eruption described by Pliny. Its crater-walls, some 5 miles in circumference, were hung with trees and brushwood, and at their base stretched a wide grassy plain, on which cattle grazed and where the wild boar lurked in the thickets. The central tract was a lower plain, covered with loose ashes and marked by a few pools of hot and saline water. At length, after a series of earthquakes lasting for six months and gradually increasing in violence, the volcano burst into renewed paroxysmal activity on 16th December 1631. Vast clouds of dust and stones, blown out of the crater and funnel of the volcano, were hurled into the air and carried for hundreds of miles, the finer particles falling to the earth even in the Adriatic and at Constantinople. The clouds of steam condensed into copious torrents, which, mingling with the fine ashes, produced muddy streams that swept far and wide over the plains, reaching even to the foot of the Apennines. Issuing from the flanks of the mountain, several streams of lava flowed down towards the west and south, and reached the sea at twelve or thirteen different points. Though the inhabitants had been warned by the earlier convulsions of the mountain, so swiftly did destruction come upon them that 18,000 are said to have lost their lives.

Since this great convulsion, which emptied the crater, Vesuvius has never again relapsed into a condition of total quiescence. At intervals, varying from a few weeks or months to a few years, it has broken out into eruption, sometimes emitting only steam, dust, and scoriæ, but frequently also streams of lava. The years 1766-67, 1779, 1794, and 1822 were marked by special activity, and the phenomena observed on each of these occasions have been fully described.

The modern cone of the mountain has been built up by successive discharges of lava and fragmentary materials round a vent of eruption, which lies a little south of the centre of the prehistoric crater. The southern segment of the ancient cone, answering to the semicircular wall of Somma on the north side, has been almost concealed, but is still traceable among the younger accumulations. The numerous deep ravines that indented the sides of the prehistoric volcano, and which still form so marked a feature on the outer slopes of Somma, have on the south side served as channels to guide the currents of lava from the younger cone. But they are gradually being filled up there and will before long disappear under the sheets of molten rock that from time to time rush into them from above. On one of the ridges between these radiating valleys an observatory for watching the progress of the volcano was established many years ago by the Neapolitan Government, and is still supported as a national institution. A continuous record of each phase in the volcanic changes has been taken, and some progress has been made in the study of the phenomena of Vesuvius, and in prognosticating the occurrence and probable intensity of eruptions. A wire-rope railway (opened in the year 1880) carries visitors from the foot of the cone up to within 150 yards of the mouth of the crater.

See *Volcanoes*, by G. P. Scrope, 1872; *Vesuvius*, by John Phillips, 1869; *Der Ausbruch des Vesuv im April 1872*, by A. Heim, 1873; *Vesuvio e la sua Storia* and *Pompei e la Regione Sotterrata dal Vesuvio nel' Anno 79*, by Prof. Palmieri, Naples, 1879; *Studien über Vulkane und Erdbeben*, by J. F. Schmidt, 1881; and "The Geology of Monte Somma and Vesuvius," by H. J. Johnstone-Lavis, 1884, in *Quart. Journ. Geol. Soc.*, vol. xl. p. 85. See also GEOLOGY, vol. x. p. 240 *sq.* (A. GE.)

VESZPRÉM, the chief town of a county of the same name in Hungary, lies between Lake Balaton and the forest of Bakony, about 65 miles south-west of Buda-Pesth. Veszprém is the seat of a Roman Catholic bishop, whose cathedral and palace, with the county hall and the gymnasium, form the chief features of the town. Veszprém is a station on the Western Railway system. Its four annual fairs are much frequented from all parts of the trans-Danubian district, and the trade in grain, wine, and home industries generally is considerable. The town is of very ancient origin, and was known to the Romans by the name of Cimbria. The queens of the Árpád dynasty used occasionally to reside here, and even now the queens of Hungary are crowned by the bishop of Veszprém. The place suffered much during the contentions between the Turks and the Hungarians and Austrians in the 16th and 17th centuries. The population numbered 14,800 in 1886.

VETERINARY SCIENCE

THIS science comprises a knowledge of the conformation and structure of all the domesticated animals, especially the horse; their physiology and special racial and individual characteristics; their humane management and utilization; their protection from, and medical and surgical treatment in, the diseases and injuries to which they are exposed; their amelioration and improvement; their relations to the human family with regard to communicable disorders; and the supply of food and other products, more particularly those derived from them for the use of mankind.

HISTORY.

There is evidence that the Egyptians practised veterinary medicine and surgery in very remote times; but it is not until we turn to the Greeks that we obtain any very definite information with regard to the state of veterinary as well as human medicine in antiquity. The writings of Hippocrates (460-356 B.C.) afford evidence of excellent investigations in comparative pathology. Diocles of Caristus, who was nearly a contemporary, was one of the first to occupy himself with anatomy, which he studied in animals. Aristotle, too, wrote on physiology and comparative anatomy, and on the maladies of animals, while many other Greek writers on veterinary medicine are cited or copied from by Varro, Columella, and Galen. And we must not overlook Mago of Carthage (200 B.C.), whose work in twenty-eight books was translated into Greek and was largely used by Varro and Columella.

Amongst the Greeks.

Until after the conquest of Greece the Romans do not appear to have known much of veterinary medicine. Varro (116-28 B.C.) may be considered the first Roman writer who deals with animal medicine in a scientific spirit, in his *De Re Rustica*, in three books, which is largely derived from Greek writers. Celsus is supposed to have written on animal medicine; and Columella (1st century) is credited with having utilized those relating to veterinary science in the sixth and seventh parts of his *De Re Rustica*, one of the best works of its class of ancient times: it treats, not only of medicine and surgery, but also of sanitary measures for the suppression of contagious diseases. From the 3d century onwards veterinary science had a literature of its own and regular practitioners, especially in the service of the Roman armies (*mulomedici, veterinarii*). Perhaps the most renowned veterinarian of the Roman empire was Apsyrtus of Bithynia, who in 322 accompanied the expedition of Constantine against the Sarmatians in his professional capacity, and seems to have enjoyed a high and well-deserved reputation in his time. He was a keen observer; he distinguished and described a number of diseases which were badly defined by his predecessors, recognized the contagious nature of several maladies, and prescribed isolation for their suppression; he also made interesting observations on accidents and diseases of horses' limbs, and waged war against certain absurd empirical practices then prevailing in the treatment of disease, indicating rational methods, some of which are still successfully employed in veterinary therapeutics, such as splints for fractures, sutures for wounds, cold water for the reduction of prolapsed vagina, hot baths for tetanus, &c. Not less eminent was Hierocles, the successor of Apsyrtus, whose writings he largely copied, but with improvements and valuable additions, especially in the hygiene and training of horses. Pelagonius again was a writer of empirical tendency, and his treatment of disease in general was most irrational. Publius Vegetius (not to be confounded with Flavius Vegetius Renatus, who wrote on the military art) was a popular author of the end of the 5th century, though less distinguished than Apsyrtus, to whom and to Pelagonius he was to a great extent indebted in the preparation of his *Mulomedicina sive Ars Veterinaria*. He appears to have been more of a horse-dealer than a veterinary practitioner, and knew next to nothing of anatomy, which seems to have been but little cultivated at that period. He was very superstitious and a believer in the influence of demons and sorcerers; nevertheless he gives some interesting observations derived from his travels. He had also a good idea of aerial infection, recognized the utility of disinfectants, and describes some operations not referred to by previous writers, such as removal of calculi from the bladder through the rectum, couching for cataract, the extirpation of certain glands, and several serious operations on the horse's foot. Though inferior to several works written by his predecessors, the *Mulomedicina* of Vegetius maintained its popularity through many centuries. Of most of the ancient veterinary writers we know little beyond what can be gathered from the citations and extracts in the two great collections of *Hippiatrica* and *Geoponica* compiled by order of Constantine Porphyrogenitus in the 10th century.

Amongst the Romans.

It is unnecessary to dwell here on the progress of the veterinary art during the Middle Ages. Towards the close of the mediæval period the subject was much cultivated in the cavalry schools of Italy; and Spain also had an organized system of good practitioners in the 15th century, who have left many books still extant. Germany was far behind, and literature on the subject did not exist until the end of the 15th century, when in 1492 there was published anonymously at Augsburg a *Pferdearzneibüchlein.* In the following century the influence of the Italian writers was becoming manifest, and the works of Fugger and Fayser mark the commencement of a new era. Fayser's treatises, *Von der Gestüterei* and *Von der Zucht der Kriegs- und Bürger-Pferde* (1529-1597), are remarkable for originality and good sense. In Great Britain animal medicine was perhaps in a more advanced condition than in Germany, if we accept the evidence of the *Ancient Laws and Institutes of Wales* (London, 1841); yet it was largely made up of the grossest superstitions.[1] Among the Celts the healer of horse diseases and the shoer were held in high esteem, as among the more civilized nations of Europe, and the court farrier enjoyed special privileges.[2] The earliest known works in English appeared anonymously towards the commencement of the 16th century, namely, *Propertees and Medcynes for a Horse* and *Mascal of Oxen, Horses, Sheepes, Hogges, Dogges.* The word "mascal" shows that the latter work was in its origin Italian. There is no doubt that in the 15th century the increasing taste for horses and horsemanship brought Italian riding-masters and farriers into England; and it is recorded that Henry VIII. brought over two of these men who had been trained by Grisone in the famous Neapolitan school. The knowledge so introduced became popularized, and assumed a concrete form in Blundeville's *Foure Chiefest Offices belonging to Horsemanship* (1566), which contains many references to horse diseases, and, though mainly a compilation, is yet enriched with original observations. In the 15th century the anatomy of the domesticated animals, formerly almost entirely neglected, began to receive attention. A work on comparative anatomy by Volcher Koyter was issued at Nuremberg in 1573; about the same time a writer in Germany named Copho or Cophon published a book on the anatomy of the pig, in which were many original remarks on the lymphatic vessels; and Jehan Hervard in France produced in 1594 his rather incomplete *Hippo-Ostéologie.* But by far the most notable work, and one which maintained its popularity for a century and a half, was that of Carlo Ruini, a senator of Bologna, published in 1598 in that city, and entitled *Dell' Anatomia e dell' Infirmità del Cavallo, e suoi Remedii.* Passing through many editions, and translated into French and German, this book was for the most part original, and a remarkable one for the time in which it was composed, the anatomical portion being especially praiseworthy. English books of the 17th century exhibit a strong tendency towards the improvement of veterinary medicine and surgery, especially as regards the horse. This is even more notable in the writings of the 18th century, among which may be particularized Gibson's *Farrier's New Guide* (1719), *Method of Dieting Horses* (1721), and (best of all) his *New Treatise on the Diseases of Horses,* besides Braken's, Burdon's, Bridge's, and Bartlet's treatises. Veterinary anatomy was greatly advanced by the *Anatomy of an Horse* (1683) of Snape, farrier to Charles II., illustrated with copperplates, and by the still more complete and original work of Stubbs, the *Anatomy of the Horse* (1766), which decidedly marked a new era in this line of study. Of foreign works it may suffice to mention that of Solleysel, *Veritable Parfait Maréschal* (1664), which passed through many editions, was translated into several languages, and was borrowed from for more than a century by different writers. Sir W. Hope's *Compleat Horseman* (1696) is a translation from Solleysel by a pupil.

[1] See *Leechdoms, Wortcunning, and Starcraft of Early England,* 3 vols. 8vo, London, 1864.

[2] See Fleming, *Horse-Shoes and Horse-Shoeing,* London, 1869.

Modern Schools and Colleges.

Veterinary schools. In France.

The most important era in the history of modern veterinary science commenced with the institution of veterinary schools. France was the first to take the great initiative step in this direction. Buffon had recommended the formation of veterinary schools, but his recommendations were not attended to. Bourgelat, an advocate at Lyons and a talented hippologist, through his influence with Bertin, prime minister under Louis XV., was the first to induce the Government to establish a veterinary school and school of equitation at Lyons, in 1761. This school he himself directed for only a few years, during which the great benefits that had resulted from it justified an extension of its teaching to other parts of France. Bourgelat, therefore, founded (1766) at Alfort, near Paris, a second veterinary school, which soon became, and has remained to this day, one of the finest and most advanced veterinary schools in the world. At Lyons he was replaced by the Abbé Rozier, a learned agriculturist, who was killed at the siege of Lyons after a very successful period of school management, during which he had added largely to agricultural and physical knowledge by the publication of his *Journal de Physique* and *Cours d'Agriculture.* Twenty years later the Alfort school added to its teaching staff several distinguished professors whose names still adorn the annals of science, such as Daubenton, who taught rural economy; Vic d'Azyr, who lectured on comparative anatomy; Fourcroy, who undertook instruction in chemistry; and Gilbert, one of its most brilliant pupils, who had veterinary medicine and surgery for his department. The last-named was also a distinguished agriculturist and published many important treatises on agricultural as well as veterinary subjects. The position he had acquired, added to his profound and varied knowledge, made him most useful to France during the period of the Revolution. It is chiefly to him that it is indebted for the celebrated Rambouillet flock of Merino sheep, for the conservation of the Tuileries and Versailles parks, and for the creation of the fine experimental agricultural establishment organized in the ancient domain of Sceaux. The Alfort school speedily became the nursery of veterinary science, and the source whence all similar institutions obtained their first teachers and their guidance. A third Government school was at a later period founded at Toulouse; and these three schools have produced thousands of thoroughly educated veterinary surgeons and many professors of high scientific repute, among whom may be named Bouley, Chauveau, Colin, Toussaint, St Cyr, Goubaux, Arloing, and Galtier.

In Germany, &c.

Soon after the Alfort school was commenced a national school for Austria was established at Vienna by order of Maria Theresa; and this, remodelled and reorganized by Joseph II., is now the largest in the country. Prussia quickly followed suit; and soon Government veterinary schools were founded in almost every other European country, except Great Britain, mostly on a munificent scale. Probably all, but especially those of France and Germany, were established as much with a view to training veterinary surgeons for the army as for the requirements of civil life.

In the United Kingdom.

In 1790 St Bel (whose real name was Vial, St Bel being a village near Lyons, where was his paternal estate), after studying at the Lyons school and teaching both at Alfort and Lyons, came to England and published proposals for founding a school in which to instruct pupils in veterinary medicine and surgery. The Agricultural Society of Odiham, which had been meditating sending two young men to the Alfort school, elected him an honorary member, and delegated a committee to consult with him respecting his scheme. Some time afterwards this committee detached themselves from the Odiham Society and formed an institution styled the Veterinary College of London, of which St Bel was appointed professor. The school was to be commenced and maintained by private subscription. In March 1792 arrangements were made for building temporary stabling for fifty horses and a forge for shoeing at St Pancras. The college made rapid progress in public estimation, notwithstanding considerable pecuniary embarrassments. As soon as the building was ready for the reception of animal patients, pupils began to be enrolled; and among the earliest were some who afterwards gained celebrity as veterinarians, as Bloxam, Blaine, R. Lawrence, Field, and Bracy Clark. On the death of St Bel in August 1793 there appears to have been some difficulty in procuring a suitable successor; but at length, on the recommendation of John Hunter and Cline, two medical men were appointed, Coleman and Moorcroft, the latter then practising as a veterinary surgeon in London. The first taught anatomy and physiology, and Moorcroft, after visiting the French schools, directed the practical portion of the teaching. Unfortunately, neither of these teachers had much experience among animals, nor were they well acquainted with their diseases; but Coleman had as a student, in conjunction with a fellow-student (afterwards Sir Astley Cooper), performed many experiments on animals under the direction of Cline. Moorcroft, who remained only a short time at the college, afterwards went to India and during a journey in 1819 was murdered in Tibet.[1] Coleman, by his scientific researches and energetic management, in a few years raised the college to a high standard of usefulness; under his care the progress of the veterinary art was such as to qualify its practitioners to hold commissions in the army; and he himself was appointed veterinary surgeon-general to the British cavalry. Owing to the lack of funds, the teaching at the college must have been very meagre, and, had it not been for the liberality of several medical men in throwing open the doors of their theatres to its pupils for instruction without fee or reward, their professional knowledge would have been sadly deficient. The board of examiners was for many years chiefly composed of eminent members of the medical profession. Coleman died in 1839, and with him disappeared much of the interest the medical profession of London took in the progress of veterinary medicine. Yet the Royal Veterinary College (first styled "Royal" during the presidentship of the duke of Kent) continued to do good work in a purely veterinary direction, and received such public financial support that it was soon able to dispense with the small annual grant given to it by the Government. In the early years of the institution the horse was the only animal to which much attention was given. But at the instigation of the Royal Agricultural Society of England, which gave £200 per annum for the purpose, an additional professor was appointed to investigate and teach the treatment of the diseases of cattle, sheep, and other animals; outbreaks of disease among these were also to be inquired into by the officers of the college. This help to the institution was withdrawn in 1875, but renewed in 1886.

This veterinary school has been the parent of other schools in Great Britain, one of which, the first in Scotland, was founded by Prof. Dick, a student of Coleman's and a man of great perseverance and ability. Commencing at Edinburgh in 1819-20 with only one student, in three years he gained the patronage of the Highland and Agricultural Society of Scotland, which placed a small sum of money at the disposal of a committee appointed by itself to take charge of a department of veterinary surgery it had formed. This patronage, and very much in the way of material assistance and encouragement, were continued to the time of Dick's death in 1866. During the long period in which he presided over the school, considerable progress was made in diffusing a sound knowledge of veterinary medicine in Scotland and beyond it. For many years his examining board, which gave certificates of proficiency under the auspices of the Highland and Agricultural Society, was composed of the most distinguished medical men in Scotland, such as Goodsir, Syme, Lizars, Ballingall, Simpson, and Knox. By his will Dick vested the college in the lord provost and town council of Edinburgh as trustees, and left a large portion of the fortune he had made to maintain it for the purposes for which it was founded. In recent years another veterinary school has been established in Edinburgh, and one in Glasgow, both of which are doing good service.

In 1844 the Royal College of Veterinary Surgeons (to be carefully distinguished from the Royal Veterinary College) obtained its charter of incorporation. The functions of this body were, until a recent date, limited almost entirely to examining students taught in the veterinary schools, and bestowing diplomas of membership on those who successfully passed the examinations conducted by the boards which sat in London and Edinburgh. Soon after the Royal College of Veterinary Surgeons obtained its charter of incorporation a difference arose between it and Dick, which resulted in the latter seceding altogether from the union that had been established and forming an independent examining board, the Highland and Agricultural Society granting certificates of proficiency to those students who were deemed competent. This schism operated very injuriously on the progress of veterinary education and on professional advancement, as the competition engendered was of a rather deteriorating nature. After the death of Dick the dualism in veterinary licensing was suppressed: the Highland Society ceased to give certificates and the only mode of admission to the profession was through the Royal College. Since then the subjects taught have been increased in number; conformably with the requirements of ever-extending science, the period of study has been enlarged so as to be nearly as long as that imposed upon medical students; the teaching is more thorough and practical; and the examinations are more frequent and searching. Candidates for admission to the schools must also give evidence of having received a good general education. Also since the suppression of the dual system an Act of Parliament has been obtained protecting the title of the graduates of the Royal College of Veterinary Surgeons, and conferring other advantages, not the least of which is the power granted to the college to remove the names of unworthy members from its register. In some respects the Veterinary Surgeons Act is superior to the Medical Act, while it places the profession on the same level as other learned bodies, and prevents the public being imposed upon by empirics and impostors. The college has instituted a higher degree, that of fellow, which can only be obtained after the graduate has been five years in practice and by passing a severe examination. Fellows only can be members of council or members of the examining boards. The graduates of the Royal College of Veterinary Surgeons who have been registered since its foundation in 1844 probably number 4000. In the British army there is a smaller mortality among the animals employed, and less loss from contagious diseases than in any other in Europe; this result, as well as the high efficiency of the horses, is largely due to the zeal, intelligence, and natural aptitude of the veterinary officers for their special duties. In no other army are they so severely tested, physically and professionally,—more than one-half of their service being foreign; and in India their skill has to be exercised on elephants, camels, bullocks, cattle, and sheep, in addition to horses. During war the strain on army veterinary surgeons is very heavy; and, while surgeons are protected in the field by the Geneva Red Cross, being considered as non-belligerents, veterinary officers are regarded as combatants, and therefore run the risk of capture, imprisonment, or death at the hands of the enemy.

In India.

In India there are one or more veterinary schools in each presidency, in which natives are trained as veterinary surgeons. The need for this will be perceived when it is stated that the loss in India from preventible animal diseases alone amounts to at least £6,000,000 annually.

In the United States.

In the United States of America veterinary science has been an exotic of very slow growth. There are veterinary schools in New York, Minneapolis, and elsewhere, but these, like those in Great Britain, are private institutions. To the Cornell, Pennsylvania, and Harvard universities veterinary schools or chairs have been attached with competent teachers. Events are at present rapidly compelling the people of the United States to realize the true value and importance of veterinary science. For many years the "lung plague" has been gradually extending itself westward, and it is now causing heavy losses. Long exempted from the more serious of the contagious diseases of animals which have scourged Europe, the United States are now invaded by all of them except two—cattle plague and the foot-and-mouth disease; and an exotic disorder of pigs, the swine plague or fever, is threatening to exterminate these animals.

The veterinary literature of this period affords striking evidence of the progress made by the science: excellent text-books, manuals, and treatises on every subject belonging to it are very numerous, and are published in every European language, while there is an abundance of periodical literature. The education—general and technical—of practitioners of veterinary medicine has, of course, been improving to a corresponding extent. The matriculation test for admission to the best veterinary schools and the fixed period for instruction in them vary but little from those of the medical schools. In Germany the veterinary schools at Berlin and Hanover have been raised to the position of universities.

Objects of the Science.

Treatment of disease.

One of the chief objects of the science is the treatment of disease in animals. Veterinary medicine has been far less exposed to the vagaries of theoretical doctrines and systems than human medicine. The explanation may perhaps be that the successful practice of this branch of medicine more clearly than in any other depends upon the careful observation of facts and the rational deductions to be made therefrom. No special doctrines seem, in later times at least, to have been adopted, and the dominating sentiment in regard to disease and its treatment has been a medical eclecticism, based on practical experience and anatomico-pathological investigation, rarely indeed on philosophical or abstract theories. In this way veterinary science has become pre-eminently a science of observation. At times indeed it has to some extent been influenced by the doctrines which have controlled the practice of human medicine—such as those of Broussais, Hahnemann, Brown, Rasori, Rademacher, and others—yet this has not been for long: experience of them when tested upon dumb unimaginative animals soon exposed their fallacies and compelled their discontinuance.

Prevention of disease.

Of more moment than the cure of disease is its prevention, and this is now considered the most important object in connexion with veterinary science. More especially is this the case with those serious disorders which depend for their existence and extension upon the presence of an infecting agent, and whose ravages for so many centuries

[1] See Moorcroft and Trebeck's *Travels in Cashmere and Thibet.*

are written largely in the history of civilization. Every advance made in medicine affects the progress of veterinary science, and the recent remarkable discoveries, some of which have been initiated by members of the veterinary profession, or developed by them, must in the end create as great a revolution in veterinary practice as in the medicine of man. In "preventive medicine" the benefits to be derived from the application of the germ theory will be immense; the sanitary police measures based on this knowledge are easily framed, and, if carried rigorously into operation, must eventually lead to the extinction of these disastrous disorders.[1] The medicine of the lower animals differs from that of man in no particular so much, perhaps, as in the application it makes of utilitarian principles. The life of man is sacred; but in the case of animals, when there are doubts as to complete restoration to health and soundness, monetary considerations generally decide against the adoption of remedial measures. This feature in the medicine of the domesticated animals brings very prominently before us the value of the old adage that "prevention is better than cure." In Great Britain the value of comparative pathology in the relations it bears to human medicine, to the public health and wealth, as well as to agriculture, has been strangely overlooked or ignored; and in consequence but little allowance has been made for the difficulties the practitioner of animal medicine has to contend with. The rare instances in which animals can be seen by the veterinary surgeon in the earliest stages of disease, and when this would prove most amenable to medical treatment; delay, generally due to the inability of those who have the care of animals to perceive these early stages; the fact that animals cannot, except in a negative manner, tell their woes, describe their sensations, or indicate what and where they suffer; the absence of those comforts and conveniences of the sick room which cannot be called in to ameliorate their condition; the violence or stupor, as well as the structural arrangements and attitude of the sick creatures, which only too frequently render favourable positions for cure impossible; the slender means generally afforded for carrying out recommendations, together with the oftentimes intractable nature of these diseases; and the utilitarian influences alluded to above,—all these considerations, in the great majority of instances, militate against the adoption of curative treatment, or at least greatly increase its difficulties.

For more than forty years most destructive plagues of animals have prevailed almost continuously in the British islands without any attempt, worthy of the name, having been made to check or extirpate them until within a very recent period. Two exotic bovine diseases alone (contagious pleuro-pneumonia or lung plague and foot-and-mouth disease) are estimated to have caused the death, during the first thirty years of their prevalence in the United Kingdom, of 5,549,780 cattle, roughly valued at £83,616,854; while the invasion of cattle plague in 1865-66 was calculated to have caused a money loss of from £5,000,000 to £8,000,000. The depredations made in South Africa and Australia by the lung plague alone are quite appalling; and in India the loss brought about by contagious diseases among animals has been stated at not less than £6,000,000 annually. The damage done by tuberculosis—a contagious disease of cattle, transmissible to several kinds of animals, and possibly also to man, by means of the flesh and milk of diseased beasts—cannot be even guessed at; but it must be enormous, when we learn how widely the malady is diffused. But that terrible pest of all ages, the cattle plague, has in its two recent invasions of England been promptly suppressed with comparatively trifling loss. The foot-and-mouth disease, which proved such a heavy infliction to British agriculture from its introduction in 1838, has been completely extirpated. Glanders, which annually caused the destruction of large numbers of cavalry horses, is now unknown in the army, and is rapidly disappearing from civilian stables. Rabies would soon be included in the category of extinct diseases if the indications of veterinary science were followed; and so with the other contagious maladies of animals. As for such diseases as depend for their development upon germs derived from the soil or herbage upon which animals live, and which cannot be directly controlled by veterinary sanitary measures, the system of protective inoculation with cultivated virus introduced by Pasteur will probably bring about their extinction, or at any rate greatly mitigate their effects.

Relations of veterinary to human medicine.

Veterinary science can also offer much assistance in the study and prevention of the diseases to which mankind are liable. Some grave maladies of the human species are certainly derived from animals, and others may yet be added to the list. In the training of the physician great benefit would be derived from the study of disease in animals,—a fact which has been strangely overlooked in England, as those can testify who understand how closely the health of man may depend upon the health of the creatures he has domesticated and derives subsistence from, and how much more advantageously morbid processes can be studied in animals than in our own species. Although as yet no chair of comparative pathology has been established in any British university, on the Continent such chairs are now looked upon as an almost indispensable item of every university. Bourgelat, towards the middle of the 18th century, in speaking of the veterinary schools he had been instrumental in forming, urged that "leurs portes soient sans cesse ouvertes à ceux qui, chargés par l'état de la conservation des hommes, auront acquis par le nom qu'ils se seront fait le droit d'interroger la nature, chercher des analogies, et vérifier des idées dont la conformation ne peut être qu'utile à l'espèce humaine." And the benefits to be mutually derived from this association of the two branches of medicine inspired Vicq d'Azyr to elaborate his *Nouveau Plan de la Constitution de la Médecine en France*, which he presented to the National Assembly in 1790. His fundamental idea was to make veterinary teaching a preliminary (*le premier degré*) and, as it were, the principle of instruction in human medicine. His proposal went so far as to insist upon a veterinary school being annexed to every medical college established in France. This idea was reproduced in the *Rapport sur l'Instruction Publique* which Talleyrand read before the National Assembly in 1790. In this project veterinary teaching was to form part of the National Institution at Paris. The idea was to initiate students of medicine into a knowledge of diseases by observing those of animals. The suffering animal always appears exactly as it is and feels, without the intervention of mind obscuring the symptomatology, the symptoms being really and truly the rigorous expression of its diseased condition. From this point of view, the dumb animal, when it is ill, offers the same difficulties in diagnosis as does the ailing infant or the comatose adult.

Of the other objects of veterinary science there is only one to which allusion need here be made: that is the perfectioning of the domestic animals in everything that is likely to make them more valuable to man. This is in an especial manner the province of this science, the knowledge of the anatomy, physiology, and other matters connected with these animals by its students being essential for such improvement.

[1] Comp. Fleming, *Veterinary Sanitary Science and Police*, London, 1875.

Diseases of Domestic Animals.

Considerations of space forbid a complete or detailed description of all the diseases, medical and surgical, to which the domesticated animals are liable. This is to be found in the current veterinary text-books. Reference will be made here only to the more important disorders of animals which are of a communicable nature, and which were not included in the article MURRAIN (*q.v.*).

Diseases of the Horse.

Every horseman should know something of the injuries, lamenesses, and diseases to which the horse is liable. Unfortunately not very much can be done in this direction by book instruction; indeed, there is generally too much doctoring and too little nursing of sick animals. Even in slight and favourable cases of illness recovery is often retarded by too zealous and injudicious medication; the object to be always kept in view in the treatment of animal patients is to place them in those conditions which allow nature to operate most freely in restoring health. This can best be rendered in the form of nursing, which sick animals greatly appreciate. However indifferent a horse may be to caressing or kind attention during health, when ill he certainly appreciates both, and when in pain will often apparently endeavour to attract notice and seek relief from those with whom he is familiar. Fresh air and cleanliness, quiet and comfort, should always be secured, if possible. The stable or loose box should be warm, without being close, and free from draughts. If the weather is cold, and especially if the horse is suffering from inflammation of the air-passages, it may be necessary to keep up the temperature by artificial means; but great care should be taken that this does not render the air too dry to breathe. The surface of the body can be kept warm by rugs, and the legs by woollen bandages. Yet a sick horse is easily fatigued and annoyed by too much clothing, and therefore it is better to resort to artificial heating of the stable than to overload the body or impede movement by heavy wrappings. If blankets are used, it is well to place a cotton or linen sheet under them, should the horse have an irritable skin. For bedding, long straw should be employed as little as possible, since it hampers movement. Clean old litter, sawdust, or peat-moss litter is the best. If the hoofs are strong, and the horse likely to be confined for some weeks, it affords relief to take off the shoes. Tying up should be avoided, if possible, unless it is urgently required, the horse being allowed to move about or lie down as he may prefer.

Nursing.

When a sick horse has lost his appetite, he should be tempted to eat by offering him such food as will be enticing to him. It should be given frequently and in small quantities, but should not be forced on him; food will often be taken if offered from the hand, when it will not be eaten out of the manger. Whether the animal be fed from a bucket or from a manger, any food that is left should be thrown away, and the receptacle well cleaned out after each meal. As a rule, during sickness a horse requires laxative food, in order to allay fever or inflammatory symptoms, while supporting the strength. The following list comprises the usual laxative food employed:—green grass, green wheat, oats, and barley, lucerne, carrots, parsnips, gruel, bran mash, linseed and bran mash, boiled barley, linseed tea, hay tea, and linseed oil. Green grass, lucerne, and similar articles of food, if cut when in a wet state, should be dried before being given. Boiled grain should be cooked with very little water, so that it may be floury and comparatively dry when ready; a little salt should be mixed with it. One gallon of good gruel may be made with a pound of meal and cold water, which should be stirred till it boils, and afterwards permitted to simmer over a gentle fire till the fluid is quite thick. To make a bran mash, scald a stable bucket, throw out the water, put in three pounds of bran and one ounce of salt, add two and a half pints of boiling water, stir up well, cover over, and allow the mash to stand for fifteen or twenty minutes until it is well cooked. For a bran and linseed mash, boil slowly for two or three hours one pound of linseed, so as to have about a couple of quarts of thick fluid, to which two pounds of bran and one ounce of salt may be added. The whole should be stirred up, covered over, and allowed to steam as before described. The thicker the mash the more readily will the horse eat it. Linseed tea is made by boiling one pound of linseed in a couple of gallons of water until the grains are quite soft. It may be economically made by using less water to cook the linseed, and afterwards making up the quantity of water to about a gallon and a half. Hay tea may be prepared by filling a bucket, after scalding it, with good sweet hay, pouring in as much boiling water as the bucket will hold, covering it over, and allowing it to stand until cold, when the fluid may be strained off and given to the horse. This forms a refreshing drink. Linseed oil, in quantities of from one quarter to half a pint daily, may be mixed with the food; it keeps the bowels in a lax condition, has a good effect on the skin and air-passages, and is useful as an article of diet. When debility has to be combated, as in low fever or other weakening diseases, strengthening and other easily digested food must be administered, though some of the foods already mentioned, such as boiled grain, answer this purpose to a certain extent. Milk, eggs, bread and biscuits, malt liquor, corn, &c., are often prescribed with this object. Milk may be given skimmed or unskimmed; a little sugar may be mixed with it; and one or two gallons may be given daily, according to circumstances. One or two eggs may be given beaten up with a little sugar and mixed with milk, three or four times a day, or more frequently; or they may be boiled hard and powdered, and mixed in the milk. A quart of stout, ale, or porter may be given two or three times a day, or a half to one bottle of port wine daily. Scalded oats, with a little salt added, are very useful when convalescence is nearly completed. As a rule, a sick horse should have as much water as he likes to drink, though it may be necessary in certain cases to restrict the quantity, and to have the chill taken off; but it should never be warmer than 75° to 80°.

Food for a sick horse.

As little grooming as possible should be allowed when a horse is very weak; it should be limited to sponging about the mouth, nostrils, eyes, and forehead with clean water, to which a little vinegar may be added. Rub the legs and ears with the hand, take off the clothing, and shake or change it once a day, and if agreeable rub over the body with a soft cloth. Exercise is of course not required during sickness or injury, and the period at which it is allowed will depend upon circumstances. Care must be taken that it is not ordered too early, or carried too far at first.

Administration of Medicine.—Much care is required in administering medicines in the form of ball or bolus; and practice, as well as courage and tact, is needed in order to give it without danger to the administrator or the animal. The ball should be held between the fingers of the right hand, the tips of the first and fourth being brought together below the second and third, which are placed on the upper side of the ball; the right hand is thus made as small as possible, so as to admit of ready insertion into the mouth. The left hand grasps the horse's tongue, gently pulls it out, and places it on that part of the right side of the lower jaw which is bare of teeth. With the right hand the ball is placed at the root of the tongue. The moment the right hand is withdrawn, the tongue should be released. This causes the ball to be carried still farther back. The operator then closes the mouth and watches the left side of the neck, to note the passage of the ball down the gullet. Many horses keep a ball in the mouth a considerable time before they will allow it to go down. A mouthful of water or a handful of food will generally make them swallow it readily. If this does not succeed, the nostrils should be grasped by the hand and held a few moments. A running halter should be used, so that the mouth may be quickly and securely closed. If the operator has not had much experience in giving balls, he should station an assistant on the near side, to aid in opening and steadying the mouth, by placing the fingers of his left hand on the lower jaw and the thumb of the right on the upper jaw. Holding the mouth in this manner facilitates the giving of the ball, and saves the operator's right hand, to a great extent, from being scratched by the horse's back teeth. It is most essential to have the ball moderately soft; nothing can be more dangerous than a hard one.

How to give a ball.

To administer a drink or drench requires as much care as giving a ball, in order to avoid choking the horse, though it is unattended with risk to the administrator. An ordinary glass or stone bottle may be used, provided there are no sharp points around the mouth; but either the usual drenching horn or a tin vessel with a narrow mouth or spout is safer. It is necessary to raise the horse's head, so that the nose may be a little higher than the horizontal line. If the horse is restless, his head must be elevated by a loop of cord inserted into the mouth over the upper jaw, the prong of a stable fork being passed through it, and the handle held steady by an assistant. The drink must be given by a person standing on the right side (the assistant being in front or on the left side of the horse), the side of the mouth being pulled out a little, to form a sack or funnel, into which the medicine is poured, a little at a time, allowing an interval now and again for the horse to swallow. If any of the fluid gets into the windpipe (which it is liable to do if the head is held too high), it will cause coughing, whereupon the head should be instantly lowered. Neither the tongue nor the nostrils should be interfered with. Powders may be given in a little mash or gruel, well stirred up.

How to give a drink or drench.

If a wide surface is to be fomented (as the chest, abdomen, or loins), a blanket or other large woollen cloth should be dipped in water as hot as the hand can comfortably bear it, moderately wrung out, and applied to the part, the heat and moisture being retained by covering it with a waterproof sheet or dry rug. When it has lost some of its heat, it should be removed, dipped in warm water, and again applied. In cases of acute inflammation, it may be necessary to have the water a little hotter; and, to avoid the inconvenience of removing the blanket, or the danger of chill when it is removed, it may be secured round the body by skewers or twine, the hot water being poured on the outside of the top part of the blanket by any convenient vessel. To foment the feet, they should be placed in a bucket or tub (the latter with the bottom resting wholly on the ground) containing warm water; a quantity of moss litter put in the tub or bucket prevents splashing and retains the heat longer.

Fomentations or bathing.

Poultices. Poultices are used for allaying pain, promoting suppuration, softening horn or other tissues, and bringing on a healthy action in wounds. To be beneficial, they should be large and always kept moist. For applying poultices to the feet, a poultice-shoe, constructed as follows, may be used with advantage. Take a circular piece of hard wood, a little longer and broader than a horseshoe, and about one and a half inches thick. Get one surface of it rounded in a lathe, so that there may be a rise of about three-quarters of an inch in the centre, while the other surface remains flat. Round the circumference of the board nail leather, so as to form a convenient boot for retaining the poultice, similar to the one in ordinary use, except that the part which comes on the ground is rounded. The fact of its being round will enable the horse to whose foot it is applied to ease the affected spot by throwing his weight on the toe, the heel, or on either quarter, as he chooses. Poultices are usually made with bran, though this has the disadvantage of drying very quickly, to remedy which it may be mixed with linseed meal or a little linseed oil. Boiled carrots or turnips mashed make a good poultice, as does linseed meal, when mixed with boiling water (with a little olive oil added) by stirring. A charcoal poultice is sometimes used when there is a bad smell to be got rid of. It is made by mixing linseed meal with boiling water and stirring until a soft mass is produced; with this some wood charcoal in powder is mixed, and when ready to be applied some more powder is sprinkled on the surface. It may be noted that, in lieu of these materials for poultices, what is known as spongiopiline can be usefully employed. A piece of sufficient size is steeped in hot water, applied to the part, covered with a large piece of oiled silk or waterproof stuff, and secured there. Even an ordinary sponge, steeped in hot water and covered with any waterproof material, makes a good poulticing medium; it is well adapted for the throat, near the head, as well as for the space between the branches of the lower jaw.

Enemata or clysters. Enemata or clysters are given in fevers, inflammation, constipation, &c., to empty the posterior part of the bowels. They are administered by a large syringe capable of containing a quart or more of water, with a nozzle about twelve inches in length, with an ox's bladder tied to a pipe, or a large funnel with a long nozzle at a right angle; but the syringe is best. Water alone is usually applied for enemata; it should be about the temperature of the body, not less, but perhaps a degree or two more. To administer an enema, one of the horse's fore-feet should be held up, while the operator pushes the end of the nozzle, smeared with a little lard or oil, very gently and steadily for a few inches into the intestine, and then presses out the water. The amount injected will depend upon the size of the animal; two or three quarts would suffice for an ordinary-sized horse.

Epizootic and Contagious Diseases.—The epizootic diseases affecting the horse are not numerous, and may generally be considered as specific, or infectious and contagious, in their nature, circumstances of a favourable kind leading to their extension by propagation of the agent upon which their existence depends. This agent, in some of the maladies, has been proved to be a micro-organism, and there can be little doubt that it is so for all of them.

Glanders. Glanders is one of the most serious diseases affecting horses, not only because it is incurable, but because it is very contagious. It is known in nearly every part of the world, except in Australasia. The virulent principle of glanders establishes itself most easily among horses kept in foul, badly-ventilated stables, or among such as are overworked, badly fed, or debilitated in any way. Glanders, however, has this in common with other contagious diseases, that it is never spontaneously developed, in the absence of the virulent agent. Carnivorous animals—as lions, tigers, dogs, and cats—have become infected through eating the flesh of glandered horses; and goats, sheep, swine, and rabbits have been successfully inoculated with the virus. Men who attend on diseased horses are liable to be infected, especially if they have any sores on the exposed parts of their bodies (see GLANDERS). Though infection through wounds is the readiest way of receiving the disease, the germ or bacillus may also obtain access through the lungs, stomach, and thin mucous membranes, such as that of the eyes, nose, and lips. Glanders is presented in two forms,—one affecting the mucous membranes of the body, more particularly those of the air-passages (glanders proper), and the other attacking the skin and the superficial lymphatic vessels (farcy). Both forms are due to the same virus, and both may be acute or chronic. The acute form is the more contagious and virulent, and either destroys life quickly or becomes chronic.

Acute form. The symptoms of acute glanders are marked by fever and its accompaniments—loss of appetite, hurried pulse and respiration, languor, and disinclination to move. Sometimes the legs or joints are swollen; but the characteristic symptoms, the classical signs, are a yellow adhesive discharge from one or both nostrils; there is also a peculiar enlarged nodulated condition of one or both lymphatic glands between the branches of the lower jaw, which, though they may be painful, very rarely suppurate; and on the mucous membrane covering the septum of the nose are little yellow pimples or pustules, running into deep ragged-edged ulcers. The discharge from the nostril adheres to its margin, because of its glutinous nature, and straw and other matters also stick to it, while the obstruction to the respiration causes the animal to snort frequently—a cause of danger to men and animals, as this nasal discharge is virulent. In addition, the lymphatic vessels of the face are often involved and appear as corded lines passing up the cheeks; they are painful on pressure. In some cases there is a cough. As the disease progresses, the ulcers in the nostrils extend in size and depth and increase in number, often completely perforating the septum, and being sometimes covered with black crusts; the nasal discharge becomes more abundant and tenacious, streaked with blood, and foul smelling, and causes the animal the greatest difficulty in breathing, so that it appears to be on the point of suffocation. Death is due either to this cause or to exhaustion.

Chronic form. Chronic glanders generally presents the same symptoms; but the animal is not so seriously ill, and may indeed appear to be in good health and be able to perform a certain amount of work. In some cases the ulceration may not be perceptible, and only the peculiar knotty enlarged gland and slight discharge from one nostril be evident. There may be uncertainty in such cases as to whether the disease is glanders, owing to the absence of ulceration; and, to prove whether it is that disease, recourse has to be had to inoculation of another animal, generally a worthless horse or ass, the latter being the best, as it develops the characteristic symptoms more rapidly and certainly.

Farcy. In farcy, instead of the symptoms being manifested in the interior of the body or head, they show themselves on the skin, where the lymphatic vessels become inflamed and ulcerate. These vessels appear as prominent lines or "cords," hard and painful on manipulation, and along their course arise little tumours (the so-called "farcy buds"). These tumours ulcerate, forming sores, from which is discharged a thin glutinous pus. When the skin of the limbs is affected, these are much swollen and the animal moves with pain and difficulty. Rarely large abscesses containing thin pus form on the body. Farcy may appear during glanders or precede it, but it generally terminates in it, though the limbs and body may be covered with ulcers before this occurs.

Treatment, &c. Medical treatment of glanders, chronic and acute, and of acute farcy should not be attempted, as the malady is incurable, while the danger of infection being transmitted to other animals or men is always real and imminent. Horses which present suspicious symptoms, or those which have been in contact or have stood in the same stable with diseased horses, should be kept apart from others, and their harness, clothing, &c., left with them. Animals which are found to be affected should be immediately destroyed and buried with proper precautions, their harness, clothing, and the utensils employed with them being either destroyed also or thoroughly cleansed, while stables and places which they have frequented should be completely disinfected. Forage and litter used by glandered horses ought to be burned or buried.

Coitus disease. The venereal or coitus disease is a malady which occurs in Arabia and continental Europe, and has recently been carried from France to the United States of America (Montana and Illinois). In some of its features it resembles human syphilis, and it is propagated in the same manner. From one to ten days after coitus, or in the stallion not unfrequently after some weeks, there is irritation, swelling, and a livid redness of the external organs of generation (in stallions the penis may shrink), followed by unhealthy ulcers, which appear in successive crops, often at considerable intervals. In mares these are near the clitoris, which is frequently erected, and the animals rub and switch the tail about, betraying uneasiness. In horses the eruption is on the penis and sheath. In the milder forms there is little constitutional disturbance, and the patients may recover in a period varying from two weeks to two months. In the severe forms the local swelling increases by intermittent steps. In the mare the vulva is the seat of a deep violet congestion and extensive ulceration; pustules appear on the perinæum, tail, and between the thighs; the lips of the vulva are parted, exposing the irregular, nodular, puckered, ulcerated, and lardaceous-looking mucous membrane. If the mare happens to be pregnant, abortion occurs. In all cases emaciation sets in; lameness of one or more limbs occurs; great debility is manifested, and this runs on to paralysis, when death ensues after a miserable existence of from four or five months to two years. In horses swelling of the sheath may be the only symptom for a long time, even for a year. Then there may follow dark patches of extravasated blood on or swellings of the penis; the testicles may become tumefied; a dropsical engorgement extends forward beneath the abdomen and chest; the lymphatic glands in different parts of the body may be enlarged; pustules and ulcers appear on the skin; there is a discharge from the eyes and nose; emaciation becomes extreme; a weak and vacillating movement of the posterior limbs gradually increases, as in the mare, to paralysis; and after from three months to three years death puts an end to loathsomeness and great suffering. This malady appears to be spread only by the act of coition. It is a purely contagious disorder, and cannot be generated by any known agency or cause. The indications for its suppression and extinction are therefore obvious. They are (1) to prevent diseased animals coming into actual contact, especially *per coitum*, with healthy ones, (2) to destroy the infected, and (3), as an additional precautionary measure, to thoroughly cleanse and disinfect the stables, clothing, utensils, and implements used for the sick horse.

Influenza. Under influenza several diseases are sometimes included, and in different invasions it may (and doubtless does) assume varying forms. It may be said to be a specific fever of a low or asthenic type, associated with inflammation of the mucous membrane lining the air-passages, and also sometimes with that of other organs. At various times it has prevailed extensively over different parts of the world, more especially during the 18th and 19th centuries. Perhaps one of the most wide-spread outbreaks recorded was that of 1872, on the American continent. It usually radiates from the district in which it first appears. The symptoms have been enumerated as follows:—sudden attack, marked by extreme debility and stupor, with increased body-temperature, quick weak pulse, rigors, and cold extremities. The head is pendent, the eyelids swollen and half closed, eyes lustreless, and tears often flowing down the face. There is great disinclination to move; the body sways on the animal attempting to walk; and the limb-joints crack. The appetite is lost and the mouth is hot and dry; the bowels are constipated and the urine scanty and high-coloured; there is nearly always a deep, painful, and harassing cough; on auscultation of the chest crepitation or harsh blowing sounds are audible; and the membrane lining the eyelids and nose assumes either a bright pink colour or a dull leaden hue. A white, yellowish, or greenish-coloured discharge flows from the nostrils. In a few days the fever and other symptoms subside, and convalescence rapidly sets in. In unfavourable cases the fever increases, as well as the prostration, the breathing becomes laboured, the cough more painful and deep, and auscultation and percussion indicate that the lungs are seriously involved, with perhaps the pleura or the heart. Clots sometimes form in the latter organ, and quickly bring about a fatal termination. When the lungs do not suffer, the bowels may, and with this complication there are, in addition to the stupor and torpor, tension and tenderness of the abdominal walls when pressed upon, manifestations of colic, great thirst, a coated tongue, yellowness of the membranes of nose and eyes, high-coloured urine, constipation, and dry fæces covered with mucus. Sometimes rheumatic swelling and tenderness take place in the muscles and joints of the limbs, which may persist for a long time, often shifting from leg to leg, and involving the sheaths of tendons. At other times acute inflammation of the eyes supervenes, or even paralysis.

In this disease good nursing is the chief factor in the treatment. Comfortable, clean, and airy stables or loose-boxes should be provided, and the warmth of the body and limbs maintained. Cold and damp, foul air and uncleanliness, are as inimical to health and as antagonistic to recovery as in the case of mankind. In influenza it has been generally found that the less medicine the sick animal receives the more likely it is to recover. Nevertheless it may be necessary to adopt such medical measures as the following. For constipation administer enemata of warm water or give a dose of linseed oil or aloes. For fever give mild febrifuge diuretics (as liquor of acetate of ammonia or spirit of nitrous ether), and, if there is cough or nervous excitement, anodynes (such as extract of belladonna). When the fever subsides and the prostration is great, it may be necessary to give stimulants (carbonate of ammonia, nitrous ether, aromatic ammonia) and tonics, both vegetable (gentian, quassia, calumba) and mineral (iron, copper, arsenic). Some veterinary surgeons administer large and frequent doses of quinine from the onset of the disease, and, it is asserted, with excellent effect. If the abdominal organs are chiefly involved, demulcents may supplement the above (linseed boiled to a jelly, to which salt is added, is the most convenient and best), and drugs to allay pain (as opium and hydrocyanic acid). Olive oil is a safe laxative in such cases. When nervous symptoms are manifested, it may be necessary to apply wet cloths and vinegar to the head and neck; even blisters to the neck have been recommended. Bromide of potassium has been beneficially employed. To combat inflammation of the throat, chest, or abdomen, counter-irritants may be resorted to, such as mustard, soap liniment, or the ordinary white liniment composed of equal parts of oil of turpentine, liquor ammoniæ, and olive oil. The food should be soft mashes and gruel of oatmeal, with carrots and green food, and small and frequent quantities of scalded oats in addition when convalescence is established.

Typhoid, gastric, or bilious fever. Typhoid, gastric, or bilious fever is often confounded with influenza, and sometimes occurs at the same time in a locality. It also appears independently in horses when shedding their coat in the autumn, in those kept in a hot, close, and impure atmosphere, and in those fed insufficiently or on badly-preserved, musty, or otherwise improper food, or supplied with water containing an excess of decomposing organic matter. Overwork or hardship predisposes to an attack. This fever seems to become contagious under certain conditions, especially in badly-ventilated insalubrious stables. Wholesome and well-aired stables are not indeed always exempt; but in them the disease is less serious and does not spread so rapidly. It is presumed that this fever is caused by some virulent principle. As "premonitory" indications of the malady, the horse appears dull and listless, and careless of food. Then signs of fever appear, in the form of staring coat, shivering, alternate heat and coldness of the surface, restlessness, a hot dry mouth, and elevation of the internal temperature of the body. The visible mucous membranes have a yellow tinge; constipation is present, and with it indications of colicky pain; the abdomen is distended, tense, and sensitive on pressure; fæces are passed in the shape of a few hard, dark-coloured pellets covered with mucus; the urine is scanty, red in colour, and after standing a short time deposits a heavy sediment. Sometimes there is sore throat, with increased respiration and a nasal discharge. In mild attacks convalescence may occur in from a week to ten days. In serious cases the pulse is small, feeble, and quick; the mouth is very hot and dry, and exhibits yellow, brown, or greenish patches; the abdomen is more tender and the bowels very irritable, diarrhœa of a fœtid character often ensuing. Prostration to an extreme degree is a very marked feature in these cases. The head is maintained in a pendent position; the eyes become sunken; the expression is haggard and listless; while the stupor may be so advanced that pinching or pricking the skin will elicit no indication of sensibility. A fatal termination usually occurs in from ten to twenty days.

The diet must be carefully attended to, and should be soft and easily digested, such as mashes of bran, sliced carrots or turnips, boiled oats or barley, freshly cut grass, and oatmeal gruel. The stable should be kept clean and sweet, fresh air being an important factor in treatment; the body of the patient must also be made comfortable by clothing. Quiet is necessary. Quinine has been found useful in large and repeated doses; and calomel has been recommended. A daily dose of Glauber's salt may be given if there is constipation; and, if this is obstinate, enemata of warm water should be administered in addition. A drachm each of chlorate or nitrate of potash and muriate of ammonia may be given three or four times daily with the water drunk; or in cases of great prostration an ounce of oil of turpentine, sulphuric ether, sweet spirits of nitre, or carbonate of ammonia may be given as well. If there is much tenderness of the abdomen, hot fomentations continued for a long time, or mustard poultices, or the application of extract of mustard should be resorted to. When convalescence sets in, three or four ounces of tincture of gentian or cinchona may be given twice daily, with muriate of iron and stimulants.

Strangles. Strangles is a specific contagious and infectious fever peculiar to ungulates, and is more especially incidental to young animals. It is particularly characterized by the formation of abscesses in the lymphatic glands, chiefly those between the branches of the lower jaw (submaxillary). Various causes are ascribed for its production, such as change of young horses from field to stable, from grass to dry feeding, from idleness to hard work, irritation of teething, and change of locality and climate. It is asserted that repeated attacks will occur in the same horse under the influence of the last-named cause. But the chief, if not the sole, cause is infection,—the malady, in some of its features, closely resembling the "mumps" of the human species. Languor and feverishness, diminution of appetite, cough, redness of the nasal membrane, with discharge from the eyes and nose, and thirst are among the earliest symptoms. Then there is difficulty in swallowing, coincident with the development of swelling between the branches of the lower jaw, which often causes the water in drinking to be returned through the nose and the masticated food to be dropped from the mouth. The swelling is hot and tender, diffused, and uniformly rounded and smooth; at first it is hard, with soft, doughy margins; but later it becomes soft in the centre, where an abscess is forming, and soon "points" and bursts, giving exit to a quantity of pus. Relief is now experienced by the animal; the symptoms subside; and recovery takes place. In some cases the swelling is so great or occurs so close to the larynx that the breathing is interfered with, and even rendered so difficult that suffocation is threatened. In other cases the disease assumes an irregular form, and the swelling, instead of softening in the centre, remains hard for an indefinite time, or it may subside and abscesses form in various parts of the body, sometimes in vital organs, as the brains, lungs, liver, kidneys, &c., or in the bronchial or mesenteric glands, where they generally produce serious consequences. Not unfrequently a pustular eruption accompanies the other symptoms. The malady may terminate in ten days or be protracted for months, often terminating fatally, especially when the animal is not well nursed and is kept in an unhealthy stable.

Good nursing is the chief part of the treatment. The strength should be maintained by soft nutritious food, and the body kept warm and comfortable; the stable or loose-box must have plenty of fresh air and be kept clean. The swelling may be fomented with warm water and poulticed. The poultice may be a little bag containing bran and linseed meal mixed with hot water, and applied warm to the tumefaction, being retained there by a square piece of calico, with holes for the ears and eyes, tied down the middle of the face and behind the ears. If the breathing is disturbed and noisy, the animal may be made to inhale steam from hot water in a bucket or from bran mash. If the breathing becomes very difficult, the windpipe must be opened and a tube inserted. Instead of the swelling being poulticed, a little blistering ointment is sometimes rubbed over it, which promotes suppuration. When the abscess points, it may be lanced, though it is generally better to allow it to open spontaneously.

It is very important to distinguish strangles from glanders; the character of the nasal discharge, the absence of ulcers from the nostrils, and the diffused soft swelling between the branches of the lower jaw establish the distinction between them.

Horse pox.

Horsepox, which is somewhat rare, is almost, if not quite, identical with cowpox, being undistinguishable when inoculated on men and cattle. It most frequently attacks the limbs, though it may appear on the face and other parts of the body. There is usually slight fever; then swelling, heat, and tenderness are manifest in the part which is to be the seat of eruption, usually the heels; firm nodules form, increasing to one-third or one-half an inch in diameter; the hair becomes erect; and the skin, if light-coloured, changes to an intense red. On the ninth to the twelfth day a limpid fluid oozes from the surface and mats the hairs together in yellowish scabs; when one of these is removed, there is seen a red, raw depression, whereon the scab was fixed. In three or four days the crusts fall off, and the sores heal spontaneously. No medical treatment is needed, cleanliness being requisite to prevent the pocks becoming sloughs. If the inflammation runs high, a weak solution of carbolic acid may be employed.

Bibliography.—Among the numerous modern popular works in English which treat of diseases of the horse, the following may be mentioned:—Robertson, *Equine Medicine* (London, 1883); Williams, *Principles and Practice of Veterinary Medicine* (2d ed., London, 1874-79), and *Principles and Practice of Veterinary Surgery* (2d ed., London, 1872-76); Courtenay, *Manual of Veterinary Medicine and Surgery* (London, 1886); Fleming, *Practical Horse-Keeper* (London, 1886); Gresswell, *Diseases and Disorders of the Horse* (Leeds, 1886); Fitzwygram, *Horses and Stables* (London, 1869); and Law, *The Farmer's Veterinary Adviser* (London, 1879).

Diseases of Cattle.

The diseases of the bovine species are not so numerous as those of the horse, and some of the more serious have been already alluded to (see MURRAIN). We will notice a few which have not been included among these.

Tuberculosis.

Tuberculosis is a most formidable and widespread disorder of cattle; it is assuming greater proportions every year in those countries in which it is prevalent, in consequence of no steps being taken to check or suppress it. It is infectious and contagious, can be conveyed to other species of animals by ingestion of the flesh and milk, as well as of the tuberculous material, and by inoculation of these, or inhalation of dried discharges from the lungs; it can also be transmitted from the affected animal to the fœtus in utero. Its infectious properties and ready communicability to other species render it a serious danger to mankind, through consumption as food of the flesh and milk of tuberculous cows. The disease owes its origin to a bacillus. The structures chiefly involved are the lymphatic glands and tissues,—the characteristic tubercles or "grapes" varying in size from that of a millet seed to immense masses weighing many pounds; they are found in all parts of the body, but generally in the chest and on its lining membrane, as well as in the abdominal cavity. The symptoms resemble somewhat the contagious pleuro-pneumonia of cattle in its chronic form (see MURRAIN), though tubercles, sometimes in large numbers, are often found after death in the bodies of cattle which exhibited no sign of illness during life, and which when killed were in excellent condition. When the lungs are involved, there are a peculiar phthisical cough, low fever, wasting and debility, and often enlarged throat glands, less frequently enlarged joints. If the animal is not killed, it perishes in a state of marasmus, from the difficulty experienced in breathing, or the profuse fœtid diarrhœa which ensues. Medical treatment is of little if any avail. Preventive measures are of the utmost importance. Animals free from the tuberculous taint should alone be bred from, and those discovered to be affected should be at once completely segregated, and if convenient destroyed. The milk of tuberculous cows should not be given to any animal as food, not at least unless well boiled. Neither should the flesh be eaten unless well cooked throughout.

Milk or parturient fever.

Milk or parturient fever is a specific malady which appears after parturition, due to the absorption of septic matter from the interior of the uterus or vagina, producing what is known as "blood-poisoning" or septicæmia. The symptoms may be briefly summarized as follows:—high fever, restlessness, intense injection of the visible mucous membranes, tympanitis, fœtid breath, stupor, swollen limbs, sanguinolent and perhaps purulent discharges from the vagina, foul-smelling diarrhœa, coma, and death. In the early stage treatment is generally successful. The uterine cavity should be thoroughly cleaned out by injections of warm water, and any adherent portions of placenta removed by hand. Then a weak solution of Condy's fluid (permanganate of potash) must be injected. Cleanliness is all-important. Diffusible stimulants in large quantity should be given, with doses of solution of sulphate of quinine, perchloride of iron, oil of turpentine, or carbolic acid.

Abortion.

There is now strong evidence that one form of abortion in cows is due to infection. Whenever a case of abortion occurs in a shed, either the cow should be at once removed from the others, if they are pregnant, and cleaning and disinfection immediately resorted to; or, better still, the pregnant cows should be quickly moved out of the shed, and every care taken to keep them away from the sick cow and the discharges from it—these and the aborted fœtus being burned or otherwise completely destroyed.

Cowpox.

Cowpox is a contagious disease of much less frequent occurrence now than formerly, probably owing to improved hygienic management. In many localities the disease appears in all heifers which have recently calved on certain farms. There is usually a slight premonitory fever, which is generally overlooked; this is succeeded by some diminution in the quantity of the milk, with some increased coagulability, and by the appearance of the eruption or "pox" on the udder and teats. In well-observed cases the udder is hot and tender on manipulation for a day or two previous to the development of small pale-red nodules about the size of peas; these increase in dimensions to from three-fourths to one inch in diameter by the eighth or tenth day, when their contents have become fluid and they present a depressed centre. This fluid, at first clear and limpid, becomes yellowish white as it changes to pus, and soon dries up, leaving a hard, button-shaped black crust, which gradually becomes detached. On the teats, owing to the handling of the milker or to the cow lying on the hard ground or on straw, the vesicles are early ruptured and sores are formed, which often prove troublesome and may cause inflammation of the udder.

Actinomycosis.

Actinomycosis, though affecting man (*cf.* vol. xviii. p. 270), horses, pigs, and other creatures, is far more common in the bovine species. The fungus (*Actinomyces*) may be found in characteristic nodules in various parts of the body, but it usually invades the bones of the jaws, upper and lower, or the soft parts in the neighbourhood of these, as the tongue, cheeks, face, throat, and glands in its vicinity. About the head the disease appears to commence with slight sores on the gums or mucous membrane of the mouth or with ulcers alongside decaying teeth, and these extend slowly into the tissues. If the jaw is affected, a large rounded tumour grows from it, the dense outer bone becoming absorbed before the increasing soft growth within. Soon the whole becomes ulcerated and purulent discharges take place, in which are found the minute, hard, yellow granules which contain the fungus. When the tongue is affected, it becomes enlarged and rigid; hence the designation of "wooden tongue" given to it by the Germans. In the course of time the surface of the organ becomes ulcerated, and yellowish masses or nodules may be seen on the surface. Sometimes the entire face is involved, the lips and nostrils becoming swollen, hard, and immovable, often rendering respiration difficult. Around the throat there are rounded dense swellings, implicating the glands. When the disease is well-defined and of slight extent, the parts involved may be removed by the knife, wholly or partially. If the latter only, then the remaining affected tissues should be dressed with tincture of iodine or iodized carbolic acid. Chromic acid has also been found useful.

Bibliography.—J. H. Steel, *Diseases of the Ox* (London, 1881); J. W. Hill, *Bovine Medicine and Surgery* (London, 1882); G. Armatage, *Clater's Cattle Doctor* (London, 1870); J. Dobson, *On the Diseases of the Ox* (London, 1864); W. Youatt, *On Cattle* (London, 1854); J. Law, *The Farmer's Veterinary Adviser* (London, 1879); G. Fleming, *Tuberculosis from a Sanitary and Pathological Point of View* (London, 1880), and *Influence of Heredity and Contagion on the Propagation of Tuberculosis* (London, 1883).

Diseases of Sheep.

The contagious diseases of the sheep are comparatively few, and two of the more serious have been described under MURRAIN.

Sheep-pox.

The formidable disorder of sheep-pox is confined chiefly to the continent of Europe. It is extremely contagious and fatal, and in these and some other characteristics resembles human smallpox. From three to twelve days after being exposed to infection the sheep appears dull and listless, and eats little if anything; the temperature rises; there are frequent tremblings; tears flow from the eyes; and there is a nasal discharge. Red patches appear inside the limbs and under the abdomen; and on them, as well as on other parts where the skin is thin, dark red spots show themselves, which soon become papules, with a deep hard base. These are generally conical, and the apex quickly becomes white from the formation of pus. This eruption is characteristic and unmistakable; and the vesicles or pustules may remain isolated (discrete pox) or coalesce into large patches (confluent pox). The latter form of the disease is serious. In bad cases the eruption may develop on the eyes and in the respiratory and digestive passages. The course of the disease lasts about three weeks or a month, and the eruption passes through the same stages as that of cowpox. The mortality may extend from 10 per cent. in mild outbreaks to 90 or 95 per cent. in very virulent ones. Diseased animals should be sheltered, and fed on nourishing food, especially gruels of oatmeal, flour, or linseed; acidulated water may be allowed. If there is sloughing of the skin or extensive sores, oxide of zinc ointment should be applied. But treatment should not be adopted unless there is general infection over a wide extent of country. All diseased animals should be destroyed, as well as those which have been in contact with them, and thorough disinfection resorted to.

Diseases of the Pig.

Swine plague or fever.

The pig may become affected with foot-and-mouth disease (see MURRAIN), and it also has its own particular variola. But the disease special to it, and which causes enormous losses, is swine plague. This scourge, known in America as hog cholera, is a specific contagious fever, or fevers, for it is extremely probable that two diseases are included under this designation. It is generally very rapid in its course, death ensuing in a very few days; and when the animal survives recovery is protracted. After a period of three or four days to a fortnight from exposure to infection, the animal exhibits signs of illness by dulness, weakness, shiverings, burying itself under the litter, disinclination to move, staggering gait, great thirst, hot dry snout, sunken eyes, loss of appetite, and greatly increased pulse, respiration, and temperature. Red and brown patches appear on the skin; there is a hacking cough; nausea is followed by vomiting; pressure on the abdomen causes extreme pain; diarrhœa ensues; the hind limbs become paralysed; stupor sets in; and the animal perishes. Treatment should not be attempted when there is danger of the infection extending to other pigs. If treatment be used, nursing ought to be the chief element; sloppy food, in which small doses of carbolic acid and oil of turpentine have been mixed, should be given, and these should be followed by tonics when convalescence sets in. To suppress the disease, kill all affected pigs, and if necessary those which have been in contact with them; burn or bury deeply the carcases and litter; and disinfect everything likely to have been contaminated by the virus.

Diseases of the Dog.

Distemper.

The contagious diseases of the dog are likewise very few, but the one which attracts most attention is common and generally serious. This is what is popularly known as distemper. It is peculiar to the canine species, for there is no evidence that it can be conveyed to other animals, though the different families of *Carnivora* appear each to be liable to a similar disease. Distemper is a specific fever which most frequently attacks young dogs, its effects being primarily developed in the respiratory passages, though the brain, spinal cord, and abdominal organs may subsequently be involved. Highly bred and pet dogs suffer more severely than the commoner and hardier kinds. It is a most infectious disease, and there is much evidence to prove that it owes its existence and prevalence solely to its virulence. One attack confers immunity from another. The symptoms are rigors, sneezing, dulness, loss of appetite, desire for warmth, and increased temperature, respiration, and pulse. The eyes are red, and the nose, at first dry and harsh, becomes smeared with the discharge which soon begins to flow from the nostrils. Suppuration also begins at the eyes; vision is more or less impaired by the mucus and pus, and often the cornea becomes ulcerated, and even perforated. There is a cough, which in some cases is so violent as to induce vomiting. Debility rapidly ensues, and emaciation is soon apparent; diarrhœa in the majority of cases sets in; the body emits an unpleasant odour; ulceration of the mouth is noticed; the nostrils become obstructed by the discharge from them; convulsions generally come on; signs of bronchitis, pneumonia, jaundice, or other complications manifest themselves; and in some instances there is a pustular or vesicular eruption on the skin. In fatal cases the animal dies in a state of marasmus. Many which recover are affected with chorea for a long time afterwards. Here, again, good nursing is all-important. Comfort and cleanliness, with plenty of fresh air, must be ensured. Debility being the most serious feature of the disease, the strength should be maintained or restored until the fever has run its course. Light broth, beef tea, or bread and milk, or these alternately, may be allowed as diet. Preparations of quinine, given from the commencement of the attack in a little wine, such as sherry, have proved very beneficial. Often a mild laxative is required. Complications should be treated as they arise. The disease being extremely infectious, precautions should be adopted with regard to other dogs.

The formidable affliction known as RABIES (*q.v.*) has been treated of under that name.

Bibliography.—J. H. Steel, *Treatise on the Diseases of the Dog*; J. W. Hill, *Management and Diseases of the Dog* (London, 1878); W. Youatt, *The Dog* (London, 1851); D. Blaine, *Canine Pathology* (London, 1851); W. Mayhew, *Diseases of the Dog* (London, 1865).

PRINCIPAL PARASITES OF DOMESTIC ANIMALS.

In horse.

Perhaps the commonest worm infesting the horse is *Ascaris megalocephala* or common lumbricoid. The males are from 6 to 8 inches long, females 7 to 17 inches. It is found in almost every part of the intestinal canal, but generally in the small intestines. The symptoms produced in the horse by this worm are colicky pains, which occur intermittently, an unhealthy condition of the skin, and staring coat. Although the animal feeds well, it does not improve in condition, but is very "tucked up," and the visible mucous membranes are very pale. In some instances pouches are formed in the coats of the intestines. There are many recipes for the expulsion of lumbricoid; among the principal remedies is a mixture of emetic tartar, oil of turpentine, and linseed oil; others are santonine, sulphate of iron, male fern, &c. *Strongylus armatus* or palisade worm was at first supposed to consist of two varieties, but it has been proved that these are simply different stages of growth of one parasite. It is a moderate-sized Nematoid worm, having a straight body, with a globular and somewhat flattened head,—males 1 to 1½ inches long, females 1½ to 2 inches. It is found in the intestines, especially the double colon and cæcum. The embryo is developed in the interior of the egg after its expulsion from the host, and is lodged in moist mud, where, according to Cobbold, it changes its first skin in about three weeks, after which it probably enters the body of an intermediate bearer, whence it is conveyed to the alimentary canal of the horse, its ultimate host, in food or water. From the stomach it bores its way into the blood-vessels, where it again changes its skin and gives rise to aneurisms. After a time it recommences its wanderings, and passes into the large intestines, where it rapidly acquires sexual maturity. It is a dung-feeder. Sometimes it passes into other tissues of the body (kidney, liver, &c.), and occasionally produces fatal results. This parasite is most dangerous to its equine host when it is migrating from one organ to another. It is principally found at the root of the anterior mesenteric artery, but it also gives rise to aneurism in the cœliac axis, the post-mesenteric and splenic arteries, and even the aorta. The common lumbricoid, the palisade worm, and the four-spined strongyle (*S. tetracanthus*) are principally productive of colic. The last-mentioned worm, of which the male and female are about the same size, ½ to ¾ inch long, is found in the cæcum, colon, and duodenum. It is a true blood-sucker, and its development is very similar to that of *S. armatus*, except that, when in the intestines in the trichonemous stage, it pierces the inner coats, encapsules itself, and forms little pill-like masses, and then again enters the tissues of the intestines before becoming mature. The symptoms of its presence are loss of condition, more or less constant colicky pains, unhealthy coat, flabby muscles, abdominal distension, diarrhœa, fœtid and watery fæces, pale mucous membranes, great weakness, more or less frequent cough, and sometimes partial or complete paralysis, due to the formation of a clot of blood causing thrombosis of one of the principal vessels of the posterior extremities, thus interfering with the circulation of blood in the part supplied by the particular vessel. The treatment by which the common lumbricoid is expelled will suffice to expel these strongyles, but care must be exercised in administering oil of turpentine, as it very often irritates the wounds caused by *S. tetracanthus* in the coats of the intestines. Of course this treatment applies to the mature stage of these worms.

Oxyuris curvula or pin worm is fusiform in shape, with smooth gently curved body (males 1⅓ to 1⅝ inches, females 3½ to 4¾ inches long). It is seated in the cæcum and colon; and, although not found in the rectum, it causes great irritation at the anus by the clusters of eggs which are deposited around that part in the form of yellowish crusts. This parasite is best treated by means of a cathartic, followed by sulphate of iron, also carbolic acid in 2½ per cent. solution.

The Cestodes of the horse are very insignificant, both as regards their size and the symptoms they create, the two principal being *Tænia perfoliata* and *T. plicata*. The former is the more common, but is only from 1 to 5 inches in length; it is found in the cæcum and colon, and is distinguished from *T. plicata*, not only by its length, but also by its rounder head. This last, which has a nearly square head, and is from 6 inches to 3 feet in length, occurs in the small intestines and stomach. Generally a horse may be proved to be infested with tape-worm by finding some of the proglottides in the fæces. The best remedy for the removal of *Tænia* is extract of male fern, with oil of turpentine and linseed oil, given three days in succession.

Gastrus equi or the common bot, though not a true helminth (see INSECTS, vol. xiii. p. 150), is classed with the parasites on account of its larval form living as a parasite. The bot-fly deposits its eggs on the hair of horses in such a position as to enable that animal, when licking itself, to take them into its mouth; there the warmth and moisture of the tongue, combined with the pressure of licking, cause them to burst, and from each egg a small grub escapes, which sticks to the tongue, and then passes down into the stomach, where it fixes itself to the cuticular lining of the organ by a hook which it has on each side of its mouth. There it undergoes no change (except that of growth, being at this time about 1 inch long) for about nine months, when it detaches itself, passes into the food, and is discharged with the fæces.

In cattle and sheep.

Of the parasites which infest cattle and sheep mention will only be made of *Fasciola hepatica* or common fluke, which gives rise to the disease called rot, and is more frequently met with in sheep than in cattle. For a full description of its anatomy and development, see TREMATODA, vol. xxiii. p. 535.

Strongylus micrurus is the husk-producing worm of cattle. The common earthworm is the intermediate bearer. *S. filaria*, or the common lung strongyle of sheep, is distinguished from *S. micrurus* by having no papillæ on its head. The males are 1 inch to 1 inch 2 lines long and the females nearly 3 inches. The development is unknown; but Cobbold thought that in its larval form the creature infested snails, &c. The symptoms of its presence in the sheep are a dull expression, quickened breathing, fœtid breath, foaming at the mouth and nostrils, violent and spasmodic cough, loss of appetite, and emaciation. Of various specific remedies the most successful is a mixture of oil of turpentine, linseed oil, and sulphuric ether, administered two mornings in succession, followed by a third dose on the fourth morning. This causes coughing, and consequent freeing of the tubes of the larvæ and mucus. Good results have been derived from inhalation of chlorine gas, &c., which acts in the same way. The intratracheal injection of oil of turpentine is said to be followed by favourable results. The system should be supported with as much good nourishing food as possible. *S. rufescens*, or gordian strongyle (males 5 to 6 inches long, females 6 to 7 inches), is very often associated with *S. filaria*.

The principal Cestode of ruminants is *Tænia expansa*, which, when fully mature, is more frequently found in sheep than in cattle. Its body consists of about one thousand segments, each more broad than long. It is the longest of all tape-worms, being (according to Cobbold) in sheep from 8 to 30 feet and in oxen from 40 to 100 feet in length. Its maximum width is $\frac{3}{4}$ inch; it is found in the large and small intestines. Cobbold thought its larval form was developed in the louse of the ox. The symptoms are emaciation, with dysentery, and loss of appetite. Male fern ought to be given in doses according to the size of the animal. For a full account of the development of *Cysticercus bovis*, the beef measle, see TAPE-WORMS, vol. xxiii. pp. 50-52. *C. ovis* is supposed by Cobbold to be the larval form of his so-called *T. tenella* of the human subject. Another bladder worm, found only in the mesentery of the sheep, is *C. tenuicollis*, the larval form of *T. marginata* of the dog. Another important hydatid of ruminants is *Cœnurus cerebralis*, which gives rise to gid; it is generally found in the brain of sheep, cattle, goats, deer, &c., and also in the soft structures of rabbits. It is the larval form of *T. cœnurus* of the dog. The symptoms of gid are these. The animal has a rotatory motion; it does not graze freely; there is paralysis on the opposite side to the vesicle; the head is elevated or depressed if the hydatid is situated in the centre; and the animal is easily frightened. Medical treatment is of no avail; but the hydatid may be removed by a surgical operation.

Trichocephalus affinis, the common whip-worm, sometimes gives rise to severe symptoms in ruminants, particularly in sheep. The males and females are each about 2 inches long.

In the pig. The helminths of the pig, although not very detrimental to the animal itself, are nevertheless of great importance in respect to the *Entozoa* of the human subject, being the intermediary bearers of some dangerous human parasites in their immature state. Allusion must be made to *Trichina spiralis* (see PARASITISM, vol. xviii. p. 270). The development of this parasite requires about three weeks after being taken into the stomach, where the capsule is digested; it then passes into the intestines of the pig, principally the duodenum, where it takes two days to become mature; then after about a week the embryos leave the body of the female worm, and immediately commence penetrating the walls of the intestines in order to pass into some voluntary muscles. About fourteen days elapse from the time they begin their wandering. Each is generally enveloped in a capsule, but two or even four have been found in one capsule. The male is $\frac{1}{16}$th, the female $\frac{1}{8}$th inch long, and the larvæ $\frac{1}{27}$th to $\frac{1}{30}$th inch. They have been known to live in their capsules from eighteen months to two years.

Cysticercus cellulosæ is the larval form of *Tænia solium* of man (see TAPE-WORMS, vol. xxiii. p. 52). "Measly pork" is caused by the presence in the tissues of the pig of this entozoon, which is bladder-like in form. It has also been discovered in the dog, ape, bear, rat, and deer. Other important parasites of the pig are *Stephanurus dentatus*, or crown-tailed strongyle, and *Echinorhynchus gigas*. This latter is the only thorn-headed or acanthocephalous worm infesting the domesticated animals (Cobbold).

In the dog. The commonest of all parasites infesting the dog is *Ascaris mystax* (males 2 to $3\frac{1}{2}$ inches, females 3 to 8 inches long). It is also found in the cat and larger canines. The symptoms are wasting, voracity, irregularity of bowels, short cough, and irritation at anus; in the cat, more particularly, large quantities of mucus, with numerous parasites, are vomited. The treatment consists of the administration of castor oil, with santonine, according to the size of the animal. *Filaria immitis*, another Nematode, infests the heart of the dog, and its larvæ circulate in the blood, giving rise to fits, which often end in death.

Tænia serrata is a moderate-sized Cestode, from 2 to 3 feet in length; it is found in about 10 per cent. of all English dogs, most frequently in sporting dogs, especially greyhounds and harriers, owing to their eating the intestines of rabbits, &c., in which the larval form (*Cysticercus pisiformis*) of this parasite dwells. It takes two months to pass through the first stage and one month to pass through the second when it is artificially produced, but much longer when produced naturally (Cobbold). *T. cœnurus* gives rise to gid in sheep, as previously stated. It is 18 to 24 inches long, and is principally seen in the small intestines. *T. marginata* is the largest Cestode infesting the dog. It varies in length from 5 to 8 feet, and is found in the small intestines of about 30 per cent. of dogs in Great Britain; its larval form, *C. tenuicollis*, is found in the mesentery, &c., of sheep. In the treatment of Cestodes extract of male fern has been found the most effectual remedy; areca nut and a pill consisting of colocynth and jalap, varying according to the size, age, and condition of the dog, have also proved efficacious. Comparatively small doses of any vermifuge have often been found to give rise to violent symptoms, and all vermifuges if taken in large doses produce death; too much care cannot, therefore, be exercised in administering vermifuges to young animals.

Dermatozoa. Another order of parasites which cause numerous diseases of the skin in the domesticated animals may be classed under two heads, viz., animal parasites or *Dermatozoa* and vegetable parasites or *Dermatophyta*. The animal parasites are those which produce scab, itch, mange, &c., in all animals. This class may be again divided into three varieties, viz., *Sarcoptes*, which burrow in the skin; *Dermatodectes*, which bite the skin; and *Symbiotes*, which simply pierce the epidermis (Gerlach). All these parasites live on serous fluids, produced by the irritation which they excite. Either one or more of these varieties infest all our domesticated animals: all three varieties have been found on the horse and sheep, the last two on the ox, and one in the pig, dog, and cat respectively. The sarcoptic variety of the horse and dog is easily transmitted to man. To distinguish between the different varieties, it is only necessary to place a few fresh scales in the sun; if *Sarcoptes* are present, they will soon be found on the under surface, whereas *Dermatodectes* are on the upper surface. Again, the *Sarcoptes* are isolated, whereas the *Symbiotes* and *Dermatodectes* live in clusters or colonies. Thirdly, the *Symbiotes* do not burrow, but merely bite the skin, and principally invade the limbs. An effectual cure for those which infest the horse is a mixture of sulphur, hellebore, oil of turpentine, whale oil, and carbolic acid, applied for three successive days, then washed off and applied again. For the dog a very useful remedy is made from creosote, olive oil, solution of potassium, and sulphur, also train oil and spirits of tar. The first is an almost sure cure for cats. A good remedy for destroying lice may be compounded from *staphysagria* powder, soft soap, and hot water, applied warm to the skin.

Dermatophyta. Vegetable parasites are of two kinds, namely, *Tinea tonsurans*, or the common ringworm, seen in most of our domesticated animals, and *Favus*, or honeycomb ringworm. The latter is seldom seen. *T. tonsurans* is due to a cryptogamic parasite, *Tricophyton*, and is lodged in the interior of the roots of the hairs, which after a time lose their elasticity and break off, leaving the fungi in the form of a greyish white bran-like incrustation. In this they differ from *Favus*, which is yellow and covers the epidermis. It may affect any part of the body, but occurs principally on the head, face, neck, and hindquarters; it is very prevalent amongst young cattle. Ringworm is very contagious, and may be communicated from one animal to another, and from animals to man. It mostly attacks badly-fed and ill-cared-for animals. The affected parts should be well washed with soft soap and warm water, removing as much as possible of the bran-like scales, and then with Stockholm tar ointment, and finally with either iodine (in tincture or ointment) or carbolic acid (in solution or ointment). (G. FL.)

VETO. By this expression (Lat. *veto*, "I forbid") is understood in public law the constitutional right of the competent authority, or in republics of the whole people in their primary assembly, to protest against a legislative or administrative act, and to prevent wholly, or for the time being, the validation or execution of the same.

It is generally stated that this right was called into existence in the Roman republic by the *tribunicia potestas*, because by this authority decisions of the senate, and of the consuls and other magistrates, could be declared inoperative. Such a statement must, however, be qualified by reference to the facts that *interdico*, *interdicimus* were the expressions used, and, in general, that in ancient Rome every holder of a magistracy could check a negotiation set on foot by a colleague, his equal in rank, by his opposition and intervention. This was a consequence of the position that each of the colleagues possessed the whole power of the magistracy, and this right of intervention must have come into existence with the introduction of colleagued authorities, *i.e.*, with the commencement of the republic. In the Roman magistracy a twofold power must be distinguished,—the positive management of the affairs of the state entrusted to each individual and the power of restraining the acts of magistrates of equal or inferior rank by his protest. As the *tribuni plebis* possessed this latter negative competence to a great extent, it is customary to attribute to them the origin of the veto.

In the former kingdom of Poland the precedent first set in 1652 was established by law as a constant right, that in the imperial diet a single deputy by his protest "Nie pozwalam," *i.e.*, "I do not permit it," could invalidate the decision sanctioned by the other members. The king of France received the right of a suspensory veto at the commencement of the French Revolution, from the national assembly sitting at Versailles in 1789, with regard to the decrees of the latter, which was only to be valid for the time being against the decisions come to and during the following national assembly, but during the period of the third session it was to lose its power if the assembly persisted in its resolution. By this means it was endeavoured to diminish the odium of the measure; but, as is well known, the monarchy was soon afterwards entirely abolished. Similarly the Spanish constitution of 1812 prescribed that the king might twice refuse his sanction to bills laid twice before him by two sessions of the cortes, but if the third session repeated the same he could no longer exercise the power of veto. The same is the case in the Norwegian constitution of 1814.

In the present French republic the president has no veto, except against decisions of the general councillors (*conseils générals du departements*), just as the prefect possesses the same power against decisions of the communal councillors. The king or queen of England has the right to withhold sanction from a bill passed by both houses of parliament. This royal prerogative has not been exercised since 1692 and may now be considered obsolete. The governor of an English colony has the power of veto against a bill passed by the legislative body of a colony, *e.g.*, Canada. In this case the bill is finally lost, just as a bill would be which had been rejected by the colonial council, or as a bill passed by the English houses of parliament would be if the crown were to exert the prerogative of refusing the royal assent. The governor may, however, without refusing his assent, reserve the bill for the consideration of the crown. In that case the bill does not come into force until it has either actually or constructively received the royal assent, which is in effect the assent of the English ministry, and therefore indirectly of the imperial parliament. Thus the colonial liberty of legislation is made legally reconcilable with imperial sovereignty, and conflicts between colonial and imperial laws are prevented.[1]

The constitution of the United States of North America contains in art. i., sect. 7, § 2, the following order:—

"Every bill which shall have passed the House of Representatives and the Senate shall, before it becomes a law, be presented to the president of the United States; if he approve, he shall sign it; if not, he shall return it with his objections to that house in which it shall have originated, who shall enter the objections at large on their journal and proceed to reconsider it. If, after such reconsideration, two-thirds of that house shall agree to pass the bill, it shall be sent, together with the objections, to the other house, by which it shall likewise be reconsidered, and, if approved by two-thirds of that house, it shall become a law. Every order, resolution, or vote to which the concurrence of the Senate and House of Representatives may be necessary (except on a question of adjournment) shall be presented to the president of the United States, and, before the same shall take effect, shall be approved by him, or, being disapproved by him, shall be repassed by two-thirds of the Senate and House of Representatives, according to the rules and limitations prescribed in the case of a bill."

In most States of the Union the governors, in the same manner or to a modified extent, possess the right of protesting against the laws and decisions of the legislature. Here therefore we have again a suspensory veto which is frequently exercised. According to the official report for 1886, the president of the United States exercised his right of veto in that year 115 times against bills, resolutions, and orders of the most different kinds. Between 1840 and 1850 the Whigs agitated for the total abolition of the power of veto. Of late an agitation has begun in the opposite direction.[2]

According to the constitution of the German empire of 1871, the imperial legislation is executed by the federal council and imperial diet; the emperor is not mentioned. In the federal council the simple majority of votes decides. But in the case of bills concerning the army, the navy, and certain specially noted taxes, as well as in the case of decisions concerning the alteration of orders for the administration, and arrangements for the execution of the laws of customs and taxes, the proposal of the federal council is only accepted if the Prussian votes are on the side of the majority in favour of the same (art. 7, sect. 3). Prussia presides in the federal council. The state of things is therefore in fact as follows: it is not the German emperor, but the same monarch as king of Prussia, who has the right of veto against bills and decisions of the federal council, and therefore can prevent the passing of an imperial law. The superior power of the presidential vote obtains, it is true, its due influence only in one legislative body, but in reality it has the same effect as the veto of the head of the empire.

The Swiss federal constitution grants the president of the Confederation no superior position at all; neither he nor the federal council possesses the power of veto against laws or decisions of the federal assembly. But in some cantons, viz., St Gall (1831), Basel (1832), and Lucerne (1841), the veto was introduced as a right of the people. The citizens had the power to submit to a plebiscite laws which had been debated and accepted by the cantonal council (the legislative authority), and to reject the same. If this plebiscite was not demanded within a certain short specified time, the law came into force. But, if the voting took place, and if the number of persons voting against the law exceeded by one vote half the number of persons entitled to vote in the canton, the law was rejected. The absent voters were considered as having voted in favour of the law. An attempt to introduce the veto in Zurich in 1847 failed. Thurgau and Schaffhausen accepted it later. Meanwhile another arrangement has quite driven it out of the field. For of late years the so-called "referendum,"—properly speaking, direct legislation by the people,—has been introduced into most of the Swiss cantons. Formerly in all cantons—with the exception of the small mountainous districts of Uri, Schwyz, Unterwalden, Zug, Glarus, and Appenzell—it was not a pure democracy, but a representative constitution that prevailed: the great councillors or cantonal councillors periodically chosen by the people were the possessors of the sovereign power, and after deliberating twice passed the bills definitively. Now they have only to discuss the bills, which are printed and sent to all voters with an explanatory message; then the people on a certain day vote for the acceptance or rejection of the law by writing "yes" or "no" on a printed voting

[1] A. V. Dicey, *Lectures Introductory to the Study of the Law of the Constitution*, p. 105 *sq.*, 2d ed., London, 1886.

[2] Rüttimann, *Das Nordamerikanische Bundes-Staatsrecht verglichen mit den politischen Einrichtungen der Schweiz*, i. 244 and 245, Zurich, 1867; D. Webster, *Works*, ii. 337 and iii. 416, Boston, 1858.

paper, which is placed in an urn under official control. In some cantons important financial resolutions involving large state expenses are also submitted to the decision of the people. In the revised federal constitution of 1874, under certain suppositions which have no further interest for us at present, a facultative referendum (*i.e.*, the possibility of demanding a plebiscite under exceptional circumstances) has been introduced for federal laws. Since that period it has often been employed and has operated like a veto. It is evident that by the compulsory referendum in the cantons the mere veto is rendered superfluous.[1]

In examining the question as to what position the veto occupies in jurisprudence, we must separate quite different conceptions which are comprised under the same name.

1. The veto may be a mere *right of intervention* on the part of a magistrate against the order of another official, or against that of an authority of equal or inferior rank. This was the case in ancient Rome. To this class belong also those cases in which, in the present French republic, the president makes his "no" valid against decisions of the general councillors, and the prefect does the same against decisions of the communal councillors. The use of the expression here is quite justifiable, and this veto is not confined to bills, but refers particularly to administrative measures. It affords a guarantee against the abuse of an official position.

2. The veto may be a safety-valve against precipitate decisions, and so a *preventive measure*. This task is fulfilled by the suspensory veto of the president of the North American Union. Similarly, to this class belong the abovementioned prescriptions of the Spanish and Norwegian constitutions, and also the veto of the governor of an English colony against decisions of the legislature; for this protest is only intended to prevent a certain want of harmony between the general and the colonial legislation, by calling forth a renewed investigation. This veto is neither an interference with the competence of an authority, nor a division of the legislative power among different factors, but simply a guarantee against precipitancy in the case of a purely legislative measure. The wisdom of establishing this veto power by the constitution is thus manifest.

3. It is wrong to apply the term veto to what is merely the *negative side of the sanctioning of the laws*, in other words, an act of sovereignty. It would not be in accordance with the nature of a constitutional monarchy to declare the monarch's consent to a law unnecessary, or make it a compulsory duty; the legislative power is divided between him and the chambers. The sovereign must therefore be perfectly at liberty to say "yes" or "no" in each single case according to his opinion. If he says the latter, we speak of it as his veto, but this—if he possesses an absolute and not merely a suspensory veto—is not an intervention and not a preventive measure, but the negative side of the exercise of the legislative power, and therefore an act of sovereignty. That this right belongs fully and entirely to the holder of sovereign power—however he may be called—is self-evident. One chamber can also by protest prevent a bill of the other from coming into force. The "placet of the temporal power for church affairs—when it occurs—also involves in this manner in itself the veto or non placet." Where in pure democracies the people in their assembly have the right of veto or referendum, the exercise of it is also a result of the sovereign rights of legislature.

The peculiar power of veto possessed by the (Prussian) president of the federal council of Germany lies on the boundary between (2) and (3). (A. V. O.)

[1] A. v. Orelli, *Das Staatsrecht der schweizerischen Eidgenossenschaft*, pp. 101 and 105, and Marquardsen, *Handbuch des öffentlichen Rechts der Gegenwart in Monographien*, vol. iv., Freiburg (in Breisgau), 1885.

VIAREGGIO, a coast town of Italy, in the province of Lucca, 13 miles by rail north-north-west from Pisa, had in 1881 a population of 10,190 (commune 12,735). The principal industry is fishing, and the place is also a favourite sea-bathing resort.

VIATICUM. This word, which in classical Latinity means "provision for a journey" (Gr. τὰ ἐφόδια), is often used by early Christian writers to denote the sacrament of the Eucharist, and sometimes even is applied to baptism. Ultimately it came to be employed in a restricted sense to denote the last communion given to the dying. The 13th canon of the council of Nice is to the effect that "none, even of the lapsed, shall be deprived of the last and most necessary viaticum (ἐφοδίου)," and that the bishop, on examination, is to give the oblation to all who desire to partake of the Eucharist on the point of death. The same principle still rules the canon law, it being of course understood that penitential discipline, which in ordinary circumstances would have been due for their offence, is to be undergone by lapsed persons who have thus received the viaticum, in the event of recovery. In extreme cases it is lawful to administer the viaticum to persons not fasting. The ritual to be observed in its administration does not differ from that laid down in the office for the communion of the sick, except in the words of the formula, which is "accipe, carissime frater (carissima soror), viaticum corporis nostri Jesu Christi, quod te custodiat ab hoste maligno, protegat te, et perducat te ad vitam æternam. Amen."

VIATKA. See VYATKA.

VIAU, or VIAUD, THÉOPHILE DE (1590-1626), more commonly called both in his own time and since simply THÉOPHILE, a poet of unfortunate life and of great but misused powers, was born at Clairac near Agen in 1590. He went to the capital in his twentieth year and ingratiated himself with at least one patron, the ill-fated duke of Montmorency, who was always constant to him. He also became acquainted with most of the literary men of the time, and in 1617 composed and produced with success the tragedy of *Pyrame et Thisbé*. This piece, written in the extravagant Spanish-Italian manner which was fashionable in the interval between the Pléiade model and the innovations of Corneille, was later the subject of much ridicule, especially directed to the passage in which a sword, reddened with the blood of its master, is said to "blush for its treason," no very unpardonable conceit in eyes less pedantic than Boileau's. Théophile's prosperity was not lasting. Only two years after the success of *Pyrame* he was accused of blasphemous and indecent writings, and was exiled to England. Returning in 1621 and joining the Roman Church (he had been a Huguenot), he served in two campaigns. But he was, rightly or wrongly, associated with the publication of the *Parnasse Satirique*, a collection of poems of the same character as those which had formerly got him into trouble, and in 1623 was tried, condemned in his absence to death, arrested, and imprisoned in the conciergerie. At length the sentence of death which hung over him was reduced to banishment, and the influence of Montmorency enabled him to hide himself in Paris till his death on 25th September 1626.

For his singular persecution, which, even if the charges had been much better established than they are, would have been surprising enough in an age of unusually loose conduct and writing, the machinations of the Jesuits are sometimes held responsible. But if Théophile had bitter enemies he had warm friends. Six years after his death Georges de Scudéry edited his work with a *Tombeau* (copy of obituary verses), and a challenge in the preface to any one who might be offended by the editor's eulogy of the poet. This was in 1632; the year before had appeared a tragedy entitled *Pasiphaé*, where the awkwardness of the subject is not redeemed by any merit of treatment; but it is by no means certainly or even probably Théophile's, and is not included in his works, the standard modern edition of which is that of Alleaume in the Bibliothèque Elzévirienne (Paris, 2 vols., 1856). These works may surprise the reader who only knows Théophile's mishaps and ill-fame; for, though varied enough, they contain in the certainly authentic part of them nothing discreditable. Besides *Pyrame et Thisbé*, the chief in point of bulk is a paraphrase, half verse half prose, after the odd fashion of the time, of the *Phædo*. There are numerous French and Latin letters, a vigorous *Apologie* rebutting the accusations against him, a promising fragment of comic prose narrative, and a large collection of occasional verses, odes, elegies, stanzas, &c. These latter, besides being very unequal, are distinguished by the faults of taste and the inelegance of language which marked the first quarter of the century. But there are occasionally bursts of real poetry; and on the whole Théophile is the superior of all his contemporaries between Regnier and Corneille. In addition to Alleaume's edition, a delightful article in Gautier's *Grotesques* should be consulted respecting him.

VIBORG, or WIBORG (Finnish, *Viipuri*), capital of a province or län of the same name in Finland, is situated at the head of the Bay of Viborg in the Gulf of Finland, at the mouth of the Saima Canal and on the railway which connects St Petersburg with Helsingfors. The Saima Canal (37 miles long), a fine engineering work, connects with the sea Lake Saima—the principal lake of Finland, 249 feet above sea-level—and a series of others, including Puruvesi, Orivesi, Höytiänen, and Kallavesi, all of which are navigated by steamers, as far north as Idensalmi in 63° 30′ N. lat. Viborg is thus the seaport of Karelia and eastern Savolaks, with the towns of Vilmanstrand (1289 inhabitants in 1880), St Michel (1432), Nyslott (1424), Kuopio (6834), and Idensalmi, with their numerous saw-mills and iron-works. Viborg stands most picturesquely on the glaciated and dome-shaped granite hills surrounding the bay, which is protected at its entrance by the naval station of Björkö and at its head by several forts. The castle of Viborg, built in 1293 by Marshal Torkel Knutson, was the first centre for the spread of Christianity in Karelia, and for establishing the power of Sweden; it is now used as a prison. Its lofty and elegant tower has fallen into decay. The court-house (1839), the town-house, the gymnasium (1641; with an excellent library), and the museum are among the principal buildings of the city. There are also a school of navigation and several primary schools, both public and private, a literary and an agricultural society, and several benevolent institutions. The population, 14,668 in 1880 and 15,800 in 1884, consists of three elements,—Finnish, Swedish, and Russian (see FINLAND). There is a strong Russian garrison. Several industrial establishments, including a foundry for the construction of steam-engines, an iron-work, and several candle-works, match-factories, and saw-mills, have risen of late at Viborg and in its neighbourhood; but the place owes its chief importance to its export trade, in which timber is the chief item. The coasting trade is also considerable.

The environs are most picturesque and are visited by many tourists in the summer. The park of Monrepos (Old Viborg), in a bay dotted with dome-shaped islands, is specially attractive. The scenery of the Saima Canal and of the Finnish lakes with the grand ås of Pungaharju; the Imatra rapids, by which the Vuoksen discharges the water of Lake Saima into Lake Ladoga, with the castle of Kexholm at its mouth; Serdobol and Valamo monastery on Lake Ladoga—all visited from Viborg—attract many tourists from St Petersburg and from other parts of Finland.

VICAR, in ecclesiastical law, is, in the words of Blackstone, "a curate, deputy, or vicegerent of the appropriator, and therefore called *vicarius* or vicar." When a benefice had become appropriated before the dissolution of the religious houses to a spiritual corporation, usually with the authority of a licence from the Chancery, the vicar was the person appointed by the appropriators for the cure of souls in the parish. He was at first generally a member of the corporation. After the dissolution in the reign of Henry VIII. these appropriated benefices became—as indeed they had been in the church in general up to the Lateran council of 1179—vested in lay impropriators,[1] but the legal position of the vicar remained the same. He was not a parson in the proper sense of the word (in fact parson and vicar are often distinguished in old statutes), and his stipend was at the discretion of the impropriator. Where he had the enjoyment of tithes, they were in most cases, apart from prescription, the small as distinguished from the great tithes, that is, such as the impropriator found it most difficult to collect. There was, however, no consistent rule in the matter: what were rectorial tithes in some parishes might be vicarial in others. The position of the vicar, at first so insecure and uncertain, was gradually ameliorated by legislation. 15 Ric. II. c. 6 provided for the sufficient endowment of the vicarage. 4 Hen. IV. c. 12 repeated this provision, and in addition enacted that the vicar should be a secular priest, not removable at the caprice of the appropriators, and canonically instituted and inducted. Among numerous other Acts may be noticed 29 Car. II. c. 8, making perpetual temporary augmentations of vicarages, and 3 Geo. IV. c. 72, enabling them to be in certain cases converted into rectories. In Scotland vicarage teinds were the subject of many Acts of the Scottish parliament. Until they became a fixed burden on the land they were payable out of minor and accidental products, were established by usage, and lost by negative prescription. 27 and 28 Vic. c. 33 provided for the commutation of those vicarage teinds of fish which had not up to then been commuted.

Perpetual Curate.—Where a benefice was appropriated *ad mensam monachorum* or was from any other cause without the services of a regular vicar, it did not fall within the statutes relating to vicars, and was served by a temporary curate, generally a regular ecclesiastic belonging to the appropriating corporation. After the dissolution the curate in charge became perpetual, inasmuch as he could not be removed except by the bishop. By 2 and 3 Vict. c. 49 every church or chapel augmented by the governors of Queen Anne's Bounty and having a district is a perpetual curacy; so, as a rule, are new churches built under the Church Building Acts. By 31 and 32 Vict. c. 117 the incumbent of every parish or new parish for ecclesiastical purposes, not being a rector, is to be styled the vicar, and his benefice is to be designated a vicarage. This Act only confers a more honourable name upon the perpetual curate; it does not in any way alter his legal position.

Vicar-general is the deputy of the archbishop of Canterbury or York. In his court the bishops of the province are confirmed. How far he has any contentious jurisdiction appears uncertain. In the confirmation of Dr Hampden as bishop of Hereford in 1848 the vicar-general of Canterbury refused to hear objections to the confirmation by the dean and chapter of Hereford, and the Court of Queen's Bench was equally divided as to whether such refusal was good in law. *Vicar-choral* is a clerk in orders who assists at cathedral services. See further ADVOWSON, BENEFICE, PARISH, PARSON, QUEEN ANNE'S BOUNTY, TITHES.

VICENTE, GIL (*c.* 1470–*c.* 1536), Portuguese dramatist, with an honourable position also in the history of Spanish literature, was born, most probably in Lisbon, about the year 1470. He was of good family, and, after studying law at the then university of Lisbon, became attached to the royal court, in what capacity is unknown. In June 1502 he produced and took the leading part in the performance of his first piece, a kind of dramatic pastoral, after the manner of Juan de la Encina, on occasion of the birth of an heir to the throne (John III.). So successful was this appearance that he soon became the recognized provider of such entertainments at court, during the reign both of Emmanuel and of John. Of his domestic history nothing is known, except that he married a lady named Branca Bezerra, by whom he had a son and a daughter. His outward circumstances, especially in his later years, if some apparently personal allusions in his works are to be literally interpreted, do not seem to have been prosperous. Almost the only personal incident that has come down to us is his successful remonstrance with the clergy of Santarem in

[1] *Appropriation* is the term for the possession of a benefice by a spiritual corporation, *impropriation* for its possession by a layman.

1531, for having taken the earthquakes of that year as a text from which to rouse orthodox fanaticism against the Jews or "Neo-Christians"; the circumstances are related by Vicente in a letter to the king. The time and place of his death are alike uncertain; most probably it occurred at Evora not much later than 1536.

Vicente published various of his pieces during his lifetime, but the first collected edition of his works, edited by his son Luis, did not appear till 1562. It is in black letter folio, and only one copy, that in the Göttingen university library, is now known to exist. A second edition, "emended by the Holy Office," appeared in 1585, of which also only a single copy is now extant (in Lisbon). The disfavour with which they were viewed by the Inquisition caused them to fall into unmerited neglect, and they do not appear to have been again reprinted till 1834, when they were carefully edited by Feio and Monteiro (Hamburg, 3 vols.). They number forty-two in all, of which seventeen are written wholly in Portuguese and ten wholly in Spanish, while in the remainder both languages are employed. The principles determining his choice of language are not easy to discover, and indeed he seems to have used either indifferently, perhaps in this accommodating himself to the aptitudes of particular actors. It may be observed, however, that, while in the 14th century it had been fashionable for all court poets in the western half of the peninsula to use Galician or Old Portuguese, the practice had changed in the days of John II. of Castile, when Castilian became the favourite speech. In writing chiefly in Portuguese Vicente thus reverted to the older practice; but, on the other hand, it is not surprising that he should have freely used Spanish at a court which stood in such intimate personal relations with that of Castile (of Emmanuel's three wives two were Castilian princesses and the third was a sister of Charles V.), and where he had taken Encina as his avowed model. According to their form the works of Vicente are conveniently divided into—(1) *obras de devoçao* or *autos*, (2) comedies and tragi-comedies, and (3) farces. The first class includes twelve autos or sacred pieces, intended for performance at Christmas, Epiphany, and other religious festivals. The plots are quaint and conceived entirely in the mediæval spirit; in their working out many touches of poetical feeling and also of sarcastic humour are introduced. There is a vein of pleasing romance in such compositions as his *Dom Duardos* and *Amadis de Gaula*, while the genuine mirthfulness of his farces (*Inez Pereira* and others), as well as their originality, well entitle him to be spoken of by his compatriots as their "father of comedy" and the national Plautus.

Some typical examples of Vicente's works may be read in Böhl von Faber's *Teatro Español anterior á Lope de Vega* (Hamburg, 1832) and in Ochoa's *Tesoro del Teatro Español* (Paris, 1838). An interesting essay, with analyses of many of the plays, occurs in vol. lxxix. of the *Quarterly Review* (1846-47); see also Ferdinand Wolf's article "Gil-Vicente" in Ersch and Gruber's *Encykl.* (sec. i. vol. lxvii.).

VICENZA, a town of Italy, capital of the province of Vicenza, lies at the northern base of the Monti Berici, on both sides of the Bacchiglione, immediately below its confluence with the Retrone, and 42 miles by rail to the west of Venice. It is surrounded by somewhat dilapidated walls, about 3 miles in circumference, and entered by six gates. Though many of the streets are narrow and irregular, the town has a number of fine public buildings, many of them the work of PALLADIO (*q.v.*). Among these are the town-hall, otherwise known as the Basilica, one of the finest works of the Renaissance period, of which Palladio himself said that it might stand comparison with the similar work of antiquity. The prefecture and the Barbarano and Chieregati Palaces are also his work; in the last-named the civic museum is housed. The Olympic theatre is also noteworthy. The cathedral, which is Gothic, dating mainly from the 13th century, consists of a nave with eight chapels on each side; it contains examples of the Montagnas and of Lorenzo da Venezia. Several of the other churches contain noteworthy paintings: thus the Romano-Gothic church of San Lorenzo has Montagnas, S. Corona Montagnas and a G. Bellini, and S. Stephano one of the most important works of Palma Vecchio. The principal square contains two columns, dating from the Venetian period, and a tall Gothic campanile. Of the Palladian villas in the neighbourhood La Rotonda or Villa Palladiana, $1\frac{1}{2}$ miles to the south-east, deserves special mention. Vicenza is the see of a bishop, and contains two gymnasia, a seminary, an academy, a public library, a botanic garden, and various hospitals. Some remains of antiquity, including ruins of a theatre and an aqueduct, have been preserved. The most important manufacture is that of silk, which employs a large proportion of the inhabitants. Great numbers of mulberry trees are grown in the neighbourhood. Woollen and linen cloth, leather, earthenware, paper, and articles in gold and silver are also made in Vicenza, and a considerable trade in these articles, as well as in corn and wine, is carried on. The population of the town in 1881 was 24,331, or, including the suburbs, 27,694.

Vicenza is the *Vicentia* or *Vicetia* of the Romans, noticed by Strabo as one of the minor towns of Venetia. It continued to be a municipal town of some importance till the fall of the Western empire, and suffered severely in the invasion of Attila, by whom it was laid waste. It was for some time during the Middle Ages an independent republic, but was subdued by the Venetians in 1405. Towards the end of the 15th century it became the seat of a school of painting, of which the principal representatives were, besides Bartolomeo Montagna, its founder, Giovanni Speranza and Benedetto Montagna. Palladio (1518-80) was a native of Vicenza.

VICH, a town of Spain, in the province of Barcelona, 38 miles by rail to the north of that town, lies in a small side valley of the Ter, about 1500 feet above sea-level. It is irregularly built on a hill slope, and has narrow ill-paved streets; there are some quaint old houses in the Plaza Mayor. The cathedral, begun about 1040, belongs chiefly to the first half of the 14th century, but with some mischievous alterations of the 18th. The interior, with three naves and a transept, is elegant, and the Gothic cloisters (1340) are particularly fine. The industries include tanning and the weaving of linen and woollen fabrics; and sausages are a speciality of the place. There are mines of copper and coal in the neighbourhood. The population within the municipal boundaries in 1877 was 12,478.

Vich, the *Ausa* of the ancient geographers, was the chief town of the Ausetani; in the Middle Ages it was called Ausona and Vicus Ausonensis, hence Vic de Osona, and simply Vich.

VICHY, a town of France, in the department of Allier, is situated on the right bank of the Allier, 227 miles by rail south-south-east from Paris and 6 south of St Germains-de-Fossés, where the railway lines to Lyons and

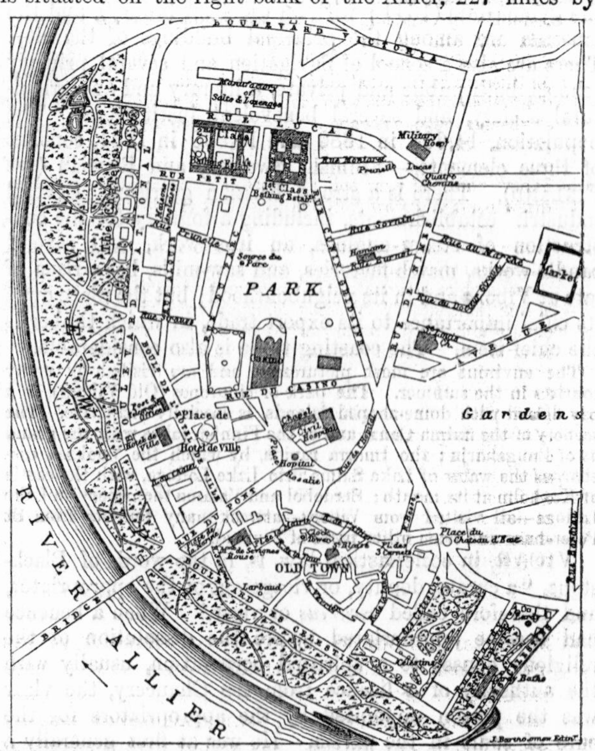

Plan of Vichy.

Nîmes separate. The population in 1881 was 8322, and in 1886 10,072.

Vichy owes its importance to its mineral waters, which were celebrated in the time of the Romans. Within the town or in its immediate vicinity there are 21 springs, 12 of which are state property (4 of these obtained by boring). The waters of those which are outside the town are brought in by means of aqueducts. The most celebrated and frequented are the Grande Grille, L'Hopital, the Célestins, and Lardy. The most copious of all, the Puits Carré, is reserved for the baths. All these, whether cold or hot (maximum temperature, 113° Fahr.), are largely charged with bicarbonate of soda (see MINERAL WATERS, vol. xvi. p. 435); some also are chalybeate and tonic. The waters, which are limpid, have an alkaline taste and emit a slight odour of sulphuretted hydrogen. They are recommended in cases of stomachic and liver complaint, also for diabetes, gravel, and gout. The thermal establishment, begun in 1787, is capable of supplying 3500 baths a day. The company by which the state baths are farmed also manufactures pastilles, barley-sugar, and digestive chocolate, as well as salts for artificial baths. A considerable trade is carried on in the natural waters. In addition to the principal establishment, Vichy has a hospital bath, the hydropathic establishments of Lardy and Larbaud, and a large military hospital, founded in 1843. Cusset (5356 inhabitants in 1886), chief-lieu of the canton, about 1 mile distant, has similar mineral waters and a bathing establishment. Vichy possesses a casino and two public parks. The promenade commands a splendid view of the mountains of Auvergne. At Vichy, Cusset, and in the neighbourhood there are cotton cloth manufactures (*toiles de Vichy*).

VICKSBURG, a city of the United States and the county seat of Warren county, Mississippi, the largest and most important city in the State, stands on the bluffs, on the east bank of the Mississippi, nearly midway between Memphis and New Orleans. It is situated in the midst of the most fertile cotton region of the country, and is one of the principal inland shipping ports of that staple. Its means of communication, besides the river, embrace three important railroad systems. The city has some manufacturing industries, particularly of lumber and cotton-seed oil and cake. The population in 1880 was 11,814, showing a slight decrease since 1870; and in 1888 it was estimated at 18,000. Nearly one-half of the population were coloured.

Prior to the Civil War Vicksburg was an important river port, having in 1860 a population of 4591. Its growth had, however, been slow. During the war it became a very strong strategic point, as it controlled the navigation of the Mississippi, and a contest for its possession was waged for several months with heavy loss of life. Finally General Grant captured it in 1863, and with it the Confederate army of General Pemberton, numbering 27,000 men. For a few years after the war the city gained rapidly in population and importance.

VICO, GIOVAN BATTISTA (1668-1744), Italian jurist and philosopher, was the son of Antonio Vico, a small bookseller, and was born at Naples on 23rd June 1668. At the age of seven he had a serious fall and severely injured his head, which produced in him "the melancholy and sour temper suited to men of talent." Afterwards he applied himself to the study of scholastic philosophy. At an early age he entered the university, and made such rapid progress, especially in jurisprudence, that he is said to have won a suit for his father at the age of sixteen. Nevertheless he preferred the study of history, literature, juridical science, and philosophy. Being appointed teacher of jurisprudence to the nephews of the bishop of Ischia, G. B. Rocca, he accompanied them to the castle of Vatolla, near Cilento, in the province of Salerno. There he passed nine studious years, chiefly devoted to classical reading, Plato and Tacitus being his favourite authors, because "the former described the ideal man and the latter man as he really is." On his return to Naples he found Cartesianism in the ascendant, and this he disliked. Belonging to no particular school or literary sect, he languished in neglect and obscurity, until in 1697 he gained the professorship of rhetoric at the university, with a scanty stipend of 100 ducats. On this he supported not only himself but his rapidly increasing family; for he had married a poor and illiterate girl, who was only able to put her mark to the nuptial contract. Meanwhile his own studies were pursued with untiring zeal, and he began to write and publish his works. Two modern authors exercised a weighty influence on his mind—Francis Bacon and Grotius. He was no follower of their ideas, indeed often opposed to them; but he derived from Bacon an increasing stimulus towards the investigation of certain great problems of history and philosophy, while Grotius proved valuable in his study of philosophic jurisprudence. In 1708 he published his *De ratione studiorum*, in 1710 *De antiquissima Italorum sapientia*, in 1720 *De universi juris uno principio et fine uno*, and in 1721 *De constantia jurisprudentis*. On the strength of these works he offered himself as a candidate for the university chair of jurisprudence then vacant, with a yearly stipend of 600 ducats. But he was rejected by the examiners, although all his competitors have remained unknown to fame. Without any sense of discouragement, he returned to his favourite studies, and in 1725 published the first edition of the work that forms the basis of his renown, *Principii d'una Scienza Nuova*. In 1730 he produced a second edition of the *Scienza Nuova*, so much altered in style and with so many substantial additions that it was practically a new work. In 1735 Charles III. of Naples marked his recognition of Vico's merits by appointing him historiographer-royal, with a yearly stipend of 100 ducats. But the philosopher derived little enjoyment from his new post. Attacked by a cruel malady, mind and memory failed. But during frequent intervals of lucidity he resumed his pen and made new corrections in his great work, of which a third edition appeared in 1744, prefaced by a letter of dedication to Cardinal Trojano Acquaviva. Vico expired on 20th January of the same year. Fate seemed bent on persecuting him to the last. A fierce quarrel arose over his burial between the brotherhood of St Stephen, to which he had belonged, and the university professors, who desired to escort his corpse to the grave. Finally the canons of the cathedral, together with the professors, buried the body in the church of the Gerolimini.

Vico has been generally described as a solitary soul, out of harmony with the spirit of his time and often directly opposed to it. In fact, though living during the later years of the 17th and the early part of the 18th century, when Locke had already given to the world the germs of the ideas afterwards developed in the philosophy of the Encyclopædists, he followed an entirely opposite line of thought. The writer who was the first to declare that great men are the representatives and personifications of their times would thus seem to have been the living contradiction of his own theory. Nevertheless a closer inquiry into the social conditions of Vico's time, and of the studies then flourishing, shows him to have been thoroughly in touch with them.

Owing to the historical past of Naples, and its social and economic condition at the end of the 17th century, the only study that really flourished there was that of law; and this soon penetrated from the courts to the university, and was raised to the level of a science. A great school of jurisprudence was thus formed, including many men of vast learning and great ability, although little known to fame. This school stood apart, as it were, from the rest of the world; the works of its representatives were inelegant, and often indeed exaggeratedly legal and scholastic in style. Accordingly they attracted little notice in upper Italy and were totally ignored beyond the Alps. But, while outside Naples scarcely anything was known of Marcello Marciano the younger, Domenico Aulisio, Duke Gaetano Argento, Niccolò Capasso, and many others, there were three men who rose to great eminence and attained to an honourable rank in general literature both in Italy and abroad. By an exposition of the political history of the kingdom, based on a study of its laws and institutions and of the legal conflicts between the state and the court of Rome, Pietro Giannone was the first initiator of what has been since known as civil history. Giovan Vincenzo Gravina, the patron and preceptor of Metastasio, and also noted as a literary critic, wrote a history of Roman law, specially distinguished for its accuracy and elegance. While Gravina studied the successive and varying forms of Roman law and sought to give them an historical explanation, Vico raised the problem to a higher plane, by tracing the origin of law in the human mind and explaining the historical changes of the one by those of the other. Thus he made the original discovery of certain ideas which constitute the modern historic method, or rather the psychologico-historic method. This problem he proceeded to develop in various works, until in his *Scienza Nuova* he arrived at a more complete solution, which may be formulated as follows. If the principle of justice and law be one, eternal, and immutable, why should there be so many different codes of legislation? These differences are not caused by difference of nationality only, but are to be noted in the history of the same people. Th_ clearest, most precise, and most constant conception of law was undoubtedly that of the Romans; nevertheless Roman jurisprudence underwent so many transformations as apparently to constitute almost different codes. How was so strange a fact to be explained? This question is touched upon in his *Orations or Inaugural Addresses* (*Orazioni o Prolusioni*) and in his *Minor Works* (*Scritti Minori*). Finally he applied himself to its solution in his *Universal Law* (*Diritto Universale*), which is divided into two books. The first of these, *De uno et universi juris principio et fine uno*, was subdivided into two parts; so likewise was the second, with the respective titles of *De constantia philologiæ* and *De constantia jurisprudentis.*

The following is the general idea derived from these researches. Vico held God to be the ruler of the world of nations, but ruling, not as the providence of the Middle Ages by means of continued miracles, but as He rules nature, by means of natural laws. If, therefore, the physicist seeks to discover the laws of nature by study of natural phenomena, so the philosopher must seek the laws of historical change by the investigation of human events and of the human mind. According to Vico, law emanates from the conscience of mankind, in whom God has infused a sentiment of justice, and is therefore in close and continual relation with the human mind, and participates in its changes. This sentiment of justice is at first confused, uncertain, and almost instinctive, is, as it were, a divine and religious inspiration instilled by heaven into the primitive tribes of the earth. It is an unconscious, universal sentiment, not the personal, conscious, and rational sentiment of the superior few. Hence the law to which it gives birth is enwrapped in religious forms which are likewise visible and palpable, inasmuch as primitive man is incapable of abstract, philosophical ideas. This law is not the individual work of any philosophical legislator, for no man was, or could be, a philosopher at that time. It is first displayed in the shape of natural and necessary usages consecrated by religion. The names of leading legislators, which we so often find recorded in the history of primitive peoples, are symbols and myths, merely serving to mark an historic period or epoch by some definite and personal denomination. For nations, or rather tribes, were then distinguished by personal names only. The first obscure and confused conception of law gradually becomes clearer and better defined. Its visible and religious forms then give way to abstract *formulæ*, which in their turn are slowly replaced by the rational manifestation of the philosophic principles of law that gains the victory in the final stage of development, designated by Vico as that of civil and human law. This is the period of individual and philosophic legislators. Thus Roman law has passed through three great periods,—the divine, the heroic, and the human,—which are likewise the three chief periods of the history of Rome, with which it is intimately and intrinsically connected. Nevertheless, on careful examination of these three successive stages, it will easily be seen that, in spite of the apparent difference between them, all have a common foundation, source, and purpose. The human and civil philosophic law of the third period is assuredly very different in form from the primitive law; but in substance it is merely the abstract, scientific, and philosophic manifestation of the same sentiment of justice and the same principles which were vaguely felt in primitive times. Hence one development of law may be easily translated into another. Thus in the varied manifestations of law Vico was able to discover a single and enduring principle (*De universi juris uno principio et fine uno*). On these grounds it has been sought to establish a close relation between Vico and Grotius. The latter clearly distinguished between a positive law differing in different nations and a natural law based on a general and unchanging principle of human nature, and therefore obligatory upon all. But Vico was opposed to Grotius, especially as regards his conception of the origin of society, and therefore of law. Grotius holds that its origin was not divine, but human, and neither collective, spontaneous, nor unconscious, but personal, rational, and conscious. He believed moreover that natural law and positive law moved on almost constant and immutable parallel lines. But Vico maintained that the one was continually progressing towards the other, positive law showing an increasing tendency to draw nearer to natural and rational law. Hence the conception that law is of necessity a spontaneous birth, not the creation of any individual legislator; and hence the idea that it necessarily proceeds by a natural and logical process of evolution constituting its history. Vico may have derived from Grotius the idea of natural law; but his discovery of the historic evolution of law was first suggested to him by his study of Roman law. He saw that the history of Roman jurisprudence was a continuous progress of the narrow, rigorous, primitive, and almost iron law of the XII. Tables towards the wider, more general, and more humane *jus gentium*. Having once derived this conception from Roman history, he was easily and indeed necessarily carried on to the next,—that the positive law of all nations, throughout history, is a continual advance, keeping pace with the progress of civilization, towards the philosophic and natural law founded on the principles of human nature and human reason.

As already stated, the *Scienza Nuova* appeared in three different editions. The divergences between the second and third are of too little moment to be recorded here. But the first and second editions are almost distinct works. In the former the author sets forth the analytical process by which the laws he discovered were deduced from facts. In the second he not only enlarges his matter and gives multiplied applications of his ideas, but also follows the synthetic method, first expounding the laws he had discovered and then proving them by the facts to which they are applied. In this edition the fragmentary and jerky arrangement, the intricate style, and a peculiar and often purely conventional terminology seriously checked the diffusion of the work, which accordingly was little studied in Italy and remained almost unknown to the rest of Europe. Its fundamental idea consists in that which Vico, in his peculiar terminology, styles "poetical wisdom" (*sapienza poetica*) and "occult wisdom" (*sapienza riposta*), and in the historical process by which the one is merged in the other. He frequently declares that this discovery was the result of the literary labours of his whole life.

Vico was the first thinker who asked, Why have we a science of nature, but no science of history? Because our glance can easily be turned outwards and survey the exterior world; but it is far harder to turn the mind's eye inwards and contemplate the world of the spirit. All our errors in explaining the origin of human society arise from our obstinacy in believing that primitive man was entirely similar to ourselves, who are civilized, *i.e.*, developed by the results of a lengthy process of anterior historic evolution. We must learn to issue from ourselves, transport ourselves back to other times, and become children again in order to comprehend the infancy of the human race. As in children, imagination and the senses prevailed in those men of the past. They had no abstract ideas; in their minds all was concrete, visible, and tangible. All the phenomena, forces, and laws of nature, together with mental conceptions, were alike personified. To suppose that all mythical stories are fables invented by the philosophers is to write history backwards and confound the instinctive, impersonal, poetic wisdom of the earliest times with the civilized, rational, and abstract occult wisdom of our own day. But how can we explain the formation of this poetic wisdom, which, albeit the work of ignorant men, has so deep and intrinsic a philosophic value? The only possible reply is that already given when treating of the origin of law. Providence has instilled into the heart of man a sentiment of justice and goodness, of beauty, and of truth, that is manifested differently at different times. The ideal truth within us, constituting the inner life that is studied by philosophers, becomes transmuted by the facts of history into assured reality. For Vico psychology and history were the two poles of the new world he discovered. After having extolled the work of God and proclaimed Him the source of all knowledge, he adds that a great truth is continually flashed on us and proved to us by history, namely, "that this world of nations is the work of man, and its explanation therefore only to be found in the mind of man." Thus poetical wisdom, appearing as a spontaneous emanation of the human conscience, is almost the product of divine inspiration. From this, by the aid of civilization, reason, and philosophy, there is gradually developed the civil, occult wisdom. The continual, slow, and laborious progress from the one to the other is that which really constitutes history, and man becomes civilized by rendering himself the conscious and independent possessor of all that in poetical wisdom remained impersonal, unconscious, came as it were from without by divine *afflatus*.

Vico gives many applications of this fundamental idea. The religion of primitive peoples is no less mythical than their history, since they could only conceive of it by means of myths. On these lines he interprets the whole history of primitive Rome. One book of the second edition of the *Scienza Nuova* is devoted to "The Discovery of the True Homer." Why all the cities of Greece dispute the honour of being his birthplace is because the *Iliad* and the *Odyssey* are not the work of one, but of many popular poets, and a true creation of the Greek people which is in every city of Greece.

And because the primitive peoples are unconscious and self-ignorant Homer is represented as being blind. In all parts of history in which he was best versed Vico pursues a stricter and more scientific method, and arrives at safer conclusions. This is the case in Roman history, especially in such portions as related to the history of law. Here he sometimes attains, even in details, to divinations of the truth afterwards confirmed by new documents and later research. The aristocratic origin of Rome, the struggle between the patricians and the plebeians, the laws of the XII. Tables, not, as tradition would have it, imported from Greece (but the natural and spontaneous product of ancient Roman customs), and many other similar theories were discovered by Vico, and expounded with his usual originality, though not always without his usual blunders and exaggerations.

Vico may be said to base his considerations on the history of two nations. The greater part of his ideas on poetical wisdom were derived from Greece. Nearly all the rest, more especially the transition from poetical to occult wisdom, was derived from Rome. Having once formulated his idea, he made it more general in order to apply it to the history of all nations. From the savage state, through the terror that gives birth to religions, through the creation of families by marriage, through burial rites and piety towards the dead, men approach civilization with the aid of poetic wisdom, and pass through three periods,—the divine, heroic, and human,—in which they have three forms of government, language, literature, jurisprudence, and civilization. The primary government is aristocratic. Patrician tyranny rouses the populace to revolt, and then democratic equality is established under a republic. Democratic excesses cause the rise of an empire, which, becoming corrupt, declines into barbarism, and, again emerging from it, retraces the same course. This is the *law of cycles*, constituting that which is designated by Vico as the "eternal ideal history, or rather course of humanity, invariably followed by all nations." It must not be held to imply that one nation imitates the course pursued by another, nor that the points of resemblance between them are transmitted by tradition from one to the other, but merely that all are subject to one law, inasmuch as this is based on the human nature common to all alike. Thus, while on the one hand the various cycles traced and retraced by all nations are similar and yet independent, on the other hand, being actually derived from Roman history, they become converted in the *Scienza Nuova* into a bed of Procrustes, to which the history of all nations has to be fitted by force. And wherever Vico's historical knowledge failed he was led into increased error by this artificial and arbitrary effort.

It has been justly observed by many that this continuous cyclical movement entirely excludes the progress of humanity towards a better future. It has been replied that these cycles are similar without being identical, and that, if one might differ from another, the idea of progress was not necessarily excluded by the law of cycles. Vico undoubtedly considered the poetic wisdom of the Middle Ages to be different from that of the Greeks and Romans, and Christianity to be very superior to the pagan religion. But he never investigated the question whether, since there is a law of progressive evolution in the history of different nations, separately examined, there may not likewise be another law ruling the general history of these nations, every one of which must have represented a new period, as it were, in the history of humanity at large. Therefore, although the *Scienza Nuova* cannot be said absolutely to deny the law of progress, it must be allowed that Vico not only failed to solve the problem but even shrank from attacking it.

He had no followers or admirers even in Naples, where the ideas of Tanucci, Filangieri, Genovesi, and Galiani prevailed, men who sometimes appear to be more French than Italian. When at last, with the German reaction initiated by Kant against the sense philosophy of the French, an entirely new philosophy arose, and many ideas started by Vico were revived on a more rigorous method, supported by more accurate research and with a wider and firmer grasp of knowledge, the name of the Neapolitan philosopher was forgotten, and no one recognized how much was owed to him. Nevertheless it may be asserted that between the close of the 17th and the early part of the 18th century, when the thought of the world was bent in a totally different direction, Vico was the first to discern and proclaim the course by which, in the present age, historical, moral, and political science was destined to make such great and assured progress.

See Cantoni, *G. B. Vico, Studii Critici e Comparativi* (Turin, 1867); Flint, *Vico* (Edinburgh and London, 1884). For editions of Vico's own works, see *Opere*, ed. Giuseppe Ferrari (Milan, 1834-35, 6 vols.), and Michelet, *Œuvres Choisies de Vico* (Paris, 1835, 2 vols.). Mamiani, Rosmini, Gioberti, and many other Italian philosophers have treated at length of Vico in their works. The most detailed account of him is Ferrari's essay, "La Mente de Vico," prefacing his edition of the *Opere*. (P. V.)

VICTOR I., St, bishop of Rome from about 190 to 202, succeeded Eleutherus and was followed by Zephyrinus. His name is chiefly associated with a display of intolerance towards the bishops of Asia Minor for the view they took in the Quartodeciman controversy (see EASTER; also POPEDOM, vol. xix. p. 489); he also excommunicated Theodotus of Byzantium on account of his doctrine as to the Person of Christ (see MONARCHIANISM).

VICTOR II., one of the series of German popes and the successor of Leo IX., was consecrated in St Peter's, Rome, on 13th April 1055. His father was a Swabian baron, Count Hartwig von Calw, and his own baptismal name was Gebhard. At the instance of Gebhard, bishop of Ratisbon, uncle of the emperor Henry III., he had been appointed while still a young man to the see of Eichstädt; in this position his great talents soon enabled him to render important services to Henry, whose chief adviser he ultimately became. His nomination to the papacy by Henry at Mainz, in September 1054, was made at the instance of a Roman deputation headed by Hildebrand, whose policy doubtless was to detach from the imperial interest one of its ablest supporters. In June 1055 Victor met the emperor at Florence, and held a council, which anew condemned clerical marriages, simony, and the alienation of the estates of the church. In the following year he was summoned to Germany to the side of the emperor, and was with him when he died at Botfeld in the Harz on 5th October 1056. As guardian of Henry's infant son, and adviser of the empress Agnes, Victor now wielded enormous power, which he began to use with much tact for the maintenance of peace throughout the empire and for strengthening the papacy against the aggressions of the barons. He died shortly after his return to Italy, at Arezzo, on 28th July 1057. His successor was Stephen IX. (Frederick of Lorraine).

VICTOR III., pope from 24th May 1086 to 16th September 1087, was the successor of Pope Gregory VII. Son of Landolfo V., prince of Benevento, he was born in 1027; in his thirtieth year he entered the cloister at Monte Cassino, changing his name of Dauferius into Desiderius. He soon became abbot of the monastery, and in 1059 Nicolas II. raised him to the cardinalate. He rendered many important services to Gregory VII., who accordingly on his deathbed indicated him to the cardinals of south Italy as his worthiest successor. He was elected on 24th May 1086, but showed genuine reluctance to accept the embarrassing honour thus thrust upon him, and after his tardy consecration, which did not take place till 9th May 1087, he withdrew at once to Monte Cassino. The countess Matilda soon afterwards induced him to return to Rome; but, owing to the presence of the antipope Clement III. (Guibert of Ravenna), who had powerful partisans, his stay there was short. In August he held at Benevento a synod of some importance, at which Clement III. was excommunicated, lay-investiture forbidden, and a kind of crusade proclaimed against the Saracens in Africa. During the synod Victor fell ill, and betook himself to Monte Cassino, where he died on 16th September 1087. His successor was Urban II.

VICTOR IV. Two antipopes have claimed this name:—(1) Cardinal Gregorio Conti, who was chosen by a party in succession to the antipope Anacletus II. in 1138, but through the influence of Bernard of Clairvaux was induced two months afterwards to make his submission to Innocent II.; and (2) Cardinal Octavianus, the Ghibelline antipope, elected in 1159, and countenanced by the emperor Frederick Barbarossa. He died at Lucca on 20th April 1164.

VICTOR, CLAUDE PERRIN (1764-1841), duke of Belluno, marshal of France, was born at La Marche (Vosges) on 7th December 1764. In 1781 he entered the army as a common soldier, and after ten years' service he received his discharge and settled at Valence. Soon afterwards he joined the local volunteers and in less than a year had risen to the command of a battalion. He greatly distinguished himself on the Italian frontier, and for his bravery at the siege of Toulon in 1793 he was raised to the rank of brigadier-general. He afterwards served for some time with the army of the eastern Pyrenees, and in the Italian campaign of 1795-97 he so acquitted himself at Mondovi, Roveredo, Porto Legnago, and many other places that he was promoted to be general of a division. After the peace of Campo Formio he for some time commanded the forces in the department of La Vendée; but in 1798 he was again in Italy and in the battle of Marengo especially took a very important part. In 1803 he became commander-in-chief of the Batavian army, and after the peace of Amiens he acted for eighteen months as French plenipotentiary at Copenhagen. On the outbreak of hostilities with Prussia he joined the fifth army corps as chief of the general staff; at the battle of Friedland he commanded the first corps in such a manner that Napoleon made him marshal of the empire on the field. After the peace of Tilsit he became governor of Prussia, and in 1808 he was created duke of Belluno. In the same year he was sent to Spain, where he took a prominent part in military affairs, until his appointment in 1812 to command the ninth army corps destined to operate in Russia. Here his most important service was in protecting the retreating army at the crossing of the Berezina. He took an active part in the wars of 1813-14, till in February of the latter year he had the misfortune to arrive too late at Montereau-sur-Yonne. The result was a scene of violent recrimination and his deprivation by the emperor, who transferred his command to Gérard. Thus wounded in his amour propre, Victor now transferred his allegiance to the Bourbon dynasty, and in December 1814 received from Louis XVIII. the command of the second military division. In 1815 he accompanied the king to Ghent, and on the second restoration he was made a peer of France and major-general of the royal guard. In 1821 he was appointed war minister and held this office for two years. After the revolution of 1830 he retired altogether into private life. His death took place at Paris on 3d March 1841.

VICTOR, Sextus Aurelius. A person of this name was made prefect of Pannonia by Julian about 360 (Amm. Marc., xxi. 10), and may be identical with the man who was consul along with Valentinian in 373 and with the prefect of the city of the same name who is mentioned in an inscription of the time of Theodosius. Four small historical works have been ascribed to him on more or less doubtful grounds—(1) *Origo Gentis Romani*, (2) *De Viribus Illustribus Romæ*, (3) *De Cæsaribus*, (4) *De Vita et Moribus Imperatorum Romanorum excerpta ex Libris Sex. Aur. Victoris*. The four have generally been published together under the name *Historia Romana*, but the fourth piece is a *réchauffé* of the third; and, though all are late, there is no sufficient reason to think that they are by one hand. The second was first printed at Naples about 1472, in 4to, under the name of Pliny (the younger), and the fourth at Strasburg in 1505. The first edition of all four was that of A. Schottus (8vo, Antwerp, 1579). The *De Cæsaribus*, which goes from Augustus to Constantius, and claims to be by a man of mean origin who rose to distinction through letters, may be the work of the Sextus Aurelius Victor known to history.

VICTOR AMADEUS, the name of three dukes of Savoy. See Savoy.

VICTOR EMMANUEL (1820-1878), king of Italy, born at Turin on 14th March 1820, was the son of Charles Albert, prince of Carignano, who in 1831 became king of Sardinia. He was brought up with some severity and as a strict Catholic; but it was not found possible to interest him in study or intellectual pursuits. In 1842 he was married to Adelaide, daughter of the Austrian grand-duke Rainer, his father at that time desiring to improve his relations with Austria. The young man took no part in politics, but showed from the first the characteristics of an energetic soldier. After the Austrian occupation of Ferrara in 1847 he was among those who pressed for an immediate declaration of war; and, when a year later hostilities broke out, he threw himself into the struggle heart and soul. At Goito, where he was wounded, his reckless bravery turned the tide of battle; and in every encounter he was to be seen in the thickest of the fight. During the armistice that followed the defeat of Custozza (25th July) he was engaged in the reorganization of the Sardinian army. The abdication of his father on the evening of the battle of Novara (23d March 1849) made him king of a ruined state. From Radetzky he obtained some mitigation of the hard terms at first demanded by the conqueror, especially in the withdrawal of the Austrian claim that the Sardinian constitution should be abolished. It was the maintenance of this constitution, at a time when reaction swept away every other vestige of representative government in Italy, that gained for Victor Emmanuel the title of the honest king (*re galantuomo*) and won for him the confidence of the Italian nation, and ultimately the Italian crown. In the bitter days that followed Novara, the king, calumniated, misunderstood, and charged like his father with treachery, showed a noble forbearance and a self-mastery that could hardly have been expected from his passionate uncultured nature. Though in D'Azeglio and Balbo he had excellent friends and advisers, it was not till 1852 that the accession of Cavour (*q.v.*) to power gave him a man of great political genius for his guide. From that time the career of Victor Emmanuel became what Cavour made it. While ecclesiastical reforms, which brought upon the king and minister the execration of the church, laid the foundation for all future social and economical advance, the alliance of Sardinia with England and France in the Crimean War secured for Italy the interest of the Western powers, which Austria by its inaction and its half-measures had forfeited. Meanwhile his mother, his wife, and his brother died within four weeks of each other; and the clericals exulted in this manifestation of an offended Providence. At the end of 1855, while the allied troops were still in the East, Victor Emmanuel visited Paris and London. In 1859 Cavour's object was attained and France united with Sardinia against Austria, the king, sorely against his will, giving his daughter Clotilda in marriage to Jerome Napoleon. Victor Emmanuel met Napoleon III. at Genoa on 13th May, and on the 30th fought at the head of a body of Sardinians and Zouaves at the battle of Palestro. After the victory of Magenta (4th June) the allied monarchs entered Milan, where Victor Emmanuel for the first time saw Garibaldi. In the crowning victory of 24th June, while the French were engaged at Solferino, the king with his Italians carried the village of San Martino. The peace of Villafranca left Venetia and the Quadrilateral to Austria. The extraordinary events of the next year united all Italy, with the exception of Rome and of what still remained to Austria, under the patriot king, who was now excommunicated by the pope (see Italy, vol. xiii. p. 490). A scene of great violence had passed between the king and Cavour when the peace of Villafranca was accepted by the former; but their old friendship was soon restored, and the death of Cavour in 1861 plunged Victor Emmanuel in the deepest grief. The Prussian alliance of 1866 incorporated Venetia with Italy. The personal desire of the king to assist Napoleon III. in the war of 1870 gave way before the wiser counsels of his ministers; and the entry of his troops into Rome after the disasters of the French army and the withdrawal of the French garrison completed Victor Emmanuel's task and the union of Italy. He lived

VICTORIA

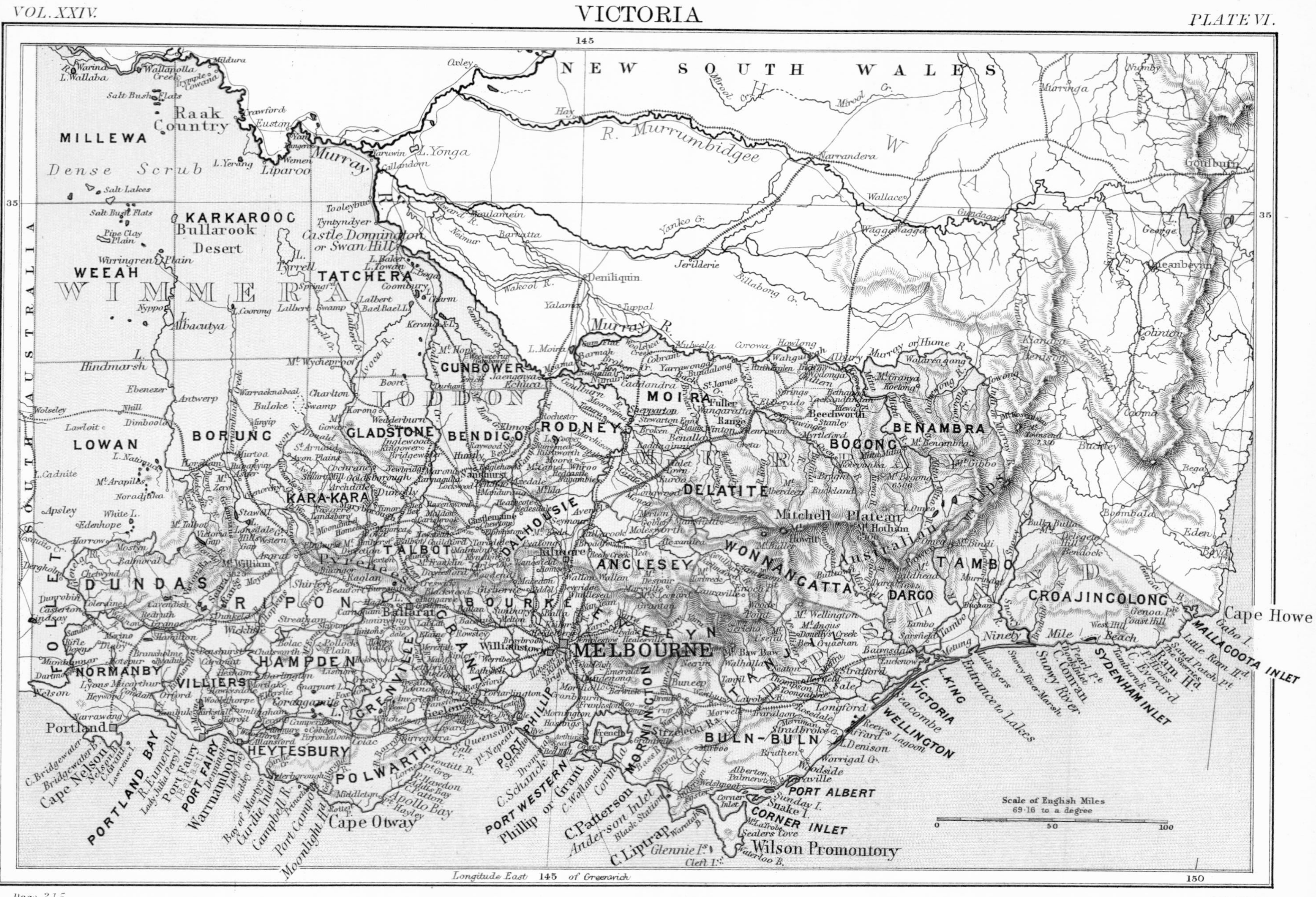

ENCYCLOPÆDIA BRITANNICA, NINTH EDITION.

W. & A. K. Johnston.

for eight years more, reigning always as a constitutional king, and preserving amidst the splendours of a great court the simple tastes of his early life. He died at Rome of a fever on 9th January 1878, and lies entombed in the Pantheon.

Plate VI. VICTORIA, a British colony occupying the south-eastern corner of Australia; its western boundary is the 141st meridian; on the east it runs out to a point at Cape Howe, in 150° E. long., being thus rudely triangular in shape; the river Murray constitutes nearly the whole of the northern boundary, its most northerly point being in 34° S. lat.; the southern boundary is the coast-line of the Southern Ocean and of Bass Strait; the most southerly point is Wilson's Promontory in 39° S. lat. The greatest length east and west is about 480 miles; the greatest width, in the west, is about 250 miles. The area is officially stated to be 87,884 square miles.

Coasts. The coast line may be estimated at about 800 miles. It begins at the 141st meridian with bold but not lofty sandstone cliffs, worn into deep caves and capped by grassy undulations, which extend inland to pleasant park-like lands. Capes Bridgewater and Nelson form a peninsula of forest lands, broken by patches of meadow. To the east of Cape Nelson lies the moderately sheltered inlet of Portland Bay, consisting of a sweep of sandy beach flanked by bold granite rocks. Then comes a long unbroken stretch of high cliffs, which owing to insetting currents have been the scene of many calamitous wrecks. Cape Otway is the termination of a wild mountain range that here abuts on the coast. Its brown cliffs rise vertically from the water; and the steep slopes above are covered with dense forests of exceedingly tall timber and tree ferns. Eastwards from this cape the line of cliffs gradually diminishes in height to about twenty to forty feet at the entrance to Port Phillip. Next comes Port Phillip Bay, a plan of which is given under MELBOURNE, vol. xv. p. 835. When the tide recedes from this bay through the narrow entrance it often encounters a strong current just outside; the broken and somewhat dangerous sea thus caused is called "the Rip." East of Port Phillip Bay the shores consist for fifteen miles of a line of sandbanks; but at Cape Schanck they suddenly become high and bold. East of this comes Western Port, a deep inlet more than half occupied by French Island and Phillip Island. Its shores are flat and uninteresting, in some parts swampy; but all the land is owned and most of it occupied. The bay is shallow and of little use for navigation. The coast continues rocky round Cape Liptrap. Wilson's Promontory is a great rounded mass of granite hills, with wild and striking scenery, tree-fern gullies, and gigantic gum-trees, connected with the mainland by a narrow sandy isthmus. At its extremity lie a multitude of rocky islets, with steep granite edges. North of this cape, and opening to the east, lies Corner Inlet, which is dry at low water. The coast now continues low to the extremity of the colony. The slight bend northward forms a sort of bight called the Ninety Mile Beach, but it really exceeds that length. It is an unbroken line of sandy shore, backed by low sand hills, on which grows a sparse dwarf vegetation. Behind these hills come a succession of lakes, surrounded by excellent land, and beyond these rise the soft blue outlines of the mountain masses of the interior. The shores on the extreme east are somewhat higher, and occasionally rise in bold points. They terminate in Cape Howe, off which lies Gabo Island, of small extent but containing an important lighthouse and signalling station.

Surface. The western half of Victoria is level or slightly undulating, and as a rule tame in its scenery, exhibiting only thinly timbered grassy lands, with all the appearance of open parks. It is here that the merino sheep are depastured whose wool secures the highest price in the markets of Europe. The north-west corner of the colony, equally flat, is dry and sometimes sandy, and frequently bare of vegetation, though in one part some seven or eight millions of acres are covered with the dense brushwood known as "mallee scrub." This wide western plain is slightly broken in two places. In the south the wild ranges of Cape Otway are covered over a considerable area with richly luxurious but almost impassable forests. This district has been reserved as a state forest and its coast forms a favourite holiday resort, the scenery being very attractive. The middle of the plain is crossed by a thin line of mountains, known as the Australian Pyrenees, at the western extremity of which there are several irregularly placed transverse ranges, the chief being the Grampians, the Victoria Range, and the Sierra Range. Their highest point is Mount Williams (3600 feet). The eastern half of the colony is wholly different. Though there is plenty of level land, it occurs in small patches, and chiefly in the south, in Gippsland, which extends from Corner Inlet to Cape Howe. But a great part of this eastern half is occupied with the complicated mass of ranges known collectively as the Australian Alps. The whole forms a plateau averaging from 1000 to 2000 feet high, with many smaller tablelands ranging from 3000 to 5000 feet in height. The highest peak, Bogong, is 6508 feet in altitude. The ranges are so densely covered with vegetation that it is extremely difficult to penetrate them; only two tracks, impassable for vehicles, intersect them from north to south. But several thousand square miles of this country are still unexplored. About fifteen peaks over 5000 feet in height have been measured, but there are probably many more. Along the ranges grow the giant trees for which Victoria is famous. The narrow valleys and gullies contain exquisite scenery, the rocky streams being overshadowed by groves of graceful tree-ferns, from amid whose waving fronds rise the tall smooth stems of the white gums. Over ten millions of acres are thus covered with forest-clad mountains too wild for settlement. The Australian Alps are connected with the Pyrenees by a long ridge called the Dividing Range (1500 to 3000 feet high).

Rivers. Victoria is fairly well watered, but its streams are generally too small to admit of navigation. This, however, is not the case with the MURRAY RIVER (*q.v.*). Echuca is the chief port of the river traffic, and about 250 vessels enter it every year, bringing down from 80,000 to 120,000 bales of wool from the interior. In the lower portion of its course the stream occupies only a narrow winding channel in the midst of its old bed, which now seems like a fertile valley hemmed in on either hand by high cliffs of clay or red earth, or sometimes of beds of oyster shells of vast extent. The navigation of the Murray is greatly impeded by "snags," or trees that have stuck fast in the bed of the river and project a little above or below the surface. But the removal of these obstacles is constantly going on, and consequently the navigation is becoming easier. Of the total length of the Murray 670 miles flow conterminous with Victoria. The Murray receives a number of tributaries from the Victorian side The Mitta Mitta, which rises in the heart of the Australian Alps, is 150 miles long. The Ovens, rising among the same mountains, is slightly shorter. The Goulburn (340 miles) flows almost entirely through well-settled agricultural country, and is deep enough to be used in its lower part for navigation. The valley of this river is a fertile grain-producing district. The Campaspe (150 miles) has too little volume of water to be of use for navigation; its valley is also agricultural, and along its banks there lie a close succession of thriving townships. The Loddon (over

200 miles) rises in the Pyrenees. The upper part flows through a plain, to the right agricultural and to the left auriferous, containing nearly forty thriving towns, including Sandhurst and Castlemaine. In the lower part of the valley the rainfall is small and droughts are frequent, but farmers are steadily pushing out into it, as the land is very fertile. Recent legislation has provided for the formation of irrigation trusts in these districts of rich soil but small rainfall. To the west of the Loddon is the Avoca river (140 miles). It is of slight volume, and though it flows towards the Murray it loses itself in marshes and salt lagoons before reaching that river.

The rivers which flow southwards into the ocean are numerous. The Snowy river rises in New South Wales and in Victoria flows entirely through wild and almost wholly unoccupied territory. The Tambo (120 miles long), which rises in the heart of the Australian Alps, crosses the Gippsland plains where the land is good, but only a small portion is occupied. The Mitchell river, rising also among the Australian Alps, is navigable to a limited extent. Its lower valley is being rapidly occupied by thriving hop plantations. The Latrobe is a deep clear stream flowing through level country. The Yarra rises in the "Black Spur" of the Australian Alps. Emerging in a deep valley from the ranges, it follows a sinuous course through the undulating plains called the "Yarra Flats," which are wholly enclosed by hills, on whose slopes are some of the best vineyards of Australia; it finds its way out of the Flats between high and precipitous but well-wooded banks, and finally reaches Port Phillip Bay below Melbourne. Owing to its numerous windings its course through that city and its suburbs is at least thirty miles. Nearer to the sea its waterway, formerly available for vessels drawing 16 feet, has now been deepened so as to be available for vessels drawing 20 feet. The Barwon, farther west, is a river of considerable length but little volume, flowing chiefly through pastoral lands. The Hopkins and Glenelg (280 miles) both water the splendid pastoral lands of the west, the lower course of the former passing through the fertile district of Warrnambool, well known throughout Australia as a potato-growing region.

Lakes.

In the west there are Lakes Corangamite and Colac, due north of Cape Otway. The former is intensely salt; the latter is fresh, having an outlet for its waters. Lakes Tyrrel and Hindmarsh lie in the plains of the north-west. In summer they are dried up, and in winter are again formed by the waters of rivers that have no outlet. In the east are the Gippsland lakes, formed by the waters of the Latrobe, Mitchell, and Tambo being dammed back by the sandhills of the Ninety Mile Beach. They are connected with Bass Strait by a narrow and shifting channel through a shallow bar; the Government of Victoria has done a great deal of late years to deepen the entrance and make it safer. The upper lake is called Lake Wellington; a narrow passage leads into Lake Victoria, which is joined to a wider expanse called Lake King. These are all fresh-water lakes, and are visited by tourists for the sake of their scenery, which, though monotonous, has a certain impressiveness. The surrounding country is being rapidly settled and utilized.

Climate.

Victoria enjoys an exceptionally fine climate. Roughly speaking, about one-half of the days in the year present a bright cloudless sky, with a bracing and dry atmosphere, pleasantly warm but not relaxing. These days are mainly in the autumn and spring. During the last twenty years there have been on an average 131 days annually on which rain has fallen more or less (chiefly in winter), but rainy days do not exceed thirty in the year. The average yearly rainfall is about 26 inches. The disagreeable feature of the Victorian climate is the occurrence of north winds, which blow on an average about sixty days in the year. In winter they are cold and dry, and have a slightly depressing effect. But in summer they are hot and dry, and generally bring with them disagreeable clouds of dust. The winds themselves blow for periods of two or three days at a time, and if the summer has six or eight such periods it becomes relaxing and produces languor. These winds cease with extraordinary suddenness, being replaced in a minute or two by a cool and bracing breeze from the south. The temperature often falls 40° or 50° Fahr. in an hour. The maximum temperature occurs in February, averaging 105°·6 Fahr. in the shade. The minimum is in July, when the thermometer registers as low as 30°. The mean for the whole year is 57°·3. The temperature never falls below freezing-point, except for an hour or two before sunrise in the coldest month. Snow has twice been known to fall in Melbourne for a few minutes, in 1849 and 1882. It is common enough, however, on the plateau: Ballarat, which is over 1000 feet high, always has a few snow storms, and the roads to Omeo among the Australian Alps lie under several feet of snow in the winter. The general healthiness of the climate is shown by the fact that the average death-rate for the last five years has been only 14·37 per thousand of the population. The rainfall of the colony varies considerably. On the table-land it averages about 40 inches, at Melbourne 25·44 inches, along the Murray basin 20 inches, and in the "Wimmera" or north-west corner not more than 15 inches.

Geology.

Victoria rests throughout on a bed of coarse granite, which is exposed in many parts by the denudation of the overlying strata. Above this lies a bed of Silurian rocks, which seems to have at one time extended over the whole area, and still forms the surface of a great portion of the colony, especially in the north-east. Other Palæozoic strata are represented by only one small patch of Devonian at Mount Tambo in the Australian Alps, and by small isolated beds of Carboniferous strata along the valley of the Mitchell river. The Mesozoic strata overlie the Silurian along the coast, being represented by beds of Upper New Red Sandstone of considerable thickness. These extend from Cape Otway as far east as Corner Inlet, and sections of them are prominent features where the coasts are rocky. The other Mesozoic strata are absent. Miocene beds occur in patches near Ballarat, near Warrnambool, and in some parts of Gippsland. These are unimportant, however, compared with the Pliocene formations, which cover a very large part of the colony, notably the great plains of the Wimmera and the Murray valley. They also occur in smaller areas over the Silurian rock, either as cappings of prominences, that were left as islands when the waves of Post-Tertiary seas washed away the rest of the beds or else as "leads," *i.e.*, the beds carved out of Silurian strata by rivers of Mesozoic periods, but filled in during Pliocene times by deposits of debris from the mountains. These have been protected by their sunken position when the great bulk of the Pliocene beds were washed away. It is from these old river beds that the alluvial gold of Victoria is got. This gold was evidently at one time contained in veins of auriferous quartz which were worn down and carried into the streams. There the heavy particles of gold gathered in the hollows, forming those collections known to miners as pockets. In some parts of Victoria vast sheets of lava overlie the Pliocene beds. These are most prominent in the south-western corner. The district round Warrnambool possesses eighty-three extinct volcanoes, and there were probably many more whose craters have been completely denuded. The volcanoes were of no great height, but from them issued sheets of glowing lava, covering the plains for hundreds of square miles. At Ballarat the mining shafts descend through four beds of basalt divided from one another by deposits of clay. These represent four distinct outflows of lava in comparatively recent geologic times.

Minerals.

During 1886 665,196 oz. of gold were obtained of the value of £2,660,780. The total yield from 1851 to 1886 was 54,393,182 oz. of the value of about £217,570,000. The number of miners is about 26,000, of whom nearly 5000 are Chinese. These devote themselves in nearly equal proportions to alluvial mining and quartz mining. But little is now done in the way of merely surface alluvial digging. The shafts are carried down to the beds of ancient rivers, where the layers of what are called "wash dirt" vary in thickness from 1 to 12 feet, yielding from ½ to 3 oz. per cubic yard. Quartz mining is rapidly increasing in extent, though the total quantity of gold obtained is steadily decreasing and the expense of getting it is increasing, for the shafts are becoming of excessive depth. One at Stawell penetrates 2409 feet below the surface; two others exceed 2000; and there are in all 17 shafts each over 1000 feet in depth. The average yield of this quartz has been of late about 10 dwts. to the ton. About one-third of the area of Victoria is supposed to be auriferous, but only 1300 square miles have as yet been worked. Besides gold, Victoria produces a little tin, copper, and antimony, and, in still smaller quantities, zinc, lead, cobalt, bismuth, and manganese. Iron ore is being smelted, but the industry has not yet reached a paying condition. Great efforts are being made to discover coalfields or to open up those that are known to exist. The total value of the coal raised in the colony up to date (1888) is only £17,000. A promising 5-foot seam is, however, now being worked in Gippsland.

Flora.

The native trees belong chiefly to the *Myrtaceæ*, being largely composed of *Eucalypti* or gum trees. There are several hundred species, the most notable being *Eucalyptus amygdalina*, a tree with tall white stem, smooth as a marble column, and without branches for 60 or 70 feet from the ground. It is singularly beautiful when seen in groves, for these have all the appearance of lofty pillared cathedrals. These trees are among the tallest in the world, averaging in some districts about 300 feet. The longest ever measured was found prostrate on the Black Spur; it measured 470 feet in length; it was 81 feet in girth near the root. *Eucalyptus globulus* or blue gum has broad green leaves, which yield the eucalyptus oil of the pharmacopœia. *Eucalyptus rostrata* is extensively used in the colony as a timber, being popularly known as red gum or hard wood. It is quite unaffected by weather, and almost indestructible when used as piles for piers or wharves. Smaller species of eucalyptus form the common "bush." Melaleucas, also of *Myrtacea* kind, are prominent objects along all the coasts, where they grow densely on the sandhills, forming "ti-tree" scrub. *Eucalyptus dumosa* is a species which grows only 6 to 12 feet high, but with a straight stem; the trees grow so close together that it is difficult to penetrate the scrub formed by them. Eleven and a half million acres of the Wimmera district are covered with this "mallee scrub," as it is called. Recent legislation has made this land easy of acquisition, and the whole of it has been taken up on pastoral leases. Five hundred thousand acres have recently been taken up as an irrigation colony on Californian principles and laid out in 40-acre farms and orchards. The *Leguminosæ* are chiefly represented by acacias, of which the wattle is the commonest. The black wattle is of considerable value, its gum being marketable and its bark worth from £5 to £10 a ton for tanning purposes. The golden wattle is a beautiful tree, whose rich yellow blossoms fill the river-valleys in early spring with delicious scent. The *Casuarinæ* or she-oaks are gloomy trees, of little use, but of frequent occurrence. Heaths, grass-trees, and magnificent ferns and fern-trees are also notable features in Victorian forests. But European and subtropical vegetation has been introduced into the colony to such an extent as to have largely altered the characters of the flora in many districts.

Fauna.

The indigenous animals belong almost wholly to the *Marsupialia*. Kangaroos are tolerably abundant on the grassy plains, but the process of settlement is causing their extermination. A smaller species of almost identical appearance called the wallaby is still numerous in the forest lands. Kangaroo rats, opossums, wombats, native bears, bandicoots, and native cats all belong to the same class. The wombat forms extensive burrows in some districts. The native bear is a frugivorous little animal, and very harmless. Bats are numerous, the largest species being the flying fox, very abundant in some districts. Eagles, hawks, turkeys, pigeons, ducks, quail, snipe, and plover are common; but the characteristic denizens of the forest are vast flocks of parrots, parakeets, and cockatoos, with sulphur-coloured or crimson crests. The laughing jackass (giant kingfisher) is heard in all the country parts, and magpies are numerous everywhere. Snakes are numerous; but less than one-fourth of the species are venomous, and they are all very shy. The deaths from snake-bite do not average 2 per annum. A great change is rapidly taking place in the fauna of the country, owing to cultivation and acclimatization. Dingoes have nearly disappeared, and rabbits, which were introduced only a few years ago, now abound in such numbers as to be a positive nuisance. Deer are also rapidly becoming numerous. Sparrows and swallows are as common as in England. The trout, which has also been acclimatized, is taking full possession of some of the streams.

Live stock.

In 1878 Victoria possessed nearly eleven millions of sheep. Victorian sheep give an exceptionally large yield of wool, and their fleeces obtain a higher price (on the average 6s. 2d.) than any other grown in Australia. The colony has one and a quarter millions of cattle, three hundred and eight thousand horses, and about a quarter of a million of pigs.

Agriculture.

There were in 1887 about 38,000 farms in the colony, containing over 2,417,157 acres of land actually cultivated; in almost all farms there is much land that is not actually tilled. Every year, however, a larger and larger proportion is brought under the plough. In the year ending March 1887 the crops were as follows:—wheat, 12,100,036 bushels; oats, 4,256,079 bushels; barley, 827,852 bushels; potatoes, 170,661 tons; and hay, 483,049 tons. The average produce per acre of wheat crop was 11½ bushels; the average per acre of oats, 23 bushels; of barley, 22 bushels; of potatoes, 3½ tons. There are 10,300 acres of vineyards, producing 986,041 gallons of wine, and this industry is fast increasing. The hop plantations in 1887 yielded 5023 cwts. of hops. The following crops are being more or less experimented with:—arrowroot, beetroot, flax, mangel wurzel, mustard, olives, poppies, oranges, and some other fruits. In the same year there were produced 12,008 cwts. of tobacco. Almost every fruit is grown more or less, but the banana and orange cannot be considered commercially successful. Apples, pears, peaches, grapes, loquats, mulberries, plums, gooseberries, strawberries, melons, apricots, raspberries, cherries, currants, quinces, almonds, figs, walnuts, all grow well and are in common use. Bananas, pine-apples, oranges, and passion fruit are cheap, but they come from the northern colonies. Tomatoes are plentiful and cheap, being easily grown in all parts of the colony.

Communication.

The central half of Victoria is well supplied with a close network of railways, whilst several long lines branch out into the less settled districts east and west. A line parallel to the coast, joining Melbourne to Bairnsdale, is sufficient for the Gippsland traffic. From Sale a number of short lines are being constructed for the convenience of the surrounding district. To the west there is a line 270 miles long joining Melbourne to Portland, giving off short branches on both sides. Three lines are being steadily pushed forward to the north-west into the Wimmera district. In 1887 there was a total length of 1880 miles open for traffic. The average cost of the lines now in operation has been £11,748 per mile, but all the more recently constructed lines have not exceeded £5000 per mile. The receipts for the year 1886-87 were £2,453,078, and the working expenses £1,427,116. All the lines are on a uniform gauge of 5 feet 3 inches, and they all belong to the state, being managed by a special board of three commissioners. Communication with Sydney, 573 miles distant, is effected by rail in 19 to 25 hours, and with Adelaide in about 20 hours.

The well-settled parts of the colony are excellently supplied with macadamized roads, which are constructed and repaired by shire councils, whose chief function it is to raise revenues, each from its own district, to support the roads in that district. The less settled districts have tracks on which riding or driving is excellent after fine weather, but not after much rain.

Victoria has 420 telegraph stations, connected by 4096 miles of line. Melbourne is connected with every town or borough in Australia, Tasmania, and New Zealand. It is also joined with London, the length of line being 13,695 miles. The shortest recorded time for the transmission of a message along this line is 32 minutes; the average time is about three hours. There are about 1300 telephone wires in use in the colony, chiefly in Melbourne.

In 1886 the colony had 1429 post-offices, through which there passed 38,392,414 letters and post-cards, 17,482,490 newspapers, and 6,926,525 packets.

Trade.

Victoria is fully committed to the system of "protection to native industry." In 1886 the value of its manufactures was £13,370,000, of which over £2,250,000 worth was exported. The number of establishments was 2770, and the number of hands employed 45,770. The total value of the exports for 1886 was £11,795,321, the chief items of which were wool, £5,028,061; gold, £4,309,535; live stock, £898,000; wheat, £408,000; flour, £318,000; sugar (brought to Victoria to be refined), £266,779; tea (brought to Melbourne to be re-exported), £395,000; machinery, £184,135. The imports in 1886 amounted to £18,530,575 in value, of which £8,741,275 were from the United Kingdom, £6,567,403 from other British colonies, and £3,221,897 from foreign countries, the United States heading the list with over half a million, chiefly manufactured goods.

Shipping.

In 1886 2307 vessels entered at Victorian ports (chiefly Melbourne) and 2324 cleared, the tonnages being 1,848,058 and 1,887,329 respectively. Of the vessels that entered 1684 and of those that cleared 1721 were colonial, their respective tonnages being 958,833 and 983,295. Of British vessels there entered 407 (648,026 tons) and cleared 382 (661,833 tons). There is no shipbuilding of importance carried on in Victoria, only 4 small vessels having been built in 1886, with a total tonnage of 420. But there is a brisk trade in repairs, there being several good yards, and the Government possesses at Williamstown a graving dock which admits vessels 500 feet long, the depth of water being 27 feet.

Banks.

Eleven banks of issue in Victoria had in 1886 notes to the extent of £1,399,208 in circulation; their deposits bearing interest amounted to £23,999,791, not bearing interest (current accounts), £7,239,681. The total liabilities amounted to £33,085,989, the assets to £41,170,989. The average rate of annual dividends is 12¼. There are, besides, six banking companies which do not issue notes, and two distinct systems of savings banks. The ordinary savings banks had in 1886 15 branches with 111,031 depositors, who owned £2,322,959 of deposits. There were 264 branches of the post-office savings banks, with 78,328 depositors, owning £1,266,957. But perhaps the most popular institution for the investment of money among persons of moderate means is the building societies, of which 60 were returned in 1886, with 19,907 members, holding £2,910,792 as deposits. These societies act as banks, and members have their current accounts with them. The total sums deposited in banks and building societies in 1888 amounted to forty millions.

Administration.

Victoria enjoys almost absolute autonomy. The practical government of the country rests with the parliament, consisting of two houses. The legislative council contains 42 members elected by 14 electoral provinces. Each member holds his seat for six years, a third of them retiring every two years but being eligible for re-election. To be eligible for election a candidate must be over thirty years of age and possessed of freehold property to the extent of £100 per annum. The electoral body consists of all citizens over twenty-one years of age, either possessing property of the yearly value of £10 or paying rates on property of not less than £25 annual value. To these are added all graduates of universities and all members of the learned professions. Members of the legislative council receive no payment. They form a sort of court of revision of the work done in the lower house. The legislative assembly consists of 86 members elected by 55 electoral districts; they are paid at the rate of £300 a year. A general election must take place every three years. In all other respects it resembles very closely the British House of Commons. Every man of the full age of twenty-one years who has taken out his elector's right has a vote for the election of a member for the district in which he resides. All voting is by ballot. The governor is appointed by the sovereign of the British empire. He has the power of assenting to or rejecting bills sent up to him from parliament, except eight classes, which he is bound to refer to the sovereign, who can disallow all bills by signifying disapproval of them within two years of their being passed by the legislature. The governor is assisted by an executive council consisting of the ministers and ex-ministers of the crown. The cabinet consists of treasurer, chief secretary, minister of public instruction, commissioner of trade and customs, minister of mines, postmaster-general, minister of lands, minister of public works, minister of agriculture, solicitor-general, attorney-general, and minister of defence. The civil service of Victoria is under the control of three commissioners, who are appointed for a term of three years by Government, but are then wholly independent. Their business is to make all appointments, determine all promotions, and watch over the administration of the Civil Service Act. Their existence has effectually abolished the evils of political patronage.

Finance. During the financial year 1885-86 the total receipts of the colony from all sources amounted to £6,945,099 and the expenditure to £6,513,539. On 30th June 1887 the public debt amounted to £33,119,164, more than twenty-three millions of which have been borrowed for the construction of railways.

Education. Victoria possesses a most efficiently organized system of state schools, where the education given is free, secular, and compulsory. The schools number 1826, with 4050 teachers, and 189,637 scholars. The average attendance is 119,488. The state awards each year for competition among boys and girls of the state schools eleven exhibitions of the yearly value of £35 each, tenable for six years, and two hundred of the value of £10 each for three years. The successful candidates of the former must go for two years to a college or grammar school and then enter the university of Melbourne; those of the latter class attend the nearest grammar school. The Roman Catholic Church supports 130 primary schools with 18,000 scholars. Secondary education is quite unconnected with the state and wholly unsupported by it; but the churches and private enterprise provide all that is needed. The Church of England has large grammar schools in Melbourne and Geelong. The Presbyterians have colleges in Melbourne, Geelong, and Ballarat, and a ladies' college in Melbourne. The Wesleyans have colleges for males and females respectively in Melbourne. The Catholics have also two institutions. Private grammar schools exist in all important towns. The university has four faculties—arts, law, engineering, and medicine—in which in 1886 the students numbered respectively 166, 61, 9, and 212. There are 14 professors and 10 lecturers. About one thousand candidates present themselves every year for matriculation, but only about 160 actually enter the university each year. A considerable number of ladies have matriculated and are pursuing their studies in the university. In 1886 the number of persons who graduated was 124 and the total from the beginning of the university (founded in 1853) has been 1169. The compulsory clause has not been in force more than ten years, and it has not yet produced its full result in raising the general standard of education. At present 94 per cent. of the children between the ages of six and fifteen attend school, but nearly a fourth of these fail to make up 40 days in the quarter. Still of persons above fifteen years of age 96 per cent. can read and 92 per cent. can both read and write. These results would be even more favourable but for the presence of 13,000 Chinese in the colony nearly all of whom are returned as illiterate, neither reading nor writing English.

Population. The population in 1886 was 1,003,043 (531,452 males and 471,591 females), of whom about one-half were born in the colony and rather less than a third in the British Isles. The estimated population at the end of 1887 was 1,035,900. In religion a third are Episcopalians, a fourth Catholics, a sixth Presbyterians, and an eighth Wesleyans.

There are now only about 780 of the aborigines left; but they never were numerous. When white men first settled in the colony, there probably were not 15,000; some estimates place them as low as 5000. Those who now remain live on stations maintained by the Government. They are allowed great freedom, with plenty of land to roam over, but each station is under the paternal care of a superintendent. Nevertheless they are steadily diminishing in numbers.

History. The eastern shore of Victoria was first explored by Surgeon Bass, who in January 1798 rounded Cape Howe from Sydney in a whale-boat. The western half was first examined in 1800-1 by Lieutenant Grant, when he discovered Port Phillip. In 1802 Flinders in charge of a British exploring expedition and Baudin at the head of one sent out by Napoleon did exploring work in the same waters.

The colony was at first known as Port Phillip, settlement being confined to the shores of that inlet. The earliest attempt to colonize this part of Australia was made in 1803, when Collins was sent out with a number of convicts and landed on the sandy peninsula to the east of the entrance to the bay. But, water being scarce, he went across to Tasmania. In 1835 John Bateman and John Pascoe Fawkner brought over from Tasmania rival pastoral companies. Previous to this the brothers Henty had formed a whaling station at Portland, and had resided there for two years. But, as this was a purely private enterprise, and not publicly known, the founding of the colony is rightly ascribed to Bateman and Fawkner. Before a year had passed about 200 persons had followed in their wake. At the end of 1839 there were 3000 persons on the banks of the Yarra; in 1841 these had increased to 11,000. In 1842 the small community began to agitate for separation from New South Wales, and in 1851, when its desires were realized, it numbered 97,000 persons. In this same year (1851) some of the Australian colonies received constitutions which rendered them self-governing, and among these the new colony of Victoria attained to the dignity of representative institutions. It was also in this year that the discovery of gold totally altered the character and prospects of Victoria. The discovery was first made in New South Wales in February 1851 by Edward Hargraves; but a month or two elapsed before it became generally known. So great was the exodus to New South Wales that a committee of leading Melbourne citizens offered a reward for the first discovery of gold in Victoria. Numerous parties scoured the colony, with the result of finding gold at Clunes. Six weeks later the wonderful field of Ballarat was discovered, and attention was drawn to Victoria as a gold-producing country. In 1852 there were 70,000 arrivals in the colony, nearly all men. In 1853 there were 54,000, in 1854 there were 90,000, and so on, the population in 1861 being six times that of 1851. In 1854 the severity with which the licence-fee of thirty shillings a month was exacted from miners, whether successful or not, led to a serious riot. A number of the ringleaders were brought to trial, but the juries acquitted them. In 1860 the ill-fated expedition of Burke and Wills left Melbourne on its bold dash across the continent. In 1863 the colony was thrown into much excitement over a constitutional struggle generally known as the "deadlock." The democratic party wished to introduce the fiscal system of protection to native industry, but, after the bill had passed the lower house, the upper rejected it. It was then tacked to an Appropriation Bill, which the upper house resolutely refused to pass. For a year all supplies were stopped, and the business of the colony was carried on without funds. In 1866 a compromise was effected; but then the struggle commenced anew. The English Government recalled the governor, Sir Charles Darling, for siding with the democracy; the lower house, thinking him ill-used, placed on the estimates a grant of £20,000 for Lady Darling, which the upper house threw out. In 1868 Sir Charles received a lucrative position elsewhere, with £5000 from the colony as arrears of salary. The later history of the colony tells only of quiet, orderly, and unbroken prosperity. (A. SU.)

VICTORIA, capital of British Columbia and the principal town of Vancouver Island, in the south-east corner of which it is finely situated (48° 25′ 20″ N. lat., 123° 22′ 24″ W. long.), on a small arm of the sea, its harbour, however, only admitting vessels drawing 18 feet. The city has some fine streets, handsome villas and public buildings, Government offices, and churches. There are several schools, public and private, a free library, a theatre, a mechanics' institute, and a public park. The water supply is good. The town, which is connected by cable with the mainland, is a favourite holiday resort for the Columbians. Till 1858 Victoria was a post of the Hudson Bay Company. The city was incorporated in 1862; and, according to the census of 1886, the population was 14,000, including Chinese and Indians, spread over an area of 4 square miles.

VICTORIA, a city of Brazil, capital of the province of Espirito Santo, 270 miles north-east from Rio de Janeiro, in 20° 18′ S. lat. and 40° 20′ W. long. Victoria, which has a white, Negro, and coloured population (1880) of 12,500, stands on the west side of an island at the head of the Bay of Espirito Santo, the entrance of which is defended by five forts, and also rendered difficult of access by several other islets and reefs rising little above high-water mark. The town is regularly laid out and well-built, with some good streets, two or three fine churches, a substantial governor's residence, and a few other conspicuous buildings. The surrounding district grows much rice, sugar, and manioc, which with other produce are here shipped, chiefly for the neighbouring coast towns.

Victoria, originally Espirito Santo, is one of the oldest Portuguese settlements on the Brazilian coast, having been founded in 1535 by Vasco Fernando Continho at a little distance from its present site, on the south side and nearer to the entrance of the bay. It took the name of Victoria in 1558 to commemorate the crushing defeat inflicted by Fernando de Sa on the allied Indian tribes of the Aimores, Tapininguins, and Goitacazes in that year. The original site is still occupied by a group of houses and buildings commonly known as the Villa Velha or "Old Town," which is separated from Victoria by the Rio Santa Maria flowing to the south-west corner of the bay.

VIDA, Marco Girolamo (*c.* 1489-1566), one of the most eminent Latin poets and scholars of the age of Leo X., was born at Cremona shortly before the year 1490. He received the name of Marcantonio in baptism, but changed this to Marco Girolamo when he entered the order of the Canonici Regolari Lateranensi. During his early manhood he acquired considerable fame by the composition of two didactic poems in the Latin tongue, on the *Game of Chess* and on the *Silkworm*. This reputation induced him to seek the papal court in Rome, which was rapidly becoming the headquarters of polite learning, the place where students might expect advancement through their literary talents. Vida reached Rome in the last years of the pontificate of Julius II. Leo X., on succeeding to the papal chair (1513), treated him with marked favour, bestowed on him the priory of St Sylvester at Frascati, and bade him compose a heroic Latin poem on the life of Christ. Such was the origin of the *Christiad*, Vida's most celebrated, if not his best, performance. It did not, however, see the light in Leo's lifetime. Between the years 1520 and 1527 Vida produced the second of his masterpieces in Latin hexameters, a didactic poem on the *Art of Poetry*. Clement VII. raised him to the rank of apostolic protonotary, and in 1532 conferred on him the bishopric of Alba. It is probable that he took up his residence in this town soon after the death of Clement; and here he spent the greater portion of his remaining years. Vida attended the council of Trent, where he enjoyed the society of Cardinals Cervini, Pole, and Del Monte, together with his friend the poet Flaminio. A record of their conversations may be studied in Vida's Latin dialogue *De Republica*. Among his other writings should be mentioned three eloquent orations in defence of Cremona against Pavia, composed upon the occasion of some dispute as to precedency between those two cities. Vida died at Alba on 27th September 1566.

Vida's fame rests almost wholly on his Latin poems. These are more remarkable for their purity and grace of style than for qualities of imagination or powerful thinking. His contemporaries were of opinion that Vida approached more nearly to the ancients in majesty and gravity of diction than his rivals. Indeed, the *Poetica* can still be read with both pleasure and instruction. Though we miss the poetic glow of Poliziano's and Pontano's Latin compositions, and the exquisite workmanship of Flaminio's lyrics, there is in Vida so facile a command of the Latin language and metre that we might fancy ourselves listening to a writer of the Augustan age. The following lines will give a fair notion of his powers:—

> Dii Romæ indigetes, Trojæ tuque auctor, Apollo,
> Unde genus nostrum cœli se tollit ad astra,
> Hanc saltem auferri tandem prohibete Latinis:
> Artibus emineat semper studiisque Minervæ
> Italia, et gentes doceat pulcherrima Roma;
> Quandoquidem armorum penitus fortuna recessit,
> Tanta Italos inter crevit discordia reges;
> Ipsi nos inter sævos destringimus enses,
> Nec patriam pudet externis aperire tyrannis.

This pious prayer was not granted in the age which followed the council of Trent.

Vida's poems were collected and printed at Oxford in 1722, and an enlarged edition appeared in 1731. For an account of his works, see Symonds's *Renaissance in Italy*, vol. ii.

VIEN, Joseph Marie (1716-1809), French painter, was not only the master but the forerunner of David, and the author of the classic movement which, inaugurated under Louis XVI., ran itself out under the first empire. He was born at Montpellier, 18th June 1716. Protected by Comte de Caylus, he entered at an early age the studio of Natoire, and obtained the great prize in 1745. He used his time at Rome in applying to the study of nature and the development of his own powers all that he gleaned from the masterpieces around him; but his tendencies were so foreign to the reigning taste that on his return to Paris he owed his admission to the academy for his picture Dædalus and Icarus (Louvre) solely to the indignant protests of Boucher. When in 1776, at the height of his established reputation, he became director of the school of France at Rome, he took David with him amongst his pupils. After his return, five years later, his fortunes were wrecked by the Revolution; but he undauntedly set to work, and at the age of eighty (1796) carried off the prize in an open Government competition. Bonaparte acknowledged his merit by making him a senator. He died at Paris on 27th March 1809, leaving behind him several brilliant pupils, amongst whom were Vincent, Regnault, Suvée, Ménageot, Taillasson, and others of high merit; nor should the name of his wife, Marie Thérèse Reboul (1728-1805), herself a member of the academy, be omitted from this list. Their son, Marie Joseph, born in 1761, also distinguished himself as a painter.

VIENNA (Germ. *Wien*), the capital and largest city of the Austrian-Hungarian empire, is situated on the right bank of the Danube, in 48° 13′ N. lat. and 16° 23′ E. long., at a height of about 550 feet above the level of the sea. It lies at the base of the last outlying spurs of the eastern Alps (the Wiener Wald), at the beginning of a plain which stretches eastwards to the Carpathians. The main channel of the Danube passes to the north of Vienna; but an arm of the river, the Danube Canal, passes through the city, dividing it into two unequal parts. Into this arm, on the east side of Vienna, flows the dirty and generally insignificant stream called the Wien, which gives its name to the city.[1] Vienna is the principal residence of the emperor, the see of an archbishop, the seat of the imperial and Cisleithan (Austrian) ministries, the meeting-place of the Austrian diet, and also the meeting-place, alternately with Buda-Pesth, of the delegations (compare Austria). Vienna is now officially divided into the following ten municipal districts,—the inner town (Innere Stadt) or old city of Vienna, Leopoldstadt, Landstrasse, Wieden, Margarethen, Mariahilf, Neubau, Josefstadt, Alsergrund, and Favoriten. The inner town, which lies almost exactly in the centre of the others, is, unlike the older parts of most European towns, still the most aristocratic quarter, containing the palaces of the emperor and of many of the nobility, the Government offices, many of the embassies and legations, the opera house, and the principal hotels. Leopoldstadt, which is the only district on the left bank of the Danube Canal, is the chief commercial quarter, and is inhabited to a great extent by Jews. Mariahilf, Neubau, and Margarethen are the chief seats of manufacturing industry. Landstrasse may be described as the district of officialism; there too are the British and German embassies. Alsergrund, with the enormous general hospital, the military hospital, and the municipal asylum for the insane, is the medical quarter. The inner city, or Vienna proper, was formerly separated from the other districts by a circle of fortifications, consisting of a rampart, fosse, and glacis. These, however, were removed in 1858-1860, and the place of the glacis has been taken by a handsome boulevard (Ring-Strasse), 2 miles in length and about 150 feet in average width. A series of external

[1] Some authorities connect the name of Vienna with Vindobona (see p. 222 below).

works, consisting of a rampart and fosse, were constructed in 1704 to surround the whole city at that time, including its suburbs; and these are still maintained as the boundary-line for the city imposts, and separate the above-named districts from the as yet unincorporated suburbs. This second girdle of fortifications is known as the Lines (Linien), and a second wide boulevard (Gürtel-Strasse) follows their course round the city.

Near the centre of the inner city, most of the streets in which are narrow and irregular, is the cathedral of St Stephen, the most important mediæval building in Vienna, dating in its present form mainly from the 14th and 15th centuries, but incorporating a few fragments of the original 12th-century edifice. Among its most striking features are the fine and lofty tower (450 feet), rebuilt in 1860-64; the extensive catacombs, in which the emperors were formerly interred; the sarcophagus (1513) of Frederick III.; the tomb of Prince Eugene of Savoy; thirty-eight marble altars; and the fine groined ceiling. A little to the south-west of the cathedral is the Hofburg, or imperial palace, a huge complex of buildings of various epochs and in various styles, enclosing several courtyards. The oldest part of the present edifice dates from the 13th century, and extensive additions are now being made according to

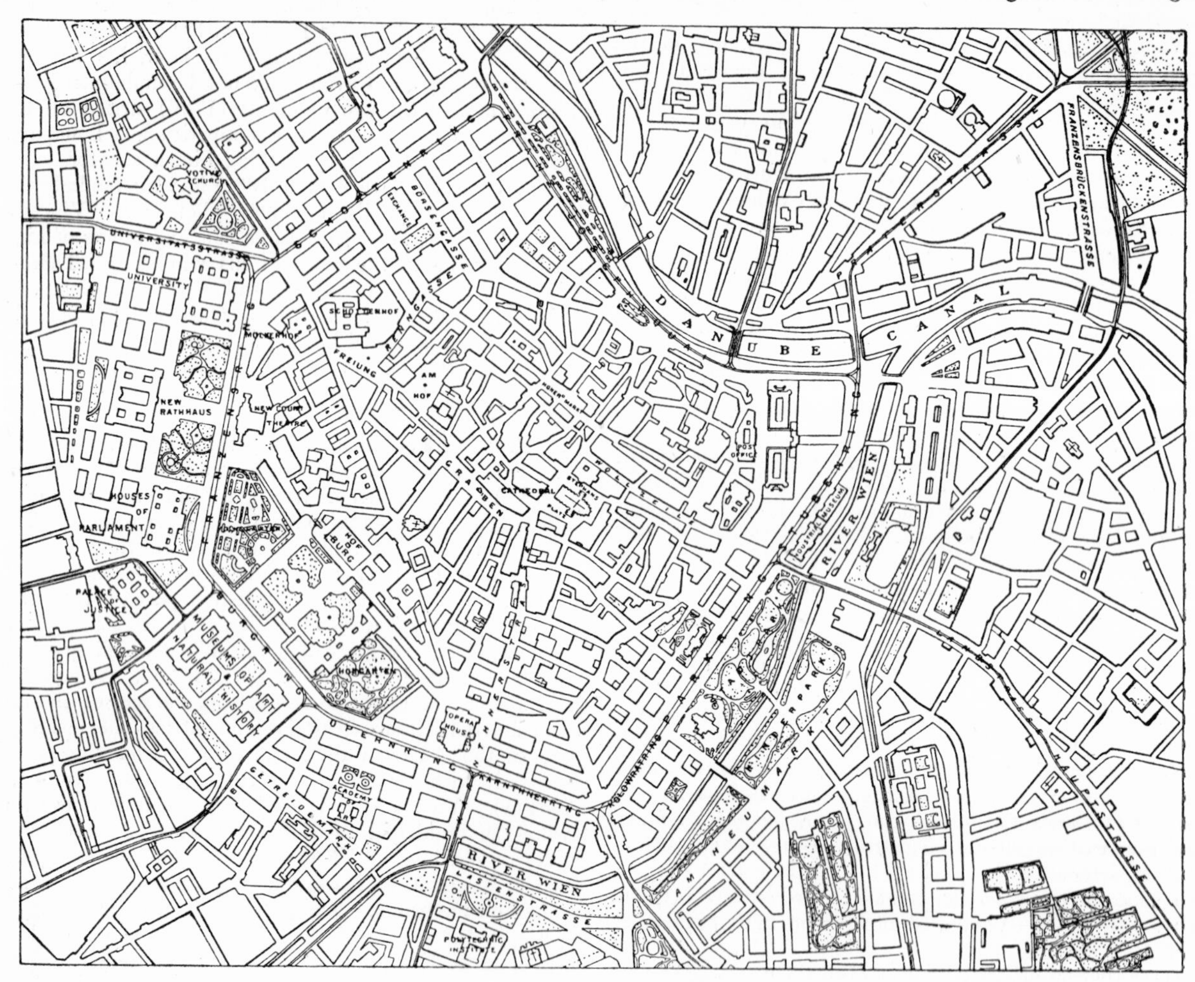

Plan of the city of Vienna.

the plans of the architect Fischer von Erlach (1656-1723). In addition to private rooms and state apartments, the Hofburg contains a library of 400,000 volumes and 20,000 MSS.; the imperial treasury, a storehouse of objects of the greatest historical interest and intrinsic value; a cabinet of coins and antiquities; and other important collections. In the old town are the two largest of the Höfe, extensive blocks of buildings belonging to the great abbeys of Austria, which are common throughout Vienna. These are the Schottenhof (once belonging to the "Scoti," or Irish Benedictines) and the Mölkerhof, adjoining the open space called the Freiung, each forming a little town of itself. As in most Continental towns, the custom of living in flats is prevalent in Vienna, where few except the richer nobles occupy an entire house. Of late the so-called "Zinspaläste" ("tenement palaces") have been built on a large and magnificent scale, often profusely adorned without and within with painting and sculpture. Some of the finest of these, a characteristic feature of Vienna architecture, are also to be seen in the old town. Other notable buildings within the line of the old fortifications are the Gothic Augustine church, containing a fine monument by Canova, the Capuchin church, with the burial vault of the Hapsburgs; the church of Maria-Stiegen, an interesting Gothic building of the 14th century; the handsome Greek church, by Hansen; and the old rathhaus. At the corner of the Graben is the "Stock im Eisen," the stump of a tree, said to be the last survivor of a holy grove round which the original settlement of Vindomina sprang up (see p. 222 below). It is full of nails driven into it by travelling journeymen.

In the number of its large and handsome modern buildings Vienna can hold its own with any European capital. Most of these are found in or adjoining the Ring-Strasse, which certainly ranks as one of the most imposing achievements of recent street architecture. Opposite the Hof burg, the main body of which is separated from the Ring-Strasse by the Hofgarten and Volksgarten, rise the handsome monument of the empress Maria Theresa and the imperial museums of art and natural history, two extensive Renaissance edifices with domes, matching each other in every particular and grouping finely with the new part of the palace. Hans Makart's painted dome in the natural history museum is the largest pictorial canvas in the world. Adjoining the museums to the west is the palace of justice (1881), and this is closely followed by the houses of parliament (1883), in which the Grecian style has been successfully adapted to modern requirements. Beyond the houses of parliament stands the new rathhaus, an immense and lavishly-decorated Gothic building, erected in 1873-83. It was designed by Friedrich Schmidt, who may be described as the chief exponent of the modern Gothic tendency, as Hansen and Semper, the creators respectively of the parliament house and the museums, are the leaders of the Classical and Renaissance styles which are so strongly represented in Viennese architecture. The central tower and the tapering steeple of the rathhaus are surmounted by a colossal bronze figure of a knight. Opposite the rathhaus, on the inner side of the Ring, is the new court theatre, another specimen of Semper's Renaissance work. To the north stands the new building of the university, a Renaissance structure by Ferstel, rivalling the rathhaus in extent. Near the university, and separated from the Ring by a garden, stands the votive church in Alsergrund, erected to commemorate the emperor's escape from assassination in 1853, one of the most elaborate and successful of modern Gothic churches, in which the efforts of the architect (Ferstel) are supported by a profusion of sculpture and stained glass windows. The other important buildings of the Ring-Strasse include the magnificent opera house, the sumptuous interior of which vies with that of Paris, the Academy of Art, the industrial museum, and the exchange. On the north side the Ring-Strasse gives place to the spacious Franz Joseph's quay, flanking the Danube Canal. The municipal districts outside the Ring also contain numerous handsome modern buildings. Among the churches may be instanced those of Wieden (St Carlo Borromeo) and Lerchenfeld, the former an 18th-century imitation of St Peter's at Rome, the latter a plain but graceful building in an early mediæval Italian style. The secular buildings include several large barracks and hospitals, various institutions connected with the university, the arsenal (with a collection of weapons), the Belvedere (see below), and the polytechnic institute, market-halls, &c. In the outlying districts are numerous villas of great taste and elegance.

Vienna is the intellectual as well as the material capital of Austria,—emphatically so in regard to the German part of the empire. Its university, established in 1365, is now attended by nearly 6000 students, and the medical faculty enjoys a world-wide reputation. Besides an adequate supply of elementary and secondary schools, the other educational institutions include a large polytechnic, an agricultural academy, a military school, Roman Catholic and Protestant theological seminaries, a conservatorium of music, a training school for aspirants to a diplomatic career, a commercial college, and numerous technical and special schools. Its scientific institutions are headed by the Academy of Science. The Academy of Art was founded in 1707. Few European capitals possess more valuable art collections than Vienna. The picture gallery in the Belvedere Palace, formerly the residence of Prince Eugene, is unsurpassed for its specimens of Rubens, Dürer, and the Venetian masters. The Lower Belvedere, at the other end of the garden, contains the famous Ambras collection of armour, curiosities, and antiquities. The private picture galleries of Prince Liechtenstein, Count Harrach, and Count Czernin are of great extent and importance; and the collection of drawings and engravings known as the "Albertina," in the palace of the archduke Albert, is familiar to all connoisseurs. The collections of the various museums, &c., which are not unworthy of the handsome buildings in which they are exhibited, and the extensive military collections of the arsenal must also be mentioned.

In 1880 the population of Vienna proper, *i.e.*, the ten municipal districts, amounted to 705,402, a number which gave it the fourth place among the cities of Europe. Including the suburbs, the total population rose to 1,082,812. The above figures are exclusive of the garrison of 20,700 men. The overwhelming majority of the inhabitants are Roman Catholics; the Jews number about 75,000, and the Protestants 26,500.

Owing to the peculiarities of its situation, the population of Vienna is of a very cosmopolitan and heterogeneous character. The German element is, of course, largely in the ascendant; but there are also large numbers of Czechs, Hungarians, and Slavs. As a general rule the Viennese are gay, pleasure-loving, and genial, and they possess a *bonhomie* which differentiates them markedly from the inhabitants of the other great German capital. The Viennese women are often distinguished by beauty and elegance; and dressing as a fine art is cultivated here with almost as great success as in Paris. As a rule the Viennese are passionately fond of dancing; and the city of Strauss, Lanner, and Gungl provides the civilized terpsichorean world with waltzes and polkas. Opera, especially in its lighter form, flourishes, and the actors of Vienna maintain with success a traditional reputation of no mean order. The above description must not be understood to convey a negation of more solid qualities, especially industry, frugality, and sobriety. Its chief place in the history of art Vienna owes to its musicians, among whom are counted Haydn, Mozart, Beethoven, and Schubert. The Viennese school of painting is of modern origin; but some of its members, for instance, Hans Makart, have acquired a European reputation.

The Prater, a vast expanse (2000 acres) of wood and park on the east side of the city, between the Danube and the Danube Canal, is greatly frequented by all classes; and here all phases of Viennese life may be studied, from the fashionable corso in the Haupt-Allee in May down to the boisterous and Derby-day-like jollity of a Sunday in the Wurstel Prater or people's Prater. The great exhibition of 1873 was held in this park, and several of its buildings, including the large rotunda, have been left standing. Smaller parks are the Hofgarten, the Volksgarten, and the Town Park, all adjoining the Ring-Strasse. The environs of the city of Vienna contain many points of beauty and interest. Among the most popular resorts are the parks and gardens belonging to the imperial châteaux of Schönbrunn and Laxenburg.

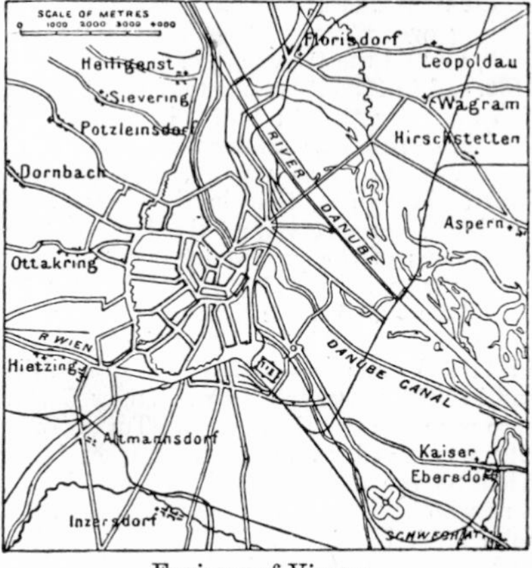

Environs of Vienna.

The position of the city on the chief European waterway running from west to east early marked out Vienna as one of the great commercial emporia of eastern Europe. The valley of the March, which river here joins the Danube, forms the natural line of communication with the Oder and the Vistula. But the Austrian Government and the corporation of Vienna, by failing to keep the Danube in a proper state for navigation, have let slip the opportunity of making the city the great Danubian metropolis which its geographical position entitles it to be. An extensive trade is nevertheless carried on from Vienna in grain, partly as a direct importation from Hungary and partly in transit between Russia and southern Germany. Other important articles are wine, cattle, colonial wares, and manufactured goods of the most varied description. Though not conspicuous among cities of its own rank as an industrial centre, Vienna nevertheless carries on a considerable number of manufactures; and some of its products, such as its bent-wood furniture and meerschaum pipes, are exported to all parts of Europe. In the number and variety of its leather and other fancy goods it rivals Paris; and among manufactures of a more solid character may be instanced machinery, ironwares, carriages, cotton and silk goods, &c. The beer of Vienna is also famous. The municipal government of Vienna is entrusted to a gemeinderath of 120 elected members, with an executive and police magistracy. The annual income of this body amounts to about one and a half millions sterling. In the national parliament the city is represented by 10 members. The climate of Vienna is changeable, and rapid falls of temperature are not uncommon. The range between January and June is about 40° Fahr. Violent storms often occur in spring and autumn; and the heat of summer is accompanied by a plague of dust. Good water is brought by an aqueduct from the Schneeberg, 50 miles to the south-west. The annual death-rate is about twenty-six per thousand.

History.—For several centuries Vienna filled an important rôle as the most advanced bulwark of Western civilization and Christianity against the Turks, for during the whole of the Middle Ages Hungary practically retained its Asiatic character. The story of Vienna begins in the earliest years of the Christian era, with the seizure of the Celtic settlement of *Vindomina* by the Romans, who changed its name to *Vindobona*, and established a fortified camp here to command the Danube and protect the northern frontier of the empire. The fortress grew in importance, and was afterwards made a municipium; and here Marcus Aurelius died in 180. On the decline of the Roman empire Vindobona became the prey of successive barbarian invaders. Attila and his Huns were among the temporary occupants of the place (5th century), and in the following century it came into the possession of the Avars, after which its name disappears from history until towards the close of the 8th century, when Charlemagne expelled the Avars and made the district between the Enns and the Wiener Wald the boundary of his empire. In the time of Otho II. (976) this "East Mark" (Ostmark, Oesterreich, Austria) was granted in fief to the Babenbergers, and in the reign of Frederick Barbarossa (1156) it was advanced to the rank of a duchy. There is no certain record that the site of Vindobona was occupied at the time of the formation of the Ostmark, though many considerations make it probable. It is not likely that the Avars, living in their "ring" encampments, destroyed the Roman municipium; and Becs, the Hungarian name for Vienna to this day, is susceptible of a Slavonic interpretation only, and would seem to indicate that the site had been occupied in Slavonic times. The frequent mention of "Wiene" in the oldest extant version of the *Nibelungenlied* points in the same direction. Passing over a doubtful mention of "Vwienni" in the annals of 1030, we find the "civitas" of Vienna mentioned in a document of 1130, and in 1156 it became the capital and residence of Duke Heinrich Jasomirgott. In 1237 Vienna received a charter of freedom from Frederick II., confirmed in 1247. In the time of the crusades Vienna increased so rapidly, in consequence of the traffic that flowed through it, that in the days of Ottocar II. of Bohemia (1251-76), the successor of the Babenbergers, it had attained the dimensions of the present inner town. A new era of power and splendour begins in 1276, when it became the capital of the Hapsburg dynasty, after the defeat of Ottocar by Rudolph of Hapsburg. From this time on it has shared the fortunes of the house of Austria. In 1477 Vienna was besieged unsuccessfully by the Hungarians, and in 1485 it was taken by Matthew Corvinus. Of more importance were the two sieges by the Turks (1529 and 1683), when the city was saved on the first occasion by the gallant defence of Nicholas von Salm, and on the second by Rüdiger von Starhemberg, who held out until the arrival of the Poles and Germans under John Sobieski of Poland. The suburbs, however, were destroyed on both occasions. In 1805, and again in 1809, Vienna was for a short time occupied by the French. In 1814-15 it was the meeting-place of the congress which settled the political affairs of Europe after the overthrow of Napoleon. In 1848 the city was for a time in the hands of the revolutionary party; but it was bombarded by the imperial forces and compelled to surrender on 30th October of the same year. Vienna was not occupied by the Prussians in the war of 1866, but the invaders marched to within sight of its towers. Since then the most important event in its history has been the exhibition of 1873.

See Weiss, *Gesch. der Stadt Wien* (2 vols., 2d ed., 1882-83), containing an ample bibliography; *Oesterreich in Wort und Bild*, &c., *Erste Abth.* (1886); Weiss, *Topographie der Stadt Wien* (1876); Victor Tissot, *Vienne et la Vie Viennoise* (Paris, 1878). (J. F. M.)

VIENNE, a department of France, formed in 1790 out of Poitou (four-fifths of its present area), Touraine (one-seventh), and Berry, lies between 46° 3′ and 47° 10′ N. lat. and 0° 6′ W. and 1° 12′ E. long., and is bounded by Deux-Sèvres on the W., Charente on the S., Haute-Vienne on the S.E., Indre on the E., Indre-et-Loire on the N.E. and N., and Maine-et-Loire on the N.W. The river Vienne, which gives its name to the department, with its tributaries the Creuse (subtributary the Gartempe) on the east and the Clain on the west, flows from south to north. The general slope of the department is in the same direction, the highest point (764 feet) being in the south-east and the lowest (115 feet) at the junction of the Vienne and the Creuse. In the south the Charente, on the north-west the Dive, and in the west some streams belonging to the basin of the Sèvre-Niortaise drain small portions of the department. The average temperature is 54° Fahr. The prevailing winds are from the south-west and west. The annual rainfall is 23 inches.

Of the total area of 1,722,478 acres arable land occupies 1,119,675, grass 76,899, vines 90,750, woods 193,322, and heath, pasture, and uncultivated land 146,971. In 1881 the live stock included 22,637 horses, 7176 mules, 9679 asses, 63,052 cattle, 155,212 sheep of native and 47,970 of improved breed, 66,655 pigs, and 21,744 goats. There were also 11,047 beehives (32½ tons of honey and as much of wax). The crops in 1884 were—wheat 4,557,146 bushels, meslin 245,641, rye 291,673, barley 1,063,647, oats 4,295,742, buckwheat 27,813, maize 51,529, potatoes 3,455,220, beetroot 54,941 tons, colza seed 668 tons, hemp 323 tons, flax 3½ tons, hay 108,955 tons, clover 54,862, lucerne 98,282, sainfoin 53,350, other fodder 10,079 tons, wine 20,288,952 gallons (average for last ten years 21,384,880 gallons). Oak, ash, alder, and birch are the principal forest trees, and among the fruit-trees are the chestnut, walnut, and almond. Iron and manganese occur, and there are numerous quarries of building and lithographic stones, lime, limestone, mill-stones, marl, and a sort of pebbles which are cut into "Châtellerault diamonds." There are sulphur and iron mineral springs. The most important industrial establishments are the national arms manufactory and the cutlery works at Châtellerault; in other parts of the department are forges, blast furnaces, wool-spinning mills (580 spindles), hemp-spinning mills (4000 spindles, of which only 1500 are in use, and 28 looms), manufactories of serges and coarse cloth, vinegar, candles, leather, tiles, and pottery, paper-works, breweries, distilleries, rope-yards, lime-kilns, and numerous plaster and flour mills. Corn, wine, brandy, vegetables, fruit, chestnuts, fodder, cattle, cutlery, and dressed hides are exported; butcher's meat, colonial produce, and coals are imported. The department has 233 miles of railway, 239 of national and 8704 of other roads, and 32 of waterway (the Vienne from Châtellerault, the Dive below Moncontour, and some miles of the Creuse being navigable). The population in 1881 was 340,295 and in 1886 342,785, an increase of 101,795 since 1801. Vienne forms part of the diocese of Poitiers, has its court of appeal and academy at Poitiers, and belongs to the Tours army corps district. The chef-lieu is Poitiers (population 34,628 in 1886), and the department is divided for purposes of administration into 5 arrondissements (Poitiers; Châtellerault, population of town 14,498 in 1886; Civray, 2464; Loudun, 4041; Montmorillon, 4155), 31 cantons, and 300 communes.

VIENNE, a town of France, chef-lieu of an arrondissement in the department of Isère, historically and industrially the first, and by population the second, city of Dauphiné, is situated on the left bank of the Rhone, at the point where it is joined by the Gère, 19 miles S. of Lyons by the railway to Marseilles. On the north, east, and south the town is sheltered by low hills. Its site is an immense mass of ancient débris, which is constantly yielding interesting antiquities. Along the Gère are traces of the ramparts of the old Roman city; on Fort Pipet, to the east of the town, are the remains of a theatre and citadel and some vestiges of a pantheon and an amphitheatre; and in the interior of the town are two arches of a theatre and the balustrade of a magnificent staircase. The ancient aqueducts, restored in 1822, still convey the waters of the Gère from a distance of 4 or 5 miles; and there are several pieces of Roman road to be seen in the neighbourhood. The Plan de l'Aiguille, a truncated quadrangular pyramid 55 feet high, resting on a portico with four arches, used to be pointed out as the tomb of Pontius Pilate (who, according to tradition, died here), but it is now recognized as having been part of the spina of a large circus, the outlines of which have been traced. The temple of Augustus and Livia, a rectangular building of the Corinthian order, was rebuilt at the end of the 2d century, and in the 5th century was converted into a church. The "festival of reason" was celebrated in it at the Revolution; and it has only lately been restored, and the houses built against it cleared away. The museum in the town-hall is very rich in antiquities. The cathedral of St Maurice, exhibiting the finest Gothic architecture in Dauphiné, was begun at the end of the 12th century in the Transitional Burgundian style, on the ruins of a church which had been finished in 1107, and it was consecrated by Pope Innocent IV. in 1251. There is neither apse nor transept, and the building (315 feet long, 118 wide, and 89 high) is a singular mixture of the Romanesque and Gothic styles. The best part is the façade, finished in 1533, which rises majestically from a terrace overhanging the Rhone. Parts of the church of St André-le-Bas, which was used as a chapel by the dukes of Burgundy, are as old as the 9th century, and most of it was built in 1152. The church of St Peter, at present (1888) undergoing restoration, is one of the oldest in France, dating from the 6th century; the porch is in the most primitive Romanesque style; and the side walls, decorated with two rows of arches resting on marble columns (9th century), are unique in France. The steeple belongs to the 12th century, and the vaults were rebuilt by Soufflot in the 18th century. Among the many tombs is that of St Mamert. In the square fronting the town-hall is a statue of Ponsard the dramatist, who was born at Vienne. The Gère supplies the motive power to numerous factories. About one million yards of cloth are annually produced, and from 8000 to 9000 hides are dressed. The other industrial establishments include a paper-mill, an iron and copper foundry (400 men), iron-works, foundries, lapidaries' workshops, glass-works, brick-works, and calcining and refining furnaces in connexion with the lead and zinc mines in the neighbourhood. Grain is an important article of commerce. A suspension bridge connects Vienne with the right bank of the Rhone, where the village of St Colombe occupies part of the site of the ancient town. Near St Romain-en-Gal is a tower built by Philip of Valois to defend the right, or French, bank, as distinguished from the left, which belonged to the empire. The population in 1881 was 22,740 (commune 26,060), and in 1886 23,011 (commune 25,480).

Vienne was originally the capital of the Allobroges, and was embellished and fortified by Julius Cæsar, who made it a colony. Tiberius granted the citizens the *jus Italicum*. The ramparts, pierced by five gates, enclosed a lower, middle, and upper town. Vienne was the residence of a prætor, had a senate, consuls, and a garrison of five legions, and was the seat of a celebrated school. A bridge of five arches connected it with the new town on the right bank. Postumus (see vol. xx. p. 776) was proclaimed Cæsar here in 259, and Vienne became the capital of a provincial empire, which under himself and his successors, Victorinus and Tetricus, lasted fourteen years. Christianity was introduced by St Crescens in the 2d century, and St Lupicin is named as the first archbishop. The archbishops of Vienne all through the Middle Ages disputed the title of primate of Gaul with those of Lyons. Vienne was conquered by the Burgundians in 438, and sacked by the Lombards in 558 and by the Saracens in 737. It was one of the residences of Boso, king of Burgundy and Provence (879), who died and was buried here. After the fall of the second kingdom of Burgundy, Vienne became the chef-lieu of a county, for which the nobility and clergy disputed, and which was finally seized by the counts of Albon. In 1349 Humbert II. ceded Vienne with all Dauphiné to France. The town was sacked in 1562 by Baron des Adrets, was claimed by both Roman Catholics and Protestants, but declared for the League in 1590, and was compelled to surrender to the duke of Montmorency, who destroyed the citadel and ramparts. The archbishopric was suppressed in 1790. Vienne was the birthplace of St Julian (3d century); and pope Calixtus II. (Guy of Burgundy; *ob.* 1124) was one of its archbishops.

VIENNE, HAUTE-, a department of France, formed in 1790 out of Limousin (three-fifths), La Marche (one-fourth), Poitou, and Berry, and formerly known as Haut-Limousin, lies between 45° 26′ and 46° 23′ N. lat. and 0° 38′ and 1° 54′ E. long., and is bounded by the Indre on the N., Creuse on the E., Corrèze on the S.E., Dordogne on the S.W., Charente on the W., and Vienne on the N.W. Haute-Vienne belongs to the central plateau of France, and drains partly to the Loire and partly to the Garonne. The highest point (2549 feet) is in the extreme south-east, and belongs to the treeless but well-watered plateau of Millevaches, formed of granite, gneiss, and mica. To the north-west of the Millevaches are the Ambazac (2300 feet) and Blond (1690 feet) Hills, both separating the valley of the Vienne from that of the Gartempe, a tributary of the Creuse. The Vienne traverses the department from east to west, passing Eymoutiers, St Léonard, Limoges, and St Junien, and receiving on the right the Maude and the Taurion. The Isle, which flows into the Dordogne, with its tributaries the Auvézère and the Dronne, and the Tardoire and the Bandiat, tributaries of the Charente, all rise in the south of the department. The altitude and inland position of Haute-Vienne, its geological character, and the northern exposure of its valleys make the winters long and severe; but the climate is milder in the west and north-west. The annual rainfall at Limoges is 36 inches.

Of the total area of 1,360,000 acres 439,215 are cultivated, 4263 are occupied by vineyards, 75,333 by chestnut trees, and 163,135 by dry underwood. The crops in 1884 were—wheat 1,242,271 bushels, meslin 34,298, rye 2,482,557, barley 13,300, oats 318,026, buckwheat 1,529,368, maize 65,579, potatoes 6,710,723, beetroot 189,000 tons, colza seed 1845 tons, hemp seed 1921, hemp 1200, linseed 93, flax 46, hay 387,192, clover 31,527, lucerne 3153, wine 111,430 gallons (average for preceding ten years 141,020 gallons). The live stock included 8371 horses of a shapely and powerful breed, 684 mules, 4975 asses, 146,131 cattle, 507,443 sheep of native and 43,593 of improved breed, 104,263 pigs, and 9642 goats. There were 36,601 beehives (104½ tons of honey and 34½ tons of wax). The department is on the whole unproductive. The chestnut is here characteristic, as the apple in Normandy, and with the potato and turnip it forms the chief food of the people. The brooks are fringed by fine meadows, and the hills are covered with heaths or forests of beech, hornbeam, oak, birch, and chestnut. The mineral wealth consists of iron, copper, tin, wolfram, antimony, serpentine, fine-grained granite, gneiss, garnets, emeralds, and a kind of porphyry, which takes a fine polish. There are inexhaustible supplies of china clay, in which an export trade is carried on with Russia and America. 5800 workmen are employed in porcelain manufactories, 650 in paper and pasteboard mills (annual product, £100,000), 560 in wool and cotton spinning mills and manufactories of flannel, druggets, woollen cloaks, and carpets, 600 in shoe-making (annual product, £100,000), 600 in manufactories of sabots, 340 in glove manufactories, 370 in tan-yards, 325 in leather-dressing works, 130 in coach-building and wheelwrights' shops, 125 in cabinet workshops, 325 in printing works, and 100 in distilleries (annual product, £480,000). In 1878 1153 tons of iron were produced, and there are forges, foundries, copper-works, and manufactories of agricultural and other implements. Porcelain, china clay, woven goods, boots and shoes, sabots, gloves, leather, cattle, horses, wood, chestnuts, hemp, and paper are exported; corn, wine, coal, raw materials, and various manufactured articles are imported. There are in Haute-Vienne 234 miles of railway, and 234 of national and 3191 of other roads. This department, with that of Corrèze, forms the diocese of Limoges; it belongs to the district of the Limoges court of appeal and army corps, has its academy at Poitiers, and is divided for purposes of administration into 4 arrondissements (Limoges, population of town 63,707 in 1886; Bellac, 4015; Rochechouart, 1829; and St Yrieix, 3556), 27 cantons, and 203 communes. The population in 1881 was 349,332 and in 1886 363,182, an increase of 117,982 since 1801. Limoges is the chef-lieu. St Yrieix has an early Gothic church of the 12th century, kaolin mines, porcelain manufactories, and tan-yards. St Junien (5454) has an interesting bridge and houses of the 13th century, and numerous manufactories of gloves, paper, porcelain, sabots, and woven goods. St Léonard (3427), the birthplace of Gay-Lussac, possesses a remarkable church of the 11th and 12th centuries, tan-yards, paper-mills, and copper-works. At Châlus (1675) Richard Cœur de Lion died.

VIERZON, a town of France, in the department of Cher, 124 miles by rail to the south of Paris. The Cher and the Yèvre unite at the foot of the hill on which lie the communes of Vierzon-Ville (population 10,514 in 1886) and Vierzon-Village (6995); Vierzon-Bourgneuf (1498) is on the left bank of the Cher. The three communes together have a population of 19,007. Vierzon has several large manufactories for the production of agricultural machines, also foundries, porcelain and earthenware works, and glass-works. A very fine technical school has just been opened.

VIETA, or VIÈTE, FRANÇOIS, SEIGNEUR DE LA BIGOTIÈRE (1540-1603), more generally known as FRANCISCUS VIETA, mathematician, was born in 1540 at Fontenay-le-Comte, in Poitou. According to F. Ritter's investigations,[1] Vieta was brought up as a Catholic, and died in the same creed; but there can be no doubt that he belonged to the Huguenots for several years. On the completion of his studies in law at Poitiers Vieta began his career as an advocate in his native town. This he left about 1567, and somewhat later we find him at Rennes as a councillor of the parlement of Brittany. The religious troubles drove him thence, and Rohan, the well-known chief of the Huguenots, took him under his special protection. He recommended him in 1580 as a "maître des requêtes" (master of requests); and Henry of Navarre, at the instance of Rohan, addressed two letters to Henry III. of France on 3d March and 26th April 1585, to obtain Vieta's restoration to his former office, but without result. After the accession of Henry of Navarre to the throne of France Vieta filled in 1589 the position of councillor of the parlement at Tours. He afterwards became a royal privy councillor, and remained so till his death, which took place suddenly at Paris in February 1603, but in what manner we do not know; Anderson, the editor of his scientific remains, speaks only of a "præceps et immaturum autoris fatum."

We know of one important service rendered by Vieta as a royal officer. While at Tours he discovered the key to a Spanish cipher, consisting of more than 500 characters, and thenceforward all the dispatches in that language which fell into the hands of the French could be easily read. His fame now rests, however, entirely upon his achievements in mathematics. Being a man of wealth, he printed at his own expense the numerous papers which he wrote on various branches of this science, and communicated them to scholars in almost every country of Europe. An evidence of the good use he made of his means, as well as of the kindliness of his character, is furnished by the fact that he entertained as a guest for a whole month a scientific adversary, Adriaan van Roomen, and then paid the expenses of his journey home. Vieta's writings thus became very quickly known; but, when Franciscus van Schooten issued a general edition of his works in 1646, he failed to make a complete collection, although probably nothing of very great value has perished.

The form of Vieta's writings is what we may call their weak side. He indulged freely in flourishes; and in devising technical terms derived from the Greek he seems to have aimed at making them as unintelligible as possible. None of them, in point of fact, has held its ground, and even his proposal to denote unknown quantities by the vowels A, E, I, O, U, Y,—the consonants B, C, &c., being reserved for general known quantities, has not been taken up. In this denotation he followed, perhaps, some older contemporaries, as Ramus, who designated the points in geometrical figures by vowels, making use of consonants, R, S, T, &c., only when those were exhausted. Vieta is wont to be called the father of modern algebra. This does not mean, what is often alleged, that nobody before him had ever thought of choosing symbols different from numerals, such as the letters of the alphabet, to denote the quantities of arithmetic, but that he made a general custom of what until his time had been only an exceptional attempt. All that is wanting in his writings, especially in his *Isagoge in artem analyticam* (1591), in order to make them look like a modern school algebra, is merely the sign of equality,—a want which is the more striking because Robert Recorde had made use of our present symbol for this purpose since 1557 and Xylander had employed vertical parallel lines since 1575. On the other hand, Vieta was well skilled in most modern artifices, aiming at a simplification of equations by the substitution of new quantities having a certain connexion with the primitive unknown quantities. Another of his works, *Recensio canonica effectionum geometricarum*, bears a stamp not less modern, being what we now call an algebraic geometry,—in other words, a collection of precepts how to construct algebraic expressions with the use of rule and compass only. While these writings were generally intelligible, and therefore of the greatest didactic importance, the *principle of homogeneity*, first enunciated by Vieta, was so far in advance of his times that most readers seem to have passed it over without adverting to its value. That principle had been made use of by the Greek authors of the classic age; but of later mathematicians only Hero, Diophantus, &c., ventured to regard lines and surfaces as mere numbers that could be joined to give a new number, their sum. It may be that the study of such sums, which he found in the works of Diophantus, prompted him to lay it down as a principle that quantities occurring in an equation ought to be homogeneous, all of them lines, or surfaces, or solids, or supersolids,—an equation between mere numbers being inadmissible. During the three centuries that have elapsed between Vieta's days and our own several changes of opinion have taken place on this subject, till the principle has at last proved so far victorious that modern mathematicians like to make homogeneous such equations as are not so from the beginning, in order to get values of a symmetrical shape. Vieta himself, of course, did not see so far as that; nevertheless the merit cannot be denied him of having indirectly suggested the thought. Nor are his writings lacking in actual inventions. He conceived methods for the general resolution of equations of the second, third, and fourth degrees different from those of Ferro and Ferrari, with which, however, it is difficult to believe him to have been unacquainted. He devised an approximate numerical solution of equations of the second and third degrees, wherein Leonardo of Pisa must have preceded him, but by a method every vestige of which is completely lost. He knew the connexion existing between the positive roots of an equation (which, by the way, were alone thought of as roots) and the coefficients of the different powers of the unknown quantity. He found out the formula for deriving the sine of a multiple angle, knowing that of the simple angle with due regard to the periodicity of sines. This formula must have been known to Vieta in 1593. In that year Adriaan van Roomen gave out as a problem to all mathematicians an equation of the 45th degree, which, being recognized by Vieta as depending on the equation between sin ϕ and sin $\frac{\phi}{45}$, was resolved by him at once, all the twenty-three positive roots of which the said equation was capable being given at the same time. Such was the first encounter of the two scholars. A second took place when Vieta pointed to Apollonius's problem of taction as not yet being mastered, and Adriaan van Roomen gave a solution by the hyperbola. Vieta, however, did not accept it, as there existed a solution by means of the rule and the compass only, which he published himself in his *Apollonius Gallus* (1600). In this paper Vieta made use of the centre of similitude of two circles. Lastly, he gave an infinite product for the number π (see SQUARING THE CIRCLE, vol. xxii. p. 434).

Vieta's collected works were issued under the title of *Opera Mathematica* by F. van Schooten at Leyden in 1646. (M. CA.)

[1] *Bolletino Boncompagni*, vol. i. p. 227, note 1, Rome, 1868.

VIGEVANO, a town of Italy, in the province of Pavia, on the right bank of the Ticino, 24 miles south-west from Milan and about the same distance north-west from Pavia. It is a mediæval walled town, with an arcaded market-place, a cathedral, and a castle of the Sforza family, dating from the 14th century and adorned with a loggia by Bramante. It is a place of some importance in the silk trade, and also produces excellent macaroni. The population in 1881 was 14,794 (commune, 20,096).

VIGIL, in its ecclesiastical sense, means the day preceding a festival. In the liturgy of the Roman Catholic Church there are special offices for the vigils of the greater feasts, and the vigil is regarded as more or less of a fast day. In the early church there was a widespread practice of celebrating festivals, of martyrs especially, by actual vigils (*vigiliæ* or *pernoctationes*, παννυχίδες) in the churches; but this led to such serious evils that the custom had to be discouraged, and now survives, if at all, only in rare, unauthorized, and considerably disguised forms. In some of the stricter religious orders the daily office is recited at various hours of the night as well as during the day; but, if these nocturnal services are spoken of as vigils, it is only in the popular meaning of that word.

VIGILANTIUS, presbyter, celebrated as the author of a work, no longer extant, against superstitious practices, which called forth one of the most violent and scurrilous of Jerome's polemical treatises, was born about 370 at Calagurris in Aquitania (the modern Saint Bertrand de Comminges in the department of Haute-Garonne), where his father kept a "statio" or inn on the great Roman road from Aquitania to Spain. While still a youth his talent became known to Sulpicius Severus, who had estates in that neighbourhood, and in 395 Sulpicius, who probably baptized him, sent him with letters to Paulinus of Nola, where he met with a friendly reception. On his return to Severus in Gaul he was ordained; and, having soon afterwards inherited means through the death of his father, he set out for Palestine, where he was received with great respect by Jerome at Bethlehem. The stay of Vigilantius lasted for some time; but, as was almost inevitable, he was dragged into the dispute then raging about Origen, in which he did not see fit wholly to adopt Jerome's attitude. On his return to the West he was the bearer of a letter from Jerome to Paulinus, and at various places where he stopped on the way he appears to have expressed himself about Jerome in a manner that when reported gave great offence to that father, and provoked him to write a reply (*Ep.*, 61). Vigilantius now settled for some time in Gaul, and is said by one authority (Gennadius) to have afterwards held a charge in the diocese of Barcelona. About 403, some years after his return from the East, Vigilantius wrote his celebrated work against superstitious practices, in which he argued against relic worship, as also against the vigils in the basilicas of the martyrs, then so common, the sending of alms to Jerusalem, and the attribution of special virtue to the unmarried state, especially in the case of the clergy. All that is known of this work is through Jerome's treatise *Contra Vigilantium*, or, as that controversialist would seem to prefer saying, "Contra Dormitantium." Notwithstanding Jerome's exceedingly unfavourable opinion, there is no reason to believe that the tract of Vigilantius was exceptionally illiterate, or that the views it advocated were different from those now held on the subjects with which it deals by most educated men outside the Roman Catholic Church, or even by many within its pale. Soon, however, the great influence of Jerome in the Western Church caused its leaders to espouse all his quarrels, and Vigilantius gradually came to be ranked in popular opinion among heretics. The year of his death is unknown.

VIGILIUS, pope from 537 to 555, succeeded Silverius and was followed by Pelagius I. He was ordained by order of Belisarius while SILVERIUS (*q.v.*) was still alive; his elevation was due to Theodora, who, by an appeal at once to his ambition and, it is said, to his covetousness, had induced him to promise to disallow the council of Chalcedon, in connexion with the "three chapters" controversy (see vol. xiii. p. 796). When, however, the time came for the fulfilment of his bargain, Vigilius declined to give his assent to the condemnation of that council involved in the imperial edict against the three chapters, and for this act of disobedience he was peremptorily summoned to Constantinople, which he reached in 547. Shortly after his arrival there he issued a document known to history as his *Judicatum* (548), in which he condemned indeed the three chapters, but expressly disavowed any intentions thereby to disparage the council of Chalcedon. After a good deal of trimming (for he desired to stand well with his own clergy, who were strongly orthodox, as well as with the court) he prepared another document, the *Constitutum ad Imperatorem*, which was laid before the so-called fifth "œcumenical" council in 553, and led to his condemnation by the heterodox majority of that body, some say, even to his banishment. Ultimately, however, he was induced to assent to and confirm the decrees of the council, and was allowed after an enforced absence of seven years to set out for Rome. He died, however, before he reached his destination, most probably in the beginning of 555.

VIGNA, PIETRO DE LA, or PETRUS DE VINEA (*c.* 1190-1249), the emperor Frederick II.'s minister, was born at Capua probably about 1190. From his own letters he would seem to have been of obscure parentage, though one of his correspondents refers to his *nobilitas*. He was perhaps educated at Bologna; but he certainly studied in a strange city and not at his own expense, though it is not till after his death that we find the story which makes him beg his bread in the streets. His name does not appear affixed to any judicial act before July 1225, at which time he was *judex magnæ curiæ*; and this continued to be his official title till April 1247, when his style was changed for that of protonotary and logothete. In 1232 he was at Rome on a mission to Gregory IX., and in 1234-35 he was in England negotiating the marriage of his master with Henry III.'s sister Isabella, after which time he seems to have kept up a friendly communication with the king, and on one occasion even begs to be reckoned "as a son and citizen of the realm." In March 1239 he was with Frederick II. at Padua when the news came of the emperor's excommunication, with reference to which he was ordered to address the people. In 1247 he was at the very height of his power and regarded as the emperor's *alter ego*. But from this height of prosperity Peter suddenly fell very early in 1249, and all kinds of stories have been invented to explain an event that puzzled his contemporaries as well as succeeding ages. He was thrown into prison and blinded, after which he was led about from place to place as a public example, "the master-councillor of the emperor, who was lord of his law and betrayed him to the pope." His death must have taken place about April 1249. There seems to be some truth in the tale that makes him die a suicide's death at Pisa. It is among the suicides that Dante meets his shade in hell.

Pietro de la Vigna's writings consist of (1) *Letters* and (2) a Latin poem on the twelve months of the year. A Latin satire directed against the Dominicans and Franciscans is also perhaps his. Besides these, many poems in the common speech are attributed to him. It is difficult to pronounce a definite opinion on his relation to the new religion or new church which it was perhaps the ambition of Frederick's most enthusiastic adherents to inaugurate. The *Letters* were first printed at Basel in 1566. See Huillard-Bréholles, *Vie et Correspondance de P. de la Vigne*, Paris, 1864.

VIGNOLA. See BAROCCHIO.

VIGNY, ALFRED DE (1799-1863), a French poet of exceptionally refined and original faculty, which was kept from voluminous production by a fastidiousness perhaps verging on affectation, was born at Loches (Indre-et-Loire) on 27th March 1799. Sainte-Beuve, in the rather ill-natured essay which he devoted to Vigny after his death, expresses a doubt whether the title of count which the poet bore was very well authenticated, and hints that no very ancient proofs of the nobility of the family were forthcoming; but it is certain that in the 18th century persons of the name occupied positions which were not open to any but men of noble birth. For generations the ancestors of Alfred de Vigny had been soldiers, and he himself joined the army at the age of sixteen. But the Revolutionary and Napoleonic wars were over, and after twelve years of life in barracks he retired, preserving, however, a very high estimate of the duties and career of the soldier. While still serving he had made his mark by the publication in 1822 of a volume of poems, and in 1826 by another, together with the famous prose romance of *Cinq-Mars*. Sainte-Beuve asserts that the poet antedated some of his most remarkable work. This may or may not be the case; he certainly did not and could not antedate the publication, and it so happens that some of his most celebrated books—*Eloa*, *Dolorida*, *Moïse*,—appeared before the work of younger members of the Romantic school whose productions strongly resemble these poems. It is quite certain that the other Alfred—Alfred de Musset—felt the influence of his elder namesake, and an impartial critic might discern no insignificant marks of the same effect in the work of Hugo himself. Even Lamartine, considerably Vigny's elder and his predecessor in poetry, seems rather to have been guided by Vigny than Vigny by him. No one can read *Dolorida* or *Le Cor* without seeing that the author had little to learn from any of his French contemporaries and much to teach them. At the same time Vigny, either from indolence, or from fastidiousness, or from being a "barren rascal," or from fear of losing the high position which he had gained, hardly attempted anything more in poetry proper during the more than thirty years of his life, and his entire poems, including posthumous fragments, form but one very small pocket volume. *Cinq-Mars*, which at least equalled the poems in popularity, will hardly stand the judgment of posterity so well. It had in its favour the support of the Royalist party, the immense vogue of the novels of Walter Scott, on which it was evidently modelled, the advantages of an exquisite style, and the taste of the day for the romance as opposed to the novel of analysis. It therefore gained a great name both in France and abroad. But any one who has read it critically must acknowledge it to be disappointing. The action is said to be dramatic; if it be so, it can only be said that this proves very conclusively that the action of drama and the action of the novel are two quite different things. To the reader who knows Scott or Dumas the story is singularly uninteresting (far less interesting than as told in history); the characters want life; and the book generally stagnates. Alfred de Vigny's admirable French and the quasi-poetical beauty of detached passages alone save it from positive dulness. Its author, though always as a kind of outsider (the phrase constantly applied to him in French literary essays and histories being that he shut himself up in a "tour d'ivoire"), attached himself more or less to the Romantic movement of 1830 and the years immediately preceding and following it, and was stimulated by this movement both to drama and to novel-writing. In the year before the revolution of July he produced at the Théâtre Français a translation or rather paraphrase of *Othello*, and an original piece, *Maréchale d'Ancre*. In 1832 he published the curious book *Stello*, and in 1835 he brought out his drama of *Chatterton*, which shocked French taste even after five years of Romantic education, by the hero's suicide, but had a considerable success. The same year saw the publication of *Servitude et Grandeur Militaires*, a singular collection of sketches rather than a connected work, in which Vigny's military experience, his idea of the soldier's duties, and his rather poetical views of history were all worked in. The subjects of *Chatterton* and *Othello* naturally suggest a certain familiarity with English, and in fact Alfred de Vigny knew English well, lived in England for some time, and married an Englishwoman. His father-in-law was, according to French gossip, so conspicuous an example of insular eccentricity that he never could remember his son-in-law's name or anything about him, except that he was a poet, by which fact and the kindness of casual Frenchmen who went through the list of the chief living poets of their country he was sometimes able to discover his daughter's husband's designation. In 1842 Alfred de Vigny was elected to the Academy, whose meetings he frequented with an assiduity rather surprising in a man of such retired habits and (still according to Sainte-Beuve) rather troublesome to his colleagues. But he produced nothing save a few scraps; and, beyond the work already enumerated, little has to be added except his *Journal d'un Poëte* and the poems called *Les Destinées*, edited, with a few fragments, by M. Louis Ratisbonne immediately after his death. Among his dramatic work, however, should be mentioned *Quitte pour la Peur* and an adaptation of the *Merchant of Venice* called *Shylock*. *Les Destinées* excited no great admiration in France, but they contain some exceedingly beautiful poetry of an austere kind, such as the magnificent speech of Nature in "La Maison du Berger" and the remarkable poem entitled "La Colère de Samson." Vigny died at Paris on 17th September 1863.

The later life of Alfred de Vigny was almost wholly uneventful, and for the most part, as has been said, spent in retirement. His reputation, however, is perfectly secure. It may, and probably will, rest only on his small volume of poems, though it will not be lessened, as far as qualified literary criticism is concerned, should the reader proceed to the rest of the work. The whole of his non-dramatic verse does not amount to 5000 lines; it may be a good deal less. But the range of subject is comparatively wide, and extraordinary felicity of execution, not merely in language, but in thought, is evident throughout. Vigny, as may be seen in the speech of Nature referred to above, had the secret,—very uncommon with French poets,—of attaining solemnity without grandiosity, by means of an almost classical precision and gravity of form. The defect of volubility, of never leaving off, which mars to some extent his great contemporary Hugo, is never present in him, and he is equally free from the looseness and disorders of form which are sometimes blemishes in Musset, and from the effeminacy of Lamartine, while once more his nobility of thought and plentifulness of matter save him from the reproach which has been thought to rest on the technically perfect work of Théophile Gautier. The dramatic work is, perhaps, less likely to interest English than French readers, the local colour of *Chatterton* being entirely false, the sentiment conventional in the extreme, and the real pathos of the story exchanged for a commonplace devotion on the poet's part to his host's wife. In the same way, the finest passages of *Othello* simply disappear in Vigny's version. In his remaining works the defect of skill in managing the plot and characters of prose fiction, which has been noticed in *Cinq-Mars*, reappears, together (in the case of the *Journal d'un Poëte* and elsewhere) with signs of the fastidious and slightly affected temper which was Vigny's chief fault as a man. In his poems proper none of these faults appear, and he is seen wholly at his best. It should be said that of his posthumous work not a little had previously appeared piecemeal in the *Revue des Deux Mondes*, to which he was an occasional contributor. The prettiest of the complete editions of his works (of which there are several) is to be found in what is called the *Petite Bibliothèque Charpentier*. (G. SA.)

VIGO, a town of Spain, in the province of Pontevedra, 486 miles by rail north-west from Madrid, is picturesquely situated on the side of a hill (Castelo) which slopes down to the southern shore of the Ria de Vigo. The Ria is the most southerly of the great fjords by which the western coast of Galicia is so deeply indented; Bayona at its mouth is 13 miles from the town of Vigo and Puente Sampayo at its head a somewhat shorter distance. Some of the former walls still remain, and there are two old castles on the hill behind the town; the older streets retain their narrow, steep, and tortuous aspect. There are some fisheries at Vigo; but the manufactures of the place are insignificant. Its activity is entirely due to its magnificent anchorage; it is a regular port of call for several international lines of steamers, and has a very important trade; the chief imports are cotton and woollen fabrics, sugar, hides, &c., while cattle, sardines, grain, and eggs are exported. The population within the municipal limits in 1877 was 13,416.

Vigo, the ancient Οὔικα (Ptolemy) or *Vicus Spacorum*, has in modern times been more than once attacked by the English,—by Drake in 1585 and 1589, and by Cobham in 1719. The Plate fleet was destroyed by the duke of Ormond and admirals Rooke and Stanhope in Vigo Bay on 22d October 1702.

VILKOMIR, or WILKOMIERZ, a district-town of Russia, in the government of Kovno, 44 miles north-east of the capital of the province, is one of the oldest cities in that part of western Russia. Founded as early as 1025, it suffered much from the attacks of the Teutonic Knights, as well as from internal wars. It flourished in the 16th century under "Magdeburg law," but soon came upon adverse times again during the wars between Poland, Russia, and Sweden. It was annexed to Russia in 1796. Its position on the principal highway from St Petersburg to Kovno gave it some trade in flax, but this is now declining. Its population increased from 7300 in 1860 to 16,240 in

1885. Vilkomir has a fine church dating from the 14th century.

VILLA DE CONTAS, a town of Brazil, in the province of Bahia, 230 miles south-west from the city of Bahia, on the Brumado (Contas-Pequeno), a head-stream of the Rio de Contas (Jussiape), which rises on the east slope of the neighbouring Serra das Almas, and flows thence to the coast at Barra do Rio Contas. This town, which has a mixed population (1880) of 10,200 whites, Negroes, half-castes, and Indians, lies in a fertile district producing much cotton, sugar, and tobacco. It was founded in 1715 by some enterprising "Paulistas," who were attracted to the district by the auriferous sands washed down by the head-streams of the Jussiape. It received the title of a town in 1724, and soon afterwards most of the inhabitants removed to the present more convenient site five miles lower down the Brumado, on the high road between Bahia and Goyaz. Villa de Contas is the capital of the department of the same name, which was detached in 1833 from the old department of Jacobina.[1]

VILLA DO RIO PARDO, a town of Brazil, in the province of Rio Grande do Sul, on the left bank of the Jacuhy at its confluence with the Pardo, about 80 miles due west from Porto Alegre, in 30° S. lat. and 52° W. long. The Jacuhy, chief affluent of the coast lagoon Dos Patos, is navigable by small steamers to this place, which is one of the most flourishing towns in the province, with a total population (1880) of 11,500, including 6000 whites, 4500 Negroes and coloured, and about 1000 civilized Indians. It had its origin in a fort built by the Portuguese at this point in 1751, but was not raised to the rank of a town till 1809. There is a large parish church founded in 1769, besides several other churches and three schools, but no noteworthy buildings. The district is fertile and well-watered, and grows an excellent flax, which supplies a number of local hand-looms. A considerable export trade is carried on by the river craft, which here ship maté (Paraguay tea), jerked meat, linen, and other products for the coast towns.

VILLANI, Giovanni (*c.* 1275-1348), Italian chronicler, was the son of Villano di Stoldo, and was born at Florence in the second half of the 13th century; the precise year is unknown. He was of good burgher extraction, and, following the traditions of his family, applied himself to commerce. During the early years of the 14th century he travelled in Italy, France, and the Netherlands, seeing men and things with the sagacity alike of the man of business and of the historian. Before leaving Florence, or rather in the interval between one journey and another, he had at least taken some part in that troubled period of civil contentions which Dino Compagni has described, and which swept Dante Alighieri into banishment. In 1301 Villani saw Charles of Valois ruining his country under the false name of peacemaker, and was witness of all the misery which immediately followed.[2] Somewhat later he left Italy, and in September 1304 he visited Flanders. It is not well ascertained when he returned to his native city. He was certainly living there shortly after the emperor Henry VII. had come to Italy in 1312, and probably he had been there for some time before. While still continuing to occupy himself with commerce, he now began to take a prominent part in public affairs. In 1316 and 1317 he was one of the priors, and shared in the crafty tactics whereby Pisa and Lucca were induced to conclude a peace with Florence, to which they were previously averse.[3] In 1317 he also had charge of the mint, and during his administration of this office he collected its earlier records and had a register made of all the coins struck in Florence up to his day. In 1321 he was again chosen prior; and, the Florentines having just then undertaken the rebuilding of the city walls, he and some other citizens were deputed to look after the work. They were afterwards accused of having diverted the public money to private ends; but Villani clearly established his innocence. He was next sent with the army against Castruccio Castracane, lord of Lucca, and was present at its defeat at Altopascio. In 1328 a terrible famine visited many provinces of Italy, including Tuscany, and Villani was appointed to guard Florence from the worst effects of that distressing period. He has left a record of what was done in a chapter of his *Chronicle*, which still remains a monument of the economic wisdom in which the mediæval Florentines were often so greatly in advance of their age.[4] In 1339, some time after the death of Castruccio, some rich Florentine merchants, and among them Villani, treated for the acquisition of Lucca by Florence for 80,000 florins, offering to supply the larger part of that sum out of their own private means; but the negotiations fell through, owing to the discords and jealousies then existing in the Government (*Chron.*, x. 143). The following year Villani superintended the making of Andrea Pisano's bronze doors of the baptistery (see vol. xix. p. 122). In the same year he watched over the raising of the campanile of the Badia, erected by Cardinal Giovanni Orsini (*Chron.*, x. 177). In 1341 the acquisition of Lucca was again under treaty, this time with Martino della Scala, for 250,000 florins. Villani was sent with others as a hostage to Ferrara, where he remained for some months (xi. 130, 133, 135). He was present in Florence during the unhappy period that elapsed between the entry of the duke of Athens and his expulsion by the Florentines (xii. 1, 2, 8, 15, 16). Involved through no fault of his own in the failure of the commercial company of the Bonaccorsi, which in its turn had been drawn into the failure of the company of the Bardi (1345), Villani towards the end of his life suffered much privation and for some time was kept in prison.[5] In 1348 he fell a victim to the plague described by Boccaccio.

The idea of writing the *Chronicle* was suggested to Villani under the following circumstances. "In the year of Christ 1300 Pope Boniface VIII. made in honour of Christ's nativity a special and great indulgence. And I, finding myself in that blessed pilgrimage in the holy city of Rome, seeing her great and ancient remains, and reading the histories and great deeds of the Romans as written by Virgil, Sallust, Lucan, Livy, Valerius, Paulus Orosius, and other masters of history who wrote the exploits and deeds, both great and small, of the Romans and also of strangers in the whole world . . . considering that our city of Florence, the daughter and offspring of Rome, is on the increase and destined to do great things, as Rome is in her decline, it appeared to me fitting to set down in this volume and new chronicle all the facts and beginnings of the city of Florence, in as far as it has been possible to me to collect and discover them, and to follow the doings of the Florentines at length . . . and so in the year 1300, on my return from Rome, I began to compile this book, in honour of God and of the blessed John, and in praise of our city of Florence."[6] Villani's work, written in Italian, makes its appearance, so to say, unexpectedly in the historical literature of Italy, just as the history of Florence, the moment it emerges from the humble and uncertain origin assigned to it by legend, rises suddenly into a rich and powerful life of thought and action. Nothing but scanty and partly legendary records had preceded Villani's work, which rests in part on them. The *Gesta Florentinorum* of Sanzanome, starting from these vague origins, begins to be more definite about 1125, at the time of the union of Fiesole with Florence. The *Chronica de Origine Civitatis* seems to be a compilation, made by various hands and at various times, in which the different legends regarding the city's origin have been gradually collected. The *Annales Florentini Primi* (1110-1173) and the *Annales Florentini Secundi* (1107-1247),

[1] Ritter, and with him nearly all other geographers, wrongly make this place still the capital of Jacobina, although Millet de Saint-Adolphe (ii. p. 404) distinctly makes the statement given in the text.

[2] See Villani, *Chronicle*, bk. viii. ch. 37, 38.

[3] *Chron.*, bk. ix. ch. 80.

[4] *Chron.*, bk. x. ch. 121.

[5] On Villani's imprisonment, see Massai's biography of Villani, mentioned below.

[6] *Chron.*, bk. viii. ch. 36.

together with a list of the consuls and podestas from 1197 to 1267, and another chronicle, formerly attributed, but apparently without good reason, to Brunetto Latini, complete the series of ancient Florentine records. To these must, however, be added a certain quantity of facts which were to be found in various manuscripts, being used and quoted by the old Florentine and Tuscan writers under the general name of *Gesta Florentinorum*. Another work which used to be reckoned among the sources of Villani is the *Chronicle of the Malespini*; but very grave doubts are now entertained as to its authenticity, and many hold that at best it is merely a remodelling, posterior to Villani's time, of old records unknown to us, from which several chroniclers may have drawn, either without citing them at all or only doing so in a vague manner. The *Cronaca Fiorentina* of Villani goes back to Biblical times and comes down to 1346. The wide universality of the narrative, especially in the times near Villani's own, while it bears witness to the author's extensive travels and to the comprehensiveness of his mind, makes one also feel that the book was inspired within the walls of the universal city. Whereas Dino Compagni's *Chronicle* is confined within definite limits of time and place, this of Villani is a general chronicle extending over the whole of Europe. Dino Compagni feels and lives in the facts of his history; Villani looks at them and relates them calmly and fairly, with a serenity which makes him seem an outsider, even when he is mixed up in them and is himself their originator. While very important for Italian history in the 14th century, this work is the cornerstone of the early mediæval history of Florence. Of contemporary events Villani has a very exact knowledge. Having been a sharer in the public affairs, and in the intellectual and economic life, of his native city, at a time when in both it had no rival in Europe, he depicts what he saw with the vividness natural to a clear mind accustomed to business and to the observation of mankind. He was Guelph, but without passion; and his book is much more taken up with an inquiry into what is useful and true than with party considerations. He is really a chronicler, not an historian, and has but little method in his narrative, often reporting the things which occurred long ago and far off just as he heard them and without criticism. Every now and then he falls into some inaccuracy; but such defects as he has are largely compensated for by his valuable qualities. He was for half a century eyewitness of his history, and provides abundant information on the constitution of Florence, its customs, industries, commerce, and arts; and among the chroniclers throughout Europe he is perhaps unequalled for the value of the statistical data he has preserved. As a writer Villani is clear and acute; and, though his prose has not the force and colouring of Compagni, it has the advantage of greater simplicity, so that taking his work as a whole he may be regarded as the greatest chronicler who has written in Italian. The many difficulties connected with the publication of this most important text have hitherto prevented the preparation of a perfect edition. The Italian Historical Institute, lately founded, has, however, undertaken to reprint on a wider scheme the great collection of Muratori.

Villani's *Chronicle* was continued by two other writers of the same name. (1) MATTEO VILLANI, his brother, of whom nothing is known save that he was twice married, and that he died of the plague in 1363, continued it down to the year of his death. Matteo's work, though inferior to Giovanni's, is nevertheless very valuable. A more prolix writer than his brother and a less acute observer, Matteo is well informed in his facts, and for the years of which he writes is one of the most important sources of Italian history. (2) FILIPPO VILLANI, the son of Matteo, flourished in the end of the 14th and the beginning of the 15th century. In his continuation, though showing greater literary ability, he is very inferior as an historian to his predecessors. His most valuable work was a collection of lives of illustrious Florentines. Twice, in 1401 and 1404, he was chosen to explain in public the *Divina Commedia* in the Florentine "studio." The year of his death is unknown.

On Giovanni Villani, as well as on Matteo and Filippo, the following books may be consulted:—Argelati, *Bibl. Mediol.* (1745); U. Balzani, *Early Chroniclers of Italy* (1883); Bellarmin-Labbé, *Script. eccl.* (1728); Brunet, *Manuel* (1864); *Classici Ital.* (1802); Fabricius, *Bibl. Med. Æv.* (1735); Gamba, *Testi Ital.* (1828); Gervinus, *Hist. Schrift.* (1833); Giovanni e Mira (Ant. di), in *Giorn. di Scienze*, xxxi; Graesse, *Trésor* (1867); Hartwig (Otto), "Giovanni Villani und die Leggenda di Messer Gianni di Procida," in Sybel, *Histor. Zeitschr.* (1871); Id., *Quellen und Forschungen zur ältesten Geschichte der Stadt Florenz* (1870); V. Le Clerc, in *Hist. Litt. France* (1862); Lorenz, *Deutsch. Geschichtsquellen* (1870); Massai (Pietro), in *Uom. Ill. Toscani* (1771); Melzi, *Anon. Ital.* (1852); Michaud, *Bibl. des Croisades* (1829); Milanesi (Gaet.), "Documenti riguardanti G. Villani e il Palazzo degli Alessi in Siena," in *Arch. Stor. Ital.* (1856); Moreni, *Bibl. Toscana* (1805); Muratori, *Rer. Ital. Script.*; Negri, *Scritt. Fiorent.* (1722); *Rev. de Paris* (1832); and Tiraboschi, *Stor. Lett. Ital.* (1807). (U. B.)

VILLARS, CLAUDE LOUIS HECTOR, DUKE OF (1653-1734), French general, was born at Moulins on 8th May 1653. After spending some time at the college of Juilly, he became a page of the *grand écurie*, and then entered the army as a volunteer. He first saw service in Holland under Louis XIV. and later under Condé, Turenne, and Luxembourg in Germany, where in 1674 he obtained the command of a troop of horse. Hostilities being brought to a close by the peace of Nimeguen in 1678, he was sent as ambassador to the courts of Vienna and Munich, in which capacity he greatly distinguished himself. In 1702 he received the command of an army in order to succour the elector of Bavaria, who had espoused the cause of France in the War of Succession. On 14th October he routed at Friedlingen Louis of Baden, the Austrian commander. In the beginning of the following year he captured Kehl and effected a junction with the army of the elector. He then conceived the daring project of marching on Vienna. The united forces defeated the Austrians under Count Styrum at Hochstädt, but his skilfully-conceived project, which had every prospect of success owing to the scattered state of the Austrian forces, had to be abandoned on account of the pusillanimous conduct of the elector. Villars was next sent to subdue the Camisards, the Protestants of the Cevennes, a task which he completed by a judicious combination of military skill and clemency. In 1705 the north-eastern frontier, which was threatened by Marlborough, was defended by Villars with such skill and ability that Marlborough was completely baffled in his attempts to penetrate into France, and even compelled to retreat. Villars took advantage of this opportunity to march into Alsace, where he captured several towns along with great quantities of war materials belonging to Marlborough and Prince Eugene. These advantages were, however, counterbalanced by Villeroy's defeat at Ramillies. After two short campaigns in 1707-8 Villars was sent (in 1709) to Flanders to oppose Marlborough and Prince Eugene. He was, however, defeated at Malplaquet and severely wounded. The weak state of his health, the consequence of his wound, prevented him during the next two years from engaging in active service. In 1712 Villars, at the head of an army raised with great difficulty by the French, defeated the Austrians under Albemarle in a brilliant action at Denain, compelled Prince Eugène to raise the siege of Landrecies, and took several fortresses and towns. This brilliant campaign raised again the almost desperate fortunes of France and led to the treaty of Utrecht (1713) and the peace of Rastadt (1714). For many years after this Villars exerted great influence at court, until he was finally supplanted by Fleury. In 1733 the war with Austria again broke out, and in the following year Villars, although over eighty years of age, was sent to take command in Italy. But after some successes he demanded his recall, either in consequence of his increasing infirmities or of disgust at the conduct of his ally, the king of Sardinia; he died on his way back to France, at Turin, on 17th June 1734.

VILLEFRANCHE DE ROUERGUE, a town of France, chef-lieu of an arrondissement in the department of Aveyron, is situated 390 miles south of Paris by the railway to Toulouse, on the right bank of the Aveyron. One of the three bridges that cross the river belongs to the 13th century, and the narrow, winding streets are full of gabled houses of the 13th and 14th centuries. The church of Notre Dame (1260-1581) has a nave and two fine rose windows of the 14th and 15th centuries. The steeple is represented by an unfinished square tower (190 feet). In the interior the stone pulpit, the rich woodwork of the choir, and tapestry of the 16th century are worthy of notice. Some parts of the Carthusian monastery, now used as a hospital, belong to the 15th and 16th centuries. The little cloister is a masterpiece of the best period of Gothic; the fine pulpit of the refectory and the Gothic architecture of some of the rooms have been preserved. Rich quarries of phosphates are worked near Villefranche

The population in 1881 was 8433 (commune 10,366), and in 1886 8092 (commune 9836).

Villefranche, founded about 1252, owes its name to the numerous immunities granted by Alphonse of Poitiers, count of Toulouse. In 1348 it was so flourishing that sumptuary laws were passed. The town fell into the hands of the Black Prince, but was the first place in Guienne to rise against the English. Charles V. granted it new privileges, which were taken away by Louis XI. In 1588 the inhabitants repulsed the League, and afterwards murdered a governor sent by Henry IV. The town was ravaged by the plague in 1463, 1558, and 1628. A revolt excited by the exactions of the intendants was cruelly repressed in 1643. Villefranche was the birthplace of Marshal de Belle-Isle.

VILLEFRANCHE-SUR-SAÔNE, a commercial and manufacturing town of France, chef-lieu of an arrondissement in the department of Rhone, is situated on the Morgon, near its junction with the Saône, 18 miles by rail nearly north of Lyons. The chief industrial establishments are factories of coarse woven goods, cotton, fustian, "molletons," prints, and blankets, tan-yards, puddling-works, spinning-mills, distilleries, foundries, and a saw-mill. The wines of Beaujolais, hemp, cloth, linen, cottons, drapery goods, and cattle are the principal articles of trade. An old Renaissance house is used as the town-hall. The church of Notre Dame des Marais, begun at the end of the 14th and finished in the 16th century, has a tower and spire (rebuilt in 1862), standing to the right of the façade (15th century), in which are carved wooden doors. Villefranche is the seat of the primary normal school of the department. The population, 12,032 (commune 13,074) in 1881, was 12,157 (commune 12,518) in 1886.

The town grew up near a tower from which the lords of Beaujeu enforced their rights of toll on the Burgundy and Lyons road. The name arose out of privileges granted by Guichard I. of Beaujeu, which were confirmed and extended by his successors. Under the dukes of Burgundy Villefranche was the capital of Beaujolais, and retained some of its privileges when united to France. Baron des Adrets sacked the town and demolished the ramparts in 1562. A well-known academy was founded here in 1695.

VILLEHARDOUIN, Geoffroy de (c. 1160–c. 1213), the first vernacular historian of France, and perhaps of modern Europe, who possesses literary merit is rather supposed than known to have been born at the château from which he took his name, near Troyes in Champagne, about the year 1160. Not merely his literary and historical importance, but almost all that is known about him comes from his chronicle of the fifth crusade, or *Conquête de Constantinople.* Nothing is positively known of his ancestry, for the supposition (originating with Du Cange) that a certain William, marshal of Champagne between 1163 and 1179, was his father appears to be erroneous. Villehardouin himself, however, undoubtedly held this dignity, and certain minute and perhaps not very trustworthy indications, chiefly of an heraldic character, have led his most recent biographers to lay it down that he was not born earlier than 1150 or later than 1164. He introduces himself to us with a certain abruptness, merely specifying his own name as one of a list of knights of Champagne who with their count, Thibault, took the cross at a tournament held at Escry-sur-Aisne at Advent 1199, the crusade in contemplation having been started by the preaching of Fulk de Neuilly, who was commissioned thereto by Pope Innocent III. The next year six deputies, two appointed by each of the three allied counts of Flanders, Champagne, and Blois, were despatched to Venice to negotiate for ships. Of these deputies Villehardouin was one and Quesnes de Béthune, the poet, another. They concluded a bargain with the seigniory for transport and provisions at a fixed price. Villehardouin had hardly returned when Thibault fell sick and died; but this did not prevent, though it somewhat delayed, the enterprise of the crusaders. The management of that enterprise, however, was a difficult one, and cost Villehardouin another embassy into Italy to prevent if possible some of his fellow-pilgrims from breaking the treaty with the Venetians by embarking at other ports and employing other convoy. He was only in part successful, and there was great difficulty in raising the charter-money among those who had actually assembled (in 1202) at Venice, the sum collected falling far short of the stipulated amount. It is necessary to remember this when the somewhat erratic and irregular character of the operations which followed is judged. The defence that the crusaders were bound to pay their passage-money to the Holy Land in one form or other to the Venetians is perhaps a weak one in any case for the attack on two Christian cities, Zara and Constantinople; it becomes weaker still when it is found that the expedition never went or attempted to go to the Holy Land at all. But the desire to discharge obligations incurred is no doubt respectable in itself, and Villehardouin, as one of the actual negotiators of the bargain, must have felt it with peculiar strength.

The crusaders set sail at last, and Zara, which the Venetians coveted, was taken without much trouble. The question then arose whither the host should go next. Villehardouin does not tell us of any direct part taken by himself in the debates on the question of interfering or not in the disputed succession to the empire of the East,—debates in which the chief ecclesiastics present strongly protested against the diversion of the enterprise from its proper goal. It is quite clear, however, that the marshal of Champagne, who was one of the leaders and inner counsellors of the expedition throughout, sympathized with the majority, and it is fair to point out that the temptation of chivalrous adventure was probably as great as that of gain. He narrates spiritedly enough the dissensions and discussions in the winter camp of Zara and at Corfu, but is evidently much more at ease when the voyage was again resumed, and, after a fair passage round Greece, the crusaders at last saw before them the great city of Constantinople which they had it in mind to attack. When the assault was decided upon, Villehardouin himself was in the fifth "battle," the leader of which was Mathieu de Montmorency. But, though his account of the siege is full of personal touches, and contains one reference to the number of witnesses whose testimony he took for a certain wonderful fact, he does not tell us anything of his own prowess. After the flight of the usurper Alexius, and when Isaac, whose claims the crusaders were defending, had been taken by the Greeks from prison and placed on the throne, Villehardouin, with Montmorency and two Venetians, formed the embassy sent to arrange terms. He was again similarly distinguished when it became necessary to remonstrate with Alexius, the blind man's son and virtual successor, on the non-keeping of the terms. Indeed Villehardouin's talents as a diplomatist seem to have been held in very high esteem, for later, when the Latin empire had become a fact, he was charged with the delicate business of mediating between the emperor Baldwin and Boniface, marquis of Montferrat, in which task he had at least partial success. He was also appointed marshal of "Romanie"—a term very vaguely used, but apparently signifying the mainland of the Balkan Peninsula, while his nephew and namesake, afterwards prince of Achaia, took a great part in the Latin conquest of Peloponnesus. Villehardouin himself before long received an important command against the Bulgarians. He was left to maintain the siege of Adrianople when Baldwin advanced to attack the relieving force, and with Dandolo had much to do in saving the defeated crusaders from utter destruction, and conducting the retreat, in which he commanded the rear-guard, and brought his troops in safety to the sea at Rodosto, and thence to the capital. As he occupied the post of honour in this disaster, so he had that (the command of the vanguard) in the expedition which the regent Henry made shortly afterwards to revenge his brother Baldwin's defeat and capture. And, when Henry had succeeded to the crown on the announcement of Baldwin's death, it was Villehardouin who fetched home his bride Agnes of Montferrat, and shortly afterwards commanded under him in a naval battle with the ships of Theodore Lascaris at the fortress of Cibotus. In the settlement of the Latin empire after the truce with Lascaris Villehardouin received the fief of Messinople (supposed to be Mosynopolis, a little inland from the modern Gulf of Lagos, and not far from the ancient Abdera) from Boniface of Montferrat, with the record of whose death the chronicle abruptly closes.

In the foregoing account only those particulars which bear directly on Villehardouin himself have been detailed; but the chronicle is as far as possible from being an autobiography, and the displays of the writer's personality, numerous as they are, are quite involuntary, and consist merely in his way of handling the subject, not in the references, as brief as his functions as chronicler will admit, to his own proceedings. The chronicle of Villehardouin is justly held to be the very best presentation we possess of the spirit of chivalry, not the designedly exalted and poetized chivalry of the romances, not the self-conscious and deliberate chivalry of the 14th century, but the unsophisticated mode of thinking and acting which brought about the crusades, stimulated the vast literary development of the 12th and 13th centuries, and sent knights-errant, principally though not wholly of French blood, to establish principalities and kingdoms throughout Europe and the nearer East. On the whole, no doubt, it is the more masculine and practical side of this enthusiastic state of mind which Villehardouin shows. No woman makes any but the briefest appearance in his pages, though in reference to this it must of course be remembered that he was certainly a man past middle life when the events occurred, and perhaps a man approaching old age when he set them down. Despite the strong and graphic touches here and there, exhibiting the impression which the beauty of sea and land, the splendour of Constantinople, the magnitude of the effete but still imposing Greek power made on him, there is not only an entire absence of dilation on such subjects as a modern would have dilated on (that was to be expected), but an absence likewise of the elaborate and painful description of detail in which contemporary *trouvères* would have indulged. It is curious, for instance, to compare the scanty references to the material marvels of Constantinople which Villehardouin saw in their glory, which perished by sack and fire under his very eyes, and which live chiefly in the melancholy pages of his Greek contemporary Nicetas, with the elaborate descriptions of the scarcely greater wonders of fabulous courts at Constantinople itself, at Babylon, and elsewhere to be found in his other contemporaries, the later *chanson de geste* writers and the earlier embroiderers of the Arthurian romances and *romans d'aventures*. And this latter contrast is all the more striking that Villehardouin agrees with, and not impossibly borrows from, these very writers in many points of style and phraseology. The brief chapters of his work have been justly compared to the *laisses* or *tirades* of a chanson in what may be called the vignetting of the subject of each, in the absence of any attempt to run on the narrative in the precise forms, and in poetical rather than prosaic word-order of the sentences. Undoubtedly this half-poetic style (animated as it is and redeemed from any charge of bastardy by the freshness and vigour which pervade it) adds not a little to the charm of the book. Its succession of word pictures, conventional and yet vigorous as the illuminations of a mediæval manuscript, and in their very conventionality free from all thought of literary presentation, must charm all readers. The sober lists of names with which it opens; the account of the embassy, so business-like in its estimates of costs and terms, and suddenly breaking into a fervent description of how the six deputies, "prostrating themselves on the earth and weeping warm tears, begged the doge and people of Venice to have pity on Jerusalem;" the story immediately following how the young count Thibault of Champagne, raising himself from a sickbed in his joy at the successful return of his ambassadors, "leva sus et chevaucha, et laz! com grant domages, car onques puis ne chevaucha que cele foiz," compose a most striking overture. Then the history relapses into the business vein and tells of the debates which took place as to the best means of carrying out the vow after the count's decease, the rendezvous, too ill kept at Venice, the plausible suggestion of the Venetians that the balance due to them should be made up by a joint attack on their enemy, the king of Hungary. Villehardouin does not in the least conceal the fact that the pope ("l'apostoilles de Rome," as he calls him in the very phrase of the chansons) was very angry with this; for his own part he seems to think of little or nothing but the reparation due to the republic, which had loyally kept its bargain and been defrauded of the price, of the infamy of breaking company on the part of members of a joint association, and perhaps of the unknightliness of not taking up an adventure whenever it presents itself. For here again the restoration of the disinherited prince of Constantinople supplied an excuse quite as plausible as the liquidation of the debt to Venice. A famous passage and one short enough to quote is that describing the old blind doge Dandolo, who had "Grant ochoison de remanoir (reason for staying at home), car viels hom ere, et si avoit les yaulx en la teste biaus et n'en veoit gote (goutte)," and yet was the foremost in fight.

It would be out of place to attempt any further analysis of the *Conquête* here. But it is not impertinent, and is at the same time an excuse for what has been already said, to repeat that Villehardouin's book, brief as it is, is in reality one of the capital books of literature, not merely for its merit, but because it is the most authentic and the most striking embodiment in contemporary literature of the sentiments which determined the action of a great and important period of history. There are but very few books which hold this position, and Villehardouin's is one of them. If every other contemporary record of the crusades perished, we should still be able by aid of this to understand and realize what the mental attitude of crusaders, of Teutonic knights, and the rest was, and without this we should lack the earliest, the most undoubtedly genuine, and the most characteristic of all such records. The very inconsistency with which Villehardouin is chargeable, the absence of compunction with which he relates the changing of a sacred religious pilgrimage into something by no means unlike a mere filibustering raid on the great scale, add a charm to the book. For, religious as it is, it is entirely free from the very slightest touch of hypocrisy or indeed of self-consciousness of any kind. The famous description of the crusades, *gesta Dei per Francos*, was evidently to Villehardouin a plain matter-of-fact description, and it no more occurred to him to doubt the divine favour being extended to the expeditions against Alexius or Theodore than to doubt that it was shown to expeditions against Saracens and Turks.

The person of Villehardouin reappears for us once, but once only, in the chronicle of his continuator, Henri de Valenciennes. There is a great gap in style, though none in subject, between the really poetical prose of the first historian of the fifth crusade and the Latin empire and the awkward mannerism (so awkward that it has been taken to represent a "disrhymed" verse chronicle) of his follower. But the much greater length at which Villehardouin appears on this one occasion shows us the restraint which he must have exercised in the passages which deal with himself in his own work. He again led the vanguard in the emperor Henry's expedition against Burilas the Bulgarian, and he is represented by the Valenciennes scribe as encouraging his sovereign to the attack in a long speech. Then he disappears altogether, with the exception of some brief and chiefly diplomatic mentions. Du Cange discovered and quoted a deed of donation by him dated 1207, by which certain properties were devised to the churches of Notre Dame de Foissy and Notre Dame de Troyes, with the reservation of life interests to his daughters Alix and Damerones, and his sisters Emmeline and Haye, all of whom appear to have embraced a monastic life. A letter addressed from the East to Blanche of Champagne is cited, and a papal record of 1212 styles him still "marshal of Romania." The next year this title passed to his son Erard; and 1213 is accordingly given as the date of his death, which, as there is no record or hint of his having returned to France, may be supposed to have happened at Messinople, where also he must have written the *Conquête*.

The book appears to have been known in the ages immediately succeeding his own; and, though there is no contemporary manuscript in existence, there are some half dozen which appear to date from the end of the 13th or the course of the 14th century, while one at least appears to be a copy made from his own work in that spirit of unintelligent faithfulness which is much more valuable to posterity than more intelligent editing. The first printed edition of the book, by a certain Blaise de Vigenère, dates from 1585, is dedicated to the seigniory of Venice (Villehardouin, it should be said, has been accused of a rather unfair predilection for the Venetians), and speaks of either a part or the whole of the memoirs as having been printed twelve years earlier. Of this earlier copy nothing seems to be known. A better edition, founded on a Netherlandish MS., appeared at Lyons in 1601. But both these were completely antiquated by the great edition of Du Cange in 1657, wherein that learned writer employed all his knowledge, never since equalled, of the subject, but added a translation, or rather paraphrase, into modern French which is scarcely worthy either of himself or his author. Dom Brial gave a new edition from different MS. sources in 1823, and the book figures with different degrees of dependence on Du Cange and Brial in the collections of Petitot, Buchon, and Michaud and Poujoulat. All these, however, have been superseded for the modern student by the editions of M. Natalis de Wailly (1872 and 1874), in which the text is critically edited from all the available MSS. and a new translation added. The charm of Villehardouin can escape no reader; but few readers will fail to derive some additional pleasure from the two essays which Sainte-Beuve devoted to him thirty years ago, and which may be found reprinted in the ninth volume of the *Causeries du Lundi*. (G. SA.)

VILLEINAGE. See COPYHOLD and SLAVERY.

VILLEMAIN, ABEL FRANÇOIS (1790-1867), historian of French literature, was born at Paris on 11th June 1790. He was educated at the lycée Louis-le-Grand, and was only twenty when he was appointed to an assistant-mastership at the lycée Charlemagne. This appointment was shortly exchanged for a post at the École Normale. He early devoted himself to the composition of the Academic prize essays which have founded the fortune of so many French men of letters, and in 1812 he gained the prize with an *éloge* on Montaigne, which was followed by other successful attempts. His second successful essay, *On Criticism*, had the honour of being read by the author before the Academy and the allied sovereigns who were then (April 1814) in Paris. Under the restoration he was appointed, first, assistant professor of modern history and then professor of French eloquence at the Sorbonne. Here he began and continued for about ten years a series of literary lectures which had an extraordinary effect on his younger contemporaries. The secret indeed of Villemain's great popularity and immense influence is only to be understood by exact observation of the time at which he came. He had no very extraordinary gift of style, nor was he a very original thinker. But he had the great advantage of coming just before the Romantic movement, of having a wide and catholic love of literature, and, at the same time, of not being an extremist. All, or almost all, the clever young men of the brilliant generation of 1830 passed under his influence; and, while he enchanted those of Romantic tendency by his constant reference to, and his frank appreciation of, the beauties of English, German, Italian, and Spanish poetry, he had not the least inclination to decry the classics —either the classics proper of Greece and Rome or the so-called classics of France. In 1819 he published a book on *Cromwell*, remarkable for a Frenchman of his day, and two years later he was elected to the Academy. The time was more favourable than any previous time had been to literary men with political inclinations, and Villemain was appointed by the restoration Government "chef de l'imprimerie et de la librairie," a post involving a kind of irregular censorship of the press, and afterwards to the office of master of requests. Like others, however, Villemain became more and more Liberal, and before the revolution of July he had been deprived of his office and had been elected deputy for Evreux. This secured his fortune under Louis Philippe's reign, and, though he did not long sit in the lower chamber, he received a peerage in 1832. He was a very important member of the council of public instruction, and was twice minister of that department, while at the same time with his elevation to the upper chamber he was made secretary of the Academy. This combination made him during the whole of the July monarchy one of the chief dispensers of literary patronage in France; and, though he never drew on himself the personal ill-will which his friend and colleague Cousin attracted, it was almost inevitable that he should displease many for every one that he gratified. Villemain's literary position had moreover been somewhat left behind by the course of events, and in politics he was something of a doctrinaire. For more than the last twenty years of his life he took no open part in public affairs, though his literary activity continued to be considerable, the books which he published being in part workings-up of his brilliant Sorbonne courses. Although he still retained a great name and an important Academic position, his later years are supposed to have been somewhat saddened by the difference of his employments and consideration, as compared with those of his middle age. Villemain, in fact, was a man who had at one time, chiefly by accident and coincidence, acquired a position to which he was not quite equal. Some reflexions on him in the "Notes et Pensées" to be found in Sainte-Beuve's *Causeries du Lundi*, vol. xi., are, as is too often the case in that collection when it refers to contemporaries, harsh. But it is certain that he had little originality of thought or definiteness of literary theory, that he was rather a clever exponent of ideas which happened to be popular than a convinced reasoner, and that he had an undue admiration of success. His death took place at Paris on 8th May 1867.

Villemain's chief work is his *Cours de la Littérature Française*, in 6 volumes, printed soon after he ceased lecturing, and reprinted long afterwards in 1864. It is a very discursive book, containing literary judgments on all sorts of subjects, and illustrating very well the fashion in which Villemain satisfied and stimulated a generation which had just become aware that literature was not limited to the productions of the men of the *grand siècle*. Almost all his later works, which are numerous, consist of collections of Academic *éloges*, lectures, and literary and historical essays. As, however, he began with a substantive historical work so did he end with one, the posthumous *History of Gregory VII.*, on which he had been known to be engaged for many years, and the long delay of which had been the cause of not a few sarcasms. Although a book of merit, it will hardly supplant Villemain's early Academic lectures as his title to remembrance and fame—such fame as is due to a teacher who succeeds in stirring up the literary faculties of men more highly gifted than himself.

VILLENA, a town of Spain, in the province of Alicante, is situated 37 miles by rail to the north-west of that town, on the right bank of the little river Vinalapo. It has narrow winding streets, and is crowned by a picturesque-looking old castle. The slopes of the surrounding hills are clothed with vines, and there are also some extensive salt lagoons. The annual fair of Villena (29th Sept.–5th Oct.), dealing in the produce of the neighbourhood, is still of considerable importance. The industries (soap-making, weaving, distilling) are not extensive. The population within the municipal boundaries in 1877 was 11,424.

VILLENEUVE-SUR-LOT, a town of France, chef-lieu of an arrondissement in the department of Lot-et-Garonne, is built on both sides of the river Lot, 22 miles north of Agen by a line which branches at Penne from the Agen and Périgueux Railway. Large portions of the 13th-century ramparts, altered and surmounted by machicolations in the 15th century, still remain, and high square towers rise above the gates to the north-east and south-west. The principal arch of the bridge (13th century) has a span of 118 feet and is 59 feet in height, and was built in the reign of Louis XIII. Arcades of the 13th century surround a square. Important markets of cattle, horses, wines, and Agen plums (£120,000 worth exported annually) are held. Boots and shoes, sausages, tinned foods, and buttons are made, and there are marble works and large mills. The population in 1881 was 9520 (commune 14,560) and in 1886 9780 (commune 14,693). Of these 1102 were prisoners at Eysses.

Villeneuve originated in a fortress built in 1264 as a refuge for the inhabitants of Pujols, whose town had been destroyed in the Albigensian War. The English held it from 1279 to 1337, and again in the 15th century. Less than a mile from Villeneuve the former abbey of Eysses, founded about the 7th century, stands on the site of the Roman town of Excisum. It is now used as a central prison, and accommodates about 1200 prisoners. On the left bank of the Lot, 2 miles south of Villeneuve, are the 13th-century walls of Pujols.

VILLIERS, George. See Buckingham, Duke of.

VILLON, Francis (1431-1461?), whose real surname is a matter of much dispute, so that he is also called Corbueil, Corbier, De Montcorbier, and Des Loges, though in literature Villon is the sole term used, was born in 1431, and, as it seems, certainly at Paris. The mixture of the real and the ironical in the singular poems called *Testaments*, which form his chief, if not his only certain, work, make it very unsafe to speak positively as to such details of his life as depend upon them. Yet the *Testaments*, with some extant documents, are the only trustworthy information that we have, the legends and anecdotes which are told respecting him being for the most part of the most dubious, if not the most certainly apocryphal, character. It appears that he was born of poor folk, that his father died in his youth, but that his mother was alive when her son was thirty years old. The very name Villon was stated, and that by no mean authority, the president Claude Fauchet, to be merely a common and not a proper noun, signifying "cheat" or "rascal"; but this seems to be a mistake. It is, however, certain that Villon was a person of loose life, and that he continued, long after there was any excuse for it in his years, the reckless way of living common among the wilder youth of the university of Paris. He appears to have derived his surname from a friend and benefactor named Guillaume de Villon, an ecclesiastic and a person of some property and position. The poet, either by his assistance or in some other way, became a student, and took the degree of bachelor in 1450 and that of master in 1452. Between this year and 1455 nothing positive is known of him, except that nothing was known against him.

On 4th June 1455 the first important incident of his life that is known occurred. Being in the company of a priest named Giles and a girl named Isabeau, he met a certain Breton, a master of arts, who was also in the company of a priest, Philippe Chermoye or Sermoise or Sermaise. A scuffle ensued; daggers were drawn; and Sermaise, who is accused of having attacked Villon and drawn the first blood, not only received a dagger thrust in return, but a blow from a stone which struck him down. Sermaise died of his wounds. Villon fled, and was sentenced to banishment,—a sentence which was remitted in January 1456, the formal pardon being extant strangely enough in two different documents, in one of which the culprit is described as "François des Loges, autrement dit Villon," in the other as "François de Montcorbier." That he is also said to have described himself to the barber-surgeon who dressed his own wounds as Michael Piton is less surprising, and hardly needs an addition to the list of his aliases. It should, however, be said that the documents relative to this affair confirm the date of his birth, by representing him as twenty-six years old or thereabouts. A year later he was again in trouble. In his first broil "la femme Isabeau" is only generally named, and it is impossible to say whether she had anything to do with the quarrel. In the second, Catherine de Vaucelles, of whom we hear not a little in the poems, is the declared cause of a scuffle in which Villon was so severely beaten that to escape ridicule he fled to Angers, where he had an uncle who was a monk. It was before leaving Paris that he composed what is now known as the *Petit Testament*, of which we shall speak presently, with the rest of his poems, and which, it should be said, shows little or no such mark of profound bitterness and regret for wasted life as its in every sense greater successor the *Grand Testament*. Indeed Villon's serious troubles were only beginning, for hitherto he had been rather injured than guilty. He left Paris for Angers in the very early spring of 1456-57, and shortly afterwards (in March) the chapel of the College of Navarre was broken open and five hundred gold crowns stolen. The inquiries set on foot discovered a gang of student robbers, one of whom, Guy Tabarie, turned king's evidence and accused Villon, who was then absent, of being the ringleader, and of having gone to Angers, partly at least, to arrange for similar burglaries there. Other crimes were confessed by the accomplice, and Villon was arrested, put to the torture, and condemned to be hanged,—a penalty which was actually inflicted later on two of his gang, and which he commemorated by anticipation in one of the most famous and remarkable of his poems, the sombre "Ballade des Pendus." He escaped Montfaucon, however, by appealing from the bishop's court, where as a clerk he had been tried, to the parlement of Paris, by which body his sentence was commuted to banishment—that is, of course, banishment from the capital. Where he went and what he did for the next four years we do not know. It is certain that at one time, and probable that at more times than one, he was in correspondence with Charles d'Orléans, and it is likely that he resided, at any rate for some period, at that prince's court at Blois. He had also something to do with another prince of the blood, Jean of Bourbon, and traces are found of him in Poitou, in Dauphiné, &c. But at his next certain appearance he is again in trouble. He tells us that he had spent the summer of 1461 in the bishop's prison (bishops were fatal to Villon) of Meung. His crime is not known; but his enemy, or at least judge, was Thibault d'Aussigny, who held the see of Orleans. Villon owed his release to a general jail delivery at the accession of Louis XI., and became a free man again on 2d October.

It was now that he wrote the *Grand Testament*, and this, the work which has immortalized him, is the last certain fact which is known of his life. If one could judge from a vague kind of internal evidence, it would seem likely that it is really a testament, and that the poet died soon afterwards. Although he was only thirty at the date of this composition (which is unmistakable, because given in the book itself), there seems to be no kind of aspiration towards a new life, nor even any hankering after the old. Nothing appears to be left him but regret; his very spirit has been worn out by excesses or sufferings or both. But, however this may be, he disappears from history. Rabelais indeed tells two stories about him which have almost necessarily been dated later. One is a countryside anecdote of a trick supposed to have been played by the poet in his old age at Saint Maixent in Poitou, whither he had retired. The other, a coarse but pointed jest at the expense of England, is told as having been addressed by Villon to King Edward V. during an exile in that country. Now, even if King Edward V. were not evidently out of the question, a passage of the story refers to the well-known scholar and man of science, Thomas Linacre, as court physician to the king, and makes Villon mention him, whereas Linacre was only a young scholar, not merely at the time of Edward V.'s supposed murder, but at the extreme date (1489) which can be assigned to Villon's life. For in this year the first edition of the poet's work appeared, obviously not published by himself, and with no sign in it of his having lived later than the date (1461) of the *Grand Testament*. It would be easy to dismiss these Rabelaisian mentions of Villon as mere humorous inventions, if it were not that the author of *Pantagruel* was born quite soon enough to have actually seen Villon if he had lived to anything that could be called old age, that he almost certainly must have known men who had known Villon, and that the poet undoubtedly spent much time in Rabelais's own country on the banks of the lower Loire.

The obscurity, the unhappiness, and the evil repute of Villon's life would not be in themselves a reason for the minute investigation to which the events of that life have been subjected, and the result of which has been summed up here. But his poetical work, scanty as the certainly genuine part of it is, is of such extraordinary interest, and marks such an epoch in the history of European literature, that he has been at all times an interesting figure, and, like all very interesting figures, has been often praised for qualities quite other than those which he really possessed. Boileau's famous verses, in which Villon is extolled for having first known how to smooth out the confused art of the old romancers, are indeed a prodigy of blundering or ignorance or both. As far as art, or the technical part of poetry goes, Villon made not the slightest advance on his predecessors, nor stood in any way in front of such contemporaries as his patron Charles d'Orléans. His two *Testaments* (so called by the application to them of a regular class-name of mediæval poetry) consist of eight-line stanzas of eight-syllabled verses, varied in the case of the *Grand Testament* by the insertion of ballades and rondeaux of very great beauty and interest, but not formally different in any way from poems of the same kind for more than a century past. What really distinguishes Villon is the intenser quality of his poetical feeling and expression, and what is perhaps arrogantly called the modern character of his subjects and thought. Mediæval poetry, with rare exceptions, and, with exceptions not quite so rare, classical poetry, are distinguished by their lack of what is now called the personal note. In Villon this note sounds, struck with singular force and skill. Again, the simple joy of living which distinguishes both periods—the mediæval, despite a common opinion, scarcely less than the ancient—has disappeared. Even the riot and rollicking of his earlier days are mentioned with far less relish of remembrance than sense of their vanity. This sense of vanity, indeed, not of the merely religious, but of the purely mundane and even half pagan kind, is Villon's most prominent characteristic. It tinges his narrative, despite its burlesque bequests, all through; it is the very keynote of his most famous and beautiful piece, the "Ballade des Dames du Temps Jadis," with its refrain "Mais où sont les neiges d'antan?" as well as of his most daring piece of realism, the other ballade of "La Grosse Margot," with its burden of hopeless entanglement in shameless vice. It is nowhere more clearly sounded than in the piece which ranks with these two at the head of his work, the "Regrets de la Belle Heaulmière," in which a woman, once young and beautiful, now old and withered, laments her lost charms. So it is almost throughout his poems, including the grim "Ballade des Pendus," and hardly excluding the very beautiful "Ballade pour sa Mère," with its description of sincere and humble piety. It is in the profound melancholy which the dominance of this note has thrown over Villon's work, and in the suitableness of that melancholy to the temper of all generations since, that his charm and power have consisted, though it is difficult to conceive any time at which his poetical merit could be ignored.

His certainly genuine poems consist of the two *Testaments* with their codicil (the latter containing the "Ballade des Pendus," or more properly "Epitaphe en Forme de Ballade," and some other pieces of a similarly grim humour), a few miscellaneous poems, chiefly ballades, and an extraordinary collection (called *Le Jargon*) of poems in *argot*, the greater part of which is now totally unintelligible, if, which may perhaps be doubted, it ever was otherwise. Besides these, certain poems of no inconsiderable interest are usually printed with Villon's works, though they are certainly, or almost certainly, not his. The chief are "Les Repues Franches," a curious series of verse stories of cheating tavern-keepers, &c., having some resemblance to those told of George Peele, but of a broader and coarser humour. These are beyond doubt, if not the poet's work, nearly contemporary with him, and may have some foundation in fact. Another of these spurious pieces is the extremely amusing monologue of the "Franc Archier de Bagnolet," in which one of the newly constituted archers or regularly trained and paid soldiery, who were extremely unpopular in France, is made to expose his own poltroonery. The third most important piece of this kind is the "Dialogue de Mallepaye et de Baillevent," a dramatic conversation between two penniless spendthrifts, which is not without merit. These poems, however, were never attributed to Villon or printed with his works till far into the 16th century.

It has been said that the first dated edition of Villon is of 1489, though some have held one or more than one undated copy to be still earlier. Between the first, whenever it was, and 1542 there were no less than twenty seven editions, the most famous being that of Clément Marot in 1533, one of whose most honourable distinctions is the care he took of his poetical predecessors. The Pléiade movement and the classicizing of the *grand siècle* put Villon rather out of favour, and he was not again reprinted till early in the 18th century, when he attracted the attention of students of old French like Duchat, La Monnoye, and Prosper Marchand. The first critical edition in the modern sense—that is to say, an edition founded on MSS. (of which there are in Villon's case several, chiefly at Paris and Stockholm)—was that of the Abbé Prompsault in 1832. The next and on the whole the most important was that of the bibliophile Jacob (P. Lacroix) in the Bibliothèque Elzevirienne (Paris, 1854). Since then Villon has been frequently reprinted, very great interest having been shown in him; but not much has been done to the text till the recent and uncompleted labours of a Dutch scholar, Dr Bijvanck, who is occupied especially on the Stockholm MS. On the other hand, from the literary and biographical view, Villon has been exhaustively studied of late, especially by MM. Campaux, Vitu, and Longnon, the researches of the last-named (Paris, 1877) having probably ascertained everything that there is to know. In England, too, attempts have been made to translate his work, especially by the late D. G. Rossetti, by Mr Swinburne, and by Mr Andrew Lang, while a complete translation has been produced by Mr John Payne. (G. SA.)

VILNA, or WILNO, a Lithuanian government of west Russia, has the Polish province of Suwałki on the W., Kovno and Vitebsk on the N. and E., and Minsk and Grodno on the E. and S. Its area is 16,421 square miles. Vilna lies on the broad marshy swelling, dotted with lakes, which separates POLAND (*q.v.*) from East Prussia and stretches east-north-east towards the Valdai Plateau. Its highest parts are a little more than 1000 feet above sea-level. On its western and eastern boundaries Vilna is deeply trenched by the valleys of the Niemen and the Dwina. Devonian limestones crop out in the north-east. Elsewhere they are concealed by the marine and freshwater limestones and sandstones of the Eocene period, which cover nearly the whole of Vilna; and these in their turn are overlain by thick layers of boulder clay, sands, and lacustrine deposits. The soil is for the most part clayey or sandy, fertile loam appearing only in the depression watered by the Vilia. Numerous lakes and marshes, partly covered with forests, and scarcely passable except when frozen, as well as wet meadow-land, occupy a large area in the central parts of Vilna. The Niemen, which flows along the southern and western borders for more than 200 miles, is the chief artery of trade for the government, and its importance in this respect is enhanced by its tributary the Vilia, which flows west for more than 200 miles through the central parts of Vilna, receiving many affluents on its course. Among the tributaries of the Niemen is the Berezina, which acquired renown during Napoleon's retreat in 1812; it flows in a marshy valley in the south-east. The Dwina for 50 miles of its course separates Vilna from Vitebsk. The combined traffic on the Niemen and the Dwina was valued at nearly £200,000 in 1883. The climate of the government is only slightly tempered by its proximity to the Baltic Sea (January 21°·8 Fahr.; July 64°·5); the average temperature at the town of Vilna is only 43°·5. But in winter the thermometer descends very low, the minimum observed during the last sixty years being − 30°. The flora and fauna are intermediate between those of Poland and middle Russia. The population of Vilna, which amounted to 1,223,260 in 1883, consists chiefly of Lithuanians (35 per cent.) in the west and north and White Russians (45 per cent.) in the south and east. Jews make up 11 per cent. of the population; and the Poles, who constitute the landed aristocracy and the artisan classes of the towns, reach 7 per cent. A few Great Russians and Tatars, descendants of Crimean prisoners, must be added to the above. Roman Catholicism is the prevailing creed among the Lithuanians and Poles; and the White Russians belong for the most part to the Greek and Nonconformist Churches.

In spite of the unfertile soil, sufficient cereals are grown for the needs of the population and to supply the distilleries. The average crops of 1882-1885 were 1,010,000 quarters of rye, 44,000 of wheat, 790,000 of various kinds of grain, and 9,840,000 bushels of potatoes. Apart from finer breeds kept by a few landowners, the cattle of the peasantry belong to inferior varieties. In 1883 there were 203,620 horses, 303,100 horned cattle, 277,800 sheep, and 238,800 pigs. More than one-third of the area is covered with forests, whence a considerable quantity of timber is exported, partly to Germany, for shipbuilding. A variety of petty trades are carried on in the villages of the forest region,—sledges, cars, wheels, and wooden ware being made by the peasants. Tar, pitch, and potash are exported. The manufactures have only begun to develop of late. In 1884 there were 300 establishments employing 3020 men, and giving an annual output valued at £885,100 (as against £200,000 in 1860). An active trade in timber, corn, and flax (exported) and in manufactured goods (imported) is carried on. Vilna is divided into seven districts, the chief towns of which (with their populations in 1883) are—Vilna (see below), Vileika (3905), Disna (8030), Lidy or Lida (7940), Oshmiany (4470), Svienciany (8510), and Troki (2440).

VILNA, or WILNO, capital of the above government, is situated 436 miles to the south-west of St Petersburg, at the junction of the Vilia with the Vileika, and at the intersection of two great railway lines, one from St Petersburg to Warsaw, the other from Libau to the mouth of the Don. It is an old town, rich in historical associations. Its imperial palace, and the cathedral of St Stanislaus, containing the silver sarcophagus of St Casimir, are fine buildings. The (Greek) cathedral of the Holy Virgin contains the remains of Prince Olgerd (baptized in 1377) and his family. The museum of antiquities has valuable historical collections of the region. The ancient castle of the Jagellones is now a mass of ruins. The old university, founded in 1576, was restored by Alexander I., but has been closed since 1832 for political reasons; the only departments which remain in activity are the astronomical observatory and a medical academy. The scientific societies of Vilna, especially the medical and archæological, are well known. In spite of the war of 1812, and the Polish risings of 1831 and 1863, the population has of late increased rapidly. In 1883 it numbered 93,760. The inhabitants are chiefly Roman Catholics in religion and Poles by nationality. The Jews are steadily increasing in numbers and now make more than one-third of the population. The town has an important trade in timber (with Prussia), as also in corn.

History.—The territory of Vilna has certainly been occupied by the Lithuanians since the 10th century, and probably much earlier; their chief fortified town, Vilna, is first mentioned in 1128. A temple to the god Perkunas stood on one of its hills till 1387, when it was destroyed by Jagello, after his baptism. After 1323, when Gedimin abandoned Troki, Vilna became the capital of Lithuania. The formerly independent principalities of Minsk and Lidy, as well as the territory of Disna, which belonged to the Polotsk principality, were annexed by the Lithuanian princes, and from that time Vilna, which was fortified by a stone wall, became the chief city of the Lithuanian empire. It was united with Poland when its prince Casimir was elected (1444) to the Polish throne. In 1519 it had a printing-office, and fifty years later the Jesuits founded there a college, which became later on a university. But the plague of 1588, a fire in 1610, and still more the wars between Russia and Poland, which began in the 17th century, checked its further growth. The Russians took Vilna in 1655, and in the following year it was ceded to Russia. The Swedes captured it in 1702 and in 1706. The Russians again took possession of it in 1788; and it was finally annexed to Russia in 1795, after the partition of Poland. Its Polish inhabitants took an active part in the risings of 1831 and 1863, for which they were severely punished by the Russian Government.

VINCENNES, a town of France, in the department of Seine, 4 miles east of Paris, with which it is connected by a railway and two tramways. The castle, formerly a royal residence, was begun by Louis VII. in 1164, and rebuilt by Philip Augustus, Philip of Valois, and Charles V. Catherine de' Medici added two pavilions, finished in 1614, which Louis XIV. connected by two covered galleries, one of which has been destroyed and the other hidden by casemates. Napoleon altered the castle into a vast magazine of war materials. Louis XVIII. added an armoury; and under Louis Philippe numerous casemates and a new fort on the east side were constructed. The population of Vincennes, 20,530 in 1881, was 22,237 in 1886.

The old castle is a rectangle of 1253 feet by 735. The enclosing wall was originally flanked by nine towers, which were cut down to its level between 1808 and 1811, and now serve as bastions. Vincennes is at once a barracks, a fortress, an arsenal, and a school of artillery, and is the scene of most new artillery experiments in France. The donjon is a square tower 170 feet high, with walls 10 feet thick. The chapel, begun by Charles V. in 1379, continued by Charles VI. and Francis I., and finished by Henry II. in 1552, has been recently restored. In the sacristy is the monument erected in 1816 to the memory of the duke of Enghien, who was shot in the castle moat in 1804. Vincennes possesses a military hospital with 642 beds, and a statue of General Daumesnil, erected in 1873. The wood of Vincennes contains various military establishments, an experimental farm, and the redoubts of Gravelle and La Faisanderie. In the latter is the normal school of military gymnastics. The wood, which now belongs to Paris, was laid out during the second empire in imitation of the Bois de Boulogne. In the Lake of Gravelle the waters of the Marne are collected in a reservoir, holding upwards of 700,000 cubic feet. The Marne flows 130 feet below. On the south border of the wood near Charenton is the asylum of Vincennes (500 beds), founded in 1855 for the benefit of convalescents from the hospitals.

VINCENNES, a city of the United States, the county seat of Knox county, Indiana, is situated on the east bank of the Wabash, which is navigable to this point. It is the centre of a fertile agricultural district, with extensive underlying coal deposits, and is an important railroad centre, where seven railroads intersect. These railroads have their workshops here, in which they employ a large number of men. Besides this there are flour-mills, a woollen mill, furniture and cigar factories, and machine-shops. The population in 1880 was 7680, an increase since 1870 of 42 per cent. Vincennes is the seat of a university, chartered in 1804.

The site of the city was settled in 1702. In 1763 the British became its possessors, and it remained a British fort until captured by Colonel G. R. Clarke in 1779. From 1800 to 1813 it was the capital of Indiana Territory.

VINCENT, or VINCENTIUS, ST, deacon and martyr, according to the Roman *Breviary*, was born of noble parents at Huesca (Osca) in Spain, and was educated by Valerius, bishop of Zaragoza, who in due time ordained him to the diaconate. Under the persecution of Diocletian he was arrested and taken to Valencia. Having stood firm in his profession before Dacianus, the governor, he was subjected to excruciating tortures and thrown into prison, where angels visited him, lighting up his dungeon with celestial light, relieving his pains, loosing his bonds, and mingling their voices with his in psalms of praise. His warders, having seen these wonders through the chinks of the wall, forthwith became Christians. He was afterwards brought out and laid upon a soft mattress that he might regain sufficient strength for new torments; but, while Dacianus was vainly meditating punishment, the saint gently breathed his last, as a crowd of bystanders kissed his feet and treasured up his blood in napkins. The tyrant exposed the body to wild beasts, but a raven miraculously descended and protected it; it was then thrown into the sea, but could not be hid, and finally received decent burial. The date assigned to his martyrdom is 304; he is commemorated on 22d January, chiefly in Spain and the patriarchate of Lisbon. Prudentius (403) devotes a hymn to the details of his martyrdom; Paulinus calls him the glory and ornament of Spain; and in more than one of his discourses St Augustine has celebrated his praise.

VINCENT, GEORGE (1796-1831?), English landscape and marine painter, was born at Norwich in June 1796. He studied art under "Old" Crome, and at the age of fifteen began to contribute to the Norwich exhibition. From 1814 till 1823 he exhibited occasionally at the Royal Academy, and also in the Water-Colour Exhibition and the British Institution. In 1819 he removed from Norwich to London, and he was a contributor to the Suffolk Street gallery from its foundation in 1824 till 1830. He possessed great artistic abilities; but unfortunately he fell into dissipation, and his works became slight and hastily executed. Finally he dropped out of sight, and he is believed to have died about 1831. His most important work, a View of Greenwich Hospital, was shown in the International Exhibition of 1862. His London from the Surrey Side of Waterloo Bridge is also a fine work.

VINCENT OF BEAUVAIS, or VINCENTIUS BELLOVACENSIS (*c.* 1190–*c.* 1264), the encyclopædist of the Middle Ages, was probably a native of Beauvais.[1] The exact dates of his birth and death are unknown. A tolerably old tradition, preserved by Louis a Valleoleti (*c.* 1413), gives the latter as 1264;[2] but Tholomæus de Luca, Vincent's younger contemporary (*ob.* 1321), seems to reckon him as living during the pontificate of Gregory X. (1272-1276). If we assume 1264 as the year of his death, the immense volume of his works forbids us to think he could have been born much later than 1190. Very little is known of his career. A plausible conjecture makes him enter the house of the Dominicans at Paris between 1215 and 1220, from which place a second conjecture carries him to the Dominican monastery founded at Beauvais in 1228-29. There is no evidence to show that the Vincent who was sub-prior of this foundation in 1246 is the encyclopædist; nor indeed is it likely that a man of such abnormally studious habits could have found time to attend to the daily business routine of a monastic establishment. It is certain, however, that he at one time held the post of "reader" at the monastery of Royaumont (*Mons Regalis*), not far from Paris, on the Oise, founded by St Louis between 1228 and 1235. St Louis read the books that he compiled, and supplied the funds for procuring copies of such authors as he required for his compilations. Queen Margaret, her son Philip, and her son-in-law Theobald V. of Champagne and Navarre are also named among those who urged him to the composition of his "little works," especially the *De Institutione Principum.* Though Vincent may well have been summoned to Royaumont even before 1240, there is no actual proof that he lived there before the return of Louis IX. and his wife from the Holy Land, early in the summer of 1254. But it is evident that he must have written his work *De Eruditione Filiorum Regalium* (where he styles himself as "Vincentius Belvacensis, de ordine prædicatorum, qualiscumque lector in monasterio de Regali Monte") after this date and yet before January 1260, the approximate date of his *Tractatus Consolatorius.* When he wrote the latter work he must have left Royaumont, as he speaks of returning from the funeral of Prince Louis (15th January 1260) "ad nostram domum," a phrase which can hardly be explained otherwise than as referring to his own Dominican house, whether at Beauvais or elsewhere.

The *Majus Speculum,* the great compendium of all the knowledge of the Middle Ages, as it left the pen of Vincent, seems to have consisted of three parts only, viz., the *Speculum Naturale, Doctrinale,* and *Historiale.* Such, at least, is Échard's conclusion, derived from an examination of the earliest extant MSS. All the printed editions, however, consist of four parts, the additional one being entitled *Speculum Morale.* This has been clearly shown to be the production of a later hand, and is ascribed by Échard to the period between 1310 and 1325. In arrangement and style it is quite different from the other three parts, and indeed it is mainly a compilation from Thomas Aquinas, Stephen de Bourbon, and two or three other contemporary writers.

The *Speculum Naturale* fills a bulky folio volume of 848 closely-printed double-columned pages. It is divided into thirty-two books and 3718 chapters. It is a vast summary of all the natural history known to western Europe towards the middle of the 13th century. It is, as it were, the great temple of mediæval science, whose floor and walls are inlaid with an enormous mosaic of skilfully-arranged passages from Latin, Greek, Arabic, and even Hebrew authors. To each quotation, as he borrows it, Vincent prefixes the name of the book and author from whom it is taken, distinguishing, however, his own remarks by the word "actor." The *Speculum Naturale* is so constructed that the various subjects are dealt with according to the order of their creation; it is in fact a gigantic commentary on Genesis i. Thus bk. i. opens with an account of the Trinity and its relation to creation; then follows a similar series of chapters about angels, their attributes, powers, orders, &c., down to such minute points as their methods of communicating thought, on which matter the author decides, in his own person, that they have a kind of intelligible speech, and that with angels to think and to speak are not the same process. The whole book, in fact, deals with such things as were with God "in the beginning." Bk. ii. treats of our own world, of light, colour, the four elements, Lucifer, and his fallen angels, thus corresponding in the main with the sensible world and the work of the first day. Bks. iii. and iv. deal with the phenomena of the heavens and of time, which is measured by the motions of the heavenly bodies, with the sky and all its wonders, fire, rain, thunder, dew, winds, &c. Bks. v.-xiv. treat of the sea and the dry land: they discourse of the seas, the ocean, and the great rivers, agricultural operations, metals, precious stones, plants, herbs, with their seeds, grains, and juices, trees wild and cultivated, their fruits and their saps. Under each species, where possible, Vincent gives a chapter on its use in medicine, and he adopts for the most part an alphabetical arrangement. In bk. vi. c. 7 he incidentally discusses what would become of a stone if it were dropped down a hole, pierced right through the earth, and, curiously enough, decides that it would stay in the centre. Bk. xv. deals with astronomy—the moon, stars, and the zodiac, the sun, the planets, the seasons, and the calendar. Bks. xvi. and xvii. treat of fowls and fishes, mainly in alphabetical order and with reference to their medical qualities. Bks. xviii.-xxii. deal in a similar way with domesticated and wild animals, including the dog, serpents, bees, and insects; they also include a general treatise on animal physiology spread over bks. xxi.-xxii. Bks. xxiii.-xxviii. discuss the psychology, physiology, and anatomy of man, the five senses and their organs, sleep, dreams, ecstasy, memory, reason, &c. The remaining four books seem more or less supplementary; the last (xxxii.) is a summary of geography and history down to the year 1250, when the book seems to have been given to the world, perhaps along with the *Speculum Historiale* and possibly an earlier form of the *Speculum Doctrinale.*

The *Speculum Doctrinale,* in seventeen books and 2374 chapters, is a summary of all the scholastic knowledge of the age and does not confine itself to natural history. It is intended to be a practical manual for the student and the official alike; and, to fulfil this object, it treats of the mechanic arts of life as well as the subtleties of the scholar, the duties of the prince, and the tactics of the general. The first book, after defining philosophy, &c., gives a long Latin vocabulary of some 6000 or 7000 words. Grammar, logic, rhetoric, and poetry are discussed in bks. ii. and iii., the latter including several well-known fables, such as the Lion and the Mouse. Bk. iv. treats of the virtues, each of which has two chapters of quotations allotted to it, one in prose and the other in verse. Bk. v. is of a somewhat similar nature. With bk. vi. we enter on the practical part of the work; it deals with the *ars œconomica,* and gives directions for building, gardening, sowing, reaping, rearing cattle, and tending vineyards; it includes also a kind of agricultural almanac for each month in the year. Bks. vii.-ix. have reference to the *ars politica*: they contain rules for the education of a prince and a summary of the forms, terms, and statutes of canonical, civil, and criminal law. Bk. xi. is devoted to the *artes mechanicæ,* namely, those of weavers, smiths, armourers, merchants, hunters, and even the general and the sailor. Bks. xii.-xiv. deal with medicine both in practice and in theory: they contain practical rules for the preservation of health according to the four seasons of the year, and treat of various diseases from fever to gout. Bk. xv. deals with physics and may be regarded as a summary of the *Speculum Naturale.* Bk. xvi. is given up to mathematics, under which head are included music, geometry, astronomy, astrology, weights and measures, and metaphysics. It is noteworthy that in this book Vincent shows a knowledge of the Arabic numerals, though he does not call them by this name. With him the unit is termed "digitus"; when multiplied by ten it becomes the "articulus"; while the combination of the articulus and the digitus is the "numerus compositus." In this chapter (xvi. 9), which is superscribed "actor," he clearly explains how the value of a number increases tenfold with every place it is moved to the left. He is even acquainted with the later invention of the "cifra" or cipher. The last book (xvii.) treats of theology or (as we should now say) mythology, and winds up with an account of the Holy Scriptures and of the fathers, from Ignatius and Dionysius the Areopagite to Jerome and Gregory the Great, and even of later writers from Isidore and Bede, through Alcuin, Lanfranc, and Anselm, down to Bernard of Clairvaux and the brethren of St Victor.

As the fifteenth book of the *Speculum Doctrinale* is a summary of the *Speculum Naturale,* so the *Speculum Historiale* may be regarded as the expansion of the last book of the same work. It consists of thirty-one books divided into 3793 chapters. The first book opens with the mysteries of God and the angels, and then passes on to the works of the six days and the creation of man. It includes

[1] He is sometimes styled Vincentius Burgundus; but, according to M. Daunou, this appellation cannot be traced back further than the first half of the 15th century.

[2] Apparently confirmed by the few enigmatical lines preserved by Échard from his epitaph—

"Pertulit iste necem post annos mille ducentos,
Sexaginta decem sex habe, sex mihi retentos."

dissertations on the various vices and virtues, the different arts and sciences, and carries down the history of the world to the sojourn in Egypt. The next eleven books (ii.-xii.) conduct us through sacred and secular history down to the triumph of Christianity under Constantine. The story of Barlaam and Josaphat occupies a great part of bk. xv.; and bk. xvi. gives an account of Daniel's nine kingdoms, in which account Vincent differs from his professed authority, Sigebert of Gembloux, by reckoning England as the fourth instead of the fifth. In the chapters devoted to the *origines* of Britain he relies on the Brutus legend, but cannot carry his catalogue of British or English kings further than 735, where he honestly confesses that his authorities fail him. Seven more books bring us to the rise of Mohammed (xxiii.) and the days of Charlemagne (xxiv.). Vincent's Charlemagne is a curious medley of the great emperor of history and the champion of romance. He is at once the gigantic eater of Turpin, the huge warrior eight feet high, who could lift the armed knight standing on his open hand to a level with his head, the crusading conqueror of Jerusalem in days before the crusades, and yet with all this the temperate drinker and admirer of St Augustine, as his character had filtered down through various channels from the historical pages of Eginhard. Bk. xxv. includes the first crusade, and in the course of bk. xxix., which contains an account of the Tartars, the author enters on what is almost contemporary history, winding up in bk. xxxi. with a short narrative of the crusade of St Louis in 1250. One remarkable feature of the *Speculum Historiale* is Vincent's constant habit of devoting several chapters to selections from the writings of each great author, whether secular or profane, as he mentions him in the course of his work. The extracts from Cicero and Ovid, Origen and St John, Chrysostom, Augustine, and Jerome, are but specimens of a useful custom which reaches its culminating point in bk. xxviii., which is devoted entirely to the writings of St Bernard. One main fault of the *Speculum Historiale* is the unduly large space devoted to miracles. Four of the mediæval historians from whom he quotes most frequently are Sigebert of Gembloux, Hugh of Fleury, Helinand of Froidmont, and William of Malmesbury, whom he uses for Continental as well as for English history.

Vincent has thus hardly any claim to be reckoned as an original writer. But it is difficult to speak too highly of his immense industry in collecting, classifying, and arranging these three huge volumes of 80 books and 9885 chapters. The undertaking to combine all human knowledge into a single whole was in itself a colossal one and could only have been born in a mind of no mean order. Indeed more than six centuries passed before the idea was again resuscitated; and even then it required a group of brilliant Frenchmen to do what the old Dominican had carried out unaided. The number of writers quoted by Vincent is almost incredible: in the *Speculum Naturale* alone no less than 350 distinct works are cited, and to these must be added at least 100 more for the other two *Specula*. His reading ranges from Arabian philosophers and naturalists to Aristotle, Eusebius, Cicero, Seneca, Julius Cæsar (whom he calls Julius Celsus), and even the Jew Peter Alphonso. But Hebrew, Arabic, and Greek he seems to have known solely through one or other of the popular Latin versions.

A list of Vincent's works, both MS. and printed, will be found in the *Histoire Littéraire de France*, vol. xviii., and in Échard. The *Tractatus Consolatorius pro Morte Amici* and the *Liber de Eruditione Filiorum Regalium* (dedicated to Queen Margaret) were printed by Amerbach at Basel in December 1480. The *Liber de Institutione Principum* has never yet been printed, and the only MS. copy the writer of this article has been able to consult does not contain in its prologue all the information which Échard seems to imply is to be found there. The so-called first edition of the *Speculum Majus*, including the *Speculum Morale*, ascribed to Mentelin and long celebrated as the earliest work printed at Strasburg, has lately been challenged as being only an earlier edition of Vincent's three genuine *Specula* (c. 1468-70), with which has been bound up the *Speculum Morale* first printed by Mentelin (c. 1473-76). (T. A. A.)

VINCENT OF LERINS, ST, an ecclesiastical writer of the Western Church, of whose personal history hardly anything is known, except that he was a native of Gaul, possibly brother of St Loup, bishop of Troyes, that he became a monk and priest in the monastery of Lerinum (island of St Honorat opposite Cannes), and that he died in or about 450. From himself we further learn that only after long and sad experience of worldly turmoil did he betake himself to the haven of a religious life. In 434, three years after the council of Ephesus, he wrote the *Commonitorium adversus profanas omnium hæreticorum novitates*, in which the famous threefold test of orthodoxy is laid down and applied,—"quod ubique, quod semper, quod ab omnibus creditum est." It is not altogether improbable that Vincent of Lerins was also the author of the Semipelagian treatise against Augustinianism which is dealt with by Prosper of Aquitania in his *Pro Augustini doctrina responsiones ad capitula objectionum Vincentianarum.*

The *Commonitorium* has been edited by Baluze (Paris, 1663, 1669, and 1684), and by Klüpfel (Vienna, 1809). It also occurs in vol. l. of Migne's *Patrol. curs. compl.* (1846).

VINCENT DE PAUL, ST (1576-1660), founder of the "Congregation of Priests of the Mission," usually known as LAZARITES (*q.v.*), was born on 24th April 1576 at Pouy near Dax (Landes), where his father owned a small farm. It was originally intended to train him for the ordinary pastoral life of the peasants of the Landes, but he soon showed other aptitudes, and after passing through the school at Dax he studied at Toulouse, and was ordained to the priesthood in 1600. Some time afterwards, while on board a felucca off Marseilles, he had the misfortune to be captured by Barbary pirates, who took him to Tunis and sold him as a slave. His third master, who happened to be a renegade Italian, he succeeded in converting, and both managed to make their escape, landing at Aigues-Mortes near Marseilles in June 1607. After short stays at Avignon and Rome, Vincent found his way to Paris, where he became favourably known to Monsieur (afterwards cardinal) de Bérulle, who was then engaged in founding the congregation of the French Oratory. At Bérulle's instance he became curate of Clichy near Paris (1611); but this charge he soon exchanged for the post of tutor to the count of Joigny at Folleville, in the diocese of Amiens, where he first developed the idea of those "missions" with which his name is associated. In 1617 he accepted the curacy of Châtillon-lès-Dombes (or sur-Chalaronne), and it was here that he received from the countess of Joigny the means by which he was enabled to found his first "confrérie." The subsequent history of the priests of the mission will be found in the article LAZARITES. Among the works of benevolence with which his name is more immediately and personally associated are the establishment of a hospital for galley slaves at Marseilles, the institution of two establishments for foundlings at Paris, and the organization of the "Filles de la Charité." He died at Paris on 27th September 1660, and was buried in the church of St Lazare. He was beatified by Benedict XIII. in 1729 and canonized by Clement XII. in 1737, his festival (duplex) being observed on 19th July.

VINCENT FERRER, ST (1355-1419), a great Spanish Dominican preacher, was born of respectable parentage at Valencia on 23d January 1355. In February 1374 he took the Dominican habit, and after spending some years in teaching, and in completing his theological studies, he was licensed to preach. He graduated as doctor of theology at Lerida in 1374, and his sermons in the cathedral of Valencia from 1385 onwards soon became famous. Cardinal Peter de Luna took him with him to Paris in 1391; and on his own election to the pontificate as antipope Benedict XIII. made Ferrer his confessor and master of the sacred palace. Finding, however, the ecclesiastical atmosphere of Avignon an uncongenial one, he in 1397 resumed his work as a preacher, and Spain, France, Italy, Germany, and Great Britain and Ireland were successively visited by him; and in every case numerous conversions were the result of his eloquence, which is described as having been singularly powerful and moving. In 1412 he was delegated by his native city to take part in the election of a successor to the vacant crown of Aragon; and in 1416 he received a special invitation to attend the council of Constance, which, however, he does not appear to have accepted. He died at Vannes on 5th April 1419, and was canonized by Calixtus III. in 1455, his festival (duplex) being observed on 5th April.

VINCI. See LEONARDO DA VINCI.

VINDELICIA, or the country of the Vindelici, is a name of the Roman province which was also called Rhætia Secunda. See RHÆTIA.

VINE. Of the grape vines (*Vitis*) *V. vinifera* is the species best known and longest cultivated; but out of ten species that grow wild in the United States four (*V. rotundifolia*, *V. Labrusca*, *V. æstivalis*, and *V. cordifolia*), according to Engelmann, are cultivated and have given origin to numerous derivatives used for wine-making purposes. Some of the American varieties have been introduced into France and other countries infested with *Phylloxera*, to serve as stocks on which to graft the better kinds of European vines, because their roots, though perhaps equally subject to the attacks of the insects, do not suffer so much injury from them as the European species. American vines should not, however, be introduced for grafting or other purposes into a vine-growing country hitherto free from *Phylloxera*, but only into those in which the insect has already spread.

Although the genus *Vitis* comprises, according to Bentham and Hooker, more than two hundred species, mostly natives of tropical or subtropical regions, yet less than half-a-dozen species have any economic value, while the great interest centres in four or five only. Vines have woody climbing stems, with alternate, palmately-lobed, or in some

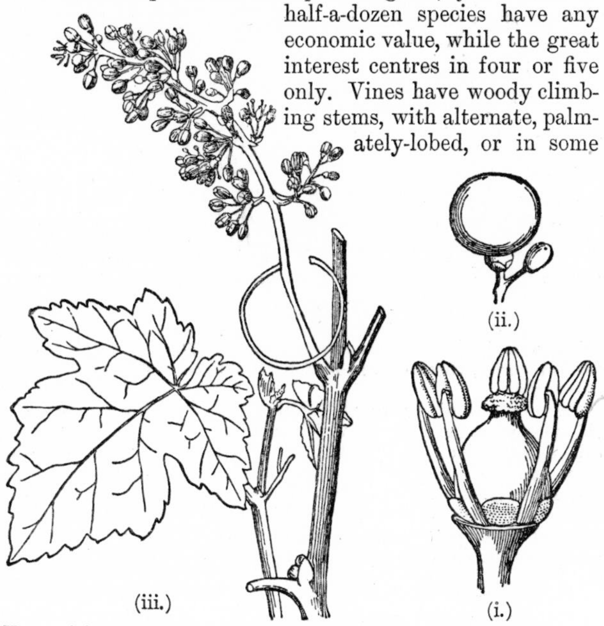

Vine. (i.) Flower after fall of petals; magnified. (ii.) Fruit; reduced. (iii.) Foliage, tendril, and inflorescence; reduced.

cases (*Ampelopsis*, *Cissus*) compound (digitate), leaves, provided at the base with small stipules. Opposite some of these leaves springs a tendril, the nature of which is obvious from the numerous transitional states it offers between the ordinary form of tendril and the inflorescence. The flowers are small, green, and fragrant, and are arranged in dense clusters. Each has a small calyx in the form of a shallow rim, sometimes four-lobed or five-lobed, or toothed. Within this is an equal number of petals, which in the true vines cohere by their tips and form a cap or hood, which is pushed off when the stamens are ripe. In other species (and as a malformation in the vine itself) the petals are free and spreading. Four or five free stamens, placed opposite the petals, spring from a fleshy ring or disk surrounding the ovary, each bearing a two-celled anther. The ovary is surmounted by a sessile stigma and is more or less completely two-celled, with two erect ovules in each cell. This ripens into the berry and seed. Planchon, in his monograph of the *Ampelideæ* (1887), divides the genus *Vitis* into numerous genera of equal rank. He retains, however, the grape vines under their original name. The cultivated vine has usually hermaphrodite flowers; but, as it occurs in a wild state, or as an escape from cultivation, the flowers manifest a tendency towards unisexuality: that is, one plant bears flowers with stamens only, or only the rudiments of the pistil, while on another plant the flowers are bisexual. Exclusively female flowers without stamens do not appear to have been observed. Seedling plants from the cultivated vines often produce unisexual flowers, thus reverting to the feral type. Perhaps the explanation of the fact that some of the cultivated varieties are, as gardeners say, "bad setters,"—*i.e.*, do not ripen their fruit owing to imperfect fertilization,—is to be sought in this natural tendency to diœcism.

The conformation of the vine stem has elicited a vast amount of explanatory comment. The most generally accepted explanation is the "sympodial" one. According to this, the shoot of the vine is a "sympode," consisting of a number of "podia" placed one over the other in longitudinal series. Each podium consists of a portion of the stem bearing one or more leaves, each with an axillary bud or buds, and terminating in a tendril or an inflorescence. In *V. Labrusca* there is a tendril opposite to each leaf, so that the podium bears only a single leaf. In other species there is a definite arrangement of the leaves, some with and others without tendrils opposite to them, the numerical order remaining constant or nearly so. These arrangements have doubtless some reference to climatic phenomena, continuity of growth being arrested by cold and promoted by warmth. In any case it is obvious that these facts might be turned to practical ends in cultivation. A vine, for instance, that produces bunches of grapes at each joint is preferable to one in which there are several barren joints, as a larger quantity can be grown within a smaller area. The practice of pruning or "stopping," as explained under HORTICULTURE (vol. xii. p. 277), is consciously or unconsciously regulated by the mode of growth. The tendril or inflorescence, according to the views above explained, though in reality terminal, is bent to one side; hence it appears to be lateral and opposite to the leaf. While the tendril is thus diverted from its orginal direct course, the axillary bud of the leaf opposite the tendril begins a new podium, by lengthening into a shoot which assumes the direction the tendril had prior to its deflexion. This new podium, now in a direct line with its predecessor, produces leaves and ends in its turn in a tendril or inflorescence. A third podium succeeds the second, and so on. Other authorities explain the formation of the tendril and its anomalous position opposite to a leaf by supposing that the end of the stem bifurcates during growth, one division forming the shoot, the other the tendril or inflorescence. It is not possible within the limits at our command to specify the facts and arguments by which these theories are respectively supported. Practically the tendrils assist the plant in its native state to scramble over rocks or trees. As in the case of similar formations generally, they are endowed with a sensitiveness to touch which enables them to grasp and coil themselves round any suitable object which comes in their way, and thus to support the plant. The tendrils of the Virginian creeper (*Vitis* or *Ampelopsis hederacea*; the *Parthenocissus quinquefolia* of Planchon) are branched, each branch terminating in a little sucker-like expansion by means of which it adheres firmly to walls or rocks. This is especially noticeable in the Japanese species now so commonly grown against walls under the name of *Ampelopsis Veitchii* (the *Parthenocissus tricuspidata* of Planchon). The extremities of these tendrils turn away from the light, and by this means they are enabled to enter crevices, inside which they expand and fix themselves, just as the lewis or key, used by stone-masons, is fixed into blocks of stone. The anomalous position of the stamens in front of the petals is explained by the abortion or non-development of an outer row of stamens, indications of which are sometimes seen on the hypogynous disk encircling the ovary. The seeds or grape stones are somewhat club-shaped, with a narrow neck-like portion beneath, which expands into a rounded and thickened portion above. On the inner or central side of the seed is a ridge bounded on either side by a shallow groove. This ridge indicates the point of union of the "raphe" or seed-stalk with the seed; it serves to distinguish the varieties of *V. vinifera* from those of other species. In the true vines the neck of the seed is much longer than in the American vines, and the ridge or "chalaza" occupies the upper half of the seed, not the middle portion, as in the American kinds. In endeavouring to trace the filiation and affinities of the vine, the characters afforded by the seed are specially valuable, because they have not been wittingly interfered with by human agency. Characters derived from the size, colour, or flavour of the berry are of less value for historical or genealogical purposes than those which are the outcome of purely natural conditions.

The native country of the European vine is considered to be the region south of the Caspian. From this presumed centre it has spread eastwards into Central Asia and westwards to both sides of the Mediterranean, Central Europe, and as far north as Belgium (Planchon). Regel has propounded the notion that the cultivated vine originated as a hybrid between *V. vulpina* and *V. Labrusca*, both North-American species; but he offers little evidence in support of his opinion, which has not received the assent of botanists generally. It is interesting to note that grape stones have been found with mummies in Egyptian tombs of not later age than 3000 years. The seeds, according to Engelmann, have the characteristics of those of *V. vinifera*, but show some very slight variations from the type of seed now prevalent. Among the Greeks in the time of Homer wine was in general use. The cultivation of the vine must also have been introduced into Italy at a very early period. In Virgil's time the varieties in cultivation seem to have been exceedingly numerous; and the varied methods of training and culture now in use in Italy are in many cases identical with those described by Columella and other Roman writers (comp. HORTICULTURE, vol. xii. pp. 223, 277). Grape stones have been found among the remains of Swiss and Italian lake dwellings of the Bronze period, and others in tufaceous volcanic deposits near Montpellier, not long before the historic era.

The vine requires a high summer temperature and a prolonged period in which to ripen its fruit. Where these are forthcoming, it can be profitably cultivated, even though the winter temperature be very low. Tchihatchef mentions that at Erivan in Russian Armenia the mean winter temperature is 7°·1 C. and falls in January to − 30° C., and at Bokhara the mean temperature of January is 4° C. and the minimum − 22° C., and yet at both places the vine is grown with success. In the Alps it is profitably cultivated up to an altitude of 1870 feet, and in the north of Piedmont as high as 3180 feet. At the present time the limit of profitable cultivation in Europe passes from Brittany, lat. 47° 30′, to beyond the Rhine by Liége and through Thuringia to Silesia in lat. 51° 55′ (Grisebach). In former centuries vines were cultivated to the north of this region, as, for instance, in Holland, in Belgium largely, and in England, where they might still be grown. Indeed experiments have lately been made in this direction near Cardiff in South Wales. The yield is satisfactory and the wine made, the variety known as Gamay noir, is described as being like still champagne. In the Middle Ages, owing to various causes, the better wines of France and Germany could not be obtained in England except at prohibitive prices; but, when this state of things ceased and foreign wine could be imported, the English consumers would no longer tolerate the inferior productions of their own vineyards. It is also probable that the English mixed sugar or honey with the wine and thus supplied artificially that sweetness which the English sun denied. It is a curious fact that at the present day much or even most of the wine of finest quality is made at or near to the northern limits of possible cultivation with profit. This circumstance is probably explained by the greater care and attention bestowed both on the cultivation of the vine and on the manufacture of the wine in northern countries than in those where the climate is more propitious. The relative inferiority of the wines made at the Cape of Good Hope and in Australia is partly due to variations of climate, the vine not yet having adapted itself to the new conditions, and partly to the deficient skill of the manufacturers. That such inferiority may be expected to disappear is suggested by the success of vine-culture in Madeira and the Canary Islands.

The development of other species of *Vitis*, such as the curious succulent species of the Soudan and other parts of equatorial Africa, or the numerous kinds in India and Cochin China, is of course possible under suitable conditions; but it is obvious that an extremely long period must elapse before they can successfully compete with the product of many centuries.

For currants and raisins, both produced by varieties of the grape-vine, see the respective articles.

Apart from their economic value, vines are often cultivated for purely ornamental purposes, owing to the elegance of their foliage, the rich coloration they assume, the shade they afford, and their hardihood. (M. T. M.)

DISEASES OF VINES.

The organic diseases which affect the vine may be divided into two categories, those caused by insects and those caused by parasitic fungi.

Diseases Caused by Insects.—Kaltenbach in 1874 enumerated thirty-two species of insects which injure the vine; and since then others have been added to the list. We here deal only with the most important. Amongst those which attack the leaves and young buds a small beetle, *Anomala vitis*, one of the *Scarabæidæ*, does great harm in some parts of southern Europe by devouring the soft tissue of the leaves. A genus of weevils, *Otiorhynchus*, contains several species which are injurious to the vine, chiefly by the adult beetle devouring the buds. *O. raucus*, *hirticornis*, *picipes*, *nigritus*, *ligustici*, and *sulcatus* are all reported from various places as doing much damage; the larva of the last-mentioned species attacks the roots of the vine, causing the shoots to be small and ultimately bringing about the death of the plant. Fortunately the members of this genus have no wings, so that the damage they cause is to a great extent localized. The same kind of injury is caused by a small Chrysomeleous beetle, *Eumolpus vitis*. The larvæ of several *Lepidoptera* attack the vine in the same way, destroying the young buds. Amongst these *Nænia typica*, *Agrotis tritici*, and *A. pronuba* may be mentioned. The larva of *Tortrix pilleriana* in the early spring weaves the young vine leaves together, and, enclosed in this nest, devours the soft tissue at leisure. The imago emerges from the chrysalis in July and shortly after lays its eggs upon the upper surface of the vine leaf. After a few weeks the caterpillars emerge and continue their work of destruction. *Lethrus cephalotes*, one of the *Scarabæidæ*, is very injurious in vineyards which have a dry sandy soil. The beetles live in pairs in holes in the ground; during the summer the beetle bites off the small young shoots and drags them away to its hole, where it is believed they serve as food for the larvæ. In this way very serious damage is caused to the vine plants. *Rhynchites betuleti*, a weevil, also does much damage to the young shoots and leaves. The grapes are attacked by the caterpillar of a moth, *Conchylis ambiguella*, which lays its egg in the young fruit; and in a similar way the larva of *Graptolitha* (*Conchylis*) *botrana* attacks the flowers and fruit. The larva of the cockchafer, *Melolontha vulgaris*, also does much damage by biting through and devouring the roots. *Coccus vitis* is a small scale insect of reddish brown colour, with irregular black spots in the female, which lives in the bark of old or neglected vines and weakens the tree.

Insect enemies.

By far the most destructive of all insect pests which attack the cultivated vine is *Phylloxera vastatrix*. This much-dreaded insect belongs to the family *Aphidæ* or plant lice of the order *Hemiptera*. The genus contains several species which live upon oak trees. Their proper home is in North America; but they have been found

Phylloxera.

in English vineries since 1863. The symptoms of the disease first appeared in France about the same time, in the neighbourhood of Tarascon. From the department of Gard the infection spread south to the sea, and east, west, and north, till the south-eastern corner of France was thoroughly infected. Another centre of infection arose a few years later near Bordeaux in Gironde, whence the disease spread till the whole of the southern half of France was more or less severely attacked. The parasite was first discovered in France in the year 1868. The *Phylloxera* has spread to Corsica; it has appeared here and there amongst the vineyards of the Rhine and Switzerland; it is found in Spain and Portugal, Austria, Hungary, Italy, and Greece; and in 1885 its presence was discovered in Australia (Victoria), at the Cape of Good Hope, and in Algeria. Hence it is no exaggeration to say that with very few exceptions its distribution is co-extensive with that of the cultivated grape-vine.

The symptoms of the disease, by means of which an infected spot may be readily recognized, are those. The vines are stunted and bear few leaves, and those small ones. When the disease reaches an advanced stage, the leaves are discoloured, yellow or reddish, with their edges turned back, and withered. The grapes are arrested in their growth and their skin is wrinkled. If the roots are examined, numerous fusiform swellings are found upon the smaller rootlets. These are at first yellowish in colour and fleshy; but as they grow older they become rotten and assume a brown or black colour. If the roots on which these swellings occur be examined with a lens, a number of minute insects of a yellowish brown colour are observed; these are the root-forms (radicola) of *Phylloxera* (fig. 1); they

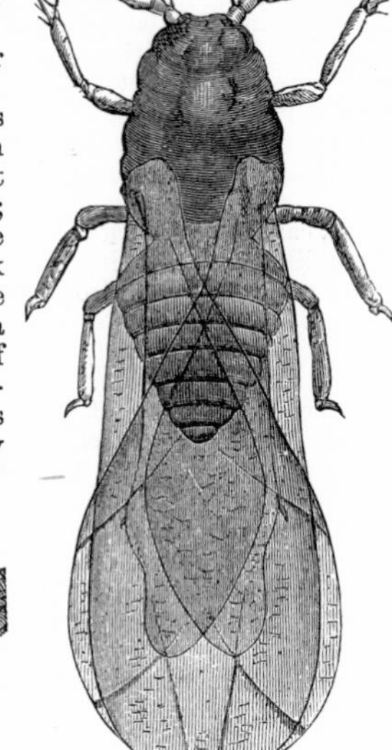

Fig. 1. Fig. 2.

Fig. 1.—Root-inhabiting form (radicola) of *Phylloxera*, with proboscis inserted into tissue of root of vine.
Fig. 2.—*Phylloxera*. Winged female which lives on leaves and buds of vine, and lays parthogenetically eggs of two kinds, one developing into a wingless female, the other into a male.

are about ·8 mm. long, of an oval outline, and with a swollen body. No distinction between head, thorax, and abdomen can be observed. The head bears small red eyes and a pair of three-jointed antennæ, the first two joints being short and thick, the third more elongated, with the end cut off obliquely and slightly hollowed out. Underneath, between the legs, lies the rostrum, which reaches back to the abdomen. The insect is fixed by this rostrum, which is inserted into the root of the vine for the purpose of sucking the sap. The abdomen consists of seven segments, and these as well as the anterior segments bear four rows of small tubercles on their dorsal surface. These root-dwelling insects are females, which lay parthenogenetic eggs. The insect is fixed by its proboscis, but moves its abdomen about and lays thirty to forty yellow eggs in small clusters. After the lapse of six, eight, or twelve days, according to the temperature, the larvæ hatch out of the eggs. These are light yellow in colour and in appearance resemble their mother, but with relatively larger appendages. They move actively

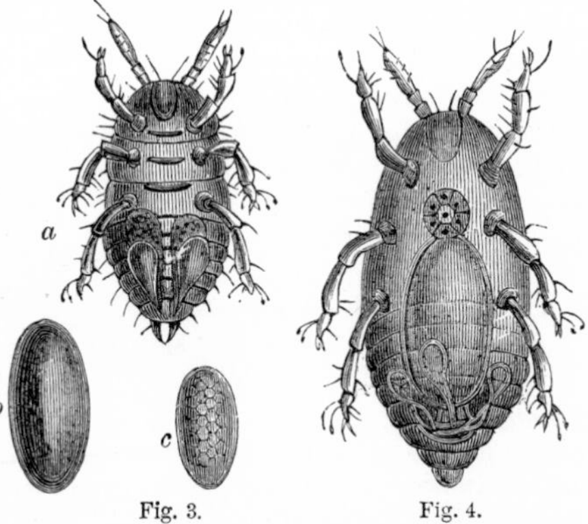

Fig. 3. Fig. 4.

Fig. 3.—*a*, Male produced from small egg *c*, laid by winged female (fig. 2); *b*, large egg; *c*, small egg.
Fig. 4.—Wingless female produced from large egg (fig. 3, *b*), laid by winged female (fig. 2).

about for a few days and then, having selected a convenient place on the young roots, insert their proboscis and become stationary. They moult five times, becoming with each change of skin darker in colour; in about three weeks they become adult and capable of laying parthenogenetic eggs. In this way the insect increases with appalling rapidity: it has been calculated that a single mother which dies after laying her eggs in March would have over 25,000,000 descendants by October. If, however, the insect were content with this method of reproduction, the disease could be isolated by surrounding the infected patches with a deep ditch full of some such substance as coal-tar, which would prevent the insects spreading on to the roots of healthy vines. The fertility of the parthenogenetically-produced insects would also diminish after a certain number of generations had been produced.

As the summer wears on a second form of insect appears amongst the root-dwellers, though hatched from the same eggs as the form described above. These are the nymphs, destined to acquire wings; their body is more slender in outline, and at first they bear well-marked tubercles. After several moults the rudiments of two pairs of wings appear, and then the insect creeps up to the surface of the earth, and on to the vine. Here it undergoes its fifth and last moult, and appears as a winged female, capable of reproducing parthenogenetically. The winged form has a slender body with distinct head (fig. 2). The eyes are well developed, with numerous facets; the antennæ have three joints, the terminal one shaped like that of the root-dwellers. The wings are transparent, with few nervures, and are well adapted for flight. The anterior pair reach far beyond the end of the abdomen; the posterior are narrower and not so long. These winged forms are about 1 mm. long. They fly about from July till October, living upon the sap of the vine, which is sucked up by the rostrum from the leaves or buds. They lay their parthenogenetically-produced eggs in the angles of the veins of the leaves, in the buds, or, if the season is already far advanced, in the bark. In very damp or cold weather the insect remains in the ground near the surface, and deposits its eggs there. The eggs are very few in number and of two sizes, small and large (fig. 4, *b* and *c*). From the larger a female (fig. 3) is hatched in eight or ten days, and simultaneously, for the first time in the life-history of the *Phylloxera*, a male (fig. 4) appears from the smaller egg. Neither male nor female has wings; the rostrum is replaced by a functionless tubercle; and there is no alimentary canal. The female is larger than the male and differs from it and the other forms in the last joint of the antennæ. The life of these sexual forms lasts but a few days, and is entirely taken up with reproduction. The female is fertilized by the male and three or four days later lays a single egg—the winter egg—and then dies. This egg is laid in the crevices of the bark of the vine, and as it is protectively coloured it is almost impossible to find it. Here the winter eggs remain undeveloped during the cold months; but in the following spring, as a rule in the month of April, they give birth to a female insect without wings, which resembles the root-dwelling forms, but has pointed antennæ. These forms are termed the stock-mothers; they creep into the buds of the vine, and, as these develop into the young leaves, insert their proboscis into the upper side. By this means a gall is produced on the under side of the leaf. The gall is cup-shaped, and its outer surface is crumpled and covered with small warts and hairs. The opening upon the upper surface of the leaf is protected by similar structures. Within this gall the stock-mother lives and surrounds herself with numerous parthenogenetically-produced eggs,—sometimes as many as two hundred in a single gall; these eggs give birth after six or eight days to a numerous progeny (gallicola), some of which form new galls and multiply in the leaves, whilst others descend to the roots and become the root-dwelling forms already described. The galls and the gall-producing form are much commoner in America than in the Old World.

Scheme of the Various Forms of Phylloxera vastatrix.

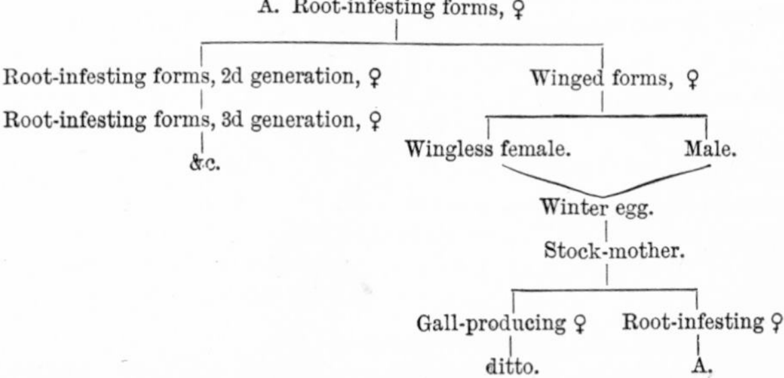

The natural enemies of the *Phylloxera* are few in number: they include some mites,—*Hoplophora arctata*, *Thyroglyphus phylloxeræ*.—and the millepede *Polyxenus lagurus*, which devours the subterranean forms. Innumerable artifices have been proposed to combat the terrible disease caused by this minute insect, but none of them seem to be completely successful. As a rule the means suggested are to render the soil uninhabitable for the root forms by injecting certain chemical poisons. Since the importance of the winter egg in the life-history of the insect was demonstrated by Balbiani, attempts have been made to destroy these eggs by rubbing the branches with a chain-armour glove, or some such contrivance for removing the outer layers of the bark, which should be burnt. Again, certain varieties of American vines, which have the reputation of being *Phylloxera* proof, have been grafted on European stocks; but this has proved to be only a doubtful success as regards the *Phylloxera*, whilst the wine made from such vines has undoubtedly deteriorated. The treatment which has been most successful is periodically to submerge the vineyard for a period of not less than forty days. Where this plan has been tried, it has been most successful; unfortunately the majority of vineyards are planted on hill-sides and other places where this method of treatment is impracticable. The root-dwelling forms do not thrive in a sandy soil; hence vines grown in a district where such soil is found usually escape the disease.

Oidium. *Fungoid Diseases.*—The most destructive form of fungoid disease which attacks the vine is caused by a Pyrenomycetous fungus, *Oidium* (*Erysiphe*) *Tuckeri.* The disease was first noticed in England in 1845; in 1848 it appeared at Versailles; by 1851 it had spread through all the wine-producing countries of Europe, being especially virulent in the lands bordering on the Mediterranean; and in the following year it made its appearance in Madeira. There is little doubt that, like the *Phylloxera*, the *Oidium* is in its origin American. The disease is characterized by the appearance of a white mycelium on the young leaves; this spreads quickly and attacks the older leaves and branches, and ultimately reaches the grapes. At first these are marked only by small brown spots; but the spots spread and fuse together, the skin of the grape is destroyed, and the flesh decays, the seed only remaining apparently untouched. The disease spreads by the mycelium growing over the epidermis of the plant. The hyphæ composing the mycelium are provided with haustoria, which project into the cells of the affected part. Some of the hyphæ which project from the leaf bear conidia, which are constricted off one at a time, and it is by their means that the fungus spreads. The perithecia have not yet been discovered in Europe. But it is not impossible that this stage of the life-history of *Oidium* exists in the United States in the form of *Uncinula spiralis*, which causes a widely spread disease amongst the American vines. The *Oidium* is in its turn attacked by a fungus of the same tribe, *Cicinnobolus Cesatii*, De By, which lives parasitically within the hyphæ of its host, and at times even succeeds in destroying it. The means which have proved most efficacious, both as a remedy and a preventative of this disease, is to scatter flower of sulphur over the vines, before the morning dew has evaporated. Another method is to boil one part of lime with three parts of sulphur, and to sprinkle the mixture over the affected plants.

Peronospora viticola. Another fungus which attacks vines, especially those of America, is *Peronospora viticola.* The mycelium spreads through the green parts of the plant, attacking the leaves, twigs, and unripe grapes. On the upper side of the leaf, where it is first visible, it forms pale green irregular spots, which become darker in colour. On the under side of the leaf these patches are white and are composed of the spore-bearing hyphæ. The leaf ultimately becomes dried up and brittle. The grapes which are attacked cease to grow, turn brown or white, and ultimately dry up and fall off. This disease has been successfully treated with a spray of copper sulphate and lime, or sulphate of iron; solutions of these salts prevent the conidia from germinating.

Anthracnose. Anthracnose is the name usually given to a disease which was formerly known as "charbon," "pech," or "brenner." This disease is caused by the parasitism of *Sphaceloma ampelinum*, one of the Pyrenomycetous fungi. The fungus assails all the green parts of the vine, and injures the leaves and young shoots as much as it does the grape itself. The first sign of its presence is the appearance of a minute spot, which is greyish in the centre, with a brown border. This spot increases in size; in the stalks it assumes an oval shape, with its long axis parallel to the stalk, whilst in the leaves and grapes it is more or less circular in outline. The centre of the spots on the grapes becomes darker as the disease advances, and a red line appears dividing the dark brown border into an outer and an inner rim and giving a very characteristic appearance to the diseased plant. The berries do not shrivel up as those do that are affected by the black rot. The mycelium of *Sphaceloma* grows just beneath the cuticle of the vine, through which it soon bursts, giving rise to a number of minute hyphæ, which bear conidia. These are minute, oval, colourless spores, which serve to spread the disease over the vineyard and from place to place. The complete life-history of this form is at present unknown; and information as to where the fungus passes the winter, and in what form, would probably afford some useful indications as to the method that should be adopted to combat the disease. Anthracnose has been known in Europe for many years, but has only been observed in America since 1881, whither it was probably imported from the Old World. As a preventative to its attacks a solution (50 per cent.) of iron sulphate has been found very useful, as well as care in planting on well-drained soil that does not lie too low, the disease seldom appearing in dry, well-exposed vineyards.

Black rot. The black rot, like the *Oidium* and *P. viticola*, is American in its origin. It has been known and observed there since 1848, but appeared for the first time in France in 1885. The disease is caused by a fungus, *Physalospora Bidwellii*, Sacc. (*Phoma uvicola*), one of the *Pyrenomycetes*, and by some authorities it has been considered to be a further stage in the life-history of *Sphaceloma.* The fungus confines its attacks to the grapes, the leaves and stems being rarely if ever affected. The grapes are not assailed until nearly full-grown, when a brownish spot appears, which spreads over the whole grape. The latter at first retains its plumpness, but on the appearance of little black pustules, which first occur on the part first affected, the grape begins to shrivel. This continues until the grape is reduced to a black hard mass, with the folds of skin pressed closely against the seed. The disease does not spread from grape to grape, so that as a rule only a certain number of grapes in a bunch are destroyed. The hyphæ of the mycelium of this fungus are septate, with numerous short branches. The pustules on the surface are due to fructifications, pycnidia, and spermagonia. The presence of conidia has also been recently demonstrated. The fungus passes the winter in the withered grapes which fall to the ground; hence every care should be taken to collect these and burn them. The use of the solutions mentioned above may also be recommended as a preventative.

Other fungi. Among the other fungi which infest the vine may be mentioned *Phyllosticta viticola* and *Ph. Labruscæ*, which, when the attack is severe, cause the destruction of the leaves, the only part they assail. These, like the foregoing, are members of the *Pyrenomycetes.* To the same class belongs also *Cercospora vitis* (*Cladosporium viticolum*), which has club-shaped spores of a green-brown colour. This also attacks the leaves; but, unless the season is extremely unfavourable, it does little harm.

A very disastrous root-disease of the vine is due to the ravages of the fungus *Dematophora necatrix*, which forms subterranean strings of mycelium—so-called rhizomorphs—the fructification of which is as yet not known; it forms conidia and sclerotia, however, and presents certain analogies to the *Discomycetes.* The diseased roots have been confounded with those attacked by *Phylloxera.* The only mode of combating the malady seems to be to uproot the plants and burn them. Isolation of the diseased areas by means of trenches has also been practised. This fungus has extended its ravages considerably in southern France and Switzerland within the last ten years. (A. E. S.)

VINEA. See VIGNA.

VINEGAR is a dilute form of acetic acid, having a flavour that varies according to the source from which it is obtained. Vinegar has been known from the earliest historical period, and its power of acting on and dissolving mineral substances rendered it an important agent in the hands of the alchemists. They were, however, unacquainted with pure acetic acid; the most concentrated solution they possessed, called *spiritus veneris*, was obtained by distillation from cupric acetate (verdigris). The nature of acetous fermentation, and the rationale of the processes by which vinegar is prepared, are explained under FERMENTATION (vol. ix. p. 98); and the acetic acid obtained by the destructive distillation of wood is dealt with under TAR (vol. xxiii. p. 57). Here we have to do only with the various kinds of vinegar used for table, medicinal, and other household purposes. Malt, wine, and beetroot vinegars are made by the slow process, whilst for the quick method dilute brandy or other spirit is most largely employed.

Malt vinegar is the preparation commonly manufactured in the United Kingdom, the high alcoholic duties there excluding the use of spirits in the industry. A fermented wort is prepared, as in brewing, which is run into casks laid on their side, bung-hole upwards, till they are three-fourths filled. These casks have a hole bored in each end near the top, and between the three holes a constant circulation of air is secured over the surface of the liquid. The casks are disposed in low-roofed vaults, artificially heated, in which free circulation of air is kept up; but sometimes the process is carried on in the open air in what is termed a vinegar field. According to the temperature (which should be about 70° Fahr.) and other conditions, the acetification of the wort may occupy from weeks to months. From the casks the vinegar is transferred to large tuns provided with false bottoms, over which a thick layer of stalks and skins of grapes and raisins, &c., termed rapes, is strewn. Through this the vinegar is filtered from one tun into another, whereby it is cleared from mucilaginous matter and the last traces of alcohol are thoroughly oxidized. *Wine vinegar* is made in France and other vine-cultivating countries from wine lees and inferior wines. The finest vinegar is yielded by white wines, the product being purer, pleasanter, and generally stronger than ordinary malt vinegar. Vinegar is also largely prepared from beet-root, from the juice of other saccharine vegetables and fruits, and from sugar; and indeed all sources of alcohol may be regarded as possible materials for making vinegar. *Quick method vinegar* is made, principally in Germany, from dilute spirit (about one of proof spirit to six of water), to which are added small proportions of sugar, honey, or malt extract. The standard liquor used by different manufacturers varies considerably. The process is also used to some extent in England for converting fermented and clarified malt wort into vinegar. Commercial vinegar varies much in strength. What is termed "proof" vinegar contains 4·6 per cent of real acetic acid; and, as it requires twenty-four grains of anhydrous carbonate of soda to neutralize each fluid ounce, it is also known as No. 24. In the same way weaker qualities are known as No. 22, No. 20, &c., these figures indicating the grains of carbonate of soda which neutralize a fluid ounce.

Vinegar is extensively consumed in the preparation of pickles and sauces, and as a table condiment, especially with salad vegetables and fish. For many culinary purposes it is flavoured with aromatic herbs and spices. Aromatic vinegar, made from glacial acetic acid and perfumes, possesses a refreshing stimulating pungency, as is familiarly known by its use in vinaigrettes. Marseilles vinegar, or thieves' vinegar, is an aromatic preparation used as a prophylactic and masker of evil odours. Vinegar is also a menstruum for several medicinal agents; and in a concentrated condition it is a valuable rubefacient and external stimulant.

VINET, ALEXANDRE RODOLPHE (1797-1847), a French critic, though not a Frenchman, was born near Lausanne on 17th June 1797. He was educated for and duly entered the ministry of the Protestant Church, the date of his ordination being 1819. He had, however, already acquired an important position as teacher of the French language and literature in the gymnasium at Basel, and during the whole of his life he was more of a critic than of a theologian, though he exercised some influence in the latter capacity, headed a secession from the national church in Vaud, was for a time professor of theology at Lausanne, and advocated an extreme toleration in the matter of religious formulas, together with the separation of church and state. As a theologian Vinet would already have been long forgotten, despite some sermons and treatises which had a certain vogue in his native country, and, being in part translated into English, exercised some influence on English-speaking adherents of Calvinism. His performances as a literary critic, which for the most part represent his academic lectures, are, however, of greater importance. By procuring for Sainte-Beuve an invitation to lecture at Lausanne on Port-Royal, he was the cause of one of the capital works of recent French literary history. But he had less indirect titles to fame in the same department than this. Like all other French writers of repute in Switzerland, he has been accused by French-born censors of that mysterious patavinity which is supposed to attach to Swiss French, and which has been illustrated in such a remarkable fashion by Rousseau, Benjamin Constant, Joseph and Xavier de Maistre, Töpffer, and others. But the persons thus branded were probably content to write French as well as Livy wrote Latin. Vinet's *Chrestomathie Française* (1829), his *Études sur la Littérature Française au XIXème Siècle* and his *Histoire de la Littérature Française au XVIIIème Siècle*, together with his *Études sur Pascal*, *Études sur les Moralistes des XVIème et XVIIème Siècles*, *Histoire de la Prédication pendant les Réformes*, and other books gave evidence of a wide knowledge of literature, a sober and acute literary judgment, and a very considerable faculty of appreciation. On the whole, he belongs to the academic school of critics rather than to the romantic-impressionist school, or to that rarer and better school than either which adjusts its theories to the work which is brought before it, and condemns nothing so long as it is good work according to the writer's own standard. He had considerable affinities with this last, and his work, having the singular advantage of being in some sort foreign criticism, without undergoing the disadvantage which attaches in French eyes to all criticism of French affairs written in a foreign language, has had a great influence on France. Vinet died on 15th May 1847 at Clarens (Vaud). A considerable part of his works was not printed till after his death.

VINNITSA, a district-town of Russia, in the government of Podolia, is situated on the Bug, 137 miles to the north-east of Kamenets-Podolsk, and 29 by rail from the Zhmerinka junction on the railway from Odessa to Lemberg. It was founded in the 14th century, but nothing now remains of its two stone forts. Its old Jesuit college is now a gymnasium. Owing to the great fertility of the neighbourhood, there are a number of distilleries; and the Vinnitsa merchants, mostly Jews, carry on trade in corn and spirits. The population in 1884 was 18,580.

VIOL. See VIOLIN.

VIOLET. The violets comprise a genus of at least one hundred, some say two hundred species, found principally in temperate regions of the northern hemisphere; a few also occur in mountainous districts of South America, while the genus is not wholly without representatives in Australia. The species are mostly low-growing herbs with alternate leaves provided with large leafy stipules. The flowers are solitary, or rarely in pairs, at the end of slender axillary flower stalks. The flowers themselves are very irregular in form, with five sepals prolonged at the base, and five petals, the lowest one larger than the others and provided with a spur. The five anthers are remarkable for the petal-like processes which extend beyond the anther cells and form a sort of cone around the style. The ovary is superior, one-celled, with three parietal placentas and numerous ovules. It is surmounted by a single style, which terminates in a dilated or hook-like stigma. The fruit is a capsule bursting loculicidally, *i.e.*, through the centre of each of the three valves. The irregular construction of the flower is evidently connected with fertilization by insect agency. To reach the honey in the spur of the flower (of the pansy), says Müller, the insect must thrust its proboscis into the flower close under the globular head of the stigma. This lies in the anterior part of a groove fringed with hairs on the inferior petal. The anthers shed their pollen into this groove, either of themselves or when the pistil is shaken by the insertion of the bee's proboscis. The proboscis, passing down this groove to the spur, becomes dusted with pollen; as it is drawn back, it presses up the lip-like valve (of the stigma) so that no pollen can enter the stigmatic chamber; but as it enters the next flower it leaves some pollen on the upper surface of the valve, and thus cross-fertilization is effected. It is curious, however, that in the common violet, *V. odorata* and other species "cleistogamic" flowers occur of a greenish colour, so that they offer no attractions to insect visiters and their form is correspondingly regular. In such flowers self-fertilization is compulsory and very effectual, as seeds in profusion are produced.

Several species of *Viola* are native to Great Britain. *V. odorata* is highly prized for its fragrance, and in cultivation numerous varieties have originated. The garden pansies or heartseases are derivatives from *V. tricolor*, a cornfield weed, *V. altaica*, and *V. grandiflora*. They are reputed to have been first raised about 1810 by Lady Mary Bennet, with the assistance of her gardener, Mr Richardson, the term pansy or *pensée* having been long attributed to *V. tricolor*. The variety and richness of colouring in these flowers are very remarkable. "Bedding violas," which differ from pansies in some slight technical details, have been raised by crossing *V. lutea* with *V. calcarata*. The violas are credited with powerful emetic and diuretic properties, on which account they have been admitted into some of the pharmacopœias; but they are now very little used.

Description of the instrument.

VIOLIN, a stringed instrument employed in orchestral and chamber music. The body is a resonant box, composed of a belly, back, and six ribs, all shaped out of thin wood to various curves, the belly and back being scooped out of solid slabs, and the ribs planed and bent. The whole is glued together upon six internal blocks. Pine is used for the belly, maple for the other parts. The external surface is covered with a fine hard varnish of a brown, red, orange, or yellow colour, which renders the box more resonant. To this box is glued a solid neck or handle, slightly inclined to the plane of the box, and along the whole instrument four gut strings are stretched by means of as many pegs and a tail-piece. They are tuned in fifths, thus— and set in vibration with a bow, strung with horsehair well rubbed with rosin, which is held in the right hand, the scale being completed by stopping the strings with the fingers of the left hand, in which the instrument is held, on an ebony finger-board glued to the handle, and projecting over the body of the fiddle. The movable bridge, across which the strings are strained, forms the spring or mechanical centre of the violin, and answers to the reed in wood wind-instruments. It has two feet, of which the treble or right-hand one rests firmly on that part of the belly which is supported by a sound-post resting on the back, thus forming a rigid centre of vibration, while the bass or left-hand foot, resting on the freely-vibrating part of the belly, communicates to it, and through it to the air in the box, the vibrations which the bow excites in the strings. The belly is strengthened, and its vibration regulated and increased, by a longitudinal bar glued inside it exactly under the bass foot of the bridge. Two incisions in the belly, called sound-holes, from their letting out the sound, also facilitate and modify the vibration. The middle pair of ribs on each side have an inward curvature, to afford the bow better access to the strings. The superficial area of the belly is divided by the bridge into two approximately equal parts, for an obvious acoustical reason;[1] but the upper half is longer and narrower than the lower, which is relatively short and broad. This device gives greater length to the vibrating portion of the strings, and hence greater compass to the instrument. It also brings the bowing place on the strings nearer to the player.

Descent of violin.

The violin, as the name imports, is a modified form of the viol, an instrument constructed on exactly similar principles, though different in every detail. It dates from the middle of the 16th century; the viol was perfected somewhat earlier. During two centuries the two instruments were in use contemporaneously; but the violin class gradually drove the viols from the field, on the principle, which governs the general history of musical instruments, of the "survival of the loudest." The primitive viol is a modified form of the lute; and the lute is an adaptation of the small lyre of classical antiquity, the name of which (*fidicula*) survives in both groups of the common names for bowed instruments (fidicula, fidula, fideille, vielle, fidel, vedel, fiedel, fiddle; in the Romance group, vidula, viula, viola, violino, violone, violoncello).

Lyre.

The fidicula or lyre consisted of a resonant box, having a yoke (*jugum* or *transtillum*) instead of a neck, and one string for each note. Obviously, by substituting for the *jugum* a handle or neck, and thus enabling the fingers of the left hand to stop the strings at will, the number of strings and the tension on the box could be diminished, the scale of notes increased, and the task of the right hand facilitated. By this improvement the class of instruments denominated lyre developed into the lute class; and by other improvements upon the original basis it developed into the harp.

Viol.

The origin of the peculiar mechanism which, when added to the lute, produced the viol, viz., the movable bridge, sound-post, and bow, is obvious. The bow is a development of the plectrum employed for sounding the lyre. The bridge was borrowed from the Greek κανών, or monochord. Movable bridges (ὑπαγωγεῖς, *subductaria, ponticuli*) were employed to divide the monochord so as to produce the intervals of the various scales.[2] The sole use of this instrument being to train the ear of singers, it may well be supposed that musicians would endeavour to render the tone continuous, the better to support the voice; and this could be readily done by substituting for the plectrum a common military bow, with the string well rubbed with rosin,[3]—a substance largely used by the Greeks and Italians.

The bow

This supposition is confirmed by the fact that the marine trumpet, the most primitive of bowed instruments, is simply a bowed monochord. Although we can point to no pictorial representation of the bow as applied to musical instruments earlier than the 10th or 11th century, it is reasonable to conclude that the bridge and bow were adapted to the monochord and fidicula during the later empire. A substitute for the bow was afterwards found in the rosined wheel and handle, doubtless first applied to the monochord, afterwards perfected in the large mediæval organistrum, and still employed in the smaller vielle or hurdy-gurdy. The bow, however, held and still holds its ground as the most convenient means of producing continuous tone from stringed instruments. The substitution of a hank of horse-hair for the single bow-string dates from very early times.

Geige, crowd, rebec, and fidel.

Except the marine trumpet or bowed monochord, we find in Europe no trace of any large bowed instruments before the appearance of the viol in the 15th century. The geige, crowd, rebec, and fidel, as the small bowed instruments of the Middle Ages were variously called, were small enough to be rested on the shoulder during performance, and were usually rather smaller than the modern violin. It is not easy to assign each of these names to any particular form of instrument. They all had in common a resonant box, either circular, oval, or semi-pear-shaped, a handle with a finger-board, a tail-piece, a bridge, and from two to four strings tuned to fourths or fifths. The pegs were set vertically to the handle above the finger-board, as in the modern guitar. The bow, which was short and clumsy, had a considerable curvature, and the string a high tension. None of these instruments can have had a deeper compass than a boy's voice. The use of the fidel in the hands of the troubadours, to accompany the adult male voice, explains the attempts which we trace in the 13th century to lengthen the oval form of the instrument. A contrary curvature, as in the guitar, was then given to the sides of the resonant box, to enable the bow to reach the strings of the enlarged instrument. This may be denominated the troubadour's fiddle.

Side-blocks and corner-blocks.

The invention next to be described formed the turning-point in the history of bowed instruments. In order to keep in place the ribs of the troubadour's fiddle, with their troublesome contrary flexures, side-blocks inside the instrument were probably used. By cutting these blocks with an angle towards the outside, dividing each side rib into three smaller ones, and giving the middle one on each side a contrary curve so as to meet the upper and

[1] In order that the vibrational impulse may be given as nearly as possible at the centre of the mass of air in the resonant box.

[2] Meibomius, *Auctores Musicæ Antiquæ*, Amsterdam, 1652, p. 89.

[3] Rosin, manufactured as now from turpentine, was generally used in Italy and Greece in the preparation of wine (Pliny, *N.H.*, xiv. 20, 25), as an ingredient in medicine, and as a cosmetic (Scribonius Largus, *Compos.*, 137 *sq.*). Violin rosin is called in French *colophane* and in German *colophonium*, from the town of Colophon; and Colophonian rosin is described by Pliny as "præ cæteris fulva, si teratur alba fit, gravior odore." Good violin rosin answers exactly to this description.

lower ribs at an angle on the block, the resonant box was greatly strengthened, its construction became easier, and it became possible to make instruments of indefinitely larger size. Corner-blocks thus converted the fidel into the viol. Single corner-blocks (contrary flexures being still given to the upper ribs) were sometimes used, and often occur later on; but double corner-blocks came at once into general use, and resulted in the construction of the viol in several sizes. The mediæval fiddle appears originally to have had a perfectly flat belly like the lute. It must early have been discovered that a belly scooped out to a slight curve offered greater resistance to the pressure of the strings transmitted by the bridge. Bellies thus scooped out probably came into general use with the invention of corner-blocks. The back continued to be, and in the viol family has always been, a piece of flat joinery. Theoretically, no doubt, this is right; for a scooped-out back is false in construction, as there is nothing for the arch of the back to carry. But, as a back thus modelled and forming a duplicate of the belly, as in the violin, produces a much more powerful tone, this consideration has come to be disregarded.

The viol family.

The viol is an instrument, or rather family of instruments, of merit and interest, though now superseded by the violin, with the exception of the double bass, which still survives as a practical instrument. The following are the points in which the viol differs from the violin:—

The Viol has—	The Violin has—
1. A flat back of joiner's work.	1. A scooped-out back, modelled like the belly.
2. Shoulders with a contrary flexure in the pattern, and an oblique slope in the back.	2. Square shoulders, and a top like the bottom.
3. A high bridge mounted on legs.	3. A low bridge with feet only.
4. C-shaped, sometimes "flaming sword," sound-holes.	4. *f*-shaped sound-holes.
5. A thin broad handle.	5. A thick narrow handle.
6. Six or seven strings, tuned by fourths and a third.	6. Four strings tuned by fifths.
7. Square or obtuse corners.	7. Acute corners.
8. Deep ribs.	8. Shallow ribs.
9. A soft penetrating tone.	9. A ringing brilliant tone.

In the matter of 4 and 7 a few viols, made after the violin had been perfected, and chiefly Italian, follow the violin. The modern double bass also follows the violin in these points and in 5. The viol was made in three main kinds,—discant, tenor, and bass,—answering to the cantus, medius, and bassus of vocal music. Each of these three kinds admitted of some variation in dimensions, especially the bass, of which three distinct sizes ultimately came to be made—(1) the largest, called the concert bass viol; (2) the division or solo bass viol, usually known by its Italian name of viola da gamba; and (3) the lyra or tablature bass viol. The normal tuning of the viols, as laid down in the earliest books, was adapted from the lute to the bass viol, and repeated in higher intervals in the rest.

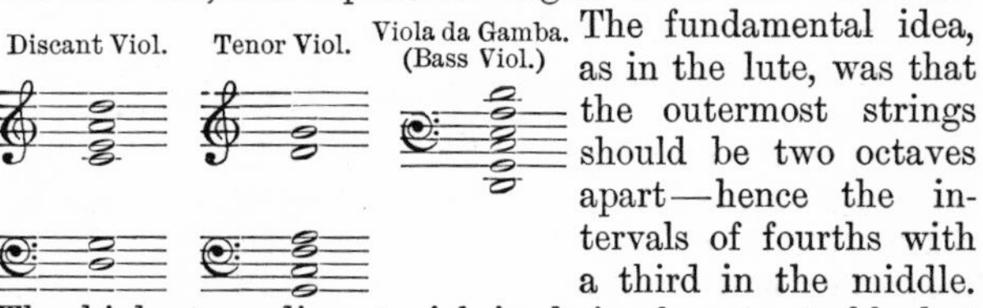

The fundamental idea, as in the lute, was that the outermost strings should be two octaves apart—hence the intervals of fourths with a third in the middle.

Discant viol.

The highest, or discant viol, is obviously not a treble but an alto instrument, the three viols answering to the three male voices. As a treble instrument, not only for street and dance music, but in orchestras, the rebec or geige did duty until the invention of the violin, and long afterwards. The discant viol first became a real treble instrument in the hands of the French makers, who converted it into the quinton.

Double bass viol.

The double bass, the largest of the viols, is not a legitimate member of the family, having no corresponding voice, and being from the purely musical point of view superfluous. It appeared, however, concurrently with the bass, as soon as the invention of corner-blocks made it possible to construct bowed instruments of a size only limited by the possibility of playing them. As the discant viol is determined in size by the proportions of the bent arm, the tenor viol by the height above the knee of a sitting player, the bass by a relative height when the instrument is held between the knees, instead of supported on them, so the double bass is determined in size by the height of the standing figure, the bottom of the resonant box resting on the ground. In this respect it corresponds with the marine trumpet, which afforded an obvious hint for its construction. Originally it was made for six strings, the tuning being as follows:—

Double Bass Viol.

In imitation probably of the largest register of pipes on the improved organs which were then being built, the double bass viol was used as a sub-bass. For this purpose the three highest strings were probably soon found to be useless, and they must have been very liable to break; and, as the pressure of useless strings impairs the resonance of the instrument, they seem to have been gradually dropped. The three lowest strings are the same as those used for the modern double bass.

Development of the viols.

The earliest use of the viols was to double the parts of vocal concerted music; they were next employed in special compositions for the viol trio written in the same compass. Many such works in the form of "fantasies" or "fancies," and preludes with suites in dance form, by the masters of the end of the 16th and 17th centuries, exist in manuscript; a set by Orlando Gibbons, which are good specimens, has been published by the English Musical Antiquarian Society. Later, the viols, especially the bass, were employed as solo instruments, the methods of composition and execution being based on those of the lute. Most lute music is in fact equally adapted for the bass viol, and *vice versa*. In the 17th century, when the violin was coming into general use, constructive innovations began which resulted in the abandonment of the trio of pure six-stringed viols. Instruments which show these innovations are the quinton, the lyre, and the viola d'amore. The first-mentioned is of a type intermediate between the viol and the violin. In the case of the discant and tenor viol the lowest string, which was probably found to be of little use, was abandoned, and the pressure on the bass side of the belly thus considerably lightened. The five strings were then spread out, as it were, to the compass of the six, so as to retain the fundamental principle of the outer strings being two octaves apart. This was effected by tuning the lower half of the instrument in fifths like the violin and the upper half in fourths. This innovation altered the tuning of the treble and tenor viols, thus—

Treble Quinton. Quinte or Tenor Quinton.

One half of the instrument was therefore a viol, the other half a violin, the middle string forming the division. The tenor viol thus improved was called in France the quinte, and the treble corresponding to it the quinton. From the numerous specimens which survive it must have been a popular instrument, as it is undoubtedly a substantially excellent one. The relief in the bass, and the additional pressure caused by the higher tuning in the treble, gave it greater brilliancy, without destroying the pure, ready, and sympathetic tone which characterizes the viol. While the tendency in the case of the discant and tenor was to lighten and brighten them, the reverse process took place in that of the bass. The richer and more sonorous tones of the viola da gamba were extended downwards by the addition of a string tuned to double bass A, thus—

Seven-stringed Viola da Gamba.

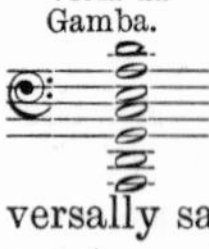

Marais, a French virtuoso, is usually credited with this improvement; and this extended compass is recognized in the classical viola da gamba writings of Sebastian Bach and De Caix d'Hervelois. The result, however, was not universally satisfactory, for Abel used the six-stringed instrument; and the seven strings never came into general use in England, where the viola da gamba was more generally employed and survived longer than elsewhere.

The want of positive power, which is the weakness of the viol and ultimately drove it from the field, must have been early noticed on a comparison of its delicate tones with the harsher notes of the rebec. Hardly had the viol appeared, when makers cast about for means of augmenting its tone. One way of doing this was by additional strings in unisons, fifths, and octaves, a device which had been already employed in the small fiddles of the Middle Ages, and is identical in principle with the augmentation of diapason tone on the organ by means of other registers. The double or treble strung viol, in various sizes, was known as the lyre (Italian, *accordo*); but this multiplication of strings proceeds on a false principle, for each additional string diminishes the resonance of the box, and at the same time hardens the tone and increases the task of the player. More ingenious and successful was the invention of sympathetic metal strings, usually steel, laid under the finger-board, as close as possible to the belly, and speaking by consonance with the notes produced on the bowed strings. From this resonance by sympathy the viol thus strung acquired the general name of *viola d'amore*. The original viola da gamba when so strung came to be called the *viola bastarda*; the seven-stringed bass, with an elaborately perfected sympathetic apparatus, was well known in the 18th century by the name of the *bordone* or baritone, and was a favourite instrument with musical epicures. Instruments made on this principle are found in all sizes; even kits are met with having sympathetic strings (*sordino d'amore*). Violins with sympathetic strings (usually five) are more rare; the viola d'amore chiefly used was of tenor size and compass. Originally tuned as to its bowed strings like the pure tenor viol, an additional string was given it, and the so-called "harp-way" tuning adopted, thus—

Sympathetic strings.

Viola d'Amore, flat tuning. Viola d'Amore, sharp tuning.

The sympathetic strings were attached to ivory pegs driven into the bottom block, passed through the lower part of the bridge, or over a low bridge of their own, as near as possible to the surface of the belly, under the fingerboard, and were strained to pitch either by means of additional pegs, or, better, by wrest-pins driven into the sides of the peg box and tuned by a key. Originally six, seven, or eight sympathetic strings were used, which were tuned to the diatonic scale of the piece in performance. Later, a chromatic set of twelve strings was employed; and instruments are met with having a double set (24) of chromatic strings, two for each semitone in the scale. With thirty-one strings to be kept in perfect tune, the task of the player must have been arduous indeed; and it is not strange that instruments so elaborate and troublesome were abandoned. In a moist climate like that of Great Britain it is practically impossible to keep a viola d'amore in playing order, the steel strings being in most of their length covered by the fingerboard and out of reach, while the slightest rust impairs the resonance, and much rust renders the instrument completely useless.

The violin.

The improvements which were to develop an ultimate bowed instrument for permanent musical use proceeded in the opposite direction to the lyre and viola d'amore: they consisted in increasing yet more the resonance of the box, by making it lighter and more symmetrical and by stringing it more lightly, instead of more heavily. This was really falling back on primitive principles, for the hints were certainly derived from old extant specimens of the crowd and the geige. Existing pictures prove that the oval and the circular geige were made with nearly flat backs and bellies of correlative pattern; and it was natural to seek to reproduce their more powerful tone in the viol by giving it shallower ribs and a back modelled like the belly, and by assimilating the top of the instrument, where the handle is added, to the bottom. This change at once transformed the box of the viol into that of the violin, and the transformation was completed by rejecting the lute tuning with its many strings and tuning the instrument by fifths, as the geige and rebec had always been tuned. The tenor viol was apparently the first instrument in which the change was made, about the middle of the 16th century, and it was so successful that it was quickly applied to the treble and bass instruments.

The question so often mooted, Who invented the violin? may therefore be dismissed. The instrument was produced by applying to the viol certain principles borrowed from its smaller predecessors. It would be equally correct to say that it was produced by applying to the geige other principles borrowed from the viol. Tradition indicates one of the Tieffenbrückers, a German family whose members for more than a century were famous lute-makers in Venetia and Lombardy, as the inventor. The earliest instrument of the violin type known to the present writer is a tenor made by Fr. Linaroli of Bergamo, at Venice, in 1563; and the earliest makers whose authentic works have descended to us in considerable numbers are Gaspar da Salò and Maggini, both of Brescia.

High and flat modelled violins.

An important distinction should be mentioned which divides violins into two classes, known respectively as the "high" and the "flat" model. On this subject much has been said and written; but it has not been discussed scientifically, nor has the prevalence of one model over the other at different times and in different places been accounted for. It is understood that, while the flat model, which has now practically driven the high model from the field, yields a tone that is more powerful and travels further, the high model yields a tone which comes out more readily, and is softer and more flute-like, although less capable of light and shade. The high model is less convenient for the player, because when the instrument is rested on the clavicle the strings are at a greater altitude in relation to the right arm, which accordingly requires to be raised. Hence the high model has become less popular as the art of violin-playing has developed, and is undoubtedly less suitable to the elaborate system now in use. These remarks apply to instruments of pronounced high model; for the distinction is in fact a matter of degree, and is purely mechanical in origin. The flattest models rise about twelve millimetres above the ribs, while the highest do not exceed twenty, and many of the best violins have an elevation between these limits. The object of the rise being to give just such a degree of resistance to the pressure of the bridge as will set the enclosed air in due vibration, and this degree being approximately the same in all violins, the amount of elevation must obviously be relative to the strength and elasticity of the fibres of the belly. The more regular the shape of the box,—that is, the flatter the model,—the more perfect and the more completely blended will be the undulations of the mass of air within, and the more uniformly sonorous and musical the tone; but owing to the pressure of the strings only strong and elastic wood can be used for this model. Wood of stiff and brittle fibre must be worked to a higher arch, or if used for the flat model must be left too thick for perfect vibration. Hence we might expect to find the flat and the high model employed respectively where different qualities of wood are available, with a corresponding result in the tone. Fine elastic pine is chiefly found on the southern slopes of the Alps; and thereabouts the best viols and violins have always been made. The famous violin-makers carried on their trade at Brescia, Cremona, Mantua, Milan, and Venice, while the Piedmontese Alps and the Apennines furnished material for some makers in Piedmont and at Bologna. High-modelled violins, and flatter instruments of thicker wood and inferior sonority, were chiefly made in Tyrol, Germany, France, and England, where the available material was less tenacious and elastic.

Early Italian makers.

The early Italian school is chiefly represented by the Brescian makers, Gaspar da Salò, Giovanni Paolo Maggini, Giovita Rodiani, and the two Zanettos (1580-1630). It is, however, misleading to denominate it the Brescian school, for its characteristics are shared by the earliest makers of Cremona and Venice. To eyes familiar with the geometrical curves of the later Cremona school most of the violins of these makers, like the early violins of England and Germany, have a rude and uncouth appearance. The height of the model varies; the pattern is attenuated; the *f*-holes share the general rudeness of design, and are set high in the pattern. Andreas Amati of Cremona, the eldest maker of that name, effected some improvements on this primitive model; but the violin owes most to his sons, Antonio and Geronimo, who were partners. Nicholas, son of Geronimo, and Antonio Stradivari, the pupil of Nicholas, each did something to perfect the model; but the substantial improvements which converted the Brescian violin into the modern instrument were the work of Antonio and Geronimo. These improvements, which were, in fact, of an artistic rather than a scientific nature, consisted in modelling the instrument in all its outlines and surfaces to regular curves. Painting and inlaying had long been employed in the decoration of stringed instruments; but the brothers Amati were the first who applied to the violin the fundamental law of decorative art, that the decorative and constructive elements should be blended in their inception: in other words, the construction should be itself decorative and the decoration itself constructive. The nature of the instrument suggested the application of this law, for all extraneous additions to the varnished wood of which it consists tend to damp the tone. Nicholas Amati (1596-1684) made some slight improvements in the Cremona model, and Antonio Stradivari (1649-1737) finally settled the typical Cremona pattern, which has been generally followed; for the majority of violins since made, whether by good or bad makers, are copies of Stradivari. Besides the last-named, the following makers worked generally on the Amati model,—Cappa, Gobetti, the Grancino family, Andreas Guarnieri, and his son Giuseppe, the Ruggieri family, and Serafin of Venice. Balestrieri, the Bergonzi family, Alessandro Gagliano, the earlier members of the Guadagnini family, Montagnana, and Panormo were pupils or followers of Stradivari. Landolfi, Storioni, and Carlo Giuseppe Testore, a pupil of Giovanni Grancino, leaned to the model of Giuseppe Guarnieri del Gesù. Some resemblances, especially in the matter of the varnish, are traceable between the works of makers who lived contemporaneously in the same town, *e.g.*, in Naples, Milan, and Venice.

German, English, and French makers.

The Amati method was adapted to the higher model by Jacob Stainer of Absam, near Hall in Tyrol, whose well-known pattern was chiefly followed by the makers of England, Tyrol, and Germany, down to the middle of the 18th century. It thenceforward fell into disuse, owing to the superior musical qualities of the Cremona violin and to improved means of communication, which enabled the violin-makers of other countries to procure wood sufficiently soft and tenacious to be worked to the flat model. The school of Stainer is represented amongst many others by Albani, Hornsteiner, the Klotz family (who made large numbers of instruments excellent in their kind), Schorn of Salzburg, and Withalm of Nuremberg. The English makers may be divided into three successive groups:—1. an antique English school, having a character of its own (Rayman, Urquhart, Pamphilon, Barak Norman, Duke of Oxford, &c.); 2. imitators of Stainer, at the head of whom stands Peter Wamsley (Smith, Barrett, Cross, Hill, Aireton, Norris, &c.); 3. a later school who leaned to the Cremona model (Banks, Duke of Holborn, Betts, the Forsters, Gilkes, Carter, Fendt, Parker, Harris, Matthew Hardie of Edinburgh, &c.). The early French makers have little merit or interest (Bocquay, Gavinies, Pierray, Guersan, &c.); but the later copyists of the Cremona models (Lupot, Aldric, Chanot the elder, Nicholas, Pique, Silvestre, Vuillaume, &c.) produced admirable instruments, some of which rank next in merit to the first-rate makers of Cremona.

The tenor violin, in compass a fifth lower than the treble violin, appears to have preceded the latter; and from

Tenor violin and violoncello.

Tenor Violin. Violoncello. Basso da Camera.

existing specimens we know that the bass violin, now termed the violoncello, with a tuning an octave below the tenor, appeared very shortly afterwards. A double bass violin, tuned a fourth below the violoncello and usually known as the *basso da camera*, completed the set of instruments in violin shape; but from the difficulty attending its manipulation it never came into general use. The celebrated double bass player, Dragonetti, occasionally used the basso da camera, and an English player named Hancock, who dispensed with the highest or E string, is still remembered for his performances on this unusual instrument.

The tenor and violoncello are made on the same general model and principles as the violin, but with certain modifications. Both are relatively to their pitch made smaller than the violin, because, if they were so constructed as to have the same relation to the pitch and tension of the strings as the violin, they would not only have an overpowering tone but would be unmanageable from their size. This relatively diminished size, both in the dimensions of the instrument and in the thickness of the wood and strings, gives to the tenor and violoncello a graver and more sympathetic tone. To some extent this reduced size is compensated by giving them a greater proportional height in the ribs and bridge; the increase is hardly perceptible in the tenor, but is very noticeable in the violoncello. Correlative to this general diminution in the size of the instrument and the tension of the strings as the bass register is entered, there is a progressive diminution in the size and tension of the strings of each instrument, the treble string having in all cases the greatest tension and being thickest in proportion, though actually the thinnest. This is partly due to the fact that the ear demands greater brilliancy and force in the higher register; but it has also a mechanical reason. The treble foot of the bridge is fixed, while the bass foot vibrates freely; additional stability is given to the rigid side and additional freedom to the bass side by lightening the tension in each string progressively towards the bass. This can be verified by the simple experiment of stringing up a violin with the strings reversed, but without altering the sound-post and bass-bar. Still further to lighten the tension on the bass side, the lowest string of the violin and the two lowest of the tenor and violoncello are specially made of thin gut and covered with fine metal wire. Such strings yield a grave tone with comparatively little tension.

Scordatura.

It is obvious that, if the lowest string, or the two lowest strings, are elevated in pitch, the tension will be greater, and the violin will produce a more powerful tone; if the bass string is lowered, the contrary will take place. By adapting the music to this altered tuning (*scordatura*) some novel effects are produced. The following are the principal *scordature* which have been occasionally employed by various players.

The violoncello is less amenable to the scordatura than the violin; the only classical instance is the tuning employed by Bach in his fifth sonata, which consists in lowering the first string by a tone.

Bach.

It is commonly said that an old violin is better than a new one. Other things being equal, and supposing

"Good" violins.

the older to be in fair preservation, this is true; it is also true that of old violins the best, as a rule, have survived. Good violins, however, have been continuously made, and are still being made, though since the middle of the 18th century the cheapness of the "trade" fiddle, made by the hundred by divided labour, has much circumscribed the business of the higher-class workman. The best workmen of different countries differ little in merit; but it is seldom that any maker out of Italy is successful in varnishing his work so as to impart to it the superior resonance which characterizes the best Italian violins. The varnish, originally merely ornamental and preservative, has become an essential part of the work, from its intimate connexion with the tone. The secret of making varnish is not lost, as is sometimes stated; the difficulty consists in applying and drying it with reference to the climate where the operation takes place. In moist climates, oil varnish, which is the best, dries too slowly; hence the use of spirit varnish, which is more manageable, but has not the effect of permeating the superficial tissues of the wood so as to increase and perpetuate its elasticity. Many well-made modern violins, notably those of some French makers, have proved failures, because they have, under a mistaken belief, been made out of old and dry wood. After a few years pine begins to lose its elasticity; the old makers used wood that was only just sufficiently seasoned, and they preserved its elasticity by applying their varnish at once.

It is also commonly said that a flat violin is preferable to a high-modelled one. This must be accepted with some modification. Instruments which are excessively flat should be avoided, for reasons above stated. A moderate height, rather less than the medium, is most favourable to vibration; what is really essential is that the sound-holes should be in horizontal planes, not in planes inclined at a considerable angle to the transverse section of the instrument. Such sound-holes, as may be proved at once by the ear, have the property of immediately letting out the vibrations of the small mass of air which lies directly under the bridge, and thus rob the great mass of air in the body of the fiddle of the impulse necessary to set it properly in vibration; hence the tone, though quickly yielded and not feeble to the ear of the player, is found at a short distance to be deficient in force and flexibility. The violins most in request are the larger specimens of the Amati family, of Stradivari and his best pupils, and of the two cousins Giuseppe Guarnieri,—the instruments of Giuseppe called "del Gesù," from his use of the sacred monogram on his tickets, being by some players preferred to those of Stradivari. For old instruments of the best class purchasers must be prepared to pay from £200 to £600, according to their quality and state of preservation. Second-class old Italian instruments, and first-rate specimens of the best school of French copyists, can usually be bought for smaller sums down to £20. The chief seats of the wholesale violin manufacture are Mirecourt in France and Markneukirchen in Saxony.

Violin bow.

The violin bow, which is made of Brazil wood, was reduced to its present admirable shape about 1780 by François Tourte of Paris (1747-1835), whose bows are still esteemed above all others. A fair Tourte bow is generally worth £10; but a fine one has been sold for £30; and one of his best violoncello bows, which are rarities, was recently sold in Paris for £44. Bows, however, which leave little to be desired are made in great numbers by English, French, and German makers. A good bow is of more importance to a player than a good violin; something may be done with an indifferent instrument, but no one can play with a bad bow.

Strings.

The best strings have always been made in Italy; the climate of northern Europe is unsuitable for the manufacture. Good strings are essential to the player, and they should be frequently changed, as they only retain their shape at the place where the bow touches them, and their elasticity, for a limited period.

For further information on the history of stringed instruments, the reader is referred to Vidal, *Les Instruments à Archet*, 3 vols. 4to (Paris, 1876-79); Rühlmann, *Gesch. der Bogen-Instrumente* (Brunswick, 1882); and the various articles in Grove's *Dictionary of Music and Musicians*. The best handbook of violin-makers is Hart's *Violin* (London, 1875-80). The process of violin-making is well described in E. H. Allen's *Violin-Making as it was and is* (London, 1885). A smaller work, which can be recommended, is Maugin's *Manuel du Luthier* (Paris, 1869). The art of playing the violin has been practically treated at length by Campagnoli, Baillot, Spohr, Ferdinand David, Alard, and many other professors of the various schools; but the only attempt to explain it systematically with reference to sound scientific theory is contained in an unpretending *brochure* by Karl Courvoisier (*Die Violin-Technik*, Cologne, 1878), which it is impossible to praise too highly. See also *Musical Instruments, Historic, Rare, and Unique*, by A. J. Hipkins (Edinburgh, 1887). (E. J. P*.)

VIOLLET-LE-DUC, Eugène Emmanuel (1814-1879), French architect and writer on archæology, was born at Paris on 27th January 1814. He was a pupil of Achille Leclère, and in 1836-37 spent a year studying Greek and Roman architecture in Sicily and Rome. His chief interest was, however, in the art of the Gothic period, and, like Sir Gilbert Scott in England, he was employed to "restore" some of the chief mediæval buildings of France, his earliest works being the abbey church of Vézelay, various churches at Poissy, St Michel at Carcassonne, the church of Semur in Côte-d'Or, and the fine Gothic town-halls of Saint-Antonin and Narbonne, all carried out between 1840 and 1850. From 1845 to 1856 he was occupied on the restoration of Notre Dame in Paris in conjunction with Lassus,[1] and also with that of the abbey of St Denis. In 1849 he began the restoration of the fortifications of Carcassonne and of Amiens cathedral; and in later years he restored Laon cathedral, the château of Pierrefonds, and many other important buildings. He was an intimate friend of Napoleon III., and during the siege of Paris (1871) gave valuable help as an engineer to the beleaguered army.[2] He held many important offices, both artistic and political, and was for many years inspector-general of the ancient buildings throughout a large part of France. His last work was the general scheme for the Paris exhibition buildings in 1878. He died on 17th September 1879.

As a designer Viollet-le-Duc occupied only a secondary place; but as a writer on mediæval architecture and the kindred arts he takes the highest rank. His two great dictionaries are the standard works in their class, and are most beautifully illustrated with very skilful drawings by his own hand. Viollet-le-Duc was a man of the most varied and brilliant abilities, endowed with a power of work which has seldom been equalled. He was at once an artist, a man of science, a learned archæologist, and a scholar. His map showing the rock contours and the glaciers of Mont Blanc is a model of its kind, which combines great artistic beauty with the accuracy of the most skilful engineer. His strong poetical fancy enabled him to reconstruct the life and buildings of the Middle Ages in the most vivid way. His principal literary works were the *Dictionnaire de l'Architecture Française du XI. au XVI. Siècle*, 1853-69; *Dictionnaire du Mobilier Français*, 1854-75; *L'Architecture Militaire au Moyen Âge*, 1854; *Habitations Modernes*, 1874-1877; *Histoire d'une Maison*, 1873; *Histoire d'une Forteresse*, 1874; *Histoire de l'Habitation Humaine*, 1875; *Le Massif de Mont-Blanc*, 1876; *L'Art Russe*, 1877; *Histoire d'un Hôtel-de-Ville et d'une Cathédrale*, 1878; *La Décoration appliquée aux Édifices*, 1879; as well as many minor works dealing with separate buildings.

VIOLONCELLO. See Violin.

VIOTTI, Giovanni Battista (1753-1824), violinist and musical composer, was born at Fontanetto in Piedmont, on 23d March 1753. He learned the rudiments of music from his father, a veterinary surgeon and an amateur horn-player; and in 1764 Giovannini taught him the violin for a year. Two years later he was placed by the Marchesa di Voghera under the violinist Pugnani at Turin. In 1780 Viotti, having already made himself a name, travelled through Germany and Poland to Russia, where the empress Catherine honoured him with marks of extraordinary favour. He next appeared in London, in company with Pugnani, and at once achieved a brilliant and lasting reputation. In 1782 he was equally successful in Paris. Two years later he was appointed leader of Prince de Soubise's private orchestra; and in 1788 he undertook the direction of the opera, raising the performances, with Cherubini's assistance, to a very high level. Viotti also joined with Feydeau-de-Brou in constructing the famous Feydeau theatre. In 1790 the Revolution compelled him to fly to England; but a charge of Revolutionary espionage drove him for a time to Hamburg, whence, however, he returned in 1795. From that time he resided almost uninterruptedly in London until 1818, when he once more settled in Paris, resumed the direction of the opera, and retired in 1822 with a pension. He died in London on 10th March 1824.

Viotti's playing was distinguished by an extreme purity of style, a magnificent tone, and an endless variety of poetical and imaginative expression. He was undoubtedly the best violinist of the age, and the best composer for his instrument. Among his works are 29 violin concertos, a series of symphonies concertantes for two violins, 45 duos, 18 trios, and 21 quartetts, and a great number of sonatas, notturnos, and other instrumental works. His school was worthily perpetuated by his pupil Rode.

[1] He published in 1867-69 a fine work showing his not very successful coloured decoration applied to the chapels of Notre Dame.

[2] See his *Mémoire sur la Défense de Paris*, 1871.

VIPER. The vipers constitute a family (*Viperidæ*) of Old-World, poisonous, viviparous snakes, which have a single movable poison fang on either side of the upper jaw, without any excavation or pit between the eye and the nostril,—thus differing from the *Crotalidæ*. They have a post-frontal and a maxillary bone, which latter is swollen and upright, articulating with the pre-frontal by a ginglymus, and short—not reaching the premaxilla. Vipers are mostly more or less thick-bodied and short-tailed, the head being entirely covered above with small scales, except in a single species. The nose is often recurved, and some scales of the head are elongated so as to form "horns" in several species. The main points in the anatomy[1] of the group have been already described in the article REPTILES, and their zoological relations stated in the article SNAKES.

There is much diversity of opinion as to the classification of the vipers, and, as Dr Alexander Strauch appears to be the author who has worked out the group with the greatest care and completeness, his classification is here provisionally adopted.

The *Viperidæ* thus consist of three genera, which are distinguished as follows:—

(1) Two rows of sub-caudal scales.................... { *Vipera* (20 species.)
(2) One row of sub-caudal scales—
  a. Gular scales smooth, body rounded or depressed, tail simple .... { *Echis* (1 species.)
  b. Gular scales strongly keeled, body compressed, tail prehensile.................... { *Atheris* (3 species.)

The common viper (*V. berus*) is easily distinguished from the harmless ring-snake by the black and white (or yellow) band behind the head, which is generally conspicuous in the latter animal. It is also distinguishable (apart from individual varieties) from the snake *Coronella*, rare in England, by having a dark V-shaped mark on its head and a dark zig-zag line down the back. It is this viper which has the top of the head covered by shields (which may be regular or irregular in outline) instead of small scales only. It is one of the most widely distributed of snakes, being found from northern Spain eastwards to the island of Saghalin, and from the northern boundary of Persia to beyond the Arctic Circle in Scandinavia, though it is not found in Ireland. It inhabits all sorts of situations, though it prefers a dry soil, and it may be met with at an elevation of 9000 feet above the sea. It seeks its prey at night, and penetrating the burrows of mice will eat their nestlings. Its bite is sometimes fatal to large dogs, and occasionally to weakly children. It brings forth in April and May from five to fourteen young, which are hatched as they are born.

The other European vipers are *V. aspis*, *V. ammodytes*, and *V. latastii*.[2] *V. aspis* is very like the common viper, save as to the scales on the head and the fact that its snout is somewhat turned up. It inhabits France, Switzerland, and Italy. *V. ammodytes* is a somewhat larger species, with a singular pointed process extending upwards from the snout end. It is found in Egypt, Syria, Asia Minor, Turkey, Greece, southern Austria, and Italy. *V. latastii* is a species intermediate between *V. aspis* and *V. ammodytes*. It inhabits Spain, Portugal, Morocco, and Algiers. Thus, of the four European vipers, two are also found in Africa and one in both Africa and Asia. There are three exclusively Indian vipers,—*V. xanthina*, *V. persica*, and *V. russellii*. *V. xanthina* is an animal about 2½ feet long. As in all the other non-European vipers, the body scales are strongly keeled. It is found in Asia Minor, Syria, and Persia. *V. persica* is, as its name implies, a Persian animal. The scales above each eye are so modified as to form a horn. *V. russellii* is hornless, but very large: it is said to attain a length of more than 6 feet. It is widely distributed, inhabiting India, Burmah, Siam, Ceylon, Sumatra, and Java.

[1] For a description of the poison fang, see vol. xx. p. 457; and for a figure of the skull, see vol. xx. p. 452.

[2] In collections wherein very many specimens are preserved it is possible to find transitional forms between all the four European species.

Two vipers are common to Asia and Africa. One of these, *V. mauritanica*, extends from Algiers to Persia. It may be nearly 5 feet long. The other species, *V. cerastes*, is a much smaller snake, never being much more than 20 inches in length. It is remarkable for two long pointed horns (which stand up over either eye), and is widely distributed in North Africa and Arabia. All the other species of the genus *Vipera* are exclusively African, and only one is found north of the Sahara. This is *V. avizennæ*. It has no horns, and only attains a length of about 16 inches. *V. superciliaris* is also a small snake, but it has a large rugose supra-orbital plate. It comes from Mozambique. The puff-adder (*V. arietans*) is a large thick snake, which may be 4 feet long. It is a very deadly animal, and is widely distributed over southern and central Africa, extending to both the east and west coast of that continent. It is without horns. *V. nasicornis* is a beautifully

FIG. 1.—*Vipera nasicornis*.

coloured, large, and bulky snake, which may be upwards of 6 feet long. Two horns project obliquely forwards from just in front of either nostril. It inhabits southern Africa. It is a very venomous animal.[3] *V. rhinoceros* is another large snake, which comes from both the east and west coasts. It has a pair of horns upstanding between its nostrils, each clothed with but a single shield. *V. cornuta* has scaly prominences, which are hardly "horns," and which consist each of a group of four or five large upright distinct scales placed above one of the eyes. It is a small snake, hardly ever more than 20 inches long. It inhabits western, southern, and eastern Africa. *V. caudalis* is a still smaller snake, which has a single scale extending upwards over either eye. It comes from southern Africa, as also does *V. schneideri*, which is like the last species, save that it has nothing at all representing horns. *V. inornata* is also hornless, though it has the supraorbital region somewhat elevated. It is a very small snake, only about 15 inches long. It is a South-African species, as also are *V. atropos* and *V. atropoides*, which are both hornless and are about 2 feet long.

The genus *Echis* consists of but one species (*E. carinata*), which has been noticed and figured in the article SNAKES (see vol. xxii. p. 198). It is a viper-like snake, which

[3] On one occasion one of these snakes, after giving birth to twenty-one young (which bit and killed mice within five minutes of being born), became very ill-tempered, and when two adult males were placed in her cage she bit one with such violence as to break off one of her fangs, which she left, about three-quarters of an inch in length, sticking in his back. He, however, appeared not to suffer the slightest inconvenience, and was never the worse for it (see *Proc. Zool. Soc.*, 1871, p. 638).

inhabits desert lands or dry plains, and extends from India through Abyssinia and North Africa to Senegal.

Fig. 2.—*Atheris burtoni*. (Length 12 inches.)

The genus *Atheris* is made up of several more or less problematical species of snakes, all of which present a great contrast to the other *Viperidæ*, in that they have long, slender, and laterally compressed bodies with prehensile tails—being altogether adapted for arboreal life. Nevertheless the head is decidedly viperine, sharply marked off from the neck, broad behind, and heart-shaped when looked at from above. These animals are assisted in climbing, not only by their prehensile tails, but also the strongly keeled scales beneath the lower jaw. All the so-called species are inhabitants of tropical Africa,—*A. burtoni*, *A. squamigera*, and *A. chloroechis* being found on the west coast. Two new species have been lately discovered, *A. anisolepis* and *A. cæviceps*,—both from the Congo.

The genus *Acanthophis* is sometimes classed with the vipers, but is here excluded on account of its large, truly colubrine head shields. See Snakes, vol. xxii. p. 198.

The *Viperidæ* are geographically distributed as follows:—

Palæarctic Region.[1]—*V. berus*, *V. aspis*, *V. ammodytes*, *V. latastii*, *V. xanthina*, *V. persica*, *V. mauritanica*, *V. cerastes*, *V. avizennæ*, *E. carinata.*

Ethiopian Region.—*V. superciliaris*, *V. arietans*, *V. nasicornis*, *V. rhinoceros*, *V. cornuta*, *V. caudalis*, *V. schneideri*, *V. inornata*, *V. atropos*, *V. atropoides*, *A. burtoni*, *A. squamigera*, *A. chloroechis.*

Indian Region.—*V. russellii*, *E. carinata.* (ST G. M.)

VIRGIL (P. Vergilius Maro) enjoyed in ancient times an unquestioned supremacy among Roman poets. His pre-eminence in poetry was as distinctly recognized as that of Cicero in prose; and among the Romans, as among all nations who have possessed a great poetical and a great prose literature, the superior power of poetry over that of any other mode of artistic expression to embody and perpetuate the true ideal of the national imagination and the deepest vein of national sentiment, was fully recognized. The veneration in which his name was held during the long interval between the overthrow of Western civilization and the revival of letters affords testimony of the depth of the impression which he made on the heart and imagination of the ancient world. The traditional belief in his pre-eminence has been on the whole sustained, though not with absolute unanimity, in modern times. By the scholars and men of letters of the 16th, 17th, and 18th centuries it was never seriously questioned. Only during the first half of the present century has his right to be ranked among the great poets of the world been disputed by eminent German and English critics. The German mind has always been more in sympathy with the art and genius of Greece than of Rome and Italy; and during the first half of the present century, when English criticism first came under German influence, there was a strong reaction from the habitual deference paid to those writers who had moulded literary taste in the previous century. The estimation of Virgil, as the most consummate representative of Latin culture, suffered most from this reaction.

In the present day the effect of this reaction shows itself only in a juster estimate of Virgil's relative position among the poets of the world. It is no longer a question whether he or Homer was best entitled to hold that "sceptre" among the great poets of antiquity which Lucretius awards to the older poet. It may still be a matter of individual opinion whether Lucretius himself was not a more powerful and original poetical force, whether he does not speak more directly to the heart and imagination of our own time. But it can hardly be questioned, on a survey of Roman literature, as a continuous expression of the national mind, from the age of Nævius to the age of Claudian, that the position of Virgil is central and commanding, while that of Lucretius is in a great measure isolated. If we could imagine the place of Virgil in Roman literature vacant, it would be much the same as if we imagined the place of Dante vacant in modern Italian, and that of Goethe in German literature. The serious efforts of the early Roman literature—the efforts of the older epic and tragic poetry—found their fulfilment in him. The revelation of the power and life of Nature, first made to Lucretius, was able to charm the Roman mind, only after it had passed into the mind of Virgil, and been brought nearer to the heart of Romans and Italians by association with the industry most congenial to them. And not only does Virgil absorb and supersede much of what went before him; he anticipates and supersedes much of what came after him. When we have read the *Æneid*, we add scarcely anything to our sense of the capacities of the Italian genius and of the Latin language by studying the artificial epics of the empire. It is enough to read any ten lines of them along with any ten lines of Virgil to feel how absolute is his superiority.

Virgil is the only complete representative of the deepest sentiment and highest mood of his countrymen and of his time. In his pastoral and didactic poems he gives a living voice to the whole charm of Italy, in the *Æneid* to the whole glory of Rome. He was in the maturity of his powers at the most critical epoch of the national life, one of the most critical epochs in the history of the world. Keeping aloof from the trivial daily life of his contemporaries, he was moved more profoundly than any of them by the deeper currents of emotion in the sphere of government, religion, morals, and human feeling which were then changing the world; and in uttering the enthusiasm of the hour, and all the new sensibilities that were stirring in his own heart and imagination, he had, in

[1] This region includes Europe, Africa north of the Sahara, and Asia north of the Himalayas.

the words of Sainte-Beuve, "divined at a decisive hour of the world what the future would love." He was also by universal acknowledgment the greatest literary artist whom Rome produced. It was an essential condition of Roman more than of any other great literature that it was based on culture and education. Not only the knowledge but the inspiration of Greek poetry—"spiritus Graiæ camenæ"—was the condition of Roman success in poetry. Virgil had not only more learning and culture, but had a more catholic sympathy with the whole range of Greek poetry, from Homer and Hesiod to Theocritus and the Alexandrians, than any one else at any period of Roman literature. Greek studies were in his time pursued with greater ardour, completeness, and thoroughness than at any previous period. The effort of the preceding generation to attain to beauty of form and finish of artistic execution found in him, at the most susceptible period of his life, a ready recipient of its influence. The rude dialect of Latium had been moulded into a powerful and harmonious organ of literary expression by the emotional ardour and vigorous understanding of a long series of orators; the rough and unhewn structure of the Latin hexameter, first shaped by Ennius to meet the wants of his own spirit and of his high argument, had been smoothed and polished by the congenial labour of Lucretius, and still more perfected by the finer ear and more careful industry of Catullus and his circle; but neither had yet attained their final development. It was left for Virgil to bring both diction and rhythm to as high a pitch of artistic perfection as has been attained in any literature.

The great work which he accomplished was the result of the steady devotion of his genius, undistracted by pleasure or business, to his appointed task. For the first half of his life he prepared himself to be the great poet of his time and country with a high ambition and unresting industry, equalled only by the ambition and industry with which Cicero prepared himself to be the greatest orator and the most accomplished exponent of philosophy among his contemporaries and countrymen. The second half of his career was a religious consecration of all his powers of heart, mind, and spirit to his high office. He was born on the 19th of October in the year 70 B.C., in a farm on the banks of the Mincio, in the district of Andes, not far from the town of Mantua. He thus belonged to a generation about thirty years younger than that to which Lucretius belonged, and about fifteen years younger than that of Catullus: but both these poets were dead before the younger poet was old enough or sufficiently known to have come into personal contact with them. But the literary impulse which gave birth to their poetry was felt in all its force in his early youth, and especially in the district north of the Po, in which a race of more imaginative susceptibility than the people of Latium, who had been the first to receive the discipline and feel the enthusiasm of Greek studies, formed part of the Latin-speaking population.[1] It was favourable to his development as a national poet that he was born and educated during the interval of comparative calm between the first and second civil wars, and that he belonged to a generation which, as the result of the social war, first enjoyed the sense of an Italian nationality. Yet it was only after Virgil had grown to manhood that the province to which he belonged obtained the full rights of Roman citizenship. It is remarkable that the two poets whose imagination seems to have been most powerfully possessed by the spell of Rome,—Ennius and Virgil,—were born outside the pale of Roman citizenship, though belonging to races who had acknowledged the sovereignty without deeply or permanently resenting the hostility of Rome.

The scenery familiar to his childhood, which he recalls with affection both in the *Eclogues* and the *Georgics*, was that of the green banks and slow windings of the Mincio and the rich pastures in its neighbourhood. Like his friend and contemporary Horace, and unlike the poets of the preceding generation, who were members either of the aristocracy or of the class closely associated with it, he sprung from the class of yeomen, whose state he pronounces the happiest allotted to man and most conducive to virtue and piety. Virgil, as well as Horace, was fortunate in having a father who, though probably uneducated himself, discerned his genius and spared no pains in nourishing it with the highest and richest culture then obtainable in the world. At the age of twelve he was taken for his education to Cremona, an old Latin colony, and from an expression in one of the minor poems attributed to him, about the authenticity of which there cannot be any reasonable doubt, it may be inferred that his father accompanied him thither as Horace's father accompanied him to Rome for the same purpose. He assumed the *toga virilis* on his sixteenth birthday, the day, according to Donatus, on which Lucretius died; and shortly afterwards he removed to Milan, where he continued engaged in study till he went to Rome two years later. The time of his removal to Rome must have nearly coincided with the publication of the poem of Lucretius and of the collected poems of Catullus, the first really artistic poems produced in the Latin language. A powerful stimulus must have been given to a youth of genius from a northern province by his arrival in the metropolis of the world at such a crisis in the national literature. The impression produced on his imagination on his first coming to Rome may be recalled to memory in the lines he puts into the mouth of Tityrus in the first eclogue,

"Urbem quam dicunt Romam Melibœe putavi," &c.

After studying under a rhetorician, who was, probably about the same time, the teacher of the future emperor, he proceeded to the study of philosophy under Siron the Epicurean, who, in common with other teachers of that sect, appears to have had the gift of inspiring enthusiasm for his subject and affection for himself. One of the minor poems written about this time in the scazon metre, which had recently been brought to the highest possible perfection by Catullus, tells of his delight at the immediate prospect of entering on the study of philosophy, and of the first stirring of that enthusiasm for philosophical investigation which haunted him through the whole of his life, but never obtained complete realization. At the end of the poem, the real master-passion of his life, the charm of the Muses—"dulces ante omnia Musæ"—reasserts itself.

Our next knowledge of him is derived from allusions to his circumstances and state of feeling contained in the *Eclogues*, and belongs to a period nine or ten years later. Of what happened to him in the interval, during which the first civil war took place and Julius Cæsar was assassinated, we have no indication from ancient testimony or from his own writings. We might conjecture that this was a time of studious leisure passed in his father's house in the country, as the life of Milton was passed after leaving Cambridge. In 42 B.C., the year of the battle of Philippi, when he was in his 28th year, we find him leading such a life, "cultivating his woodland Muse," and enjoying the protection of Asinius Pollio, the governor of the district north of the Po. In the following year the famous confiscations of land for the benefit of the soldiers of the triumvirs took place. Of the impression produced

[1] *Cf.* Cic., *Pro Archia*, iii. 5—"Erat Italia tunc plena Græcarum artium ac disciplinarum, studiaque hæc et in Latio vehementius tum colebantur quam nunc iisdem in oppidis, et hic Romæ propter tranquillitatem reipublicæ non neglegebantur."

on Virgil by these confiscations, and of the effect they had on his fortunes, we have a vivid record in the poem which stands first in his collected works. Mantua, in consequence of its vicinity to Cremona, which had been faithful to the cause of the republic, was involved in this calamity; and Virgil's father was driven from the farm which he had acquired by the thrift and industry of his early years. By the influence of his powerful friends, and by personal application to the young Octavianus, already practically master of the Western world, Virgil obtained the restitution of his land; but, on attempting to resume possession of it, he was exposed to imminent personal danger, and had to swim across the river to escape from the violence of the soldier to whom it had been allotted. Immediately afterwards he took his father and family with him to the small country house of his old teacher Siron

("Villula quæ Sironis eras, et pauper agelle," &c., *Catal.*, x.),

which may have become his own by gift or inheritance. Soon afterwards we hear of him living in Rome, enjoying, in addition to the patronage of Pollio, the favour of Mæcenas, intimate with Varius, who was at first regarded as the rising poet of the new era, and soon afterwards with Horace, who had just returned from his unfortunate adventure with the army of Brutus. His friendship with Gallus, for whom he indicates a warmer affection and more enthusiastic admiration than for any one else, was formed before his second residence in Rome, in the Cisalpine province, with which Gallus also was connected both by birth and office. The pastoral poems, or "eclogues," as they are usually called, though that name is never given to them by himself, commenced in his native district, were finished and published in Rome, probably in 37 B.C. Soon afterwards he withdrew from habitual residence in Rome, and lived chiefly in Campania, either at Naples or in a country house in the neighbourhood of Nola. He resided also for some time in Sicily; and there is in the fourth *Georgic* distinct evidence of his familiarity with the neighbourhood of Tarentum. He was one of the companions of Horace in the famous journey to Brundisium; and it seems not unlikely that, sometime before 23 B.C., he made the voyage to Athens which forms the subject of the third ode of the first book of the *Odes* of Horace.

The seven years from 37 to 30 B.C. were devoted to the composition of the *Georgics*. In the following year he read the poem to Augustus, on his return from Asia. The remaining years of his life were spent on the composition of the *Æneid*. In the course of its composition, in 23 B.C., the year of the death of the young Marcellus, he read three books, the 2nd, 4th, and 6th, to the emperor and the members of the imperial family. In 19 B.C., after the *Æneid* was finished but not finally corrected, he set out for Athens, intending to pass three years in Greece and Asia, and to devote that time to perfecting the workmanship of the poem. At Athens he met Augustus and was persuaded by him to return with him to Italy. While visiting Megara under a burning sun, he was seized with illness, and, as he continued his voyage without interruption, he grew rapidly worse, and died on the 21st of September, in his fifty-first year, a few days after landing at Brundisium. In his last illness he called for the cases containing his manuscripts, with the intention of burning the *Æneid*. He had previously left directions in his will that his literary executors, Varius and Tucca, should publish nothing of his which had not already been given to the world by himself. This pathetic desire that the work to which he had given so much care, and of which such great expectations were formed, should not survive him has been used as an argument to prove his own dissatisfaction with the poem. A passage from a letter of his to Augustus is also quoted, in which he speaks as if he felt that the undertaking of the work had been a mistake. Virgil does not indeed show that sanguine confidence in the result of his labours which Horace expresses on the completion of the three books of lyrical poetry to which he devoted the best years of his life; but the lines (*Æn.*, ix. 444, &c.),

"Fortunati ambo si quid mea carmina possunt," &c.,

though with less self-assertion, imply a similar assurance that his work would endure as long as the Roman state and empire. The dissatisfaction with his work, increased by the depression of his last illness and the fatigue of the long tension of mind, heart, and imagination upon it, may more probably be ascribed to his passionate craving for a perfection of workmanship which death prevented him from attaining than to any sense either of the unworthiness of his subject or of his own inadequacy to do justice to it. The commands of Augustus fortunately intervened to prevent the loss of some of the noblest poetry of antiquity and of the most enduring monument of the greatness and glory of Rome.

He was buried at Naples, where his tomb was long regarded with religious veneration, and visited as a temple. That veneration was a survival of the feeling with which he was regarded in his lifetime, and is greater than what we find attaching to the actual memory of any other ancient poet, though the mystery connected with the personality of Homer excited a greater curiosity. Horace is our most direct witness of the affection which he inspired among his contemporaries. The qualities by which he gained their love were, according to his testimony, "candor,"—that sincerity of nature and goodness of heart which, along with "fides" or loyalty, the Romans valued most among the qualities which attach men to one another; and "pietas,"—the deep affection for kindred, friends, and country, combined with a reverent spirit, which they prized above all personal qualities. The statement of his biographer, that he was known in Naples by the name "Parthenias," is a testimony to the exceptional purity of his life in an age of licence. These direct testimonies are confirmed by the indirect testimony of his works. Scarcely any poet in any age seems to deserve so high a rank among those whom he himself characterizes as "pii vates et Phœbo digna locuti." The seclusion of his life and his devotion to his art touched the imagination of his countrymen as the finer qualities of his nature touched the heart of his friends. It had been, from the time of Cicero,[1] the ambition of the men of finest culture and most original genius in Rome to produce a national literature which might rival that of Greece; and the feeling that at last a poem was about to appear which would equal or surpass the greatest among all the works of Greek genius found a voice in the lines of Propertius—

"Cedite Romani scriptores, cedite Graii;
Nescio quid majus nascitur Iliade."

The feeling which his countrymen and contemporaries entertained towards him seems justified by the personal impression which he produces on modern readers,—an impression of sanctity, as of one who habitually lived in a higher and serener sphere than that of this world. The reverential love inspired by him is something distinct from the affection felt for Horace as a familiar friend, a wise

[1] *Cf. Tusc. Disp.*, ii. 2: "Quamobrem hortor omnes qui facere id possunt, ut hujus quoque generis laudem jam languenti Græciæ eripiant," &c. These words apply specially to philosophical literature, but other passages in the same and in other works imply that Cicero thought that the Romans had equal aptitudes for other departments of literature; and the practice of the Augustan poets in each appropriating to himself a special province of Greek literary art seems to indicate the same ambition.

counsellor, and genial companion, sharing the ordinary interests and pleasures of life, liable to the same weaknesses and endeared by the same social charm as those who are best liked in the intercourse of our own day.

Virgil's fame as a poet rests on the three acknowledged works of his early and mature manhood—the pastoral poems or *Eclogues*, the *Georgics*, and the *Æneid*—all written in that hexameter verse which he received from his immediate predecessors, still lacking something in variety and smoothness of cadence, and which he left to the world, in the words of a poet, who, if any one, is entitled to speak with authority on such a subject,

"The noblest metre ever moulded by the lips of man."

But other poems were attributed to him in ancient times, and have been incorporated with his acknowledged works. These are (1) a collection of short poems, under the name "Catalepton," most of them in the style of the short poems of Catullus, and composed in various forms of the iambic metre (chiefly the scazon), and in elegiacs; and (2) some longer poems, the *Culex*, *Ciris*, *Copa*, *Moretum*, to which sometimes the *Ætna* and *Diræ* are added, all with one exception written in hexameters. As the younger Pliny mentions Virgil among the men of grave character by whose authority he justifies his own occasional indulgence in the composition of slight, playful, and somewhat indecorous verses, it is quite possible that two or three pieces of that kind found in the *Catalepton* may have been written by Virgil when fresh from the first reading of Catullus. The fifth, written in the couplet most used in the *Epodes* of Horace, and the most bitter in tone and coarsest in expression, it is impossible to attribute to him. But there are others among them of which there is no reason to question the authenticity, and which are interesting as an immediate expression of the poet's personal feelings at various periods of his life. Of the longer poems attributed to him in ancient times it is clear from internal evidence that the *Ciris* and *Diræ*, though belonging to the Augustan age, are not his. The *Ætna* has been shown to have been written in the age of Nero. The *Moretum* and the *Copa* are interesting as graphic and sharply defined pictures from common or homely life. But they have nothing in common with the idealizing art of Virgil, and the tone and sentiment of the *Copa* especially are quite alien from the tone and sentiment of his acknowledged work. But there has been more controversy about the authenticity of the *Culex*. The ambitious saying, not to apply to it a harsher epithet, attributed by his biographer to Lucan, "et quantum mihi restat ad Culicem," shows that in his time it was believed that Virgil had written a poem of that name. Martial (xiv. 185) writes of a *Culex* as the undoubted work of Virgil. He believes in it as unhesitatingly as he does in the "Passer Catulli," and speaks as if it were only the patronage of Mæcenas that enabled Virgil to rise to higher themes. Virgil's biographer speaks of the poem as having been written by him at the age of sixteen, though the saying of Lucan seems to imply that he supposed it to have been written when he was ten years older. The poem has no trace of the charm and variety of Virgil's style and rhythm, and is even less like the style and metre of the *Eclogues* than of his later poems. On the other hand, there is a technical correctness and regularity in the metre which was not possible until after the art of Virgil had made the knack of writing hexameters as attainable by all educated men as the art of Pope made the writing of the heroic couplet; and the writing of such verse seems to have become a regular part of a liberal education. It is to be remembered that in the same soil and under the same air under which the genius of Virgil and Horace expanded to such stately proportions, there was a great undergrowth of minor poets who are the frequent butts of Horace's good-natured satire. Descriptions of nature to which they were trained by the reading of Lucretius and Virgil, and mythological commonplace, were apparently the chief materials of their verse exercises. The descriptions in the *Culex* show the careful study both of Lucretius and of the *Eclogues* and *Georgics*, and, though too diffuse and diluted, are not without a real perception of, and feeling for, Italian nature. But it is very difficult to believe that the poem was ever edited by or acknowledged by Virgil in his lifetime. Nothing is more alien to his character than such immature ambition. It is difficult also to believe that it is a crude effort of his boyhood, accidentally preserved, and given to the world after his death by an authorized editor. It seems more probable that it is the composition of some young and enthusiastic admirer of Virgil, who, some time after his death, and, perhaps, after the death of his immediate contemporaries, succeeded in palming off his own imitative concoction as an early composition of the great master. The dedication to the "revered Octavius," if the person addressed is the "young Augustus," and not the poet and historian mentioned by Horace, and the lines—

"Posterius graviore sono tibi musa loquetur
Nostra, dabunt cum maturos mihi tempora fructus"—

seem like not very ingenious artifices to secure acceptance for the poem, and to represent Virgil as already in boyhood closely connected with the future emperor, and conscious of his own genius and of the great future that awaited both himself and the young friend whom he addresses as "sancte puer."

Eclogues.

The pastoral poems or *Eclogues*—a word denoting short selected pieces—were composed between the years 42 and 37 B.C., when Virgil was between the age of twenty-eight and thirty-three. By his invocation to the "Sicelides Musæ" and "Arethusa," by the names "Daphnis" and "Menalcas," "Thyrsis" and "Corydon," &c., which he gives to his shepherds, by his mention of "Arcadians" and of "Eurotas," and by many other indications, he avows the purpose of eliciting from the strong Latin language the melody which the "Sicilian shepherd" drew out of the "Doric reed," of peopling the familiar plains and river-banks of his native land with the picturesque figures of the old Greek pastoral, and of expressing that tender feeling for the beauty of Italian scenes which Theocritus had expressed for the beauty of Sicily. The position of Virgil indicated in the *Eclogues* was not unlike that indicated in the idylls of Theocritus,—that of a youth of genius with all the refinement of a rich culture, but with rustic tastes and habits, living his life among other young poets of his native province, cultivating his art by friendly rivalry with them, and nourishing his genius by communion with the spirit of nature as revealed in the scenes around him and in the melodies of older poets. It was as natural under these circumstances that he should aspire to be the Italian Theocritus as that Horace, with his more social and versatile temperament, and with the more adventurous experience of his youth, should aspire to be the Roman Alcæus.

The earliest poems in the series were the second, third, and fifth; and these, along with the seventh, are the most purely Theocritean in character. The first and ninth, which probably were next in order, are much more Italian in sentiment, are much more an expression of the poet's own feelings, and have a much more direct reference both to his own circumstances and the circumstances of the time. The first is a true poetical reflex of the distress and confusion which arose out of the new distribution of lands, and blends the poet's own deep love of his home, and of the sights and sounds familiar to him from childhood, with his Italian susceptibility to the beauty of nature. The ninth is immediately connected in subject with the first. It contains the lines which seem accurately to describe the site of Virgil's farm, at the point where the range of hills which accompany the river for some distance from the foot of the Lago di Garda sinks into the plain about 14 or 15 miles above Mantua—

"Qua se subducere colles
Incipiunt mollique jugum demittere clivo."

The sixth is addressed to Varus, who succeeded Pollio as governor of the Cisalpine district. Its theme is the creation of the world (according to the Epicurean cosmogony), and the oldest tales of mythology.[1] The fourth and eighth are both closely associated with the name of Virgil's earliest protector, Pollio. The fourth celebrates the consulship of his patron in 40 B.C., and perhaps also the birth of his son, though it was disputed in antiquity, and still is disputed, who was meant by the child whose birth was to be coincident with the advent of the new era, and who, after filling the other great offices of state, was to "rule with his father's virtues the world at peace." The main purpose of the poem, however, is to express, in connexion with pastoral associations, the longing of the world for a new era of peace and happiness, of which the treaty of Brundisium seemed to hold out some definite hopes. There is no trace in this poem of Theocritean influence. The rhythm recalls the stately monotonous movement of the longest poem of Catullus, not the vivacity of the idyllic rhythm. The ideas are derived partly from Greek representations of the Golden Age, and partly, it is supposed, from the later Sibylline prophecies, circulated after the burning in the time of Sulla of the old Sibylline books, and possibly tinged with Jewish ideas. Some of the phraseology of the poem led to a belief in the early Christian church that Virgil had been an unconscious instrument of inspired prophecy. The date of the eighth is fixed by a reference to the campaign of Pollio against the Dalmatians in 39 B.C. It is founded on the Φαρμακευτρία of Theocritus, but brings before us, with Italian associations, two love tales of homely Italian life. The tenth reproduces the Daphnis of Theocritus, and is a dirge over the unhappy love of Gallus and Lycoris. As in the other poems, the second and eighth, of which love is the burden, it is to the romantic and fantastic melancholy which the passion assumes in certain natures that Virgil gives a voice. Nothing can be more unreal than the association of such a feeling with an ordinary *liaison* like that of Gallus, the adventurous and ambitious soldier, and Cytheris, the notorious actress and discarded mistress of Antony. But there is no representation in ancient poetry of an ideal and chivalrous passion so tender and true as that of the Gallus of Virgil.

There is no important work in Latin literature, with the exception of the comedy of Terence, so imitative as the *Eclogues*. But they are not, like the comedies of Terence, purely exotic as well as imitative. They are rather composite, partly Greek and partly

[1] In the *Georgics* also Virgil attempts to combine science with the poetic fancies which filled its place in older times.

Italian, and, as a vehicle for the expression of feeling, hold an undefined place between the objectivity of the Greek idyll and the subjectivity of the Latin elegy. For the most part, they express the sentiment inspired by the beauty of the world, and the kindred sentiment inspired by the charm of human relationships. Virgil's susceptibility to the beauty of nature was fostered by the sympathetic study of Theocritus, but it was also native to himself. The originality of his representation appears in the truth with which it suggests the charm of Italy—the fresh and tender life of an Italian spring, the grace and delicate hues of the wild flowers, and the quiet beauty of the green pastures and the rich orchards of his native district. The representative character of the poems is enhanced by the fidelity and grace with which he has expressed the Italian peasant's love of his home and of all things associated with it. But, whatever detraction may have to be made from the originality of the substance and form of these poems, the supreme charm of the medium of diction and rhythm through which the poet's feeling has found utterance is universally recognized. The power of varied harmony is as conspicuous in Virgil's earliest poems as in the maturer and more elaborate workmanship of the *Georgics* and *Æneid*. The Italian language, without sacrifice of the fulness, strength, and majesty of its tones, acquired a more tender grace and more liquid flow, which reappeared long after in the poets of modern Italy, from the gift—the "molle atque facetum"—which the Muses of country life bestowed on Virgil.

Georgics. But these Muses had a more serious and dignified function to fulfil than that of glorifying the picturesque pastime, the "dolce far niente," the "otia dia," of rural life. The Italian imagination formed an ideal of the happiness of a country life nobler than that of passive susceptibility to the sights and sounds of the outward world. In the idyllic picture in which Horace enumerates the various delights of the countryman's condition (*Epode* 2), while the pleasures to eye and ear are not wanting, more stress is laid on the labours by which man co-operates with nature, and on the joy with which he contemplates the results of his toil. It was the aim of the more serious Roman writers to invest objects which minister to practical utility with the glory and charm of poetry. Suetonius tells us that Augustus valued nothing so much in literature as "præcepta et exempla publice vel privatim salubria." It is stated that Mæcenas, acting on the principle of employing the poets of the time in favour of the conservative and restorative policy of the new government, directed the genius of Virgil to the subject of the *Georgics*. From a moral, social, and national point of view, no object could be of more consequence in the eyes of a statesman whose master inherited the policy of the popular leaders than the revival of the great form of national industry, associated with the older and happier memories of Rome, which had fallen into abeyance owing to the long unsettlement of the revolutionary era as well as to other causes. Virgil's previous life and associations made it natural for him to identify himself with this object, while his genius and artistic accomplishment fitted him to enlist the imagination of his countrymen in favour of so great a practical reform. It would be a most inadequate and false view of his purpose to suppose that, like the Alexandrian poets or the didactic poets of modern times, he desired merely to make useful information and practical precepts more attractive by the aid of poetical rhythm and diction. His aim was rather under the form of practical instruction to describe with realistic fidelity, and at the same time to surround with an atmosphere of idealizing poetry, the annual round of labour in which the Italian yeoman's life was passed; to bring out the intimate relation with the manifold aspects and processes of nature into which man was brought in the course of that life, and to suggest the delight to heart and imagination which he drew from it; to contrast the simplicity, security, and sanctity of such a life with the luxury and lawless passions of the great world; and to associate the ideal of a life of rustic labour with the varied beauties of Italy and the historic glories of Rome. Thus a speculative and religious, an ethical and patriotic, motive enlarges and supersedes the apparent motive of conveying instruction. This larger conception of the dignity of his subject separates the didactic poem of Virgil from all other didactic, as distinct from philosophic, poems. He has produced in the *Georgics* a new type of didactic, as in the *Æneid* he has produced a new type of epic, poetry.

The subject which is unfolded in the four opening lines—

> "Quid faciat lætas segetes, quo sidere terram
> Vertere, Mæcenas, ulmisque adjungere vites
> Conveniat; quæ cura boum, qui cultus habendo
> Sit pecori, apibus quanta experientia parcis"—

is treated in four books, varying in length from 514 to 566 lines. The first treats of the tillage of the fields, of the constellations, the rise and setting of which form the farmer's calendar, and of the signs of the weather, on which the success of his labours largely depends. The second treats of the cultivation of trees, and especially of the vine and olive, two great staples of the national wealth and industry of Italy; the third of the rearing of herds and flocks and the breeding of horses; the fourth of the tending of bees. The treatment of these homely subjects is relieved by various episodes, introduced at various places, but mainly at the end of the different books, which serve to bring out the intimate connexion of his theme with his national and ethical purpose.

As he had found in Theocritus a model for the form in which his idler fancies were expressed, he turned to an older page in Greek literature for the outline of the form in which his graver interest in rural affairs was to find its outlet; and, though the *Works and Days* of Hesiod could not supply an adequate mould for the systematic treatment of all the processes of rural industry, and still less for the treatment of the larger ideas to which this systematic treatment of the subject is subsidiary, yet that Virgil considered him as his prototype is shown by the line which concludes one of the cardinal episodes of the poem—

> "Ascræumque cano Romana per oppida carmen."

By the use which he makes of his quaint phraseology Virgil attracts attention to the relation which he wishes to establish between himself and Hesiod; and in the religious spirit with which they each regard man's labours and condition in the world there is a real affinity between the primitive Bœotian bard and the refined artist of the Augustan age. Virgil accepts also the guidance of other models of the decadence of Greek literature, the Alexandrian poets who treated the science of their day—astronomy, natural history, and geography—in the metre and diction of epic poetry. But, in availing himself of the work of the Alexandrians, Virgil is like a great master making use of mechanical assistants. From the comparison of passages in the *Georgics* with passages in those authors which suggested them, we learn to appreciate the immeasurable superiority of the poetical language of Rome at the maturity of its development over the exotic diction produced in the decay of Greek creative imagination. But a more powerful influence on the form, ideas, sentiment, and diction of the *Georgics* was exercised by the great philosophical poem of Lucretius, of which Virgil had probably been a diligent student since the time of its first appearance, and with which, in the phrase of the English editor of the older poet, his mind was "saturated" when he was engaged in the composition of the *Georgics*. In Virgil we find the spirit of Hesiod in conflict with the spirit of Lucretius. He is at once attracted and repelled by the genius and attitude of the philosophic poet. He is possessed by his imaginative conception of nature, as a living all-pervading power; he shares with him the Italian love of the beauty of the world, and the pathetic sympathy with animal as well as human life. He recognizes with enthusiasm his contemplative elevation above the petty interests and passions of life. But he is repelled by his apparent separation from the ordinary beliefs and pleasures, the hopes and fears, of his fellow men. Virgil is in thorough sympathy with the best restorative tendencies—religious, social, and national—of his time; Lucretius was driven into isolation by the anarchic and dissolving forces of his.

So far as any speculative idea underlying the details of the *Georgics* can be detected, it is one of which the source can be traced to Lucretius—the idea of the struggle of human force with the forces of nature. In Virgil this idea is modified by Italian piety and by the Italian delight in the results of labour. In the general plan of the poem, and the systematic arrangement of his materials, Virgil follows the guidance of Lucretius rather than of any Greek model. The dedication and personal appeals to Mæcenas are parallel to those addressed to Memmius. The distinction between a poem addressed to national and one addressed to philosophical sympathies is marked by the prominence assigned in the one poem to Cæsar as the supreme personality of the age, in the other to Epicurus as the supreme master in the realms of mind. The invocation to the "Di agrestes," to the old gods of mythology and art, to the living Cæsar as the latest power added to the pagan Pantheon, is both a parallel and a contrast to the invocation to the all-pervading principle of life, personified as "Alma Venus." In the systematic treatment of his materials, and the interspersion of episodes dealing with the deeper poetical and human interest of the subject, Virgil adheres to the practice of the older poet. He makes use of his connecting links and formulas, such as "principio," "quod superest," "his animadversis," "nunc age," &c. Virgil indeed uses these more sparingly, so as to make the logical mechanism of the poem less rigid, while he still keeps up the liveliness of a personal address. He shows his artistic superiority by passing lightly over details which it is impossible to invest with beauty. All his topics admit of being vitalized by attributing the vivacity of human relationships and sensibility to natural processes, and by association with the joy which the ideal farmer feels in the results of his energy. Much of the argument of Lucretius, on the other hand, is as remote from the genial presence of nature as from human associations. Virgil makes a much larger use than Lucretius of ornament borrowed from older poetry, art, science, and mythology. There is uniformity of chastened excellence in the diction and versification of the *Georgics*, contrasting with the imaginative force of isolated expressions and the majesty of isolated lines and passages in Lucretius. The "vivida vis" of imagination is more apparent in the older poet; the artistic perfection of Virgil is even more conspicuous in the *Georgics* than in the *Eclogues* or the *Æneid*.

The principal episodes of the poem, in which the true dignity and human interest of the subject are brought out, occur in the first and second books. Other shorter episodes interspersed through the different books add variety to the didactic disquisition. These episodes, as is the case still more with the episodes of Lucretius, are not detached or isolated ornaments, but give a higher unity to the poem, and are the main ground of its permanent hold upon the world. There is indeed one marked exception to this rule. The long episode with which the whole poem ends,—the tale of the shepherd Aristæus, with which is connected the more poetical fable of Orpheus and Eurydice, has only the slightest connexion with the general ideas and sentiment of the poem. It is altogether at variance with the truthful realism and the Italian feeling which prevade it. If we suppose that Virgil originally thought it necessary to relieve the interest and keep the attention of his readers by appealing to their taste for those mythological tales, which in an earlier part of the poem he had decried as "omnia jam volgata," it would be difficult to acquit even so great an artist of some forgetfulness of the requirement of unity of impression in a work of art, especially in such a "templum de marmore" as the *Georgics*. But we are distinctly told that the concluding episode, from the middle till the end of the fourth book, had contained the praises of Gallus, the friend of Virgil's youth, who, about the time when Virgil was finishing the poem, had gained distinction in the war against Cleopatra, and had in consequence been made the first governor of the new province of Egypt. It is difficult to see how such a statement could have been invented if it were not true. Such a conclusion might well have been in keeping with the main purpose of the poem. As the first book ends with a dirge over the national fortunes before the outbreak of the war with Antony and Cleopatra, the last book might well have ended with a hymn of triumph over the successful end of that war, in which the hero of Virgil's youthful enthusiasm played so distinguished a part. After the fall of Gallus, owing to his ambitious failure in his Egyptian administration, and his death in 26 B.C., the poet, according to the story, in obedience to the command of the emperor, substituted for this encomium the beautiful but irrelevant fable of Orpheus and Eurydice, in which he first displayed the narrative skill, the pathos, and the magical power of making the mystery of the unseen world present to the imagination, which characterize the *Æneid*.

The cardinal episodes of the poem, as it now stands, are the passages in bk. i. from line 464 to the end, and in bk. ii. from 136 to 176 and from 475 to 542. The first, introduced in connexion with the signs of the weather, recounts the omens which accompanied the death of Julius Cæsar, and shows how the misery of Italy and the neglected state of the fields, for which the poem seeks to find a remedy, are the punishment for the great sin of the previous generation. In the second of these passages the true keynote of the poem is struck in the invocation to Italy—

> "Salve, magna parens frugum, Saturnia tellus,
> Magna virum.

The thought of the varied beauties of the land, of the abundance and variety of its products, of its ancient cities and mighty works of man, its brave and hardy races, the great men and great families who had fought for her and saved her in old times, and of him, the greatest among her sons, who was then defending Rome against her enemies in the farthest East, inspires the poet, and gives dignity to the trivial details which seem sometimes to clog his high ambition. But a still higher and more catholic interest is given to the subject in the greatest of the episodes,—the most perfect passage in all Latin poetry,—that from line 458, "O fortunatos nimium," to the end. The subject is there glorified by its connexion not only with the national wellbeing but with the highest life and purest happiness of man. An ideal is held up to the imagination in which the old realistic delight in the labours of the field blends with the new delight in the beauty of nature, and is associated with that purity and happiness of family life which was an Italian ideal, and with the poetry of those religious beliefs and observances which imparted a sense of security, a constantly recurring charm, and a bond of social sympathy to the old rustic life.

The *Georgics* is not only the most perfect in art, but is the most native in sentiment and conception of all the works of the ancient Italian genius. It is essentially Italian in idea, in detail, in religious and ethical feeling, in colouring and sentiment, in its solid and massive composition. Though the form was borrowed from the Greek, yet we have to remember that it was only by becoming a province of Roman art that the didactic poem acquired dignity and the capacity of treating a great theme. Even where he borrows from Greek originals, Virgil, like a conqueror, makes the Greek mind tributary to his national design. The *Georgics*, the poem of the land, is as essentially Italian as the *Odyssey*, the poem of the sea, is essentially Greek. Nature is presented to us as she is revealed in the soft and rich luxuriance of Italian landscape, not in the clearly defined forms of Greek scenery. The ethical and religious ideal upheld is an Italian one. As a work of art, while showing in the largest degree the receptivity of the Greek feeling for form and symmetry which was the primary condition of all Roman success in literature, the poem shows equally the Italian susceptibility to the beauty of the outward world, the dignity and sobriety of the Italian imagination, the firm and enduring structure of all Roman workmanship.

Æneid.

The work which yet remained for Virgil to accomplish was the addition of a great Roman epic to literature. This had been the earliest effort of the national imagination, when it first departed from the mere imitative reproduction of Greek originals. The work which had given the truest expression to the genius of Rome before the time of Virgil had been the *Annales* of Ennius. This work had been supplemented by various historical poems but had never been superseded. It satisfied the national imagination as an expression of the national life in its vigorous prime, but it could not satisfy the newly developed sense of art; and the expansion of the national life since the days of Ennius, and the changed conditions into which it passed after the battle of Actium, demanded a new and ampler expression. It had been, as we learn both from his biographer and from himself—

> "Cum canerem reges et prœlia"—

Virgil's earliest ambition to write an heroic poem founded on the traditions of Alba Longa; and he had been repeatedly urged by Augustus to celebrate his exploits. The problem before him was to compose a work of art on a large scale, which should represent a great action of the heroic age, and should at the same time embody the most vital ideas and sentiment of the hour,—which in substance should glorify Rome and the present ruler of Rome, while in form it should follow closely the great models of epic poetry and reproduce all their sources of interest. It was his ambition to be the Homer as he had been the Theocritus and Hesiod of his country.

Various objects had thus to be combined in a work of art on the model of the Greek epic:—the revival of interest in the heroic foretime; the satisfaction of the national and imperial sentiment; the expression of the enthusiasm and of the deeper currents of emotion of the age; the personal celebration of Augustus. A new type of epic poetry had to be created, as a new type of didactic poetry had been realized in the *Georgics*. It was desirable to select a single heroic action which should belong to the cycle of legendary events celebrated in the Homeric poems, and which should be associated with the whole fortunes of Rome and with the supreme interests of the hour. The only subject which in any way satisfied these apparently irreconcilable conditions was that of the wanderings of Æneas and of his final settlement in Latium. The story, though not of Roman origin but of a composite growth, had been familiar to the Romans from the beginning of their literature, and had been recognized by official acts of senate and people as associated with the national fortunes. The subject enabled Virgil to tell over again and to give novelty to the tale of the fall of Troy, and to tell a tale of sea-adventure similar to that of the wanderings of Odysseus. But the special applicability of his subject to his purposes was determined by the claim which the Julii, a patrician family of Alban origin, made to descent from Iulus, the supposed son of Æneas and founder of Alba Longa. The personal, as distinct from the national and artistic, motives of the poem could be satisfied by this subject alone.

The *Æneid* is thus at once the epic of the national life under its new conditions and an imitative epic of human actions, manners, and character. The true keynote of the poem is struck in the line with which the proem closes—

> "Tantæ molis erat Romanam condere gentem."

The idea which underlies the whole action of the poem is that of the great part played by Rome in the history of the world, that part being from of old determined by divine decree, and carried out through the virtue of her sons. The idea of universal empire is thus the dominant idea of the poem. With this idea that of the unbroken continuity of the national life is intimately associated. The reverence for antiquity, for old customs and the traditions of the past, was a large element in the national sentiment, and has a prominent place in the *Æneid*. So too has the feeling of local attachment and of the power of local association over the imagination. This feeling is specially appealed to in the eighth book, which has been called the most purely Roman in the poem. The poem is also characteristically Roman in the religious belief and observances which it embodies. Behind all the conventional and artistic machinery of the old Olympic gods there is the Roman apprehension of a great inscrutable power, manifesting itself by arbitrary signs, exacting jealously certain observances, alienated for a time by neglect, and again appeased by compliance with its will, working out its own secret purposes through the agency of Roman arms and Roman counsels.

The word by which Virgil recognizes this power is Fatum (or Fata in the plural). The hero of the *Æneid* is an instrument in their hands, and the living emperor is regarded as fulfilling the same function in the actual world. The predominance of this idea gives coherence to the action, and establishes its relation to the whole national life. The poem is thus a religious as well as a national epic, and this explains the large part played in the development of the action by special revelation, omens, prophecies, ceremonial usages, and prayer. But, while the predominant religious idea of the poem is that of a divine purpose carried out regardlessly of human feeling, in other parts of the poem, and especially in that passage of the sixth book in which Virgil tries to formulate his deepest convictions on individual destiny, the agency of fate seems to yield to that of a spiritual dispensation, awarding to men their portions according to their actions.

The idealization of Augustus is no expression of servile adulation. It is through the prominence assigned to him that the poem is truly representative of the critical epoch in human affairs at which it was written. The cardinal fact of that epoch was the substitution of personal rule for the rule of the old commonwealth over the Roman world. Virgil shows the imaginative significance of that fact by revealing the emperor as chosen from of old in the counsels of the supreme ruler of the world to fulfil the national destiny, as the descendant of gods and of heroes of old poetic renown, as one, moreover, who, in the actual work done by him, as victor in a great decisive battle between the forces of the Western and the Eastern world, as the organizer of empire and restorer of peace, order, and religion, had rendered better service to mankind than any one of the heroes who in an older time had been raised for their great deeds to the company of the gods.

Virgil's true and yet idealizing interpretation of the imperial idea of Rome, in its national, religious, and personal significance, is the basis of the monumental greatness of the *Æneid* as a representative poem. It is on this representative character and on the excellence of its artistic execution that the claim of the *Æneid* to rank as one of the great poems of the world mainly rests. The inferiority of the poem to the *Iliad* and the *Odyssey* as a direct representation of human life is so unquestionable that we are in greater danger of underrating than of overrating the real though secondary interest which the poem possesses as an imitative epic of human action, manners, and character. What are the main sources of human interest in the poem can only be briefly indicated. In the first place, the action is chosen not only as suited to embody the idea of Rome and the dominant sentiment of a great and critical epoch in human affairs, but as having a peculiar nobleness and dignity of its own. It brings before us the spectacle, but restored by the light of a romantic imagination cast upon dim traditions, of the destruction of the city of greatest name in poetry or legend, the supposed seat of a prehistoric empire, of the foundation of the imperial city of the Western seas, in which Rome had encountered her most powerful and dangerous antagonist in the whole course of her long struggle for supremacy, and that of the first rude settlement on the hills of Rome itself. The scenes through which the action is carried are familiar, yet full of great memories and associations,—Troy and its neighbourhood, the seas and islands of Greece, the coasts of Epirus, familiar to all travellers between Italy and the East, Sicily, the site of Carthage, Campania, Latium, the Tiber, and all the country within sight of Rome. The personages of the action are prominent in poetry and legend, or by their ethnical names stir the sentiment of national enthusiasm,—Æneas and Anchises, Dido, Acestes, Evander, Turnus. The spheres of activity in which they are engaged are war and sea-adventure, the themes of the oldest and greatest of epic poems. The passion of love, which had played a great part in Attic tragedy and in the epic and elegiac poets of Alexandria, is a powerful addition to the older sources of interest which Virgil derives from the Homeric poems. The *Æneid*, like the Alexandrian epic, revives, by a conventional compromise between the present and the remote past, some image of the old romance of Greece; it creates the romance of "that Italy for which Camilla the virgin, Euryalus, and Turnus and Nisus died of wounds." It might be said of the manner of life represented in the *Æneid*, that it is no more true to any actual condition of human society than that represented in the *Eclogues*. But may not the same be said of all idealizing restoration of a remote past in an age of advanced civilization? The life represented in the *Œdipus Tyrannus* or in *King Lear* is not the life of the Periclean nor of the Elizabethan age, nor is it conceivable as the real life of a prehistoric age. The truth of such a representation is to be judged, not by its relation to any actual state of things ever realized in the world, but by its relation to an ideal of the imagination,—the ideal conception of how man, endowed with the gifts and graces of a civilized time, but who had not yet lost the youthful buoyancy of a more primitive age, might play his part under circumstances which would afford scope for the passions and activities of a vigorous personality, and for the refined emotions and subtle reflexion of an era of high intellectual and moral cultivation. The verdict of most readers of the *Æneid* will be that Virgil does not satisfy this condition, as it is satisfied by Sophocles and Shakespeare. Yet there is a considerable attraction in the compromise which Virgil has produced between the life which he knew by experience and that which he saw in the past of his imagination. There is a courtesy, dignity, and consideration for the feelings of others in the manners of his chief personages, such as might be exhibited by the noblest and most commanding natures in an age of chivalry and in an age of culture. The charm of primitive simplicity is present in some passages of the *Æneid*, the spell of luxurious pomp in others. The actual delight of voyaging past beautiful islands, familiar to travellers in the Augustan age, is enhanced by the suggestion of the adventurous spirit which sent the first explorers abroad in search of unknown settlements. Where Virgil is least real, and least successfully ideal, and where consequently he is most purely imitative, is in the battle-scenes of the later books. They afford scope, however, to his patriotic desire to do justice to the martial energy of the Italian races; and some of them have a peculiar beauty from the pathos with which the death of some of the more interesting personages of his story is described.

But the adverse criticisms of the *Æneid* are chiefly based on Virgil's supposed failure in the crucial test of a great poem of action, the creation of character. And his chief failure is pronounced to be in the protagonist of the poem, the "pious Æneas." Is this charge true? Is Æneas a worthy and interesting hero of a great poem of action? Not, certainly, according to the ideals realized in Achilles and Odysseus, nor according to the modern ideal of gallant and adventurous heroism. A blameless character, patiently enduring much suffering, cannot arouse the same personal interest as a more energetic and impulsive character, relying on his own resources, and stirred by ordinary human passions. It is well said of Æneas by a French critic—"Sa vertu doit être une haute et froide impersonalité, qui fasse de lui non un homme mais un instrument des dieux." Virgil wishes to hold up in Æneas an ideal of pious obedience, steadfast endurance, persistent purpose,—a religious ideal belonging to the ages of faith combined with the humane and self-sacrificing qualities belonging to an era of moral enlightenment. The virtues of the natural man—chivalry and daring courage—he represents in Turnus. His own sympathy is with his religious ideal rather than with that which better satisfies modern sentiment, nursed on the traditions of chivalrous romance. Yet that there was in his own imagination, more than in that of any other Roman writer, a chord responsive to the chivalrous emotion of a later time is seen in the love and pathos which he has thrown into his delineations of Pallas, Lausus, and Camilla. But, with all his sympathies with the "Itala virtus"—the martial virtues of the old Italian race and the martial prowess of Rome,—he felt that the deepest need of his time was not military glory, but peace, reconciliation, the restoration of law, order, and piety.

Among the personages of the *Æneid* the only one which entitles Virgil to rank among great creators is Dido, an ideal of a true queen and a true woman. She is the sole creation which Roman poetry has added to the great gallery of men and women filled by the imaginative art of different times and peoples. There are the outlines of a great creation in Mezentius; but Dido alone is a life-like and completed picture. On the episode of which she is the heroine the most passionate human interest is concentrated. It has been objected that Virgil does not really sympathize with his own creation, that he gives his approval to the cold desertion of her by her "false friend." Whether he sympathizes with his own creation or not, he is entirely possessed by it. If he does not condemn his hero, he sees in the desertion and death of Dido a great tragic issue in which a noble and generous nature is sacrificed to the larger purpose of the gods. But that Virgil really sympathized with the creation of his imagination appears, not only in the sympathy which she still inspires, but in the part which he assigns to her in that shadowy realm in which he conceives that the "world's great wrongs" are at last righted—

> "Conjunx ubi pristinus illi
> Respondet curis, æquatque Sychæus amorem."

Even those who have been insensible to the representative and to the human interest of the *Æneid* have generally recognized the artistic excellence of the poem. This is conspicuous both in the conception of the action and the arrangement of its successive stages and in the workmanship of details. In variety of interest and finish of execution the first eight books are superior to the last four. Each of the former has a large and distinct sphere of interest, and they each contribute to the impression of the work as a whole. In the first book we have the interest of the storm, of the prophecy of Jove, and of the building of Carthage; in the second the spectacle of the destruction of Troy; in the third the voyage among the islands and coasts of the Mediterranean; in the fourth the tragedy of Dido; in the fifth the rest in the Sicilian bay, at the foot of Mount Eryx; in the sixth the revelation of the spiritual world of Virgil's imagination, and of the souls of those who built up the greatness of Rome in their pre-existent state, in their shadowy dwelling-place; in the seventh the arrival of the Trojans at the mouth of the Tiber and the gathering of the Italian clans; in the eighth the first sight of the hills of Rome, and the prophetic representation of the great crises in Roman history, leading up to the greatest of them all, the crowning victory of Actium. Among these books we may infer that Virgil assigned the palm to the second, the fourth, and the sixth, as he selected them to read to Augustus and the members of the imperial family. The interest flags in the last

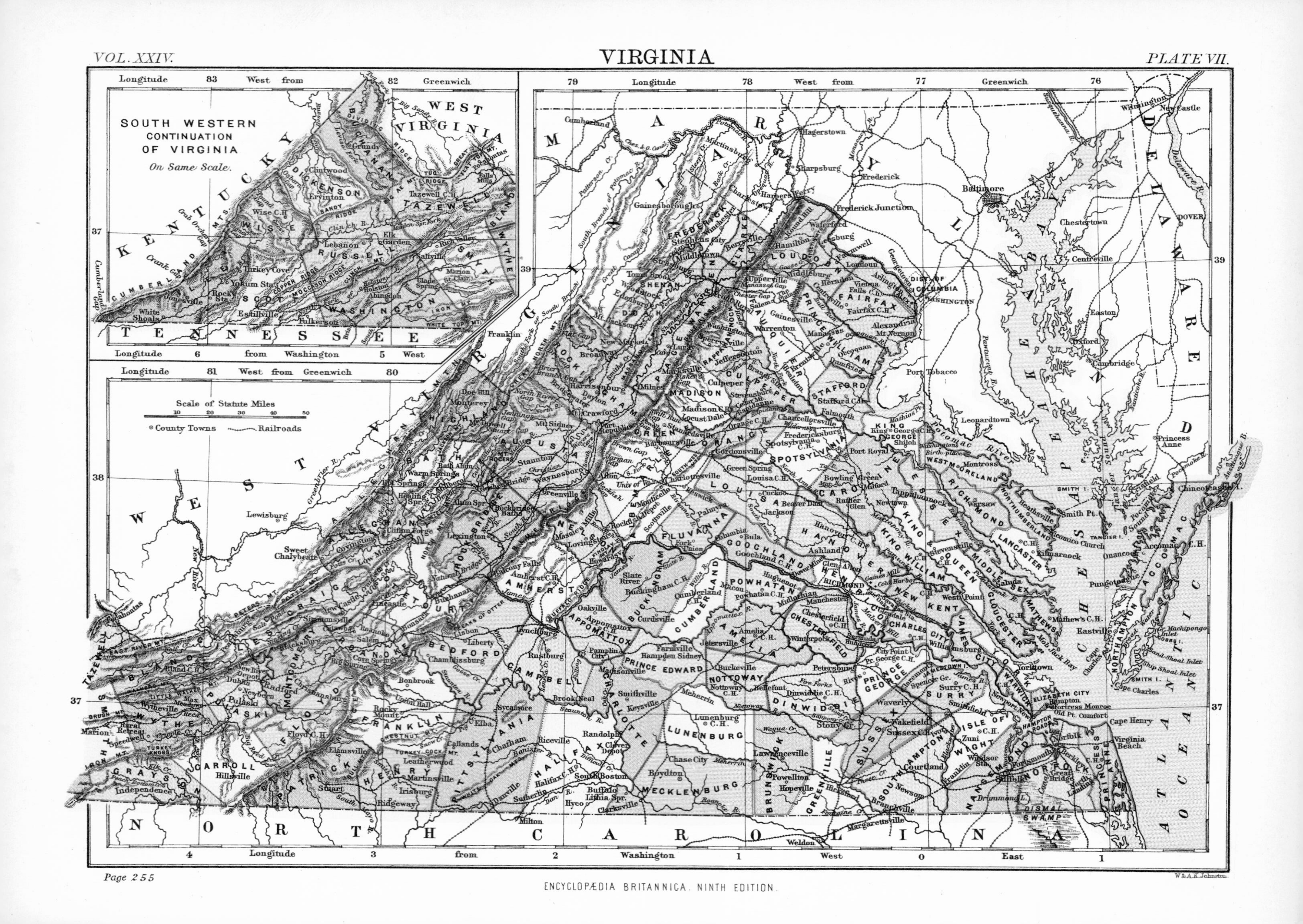

ENCYCLOPÆDIA BRITANNICA. NINTH EDITION.
W. & A. K. Johnston.

four; nor is it possible to feel that culminating sympathy with the final combat between Turnus and Æneas that we feel with the combat between Hector and Achilles. Yet a personal interest is awakened in the adventures and fate of Pallas, Lausus, and Camilla. Virgil may himself have become weary of the succession of battle-scenes—"eadem horrida bella,"—which the requirements of epic poetry rather than the impulses of his own genius or the taste of his readers called upon him to pourtray; and this may partly account for the sense of discouragement which he is supposed to have felt at the end of his labours. There is not only a less varied interest, there is greater inequality of workmanship in the later books, owing to the fact that they had not received their author's final revisal. Yet in them there are many lines and passages of great power, pathos, and beauty. Virgil brought the two great instruments of varied and continuous harmony and of a rich, chastened, and noble style to the highest perfection of which the Latin tongue was capable. The rhythm and style of the *Æneid* is more unequal than the rhythm and style of the *Georgics*, but is a larger and more varied instrument. The note of his supremacy among all the poetic artists of his country is that subtle fusion of the music and the meaning of language which touches the deepest and most secret springs of emotion. He touches especially the emotions of reverence and of a yearning for a higher spiritual life, and the sense of nobleness in human affairs, in great institutions, and great natures; the sense of the sanctity of human affections, of the imaginative spell exercised by the past, of the mystery of the unseen world. This is the secret of the power which his words have had over some of the deepest and greatest natures both in the ages of faith and in more positive times. No words more subtly and truly express the magic of his style than those in which Dr Newman characterizes "his single words and phrases, his pathetic half-lines, giving utterance as the voice of nature herself to that pain and weariness, yet hope of better things, which is the experience of her children in every age."

The most important of the recent editions of Virgil are those of Heyne and the revised edition by Wagner, that of Forbiger, of Ribbeck, of E. Benoist, and of Conington. Among recent works bearing on the literary criticism of Virgil are Sainte-Beuve's *Étude sur Virgile*, M. G. Boissier's *La Religion Romaine d'Auguste aux Antonins*, Comparetti's *Virgilio nel Medio Evo*, *Vergil und die epische Kunst*, by Theodor Plüss, various works by Prof. Nettleship, and Prof. Sellar's *Roman Poets of the Augustan Age*. The best critical estimate of the genius and art of Virgil in English is that of Mr F. Myers. Among recent translations of the *Æneid* are those of Conington, Mr W. Morris, and Lord Justice Bowen in verse, and of Conington and Mr J. W. Mackail in prose. (W. Y. S.)

VIRGIL, POLYDORE (*c.* 1470–1555), author of the *Historia Anglica*, otherwise known as P. V. CASTELLENSIS, was a kinsman of Cardinal Hadrian Castellensis, a native of Castro in Etruria. His father's name is said to have been George Virgil; his great-grandfather, Anthony Virgil, "a man well skilled in medicine and astrology," had professed philosophy at Paris, as did Polydore's own brother and protégé, John Matthew Virgil, at Pavia, in 1517. A third brother was a London merchant in 1511. Polydore is said to have been educated at Bologna, and was probably in the service of Guido Ubaldo, duke of Urbino, before 1498, as in the dedication of his first work, *Liber Proverbiorum* (April 1498), he styles himself this prince's client. Polydore's second book, *De Inventoribus Rerum*, is dedicated to Guido's tutor, Ludovicus Odaxius, from Urbino, in August 1499. After being chamberlain to Alexander VI. he came to England in 1501 as deputy collector of Peter's pence for the cardinal. As Hadrian's proxy, he was enthroned bishop of Bath and Wells in October 1504. It was at Henry VII.'s instance that he commenced his *Historia Anglica*—a work which, though seemingly begun as early as 1505, was not completed till August 1533, the date of its dedication to Henry VIII., nor published till 1534. In May 1514 he and his patron the cardinal are found supporting Wolsey's claims to the cardinalship, but he had lost the great minister's favour before the year was out. A rash letter, reflecting severely on Henry VIII. and Wolsey, was intercepted early in 1515, after which Polydore was cast into prison and supplanted in his collectorship (March and April). He was not without some powerful supporters, as both Catherine de' Medici and Leo X. wrote to the king on his behalf. From his prison he sent an abject and almost blasphemous letter to the offended minister, begging that the fast approaching Christmas—a time which witnessed the restitution of a world—might see his pardon also. He was set at liberty before Christmas 1515, though he never regained his collectorship. In 1525 he published the first edition of Gildas, dedicating the work to Tunstall, bishop of London. Next year appeared his *Liber de Prodigiis*, dedicated from London (July) to Francesco Maria, duke of Urbino. Somewhere about 1538 he left England, and remained in Italy for some time. Ill-health, he tells us, forbade him on his return to continue his custom of making daily notes on contemporary events. About the end of 1551 he went home to Urbino, where he appears to have died in 1555. He had been naturalized in October 1510, and had held several clerical appointments in England. In 1508 he was appointed archdeacon of Wells, and in 1513 prebendary of Oxgate in St Paul's Cathedral, both of which offices he held after his return to Urbino.

The first edition of the *Historia Anglica* (twenty-six books) was printed at Basel in 1534; the twenty-seventh book, dealing with the reign of Henry VIII. down to the birth of Edward VI. (October 1536), was added to the third edition of 1555. Polydore claims to have been very careful in collecting materials for this work, and takes credit for using foreign historians as well as English; for which reason, he remarks, the English, Scotch, and French will find several things reported in his pages far differently from the way in which they are told in current national story. In his search after information he applied to James IV. of Scotland for a list of the Scottish kings and their annals; but not even his friendship for Gavin Douglas could induce him to give credit to the historical notions of this accomplished bishop, who traced the pedigree of the Scots down from the banished son of an Athenian king and Scotta the daughter of the Egyptian tyrant of the Israelites. A similar scepticism made him doubt the veracity of Geoffrey of Monmouth, and thus called forth Leland's *Defensio Gallofridi* and *Assertio Incomparabilis Arturii*. This doubting instinct led to his being accused of many offences against learning, such as that of burning cartloads of MSS. lest his errors should be discovered, of purloining books from libraries and shipping them off by the vesselful to Rome. As a matter of fact, it is of course mainly from the time of Henry VI., where our contemporary records begin to fail so sadly, that Polydore's work is useful. He must have been personally acquainted with many men whose memories could carry them back to the beginning of the Wars of the Roses. Dr Brewer speaks somewhat harshly of him as an authority for the reign of Henry VIII., and indeed his spite against Wolsey is evident; but it is impossible to read his social and geographical accounts of England and Scotland without gratitude for a writer who has preserved so many interesting details. Polydore's *Adagia* (Venice, April 1498) was the first collection of Latin proverbs ever printed; it preceded Erasmus's by two years, and the slight misunderstanding that arose for the moment out of rival claims gave place to a sincere friendship. A second series of Biblical proverbs (553 in number) was dedicated to Wolsey's follower Richard Pace, and is preceded by an interesting letter (June 1519), which gives the names of many of Polydore's English friends, from More and Archbishop Warham to Linacre and Tunstall. The *De Inventoribus*, treating of the origin of all things whether ecclesiastical or lay (Paris, 1499), originally consisted of only seven books, but was increased to eight in 1521. It was exceedingly popular, and was early translated into French (1521), German (1537), English (1546), and Spanish (1551). All editions, however, except those following the text sanctioned by Gregory XIII. in 1576, are on the Index Expurgatorius. The *De Prodigiis* also achieved a great popularity, and was soon translated into Italian (1543), English (1546), and Spanish (1550). This treatise takes the form of a Latin dialogue between Polydore and his Cambridge friend Robert Ridley. It takes place in the open air, at Polydore's country house near London. Polydore's duty is to state the problems and supply the historical illustrations; his friend's to explain, rationalize, and depreciate as best he can. Here, as in the *Historia Anglica*, it is plain that the writer plumes himself specially on the excellence of his Latin, which in Sir Henry Ellis's opinion is purer than that of any of his contemporaries.

VIRGINAL. See PIANOFORTE, vol. xix. pp. 67, 68.

VIRGINIA, one of the original thirteen States of the North American Union, extends from 36° 31′ to 39° 27′ N. lat., and from 75° 13′ to 83° 37′ W. long. It is rudely triangular in form,—its southern boundary, the base of the triangle, a nearly east to west line, being 440 miles long, the north-western 565, the northern and north-eastern 230, and the eastern 125 miles. On the S. it is bounded by North Carolina and Tennessee, on the W. and N.W. by Kentucky and West Virginia, on the N. and N.E. by

Plate VII.

Maryland, and on the E. by the Virginian Sea of the Atlantic Ocean. Its greatest length from east to west is 476 miles, its greatest breadth from north to south 192 miles. It is subdivided into 100 counties. The area is variously stated at about 44,500 and 42,450 square miles; the latter extent is that given at the census of 1880. Of the 1,512,565 inhabitants of Virginia (1,059,034 of them over ten years of age) in 1880, 494,240 were engaged in gainful occupations,—254,099, or over 50 per cent., in agriculture, 30,418 in trade and transportation, and 63,059 in manufactures and mining and mechanical industries; but now (in 1888) a very much larger proportion of the industrial population is engaged in mining, manufacturing, trade, and transportation, in consequence of the opening of mines, the erection of blast-furnaces, coke ovens, and various manufacturing establishments since 1880.

Physical features.

Physical Features.—Speaking broadly, Virginia may be divided into a lowland and a highland country. Its south-eastern part—over 23,000 square miles, or more than half of the whole—has the aspect of a broadly undulating plain, that, with but few marked variations of relief, rises from the sea-level to from 400 to 800 feet above it. The north-western portion is a region composed of approximately parallel mountain ranges, running entirely across the State from north-east to south-west, separated by nearly parallel valleys,—the whole presenting all the varieties of relief peculiar to the Appalachian country between the levels of 800 and 5700 feet. To speak more accurately, the State is naturally divided into seven grand divisions or belts, each with marked characteristics of relief and geological structure, and each succeeding the other, somewhat as a more or less ascending stairway, from the sea to the north-west.

1. Tidewater Virginia is the marine plain, of Quaternary and Tertiary structure, 10,850 square miles in area, that extends westward, for nearly 100 miles, from the Atlantic border to "The Ridge," the granitic escarpment which by its rise determines the tidal limit in the great rivers of the State. This Tidewater plain, rectangular in form, is divided by Chesapeake Bay and the great estuaries of the Potomac, the Rappahannock, the York, and the James rivers, into five large peninsulas, which are subdivided by arms of the bay and tidal branches of the rivers into hundreds of smaller peninsulas, thus giving to the region great wealth of tidal shore outline—fully 2000 miles—so that nearly every square mile of its surface can be reached by tide-borne vessels. The nearly level surface of its north to south trending peninsulas, those of the eastern marine plain, the Quaternary ones, averages about 12 feet above sea-level; their low-lying semi-insular position and their warm finely comminuted soils make these the highly favoured great market-garden or "trucking" portions of Tidewater. The north-west to south-east trending peninsulas, those of the western marine plain, the Tertiary ones, have more broken surfaces that vary in altitude from sea-level to about 100 feet, and are disposed in flat watershed ridges and slopes, terraces, and swamps, all deeply trenched by the secondary drainage.

2. Midland Virginia is the triangular area (12,470 square miles) which, 25 miles wide along the Potomac and 100 wide along the North Carolina line, extends from the Tidewater escarpment westward to the eastern base of the Atlantic coast range, the broken eastern range of the Appalachian Mountains. The elevation here varies from 100 to 200 feet above sea-level in the east to from 700 to 800 in the west; once a gently eastwardly sloping plain, mostly underlaid by steeply dipping granitic and other Archæan rocks—with included areas of Jura-Trias—striking north-east to south-west, the rivers have deeply trenched into this, and so given it a greatly broken and varied relief through a moderate range of altitude; it abounds in stream-valleys. This, with Piedmont and the Blue Ridge, was the first dry land, the oldest portion of Virginia.

3. Piedmont Virginia is the area (6680 square miles) of greatly diversified country, some 250 miles in length and 20 to 30 miles in width, that stretches between the Blue Ridge and the Coast Range mountains, including all of the latter and the eastward spurs and slopes of the former; its valleys, coves, and plains vary in altitude from 300 to 700 feet in the north-east to from 500 to 1000 in the south-west, while its included and bordering mountains range through all gradations from above 4000 feet down to the levels of its valleys. It is charmingly varied and picturesque, and adapted to a great variety of productions.

4. Blue Ridge Virginia is the Virginian portion (300 miles in length) of the great mountain chain of that name, with its numerous tablelands—especially the Floyd-Carroll-Grayson plateau (1230 square miles) in the south-west, having an altitude of from 916 to 5700 feet. It is, for most of its length, a chain of two ranges: the eastern, the chief, in which numerous rivers have their origin, is a grand mountain mass, carved from the Archæan and eruptive rocks, forming the most striking feature of thousands of square miles of Virginia landscape; the western is mainly composed of short ridges, formed from the easterly out-crops of the Palæozoic rocks, flanking the western slopes of the main range.

5. The Valley of Virginia is the Virginian portion (300 miles) of the length of the great limestone or Appalachian valley of the Atlantic highlands, one that, made up of numerous subordinate valleys, extends with unbroken continuity from Canada to Alabama, and has for its whole length, with varying local names, the Blue Ridge on its eastern and the Kittatinny or Great North Mountain on its western border. In Virginia this is a plateau-valley,—embracing 7550 square miles,—its greatly varied tillable surface ranging in altitude from about 500 to over 2500 feet and averaging fully 1000. Carved from the limestones and limy shales and slates of the Cambrian group into an almost endless variety of valley and upland forms, the higher ones in gracefully rounded outline, all blending into one or more broad valleys, and bounded by grand mountain chains, this is indisputably one of the most desirable regions in the United States.

6. Appalachia (4500 square miles), a region of alternating "rich" and "poor" valleys (according as they are carved from the lime-abounding or from the slaty sandstone rocks of the Silurian or the Devonian groups), is Virginia's portion of the Appalachian Mountains region proper, the one that lies between the Great Valley on the east and the great Carboniferous escarpment of the Trans-Appalachia plateau. Its general features are repetitions of long, parallel, straight, and level-crested mountain ranges—many of them over 4000 feet—succeeding one another in echelon, with narrow, trough-like valleys,—ranging from 800 to 2700 feet,—but these are diversified by the occasional dying out of some mountain ranges and the consequent widening of valleys, and by the widening of ranges into plateaus or their opening into double crests or lovely mountain "coves" and "gardens." It is a noted grazing and timber region.

7. Trans-Appalachia (mainly the 1200 square miles in Buchanan, Dickenson, and Wise counties) is the Virginian portion of the tableland that extends westward from the great Carboniferous escarpment or Alleghany "backbone." It is eroded from the Carboniferous rocks, and so is the great coal-bearing portion of the State.

Climate.

Climate.—The State lies in the middle latitudes. It is open to the sea on the east; its great mountain chains guard it on the north and west; and it has accordingly as nearly a climate of means as any of the Atlantic-bordering States can have. Its position and physical structure also give great variety to its climate: that of its bordering sea islands and large peninsulas is insular; that of its great Tidewater and Midland plains is warm temperate; that of Piedmont and the Great Valley is typically mild temperate; and that of the Blue Ridge plateau and of the high valleys and tablelands of Appalachia is more uniformly cool temperate than in higher latitudes. Its climatic range, in the average latitude of 38° N., is from the sea-coast to 500 miles inland, and from the sea-level to 5700 feet, a range that is equivalent to 19° of latitude, and that gives to Virginia all the adaptations for production embraced between 36° 30′ and 59° N. lat. This wide range finds expression in the market-gardens and temperate fruits and trees and the extensive sweet potato, cotton, and peanut fields of Tidewater; in the large plantations of tobacco, hard-grained winter wheat, and the dented-seed (the large variety) Indian corn, and in great forests of pitch-pines, oaks, &c., in Midland and Piedmont, and in the lower portions of the Valley and Appalachia; in the productive vineyards and orchards of Piedmont and the adjacent slopes of the Blue Ridge; in the perennial pasture-lands—the native homes of the rich blue grass—of the higher levels of Piedmont, of the crests and plateaus of the eastern Blue Ridge, of the Great Valley, and of the extensive limestone valleys and ridges of Appalachia; in the large cereal crops and dairy products of the Valley; in the big cattle farms and ranges of Appalachia, the Blue Ridge, and the more elevated parts of the Valley; in the flax, buckwheat, Irish potato, cabbage, and other north-country crops that flourish in the Blue Ridge, the higher parts of the Valley, and Appalachia; and in the north-land balsams and other cold climate trees and vegetation that clothe the higher levels of the Blue Ridge and of Appalachia.

The mean annual temperature zones of Virginia are—60° to 65° in eastern Tidewater; 55° to 60° in western Tidewater, and most of Midland; 50° to 55° in the higher parts of Midland, in most of Piedmont, and in the lower parts of the Valley and Appalachia; 45° to 50° in north-east Piedmont, in most of the Valley, and in the lower valleys of Appalachia; and 40° to 45° on the Blue Ridge, on and near the high levels of the Valley, and in most of Appalachia. The average for the State is near 56°, ranging from 48° in the highlands to 64° in the lowlands—from the mean adapted to grass to that suitable for cotton. The changes of temperature are great, but not so sudden or so extreme as they are in the regions to the north-east and north-west.

The prevailing winds are from the south quadrants, generally shifting between south and west; next in frequency are those between north and west; high winds are rare, except along the coast. The rainfall is abundant and well distributed throughout the seasons in every part, there being two sources of supply, one from the Gulf by the south-west and one from the Atlantic by the south-east winds; the average annual precipitation is from 32 to 44 inches, except in a belt extending north-west from the mouth of Chesapeake Bay towards Staunton, in which it is from 44 to 56 inches; there is a gradual decrease in the rainfall from the coast westward. The snowfall is generally light, some winters insignificant; and the snow soon melts, save in the elevated regions.

Virginia is noted for the clearness of its skies, the purity of its air, and its freedom from great storms. Its climate is moist without being damp, and so mild as to invite to living much in the open air; its winters are short, its periods of seedtime and harvest long; and its healthfulness is attested by the vigour and longevity of its people.

Geology.

Geology.—The subjoined table of the geological formations found in Virginia, correlated with those of Pennsylvania and New York, and with the general groups and systems of the American geological scale, follows, in the main, the late Prof. William B. Rogers:—

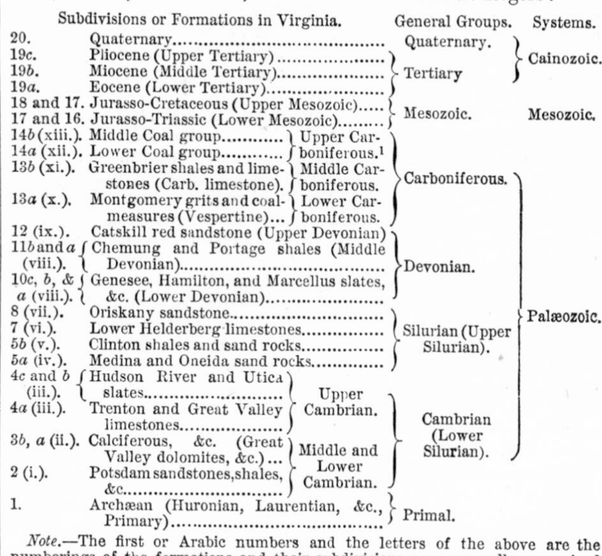

	Subdivisions or Formations in Virginia.		General Groups.	Systems.
20.	Quaternary		Quaternary.	Cainozoic.
19*c*.	Pliocene (Upper Tertiary)		Tertiary	
19*b*.	Miocene (Middle Tertiary)			
19*a*.	Eocene (Lower Tertiary)			
18 and 17.	Jurasso-Cretaceous (Upper Mesozoic)		Mesozoic.	Mesozoic.
17 and 16.	Jurasso-Triassic (Lower Mesozoic)			
14*b* (xiii.).	Middle Coal group	Upper Carboniferous.[1]	Carboniferous.	Palæozoic.
14*a* (xii.).	Lower Coal group			
13*b* (xi.).	Greenbrier shales and limestones (Carb. limestone).	Middle Carboniferous.		
13*a* (x.).	Montgomery grits and coal-measures (Vespertine)	Lower Carboniferous.		
12 (ix.).	Catskill red sandstone (Upper Devonian)		Devonian.	
11*b* and *a* (viii.).	Chemung and Portage shales (Middle Devonian)			
10*c*, *b*, & *a* (viii.).	Genesee, Hamilton, and Marcellus slates, &c. (Lower Devonian)			
8 (vii.).	Oriskany sandstone		Silurian (Upper Silurian).	
7 (vi.).	Lower Helderberg limestones			
5*b* (v.).	Clinton shales and sand rocks			
5*a* (iv.).	Medina and Oneida sand rocks			
4*c* and *b* (iii.).	Hudson River and Utica slates	Upper Cambrian.	Cambrian (Lower Silurian).	
4*a* (iii.).	Trenton and Great Valley limestones			
3*b*, *a* (ii.).	Calciferous, &c. (Great Valley dolomites, &c.)	Middle and Lower Cambrian.		
2 (i.).	Potsdam sandstones, shales, &c.			
1.	Archæan (Huronian, Laurentian, &c., Primary)		Primal.	

Note.—The first or Arabic numbers and the letters of the above are the numberings of the formations and their subdivisions now generally recognized and used in North America; the Roman numbers in brackets are the equivalent formations as numbered and used by the Rogers Brothers in the Pennsylvania and Virginia reports.

As the accompanying geological map shows, Midland, Piedmont, and the Blue Ridge grand divisions, over 20,000 square miles, or about half the land area of the State, are underlain by the Archæan or old Primary and metamorphic rocks; within this Archæan area are a dozen or more patches, large and small, of the Jura-Trias (formations 16, 17, and 18) or Mesozoic rocks, some of them with valuable coal-beds, that in later times were deposited in depressions, lake-like basins, in the Archæan rocks. The Cambrian (Lower Silurian) areas, the Virginia formations i., ii., and iii., include all the Great Valley (limestone) and numerous limestone valleys of Appalachia, some of them, like that of Clinch river, quite large—in all some 10,000 square miles of surface—having within them detached mountain ranges of more recent formations. The Silurian (Upper Silurian) areas, those where the Virginia formations iv., v., vi., and vii. outcrop, are

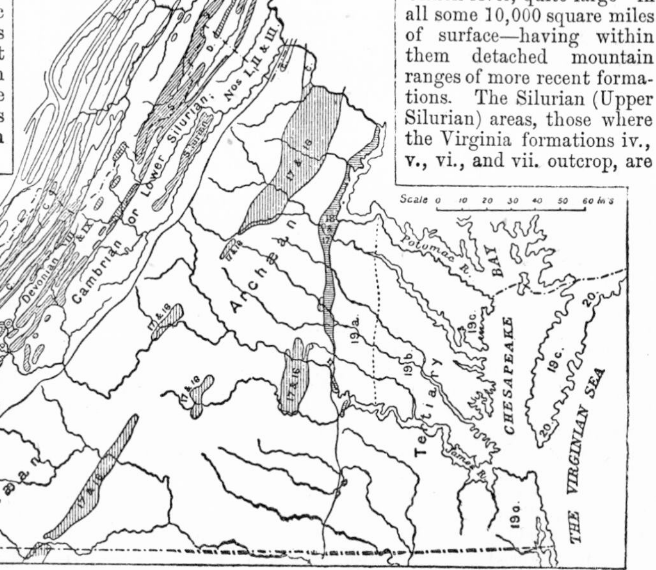

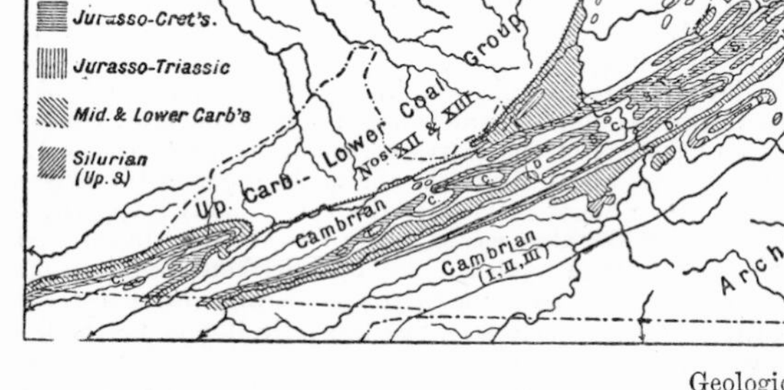

Geological Map of Virginia.

mountain ranges, detached once in the Great Valley, and ranges and chains of them in Appalachia, for these formations, made up largely of massive sand-rocks, are mountain-builders. The Devonian areas, Virginia formations viii. and ix., are principally those of the slaty or "poor" valleys of Appalachia, No. viii. being a formation from which stream-valleys are liberally carved, though ix., chiefly sand-rocks, often holds it up to included or bordering ridges. The Lower and the Middle Carboniferous rocks, Virginia formations x. and xi., outcrop in long and narrow belts or strips of Greenbrier shales and limestones (xi.), and adjacent narrow and long mountain ranges of Montgomery grits and coal-measures (x.), in south-west portions of the Valley and of Appalachia, and in small mountain areas elsewhere in Appalachia. The Upper Carboniferous, Virginia formations xii. and xiii., the Lower (xii.) and the Middle (xiii.) Coal groups, underlie all the thousand square miles of Trans-Appalachia, where the semi-bituminous coking coals of the Lower Coal group are exposed, above water-level, in their best conditions of purity (high in carbon, low in volatile matter,

1 Formations xiv., xv., and xvi., the Upper Coal group, are not known in the present limits of Virginia.

and very low in ash, sulphur, and phosphorus) for metallurgical purposes, and in beds of remarkable thickness, and where the bituminous coals of the Middle Coal group also have a maximum of development combined with remarkable purity of composition, adapting them to gas and domestic uses. Tertiary rocks (19*a*, *b*, *c*) underlie all Tidewater (the new Virginia of geology, though the old one of colonial history),—the Lower or Eocene outcropping, approximately, in a line a little west of 77° W. long., the Middle or Miocene between that and a little east of 76° 30′ W., and the Upper or Pliocene in the remaining east part, except where covered by recent or Quaternary (20) deposits.

Minerals.

Minerals.—The varied and abundant mineral resources of the State are as yet but imperfectly developed. Her medicinal mineral springs are numerous, and many of them well known. Tidewater abounds in fertilizing marls, and in choice brick-clays, sands, and shell-limestones for building. Lime-burning, from oyster shells, is an important industry. Midland abounds in superior granites, which are extensively quarried near Richmond and Petersburg; in the best of slates for roofing and other purposes, especially in Albemarle and Buckingham counties; in Jura-Trias brownstones and sandstones; in trap for Belgian blocks; in soapstones (steatites), limestones, and in brick-, plastic-, and fire-clays. Thick beds of excellent bituminous coal and of natural coke are found in the Jura-Trias of Chesterfield and adjacent counties, which have long been mined; ochre beds are worked in Chesterfield county; thick beds of magnetic, specular, and limonite iron-ores, and of gold, silver, and copper-bearing rocks, traverse its whole length from north-east to south-west. Its gold belt, from 15 to 20 miles wide, rich in free, quartz, and pyritous-rock gold, traverses the whole western tier of Midland counties, for more than 200 miles, from the Potomac to the Dan; in this belt, in Louisa county, at the Arminius copper mines, veins of white pyrites, 42 feet, bearing 46 per cent. of sulphur and considerable yellow copper, have been opened and reduction works erected for a 300 tons daily output; 12,000 tons of pyrites were shipped in 1886. Manganese, mica, plumbago, titanium, cyanite, garnets, emeralds, quartz, and other Archæan and Jura-Trias minerals are found at many points. The minerals and metals now exploited are gold, iron and copper pyrites, manganese, hæmatites, magnetites, and limonites, mica, slates, granites, brownstones, and trap-rock. Piedmont has extensive beds of magnetic, specular, and limonite iron ore throughout its length; chromic iron ore is found in the north-east; copper ores abound especially along the west border in spurs of Blue Ridge; manganese deposits have been worked at various points; the same Archæan and Jura-Trias building stones and minerals are found here as in Midland, the marbles of Bedford and Loudoun counties of fine quality. Iron ores, manganese, slates, and marbles are now exploited. The Blue Ridge abounds in copper and iron ores for its whole length in Virginia; these as well as pyritous silver, copper, and iron ores, are especially abundant in the Floyd-Carroll-Grayson or south-west plateau, where also auriferous quartz is milled; tin mines have been opened in Rockbridge county; the great Potsdam or primordial iron belt, with its vast deposits of ore, flanks the western base of the Blue Ridge in Virginia for nearly 300 miles, and from the rich deposits of manganese in the same belt two-thirds of the manganese output of the United States in 1886 was mined; glass-sand of the best quality and fire and other clays are abundant, and so are building sandstones in the western Blue Ridge. Mining operations are now extensively conducted in iron and manganese ores. The Great Valley is all underlain by limestones suitable for ornamental, building, and agricultural purposes; its cement (hydraulic) and architectural, fluxing, and agricultural limes are noted for their purity; extensive beds of iron-ore are found among its hills; marbles, barytes, brick- and fire-clays, and travertine marls are abundant; there are large deposits of lead and zinc ores, especially in the south-west, in Pulaski and Wythe counties, where they accompany the great iron-ore deposits of the Cripple Creek region; from the Vespertine (No. x.) beds of the Lower Carboniferous, in Montgomery and Pulaski counties, from 15,000 to 20,000 tons of semi-anthracite coal are annually mined; ochres are mined in Page and Augusta counties; iron, manganese, zinc, and lead ores are now mined on quite an extensive scale, and lime-burning is an important industry. Appalachian Virginia abounds in very remarkable beds of limonite iron ores, found (often, under large areas, in a more or less stratified condition) in the Hudson river (iii.), Clinton (v.), and Oriskany (vii.) formations of Cambrian and Silurian age; there are also deposits of magnetic hæmatites in Craig and Giles counties; limestones of the Valley (ii.), Trenton (iii.), and Lower Helderberg (vi.) formations, underlying the "rich" valleys and ridges, abound, and furnish the best of materials for building, lime-burning, and blast-furnace fluxing purposes, as well as for beautiful encrinal and other fancy marbles; in its Vespertine (x.) areas are numerous patches of anthracite and semi-anthracite coals, worked and workable for local use; in the Appalachian portions of Smyth and Washington counties are large deposits of rock-salt and gypsum; travertine marls, caves abounding in nitrous earths, and chalybeate, sulphur, alum, hot, warm, and other mineral springs are common; sandstones and slates for building purposes are plentiful. The iron-ores of Alleghany county and those of the Appalachian portions of Rockbridge and Botetourt counties are extensively mined for local blast-furnaces; marbles and gypsum are quarried; considerable salt is manufactured, and semi-anthracite coal in Pulaski for use in local zinc furnaces. Trans-Appalachia is Virginia's 1000 square miles of the Great Coal Basin of the Ohio, or the Trans-Appalachian Coal Basin (the one usually, but improperly, called the Great Appalachian Coal Basin); this is all underlain by thick and easily accessible beds of the best of semi-bituminous and bituminous coals, those of the Lower (xii.) and of the Middle (xiii.) Coal groups of the Carboniferous. Only the semi-bituminous coking, steam, and domestic coal of this region is now mined for exportation at Pocahontas, Tazewell county, from which 639,751 tons (93,550 of them converted into coke) were shipped in 1886, the traffic having begun with the shipment of 105,805 tons in 1883. From the Flat-top coalfield, including the Pocahontas and some adjacent mines in West Virginia, 1,314,700 tons of coal were mined in 1887, part of which was made into about 145,000 tons of coke, equal in quality to any made in the United States. This fuel is remarkably high in fixed carbon and low in ash and sulphur, and therefore admirably adapted for metallurgical purposes. Twenty mineral springs of Virginia, used medicinally, were reported to the United States Geological Survey in 1886 (Tidewater 1, Midland 4, Blue Ridge 2, Valley 5, Appalachia 8); they were reported as chalybeate, alum, white sulphur, red sulphur, blue sulphur, warm sulphur, cold sulphur, hot sulphur, lithia, healing, ague, and sweet chalybeate. These and many others not reported are visited as health resorts, and many of them ship to market large quantities of their waters.

Virginia produced—of coal 300,000 tons in 1884, 1,000,000 in 1886, and about 1,250,000 in 1887; of coke 25,340 tons in 1884, about 122,352 tons in 1886; of pig iron, 29,934 tons in 1880, 152,907 in 1883, 156,250 in 1886, and 156,698 in 1887; of rolled iron 40,581 tons, and of cut nails 212,552 kegs of 100 ℔ in 1886; of manganese 3661 tons in 1880 and 20,567 tons in 1886; of pyrites 12,000 tons in 1886; of ochre 1750 tons in 1886; of salt, gypsum, lead, zinc, granite, slates, lime, limestone for blast-furnace flux, cement, brownstone, mineral waters, and iron-ore for export large quantities were produced in 1886, and still larger in 1887, when the mining industries of this State were in a healthy condition of development.

Vegetation.

Vegetation.—The variety of vegetation in Virginia is very great, the range being from a profitable growth of semi-tropical cotton to semi-arctic pines and balsams. From one-half to two-thirds of the State is now covered by forests of native evergreen and deciduous trees. Hard and soft woods, in nearly equal proportions, form the original forests of Tidewater and Midland,—the plain regions; hard woods predominate in the high country divisions; the park-like hardwood forests of the Great Valley have grown up since its occupation by white men.

The census report of 1880, in its natural divisions of North American forests, assigns the east maritime plain of Tidewater to the coast-pine division; the north-east portions of Blue Ridge, Valley, and Appalachia to the northern-pine division; and the rest of the State to that of deciduous trees. The principal timber trees, found in varying abundance in all parts, are white, Spanish, black, chestnut, red, post, and swamp oaks; tulip-poplar and cucumber; white (or shell), bark, and pignut hickories; yellow or pitch pine; red or Virginia cedar; beech, elm, black and white walnuts, sycamore, mulberry, locust, sassafras, and gum; sugar, red, and white maples; black, red, and yellow birches; wild cherry, persimmon, dogwood, ironwood; white, red, black, and water ashes; chestnut, and willows. Cypress, juniper, long-leaved pine, holly, sweet gum, and some live oaks are confined mainly to Tidewater and east Midland; white pine, hemlock, black spruce, rock chestnut oak, and balsams to the mountain regions; the oaks of the Valley are of rare excellence, and the tulip-poplars and oaks of Trans-Appalachia and its borders are of remarkable size; sumachs, millions of pounds of the leaves of which are gathered for their tannin, are everywhere plentiful. From the sugar-maple considerable quantities of sugar are made in the Valley and the Appalachias; the forests of Tidewater, easily reached by vessels, furnish large quantities of fuel and lumber to seaboard markets; railways reach the other timber regions of the State; lumbering, charcoal-making, the cutting of railway sleepers, and the collection of tan-bark are important industries. Wild fruits and nuts, gooseberries, blackberries, whortleberries, cranberries, strawberries, haws, serviceberries, persimmons, plums, crab and thorn apples, cherries, various wild grapes, chestnuts, chinquapins, black and white walnuts, hickory nuts, hazel and beech nuts, acorns, &c., are nearly all found in all parts. Medicinal roots (ginseng, sarsaparilla, snake-root, mandrake, &c.) are gathered in large quantities in the Appalachias; oil from sassafras roots is made in quantities in Midland and Piedmont. All the cultivated fruits of temperate climates flourish; apples, pears, peaches, grapes, plums, cherries, currants, and other small fruits are everywhere plentifully grown; the peach, pear, and apple orchards of Midland, Piedmont, Blue Ridge, and the Valley are noted; the vineyards of Midland, Piedmont, and Blue Ridge are becoming well known for both grapes and wines in variety; in Tidewater and eastern Midland figs, apricots, nectarines, and other warm-country fruits flourish, and the scuppernong grapes and wines of Tidewater are also worthy of mention. The flora of Virginia includes nearly every species of plant found in the United States east of the Mississippi, excepting only the extreme south. The cleared lands of the State, about two-sevenths of the whole, are devoted to orchards, vineyards, meadows, and pastures, to market and other gardens, and to crops of maize (Indian corn), wheat, oats, rye, buckwheat, barley, pease, beans, peanuts, round (Irish) and long (sweet) potatoes, turnips, cabbage, clover, flax, hemp, cotton, tobacco, &c. Cereal and root crops are abundantly grown in all parts, as also are tobacco, hay, clover and grass seeds, flax and flaxseed, hops, hemp, and cotton. Nearly half the State, part of Piedmont, and all Blue Ridge, the Valley, and the Appalachias is a natural grass country—half of it the habitat of the famous blue grass—and well adapted to grazing and dairy-farming; the special crops of Tidewater are those of market-gardens, early vegetables, and round and sweet potatoes in the east, and of peanuts and cotton in the west; tobacco is a specialty of south-west Midland and Piedmont.

Animals.

Fauna.—The buffalo and elk, common when white men first settled here, are now extinct; deer, red and grey foxes, rabbits, hares, ground-hogs or woodchucks, red, grey, and ground squirrels, opossums, polecats, muskrats, martens, minks, weasels, bats, rats, and mice are found everywhere; otters and beavers, once numerous in all parts, are again becoming common in south Midland and elsewhere; black bears frequent the Appalachian and borders of the adjacent Valley divisions; wild-cats, catamounts, and the small wolves are occasionally met in unfrequented portions of the mountain regions. Of game or food birds, partridges (quails), pigeons, wood doves, grouse (pheasants), larks, thrushes, snipe, wild turkeys, and several kinds of wild ducks are found in nearly all parts; the coasts, the inland bays, the great estuary rivers, and the marshes of Tidewater fairly swarm, especially during the colder months, with canvas-back, mallard, creek, redhead, bald-face, teal, and other wild ducks, and with wild geese, swans, snipe, and other water and water-side fowl; gulls and other sea birds frequent the coast. Song-birds, including mocking-birds, orioles, bobolinks, robins, catbirds, bluebirds, wrens, tanagers, sparrows, &c., abound; the English sparrow is domiciled in all the cities and towns; humming-birds are plentiful. The common birds of prey, eagles, hawks, owls, a vulture (the turkey-buzzard); the wading birds (herons, grass snipes, fly-up-the-creeks, &c.) and the various swimming birds are abundant. The common reptiles include land and water tortoises, or turtles and terrapins (some highly prized for food), and harmless snakes, useful in the destruction of vermin, frogs, toads, salamanders, &c.; the poisonous rattlesnakes, copperheads, and moccasins are sometimes encountered, but are not numerous; the comparatively harmless black snakes are more common. Of edible saltwater fishes, more than thirty kinds are taken in quantities in Chesapeake Bay waters, including sturgeon, rock-fish, trout, chub, sheepshead, spot, sunfish, bluefish, shad, herring, anchovy, Spanish mackerel, cod, bonito, drum, menhaden, bass, sea-eels, and hog-fish; while dozens of kinds not used for food are known. The freshwater fishes are perch, pickerel, cat-fish, chub, bass, sucker, fall-fish, salmon, hog-fish, red-horse, red-eye, carp, mullet, sun-fish, eels, and trout in the mountain streams. Of the abounding crustaceans, edible crabs and lobsters are caught in great numbers in the marine waters, and millions of bushels of oysters, clams, and other shell-fish are annually sent to market.

Government.

Government.—The government is entrusted to three departments, each with distinct and separate powers. (1) The legislative authority is vested in a general assembly, composed of a house of delegates of 100 and a senate of 40 members which meets biennially at Richmond; the members of the house of delegates are elected for two years, those of the senate for four,—half the latter being elected biennially. (2) The executive authority is vested in a governor, elected by the people for four years. A lieutenant-governor is elected at the same time, who is president of the senate, and should a vacancy occur during the term of office becomes governor. The other executive officers are a secretary of the commonwealth, a treasurer, first and second auditors of public accounts, a superintendent of public printing, a superintendent of the penitentiary, a railroad commissioner, a commissioner of agriculture, a registrar of the land office, and a superintendent of public instruction. (3) The judicial authority is vested—(*a*) in justices of peace, three in each of the magisterial districts into which the counties are subdivided; (*b*) in judges of county courts; (*c*) in judges of the seventeen circuit courts into which the State is divided, and judges of city courts; and (*d*) in a supreme court of appeals of five judges. The right of appeal, with specified limitations, is provided for from each of the above courts to the other, in the order named; the supreme court has only appellate jurisdiction save in cases of habeas corpus, mandamus, and prohibition. The justices of the peace, a supervisor, a constable, and an overseer of the poor are elected by the voters of each magisterial district to serve two years; the general assembly elects the county judges for terms of six years, the circuit judges for terms of eight years, and the judges of the supreme court of appeals for terms of twelve years. An attorney-general for the State is elected at and for the same time as the governor. In the Congress of the United States, Virginia has two senators and ten representatives. Aliens can acquire and hold any property in Virginia on the same footing as citizens.

Population.

Population.—The population of Virginia before the separation of West Virginia in 1862 is shown by the following table:—

Census.	Population.	Increase per cent.	Persons per sq. m.	Census.	Population.	Increase per cent.	Persons per sq. m.
1790	747,610	...	11·5	1830	1,211,405	13·7	18·7
1800	880,200	17·7	13·6	1840	1,239,797	2·3	19·1
1810	974,600	10·7	15·0	1850	1,421,661	14·6	21·9
1820	1,065,116	9·2	16·4	1860	1,596,318	12·2	24·6

In 1870 the population of Virginia was 1,225,163, and that of West Virginia 442,014. In 1880, while West Virginia had 618,457 inhabitants (39·9 per cent. increase), Virginia had 1,512,565 (745,589 males, 766,976 females),—an increase of 23·4 per cent., with 37·7 persons to the square mile.

The accompanying table shows the distribution of the population in 1880 according to the grand divisions. There were in addition 6 Chinese and 85 Indians. The number of foreign-born, 14,696, does not amount to 1 per cent. of the population.

	White.	Coloured.
Tidewater	201,578	213,691
Midland	198,140	245,151
Piedmont	148,138	103,620
Blue Ridge	37,029	2,617
The Valley	199,628	51,478
The Appalachias	96,345	9,059
Virginia	880,858	631,616

The original stock of the whites was mainly English, Scottish, and Huguenot French in Tidewater, Midland, and Piedmont, and Scottish (largely Scoto-Irish from migrating by way of Ireland), German, and English in the remainder of the State—in proportions in the order named.

Cities.

Virginia has six cities with over 10,000 inhabitants. In 1880 Richmond, the State capital, had 63,600, Norfolk 21,966, Petersburg 21,656, Lynchburg 15,959, Alexandria 13,659, and Portsmouth 11,390,—Danville coming next with 7526.

Education.

Education.—The public school system of the State, organized in 1870, provides (1) primary and (2) intermediate instruction in the common branches of education, including preparation for college, by graded primary and high schools—the latter confined to cities, towns, and large villages—free to all between the ages of five and twenty-one inclusive; (3) advanced instruction and training in scientific and professional studies, by a military institute, an agricultural and mechanical college, male and female normal schools, and an institution for the deaf-mutes and the blind—all for whites, and by a normal and agricultural institute and normal college for coloured pupils,—tuition free to a selected number from all parts of the State; and (4) higher instruction, in the complete academic, scientific, technical, and professional schools of the university of Virginia, its academic department tuition free to all young men of Virginia, over eighteen years of age, under restrictions in regard to culture. The State schools confer no honorary degrees. Equal provision, but in entirely separate schools, is made by law for white and coloured.

The public free school system is in charge of a board of education. In 1887 the school population, those between five and twenty-one, numbered 610,271 (345,022 white and 265,249 coloured); 7140 schools (5047 white and 2093 coloured) were open, including 458 graded schools; 7161 teachers (2416 white males, 2889 white females, 1023 coloured males, and 833 coloured females) were employed; 325,184 pupils (209,638 white and 115,546 coloured) were enrolled, and 184,520 (121,571 white and 62,949 coloured) were in average daily attendance. The school districts owned 4365 schoolhouses, and their school property was valued at $1,907,775; the expense of the free school system in 1887 was $1,381,690, besides $153,600 spent on permanent improvements. The State makes liberal grants to the military institute, the agricultural and mechanical college, the normal and agricultural institute, the three normal schools, and the university.

Private and corporate schools embrace academies and high schools for boys, preparatory for college or university; female colleges, mainly under denominational control; and the well-known colleges of St John's in Tidewater; Hampden-Sidney, Randolph-Macon, Richmond, and Virginia Medical in Midland; and Roanoke, Emory and Henry, and Washington and Lee University in the Valley. The college of William and Mary (founded in 1693), suspended by reason of losses during the civil war, is now a normal school.

Crime.

Prisons.—One penitentiary, at Richmond, provides for all convicted of serious crimes in Virginia; during 1885–86 it received 337 convicts (80 white, 257 coloured); its expenses were $98,978, and the labour of the convicts yielded $78,000. Each county has a jail for persons committed for petty offences or awaiting trial.

Lunacy.

Lunacy, &c.—There are four first-class lunatic asylums,—at Williamsburg, Staunton, and Marion, and (for coloured patients) at Petersburg. In 1885–86 there were 1479 patients in the State's three asylums, for which it contributed $345,077. The census of 1880 returned 2411 insane,—1171 males,1240 females, 1719 white, and 692 coloured.

Pauperism.

Pauperism is not common in Virginia; in 1870 there were only 3890 paupers, supported by public charity at a cost of $303,081; in 1880 the total number was 3138, 2117 of these being in almshouses, of whom 1027 were coloured.

Deaf-mutes and blind.

Deaf-mutes and blind are well cared for in a noble institution at Staunton, which trained during 1885–86 78 deaf-mutes and 44 blind, with an annual grant of $35,000. The disabled Confederate soldiers of Virginia are aided by the State ($83,040 in 1885–86). There is also, near Richmond, a soldiers' home.

Agriculture.

Agriculture.—More than 50 per cent. of the labouring population was in 1880 engaged in agriculture. According to that year's census the land area was 25,680,000 acres, 19,835,785 of which (0·772 of the whole) were embraced in 118,517 farms, although only 8,510,113 acres of such area (only two-sevenths of the whole) were under cultivation (leaving 57·1 per cent. of land in farms unimproved), yet the number of farms increased 60·5 per cent. and the acreage in farms 9·3 per cent. from 1870. Seventh-tenths of its farms were cultivated by owners; over half of the remainder were rented for a share of the crop, and the other part for a fixed money rental. The average size of farms was 167 acres; but there were 53,101 containing from 100 to 500 acres, 5561 with from 500 to 1000 acres, and 1563 containing over 1000 acres each,—so that more than half the farms contained from 100 to over 1000 acres each, or a probable average of 300 acres each, large farms being the rule. The farms and their improvements were valued at $216,028,107, their farming implements at $5,495,114, the live stock at $25,953,315; for improvements $1,697,180 and for manures $2,137,283 were spent, and the value of their products was estimated at $45,726,221. The live stock comprised 218,838 horses, 33,598 mules and asses, 54,709 working oxen, 243,061 milch cows, 388,414 other cattle, 497,289 sheep, and 956,451 swine. The wool clip was 1,836,673 ℔; 1,224,469 gallons of milk were sold; 11,470,923 ℔ of butter and 85,535 of cheese were made; 859 acres of barley yielded 14,223 bushels; 16,463 of buckwheat 136,004; 1,768,127 of Indian corn 29,119,761; 563,443 of oats 5,333,181; 48,746 of rye 324,431; 901,177 acres of wheat yielded 7,826,174 bushels; 45,040 acres of cotton 19,595 bales; the flax crop was 4526 bushels of seed, 16,430 tons of straw, and 66,264 ℔ of fibre; the sorghum crop was 143 ℔ of sugar and 564,558 gallons of molasses; from the sugar maple were made 85,693 ℔ of sugar and 7518 gallons of molasses; of hay 286,823 tons were grown on 336,289 acres; 17,806 bushels of clover seed and 41,722 bushels of grass seed were raised; there were 1,987,010 barn-yard and 660,147 other fowls, and 8,950,629 dozen eggs were produced during the year; 1,090,451 ℔ of honey and 53,200 of beeswax were made; on 140,791 acres were grown 79,988,868 ℔ of tobacco; 2,016,766 bushels of Irish potatoes were raised, and on 23,755 acres 1,901,521 bushels of sweet ones; orchard products were valued at $1,609,663, and market-garden products at $837,609; 2,177,770 cords of wood, valued at $3,053,149, were cut; the wool clip was valued $1,836,673; 12 acres of hops yielded 1599 ℔, and 127,976 ℔ of broom corn were grown; the crop of pease was 77,758 bushels, and that of beans 45,411. Of the 8,510,113 acres of improved land, 1,152,083 were in permanent meadows, pastures, orchards, and vineyards, and 7,358,030 were under tillage; of the 11,325,672 acres unimproved in farms, 9,126,601 were in woodland and forest, and 2,199,071 in old fields, &c. Virginia was one of the twenty States that produced over 20,000,000 bushels of Indian corn each, ranking thirteenth; it stood second to Kentucky in acreage and quantity of tobacco grown. The United States commissioner of agriculture estimates that in 1884 Virginia had 4,071,401 acres in crops, producing 44,000,000 bushels of cereals, 2,061,000 bushels of potatoes, 99,763 ℔ of tobacco, 366,389 tons of hay, and 13,500 bales of cotton, valued at $39,050,052; and had on its farms 2,127,023 domestic animals, worth $39,608,536.

Manufactures.

Manufactures.—Though Virginia has great natural advantages for becoming a leading manufacturing State, in 1870 less than 12 per cent. of its population was engaged in manufacturing industries. In 1880, however, its 5710 establishments had invested $26,968,990, employed 40,184 persons (28,779 men), paid $7,425,261 for wages and $32,883,933 for materials, and produced to the value of $51,780,992,—a gain of nearly 60 per cent. in ten years. It is estimated[1] that the value of the products in 1885 was $75,000,000, —a gain of over 44 per cent. in five years. The sales of products of the manufacturing establishments of Richmond city alone amounted in 1887 to $27,887,340. The pig-iron output in 1887 was worth over $3,000,000. The more important manufactures are those of iron, tobacco, leather, coke, cotton, manures, paper, agricultural implements and machinery, builders' materials, vehicles, lumber, lime, tanning extracts, railway cars and locomotives, flour and mill products, spelter, salt, distilled spirits, canned fruits, vegetables, &c.

Communication.

Communication.—The navigable tidal bays, creeks, rivers, harbours, and roads of Tidewater Virginia furnish more than a thousand miles of channels for commerce; Richmond, at the head of the tidal waters of the James, 117 miles from Chesapeake Bay, is reached by ocean ships drawing 15 feet of water; West Point, at York Head, 41 miles from the bay, has 18 feet of depth; Elizabeth river gives to the fine harbour of Norfolk a channel 25 feet deep; while Hampton Roads, with its 400 square miles of area, is the largest as well as the most central and commodious landlocked harbour on the Atlantic coast of the United States. Ship canals connect the great waterways of Virginia with those of North Carolina and beyond to the southward; and, similarly, northward the head of Chesapeake Bay is connected with Delaware Bay. At the beginning of 1888 there were 35 railway companies working 2540 miles of road, all of standard 4 feet 9 inches gauge, except some 256 miles of narrow-gauge short lines. The Virginia railways earned $13,825,909 in 1885 at an outlay of $8,999,853, the work done being equivalent to 971,477,375 mile-tons. Virginia early took part in the construction of railways, investing many millions in the stocks of the various lines now reaching nearly every part of the State; beginning about 1830, it had 147 miles of railway in 1840, 384 in 1850, 1350 in 1860, 1449 in 1870, 1893 in 1880, 2430 in 1885, and 2540, with some 200 miles more in course of construction, at the beginning of 1888. Eight great through railway lines connect its trade and manufacturing centres with those of other States.

Finance.

Finance.—For the year ending September 30, 1886, the assessed value of the real estate of Virginia was $257,607,935, and of personal property $83,152,971, or $340,760,906 of taxable valuation; the taxes were $1,029,936 on real estate, $336,366 on personal property, $39,112 on incomes, $316,293 capitation, $141,755 from railways on a valuation of $34,614,427, $299,343 from liquor and $400,325 from other licences. The receipts of the State were $2,773,437, and its expenses of all kinds $2,755,036; of these $657,610 went to the support of the free public schools and $1,064,097 to the support of the State Government. The rate of taxation is low, and on a low property valuation. The State debt at January 1, 1885, was $28,961,829.

Militia.

Militia.—In 1880 the natural militia (male persons from eighteen to forty-four years of age inclusive) was 264,033 (102,426 of them coloured) in a male population of 745,589. The organized militia force is small. In 1885–86 there were 51 equipped volunteer companies of active militia under the orders of the State,—mainly in its cities and larger towns,—43 of infantry (18 of them coloured), 5 of artillery, and 3 cavalry,—mustering in all 2904 men. The Virginia military fund is about $11,000 a year.

History.

History.—The mound-builders of the Mississippi valley had outposts, as evidenced by remains of their earth-works, in the mountain passes of Appalachia. At the time of the arrival of the whites the Powhatans held most of Tidewater, the Mannahoacks the north-east and the Monacans the south-west of Midland and Piedmont; the Cherokees held the Tennessee basin parts of the Valley and Appalachia, and Algonkin tribes—Shawnees, Delawares, &c.—the rest of those divisions. Many of the place names are still Indian. Cabot probably entered Chesapeake Bay in 1498; when Raleigh's ships, in 1584, brought to England glowing accounts of the Albemarle Sound region, the whole country was named Virginia in honour of Elizabeth, the virgin queen. The first permanent English settlement in America was made at Jamestown, Virginia, May 13, 1607, by one hundred settlers sent from England by Sir Thomas Gates and Company, who had obtained in April 1606 a charter from James I. to plant two colonies in Virginia,—a southern somewhere between 34° and 41°, and a northern between 38° and 45° N. lat., but at places not less than 100 miles apart. In 1609 the London Company superseded Gates's, which had merely held its settlement and given to the world the romantic adventures of Captain John SMITH (*q.v.*). King James gave the London Company, by charter, a sea-front of 400 miles,—200 north and 200 south from Point Comfort,—all islands within 100 miles of the coast, and all the country back from this 400 miles of frontage "throughout from sea to sea," and to its colonists all the rights of natural-born Englishmen; under this charter Virginia had jurisdiction over her imperial colonial territory, and under it holds the fragment of that colony now called Virginia. The colony of the London Company grew and prospered, and in 1619 Governor Yardley organized at James City, the capital, a few miles inland from Jamestown, the first legislative body that met in North America; in 1621 the London Company granted the colony a liberal constitution, the general form of which Virginia has always preserved. In August 1619 a Dutch man-of-war sold at Jamestown twenty African negroes, and introduced negro slavery. In 1624 James I. arbitrarily deprived the London Company of its charter, and Virginia became a royal colony, which was, till the revolution, a favourite and generally a loyal royal province governed

[1] *United States Internal Commerce Report* for 1886.

by the constitution of 1621, the king appointing the governor and council and the people electing the members of the house of burgesses. In 1698 the capital was transferred to Williamsburg, where, under royal patronage, William and Mary College had been established in 1693. The colony soon occupied most of Tidewater and its Midland border; in 1716 Governor Spotswood crossed the Blue Ridge, and was, so far as known, the first white man to enter the Great Valley, which was soon thereafter occupied by large numbers of Scottish and some German and English settlers. Indian wars followed as settlers moved westward, but in 1744 Virginia purchased from the Indians the right to make settlements to the Ohio, and built a fort where Pittsburgh now stands; the French captured this in 1754, and the long French and Indian war followed, until the 1763 treaty of Paris ended it and made the Mississippi the western boundary of Virginia. During that war, in 1755, Braddock was defeated; and in 1758 Fort Duquesne, which under the French had taken the place of Pittsburgh, was captured and renamed Fort Pitt. In 1773 the general assembly of Virginia resolved for an "inter-colonial committee of correspondence," and was dissolved by Lord Dunmore, the royal governor. In May 1774 it again met and protested against the closing of the port of Boston; Dunmore again dissolved it, but the burgesses, the members elected by the people, reassembled and passed resolutions denouncing British taxation and recommending to the other colonies an annual congress of delegates,—leading in this as it had in recommending committees of correspondence. Virginia took a leading part in the subsequent war of independence, but the various steps of her policy need not be detailed here (see United States, and compare also Jefferson and Washington).

The great territory of Virginia, reaching from the Atlantic to the Mississippi, and now divided into five large States, made the other States of the Union apprehensive of her future domination. In 1781, to promote harmony, she offered to cede to the general Government all her territory beyond the Ohio, and in 1784 she made the cession, only stipulating that the territory thus voluntarily given up should, when peopled, be divided into new States, in which slavery should be for ever prohibited, and that the remainder of her territory—that from the Atlantic to the Ohio—should remain inviolably hers. In 1787 the convention of the States, at Philadelphia, presided over by Washington, adopted the present constitution of the United States, and this Virginia, in convention, ratified in 1788. In the war of 1812–14 with England Virginia bore a conspicuous part, as also in that of 1846–47 with Mexico. The civil war of 1861–65 was more disastrous in its consequences to Virginia than to any other State of the Union; from first to last its territory was overrun, hundreds of battles and minor engagements took place within its borders, and all the destruction incident to gigantic military operations fell upon it; tens of thousands of its best men were killed in battle; its territory was dismembered, and a third part of it cut off, while more than three hundred million dollars' worth of property was destroyed in what remained.

For some time after 1865 Virginia was under Federal military control as "District No. 1"; but on December 3, 1867, a convention, elected by the people, under an Act of the United States Congress, met and framed a new constitution, prohibiting slavery and accepting the results of the war; this was ratified by a popular vote, July 6, 1869, at which time members of a general assembly and State officers were also elected. The chosen governor was inaugurated September 21, 1869; the general assembly met October 5, 1869, and ratified the fourteenth and fifteenth amendments to the constitution of the United States; and on January 26, 1870, Virginia was readmitted to representation in Congress, and released from military control. (J. H*.)

VIRGINIA CITY, the county seat of Storey county, Nevada, U.S., and the largest and most important city of the State, is situated upon the steep rugged eastern slope of Mount Davidson, about 6300 feet above sea-level. A branch line connects it with the Central Pacific Railroad at Reno. Virginia City is built over the great Comstock lode, the mineral vein which has yielded probably more of the precious metals than any other single deposit in the world (see vol. xxiii. p. 815). With the varying fortunes of this lode the prosperity of Virginia City is intimately connected. It was founded in 1859, and in 1860 its inhabitants numbered 2345. In 1861 it received a city charter. It continued to increase until towards the end of that decade, when the falling off in the receipts from the mines caused a partial exodus from the town, and the census of 1870 showed only 7048 inhabitants. The discovery of the "great bonanza" in 1875 produced a return of prosperity, but this was but transient, and before the next census the city was again on the wane. In 1880 the census showed 10,917 inhabitants,—nearly half of foreign birth, and about 5 per cent. Chinese. Since the last census the population has, in all probability, not increased. The city is laid out rather irregularly, conforming to some extent to the surface of the mountain side. Some streets have been graded, at great expense, as it involved much rock cutting.

VIRGIN ISLANDS, a group of small West India Islands (see West Indies), about one hundred in number, for the most part uninhabited, extending eastward from Porto Rico, and lying between 17° and 18° 50′ N. lat., and 64° 10′ and 65° 30′ W. long. Their total area may be estimated at about 465 square miles, and their population at 67,000. For the most part they are rocky or sandy and barren, but the cultivable portions yield sugar, maize, coffee, cotton, indigo, and tobacco. Guinea grass grows abundantly on the hillsides, and the rich natural grass affords excellent pasturage; the forests include many useful trees, among which are mahogany and fustic. Fish are very plentiful on the coasts. The westerly portion of the group belongs to Spain, the central to Denmark, and the easterly to Great Britain. The chief of the Spanish islands are Culebra or Snake Island, and Bieques or Crab Island; they have in all an area of about 150 square miles, with a population of 2600. The Danish Virgin Islands, which include St Thomas (*q.v.*), St Croix (*q.v.*), and St John, have a total of about 240 square miles, with about 34,000 inhabitants. The principal of the British portion of the group are Tortola, Anegada, and Virgen Gorda or Spanish Town, and Jost van Dyke (total area 57 square miles, and population 5287 in 1881, of whom more than one-half are in Tortola). They are subject to a lieutenant-governor, under the governor-in-chief of the Leeward Islands, and are governed by an administrative council of six elective and three non-elective members, presided over by the governor for the time being. In 1886 the revenue and expenditure were respectively £1448 and £1676. The customs revenue was £823, and there was no public debt. In the same year 1710 vessels entered, of 10,764 tons burden (exclusive of coasting trade), and 1779 vessels cleared, of 8444 tons; the total value of the imports was £3603, and of the exports £4103.

The Virgin Islands were discovered by Columbus on his second voyage, in 1494, and named Las Virgenes, in honour of St Ursula and her companions. In 1666 the English established themselves on Tortola, which has ever since remained in their possession. In the 17th century the Virgin Islands were favourite resorts of the Buccaneers (*q.v.*). The Danish islands of St Thomas and St John were taken by the British in 1801, but restored the following year. In 1807 they surrendered to the British, and continued in their hands till 1815, when they were again restored. The constitution of the British Virgin Islands was amended in 1854.

VISCONTI. See Milan, vol. xvi. p. 293.

VISCOUNT (Latin *vice-comes*), a titled rank of nobility, the fourth in the order of the British peerage, and consequently intervening between the dignities of earl and baron. The first English viscount, as that term now is used and understood, was John, Baron Beaumont, K.G., who, by letters patent dated 12th February 1440, by Henry VI. was created Viscount Beaumont. The title *vice-comes*, however, existed in England certainly as early as the Domesday survey; and in those early times it was borne by a county officer, who was deputy to the *comes* or earl, in accordance with the feudal system, which knew no titles independent of offices. The *vice-comes*, whose title from the first may fairly be translated "viscount," and who acted in the absence of the earl, may be considered to have been identical with the functionary known by the English term "shire-reeve" or "sheriff," or, as we now should say, "high-sheriff." During the reigns of the Anglo-Norman monarchs this office of *vice-comes* was commonly hereditary; after a while it was granted for several successive years to the same personage at the king's pleasure; and, finally, the modern practice obtained of appointing a new high-sheriff every year. A viscount is "Right Honourable," and is styled "My Lord." His wife, also "Right Honourable," is a "Viscountess," and is styled "My Lady." All their sons and daughters are "Honourable." The coronet first granted by James I. has on the golden circlet a row of fourteen small pearls set in contact, of which number in representations nine are shown. The scarlet parliamentary robe of a viscount has two and a half doublings of ermine.

VISHNU. See BRAHMANISM, vol. iv. p. 207.

VISTULA. See POLAND, vol. xix. p. 307.

VITALIANUS, bishop of Rome from 657 to 672, succeeded Eugenius I. and was followed by Adeodatus. In the monothelite controversy then raging he acted with cautious reserve, refraining at least from express condemnation of the *Typus* of Constans II. (see vol. xvi. p. 758). The chief episode in his uneventful pontificate was the visit of Constans to Rome; the pope received him "almost with religious honours," a deference which he requited by stripping all the brazen ornaments of the city—even to the tiles of the Pantheon—and sending them to Constantinople. Archbishop Theodore was sent to Canterbury by Vitalian.

VITEBSK, a government of western Russia, with Livonia and Pskoff on the N., Smolensk on the E., Moghileff, Minsk, and Vilna on the S., and Courland on the W., has an area of 17,440 square miles. Except on its south-eastern and northern borders, where there are low hills, deeply eroded by the rivers, its surface is mostly flat, or slightly undulating, and more than a million of acres are occupied by immense marshes, with as many as 2500 small lakes. The Devonian limestones and red sandstones of which it is built up are covered with thick layers of Glacial and Lacustrine deposits,—the Glacial boulder-clay, with immense numbers of boulders, covering extensive areas. The rest consists of Lacustrine clays or sands. The soil is thus for the most part unproductive.

The Düna, or West Dwina, rises not far from the north-eastern angle of the government, and flows through it, or along its southern boundary, for 530 miles. From its junction with the Kasplya, *i.e.*, for more than 450 miles, it is navigable; and, through a tributary, the Ulla, it is connected with the Dnieper by the Berezina Canal. The Mezha and Kasplya, tributaries of the Düna, are navigable in spring. The climate is relatively mild, the average yearly temperature at Vitebsk being 40° F. (January, 16°·4; July, 64°·3).

The population, 1,204,950 in 1884, is chiefly White Russian (61 per cent.) and Lettish (21 per cent.); Jews come next (10 per cent.). The Poles make only about 2·3 per cent. of the population, and there are moreover about 10,000 Germans in the north-west. The Great Russians number only a few thousands. Nearly two-thirds of the inhabitants are Orthodox or Raskolnik, the remainder being Catholics, Jews, or Lutherans.

Agriculture is the chief industry, but the yearly produce rarely suffices for the wants of the population, and corn has to be imported from Smolensk. Rye, oats, and potatoes are the chief crops, occupying about a third of the area. Flax is an important crop for export. Cattle-breeding is only moderately prosperous. Manufactures in 1884 occupied only some 3000 persons, and their aggregate production reached only about £788,700 (as against £84,000 in 1860); the most important branches are represented by distilleries, flour-mills, and tanneries. As a rule, the White Russian population of the villages is very poor, and great numbers of the peasants are compelled every year to leave their homes in search of work. Of domestic trades, the manufacture of wooden wares, as well as some boat-building and flax-combing, may be mentioned. The principal exports are flax, linseed, timber, and hides. There is a brisk water-traffic on the Düna by boats to Riga, Vitebsk loading-places contributing 1,128,500 cwts. (483,000 roubles value) loaded and 630,000 cwts. discharged in 1883.

Vitebsk is divided into twelve districts, the chief towns of which, with populations in 1885, are Vitebsk (54,680), Drissa (3490), Dünaburg, a fortress on the Düna (69,030), Gorodok (5620), Lepel (6000), Lutsin (5460), Nevel (7310), Polotsk (19,130), Ryezhitsa (10,150), Sebezh (3820), Surazh (5085), and Velizh (16,370).

VITEBSK, capital of the above government, stands on both banks of the Düna, on the railway from Smolensk to Riga, 345 miles west of Moscow. It is an old town, with decaying mansions of the old nobility, and dirty Jewish quarters, half of its 54,680 inhabitants being Jews. Its manufactures are insignificant, and the poorer classes support themselves by gardening, boat-building, and the flax trade, while the merchants carry on an active business with Riga in corn, flax, hemp, tobacco, sugar, and timber.

Vitebsk (Dbesk, Vitbesk, and Vitepesk) is mentioned for the first time in 1021, when it made part of the Polotsk principality. Eighty years later it became the chief town of a separate principality, and so continued until 1320, when, after having taken an active part in the internal wars of the Russian princes, it came under the dominion of the Lithuanians. In the 16th century it fell to Poland. Under the privileges given to the city by the Polish sovereigns it flourished, but it soon began to suffer from the wars between Russia and Poland, during which it was thrice taken by the Russians and burned. Russia annexed it finally in 1772.

VITELLIUS, AULUS, the ninth of the twelve Cæsars, and Roman emperor during the greater part of 69 A.D., was the son of Lucius Vitellius, who had been consul and governor of Syria under Tiberius, and distinguished for his gross and ridiculous flattery under Caius (Caligula) and Claudius, which the senate, who gave him a public funeral, recognized by a statue with the inscription "Pietatis immobilis erga principem." He was one of the intimate companions of Tiberius at Capreæ; he had driven chariots in the circus with Caius, had played dice with Claudius, had induced the young Nero to sing at a public entertainment, and had been a censor once and a consul three times. He had been governor of Africa, and had there, according to Suetonius (*Vitellius*, 5), acquitted himself creditably. Under Galba, to the general astonishment, he was chosen to command the army of Lower Germany, and here he made himself popular with his subalterns and with the soldiers by an outrageous prodigality and an excessive good nature, which soon proved quite fatal to order and discipline. Far from being an ambitious or scheming man, he was lazy and self-indulgent, fond of eating and drinking, and he was in fact drifted into empire by the promptings of Cæcina and Valens, commanders of two legions on the Rhine. Through these two men a military revolution was speedily accomplished, and early in 69 Vitellius was proclaimed emperor at Cologne, or, to speak more accurately, emperor of the armies of Upper and Lower Germany. In fact, he was never acknowledged as emperor by the entire Roman world, though at Rome the senate accepted him and decreed to him the usual imperial honours. But after all he was only emperor in name. It was noted as a bad omen that he received the title of supreme pontiff on the anniversary of the day of Allia, 390 B.C., on which Rome was all but utterly overthrown by the Gauls. His advance into Italy at the head of a licentious and ruffianly soldiery was as horrible and calamitous as civil war could possibly be; there was fighting and bloodshed within 7 miles of Rome, and amid riot and massacre and gladiatorial shows and extravagant feasting and a waste of seven millions of money (Tacitus, *Hist.*, ii. 95) the capital of the empire was a scene of horror and infamy such as had never been witnessed in the most savage revolutions of past days. As soon as it was known that the armies of the East, Dalmatia, and Illyricum had declared for Vespasian, Vitellius, finding himself deserted by many of his adherents, was for resigning the title of emperor; so crestfallen was he, so dull and lethargic, that, to quote Tacitus (*Hist.*, iii. 63), "had not others remembered he had been an emperor, he would have forgotten it himself." On the entrance into Rome of Vespasian's troops he was dragged out of some miserable hiding-place, and, with his hands tied behind him, insulted unpitied, driven to the fatal Gemonian stairs, and there struck down amid a shower of fierce eager blows. "Yet I was once your emperor," were the last, and, as far as we know, the noblest words of Vitellius. He perished thus miserably in his 57th year.

The *Histories* of Tacitus and the biography of Suetonius give us in full detail the story of Vitellius. In Merivale's *History of the Romans under the Empire* (chaps. 56, 57) the period is fully and vividly described.

VITERBO, a city of Italy, capital of a circondario in the province of Rome, lies 1200 feet above sea-level, on the Arcione, at the north-western base of Monte Cimino (3450 feet), on the high road between Florence and Rome, 42 miles north-north-west of the latter city; a branch line ($24\frac{3}{4}$ miles) connects it with the Attigliano station on the railway. It is picturesquely surrounded by luxuriant gardens, and enclosed by walls and towers, which date partly from the Lombard period. The streets are paved with large lava blocks, and the town has many handsome edifices, and some elegant fountains; among the latter may be mentioned the Fontana della Rocca by Vignola (1566). The cathedral, a fine basilica, with 13th-century restorations, contains the tombs of Popes Alexander IV., Clement IV., and John XXI. In 1271 it was the scene of the murder, on the steps of the high altar, during public worship, of Henry, son of Richard of Cornwall, by Guy de Montfort (see Dante, *Inf.*, xii. 118). In the sacristy is a Madonna with saints by Lorenzo di Viterbo. The old episcopal palace is a Gothic building of the 13th century, in which numerous conclaves have been held. The church of St Rosa exhibits the embalmed body of that saint, a native of Viterbo, who died in her eighteenth year, after working various miracles and having distinguished herself by her invectives against Frederick II. (1251). St Francesco contains the tomb of Pope Adrian V., and has an important work by Sebastiano del Piombo; the Gothic cloisters of St Maria della Verità are strikingly beautiful. The town-hall contains some Etrurian sarcophagi and a few good paintings. The inhabitants of Viterbo (15,279 in 1881) are chiefly dependent on agriculture; hemp is a specialty of the district, and tobacco and various grains are largely grown, as well as the olive and vine. There are in the vicinity numerous mineral springs; the warm sulphur spring of Bulicame, about 2 miles off, is alluded to by Dante (*Inf.*, xiv. 79).

Viterbo has sometimes, but very doubtfully, been identified with the *Fanum Voltumnæ*, where the general assembly of the Etruscans used to be held. It was fortified by the Lombards, and in the Middle Ages became a favourite papal residence. Popes Urban IV. (1261), Gregory X. (1271), John XXI. (1276), Nicholas III. (1277), and Martin IV. (1281) were elected here, and it was at Viterbo that Alexander IV. (1261), Clement IV. (1268), Adrian V. (1276), and John XXI. (1277) died.

VITORIA, a town of Spain, capital of the Basque province of Alava, stands at a height of about 1750 feet above sea-level, on a small hill commanding the plain of Alava, 234 miles by rail north-north-east of Madrid. The oldest part of the town, the Campillo or Villa-Suso, occupies the top of the hill; some of the walls and towers by which it was formally defended still remain, but it is now almost deserted, and chiefly occupied by gardens. Below it is "Vitoria Antigua," with narrow tortuous lanes; on the lower level ground is the modern town, with wide streets, an arcaded market place, and shady promenades. The cathedral of St Mary in the Campillo dates its foundation from 1181, and has some good Gothic arches, but has been considerably spoiled by late additions; the church of San Miguel also dates from the 12th century, but does not possess any features of special interest. Vitoria, from its favourable position, is an important centre of trade in wine, wool, horses, mules, and hardware; the chief industries are paper-making, carriage-building, cabinet-making, tanning, and the manufacture of earthernware. The population within the municipal boundaries in 1877 was 25,039.

Though an obscure village seems to have occupied the site from an early period, the existence of Vitoria as a town dates from 1181, when Sancho the Wise of Navarre granted a "fuero" similar to that of Logroño, and fortified the place. A decisive victory was here gained by the Anglo-Spanish army under Wellington over the French under Joseph Bonaparte and Jourdan on June 21, 1813.

VITRÉ, a town of France, chef-lieu of an arrondissement in the department of Ille-et-Vilaine, stands on a hill rising from the left bank of the Vilaine, 24 miles east of Rennes by the railway to Paris. The town has preserved as many features of the Middle Ages as any in France, and viewed from the north its feudal aspect is striking. The streets are formed of confused masses of wooden houses, full of projections and curves, covered with coarse slate overgrown with moss and lichen, and are bordered by covered galleries on a level with the ground, out of which dark shops open. Most of the curious houses, ornamented with statuettes and sculptures, are older than the first half of the 17th century. Only one vault remains of the original castle, founded towards the end of the 11th century; the rest was rebuilt in the 14th and 15th centuries (the best period of Breton military architecture in Brittany), and all has been recently restored. It is now occupied by a prison, a museum of natural history and painting, and the town library (6000 volumes). In the court is the former collegiate church, some of it older than the 12th century. The church of Notre Dame, formerly a priory of the abbey of St Mélaine of Rennes, dates from the 15th and 16th centuries. An outside stone pulpit is a fine example of 16th-century sculpture. Parts of the ramparts are still standing, and other parts are built into the houses of the town. There is a well-wooded botanical garden, and the remains of a castle destroyed at the Revolution. The chief articles of trade are cloth, hosiery, and thick clothing made of goats' skins. The chateau of Les Rochers, celebrated through Madame de Sévigné, stands 3 miles from the town. The population in 1886 was 8957 (commune 10,447).

Vitré was formerly a Breton barony, and belonged in the 10th century to the younger branch of the counts of Rennes. In 1295 it passed to Guy IX. baron of Laval, on his marriage with the heiress, and afterwards successively belonged to the families of Rieux, Coligny, and La Trémoille. The town was seized by Charles VIII. in 1488. Protestantism spread under the rule of the houses of Rieux and Coligny; Vitré became a Huguenot stronghold; and a Protestant church was established, which was not suppressed till the revocation of the edict of Nantes in 1685. Mercœur, the head of the members of the League in Brittany, besieged the town in vain for five months in 1589, and was forced to withdraw by the army under the Prince de Dombes. The estates of Brittany, over which the barons of Vitré and of Léon alternately presided, met here several times, and Madame de Sévigné gives interesting details of such an occasion. Vitré was the birthplace of Pierre Landais, the favourite minister of Francis II., duke of Brittany (hanged in 1485), of his nephew Cardinal Guibé, and of Bertrand d'Argentré, jurist and the historian of Brittany.

VITRIFIED FORTS is the name given to certain rude stone enclosures whose walls bear traces of having been subjected to the action of fire. They are generally situated on elevated hills, which occupy strong and easily defended positions. Their form is irregular, and seems to have been determined rather by the contour of the flat summits which they enclose than by any definite architectural plan. The walls vary in size, some being comparatively small, while a few are upwards of 12 feet high, and are so broad that they present the appearance of huge embankments. Weak and exposed parts in the defence are strengthened by double or triple walls, and occasionally vast lines of ramparts, composed of large blocks of unhewn and unvitrified stones, are drawn around the fortified hills at some distance from the vitrified centre. No lime or cement has been found in any of these structures, but all of them present the peculiarity of being more or less consolidated by the fusion of the rocks of which they are built. This fusion, which has been caused by the application of intense heat, is not equally complete and regular in the various forts, or even in the walls of the same fort. In some cases the stones are only partially melted and calcined; in others their adjoining edges are fused so that they are firmly cemented together; in many instances pieces of rock are enveloped in a glassy enamel-like coating which binds them into a uniform whole; and at times, though rarely, the entire length of the wall presents one solid mass of vitreous substance.

Since John Williams—one of the earliest of British geologists, and author of *The Mineral Kingdom*—first described, in 1777, these singular ruins, about fifty examples have been discovered in different parts of Scotland. The most remarkable are Dun Mac Uisneachain, the ancient Beregonium, north of Oban; Tap o' Noth, in Aberdeenshire; Craig Phadraic and Dun Dhardhail, in Inverness; Knockfarrail, near Strathpeffer; Dun Creich, in Sutherland; Findhaven, near Aberlemno; Barryhill, in Perthshire; Laws, near Dundee; Dun Gall and Burnt Island, in Buteshire; Anwoth, in Kirkcudbright; and Cowdenknowes, in Berwickshire. Dun Mac Uisneachain is the largest in area, being 250 yards long by 50 yards broad. The strongest and most cyclopean is the Tap o' Noth: here the walls are about 8 feet high, and between 20 and 30 feet thick. In Dun Mac Uisneachain, Barryhill, and Laws the remains of small rectangular huts or dwellings have been found.

For a long time it was supposed that these forts were limited in their range to Scotland; but they are now known to exist in Londonderry and Cavan, in Ireland; in Upper Lusatia, Bohemia, Silesia, Saxony, and Thuringia; in the provinces on the upper banks of the Rhine, especially in the neighbourhood of the Nahe; in the Ucker Lake, in Brandenburg, where the walls are formed of burnt and smelted bricks; and in several places in France, such as Châteauvieux, Peran, La Courbe, Saint Suzanne, Puy de Gaudy, and Thauron. They have not been found in England or Wales; and Worsaae, Herbst, Rygh, Hildebrand, and Stephens assert that they do not exist in Denmark or in Scandinavia.

All the examples yet described present a general similarity in form and structure. In some of the Continental forts the vitrified walls are supported by masses of unvitrified stone built up on each side. This, in all probability, constituted an essential feature in the Scottish forts. Except on the hypothesis of buttresses of a similar kind, it is impossible to explain the vast quantities of loose stones which are found both inside and outside many of the vitrified walls.

The method by which the fusion of such extensive fortifications was produced has always excited much interest and conjecture. Williams, when he first directed attention to the subject, maintained that the builders of the forts, whoever they were, found out, either during the process of smelting bog-ore, or whilst offering sacrifices, the power of fire in vitrifying stone, and that they improved upon this discovery by using it for the purpose of cementing and strengthening their strongholds. This view has been keenly controverted, and other theories have been suggested. It has been held that the vitrified summits were not forts at all, but the craters of extinct volcanoes (West, Pennant, and Cordiner), an hypothesis long since abandoned as unscientific; that the vitrified summits are not so much vitrified forts as vitrified sites, and that the vitrescence was produced by beacon fires lighted during times of invasion, or by bonfires kindled on hill tops in religious celebrations (Sir George Mackenzie, Dr S. Hibbert, and Principal Daniel Wilson); and, lastly, that if they were forts they must have originally been built of wood and stone, and that their present vitrified appearance is not due to design, but to their being set on fire by a besieging enemy (A. Fraser Tytler, Forbes Leslie, Von Cohausen, and Dr Joseph Anderson). The theory of Williams—which has, with modifications, been accepted by all the principal British and Continental authorities, such as MacCulloch, Hugh Miller, Virchow, Schaaffhausen, Thuot, and Montaiglon—is likely to hold the field. It is supported by the following facts:—

(1) The idea of strengthening walls by means of fire is not singular, or confined to a distinct race or area, as is proved by the burnt-earth enclosure of Aztalan, in Wisconsin, and the vitrified stone monuments of the Mississippi valley. (2) Many of the Primary rocks, particularly the schists, gneisses, and traps, which contain large quantities of potash and soda, can be readily fused in the open air by means of wood fires,—the alkali of the wood serving in some measure as a flux. (3) The walls are chiefly vitrified at the weakest points, the naturally inaccessible parts being unvitrified. (4) When the forts have been placed on materials practically infusible, as on the quartzose conglomerates of the Old Red Sandstone, as at Craig Phadraic, and on the limestones of Dun Mac Uisneachain, pieces of fusible rocks have been selected and carried from a considerable distance to the top. (5) The vitrified walls of the Scottish forts are invariably formed of small stones which could be easily acted upon by fire, whereas the outer ramparts, which are not vitrified, are built of large blocks. (6) Many of the Continental forts are so constructed that the fire must have been applied internally, and at the time when the structure was being erected. (7) Daubrée, in an analysis which he made on vitrified materials taken from four French forts, and which he submitted to the Academy of Paris in February 1881, found the presence of natron in such great abundance that he inferred that sea-salt was used to facilitate the original fusion. (8) In Scandinavia, where there are hundreds of ordinary forts, and where for centuries a system of signal fires was enforced by law, no trace of vitrifaction has yet been detected.

A great antiquity has been assigned to vitrified forts, but without sufficient proof. Articles of bronze and iron have been found in the Scottish forts, while in Puy de Gaudy a Roman tile has been discovered soldered to a piece of vitrified rock. In a few of the German forts Prof. Virchow found some of the short logs of oak used as fuel in vitrifying the walls, and he concluded from the evenness of their cut surfaces that iron and not stone implements must have been used. These results indicate that these structures are the products of a high civilization, and were possibly in use as late as the early centuries of our era. It has been suggested that they were built as temporary refuges against the invasions of the Norsemen in Europe. There is much in the situation and character of the forts which favours this supposition. This is especially the case with reference to the Scottish forts. Here the vitrified summits are invariably so selected that they not only command what were, as we learn from the sagas, the favourite landing places of the vikings, but are the best natural defences against attacks made from the direction of the sea-coast. In Saxony and Lusatia the forts are known as *Schwedenburgen*, and in the Highlands of Scotland as the fortresses of the *Feinne*—designations which also seem to point to an origin dating back to the times of the vikings.

It may be interesting, as throwing light on the influence of high temperature on rocks, to notice some of the forms exhibited by the fused substances. Schistose gneiss is resolved into a kind of green glass; mica is converted into a grey glassy stone of great hardness; quartz is reduced to the condition of pumice; trap rock becomes glazed like bottle glass; sandstone is transformed into a compact quartzite; and the felspar of granite is changed into coarse porcelain. Some of the materials have assumed, probably during the process of cooling, the prismatic structure, with four or six sides; while others, owing to the iron peroxide being reduced, have become distinctly magnetic.

The following are some of the more important treatises and references:—Williams, *An Account of some Remarkable Ancient Ruins*; A. Fraser Tytler, *Edin. Phil. Trans.*, vol. ii.; Sir George Mackenzie, *Observations on Vitrified Forts*; Hibbert, *Arch. Scot.*, vol. iv.; MacCulloch, *Highlands and Western Islands*, vol. i.; Miller, *Rambles of a Geologist*, chap. ix.; Wilson, *Archæology*, and *Prehistoric Annals*, vol. ii.; J. H. Burton, *History of Scotland*, vol. i.; R. Angus Smith, *Loch Etive and the Sons of Uisneach*; Anderson, *Scotland in Pagan Times*; C. MacLagan, *The Hill Forts of Ancient Scotland*; Thomas Aitken, *Trans. Inverness Scientific Soc.*, vol. i.; Charles Proctor, *Chemical Analysis of Vitrified Stones from Tap o' Noth and Dunideer* (Huntly Field Club); various papers in published *Proceedings of Soc. Antiq. Scot.* and *Proceedings of Royal Irish Academy*; Leonhard, *Archiv für Mineralogie*, vol. i.; Virchow, *Ztschr. für Ethnologie*, vols. iii. and iv.; Schaaffhausen, *Verhandlungen der deutsch. anthrop. Gesellschaft* (1881); Köhl, *Verhand. d. deutsch. anthrop. Gesellschaft* (1883); Thuot, *La Forteresse vitrifiée du Puy de Gaudy, &c.*; De Nadaillac, *Les Premiers Hommes*, vol. i.; *Mémoires de la Soc. Antiq. de France*, vol. xxxviii.; and Hildebrand, *De förhistoriska folken i Europa* (Stockholm, 1880). (R. MU.)

VITRIOL, a name formerly and sometimes still given to sulphuric acid and to certain sulphates (see SULPHUR, vol. xxii. p. 636). Oil of vitriol is concentrated sulphuric acid. Blue vitriol is sulphate of copper; green vitriol, sulphate of iron (copperas, ferrous sulphate); and white vitriol, sulphate of zinc.

VITRUVIUS,[1] a Roman architect and engineer, whose full name was MARCUS VITRUVIUS POLLIO, the author of a very celebrated work on architecture. Nothing is known about his personal history, except what can be gathered from incidental remarks in his own writings. Owing to the discovery of a number of inscriptions relating to the Gens Vitruvia at Formiæ in Campania (Mola di Gaeta), it has been suggested that he was a native of that city, and he has been less reasonably connected with Verona on the strength of an existing arch of the 3d century, which is inscribed with the name of a later architect of the same family name—"Lucius Vitruvius Cerdo, a freedman of Lucius." From Vitruvius himself we learn that he was appointed, in the reign of Augustus, together with three others, a superintendent of *balistæ* and other military engines, a post which, he says, he owed to the friendly influence of the emperor's sister, probably Octavia (*De Architectura*, i. pref.). In another passage (v. 1) he describes a basilica and adjacent ædes Augusti, of which he was the architect. From viii. 3 it has been supposed that he had served in Africa in the time of Julius Cæsar, probably as a military engineer, but the words will hardly bear this interpretation. He speaks of himself as being low in stature, and at the time of his writing bowed down by age and ill-health (ii. pref.). He appears to have enjoyed no great reputation as an architect, and, with philosophic contentment, records that he possessed but little fortune. Though a great student of Greek philosophy and science, he was unpractised in literature, and his style is very involved and obscure. To a great extent the theoretical and historical parts of his work are compiled from earlier Greek authors, of whom he gives a list at i. 1 and viii. 3. The practical portions, on the contrary, are evidently the result of his own professional experience, and are written with much sagacity, and in a far clearer style than the more pedantic chapters, in which he gives the somewhat fanciful theories of the Greeks. Some sections of the latter, especially those on the connexion between music and architecture, the scale of harmonic proportions, and the Greek use of bronze vases to reverberate and strengthen the actors' voices in the theatre, are now almost wholly unintelligible.

The *De Architectura* is divided into ten books, each with a preface, in which occur most of the personal facts about himself. It is dedicated to Augustus, and that fact is really all that is known with regard to the date at which Vitruvius lived, though many attempts have been made to gather more minute indications from the internal evidence of his writings: for example, the omission of any mention of the Pantheon in Rome has been taken as an argument to show that he wrote before it was built in 27 B.C. This, however, and other arguments of the same kind are obviously of but little weight. Vitruvius's name is mentioned by Frontinus in his work on the aqueducts of Rome; and most of what Pliny says (*H.N.*, xxxv. and xxxvi.) about methods of wall-painting, the preparation of the stucco surface, and other practical details in building is taken almost word for word from Vitruvius, especially from vi. 1, though without any acknowledgment of the source.

From the early Renaissance down to a comparatively recent time the influence of Vitruvius's treatise has been remarkably great. Throughout the period of the classical revival Vitruvius was the chief authority studied by all architects, and in every point his precepts were accepted as final. In some cases a failure to understand his meaning led to curious results; for example, the mediæval custom, not uncommon in England, of placing rows of earthenware jars under the floor of the stalls in church choirs appears to have been an attempt to follow out Vitruvius's remarks about the advantages of placing bronze vases round the auditorium of theatres. Bramante, Michelangelo, Palladio, Vignola, and earlier architects were careful students of Vitruvius's work, which through them has largely influenced the architecture of almost all European countries down to the present century, a very remarkable instance of the success and influence of a book being actively redeveloped a very long time—about fifteen centuries—after its author's lifetime. There is no reason to suppose that the book was either popular or influential among the ancient Romans, and yet in more modern times its influence has been unbounded. Its archæological value is very great, as without it we should find it very difficult to understand the uses of the various parts of such houses as those at Pompeii, and many interesting details with regard both to construction and design would have remained unintelligible.

Bk. i. opens with a dedication to Augustus. C. 1 is on the science of architecture generally, and the many different branches of knowledge with which the trained architect ought to be acquainted, viz., grammar, music, painting, sculpture, medicine, geometry, mathematics, and optics; c. 2 is on the general principles of architectural design; c. 3 on the considerations which determine a design, such as strength, utility, beauty, and the like; c. 4 on the nature of different sorts of ground for sites; c. 5 on walls of fortification; c. 6 on aspects towards the north, south, and other points; c. 7 on the proper situations of temples dedicated to the various deities. Bk. ii. relates to materials (preface about Dinocrates, architect to Alexander the Great). C. 1 is on the earliest dwellings of man; c. 2 on systems of Thales, Heraclitus, Democritus, &c.; c. 3 on bricks; c. 4 on sand; c. 5 on lime; c. 6 on pozzolana; c. 7 on kinds of stone for building; c. 8 on methods of constructing walls in stone, brick, concrete, and marble, and on the materials for stucco; c. 9 on timber, time for felling it, seasoning, &c.; and c. 10 on the fir trees of the Apennines. Bk. iii., on styles, has a preface on ancient Greek writers. C. 1 is on symmetry and proportion; c. 2 on various forms of Greek temples, *e.g.*, in antis, prostyle, peripteral, dipteral, hypæthral;[2] c. 3 on intercolumniation—pycnostyle, systyle, eustyle, &c.; c. 4 on foundations, steps, and stylobates; c. 5 on the Ionic order, its form and details. Bk. iv., on styles and orders, has a preface to Augustus on the scope of the work. The subjects of its nine chapters are—(1) the Corinthian, Ionic, and Doric orders; (2) the ornaments of capitals, &c.; (3) the Doric order; (4) proportions of the cella and pronaos; (5) sites of temples; (6) doorways of temples and their architraves; (7) the Etruscan or Tuscan order of temples; (8) circular temples; (9) altars. Bk. v., on public buildings, has a preface on the theories of Pythagoras, &c. Its twelve chapters treat (1) of fora and basilicæ, with a description of his own basilica at Fanum;

[1] The references in this article follow the divisions into books and chapters adopted in the more recent German editions.

[2] The excavations made in 1887 have shown that Vitruvius was right in describing the great temple of Olympian Zeus at Athens as being octastyle. The previously almost universal opinion that it was decastyle had led to the needless theory that the passage containing this statement was corrupt.

(2) of the adjuncts of a forum (ærarium, prison, and curia); (3) of theatres, their site and construction; (4) of laws of harmonics; (5) of the arrangement of tuned bronze vases in theatres for acoustic purposes; (6) of Roman theatres; (7) of Greek theatres; (8) of the selection of sites of theatres according to acoustic principles; (8) of porticus and covered walks; (9) of baths, their floors, hypocausts, the construction and use of various parts; (11) of palæstræ, xysti, and other Greek buildings for the exercise of athletes; (12) of harbours and quays. Bk. vi. is on sites and planning, and the preface treats of various Greek authors. C. 1 is on selection of sites; c. 2 on the planning of buildings to suit different sites; c. 3 on private houses, their construction and styles, the names of the different apartments; c. 4 on the aspects suited for the various rooms; c. 5 on the various sorts of buildings fitted for special positions; c. 6 on farms and country houses; c. 7 on Greek houses and the names of various parts; c. 8 on construction of houses in wood, stone, brick, or concrete. Bk. vii., mostly on methods of decoration, has a preface (as usual) on the opinions of ancient Greek writers, with lists of Greek sculptors, architects, and writers on architecture, and of Roman architects. C. 1 has for its subject pavements and roads, their construction, mosaic floors; c. 2 is on white stucco for walls (*opus albarium*); c. 3 on concrete vaults, gypsum mouldings, stucco prepared for painting; c. 4 on building of hollow walls to keep out the damp, wall decoration by various processes; c. 5 on methods and styles of wall painting, the debased taste of his time; c. 6 on fine stucco made of pounded marble,—three coats to receive wall paintings; c. 7 on colours used for mural decoration; c. 8 on red lead (*minium*) and mercury, and how to use the latter to extract the gold from worn-out pieces of stuff or embroidery; c. 9 on the preparation of red lead and the method of encaustic painting with hot wax, finished by friction; cc. 10–14 on artificial colours—black, blue, purple; c. 10 white lead and *ostrum*, *i.e.*, murex purple, and imitations of murex dye. Bk. viii. is on hydraulic engineering, and the preface on theories of the ancients. C. 1 treats of the finding of good water, its quality according to the soil it runs through; c. 2 of rain-water and rivers—rivers in various countries; c. 3 of hot springs, mineral waters, with an account of the chief medicinal springs of the world; c. 4 of selection of water by observation and experiment; c. 5 of instruments for levelling used by aqueduct engineers; c. 6 of construction of aqueducts, pipes of lead, clay, &c., cisterns, fountains, poisoning from lead pipes, hydraulic cement, settling tanks, and other valuable matter on the subject of water-supply. Bk. ix. is on astronomy. The preface treats of Greek sciences, geometry, the discovery of specific gravity by Archimedes, and other valuable discoveries of the Greeks, and of Romans of his time who have vied with the Greeks—Lucretius in his poem *De Rerum Natura*, Cicero in rhetoric, and Varro in philology, as shown by his *De Lingua Latina*.[1] The subjects of the eight chapters are (1) the signs of the zodiac and the seven planets; (2) the phases of the moon; (3) the passage of the sun through the zodiac; (4) and (5) various constellations; (6) the relation of astrological influences to nature; (7) the mathematical divisions of the gnomon; (8) various kinds of sun-dials and their inventors. Bk. x. is on machinery, with a preface concerning a law at ancient Ephesus compelling an architect to complete any public building he had undertaken; this, he says, would be useful among the Romans of his time.[2] The chapters are—(1) on various machines, such as scaling-ladders, windmills, &c.; (2) on windlasses, axles, pulleys, and cranes for moving heavy weights, such as those used by Chersiphron in building the great temple of Diana at Ephesus, and on the discovery by a shepherd of a quarry of marble required to build the same temple; (3) on dynamics; (4) on machines for drawing water; (5) on wheels for irrigation worked by a river; (6) on raising water by a revolving spiral tube; (7) on the machine of Ctesibius for raising water to a height; (8) on a very complicated water engine, the description of which is not intelligible, though Vitruvius remarks that he has tried to make the matter clear; (9) on machines with wheels to register the distance travelled, either by land or water; (10) on the construction of *scorpiones* for hurling stones; (11) and (12) on *balistæ* and catapults; (13) on battering-rams, and other machines for the attack of a fortress; (14) on shields (*testudines*) to enable soldiers to fill up the enemy's ditches; (15) on other kinds of *testudines*; (16) on machines for defence, and examples of their use in ancient times.

The first MS. of the *De Architectura* which attracted much attention was a fine codex on vellum preserved in the Benedictine monastery of Monte Cassino. The first printed edition is that issued in Rome by George Herolt about 1485–86, but without indication of place or date; it is a small folio with thirty-four lines to the page, and has neither signatures, catchwords, nor numbering of the leaves. It was edited by J. Sulpicius, and with it is printed Frontinus *De Aquæductibus*; this second work occurs as an addition in many early editions of Vitruvius, of which a very large number were printed at various places in Italy within a few years after the publication of the *editio princeps*.[3] On the whole the best edition of Vitruvius's text is that edited by Schneider, Leipsic, 1807, 3 vols. 8vo, with good notes, but no plates. An immense number of translations have also been published in most European languages—the first Italian translation at Como in 1521; French, at Paris in 1547; German, at Nuremberg in 1548; and the first English translation in London in 1692. The best English translation is that of Gwilt, 1826, improved edition, 1860. That of Wilkins (1812) is merely a fragment of some of the books, but it is copiously illustrated with engraved plates.

The name of Vitruvius has been given to several handsome works on modern architecture, such as Campbell, *Vitruvius Britannicus*, London, 1715–71, a series of illustrations of the chief buildings of the 18th century in England, including many works of the brothers Adam; one of these brothers, William Adam, produced a similar work illustrating the buildings which he had designed for Scotland, of which he was a native, under the title of *Vitruvius Scoticus*, Edinburgh, 1790. Thurah, *Le Vitruve Danois*, Copenhagen, 1746–49, is a similar collection of modern buildings in Denmark.

The biographies of Vitruvius as usually published are very untrustworthy, and contain many statements which rest upon no authority whatever. (J. H. M.)

[1] Vitruvius names Cicero and Lucretius as "post nostram memoriam nascentes." [2] The architect being at that time also the contractor.

[3] One of the earliest commentators on Vitruvius was the monk-architect Fra Giocondo, a man of extraordinary talent (see VERONA).

VITTORIA, an inland town of Sicily, in the Italian province of Syracuse, about 18 miles by road east-south-east from Terranova, stands in the midst of a rich vine and olive district, which also produces silk, rice, and honey. The population in 1881 was 21,755. It is quite a modern town,—founded towards the beginning of the 17th century. The principal church (San Giovanni) dates from 1854.

VITUS, ST, according to the Roman Breviary, while still a very young boy, had been baptized without the knowledge of his father, who, on learning this, spared no effort to bring about his return to paganism. After other severe measures had been tried in vain he was delivered to Valerian to be scourged, but even this had no effect, and he was handed back to his father. Admonished by an angel, Vitus, accompanied by Modestus and Crescentia, by whom he had been brought up, now took refuge abroad, where his fame for sanctity became so great that he was summoned by Diocletian to heal his child, who was grievously vexed with a devil. Successful in this he was urged by the ungrateful emperor to worship the pagan deities, and on his refusal was cast into prison. Along with Modestus and Crescentia he was sentenced to be plunged into a cauldron of molten lead, resin, and pitch, but here their experience was that of the three Hebrew children. Next they were cast before the lion, but the wild beast fawned upon them and licked their feet. Finally they were torn limb from limb. The three are commemorated on June 15. The more extended legend of St Vitus relates that, on one occasion when he had been shut up in a dungeon, his father looking through a chink in the door beheld him dancing with seven beautiful angels; so dazzled was he by the sight that he became blind, and recovered only through the intercession of his son. St Vitus is accordingly the patron saint of dancers and actors, and is invoked against the disease known as ST VITUS'S DANCE (*q.v.*). He is the patron of Saxony, Bohemia, and Sicily, and throughout Germany ranks as one of the fourteen "Nothhelfer" of the church.

VIVARINI, the surname of a family of painters of Murano (Venice), who produced a great quantity of work in Venice and its neighbourhood in the 15th century, leading on to that phase of the school which is represented by Carpaccio and the Bellinis.

ANTONIO VIVARINI was probably the earliest of this family. He came from the school of Andrea da Murano, and his works show the influence of Gentile da Fabriano. The earliest known date of a picture of his, an altar-piece in the Venetian academy, is 1440; the latest, in the Lateran museum, 1464. He worked in company with a certain "Joannes de Alemania." By some writers Joannes has been regarded as himself a Vivarini, but this appears improbable: no trace of him exists of a date later than 1447. After 1447 Antonio painted either alone or in combination with his younger brother Bartolommeo. The works of Antonio are well drawn for their epoch, with a certain noticeable degree of softness, and with good flesh and other tints. Three of his principal paintings are the Virgin Enthroned with the Four Doctors of the Church, the Coronation of the Virgin, and Sts Peter and Jerome. The first two (in which Joannes co-operated) are in the Venetian academy, the third in the London National Gallery.

Bartolommeo Vivarini is known to have worked from 1450 to 1499. He learned oil-painting from Antonello da Messina, and is said to have produced, in 1473, the first oil picture done in Venice. This is in the church of Sts John and Paul,—a large altar-piece in nine divisions, representing Augustine and other saints. Most of his works, however, including one in the National Gallery, are in tempera. His outline is always hard, and his colour good; the figures have much dignified and devout expression. As "vivarino" means in Italian a goldfinch, he sometimes drew a goldfinch as the signature of his pictures.

Luigi or Alvise Vivarini painted in 1490 and on to 1505. It has sometimes been supposed that, besides the Luigi who was the latest of this pictorial family, there had also been another Luigi who was the earliest, this supposition being founded on the fact that one picture is signed with the name, along with the date 1414. There is good ground, however, for considering this date to be a forgery of a later time. The works of Luigi show an advance on those of his predecessors, his best work being one which he executed for the Scuola di S. Girolamo in Venice, representing the saint caressing his lion, and some monks decamping in terror. The architecture and perspective in this work are superior. Other works by Luigi are in Treviso and in Milan.

VIVES, Juan Luis (or Ludovicus) (1492–1540), a well-known scholar of the third and fourth decades of the 16th century, was born at Valencia, in Spain, in March 1492. He studied at Paris and Louvain, ultimately becoming professor of humanity at the latter university. At the instance of his friend Erasmus he prepared an edition of Augustine's *De Civitate Dei*, which was published in 1522 with a dedication to Henry VIII. of England. Soon afterwards he was invited to England and appointed tutor to the Princess Mary, for whose benefit he wrote *De Ratione Studii Puerilis Epistolæ Duæ*. While in England he resided a good deal at Oxford, where he was made doctor of laws and lectured on philosophy. Having openly declared himself against the king's divorce, he lost the royal favour and was thrown into prison, where he remained for six months. On his release he went to Spain and afterwards to the Low Countries, finally settling in Bruges, where he married and devoted himself to the composition of his numerous works, which were chiefly directed against the scholastic philosophy and the preponderant authority of Aristotle. He died on May 6, 1540.

A complete edition of his works was published at Basel in 1555 (2 vols. fol.), and another at Valencia in 1782.

VIZAGAPATAM, a British district of India, in Madras presidency, lying between 17° 14′ 30″ and 18° 58′ N. lat. and 82° 19′ and 83° 59′ E. long., with an area of 3477 square miles. Including the Jáipur and Vizianagram zamindaries, which are under British administration, the area is 17,380 square miles. Vizagapatam is bounded on the N. by Ganjam district, on the E. by Ganjam and the sea, on the S. by the sea and Godávari district, and on the W. by the Central Provinces. It is a beautiful, picturesque, and hilly country, forming part of the large extent of shore known as the Orissa coast, but for the most part it is unhealthy. The surface of the country is generally undulating, rising towards the interior, and crossed by streams, which are dry except during the rainy season. The main portion is occupied by the Eastern Gháts. The slopes of these mountains are clothed with luxuriant vegetation, amid which rise many tall forest trees, while the bamboo grows profusely in the valleys. The drainage on the east is carried by numerous streams direct to the sea, and that to the west flows into the Godávari through the Indravati or through the Sabari and Sillar rivers. To the west of the range is situated the greater portion of the extensive zamindari of Jáipur, which is for the most part very hilly and jungly. The north and north-west of the district is also mountainous. In the extreme north a remarkable mass of hills, called the Nimgiris, rise to a height of 4972 feet, and these are separated by valleys of not more than 1200 feet from the neighbouring ranges of Gháts. The plain along the Bay of Bengal is exceedingly rich and fertile. It is described as a vast sheet of cultivation, green with rice fields and gardens of sugar-cane and tobacco. There are great varieties of climate in the district. Along the coast the air is soft and relaxing, the prevailing winds being south-easterly. The average annual rainfall at Vizagapatam exceeds 40 inches.

The census of 1881 returned the population of the district, exclusive of the agency tracts, at 1,790,468 (males 897,116, females 893,352). Including the Jaipur and Vizianagram dependencies, the total population of the district was 2,485,141 (males 1,254,850, females 1,230,291), of whom 2,460,474 were Hindus, 20,403 Mohammedans, and 3410 Christians. There are five towns with populations of more than 10,000, viz.:—Vizagapatam and Vizianagram (*q.v.*); Anakapalle, 13,341; Bobbili, 14,943; and Salur, 11,856. The chief crops are rice, which is the staple product of the country, and sugar. The cultivation of indigo is also successfully carried on. The actual area under cultivation in 1885–86 amounted to 168,559 acres, besides 10,833 acres of forests. The gross revenue of the district in 1885–86 was £201,699, of which the land yielded £139,200. There are few industries, the principal being cotton cloths and the beautiful fancy wares of Vizagapatam towns. On the dissolution of the Mughal empire Vizagapatam occupied a portion of the territory known as the Northern Circars, which were ceded to the East India Company by treaty in 1768. On the introduction of the permanent settlement in 1802 it was formed into a separate collectorate, and since then several changes have been made in its administration.

VIZAGAPATAM, a municipal and seaport town, the administrative headquarters of the above district, with a population in 1881 of 30,291. It lies on a small bay, the south extremity of which is bounded by a promontory known as the Dolphin's Nose, and its northern extremity by the suburb of Waltair. The town or fort, as it is called, is separated from the Dolphin's Nose by a small river, which forms a bar where it enters the sea, but is passable for vessels of 300 tons during spring tides. Vizagapatam is the residence of a Roman Catholic vicar apostolic. It contains some good streets, has a handsome hall, library, and reading-room, an excellent hospital and dispensary, and maintains a great many schools. The principal exports are grain and sugar, and the principal industries of the town are elk horn and ivory knick-knacks and gold and silver filigree work.

VIZIADRUG, or Gheria, a port in Ratnágiri district, Bombay presidency, India, about 30 miles south of Ratnágiri town and 170 miles south of Bombay city, in 16° 33′ 40″ N. lat. and 73° 22′ 10″ E. long. It is one of the best harbours on the western coast of India, being without any bar, and may be entered in all weathers; even to large ships it affords safe shelter during the south-west monsoon. The chief interest of the place centres in its fort, which is one of the strongest Mohammedan fortresses in the Concan, and rises grandly about 100 feet above the river.

About 1698 the pirate chief Angria made Viziadrug the capital of a territory stretching for about 150 miles along the coast, and from 30 to 60 miles inland. The fort surrendered to the English fleet in 1756, and was given over to the peshwá. In May 1818 an unsuccessful attempt was made to take Viziadrug, but, the whole of the district of Ratnágiri having now passed into the hands of the British, the fortress surrendered in June.

VIZIANAGRAM, one of the most ancient and extensive estates or zamindaries in India, included in the Vizagapatam district of the Madras presidency, with an area of about 3000 square miles, and a population (1881) of 844,168. The chief town, Vizianagram, had in 1881 a population of 22,577.

The zamindari first came under the charge of the English authorities in 1817, with a very heavy debt, but it was restored to the rájá five years afterwards clear of all incumbrances. It again came under their charge in 1827, during a minority, but on the rájá's coming of age it was again restored with a surplus.

VIZIER (Arabic *Wazîr*), literally the "burden bearer" of the sovereign. The office of vizier, which spread from the Arabs to the Persians, Turks, Mongols, and other Oriental peoples, arose under the first Abbasid caliphs, and took shape under their great ministers the Barmecides (see vol. xvi. p. 591). The vizier stood between sovereign and subjects, representing the former in all matters touching the latter. This withdrawal of the head of the state from direct contact with his people was unknown to the Omayyads, and was certainly an imitation of Persian usage; it has even been plausibly conjectured that the name is but the Arabic adaptation of a Persian title.[1] It appears, however, in the Koran (xx. 30, xxv. 37), where Aaron is called the *wazîr* of Moses, and these passages are appealed to by Arabic writers as giving divine sanction to the institution. The title of *wazîr* was often given to ministers of a special department, such as the treasury or the police, but *the wazîr* (the grand vizier, as Europeans say) bore the whole burden of the state, and, although his position was absolutely uncertain, depending on the mere will of the sovereign, his power was unlimited. His place was one of dizzy grandeur but of extreme difficulty. He was expected to be able to answer all questions, realize every wish of the caliph, keep the coffers of the state full, and yet find time to cultivate the personal favour of the sovereign by the display of social gifts. Such were the Barmecide viziers, the brilliant type of which all subsequent Oriental ministers are more or less imperfect copies. Ultimately under the caliph Râḍî the grand vizier gave way to a mayor of the palace called the *amîr al-omarâ*, but the old office and title were continued at the courts of the princes who rose on the decline of the caliphate. In Spain, where the chamberlain (*ḥâjib*) was the greatest officer of state, the title of *wazîr* was given to governors of towns, and in this sense the word was the parent of the Spanish *alguazil*.

VIZZINI, an inland town of Sicily, in the Italian province of Catania, 39 miles E.N.E. of Terranova and 34 miles W.N.W. of Syracuse, is a prosperous country place of 13,966 inhabitants (1881). It has several churches (S. Gregorio, Minori Osservanti, S. Maria de' Greci), with pictures of some artistic or antiquarian interest.

VLACHS. Vlach, otherwise written Wallack, is a general name for all the members of the Latin-speaking race inhabiting eastern Europe. The name is in its origin identical with our "Welsh," "Welshman," and represents a Slavonic adaptation of a generic term applied by the Teutonic races at the time of the migration of peoples to all Roman provincials. It thus finds its analogies in the German name for Italy—Welschland (Wälischland), in the Walloons of the Low Countries, the "Wallgau" of Tyrol, &c. An early instance of its application to the Roman population of the Eastern empire is found in the *Traveller's Song*, where in a passage which in all probability connects itself with the early trade-route between the Baltic staple of Wollin and Byzantium, the gleeman speaks of Cæsar's realm as *Walaric* = "Welshry." In verse 140 he speaks of the "Rum-walas," and it is to be observed that "Rum" is one of the words by which the Vlachs of eastern Europe still know themselves.

The Slavs, at least in their principal extent, first knew the Roman empire through a Teutonic medium, and adopted their terms Vlach, Voloch, from the Ostro-Gothic equivalent of the Anglo-Saxon "Wealh." The name is thus of foreign origin, the native Vlachs continuing to this day to call themselves "*Rumeni*," *Romeni*, or even *Romani*; and it is from the native pronunciation of the Roman name that we have the equivalent expression *Rouman*, a word which must by no means be confined to that part of the Vlach race inhabiting the present kingdom of Roumania. This Vlach or Rouman race constitutes a distinct division of the Latin family of peoples, widely disseminated throughout eastern Europe, both north and south of the Danube. North of the Danube the Roumans inhabit, besides Walachia and Moldavia, Bessarabia and the adjoining South-Russian districts, a large part of Transylvania and the Hungarian Banat, and extend sporadically from the Bug to the Adriatic. South of the Danube the central glens of Pindus form the principal nucleus of Rouman habitation, but there is besides a considerable colony in the Epirote district of Musakja, in Ætolia and Acarnania, in various districts of Albania, Thessaly, Macedonia, and the Bulgarian principality. In Servia this element is preponderant in the Timok valley, while in Istria it is represented by the Cici, at present largely Slavonized, as are now entirely the kindred Morlachs of Dalmatia.

The centre of gravity of the Vlach or Rouman race is at present unquestionably north of the Danube, and corresponds roughly to the limits of Trajan's Dacian province. From this circumstance the popular idea has arisen that the race itself represents the descendants of the Romanized population of Trajan's Dacia, which was assumed to have maintained an unbroken existence in Walachia, Transylvania, &c., beneath the dominion of a succession of invaders. The Vlachs of Pindus, &c., on this hypothesis, were to be regarded as later immigrants from the lands north of the Danube. In 1871 Roesler published, in a collective form, a series of essays, in which he absolutely denied the claim of the Roumanian and Transylvanian Vlachs to be regarded as Dacian autochthones. He laid stress on the statements of Vopiscus and others as implying the total withdrawal of the Roman provincials from Trajan's Dacia by Aurelian, and on the non-mention by historians of a Latin population in the lands on the left bank of the lower Danube, during their successive occupation by Goths, Huns, Gepidæ, Avars, Slavs, Bulgars, and other barbarian races. He found the first trace of a Rouman settlement north of the Danube in a Transylvanian diploma of 1222. Roesler's thesis has been generally regarded as an entirely new departure in critical ethnography. As a matter of fact, his conclusions had to a great extent been already anticipated by Sulzer in his *Geschichte des Transalpinischen Daciens*, published at Vienna in 1781, and at a still earlier date by the Dalmatian historian Lucius of Traü in his work *De Regno Dalmatiæ et Croatiæ*, 1666.

The theory of the later immigration of the Roumans into their present abodes north of the Danube, as stated in its most extreme form by Roesler, commanded wide acceptance, and in Hungary it was politically utilized as a plea for refusing parity of treatment to a race of comparatively recent intruders. In Roumania itself Roesler's views were resented as an attack on Rouman nationality. Outside Roumania they found a determined opponent in Dr Jung, of Innsbruck, who in his *Anfänge der Romänen* upheld the continuity of the Roman provincial stock in Trajan's Dacia, disputing from historic analogies the total withdrawal of the provincials by Aurelian; and the reaction against Roesler was carried still further by T. Lad. Pič (*Ueber die Abstammung der Rumänen*, 1880) and Prof. A. D. Xenopol of Jassy (*Les Roumains au Moyen Âge*, 1885).

On the whole,—as often in controversies,—it may be said that the truth lies between the two extremes. Roesler is no doubt so far right that at the time of the migration of peoples, and indeed throughout the early Middle Ages, the bulk of the Rouman people lay south of the Danube.

[1] See Lagarde, *Armenische Studien*, p. 147, and Nöldeke's translation of Tabari, pp. 53 n, 444 n.

Pič's view that the population of the Roman provinces of Mœsia, &c., were Hellenized rather than Romanized, and that it is to Trajan's Dacia alone that we must look for the Roman source of the Vlach race, conflicts with what we know of the Latinizing of the Balkan lands from inscriptions, martyrologies, Procopius's list of Justinian's Illyrian fortresses, and other sources. This Roman element south of the Danube had further received a great increase at the expense of Trajan's colonial foundation to the north when Aurelian established his New Dacia on the Mœsian side of the river. On the other hand, the analogy supplied by the withdrawal of the Roman provincials from Riparian Noricum tells against the assumption that the official withdrawal of the Roman colonists of Trajan's Dacia by Aurelian entailed the entire evacuation of the Carpathian regions by their Latin-speaking inhabitants. As on the upper Danube the continuity of the Roman population is attested by the *Vici Romanisci* of early mediæval diplomas and by other traces of a Romanic race still represented by the Ladines of Tyrol, so it is reasonable to suppose a Latin-speaking population continued to exist in the formerly thickly colonized area embracing the present Transylvania and Little Walachia, with adjoining Carpathian regions. Even as late as Justinian's time, the official connexion with the old Dacian province was not wholly lost, as is shown by the erection or restoration of certain *têtes-de-pont* and *castella* on the left bank of the lower Danube.

We may therefore assume that the Latin race of eastern Europe never wholly lost touch of its former trans-Danubian strongholds. It was, however, on any showing greatly diminished there. The open country, the broad plains of what is now the Roumanian kingdom, and the Banat of Hungary were in barbarian occupation. The centre of gravity of the Roman or Romance element of Illyricum had now shifted south of the Danube. By the 6th century a large part of Thrace, Macedonia, and even of Epirus, had become Latin-speaking.

What had occurred in Trajan's Dacia in the 3d century was consummated in the 6th and 7th throughout the greater part of the South-Illyrian provinces, and the Slavonic and Avar conquests severed the official connexion with eastern Rome. The overthrow of civic life and break-down of provincial organization was complete. The Roman element was uprooted from its fixed seats, and swept hither and thither by the barbarian flood. Nomadism became an essential of independent existence. On the other hand, large masses of homeless provincials were dragged off as captives in the train of their barbarian conquerors, to be distributed in servile colonies. They were thus in many cases transported by barbarian chiefs—Slav, Avar, and Bulgarian—to trans-Danubian and Pannonian regions. In the *Acts* of St Demetrius of Thessalonica we actually find an account of such a Roman colony, which, having been carried away from South-Illyrian cities by the Avar khagan, and settled by him in the Sirmian district beyond the Save, revolted after seventy years of captivity, made their way once more across the Balkan passes, and finally settled as an independent community in the country inland from Salonica. Others, no doubt, thus transported northwards never returned. It is certain that the earliest Hungarian historians who describe the Magyar invasion of the 9th century speak of the old inhabitants of the country as Romans, and of the country they occupied as *Pascua Romanorum*; and the Russian Nestor, writing about 1100, makes the same invaders fight against Slavs and Vlachs (Volochi) in the Carpathian Mountains. So far from the first mention of the Vlachs north of the Danube occurring only in 1222, as Roesler asserts, it appears from a passage of Nicetas of Chonæ that they were to be found already in 1164 as far afield as the borders of Galicia.

It is nevertheless true that throughout the early Middle Ages the bulk of the Rouman population lay south of the Danube. It was in the Balkan lands that the Rouman race and language took their characteristic mould. It is here that this new Illyrian Romance first rises into historic prominence. Already in the 6th century, as we learn from the place names, such as Sceptecasas, Burgualtu, Clisura, &c., given by Procopius, the Rouman language was assuming, so far as its Latin elements were concerned, its typical form. In the somewhat later campaigns of Commentiolus (587) and Priscus, against the Avars and Slovenes, we find the Latin-speaking soldiery of the Eastern emperor making use of such Romance expressions as "torna, frate!" (turn, brother!), or "sculca" (out of bed) applied to a watch (*cf.* Rouman "a se culca" = Italian "coricarsi" + ex-(s-) privative). Next we find this warlike Rouman population largely incorporated in the Bulgarian kingdom, and, if we are to judge from the names Paganus and Sabinus, already supplying it with rulers in the 8th century. The blending and close contact during this period of the surviving Latin population with the Slovene settlers of the peninsula impregnated the language with its large Slavonic ingredient; and the considerable Albanian element in Rouman, as well as the still greater element of Rouman in Albanian, is alone sufficient to show that the two languages took their characteristic shapes in a contiguous area. The fact that these peculiarities are common to the Roumans north of the Danube, whose language differs dialectically from that of their southern brothers, shows that it was this southern branch that throughout the early periods of Rouman history was exercising a dominating influence. Migrations, violent transplantation, the intercourse which was kept up between the most outlying members of the race, in its very origin nomadic, at a later period actual colonization *en masse* and the political influence of the Bulgaro-Vlachian empire, no doubt contributed to propagate these southern linguistic acquisitions throughout that northern area to which the Rouman race was destined almost imperceptibly to shift its centre of gravity.

Byzantium, which had ceased to be Roman, and become Romaic, renewed its acquaintance with the descendants of the Latin provincials of Illyricum through a Slavonic medium, and applied to them the name of "Vlach," which the Slav himself had borrowed from the Goth. The first mention of Vlachs in a Byzantine source is about the year 976, when Cedrenus (ii. 439) relates the murder of the Bulgarian czar Samuel's brother "by certain Vlach wayfarers," at a spot called the Fair Oaks, between Castoria and Prespa. From this period onwards the Rouman inhabitants of the Balkan peninsula are constantly mentioned by this name, and we find a series of political organizations and territorial divisions connected with the name of "Vlachia." Within the limits of the present article it is impossible to give more than a short synopsis of the most important of these, while for a history of the later Rouman principalities of Walachia and Moldavia the reader is referred to the article Roumania.

1. *The Bulgaro-Vlach Empire.*—After the overthrow of the older Bulgarian czardom by Basil Bulgaroktonos, the Vlach population of Thrace, Hæmus, and the Mœsian lands passed once more under Byzantine dominion; and in 1185 a heavy tax, levied in kind on the cattle of these warlike mountain shepherds, stirred the Vlachs to revolt against the emperor Isaac Angelus, and under the leadership of two brothers, Peter and Asen, to found a new Bulgaro-Vlachian empire, which ended with Kaliman II. in 1257. The dominions of these half-Slavonic half-Rouman emperors extended north of the Danube over a great deal of what is now Roumania, and it was during this period that the Vlach population north of the river seems to have been most largely reinforced. The French traveller Rubruquis speaks of all the country between Don and Danube as "Asen's land" or "Blakia."

2. *Great Walachia* (Μεγάλη Βλαχία).—It is from Anna Comnena, in the second half of the 11th century, that we first hear of

a Vlach settlement, the nucleus of which was the mountainous region of Thessaly. Benjamin of Tudela, in the succeeding century, gives an interesting account of this Great Walachia, which was then completely independent. It embraced the southern and central ranges of Pindus, and extended over part of Macedonia, thus including the region in which the Roman settlers mentioned in the *Acts* of St Demetrius had fixed their abode. After the Latin conquest of Constantinople Great Walachia was included in the enlarged despotate of Epirus, but it soon reappears as an independent principality under its old name, which, after passing under the yoke of the Serb emperor Dushan, was finally conquered by the Turks in 1393. Many of their old privileges were still accorded to the inhabitants, and their taxes were limited to an annual tribute to the sultana Valide. Since this period the Megalovlachites have been largely Hellenized, but they are still represented by the flourishing Tzintzar settlements of Pindus, and traces are at present perceptible among them of a national Rouman reaction.

3. *Little Walachia* (Μικρὰ Βλαχία) was a name applied by Byzantine writers to the Rouman settlements of Ætolia and Acarnania, and with it may be included "Upper Walachia" or Ανώβλαχα. Its inhabitants are still represented by the Tzintzars of the Aspropotamo and the Karaguni (Black Capes) of Acarnania.

4. *The Morlachs* (*Mavrovlachi*) *of the West*.—These are already mentioned as *Nigri Latini* by the Presbyter of Dioclea (*circ.* 1150) in the old Dalmatian littoral and the mountains of what is now Montenegro, Herzegovina, and North Albania. Other colonies extended through a great part of the old Servian interior, where is a region still called Stara Vlaška or "Old Walachia." The great commercial staple of the east Adriatic shores, the republic of Ragusa, seems in its origin to have been a Rouman settlement, and many Vlach traces survived in its later dialect. Philippus de Diversis, who described the city as it existed in 1440, says that "the various officers of the republic do not make use either of Slav or Italian, with which they converse with strangers, but a certain other dialect only partially intelligible to us Latins," and cites words with strong Rouman affinities. In the mountains above Ragusa a number of Vlach tribes are mentioned in the archives of that city, and the original relationship of the Ragusans and the nomadic Alpine representatives of the Roman provincials, who preserved a traditional knowledge of the old lines of communication throughout the peninsula, explains the extraordinary development of the Ragusan commerce. In the 14th century the Mavrovlachi or Morlachs extended themselves towards the Croatian borders, and a large part of maritime Croatia and northern Dalmatia began to be known as "Morlacchia." A "Major Vlachia" was formed about the triple frontier of Bosnia, Croatia, and Dalmatia, and a "Little Walachia" as far north as Posega. The Morlachs have now become Slavonized.

5. *Cici of Istria.*—The extreme Rouman offshoot to the northwest is still represented by the Cici of the Val d'Arsa and adjoining Istrian districts. They represent a 15th-century Morlach colony from the Isle of Veglia, and had formerly a wider extension to Trieste and the counties of Gradisca and Gorizia. The Cici are at present rapidly losing their native tongue, which is the last remaining representative of the old Morlach, and forms a connecting link between the Daco-Roman (or Roumanian) and the Macedo-Roman (or Tzintzar) dialects.

6. *Roumans of Transylvania and Hungary.*—As already stated, a large part of the Hungarian plains were, at the coming of the Magyars in the 9th century, known as *Pascua Romanorum*. At a later period privileged Rouman communities existed at Fogaras, where was a *Silva Vlachorum*, at Marmaros, Deva, Hatzeg, Hunyad, and Lugos, and in the Banat were seven Rouman districts. Two of the greatest figures in Hungarian history—John Corvinus of Hunyad, and his son King Matthias—were due to this element. Oppressed by the dominant race, which had deprived them of their ancient privileges, the Roumans of Transylvania and the Banat rose in 1785 under Horia, Closca, and Crischanu. This Rouman "Jacquerie" was suppressed, but Joseph II. declared the peasants free. Since that date the Rouman element in this part of the old Dacian region has largely increased in numbers, though it has hitherto failed to secure its political rights. The contiguous district of the Bukovina, a part of Moldavia annexed to the Hapsburg dominions in 1775, remains under the Austrian Government.

The present numerical strength of the Roumanians may approximately be given as follows:—

Southern or Tzintzar branch in Pindus, &c.	225,000
Roumans of Tirnok district	150,000
Roumanians	4,500,000
In Austria-Hungary	3,500,000
In Bessarabia and South Russia	600,000
Total	8,975,000

In features the Vlachs especially of the Carpathian valleys present decidedly Roman characteristics, and it is not unfrequent to find types which occur in North Italy and amongst Spaniards and Provençals. They are usually short and dark. Those of Pindus have sharper-cut features and some Slovene traits in their physiognomy. The race has a great natural capacity for trade and manufacture. The Vlachs excel as builders and artisans, but notably as workers in metal; their financial enterprise is also remarkable, and some of the principal banking establishments in Vienna are due to members of this race. An extraordinary example of their successful enterprise in the Balkan peninsula is supplied by the history of Moschopolis on the Epirote side of Pindus, which was founded by a Vlach colony in the 16th century, and which not only became a populous commercial staple but a centre of literary culture. Moschopolis possessed a large public library, flourishing schools, and a printing press, from which issued both Greek and Rouman books of a religious and scholastic nature. Joannina, since completely Hellenized, was also of Rouman origin. Metzovo (Minciu) is another flourishing Rouman colony in the same region, and, though Moschopolis has fallen a victim to the ravages of the wild Arnauts, a local successor has sprung up in the rising town of Gjurtza. The Roumans make good soldiers, as was seen at Plevna. In their customs and folk-lore both Latin and Slavonic traditions assert themselves as in their language. Of their Roman traditions the Trajan saga, the celebration of the Rosalia and Kalendæ, the belief in the "striga" (witch), the names of the months and days of the week, may be taken as typical examples. Some Roman words connected with the Christian religion, like biserica (basilica) = a church, botez = baptizo, duminica = Sunday, preot (presbyter) = priest, point to a continuous tradition of the Illyrian church, though most of their ecclesiastical terms, like their liturgy and alphabet, were derived from the old Slovene. In most that concerns political organization the Slavonic element is also preponderant, though there are words like impărat = imperator, and domn = dominus, which point to the old stock. Many words relating to kinship are also Latin, some like vitrig (vitricus) = father-in-law being alone preserved by this branch of the Romance family. Although of the actual vocabulary only about one-fifth is Latin, and two-fifths, or about double the amount, Slavonic (see Cihac, *Dictionnaire d' Étymologie Daco-Romaine*), the greater proportion of the words in common use is still Latin. Many words, however, of common and indispensable use, those even connected with ideas nearest to the heart, as for instance the Rouman iubesc = to love, and máică = a mother, are themselves of Slavonic origin. Alike in the dwellings, customs, and costumes of the Vlach race we encounter at every turn the dominating influence of the Slav peoples by whom they were surrounded. This external influence, however, has not by any means affected the strong pride of Roman origin which is the heirloom of all members of the Rouman race. Hellenization itself, hitherto successful among the southern Roumans, has received a check in the Pindus region, while north of the Danube the Rouman race is continually gaining at the expense of its neighbours. A glance at the ethnographic map of eastern Europe shows that the reconquest of Trajan's Dacia by the Latin race is already practically completed, and with the triumphant progress of the principle of nationality in the Danubian lands the reunion of *Dacia Romana* under a single sceptre cannot long be deferred. (A. J. E.)

VŁADIKAVKAZ, a fortified town of Russia, in the province of Terek, is advantageously and picturesquely situated at the northern base of the Great Caucasus chain, on a raised plain, 2230 feet above the sea-level, where the gorge of the Terek emerges from the mountain tracts. It is the present terminus of the railway from ROSTOFF (*q.v.*), which is intended ultimately to cross the main ridge. The fortress, formerly but a small redoubt, erected in 1784 at the northern entrance of the pass by which the Caucasus used to be crossed, now stands higher up, and is connected by a bridge with the town proper. Vładikavkaz is now the capital of the province. It is tidily built, and its population since it became an entrepôt for trade between Russia and Caucasus has rapidly grown (32,340 in 1883). The transport of merchandise is the principal occupation of the place, 400,000 cwts. of goods annually arriving by rail to be forwarded to Tiflis, while 160,000 cwts. are sent from Vładikavkaz northwards.

VLADIMIR, a government of middle Russia, bounded by Moscow and Tver on the W., Yarosłav and Kostroma on the N., Nijniy Novgorod on the E., Tamboff and Ryazañ on the S., has an area of 18,864 square miles. It extends over the eastern parts of the central plateau of middle Russia, which has an average elevation of from 800 to 950 feet above the sea, and is grooved by river valleys to a depth ranging from 300 to 450 feet below the general level, so that the country has a hilly appearance on the banks of the chief rivers. The lacustrine depression of the middle Volga and Oka extends into the eastern parts of the government. The Upper Carboniferous limestones, of which it is mostly built up, are covered with Permian sandstones towards the east, and patches of Jurassic clays—denuded remnants of formerly extensive deposits—are scattered over its surface. Cretaceous deposits are supposed to make their appearance in the south. The whole is covered with a thick sheet of boulder clay, considered as the bottom-moraine of the North-European ice-sheet, and overlaid, in its turn, in the depressions, by extensive Lacustrine clays and sands. The soil is thus for the most part unfertile, save in the district of Yurieff, where are found patches of black earth, which of late have occasioned a good deal of discussion among Russian geologists. Iron-ore is widely diffused, and china clay and gypsum are met with in several places. Peat is of common occurrence. As for coal, it is certain that the coal-bearing Lower Carboniferous strata of the Moscow basin would be encountered by boring to a certain depth; no such explorations, however, have yet been made, as forests still cover extensive tracts in the south-east, and the numerous manufactures of Vladimir suffer from no lack of fuel. The climate resembles that of Moscow, but is a little colder, and still more continental; the average yearly temperature at Vladimir is 38° F. (January, 16°; July, 66°·5).

The Oka flows through the government for 85 miles, and is navigable throughout. Of its tributaries, the Klyasma is navigable to Kovroff, and even to Vladimir in summer; and timber is floated on the Teza. Small lakes are numerous; that of Plescheyevo or Pereyasłavl (5 miles in length) has historical associations, Peter I. having here acquired in his boyhood his first experiences in navigation. Marshes cover more than half a million acres.

The population (1,359,330 in 1883) is thoroughly Great Russian; the Finnish tribes, Muroma and Merya, which formerly inhabited the region, have been absorbed by the Slavonians, as also have the Karelians who are supposed to have formerly inhabited the territory; the descendants of the few hundred Karelian families, which were settled by Peter I. on the shores of Lake Pereyasłavl, still, however, maintain their language. Agriculture is carried on everywhere, but is in a prosperous state only on the left bank of the Klyasma, and corn is imported. The culture of flax, both for local manufactures and for export—especially about Melenki—is important; so also are that of hemp and gardening. Natural pastures being by no means deficient, the number of cattle is greater than might be expected in a province so backward in agriculture. The average crops of the years 1883–85 were—rye, 1,400,300 quarters; oats, 1,097,000; wheat, 36,400; barley, 63,000; other grains, 250,800; and potatoes, 52,300. In 1883 there were 323,000 cattle, 210,050 horses, and 330,050 sheep.

A distinctive feature of Vladimir is the great variety of petty trades carried on in its villages by peasants who still continue to cultivate their allotments and thus combine manufacture with agriculture. Nearly every village has its own specialty, and, while in some of them almost all the male population leave their homes and go in numerous *artels* (see vol. xxi. p. 84) all over Russia as carpenters, masons, iron-roof makers, or as *ofeni* (pedlars or travelling merchants), other villages have their specialties in some branch of manufactured produce. Nearly 30,000 carpenters leave Vladimir every year. Whole villages are engaged in painting sacred pictures or ikons, and there are weekly fairs, where no fewer than 130 cart-loads of planks for such works are bought every week during winter. Although the ikons are sold at a shilling the hundred, the aggregate trade is valued at £150,000 a year; and the Vladimir (or rather Suzdal) pictures spread all over Russia and the Balkan peninsula. In other villages some 1200 men are employed in making sickles, knives, or locks. Wooden vessels, boxes, and baskets, *lapti* (shoes made of lime-tree bark which are worn in Great Russia, and are produced by the million), wheels and sledges, sieves, combs, woollen stockings and gloves, sheepskins and sheepskin gloves for peasants, felt, all kinds of toys, earthenware, and finally all kinds of woven fabrics, are so many specialties of separate villages. In 1884 102,500 persons were directly engaged in petty trades, in which indeed Vladimir occupies the first rank in Russia, the annual production (63,000,000 roubles) being one-third of the total for the whole country, Moscow coming next with 37,300,000 roubles.

The manufactures of Vladimir are equally important: out of the aggregate production of the fifty governments of European Russia (1,329,602,000 roubles in 1884), Vladimir was returned for 88,827,000 roubles, exclusive of numerous minor manufactures not included in the census. In the number of workmen employed in manufactures (102,900) Vladimir is second only to Moscow, and in its production it is second only to Moscow and St Petersburg. The chief industrial establishments are cotton and linen factories, glass, chemical, and iron works, distilleries, and tanneries.

Vladimir is divided into fourteen districts, the chief towns of which (with populations in 1884) are VLADIMIR (*q.v.*), 18,420; Alexandroff, 6915; Ivanovo-Voznesensk, 14,060; Kovroff, 8050; Melenki, 6470; MUROM (*q.v.*), 13,680; Pereyasłavl Zalyesskiy, 7470; Pokroff, 2700; SHUYA (*q.v.*), 21,430; Sudogda, 1880; Suzdal, 6770; Vyazniki, 6015; and Yurieff Polskiy, 5400. Kirzhatch (3285), Voznesensk (6000), and Gavriłovsk (1780) have also municipal institutions. Ivanovo, Gusevsk, Khołui, and several others, though mere villages, are more important than some district towns.

VLADIMIR, capital of the above government, is known in history as Vladimir-on-the-Klyasma, to distinguish it from Vladimir in Volhynia. It is picturesquely situated on the Klyasma and Lybed, 114 miles by rail to the east of Moscow. The Lybed divides it into two parts. Extensive cherry gardens occupy the surrounding slopes, each with its small watch-tower, having cords drawn in all directions to be shaken by the watcher when birds alight. The kreml stands on a hill and contains two very old cathedrals—the Uspenskiy (1150), where all princes of Vladimir have been buried, and the Dmitrievskiy, restored in 1834 in its old style. Several churches date from the 12th century. The "Golden Gate"—a triumphal gate surmounted by a church—was built by Andrei Bogolubskiy in 1158. On the whole Vladimir is a decaying place; its population has only risen to 18,420 in 1884 from 13,865 in 1859. The manufactures are for the most part insignificant, and trade has not the importance it has in some of the district towns.

Vladimir was founded in the 12th century. It first comes into notice in 1151, when Andrei Bogolubskiy secretly left Vyshgorod—the domain of his father in the principality of Kieff—and migrated to the newly settled land of Suzdal, where he became (1157) grand-prince of the principalities of Vladimir, Suzdal, and Rostoff. During the next century Vladimir became the chief town of the Russian settlements in the basin of the Oka, and till 1328 it disputed the superiority with the new principality of Moscow (*q.v.*). In the 14th century it began to fall to decay; and, like Pskoff, it is now one of the less important provincial cities of Russia.

VŁADIVOSTOK, the chief naval station of Russia on the Pacific, is situated in 43° 7′ N. lat. and 131° 55′ E. long., on the Gulf of Peter the Great in the Sea of Japan. This gulf, which has a length of nearly 50 miles, and a width at its entrance of 112 miles, is divided into two large bays—Amur and Usuri—by the hilly peninsula of Muravioff-Amurskiy, continued in a group of islands, of which the Kozakevitch or Russkiy (Johanga-tun) is the largest. A narrow strait, which has received the high-sounding name of the Eastern Bosphorus, separates this from the peninsula, and Vładivostok occupies the northern shore of one of its horn-like expansions, which the Russians have called the Golden Horn (*Zolotoi Rog*). The depth of the Eastern Bosphorus ranges from 13 to 20 fathoms, and that of the Golden Horn from 5 to 13, the latter thus affording a spacious harbour, —one of the finest, indeed, in the world. The hills are covered with forests of oak, lime, birch, maple, cork, walnut, acacia, ash, aspen, poplar, elm, apple, pear, and wild cherry, with a rich undergrowth of the most varied shrubs. Excellent timber is supplied by oak and cedar forests not far off. The climate, however, is severe, if compared with that of corresponding latitudes in Europe. Though standing in almost the same parallel as Marseilles, Vładivostok has an average annual temperature of only

Environs of Vładivostok.

38°·5 F., and, although the gulf itself never freezes, a thin ice-crust forms along the shores in December, keeping ships ice-bound for from thirty to forty-five days.

The settlement of Vładivostok, though founded only in 1861, had in 1886 12,500 inhabitants, chiefly military; and for hundreds of miles inland the sole population consists of the small military posts by which communication is maintained up the Suifun to Lake Khangka and the Cossack settlements on the Usuri. Vładivostok is connected with headquarters by telegraph.

Since the transference of the navy workshops from Nikolaievsk the place has gained in importance. It has a pro-gymnasium for boys (60 pupils), a club, and a newspaper. The imports of both Russian and foreign goods during the last five years have reached an average of from 2½ to 3 millions of roubles; but the exports are insignificant. Some 3000 or 4000 Coreans find employment in the Gulf of Peter the Great in gathering the edible seaweed *Laminaria saccharina*, of which about 70,000 cwts. (£45,000) are sent to China annually. The discovery of gold in the neighbouring alluvial deposits brought together some hundreds of Chinese, but the Russian Government compelled them to withdraw. The amount of gold is, however, not believed to be remunerative.

The Gulf of Peter the Great was discovered in 1852 by the French corvette "Capricieuse," and named the Golfe d'Anville. Two years later Count Putyatin, on board the frigate "Pallada," described the south-western part of the gulf and the Bay of Possiet. In 1855 an English squadron mapped its middle portion as far as Lefu (Askold) Island, and gave it the name of Victoria Bay. The whole gulf was mapped in 1859 by the Russian ships "America" and "Stryelok," and two years later a Russian post, which afterwards received the name of Vładivostok, was established.

VOGELWEIDE. See WALTER VON DER VOGELWEIDE.

VOGHERA (*Vicus Iriæ*), a town of Italy, in the province of Pavia, and 19 miles by rail to the south-south-west of that city, on the Staffora, formerly the Iria (a tributary of the Po), here crossed by a fine bridge. The fortifications erected by the Visconti in the Middle Ages have given place to a series of shady promenades. The large church of San Lorenzo dates its foundation from the 11th century, but was remodelled in the baroco style about the beginning of the 17th. The neighbourhood is fertile and produces much silk, in which, as well as in corn and wine, an active trade is carried on. The population in 1881 was 10,785.

VOGLER, GEORG JOSEPH (1749–1814), usually known as Abbé Vogler, organist and composer, was born at Würzburg, June 15, 1749. His father, a violin maker, while educating him for the church, took every opportunity of encouraging his musical talent, which was so marked that at ten years old he could not only play the organ well, but had also acquired a fair command of the violin and some other instruments without instruction. In 1769 he prosecuted his higher studies at Bamberg, removing thence in 1771 to Mannheim. Here he composed a ballet for the elector Karl Theodor, who, charmed with his talent, sent him to Bologna, to study under the Padre Martini. Unsatisfied with the method of that learned theorist, he studied for five months under Valotti, at Padua, and afterwards proceeded to Rome, where he was ordained priest in 1773, admitted to the famous academy of Arcadia, made a knight of the Golden Spur, and appointed protonotary and chamberlain to the pope.

On his return to Mannheim in 1775 Vogler was appointed court chaplain and second "maestro di cappella." He now established his first great music school, to which Winter, Ritter, Kraus, Danzi, and Knecht came for instruction. His pupils were devoted to him, but he made innumerable enemies, for the principles upon which he taught were confessedly opposed to those of all other teachers whatsoever. He had invented a new system of fingering for the harpsichord, a new form of construction for the organ, and a new system of musical theory founded upon that of Valotti. Mozart condemned the fingering as "miserable." The proposed change in the construction of the organ consisted in simplifying the mechanism, introducing free-reeds in place of ordinary reed-stops, and substituting unisonous stops for the great "mixtures" then in vogue.[1] The theoretical system, though professedly based upon Valotti's principles, was to a great extent empirical, and, like the scheme for revolutionizing the organ, has long been forgotten. Nevertheless, a certain substratum of truth seems to have underlain all his new heresies; and, by virtue of this, in spite of a rage for reform amounting almost to madness, Vogler undoubtedly exercised a powerful influence over the progress of musical science, and numbered among his disciples some of the greatest geniuses of the period.

In 1778 the elector removed his court to Munich. Vogler followed him thither in 1780, but, dissatisfied with the reception accorded to his dramatic compositions, soon quitted his post, and travelled for some years in Spain, Greece, Armenia, remote districts of Asia and Africa, and even Greenland, in search of uncorrupted forms of national melody. In 1786 he was appointed "kapellmeister" to the king of Sweden, founded his second music school at Stockholm, and attained extraordinary celebrity by his performances on an instrument called the "orchestrion,"—a species of organ invented by himself. In 1790 he brought this instrument to London, and performed upon it with great effect at the Pantheon, for the concert-room of which he also constructed an organ upon his own principles. Gerber alleges that organ pedals were unknown in England until Vogler introduced them, during his residence in London. This assertion is disproved by a MS. Concerto, by Handel, now in the Royal Library at Buckingham Palace, dated February 17, 1740, and containing an *obbligato* pedal part; nevertheless, it is certain that the abbé's pedal-playing excited great attention. His most popular pieces were a fugue on themes from the "Hallelujah Chorus," composed after a visit to the Handel festival at Westminster Abbey, and *A Musical Picture for the Organ*, by Knecht, containing the imitation of a storm.

From London Vogler proceeded to Rotterdam and the chief towns on the Rhine. At Esslingen he was presented with the "wine of honour" reserved for the use of sovereigns. At Frankfort he attended the coronation of the emperor Leopold II. He then visited Stockholm, and after a long residence there, interrupted by endless wanderings, once more established himself in Germany, where his compositions, both sacred and dramatic, received at last the full credit that was due to them. To trace his journeys from end to end of Europe would be impossible. We hear of him at Berlin in 1800, at Vienna in 1804, and at Munich in 1806. But while at Frankfort in 1807 he received an invitation from Louis I., grand-duke of Hesse-Darmstadt, offering him the appointment of "kapellmeister," with the order of merit, the title of privy councillor, a salary of 3000 florins, a house, a table supplied from the duke's own kitchen, and other privileges, which determined him to bring his wanderings at last to a close.

At Darmstadt he opened his third and most famous music school, the chief ornaments of which were Gänsbacher, Weber, and Meyerbeer. Gänsbacher had been his pupil at Vienna. Weber had studied under him in 1803, and once more sought his old master's help in 1810, though rather in the way of advice than instruction. Meyerbeer had been first introduced to him by means of a fugue which he criticized very severely, though he saw in it so much talent that he invited the composer to become his pupil. The three young students were inseparable, and their affection for their old master was unbounded.

[1] An organ built on the "unisonous system" stood for many years in Wornum's Music Hall, Store Street, London.

One of Vogler's latest exploits was a journey to Frankfort in 1810, to witness the production of Weber's *Sylvana.* He continued hard at work, genial and pleasant to the last, and died suddenly of apoplexy at Darmstadt, May 6, 1814.

Opinions are strangely divided as to the reality of Vogler's vocation. Some have pronounced him a genius, others a charlatan. Mozart was strongly prejudiced against him. That he was a brilliant and accomplished performer no one denies. It is certain that he was an excellent, if an eccentric, teacher. But his theories were visionary, and of his numberless compositions not one has survived to the present day.

VOICE is produced by the vibrations of the vocal cords, two ligaments or bands of fibrous elastic tissue situated in the larynx. It is to be distinguished from *speech*, which is the production of sounds intended to express ideas. Many of the lower animals have voice, but none have the power of speech in the sense in which man possesses that faculty. There may be speech without voice, as in whispering, whilst in singing a scale of musical tones we have voice without speech. Regarding speech, see PHONETICS and SPEECH-SOUNDS; also the articles on the various letters of the alphabet.

1. *Physiological Anatomy.*—The organ of voice, the *larynx*, is situated in man in the upper and fore part of the neck, where it forms a well-known prominence in the middle line. It opens below into the trachea or windpipe, and above into the cavity of the pharynx, and it consists of a framework of cartilages, connected by elastic membranes or ligaments, two of which constitute the true vocal cords. These cartilages are movable on each other by the action of various muscles, which thus regulate the position and the tension of the vocal cords. The trachea conveys the blast of air from the lungs during expiration, and the whole apparatus may be compared to an acoustical contrivance in which the lungs represent the wind chest and the trachea the tube passing from the wind chest to the sounding body contained in the larynx. Suppose two tight bands of any elastic membrane, such as thin sheet india-rubber, stretched over the end of a wide glass tube so as to leave a narrow chink between the free borders of the membrane, and that a powerful blast of air is driven through the tube by a bellows. The pressure would so distend the margins of the membrane as to open the aperture and allow the air to escape; this would cause a fall of pressure, and the edges of the membrane would spring back by their elasticity to their former position; again the pressure would increase, and again the edges of the membrane would be distended; and those actions would be so quickly repeated as to cause the edges of the membrane to vibrate with sufficient rapidity to produce a musical tone, the pitch of which would depend on the number of vibrations executed in a second of time. The condensation and rarefaction of the air thus produced are the chief cause of the tone, as Von Helmholtz has pointed out, and in this way the larynx resembles the syren in its mode of producing tone (see ACOUSTICS). It is evident also that the intensity or loudness of the tone would be determined by the amplitude of the vibrations of the margins of the membrane, and that its pitch would be affected by any arrangements effecting an increase or decrease of the tension of the margins of the membrane. The pitch might also be raised by the strength of the current of air, because the great amplitude of the vibrations would increase the mean tension of the elastic membrane. With tones of medium pitch, the pressure of the air in the trachea is equal to that of a column of mercury of 160 mm.; with high pitch, 920 mm.; and with notes of very high pitch, 945 mm.; whilst in whispering it may fall as low as that represented by 30 mm. of water. Such is a general conception of the mechanism of voice.

The *cartilages* form the framework of the larynx. They consist of three single pieces (the thyroid, the cricoid, and the cartilage of the epiglottis) and of three pairs (two arytenoids, two cornicula laryngis or cartilages of Santorini, and two cuneiform cartilages or cartilages of Wrisberg), see figs. 1 and 2. The epiglottis, the

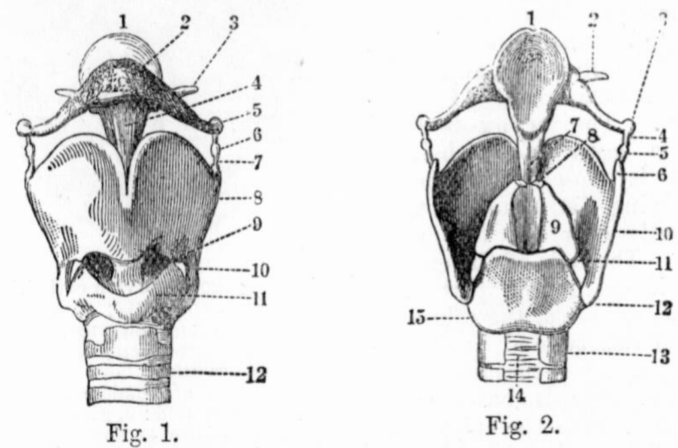

Fig. 1. Fig. 2.

FIG. 1.—Cartilages and ligaments of the larynx seen from the front; half natural size. 1, epiglottis; 2, hyoid bone; 3, small cornu of hyoid bone; 4, middle thyro-hyoid ligament; 5, great cornu of hyoid bone; 6, small nodules of cartilage (*cartilago triticea*); 7, the lateral thyro-hyoid ligament; 8, left lamina or wing of thyroid cartilage; 9, cricoid cartilage; 10, lower cornu of thyroid cartilage; 11, part of cricoid united to the thyroid by the middle crico-thyroid ligament; 12, second ring of trachea. (From Krause.)

FIG. 2.—Cartilages and ligament of larynx seen from behind; half natural size. 1, epiglottis; 2, lesser cornu of hyoid bone; 3, greater cornu of hyoid; 4, lateral thyro-hyoid ligament; 5, cartilago triticea; 6, upper cornu of thyroid; 7, thyro-epiglottic ligament; 8, cartilages of Santorini; 9, arytenoid cartilages; 10, left lamina of thyroid; 11, muscular process of arytenoid cartilage; 12, inferior cornu of thyroid; 13, first ring of trachea; 14, posterior membranous wall of trachea; 15, lamina of cricoid cartilage. (From Krause.)

cornicula laryngis, the cuneiform cartilages, and the apices of the arytenoids are composed of yellow or elastic fibro-cartilage, whilst the cartilage of all the others is of the hyaline variety, resembling that of the costal or rib cartilages. These cartilages are bound together by ligaments, some of which are seen in figs. 1 and 2, whilst the remainder are represented in fig. 3. The ligaments specially concerned in the production of voice are the *inferior thyro-arytenoid ligaments*, or true vocal cords. These are composed of fine elastic fibres attached behind to the anterior projection of the base of the arytenoid cartilages, *processus vocalis*, 3 in fig. 3, and in front to the middle of the angle between the wings or laminæ of the thyroid cartilage. They are practically continuous with the lateral crico-thyroid ligaments, 6 in fig. 3.

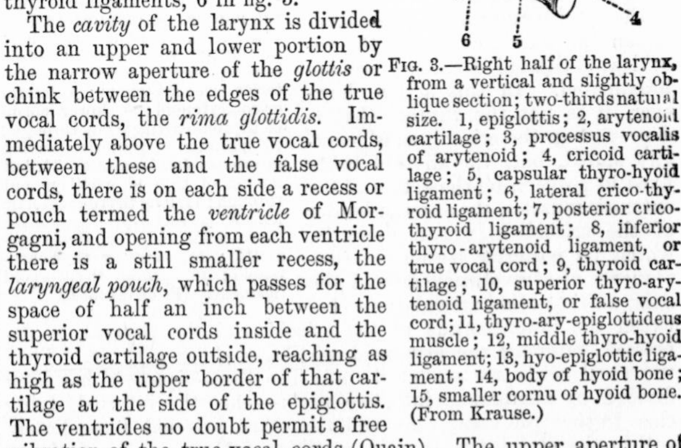

FIG. 3.—Right half of the larynx, from a vertical and slightly oblique section; two-thirds natural size. 1, epiglottis; 2, arytenoid cartilage; 3, processus vocalis of arytenoid; 4, cricoid cartilage; 5, capsular thyro-hyoid ligament; 6, lateral crico-thyroid ligament; 7, posterior crico-thyroid ligament; 8, inferior thyro-arytenoid ligament, or true vocal cord; 9, thyroid cartilage; 10, superior thyro-arytenoid ligament, or false vocal cord; 11, thyro-ary-epiglottideus muscle; 12, middle thyro-hyoid ligament; 13, hyo-epiglottic ligament; 14, body of hyoid bone; 15, smaller cornu of hyoid bone. (From Krause.)

The *cavity* of the larynx is divided into an upper and lower portion by the narrow aperture of the *glottis* or chink between the edges of the true vocal cords, the *rima glottidis.* Immediately above the true vocal cords, between these and the false vocal cords, there is on each side a recess or pouch termed the *ventricle* of Morgagni, and opening from each ventricle there is a still smaller recess, the *laryngeal pouch*, which passes for the space of half an inch between the superior vocal cords inside and the thyroid cartilage outside, reaching as high as the upper border of that cartilage at the side of the epiglottis. The ventricles no doubt permit a free vibration of the true vocal cords (Quain). The upper aperture of the glottis is triangular, wide in front and narrow behind; and, when seen from above by means of the laryngoscope, it presents the view represented in fig. 4. The aperture is bounded in front by the epiglottis, *e*, behind by the summits of the arytenoid cartilages, *ar*, and on the sides by two folds of mucous membrane, the aryteno-epiglottic folds, *ae*. The rounded elevations corresponding to the cornicula laryngis and cuneiform cartilages, *c*, and also the cushion of the epiglottis, *e*, are readily seen in the laryngoscopic picture. The glottis, *o*, is seen in the form of a long narrow fissure, bounded by the true vocal cords, *ti*, whilst above them we have the false vocal cords, *ts*, and between the true and false cords the opening of the ventricle, *v*. The *rima glottidis*, between the true vocal cords, in the adult male measures about 23 millimetres, or nearly an inch, from before backwards, and from 6 to 12 millimetres across its widest part, according to the degree of dilatation. In females and in males before puberty the antero-posterior diameter is about 17 millimetres and its transverse diameter about 4 millimetres. The vocal cords of the adult male are in length about 15 millimetres, and of the adult female about 11 millimetres. The larynx is lined with a layer of epithelium, which is closely adherent to underlying structures, more especially over the true vocal cords. The cells of the epithelium, in the greater portion of the larynx, are of the columnar ciliated variety, and by the vibratory action of the cilia mucus is driven upwards, but over the true vocal cords the epithelium is squamous. Patches of squamous epithelium are also found in the ciliated tract above the glottis, on the under surface of the epiglottis, on the inner surface of the arytenoid cartilages, and on the free border of the upper or false cords. Numerous mucous glands exist in the lining membrane of the larynx, more especially in the epiglottis. In each laryngeal pouch there are sixty to seventy such glands, surrounded by fat.

Fig. 4.—Laryngoscopic view of the glottis. *l*, tongue; *e*, epiglottis; *pe*, pharyngo-epiglottic fold; *g*, pharyngo-laryngeal groove; *ae*, aryteno-epiglottic fold; *c*, cuneiform cartilage, or cartilage of Wrisberg; *ar*, arytenoid cartilage; *r*, inter-arytenoid fold; *o*, glottis; *v*, ventricle; *ti*, inferior or true vocal cord; *ts*, superior or false vocal cord. (From Mandl.)

We are now in a position to understand the action of the *muscles* of the larynx by which the vocal cords, forming the *rima glottidis*, can be tightened or relaxed, and by which they can be approximated or separated. Besides certain extrinsic muscles—sterno-hyoid, omo-hyoid, sterno-thyroid, and thyro-hyoid—which move the larynx as a whole, there are *intrinsic* muscles which move the cartilages on each other. Some of these are seen in fig. 5. These muscles are (*a*) the crico-thyroid, (*b*) the posterior crico-arytenoid, (*c*) the lateral crico-arytenoid, (*d*) the thyro-arytenoid, (*e*) the arytenoid, and (*f*) the aryteno-epiglottidean. Their actions will be readily understood with the aid of the diagrams in fig. 6. (1) The *crico-thyroid* is a short thick triangular muscle, its fibres passing from the cricoid cartilage obliquely upwards and outwards to be inserted into the lower border of the thyroid cartilage and to the outer border of its lower horn. When the muscle contracts, the cricoid and thyroid cartilages are approximated. In this action, however, it is not the thyroid that is depressed on the cricoid, as is generally stated, but, the thyroid being fixed in position by the action of the extrinsic muscles, the anterior border of the cricoid is drawn upwards, whilst its posterior border, in consequence of a revolution around the axis uniting the articulations between the lower cornua of the cricoid and the thyroid, is depressed, carrying the arytenoid cartilages along with it. Thus the vocal cords are stretched. (2) The *thyro-arytenoid* has been divided by anatomists into two parts—one, the internal, lying close to the true vocal cord, and the other, external, immediately within the ala of the thyroid cartilage. Many of the fibres of the anterior portion pass from the thyroid cartilage with a slight curve (concavity inwards) to the processus vocalis at the base of the arytenoid cartilage. They are thus parallel with the true vocal cord, and when they contract the arytenoids are drawn forwards, carrying with them the posterior part of the cricoid and relaxing the vocal cords. Thus the thyro-arytenoids are the antagonists of the crico-thyroids. Ludwig has pointed out that certain fibres (*portio-ary-vocalis*) arise from the side of the cord itself and pass obliquely back to the processus vocalis. These will tighten the parts of the cord in front and relax the parts behind their points of attachment. Some of the fibres of the outer portion run obliquely upwards from the side of the crico-thyroid membrane, pass through the antero-posterior fibres of the inner portion of the muscle, and finally end in the tissue of the false cord. These fibres have been supposed to render the edge of the cord more prominent. Other fibres inserted into the processus vocalis will rotate slightly the arytenoid outwards, whilst a few passing up into the aryteno-epiglottidean folds may assist in depressing the epiglottis (Quain).

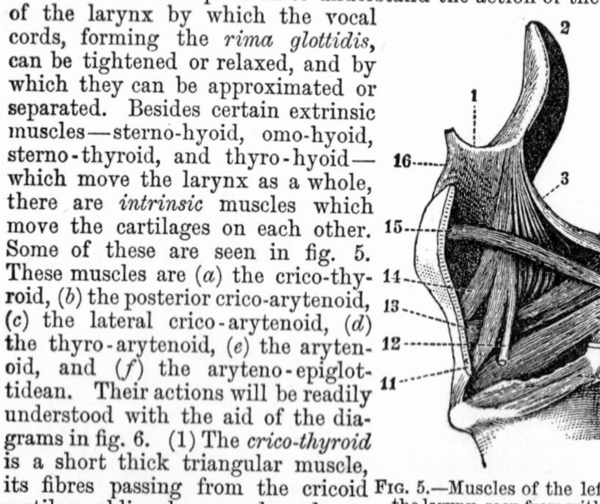

Fig. 5.—Muscles of the left side of the larynx, seen from within; two-thirds natural size. 1, hyo-epiglottic ligament, seen in profile; 2, epiglottis; 3, aryteno-epiglottic muscle; 4, Santorini's cartilage; 5, oblique arytenoid muscle; 6, transverse arytenoid muscle, seen in profile; 7, posterior crico-arytenoid; 8, lateral crico-arytenoid; 9, lower cornu of thyroid cartilage cut through; 10, insertion of posterior portion of crico-thyroid muscle; 11, left lamina of thyroid cartilage cut through; 12, long thyro-epiglottic muscle (a variety); 13, inferior thyro-arytenoid: 14, thyro-epiglottic; 15, superior thyro-arytenoid; 16, median thyro-hyoid ligament. (From Krause.)

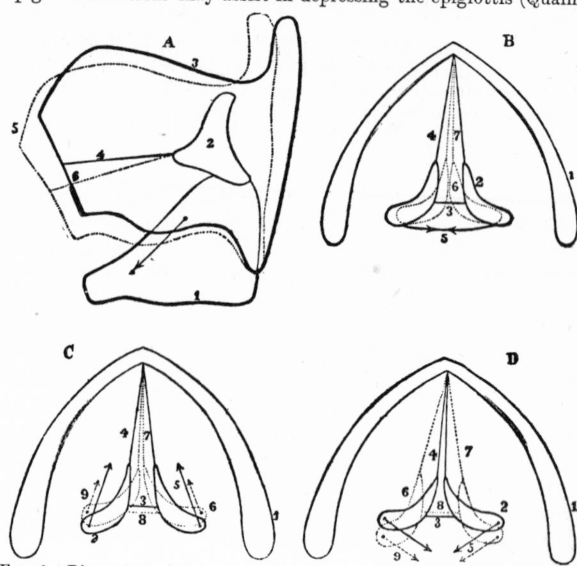

Fig. 6.—Diagrams explaining the action of the muscles of the larynx. The dotted lines show the positions taken by the cartilages and the true vocal cords by the action of the muscle, and the arrows show the general direction in which the muscular fibres act. A, Action of crico-thyroid: 1, cricoid cartilage; 2, arytenoid cartilage; 3, thyroid cartilage; 4, true vocal cord; 5, thyroid cartilage, new position; 6, true vocal cord, new position. B, Action of arytenoid: 1, section of thyroid; 2, arytenoid; 3, posterior border of epiglottis; 4, true vocal cord; 5, direction of muscular fibres; 6, arytenoid, new position; 7, true vocal cord, new position. C, Action of lateral crico-arytenoid; same description as for A and B; 8, posterior border of epiglottis, new position; 9, arytenoid in new position. D, Action of posterior crico-arytenoid; same description. (From Beaunis and Bouchard.)

(3) The *posterior* and *lateral crico-arytenoid* muscles have antagonistic actions, and may be considered together. The *posterior* arise from the posterior surface of the cricoid cartilage, and passing upwards and outwards are attached to the outer angle of the base of the arytenoid. On the other hand, the *lateral* arise from the upper border of the cricoid as far back as the articular surface for the arytenoid, pass backwards and upwards, and are also inserted into the outer angle of the base of the arytenoid before the attachment of the posterior crico-arytenoid. Imagine the pyramidal form of the arytenoid cartilages. To the inner angle of the triangular base are attached, as already described, the true vocal cords; and to the outer angle the two muscles in question. The posterior crico-arytenoids draw the outer angles backwards and inwards, thus rotating the inner angles, or processus vocalis, outwards, and, when the two muscles act, widening the rima glottidis. This action is opposed by the lateral crico-thyroids, which draw the outer angle forwards and outwards, rotate the inner angles inwards, and thus approximate the cords. (4) The *arytenoids* pass from the one arytenoid cartilage to the other, and in action these cartilages will be approximated and slightly depressed. (5) The *aryteno-epiglottidean* muscles arise near the outer angles of the arytenoid; their fibres pass obliquely upwards, decussate, and are inserted partly into the outer and upper border of the opposite cartilage, partly into the aryteno-epiglottic fold, and partly join the fibres of the thyro-arytenoids. In action they assist in bringing the arytenoids together, whilst they also draw down the epiglottis, and constrict the upper aperture of the larynx. The vocal cords will be also relaxed by the elasticity of the parts.

2. *General Physiological Characters.*—As already stated, the *intensity* or *loudness* of voice depends on the amplitude of the movement of the vocal cords. *Pitch* depends on the number of vibrations per second; and the length, size, and degree of tension of the cords will determine the number of vibrations. The more tense the cords the higher the pitch, and the greater the length of the cords the lower will be the pitch. The *range* of the human voice is about three octaves, that is from fa_1 (87 vibrations per second) to sol_4 (768 vibrations). In men, by the development of the larynx, the cords become more elongated than in women, in the ratio of 3 to 2, so that the male voice is of lower pitch and is usually stronger. At the age of puberty the larynx grows rapidly, and the voice of a boy "breaks"

in consequence of the lengthening of the cords, generally falling an octave in pitch. A similar change, but very much less in amount, occurs at the same period in the female. At puberty in the female there is an increase of about one-third in the size of the glottis, but it is nearly doubled in the male, and the adult male larynx is about one-third greater than that of the female. In advanced life the upper notes of the register are gradually weakened and ultimately disappear, whilst the character of the voice also changes, owing to loss of elasticity caused by ossification, which first begins about middle life in the thyroid cartilage, then appears in the cricoid, and much later in the arytenoid. Eunuchs retain the voices of childhood; and by careful training it is possible in normal persons to arrest the development of the larynx so that an adult male can still sing the soprano parts sometimes used in cathedral choirs. The ranges of the different varieties of voice are shown in the following diagram, where the dotted lines give the range of certain remarkable voices, and the figures represent vibrations per second.

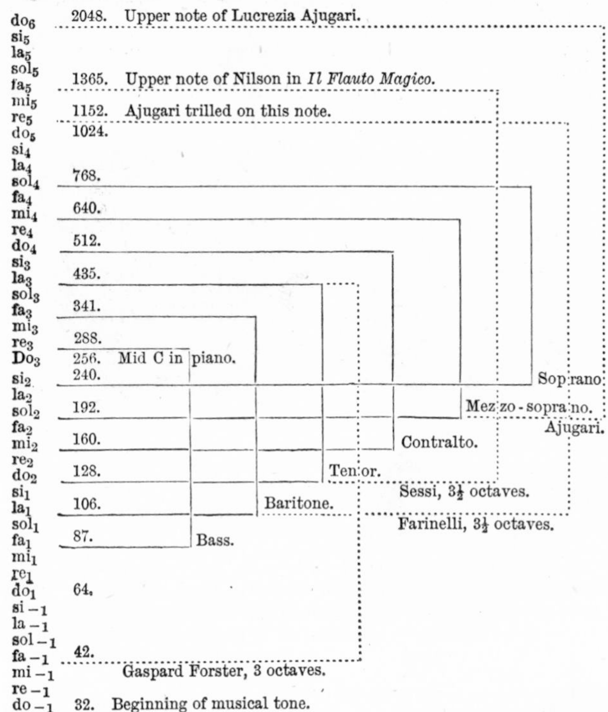

There is thus a range for ordinary voices of nearly two octaves, and certain rare voices may have a range of three and a half octaves. A basso named Gaspard Forster passed from fa_{-1} to la_3; the younger of the sisters Sessi had a contralto voice from do_2 to fa_5; the voice of Catalani ranged three and a half octaves; a eunuch singer, Farinelli, passed from la_1 to re_5; Nilson, in *Il Flauto Magico*, can take fa_5; and Mozart states that he heard in Parma in 1770 a singer, Lucrezia Ajugari, range from sol_2 to do_6, which she gave purely, whilst she could execute trills on re_5. The latter is the most highly pitched voice referred to in musical literature, an octave and a half above the highest ordinary soprano. The range of these voices is shown in dotted lines in the accompanying diagram, and the number of vibrations per second is also noted, taking the middle C of the piano as 256 vibrations per second. It will be observed that the lowest note of Gaspard Forster's voice is not much above the pitch at which the perception of musical tone begins, and that from this note to the upper note of Lucrezia Ajugari there is a range of nearly six octaves, whilst the extreme range of ordinary voices, from the lowest bass to the highest soprano, is a little over three octaves. It is also interesting to observe in connexion with this that the range of the human ear for the perception of musical tone is from do_{-1} to do_{10}, or from about 32 to 33,768 vibrations per second,—eleven octaves.

The *quality* of the human voice depends on the same laws that determine the quality, clang-tint, or timbre of the tones produced by any musical instrument. Musical tones are formed by the vibrations of the true vocal cords. These tones may be either pure or mixed, and in both cases they are strengthened by the resonance of the air in the air-passages and in the pharyngeal and oral cavities. If mixed—that is, if the tone is compounded of a number of partials—one or more of these will be strengthened by the cavities above the cords acting as a resonator; and so strongly may these partials be thus reinforced that the fundamental one may be obscured, and a certain quality or timbre will be communicated to the ear. Further, Von Helmholtz has shown that special forms of the oral cavity reinforce in particular certain partials, and thus give a character to vowel tones,—indeed to such an extent that each vowel tone may be said to have a fixed pitch. This may be proved by putting the mouth in a certain form, keeping the lips open, and bringing various tuning forks sounding feebly in front of the opening. When a fork is found to which the resonant cavity of the mouth corresponds, then the tone of the fork is intensified, and by thus altering the form and capacity of the oral cavity its pitch in various conditions may be determined. Thus, according to Von Helmholtz, the pitch corresponding to the vowels may be expressed:—

Vowels	OU	O	A	AI	E	I	EU	U
Tone	fa_2	$si\flat_3$	$si\flat_4$	sol_5 or re_4	$si\flat_5$ or fa_3	re_6 or fa_2	do_5 or fa_3	sol_5 or fa_2
No. of vibrations	170	470	940	1536 or 576	1920 or 341	2304 or 170	1024 or 341	1536 or 170

Koenig has fixed the pitch of the vowels differently, thus:—

Vowels	OU	O	A	E	I
Tone	$si\flat_2$	$si\flat_3$	$si\flat_4$	$si\flat_5$	$si\flat_6$
No. of vibrations	235	470	940	1880	3760

Donders has given a third result, differing from each of the above; and there is little doubt that much will depend on the quality of tone peculiar to different nationalities. By means of Koenig's manometric flames with revolving mirror the varying quality of tone may be illustrated: with a pure tone, the teeth in the flame-picture are equal, like the serrations of a saw, whilst usually the tone is mixed with partials, which show themselves by the unequal serrations. It is thus certain that quality of voice depends, not merely on the size, degree of elasticity, and general mobility of the vocal cords, but also on the form of the resonating cavities above, and there can be no doubt that very slight differences in these may produce striking results.

3. *Condition of the Larynx in the Various Registers.*—In singing, one can readily observe that the tone may appear to come chiefly from the chest, from the throat, or from the head, or it may show the peculiar quality of tone termed falsetto. Authorities differ much in the nomenclature applied to these varieties of the voice. Thus the old Italian music masters spoke of the voce di petto, voce di gola, and voce di testa. Madam Seiler describes five conditions, namely, the first series of tones of the chest register, the second series of tones of the chest register, the first series of tones of the falsetto register, the second series of tones of the falsetto register, and the head register. French writers usually refer to two registers only, the chest and the head; whilst Behnke gives three registers for male voices (lower thick, upper thick, and upper thin), and five for the voices of women and children (lower thick, upper thick, lower thin, upper thin, and small).[1] These

[1] See *Voice, Song, and Speech*, by Lennox Browne and Emil Behnke, 1883, p. 171.

distinctions are of more importance practically than as implying any marked physiological differences in the mechanism of the larynx during the production of the tones in the different registers. By means of the laryngoscope it is possible to see the condition of the rima glottidis and the cords in passing through all the range of the voice.

In 1807 Bozzini first showed that it was possible to see into the dark cavities of the body by illumining them with a mirror, and in 1829 Babington first saw the glottis in this way. In 1854 Garcia investigated his own larynx and that of other singers, and three years later Türck and especially Czermak perfected the construction of the laryngoscope. In 1883 Lennox Browne and Emil Behnke obtained photographs of the glottis in the living man. The laryngoscope is a small mirror, about the diameter of a shilling, fixed to the end of a long handle at an angle of 125° to 130°. This mirror is gently pushed towards the back of the throat, and if sufficient light be thrown into the mouth from a lamp, and if the eye of the observer be in the proper position, by angling the small mirror it is not difficult to get a view of the glottis. The light from the lamp is reflected by the mirror down on the glottis, from this it is reflected back to the mirror, and then by the mirror it is finally reflected to the eye of the observer. Usually the observer has in front of his eye a mirror by which a powerful beam of light can be thrown from a lamp into the mouth and throat. In the centre of the mirror there is a small hole through which the eye of the observer sees the image in the small mirror at the back of the throat. By placing a second plane mirror in front of the face, an observer can easily study the mechanism of his own larynx.[1]

Suppose the picture of the larynx to be examined in the small mirror at the back of the throat, an image will be seen as in fig. 4. During calm breathing, the glottis is lance-shaped, between the yellowish white cords. A deep inspiration causes the glottis to open widely and in favourable circumstances one may look into the trachea. When a sound is to be made, the vocal cords are brought close together, either along their whole length, as in fig. 7, or only along the ligamentous portion, the space between

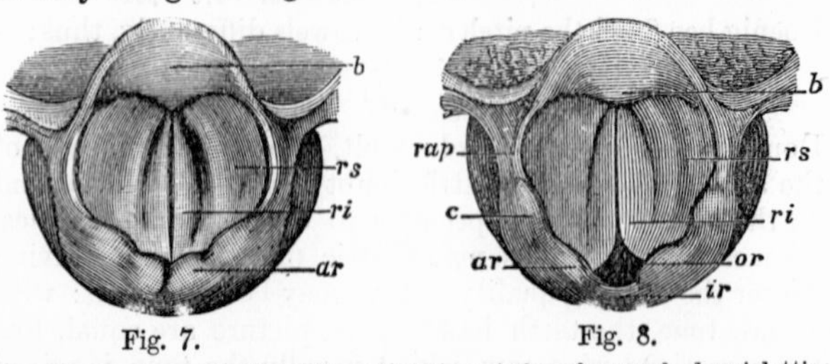

Fig. 7. Fig. 8.

Fig. 7.—Arrangement of glottis previous to emission of a sound. *b*, epiglottis; *rs*, false cord; *ri*, true vocal cord; *ar*, arytenoid cartilages. (From Mandl.)
Fig. 8.—Closure of the ligamentous portion of glottis. *b*, epiglottis; *rs*, false cord; *ri*, true vocal cord; *or*, space between arytenoids; *ar*, arytenoid cartilages; *c*, cuneiform cartilages; *rap*, ary-epiglottic fold; *ir*, inter-arytenoid fold. (From Mandl.)

the arytenoids being still open, as in fig. 8. Then when the sound begins the glottis opens (fig. 4), the form of the opening influencing the kind of voice, whilst the degree of tension of the cords will determine the pitch.

During inspiration the edges of the true vocal cords may occasionally be close together, as in sobbing, and it has been pointed out by various observers that during inspiration the false cords are easily separated, even when they touch, and during expiration, owing to dilatation of the ventricles, they come together and may readily close. Thus, from the plane of the cords, the true cords are most easily closed during inspiration and the false cords during expiration. Wyllie clearly showed in 1865 that the false vocal cords play the chief part in closure of the glottis during expiration (*Edin. Med. Jour.*, 1866). Lauder Brunton and Cash have confirmed Wyllie's results, and have shown further that the function of the false cords is to close the glottis and thus fix the thorax for muscular effort; and they adduce many facts from comparative anatomy in favour of this view, these cords being strongly developed in those animals whose habits render fixation serviceable, whilst, on the other hand, they are absent or weakly developed in animals where fixation is of little or no service (*Jour. Anat. and Physiol.*, vol. xvii.).

During the production of the *chest* voice, the space between the arytenoid cartilages is open, and between the vocal cords there is an ellipsoidal opening which gradually closes as the pitch of the sound rises (see figs. 9, 10, 11).

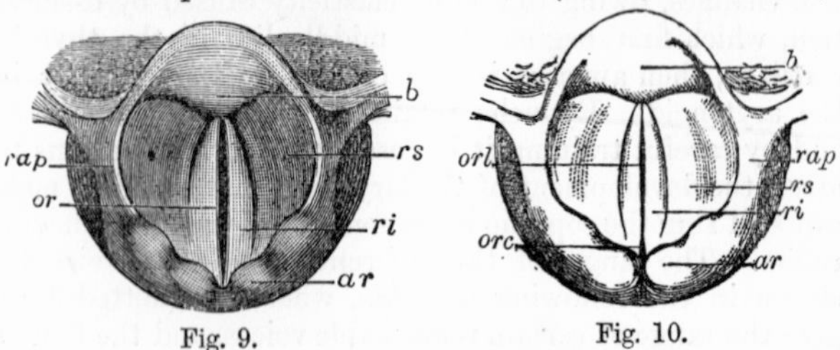

Fig. 9. Fig. 10.

Fig. 9.—Chest voice, deep tone. *b*, epiglottis; *or*, glottis; *rs*, false vocal cord; *ri*, true vocal cord; *rap*, ary-epiglottidean fold; *ar*, arytenoid cartilages. (From Mandl.)
Fig. 10.—Chest voice, medium tone. *orl*, ligamentous portion of glottis; *orc*, portion of glottis between arytenoids; remaining description as in fig. 7. (From Mandl.)

During *head* voice, the opening between the arytenoids is completely closed; the portion between the vocal cords is

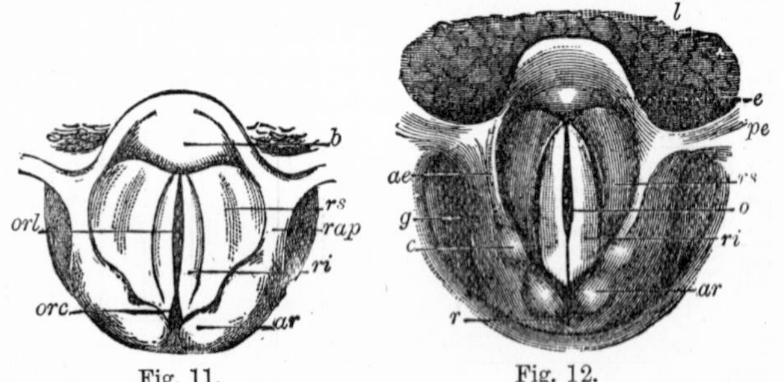

Fig. 11. Fig. 12.

Fig. 11.—Chest voice, high tone; description same as for figs. 7 and 8. (From Mandl.)
Fig. 12.—Head voice, deep tones. *l*, tongue; *e*, epiglottis; *pe*, pharyngo-epiglottidean folds; *ae*, ary-epiglottic folds; *rs*, false cords; *ri*, true vocal cords; *g*, pharyngo-laryngeal groove; *ar*, arytenoid cartilages; *c*, cuneiform cartilages; *o*, glottis; *r*, inter-arytenoid folds. (From Mandl.)

open, but in place of being almost a narrow straight slit as in chest voice, it is wide open so as to allow an escape of more air (see fig. 12). The condition of the cords during *falsetto* is, according to Müller, one in which the cords can only vibrate at their margins, and especially in the middle, in consequence of the false cords pressing downwards upon them. Oertel, on the other hand, states that in falsetto the cords vibrate throughout their length, "but that they form nodal lines parallel to the free borders of the loops or bellies of vibration" (Beaunis). Probably in these circumstances the membranes become much thinner. Oertel also found that during the falsetto voice the epiglottis became erect, the apices of the arytenoids were directed backwards, and the whole larynx became narrower but longer from before backwards. Behnke says that, in the production of the "small register," the mechanism "consists in the formation of an oval orifice in the front part of the glottis which contracts the more the higher the voice ascends, the vocal ligaments being, in the hinder part, pressed together so tightly that scarcely any trace of a slit remains" (Lennox Brown and Behnke, *op. cit.*). Illingworth is of opinion that falsetto (and even the ordinary voice) is produced in the "same way as the mouth is used in whistling" (see *Edin. Med. Jour.*, 1876). This view may be true to some extent as regards falsetto, but it will not hold good for the ordinary voice.

The crico-thyroid muscle is supplied by the superior laryngeal branch of the pneumogastric nerve, and all the other muscles by the inferior or recurrent laryngeal branch

[1] A cheap and efficient form of auto-laryngoscope was constructed by the late Dr David Foulis, and may be had from Messrs. W. B. Hilliard & Son, 65 Renfield Street, Glasgow.

of the same nerve. The superior laryngeal is also the sensory nerve of the larynx. Stirling has found ganglionic cells in the course of this nerve. Paralysis of the motor fibres causes aphonia, or loss of voice. If one cord is paralysed the voice may be lost or become falsetto in tone. Sometimes the cords may move in breathing or during coughing, but be motionless during an attempt at the production of voice. Rarely, incomplete unilateral paralysis of the recurrent nerve, or the existence of a tumour on each cord, thus making them unequal in length, may cause a double tone, or *diphthongia* (Türck). Hoarseness is caused by roughness or swelling of the cords.

On the history of the theories of voice production, see Longet's *Traité de Physiologie*, 1869, vol. ii. p. 733, and Gavarret's *Phonation et Audition*, 1877, p. 541. An excellent bibliography is given in Beaunis's *Physiologie Humaine*, 1881, vol. ii. p. 946; also in Quain's *Anatomy*, 1882, vol. ii. p. 538. (J. G. M.)

VOIRON, a manufacturing town of France, in the department of Isère, stands on the banks of the Morge (a tributary of the Isère) and on the lower slopes of a mountain nearly 2500 feet high, 15 miles north-north-west of Grenoble on the Lyons railway. Some 30 or 35 factories, employing from 4000 to 5000 persons, are engaged in the production of a kind of cloth that takes its name from the town (toiles de Voiron), and the industry is carried on in the neighbourhood also, every inhabitant having his loom. Table linen, silk stuffs (2000 looms), and liqueurs are also made, and there are paper-mills, bleachworks, foundries, edge-tool factories, and building sheds. The monks of La Grande Chartreuse have stores at Voiron in connexion with the railway. A fine modern church was built from 1864 to 1873 in the style of the 13th century. The chief attraction of the town lies in the fine views it possesses of the mountains of Grenoble and the valley of the Isère. The population in 1886 was 8575.

VOITURE, VINCENT (1598–1648), the best writer of *vers de société* that France has yet produced, and one of the most influential preceptors of classical French prose, was born at Amiens in 1598. His father was a well-to-do wine merchant, who had connexions with the court, and it is one of the charges brought against Voiture that he was unnecessarily ashamed of his origin. At any rate he soon obtained a position in society, being appointed by Gaston d'Orléans to various offices in his household. Voiture had been well educated, and had profited both by his education and by the school friendships which it enabled him to make. He was early introduced to the Hôtel de Rambouillet, and travelled in the suite of Monsieur, or on missions, a good deal both in and out of France, on one occasion extending his journeyings as far as Ceuta, whence he wrote a letter of elaborate gallantry to Mademoiselle Paulet. Although a follower of Gaston, he made friends with Richelieu, and was one of the earliest Academicians. He also received appointments and pensions from Louis XIII. and Anne of Austria, and became altogether a very prosperous person. During his lifetime he, like most of the literary men of his time who were not either dramatists or serious scholars, published nothing in book form, but his verses and his prose letters were the delight of the coteries, and were copied, handed about, and admired more perhaps than the work of any contemporary. This coterie success has, it would seem, done them more harm than good in the eyes of posterity. When the long and rather wearisome history of the quarrel between the Uranistes and the Jobelins (partisans of the respective merits of a sonnet of Voiture addressed to a certain Uranie and of another composed by his younger rival Benserade on the subject of Job) is mentioned, the modern reader is apt to suppose that the interest of the affair is merely one of antiquarian gossip. Yet it is difficult to think of any living writer who could surpass, or of any writer living during the last two centuries who could have surpassed, the mixture of gallantry and sincerity in the Uranie sonnet. Another famous piece of his of the same kind, "La Belle Matineuse," is less exquisite, but still very admirable, and, generally speaking, Voiture deserves the praise given to him at the head of this article. His prose letters, if less interesting to the present generation, are full of lively wit, and are historically even more important. He ranks with Jean de Balzac as the chief director of the reform in French prose which accompanied that of Malherbe, and preceded that of Corneille, in French verse. Nor is there any one to whom more than to Voiture (who was for many years almost an *arbiter elegantiarum* in literary matters) the escape of French prose from the over-legislation which had such injurious effect on French verse can be ascribed. The fault of the century—a tendency to elaborate and "metaphysical" turns of phrase—affected him to a certain extent, but in a mild form; and, on the whole, he was the Frenchman of letters of the old school who has been least favourably treated by the resurrection of taste for that old school which the present century has seen. It may seem absurd, but is probably just, to ascribe this absence of enthusiasm in part to the fact that the most unjust censures of the extreme classical school passed harmless by him. Boileau had no abuse for him, and the 18th century read him with pleasure. The militant spirit of Romanticism had therefore nothing to avenge. Voiture lived a careless and Epicurean life for just fifty years, and died at the outbreak of the Fronde, which killed the society to which he was accustomed, on the 26th of May 1648. His works were first published two years later, and a characteristic and rather absurd literary quarrel, which made a great noise at the time, broke out, on the subject of his literary merits, between his friend Costar and a certain Sieur de Griac. The standard modern edition of Voiture is that of Ubicini, 2 vols., Paris, 1855.

VOLCANOES. See GEOLOGY, vol. x. pp. 240–254.

VOLE (Germ. *Wühlmaus*, Fr. *Campagnol*). This word, little known as it is to the majority of English people, is the proper name for a genus containing three of the commonest of our English mammals, namely, the water, bank, and field voles,—animals generally called "water-rat," "red field-mouse," and "short-tailed field-mouse" respectively. The scientific name for the group is *Arvicola*, a genus which, with the lemmings and two or three other genera, forms the subfamily *Arvicolinæ* of the great Rodent family *Muridæ*, whose proper place in the general system is shown under MAMMALIA (vol. xv. p. 419).

The voles, as a whole, are distinguished by their squat and heavy shape, their slower and less graceful movements, very small eyes, blunt snout, inconspicuous ears, and shortened limbs and tail, in all of which points they are markedly contrasted with the true rats and mice of the genus *Mus*, the only animals with which they can be confounded. But by far the most important characteristic of the voles lies in their molar teeth, which have been said to form "the perfection of Rodent dentition" from their wonderful specialization and adaptation to the purpose of grinding vegetable substances. These teeth, three in number on each side of each jaw, are rootless, that is to say, they go on growing during the whole life of the animal at the same rate

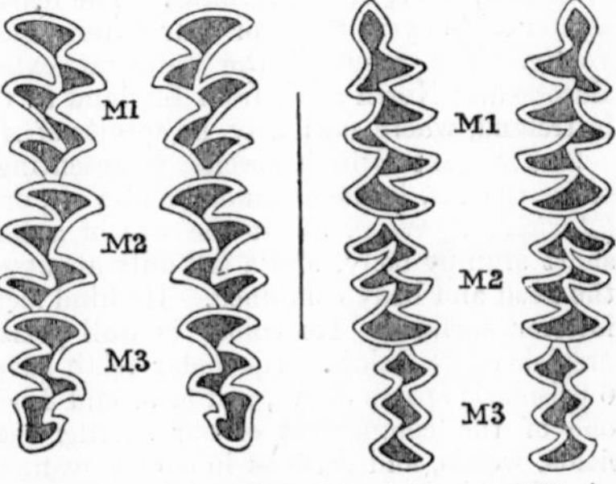

Molars of Water-Vole (*Arvicola amphibius*); top view.

that they are worn down by use, just as is the case with the incisors, whose rootless condition is a characteristic of the whole Rodent order. Each tooth consists of a variable number of prismatic pillars formed externally of enamel and internally of the softer dentine, their section, as produced naturally by wear, being as is shown in the woodcut, a figure which may be compared with that given of the true murine dentition under MOUSE (vol. xvii. p. 5). The general prismatic appearance of the teeth, however, is only due to the bending in at regular distances of the external enamel walls of the tooth, to such an extent that the enamel touches that at the opposite side of the tooth and thus shuts off a greater or less number of dentinal spaces, triangular in section. Owing to the manner of growth of the teeth their general pattern of spaces and angles is but little affected by age and wear, remaining practically the same throughout the life of the animal. On this account the variations in the pattern have been very generally used as a means of characterizing the different genera, subgenera, and species of the group, although their value for this purpose has of late been questioned, and a new classification proposed, entirely ignoring the tooth-characters, and based more upon external peculiarities.

Without entering into the characters of the different sub-groups of the voles, it may suffice to say that each of the three species found in Great Britain belongs to a distinct subgenus of *Arvicola*, and therefore the three together give a fair idea of the extent to which the subgenera differ from one another. These three species are the following:—

1. The common Water-Vole (*Arvicola amphibius*) is as large as the house-rat, with which it is so often confused, but possesses of course the bluff-headed appearance and short tail characteristic of the voles. Its fur is long, soft, and thick, of a uniform grizzled brown all over, except when, as is not uncommon, it is wholly black. Its tail is about half the length of its head and body, and its hind feet are unusually long and powerful, although not webbed, and have five rounded pads on their lower surfaces. Its molar teeth (see woodcut) present the following number of prismatic spaces:—in the upper jaw the first, or anterior, has 5, the second 4, and the third 4, of which the last is very irregular in shape, and is sometimes itself divided into two, making 5 in all; in the lower jaw the first has 7 spaces, of which the 3 anterior are generally not fully separated from one another, the second has 5, and the third 3. These numbers for the different teeth are taken as the characters of the subgenus *Paludicola* of Dr Blasius, by whom this method of subdividing the group was first introduced. The water-vole is one of the commonest English mammals, and is perhaps the most often actually seen of all, owing to its diurnal instead of nocturnal habits. It frequents rivers and streams, burrowing deeply into their banks, and in this way often causing considerable damage. Its food consists almost wholly of water-weeds, rushes, and other vegetable substances, but, like so many other rodents, it will also eat animal food on occasion, in the shape of insects, mice, or young birds. The female has during the warm season of the year three or four litters, each of from two to seven young. The range of the water-rat extends over the whole of Europe and North Asia, from England to China, but is not found in Ireland, where, curiously, no species of *Arvicola* is indigenous.

2. The next British species, representing the subgenus *Agricola* of Dr Blasius, is the common Field-Vole, or short-tailed field-mouse (*Arvicola agrestis*), about the size of a house-mouse, but with a short stumpy body, and a tail only about one-third the length of the head and body combined. Its hind feet have six pads on their inferior surfaces. Its colour is dull grizzled brown above, and greyish-white below. Its molar teeth have respectively 5, 5, and 6 prismatic spaces above, and 9, 5, and 3 below. The field-vole is one of the commonest of our smaller mammals, and frequents fields, woods, and gardens in enormous numbers, often doing very considerable damage in the latter owing to its fondness for garden produce of all kinds. It is spread over the whole of Great Britain from the Hebrides southwards. Abroad its range extends from Finland to North Italy and from France and Spain to Russia.

3. The Bank-Vole (*Arvicola glareolus*) is of much the size and general appearance of the common field-vole, but may be distinguished by its more or less rusty or rufous-coloured back, its larger ears, and its comparatively longer tail, which attains to about half the length of the head and body. Its molar teeth present characters so different from those of all other voles as to have caused it to be often looked upon as belonging to an entirely distinct genus, for which the name of *Evotomys* is used. Their chief distinction lies in the fact that, unlike those of all other voles, their pulp-cavities close up in adult life, and they form distinct roots, more resembling those of the ordinary rats and mice. The enamel spaces of these teeth number respectively 5, 4, and 5 above, and 7, 3, and 3 below. The habits of this species are in every way similar to those of the field-vole. Its range in Great Britain extends northwards to Morayshire, beyond which it has not yet been observed. Abroad it is found all along the north temperate zone from France to China, and is replaced in North America by a closely allied animal known as *Arvicola gapperi*. It is probable, however, that both these forms, *A. gapperi* and *A. glareolus*, are only southern climatic offshoots of a still more northern species, the *Arvicola rutilus* of northern Europe, Siberia, and Arctic America.

The foreign species of vole number about 40, of which about 10 are European, 20 Asiatic, and 10 North American, none being found either in Africa, India (except in the extreme north), Australia, or South America. The group is therefore one peculiarly characteristic of the temperate parts of the northern hemisphere. (O. T.)

VOLGA, THE, the chief river of European Russia, rises in the Valdai plateau of Tver in north-western Russia, and after a winding course of 2325 miles (1040 in a straight line) falls into the Caspian at Astrakhan. It is by far the largest river of Europe, those next in length, the Danube and the Ural, being only 1735 and 1478 miles respectively, while the Rhine (825 miles) is shorter even than two of the chief tributaries of the Volga,—the Oka and the Kama. Its drainage area, which includes the whole of middle and eastern as well as part of south-eastern Russia, amounts to 563,300 square miles, thus exceeding the aggregate superficies of Germany, France, and the United Kingdom. A hundred tributaries of the Volga are navigable for an aggregate length of 14,600 miles, a distance greater than the aggregate length of all the railways of England and Wales. The drainage area embraces twenty-one provinces of the Russian empire, or, in other words, nearly the whole of Great Russia proper, and has a population of nearly 40,000,000. The most populous regions of Great Russia are situated within the Volga basin, and cities like Moscow, Nijni-Novgorod, Saratoff, Simbirsk, and Kazañ, as well as many others, are indebted for their growth and present importance to their situation on the Volga or its tributaries. But the real "basin" of the Volga is not limited to its drainage area. By a system of canals which connects the upper Volga with the Neva, the commercial mouth of the Volga has been transferred, so to speak, from the Caspian to the Baltic, thus making St Petersburg, the capital and chief seaport of Russia, the chief port of the Volga basin as well. Other less important canals connect it with the Düna and the White Sea (Riga and Archangel); while a railway only 40 miles in length joins the Volga with the Don and the Sea of Azoff, and three great trunk lines bring its lower parts into connexion with the Baltic and western Europe. Traffic on the river and its tributaries is carried on by more than 760 steamers, 20,000 barges and boats, and 50,000 rafts; upwards of 4,000,000 tons of various goods, valued at 500,000,000 roubles (in weight one half and in value three-fourths of the total merchandise on Russian rivers) are carried. If in addition some 50,000 rafts of timber not included in the preceding statistics are reckoned, the timber floated in the basin of the Volga exceeds by nearly a million tons the total weight of merchandise carried on the 13,000 miles of Russian railways.[1]

See vol. xxi. Plate II.

The Volga rises in the extensive marshes covering the western parts of the Valdai plateau, where the Düna also has its origin. Small streamlets languidly circulate from marsh to marsh, so that

[1] See "The Volga as a Means of Communication," by Prof. Boguslavskiy, St Petersburg, 1887 (Russian), being vol. ix. of the *Sbornik* of the Institute of Roads and Communications. The above length of the Volga is taken from this work, based on recent surveys, and is therefore more accurate than the length given by M. Strelbitzky (1978 miles) and Gen. Tillo (2108 miles).

it is very difficult to say which of these ought to be regarded as the real source. Lake Seliger was formerly so considered; but at present that distinction is given to a small spring trickling into a wooden trough from beneath a small chapel in the midst of an extensive marsh to the south of Seliger (57° 10′ N. lat.). The honour has also been claimed of late, not without plausibility, for the Runa rivulet.[1] Recent exact surveys have shown those marshes to be no more than 665 feet above sea-level. The stream first traverses several small lakes, all having the same level, and, after its junction with the Runa, enters Lake Volgo. A dam recently erected a few miles below that lake, with a storage of 350 million cubic yards of water, makes it possible to raise the level of the Volga as far as the Sheksna, thus rendering it navigable, even at low water, from its 65th mile onwards. Unlike most other great rivers, the Volga has thus no "upper course" among the mountains. From the Valdai plateau, however, its descent is rapid, until at Tver its level is only 420 feet. Before reaching this point it has received numerous small tributaries, so as to be already 300 yards in breadth, with a volume of more than 4000 cubic feet per second, and a minimum depth at low water of 19 inches. The Tvertsa is connected by the Vyshniy-Vołotchok Canal with the Tsna, a tributary to the Msta and Volkhoff, which flows to Lake Ladoga,—the first of the three systems of canals which, as already remarked, have removed the commercial mouth of the Volga to the Baltic. From Tver the Volga is regularly navigated, although not without some difficulties on account of the shallows and sandbanks. It flows north-east along a broad valley to join the Mołoga and the Sheksna, two important tributaries connected by the Tikhvinsk and Mariinsk Canals with the tributaries of Lake Ladoga. Of these two systems the latter is much the more important, and the town of Rybinsk, at the mouth of the Sheksna, has therefore become the chief port of the upper Volga.

From its junction with the Sheksna the Volga flows with a very gentle descent towards the south-east, past Yarosłavl and Kostroma, along a broad valley hollowed to a depth of some 150 and 200 feet in the Permian and Jurassic deposits. In fact, its course is through a succession of depressions formerly filled with wide lakes, and connected by links. When the Volga assumes a due south-east direction it is already a large river (8250 cubic feet per second, rising occasionally in high flood to as much as 178,360 cubic feet); of its numerous tributaries, the Unzha (365 miles, 330 navigable), from the north, is the most important.

The next great tributary is the Oka, which comes from the south-west after having traversed, on its course of 920 miles, all the Great Russian provinces of central Russia. It rises in Orel among hills which also send tributaries to the Dnieper and the Don, and receives on the left the Upa, the Jizdra, the Ugra (300 miles), navigable up to Kozelsk, the Moskva, on which steamers ply up to Moscow, the Klyazma (395 miles), on whose banks arose the Middle Russian principality of Suzdal, and on the right the navigable Tsna (255 miles) and Moksha. Every one of these tributaries is connected with some important event in the history of Great Russia, and the drainage area of the Oka is a territory of 97,800 square miles. It has been maintained of late that, of the two rivers which unite at Nijni-Novgorod, the Oka, not the Volga, is the chief; and the fact is that both in length (818 miles) and in drainage area above the junction (89,500 square miles), as well as in the aggregate length of its tributaries, the Volga is the inferior. But, on the other hand, the Volga contributes on the whole the largest volume of water, although in flood the Oka here also has the advantage.

At its junction with the Oka the Volga enters the broad lacustrine depression (see RUSSIA) which must have communicated with the Caspian during the Post-Pliocene period by means of at least a broad strait. Its level at low water is only 190 feet above that of the ocean. Immediately below the junction its breadth ranges from 350 to 1750 yards, and even at the lowest water (in 1873) it had a minimum depth of 5½ feet. The valley, which is nearly 7 miles wide, but at several places is narrowed to less than 2 miles, shows evident traces of having originated from a succession of elongated lakes, the shores of which bear numerous traces of the dwellings of prehistoric man from the Stone Age. There are many islands which change their appearance and position after each inundation. On the right it is joined by the Sura, which drains a large area and brings a volume of from 2700 to 22,000 cubic feet of water per second, the Vetluga (465 miles long, of which 365 are navigable), from the forest-tracts of Yarosłavl, and many smaller tributaries; then it turns south-east and descends to another lacustrine depression, where it receives the Kama below Kazañ, 300 miles below its junction with the Oka, and only 110 feet above the sea. Remains of molluscs still extant in the Caspian occur extensively throughout this depression and up the lower Kama.

The Kama, which brings to the Volga a contribution ranging from 52,500 to 144,400 cubic feet and occasionally reaching even 515,000 cubic feet per second, might again be considered as the more important of the two rivers. It rises in Vyatka, takes a wide sweep towards the north and east, and then flows south and south-west to join the Volga after a course of no less than 1120 miles. A great number of important rivers join it:—the Wishera, coming from the depth of the forest region; the Kosva, so important for the export of metallic wares from the Ural works; the Tchusovaya (430 miles), which receives the Sylva and connects the Ekaterinburg mining district with central Russia; and finally the Byełaya (800 miles), which, together with the Ufa, its tributary, waters the fertile lands of the Bashkirs, rapidly being settled now by the Russians. A territory larger than France is thus brought into connexion with the great artery of Russian industrial life.

Along the next 738 miles of its course the Volga—now from 580 to 2600 yards wide—flows south-south-west, with but one great bend at Samara. At this point, where it pierces a range of limestone hills, the course of the river is very picturesque, fringed as it is by high cliffs which rise about 1000 feet above the level of the water (which is only 54 feet above the sea at Samara). Along the whole of the Samara bend the Volga is accompanied on its right bank by high cliffs, which it is constantly undermining, while wide lowland areas extend on the left or eastern bank, and are intersected by several old beds of the Volga. At SARATOFF (*q.v.*) the cliffs are being undermined so rapidly that a broad beach now separates the chief channel of the river from the city. Very few streams of any importance join the Volga in this part of its course. Still, at Ekaterinenstadt, a few miles above Saratoff, the volume per second for the two years 1884 and 1885 appears to have been as much as 384,000 cubic feet. In flood 1,427,000 cubic feet per second has been recorded (Boguslavskiy). In the lower portion of this section the Volga has already passed below sea-level (58 feet below at Tsaritsyn).

At Tsaritsyn the Volga reaches its extreme south-western limit, where it is separated from the Don by an isthmus of only 40 miles in width. The isthmus is too high to be crossed by means of a canal, but a railway at Duboffka brings the Volga into some sort of connexion with the Don and the Sea of Azoff. At Tsaritsyn the river takes a sharp turn in a south-easterly direction towards the Caspian; it enters the Caspian steppes, and some 50 miles below Tsaritsyn sends off a branch—the Akhtuba—which accompanies it for 330 miles before falling into the Caspian. Here the Volga receives no tributaries; its right bank is skirted by low hills, but on the left it spreads freely, joining the Akhtuba by many branches when its waters are high, and flooding the country for from 15 to 35 miles. The width of the main branch ranges from 520 to 3500 yards, and the depth exceeds 80 feet. The delta proper begins 40 miles above Astrakhan, and the branches subdivide so as to reach the sea by as many as 200 separate mouths. Below Astrakhan navigation is difficult, and on the sand-bars at the mouth the maximum depth is only 12 feet in calm weather,—a depth increased or diminished by a few feet according to the force and direction of the wind.

The figures given above, showing as they do how immensely different in volume is the river at different periods, help to indicate the greatness of the changes which are constantly going on in the channel and on its banks. Not only does its level occasionally rise in flood as much as 50 feet and cover its low-lying banks for a distance ranging from 5 to 15 miles; even the level of the Caspian is considerably affected by the sudden influx of water brought by the Volga. The amount of suspended matter brought down is of course correspondingly great; and, were it not for the action of the wind in driving back masses of water at the mouth of the Volga and thus filling up lakes where the mud is deposited, the bar at Astrakhan would soon become so silted up as completely to prevent navigation. All along its course the Volga wastes its banks with great rapidity; towns and loading ports have constantly to be shifted farther back. The shoals and shallows are continually changing, and maps of the river made for a series of consecutive years are of the greatest interest to the physical geographer.

The question as to the gradual desiccation of the Volga, and its causes, has often been discussed, and in 1838 a committee which included Karl Baer among its members was appointed by the academy of sciences to investigate the subject; no positive result has, however, been arrived at, principally on account of the want of regular measurements of the volume of the Volga and its tributaries, —measurements which began to be made on scientific principles only in 1880. Still, it may be regarded as established that during the last thirty years new shallows have appeared in the upper Volga, and the old ones have increased in size; while if we go back two or three centuries it is indisputable that rivers of the Volga basin which were easily navigable then are now hardly accessible to the smallest craft. The desiccation of the rivers of Russia has been often attributed to the steady destruction of its forests. But it is obvious that there are other general causes at work much more important,—causes to which the larger phenomena of the general desiccation of all rivers of the northern hemisphere in the deserts of Siberia and Turkestan, as well as in Russia, must be attributed. The gradual elevation of the whole of northern Russia and Siberia,

[1] Ragozin, *The Volga*, St Petersburg, 1881, 3 vols. (Russian), summarized in Roskoschny's *Die Wolga und ihre Zuflüsse*, Leipsic, 1887.

and the consequent draining of the marshes (see NOVGOROD), is one of them; the drying-up of lakes all over the northern hemisphere, a process which is going on so rapidly (see TOMSK), in consequence of the deepening of the outflows of lakes and the cessation of supply to the lakes which remained after the glaciation of the northern hemisphere, is another; and both causes are amply sufficient to explain the known phenomena throughout the historical period. The desiccation of the Russian rivers is only one instance of the general desiccation of the northern parts of the Old World, of which so many instances have been given under RUSSIA, TURKESTAN, TRANSCASPIAN REGION, and SIBERIA.

Fisheries.—The network of shallow and still *limans* or "cut-offs" in the delta of the Volga and the shallow waters of the northern Caspian, sweetened as these are by the water of the Volga, the Ural, the Kura, and the Terek, is exceedingly favourable to the breeding of fish, and as a whole constitutes one of the richest fishing grounds of the world. As soon as the ice breaks up in the delta innumerable shoals of roach (*Leuciscus rutilus*) and trout (*Luciotrutta leucichthys*) rush up the river. They are followed by the great sturgeon (*Acipenser huso*), the pike, the bream, and the pike perch (*Leucioperca sandra*). Later on appears the Caspian herring (*Clupea caspia*), which formerly was neglected, but has now become more important than the various species of sturgeon; the sturgeon (*A. stellatus*) and "wels" (*Silurus glanis*, see vol. xxii. p. 67) follow, and finally the sturgeon *Acipenser güldenstädtii*, so much valued for its caviare. In search of a gravelly spawning-ground the sturgeons go up the river as far as Sarepta (250 miles). The lamprey, now extensively pickled, the sterlet (*A. ruthenus*), the tench, the gudgeon, and other river species also appear in immense numbers. No less than 15,000 men, partly from central Russia, are engaged in the fisheries of the lower Volga and its delta, while on the waters of the northern Caspian there are as many as 3000 fishing-boats, giving employment to something like 50,000 persons. From the end of June onwards immense trawl-nets, sometimes a mile in length, and occasionally taking at one haul as many as 40,000 bream, 150,000 roach, and 200,000 herrings, are continually at work, and it is estimated that 3,600,000 cwts. of various fish, of the value of 15,000,000 roubles, are taken annually in the four fishing districts of the Volga, Ural, Terek, and Kura. Seal-hunting is also carried on off the Volga, and every year about 40,000 of the *Phoca vitulina* are killed to the north of the Manghishlak peninsula. Fishing is extensively carried on along the entire course of the Volga and its tributaries, as also in the lakes of its upper basin.

Ice-Covering.—In winter the numberless tributaries and sub-tributaries of the Volga become so many highways for sledges. The ice lasts from 90 to 160 days according to the climatic conditions, and breaks up earlier in its upper course than in some parts lower down. The average date of the break-up is April 11th at Tver, and 14 days later about Kostroma, from which point a regular acceleration is observed (April 16th at Kazañ, April 7th at Tsaritsyn, and March 17th at Astrakhan). Similarly, the average dates of freezing are November 23d at Tver, November 20th about Kostroma, December 7th at Kazañ, 20th at Tsaritsyn, and 17th at Astrakhan. Thus the river is open for an average of 226 days at Ostashkoff and Tver, 215 days at Kostroma, and 209 at Kineshma; from Nijni-Novgorod, where the average is 224 days, there is a regular increase (235 days at Kazañ, 241 at Samara, 257 at Tsaritsyn, and 275 at Astrakhan). There are, however, great fluctuations, the navigation in some years having lasted only 182 days in the upper course, 169 at Kostroma, and 243 at Tsaritsyn; while within the last eighty years maxima of 260 days in the upper course and 288 in the lower course have been observed. The tributaries are navigable for periods ranging from 180 to 246 days.

Traffic.[1]—The chief Volga traffic is up river, the amount of merchandise which reaches Astrakhan being nearly fifteen times less than that reaching St Petersburg by the Volga canals. The details of this traffic are highly characteristic of the present economic life of Russia. Ten million cwts. of fish, salt, and naphtha are despatched from Astrakhan; this contingent is soon swelled to 12 millions at Tsaritsyn by the salt brought by rail from the Baskuntchak salt-lakes. From Tsaritsyn 7 million cwts. of fish, salt, and naphtha are despatched by the first of the three railways which traverse Russia from south-east to north-west and connect the lower Volga with the Baltic. Considerable amounts of corn are added to this total on its way towards the north-west; and, while salt, fish, and naphtha are discharged for use at various points in middle Russia, the flow of corn continues to swell; portions of it are sent to Moscow from Gryazi and Orel, but the remainder goes north-west, so as to reach Riga to the amount of 9,300,000 cwts., chiefly of corn and flax.

By the Volga itself only 5,100,000 cwts., chiefly of fish, salt, and naphtha, leave Tsaritsyn, but before this ascending traffic reaches Saratoff it has increased to 6,300,000 cwts., chiefly by the addition of corn from the Saratoff steppes. There the current of merchandise divides again; 3 million cwts. of corn, fish, &c., leave the Volga to be carried north-westwards towards Tamboff, while the remainder is carried on farther north, up the Volga, receiving on the way considerable additions of corn from the fertile tracts of Samara and the steppes of Orenburg, which are connected with Samara by rail. At Samara the flow again divides, and part of it is sent again north-west, *via* Penza, to Ryazhsk; there the three north-western currents which leave the Volga respectively at Tsaritsyn, Saratoff, and Samara reunite after having taken in corn from the fertile regions of Tamboff and Ryazañ, so that nearly 20 million cwts. of corn and other produce leave Ryazhsk to be carried on to Moscow. But the flow of corn ascending the Volga does not diminish, and Samara sends farther north no less than 14 million cwts., chiefly corn. At Kazañ the volume of traffic is 16,200,000 cwts. (13 million cwts. of corn). Here a new mass, consisting of 11 million cwts. of corn, 3½ of various metals, 4 of salt, and 6½ of miscellaneous merchandise, all shipped down the Kama, joins the former, so that the total amount of merchandise forwarded from Kazañ up the Volga reaches 35 million cwts. The Sura, the Oka, and the Vetluga add their corn, timber, and manufactured goods, and the volume reaching Nijni-Novgorod amounts to 38 million cwts. Here the stream divides once more: while manufactured goods brought in to the Nijni-Novgorod fair are dispersed from it all over Russia, nearly 10 million cwts. of various merchandise (4 million of corn) are sent by rail to Moscow, but the great bulk (28 million cwts.) continues to move up the river, receiving on the way more timber from the Unzha, and sending some corn northwards to Vologda and Archangel.

When the traffic reaches Rybinsk, we find that it consists of 20 million cwts. of corn and flax, and 5½ million of metals, metallic and manufactured goods, hides, leather, and so on. At Rybinsk it again subdivides into three branches; one (6,300,000 cwts., chiefly of corn) is discharged and sent by rail to St Petersburg; another (2,800,000 cwts.) continues up the Volga to enter the Vyshniy Volotchok and Tikhvinsk canal-systems; and the third and largest (16 million cwts., almost entirely corn and flax) moves along the Mariinsk system towards Lake Ladoga and St Petersburg. Masses of timber and wood for fuel are added to it from the forest tracts of the lake district,—the Syas and the Volkhoff bringing together nearly 17 million cwts., chiefly wood, so that finally 14,000,000 cwts. of corn and flax, 31,300,000 of timber and wood, 16,000,000 of building materials, and 4,000,000 of miscellaneous goods reach St Petersburg, which thus is the real seaport of the Volga basin.

The goods traffic down the river is much less important in weight, but relatively greater in value. Its prominent feature is the amount of wood sent to supply the provinces of Samara, Saratoff, and Astrakhan, as well as the lower Don, which now have very few or no forests. But the 8½ million cwts. of wood and timber which reach Samara on boats are but a trifle in comparison with what is floated in the shape of rafts. The down traffic in manufactured goods is still more important. The great bulk of those exported from St Petersburg is sent to Moscow by rail, and thence distributed by rail over central Russia; but part of it is sent by rail to Rybinsk, and thence shipped down the Volga. Moscow sends its goods for the same purpose, partly to Yaroslavl, and partly to Nijni-Novgorod (by rail), as also does Vladimir. Nijni-Novgorod distributes the merchandise all over eastern Russia, sends it up the Kama to Siberia, and ships nearly 2 million cwts. down the Volga. This quantity is increased by the additions brought by rail to Samara, Saratoff, and Tsaritsyn.

According to official returns the aggregate amount of goods loaded in the basin of the Volga amounts to nearly 4 million tons, valued at 150 million roubles (2 million tons, 100 millions worth, on the Volga proper); trustworthy authorities, however, consider the real value of goods loaded in the basin of the Volga to be not less than 500 million roubles, exclusive of nearly 34 million tons of timber and fuel.

Formerly tens of thousands of "burlaki" were employed in dragging boats up the Volga and its tributaries, but this method of traction has disappeared unless from a few of the tributaries. Horse-power is still extensively resorted to along the three canal systems. The first large steamers of the American type were built in 1872. Steamers are now very common; in 1885 as many as 766 were already in use on the Volga and its tributaries, and of these only one-eighth were not built within the Volga basin itself. One-third of them used naphtha as fuel. Of barges and other light vessels an immense variety of types are now in use; during 1885 no fewer than 20,610 vessels were afloat, and during the last thirteen years the annual average of vessels built on the Volga and its tributaries has been 5030 (4,130,000 roubles). Large numbers of them are broken up after a single voyage.

History.—The Volga was not improbably known to the early Greeks, though it is not mentioned by any of the writers previous to Ptolemy, who all confounded the Caspian with a gulf of the Arctic Ocean. According to Ptolemy, the Rha is a tributary of an interior sea, formed from the confluence of two great rivers, the sources of which are separated by twenty degrees of longitude; but

[1] See *Sbornik* of the Ministry of Roads and Communications, vols. xi. and xii., 1885 and 1887: Graphical Maps of the Movement of Goods in 1882 and 1883.

it is scarcely possible to judge from his statements how far the Slavonians had by that time succeeded in penetrating into the basin of the Volga. The Arabian geographers also throw but little light on the condition of the Volga (which they knew under the names of Itil, Etil, or Atel) during the great migrations of the 3d century, or subsequently under the invasion of the Huns, the growth of the great Khazar empire in the southern steppes, and of that of Bulgaria on the middle Volga. But we know that in the 9th century the Volga basin was occupied by Finnish stems in the north, and by Khazars and various Turkish stems in the south. The Slavonians, driven perhaps to the west, had only the Volkhoff and the Dnieper, while the Mohammedan Bulgarian empire, at the confluence of the Volga with the Kama, was so strong that for some time it was an open question whether Islam or Christianity was to gain the upper hand among the Slavonian idolaters. But, while the Russians were driven from the Black Sea by the Khazars, and later on by a tide of Ugrian migration from the north-east to the south-west (see p. 5 *supra*), a stream of Slavonians slowly moved towards the north-east, down the Oka, into the borderland between the Finnish and Turkish stems. After two centuries of struggle the Russians succeeded in colonizing the fertile valleys of the Oka basin; in the 12th century they built a series of fortified towns on the Oka and Klyazma, and finally they reached the mouth of the Oka, there founding (in 1222) a new Novgorod—the Novgorod of the Lowlands, now Nijni-Novgorod. The great lacustrine depression of the middle Volga was thus reached. Under the protection of the forts in the north-east, of the forests of Ryazañ in the south, and of the marshes of Novgorod and Tver in the north, the Great-Russian nationality freely developed in the fertile valleys of the Oka, absorbing the feeble Finnish tribes which formerly peopled them; and when the Tartar-Mongolian invasion came it encountered in the Oka basin a dense agricultural population with many fortified and wealthy towns,—a population which the Mongols found they could conquer, indeed, but were unable to drive before them as they had done with so many of the Turkish stems. This invasion only checked but did not stop the further advance of the Russians down the Volga; nay, it partly facilitated it, because it weakened the Bulgarian empire, and, by keeping up on the lower Volga a continual flow and ebb of nomads, prevented the development there of any settled population which might ultimately have opposed the further advance of the Russians towards the Caspian. Two centuries elapsed before the Russians covered the 300 miles which separate the mouths of the Oka and the Kama, and took possession of Kazañ. But in the meantime a flow of Novgorodian colonization had moved eastward, in the upper portions of the left-bank tributaries of the Volga, and had reached the Urals, thus opening the way to Siberia.

With the capture of Kazañ the Russians found the lower Volga open to their boats, and eight years afterwards they were already masters of the mouth of the river at Astrakhan. The Tartars and Turks of the steppes between the Dnieper and the Volga were thus encircled; the Little Russians endeavoured to take possession of the lower Dnieper, and the Great Russians already had a firm footing on the lower Volga. The possession of the latter opened a free passage to the Don, up the little river Kamyshinka (now dried up but then navigable), which gave easy means of crossing the narrow isthmus between the Don and the Volga. Thus the lower Don was colonized. But two centuries more elapsed before the Russians opened for themselves a free passage to the Black Sea and became masters of the Sea of Azoff and the Crimea; the Volga, however, was their route. During these two centuries they fortified the lower river, settled it, and penetrated also farther eastward into the steppes, towards the upper Ural and thence to the upper parts of the Tobol and the other great Siberian rivers. They penetrated also into the northern parts of the Caucasus isthmus, while another stream of armed colonization moved up the Kama and its numerous tributaries; finding the sources of these close to those of the Ob and Tobol, they crossed the low watersheds of the Urals and spread over northern Siberia, always following the river courses and taking advantage of the portages for penetrating from one basin into the next. The entire growth of Russia towards the east went on from the Volga and its tributaries, and the long line of water communication (nearly 1000 miles) which flows from the upper Kama (60° N. lat.) to Astrakhan (46° 4′), between Europe and Asia, and extends as far south as Astrabad on the Caspian (36° 51′ N. lat.), became the basis for all further advance of Russia into Asia.

Bibliography.—Semenoff's *Geographical and Statistical Dictionary*, 5 vols., 1863–1885, contains a full bibliography of the Volga and tributaries up to date. See also Baer's *Kaspische Studien*, 1837 *sq.*; Haxthausen's *Studien über Russland*; Baer and Helmersen's *Beiträge*; *Spiski naselennykh myest* of Volga provinces; V. Ragozin's *Volga*, 3 vols., 1880–81, with atlas (Russian); N. Bogoluboff, *The Volga from Tver to Astrakhan* (Russian), 1876; S. Monastyrskiy, *Illustrated Handbook of the Volga* (Russian), Kazañ, 1884; *Nijegorodskiy Sbornik* (Russian); Reclus's *Géographie Universelle*, vol. v.; Roskoschny, *Die Wolga und ihre Zuflüsse*, Leipsic, 1887, vol. i. (history, ethnography, hydrography, and biography, with rich bibliographical information); N. Boguslavskiy, *The Volga as a Means of Communication* (Russian), 1887, with detailed profile and maps; M. Bogdanoff, *Birds and Mammals of the Black-Earth Region of the Volga*, 1869; Id., "Fauna of Volga," in *Mem. Kazan Natur.*, 1872; Peretyatkovitch, *Volga Region in the 15th and 16th Centuries*, 1877; Klopoff, *Results of Exploration of Volga Corn Trade*, 1887. For geology, see the publications of the Geological Committee and Mineral Society (maps of Yarosłavl and lower Volga), and *Memoirs* of Astrakhan Statistical Committee for fishing. (P. A. K.)

VOLHYNIA, a government of south-western Russia, bounded by the Polish provinces of Lublin and Siedlce on the W., Grodno and Minsk on the N., Kieff on the E., and Podolia and Galicia (Austria) on the S., has an area of 27,731 square miles. A broad and flat spur of the Carpathians—the Avratynsk plateau—which enters from the west and spreads eastward towards the Dnieper, occupies its southern portion, reaching a maximum elevation of 1200 feet; another branch of the Carpathians in the west of the government ranges between 700 and 900 feet at its highest points. Both are deeply grooved in some places, and the crags give a hilly aspect to the districts where they occur. The remainder of the government, which is quite flat, with an imperceptible slope towards the marshes of Pinsk, is known as the Polyesie (see MINSK). It is covered by impassable marshes (sometimes as much as 400 square miles in extent), sparsely interspersed with forests and traversed by languid streams, with low, almost inaccessible banks, here and there diversified by sandy dunes. The drainage of the Polyesie is, however, being vigorously carried on, and large tracts of meadow land have already been reclaimed by extensive operations recently undertaken by Government. Among the marshes are many small lakes. Volhynia is copiously watered by a number of comparatively unimportant rivers which rise in the Avratynsk Hills and flow northwards towards the Dnieper; the Pripet with the Turia, the Styr, the Goryñ, the Slutch, and other smaller tributaries of the Dnieper are navigable by small boats, and considerable quantities of timber and firewood are floated. By the western Bug, which separates Volhynia from Poland, timber is floated and corn and various goods shipped to Prussia.

The geological formation of Volhynia is very simple. The Avratynsk Hills, consisting of granite and various crystalline rocks, are covered with the Chalk, above which in turn are Tertiary sandstones, sands, and clays containing lignite. The whole is covered by Glacial deposits and Lacustrine clays, reaching a great thickness in the north. Kaolin, pottery clay, and iron ore are the chief mineral products; amber also is occasionally found in the Tertiary sands. The climate of Volhynia, notwithstanding the influence of its marshes, is much milder than that of central Russia within the same latitudes. The vegetation on the southern slopes of the Avratynsk Hills begins to show something of a West-European character; oaks, maples, and limes prevail, while on the northern slope there are immense forests of Scotch fir. The forests cover more than one-third of the entire area, and it is reckoned that 2,500,000 acres yield timber for building purposes.

The population of Volhynia in 1884 was 2,096,475, of whom nearly four-fifths were Little Russians (from 70 to 91 per cent. in various districts); there were 30,000 White Russians and some 10,000 Great Russians. Next in importance to the Russians come the Jews, who numbered about 12 per cent. of the population. The Poles are variously estimated at from 120,000 to 170,000, but are certainly under 7 per cent. of the total population. The Germans number about 30,000. Agriculture cannot be said to flourish except on the Avratynsk plateau and its slopes, but is still the chief occupation, and more than one-third of the area is under crops. The fertile soil of the south produces a surplusage of corn, which is either used in distilleries or exported; the average crops from 1883 to 1885 were 1,606,000 quarters of rye, 550,000 of wheat, 1,145,000 of oats, 394,000 of barley, and 1,032,000 of potatoes. Hay is exported, but cattle-breeding has been almost stationary since 1850. In 1883 there were 506,500 horses, 655,050 cattle, and 571,500 sheep. Wool is exported. Beet is largely grown for sugar (38,000 acres, producing 4,800,000 cwts., having been under this crop in 1885). The culture of tobacco is rapidly extending (7000 tobacco plantations yielding about 8000 cwts. of tobacco in 1885). In the Polyesie the principal occupations are connected with the export of timber and firewood, the preparation of pitch, tar, potash, and various wooden wares, and boat-building. The wild boar, bear, fox, and hare are hunted.

The manufactures in 1884 yielded 18,884,000 roubles, as against only 2,856,000 in 1860. The goods principally produced are sugar spirits, woollen cloth, paper, china, and metal wares. Wool, corn, hides, and tallow are partly manufactured within the government, and partly exported to Riga and Poland. Volhynia is traversed by a railway from Kieff *via* Berditcheff to Brest-Litovsk, with branches to Lublin and to Lemberg. The traffic by this line is considerable, and the Radziviloff custom-house, on the Austrian frontier, is one of the most important in Russia.

Volhynia is divided into twelve districts, the chief towns of which are Zhitomir (*q.v.*), which had 54,830 inhabitants in 1884, Dubno (7255), Kovel (13,980), Kremenets (10,560), Lutsk (13,770), Novgrad Volhynskiy (13,590), Ostrog (16,520), Ovrutch (6480), Radziviloff (7350), Rovno (7300), Staro-Konstantinoff (17,980), and Zaslavl (10,120).

Volhynia has been inhabited by Slavonians from a remote antiquity. In Nestor's *Annals* its people are mentioned under the name of Dulebs, and later in the 12th century they were known as Velhynians and Buzhans (dwellers on the Bug). From the 9th century the towns of Volhynia—Vladimir, Ovrutch, Lutsk, and Dubno—were ruled by descendants of Rurik, and the land of Volhynia remained independent until the 14th century, when it fell under Lithuania. In 1659 it was annexed to Poland, and so remained until 1795, when it was taken possession of by Russia.

VOLNEY, Constantin François Chassebœuf, Comte de (1757–1820), was born at Craon, on February 3, 1757, of a good but not noble family, and educated first at the neighbouring provincial towns of Ancenis and Angers, then at Paris. According to the common and curious habit of the time and country he was at first surnamed Boisgirais, but afterwards assumed the name of Volney. When he was about four and twenty he acquired some reputation by an essay on the chronology of Herodotus, and was introduced into literary and philosophical society. He then did what was at the time not common, common as it has become since. Having inherited a sum of money, he visited the East and spent some four years in Egypt and Syria, writing the history of his travels when he returned, and publishing it in 1787. He had not merely travelled but had learnt Arabic, and had studied the politics as well as the topography of the countries he visited. Of the former study he gave evidence the year before the Revolution by some *Considerations* on the war between Russia and Turkey. He was a member both of the States-General and of the Constituante, and distinguished himself as an ardent reformer. In 1791 appeared the book *Les Ruines*, by which he is known to a great many people who have never read it. It is a kind of essay on the philosophy of history written from the *philosophe* point of view, and of course containing some direct and much oblique manifestation of *philosophe* antipathy to religion. It is probable, however, that those who, after the lapse of a century, read it under the impression of the strong denunciations of it by some orthodox writers of its own and immediately succeeding times will be not a little surprised. The book, of which the full title is *Les Ruines, ou Méditation sur les Révolutions des Empires*, purports to contain the discourses of a traveller among the ruins of Palmyra with a very 18th-century genius. Volney was a good deal more than a mere author. He tried to put his politico-economic theories into practice in Corsica, where in 1792 he bought an estate and made an attempt to cultivate colonial produce. He was thrown into prison during the Jacobin triumph, but escaped the guillotine. He was some time professor of history at the newly-founded École Normale, lectured there, and published his lectures. Then he undertook a journey to the United States, the result of which took form in a book (chiefly geographical) published in 1803. Next year he republished and much enlarged his early essay on Herodotus. He was not a partisan of Napoleon, but, being a moderate man, a savant, and a Liberal, was impressed into service by the emperor, who made him a count and put him into the senate, of which he was one of the least servile members. The restoration in the same way recruited him against his will, and he became a peer of France. He was a member of the Institute and latterly of the Academy proper, and, besides his historical, political, and (as the 18th century understood philosophy) philosophical studies, was a philologist of some power. He died at Paris on April 25, 1820, and his complete works appeared soon afterwards in 8 volumes.

Volney has been called the last of the *philosophes*, and so, if date and eminence together be considered, he was. It may, as in many such cases, be doubted whether his identification with a powerful but one-sided movement was more of service than of disservice to him. No doubt it stimulated his work, but it also cramped and distorted it,—the curious and not wholly intelligible attitude of the whole school towards Christianity showing itself distinctly in him as a prejudicing and narrowing force. He was, however, an accurate observer, a thinker of acuteness and originality if not of great width or depth, and master of his pen in no ordinary degree. His style suffers from the general defects of 18th-century French prose, in being thin, colourless, and devoid of flavour despite its clearness and brilliancy. But it serves him as a most excellent vehicle both of description and of argument.

VOLO, a town and seaport of Greece, on the east coast of Thessaly, at the head of the gulf to which it gives its name. Volo lies just below the mouth of the little river Orchestus, near the west foot of Mount Pelion, on the southern verge of an undulating and extremely fertile plain, which stretches thence northwards beyond Larissa, and which is skirted on the east by the chain above which tower Pelion, Ossa, and Olympus. The town, which has a mixed population (1884) of 4000, comprises three distinct quarters:—the kastro, enclosed by walls and inhabited chiefly by Turks; the scala, or port, centre of the trade and shipping; and the squalid Græco-Jewish suburb, which stretches from near the kastro to the coast. Volo, which is regularly visited by the Austrian, French, and Greek steamers plying weekly between the Piræus and Constantinople, is the only outlet for the produce of northern Greece. The exports (tobacco, hides and skins, fruits, olive oil, raw silk and cocoons, &c.) were valued in 1886 at £31,000, while the imports (cereals, cotton goods, petroleum, sugar, hardware, &c.) amounted to £259,000.

The castle of Volo stands on or close to the site of Pagasæ, whence the gulf took the name of Sinus Pagasæus or Pagasicus, and which was one of the oldest places of which mention occurs in the legendary history of Greece. From this port the Argonautic expedition was said to have sailed, and it was already a flourishing place under the tyrant Jason, who from the neighbouring Pheræ ruled over all Thessaly. Two miles farther south stand the ruins of Demetrias, founded (290 B.C.) by Demetrius Poliorcetes, and for some time a favourite residence of the Macedonian kings. On the opposite side of the little inlet at the head of the gulf rises the hill of Episcopi, on which stood the ancient city of Iolcus. Here Dr Lolling discovered in 1883 some underground sepulchral chambers resembling those of Mycenæ and Orchomenus.

VOLOGDA, a government of north-eastern Russia, having Archangel on the N., Tobolsk on the E., Perm, Vyatka, Kostroma, and Yaroslavl on the S., Novgorod and Olonetz on the W. This immense government, which comprises an area of 155,500 square miles, stretches in a north-easterly direction for 800 miles, from Novgorod to the Urals, including the broad depression drained by the Sukhona from the S.W. and the Vytchegda from the N.E., head-waters of the Dwina. From the basin of the Volga it is separated by a flat, swampy, and wooded swelling, where the heads of tributaries belonging to both Arctic and Caspian drainage-areas are closely intermingled. The eastern boundary of Vologda follows the main water-parting of the Urals, which has but few points over 3000 feet; wide *parmas*, or woody plateaus, fill up the space between the main Urals and the southern spurs of the Timansk Mountains, in the upper basin of the Petchora, and it is above the parmas—especially over those which are nearest to the Urals proper—that the highest summits of the Urals rise in the form of dome-shaped mountains (Tellpöss, 5540 feet above sea-level; Hoste-piär, 4955 feet;

Idjed-kashem, 4225 feet). The Timansk Mountains are a swampy plateau, where the rivers flowing either to the Dwina or to the Petchora take their rise in common marshes; so that on the Myťva portage boats have to be dragged only a distance of three miles through marshy forests to be transported from one system to the other.

Permian sandstones and cupriferous slates cover most of the territory; only a few patches of Jurassic clays overlie them; while in the east, in the Ural *parmas*, coal-bearing Carboniferous, Devonian, and Silurian slates and limestones appear, covering the crystalline slates of the main ridge. Vast layers of boulder clay and Lacustrine deposits cover the whole. Rock-salt and salt springs, iron ore, millstones, and grindstones are the chief mineral products; but mining is in its infancy.

Vologda is profusely watered; as many as 4800 rivers and streams have been counted on its maps. The Sukhona, which rises in the south-west and flows north-east past Vologda, Totma, and Velikiy Ustyug, is navigable for 375 miles. After its junction with the Yug (390 miles long), which comes from the south, it becomes the Dwina, which flows north-west, and receives the Vytchegda, another great river, 740 miles long and navigable for 570 miles, which, however, waters a nearly uninhabited region. The Luza, a tributary of the Yug, is also navigated for more than 250 miles. The Petchora, which flows through eastern Vologda, is an artery for the export of corn and the import of fish in the Petchora region, otherwise difficult of access. The Pinega, the Mezeñ, and the Vaga, all belonging to the Arctic basin, rise in northern Vologda. In the south-west the Sukhona is connected by means of Lake Kubenskoye and the canal of Alexander of Würtemberg with the upper Volga. Numberless smaller lakes occur, and marshes cover a considerable part of the surface.

The climate is severe, the average yearly temperature being 36° F. at Vologda (Jan., 10°·7; July, 63°·5) and 32°·5 at Ust-Sysolsk (Jan., 4°·8; July, 61°·7).

The flora and the physical aspects present a great variety of characters as the traveller moves north-east down the Sukhona and up the Vytchegda, towards the *parmas* of the Petchora. In the south-west the forests are cleared, and the dry slopes of the hills are covered with fields and meadows; the population is relatively dense, and nearly one-quarter of the area is under crops. There is a surplus of grain, which is used for distilleries; and apples are extensively cultivated. The flora is middle-Russian. Farther to the north-east the climate grows more severe; but still, until the Dwina is reached, corn succeeds well, and there is no lack of excellent meadows on the river-terraces. Flax is cultivated for export; but only 4 per cent. of the area is tilled, the remainder being covered with thick fir forests, with occasional woods of deciduous trees (birch, aspen, elder). At about the 46th degree of east longitude the larch appears and soon supersedes the fir. Several plants unknown in western Russia make their appearance (*Silene tartarica*, *Anthyllus vulneraria*, *Euphorbia palustris*, *Filago arvensis*, *Lycopodium complanatum*, *Sanguisorba officinalis*). The *Veratrum* is especially characteristic: it sometimes encroaches on the meadows to such an extent as to compel their abandonment. The region of the upper Mezeñ (the Udora) again has a distinctive character. The winter is so protracted, and the snowfall so copious, that the Zyrians are sometimes compelled to clear away the snow from their barley-fields. But the summer is so hot (a mean of 54° for the three summer months) that barley ripens within forty days after being sown. The Timansk plateaus are a marked boundary for the middle-Russian flora. Those to the east of them are uninhabitable; even on the banks of the rivers the climate is so severe, especially on account of the icy northern winds, that rye and barley are mostly grown only in orchards. The whole is covered with quite impenetrable forests, growing on a soil permeated with water. Mosquitoes swarm in the forests; birds are rare. The Siberian cedar begins, and the lime-tree disappears. Fir, cedar, pine, and larch chiefly compose the forests, with birch and aspen on their outskirts. Hunting is the chief occupation of the Zyrian inhabitants.

The population (1,172, 250 in 1883 as against 960,850 in 1861), consists chiefly of Great Russians (88 per cent.), and Zyrians (12 per cent.; only 7 per cent. according to Rittich). The Zyrians —a Finnish stem akin to the Permians—constitute the bulk of the population on the Ural slopes. They formerly inhabited the Kama and Vyatka basins, and call themselves Komi-yurt, or Komi-yas, and in the 14th century the Russians hardly distinguished them from the Permians; but they were compelled to migrate northwards into the basins of the Dwina and Petchora, and even across the Urals, by the religious fanaticism of the earlier Christian missionaries. A portion of them now live in Archangel (about 15,000), and their aggregate numbers are estimated at from 100,000 to 120,000, but the figures are very uncertain, as they are often hardly distinguishable from the Russians, whose religion and habits they have assumed. They differ widely from the western Finns in having dark eyes and hair; their honesty is proverbial, as also is their industry. They grow corn amidst the forests, after having patiently cleared them, and rear cattle, but are pre-eminently hunters. Their "artels," guided by a primitive compass, penetrate hundreds of miles into the virgin forests, and bring in vast quantities of squirrel furs and feathered game; they fell timber for export, and gather cedar-nuts, but in doing so are rapidly destroying the cedar-tree.

The chief occupation of the Russians is agriculture, and the average crops of 1883 to 1885 were rye, 785,000 quarters; barley, 926,000; oats, 925,000; other grains, 197,000; and potatoes, 107,000 quarters. In 1883 they had 229,500 horses, 520,200 cattle, and 392,900 sheep. They also fell timber, prepare tar, pitch, and potash, and manufacture wooden utensils. In the south-west they pursue a variety of domestic trades (spinning, weaving, sewing of plain cloth, &c.). The manufacturing industry is represented by a few ironworks, distilleries, paper-mills, and a variety of small manufactures; their aggregate production was only £274,500 in 1884. Salt was raised in 1881–84 to the average amount of 65,000 cwts. Flax, linen cloth, linseed, butter, tar, pitch, timber, and furs are the main items of export, the chief centres for trade being Vologda, Verkhovajsk, and Ustyug.

Vologda is divided into ten districts, the chief towns (with populations in 1881) being VOLOGDA (17,025), Gryazovets (2225), Kadnikoff (1520), Nikolsk (1880), Solvytchegodsk (1320), Totma (3380), Ustyug Velikiy (7980), Ust-Sysolsk (4100), Velsk (1410), and Yarensk (1250). (P. A. K.)

VOLOGDA, capital of the above government, is situated in its south-western corner, 302 miles to the north-east of Moscow, with which it is connected by rail *via* Yarosťavl. It is an old town, having many relics of the past in its churches, including one which dates from the 12th century, and the cathedral founded in 1565. The educational institutions are in a better state than in many other provincial towns. Vologda, though a place of only 17,025 inhabitants in 1881, is a considerable commercial centre,—flax, linseed, oats, hemp, butter, and eggs being bought to a large amount in the neighbouring districts and in Vyatka, and exported both to St Petersburg and Archangel.

Vologda existed as a place of commerce as early as the 12th century. It was a colony of Novgorod, and, owing to its advantageous position and the enterprise of the Novgorod merchants, it grew to be a populous city. It carried on a brisk trade in flax, tallow, and furs, which were sent in from Ustyug Velikiy,—another important colony of Novgorod; while the Byelo-ozero merchants brought to Vologda and Ustyug corn, leather, and various manufactured goods to be bartered against furs, or to be shipped to Kloťmogory, at the mouth of the Dwina. In 1273 it was plundered by the prince of Tver in alliance with the Tartars, but soon recovered. Moscow disputed its possession with Novgorod until the 15th century; the Moscow princes intrigued to find support amidst the poorer inhabitants against the richer Novgorod merchants, and four successive times Vologda had to fight against its metropolis. It was definitely annexed to Moscow in 1447. When Archangel was founded, and opened for foreign trade in 1553, Vologda became the chief depôt for goods exported through that channel. They were brought on sledges from Moscow, Yarosťavl, and Kostroma; and special *yams*, or post stations, were maintained to connect Vologda with Moscow. Many foreigners lived at Vologda; Fletcher, the British envoy, stayed there, and the first Russian envoy to Britain came originally from Vologda. Polish bands plundered it in 1613, and the plague of 1648 devastated it; but it maintained its commercial importance until the foundation of St Petersburg, when Russian foreign trade took another channel.

VOLSCI. See ITALY, vol. xiii. p. 445, and ROME, vol. xx. p. 739–741.

VOLSK, or VOLJSK, a district town of Russia, in the government of Saratoff, and 90 miles to the north-east of that town, on the right bank of the Volga, was a century ago but a small village (Maťykovo); recently, however it has grown to be one of the important towns on the lower Volga, and its population has rapidly increased from 23,500 in 1860 to 36,315 in 1885. It is built in a narrow valley between chalk cliffs, and has a large cathedral and a market; it is surrounded by gardens, the produce of which is exported to Nijni-Novgorod—gardening being also a distinctive feature of the wealthy and populous neighbouring villages.

VOLTA, Alessandro (1745–1827), was born at Como on February 18, 1745. In 1774 he was appointed professor of physics in the gymnasium of Como, and in 1777 he left his native town for the first time to travel through Switzerland, where he formed an intimate friendship with De Saussure. In 1779 a chair of physics was founded in Pavia, and Volta was chosen to occupy it. In 1782 he undertook a journey through France, Germany, Holland, and England, and became acquainted with nearly all the scientific celebrities of that day. In 1791 he received the Copley medal of the Royal Society. In 1801 Napoleon called him to Paris, to show his experiments on contact electricity, and a medal was struck in his honour. He was made a senator of the kingdom of Lombardy. In 1815 the emperor of Austria made him director of the philosophical faculty of Padua. In 1819 he retired, and settled down again in his native town. He died on March 5, 1827.

The first published paper of Volta (*De Vi Attractiva Ignis Electrici*) dates from 1769; it contains no new facts, but deserves our attention as showing us the knowledge with which Volta set out on his journey of discoveries, and the theoretical speculations which seem to have given him the first impulse to experimental work. Franklin, who was then justly considered the great authority on these matters, had endeavoured to explain electrical phenomena by the mutual repulsion of the particles of an electrical substance and the attraction between that electrical substance and ordinary matter. Volta tried to simplify the theory by assuming an action only between the electrical substance and matter, and he tells us that he explained his views in a letter to the Abbé Nollet when he was nineteen years old. The way in which he endeavoured to account for the phenomena of attraction and repulsion and the phenomena of the Leyden jar have no interest for us to-day, but that part of his paper in which he showed the application of his theory to the generation of electricity is of historical importance, for in it we can trace the germ of many future discoveries. He imagines all bodies in the natural state to contain electricity in such proportion that they are in electrical equilibrium. He believes that his experimental results obtained by rubbing metals with each other show this. But when bodies are brought into close contact, as, for instance, in friction, adopting the views of Boscovich, according to which attraction and repulsion alternate at small distances, he considers that the attractions of electricity and matter may alter and a new electrical equilibrium will establish itself. He asks the question whether during the progress of chemical action, such as solution, mixture of fluids, combustion, in which the particles of matter change their position, there is no disturbance of electrical equilibrium. He expresses his conviction that this is the case, and explains the experimental difficulties which prevent a proof, but expresses a hope that he will succeed in obtaining signs of electrical action during chemical operations. He shows how atmospheric electricity might be accounted for in accordance with these views.

The principal point of interest in his second paper (*Novus ac Simplicissimus Electricorum Tentaminum Apparatus*) is the attempt to explain electrical insulation by a repulsion between the insulating matter and electricity. The influence of Boscovich in this attempt to explain everything by forces and centres of force is here apparent. Theory thus seems to have given Volta the first impulse to his electrical inquiries; but as he went on with his experimental work the firm establishment of facts took the first place in his mind, and after the first two papers we find hardly anything speculative in his writings.

On June 10, 1775, Volta announced the construction of the electrophorus in a letter to Priestley, asking him, as the historian of electricity, how far the discovery was new. The remainder of the year seems to have been taken up with improvements in the mechanical construction of the apparatus. A letter to De Saussure in 1778 treats of the electrostatic capacity of conductors. Although we now know that Cavendish had treated the same subject in a much more complete way, the researches of Cavendish have only recently been published, and Volta's experiments are a great advance on anything that had been published at the time. The construction of the condenser, and its applications to the study of electrical phenomena, were first published in the *Philosophical Transactions* (1782). By means of the delicate apparatus at his disposal he returned to the ideas announced in his first paper, and tried to discover signs of electricity during the processes of evaporation and ebullition, and during changes of temperature; after repeated failure he at last believed himself to have succeeded in obtaining electrical effects during the evaporation of water. The first successful experiments were made in Paris in the presence of Lavoisier and Laplace. We know now that evaporation by itself does not cause a difference in electric potential, and that Volta's effect was due to friction of the vapour generated against the sides of the vessel; but this has only been established quite recently.

The results on electrical effects due to evaporation led Volta to the closer investigation of the phenomena of atmospheric electricity, a subject which seems always to have had a special attraction for him. Between 1788 and 1790 he wrote nine letters on *Meteorologia Elettrica* addressed to Lichtenberg. The first two letters treat of electrical measurements. For the pith ball electroscope he substitutes the straw electrometer, in which the angle of divergence of two electrified straws is measured. Different electrometers of various sensitiveness are carefully graduated and compared with each other. Nor is this all: Volta has never as yet received the credit of having constructed the first absolute electrometer, and for having compared his other instruments with it, so that it would be possible now to refer all his measurements to absolute units. His electrometer consisted of a balance, one pane of which was a flat round disk. Below this disk was placed a larger parallel plate, conducted away to earth, and stops were arranged so that the disk could not approach the plate nearer than 2 inches. In the unelectrified state the balance was in a state of equilibrium. When the disk is electrified it is attracted towards the plate but kept at its proper distance by the stops; weights are then added in the other plate of the balance until the disk is torn away from the stops.

The remaining letters addressed to Lichtenberg contain observations on atmospheric electricity and on the action of points and flames in discharging electricity. The reader cannot help feeling how very little more we now know about these matters than Volta did.

It was probably in 1790 that Galvani first made the observations which have rendered him celebrated. He was struck by the muscular contractions of a frog which had recently been killed and skinned, and was lying on a table near an electrical machine, which was accidentally set to work. In order to see whether he could obtain similar contraction from atmospheric electricity, he suspended the thigh of a frog by means of a hook from an iron railing, and found the contraction whenever the muscle touched the railing. He tried to account for the observation by assuming that the nerves and muscles of the animal body formed a kind of Leyden jar, which was discharged whenever an external circuit brought them into electrical contact. Volta at first agreed to this explanation, but his own experiments soon led him to change his opinion. It is very instructive to read the various letters and essays in which Volta describes his observations and his reasoning which gradually led him up to the construction of the electrical pile. His whole experimental training as well as the speculations of his early youth seemed to force him on in the right path, and in this work, as indeed in his whole career, none of the discoveries seems due to chance. The muscle of the frog soon appeared to him to be nothing but a very delicate electrometer, and he made use of it as such. The conductors he divided into two classes. Conductors of the first kind, to which carbon and the metals belong, he showed to become electrified by contact, but in such a way that equilibrium is established in each circuit, so that no current of electricity can be produced by any arrangement containing conductors of this class only. Conductors of the second kind are what we should now call electrolytes. An electric current is produced whenever a circuit is arranged between two conductors of the first kind and one of the second kind. It is impossible here to enter into the history of this now celebrated contact theory, but, although opinions may differ on the interpretation of some of the experiments, there is not much in Volta's writings on this subject which could be called incorrect even at the present day. Volta's electric pile was first described in a letter to Sir J. Banks, then president of the Royal Society. The letter is dated March 20, 1800, and it was read before the Society on June 26 of the same year. The pile consisted of a number of disks of tin and an equal number of disks of silver or copper. The zinc and tin plates are in contact, and each pair is separated by some porous matter which is kept moist. He describes a number of experimental results obtained with this pile, and finally shows that all the effects produced are the same as those which can be obtained from electrical machines, and that therefore "galvanism" and "electricity" are identical. Volta lived to see the remarkable development of his science at the hands of Sir Humphry Davy, Oersted, and Ampère, but he was no mathematician, and the subject grew beyond his powers. He recognized this with that frank honesty which is apparent in all his writings, and during the last twenty-five years of his life he published nothing on electrical subjects.

A complete history of Volta's writings ought to take in much which must be omitted here. His investigations on gas analysis, and his very interesting paper on the expansion of gases by heat, deserve, however, to be mentioned. He showed the causes which had led different experimenters to such inconsistent results, and established independently what is now known as the law of Charles.

(A. S.*)

VOLTAIRE, François Marie Arouet de (1694–1778), whose real name was François Marie Arouet simply, was born on the 21st of November 1694 at Paris, and was baptized the next day. His father was François Arouet, a notary; his mother was Marie Marguerite Daumart (sometimes, but less correctly, spelt D'Aumard, apparently because her family was noble). Both father and mother were of Poitevin extraction, but the Arouets had been for two generations established in Paris, the grandfather being a prosperous tradesman, and the father, as has been said, a still more prosperous notary. The Arouet family are heard of in Poitou as far back as the early 16th century, and appear to have always belonged to the yeoman-tradesman class. Their special home was the town of St Loup. Voltaire was the fifth child of his parents—twin boys (of whom one survived), a girl, Marguerite Catherine, and another boy who died young, having preceded him. Not very much is known of the mother, who died when Voltaire himself was but seven years old. She seems, however, to have had delicate health, and she pretty certainly was the chief cause of Voltaire's early introduction to good society, the Abbé de Châteauneuf (his sponsor in more ways than one) having been her friend. The father appears to have been somewhat peremptory in temper, but neither inhospitable nor tyrannical. Marguerite Arouet, of whom her younger brother was very fond, married early; the elder brother Armand was a strong Jansenist, and there never was any kind of sympathy between him and François.

Voltaire appears to have received no very regular education till he was ten years old; but the Abbé de Châteauneuf instructed him pretty early in belles lettres and deism, and he showed when quite a child the unsurpassed faculty for facile verse-making which always distinguished him, and to which the literary tastes and models of the time lent themselves with especial readiness. But at the age just mentioned he was sent to the Collége Louis-le-Grand, which was under the management of the Jesuits. This was in 1704. He remained there till 1711. It was his whim, as part of his general liberalism, to depreciate the education he received; but it seems to have been a very sound and good education, which beyond all doubt formed the basis of his extraordinarily wide, though never extraordinarily accurate, collection of knowledge subsequently, and (a more important thing still) disciplined and exercised his literary faculty and judgment. Nor can there be much doubt that the great attention bestowed on acting—the Jesuits kept up the Renaissance practice of turning schools into theatres for the performance of plays both in Latin and in the vernacular—had much to do with Voltaire's lifelong devotion to the stage. It must have been in his very earliest school years that the celebrated presentation of him by his godfather to Ninon de Lenclos took place, for Ninon died in 1705. She left him two thousand livres "to buy books with." Voltaire's school experience appears to have been much more like that of English schoolboys than like the dreary imprisonment of which in later days Frenchmen have generally complained. He worked fairly, played fairly, lived comfortably, made good and lasting friends. Some curious traits are recorded of this life—one being that in the terrible famine year of Malplaquet a hundred francs a year were added to the usual boarding expenses, and yet the boys had to eat *pain bis*.

His troubles began when, in August 1711, at the age of 17, he came home, and the usual battle began between a son who desired no profession but literature and a father who, in those days not quite unreasonably, refused to consider literature a profession at all. For a time Voltaire submitted, and read law at least nominally, doing quite other things besides or instead of that study. The Abbé de Châteauneuf died before his godson left school, but he had already introduced him to the famous coterie of the Temple, of which the grand prior Vendôme was the head, and the poets Chaulieu and La Fare the chief literary stars, and which chiefly existed for purposes of sometimes elegant and sometimes by no means elegant dissipation. It does not appear that Voltaire got into any great scrapes, and the anecdotes recorded of this wild oats time of his are harmless enough. But his father naturally prognosticated little good to him from such society, and tried to break him off from it, by sending him first to Caen and then in the suite of the Marquis de Châteauneuf, the abbé's brother, to the Hague. Here, however, he got into what, in the paternal eyes at least, was a far worse scrape than staying out at night or wasting his substance on the purchase of coaches and horses. He met a certain Olympe Dunoyer ("Pimpette"), a girl apparently of respectable character and not bad connexions, but a Protestant, penniless, and daughter of a literary lady whose literary reputation was not spotless. The mother discouraged the affair, and, though Voltaire, with an early display of his afterwards famous cunning, tried to avail himself of the mania for proselytizing which then distinguished France, his father would not hear of the match, and stopped the whole affair by procuring a *lettre de cachet*, which, however, he did not use. Voltaire, who had been sent home, submitted, and for a time pretended to work in a Parisian lawyer's office. But he again manifested a faculty for getting into trouble,—this time in the still more dangerous way of writing libellous poems,—so that his father was glad to send him to stay for nearly a year (1714–1715) with Louis de Caumartin, Marquis de St Ange, in the country. Here he was still supposed to study law, but as usual really devoted himself in part to literary essays, in part to storing up that immense treasure of gossiping history which was afterwards one of his most unique possessions. Almost exactly at the time of the death of Louis XIV. he returned to Paris, to fall once more into literary and Templar society, and to make the tragedy of *Œdipe*, which he had already written, privately known. He was now introduced to a less questionable and even more distinguished coterie than Vendôme's, to the famous "court of Sceaux," the circle of the beautiful and ambitious Duchesse du Maine. It seems, though it is not certainly known, that Voltaire lent himself to the duchess's frantic hatred of the regent Orleans, and helped to compose lampoons on that prince. At any rate, in May 1716 he was exiled, first to Tulle, then to Sully. He was allowed to return, but again fell under suspicion of having been concerned in the composition of two violent libels,—one in Latin and one in French,—called from their first words the *Puero Regnante* and the *J'ai vu*, was inveigled by a spy named Beauregard into a real or burlesque confession, and on May 16, 1717, was arrested and sent to the Bastille. He remained there for eleven months, recast *Œdipe*, began the *Henriade*, and determined to alter his name. Ever after his exit from the Bastille in April 1718 he was known as Arouet de Voltaire, or simply Voltaire, though legally he never abandoned his patronymic. The origin of the famous name has been much debated, and attempts have been made to show that it actually existed in the Daumart pedigree or in some territorial designation. The balance of opinion has, however, always inclined to the hypothesis of an anagram on the name "Arouet le jeune," or "Arouet l. j.," *u* being changed to *v* and *j* to *i* according to the ordinary rules of the game. If it be so, the much despised art of the anagrammatist has the triumph of producing one of the dozen or score most famous names in literary history.

A further "exile" at Châtenay and elsewhere succeeded

the imprisonment, and though Voltaire was admitted to an audience by the regent and treated graciously it is clear that he was not trusted, and the inconveniences he had suffered for a time induced even his incorrigibly mischievous nature to keep quiet. *Œdipe* was acted at the Théâtre Français on 18th November of the year of release, and was very well received, a not dissimilar rivalry between parties to that which not long before had helped Addison's *Cato* assisting its success. It had a run of forty-five nights, was acted at court, and brought the author not a little money in profits and presents, besides a gold medal from the regent. Voltaire seems to have begun with these gains his long and (among authors) almost unique series of successful financial speculations. But adversity had by no means done with him. In the spring of next year the production of Lagrange-Chancel's libels, entitled the *Philippiques*, again brought suspicion on him. He was informally exiled, and spent much time with Marshal Villars, again increasing his store of "reminiscences." He returned to Paris in the winter, and his second play, *Artémire*, was produced in February 1720. It was a failure, and though it was recast with some success Voltaire never published it as a whole, and used parts of it up in other work. He again spent much of his time with Villars, listening to the marshal's stories and making harmless love to the duchess. In December 1721 his father died, leaving him property (rather more than four thousand livres a year), which was soon increased by a pension of half the amount from the regent. In return for this, or in hopes of more, he offered himself as a spy—or at anyrate as a secret diplomatist—to Dubois. He had, however, an awkward brush with a fellow-servant in this honourable kind of work, for, meeting his old enemy Beauregard in one of the minister's rooms and making an offensive remark, he was waylaid by Beauregard some time after in a less privileged place and soundly beaten. This unpleasant proceeding was only a preliminary to Voltaire's second and most important experience of "Black Will with a cudgel," to use Rochester's phrase as to the proper mode of dealing with troublesome men of letters. His visiting espionage, as unkind critics put it—his secret diplomatic mission, as he would have liked to have it put himself—began in the summer of 1722, and he set out for it *en bonne fortune*,—in company, that is to say, with a certain Madame de Rupelmonde, to whom he as usual made love, though it may perhaps be platonic love only (for Voltaire was not fortunate in this way), taught deism, and served as an amusing travelling companion. He stayed at Cambray for some time, where European diplomatists were still in full session, journeyed to Brussels, where he met and quarrelled with Jean Baptiste Rousseau, went on to the Hague, and then returned. It does not seem that he did anything diplomatically important, but from that day to this French Governments have had an amiable weakness for paying the travelling expenses of men of letters who feel inclined to see the world. The *Henriade* had got on considerably during the journey, and, according to his lifelong habit, the poet, with the help of his friend Thiériot and others, had been "working the oracle" of puffery after a fashion not particularly creditable, but perhaps recommended by a knowledge of mankind. During the late autumn and winter of 1722-23 he abode chiefly in Paris, taking a kind of lodging in the town house of M. de Bernières, a nobleman of Rouen, and endeavouring to procure a "privilege" for his poem. In this he was disappointed, but he had the work printed at Rouen nevertheless, and spent the summer of 1723 revising it. In November he caught smallpox and was very seriously ill, so that the book was not given to the world till the spring of 1724 (and then of course, as it had no privilege, appeared privately). Almost at the same time, March 4, his third tragedy, *Mariamne*, appeared, at first with great success, but before the curtain fell complete damnation fell on it. The regent had died shortly before, not to Voltaire's advantage; for though that rather hardly treated person had little reason to love the poet he had been a generous patron to him. Voltaire had made, however, a useful friend in another *grand seigneur*, as profligate and nearly as intelligent, the duke of Richelieu, and with him he passed 1724 and the next year chiefly, recasting *Mariamne* (which was now successful), writing the comedy of *L'Indiscret*, and courting the queen, the ministers, the favourites, and everybody who seemed worth courting. The end of 1725 brought a disastrous close to this period of his life. He was insulted in one way or another by the Chevalier de Rohan, replied with his usual sharpness of tongue, and shortly afterwards, when dining at the Hôtel Sully, was called out and bastinadoed by the chevalier's hirelings, Rohan himself looking on. Nobody would take his part, and at last he challenged Rohan, who accepted the challenge, but on the morning appointed for the duel Voltaire was arrested and sent for the second time to the Bastille. This was nearly three months after the outrage. Voltaire had been ostentatiously taking lessons in fencing meanwhile, and it requires some effort to sympathize with him in all the circumstances. He was only kept in confinement a fortnight, and was then packed off to England in accordance with his own request. In the then state of social matters in France this was probably the best end of the matter, and nobody comes out of it so badly as the duke of Sully, who, by the code of gentlemen of all ages, was clearly bound to take the part of the guest who had been trepanned from his own table, and did not take it. But here also Voltaire took the best means of putting himself in the wrong and his enemies in the right by cutting Maximilien de Béthune's name out of the *Henriade*.

No competent judges have ever mistaken the importance of Voltaire's visit to England, and the influence it exercised on his future career. In the first place, the ridiculous and discreditable incident of the beating had time to blow over; in the second (as a previous experience of J. B. Rousseau's, which a good man of business like Voltaire was not likely to forget, had shown), England was a very favourable place for Frenchmen of note to pick up guineas; in the third, and most important of all, his contact with a people then far more different in every conceivable way from their neighbours than any two peoples of Europe are different now, acted as a sovereign tonic and stimulant on his intellect and literary faculty. Before the English visit Voltaire had been an elegant trifler, an adept in the forms of literature popular in French society, a sort of superior Dorat or Bouffiers of earlier growth. He returned from that visit one of the foremost literary men in Europe, with views, if not profound or accurate, yet wide and acute on all *les grands sujets*, and with a solid stock of money to make him independent of those great men of his own country who had taught him how dearly their patronage was to be purchased. The visit lasted about three years, from 1726 to 1729; and, as if to make the visitor's luck certain, George I. died and George II. succeeded soon after his arrival. The new king was not fond of "boetry," but Queen Caroline was, and the international jealousy (which, though there was no actual war, was never stronger than then) was pleased at the thought of welcoming a distinguished exile from French illiberality. The Walpoles, Bubb Dodington, Bolingbroke especially, Sir Everard Falkener, a merchant and a diplomatist, Young, Congreve, Sarah Marlborough, Pope, were among his English friends. He at least tried to appreciate Shakespeare, and at least attained to the length of now copying and now reviling him. He was much struck (and it would appear not unfrequently hoaxed) by English manners, was deeply penetrated by English toleration for personal freethought and eccentricity, and (though the amount is very variously stated) certainly gained some thousands of pounds from an authorized English edition of the *Henriade* dedicated to the queen. But he visited Paris now and then, without permission (at other times he obtained permission to go without visiting it), and his mind, like the mind of every exiled Frenchman, was always set thereon. He at last gained full licence to return in the spring of 1729.

He was full of literary projects, and immediately after his return he is said to have increased his fortune immensely by a lucky lottery speculation. The *Henriade* was at last licensed in France; *Brutus*, a play which he had printed in England, was accepted for performance, but kept back for a time by the author; and he began the celebrated poem of the *Pucelle*, the amusement and the torment of great part of his life. But he had great difficulties with two of his chief works which were ready to appear, and did after a fashion appear in 1731,—to wit, *Charles XII.* and the *Lettres sur les Anglais.* With both he took all imaginable pains to avoid offending the censorship; for Voltaire had, more than any other man who ever lived, the ability and the willingness to stoop to conquer. At the end of 1730 *Brutus* did actually get acted with not inconsiderable but gradually decreasing success. Then in the spring of the next year he went to Rouen to get *Charles XII.* surreptitiously printed, which he accomplished. In all this nomadic life of his, which had now reached more than "the middle of the way," he had never had a house of his own, nor had he now, though for a rather unusually long time he was half-guest half-boarder with the Comtesse de Fontaine-Martel. In 1732 another tragedy, *Ériphile*, appeared with the same kind of halting success which had distinguished the appearance of its elder sisters since *Œdipe*. But at last, on August 13, 1732, he produced *Zaïre*, the best (with *Mérope*) of all his plays, and one of the ten or twelve best plays of the whole French classical school. Its motive was borrowed to some extent from *Othello*, but that matters little. In the following winter the death of his hostess turned him out of a comfortable abode. He still, however, did not set up housekeeping, but took lodgings with an agent of his, one Demoulin, in an out-of-the-way part of Paris, and was, for some time at least, as much occupied with contracts, speculation, and all sorts of means of gaining money as with literature.

It was in the middle of this period, however, in 1733, that two important books, the *Lettres Philosophiques sur les Anglais* and the *Temple du Goût* appeared. Both were likely to make bad blood, for the latter was, under the mask of easy verse, a satire on contemporary French literature, especially on J. B. Rousseau, and the former was, in the guise of a criticism or rather panegyric of English ways, an attack on everything established in the church and state of France. It was published with certain "remarks" on Pascal, more offensive to orthodoxy than itself, and no mercy was shown to it. The book was condemned (June 10, 1734), the copies seized and burnt, a warrant issued against the author, and his dwelling searched. He himself, as usual henceforward, took care to be out of the way of danger, and was safe in the independent duchy of Lorraine with Madame du Châtelet, not having taken, but very shortly about to take, up his abode with that "respectable Emily" at her famous chateau of Cirey.

If the English visit may be regarded as having finished Voltaire's education, the Cirey residence may be justly said to be the first stage of his literary manhood. He had written important and characteristic work before; but he had always been in a kind of literary *Wanderjahre.* He now obtained a settled home for many years, and, taught by his numerous brushes with the authorities, he began and successfully carried out that system of keeping out of personal harm's way, and of at once denying any awkward responsibility, which made him for nearly half a century at once the chief and the most prosperous of European heretics in regard to all established ideas. He was in no great or immediate danger on this particular occasion, especially as he was perfectly ready to deny his authorship, and he travelled about for some time, visiting the camp at Philippsburg, where some not very important fighting, notable only for being the last campaign of Eugene, was going on. It was not till the summer of 1734 that Cirey, a half-dismantled country house on the borders of Champagne and Lorraine, was fitted up with Voltaire's money and became the headquarters of himself, of his hostess, and now and then of her accommodating husband. Many pictures of the life here, some of them not a little malicious, survive. It was not entirely a bed of roses, for the "respectable Emily's" temper was violent, and after a time she sought lovers who were not so much *des cérébraux* as Voltaire. But it provided him with a safe and comfortable retreat and with something of the same kind of convenience for literary work which matrimony provides for more commonplace or more scrupulous men of letters. In March 1735 the ban was formally taken off him, and he was at liberty to return to Paris, a liberty of which he availed himself but sparingly now and ever afterwards, finding himself better away from the capital. At Cirey he wrote indefatigably and did not neglect business. The principal literary results of his early years here were the play of *Alzire* (1736) and a long treatise on the Newtonian system which he and Madame du Châtelet—an expert mathematician—wrote together. But as usual Voltaire's extraordinary literary industry was rather shown in a vast amount of fugitive writings than in substantive works, though for the whole space of his Cirey residence he was engaged in writing, adding to, and altering the *Pucelle.* In the very first days of his sojourn he had thus written a pamphlet with the imposing title of "Treatise on Metaphysics." Of metaphysics proper Voltaire neither now nor at any other time understood anything, and the subject, like every other, merely served him as a pretext for laughing at religion with the usual reservation of a tolerably affirmative deism. In March 1736 one of the least creditable events of his life, yet still not wholly discreditable, happened. An avowal of the *English Letters* was got out of him privately and then used publicly as an engine of extortion. In the same year he received his first letter from Frederick of Prussia, then crown prince only. He was soon again in trouble, this time for the poem of the *Mondain*, and he at once crossed the frontier and then made for Brussels. He spent about three months in the Low Countries, and in March 1737 returned to Cirey, and continued writing, making experiments in physics (he had at this time a large laboratory), and busying himself not a little with iron-founding, the chief industry of the district. The best known accounts of Cirey life, those of Madame de Grafigny, date from the winter of 1738–39; they are, as has been said, somewhat spiteful but very amusing, depicting the constant quarrels between Madame du Châtelet and Voltaire, his intense suffering under criticism, his constant dread of the surreptitious publication of the *Pucelle* (which nevertheless he could not keep his hands from writing or his tongue from reciting to his visitors), and so forth. The chief and most galling of his critics at this time was the Abbé Desfontaines, and the chief of Desfontaines's attacks was entitled *La Voltairomanie*, in reply to a libel of Voltaire's called *Le Préservatif.* Both combatants had, according to the absurd habit of the time, to disown their works, Desfontaines's disavowal being formal and procured by the exertion of all Voltaire's own influence both at home and abroad. For he had as little notion of tolerance towards others as of dignity in himself. In April 1739 a journey was made to Brussels, to Paris, and then again to Brussels, which was the headquarters for a considerable time owing to some law affairs of the Du Châtelets. Frederick, now king of Prussia, made not a few efforts to get Voltaire away from Madame du Châtelet, but unsuccessfully, and the king earned the lady's cordial hatred by persistently refusing or omitting to invite her. At last, in September 1740, master and pupil met for the first time at Cleves, an interview followed three months later by a longer visit at Remusberg. Brussels was again the headquarters in 1741, by which time Voltaire had finished the best and the second or third best of his plays, *Mérope* and *Mahomet. Mahomet* was played first in the year and at the place just mentioned; it did not appear in Paris till August next year, and *Mérope* not till 1743. This last was and deserved to be the most successful of its author's whole theatre. It was in this same year that he received the singular diplomatic mission to Frederick which nobody seems to have taken seriously, and after his return the oscillation between Brussels, Cirey, and Paris was resumed, in a manner rather difficult to record in a short biography. During these years Voltaire's production of miscellanies was as constant as usual, but his time allotted to serious work was chiefly given to history and much of the *Essai sur les Mœurs* and the *Siècle de Louis XIV.* was now composed. He also returned, not too well-advisedly, to the business of courtiership, which he had given up since the death of the regent. He was much employed, owing to Richelieu's influence, in the fêtes of the dauphin's marriage, and was rewarded on New Year's day 1745 by the appointment to the post of historiographer-royal, once jointly held by Racine and Boileau. The situation itself and its accompanying privileges were what Voltaire chiefly aimed at, but there was a salary of two thousand livres attached, and he had the year before come in for three times as much by the death of his brother. In the same year he wrote a poem on Fontenoy, he received medals from the pope, and dedicated *Mahomet* to him, and he wrote court *divertissements* and other things to admiration. But he was not a thoroughly skilful courtier, and one of the best known of Voltairiana is the contempt or at least silence with which Louis XV.—a sensualist but no fool—received the maladroit and almost insolent inquiry *Trajan est-il content?* addressed in his hearing to Richelieu at the close of a piece in which the emperor had appeared with a transparent reference to the king. All this assentation had at least one effect. He who had been for years admittedly the first writer in France had been repeatedly passed over in elections to the Academy. He was at last elected in the spring of 1746, and received on May 9. Then the tide began to turn. His favour at court had naturally exasperated his enemies; it had not secured him any real friends, and even a gentlemanship of the chamber was no solid benefit, except from the money point of view. He did not indeed hold it very long, but was permitted to sell it for a large sum, retaining the rank and privileges. He had various proofs of the instability of his hold on the king during 1747 and in 1748. He once lay in hiding for two months at Sceaux, and afterwards for a time lived chiefly at Lunéville, where Madame du Châtelet had established herself at the court of King Stanislaus, where she carried on her flirtations with Saint Lambert, and where, in September 1749, she died, not in, but about four days after, childbirth.

The death of Madame du Châtelet is another turning point in the history of Voltaire. He was now not a young man—indeed he was fifty-five—but he had nearly thirty years more to live, and he had learnt much during what may be called his Cirey cohabitation. On the one hand, he had discovered that it was undesirable that a man should not have a household; on the other, he had discovered that it was still more undesirable that a man should put himself under illegitimate petticoat government. For some time, however, after Madame du Châtelet's death he was in a state of pitiable unsettlement. At first, after removing his goods from Cirey, he hired the greater part of the Châtelet town house and then the whole. He had some idea of settling down in Paris, and might perhaps have done so if mischief had not been the very breath of his nostrils. He could not bring himself to testify in any open and dangerous manner for what he thought to be the truth; he could not bring himself to refrain from attacking, by every artifice and covert enginery, what he thought to be falsehood. He went on writing tales like *Zadig.* He engaged in a foolish and undignified struggle with Crébillon *père* (not *fils*), a dramatist who, in part of one play, *Rhadamiste et Zénobie*, has struck a note of tragedy in the grand Cornelian strain, which Voltaire could never hope to echo, and who, in most of his other efforts, was and is mainly futile. He used the most extraordinary efforts to make himself more popular than he was, but he could not help being uncomfortable in a city where the court all but threatened, and where the city did more than all but laugh.

All this time Frederick of Prussia had been continuing his invitations, and the "respectable Emily" was no longer in the way. It does not appear that, at any rate at first, Frederick made any real difficulty as to money. Indeed he behaved on the whole very generously. Voltaire left Paris on the 15th June 1751, and reached Berlin on the 10th July.

This Berlin visit might itself be treated, without undue extension, at the length of the present article; but its circumstances may be presumed to be already more or less familiar to most English readers from the two great essays of Macaulay and Carlyle as well as from the *Frederick* of the latter. It is desirable, if not altogether necessary, to say that these two masters of English were not perhaps the best qualified to relate the story. Both were unjust to Voltaire, and Macaulay was unjust to Frederick as well. It is quite certain that at first the king behaved altogether like a king to his guest. He pressed him to remain; he gave him (the words are Voltaire's own) one of his orders, twenty thousand francs a year, and four thousand additional for his niece, Madame Denis, in case she would come and keep house for her uncle. But Voltaire's conduct was from the first Voltairian. He sent a letter, in which Madame Denis pleaded with him to return, to Frederick—an odd way of ingratiating his niece with that monarch. He insisted on the consent of his own king, which was given without delay and on very liberal terms, —Louis XV., if gossip is to be trusted, pointing out with considerable shrewdness that it was not his fault if Voltaire would put himself constantly in hot water, and still less his fault that there were so few men of letters in Prussia that it suited the king of Prussia to ask them to dinner, and so many in France that it was quite impossible for the king of France to do so. Frenchmen, always touchy on such a point, regarded Voltaire as something of a deserter; and he was not long before he bitterly repented his desertion, though his residence in Prussia actually lasted for nearly three years. It was quite impossible that Voltaire and Frederick should get on together for long. Voltaire was not humble enough to be a mere butt, as many of Frederick's led poets were; he was not enough of a gentleman to hold his own place with dignity and discretion; he was constantly jealous both of his equals in age and reputation, such as Maupertuis, and of his juniors and inferiors, such as Baculard D'Arnaud. He was greedy, restless, and in a way Bohemian. Frederick, though his love of teasing for teasing's sake has been exaggerated by Macaulay, was anything but amiable in disposition, was a martinet of the first water, had a sharp though one-sided idea of justice, and had not the slightest intention of allowing Voltaire to insult or to tyrannize over his other guests and servants. If he is to be blamed in this particular matter, the blame must be chiefly confined to his imprudence in inviting Voltaire at the beginning and to the brutality of his conduct at the end. Within Voltaire there was always a mischievous and ill-behaved child; and he was never more mischievous, more ill-behaved, and more childish than in these years. But, knowing as we do what he was, there is much excuse for him. He tried to get D'Arnaud exiled and succeeded. He got into a quite unnecessary quarrel with Lessing, the most distinguished, or at least the most gifted, German author of the day. He had not been in the country six months before he engaged in a discreditable, and in Prussia directly illegal, piece of financial gambling with Hirsch, the Dresden Jew. He had the extreme unwisdom and meanness to quarrel with this agent of his about money, and was at least accused of something like downright forgery—that is to say, of altering a paper signed by Hirsch after he had signed it. The king's very well justified disgust at this affair (which came to an open scandal before the tribunals) was so great that he was on the point of ordering Voltaire out of Prussia, and Darget the secretary had no small trouble in arranging the affair (February 1751). Then it was Voltaire's turn to be disgusted with an occupation he had undertaken himself—the occupation of "buckwashing" the king's French verses. However, he succeeded in finishing and printing the *Siècle de Louis XIV.*, while the *Dictionnaire Philosophique* is said to have been devised and begun at Potsdam. But Voltaire's restless temper was brewing up for another storm. In the early autumn of 1751 La Mettrie, one of the king's parasites, and a man of much more talent than is generally allowed, horrified Voltaire by telling him that the king had in conversation applied to him, Voltaire, a proverb about "sucking the orange and flinging away its skin;" and about the same time the dispute with Maupertuis, which had more than anything else to do with his exclusion from Prussia, came to a head. No one quite knows how it began, though it is probably enough to say that Maupertuis and Voltaire had been of old quasi-rivals in the favour of the "divine Émilie," that as president of the Berlin Academy Maupertuis was in a manner Voltaire's literary superior, that he was a man of rough and boorish manners, and that he is said at least to have refused his aid in the Hirsch affair. He also seems to have had something at least to do with a tedious and complicated squabble arising from the work of a certain La Beaumelle, a literary hack of the time, not without ability, who chose to visit Berlin and court Voltaire. The final rupture was provoked by Maupertuis himself, though indirectly, by a dispute into which he got with one König. The king took his president's part; Voltaire (unluckily for him, but with sufficient adroitness to make no open breach) took König's. But Maupertuis must needs write his *Letters*, and thereupon (1752) appeared one of Voltaire's most famous, though perhaps not one of his most read works, the *Diatribe du Docteur Akakia*. Even Voltaire did not venture to publish this lampoon on a great official of a prince so touchy as the king of Prussia without some permission, and if all tales are true he obtained this by another piece of something like forgery—getting the king to endorse a totally different pamphlet on its last leaf, and affixing that last leaf to *Akakia*. Of this Frederick was not aware; but he did get some wind of the *Diatribe* itself, sent for the author, heard it read to his own great amusement, and either actually burned the MS. or believed that it was burnt. In a few days printed copies appeared. Now Frederick did not like disobedience, but he still less liked being made a fool of, and he put Voltaire under arrest. But again the affair blew over, which is at least a proof that the king was not wanting in long-suffering. He believed that the edition of *Akakia* confiscated in Prussia was the only one. Alas! Voltaire, according to his usual fashion, had sent copies away; others had been printed abroad; and the thing was irrecoverable. Of course it could not be proved that he had ordered the printing, and all Frederick could do was to have the pamphlet burnt by the hangman. Things were now drawing to a crisis. One day Voltaire sent his orders, &c., back; the next Frederick returned them, but Voltaire had quite made up his mind to fly. A kind of reconciliation occurred in March, and after some days of good-fellowship Voltaire at last obtained the long-sought leave of absence and left Potsdam on the 26th of the month (1753). It was nearly three months afterwards that the famous, ludicrous, and brutal arrest was made at Frankfort, on the persons of himself and his niece, who had met him meanwhile. There was some faint excuse for Frederick's wrath. In the first place, after a plea of business in Paris, of the necessity of the waters of Plombières, and so forth, it was a little incongruous that the poet should linger at Leipsic. In the second place, in direct disregard of a promise given to Frederick, a supplement to *Akakia* appeared, more offensive than the main text, and was followed by a paper war of letters with Maupertuis. But the king cooked his spleen and bided his time. From Leipsic, after a month's stay, Voltaire moved to Gotha, and seemed once more in no hurry to go on, his excuse being the compilation of *Annals of the Empire*, asked of him by the duchess of Saxe-Weimar. Once more, on May 25, he moved on to Frankfort, and here the blow fell. Frankfort, nominally a free city, but with a Prussian resident who did very much what he pleased, was not like Gotha and Leipsic. An excuse was provided in the fact that the poet had a copy of some unpublished poems of Frederick's, and as soon as Voltaire arrived the thing was done, at first with courtesy enough. The resident, Freytag, was not a very wise person (though he probably did not, as Voltaire would have it, spell "poésie" "poéshie"); constant references to Frederick were necessary; and the affair was prolonged so that Madame Denis had time to join her uncle. At last Voltaire did the unwisest thing he could have done by trying to steal away. He was followed, arrested, his niece seized separately, and sent to join him in custody; and the two, with the secretary Collini, were kept close prisoners at an inn called the Goat. This situation lasted some time (a time, indeed, since the "œuvre de poéshie" was at once recovered, rather unintelligible except on the score of Freytag's folly), and was at last put an end to by the city authorities, who probably felt that they were not playing a very creditable part. Voltaire left Frankfort on July 7th, travelled safely to Mainz, and thence to Mannheim, Strasburg, and Colmar. The last-named place he reached (after a leisurely journey and many honours at the little courts just mentioned) at the beginning of October, and here he proposed to stay the winter, finish his *Annals of the Empire*, and look about him.

Voltaire's second stage was now over, and he was about to try what an Englishman would have tried long before—complete independence of hosts and patrons, mistresses and friends. Even now, however, in his sixtieth year, it required some more external pressure to induce him to take this apparently obvious step. He had been, in the first blush of his Frankfort disaster, refused, or at least not granted, permission even to enter France proper,—a rebuff probably due in about equal parts to a wish not to displease or disoblige Frederick, and a wish to punish Voltaire himself for selecting Prussia as a home. At Colmar he was not safe, especially when in January 1754 a pirated edition of the *Essai sur les Mœurs*, written long before, appeared. Permission to establish himself in France was now absolutely refused; and even Madame de Pompadour was powerless, if indeed she cared greatly to exert her power. Nor did an extremely offensive performance of Voltaire's—the solemn partaking of the eucharist at Colmar after due confession—at all mollify his enemies. His exclusion from France, however, was chiefly metaphorical, and really meant exclusion from Paris and its neighbourhood. In the summer he went to Plombières, and after returning to Colmar for some time journeyed in the beginning of winter to Lyons, and after a month there went, as it may almost be said, "home"—to a home which he had never yet visited, but which was, with slight changes of actual domicile, but with no change of neighbourhood, to shelter him for the rest of his life.

His first resting-place, Geneva, was reached in the middle of December; but Voltaire had no purpose of remaining in the city, and almost immediately bought a country house just outside the gates, to which he gave the name of Les Délices. This, the first house of his own which he can be said to have possessed, is still standing, though now absorbed in the suburbs. It was pretty, with fine views; but it had advantages of a non-æsthetic kind for its owner, of which he made no secret. He was here practically at the meeting-point of four distinct jurisdictions—Geneva, the canton Vaud, Sardinia, and France, while other cantons were within easy reach. Before finally settling in Ferney he bought other houses dotted about these territories, so as never to be without a refuge close at hand in case of sudden storms. At Les Délices he set up a considerable establishment, which his great wealth (obtained chiefly by speculation in the manner already more than once hinted at) made him able easily to afford. He kept open house for visitors; he had printers close at hand in Geneva; he fitted up a private theatre in which he could enjoy what was perhaps the greatest pleasure of his whole life—acting in a play of his own, stage-managed by himself. His residence at Geneva brought him into correspondence (at first quite amicable) with the most famous of her citizens, J. J. Rousseau. His *Orphelin de la Chine*, performed at Paris in 1755, was very well received; and the earthquake at Lisbon, which appalled other people, gave Voltaire an excellent opportunity for ridiculing the beliefs of the orthodox, first in verse (1756) and later in the (from a literary point of view) unsurpassable tale of *Candide* (1759). All was, however, not yet quite smooth with him. Geneva had a law expressly forbidding theatrical performances in any circumstances whatever. Voltaire, as has been said, had infringed this law already as far as private performances went, and he had thought of building a regular theatre, not indeed at Geneva but at Lausanne. In July 1755 a very polite and, as far as Voltaire was concerned, indirect resolution of the consistory declared that in consequence of these proceedings of the Sieur de Voltaire the pastors should notify their flocks to abstain, and that the chief syndic should be informed of the consistory's perfect confidence that the edicts would be carried out. Voltaire obeyed this hint as far as Les Délices was concerned, and consoled himself by having the performances in his Lausanne house. But he never was the man to take opposition to his wishes either quietly or without retaliation. He undoubtedly instigated D'Alembert to include a censure of the prohibition in his *Encyclopédie* article on "Geneva," a proceeding which provoked Rousseau's celebrated *Lettre à D'Alembert sur les Spectacles*. As for himself, even still restless, he looked about for a place where he could combine the social liberty of France with the political liberty of Geneva, and he found one. At the end of 1758 he bought the considerable property of Ferney, on the shore of the lake, about four miles from Geneva, and on French soil. At Les Délices (which he sold in 1765) he had become a householder on no small scale; at Ferney (which he increased by other purchases and leases) he became a complete country gentleman. He set about establishing himself handsomely in his new abode, and though he did not absolutely abandon his other houses he was henceforward known to all Europe as squire of Ferney, hardly less than as author of the *Henriade* and the *Pucelle*, of *Charles XII.* and *Akakia*.

From this time forward many of the most celebrated men of Europe visited him there, and large parts of his usual biographies are composed of extracts from their accounts of Ferney. His new occupations by no means quenched his literary activity, but on the contrary stimulated it. He did not make himself a slave to his visitors, but appeared only occasionally and reserved much time for work and for his immense correspondence, which had for a long time once more included Frederick, the two getting on very well when they were not in contact. Above all, he now, being comparatively secure in position, engaged much more strongly in public controversies, and, without wholly abandoning, resorted less to, his old labyrinthine tricks of disavowal, garbled publication, and private libel. The suppression of the *Encyclopédie*, to which he had been a considerable contributor, and whose conductors were his intimate friends, drew from him a shower of lampoons directed now at "l'infâme" (see *infra*) generally, now at literary victims, such as Le Franc de Pompignan (who had written one piece of verse so much better than anything serious of Voltaire's that he could not be forgiven), or Palissot (who had boldly gibbeted most of the *philosophes* in his play of that name, but had not included Voltaire), now at Fréron, an excellent critic and a dangerous writer, who had attacked Voltaire from the conservative side, and at whom the patriarch of Ferney, as he now began to be called, levelled in return the very inferior farce-lampoon of *L'Écossaise*, of the first night of which Fréron himself did an admirably humorous criticism.

How he built a church and got into trouble in so doing at Ferney, how he put "Deo erexit Voltaire" on it (1760–61) and obtained a relic from the pope for his new building, how he entertained a grand-niece of Corneille, and for her benefit wrote his well-known "commentary" on that poet, are matters of interest, but to be passed over briefly. Here, too, he began that series of interferences on behalf of the oppressed and the ill-treated which, whatever mixture of motives may have prompted it, is certainly an honour to his memory. Volumes and almost libraries have been written on the Calas affair, and it is impossible here to give any account of it or of the only less famous cases of Sirven (very similar to that of Calas, though no life was actually lost), Espinasse (who had been sentenced to the galleys for harbouring a Protestant minister), Lally (the son of the unjustly treated but not blameless Irish-French commander in India), D'Étalonde (the companion of La Barre), Montbailli, and others.

In 1768 he entered, it would seem out of pure wantonness, into an indecent controversy with the bishop of the diocese (who, like an honest man, was not particularly well satisfied with his occasional conformity); he had differences with the superior landlord of part of his estate, the president De Brosses; and he engaged in a long and tedious return match with the republic of Geneva, in which the scoring was alternate and rather bewildering, Geneva playing at one time an insult to Voltaire's friend and patron Catherine of Russia, and Voltaire replying at another by setting up a rival colony of watchmakers at Ferney. The match went on the whole in favour of Voltaire, for during its course a theatre was authorized in the city, and he himself, a kind of exile from it, was applied to to mediate between different classes of the community. But the general events of this Ferney life are somewhat of that happy kind which are no events—the distractions and employments of a man who has nothing serious to occupy himself about.

In this way things went on for many years, and Voltaire, who had been an old man when he established himself at Ferney, became a very old one almost without noticing it. The death of Louis XV. and the accession of Louis XVI. excited even in his aged breast the hope of re-entering Paris, but he did not at once receive any encouragement, despite the reforming ministry of Turgot. A much more solid gain to his happiness was the adoption, or practical adoption, in 1776 of Reine Philiberte de Varicourt, a young girl of noble but poor family, whom Voltaire rescued from the convent, installed in his house as an adopted daughter, and married to the Marquis de Villette. Her pet name was "Belle et Bonne," and nobody had more to do with the happiness of the last years of the "patriarch" than she had. It is doubtful whether his last and fatal visit to Paris was due to his own wish or to the instigation of his niece, Madame Denis; but it is fair to say that this lady—a woman of disagreeable temper, especially to her inferiors—appears to have been rather hardly treated by Voltaire's earlier, and sometimes by his later, biographers. The suggestion which has been made that the success of Beaumarchais piqued him has nothing impossible in it. At any rate he had, at the end of 1777 and the beginning of 1778, been carefully finishing a new tragedy—*Irène*—for production in the capital; he started on the 5th of February, and five days later arrived at the city which he had not seen for eight and twenty years.

Abundant as is the information respecting the whole, or almost the whole, of his life, it is nowhere more abundant than in respect to these last months. He was received with immense rejoicings, not indeed directly by the court, but by the Academy, by society, and by all the more important foreign visitors. About a fortnight after his arrival age and fatigue made him seriously ill, and a confessor was sent for. But he recovered, scoffed at himself as usual, and prepared more eagerly than ever for the first performance of *Irène*, on March 16. At the end of the month he was able to go out and attend a performance of it, which has often been described, and was a kind of apotheosis. He was crowned with laurel in his box, amid the plaudits of the audience, and did not for the moment seem to be the worse for it, enjoying several other triumphs, during one of which he had, in full Academic *séance*, to embrace Franklin after the French manner. He even began or proceeded with another tragedy,—*Agathocle*,—and attended several Academic meetings. But such proceedings in the case of a man of eighty-four were impossible. To keep himself up he exceeded even his usual excess in coffee, and about the middle of May he became very ill. For about a fortnight he was alternately better and worse; but on May 30 the priests were once more sent for,—to wit, his nephew the Abbé Mignot, the Abbé Gaultier, who had officiated on the former occasion, and the parish priest, the curé of St Sulpice. He was, however, in a state of half insensibility, and petulantly motioned them away. The legends set afloat about his dying in a state of terror and despair are certainly false; but it must be regarded as singular and unfortunate that he who had more than once gone out of his way to conform ostentatiously and with his tongue in his cheek should have neglected or missed this last opportunity. The result was a difficulty as to burial which was compromised by hurried interment at the abbey of Scellières in Champagne, anticipating the interdict of the bishop of the diocese by an hour or two. On July 10, 1791, the body was transferred to the Pantheon, but it was not to rest there, and during the Hundred Days it was once more, it is said, disentombed, and stowed away in a piece of waste ground. His heart, taken from the body when it was embalmed, and given to Madame Denis and by her to Madame de Villette, was preserved in a silver case, and when it was proposed (in 1864) to restore it to the other remains the sarcophagus at Sainte Geneviève (the Pantheon) was opened and found to be empty.

In person Voltaire was not engaging, even as a young man. His extraordinary thinness is commemorated, among other things, by the very poor but well-known epigram attributed to Young, and identifying him at once with "Satan, Death, and Sin." In old age he was a mere skeleton, with a long nose and eyes of preternatural brilliancy peering out of his wig. He never seems to have been addicted to any manly sport, and took little exercise. He was sober enough (for his day and society) in eating and drinking generally; but drank coffee, as his contemporary, counterpart, and enemy, Johnson, drank tea, in a hardened and inveterate manner. It may be presumed with some certainty that his attentions to women were for the most part platonic; indeed, both on the good and the bad side of him, he was all brain. He appears to have had no great sense of natural beauty, in which point he resembled his generation (though one remarkable story is told of his being deeply affected by Alpine scenery); and, except in his passion for the stage, he does not seem to have cared much for any of the arts. Conversation and literature were, again as in Johnson's case, the sole gods of his idolatry. As for his moral character, the wholly intellectual cast of mind just referred to makes it difficult to judge that. His beliefs or absence of beliefs emancipated him from conventional scruples; and it must be admitted that he is not a good subject for those who maintain that a nice morality may exist independently of religion. He was good-natured when not crossed, generous to dependants who made themselves useful to him, and indefatigable in defending the cause of those who were oppressed by the systems with which he was at war. But he was inordinately vain, and totally unscrupulous in gaining money, in attacking an enemy, or in protecting himself when he was threatened with danger. In these three cases he stuck at no lie, found no weapons too foul to use, and regarded no gain as too dirty to pouch. His peculiar fashion of attacking the popular beliefs of his time has also failed to secure the approval of some who have very little sympathy with those beliefs, of not a few even who go so far as to approve of ridicule and indeed of mere ribaldry being used to wean those who hold things sacred from their belief in them. The only excuse made for the alternate cringing and insult, the alternate abuse and lying, which marked his course in this matter, has been the very weak plea that a man cannot fight with a system,—a plea which is sufficiently answered by the retort that a great many men have so fought and have won. But this comes so closely to the discussion of Voltaire's works and intellectual character that it may be dismissed for the present with only one more remark, by no means new, but it would seem constantly requiring repetition. Voltaire's works, and especially his private letters, constantly contain the word "l'infâme" and the expression in full or abbreviated "écrasez l'infâme." This has been misunderstood in many ways,—the mistake going so far as in some cases to suppose that Voltaire meant Christ by this opprobrious expression. No careful and competent student of his works, whatever that student's sympathies, has ever failed to correct this gross misapprehension. "L'infâme" is not God; it is not Christ; it is not Christianity; it is not even Catholicism. Its briefest equivalent may be given as "persecuting and privileged orthodoxy" in general, and, more particularly, it is the particular system which Voltaire saw around him, of which he had felt the effects in his own exiles and the confiscations of his books, and of which he saw the still worse effects in the hideous sufferings of Calas and La Barre, and in the less hideous but still severe miseries of persons perfectly guiltless, even according to their tormentors, such as the families of Calas and Sirven.

Vast and various as the work of Voltaire is, no article such as the present could be even approximately complete without some attempt to give an outline of its general contents and characteristics, for its vastness and variety are of the essence of its writer's peculiar quality. The divisions of it have long been recognized, and may be treated in order.

The first of these divisions in order, not the least in bulk, and, though not the first in merit, inferior to none in the amount of congenial labour spent on it, is the *theatre* of Voltaire. Between fifty and sixty different pieces (including a few which exist only in fragments or sketches) are included in his writings, and they cover the entire stretch of his literary life. It is at first sight remarkable that Voltaire, whose comic power was undoubtedly far in excess of his tragic, should have written many tragedies of no small excellence in their way but only one fair second-class comedy, *Nanine*. His other efforts in this latter direction are quite inferior, being either slight and almost insignificant in scope, or, as in the case of the somewhat famous *Écossaise*, deriving all their interest from being personal libels. His tragedies, on the other hand, though they can never fully satisfy those who have been accustomed to the stronger meat of romantic drama, are works of extraordinary merit in their own way. Although Voltaire had neither the perfect versification of Racine nor the noble poetry of Corneille, he surpassed the latter certainly, and the former in the opinion of some not incompetent judges, in playing the difficult and artificial game of the French tragedy. *Zaïre*, among those where love is admitted as a principal motive, and *Mérope*, among those where this motive is excluded and kept in subordination, yield to no plays of their class in such sustaining of interest as is possible on the model, in adaptation of that model to stage effect, and in uniform, if never very transporting or extraordinary, literary merit. Voltaire was an enthusiastic lover of the stage; he was intimately acquainted with its laws; he knew that the public opinion of his time reserved its highest prizes for a capable and successful dramatist; and he was determined to win those prizes. He therefore set all his wonderful cleverness to the task, going so far as to adopt a little even of that romantic disobedience to the strict classical theory which he condemned, and no doubt sincerely, in Shakespeare. The consequence is that his work in its kind is unlikely ever to be surpassed.

It is very different with his *poems* proper, of which there are two long ones, the *Henriade* and the *Pucelle*, besides smaller pieces, of which it is enough to say that a bare catalogue of them fills fourteen royal octavo columns. The value of these is very unequal. The *Henriade* has by universal consent been relegated to the position of a school reading book, and perhaps does not hold even that very securely. Constructed and written in almost slavish imitation of Virgil, employing for medium a very unsuitable vehicle—the alexandrine couplet (as reformed and rendered monotonous for dramatic purposes)—and animated neither by enthusiasm for the subject nor by real understanding thereof, it could not but be an unsatisfactory performance to posterity. The *Pucelle*, if morally inferior, is from a literary point of view of far more value. It is desultory to a degree; it is a base libel on religion and history; it differs from its model Ariosto in being, not, as Ariosto is, a mixture of romance and burlesque, but a sometimes tedious tissue of burlesque pure and simple; and it is exposed to the objection—often and justly urged—that much of its fun depends simply on the fact that there were and are many people who believe enough in Christianity to make its jokes give pain to them, and to make their disgust at such jokes piquant to others. Nevertheless, with all the *Pucelle's* faults, it is amusing—less so indeed than its author's prose tales, but still amusing. The minor poems are as much above the *Pucelle* as the *Pucelle* is above the *Henriade*. It is true that there is nothing, or hardly anything, that properly deserves the name of poetry in them—no passion, no sense of the beauty of nature, only a narrow "criticism of life," only a conventional and restricted choice of language, a cramped and monotonous prosody, and none of that indefinite suggestion which has been rightly said to be of the poetic essence. But there is immense wit, a wonderful command of such metre and language as the taste of the time allowed to the poet, occasionally a singular if somewhat artificial grace, and a curious felicity of diction and manner on occasions proper to the poet's genius.

The third division of Voltaire's works in a rational order (though it is usually placed later in the editions) consists of his *prose romances* or *tales*. These productions—incomparably the most remarkable and most absolutely good fruit of his genius—were usually, if not always, composed as pamphlets, with a purpose of polemic in religion, politics, or what not. Thus *Candide* attacks religious and philosophical optimism, *L'Homme aux Quarante Écus* certain social and political ways of the time, *Zadig* and others the received forms of moral and metaphysical orthodoxy, while some are mere lampoons on the Bible, the unfailing source of Voltaire's wit. But (as always happens in the case of literary work where the form exactly suits the author's genius) the purpose in all the best of them disappears almost entirely. It is in these works more than in any others that the peculiar quality of Voltaire—ironic style without exaggeration—appears. That he learned it partly from St Évremond, still more from Anthony Hamilton, partly even from his own enemy Le Sage, is perfectly true, but he gave it perfection and completion. There is no room to analyse it here; but, if one especial peculiarity can be singled out, it is the extreme restraint and simplicity of the verbal treatment. Voltaire never dwells too long on his point, stays to laugh at what he has said, elucidates or comments on his own jokes, guffaws over them, or exaggerates their form. The famous "pour encourager les autres" (that the shooting of Byng did "encourage the others" very much is not to the point) is a typical example, and indeed the whole of *Candide* shows the style at its perfection.

The fourth division of Voltaire's work, as we shall rank it here, his *historical work*, is the bulkiest of all except his correspondence, and some parts of it are or have been among the most read, but it is far from being the best, or even among the best. The universally known small treatises on Charles XII. and Peter the Great are indeed models of clear narrative and ingenious if somewhat superficial grasp and arrangement in little of considerable subjects. The so-called *Siècle de Louis XIV.* and *Siècle de Louis XV.* (the latter inferior to the former but still valuable) contain a great miscellany of interesting matter, treated by a man of great acuteness and unsurpassed power of writing, who had also had access to much important private information. But even in these books defects are present, which appear much more strongly in the singular *olla podrida* entitled *Essai sur les Mœurs*, in the *Annales de l'Empire*, and in the minor historical works of which there are many. These defects are an almost total absence of any comprehension of what has since been called the philosophy of history, the constant presence of gross prejudice, frequent inaccuracy of detail, and, above all, a complete incapacity to look at anything except from the narrow standpoint of a half pessimist and half self-satisfied *philosophe* of the 18th century. Attempts have been made to argue that Voltaire's admitted want of catholicity and appreciation was merely the fault of his time; but, while this would be an insufficient plea if granted, it is not the fact. Montesquieu, to name no other of his contemporaries, had if not a perfect yet a distinct sense of the necessity of dealing with other times and other manners so as to take to some extent the point of view of the actors; Voltaire had none. And, though he was very far from being an idle man, he cannot be said to have been extraordinarily anxious to secure accuracy of fact.

His work in *physics* concerns us less than any other here; it is, however, not inconsiderable in bulk, and is said by experts to give proof of aptitude.

To his own age Voltaire was pre-eminently a poet and a philosopher; the unkindness of succeeding ages has sometimes questioned whether he had any title to either name and especially to the latter. His largest *philosophical* work, at least so-called, is the curious medley entitled *Dictionnaire Philosophique*, which is compounded of the articles contributed by him to the great *Encyclopédie* and of several minor pieces. No one of Voltaire's works shows his anti-religious or at least anti-ecclesiastical animus more strongly. The various title-words of the several articles are often the merest stalking horses, under cover of which to shoot at the Bible or the church, the target being now and then shifted to the political institutions of the writer's country, his personal foes, &c., and the whole being largely seasoned with that acute, rather superficial, common-sense, but also commonplace, ethical and social criticism which the 18th century called philosophy. The book ranks perhaps second only to the novels as showing the character, literary and personal, of Voltaire; and despite its form it is nearly as readable. The minor philosophical works are of no very different character. In the brief *Traité de Métaphysique* the author makes his grand effort, but scarcely succeeds in doing more than show that he had no real conception of what metaphysic is. His *Philosophe Ignorant* is a clever skit on the contradictions of philosophers, his *Lettres de Memmius* a fair instance of his habit of taking oblique shots at one thing under cover of another and while apparently aiming at a third. And all the minor works commonly called philosophical, though they are voluminous enough, come to little more than the same result.

In general *criticism* and *miscellaneous* writing Voltaire is not inferior to himself in any of his other functions. Almost all his more substantive works, whether in verse or prose, are preceded by prefaces of one sort or another, which are models of his own light pungent *causerie*; and in a vast variety of nondescript pamphlets and writings he shows himself a perfect journalist. In literary criticism pure and simple his principal work is the *Commentaire sur Corneille*, though he wrote a good deal more of the same kind—sometimes (as in his *Life* and notices of Molière) independently, sometimes as part of his *Siècles*. Nowhere, perhaps, except when he is dealing with religion are Voltaire's defects felt more than here. His great acquaintance with stage matters often enabled him to make valuable technical criticism in that department, and his unrivalled acuteness of course served him in literary as in other matters. But he was quite unacquainted with the history of his own language and literature, and more here than anywhere else he showed the extraordinarily limited and conventional spirit which accompanied the revolt of the French 18th century against limits and conventions in theological, ethical, and political matters.

There remains only the huge division of Voltaire's *correspondence*, which fills some three thousand pages, double-columned, large, and closely printed, in the compactest editions, which is constantly being augmented by fresh discoveries, and which, according to M. Georges Bengesco, the best living authority, has never been fully or correctly printed, even in some of the parts longest known. In this great mass Voltaire's personality is of course best shown, and perhaps his literary qualities not worst. His immense energy and versatility, his adroit and unhesitating flattery when he chose to flatter, his ruthless sarcasm when he chose to be sarcastic, his rather unscrupulous business faculty, his more than rather unscrupulous resolve to double and twist in any fashion so as to escape his enemies,—all these things appear throughout the whole mass of letters.

After giving an account of Voltaire's personal character, and a sketch of the characteristics of the different sections of his work, his intellectual and literary position in history can be briefly summed up, though the summary is not one to be lightly undertaken. Most judgments of him have been unduly coloured by sympathy with or dislike of what may be briefly called his polemical side. When sympathy and dislike are both carefully discarded or allowed for, he remains certainly one of the most astonishing, if not exactly one of the most admirable, figures of letters. That he never, as Carlyle complains, gave utterance to one great thought is strictly true. That his characteristic is for the most part an almost superhuman cleverness rather than positive genius is also true. But that he was merely a mocker, which Carlyle and others have also said, is not strictly true or fair. In politics proper he seems indeed to have had few or no constructive ideas, and to have been entirely ignorant or quite reckless of the fact that his attacks were destroying a state of things for which as a whole he neither had nor apparently wished to have any substitute. In religion he protested stoutly, and no doubt sincerely, that his own attitude was not purely negative; but here also he seems to have failed altogether to distinguish between pruning and cutting down. Both here and elsewhere his great fault was an inveterate superficiality. But this superficiality was accompanied by such wonderful acuteness within a certain range, by such an absolutely unsurpassed literary aptitude and sense of style in all the lighter and some of the graver modes of literature, by such untiring energy and versatility in enterprise, that he has no parallel among ready writers anywhere. Not the most elaborate work of Voltaire is of much value for matter; but not the very slightest work of Voltaire is devoid of value as form. In literary craftsmanship, at once versatile and accomplished, he has no superior and scarcely a rival.

The bibliography of Voltaire is a very large subject, and it has for years been the special occupation of a Roumanian diplomatist of much erudition and judgment, M. Georges Bengesco, the first volume of whose work was published at Paris in 1882. The latest, and on the whole the best, edition of the works is that completed not long ago by M. Louis Moland in 52 volumes (Paris, Garnier); the handiest and most compact is that issued in 13 volumes royal octavo some fifty years ago by Furne, and kept in print by the house of Didot. Of the earlier editions, though their bulk is an objection, several are interesting and valuable. Especially may be noticed the so-called edition of Kehl, in which Voltaire himself, and later Beaumarchais, were concerned (70 vols., 1785-89); those of Dalibon and Baudouin, each in 97 vols. (from which "the hundred volumes of Voltaire" have become a not infrequent figure of speech); and the excellent edition of Beuchot (1829) in 72 volumes. Editions of separate or selected works are innumerable, and so are books upon Voltaire. There is no really good detailed life of him, with complete examination of his work, in any language as yet, though the works containing materials for such are numerous, and (especially in the case of M. Desnoiresterres) sometimes excellent. In English the essays of Carlyle and Mr John Morley are both in their way invaluable, and to a great extent correct one another. The principal detailed life in our language is that of an American writer, Mr James Parton, which gives the facts with very considerable detail and fair accuracy, but with no power of criticism. Fresh correspondence of Voltaire is constantly being discovered, sometimes showing that his published works have been considerably garbled, so that an *édition définitive* from such manuscripts as exist, and containing all the variants of his own constantly altered issues, is likely to be a matter long delayed. (G. SA.)

VOLTERRA, a town of Italy, in the province of Pisa, 51 miles by rail east-south-east from Leghorn, and 35 by road west-north-west from Siena, stands on a commanding olive-clad eminence about 1600 feet above sea-level, and is surrounded by the massive remains of its ancient walls, some 4½ miles in circuit. The most important relic of its Etrurian period is the Porta dell' Arco, an archway of dark grey stone, about 20 feet in height, the corbels of which are adorned with almost obliterated heads, probably representing the guardian deities of the city. Volterra possesses several public buildings of interest, dating from the period of its republican independence in the 13th century. The Palazzo dei Priori, or Palazzo Pubblico (1208–57), is a handsome building, unfortunately somewhat modernized in its windows and mouldings; it contains a very valuable collection of Etruscan antiquities, especially cinerary urns. The cathedral, consecrated in 1120, but enlarged and adorned by Niccolo Pisano in 1254, has a fine pulpit of that period, and on the high altar are sculptures by Mino da Fiesole; in the transept is a remarkably fine Annunciation by Luca Signorelli. The baptistery also, supposed to date in part from the 7th century, largely belongs to the 13th; the font is by Andrea di Sansovino, and the ciborium by Mino da Fiesole. The citadel, now a house of correction, consists of two portions, the Rocca Vecchia, built in 1343 by Walter de Brienne, duke of Athens, and the Rocca Nuova, built by the Florentines (1472). The inhabitants are chiefly employed in the manufacture of vases and other ornaments from alabaster, of good quality, found in the vicinity of Volterra and near Leghorn. The population in 1881 was 5347 (commune 14,063).

Volaterræ (Etrurian *Velathri*) appears to have been one of the twelve confederate cities of Etruria (see ETRURIA, vol. xiii. p. 636). It received a military colony under the triumvirate, but is included by Pliny among the municipal towns of Etruria. It was destroyed in the 10th century, and rebuilt under the Othos. In the 12th and 13th centuries it enjoyed free institutions; in the 14th it fell under the power of Florence. Persius the satirist and Daniele da Volterra (see RICCIARELLI) were both natives of the town.

VOLUNTEERS. Although it would be difficult to assign a period when the principle of volunteer organization for national defence was first adopted in England, it is certain that societies to promote this object existed in various parts of the country in the reign of Henry VIII., who in fact granted a charter in 1537 to the "Fraternity or Guylde of Saint George: Maisters and Rulars of the said Science of Artillary as aforesaid rehearsed for long-bowes Cros-bowes and Hand-Gonnes." This ancient volunteer corps is now the Honourable Artillery Company of London, whose muster-rolls have borne the names of many distinguished personages, including John Milton. Although the Honourable Artillery Company has always been a distinct volunteer association, it was at one time (notably during the wars of the Commonwealth) a centre of instruction for the City trained bands, whose officers indeed were required by statute to be members also of the company. It is an interesting fact in connexion with this company that there exists at Boston, U.S., a volunteer corps bearing the name of the "Antient and Honorable Artillery Company of Massachusetts." This legacy of the pilgrim-fathers was formed in 1638 after its London prototype, and its Puritan origin is still recognized in the "election sermon" which celebrates the anniversary of its formation.

It was not, however, until 1779 that volunteer organization became an integral part in national defence. In that year, Ireland being threatened with invasion by France and Spain, a levy of 40,000 Protestants was made by the gentry in the north. The energy and patriotism thus promptly manifested no doubt averted the impending danger, but not without unexpected results, for the volunteers then enrolled availed themselves of the opportunity to assert claims on their own account for the extension of civil liberty. The close of the 18th and the early part of the present century saw in Great Britain itself a more complete development of the national instinct for self-defence, when the aggressive wars of France, following upon the Revolution of 1789, threatened the safety of the United Kingdom. Between 1794 and 1804 successive Acts of Parliament were passed providing for the administration and discipline of the volunteer force, which, in 1805, when invasion by the first Napoleon was imminent, amounted to 429,165 men (70,000 of whom were Irish). When peace, however, was restored, this force was disbanded, with the exception of the yeomanry or volunteer cavalry, which continues to this day.

After an interval of nearly half a century the warlike attitude of France, under Napoleon III., caused the British once more to arm for the protection of their country. This long interval, however, had been used differently by the respective nations. England, from a questionable economy, had allowed both army and navy to decline in strength and efficiency; France on the other hand, by the energetic development of her military and naval power, and the early application of steam to ships of war, brought the possibilities of the invasion of England in 1846 within measurable distance, while a feeling of hostility was fostered and inflamed by her political writers. England at this time was awakened to the gravity of the situation by the publication of a well-known letter from the duke of Wellington, then commander-in-chief, to Sir John Burgoyne,[1] followed by a well-timed pamphlet by General Sir Charles Napier, entitled *The Defence of England by Volunteer Corps and Militia*. This characteristic sketch of the true principles of defence for a free people became seven years later the basis of the volunteer organization.

In 1857 the French press became more and more menacing. The United States had dismissed the resident British minister, and in consequence reinforcements had to be sent to Canada and New Brunswick. The war going on in China required an army and employed a fleet. The Indian Mutiny taxed the resources of England to the uttermost, while at home (save the actual garrisons) an unsatisfactory reserve of barely 36,000 militia was all that could be counted on. This threatening condition of affairs tended to aggravate, if not to produce, a serious commercial panic. It was then that the volunteer movement began, and by a popular impulse.

A circular letter, dated 12th May 1859, from the secretary for war to the lord-lieutenants of counties in Great Britain, authorized the formation of volunteer corps. The statute under which the general enrolment took place was the same that had governed the organization of the volunteer force in the beginning of the century.[2] The main provisions of that Act, however, were found inapplicable to the altered conditions under which invasion was now possible (through the application of steam); they failed also to meet the new system entertained of maintaining the volunteer force on a permanent footing in peace. A new Act was therefore passed, the most important provision of which[3] was that apprehended invasion should constitute a sufficient reason for the sovereign to call out the volunteers for service, in lieu of the old condition which required the actual appearance of the enemy upon the coast. To carry this provision into effect, the apprehension has to be first communicated to parliament, or if parliament is not sitting declared by the queen in council and notified by proclamation. The volunteers are thereupon bound to serve in Great Britain until released by a proclamation declaring the occasion to have passed. When so called out, they receive pay on the army scale.

The force thus brought into existence is composed of corps of light horse, artillery, engineers, mounted rifles, and rifle volunteers. There exist also in connexion with the Admiralty special volunteer corps for the defence of the coast-line, called "Royal Naval Artillery Volunteers." The term "corps" possesses no tactical signification. Any body of persons, great or small, whose offer of service the queen has accepted constitutes a "corps." The property belonging to the corps is vested in the commanding officer, and is administered by a committee of officers under the rules of the corps. These rules are in the first instance agreed on at a general meeting of officers and men, and, having received the queen's approval, become legal, and may be enforced by a magistrate's order. The commanding officer has power to dismiss a man from the corps, and a volunteer not on actual service may terminate his engagement on giving fourteen days' notice.

Volunteers, when assembled under arms, whether for actual service or for exercise, are under the command of the commander-in-chief or of general or other field-officers of the regular army appointed to command them, who must be senior in rank to every officer of the volunteers present. But it is a fundamental law that volunteers are to be led by their own officers. For the purposes of training, a permanent staff of adjutants and sergeant-instructors is provided from the regular army.

The formation of corps constituted as described was so rapid that in the course of a few months in 1859–60 a force of 119,000 volunteers was created. For administrative purposes, and for instruction, small corps were grouped in their several counties into "administrative battalions." This provisional arrangement has since been abolished (a questionable measure), and the small "corps," deprived of much of the status necessary as nuclei of battalions in time of war, are converted into constituent parts or companies of what had been their administrative battalions. These latter are now not only constituted "corps" in the meaning of the Act, but are called "consolidated corps," though their constituent parts are widely scattered. Though this arrangement is convenient during peace, confusion would probably result under pressure of apprehended invasion.

On the 7th March 1860 the queen held a levee in London, at which 2500 officers of volunteers were presented. On the 23d June a royal review was held in Hyde Park, when 21,900 volunteers marched past; and at Edinburgh on the 7th August another royal review took place, at which 22,000 volunteers from the northern corps were under arms.

Public confidence was thus restored, but yet more remained to be done. An end had to be put to the ever-recurring panics that paralysed from time to time the commercial system of the country. The Government, which in the beginning had tolerated rather than encouraged the movement, now followed the lead of public opinion, and decided on maintaining the volunteer force as a part of the regular defensive system of the country. The *personnel* of the volunteer corps (with a few essential exceptions) thereupon underwent a change. The wealthy and professional classes, who had at first joined the ranks in anticipation of war, cared no longer to bear arms. Their places were taken by the artisan class, which added

[1] *Life and Letters of Field-Marshal Sir John Burgoyne.*
[2] 44 Geo. III. cap. 54. [3] Volunteer Act, 1863, s. 17.

materially to the number and permanence of the force. But, as contributions and subscriptions now flagged, it became evident that public grants would have to be voted for its maintenance. A Royal Commission was therefore appointed in 1862 to inquire into the requirements of the volunteers, as well as to determine the conditions on which the public grant should be given, and a scale of ordinary and special capitation allowances, subject to regulation, was fixed on that commission's recommendation.

It was not to be expected that this so-called mushroom army should escape a certain amount of professional ridicule, which the inefficiency of the old volunteers associated with the name. Nor was this tendency unmixed with apprehension in certain quarters that the public grants voted for the force might in some way affect the interests of the regular army. But a generous appreciation and sympathy took the place of adverse criticism, as the earnestness of the volunteers and their devoted loyalty became apparent. Nor were they unsuccessful in their own efforts to keep pace with modern military training, and even to introduce improvements. Lord Elcho, a prominent leader of the volunteer movement, revived in the National Rifle Association the ancient English pastime of practising at the butts. The queen herself fired the first shot (a bull's-eye) at Wimbledon in 1860, and thus inaugurated those great national meetings where many thousands compete annually for prizes, the aggregate value of which has now reached £14,680, with 126,463 entries.

Colonel Harcourt followed Lord Elcho in establishing the National Artillery Association, whose meetings are held annually at the School of Gunnery at Shoeburyness. The volunteers in this arm of the force are more than 40,000 strong, and belong chiefly to the mechanic class. Their aptitude to learn the use of the great modern ordnance which their presence at the School of Gunnery encourages, and their steady discipline when in garrison, have impressed the officers of the Royal Artillery with their value as a reserve for manning the coast defences, as well as for the equipment of field batteries. Special provision has now been made for the latter, on the condition that the batteries are fully horsed by the volunteers, and that three complete detachments of men per gun are maintained in training.

The regular attendance of detachments of colonial volunteers at these great annual national competitions has exercised for some years past a silent and beneficial influence, by fostering the military sympathy of the colonies with the mother country as regards the interests of imperial defence. This feeling found practical expression in the expedition to the Soudan in 1885.

A novel and peculiarly national arm was also introduced in 1860 by Colonel Bower, then master of the Hambledon hounds at Droxford, who trained members of the hunt as a corps of mounted riflemen to occupy ground from point to point across country.

When the number of hunting men in Great Britain is considered, all of whom would be ready to turn out, thus equipped, to harrass the flank of an invader, beyond reach even of his cavalry, some estimate may be formed of the value of this contribution to the plan of defence.

The late Lord Ranelagh, another leader of mark among volunteers, initiated the great Easter volunteer field-days at Brighton and elsewhere. His views, at first opposed, are now officially acted on, and the annual Easter assemblies have developed into manœuvres, interesting as well as instructive to all engaged. The Easter holidays afford also opportunity to artillery volunteers to go into garrison in forts, as at Sheerness and other coast works, where means of practising are available. Facilities in camp instruction are also extended to volunteers in summer, an arrangement which enables the small scattered corps to unite for drill. As many as 100,000 volunteers were in camp in 1887.

Perhaps the most important organization of all, alike for the service of the army and the auxiliary forces, is that known as the "Engineer and Railway Transport Corps," formed by the patriotic exertions of the late Charles Manby, civil engineer, and a lieutenant-colonel in the corps. The term "corps" presents in this case a council of officers composed of the following elements:—(1) eminent civil engineers; (2) the general managers of the main lines of railway; (3) the chief employers of labour. These officers have the rank of lieutenant-colonel. There are also other officers of the same classes, subordinate to the above, and not belonging to the council. The functions of the corps include (*a*) the arrangement and the carrying into effect of any sudden and general concentration of troops to oppose invasion, and (*b*) the rapid execution of works upon the railways and lines of defence by the means at the disposal of the great contractors directed by the civil engineers. The ready labour power of this useful corps is estimated at from 12,000 to 20,000 navvies, with tools, barrows, and commissariat complete. It has already performed important service in tabulating, and printing at great private cost, complete time-tables and special reports for six general concentrations against possible invasion. A special return was also prepared by the corps (the first of its kind) of the entire rolling stock of all the railways in Great Britain. This important work—which is corrected and republished annually—shows where the requisite numbers of carriages of every description can be obtained for the composition of troop trains.

The opinion of military judges has been that the main weakness of the whole volunteer system rests with the officers. But this judgment has undoubtedly been modified of late years by the eagerness displayed by the officers of all ranks to become capable leaders of their men. While advantage is taken of the facilities provided by the Government—such as schools of instruction, temporary attachment to regular and militia regiments, and half-yearly examinations in tactics—officers of volunteers are making progress among themselves by initiating societies in various parts of the country for the study and discussion of military subjects, war games, &c. Individually, some officers have already taken a prominent position as students in the art of war. One of these, Colonel Macdonald, C.B., commanding the Edinburgh Rifle Volunteers, has originated important improvements in the system of infantry drill, and his modifications have been approved in principle by the adjutant-general. An ambulance service has been organized, and a scheme for battalion transport brought out.

The foregoing organization has not exhausted the resources of volunteer national defence. Science and commercial wealth combined are now creating an outer line,—the former for the defence of the Humber, Tees, Tyne, Mersey, &c., by means of volunteer marine mining corps, and the latter by the institution of the Naval Volunteer Defence Association, having for its object the protection of merchant ships, by fitting out in British ports a number of merchant vessels to serve in time of war as a cordon around the coasts of the kingdom, within which the shipping may pass in security.

There is yet another weak point, of equal importance, in the personal equipment of the volunteers, which, as a rule, is deficient for field service. But now that the jurisdiction has been transferred from the lord-lieutenants of counties to the crown, the whole subject of equipment for the field is entrusted to direct and responsible military authority.

The still graver question arises as to the issue of warlike stores in general in the time of national danger. Notwithstanding that such stores are already partially in possession of the services, the issue to the *levée en masse* (or augmentation of the volunteer force) alone will be a matter of extreme difficulty for one arsenal to manage. This difficulty will be best understood by the following statement. The volunteer force in Great Britain at the beginning of the century numbered 359,165. Since then, however, the population has nearly doubled. Therefore, supposing all other conditions to be equal, the number that would now come forward to defend the country would be about 700,000, or 481,800 more than the present peace footing of the volunteer force. One arsenal is not sufficient to sustain the strain that would then be put upon it. Strategically considered also, the situation of that at Woolwich is not such as to justify the accumulation there of all the warlike material the nation would have to depend on. A central arsenal, if not a northern one as well, appears to be a national necessity.

The existence of the volunteer force averts conscription for the country's defence, and it forms, as the first Lord Brougham characterized it, a "national insurance." The cost to the country is trifling compared with the magnitude of the issues, being in 1885 £767,400 for 218,000 "efficient" volunteers entitled to the public grant, that is £3, 8s. 6d. per volunteer, or barely 6d. per head of the population to be defended. The value of the volunteer force is not, however, to be estimated by the numbers actually enrolled. It is in fact, in its present form, a great training school of citizen soldiers, through which thousands pass annually into a reserve ready to join in case of need. And every year of its valuable service confirms the wisdom of Sir Charles Napier's last words of advice to his countrymen, viz., "Militia and volunteers are the proper forces to prepare for danger in time of peace." (M. M'M.)

VOLUSENUS, Florentius (that is, Florence Wilson or Wolsey, though in an English letter he writes himself Voluzene), a Scottish humanist of the first half of the 16th century, whose elegant Latinity, but still more the thoughtful beauty of his Christian philosophy, claims for him a high place among the scholars of his age. That he was born near Elgin, and studied philosophy at Aberdeen, as is stated in the notice of his life published in 1619 by Thomas Wilson in *Adamsoni Poemata Sacra*, may be only an inference (though probably a just one) from a passage in the dialogue *De Tranquillitate Animi*, more than half of which consists of a description of the abode of tranquillity, based on a dream that, as we are told, came to the author, when he had been a student of philosophy for four years, after a conversation on the pleasant banks of the Lossie with John Ogilvy, afterwards rector of Cruden. Proceeding to Paris, he became tutor to a nephew (or really a bastard son) of Cardinal Wolsey, and this connexion led to repeated visits to England, where he was well seen by the king, and formed, with men like John Fisher, Stephen Gardiner, and Thomas Cromwell, connexions that were not dissolved by Wolsey's fall, for he was in England as late as 1534. In Paris he knew George Buchanan, who afterwards wrote a graceful epitaph on his friend's death, and found patrons in the cardinals Jean de Lorraine (to whom he dedicated in 1531 a Latin exposition of Psalm xv.) and Jean du Bellay. With the latter he started in 1534 for Italy, but, being detained by sore sickness at Avignon, found a new patron in the bishop of the diocese, the learned and pious Sadolet, who procured for him the mastership of the school at Carpentras, with a salary of seventy crowns. Volusenus felt himself a little out of place in a grammar school, all his tastes leaning to philosophy, and it would seem that from Carpentras he made repeated visits to Lyons (where Gesner saw him, still a young man, in 1540), probably also to Italy, where he made many friends, perhaps even to Spain, for Alciat tells us that he had acquired French, Italian, and Spanish "par frequentation des nations." A letter of Sadolet from Rome in 1546 shows that he had then resolved to return to Scotland, and was concerned to know what course he should hold in the religious dissensions of the time. He died on the journey, however, at Vienne in Dauphiné.

The authorities for the life of Wilson are well brought together by Irving in the *Lives of Scottish Writers* (1839); with the exception of two letters in the *Bannatyne Miscellany*, vol. i., the most important of them had already been collected in Wishart's edition of the *De Tranquillitate* (8vo, Edin., 1751). Irving, however, overlooked Wilson's earliest works, *Fl. Vol. ad illustr. Dom. Card. Lotharingorum Ps. xv. Enarratio* (4to, Paris, 1531) and *Fl. Vol. Britanni in Psalmum nobis 50 Hebræis vero 51 ad . . . Stephanum Wintoniensem Episcopum Enar.* (4to, Paris, 1532). These show that his linguistic studies embraced Hebrew as well Greek and Latin. Wilson's reputation, however, rests on the beautiful dialogue already cited, and first printed by Gryphius at Lyons in 1543. From internal evidence it appears to have been composed about that time, but the subject had exercised the writer for many years. The dialogue shows us Christian humanism at its best, not yet breaking with the church and somewhat afraid of authority, but open to new light, tolerant and yet believing. Volusenus is a great admirer of Erasmus, but censures in him a lack of purity in his Latin and a certain want of philosophy. Latinity and philosophical training are his own distinguishing points, but his philosophy is Christian and Biblical rather than classical or scholastic. To analyse his argument would here be out of place; the title of the dialogue itself shows that he takes a fresh and independent view of the chief good of Christian ethics, and it is sufficient to observe that from this point of view he ultimately reaches a doctrine as to the witness of the Spirit and the assurance of grace which breaks with the traditional Christianity of his time and contains ethical motives akin to, though not identical with, those of the German Reformation. The verses which occur in several parts of the dialogue, and the poem which concludes it, give Wilson a place among Scottish poets, but not nearly so high as that which he occupies among philosophical writers on Christianity.

VONDEL, Joost van der (1587–1679), Dutch poet See Holland, vol. xii. p. 94.

VORAGINE, Jacobus de (*c.* 1230–1298), archbishop of Genoa, is said to have been born at the little village of Varaggio, near Savona, about the year 1230. He entered the order of St Dominic in 1244, and is said to have preached with great success in many parts of Italy, as well as to have taught in the schools of his own fraternity. From the office of prior in 1267 he was raised to be provincial of all Lombardy. This post he held till 1286, when he was removed at the meeting of the order in Paris. He also represented his own province at the councils of Lucca (1288) and Ferrara (1290). On the last occasion he was one of the four delegates charged with signifying Nicholas IV.'s desire for the deposition of Munio de Zamora, who had been master of the order from 1285, and was deprived of his office by a papal bull dated April 12, 1291. In 1288 Nicholas empowered him to absolve the people of Genoa for their offence in aiding the Sicilians against Charles II. Early in 1292 the same pope, himself a Franciscan, summoned James to Rome, intending to consecrate him archbishop of Genoa with his own hands. James reached Rome on Palm Sunday (March 30), but only to find his patron ill of a deadly sickness, from which he died on Good Friday (April 4). The cardinals, however, "propter honorem Communis Januæ," determined to carry out this consecration on the Sunday after Easter, and thus, to quote his own words, "he returned with joy to his own city, and was reverently received by the people." If we may trust Echard, he was a model bishop, and especially distinguished himself by his efforts to appease the civil discords of Genoa. His death seems to have taken place in June 1298. He was buried in the Dominican church at Genoa. A story, mentioned by Echard as unworthy of credit, makes Boniface VIII., on the first day of Lent, cast the ashes in the archbishop's eyes instead of on his head, with the words, "Remember that thou art a Ghibelline, and with thy fellow Ghibellines wilt return to naught."

Jacobus de Voragine has left us a list of his own works. Speaking of himself in his *Chronicon Januense*, he says, "While he was in his order, and after he had been made archbishop, he wrote many works. For he compiled the legends of the saints (*Legendæ Sanctorum*) in one volume, adding many things from the *Historia Tripartita et Scholastica*, and from the chronicles of many writers." The other writings he claims are two volumes of "Sermons concerning all the Saints"[1] whose yearly feasts the church celebrates. Of these volumes, he adds, one is very diffuse, but the other short and concise. Then follow *Sermones de Omnibus Evangeliis Dominicalibus* for every Sunday in the year; *Sermones de Omnibus Evangeliis, i.e.*, a book of discourses on all the Gospels, from Ash Wednesday to the Tuesday after Easter; and a treatise called "*Marialis*, qui totus est de B. Maria compositus," consisting of about 160 discourses on the attributes, titles, &c., of the Virgin Mary. In the same work the archbishop claims to have written his *Chronicon Januense* in the second year of his pontificate (1293), but it extends to 1296 or 1297. To this list Echard adds several other works, such as a defence of the Dominicans, printed at Venice in 1504, and a *Summa Virtutum et Vitiorum Guillelmi Peraldi*, a Dominican who died about 1250. James is also said to have translated the Old and New Testaments into his own tongue. "But," adds Echard, "if he did so, the version lies so closely hid that there is no recollection of it."

His two chief works are the *Chronicon Januense* and the *Golden Legend* or *Lombardica Hystoria*. The former is partly printed in Muratori (*Scriptores Rer. Ital.*, ix. 6). It is divided into twelve parts. The first four deal with the mythical history of Genoa from the time of its founder, Janus the first king of Italy, and its enlarger, a second Janus, "citizen of Troy," till its conversion to Christianity "about twenty-five years after the passion of Christ." Part v. professes to treat of the beginning, the growth, and the perfection of the city; but of the first period the writer candidly confesses he knows nothing except by hearsay. The second period includes the Genoese crusading exploits in the East, and extends to their victory over the Pisans (*c.* 1130), while the third reaches down to the days of the author's archbishopric. The sixth part deals with the constitution of the city, the seventh and eighth with the duties of rulers and citizens, the ninth with those of domestic life. The tenth gives the ecclesiastical history of Genoa from the time of its first known bishop, St Valentine, "whom we believe to have lived about 530 A.D.," till 1133, when the city was raised to archiepiscopal rank. The eleventh contains the lives of all the bishops in order, and includes the chief events during their pontificates; while the twelfth deals in the same way with the archbishops, not forgetting the writer himself.[2]

The *Golden Legend*, one of the most popular religious works of the Middle Ages, is a collection of the legendary lives of the greater saints of the mediæval church. The preface divides the ecclesiastical year into four periods corresponding to the various epochs of the world's history, a time of deviation, of renovation, of reconciliation, and of pilgrimage. The book itself, however, falls into five sections:—(*a*) from Advent to Christmas (*cc.* 1–5); (*b*) from Christmas to Septuagesima (6–30); (*c*) from Septuagesima to Easter (31–53); (*d*) from Easter Day to the octave of Pentecost (54–76); (*e*) from the octave of Pentecost to Advent (77–180). The saints' lives are full of puerile legend, and in not a few cases contain accounts of 13th-century miracles wrought at special places, particularly with reference to the Dominicans. The author is very particular in giving the derivation of proper names, and indeed generally supplies a copious choice of alternatives. He is nearly always careful to assign a yearly date to the saints he treats of, but seldom, if ever, mentions their feast days. As he reaches the great seasons of the year he inserts treatises dealing with their significance and interpretation. These we have for Advent, Christmas, Good Friday, Easter, Whitsunday, &c. The last chapter but one (181) "De Sancto Pelagio Papa," contains a kind of history of the world from the middle of the 6th century; while the last (182) is a somewhat allegorical disquisition, "De Dedicatione Ecclesiæ."

The *Golden Legend* was translated into French by Jean Belet de Vigny in the 14th century. It was also one of the earliest books to issue from the press. A Latin edition is assigned to about 1469; and a dated one was published at Lyons in 1473. Many other Latin editions were printed before the end of the century. A French translation by Master John Bataillier is dated 1476; Jean de Vigny's appeared at Paris, 1488; an Italian one by Nic. Manerbi (? Venice, 1475); a Bohemian one at Pilsen, 1475-9, and at Prague, 1495; Caxton's English versions, 1483, 1487, and 1493; and a German one in 1489. Several 15th-century editions of the *Sermons* are also known, and the *Mariale* was printed at Venice in 1497 and at Paris in 1503.

VORARLBERG, the most western division of the Austrian-Hungarian monarchy, is bounded on the N. by Bavaria, on the W. by the Lake of Constance Liechtenstein, and Switzerland, on the S. by Switzerland, and on the E. by Tyrol. Though united for administrative purposes with Tyrol, it enjoys a constitution of its own, and ranks as a separate member of the empire. It is emphatically an Alpine region, being traversed by various spurs of the Rhætian Alps (Arlberg, Bregenzer Wald, &c.), attaining a height of 6000 to 9000 feet, and even possessing a few small glaciers. The name is derived from the Arlberg Pass (*i.e.*, Adlerberg, or Eagle's Mountain, 5895 ft.), separating it from Tyrol and forming the means of communication between Innsbruck and the Lake of Constance. The pass is now traversed by a railway, the tunnel under the Arlberg itself (opened Oct. 1884), being 6½ miles in length. Vorarlberg is watered by numerous small streams, most of them flowing into the Rhine, which is in contact with the west side of the crownland for a distance of about 20 miles. About one-third of the surface (almost exactly 1000 square miles in extent) is occupied by pasture, upwards of one-sixth by forests, one-seventh by meadows, and only one-twentieth by arable land. In correspondence with these figures, we find that the chief employments of the inhabitants are cattle-rearing, dairy-farming, and forestry.

In 1881 the district contained 61,115 cattle, and cheese is produced in large quantities. Grain is cultivated in the valley-bottoms, but not more than enough is raised to cover the home consumption; potatoes, fruit, and wine are also produced. The manufacturing industry is also by no means unimportant, occupying nearly 30 per cent. of the population. The chief branch is the spinning and weaving of cotton, which is carried on with special vigour in the neighbourhood of the towns and larger villages. A characteristic industry is the construction of wooden chalets, which are exported to Switzerland by water. Many of the men spend the summer in Switzerland as masons and labourers, returning to their homes in winter. In 1881 the population numbered 107,373, nearly all of Teutonic stock and the Roman Catholic faith. The chief towns, none of which are large, are Bregenz (4736 inhabitants), the capital, and the port of Austria on the Lake of Constance, Bludenz (3150 inhabitants), Feldkirch (3600), and Dornbirn. Vorarlberg belongs to the see of Brixen, the prince-bishop of which is represented by a vicar-general at Feldkirch. The provincial diet consists of twenty-one members, including the vicar-general. The crownland sends two representatives to the imperial parliament.

Vorarlberg is formed out of the old duchies and countships of Bregenz, Feldkirch, Bludenz, Sonnenberg, and Hohenems, all of which had come into the possession of the house of Austria by the 14th century, chiefly by purchase. Prior to 1782 it was counted part of Hither Austria, but since then it has been administratively united with Tyrol. The peace of Pressburg (1805) assigned it to Bavaria, along with northern Tyrol, but it was restored to its old allegiance in 1814.

VORONEZH, a government of southern Russia, is bounded by Tamboff on the N., Saratoff and the Don Cossacks on the E., Kharkoff on the S., and Kursk and Orel on the W., and has an area of 25,448 square miles. It occupies the southern slopes of the Middle-Russian plateau, and its average elevation is from 450 to 700 feet above sea-level. The surface is hilly, and broken by ravines in the west (where two ranges of chalk hills separated by a broad valley run north and south), but flat and low to the east of the Don. Devonian sandstones crop out in the north, but farther south these are covered with chalk. Glacial clays with northern erratics spread as far south as Voronezh, and extensive areas are covered with Lacustrine clays and sands. The soil is very fertile, owing to the large prevalence of the black earth; it becomes, however, sandy towards the east. Voronezh lies on the border between the forest and meadow-region of Middle Russia and the southern steppes; the forests rapidly disappear as one advances south, and those which in the time of Peter the Great still covered the upper parts of the tributaries of the Don, and were used for shipbuilding, are now almost entirely destroyed. Less

[1] Printed without name or place, 1484.

[2] The adjective "golden" has been transferred from this to other works of the author.

than one-tenth of the entire area is under wood, and both timber and firewood have to be imported.

The Don traverses Voronezh from north to south-east, watering it for more than 400 miles; it is an important channel for the export of corn, tallow, and other raw produce, as well as for the import of wood, floated from the north. Its tributary the Voronezh is also navigated, and another large tributary, the Vorona, flows through the eastern part of the government. Many other small streams flowing into the Don intersect the territory, but the influence of the dry steppes begins to make itself felt; there are no lakes, and marshes persist only in the valleys. The climate is therefore continental, and, although the mean temperature at Voronezh is 42°·7 F., that of January is as low as 8°·3 and that of July as high as 74°·2.

The population is steadily increasing, and reached 2,532,840 in 1883 as against 1,974,400 in 1860. It is Little Russian in the south-west (from 35 to 40 per cent., according to different estimates), and Great Russian elsewhere. There are also a few German colonies with some 3500 inhabitants, and a few Poles (2000).

Agriculture is the chief occupation, and corn is exported to a considerable amount. The average crops from 1883 to 1885 reached 3,467,800 quarters of rye, 901,600 of wheat, 958,000 of oats, 1,680,000 of various grains, and 960,100 of potatoes. 17,000 acres were under beet (176,000 cwts. in 1885); tobacco is also largely cultivated, and the crop of 1885 yielded 1,723,000 lb. The sunflower has also been much cultivated of late for oil. The Voronezh horses enjoy a high reputation in Russia, as also do its cattle, and cattle-breeding has advanced during the last thirty years. In 1883 there were 535,500 horses, 649,100 cattle, and 1,348,100 sheep. Bees are kept in many villages, and honey is gathered to the annual amount of more than 10,000 cwts. Market-gardening and fishing are also of importance. The manufactures are of recent growth; the production reached £2,066,000 in 1884, the chief products being spirits, oil, sugar, woollens, and tallow. Wheat and other grains, flour, flax, tallow and hides, wool, and cattle are the chief items of export.

Voronezh is divided into twelve districts, the chief towns of which are Voronezh (56,185 inhabitants in 1885), Biryutch (4435), Bobroff (3660), Bogutchary (4230), Korotoyak (1840), Nijne-Dyevitsk (2635), Novokhopersk (8015), Ostrogozhsk (8610), Pavlovsk (8390), Valuiki (4425), Zadonsk, with a great monastery (9940), and Zemlyansk (3870). These are mostly mere administrative centres; and several villages, such as Buturlinovka (21,700), Kalatch (13,000), and Vorontsovka (12,000), have larger populations and more commerce.

VORONEZH, capital of the above government, is situated on a high bank of the river of the same name, 365 miles by rail to the south of Moscow. It is almost entirely built of wood, and only recently began to re-acquire importance as an entrepôt on the railway which connects Moscow with the Sea of Azoff. It has a military school of cadets, gymnasiums for boys and girls, and a number of schools for elementary education. Its theatre, now rebuilt, has a name in the history of the Russian stage, and the town was also the birthplace of two peasant poets, to whom we owe some of the finest examples of Russian poetry—Koltsoff and Nikitin. A memorial to the former has been erected on a public promenade. A few factories for cleansing wool and for the preparation of tallow and oil, as well as some distilleries, have arisen of late. The population of the town increased from 39,800 in 1860 to 56,185 in 1885. It is now an important entrepôt for corn, flax, tallow, hides, sugar, wood, and coal from the Don; the railway traffic amounts to 2½ million cwts., and that of the Razdelnaya junction, close by, is nearly thrice that amount.

Voronezh was founded in 1586, as a fort against Tartar raids, on a site which had been occupied from the 11th century by a Khazar town, but had been deserted during the 14th and 15th centuries. Four years afterwards it was burned by the Tartars, but again rebuilt, and soon became an important trading place. Its wooden fort was rebuilt in 1672. Peter I. recognized its importance, and in 1694 erected on an island of the river a wharf, where a flotilla of sixty-six boats (2546 guns and 17,000 men) was built, under the direction of Dutch shipbuilders, for the conquest of Azoff. It thus became the basis of further advances towards the Black Sea. The town was almost completely destroyed by fire in 1703, 1748, and 1773, but was always rebuilt and has steadily developed.

VORTEX MOTION. See HYDROMECHANICS, vol. xii. p. 450 *sq.*

VOSGES, a mountain range of central Europe, stretching along the west side of the Rhine valley in a north-north-east direction, from Basel to Mainz, for a distance of 150 miles. Since 1871 the southern portion, from the Ballon d'Alsace to Mont Donon, has been the political boundary between France and Germany. There is a remarkable similarity between the Vosges and the corresponding range of the Black Forest on the other side of the Rhine: both lie within the same degrees of latitude and have the same geological formation; both are characterized by fine forests on their lower slopes, above which are open pasturages and rounded summits of a uniform altitude; both have a steep fall to the Rhine and a gradual descent on the other side. The Vosges in their southern portion are mainly of granite, with some porphyritic masses, and of a kind of red sandstone (occasionally 1640 feet in thickness) which on the western versant bears the name of "grès Vosgien."

Orographically the range is divided from south to north into four sections:—the Grandes Vosges (62 miles), extending from Belfort to the valley of the Bruche; the Central Vosges (31 miles), between the Bruche and the Col de Saverne; the Lower Vosges (30 miles), between the Col de Saverne and the source of the Lauter; and the Hardt (25 miles). The rounded summits of the Grandes Vosges are called "ballons." The departments of Vosges and Haute Saône are divided from Alsace and the territory of Belfort by the Ballon d'Alsace or St Maurice (4100 feet). Thence northwards the average height of the range is 3000 feet, the highest point of all, the Ballon de Guebwiller (Gebweiler) or Soultz, rising on the east to a height of 4680 feet. The Col de Saales, between the Grandes Vosges and the central section, is 1900 feet high; the latter is both lower and narrower than the Grandes Vosges, the Mont Donon and other chief heights not exceeding 3300 feet. The railway from Paris to Strasburg and the Rhine and Marne Canal traverse the Col de Saverne (1085 feet). No railway crosses the Vosges between Saverne and Belfort, but there are very good carriage roads over the passes of Bussang (2410 feet) from Remiremont to Thann, the Schlucht (3746 feet) from Gérardmer to Munster, the Bon Homme (3100 feet) from St Dié to Colmar, and from St Dié to St Marie-aux-Mines (2625 feet). The Lower Vosges are a sandstone plateau ranging from 1000 to 1850 feet high, and are crossed by the railway from Hagenau to Sarreguemines, defended by the fort of Bitche. The Hardt, a sterile region, covered with heath and low brushwood, has for its highest point the Donnersberg (Mont Tonnerre), 2264 feet high; it is traversed through deep ravines by the railways from Deux-Ponts to Landau, and from Kaiserslautern to Spires and Worms. Meteorologically, the difference between the eastern and western versants of the range is very marked, the annual rainfall being much higher and the mean temperature being much lower in the latter than in the former. On the eastern slope the vine ripens to a height of 1300 feet; on the other hand, its only rivers are the Ill and other shorter streams, which afford water-power rather by their rapid fall than by their abundance. The Moselle, Meurthe, and Sarre all rise on the Lorraine side. Moraines, boulders, and polished rocks testify the existence of the glaciers which formerly covered the Vosges. The lakes, surrounded by pines, beeches, and maples, the green meadows where hundreds of cows with tinkling bells peacefully graze, and the fine views of the Rhine valley, Black Forest, and snow-covered Swiss mountains combine to make the district charmingly picturesque. The lower heights and buttresses of the main chain on the Alsatian side are covered with numerous castles, generally in ruins, in connexion with which curious legends and interesting historical incidents are told. At several points on the main ridge, especially at St Odile above Ribeauvillé (Rappoltsweiler), are the remains of a wall of unmortared stone with tenons of wood, 6 to 7 feet thick and 4 to 5 feet high, called the pagan wall (Mur Payen). It was certainly used for local defence in the Middle Ages, and archæologists are divided as to whether it was built for this purpose by the Romans, or before their arrival.

VOSGES, a frontier department of eastern France, was formed in 1790, for the most part of territory previously belonging to Lorraine, with fragments of Franche-Comté, Champagne, and Alsace. The portion belonging to Alsace was ceded to Germany in 1871. Lying between 47° 48′ and 48° 32′ N. lat., and 5° 22′ and 7° 10′ E. long., the department is bounded by Alsace-Lorraine on the E. and by the departments of Meurthe-et-Moselle on the N., Meuse on the N.W., Haute-Marne on the W., and Haute-Saône on the S. The Vosges Mountains form a natural boundary on the E. The highest point is the Hohneck (4482 feet) near the Schlucht. The south of the department is traversed by the Monts Faucilles (2000 feet), which form part of the European watershed, separating the basins of the Rhine and the Rhone. The Moselle and the Meuse, tributaries of the Rhine, have the largest drainage areas in the department; a small district in the north-west belongs to the basin of the Seine (Ornain and Marne), the rest to that of the Rhone. The Moselle rises in the Col de Bussang, and in a N.W. course of 75 miles receives the Moselotte and Vologne on the right; the Mortagne and the Meurthe on the right and the Madon on the left bank also belong to Vosges, though they join the Moselle outside the department. The source of the Saône is on the south-east slope of the Monts Faucilles, and the Canal de l'Est follows the course of the Coney, a tributary of the left bank. The height above the sea, the northward exposure of the valleys, and the impervious subsoil combine to make the climate severe; the average temperature at Épinal (1070 feet) is 49° F. The annual rainfall is 24 inches at Épinal, 31 at St Dié, and more in the mountains.

Of a total area of 1,452,181 acres, arable land occupies 603,201 acres, grass 199,839, wood 361,526, heath, pasture, and uncultivated land 81,486, and vineyards 12,054. The live stock in 1881 included 31,811 horses (of a small but strong breed), 357 asses and mules, 143,827 cattle, 45,634 sheep, 81,488 pigs, 19,615 goats, more than 17,000 dogs, 500,000 head of poultry; 17,952 beehives yielded 43 tons 7 cwts. of honey and 18 tons 11 cwts. of wax. 872 tons of cheese were made at Gérardmer. The crops in 1884 were—wheat 1,911,470 bushels, meslin 494,483, rye 710,627, barley 103,262, oats 3,225,755, buckwheat 63,409, potatoes 17,787,404, dry vegetables 45,974, fodder beetroot 25,060 tons, tobacco 33 tons, hops 79 tons, hemp seed 138 tons, hemp 99 tons, linseed 39 tons, flax 22 tons, hemp, flax, and poppy oils 94 tons, colza seed 206 tons, fodder 457,383 tons, wine 2,869,000 gallons (average of preceding ten years 3,964,441). The department stands first in France for the extent and importance of the woods under forest rule, though only third for the actual area of forest land. The state owns one-third of the forests, private individuals one-fifth, and the communes the rest. Oaks, beeches, hornbeams, birches, aspens, and maples thrive on the plains, beeches and oaks on the higher grounds, and firs, beeches, and pines on the mountains. The annual value of timber produced is £280,000, and 9,000,000 fir planks, besides other kinds, are annually cut in 300 sawmills. Traces of gold are found, and the department contains silver and lead mines, copper ore, iron ore (4530 tons of iron annually), zinc, manganese, cobalt, and antimony. In 1884, 681 tons of coal were mined, and in 1882 1595 tons of peat were dug; 1336 persons are employed in 432 quarries of marble, sandstone, granite, and building and lithographic stones. The department is rich in hot, cold, sulphate, sodic, calcium, iron, bicarbonate, and gaseous mineral springs. Those at Plombières were known to the Romans. 37,000 hands are employed in the manufacture of pig and cast iron (for all which wood is the chief fuel) and wares of iron and steel. The cotton industry (135,000 looms and 423,724 spindles) has been largely developed since 1871; canvas and linen are woven at Gérardmer (3000 looms). The manufacture of cloth employs 500 workmen, of lace 1000, embroidery by the hand and loom 40,000 workwomen, silk spinning 1000 spindles. Wool is spun and hosiery manufactured. Coopers' work (over 300 tons) is exported, as are also sabots. At Épinal several hundred workmen are engaged in the manufacture of images; and musical instruments are made at Mirecourt. 1000 workmen are employed in glass-works, and 1937 in paper-mills (10,000 tons of paper and cardboard). The department contains in all 409 industrial establishments; 200,000 tons of coal are imported. There are 281 miles of railway, 177 of national roads, and 3096 of other roads. The Eastern Canal connects the Saône with the Moselle and Meuse. The population in 1881 was 408,862, of whom 189,176 were engaged in agriculture and 131,253 in manufactures; the population in 1886 was 413,707. The department forms the diocese of St Dié, has its court of appeal and academy at Nancy, belongs to the district of the corps d'armée of Châlons-sur-Marne, and is divided for administrative purposes into 5 arrondissements (Épinal, Mirecourt, Neufchâteau, Remiremont, St Dié), 29 cantons, and 530 communes. The chef-lieu is Épinal.

VOSS, JOHANN HEINRICH (1751–1826), German poet, archæologist, and translator, was born at Sommersdorf in Mecklenburg on the 20th February 1751. In the same year his father, a farmer, removed from Sommersdorf to Penzlin. From 1766 to 1769 Voss attended school at Neubrandenburg. In the latter year, in consequence of misfortunes which had overtaken his father, he was obliged to accept a tutorship in the family of a private gentleman near Penzlin. He went to Göttingen in 1772, in response to the invitation of Boie, whose attention he had attracted by poems contributed to the Göttingen *Musenalmanach*. At Göttingen he studied with enthusiasm ancient and modern literature, and became one of the leading members of the famous "Dichterbund." In 1775 Boie made over to him the editing of the *Musenalmanach*, which he continued to issue for many years. He married Boie's sister, Ernestine, in 1777, and in the following year he accepted the position of rector at Ottendorf in Hanover. As the climate of Ottendorf did not suit his health, he resigned this office in 1782, and went as rector to Eutin, where he remained until 1802. He then lived for some time in Jena, but in 1805 he accepted a call to a professorship at Heidelberg. He died at Heidelberg on March 29, 1826.

Voss was a man of a remarkably independent and vigorous character, and he achieved distinction in several kinds of literary activity. In 1785-95 he published in two volumes a collection of original poems, to which he afterwards made many additions. The best of these works is his idyllic poem "Luise," in which he sought, with much success, to apply the style and methods of classical poetry to the expression of modern German thought and sentiment. In his *Mythologische Briefe* (2 vols., 1794), in which he attacked the ideas of Heyne, in his *Antisymbolik* (2 vols., 1824–26), written in opposition to Creuzer, and in other writings he made important contributions to the study of mythology. He was also prominent as an advocate of the right of free judgment in religion, and at the time when some members of the Romantic school were being converted to the Roman Church he produced a strong impression by a powerful article, in *Sophronizon*, on his friend Friedrich von Stolberg's repudiation of Protestantism. It is, however, to his work as a translator that Voss chiefly owes his place in German literature. All his renderings of the works of ancient writers indicate not only sound scholarship but a thorough mastery of the laws of German diction and rhythm. The most famous of his translations are those of Homer, which were published together, in 4 volumes, in 1793. Of these the one generally preferred is the translation of the *Odyssey*, as originally issued in 1781. He also translated Hesiod, Theocritus, Bion and Moschus, Virgil, Horace, Tibullus, Propertius, and other classical poets, and he prepared a critical edition of Tibullus. In 1818–29 was published, in 9 volumes, a translation of Shakespeare's plays, which he completed with the help of his sons Heinrich and Abraham, both of whom were scholars and writers of considerable ability.

See Paulus, *Lebens- u. Todeskunden über J. H. Voss* (1826), and Herbst, *J. H. Voss* (2 vols., 1872–76).

VOSSIUS, GERARDUS JOHANNES (1577–1649), classical scholar and theologian, was born near Heidelberg in 1577. His father Johannes Vos, a native of the Netherlands, had fled as a Protestant from the persecutions in his own country into the Palatinate, and became pastor in the village near Heidelberg where Gerard was born; but, as he was a Calvinist, the strict Lutherans of the Palatinate caused him once more to become a wanderer. In 1578 he settled at Leyden as student of theology in the university, and finally as pastor at Dort, where he died in 1586, leaving Gerard an orphan. Here the boy received his education, until he entered the theological college and then the university of Leyden. He there became the lifelong bosom friend of Hugo Grotius, and pursued with great zest the study of the classics, Hebrew, ecclesiastical history, and theology. In 1600 he was made rector of the high school at Dort, where he devoted himself to philology and historical theology. From 1614 to 1619 he filled the office of director of the theological college at Leyden. The moderation of his theological views and his abstention from controversy brought him under the suspicion of heresy, in consequence of which he escaped expulsion from his office only by resignation (1619). The year before he had published his valuable work the *Historia Pelagiana*, which his enemies considered favoured the views of the Arminians or Remonstrants. But in the year 1622 he received the appointment of professor of rhetoric and chronology, and subsequently of Greek, in the university. In 1624 the university of Cambridge offered him a professorship, which he declined. Two years afterwards another unsuccessful effort was made to induce him to settle in England, but he accepted from Archbishop Laud a prebend in Canterbury cathedral of the value of £100 per annum, without residence, coming over to England to be installed in 1629, when he was made LL.D. at Oxford. In 1632 he left Leyden to take the post of professor of history in the newly founded Athenæum at Amsterdam, which he held till his death, March 17, 1649.

He was one of the great scholars of the world, and his character added lustre to his learning. His works, of which a complete edition appeared at Amsterdam, 1695-1701, in 6 vols. fol., are philological, historical, and theological. He made invaluable contributions to the correct study of Latin grammar and of the Greek and Latin historians. He was amongst the first to treat theological dogmas and the heathen religions from the historical point of view. His principal works are *Historia Pelagiana* (1618); *Etymologicum Linguæ Latinæ* (1662); *Commentariorum Rhetoricorum Libri VII.* (1606); *De Historicis Græcis Libri III.* (1624); *De Historicis Latinis Libri III.* (1627); *De Theologia Gentili* (1642); *Dissertationes Tres de Tribus Symbolis, Apostolico, Athanasiano, et Constantinopolitano* (1642).

See Nicéron, *Mémoires pour servir à l'Histoire des Hommes Illustres*, vol. xiii., Paris, 1730; Herzog's *Realencyklopädie*, art. "Vossius."

VOSSIUS, Isaac (1618–1689), son of the preceding, was born at Leyden in 1618, and was carefully educated by his father. After three years spent on a learned tour through England, France, and Italy, which he used in making the acquaintance of the first scholars and the great libraries of those countries, and from which he brought back many valuable MSS., he accepted in 1648 an invitation to the court of the brilliant Queen Christina of Sweden, whom he taught Greek. He declined the offer of the chair of history at Amsterdam vacated by his father's death, and continued for some years in Sweden, with occasional visits to Holland. In 1658 he finally left Sweden. His father's merits and his own learning procured him favour with Louis XIV. of France and in England. In 1670 he came to reside in England, was made LL.D. of Oxford, and in spite of notorious looseness of morals and levity of character received a canonry at Windsor from Charles II. in 1673, residing in the castle, where he died in February 1689.

His learning was great, and he rendered valuable services in connexion with ancient history, antiquities, chronology, and geography, though they were marred by the admixture of great levity and want of judgment. To him is owing the first Greek text of the six shorter epistles of Ignatius (1646). He published valuable editions of the geographer Scylax (1639), of Justin (1640), of Pomponius Mela (1648), and of Catullus (1684). In his various dissertations on chronology he maintained the greater accuracy of the system of the Septuagint in comparison with that of the Hebrew text, and generally asserted the greater genuineness of the Greek translation as compared with the Massoretic text. He inherited his father's valuable library, which, to the great sorrow of Evelyn, went after his death back to Holland.

Comp. Nicéron's *Mémoires*, vol. xiii.

VOTKINSK, an iron-work in the Urals, in the Russian government of Vyatka, 47 miles north of Sarapul, and 8 miles from the Kama, was founded in 1756. Its population reached 15,480 in 1885. Together with the Kamsk iron-work, Votkinsk was till lately one of the chief Government establishments for the construction of steamers for the Caspian flotilla, as well as of locomotives for the Siberian railway, and it has long been renowned for its excellent tarantasses and other smaller iron-wares, as well as for its knitted goods. No large orders having been received from the Government, a number of workmen recently united into an "artel" or co-operative society for the manufacture of agricultural machinery, already known throughout Russia for its excellence and cheapness.

VOUET, Simon (1590–1649), French painter, born at Paris, January 9, 1590, passed many years in Italy, where he married, and established himself at Rome, enjoying there a high reputation as a portrait painter. Louis XIII. recalled him to France, lodged him in the Louvre with the title of First Painter to the Crown, and gave him a considerable salary. All royal work for the palaces of the Louvre and the Luxembourg was placed in his hands; the king became his pupil; he formed a large school, and renewed the traditions of that of Fontainebleau. Amongst his scholars was the famous Lebrun (who raised on the foundations laid by his master the tyranny by which he dominated the whole artistic world during the reign of Louis XIV.), Lebrun's rival Errard, Louis Lerambert, the two Testelins, Poerson, and Dorigny. Vouet was an exceedingly skilful painter, especially in decoration, and executed important works of this class for Cardinal Richelieu (Rueil and Palais Royal) and other great nobles. His better easel pictures bear a curious resemblance to those of Sassoferrato, but, being much in demand, he fell into mannerisms, and of the enormous quantity of work produced by himself or with the aid of his pupils little has survived worth study. Almost everything he did was engraved by his sons-in-law Tortebat and Dorigny.

VOW, a solemn undertaking to do something which is held to be acceptable to the Deity. In the antique religions mere prayer, without some material expression of homage, was not held to be a complete or normal act of worship (*cf.* Sacrifice). Supplications, therefore, were generally presented to the Deity in connexion with a sacrifice, or, if the moment of need was one at which a ritual offering could not well be presented, the prayer for help was naturally accompanied by a promise to present a gift at a future time. Thus prayer together with a vow is a sort of imperfect act of worship, which has to be completed by the discharge of the vow at the sanctuary. So in Greek the same word εὐχή is equally applicable to the prayer which opened a service of sacrifice and to a vow taken at the commencement of an enterprise or in other time of need. So too the Latin *votum* means both "vow" and "desire." In the Old Testament, in like manner, it is generally a sacrifice or gift at the sanctuary which is promised in vows, and the word "vow" (*nédhr*) means also "a votive sacrifice," as distinguished from obligatory sacrifices (piacular offerings and stated festal sacrifices; 1 Sam. i. 21).

The vows of which we read in the Old Testament and in classical authors are generally conditional on the fulfilment of the petition with which they are coupled. Such vows are made on occasions of special need, or difficulty (Ps. lxvi. 13 *sq.*; Pliny, *H. N.*, viii. 21 [57], "tum præcipuus votorum locus est cum spei nullus est"), as before a perilous enterprise (Gen. xxviii. 20; Judg. xi. 30). The payment offered may be a victim for the altar, or any other gift which the ritual of the religion acknowledges as acceptable. But, as vows are generally made on extraordinary occasions, the thing promised will often be exceptional in kind or magnitude. The vow of Jephthah (Judg. xi.) is a case in point, and also illustrates by an extreme example the principle that a vow once taken must be fulfilled at any cost. This principle was so far modified in later times, in Israel, that exceptional vows were by law redeemed at a valuation (Lev. xxvii.). Hannah's vow, devoting her unborn son to the service of the sanctuary (1 Sam. i. 11), would have fallen under this law. Moreover, the law provided that the vow of an unmarried daughter or of a wife might be disallowed by the father or husband respectively (Numb. xxx.). On the other hand, a widow or a divorced woman was free to make what vow she pleased. These provisions are important evidence of the legal position of woman in Hebrew society, and also, *ex silentio*, as implying that Hebrew sons (at least after infancy) were not subject to *patria potestas* of the Roman kind.

Of ordinary vows a common type in antiquity was a promise made in peril by sea, sickness, or other straits, to suspend in a temple a picture or other symbol of the danger against which the Divine aid was implored. This usage passed into Christianity and survives in Catholic countries, where votive pictures and models of eyes, hands, &c., cured in answer to prayer, are still seen in churches. At the council of Lestines (743 A.D.) the use of such models was condemned as a pagan practice.

In point of obligation, vows were analogous to oaths (Numb. xxx. 2); their sanction was not human but Divine (Deut. xxiii. 21). Thus slackness or fraud in the fulfilment of vows is the mark of an age of declining faith (Mal. i. 14; Ḥárith, *Moall.*, l. 69 Arnold; Lucian, *Jupiter Trag.*, c. 15; *cf.* Eccles. v. 4). Among the Arabs the speedy fulfilment of vows was favoured by a rule of abstinence from certain enjoyments and conveniences (*iḥrām*), which custom imposed till the vow was fulfilled. This appears to have been the ancient practice of other Semitic nations also; among the Hebrews it survives in the Nazarite vow (see NAZARITE), and probably also in the *esār* or *issār* (interdict), which is mentioned along with vows in Numb. xxx., and is described in verse 13 as "an oath of abstinence to afflict the soul,"—words which seem to show that fasting is specially contemplated. As there is no ascetic tendency in Hebrew religion, in which fasting and similar observances have not positive religious value, but are only expressions of penitent supplication, it seems reasonable to interpret the oath of abstinence by the aid of the examples in Psalm cxxxii. 2 *sq.*, Acts xxiii. 12 (*cf.* also 1 Sam. xiv. 24 *sq.*), and to understand it, like the Arabian *iḥrām*, as an obligation of abstinence till a positive vow was fulfilled. The detail in the Psalm, "I will not enter my house or rest in my bed till," &c., has its parallel in Arabia and in Syrian heathenism (Sūr. ii. 185—where to enter the house from behind is an evasion of the rule; Lucian, *Dea Syr.*, § 55; *cf.* Wellhausen, *Skizzen*, iii. 117). It is to be observed that in Arabia, where there was little or no development of obligatory ritual sacrifices, offerings were usually votive, and vows were often simple and not conditional promises; so too in Deut. xxiii. 23, Lev. vii. 16, vows are closely associated with free-will offerings. A purpose of sacrifice formed at a distance from a sanctuary naturally found expression in a vow. Occasions of sacrifice are not frequent in nomad life and it may be conjectured that the earliest vows were simply deferred sacrifices, without the element of bargaining with the Divinity which is prominent in later times. The simple vow presupposes that the sanctuary or the customary day of sacrifice is remote; the conditional vow, on the other hand, may often be made at the sanctuary itself, where the Godhead is nearest to man (Gen. xxviii. 20; 1 Sam. i. 11; *Iliad*, vii. 93).

In Christian times vows to present a material gift (*vota realia*) have been less important than vows to adopt a certain course of life (*vota personalia*), a change which naturally followed from the modification of the idea of sacrifice in Christianity (see SACRIFICE). The personal vows recognized by the Catholic church are of various kinds, covering all manner of actions religiously meritorious (*e.g.*, pilgrimage or crusading); but the most prominent have been vows of abstinence (fasting, chastity), to which the growth of asceticism gave a positive value. Most important of all is the monastic vow of poverty, chastity, and obedience (see MONACHISM). The presupposition of all such vows is that there is a higher life of godliness, which cannot be attained to by Christians at large, and which all are not bound to attempt, although there is merit in consecrating oneself to it. From this point of view it came about in process of time that vows of self-consecration were viewed as necessarily perpetual. To fall back from a purpose of higher life was not at all the same thing as never to have formed such a purpose. Hence, *e.g.*, the vow of chastity, which Cyprian still regards as terminable by marriage in the case of virgins who have not strength to persevere in continence, was declared to be of perpetual obligation as early as the council of Ancyra (314 A.D.). On the other hand, the church was careful to guard against the rash assumption of vows, by requiring certain formalities in the act, and by the institution of the noviciate, as a period of probation. The power of the pope to dispense from vows, which appears in the *Decretals*, was of later growth. Protestantism, denying the superior merit of the ascetic life, rejects all perpetual vows, and indeed shows little favour to vows of any kind. (W. R. S.)

VRANCX, SEBASTIAN, born about 1572, was a painter of the Antwerp school, of very moderate ability. Most of his pictures represent scenes of war, such as the sack of towns, cavalry combats, and the like. Though occasionally vigorous in drawing, his paintings are dull and heavy in tone. The date of his death is uncertain.

VULCAN, the old Roman fire-god, answering to the Greek HEPHÆSTUS (*q.v.*), with whom he was confounded by the ancients. The etymology of the name is uncertain: it has been proposed to derive it from the root *var*, "warm"; *ulka* in Sanscrit is a firebrand. How closely Vulcan was identified with the fire, regarded as a person, appears from the stories of the birth of Cæculus and Servius Tullius, both of whom were called sons of Vulcan, and were supposed to have been conceived by virgins who had been impregnated by sparks of fire from the hearth. At Rome his temple was in the Campus Martius outside the city walls. But there was also a place sacred to him in the comitium. It was not a temple, but only a raised area, called the Volcanal. It was said to have been founded by Romulus, and a lotus tree in it was thought to be as old as the city. Statues of persons who or whose statues had been struck by lightning were sometimes set up in the Volcanal. There was a festival of Vulcan called the Volcanalia on August 23d, in which the people threw animals into the fire instead of themselves. On the 7th of June there was a fishermen's festival, with games, held under the superintendence of the "prætor urbanus," and the fish were brought to the Volcanal and sacrificed to the god instead of human victims. Another festival of Vulcan was the Tubilustria, or purification of trumpets, on May 23d, Vulcan being regarded as the father of trumpets. At Ostia there was a festival of Vulcan (Volcanalia) presided over by a "prætor sacris Volcani faciundis," and at Ostia there were also a temple and a pontifex of Vulcan. At Rome there was a "flamen" of Vulcan, who sacrificed to Maia, wife of Vulcan, on the 1st of May. According to others the name of Vulcan's wife was Majesta.

VULCANO. See LIPARI ISLANDS, vol. xiv. p. 682.

VULGATE. See BIBLE, vol. iii. p. 647.

VULTURE, the name of certain birds whose best-known characteristic is that of feeding upon carcases, and these birds, owing to this obscene habit, are in many hot countries regarded with favour as useful scavengers. The genus *Vultur*, as instituted by Linnæus, is now restricted by ornithologists to a single species, *V. monachus*, of which more presently, the other species included therein by him, or thereto referred by succeeding systematists, being elsewhere relegated (*cf.* LÄMMERGEYER); but the most important taxonomic change that has been introduced is that by Prof. Huxley (*Proc. Zool. Society*, 1867, pp. 462–464), who pointed out the complete structural difference between the Vultures of the New World and those of the Old, regarding the former as constituting a distinct Family, *Cathartidæ* (which, however, would be more properly named *Sarcorhamphidæ*), while he united the latter with the ordinary diurnal Birds-of-Prey as *Gypaetidæ*. This arrangement seems to overlook the signification of some considerable distinctions, and to the present writer it would appear more reasonable to recognize the existence of a Family *Vulturidæ*, confined to the true Vultures of the Ancient Continent, equal in rank to the *Falconidæ*, while fully admitting the claim made on behalf of the New-World forms for the same standing.

The American Vulture may be said to include four genera:—(1) *Sarcorhamphus*, the gigantic Condor, the male distinguished by a large fleshy comb and wattles; (2) *Gypagus*, the King-Vulture, with its gaudily-coloured head and nasal caruncle; (3) *Catharista*, containing the so-called Turkey-Buzzard of English-speaking Americans with its allies; and (4) *Pseudogryphus*, the great Californian Vulture—of very limited range on the western slopes of North America, and threatened with speedy extinction through the use of poison. Though all these birds are structurally so different from the true Vultures of the Old World, in habits the *Vulturidæ* and *Sarcorhamphidæ* are much alike, and of several of the latter—

King-Vulture (*Gypagus papa*).

particularly of the Condor and the Turkey-Buzzard—we possess rather elaborate accounts by excellent observers, as Darwin, Alexander Wilson, and Mr Gosse—whose works are readily accessible.

The true Vultures of the Old World, *Vulturidæ* in the restricted sense, are generally divided into five or six genera, of which *Neophron* has been not unjustifiably separated as forming a distinct Subfamily, *Neophroninæ*,—its members, of comparatively small size, differing both in structure and habit considerably from the rest. One of them is the so-called Egyptian Vulture or Pharaoh's Hen, *N. percnopterus*, a bird whose delicacy of build and appearance contrast forcibly with its choice of the most filthy kind of food. It is a well-known species in some parts of India,[1] and thence westward to Africa, where it has an extensive range. It also occurs on the northern shores of the Mediterranean, and on three occasions has strayed to such a distance from its usual haunts as to have twice suffered capture in England, and once even in Norway. Of the genera composing the other Subfamily, *Vulturinæ*, space is wanting to say much. *Gyps* numbers seven or eight local species and races, on more than one of which the English name Griffon has been fastened. The best known is *G. fulvus*, which by some authors is accounted "British," from an example having been taken in Ireland, though under circumstances which suggest its appearance so far from its nearest home in Spain to be due to man's intervention. The species, however, has a wider distribution on the European continent (especially towards the north-east) than the Egyptian Vulture, and in Africa nearly reaches the Equator, extending also in Asia to the Himalaya; but both in the Ethiopian and Indian Regions its range inosculates with that of several allied forms or species. *Pseudogyps* with two forms—one Indian, the other African—differs from *Gyps* by having 12 instead of 14 rectrices. Of the genera *Otogyps* and *Lophogyps* nothing here need be said; and then we have *Vultur*, with, as mentioned before, its sole representative, *V. monachus*, commonly known as the Cinereous Vulture, a bird which is found from the Straits of Gibraltar to the sea-coast of China.[2] Almost all these birds inhabit rocky cliffs, on the ledges of which they build their nests.

The question whether Vultures in their search for food are guided by sight of the object or by its scent has long excited much interest, and the advocates of either opinion have warmly contended in its behalf. Without denying to them the olfactory faculty, it seems to be now generally admitted, notwithstanding the assertions to the contrary of Waterton and a few more, that the sense of sight is in almost every case sufficient to account for the observed facts. It is known that, directly a camel or other beast of burden drops dead, as the caravan to which it belonged is making its way across the desert, Vultures of one sort or another appear, often in considerable numbers, though none had before been observed by the ordinary traveller, and speedily devour the carcase over which they are gathered together. The mode in which communication is effected between the birds, which are soaring at an immense height, seems at first inexplicable, but Canon Tristram has suggested (*Ibis*, 1859, p. 280) the following simple solution of the supposed mystery:—

"The Griffon who first descries his quarry descends from his elevation at once. Another, sweeping the horizon at a still greater distance, observes his neighbour's movements and follows his course. A third, still further removed, follows the flight of the second; he is traced by another; and so a perpetual succession is kept up so long as a morsel of flesh remains over which to consort. I can conceive no other mode of accounting for the number of Vultures which in the course of a few hours will gather over a carcase, when previously the horizon might have been scanned in vain for more than one, or at the most two, in sight."

The Canon goes on to suppose that in this way may be explained the enormous congregation of Vultures in the Crimea during the siege of Sevastopol, where they had before been scarce:—"the habit of watching the movements of their neighbours" may "have collected the whole race from the Caucasus and Asia Minor"—he might have added the Balkans—"to enjoy so unwonted an abundance." Doubt may be entertained whether the last supposition be correct, but none as to the accuracy of the first. (A. N.)

VYATKA, or **Viatka**, a government of north-eastern Russia, with Vologda on the N., Perm on the E., Ufa and Kazañ on the S., and Nijni Novgorod and Kostroma on the W., has an area of 59,124 square miles. It has on its northern boundary the flat water-parting which separates the basins of the Northern Dwina and Volga, and its surface is an undulating plateau of from 800 to 1400 feet above sea-level, deeply grooved by rivers and assuming a hilly aspect on their banks, broken up as they are by ravines. Permian sandstones, marls, and limestones cover it; over these is boulder clay, with extensive forests and marshes. The Kama rises in the north-east, and, after making a wide sweep through Perm, flows along its south-eastern boundary, while the whole of the government is watered by the Vyatka and its numerous tributaries. Both the Kama and the Vyatka are navigable, as also are several of their tributaries; the Izha and Votka, which flow into the latter, have important iron-works on their banks. As many as 1,700,000 cwts. of corn, iron, hides, leather, tallow, timber, and wooden wares were loaded in 1883 at the landing-places of Vyatka, while the traffic on the Kama is still more important. There are no railways, but the province is traversed by the great highway to Siberia, and two other roads by which goods from the south are transported to

[1] In the eastern part of the Indian peninsula it is replaced by a smaller race or (according to some authorities) species, *N. gingianus*, which has a yellow instead of a black bill.

[2] The geographical range of the various species of Vultures has been exhaustively treated by Mr Sharpe (*Journ. Linn. Society*, Zoology, xiii. pp. 1-26, pls. i.-ix.).

loading-places on the Vytchegda and the Yug to be shipped farther north to Archangel. Lakes are numerous, and vast marshes are met with everywhere, especially in the north; three-quarters of the area are under forests. The climate is very severe, the average yearly temperature being 36° F. at Vyatka (January, 8°·2; July, 67°·0), and 35° at Slobodskoi (January, 3°·5; July, 65°·3).

The population (2,859,000 in 1883, as against 2,170,221 in 1861), though sparse on the average, is somewhat dense in the better-situated valleys. The bulk consists of Great Russians (81 per cent.), but there are also considerable remains of the aboriginal Votiaks (250,000), Tcheremisses (about 150,000), Tartars, Tepters, Permians, and even Bashkirs. Mohammedans number about 100,000, and pagans (Tcheremisses and Votiaks) about 11,000. The Votiaks (Otiaks), a Finnish stem of the Permian group, call themselves Ot, Ut, or Ud, and the Tartars call them Ar, so that it is supposed that they may be akin to the Ars of the Yenisei. They are middle-sized, with fair hair and eyes, often red-haired; and the general structure of the face and skull is Finnish. By their dialect they belong to the same branch as the Permians. They are excellent agriculturists, very laborious, and excel in bee-keeping.

The soil is fertile, especially in the valleys of the south; rye, barley, oats, buckwheat, and to some extent wheat are grown. The crops of 1885 were—rye, 4,006,000 quarters; oats, 3,957,000; barley, 734,000; wheat, 98,000; potatoes, 231,000 quarters. Corn is exported to the Kama or to the north, as also are flax and hemp. There is no want of natural meadows in the south, and cattle-rearing prospers. The Vyatka horses, a fine breed, though rather small, are well known throughout Russia. There were in 1883 706,600 horses, 925,100 cattle, and 1,446,400 sheep. Attempts are being made to introduce finer breeds of cows and sheep.

Industries are developing steadily, there having been in 1884 684 establishments, which employed 9700 workmen, and showed a yearly return of £1,510,000. They include distilleries (£885,600), iron-works, chemical works, tanneries, soap and glass works, and cotton and paper mills. VOTKINSK (*q.v.*) has a considerable yearly production of agricultural machinery and steam-engines. The crown manufactory of guns at Izhevsk works up yearly 10,000 cwts. of steel. Domestic trades give occupation to more than 40,000 persons, and their returns in 1884 reached £706,800. The manufacture of wooden vessels, window frames, doors, furniture, sledges, and carts supplies a considerable export trade to the steppe provinces of the lower Volga. Domestic weaving produces, it is estimated, about 5,400,000 yards of linen every year. Many peasants have nevertheless to leave their homes in search of work, either as "burlaki" for shipping and dragging boats or as porters; hunting and bird-catching still have some importance in the forest tracts.

Trade is considerable,—iron, copper, tar, pitch, glass, leather, paper, timber, and wooden wares, as also corn, hides, flax, linseed, honey, and other raw produce being exported to Nijni Novgorod, Orenburg, and Siberia; while groceries and various manufactured goods are imported.

Vyatka is one of those few governments of Russia where the *zemstvo*, consisting to a great extent of representatives of the peasantry, has succeeded in creating a series of educational institutions without incurring the displeasure of the Government. It distinguishes itself very favourably by its schools, libraries, surgeons, and hospitals in villages, and by its elaborate house-to-house statistical descriptions of several districts, and statistical publications. There were in 1884 641 primary and 22 secondary schools.

Vyatka is divided into eleven districts—those of VYATKA (24,480 inhabitants in 1885); Elabuga (9750); Głazoff (1945); Kotelnitch (4490); Małmyzh (3400); Nolinsk (3990); Orłoff (3380); Sarapul (12,370); Słobodskoi (9225); Urzhum (5100); Yaransk (2855). VOTKINSK (*q.v.*) has 15,480 inhabitants, and Izhevsk has 21,500.

VYATKA, capital of the above government, is situated on the Vyatka river, 653 miles to the north-east of Moscow. It is built mostly of wood, on the steep hills which rise above the river, as well as on their slopes and at their base. Its old walls have been demolished, and its old churches built anew. Two public gardens, a small public library, and the usual educational institutions of a Russian provincial town are all that it can boast of. Its manufactures are insignificant, but its trade in corn, leather, tallow, candles, soap, wax, paper, and furs (exported), and in all kinds of manufactured and grocery wares (imported), is important. The population in 1885 was 24,480.

Vyatka was founded in 1181 by the Novgorodians, under the name of Khłynoff, for the purpose of maintaining their dominion among the Votiaks, Tcheremisses, and Tartars. The squirrel and beaver furs, especially the latter (beaver being then common in the region), and the Vyatka horses, as also wax and honey, were the chief attractions for trade; and, notwithstanding the dangers then encountered on the route to Vyatka and Perm, *via* Vologda, the Novgorod merchants and *ukshuiniki* (plundering merchants) willingly visited Vyatka and settled there. The town soon grew around the fort, and had to be enclosed within new walls. In 1391 it was plundered by the Tartars, and again in 1477. The power of Novgorod was decaying, and the Moscow princes, always pursuing the same policy of intrigue, and showing themselves ready to take up the cause of the poorer classes against the richer merchants, made advantageous use of internal struggles, and annexed Khłynoff to Moscow in 1489. It received the name of Vyatka in 1780.

VYAZMA, a district town of Russia, in the government of Smolensk, and 109 miles by rail to the north-east of that town, was a populous place as early as the 11th century, and carried on a lively trade with Narva on the Gulf of Finland. In the 15th century it fell under the dominion of the Lithuanian princes, but was too close to Moscow to remain in their hands, and was retaken by the Russians by the end of the century. The Poles took it again, however, during the outbreak of 1611, and kept it till the peace of 1634. At present it is an important centre for the trade of Smolensk; corn, hemp, linseed and hemp seed, tallow, and hides are exported to St Petersburg and Riga, while fish, metals, and manufactured goods are supplied to the neighbouring region chiefly by the Vyazma merchants. The population was 13,000 in 1882.

VYERNYI, formerly AŁMATY, capital of the Russian Central-Asian province of Semiryetchensk, is situated on a plateau at the base of the Trans-Ili Alatau, in 43° 16′ N. lat., 47 miles to the south of the Ili river. It was founded in 1854 as a small blockhouse, but from the advantages of its situation—the fertility of the surrounding country, the ample water-supply from the Ałmatinka river, and of timber and firewood from the valleys of the Alatau—it rapidly increased; in 1884 the population numbered 17,545, nearly 3000 of them military. Around the central blocks are several suburbs of wooden and brick houses; the streets are broad and planted with trees. Most of the houses are surrounded by thick growths of poplar and elm as well as by fruit-gardens, and the streets and squares are refreshed by channels of running water. The Little Russian, Kirghiz, and Tarantchi villages which surround the town, and have excellent orchards, amply supply Vyernyi with all necessaries. The Tarantchis proved specially helpful to the young settlement on account of their laborious habits and their acquaintance with the agriculture of the steppes. Situated as it is on the site of the old Ałmaty, at the crossing of two roads—from Kuldja to Tashkend, and from Semipalatinsk to Kashgar—Vyernyi carries on an active trade in wheat, rice, corn, tea, oil, and tobacco. The dislocation of the rocks on the northern slope of the Alatau Mountains is the cause of severe earthquakes, the last of which, on June 9, 1887, destroyed or damaged nearly a thousand stone houses in Vyernyi and its neighbourhood, killing 326 persons. Slighter shocks were felt up till February 1888.

VYSHNIY VOŁOTCHOK, a district town of Russia, in the government of Tver, 82 miles by rail to the north-west of that city, owes its importance to its situation in the centre of the Vyshne-Vołotsk navigation system, which connects the upper Volga with the Neva. The portage (*vołok*) of less than 17 miles between the Tvertsa, a tributary of the Volga, and the Tsna, which flows into the Msta and the Volkhoff (Lake Ladoga), had long been used for transporting boats from the one basin to the other, and the canal, which was afterwards dug, soon became one of the most important links of connexion between the Volga and the Neva; now, however, the boats prefer the Mariinsk system, and the prosperity of Vyshniy Vołotchok is declining. The inhabitants (11,590 in 1884) support themselves chiefly by shipping, and partly by the cotton industry. The trade is still considerable.

W

W is simply double *v*, so far as the form goes; but its value, like its name, is double *u*, and it dates back to a time when *u* and *v* had not been fully differentiated, one into a vowel, the other into a consonant (see under U). The oldest form of the letter was *uu*, sometimes *u* only; *e.g.*, uulfheard, uilfrith, in the *Liber Vitæ*, 9th century. Later, a peculiar symbol appears, ƿ, called "wen"; this belonged to the runic alphabet, which the Latin superseded: it undoubtedly represented the *w*-sound. It died out about 1300, probably through the influence of French copyists. As early as the 11th century we find *vv*, later *w*.

The sound denoted by W is a voiced labial, formed by rounding the lips so much that the voice cannot escape without friction. In the nature of the case no hard and fast line can be drawn between it and the vowel *u* (any more than between *i* and *y*): it is impossible to say exactly at what point the open position of the lips for *u* ceases and sufficient closure for a definite consonant begins. We may perhaps mark out three noticeable sounds:—(1) the clear vowel *u*; (2) a consonant *u*, equivalent to a "glide" in the diphthongs "eu," "ou," &c., *i.e.*, a sound which is held not long enough to be a vowel as forming a syllable by itself, yet without sufficient friction to make a consonant; (3) the consonant *w*. The difference between (2) and (3) may be illustrated by the initial sounds of French "oui" and English "we"; the *ou* in "oui" is a consonant *u*; it does not make a syllable distinct from the following *i*, and so it is not a vowel; yet it is quite distinguishable from the *w* in "we." It is probable, from some slight indications, principally in Sanskrit, that both (2) and (3) were sounds of the Indo-European language. But it could hardly be supposed that they would be kept rigorously distinct in the derived languages; they lie too near together.

It has been already pointed out (see article U) that the representatives of the sound *w* varied much in the different languages. In Greek we find ϝ and sometimes υ (as in εὔαδε, &c.); in Latin there was no symbol to distinguish it from the vowel *u*. The English varieties are mentioned above.

For the history of this sound in connexion with the velar *k* of the original speech see article Q. This sound died out in most of the derived languages, but left traces in Greek—(1) in the symbol koppa, (2) in the phonetic change called "labialism," by which the slight labial of the original sound developed and eventually changed the guttural explosive into a labial, *e.g.*, k^{w}ou became ποῦ. Similarly in Italy the Latin *qu* of "qui," "quantus," &c., preserved the original symbol and sound, whereas the Oscan and Umbrian agreed with the Greek in labializing.

In English the *w*-sound has commonly held its own. It has survived in writing, even in the almost impossible combination *wr*, as in "wrath," "write," "wreck," "wretch," but the sound is lost. In several Old English words the combination *cw* was exchanged for *qu*, as was natural under French influence, *e.g.*, quoth (O.E. cwæð), quell (O.E. cwellan), queen (O.E. cwên).

The digraph *wh* denotes the voiceless sound corresponding to the voiced *w*. In the great majority of cases where it occurs it represents original k^{w}, as in who, what (original base $k^{w}a$); these were originally written hwá, hwæt; so also "while" was "hwil," "wheeze" was "hwæs" (Lat. ques-tus). In similar combinations with *l* and *r* the *h* has been lost, as in "loud," formerly "hlúd" (κλυτός), raven (hræfn), ring (hring); and in *hw* the *h* seems to have robbed the *w* of its voice (a result denoted by the writing *wh*), and then fallen off here also as an independent sound.

WACE, whom most modern writers without any authority call ROBERT, but who simply calls himself "MAISTRE WACE," was a clerk ("clerc lisant") and trouvère of the 12th century, who was born in Jersey, studied at Caen, and received from Henry II. a prebend at Bayeux with other gifts. Nothing is known certainly of the dates of his birth or death; but the one is conjecturally put at about 1120 and the other at about 1180. He seems to have been much about the reigning house of Normandy and England: he boasts of the kindness of Henry to him (he knew, he says, three Henrys, the third being Prince Henry, the eldest son of Henry II.), and is said by Layamon to have dedicated his *Brut* to Eleanor of Aquitaine. This shadowy personality is partly compensated by a considerable literary work. Wace has left two long romances, the *Roman de Brut* and the *Roman de Rou*, both of which are interesting monuments of Norman French, while the latter is a document of some importance for English history, the writer informing us that he got some direct information from his father, who no doubt was not his only source. The *Roman de Brut*, the longer of the two, is in octosyllabic couplets of a facile and somewhat undistinguished kind. It has generally been regarded as a mere versifying of Geoffrey of Monmouth, a point which turns to some extent of course on the vexed question of Geoffrey's own originals. The *Roman de Rou*, a chronicle of the Norman dukes, is much more interesting and much more vigorously written. The greater part of it is also in octosyllables, but there is a large insertion of assonanced alexandrines in something like the form of the chansons de geste. Wace is not in mere poetical value a very good example of the trouvères, but his subjects give him interest, especially for Englishmen.

The first and hitherto the only edition of the *Brut* is that of Le Roux de Lincy (1838); the *Rou*, after being edited by Pluguet in 1827, has been recently (1877) re-edited by Dr Hugo Andresen.

WACO, a city and the county seat of M'Lennan county, Texas, U.S., is situated on the west bank of the Brazos river, at the mouth of the Bosque, in an agricultural and pastoral region. It contains Waco university (Baptist) and a female college. The population in 1880 was 7295, more than one-third being negroes.

WADAI. See SOUDAN, vol. xxii. p. 279.

WADDING, LUKE (1588–1657), ecclesiastical historian, born at Waterford in 1588, emigrated with his parents to Spain in early youth, and from Spain passed to Portugal, to study at the Irish College in Lisbon. While still a student, he entered the order of Cordeliers, or Friars Minim, in 1604, taking the name Michael Angelo of St Romulus, and his early reputation for learning soon obtained for him a professorship of theology at Salamanca. Philip III. of Spain was anxious to procure the formal definition of the Immaculate Conception B. V. M., which had been left open by the council of Trent, and sent Diego de Torres, bishop of Cartagena, as ambassador to the pope for that purpose. Torres, being himself a Cordelier, made choice of Wadding to accompany him on his embassy, and the young divine created so favourable an impression at Rome that another chair of theology was bestowed upon him there, and he was made vice-commissary and procurator-general of his order. He made Rome his headquarters for the remainder of his life, dying there as principal of the Irish College of St Isidore in 1657.

His earliest publication was an account of the embassy in which he had taken part, Πρεσβεία, *sive Legatio Philippi III. et IV., Hispaniarum Regum, ad Summos Pontifices Paulum V., Gregorium XV., et Urbanum VIII., pro definienda Controversia Immaculatæ*

Conceptionis Beatæ Mariæ Virginis (Louvain, 1624, fol.). He contributed, many years later, a work to this question himself, *Immaculatæ Conceptionis Beatæ Mariæ Opusculum* (Rome, 1655, 8vo), now of extreme rarity. He was also author of a treatise on the Hebrew language and other occasional writings, but his literary reputation rests chiefly upon the important works he published in connexion with the Franciscan order. The principal of these are *Annales Ordinis Minorum*, 8 vols. folio (Lyons and Rome, 1628–1654), a book of high repute, recast and enlarged by Fonseca, 19 vols. folio (Rome, 1731–1745), and since continued by Michelesi, 1794, and Melchiori de Ceretto, 1844; *Scriptores Ordinis Minorum* (Rome, 1650), to which is subjoined a reprint of a *Syllabus FF. Minorum*, a list of the English Franciscans who were put to death in Tudor days, which had become extremely rare, because most of the original impression was sent to England during the legateship of Cardinal Pole, and was seized and destroyed by order of Queen Elizabeth, because of its reflexions upon the character of Henry VIII.; an edition of the *Concordantiæ Bibliorum Hebraicæ* of Calasio, 4 vols. folio (Rome, 1621); *Opera Omnia Joannis Duns Scoti*, 12 vols. in 11, folio (Lyons, 1639); *Sti Francisci Assisiatis Opuscula* (Antwerp, 1623); and *Sti Antonii Paduani Concordantiæ Morales* (Rome, 1624).

WAFERS, as articles of stationery, consist of thin, brittle, adhesive disks, used for securing papers together, and for forming a basis for impressed official seals. Wafers are made of a thin paste of very fine flour, baked between "wafer irons" over a charcoal fire till the thin stratum of paste becomes dry and brittle, and the flour starch is partly transformed into glutinous adhesive dextrin. The cake is cut into round disks with suitable steel punches. Bright non-poisonous colouring matter is added to the paste for making coloured wafers. Wafers of gelatin are also made.

WAGER. The law of wagers may be divided for purposes of convenience into two great classes, dealing respectively with procedure and with substantive law. In both classes the legal importance of the wager has tended to diminish.

Procedure.—Determination of cases, civil and criminal, by means of wager or analogous forms of procedure is a characteristic feature of archaic law. The *legis actio sacramenti* at Rome—at first a real, then a fictitious wager—the wager of battle and of law in England, of the highest antiquity in their origin, survived up to a comparatively late period in the history of both legal systems. The form of the wager survived long after its reason had been forgotten. The general prevalence of the wager form of proceeding is perhaps to be attributed to the early conception of a judge as a mere referee who decided the dispute submitted to him, not as an executive officer of the state, but as an arbitrator casually called in (see Maine, *Ancient Law*, c. x.). Wager of battle in England was a mode of trial which was allowed in certain cases, viz., on a writ of right (see WRIT), and on appeals of treason and felony (see APPEAL). A full account of the judicial combat will be found under DUEL and ORDEAL. Wager of law (*vadiatio legis*) was a right of a defendant in actions of simple contract debt and of detinue. It superseded the ordeal (itself called *lex* in the Assize of Clarendon and other ancient constitutional records). The mode of proceeding in a wager of law was an interesting relic of that system of compurgation—traced by Blackstone to the Mosaic law, Ex. xxii. 10—which was employed in many legal systems, especially the Scandinavian, and had probably an appreciable effect on the development of the English JURY (*q.v.*). It also has some points of resemblance, perhaps some historical connexion, with the *sponsio* and the decisory oath of Roman law, and the reference to oath of Scots law (see OATH). The use of the oath instead of the real or feigned combat—real in English law, feigned in Roman law—no doubt represents an advance in legal development. The technical term *sacramentum* is the bond of union between the two stages of law. In the wager of law the defendant, with eleven compurgators, appeared in court, and he swore that he did not owe the debt or (in detinue) that he did not detain the plaintiff's chattel; while the compurgators swore that they believed that he spoke the truth. It was an eminently unsatisfactory way of arriving at the merits of a claim, and it is therefore not surprising to find that the policy of the law was in favour of its restriction rather than of its extension. Thus it was not permitted where the defendant was not a person of good character, where the king sued, where the defendant was the executor or administrator of the person alleged to have owed the debt, or in any actions other than those named, even though the cause of action were the same. No wager of law was allowed in *assumpsit*, even though the cause of action were a simple debt. This led to the general adoption of *assumpsit*—proceeding originally upon a fictitious averment of a promise by the defendant—as a means of recovering debts. Where a penalty was created by statute, it became a common form to insert a proviso that no wager of law was to be allowed in an action for the penalty. Wager of law was finally abolished by 3 and 4 Will. IV. c. 42. Another form of the judicial wager in use up to 1845 was the feigned issue by which questions arising in the course of Chancery proceedings were sent for trial by jury in a common law court. The plaintiff averred the laying of a wager of £5 with the defendant that a certain event was as he alleged; the defendant admitted the wager, but disputed the allegation; on this issue was joined. 8 and 9 Vict. c. 109 enabled such questions to be referred by the Chancery to the common law courts in a direct manner.

Substantive Law.—A wager may be defined as "a promise to pay money or transfer property upon the determination or ascertainment of an uncertain event" (Anson, *Law of Contract*, p. 171). At common law wagers were legally enforceable, subject to certain rules dictated by considerations of public policy, *e.g.*, that they did not lead to immorality or breach of the peace, or expose a third person to ridicule. Actions or wagers were not favoured by the judges; and, though a judge could not refuse to try such an action, he could, and often did, postpone it until after the decision of more important cases. Parliament gradually intervened to confine the common law within narrower limits, both in commercial and non-commercial wagers, and both by general and temporary enactments. An example of the latter was 7 Anne c. 16, avoiding all wagers and securities relating to the then war with France. The earliest general enactment was 16 Car. II. c. 7, prohibiting the recovery of a sum exceeding £100 lost in games or pastimes, or betting on the sides or hands of the players, and avoiding securities for money so lost. 9 Anne c. 19 avoided securities for such wagers for any amount, even in the hands of *bona fide* holders for value without notice, and enabled the loser of £10 or upwards to sue for the money he had lost within three months. The hardship of the Act, as it affects securities in the hands of *bona fide* holders, was remedied by 5 and 6 Will. IV. c. 41, which enacted that such securities should be taken to be held for illegal consideration. Finally, 8 and 9 Vict. c. 109, § 18, enacted "that all contracts or agreements, whether by parole or in writing, by way of gaming or wagering shall be null and void; and that no suit shall be brought or maintained in any court of law or equity for recovering any sum of money or valuable thing alleged to be won upon any wager, or which shall have been deposited in the hands of any person to abide the event on which any wager shall have been made; provided always that this enactment shall not be deemed to apply to any subscription, or contribution, or agreement to subscribe or contribute, for or towards any plate, prize, or sum of money to be awarded to the winner or winners of any lawful game, sport, pastime, or exercise."

What is a lawful game depends upon numerous statutes from 33 Hen. VIII. c. 9 downwards, among which may be classed the Lottery Acts (see LOTTERIES). A curious exception is made in some of the statutes in favour of unlawful games if they are played in a royal palace. The mere making of a wager is not now illegal, as it was under the earlier statutes; it is simply unenforceable. The winner has no legal remedy against the loser or the stakeholder. The loser can recover his stake where it still remains in the stakeholder's hands or has been paid over to the winner after notice from the loser to the stakeholder not to pay it over. He cannot recover where it has been paid over to the winner without notice. The agent in a wagering contract may have legal rights against his principal, though the principal has none against the other party. Agreements between buyers and sellers of stocks and shares to pay or receive differences only (sometimes known as "time-bargains") are within 8 and 9 Vict. c. 109, but a broker employed to speculate on the understanding that only differences should be paid by his principal may recover indemnity against the principal. Employment of an agent to bet in his own name may imply an authority to pay the bet if lost, an authority that may become irrevocable after payment to the winner. Though wagers themselves are now void and not illegal, securities for wagers, by the combined effect of 5 and 6 Will. IV. c. 41 and 8 and 9 Vict. c. 109, are still either illegal (as a bet on the result of a game) or void (as a bet on the result of something other than a game, such as a contested election). This difference is important as affecting the question of burden of proof in actions on securities originally given for wagering purposes. Where the consideration is illegal, the plaintiff must show affirmatively that he gave value, but the mere absence of consideration throws on him no such duty. In commercial matters the most important examples are wagering policies of insurance, that is, policies made by persons having no insurable interest, and made void by statute (see INSURANCE). Sir John Barnard's Act, 7 Geo II. c. 8 (called "An Act to prevent the infamous practice of stock-jobbing"), prohibited contracts for liberty to accept or refuse any public stocks or securities, and wagers relating to the stocks.

In Scotland the courts refuse to try actions on wagers, as being *sponsiones ludicræ*, unbecoming the dignity of the courts. 9 Anne c. 19 and 5 and 6 Will. IV. c. 41 extend to Scotland, but the weight of judicial opinion is that 8 and 9 Vict. c. 109 does not. In the United States the loser may, by the legislation of some States, recover his money if he sue within a limited time, as he might have done in England under 9 Anne c. 19.

Definition.

WAGES. Wages, although one of the most common and familiar terms in economic science, is at the same time one of the most difficult to define accurately. The natural definition is that wages is the "reward for labour," but then we are at once confronted with the difficulty so well stated by Adam Smith:—"The greater part of people understand better what is meant by a quantity of a particular commodity than by a quantity of labour; the one is a plain palpable object, the other an abstract notion, which, though it can be made sufficiently intelligible, is not altogether so natural and obvious." If we regard wages as the reward for a quantity of labour, it is clear that to make the meaning precise we must give a precise meaning to this abstract notion of Adam Smith. From the point of view of the labourer the quantity of labour refers not so much to the work accomplished (*e.g.*, raising so many foot-pounds) as to "all the feelings of a disagreeable kind, all the bodily inconvenience or mental annoyance, connected with the employment of one's *thoughts* or muscles or both in a particular occupation" (J. S. Mill). But this analysis seems only to make the task of definition more difficult, for the class of labourers, in this wide sense of the term labour, would include the capitalist who racks his brains in making plans just as much as the navvy who digs with the sweat of his brow. Thus "profits," in the ordinary sense of the term, instead of being contrasted, would to a large extent be classified with wages, and in fact the wages of superintendence or of management is one of the recognized elements in the classical analysis of profits. It is, however, only when we refer to the list of "occupations" in any civilized country that we can really form an adequate idea of the variety of classes to which the term labour, as defined by Mill, may be extended. In the *General Report* of the census (1881) in England and Wales (published 1883) an analysis is given of the "unoccupied class." After deducting children and young persons under fifteen, persons over sixty-five years of age, who for the most part had been engaged in work of some kind previously, and those between the ages of fifteen and twenty, who might be considered as training for work, there remained 4,641,190 between the ages of twenty and sixty-five without specified occupation. But of these 4,458,908 were "women, of whom by far the greater part were married and engaged in the management of domestic life," and thus the number of males in the working period of life (20–65) of the "unoccupied" class was reduced to 182,282. Thus practically nearly the whole of the efficient male population of the country was engaged in some form of "labour" and in receipt of some form of "wages."

It may be granted that in certain economic inquiries it is extremely useful to bring out the points of resemblance between "workers" at the various stages of the social scale, and it is especially serviceable in showing that the opposition between "employer" and the "employed," and the "classes" and the "masses," is often exaggerated. At the same time, however, the differences, if not in kind at any rate in degree, are so great that if the analogy is carried very far it becomes misleading. Accordingly it seems natural to adopt as the preliminary definition of "wages" something equivalent to that of Prof. Walker in his work on the *Wages Question* (the best book on the subject as a whole), viz., "the reward of those who are employed in production with a view to the profit of their employers and are paid at stipulated rates." Even as thus restricted the "working or wage-earning classes" represent probably two-thirds of the population of the United Kingdom. It may be observed that by extending the meaning of production, as is now done by most economists, to include all kinds of labour, and by substituting benefit for profit, this definition will include all grades of wages.

Nominal and real wages.

Having thus limited the class of those who earn "wages," the next point is to consider the way in which the wages ought to be measured. The most obvious method is to take as the rate of *time-wages* the amount of *money* earned in a certain *time*, and as the rate of *task-wages* the amount of *money* obtained for a given amount of *work* of a given quality; and in many inquiries this rough mode of measurement is sufficient. But the introduction of money as the measure at once makes it necessary to assume that for purposes of comparison the value of the money to the wage-earners may be considered constant. This supposition, however, does not hold good even between different places in the same country at the same time, and still less with variations in time as well as place. To the labourers, however, the amount of money they obtain is only a means to an end, and accordingly economists have drawn a sharp distinction between *nominal* and *real* wages. "Labour, like commodities," says Adam Smith, "may be said to have a real and a nominal price. Its real price may be said to consist in the quantity of the necessaries and conveniences of life which are given for it; its nominal price in the quantity of money. The labourer is rich or poor, is well or ill rewarded, in proportion to the real not to the nominal price of his labour."

Variations in real wages.

Prof. Walker (*op. cit.*, p. 12 *sq.*) has given a full analysis of the principal elements which ought to be taken into account in estimating the *real* wages of labour. They may be classified as follows. (1) Variations in the purchasing power of money may be due in the first place to causes affecting the general level of prices in a country. Such, for instance, is a debasement of the coinage, of which a good example is furnished in English history in the reigns of Henry VIII. and Edward VI. Prof. Thorold Rogers has ascribed much of the degradation of labour which ensued to this fact; and Lord Macaulay has given a graphic account of the evils suffered by the labouring classes prior to the recoinage of 1696. The issues of inconvertible paper notes in excess have frequently caused a disturbance of real wages, and it is generally asserted that in this case wages as a rule do not rise so quickly as commodities. A general rise in prices due to great discoveries of the precious metals would, if nominal wages remained the same, of course cause a fall in real wages. There are, however, good grounds for supposing that the stimulus given to trade in this case would raise wages at least in proportion; and certainly the great gold discoveries in Australia and California raised wages in England, as is shown in Tooke's *History of Prices*, vol. v. p. 284. Similarly it is possible that a general fall in prices, owing to a relative scarcity of the precious metals, may lower the prices of commodities before it lowers the price of labour, in which case there is a rise in real wages. In the controversy as to the possible advantages of bimetallism this is one of the points most frequently discussed. It is impossible to say *a priori* whether a rise or fall in general prices, or a change in the value of money, will raise or lower real wages, since the result is effected principally by indirect influences. But, apart from these general movements in prices, we must, in order to find the real value of nominal wages, consider variations in local prices, and in making this estimate we must notice the principal items in the expenditure of the labourers. Much attention has been given recently by statisticians to this subject, with the view of finding a good "index number" for real wages. (2) Varieties in the form of payment require careful attention. Sometimes the payment is only partly in money, especially in agriculture in some places. In many parts of Scotland the labourers receive meal, peats, potatoes, &c. (3) Opportunities for extra earnings are sometimes of much importance, especially if we take as the wage-earning unit the family and not the individual. At the end of last century Arthur Young, in his celebrated tours, often calls attention to this fact. At the present time, in Northumberland and other counties a "hind" (*i.e.*, agricultural labourer) is more valued if he has a large working family, and the family earnings are relatively large. (4) Regularity of employment is always, especially in modern times, one of the most important points to be considered. Apart from such obvious causes of fluctuation as the nature of the employment, *e.g.*, in the case of fishermen, guides, &c., there are various social and industrial causes (for a particular and able investigation of which the reader may consult Prof. Foxwell's essay on the subject). Under the system of production on a large scale for foreign markets, with widely-extended division of labour, it seems impossible to adjust accurately the supply to the demand, and there are in consequence constant fluctuations in the employment of labour. A striking example, happily rare, is furnished by the cotton famine during the American civil war. (5) In forming a scientific conception of real wages we ought to take into account the longer or the shorter duration of the power to labour: the man whose employment is healthy and who lives more comfortably and longer at the same nominal rate of wages may be held to obtain a higher real wage than his less fortunate competitor. It is worth noting, in this respect, that in nearly every special industry there is a liability to some special form of disease: *e.g.*, lace-workers often suffer from diseases of the eyes, miners from diseases of the lungs, &c. (For further illustration the reader may consult the excellent works of Mr Bevan on *Industrial Classes and Industrial Statistics.*) Thus, in attempting to estimate real wages, we have to consider all the various discomforts involved in the "quantity of labour" as well as all the conveniences which the nominal wages will purchase and all the supplements in kind.

General rate of wages in any country at any time.

In a systematic treatment of the wages question it would be natural to examine next the causes which determine the general rate of wages in any country at any time. This is a problem to which economists have given much attention, and is one of great complexity. It is difficult, when we consider the immense variety of "occupations" in any civilized country and the constant changes which are taking place, even to form an adequate conception of the general rate of wages. At the census in 1881 in the United Kingdom, the commissioners found it necessary to make a small dictionary of the words by which different classes of workers described their callings, and without a special dictionary it would be impossible to classify such as the following: "blabber," "doctor-maker," "fluker," "egger," "lurer," "toother," &c., &c. There are thousands of occupations of various kinds, and at first sight it may seem impossible to determine, in a manner sufficiently accurate for any useful purpose, an average or general rate of wages, especially if we attempt to take real and not merely nominal wages. At the same time, however, in estimating the progress of the working-classes, or in comparing their relative positions in different countries, it is necessary to use this conception of a general rate of wages in a practical manner. The difficulties presented are of the same kind as those met with in the determination of the value of money or the general level of prices, and may be overcome to some extent by the same methods. An "index number" may be formed by taking various kinds of labour as fair samples, and the nominal wages thus obtained may be corrected by a consideration of the elements in the real wages to which they correspond. Care must be taken, however, that the quantity and quality of labour taken at different times and places are the same, just as in the case of commodities similar precautions are necessary. Practically, for example, errors are constantly made by taking the rate of wages for a short time (say an hour), and then, without regard to regularity of employment, constructing the annual rate on this basis; and again, insufficient attention is paid to Adam Smith's pithy caution that "there may be more labour in an hour's hard work than in two hours' easy business." But, however difficult it may be to obtain an accurate measure of the general rate of wages for practical purposes, there can be no doubt as to the value and necessity of the conception in the theory of political economy. For, as soon as it is assumed that industrial competition is the principal economic force in the distribution of the wealth of a community, and this is in reality the fundamental assumption of modern economic science, a distinction must be drawn between the most general causes which affect all wages and the particular causes which lead to differences of wages in different employments. In other words, the actual rate of wages obtained in any particular occupation depends partly on causes affecting that group compared with others, and partly on the general conditions which determine the relations between labour, capital, and production over the whole area in which the industrial competition is effective.

Wages-fund theory

Thus the theory of the wages question consists of two parts, or gives the answers to two questions:—(1) What are the causes which determine the general rate of wages? (2) Why are wages in some occupations and at some times and places above or below this general rate?

With regard to the first question, Adam Smith, as in almost every important economic theory, gives an answer which combines two views which were subsequently differentiated into antagonism. "The produce of labour constitutes the natural recompense or wages of labour," is the opening sentence of his chapter on wages. But then he goes on to say that "this original state of things, in which the labourer enjoyed the whole produce of his own labour, could not last beyond the first introduction of the appropriation of land and the accumulation of stock." And he thus arrives at the conclusion that "the demand for those who live by wages, it is evident, cannot increase but in proportion to the increase of the *funds* which are *destined* to the payment of wages." This is the germ of the celebrated wages-fund theory which was carried to an extreme by J. S. Mill and others; and, although Mill abandoned the theory some time before his death, he was unable to eradicate it from his systematic treatise and to reduce it to its proper dimensions. It is important to observe that in the hands of Mill this theory was by no means, as was afterwards maintained by Prof. Cairnes, a mere statement of the problem to be solved. According to Cairnes (*Leading Principles of Political Economy*, bk. ii.), the wages-fund theory, as given in Mill's *Principles* (bk. ii. ch. xi. § 1), embraces the following statements:—(1) the wages-fund is a general term used to express the aggregate of all wages at any given time in possession of the labouring population; (2) the average wage depends on the proportion of this fund to the number of people; (3) the amount of the fund is determined by the amount of general wealth applied to the direct purchase of labour. These propositions Cairnes easily reduces to mere verbal statements, and he then states that the real difficulty is to determine the causes which govern the demand and supply of labour. But the most superficial glance, as well as the most careful survey, will convince the reader of Mill's chapters on wages that he regarded the theory not as the statement but as the solution of the problem. For he applies it directly to the explanation of movements in wages, to the criticism of popular remedies for low wages, and to the discovery of what he considers to be legitimate and possible remedies. In fact, it was principally on account of the application of the theory to concrete facts that it aroused so much opposition, which would have been impossible if it had been a mere statement of the problem.

Analysis of the theory.

The wages-fund theory as a real attempt to solve the wages question may be resolved into three propositions, which are very different from the verbal truisms of Cairnes. (1) In any country at any time there is a determinate amount of capital unconditionally destined for the payment of labour. This is the wages-fund. (2) There is also a determinate number of labourers who must work independently of the rate of wages,—that is, whether the rate is high or low. (3) The wages-fund is distributed amongst the labourers solely by means of competition, masters competing with one another for labour, and labourers with one another for work, and thus the average rate of wages depends on the proportion between wage-capital and population. It follows then, according to this view, that wages can only rise either owing to an increase of capital or a diminution of population, and this accounts for the exaggerated importance attached by Mill to the Malthusian theory of population. It also follows from the theory that any restraint of competition in one direction can only cause a rise of wages by a corresponding fall in another quarter, and in this form it was the argument most frequently urged against the action of trade unions. It is worth noting, as showing the vital connexion of the theory with Mill's principles, that it is practically the foundation of his propositions on capital in his first book, and is also the basis of the exposition in his fourth book of the effects of the progress of society on the condition of the working-classes.

It has often been remarked that, in economics as in other sciences, what eventually assumes the form of the development of or supplement to an old theory at first appears as if in direct antagonism to it, and there is reason to think that the criticism of the wages-fund theory was carried to an extreme, and that the essential elements of truth which it contains were overlooked. In many respects the theory may be regarded as a good first approximation to the complete solution of the problem. The causes which it emphasizes too exclusively are after all *veræ causæ*, and must always be taken into account. There can be no doubt, for example, that under certain conditions a rapid increase in the labouring population may cause wages to fall, just as a rapid decline may make them rise. The most striking example of a great improvement in the condition of the labouring classes in English economic history is found immediately after the occurrence of the Black Death in the middle of the 14th century. The sudden and extensive thinning of the ranks of labour was manifestly the principal cause of the great improvement in the condition of the survivors.

Apparent truth of it.

Again, as regards the amount of capital competing for labour, the reality of the cause admits of no dispute, at any rate in any modern society. The force of this element is perhaps best seen by taking a particular case and assuming that the general wages-fund of the country is divided into a number of smaller wages-funds. Take, for example, the wages of domestic servants when the payment of wages is made simply for the service rendered. We may fairly assume that the richer classes of the community practically put aside so much of their revenue for the payment of the wages of their servants. The aggregate of these sums is the domestic wages-fund. Now, if owing to any cause the amount available for this purpose falls off, whilst the number of those seeking that class of employment remains the same, the natural result would be a fall in wages. It may of course happen in this as in other cases that the result is not so much a direct fall in the rate of wages as a diminution of employment—but even in this case, if people employ fewer servants, they must do more work. Again, if we were to seek for the reason why the wages of governesses are so low, the essence of the answer would be found in the excessive supply of that kind of labour compared with the funds destined for its support. And similarly through the whole range of employments in which the labour is employed in perishable services and not in material products, the wages-fund theory brings into prominence the principal causes governing the rate of wages, namely, the number of people competing, the amount of the fund competed for, and the effectiveness of the competition. This view also is in harmony with the general principles of demand and supply. If we regard labour as a commodity and wages as the price paid for it, then we may say that the price will be so adjusted that the quantity demanded will be made equal to the quantity offered at that price,—the agency by which the equation is reached being competition.

Apparent failure of it.

But when we turn to other facts for the verification of the theory we easily discover apparent if not real contradictions. The case of Ireland after the potato famine affords an instance of a rapidly declining population without any corresponding rise in wages, whilst in new countries we often find a very rapid increase of population accompanied by an increase in wages. In a similar manner we find that the capital of a country may increase rapidly without wages rising in proportion—as, for example, seems to have been the case in England after the great mechanical improvements at the end of last century up to the repeal of the Corn Laws—whilst in new countries where wages are the highest there are generally complaints of the scarcity of capital. But perhaps the most striking conflict of the theory with facts is found in the periodical inflations and depressions of trade. After a commercial crisis, when the shock is over and the necessary liquidation has taken place, we generally find that there is a period during which there is a glut of capital and yet wages are low. The abundance of capital is shown by the low rate of interest and the difficulty of obtaining remunerative investments. Accordingly this apparent failure of the theory, at least partially, makes it necessary to examine the propositions into which it was resolved more carefully, in order to discover, in the classical economic phraseology, the "disturbing causes." As regards the first of these propositions—that there is always a certain amount of capital destined for the employment of labour—it is plain that this destination is not really unconditional. In a modern society whether or not a capitalist will supply capital to labour depends on the rate of profit expected, and this again depends proximately on the course of prices. But the theory as stated can only consider profits and prices as acting in an indirect roundabout manner upon wages. If profits are high then more capital can be accumulated and there is a larger wages-fund, and if prices are high there may be some stimulus to trade but the effect on real wages is considered to be very small. In fact Mill writes it down as a popular delusion that high prices make high wages. And if the high prices are due purely to currency causes the criticism is in the main correct, and in some cases, as was shown above, high prices may mean low real wages. If, however, we turn to the great classes of employments in which the labour is embodied in a material product, we find on examination that wages vary with prices in a real and not merely in an illusory sense. Suppose, for example, that, owing to a great increase in the foreign demand for our produce, a rise in prices takes place, there will be a corresponding rise in nominal wages, and in all probability a rise in real wages. Such was undoubtedly the case in Great Britain on the conclusion of the Franco-German war.

On the other hand, if prices fall and profits are low, there will so far be a tendency to contract the employment of labour. At the same time, however, to some extent the capital is applied unconditionally,—in other words, without obtaining what is considered adequate remuneration, or even at a positive loss. The existence of a certain amount of fixed capital practically implies the constant employment of a certain amount of labour.

Nor is the second proposition perfectly true, namely, that there is always a certain amount of labourers who must work independently of the rate of wages. For the returns of pauperism and other statistics show that there is always a proportion of "floating" labour sometimes employed and sometimes not. Again, although, as Adam Smith says, man is of all luggage the most difficult to be transported, still labour as well as capital may be attracted to foreign fields. The constant succession of strikes resorted to in order to prevent a fall in wages shows that in practice the labourers do not at once accept the "natural" market rate. Still, on the whole, this second proposition is a much more adequate expression of the truth than the first; for labour cannot afford to lie idle or to emigrate so easily as capital.

The third proposition, that the wages-fund is distributed solely by competition is also found to conflict with facts. Competition may be held to imply in its positive meaning that every individual strives to attain his own economic interests regardless of the interests of others. But in some cases this end may be attained most effectively by means of combination, as, for example, when a number of people combine to create a practical monopoly. Again, the end may be attained by leaving the control to Government, or by obeying the unwritten rules of long-established custom. But these methods of satisfying the economic instincts are opposed to competition in the usual sense of the term, and certainly as used in reference to labour. Thus on the negative side competition implies that the economic interests of the persons concerned are attained neither by combination, nor by law, nor by custom. Again, it is also assumed, in making competition the principal distributing force of the national income, that every person knows what his real interests are, and that there is perfect mobility of labour both from employment to employment and from place to place. Without these assumptions the wages-fund would not be evenly distributed according to the quantity of labour. It is, however, obvious that, even in the present industrial system, competition is modified considerably by these disturbing agencies; and in fact the tendency seems to be more and more for combinations of masters on one side and of men on the other to take the place of the competition of individuals.

Wages paid from the produce of labour.

The attempted verification of the wages-fund theory leads to so many important modifications that it is not surprising to find that in recent times the tendency has been to reject it altogether. And thus we arrive at the development of Adam Smith's introductory statement, namely, that the produce of labour constitutes the natural recompense or wages of labour. The most important omission of the wages-fund theory is that it fails to take account of the quantity produced and of the price obtained for the product. If we bring in these elements, we find that there are several other causes to be considered besides capital, population, and competition. There are, for example, the various factors in the efficiency of labour and capital, in the organization of industry, and in the general condition of trade. To some extent these elements may be introduced into the old theory, but in reality the point of view is quite different. This is made abundantly clear by considering Mill's treatment of the remedies for low wages. His main contention is that population must be rigidly restrained in order that the average rate of wages may be kept up. But, as several American economists have pointed out, in new countries especially every increase in the number of labourers may be accompanied by a more than proportionate increase in the produce and thus in the wages of labour. Again, the older view was that capital must be first accumulated in order afterwards to be divided up into wages, as if apparently agriculture was the normal type of industry, and the workers must have a store to live on until the new crop was grown and secured. But the "produce" theory of wages considers that wages are paid continuously out of a continuous product, although in some cases they may be advanced out of capital or accumulated stores. According to this view wages are paid out of the annual produce of the land, capital, and labour, and not out of the savings of previous years. There is a danger, however, of pushing this theory to an untenable extreme, and overlooking altogether the function of capital in determining wages; and the true solution seems to be found in a combination of the "produce" theory with the "fund" theory.

An industrial society may be regarded, in the first place, as a great productive machine turning out a vast variety of products for the consumption of the members of the society. The distribution of these products, so far as it is not modified by other social and moral conditions, depends upon the principle of "reciprocal demand." In a preliminary rough classification we may make three groups—the owners of land and natural agents, the owners of capital or reserved products and instruments, and the owners of labour. To obtain the produce requisite even for the necessary wants of the community a combination of these three groups must take place, and the relative reward obtained by each will vary in general according to the demands of the others for its services. Thus, if capital, both fixed and circulating, is scanty, whilst labour and land are both abundant, the reward of capital will be high relatively to rent and wages. This is well illustrated in the high rate of profits obtained in early societies. According to this view of the question the aggregate amount paid in wages depends partly on the general productiveness of all the productive agents and partly on the relative power of the labourers as compared with the owners of land and capital (the amount taken by Government and individuals for taxes, charity, &c., being omitted). Under a system of perfect industrial competition the general rate of wages would be so adjusted that the demand for labour would be just equal to the supply at that rate.

Relative wages.

If all labour and capital were perfectly uniform it would not be necessary to carry the analysis further, but as a matter of fact, instead of two great groups of labourers and capitalists, we have a multitude of subdivisions all under the influence of reciprocal demand. Every subgroup tries to obtain as much as possible of the general product, which is practically always measured in money. The determination of relative wages depends on the constitution of these groups and their relations to one another. Under any given social conditions there must be differences of wages in different employments, which may be regarded as permanent until some change occurs in the conditions; in other words, certain differences of wages are stable or normal, whilst others depend simply on temporary fluctuations in demand and supply. A celebrated chapter in the *Wealth of Nations* (bk. i. ch. x.) is still the best basis for the investigation of these normal differences,—which, as stated above, is the *second* principal problem of the wages question. First of all, a broad distinction may be drawn between the natural and artificial causes of difference, or, in Adam Smith's phraseology, between those due to the nature of the employments and those due to the policy of Europe.

Natural causes of difference.

In the former division we have (1) the agreeableness or disagreeableness of the employment, illustrated by two classical examples—"honour makes a great part of the reward of all honourable professions," and "the most detestable of all employments—that of public executioner—is, in proportion to the work done, better paid than any common trade whatever." There is, however, much truth in Mill's criticism, that in many cases the worst paid of all employments are at the same time the most disagreeable, simply because those engaged in them have practically no other choice. (2) The easiness and cheapness or the reverse of learning the business. This factor operates in two ways. A difficult business implies to some extent peculiar natural qualifications, and it also involves the command of a certain amount of capital to subsist on during the process of learning, and thus in both respects the natural supply of labour is limited. (3) The constancy or inconstancy in the employment,—a point already noticed under real wages. (4) The great or small trust reposed in the workmen, an important consideration in all the higher grades of labour, *e.g.*, bankers, lawyers, doctors, &c. (5) The chance of success or the reverse. Here it is to be observed that, owing to the hopefulness of human nature and its influence on the gambling spirit, the chance of success is generally over-estimated, and therefore that the wages in employments where the chance of success is really small are lower than they ought to be. The most striking instance is furnished by the labour in gold mines, diamond fields, and the like, and the same cause also operates in many of the professions.

All these causes of differences of wages in different employments may be explained by showing the way in which they operate on the demand and supply of labour in the particular group. If the "net advantages," to adopt Prof. Marshall's phraseology, of any group are relatively high, then labour will be directly attracted to that group, and the children born in it will be brought up to the same occupation, and thus in both ways the supply of labour will be increased. But the "net advantages" embrace the conditions just enumerated. Again, if the other members of the community require certain forms of labour to a greater extent, there is an increase in the demand and a rise in their price.

Artificial causes of difference.

In addition to these so-called natural causes of difference, there are those arising from law, custom, or other so-called artificial causes. They may be classified under four headings. (1) Certain causes artificially restrain industrial competition by limiting the number of any particular group. Up to the close of last century, and in many instances to a much later date, the regulations of guilds and corporations limited the numbers in each trade (*cf.* Brentano, *Guilds and Trade Unions*). This they did by making a long apprenticeship compulsory on those wishing to learn the craft, by restricting the number of apprentices to be taken by any master, by exacting certain qualifications as to birth or wealth, by imposing heavy entrance fees, either in money or in the shape of a useless but expensive masterpiece. Some of these regulations were originally passed in the interests of the general public and of those employed in the craft, but in the course of time their effect was, as is stated by Adam Smith, simply to unduly restrain competition. The history of the craft-guilds is full of instructive examples of the principles governing wages. No doubt the regulations tended to raise wages above the natural rate, but as a natural consequence industry migrated to places where the oppressive regulations did not exist. In the time of the Tudors the decay of many towns during a period of rapid national progress was largely due to those "fraternities in evil," as Bacon called the guilds. At present one of the best examples of the survival of this species of artificial restriction is the limitation of the number of teachers qualifying for degrees in certain universities. (2) In some employments, however, law and custom tend unduly to increase the amount of competition. This was to a great extent the case in the church and the scholastic professions owing to the large amount of charitable education. Adam Smith points out that even in his day a curate was "passing rich on forty pounds a year," whilst many only obtained £20,—below the wages earned by a journeyman shoemaker. In the same way state-aided education of a commercial and technical kind may result in lowering the rates (relatively) of the educated business classes. It is said that one reason why the Germans replace Englishmen in many branches is that, having obtained their education at a low rate, there are more of them qualified, and consequently they accept lower wages. The customary idea that the position of a clerk is more genteel than that of an artisan accounts largely for the excessive competition in the former class, especially now that education is practically universal. (3) In some cases law and custom may impede or promote the circulation of labour. At the time Adam Smith wrote the laws of settlement were still in full operation. "There is not a man of forty who has not felt most cruelly oppressed by this ill-contrived law of settlement." Differences in wages in different parts of the same country and in different occupations are still largely due to impediments in the way of the movement of labour, which might be removed or lessened by the Government making provisions for migration or emigration. (4) On many occasions in the past the law often directly interfered to regulate wages. The Statute of Labourers, passed immediately after the Black Death, was an attempt in this direction, but it appears to have failed, according to the investigations of Prof. Thorold Rogers. The same writer, however, ascribes to the celebrated Statute of Apprentices (5th of Elizabeth) the degradation of the English labourer for nearly three centuries (*Agriculture and Prices*, vol. v.). This, he asserts, was due to the wages being fixed by the justices of the peace. It is, however, worth noting that Brentano, who is equally sympathetic with the claims of labour, asserts that so long as this statute was actually enforced, or the customs founded upon it were observed, the condition of the labourers was prosperous, and that the degradation only began when the statute fell into disuse (*Origin of Guilds and Trade Unions*).

State regulation of wages.

It is impossible in the limits of this article to discuss this particular case, but something must be said as to the power of the state to regulate wages. As far as any direct regulation is concerned, it seems to be only possible within narrow limits. The state might of course institute certain complex sliding-scales for different classes of labour and make them compulsory, but this would rather be an official declaration of the natural market rate than a direct regulation. Any rate which the state of trade and prices would not bear could not be enforced: masters could not be compelled to work at a loss or to keep their capital employed when it might be more advantageously transferred to another place or occupation. Thus the legal rate could not exceed to any considerable extent the market rate. Nor, on the other hand, could a lower rate in general be enforced, especially when the labourers have the right of combination and possess powerful organizations. And even apart from this the competition of capitalists for labour would tend to raise wages above the legal rate, and evasion would be extremely easy.

Poor relief in aid of wages.

The best illustration of the failure to raise the rate of wages directly by authority is found in the English poor law system between 1796 and 1834. "In the former year (1796) the decisively fatal step of legalizing out-relief to the able-bodied, and *in aid of wages*, was taken," and "in February 1834 was published perhaps the most remarkable and startling document to be found in the whole range of English, perhaps indeed of all social, history" (Fowle's *Poor Law*). The essence of the system was in the justices determining a natural rate of wages, regard being paid to the price of necessaries and the size of the labourer's family, and an amount was given from the rates sufficient to make up the wages received to this natural level. The method of administration was certainly bad, but the best administration possible could only have kept the system in existence a few years longer. In one parish the poor-rate had swallowed up the whole value of the land, which was going out of cultivation, a fact which has an obvious bearing on land nationalization as a remedy for low wages. The labourers became careless, inefficient, and improvident. Those who were in regular receipt of relief were often better off (in money) than independent labourers. But the most important consequence was that the real wages obtained were, in spite of the relief, lower than otherwise they would have been, and a striking proof was given that wages are paid out of the produce of labour. The *Report of the Poor Law Commissioners* (1834) states emphatically (p. 48) that "the severest sufferers are those for whose benefit the system is supposed to have been introduced and to be perpetuated, the labourers and their families." The independent labourers suffered directly through the unfair competition of the pauper labour, but, as one of the reporters stated, in every district the general condition of the independent labourer was strikingly distinguishable from that of the pauper and superior to it, though the independent labourers were commonly maintained upon less money.[1]

Factory legislation.

But, although the direct intervention of the state, with the view of raising the nominal rates of wages, is, according to theory and experience, worse than useless, still, when we consider real wages in the evident sense of the term, there seems to be an almost indefinite scope for state interference. The effect of the Factory Acts and similar legislation has been undoubtedly to raise the real wages of the working-classes as a whole, although at first the same arguments were used in opposition to these proposals as in the case of direct relief from the poor-rates. But there is a vital difference in the two cases, because in the former the tendency is to increase whilst in the latter it is to diminish the energy and self-reliance of the workers. An excellent summary of the results of this species of industrial legislation is given by Mr John Morley (*Life of Cobden*, vol. i. p. 303):—

"We have to-day a complete, minute, and voluminous code for the protection of labour: buildings must be kept pure of effluvia; dangerous machinery must be fenced; children and young persons must not clean it while in motion; their hours are not only limited but fixed; continuous employment must not exceed a given number of hours, varying with the trade but prescribed by the law in given cases; a statutable number of holidays is imposed; the children must go to school, and the employer must have every week a certificate to that effect; if an accident happens notice must be sent to the proper authorities; special provisions are made for bakehouses, for lace-making, for collieries, and for a whole schedule of other special callings; for the due enforcement and vigilant supervision of this immense host of minute prescriptions there is an immense host of inspectors, certifying surgeons, and other authorities whose business it is to 'speed and post o'er land and ocean' on sullen guardianship of every kind of labour, from that of the woman who plaits straw at her cottage door to the miner who descends into the bowels of the earth and the seaman who conveys the fruits and materials of universal industry to and fro between the remotest parts of the globe."

The analysis previously given of real wages shows that logically all these improvements in the conditions of labour, by diminishing the "quantity of labour" involved in work, are equivalent to a real rise in wages. Experience has also shown that the state may advantageously interfere in regulating the methods of paying wages. A curious poem, written about the time of Edward IV., on England's commercial policy (*Political Songs and Poems*, Rolls Series, vol. ii. p. 282), shows that even in the 15th century the "truck" system was in full operation, to the disadvantage of the labourers. The cloth-makers, in particular, compelled the workers to take half of their wages in merchandise which they estimated at higher than its real value. The writer proposes that the "wyrk folk be paid in good moné," and that a sufficient ordinance be passed for the purpose, and a law to this effect was enacted in the 4th year of Edward IV. At the present day the Truck Act (1st and 2d William IV.) is in full operation, and has quite recently been extended. Again, the legislation directed against the adulteration of all kinds of goods, which also finds its prototypes in the Middle Ages is in its effects equivalent to a rise in real wages.[2]

Trade unions and wages.

The power of trade unions in regulating wages is in most respects analogous in principle to that of legislation just noticed. Nominal wages can only be affected within comparatively narrow limits, depending on the condition of trade and the state of prices, whilst in many cases a rise in the rate in some trades or places can only be accomplished by a corresponding depression elsewhere. At the same

[1] For a general criticism of the Allowance System, *cf.* Mill's *Principles*, bk. ii. ch. xi. § 3.

[2] On this subject compare Jevons, *The State in Relation to Labour*.

time, however, it can hardly be questioned that through the unions nominal wages have on the whole risen at the expense of profits,—that is to say, that combinations of labourers can make better bargains than individuals. But the debatable margin which may make either extra profits or extra wages is itself small (*cf.* Atkinson on the *Distribution of Products*), and at present the principal direct effect of trade unions is to make wages fluctuate with prices, a rise at one time being compensated by a fall at another. The unions can, however, look after the interests of their members in many ways which improve their general condition or raise the real rate of wages, and when nominal wages have attained a natural maximum, and some method of arbitration or sliding-scale is in force, this indirect action seems the principal function of trade unions. The effects of industrial partnership (*cf.* Sedley Taylor's *Profit Sharing*) and of productive co-operation (*cf.* Holyoake's *History of Co-operation*) are at present small in amount (compared with the total industry of any country) though excellent in kind, and there seem to be no signs of the decay of the *entrepreneur* system.

Effects of machinery on wages.

The industrial revolution which took place about the end of last century, involving radical changes in production, destroyed the old relations between capital and labour, and perhaps the most interesting part of the history of wages is that covered by the present century. For fifty years after the introduction of production on a large scale, the condition of the working-classes was on the whole deplorable, but during the last fifty years great progress has been made. The principal results may be summed up under the effects of machinery on wages,—taking both words in their widest sense. Machinery affects the condition of the working-classes in many ways. The most obvious mode is the direct substitution of machinery for labour. It is clear that any sudden and extensive adoption of labour-saving machinery may, by throwing the labourers out of employment, lower the rate of wages, and it is easy to understand how riots arose repeatedly owing to this cause. But as a rule the effect of labour-saving machinery in diminishing employment has been greatly exaggerated, because two important practical considerations have been overlooked. In the first place, any radical change made in the methods of production will be only gradually and continuously adopted throughout the industrial world; and in the second place these radical changes, these discontinuous leaps, tend to give place to advances by small *increments of invention.* We have an instance of a great radical change in the steam-engine. Watt's patent for "a method of lessening" the consumption of steam and fuel in fire-engines was published on January 5, 1769, and it may be said that the movement of substituting steam as a motive power is not yet over. Every day we hear of steam being extended to some new employment and to some out-of-the-way district. The history of the power-loom again shows that the adoption of an invention is comparatively slow. In 1813 there were not more than 2400 power-looms at work in England. In 1820 they increased to 14,150. In 1853 there were 100,000, but the curious thing is that during this time the number of hand-looms had actually *increased* to some extent (Porter's *Progress of the Nation*, p. 186). The power-loom also illustrates the gradual continuous growth of improvements. This is clearly shown by Porter. A very good hand-weaver, twenty-five or thirty years of age, could weave two pieces of shirting per week. In 1823 a steam-loom weaver, about fifteen years of age, attending two looms, could weave nine similar pieces in a week. In 1826 a steam-loom weaver, about fifteen, attending to four looms, could weave twelve similar pieces a week. In 1833 a steam-loom weaver, from fifteen to twenty, assisted by a girl of twelve, attending to four looms, could weave eighteen pieces. This is only one example, for, as Porter remarks, it would fill many large volumes to describe the numerous inventions which during the present century imparted facility to manufacturing processes, and in every case we find a continuity in the improvements. This twofold progressive character of invention operates in favour of the labourer,—in the first place, because in most cases the increased cheapness of the commodity consequent on the use of machinery causes a corresponding extension of the market and the amount produced, and thus there may be no actual diminution of employment even temporarily; and secondly, if the improvement takes place slowly, there is time for the absorption of the redundant labour in other employments. It is quite clear that on balance the great increase in population in this century has been largely caused, or rather rendered possible, by the increased use of labour-saving machinery. The way in which the working-classes were at first injured by the adoption of machinery was not so much by a diminution in the number of hands required as by a change in the nature of the employment. Skilled labour of a certain kind lost its peculiar value, and children and women were able to do work formerly only done by men. But the principal evils resulted from the wretched conditions under which, before the factory legislation, the work was performed; and there is good reason to believe that a deterioration of the type of labourer, both moral and physical, was effected. It is, however, a mistake to suppose that on the whole the use of machinery tends to dispense with skill.

Progress of the working classes.

On the contrary, everything goes to prove that under the present system of production on a large scale there is on the whole far more skill required than formerly,—a fact which has been well brought out by Mr Giffen in his essay on the progress of the working-classes (*Essays on Finance*, vol. ii. p. 365). The two lowest classes of labour, which constituted each about one-third of the whole manual-labour class of the United Kingdom fifty years ago, now constitute only one-eighth each, and the remaining highest-paid class, which was only one-third fifty years ago, is now three-fourths of the whole. Taking this fact into consideration, it is easy to understand the estimate that the money wages of labour have on the whole risen 100 per cent. during this period. There seems every reason to believe that this rise in real wages will continue with every extension of the power of man over nature.

Tendency of profits to fall and wages to rise.

For, taking the most general view of the subject, the more there is produced or acquired in exchange from other countries, so much more is there to consume. But this very improvement in the production and acquisition of wealth facilitates the creation of new capital, and increases the rate of accumulation, and thus there is a greater intensity in the demand of capital for labour, and the rate of profits falls whilst the rate of wages rises.[1] (J. S. N†.)

Law Relating to Wages.

The legislature has often dealt with wages in a manner which modern political economy would not endorse. The amount was fixed by the Statute of Labourers in 1349, and by many succeeding statutes (see Labour). The policy of these Acts is now obsolete, although the British parliament has never gone as far as the constitution of Louisiana, and expressly provided that no law is to fix the price of manual labour. To conspire to effect an alteration in wages is now no longer an offence. It was formerly punished very severely both at common law and under the provisions of various statutes, especially 2 and 3 Edw. VI. c. 15. Existing legislation on the subject of wages deals with the mode of their payment and recovery, and their protection from attachment and from the

[1] For further information on this branch of the subject compare Atkinson, *Distribution of Products* and *The Margin of Profits*; Leroy-Beaulieu, *Repartition des Richesses*; Nicholson, *Effects of Machinery on Wages*; and Marshall, *Economics of Industry.*

bankruptcy laws. They must (except in the case of farm servants) be paid in money, and the payment must not be made in a public house (see PAYMENT). The recovery of wages by SEAMEN (*q.v.*) is the subject of special legislation. In other cases statutory authority is given to county courts and courts of summary jurisdiction to deal with claims for wages. See especially the Employers and Workmen Act, 1875. The County Courts Acts enable an infant to sue in a county court for wages not exceeding £50 as though he were of age. Wages are as a rule privileged debts (see PRIVILEGE). By 33 and 34 Vict. c. 30 the wages of a servant, labourer, or workman cannot be attached by order of a court of record or inferior court. In Scotland wages are exempt from arrestment on process under the Small Debt Acts and in any case up to 20s. a week by 8 and 9 Vict. c. 39 and 33 and 34 Vict. c. 63. The English Bankruptcy Act, 1883, gives priority in the distribution of a bankrupt's estate to wages of clerks, servants, labourers, and workmen up to the extent of £50. The Scottish Bankruptcy Act, 1856 (as amended in 1875), is in similar terms.

WAGNER, RUDOLPH (1805-1864), anatomist and physiologist, was born in June 1805 at Baireuth, where his father was a professor in the gymnasium. He began the study of medicine at Erlangen in 1820, and finished his curriculum in 1826 at Würzburg, where he had attached himself mostly to Schönlein in medicine and to Heusinger in comparative anatomy. Aided by a public *stipendium*, he spent a year or more studying in the Jardin des Plantes, under the friendly eye of Cuvier, and in making zoological discoveries at Cagliari and other places on the Mediterranean. On his return he set up in medical practice at Augsburg, whither his father had been transferred; but in a few months he found an opening for an academical career, on being appointed prosector at Erlangen. In 1832 he became full professor of zoology and comparative anatomy there, and held that office until 1840, when he was called to succeed Blumenbach at Göttingen. At the Hanoverian university he remained till his death in 1864, being much occupied with administrative work as pro-rector for a number of years, and for nearly the whole of his residence troubled by ill-health (hereditary phthisis). In 1860 he gave over the physiological part of his teaching to a new chair, retaining the zoological, with which his career had begun. While at Frankfurt, on his way to examine the Neanderthal skull at Bonn, he was struck with paralysis, and died at Göttingen a few months later (May 1864) in his 59th year.

Wagner's activity as a writer and worker was enormous, and his range extensive, most of his hard work having been done at Erlangen while his health was good. His graduation thesis was on the ambitious subject of "the historical development of epidemic and contagious diseases all over the world, with the laws of their diffusion," which showed the influence of Schönlein. His first treatise was *Die Naturgeschichte des Menschen* (in 2 vols., Kempten, 1831). Frequent journeys to the Mediterranean, the Adriatic, and the North Sea gave him abundant materials for research on invertebrate anatomy and physiology, which he communicated first to the Munich academy of sciences, and republished in his *Beiträge zur vergleichenden Physiologie des Blutes* (Leipsic, 1832-33, with additions in 1838). In 1834-35 he brought out a text-book on the subject of his chair (*Lehrbuch der vergleichenden Anatomie*, Leipsic), which recommended itself to students by its clear and concise style. A new edition of it appeared in 1843 under the title of *Lehrbuch der Zootomie*, of which only the vertebrate section was corrected by himself. The precision of his earlier work is evidenced by his *Micrometric Measurements of the Elementary Parts of Man and Animals* (Leipsic, 1834). His zoological labours may be said to conclude with the atlas *Icones Zootomicæ* (Leipsic, 1841). In 1835 he communicated to the Munich academy of sciences his researches on the physiology of generation and development, including the famous discovery of the germinal vesicle of the human ovum. These were republished under the title *Prodromus Historiæ Generationis Hominis atque Animalium* (Leipsic, 1836). As in zoology, his original researches in physiology were followed by a students' text-book, *Lehrbuch der speciellen Physiologie* (Leipsic, 1838), which soon reached a third edition, and was translated into French and English. This was supplemented by an atlas, *Icones Physiologicæ* (Leipsic, 1839). To the same period belongs a very interesting but now little known work on medicine proper, of a historical and synthetic scope, *Grundriss der Encyklopädie und Methodologie der medicinischen Wissenschaften nach geschichtlicher Ansicht* (Erlangen, 1838), which was translated into Danish. About the same time he worked along with Will at a translation of Prichard's *Natural History of Man*, and edited various writings of Sömmering, with a biography of that anatomist (1844), which he himself fancied most of all his writings. In 1843, after his removal to Göttingen, he began his great *Handwörterbuch der Physiologie, mit Rücksicht auf physiologische Pathologie*, and brought out the fifth (supplementary) volume in 1852; the only contributions of his own in it were on the sympathetic nerve, nerve-ganglia, and nerve-endings, and he modestly disclaims all merit except as being the organizer. While resident in Italy for his health from 1845 to 1847, he occupied himself with researches on the electrical organ of the torpedo and on nervous organization generally; these he published in 1853-54 (*Neurologische Untersuchungen*, Göttingen), and therewith his physiological period may be said to end. His next period was stormy and controversial. He entered the lists boldly against the materialism of "Stoff und Kraft," and avowed himself a Christian believer, whereupon he lost the countenance of a number of his old friends and pupils, and was unfeelingly told that he was suffering from an "atrophy of the brain." His quarrel with the materialists began with his oration at the Göttingen meeting of the Naturforscher-Versammlung in 1854 on "Menschenschöpfung und Seelensubstanz." This was followed by a series of "Physiological Letters" in the *Allgemeine Zeitung*, by an essay on "Glauben und Wissen," and by the most important piece of this series, "Der Kampf um die Seele" (Göttingen, 1857). Having come to the consideration of these philosophical problems late in life, he was at some disadvantage; but he endeavoured to join as he best could in the current of contemporary German thought. He had an exact knowledge of classical German writings, more especially of Goethe's, and of the literature connected with him. In what may be called his fourth and last period, Wagner became anthropologist and archæologist, occupied himself with the cabinet of skulls in the Göttingen museum collected by Blumenbach and with the excavation of prehistoric remains, corresponded actively with the anthropological societies of Paris and London, and organized, in co-operation with the veteran Von Baer, a successful congress of anthropologists at Göttingen in 1861. His last writings were memoirs on the convolutions of the human brain, on the weight of brains, and on the brains of idiots (1860-62).

See memoir by his eldest son in the *Göttinger gelehrte Anzeigen*, "Nachrichten" for 1864.

WAGNER, WILHELM RICHARD (1813-1883), dramatic composer and reformer of the musical drama, was born at Leipsic on May 22, 1813. In 1822 he was sent to the Kreuzschule at Dresden, where he did so well that, four years later, he translated the first 12 books of the *Odyssey* for amusement. In 1828 he was removed to the Nicolaischule at Leipsic, where he was less successful. His first music-master was Gottlieb Müller, who thought him self-willed and eccentric; and his first important composition was an "Overture in B♭," performed at the Leipsic theatre in 1830. In that year he matriculated at the university, and took lessons in composition from Theodor Weinlig, cantor at the Thomasschule. His "First Symphony" was performed at the Gewandhaus concerts in 1833, and in the following year he was appointed conductor of the opera at Magdeburg. The post was an unprofitable one, and Wagner's life at this period was very unsettled. He had composed an opera called *Die Feen*, adapted from Gozzi's *La Donna Serpente*, and another, *Das Liebesverbot*, founded on Shakespeare's *Measure for Measure*, but these were never performed, and for some considerable time the young composer found it difficult to obtain a hearing.

In 1836 Wagner married Fräulein Wilhelmina Planer, an actress at the theatre at Königsberg. He had accepted an engagement there as conductor, but, the lessee becoming bankrupt, the scheme was abandoned in favour of a better appointment at Riga. Accepting this, he remained actively employed until 1839, when he made his first visit to Paris, taking with him an unfinished opera, for which he had himself prepared a libretto, upon the lines of Lord Lytton's novel *Rienzi*. The venture proved a most unfortunate one. Wagner was unsuccessful in all his attempts to achieve popularity, and *Rienzi*, destined for the Grand Opéra, was relentlessly rejected. He completed it, however, and in 1842 it was produced at the court theatre in Dresden, where, with Madame Schroeder Devrient and Herr Tichatschek in the principal parts, it achieved an immense success, and undoubtedly laid the foundation of the great composer's fame.

Though, in completing *Rienzi*, Wagner had put forth all the strength he then possessed, that work was far from representing his preconceived ideal. This he now endeavoured to embody in *Der Fliegende Holländer*, for which, as before, he composed both the libretto and the music. In this fine work we find the first sign of his determination to sacrifice all considerations of traditional form and symmetrical construction to the dramatic exigencies of the story. It is true, this great principle was but very faintly announced in the new work, and in an evidently tentative form; but the success of the experiment was incontestable, though it took some time to convince the world of the fact. The piece was warmly received at Dresden, January 2, 1843; but its success was by no means equal to that of *Rienzi*. Spohr, however, promptly discovered its merits, and produced it at Cassel some months later, with very favourable results.

Wagner was now fairly launched upon his arduous career. On February 2, 1843, he was formally installed as hofkapellmeister at the Dresden theatre, and he celebrated the event by at once beginning the composition of a new opera. For the subject of this he selected the legend of Tannhäuser, collecting his materials from the ancient "Tannhäuser-Lied,"[1] the *Volksbuch*, Tieck's poetical *Erzählung*, Hoffmann's story of *Der Sängerkrieg*, and the mediæval poem on *Der Wartburgkrieg*. This last-named legend introduces the incidental poem of "Loherangrin," and led to the study of Wolfram von Eschenbach's *Parzival und Titurel*, with strange effect upon Wagner's subsequent inspirations. But for the present he confined himself to the subject in hand; and on October 19, 1845, he produced his *Tannhäuser*, with Madame Schroeder Devrient, Fräulein Johanna Wagner,[2] Herr Tichatschek, and Herr Mitterwurzer in the principal parts. Notwithstanding this powerful cast, the success of the new work was not brilliant, for it carried still farther the principles embodied in *Der Fliegende Holländer*, and these principles were not yet understood either by the public or the critics. But Wagner boldly fought for them, and would probably have gained the victory much sooner than he did had he not taken a fatally prominent part in the political agitations of 1849, after which his position in Dresden became untenable. In fact, after the flight of the king, and the subsequent suppression of the riots by troops sent from Berlin, a formal act of accusation was drawn up against him, and he had barely time to escape to Weimar, where Liszt was at that moment engaged in preparing *Tannhäuser* for performance at the court theatre, before the storm burst upon him with a violence that seriously alarmed both his friends and himself.

Without the loss of a moment Liszt procured a passport, and escorted his guest as far as Eisenach. Wagner proceeded in all haste to Paris, and thence to Zurich, where, with few interruptions, he lived in strict retirement until the autumn of 1859. And it was during this period that most of his literary productions—including *Oper und Drama*, *Ueber das Dirigiren*, *Das Judenthum in der Musik*, and other like works—were given to the world.

We have spoken of Wagner's incidental study of the legends of "Loherangrin" and "Parzival" during the time that he was preparing the libretto of *Tannhäuser*. After the production of that opera he again recurred to the subject, chose *Lohengrin* as the title for his next opera, and elaborated the conception with his usual minute and affectionate care, carrying out his new principles somewhat farther than he had hitherto ventured to do. He had completed the work before he fled from Dresden, but could not get it produced. Hoping against hope, he took the score with him to Paris, and, as he himself tells us, "when ill, miserable, and despairing, I sat brooding over my fate, my eye fell on the score of my *Lohengrin*, which I had totally forgotten. Suddenly I felt something like compassion that the music should never sound from off the death-pale paper. Two words I wrote to Liszt; his answer was the news that preparations were being made for the performance of the work, on the grandest scale that the limited means of Weimar would permit. Everything that care and accessories could do was done to make the design of the piece understood. Liszt saw what was wanted at once, and did it. Success was his reward; and with this success he now approaches me, saying, 'Behold we have come thus far; now create us a new work, that we may go farther'."

Lohengrin was, in fact, produced at Weimar, under Liszt's direction, on August 28, 1850. It was a severe trial to Wagner not to be permitted to hear his own work, but he knew that all that could be done for it was done, and he responded to Liszt's appeal for a new creation by meditating upon his famous tetralogy, *Der Ring des Nibelungen*, the four divisions of which—*Das Rheingold*, *Die Walküre*, *Siegfried*, and *Götterdämmerung*—though each as long as an ordinary opera, are in reality but parts of one colossal whole. At this time, also, he first began to lay out the plan of *Tristan und Isolde*, and to think over the possibilities of *Parsifal*.

It is in these later works, and in *Die Meistersinger von Nürnberg*, the first sketch for which had been made at Dresden in 1845, that the genius of Wagner reaches its culminating point; and it is in these only that his great plan for the reformation of the musical drama is fully and honestly carried out. In order to understand this plan, we must first inquire what kind of reformation was needed. What were the abuses that demanded redress? What were the causes that had led to the decline of the opera from a higher state of perfection than that which it exhibited in the middle of the 19th century—if, indeed, it ever did exhibit a higher state of perfection than that? What, in short, had been the history of the musical drama during the two centuries and a half that had elapsed between its first invention and its arrival at the condition in which Wagner found it when he first began to compose for the stage? The story is a very simple one, and may be told in a very few words; but it was not without an immensity of deep thought and earnest consideration that Wagner was able to grapple with the gigantic practical difficulties with which the case was surrounded.

The possibility of constructing a musical drama on reasonable principles was first seriously discussed during the closing years of the 16th century, at certain *réunions* of literary and artistic dilettanti, who were accustomed to meet periodically at the palazzo of Giovanni Bardi, Conte di Vernio, in Florence. The principal members of the little society were Ottavio Rinuccini the poet, Vincenzo Galilei the father of the great astronomer, Giulio Caccini, Jacopo Peri, Pietro Strozzi, and the Conte di Vernio himself. All these earnest savants were deeply embued with the principles of the Renaissance, and regarded the traditions of classical antiquity with a reverence which led them to hold the greatest creations of modern art in undisguised contempt. The music of Palestrina and the great composers of the contrapuntal schools they utterly despised; and their one idea was to revive the system of declamation peculiar to Greek tragedy, and by means of that to produce a form of drama which could be consistently sung throughout as the trilogies of Æschylus and Sophocles were sung by the Greeks. So far their aim was identical with Wagner's. The difference lay in the means by which this aim was to be attained. Wagner himself tells us that, while occupied upon *Lohengrin*, he looked upon his work as "an experiment towards determining whether or not opera was possible." And in other places he speaks of the question whether or not the modern spirit can produce a theatre that shall stand in relation to modern culture as the theatre of Athens stood in relation to the culture of ancient Greece. He believed that this might be accomplished by reforming the opera from the standpoint of Beethoven's music. The friends of the Conte di Vernio had hoped to accomplish it by restoring the actual music of the Greek drama. But this was impossible. For Greek music was based upon a system of tonality which, even in the time of Galilei, had been obsolete for centuries. The Greek scales and tunes differ so widely in their radical construction that no vocalist accustomed

[1] Preserved in Uhland's *Alte hoch- u. nieder-deutsche Volkslieder*.

[2] The composer's niece.

to the one could by any possibility sing the other. Even Peri and Vincenzo Galilei must have known this. But, pretending to ignore the fact, they made a compromise, and endeavoured to imitate what they fondly conceived to be the Greek method of recitative, in the tonality of the modern scales; and in this way they struck, not upon the form of which they were in search—for that was irretrievably lost—but a new one, which rapidly developed itself into the kind of music now called recitative. This recitative —the most valuable artistic invention of the 17th century—they used as the basis of their musical drama; and, after the lapse of two centuries and a half, Wagner determined that this, and none other, must be the basis of his. Enriching it with all the beautiful accessories that had been amassed by composer after composer during its long period of progressive development, and notably with other very important accessories of his own invention, he built his drama upon it as completely as the first dramatic music was built upon it by the frequenters of the Palazzo Bardi. And in this great fact lies the secret of his gigantic reform.

The first Italian opera ever publicly performed was Jacopo Peri's *Euridice*, composed to a libretto written by Ottavio Rinuccini, and produced at Florence in 1600, in honour of the marriage of Henry IV. of France with Maria de' Medici. This most interesting work, a rare printed copy of which is preserved in the British Museum, is entirely in recitative; and the music is so constructed throughout as to aid in the true dramatic expression of the words, at the expense of all attempt at what is now called melody. The operas of Monteverde, Cesti, Cavalli, and all the earlier composers of the 17th century were conceived upon the same principle. But Alessandro Scarlatti (1659–1725), aiming at higher musical perfection, and willing to sacrifice no small amount of dramatic truth to its exigencies, introduced certain constructive forms—notably that called the "da capo"—which, while adding to the symmetrical beauty of the aria, tended eventually entirely to destroy its dramatic force and its logical consistency as an exponent of the situation presented upon the stage. Later composers carried this abuse very much farther. Handel's strong dramatic instinct kept him above the errors of his time; but his contemporaries sinned more and more deeply until, for the sake of obtaining popularity, they were ready to fill their operas with unmeaning passages, introduced solely for the purpose of showing off the skill of the favourite vocalists of the period. And so the abuse proceeded from worse to worse until, under Porpora (1686–1766) and Hasse (1699–1783), the opera at Naples and Dresden became a mere concert sung upon the stage without any trace of dramatic propriety whatever.

And now arose a reformer whose work will be remembered as long as the musical drama continues to exist. Christoph Willibald Gluck (1714–1785), disgusted with his own want of success while writing in the vicious style of the period, determined to reform it upon true dramatic principles; and in the preface to his *Alceste* (1767) he set forth those principles with a clearness which cannot possibly be misunderstood. The history of his great reform has already been narrated in detail (see GLUCK). A careful comparison of the argument laid down in the preface to *Alceste* with that set forth in Wagner's *Oper und Drama* will prove the aim of the two reformers to have been absolutely identical. That a less perfect identity should have existed with regard to the means they used for the attainment of their common end was naturally to be expected. At the outset of their career both Gluck and Wagner freely employed all the resources at their command, adding to them afterwards as circumstances permitted. But between the production of Gluck's latest and Wagner's first masterpiece art had made enormous strides; the advantage, therefore, in this respect was immeasurably on Wagner's side.

In France Gluck's principles were carried out more or less conscientiously by Méhul, Cherubini, and Spontini. In Germany they bore still richer fruit. Glorified by the genius of Mozart and Beethoven, and accepted without reserve by Weber, Spohr, Marschner, and the most enlightened of their followers in the German romantic school, they were professed, if not fully carried out, by composers of every degree. But in Italy they produced no effect whatever. Though Rossini sometimes invested his situations with a certain amount of dramatic colouring, he never attempted anything farther than this; while Mercadante, Bellini, Donizetti, and their imitators regarded melody, pure and simple, as the highest, if not the only really important, attribute of art. Under their rule the opera once more descended to the level of a concert on the stage. The effect of their example upon the lower class of German composers was fatal, and ended in the production of a form of *Singspiel*, lacking all the freshness of the Italian *Cantilena*, and noticeable only for its intolerable vapidity. Notwithstanding the attempts of Halévy and Meyerbeer to perpetuate in France the traditions of a purer epoch, the musical drama sank, under Auber and his imitators, to the level of a string of dance tunes. The 19th century had witnessed the birth of abuses as flagrant as those against which Gluck had protested in the 18th. It was Wagner's turn now to effect the desired reform, and he effected it as completely as his predecessor had done—but not in the same way. Gluck had begun by propounding a theory, and carried on the good work by consistently putting it into practice. Wagner theorized also; but for his ultimate triumph he was indebted to the power of his own creative genius—to his ceaseless endeavour to realize the preconceived ideal which neither theory nor desire for reform could ever tempt him to forget. "The nature of the subject," he says, "could not induce me, in sketching my scenes, to consider in advance their adaptability to any particular musical form, the kind of musical treatment being, in every case, suggested by the scenes themselves. I never contemplated on principle, and as a deliberate reformer, the destruction of the aria, the duet, or any other operatic form; but the disuse of these forms followed naturally from the character of my subjects." Surely no frame of mind could be more free from prejudice than this.

While exercising this unrestrained freedom of thought and action, Wagner found one particular form more useful to him than any other. Mozart in *Don Giovanni*, and Weber in *Der Freischütz*, *Euryanthe*, and *Oberon*, had availed themselves of certain characteristic musical phrases as exponents of emotional or scenic complications of peculiar interest, and had emphasized their meaning by repeating them at every recurrence of the dramatic situation. In modern musical terminology a musical phrase of this kind is now called a "leading theme" ("Leitmotif"). Wagner has employed this expedient more freely than any other composer, and in a way peculiarly his own. Not only has he introduced in his later works a leading theme for every one of the *dramatis personæ*, and for every prominent feature in the scenery or action of the play, but in many cases he even indicates the changing moods and passions of his principal characters by distinct phrases, which he combines together with a power of part-writing truly marvellous, interweaving them—as in "Siegfried's Trauermarsch," in the *Götterdämmerung*—in such sort as to present the whole story of a life and mission in the music of a single scene. Short-sighted critics have dwelt too much upon the technical ingenuity displayed in scenes of this description, and too little upon the expression thrown into them by the power of Wagner's genius. A diligent student may acquire sufficient mastery over the art of part-writing to enable him to interweave his themes with any amount of mechanical perfection, yet without a trace of the beauty displayed by Sebastian Bach in the involutions of his counter-subjects, or by Wagner in labyrinthine combinations used, not for the sake of vaunting his scholarship, but as his most potent engines of dramatic expression. The plaintive wail of the "Trauermarsch" appeals to hearers who know nothing at all of its ingenious construction, and tells its tale to them beyond all possibility of misunderstanding. It is at this point that genius steps in; and the power of Wagner's genius is irresistible.

It was during the period of his exile that Wagner matured his plans and brought his style to its culminating point of perfection; but it was not until some considerable time after his return that any of the works he then meditated were placed upon the stage. In 1855 he accepted an invitation to London, where he conducted the concerts of the Philharmonic Society with great success. In 1857 he completed the libretto of *Tristan und Isolde* at Venice, taking as the basis of his scheme the Celtic legend modified by Gottfried of Strasburg's mediæval treatment of the subject (see GOTTFRIED and ROMANCE). But the music was not completed till 1859. In that year Wagner visited Paris for the third time; and after much negotiation, in which he was nobly supported by the Prince and Princess Metternich, *Tannhäuser* was accepted at the Grand Opéra. Magnificent preparations were made for its production. It was rehearsed 164 times, 14 times with the full orchestra; and the scenery, dresses, and stage accessories generally were placed entirely under the composer's direction. More than £8000 was expended upon the venture; and the work was performed for the first time in the French language on March 13, 1861. But, for political reasons, a powerful clique determined to suppress both the piece and its composer. A scandalous riot was inaugurated by the members of the Parisian Jockey Club, who interrupted the performance with howls and dog-whistles; and so great was the disturbance that after the third representation the opera was withdrawn to reappear no more. Wagner was broken-hearted. But the Princess Metternich continued to befriend him, and in 1861 he received through her intercession a pardon for his political offences, with permission to settle in any part of Germany except Saxony. Even this restriction was removed in 1862.

Wagner now settled for a time in Vienna, where *Tristan und Isolde* was accepted, but abandoned after 57 rehearsals, through the incompetence of the tenor, Herr Ander. *Lohengrin* was, however, produced on May 15, 1861, when Wagner heard it for the first time. His circumstances were now extremely straitened; but better times were at hand. In 1863 he published the libretto of *Der Ring des Nibelungen.* King Louis II. of Bavaria was much struck with it, and in 1864 sent a private secretary to Wagner, who was then at Stuttgart, with an invitation to come to Munich and carry on his work there. The invitation was accepted with joy by the then almost despairing composer. The king gave him an annual grant of 1200 gulden (£120), considerably enlarging it before the end of the year, and placing a comfortable house in the outskirts of the city at his disposal. The master celebrated his good fortune by composing a "Huldigungsmarsch." In the autumn he was formally commissioned to proceed with the tetralogy, and to furnish proposals for the building of a theatre and the foundation of a Bavarian music school. All seemed to promise well, but no sooner did his position seem assured than a miserable court intrigue was formed against him. His political misdemeanours at Dresden were quoted to his discredit and made the excuse for bitter persecutions, and, notwithstanding King Louis's undiminished favour, the opposition was too strong to be resisted, and Wagner was obliged to retire to Triebschen, near Lucerne, where he spent the next six years in uninterrupted study.

Der Fliegende Holländer was performed at Munich in 1864; and on June 10, 1865, *Tristan und Isolde* was produced for the first time, with Herr and Frau Schnorr in the principal parts. *Die Meistersinger von Nürnberg*, first sketched in 1845, was completed in 1867, and first performed at Munich under the direction of Herr von Bülow, June 21, 1868. The story, though an original one, is founded on an episode in the life of Hans Sachs, the poet-cordwainer of Nuremberg; and Wagner has combined its incidents with infinite ingenuity and humour. The success of the opera was very great; but the production of the tetralogy was still impracticable. The scheme for the new theatre, which was to have been designed by the architect Semper, having been abandoned, there was no opera-house in Germany fit for the production of a work designed on so colossal a scale. A project was therefore started for the erection of a suitable building at Baireuth. Wagner laid the first stone of this in 1872, and the edifice was completed, after almost insuperable difficulties, in 1876.

After this Wagner resided permanently at Baireuth, in a house named Wahnfried, in the garden of which he himself built the tomb in which his remains now rest. His first wife, Wilhelmina (*née* Planer), having died in 1866, he was united in 1870 to Liszt's daughter Cosima, who had previously been the wife of Herr von Bülow. Meantime *Der Ring des Nibelungen* was rapidly approaching completion, and on August 13, 1876, the introductory portion, *Das Rheingold*, was performed at Baireuth for the first time, followed on the 14th by *Die Walküre*, on the 16th by *Siegfried*, and on the 17th by *Götterdämmerung*. The success of the work, the story of which is founded on the famous *Nibelungenlied*, was very great; and the performance, directed by Herr Hans Richter, excited extraordinary attention, but the expenses attendant upon its production were enormous, and burdened the management with a debt of £7500. A portion of this was raised by performances at the Albert Hall, in London, at which the composer himself was present, in 1877. The remainder was met by the profits upon performances of the tetralogy —or, as Wagner himself called it, the "Bühnenfestspiel"— at Munich.

Wagner's next, last, and perhaps greatest work was *Parsifal*, based upon the legend of the Holy Grail, as set forth, not in the legend of the *Mort d'Arthur*, which fixes the home of the sacred vessel at Glastonbury, but in the poems of Chrestien de Troyes and Wolfram von Eschenbach, written in the 12th and 13th centuries, and other less-known works (see the article ROMANCE, in which the subject is treated in its various aspects). The libretto was complete before his visit to London in 1877. The music was begun in the following year, and completed at Palermo, January 13, 1882. The first sixteen performances took place at Baireuth, in July and August 1882, under Wagner's own directing, and fully realized the expectations that had been formed of them. There can indeed be no doubt that this last work, called by Wagner a "Bühnenweihfestspiel," in allusion to its mystically religious character, forms a fitting crown to his already brilliant reputation. Unhappily, the exertion of directing so many consecutive performances seems to have been too much for the veteran master's already failing strength, for towards the close of 1882 his health began to decline rapidly. He spent the autumn at Venice, in the Palazzo Vendramini, on the Grand Canal, and was well enough on Christmas Eve to conduct his own first symphony (composed in 1833), at a private performance given at the Liceo Marcello. But late in the afternoon of February 13, 1883, he was seized with a sudden attack of faintness, and on that evening he calmly breathed his last.

Wagner was buried at Wahnfried, in the tomb he had himself prepared, on February 18, and a few days afterwards King Louis rode to Baireuth alone, and at dead of night, to pay his last tribute of respect to the master he had so generously befriended.

In private life Wagner was beloved and respected by all who knew him, though in his public character he made himself innumerable enemies, and provoked an immense amount of hatred—it must be confessed, not wholly undeserved—by the violent and intemperate character of his writings. Though Meyerbeer had been extremely kind to him in Paris, he spoke of him in *Oper und Drama* with the grossest disrespect. His utterly groundless prejudice against Liszt was ultimately conquered by that great master's beautiful forbearance alone. But these things will be forgotten, while the brightness of his genius will remain the lasting heritage of art. In person he was rather below the middle height, erect in carriage, with commanding aspect and remarkable quickness of speech and gesture. That his manners were to some extent unconventional there can be no doubt, but those who knew him best deny that there was even the semblance of truth in the absurd stories that were circulated with regard to his extraordinary eccentricities.

Besides the great dramatic works we have mentioned, Wagner composed the choral music for Weber's funeral (Dresden, 1844), *Das Liebesmahl der Apostel* (Dresden, 1847), *Eine Faustovertüre* (Paris, 1839), *Kaisermarsch* (1871), *Siegfried Idyl* (1871), and a not very numerous collection of smaller pieces. His literary works, published at Leipsic in 1871, fill nine thick volumes. (W. S. R.)

WAGTAIL (*Wagsterd* and *Wagstyrt*, 15th century, *fide* Th. Wright, *Vol. Vocabularies*, ii. pp. 221, 253; *Uuagtale*, Turner, 1544, p. 53), the little bird that delights us equally by its neat coloration, its slender form, its nimble actions, and its sprightly notes. Since it is so generally dispersed, especially in summer, throughout the British Islands, it seems to need no further description.

The Pied Wagtail of authors, it is the *Motacilla lugubris* of modern ornithology, or *M. yarrelli* of some writers, and has for its very near ally—if indeed it be not considered merely a local race or subspecies of—the *M. alba* of Linnæus, which has a wide range in Europe, Asia, and Africa, visiting England almost yearly, and chiefly differing from the ordinary British form in its lighter-coloured tints,—the cock especially having a clear grey instead of a black back. Eleven other more or less nearly-allied species are recognized by Mr Sharpe (*Cat. B. Brit. Museum*, x. pp. 456–496), who has laboriously treated the complicated synonymy of this group of birds. Eight of these are natives of Asia, several of them wintering in India, and one, *M. ocularis*, even occasionally reaching the west coast of North America, while the rest are confined to Africa. No colours but black, grey, or white enter into the plumage of any of the foregoing; but in the species peculiar to

Madagascar, *M. flaviventris*, as well as in that which it much resembles, the so-called Grey Wagtail of Britain, *M. melanope* (*M. boarula* or *sulphurea* of some authors), a great part of the lower surface is yellow. The species last mentioned is one of the most graceful of birds, and though having a very wide range in the world at large is curiously local in its distribution in Britain, being almost wholly confined in the breeding-season to the neighbourhood of rocky streams in the west and north, and a line drawn from the Start Point, slightly curving to round the Derbyshire hills, and ending at the mouth of the Tees, will, it is believed, mark off its breeding-range in England. Then there is a section which by some systematists has been raised to the rank of a genus, *Budytes*, containing the Wagtails in which yellow takes a still more prominent part in their coloration. Of these, 8 species, besides several subspecies, are recognized by Mr Sharpe (*ut supra*, pp. 503–532). One of these is the common Yellow Wagtail of England, *M. raii* (by some mistakenly called *M. campestris*), which, though very generally distributed throughout the country, is much less numerous than the Pied Wagtail, and more addicted to wet meadows; but, just as *M. lugubris* is regarded by some as a local form of the more widely-ranging *M. alba*, so does *M. raii* hold the same relation to *M. flava*, the Blue-headed Wagtail, which has a very extensive distribution in the Old World, and even crosses the Pacific to Alaska, presenting also a great number of varieties or races (most of which are treated by Mr Sharpe as real species) differing from each other chiefly, if not solely, in the colour of the head, a character which in this section can hardly be deemed specific, while their geographical range intersects and inosculates in a most puzzling manner. Much credit is due to the author just named for the enormous trouble he has taken, after study of a vast series of specimens, to clear up the questions herein involved; but it will probably be long before ornithologists can agree on many of the disputed points, and it is certain that the last word has by no means been spoken concerning them.

The genus *Motacilla* (an exact rendering of the English "Wagtail," the Dutch *Kwikstaart*, the Italian *Codatremola* and other similar words), which, as originally founded by Linnæus, contained nearly all the "soft-billed" birds of early English ornithologists, was restricted by various authors in succession, following the example set by Scopoli in 1769, until none but the Wagtails remained in it. Most of the rest are now commonly classed as *Sylviidæ* (*cf.* WARBLER), while the Wagtails with the PIPITS (*q.v.*) constitute the Family *Motacillidæ*. (A. N.)

WAHABEES, or WAHHÁBÍS. See ARABIA, vol. ii. p. 260.

WAINEWRIGHT, THOMAS GRIFFITHS (1794–*c.* 1852), journalist and subject-painter, was born at Chiswick in October 1794. He was educated by his distant relative Dr Charles Burney, and served as an orderly officer in the guards, and as cornet in a yeomanry regiment. In 1819 he entered on a literary life, and began to write for *The Literary Pocket-Book*, *Blackwood's Magazine*, and *The Foreign Quarterly Review*. He is, however, most definitely identified with *The London Magazine*, to which, from 1820 to 1823, he contributed some smart but most flippant art and other criticisms, under the signatures of "James Weathercock," "Mr Bonmot," and "Herr Vinkbooms." He was a friend of Charles Lamb,—who thought well of his literary productions, and in a letter to Bernard Barton, styles him the "kind, light-hearted Wainewright,"—and of the other brilliant contributors to the journal. He also practised as an artist, designing illustrations to Chamberlayne's poems, and from 1821 to 1825 exhibiting in the Royal Academy figure pictures, including a Romance from Undine, Paris in the Chamber of Helen, and the Milk Maid's Song. Owing to his extravagant habits, Wainewright's affairs became deeply involved; and in 1830 he insured the life of his sister-in-law in various offices for a sum of £18,000. The lady died in the December of the same year, and payment of the amount was declined by the companies on the ground of their having been misrepresentation when the insurance was effected. Wainewright now retired to France, but here he was seized by the authorities as a suspected person, and imprisoned for six months. On his being examined there was found upon his person a quantity of strychnine, a poison by means of which it was afterwards found he had destroyed, not only his sister-in-law, but also his uncle, his mother-in-law, and a Norfolkshire friend. He returned to London in 1837, but was at once arrested on a charge of forging, thirteen years before, a transfer of stock, and was sentenced to transportation for life. He died of apoplexy in Hobart Town hospital, about the year 1852.

The *Essays and Criticisms* of Wainewright were published in 1880, with an account of his life, by W. Carew Hazlitt; and the history of his crimes suggested to Dickens his story of "Hunted Down," and to Bulwer Lytton his novel of *Lucretia*.

WAITZ, GEORG (1813–1886), one of the most distinguished of modern German historians, was born at Flensburg, in the duchy of Schleswig, on October 9, 1813. He was educated at the Flensburg gymnasium and the universities of Kiel and Berlin. His strong bent to historical studies and the influence of Ranke early diverted him from his original purpose of studying law, and while still a student he began that series of researches in German mediæval history which was to be the occupation of his life. On graduating at Berlin in August 1836, Waitz went to Hanover to assist Pertz in the great national work of publishing the *Monumenta Germaniæ Historica*; and the energy and learning he displayed in that position won him a summons to the chair of history at Kiel in 1842. The young professor soon began to take an interest in politics, and in 1846 entered the provincial diet as representative of his university. His leanings were strongly German, so that he became somewhat obnoxious to the Danish Government, a fact which made an invitation in 1847 to become professor of history at Göttingen peculiarly acceptable. The political events of 1848–49, however, delayed his appearance in his new chair. When the German party in the northern duchies rose against the Danish Government, Waitz hastened to place himself at the service of the provisional Government. He was sent to Berlin to represent the interests of the duchies there, and during his absence he was elected by Kiel as a delegate to the assembly at Frankfort. Waitz was an adherent of the party who were eager to bring about a union of the German states under a German emperor; and when the king of Prussia declined the imperial crown the professor withdrew from the assembly in disappointment, and ended his active share in public life. In the autumn of 1849 Waitz began his lectures at Göttingen. His style of speaking was dry and uninteresting; but the matter of his lectures was so practical and his teaching so sound that students were attracted in crowds to his lecture-room, and the reputation of the Göttingen historical school spread far and wide. At the same time Waitz's pen was not idle, and his industry is to be traced in the list of his works and in the *Proceedings* of the different historical societies to which he belonged. In 1875 Waitz removed to Berlin to succeed Pertz as principal editor of the *Monumenta Germaniæ Historica*. In spite of advancing years the new editor threw himself into the work with all his former vigour, and took journeys to England, France, and Italy to collate works preserved in these countries. He died at Berlin on May 24, 1886. He was twice married,—in 1842 to a daughter of Schelling the philosopher, and in 1858 to a daughter of General Von Hartmann.

Waitz is often spoken of as the chief disciple of Ranke, though perhaps in general characteristics and mental attitude he has more affinity with Pertz or Dahlmann. He is an industrious and painstaking historian, who, without troubling himself about the graces of style, has collected and published an immense quantity of valuable and carefully sifted material. His special domain was mediæval German history, and he rarely travelled beyond it.

Waitz's chief works are—*Deutsche Verfassungs-Geschichte*, 8 vols., Kiel, 1844–78; 2d ed., 2 vols. only, 1865–70; *Schleswig-Holsteins Geschichte*, 2 vols., Göttingen, 1851–54 (the 3d vol. was never published); *Lübeck unter Jürgen Wullenwever und die Europäische Politik*, 3 vols., Berlin 1855–56; and *Grundzüge der Politik*, Kiel, 1862. Among his smaller works, which, however, indicate the line of his researches, are the following:—*Jahrbücher des deutschen Reichs unter Heinrich I.*, Berlin, 1837, 3d ed., 1885; *Ueber das Leben und die Lehre des Ulfila*, Hanover, 1840; *Das alte Recht der Salischen Franken*, Kiel, 1846; and *Deutsche Kaiser von Karl dem Grossen bis Maximilian*, Berlin, 1872. In conjunction with other scholars Waitz took a leading part in the publication of the *Forschungen zur deutschen Geschichte*, Munich, 1862 *sq.*, and in the *Nordalbingische Studien*, published in the proceedings of the Schleswig-Holstein Historical Society, Kiel, 1844–51. It is impossible here to do more than refer to his numerous and valuable contributions to the *Monumenta*, and to his numerous papers and criticisms published in periodicals and the proceedings of historical societies. A *Bibliographische Uebersicht über Waitz's Werke* was published by E. Steindorff at Göttingen in 1886.

Obituary notices of Waitz are to be found in the *Historische Zeitschrift*, new series, vol. xx.; in the publications for 1886 of the Berlin Academie der Wissenschaften, the Göttingen Gesellschaft der Wissenschaften, and the Hansische Geschichtsverein; in the *Historisches Jahrbuch der Görres Gesellschaft*, vol. viii.; and in the *Revue Historique*, vol. xxxi.

WAKEFIELD, a municipal and parliamentary borough and market-town of England, in the West Riding of Yorkshire, of which division it is the shire-town, is pleasantly situated on the Calder, and on the Lancashire and Yorkshire, Great Northern, and North-Eastern Railway lines, 9 miles south of Leeds and 175½ miles from London. It has water communication (*via* Goole) with Hull by the Calder, which also communicates with the Lancashire canals. The streets are spacious; and, if the town has a somewhat old-fashioned appearance, and is less regularly built than several of the other large towns in Yorkshire, it enjoys the advantage of an atmosphere less polluted by smoke. The Calder is crossed by a fine bridge of eight arches, on which stands the chantry of St Mary, a beautiful Gothic structure, 30 feet long by 24 feet wide, endowed by Edward IV. in memory of his father Richard, duke of York, killed at the battle of Wakefield in 1460; it was restored in 1847 at a cost of £3000. The parish church of All Saints, consecrated by Archbishop William de Melton in 1329, but almost wholly rebuilt in the 15th century, is a beautiful building, partly Early English and partly Perpendicular, consisting of chancel, nave, and tower surmounted by a fine spire rebuilt in 1860–61, the total height being 247 feet. The whole building was restored in 1857–86 from designs of the late Sir Gilbert Scott, at a cost of about £30,000. The other churches are without special interest. The Elizabethan grammar school founded in 1592 was rebuilt in 1829; it is now regulated by a scheme formed by the charity commissioners. Among the principal public buildings of Wakefield are the corn exchange, erected in 1837, enlarged in 1862, and including a public concert-room; the town-hall, in the French Renaissance style, opened in 1880 at a cost of £80,000; the large prison for the West Riding of Yorkshire; the West Riding sessions house; the borough police station (1879); the office of probate (1863); the mechanics' institution, with large library; the church institute and library; the fine art institution; and the public baths. The benevolent institutions include the Clayton hospital, built on the pavilion system, opened in 1879 at a cost of £25,000, and the West Riding pauper lunatic asylum, with accommodation for upwards of 1400 patients. Formerly Wakefield was the great emporium of the cloth manufacture in Yorkshire, but it has within the present century been superseded in this respect by Leeds. Foreign weavers of cloth were established at Wakefield by Henry VII.; and Leland, writing in the time of Henry VIII., states that its "whole profit standeth by coarse drapery." During the 18th century it became noted for the manufacture of worsted yarn and woollen stuffs. Although its manufacturing importance is now small in comparison with that of several other Yorkshire towns, it possesses large mills for spinning worsted and carpet yarns, cocoa fibre, and China grass. It has also rag-crushing mills, chemical works, soap-works, and iron-works; and there are a large number of collieries in the neighbourhood. Wakefield is the chief agricultural town in the West Riding, and has one of the largest corn-markets in the north of England. It possesses large agricultural implement and machine works, corn and flour mills, malt-works, and breweries. A large trade in corn is carried on by means of the Calder, and the building of boats for inland navigation is also a considerable industry. There are very extensive market-gardens in the neighbourhood. Wakefield is the seat of the court of probate for the Wakefield district. It is governed by a mayor, eight aldermen, and twenty-four councillors. The erection of a new diocese of Wakefield was sanctioned in 1878, and the first bishop was appointed in February 1888. The population of the municipal and parliamentary borough (area 1553 acres) in 1871 was 28,069, and in 1881 it was 30,854. By the Act of 1885 the parliamentary borough was enlarged by the addition of the suburb of Bellevue.

Wakefield is supposed by some to occupy the site of a Roman station. In Domesday the name occurs as Wackefield. Originally it consisted of three hamlets—Northgate, Kirkgate, and Westgate. The manor of Wakefield soon after the Conquest was granted to William, third earl of Warren. It formed an extensive baronial liberty extending westwards to the borders of Lancashire and Cheshire. On the death without male issue (30th June 1347) of John, eighth earl of Warren, it reverted to the crown, and by Edward III. it was given to his fifth son, Edward de Langley, whom he created earl of Cambridge, and who in the reign of Richard II. was created duke of York. After the battle of Wakefield in 1460 it remained in the possession of the crown till the reign of Charles I., who granted it to Henry, earl of Holland. It became the marriage portion of the earl's daughter when she married Sir Gervaise Clifton of Clifton in the county of Nottingham. About 1663 Sir Gervaise Clifton sold it to Sir Christopher Clapham, whose heirs in the year 1760 sold it to the duke of Leeds, and it still remains in the possession of that family. Near Wakefield Queen Margaret inflicted a memorable defeat on Richard, duke of York (31st December 1460). The town has possessed a corn-market since the time of the Saxons. It obtained a charter for a cattle-market 1st March 1765. It was incorporated by Charles I. in 1626, and was governed by a constable, until it obtained a new charter under the Municipal Act, 11th March 1848. Since 1832 it has returned a member of parliament. Under an Improvement Act obtained in 1877, the corporation were empowered to purchase the waterworks belonging to a company which had been formed in 1835. In 1880 an Act was granted for obtaining a supply from Rishworth Moors, near Halifax, and the works were completed in 1888 at a cost of about £500,000.

WAKEFIELD, Edward Gibbon (1796–1862), colonial statesman, was born in London, March 20, 1796, of an originally Quaker family. His father, Edward Wakefield, author of *Ireland, Statistical and Political*, was a surveyor and land agent in extensive practice; his grandmother, Priscilla Wakefield, was a popular author for the young, and one of the first introducers of savings banks. Wakefield was for a short time at Westminster School, and was brought up to his father's profession, which he relinquished on occasion of his elopement at the age of 20 with Miss Pattle, the orphan daughter of an Indian civil servant. The young lady's relatives ultimately became reconciled to the match, and procured him an appointment as attaché to the British legation at Turin. He resigned this post in 1820, upon the death of his wife, to whom he was fondly attached, and, though making some efforts to connect himself with journalism, spent the years immediately succeeding in idleness, residing for the most part in Paris. In 1826 he appeared before the public as the hero of a most extraordinary adventure, the abduction of Miss Ellen Turner, daughter of William Turner, of Shrigley Park, Cheshire. Miss Turner was decoyed from school by means of a forged letter, and made to believe that she could only save her father from ruin by marrying Wakefield, whom she accordingly accompanied to Gretna Green. This time the family refused to condone his proceedings; he was tried with his confederates at Lancaster assizes, March 1827, convicted, and sentenced to three years' imprisonment in Newgate. The marriage, which had not been consummated, was dissolved by a special Act of Parliament. A disgrace which would have blasted the career of most men made Wakefield a practical statesman and a benefactor to his country. Meditating, it is probable, emigration upon his release, he turned his attention while in prison to colonial subjects, and acutely detected the main causes of the slow progress of the Australian colonies in the enormous size of the landed estates, the reckless manner in which land was given away, the absence of all systematic effort at colonization, and the consequent discouragement of immigration and dearth of labour. He proposed to remedy this state of things by the sale of land in small quantities at a sufficient price, and the employment of the proceeds as a fund for promoting immigration. These views were expressed with extraordinary vigour and incisiveness in his *Letter from Sydney* (1829), published while he was still in prison, but composed with such graphic power that it has been continually quoted as if written on the spot. After his release Wakefield seemed disposed for a while to turn his attention to social questions at home, and produced a tract on the *Punishment of Death*, with a terribly graphic picture of the condemned sermon in Newgate, and another on incendiarism in the rural districts, with an equally powerful exhibition of the degraded condition of the agricultural labourer. He soon, however, became entirely engrossed with colonial affairs, and, having impressed Stuart Mill, Colonel Torrens, and other leading economists with the value of his ideas, became a leading though not a conspicuous manager of the South Australian Company, by which the colony of South Australia was ultimately founded. In 1833 he published anonymously *England and America*, a work primarily intended to develop his own colonial theory, which is done in the appendix entitled "The Art of Colonization." The body of the work, however, is fruitful in seminal ideas, though some statements may be rash, and some conclusions extravagant. It contains the distinct proposal that the transport of letters should be wholly gratuitous—the precursor of subsequent reform—and the prophecy that, under given circumstances, "the Americans would raise cheaper corn than has ever been raised." In 1836 Wakefield published the first volume of an edition of Adam Smith, which he did not complete. In 1837 the New Zealand Association was established, and he became its managing director. Scarcely, however, was this great undertaking fairly commenced when he accepted the post of private secretary to Lord Durham on the latter's appointment as special commissioner to Canada. The Durham Report, the charter of constitutional government in the colonies, though drawn up by Charles Buller, embodied the ideas of Wakefield, and the latter was the means of its being given prematurely to the public through the *Times*, to prevent its being tampered with by the Government. He acted in the same spirit a few months later, when (about July, 1839), understanding that the authorities intended to prevent the despatch of emigrants to New Zealand, he hurried them off on his own responsibility, thus compelling the Government to annex the country just in time to anticipate a similar step on the part of France. For several years Wakefield continued to direct the New Zealand Company, fighting its battles with the colonial office and the missionary interest, and secretly inspiring and guiding many parliamentary committees on colonial subjects, especially on the abolition of transportation. The company was by no means a financial success, and many of its proceedings were wholly unscrupulous and indefensible; its great object. however, was attained, and New Zealand became the Britain of the south. In 1846 Wakefield, exhausted with labour, was struck down by apoplexy, and spent more than a year in complete retirement, writing during his gradual recovery his *Art of Colonization*. The management of the company had meanwhile passed into the hands of others, whose sole object was to settle accounts with the Government, and wind up the undertaking. Wakefield seceded, and joined Lord Lyttelton and Mr Godley in establishing the Canterbury settlement as a Church of England colony. A portion of his correspondence on this subject has been published by his son, and is perhaps the most adequate memorial extant of the vigour and sagacity of his intellect. As usual with him, however, he failed to retain the confidence of his coadjutors to the end. In 1853, after the grant of a constitution to New Zealand, he took up his residence in the colony, and immediately began to act a leading part in colonial politics. In 1854 he appeared in the first New Zealand parliament as extra-official adviser of the acting governor, a position which excited great jealousy, and as the mover of a resolution demanding the appointment of a responsible ministry. It was carried unanimously, but difficulties, which will be found detailed in Swainson's *New Zealand and its Colonization* (ch. 12), prevented its being made effective until after the mover's retirement from political life. In December 1854, after a fatiguing address to a public meeting, followed by prolonged exposure to a south-east gale, his constitution entirely broke down. He spent the rest of his life in retirement, dying at Wellington on 16th May 1862.

Wakefield was a man of large views and lofty aims, and in private life displayed the warmth of heart which commonly accompanies these qualities. His main defect was unscrupulousness: he hesitated at nothing necessary to accomplish an object, and the conviction of his untrustworthiness gradually alienated his associates, and left him politically powerless. Excluded from parliament by the fatal error of his youth, he was compelled to resort to indirect means of working out his plans by influencing public men. But for a tendency to paradox, his intellectual powers were of the highest order, and as a master of nervous idiomatic English he is second to Cobbett alone. After every deduction it remains true that no contemporary showed equal genius as a colonial statesman, or in this department rendered equal service to his country.

For an impartial examination of the Wakefield system, see Leroy-Beaulieu, *De la Colonisation chez les Peuples Modernes* (3d ed., pp. 562–575 and 696–700). (R. G.)

WAKEFIELD, Gilbert (1756–1801), classical scholar, theologian, and politician, was born at Nottingham, February 22, 1756, and was the son of the Rev. George Wakefield, rector of St Nicholas. After being educated at various private schools, he proceeded at the age of sixteen to Jesus College, Cambridge, where he cultivated his classical studies diligently, but imbibed a thorough distaste for logic and mathematics. He became, however, fellow of his college in 1776, and in 1778 was ordained by the bishop of Peterborough, in a frame of mind which led him afterwards to declare that he regarded his subscription to the Articles as the most disingenuous action of his life. He held, however, curacies for a short time at Stockport and Liverpool, but in 1779, the year of his marriage, quitted the church, and accepted the post of classical tutor at the Nonconformist academy at Warrington. The institution was already on the decline, and Wakefield's pugnacious temper was not likely to contribute to restore it. "It survived my arrival," he says, "four years." During this short period he published translations of Matthew and the first epistle to the Thessalonians, and treatises on inspiration and baptism, the latter of which was entirely written in nine days. He apologizes for this precipitancy as the result of "a constitutional ardour which will not suffer me to dwell long on the same subject." However inevitable, this was the source of most of his failures and mistakes. After the dissolution of the academy, he resided successively at Bramcote in Nottinghamshire, at Richmond, and at Nottingham, taking pupils and persevering in his theological and classical studies, which were considerably retarded by ill health. His most important production at this time was the *Silva Critica*, "illustrating the Scriptures by light borrowed from the philology of Greece and Rome." Three parts of this work were printed at the Cambridge university press, but, the authorities declining to proceed further with it, the author was obliged to complete it himself. In 1790 he was appointed professor of classics at the newly-founded Unitarian college at Hackney. Here he speedily became uncomfortable; his proposals for reform in the course of instruction were unacceptable to his colleagues, and his dislike to the religious services, which he carried to the length of objecting to all social worship, occasioned his resignation in June 1791. The publication of his views on public worship deprived him of all his private pupils, and his time was henceforth devoted to authorship and the education of his children. His next important work was a new translation of the New Testament, retaining as much of the language of the Authorized Version as he deemed consistent with accuracy. This soon reached a second edition. He commenced an edition of Pope, which he was prevented from completing by the competition of Warton, but the notes were published separately. His edition of Lucretius, a work of high pretensions and little solid performance, appeared in 1796. It gained for the editor a very exaggerated reputation, but Wakefield suffered himself to be allured from the paths of literature into those of political and religious controversy. After assailing with equal acerbity writers so diverse in their principles as Wilberforce and Thomas Paine, he in January 1798 "employed a few hours" in drawing up a reply to Bishop Watson's *Address to the People of Great Britain.* These few hours procured him two years' imprisonment in Dorchester jail. He was convicted in February 1799 of having published a seditious libel, an offence which he had assuredly no intention of committing, and his eloquent defence was naturally thrown away upon the same jurymen who had already convicted the printer. The sympathy excited for him, however, led to a subscription, amounting to no less than £5000, and forming a sufficient provision for his family upon his death, which occurred September 9, 1801, shortly after his liberation, from an attack of typhus fever. He had occupied himself while in prison with the preparation of classical lectures and an English-Greek lexicon, and had corresponded on classical subjects with Charles James Fox. The letters were subsequently published.

Wakefield was one of the most honest of men, but also one of the most precipitate, narrow-minded, and presumptuous. His extreme ardour and his consciousness of integrity produced an uncharitableness verging on offensiveness, little in harmony with the many magnanimous and amiable features of his character. Rashness, opinionativeness, and contentiousness grievously marred in him the character of patriot and scholar, though they could not destroy his claim to be numbered among both.

The principal authority for his life is the second edition of his *Memoirs*, in two volumes (London, 1804). The first volume is autobiographical; the second, compiled by the editors, Rutt and Wainwright, includes several estimates of his character and performances from various sources, the most remarkable being one by Dr Parr.

WAKIDI. See TABARI.

WALACHIA. See ROUMANIA and VLACHS.

WALAFRID[1] STRABO (or STRABUS, *i.e.*, "squint-eyed") was born in Germany (808–9), but the exact place is unknown. His taste for literature early displayed itself, and by the age of eighteen he had already achieved a reputation among the learned men of his age. He was educated at the monastery of Reichenau, near Constance, where he had for his teachers Tatto and Wettin, to whose visions he devotes one of his poems. Later on in life (*c.* 826–829) he passed to Fulda, where he studied for some time under Hrabanus Maurus before returning to Reichenau, of which monastery he was made abbot in 838. There is a story, based, however, on no good evidence, that Walafrid devoted himself so closely to letters as to neglect the duties of his office, owing to which he was expelled from his house; but, from his own verses, it seems that the real cause of his flight to Spires was that, notwithstanding the fact that he had been tutor to Charles the Bald, he espoused the side of his elder brother Lothair on the death of Louis the Pious in 840. He was, however, restored to his monastery in 842, and died August 16, 849, on an embassy to his former pupil. His epitaph was written by Hrabanus Maurus, whose elegiacs praise him for being the faithful guardian of his monastery.

Walafrid Strabo's works may be divided into three classes,—theological, historical, and poetical.

1. The first class includes the *Glossa Ordinaria*,[2] a large commentary on the Bible and part of the Apocrypha. This is of course to a great extent a compilation from St Jerome, St Augustine, St Isidore, Bede, Hrabanus Maurus, &c. Under the same heading come the exposition of the first twenty Psalms, published by Pez (*Anecdota Nova*, iv.), and an epitome of Hrabanus Maurus's commentary on Leviticus. An *Expositio Quatuor Evangeliorum* is also ascribed to Walafrid. The treatise *De Rebus Ecclesiasticis*, dedicated to Regenbert the librarian, gives not only explanations and directions for the erection and embellishment of churches, but also instructions as regards such questions as the method of taking the holy communion and the payment of tithes. Walafrid approves of the use of images and pictures in churches, "quia pictura est quædam literatura illiterata." He had himself seen "simple folk and idiots," whom words could hardly bring to a realization of what they were told, so touched by representations of our Lord's passion that the tears ran down their faces. Last among Walafrid's theological treatises must be mentioned the *De Subversione Jerusalem Tractatus*.

2. Walafrid's chief historical works are—(*a*) the *Vita Sancti Galli*, which, though written nearly two centuries after this saint's death, is still the primary authority for his life, and (*b*) a much shorter life of St Othmar, abbot of St Gall (d. 759). Both these lives were based on previous ones written by Abbot Gotzbert of St Gall (from 816–837).[3]

3. Walafrid's poetical works include a short life of St Blaithmaic, a high-born monk of Iona, murdered by the Danes in the first half of the 9th century; a life of St Mammes; and a *Liber de Visionibus Wettini*. This last poem, like the two preceding ones written in hexameters, was composed at the command of "Father" Adalgisus, and based upon the prose narrative of Heto, abbot of Reichenau from 806 to 822. It is dedicated to Wettin's brother Grimald. At the time he sent it to Grimald Walafrid had, as he himself tells us, hardly passed his eighteenth year, and he begs his correspondent to revise his verses, because, "as it is not lawful for a monk to hide anything from his abbot," he fears he may be beaten with deserved stripes. In this curious vision Wettin saw Charles the Great suffering purgatorial tortures because of his incontinence. The name of the ruler alluded to is not indeed introduced into the actual text, but "Carolus Imperator" form the initial letters of the passage dealing with this subject. Many of Walafrid's other poems are, or include, short addresses to kings and queens (Lothair, Charles, Louis, Pippin, Judith, &c.) and to friends (Einhard, Grimald, Hrabanus Maurus, Tatto, Ebbo, archbishop of Rheims, Drogo, bishop of Metz, &c.). His most famous poem is the *Hortulus*, dedicated to Grimald. It is an account of a little garden that he used to tend with his own hands, and is largely made up of

[1] In the oldest MSS. this is always spelt "Walahfrid."

[2] This commentary was the one in general use during the Middle Ages, when it went by the name of *Glossa* simply.

[3] Walafrid also edited Thetmar's *Life of Louis the Pious*, prefixing a preface and making a few additions, and divided Einhard's *Vita Caroli* into chapters, adding an introduction.

descriptions of the various herbs he grows there and their medicinal and other uses. Sage holds the place of honour; then comes rue, the antidote of poisons; and so on through melons, fennel, lilies, poppies, and many other plants, to wind up with the rose, "which in virtue and scent surpasses all other herbs, and may rightly be called the flower of flowers." The curious poem *De Imagine Tetrici* takes the form of a dialogue.

WALCH, the name of a family of scholars.

I. JOHANN GEORG WALCH (1693–1775) was born at Meiningen, and studied at Leipsic and Jena under Olearius and Buddæus. From 1716 he was professor at Jena of philosophy, rhetoric, and poetry successively, and afterwards (from 1724) of theology. He married the only daughter of Buddæus, and in his learned and theological career followed in the footsteps of his father-in-law. His theological position was that of a very moderate orthodoxy, which had been influenced greatly by the philosophy and controversies of the Deistic period. His university lectures and published works ranged over the wide fields of ecclesiastical history in its various branches, particularly the literature and the controversies of the church, dogmatics, ethics, and pastoral theology.

Of his works the most valuable were *Bibliotheca Theologica* (1757–64); *Bibliotheca Patristica* (1770, new ed. 1834); his edition of Luther's works in 24 vols. (1740–52); *Historische und theologische Einleitung in die religiösen Streitigkeiten ausserhalb der Lutherischen Kirche*, 5 vols. (1734–36); and the companion work to this, *Streitigkeiten der Evangel. Luth. Kirche* (1730–39). His life, with a complete list of his writings, which amounted to 287, *Leben und Charakter des Kirchenraths J. G. Walch*, was published by his son C. W. F. Walch (Jena, 1777). Comp. Gass, *Protestantische Dogmatik*, iii. p. 205 *sq.*

II. JOHANN ERNST IMMANUEL WALCH (1725–1778), son of the above, born at Jena in 1725, became professor of philosophy in the university in 1750, and of rhetoric and poetry in 1759. He died in 1778. He was distinguished for his philological, antiquarian, and mineralogical acquirements.

See *Lebensgeschichte Johann Ernst Im. Walch*, Jena, 1780, and Meusel's *Lexicon verstorbener deutscher Schriftsteller*, vol. xiv.

III. CHRISTIAN WILHELM FRANZ WALCH (1726–1784), younger brother of J. E. I. Walch, was born at Jena December 25, 1726. He was educated at Jena under his father's direction, and as early as 1745–1747 lectured in the university in branches of exegesis, philosophy, and history. He then travelled with his brother J. E. I. Walch for a year through the Continent, making the acquaintance of the learned men of each country. On his return he was made professor of theology in Jena, but in 1753 he accepted an invitation to Göttingen, where he spent his life as professor of theology. He lectured on dogmatics, church history, ethics, polemics, natural theology, symbolics, the epistles of Paul, Christian antiquities, historical theological literature, ecclesiastical law, and the fathers. His permanent place amongst learned theologians rests on his works on ecclesiastical history. He here holds the third place in the important trio Semler, Mosheim, Walch. Semler was much his superior in originality and boldness, and Mosheim in clearness, method, and elegance. But to his wide, deep, and accurate learning, to his conscientious and impartial examination of the facts and the authorities at first hand, and to "his exact quotation of the sources and works illustrating them and careful discussion of the most minute details" all succeeding historians are deeply indebted. His method is critical and pragmatic, "pursuing everywhere the exact facts and the supposed causes of the outward changes of history," leaving wholly out of sight the deeper moving principles and ideas which influence its course. He speaks of history as consisting of "the accidental changes of accidental matters." But, although he thus failed to reach the modern standard of an historian, the results of his industry and research remain as permanent historical materials.

His principal work was his *Entwurf einer vollständigen Historie der Ketzereien, Spaltungen, und Religionsstreitigkeiten, bis auf die Reformation*, 11 vols., Leipsic, 1762–85. It was a great advance in theological liberality that he defined a heretic on the one hand as a Christian and on the other as one in fundamental error. He thus claimed for the heretic a place in the church, while he declined to treat as heretical such differences as divided great sections of Christians. Of his other valuable works may be mentioned *Entwurf einer vollständigen Historie der Römischen Päpste* (1756, 2d ed. 1758), *Entwurf einer vollständigen Historie der Kirchenversammlungen* (1759), *Bibliotheca Symbolica Vetus* (1770), *Kritische Untersuchung vom Gebrauch der heiligen Schrift unter den alten Christen* (1779), occasioned by the controversy between Lessing and Goeze, and to which Lessing began an elaborate reply just before his death.

On C. W. F. Walch as historian see Baur, *Epochen der kirchlichen Geschichtschreibung* (1852), p. 145 *sq.*, and *Dogmengeschichte*, p. 38 *sq.* (1867, 3d ed.); Gass, *Geschichte der Protestantischen Dogmatik*, iii. p. 267 *sq.*; Meusel, *Lexicon verstorbener deutscher Schriftsteller*, vol. xiv.

IV. CARL FRIEDRICH WALCH (1734–1799), brother of the last-named, was professor of jurisprudence at Jena, and the author of several valuable legal works. He died at Jena in 1799. His son Georg Ludwig (1785–1838) was for a time professor in the Kloster gymnasium of Berlin and afterwards in the university of Greifswald. He edited valuable editions of Tacitus's *Agricola* and *Germania*.

WALCHEREN. See ZEALAND.

WALDECK-PYRMONT, a small principality in the north-west of Germany, is the eighteenth factor of the German empire in point of area, and the twenty-fourth in point of population. It consists of two separate portions lying about 30 miles apart, viz., the county (grafschaft) of Waldeck, embedded in Prussian territory between the provinces of Westphalia and Hesse-Nassau, and the principality (fürstenthum) of Pyrmont, farther to the north, between Lippe, Brunswick, and Hanover. Waldeck, with 48,580 inhabitants, comprises an area of 407 square miles, covered for the most part with hills, which culminate in the Hegekopf (2807 feet). The centre is occupied by the plateau of Corbach. The chief rivers are the Eder and Diemel, both of which eventually find their way into the Weser. Pyrmont, only 26 square miles in extent, with 8123 inhabitants, is also mountainous. The Emmer, also belonging to the Weser system, is its chief stream. The united area is thus 433 square miles, or about half the size of Cambridgeshire in England, and the united population in 1885 was 56,703. Agriculture and cattle-rearing are the main resources of the inhabitants in both parts of the principality, but the soil is nowhere very fertile. Only 55½ per cent. of the area is occupied by arable land and pasture; forests, one-tenth of which are coniferous, occupy 36 per cent. Rye is the principal crop; but oats, potatoes, and flax are also grown in considerable quantities. In 1883 the principality contained 5956 horses, 20,249 cattle, 66,704 sheep, 17,735 pigs, and 7332 goats. Iron, slate, and building-stone are worked at various points, and, along with horses, cattle, sheep, pigs, wool, and timber, form the chief exports. A few insignificant manufactures (cigars, liqueurs, earthenware, linen, knitted stockings) are carried on in some of the little towns, but both trade and manufactures are much retarded by the almost complete isolation of the country from railways. Wildungen in the extreme south of Waldeck is the terminus of a branch line, and a narrow part of Pyrmont is intersected by an unimportant line.

The capital and the residence of the prince is Arolsen (2442 inhabitants) in Waldeck; twelve smaller "towns" and about one hundred villages are also situated in the county. The only town in Pyrmont is Bad Pyrmont, with about 1500 inhabitants, at one time a highly fashionable watering-place on account of its chalybeate and saline springs. The annual number of visitors is still estimated at 13,000. Wildungen is also a spa of some repute. The inhabitants to the north of the Eder are of Saxon stock, to the south of Franconian,—a difference which is distinctly marked in dialect, costumes, and manners. Nearly all are Protestants. In 1880, when the population was 56,522, there were 53,995 Protestants, 1576 Roman Catholics, 854 Jews, and 97 others.

Waldeck-Pyrmont has one vote in the federal council and one in the imperial diet. The constitution, dating from 1852, is a reactionary modification of one carried in 1849, which in its turn had been a considerable advance upon one granted in 1816. The single chamber consists of fifteen members (three of whom represent Pyrmont), elected indirectly for three years. In the event of the male line of the present ruling family becoming extinct the female line succeeds in Waldeck, but Pyrmont falls to Prussia. In terms of a treaty concluded in 1868 for ten years and renewed in 1878 for a similar period, the finances and entire government of Waldeck-Pyrmont are managed by Prussia, the little country having found itself unable to support unassisted the military and other burdens involved by its share in the North-German Confederation. The government is conducted in the name of the prince by a Prussian "landes-director," while the state-officials are "Prussian subjects," and take the oath of allegiance to the king of Prussia. The prince of Waldeck reserves his whole rights as head of the church, and also the right of granting pardons, and in certain circumstances may exercise a veto on proposals to alter or enact laws. Education, the administration of justice, and similar matters are thus all conducted on the Prussian model; a previous convention had already handed over military affairs to Prussia. The budget for 1886 showed a revenue of £52,530 and an expenditure of £48,680. The public debt was £117,550, paying interest at 4 per cent. The prince is supported by the income derived from crown-lands.

The princes of Waldeck-Pyrmont are descendants of the counts of Schwalenberg, the earliest of whom known to history was Wittekind, who died in 1137. His grandson seems to have been the first count of Waldeck. For many centuries the original possessions of the Schwalenbergs were divided among several collateral lines of counts (Waldeck, Landau, Wildungen, Eisenberg); and about 1428 Hesse obtained a right of superiority over Waldeck, in return for its protection during those troublous times. This right gave rise to important claims on the part of Hesse, which were not finally set aside until 1847, when the German diet decided that the right had come to an end with the extinction of the empire. In 1685 a *pactum primogenituræ* was made between the two surviving lines, which took effect in 1692, when the Eisenberg branch became extinct with the death of George Frederick, who had served with distinction as an imperial field-marshal, and had received the title of prince. Pyrmont had also originally belonged to a branch of the Schwalenberg family; but it had successively been held by the counts of Lippe (from 1557) and Gleichen (from 1584), before it finally fell back to Waldeck in 1625. From 1692 the lands have remained undivided under the Wildungen line, with the exception of a brief period (1805–1812) when Waldeck and Pyrmont were held by two brothers. Frederick Anthony Ulrich, who succeeded in 1706, was made prince by the emperor Charles VI. In 1807 Waldeck was a member of the Confederation of the Rhine; and in 1814 it entered the German Confederation. Its first constitution was granted in 1816 by Prince George Henry (1813–1845). George Victor, the present prince (1888), succeeded in 1845 at the age of 14, and assumed the government in 1852. The most important incident in the recent history of the principality is the conclusion of the above-mentioned treaty with Prussia, with whom it sided in the war against Austria.

WALDENBURG, an active industrial town in Prussian Silesia, is situated on the Polsnitz, 39 miles south-west of Breslau. It contains a handsome modern town-house and two churches. Among the chief industrial establishments are a large porcelain and stoneware factory, extensive fire-clay works, glass-works, and a china-painting establishment; and there are numerous flax-spinneries and linen-factories in the neighbourhood. Adjoining the town on the south is the village of Oberwaldenburg, with a chateau. Waldenburg lies in the centre of the extensive and productive coal-district of the Waldenburger Gebirge, a branch of the Sudetic chain. The town, which received municipal rights in the 16th century, had a population of 12,999 in 1885; in 1816 the population was 1768. There are villages of the same name in Saxony and Würtemberg.

WALDENSES, THE, a name given to the members of an heretical sect which arose in the south of France about 1170. The history of the sects of the Middle Ages is obscure, because the earliest accounts of them come from those who were concerned in their suppression, and were therefore eager to lay upon each of them the worst enormities which could be attributed to any. In later times the apologists of each sect reversed the process, and cleared that in which they were interested at the expense of others. In early times these sectaries produced little literature of their own; when they produced a literature at the beginning of the 15th century they attempted to claim for it a much earlier origin. Hence there is confusion on every side; it is difficult to distinguish between various sects and to determine their exact opinions or the circumstances under which they came into being. The polemical conception which has done much to perpetuate this confusion is that of the historical continuity of Protestantism from the earliest times. According to this view the church was pure and uncorrupt till the time of Constantine, when Pope Sylvester gained the first temporal possession for the papacy, and so began the system of a rich, powerful, and worldly church, with Rome for its capital. Against this secularized church a body of witnesses silently protested; they were always persecuted but always survived, till in the 13th century a desperate attempt was made by Innocent III. to root them out from their stronghold in southern France. Persecution gave new vitality to their doctrines, which passed on to Wycliffe and Huss, and through these leaders produced the Reformation in Germany and England.

This view rests upon a series of suppositions, and is entirely unhistorical. So far as can be discovered the heretical sects of the Middle Ages rested upon a system of Manichæism which was imported into Europe from the East (see MANICHÆISM). The Manichæan system of dualism, with its severe asceticism, and its individualism, which early passed into antinomianism, was attractive to many minds in the awakening of the 11th century. Its presence in Europe can first be traced in Bulgaria soon after its conversion in 862,[1] where the struggle between the Eastern and Western churches for the new converts opened a way for the more hardy speculations of a system which had never entirely disappeared, and found a home amongst the Paulicians in Armenia. The name of Cathari, taken by the adherents of this new teaching, sufficiently shows the Oriental origin of their opinions, which spread from Bulgaria amongst the Slavs, and followed the routes of commerce into central Europe. The earliest record of their presence there is the condemnation of ten canons of Orleans as Manichees in 1022, and soon after this we find complaints of the prevalence of heresy in northern Italy and in Germany. The strongholds of these heretical opinions were the great towns, the centres of civilization, because there the growing sentiment of municipal independence, and the rise of a burgher class through commerce, created a spirit of criticism which was dissatisfied with the worldly lives of the clergy and their undue influence in affairs.

The system of Catharism recognized two classes of adherents, *credentes* and *perfecti*. The *perfecti* only were admitted to its esoteric doctrines and to its superstitious practices. To the ordinary men it seemed to be a reforming agency, insisting on a high moral standard, and upholding the words of Scripture against the traditions of an

[1] Schmidt, *Histoire des Cathares*, i. 7.

overgrown and worldly church. Its popular aim and its rationalistic method made men overlook its real contents, which were not put clearly before them. It may be said generally that Catharism formed the abiding background of mediæval heresy. Its dualistic system and its anti-social principles were known only to a few, but its anti-ecclesiastical organization formed a permanent nucleus round which gathered a great deal of political and ecclesiastical discontent. When this discontent took any independent form of expression, zeal, which was not always accompanied by discretion, brought the movement into collision with the ecclesiastical authorities, by whom it was condemned as heretical. When once it was in conflict with authority it was driven to strengthen its basis by a more pronounced hostility against the system of the church, and generally ended by borrowing something from Catharism. The result was that in the beginning of the 13th century there was a tendency to class all bodies of heretics together: partly their opinions had coalesced; partly they were assumed to be identical.

Most of these sects were stamped out before the period of the Middle Ages came to a close. The Waldenses, under their more modern name of the Vaudois, have survived to the present day in the valleys of Piedmont, and have been regarded as at once the most ancient and the most evangelical of the mediæval sects. It is, however, by no means easy to determine their original tenets, as in the 13th and 14th centuries they were a body of obscure and unlettered peasants, hiding themselves in a corner, while in the 16th century they were absorbed into the general movement of the Reformation. As regards their antiquity, the attempts to claim for them an earlier origin than the end of the 12th century can no longer be sustained. They rested upon the supposed antiquity of a body of Waldensian literature, which modern criticism has shown to have been tampered with. The most important of these documents, a poem in Provençal, "La Nobla Leyczon," contains two lines which claimed for it the date of 1100:—

> Ben ha mil e cent anez compli entieramant
> Que fo scripta l'ora, car sen al derier temp.

But it was pointed out[1] that in the oldest MS. existing in the Cambridge university library the figure 4 had been imperfectly erased before the word "cent," a discovery which harmonized with the results of a criticism of the contents of the poem itself. This discovery did away with the ingenious attempts to account for the name of Waldenses from some other source than from the historical founder of the sect, Peter Waldo or Valdez. To get rid of Waldo, whose date was known, the name Waldenses or Vallenses was derived from Vallis, because they dwelt in the valleys, or from a supposed Provençal word Vaudes, which meant a sorcerer.

Putting these views aside as unsubstantial, we will consider the relation of the Waldenses as they appear in actual history with the sects which preceded them. Already in the 9th century there were several protests against the rigidity and want of spirituality of a purely sacerdotal church. Thus Berengar of Tours (999–1088) upheld the symbolic character of the Eucharist and the superiority of the Bible over tradition. The Paterines in Milan (1045) raised a protest against simony and other abuses of the clergy, and Pope Gregory VII. did not hesitate to enlist their Puritanism on the side of the papacy and make them his allies in imposing clerical celibacy. In 1110 an apostate monk in Zeeland, Tanchelm, carried their views still further, and asserted that the sacraments were only valid through the merits and sanctity of the ministers. In France, at Embrun, Peter de Bruys founded a sect known as Petrobrusians, who denied infant baptism, the need of consecrated churches, transubstantiation, and masses for the dead. A follower of his, a monk, Henry, gave the name to another body known as Henricians, who centred in Tours. The teachers of these new opinions were men of high character and holy lives, who in spite of persecution wandered from place to place, and made many converts from those who were dissatisfied at the want of clerical discipline which followed upon the struggle for temporal supremacy into which the reforming projects of Gregory VII. had carried the church.

It was at this time (1170) that a rich merchant of Lyons, Peter Waldo, sold his goods and gave them to the poor; then he went forth as a preacher of voluntary poverty. His followers, the Waldenses, or poor men of Lyons, were moved by a religious feeling which could find no satisfaction within the actual system of the church, as they saw it before them. Like St Francis, Waldo adopted a life of poverty that he might be free to preach, but with this difference that the Waldenses preached the doctrine of Christ while the Franciscans preached the person of Christ, Waldo reformed teaching while Francis kindled love; hence the one awakened antagonisms which the other escaped. For Waldo had a translation of the New Testament made into Provençal, and his preachers not only stirred up men to more holy lives but explained the Scriptures at their will. Such an interference with the ecclesiastical authorities led to difficulties. Pope Alexander III., who had approved of the poverty of the Waldensians, prohibited them from preaching without the permission of the bishops (1179). Waldo answered that he must obey God rather than man. The result of this disobedience was excommunication by Lucius III. in 1184. Thus a reforming movement became heresy through disobedience to authority, and after being condemned embarked on a course of polemical investigation how to justify its own position. Some were readmitted into the Catholic Church, and one, Durandus de Osca (1210), attempted to found an order of Pauperes Catholici, which was the forerunner of the order of St Dominic. Many were swept away in the crusade against the ALBIGENSES (*q.v.*). Others made an appeal to Innocent III., protesting their orthodoxy. Their appeal was not successful, for they were formally condemned by the Lateran council of 1215.

The earliest definite account given of the Waldensian opinion is that of the inquisitor Sacconi about 1250.[2] He divides them into two classes, those north of the Alps and those of Lombardy. The first class hold (1) that oaths are forbidden by the gospel, (2) that capital punishment is not allowed to the civil power, (3) that any layman may consecrate the sacrament of the altar, and (4) that the Roman Church is not the church of Christ. The Lombard sect went farther in (3) and (4), holding that no one in mortal sin could consecrate the sacrament, and that the Roman Church was the scarlet woman of the Apocalypse, whose precepts ought not to be obeyed, especially those appointing fast-days. This account sufficiently shows the difference of the Waldenses from the Cathari: they were opposed to asceticism, and had no official priesthood; at the same time their objection to oaths and to capital punishment are closely related to the principles of the Cathari. Their other opinions were forced upon them by their conflict with the authority of the church. When forbidden to preach without the permission of the bishop, they were driven to assert the right of all to preach, without distinction of age or sex. This led to the further step of setting up personal merit rather than ecclesiastical ordination as the ground of the priestly office. From this

[1] Bradshaw, in *Transactions of Cambridge Antiquarian Society*, 1842. The text edited by Montet, 4to, 1887.

[2] D'Argentré, *Collectio Judiciorum de Novis Erroribus*, i. 50, &c.

followed again the conclusion that obedience was not due to an unworthy priest, and that his ministrations were invalid.

These opinions were subversive of the system of the mediæval church, and were naturally viewed with great disfavour by its officials; but it cannot fairly be said that they have much in common with the opinions of the Reformers of the 16th century. The mediæval church set forth Christ as present in the orderly community of the faithful; Protestantism aimed at setting the individual in immediate communion with Christ, without the mechanical intervention of the officers of the community; the Waldenses merely set forward a new criterion of the orderly arrangement of the church, according to which each member was to sit in judgment on the works of the ministers, and consequently on the validity of their ministerial acts. It was a rude way of expressing a desire for a more spiritual community. The earliest known document proceeding from the Waldensians is an account of a conference held at Bergamo in 1218 between the Ultramontane and the Lombard divisions, in which the Lombards showed a greater opposition to the recognized priesthood than did their northern brethren.[1]

As these opinions became more pronounced persecution became more severe, and the breach between the Waldenses and the church widened. The Waldenses withdrew altogether from the ministrations of the church, and chose ministers for themselves whose merits were recognized by the body of the faithful. Election took the place of ordination, but even here the Lombards showed their difference from the Ultramontanes, and recognized only two orders, like the Cathari, while the northern body kept the old three orders of bishops, priests, and deacons. Gradually the separation from the church became more complete: the sacraments were regarded as merely symbolical; the priests became helpers of the faithful; ceremonies disappeared; and a new religious society arose equally unlike the mediæval church and the Protestantism of the 16th century.

The spread of these heretical sects led to resolute attempts at their suppression. The crusade against the Albigensians could destroy prosperous cities and hand over lands from a heedless lord to one who was obedient to the church; but it could not get rid of heresy. The revival of preaching, which was the work of the order of St Dominic, did more to combat heresy, especially where its persuasions were enforced by law. The work of inquisition into cases of heresy proceeded slowly in the hands of the bishops, who were too busy with other matters to find much time for sitting in judgment on theological points about which they were imperfectly informed. The greatest blow struck against heresy was the transference of the duty of inquiry into heresy from the bishops to Dominican inquisitors. The secular power, which shared in the proceeds of the confiscation of those who were found guilty of heresy, was ready to help in carrying out the judgments of the spiritual courts. Everywhere, and especially in the district round Toulouse, heretics were keenly prosecuted, and before the continued zeal of persecution the Waldenses slowly disappeared from the chief centres of population and took refuge in the retired valleys of the Alps. There, in the recesses of Piedmont, where the streams of the Pelice, the Angrogne, the Clusone, and others cleave the sides of the Alps into valleys which converge at Susa, a settlement of the Waldensians was made who gave their name to these valleys of the Vaudois. In the more accessible regions north and south heresy was exposed to a steady process of persecution, and tended to assume shifting forms. Among the valleys it was less easily reached, and retained its old organization and its old contents. Little settlements of heretics dispersed throughout Italy and Provence looked to the valleys as a place of refuge, and tacitly regarded them as the centre of their faith. At times attempts were made to suppress the sect of the Vaudois, but the nature of the country which they inhabited, their obscurity, and their isolation made the difficulties of their suppression greater than the advantages to be gained from it. However, in 1487 Innocent VIII. issued a bull for their extermination, and Alberto de' Capitanei, archdeacon of Cremona, put himself at the head of a crusade against them. Attacked in Dauphiné and Piedmont at the same time, the Vaudois were hard pressed; but luckily their enemies were encircled by a fog when marching upon their chief refuge in the valley of the Angrogne, and were repulsed with great loss. After this Charles II., duke of Piedmont, interfered to save his territories from further confusion, and promised the Vaudois peace. They were, however, sorely reduced by the onslaught which had been made upon them, and lost their ancient spirit of independence. When the Lutheran movement began they were ready to sympathize with it, and ultimately to adapt their old beliefs to those of the rising Protestantism. Already there were scattered bodies of Waldenses in Germany who had influenced, and afterwards joined, the Hussites and the Bohemian Brethren.

The last step in the development of the Waldensian body was taken in 1530, when two deputies of the Vaudois in Dauphiné and Provence, Georges Morel and Pierre Masson, were sent to confer with the German and Swiss Reformers. A letter addressed to Œcolompadius[2] gives an account of their practices and beliefs at that time, and shows us a simple and unlettered community, which was the survival of an attempt to form an esoteric religious society within the mediæval church. It would appear that its members received the sacraments of baptism and the holy communion from the regular priesthood, at all events sometimes, but maintained a discipline of their own and held services for their own edification. Their ministers were called *barba*, a Provençal word meaning *guide*. They were chosen from among labouring men, who at the age of twenty-five might ask the body of ministers to be admitted as candidates. If their character was approved they were taught during the winter months, when work was slack, for a space of three or four years; after that they were sent for two years to serve as menial assistants at a nunnery for women, which curiously enough existed in a recess of the valleys. Then they were admitted to office, after receiving the communion, by the imposition of hands of all ministers present. They went out to preach two by two, and the junior was bound absolutely to obey the senior. Clerical celibacy was their rule, but they admit that it created grave disorders. The ministers received food and clothing from the contributions of the people, but also worked with their hands; the result of this was that they were very ignorant, and also were grasping after bequests from the dying. The affairs of the church were managed by a general synod held every year. The duties of the barbas were to visit all within their district once a year, hear their confessions, advise and admonish them; in all services the two ministers sat side by side, and one spoke after the other. In point of doctrine they acknowledged the seven sacraments, but gave them a symbolical meaning; they prayed to the Virgin and saints, and admitted auricular confession, but they denied purgatory and the sacrifice of the mass, and did not observe fasts or festivals. After giving this account of themselves they ask for information about several points in a way which shows the exigencies of a rude and isolated society, and finally they say that they have been much disturbed by the

[1] Preger, *Beiträge zur Geschichte der Waldesier.*

[2] Scultetus, *Annales*, ii. 294, &c.

Lutheran teaching about freewill and predestination, for they had held that men did good works through natural virtue stimulated by God's grace. and they thought of predestination in no other way than as a part of God's foreknowledge.

Œcolampadius gave them further instruction, especially emphasizing the wrongfulness of their outward submission to the ordinances of the church: "God," he said, "is a jealous God, and does not permit his elect to put themselves under the yoke of Antichrist." The result of this intercourse was an alliance between the Vaudois and the Swiss and German Reformers. A synod was held in 1532 at Chanforans in the valley of the Angrogne, where a new confession of faith was adopted, which recognized the doctrine of election, assimilated the practices of the Vaudois to those of the Swiss congregations, renounced for the future all recognition of the Roman communion, and established their own worship no longer as secret meetings of a faithful few but as public assemblies for the glory of God.

Thus the Vaudois ceased to be relics of the past, and became absorbed in the general movement of Protestantism. This was not, however, a source of quiet or security. In France and Italy alike they were marked out as special objects of persecution, and the Vaudois Church has many records of martyrdom. The most severe trial to which the Vaudois of Piedmont were subjected occurred in 1655. The Congregation *de Propaganda Fide* established, in 1650, a local council in Turin, which exercised a powerful influence on Duke Charles Emmanuel II., who ordered that the Vaudois should be reduced within the limits of their ancient territory. Fanaticism took advantage of this order; and an army, composed partly of French troops of Louis XIV., partly of Irish soldiers who had fled before Cromwell, entered the Vaudois valleys and spread destruction on every side. They treated the people with horrible barbarity, so that the conscience of Europe was aroused, and England under Cromwell called on the Protestant powers to join in remonstrance to the duke of Savoy and the French king. The pen of Milton was employed for this purpose, and his famous sonnet is but the condensation of his state papers. Sir Samuel Morland was sent on a special mission to Turin, and to him were confided by the Vaudois leaders copies of their religious books, which he brought back to England, and ultimately gave to the university library at Cambridge. Large sums of money were contributed in England and elsewhere, and were sent to the suffering Vaudois.

By this demonstration of opinion peace was made for a time between the Vaudois and their persecutors; but it was a treacherous peace, and left the Vaudois with a hostile garrison established among them. Their worship was prohibited, and their chief pastor, Leger, was obliged to flee, and in his exile at Leyden wrote his *Histoire Génèrale des Églises Vaudoises* (1684). The revocation of the edict of Nantes in 1685 began a new period of persecution, which aimed at entire extermination. This was found so difficult that the remnant of the Vaudois, to the number of 2600, were at last allowed to withdraw to Geneva. But the love of their native valleys was strong among the exiles, and in 1689 one of their pastors, Henri Arnaud, led a band of 800 men to the reconquest of their country. His first attempts against the French were successful; and the rupture between Victor Amadeus, duke of Savoy, and Louis XIV. brought a sudden change of fortune to the Vaudois. They were recognized once more as citizens of Savoy, and in the war against France which broke out in 1696 the Vaudois regiment did good service for its duke. The peace of Utrecht saw the greater part of the French territory occupied by the Vaudois annexed to Savoy, and though there were frequent threatenings of persecution, the idea of toleration slowly prevailed in the policy of the house of Savoy. The Vaudois, who had undergone all these vicissitudes, were naturally reduced to poverty, and their ministers were partially maintained by a subsidy from England, which was granted by Queen Anne. The 18th century, however, was a time of religious decadence even among the Alpine valleys, and the outbreak of the French Revolution saw the Vaudois made subjects of France. This led to a loss of the English subsidy, and they applied to Napoleon for an equivalent. This was granted, and their church was organized by the state. On the restoration of the house of Savoy in 1816 English influence was used on behalf of the Vaudois, who received a limited toleration. From that time onwards the Vaudois became the objects of much interest in Protestant countries. Large sums of money were collected to build hospitals and churches among their valleys, and they were looked upon as the possible centre of a Protestant church in Italy. Especially from England did they receive sympathy and help. An English clergyman, Dr Gilly, visited the valleys in 1823, and by his writings on the Vaudois Church attracted considerable attention, so that he was enabled to build a college at La Torre. Moreover, Dr Gilly's book (*A Visit to the Valleys of Piedmont*), chancing to fall into the hands of an officer who had lost his leg at Waterloo, Colonel Beckwith, suggested an object for the energies of one who was loth at the age of twenty-six to sink into enforced idleness. Beckwith visited the valleys, and was painfully struck by the squalor and ignorance of a people who had so glorious a past. He settled among them, and for thirty-five years devoted himself to promote their welfare. During this period he established no fewer than 120 schools; moreover he brought back the Italian language which had been displaced by the French in the services of the Vaudois Church, and in 1849 built a church for them in Turin. He lived in La Torre till his death in 1862, and the name of the English benefactor is still revered by the simple folk of the valleys.

According to the latest official returns the Waldensian Church had, in 1887–88, 44 churches and 44 mission stations throughout Italy. The ordained pastors numbered 38, evangelists 8, and male and female teachers 57, the total number of salaried agents being 128. The mission church had 4074 members, and the day schools were attended by 2323 scholars, the Sunday schools by 2621. The total income, about three-fourths of it contributions from the United Kingdom and other Protestant countries of northern Europe and from America, amounted to upwards of £10,000.

The parent church in the valleys is ecclesiastically governed by a court for internal affairs called the "Table," after the old stone table round which the ancient barbas used to sit, and a mission board, with an annual synod to which both the home and mission boards are subject. There are 18 parishes, 22 pastors, 206 teachers, 13,289 members, 202 primary and 88 Sunday schools, with 5052 day and 3437 Sunday scholars, a normal school and preparatory college at Torre Pellice in the valleys and a fully equipped theological college in Florence, a school for young ladies, an orphanage, a hospital, and an industrial school. They have also a mission in South Africa, and a colony in Uruguay. The home work of the Waldensian Church is carried on without foreign assistance.

The literature on the subject of the Waldensian and other sects is copious. For their rise the most important authorities are to be found in Moneta, *Adversus Catharos et Waldenses*; D'Argentré, *Collectio Judiciorum de Novis Erroribus*; Alanus, *Adversus Hæreticos*; D'Achery, *Spicilegia*, vol. i.; Gretser, *Opera*, vol. x.; Limborch, *Historia Inquisitionis*, at the end of which is the *Liber Sententiarum* of the Inquisition of Toulouse from 1307–1322. Of modern books may be mentioned Schmidt, *Histoire des Cathares*; Hahn, *Geschichte der neu-manichäischen Ketzer*; Dieckhoff, *Die Waldenser im Mittelalter*; Preger, *Beiträge zur Geschichte der Waldesier*; Cantù, *Gli Eretici in Italia*; Comba, *Storia della Riforma in Italia*, and *Histoire des Vaudois d'Italie*; Tocco, *L'Eresia nel Medio Evo*; Montet, *Histoire littéraire des Vaudois*; Lea, *History of the Inquisition of the Middle Ages*. Amongst books dealing with the more modern history of the Vaudois specially are Léger, *Histoire des l'Églises Vaudoises*; Arnaud, *Histoire de la Rentrée des Vaudois*; Perrin, *Histoire des Vaudois*; Monastier, *Histoire de l'Église Vaudoise*; Muston, *L'Israel des Alpes*; Gilly, *Excursion to the Valleys of Piedmont*, and *Researches on the Waldensians*; Todd, *The Waldensian Manuscripts*; Melia, *Origin, Persecution, and Doctrines of the Waldensians*. (M.C.)

WALDO, VALDO, or VALDEZ, PETER. See p. 323 *supra*.

WALES, See ENGLAND.

WALKER, a town of Northumberland, England, on the north bank of the river Tyne, 2 miles east of Newcastle-on-Tyne, with which it is connected by railway. Christ Church, in the Perpendicular style, erected in 1848, consists of chancel, nave, aisles, and tower with beautiful illuminated clock erected in 1887. The windows of the church are all monumental stained glass. There is a large colliery, in which at one time was a salt spring, which was used in the manufacture of soda, begun by permission of the Government in 1795, by a company who may be regarded as the first producers of mineral alkali and soda in England. Along the banks of the Tyne there are large iron and chemical works, coal staiths, ship- and boat-building establishments, and brick and tile works. The corporation of Newcastle-on-Tyne are lords of the manor. The town is formed of what were formerly the villages of Walker, Low Walker, and Walker Quay. It is governed by a local board of health of twelve members. The population of the urban sanitary district (area 1200 acres) in 1871 was 8888, and in 1881 it was 9527.

WALKER, FREDERICK (1840-1875), subject painter, was born in Marylebone, London, on May 24, 1840. While very young he began to draw from the antique in the British Museum, and at the age of sixteen he was placed in the office of Baker, an architect. The occupation proved uncongenial; at the end of eighteen months he resumed his work from the Elgin marbles at the Museum, attending art classes; and in March 1858 he was admitted a student of the Royal Academy. He soon turned his attention to designing for the wood-engravers, and served an apprenticeship of three years with J. W. Whymper. His earliest book-illustrations appeared in 1860 in *Once a Week*, a periodical to which he contributed largely, as also to the *Cornhill Magazine*, where his admirable designs to the works of Thackeray and those of his daughter appeared. These woodcuts are among the most spirited and artistic works of their class, and entitle Walker to rank with Millais at the very head of the draughtsmen of our time who have dealt with scenes of contemporary life. In the intervals of work as a book-illustrator he practised painting in water-colours, his subjects being frequently more considered and refined repetitions in colour of his black-and-white designs. Among the more notable of his productions in water-colour are Spring, a Fishmonger's Shop, the Ferry, and Philip in Church, which gained a medal in the Paris International Exhibition of 1867. He was elected an associate of the Society of Painters in Water Colours in 1864, and a full member in 1866; and in 1871 he became an associate of the Royal Academy. His first oil picture, the Lost Path, was exhibited in the Royal Academy in 1863, where it was followed in 1867 by the Bathers, one of the artist's finest works, in 1868 by the Vagrants, now in the National Gallery, in 1869 by the Old Gate, and in 1870 by the Plough, a powerful and impressive rendering of ruddy evening light, of which the landscape was studied in Somerset. In 1871 he exhibited his tragic life-sized figure of a Female Prisoner at the Bar, a subject which now exists only in a finished oil study, for the painter afterwards effaced the head, with which he was dissatisfied, and was prevented by death from again completing the picture. The last of his fully successful works was the Harbour of Refuge, shown in 1872, for the Right of Way, exhibited in 1875, bears evident signs of the artist's failing strength. In the end of 1873 he made a journey to Algiers for his health, but, returning in the bitter English spring, he was again prostrated; and on June 5, 1875, he died of consumption at St Fillan's, Perthshire.

The works of Frederick Walker are thoroughly original and individual, both in the technique of their colour and execution and in their view of nature and humanity. His colour, especially in his water-colours, is pure, powerful, and full of delicate gradations; he had an admirable sense of design, and the figures of his peasants at their daily toil show a grace and sweeping largeness of line which recalls the antique; while the sentiment of his subjects is unfailingly refined and poetic.

WALKER, SEARS COOK (1805-1853), astronomer, was born at Wilmington, Massachusetts, U.S., on March 28, 1805. He kept a school at Philadelphia till 1845, when he was appointed assistant at the Washington observatory. Shortly afterwards he took charge of the astronomical department of the United States Coast Survey, where he was among the first to make use of the electric telegraph for the purpose of determining the difference of longitude between two stations, and he introduced the method of registering transit observations electrically by means of a chronograph. He also investigated the orbit of the newly discovered planet Neptune. He died at Cincinnati on January 30, 1853.

WALLACE, SIR WILLIAM, the most popular national hero of Scotland, is believed to have been the second son of Sir Malcolm Wallace of Elderslie and Auchinbothie, in Renfrewshire. The date of his birth is not certainly ascertained, but is usually given as 1270. The only authority for the events of his early life is the metrical history of Blind Harry. That authority cannot be implicitly relied on, though we need not conclude that the minstrel invented the stories he relates. He lived about two centuries later than Wallace, during which a considerable body of legend had probably gathered round the name, and these popular "gestis" he incorporates in his narrative. At the same time he professes to follow as his "autour" an account that had been written in Latin by John Blair, the personal friend and chaplain of Wallace himself. As Blair's account has perished, we cannot tell how far the minstrel has faithfully followed his authority, but some comparatively recent discoveries have confirmed the truth of portions of the narrative which had previously been doubted. At best, however, his authority must be regarded with suspicion, except when it is confirmed by other and more trustworthy evidence.

Only for a period of less than two years in his life—from the beginning of the insurrection in 1297 to the battle of Falkirk—does Wallace come before us in the clearest historical light. With the exception of one or two glimpses of him that we obtain from authentic historical documents, the recorded events of his later as of his earlier life rest on no more certain authority than that of Blind Harry.

In his boyhood, according to the usual accounts, he resided for some time at Dunipace, in Stirlingshire, with an uncle, who is styled "parson" of the place. By this uncle he was partially educated, and from him he imbibed an enthusiastic love of liberty. His education was continued at Dundee, where he made the acquaintance of John Blair. On account of an incident that happened at Dundee—his slaughter of a young Englishman named Selby, for an insult offered to him—he is said to have been outlawed, and so driven into rebellion against the English. Betaking himself to the wilds of the country, he gradually gathered round him a body of desperate men whom he led in various attacks upon the English. In consequence of the success of these early enterprises his following largely increased, several of the more patriotic nobles—including the steward of Scotland, Sir Andrew Moray, Sir John de Graham, Douglas the Hardy, Wishart, bishop of Glasgow, and others—having joined him. His insurrection now became more open and pronounced, and his enterprises of greater importance. An attack was made upon the English justiciar, Ormsby, who was holding his court at Scone. The justiciar himself escaped, but many of his followers were captured or slain. The burning of the Barns of Ayr, the quarters of English soldiers, in revenge for the treacherous slaughter of his uncle, Sir Ronald Crawford, and other Scottish noblemen, followed. The success of these exploits induced the English king to take measures for staying the insurrection. A large army, under the command of Sir Henry Percy and Sir Robert Clifford, was sent against the insurgents, and came up with them at Irvine. Dissensions broke out among the Scottish leaders, and all Wallace's titled friends left him and made submission to Edward, except the ever faithful Sir Andrew Moray. The treaty of Irvine, by which these Scottish nobles agreed to acknowledge Edward as their sovereign lord, is printed in Rymer's *Fœdera*. It is dated 9th July 1297, and is the first public document in which the name of Sir William Wallace occurs. Wallace retired to the north, and although deserted by the barons was soon at the head of a large army. The vigour and success of his operations was such that in a short time he succeeded in recovering almost all the fortresses held by the English to the north of the Forth. He had begun the siege of Dundee when he received information that an English army, led by the earl of Surrey and Cressingham the treasurer, was on its march northward. Leaving the citizens of Dundee to continue the siege of the castle, he made a rapid march to Stirling. Encamping in the neighbourhood of the Abbey Craig—on which now stands the national monument to his memory—he watched the passage of the Forth. After an unsuccessful attempt to bring Wallace to terms, the English commander, on the morning of 11th September 1297, began to cross the bridge. When about one-half of his army had crossed, and while they were still in disorder, they were attacked with such fury by Wallace, that almost all—Cressingham among the number—were slain, or driven into the river and drowned. Those on the south side of the river were seized with panic and fled tumultuously, having first set fire to the bridge. The Scots, however, crossed by a ford, and continued the pursuit of the enemy as far as Berwick. Sir Andrew Moray fell in this battle. The results of it were important. The English were everywhere driven from Scotland. To increase the alarm of the English, as well as to relieve the famine which then prevailed, Wallace organized a great raid into the north of England, in the course of which he devastated the country to the gates of Newcastle. On his return he was elected guardian of the kingdom. In this office he set himself to reorganize the army and to regulate the affairs of the country. His measures were marked by much wisdom and vigour, and for a short time succeeded in securing order, even in the face of the jealousy and opposition of the nobles. Edward was in Flanders when the news of this successful revolt reached him. He hastened home, and at the head of a great army entered Scotland in July 1298. Wallace was obliged to adopt the only plan of campaign which could give any hope of success. He slowly retired before the English monarch, driving off all supplies and wasting the country. The nobles as usual for the most part deserted his standard. Those that remained thwarted his councils by their jealousies. His plan, however, came very near being successful. Edward, compelled by famine, had already given orders for a retreat when he received information of Wallace's position and intentions. The army, then at Kirkliston, was immediately set in motion, and next morning (July 22, 1298) Wallace was brought to battle in the vicinity of Falkirk. After an obstinate fight the Scots were overpowered and defeated with great loss. Among the slain was Sir John de Graham, the bosom friend of Wallace, whose death, as Blind Harry tells, threw the hero into a frenzy of rage and grief. The account of his distress is one of the finest and most touching passages in the poem. With the remains of his army Wallace found refuge for the night in the Torwood —known to him from his boyish life at Dunipace. He then retreated to the north, burning the town and castle of Stirling on his way. He resigned the office of guardian, and betook himself again to a wandering life and a desultory and predatory warfare against the English. At this point his history again becomes obscure. He is known to have paid a visit to France, with the purpose of obtaining aid for his country from the French king. This visit is narrated with many untrustworthy details by Blind Harry; but the fact is established by other and indisputable evidence. When in the winter of 1303–4 Edward received the submission of the Scottish nobles, Wallace was expressly excepted from all terms. And after the capture of Stirling Castle and Sir William Oliphant, and the submission of Sir Simon Fraser, he was left alone, but resolute as ever in refusing allegiance to the English king. A price was set upon his head, and the English governors and captains in Scotland had orders to use every means for his capture. On the 5th August 1305 he was taken—as is generally alleged, through treachery—at Robroyston, near Glasgow, by Sir John Menteith, carried to the castle of Dumbarton, and thence conveyed in fetters and strongly guarded to London. He reached London on the 22d August, and next day was taken to Westminster Hall, where he was impeached as a traitor by Sir Peter Mallorie, the king's justice. To the accusation Wallace made the simple reply that he could not be a traitor to the king of England, for he never was his subject, and never swore fealty to him. He was found guilty and condemned to death. The sentence was executed the same day with circumstances of unusual cruelty.

The cause of national independence was not lost with the life of Wallace. Notwithstanding the cruelty and indignity amid which it terminated, that life was not a failure. It has been an inspiration to his countrymen ever since. The popular ideas regarding his stature, strength, bodily prowess, and undaunted courage are confirmed by the writers nearest his own time—Wyntoun and Fordun. And indeed no man could in that age have secured the personal ascendency which he did without the possession of these qualities. The little we know of his statesmanship during the short period he was in power gives proof of political wisdom. His patriotism was conspicuous and disinterested. He was well skilled in the modes of warfare that suited the country and the times. That he failed in freeing his country from the yoke of England was due chiefly to the jealousy with which he was regarded by the men of rank and power. But he had a nobler success in inspiring his countrymen with a spirit which made their ultimate conquest impossible. (A. F. H.)

WALLACE, William (1768–1843), mathematician, was born on September 23, 1768, at Dysart, in Fifeshire, where he received his school education. In 1784 his family removed to Edinburgh, where he himself was set to learn the trade of a bookbinder; but his taste for mathematics had already developed itself, and he made such use of his leisure hours that before the completion of his apprenticeship he had made considerable acquirements in geometry, algebra, and astronomy. He was further assisted in his studies by Professors Robison and Playfair, to whom his abilities had become known. After various changes of situation, dictated mainly by a desire to gain time for study, he became assistant teacher of mathematics in the academy of Perth in 1794, and this post he exchanged in 1803 for a mathematical mastership in the Royal Military College at Great Marlow (afterwards at Sandhurst). In 1819 he was chosen to succeed Playfair in the chair of mathematics at Edinburgh, and in 1838, when compelled by ill-health to retire, he received a Government pension for life. He died in Edinburgh, after a lingering illness, on April 28, 1843.

In his earlier years Wallace was an occasional contributor to Leybourne's *Mathematical Repository* and to the *Gentleman's*

Mathematical Companion. Between 1801 and 1810 he contributed the articles "Algebra," "Conic Sections," "Trigonometry," and several others in mathematical and physical science to the fourth edition of the *Encyclopædia Britannica*, and some of these were retained in subsequent editions from the fifth to the eighth inclusive. He was also the author of the principal mathematical articles in the *Edinburgh Encyclopædia*, edited by Brewster (1808–30). Subjoined is a list of his more important papers contributed to the *Transactions* of the Royal Society of Edinburgh:—"Geometrical Porisms, with Examples of their Applications to the Solution of Problems" (1796); "A new Method of expressing the Coefficients in the Development of the Formula which represents the Mutual Perturbation of two Planets" (1802); "New Series for the Quadrature of the Conic Sections, and the Computation of Logarithms" (1808); "Investigation of Formulæ for finding the Logarithms of Trigonometrical Quantities from one another" (1823); "Account of the Invention of the Pantograph, and a Description of the Eidograph," the latter being an instrument of his own invention (1831); "Analogous Properties of Elliptic and Hyperbolic Sectors" (1839); and "Solution of a Functional Equation, with its Application to the Parallelogram of Forces and the Curve of Equilibration." In 1836 he contributed "Two Elementary Solutions of Kepler's Problem by the Angular Calculus" to the Royal Astronomical Society; and for the Cambridge Philosophical Society he wrote a paper on "Geometrical Theorems and Formulæ, particularly applicable to some Geodetical Problems."

WALLASEY, a town of Cheshire, England, on rising ground near a branch of the Mersey called Wallasey Pool, which bounds it on the S.E., while to the N.W. is the Irish Sea. It is about 2 miles north-west of Birkenhead, of which part of it is practically a suburb, and Wallasey Pool is now occupied by the Great Float, forming an immense dock of about 150 acres. The church of St Hilary, rebuilt in the 18th century, with the exception of the tower bearing date 1536, having been gutted by fire in 1857, the whole, except the tower, was rebuilt in the Early English style. The free grammar school, built and endowed by Major Henry Meols in 1656–57, was re-established under a scheme of the charity commissioners, and reopened in 1876. On the shore of the Irish Sea is Leasowe Castle, once known as Mock-Beggar Hall, and supposed to have been erected by the earls of Derby in the reign of Elizabeth, in order to witness the races. On the sides of Wallasey Pool are remains of a submarine forest bed, in which various animal skeletons have been found. The population of the urban sanitary district (which includes Liscard and Poulton, with Seacomb, the total area being 3408 acres) in 1871 was 14,944, and in 1881 it was 21,192.

At the Conquest Wallasey formed part of the possessions of Robert de Rhuddlan, and on his decease became part of the fee of Halton. In the reign of Elizabeth it had a small port, to which there belonged three barques and fourteen men. In 1668 the manor was possessed by the earl of Derby, but various parts afterwards became alienated. For a considerable time the horse races held on what was then a common had considerable reputation, but they were discontinued in 1760. At these races the duke of Monmouth, son of Charles II., once rode his own horse and won the plate.

WALLA WALLA, a city and the county seat of Walla Walla county, Washington Territory, United States, is situated in a valley on Mill Creek, a tributary of the Walla Walla, in a fertile agricultural region, devoted mainly to the growth of wheat, fruit, and vegetables. The population, which in 1880 was 3588, was estimated at 5000 in 1888.

WALLENSTEIN (properly WALDSTEIN), ADALBERT EUSEBIUS VON (1583–1634), duke of Friedland, Sagan, and Mecklenburg, was born on the hereditary estate of his family, Hermanic, in Bohemia, on 15th September 1583. His parents were Protestants, and in early youth he attended the school of the Brothers of the Common Life at Koschumberg. After the death of his parents he was sent by his uncle, Slawata, to the Jesuit college at Olmütz, where he joined the Roman Catholic Church. In 1599 he went to the university of Altdorf, which he had to leave in consequence of some boyish follies. Afterwards he studied at Bologna and Padua, and, according to the custom of the young nobles of the time, visited many places in southern and western Europe. While in Padua, he gave much attention to astrology, and during the rest of his life he seems never to have wavered in the conviction that he might trust to the stars for indications as to his destiny.

For some time Wallenstein served in the army of the emperor Rudolph II. in Hungary. In 1606 he returned to Bohemia, and soon afterwards he married a rich widow, Lucretia Nikossie von Landeck, whose lands in Moravia he inherited after her death in 1614. Supporting the archduke Ferdinand in his war with Venice, he became favourably known at court, and his influence was increased by his marriage with Isabella Katharina, daughter of Count Harrach, a confidential adviser of the emperor Matthias.

In the disturbances which broke out in Bohemia in 1618 —disturbances which proved to be the beginning of the Thirty Years' War—advances were made to Wallenstein by the revolutionary party; but he preferred to associate himself with the imperial cause, for which he repeatedly fought with marked success. In 1620 he was made quartermaster-general of the army of the League, commanded by Tilly. Wallenstein was not present at the battle of the Weissenberg (1620), but soon afterwards he did brilliant service as second in command of the army which opposed Bethlen Gabor in Moravia.

The battle of the Weissenberg placed Bohemia absolutely at the mercy of the emperor Ferdinand; and Wallenstein, who was a man of insatiable ambition, knew how to turn the prevailing confusion to his own advantage. Through no very honourable means he secured the inheritance of the great estates belonging to his mother's family, and the emperor sold to him on easy terms vast tracts of confiscated lands. His possessions he was allowed to form into a territory called Friedland, and he was raised in 1622 to the rank of an imperial count and palsgrave, in 1623 to that of a prince. In 1625 he was made duke of Friedland. In the government of his principality he displayed much vigour and foresight. He not only placed the administration of justice on a firm basis, but by many wise measures developed agriculture and mining and manufacturing industries.

The early successes of the emperor Ferdinand in the Thirty Years' War were due chiefly to the army of the League, which he could only indirectly control. When he was threatened with a coalition of the Protestant powers, with Christian IV. of Denmark as his most active enemy, he was anxious to have an army of his own, which should be more devoted than that of the League to the interests of his dynasty. He had not, however, the means of securing the fulfilment of his wish. In these circumstances Wallenstein saw that he might have an opportunity of playing a great part in the events of the age; and accordingly, early in 1626, he offered to raise an army for the imperial service. After some negotiations the offer was accepted, the understanding being that the troops were to be maintained at the cost of the countries they might occupy. Wallenstein had always been a popular commander, and great numbers of recruits flocked to his standard, so that he soon found himself at the head of an army of 30,000 men. With this force he marched northwards for the purpose of co-operating with Tilly against Christian IV. and Mansfeld. No engagement was fought in 1625; but on April 25, 1626, Wallenstein defeated Mansfeld at the bridge of Dessau, and later in the year Christian IV. was defeated by Tilly at Lutter. Wallenstein pursued Mansfeld into Hungary, where the Protestant general effected a junction with Bethlen Gabor. Before the end of the year Mansfeld died, and Bethlen Gabor came to terms with the emperor.

Having established peace in Hungary, Wallenstein proceeded, in 1627, to clear Silesia of some remnants of Mansfeld's army; and at this time he bought from the emperor the duchy of Sagan, his outlay in the conduct of the war being taken into account in the conclusion of the bargain. He then joined Tilly in the struggle with Christian IV., and afterwards took possession of the duchy of Mecklenburg, which was granted to him in reward for his services, the hereditary dukes being displaced on the ground that they had helped the Danish king. He failed to capture Stralsund, which he besieged for several months in 1628. This was his first important reverse, and it caused him bitter disappointment, for he had hoped that by obtaining free access to the Baltic he might be able to make the emperor as supreme at sea as he seemed to be on land. It was a part of Wallenstein's scheme that he should obtain possession of the Hanseatic towns, and through them destroy the naval power of the Scandinavian kingdom, the Netherlands, and England. This plan completely broke down when he was compelled to withdraw his troops from the brave city which he had sworn to take even if it were bound with chains to heaven. Notwithstanding this check, the imperial cause prospered; and early in 1629 Christian IV. was obliged to accept terms of peace. About the same time Ferdinand issued the famous edict of restitution, which excited deep resentment in every Protestant state in the realm.

Meanwhile Wallenstein had made for himself a host of enemies among the princes of the empire. They regarded him as an upstart, and complained of the incessant exactions of his army. Moreover, it was by no means clear what he intended to do with the great force he had gathered around him. He was sometimes heard to speak ominously of the arrogance of the princes, and it appeared probable that he might try to bring them, Catholics and Protestants alike, into rigid subjection to the crown. Again and again, therefore, the emperor was advised to dismiss him from his command. Ferdinand was very unwilling to part with one who had served him so well; but the demand was pressed so urgently by the electors in 1630 that he had no alternative, and in September of that year envoys were sent to Wallenstein to announce his removal. Had the emperor declined to take this course, the princes would probably have combined against him; and the result would have been a civil war even more serious than that which had already brought so many disasters upon the country. This was perfectly understood by Wallenstein, who therefore accepted the emperor's decision calmly, and retired to Gitschin, the capital of his duchy of Friedland.

Some months before the dismissal of Wallenstein, Gustavus Adolphus had landed in Germany, and it soon became obvious that he was by far the most formidable of the enemies with whom the emperor had yet had to contend. Tilly was defeated at Breitenfeld and in the battle of the Lech, where he received a mortal wound; and Gustavus advanced to Munich, while Bohemia was occupied by his allies the Saxons. After the battle of Breitenfeld the emperor entreated Wallenstein to come once more to his aid. Wallenstein at first declined; he had, indeed, been secretly negotiating with Gustavus Adolphus, in the hope that he might thus be able to maintain his hold over his great possessions. In the end, however, he accepted the offers made to him by Ferdinand, and in the spring of 1632 he took the field with an army of more than 40,000 men. This army was placed absolutely under his control, so that he assumed the position of an independent prince rather than of an ordinary subject.

His first aim was to drive the Saxons from Bohemia,—an object which he accomplished without serious difficulty. Then he advanced against Gustavus Adolphus, who attacked him near Nuremberg on the 3d of September, but was driven back. On the 16th of November 1632 a decisive battle was fought at Lützen, in Saxony. In this battle the imperialists were routed, but Gustavus Adolphus was killed.

To the dismay of Ferdinand, Wallenstein made no use of the opportunity provided for him by the death of the Swedish king, but withdrew to winter quarters in Bohemia. In the campaign of 1633 much astonishment was caused by his apparent unwillingness to attack the enemy. The truth was that he was preparing to desert the emperor. That he sincerely desired to secure for Germany the benefits of peace is probable enough, but it is certain that he was also resolved to make for himself a position of commanding importance. He entered into negotiations with Saxony, Brandenburg, Sweden, and France; and one of his conditions was that the possession of the kingdom of Bohemia should be guaranteed to him. He had vast and somewhat vague schemes for the reorganization of the entire constitutional system of the empire, and he himself was to have supreme authority in determining the political destinies of his country.

Irritated by the distrust excited by his proposals, and anxious to make his power felt, he at last assumed the offensive, and in October he defeated the Swedes at Steinau. Soon afterwards he entered Lusatia and took Görlitz and Bautzen, and despatched a troop of cavalry as far as Berlin. He then resumed the negotiations, and pressed for a full and final acceptance of his plans. In December he retired with his army to Bohemia, fixing his headquarters at Pilsen.

It had soon been suspected in Vienna that Wallenstein was playing a double part, and the emperor, encouraged by the Spaniards at his court, anxiously sought for means of getting rid of him. Wallenstein was well aware of the designs formed against him, but displayed little energy in his attempts to thwart them. This was due in part, no doubt, to ill health, in part to the fact that he trusted to the assurances of his astrologer, Seni, with whom he often conferred. He also felt confident that when the time came for his army to decide between him and the emperor the decision would be in his own favour.

His principal officers assembled around him at a banquet on the 12th January 1634, when he submitted to them a declaration to the effect that they would remain true to him. This declaration they signed. More than a month later a second paper was signed; but on this occasion the officers' expression of loyalty to their general was associated with an equally emphatic expression of loyalty to their emperor. By this time Wallenstein had learned that he had too easily allowed himself to be lulled into a sense of security, and that he needed to act warily. On the 24th of January the emperor had signed a secret patent removing him from his command and requiring the army to obey Count Gallas; and imperial agents had been labouring to undermine Wallenstein's influence. Another patent charging Wallenstein and two of his officers with high treason, and naming the generals who were to assume the supreme command of the army, was signed on the 18th February, and published in Prague.

When Wallenstein heard of the publication of this patent, he realized the full extent of his danger, and on the 23d February, accompanied by several of his most intimate friends, and guarded by about 1000 men, he went from Pilsen to Eger, hoping to obtain the protection of the Protestant general Bernard of Weimar. After the arrival of the party at Eger, Colonel Gordon, the commandant, and Colonels Butler and Leslie agreed to rid the emperor of his enemy. On the evening of the 25th February Wallenstein's supporters Illo, Kinsky, Terzky, and Neumann were received at a banquet by the three colonels, and murdered by several dragoons. Butler, accompanied by Captain Devereux and a number of soldiers, then hurried to the house where Wallenstein was staying, and broke into his room. He had just taken a bath, and was standing in his shirt ready to go to bed. He was instantly killed by a thrust of Devereux's partisan. The body was taken to the citadel, and laid beside those of his murdered comrades. Wallenstein was buried at Gitschin, but in 1732 the remains were removed to the castle chapel of Münchengrätz.

No direct orders for the murder of Wallenstein had been issued, but it was well understood that tidings of his death would be welcome at court. The murderers were handsomely rewarded for what they had done, and their deed was commended as a necessary act of justice.

Wallenstein was tall, thin, and pale, with reddish hair, and eyes of remarkable brilliancy. He was of a proud and imperious temper, and was seldom seen to laugh. He worked hard, and invariably acted on the motto that if speech is silvern silence is golden. In times of supreme difficulty he listened carefully to the advice of his counsellors, but the final decision was always his own, and he rarely revealed his thoughts until the moment for action arrived. Few generals have surpassed him in the power of quickly organizing great masses of men and of inspiring them with confidence and enthusiasm; and as a statesman he was distinguished for the boldness of his conceptions and the liberality of his sentiments. All his good qualities were, however, marred by a furious lust for power, in the gratification of which he allowed no scruples to stand in his way.

See Förster, *Albrecht von Wallenstein* (1834); Barthold, *Geschichte des grossen deutschen Kriegs* (1842-43); Aretin, *Wallenstein* (1846); Helbig, *Wallenstein und Arnim, 1632-34* (1850), and *Kaiser Ferdinand und der Herzog von Friedland, 1633-34* (1853); Hurter, *Zur Geschichte Wallensteins* (1855); Fiedler, *Zur Geschichte Wallensteins* (1860); L. von Ranke, *Geschichte Wallensteins* (3d ed., 1872); Gindely, *Geschichte des dreissigjährigen Kriegs* (1869). (J. SI.)

WALLER, EDMUND (1605-1687), enjoyed in the latter half of his long life a high reputation as a poet, which has been partly fixed by the compliments of Dryden and Pope. Waller is a singular and piquant figure in the history of the 17th century; his relations with Charles I., with the Long Parliament, with Cromwell, with Charles II., his position as a poet, as a courtier, as a privileged water-drinker among the bibulous Restoration wits, form a combination that has no parallel. The character might be paralleled, but the run of incidents is unique. He was born at Coleshill, in Hertfordshire, March 3, 1605, and came of distinguished ancestry, landed gentry, with estates in Kent and other counties, and prominent places in the public service from the reign of Henry V. downwards. He inherited a position of difficulty in view of the civil strife that began when he reached manhood; his mother was herself an ardent Royalist, but was connected by blood with Hampden and by marriage with Cromwell. His father died when he was eleven years old. He entered parliament at sixteen, and sat also in the first and in the third parliaments of Charles I. He was thus, as Clarendon put it, nursed in parliament, and this early experience helped him to make a figure afterwards; but he took no active part at the time, the chief use that he made of his advantages as a courtier and a youth of fashion being to marry a wealthy city heiress. With this addition to the handsome fortune left him by his father, he retired to his estate at Beaconsfield and studied literature. This was about 1632.

When he first began to write verses is a doubtful and disputed point. Clarendon says that he began at an age when most men leave off, and if we put this at thirty there is no published or even probable evidence to the contrary; but, on the other hand, it is argued that he began at the age of eighteen, in 1623, this being the date of the subject of his first poem,—Prince Charles's escape from a storm at St Andero. This earliest date must be increased by at least two years, the whole point of the poem being Charles's marriage with his queen Henrietta, which took place in 1625. The exact date of his beginning acquires some interest from Johnson's dictum that he wrote as smoothly at eighteen as at eighty, "smoothness" being his established merit; and the difficulty of determining the date arises from his not having "gathered his sticks into a faggot" and published till 1645. The incidents that furnished him with themes for his peculiar artificial and decorative treatment occurred long before,—for example, the duke of Buckingham's death in 1628, the taking of Salle in 1632, the repair of St Paul's in 1633, the death of the earl of Carlisle in 1636, his courtship of Lady Dorothy Sidney—"Saccharissa"—between the death of his first wife in 1634 and Saccharissa's marriage to another in 1639. But that the poems, as we now have them, were written immediately after the incidents glorified in his verse is an uncertain assumption, considering his elaborating habits, the strongly Royalist tone of his verses on public events, and the express statement of Clarendon, who was likely to have known if copies had been circulated in the society of the court long before they appeared in print. If they were at least retouched by him between the ages of thirty and forty, the wonder of his uniformity of manner from first to last—which, after all, has been somewhat exaggerated—is considerably lessened.

In the struggle between king and parliament, Waller tried at first to mediate, holding the king's demands unconstitutional, but endeavouring through his advisers to induce him to modify them. He made such a mark as a speaker in the Short Parliament that at the opening of the Long Parliament he was chosen by the Commons to conduct the impeachment of Judge Crawley for his ship-money decision. Thereafter, as the struggle became fiercer, with a view apparently to prevent parliament from proceeding to extremities, he engaged in what was known as Waller's plot. The object of the plot seems to have been to restrain the extreme Parliamentarians by some public declaration of moderate opinion, but it was complicated with another plot, the object of which was to assist the king with armed force. All Waller's relations, except his mother, were anti-Royalist, and it is said that his complicity was discovered by domestic treachery. He behaved with the most abject meanness when arrested by order of Pym on May 31, 1643, saved himself by at once turning informer and making disclosures that were at least unreserved, and was let off eventually with a fine of £10,000 and banishment. It was from his exile in Paris, in 1645, that he directed his first publication of poems. He lived there in high repute as a wit and a munificent host till 1654, when Cromwell, at the intercession of his anti-Royalist relatives, allowed him to return to England, and try to mend his impaired estate. He celebrated the Protector's greatness in a lofty panegyric, and Cromwell is said to have relished his pleasant qualities as a companion. It deserves to be noted, as evidence of a real admiration, that he wrote also a lament "Upon the Death of the Lord Protector," when the sincerity of his panegyric was less open to question. The poem contains two famous lines of bathos—

> Under the tropic is our language spoke
> And part of Flanders hath received our yoke.

But otherwise it does not fall beneath the poet's steady level.

Upon the Restoration Waller hastened to express his joy, mingled with trembling, "Upon His Majesty's Happy Return," and found little difficulty in making his peace. He met the king's complaint that his congratulation was inferior to his panegyric on the Protector with the famous retort, "Poets, Sire, succeed better in fiction than in truth." He was soon on such terms with Charles that he applied for the provostship of Eton; the king agreed, but Clarendon refused, on the ground that he was a layman, and the refusal was sustained by the council. He thus failed in his only application for substantial evidence of the king's favour, but in every other respect the changed state of things made his old age happy and glorious. He entered parliament again, and became, Burnet says, "the delight of the House, and, though old, said the liveliest things of any of them." His witty sayings were circulated through the town, and, as Johnson suspects, good things were fathered on him,—a tribute to his reputation. Although a water-drinker, he was a boon companion with the roystering wits, Dorset saying that "no man in England should sit in his company without drinking, except Ned Waller." Further, surviving all his early contemporaries, he found himself in higher reputation than ever as a poet. His poems now went through several editions, each increased by new productions, though the bulk was never large. He wrote in his formed eulogistic fashion on topics of the day, on St James's Park, on Somerset House, the victory over the Dutch, the queen's birthday, the beauties, and other celebrities of the time. He fitted *The Maid's Tragedy* with a happier ending in rhymed couplets, assisted Dorset and Godolphin in the translation of the *Pompey* of Corneille, and wound up his career becomingly with *Divine Poems*, continuing to write to the last. He died in 1687, at the age of eighty-two, and at the height of his poetic reputation. Rymer of the *Fœdera*, the savage critic of Shakespeare, wrote the epitaph for his tomb at Beaconsfield, in which it is recorded that "inter poetas sui temporis facile princeps, lauream, quam meruit adolescens, octogenarius haud abdicavit." Fenton, Pope's coadjutor in the translation of the *Odyssey*, edited and commented on his poems after his death, justifying the pains bestowed by comparing him to Petrarch and Malherbe.

There can be no doubt that as a panegyrical poet, ready to overlay any subject, entirely irrespective of its intrinsic worth, with a cleverly woven and tastefully coloured garment of words and images, Waller deserved all the admiration he received, and would be hard to beat in our literature. Fenton showed true discernment in urging that his excellence lay in commendation, whether or not he was right in adding that any ill-natured person could be a satirist. And complimentary poetry was so much in fashion when poets were courted and munificently rewarded by politicians that Waller's fame from the Restoration till the time of Walpole, who dispensed with the aid of complimentary poets, is easy to understand. But Mr Gosse's recent contention that Waller must be regarded as the founder of the classical school, and that his influence changed the course of our literature for a century, must pass as a hurried exaggeration. He was so eminently successful that he influenced minor poets at the close of his life and for a generation afterwards, but his range of subjects as well as his art was extremely limited, and much larger and wider influences were at work. He is an example of one of the tendencies, but it is absurd to represent him as a commanding influence, except in a very humble field. He influenced panegyrical writing, and, inasmuch as this fell in with and influenced the tendency "to dress nature to advantage," "to raise sentiments above the vulgar pitch" with the borrowed riches of genuinely impassioned poetry, it might be argued that Waller's influence extended beyond his own narrow circle of aims. But his effect on Dryden or on Pope was infinitesimal. Even on the form of the favourite "classical" couplet Waller's single example cannot be held to have told in any considerable degree. It was already an established form for complimentary verse when he began to write. "Waller was smooth," it is true, but Pope at once qualifies the compliment with a reference to his want of variety. And Pope is also strictly correct in confining Waller's metrical improvements to his post-Restoration verse. When we place Waller's later couplets side by side with his earlier, say *The Triple Combat* or *The Divine Poems*, with *His Majesty's Escape*, or *The Countess of Carlisle in Mourning*, or *The Death of Lady Rich*, we become aware of a marked change in his metrical scheme, notwithstanding the current opinion to the contrary. It is only in his later couplets that he aims, under French influence, as Pope justly implies, at making each distich complete in itself, varying this only with a stave of four, generally with a break in the third line. His earlier couplets are less monotonous, and were obviously modelled on the *Hero and Leander* of Marlowe and Chapman. To that noble poem, indeed, which was not known in the days when Waller's rhythm was so admired, he owed a large part of his panegyrical stock-in-trade, as anybody familiar with it can trace, not merely in his "classical" allusions, but also in his diction and his earlier metre. As regards smoothness and balance, there are no couplets in the edition of 1645 that could not be paralleled from the verses of his contemporaries, George Sandys and Cowley. (W. M.)

WALLIS, JOHN (1616–1703), an eminent English mathematician, logician, and grammarian, was born on the 23d November 1616 at Ashford, in Kent, of which parish his father was then incumbent. Having been previously instructed in Latin, Greek, and Hebrew, he was in 1632 sent to Emmanuel College, Cambridge, and afterwards was chosen fellow of Queen's College. Having been admitted to holy orders, he left the university in 1641 to act as chaplain to Sir William Darley, and in the following year accepted a similar appointment from the widow of Sir Horatio Vere. It was about this period that he displayed surprising talents in deciphering the intercepted letters and papers of the Royalists. His adherence to the Parliamentary party was in 1643 rewarded by the living of St Gabriel, Fenchurch Street, London. In 1644 he was appointed one of the scribes or secretaries of the Assembly of Divines at Westminster. During the same year he married Susanna Glyde, and thus vacated his fellowship; but the death of his mother had left him in possession of a handsome fortune. In 1645 he attended those scientific meetings which led to the establishment of the Royal Society. When the Independents obtained the superiority, Wallis adhered to the Solemn League and Covenant. The living of St Gabriel he exchanged for that of St Martin, Ironmonger Lane; and, as rector of that parish, he in 1648 subscribed the Remonstrance against putting Charles I. to death. Notwithstanding this act of opposition, he was in June 1649 appointed Savilian professor of geometry at Oxford. In 1654 he there took the degree of D.D., and four years later succeeded Dr Langbaine as keeper of the archives. After the Restoration he was named one of the king's chaplains in ordinary. While complying with the terms of the Act of Uniformity, Wallis seems always to have retained moderate and rational notions of ecclesiastical polity. He died at Oxford on the 28th of October 1703, in the eighty-seventh year of his age.

The works of Wallis are numerous, and relate to a multiplicity of subjects. His *Institutio Logicæ*, published in 1687, was very popular, and in his *Grammatica Linguæ Anglicanæ* we find indications of an acute and philosophic intellect. The mathematical works are published some of them in a small 4to volume, Oxford, 1657, and a complete collection in three thick folio volumes, Oxford, 1695–93–99. The third volume includes, however, some theological treatises, and the first part of it is occupied with editions of treatises on harmonics and other works of Greek geometers, some of them first editions from the MSS., and in general with Latin versions and notes (Ptolemy, Porphyrius, Briennius, Archimedes, Eutocius, Aristarchus, and Pappus). The second and third volumes include also two collections of letters to and from Brouncker, Frenicle, Leibnitz, Newton, Oldenburg, Schooten, and others; and there is a tract on trigonometry by Caswell. Excluding all these, the mathematical works contained in the first and second volumes occupy about 1800 pages. The titles in the order adopted, but with date of publication, are as follows:—"Oratio Inauguralis," on his appointment (1649) as Savilian professor, 1657; "Mathesis Universalis, seu Opus Arithmeticum Philologice et Mathematice Traditum, Arithmeticam Numerosam et Speciosam Aliaque Continens," 1657; "Adversus Meibomium, de Proportionibus Dialogus," 1657; "De Sectionibus Conicis Nova Methodo Expositis," 1655; "Arithmetica Infinitorum, sive Nova Methodus Inquirendi in Curvilineorum Quadraturam Aliaque Difficiliora Matheseos Problemata," 1655; "Eclipsis Solaris Observatio Oxonii Habita 2d Aug. 1654," 1655; "Tractatus Duo, prior de Cycloide, posterior de Cissoide et de Curvarum tum Linearum Εὐθύνσει tum Superficierum Πλατυσμῷ," 1659; "Mechanica, sive de Motu Tractatus Geometricus," three parts, 1669–70–71; "De Algebra Tractatus Historicus et Practicus, ejusdem originem et progressus varios ostendens," English, 1685; "De Combinationibus Alternationibus et Partibus Aliquotis Tractatus," English, 1685; "De Sectionibus Angularibus Tractatus," English, 1685; "De Angulo Contactus et Semicirculi Tractatus," 1656; "Ejusdem Tractatus Defensio," 1685; "De Postulato Quinto, et Quinta Definitione, Lib. VI. Euclidis, Disceptatio Geometrica," ?1663; "Cuno-Cuneus, seu Corpus partim Conum partim Cuneum Representans Geometrice Consideratum," English, 1685; "De Gravitate et Gravitatione Disquisitio Geometrica," 1662 (English, 1674); "De Æstu Maris Hypothesis Nova," 1666–69.

The *Arithmetica Infinitorum* relates chiefly to the quadrature of curves by the so-called method of indivisibles established by Cavalleri, 1629, and cultivated in the interval by him, Fermat, Descartes, and Roberval. The method is substantially that of the integral calculus; thus, *e.g.*, for the curve $y=x^2$ to find the area from $x=0$ to $x=1$, the base is divided into n equal parts, and the area is obtained as $=\frac{1}{n^3}(1^2+2^2 \ldots + n^2)$, $=\frac{1}{6n^3}n(n+1)(2n+1)$, which, taking n indefinitely large, is $=\frac{1}{3}$. The case of the general parabola $y=x^m$ (m a positive integer or fraction), where the area is $\frac{1}{m+1}$, had been previously solved. Wallis made the important remark that the reciprocal of such a power of x could be regarded as a power with a negative exponent $\left(\frac{1}{x^m}=x^{-m}\right)$, and he was thus enabled to extend the theorem to certain hyperbolic curves, but the case m a negative value larger than 1 presented a difficulty which he did not succeed in overcoming. It should be noticed that Wallis, although not using the notation x^m in the case of a positive or negative fractional value, nor indeed in the case of a negative integer value of m, deals continually with such powers, and speaks of the positive or negative integer or fractional value of m as the index of the power. The area of a curve, $y=$ sum of a finite number of terms Ax^m, was at once obtained from that for the case of a single term; and Wallis, after thus establishing the several results which would now be written $\int_0^1 (x-x^2)^0 dx=1$, $\int_0^1 (x-x^2)^1 dx=\frac{1}{6}$, $\int_0^1 (x-x^2)^2 dx=\frac{1}{30}$, $\int_0^1 (x-x^2)^3 dx=\frac{1}{140}$, &c., proposed to himself to interpolate from these the value of $\int_0^1 (x-x^2)^{\frac{1}{2}} dx$, which is the expression for the area ($=\frac{1}{8}\pi$) of a semicircle, diameter $=1$; making a slight transformation, the actual problem was to find the value of $\square\left(=\frac{4}{\pi}\right)$, the term halfway between 1 and 2, in the series of terms 1, 2, 6, 20, 70, . . . ; and he thus obtained the remarkable expression $\pi=\frac{2.4.4.6.6.8.8\ldots}{3.3.5.5.7.7.9\ldots}$, together with a succession of superior and inferior limits for the number π.

In the same work Wallis obtained the expression which would now be written $ds=dx\sqrt{1+\left(\frac{dy}{dx}\right)^2}$ for the length of the element of a curve, thus reducing the problem of rectification to that of quadrature. An application of this formula to an algebraical curve was first made a few years later by W. Neil; the investigation is reproduced in the "Tractatus de Cissoide, &c." (1659, as above), and Wallis adds the remark that the curve thus rectified is in fact the semicubical parabola.

The *Mathesis Universalis* is a more elementary work intended for learners. It contains copious dissertations on fundamental points of algebra, arithmetic, and geometry, and critical remarks.

The *De Algebra Tractatus* contains (chapters 66–69) the idea of the interpretation of imaginary quantities in geometry. This is given somewhat as follows: the distance represented by the square root of a negative quantity cannot be measured in the line backwards or forwards, but can be measured in the same plane above the line, or (as appears elsewhere) at right angles to the line either in the plane, or in the plane at right angles thereto. Considered as a history of algebra, this work is strongly objected to by Montucla on the ground of its unfairness as against the early Italian algebraists and also Vieta and Descartes, and in favour of Harriot; but De Morgan, while admitting this, attributes to it considerable merit.

The two treatises on the cycloid and on the cissoid, &c., and the *Mechanica* contain many results which were then new and valuable. The latter work contains elaborate investigations in regard to the centre of gravity, and it is remarkable also for the employment of the principle of virtual velocities. The cuno-cuneus is a highly interesting surface; it is a ruled quartic surface, the equation of which may be written $c^2y^2=(c-z)^2(a^2-x^2)$.

Among the letters in volume iii., we have one to the editor of the Leipsic *Acts*, giving the decipherment of two letters in secret characters. The ciphers are different, but on the same principle: the characters in each are either single digits or combinations of two or three digits, standing some of them for letters, others for syllables or words,—the number of distinct characters which had to be deciphered being thus very considerable.

For the prolonged conflict between Hobbes and Wallis, see HOBBES, vol. xii. pp. 36–38. (A. CA.)

WALLON, or WALLOON, the collective name of the inhabitants of the south-eastern division of Belgium, who are distinguished from the rest of the population chiefly by their Romance speech and darker complexion. The Wallon domain comprises the four provinces of Hainault, Namur, Liége, and Luxemburg, besides about one-third of Brabant. It forms a nearly regular right-angled triangle, with apex at Maestricht within the Dutch frontier, and base stretching along the French frontier in a south-easterly direction, from the neighbourhood of Lille to Longwy at the south-west corner of German Luxemburg. It coincides almost exactly with the section of the Meuse basin comprised within Belgian territory, and has a total area of 6000 square miles, or about one-half of the kingdom, with a population (1886) of 2,780,000, or considerably less than half of the entire Belgian population. But from the following figures it is evident that the Romance is steadily gaining on the Flemish (Teutonic) section and will soon be in a majority. In 1830 the Wallon population numbered 1,360,000 as against 1,860,000 Flemish; in 1866 the corresponding figures were 2,040,000 and 2,406,000; and in 1886 they were 2,780,000 and 3,060,000.

This north-eastern extremity of ancient Gaul, originally inhabited by the Aduatici, Eburones, Tungri, and other Belgic nations, was reduced by Cæsar (51 B.C.), and early brought within the sphere of Roman culture. Hence the Latin language was already too firmly established to be supplanted by the Teutonic when the country was occupied in the 5th century by the Franks previous to their conquest of the more central provinces. But about the same time Roman institutions and speech were entirely supplanted in the more open low-lying districts of western Belgium by the same Franks penetrating from the east, and by the roving Saxon and Frisian tribes arriving by sea on the *Litus Saxonicum*. Since that time the two elements have remained, without much further change, in close proximity, or separated only by intervening strips of "marches" or border-lands formed by the uncleared forest formerly known as the *Silva Carbonaria*.

The Wallons, allowing for inevitable intermingling, especially towards the German frontier, are thus Romanized Gauls, lineal representatives of the ancient Belgæ, in a much truer sense than their Flemish neighbours, although accepting from them this name of "Wallon," that is, *Welsh* or *Foreign*, just as the Saxon intruders in Britain imposed the same designation on its primitive inhabitants. Their Gallic descent is shown specially in their much darker complexion, as clearly established by the anthropological statistics collected by Dr Beddoe.[1] In other respects the Wallons contrast favourably with the Teutonic-speaking populations of Belgium. They are physically a stronger race, more bony, angular, and taller, and also more long-lived and exempt from disease, as shown by the much lower death-rate in the province of Namur (18 per 1000) than in West Flanders (25 per 1000). The cause of this superiority has been attributed by some writers to a greater inherent vitality of the Wallons, but by others with more probability to their greater general comfort, and particularly to the more salubrious climate of their elevated and more hilly territory. In mediæval times the Flemings were certainly far superior in wealth, culture, and public spirit. But the great centres of industry have since been shifted from Bruges and Ghent (Flanders) to Liége and Namur, and the Wallons now take the lead in all these respects,—in fact, in everything except music, painting, and the fine arts generally.

The Wallon language is a very marked dialect of the Langue d'Oïl (Northern French), betraying strong affinities to the neighbouring idioms of Picardy and Lorraine, but still distinct from both. Being little cultivated, and possessing no literary standard, it has developed several varieties, the chief of which are—(1) the *Liégeois*, current throughout the districts bordering on Rhenish Prussia, and largely affected by German influences; (2) the *Namurois* of the central districts and the Ardennes, with several local patois; (3) the *Hennuyer* of Hainault and the western districts, so named from the town of Hennuyères, where it is spoken with the greatest purity. But since French has been accepted as the written standard and the official language of the whole kingdom Wallon is gradually receding from the large towns and assuming more and more the character of a purely rural patois. It possesses no literary remains of any consequence, and its earliest extant monument appears to be the "Declaration des Provost, Juret, Eskievin de Valenchienes" of the year 1256.

[1] In Namur, a central point of the Wallon domain, the proportion of dark eyes is 47 and of dark hair 57·5 per cent. as compared with 24 and 20 respectively in Mechlin, a corresponding central point in the Flemish domain.

WALLSEND, a town of Northumberland, England, on the north bank of the Tyne and on the Newcastle and Tynemouth Railway, 4 miles east-north-east of Newcastle. The church of St Peter, erected in 1809 at a cost of £5000, has a tower surmounted by a spire. There are still some remains of the old church of the 11th century in the Transition Norman style. The church of St Luke was erected in 1886 at a cost of £4000. At an early period Wallsend was famous for its coals, but the name has now a general application to coal that does not go through a sieve with meshes $\frac{5}{8}$ths of an inch in size. The colliery, which was opened in 1807, has frequently been the scene of dreadful accidents. There are also ship and boat building yards, engineering works, lead and copper smelting works, cement works, and brick and tile works. The ecclesiastical commissioners are lords of the manor. The town is governed by a local board of twelve members. The population of the urban sanitary district (area 1202 acres) in 1871 was 4169, and in 1881 it was 6351.

Wallsend derives its modern name from its position at the extremity of HADRIAN'S WALL (*q.v.*); originally it was the Roman station *Segedunum*. It had a quay, of which remains have been discovered, and possessed a magazine of corn and other provisions for the supply of the stations in the interior.

WALNUT (*Juglans*), a genus of seven or eight species, natives of the temperate regions of the northern hemisphere, some even extending into Mexico and the West Indies. They are all trees, usually of large size, with alternate, stalked, unequally pinnate leaves, and abounding in an aromatic resinous juice. The scars left by the fallen leaves are unusually large and prominent. The buds are not unlike those of the ash; and it frequently happens that in the axils of the leaves, instead of one, several buds may be formed. The utility of this is seen in seasons when the shoot produced from the first bud is killed by frost; then one of the supplementary buds starts into growth, and thus replaces the injured shoot. The flowers are unisexual and monœcious, the numerous males borne in thick catkins proceeding from the side of last year's shoot. The female flowers are solitary or few in number, and borne on short terminal spikes of the present season's growth. In the male flower the receptacle is "concrescent" or inseparate from the bract in whose axil it originates. The receptacle is, in consequence, extended more or less horizontally, so that the flowers appear to be placed on the upper surface of horizontally-spreading stalks. The perianth consists of five or six oblong greenish lobes, within which is found a tuft, consisting of a large number of stamens, each of which has a very short filament and an oblong two-lobed anther bursting longitudinally, and surmounted by an oblong lobe, which is the projecting end of the connective. There is usually no trace of ovary in the male flowers, though by exception one may occasionally be formed.

The female flower consists of a cup-like receptacle, inseparate from the ovary, and bearing at its upper part a bract and two bracteoles, uplifted with the receptacle. From the margin of this latter organ springs a perianth of four short lobes. The one-celled ovary is immersed within the receptacular tube, and is surmounted by a short style with two short ribbon-like stigmatic branches. The solitary ovule springs erect from the base of the ovarian cavity. The fruit is a kind of drupe, the fleshy husk of which is the dilated receptacular tube, while the two-valved stone represents the two carpels. The solitary seed has no perisperm or albumen, but has two large and curiously crumpled cotyledons concealing the plumule, the leaves of which, even at this early stage, show traces of pinnæ.

The species best known is *J. regia*, the Common Walnut, a native of the mountains of Greece, of Armenia, of Afghanistan and the north-west Himalayas, and also found in Japan. Traces of the former existence of this or of a very closely-allied species are found in the Post-Tertiary deposits of Provence and elsewhere, proving the former much wider extension of the species. At the present day the tree is largely cultivated in most temperate countries for the sake of its timber or for its edible nuts. The timber is specially valued for cabinet work and for gun-stocks, the beauty of its markings rendering it desirable for the first-named purpose, while its strength and elasticity fit it for the second. The leaves and husk of the fruit are resinous and astringent, and are sometimes used medicinally as well as for dyeing purposes. It is stated that sugar is prepared from the sap in a similar manner to that obtained from the maple *Acer saccharinum* in Canada. The young fruits are used for pickling. When ripe the seeds are much esteemed as a delicacy, while in France much oil of fine quality is extracted from them by pressure. There are several varieties in cultivation, varying in the degree of hardihood, time of ripening, thickness of shell, size, and other particulars. In the climate of Great Britain a late variety is preferable, as securing the young shoots against injury from frost, to which otherwise they are very subject. The kernel of the large-fruited variety is of very indifferent quality, but its large shells are made use of by the French as trinket-cases.

Among the American species *J. nigra*, the Black Walnut, is especially noteworthy as a very handsome tree, whose timber is of great value for furniture purposes, but which is now becoming scarce. In Britain it forms a magnificent tree. The White Walnut, *J. cinerea*, is a smaller tree; its leaves are used medicinally.

Closely allied to the walnuts and sometimes confounded with them are the hickories (see HICKORY). See also vol. xii. p. 278.

WALPOLE, HORACE (1717–1797), who was born on 24th September 1717, was accepted and recognized throughout his life as the youngest of the five children of Sir Robert Walpole by Catherine Shorter, but by some of the scandal-mongers of a later age, Carr, Lord Hervey, the half-brother of the peer who wrote the *Memoirs of the Court of George the Second*, has been called his father. This parentage has been assigned to him partly through the circumstance that the first wife of Sir Robert Walpole lived for some time estranged from her husband and on terms of friendship with Carr, Lord Hervey, not the least clever or unprincipled member of a family notorious for ability and for laxity of morals, and partly through the antagonism of the qualities shown by Horace Walpole to those of the prime minister, and through their affinity with the talents of the Herveys. If this rumour be correct, no such suspicion ever entered into the mind of Horace Walpole. To his mother he erected a monument, with an inscription couched in terms of sincere affection, in the chapel of Henry VII. in Westminster Abbey, and from the beginning to the end of his life his sarcasms never spared the Newcastles and the Hardwickes, who had shown, as he thought, lukewarmness in support of his father's ministry. About 1728 he was sent to Eton, and in 1735 matriculated at King's College, Cambridge. Two years (1739–41) were spent in the recognized grand tour of France and Italy, in company with Gray the poet, whose acquaintance had been made amid the classic groves of Eton and Cambridge. They stopped a few weeks in Paris, and lingered for three months under the shadow of the magnificent portals of the cathedral of Rheims, on the pretence of learning the French language. Henry Seymour Conway, whose mother was a sister of Lady Walpole, shared their society in the French city, and retained Horace Walpole's warm friendship during life. The other two members of this little circle next proceeded to Florence, where Walpole rested for more than a year in the villa of Horace Mann, the British envoy-extraordinary for forty-six years to the court of Tuscany. Mann's family had long been on terms of the closest intimacy with his guests, as Robert Mann was concerned in the contract for which Sir Robert Walpole was expelled from the House of Commons in 1712, and the envoy continued the correspondent of Walpole until 1786, for as they never met again their friendship remained unbroken. At Reggio Walpole and Gray parted in resentment. The latter was shy in manners and absorbed in literature, while his more opulent companion lived in society, and only dabbled in antiquities for pleasure's sake. Walpole in after years took the blame of these differences on himself, and it is generally believed that the quarrel arose from his laying too much stress on his superiority in position. In 1744 the two friends were nominally reconciled, but the breach was not cemented.

During Walpole's absence he was returned to parliament in 1741 for the Cornish borough of Callington, over which his elder brother, through his marriage with the heiress of the Rolles, exercised supreme influence. He represented three constituencies in succession, Callington 1741–54, the family borough of Castle Rising from 1754 to 1757, and the more important constituency of King's Lynn, for which his father had long sat in parliament, from the latter date until 1768. In that year he retired, probably because his success in political life had not equalled his expectations, but he continued until the end of his days to follow and to chronicle the acts and the speeches of both Houses of Parliament. Through his father's influence he had obtained three lucrative sinecures producing at least £5000 a year, and for many years (1745–84) he enjoyed a share, estimated at about £1500 a year, of a second family perquisite, the collectorship of customs. The possession of these ample endowments and of a leasehold house in Arlington Street, which was left to him by his father, enabled him, a bachelor all his days, to gratify every expensive luxury and every costly taste. He purchased in 1747 the charmingly situated villa of Strawberry Hill, near Twickenham, on the banks of the Thames, and six years later began a series of alterations in the Gothic style, not completed for nearly a quarter of a century later, under which the original cottage became transformed into a building without parallel in Europe. Some years after this purchase he established a printing-press there for the gratification of his literary tastes, and many of the first editions of his own works were struck off within its walls. At this press were produced in 1753 the clever, if eccentric, designs of Richard Bentley (the youngest child of the great doctor, and for some time a protegé of Horace Walpole) for the poems of Gray; and among the reprints of Strawberry Hill were the *Life of Lord Herbert of Cherbury*, *Memoirs of Grammont*, Hentzner's *Journey into England*, and Lord Whitworth's *Account of Russia.* The rooms of this whimsical edifice were crowded with curiosities of every description, and the house and its contents were shown, by tickets to admit four persons, between 12 and 3 from May to October, but only one party was admitted on each day, and the owner, although enamoured of notoriety, simulated discontent at this limited intrusion into his privacy. His nephew, the reckless third earl, died in 1791, and Horace succeeded to the peerage, but he never took his place in the House of Lords, and sometimes signed his name as "the uncle of the late earl of Orford." All his life long he was the victim of the gout, but he lived to extreme old age, and died unmarried, in Berkeley Square, London, March 2, 1797, when his body was buried privately at Houghton. The ancient estate of the family descended to the earl of Cholmondeley, whose ancestor had married Horace Walpole's younger sister. All Walpole's printed books and manuscripts were left to Robert Berry and his two daughters, Mary and Agnes; their friendship had been very dear to the declining days of Walpole, who, it has even been said, wished to marry Mary Berry. By his will each of the ladies obtained a pecuniary legacy of £4000, and for their lives the house and garden, formerly the abode of Kitty Clive, which adjoined Strawberry Hill. Strawberry Hill went to Mrs Anne Damer, daughter of his lifelong friend General Conway, for her life, but it was entailed on the countess dowager of Waldegrave and her heirs. Walpole died worth £91,000 in the three per cents, and gave the whole of it away, the chief legacy being £10,000 for his niece the duchess of Gloucester. The collections of Strawberry Hill, which he had spent nearly fifty years in amassing, were dispersed under the hammer of George Robins in 1842. They are described in a catalogue of that date, and in a series of articles in the *Gentleman's Magazine* for that year.

The pen was ever in Horace Walpole's hands, and his entire compositions would fill many volumes. His two works of imagination, the romance of the *Castle of Otranto* and the tragedy of the *Mysterious Mother*, are now all but forgotten. The former, which purported to be a story translated by William Marshal, gent., from the original Italian of Onuphrio Muralto, canon of the church of St Nicholas at Otranto, was often reprinted in England, and was translated into both French and Italian. By Sir Walter Scott it was lauded to the skies for its power in raising the passions of fear and pity; from Hazlitt it met with intense condemnation. The *Mysterious Mother*, a tragedy too horrible for representation on any stage, was never intended for performance in public, and only fifty copies of it were printed at Strawberry Hill. By Byron, who, like Horace Walpole, affected extreme liberalism, and like him never forgot that he was born within the purple, this tragedy was pronounced "of the highest order." Several of Walpole's antiquarian works merit high praise. The volume of *Historic Doubts on the Life and Reign of King Richard the Third*, one of the earliest attempts to rehabilitate a character previously stamped with infamy, showed acuteness and research. These doubts provoked several answers, which are criticized in a supplement edited by Dr Hawtrey for the Philobiblon Society. A work of more lasting reputation, which has retained its vitality for more than a century, is entitled *Anecdotes of Painting in England, with some Account of the Principal Artists; collected by George Vertue, and now digested and published from his original manuscripts by Horace Walpole* (4 vols., 1762–71). Its value to art students and to admirers of biographical literature demanded its frequent reproduction, and it had the good fortune to be re-edited with additions by the Rev. James Dallaway in five volumes (1826–28), and then again was revised and edited by R. N. Wornum in 1849. A cognate volume, also based on the materials of Vertue, is entitled the *Catalogue of Engravers Born and Resident in England*, which, like its more famous predecessor, often passed through the press. On the *Catalogue of Royal and Noble Authors of England* Walpole, whose professed liberalism only stopped short of the principles of republicanism, spent many hours of toilsome research. The best edition is that which appeared in five volumes, in 1806, under the competent editorship of Thomas Park, who carefully verified and diligently augmented the labours of the original author. As a senator himself, or as a private person following at a distance the combats at St Stephen's, Walpole recorded in a diary the chief incidents in English politics. For twenty-seven years he studied, a silent spectator for the most part, the characters of the chief personages who trod the stage of politics, and when he quitted the scene he retained the acquaintance of many of the chief actors. If he was sometimes prejudiced, he rarely distorted the acts of those whom he disliked; and his prejudices, which lie on the surface, were mainly against those whom he considered the traitors of his father. These diaries extend from 1750 to 1783, and cover a period of momentous importance in the annals of the national history. The *Memoirs of the Last Ten Years of the Reign of George II.* was edited by Lord Holland; its successor, *Memoirs of the Reign of King George III.*, was published under the editorial care of Sir Denis Le Marchant, who poured into his annotations a vast store of information; the last volumes of the series, *Journal of the Reign of George III. from 1771 to 1783*, were edited and illustrated by Doran; and to these works should be added the *Reminiscences*, which Walpole wrote in 1788 for the gratification of the Misses Berry. These labours would in themselves have rendered the name of Horace Walpole famous for all time, but his delightful *Letters* are the crowning glory of his life. His correspondents were numerous and widespread, but the chief of them were Cole the clerical antiquary of Milton, Robert Jephson, an obscure play-writer in Ireland, Mason the poet, Lord Hertford during his embassy in Paris, the countess of Ossory, Lord Harcourt, George Montagu, one of his earliest friends, Conway, and Sir Horace Mann. With most of these friends he quarrelled, but the friendship of the last two, in the former case through genuine liking, and in the latter through his fortunate absence from England, was never interrupted. The *Letters* were published at different dates, but the standard collection is that by Peter Cunningham (9 vols., 1857–59), and to it should be added the volumes of the letters addressed to Walpole by his old friend Madame du Deffand (1810, 4 vols.), and the publication of Dr Doran, *Mann and Manners at the Court of Florence*, which is founded on the epistles sent in return to Walpole by the envoy-extraordinary. A handsome little volume, *Horace Walpole and his World*, consisting of select passages from his letters, extracted and strung together in a simple narrative by Mr L. B. Seeley, was issued in 1884. Walpole has been called "the best letter-writer in the English language"; and few indeed are the names, possibly none save Swift and Cowper, which can compare with his. In these compositions his very foibles are penned for our amusement, and his love of trifles—for, in the words of another Horace, he was ever "nescio quid meditans nugarum et totus in illis"—minister to our instruction. To these friends he communicated every fashionable scandal, every social event, and the details of every political struggle in English life. The politicians and the courtiers of his day were more akin to his character than were the chief authors of his age, and the weakness of his intellectual perceptions stands out most prominently in his estimates of such writers as Johnson and Goldsmith, Gibbon and Hume. On many occasions he displayed great liberality of disposition, and he bitterly deplored for the rest of his days his neglect of the unhappy Chatterton.

Abundant information about Horace Walpole will be found in the *Memoirs* of him and of his contemporaries edited by Eliot Warburton, Jesse's *George Selwyn and his Contemporaries*, and the extracts from the journals and correspondence of Miss Berry; and it would be unpardonable to omit mention of Macaulay's sketch of Walpole's life and character. (W. P. C.)

WALPOLE, Sir Robert, Earl of Orford (1676–1745), prime minister of England from 1721 to 1742, was the third but eldest surviving son of Robert Walpole, M.P., of Houghton in Norfolk,[1] by Mary, only daughter and heiress of Sir Jeffery Burwell, of Rougham, in Suffolk. The father, a jolly old squire who revelled in outdoor sport and the pleasures of the table, transmitted to his son the chief traits in his own character. The future statesman was born at Houghton on 26th August 1676, and was sent to Eton and to King's College, Cambridge, where he was admitted as scholar on 22d April 1696. At this time he was destined, as a younger son, for the church, but his two elder brothers died young and he became the heir to an estate producing about £2000 a year, whereupon in May 1698 he resigned his fellowship, and was soon afterwards withdrawn by his father from the university. His education lasted sufficiently long, however, to enable him to gratify the tastes of the county members in parliament with the usual quotations from Horace, though in classical attainments he was excelled by Pulteney, Carteret, and many others of his contemporaries in politics. On his father's decease the electors of the family borough of Castle Rising returned him in January 1701 to the House of Commons as their representative, but after two short-lived parliaments he sought the suffrages of the more important constituency of King's Lynn (1702), and was elected as its member at every subsequent dissolution until he left the Lower House. From the first he took a keen interest in the business of the House, and not many months passed away before his shrewdness in counsel and his zeal for the interests of the Whigs were generally recognized. In March 1705, according to the statement of Archdeacon Coxe, he was appointed one of the council to Prince George of Denmark, the inactive husband of Queen Anne, and then lord high admiral of England. Complaints against the administration of the navy were then loud and frequent (Burton's *Queen Anne*, ii. 22–31), and the responsibilities of his new position tested his capacity for public life. His abilities proved equal to the occasion, and justified his advancement, in succession to his life-long rival Henry St John, to the more important position of secretary-at-war (February 1708), an office of recent creation but in time of war of great responsibility, which brought him into immediate contact with the duke of Marlborough and the queen. With this post he held for a short time (1710) the treasurership of the navy, and by the discharge of his official duties and by his skill in debate became admitted to the inmost councils of the ministry. He could not succeed, however, in diverting Godolphin from the great error of that statesman's career, the impeachment of Sacheverell, and when the committee was appointed for elaborating the articles of impeachment Walpole was called upon to act as one of the managers for the House of Commons. On the wreck of the Whig party which ensued upon this fatal mistake, Walpole shared in the general misfortune, but neither cajolery nor menace could induce him to retain office, and he took his place with his friends in opposition. His energies now shone forth with irresistible vigour; both in debate and in the pamphlet press he took up the cause of the ejected ministry, and in revenge for his zeal his political opponents brought against him an accusation of personal corruption. On these charges, now universally acknowledged to have proceeded from party animosity, he was in the spring of 1712 expelled from the House and committed to the Tower. His prison cell now became the rendezvous of the Whigs among the aristocracy, while the populace heard his praises commemorated in the ballads of the streets. The ignominy which the Tories had endeavoured to inflict upon him was turned into augmented reputation. At the dissolution of 1713 the faithful electors of King's Lynn again placed their trust in him, and during this parliament, the last summoned by Queen Anne, he took the leading part in defence of Steele against the attacks of the Tories.

With the accession of George, the Whigs regained their supremacy, and for nearly half a century they retained the control of English politics. The prizes fell to the victors, and Walpole obtained the lucrative if unimportant post of paymaster-general of the forces in the administration which was formed under the nominal rule of Lord Halifax, but of which Stanhope and Townshend were the guiding spirits. A committee of secrecy was appointed to inquire into the acts of the late ministry, and especially into the peace of Utrecht, and to Walpole was entrusted the place of chairman. Most of his colleagues in office were members of the House of Lords, and the lead in the Commons quickly became the reward of his talents and assiduity. Halifax died, and after a short interval Walpole was exalted into the conspicuous position of first lord of the treasury and chancellor of the exchequer (11th October 1715). Jealousies, however, prevailed among the Whigs, and the German favourites of the new monarch quickly showed their discontent with the heads of the ministry. Townshend was forced into resigning his secretaryship of state for the dignified exile of viceroy of Ireland, but he never crossed the sea to Dublin, and the support which Sunderland and Stanhope, the new advisers of the king, received from him and from Walpole was so grudging that Townshend was dismissed from the lord-lieutenancy (April 1717), and Walpole on the next morning withdrew from the ministry. They plunged into opposition with unflagging energy, and in resisting the measure by which it was proposed to limit the royal prerogative in the creation of peerages Walpole exerted all his powers. This display of ability brought about a partial reconciliation of the two parties among the Whigs. To Townshend was given the presidency of the council, and Walpole once again assumed the paymastership of the forces (June 1720). On the financial crash which followed the failure of the South

[1] The head of a family whose ancestors and descendants are recorded in an elaborate pedigree published in the *Proceedings of the Norfolk and Norwich Archæol. Soc.*, i. 363–79.

Sea scheme, the public voice insisted that he should assume a more prominent place in public life. At this crisis in England's fortunes Stanhope and Craggs were seized by death, Aislabie, the chancellor of the exchequer, was committed to the Tower, and Sunderland, though acquitted of corruption, was compelled to resign the lead. Walpole, as first lord of the treasury and chancellor of the exchequer (April 1721), became with Townshend responsible for the country's government (though for some years they had to contend with the influence of Carteret), and during the rest of the reign of George I. they remained at the head of the ministry. The hopes of the Jacobites, which revived with these financial troubles, soon drooped in disappointment. Atterbury, their boldest leader, was exiled; Bolingbroke, in dismay at their feebleness, sued for pardon, and was permitted to return to his own country. The troubles which broke out in Ireland over Wood's patent for a copper coinage were allayed through the tact of Carteret, who had been banished as its lord lieutenant by his triumphant rivals. The Continent was still troubled with wars and rumours of wars, but a treaty between England, Prussia, and France was successfully effected at Hanover in 1725. England was kept free from warfare, and in the general prosperity which ensued Walpole basked in the royal favour. His eldest son was raised to the peerage as Baron Walpole (10th June 1723), and he himself became a knight of the Bath in 1725, and was rewarded with the Garter in 1726. Next year the first King George died, and Walpole's enemies fondly believed that he would be driven from office, but their expectations were doomed to disappointment. The confidence which the old king had reposed in him was renewed by his successor, and in the person of Queen Caroline, the discreet ruler of her royal spouse, the second George, the Whig minister found a faithful and life-long friend. For three years he shared power with Townshend, but the jealous Walpole brooked no rival near the throne, and his brother-in-law withdrew from official life to the groves of Norfolk in May 1730. Before and after that event the administration was based on two principles, sound finance at home and freedom from the intrigues and wars which raged abroad. On the Continent congresses and treaties were matters of annual arrangement, and if the work of the plenipotentiaries soon faded it was through their labours that England enjoyed many years of peace. Walpole's influence received a serious blow in 1733. The enormous frauds on the excise duties forced themselves on his attention, and he proposed some arrangements by which the income resulting to the national exchequer from the duties on wine and tobacco might be largely increased. His opponents fastened on these proposals with irresistible force, and so serious an agitation stirred the country that the ministerial measure was dropped amid general rejoicing. Several of his most active antagonists were dismissed from office or deprived of their regiments, but their spirit remained unquenched, and when Walpole met a new House of Commons in 1734 his supporters were far less numerous. The Gin Act of 1736, by which the tax on that drink was raised to an excessive amount, led to disorders in the suburbs of London; and the imprisonment of two notorious smugglers in the Tolbooth at Edinburgh resulted in those Porteous riots which have been rendered famous in the *Heart of Midlothian*. These events weakened his influence with large classes in England and Scotland, but his parliamentary supremacy remained unimpaired, and was illustrated in 1737 by his defeat of Sir John Barnard's plan for the reduction of the interest on the national debt, and by his passing of the Playhouse Act, under which the London theatres are still regulated. That year, however, heralded his fall from power. His constant friend Queen Caroline died, and the prince of Wales, long discontented with his parents and their minister, flung himself into active opposition. Many of the boroughs within the limits of the duchy of Cornwall were obedient to the prince's will, and he quickly attracted to his cause a considerable number of adherents, of whom Pitt and the Grenvilles were the most influential. The leading orators of England thundered against Walpole in the senate, and the press resounded with the taunts of the poet and pamphleteer, illustrious and obscure, who found abundant food for their invectives in the troubles with Spain over its exclusive pretensions to the continent of America and its claim to the right of searching English vessels. The minister long resisted the pressure of the opposition for war, but at the close of 1739 he abandoned his efforts to stem the current, and with a divided cabinet was forced, as the king would not allow him to resign, into hostility with Spain. The Tory minority had seceded from parliament, but at the commencement of the session, in November 1739, they returned to their places with redoubled energies. The campaign was prosecuted with vigour, but the successes of the troops brought little strength to Walpole's declining popularity, and when parliament was dissolved in April 1741 his influence with his fellow-countrymen had faded away. His enemies were active in opposition, while some of his colleagues were lukewarm in support. In the new House of Commons political parties were almost evenly balanced. Their strength was tried immediately on the opening of parliament. The Bossiney election went against him by six votes; a member of the opposition was elected as chairman of committees by a majority of four; and the ministry was twice defeated over the Westminster election. The voting on the return for Chippenham was accepted as a decisive test of parties, and, as Walpole was beaten on a preliminary point in connexion with the return, he resolved upon resigning his places. On the 9th of February 1742 he was created earl of Orford, and two days later he ceased to be prime minister. A committee of inquiry into the conduct of his ministry for the previous ten years was ultimately granted, but its deliberations ended in nought, and Walpole was allowed to spend the rest of his days in retirement at Houghton. There he died 18th March 1745, and in its parish church he was buried on March 25. With the permanent places, valued at £15,000 per annum, which he had secured for his family, and with his accumulations in office, he had rebuilt the mansion at great expense, and formed a gallery of pictures within its walls at a cost of £40,000, but the collection was sold by his grandson for a much larger sum in 1779 to the empress of Russia, and the estate and house of Houghton, a vast and gloomy edifice described in the *Art Journal* for March 1887, passed to Lord Cholmondeley, the third earl having married the premier's younger daughter. Walpole was twice married,—in 1700 to Catherine, eldest daughter of John Shorter, who died in 1737, having had issue three sons and two daughters, and in 1738 to Maria, daughter of Thomas Skerret, a lady often mentioned in the letters of Lady Mary Wortley Montague.

Civil wars at home and the protracted struggle with France on the Continent had produced in Englishmen an intense desire for peace, and, in their remembrance of the constant disputes under the previous two sovereigns over the succession to the throne, the great majority of them cheerfully consented to the rule of the electors of Hanover. Walpole knew the disposition of his countrymen, and he gratified their tastes by consistently acting both in ecclesiastical and civil affairs on the principle *quieta non movere*. He had profited by the lesson of the ill-fated prosecution of Sacheverell, and while he was prime minister the Church of England slept in peace without fear of danger from her enemies. The followers of dissent ranged themselves behind his banner, but they were fed by promises rather than by actual concessions, and the wisest among them were contented with permission to worship undisturbed. His aim ever was to maintain peace abroad and quiet at home, and the chief blot on his ministerial career is that through love of office he allowed himself to be drawn into the war with Spain. In business matters he was methodical; his judgment was sound in financial affairs; and his speeches were marked by clearness of expression. Pope, who loved him not, has borne witness to his merits "in the happier hours of social pleasure," but neither in private nor in public life were his manners refined or his estimates of men and women exalted. "All these men have their price" was his estimate of members of the House of Commons, and although he gathered together at Houghton many of the masterpieces of painting he was not a lover either of art or of letters. All the eminent writers of the day were opposed to his rule, and at his fall his jealous spirit had driven into opposition every politician of repute. Great as his faults were, his character was suited to the temperament of the period within which he lived, and during his tenure of office his country advanced in prosperity by leaps and by bounds.

His life is written by Archdeacon Coxe in three ponderous folios, and has more recently been described in one volume by Mr Ewald. (W. P. C.)

WALPURGIS, Walpurga, or Walburga,[1] St, was born in Sussex about the end of the 7th or the beginning of the 8th century, and was educated at Winburn, Dorset, where, after taking the veil, she remained for twenty-seven years. She then at the instance of her uncle, St Boniface, and her brother, St Wilibald, set out along with some other nuns to found religious houses in Germany. Her first settlement was at Bischofsheim in the diocese of Mainz, and two years later (754) she became abbess of the Benedictine nunnery at Heidenheim, within her brother Wilibald's diocese of Eichstädt in Bavaria, where also another brother, Winebald, had at the same time been made head of a monastery. On the death of Winebald in 760 she succeeded him in his charge also, retaining the superintendence of both houses until her death on February 25, 779. Her relics were translated to Eichstädt, where she was laid in a hollow rock, from which exuded a kind of bituminous oil afterwards known as Walpurgis oil, and regarded as of miraculous efficacy against disease. The cave became a place of pilgrimage, and a fine church was built over the spot. She is commemorated at various times, but principally on May 1, her day taking the place of an earlier heathen festival, which was characterized by various rites marking the commencement of summer. In art she is represented with a crozier, and bearing in her hand a flask of balsam.

WALRUS, or Morse.[2] In the article Mammalia (vol. xv. p. 442) it was shown that the existing members of the Pinniped division of the order *Carnivora* are divided into three very distinct groups, the true seals (*Phocidæ*), the sea-bears or eared seals (*Otariidæ*), and the *Trichechidæ*, containing the walrus alone, in some respects intermediate between the other two, but also possessing, especially in its greatly modified dentition, peculiar characters of its own.

Trichechus is the almost universally accepted generic name by which the walrus is known to zoologists, but lately some confusion has been introduced into literature by the revival of the nearly obsolete terms *Rosmarus* by some authors and *Odobænus* by others. *T. rosmarus* is the name of the species met with in the Arctic seas; that of the North Pacific, if distinct, is *T. obesus*. The following description will apply equally to both. A full-grown male walrus measures from ten to eleven feet from the nose to the end of the very short tail, and is a heavy, bulky animal, especially thick about the shoulders. The head is rounded, the eyes rather small, and there are no external ears. The muzzle is short and broad, with, on each side, a group of very stiff, bristly whiskers, which become stouter and shorter in old animals. The tail scarcely projects beyond the skin. The fore-limbs are free only from the elbow; the hand is broad, flat, and webbed, the five fingers being of nearly equal length, the first slightly the longest. Each finger has a small, flattened nail, situated on the dorsal surface at a considerable distance from the end. The hind-limbs are enclosed in the skin of the body almost to the heel. The free portion, when expanded, is fan-shaped, the two outer toes (first and fifth) being the longest, especially the latter. Cutaneous flaps project considerably beyond the bones of the toes. The nails of the first and fifth toes are minute and flattened; those of the second, third, and fourth elongated, sub-compressed, and pointed. The soles of both fore and hind feet are bare, rough, and warty. The surface of the skin generally is covered with short, adpressed hair of a light, yellowish-brown colour, which, on the under parts of the body and base of the flippers, passes into dark reddish-brown or chestnut. In old animals the hair becomes more scanty, sometimes almost entirely disappearing, and the skin shows ample evidence of the rough life and pugnacious habits of the animal in the innumerable scars with which it is usually covered. It is everywhere more or less wrinkled, especially over the shoulders, where it is thrown into deep and heavy folds.

Walrus.

One of the most striking external characteristics of the walrus is the pair of tusks which descend almost directly downwards from the upper jaw, sometimes attaining a length, in old animals, of 20 inches, or even more. In the female they are as long or sometimes longer than in the male, but less massive. In the young of the first year they are not visible. These tusks correspond to the upper canine teeth of other mammals. All the other teeth, including the lower canines, are much alike—small, simple, and one-rooted, and with crowns, rounded at first, but wearing to a flat or concave surface. The complete dentition appears to be $i\ \frac{3}{3}$, $c\ \frac{1}{1}$, $pm\ \frac{4}{4}$, $m\ \frac{1}{0} = \frac{9}{8}$, total 34. Many of these teeth are, however, lost early, or remain through life in a rudimentary state concealed beneath the gum. The teeth which are usually functionally developed are $i\ \frac{1}{0}$, $c\ \frac{1}{1}$, $pm\ \frac{3}{3} = \frac{5}{4}$, total 18. The tusks are formidable weapons of defence, but their principal use seems to be scraping and digging among the sand and shingle for the molluscs and crustaceans on which the walrus feeds. They are said also to aid in climbing up the slippery rocks and ledges of ice on which so much of the animal's life is passed. Although this function of the tusks is affirmed by numerous authors, some of whom appear to have had opportunities of actual observation, it is explicitly denied by Malmgren.

Walruses are more or less gregarious in their habits, being met with generally in companies or herds of various sizes. They are only found near the coast or on large masses of floating ice, and

[1] French forms of the name are Gualbourg, Falbourg, Vaubourg, and Avougourg.

[2] The former word is a modification of the Scandinavian *vallross* or *hvalros* ("whale-horse"), the latter an adaptation of the Russian name for the animal.

rarely far out in the open sea; and, though often moving from one part of their feeding ground to another, they have no regular seasonal migrations. Their young are born between the months of April and June, usually but one at a time, never more than two. Their strong affection for their young, and their sympathy for each other in times of danger, have been particularly noticed by all who have had the opportunity of observing them in their native haunts. When one of their number is wounded, the whole herd usually join in a concerted and intelligent defence. Although harmless and inoffensive when not molested, they exhibit considerable fierceness when attacked, using their great tusks with tremendous effect either on human enemies who come into too close quarters or on polar bears, the only other adversary they can meet with in their own natural territory. Their voice is a loud roaring, and can be heard at a great distance; it is described by Dr Kane as "something between the mooing of a cow and the deepest baying of a mastiff, very round and full, with its bark or detached notes repeated rather quickly seven or nine times in succession."

The principal food of the walrus consists of bivalved molluscs, especially *Mya truncata* and *Saxicava rugosa*, two species very abundant in the Arctic regions, which it digs up from the mud and sand in which they lie buried at the bottom of the sea by means of its tusks. It crushes and removes the shells by the aid of its grinding teeth and tongue, and swallows only the soft part of the animal. It also feeds on other molluscs, sand-worms, star-fishes, and shrimps. Portions of various kinds of algæ or sea-weeds have been found in its stomach, but whether swallowed intentionally or not is still doubtful.

The commercial products of the walrus are its oil, hide (used to manufacture harness and sole-leather and twisted into tiller ropes), and tusks. The ivory of the latter is, however, inferior in quality to that of the elephant. Its flesh forms an important article of food to the Eskimo and Tchuktchis. Of the coast tribes of the last-named people the walrus forms the chief means of support. "The flesh supplies them with food, the ivory tusks are made into implements used in the chase and for other domestic purposes, as well as affording a valuable article of barter, and the skin furnishes the material for covering their summer habitations, harness for their dog-teams, and lines for their fishing gear" (Scammon).

Geographically the walrus is confined to the northern circum-polar regions of the globe, extending apparently as far north as explorers have penetrated, but its southern range has been much restricted of late in consequence of the persecutions of man. On the Atlantic coast of America it was met with in the 16th century as low as the southern coast of Nova Scotia and in the last century was common in the Gulf of St Lawrence and on the shores of Labrador. It still inhabits the coast round Hudson's Bay, Davis Straits, and Greenland, where, however, its numbers are daily decreasing. It is not found on the Arctic coast of America between the 97th and 158th meridians. In Europe, occasional stragglers have reached the British Isles, and it was formerly abundant on the coasts of Finmark. It is rare in Iceland, but Spitzbergen, Nova Zembla, and the western part of the north coast of Siberia are still constant places of resort, in all of which a regular war of extermination is carried on. The North Pacific, including both sides of Behring's Strait, northern Kamchatka, Alaska, and the Pribyloff Islands are also the haunts of numerous walruses, which are isolated from those of the North Atlantic by the long stretches of coast, both of Siberia and North America, in which they do not occur. The Pacific walrus appears to be as large as, if not larger than, that of the Atlantic; its tusks are longer and more slender, and curved inwards; the whiskers are smaller, and the muzzle relatively deeper and broader. These and certain other minor differences have induced some naturalists to consider it specifically distinct under the name of *Trichechus obesus*. Its habits appear to be quite similar to those of the Atlantic form. Though formerly found in immense herds, it is rapidly becoming scarce, as the methods of destruction used by the American whalers, who have systematically entered upon its pursuit, are far more certain and deadly than those of the native Tchuktchis, to whom, as mentioned before, the walrus long afforded the principal means of subsistence.

Fossil remains of walruses and closely allied animals have been found in the United States, and in England, Belgium, and France, in deposits of Quaternary and late Tertiary age.

An exhaustive account of this animal, with references to all the authors who have written upon it, will be found in Allen's *History of North American Pinnipeds*, 1880. (W. H. F.)

WALSALL, a municipal and parliamentary borough and market-town of Staffordshire, England, is situated chiefly on an eminence above a rivulet tributary to the Tame, on various canals and branch railway lines, 8 miles north-north-west of Birmingham and 123 north-west of London. The principal street is spacious and regular, and, although the side streets are generally crooked and mean, the suburbs are for the most part built with regularity and neatness. The parish church of St Matthew, occupying a prominent position on an eminence, is a handsome modern building in the Transition style. The other five parish churches are also all modern. The schools include the grammar school, founded in 1554 for the education of boys, natives of Walsall, in the classics, the blue coat and national infant schools, and several board schools. The public library, established in 1859, enlarged in 1872, contains about 12,000 volumes; the scientific and art institution was established in 1854, and the literary institute in 1883. Among the principal public buildings are the town-hall in the Italian style, erected in 1866; the guild hall (1773), the theatre (formed out of the old agricultural hall in 1881), the drill hall (1866), the temperance hall (1866), the county court-house (1869), and the post-office (1879). The charitable institutions include the corporation almshouses (1825); Harper's almshouses for six women, founded in the reign of James I. and rebuilt in 1793; the Henry Boy's almshouse, opened in 1887; the memorial cottages at Caldmore, erected in 1868 by private benefaction of two townspeople, for twelve poor couples or widows; the Walsall cottage hospital (1863); the epidemic hospital (1872); and a number of minor charities. In the vicinity of the town are extensive coal-mines and limestone quarries. Ironstone is also obtained, and brick clay is dug. The town possesses iron and brass foundries, corn mills, and tanneries. One of the staple industries is the manufacture of the various kinds of ironmongery required in the construction of harness and carriages. Locks and keys, bolts, pulleys, and other hardware goods are also largely manufactured. The town is governed by a mayor, six aldermen, and eighteen councillors. The area of the municipal borough was extended in 1877 to 6929 acres; the population in 1871 was 46,447 (estimate of that in the extended area 49,018), and in 1881 it was 58,795. The population of the parliamentary borough (area 7478 acres) in 1871 was 49,018, and in 1881 it was 59,402.

In the early part of the 10th century Walsall was fortified by Ethelfleda, daughter of Alfred the Great and countess of Mercia. At the time of the Conquest it was retained by William as a royal demesne for about twenty years, until it was bestowed on Robert, son of Asculpus, who had accompanied the Conqueror to England. Subsequently it was owned by Richard Neville, earl of Warwick, the king-maker, and it was held successively by Henry VII. and Henry VIII. By the latter it was granted to John Dudley, duke of Northumberland, on whose attainder and execution in the reign of Mary it was forfeited and came into the possession of the Wilbrahams, from whom it passed by marriage to the Bridgmans. It is spoken of by Camden as "none of the meanest of market towns." Queen Elizabeth visited Walsall in the 28th year of her reign, and made a grant of lands to the town. Walsall was the residence of Henrietta Maria for a short time in 1643. It is a borough by prescription, but received charters from Edward III. and Henry IV., confirming the privileges and immunities conferred on it by previous sovereigns. Its oldest charter is that bestowed in the 3d of Charles I., which was confirmed in the 13th of Charles II. It is now governed under the Municipal Act of 1835. It was constituted a parliamentary borough by the Reform Act of 1832, and returns one member to parliament.

WALSH, William (1663–1709), is included among Johnson's *Most Eminent English Poets*, but is justly said to be "known more by his familiarity with greater men than by anything done or written by himself." It was he who gave Pope in his boyhood the advice to study correctness. The value of his counsel is acknowledged in the *Essay on Criticism* (l. 729). He was a native of Worcestershire, represented his native county in several parliaments, and was gentleman of the horse to Queen Anne.

WALSINGHAM, Sir Francis (c. 1536–1590), secretary of state under Elizabeth, was descended from an old Norfolk family, and was the third and youngest son of William Walsingham of Scadbury, Chislehurst, Kent, where he was born about 1536. After a good private education he entered King's College, Cambridge, but did not take a degree. He remained abroad during the reign of Mary, and the knowledge of foreign languages he thus acquired is said to have commended him to the notice of Cecil, Lord Burghley. In the parliament which met in January 1558–59 he was returned for Banbury, and in that which met in January 1562–63 for both Banbury and Lyme Regis; he decided to sit for the latter place. Nothing further is known of his political history, till in 1568 he wrote to Cecil a letter on the Darnley murder, which shows that he enjoyed the confidence of Cecil and the regent Murray, and was fully convinced of Queen Mary's guilt. In the following year Ridolfi, the papal agent, was confined, under suspicion of conspiracy, in Walsingham's house. In August 1570 Walsingham was selected as special ambassador to France in connexion with the negotiations for the toleration of the Huguenots, and in December took up his residence as permanent ambassador at Paris. On the 19th April 1572 he was successful in obtaining the signature of a treaty of peace between England and France, but the beneficial results of his skilful diplomacy in connexion with the negotiations for the Anjou and Alençon marriages were neutralized by the uncertain and changeable moods of Elizabeth, and finally frustrated by the massacre of St Bartholomew. He took his leave of the king of France on 23d May 1573, and on 20th December of the same year he was made secretary of state. On 1st December 1577 he was knighted, and on 22d April of the following year made chancellor of the order of the garter. In June following, along with Lord Cobham, he was sent to the Netherlands to assist in arranging a pacification of the States, but the extraordinary vacillation of Elizabeth rendered his mission a total failure. In July 1581 he was again sent on an embassy to Paris, but his instructions were of a kind both so dishonourable and so foolish that he said he wished rather the queen had sent him to the Tower. In such circumstances he could only endeavour to temper and qualify the policy of Elizabeth in such a manner as to prevent a fatal breach in the relations between the two countries, and in this he was successful. His embassy to Scotland in 1583 to endeavour to persuade James to dismiss the earl of Arran was also, as he prognosticated, a failure. He therefore recommended that the purpose of Elizabeth should be effected by fostering a conspiracy among the Scottish nobles, but the project was not carried out for some time afterwards. In 1584 Walsingham was appointed *custos rotulorum* of Hants and recorder of Colchester, and in 1585 high steward of Winchester. On 23d November 1586 he was returned member for Surrey, and again on 29th October 1587.

From the first Walsingham, equally with Cecil, Lord Burghley, was strongly hostile to Queen Mary of Scotland. By constant watchfulness and the skilful use of spies he succeeded in discovering the inmost secrets of her policy and plans. He permitted the Babington conspiracy to develop until letters passed between Babington and Mary which, if they are to be accepted as genuine, proved that the scheme for the assassination of Elizabeth had Mary's full approval. Mary and her friends declared that Walsingham had counterfeited her ciphers; but that Babington sent her letters informing her of the assassination scheme is beyond denial. Mary's friends, without any proof but her own asseveration, affirm that the letters never reached her, and that Mary's letters in reply, the authenticity of which Babington to the last never doubted, were forged by the agents of Walsingham. The asseveration of Mary is, however, robbed of all value by the fact that, in addition to denying the authenticity of the letters, she denied all knowledge of the Babington conspiracy; for Mendoza, the Spanish ambassador, while the plot was in progress, wrote to Philip II. that Mary had informed him she was fully acquainted with it. The accusation against Walsingham, that he was an accomplice in bringing Mary to the block on false and forged evidence, cannot therefore be entertained, although there cannot be any doubt that he regarded her execution as a happy deliverance from a position of great political embarrassment. He was one of the commissioners on her trial, and on Mary hinting that the incriminating letters had been written by him, called God to witness that he "had done nothing unbecoming an honest man."

By becoming surety for the debts of Sir Philip Sidney, Walsingham, on account of a flaw in the power of attorney left by Sidney, found himself on Sidney's death unexpectedly involved in pecuniary ruin. But, although one of the ablest and wisest of Elizabeth's councillors, his honesty had frequently ruffled her self-esteem, and she witnessed his embarrassments without deigning to lend him the smallest help. He died at his house in Seething Lane, London, 6th April 1590, in circumstances of so great poverty that his friends buried him in St Paul's at night to save the expense of a public funeral. Walsingham was a Puritan in his religious principles, but was unable to obtain for the Puritans the consideration from Elizabeth he desired. He established in 1586 a divinity lectureship at Oxford; he was a general patron of learning; and he encouraged Sir R. Hakluyt and other navigators in their voyages of discovery. By Spenser he is described as

> "The Great Mæcenas of this age
> As well to all that civil acts professe
> As those that are inspired with martial rage."

A large number of Walsingham's letters and state documents are in the library of the British Museum and State Paper Office. An account of his embassies to France with letters and despatches is contained in the *Compleat Ambassador*, edited by Sir Dudley Digges, 1655; the "Heads of a Conference between James VI. and Sir Frances Walsingham, September 1853," is published in vol. i. of the *Bannatyne Miscellany*; and his "Journal from December 1570 to April 1583" is published in vol. vi. of the *Camden Miscellany* (1871). The *Arcana Aulica, or Walsingham's Prudential Maxims for the Statesman and the Courtier*, London, 1655, said to have been translated from the Spanish, was probably translated by another Walsingham than Sir Francis. In Sir Robert Cotton's *Cottoni Posthuma* is a short article entitled "Sir Francis Walsingham's Anatomizing of Honesty, Ambition, and Fortitude."

WALTHAM, a city in Middlesex county, Massachusetts, United States, like the other so-called cities and towns of New England is in effect a township, containing several bodies of urban population, together with rural districts. It is situated about 9 miles west-north-west from Boston, being in fact a suburb of that city, in a country of rounded hills of glacial gravel. Besides the large village of Waltham, there are comprised in the city five others, viz., Bleachery, Chemistry, New Church, Prospectville, and Robert's Crossing. These have absorbed nearly all the population of the city, the rural inhabitants being comparatively few in number. The population, by the State census of 1885, was 14,609, about one-fourth being of foreign birth. Waltham is known all over the world for its machine-made watches, of which over 1400 are turned out daily. It has also a cotton-mill, a bleachery, and watch-tool manufactories.

The present area of Waltham was settled in 1630 by Puritans. In 1783 the town was incorporated, and in 1884 it received a city charter.

WALTHAM ABBEY, or WALTHAM HOLY CROSS, a market-town of Essex, England, on the borders of Hertfordshire and Middlesex, is situated on the Lea, near the great northern road, and on the Cambridge branch of the Great Eastern Railway, 13 miles north of Liverpool Street station, London. The town lies in a hollow, with streets for the most part crooked and narrow, and although many additions have lately been made it still retains much of the characteristic appearance of an old country town. Of the former magnificent abbey church the only portion of importance now remaining is the nave, forming the present parish church, the two easternmost bays of the nave being converted into the chancel. It is a very fine specimen of

Norman, and in the opinion of Mr Freeman forms part of the original building of Harold, although others assign its date to the time of Henry I. Only the western supports of the ancient tower now remain. A tower corresponding with the present size of the church was erected in 1556 and restored in 1798. On the south side of the church is a lady chapel of about the end of the reign of Edward II. or beginning of that of Edward III., containing some good decorated work. Bishop Hall became curate of Waltham in 1612, and Thomas Fuller was curate from 1648 to 1658. At Waltham Cross on the great northern road, about a mile west of Waltham, is the beautiful cross erected (1291–94) by Edward I. at one of the resting-places of the corpse of Queen Eleanor on its way to burial in Westminster Abbey. It is of Caen stone and is supposed to have been designed by Pietro Cavalini, a Roman sculptor. It is hexagonal in plan, and consists of three stages, decreasing towards the top, which is finished by a crocketed spirelet and cross. The lower stage is divided into compartments enclosing the arms of England, Castile and Leon, and Ponthieu. It underwent restoration in 1833, and a scheme for the same object was started in 1885. The old Elizabeth market-house that formerly stood in the market-square of Waltham was taken down in 1852. The town is the seat of a county court for Epping division of Essex, and possesses a court-house erected in 1849. The royal gunpowder factory is in the immediate vicinity; and the town possesses gun-cotton and percussion-cap factories, flour-mills, malt kilns, and breweries. Watercresses are largely grown in the neighbourhood, and there are extensive market-gardens and nurseries, including Paul's famous rose nursery. The area of the urban sanitary district of Waltham Holy Cross, which is identical with the parish of Waltham Abbey and is in the civil county of Essex and registration county of Middlesex, is 11,017 acres. the population being 5197 in 1871 and 5368 in 1881.

Waltham appears first in history as the hunting seat of the Danish thane Tovi or Tofi, the royal standard-bearer at whose wedding feast Hardicanute died. The great forest on the edge of which it was built was long known as the forest of Waltham, but the only portion of it now remaining is called Epping forest. A wonderful cross which had been found in Tovi's land at Montacute, Somerset, was brought to Waltham, and Tovi built a church for its reception, which was named the Church of the Holy Cross. When the estate after being confiscated to the crown came into the possession of Harold, he pulled down Tovi's church and built a new one of great magnificence, which was consecrated in 1060. He also founded a great secular college, which, though usually referred to as an abbey, did not, as is pointed out by Mr Freeman, become a religious house till the reign of Henry II. Shortly before the fatal battle of Hastings, Harold made a pilgrimage to Waltham, bringing with him many gifts. His body, which was first buried under a cairn at Hastings, was subsequently brought to Waltham and buried in the place of honour by the high altar. The tomb was destroyed about 1540. The site and property of the abbey were given by Henry VIII. to Sir Anthony Denny, whose grandson, Sir Edward Denny, was created by James I. baron of Waltham, and by Charles I. earl of Norwich. The town obtained a grant of a market from Henry III.

See "Architecture and Early History of Waltham Abbey Church," by E. A. Freeman, and other papers in vol. ii. of *Transactions of the Essex Archæological Society*; Thomas Fuller's *History of Waltham Abbey*; Stubbs's *Foundation of Waltham Abbey*; and Freeman's *Norman Conquest*.

WALTHAMSTOW, a town of Essex, England, now practically a suburb of London, is situated a short distance east of the river Lea, on a branch of the Great Eastern Railway, 6 miles north of Liverpool Street station. The original village grouped round the church is of comparatively small dimensions, but a large number of houses and villas have been built along the high road, from which diverge a number of streets and "ends." The church of St Mary existed at a very early period, but the present building, chiefly of brick, was erected in 1535 by Sir George Monoux, lord mayor of London, and has undergone frequent alteration and improvement. Besides other old brasses it contains in the north aisle the effigies in brass of Sir George Monoux and Anne his wife. Among the other public buildings are the town hall, erected in 1876 at a cost of £4500, the literary institute, founded in 1882, and the working men's club and institute. There are a number of educational institutions, including a school of art connected with the science and art department of South Kensington, the Monoux grammar school, the Forest school, founded in 1834 in connexion with King's College, and the home for orphan boys. The benevolent and charitable institutions include the public dispensary (1873), the Leyton and Walthamstow hospital home for children (1877), Sir George Monoux's almshouses for thirteen poor men (1527), the Collard almshouses for ten married couples (1851), and the Squire almshouses for widows of decayed tradesmen. In the vicinity are the reservoirs of the East London Waterworks Company. On the banks of the Lea there are flour-mills and an oil-mill. The population of the urban sanitary district (area 4374 acres) in 1871 was 10,692, and in 1881 it was 21,715.

In Domesday the name occurs as Welamestun. In the reign of Edward the Confessor it belonged to Waltheof, son of Siward, earl of Northumberland, who married Judith, niece of the Conqueror, who betrayed him to his death in 1075. The estate subsequently passed to Guy de Beauchamp, earl of Warwick, and on the attainder of Earl Thomas in 1396 reverted to the crown. Afterwards it came into the possession of Edmund Beaufort, duke of Somerset; from the Somersets it passed to Sir George Rodney, and subsequently it came to the Maynard family. It is supposed to have been the birthplace of George Gascoigne the poet (d. 1577). Sir William Patten, commissioner of the navy, the friend of Pepys, had his seat at Walthamstow, and was frequently visited there by Pepys.

WALTHER, BERNHARD (1430–1504), astronomer, was born at Nuremberg in 1430. He was a man of large means, which he devoted to scientific pursuits. When REGIOMONTANUS (*q.v.*) settled at Nuremberg in 1471, Walther built for their common use an observatory and a printing office, from which numerous calendars and ephemerides were issued, which became of great importance for the voyages of discovery. At this, the first German observatory, clocks driven by weights were first used in astronomical observations in 1484. The observations, continued until Walther's death in May 1504, were published by Schoner in 1544, and by Snell in 1618, as an appendix to his edition of Landgrave William's observations.

WALTHER VON DER VOGELWEIDE (*c.* 1170–*c.* 1230), the most illustrious of the German minnesänger, was born in Tyrol between 1165 and 1170. He belonged to a noble family, but had no hereditary possessions. At an early age he seems to have given evidence of an aptitude for poetry, and his genius was developed under the influence of the older poet Reinmar, whom he soon far surpassed. His earliest patron was the young and brilliant Duke Frederick of Austria, at whose court in Vienna he spent several years. After Duke Frederick's death Walther betook himself to King Philip, at whose coronation in Mainz, on the 8th September 1198, he was present. King Philip appreciated his genius, but nothing is definitely known as to their relations to one another, or as to the causes which brought their connexion to an end. After a short stay at the court of Duke Leonhard of Carinthia Walther went to Eisenach, where poets were always welcomed by the landgrave Hermann. Here he remained until 1211, when the landgrave, in deference to the pope, joined some other princes in an attempt to secure the crown for the prince afterwards known as Frederick II. Walther, who disapproved of this policy, soon afterwards entered the service of the emperor Otho; but, the emperor having proved unfriendly towards him, he associated himself with the cause of Frederick, who greatly pleased him by granting him a small fief near Würzburg, thereby gratifying a wish the poet had often expressed. He might now have led a settled life, but he had so long been accustomed to go from court to court that it was apparently hard for him to live without the excitement of travel and adventure. In 1217 he was at the court of Duke Leopold of Austria, after whose departure for the Holy Land he appears to have been received first by the duke's uncle, Henry of Medlik, then by Berthold of Andechs, the patriarch of Aquileia. On the return of Duke Leopold Walther again spent some time with him; but in 1220 he joined the retinue of the imperial vicar Engelbert of Cologne and Frederick II.'s son, Henry, to whom he seems to have acted as tutor. In 1224 Walther retired to Würzburg, where, although living in privacy, he watched closely the course of public affairs. He may have taken part in the crusade of 1228, but he certainly did not reach Palestine. He died about 1230 at Würzburg, where, under a tree in the Laurence garden of the new minster, a stone was long pointed out as that which, according to tradition, marked his grave. A new monument to him was erected at Würzburg in 1843, and a statue of him was unveiled at Innsbruck in 1877.

Walther von der Vogelweide was a poet not only of exquisite sensibility, but of a frank, independent, and manly character. He lived in a troubled age, when church and state were often in deadly conflict. In this struggle, in which he took keen interest, his sympathy was wholly with the imperial cause, and he did much to influence opinion by the vigour with which he attacked the extravagant pretensions of the papacy. While defending the rights of secular rulers, he did not forget their duties, and many of his verses—considering the period to which they belong—display a remarkably clear and generous conception of the principles of humanity and freedom. In writing of love, the favourite subject of the minnesänger, he had all the brightness, freshness, and gaiety of the best of his contemporaries, and he excelled them in his delicate appreciation of the noblest womanly qualities. His love of nature, especially in the season of spring, was an essential element of his intellectual and emotional life, and gives an enduring charm to the poems in which it is incidentally or indirectly expressed. He was a master of all the forms of verse used in Middle High German, and the perfection of his rhythm and diction, combined with the depth and wide range of his ideas, secures for him an enduring place in the front rank of the lyrical poets of his country.

A critical edition of his poems was issued by Lachmann in 1827, and there have been later editions by Wackernagel, Rieger, and Pfeiffer. There are renderings into modern German by Simrock, Koch, and Weiske. An admirable biography of the poet was written by Uhland (1822). Biographical and critical studies have also been written by Reuss, Rieger, Menzel, and Böse.

WALTON, or WALTON-LE-DALE, a township of Lancashire, is situated on the south bank of the Ribble, $1\frac{1}{2}$ miles south-east of Preston. The township includes the town of Walton-le-Dale, the villages of Bumber Bridge and Higher Walton, and several hamlets. The Ribble is crossed by a stone bridge of three arches erected in 1782, connecting Walton-le-Dale with Preston. The church of St Leonard, situated on an eminence to the east of the town, was originally erected in the 11th century. The earliest portions of the present building are the chancel and tower, in the Perpendicular style, the nave having been rebuilt in 1798, while the transepts were erected in 1816. The nave was re-pewed in 1855 and the chancel restored in 1864. There are a number of interesting old brasses and monuments. A working men's institute was built in 1881. Cotton-spinning is carried on, and there are market-gardens in the vicinity. The population of the urban sanitary district (area 4683 acres) was 8187 in 1871 and 9286 in 1881.

Walton occupies the site of a Roman station, probably that of *Coccium*. The manor was granted by Henry de Lacy about 1130 to Robert Banastre. It afterwards passed by marriage to the Langtons, and about 1592 to the Hoghtons of Hoghton. Walton was the principal scene of the great battle of Preston, fought on the 17th August 1648 between Cromwell and the duke of Hamilton. In 1701 the duke of Norfolk, the earl of Derwentwater, and other Jacobites incorporated the town by the style of the "mayor and corporation of the ancient borough of Walton." In 1715 the passage of the Ribble was bravely defended against the Jacobites by Parson Woods and his parishioners.

WALTON, or WALTON-ON-THE-HILL, a township of Lancashire, England, now practically a suburb of Liverpool, 3 miles north-east of the central station. It consists largely of villas and the better class residences, but a considerable portion of the Parish Church district is occupied by labourers and artisans. The parish church, dedicated to St Mary, was originally founded in 1326, but has all been rebuilt within recent times, the nave in 1742, the chancel in 1810, and the embattled western tower in 1831–32. There are also situated within the township the West Derby union workhouse, erected in 1868 at a cost of £10,000; the borough prison, 1855, £180,000 (which, however, is by a special Act of Parliament included within the borough of Liverpool); and the county police station, 1885, £8000. One of the attractions of Walton is Stanley Park, 100 acres in extent, opened in 1870 at a cost of £200,000. In the neighbourhood are also the Liverpool parochial cemetery, the Anfield Park cemetery, and the Kirkdale cemetery. The population of the urban sanitary district (area 1907 acres) in 1871 was 6449, and in 1881 it was 18,536.

The parish of Walton originally included Liverpool, which was separated from the mother church in 1699. At Domesday it was held by a Saxon named Winestan, and subsequently it was for some centuries in the possession of a family who took from it their name. The earl of Sefton is now lord of the manor.

WALTON, BRIAN (1600–1661), bishop of Chester, and editor of the great London Polyglott Bible, was born at Seymour, in the district of Cleveland, Yorkshire, in 1600. He went to Cambridge as a sizar of Magdalene College in 1616, migrated to Peterhouse in 1618, was bachelor in 1619, and master of arts in 1623. After holding a school mastership and two curacies he was in 1626 made rector of St Martin's Orgar in London (1626), where he took a leading part in the contest between the London clergy and the citizens about the city tithes, and compiled a treatise on the subject, which is printed in Brewster's *Collectanea*, 1752. His conduct in this matter displayed his ability, but his zeal for the exaction of ecclesiastical dues was remembered to his hurt in 1641 in the articles brought against him in parliament, which appear to have led to the sequestration of his very considerable preferments.[1] He was also charged with Popish practices, but on frivolous grounds, and with aspersing the members of parliament for the city. Up to this time he was perhaps more an active ecclesiastic than an eager student. In 1642 he was ordered into custody as a delinquent; thereafter he took refuge at Oxford, and ultimately returned to London to the house of Dr Fuller, dean of Ely, whose daughter Jane was his second wife. In this retirement he planned and executed his great work, a Polyglott Bible which should be completer, cheaper, and provided with a better critical apparatus than any previous work of the kind (see POLYGLOTT). The proposals for the Polyglott appeared in 1652, and the book itself came out in six great folios in 1657, having been printing for five years. England had at this time a band of Biblical and Oriental scholars of unusual distinction, and Walton could reckon among his active helpers Usher, Lightfoot, and Pococke, Castle, Wheelock, and Patrick Young, Hyde, Thomas Greaves, and others of less note. The great undertaking was supported by liberal subscriptions, and Walton's political opinions did not deprive him of the help of the Commonwealth; the paper used was freed from duty, and the interest of Cromwell in the work was acknowledged in the original preface, part of which was afterwards cancelled to make way for more loyal expressions towards that restored monarchy under which Oriental studies in England immediately began to languish. To Walton himself, however, the Reformation

[1] He was from January 1635–36 rector of Sandon, in Essex, where his first wife, Anne Claxton, is buried. He appears to have also been a prebendary of St Paul's, and for a very short time he had held the rectory of St Giles in the Fields.

brought no disappointment. He was consecrated bishop of Chester in December 1660. In the following spring he was one of the commissioners at the Savoy Conference, but took little part in the business. In the autumn of 1661 he paid a short visit to his diocese, and returning to London he fell sick and died on 29th November.

However much Walton was indebted to his helpers, the Polyglott Bible is a great monument of industry and of capacity for directing a vast undertaking, and the *Prolegomena* (separately reprinted by Dathe, 1777, and Wrangham, 1825) show judgment as well as learning. The same qualities appear in Walton's *Considerator Considered* (1659), a reply to Dr John Owen's *Considerations*, who thought that the accumulation of material for the revision of the received text tended to atheism. Among Walton's works must also be mentioned an *Introductio ad Lectionem Linguarum Orientalium* (1654, 2d ed. 1655), meant to prepare the way for the Polyglott.

See Henry J. Todd, *Memoirs of the Life and Writings of Walton*, London, 1821, in 2 vols., of which the second contains a reprint of Walton's answer to Owen.

WALTON, IZAAK (1593–1683), author of *The Compleat Angler*, hooked a much bigger fish than he angled for when he offered his quaint treatise to the public. There is hardly a name in our literature, even of the first rank, whose immortality is more secure, or whose personality is the subject of a more devoted cult. Not only is he the *sacer vates* of a considerable sect in the religion of recreation, but multitudes who have never put a worm on a hook—even on a fly-hook—have been caught and securely held by his picture of the delights of the gentle craft and his easy leisurely transcript of his own simple, peaceable, lovable, and amusing character.

A succession of devotees have supplemented by patient inquiry what he tells us of himself. He was born at Stafford in August 1593; the register of his baptism gives his father's name as Jervis, and nothing more is known of his parentage. He settled in London as a shopkeeper, and at first had one of the small shops, seven and a half feet by five, in the upper story of Gresham's Royal Burse or Exchange in Cornhill. In 1624 he had a shop in Fleet Street opposite the Temple, and was described as a linen-draper. In 1632 he bought a lease of a house and shop in Chancery Lane, and was described as a "sempster" or milliner.[1] His first wife, married in December 1626, was Rachel Floud, a great-great-niece of Archbishop Cranmer.[2] She died in 1640. He married again soon after, his second wife being also of distinguished clerical connexion, Anne Ken—the pastoral "Kenna" of *The Angler's Wish*—sister of Thomas Ken, afterwards bishop of Bath and Wells. When the civil war broke out, he retired from business. He had bought some land near his birthplace, Stafford, and he went to live there, but, according to Wood, spent most of his time "in the families of the eminent clergymen of England, of whom he was much beloved." His second wife died in 1662, and was buried in Worcester cathedral church, where there is a monument to her memory. One of his daughters married Dr Hawkins, a prebendary of Winchester, in whose house he died in December 1683, at the age of ninety. The last forty years of his long life seem to have been spent in ideal leisure and occupation, the old man travelling here and there, visiting his "eminent clergymen" and other brethren of the angle, compiling the biographies of congenial spirits, and collecting here a little and there a little for the enlargement of his famous treatise.

The first edition of *The Compleat Angler* was published in 1653, but the peaceful angler continued to add to its completeness in his leisurely way for a quarter of a century. There was a second edition in 1656, a third in 1661 (identical with that of 1664), a fourth in 1668, and a fifth in 1676. In this last edition the thirteen chapters of the original have grown to twenty-one, and a second part was added by his loving friend and brother angler Charles Cotton, who took up "Venator" where Walton had left him and completed his instruction in fly-fishing and the making of flies.

[1] There was more millinery in men's clothes in those days; hence his location near the fashionable Temple.

[2] See *Notes and Queries*, Nov. 15, 1873.

Walton did not profess to be an expert with the fly; the fly-fishing in his first edition was contributed by Mr Thomas Barker, a retired cook and humorist, who produced a treatise of his own in 1659; but in the use of the live worm, the grasshopper, and the frog "Piscator" himself could speak as a master. The famous passage about the frog—often misquoted about the worm— "use him as though you loved him, that is, harm him as little as you may possibly, that he may live the longer"—appears in the original edition. The additions made as the work grew were not merely to the didactic part; happy quotations, new turns of phrase, songs, poems, and anecdotes were introduced as if the leisurely author, who wrote it as a recreation, had kept it constantly in his mind and talked it over point by point with his numerous brethren. There were originally only two interlocutors in the opening scene, "Piscator" and "Viator"; but in the second edition, as if in answer to an objection that "Piscator" had it too much in his own way in praise of angling, he introduced the falconer, "Auceps," changed "Viator" into "Venator," and made the new companions each dilate on the joys of his favourite sport.

Although *The Compleat Angler* was not Walton's first literary work, his leisurely labours as a biographer seem to have grown out of his devotion to angling. It was probably as an angler that he made the acquaintance of Sir Henry Wotton, but it is clear that Walton, whatever his education and breeding may have been, must have had more than a love of fishing and a humorous temper to recommend him to the friendship of the accomplished ambassador. At any rate, Wotton, who had intended to write the life of John Donne, left the task to Walton, who had lamented his pastor's death in an *Elegy* in 1633, and now completed and published the life, much to the satisfaction of the most learned critics, in 1640. Sir Henry Wotton dying in 1639, Walton undertook his life also; it was finished in 1642, and published in 1651. His life of Hooker was published in 1662, George Herbert in 1670, and Bishop Sanderson in 1678. All these subjects were endeared to the biographer by a certain gentleness of disposition and cheerful piety; three of them at least, Donne, Wotton, and Herbert, were anglers. Their lives were evidently written with loving pains, in the same leisurely fashion as his *Angler*, and like it are of value less as exact knowledge than as harmonious and complete pictures of character. Walton also rendered affectionate service to the memory of his friends Sir John Skeffington and John Chalkhill, editing with prefatory notices Skeffington's *Hero of Lorenzo* in 1652, and Chalkhill's[3] *Thealma and Clearchus* a few months before his own death in 1683. Two political letters, published in 1680, under the title *Love and Truth*, though conciliatory enough in temper to be Walton's, are ascribed to him on somewhat doubtful authority (see Zouch's *Lives*, vol. ii. p. 387, ed. 1817).

There are biographies of Walton himself by Sir John Hawkins (prefixed to an edition of the *Angler*, 1760), Dr Zouch (appended to an edition of the *Lives*, 1796), and Sir Harris Nicolas (prefixed to an edition of the *Angler*, 1836). There are notices also, with additional scraps of fact, annexed to two great American editions, Bethune's (1847, particularly splendid) and Dowling's (1857). A facsimile of the original edition of the *Angler* was issued by Bagster in 1810, another by Elliot Stock in 1876. (W. M.)

WĂN-CHOW-FU, a prefectural city in the Chinese province of Chĕ-keang, and one of the ports opened by treaty to foreign trade, is situated (28° 1′ N. lat. and 120° 31′ E. long.) on the south bank of the river Gow, about 20 miles from the sea. The site is said to have been chosen by Kwo P'oh (276–324 A.D.), a celebrated antiquary who recognized in the adjacent mountain peaks a correspondence with the stars in the constellation of the Great Bear, from which circumstance the town was first known as the Tow, or Great Bear, city. Subsequently, however, the appearance in its vicinity of a white deer carrying a flower in its mouth was deemed to be so favourable an omen as to more than justify the change of its name to Luh, or Deer, city. Its present name, which signifies the "mild district," and which is correctly descriptive of the climate, though not of the inhabitants, was given to it during the last dynasty (1368–1644). The walls, which were built in the 10th century, are about 6 miles in circumference, 35 feet in height, and 12 feet broad at the top. The gates, seven in number, were put up in 1598. Wăn-chow is about 1563 miles by road from Peking and 600 from Hankow. The country in the neighbourhood of the town is hilly and pretty, while opposite the north-west

[3] The existence of Chalkhill was called in question by S. W. Singer in 1820, and the pastoral supposed to be Walton's own. There can be little doubt that the poet is the same person whose tomb is in Winchester cathedral, and that Walton was simply mistaken in describing him as "an acquaintant and friend of Edmund Spenser."

gate "Conquest Island" forms a picturesque object. The island is, however, more beautiful than healthy. The port, which was opened to foreign trade in 1876, has not justified the great expectations which were formed of its probable success as a commercial centre.

In 1886 the imports (excluding treasure) were valued at £118,710, and the exports at £25,751; 44 vessels entered, of which one only was British, and 45 cleared. A noticeable feature in the year's return is the falling off in the quantity of opium imported,—only 25 piculs, 62 per cent. less than the average of the previous three years. The principal item of import is cotton goods, which showed an increase of 12 per cent. over the same average. Kerosene oil, matches, window-glass, sugar, dates, and old iron are among the chief goods imported; while among the exports kittysols or umbrellas, timber, oranges, and tea figure prominently.

WANDERING JEW. See JEW, WANDERING.

WANSTEAD, a village of Essex, England, now really a London suburb, is situated on a branch of the Great Eastern Railway (Snaresbrook station), 8 miles by rail north-east of Liverpool Street station. It possesses the usual characteristics of the better-class eastern suburbs of London. Wanstead Park, 184 acres in extent, was opened in 1882. A feature of Wanstead is Eagle Pond or Lake, 10½ acres in extent. At Lake House Hood wrote *Tylney Hall.* The population of the urban sanitary district (area about 1072 acres) is estimated to have been 4311 in 1871; in 1881 it was 5362.

Wanstead is supposed to have been a Roman station. It belonged to the monks of St Peter's, Westminster, and afterwards to the bishop of London, of whom it was held at Domesday by Ralph Fitz Brien. In the reign of Henry VIII. it came into the possession of the crown, and in 1549 it was bestowed by Edward VI. on Lord Rich, whose son sold it in 1577 to Robert, earl of Leicester. The original manor house was rebuilt by Lord Chancellor Rich, who was here visited by Queen Elizabeth in 1561, and for her entertainment Sir Philip Sidney wrote a dramatic interlude which was played before the queen at Wanstead garden, and is printed at the end of the *Arcadia.* Sir Richard Child, afterwards earl of Tylney, built the splendid mansion of Wanstead House in 1715 (demolished in 1822), in which the prince of Condé and others of the Bourbon family resided during the reign of the first Napoleon.

WAR

WHATEVER definition of the word "army" (see ARMY) be adopted, the fact that it is a body of men organized for the effective employment of *arms* is the essence of it. Hence the nature of the most effective organization and employment of armies in active warfare at any given period has always turned upon the nature of the arms in use at the time. The laboratory and workshops of science in recent years have in fact produced and forced on a change in the nature of fighting, of a kind which it is safe to say never entered the mind of any one of the inventors whose skill made it necessary. And yet the change is of such a kind that, though due to the development of very material things, as, for instance, the greater rapidity of fire, the greater range of weapons, and the like, it is much more remarkable in its effect on the spirit of armies and the nature of fighting discipline than in almost any other aspect.

Modern changes in the art of war.

An army an organism, not a machine.

In all periods of war, under all conditions of arms, the moral forces which affect armies have been the great determining factors of victory and defeat. From a date much earlier than the day when Cæsar, defeated at Dyrrachium, gained the empire of the world by so acting as to restore the *morale* of his army before the great contest at Pharsalia, it has been on this nice feeling of the moral pulse of armies that the skill of great commanders has chiefly depended. In that respect there is nothing new in the modern conditions of war. But the sequence by which the development of arms has changed the moral pivot of military power in our own times is so remarkable that it deserves to receive a somewhat careful historical statement at the outset of this article. Unless it is understood the lessons of modern fighting cannot be learnt; for there has not yet occurred a modern war in which the principles of modern fighting, as they are now universally understood among the most thoughtful soldiers of all nations, have been deliberately applied to action, after those principles have been realized and worked out in practice during peace time. And yet it is among the first of these principles that for success in our days careful peace practice, adapted to the actual conditions of fighting, must precede the entry on a campaign. When letters from the seat of war in 1866 brought home to Europe the effect which the breech-loader was producing in determining the contest, the first impression was that of simple consternation. It was supposed that Prussia, by the possession of that weapon alone, had made herself mistress of Europe. Gradually it came to be known that the secret of Prussian power lay, not in her breech-loader alone, but at least as much in her perfect organization. In 1870 her scarcely less startling successes tended for a time to produce an effect almost as blinding upon the eyes of those who watched them. There was a disposition to assume that whatever had been done in the war by the Prussians was, by the deliberate choice and determination of the best and most successful soldiers in Europe, shown to be the best thing that could be done under the circumstances. The exhaustive statement of facts contained in the Prussian official narrative and in the regimental histories, and the evidence of eye-witnesses innumerable, have, however, gradually made it evident that, valuable as the experiences of the 1870 campaign unquestionably are for soldiers of all nations, the Prussian successes were certainly not due to the carrying out of what are now regarded by the best Prussian officers themselves as the principles of action which ought to determine practice in future wars. But during the course of the war itself the Prussian army, prepared by the soundest peace training to adapt itself to whatever conditions it met with, was continually and progressively modifying its practice under the experience of conditions which it had been impossible fully to anticipate.

It is upon the surface of the facts that the extreme loss of life suddenly occasioned at particular points by the effectiveness of the fire of the new weapons, both of artillery and infantry, compelled the gradual abandonment of close formations of men, massed together in dense columns or even in closed lines, and the gradual adoption of what are known as "skirmishing" or open order formations. In other words, when the French fire fell upon the solid columns of the advancing Prussians, the column instinctively scattered. The officers and non-commissioned officers were often lost in very large proportion, and during the actual course of the fighting, without any preconceived idea on the subject, a method of attack was adopted which proceeded by successive swarms of dispersed men taking advantage of such shelter as the ground permitted. The noise of the rapid breech-loader, and the crash of an artillery able to fire much more frequently than in former campaigns, and, moreover, accumulated in much greater masses than had ever been the case before, made words of command inaudible at a distance. Hence it came to pass that small parties of men, once launched into an infantry fight, were virtually beyond all control on the part of superior officers. All that these could do to influence the action was to determine the direction and object of the first attack of each fraction, and then to furnish it with fresh supports at the proper moment, sending them forward in such a way as to cause their blows to be delivered in the most telling direction.

Here then was the great change which had come about, produced, as has been said, by the efficiency of the new weapons, but rendered possible by those changes in the characteristics of the men of whom armies are composed, which had arisen from altogether different circumstances, such as the high educational standard of the Prussian nation, and the introduction into the ranks of highly cultivated classes. The army, at all events in battle, was and could be no longer a mere mechanical weapon in the hands of its commander. If this latter could not infuse into it a spirit of hearty willing co-operation and intelligent subordination, chaos and chaos only must ensue. For the very essence of the old forms of fighting in battle, as they had been inherited from the time of Frederick the Great, and, though modified by Napoleon, had yet in this respect remained the same, was that battle movements were led up to and prepared for by an elaborate system of drill, so arranged that by the issue of predetermined words of command the officer leading at least a division of an army could decide precisely the formation it was to assume and the movements it was to make in battle. Now, though no doubt many of the preliminary movements could still be accomplished in accordance with the old drill, yet, for at least the very mile and a half over which the issue had actually to be fought out, drill had vanished, as far at all events as the infantry were concerned. All effective movements and co-operation depended on perfect organization, and on a training which made every officer and every man know almost instinctively what to do and what decisions to form as each emergency arose. The Germans had in the largest sense perfected their organization, not merely in its form, itself a matter of no small importance, but in its preparedness for battle action. This had been done chiefly by keeping and training together much larger units of command than had ever been organically worked together before. By "organic working" we specifically mean such work as leads each man to know by long habit what the part assigned to him is, and how to contribute his share in bringing about the result desired by his general. In the article ARMY will be found an exhaustive statement of the successive *forms* which army organization has assumed at different periods of history. With regard to these forms, representing as they do the condition of an army in a state of rest, suffice it to say that the ancient proverb about new wine and old bottles applies perfectly. It would not have been possible for the Germans to have secured a complete correspondence of working, a unity amid great diversity, without having devised a form of organization which assigned to every man an adequate share of work and of responsibility, by bringing a limited number of men at each step under the authority of one, those so placed in authority being themselves at the next stage, in limited number, also under one man's authority. But the very idea of organization implies more than this mere perfection of form. It implies also, as animating the whole body, a spirit developed by careful training, a mutual reliance on the certainty of the adherence of all to known principles of action.

Subordination of drill to organization.

The essential change, then, which appears to have come over modern war may be stated thus. Under the conditions of the past, the general in command of an army relied upon its perfection in drill and in formal manœuvres for enabling him to direct it with success against the weak points of an adversary. Now he must depend instead upon the perfection of its organization and of a training adapted to make each man ready when required to apply sound principles in every emergency, and, above all, as soon as possible voluntarily to place himself under authority again so as to secure unity of action. To summarize this statement in a single sentence, and employing the word organization in the larger sense explained above, the change consists in the substitution of organization for drill as a means of battle-action. In other words, a living organism must take the place of a mechanical instrument.

It will be seen at once that the perfection aimed at, involving as it does not merely a mechanical learning, by rote and drill-sergeant, of required changes of position, is of a much higher order both for the individual man and for the whole body than was the case under the old conditions. On the other hand, it is not possible that the practical performance should so nearly approach the ideal as happened formerly. Hence, great as was the excellence of the Prussian army in 1870 as a whole, yet the more thoroughly that campaign is studied the more manifest will be the mistakes in point of details committed by subordinate actors. It is in the nature of things impossible that this should ever be otherwise under the conditions of war which are now established. When the choice of action in detail is left to so many hands the possibilities of error are multiplied indefinitely.

Application of past experience to strategy and tactics.

It is clear from what has been said that a change of the most complete character has come over the very principle by which armies are held together. It is by no means surprising, therefore, that a few soldiers should have arrived at the conclusion that, because of the importance of this change, all past experience of fighting has ceased to be of any importance to him who would understand the principles of war as they exist to-day. On the other hand, others of far higher authority have declared it to be certain that change has only affected that branch of the art of war which is called tactics, and that the other branch, or strategy, is in no way affected. We are not able to subscribe absolutely to either of these statements. But before stating our views it will be convenient to define the terms employed. By strategy we understand "the art of rightly directing the masses of troops towards the object of the campaign." Of modern tactics no better definition perhaps has ever been given than that of Sir Edward Hamley. After defining the limits of either subject thus—"the theatre of war is the province of strategy, the field of battle is the province of tactics,"[1] he describes the manœuvres of a modern battle-field as "the quick orderly change of highly trained and flexible masses of men from one kind of formation to another, or their transference from point to point of a battle-field for purposes which become suddenly feasible in the changing course of action."

It is necessary, in discussing the application of past experience to modern war, to make intelligible the distinction between these two fields of experience, because undoubtedly the changes wrought by time affect the two great parts of the art of war in very different ways and in a very different degree. But in fact there are many parts of the study of tactics which are not strictly included within its province when that is limited to the field of battle. The distinction between the two provinces having been understood as a general idea, it will be seen at once how it has happened that in the varied incidents of warfare it has become necessary to apply the terms "tactics" and "strategy" to other matters. For no army can determine for itself or know beforehand absolutely what will be a field or a day of battle. Hence it is necessary throughout almost the entire course of a campaign to take those precautions and to take into account those considerations

[1] *Operations of War*, 4th ed., pt. iii. ch. i.; pt. vi. ch. i.

which apply properly to the period of actual combat. Thus, though an enemy may in fact be many marches distant, it is necessary to provide against his possible attack, by having some troops always on the alert whilst others are marching with all the ease and security which the protection of these procures for them. It is necessary also in a similar manner to have protection for the repose of an army, and to detail troops for this purpose. All the questions, then, which concern the fixing of "advanced guards" and "rear guards," which protect the front and rear of an advancing army, and the "outposts," which protect an army at rest, are usually included in the study of tactics, though in many instances they may have nothing to do with a battle-field. But again, though the campaign —the large field of war which concerns the marches and movements of armies striving against one another to obtain positions of vantage for the actual combat—is the province of strategy, yet it may well happen that on the actual battle-field it is necessary to take account, not only of those circumstances which will help to secure victory in the fight, but of the effect which victory or defeat will have upon the campaign. All these considerations we necessarily regard as "strategical," even though they occupy our minds on a battle-field.

The art of war as a study.

For it must be emphatically asserted that there does not exist, never has existed, and never, except by pedants, of whom the most careful students of war are more impatient than other soldiers, has there ever been supposed to exist, an "art of war" which was something other than the methodic study of military history. Those who have most assisted in making the study sufficiently methodic to enable it to be of practical profit in their own profession to soldiers for future use, or to historical students in watching the play of mind between great commanders, have been invariably the most emphatic in denouncing all attempts to formulate a systematic series of "rules of war." Among generals, Mack, the unfortunate Austrian who surrendered at Ulm to Napoleon, and in our own time Count Palikao, who had made himself the laughing-stock of the English staff during the advance on Peking, and who was afterwards responsible for bringing about the catastrophe of Sedan, have been the great sticklers for the "rules of war." At least once Count Palikao, in China, came without his sword to look on at the success of operations which he had denounced as "contrary to every maxim of war." On the other hand, Sir Edward Hamley, who has done more than any other Englishman to make known to English officers the value of a methodical treatment of the study of campaigns, has most vigorously denounced such talk as this.

"Nothing is more common," he writes "than to find in writings on military matters reference to the 'rules of war,' and assertions such as that some general 'violated every principle of war,' or that some other general owed his success to 'knowing when to dispense with the rules of war.' It would be difficult to say what these rules are, or in what code they are embodied; and an inquirer, who is somewhat puzzled, perhaps, to understand how the highest proficiency can be displayed in a science by defiance of its principles, had better resolve to base his own conclusions upon fact and reason alone, when he will probably discover that such criticisms have only very vague ideas for their foundation."

Jomini, a very eminent authority in his day, though not a little disposed to somewhat exact definition, and perhaps sometimes to over-pedantic statement, has with very little difference expressed the same view. Clausewitz, probably the most profound of all military students, has even more emphatically declared that the theory of the art of war is valuable, just in so far as it assists to guide a man through the vast labyrinth of military experience, and to prepare his mind to be ready to act for itself under the emergencies of actual war; but, he adds, "it must renounce all pretension to accompany him on to the field of battle." Both he and Jomini agree in asserting that it must have become with him an instinct, almost absorbed into his blood, to be of any value to him. "The wise teacher," says Clausewitz, "restricts himself to the work of directing and assisting the mental development of his pupil, and does not try to keep him in leading-strings throughout his career." Thus from all countries those who have come to be accepted as authorities on the study of war, the very men who, if any, ought to be tempted to magnify their office, have cried aloud against the abuse of such study. It is not from them, but from non-military writers like Macaulay, that the notion of some formal code of the rules of war has been derived. Macaulay's expression about Peterborough winning battles by violating the rules of war cannot be characterized otherwise than as worthless rhetoric, not only unsupported, but absolutely contradicted by fact. So thoroughly reasoned and so entirely worked out on a principle were Peterborough's campaigns that they have in our own day served to guide one of the most brilliant of English soldiers in the conduct of one of his most successful wars. The campaigns by which Colonel Gordon saved China were largely assisted in their conception by his careful study of Peterborough's generalship in Spain.

On the other hand, it is not from writers on war, but from the greatest generals, that the most emphatic statements have come as to the paramount importance to a soldier of the careful study of past campaigns. The classical instance of the most authoritative dictum on this subject is surrounded by circumstances of dramatic interest. Napoleon in 1813, sitting after dinner surrounded by his marshals, between the first and the second battle of Dresden, was drawn to speak on this subject by Marmont, the one who, in Napoleon's own judgment and that of others, had himself the most complete knowledge of war as an art. Marmont, observing how difficult it was, during the continued strain of war itself, to improve in its practice, maintaining that rather in peace than in war could war be best studied, said to Napoleon that he thought that Napoleon's own first campaign in Italy was the most brilliant in its conception of any that he had ever fought; so that sixteen years of high command had hardly made his knowledge of war as an art more perfect. Napoleon at once admitted the truth of this, and in reply said, "Yes; Turenne was the only one of us all who constantly improved in the management of his campaigns as he advanced in years." This reply is especially remarkable, because Napoleon was not only the greatest captain of his own age, but he was by far the most careful student that the world has known of the great generals of all ages. It is an unanswerable assertion that only by study of the past experience of war has any great soldier ever prepared himself for commanding armies.

It must, however, be always a question how far the circumstances of our own time have so changed as to limit the period within which it is worth while to devote very careful study to the wars of the past. On the one hand, the greater number of officers in any army will never find time exhaustively to study all the great campaigns which would be of value if they had really so known them as to acquire the experience, as far as may be, of the various actors in them, and it is therefore of special importance that the most modern experiences at least should be completely known to them. On the other hand, even after all the campaigns which have taken place since breech-loaders and rifle-guns have become the determining factors of battles have been carefully studied, it can hardly be claimed for them that they present a picture approximately complete of all the possibilities of modern war. To any one who tells us that nothing applicable to the wars of the future is now to be learnt from the campaigns of Napoleon, or even from the events of the Peninsular War, we are prepared to reply by adducing, either from almost any one of Napoleon's most important campaigns or from the Peninsula, specific lessons, for the most part experiences of human nature, and illustrations of the mistakes which men are liable to make, which have in no wise been diminished in value by the changes which have come over the face of war.

As an instance in point, reference may here be made to a recently published study of the campaign of Fredericksburg during the civil war in America. It deals in a sound and useful manner with both strategy and tactics, and yet it is based entirely on conclusions drawn from a period of war prior to the introduction of the breech-loader We are disposed to put it forward as a very powerful illustration of the kind of lessons which a careful student may draw from one condition of tactics and apply to another. What is most interesting in the work is perhaps the way in which those lessons are made to apply with exceptional force to the peculiar and special conditions involved in breech-loader fighting. It seems impossible for any one who has appreciated its excellence not to perceive that in a similar manner, with the like wise appreciation of those things which are permanent and those things which change, sound deductions may be drawn from even the tactical experiences of the Napoleonic era. Nay, the statement of the most brilliant and successful general in the British army of to-day appears to be indisputable, that a perusal of the words of even Cæsar himself will suggest to any thoughtful soldier, who knows something also of modern war, reflexions that he may afterwards recall with advantage as applicable to modern campaigns.

That tactics have been first and most directly affected by the changes which have recently taken place in the conditions of modern war it is impossible to doubt. The nature of tactics has been always of a kind more tending to admit of rapid change, and more frequently suggesting to a commander of originality new developments. Napoleon indeed declared that tactics should be changed every ten years. Strategy has always, on the other hand, been assumed to possess a more permanent character. All important changes in armament immediately affect tactics. No one now disputes the general character of the tactical changes which have been produced by the introduction of the breech-loader and the development of artillery. Indeed, when we come to describe the broad features of modern tactics, we shall be dealing with matters as to which, except as to a few specific points, it may be said that practically the military world of Europe is agreed; but we confess that we are not prepared to accept the assumption that tactics only have been changed, and that he who would be ready for future war on the grand scale must not also look for some change in the general character of strategy.

Sir E. Hamley, in his *Operations of War*, has graphically described how it was that armies lived in the days of Edward III.; how they depended absolutely upon the food and supplies which they found in the country through which they moved; and how, when they had exhausted that country, and were opposed by an enemy holding a strong position, which they could not venture to assail, they were obliged to fall back simply because they had no arrangements for obtaining supplies regularly from their own land. Now the great strategic movements of armies have depended always upon this question of food and of warlike supplies in the first instance. It will therefore be evident at once that the character of strategy changed from the moment when a system was devised by which along a regular chain of posts, or "line of communications," an army received its supplies of food, warlike implements, and reinforcements, from either its own country or some other source which came to be known as its "base of supply." It began to be the object of generals to manœuvre in such a way as to interfere with the lines by which their opponents were receiving their supplies and to protect their own. In many respects, no doubt, even the Roman armies in the time of Hannibal acted on strategical principles that are applicable in our own time. Yet the change in the conditions under which armies began to live in the field was so great from the moment when, in order to facilitate and hasten their movements, they began to be thus supplied from a particular "base," and along these "lines of communication," that the art of handling them in campaigns changed almost as completely as tactics ever changed. New combinations became possible. Skill was turned into a new direction. In other words, strategy, like tactics, changes when its implements or weapons change. If now it be asked whether since the days of Napoleon and Wellington the implements of strategy have not changed almost as completely as those of tactics, it must be answered that the change has been even more complete.

Changes in the general conditions of war

Since 1815 the face of Europe has been more altered than it had been in five previous centuries. It is now covered with a network of railways and telegraphs. The commerce of the world and its means of intercommunication have developed in a manner that has everywhere revolutionized the conditions of life. The advance of science has operated in a thousand forms upon the circumstances under which armies exist in the field. The conditions of sea transport and of sea warfare are even more completely changed than those of land. Further, it must be remembered that battle-action is itself one of the determining factors of strategy. If, in their general character, the nature of battles and the circumstances under which battles have to be fought change very materially, that in itself involves a further change in the combinations which are open for manœuvres in the field of which the ultimate object is to lead up to battle. Once more, the size of the armies which will enter into the next great campaign in Europe will be so vastly different from those which fought out the great wars of the past that their manœuvring in campaigns must necessarily be very different from anything that Napoleon undertook. Now, even during the later wars of Napoleon, Jomini was obliged to admit that many of the experiences of the past must be materially modified as armies increased in size. One of the most familiar forms in which Napoleon exercised his strategic skill lay in defeating with his own entire army a fraction of the forces opposed to him, before it could be reinforced by the remainder of the enemy. Thus the element of time essentially entered into the question. Even during the great campaign of 1813, when Napoleon, holding a central position on the Elbe, endeavoured to strike from thence against the masses of the allies formed in a great circle round him at Berlin, in Silesia, and in Bohemia, experience showed that it was by no means easy to crush with sufficient rapidity armies of 120,000 men so as to prevent them from being supported in time by others. As the allies gradually closed in on him, and the distances between their different forces diminished, this became continually more and more apparent. In fact, it became clear, if it had been doubtful beforehand, that the question was altogether a matter of proportion between time, distance, and the resisting power of the several armies concerned. On the other hand, in 1814, when the nature of the country invaded caused a reduction in the size of the armies moving forward separately, Napoleon was able as of old to strike his blows right and left with telling effect.

Now, if it were possible for an army of our day, supplied with all the implements with which modern science has provided it, to meet any army of equal members, equipped as Napoleon's armies were equipped, the difference in power of the modern army would be such that it would almost be able to deal with its enemy as civilized armies provided with fire-arms were at first able to deal with savages possessed only of bows and arrows. The artillery of the days of Napoleon would not be able to act at all, for our modern infantry can fire with effect at a distance greater than could Napoleon's big guns. Our artillery would be able to destroy Napoleon's army before either his artillery or infantry could act against us. Thus an army of 50,000 men of our own time must be reckoned as possessing at least the resisting power of 100,000 of the days of Napoleon. It is obvious therefore that the relationship between time, distance, and the resisting power of armies has been greatly affected by the change in the character of weapons, and that calculations as to what a superior army can do in a given time to break up the force of an army opposing it, and to be free to deal with another army, are greatly modified.

There is another element which has largely to be taken into account in our modern battles. The expenditure of ammunition is, from the rapidity of fire, enormous. Even in the days of Napoleon it was extremely difficult, as his own words after the battle of Ligny show, for a victorious army rapidly to turn upon a second force which had not been engaged, because of the time required for filling up the empty ammunition waggons and the men's cartouches. These difficulties under our conditions of warfare are therefore immeasurably increased.

Again, in order that an army may nowadays be isolated in the way in which Napoleon in 1805 cut off the army of Mack in Ulm and utterly destroyed it, many conditions have to be secured which were not needed then. The telegraph is a formidable enemy to such an operation. The newspapers are a still greater. When MacMahon in 1870 attempted his disastrous march to the relief of Bazaine in Metz, to the success of which secrecy was essential, his movements first became known to the Prussian headquarters through French and English journals. Thus the rapid intercommunication between town and town, capital and capital, which is now extended in all directions over Europe to an extent that makes it extremely difficult to completely prevent news of all kinds from leaking out, is an element that cannot be neglected in any strategical calculations. The change in this respect is strikingly shown by the fact that seven weeks elapsed before the news of Trafalgar reached Naples. Furthermore, distant parts of an army may, under certain conditions, be in point of time much more closely connected than they formerly were because of the facilities afforded by railways and telegraphs. There are a variety of other elements less important individually than as all contributing to the same result, which must not be ignored,—the facilities afforded for the supply of armies by compressed food and compressed forage, the enormously extended area which caters for the feeding of the European populations and the organization of the commerce of the world rendering all which that area yields rapidly available, and, lastly, the continually improving methods of machine transport by road, bicycles, tricycles, &c., making it possible to effect rapid movements without forage at all.

Furthermore, not only have we to deal with new material conditions, but, as already observed, the armies which have to be led under these new circumstances have themselves been profoundly changed, not only in their armament but in the very spirit, discipline, and organization by which they are held together. What is true of the private, of the sergeant, of the captain, in his relations with superiors, is even truer of the leader of the brigade, of the division, of the army-corps, of the co-operating army. The whole method of the Prussian discipline and organization, as it showed itself in 1870, implied an intelligent independence of action in all ranks that most seriously affected the strategical operations. In fact, in that campaign two very noteworthy points may be observed. From the first battle at Weissenburg up to and including Gravelotte, the peculiar feature of the war was that the German successes at each action—Weissenburg, Wörth, Spicheren, Colombey-Nouilly, Mars-la-Tour—were much more important in their strategical than in their tactical aspect,—much more important, that is to say, in their general influence on the campaign than in the severity of the losses in men and material inflicted on the enemy. The losses in battle were in fact greater on the side of the victors than on that of the vanquished. Yet, secondly, each of these actions, up to but not including Gravelotte, was brought on by the determination of subordinate leaders, and was not designed beforehand either by the king's headquarters or by the headquarters of any one of the three armies. It cannot of course be denied that there was an element of danger in this way of managing a campaign. But the general who attempts to carry out a modern campaign without having realized the nature of this strictly strategical experience is reckoning without his host. Armies now occupy, even when in numbers similar to those of the past, distances vastly greater than was the case in former times. One of two things must happen: either a general must attempt to prescribe the action of his subordinate leaders with a rigidity which nowadays will continually prevent them from carrying out what would be his wishes could he be on the spot to advise them; or he will find that he has, as best he may, to make his strategical movements fit into events which have not been previously designed by himself. The Prussian headquarters, realizing fully the dangers involved in the plan which they, in fact yielding to necessity, accepted, found no fault with the generals who had initiated battles which had proved successful, fearing to do more injury to the spirit of the army than would be compensated by any other advantage. Nevertheless the notes of warning thrown out in the official history of the war are clear and unmistakable. To us it appears that this condition of things is an element in modern war to be foreseen and prepared for, that it represents, not an accident of the 1870 campaign, but an almost inevitable consequence of the present condition of armies. It was their high spirit, their high training, their knowledge of war, which made the German leaders so hard to keep within the leash when they saw the prey before them, and realized that it was a matter of moments whether it could be seized or not. There is nothing like this campaign, in the peculiar mode in which its strategical aspects developed, in all the past history of war.

Changes since time of Napoleon.

It would appear, therefore, that it tends to mislead a man who is anxious to consider what combinations are open to a general in the field in our day, to assure him that strategy has undergone no change since the days of Napoleon. No doubt a soldier who had never considered how or why Napoleon triumphed over his opponents, and when and why he failed, would have very little chance of solving aright the problems of a modern campaign. The handling of armies is, before all things, in the infinite variety of its elements, a dealing with human nature, under certain peculiar conditions, a play of mind against mind, and only by a study of the masters of the game can some of its experiences be gathered. If the changed conditions under which a modern war now takes place have been realized, then all study of the martial experiences of the past will in its own degree have value. We doubt extremely if any man can fairly appreciate the character of the campaign of

1866, or the campaign of 1870, who knows nothing of the campaigns of Napoleon. To take, for instance, the earlier of the two, the Prussian strategy in it has been the subject of much dispute; and those who think that questions of war can be settled by quoting maxims of Napoleon, or of other great generals, find no difficulty in picking out sayings of his that would condemn without excuse the scheme of the Prussian campaign. Certainly we should ou selves be sorry to suggest that it is the one satisfactory model for future guidance under analogous circumstances. To us it seems that its value, as a sample of what may be done in war, depends on a careful comparison of the handling of the Prussian armies, under the conditions in which they had to act, with the mode in which Napoleon and other great generals acted under their own conditions. The point in which the Prussians offended against the received maxims of Napoleon lay in their attempting to pass the Bohemian mountains in two separate armies,—one from Silesia, one from Saxony and Prussia. The Prussian headquarters remained at Berlin in telegraphic connexion with both armies up to the moment when the junction of the two had been so far effected that they were able to communicate with each other. Now Napoleon in many letters, more especially those addressed to his brother Joseph in Spain, has condemned the attempt to arrange complicated schemes for the co-operation of armies acting from different bases of supply. His reason is that such complicated schemes are rarely worked out as they are intended to be. For our own part we do not believe that the warning from the vast experience on which Napoleon's views were based has ceased to be of practical importance. We think that it ought to be present to the minds of all who are working out the plan of a campaign, and that the simpler, the less complicated, the less dependent on the successful combination of a number of different elements the plan is the more likely is it to be successful. But we think also that the actual circumstances of each case as a whole must be taken into account, and that in the instance of the campaign under consideration the Prussian headquarters were fully justified in the method they adopted. Such an operation indeed would not have been safe or wise in the days of Napoleon (see below); but for the moment our contention is that the modifications of the art of war which are necessitated by modern conditions extend to all its branches, and that criticism of modern campaigns which is based upon maxims derived from the past, without taking account of those new circumstances, is unsound and untrue. Few things are more unsafe in war than to judge by isolated cases of success alone, as to the soundness of the principles and the capacity of the leaders concerned in bringing about the successful result. The importance of military success is, in Britain more especially, apt to be measured much more by the national interest and national excitement which the result occasions than by any careful estimate of the difficulties actually overcome and the capacity for future command exhibited by the triumphant leader. To take illustrations sufficiently distant from our own days:—scarcely any victory, naval or military, has ever excited wilder enthusiasm in England than the capture of Porto Bello by Vernon in 1725; scarcely any disaster, the most disgraceful that ever occurred, caused greater horror and alarm in England than the return of Moore's expedition from Corunna in January 1809. Yet, as subsequent events showed, Vernon was by no means a very able admiral; and, on the other hand, as all who have really studied the Corunna campaign well know, few have been ever conducted with more conspicuous ability or would have justified a higher confidence in the general. It is thus of the greatest importance that statesmen at least should not be carried away by the sort of hasty criticism which deals in glib phrases, and avoids reasoned examination of facts. The maxims of Napoleon may be as easily kiln-dried and deprived of life as those of Frederick had been by the Prussian army of Jena, which was so sure of defeating the upstart aspirant to military supremacy.

Merit not necessarily to be estimated by success.

To sum up, then, what has been said on the art of war. There is no royal road to the knowledge of the art of handling armies any more than to that of any other branch of human activity. All that the best summary on that subject can profess to do for a reader is to assist him in undertaking a methodic study for himself of the principles which have guided great commanders, of the experiences of those who have fought in great battles and great campaigns, in endeavouring to put himself in their place so as to see with their eyes, hear with their ears, and realize the passions which influenced them, and the circumstances under which their decisions had to be formed.

It is not to be forgotten that even a commonplace critic may find it easy, when all the facts are fairly laid before him, to judge what ought to have been done in a given emergency. "La critique est facile, l'art est difficile," was the motto which Muffling, the very able representative of the Prussian army at Wellington's headquarters in 1815, chose for the title-page of his studies of war. The historical student has at least one advantage which is always and absolutely denied to the general. He may never, for many reasons, have an altogether correct and a completely true picture of all the circumstances which occurred on a given day, but he has a far more complete one than could possibly be before the general at the moment when he formed his decisions. Still more, he has far better materials for judgment than any of the minor actors who had themselves to decide what they ought to do, within the limitations of the orders they received, on most incomplete knowledge of what others were doing at distant parts of the field, of the positions and designs of the enemy, and of many other facts which may now be known with certainty by any one who will read what happened. He who would prepare himself in any measure for criticizing aright must put himself in the place of the soldier who has to choose,—must realize the conditions of personal danger, of noise, of passion, of incomplete and constantly misleading information, of disorder, confusion, panic, excitement, under which decisions are to be formed that must be calm and cool though they involve the lives of thousands of men, the fate of nations, and the course of history, and yet must be given then and there, for the lost moment will not return. Then he will perhaps perceive that after all the question whether he would himself have given the right decision, no matter what his previous training may have been, will be more a question of character than of knowledge. Nevertheless he is much more likely to decide aright if he has in his mind some large knowledge of the accumulated experience of the past than if, without anything to guide him, he judges by a so-called "common sense" which has already led him to ignore the earnest advice of those who have been themselves most successful in war. He is still more likely to decide aright, if, after he has acquired some general knowledge of the experience of the past, his judgment has been exercised by considering under assigned conditions what course he would actually choose to adopt. This is the method of peace preparation for war in which the Prussian officers of our day have been most carefully trained. In all their current works on the study of war they insist on the importance of this formation of the judgment and this training of choice as a matter of the utmost importance. All their most important military educational works take the form of "studies" or problems. The use of the war game and the training given by peace-manœuvres, as well as all regimental instruction, are adapted to the same end.[1]

STRATEGY.

The character of all military operations, whether those of strategy or tactics, is mainly determined by the nature of the armies engaged in them. An army as it exists in the field owes its constitution largely to those military institutions which have been fully described for each of the armies of our time under ARMY. But an army in the field differs considerably in each case from that which has been described as "the machine in a state of rest." This will be obvious at once if we consider the first question which attracts the attention of a commander about to lead an army in war. He has to choose the line of operations along which his army will act. The considerations which determine his choice are mainly connected with the necessity he is under of providing at all times for the supply of his army with food, forage, and ammunition, whilst he directs it against the point at which he is to strike.

Supplies.

In order that, for actual fighting purposes and during war, "that vast and complicated machine," an army, may so act "that the whole aggregate force of its numerous parts may be exerted in any direction and on any point required," the necessities of the individual soldier must be so provided for as not to hamper its working. A body of even thirty thousand men occupies a very considerable space, and requires an amount of food that completely disturbs the ordinary peace arrangements of most places at which it arrives in the course of its movements. Hence, apart from the large means of transport, such as a great fleet or ample railway communication, which may be sometimes used to carry a whole army to a given destination, an army requires what is known as "transport" for an altogether different purpose. The food and ammunition must be distributed to the several battalions of soldiers composing the army from the points at which it has been collected, and within the battalions it will often be necessary to distribute it by transport to the men. Similarly for the conveyance of the sick and wounded of an army transport is required. In former days the arrangements which were made to provide an army with what was needed in this way were clumsy in the extreme. It will be remembered that during the Peninsular War the Duke of Wellington was necessarily so much occupied with this question of food and supply that he used humorously to say that he did not know that he was much of a general, but he prided himself upon being a first-rate commissariat officer. As long as all armies depended upon the services of country carts and undisciplined drivers it was always possible to carry on war by these means. An army which, like the British in the Peninsula, fought continuously in the same country for six years, gained an enormous advantage by the gradual training and discipline of its transport drivers and commissariat employés. But now that the great nations of the continent of Europe have adopted a system by which all the population is available for military service, the result is that from the moment of declaration of war a modern army enters upon a campaign with the whole of its "transport," using the term in the sense we have employed, as definitely a part of the disciplined army as its infantry, its cavalry, or artillery are. It is scarcely possible to exaggerate the importance of this change in facilitating the operations of an army in the field. The British army stands at a very great disadvantage in this respect, from the fact that the population outside the fighting ranks is not, like that of Germany or France, ready to take up its place in the departments which cater for supply and transport. This modern perfecting of the efficiency of the interior transport of an army is a new strategical weapon in the hands of a general, to be reckoned among those spoken of in the earlier part of this article. Whether with the British army in an imperfect degree, or in a Continental army more completely, this transport must be understood to be as much a part of a modern army as any of its "arms." When, during a campaign, an infantry battalion is moved by train, it, unless for a very especial emergency, requires to have with it the waggons and carts which form what is called its "regimental transport." Other transport is required to carry the more general stores needed for a brigade, a division, or an army-corps. Thus each unit of an army, if it is to remain in a condition of fighting efficiency, requires to have with it a great number of horses and carts. It is impossible to realize the nature of the problems involved in the movements of armies unless this condition is kept in mind. For instance, when the British were moving to Ismailia in 1882, it was no uncommon assumption of the critics who at home watched the operations as they went on that within a day or two at the outside the small force, not exceeding about 10,000 men, which at first moved thither from Alexandria, had effected its landing. Had it been a body of 10,000 travellers landing from a variety of ships, to be provided for by the civil arrangements of the country after they had landed, that might not have been an exaggerated estimate of what was possible. But in fact the great ships were carrying not only 10,000 travellers,[2] but great quantities of stores of all kinds, of ammunition, of railway rolling-stock, of engineer equipment, of waggons and of horses. The landing of these and their passage up a narrow causeway was necessarily a very elaborate and slow operation. The whole scheme of the campaign had to take account of the time which such work would take, and, in fact, as a consequence of it, more than half the force to be ultimately employed was left either at Alexandria or at sea, and only arrived at Ismailia many days afterwards, when the landing of the first part had advanced considerably.

Transport.

The same difficulty in rapidly transferring an army, chiefly because of its attendant departments, affects all strategical movements by railway. The embarking of troops on a railway, and their disembarking from the carriages, is an operation of such slowness that for comparatively short journeys it is actually quicker for troops to march than to move by railway. The miscalculations and mistakes which were made so recently as 1870 by the French army, from failure to understand these facts, led often to the most disastrous consequences. In one instance Gambetta, insisting on sending troops by railway which Aurelle de Palladines had wished to march, hampered the operations of that veteran by the delay which was thus imposed upon certain portions of the army. There is, in fact, between the distance to be moved over and the number of troops to be moved by a line of railway a proportion which determines whether it is a more rapid operation to march or to travel by railway. In a pamphlet published shortly after the war the French emperor attributed his disasters to the general ignorance of his army as to the conditions involved in railway transport.

Continuity of supplies.

An army in the field, however, in addition to having transport present with it for distribution, needs to be able to replenish its supplies; and, though in fertile countries like France the feeding of the army may be greatly assisted by requisitions or by opening markets, it is impossible to depend for existence on these alone.

[1] We are indebted to the Volunteer Tactical Society of Manchester for by far the best essay we have seen in any language on the history and use of the war game—that by Captain Spenser Wilkinson—and for the beginning of a series of translations of exercises in strategy and tactics by some of the ablest German soldiers of the day.

[2] The entire army employed in Egypt was about 30,000 strong. Only the force which first landed at Ismailia is here spoken of.

Fresh supplies of ammunition at least must be continually received from a secure source, and the means must be available for feeding the army in case the resources of the country fail. Nowadays, and in most countries, the main line of supply is carried along lines of railway; but, as these are always liable to be destroyed by a retreating enemy, transport, independent of that which is required merely for distribution, must be provided in the form of waggons, carts, or pack animals sufficient to supply, for at least some days, the entire army.

Line of communications.

The source from which an army is supplied is usually spoken of as its "base" or its "base of supply." The direction in which, looking forward, a general proposes to advance, and along which it will be necessary to arrange for supply, is spoken of as his "line of operations." The direction along which the army, having already advanced to some distance from its base, is supplied, is spoken of as its "line of communications." Now, as the line of communications may come to be of great length as an army advances, and as the army needs to have its fighting strength available in the front when it is engaged with the enemy, it is clear that the long lines of road or railway along which the food and ammunition are moving forward, while parties of sick and wounded men are going backward, become weak points in its condition, which must be jealously guarded, but are difficult adequately to protect throughout their length, without detracting too much from the force in the front. In modern war the effort of the general is directed to maintaining in its full efficiency "the vast and complicated machine" which he handles, and to breaking up and destroying the efficiency of that to which he is opposed. This is the central fact to be kept in mind. Generals and soldiers, long accustomed to look at war from this point of view, frequently embody their whole conception of strategy in a phrase which to a reader, taking it in its simple form, is apt to seem like a mere truism—that the great principle of strategy is to concentrate the largest possible force at the right moment at the decisive point. So stated, strategy may seem to have nothing exceptional in its nature, and to involve no study of the nature of the great organizations of men with which it is concerned. But, in fact, this study and this knowledge are presupposed by those who thus explain their art. It is because armies are not mere gatherings of armed men, but have a vitality of their own, that some very heavy blows may be struck against them without affecting a vital point, whilst a more skilfully directed stroke may destroy their whole future power of action. An army then, as it stands in the field, is of this character, that, while the fighting force directly opposed to the enemy is an organism which depends for its vitality upon the trained spirit of order, discipline, and enthusiasm or devotion which holds it together, and on the trained capacity for mutual and effective fighting co-operation which makes it act like one man, it has also, reaching far behind it, a long and weak tail, on the safety of which its very existence depends.

Now, if by employing a large portion, or the whole of his own force, against a smaller portion of the enemy's, a general can break up and defeat it, the advantage gained depends on the fact that he has broken up the organic unity of this portion. Even if, as may easily happen, he has lost more men than the enemy during the effort, that very little affects the importance of the result on the future of the campaign. The strength of armies cannot be measured by counting heads within the theatre of war. It depends upon the organized force that the general is able to use and to direct. During the earlier battles of the 1870 campaign, for instance, the Germans lost very many more men than the French, but at Weissenburg they broke up the organic efficiency of a French division of about 8000 men. At Wörth they broke up the organic efficiency of 40,000 men at least. After Wörth the French army which had fought there had for the time being ceased to be an effective fighting body at all. Throughout the campaign it never recovered efficiency. The German forces, on the other hand, though they had lost more fighting men than the French, had actually increased their own effective power. Their organic unity was retained, and the spirit which inspired it had been incalculably raised by victory. But if a general can in any way interfere with the source from which an enemy is obtaining his supplies of food, ammunition, and fresh men, he can diminish his fighting power as effectually as if he broke up the organic unity in battle. A body of men who are starving can as little be held in the bonds of organization as a body of men who are dispersed. Hence the slightest movement which threatens that long and weak tail already described obliges the general whose line of communications is threatened to take steps for its protection.

At first sight it is not very obvious, since each army possesses lightly movable troops—cavalry, mounted infantry, and the like—why these should not be able to pass round the front of the opposing army, and get at the unguarded parts of the roads and railways along which the supplies are moving. To some extent, during the American civil war, this was actually done by the great leaders of horsemen on either side,—Sheridan and Longstreet. In all probability a similar attempt will be made in future wars by the great bodies of Russian Cossacks, and perhaps by the cavalry of Germany, France, and Austria. But what facilitated the raids of the American cavalry of either army was the fact that they were moving in a country where all the people spoke the same language as themselves, and where they were sure to find sympathizers to supply them with needed information. Under ordinary circumstances the difficulty is that each army faces the other without any approach to complete knowledge of the distribution of the troops opposed to it. The part of the enemy's line of communication which is nearest to you is also the part nearest to the main body of that enemy's own army. In order to get at some parts of his communications which would be out of reach of support from the main army, it would be necessary to send the assailing light troops to points several marches in rear. This involves a long détour, an elaborately prepared march, and the risk that the enemy may become aware of what is designed. In fact, to use the forcible illustration which Clausewitz has employed to explain the situation in which the leader of such a raid finds himself, he is like a man entering a dark room full of assailants, never knowing when or whence a blow may be struck against him.

The situation is altogether changed if, instead of the two armies fronting one another directly, one of the two is able to make its movements in such a way that, while it securely covers its own line of communications, its direct march forward threatens to strike the line of communications of the enemy. Then the light troops can at once strike the most exposed parts in all security. Under those circumstances the army whose communications are threatened is obliged immediately, for fear of losing its means of existence, to turn to face its opponents. The advantage so gained by the army which has obliged its enemy to conform to its movement is very great. For the choice of position can no longer be made by the assailed army solely with the view to gaining success in battle. It may be obliged to fight in a position tactically disadvantageous, and if it is defeated the defeat is almost certain to be fatal: for it will be driven away from the means of replenishing supplies. On the other hand, the army to which it is opposed, if obliged by ill-success in action to retreat, falls securely back upon fresh supplies, and suffers only in proportion to the extent of its actual defeat on the battle-field.

Aims of strategy.

Thus the aims of strategy directed against the actual condition of the armies of our time are twofold,—first, to break up the organic force of the opposing army by dealing in concentrated force with fractions of the enemy, and secondly, to threaten, and if possible to destroy, the enemy's connexion with the sources from which he draws his supplies. Failing either of these opportunities, a superior army may nevertheless endeavour to force on a decisive action in order to make its superiority tell. In other words, in that case the aim of strategy becomes that of securing a decided tactical advantage. It might be supposed, since these facts are known to all men who are at all likely to be placed in the command of armies in the field, that opportunities would rarely occur for delivering blows of the kind described. In fact, the difficulties in the arrangements for the movement of armies are so great, and the difficulties in obtaining information of what is going on in a theatre of war are so serious, that such chances are presented in almost every campaign. Thus in the 1870 campaign the Germans, after first breaking up comparatively small fractions of the French army at Weissenburg, Wörth, and Spicheren, succeeded in separating one great mass of the French army under Bazaine from the other under MacMahon, and in separately crushing them. In the 1877–78 campaign the Russian army in Asia Minor advanced westwards past Kars against Erzeroum, driving Mouktar Pasha back before it; but the arrival of a fresh hostile force from the neighbourhood of Van in the south, which, marching northwards upon Bayazid, struck directly upon the line of communications of the Russian army, produced an immediate collapse of the whole movement. The Russian army was obliged to fall back at once. Similarly, in Europe the Russian forces advancing from Tirnova had pushed their advance across the Balkans towards Adrianople, when the arrival of Osman Pasha's army, moving from Widdin upon Plevna at right angles to their line of communications, caused the whole movement to collapse, and obliged the Russians to turn their attention to the force which thus threatened them.

Relations of strategy and tactics illustrated.

This movement of Osman Pasha's illustrates very happily several points in the relation between strategy and tactics. In the first place, Osman's move was obviously in its general character, in what we call its strategical aspect, an offensive one directed against the most vital point of the Russian field of campaign, the bridge by which they had passed the Danube at Sistova. The threatening character of the position he took up obliged the Russians in some way to dispose of his force. Very unwisely they engaged in a series of ill-prepared and ill-directed attacks upon him. The result was so completely to shatter their forces that, had Osman advanced, after his final success, against Sistova, the small Russian remnant between him and the Danube must have been driven into the river, and in all probability all the Russian forces which had crossed it would have been destroyed. But, as he remained obstinately within his field fortress at Plevna, the Russians in their turn gradually succeeded in cutting off his communications, and in obliging him to surrender that which they could not take. Thus it is clear how a site for an army may be so chosen as, from its strategical character, to induce if not to compel an enemy to attack it. It is also clear that an army fighting in a well-chosen and well-fortified position, acting on the defensive, may inflict serious defeat upon forces superior to it in numbers. Finally, it is clear that such an army will, in the long run, lose all the advantages of its success, if it is not able to advance and to act offensively when the opportunity is presented to it. It has been convenient to illustrate these points from the most recent campaign in Europe, but they had been already deduced and were fully understood long before that campaign had been entered on. They illustrate the way in which the experience of the past indicates what will happen in future war. The arrival of Osman Pasha at Plevna was a complete surprise to the Russians. Its disastrous effect for them was largely due to this cause. Apparently the same thing is true of the arrival of the Van forces at Bayazid. Yet, at the time, the existence of the Turkish forces both at Van and Plevna was known in London. The want of information at the Russian headquarters appears therefore to suggest the most extraordinary negligence on the part of the Russian staff. In any case, the vital effect upon a campaign of being able to procure the best information in any way obtainable can hardly be exaggerated. Cavalry being the arm employed to spread round an army in all directions, to gain information and to conceal the movements of the army, is on this account often justly called the strategical arm.

Secrecy of operations essential

In whatever way strategy is employed surprise and concealment are essential to its success. On this account it will continually happen, in selecting a line of operations or a scheme of campaign, that the most important point of all is to carry out just what an enemy does not expect. Very often successful campaigns, the method of which has been subsequently much criticized, have owed their success to the fact that, from a nice calculation of time and distance, the successful general has seen that he could carry through an operation dangerous in itself but sure not to be the one expected by his opponent. For the same reason, in all the most brilliant and successful efforts of strategic skill, steps have been taken beforehand to carry out the preliminary movements of an army in such a way as to leave an enemy up to the last moment uncertain in what direction the blow would be struck. Usually also some special effort has been made to induce the enemy to believe that he would be attacked in some very different direction from that intended.

One of the means by which this has been most successfully accomplished is the selection of the point of concentration prior to the opening of a campaign. The motives and causes for this "concentration" require, however, some explanation. It is much more easy to feed and supply an army which is distributed over a considerable area than one which is closely concentrated for the purposes of action. Furthermore, armies when moving along roads occupy a very great length. The head of the column is more or less distant from the rear in proportion to the number of troops, waggons, and animals that march by the same road. Hence it follows that the more roads an army can employ in its march the more easy will it be for its several parts to reach a required point at the same moment. Therefore, for facility of supply and for facility of movement, as long as an army is out of reach of an enemy, a considerable dispersion is advisable. But it is vitally necessary to an army entering on a campaign to be able to get all its parts together before there is any possibility of an enemy's attacking it. Otherwise it would be in the position of exposing some of its fragments to the danger of being separately attacked by superior forces of the enemy, and having their efficiency destroyed before they could be supported. Hence a concentration out of reach of an enemy's concentrated army is the preliminary necessity of every campaign.

Though it is nearly always to the advantage of a body of troops which comes in contact with a hostile force inferior to it in fighting power to fight with it and

Detention of a large force by a small one.

destroy its organic unity, yet a small force may for a time succeed in delaying the movements of one very superior to it. The fighting power of an army depends upon the number of weapons that it is able to bring to bear upon its enemy. Now, as for rapid movement that does not fatigue the men an army is ordinarily obliged to march along roads, it follows that the number of weapons available for fighting in front of the line of march is very small. Hence, though a general may have under his command a very large body of troops, representing a very great amount of power when that power is developed, yet as long as he is simply marching forward he cannot immediately use that power at the point which the head of his column has reached. In order to do so he must bring those men who are far away from the front up to a position in which they can use their arms. Such an operation often takes a very long time. The time becomes much longer if, instead of marching on a road through open country or between hedge-rows, he has great mountain precipices on either side of him, so that he cannot easily get his men out of the path in which they are. Or again, if he finds that it is necessary for him to develop the power of his army in order to force his way across a bridge over a river, it may be necessary for him in the first instance to extend his artillery and infantry along the side of the stream nearest him in order to use his weapons; and then, when he wants to resume his march, he may have to bring them back again to the bridge. These are instances of the delay which is imposed upon armies which have to force their way through "defiles."

Now, if a small force is employed in delaying a larger one, which it does not intend seriously to engage, its object almost always is to induce the larger one thus to "deploy" its force from the march to a position for fighting, purposing itself to escape before the enemy seriously attacks it. It may seem at first that, as the small force has itself necessarily to pass from the march formation to the fighting position and to return again to the march, there is no gain of time. But, in fact, if the successive positions be judiciously chosen for the small force, it is extremely difficult for the general commanding the superior army to know what number of enemies he has before him. If, not wishing to delay the movement of his army, he deploys too small a force, the defender may use his whole power to inflict a crushing defeat upon this before it can be supported. If, on the other hand, he deploys a force sufficient to destroy the body opposed to him, this must involve a long delay, and very probably he will find, when he moves to attack, that the defensive force is already gone, or has left only some light troops to make a show up to the last. By such means again and again in war a small force employed in well-chosen ground has been able to hamper the movements of a superior body and to gain time for other operations. The different applications of this detaining power of small bodies are so numerous that hardly any problems either of strategy or tactics are intelligible unless its nature is understood. The essence of it lies in the smaller body not allowing itself to become so engaged as to have its organic unity destroyed by defeat.

The simplest application of this detaining power of small bodies occurs in this way. Suppose, as often happens, that two allied armies, or two parts of the same army, are moving to unite against an enemy. It may happen that by skilful dispositions or the chance of war the general engaged against them is able to interpose between them whilst they are still several marches apart from one another. Suppose now that in a country favourable to such an operation he employs a small portion of his own force to delay the march of one of his opponents, whilst he throws the bulk of his forces against the other. In attempting to defeat this body before it can receive support he holds a position of very great advantage. This is the situation which is commonly described by saying that the general in question is acting on "interior lines" against the two armies opposed to him. But it is vitally important to his success in this matter that he shall succeed in defeating one of his opponents whilst the other is still some marches off, otherwise their union against him on the field of battle may, from the very fact of their striking his position from different directions, prove even more disastrous to him than if he had allowed them to unite before he attacked them. Thus when Napoleon, during the Waterloo campaign, had broken in at Charleroi upon the intended point of concentration of the allied armies, he, with Ney opposing Wellington at Quatre-Bras long before the English army was concentrated, and himself able to act with the bulk of his forces against Blücher at Ligny before the Prussian army was fully concentrated, was acting in the most perfect way upon interior lines. But, when at Waterloo, whilst he was still engaged with Wellington in his front, Blücher broke in upon his flank, though the bulk of the French army was still between its opponents, that was a position of disaster. During the 1866 campaign the Prussians crossed the Bohemian mountains in two separate armies,—one from Silesia under the crown prince, one from Saxony and Prussia under Prince Frederick Charles. Had the army under the Austrian commander Benedek been concentrated in Bohemia, so that, whilst one part of his forces detained either the crown prince or Prince Frederick Charles, the main body had been thrown against the other, the general would have gained all the advantages of interior lines. But, when on the field of Sadowa, whilst Benedek was still fiercely engaged against the army of Frederick Charles in front, the crown prince broke upon his flank, though the Austrian army was still in one sense between the two Prussian armies, it was so only in a sense disastrous for it. This event, in which an army attempting to take advantage of the separation of two opponents is crushed between them on the field of battle, is described by German soldiers by the phrase that such an army is taken "tactically between them" ("in der taktischen Mitte").

The operation of acting on interior lines was the favourite form of Napoleon's strategy. He would have condemned unhesitatingly the attempt to carry out any plan of campaign which involved such a combination as the Prussians attempted in 1866. But in his day armies were not connected by telegraph. In speaking of the concentration of armies prior to a campaign as necessarily made out of reach of a concentrated enemy there is this reservation to be noted. If two armies acting against a third can so nicely time their union as to strike against the enemy on the field of battle within a few hours of one another, they gain all the advantage of getting their enemy "tactically between them." The difficulties, however, of this nice adjustment of time are so great that no prudent commander would deliberately beforehand arrange his general concentration in this way on the field of battle. Nevertheless, the fact that it is sufficient for the armies to have effected their junction so nearly as to be within reach of mutual support on a field of battle considerably enlarges the area within which their union can be accomplished. Thus at the beginning of the 1866 campaign the Prussians had fixed the point of junction of their two armies at Gitchin; but, though it would have been possible for them to have joined their forces on June 30, they did not carry out this actual meeting. They were content with the fact that the two armies were by June 30 in close supporting distance of one another.

They only actually met on the field of battle of Sadowa. The effect of the selection of a point of concentration, as tending to leave an enemy uncertain as to the direction which a general purposes afterwards to take, can hardly be better illustrated than by Napoleon's concentration in the Waterloo campaign. By gathering his army at Philippeville, Beaumont, and Solre, he threatened Mons more directly than he threatened Charleroi, and thereby tended to prevent his enemies from concentrating against the point of his intended attack.

Depôts of supplies.

There is a peculiarity in the strategical aspect of British campaigns beyond sea against savage tribes which requires a short explanation. Usually the difficulty lies in transporting from the base towards the front a sufficient quantity of provisions without eating them up on the road. Since the animals and men employed in transporting food and ammunition must themselves be fed, it is evident that if we send supplies for a day's journey forward the balance available for feeding the troops will be the amount the transport can carry, less two days' food for themselves, that is one day forward and one day in coming back. Similarly, for a journey of eight days to the front sixteen days' food for the carrying animals and men will have to be deducted. In fact, more than this will be required, because when the journey is extended beyond a certain limit there must be occasional rest days. It is clear that if, as was the case in Abyssinia, in Ashantee, in the movement on Sikukuni's country, and, though with different transport, on the Nile and in Egypt, a march of many days beyond all supplies of food not carried by the transport has to be made, a point will be reached at which the animals begin to eat up all the food they carry. This can only be met by the system of depôting. That is to say, an accumulation of large supplies of food is made as far forward on the road as possible, and then from that point it is again pushed forward by one relay of transport whilst others fill it up from behind. But here again another point arises. If the whole army to be employed on the expedition were pushed forward to the front where the supplies are being accumulated, these supplies would be eaten up as fast as they arrived. The fewer the troops in the front the more rapid will be the accumulation. Hence the great secret of a rapid advance in this case is to keep in front only as many troops as are necessary, when well entrenched, to guard the accumulation of supplies. The more completely all others are kept back from the front the sooner will the expedition achieve the object for which it is employed. These are incidents which repeat themselves on every English expedition, while at the same time complaints are continually being made of the generals during the course of the campaign for the delay involved in their doing the very thing which hastens achievement.

Tactics.

In speaking of the changes which have affected strategy, we declared our belief that the *weapons* of strategy have changed since the Napoleonic era even more completely than those of tactics. It now becomes necessary to define the limits of what this statement implies. We have shown how, even in questions of strategy, the spirit of subordination and the nature and kind of co-operation which a minor leader has to give to his commander-in-chief have been affected by the changes in the size of armies, the scope of operations, and the developed facilities of communication and supply. This change, however, of the spirit of organization is, in so far as regards strategy, a comparatively secondary matter. Among the few men engaged in the actual command of armies and army corps, it is almost an affair of personal arrangement and of mutual understanding how far the subordinate acts independently, and how far he merely carries out the precise directions of his superior. Where men are so well known to one another as were, for instance, the leaders of armies and army corps of the Germans during the campaign of 1870, the generals of such great bodies as these could judge from personal knowledge of the characters of those under whom they were acting what degree of latitude to allow themselves in the interpretation of orders. We see the evidence of this everywhere. This personal confidence, this mutual knowledge of one another among the higher leaders of armies, has become an essential instrument of modern war. The general who has men under him whom he does not know and cannot trust suffers now in a degree in which he never suffered before.

But when we come to compare the effect of modern changes on the spirit of strategy, in these matters of discipline, with its effect on tactics, there is no proportion between the two.

Importance of mechanical drill.

Discipline is the very life-blood of an army, and it is on the field of battle, that is, within the province of tactics, that it shows its potency. To interfere in any way with this spirit, as it determines the power of the commander over his men in the presence of the enemy and under the stress of battle, to introduce the least malignant influence into it, is to blood-poison the army. Therefore, as no army can nowadays hope, in presence of a modern enemy armed with the weapons of to-day, to carry out a system of manœuvres in which discipline can be maintained with the old facility, and under conditions so favourable to it as those of the past, we must approach the subject with a caution proportioned to its vital importance. Curiously enough it is from an English scientific author, from Mr Darwin, that one of the ablest of recent German writers on war has borrowed the penetrating phrase which sums up the essential element, common to the discipline of the past with that of the present, which it is vital to us not to shake or to impair. The engrained habit of mutual confidence among all ranks of a regiment is the factor in its strength which attracted Mr Darwin's attention as the cause of its incalculable superiority in power over an armed mob. Baron von der Goltz accepts the statement as true, without reserve. When, however, we come to consider what has enabled armies to acquire this engrained habit, we are met by some very curious experiences. In the first place, the instinctive habit of obedience to a word of command, as coming from one who has the right and the duty to give that command, has to be carried into the very limbs of a man. When cultivated men of mature years entered the ranks of the British volunteers during the early stages of the movement, some very amusing protests appeared in print as to the dreary monotony of the mechanical contortions which represent the early phases of recruit drill. A certain pity or sympathy was expressed for the poor soldiers who had to spend their lives in such uninteresting tasks It would hardly be too much to say that the complaints of these very superior persons showed a want of philosophic acuteness, which is entirely absent from the minds of the most zealous volunteers of our day. No one understands better than these the fact that in the dull mechanical routine of those incidents of recruit drill is laid the foundation of all military power. The zealous barrister, who at thirty-five always found himself turning by mistake to the right when he was ordered to turn to the left, who found it impossible to supple his limbs in the required "extension motions," was unconsciously illustrating the weakness of the most zealous untrained armed man. With the best of wishes his body was so little under the command of his own mind and will that he could not, much as he wished it, place it at once under the command of anyone else. Much less could he cut out that disturbing element himself so far as to obey instinctively, and without a certain element of resisting individuality, the command he received.

Now the capacity to act together under the orders of one man can never be dispensed with under any of the conditions of modern war. The instinctive obedience of a rank of soldiers to the order to turn "Right about," when that order sends them back into the ground where shells are bursting and where bullets are raining, has been a power in fighting too great for us ever willingly to throw it away. Some humorous illustrations of its effect on soldiers, and of the victory-winning power which an even apparently unintelligent submission to this authority of instinct has given, more especially to English soldiers, are mentioned in the article ARMY (vol. ii. p. 589). In proportion as men understand war they value this effect, and would be unwilling even to diminish at a given moment actual loss of life if that diminution were secured by any sacrifice of this power. An old English battalion trained to the absolute perfection of such mechanical obedience was a splendid fighting instrument. No training, however perfect, to take advantage of ground, to seek cover, to glide on to the weak points of an enemy, will compensate, even in these days, a deficiency in that habit of utter self-abnegation, of entire subordination to the one purpose of united action under assigned orders. But, under the modern conditions of war, the loss inflicted within a given time by the terrible weapons now in the hands of all armies is so great that the very formations under which on a parade ground the armies of the past prepared to move in actual fighting under the orders of their commanders are mechanically as much as morally dissolved. Not even can the voice of the captain or the subaltern be heard, much less that of the lieutenant-colonel, above the din of breech-loaders and of shrapnel shells. It is not therefore with a light heart, not willingly, not as thinking that a dispersed order of fight is something in itself more powerful or more advantageous than a rigid formation in which ordered and orderly movement is easy, in which force can be concentrated, in which the habits of discipline can be more certainly maintained, but of dire necessity, that the most experienced soldiers of our day have come to the absolute conviction that only by preparing armies for fighting in dispersed order can discipline be maintained at all. The great problem of modern tactics, in so far as it concerns actual fighting, which regulates everything else, is how to maintain the old unity under the new conditions which make it so difficult.

Further training now necessary.

Infantry.

This much at least we know, that from the moment that infantry are actually involved in a modern breech-loader fight all manœuvring has ceased to be possible. The natural and the necessary deduction from this is that the only influence which can be exercised upon such a fight by any but very subordinate leaders is to throw into it fresh bodies of men who till then have been retained in close formations. Now the experience of the 1870 battles showed clearly that the effect of fresh bodies thus thrown into a fight is very great indeed. Moreover, that experience showed further that the direction in which the fresh force is thrown into a contest already engaged between two bodies of infantry is vitally important in determining how great the effect of the blow so delivered will be. The tendency of any great fight is to break up into a series of partially independent actions. Therefore it almost always happens that in each of these there are on both sides certain weak points, which present opportunities to a skilful assailant. These arise either from circumstances of ground or from the inevitable disconnexion produced by isolated action of particular bodies of troops. Skill now consists in taking advantage of these opportunities, in anticipating the conditions under which they are likely to occur, in preparing to escape from similar dangers, and in pressing home a success. Here then is the way in which the organization spoken of above as the means of battle action makes itself felt. It is impossible now for the commander-in-chief of a great army to be ready at each part of a battle for one of these emergencies. Scarcely can the commander of a division of 10,000 men, or even the commander of 3000, meet all the local incidents that occur. At each stage of the hierarchy there is needed a man who, in proportion to the extent of the opportunity or the danger, is ready to seize or to meet it.

But among the means of doing this which the practical experience of the Prussians taught them is one which tends more and more to be forgotten as the experiences of the great campaign are lost in the distance of the past. As the phases of any battle now succeed one another a time comes when the fight sways forward, and many men are left behind out of the immediate region of the combat. Often these stragglers are more numerous than the men engaged in the actual shooting line. They may be in a wood or for some other reason out of the reach of the enemy's projectiles, or they may at all events not be severely exposed to them. What is wanted is to take advantage of this wasted power and to throw it into the fight. This can only be done effectively by getting the men into closed bodies, and so bringing them again under orders and discipline. This was what the Germans—or, to speak more accurately, the Prussians, who in all these respects were head and shoulders over all their German compatriots—habitually did.

The study then of the mode of preparing infantry for the fights of the future does not in these inner circumstances of battle consist in training them for some particular forms of attack nearly so much at least as in the following points:—

1. In accustoming the men, as soon as from any cause they find themselves thrown out of the actual fighting line and out of the stress of fire, to place themselves instinctively and as quickly as possible under the orders of some officer who can get them into order, and either lead them on or await the moment when the services of a formed body of men will become invaluable;

2. In accustoming officers to seek all opportunities for re-forming dispersed men at the earliest possible moment;

3. In maintaining such close order as is possible as long as it can be maintained without risking overwhelming loss of life and dire confusion,—hence therefore the breaking up into such small organized bodies as, by taking advantage of ground or other means, may be able to preserve unity of action longer than would be possible with greater masses;

4. In keeping up, by the action of the higher ranks of the military hierarchy, the fighting connexion between these bodies, by the judicious employment of fresh force or of reserves that have been made up out of men that have been already engaged;

5. In providing for the continual replenishment of ammunition close to the fighting line of at least all those who are not actually engaged in it, and the continually thrusting into the fighting line of men well supplied with ammunition to push forward the line, so that those who have exhausted their ammunition may be resupplied without having to fall back; and

6. Above all, in practice and training during peace in a mode of action which cannot be simply learnt on a parade-ground by help of drill-sergeant and words of command taught by rote.

We have taken first this question of the change which has taken place in infantry fighting, because it is on the forms of infantry fight that the changes in armament have produced their greatest effect, because the main substance of an army always consists of infantry, and because the changes which have occurred in the use of the other arms, artillery and cavalry, have been determined by the changes in infantry tactics and arms more than by any other cause, though the development of artillery armament has also affected them.

Now the danger which faces any British army under present conditions in preparing for modern battle lies in the fact that a long peace following upon the great wars of the end of the last and the beginning of the present century has tended to stereotype forms which were originally based upon the battle-experience of the past. There is a dread of change where change is required, because officers and men have come to look upon the great traditions of the past as sacred. In England men wish to follow in the footsteps of the soldiers who acquired an experience under Wellington such as no men since then have had. It is in its essence a sound and healthy feeling. But there is the greatest danger lest names should be put for facts, lest in the very act of servilely copying forms we should ignore altogether the principle which determined the action of our forefathers. They started from the experiences and necessities of the battle-field as these existed in their own day. They based their forms upon those necessities. If we would really imitate them we must in this do as they did. We cannot take their forms based on the battles of their own time, and then work forward from these forms to what we shall do on the battle-field now. We must frankly face the fact that, the character of battles having changed, we must work back from the conditions of our present battle-fields to the peace-forms which will prepare our soldiers for them.

Practical work.

Terms under such circumstances become confused. Men talk about the practice of forms in which their life is spent as "practical work." They look upon all experience gathered from the fields where shells actually burst and where infantry firearms are used to kill as "theoretical." The truth is exactly the opposite. Such merit as the older drill at present has is due to certain theoretical considerations which were at one time soundly deduced from practice in the past. The only practical work is that which tends to prepare men, not for the inspection of some general on a parade ground, but for actual war. An army is doing "practical" work in the preparation for its real duty, that of winning battles. It is employed on mischievous theoretical work, on false theory, whenever it is doing anything else.

Control drill.

Now this one thing is certain, that, whereas the great fighting formation of the past for British infantry was the line, that formation can be used no longer in actual fighting against troops armed with modern weapons, unless exceptionally in purely defensive positions, where its trained cohesion is of little importance, because cohesion is in any case easy. All rigid drill is at present based on the assumption that wheels of parts of this line are necessary in order to enable the troops to keep together shoulder to shoulder. What is required is not this, but that we shall obtain by complete organization down to the lowest units a command of fire and a command of groups. Of all the incidents of a modern fight that of which it is the hardest to give any conception to a man who has not seen infantry possessed of the enormous facilities for firing which are supplied by modern arms is the intense absorption in the mere fact of firing, which almost like a catalepsy takes possession of the man who is using his weapon against an enemy, or, as may often happen in close country, against nothing at all. Many of the rifles that were picked up on Majuba Hill were found, at the last moment when the Boers were closing, sighted to 800 yards. It is noted as a quite remarkable instance of presence of mind on the part of a Prussian sergeant during the attack on St Privat, that he personally took care that the men reduced their sights to the proper range as they advanced. Now this illustrates perfectly the kind of trained habit which we need by our modern drill to induce in men in action. We want to educate men so that they do not fire under the conditions of a catalepsy. Now experience has shown that this can only be done by having men who are not themselves firing trained to look after those who are firing, so that the fire may be regulated, effective, and deliberate. The men themselves must be trained to fire only under orders, and not under the influence of a tendency to fire merely to relieve their feelings. We cannot put better what is involved in these necessities than in the following words of Colonel J. H. A. Macdonald of the Queen's Edinburgh Rifle Volunteer Brigade:—

"How is this to be done? How but by so regularly, consistently, and persistently putting the soldier through the action of firing by orders that it shall be a second nature to fire his rifle only under control of his superior, and not otherwise. What is wanted is the conviction in the mind of every instructor, from the highest to the lowest, that his men should never leave a parade without having gained something in fire discipline,—that is, that fire control drill be one of the main points in view as a necessary part of the work to be performed on every occasion when men are being drilled, exercised, or inspected, from the moment that they know the rifle exercises until the day when they leave the service. Let some of the time which formerly was spent in a perpetual *form* drill to produce a military machine that had a steadiness in formation which nothing could shake be now spent in producing by a perpetual *control* drill a firing organism which shall have a steadiness in the use of fire which nothing can shake. The troops that shall be found most in the hands of the commander in the matter of fire will, *cæteris paribus*, be invincible."[1]

But in order that we may secure this end it is essential that the organization be carried down to the smallest groups within a company, and our drill must be adapted to deliver such groups as methodically and regularly as possible within the zone of fighting.

It does not appear that any adequate experiments have as yet been made to determine the means by which this can best be done. Experiments during peace time are in no sense wholly satisfactory. In order that they may be worked out properly they require to be watched at every stage by men who have closely studied the experiences of modern war, and know what has been done by other armies, who have learned from those experiences not slavishly to copy what was done by men who were themselves experimenting under the dread conditions of actual warfare, but to extract from them sound lessons for future guidance. To quote again from Colonel Macdonald.

"Would it not be wise to do what is done in other departments of military science, and give some facility for practical and exhaustive experiment? In all other departments practical experiment goes merrily and expensively on. Thousands of pounds are spent on a gun which penetrates another inch or two of armour. New and thicker plates are rolled. A new 'Big Will' is built, and again crashes through the armour with its first shot, and perhaps blows off its own muzzle with the second. Treasure-devouring sea monsters are built superseding one another at short intervals. Torpedoes, torpedo boats, and machine guns are subjected to crucial experiments. But from the nature of the material with which experiment has to be conducted in the case of the most important land fighting machine — the infantry—the circumstances are exactly reversed. Experiment would cost nothing; but, while inventors can experiment in armour metal, gun building, and rifling and explosives, before offering appliances to the Government, there can be no practical experiment with the only material out of which the infantry machine of war is made without order from authority. It is only by leave of the state, through its officers, that any proposals to improve the working can be tested, and—as is the case in all inventions—not only tested, but developed and improved by experiment. Almost all successful invention is the result of alternate thought and experiment. There is also the further difficulty that the proposers of tactical improvements are not independent men, but servants of the owners of the material. They cannot consistently with discipline proceed as other inventors are able to do. They cannot canvass higher officials, or exert extraneous influence. They may not use the soldiers who happen to be under their control as material for experiment.

"Further, even if it be permitted to them to exhibit these ideas experimentally, the material with which they must do so is not dead material, plastic and absolutely passive. They have to test

[1] *Common Sense on Parade, or Drill without Stays* (p. 118), by Colonel the Right Hon. J. H. A. Macdonald C.B., M.P., 1886.

their invention with materials which have been turned into a machine already on a different system, and have therefore a way of working which unconsciously at first militates against the display to the best advantage of the new idea."

These conclusions appear unanswerable. Though, for the reasons which are implied in the very sentences we have quoted, we are not as yet prepared absolutely to advocate any specific system, it appears to us that the method of working which has been suggested by Col. Macdonald promises such valuable results that it ought at least to be fairly tried on a large scale. It has received the warmest possible support from the best infantry soldiers of the English army—from Lord Wolseley, from Sir Donald Stewart, and many more. It has been approved in principle by many others, who have not had the opportunity of examining its practice. It has been successfully tried and experimented upon so far as peace-trials go, both at home and in the colonies, and has been greatly appreciated by those who have tried it. It consists in a method of permanently arranging a company in four ranks, so that from these the successive bodies of firing line supports and reserves may be successively sent forward. It has several important recommendations. It limits the front of a captain's command. By forming groups of eight men of those who stand side by side in the fours it carries organization down to the lowest point, while it tends to bind together, by the principle of comradeship, the supports who successively arrive to the men who are in front. By making this comradeship apply to those who form the two adjacent groups of four of the company when in line, it ought certainly to facilitate the re-formation of the company. At present if one man is lost in the front rank of a company, the whole have to be numbered again in order to enable it to form in a column of fours at all. On Col. Macdonald's system each group of eight being fixed, the company can be fitted together by the gathering of these groups in any order, so long as all are in their proper places within their own group of eight.

In any case, going back once more to the experience of the past, we are now at a time in these matters very like that which preceded the Peninsular War. The drill which was employed in the Peninsula was in all essentials worked out by Sir John Moore in a series of experiments conducted at the camp of Shorncliffe. No more important results were ever obtained by peace-training for war than those which were deduced from these experimental exercises. If we really reverence the great soldiers of the Peninsula, this is the way in which we shall honour them. We shall not do what they did not. We shall not accept from the traditions of the past forms which are not adapted to actual warfare. We shall not write drill books in the study or the bureau, and force field movements into conformity with them. We shall employ for the work of our great camps of exercise generals who have made an exhaustive study of the present conditions of warfare, and staff-officers who can assist them in their work. We shall experimentally try "those suggestions which have upon them any reasonably good stamp of approval by military men of skill." We shall really and crucially investigate them, "with opportunity afforded to proposers to meet difficulties that may be suggested." "Those proposals which can be defended from serious theoretical objections should be submitted to a few months' experiment in selected regiments, and reported on as to their practical working in the essential points of simplicity and uniformity of manœuvre, adaptability to circumstances arising, maintenance of order, retention of unity of commands, rapid recovery of exact tactical form, and fire control. Then let authority take what is best, it may be adopting here one detail and there another."[1]

[1] Colonel Macdonald, as above, p. 127.

The Russians at one time adopted and abandoned a system of working by groups of four. So far as we are able to perceive, Colonel Macdonald's system is not open to the objection which led the Russians to abandon their method of fours. They found that, when they had formed their groups under a "father" who became the leader, the men were so much attached to one another that as soon as one was wounded all remained with him, so that every time the enemy wounded one man four were put *hors de combat*. It is clear, on the one hand, that this is an objection that would not present itself in mere peace practice at all, so that the necessity for criticism applied at the time from actual experience of fighting shows itself forcibly. On the other hand, it by no means follows that the difficulty would not be overcome by such a closer association of groups as Colonel Macdonald's system appears to promise, and by a trained habit of trusting that the wounded will be properly cared for by the men assigned for that purpose, and a knowledge that the business of all those who are able to continue the fight is to ensure the safety of the wounded by securing victory.

It will be obvious from what we have already said that we do not believe that any army in Europe has as yet solved the question of the most effective mode of delivering infantry within the area of modern fight, and that nevertheless we believe that data now exist from which, with proper experiments, a method might be adopted which would at least give to that army which adopted it incalculable advantages in the earlier battles of a modern war. The one point that must be thoroughly realized is that the firearm of the present day has become the determining weapon, for the development of the efficiency of which all tactics must prepare the way.

That brings us to another matter of vital importance. As long as the shock tactics of the past were possible, the neat drills of the parade ground were the essence of soldiering, and therefore, when a few rifle regiments at first, and afterwards the army generally, had liberty to practise shooting, that was looked upon as an accidental and exceptional thing unconnected with the real business of the soldier, and therefore with his everyday life. This unfortunate divorce between the work at the butts and on the manœuvre-ground, once established in the habits of an army, cannot for many years be cured. It exists still. Yet every manœuvre in which careless aiming, careless expenditure of ammunition, and wrongly adjusted sights are permitted is a direct injury to the fighting efficiency of the force which manœuvres. Nothing else can compensate for the evil so done. Good shooting, and movements tending to give to good shooting and good weapons the greatest possible advantage, are next to a healthy morale the essence of modern fight.

Nevertheless, it is the training of the spirit of an army, the bringing home to all ranks of the objects now to be aimed at, that is the difficulty in all these matters. The very strength and power of discipline in its formation and engraining of habits is that which makes an army so hard to deal with when habits have to be changed.

In the present condition of the tactical question it has seemed to us essential to devote so much space and pains to the enforcing of these points that we can only lightly touch on several questions that have been most eagerly discussed in relation to infantry tactics.

Long-ra and reserved

The question of long-range fire against reserved fire is mainly a question between material and moral effect. It seems no doubt a strange thing, when we have enormously increased the range of modern weapons, that we should throw away that advantage, and allow an enemy without firing a shot at him to pass over a large area of ground where we could inflict loss on him. Undoubtedly, in so far as we can train picked shots to fire at long ranges, so as to disturb the movements of columns, and to interfere with artillery, it is well worth our while to do so. But with the utmost training that we can give them the mass of men in the ranks of an army never will become good shots at long ranges. Almost all fire, therefore, at long ranges becomes unaimed fire, and an enemy can to a great extent avoid exposing himself on the ground where the fortuitous rain of bullets is falling. Meantime the mere fact of firing having begun puts the troops who are firing almost beyond the reach of orders. Their own excitement and the noise together make it most difficult to give them any directions. Sights that have been fixed for the long range are not changed to the short. The fact that, despite all their efforts, the enemy continues to advance demoralizes them, and despite his losses encourages him. These are considerations which are not taken into account in the arguments of those who base their conclusions merely on the amount of loss which may be inflicted at very long ranges. Yet, at all events up to 1877, they had in actual fighting proved supreme. It may be the case that a very highly trained army, using long-range volley firing under effective control, might produce such loss upon an enemy approaching that it would make his actual attack upon a position impossible. What is certain is that, up to 1877, there had been no experience in war which proved that such long-ranged fire was as effective as fire carefully reserved for the ranges within which infantry can use their arm with the greatest effect.

Such at all events was the experience of the 1870 campaign, and it confirmed the experience of previous wars in certain respects which, as will have been seen from the above account, depend rather on the condition of men's minds than on the efficiency of weapons. Both, however, in the German army and in the French an immense impression was produced by the incidents of the attack on Plevna. There is no doubt that there the certainly unaimed fire of the Turks produced an enormous effect. Skobeleff, when he had at last succeeded in reaching the "Green Hill" in one of his own most brilliant efforts, found that there were no troops behind the slender line of skirmishers whom he had actually with him. All his reserves had melted away under the storm of bullets. If this experience could be accepted as representing a normal phase of a modern battle, the conclusion would be inevitable that so long as there are ample supplies of ammunition the effect of long-range fire may be so great as to be decisive. It would be madness altogether to reject such an experience. Where analogous conditions occur no doubt a better regulated long-range fire is too important an element of power to be ignored. But it is necessary to realize what the conditions were. In the first place, the whole attack was one that never ought to have been made. It never would have been made had not the commanding archduke overriden the advice of all the best soldiers he had, and in mere obstinacy and ignorance dashed his men against a position that ought never to have been so assailed. It was an attempt of a field army against what had almost become a fortress. The Russians were unsupported by any adequate artillery for its reduction. The ground was unusually open and exposed to the full range of the Turkish fire. The Russians showed here just the same incapacity for taking advantage of ground, so far as the smaller groups were concerned, which they had shown in the Crimea. They huddled together in great masses, more unwieldy than any regular column, but just as much exposed to unaimed fire. There was therefore nothing to show that a properly conducted skirmishing attack might not have found means of reaching the position which Skobeleff actually secured.

Nevertheless, when all these allowances have been made, and while it seems as important as ever to realize what advantages the sudden effect of reserved fire may secure, the fact remains that under certain very possible conditions of fighting an extensive employment of long-range fire may be advisable, and it is therefore right that every army should prepare for such an event.

For instance, in an attack on the *forts d'arrêt* with which the French have covered their frontier, it is extremely probable that the Germans, being close to their own magazines, and therefore able to employ a practically unlimited amount of ammunition, will overwhelm these places with long-range infantry as well as with artillery fire. There is no doubt that their infantry has been practised in firing volleys at very long range, and for such purposes it would be certainly comparatively easy to ensure the delivery of actual volleys. It may even be the case that in defensive positions, where the extent of ground open to view is considerable, long-range infantry fire regulated by volleys may be attempted. We cannot, however, see how it would be possible to attempt this during an attack unless one special body of troops be assigned for the work of long-range fire, in order to occupy the attention of the enemy while other forces advance to the attack. On the one hand, the discipline of the French army was so loose during the campaign of 1870 that it is quite possible that long-range fire might be much better brought under control than it was by them; on the other, it is emphatically necessary to assert that the difficulties involved in a free employment of long-range fire are not merely those of an adequate supply of ammunition, but that those considerations to which we have drawn attention must be taken into account. If an army is sufficiently well in hand for the choice between long-range fire and reserved fire to be in the option of the general who commands, then undoubtedly cases will arise when each may be used with advantage. Certainly it would not be a wise or safe thing for an army to enter the field without having ever practised the regulated fire by volleys at long range against an army which had practised it. It is clear that the tendency in that case would be for the unpractised to indulge in much unregulated long-range firing. With an army trained to both methods of action, the general who realizes the risks and advantages of either will be able to exercise a sounder choice than the man who has become an inveterate pleader for either system, and cannot therefore adapt himself to the cases that arise.

Volley firing.

The general question of volley firing as against individual shooting is independent of the special use of volleys for very long-range shooting to which we have above referred. It may obviously be possible to ensure the regular delivery of volleys at very long ranges, such as the French are now practising, 3000 yards or more, without its being possible to do so in anything that can properly be called an engaged fight. The effect produced by a well-delivered volley is out of all proportion great as compared with the effect of isolated shots. Moreover, it is a curious fact that apparently men aim better when they fire together than when they fire each by himself one after another. It is constantly found at the butts that the greatest number of shots has been delivered by the "best volley," that is, the one in which all the arms go off most like one. But it is a matter of great doubt whether in war it is practically possible under most circumstances to deliver a volley at all. Captain May, the author of the "tactical retrospect" on the 1866 campaign, denied that any volleys had been fired in that campaign. The cases of its employment in the 1870 campaign, which are sufficiently established not to fall under such criticism as he applied to the nominal volleys of 1866, are not very numerous. We may leave the question with the remark that the moral effect produced by a volley is too great for the attempt to use it ever to be willingly thrown away, but that it would be now rash to take for granted that on service the best troops can be depended on to deliver during close fighting accurate volleys, unless it be in small parties. The possibility of even the fire of groups is disputed by Von der Goltz. It is obvious that, if he be correct in this respect, all attempt at regulating fire in action is

> "An effort only and a noble aim,
> Still to be sought for, never to be won."

We incline to think that all war experience tends to this conclusion, and it is a reservation which we must therefore append to our cordial agreement with the passages we have quoted from Colonel Macdonald.

Cavalry.

Of all tactical facts, the one which needs most study for practical purposes is the relation of the size of men, on foot, mounted, in mass, and in different formations, to the undulations and features of ground. There is nothing which the untrained eye so little realizes as the extent to which concealment and cover for men, even for mounted men, exists on the apparently most level plain. This fact, which is important for both the other arms, is for cavalry vital to its present use. Nothing is more certain than that under the present condition of arms cavalry cannot successfully assail in front either artillery or infantry in any formation in which the artillery or infantry are able to use their arms and can observe the approach of cavalry over long distances.

On the other hand, cavalry striking by sudden surprise on the flank of unprepared infantry or artillery, engaged with other enemies, may produce an effect, great to an extent of which as yet we have no adequate example in modern war. That is the conclusion drawn from their own experiences of the 1870 campaign by the most experienced leaders who were employed in it. Count Von Moltke in 1882, and Prince Kraft of Hohenlohe-Ingelfingen in his letters on cavalry published in 1887, have alike pronounced decisively on the subject, and it would be easy to show that the whole weight of the best military opinion in all countries except Russia is on the same side.

The practical possibility on most fields of battle of cavalry being thus employed depends on two facts,—on the one hand the extent to which almost all ground presents opportunities to a skilful leader for moving his men unobserved from point to point of a great battle-field, and on the other that absorption in the intense excitement of a modern fight which prevents men from observing what is taking place anywhere beyond the immediate range of their own employment.

It follows from this that the utmost possible skill in the handling of cavalry as a mounted arm will be required if cavalry is to take advantage of such chances as modern fight will present to it. Now, in all periods since the invention of firearms, there has been a tendency, as improvement in weapons has taken place, to attempt to put cavalry on a level in point of firearms with the infantry with which it has had to contend. Invariably, when that rare development of armies, a great cavalry leader, has arisen, he has swept away all attempts of the kind, and has employed his cavalry with their proper weapon, the "arme blanche," sword or lance.

The reason of this is easy to explain, and the explanation is one that shows that the principle is as applicable to the present condition of warfare as to any preceding one. The effective action of cavalry as cavalry depends on ruse, on surprise, on skilful manœuvring, and on the impetuous power and moral effect of the man and horse, glued to one another as though they together formed the old ideal of the arm, the centaur. Now, the dash and vigour with which an actual cavalry charge takes place depends on the moral condition of that part of the centaur in whose hands it is the great purpose and effect of high training to place the guiding of the composite animal. Never has it been possible to train a great body of fighting men in two opposite directions at once. Balanced judgment, and an appreciation of the powers and uses of each part of the force he has to employ, are the duties of a general. But if a body of infantry, dispersed in scattered groups, or isolated men, are to repel successfully a body of charging cavalry, they must have acquired sufficient sang-froid to calmly fire at the great and overwhelming avalanche which they see moving down on them. To that end they must have acquired confidence in their weapon, the firearm, and must have learnt to believe that its power is so great that it gives them plenty of time to bring down the mighty-looking horseman before he closes with them. Similarly, if cavalry is successfully to be led by skilful manœuvring into a fight where firearms are creating the most horrible appearance of danger, they must have acquired a confidence in the skill of their leaders, in their own power of combined action, and in the effects of their sudden appearance, which will carry them on though leaders fall, and though death and destruction seem to await them. In other words, they must have learnt to despise the firearm when pitted against their own skill in evading its danger and in delivering home their blows. All attempts, therefore, to train cavalry not to employ their skill in manœuvring as the weapon to which they trust, but, on the contrary, to be always ready to jump off their horses and begin firing, tends directly to weaken and destroy the very spirit and quality on which the efficiency of true cavalry depends.

Now, the great leaders to whom we have referred believe absolutely in the possibility of true cavalry properly trained being able to play its part on the field of battle. Prince Kraft's 7th letter on this subject is so admirable in its analysis of past experience that all who would understand the subject should study it in its integrity. His conclusion is—"From all that I have stated in this long letter I draw the conclusion that cavalry will, in the future, also be able to play a decisive part in battle if they can be led in such a manner that they can break out round a flank, and can thus, up to the last moment, take advantage of the fire effect of their own line of battle. But to do so will sometimes require from the cavalry that they shall be able to advance as much as four miles, at a rapid pace, before they deliver their charge."[1]

Mounted infantry.

There is, however, another necessity of modern warfare which is altogether distinct from the question of supplying firearms to cavalry in order to make up to them for the increased power of infantry. Powerful as modern infantry is, it is very slow in its movements. It is very difficult for a general to have it at the very place where he wants it. Hence the idea of mounting infantry and of sending them forward either on horseback or in carts, or where there are numerous roads on bicycles and tricycles, is one that is of the greatest importance. The so-called cavalry of the American civil war were all of this character. Most of them had been accustomed to rifle-shooting from their childhood and could ride. They had had no opportunity whatever of acquiring the manœuvring facilities of European cavalry. Probably European cavalry would have been altogether unsuited to the country in which they had to work. The essential condition of the efficiency of mounted

[1] Translation in *Royal Artillery Institution Proceedings*, April 1888, p. 40. See also *Die Kavallerie-Division als Schlachtenkörper*, 1884.

infantry, which these men in fact were, is that, while they can ride well enough to get over such ground as is required, they waste no time in learning manœuvres which they could not master, but look altogether to fighting with firearms and on foot whenever collision becomes necessary. The Boers represented an almost ideal body of this kind. British wars have supplied most valuable bodies of mounted infantry, who have been always picked men, picked shots, and excellent infantry. As a general principle, it is safe to say that they ought to be under infantry and not under cavalry officers, as to their immediate command,—though very often indeed they will be a most valuable auxiliary for any cavalry commander, who will in that case of course have the whole body under his orders. In so far as their presence tends to save cavalry from the disastrous necessity which occasionally befalls them of having to employ their men in fighting on foot, their presence with cavalry is always valuable. But, as the time when all their best training is required is when they are actually fighting on foot, it is far better that they should then find themselves under the orders of an officer whose training tends to make him accustomed to handling men on foot, rather than to one all whose experience ought to have accustomed him to handle men on horseback, and to hate making them jump off their horses.

The difficulty in enforcing these principles lies in the fact that it is only the experience of war on a large scale which brings home to cavalry officers the disastrous consequences of injuring their own power by continually trying to take up the rôle of mounted infantry. They find themselves at peace manœuvres continually put *hors de combat*, because they have come under the fire of infantry. They can very often get into positions where, if they were infantry and in large numbers, their effect would be most telling. Their rapidity of movement enables them to do this. A narrow deduction from a very incomplete knowledge of the experiences of cavalry charges during the 1870 campaign led to the conclusion that cavalry could not be employed on a modern battle-field in their proper work. That conclusion is utterly rejected by all those authorities who have had the best means of analysing the experiences on which it was based; yet it remains a tradition which unfortunately affects the minds of many cavalry officers as well as those of many other officers in the army.

It is safe to say, in conclusion on this matter, that the two forces of cavalry and mounted infantry are each of the greatest value, provided they each adhere to their own proper function. As soon as mounted infantry begins to attempt manœuvres on horseback it necessarily becomes a very inferior cavalry. As soon as cavalry takes to dismounting, its equipment, its training, and usually its arms are sure to make it into a very inefficient body. Every year adds to the necessity of high shooting training for infantry, and of every hour of their work being connected with the efficient use of their arm. Every hour devoted by cavalry to shooting which subtracts anything from training in their own proper work, or which leads them to compete with the other arm in that way, weakens them. By no process can they compete with infantry if they measure themselves with them under the conditions favourable to infantry fighting. Nothing is more fallacious than the notion that because during the latter part of the 1870 campaign the German cavalry often fought on foot the Germans therefore consider that the proper employment of the arm.

Prince Kraft emphatically says—"The circumstances of the latter campaigns of this war were so abnormal that no rules for the employment of the arms can be deduced from them." "No cavalry could perform the duty" the German cavalry here did, of saving their own infantry by acting on the wings against the French infantry, "except in the case where they were engaged with an enemy whose hastily collected and undrilled masses had not the full value of regular troops."

We may also mention as an illustration of at least the views of the German leaders that during some manœuvres in 1879 a regiment of lancers by sudden surprise charged from behind some rising ground at four battalions of infantry, who did not see the cavalry till these were on their flank at a distance of 200 yards already in full charge. Scarcely a shot was fired before the cavalry were among the infantry. The emperor and Count Von Moltke were present, and the decision was that three battalions were *hors de combat*. Now, when it is remembered that a cavalry regiment numbers about 400 men and three battalions about 3000, the difference between the effect produced under such circumstances by a body of cavalry and an equivalent body of mounted infantry, who could not have dismounted at most more than 300 men, who would certainly have been destroyed, is too great not to be realized. In this case an instance occurred of what Prince Kraft mentions as a possibility continually illustrated by the experiences of the 1870 campaign. The colonel commanding the lancers, having moved personally to a well-chosen spot, had been quietly observing the movements of the infantry, himself unseen up to the moment when by a signal he gave the order for his regiment to advance at a gallop, and then charge.

Artillery.

Here the first point it is necessary to insist on is that the tendency to a divorce between firing practice and drill manœuvre has been inherited by the artillery from the past as it has been by the infantry. Napoleon's formation for the battle of Austerlitz placed his artillery guns between his infantry brigades and on their flank. The artillery advanced nearly in line with the infantry and rather in advance of it. As long as it was possible for artillery thus to move up to close quarters with the infantry, exact accuracy of fire training was of little importance. The distance was so short that the round shot were bound to produce their effect. But, when the range of both infantry and artillery fire were greatly extended, a change took place which required a change of habit in the artillery, for which the long training of the past had as little prepared them as had been the case with the infantry. The horse artillery, and at a much later date the field batteries, had acquired a mobility which enabled them very rapidly to take up assigned positions. But the habit of thinking that drill movements, irrespective of accuracy of fire, were the business on which a soldier's mind should be set continued to operate long after all idea of moving artillery cheek by jowl with infantry or cavalry had been abandoned. The practice grounds of artillery for actual shell fire are necessarily much fewer and more difficult to select than the ranges for infantry. Hence what we have said of the tendency in infantry manœuvres to separate the effective fire of the ranges and the butts from drill and manœuvres applies with tenfold force to the artillery. Moreover, in the case of the artillery this tendency has been aggravated by a certain fear among generals and their staff officers of interfering in the detail work of a special arm. As long as a battery is seen to manœuvre rapidly, to take up an assigned and telling position, and to fire off a puff of smoke, the superintending general is apt to think that he may assume that all has been done that ought to have been done.

Unfortunately, it may happen that the battery which thus appears to have acted in the very smartest possible way may have all the time been learning to do just what will injure it for war service. Nothing is more noteworthy throughout the 1870 campaign than the extraordinary superiority of the German artillery over the French. There were no doubt certain technical reasons for this; but by far the most important reasons were these:—(1) the German batteries had been trained habitually so to co-operate that a French battery almost always found itself opposed to a German brigade of six batteries when it came to fighting; and (2) at all their manœuvres the Germans had been training for war, while the French artillery had not. The German artillery had never fired off a gun which had not been properly laid at an assigned object, with the range determined, the nature of the projectile declared, and the fuse to burst the shell so far fixed that, had it been necessary actually to fire in earnest, every man would have gone through an almost exactly similar experience. The French, on the other hand, had piqued themselves on their dashing battery manœuvres, and had been content to fire off a blank cartridge as rapidly as possible, no matter how the gun was laid, or what would have happened about the shell.

The same two schools at this moment exist among British artillery officers. The unfortunate tendency at present is for the officer commanding a battery who tells his subalterns, "Never mind how you fire; get off a puff of smoke, just to show where you are," to *seem* much smarter than the man who insists upon every gun being properly laid at an assigned object, and on having every possible condition fulfilled as it would be in war. The general who at a mile's distance sees the two puffs of smoke cannot tell the difference, though, if he rode into the battery which has so promptly puffed off its smoke, he would probably find that one gun was inclined high in air and the next shooting into the ground ten paces in front of the muzzle. It is not too much to say that this latter battery has been in every respect acquiring inefficiency by the day's work. It will be slow when it comes to action, because the men have never been trained to be as quick as the circumstances of action permit, have acquired no practice in rapidity under those conditions. It will have acquired no practice in actual shooting except its few annual shots on the practice ground, which are sure with it to have been regarded as a most inconvenient interruption to the show drill and show manœuvres on which it has been employed throughout the year. This is the point of artillery tactics without which everything else is utterly valueless. As Prince Kraft of Hohenlohe-Ingelfingen puts it, "The artillery must in the first place *hit*, in the second place *hit*, and in the third place *hit*."

It depends far more in England upon generals commanding districts and divisions and on their staffs than upon artillery officers whether this result is attained or not. It is almost impossible for the most zealous artillery officer to keep up the confidence and spirits of his battery and to keep their work to the proper level if on every occasion they find that, because he insists on work being properly done, some other battery which is amusing itself with sham firing gets all the credit of superior smartness. The matter is therefore vital to the efficiency of this arm of the service. The infantry and cavalry will find in action that they rely on the support of a broken reed if the artillery generally has not brought the most efficient technical and practice-ground work into the closest relation with field manœuvring. Given that this has been done in the sense here described, Prince Kraft's next condition may be briefly stated, because its importance will be easily understood. "It must next be in a condition to come into position at the right moment, and, with this object it must practise itself in getting over distances of many miles, and even forced marches of a day or so, at rapid pace. If," he adds,[1] "it can satisfy these claims, it will give us everything which is needed as to its fitness for employment in battle."

Massed artillery fire.

So far we have spoken of conditions in which the tactical necessities of modern artillery are very similar to those of modern infantry. In the next point the contrast is as sharp as the analogy was close in the former instance. Infantry, as we have seen, once committed to a fight, is beyond the control of all officers not actually leading them at the time. Artillery under all but the rarest circumstances can be almost as easily moved from one point to another of a battle-field out of action in which it is fiercely engaged as if it were not employed in firing at all. Therefore the rule is now accepted in all armies that every gun that can be employed should as soon as possible be brought to bear on the enemy. The shorter time artillery is limbered up and the longer it is employed in action the more effective is its work. With a very large army Prince Kraft, whose authority on such a subject is probably the highest we have, makes a rather hesitating exception in this sense that ordinarily the commander-in-chief of a very large army will have whole army corps designed for a particular work, usually for striking at the decisive point of a field of battle. With these their own artillery will naturally move. But so far as artillery is available on any part of a field of action, even including that of divisions and army corps kept back from the actual fight, as long as these are stationary, every possible gun will be pushed forward. The altogether overwhelming effect of a concentrated and massed artillery fire is so enormous that whatever tends to increase the number of guns employed tends to give that superiority over the enemy's artillery which it is one of a general's first objects to secure.

Ordinarily a battle will now begin by artillery opening fire at a range which is fixed by the necessity of the attacking artillery not exposing itself during the time that it is coming up to the enemy's effective fire with shrapnel shell. This is reckoned at about 3800 yards. From that point the artillery, as soon as it has been able sufficiently to occupy the fire of the enemy to make further advance possible, pushes in to a distance of from 2200 yards to 2700 yards. Infantry in the meantime will have been pushed on sufficiently to protect the ground thus to be occupied by the artillery from direct attacks from the enemy. At this point an artillery duel is practically the certain beginning of the regular battle. The artillery will fire at any of the other arms as soon as it is able to bring any effective fire to bear on them. It is no easy matter for infantry to attack other infantry until the artillery has prepared the way for them by a heavy fire. But the artillery will hardly ever be able to do this until it has established such an ascendency over the enemy's artillery that the latter is either silenced or at least temporarily withdrawn.

Regulation battery fire.

No matter how great the mass of artillery that is gathered together, Prince Kraft, basing his conclusions upon the soundest reasoning, condemns altogether the independent fire of individual guns within a battery, and, unless exceptionally for the purpose of ascertaining a range, all salvoes of artillery by batteries or otherwise. Nothing is gained in point of the number of shell that can be thrown in a given time by firing battery salvoes instead of firing steadily gun by gun from the flank of a battery. After a salvo an interval of from 36 to 48 seconds at least is required before another can be fired,

[1] We quote from his correspondent's summary of his views, and from the translation given by Major Walford, R.A. These words occur in the 17th letter, *Royal Artillery Institution Proceedings*, August 1887. p. 187.

while with very rapid firing from the flank an interval of from 6 to 8 seconds allows a shell to traverse a range of from 2500 to 3000 yards, so that the effect of each shell can be seen.[1] The effect of this is to enable the officer commanding the battery to have his fire under control, and to induce much more careful firing by each gun. Indeed, if a German battery is seen to be firing, not from the flank but irregularly, it may be taken for granted that it is being mastered by the hostile fire, and is out of hand.

Supply of ammunition.

The duty of each commanding officer of a battery is to be continually watching over the replenishment of his ammunition, and therefore as long as possible to draw upon his waggons for ammunition, keeping the ammunition in his limbers as a last reserve. If this cannot be done, the limbers must be filled up as rapidly as possible. If, however, by misfortune all ammunition is exhausted, the artillery must not retire, but must, for the sake of the moral effect, remain without firing rather than produce the encouragement to the enemy and discouragement to their own troops of withdrawing without express orders.

Summary.

We shall complete this sketch of the duties of artillery in action by quoting the following summary from Prince Kraft of Hohenlohe-Ingelfingen :—

On the Offensive.—(*a*) Artillery, after it has silenced the enemy's artillery, must not as a rule approach nearer than from 1600 to 1700 yards to infantry of the enemy which is as yet intact and is not engaged with other troops. (*b*) If the enemy's infantry is held in check by another force of artillery, or by infantry, it is not only advisable, but it is the duty of artillery to advance to a range of from 1100 to 1200 yards. (*c*) At the most decisive moment of the action artillery must not shun the very closest range. (*d*) As soon as the main attack has proved successful, the artillery must hasten up to secure the captured position by its fire; at such a moment, its proper place, in most cases, is in the line of skirmishers.

On the Defensive.—(*a*) The normal post for artillery in a defensive position (though this may be modified by the character of the ground) is 500 yards in rear of the foremost infantry position, provided always that the latter leaves the field of fire of the artillery open. (*b*) Artillery must never abandon its position, even if the enemy come up to the muzzles of the guns, unless the officer commanding the troops has given orders for a general retreat. But this does not imply that artillery, acting on the defensive, are forbidden, if the assailant begins to get the advantage in the artillery duel, to cease firing for a time, and to withdraw their guns under cover, with the object of suddenly coming into action again at the most critical moment. (*c*) If the order to retreat is given, the only possible moment at which it can be commenced is either when the enemy has not yet advanced to the attack, or when he is preparing a second attack after having been repulsed in the first.

Horse Artillery in a Cavalry Action.—(*a*) As a rule horse artillery should go in at once to a decisive range for the artillery duel, since the considerations which compel artillery when engaged with infantry to fight at longer ranges lose their force in this case, owing to the speed at which cavalry can move. From this position it will silence the enemy's artillery, and immediately afterwards, or as soon as it can see them, it will turn its fire on the enemy's cavalry. (*b*) During the charge of its own cavalry it will fire on that of the enemy, or, if that be not possible, on his artillery. If it has nothing to fire at, it will remain in position with loaded guns (common shell and not shrapnel should be used), in order, in case of the failure of the charge, to give support to its retiring cavalry, and to show them where they are to rally. (*c*) The horse artillery requires a special escort on that flank of its position only on which the cavalry fight is not taking place, and even there it requires it merely for the purpose of scouting; a section will therefore be sufficient. (*d*) If the charge succeeds, the horse artillery must gallop up to the spot where it took place, in order to secure its possession with their fire, and to assist in the pursuit.

The Combined Action of the Three Arms.

So far we have spoken of what may properly be called the minor tactics of the three arms, though that name is often applied in quite a different sense. There can be little doubt that it is in that portion of tactics that the complexity and difficulty of the present stage of the question lie. As regards the larger handling of armies, the tendency of recent wars has been rather to simplification than to increased difficulty. The employment of artillery in great masses, never in isolated batteries, is, so far as that arm is concerned, its most important law. So much so is this the case that, even when as many as eighty-four guns were collected together at Wörth, the Germans found it answer best to turn all of them at once upon a single French battery, and then upon another, and so on. Wherever possible, some at least of the guns will take up an enfilading position; that is, they will fire from flank to flank of the troops they assail, in preference to firing directly at them. It is always advantageous to the fire of artillery to have great depth rather than great extent to fire at, because range is much more difficult to fix correctly than direction.

Prince Kraft regards it as doubtful whether artillery can be employed in crossing its fire, the right of a long line of guns firing at an enemy's right and the left at the left, which would give to each a certain advantage in the direction of their fire. But it is clear that, if the whole of a long line of guns be employed, as at Wörth, first against one object and then against another, many of the batteries will not be firing directly to their front, but at an angle, sometimes a very sharp one, to their own front.

Normal course of a modern battle.

In any case the earlier stages of a modern battle are sure to begin with a heavy fire of artillery, following either on some slight affairs of outposts or on the cavalry having ascertained the position of the enemy at least approximately. Then may perhaps follow, what we have already suggested as one of the alternatives, a carefully regulated long-range fire of infantry; then probably a gradual development of the infantry of the assailing army in front of the position to be attacked and certain tentative movements designed to feel the strength of an enemy's position. Then, as soon as the point to be carried at any cost has been determined on, every effort will be made to distract the enemy's attention from this, to occupy him at other points, and by engaging him all along the line to prevent him from reinforcing the point which it is essential to carry. At present the attempt will be, when possible, almost certainly to attack a flank. But, as the necessity of this becomes thoroughly realized as it now is on both sides, and a tendency arises towards continual extension of the space occupied in order to meet outflanking movements, it is almost certain that on one side or other the extension will exceed the limits of defensive power, and that then blows will be struck with the object of breaking the too extended line. All the cavalry not employed in mere reconnoitring duties, or for keeping up the connexion between different parts of the army, will ordinarily be kept under the control of the commander-in-chief until he is able to define the part of the battle in which it can be most effectually used. Then, when he has so far decided its direction, he will be obliged to leave all details to the cavalry leader, who will choose his own time and opportunity for delivering his blow. The local defensive power conferred by the present arms will be used on both sides. The assailant will endeavour by employing it at unimportant parts of his line to gain the advantage of the superiority of force necessary for striking at the decisive point. The defendant will naturally employ it to the full. Both on one side and the other, however, the effort will be to keep strong forces of all arms for the decisive period of the action.

So far as Continental warfare is concerned, the enormous development of modern armies makes it very uncertain how far elaborate strokes of tactical skill can ever again be delivered in the way they were by Napoleon,—for instance, at Austerlitz and Dresden. The experience of recent wars supplies us at all events with nothing of the kind. The enormous masses and the enormous extent of ground to be covered almost force a general into the simplest possible arrangements on the larger scale, leaving

[1] See the prince's 15th letter, *Royal Artillery Institution Proceedings*, p. 171.

it to his subordinates to work out the development with such local skill as the circumstances permit. Nevertheless, it would be rash to say that, as incidents of a great campaign, many battles may not be fought, the effect of which on the conduct of the general operations will be very decisive, where comparatively small numbers are engaged. For the conduct of these at least there are many lessons to be gathered from the tactical experiences of earlier wars.

Choice of position.

In the taking up of positions it may be assumed generally that the conditions to be sought are freedom for manœuvre, free scope for fire both of artillery and infantry, and, as a rule, for that end gentle glacis slopes like those of St Privat and Gravelotte, rather than precipitous heights like that of the Red Hill at Spicheren. There is nothing as to which war experience and popular assumptions differ more than as to the relative strength of different positions. As a rule, steep heights give a great deal of cover from fire. Their lower slopes can only be seen from the edge, and that edge cannot be held because it is completely exposed to the enemy's fire from many points below. It is better to have a difficult climb than to be shot by a bullet. It has constantly happened that positions have fallen because the defenders have trusted to physical difficulties of access rather than to the effect of ground upon the use of arms for their defence. Whatever tends to oblige an enemy to debouch on a narrow front against a wide front of fire is most valuable to the defence; but it is upon considerations like these of the use of arms that the strength of a position must be determined. Similarly, whatever tends to facilitate communication between one part and another of your own troops, and to cause an enemy to separate his, adds greatly to the strength of your position. The element of time also has here, as in the province of strategy, to be always taken into account. Where ground tends to make movements slow and difficult, there it will be safe to economize men by employing small forces, in order to gain time for decisive blows in other directions. Whatever in an enemy's rear will prevent his safe retreat, and therefore either locally or throughout a position will make successful attack decisive, is greatly in favour of the army which, whether at first on the defensive or offensive, can attack an enemy in such a position. The application of these principles is almost infinite in its variety. It is impossible here to do more than indicate their general character.

Provision against outflanking movements.

The proposition has been advanced that it would be best to meet the effort of an assailant to outflank a position by employing detached bodies to manœuvre outside the position, so that when an assailant has committed himself to an outflanking movement, and has moved up his enveloping troops, the detached body could fall upon these unexpectedly from their rear. Twice during the 1870 campaign the Germans designed a movement of this kind. In neither case was there an opportunity for putting it to the test. Such a movement successfully executed could hardly fail to have great results. On the other hand, a well-handled cavalry, searching all the country round prior to an action, might not improbably discover the isolated corps placed for the purpose, and in that case it ought not to be difficult for the assailant to keep it apart from the main army and to destroy it.

A proposal of a somewhat kindred kind, but involving a different principle, was made by Sir E. Hamley as a deduction from the 1870 campaign, and was applied in practice by the Russians in Asia in 1877. He suggested that the defensive strength of comparatively small bodies was now so great that a general would be tempted to detach, or to connect with his main body only by a telegraphic wire, a body of troops, who, passing round an enemy to be attacked, should take up a strong position in his rear, and should thus become the anvil on which the main assailing army should act as hammer, grinding the enemy between them to powder. This was actually done by the Russians, who in October 1877 destroyed Moukhtar Pasha's army by this very means.

Both these forms of operation—the detached force to the flank and the detached force to the rear—partake of the nature of the attempt of Napoleon to destroy the allied armies, after the battle of Dresden in 1813, by previously detaching Vandamme to intercept their retreat. As a matter of fact, that manœuvre was one of the most disastrous that Napoleon ever attempted, but the disaster was probably due to a failure of Napoleon's own wonted activity arising from illness. The telegraph might then have made a very great difference in the result of the operation. In any case, these suggestions indicate possibilities of action, due to the present condition of arms and of science, which may have much wider application in the hands of skilful commanders. Everything will depend on their execution, and on the skill with which they are met. It may at least be asserted that, with the possibilities of such manœuvres being employed against him, it will ordinarily be extremely rash for a general to commit himself to the actual turning movement by which he wheels up a portion of his army to attack an exposed flank, without having searched the ground with his cavalry far beyond the point which he proposes to assail. This was actually done by the German cavalry under express orders from headquarters, prior to and during the great turning movement at the battle of Gravelotte.

Marches.

Marches.—The principles regulating the marches of armies which precede battles are determined by the conditions of a modern battle itself. As a rule nowadays the cavalry of an army will be certainly pushed far forward in advance of the main body. Therefore, with the exception of small parties of horsemen employed as orderlies, for keeping up the connexion between one part of an army and another, and to aid the infantry in the immediate work of local security, the marching body will in ordinary country consist of artillery and infantry. The tendency for every action to begin by artillery fire continually leads more and more to the pushing forward of that arm to the front of the column, only sufficient infantry being placed before it on the road to give protection in case of sudden attack, and to furnish the necessary troops for the defence of the guns at the beginning of an action. The exact order of march will therefore necessarily vary with the character of the country through which the army moves. In very mountainous districts, in which collision with an enemy may occur at any moment, it may be necessary to push forward infantry instead of cavalry. In all cases where mountain defiles have to be passed, detached infantry must gain possession of the heights before the main body enters the defile.

Since the great object of all marches is to deliver the army in fighting order on the battle-field, it is necessary that the force should not be dispersed too widely on the march, but it is quite as necessary with large bodies of troops that the march should not be made upon too few roads. An army corps with its attendant waggons occupies in depth about 25 miles on a single road. As under most circumstances a day's march is about 13 or 14 miles, it is clear that, if an army corps were moving in the ordinary road formation on a single road, the rear of the column would scarcely be able to arrive on the same day that the head of the column was first involved in action. Nor is it always possible to place the whole of the fighting force in front and to leave the whole mass of waggons in rear. Ambulances and surgeons at least, as well as ammunition columns, are required at the very moment of battle. Therefore it is advisable to employ as many roads as possible that are within convenient reach of one another. The difference between the lengths of march that have been done by troops under favourable and unfavourable conditions is so great that it is impossible to fix any specific length as the march that can under all circumstances be relied on. Good spirits, good roads, high training, and favourable weather on the one hand, and depression, deep mud, storms, and want of marching condition on the other, are elements that must be taken into account in all such matters. Of the difficulties which a large number of troops marching on a single road encounter a striking illustration is afforded by an incident of the 1866 campaign. According to the Austrian official account, the men marched eight abreast in order to diminish the length of road occupied. Yet, though this unusually wide marching front was taken up by the infantry, and corresponding formations were as far as possible taken by the other arms, the length of the longest column, according to Von der Goltz, was, when actually on the road, from front to rear 67½ miles in length. In this case about three corps were marching together. Hence it is always desirable when possible to allow one road at least to each division. Another striking illustration both of the size of modern armies and of the length occupied by troops on a road is given by Von der Goltz. He calculates that, if the present German army were placed on one road, it would reach from Mainz to the Russian frontier, the whole distance being densely packed with men, guns, and waggons. Again, he shows that either the present French or German army extended in battle array would occupy the entire length of the common frontier of the countries.

Advanced and rear guards.

Advanced and Rear Guards.—The questions involved in the proper use and employment of advanced and rear guards would occupy more space than we can possibly afford for them. In general terms it may be said that, with both advanced and rear guards, artillery (perhaps with machine and quick-firing guns), cavalry, and mounted infantry will play the principal parts. It is tolerably certain, though opinion is much divided on the subject, that the enormous advanced guards employed by the Germans during the 1870 campaign, in which the advanced guard of an army corps sometimes consisted of about half the whole force, would be for most campaigns a mistake. The tendency of very large advanced guards is, as that campaign showed, to bring on actions prematurely. Artillery or mounted corps can be easily drawn out of a premature action. Infantry cannot be so withdrawn. If the advanced guard is large enough to give time to the marching body to form upon suitable ground before it is attacked, it possesses all the strength that is necessary.

The task of a rear guard retiring before a victorious enemy, and covering the retreat of a beaten army, is one of the most delicate of operations. It depends for its proper execution on the full employment of those means for gaining time by forcing an enemy to deploy on unfavourable ground which have been described under the general heading.

Outposts.

Outposts.—The subject of outposts is also one which, for its full explanation, would require a volume to itself. The general principle on which their use is based is that a slender cordon of men shall so surround an army when at rest that no enemy can approach its quarters unobserved, and that this cordon shall be supported by piquets from which the actual sentries for the cordon are taken, and these again by stronger but less numerous bodies, serving to connect together the different parts, so that, if the enemy attempts to drive in the outposts at any point, he meets with a continually increasing resistance. In this broad indication of the method, the principle is equally applicable to cavalry and to infantry outposts. In general, however, the security of a modern army, when not in actual contact with an enemy preparatory to battle, depends chiefly on the early information gained by cavalry pushed far out beyond the rest of the army. The cavalry will be at a distance of at least one or two days' march in advance and on the flanks scouring the country in all directions.

It is practically certain that during the earlier stages of a campaign the collisions that will occur will be between bodies of cavalry pushed forward from both sides, supported by horse artillery and by such infantry as can be rapidly transported to the front. The circumstances of the collision of the main armies must depend in the first instance upon what happens in these encounters, in which cavalry will be the most important arm. Both sides will endeavour to use their cavalry to obtain all the information they can and to prevent the enemy from obtaining information of their own movements. At the same time, in the case of two great neighbouring powers like France and Germany, it is probable that attempts will be made by the cavalry on both sides to interfere with the mobilization of the armies across the frontier. These efforts promise to result in contests on a scale and of a kind such as we have never yet seen, and of the nature of which it is difficult to judge from any past experience of war. It seems certain, however, that the body which will gain victory in these encounters will be the most highly trained and numerous cavalry, supported by its sister arm the horse artillery. But the value of a body of mounted infantry, and perhaps a strong force of cyclists, pushed forward to support the cavalry, can hardly be doubted when it is remembered how often defiles will have to be seized, bridges held, and important stations permanently secured. No doubt, when such infantry is not available, cavalry will at times have to be employed on foot for these purposes. So long as such employment is looked on as exceptional and a necessity to be regretted, it need do no harm. In any case no rules must prevent the securing of the actual object for the time being.

Reconnaissance and Intelligence.—The vital necessity of obtaining all possible information of what an enemy is doing makes the reconnaissances continually carried out by cavalry all round an army, and the occasional special reconnaissances conducted by single officers and small parties or strong bodies employed for the purpose, some of the most important operations of war. It is, however, difficult in brief space to lay down rules for their guidance, because the essence of the value of such work depends on officers being trained in all parts of the art of war so as to know what to look for and what to report. The principles of such reconnaissance are determined by the general principles of both strategy and tactics, and are not in themselves independent. Nevertheless, it is very important that it should be realized, by men who are sending in reports from some one point of a large circle, that information in itself apparently unimportant may be of the greatest value when it is collated with other facts either already known or simultaneously gathered from other quarters. Thus, for instance, a newspaper advertisement, or a reference to a particular man or officer as not being with his regiment, may give negative evidence of the position of that regiment which may become of great importance. The sifting, therefore, of information should be chiefly left to the department at headquarters which has charge of that work. Spies and deserters will supply evidence the value of which usually depends on the power of the department to check their assertions by a number of minute facts already known. Any information about the enemy or the country which may assist to that end should be carefully gathered and reported. Numerous forms and rules have been drawn up to supply hints as to the kind of information about roads, rivers, railways, villages, &c., which should be gathered. Lord Wolseley's *Pocket-Book* and Colonel Harrison's *Handbook* are the best for these purposes.

Literature.—The following books may be recommended as the most recent and most valuable on matters of military art. (1) On tactics, to which modern military literature has been chiefly devoted, see Prince Kraft of Hohenlohe-Ingelfingen's *Letters* on cavalry, infantry, and artillery, especially those on the last-named. These are being now translated in the *Proceedings* of the Royal Artillery Institution. (2) On cavalry tactics two anonymous works by the same writer appeared in Germany in 1884: *Die Kavallerie-Division als Schlachtenkörper*, and *Ueber die Bewaffnung, Ausbildung, und Verwendung der Reiterei.* The former has been translated into French in the *Revue de Cavalerie* of successive months of 1885–86, and we have no hesitation in saying that it is a book that ought to be known to every officer of every arm of the service, but more especially to every cavalry officer. See also *Das Volk in Waffen* ("The Nation in Arms"), by Baron von der Goltz, which has been completely translated into French under the title of *La Nation armée—organisation militaire et grande tactique modernes* (1884); parts of it have been translated by Sir Lumley Graham in the *Journal* of the United Service Institution, No. 138, vol. xxxi. (1887). (3) On infantry tactics the books are legion. They should be read in conjunction with the actual history of the battles on which their conclusions are based, and if possible with a study of them on the ground on which they were fought. Perhaps the most important are Von Scherff's *Studien zu neuen Infanterie-Taktik* (1873), translated by Sir Lumley Graham, *New Tactics of Infantry*, 1875; Verdy du Vernois's *Studien über Felddienst* (1886), and his *Studien über Truppen-Führung* (1873–75), and the numerous strategical and tactical studies recently published in Germany,—many by Von Gizycki, and in some cases translated as we have noted above by Captain Spenser Wilkinson, and published by the Manchester Tactical Society. We should also recommend a perusal of Col. the Right Hon. J. H. A. Macdonald's *Common Sense on Parade* (1886), from which we have given several extracts. (4) On strategy Prince Kraft's "strategical letters" have already been alluded to. Sir Edward Hamley's *Operations of War* (4th ed., 1878) remains without a rival in the English language on questions of strategy. We cannot think that Clausewitz's great book, *On War*, translated by Col. J. J. Graham, 1873, has ceased to be of value. Mekler's *Taktik*, which represents the course for the German war school, has not as yet been translated; it is a most important work. No soldier can read Major Adams's *Great Campaigns* without advantage. But on these matters we must conclude by expressing our conviction that an exhaustive study of at least a single campaign carried out pretty nearly on the principles laid down, for the purposes of the study of general history, by Dr Arnold, in his *Lectures on History*, but with just such modifications as apply to war study, is almost indispensable to a soldier who would derive much value from those books which examine the whole field of war, and that that cultivation of the judgment of which we have spoken must follow, if any real use is to be made of either one or the other. (J. F. M*.)

NAVAL STRATEGY AND TACTICS.

The introduction of steam, armour, the torpedo, and other modern changes must necessarily have produced modifications in naval strategy and tactics since the days of the last great naval war. In the course of the last eighty years wars on land, both in Europe and elsewhere, have been frequent, and soldiers have thus been enabled to keep pace with modern inventions, and to accommodate their strategy and tactics to the ever-changing conditions of the problem. But since 1805, when Great Britain, by her crowning victory of Trafalgar, placed herself in undisputed command of the seas, and, having rendered herself superior to all possible combinations against her, was thus enabled to found unmolested her unrivalled colonial empire, the world has seen no naval war of sufficient magnitude to enable seamen to lay down maxims of strategy and tactics founded on actual experience. It does not follow, however, that we must necessarily give up the problems as insoluble; we are entitled to reason by analogy. The lessons of history, if not followed too slavishly, will act as a useful guide; and when we have made due allowance for the superseding of sail by steam power, and the consequent limits to the mobility of all fighting ships dependent on their supply of coal, when we have taken into consideration the cutting of the Suez Canal and the possibility of another through Panama, and when we have given due weight to the possession by various nations of certain strategic points on the surface of the globe where coal may be obtained, we shall be able to construct some not altogether imaginary theories of future naval strategy, and shall probably find that the problem, at least as between Great Britain and her maritime rivals, bears a striking family resemblance to that which presented itself in the past. The geographical factors are not greatly altered. Some new naval powers have sprung into existence, and must be taken account of, whilst some of those which figured conspicuously in the beginning of the century have dwindled into insignificance; but the relative interests of the two great maritime rivals, Great Britain and France, are practically unchanged.

Strategy.

Strategy.—The great continental powers of Europe, in consequence of their land frontiers, have to depend mainly on their armies to defend their position, and maintain their independence, and they have all been constrained to adopt a system of forced military service, and to support great standing armies, with prodigious reserves, and vast stores of war material constantly at hand. For them the problems with which we are now dealing are questions of minor importance, and must be held entirely subordinate to their military requirements. Italy is probably the only one of them which has reason to fear invasion by sea, or descents and raids upon her extended coast line; and she has lately been making gigantic efforts to supply herself with a powerful war navy, though she is still far behind France, the only power from whom she has any cause to apprehend attack. To Great Britain alone of the great powers of Europe are the problems of naval strategy of paramount importance. Upon a thorough knowledge and just appreciation of them, with a sufficient provision of physical force to secure their successful development in her own interests, depends the existence of the British empire.

Strategic problems of paramount importance to Great Britain.

The two primary factors which must decide the future naval strategy of Great Britain are the command of the English Channel and the protection of her mercantile marine. Upon the former depends her own safety from invasion, or from partial but disastrous raids upon her open commercial cities and coast towns; and upon the latter depends the no less vital consideration of the uninterrupted supply of food and of raw material for manufacture.

Her naval supremacy in the Mediterranean is of vast importance, for upon it will depend the freedom of her principal route to India and Australia, and also the eventual retention of Malta, Gibraltar, and Cyprus, and of that priceless possession vaguely termed naval prestige, upon which alone she can found a claim to be classed amongst the great powers of Europe. But, notwithstanding the importance to Great Britain of being able to hold her own in the Mediterranean, either with or without allies, in the event of a war with France, or with France and Russia combined, it cannot be considered as vital to the existence of the empire; and it is possible to conceive circumstances in which she might be driven from that sea, or for strategic reasons be induced temporarily to withdraw her ships, and yet, if she could keep open her alternative trade route by the Cape of Good Hope, and protect her food supplies from America, she might secure time to develop her unrivalled maritime resources, and eventually, notwithstanding the enormous temporary loss of prestige, regain her wonted supremacy on all seas.

The naval strategy of the past was necessarily a somewhat inexact and haphazard business. The fact that fleets had to depend entirely for locomotion upon the fickle and uncertain power of wind rendered it impossible to form accurate schemes of combination, and thus the most carefully planned expeditions and enterprises were often frustrated and rendered abortive almost at the moment of consummation by a foul wind or storm. All this is now changed; the present development of steam-power renders fleets practically independent of wind, and even storms can only slightly affect them. The limit to their range of operations dependent on their coal supply, with the question of the possibility of replenishing, adds another element of certainty to the data upon which we can form accurate calculations as to the power and mobility of fleets. It has become possible, therefore, to say that naval strategy is no longer the inexact and haphazard business, depending largely on chance, which it was of old, but an accurate and most interesting science, worthy of the close attention and practical study of the most skilled experts.

The two principal objects of the naval strategy of Great Britain—the command of the narrow seas around her coasts, and the protection of her mercantile marine—are to a certain extent different, though not actually independent of each other. Thus she might, by providing an overwhelming fleet of iron-clads, and neglecting to build a sufficiency of fast cruisers, retain undisputed command of the narrow seas, and yet have her commerce swept off the ocean by an enemy provided with numerous fast, far-ranging cruisers; and on the other hand, it would be useless for her to provide vast numbers of vessels of the latter class to protect her commerce all over the world, if by neglecting her iron-clads she lost command of the narrow seas, and saw her merchant ships captured in sight of their ports. It is obvious, therefore, that her only safety depends upon an ample supply of both.

Blockade of enemy's ports.

The naval strategy of the last war may be briefly but comprehensively described as a blockade of the enemy's ports. The question which now exercises the minds of seamen is whether blockade is at present possible, and if so under what conditions; and the conclusion which seems to have been arrived at by the ablest naval strategists of the present day appears to be that a close blockade, carried on under the old system, is, for various reasons, no longer possible. What is now practicable is observation, or watching by a chain of look-out vessels in connexion with a superior fleet, in such a way that the squadron in port would be masked (to use a military term), or in other words, that they would be unable to leave the port without the extreme probability of being obliged to meet and engage with a superior force. The distance at which the masking fleet should remain from the blockaded port, and the question whether they should be kept under weigh, or at anchor at some suitable anchorage, are points of detail which come more under the head of tactics, and must be decided in each individual case in accordance with local circumstances, and with such considerations as the prospect of the blockading fleet being or not being subjected to the attacks of torpedo boats and coast defenders, which, although not strictly speaking sea-going vessels, are yet capable of exercising potent energies within a certain zone of their port, by selecting the most suitable time and weather for their operations. Such considerations render it obvious that the blockading ships must greatly exceed the sea-going force in the port blockaded, as they render themselves liable to all sorts of subsidiary but very effective attacks from comparatively insignificant forces, which, in consequence of their own distance from their base of operations, they would be unable to reply to in a similar manner. If the blockading force is to be kept constantly under weigh, its numbers must be still further increased, as in that case a certain proportion of the ships, variously estimated at from one-sixth to one-third, must be continually absent from their station for the purpose of replenishing their coal supply, and of making those repairs to machinery which are incidental to steam ships kept constantly under weigh.

Swift cruisers.

The effective blockade of an enemy's ports would of itself provide for the protection of commerce, for if no hostile ships could escape there would be nothing to prey upon the commerce. Such experience, however, as was gained during the American civil war, supported by numerous peace trials and general nautical experience on the subject, tends to show that a perfectly effectual blockade is impossible, as against steamers: some vessels of high speed will certainly find means of escaping on dark nights or during thick weather, so that it becomes necessary for a rich commercial nation, whose merchant ships cover every sea, to make arrangements for providing at least two cruisers of superior speed and greater coal endurance, to look after every one of the hostile raiders which may escape the blockade and endeavour to adopt the tactics of the famous "Alabama." Some half-dozen Confederate cruisers of feeble power and insignificant speed succeeded in driving the merchant flag of the United States off the ocean, and deprived that country of the large share of the carrying trade of the world which it then possessed. A similar disaster to Great Britain in her present unique position would, it is almost superfluous to point out, have far wider consequences.

Some high political authorities have given it as their opinion that no fleet of fast cruisers which it would be possible to provide would suffice for the protection of Great Britain's commerce in case of war with a maritime power. This may or may not be the case, but it is a view not generally shared by the highest naval authorities, who take into consideration the possession by Great Britain of the principal coaling stations of the world.

A novel but apparently not unpractical proposition has been made by one of the ablest and most thoughtful admirals of the British navy, with a view to prevent the wholesale transfer of the mercantile marine to a neutral flag on the outbreak of war with a maritime power. It is to the effect that the national exchequer should guarantee to make good all war losses, provided owners conformed to a few simple but not too harassing regulations as to routes and times of sailing, to be laid down by the Admiralty from time to time. It is quite possible that the call on the national purse might be enormous, perhaps a hundred millions sterling during the first six months of the war; but no mulct it would be reasonable to conceive would equal the amount of the indirect national loss which would accrue from the wholesale transfer of the carrying trade of the country to a foreign flag.

The subject is worthy of the attentive consideration of all those who essay to deal with the great questions of naval strategy, as the protection of the mercantile marine of the country from either direct or indirect destruction is one of the principal factors in the problem.

Changes in naval tactics.

Tactics.—If naval strategy has been modified by the recent inventions and alterations in warlike materials and the motive power of ships, it is certain that the same causes have had a still greater effect upon all preconceived notions of naval tactics.

Weather gauge will no longer be sought for as an advantage. In fact in all cases of attack by surprise, such as an assault by torpedo boats, or other light craft, for the purpose of harassing a fleet, the attacking force would certainly approach from the leeward, by which tactics the smoke from every gun fired by the fleet would act as a screen to hide their movements, and protect them from machine gun fire; for not even the beams of the electric light can penetrate smoke.

A large amount of speculative writing has lately been indulged in, by both English and French writers, as to the naval tactics of the future. We hear of "ramming tactics," "the end-on attack," "the melée," and various other somewhat vague phrases, used to express the views of theorists as to the probable tactics of a future naval battle; and, whilst the torpedoist tells us that his weapon (meaning the locomotive torpedo) will certainly decide an action, and forbid ships to approach near enough for ramming, the artillerist laughs to scorn the inaccuracy and limited range of torpedoes moving in such a dense medium as water, and maintains that his weapon, of far greater accuracy, almost equal destructive power, and immensely greater range, will as of old decide the battle.

It is probable that all three weapons, ram, gun, and torpedo, will play a part in future naval battles, though many thoughtful and practical seamen seem to be coming to the conclusion that the ram will not be deliberately used, except perhaps to give the *coup de grace* to a ship with her engines already disabled; and this even would appear to be a wanton destruction of a ship which might become a valuable prize, and an inhuman sacrifice of lives no longer capable of exercising any material influence on the battle.

Ramming.

It seems to be thought that ramming when it takes place in action will be as often accidental as deliberate; and indeed the present high speed and great size and weight of iron-clads would probably forbid practical seamen from adopting that mode of attack. Two ships of from ten to thirteen thousand tons, meeting end-on at a speed of 28 knots an hour (assuming the speed of each to be 14 knots), would certainly produce mutual destruction, with loss of the lives of almost all on board, and it seems difficult to believe that any two men who still retained calm judgment and reason would deliberately adopt such a suicidal method of fighting, if indeed it be possible to steer two large ships at high speed with such accuracy as to cause a direct collision,—a point which many practical seamen doubt.

On the other hand, a ship striking another on the broadside, or at any angle approaching a right angle, would probably cause the destruction of the latter, with but trifling injury to herself, supposing her bows to be properly constructed for ramming; but, in order to place a ship in a situation to strike such a blow (both ships proceeding at speed), she would herself have to assume a very critical position; that is to say, she would have to expose her broadside, or in other words, she would have to place herself almost as much across the assumed path of her adversary as the adversary was across hers; in which position the miscalculation of a few seconds in time, a knot or two in speed, or even a small touch of the helm of either ship at the last moment, would turn the would-be rammer into the victim. It is probable therefore that, if ramming takes place in action, it will be more frequently by accident than design.

Much has been made by the advocates of ramming tactics of the incident of the battle at Lissa, where the Austrian wooden ship "Ferdinand Max" rammed and sank the Italian iron-clad "Re d'Italia"; but it has been stated on high authority that the brave Tegethoff himself has disclaimed any preconceived design in the matter, further than that he suddenly observed through the smoke a grey object in front of him, which he took to be an enemy, that he ordered his ship's engines to be put "full speed a-head" and his ship to be steered for the object, and that he then found he had rammed and sunk the "Re d'Italia."

In some instances modern ships have been designed and built with a view to carrying out some special plan of tactics. Thus in the British navy several ships have been built for the "end-on attack," as it is called, a somewhat vague term for expressing the desire of some officers to fight their ships end-on to the enemy,—tactics, however, which can only be consistently carried out if the enemy consents to run away; otherwise it is evident that, if both ships continue to advance towards each other, they will meet, and if they do not strike and sink each other, they must pass from the "end-on" to the "broadside-on," then "stern-on," and then, unless they mutually agree to run away from each other, they must pass through the "broadside-on" position again before they resume the "end-on" or bow attack.

It would seen therefore to be wise not to construct the ordinary battle ships for any particular method of attack, whilst the whole subject is in such an untried and speculative condition, and so much necessarily depends on the tactics of the enemy, but rather to make ships as strong all over, both offensively and defensively, as it is possible to do upon a given displacement and at a certain cost.

Tactical formations. The principal tactical formations for modern fleets are—single column in line ahead; two and three columns in line ahead; the same in line abreast; quarter line or line of bearing; indented line; and the group formation. In the last-named, a group of three ships becomes the tactical unit instead of the single ship; there is a leader with a ship on each quarter at different angles and different distances; and in this, and also in the indented line formation, the object is to keep the broadsides of the ships open or clear of consorts; but, in consequence of the more recent battle ships not being built specially with a view to broadside fire, these somewhat complicated formations are not generally popular.

Science and the ingenuity of inventors are day by day adding fresh weapons of more terribly destructive energy to the already prodigious list of war material, and the attack may be said to keep always well ahead of the defence, so that it becomes more difficult to lay down fixed rules for tactics than for strategy. Much will depend upon the personal genius, nerve, and happy inspirations of the individual admirals and captains who first find themselves engaged in a modern naval battle; and national instincts, and practical experience in handling steam ships at high speed, will count for much towards the issue. (C. C. P. F.)

WARANGAL, or WORUNGUL, an ancient town in the Nizam's Dominions, or Hyderabad state, situated 86 miles north-east of Hyderabad city, in 17° 58′ N. lat. and 79° 40′ E. long., and containing in 1881 a population of 3347. It was the ancient capital of the Hindu kingdom of Telingána, founded by the Narapati Andhras, of which now little remains to denote its former grandeur except the four gateways of the temple of Siva. These are still in a state of tolerable preservation.

WARASDIN. See VARASD.

WARBLER, in ornithology, the name bestowed in 1773 by Pennant (*Genera of Birds*, p. 35)[1] on the birds removed, in 1769, by Scopoli from the Linnæan genus *Motacilla* (*cf.* WAGTAIL) to one founded and called by him *Sylvia*,—the last being a word employed by several of the older writers in an indefinite way,—that is to say, on all the species of *Motacilla* which were not Wagtails. "Warbler" has long been used by English technical writers as the equivalent of *Sylvia*, and consequently generally applied to all members of the Family *Sylviidæ* thereon raised, which has since been so much subdivided as to include a vast number of genera, while species almost innumerable have from time to time been referred to it.

Until recently ornithologists had come to agree pretty well as to which forms should be considered to belong to the Family *Sylviidæ*, —the "American Warblers" (*Mniotiltidæ*), to be presently considered, being therefrom segregated; but some writers, seeing the difficulty of separating the remainder from the *Turdidæ* (*cf.* THRUSH), tried to get over it by proposing to erect an intermediate Family for the WHEATEAR (*q.v.*) and some similar forms, under the name *Saxicolidæ*. In truth the difficulty was thereby doubled, for, if it was before hard to distinguish between *Sylviidæ* and *Turdidæ*, it has since become harder to distinguish on the one hand between *Sylviidæ* and *Saxicolidæ*, and on the other between *Saxicolidæ* and *Turdidæ*. The confusion thus caused is chiefly due to the adoption in a more or less modified form of the views put forth by Sundevall in 1872, and revised by him in 1874 (*cf.* ORNITHOLOGY, vol. xviii. p. 38). For him, however, it is to be said that he at least proceeded in a fashion that had long been recognized, and gave reasons, whether good or bad, for the system he propounded; but his imitators have omitted so obvious a requirement, and leave to any one who would use their results the task of discovering how they have been reached. Hence it has been suggested that some of the alterations introduced since Sundevall's time have been purely arbitrary, if indeed they did not proceed from considerations of personal convenience, or occasionally even through mischance. Still the greatest allowance must be made for those who attempt to reduce to order such a multitudinous assemblage of forms—forms which present an almost endless variety of small differentiating characters, pointing in numerous directions—while the essential structure of all is apparently so similar that at present there is no hope of assistance from the anatomist or the morphologist. But the affinity, seeming or real, to the *Turdidæ* does not offer the only difficulty. The resemblance which some other forms, often placed with the *Sylviidæ*, bear to the *Timeliidæ*[2]—the *Crateropodidæ* of some systematists—is equally if not more puzzling. It is admitted by many systematists that the *Timeliidæ* form a group that has been made a "refuge for the destitute," a group into which genera and species that were troublesome to classify have been thrust; and, as a natural consequence, the limits of such a "Family" or group have scarcely been plausibly defined.[3] It appears that the so-called *Timeliidæ* lead off to other groups, as the *Laniidæ* (*cf.* SHRIKE) and what not, and their existence as a separate "Family" can hardly be taken for a certainty. Again, a small group of birds, almost wholly peculiar to the Australian region, have been sometimes separated as *Maluridæ*, and of these more must be said presently. Lastly, there are certain genera that, though formerly included without hesitation among the *Sylviidæ*, have lately been designated "Fly-catchers," on grounds, however, that have not been explained.

To deal with this theme in satisfactory detail would require far more space than can here be allowed, for the failures of later systematists would have to be shewn by a series of minute criticisms of a kind that would be only acceptable to specialists, and hardly understood by others than experts. All things then considered, it would seem to be best for our present purpose to regard the "Warblers"—without pledging our faith to the recognition of a "Family" *Sylviidæ*—from the point of view which obtained before the more recent and perplexing (because ill-defined) opinions were introduced, and that aspect is afforded by the scheme furnished by Canon Tristram to Mr Wallace, and by him adopted in his *Geographical Distribution of Animals* (ii. pp. 257-260); but our limits will only allow us to touch upon a few of the most prominent members in addition to those which have already been or will form the subject of separate articles. In this sense then the first that may be mentioned are those forming a group of more or less aquatic habit, usually called *Calamoherpinæ* but more correctly *Acrocephalinæ*, the commonest of which in England is the well-known Sedge-bird or Sedge-Warbler, *Acrocephalus schœnobænus*, whose chattering song resounds in summer-time from almost every wet ditch in most parts of Britain. As is the case with so many of its allies, the skulking habits of the bird cause it to be far more often heard than seen; but, with a little patience, it may be generally observed flitting about the uppermost twigs of the bushes it frequents, and its mottled back and the yellowish-white streak over its eye serve to distinguish it from its ally the Reed-Wren or Reed-Warbler, *A. streperus*, which is clad in a wholly mouse-coloured suit. But this last can also be recognized by its different song, and comparatively seldom does it stray from the reed-beds which are its favourite

[1] For this reference, not before precisely given, the writer is indebted to the Rev. G. M'Arthur.

[2] These are exotic birds, having no recognized English name. Those of "Babblers," "Bush-Babblers," and "Babbling-Thrushes" have been applied to them by some writers, who consider them to be sufficiently characterized by their short, rounded, and incurved wings.

[3] *Cf.* Mr Sharpe's meritorious efforts, *Cat. B. Brit. Museum*, vols. vi. and vii.

haunts. In them generally it builds one of the most beautiful of nests, made of the seed-branches of the reed and long grass, wound horizontally round and round so as to include in its substance the living stems of three or four reeds, between which it is suspended at a convenient height above the water, and the structure is so deep that the eggs do not roll out when its props are shaken by the wind. Of very similar habits is the Reed-Thrush or Great Reed-Warbler, *A. arundinaceus*, a loud-voiced species, abundant on the Continent but very rarely straying to England. Much interest also attaches to the species known as Savi's Warbler, *A. luscinioides*, which was only recognized as a constant inhabitant of the Fen-district of England a few years before its haunts were destroyed by drainage. The last example known to have been obtained in this country was killed in 1856. The nest of this species is peculiar, placed on the ground and formed of the blades of a species of *Glyceria* so skilfully entwined as to be a very permanent structure, and it is a curious fact that its nests were well known to the sedge-cutters of the district which it most frequented, as those of a bird with which they were unacquainted, long before the builder was recognized by naturalists. In coloration the bird somewhat resembles a Nightingale (whence its specific name), and its song differs from that of any of those before mentioned, being a long smooth trill, pitched higher but possessing more tone than that of the Grasshopper-Warbler, *A. nævius*—the *Salicaria locustella* of many authors—which is a widely-distributed species throughout the British Isles, not only limited to marshy sites, but affecting also dry soils, inhabiting indifferently many kinds of places where there is tangled and thick herbage, heather, or brushwood. In those parts of England where it was formerly most abundant it was known as the Reeler or Reel-bird, from its song resembling the whirring noise of the reel at one time used by the spinners of wool. The precise determination of this bird—the Grasshopper Lark, as it was long called in books, though its notes if once heard can never be mistaken for those of a grasshopper or cricket, and it has no affinity to the Larks—as an English species is due to the discernment of Gilbert White in 1768. In its habits it is one of the most retiring of birds, keeping in the closest shelter, so that it may be within a very short distance of an eager naturalist without his being able to see it,—the olive-colour, streaked with dark brown, of its upper plumage helping to make it invisible. The nest is very artfully concealed in the thickest herbage. The foreign forms of Aquatic Warblers are far too numerous to be here mentioned.

In the scheme already mentioned, a Subfamily *Drymœcinæ*, with 15 genera and nearly 200 species, is recognized. That such a natural group may exist is quite likely, but about its composition and limits much doubt cannot fail to be entertained. If its existence be acknowledged, the remarkable genera *Orthotomus* with about 12 and *Cisticola* with some 30 species may be fairly admitted as belonging to it. The former includes the Tailor-birds of the Indian region of which all have heard or read, for their habit of sewing together the leaves of plants so as to form a cone in which to build their nests has often been described and the fabric figured. Jerdon (*B. India*, ii. p. 166) writes of the common Indian Tailor-bird, *O. longicauda*, that it "makes its nest of cotton, wool, and various other soft materials," and "draws together one leaf or more, generally two leaves, on each side of the nest, and stitches them together with cotton, either woven by itself, or cotton thread picked up; and, after passing the thread through the leaf, it makes a knot at the end to fix it." *Cisticola*, of which one species inhabits the south of Europe, follows the same trade on stems of grass, confining them by stitches above the nest, which assumes a globular form.

In the same group *Drymœcinæ* is placed by some authors the Australian genus *Malurus*, to which belong the birds known as "Superb Warblers," and they are not inaptly so named, since in beauty they surpass any others of their presumed allies. Part of the plumage of the cocks in breeding-dress is generally some shade of intense blue, and is so glossy as to resemble enamel, while black, white, chestnut, or scarlet, as well as green and lilac, are also present in one species or another, so as to heighten the effect. But, as already stated, there are systematists who would raise this genus, which contains some 15 species, to the rank of a distinct Family, though on what grounds it is hard to say.

Of the other Subfamilies, *Saxicolinæ*, *Sylviinæ*, and *Phylloscopinæ*, will be conveniently treated under WHEATEAR, WHITETHROAT, and [Willow-] WREN (*qq.v.*), while the *Ruticillinæ* have been already mentioned under NIGHTINGALE, REDBREAST, and REDSTART, and the *Accentorinæ* under [Hedge-] SPARROW.

The birds known as "American Warblers," forming what has now for a long while been almost universally recognized as a distinct Family, *Mniotiltidæ*, remain for consideration. They possess but nine instead of ten primaries, and are peculiar to the New World. More than 130 species have been described, and these have been grouped in 20 genera or more, of which members of all but three are at least summer-visitants to North America. As a whole they are much more brightly coloured than the *Sylviidæ* (*Malurus*, if it belongs to them, always excepted); for, though the particular genus *Mniotilta* (from which, as the fortune of nomenclature will have it, the Family takes its right name)[1] is one of the most abnormal—its colours being plain black and white, and its habits rather resembling those of a TREE-CREEPER (*q.v.*)—in other groups chestnut, bluish-grey, and green appear, the last varying from an olive to a saffron tint, and in some groups the yellow predominates to an extent that has gained for its wearers, belonging to the genus *Dendrœca*, the name of "Golden" Warblers. In the genus *Setophaga*, the members of which deserve to be called "Fly-catching" Warblers, the plumage of the males at least presents yellow, orange, scarlet, or crimson. Dr Coues (*Key N.-Am. Birds*, ed. 2, p. 288), following on the whole the arrangement of Baird, Brewer, and Ridgway (*N.-Am. Birds*, i. p. 178), separates the whole Family (for which he arbitrarily retains the name *Sylvicolidæ*) into three Subfamilies, *Sylvicolinæ* (=*Mniotiltinæ*), *Icteriinæ*, and *Setophaginæ*, grouping the genera *Mniotilta*, *Parula*, and *Peucedromus* as "Creeping Warblers"; *Geothlypis*, *Oporornis*, and *Siurus* as "Ground-Warblers"; *Protonotaria*, *Helminthotherus*, and *Helminthophila* as "Worm-eating Warblers"; *Setophaga*, *Cardellina*, and *Myiodioctes* as "Fly-catching Warblers"; *Icteria*, which perhaps may not belong to the Family, standing alone; and *Dendrœca* as "Wood-Warblers."

The *Mniotiltidæ* contain forms exhibiting quite as many diverse modes of life as do the *Sylviidæ*. Some are exclusively aquatic in their predilections, others affect dry soils, brushwood, forests, and so on. Almost all the genera are essentially migratory, but a large proportion of the species of *Dendrœca*, *Setophaga*, and especially *Basileuterus*, seem never to leave their Neotropical home; while the genera *Leucopeza*, *Teretristis*, and *Microligia*, comprising in all but 5 species, are peculiar to the Antilles. The rest are for the most part natives of North America, where a few attain a very high latitude,[2] penetrating in summer even beyond the Arctic Circle, and thence migrate southward at the end of summer or in the fall of the year, some reaching Peru and Brazil, but a few, as, for instance, *Parula pitiayumi* and *Geothlypis velata* seem to be resident in the country last named.

To return, in conclusion, to the *Sylviidæ*, or true Warblers, it is to be hoped that before long some competent ornithologist will take on himself the task, necessary if toilsome and perhaps ungrateful, of revising the work that has lately been done upon them and upon the *Turdidæ*, and, setting aside all preconceived notions except that of aiming at the truth, without prejudice fix the limits of the two Families, if Families they be, and at the same time adjust the relations of the hitherto very indefinite group *Timeliidæ*. (A. N.)

WARBURTON, ELIOT BARTHOLOMEW GEORGE (1810–1852), traveller and novelist, born in 1810 near Tullamore, Ireland, made a hit with his first book, *The Crescent and the Cross*. It was a book of Eastern travel, in Turkey, Syria, Palestine, and Egypt, and fairly divided public attention with Mr Kinglake's *Eothen*, which appeared in the same year, 1844. Interest was centred in the East at the time, and Warburton had popular sympathy with him in his eloquent advocacy of the annexation of Egypt; but, apart from this harmony with the tastes of the time, the traveller had so many adventures, told them with such spirit, described what he saw with such picturesque vigour, and sketched character with such animation and generosity, that the success of the book on its merits was perfectly legitimate. Warburton was an Irishman, with an Irishman's rhetoric and spirit of adventure, who, after an education at Cambridge, was called to the Irish bar, tried to settle down on his paternal estate, but very soon abandoned the management of his tenants for a life of nobler excitement. His first success as an author tempted him to try again, but he had unhappily a short career, and did not again equal *The Crescent and the Cross*. His most substantial work was a *Memoir of Prince Rupert*, published in 1849, enriched with original documents, and written with eloquent partiality for the subject. This was followed in 1850 by a novel, *Reginald Hastings*, the scenes of which

[1] By some writers the Family is called *Sylvicolidæ*, a practice which contravenes the ordinary usage of nomenclaturists, since the name *Sylvicola* in ornithology is preoccupied by its employment in conchology.

[2] Seven species have been recorded as wandering to Greenland, and one, *Dendrœca virens*, is said to have occurred in Europe (*Naumannia*, 1858, p. 425)

were laid in the same period of civil war. It was much more commonplace than his travels, and showed no power of construction or felicity in the creation of character. He produced another historical novel, *Darien, or The Merchant Prince* (1851). The knowledge therein shown of the inhabitants of the isthmus led to his selection by the Atlantic and Pacific Company to explore the country and negotiate a treaty with the Indian tribes. He sailed on this mission in the "Amazon," which perished by fire with nearly all on board on the 4th of January 1852.

His *Life of the Earl of Peterborough* was published posthumously in 1853. To the *Memoirs of Horace Walpole* (1851), nominally edited by him, he contributed, as he avowed in the preface, only his advice to the anonymous author and the countenance of his name.

WARBURTON, WILLIAM (1698–1779), bishop of Gloucester, was the son of the town clerk of Newark, where he was born on December 24, 1698. He was educated at Oakham and Newark grammar schools, but, being intended for his father's profession, does not seem to have addicted himself especially to the classics, or to have manifested extraordinary proficiency in any study. He lost his father while a boy, and in 1714 he was articled to Mr Kirke, attorney at Great Markham, in Nottinghamshire, and after serving his time with him returned to Newark with the intention of practising as a solicitor. Whether he ever did seems uncertain, but a very short time afterwards he is found studying Latin and Greek under the master of Newark school, who frequently sat up till late at night with his pupil. In 1723 he was ordained deacon by the archbishop of York, and on March 1, 1727, received priest's orders from the bishop of London. He had occupied the interval in various literary labours, the most important being the notes he contributed to Theobald's edition of Shakespeare, and an anonymous pamphlet on a question which had arisen concerning the jurisdiction of the Court of Chancery. Warburton had undertaken to answer another anonymous pamphlet, which proved to be the composition of no less a person than Mr Yorke, afterwards Lord Chancellor Hardwicke, and the impression which he made upon his antagonist was evinced by the pains the latter took with his reply. He now received from Sir Robert Sutter the small living of Griesley, in Nottinghamshire, exchanged next year for that of Brant Broughton, in Lincolnshire, and was made an honorary M.A. of Cambridge. Here for eighteen years he spent his time in intense study, the first result of which was his celebrated treatise on the alliance between church and state, published in 1736. The work was probably intended, and certainly admirably adapted, to afford the ministry of the day an excuse for omitting to redeem their promise to the Dissenters of freeing them from the bondage of the Test and Corporation Acts. To this end the test is represented as the only possible means of reconciling the principle of a religious establishment with that of a free toleration, a piece of logic which, now that religious tests are no longer held a qualification for civil office, would excite most opposition where it originally gained most favour. It fully answered its temporary purpose, and equally subserved the author's real end by gaining him credit at court. It would appear that he only missed immediate preferment by the death of Queen Caroline. His next performance, the famous *Divine Legation of Moses Demonstrated on the Principles of a Religious Deist*, the first part of which was published in 1738, will long preserve his name as the author of the most daring and ingenious of theological paradoxes. The deists had made the absence of any inculcation of the doctrine of a future life an objection to the divine authority of the Mosaic writings. Warburton boldly admits the fact and turns it against the adversary. No human legislator, he contends, would have omitted such a sanction of morality; *ergo*, the legislation was divine. It may be doubted whether the argument ever convinced any one; and its cogency was not assisted by the multitude of minor paradoxes with which it was interwoven, such as the identification of the scenery of the sixth book of the *Æneid* with the exhibitions of the Eleusinian mysteries. But the author's extraordinary power, learning, and originality were acknowledged on all hands, though he excited censure and suspicion by a circumstance highly honourable to him, his tenderness to the alleged heresies of Conyers Middleton. The second volume of the work appeared in 1741.

Warburton's next undertaking, though still theological, brought him into the field of general literature. Either in quest of another paradox, or actually unable to recognize the Spinozistic tendency of Pope's *Essay on Man*, he entered upon its defence against Crousaz, in a series of articles contributed to *The Republic of Letters*. Whether Pope had really understood the tendency of his own work has always been a question, but there is no question that he was glad of an apologist, or that Warburton's *jeu d'esprit* (for him it was hardly more) in the long run did more for his fortunes than all his erudition. It occasioned a sincere friendship between him and Pope, whom he persuaded to add a fourth book to the *Dunciad*, and substitute Cibber for Theobald as the hero of the poem. Pope bequeathed him the copyright and the editorship of his works, and contributed even more to his advancement by introducing him to Murray, afterwards Lord Mansfield, who obtained for him the preachership of Lincoln's Inn, and to Ralph Allen, who, says Johnson, "gave him his niece and his estate, and, by consequence, a bishopric." The marriage took place in 1745, and from that time Warburton resided principally at his father-in-law's estate at Prior Park, in Gloucestershire, which he inherited on Allen's death in 1764. In 1747 appeared his edition of Shakespeare, into which, as he expressed it, Pope's previous edition was melted down. He had previously entrusted notes and emendations on Shakespeare to Sir Thomas Hanmer, whose unauthorized use of them led to a warm controversy. Warburton was further kept busy by the attacks on his *Divine Legation* from all quarters, by a dispute with Bolingbroke respecting Pope's behaviour in the affair of Bolingbroke's *Patriot King*, and (1750) by a work of more importance in vindication of the alleged miraculous interruption of the rebuilding of the temple of Jerusalem undertaken by Julian. Here again Warburton shows his habitual intrepidity as a controversialist, and places himself upon ground where few at the present day would care to follow him. His defence of revelation was continued in his *View of Bolingbroke's Posthumous Writings* (1754), universally allowed to be a most masterly performance. Warburton's manner of dealing with opponents would be in our day considered both insolent and rancorous, but it did him no disservice in his own. In 1757 he was made dean of Bristol, and in 1760 bishop of Gloucester.

Mr Abbey characterizes Warburton as an inactive bishop, and the partial Hurd can say no more than that "he performed the duties of his office with regularity, but further than this he could not prevail with himself to go." Nor did he ever seek to shine in parliament. He continued, however, active with his pen, so long as the infirmities of age allowed, collecting and publishing his sermons, reprinting his principal works with large additions, toiling to complete the *Divine Legation*, the last book of which appeared after his death, and writing (1762) a vigorous attack on Methodism under the title of *The Doctrine of Grace*. Of this work his friend and biographer Hurd says, with curious infelicity, "the sect will find a sort of immortality in this discourse." The reverse has proved true, yet the book ranks among the author's most powerful productions. He also engaged in a keen controversy with Bishop Lowth on the book of Job, which even his admiring biographer wishes forgotten. His last important act was to found, in 1768, the Warburtonian lecture, "to prove the truth of revealed religion from the completion of the prophecies in the Old and New Testament which relate to the Christian church, especially to the apostacy of Papal Rome." "On the right determination of the prophecies relating to Antichrist," he said, "one might rest the whole truth of the Christian religion,"—another opinion which finds little support in the 19th century. The principal authority for his latter years is his correspondence with his friend Bishop Hurd, an important contribution to the literary history of the period. After the death of his only son in 1776 he fell into a lethargic languor, which was terminated by death on June 7, 1779.

Warburton was undoubtedly a great man, but his intellect, marred by wilfulness and the passion for paradox, has effected no result in any degree adequate to its power. He disdained to persuade unless he could at the same time astonish, and in endeavouring to amaze he has failed to convince. None of the propositions with which his name is chiefly connected have found acceptance with posterity, and while abundantly demonstrating his own learning he has failed to make any considerable addition to the stock of human knowledge, or to leave any signal mark on the history of opinion. He was rather a gladiator than a warrior, an exhibitor of brilliant fence leading to no definite end. Though always faithful to his convictions, he argued for victory rather than truth, and wasted upon advocacy powers which would have produced great results if they had been employed in serious and dispassionate investigation. His rude and arrogant style of controversy deserved and received severe reprehension; it was at all events free from pettiness and malignity; and his faults were in general those of an aspiring and magnanimous nature. He was a warm and constant friend, and gave many proofs of gratitude to his benefactors. As an editor and critic he displayed much force of mind, but his standard of research was not high, and his literary taste was that of the 18th century. (R. G.)

WARD. See INFANT.

WARD, EDWARD MATTHEW (1816–1879), history and *genre* painter, was born at Pimlico, London, in 1816. Among his early boyish efforts in art was a series of clever illustrations to the *Rejected Addresses* of his uncles Horace and James Smith, which was followed soon afterwards by designs to some of the papers of Washington Irving. In 1830 he gained the silver palette of the Society of Arts; and in 1835, aided by Wilkie and Chantrey, he entered the schools of the Royal Academy, having in the previous year contributed to its exhibition his portrait of Mr O. Smith, the comedian, in his character of Don Quixote. In 1836 he went to Rome, where in 1838 he gained a silver medal from the Academy of St Luke for his Cimabue and Giotto, which in the following year was exhibited at the Royal Academy. The young artist now turned his thoughts to fresco-painting, which he studied under Cornelius at Munich. In 1843 he forwarded his Boadicea Animating the Britons previous to the Last Battle against the Romans to the competition for the decoration of the Houses of Parliament,—a work upon which he was afterwards engaged, having in 1853 been directed by the fine art commissioners to execute eight subjects in the corridor of the House of Commons. The success of his Dr Johnson in Lord Chesterfield's Ante-Room—now in the National Gallery, along with the Disgrace of Lord Clarendon (the smaller picture) (1846), the South Sea Bubble (1847), and James II. receiving the News of the Landing of the Prince of Orange (1850)—secured his election as an associate of the Royal Academy in 1847, and in 1855 he gained full academic honours. Among the more important of his other works may be named Charlotte Corday Led to Execution (1852), the Last Sleep of Argyll (1854), the Emperor of the French Receiving the Order of the Garter (1859), painted for the queen, the Antechamber at Whitehall during the Dying Moments of Charles II. (1861), Dr Johnson's First Interview with John Wilkes (1865), and the Royal Family of France in the Temple, painted in 1851, and usually considered the artist's masterpiece. For several years before his death Ward suffered from ill-health and mental depression, which led to temporary aberration of intellect. He died at Windsor, on January 15, 1879.

Ward's pictures have been extremely popular, and the engravings which reproduce so many of them have had a wide circulation His works are generally interesting in subject; they tell their story with point and clearness, are correct and learned in costume, and full of observation and character. In purely technical qualities, in lighting, tone, colour, and draughtsmanship, they are more frequently open to exception.

WARD, JAMES (1769–1859), animal painter and engraver, was born in Thames Street, London, on October 23, 1769. At the age of twelve he was bound apprentice with J. Raphael Smith, but he received little attention and learnt nothing from this engraver. He was afterwards instructed for over seven years by his elder brother, William Ward, and he engraved many admirable plates, among which his Mrs Billington, after Reynolds, occupies a very high place. He presented a complete set of his engravings, in their various states, numbering three hundred impressions, to the British Museum. While still a youth he made the acquaintance of George Morland, who afterwards married his sister; and the example of this artist's works induced him to attempt painting. His early productions were rustic subjects in the manner of Morland, which were frequently sold as the work of the more celebrated painter. His Bull-Bait, an animated composition, introducing many figures, attracted much attention in the Royal Academy of 1797. A commission from Sir John Sinclair, president of the new agricultural society, to paint an Alderney cow led to much similar work, and turned Ward's attention to animal-painting, a department in which he achieved his highest artistic successes, his renderings of cattle being unrivalled in the English school, and worthy to rank with the pictures of the great animal-painters of Holland. His Landscape with Cattle, acquired for the National Gallery at a cost of £1500, was painted in 1820–22 at the suggestion of West, in emulation of the Bull of Paul Potter at The Hague. His Boa Serpent Seizing a Horse was executed in 1822, and his admirable Grey Horse, shown in the Old Masters' Exhibition of 1879, dates from 1828. Ward also produced portraits, and many landscapes like the Gordale Scar and the Harlech Castle in the National Gallery. Sometimes he turned aside into the less fruitful paths of allegory, as in his unsuccessful Pool of Bethesda (1818), and Triumph of the Duke of Wellington (1818). He was a frequent contributor to the Royal Academy and the British Institution, and in 1841 he collected one hundred and forty examples of his art, and exhibited them in his house in Newman Street. He was elected an Associate of the Royal Academy in 1807, and a full member in 1811, and died at Cheshunt on the 23rd of November, 1859.

Ward compiled an autobiography, of which an abstract was published in the *Art Journal* in 1849.

WARD, WILLIAM (1766–1826), mezzotint-engraver, an elder brother of James Ward (see above), was born in London in 1766. He was the most distinguished pupil of J. Raphael Smith, and executed a great part of many of the plates which bear the name of that excellent engraver. In 1795 he began to exhibit in the Royal Academy, of which in 1814 he was elected an associate engraver. He also held the appointment of mezzotint-engraver to the prince regent and the duke of York. He executed six plates after Reynolds, engraved many of the works of his brother-in-law, George Morland, and his mezzotints after Andrew Geddes, which include the full-lengths of Sir David Wilkie and of Patrick Brydone, are of great merit. His engravings are full of artistic spirit, and show fine feeling for colour; and they are excellently tender and expressive in their rendering of flesh. He died suddenly at Mornington Place, on December 1, 1826.

WARDHÁ, or WURDA, a British district in the chief commissionership of the Central Provinces of India, with an area of 2401 square miles. It lies between 20° 18′ and 21° 21′ N. lat. and 78° 4′ 30″ and 79° 15′ E. long., and forms a triangle with its apex towards the north-west, the base resting on Chanda district; on the east it is bounded by Nágpur, and on the west the Wardhá river separates it from Berar. Wardhá is hilly in the north, and intersected by spurs from the Satpura range. The central portion includes the three peaks of Málegáon (1726 feet), Nándgáon (1874 feet), and Jaitgarh (2086 feet). From this cluster of hills numerous small streams lead to the Wardhá river on the one side, while on the other the Dham, Bor, and Asodá *nálá* flow down the length of the district in a south-easterly direction. The Wardhá, and its affluent the Waná, are the only rivers of any importance. To the south the country spreads out in an undulating plain, intersected by watercourses, and broken here and there by isolated hills rising abruptly from the surface. In general the lowlands are well wooded. Leopards, hyænas, wolves, jackals, and wild hogs abound in the district; other animals found are the spotted deer, *nilgai*, wild goat, and antelopes. Among birds are the bustard, partridge, quail, and rock pigeon. There are numerous roads and 65 miles of railway. The district is subject to great variations of climate, and the rainfall at Wardhá town averages nearly 40 inches.

The census of 1881 disclosed a population of 387,221 (males 195,564, females 191,657), Hindus numbering 328,523, Mohammedans 14,200, Christians 96, and aboriginals 41,933. The district contains five towns with a population exceeding 5000. Wardhá (5816), the chief town, has wide and regular streets, having been built in 1866. Of the total area 1500 square miles are cultivated; while of the portion lying waste 380 square miles are returned as cultivable. The chief crops are cotton, wheat, other food-grains, and oil-seeds. The only manufacture of any importance is cotton cloth, the greater part of which is exported to Berar and to the districts farther west. Cotton thread, blankets, gunny, and rope are also made, and since the completion of the railway a considerable trade has also sprung up in butter, which finds a ready sale in the Bombay market. But by far the most important article exported is the raw cotton known as "Hinganghâts," from the cotton mart of that name. The principal imports are salt, English piece goods, hardware, and spices. In 1886–87 the gross revenue of the district amounted to £99,955, of which the land yielded £51,494. The history of Wardhá forms part of that of Nágpur district, from which it was separated in 1862 for administrative purposes.

WARE, an ancient market-town of Herts, England, is situated in a valley on the north side of the river Lea, and on a branch of the Great Eastern Railway, 2 miles east-north-east of Hertford, and 22¼ north of London by rail. The principal street is the spacious High Street, running east and west by the river. The houses are chiefly modern, but there are a few of the old timber frame-houses. The Lea, by means of which there is good water communication, is crossed by an iron bridge erected in 1845. The New River Head is half a mile distant. The parish church of St Mary is a large and handsome cruciform building of flint and stone in the Perpendicular style, consisting of chancel (built, it is supposed, by Lady Margaret Beaufort, countess of Richmond, and mother of Henry VII.), lady chapel to the south (about 1380), nave of five bays of the time of Richard II., transepts, aisles, south porch, and embattled tower of the time of Edward III. There is an elaborate font of the time of Henry IV., and a few old brasses and monuments. The church has undergone restoration in 1848, 1881, and 1885–86. The modern mansion of the Priory, to the west of the town, occupies the site of a priory of the order of St Francis, founded by Margaret, countess of Leicester, sister of Henry III., who was then lady of the manor of Ware. A considerable portion of the original building is incorporated in the modern one. Among the modern public buildings are the corn exchange and the town-hall, which includes a literary institute and library. There is a recreation ground 6 acres in extent, and a cemetery of 4 acres. The famous "great bed of Ware" referred to in Shakespeare's *Twelfth Night*, which formerly was at the Saracen's Head, has been removed to Rye House, 2 miles distant. The town possesses breweries and brick-fields, and there is a large trade in malt. The population of the urban sanitary district (area about 641 acres) in 1871 was 4917, and in 1881 it was 5277.

Roman remains have been discovered at various times in the neighbourhood of Ware, and the Ermine Street crossed the Lea valley just a little above it. At the time of the Domesday survey the town had 130 inhabitants, and belonged to Hugh de Grentemaisnil. In the reign of John it came into the possession of Saier de Quincy, earl of Winchester, who, by forcing the thoroughfare of the bridge by breaking the chain, and thus freeing the bridge of toll, greatly increased the trade of the town. The tolls were, however, again imposed. They were granted by Charles I. to William, earl of Salisbury, and they are still collected from non-resident traders. Robert de Quincy in 1254 received for the town the grant of a market and fair from Henry III. In the 15th century it came into the possession of the earl of Warwick, the king-maker. On the death of Richard, duke of Gloucester, it was settled by Henry VII. on his mother, the countess of Richmond. It was then granted to Margaret Plantagenet, countess of Salisbury, on whose execution in 1541 it reverted to the crown. Queen Mary on her accession restored it to Catherine, countess of Huntingdon, granddaughter of the countess of Salisbury, who about 1570 sold it to Thomas Fanshawe, remembrancer in the exchequer. About 1700 the manor was sold to Sir Thomas Byde, a London brewer, in whose family it remained till 1846. Ware is the "town of fame" alluded to by Cowper in his "John Gilpin." William Godwin was for some time minister of the Independent chapel there. William of Ware was the teacher of Duns Scotus.

WARMINSTER, an ancient market-town of Wiltshire, England, is situated on elevated ground, at the western extremity of Salisbury Plain, near the Somerset border, on the river Wily, and on a branch of the Great Western Railway, 17 miles south-west of Devizes, 21 north-west of Salisbury, and 105 south-south-west of London by rail. It consists chiefly of one street about a mile in length. The parish church of St Denys is an ancient stone structure of various styles, the south porch and tower being of the time of Edward III., the chancel Perpendicular, and the nave of the 18th century. It is now (1888) undergoing complete restoration at a cost of £9000, the nave being in process of entire reconstruction. The town-hall was erected by the marquis of Bath in 1830. Among the benevolent institutions are the free school, established in 1707 by the first Viscount Weymouth, the missionary college of St Boniface (1860), the community of St Denys home (1866) for training young women to assist in missionary work, the Wilts reformatory for boys (1856), the cottage hospital (1866), the almshouses for four aged women (1873), and an orphanage. The town possesses a large silk mill, engineering and agricultural implement works, and malt-works. There is a considerable agricultural trade. The population of the urban sanitary district (area 6370 acres) in 1871 was 5786, and in 1881 it was 5640.

Warminster is probably of ancient British origin, and the neighbourhood is remarkable for the number of its barrows. The old Roman road from Old Sarum to Bath skirted Warminster to the north. Camden supposes it to have been the Roman *Verlucio*, and, although this conjecture is probably wrong, there can be no doubt that it was a Roman station of importance. The barrows within the entrenchments at Battlesbury camp, a little to the east, indicate an earlier than Roman occupation, but the entrenchments were probably themselves the work of the Romans. A great variety of Roman remains have been found in the neighbourhood of the town. Warminster was a royal manor in the time of Edward the Confessor, and as such was free of taxes and assessments. In Domesday the name occurs as Guerminster. It then possessed 30 burgesses and probably a total population of over 400. It was bound to provide a night's lodging for the king and all his retinue. Its early importance was chiefly owing to its situation at the junction of the roads from Bath, Frome, Salisbury, and Shaftesbury. It remained a royal manor till the reign of Henry II.

WARRANT, in law, is an authority empowering a person to act in a way which would not be lawful without such authority. The term occurs very early in constitutional documents: it is found in the Assize of Clarendon and the Assize of the Forest, both in the reign of Henry II. A warrant must be under the hand and seal of the person issuing it, unless such formalities be dispensed with by statute. Warrants are of several kinds, and may be conveniently divided into four classes, which may be called the executive, the judicial, the financial, and the private.

Executive.—A warrant under the sign-manual of the king, countersigned by the lord chancellor or a secretary of state, is still in use for some purposes. It is the means of granting PARDON (*q.v.*) and letters patent (except those for inventions), and of framing certain regulations for the forces. It was by royal warrant (afterwards confirmed by Act of Parliament) that purchase of commissions in the army was abolished in 1871.[1] By 18 Hen. VI. c. 1 letters patent are to bear the date of the king's warrant delivered to the lord chancellor. The issue of warrants under the sign-manual has been recently regulated by the Great Seal Act, 1884. Such a warrant must bear a ten-shilling stamp. Royal warrants were at one time in considerably more frequent use than they are at present. For instance, in 1602 the censorship of the stage was committed to the poet Daniel by royal warrant (see THEATRE). A false representation that any goods were made by a person holding a royal warrant is now punishable under the Merchandise Marks Act, 1887. The issue of warrants under the hand of a secretary of state is now, with two exceptions, confined to cases in which there is suspicion of treason or treasonable practices, and the warrant must name the person whom it is intended to arrest. The exceptions are the cases of bringing up a prisoner to give evidence under 16 and 17 Vict. c. 30, and warrants issued under the Extradition Act (see EXTRADITION). By 16 Car. I. c. 10, if any person be imprisoned by warrant of the king in person, of the council board, or any of the privy council, he is entitled to a writ of *habeas corpus*. By the Habeas Corpus Act, 31 Car. II. c. 2, detention on a legal warrant is good ground for refusing discharge to the prisoner on return to a writ of *habeas corpus*. General warrants of a secretary of state were decided to be illegal in 1763. A named person may still be committed by a secretary of state's warrant, but his papers cannot be seized (see PRESS LAWS). Power to issue warrants to search for arms and to arrest for treason or treasonable practices in Ireland has been given by various Acts, *e.g.*, 44 Vict. cc. 4, 5, and by the Criminal Law and Procedure Act, 1887. The right of a secretary of state or the lord lieutenant in Ireland by warrant to detain or open letters in the post-office still exists, and has been recognized by orders in council and proclamations in the 17th century, and more recently by various Post-Office Acts, such as 9 Anne c. 10, 35 Geo. III. c. 62, 7 Will. IV. and 1 Vict. c. 36. The right was finally established by the reports of committees of both houses appointed in 1844 on a complaint by Mazzini and others that Sir James Graham, then home secretary, had opened their letters. It was exercised as recently as 1881 over the letters of persons suspected of treasonable correspondence in Ireland. Committal for breach of privilege of the House of Commons is by warrant of the speaker. A warrant of a law officer of the crown for sealing letters patent for invention was necessary under the old patent law, but has been superseded by other procedure since the Patents Act, 1883. The lowest form of executive warrant is the warrant of a sheriff to his bailiff in pursuance of a writ.

Judicial.—Warrants of this kind are used in either civil or criminal procedure. The only kind used in both seems to be that issued by a judge of the High Court, who has the same jurisdiction as a secretary of state under 16 and 17 Vict. c. 30. In civil procedure the warrant in a county court corresponds very nearly to the WRIT (*q.v.*) in the High Court. Examples of county court warrants are those of attachment, delivery, execution, and possession. The warrant of arrest in Admiralty is a form of procedure confined to Courts of Admiralty jurisdiction. The most important and frequent use of the warrant is for the apprehension of an accused person to be brought before a court of summary jurisdiction, either in the first instance or on failure to obey a summons (see SUMMARY JURISDICTION, SUMMONS). Such warrants are usually issued by a justice of the peace; when issued by the court they are called bench warrants. Where issued by a justice for execution out of his jurisdiction, a warrant must usually be backed by another justice having jurisdiction where it is to be executed. The warrant of a justice may also issue in some non-judicial matters, *e.g.*, for the compul sory supply of carriages under the Army Act, 1881. There are certain warrants which by common law or statute extend much further than ordinary judicial warrants. Those issued under the Fugitive Offenders Act, 1881, if duly backed, extend throughout the British empire. Warrants of a court having jurisdiction in bankruptcy run throughout the United Kingdom. A judge of the Queen's Bench Division has, both at common law and by statute, authority to issue a warrant in certain cases. Such a warrant is valid throughout England. Execution of the decisions of a court of summary jurisdiction is secured by warrants, part of the process of the court, such as warrants of distress or commitment. A warrant may also issue for the apprehension of a witness whose attendance cannot be otherwise assured. A search warrant may be granted for the purpose of searching suspected premises for stolen goods. Special powers for issuing such warrants are given by the Army, Merchant Shipping, Customs, Pawnbrokers, Stamp, and other Acts. The Criminal Law Amendment Act, 1885, allows the issue of search warrants where it is suspected that a female is unlawfully detained for immoral purposes. As a general rule no one can be arrested without warrant. To this rule there are certain exceptions either at common law or by statute. At common law a justice of the peace, a sheriff, a coroner, a constable, and even a private person, may arrest any one without warrant for a treason, felony, or breach of the peace committed, or attempted to be committed, in his presence. A constable (whether a constable at common law or a police constable appointed under the Police Acts) may arrest a person indicted for felony; a constable or a private person may arrest on reasonable suspicion that he who is arrested has committed a felony. But in the latter case he does so at his peril, for he must prove (what the constable need not) that there has been an actual commission of the crime by some one, as well as a reasonable ground for suspecting the particular person. What is a reasonable ground it is of course impossible to define, but, in the case of a constable, a charge by a person not manifestly unworthy of credit is generally regarded as sufficient. An accused person who

[1] The warrant officer (so called no doubt from the mode of his appointment) is a distinct rank in both the army and navy. For the warrant officer in the navy, see vol. xvii. p. 293.

has been bailed may be arrested by his bail, and the police may assist in the arrest. In neither case is a warrant necessary. Nor is it necessary for the apprehension of one against whom the hue and cry is raised (see THEFT). The king cannot arrest in person or by verbal command, as no action would lie against him for wrongful arrest. Statutory powers of arrest without warrant are given to both constables and private persons by numerous Acts of Parliament, for instance, the Game Act of 9 Geo. IV. c. 69, various Police Acts, the Criminal Law Consolidation Acts of 1861, the Prevention of Crime Act, 1871. The possession of a legal warrant by a peace officer on arrest is of great importance in determining whether the person resisting apprehension is justified or not in so doing. Should the officer attempt to apprehend him on an illegal warrant, or without a warrant in a case where a warrant is necessary, and be killed in the attempt, the killing would probably be held to be manslaughter and not murder. The authorities on this point are, however, conflicting. In an action against a peace officer for arrest on an illegal warrant, he is, by 24 Geo. II. c. 44, entitled to demand perusal and a copy of the warrant. Execution of warrants in border counties of England and Scotland, and backing and execution of warrants issued in one part of the kingdom by justices and officers of another part, are specially provided for by numerous Acts of Parliament. Forms of warrants will be found in the schedule to the rules under the Summary Jurisdiction Act and the appendix to the County Court Rules, 1886.

Financial.—Payment out of the Treasury is generally made upon warrant. Treasury warrants are regulated by many of the Acts dealing with the national debt. Payment of dividends by trading corporations and companies is generally made by means of dividend warrants.

Private.—Warrants issued by private persons are either mercantile or non-mercantile. Mercantile warrants are negotiable instruments giving a right to the delivery of goods, generally those deposited at a dock or warehouse, and by mercantile custom regarded as documents of title to the goods to which they relate. They have been recognized by the legislature, especially in the Factors Acts (see FACTOR). Thus the interpretation clause of one of those Acts, 5 and 6 Vict. c. 39, included under the head of documents of title India warrants, dock warrants, and warehouse keepers' warrants. The forgery of any warrant or endorsement or assignment of any warrant of this kind is by 24 and 25 Vict. c. 98 punishable with a maximum penalty of penal servitude for life. The stamp on such a warrant is, with certain exceptions, threepence. Among private warrants of a non-mercantile kind those in the most frequent use are warrants of distress, by which a landlord empowers his agent to distrain for arrears of rent.

Warrant of Attorney to confess judgment is a security for money (now practically obsolete) in the form of a warrant to a solicitor named by the creditor, empowering him to sign judgment in an action against the debtor for the sum due, with a defeasance, or clause that the warrant shall not be put into force in case of due payment of the money secured. It was often used as a collateral security for the payment of an annuity. The Debtors Act, 1869, contained various provisions for making known to the debtor the extent of the liability incurred by him, among others that the warrant must be executed in the presence of a solicitor named by the debtor, and that it and the defeasance must be written on the same paper. A warrant of attorney must be duly stamped, generally as a MORTGAGE (*q.v.*), and must be registered as a judgment in the central office of the Supreme Court.

QUO WARRANTO (*q.v.*) is a means of determining the right of a person to continue to hold an office.

Scotland.—By Art. xxiv. of the Articles of Union royal warrants were to continue to be kept as before the union. The Secretary for Scotland Act, 1885, enabled the crown by royal warrant to appoint the secretary to be vice-president of the Scotch Education Department. The lord advocate's warrant runs throughout the whole of Scotland. Warrants issued by courts of summary jurisdiction agree in the main with those in use in England, though their names are not the same (see SUMMARY JURISDICTION). There are numerous statutory provisions as to warrants of other kinds. By 1 and 2 Vict. c. 114 warrants for diligence, and to charge the debtor under pain of imprisonment, may be inserted in an extract of decree; and in a summons concluding for payment of money a warrant to arrest the movables, debts, and money of the defender may be included. By 31 and 32 Vict. c. 100 a warrant of inhibition may be inserted in the will of a summons. A crown writ is a warrant for infeftment (31 and 32 Vict. c. 101). The same Act gives forms of warrants of REGISTRATION (*q.v.*). The practice as to warrants of citation and commitment in the High Court of Justiciary and the sheriff court now depends chiefly on the Criminal Procedure Act, 1887, 50 and 51 Vict. c. 35. The *meditatio fugæ* warrant is a judicial warrant on which imprisonment may follow until the debtor give *cautio judicio sisti*. It corresponds to some extent to the writ *ne exeat regno* of English practice, but it may be issued by a sheriff (1 and 2 Vict. c. 119). A border warrant for arresting a debtor on the English side of the border is another kind of judicial warrant. The warrant of attorney is not known in Scotland, its place being taken by the clause of registration, which has this advantage over the warrant of attorney that it is not avoided, as is the warrant, by the death of the person giving it.

United States.—By the constitutions of the United States and of almost all the States, warrants are not to issue but upon probable cause, supported by oath or affirmation, and particularly describing the place to be searched and the persons or thing to be seized. These provisions have been held not to mean that there shall be no arrest without warrant, but to confine the right of arrest to circumstances similar to those which justify it in English law. The constitutions of some States forbid general warrants. A warrant is generally necessary for the payment of money out of the United States or a State treasury. (J. W†.)

WARRANTY is etymologically another form of GUARANTEE (*q.v.*). It is used, however, in a rather different sense. The sense common to both words is that of a collateral contract, under which responsibility for an act is incurred, and for the breach of which an action for damages lies. Warranty generally expresses the responsibility of the person doing the act, guarantee the responsibility of some other person on his behalf. A warranty may be defined, in the words of Lord Abinger, as "an express or implied statement of something which the party undertakes shall be part of the contract, and, though part of the contract, collateral to the express object of it" (Chanter *v.* Hopkins, 4 *Meeson and Welsby's Reports*, 404). It differs from a condition in that a condition forms the basis of the contract and a breach of it discharges from the contract, and from a representation in that the latter does not affect the contract unless made a part of it expressly or by implication, as in contracts of insurance and other contracts *uberrimæ fidei*, or unless it be fraudulent. These distinctions are not always accurately maintained. Thus in 8 and 9 Vict. c. 106, § 4, condition seems to be used for warranty.

Warranty as it affected the law of real estate was, up to half a century ago, a matter of the highest importance. A warranty in a conveyance was a covenant real annexed to an estate of freehold, and either expressed in a clause of warranty or implied in cases where a feudal relation might exist between feoffor and feoffee. The warranty, as described by Littleton, § 697, was an outgrowth of feudalism, and something very like it is to be found in the *Liber Feudorum*. At the time of Glanvill the heir was bound to warrant the reasonable donations of his ancestor. Warranty was one of the elements in Bracton's definition of homage, 78*b*, "juris vinculum quo quis astringitur ad warrantizandum defendendum et acquietandum tenentem suum in seisina versus omnes." For an express warranty the word *warrantizo* or warrant was necessary. The word "give" implied a warranty, as did an exchange and certain kinds of partition. In order to bind heirs a clause of warranty was required. This was either lineal, collateral, or commencing by disseisin. The differences between the three kinds were very technical, and depended on abstruse and obsolete learning. They are treated at great length in old works on real property, especially Coke upon Littleton by Butler, 364*b*. The feoffor or his heirs were bound by voucher to warranty or judgment in a writ of *warrantia chartæ* to yield other lands to the feoffee in case of the eviction of the latter. Vouching to warranty was a part of the old fictitious proceedings in a common recovery in use for the purpose of barring an entail before the Fines and Recoveries Act (see ENTAIL). Warranty of this nature, as far as it relates to the conveyance of real estate, though not actually abolished in all possible cases, is now superseded by covenants for title. The more usual of these are now by the Conveyancing Act, 1881, deemed to be implied in conveyances (see REAL ESTATE). For the implied warranties of title and quality see SALE. Vouching to warranty was at one time important in the law of personalty as well as of realty. The procedure is fully described in Glanvill. The right of calling on the holder of lost or stolen goods to vouch to warranty (*interciare*), *i.e.*, to give up the name of the person from whom he received them, under pain of forfeiture, was often granted under the name of *theam* as a local franchise (see THEFT). Warranty, as it exists at present in the law of personalty, is either express or implied. There is no general rule as to what constitutes a warranty. It is not necessary that an express warranty should be in writing, the law being that every affirmation at the time of sale of personal chattels is a warranty, provided that it appears to have been so intended. The principal cases of implied warranty occur in the contracts of sale and INSURANCE (*q.v.*). There is also an implied warranty in other kinds of contract, *e.g.*, of seaworthiness by the shipowner in a contract between him and a charterer for the hire of a ship. In all cases of implied warranty the warranty may be excluded by the special terms of the contract. For breach of warranty an action may be brought directly, or the breach may be used as ground for a counter claim or for reduction of damages, but the breach will not in the case of a warranty proper entitle the person suffering by it to a rescission of the contract. Thus in a sale the property passes although the warranty be broken. In some cases warranties on sale are the subject of statutory enactments. By the Merchandise Marks Act, 1887, a vendor is deemed to warrant that the trade mark or trade description on any goods sold is genuine. The Chain Cables and Anchors Act, 1874, enacts that every contract for the sale of a chain cable shall (in the absence of any stipulation to the contrary) imply a warranty that the cable has been duly tested and stamped. In some other Acts, such as the Bills of Exchange Act, 1882, the term warranty does not occur, but the practical effect is the same.

Scotland.—The term corresponding to warranty in the law of heritable property is "warrandice." Warranty, strictly speaking, seems confined to movables. Warrandice appears early in Scots law, the heir by *Regiam Majestatem* being bound to warrant the reasonable donations of his ancestor. Warrandice in the existing law is either real or personal. Real warrandice is that whereby warrandice lands are made over, as indemnity for those conveyed, to assure the person to whom they were conveyed from loss by the appearance of a superior title. Real warrandice is implied in excambion. Its effect is that the excamber, in case of eviction, may recover possession of his original lands. This is not in accordance with the English law in exchange. Personal warrandice is either express or implied. There is an implied warrandice in every onerous deed, and an absolute warrandice presumes an onerous consideration. Express warrandice is either simple, against the future acts of the vendor, from fact and deed, against acts whether past or future, or absolute, or against all deadly, that is, on any ground existing before the sale. A clause of warrandice is the Scottish equivalent of the English covenants for title. By 32 and 33 Vict. c. 116 a clause of warrandice in the form given in the schedule to the Act imports absolute warrandice as regards the lands and the title-deeds thereof, and warrandice from fact and deed as regards the rents. For the warranty in the sale of movables see SALE.

United States.—Warranty in conveyances of real estate is expressly abolished by statute in many States. In some States warranty is implied on the transfer and indorsement of negotiable instruments. (J. W†.)

WARREN, SAMUEL (1807-1877), author of *Ten Thousand a Year*, was born in Denbighshire in 1807. After a curriculum at the university of Edinburgh, of such distinction that he made the acquaintance of "Christopher North" through his undergraduate fame, he began the study of medicine, but soon abandoned it for the English bar. He entered at the Inner Temple in 1828, and was successful in his profession. He took silk in 1851, was made recorder of Hull in 1854, represented Medhurst in parliament for three years (1856-59), and was rewarded by his party leaders in 1859 with a mastership in lunacy. Meantime he had made a much more brilliant success in fiction-writing. Very early in his career, before he was called to the bar, he had begun to write for *Blackwood*. His *Passages from the Diary of a Late Physician* appeared in that magazine between August 1830 and October 1831, being collected into two volumes in 1832. A third volume was published in 1838, the contents of which appeared originally in the same magazine between September 1832 and August 1837. These short stories, most of them of a horrible character, with morbid interest shielded under a moral purpose, were extremely popular, and so realistic that as long as the writer remained anonymous it was customary for doctors to declare that some brother must be making capital of the secrets of his profession. Warren's brief experience as a medical student thus stood him in good stead. But his great success was *Ten Thousand a Year*, which ran in *Blackwood* from October 1839 to August 1841, and was published separately immediately on its conclusion. Critics complained of the coarseness of the workmanship, of the banality of the moralizing, the crudeness of the pathos, the farcical extravagance of the humour; but meantime the work established itself as one of the most popular novels of the century. Of the higher qualities of imagination and passion Warren was destitute, but his sketches of character, especially farcical character,—Tittlebat Titmouse, Oily Gammon, Mr Quicksilver (an open caricature of Lord Brougham),—are bold and strong, forcibly imprinted on the memory, and the interest of the story is made to run with a powerful current. For several years Warren was content to be known as the author of *Ten Thousand a Year*, and many tales were told of his open pride in the achievement. In 1847 he made another venture, but *Now and Then* was not a success. *The Lily and the Bee*, a squib on the Crystal Palace, published in 1851, though it had the honour of translation into Italian, was a signal failure. A pessimistic dissertation on *The Intellectual and Moral Development of the Age*, published in 1853, also fell flat, and thenceforth Warren, after publishing his *Works, Critical and Imaginative*, in four volumes in 1854, retired on his laurels. He died at London, July 29, 1877.

Besides his novels and other contributions to *Blackwood*, Warren wrote several legal works of repute—*Introduction to Law Studies* (1835), *Extracts from Blackstone* (1837), *Manual of Parliamentary Law* (1852).

His whole attitude towards the subject of insanity in its legal relations was determined by his clear perception and tenacious grasp of the fact that the disease insanity is merely one of the indicia of legal "unsoundness of mind;" he thus reduced medical expertism to its proper proportions, by treating the alienist as a witness and not a judge. The masterly brevity with which he addressed the jury in the Windham inquiry branded as practically irrelevant the mass of the evidence produced at the trial, and prepared the public mind for the third section of the Lunacy Regulation Act of 1862.[1] To the doctrine of moral insanity he offered an uncompromising but ineffective and, it must be confessed, an ignorant opposition. It is doubtful whether he understood the meaning, and it is certain that he had never studied the evidences, of the theory which he so severely condemns. A writer who imagined that the cases of Oxford and MacNaughten bore any resemblance to the "observations" of Pinel was hardly qualified to criticize even the less worthy of his disciples. Yet this hostility was not altogether irrational. Exaggerating, indeed mistranslating, the language of Pinel, in whose work moral insanity appears as "manie sans délire," the English alienists had pressed into their service cases which were far less closely allied to insanity than to crime, and had claimed, in the name of science, to return the verdict whenever mental incompetence existed or was presumed. Against these extravagant pretensions the school of Alderson and Rolfe arose in healthy revolt. Ignorant of, or possibly not caring to sift, the residuum of fact which undoubtedly they would have

[1] It is substantially as follows:—Under every commission, the inquiry shall be confined to the question whether or not the alleged lunatic is, at the time of such inquiry, of unsound mind, and no evidence as to his acts, demeanour, or state of mind at any time being more than two years before the date of the inquiry shall be receivable in proof of insanity, unless the judge or master shall otherwise direct.

found in the standard literature of "manie sans délire," they believed moral insanity to be nothing more than the immoral and illogical plea with which English alienists had made them familiar, and they sternly refused to recognize it. To the exertions of this school, of which Samuel Warren was a distinguished member, we owe the wise jealousy with which the defence of moral insanity is now regarded by alienists themselves. See Warren's *Miscellanies*, vol. ii., "High Treason and Murder—Moral Insanity" (1854); also *The Windham Trial*, published by Wm. Olliver.

WARRINGTON, a municipal and parliamentary borough and market-town of England, chiefly in Lancashire but partly in Cheshire, is situated on the Mersey, near the Sankey Canal, and on the London and North-Western main line and several branch lines of other railways, 18 miles west-south-west of Manchester, 20 east of Liverpool, and 182 from London. The bridge across the Mersey, formerly forming the chief passage over the river from Lancashire to Cheshire, was partly destroyed on the approach of the rebels in 1745, was restored with a watch tower in the middle by parliament in 1747, was replaced by a wooden structure in 1812, and was rebuilt of stone in 1836 at a cost of £6000. The parish church of St Elphin, a cruciform building in the Decorated style, occupies the site of the ancient church, which was taken down about the beginning of the 15th century, the crypt being all of the old structure that now remains. The church now consists of chancel with chapels, nave, aisles, crypt, and embattled central tower and spire rising to the height of 300 feet. It was restored in 1859–67 at a cost of over £15,000. Among the principal modern public buildings are the town-hall, formerly the seat of Colonel Wilson-Patten, now Lord Winmarleigh, purchased in 1872 at a cost of £20,000; the museum and library, erected in 1857, enlarged by the addition of an art gallery and lecture-room in 1876, and again extended in 1881; the market hall (1857); the large covered market shed (1879, enlarged 1885); the public hall (1862); the public baths (1866); the school of art (1883); the infirmary and dispensary (1872); the infectious diseases hospital; and the Warrington clergy orphan institution (1697). The educational institutions include a free grammar school, founded by one of the Boteler family in 1526, and a blue coat school.

Warrington, in the period before the introduction of railways, possessed special advantages through its connexion with the Mersey and Irwell navigation, and it now enjoys unusual facilities for the transit of heavy goods both by canal and railway, while its situation midway between Manchester and Liverpool, and on the main line of the London and North-Western Railway, forms one of the chief sources of its prosperity. It was referred to by Blome in 1683 as "a very fine and large town which hath a considerable market on Wednesday for linen cloth, corn, cattle, provisions, and fish, being much resorted to by the Welshmen." It was among the earliest of the manufacturing towns of Lancashire,—coarse linens and checks being the manufactures which at first formed its staple goods, and afterwards sailcloth and sacking. Perhaps it is now best known for its trade in heavy leather, the tanneries in its immediate neighbourhood consuming on an average about 10,000 hides a week. It has also a great variety of important iron manufactures, including iron in bar, hoop, and wire rod, and files and tools and pins. There are, besides, soap factories, breweries, maltings, cotton mills, and glass-works. The town is divided into five wards, four of which are in Warrington proper, and one in Latchford. The corporation act as the urban sanitary authority. There is a commission of the peace and a police force. The gas supply is managed by the corporation, but the water supply is in the hands of a company. The population of the parliamentary borough (area 3783 acres) in 1871 was 33,050, and in 1881 it was 45,253. The population of the municipal borough (area 1442 acres) in the same years was 32,144 and 41,452.

Warrington is stated to have been an ancient British and Roman town, but there are no traces of a Roman settlement on the north side of the Mersey. On the south side, however, near Wilderspool there are a considerable variety of remains, which some identify with the station *Condate*. At Domesday, Warrington, under the name of Walintune, was at the head of a hundred now merged in West Derby. Its present name first occurs in the 12th century, when Matthew de Vilers gave the church of Warrington to the priory of Thurgarton. Shortly afterwards Warrington came into the family of Pincerna, or Boteler, the progenitors of the Butlers, earls and dukes of Ormonde. Sir William Boteler, who was high sheriff of the county, and governor of the castle of Lancaster, obtained for it, in 1255, from Henry III. the grant of a fair of three days' duration. In the 5th of Edward I. (1277) the charter was renewed, and another was obtained in 1285. About 1592 it was bought by the Irelands, and in 1631 it came into the possession of William Booth, father of Sir George Booth, first Lord Delamere. During the civil war it was held, in 1643, for the king by James, Lord Strange, seventh earl of Derby, who fortified it at great expense, and made it a centre for Royalist excursions, but after a siege of five days it surrendered to the Parliamentary troops. After the battle of Preston in 1648, the remnant of the duke of Hamilton's army under General Baillie rallied at Warrington, and possessed themselves of the bridge, but surrendered on the approach of Cromwell. Henry Booth, second Lord Delamere, was created earl of Warrington on his retirement from the chancellorship of the exchequer in 1690. The town received parliamentary representation in 1832, and was incorporated in 1847. Among persons of eminence connected with Warrington are Dr Aikin, editor of the *Dictionary of General Biography*, Lucy Aikin, Mrs Barbauld, John Kay, the clockmaker who assisted Arkwright in his mechanical experiments, and Dr Joseph Priestley.

See *Warrington in 1465*, in Chetham Society's Publications, vol. xvii.; *Annals of the Lords of Warrington during the first Five Centuries after the Conquest*, *ibid.*, vols. lxxxvi. and lxxxvii.; *Homage Roll of the Manor of Warrington, 1491–1517*, in the publications of the Manchester Record Society, 1885; Kendrick, *Profiles of Warrington Worthies*, 1859.

WARSAW, a government of Russian Poland, occupies a narrow strip of land to the left of the lower Bug and of the Vistula from its junction with the Bug to the Prussian frontier, and is bounded by the Polish governments of Płock and Łomza on the N., Siedlce on the E., and Radom, Piotrkow, and Kalisz on the S. It has an area of 5623 square miles and in 1885 the population was 971,730, of whom 384,000 were then reckoned as living in the capital. It occupies the great plain of central Poland and Mazovia, and is low and flat, with only a few hills in the south, and along the course of the Vistula in the north-west, where the terraces on the left bank descend by steep slopes to the river. Terrible inundations often devastate the region adjacent to the confluence of the Vistula with the Narew and Bug, and marshes cover the low-lying grounds. The soil, which consists chiefly either of boulder clay, lacustrine clays, or sandy fluviatile deposits, is not particularly fertile. The Vistula traverses the government from south-east to north-west, and is joined by the Narew and Bug from the right, and by the Bzura from the left. It is an important channel of communication (see POLAND, vol. xix. p. 307).

The population consists of Poles and Mazurs (Roman Catholics, 76 per cent.), Jews (15 per cent.), and Germans (9 per cent.). The Great and Little Russians number only a few thousands, and the former are gathered chiefly in the towns.

Of the 3,256,800 acres registered, nearly two-thirds of which are arable land, 1,197,000 acres belong to the peasantry (70,724 households), 257,000 to the crown, and the remainder to 4526 small and 1190 large proprietors; 118,000 acres are under forests. In the west the Germans are rapidly colonizing the country, and it was reckoned in 1885 that no less than 373,000 acres, *i.e.*, nearly one-eighth of the territory, and a still larger proportion of the arable land, belonged to 4260 foreigners, chiefly Germans. Agriculture is the prevailing occupation, and reaches great perfection on some estates. Beet is extensively grown. Cattle-breeding is also of importance.

Manufactures have developed rapidly of late, especially in Warsaw and its vicinity. In 1885 there were 1575 establishments, employing 35,400 operatives, with an output valued at 54,700,000 roubles. Sugar works occupied a prominent place. In 1886 nineteen sugar works and refineries employed 8925 operatives, and produced 6,450,000 cwts. of raw and 3,220,000 of refined sugar. Plated silver, carpets, woollen cloth, machinery, boots and shoes, spirits and beer are among the other items produced.

The government is divided into thirteen districts, the chief towns of which are WARSAW (*q.v.*), Błonie (1370 inhabitants), Góra Kalwaria (2630), Gostynin (8870), Grojec (3500), Kutno (13,210), Łowicz (8720), Novo-Minsk (1830), Radziejewo (7680), Radzymin (4200), Skiernewice (3720), Sochaczew (5130), and Włocławek (20,660). Novy Dwor (4420), Neszawa (2330), Gombin (3000), and several others have municipal institutions.

WARSAW (*Warszawa*), capital of Poland, and chief town of the above government, is beautifully situated on the left bank of the Vistula, 395 miles to the east of Berlin, and 700 miles to south-west of St Petersburg. It stands on a terrace nearly 100 feet in height, which stretches far to the westward, and descends by steep slopes

Plan of Warsaw.

towards the river, leaving a broad beach at its base. The suburb of Praga on the right bank of the Vistula, here from 450 to 880 yards broad, is connected with Warsaw by two bridges,—the railway bridge, which passes right under the guns of the Alexandrovsk citadel to the north, and the Alexandrovsk bridge in the centre of the town.

With its population of nearly 450,000, its beautiful river, its ample communications and its commerce, its university and scientific societies, its palaces and numerous places of amusement, Warsaw is one of the most pleasant as well as one of the most animated cities of eastern Europe. In Russia it is excelled in importance by the two Russian capitals only; and doubtless it would have attained even a larger population, and a yet higher place in the world of commerce and intellect, were it not for its sad and chequered history, and the foreign domination of which the traveller is reminded at every step.

Situated in a fertile plain, on a great navigable river, below its junction with the Pilica and Weprz, which water southern Poland, and above its junction with the Narew and Bug, which water a wide region in the east, it became in mediæval times the chief entrepôt for the trade of those fertile and populous valleys with western Europe. Its position in the territory of Mazovia, which was neither Polish nor Lithuanian, and, so to say, remained neutral between the two rival powers which constituted the united kingdom, it became the capital of both, to the detriment of the purely Polish Cracow and the Lithuanian Vilna. And now, connected as it is by six trunk lines with Vienna, south-western Russia, Moscow, St Petersburg, Dantzic, and Berlin (*via* Bromberg), it has become one of the most important commercial cities of eastern Europe. The south-western railway connects it with Łodz, the Manchester of Poland, as also with the rich coal fields of Kielce, which supply its steadily growing manufactures with coal and iron, so that Warsaw and its neighbourhood have become a centre for all kinds of manufactures, greatly aided in their development by the high technical training and general superiority of the engineers of the Polish capital, as well as by the skill, taste, and intelligence of its artisans. The periodical wholesale deportations of Warsaw artisans, who never failed to take an active part in the Polish insurrections, especially in 1794, 1831, and 1863, considerably checked, but could not wholly stop the industrial progress of the town; but the lines of customhouses which surround Poland, and thus limit the Warsaw market, as also the Russian rule, which militates against the progress of Polish science, technology, and art, are so many obstacles to the development of its natural resources. The population of Warsaw has nevertheless grown rapidly of late, having risen from 161,008 in 1860, and 276,000 in 1872, to 436,570 in 1887; of these more than 25,000 are Germans, and one-third are Jews (43,000 in 1860, and 117,300 in 1879). The Russian garrison amounts to nearly 20,000 men.

The streets of Warsaw are very animated, and are adorned with many fine buildings—partly due to the old Polish nobility's love of display (there are more than 160 palaces, 60 of which have been confiscated by the Russian Government), partly churches and cathedrals (179 Catholic, 6 Greek, and 2 Lutheran, several synagogues, 14 monasteries, and 4 nunneries), and partly public buildings,—schools, hospitals, scientific societies,—erected at great expense by the municipality or by private bodies. Fine public gardens and several monuments further embellish the city. The present university, founded as the "Glawnaja Szkoła," in 1816, but closed in 1832, was again opened in 1864; it has a remarkable library of more than 350,000 volumes, rich natural history collections, a fine botanic garden, and an observatory well known for its astronomical work. There are 75 professors and nearly 1000 students. The teaching is in Russian, and mostly by Russians, and the close intercourse which used to exist between the university and the educated classes of Poland is becoming a thing of the past. The rich university library, one of the largest in the world, was confiscated in 1794, and transferred to St Petersburg, where it became the nucleus of the present imperial public library; and, after the insurrection of 1831, it was again ransacked for the same purpose. The medical school, which enjoys high repute in the scientific world, still retains the right of teaching in Polish, and has about 220 students. The same privilege is enjoyed by the school of arts, the academy of agriculture and forestry, and the conservatory of music, all of which are high-class institutions. There are, besides, six classical gymnasia, two "real" schools, and numerous elementary schools. The museum of the society of fine arts is rich in examples of ancient and modern art. The association of the friends of science and the historical and agricultural societies of Warsaw were once well known, but all were closed after the insurrections, and now they live but a precarious life, the scientific works which continue to be produced in Poland being partly published at Cracow.

The great theatre for Polish drama and the ballet is a fine building which really includes two theatres under the same roof; but the pride of Warsaw is its theatre in the Łazienki gardens, which were laid out in an old bed of the Vistula by Stanislaus Augustus Poniatowski, and have beautiful shady alleys, artificial ponds, an elegant little palace with ceilings painted by Bacciarelli, several imperial villas, and a monument to Sobieski. An artificial ruin on an island makes an open-air theatre, the stage of which is separated from the auditorium by a channel of water, and the decorations of which blend with the parks and the palace behind. Two other public gardens, with alleys of old chestnut trees, are situated in the centre of the city. One of these, the Saski Ogrod, or Saxon garden (17 acres), which has a summer theatre and excellent fountains, and is richly adorned with statues and flowers, is one of the most beautiful in Europe; it is the resort of the Warsaw aristocracy. The Krasinski garden, now somewhat less frequented, and many other smaller squares and gardens in the theatres of which Polish and German companies give their summer representations, contribute very much to the enlivenment of the streets of Warsaw; while the variety of smart national costumes still worn by the Polish peasantry gives colour and brightness to the crowds which throng them.

Warsaw is semicircular in plan, the diameter, nearly 5 miles in length, lying along the Vistula. The central point of the life of the place is the castle (Zamek Królewski) on Sigismund Square. It was built by the dukes of Mazovia, enlarged by Sigismund III. (whose memorial stands opposite) and Ladislaus IV., and embellished by Stanislaus Augustus. At present it is inhabited by the "governor-general of the provinces on the Vistula," and its pictures and other art treasures have been removed to St Petersburg. Four main thoroughfares radiate from it: one, the Krakowskie Przedmiescie, the best street in Warsaw, runs southward. It is continued by the Nowy Swiat and the Ujazdowska Aleja avenue, which leads to the Łazienki gardens. Many fine buildings are found in these two streets:—the church of the Bernardine convent; the house of the benevolent society; the Carmelite church, now closed, where the crown archives of Poland are still kept; the rich Radziwill palace, now inhabited by the governor-general; the university, Saxon Square, on which Nicholas I. ordered the erection of a memorial to the Polish generals who refused to take part in the insurrection of 1831 and were therefore shot by the insurgents; the Saxon garden behind the square; the fine palaces of the Potockis, the Oginskis, the Uruskis, &c.; the church of the Holy Cross, erected in 1682–96, the richest in Warsaw; the palace of the Krasinskis, with library and museum; the statue of Copernicus, by Thorwaldsen, erected in 1822 by national subscription; the house of the friends of natural history, now a gymnasium; the palace of the Zamojskis, now confiscated and transformed into a building for subalterns of the garrison; the church of St Alexander, erected to commemorate the re-establishment of the kingdom of Poland; and the deaf and dumb asylum. The Ujazdowska Aleja avenue, planted with lime-trees and surrounded by cafés and various places of amusement, is the Champs Elysées of Warsaw. It leads to the Łazienki park, and to the Belvedere palace, now the summer residence of the governor-general, and farther west to the Mokotowski parade ground, which is surrounded on the south and west by the smoky chimneys of the manufacturing district. Another great street, the Marszałkowska, runs parallel to the Ujazdowska from the Saxon garden to this parade ground, on the south-east of which are the Russian barracks. The above-mentioned streets are crossed by another series running west and east, the chief of them being the Senatorska, which begins at Sigismund Square and contains the best shops. The palace of the archbishops of Gnesen and primates of Poland, confiscated by the Prussian Government, and now used by the ministry of education, the bank of Poland, the fine mansion-house burned in 1863 and now rebuilt as police bureau, the small Pod Blachoi palace, now occupied by a chancery, the theatre, the old mint, the chief post-office, the beautiful Reformed church, the exchange, the school of subaltern officers, and several palaces are grouped in Senators' Street, which is joined from the north by Miodowa Street, in which are situated the fine church of the Capuchins, erected in 1683 to commemorate the victory of John Sobieski over the Turks, the palace of the archbishops of Warsaw, and the Russian cathedral.

To the west Senators' Street is continued by Electors' Street, where is the very elegant modern church of St Charles Borromeo and the Chłodna leading to the suburb of Wola, with a large field where the kings of Poland used to be elected. In Leshno Street, which branches off from Senators' Street, are the Zelazna Brama, or Iron Gate, in the market-place, the gostinyi dvor or bazaar, the arsenal, and the Wielopolski barracks. The cemeteries, the summer barracks of the troops (Powonzski lager), and the artillery barracks lie to the north-west.

To the north of Sigismund Square is the old town—Staro Miasto—the Jewish quarter, and farther north still the Alexandrovsk citadel. The old town very much recalls old Germany by its narrow streets and old buildings; it has the church of St John at its entrance, and farther down the cathedral, which is the oldest church of Warsaw, having been built in the 13th century and restored in the 17th. The citadel, erected in 1832–35 as a punishment for the insurrection of 1831, is of the old type, with six forts too close to the walls of the fortress to be useful in modern warfare. The railway bridge, built in 1865 and 570 yards long, begins under the walls of the citadel and is protected on the right bank of the Vistula by the Sliwnicki *tête de pont*.

The suburb of Praga, on the right bank of the Vistula, is poorly built and often flooded; but the bloody assaults which led to its capture in 1794 by the Russians under Suwaroff, and in 1831 by Paskevitch, give it a name in history.

Industry and Trade.—Warsaw has of late become industrially important, and now has more than 320 establishments employing nearly 20,000 workmen, and producing to the amount of nearly 40 million roubles annually. The leading industries are the production of plated silver ware, with a wide market throughout Russia, machinery and engines, chemicals, musical instruments, especially pianos, carpets, boots, and shoes, largely exported, carriages, woollen cloth, leather wares, spirits, and beer. The trade of Warsaw is considerable. Nearly 14,000,000 cwts. of coal and 4,800,000 cwts. of miscellaneous goods are imported by rail from the south-west (Kielce, Łodz, and Galicia), and 3,200,000 cwts. of manufactured goods, corn, flax, &c., are exported in the same direction. Corn and flax are imported to the amount of 7,000,000 cwts. from the south-east and east, and exported to Prussia to the amount of 5,300,000 cwts. by rail and partly down the Vistula, while the total railway traffic is represented by 34,400,000 cwts. of merchandise brought in and 18,000,000 cwts. sent away. To all this must be added the traffic on the Vistula (about 3,000,000 cwts.). A great proportion of the trade is in the hands of Germans, especially of Jews.

The suburbs of Warsaw are surrounded by villas, palaces, and battlefields. Wilanow, the palace of John Sobieski, now belonging to the Potockis, was partly built by Turkish prisoners in a fine Italian style, and is now renowned for its historical portraits and pictures. It is situated to the south of Warsaw, together with many other fine villas (Morysin, Natolin, Krolikarnia, which also has a picture gallery, &c.). The Marymont, an old country residence of the wife of John Sobieski, and the Kaskada, much visited by the inhabitants of Warsaw, in the north, the Saska Kempa on the right bank of the Vistula, and the castle of Jabłona down the Vistula are among others that deserve mention.

The events associated with the name of Praga have been already alluded to. Among other battlefields in the neighbourhood of Warsaw is that of Grochowo, where the Polish troops were defeated in 1831 after a gallant fight. Raszyn saw its fields covered with blood in the war of 1809 with Austria; at Maciejowice, 50 miles up the Vistula, Kosciuszko was wounded and taken by the Russians in 1794; and 20 miles down the river stands the fortress of Modlin, now Novogeorgievsk, fortified by Napoleon, taken in 1813 by the Russians, and the last stronghold of the Poles during the insurrection of 1831.

History.—The history of Warsaw from the 16th century onwards is intimately connected with that of POLAND (*q.v.*). The precise date of the foundation of the town is not known. The banks of the Vistula between the Pilica and the Narew must have been inhabited from a very early period, and it is supposed that Conrad, duke of Mazovia, erected a castle on the present site of Warsaw as early as the 9th century. Casimir the Just is supposed to have fortified it in the 11th century, but Warsaw is not mentioned in annals before 1224. Until 1526 it was the residence of the dukes of Mazovia, but when their dynasty was extinguished the land of the Mazurs, till then independent, was annexed to Poland. When Poland and Lithuania became united, it was chosen as the royal residence. Sigismund Augustus (Wasa) made it the real capital of Poland, and from 1572 onwards the election of the kings of Poland took place on the field of Wola. From the 17th century possession of it was continually disputed by the Swedes, the Russians, and the Brandenburgers and the Austrians. Charles Gustavus of Sweden took it in 1655 and kept it for a year; the Poles retook it in July 1656 but lost it again almost immediately. Augustus II. and Augustus III. did much for its embellishment, but it had much to suffer during the northern war. Charles XII. took it in 1702, but in the following year peace was made between the Swedes and Stanislaus Lezczynski, and it became free again. The disorderly rule of the Rzec Pospolita opened a large field for Russian intrigue, and in 1764 the Russians took possession of it and secured the election of Stanislaus Poniatowski, which led in 1773 to the first partition of Poland. In November 1794 the Russians took it again, after the bloody assault on Praga, but next year, in the third partition of Poland, Warsaw was given to Prussia. In November 1806 the town was occupied by the troops of Napoleon, and after the peace of Tilsit was made the capital of the independent duchy of Warsaw; but the Austrians took it on April 21, 1809, and kept it till June 2, when it once more became independent, but only for a few years. The Russians finally took it on February 8, 1813, since which time they have always retained it. On November 29, 1830, Warsaw gave the signal of the great but unsuccessful insurrection which lasted nearly one year; it was taken after great bloodshed by Paskevitch, on September 7, 1831. Deportations on a large scale, executions, and confiscation of the domains of the nobility followed, and until 1856 Warsaw remained under severe military rule. In 1862 a series of demonstrations began to be made in Warsaw in favour of the independence of Poland, and after a bloody repression a general insurrection followed in January 1863, the Russians remaining, however, masters of the situation. The Russian Government now decided to take the most stringent measures to crush the powers of the clergy, the landed nobility, and the turbulent Warsaw artisans and educated classes. Executions, banishment to the convict prisons of Siberia, and confiscation of estates followed. Deportation to Siberia and the interior of Russia was carried out on an unheard-of scale. Scientific societies and high schools were closed; monasteries and nunneries were emptied. Hundreds of Russian officials were called in to fill up administrative posts, the schools, and the university; the Russian language was rendered obligatory in official acts, in all legal proceedings, and even, to a great extent, in trade. The very name of Poland was expunged from official writings, and, while the old institutions were abolished, the Russian tribunals and administrative institutions were introduced. The serfs were liberated. See POLAND.

Officially, Warsaw is now simply the chief town of the government of Warsaw, the residence of the governor-general of the provinces on the Vistula and the commander of the Warsaw military district, and the see of the Roman and Greek archbishops. But it continues to be the heart of the Polish nationality. (P. A. K.)

WART is a papillary excrescence of the surface, most commonly of the skin, but in special circumstances also of the transitional and mucous membranes. The ordinary broad and flat warts of the skin occur mostly upon the hands of children and young persons; a long pendulous variety occurs about the chin or neck of children who are constitutionally delicate (it used to be thought a mark of scrofula) and on the scalp in adults. Both the broad sessile warts of the fingers or hands and the thin hanging warts of the neck and head are apt to come out in numbers at a time; a crop of them suddenly appears, to disappear after a time with equal suddenness. Hence the supposed efficacy of charms. A single wart will sometimes remain when the general eruption has vanished. The liability to crops of warts runs in families. In after life a wart on the hands or fingers is usually brought on by some irritation, often repeated, even if it be slight. A special form has been observed on the hands of those much occupied with anatomical dissection. Chimney-sweeps and workers in coal-tar, petroleum, &c., are subject to warts, which often become cancerous. Ordinary innocent warts occur singly in later life on the nose or lips or other parts of the face, sometimes on the tongue. Towards old age there are apt to be broad and flattened patches of warts on the back, of a greasy consistence and brownish colour.

A wart consists essentially of a framework or ground-plan of small blood-vessels supported by bands of fibrous tissue, and a more or less thick covering of epidermic scales. When the wart is young, the surface is a rounded and even knob; as it gets rubbed and worn the surface appears cleft into thread-like projecting points. The blood-vessels, whose outgrowth from the surface really makes the wart, may either be in a cluster of parallel loops, in which case we have the common broad and sessile wart, or the vessels may branch from a single stem, making the dendriform pattern of the long, slim, and pendulous warts of the chin and neck. The same two kinds of pattern occur also in warts of the transitional or mucous surfaces. (For a figure of a dendriform wart, see PATHOLOGY, vol. xviii. fig. 43, p. 379.) A wart of either pattern is a projection of the system of cutaneous blood-vessels beyond the surface. It is owing to its vascular ground-plan that a wart is liable to come back after being shaved off; the vessel or vessels are cut down to the level of the skin, but the current of blood is still forced into the stem, and the branches tend to be thrown out beyond the surface as before. This fact has a bearing on the treatment of warts. If they are shaved or snipped off, the blood-vessels of the stem should be destroyed at the same time by caustic, or made to shrivel by an astringent. The same end is served by a gradually tightening ligature (such as a thread of elastic pulled out from an old brace) round the base or neck of the wart; an ordinary thread is apt to cut too deep and may cause suppuration. The best treatment is to rub an astringent, or acid, or caustic substance into the surface of the wart. Glacial acetic acid may be applied on the end of a glass rod, or by a camel-hair brush, care being taken not to touch the adjoining skin. A solution of perchloride of iron is also effective in the same way. Nitrate of silver is objectionable, owing to the black stains left by it. A simple domestic remedy, often effectual, is the astringent and acrid juice of the common stonecrop (*Sedum acre*) rubbed into the wart, time after time, from the freshly gathered herb. The result of these various applications is that the wart loses its turgor or firmness, shrivels up, and eventually falls off.

A peculiar form of wart, known as *verrugas*, occurs endemically in certain valleys of the Peruvian Andes, especially in the region of the Cerro de Pasco. It is believed to have been one of the causes of the excessive mortality from hæmorrhages of the skin among the troops of Pizarro. In recent times attention was called to it by Dr Archibald Smith in 1842; in 1874, during the making of the Trans-Andean Railway, it caused a considerable loss of life among English navvies and engineers. Strangers of the white race suffer much more severely from it than the acclimatized or the natives. It is sometimes epidemic and peculiarly fatal. Its endemic seats are certain deep and narrow valleys traversed by a mountain stream or torrent and covered with luxuriant vegetation; where the valley widens the endemic influence is no longer felt. The warts may be few or many, up to several hundreds; they occur on internal mucous membranes as well as on the skin. Their outbreak is preceded for some weeks by a feverish state and by pains in the limbs. These symptoms disappear when the warts come out; they are at first reddish spots about the size of a pea, but grow to be rounded or conical excrescences as large as a raspberry or filbert, or pigeon's egg; after a time the surface becomes ragged or fissured (as in an ordinary wart), especially when rubbed or chafed, and blood begins to ooze, which may amount to considerable hæmorrhage. Death (in about 10 per cent. of cases) is due to loss of blood, or to the protracted ulceration following the fall of the warts. The disease lasts usually several months; but a feeble state of the system may remain long after the warts are all gone. The excrescences (besides those of the internal membranes) occur in the favourite situations of common warts—the fingers and back of the hand (also the toes and back of the foot), the face and neck, and among the hair of the head.

See Hirsch, *Geographical and Historical Pathology*, vol. ii., Engl. trans., 1885.

WARTON. Three authors of this name, a father and two sons, were leaders of reaction against the didactic poetry of Pope's school, and did much to help forward the descriptive and romantic revival.

THOMAS WARTON (1688–1745), satirized in *Terræ Filius* (February 18, 1721) as "squinting Tom of Maudlin," was vicar of Basingstoke in Hampshire, and professor of poetry at Oxford. He published nothing during his lifetime, but after his death his son Joseph published some of his poetry under the title *Poems on Several Occasions*, 1748.

JOSEPH WARTON (1722–1800), eldest son of the preceding, was born at Dunsford, in Surrey, in 1722, and sent to Winchester school in 1736. Collins was already there, and the school seems to have been at the time quite a nest of singing birds, quickened into unusual ambition by a visit from Pope. Collins and Warton became close friends, read Milton and Spenser together, and wrote verses which they sent to the *Gentleman's Magazine*, verses of such promise that Johnson formally criticized them. The two friends went to Oxford together, and took the degree of B.A. in the same year (1743). Warton was far from having the genius of Collins, but he had abundance of poetical enthusiasm, and they were at one in their impatience under the prevailing taste for moral and ethical poetry. Whoever wishes to understand how early the discontent under Pope's ascendency began should read Warton's *The Enthusiast*, or *The Love of Nature*, and remember that it was written by an undergraduate in 1740, while Pope was still alive. Warton sounded a bold note in 1746, in the preface to his *Odes on Several Subjects*. "As he is convinced," he wrote, "that the fashion of moralizing in verses has been carried too far, and as he looks upon invention and imagination to be the chief faculties of a poet, so he will be happy if the following odes may be looked upon as an attempt to bring back poetry into its right channel." Warton thereafter married, became a country clergyman, a master in Winchester school, eventually for thirty years (1766–96) a much respected headmaster, but all his leisure was given to literature, and he remained constant to his conception of the "right channel" in poetry, though he soon abandoned the idea of setting the world right by his own example. He became an active and prominent man of letters, produced an edition of Virgil, in 1753, with distinguished coadjutors, and a translation of the *Eclogues* and the *Georgics*, and a preparatory essay by himself; made the acquaintance of Johnson, and wrote papers on Shakespeare and Homer in *The Adventurer*; published the first part of an essay on Pope in 1756, an essay regarded at the time as revolutionary, by Dictator Johnson at least, because it put Pope in the second rank to Shakespeare, Spenser, and Milton, on the ground that moral and ethical poetry, however excellent, is an inferior species; held his own against Johnson in the Literary Club; and, after enduring many jests about the promised second part and the delay in its appearance, published it at last, retracting nothing, in 1782. Of this essay Campbell justly says that "it abounds with criticism of more research than Addison's, of more amenity than Hurd's or Warburton's, and of more insinuating tact than Johnson's." Warton's edition of Pope was the work of his old age; when published in 1797, it found a larger number of sympathizers with his criticism of the poetic idol of the 18th century than had welcomed his first essay forty years before in the same vein. The last three years of the critic's life were spent in preparing an edition of Dryden, which was completed and published by his son in 1811. He died in London in February 1800, at the age of seventy-eight.

THOMAS WARTON (1728–1790), the younger brother of Joseph, at least as active and influential as he in enlarging the poetic ideas of the 18th century, was born at Basingstoke in 1728. He was still more precocious as a poet than his brother—translated one of Martial's epigrams at nine, and wrote *The Pleasures of Melancholy* at seventeen —and he showed exactly the same bent, Milton and Spenser being his favourite poets, though he "did not fail to cultivate his mind with the soft thrillings of the tragic muse" of Shakespeare. He wrote as follows in 1745:—

> Through Pope's soft song though all the Graces breathe,
> And happiest art adorn his Attic page,
> Yet does my mind with sweeter transport glow
> As, at the root of mossy trunk reclined,
> In magic Spenser's wildly warbled song
> I see deserted Una, &c.

In the same poem he shows the delight in Gothic churches and ruined castles which inspired so much of his subsequent work in romantic revival. Most of Warton's poetry, humorous and serious,—and the humorous mock heroic was better within his powers than serious verse,—was written before the age of twenty-three, when he took his M.A. degree and became a fellow of his college (Trinity, Oxford). He did not altogether abandon verse; his sonnets, especially, which are the best of his poems, were written later, and during the last six years of his life he was poet-laureate, and one of the happiest in the execution of the delicate duties that have ever held the office. But his main energies were given to omnivorous poetical reading and criticism. He was the first to turn to literary account the mediæval treasures of the Bodleian Library. It was through him, in fact, that the mediæval spirit which always lingered in Oxford first began to stir after its long inaction, and to claim an influence in the modern world. Warton, like his brother, entered the church, and held, one after another, various livings, but he did not marry. He gave little attention to his clerical duties, and Oxford always remained his home. He was a very easy and convivial as well as a very learned don, with a taste for pothouses and crowds as well as dim aisles and romances in manuscript and black letter. The first proof that he gave of his extraordinarily wide scholarship was in his *Observations on the Poetry of Spenser*, published in 1754, when the author was twenty-six. Three years later he was appointed professor of poetry and held the office for ten years, sending round, according to the story, at the beginning of term to inquire whether anybody *wished* him to lecture. The first volume of his monumental work, *The History of English Poetry*, appeared twenty years later, in 1774, the second volume in 1778, and the third in 1781. A work of such enormous labour and research could proceed but slowly, and it was no wonder that Warton flagged in the execution of it, and stopped to refresh himself with annotating the minor poems of Milton, pouring out in this delightful work the accumulated suggestions of forty years. Specialists may here and there detect errors and imperfections in Warton's *History*, but its miscellaneous and curious lore must make it always an interesting book, while its breadth and exactness of scholarship must always command wonder and respect. Through this work Warton became the veritable literary father of Sir Walter Scott; if he could have lived to read the *Lay* and *Marmion* he would have found realized there what he vaguely desiderated in modern poetry. Among Warton's minor works were a selection of Roman metrical inscriptions (1758); the humorous Oxford *Companion to the Guide* and *Guide to the Companion* (1762); *The Oxford Sausage* (1764); an edition of Theocritus (1770); lives of Thomas Pope and Bathurst, college benefactors; a *History of the Antiquities of Kiddington Parish*, of which he held the living (1781); and an *Inquiry into the Authenticity of the Poems attributed to Thomas Rowley* (1782). His busy and convivial life was ended by a paralytic stroke in May 1790. (W. M.)

WARWICK, a midland county of England, is bounded on the N. by Stafford, on the E. by Leicester and Northampton, on the S. by Oxford and Gloucester, and on the W. by Worcester. Its greatest length from north to south is 50 miles, and its greatest breadth 33 miles. Its area is 566,458 acres, or about 885 square miles. Camden describes it as being "divided into two parts, the *Feldon* and *Woodland* [or Arden], that is into a plain champain and a woody country; which parts, the Avon, running crookedlie from north-east to south-west, doth, after a sort, sever one from the other."

Plate VIII.

Surface and Geology.—The surface of the county is of a gently undulating nature. For a description of the scenery and early history the reader is referred to the article SHAKESPEARE, vol. xxi. pp. 738 *sq.*

The chief elevations are the Edge Hills on the southern border of the county, where they rise in some places to about 800 feet above sea-level. In the same neighbourhood are the Burton Dassett and Farnborough Hills; north-east of these are the Napton and Shuckburgh Hills, and

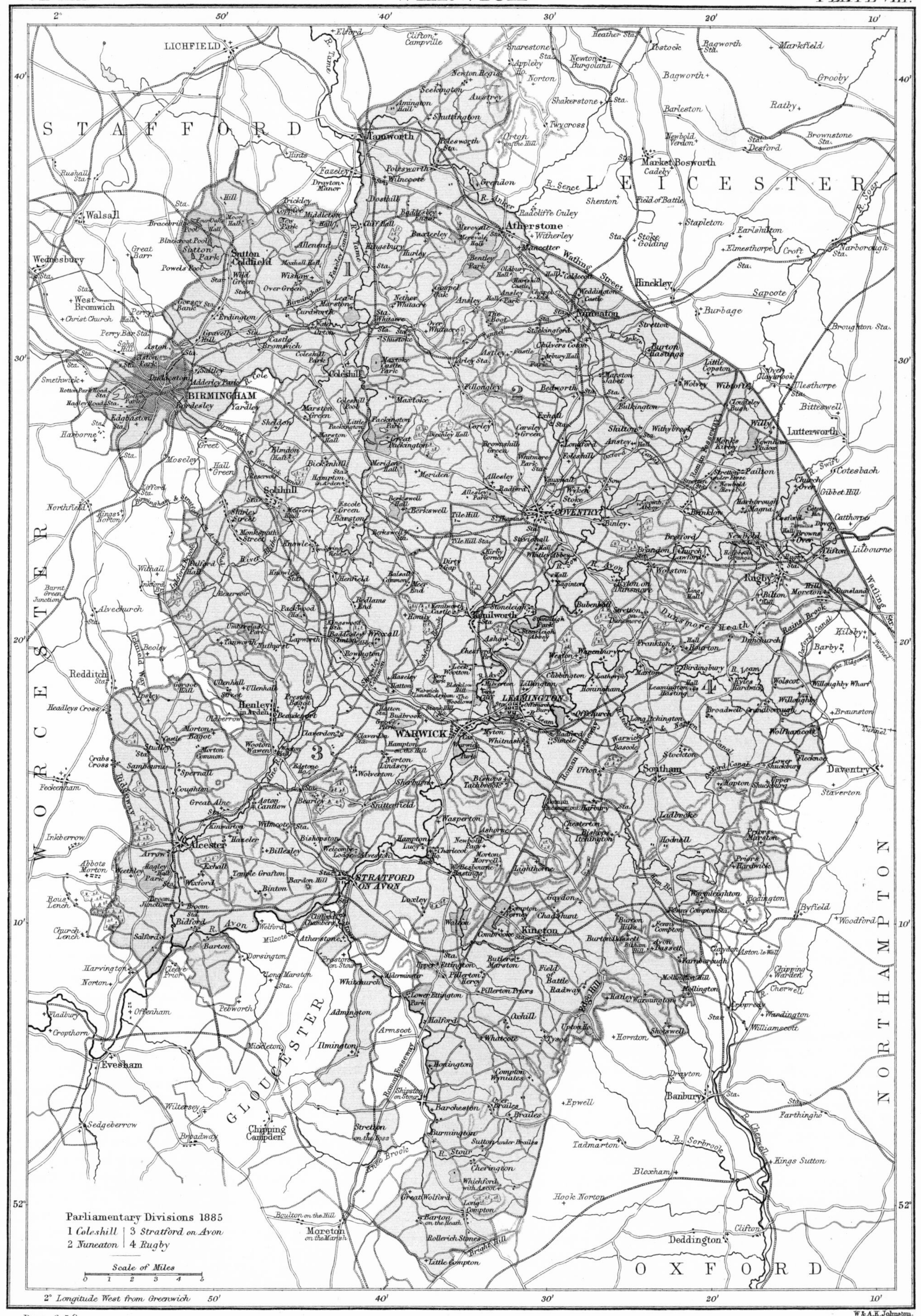
STAFFORD
LEICESTER
WORCESTER
GLOUCESTER
NORTHAMPTON
OXFORD
BIRMINGHAM
COVENTRY
WARWICK
LEAMINGTON
STRATFORD ON AVON
Parliamentary Divisions 1885
1 Coleshill
2 Nuneaton
3 Stratford on Avon
4 Rugby
Scale of Miles
2° Longitude West from Greenwich
W. & A. K. Johnston.

south-west of the Edge Hills is Brailes Hill. Some elevated land is found at Corley, Oldbury, Hartshill, &c., in the north of the county.

The lofty elevation of the county in general is evidenced by the fact that rivers flow from it in several directions, contributing to each of the three systems of the Severn, Trent, and Thames. The Avon rises in Northamptonshire, and flowing south-west through the county receives on its way the Swift, Sowe, Leam, Itchene, Stour, Alne, and other tributaries, and falls into the Severn at Tewkesbury. It is navigable for barges up to Stratford, and is rich in its associations with Shakespeare. The Tame rises in Staffordshire, and flowing through the northern portion of Warwickshire takes in the Cole, Blythe, Anker, Rea, and other minor streams. A few small rivulets in the south of the county fall into the Cherwell, a tributary of the Thames.

The New Red Sandstone is the principal geological formation of the county, but towards the south the Lias prevails. In the north central district there is a large deposit of gravel, which consists of "small boulders and sea-worn pebbles, and ancient rocks traceable to the parent beds in Yorkshire, Cumberland, and Scotland, and commonly known as the northern drift. Quartz pebbles especially abound in it; granite, gneiss, syenite, porphyry, slate, mica schist, trap, and almost every other variety of the primary rocks may be collected." The Lias is near Edge Hill; the strata immediately below it consist of clay and ironstone, rich in iron ore. The Upper Lias crosses the county by Henley-in-Arden, Stratford, Kineton, Southam, and Rugby. With the exception of one coal-field, small but rich, extending from Tamworth to near Wyken, about 15 miles, the New Red Sandstone and Permian occupy the whole of the central part of the county. In the north Upper Cambrian quartzites and shales are found, together with some volcanic rocks. The Coal-Measures dip under the Lower Permian rocks, and in the southern part of the field underlie the Trias. According to the report of the Coal Commission in 1871, the area of the Warwickshire coal-field is 30 square miles, the thickness of the coal being from 26 to 30 feet. The quantity raised in 1870 was 647,540 tons, and in 1885 it was 1,281,724.

The minerals of the county are limestone, freestone, iron, blue flagstone, marl, and blue clay. The blue flagstone is found in many places, and ironstone at Bedworth, Oldbury, and Merevale. The limestone quarries are principally at Bearley, Grafton Court, Stretton, Princethorpe, Ufton, Harbury, Arlescote, Bidford, Newbold-on-Avon, Stockton, and Southam; freestone is found largely about Warwick, Leamington, Kenilworth, and Coventry.

Climate and Agriculture.—The climate is generally mild and healthy. The soil is on the whole good, and consists of various loams, marls, gravels, and clays, well suited for most of the usual crops. It is rich in pasture-land, and dairy farming is increasing. It has excellent orchards and market gardens, and possesses some of the finest woodlands in England. Nearly all the farm buildings are good; and many of the cottages of the labourers are exceedingly picturesque. There are many charming villages in the county. According to the agricultural returns, out of a total area of 566,458 acres there were 496,429 acres under cultivation in 1887, corn crops occupying 105,039 acres, green crops 31,411, rotation grasses 40,783, permanent pasture 308,689, and fallow 10,493; of the corn crops much the largest area was under wheat, which occupied 43,728 acres, barley occupying 16,290, oats 26,297, rye 256, beans 14,050, and pease 4418. Of the green crops turnips occupied 16,913 acres, potatoes 4936 acres, while 4198 were under mangolds, 114 under carrots, 971 under cabbage, &c., and 4279 under vetches and other green crops.

The number of horses in 1887 was 20,769, cattle 107,555, of which 37,080 were cows and heifers in milk or in calf, sheep 294,442, 172,151 of them one-year-old and above, and pigs 37,092.

According to the *Return of Owners of Land*, 1873, the total number of proprietors in the county was 51,516, possessing 541,022 acres, with a gross annual rental of £3,318,304, or about £6, 2s. 8d. per acre all over. Of these owners of land only 4622 had one acre and upwards. Of waste or common land there was 1833 acres. The following possessed over 5000 acres:—Lord Leigh, 14,892 acres; Lord Willoughby de Broke, 12,621; earl of Aylesford, 12,159; marquis of Hertford, 10,282; earl of Craven, 8448; earl of Warwick, 8263; Sir N. W. Throckmorton, 7619; duke of Buccleuch, 6881; H. J. Lucy, 5766; W. S. Dugdale, 5689; Sir G. R. Philips, 5397; and C. N. Newdegate, 5318.

Manufactures.—The principal seats of manufacture in the county are BIRMINGHAM and COVENTRY (*qq.v.*). Suffice it to say here that in Birmingham almost every article of use, from a pin to a steam engine, is produced, and that Coventry has long been famous for its ribbons and watches, and has recently won a well-merited reputation for bicycles and tricycles.

Communication.—The county is well supplied with excellently preserved roads. There are also a great number of canals giving access to the Trent, the Mersey, the Thames, and the Severn. The London and North-Western, the Great Western, the Midland, and various branch railways traverse the county in various directions.

Population and Administration.—The population in 1871 was 634,189, and in 1881 737,339 (357,146 males and 380,193 females). More than half the population is contained in the borough of Birmingham. The county is divided into four hundreds:—(1) Hemlingford, (2) Knightlow, (3) Barlichway, (4) Kineton. It has one city, Coventry (42,111), which is also a municipal borough; five other boroughs—Birmingham (400,774), Leamington (22,979), Stratford-on-Avon (8054), Warwick (11,800), and Sutton Coldfield (7737); and, besides the boroughs, ten market towns, viz., Alcester (2430), Atherstone (4645), Coleshill (2356), Henley in Arden (1119), Kenilworth (4150), Kineton (1053), Nuneaton (8465), Rugby (9891), Solihull (5280), and Southam (1784). It is mostly in the diocese of Worcester. It is in the midland judicial circuit, has one court of quarter sessions, and is divided into fourteen petty and special sessional divisions. The boroughs of Birmingham and Warwick have separate courts of quarter sessions and commissions of the peace, and the city of Coventry and the boroughs of Leamington and Stratford-on-Avon have commissions of the peace.

By the Redistribution Bill of 1885 Warwickshire was for parliamentary purposes divided into four boroughs and four county divisions. The boroughs are Birmingham, Aston Manor, Coventry, and Warwick and Leamington united. Birmingham has seven divisions, each returning a member—Bordesley, Central, East, Edgbaston, North, South, and West; the other three boroughs return one member each. The county divisions (Nuneaton, Rugby, Stratford-on-Avon, and Tamworth) each return one member.

History and Antiquities.—Warwickshire was occupied by the British tribes Cornavii and Dobuni. The Romans named this part of England Flavia Cæsariensis, and many evidences of their occupation and works exist in the county. It was crossed by the three great roads—Watling Street, the Fosse Way, and Icknield Street; the last-named gives its name to a street in Birmingham which is on the lines of the old Roman road. The Ridgeway borders a part of Warwickshire on the west. Roman stations or camps were at Mancetter, High Cross, Alcester, Chesterton, and other places; coins, pottery, and other remains have been found at Warwick, Willoughby, Hampton-in-Arden, Birmingham, and elsewhere. The Teutons followed the Romans, and after suffering many changes Warwickshire became part of Mercia. From 593 to 918 it was the scene of frequent invasions, conquests, and reconquests.

Although Mercia was for the most part peopled by Angles, the Saxons seem to have occupied the portion now known as Warwickshire in very considerable numbers; for, if we except Alcester, Mancetter, and a few other places, nearly all the towns and villages have Saxon names. Of the three hundred and sixty places in the county mentioned in Domesday nearly all are of Saxon origin. As Verstegan says,

> "In Foord, in Ham, in Ley, in Tun,
> The most of English surnames run."

And these terminations are found in the vast majority of the names of places in Warwickshire. This prevalence of the Saxons here is also confirmed by the fact that Mr Kemble discovered no fewer than thirty-one Mark names in places in Warwickshire. The Danes, although they made inroads into Warwickshire several times, seem to have made no settlements in the county, the only names bearing the Danish suffix *by* being on the north-east border. In later times the "king-maker" earl of Warwick made the county memorable by the part he took in the Wars of the Roses. In the civil war under Charles I. "scarcely a place of any note escaped" without a struggle: at Edge Hill the first engagement was fought; Aston Hall was besieged; Birmingham was sacked and burned by Prince Rupert; Coventry endured a siege; Warwick was the centre of several encounters; and a skirmish took place near Southam.

Few remains of Saxon architecture are to be found in the county, and these are of minor importance. Saxon jewels have been found at Compton-Verney; a fine burial urn filled with ashes, an iron sword, a spear head, and other relics, at Church Over; in a tumulus or barrow, at Marston, were found two sepulchral urns, one of them containing bones, a fibula, a pin, part of a sword, and two spear heads. In 1824 an Anglo-Saxon cemetery was discovered on Watling Street, near Bensford Bridge, in which a large number of articles, both of use and ornament, were found. Other burial places have been opened, and similar remains found. Some good examples of Norman work exist in the churches at Kenilworth, Ryton, Stoneleigh, Berkeswell, Wolston, and Beaudesert. Of famous and interesting places may be mentioned the noble structure Warwick Castle; the ruins of Kenilworth Castle and Maxstoke Priory; Maxstoke Castle; Compton Wyniates; Temple Balsall church; the "three tall spires" at Coventry, with the beautiful churches of St Michael, Holy Trinity, and St John Baptist; Ragley Hall, Combe Abbey, Wroxhall Abbey, Newnham Padox, Astley Castle, Arbury Hall, Walton Hall, Guy's Cliff, Baddesley Clinton, Tamworth Castle and church, Packington Hall, and Stoneleigh Abbey.

Among the eminent persons connected with Warwickshire besides William Shakespeare are John Rogers the martyr, Michael Drayton, Sir W. Dugdale, Dr Parr, Dr Joseph Priestley, Matthew Boulton, John Baskerville, Walter Savage Landor, and Marian Evans ("George Eliot").

See Dugdale, *Antiquities of Warwickshire*, Thomas's edition (2 vols. fol., 1730); Brewer, *Description of Warwickshire* (8vo, 1810); Murray, *Agriculture of Warwickshire* (8vo, 1813); Smith, *History of Warwickshire* (4to, 1830); Langford, *Staffordshire and Warwickshire* (4 vols. 4to, 1868); Langford, "The Saxons in Warwickshire" (*Birmingham Archæological Society*, 4to, 1881).

WARWICK, the county town of Warwickshire, and a municipal and parliamentary borough, is finely situated on the Avon, on the Warwick and Birmingham and Warwick and Napton Canals, and on a branch of the Great Western Railway, 8 miles north-east of Stratford-on-Avon and 108 north-west of London. The glory of Warwick is still its castle, which has been truly pronounced to be the "most magnificent of the ancient feudal mansions of the English nobility still used as a residence." Its position is at once commanding and picturesque, standing as it does on a rock overhanging the Avon. Its principal features are Cæsar's Tower, 147 feet high, built in the 14th century; the Gateway Tower, in the centre; and Guy's Tower, 128 feet, also of the 14th century. There is a fine collection of pictures. The Great Hall and the family apartments were destroyed by fire in 1871, but have been restored. In the collegiate church of St Mary Warwick possesses one of the most interesting ecclesiastical buildings in the country. We learn from Domesday that a church existed before the Conquest, but of its foundation nothing is really known. It was made collegiate by Roger de Newburgh, the second Norman earl. It was dissolved by Henry VIII. in 1545, by whom it was granted to the burgesses of the town, with an estate then worth £58, 14s. 4d. to maintain it, together with the king's school. A great part of the church was destroyed by fire in 1694, and afterwards rebuilt. The glory of this church, however, is the Beauchamp Chapel, founded by Earl Richard Beauchamp by will, and commenced in 1443 and completed 1464. It is one of the finest examples of pure Gothic in the kingdom. In the centre of the chapel is the splendid tomb of the earl. The church of St Nicholas, near the entrance to the castle grounds, is modern, with a tower and spire, and was erected towards the end of the 18th century. St Paul's is new. The priory of St Sepulchre was founded by Henry de Newburgh on the site of an ancient church for a society of canons regular. It is now a private residence. One of the most interesting places in Warwick is the hospital of Robert Dudley, earl of Leicester, one of the most picturesque examples of half-timber buildings in England. It was originally used as the hall of the united guilds of the Holy Trinity, the Blessed Virgin, and St George the Martyr. The earl of Leicester, by an Act of Incorporation obtained in 1571, founded the hospital for the reception of twelve poor men possessing not more than £5 a year, and a master. The first master, appointed by the earl himself, was the famous Puritan, Thomas Cartwright. There are numerous charities in the town, the principal being those of Henry VIII., Sir Thomas White, and Thomas Oken. The first is derived from the tithes of St Mary, St Nicholas in Warwick, the parish of Budbrooke, and Chaddesley Corbett, Worcestershire, together with the rents of houses and lands in the borough. It produces about £3000 a year, and is used for paying the stipends of the vicar and an assistant minister for St Mary's, the vicars of St Nicholas and Budbrooke, the mayor, the town-clerk, yeoman, serjeant-at-mass, and a beadle; while £460, 10s. is annually given in aid of the king's school. By the charity of Sir Thomas White the sum of £100 is lent, without interest, to young tradesmen for a period of nine years. From the funds left for that purpose by Thomas Oken, allowances are made to the poor. The area of the borough is 5512 acres; the population in 1861 was 10,570, in 1871 10,986, and in 1881 11,800.

A fortress is said to have been erected here as early as the year 50, by P. Octavius Scapula, and it is supposed to have been the præsidium Romanorum at which a cohort of Dalmatian horse was stationed. It was destroyed by the Danes in one of their incursions into Mercia, and in 915 Alfred's daughter Ethelfleda built the fortress on which the castle now stands. The town is mentioned in Domesday, where we learn that "in the borough the king has in his demesne 113 houses, and the king's barons have 112, from which the king receives Danegeld. The bishop of Worcester has 9 dwellings, the bishop of Chester 7, the abbot of Coventry 36, and four were destroyed to enlarge the castle." In the time of Edward the Confessor the sheriffwick of Warwick, with the borough and royal manors, rendered £65, and "thirty-six sextars of honey, or £24, 6s. instead of honey (*pro omnibus quæ ad mel pertinebant*). Now, with the *forra* of the royal manors and pleas of the county, it pays per annum £145 by weight, £23 for the custom of dogs, 20s. for a sumpter horse, £10 for a hawk, and 100s. for Queengold. Besides this it renders twenty-four sextars of honey of the larger measure, and from the borough six sextars of honey, at the sextar for 15d." The celebrated Thurkill (or Turchill) was the last Saxon earl of Warwick.

William the Conqueror began his first northern campaign in 1068, and the first place where his presence is distinctly recorded is Warwick. He erected here one of his strong fortifications on the site of the old one. Not a vestige of it now exists, but, as Mr Freeman writes, "the mound itself still remains, a monument of the wisdom and energy of the mighty daughter of Ælfred, while the keep of William has so utterly perished that its very site can only now be guessed at."

Of the earls of Warwick who may be noticed, of course the legendary Guy, with the numerous traditions relating his wonderful achievements, stands first. In proof of his prowess do not his gigantic helmet, his furnace-like pot, and his mighty fork remain in the castle to this day, to testify against all unbelievers? Prominently in history we have Guy de Beauchamp, who came to the title in 1298, and who was called by the favourite Piers Gaveston "the Black Hound of Arden." He was instrumental in taking Piers prisoner, and in leading him to Blacklow Hill, close to Warwick, and there beheading him in 1311. Richard Nevil, the famous "king-maker" (see below), assumed the title in right of his wife Anne, and was slain at the battle of Barnet, 1471. Then the unfortunate George Plantagenet, duke of Clarence, was created earl by his brother Edward IV., but afterwards perished, it is said, by being drowned in a butt of Malmsey wine. The title has frequently lain dormant. In 1547 it was revived in favour of the Dudleys, when Viscount Lisle was created earl by Edward VI. It became extinct in 1589, and in 1618 was renewed in the person of Robert, Lord Rich, whose eldest son was lord high admiral for the Commonwealth. Again the title became extinct in 1759. The castle had long been in the possession of the Greville family, having been granted to Sir Fulke Greville, Lord Brooke, by James I. when it was in a ruinous condition, and he restored it, at a cost, it is said, of £20,000. Dugdale says he made it "not only a place of great strength, but extraordinary delight, with most pleasant gardens, walks, and thickets, such as this part of England can hardly parallel; so that now it is the most princely seat that is within the midland parts of this realm." He died from the effects of a wound inflicted by his own servant, September 8, 1628. His successor, Robert Greville, was the son of Fulke's first cousin, and is the Lord Brooke who is famous in the civil war between Charles and the Parliament, and was appointed commander-in-chief of the Parliamentary forces of Warwickshire and Staffordshire. He was engaged in the first fight of the war at Edge Hill, and was killed at the siege of Lichfield cathedral, on March 1, 1643. The title of earl of Warwick was bestowed on Francis, eighth Lord Brooke, by George II. in 1746. His son George, who succeeded to the title in 1773, was a great benefactor of the borough, and was lavish in his expenditure on the castle.

WARWICK, Richard Nevil, Earl of (*c.* 1420–1471), was born between 1420 and 1430. He was descended from a family of note in the north of England, that of the Nevils, who enjoyed for many generations the title of earls of Westmorland. His grandmother on the father's side was Joan, daughter of John of Gaunt. He inherited the title of earl of Salisbury from his father, a younger son of Ralph Nevil, and by his marriage with Anne, daughter of Richard Beauchamp, he became earl of Warwick. His descent from John of Gaunt made him naturally a member of the Lancastrian party, but the marriage of his aunt, Cicely Nevil, to Richard, duke of York, connected him also with the Yorkist house. As first cousin of Edward IV. and second cousin of Henry VI. he was well fitted for the double part which he was destined to play in English history.

When the struggle between the Roses began, he and his father threw in their lot with the Yorkists. The first attempt of the duke of York (in 1450) to assert his claims proved unsuccessful, but three years later the final loss of Guienne, coupled with the king's imbecility, enabled him to renew his efforts. The duke became protector, but the king's recovery drove him from power and forced him to take up arms a second time. He was now joined actively by Warwick and his father, the former of whom raised a body of troops and contributed largely to the Yorkist victory at St Albans (1455). Warwick was rewarded for his services with the governorship of Calais. This important post gave him the control of the narrow seas, and supplied him with a harbour of refuge whither he could safely retire in case of a change of affairs in England. In the latter capacity Calais soon proved useful.

In 1457, when Henry had recovered his senses, Warwick attended a council at Coventry, at which he took an oath of fealty to the king. Next year he attended a great meeting in London, summoned for the purpose of reconciling the two parties. He was followed on this occasion by six hundred men clad in his livery, and wearing red coats embroidered with ragged staves, the badge of the house of Warwick. An apparent reconciliation was effected, but Warwick, accused of misconduct in attacking a fleet of North Sea merchant-ships near Calais, took advantage of an affray between his followers and some of the king's men to assert that a plot was laid against his life, and retired to his fortress across the Channel. When in 1459 the duke of York took up arms for the third time, Warwick and his father, the earl of Salisbury, joined him at Ludlow. The confederates were strongly posted, but, being deserted by Sir Andrew Trollop, they lost heart and dispersed, Salisbury and Warwick again taking refuge at Calais. A parliament which met at Coventry now attainted Warwick and his father, with other leaders, of high treason, and Somerset was sent to supersede Warwick in his command. The latter, however, made a strong resistance, repelled Somerset, and took his ships, after which he sailed to Dublin to concert further measures with the duke of York. The results of this negotiation were seen early in 1460, when the duke of York issued a manifesto to rouse the people against the Government, and Warwick, landing in Kent, marched on London. The king retired northward and intrenched himself at Northampton, where he was defeated with much loss by Warwick, and taken prisoner. Warwick returned with his captive to London, and the duke of York at once claimed the crown. After much debate the king was induced to consent to a compromise, by which he was to retain the crown during life, and the duke of York and his heirs were to succeed him. The queen, however, refused to sanction this arrangement, and assembled an army in the north. The duke of York, marching against her, was defeated and killed at Wakefield (December 1460), and the earl of Salisbury was taken and beheaded shortly after. The Yorkist victory of Mortimer's Cross (1461) did not stop the queen's march on London, and Warwick, attempting to bar her progress, was entirely defeated at the second battle of St Albans. The king fell into the hands of his own party, but Warwick escaped. The Lancastrian triumph was, however, short-lived. The citizens of London, already devoted to the house of York, were exasperated by the excesses of the Lancastrian troops, and when Warwick, with Edward, earl of March, raised another army and marched towards the capital, the queen was forced to retire to the north. Warwick and Edward entered the city, and the latter was proclaimed king under the title of Edward IV. The sanguinary battle of Towton (March 1461), in which the victory was greatly due to the skill and energy of Warwick, secured the crown for Edward, and gave the nation peace for several years.

Honours and emoluments were showered on Warwick. The governorship of Guisnes and Dammes, with the lieutenancy of the marches there, was added to his command at Calais; he became warden of the western marches towards Scotland, constable of Dover, and lord high chamberlain. The revenue derived from these employments was calculated at 80,000 crowns a year. His brother, John, Lord Montague, was made earl of Northumberland and warden of the eastern marches, and his brother George became archbishop of York and lord chancellor. For some time Warwick did his best to maintain Edward on his throne. An attempt on the part of the Lancastrians in 1463 to recover their power was put down by the united efforts of the Nevils. Montague defeated Percy at Hedgley Moor and Somerset at Hexham, while Warwick besieged and took Bamborough Castle, which was held by Sir Ralph Grey. Soon afterwards Henry VI. was taken prisoner and was lodged by Warwick in the Tower.

But the power and ambition of Warwick were too great to allow the good understanding between the king-maker and the king to be of long duration. The first difference between them arose on the question of the king's marriage. In 1464 Warwick was employed to treat for peace with France, and was anxious to establish it on the firm basis of a matrimonial alliance. His plans were frustrated by Edward's marriage with Elizabeth Woodville. At this time Warwick is said to have been negotiating for a marriage between the king and Bona of Savoy, niece of Louis XI. According to another authority, the princess proposed was Isabella of Castile. Whatever may be the truth of these reports, it is clear that Edward's marriage was not approved by Warwick, and that on the question of foreign policy they followed divergent aims. The rapid advancement of the queen's family contributed to widen the breach. When in 1467 a marriage was proposed between the king's sister Margaret and Charles of Burgundy, Warwick, true to his policy of reconciling England and France, vigorously opposed the match, and suggested in its stead a marriage with a French prince. For a time Edward seemed willing to yield, and Warwick was sent over to treat with the French king. He met him at Rouen, and was received with unusual marks of respect. The result of the conference was that ambassadors were sent by Louis to offer Edward a treaty on favourable terms. But the latter, who had already shown his displeasure by depriving the archbishop of his chancellorship, rejected the offer, and Warwick retired in disgust to one of his castles in the north. Shortly afterwards the marriage between Charles and Margaret took place. An apparent reconciliation between Edward and Warwick was now effected, but its hollowness was shown by the marriage of Isabella, eldest daughter of Warwick, with George, duke of Clarence, a match which Edward strenuously but vainly opposed (1468). A period of intrigue and insurrection followed. A rising in the north, under Robin of Redesdale, was at first defeated by Montague, but the rebels were allowed to make head again. They were soon joined by Warwick and his party, who, if they did not originate, at all events encouraged the rebellion. Edward, whose troops were defeated at Edgecote, fell into Warwick's hands, and was removed to his castle at Middleham. When, however, the Lancastrians took advantage of this state of affairs and rose in arms, they were speedily put down by Warwick. Edward was released and a formal reconciliation followed (1469).

The situation had, however, by this time become intolerable. A fresh insurrection broke out in Lincolnshire, and the confessions of the leaders, who were taken by the royal troops, showed that it had been instigated by Clarence and Warwick. The king at once marched against the conspirators, who in vain attempted to collect sufficient forces, and with some difficulty escaped from the country. Warwick made for his old stronghold at Calais, but his lieutenant proved faithless, and turned his guns against him. Thereupon he took refuge at the court of France and resolved to side openly with the Lancastrians. A treaty was made between Warwick and Queen Margaret, which was cemented by the marriage of Prince Edward with Warwick's daughter Anne. This change of front naturally caused a coolness between Warwick and Clarence; but, before the latter could trim his course anew, Warwick, having obtained assistance from Louis XI., landed in the south of England. Edward was taken by surprise, and, unable to make any resistance, fled to Flanders. Warwick at once marched to London, released Henry VI. from captivity, and replaced him on the throne. A general restoration of property and position to the Lancastrians took place. Warwick and his brothers resumed their offices, and Clarence was recognized as successor to the throne in default of heirs-male to Henry VI. (1470).

But this turn of fortune was as brief as it was sudden. The house of Lancaster was finally overthrown by another revolution as capricious and inexplicable as any of those which had already marked this extraordinary conflict. Henry VI. had only been a few months on the throne when Edward, with the assistance of the duke of Burgundy, landed in Yorkshire, and, gathering troops as he went, marched upon London. He was joined by "false, fleeting, perjured" Clarence, and admitted into the capital by Warwick's brother the archbishop. On Easter-Day 1471 the forces of the king and the earl met at Barnet, and the former won a complete victory. The earl and his brother Montague were slain. Soon afterwards the battle of Tewkesbury and the death of Prince Edward extinguished the last hopes of the Lancastrian party.

The career of the king-maker is chiefly remarkable as illustrating the grandeurs and the evils of feudalism. Warwick's landed property was enormous, comprising, according to the deed by which his widow made it over to Henry VII., upwards of 110 manors in 21 counties, besides the city of Worcester, the islands of Guernsey, Jersey, Alderney, and Sark, and various places in Wales. Commynes tells us that at Calais he was so popular that every one wore his badge, "no man esteeming himself gallant whose head was not adorned with his ragged staff." Stow (*Annals*) says that "at his house in London six oxen were usually eaten at a breakfast, and every tavern was full of his meat, for who that had any acquaintance in his family should have as much sodden and roast as he could carry on a long dagger." In a time of civil war and a disputed title to the throne, such a man was naturally too strong for a subject. The restoration of order and the maintenance of the sovereignty of the state rendered inevitable the disappearance of the class so vigorously represented by the "Last of the Barons."

See Dugdale, *Baronage of England*; P. de Commynes, *Memoirs*; Lingard, *History of England*; Pauli, *Geschichte England's*. (G. W. P.)

WASHINGTON, the seat of government of the United States, forms a part of the District of Columbia, which is under the immediate government of the United States. The city of Washington as a corporation has had no existence since 1871, when Congress abolished the charters of that city and of Georgetown (also within the District of Columbia), and placed the entire District under one government.

The District of Columbia occupies an area of about 70 square miles, on the north-eastern bank of the Potomac, about 100 miles above its mouth, and at the head of tide and of navigation. Most of its area is a plateau, elevated 300 to 400 feet above the river, and traversed by the Anacostia river and Rock creek. Just above the mouth of the former stream, the bluffs, which form the descent from the plateau, recede from the river, leaving an area of bottom land about 6 square miles in extent between that stream and the Potomac. This bottom land is undulating, much of it being but slightly elevated above the river, while the highest parts are scarcely more than 100 feet above high tide. The city of Washington is built upon this bottom land, while its immediate suburbs extend up the bluffs and over the plateau to the northward. The bluffs return to the river immediately above the city, and upon their slopes is built the old city of Georgetown, which is practically continuous with Washington. There are several suburban villages scattered over the district, including Mount Pleasant, Tenallytown, Brightwood, Le Droit Park, and Uniontown.

The climate of Washington is characterized by great humidity, long-continued but not excessive heat in summer, with mild winters. Snow does not often fall, and never lies long on the ground.

Three railroads enter the city, the Baltimore and Ohio and the Pennsylvania, which afford communication with the north and west, and the Richmond and West Point Terminal, which extends southward. Besides its railroad connexions, regular lines of steamers ply to northern and southern ports during most of the year.

The plan of the city is regular and symmetrical. Radiating from the Capitol are three streets, running north, south, and east, and known respectively as North, South, and East Capitol Streets. These, together with a line of public parks running west from the Capitol, divide the city into quarters, known as the north-west, north-east, south-east, and south-west quarters. The streets run in the cardinal directions, the north and south ones being designated by numbers, and the east and west ones by the letters of the alphabet,—the numbers increasing eastward and westward from the meridian of the Capitol, the letters progressing northward and southward from a parallel through that building. In addition to these streets, there is a system of avenues, which run diagonally to the cardinal directions, and which bear the names of States. The intersections of the streets and avenues have given opportunity for the construction of many small parks in the forms of triangles, circles, quadrilaterals, &c., which, with the numerous larger parks scattered about the city, add greatly to its beauty and healthfulness. The streets have a total length of 233½ miles. They are wider than in any other city on the globe, the avenues ranging in width from 120 to 160 feet, while the streets range from 80 to 120 feet. The area comprised in the streets, avenues, and public parks is considerably more than half the area of the city. As the width of the streets is in most cases in excess of the demands of travel, a portion of this width has, in the residence streets, been left between the side walks and the houses, and has been improved as a public parking. In some cases, similar parking has been left in the middle of the streets. Of the 233½ miles of streets, 30 per cent. are paved with smooth pavements, either asphalt, coal-tar, concrete, or asphalt blocks; 10 per cent. are paved with granite or trap blocks, and an equal extent with cobble or rubble; 4½ per cent. are macadamized, and 14 per cent. are gravelled, while the remainder are unimproved. The paved streets are swept by machinery at frequent intervals. With the exception of the business streets every street is lined with shade trees, which, arching over the pavements, form continuous shade for miles. The trees are mainly elms and maples.

The river is crossed by three bridges,—the Long Bridge, by which the city is directly connected with the Virginia shore, the Aqueduct Bridge, so named because it formerly carried the Chesapeake and Ohio Canal, and the Chain Bridge, farther up the river.

The water supply of the District comes from the Potomac. It is taken out of the river at the head of a cataract, known as Great Falls, about 16 miles above the city. It is brought to the distributing reservoir, just above Georgetown, in an aqueduct, passing through a receiving reservoir on the way, and is thence brought to Washington and Georgetown through iron mains. No pumping is done, except to supply the suburbs on the bluffs. The water is excellent, and the supply ample. In order to give a stronger head in certain sections of the city, a tunnel has been constructed to conduct a part of the supply from the distributing reservoir to a third reservoir, north of the middle of the city. The sewer system of the city was not, like its streets, planned in advance, but was suffered to grow up, and is in consequence imperfect. There are three main outlet sewers, one emptying into the Potomac just above the Long Bridge, another near the mouth of the Anacostia, while the third, after skirting the city at the base of the bluffs, empties into the Anacostia. The houses are generally

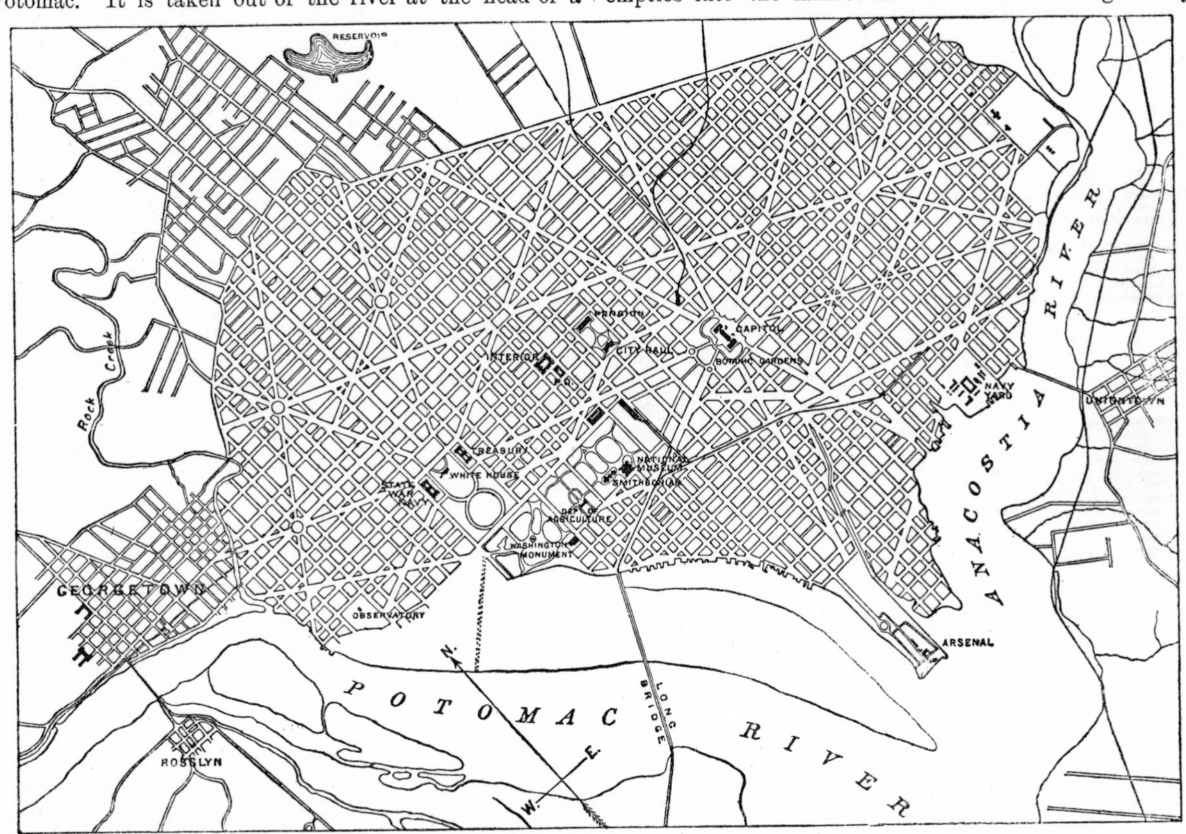

Plan of Washington.

connected with the sewers. The city is fairly well lighted with gas and electric lights.

The District has an excellent common school system, modelled after that of New England; it is managed by a board of trustees appointed by the commissioners. Separate schools are maintained for white and coloured pupils.

The District of Columbia is governed by three commissioners, appointed by the president of the United States. They perform the executive duties, the various departments of the civic government being apportioned among them. Legislation for the District is enacted by Congress. The District has courts of its own, the judges being appointed by the president. The people have no voice in the management of affairs. Thus is presented the singular spectacle of the capital of a great republic governed by an absolute monarchy. Still more singular, perhaps, is the fact that this is the best governed municipality in the United States. The assessed valuation of the District in 1886 was $234,039,436. Of this, nearly one-half, or $113,803,090, was non-taxable, the exemptions being as follows:—property of the United States, $105,389,684; property of the District of Columbia, $2,058,772; private property, $6,354,634. The net debt was $21,279,600, and the rate of taxation $1·50 per $100. This enormous indebtedness was incurred in building up a beautiful city from a swampy waste. One-half of the interest upon it, as well as one-half of the current expenses of the District, is borne by the United States. Washington is unique in the fact that it was planned and constructed solely for the purpose of serving as the seat of government. It is therefore not surprising that it is without commerce or manufactures, excepting such as are required for the support of its inhabitants.

The population of the District by the last census, taken in 1885, was 203,459 (136,271 white and 67,188 coloured, the two races being in about the proportion of two to one). The population comprised within the old corporate limits of Washington was 173,606. The death-rate of the District in 1886 was—for whites 17·96, for negroes 32·35, and for all inhabitants 22·80 per thousand. The death-rate among the white population is less than in any other American city approaching Washington in size.

The public buildings are scattered widely over the city. The Capitol (see vol. ii. p. 454) stands upon an eminence towards the eastern edge of the thickly settled portion, in the midst of extensive grounds. It consists of a central building, surmounted by a dome, and flanked by two wings, in which are the chambers of the two houses of Congress. The length of the building is 751 feet, while its breadth ranges in different parts from 121 to 324 feet. It covers nearly 3½ acres. Its extreme height, from the ground to the top of the statue of Liberty, which stands upon the dome, is 307½ feet. The material of the central building is sandstone, that of the wings marble, while the dome is of iron. The entire cost of the building has been $13,000,000. Besides the two houses of Congress, the Capitol is occupied by the United States Supreme Court and the library of Congress. For the latter a separate building is now in process of erection, upon ground just east of the Capitol.

The Treasury is situated 1½ miles west of the Capitol, at the corner of 15th Street and Pennsylvania Avenue; it is built mainly of granite, in the Ionic style, and measures 468 by 264 feet, with a court in the interior. It contains some 500 rooms, and cost $6,000,000. The building occupied by the state, war, and navy departments is just west of the Treasury, separated from it by the president's residence, which is known as the White House. It is

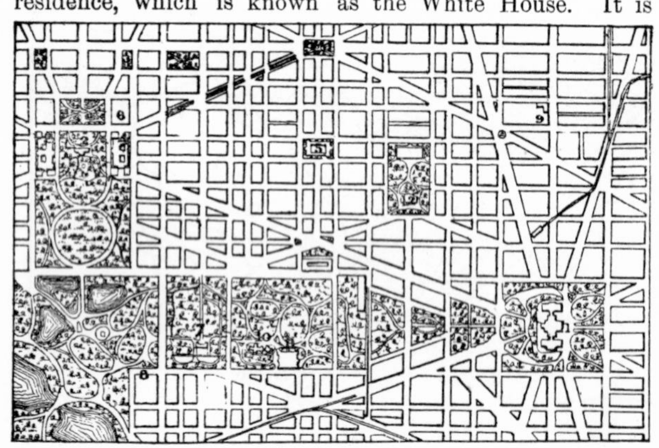

Washington—Central Portion.

1. Capitol.
2. White House.
3. State, War, and Navy Departments.
4. Treasury.
5. Interior Department.
6. Department of Justice.
7. Department of Agriculture.
8. Bureau of Engraving and Printing.
9. Government Printing Office.
10. Smithsonian Inst.
11. National Museum.
12. City Hall.

built entirely of granite, is 567 feet long by 471 feet wide, and 128 feet in height, and cost $10,000,000. The interior department building is on F Street North, nearly equidistant from the Capitol and Treasury. It occupies two squares of the city, being 453 by 331 feet, with an interior court. It is simple in its proportion, and in the Doric style. It is built in part of freestone, in part of marble, while the interior is of granite. This building cost $2,700,000. The post-office department building is directly opposite the interior department, and occupies a whole square. The style is Corinthian, and the material is marble. The dimensions are 300 by 204 feet, with an interior court, and its cost was $1,700,000.

Running westward from the Capitol grounds to the river is a line of public reservations, having a breadth of four squares, from B Street North to B Street South. Within these extensive grounds are several public structures,—the botanic gardens, the buildings of the Fish Commission, the army medical museum, the national museum, the Smithsonian Institution, the department of agriculture, and the Washington monument. All these are of brick, with the exception of the Smithsonian Institution, which is of brown sandstone, and the monument, which is of marble. This is a plain obelisk, 55 feet square at the base and 555 feet in height. The White House is situated between the Treasury and the building of the state, war, and navy departments, on Pennsylvania Avenue, in the midst of ample grounds. It is of sandstone, 170 feet long by 86 feet wide. Among the other public buildings are the naval observatory, the Government printing office, the navy yard, artillery barracks, marine barracks, naval hospital, the city hall, the bureau of engraving and printing, and the pension office. Outside the former city limits are the Government asylum for the insane, the national college for the deaf and dumb, the reform school, and in the midst of a large and beautiful public park the soldiers' home, a retreat for aged and disabled soldiers.

It was the design of those who laid out the city that its principal growth should be east of the Capitol. Certain causes, however, prevented this result, and sent the wealth and fashion into the north-western quarter. This quarter contains at present more than half the population and over three-quarters of the taxable property of the District. In this section are many thousands of residences of fine and varied architecture, the display of which has been much encouraged by the freedom of the building regulations.

Washington is one of the most cosmopolitan of cities. Its population is not only drawn from all parts of the United States, but every civilized nation has its representatives there. Its social life is characterized by a degree of variety and freedom rarely enjoyed elsewhere. It has become in recent years the American centre of scientific thought, and is rapidly gathering men of letters.

Washington was selected as the site for the federal capital in 1790. The States of Maryland and Virginia had ceded to the general Government a tract of land 10 miles square, lying on both sides of the Potomac, for that purpose. The Virginia portion was subsequently re-ceded to that State. In 1790 Georgetown was a city of considerable importance, but upon the site of Washington there were very few settlers. The plan of the city was drawn by Major l'Enfant, and the city laid out in accordance therewith by Andrew Ellicott. At that time the greater part of the site lying west of the Capitol was a morass, well-nigh impassable. The machinery of the government was moved to Washington in 1800, when it was "a backwoods settlement in the wilderness." It existed principally upon paper, and the magnificence of the plan only served to emphasize the poverty of the execution. In 1814, during the second war with Great Britain, it was captured by the British troops, and the Capitol, together with most of the other public buildings, was burned. In 1839 it was described as a "large straggling village reared in a drained swamp." Indeed, in 1871, although it had attained to considerable size, it was exceedingly backward in all municipal improvements. The public buildings and grounds were neglected. The streets were deep in mud, or clouded with dust; the unbuilt portions were morasses; and the sewerage was worse than useless. In that year Congress abolished the charters of the two cities, and instituted a form of territorial government, with a governor and a legislative assembly. The matter of municipal improvement was placed in the hands of a board of public works, with authority to carry out a comprehensive scheme. The work was commenced and pushed forward with the greatest energy, and almost fabulous results were achieved. In a very few years the appearance of the city was revolutionized. The cost of these improvements, was, however, enormous, and it was increased greatly by the rapidity with which the work was done. Much of it, too, was badly executed, so that it has been necessary to replace it. But, in spite of these drawbacks, the fact that Washington is one of the most beautiful and comfortable cities in the world is principally due to the first governor of the District and his board of public works. This government lived too fast to live long. In 1874 Congress abolished the territorial form, and established the present government by three commissioners.

The following figures illustrate the growth of the District in population:—1800, 14,093; 1820, 33,039; 1840, 43,712; 1860, 75,080; 1870, 131,700; 1880, 177,624; 1885, 203,459. Washington had 109,199 inhabitants in 1870, and 147,293 in 1880. (H. G*.)

See vol. xvii. Plate XXIV.

WASHINGTON, a Territory of the United States, is the extreme north-western political subdivision of the Union (except the detached Alaska), and is bounded on the N. by the Canadian province of British Columbia, on the E. by Idaho Territory, on the S. by Oregon, and on the W. by the Pacific Ocean. It lies between 45° 40′ and 49° 0′ N. lat. and 117° 0′ and 124° 44′ W. long., and has a total land area within its boundaries of 66,880 square miles and a water area of 3114 square miles; its average length from east to west is 330 miles and from north to south is 220 miles. The Territory is divided by the Cascade Mountains into two unequal sections, which have very different climatic and physical characteristics and commercial and business interests. The climate is very mild, on account of the warm oceanic current from Japan which flows south along the coast. The moisture-bearing winds moving inland from the ocean are chilled against the Cascade Mountains, and cause the western section of the Territory to have a very heavy annual rainfall (about 53 inches), which is quite evenly distributed throughout the year. The summers are cool and pleasant and the winters mild; flowers bloom in the open air every month in the year, and the nights are always cool and refreshing. The climate in the western section is similar to that of Scotland. That of the eastern section is remarkable for clearness and brightness; it is hot and dry in summer, and has a brief and severe winter. The climate is tempered by a remarkable balmy wind, called the Chinook wind, coming over the mountains from the great Japanese current of the Pacific. In the summer it is a cool wind tempering the heat, and in the winter it is a warm wind, before which snow and ice disappear with marvellous rapidity.

The Cascade range is the local name of the extension through the Territory of the Sierra Nevada, the great and sharply-defined mountain chain which extends at a distance from shore of about 100 miles through the Pacific States and Territories (see vol. xxiii. pp. 800–1). To the north of the Columbia river the range widens out considerably into a region of high grassy mountain plateaus, of deep cañons, heavily timbered slopes, and high peaks of volcanic origin, furnishing mountain scenery of indescribable grandeur. The western slopes are covered with magnificent forests, principally of fir, the trees growing to an immense size. The mountain plateaus are from 3000 to 5000 feet in elevation, untimbered and covered with excellent grass, furnishing a large extent of valuable pasture-land. On the eastern slope the forests are more open, and consist principally of blue and yellow pine, tamarack, fir, and white cedar. The Northern Pacific Railroad reaches the sea by two routes, one of which goes down the Columbia river, and the other crosses the Cascade range by the Yakima Pass in 47° 20′ N. lat.; this pass has an elevation of 3600 feet, and is in a region of beautiful deeply-embosomed lakes, the high cliff-like banks of which are crowned with splendid evergreen forests. To the north of the Yakima Pass the range becomes higher, and more rough and rugged than it is farther south. There seems to have been a volcanic centre between the Yakima and Wenatchee and about midway between the upper Yakima lakes and the Columbia, the highest peak of which is known as Mount Stuart, from which poured a grand flood of lava to the east and south, forming the elevated range between the Yakima and Wenatchee known as the Wenatchee Mountains, and crossing the present channel of the Columbia and forming Badger Mountain on the east. To the north of the 48th parallel, which is about the line of the Spokane river and the westward-flowing portion of the upper Columbia, the country changes, becoming more independent in its mountain formations, and the eastern jutting ranges of the Cascades meet and join with the earlier rock materials of the western spurs of the Rocky Mountains. Here the great interior basin may be considered as ending, for to the north the Rocky and Cascade ranges approach, and are blended in inextricable confusion. The principal rivers having their sources in the Cascade Mountains on the west are the Nooksack, Skagit, Steilaguamish, Snohomish, Puyallup, and Nisqually flowing into Puget Sound, the Chehalis flowing into Gray's Harbour, and the Cowlitz and Lewis rivers flowing into the Columbia; while on the east are the Methow, Chelan, Wenatchee, Yakima, and Klickitat, flowing into the Columbia. The mountains are well stocked with large game, as deer, bear, mountain sheep, mountain goats, wolves, panthers, foxes, &c., the valleys, plateaus, and lakes with feathered game, and the streams and lakes with trout and salmon.

The western section of the Territory lying between the Cascades and the ocean is the smaller of the two, and is covered with timber throughout nearly its entire extent. The principal natural feature is Puget Sound—one of the most beautiful sheets of salt water in the world, if not indeed *the* most beautiful. It is an arm of the sea joining the waters of the Gulf of Georgia and Strait of Juan de Fuca, and stretching about a hundred miles to the south into the heart of the country; it has a great number of bays, coves, inlets, and channels branching off from the main sound, altogether forming a collection of harbours unsurpassed in the world. The total area of the Sound is about 2000 square miles, with a shore-line of about 1600 miles. The water is very deep, in places more than 800 feet, the ordinary depths in the inlets and channels being from 300 to 600 feet. These depths in some places continue right up to the shore, so that vessels of the deepest draught could go and tie up to the trees on the banks as to a wharf. The tides in Puget Sound vary ordinarily from about 9 feet at Port Townsend to 15 feet or more at Olympia and the remote inlets. Along the shores, and for many miles back, the country is covered with the densest growth of very fine timber. The region of the Olympic Mountains lying between Puget Sound and the Pacific has never been explored to any extent, owing to the enormous difficulties of penetrating the forests, which, besides the standing trees, consist of masses of fallen timber and undergrowth. No rivers or creeks navigable for canoes penetrate any distance into it. There is no doubt that Puget Sound once extended much farther south, and occupied the Willamette valley of Oregon. Its retrogression has left large areas of low-lying land bordering the Sound and between it and the Columbia, which, when brought under cultivation, are found to be remarkably fertile. There are large areas of these low-lying lands covered with water at the highest tides which could be easily reclaimed by dyking; about 30,000 acres have been so reclaimed, and it is estimated that 150,000 acres besides can be thus improved. There are no good harbours along the Pacific coast of the Territory; but on the Straits of Juan de Fuca several fine ones exist. Western Washington is specially adapted to raising all the grasses, oats, hops, the root-crops, and fruits; whatever requires great heat does not ripen well.

Eastern Washington Territory differs in a very marked manner and in almost every material respect from the western section. South of the 48th parallel and east of the Cascades it is essentially a prairie country, which owes its origin to the great lava flow that covered eastern Oregon and northern California. This lava has disintegrated in the course of ages, and produced a soil which is unsurpassed in the world for richness. The region lying between the Blue Mountains and the Snake river, known as the Walla Walla country, and that between the Snake and the Spokane, known as the Palouse and Spokane countries, are noted for their fertility. This is also the case with the regions along the eastern foot-hills of the Cascades known generally as the Yakima and Kittitass countries. In these regions there is sufficient rainfall to enable the agriculturist to raise almost every product of the temperate zone of the finest quality and in the greatest abundance. Besides the cereals, such as wheat, oats, barley, flax, &c., there are grown grapes, apples, cherries, peaches, prunes, potatoes, both white and sweet, tobacco, cotton, broom corn, sorghum, peanuts, egg plants, &c. Over a large part of this eastern section, however, the rainfall is not sufficient, and irrigation must be resorted to. With irrigation properly conducted it is safe to say that nearly every foot of land now classed as desert will be found to be as productive as the regions more favoured by rain.

That part of eastern Washington Territory north of the Columbia and Spokane rivers is a region of low-timbered mountains and fertile valleys. This is mostly given up to the Indians, there being the two large reservations called the Columbia and Colville reservations stretching from the Cascade Mountains eastward to the southward-flowing portion of the Columbia, and embracing 7880 square miles of land. North of the Spokane river is the Colville country, which is open to settlement, and in which are much good land and large quantities of valuable timber.

The most important feature of eastern Washington is the Columbia river, which enters the Territory from British Columbia at about 117° 30′ W. long., and pursues nearly a southerly course to the "Big Bend," a distance of 110 miles, where it takes a westerly course, which it keeps for 93 miles until it receives the waters of the Okinakane, where it changes its course again to the south, keeping it for 224 miles, until it unites with its greatest tributary, the Snake river; from this point it keeps a westerly course, breaking through the Cascades, and entering the Pacific in lat. 46° 15′. It forms the boundary between Washington Territory and Oregon for this latter part of its course. The lower portion of the Columbia is described under OREGON (*q.v*). The upper part may be briefly described as a deeply cañoned river with numerous rapids and falls, which make it unnavigable and in all probability incapable of improvement. The Kettle Falls, near the northern boundary, are the most marked on the river, being about 25 feet at low water. Here each year the Indians from all directions gather on neutral ground to take salmon for their next year's subsistence. A salmon chief is elected, whose duties are to keep order and to divide equitably all the fish taken. The fish are taken in baskets as they try to jump the falls, those that fail falling back into the baskets. That part of the Columbia from the northern boundary-line to the "Big Bend" is the most beautiful portion of the river within the Territory, except where it breaks through the Cascades. Throughout this portion there is considerable bottom-land, and this and the neighbouring hills and mountains are well covered with fine open timber, with charming little grassy prairies scattered here and there. Below the Big Bend the cañon of the Columbia becomes more prominent, the timber recedes from the banks, and the channel narrows between basalt rocks, and in places is highly dangerous to anyone who entrusts himself upon the waters. The general depth of the cañon is about 2000 feet. Much gold is found in the sand bars and low terraces along the river.

The principal tributaries of the Columbia within the Territory are Clarke's Fork, the outlet of Lake Pend d'Oreille, an unnavigable stream flowing through a deep cañon, which enters the Columbia just above the northern boundary of the Territory. The Spokane river, one of the most important tributaries, is the outlet of Lake Cœur d'Alene, which drains a large extent of the Bitter Root Mountains. The Spokane, from the lake to Spokane Falls, a distance of about 30 miles, flows just below the level of a lovely prairie country; at the falls the river takes a plunge of 156 feet, and from there to the Columbia it flows through a deep cañon. These falls of the Spokane furnish one of the finest, most accessible, and most easily controlled water-powers in the world, and already they are utilized to a considerable extent for manufacturing purposes. The Okinakane is the next important tributary; it rises in British Columbia and flows southward through Lakes Okinakane and Osoyoos, and enters the Territory in 119° 30′ W. long. Its course lies through a rich and inviting country. At its mouth was one of the most important of the old Hudson's Bay Company's trading posts. The Methow river, Lake Chelan and its outlet, and the Wenatchee are rivers of considerable magnitude, draining the eastern slopes of the Cascades. They are in a mountainous country presenting few attractions to the settler. The Yakima, which also comes from the Cascades, is of far greater importance, as about its headwaters is a large amount of fine agricultural land, and the river itself and its tributaries will ultimately furnish the water for irrigating an enormous extent of very fine land now virtually desert. Already large irrigating canals, having a total length of 325 miles, are projected, and work on them has been commenced.

The largest tributary of the Columbia, the Snake, joins it about 8 miles below the mouth of the Yakima. The Snake is navigable for the whole 150 miles of its course through the Territory, but has some difficult rapids. It flows through a cañon 1000 to 2000 feet deep, which it has cut for itself through the lava deposits.

An area nearly encircled by the Columbia, below the Big Bend, and the Snake, in the last 50 miles of its course, is known as the Great Plain of the Columbia. Its southern part is an alkaline nearly waterless desert, the principal vegetation being sage brush; the northern part is somewhat more elevated, and is for the most part a rich rolling grassy country intersected here and there by *coules*, or deep and almost vertical cuts, through the basalt rock underlying the soil. They indicate the former presence of large streams of water.

Forests.—Very valuable forests exist in every part of western Washington and in the northern part of eastern Washington The sawmills on Puget Sound have a capacity of 350,000,000 feet per year, and the total capacity of the mills of the Territory is over 650,000,000 feet per year. The principal timber is yellow and red fir, ordinarily known as "Oregon pine," which constitutes the bulk of the forests; white and red cedar, spruce, and larch also abound. White pine of magnificent size grows on the upper benches of the Cascade Mountains; white fir and hemlock are also found. Alder, maple, ash, oak, and cottonwood occur in abundance on the bottom-lands of western Washington, but are not equal to timber of the same names in the east. Bull pine, yellow pine, and tamarack grow on the eastern slopes of the Cascade range, and constitute the bulk of the forests of eastern Washington. They make a fair quality of lumber, but greatly inferior to the products of the western slopes and the Pacific coast regions.

Fisheries.—The salmon fisheries of the Columbia river, Shoalwater Bay, Gray's Harbour, and Puget Sound form one of the leading industries of the Territory. The preservation of salmon in cans was commenced in 1866 on the Columbia river, and the business rapidly increased, so that now the annual value of the pack is from 2 to 2½ million dollars.

Mines and Mining.—The mineral resources of the Territory are very great upon both sides of the Cascade Mountains. There are large tracts of valuable coal-lands between Puget Sound and the Cascades, stretching all the way from Bellingham Bay on the north to the Chehalis valley on the south. The veins at present worked vary from 5 to 12 feet in thickness, and in quality from lignite to bituminous coal, some of which produces gas and coke of superior excellence. Mines are also worked on the eastern slope of the Cascades about the head of the Yakima river. The present known area of coal-lands in the Territory is about 180,000 acres, and the total shipments for the year ending June 30, 1887, amounted to 525,705 tons. The supply of coal for the Pacific coast is mainly drawn from the beds in Washington Territory and their continuation in British Columbia.

There are large deposits of valuable iron ore in the western part of the Territory and in the Snoqualmie Pass. Brown hæmatite iron ore is found in Skagit county, magnetic ore in King county, and bog iron ore of the best quality in several counties, notably Jefferson, King, and Pierce; but these deposits have not yet been worked to any great extent. There can be no question, however, that the existence of coal, iron, and timber in the near vicinity of Puget Sound must make this a great manufacturing and shipbuilding centre. Limestone is found in great abundance on San Juan Island, in the Puyallup valley, and in the north-eastern part of the Territory. Copper and lead are found in different localities.

The northern part of eastern Washington abounds in mines of the precious metals, and these are now being worked on quite an extensive scale. In the Colville district (between the Columbia, Clarke's Fork, and Spokane rivers) the prevailing country rock is limestone, and the prevailing mineral is argentiferous galena; at some points grey copper ore is found carrying both silver and lead, and in others silver chlorides are found. The development of these mines has been delayed by lack of railway facilities, but this will be remedied in a short time by lines now projected and incorporated.

The Kettle river district lies to the west of the Columbia, and in regions about the headwaters of the river. The mines are very varied in their character, comprising placer gold, gold quartz, copper, and galena with carbonates. Some of the placer mines have yielded heavily, the gold being coarse and obtained by ground sluicing.

Very valuable quartz ledges, assaying 80 to 2000 ounces of gold per ton, have been discovered in a formation of granite and slate.

The Okinakane district comprises the mines in the vicinity of the Okinakane, Salmon, and the Similkameen rivers and Osoyoos lake. Here the formation is granite, syenite, and porphyry, and the ores are galena, grey copper, and quartz, carrying sulphurets and native silver.

The city of Spokane Falls, on the Northern Pacific Railroad, is the distributing point for all these mines, as well as for the Cœur d'Alene mines in northern Idaho.

Shipbuilding.—Shipyards exist at Seattle and Tacoma, and at other points on Puget Sound, at Gray's Harbour and Shoalwater Bay, and on the Columbia river. The vessels constructed are mainly schooners for the lumber-carrying trade; many of them also are provided with auxiliary steam-power. All raw materials for their construction are found in the vicinity. The yellow fir of the northern Pacific ranks next to oak for strength and durability, and constitutes excellent material for shipbuilding. Vessels of 4854 tons were built during 1886, and the industry is rapidly growing.

Commerce.—The principal articles of export are lumber, coal, wheat, and salmon, and their annual value is from 8 to 10 millions of dollars. In the year from July 1886 to June 1887 the total entrances at Puget Sound were 994 vessels (539,597 tons), and the clearances 988 (514,441 tons).

Railways.—Washington Territory was the last of the political subdivisions of the United States to be reached by railroads. In 1883 the Northern Pacific was completed and direct rail connection secured with the east.

Education.—There are about a thousand common schools in the Territory, under the supervision of a superintendent of public instruction and a board of education of three persons, all of whom are appointed by the governor. In each county, county superintendents and a board of county examiners visit the schools and report to the superintendent of public instruction. There is held each year a territorial teachers' institute, and local teachers' institutes are also held in different sections. These common schools are supported by county taxes and by certain criminal fines. Special taxes are also permitted in counties under certain conditions. There are at present about 65,000 children under instruction, at a cost of about $500,000 per annum.

The general Government has set aside for educational purposes one-eighteenth of all the land in the Territory, comprising about 2½ million acres. This land, however, does not become available until the Territory becomes a State. All children must attend school at least three months in the year.

There is a university at Seattle, supported by large annual appropriations of the legislature. It has four departments at present:—literature, science, and the arts; law; medicine; and military instruction. There are also twenty-four higher institutions of learning scattered throughout the Territory, consisting of colleges, seminaries, and academies, most of which are under sectarian control, and some of which have already a liberal endowment.

Churches.—All the leading Christian sects are well represented in the Territory, their membership and value of church property being about in the order given below:—Methodist Episcopal, Roman Catholic, Protestant Episcopal, Congregational, Baptist, Presbyterian, Christian, Lutheran, German Reformed, and Unitarian.

Government.—The administrative affairs of the Territory are in the hands of a governor, secretary, and chief justice, all appointed by the president of the United States, and a treasurer and comptroller and an upper and lower legislative house elected by the people. The Territory is represented in Congress by a delegate also elected by the people.

Population.—The total population, 75,116 in 1880, was 143,669 (84,470 males, 59,199 females) according to the census taken in 1886 and 1887, classified as follows:—whites, 137,430; blacks, 254; mulattoes, 69; Chinese, 2584; Indian half-breeds, 3288; and Kanakas, 44. In addition to these there are about 11,000 Indians. The total population is now (1888) about 175,000. The capital is Olympia, and the chief city Seattle, both on Puget Sound.

Banks.—There are in the Territory 18 national banks, with a capital of $1,430,000, 5 territorial banks, with a capital of $355,000, and also a number of private banks.

History.—The first event in history relating to Washington Territory was the discovery, in 1592, of the Strait of Juan de Fuca by an old Greek pilot of that name in the service of Spain. In 1775 Captain Hecata, a Spanish navigator, discovered the mouth of the Columbia, but was unable to enter the river. Captain Kendrick, an American navigator, in 1789 sailed into the Strait of Fuca and through the Gulf of Georgia and Queen Charlotte Sound to the Pacific, and was the first to clearly make known the character of these inland waters. On the 11th of May 1792 Captain Gray, of the American ship "Columbia," sailed into and explored for about 15 miles the great river to which he gave the name of his ship. This first entrance into the Columbia river gave the United States their principal claim to the territory drained by the river, and is thus a very important episode in the history of the Oregon region, which formerly comprised the present State of Oregon and the Territories of Washington and Idaho. In October of the same year (1792) an Englishman, Lieutenant Broughton, sailed up and examined the Columbia for about 100 miles from its mouth. The coast soon became quite well known, and the Government of the United States fitted out a number of expeditions to obtain a knowledge of the interior. The most important of these was that of Lewis and Clarke, who were directed to ascend the Missouri, cross the Rocky Mountains, and trace the Columbia from its sources to the sea. They began the ascent of the Missouri in 1804, and spent the winter of 1804-5 at Fort Mandan. In the next season, after incredible hardships and great sufferings, they crossed the Rocky Mountains, and reached the Clearwater river. Here they made boats, and proceeded down it, the Snake river, and the main Columbia, reaching the Pacific in December 1805. They returned by nearly the same route.

The next important era in the history of the Territory was the attempt of J. J. Astor to establish a fur-trading empire on the Columbia and its tributary lands and streams. Two expedition were sent out in 1810 for this purpose, one by land and one by sea. The latter reached the Columbia in 1811, and established a trading post at Astoria near the mouth of the river. The land expedition reached this post in 1812. In the meantime, in hopes of forestalling Astor's expeditions, the North-West Fur Company sent a party in 1810 to cross the mountains and reach the mouth of the Columbia before them. This expedition experienced great difficulty in crossing the mountains in 52° N. lat., but in the spring of 1811 they reached the Columbia, and went down to its mouth, where they found Astor's sea party already established. This North-West Fur Company's expedition was the first to navigate the upper Columbia, or to traverse any part of the country drained by it. In 1813 the fortunes of war compelled the transfer of the Astor Fur Company to the North-West Fur Company. Henceforward for many years the history of the Territory is the history of the operations of the great North-West and Hudson's Bay Companies, and of the effort of private parties to get a share in the profits of the fur trade. A number of trading posts were built, and exploring and trading expeditions sent into all parts of the country. Missionaries began to arrive, and emigrants to drift in by sea and land.

During all the years in which this region was first being explored and settled, a dispute had been going on between the United States and Great Britain in regard to its ownership, which at different times waxed so fierce as to threaten war. Finally an arrangement was arrived at, and in 1846 the treaty was signed fixing the boundary-line at the 49th parallel. The Territory of Oregon (comprising Washington, Idaho, and Oregon) was formed in 1848, and General Joseph Lane, the first Territorial governor, arrived in 1849, after which United States courts were established. The present Territory of Washington was established in 1853, and its first governor was Isaac I. Stevens.

The settlement of the Territory has been slow, on account of its remoteness and the fact that it has had no great mining excitement to attract adventurous settlers. Since the advent of railroads, however, its development has been rapid. (T. W. S.)

WASHINGTON, George (1732-1799), the first president of the United States, was born in Westmoreland county, Virginia, February 22 (Old Style, Feb. 11), 1732. One lawless genealogist has traced his ancestry back to Odin. Another genealogy, since given up with much regret, connected the family with the Washingtons of Northumberland or Durham, England. The ancestry of Washington can be traced no farther back than his great-grandfather, John Washington, who settled in Virginia about 1657. His eldest son, Lawrence, had three children—John, Augustine, and Mildred. Augustine Washington married twice. By the first marriage, with Jane Butler, there were four children, two of whom, Lawrence and Augustine, grew to manhood. By the second marriage, with Mary Ball, in 1730, there were six children—George, Betty, Samuel, John, Augustine, Charles, and Mildred. The father died when George was but twelve years old; Lawrence inherited the estate now known as Mount Vernon, and George his father's usual residence, nearly opposite Fredericksburgh.

Very little is known of Washington's early life, probably because there was little unusual to tell. The story of the hatchet and the cherry-tree, and similar tales, are quite apocryphal, having been coined by Washington's most popular biographer, Weems. The boy's life was not different from that common to Virginia families in easy circumstances; hunting, fishing, plantation affairs, and a little reading made up its substance. His education was but elementary and very defective, except in mathematics, in which he was largely self-taught. Sparks has "edited" the spelling, grammar, and rhetoric of Washington's *Writings* to such an extent as to destroy their value as evidence. About 1748 we begin to know something of Washington's life. He was then at Mount Vernon with his half-brother Lawrence, who was his guardian. Lawrence was the son-in-law of his neighbour Lord Fairfax, with whom he had served at Carthagena, and had made the acquaintance of Admiral Vernon, from whom Mount Vernon was named. A commission as midshipman was obtained for George through the admiral, but the opposition of the boy's mother put an end to the scheme. As a substitute, the appointment as surveyor of the enormous Fairfax property was given to Washington at the age of sixteen; and the next three years of his life were spent in this service. He always retained a disposition to speculate in Western lands; many of his later investments were of this kind, and they are treated in Butterfield's *Washington-Crawford Letters.* He seems already to have impressed others with a belief in his force of mind and character, for at the age of nineteen, when the first indications of the "French and Indian war" appeared, he was appointed adjutant of the Virginia troops, with the rank of major; on the death of his half-brother Lawrence in the following year he was executor under the will, and residuary heir of Mount Vernon; and in 1753, when he had barely attained his majority, the young man was made commander of the northern military district of Virginia by the new lieutenant-governor, Dinwiddie. It is at this point in his career that Washington appears in Thackeray's *Virginians*, but the portrait there drawn of a "shrewd young man" on the lookout for a rich wife is not accepted as life-like by Americans.

At the outbreak of the French and Indian war in 1753–54 Washington was the agent sent by Governor Dinwiddie to warn the French away from their new forts in western Pennsylvania; the command of the Virginia troops who began hostilities fell to him, and his vigorous defence of Fort Necessity (see UNITED STATES, vol. xxiii. pp. 734–35) made him so prominent a figure that in 1755, at the age of twenty-three, he was commissioned commander-in-chief of all the Virginia forces. He served in Braddock's campaign, and in the final defeat showed for the first time that fiery energy which always lay hidden beneath his calm and unruffled exterior. He ranged the whole field on horseback, making himself the most conspicuous mark for Indian bullets, and, in spite of what he called the "dastardly behaviour" of the regular troops, brought the little remnant of his Virginians out of action in fair order. In spite of this reckless exposure he was one of the few unwounded officers. For a year or two his task was that of "defending a frontier of more than 350 miles with 700 men;" but in 1758 he had the pleasure of commanding the advance guard of the expedition which captured Fort Du Quesne and renamed it Fort Pitt. The war in Virginia being then at an end, he resigned his post, married Mrs Custis, a widow, and settled at Mount Vernon.

Washington's life for the next twenty years was merely that of a typical Virginia planter, a consistent member of the Established (Episcopal) Church, a large slaveholder, a strict but considerate master, and a widely trusted man of affairs. His extraordinary escape in Braddock's defeat had led a colonial minister to declare in a sermon his belief that the young man had been preserved to be "the saviour of his country." If there was any such impression it soon died away, and Washington gave none of his associates reason to consider him an uncommonly endowed man. His marriage had brought him an increase of about $100,000 in his estate; and his diaries show comparatively little reading, a minutely methodical conduct of business, a wide acquaintance with the leading men of the country, but no strong indications of what is usually considered to be "greatness." As in the case of Lincoln, he was educated into greatness by the increasing weight of his responsibilities and the manner in which he met them. Like others of the dominant caste in Virginia, he was repeatedly elected to the legislature, but he is not known to have made any set speeches in that body, or to have said anything beyond a statement of his opinion and the reasons for it. That he thought a great deal, and took full advantage of his legislative experiences as a political education, is shown by his letter of April 5, 1769, to his neighbour George Mason, communicating the Philadelphia non-importation resolutions, which had just reached him. He considers briefly the best peaceable means of resistance to the policy of the ministry, but even at that early date faces frankly and fully the probable final necessity of resisting by force, and endorses it. Without speech-making, he took a prominent part in struggles of his legislature against Governor Dunmore, and his position was always a radical one. He even opposed petitions to the king and parliament, on the ground that the question had been put by the ministry on the basis of right, not of expediency, that the ministry could not abandon the right and the colonists could not admit it, and that petitions must be, as they had been, rejected. "Shall we," says he in a letter, "after this whine and cry for relief?" In 1774 the Virginia Convention, appointing seven of its members as delegates to the Continental Congress, named Washington as one of them; and with this appointment his national career begins.

Washington's letters during his service in Congress show that he was under no delusions as to the outcome of the taxation struggle, and that he expected war. In one letter he says that if the ministerial policy is persisted in "more blood will be shed than history has ever yet furnished instances of in the annals of North America." His associates in Congress recognized his military ability at once, and most of the details of work looking towards preparations for armed resistance were by common consent left to him. Even in the intervals of his Congressional service he was occupied in urging on the formation, equipment, and training of Virginia troops, and it was generally understood that, in case of war, Virginia would expect him to act as her commander-in-chief. History was not to be cheated in that fashion. The two most powerful colonies were Virginia and Massachusetts. War began in Massachusetts; New England troops poured in almost spontaneously; it was necessary to ensure the support of the colonies to the southward; and the Virginia colonel who was at the head of all the military committees was just the man whom the New England delegates desired. When Congress, after the fights at Lexington and Concord, resolved to put the colonies into a state of defence, the first practical step was the unanimous selection, on motion of John Adams of Massachusetts, of Washington as commander-in-chief of the armed forces of the United Colonies. Refusing any salary, he accepted the position, asking "every gentleman in the room," however, to remember his declaration that he did not believe himself to be equal to the command, and that he accepted it only as a duty made imperative by the unanimity of the call. He reiterated this belief in private letters even to his wife; and there seems to be no doubt that, to the day of his death, he was the most determined sceptic as to his fitness for the positions to which he was called in succession. He was commissioned June 19, 1775, and reached Cambridge, Mass., July 2, taking command of the levies there assembled for action against the British garrison of Boston. The battle of Bunker Hill had already taken place, and Washington's work until the following spring was to bring about some semblance of military discipline, to obtain ammunition and military stores, to correspond with Congress and the colonial governors, to guide military operations in the widely separated parts of a great continent, to create a military system and organization for a people who were entirely unaccustomed to such a thing and impatient under it, and to bend the course of events steadily towards driving the British out of Boston. It is not easy to see how Washington survived the year 1775; the colonial poverty, the exasperating annoyances, the selfishness or stupidity which cropped out again and again from the most patriotic of his coadjutors, were enough to have broken down most men. They completed his training. The change in this one winter is very evident. If he was not a great man when he went to Cambridge, he was a general and a statesman in the best sense when he drove the British out of Boston in March 1776. From that time until his death he was the foremost man of the continent.

The military operations of the remainder of the war are given elsewhere (see UNITED STATES, vol. xxiii. pp. 743–745). Washington's retreat through the Jerseys; the manner in which he turned and struck his pursuers at Trenton and Princeton, and then established himself at Morristown so as to make the way to Philadelphia impassable; the vigour with which he handled his army at Chad's Ford and Germantown; the persistence with which he held the strategic position of Valley Forge through the dreadful winter of 1777–78, in spite of the misery of his men, the clamours of the people, and the impotence of the fugitive Congress,—all went to show that the fibre of his public character had been hardened to its permanent quality. The Valley Forge winter was said to be "the time that tried men's souls:" Washington's had no need to fear the test. It was a serious addition to his burdens that the spirit which culminated in Benedict Arnold chose this moment to make its appearance. Many of the American officers had been affronted by the close personal friendship which had sprung up between La Fayette and Washington, and by the diplomatic deference which the commander-in-chief felt compelled to show to other foreign officers. Some of the latter showed no gratitude. The name of one of them, Conway, an Irish soldier of fortune from the French service, is attached to what was called "Conway's Cabal." He formed a scheme for replacing Washington in the command by Gates, who had just succeeded in forcing Burgoyne to surrender at Saratoga; and a number of officers and men in civil life were mixed up in it. The methods employed were the lowest forms of anonymous slander, and at the first breath of exposure every one concerned hurried to cover up his part in it, leaving Conway to shoulder all the responsibility. The treaty of 1778 with France put an end to every such plan. It was a flat absurdity to expect foreign nations to deal with a second-rate man as commander-in-chief while Washington was in existence, and he seems to have had no more trouble of this kind. The prompt and vigorous pursuit of Clinton across the Jerseys towards New York, and the battle of Monmouth, in which the plan of battle was thwarted by Charles Lee, another of the foreign officers, closed the direct military record of Washington until the end of the war. The enemy confined their movements to other parts of the continent, and Washington did little more than watch their headquarters in New York city. It was more than appropriate, however, that he who had been the mainspring of the war, and had borne far more than his share of its burdens and discouragements, should end it with the campaign of Yorktown, conceived by himself, and the surrender of Cornwallis. The war was then really over, but the commander-in-chief retained his commission until December 28, 1783, when he returned it to Congress, then in session at Annapolis, Md., and retired to Mount Vernon.

By this time the canonization of Washington had fairly begun. He occupied such a position in the American political system as no man could possibly hold again. He had become a political element, quite apart from the Union, the States, or the people of either. In a country where communication was still slow and difficult, the general knowledge that Washington favoured anything superseded argument and the necessity of information with very many men. His constant correspondence with the governors of the States gave him a quasi-paternal attitude towards government in general. On resigning his commission, for example, he was able to do what no other man could have done with propriety or safety: he addressed a circular letter to the governors of the States, pointing out changes in the existing form of government which he believed to be necessary. His refusal to accept a salary, as general or as president, would have been taken as affectation or impertinence in anyone else; it seemed natural and proper enough in the case of Washington, but it was his peculiar privilege. It is possible that he might have had a crown if he had even been willing. The army, at the end of the war, was justly dissatisfied with its treatment. The officers were called to meet at Newburgh, and it was the avowed purpose of the leaders of the movement that the army should march westward, appropriate vacant lands, leave Congress to negotiate for peace without an army, and "mock at their calamity and laugh when their fear cometh." It was the less publicly avowed purpose to make their commander-in-chief king, if he could be persuaded to aid in establishing a monarchy. Washington put a summary stop to the whole proceeding. Their letter to him detailed the weakness of a republican form of government as they had experienced it, their desire for "a mixed government," with him at its head, and their belief that "the title of king" would be objectionable to few and of material advantage to the country. His reply was peremptory, and even angry. He stated in plain terms his abhorrence of the proposal; he was at a loss to conceive what part of his conduct could have encouraged their address; they could not have found "a person to whom their schemes were more disagreeable;" and he threatened them with exposure unless the affair was stopped at once. His influence, and that alone, secured the quiet disbanding of the discontented army. His influence was as powerful after he had retired to Mount Vernon as before his resignation. He was in constant correspondence with public men in every part of the country. He received from them such a store of suggestions as came to no other man, digested it, and was able from it to speak with what seemed infallible wisdom. In the midst of his voluminous correspondence, the minute details in his diaries of tree-planting and rotation of crops, and his increasing reading on the political side of history, he found time for a stream of visitors. Among these, in March 1785, were the commissioners from Virginia and Maryland, who met at Alexandria to form a commercial code for Chesapeake Bay, and made an opportunity to visit Mount Vernon. From that moment the current of events, leading into the Annapolis convention of 1786 and the final convention of the next year, shows Washington's close supervision at every point.

When the Federal Convention met at Philadelphia in May 1787 to frame the present constitution he was present as a delegate from Virginia, though much against his will; and a unanimous vote at once made him its presiding officer. He took no part in the debates, however, beyond such suggestive hints as his proposal to amend a restriction of the standing army to 5000 men by forbidding any enemy to invade the United States with more than 3000. He approved the constitution which was decided upon, believing, as he said, "that it was the best constitution which could be obtained at that epoch, and that this or a dissolution awaits our choice, and is the only alternative." All his influence was given to secure its ratification, and his influence was probably decisive. When it had been ratified, and the time came to elect a president, there was no more hesitation than if the country had been a theocracy. The office of president had been "cut to fit the measure of George Washington," and no one thought of any other person for it. The unanimous vote of the electors made him the first president of the United States; their unanimous vote re-elected him in 1792–93; and, even after he had positively refused to serve for a third term, two electors obstinately voted for him in 1796–97. The public events of his presidency are given elsewhere (see UNITED STATES, vol. xxiii. pp. 752–755). One can hardly follow them without receiving the conviction that the sudden success of the new system was due mainly to the existence at that time of such a character as Washington. He held the two natural parties apart, and prevented party contest until the new form of government had been firmly established. It seems hardly possible that the final result should have been baulked, even if "blood and iron" had been necessary to bring it about. It would be unwise to attribute the quiet attainment of the result to the political sense of the American people alone, or to use it as an historical precedent for the voluntary assumption of such a risk again, without the advantage of such a political factor as Washington.

No greater mistake could be made, however, than to think that the influence of the president was fairly appreciated during his term of office. He attempted to balance party against party, to divide his cabinet between them, and to neutralize the effects of parties in that way. The consequence was that the two leading members of the cabinet soon occupied the position, to use the words of one of them, of "two game-cocks in a pit." The unconscious drift of Washington's mind was toward the Federal party; his letters to La Fayette and Henry, in December 1798 and January 1799, are enough to make that evident. When the Republican party was formed, about 1793, it could not have been expected that its leaders would long submit with patience to the continual interposition of Washington's name and influence between themselves and their opponents; but they maintained a calm exterior. Some of their followers were less discreet. The president's proclamation of neutrality between France and Great Britain excited them to anger; his support of Jay's treaty with Great Britain roused them to fury. Forged letters, purporting to show his desire to abandon the revolutionary struggle, were published; he was accused of drawing more than his salary; hints of the propriety of a guillotine for his benefit began to appear; some spoke of him as the "stepfather of his country." The attacks embittered the close of his term of service; he declared, in a cabinet meeting in 1793, that "he had never repented but once the having slipped the moment of resigning his office, and that was every moment since." Indeed, the most unpleasant portions of Jefferson's *Ana* are those in which, with an air of psychological dissection, he details the storms of passion into which the president was hurried by the newspaper attacks upon him. These attacks, however, came from a very small fraction of the politicians; the people never wavered in their devotion to the president, and his election would have been unanimous in 1796, as in 1789 and 1792, if he had been willing to serve.

All accounts agree that Washington was of imposing presence. He measured just 6 feet when prepared for burial; but his height, in his prime, as given in his orders for clothes from London, was 3 inches more. La Fayette says that his hands were "the largest he ever saw on a man." Custis says that his complexion was "fair, but considerably florid." His weight was about 220 ℔. The various and widely-differing portraits of him find exhaustive treatment in the seventh volume of Winsor's *Narrative and Critical History of the United States.* The editor thinks that "the favourite profile has been unquestionably Houdon's, with Stuart's canvass for the full face, and probably Trumbull's for the figure." Stuart's face, however, gives the popular notion of Washington, though it has always been a subject of curious speculation to some minds how much of the calm and benign expression of the face was due to the shape of Washington's false teeth.

Washington was childless: said the people of his time, he was the father only of his country. Collateral branches of the family have given the Lees, the Custises, and other families a claim to an infusion of the blood; but no direct descendants of Washington can claim his honours, or disgrace his name. His estate of Mount Vernon was acquired in 1858 by an association, and has been practically national property ever since.

Retiring from the presidency in 1797, Washington resumed the plantation life which he most loved, the society of his family, and the care of his slaves. He had resolved some time before never to obtain another slave, and "wished from his soul" that his State could be persuaded to abolish slavery; "it might prevent much future mischief." He was too old, however, to attempt further innovations. In 1798 he was made commander-in-chief of the provisional army raised in expectation of open war with France, and was fretted almost beyond endurance by the quarrels of Federalist politicians about the distribution of commissions. In the midst of his military preparations, he was struck down by sudden illness, which lasted but for a day, and he died at Mount Vernon, December 14, 1799. The third of the series of resolutions introduced in the house of representatives five days after his death, by John Marshall, and passed unanimously, states exactly, if a trifle rhetorically, the position of Washington in American history: "first in war, first in peace, and first in the hearts of his countrymen."

Washington's disorder was an œdematous affection of the wind-pipe, contracted by careless exposure during a ride in a snow-storm, and aggravated by neglect afterwards, and by such contemporary remedies as excessive bleeding, gargles of "molasses, vinegar, and butter" and "vinegar and sage tea," which "almost suffocated him," and a blister of cantharides on the throat. He died without theatrical adieus; his last words were only business directions, affectionate remembrances to relatives, and repeated apologies to the physicians and attendants for the trouble he was giving them. Just before he died, says his secretary, Mr Lear, he felt his own pulse; his countenance changed; the attending physician placed his hands over the eyes of the dying man, "and he expired without a struggle or a sigh."

Any complete bibliography of books relating to Washington would be voluminous. Lives have been written by Weems, Marshall (1804–7), Ramsay (1807), A. Bancroft (1826), and Irving (1855). See also Sparks's *Writings of Washington* (1834–37); Rush's *Domestic Life of Washington* (1857); G. W. P. Custis's *Recollections of Washington* (1860); Baker's *Character Portraits of Washington* (1887); *Science*, December 11, 1885 (an attempt to make a composite portrait of Washington); Winsor's *Narrative and Critical History of the United States* (editor's article); Bancroft's *United States* (final revision); Schouler's *United States*; M'Master's *United States*. (A. J.)

WASPS. The order *Hymenoptera* is divided into two sub-orders, the *Terebrantia* and the *Aculeata*. The latter is subdivided into several sub-sections, one of which, the *Diploptera* (Latreille), includes all the true wasps.

The *Diploptera* are in their turn divided into three families—(1) the *Vespidæ*, (2) the *Eumenidæ*, and (3) the *Masaridæ*, which together comprise some 1000 different species. They are characterized by their wings, which are present in both sexes and also in the neuters, being longitudinally folded when at rest. The antennæ are usually elbowed, and contain twelve or thirteen joints; in some cases they are clavate. A pair of notched faceted eyes are present, and three ocelli in the top of the head. The mouth-parts are arranged for sucking, but have not reached that degree of perfection found amongst the bees. Hence wasps cannot obtain the sugary secretion from deeply-seated nectaries, and their visits to flowers are confined to such as are shallow or widely opened; they particularly frequent the *Umbelliferæ*. The maxillæ are elongated, and compressed, the maxillary palp six-jointed. The labium bears a tongue which is glandular at the tip; the paraglossæ are linear. The labial palp has three or four joints. The thorax is oval, and its sides prolonged backward to the base of the wings. The fore wing has two or three sub-marginal cells. The legs are not provided with any adaptations for collecting pollen. The abdomen is sometimes pedunculate, its anterior segment being drawn out into a long stalk, which connects it with the thorax. The females and the neuters are armed with a powerful sting. The usual colour of these insects is black, relieved to a greater or less degree by spots and patches of yellow or buff.

The *Diploptera* may be subdivided into two groups in accordance with the habits of life of the insects comprising the section. One of the groups includes the family *Vespidæ*, which is composed of social wasps, and includes the hornet (*Vespa crabro*) and the common wasp (*V. vulgaris*). The other group contains two smaller families, the *Eumenidæ* and the *Masaridæ*, the members of which are solitary in their mode of life.

Family I. *Vespidæ*.—In addition to their social habits the members of this family are characterized by certain structural features. The anterior wings have three sub-marginal cells. The antennæ have thirteen joints in the males and twelve in the females; the claws of the tarsi are simple; the anterior four tibiæ have two spines at the tip; the abdomen is but rarely pedunculated, and the posterior segments are often very contractile.

The members of this family approximate very closely to bees in their social manner of life. The communities are composed of males, females, and neuters or workers. The latter are females in which the ovary remains undeveloped; they resemble the perfect female in external appearance, but are slightly smaller. Unlike the bees', the wasps' community is annual, existing for one summer only. Most of the members die at the approach of autumn, but a few females which have been fertilized hibernate through the winter, sheltered under stones or in hollow trees. In the spring and with the returning warm weather the female regains her activity and emerges from her hiding-place. She then sets about finding a convenient place for building a nest and establishing a new colony. The common wasp (*V. vulgaris*) usually selects some burrow or hole in the ground, which, if too small, she may enlarge into a chamber suitable for her purpose. She then commences to build the nest. This is constructed of small fibres of old wood, which the wasp gnaws, and kneads, when mixed with the secretion from the salivary glands, into a sort of papier-mâché pulp. Some of this is formed into a hanging pillar attached to the roof of the cavity, and in the lower free end of this three shallow cup-like cells are hung. In each of these an egg is laid. The foundress of the society then continues to add cells to the comb, and as soon as the grubs appear from the first-laid eggs she has in addition to tend and feed them.

The grubs are apodal, thicker in the middle than at either end; the mandibles bear three teeth; the maxillæ and labium are represented by fleshy tubercles. The body, including the head, consists of fourteen segments, which bear lateral tubercles and spiracles. They have no anus. They are suspended with the head downwards in the cells, and require a good deal of attention, being fed by their mother upon insects which are well chewed before they are given to the larvæ, or upon honey. At the same time the mother is enlarging and deepening the cells in which they live, building new cells, and laying more eggs, which are usually suspended in the same angle of each cell. The development within the egg takes eight days.

After about a fortnight the grubs cease to feed, and, forming a silky cover to their cells, become pupæ. This quiescent stage lasts about ten days, at the end of which period they emerge as the imago or perfect insect. The silky covering of the cell is round or convex outwards; and to leave the cell the insect either pushes it out, when it opens like a box lid, or gnaws a round hole through it. As soon as the cell is vacated it is cleaned out and another egg deposited. In this way two or three larvæ occupy successively the same cell during the summer. The first wasps that appear in a nest are neuters or workers, and these at once set to work to enlarge the comb, and feed the larvæ, &c.

The material which forms the substance of the nest is usually dried wood, worked by the mandibles of the wasp, with the addition of its salivary secretion, into a pulp, which can easily be moulded whilst moist; it dries into a substance of a papery appearance, but possessing considerable tenacity. Sometimes paper itself, such as old cartridge cases, is used. The combs are arranged horizontally; each contains a single layer of cells opening downwards. The second comb is suspended from the first by a number of hanging pillars which are built from the point of union of three cells. The space between two combs is just sufficient to allow the wasps to cross each other. The combs are roughly circular in outline, and increase in size for the first four or five layers, after which they begin to decrease; the whole is covered by a roughly made coating of the same papery substance which composes the combs. This at first forms a cap-shaped protection, but as each comb is built it is continued down until finally it forms a roughly spherical covering for the whole, but not giving any support to the combs, which are independent of it. The covering is pierced by apertures for the passage of the wasps. The cells are hexagonal at their mouths, but above become more rounded in their cross section.

During the first half of the summer only workers are produced, but, as fruit ripens and food becomes more abundant, fully developed females and males appear, the latter from parthenogenetically developed eggs of the later broods of workers. The males and females are larger than the workers, and require larger cells for their development; these are usually kept apart from one another and from those of the workers. The males may be distinguished by their longer antennæ, by the more elongated outline of their body, and by the absence of a sting.

In a favourable season, when the weather is warm and food plentiful, a nest may contain many thousands of cells full of wasps in various stages of development; and, as each cell is occupied two or three times in the course of a summer, those authorities who put the number of the members of the community as high as 30,000 are probably not far wrong.

At the approach of autumn the society begins to break up; the males fertilize the females whilst flying high in the air. They then die, often within a few hours. The workers leave the nest, carrying with them any grubs that remain in the cells, and both soon perish. The nest is entirely deserted. The females which have been fertilized creep into crevices under stones or trees, or hide amongst moss, and hibernate until the warmth of the following spring induces them to leave their hiding-places and set about founding a new community.

There are altogether seven species of *Vespa* met with in Britain. *V. vulgaris*, the common or ground wasp, *V. rufa*, the red wasp, distinguished by its reddish-yellow legs, and *V. germanica*, the German wasp, with three black spots upon its first abdominal segment, are classed together as ground wasps. They build their nests in burrows in the ground, but this is not an invariable rule; they may be distinguished from the tree wasps by the first joint in the antennæ of the female being black. The tree wasps build stouter nests upon branches of trees; the first joint of the antennæ of the females is yellow in front. The tree wasps are *V. arborea*, *sylvestris*, *norwegica*, and *crabro*.

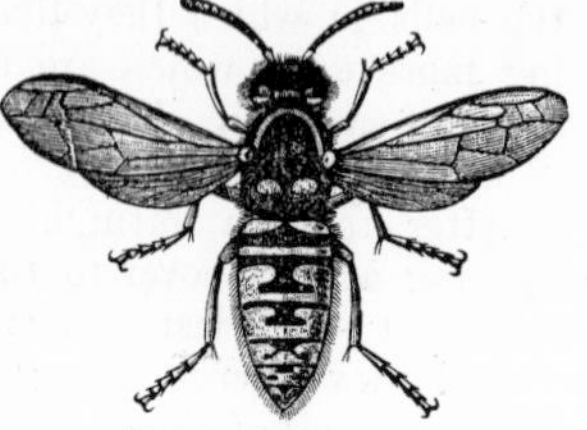

Fig. 1.—*Vespa rufa.*

The hornet, *V. crabro*, is the largest species occurring in Great Britain. They have a more distinctly red colour than the common wasp, and a row of red spots upon each side of the abdomen. They occur much more rarely than the common wasp, and appear to be almost confined to the southern half of England. Their nests resemble those described above, but are larger; they are found in hollow trees or deserted outhouses. Their communities are smaller in number than those of wasps.

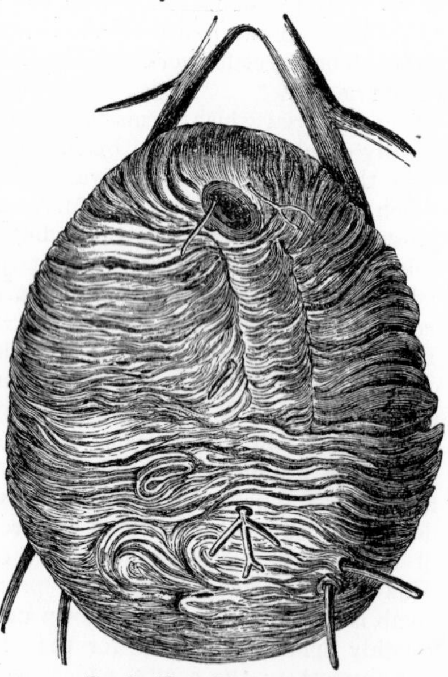

Fig. 2.—Nest of *Vespa sylvestris.*

The hornet, where it occurs in any number, does a considerable amount of damage to forest trees, by gnawing the bark off the younger branches to obtain material for constructing its nest. It usually selects the ash or alder, but sometimes attacks the lime, birch, and willow. Like the wasp, it does much damage to fruit, upon the juices of which it lives. On the other hand, the wasp is useful by keeping down the numbers of flies and other insects. It catches these in large numbers, killing them with its jaws and not with its sting. It then tears off the legs and wings, and bears the body back to its nest as food for the larvæ. Wasps also act to some extent as flower fertilizers, but in this respect they cannot compare with bees; they visit fewer flowers, and have no adaptations on their limbs for carrying off the pollen.

The genus *Vespa* is very widely spread; it contains over forty species, distributed all over the world. Some of the largest and handsomest come from eastern Asia. *V. mandarina* of China and Japan, and *V. magnifica* of the East Indies and Nepal, measure 2 inches across the wings; *V. orientalis*, found in Greece, Egypt, and the East, builds its nest of clay.

The only other genus of *Vespidæ* which is found in Europe is *Polistes*, which occurs in the countries bordering the Mediterranean. The colonies of this genus are much smaller than those of *Vespa*. Each nest consists of a single tier of cells in the form of a round plate, supported in the middle by a single stalk. This comb is sometimes vertical, the cells then being horizontal or slightly oblique. Some of the members of this genus store up honey, which in the case of a South-American species is poisonous, from the nature of the flowers from which it is gathered. The members of this genus have a slender body; the thorax is more oblong than in the genus *Vespa*, the palps stouter, and the abdomen more distinctly pedunculate.

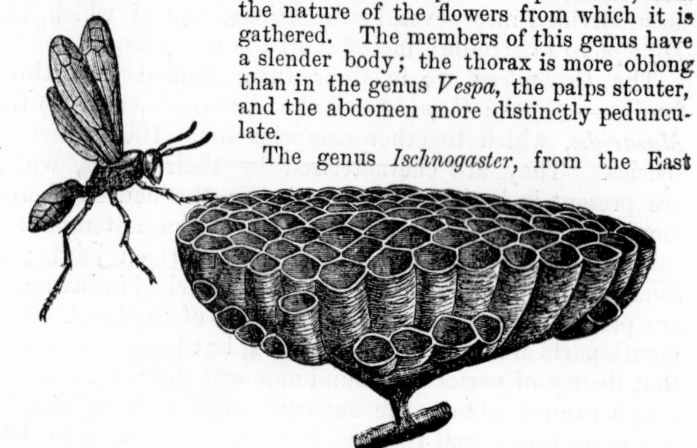

Fig. 3.—*Polistes tepidus* and nest.

The genus *Ischnogaster*, from the East Indies, has many structural features in common with the *Eumenidæ*, but the character of its communities, and its nest, which is very small, justify its position amongst the social wasps.

The genus *Icaria*, common in Australia and the East Indies, builds very small nests, of two or three rows of cells, hanging on one side from a stalk.

Synœca is a South-American genus, which builds large nests, sometimes 3 feet in length, closely applied to the branch of a tree; they never contain more than one layer of cells, which are horizontally placed. The whole nest is built of coarse material, chiefly small pieces of bark; and there is only one opening, at the lower end.

Another South-American genus, *Chartergus*, makes a tough nest, pendant from boughs of trees, and opening to the exterior below by a median aperture. The combs are arranged, somewhat like funnels, inside one another, but with spaces between. The apex of each comb is pierced by a hole for the wasps to pass from one gallery to another.

The nest of *Tatua*, which occurs in Mexico and South America, is also pendant, but the combs are horizontal; the opening from the exterior is at the side, and the passage from one gallery to another is also lateral.

The external appearance of the nest of *Nectarina*, found in Brazil and other parts of South America, resembles that of the common wasp, but is rougher. Internally the combs are arranged concentrically, more or less parallel with the external covering which affords them support.

The members of the two remaining families, the *Eumenidæ* and the *Masaridæ*, resemble one another in their solitary mode of life; only males and females exist,—no workers or neuters being found.

Family II. *Eumenidæ.*—Solitary species, with three submarginal cells in the fore wing; antennæ with thirteen joints in the male, twelve in the female; abdomen sometimes pedunculate, posterior segments contractile. In the foregoing structural features the *Eumenidæ* resemble the *Vespidæ*, but they differ in having bifid claws on their tarsi, and the four anterior tibiæ have but one spine at the tip. The mandibles are elongated, and form a kind of rostrum, in this respect approaching the *Fossores.*

Eumenes coarctata is the only British species of this genus. The female is half an inch long, the male somewhat shorter. The abdomen is connected with the thorax by a long peduncle. The colour is black, relieved by spots of yellow. It constructs small spherical cells of mud, which are found attached to stems of plants, very generally to the heath. At first the cell opens to the exterior by means of a round pore; one egg is deposited in each cell, and a store of honey as food for the larva when hatched; the cell is then closed with mud. The larva of some species are carnivorous, and then the food supply stored up in the cell consists of caterpillars and other insect larvæ which have been paralysed by the parent wasp stinging them through the cerebral ganglion; when the larva of the *Eumenes* emerges from the egg it sets upon these and devours them.

Fig. 4.—*Eumenes smithii.*

The genus *Odynerus* contains a very large number of species, found in all parts of the world. The members of this genus are about the size of a fly, and they differ from *Eumenes* in having a sessile abdomen. Some of the species construct their cells in sand heaps, lining them with agglutinated grains of sand; others live in cavities of trees lined with the same material, whilst others build their nests of mud. Like some of the species of *Eumenes*, they store up paralysed Lepidopterous and Chrysomeleous larvæ as food for their carnivorous grubs.

Family III. *Masaridæ.*—The members of the third family, the *Masaridæ*, are sharply distinguished by the possession of only two submarginal cells in the fore wing. Their antennæ are frequently clavate, particularly so in the genus *Celonites*; they are twelve-jointed, but as the terminal joints are almost fused they appear to be composed of only eight joints. The wings are not so completely folded as in the other two families, and the abdomen is but slightly contractile. The maxillæ are short and their palps very small, with but three or four joints.

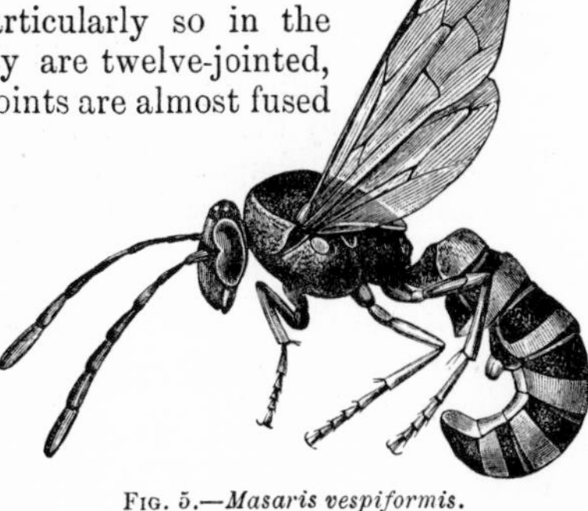

Fig. 5.—*Masaris vespiformis.*

The number of genera comprised in this family is small; none occur in Britain, but in southern Europe some species are found. They make their nest in cavities in the earth, generally in a bank, and construct an irregular gallery leading down to it.

During hot fine summers wasps cause a good deal of loss to market gardeners and fruit growers. During this time of year they live almost exclusively upon the sweet juices of ripe fruit, occasionally carrying off small particles of the flesh. At the same time they have not entirely lost their carnivorous tastes, for they frequently attack the meat in butcher's shops, but render compensation by killing and carrying off to feed their grubs considerable numbers of blow-flies. Wasps also perform an important service in keeping down the numbers of caterpillars. The larvæ are almost exclusively carnivorous, living upon insects captured by their parents and reduced by them to a pulp before being given to the young. During the spring the first broods that appear live largely upon honey; and this forms the staple food of the genus *Polistes* throughout their whole life.

In attempting to rid a district of wasps, unless the nest can be taken, there is little good in killing stray members of the community. On the other hand, the killing of wasps in early spring probably means that the formation of a nest and the production of a society whose members are counted by thousands is in each case prevented.

The number of wasps is kept down by numerous enemies. The most effective of these live in the nests and devour the larvæ; among them are two species of beetle, *Rhipiphorus paradoxus* and *Lebia linearis*. Two species of *Ichneumon*, a species of *Anthomyia*, and the larva of a *Volucella* also infest the nests of wasps and prey upon the grubs. The last-named is also found in beehives. In the tropics some species are attacked by fungi, the hyphæ of which protrude between the segments of the abdomen, and give the wasp a very extraordinary appearance. (A. E. S.)

WASTE (*Vastum*) is used in law in several senses, of which four are the most important. (1) Waste of a manor is that part of a manor subject to rights of common, as distinguished from the lord's demesne (see Commons, Manor). (2) Year, day, and waste was a part of the royal prerogative, acknowledged by the statute *De Prærogativa Regis*. The king had the profits of freehold lands of those attainted of felony and petit treason and of fugitives for a year and a day with a right of committing waste in sense (3) thereon. After the expiration of a year and a day the lands returned to the lord of the fee. Attainder for felony being now abolished, the right has ceased to exist (see Felony, Treason). (3) The most usual signification of the word is "any unauthorized act of a tenant for a freehold estate, not of inheritance or for any lesser interest, which tends to the destruction of the tenement, or otherwise to the injury of the inheritance" (Pollock, *Law of Torts*, p. 285). Waste is either voluntary or permissive. Voluntary waste is by act of commission, as by pulling down a house, cutting down trees, opening new quarries or mines (though not continuing the working of existing ones), or doing anything which may destroy evidence, such as conversion of arable into meadow land. Permissive waste is by act of omission, such as allowing buildings to fall out of repair. A fermor, by the Statute of Marlbridge, 52 Hen. III. c. 23, may not commit waste without licence in writing from the reversioner. The same statute mentions a form of waste which has long become extinct, viz., exile (*exilium*), or the impoverishment of villeins or tenants at will on an estate. In case a tenant for life or for any smaller interest holds (as is often the case by the terms of a will or settlement) without impeachment of waste, his rights are considerably greater, and he may use the profits *salva rerum substantia* (to use the language of Roman law). For instance, he may cut timber in a husband-like manner and open mines, but he may not commit what is called equitable waste, that is, pull down or deface the mansion or destroy ornamental timber. Acts of equitable waste were, before 1875, not cognizable in courts of common law, but it is now provided by the Judicature Act, 1873, § 25 (3), that in the absence of special provision to that effect an estate for life without impeachment of waste shall not confer upon the tenant for life any legal right to commit equitable waste. Removal of fixtures, which would be *prima facie* waste, is recognized by the law to a limited extent (see Fixtures). A copyholder may not commit waste unless allowed by the custom of the manor (see Copyhold). Various remedies for waste have been given to the reversioner at different periods of law. At common law only single damages seem to have been recoverable. This was altered by the legislature, and for some centuries waste was a criminal or quasi-criminal offence. Magna Charta enacted that a guardian committing waste of the lands in his custody should make amends and lose his office. The Statute of Marlbridge made a fermor committing waste liable to grievous amerciament as well as to damages, and followed Magna Charta in forbidding waste by a guardian. The Statute of Gloucester, 6 Edw. I. c. 5, enacted that a writ of waste might be granted against a tenant for life or years or in courtesy or dower, and on being attainted of waste the tenant was to forfeit the land wasted and to pay thrice the amount of the waste. In addition to the writ of waste the writ of estrepement (said to be a corruption of *exstirpamentum*) lay to prevent injury to an estate to which the title was disputed. Numerous other acts dealt with remedies for waste. The writ of waste was superseded at common law by the mixed action of waste, itself abolished by 3 and 4 Will. IV. c. 27, and the action of trespass on the case (see Tort, Trespass). The Court of Chancery also established a jurisdiction by suit or injunction, especially to restrain equitable waste. At present proceedings may be taken either by action for damages, or by application for an injunction, or by both combined, and either in the Queen's Bench or Chancery Division. By the Judicature Act, 1873, § 25 (8), the old jurisdiction to grant injunctions to prevent threatened waste is considerably enlarged. The rules of the Supreme Court, 1883, Ord. xvi. r. 37, enable a representative action to be brought for the prevention of waste. In order to obtain damages or an injunction, substantial injury or danger of it must be proved. In England only the High Court (unless by agreement of the parties) has jurisdiction in questions of waste, but in Ireland the civil bill courts and courts of summary jurisdiction have co-ordinate authority to a limited extent. The law of waste as it affects ecclesiastical benefices will be found under DILAPIDATIONS. (4) Waste of assets or *devastavit* is a squandering and misapplication of the estate and effects of a deceased person by his executors or administrators, for which they are answerable out of their own pockets as far as they have or might have had assets of the deceased. The legal liability of the representatives of the deceased is recognized by 30 Car. II. c. 7 and 4 W. and M. c. 24.

In Scots law waste is not used as a technical term, but the respective rights of fiar and liferenter are much the same as in England. The latter, however, has not the right of continuing the working of existing mines unless the deed specially confers it upon him. Interdicts have in strong cases been granted against the sale of ornamental timber.

In the United States, especially in the western States, many acts, such as the felling of timber, are not considered waste which would be waste in England. In some States waste is a cause of forfeiture; in some it gives a right to treble damages. The writ of estrepement is still in use.

WATCH. Timepieces moved by a spiral spring instead of a weight were made as early as the 16th century, though the law which governs the mechanical theory of springs was first enunciated by Huygens in the 17th century (*ut tensio sic vis*); this, however, is not invariable.

Fig. 1 shows the general arrangement of a watch or chronometer (both of which are here considered together). The barrel and fusee will be recognized at once. The fusee is a sort of grooved hollow-sided cone; the more rapid swell towards the thick end is required, because one turn of the fusee, when the chain is at that end, takes much more of it off the barrel than at the thin end; and on the assumption that the force of the spring varies as its tension the radius of the cone must increase more rapidly, in order to make the increase of leverage keep pace with the decrease in the force of the spring as it unwinds with an increasing velocity off the thick end of the fusee. The fusee itself is connected with the great wheel by a ratchet and click and going ratchet (of which the spring and click are strongly shown in the figure), just as described under CLOCKS (vol. vi. p. 22). Something is also required to prevent the watch from being overwound, or the chain strained so as to break. This is done by means of a hooked lever, set on a hinge in the upper frame-plate (which is taken off in this drawing); and when the watch is nearly wound up the chain moving upwards reaches this lever, and moves it into such a position that its hook catches hold of the long tooth projecting from the thin end of the fusee; and thus the winding is stopped without any strain on the chain by the sudden check.

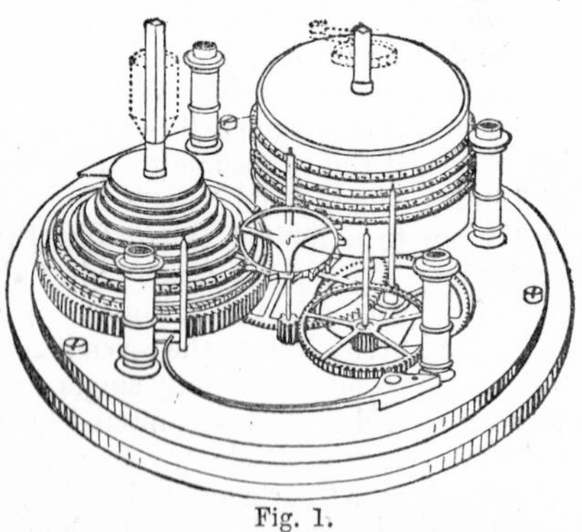
Fig. 1.

By far the greater number of watches now made both on the Continent and in America have the mechanism known as the going barrel in substitution for the chain and fusee. In the going barrel the mainspring is of great length, and only a few coils of it are brought into action. To the going barrel itself the main wheel is attached, and thus the force of the mainspring is transmitted direct to the escapement. The general adoption of the going barrel mechanism is due to the introduction of keyless winding, which can only be adapted to the fusee watches with difficulty, and to the greater cheapness of the arrangement. Moreover, it is found that for three or four coils of a long spring, at a certain degree of winding up, the tension varies very little. The going barrel is not used in the best English work, in which absolute uniformity of motion is aimed at; but for ordinary purposes it is not of so much consequence that the same rate from hour to hour should be maintained provided the daily rate is uniform.

In watches without a fusee the apparatus for preventing overwinding is different from that in the old form of watch; it goes by the name of the Geneva stop, and the principle of it is simple. If two wheels work together, of which one has the spaces between some two or more adjacent teeth filled up, it is evident that that wheel cannot be turned quite round. And it will be the same thing if one of the wheels is only a cylinder with a single tooth in it, and the other has a certain number of notches, not going all round, through which that tooth can pass. If, therefore, a one-toothed wheel of this kind is fixed to the barrel arbor, which is turned by the key, and works into a wheel with only 4 or 5 notches in it and a blank space through which the tooth cannot pass, it will evidently allow the barrel to be wound up the 4 or 5 turns and no more; and as it unwinds it turns the stopping wheel back again with it.

The other parts of a watch do not differ from those of a clock, except in size, and the position in which they are arranged, to bring them within the circle of the dial, until we come to the escapement; and there a different state of things arises, mainly from the fact that the balance of a watch revolves through sometimes as much as 270°, while a clock pendulum only vibrates through 4° or 5°. The balance being common to all the watch escapements, it will be proper first to describe that, and the conditions to which it is subject. The two equal arms, with equal weights at each end, in fig. 3 of article CLOCKS (vol. vi. p. 17) are really a balance just as much as the wheel which is commonly used as the more convenient form. But in that figure there is not to be seen that essential element of a modern balance—the thin spiral spring, opening and closing itself at every vibration. The outer end of this spring is attached to the frame by a cock R (fig. 2), and the inner to the balance at S; and the time of vibration depends only on the strength of the spring and the moment of inertia of the balance, and not at all upon the extent or angle of the vibration. And, as the force of a spring varies (approximately) inversely as its length, this suggests a ready method of regulating the watch; for it is easy to make a pointer or index, or "regulator" PT, turning on a ring fixed to the watch plate, concentric with the balance, and having two pins in it at P, called *curb pins*, just close enough together to embrace the spring, so that, as the index is moved one way or the other, the length of the spring which is free to vibrate may become shorter or longer. When the regulator has been moved as far as it can go towards *fast*, suppose, and the watch still loses, the spring has to be shortened at the cock R into which its outer end is pinned; and, in order that the balance may be capable of alteration, so as still to stand square with the escapement when the spring is in its neutral state, the other end is not actually pinned to the balance, but the cock S is on a small ring which is set on the axis or *verge* of the balance pretty tight by friction, but capable of being turned by hand. An index-plate like that in fig. 2 enables one to see smaller movements of the index than radial marks.

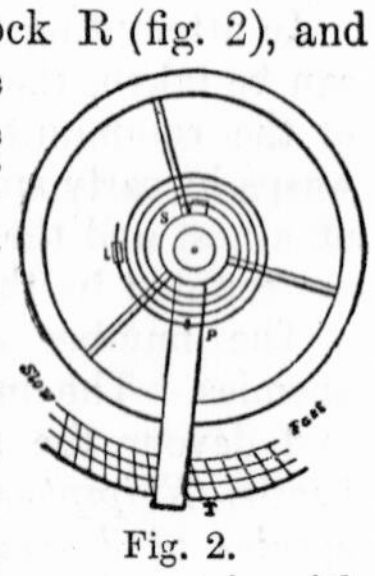

Fig. 2.

It is almost impossible to move such a regulator little enough, and with sufficient accuracy, for a very small variation of rate. One way of obtaining greater accuracy, and probably the best, is to make the regulator movable by a tangent screw acting on its end, and capable of being turned by the watch key. Another mode of giving a small motion to the regulator is by putting a portion of a wheel with teeth on it, and turning it by a small pinion with the index attached to it, so that the motion of the index exceeds that of the regulator itself as much as the radius of that wheel exceeds the radius of the pinion. Chronometers are regulated in a different way altogether. It is not expedient to alter the effective length of the spring after its length is once fixed. For it has long been ascertained that a spring does not give isochronous vibrations at all lengths, but only at certain intervals; and therefore it is necessary in an accurate timekeeper to use only one of those lengths of the spring which are found to be isochronous for different arcs of vibration; and, that being fixed, the timing of the balance can only be done by altering its moment of inertia, and this is done in chronometers by screws with heavy heads in the rim of the balance, set farther in or out as it is wanted to go faster or slower. In marine chronometers, where there is plenty of room for it, the balance-spring is generally made in a cylindrical form, with the coils all of the same diameter, instead of the flat spiral used in watches,—though it does not seem to be quite clear that the cylindrical form is materially better than the other.

The timing of a watch for position, as it is called, is a matter which requires some attention. If the balance is not exactly poised on its axis, it will have a tendency to take one position when the watch is carried vertically, as it always is in the pocket; and the time of vibration will be affected by its disposition thus to act as a pendulum. The watch ought therefore to be tried with XII, IX, VI, and III successively upwards, and if it does not keep the same rate the balance is not properly poised. Marine chronometers, indeed, being set in *gimbals* (a ring with the two pivots into the box at right angles with the pivots which carry the chronometer), will remain horizontal, though not without some degree of motion under the motion of the ship; and this gives the balance the further advantage of having its weight resting only on the end of the axis or verge, a position in which there is much less friction than that of a watch carried in the pocket; but there it is not of so much consequence, because the balance is so much lighter than a chronometer balance.

Compensated Balances.—A pendulum requires scarcely any compensation except for its own elongation by heat; but a balance requires compensation, not only for its own expansion, which increases its moment of inertia just like the pendulum, but far more on account of the decrease in the strength of the spring under increased heat. Dent, in a pamphlet on compensation balances, gave the following results of some experiments with a glass balance, which he used for the purpose on account of its less expansibility than a metal one:—at 32° F., 3606 vibrations in an hour; at 66°, 3598·5; and at 100°, 3599. If therefore it had been adjusted to go right (or 3600 times in an hour) at 32°, it would have lost 7½ and 8½ seconds an hour, or more than three minutes a-day, for each successive increase of 34°, which is about fifteen times as much as a common wire pendulum would lose under the same increase of heat; and if a metal balance had been used instead of a glass one the difference would have been still greater.

The necessity for this large amount of compensation having arisen from the variation of the elasticity of the spring, the first attempts at correcting it were by acting on the spring itself in the manner of a common regulator. Harrison's compensation consisted of a compound bar of brass and steel soldered together, having one end fixed to the watch-frame and the other carrying two curb pins which embraced the spring, as was described at fig. 2. As the brass expands more than the steel, any increase of heat made the bar bend; and so, if it was set the right way, it carried the pins along the spring, so as to shorten it. This contrivance is called a *compensation curb*; and it has often been reinvented, or applied in a modified form. But there are two objections to it: the motion of the curb pins does not correspond accurately enough to the variations in the force of the spring, and it disturbs the isochronism, which only subsists at certain definite lengths of the spring.

The compensation which was next invented left the spring untouched, and provided for the variations of temperature by the construction of the balance itself. Fig. 3 shows the plan of the ordinary compensation balance. Each portion of the rim of the balance is composed of an inner bar of steel with an outer one of brass soldered upon it, and carrying the weights b,b, which are screwed to it. As the temperature increases, the brass expanding must bend the steel inwards, and so carries the weights farther in, and diminishes the moment of inertia of the balance. The metals are generally soldered together by pouring melted brass round a solid steel disk, and the whole is afterwards turned and filed away till it leaves only the crossbar in the middle lying flat and the two portions of the rim standing edgeways. The first person who practised this method of uniting them appears to have been Thomas Earnshaw, who brought the chronometer to the state in which it has remained for the last century, with scarcely any alteration except more complete compensation.

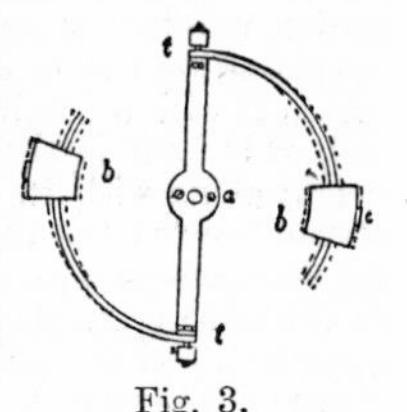

Fig. 3.

The adjustment of a balance for compensation can only be done by trial, and requires a good deal of time. It must be done independently of that for time,—the former by shifting the weights, because the nearer they are to the crossbar the less distance they will move over as the rim bends with them. The timing is done by screws with heavy heads (t,t, fig. 3), which are just opposite to the ends of the crossbar, and consequently not affected by the bending of the rim. The compensation may be done approximately by the known results of previous experience with similar balances; and many watches are sold with compensation balances which have never been tried or adjusted, and sometimes with a mere sham compensation balance, not even cut through.

Secondary Compensation.—When chronometers had been brought to great perfection it was perceived that there was a residuary error, which was due to changes of temperature, but which no adjustment of the compensation would correct. For, if the compensation was adjusted for two extreme temperatures, such as 32° and 100°, then the chronometer gained at mean temperatures; and, if adjusted for any two mean temperatures, it would lose for all beyond them. This error was observed, and attempts were made to correct it before anybody had pointed out how it arose: this appears to have been first done in a paper in the *Nautical Magazine* by E. J. Dent in 1833; and he gave the following illustration of it. The variation of the force of the spring proceeds uniformly in proportion to the temperature, and therefore may be represented by a straight line inclined at some angle to another straight line divided into degrees of temperature. But the inertia of a balance of the common construction cannot be made to vary uniformly according to the temperature, but will vary more rapidly in cold than heat; and consequently its rate of variation can only be represented by a curve, and the curve can only be made to coincide with the straight line representing the rate of variation of the spring in two points,—either two extremes, or two means, or one extreme and one mean point.

The same thing may be shown mathematically, as follows. Let r be the distance of the compensation weights b, b, in fig. 3 (which we may assume for convenience to be the whole mass M of the balance) from the centre at some mean temperature, and let dr be their increase of distance due to a decrease of some given number of degrees of heat, under the action of the compensation bars. Then the new moment of inertia will be $M(r^2+2rdr+dr^2)$, and the ratio of the new to the old will be $1+\frac{2dr}{r}+\left(\frac{dr}{r}\right)^2$; and the term $\left(\frac{dr}{r}\right)^2$ is now too large to be disregarded, as it might be in pendulums, where the compensation $\frac{dl}{l}$ is only required to be about $\frac{2}{20}$th of the $\left(\frac{dr}{r}\right)$ in a balance. It is found that an equal increase of temperature will produce an equal or rather a less motion $(-dr)$ of the weights towards the centre than from it at any given point; but, calling it only equal, the ratio of the decreased moment of inertia to the original one will be $1-\frac{2dr}{r}+\left(\frac{dr}{r}\right)^2$, so that the increase and the decrease from the mean amount differ by twice $\left(\frac{dr}{r}\right)^2$; in other words, the moment of inertia of the balance varies less in passing from mean to hot temperature than from mean to cold; and consequently if it is adjusted for mean and cold it will not have decreased enough at an equal increase from mean to hot, or the chronometer will lose, and if adjusted for the two extremes it will gain at mean temperatures.

The correction of this error is called the *secondary compensation*,

We shall give a short description of the principal classes of inventions for this purpose.

The first that was disclosed was Eiffe's (sometimes called Molyneux's), communicated to the astronomer-royal in 1835. In one of several methods proposed by him a compensation curb was used; and, though, for the reasons given before, this will not answer for the primary compensation, it may for the secondary, where the motion required is very much smaller. In another the primary compensation bar, or a screw in it, was made to reach a spring set within it with a small weight attached at some mean temperature, and, as it bent farther in, it carried this secondary compensation weight along with it. The obvious objection to this is that it is discontinuous; but the whole motion is so small, not more than the thickness of a piece of paper, that this and other compensations on the same principle appear to have been on some occasions quite successful. Molyneux took a patent for a secondary compensation exactly the same as this of Eiffe's, then before the astronomer-royal.

Another large class of balances, all more or less alike, may be represented by E. J. Dent's, which came next in order of time. He described several forms of his invention; the following description applies to the one he thought the best. In fig. 4 the flat crossbar *rr* is itself a compensation bar which bends upwards under increased heat; so that, if the weights *v*, *v* were merely set upon upright stems rising from the ends of the crossbar, they would approach the axis when that bar bends upwards. But, instead of the stems rising from the crossbar, they rise from the two secondary compensation pieces *stu*, in the form of staples, which are set on the crossbar; and, as these secondary pieces themselves also bend upwards, they make the weights approach the axis more rapidly as the heat increases; and by a proper adjustment of the height of the weights on the stems the moment of inertia of the balance can be made to vary in the proper ratio to the variation of the intensity of the spring. The cylindrical spring stands above the crossbar and between the staples.

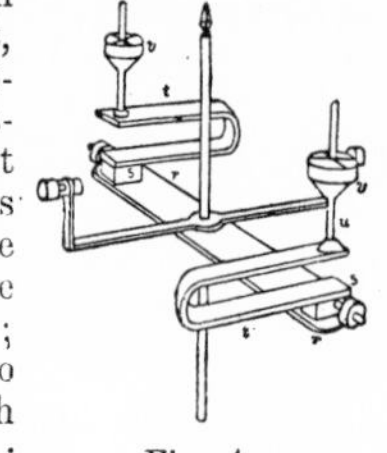
Fig. 4.

Fig. 5 represents Loseby's mercurial compensation balance. Besides the weights D, D, set near the end of the primary compensation bars B, B, there are small bent tubes FE, FE with mercury in them, like a thermometer, the bulbs being at F, F. As the heat increases, not only do the primary weights D, D and the bulbs F, F approach the centre of the balance, but some of the mercury is driven along the tube, thus carrying some more of the weight towards the centre, at a ratio increasing more rapidly than the temperature. The tubes are sealed at the thin end, with a little air included. The action is here equally continuous with Dent's, and the adjustments for primary and secondary compensation are apparently more independent of each other; and this modification of Le Roy's use of mercury for compensated balances (which does not appear to have answered) is certainly very elegant and ingenious. Nevertheless an analysis of the Greenwich lists for seven years of Mr Loseby's trials proved that the advantage of this method over the others was more theoretical than practical; Dent's compensation was the most successful of all in three years out of the seven, and Loseby's in only one. Loseby's method has never been adopted by any other chronometer-maker, whereas the principles both of Eiffe's and of Dent's methods have been adopted by several other makers.

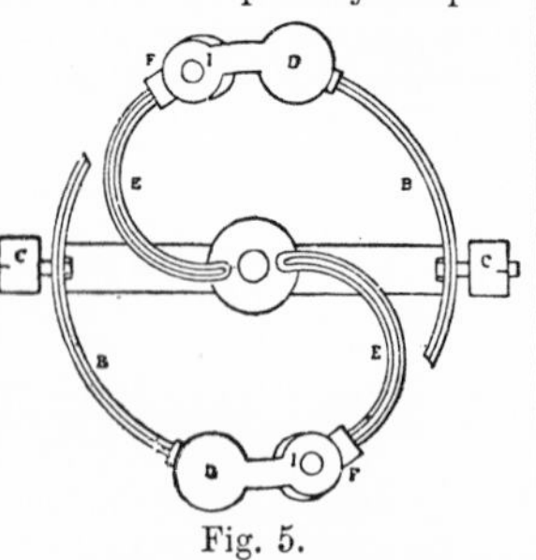
Fig. 5.

A few chronometers have been made with glass balance-springs, which have the advantage of requiring very little primary and no secondary compensation, on account of the very small variation in their elasticity, compared with springs of steel or any other metal.

Dent also invented a very different method of effecting the primary and secondary compensation at once, and without any additional appendage to the balance or addition to the cost. He called it the *prismatic balance*, from the shape of the steel rim, of which the section is shown in fig. 6, BC being the brass, and the dark triangle within it the section of the steel part of the rim. A prism of cast-steel will bend more easily from the edge than the other way, and consequently the motion is greater when it is being curved by heat than when it is pulled straighter by cold, which is exactly what is wanted. The difference is not quite so great as it ought to be for complete secondary compensation for a very wide range of temperature, but it is enough to give the requisite compensation for all ordinary variations of temperature, and chronometers so compensated were found to be also more than usually steady in their rate, for even in the best chronometers there appear every now and then quite capricious variations.

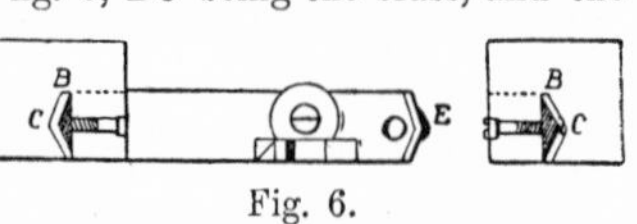

Fig. 6.

Several other forms of secondary compensation have been invented and found successful, all on the same principle of so arranging the compound bars that the weights move more under any given change of temperature in hot weather, or when they are nearest to the axis of the balance, than in cold when they are farthest off. Notices of these may be seen in various volumes of the *Horological Journal*.

The best chronometers, with all these improvements, cannot be relied on to keep a rate equal to that of a good astronomical clock of the usual kind, though they occasionally do so for a short time.

Watch Escapements.—The escapements in practical use are—(1) the old *vertical* escapement, now almost disused; (2) the *lever*, very much the most common in English watches; (3) the *horizontal* or *cylinder*, which is equally common in foreign watches, though it was of English invention; (4) the *duplex*, which used to be more in fashion for first-rate watches than it is now; and (5) the *detached* or *chronometer* escapement, so called because it is always used in marine chronometers.

The *vertical* escapement is simply the original clock escapement (see CLOCKS, fig. 3) adapted to the position of the wheels in a watch and the balance, in the manner exhibited in fig. 7. As it requires considerable thickness in the watch, it is inferior in going to all the others, and no cheaper than the lever escapement can now be made; and for these reasons it has gone out of use.

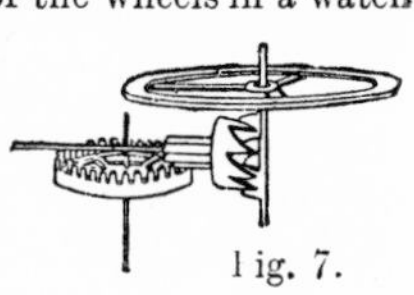

Fig. 7.

The *lever* escapement, as it is now universally made, was invented late in the last century by Thomas Mudge. Fig. 8 shows its action. The position of the lever with reference to the pallets is immaterial in principle, and is only a question of convenience in the arrangement; but it is generally such as we have given it. The principle is the same as in the dead-beat escapement clock (see CLOCKS, fig. 5), with the advantage that there is no friction on the dead faces of the pallets beyond what is necessary for locking. The reason why this friction cannot be avoided with a pendulum is that its arc of vibration is so small that the requisite depth of intersection cannot be got between the two circles described by the end S of the lever and any pin in the pendulum which would work into it; whereas, in a watch, the pin P, which is set in a cylinder on the verge of the balance, does not generally slip out of the nick in the end of the lever until the balance has got 15° past its middle position. The pallets are undercut a little, as it is called, *i.e.*, the dead faces are so sloped as to give a little recoil the wrong way, or slightly to resist the unlocking, because otherwise there would be a risk that a shake of the watch would let a tooth escape while the pin is disengaged from the lever. There is also a further provision added for safety. In the cylinder which carries the impulse pin P there is a notch just in front of P, into which the other pin S on the lever fits as they pass; but when the notch has got past the cylinder it would prevent the lever from returning, because the safety-pin S cannot pass except through the notch, which is only in the position for letting it pass at the same time that the impulse-pin is engaged in the lever. The pallets in a lever escapement (except bad and cheap ones) are always jewelled, and the scape-wheel is of brass. The staff of the lever also has jewelled pivot-holes in expensive watches, and the scape-wheel has in all good ones. The holes for the balance-pivots are now always jewelled, if nothing else is. The scape-wheel in this and most of the watch escapements generally beats five times in a second, in large chronometers four times; and the wheel next to the scape-wheel carries the seconds-hand. Macdowall's single-pin escapement was adapted to watches exactly as the dead escapement of clocks is turned into the lever escapement of watches.

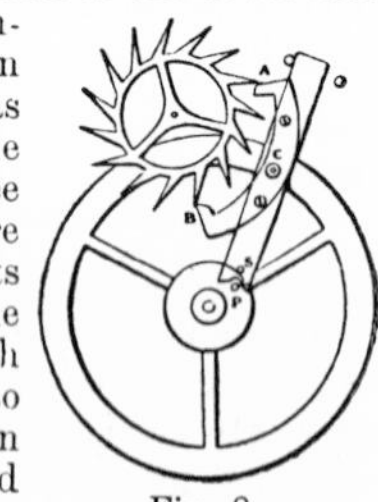
Fig. 8.

Fig. 9 is a plan of the *horizontal* or *cylinder* escapement, cutting through the cylinder, which is on the verge of the balance, at the level of the tops of the teeth of the escape-wheel; for the triangular pieces A, B are not flat projections in the same plane as the teeth, but are raised on short stems above the plane of the wheel; and still more of the cylinder than the portion shown at ACD is cut away where the wheel itself has to pass. The author of this escapement was Graham, and it resembles his dead escapement in clocks in principle more than the lever escapement does, though much less in appearance, because in this escapement there is the dead friction of the teeth against the cylinder, first on the outside, as here represented, and then on the inside, as shown by the dotted lines, during the whole vibration of the balance, except that portion which belongs to the impulse. The impulse is given by the oblique outside edges A*a*, B*b*

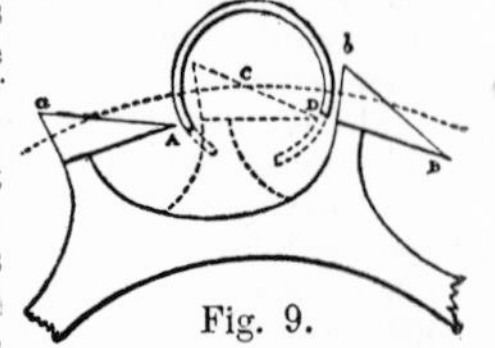
Fig. 9.

of the teeth against the edges A, D of the cylinder alternately. The portion of the cylinder which is cut away at the point of action is about 30° less than the semicircle. The cylinder itself is made either of steel or ruby, and, from the small quantity of it which is left at the level of the wheel, it is evidently a very delicate affair; and probably this has been the main reason why, although it is an English invention, it has been almost entirely abandoned by the English watchmakers in favour of the lever, which was originally a French invention, though very much improved by Mudge, for before his invention the lever had a rack or portion of a toothed wheel on its end, working into a pinion on the balance verge, and consequently it was affected by the dead friction, and that of this wheel and pinion besides. This used to be called the rack lever, and Mudge's the detached lever; but, the rack lever being now quite obsolete, the word "detached" has become detached from the lever escapement, and confined to the chronometer, to which it is more appropriate, as will be seen presently. The Swiss watches have almost universally the horizontal escapement. It is found that—for some reason which is apparently unknown, as the rule certainly does not hold in cases seemingly analogous—a steel scape-wheel acts better in this escapement than a brass one, although in some other cases steel upon steel, or even upon a ruby, very soon throws off a film of rust, unless they are kept well oiled, while brass and steel, or stone, will act with scarcely any oil at all, and in some cases with none.

The *duplex* escapement (fig. 10) is probably so called because there is a double set of teeth in the scape-wheel,—the long ones (like those of the lever escapement in shape) for locking only, and short ones (or rather upright pins on the rim of the wheel) for giving the impulse to the pallet P on the verge of the balance. It is a single-beat escapement; *i.e.*, the balance only receives the impulse one way, or at every alternate beat, as in the chronometer escapement, and in a few clock escapements which have never come into use. When the balance is turning in the direction marked by the arrow, and arrives at the position in which the dotted tooth *b* has its point against the triangular notch V, the tooth end slips into the notch, and, as the verge turns farther round, the tooth goes on with it till at last it escapes when the tooth has got into the position A; and by that time the long tooth or pallet which projects from the verge has moved from *p* to P, and just come in front of the pin T, which stands on the rim of the scape-wheel, and which now begins to push against P, and so gives the impulse until it also escapes when it has arrived at *t*; and the wheel is then stopped by the next tooth B having got into the position *b*, with its point resting against the verge, and there is evidently what we have called dead friction between them; but, as the verge is smaller than the cylinder of the horizontal escapement, and is also made of a jewel, the friction does not seriously affect the motion of the balance. The impulse is also given very directly across the line of centres, and therefore with very little friction, as in the three-legged dead escapement for clocks and in the chronometer escapement. A little impulse is also received from the long teeth on the notch; but the greatest part of that motion is wasted. As the balance turns back, the nick V goes past the end of the tooth *b*, and in consequence of its smallness, it passes without visibly affecting the motion of the scape-wheel, though of course it does produce a very slight shake in passing. It is evident that, if it did not pass, the tooth could not get into the nick for the next escape. The objection to this escapement is that it requires very great delicacy of adjustment, and the watch also requires to be worn carefully; for, if by accident the balance is once stopped from swinging back far enough to carry the nick V past the tooth end, it will stop altogether, as it will lose still more of its vibration the next time from receiving no impulse. The performance of this escapement, when well made, and its independence of oil, are nearly equal to those of the detached escapement; but, as lever watches are now made sufficiently good for all but astronomical purposes, for which chronometers are used, and they are cheaper both to make and to mend than duplex ones, the manufacture of duplex watches has almost disappeared.

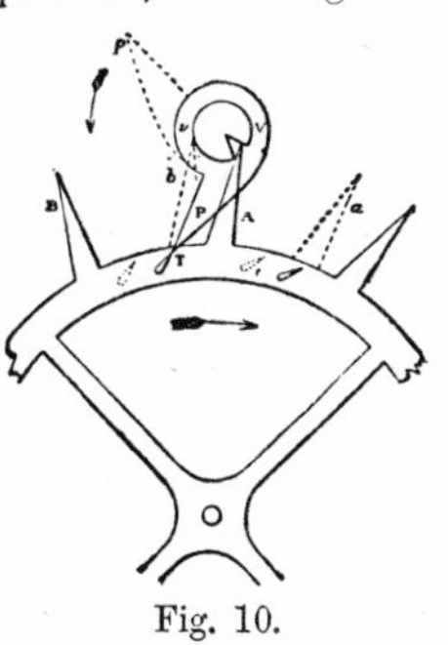
Fig. 10.

The *chronometer* or *detached* escapement is shown at fig. 11, in the form to which it was brought by Earnshaw nearly a century ago, and in which it has remained ever since, with the very slight difference that the pallet P, on which the impulse is given (corresponding exactly to the pallet P in the duplex escapement), is now generally set in a radial direction from the verge, whereas Earnshaw made it sloped backward, or undercut, like the scape-wheel teeth. The early history of escapements on this principle does not seem to be very clear. They appear to have originated in France; but there is no doubt that they were considerably improved by the first Arnold, who died in 1799. Earnshaw's watches, however, generally beat his in trials.

In fig. 11 the small tooth or cam V, on the verge of the balance, is just on the point of unlocking the detent DT from the tooth T of the scape-wheel; and the tooth A will immediately begin to give the impulse on the pallet P, which, in good chronometers, is always a jewel set in the cylinder; the tooth V is also a jewel. This part of the action is so evident as to requir no further notice. When the balance returns, the tooth V has to get past the end of the detent, without disturbing it; for, as soon as it has been unlocked, it falls against the banking-pin E, and is ready to receive the next tooth B, and must stay there until it is again unlocked. It ends, or rather begins, in a stiffish spring, which is screwed to the block D on the watch frame, so that it moves without any friction of pivots, like a pendulum. The passing is done by means of another spring TV, called the passing spring, which can be pushed away from the body of the detent towards the left, but cannot be pushed the other way without carrying the detent with it. In the back vibration, therefore, as in the duplex escapement, the balance receives no impulse, and it has to overcome the slight resistance of the passing spring besides; but it has no other friction, and is entirely *detached* from the scape-wheel the whole time, except when receiving the impulse. That is also the case in the lever escapement; but the impulse in that escapement is given obliquely, and consequently with a good deal of friction; and, besides, the scape-wheel only acts on the balance through the intervention of the lever, which has the friction of its own pivots and of the impulse pin. The locking-pallet T is undercut a little for safety, and is also a jewel in the best chronometers; and the passing spring is of gold, as steel will rust. In the duplex and detached escapements, the timing of the action of the different parts requires great care, *i.e.*, the adjusting them so that each may be ready to act exactly at the right time; and it is curious that the arrangement which would be geometrically correct, or suitable for a very slow motion of the balance, will not do for the real motion. If the pallet P were really set so as just to point to the tooth A in both escapements at the moment of unlocking (as it has been drawn, because otherwise it would look as if it could not act at all), it would run away some distance before the tooth could catch it, because in the duplex escapement the scape-wheel is then only moving slowly, and in the detached it is not moving at all, and has to start from rest. The pallet P is therefore, in fact, set a little farther back, so that it may arrive at the tooth A just at the time when A is ready for it, without wasting time and force in running after it. This, however, seems now to be doubted in practice. The detached escapement has also been made on the duplex plan of having long teeth for the locking and short ones or pins nearer the centre for the impulse; but the advantages do not appear to be worth the additional trouble, and the force required for unlocking is not sensibly diminished by the arrangement, as the spring D must in any case be pretty stiff, to provide against the watch being carried in the position in which the weight of the detent helps to unlock it.

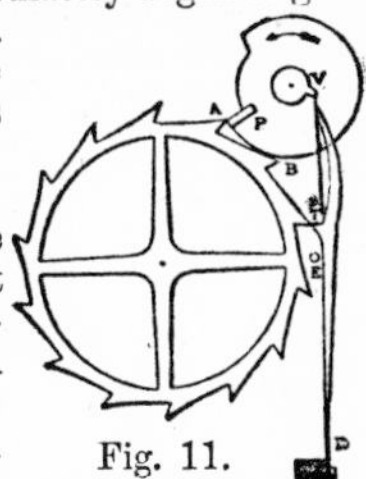
Fig. 11.

An escapement called the *lever chronometer* has been several times reinvented, which implies that it has never come into general use. It is a combination of the lever as to the locking and the chronometer as to the impulse. It involves a little drop and therefore waste of force as a tooth of the wheel just escapes at the "passing" beat where no impulse is given. But it should be understood (as it is not by some who write on clock-work) that a single-beat escapement involves no more loss of force and the escape of no more teeth than a double one, except the slight drop in the duplex and this lever chronometer or others on the same principle.

There have been several contrivances for *remontoire* escapements; but there are defects in all of them; and there is not the same advantage to be obtained by giving the impulse to a watch-balance by means of some other spring instead of the mainspring as there is in turret-clocks, where the force of the train is liable to very much greater variations than in chronometers or small clocks.

Tourbillon escapements, and a few other things not necessary to notice here, are described in the 7th edition of Sir E. Beckett's (now Lord Grimthorpe) *Rudimentary Treatise on Clocks, Watches, and Bells.*

Repeaters, Keyless Watches, &c.—Repeating-watches, *i.e.*, watches which strike the hours and quarters on pushing in the handle, are now scarcely ever made in England, and with very good reason, for it is almost impossible to crowd into the space of even a large-sized watch the quantity of wheels and other things required for the repeating work without unduly interfering with the going part, and, besides that, the striking work itself is very liable to get out of order.

The winding of watches without a key is an object for which there have been several inventions, and it possesses a considerable advantage, besides the mere convenience of being independent of a key, for, as there is then no occasion to open it, the case may be made to fit more closely, and the air is more completely excluded.

and consequently the watch will go longer without cleaning; and it also saves the thickness and the cost of a double back to the case. The first plan of the kind was that of pulling out the knob of the handle, which went into the watch, and had a gathering click attached to it which wound up the fusee, or the barrel, by means of a ratchet. But this was not found to answer: it was liable to get out of order; and, moreover, at every time of winding fresh air was pumped into the watch, which soon produced injurious effects. A far better plan is that of combining the two objects of winding and setting the hands by means of the handle, in the manner we shall now describe. In fig. 12 d is a wheel on the barrel, with bevelled teeth, and there is another small bevelled wheel on a spindle b, which ends in a milled head a, within the handle or pendant; these two wheels cannot conveniently be arranged so as to work into each other without the intervention of a third between them, which is marked e in the left-hand section. It is easy to see that turning the milled head will wind up the barrel. The same arrangement might of course be applied to the fusee, though it would increase the size; but in fact these watches are made without one, and the practice is increasing. The winding wheel d is also made with the well-known contrivance of Breguet, known by the name of the "tipsy key" when applied to a common winding key, which enables you to turn the handle the wrong way without doing anything except moving a ratchet-wheel over its click, and consequently without straining the watch in attempting to wind it the wrong way. The same handle and wheels are also made use of to set the hands, thus:—there is a small wheel f which turns on a stud at the end of the lever fgh, and as the lever turns on a pivot at g, when its end h, which just projects through the rim of the watch, is pushed on one side, the wheel f will then be thrown into gear with the winding wheel d and the hour pinion in the middle of the watch; and consequently, if the handle is then turned, it will alter the hands, just as they are usually altered from the back by a key in foreign watches, so that the face need never be opened. Of course, while this is doing, you do at the same time wind up the watch a little if the hand has to be turned the way for winding; but that is of no consequence, except that you cannot put the hands forward immediately after you have completely wound up the watch. There are various other arrangements for winding and setting by the handle substantially on the same principle. The ring is difficult to fix firmly when flexible on a stud perforated for the winding arbor, as no screw can go through it. The ring and the stud should be made in one piece. There is no use in it being hinged, as usual.

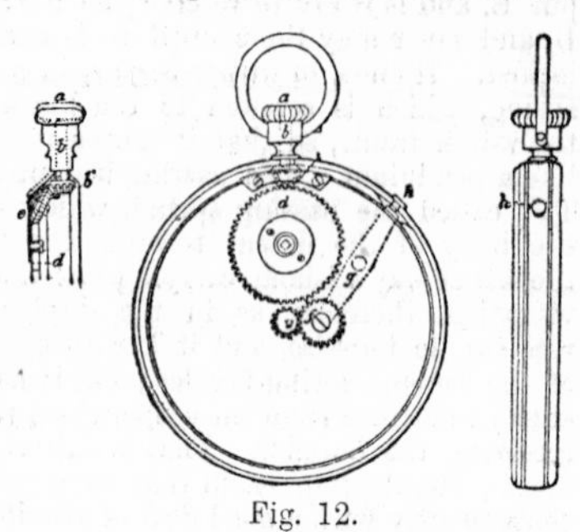

Fig. 12.

In the chronograph watch there is, in addition to the centre seconds-hand, an independent seconds-hand which, when not in operation, stands at zero. Pressure on the crown-piece acts successively (1) on a starting motion, (2) on a stopping motion, and (3) on a motion which sends the hand back by the shortest path to zero.

Watches are also made with what are called *split seconds*-hands,—the two hands being in their ordinary state together and appearing as one, but when you push in a knob one of them is stopped, while the other goes on; the time shown by the stopped one is of course the time of the observation. Sometimes this is done by merely connecting the hands by a very slight spiral spring, which will allow itself to be untwisted one or two coils without stopping the watch; and, as it cannot be of any use to stop the seconds-hand longer than a minute, this seems to answer. There is, however, another plan, in which these two hands, or at least the socket of one and the arbor of the other, are connected by a pair of disks set obliquely on the arbor and the socket respectively, so that, whenever the spring which keeps them together is allowed to act, it brings the loose hand up to the hand fixed on the arbor; and it does not signify how long it may be stopped by throwing the disks out of contact. One of the disks is heart-shaped, and is connected with the other by a spring, forming what is called a *jumper*.

For the use of electrical engineers and others who are brought within the influence of powerful electrical machinery, it has been found necessary to introduce non-magnetizable watches. At present this is best secured by making the balance of silver or platinum alloy, and the balance spring of gold or palladium. The use of steel in moving parts of the works is carefully avoided, and thus fairly good timekeepers indifferent to magnetic influences are produced.

The introduction of machinery for the manufacture of watch movements has had the effect of greatly cheapening the commoner class of watches, and yet supplying a fairly satisfactory timekeeper. It is in America that the application of machinery to watchmaking has found its greatest development, and its success has enabled the American manufacturers to obtain considerable foothold in the European market for cheap watches. But watch movements are also now very extensively made by machinery in Birmingham, Coventry, and several Lancashire towns.

Under the auspices of the Royal Society a department has been established at Kew observatory for the testing and certifying of watches in respect of their compensation for variations of temperature, and their uniformity of motion in different positions. Watches which obtain certificates of the first class have also awarded to them merit marks up to 40 for complete absence of variation in daily rate, 40 for absolute freedom from change of rate in different positions, and 20 for perfect compensation for variations of temperature. The testing establishment has only been instituted for a few years; but its services are being largely sought by manufacturers of the high class of watches, who have laboured with equal zeal and success to keep the English-made watch unapproached by the product of any other nation. (G.)

WATER,[1] as everybody knows, is a generic term which includes a great variety of different substances. But when we compare any two species we always find more of agreement than of difference in properties which suggest that all waters consist essentially of the same thing, which is only modified differently in the several varieties by the nature or proportion of impurities. This surmise is confirmed by the results of scientific inquiry. In all ordinary waters, such as are used for primary purposes, the impurities amount to very little by weight—as a rule to less than $\frac{1}{10}$th of 1 per cent.

Of all natural stores of water the *ocean* is by far the most abundant, and from it all other water may be said to be derived. From the surface of the ocean a continuous stream of vapour is rising up into the atmosphere to be recondensed in colder regions and precipitated as rain, snow, or sleet, &c. Some $\frac{8}{11}$ths of these precipitates of course return directly to the ocean; the rest, falling on land, collects into pools, lakes, rivers, &c., or else penetrates into the earth, perhaps to come to light again, or to be brought to light, as springs or wells.

As all the saline components of the ocean are non-volatile, rain-water, in its natural state, can be contaminated only with atmospheric gases—oxygen, nitrogen, and carbonic acid. So we should presume, and so it is, except that these gases, having different rates of solubility, are not associated in rain-water (or natural water generally) in the proportions characteristic of their source. Thus, for instance, while atmospheric air contains 21 per cent. by volume of oxygen, a solution of air in water contains about 34·0 per cent. of that gas. Besides, rain-water, for the reason stated, contains perceptible traces of ammonia, combined as a rule, at least partly, with nitric acid, which latter is being produced wherever an electric discharge pervades the atmosphere. This electrically-produced nitrate of ammonia forms no doubt the primary source of all organic nitrogen.

Lake waters, as a class, are relatively pure, especially so if the mountain slopes over which the rain collects into a lake are relatively free of soluble components. As an example we may refer to the water of Loch Katrine (Scotland), which is almost chemically pure, apart from small, but perceptible, traces of richly carboniferous matter taken up from the peat of the surrounding hills, which impart to it a faint brownish hue, while really pure water is blue.

River water varies very much in composition even in the same bed, as a river in the course of its journey towards the ocean passes from one kind of earth to others; while, compared with spring-waters, relatively poor in dissolved salts, rivers are liable to be contaminated with more or less of suspended matter.

Spring waters, having been filtered through more or

[1] Compare CHEMISTRY, vol. v. pp. 483–485, and SEA WATER.

less considerable strata of earth, are, as a class, clear of suspended, but rich in dissolved, mineral matter. Of ordinarily occurring minerals only a few are perceptibly soluble in water, and of these carbonate of lime, sulphate of lime, and common salt are most widely diffused. Common salt, however, in its natural occurrence, is very much localized; and so it comes that spring and well waters are contaminated *chiefly* with carbonate and sulphate of lime. Of these two salts, however, the former is held in solution only by the carbonic acid of the water, as bicarbonate of lime. But a carbonate-of-lime water, if exposed to the atmosphere, even at ordinary temperatures, loses its carbonic acid, and the carbonate of lime crystallizes out. The fantastically shaped "stalactites" which adorn the roofs and sides of certain caverns are produced in this manner.

In the relatively rare cases where a spring water in the course of its migrations meets with a deposit of common salt or other soluble salts, it dissolves more or less of these and becomes a salt-water. Most salt-waters are substantially solutions of common salt (chloride of sodium), associated with only little of salts of potash and magnesia. But there are exceptions; in the so-called "bitter waters" the dissolved matter consists chiefly of sulphate of magnesia and other magnesia salts.

Immense quantities of carbonic acid gas are being constantly produced in the interior of the earth, probably by the action, at high temperatures, of steam on the carbonates of lime and magnesia. Some of it collects and is stored up temporarily in cavities, but the bulk streams out into the atmosphere, invisibly as a rule, through what one might call the capillaries of the earth's body; but here and there it unites into veins and arteries and comes forth, it may be, as a mighty carbonic acid spring. Carbonic acid being one and a half times as heavy as atmospheric air, it may collect into pools or even lakes; the "Dog's Grotto," near Naples, and the "Valley of Death," in Asia Minor, are illustrative examples; but, carbonic acid being a gas, and consequently diffusible, such lakes can maintain their level only if there is a constant and abundant supply of the gas from below.

A far more frequent occurrence is that a mass of water and a mass of carbonic acid meet within the earth. As a rule, the pressure on the gas is more than one atmosphere, and the supply of the gas is abundant. The water then takes up considerably more carbonic acid than it would under ordinary atmospheric pressure, and if an outlet be provided, perhaps artificially by a boring, a frothy mass of carbonic-acid water comes forth as a fountain, sometimes of great volume. Such carbonic-acid waters are met with in many parts of the world,—chiefly, however, in Germany. The well-known Apollinaris water is an example. In this connexion we may refer also to the *soffioni* of Tuscany—jets of steam charged with ammonia or vapour of boric acid, which condense in the air and collect into "lagoons" of (substantially) a very dilute solution of boric acid. Boric acid waters, however, appear to be entirely confined to a limited district in Tuscany to the south of Volterra.

In addition to its natural components, water is liable to be contaminated through accidental influxes of foreign matter. Thus, for instance, all the Scottish Highland lochs are brown through the presence in them of dissolved peaty matter. Rivers flowing through, or wells sunk in, populous districts may be contaminated with excrementitious matter, discharges from industrial establishments, &c. Our instinct rebels against the drinking of a contaminated water, and it guides us correctly. Not that those organic compounds are in themselves hurtful. An otherwise pure water, contaminated with, say, one ten thousandth of its volume of urine, might be drunk with perfect confidence. Yet the presence of especially nitrogenous organic matter is a serious source of danger, inasmuch as such matter forms the natural food or soil for the development of micro-organisms, including those kinds of bacteria which are now supposed to propagate infectious diseases. Happily nature has provided a remedy. The nitrogenous organic matter dissolved in (say) a river speedily suffers disintegration by the action of certain kinds of bacteria, with formation of ammonia and other (harmless) products of simple constitution; and the ammonia, again, is no sooner formed than, by the conjoint action of other bacteria and atmospheric oxygen, it passes first into (salts of) nitrous and then nitric acid. A water which contains combined nitrogen in the form of nitrates only is, as a rule, safe organically; if nitrites are present it becomes liable to suspicion; the presence of ammonia is a worse symptom; and if actual nitrogenous organic matter is found in more than microscopic traces the water is possibly (not necessarily) a dangerous water to drink.

Wanklyn's method of water analysis is based upon these ideas. Starting with half a litre of the water, he distils it with a small quantity of carbonate of soda, and in the distillate determines the ammonia colorimetrically with Nessler's reagent (see MERCURY, vol. xvi. p. 34). When all the saline ammonia (the *free* ammonia) is thus eliminated, alkaline permanganate of potash is added to the residue and the distillation resumed. Part of the nitrogen of the organic matter is eliminated as ammonia; it is determined in the distillate, by Nessler's reagent, and reported as *albumenoid* ammonia. The results are customarily referred to one million parts of water analysed. To give an idea of the order of quantities here dealt with, let us say that a water yielding 0·1 part of free and 0·1 part of albumenoid ammonia would be condemned by any chemist, as possibly dangerous. The peaty waters of the Scottish Highlands, however, contain much of both ammonias, and yet are drunk by the natives with perfect impunity.

All waters, unless very impure, become safe by boiling, which process kills any bacteria or germs that may be present.

Of the ordinary saline components of waters, soluble magnesia and lime salts are the only ones which are objectionable sanitarily if present in relatively large proportion. Carbonate of lime is harmless; but, on the other hand, the widely diffused notion that the presence of this component adds to the value of a water as a drinking water is a mistake. The farinaceous part of food alone is sufficient to supply all the lime the body needs; besides, it is questionable whether lime introduced in any other form than that of phosphate is available for the formation of, for instance, bone tissue.

The fitness of a water for washing is determined by its degree of softness. A water which contains lime or magnesia salts decomposes soap with formation of insoluble lime or magnesia salts of the fatty acids of the soap used. So much of the soap is simply wasted; only the surplus can effect any cleansing action. An excellent and easy method for the determination of the hardness of a water has been devised by Clark. A measured volume of the water is placed in a stoppered bottle, and a standard solution of soap is then dropped in from a graduated vessel, until the mixture, by addition of the last drop of soap, has acquired the property of throwing up a peculiar kind of creamy froth when violently shaken, which shows that all the soap-destroying components have been precipitated. The volume of soap required measures the hardness of the water. The soap-solution is referred to a standard by means of a water of a known degree of hardness prepared from a known weight of carbonate of lime by converting it into neutral chloride of calcium, dissolving this in water and diluting to a certain volume. A water is said to have "1, 2, 3, . . . *n* degrees of hardness," if it is equivalent in soap-destroying power to a solution of carbonate of lime containing 1, 2, 3, . . . *n* grains of this salt per imperial gallon.

That part of the hardness of a water which is actually owing to carbonate of lime (or magnesia) can easily be removed in two ways. (1) By boiling, the free carbonic acid goes off with the steam, and the carbonate of lime, being bereft of its solvent, comes down as a precipitate which can be removed by filtration, or by allowing it to settle, and decanting off the clear supernatant liquor. (2) A method of Clark's is to mix the water with just enough of milk of lime to convert the free carbonic acid into carbonate. Both this and the original carbonate of lime are precipitated, and can be removed as in the first case. See p. 409 *infra*.

From any uncontaminated natural water pure water is easily prepared. The dissolved salts are removed by distillation; if care be taken that the steam to be condensed is dry, and if its condensation be effected within a tube made of a suitable metal (platinum or silver are best, but copper or block tin work well enough for ordinary purposes), the distillate can contain no impurities except atmospheric gases, which latter, if necessary, must be removed by boiling the distilled water in a narrow-necked flask until it begins to "bump," and then allowing it to cool in the absence of air. This latter operation ought, strictly speaking, to be performed in a silver or platinum flask, as glass is appreciably attacked by hot water. For most purposes distilled water, taken as it comes from the condenser, is sufficiently pure.

Pure water, being so easily procured in any quantity, is used largely as a standard of reference in metrology and in the quantitative definition of physical properties. Thus a "gallon" is defined as the volume at 62° F. of a quantity of water whose uncorrected mass, as determined by weighing in air of 30-inch pressure and 62° F. of temperature, is equal to 10 ℔ avoirdupois. The kilogramme in like manner is the mass of 1 cubic decimetre of water, measured at the temperature corresponding to its maximum density (4° C.). The two fixed points of the thermometer correspond—the lower (0° C., or 32° F.) to the temperature at which ice melts, the upper (100° C. or 212° F.) to that at which the maximum tension of steam, as it rises from boiling water, is equal to 760 mm. or 30-inch mercury pressure. 30 inches being a little more than 760 mm., 212° F. is, strictly speaking, a higher temperature than 100° C., but the difference is very trifling. Specific heats are customarily measured by that of water, which is taken as = 1. All other specific heats of liquids or solids (with one solitary exception, formed by a certain strength of aqueous methyl alcohol) are less than 1. The temperate character of insular climates is greatly owing to this property of water. Another physiographically important peculiarity of water is that it expands on freezing (into ice), while most other liquids do the reverse. 11 volumes of ice fuse into only 10 volumes of water at 0° C.; and the ice-water produced, when brought up gradually to higher and higher temperatures, again exhibits the very exceptional property that it contracts between 0° and 4° C. (by about $\frac{1}{10000}$ of its volume) and then expands again by more and more per degree of increase of temperature, so that the volume at 100° C. is 1·043 times that at 4° C. Imagine two lakes, one containing ordinary water and another containing a liquid which differs from water only in this that it has no maximum density. Imagine both to be, say, at 5° C., and cold winter weather to set in. Both lakes become colder, being cooled down by convection until they are at 4° C. The imaginary lake then continues losing heat in the same way; in the real lake the colder water floats on the surface and the underlying mass of water can lose heat only by the slow process of conduction. The real lake retains its heat more tenaciously, but for the reason stated will draw a sheet of ice, while the imaginary lake is still on its way to 0° C. The latter, indeed, if the winter is short, may fail to freeze altogether, while the former does freeze superficially. In either the freezing is a slow process, because for every pound of ice produced 80 pound-centigrade units of heat are set free. Let us now assume that, after even the imaginary lake had drawn a sheet of ice, warm weather sets in. In either case a layer of liquid water of 0° C. is formed on the ice, and through it the heat from the air travels, in the imaginary case by slow conduction, in the real case by quick convection. The real ice is the first to disappear, and the upper strata of relatively cold water will soon come up to 4° C. by the prompt effect of convection, while in the case of the imaginary lake it takes a far longer time before all the mass has come up to 4° C. by conduction. From 4° C. upwards, heat is taken in at the same rate on both sides.

In former times water was viewed as an "element," and the notion remained in force after this term (about the time of Boyle) had assumed its present meaning, although cases of decomposition of water were familiar to chemists. In Boyle's time it was already well known that iron, tin, and zinc dissolve in aqueous muriatic acid or vitriol with evolution of a stinking inflammable gas. Even Boyle, however, took this gas to be ordinary air contaminated with inflammable stinking oils. This view was held by all chemists until Cavendish, before 1784, showed that the gas referred to, if properly purified, is free of smell and constant in its properties, which are widely different from those of air,—the most important point of difference being that the gas when kindled in air burns with evolution of much heat and formation of water. Cavendish, however, did not satisfy himself with merely proving this fact qualitatively; he determined the quantitative relations, and found that it takes very nearly 1000 volumes of air to burn 423 volumes of "hydrogen" gas; but 1000 volumes of air, again, according to Cavendish, contain 210 volumes of oxygen; hence, very nearly, 2 volumes of hydrogen take up 1 volume of oxygen to become water. This important discovery was only confirmed by the subsequent experiments of Humboldt and Gay-Lussac, which were no more competent than Cavendish's to prove that the surplus of 3 units (423 volumes instead of 420) of hydrogen was an observational error.

(W. D.)

WATERBURY, a city in Newhaven county, Connecticut, United States, is situated on the Naugatuck river, 77 miles north-east of New York, at the junction of three railroads connecting it with Bridgeport, Hartford, and Meriden. It was settled by colonists from Hartford in 1677, and bore at first the Indian name of Mattatuck. The land, rocky and hilly, was poor for farming, and the inhabitants began to turn to manufacturing pursuits, in a humble way, before 1800. But the growth in population and business was very slow, till the civil war created such a demand for brass and manufactured articles of that metal that the small factories rapidly grew in number and size, and Waterbury has now become the centre of the brass industry in the United States. Its factories represent an outlay of 10 million dollars, and turn out a great quantity of sheet brass and copper, wire, and tubing, with a multitude of small articles—clocks, watches, lamps, pins, silver-plated ware, &c. The population, which is largely German and Irish, was 17,806 in 1880, and is now (1888) believed to approach 27,000. The city is well lighted by electric lights, and supplied with pure water from a spring-fed reservoir 6 miles distant. A free loan and reference library, founded in 1868, contains 42,000 volumes. Waterbury was incorporated as a city in 1853.

WATERFORD, a maritime county of Ireland, in the province of Munster, is bounded E. by Waterford Harbour, separating it from Wexford, N. by Kilkenny and by Tipperary, W. by Cork, and S. by the Atlantic. Its greatest length from east to west is 52 miles, and its greatest breadth from north to south is 28 miles. The total area is 461,552 acres, or about 721 square miles. The coast-line is in some parts bold and rocky, and is indented by numerous bays and inlets, the principal being Waterford Harbour; Tramore Bay, with picturesque cliffs and some extensive caves, and noted for its shipwrecks, on account of the rocky character of its bed; Dungarvan Harbour, much frequented for refuge in stormy weather; and Youghal Harbour, partly separating county Waterford from county Cork. The surface of the county is to a large extent mountainous, especially towards the west and north-west, consisting chiefly of metamorphosed Lower Silurian rocks, the valleys being occupied by Carboniferous Limestone. There is also evidence on an extensive scale of former glacial action. The Knockmealdown Mountains, which attain a height of 2609 feet, form the northern boundary with Tipperary. A wide extent of country between Clonmel and Dungarvan is occupied by the two ranges of the Commeragh and Monavallagh Mountains, reaching in Knockanarian a height of 2478 feet. To the south of Dungarvan there is a lower but very rugged range, called the Drum Hills. The south-eastern division of the county is for the most part level, consisting chiefly of clay slate interrupted by patches of primitive limestone, and also by conglomerate and basalt, forming in some parts of the coast lofty columnar cliffs. Coal and iron were formerly wrought, but the only mineral product now of importance is copper, the mines at Knockmahon ranking next in Ireland to those at Berehaven. Lead mining, formerly prosecuted with some success, has now practically ceased. Lime is abundant, and coralline sea-sand is obtained. Slate is quarried in considerable quantities at Lismore, and there are also quarries of valuable sandstone and of marble. Ochres and clays for the manufacture of earthenware are also obtained. Though Waterford has benefited in its communications by the important rivers in its vicinity, the only large river it can properly claim as belonging to it is the Blackwater. This enters the county to the east of Fermoy, and flows eastward along a trough of Carboniferous Limestone to Cappoquin, where it turns abruptly southwards, to fall into the sea at Youghal Harbour. At its junction with the Bride below Cappoquin it is navigable for vessels of 100 tons burden. Waterford Harbour may be called the estuary of three important rivers, the Suir, the Nore, and the Barrow, but neither of the last two touches the county. The Suir reaches it at its union with the Nier about 8 miles from Clonmel, and thence forms its northern boundary with Tipperary and Kilkenny. It is navigable for vessels of 800 tons burden to Waterford, for barques and large lighters to Carrick-on-Suir, and for boats of 50 tons to Clonmel.

Agriculture.—The land is generally better adapted for pasturage than for tillage, although there are considerable tracts of rich soil in the south-eastern districts. The total number of holdings in 1886 was 10,188, of which 26 were above 500 acres in extent, 1029 between 100 and 500 acres, 1660 between 50 and 100 acres, 2726 between 15 and 50 acres, 2530 between 1 and 15 acres, and 2217 did not exceed 1 acre. Out of a total of 456,198 acres only 83,968 acres, or 18·4 per cent., were under crops, 235,801 acres, or 51·7 per cent., were under grass; 330 acres fallow; 19,317 acres, or 4·2 per cent., woods and plantations; 22,791 acres, or 5·0 per cent., bog and marsh; 76,137 acres, or 16·7 per cent., barren mountain land; and 17,854, or 3·9 per cent., water, roads, fences, &c. Since 1859 the area under crops has decreased nearly a third, the amount in that year being 116,940 acres. Corn crops occupied 59,848 acres in 1859 and only 35,461 in 1886, the areas under wheat in these years being respectively 23,671 and 1326 acres, under oats 32,526 and 32,795 acres, and under barley, bere, &c., 3651 and 1340 acres. The area under green crops in 1859 was 38,213 acres, and in 1886 it was 24,436 acres, the areas under potatoes in these years being respectively 23,385 and 14,361 acres, under turnips 10,886 and 6171 acres, and under other green crops 4042 and 3904 acres. Horses between 1859 and 1886 diminished from 14,184 to 12,794, of which 9122 were two years old and upwards, but cattle increased from 84,440 to 102,878, of which 39,428 were milch cows, and sheep from 42,408 to 55,805, while pigs decreased from 55,701 to 44,510. The number of mules in 1886 was 942, of asses 4319, of goats 5510, and of poultry 258,058.

In 1876, according to the *Return of Owners of Land*, Waterford was divided among 814 proprietors, possessing 454,937 acres at an annual valuation of £276,642, or an average of about 12s. 2d. per acre. The estimated extent of waste lands was 880 acres. Of the owners 600 possessed one acre and upwards. The number of large estates is exceptionally great. The following possessed upwards of 8000 acres:—marquis of Waterford, 39,884; Lord Stuart de Decies, 30,823; duke of Devonshire, 27,484; R. A. Chearnley, 18,166; Edmond De La Poer, 13,448; John Palisser, 9825; Lord Ashtown, 9435; Sir J. H. Keane, Bart., 8909; and Sir R. J. Musgrave, Bart., 8282.

Manufactures and Trade.—The woollen manufacture, except for private use, is now practically extinct, but the cotton manufacture is still of some importance. There are also breweries, distilleries, and a large number of flour-mills. Sea-fishing is prosecuted chiefly at Dungarvan. There are valuable salmon fisheries on the Blackwater and the Suir.

Railways.—From the city of Waterford the Waterford and Central Ireland line goes northwards by Kilkenny, the Waterford and Limerick by Carrick-on-Suir and Clonmel to Limerick, the Waterford and Tramore to Tramore, and the Waterford, Dungarvan, and Lismore to Lismore, where it joins a branch of the Great South-Western.

Administration and Population.—From 119,457 in 1812 the population increased by 1841 to 196,187, but by 1861 it diminished to 134,252, by 1871 to 123,310, and by 1881 to 112,768 (males 54,618, females 58,150), or 8·5 per cent. less than in 1871. The total number of emigrants from 1st May 1857 to 31st December 1878 was 67,080, and to 31st December 1885 it was 79,240. In 1880 the number reached 2675, and in 1885 it was 1333. The county is divided into 8 baronies, with 82 parishes and 1557 townlands. The principal towns are Waterford (population 29,181), Dungarvan (6306), Tramore (2036), Portlaw (1891), and Lismore (1860). Before the Redistribution Act of 1885 the county returned two members to parliament, the borough of Waterford two, and Dungarvan one,—Clonmel, which is partly in Waterford, also returning one. The county now returns two members, for the East and West Divisions respectively, while the county of the city of Waterford returns one member, and Dungarvan and Clonmel have been disfranchised. It is in the Leinster circuit, and assizes are held at Waterford, and quarter sessions at Lismore, Dungarvan, and Waterford. It is in the Cork military district, and there is a brigade depôt at Clonmel, and barrack stations at Dungarvan and Waterford. The Catholics formed 94·8 per cent. of the population in 1871 and 95·0 in 1881, the Episcopalians in the same years 4·1 per cent. The proportion of persons who could read and write in 1871 was 35·7 per cent., and in 1881 it was 45·8; in 1881 10·6 per cent. could read but could not write, and 43·6 could neither read nor write,—14·3 per cent. being under seven years of age.

History and Antiquities.—In the 9th century the Danes landed in the district, and afterwards made a permanent settlement there. There are in the county a considerable number of barrows, duns, cromlechs, and similar relics of the ancient inhabitants. At Ardmore there is a round tower 97 feet in height, and near it a huge rath and a large number of circular entrenchments. Waterford was one of the twelve counties into which King John, in 1205, divided that part of Ireland which he nominally annexed to the English crown. On account of the convenience of the city as a landing place, many subsequent expeditions passed through the county directed against disaffected or rebellious tribes. In 1444 the greater part of it was granted to James, earl of Desmond, and in 1447 it was bestowed on John Talbot, earl of Shrewsbury, who was created earl of Waterford. The county suffered severely during the Desmond rebellion, in the reign of Elizabeth, as well as in the rebellion of 1641 and during the Cromwellian period. Among the old castles special mention may be made of Lismore, originally erected by John, afterwards king of England, in 1185, but now in great part comparatively modern. The chief ecclesiastical remains are those of the chancel and nave of the cathedral of Ardmore, where a monastery and oratory were founded by St Declan in the 7th century. The see of Ardmore was abolished in the 12th century.

WATERFORD, a city, county of a city, municipal and parliamentary borough, and the chief town of the above county, is finely situated on the south bank of the Suir 4 miles above its junction with the Barrow, at the head of the tidal estuary called Waterford Harbour, and on several railway lines, which afford it convenient communication with all parts of Ireland. It is 32 miles west of Wexford, 76 north-east of Cork, and 97 south-south-west of Dublin. The Suir is crossed by a wooden bridge of thirty-nine arches, and 832 feet long, connecting Waterford with the suburb of Ferrybank. The town is built chiefly along the banks of the river, occupying for the most part low and level ground except at its western extremity. The modern Protestant cathedral of the Holy Trinity, generally called Christ Church, a plain structure with a lofty spire, occupies the site of the church built by the Danes in 1096. Near it are the episcopal palace and deanery. There is a handsome Catholic cathedral, erected at a cost of £20,000; and the training seminary for priests called St John's College deserves notice. The principal secular buildings are the town-hall, the county and city courts and prisons, the new custom-house, erected in 1876, at a cost of £9000, the barracks, and the union workhouse. At the extremity of the quay is a large circular tower, called Reginald's Tower, forming at one time a portion of the city walls, and occupying the site of the tower built by Reginald the Dane in 1003. Near the summit one of the balls shot from the cannon of Cromwell while besieging the city is still embedded in the wall. There are a number of hospitals and similar benevolent institutions, including the leper house founded in the reign of King John, now possessing an income of £1000 a year, and made use of practically as an infirmary. The town possesses breweries, salt-houses, foundries, and flour-mills; and there is a large export trade in cattle, sheep, and pigs, and in agricultural produce. The population of the city (area 10,059 acres) in 1871 was 29,979, and in 1881 it was 29,181.

Waterford Harbour is a winding and well-sheltered bay, formed by the estuary of the river Suir, and afterwards by the joint estuary of the Nore and Barrow. Its length to the sea is about 15 miles. Its entrance is about 2½ miles wide, and is well lighted by a fixed bright light on the ancient donjon of Hook Tower (139 feet in height), by a red light on Dunmore pier, and by two leading lights at Duncannon. The quay, at which vessels of 2000 tons burden can discharge, was enlarged in 1705 by the removal of the city walls, and is about 1¼ miles in length. At Ferrybank, on the Kilkenny side of the river, there is a shipbuilding yard with patent slip and graving dock. By the Suir there is navigation for barges to Clonmel, by the Barrow for sailing vessels to New Ross and thence for barges to Athy, and by the Nore for barges to Inistiogue. The total number of vessels connected with the port in 1885 was 33, of 5246 tons. The number of British and foreign vessels that entered the port in the same year was 1784 of 530,092 tons, while 1255 of 412,326 tons cleared.

Anciently Waterford was called *Cuan-na-groith*, the haven of the sun. By early writers it was named Menapia. It is supposed to have existed in very early times, but first acquired importance under the Danes, of whom it remained one of the principal strongholds until its capture by Strongbow in 1171. On 18th October 1172 Henry II. landed near Waterford, and he here received the hostages of the people of Munster. It became a cathedral city in 1096. Prince John, afterwards king of England, who had been declared lord of Ireland in 1177, landed at Waterford in 1185. After ascending the English throne he in 1204 granted it a fair, and in 1206 a charter of incorporation. He landed at Waterford in 1210, in order to establish within his nominal territories in Ireland a more distinct form of government. The city received a new charter from Henry III. in 1232. Richard II. landed at Waterford in October 1394 and again in 1399. In 1447 it was granted by Henry VI. to John Talbot, earl of Shrewsbury, who was created earl of Waterford. In 1497 it successfully resisted an attempt of Perkin Warbeck to capture it, in recognition of which it received various privileges from Henry VII., who gave it the title of *urbs intacta*. In 1603, after the accession of James I. to the English crown, the city, along with Cork, took a prominent part in opposition to the Government and to the Protestant religion, but on the approach of Mountjoy it formally submitted. From this time, however, the magistrates whom it elected refused to take the oath of supremacy, and, as by its charter it possessed the right to refuse admission to the king's judges, and therefore to dispense with the right of holding assizes, a rule was obtained in the Irish chancery for the seizure of its charter, which was carried into effect in 1618. In 1619 an attempt was made to induce Bristol merchants to settle in the city and undertake its government, but no one would respond to the invitation, and in 1626 the charter was restored. The city was unsuccessfully attacked by Cromwell in 1649, but surrendered to Ireton 10th August 1650. After the battle of the Boyne James II. embarked at it for France (July 1690). Shortly afterwards it surrendered to William, who sailed from it to England. It sent two members to parliament from 1374 to 1885, when the number was reduced to one.

WATER-GLASS. See SILICA, vol. xxii. pp. 53, 54.

WATER-HEN. See MOOR-HEN.

WATER-LILY, a somewhat vague term, given to almost any floating plant with conspicuous flowers, but applying more especially to the species of *Nymphæa* and *Nuphar*. These are aquatic plants with their thick fleshy rootstocks or tubers embedded in the mud, and throwing up to the surface circular shield-like leaves, and leafless flower-stalks, each terminated by a single flower, often of great beauty, and consisting of four or five sepals, and numerous petals gradually passing into the very numerous hypogynous or perigynous stamens without any definite line of demarcation between them. The ovary consists of numerous carpels united together and free, or more or less embedded in the top of the flower-stalk. The ovary has many cavities with a large number of ovules attached to its walls, and is surmounted by a flat stigma of many radiating rows as in a poppy. The fruit is baccate, and the seeds are remarkable for having their embryo surrounded by an endosperm as well as by a perisperm. The anatomical construction of these plants presents many peculiarities which have given rise to discussion as to the allocation of the order among the dicotyledons or among the monocotyledons, the general balance of opinion being in favour of the former view. The leaf-stalks and flower-stalks are traversed by longitudinal air-passages, whose disposition varies in different species. The species of *Nymphæa* are found in every quarter of the globe. Their flowers range from white to rose-coloured, yellow, and blue. Some expand in the evening only, others close soon after noon. *Nymphæa alba* is common in some parts of Britain, as is also the yellow *Nuphar luteum*. The seeds and the rhizomes contain an abundance of starch, which renders them serviceable in some places for food.

Under the general head of water-lily are included the lotus of Egypt, *Nymphæa Lotus*, and the sacred lotus of India and China, *Nelumbium speciosum*, formerly a native of the Nile, as shown by Egyptian sculptures and other evidence, but no longer found in that river. The gigantic *Victoria regia*, a native of tropical South America, also belongs to this group.

WATERLOO, a village of Belgium, in the province of Brabant, 9½ miles to the south-south-east of Brussels, was the headquarters of the duke of Wellington from 17th to 19th June 1815, and has given its name throughout the English-speaking world to the famous battle fought in its neighbourhood on June 18, 1815. See NAPOLEON, vol. xvii. pp. 224–25.

WATERLOO, a city and the county seat of Black Hawk county, Iowa, United States, is situated in a rich farming and stock-raising country, on both sides of the Cedar river, which here furnishes a valuable water power. The population in 1885 was 6479, of whom 1048 were foreign-born.

WATERLOO-WITH-SEAFORTH, a watering-place of Lancashire, England, on the Irish Sea, at the mouth of the Mersey, nearly opposite New Brighton in Cheshire, and on the Liverpool, Crosby, and Southport Railway, 4 miles north by west of Liverpool. On account of its facilities for bathing, firm sands, pleasant scenery, and nearness to Liverpool, of which indeed it may now be considered a suburb, it is much frequented during the summer months. It is well and regularly built, and possesses the usual characteristics of a rising watering-place. The population of the urban sanitary district (area 740 acres) was 9118 in 1881.

WATERPROOF. See INDIA-RUBBER, vol. xii. p. 842.

WATERSPOUT. See METEOROLOGY, vol. xvi. p. 130.

WATER-SUPPLY. An ample supply of pure water is of the utmost importance for the healthiness of towns. When the population of a district is scattered it is possible to supply individual wants by means of streams, springs, or shallow wells; but when a number of people are congregated within the limited area of a town the natural supply of water in this area is liable to be insufficient, and is also in danger of being contaminated by sewage and house refuse. Accordingly, works for the collection, storage, purification, and distribution of water are indispensable necessities in towns, for the preservation of health and the promotion of cleanliness. The remains of aqueducts near Rome and at other places (see AQUEDUCT) show that important works for providing water were undertaken many centuries ago; and water for irrigation and other purposes has for ages been stored, in the rainy season, in tanks by the natives of India. Artificial provisions for the supply of water were, however, entirely neglected in Europe during the Middle Ages, and the colossal works of earlier times were allowed to fall into decay; and most of the present systems of water-supply are of comparatively modern date.

ORIGIN OF SUPPLY.

Rainfall.—All supplies of fresh water come primarily from the clouds, though portions may eventually be drawn from the bowels of the earth. Water when distilled is obtained in its purest form; and the heat of the sun is continually drawing up large quantities of moisture from sea and land, forming clouds which return it as rain to the earth. Some of the rain is quickly evaporated from the surface of the earth, and returned to the clouds; some sinks into the ground to feed springs and underground stores of water; and some passes into streams and rivers, whence it flows into the sea, from which the greater portion of the rain is derived. The available water-supply of any district, accordingly, principally depends on the rainfall of the locality and the extent of the gathering ground. The rainfall varies greatly in different places, and at different periods of the year (see METEOROLOGY); and, in England alone, the average annual rainfall at the Stye, the wettest part of the lake district in Cumberland, is about eight times the rainfall at Hunstanton, the driest locality in Norfolk. The rainfall, moreover, varies from year to year; and the driest years must be taken into consideration in estimating the available water-supply.

Evaporation.—The proportion of the rainfall which is actually serviceable for water-supply depends greatly upon the season of the year in which the rain falls; for evaporation is very active in the hot season, whereas in the cold season its influence is slight. Accordingly, for hydrological purposes, the year may be divided into two seasons in the latitudes of the British Isles,—the warm season, extending from the beginning of May to the end of October, and the cold season, embracing the other half of the year. Comparatively little effect is produced by variations in the amount of rain in the warm season, except in extreme cases, owing to the large proportion drawn off by evaporation, whereas the rainfall during the cold season is of the utmost importance for replenishing the sources of supply which have been drained during the summer. The period of the year, therefore, in which the rain falls is of more consequence than the total amount in the year; and a drought is much more likely to result from a dry winter than from a dry summer. Any deficiency in the supply is generally felt towards the close of the warm season, when the reserves of water, furnished by the rains of the preceding cold season, have been reduced to their lowest level by the demands of the summer.

Other circumstances also modify the influence of evaporation. Rain descending in a heavy continuous fall, by sinking into the ground or escaping into the watercourses, is less exposed to diminution by evaporation than several separate showers of rain, equivalent in total volume, but spread over a longer period. Forests and vegetation shelter the ground from the influence of evaporation; and thereby, in spite of abstracting some of the moisture for their own requirements, they augment the proportion of available rainfall. The nature and slope of the surface stratum, moreover, notably affect the loss from evaporation. Rain falling on an impermeable stratum is almost wholly evaporated in hot weather, when the surface is flat; but it flows off from a steep slope before evaporation can produce its full effect. Rain readily sinks into a porous stratum; and when a depth of three or four feet below the surface is reached it is to a great extent withdrawn from the influence of evaporation.

Percolation.—The percolation of rain through porous strata is the origin of springs and subterranean reservoirs of water, from whence so many supplies are derived. Sand, gravel, chalk, and sandstone are very absorbent strata; whilst the oolites and other limestones are permeable to a smaller extent. The excess of rainfall over evaporation sinks into the ground till it reaches the level of saturation of the stratum by previous rainfalls, and adds to the underground supply. The water thus introduced is prevented from sinking lower down into the earth by encountering an underlying impermeable stratum; and it is hindered in flowing away to the lowest point of the outcrop of the permeable stratum by friction, which causes the surface of saturation to slope towards its outlet, the inclination varying with the head of water and the resistance offered to its flow. The amount of percolation depends upon the rainfall, the porosity of the stratum, and the extent of its exposed surface; and it varies inversely as the evaporation, being greatest in winter and during heavy long-continued rainfalls, and least in the summer and with short showers of rain.

Watercourses.—On impermeable strata, the whole of the rain not removed by evaporation finds its way into the watercourses. The streams, however, draining these strata have a very variable discharge, as they are rapidly swollen after a heavy fall of rain, and soon subside (see River Engineering), whilst in fine summer weather they are liable to be dried up. Accordingly, torrential streams, in their natural condition, are not suitable for water-supply, as they tend to fail when they are most wanted, and owing to their rapid flow they carry along a large quantity of matter in suspension. The flow of streams draining permeable strata is more regular, both on account of the smaller fall generally of the river-bed, and also owing to the rainfall being delayed by percolation in its passage to the river. Some of the rain sinking into a permeable stratum tends to find an outlet outside the valley in which it falls, but most of it reappears again in the form of springs which feed the river gradually at a lower part of its course; and the loss which may occur is more than compensated for by the greater regularity of flow. In olden times, towns, villages, and monasteries were established on the banks of these streams, owing to the ready, ample, and never-failing water-supply thus ensured.

Sources of Supply.

Tanks.—The simplest method of procuring pure water is to collect the rain as it falls from the clouds; and this method is a necessity where, as in tropical countries, there is an excessive rainfall during one period of the year, followed by a long drought, unless the rain sinks into a permeable stratum whence it can subsequently be drawn. These open tanks, however, excavated in the ground, have to be numerous, and often large in extent, to collect sufficient rain to supply the wants of the surrounding population for several months; and the water in them is subject to loss from evaporation during the dry season.

The collection of rain-water is also advantageous in the rural districts of temperate regions, especially for large institutions and isolated mansions and farms, where, by a simple arrangement of gutters and pipes, a large proportion of the rain falling on the sloping roofs can be stored in underground tanks. In large towns, the rain-water is liable to contamination by smoke, dust, and other impurities, and is only serviceable for gardens and water-closets, or where softness is of more consequence than purity.

Springs.—A very valuable source of water-supply is provided by springs. These springs appear at the lowest point S of the outcrop of a permeable stratum, where it rests upon an impermeable stratum (fig. 1); and they constitute the outflow of the rain which has percolated

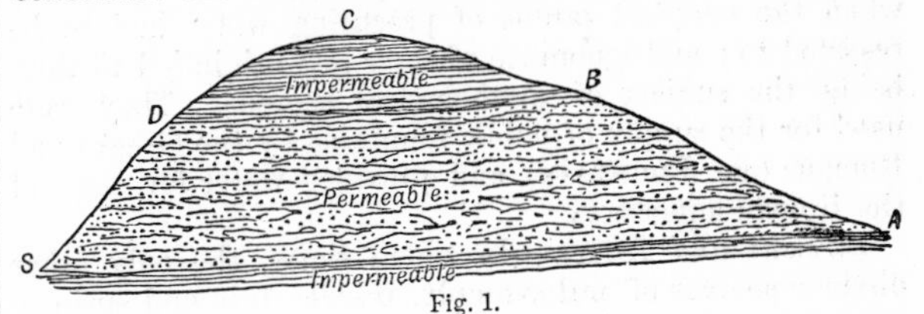

Fig. 1.

through that stratum. A spring depends for its supply upon the extent of the underground reservoir furnished by the permeable stratum; and its discharge is regulated by its level in relation to the line of saturation of the stratum and the resistance offered to its flow. The gathering ground of a spring consists of the portions AB, DS of the permeable stratum drained by it which are actually exposed at the surface, provided the surface slope is not very steep, and also of any impermeable surface strata BCD sloping from a higher level towards the permeable outcrop. The position of the spring is determined by the dip AS of the underlying impermeable stratum and the line of least resistance to the underground flow. When the permeable stratum covers the surface, and is of small extent, as when it forms a thin cap to a hill, an outflow only occurs after a fall of rain. Where a permeable stratum, with a limited gathering ground, has a sufficient depression at some point to cause the line of saturation to sink occasionally below the level of the outcrop, the outflowing spring is intermittent; and the time of the appearance of such springs (or bournes, as they are termed) can be accurately predicted by observing the rise of the water in the neighbouring wells sunk into these permeable strata. A spring is generally clear, and free from organic impurities, as particles in suspension are removed by the natural filtration, and organic matters are oxidized and eliminated in the passage of the water through the ground. The water, however, collects any soluble gases and salts which exist in the strata through which it flows; and most springs contain some inorganic compounds in solution, depending upon the nature of the strata and the distance traversed. Occasionally springs are so strongly impregnated with certain substances as to receive specific names, such as sulphuretted, chalybeate, and saline springs; but in such cases they are of more value for medicinal purposes than as sources of water-supply. The abundant springs derived from the chalk, though containing considerable quantities of carbonate of lime, are quite suitable for domestic purposes. Springs from large underground supplies possess the advantage of a fairly constant temperature, as their sources are protected from atmospheric changes; but underground waters are subject to the rise of temperature, experienced in descending below the surface of the earth, of 1° F., on the average, for each 52 feet of depth.

Small springs frequently supply little hamlets; and a shallow tank, formed at the spring, into which the water trickles, serves as a reservoir, which is gradually filled, and from which water is readily drawn. Large springs may afford adequate supplies for towns; but before relying upon such a source it is essential to gauge their discharge at the close of the autumn, in a dry year, so as to ascertain their sufficiency under unfavourable conditions. When springs have been selected, it only remains for the engineer to design suitable conduits for conveying the water to the place to be supplied. The fine chalk-water springs of Amwell and Chadwell, in Hertfordshire, have been thus utilized by the New River Company for supplying London, by means of a conduit 40 miles long, completed in 1613; and the springs issuing from the Malvern Hills furnish Malvern with a plentiful supply of the purest water.

Springs were naturally much prized in ancient times, when the simplest means of procuring water had to be resorted to; and ignorance of their real origin led to their being the subject of mythological legends. They were used for the supply of public fountains by the Greeks and Romans (see FOUNTAIN), and provided water for some of the Roman aqueducts.

Streams and Rivers.—In olden times, the only other obvious sources of water-supply, besides rain and springs, were the watercourses which carried off the surplus rainfall. Streams and rivers afford the most ample supply, but they become turbid in flood-time; and when they have a rapid fall, and drain an impermeable basin, they fail in times of drought. These objections have, however, been overcome by settling-tanks, filter-beds, and storage-reservoirs,—so that now the principal supplies are drawn from these sources. The increase, indeed, of population, and especially the introduction of the system of discharging the sewage of towns into the adjacent streams, have polluted many rivers. Fortunately, in process of time, some of the organic impurities are removed by aquatic animals and plants, and some become oxidized and thus rendered innocuous (see WATER),—so that, after a sufficient length of unpolluted flow, the river again becomes suitable for supply. The enactments against river-pollution have attacked this evil at its source; but some rivers, passing through large manufacturing centres, are hopelessly contaminated with refuse products. The best sources of water are found in streams draining uncultivated mountainous districts, where a plentiful rainfall on steep impervious strata affords a very pure though somewhat intermittent supply. The freedom from habitations, the rapid flow of rain off the surface, the absence of organic impurities and of soluble salts, prevent any chance of contamination beyond occasional discoloration by peat. Distance, however, from hilly regions and a considerable population render it frequently necessary to resort to larger rivers, which, passing towns and villages in their course, become more or less contaminated, and, being fed by springs from permeable strata, contain the salts dissolved by those springs. London, for instance, draws its principal supplies from the Thames and the Lea; and, though microscopical investigations and the reports of the water-examiners are not always reassuring about the qualities of the water thus supplied and the recuperative powers of nature, waters containing some organic matters and certain kinds of micro-organisms do not appear to be injurious, as is evidenced by the general absence of specific diseases in the inhabitants supplied from these sources.

Wells.—There are two distinct kinds of wells, namely, shallow wells, sunk into a superficial permeable stratum; and deep wells, sunk through an impermeable stratum into an underlying permeable stratum. Both kinds of wells tap the underground waters which are the sources of springs, and furnish artificial outlets for waters which would either find a natural outlet in springs at the outcrop, or which, owing to a depression of the strata, may not possess a natural outlet at a low enough level ever to drain the lower part of the underground reservoir.

Shallow wells, sunk in the ordinary manner, have long been used for collecting moderate supplies of water, where a permeable stratum, such as the Bagshot sands, or the gravel covering parts of the London basin, overlies a watertight stratum such as the London Clay, especially where a slight depression in the impervious stratum towards the centre, or a considerable expanse of the surface stratum, prevents a ready outflow from the permeable beds. Many parts of London were supplied for a long time in this manner; for the rain percolating the bed of gravel flowed into the wells sunk in it, from whence the water could be drawn up. Indeed, as pointed out by Professor Prestwich, the growth of London was restricted, till the regular establishment of waterworks, to those districts possessing a gravel subsoil, in which water could be readily procured, as no such facilities existed where the clay rose to the surface. The sites also of many of the older towns and villages were doubtless determined by similar considerations. Shallow wells are still very useful in supplying scattered populations, but they are exposed to the worst forms of contamination when the houses are near together. Any surface impurities are washed in with the rain; frequently cesspools are given an outlet into the permeable stratum from which the water-supply is derived; and pumping in the well, to increase the supply, creates a flow from the contaminated areas to the well. Such utter neglect of sanitary precautions has led to serious outbreaks of illness; and the sparkling water from some of the old wells in the City of London has proved very deleterious, from the infiltration into them of the decaying matter from graveyards and elsewhere. Shallow wells, in fact, must be resorted to with great caution, and only when an absence of habitations, or a thorough inspection of the district drained by the well, affords assurance of freedom from organic pollution.

Deep wells, passing generally through impervious beds into a permeable water-bearing stratum to a depth at which an adequate supply of water is obtained, are mostly free from organic impurities, partly owing to the protection of the superincumbent impervious stratum, and partly to the filtration any impurities must undergo before reaching the well. The wells are usually formed by sinking a shaft lined with brick for the upper portion, and then carrying down a boring below to the requisite depth. The level of the water in the well depends upon the water-level in the stratum; and generally the water has to be raised by pumping to the surface. Occasionally, owing to a depression of the strata, the top of the well is below the level of the lowest part of the outcrop of the permeable stratum into which the well is sunk, and the water rises in the well directly this stratum is reached, and flows over if the hydrostatic pressure is sufficient to overcome the friction. These latter wells, known as Artesian wells, have been already described (see ARTESIAN WELLS); and the methods of boring other deep wells are precisely similar. The most favourable strata for deep wells in England are the Chalk, Oolites, New Red Sandstone, and Lower Greensand. The yield of these wells depends upon the extent of the portion of the underground reservoir which they can drain; and the reservoir depends for its supply, as in the case of springs, on the extent of the stratum exposed at the surface, the drainage it may receive from adjoining impermeable strata, and the amount of rainfall over these areas. As these points can only be roughly estimated, it is impossible to judge of the yield beforehand; and much depends on the fissures the well may happen to pierce, as the main flow in many rocks takes place along their fissures. It is disadvantageous to sink a well where the superincumbent impervious stratum is very thick, not merely because of the depth that has to be sunk before reaching water, but also on account of the slow rate of the underground flow at a long distance from the outcrop, and owing to the compression of the porous stratum by the mass above it. For instance, the deep well on Southampton Common, sunk through 465 feet of impervious beds, has only yielded a small supply of water, though carried 852 feet into the chalk. A well may also prove a failure owing to a fault or an impervious barrier interrupting the underground flow, if it is sunk on the side of the fault or barrier away from which the dip of the stratum inclines. Thus a well sunk at A (fig. 2) will receive the water flowing along

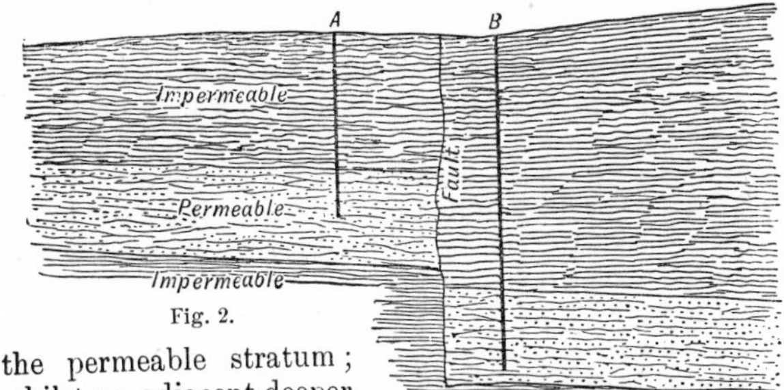

Fig. 2.

the permeable stratum; whilst an adjacent deeper well at B will yield no water, on account of the interruption of the flow. As there is a limit to the underground waters, only a limited number of wells can be advantageously sunk within a certain area; and a multiplication of wells, such as has occurred in the London basin, permanently lowers the water-level of the underground reservoir, and involves an increased lift in pumping to maintain the supply. Wells drawing their supplies from the same sources as springs reduce the yield of the springs issuing from the strata which they pierce; and when these springs feed rivers the volume of these rivers is thereby somewhat diminished. Wells, however, sunk into strata draining to the sea-coast merely intercept water which otherwise would be absolutely lost. A useful well for small supplies is a tube well, which consists of a series of strong wrought-iron pipes, between 1 and 2 inches in diameter, the bottom length being terminated in a point, and perforated with little holes for a short distance up. The point is driven into the ground by a falling weight, as in pile-driving; and, as the tube descends, fresh lengths of pipe are screwed on the top. When the perforated pipe reaches a water-bearing stratum, the water enters through the holes and is raised by a pump (compare descriptions and diagrams of tube-wells under PETROLEUM, vol. xviii. pp. 716–718).

EXTENSION OF SUPPLY.

A supply obtained from wells may be increased by reaching the water flowing through undrained fissures or lying in untouched cavities, either by sinking fresh wells, or by driving headings from the bottom of existing wells in various directions, both of which courses were adopted for extending the Brighton water-supply. Continued pumping sometimes improves the supply when the stratum is well saturated and the drain is not sufficient to lower the water-level permanently. This result is due to the steepening of the gradient of flow towards the well by the depression of the water-level in the well, which increases the velocity of flow, whereby the channels of access are cleared out and enlarged, so that the water flows more readily and quickly into the well than at the commencement.

The supply from springs and streams can only be increased by storing up the excess of supply in the wet season, to make up for the deficiency in the dry season. This can be accomplished by means of storage reservoirs, which sometimes are found suitably provided by nature in the form of lakes, or may be constructed in mountain valleys by means of dams.

RESERVOIRS.

Lakes as Reservoirs.—A lake is a natural reservoir of water, caused by the influx of a stream into a depression of an impermeable stratum, which is barred to a certain height by a ridge across its outlet, over which the water has to rise before it can flow away (see LAKE). The water of lakes is generally of exceptional purity, owing to its being usually supplied by the drainage from the impervious uncultivated ground of uninhabited mountainous districts, and its general freedom from pollution, and on account of the lake serving as a deep subsiding reservoir for any matters in suspension contained in the inflowing streams, of which the Lake of Geneva in relation to the turbid upper Rhone is a notable instance. Glasgow is supplied with excellent water from Loch Katrine (see AQUEDUCT, vol. ii. p. 224); it was at one time proposed to supply Edinburgh from St Mary's Loch, and London from Bala Lake; and works for the conveyance of water from Thirlmere, in Cumberland, to Manchester are in progress. To increase the storage capacity of a lake intended to serve as a reservoir, and avoid injury to vested interests, the ordinary water-level of the lake has to be raised by heightening the barrier at its outlet. By this means the lake is not unduly lowered by the drain upon it during the dry season, and compensation water is provided to supply the water-rights along the stream below. The extent to which the water-level of the lake has to be raised depends upon the area of the lake, the influx into it, and the supply drawn off; thus Loch Katrine, with an area of 3000 acres, needed only a rise of 4 feet in order that, with a maximum lowering of 7 feet, it might provide a storage of 5687 million gallons for a supply of fifty million gallons per day; whereas the water-level of Thirlmere, with an existing area of only 350 acres, requires raising 50 feet to furnish a storage of 8100 million gallons for a similar daily supply. The amount of water that can be collected depends on the catchment area, and the rainfall of the driest years, less the loss from evaporation; and the supply which can be relied upon from any definite gathering ground is given by the formula $Q = 62.15\ A\ (\frac{4}{5} R - E)$, where Q is the daily supply in gallons, A is the catchment area in acres, R is the average annual rainfall and E the loss from evaporation, both in inches.[1] The storage capacity must be regulated by the number of consecutive days, in time of drought, that the supply might have to be drawn from the reservoir without its receiving any accession of water. This period has been variously estimated at from 70 to 300 days according to the locality; for, owing to the smaller fluctuations in the rainfall and in the periods of drought in very rainy districts, and the less amount of evaporation, a much smaller storage suffices for very wet districts than for very dry ones.

Storage Reservoirs.—Where no natural lake is available for a reservoir, an artificial lake may be formed by constructing a dam across a narrow gorge of a mountainous valley, thereby impounding, in the winter, the stream draining the valley, and storing up a supply for the following summer. To prevent an escape of the water thus impounded, the reservoir must be formed on an impervious stratum, and all cracks and fissures closed, or the bed and banks must be rendered watertight by a surface layer of impervious material. Occasionally the configuration of the ground and the amount of storage required render it necessary to form a series of impounding reservoirs at different levels along a valley, thereby increasing the number, but keeping down the height of the dams. For instance, in supplying Manchester from the Longdendale valley, six large reservoirs, having a total area of 497 acres, and a capacity of 4160 million gallons, were formed in steps by dams from 70 to 100 feet high (see AQUEDUCT, vol. ii. p. 224).

RESERVOIR DAMS.

The capacity of a reservoir depends upon the form and levels of the valley in which it is situated, and the height of the dam retaining it. As, however, the extent of the water surface is considerably increased by raising the water-level, an additional height of dam adds largely to the capacity of a reservoir. Thus Thirlmere, with an existing maximum depth of 108 feet, will have its area increased from 350 to 800 acres by raising the barrier at its outlet 50 feet. Accordingly, dams of considerable height are sometimes erected: as, for instance, the Entwistle embankment of the Bolton waterworks, retaining a reservoir 120 feet deep, the Villar dam, for the supply of Madrid, founded $158\frac{1}{2}$ feet below the water-level of its reservoir (fig. 7), and the Furens dam, near St Étienne, with a height of 164 feet at the water-level (fig. 5); whilst the Gileppe dam, near Verviers, was made $147\frac{3}{4}$ feet high (fig. 6) in preference to four dams of 95 feet.

A reservoir dam is constructed either with earthwork in an embankment sloped on each side, and with a watertight puddle or concrete trench along the centre, or of masonry. Earthwork embankments have, till within the last three or four years, been exclusively adopted in Great Britain; whilst masonry dams have been long ago constructed in Spain, and more recently introduced into France.

Earthen Embankments.—In moist climates, and for moderate heights, embankments of earth are adopted with advantage for reservoir dams, more especially when ample materials can be readily obtained, either by excavations in the reservoir, thus enlarging its capacity, or elsewhere near at hand, and where a rock foundation is not easily attainable. All loose material must be removed from the site of the dam; and the puddle trench in the centre must be carried down to a solid impervious bed (fig. 3). The embankment must be brought up in thin layers carefully punned or rolled, the most retentive materials being placed near the middle, and the looser materials towards the outside. The inner slope, facing the reservoir, is usually made 3 to 1, and pitched on the surface to protect it from the wash of the waves. The outer slope is formed to the angle of stability of the material employed, generally 2 to 1; and occasionally berms are introduced, diminishing the liability to slips (fig. 4). The best puddled clay is used for the central trench; but the remainder of the embankment should not be composed exclusively of clay, as stiff clay under the influence of the weather, especially on the exposed outer slope, tends to slip. An earthen dam possesses ample stability if it is perfectly solid; but it may fail from the infiltration of water through it, owing to faulty construction, or from settlement, leading to its overtopping by the water in the reservoir.

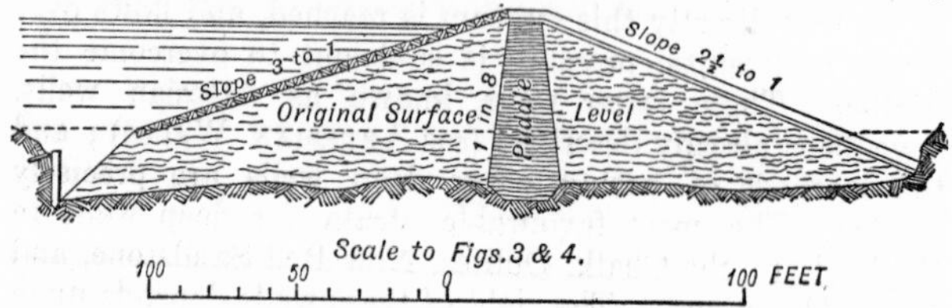

FIG. 3.—Nethertrees Reservoir Embankment, Paisley.

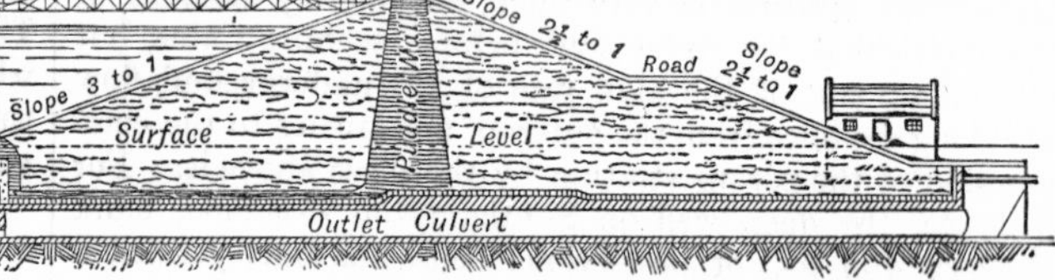

FIG. 4.—Gladhouse Reservoir Embankment, Edinburgh.

Masonry Dams.—In hot dry countries, an earthen embankment is liable to crack and become somewhat disintegrated; and high embankments, owing to their flat side slopes, require a very large amount of material. Accordingly, in Spain, masonry dams have been adopted; and they are preferable to earthen dams when the height exceeds about 80 feet, and where a rock foundation can be secured. The Spanish masonry dam of Puentes (Lorca), 164 feet high, was indeed built upon piles; but it was eventually undermined, and settled; and the outburst of the water from the reservoir on its failure in 1802 caused the loss of 608 lives. Besides a solid rock foundation, the conditions of stability of a masonry dam are that the maximum pressure shall not exceed the limit that the masonry can sustain without injury, and that the lines of resultant pressures, with the reservoir empty and full, shall not anywhere pass outside the middle third of the section of the dam, so as to prevent the possibility of tension at the faces. With the reservoir empty, the pressures on the dam are merely those due to its weight; and the line of resultant pressures is the locus of the points of intersection of the verticals from the centres of gravities of the several portions of the dam above a series of horizontal lines, with the base lines of those portions (figs. 5 and 8). With the reservoir full, the water exerts a horizontal thrust against the inner face of the dam, equal to the weight of a column of water having the depth of the water resting against the dam, and acting at the centre of pressure, which is at two-thirds of the depth down from the water-level. The line of resultant pressures, in this case, is the locus of the points obtained by the intersection of the resultant lines of the pressures of the masonry and

[1] *Theory and Practice of Hydro-Mechanics*, Inst. C. E., p. 44.

the water on the portions of dam, at different distances from the top, with the horizontal base lines of these portions (figs. 5 and 8). The direction and amount of the resultant are readily obtained graphically by the parallelogram of forces, the point of application being at the intersection of the vertical from the centre of gravity with the horizontal line one-third up from the base; for, by drawing the horizontal and vertical lines proportionate in length to the water-pressure and weight of the dam respectively, the diagonal represents the resultant of these forces both in magnitude and direction. When the inner face of the dam is battered, the weight of water resting on this face must be added to the weight of the dam when the reservoir is full. The resultant pressures necessarily increase with the depth; and the maximum pressure is at or near the base of the inner face when the reservoir is empty, and of the outer face when the reservoir is full. The top has only to be made wide enough to resist the shock of the waves and floating ice in the reservoir; but the base, having to bear the weight of the dam together with the water-pressure, requires widening out adequately for the safe limit of pressure on the masonry not to be exceeded; and, as the water-pressure with the full reservoir deflects the resultant towards the outer face, this face is given a considerable batter (fig. 5). All dams have to be raised high enough not to be overtopped by the highest waves in a storm, depending on the size and exposure of the reservoir.

Sections of three of the largest masonry dams erected within the last twenty-five years, namely, Furens, Gileppe, and Villar (figs. 5, 6, and 7), as well as the Vyrnwy rubble concrete dam, now in course of construction (fig. 8), drawn to the same scale, illustrate the forms adopted for these dams. The Furens and Villar dams follow closely the theoretical requirements; whilst the Gileppe and Vyrnwy dams, with their excess of thickness, impose an unnecessary weight on the base, and absorb extra material, without any adequate compensating advantage. Provision, however, was made in the section of the Gileppe dam to admit of its being raised at some future time, and for a roadway along the top, which in some measure accounts for its excess of width; and the Gileppe and Vyrnwy dams are the first examples of such structures in Belgium and Great Britain.

The Furens dam (fig. 5), constructed in 1859–66, across the Gouffre d'Enfer, for forming a reservoir with a capacity of 56½ million cubic feet, has a maximum height of 183 feet, and a length along the top of 337 feet; and the maximum pressure on the masonry is 6·1 tons per square foot on the inner face, a few feet above the base, with the reservoir empty; whereas, with the reservoir full, the maximum pressure on the outer face is under 6 tons. No allowance was made for the arched form of the dam, in plan, towards the reservoir, which reduces the pressure, due to the head of water, at the lower part where the valley is very contracted, and would have admitted of the omission of the projecting outer portion for the bottom 60 feet. A very low limit of pressure, in addition to the excess of strength

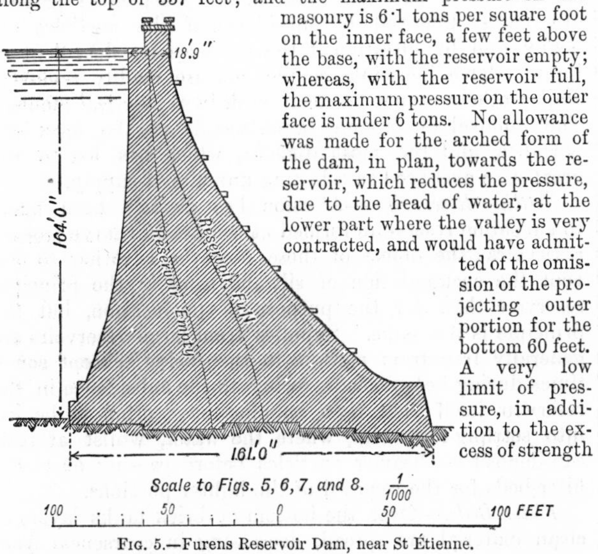

Fig. 5.—Furens Reservoir Dam, near St Étienne.

just referred to, was adopted, owing to the unprecedented height and type of the Furens dam. By raising, however, the limit to 6·6 tons per square foot, it was possible to reduce the section of the Ban dam, 138 feet in height at the water-line, making it 110¼ feet wide at the base, as compared with 116½ feet for the Furens dam at the same depth; whilst with the same limit applied to a dam of the full height of the Furens dam, the reduction in width at the base would be from 161 feet to 154 feet.[1] Any further raising of the limit of pressure, which might be safely effected, would be of little advantage for dams down to a depth of about 100 feet, as the reduction in width is restricted by the condition of the middle third; but beyond that depth the width is regulated by the pressure.

The Gileppe dam (fig. 6), built in 1869–75, having a maximum height of 154 feet, and a length along the top of 771 feet, retains a reservoir with a capacity of 423¾ million cubic feet. The average pressure on the base is 8·2 tons per square foot; so that, even allowing for the specific gravity of the masonry being about one-seventh greater at Gileppe than at Furens, the maximum pressure on the Gileppe dam

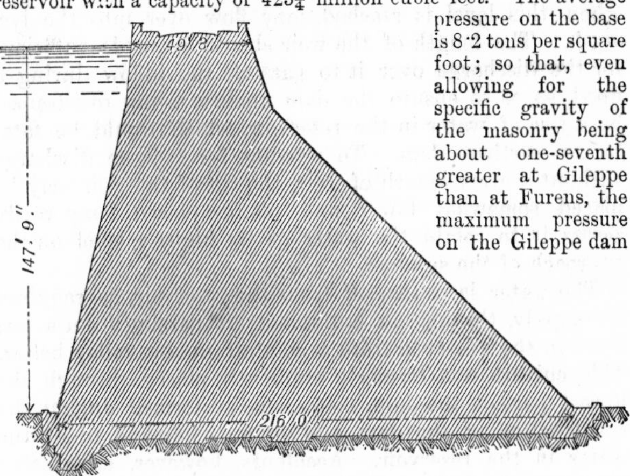

Fig. 6.—Gileppe Reservoir Dam, near Verviers.

is considerably greater than on the Furens dam, in spite of its greater base and the smaller head of water (compare figs. 5 and 6), owing to the excess of material employed in its construction.

The Villar dam (fig. 7), built across the river Lozoya in 1870–78, convex towards the reservoir as at Furens and Gileppe, has a maximum height of 168⅔ feet, and a length along the top of 546 feet; and it forms a reservoir having a capacity of 70⅔ million cubic feet. It differs very little in height and type from the Furens dam; but the form given to the batter of the outer face is calculated to render the pressures more uniform towards the base.

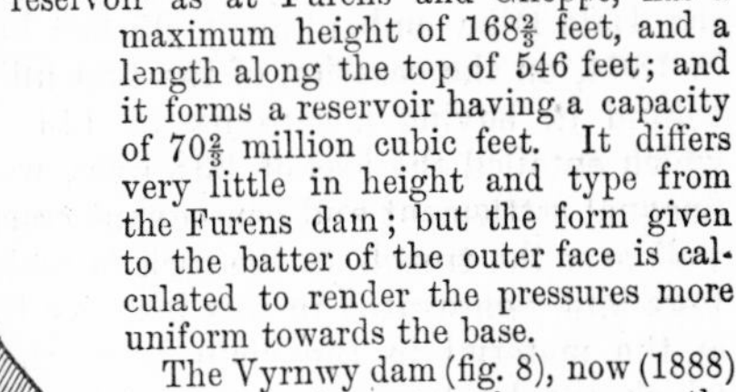
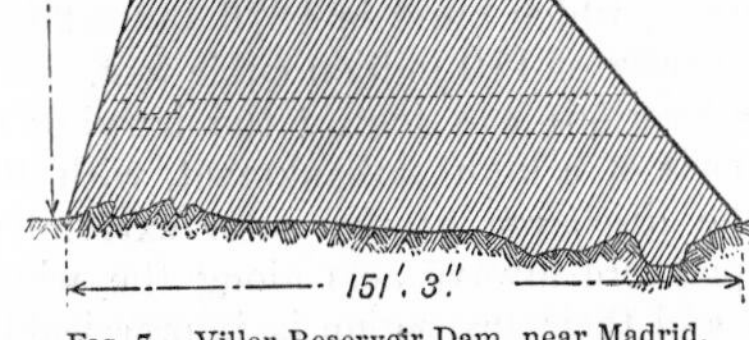

Fig. 7.—Villar Reservoir Dam, near Madrid.

The Vyrnwy dam (fig. 8), now (1888) in course of construction, across the Vyrnwy in Montgomeryshire, for forming a reservoir, 1100 acres in area, to supply 40 million gallons per day to Liverpool, is to sustain a maximum head of water of only 70½ feet; but, as it has to be carried down about 60 feet below the surface, in the centre of the valley, to reach solid rock, its maximum height is about 140 feet, and its length along the top is 1350 feet. The maximum pressure on the inner face with the reservoir empty has been estimated at 8·7 tons per square foot, and with the reservoir full at 6·7 tons on the outer face. These pressures are considerably in excess of the maxima pressures on the Furens dam, though the head of water to be supported is much less, and the width at the base is greater in proportion to the depth. The pressures at the base in the Vyrnwy and Gileppe dams show that a superabundant mass of material in a masonry dam, whilst involving a larger outlay, imposes a greater pressure upon the masonry, whereas the stability is ample in the Furens type; and the oozing of water through the dam should be provided against by the quality of the materials and workmanship, rather than by an extra thickness of masonry.

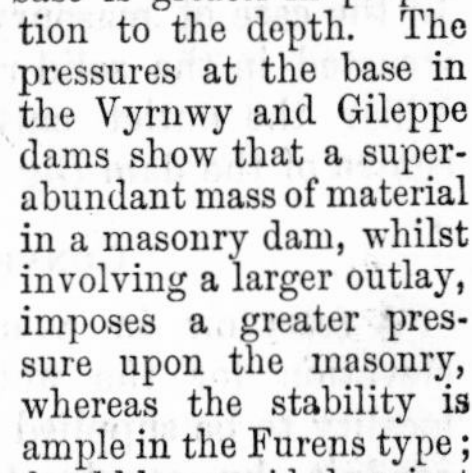

Fig. 8.—Vyrnwy Reservoir Dam.

[1] *Annales des Ponts et Chaussées*, 4th ser., vol. xii. pl. 127.

Accessory Works.—Sometimes a small dam is placed across the upper end of a reservoir, so as to form a small settling reservoir, in which the inflowing stream can deposit any sediment before passing into the main reservoir.

A waste weir is provided at a suitable place in the dam with its sill slightly lower than the highest proposed water-level in the reservoir, so that the surplus water, when this level is reached, may flow over into the lye-wash. The length of the weir should be made sufficient for the discharge over it to pass off the inflow during a flood, so as to ensure the dam against being overtopped by a rise of water in the reservoir, which would be fatal to an earthen dam. To provide for a large discharge without a great length of weir, the sill of the weir may be placed somewhat lower, and planks placed temporarily across it to retain the water at its highest level on the approach of the summer.

The water is drawn off from the reservoir, as required for supply, through an outlet culvert passing from a low level in the reservoir into a conduit in the valley below. This culvert was formerly frequently placed through the lowest part of the dam, being readily formed during the construction of the dam, and giving command of all the water in the reservoir. Accidents, however, have often been traced to the unequal settlement of the earthen embankment near the culvert, or to infiltration of water into the embankment, either by escaping from the culvert fractured by settlement, or by finding a passage along the outside line of the culvert or pipes. Thus the bursting of the Dale Dike embankment, 95 feet high, near Sheffield, in 1864, on the occasion of the first filling of the reservoir behind it, having a capacity of 114 million cubic feet, which entailed the loss of 238 lives, was attributed to the unequal settlement and consequent cracking of the puddle wall over the trench in the rock in which the outlet pipes were laid, aggravated in this instance by the defectiveness of the material in the main bank, the rough manner in which the bank was raised, and the rapid filling of the reservoir. The percolation of the water under pressure along the line of outlet pipes was the cause of the gradual failure of the embankment, 41 feet high, across the Lynde Brook, Worcester, Mass., which burst in 1876 and set free a reservoir with a capacity of 110 million cubic feet.

No possible considerations can justify the burying of outlet pipes at the base of a high embankment, with the valves regulating the discharge at the outer extremity, whereby the water-pressure always acts along the whole length of the pipes, and their inspection is impracticable. In some cases a valve-tower is erected in the centre of the embankment, by which means the water can be shut off from a portion of the pipes. If, however, the outlet pipes are carried under the embankment, they should be laid in the solid ground, and should be commanded along their entire length by a valve-tower placed at the inner toe of the embankment (fig. 4). Nevertheless, it is far safer to carry the outlet pipes in a tunnel constructed through the side of the valley, beyond one end of the embankment. In the case of masonry dams, the outlet is generally constructed in the solid rock distinct from the dam; but at Villar the outlet culvert has been carried through the centre of the dam (fig. 7).

Conveyance of Supply.

A reservoir in a mountain valley is at a sufficient elevation for the water to flow by gravitation to the locality to be supplied; and it is only necessary to form a conduit by canals, tunnels, aqueducts, and pipes, of adequate size in relation to the gradient, to convey the daily supply required (see Hydromechanics). In olden times hills were contoured, and valleys were crossed by colossal aqueducts, at great expense, to obtain a regular inclination, which was reduced by the circuitous route that had to be taken (see Aqueduct). Now, however, hills are pierced by tunnels; and, by the employment of cast-iron, deep wide valleys can be crossed by inverted siphons following the depressions of the land,—so that a much straighter course is attainable, affording better gradients, and therefore enabling smaller conduits to be adopted, which is of great importance when long distances have to be traversed. Thus the waters of Thirlmere, after being discharged through a tunnel formed under the Kirkstone Pass at the south end of the lake, instead of at the natural outlet to the north, will be conveyed to Manchester by a conduit 96 miles long, with a total fall of 178 feet. Portions of the route are in tunnels, 7 feet square, the longest tunnel being a little over 3 miles long; and there are several inverted siphons, to be formed of five cast-iron pipes, each $3\frac{1}{3}$ feet in diameter, the longest siphon being $3\frac{1}{3}$ miles, and that under the river Lune having to bear a water-pressure of 416 feet. The water from the Vyrnwy reservoir will be conveyed to Liverpool in a conduit 67 miles long, of which 4 miles will be in tunnel, and will furnish a supply of 40 million gallons per day. A large supply of water from the river Verdon for the district round Aix, serving for irrigation and manufactures, as well as for domestic purposes, is conveyed across the valley of St Paul in an inverted siphon formed of two wrought-iron tubes, each $5\frac{3}{4}$ feet in diameter.

The water obtained from rivers in low districts, and from wells, has to be raised by pumping to the height necessary to obtain a proper pressure for supply; and the pumps have to be in duplicate, to prevent a failure in the supply in the event of a break-down. Thus the water-supply of London has to be raised by pumping to fill the service reservoirs.

Purification.

The water obtained for supply is frequently not sufficiently pure to be at once distributed for domestic purposes. The impurities to which water is liable are of three kinds, namely, particles of matter in suspension, inorganic substances in solution, and organic matters in solution or of extreme minuteness. Suspended matters are readily removed by subsidence if the particles are heavy, and by filtration if the particles are flocculent or light. Some inorganic compounds are readily removed, whilst others cannot be dealt with in a practical manner. The removal of organic impurities is of the most importance, and the most difficult, which has led to the great care exercised in selecting unpolluted supply.

Settling-Reservoirs.—Allusion has already been made to subsiding reservoirs formed at the head of large storage reservoirs; the object of these, however, is rather to prevent the accumulation of silt and sand in the principal reservoir than for the purpose of purification, but the principle is the same. Supplies from large reservoirs are generally free from matters in suspension, except sometimes during heavy floods, owing to the subsidence in the reservoir itself; but river supplies have often to be led into settling-reservoirs, where the water, whilst at rest, can deposit its heavier particles before passing on to the filter-beds for the removal of the lighter portions.

Filter-Beds.—Over the bottom of brick tanks layers of clean material are spread, decreasing in coarseness from small rubble to sharp sand, with a total average thickness of about 4 feet. The actual filtration is effected by the upper layer of sand; and the lower layers allow the passage of the water unaccompanied by the sand. The efficiency of the filtration depends upon the slowness of the passage of the water, which should not exceed a flow of from 2½ to 3 gallons per square foot of area per hour. The filter must periodically be cleaned by scraping off the top surface of the sand, which becomes choked with the matter removed from the water; and after a time a fresh layer of sand has to be provided. Filtration, though in itself a purely mechanical operation, has been found to reduce the organic impurities in the water, which must be due either to their oxidation from exposure in thin layers to the air in the process of filtering or to the actual removal of very minute organisms floating in the water, or probably to both causes combined.

Filters of spongy iron mixed with gravel were set up at the Antwerp waterworks in 1881, and arrested a quantity of matter which had passed through an upper layer of sand, and proved very efficient agents for purification. Their large cost, however, their becoming rapidly clogged and caked on the top, necessitating the removal of the upper layer of sand to break up the hard top iron crust, and the rather frequent renewal of the iron required, as compared with sand, were a bar to the extension of the system, which had become inadequate for its work. Eventually, it was found that the purification could be effected more economically and rapidly, and quite as effectually, by scattering cast-iron borings in the water as it flowed through horizontal revolving cylinders, furnished with projecting plates fastened at intervals round the inside, which, in revolving, scooped up the iron at the bottom, which had fallen through the water, and discharged it on reaching the top. The iron is first converted into ferrous oxide, FeO, which dissolves, at least partly, as bicarbonate, and then by further oxidation into ferric oxide, Fe_2O_3, which readily precipitates, and is easily removed by filtration through sand, a small portion only of the oxide remaining in solution. Iron appears to purify water from organic matter, partly by its fatal influence on the growth and even life of micro-organisms, and partly by dragging down the floating organisms in the process of precipitation.

Softening Water.—Many waters drawn from springs, wells, and rivers fed by springs contain inorganic salts in solution, and, though innocuous and pleasant for drinking, are not good for general domestic and manufacturing purposes, owing to their curdling soap and encrusting kettles, boilers, and pipes. This quality, known as *hardness*, is mainly due to salts of lime, which are found in large quantities in waters drawn from the chalk. Most of the lime in solution is in the form of bicarbonate, $CaO.2CO_2$, having been produced from the very slightly soluble carbonate of lime, $CaO.CO_2$, of which chalk and other limestones are mainly composed, by combination with free carbonic acid, CO_2. It is only therefore necessary to remove half of the carbonic acid from the bicarbonate to reconvert it into the insoluble carbonate. This can be done either by boiling, which drives off the excess of carbonic acid, depositing the carbonate of lime which forms the troublesome incrustation in pipes and boilers where chalk water is used, or by adding caustic lime, CaO, to the water, which, combining with the excess of carbonic acid, reduces the bicarbonate, forming carbonate of lime, which is precipitated. This reaction is indicated by the formula $CaO + CaO.2CO_2 = 2CaO.CO_2$, and is the basis of Dr Clark's process for softening water. To indicate the degree of hardness of various waters, Dr Clark's scale of 1 degree of hardness for each grain of chalk in 1 gallon of water is employed. Some waters have 22°, or even more degrees of hardness; and all waters are termed hard which contain more than 5°; but by the softening process waters of 22° of hardness can be reduced to about 5°. The remaining or permanent hardness consists of sulphate of lime and other soluble salts. The conversion of the bicarbonate in the process of softening is rapid; but the difficulty of dealing with the fine precipitate, which requires time to settle, has hindered the general adoption of the process, though it has been applied successfully at various works deriving their supply from chalk wells. The precipitation of the carbonate of lime in the softening process has been observed to remove to a great extent the micro-organisms in the water, confirming the view expressed above, that precipitation sweeps down with it the minute germs, as in this case the chemical action could not influence them. The waters obtained from mountainous districts are very soft, and therefore very valuable for manufacturing districts; but they have more action upon lead, and are more liable to absorb organic impurities than water highly charged with inorganic salts.

Storage.

Quantity of Daily Supply.—The water-supply required is estimated in gallons per head of population, with additions in manufacturing districts for trade purposes. The consumption varies greatly in different towns, ranging from about 12 to 50 gallons per head per day; and it depends more upon the fittings and other sources of waste than upon the habits of the population, though the consumption per head is greater in the wealthier quarters. An ample supply, for domestic and general requirements, is from 20 to 25 gallons per head daily. The actual rate of consumption varies with the time of day, and also with the period of the year, being greatest between 7 and 10 A.M., and in June, July, and August, and least from 9 P.M. to 5 A.M., and in January, February, and March.

Where the quality of the supply drawn from different sources varies, as in London (the water from the deep wells in the chalk being far superior to that derived from the Lea), and where filtration has to be largely adopted, it is unfortunate that the best supply cannot be devoted to drinking and cooking, and the inferior in quality and unfiltered waters used for cleaning, for gardens, stables, water-closets, flushing sewers, watering the streets, and extinguishing fires. Besides, however, the cost of a duplicate system of mains and pipes, with the addition, in London, of difficulties between independent companies, the carelessness of persons in drawing from the two supplies has been considered a bar to this separation. It is possible, however, that, when the population becomes still more dense, and pure water more difficult to obtain, these objections may be overruled, and the purest supply devoted to special uses.

Service-Reservoir.—To provide a sufficient reserve for sudden demands, such as for a fire, and to ensure an adequate supply to every house, a service-reservoir has to be constructed, into which the water from the source of supply is led. The reservoir consists generally of a brick or concrete tank, rendered inside with cement, sunk in the ground, and roofed over with brick arches resting on the side walls and intermediate pillars, over which a covering of earth is spread. By this means light and heat are excluded, which, together with a depth of at least 15 feet of water, prevents the growth of minute aquatic plants, of which the germs are found in some well waters, particularly from the New Red Sandstone, and maintains the water at a tolerably even temperature. The reservoir should have a capacity of not less than twenty-four hours' supply, and should be at a sufficient elevation to command the whole of the district it serves, and if possible afford a good pressure on the fire-hydrants. Where a town stands at very different levels, separate reservoirs at different elevations for supplying the high-level and low-level districts are advisable, to equalize the pressure.

DISTRIBUTION.

The water is led from the service-reservoir through cast-iron mains to the branch mains, from which the service pipes convey it to the several houses. Lead is generally preferred for house connexions, owing to the facility with which it can be adapted to structural requirements. The only objection to it is that it is attacked by some very soft waters, oxide of lead being formed, which is partially soluble and very injurious to health. With free carbonic acid, however, the pipe becomes coated with carbonate of lead, which is insoluble in water and protects the pipe from further action. Peat also in water protects the lead pipes, by depositing a surface film. In the case of hard waters, the lead soon becomes coated with sulphate of lime. Accordingly, it is only under exceptional conditions that the employment of lead for pipes is deleterious; but it should be prohibited for the lining of cisterns where the water may be stored for long periods.

Domestic filters are very valuable for local well and spring supplies, and afford an additional safeguard against accidental impurities in public supplies (see FILTER).

Intermittent and Constant Supply.—Formerly the common form of supply was on the intermittent system. On this plan, each house is provided with a cistern, into which water from the main is admitted for a short period, once or twice a day, by means of a valve on each service main, which is opened and closed by the turncock for each separate district. When the cistern is filled, the inlet pipe is closed by the rising of the floating ball shutting the ball tap. The supply is, accordingly, limited to the contents of the cistern, except during the short period the water is turned on; and the cistern is proportioned to the accommodation of the house. The water in these open cisterns is liable to contamination from impurities of various kinds settling in them and not being cleaned out; and it is often exposed to heat, a smoky atmosphere, and dust, and sometimes to sewage gas. Moreover, in the event of a fire, the turncock has to be summoned before a supply of water can be obtained. Accordingly, the adoption of the constant system has been urged, and in many places carried out. The advantages of drawing a fresh supply always direct from the main, and of having an ample supply constantly at hand to meet any emergency are unquestionable; but the constant supply of water necessitates the strengthening and very careful inspection of the pipes, joints, and fittings, to prevent fracture and avoid leakage under a continual and increased pressure, and is liable to lead to a careless waste of water if unchecked by a meter. Before substituting a constant for an intermittent supply, it is essential to overhaul thoroughly the pipes and joints, and to substitute screw-down taps, which close gradually, for the leaky suddenly-closing plug-taps, which throw a sudden pressure on the pipes. Waste in water-closets can be stopped by the insertion of a waste preventer, which only allows a definite quantity of water to pass each time the plug is raised (see SEWERAGE). The detection of accidental waste from leakages has been much facilitated by the introduction of a waste-water meter, which records graphically, on a revolving cylinder, the amount of water which is passing the place where the meter is fixed. By fixing the meter on one of the district mains at night, when most of the recorded flow is running to waste, and shutting off successively the service pipes through which water is heard to be flowing, the change in the diagram of flow at each closing of a service pipe localizes the position and extent of each source of waste, showing at what places leaks must be occurring, and which are the worst, needing attention first. This method of inspection was first adopted at Liverpool in 1873; and, besides effecting a considerable economy, it enabled the constant service to be restored, which the previous waste had rendered impracticable.

Water-Meters.—There are two classes of water-meters, —the positive and the inferential. The positive meter, such as Kennedy's and Frost's piston meters, measures the actual quantity of water passed through it, as recorded by the strokes of a piston working in the cylinder, which is successively filled from the top and bottom, and affords a measure of the water introduced; whilst the inferential meter, such as that of Siemens, measures only the revolutions of a turbine actuated by the flow of the passing water, of which the quantity is deduced from the velocity. The positive meter is more accurate, and measures very small flows; whereas the turbine meter may sometimes not be turned by very small flows which are gradually increased. Measurement by meter would seem naturally to follow the adoption of the constant service for domestic supply, as well as for manufactories. Its general adoption has, however, been hindered by the fear that a charge by quantity, instead of by rental, might press unduly upon the poorer classes, and induce them to stint themselves of a proper supply, and also the difficulty of obtaining a very cheap and at the same time a perfectly trustworthy meter of adequate durability. To avoid the possibility of checking a sufficient use of water in the poorer tenements, it has been proposed to allow a definite supply at the ordinary rate, and only to charge by meter for any excess over this amount. (L. F. V.-H.)

WATERTON, CHARLES (1782–1865), naturalist and traveller, descended from a very ancient English family, was born at Walton Hall, near Pontefract, Yorkshire, in 1782. After being educated at the Roman Catholic college of Stonyhurst, and travelling a short time on the Continent, he went to Demerara to manage some estates belonging to his family. He continued in this occupation for about eight years, when he began those wanderings upon the results of which his fame as a naturalist principally rests. In his first journey, which began in 1812, and the principal object of which was to collect the poison known as curari, he travelled through British Guiana by the Demerara and Essequibo rivers to the frontiers of Brazilian Guiana, making many natural history collections and observations by the way. After spending some time in England he returned to South America in 1816, going by Pernambuco and Cayenne to British Guiana, where again he devoted his time to the most varied observations in natural history. For the third time, in 1820, he sailed from England for Demerara, and again he spent his time in similar pursuits. Another sojourn in England of about three years was followed by a visit to the United States in 1824; and, having touched at several of the West India islands, he again went on to Demerara, returning to England at the end of the year. In 1828 he published the results of his four journeys, under the title of *Wanderings in South America*, —consisting largely of a collection of observations on the appearance, character, and habits of many of the animals to be found in British Guiana. Waterton was a keen and accurate observer, and his descriptions are of a graphic and humorous character, rarely to be found in works on natural history. He married in 1829, and from that time lived mostly at Walton Hall, devoting himself to the improvement of his estate, to country pursuits, and to natural history observations. Waterton also published three series of essays on various subjects connected with natural history. He died May 27, 1865, from the result of an accident.

WATERTOWN, a city of the United States, the county seat of Jefferson county, New York, is situated upon both sides of Black River, 7 miles above its mouth, and is 140 miles north-west of Albany. It is laid out rather irregularly, with 60 miles of streets, is supplied with water by pumping, water-power being used, and is well sewered. The population in 1880 was 10,697, including 2444 of foreign birth. The river at this point is 60 yards wide. It falls 112 feet in two miles, and flows through the city in a succession of rapids, furnishing a magnificent water-power to the numerous paper, woollen, and cotton mills and machine shops which line its banks.

The first settlement was made in 1800, and the town had a rapid growth from the start. The city was chartered in 1869.

WATERTOWN, a city in Jefferson and Dodge counties, Wisconsin, United States, is situated upon both sides of Rock river, in a rich farming region. Its population in 1880 was 7883, 3072 of them of foreign birth. The river furnishes a valuable water-power for extensive manufactures. Watertown contains the North-Western University, a Lutheran institution, and a Roman Catholic seminary. About two-thirds of the present population are Germans or their direct descendants.

WATERWORKS. See WATER-SUPPLY.

WATFORD, an ancient market town of Herts, is situated on a ridge of gravel overlooking the river Colne, on the Grand Junction Canal and on the London and North-Western Railway, branches of which here diverge to St Albans and to Rickmansworth, 8 miles south-west of St Albans and 17¾ north-west of London by rail, the distance by road from Charing Cross being 15 miles. It consists chiefly of one spacious street, about 1½ mile in length, running north-westwards from the river. A bridge connects it with Bushey on the south side of the river, a suburb chiefly of villas. The church, dedicated to St Mary, with embattled tower, and spire 100 feet high, was restored in 1871 at a cost of £11,000. The other principal public buildings are the masonic hall (1873), the public library and school of art, a building of brick in the Gothic style, erected in 1873–74 at the cost of £3400, the county court and sessions-house, the agricultural hall, and the literary institute. Among the benevolent institutions are the London Orphan Asylum, founded in 1813, rebuilt in 1870 in the Elizabethan style, and having accommodation for 600 children; the almshouses of the Salters Company, London, and the almshouses erected in 1876 by the countess of Essex for superannuated servants. There is a cemetery of 14 acres laid out in 1858. For the water-supply of the town a reservoir capable of containing one million gallons has lately been constructed. The town possesses corn-mills, breweries, malt-kilns, and an iron foundry. The population of the urban sanitary district (area 530 acres) in 1871 was 7461, and in 1881 it was 10,073. In 1882 the area of the urban sanitary district was extended to 871 acres; the population of that area in 1881 was 12,162.

Watford is not mentioned in Domesday, being then included in the manor of Cashio, belonging to the abbey of St Albans. The town received the grant of a market from Henry I. When the abbey of St Albans was dissolved in 1549, Watford fell to the crown. In 1609 it came into the possession of Thomas Marbury, and it has belonged to the earls of Essex since 1767.

WATSON, RICHARD (1737–1816), bishop of Llandaff, was born in August 1737 at Heversham, in Westmorland, and was the son of the master of the grammar school of that place. He was entirely educated by his father, who sent him in 1754 to Trinity College, Cambridge, with "a considerable stock of classical learning, a spirit of persevering industry, and an obstinate provincial accent." He was elected a fellow of Trinity in 1760, and about the same time had the offer of the post of chaplain to the factory at Bencoolen. "You are too good," said the master of Trinity, "to die of drinking punch in the torrid zone," and Watson, instead of becoming, as he had flattered himself, a great Orientalist, remained at home to be elected professor of chemistry, a science of which he did not at the time possess the simplest rudiments. "I buried myself," he says, "in my laboratory, and in fourteen months read a course of chemical lectures to a very full audience." Not the least of his services was to procure an endowment for the chair, which served as a precedent in similar instances.

In 1771 he became a candidate for the regius professorship of divinity, and at the age of thirty-four gained what he calls "the first place for honour in the university," "and," he adds, "exclusive of the mastership of Trinity College, I have made it the first for profit. I found it not worth £330 a year; it is now (1814) worth £1000 at the least." He did not entirely renounce the study of chemistry: in 1768 he had published *Institutiones Metallurgicæ*, intended to give a scientific form to chemistry by digesting facts established by experiment into a connected series of propositions. In 1781 he followed this up with a volume of *Chemical Essays*, which Davy told De Quincey remained as late as 1813, after all recent discoveries, unsurpassed as a manual of introductory discipline. But on the day on which he composed his preface he burned all his chemical manuscripts, and never returned to the subject. His course as professor of divinity was no less decisive. "I reduced the study of divinity into as narrow a compass as I could, for I determined to study nothing but my Bible." He produced several anonymous pamphlets on the liberal side in the subscription controversy and other topics of the day, and some sermons, one of which was thought likely to have involved him in a prosecution, but which, Dunning said, contained "just such treason as ought to be preached once a month at St James's." It is said to have prevented his obtaining the provostship of Trinity College, Dublin. In 1776 he answered Gibbon's chapters on Christianity, and had the honour of being one of the only two opponents whom Gibbon treated with respect. In 1781 he was prostrated with a malignant fever, from the effects of which he never wholly recovered, and which served as an excuse for that neglect of many duties which remains the chief stain upon his character. He had always opposed the American War, and when the accession of Lord Shelburne to power in 1782 afforded the then unfrequent opportunity of advancing a Liberal in politics and religion to a bishopric, Watson was made bishop of Llandaff, being permitted to retain his other preferments on account of the poverty of the see. Shelburne, he says, expected great service from him as a pamphleteer, but Watson proved from the ministerial point of view a most impracticable prelate. He immediately brought forward a scheme for improving the condition of the poorer clergy by equalizing the incomes of the bishops, the reception of which at the time may be imagined, though it was substantially the same as that carried into effect by Lord Melbourne's Government fifty years later. Watson now found that he possessed no influence with the minister, and that he had destroyed his chance of the great object of his ambition, promotion to a better diocese. Neglecting both his see and his professorship, to which latter he appointed a deputy described as highly incompetent, he withdrew to Calgarth Park, in his native county, where he occupied himself largely in forming plantations and the improvement of agriculture. He nevertheless frequently came forward as a preacher and a speaker in the House of Lords, but his only very conspicuous appearance before the public was his warm support of the prince of Wales's unqualified claim to the regency on the insanity of the king in 1788, which completed his disgrace at court. In 1796 he published his *Apology for the Bible*, in answer to Thomas Paine, at present the best known of his numerous writings. It was most effective in its day; in ours Christianity would hardly be attacked or defended by the arms employed by either disputant. Undismayed by the displeasure of the court, or perhaps hoping to overcome it, Watson continued to exert his pen with vigour, and in general to good purpose, denouncing the slave trade, advocating the union with Ireland, and offering financial suggestions to Pitt, who seems to have frequently consulted him. In 1798 his *Address to the People of Great Britain*, enforcing resistance to French arms and French principles, ran through fourteen editions, but estranged him from many old friends, who accused him, probably with injustice, of aiming to make his peace with the Government. In 1807 the advent of a Whig ministry almost brought the coveted preferment within reach. Had Dr Markham died a few months sooner Watson would have been archbishop of York. Such a disappointment might palliate the querulous strain of his conversation and published references to himself, though it could not render it dignified or decorous. De Quincey, however, who knew the bishop personally in his latter years, while severely criticizing his complaints, allows that his temper had not been soured by disappointment. "His lordship was a joyous, jovial, and cordial host." He died on July 2, 1816, having occupied his latter years in the composition and revision of an autobiography, which, with all its egotism and partiality, is a valuable work, and the chief authority for his life.

As an advocate of liberal principles in church and state, Watson stands almost alone among the prelates of his day; and it cannot be said that his longing for preferment, violent and unbecoming as it was, seduced him into mean actions or unworthy compliances. His character is high enough to make it cause for regret that it should stand no higher, as it easily might if he had possessed a nicer sense of dignity and had not measured success so exclusively by the attainment of wealth and station. Hard-headed and pushing, he yet had an intellectual conscience; the two main elements of his character stood in each other's way: he failed as a courtier, and did not leave a wholly unblemished reputation as a patriot. As a bishop he neither was nor endeavoured to be anything; as an ecclesiastical statesman it was his misfortune to have been born fifty years too soon. His massive but unoriginal intellect is justly characterized by De Quincey as "robust and commonplace." (R. G.)

WATT, James (1736–1819), the inventor of the modern condensing steam-engine, was born at Greenock on the 19th of January 1736. His father was a small merchant there, who lost his trade and fortune by unsuccessful speculation, and James was early thrown on his own resources. Having a taste for mechanics he made his way to London, at the age of nineteen, to learn the business of a philosophical-instrument maker, and became apprenticed to one Morgan, in whose service he remained for twelve months. From a child he had been extremely delicate, and the hard work and frugal living of his London pupilage taxed his strength so severely that he was forced at the end of a year to seek rest at home, not, however, until he had gained a fair knowledge of the trade and become handy in the use of tools. Before going to London he had made acquaintance with some of the professors in Glasgow college, and on his return to Scotland in 1756 he sought them out and obtained work in repairing astronomical instruments. He next tried to establish himself as an instrument maker in Glasgow, but the city guilds would not recognize a craftsman who had not served the full term of common apprenticeship, and Watt was forbidden to open shop in the burgh. The college, however, took him under its protection, and in 1757 he was established in its precincts with the title of mathematical-instrument maker to the university.

Before many months Black, the discoverer of latent heat, then lecturer on chemistry, and Robison, then a student, afterwards professor of natural philosophy, became his intimate friends, and with them he often discussed the possibility of improving the steam-engine, of which at that time Newcomen's was the most advanced type. The engine was then applied only to pumping water,—chiefly in the drainage of mines; and it was so clumsy and wasteful of fuel as to be but little used. Some early experiments of Watt in 1761 or 1762 led to no positive result, but in 1764 his attention was seriously drawn to the matter by having a model of Newcomen's engine, which formed part of the college collection of scientific apparatus, given him to repair. Having put the model in order, he was at once struck with its enormous consumption of steam, and set himself to examine the cause of this and to find a remedy.

In Newcomen's engine the cylinder stood vertically under one end of the main lever or "beam" and was open at the top. Steam, at a pressure scarcely greater than that of the atmosphere, was admitted to the under side; this allowed the piston to be pulled up by a counterpoise at the other end of the beam. Communication with the boiler was then shut off, and the steam in the cylinder was condensed by injecting a jet of cold water from a cistern above. The pressure of the air on the top of the piston then drove it down, raising the counterpoise and doing work. The injection water and condensed steam which had gathered in the cylinder were drained out by a pipe leading down into a well.

Watt at once noticed that the alternate heating and cooling of the cylinder in Newcomen's engine made it work with tedious slowness and excessive consumption of steam. When steam was admitted at the beginning of each stroke, it found the metal of the cylinder and piston chilled by contact with the condensed steam and cold injection water of the previous stroke, and it was not until much steam had been condensed in heating the chilled surfaces that the cylinder was able to fill and the piston to rise. His first attempt at a remedy was to use for the material of the cylinder a substance that would take in and give out heat slowly. Wood was tried, but it made matters only a little better, and did not promise to be durable. Watt observed that the evil was intensified whenever, for the sake of making a good vacuum under the piston, a specially large quantity of injection water was supplied.

He then entered on a scientific examination of the properties of steam, studying by experiment the relation of its density and pressure to the temperature, and concluded that two conditions were essential to the economic use of steam in a condensing steam-engine. One was that the temperature of the condensed steam should be as low as possible, 100° F. or lower, otherwise the vacuum would not be good; the other was, to quote his own words, "that the cylinder should be always as hot as the steam which entered it." In Newcomen's engine these two conditions were incompatible, and it was not for some months that Watt saw a means of reconciling them. Early in 1765, while walking on a Sunday afternoon in Glasgow Green, the idea flashed upon him that, if the steam were condensed in a vessel distinct from the cylinder, it would be practicable to make the temperature of condensation low, and still keep the cylinder hot. Let this separate vessel be kept cold, either by injecting cold water or by letting it stream over the outside, and let a vacuum be maintained in the vessel. Then, whenever communication was made between it and the cylinder, steam would pass over from the cylinder and be condensed; the pressure in the cylinder would be as low as the pressure in the condenser, but the temperature of the metal of the cylinder would remain high, since no injection water need touch it. Without delay Watt put this idea to the test, and found that the separate condenser did act as he had anticipated. To maintain the vacuum in it he added another new organ, namely, the air-pump, the function of which is to remove the condensed steam and water of injection along with any air that gathers in the condenser.

To further his object of keeping the cylinder as hot as the steam that entered it, Watt supplemented his great invention of the separate condenser by several less notable but still important improvements. In Newcomen's engine a layer of water over the piston had been used to keep it steam-tight; Watt substituted a tighter packing lubricated by oil. In Newcomen's engine the upper end of the cylinder was open to the air; Watt covered it in, leading the piston rod through a steam-tight stuffing-box in the cover, and allowed steam instead of air to press on the top of the piston. In Newcomen's engine the cylinder had no clothing to reduce loss of heat by radiation and conduction from its outer surface; Watt not only cased it in non-conducting material, such as wood, but introduced a steam-jacket, or layer of steam, between the cylinder proper and an outer shell. All these features were specified in his first patent, in words which have been quoted in the article STEAM-ENGINE, vol. xxii. p. 475 (*q.v.*).

This patent was not obtained till January 1769, nearly four years after the inventions it covers had been made. In the interval Watt had been striving to demonstrate the merits of his engine by trial on a large scale. His earliest experiments left him in debt, and, finding that his own means were quite insufficient to allow him to continue them, he agreed that Dr Roebuck, founder of the Carron iron-works, should take two-thirds of the profits of the invention in consideration of his bearing the cost. An engine was then erected at Kinneil, near Linlithgow, where Roebuck lived, and this gave Watt the opportunity of facing many difficulties in details of construction. But the experiments made slow progress, for Roebuck's affairs became embarrassed, and Watt's attention was engaged by other work. He had taken to surveying, and was fast gaining reputation as a civil engineer. In 1767 he was employed to make a survey for a Forth and Clyde canal, —a scheme which failed to secure parliamentary sanction. This was followed during the next six years by surveys for a canal at Monkland, for another through the valley of Strathmore from Perth to Forfar, and for others along the lines afterwards followed by the Crinan and Caledonian Canals. He prepared plans for the harbours of Ayr, Port-Glasgow, and Greenock, for deepening the Clyde, and for building a bridge over it at Hamilton. In the course of this work he invented a simple micrometer for measuring distances, consisting of a pair of horizontal hairs placed in the focus of a telescope, through which sights were taken to a fixed and movable target on a rod held upright at the place whose distance from the observer was to be determined. The micrometer was varied in a number of ways; and another fruit of his ingenuity about the same time was a machine to facilitate drawing in perspective.

Meanwhile the engine had not been wholly neglected. Watt had secured his patent; the Kinneil trials had given him a store of valuable experience; Roebuck had failed, but another partner was ready to take his place. In 1768 Watt had made the acquaintance, through his friend Dr Small, of Matthew Boulton, a man of energy and capital, who owned the Soho engineering works at Birmingham. Boulton agreed to buy Roebuck's share in the invention, and to join Watt in applying to parliament for an Act to prolong the term of the patent. The application was successful. In 1775 an Act was passed continuing the patent for twenty-five years. By this time the inventor had abandoned his civil engineering work and had settled in Birmingham, where the manufacture of steam-engines was begun by the firm of Boulton and Watt. The partnership was a singularly happy one. Boulton had the good sense to leave the work of inventing to Watt, in whose genius he had the fullest faith; on the other hand, his substantial means, his enterprise, resolution, and business capacity, supplied what was wanting to bring the invention to commercial success.

During the next ten years we find Watt assiduously engaged in developing and introducing the engine. Its first and for a time its only application was in pumping; it was at once put to this use in the mines of Cornwall, where Watt was now frequently engaged in superintending the erection of engines. Further inventions were required to fit it for other uses, and these followed in quick succession. Watt's second steam-engine patent is dated 1781. It describes five different methods of converting the reciprocating motion of the piston into motion of rotation, so as to adapt the engine for driving ordinary machinery. The simplest way of doing this, and the means now universally followed, is by a crank and fly-wheel; this had occurred to Watt but had meanwhile been patented by another, and hence he devised the "sun and planet wheels" and other equivalent contrivances. A third patent, in 1782, contained two new inventions of the first importance. Up to this time the engine had been single-acting; Watt now made it double-acting; that is to say, both ends of the cylinder, instead of only one, were alternately put in communication with the boiler and the condenser. Up to this time also the steam had been admitted from the boiler throughout the whole stroke of the piston; Watt now introduced the system of expansive working, in which the admission valve is closed after a portion only of the stroke is performed, and the steam enclosed in the cylinder is then allowed to expand during the remainder of the stroke, doing additional work upon the piston without making any further demand upon the boiler until the next stroke requires a fresh admission of steam. He calculated that, as the piston advanced after admission had ceased, the pressure of the steam in the cylinder would fall in the same proportion as its volume increased,—a law which, although not strictly true, does accord very closely with the actual behaviour of steam expanding in the cylinder of an engine. Recognizing that this would cause a gradual reduction of the force with which the piston pulled or pushed against the beam, Watt devised a number of contrivances for equalizing the effort throughout the stroke. He found, however, that the inertia of the pump-rods in his mine engines, and the fly-wheel in his rotative engines, served to compensate for the inequality of thrust sufficiently to make these contrivances unnecessary. His fourth patent, taken out in 1784, describes the well-known "parallel motion," an arrangement of links by which the top of the piston-rod is connected to the beam so that it may either pull or push, and is at the same time guided to move in a sensibly straight line. "I have started a new hare," he writes to Boulton in June of that year; "I have got a glimpse of a method of causing a piston-rod to move up and down perpendicularly by only fixing it to a piece of iron upon the beam, without chains or perpendicular guides or untowardly frictions, arch-heads, or other pieces of clumsiness. I think it a very probable thing to succeed, and one of the most ingenious simple pieces of mechanism I have contrived."

Still a later invention was the throttle-valve and centrifugal governor, by which the speed of rotative engines was automatically controlled. One more item in the list of Watt's contributions to the development of the steam-engine is too important to be passed without mention: the indicator, which draws a diagram of the relation of the steam's pressure to its volume as the stroke proceeds, was first used by Boulton and Watt to measure the work done by their engines, and so to give a basis on which the charges levied from their customers were adjusted. It would be difficult to exaggerate the part which this simple little instrument has played in the evolution of the steam-engine. The eminently philosophic notion of an indicator diagram is fundamental in the theory of thermodynamics; the instrument itself is to the steam-engineer what the stethoscope is to the physician, and more, for with it he not only diagnoses the ailments of a faulty machine, whether in one or another of its organs, but gauges its power in health.

The commercial success of the engine was not long in being established. By 1783 all but one of the Newcomen pumping-engines in Cornwall had been displaced by Watt's. The mines were then far from thriving; many were even on the point of being abandoned through the difficulty of dealing with large volumes of water; and Watt's invention, which allowed this to be done at a moderate cost, meant for many of them a new lease of life. His engine used no more than a fourth of the fuel that had formerly been needed to do the same work, and the Soho firm usually claimed by way of royalty a sum equivalent to one-third of the saving—a sum which must have been nearly equal to the cost of the fuel actually consumed. Rival manufacturers came forward, amongst whom Bull and Hornblower are the most conspicuous names. They varied the form of the engine, but they could not avoid infringing Watt's patent by the use of a separate condenser. When action was taken against them on that ground, they retaliated by disputing the validity of the fundamental patent of 1769. In the case of Boulton and Watt *v.* Bull the court was divided on this point, but in an action against Hornblower the patent was definitely affirmed to be valid by a unanimous finding of the Court of King's Bench. This was in 1799, only a year before the monopoly expired, but the decision enabled the firm to claim a large sum as arrears of patent dues. In connexion with these trials Watt himself, as well as his early friends Black and Robison, drew up narratives of the invention of the steam-engine, which are of much interest to the student of its history.[1]

Before Watt's time the steam-engine was exclusively a steam-pump, slow-working, cumbrous, and excessively wasteful of fuel. His first patent made it quick in working, powerful, and efficient, but still only as a steam-pump. His later inventions adapted it to drive machinery of all kinds, and left it virtually what it is to-day, save in three respects. In respect of mechanical arrangement the modern engine differs from Watt's chiefly in this, that the beam, an indispensable feature in the early pumping-engines, and one which held its place long after the need for it had vanished, has gradually given way to more direct modes of connecting the piston with the crank. Another difference is in the modern use of high-pressure steam. It is remarkable that Watt, notwithstanding the fact that his own invention of expansive working must have opened his eyes to the advantage of high-pressure steam, declined to admit it into his practice. He persisted in the use of pressures that were little if at all above that of the atmosphere. His rivals in Cornwall were not so squeamish. Trevithick ventured as far as 120 ℔ on the square inch, and a curious episode in the history of the steam-engine is an attempt which Boulton and Watt made to have an Act of Parliament passed forbidding the use of high pressure on the ground that the lives of the public were endangered. The third and only other respect in which a great improvement has been effected is in the introduction of compound expansion. Here, too, one cannot but regret to find the Soho firm hostile, though the necessity of defending their monopoly makes their action natural enough. Hornblower had in fact stumbled on the invention of the compound engine, but as his machine employed Watt's condenser it was suppressed, to be revived after some years by Woolf. In one of his patents (1784) Watt describes a steam-locomotive, but he never prosecuted this, and when Murdoch, his chief assistant (famous as the inventor of gas-lighting), made experiments on the same lines, Watt gave him little encouragement. The notion then was to use a steam-carriage on ordinary roads; its use on railways had not yet been thought of. When that idea took form later in the last years of Watt's life, the old man refused to smile upon his offspring; it is even said that Watt put a clause in the lease of his house that no steam-carriage should on any pretext be allowed to approach it.

On the expiry in 1800 of the Act by which the patent of 1769 had been extended, Watt gave up his share in the business of engine-building to his sons, James, who carried it on along with a son of Boulton for many years, and Gregory, who died in 1804. The remainder of his life was quietly spent at Heathfield Hall,[2] his house near Birmingham, where he devoted his time, with scarcely an interruption, to mechanical pursuits. His last work was the invention of machines for copying sculpture,—one for making reduced copies, another for taking facsimiles by means of a light stiff frame, which carried a pointer over the surface of the work while a revolving tool fixed to the frame alongside of the pointer cut a corresponding surface on a suitable block. We find him in correspondence with Chantrey about this machine not many months before his death, and presenting copies of busts to his friends as the work "of a young artist just entering on his eighty-third year." His life drew to a tranquil close, and the end came at Heathfield on the 19th of August 1819. His remains were interred in the neighbouring parish church of Handsworth.

Watt was twice married,—first in 1763 to his cousin Miss Miller, who died ten years later. Of four children born of the marriage, two died in infancy; another was James, who succeeded his father in business; the fourth was a daughter who lived to maturity, but died early, leaving two children. His second wife, Miss Macgregor, whom he married before settling in Birmingham in 1775, survived him; but her two children, Gregory and a daughter, died young.

Some of Watt's minor inventions have been already noticed. Another, which has proved of great practical value, was the letter-copying press, for copying manuscript by using a glutinous ink and pressing the written page against a moistened sheet of thin paper. He patented this in 1780, describing both a roller press, the use of which he seems to have preferred in copying his own correspondence, and also the form of screw press now found in every merchant's office.

In the domain of pure science Watt claims recognition not only as having had ideas greatly in advance of his age regarding what is now called energy, but as a discoverer of the composition of water. Writing to Priestley in April 1783, with reference to some of Priestley's experiments, he suggests the theory that "water is composed of dephlogisticated air and phlogiston deprived of part of their latent or elementary heat." It is difficult to determine the exact meaning attached to these antiquated terms, and to say how far Watt's suggestion anticipated the fuller discovery of Cavendish. Watt's views were communicated to the Royal Society in 1783, Cavendish's experiments in 1784, and both are printed in the same volume of the *Philosophical Transactions.*

The early and middle part of Watt's life was a long struggle with poor health: severe headache prostrated him for days at a time; but as he grew old his constitution seems to have become more robust. His disposition was despondent and shrinking; he speaks of himself, but evidently with unfair severity, as "indolent to excess." "I am not enterprising," he writes; "I would rather face a loaded cannon than settle an account or make a bargain; in short, I find myself out of my sphere when I have anything to do with mankind." He was a man of warm friendships, and has left a personal memorial of the greatest interest in his numerous letters to Dr Small and others. They are full of sagacity and insight: his own achievements are told with a shrewd but extremely modest estimate of their value, and in a style of remarkable terseness and lucidity, lightened here and there by a touch of dry humour. In his old age Watt is described by his contemporaries as a man richly stored with the most various knowledge, full of anecdote, familiar with most modern languages and their literature, a great talker. Scott speaks of "the alert, kind, benevolent old man, his talents and fancy overflowing on every subject, with his attention alive to every one's question, his information at every one's command."

See J. P. Muirhead, *Origin and Progress of the Mechanical Inventions of James Watt*, 3 vols., 1854 (vols. i. and ii. contain a memoir and Watt's letters; vol. iii. gives a reprint of his patent specifications and other papers); Muirhead, *Life of Watt*, 1858; Smiles, *Lives of Boulton and Watt*; Williamson, *Memorials of the Lineage, &c., of James Watt*, published by the Watt Club, Greenock, 1856; *Correspondence of the late James Watt on his Discovery of the Theory of the Composition of Water*, edited by Muirhead, 1846; Cowper, "On the Inventions of James Watt and his Models preserved at Handsworth and South Kensington," *Proc. Inst. Mech. Eng.*, 1883; article "Watt" in the *Encyclopædia Britannica*, 6th edition (1823), by James Watt, junior; Robison, *Mechanical Philosophy*, vol. ii., 1822 (letters and notes by Watt on the History of the Steam-Engine). (J. A. E.)

WATTEAU, Antoine (1684–1721), French painter, was born at Valenciennes in 1684. Thrown on his own resources at an early age, the boy went moneyless and

[1] Another narrative of the utmost interest was written by Watt in 1814 in the form of a footnote to Robison's article "Steam-Engine," from the fourth edition of the *Encyclopædia Britannica*, which Watt revised before it was reprinted in the collected edition of Robison's works. See Robison's *Mechanical Philosophy*, vol. ii.

[2] His workroom at Heathfield (now in the possession of Mr Tangye) has been preserved full of his tools and models of his inventions. These are described, along with other Watt relics now at South Kensington, in an interesting paper by Mr E. A. Cowper, *Proc. Inst. Mech. Eng.*, Nov. 1883.

ragged alone to Paris. There, after a hard struggle, he succeeded in getting work with a painter of saints for country customers, who assigned to Watteau, the future limner of gallant feastings, the repetition of dozens of St Nicholas. The saint brought him food and shelter, and in his few holidays Watteau sketched and drew. From this shop he passed to the studio of Gillot, whose influence helped him to follow the true direction of his own special gifts, but he left him, finding employment with Audran the decorator, then at work in the Luxembourg. Then Watteau quarrelled with Audran and went his way, fancying that Audran had blamed his first picture, the Departing Regiment, out of jealousy; and, flushed with success (for he had sold the work), he went off to show himself in his native Valenciennes. There Watteau produced a second work, a Regiment Halting, which also sold in Paris, so thither he returned, and, welcomed by the celebrated Crozat, received fresh inspiration from his taste and the study of his immense collections. In 1709 he competed for the great prize, and, standing only second, applied for a crown pension to enable him to go to Italy. As proofs of his deserts, he carried to the Academy his first two pictures. His cause was warmly espoused by De la Fosse, and he was instantly made an associate of that body, becoming a full member in 1717. His diploma picture, Embarkation for the Isle of Venus, is now in the Louvre. Suffering always from lung disease, and of a highly nervous temperament, Watteau was, however, unfitted to live and work with others, and, in spite of his professional success and his assured reputation, he held himself apart, ill at ease with himself and seldom happy in his work, which suffered in sympathy with his changing moods. A visit to London further disturbed his health, and in 1721 he returned to Paris, establishing himself for a while in the house of his friend Gersaint, the picture dealer, for whom he painted a sign-board which had an extraordinary success (a fragment in the collection Schwitzer). Hoping to find rest and some alleviation to his increasing sufferings from country air, he accepted a lodging at Nogent, in the house of M. Lefebvre, which had been obtained for him through his constant friend the abbé Haranger, canon of St Germain l'Auxerrois. At Nogent, shortly after his arrival, on 18th July 1821, Watteau died, having bequeathed to the abbé, to Gersaint, to M. Henin, and to M. Julienne the vast quantity of drawings which constituted almost the whole of his fortune.

No greater contrast can be found than that which Watteau's work presents to the painful condition under which he lived his life, a contrast such as that which the boyish glee of Caldecott's designs showed in comparison to the physical misery against which his gallant spirit made so brave a stand. Watteau sought refuge, as it were, from his bodily pain in that fairyland which he created, where the pompous art of the "Grand Siècle" still cumbered the ground. His work, always conceived in a poetical spirit, lived in spite of the artificial atmosphere of the mock pastoral style of the day, and lives in virtue of the exquisite precision of his observation and of the extraordinary brilliancy and lightness of his art.

WATTS, Isaac (1674–1748), theologian and hymn writer, was born at Southampton 17th July 1674. He was the eldest of nine children, and was named after his father, who kept a boarding establishment at Southampton. The father also wrote poetry, and a number of his pieces were included by mistake in vol. i. of the son's *Posthumous Works*. Young Watts is stated to have entered on the study of the classics when only in his fifth year, and at the age of seven or eight to have composed some devotional pieces to please his mother. His nonconformity precluded him from entering either of the universities, but in his sixteenth year he went to study at an academy in London kept by the Rev. Thomas Rowe, minister of the Independent meeting at Haberdashers' Hall. In his *Improvement of the Mind* (1741) Watts has expounded his method of study, but the precepts there laid down can hardly be said to be justified by his example, for it is overwork at this period of his life that is believed to have caused the weak and uncertain health of his subsequent years. Probably it was as much from this cause as from diffidence that he deferred preaching his first sermon till the day he entered on his twenty-fourth year. Meantime he resided as tutor in the family of Sir John Hartopp at Stoke Newington, where he probably prepared the materials of his two educational works,—*Logick, or the Right Use of Reason in the Enquiry after Truth* (1725), and *The Knowledge of the Heavens and the Earth Made Easy, or the First Principles of Geography and Astronomy Explained* (1726). His *Logic*, Dr Samuel Johnson states, "had been received into the universities," but this must be regarded rather as an indication of the decadence of logical studies there than a proof of the special excellence of the work. What merits it possesses are of a hortatory and moral kind, and, as Sir William Hamilton says, it is "not worth reading as a book of logic." In his twenty-fourth year Watts was chosen assistant to Dr Chauncy, pastor of the Independent congregation, Mark Lane, London, and two years later he succeeded as sole pastor. The state of his health led to the appointment of an assistant in 1703. In 1704 the congregation removed to Pinner's Hall, and in 1708 they built a new meeting-house in Bury Street. In 1712 Watts took up his residence with Sir Thomas Abney of Abney Park, where he spent the remainder of his life, the arrangement being continued by Lady Abney after her husband's death. Watts preached only occasionally, devoting his leisure chiefly to the writing of hymns, the preparation of his sermons for publication, and the composition of theological works. Being little over 5 feet in height, and far from robust in health, he did not specially excel as an orator, although the felicity of his illustrations, his transparent sincerity, and his benevolent wisdom gave to his preaching an exceptional charm. His religious opinions were more liberal in tone than was at that time common in the community to which he belonged; his views regarding Sunday recreation and labour were scarcely of Puritanical strictness; his Calvinism was modified by his rejection of the doctrine of reprobation, and he was in the habit of representing the heaven of the Christian as affording wide scope for the exercise of the special habits and tastes formed by the employments of earth. For an estimate of Watts as a hymn writer, see Hymns, vol. xii. p. 593. He died 25th November 1748, and was buried at Bunhill Fields, where a tombstone was erected to his memory by Sir John Hartopp and Lady Abney. A memorial was also erected to him in Westminster Abbey, and a memorial hall, erected in his honour at Southampton, was opened 6th May 1875.

In 1706 appeared his *Horæ Lyricæ*, of which an edition, with memoir by Robert Southey, forms vol. ix. of *Sacred Classics* (1834); in 1707 a volume of *Hymns*; in 1719 *The Psalms of David*; and in 1720 *Divine and Moral Songs for Children*. Various collected editions of his sacred poetry have been published, and in 1869 an edition appeared with music for four voices. Among the theological treatises of Watts, in addition to volumes of sermons, are *Doctrine of the Trinity* (1726); *Treatise on the Love of God and on the Use and Abuse of the Passions* (1729); *Catechisms for Children and Youth* (1730); *Essays towards a Proof of a Separate State for Souls* (1732); *Essay on the Freedom of the Will* (1732); *Essay on the Strength and Weakness of Human Reason* (1737); *Essay on the Ruin and Recovery of Mankind* (1740); *Glory of Christ as God-Man Unveiled* (1746); and *Useful and Important Questions concerning Jesus Christ* (1746). He was also the author of a variety of miscellaneous treatises. His *Posthumous Works* appeared in 1773, and a further instalment of them in 1779. Several editions of his collected works, with memoirs, have also been published.

The *Life and Times* of Watts by Milner appeared in 1834; a life is also included in Johnson's *Lives of the Poets*.

WAVE. By this term is commonly understood a state of disturbance which is propagated from one part of a medium to another. Thus it is energy which passes, and not matter,—though in some cases the wave permanently displaces, usually to a small amount only, the medium through which it has passed. Currents, on the other hand, imply the passage of matter associated with energy.

The subject is one which, except in a few very simple or very special cases, has as yet been treated only by approximation even when the most formidable processes of modern mathematics have been employed,—so that this sketch, in which it is desired that as little as possible of higher mathematics should be employed, must be confined mainly to the statement of results. And the effects of viscosity, though very important, cannot be treated.

There are few branches of physics which do not present us with some forms of wave, so that the subject is a very extensive one:—tides, rollers, ripples, bores, breakers, sounds, radiations (whether luminous or obscure), telegraphic and telephonic signalling, earthquakes, the propagation of changes of surface-temperature into the earth's crust—all are forms of wave-motion. Several of these phenomena have been treated in other parts of this work, and will now be but briefly referred to; others require more detailed notice.

When a medium is in stable equilibrium, it has no kinetic energy, and its potential energy is a minimum. Any local disturbance, therefore, in general involves a communication of energy to part of the medium, and it is usually by some form of wave-motion that this energy spreads to other parts of the medium. The mere withdrawal of a quantity of matter (as by lifting a floating body out of still water), local condensation of vapour in the air, the crushing of a hollow shell by external pressure, the change of volume resulting from an explosion, or from the sudden vaporization of a liquid—are known to all as common sources of violent wave-disturbance.

Waves may be *free* or *forced*. In the former class the disturbance is produced once for all, and is then propagated according to the nature of the medium and the form of the disturbance. Or the disturbance may be continued, provided the waves travel faster than does the centre of disturbance. In forced waves, on the other hand, the disturbing force continues to act so as to modify the propagation of the waves already produced. Thus, while a gale is blowing, the character of the water-waves is continually being modified; when it subsides, we have regular oscillatory waves, or rollers, for the longer ones not only outstrip the shorter but are less speedily worn down by fluid friction. The huge mass of water which some steamers raise, especially when running at a high speed, is an excellent example of a forced wave. The ocean-tide is mainly a forced wave, depending on the continued action of the moon and sun; but the tide-wave in an estuary or a tidal river is practically free,—being almost independent of moon and sun, and depending mainly upon the configuration of the channel, the rate of the current, and the tidal disturbance at the mouth.

In what follows we commence with a special case of extreme simplicity, where an *exact* solution is possible. This will be treated fully, partly on account of its own interest, partly because its results will be of material assistance in some of the less simple, and sometimes apparently quite different, cases which will afterwards come up for consideration.

(1) *Transverse Waves on a Stretched Wire.*—In the article MECHANICS, § 265, it has been proved by the most elementary considerations that an inextensible but flexible rope, under uniform tension, when moving at a certain definite rate through a smooth tube of any form, exerts no pressure on the interior of the tube. In fact, the rope must press with a force T/r (where T is the tension and r the radius of curvature) on the unit of length in consequence of its tension, and with a force $-\mu v^2/r$ (where v is the speed, and μ the mass of unit length) in consequence of its inertia. That there may be no pressure on the tube, *i.e.*, that it may be dispensed with, we must therefore have $T-\mu v^2=0$, or $v=\sqrt{T/\mu}$. From this it follows that a disturbance of *any* form (of course with continuous curvature) runs along a stretched rope at this definite rate, and is unchanged during its progress. In the proof, the influence of gravity was left out of consideration, and this result may therefore be applied to the motion of a transverse disturbance along a stretched wire, such as that of a pianoforte, where the tension is very great in comparison with the weight of the wire. But the italicized word *any*, above, gives an excellent example of one of the most difficult parts of the whole subject, viz., the possibility of a *solitary* wave. This is a question upon which we cannot here enter.

If we restrict ourselves to slight disturbances only, theory points out and trial verifies that they are superposable. In fact, in the great majority of investigations which have been made with regard to waves, the disturbances have been assumed to be slight, so that we can avail ourselves of the principle of *superposition of small motions* (MECHANICS, § 73), which is merely an application of the mathematical principle of "neglecting the second order of small quantities." The verification by *trial* is given at once by watching how the ring-ripples produced by two stones thrown into a pool pass through one another without any alteration; that by *observation* is evident to any one who sees an object in sunlight, when the whole intervening space is full of intense wave-motion.

Returning to our wire, let us confine ourselves to a small transverse disturbance, in one plane, and try to discover what happens when the disturbance reaches one of the fixed ends of the wire. Whether a point of the wire be fixed or not does not matter, provided it *do not move*. In the figure below, two disturbances are shown, moving in opposite directions (and of course with equal speed). Of these, either is the *perversion*, as well as the inversion, of the other. When any part of the one reaches O,

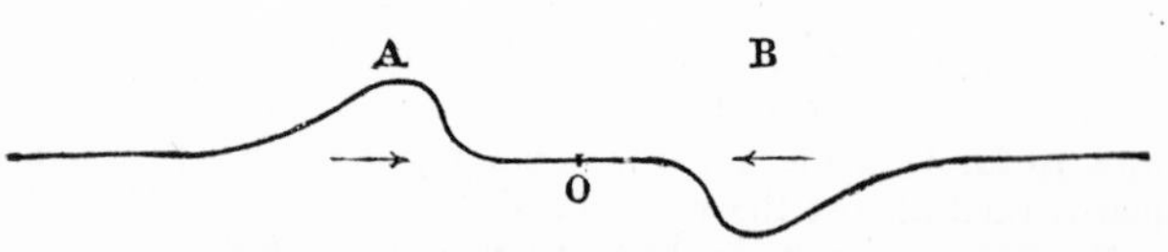

the point halfway between them, so as to displace it upwards, the other contributes an exactly equal displacement downwards. Thus O remains permanently at rest, while the two waves pass through it without affecting one another; and we may therefore assert that the wave A when it reaches the end of the wire is reflected as B, or rather that each part of A when it reaches O goes back as the corresponding part of B. B, in the same way, is seen to be reflected from O as A.

Now we can see what happens with a pianoforte wire. Any disturbance A is reflected from one end O as B, and at the other end is reflected as A again. Hence the state of the wire, whatever it may be, recurs *exactly* after such an interval as is required for the disturbance to travel, twice over, the length of the string.

Remembering that the displacements are supposed to be very small, our fundamental result may now be expressed by saying that the force acting on unit length of the disturbed wire, to restore it to its undisturbed position, is T/r or $\mu v^2/r$. Thus the *ratio of the acceleration of each element to its curvature is the square of the rate of propagation of the wave.* It will be shown below that this is the immediate interpretation of the differential equation of the wave-motion.

Let us express the position of a point of the wire, when undisturbed, by x its distance (say) from one end. Let y represent its transverse displacement at time t. Then, bearing in mind that the disturbance travels with a constant speed v, the nature of the motion, so far as we have yet limited it, will be expressed by saying that the value of y, at x, at time t, will be the value of y, at $x+v\tau$, at time $t+\tau$; or, simply,

$$y=f(vt-x).$$

For this expression, whatever be the function f, is unchanged in value, if $t+\tau$ be put for t, and $x+v\tau$ for x; and no other expression possesses this special property. If there be a disturbance running the opposite way along the wire, we easily see that it will be represented by an expression of the form

$$F(vt+x).$$

These disturbances are superposable, so that

$$y=f(vt-x)+F(vt+x) \quad . \quad . \quad . \quad . \quad . \quad . \quad (1)$$

expresses the most general state of disturbance which the wire can suffer under the limitations we have imposed. Before going farther we may use this to reproduce the results given above.

Now $x=0$ is one end of the wire, and *there* y is necessarily always zero. Hence

$$0=f(vt)+F(vt),$$

so that the functions f and F differ only in sign. This condition, inserted in (1), gives us at once the state of matters indicated by the cut above.

If $x=l$ be the other end of the wire, we have the new condition

$$0=f(vt-l)-f(vt+l).$$

The meaning of this is simply that the disturbance is periodic, the period being $2l/v$, the other result already obtained.

Fourier's theorem (see HARMONIC ANALYSIS, or MECHANICS, § 67) now shows that the expression f may be broken up into one definite series of sines and cosines, whence the usual results as to the various simple sounds which can be produced, together or separately, from a free stretched string.

It may be asked, and very naturally, How can this explanation of the nature of all possible transverse motions of a harp or pianoforte wire, as the result of sets of equal disturbances *running along it* with constant speed, be consistent with the appearance which it often presents of vibrating as a whole, or as a number of equal parts separated from one another by *nodes* which remain apparently at rest in spite of the disturbances to which, if the explanation be correct, they are constantly subjected? The answer is given at once by a consideration of the expression

$$y=\sin\frac{i\pi}{l}(vt-x)-\sin\frac{i\pi}{l}(vt+x)$$

(where i is any integer), which is a particular case of the general expression (1), limited to the circumstances of a wire of length l. This indicates, as we have seen, two exactly similar and equal sets of simple harmonic waves running simultaneously, with equal speed, in opposite directions along the wire. By elementary trigonometry we can put the expression in the form

$$y=-2\sin\frac{i\pi x}{l}\cos\frac{i\pi vt}{l}.$$

This indicates—*first*, that the points of the string where x has the values

$$0,\ l/i,\ 2l/i,\ .\ .\ .\ ,\ l$$

remain constantly at rest (these are the ends, and the $i-1$ equidistant nodes by which the wire is divided into i practically independent parts); *second*, that the form of the wire, at any instant, is a curve of sines, and that the ordinates of this curve increase and diminish simultaneously with a simple harmonic motion,—the wire resuming its undisturbed form at intervals of time l/iv.

This discussion has been entered into for the purpose of showing, from as simple a point of view as possible, the production of a *stationary* or *standing* wave. The same principle applies to more complex cases, so that we need not revert to the question.

Recurring to the general expression for y in (1), it is clear that if we differentiate it twice with respect to t, and again twice with respect to x, the results will differ only by the factor v^2 which occurs in each term of the first. Thus

$$\frac{d^2y}{dt^2}=v^2\frac{d^2y}{dx^2}=\frac{T}{\mu}\frac{d^2y}{dx^2} \quad . \quad . \quad . \quad . \quad . \quad . \quad (2)$$

is merely another way of writing (1). But in this new form it admits of the immediate interpretation given above in italics. For $\frac{d^2y}{dt^2}$ is the acceleration, and $\frac{d^2y}{dx^2}$ the curvature.

(2) *Longitudinal Waves in a Wire or Rod.*—If the displacements of the various parts of the wire be longitudinal instead of transverse, we may still suppose them to be represented graphically by the figure above—by laying off the longitudinal displacement of each point in a line through that point, in a definite plane, and perpendicular to the wire. In the figure a displacement to the right is represented by an upward line, and a displacement to the left by a downward line. The extremities of these lines will, in general, form a curve of continued curvature. And it is easy to see that the tangent of the inclination of the curve to the axis (*i.e.*, its steepness at any point) represents the elongation of unit length of the wire at that point, while the curvature measures the rate at which this elongation increases per unit of length. The force required to produce the elongation bears to the elongation itself the ratio E, viz., Young's modulus. The acceleration of unit length is the *change* of this force per unit length, divided by μ. Hence, by the italicized statement in (1), we have $v=\sqrt{E/\mu}$ (MECHANICS, § 270). All the investigations above given apply to this case also, and their interpretations, with the necessary change of a word or two, remain as before.

Thus, according to our new interpretation of the figure, the front part of A indicates a wave of compression, its hind part one of elongation, of the wire,—the displacement of every point, however, being to the right. B is an equal and similar wave, its front being also a compression, and its rear an elongation, but in it the displacement of each point of the wire is to the left.

Hence the displacements of O continually compensate one another; and thus a wave of compression is reflected from the fixed end of the wire as a wave of compression, but positive displacements are reflected as negative.

If we now consider a free rod, set into longitudinal vibration by friction, we are led to a particular case of reflection of a wave from a *free* end. The condition is obviously that, at such a point, there can be neither compression nor elongation. To represent the reflected wave we must therefore take B of such a form that each part of it, when it meets at O the corresponding part of A, shall just annul the compression. On account of the smallness of the displacements, this amounts to saying that the successive parts of B must be equally inclined to the axis with the corresponding parts of A, but *they must slope the other way.* Thus the proper figure for this case is

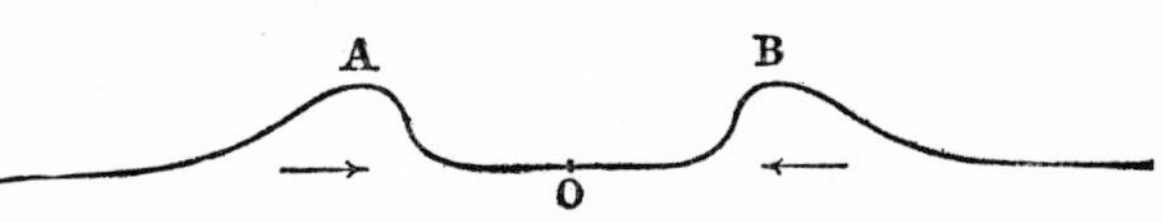

and the interpretation is that a wave of compression is reflected from a free end as an equal and similar wave of elongation; but the disturbance at each point of the wire in the reflected wave is to the same side of its equilibrium position as in the incident wave.

This enables us to understand the nature of reflexion of a wave of sound from the end of an open organ pipe, as the former illustration suited the corresponding phenomenon in a closed one.

(3) *Waves in a Linear System of Discrete Masses.*—Suppose the wire above spoken of to be massless, or at least so thin, and of such materials, that the whole mass of it may be neglected in comparison with the masses of a system of equal pellets, which we now suppose to be attached to the wire at equal distances from one another. The weights of these pellets may be supported by a set of very long vertical strings, one attached to each, so that the arrangement is unaffected by gravity. The wire may be supposed to be stretched, as before, with a definite tension which is not affected by small transverse disturbances. We will take the case of transverse disturbances only, but it is easy to see that results of precisely the same form will be obtained for longitudinal

disturbances. A moment's thought will convince the reader that there must be a limit to the frequency of the oscillations which can be transmitted along a system like this, though there was none such with the continuous wire. It is not difficult to find this limit.

Let the transverse displacement, at time t, of the nth pellet of the series, be called y_n; and let T be the tension of the wire, m the mass of a pellet, and a the distance from one pellet to the next. Then the equation of motion is obviously

$$m\frac{d^2y_n}{dt^2} = \mathrm{T}\frac{y_{n+1}-y_n}{a} - \mathrm{T}\frac{y_n-y_{n-1}}{a},$$

$$= \frac{\mathrm{T}}{a}\left(\mathrm{D}-2+\frac{1}{\mathrm{D}}\right)y_n,$$

where D stands for $\varepsilon^{a\frac{d}{dx}}$.

[We remark in passing that, if a be very small, this equation tends to become

$$m\frac{d^2y}{dt^2} = \frac{\mathrm{T}}{a}a^2\frac{d^2y}{dx^2}.$$

But in this case we have ultimately $m = a\mu$; so that we recover the equation for transverse vibrations of a uniform wire.]

Suppose

$$y_n = \mathrm{A}\cos(pt-qx)$$

(where $x = na$) to be a possible free motion of the system. When this value is substituted in the equation above it gives

$$-mp^2\cos(pt-qx) = \frac{\mathrm{T}}{a}\Big[\cos(pt-q.\overline{x+a}) + \cos(pt-q.\overline{x-a}) - 2\cos(pt-qx)\Big]$$

$$= -\frac{2\mathrm{T}}{a}\cos(pt-qx).(1-\cos qa),$$

so that

$$mp^2 = \frac{4\mathrm{T}}{a}\sin^2 qa/2.$$

It appears from the form of this expression that the greatest value of p is $2\sqrt{\mathrm{T}/am}$; or $2v/a$, if v be the speed of a disturbance in a uniform wire under the same tension, and of the same actual mass per unit of length. The time of oscillation of a pellet is $2\pi/p$, and cannot therefore be less than

$$\pi\sqrt{am/\mathrm{T}}, \text{ or } \pi a/v.$$

The result is that, if v be the speed of propagation of a disturbance in a uniform wire with the same tension and same mass, the period of the quickest simple harmonic transverse oscillation which can be freely transmitted in such a system is π times the time of running from one pellet to the next with speed v.

Instead of pellets on a tended wire, we might have a series of equal bar magnets, supported horizontally at proper distances from one another, in a line. The magnetic forces here take the place of the tension; and by arranging the magnets with their like poles together, *i.e.*, by inverting the alternate ones, we can produce the equivalent of pressure instead of tension along the series. If the magnets have each bifilar suspension, their masses will come in, as well as their moments of inertia, in the treatment of transverse disturbances.

This question is closely connected with Stokes's explanation of fluorescence (see LIGHT, vol. xiv. p. 602), for the effect of a disturbing force, of a shorter period than the limit given above, applied continuously to one of the pellets, would be to accumulate energy mainly in the immediate neighbourhood; and this, if we suppose the disturbing force to cease, would be transmitted along the system in waves of periods equal at least to the limit. These would correspond to light of lower refrangibility than the incident, but having as characteristic a definite upper limit of refrangibility.

Such investigations, with their results, prepare us to expect that the usual mode of investigating the propagation of sound, to which we proceed, cannot be correct in the case of exceedingly high notes if the medium consist of discrete particles.

(4) *Waves of Compression and Dilatation in a Fluid; Sound; Explosions.*—Consider the case of plane waves, where each layer of the medium moves perpendicularly to itself, and therefore may suffer dilatation or compression. The case is practically the same as that treated in (2) above, and can be represented by the same graphic method. For we may obviously consider only the matter contained in a *rigid* cylinder of unit sectional area, whose axis is parallel to the displacements. The only point of difference is in the law connecting pressure and consequent compression, and that, of course, depends upon the properties of the medium considered.

(*a*) If the medium be a liquid, such as water, for instance, the compression may be taken as proportional to the pressure. Thus the acceleration on unit length of the column, multiplied by its mass (which in this case is simply the density of the medium), is equal to the increase of pressure per unit length, *i.e.*, to the increase of condensation per unit length, multiplied by the resistance to compression, R. Thus the speed of the wave is $\sqrt{\mathrm{R}/\rho}$, which is exactly analogous to the forms of (1) and (2). The density, ρ, of water is 62·3 ℔ per cubic foot, and for it R is about 20,000 atmospheres at 0° C., so that the speed of sound at that temperature is about 4700 feet per second.

That even intense differences of pressure take time to adjust themselves over very short distances in water was well shown by the damage sustained by the *open* copper cases of those of the "Challenger" thermometers which were crushed by pressure in the deep sea. When a strong glass shell (containing air only) is enclosed in a stout open iron tube whose length is two or three of its diameters, and is crushed by water pressure, the tube is flattened by excess of external pressure before the relief can reach the outside.

(*b*) In the case of a gas, such as air, we must take the adiabatic relation between pressure and density. The pressure increases faster than, instead of at the same rate with, the density, as it would do if the gas followed Boyle's law. Thus the changes of pressure, instead of being equal to the changes of compression (multiplied by the modulus), exceed them in the proportion of the specific heat at constant pressure (K) to that at constant volume (N). Thus the speed of sound is $\sqrt{\mathrm{K}/\mathrm{N}.p/\rho}$, where p is the pressure and ρ the density in the undisturbed air. The ratio of the two latter quantities, as we know, is very approximately proportional to the absolute temperature.

The questions of the gradual change of type or the dying away even of plane waves of sound, whether by reason of their form, by fluid friction, or by loss of energy due to radiation, are much too complex to be treated here.

In all ordinary simple sounds even of very high pitch the displacements are extremely small compared with the wave length, so that the approximate solution gives the speed with considerable accuracy. And a very refined experimental test that this speed is independent of the pitch consists in listening to a rapid movement played by a good band at a great distance. But there seems to be little doubt that, under certain conditions at least, very loud sounds travel a great deal faster than ordinary sounds.

The above investigation gives the speed of sound relatively to the air. Relatively to the earth's surface, it has to be compounded with the motion of the air itself. But, as the speed of wind usually increases from the surface upwards, at least for a considerable height, the front of a sound-wave, moving *with* the wind, leans forward, and the sound (being propagated perpendicularly to the front) moves downwards; if *against* the wind, upwards.

In the case of a disturbance in air due to a very sudden explosion, as of dynamite or as by the passage of a flash of lightning, it is probable that for some distance from the source the motion is of a projectile character;

and that part at least of the flash is due to the heat developed by practically instantaneous and very great compression of each layer of air to which this violent motion extends.

(5) *Gravitation and Surface-Tension Waves in Liquids.*—Leaving out of consideration, as already sufficiently treated in a special article, the whole subject of TIDES, whether in oceans or in tidal rivers, there remain many different forms of water-waves all alike interesting and important. The most usual division of the free waves is into long waves, oscillatory waves, and ripples. The first two classes run by gravity, the third mainly by surface-tension (see CAPILLARY ACTION). But, while the long waves agitate the water to nearly the same amount at all depths, the chief disturbance due to oscillatory waves or to ripples is confined to the upper layers of the water, from which it dies away with great rapidity in successive layers below. We will treat of these three forms in the order named.

(6) *Long Waves.*—The first careful study of these waves was made by Scott RUSSELL (*q.v.*) in the course of an inquiry into traffic on canals. He arrived at the remarkable result that there is a definite speed, depending on the depth of the water, at which a horse can draw a canal-boat more easily than at any other speed, whether less or greater. And he pointed out that, when the boat moves at this speed, it agitates the water less, and therefore damages the banks less, than at any lower. This particular speed is thus, in fact, that of free propagation of the wave raised by the boat; and, when the boat rides, as it were, on this wave, its speed is maintained with but little exertion on the part of the horse. If the boat be made to move slower, it leaves behind it an ever-lengthening procession of waves, of course at the expense of additional labour on the part of the horse.

The theory of the motion of such a wave is based on the hypothesis that all particles in a transverse section of the canal have, at the same instant, the same horizontal speed. However great this horizontal motion may be, the vertical motion of the water may be very small, for it depends on the change of horizontal speed from section to section only. In the investigation which follows, the energy of this vertical motion will be neglected (even at the surface, where it is greatest) in comparison with that of the horizontal motion. The hypothesis is proved to be well grounded by the actual observation of the motion of the water when a long wave of slight elevation or depression passes. A long box, with parallel sides of glass, partly filled with water, represents the canal; and the wave is produced by slowly and slightly tilting the box, and at once restoring it to the horizontal position. The nature of the motion of the water is shown by particles of bran suspended in it. Such an apparatus may be usefully employed in verifying the theoretical result below, as to the connexion between the speed of the wave and the depth of the water,—observations of the passage of the crest being made with great exactness by means of a ray of light reflected from the surface of the water in a vertical plane parallel to the length of the canal. It may also be employed, by tilting it about an inclined position, for the study of the changes which take place in the wave as it passes from deeper to shallower water, or the reverse.

The statement of (1) above is immediately applicable to this question. For, if h be the (undisturbed) depth of the water, ρ its density, y and y' the elevations in two successive transverse sections at unit distance from one another, the difference of pressures (at the same level) in the two sections is $g\rho(y'-y)$. The acceleration of a horizontal cylinder of unit section is the difference of pressures divided by ρ. But the whole depth is increased at each point in proportion as the thickness of a transverse slice is diminished. Hence, by the reasoning in (2) above,

$$\frac{g\rho(y'-y)}{\rho}=\frac{p'-p}{\rho}=v^2\frac{y'-y}{h},$$

or

$$v^2=gh;$$

and the speed of propagation of the wave is that which a stone would acquire by falling through half the depth of the water. That the speed ought to be independent of the density of the liquid is clear from the fact that it is the weight of the disturbed portion which causes the motion, and that this (for equal waves in different liquids) changes proportionally to the mass to be moved.

Since we have made no hypothesis as to the form of the wave, our only assumptions being that the vertical motion is not only small in comparison with the depth, but inconsiderable in comparison with the horizontal motion, while the latter is the same at all depths in any one transverse section, it is clear that, under the same limitations, a wave of depression will run at the same speed as does a wave of elevation.

A solitary wave of elevation obviously carries across any fixed transverse plane a quantity of water equal to that which lies above the undisturbed level. If H be the mean height of this raised water, b the breadth of the canal (supposed rectangular), and λ the length of the wave, the volume of this water is $b\lambda H$. But all particles in the transverse section behave alike; and, when the wave has passed, the particles in *all* transverse sections have been treated alike. Hence the final result of the passage of the wave is that the whole of the water of the canal has been translated, in the direction of the wave's motion, through the space $b\lambda H/bh$, or $\lambda H/h$. If the wave had been one of depression, the translation of the water would have been in the opposite direction to that of the wave's motion. Hence, when the wave consists of an elevation followed by a depression of equal volume, it leaves the water as it found it. Thus any permanent displacement of the water is due to inequality of troughs and crests.

A hint, though a very imperfect one, as to the formation of breakers on a gently sloping beach, is given by considering that in shallow water the front and rear of an ordinary surface-wave must move at different rates, the front being in shallower water than the rear and therefore allowing the rear to gain upon it.

(7) *Oscillatory Waves.*—The typical example of these waves is found in what is called a "swell," or the regular rolling waves which continue to run in deep water after a storm. Their character is essentially periodic, and this feature at once enables us to select from the general integrals of the equations of non-rotatory fluid-motion the special forms which we require. The investigation may, without sensible loss of completeness for application, be still further simplified by the assumption that the disturbance is two-dimensional, *i.e.*, that the motion is precisely the same in any two vertical planes drawn parallel to the direction in which the waves are travelling. The investigation is, unfortunately, very much more simple in an analytical than in a geometrical form.

If the axis of x be taken in the surface of the undisturbed water, in the direction in which the waves are travelling, and that of y vertically *downwards*, the equation for the velocity-potential (see HYDROMECHANICS) is simply

$$\frac{d^2\phi}{dx^2}+\frac{d^2\phi}{dy^2}=0.$$

This is merely the "equation of continuity,"—the condition that no liquid is generated, and none annihilated, during the motion.

The type of solution we seek, as above, is represented by

$$\phi=\text{Y}\cos(mt-nx),$$

where Y depends on y alone. If this can be made to satisfy the equation of continuity, we may proceed to further tests and restrictions of it. Substitution leads to

$$\frac{d^2Y}{dy^2} - n^2Y = 0,$$

so that $Y = A\varepsilon^{ny} + B\varepsilon^{-ny}$, where A and B are arbitrary constants.

(*a*) If the depth of the water be unlimited, the value of A must be zero, for otherwise we should be dealing with disturbances which increase, without limit, as we go farther down. Hence, in this case, a particular integral of the equation, corresponding to a disturbance which can exist by itself, is

$$\phi = B\varepsilon^{-ny}\cos(mt - nx).$$

We will now avail ourselves of the supposition under which, as we have seen, disturbances are necessarily superposable, *i.e.*, assume terms in B^2 to be negligible. The ordinary kinetic equation (HYDROMECHANICS) then becomes

$$C + p/\rho = gy - \left(\frac{d\phi}{dt}\right)$$
$$= gy + mB\varepsilon^{-ny}\sin(mt - nx).$$

If we differentiate this expression with regard to t, and apply the result to the surface only, where v is constant, and remember that $\frac{dy}{dt} = \left(\frac{d\phi}{dy}\right)$, we have simply

$$0 = -ng + m^2,$$

which is the condition that no water *crosses* the bounding surface. This determines n, without ambiguity, when m is given, and thus gives a relation between the period of a wave and its length, or between the period or the length and the speed of propagation. For we may write

$$mt - nx = \frac{2\pi}{\lambda}(vt - x),$$

where λ is the wave-length, and v the speed; so that

$$m = \frac{2\pi v}{\lambda}, \quad n = \frac{2\pi}{\lambda}.$$

Thus we have

$$v^2 = \frac{g\lambda}{2\pi},$$

and the longer waves move faster, even when the vertical displacement is small in both. This is quite different from the result for sound-waves.

The components of the velocity of the particle of water whose mean position is x, y are

$$\left(\frac{d\phi}{dx}\right) = Bn\varepsilon^{-ny}\sin(mt - nx), \text{ parallel to } x,$$

and

$$\left(\frac{d\phi}{dy}\right) = -Bn\varepsilon^{-ny}\cos(mt - nx), \text{ parallel to } y.$$

Hence the path is a circle whose radius is

$$B\frac{n}{m}\varepsilon^{-ny}, \text{ or } B\frac{m}{g}\varepsilon^{-ny}.$$

At the surface this is Bm/g, as in fact we see at once by the equation for the pressure, which gives for the form of the surface

$$C = g\eta + mB\sin(mt - nx).$$

Each surface-particle is at the highest point of its circular path, and moving forwards, when the crest of the wave passes it. When the trough passes, it is at the lowest point of its circle and moving backwards. The radii of the circles diminish in geometrical progression at depths increasing in arithmetical progression. The factor is $\varepsilon^{-ny} = \varepsilon^{-2\pi y/\lambda}$, so that at a depth of *one* wave-length only the disturbance is reduced to $\varepsilon^{-2\pi}$ or about 1/535 of its surface-value.

From the investigation above we see that Atlantic rollers, of a wave-length of (say) 300 feet, travel at the rate of about 40 feet per second, or 27 miles an hour. But, even if they be of 40 feet height from trough to crest (which is probably an exaggerated estimate), the utmost disturbance of a water particle at a depth of 300 feet is not quite half an inch from its mean position. This shows, in a very striking manner, what a mere surface-effect is in this way due to winds, and how the depths of the ocean are practically undisturbed by such causes.

This investigation has been carried to a second, and even to a third, approximation by Stokes, with the result that the form of a section of the surface is no longer the curve of sines, in which the crests and troughs are equal. The crests are steeper and higher, and the troughs wider and shallower, than the first approximation shows. Also the forward horizontal motion of each particle under the crest is no longer quite compensated for by its backward motion under the trough, so that what sailors call the "heave of the sea" is explained. The water is permanently displaced forwards by each succeeding wave. But this effect, like the whole disturbance, is greatest in the surface-layer and diminishes rapidly for each lower layer. The third approximation shows that the speed of the waves is greater than that above assigned, by a term depending on the square of the ratio of the height to the length of a wave.

(*b*) When the depth of the water is limited, we cannot make the simplification adopted in the last investigation.

If h be the depth of the water, our condition is that the vertical motion vanishes at that depth, and the relation between m and n is now

$$m^2 = ng(\varepsilon^{nh} - \varepsilon^{-nh})/(\varepsilon^{nh} + \varepsilon^{-nh}).$$

If h be regarded as infinite this gives as before

$$m^2 = ng.$$

If, on the other hand, h be small compared with the wave-length, the equation approximates to

$$m^2 = n^2gh,$$

or

$$v^2 = gh;$$

and we have the formula for long waves again. Thus the expression above includes both extremes,—though, so far as long waves go, it limits them to harmonic forms of section.

The surface-section is still the curve of sines, but the paths of the individual particles are now ellipses whose major axes are horizontal. Both axes decrease with great rapidity for particles considered at gradually increasing depths; but the minor axes diminish faster than the major, so that the particles at the bottom oscillate in horizontal lines.

(8) *Ripples.*—Stokes in 1848 pointed out that the surface-tension of a liquid should be taken account of in finding the pressure at the free surface, but this seems not to have been done till 1871, when W. Thomson discussed its consequences. If T be the surface-tension, and r the radius of curvature of the (cylindrical) surface, in the case of oscillatory waves, the pressure at the free surface must be considered as differing from that in the air by the quantity T/r (CAPILLARY ACTION). As $T/g\rho$ is usually a small quantity, this term will be negligible unless r is very small. If the waves be oscillatory, this means that their lengths must be very short, so that the depth of the fluid may be treated as infinite in comparison.

The curvature is practically $d^2\eta/dx^2$, because η/λ is small; so that the term $-Td^2\eta/dx^2$ must be introduced into the kinetic equation along with p. The result is that

$$m^2 = ng + \frac{n^3T}{m\rho},$$

or

$$v^2 = \frac{g\lambda}{2\pi} + \frac{2\pi}{\lambda}\frac{T}{\rho}.$$

Thus the speed is, in all cases, increased by the surface-tension; and the more so the shorter is the wave-length. Hence, as the speed increases indefinitely with increase of wave-length when gravity alone acts, and also increases indefinitely the shorter the wave when surface-tension alone acts, there must be a *minimum* speed, for some definite wave-length, when both causes are at work. It is easily seen that v^2 is a minimum when

$$\lambda = \lambda_0 = 2\pi\sqrt{T/g\rho},$$

and that the corresponding value of v^2 is

$$2\sqrt{gT/\rho}.$$

In the case of water the value of λ_0 is about 0·68 inch, and v_0 is 0·76 in feet-seconds, nearly.

This slowest-moving oscillatory wave may therefore be regarded as the limit between waves proper and ripples. That ripples run faster the shorter they are is easily seen by watching the apparently rigid pattern of them which precedes a body moving uniformly through still water. The more rapid the motion the closer do the ripple-ridges approach one another. Excellent examples of ripples are produced by applying the stem of a vibrating tuning-fork to one side of a large rectangular box full of liquid. From the pitch of the note, and the wave-length of the ripples, we can make (by the use of the above formula) an approximate determination of surface-tension, a quantity somewhat difficult to measure by statical processes.

The conditions of production of ripples by wind, or generally in a surface of separation of two fluids, each of which has any motion parallel to this surface, are given in HYDROMECHANICS.

(9) *Interference of Waves.*—While the disturbances considered are so small as to be superposable, *i.e.*, independent of one another, the effect of superposition is merely a kinematical question, and, as such, has been very fully treated under MECHANICS (§§ 56–67). See also ACOUSTICS, LIGHT, and WAVE THEORY. Thus ripple-patterns, ordinary beats of musical sounds, composition of lunar and solar ocean tides, diffraction, phenomena of polarized light in crystals or in transparent bodies in the magnetic field, &c., are all, in *principle* at least, simple kinematical consequences of superposition. But the phenomena called Tartini's beats, breakers, a bore, a jabble, and (generally) cases in which a sufficient approximation cannot be obtained by omitting powers of the displacements higher than the first, are not of this simple character.

As a single illustration, take one case of the first of these phenomena. The *fact* to be explained is that when two pure musical sounds, of frequencies 2 and 3 (say), that is, forming a "perfect fifth," are sounded together, we hear in addition to them a graver note, viz., that of which the first sound is the octave and the second the twelfth. When a resonator, carefully tuned to this graver note, is applied to the ear the note is usually not heard. Hence Helmholtz attributes its production to the fact that the drum of the ear (in consequence of the attachments of the ossicles) has different elastic properties for inward and for outward displacements.

The force tending to restore the drum from a displacement x may therefore be represented approximately by

$$-p^2x+qx^2.$$

Thus, when the drum is exposed to the two sounds above mentioned, its equation of motion is

$$\frac{d^2x}{dt^2}+p^2x=qx^2+a\sin 3mt+b\sin(2mt+\beta).$$

By successive approximations, it is found that there is a term in the value of x of the form

$$\frac{abq\cos(mt-\beta)}{(p^2-9m^2)(p^2-4m^2)(p^2-m^2)},$$

which is the "difference-tone" referred to. This, of course, is communicated to the internal ear.

Helmholtz points out, however, that such sounds may be produced objectively, provided the interfering disturbances are sufficiently great. No one seems yet to have obtained any really accurate notion of the smallness of the disturbances of air which can be heard as sound. That they are excessively small has long been shown by many processes, but even more perfectly by the comparatively recent invention of the telephone.

(10) *Waves in an Elastic Solid.*—Some of the more elementary parts of this very difficult question have been treated from a theoretical point of view in the article ELASTICITY. From an observational and experimental point of view some are treated under EARTHQUAKE. See also LIGHT, and WAVE THEORY, for the luminiferous medium appears to behave like an elastic solid.

(11) *Waves of Temperature and of Electric Potential.*—In HEAT (§ 78), and specially in the mathematical appendix to that article, will be found Fourier's treatment of heat-waves produced by periodic sources of various characters. It is sufficient to call attention here to the form of the equation for the linear motion of heat (which is the same as that for electricity and for diffusion), viz.,

$$c\frac{dv}{dt}=\frac{d}{dx}\left(k\frac{dv}{dx}\right),$$

where v represents temperature, c specific heat, and k thermal conductivity.

When c and k are constants, this takes the very simple form

$$\frac{dv}{dt}=\kappa\frac{d^2v}{dx^2}.$$

If plane harmonic waves of the type

$$v=X\cos(mt-nx)$$

are to be transmitted, we must have simultaneously

$$\frac{d^2X}{dx^2}-n^2X=0\,,\quad 2\kappa n\frac{dX}{dx}=-mX.$$

The first gives

$$X=A\epsilon^{nx}+B\epsilon^{-nx};$$

and the second, by means of this, gives

$$2\kappa n^2(A\epsilon^{nx}-B\epsilon^{-nx})=-m(A\epsilon^{nx}+B\epsilon^{-nx}).$$

Thus A vanishes, which implies that the amplitude of the waves must continuously diminish as they progress. Also

$$2\kappa n^2=m,$$

so that

$$v=B\epsilon^{-nx}\cos(2\kappa n^2t-nx).$$

If the conductivity be not constant, then, even in the simple case of

$$k=k_0(1+\alpha v),$$

where α is small, the wave throws off others of inferior amplitude and of a different period.

12. *Works and Memoirs on Waves.*—The literature is very extensive, so a few references only are given. The works of Lagrange, Laplace, Poisson, and Cauchy may be specially cited. Weber's *Wellenlehre*, and Scott Russell's papers, contain valuable experimental details. Theoretical papers of importance by Earnshaw, Kelland, Green, &c., treat of long waves. The collected works of Rankine, and particularly those of Stokes, deal in part with oscillatory waves. Stokes's "Reports on Hydrodynamics," in the *Trans. of the British Association*, are of great value in themselves, and contain numerous references. A very complete discussion of the mathematics of the subject is given by Professor Greenhill in the *American Journal of Mathematics*. Lord Rayleigh's *Sound*, and the memoirs of De St Venant and Von Helmholtz, together with a remarkable series of papers by Sir W. Thomson, in recent volumes of the *Phil. Mag.* and *Proc. R. S. E.*, may fitly conclude the list. (P. G. T.)

WAVERTREE, a township of Lancashire, partly included within the parliamentary limits of Liverpool, 3 miles south-east of Liverpool Exchange. The churches are all modern. There is a small circle of monoliths on the south-east boundary of the township, called the Calder Stones. A cemetery of the Neolithic period was opened a few years ago. The town possesses roperies and a brewery. An extensive pumping station connected with the Liverpool water-works is in the vicinity. The population of the urban sanitary district (area 1838 acres) in 1871 was 7810, and in 1881 it was 11,097.

WAVE THEORY OF LIGHT

Various forms of wave theory.

§ 1. A GENERAL statement of the principles of the undulatory theory, with elementary explanations, has already been given under LIGHT, and in the article on ETHER the arguments which point to the existence of an all-pervading medium, susceptible in its various parts of an alternating change of state, have been traced by a master hand; but the subject is of such great importance, and is so intimately involved in recent optical investigation and discovery, that a more detailed exposition of the theory, with application to the leading phenomena, was reserved for a special article. That the subject is one of difficulty may be at once admitted. Even in the theory of sound, as conveyed by aerial vibrations, where we are well acquainted with the nature and properties of the vehicle, the fundamental conceptions are not very easy to grasp, and their development makes heavy demands upon our mathematical resources. That the situation is not improved when the medium is hypothetical will be easily understood. For, although the evidence is overwhelming in favour of the conclusion that light is propagated as a vibration, we are almost entirely in the dark as to what it is that vibrates and the manner of vibration. This ignorance entails an appearance of vagueness even in those parts of the subject the treatment of which would not really be modified by the acquisition of a more precise knowledge, *e.g.*, the theory of the colours of thin plates, and of the resolving power of optical instruments. But in other parts of the subject, such as the explanation of the laws of double refraction and of the intensity of light reflected at the surface of a transparent medium, the vagueness is not merely one of language; and if we wish to reach definite results by the *a priori* road we must admit a hypothetical element, for which little justification can be given. The distinction here indicated should be borne clearly in mind. Many optical phenomena must necessarily agree with any kind of wave theory that can be proposed; others may agree or disagree with a particular form of it. In the latter case we may regard the special form as disproved, but the undulatory theory in the proper wider sense remains untouched.

Elastic solid theory.

Of such special forms of the wave theory the most famous is that which assimilates light to the transverse vibrations of an elastic solid. *Transverse* they must be in order to give room for the phenomena of polarization. This theory is a great help to the imagination, and allows of the deduction of definite results which are at any rate mechanically possible. An isotropic solid has in general two elastic properties—one relating to the recovery from an alteration of volume, and the other to the recovery from a state of shear, in which the strata are caused to slide over one another. It has been shown by Green that it would be necessary to suppose the luminiferous medium to be incompressible, and thus the only admissible differences between one isotropic medium and another are those of *rigidity* and of *density*. Between these we are in the first instance free to choose. The slower propagation of light in glass than in air may be equally well explained by supposing the rigidity the same in both cases while the density is greater in glass, or by supposing that the density is the same in both cases while the rigidity is greater in air. Indeed there is nothing, so far, to exclude a more complicated condition of things, in which both the density and rigidity vary in passing from one medium to another, subject to the one condition only of making the ratio of velocities of propagation equal to the known refractive index between the media.

When we come to apply this theory to investigate the intensity of light reflected from (say) a glass surface, and to the diffraction of light by very small particles (as in the sky), we find that a reasonable agreement with the facts can be brought about only upon the supposition that the rigidity is the same (approximately, at any rate) in various media, and that the density alone varies. At the same time we have to suppose that the vibration is perpendicular to the plane of polarization.

Up to this point the accordance may be regarded as fairly satisfactory; but, when we extend the investigation to crystalline media in the hope of explaining the observed laws of double refraction, we find that the suppositions which would suit best here are inconsistent with the conclusions we have already arrived at. In the first place, and so long as we hold strictly to the analogy of an elastic solid, we can only explain double refraction as depending upon anisotropic rigidity, and this can hardly be reconciled with the view that the rigidity is the same in different isotropic media. And if we pass over this difficulty, and inquire what kind of double refraction a crystalline solid would admit of, we find no such correspondence with observation as would lead us to think that we are upon the right track. The theory of anisotropic solids, with its twenty-one elastic constants, seems to be too wide for optical double refraction, which is of a much simpler character.[1]

For these and other reasons, especially the awkwardness with which it lends itself to the explanation of dispersion, the elastic solid theory, valuable as a piece of purely dynamical reasoning, and probably not without mathematical analogy to the truth, can in optics be regarded only as an illustration.

Electromagnetic theory.

In recent years a theory has been received with much favour in which light is regarded as an electromagnetic phenomenon. The dielectric medium is conceived to be subject to a rapidly periodic "electric displacement," the variations of which have the magnetic properties of an electric current. On the basis of purely electrical observations Maxwell calculated the velocity of propagation of such disturbances, and obtained a value not certainly distinguishable from the velocity of light. Such an agreement is very striking; and a further deduction from the theory, that the specific inductive capacity of a transparent medium is equal to the square of the refractive index, is supported to some extent by observation. The foundations of the electrical theory are not as yet quite cleared of more or less arbitrary hypothesis; but, when it becomes certain that a dielectric medium is susceptible of vibrations propagated with the velocity of light, there will be no hesitation in accepting the identity of such vibrations with those to which optical phenomena are due. In the meantime, and apart altogether from the question of its probable truth, the electromagnetic theory is very instructive, in showing us how careful we must be to avoid limiting our ideas too much as to the nature of the luminous vibrations.

§ 2. *Plane Waves of Simple Type.*

Whatever may be the character of the medium and of its vibration, the analytical expression for an infinite train of plane waves is

$$A\cos\left\{\frac{2\pi}{\lambda}(Vt-x)+\alpha\right\} \quad . \quad . \quad . \quad . \quad . \quad (1),$$

in which λ represents the wave-length, and V the corresponding velocity of propagation. The coefficient A is called the amplitude, and its nature depends upon the medium and must therefore here be left an open question. The phase of the wave at a given time and place is represented by α. The expression retains the same value whatever integral number of wave-lengths be added to or subtracted from x. It is also periodic with respect to t, and the period is

$$\tau=\lambda/V \quad . \quad . \quad . \quad . \quad . \quad . \quad . \quad (2).$$

In experimenting upon sound we are able to determine independently τ, λ, and V; but on account of its smallness the periodic time of luminous vibrations eludes altogether our means of observation, and is only known indirectly from λ and V by means of (2).

There is nothing arbitrary in the use of a circular function to represent the waves. As a general rule this is the only kind of wave which can be propagated without a change of form; and, even in the exceptional cases where the velocity is independent of wave-length, no generality is really lost by this procedure, because in accordance with Fourier's theorem any kind of periodic wave may be regarded as compounded of a series of such as (1), with wave-lengths in harmonical progression.

Composition of waves of like period.

A well-known characteristic of waves of type (1) is that any number of trains of various amplitudes and phases, but of the *same wave-length*, are equivalent to a single train of the same type. Thus

$$\Sigma A\cos\left\{\frac{2\pi}{\lambda}(Vt-x)+\alpha\right\}$$

$$=\Sigma A\cos\alpha\,.\cos\frac{2\pi}{\lambda}(Vt-x)-\Sigma A\sin\alpha\,.\,\sin\frac{2\pi}{\lambda}(Vt-x)$$

$$=P\cos\left\{\frac{2\pi}{\lambda}(Vt-x)+\phi\right\} \quad . \quad . \quad . \quad . \quad . \quad (3),$$

where

$$P^2=(\Sigma A\cos\alpha)^2+\Sigma(A\sin\alpha)^2 \quad . \quad . \quad . \quad . \quad (4),$$

$$\tan\phi=\frac{\Sigma(A\sin\alpha)}{\Sigma(A\cos\alpha)} \quad . \quad . \quad . \quad . \quad . \quad . \quad (5).$$

Two trains of waves.

An important particular case is that of two component trains only.

$$A\cos\left\{\frac{2\pi}{\lambda}(Vt-x)+\alpha\right\}+A'\cos\left\{\frac{2\pi}{\lambda}(Vt-x)+\alpha'\right\}$$

$$=P\cos\left\{\frac{2\pi}{\lambda}(Vt-x)+\phi\right\},$$

where

$$P^2=A^2+A'^2+2AA'\cos(\alpha-\alpha') \quad . \quad . \quad . \quad . \quad (6).$$

[1] See Stokes, "Report on Double Refraction," *Brit. Assoc. Report*, 1862, p. 253.

The composition of vibrations of the same period is precisely analogous, as was pointed out by Fresnel, to the composition of forces, or indeed of any other two-dimensional vector quantities. The magnitude of the force corresponds to the amplitude of the vibration, and the inclination of the force corresponds to the phase. A group of forces, of equal intensity, represented by lines drawn from the centre to the angular points of a regular polygon, constitute a system in equilibrium. Consequently, a system of vibrations of equal amplitude and of phases symmetrically distributed round the period has a zero resultant.

According to the phase-relation, determined by $(\alpha-\alpha')$, the amplitude of the resultant may vary from $(A-A')$ to $(A+A')$. If A' and A are equal, the minimum resultant is zero, showing that two equal trains of waves may neutralize one another. This happens when the phases are opposite, or differ by half a (complete) period, and the effect is usually spoken of as the *interference* of light. From a purely dynamical point of view the word is not very appropriate, the vibrations being simply *superposed* with as little interference as can be imagined.

§ 3. *Intensity.*

The intensity of light of given wave-length must depend upon the amplitude, but the precise nature of the relation is not at once apparent. We are not able to appreciate by simple inspection the relative intensities of two unequal lights; and, when we say, for example, that one candle is twice as bright as another, we mean that two of the latter burning independently would give us the same light as one of the former. This may be regarded as the definition; and then experiment may be appealed to to prove that the intensity of light from a given source varies inversely as the square of the distance. But our conviction of the truth of the law is perhaps founded quite as much upon the idea that something not liable to loss is radiated outwards, and is distributed in succession over the surfaces of spheres concentric with the source, whose areas are as the squares of the radii. The something can only be energy; and thus we are led to regard the rate at which energy is propagated across a given area parallel to the waves as the measure of intensity; and this is proportional, not to the first power, but to the *square* of the amplitude.

Photometry.

Practical photometry is usually founded upon the law of inverse squares (LIGHT, vol. xiv. p. 583); and it should be remembered that the method involves essentially the use of a diffusing screen, the illumination of which, seen in a certain direction, is assumed to be independent of the precise direction in which the light falls upon it; for the distance of a candle, for example, cannot be altered without introducing at the same time a change in the apparent magnitude, and therefore in the incidence of some part at any rate of the light.

With this objection is connected another which is often of greater importance, the necessary enfeeblement of the light by the process of diffusion. And, if to maintain the brilliancy we substitute regular reflectors for diffusing screens, the method breaks down altogether by the apparent illumination becoming independent of the distance of the source of light.

The use of a revolving disk with transparent and opaque sectors in order to control the brightness, as proposed by Fox Talbot,[1] may often be recommended in scientific photometry, when a great loss of light is inadmissible. The law that, when the frequency of intermittence is sufficient to give a steady appearance, the brightness is proportional to the angular magnitude of the open sectors appears to be well established.

§ 4. *Resultant of a Large Number of Vibrations of Arbitrary Phase.*

We have seen that the resultant of two vibrations of equal amplitude is wholly dependent upon their phase-relation, and it is of interest to inquire what we are to expect from the composition of a large number (n) of equal vibrations of amplitude unity, and of arbitrary phases. The intensity of the resultant will of course depend upon the precise manner in which the phases are distributed, and may vary from n^2 to zero. But is there a definite intensity which becomes more and more probable as n is increased without limit?

The nature of the question here raised is well illustrated by the special case in which the possible phases are restricted to two *opposite* phases. We may then conveniently discard the idea of phase, and regard the amplitudes as at random *positive or negative.* If all the signs are the same, the intensity is n^2; if, on the other hand, there are as many positive as negative, the result is zero. But, although the intensity may range from 0 to n^2, the smaller values are much more probable than the greater.

The simplest part of the problem relates to what is called in the theory of probabilities the "expectation" of intensity, that is, the mean intensity to be expected after a great number of trials, in each of which the phases are taken at random. The chance that all the vibrations are positive is 2^{-n}, and thus the expectation of intensity corresponding to this contingency is $2^{-n}.n^2$. In like manner the expectation corresponding to the number of positive vibrations being $(n-1)$ is

$$2^{-n}.n.(n-2)^2,$$

and so on. The whole expectation of intensity is thus

$$\frac{1}{2^n}\left\{1.n^2+n.(n-2)^2+\frac{n(n-1)}{1.2}(n-4)^2+\frac{n(n-1)(n-2)}{1.2.3}(n-6)^2+\ldots\right\} \quad \ldots \quad (1).$$

Now the sum of the $(n+1)$ terms of this series is simply n, as may be proved by comparison of coefficients of x^2 in the equivalent forms

$$(e^x+e^{-x})^n=2^n(1+\tfrac{1}{2}x^2+\ldots)^n$$
$$=e^{nx}+ne^{(n-2)x}+\frac{n(n-1)}{1.2}e^{(n-4)x}+\ldots$$

The expectation of intensity is therefore n, and this whether n be great or small.

The same conclusion holds good when the phases are unrestricted. From (4), § 2, if $A=1$,

$$P^2=n+2\Sigma\cos(\alpha_2-\alpha_1) \quad \ldots \quad (2),$$

where under the sign of summation are to be included the cosines of the $\frac{1}{2}n(n-1)$ differences of phase. When the phases are arbitrary, this sum is as likely to be positive as negative, and thus the mean value of P^2 is n.

The reader must be on his guard here against a fallacy which has misled some high authorities. We have not proved that when n is large there is any tendency for a single combination to give the intensity equal to n, but the quite different proposition that in a large number of trials, in each of which the phases are rearranged arbitrarily, the *mean* intensity will tend more and more to the value n. It is true that even in a single combination there is no reason why any of the cosines in (2) should be positive rather than negative, and from this we may infer that when n is increased the sum of the terms tends to vanish in comparison with the number of terms. But, the number of terms being of the order n^2, we can infer nothing as to the value of the sum of the series in comparison with n.

Indeed it is not true that the intensity in a single combination approximates to n, when n is large. It can be proved[2] that the probability of a resultant intermediate in amplitude between r and $r+dr$ is

$$\frac{2}{n}e^{-r^2/n}r\,dr \quad \ldots \quad (3).$$

The probability of an amplitude less than r is thus

$$\frac{2}{n}\int_0^r e^{-r^2/n}r\,dr=1-e^{-r^2/n} \quad \ldots \quad (4).$$

or, which is the same thing, the probability of an amplitude greater than r is

$$e^{-r^2/n} \quad \ldots \quad (5).$$

The accompanying table gives the probabilities of intensities less than the fractions of n named in the first column. For example, the probability of intensity less than n is ·6321.

·05	·0488	·80	·5506
·10	·0952	1·00	·6321
·20	·1813	1·50	·7768
·40	·3296	2·00	·8647
·60	·4512	3·00	·9502

It will be seen that, however great n may be, there is a fair chance of considerable relative fluctuations of intensity in consecutive combinations.

The *mean* intensity, expressed by

$$\frac{2}{n}\int_0^\infty e^{-r^2/n}.r^2.r\,dr,$$

is, as we have already seen, equal to n.

It is with this mean intensity only that we are concerned in ordinary photometry. A source of light, such as a candle or even a soda flame, may be regarded as composed of a very large number of luminous centres disposed throughout a very sensible space; and, even though it be true that the intensity at a particular point of a screen illuminated by it and at a particular moment of time is a matter of chance, further processes of averaging must be gone through before anything is arrived at of which our senses could ordinarily take cognizance. In the smallest interval of time during which the eye could be impressed, there would be opportunity for any number of rearrangements of phase, due either to motions of the particles or to irregularities in their modes of vibration. And even if we supposed that each luminous centre was fixed, and emitted perfectly regular vibrations, the manner of composition and consequent intensity would vary rapidly from point to point of the screen, and in ordinary cases the mean illumination over the smallest appreciable area would correspond to a thorough averaging of the phase-relationships. In this way the idea of the intensity of a luminous source, independently of any questions of phase, is seen to be justified, and we may properly say that two candles are twice as bright as one.

[1] *Phil. Mag.*, v. p. 331, 1834.

[2] *Phil. Mag.*, Aug. 1880.

§ 5. *Propagation of Waves in General.*

It has been shown under OPTICS that a system of rays, however many reflexions or refractions they may have undergone, are always normal to a certain surface, or rather system of surfaces. From our present point of view these surfaces are to be regarded as wave-surfaces, that is, surfaces of constant phase. It is evident that, so long as the radius of curvature is very large in comparison with λ, each small part of a wave-surface propagates itself just as an infinite plane wave coincident with the tangent plane would do. If we start at time t with a given surface, the corresponding wave-surface at time $t+dt$ is to be found by prolonging every normal by the length Vdt, where V denotes the velocity of propagation at the place in question. If the medium be uniform, so that V is constant, the new surface is *parallel* to the old one, and this property is retained however many short intervals of time be considered in succession. A wave-surface thus propagates itself *normally*, and the corresponding parts of successive surfaces are those which lie upon the same normal. In this sense the normal may be regarded as a *ray*, but the idea must not be pushed to streams of light limited to pass through small apertures. The manner in which the phase is determined by the length of the ray, and the conditions under which energy may be regarded as travelling along a ray, will be better treated under the head of Huygens's principle, and the theory of shadows (§ 10).

Fermat's principle.

From the law of propagation, according to which the wave-surfaces are always as far advanced as possible, it follows that the course of a ray is that for which the time, represented by $\int V^{-1}ds$, is a minimum. This is Fermat's principle of least time. Since the refractive index (μ) varies as V^{-1}, we may take $\int \mu ds$ as the measure of the retardation between one wave surface and another; and it is the same along whichever ray it may be measured.

Law of magnifying.

The principle that $\int \mu ds$ is a minimum along a ray lends itself readily to the investigation of optical laws. As an example, we will consider the very important theory of magnifying power. Let A_0, B_0 be two points upon a wave-surface before the light enters the object-glass of a telescope, A, B the corresponding points upon a wave-surface after emergence from the eye-piece, both surfaces being plane. The value of $\int \mu ds$ is the same along the ray A_0A as along B_0B; and, if from any cause B_0 be slightly retarded relatively to A_0, then B will be retarded to the same amount relatively to A. Suppose now that the retardation in question is due to a small rotation (θ) of the wave-surface A_0B_0 about an axis in its own plane perpendicular to AB. The retardation of B_0 relatively to A_0 is then $A_0B_0.\theta$; and in like manner, if ϕ be the corresponding rotation of AB, the retardation is $AB.\phi$. Since these retardations are the same, we have

$$\frac{\phi}{\theta}=\frac{A_0B_0}{AB},$$

or *the magnifying power is equal to the ratio of the widths of the stream of light before and after passing the telescope.*

Prisms.

The magnifying power is not necessarily the same in all directions. Consider the case of a prism arranged as for spectrum work. Passage through the prism does not alter the vertical width of the stream of light; hence there is no magnifying power in this direction. What happens in a horizontal direction depends upon circumstances. A single prism in the position of minimum deviation does not alter the horizontal width of the beam. The same is true of a sequence of any number of prisms each in the position of minimum deviation, or of the combination called by Thollon a couple, when the deviation is the least that can be obtained by rotating the couple as a *rigid system*, although a further diminution might be arrived at by violating this tie. In all these cases there is neither horizontal nor vertical magnification, and the instrument behaves as a telescope of power unity. If, however, a prism be so placed that the angle of emergence differs from the angle of incidence, the horizontal width of the beam undergoes a change. If the emergence be nearly grazing, there will be a high magnifying power in the horizontal direction; and, whatever may be the character of the system of prisms, the horizontal magnifying power is represented by the ratio of widths. Brewster suggested that, by combining two prisms with refracting edges at right angles, it would be possible to secure equal magnifying power in the two directions, and thus to imitate the action of an ordinary telescope.

Apparent brightness.

The theory of magnifying power is intimately connected with that of apparent brightness. By the use of a telescope in regarding a bright body, such, for example, as the moon, there is a concentration of light upon the pupil in proportion to the ratio of the area of the object-glass to that of the pupil.[1] But the apparent brightness remains unaltered, the apparent superficial magnitude of the object being changed in precisely the same proportion, in accordance with the law just established.

These fundamental propositions were proved a long while since by Cotes and Smith; and a complete exposition of them, from the point of view of geometrical optics, is to be found in Smith's treatise.[2]

§ 6. *Waves Approximately Plane or Spherical.*

A plane wave of course remains plane after reflexion from a truly plane surface; but any irregularities in the surface impress themselves upon the wave. In the simplest case, that of perpendicular incidence, the irregularities are *doubled*, any depressed portion of the surface giving rise to a retardation in the wave front of twice its own amount. It is assumed that the lateral dimensions of the depressed or elevated parts are large multiples of the wave-length; otherwise the assimilation of the various parts to plane waves is not legitimate.

In like manner, if a plane wave passes perpendicularly through a parallel plate of refracting material, a small elevation t at any part of one of the surfaces introduces a retardation $(\mu-1)t$ in the corresponding part of the wave-surface. An error in a glass surface is thus of only one-quarter of the importance of an equal error in a reflecting surface. Further, if a plate, otherwise true, be distorted by bending, the errors introduced at the two surfaces are approximately opposite, and neutralize one another.[3]

Symmetrical aberration.

In practical applications it is of importance to recognize the effects of a small departure of the wave-surface from its ideal plane or spherical form. Let the surface be referred to a system of rectangular coordinates, the axis of z being normal at the centre of the section of the beam, and the origin being the point of contact of the tangent plane. If, as happens in many cases, the surface be one of symmetry round OZ, the equation of the surface may be represented approximately by

$$z=r^2/2\rho+Ar^4+ \quad . \quad . \quad . \quad . \quad . \quad . \quad (1),$$

in which ρ is the radius of curvature, or focal length, and $r^2=x^2+y^2$. If the surface be truly spherical, $A=1/8\rho^3$, and any deviation of A from this value indicates ordinary symmetrical spherical aberration.

Unsymmetrical aberration.

If, however, the surface be not symmetrical, we may have to encounter aberration of a lower order of small quantities, and therefore presumably of higher importance. By taking the axis of x and y coincident with the directions of principal curvature at O, we may write the equation of the surface

$$z=\frac{x^2}{2\rho}+\frac{y^2}{2\rho'}+\alpha x^3+\beta x^2y+\gamma xy^2+\delta y^3 \quad . \quad . \quad . \quad . \quad (2),$$

ρ, ρ' being the principal radii of curvature, or focal lengths. The most important example of unsymmetrical aberration is in the spectroscope, where (if the faces of the prisms may be regarded as at any rate surfaces of revolution) the wave-surface may by suitable adjustments be rendered symmetrical with respect to the horizontal plane $y=0$. This plane may then be regarded as primary, ρ being the primary focal length, at which distance the spectrum is formed. Under these circumstances β and δ may be omitted from (2), which thus takes the form

$$z=\frac{x^2}{2\rho}+\frac{y^2}{2\rho'}+\alpha x^3+\gamma xy^2 \quad . \quad . \quad . \quad . \quad . \quad (3).$$

The constants α and γ in (3) may be interpreted in terms of the differential coefficients of the principal radii of curvature. By the usual formula the radius of curvature at the point x of the intersection of (3) with the plane $y=0$ is approximately $\rho(1-6\alpha\rho x)$. Since $y=0$ is a principal plane throughout, this radius of curvature is a principal radius of the surface; so that, denoting it by ρ, we have

$$\alpha=\frac{1}{6}\frac{d\rho^{-1}}{dx} \quad . \quad . \quad . \quad . \quad . \quad . \quad . \quad . \quad (4).$$

Again, in the neighbourhood of the origin, the approximate value of the product of the principal curvatures is

$$\frac{1}{\rho\rho'}+\frac{6\alpha x}{\rho'}+\frac{2\gamma x}{\rho}.$$

Thus

$$d\left(\frac{1}{\rho\rho'}\right)=-\frac{d\rho}{\rho^2\rho'}-\frac{d\rho'}{\rho'^2\rho}=\frac{6\alpha x}{\rho'}+\frac{2\gamma x}{\rho};$$

whence by (4)

$$\gamma=\tfrac{1}{2}\frac{d\rho'^{-1}}{dx} \quad . \quad . \quad . \quad . \quad . \quad . \quad . \quad . \quad (5).$$

The equation of the normal at the point x, y, z is

$$\frac{\zeta-z}{-1}=\frac{\xi-x}{\rho^{-1}x+3\alpha x^2+\gamma y^2}=\frac{\eta-y}{\rho'^{-1}y+2\gamma xy} \quad . \quad . \quad . \quad (6);$$

[1] It is here assumed that the object-glass is large enough to fill the whole of the pupil with light; also that the glasses are perfectly transparent, and that there is no loss of light by reflexion. For theoretical purposes the latter requirement may be satisfied by supposing the transition between one optical medium and another to be gradual in all cases.

[2] Smith, *Compleat System of Optics*, Cambridge, 1738. The reader may be referred to a paper entitled "Notes, chiefly Historical, on some Fundamental Propositions in Optics" (*Phil. Mag.*, June 1886), in which some account is given of Smith's work, and its relation to modern investigations.

[3] On this principle Grubb has explained the observation that the effects of bending stress are nearly as prejudicial in the case of thick object-glasses as in the case of thin ones.

Primary focal line. and its intersection with the plane $\zeta=\rho$ occurs at the point determined approximately by

$$\left.\begin{array}{l}\xi=-\rho(3\alpha x^2+\gamma y^2)\\ \eta=\dfrac{(\rho'-\rho)y}{\rho'}-2\rho\gamma xy\end{array}\right\} \quad . \quad . \quad . \quad . \quad . \quad . \quad (7),$$

terms of the third order being omitted.

According to geometrical optics, the thickness of the image of a luminous line at the primary focus is determined by the extreme value of ξ; and for good definition in the spectroscope it is necessary to reduce this thickness as much as possible. One way of attaining the desired result would be to narrow the aperture; but, as we shall see later, to narrow the horizontal aperture is really to throw away the peculiar advantage of large instruments. The same objection, however, does not apply to narrowing the *vertical* aperture; and in many spectroscopes a great improvement in definition may be thus secured. In general, it is necessary that both γ and α be small. Since the value of ξ does not depend on ρ', it would seem that in respect of definition there is no advantage in avoiding astigmatism.

The width of the image when $\eta=0$ (corresponding to $y=0$) is $3\alpha\rho x^2$, and vanishes when $\alpha=0$, *i.e.*, when there is no aberration for rays in the primary plane. In this case the image reduces to a linear arc. If further $\gamma=0$, this arc becomes straight, and then the image at the primary focus is perfect to this order of approximation. As an example where $\alpha=0$, the image of a luminous point, formed at an equal distance on the further side of a sloped equi-convex lens, may be mentioned.

Secondary focal line. At the secondary focus, $\zeta=\rho'$, and from (6)

$$\xi=x\frac{\rho-\rho'}{\rho}, \quad \eta=-2\rho'\gamma xy \quad . \quad . \quad . \quad . \quad . \quad (8).$$

If $\gamma=0$, the secondary focal line is formed without aberration, but not otherwise. Both focal lines are well formed when parallel rays fall upon a plano-convex lens, sloped at about 30°, the curved side of the lens being turned towards the parallel rays.

§ 7. *Interference Fringes.*

We have seen (§ 2) that, when two trains of parallel waves of equal wave-length are superposed, the intensity of the resultant depends upon the phase-relation of the components; but it is necessarily the same at all points of the wave-front. It not unfrequently happens that the parallelism of the component trains is approximate only, and there then arises the phenomenon known as interference fringes. If the two directions of propagation be inclined on opposite sides to the axis of x at small angles α, the expressions for two components of equal amplitudes are

$$\cos\frac{2\pi}{\lambda}\left\{Vt-x\cos\alpha-y\sin\alpha\right\},$$

and

$$\cos\frac{2\pi}{\lambda}\left\{Vt-x\cos\alpha+y\sin\alpha\right\};$$

so that the resultant is expressed by

$$2\cos\frac{2\pi y\sin\alpha}{\lambda}\cos\frac{2\pi}{\lambda}(Vt-x\cos\alpha) \quad . \quad . \quad . \quad . \quad (1);$$

from which it appears that the vibrations advance parallel to the axis of x, unchanged in type, and with a uniform velocity $V/\cos\alpha$. Considered as depending on y, the vibration is a maximum when $y\sin\alpha$ is equal to 0, λ, 2λ, 3λ, &c., corresponding to the centres of the bright bands, while for the intermediate values $\frac{1}{2}\lambda$, $\frac{3}{2}\lambda$, &c., there is no vibration. This is the interference of light proceeding from two similar homogeneous and very distant sources.

Fresnel's experiment. In the form of experiment adopted by Fresnel the sources O_1, O_2[1] are situated at a finite distance D from the place of observation (LIGHT, vol. xiv. p. 606). If A be the point of the screen equidistant from O_1, O_2, and P a neighbouring point, then approximately

$$O_1P-O_2P=\sqrt{\{D^2+(u+\tfrac{1}{2}b)^2\}}-\sqrt{\{D^2+(u-\tfrac{1}{2}b)^2\}}=ub/D,$$

where $O_1O_2=b$, $AP=u$.

Thus, if λ be the wave-length, the places where the phases are accordant are given by

$$u=n\lambda D/b \quad . \quad . \quad . \quad . \quad . \quad . \quad . \quad . \quad (2),$$

n being an integer.

If the light were really homogeneous, the successive fringes would be similar to one another and unlimited in number; moreover there would be no place that could be picked out by inspection as the centre of the system. In practice λ varies, and the only place of complete accordance for all kinds of light is at A, where $u=0$. Theoretically, there is no place of complete discordance for all kinds of light, and consequently no complete blackness. In consequence, however, of the fact that the range of sensitiveness of the eye is limited to less than an "octave," the centre of the first dark band (on either side) is sensibly black, even when white light is employed; but it should be carefully remarked that the existence of even one band is due to selection, and that the formation of several visible bands is favoured by the capability of the retina to make chromatic distinctions within the visible range.

[1] It is scarcely necessary to say that O_1, O_2 must not be distinct sources of light; otherwise there could be no fixed phase-relation and consequently no regular interference. In Fresnel's experiment O_1, O_2 are virtual images of one real source O, obtained by reflexion in two mirrors. The mirrors may be replaced by a bi-prism. Or, as in Lloyd's arrangement, O_1 may be identical with O, and O_2 obtained by a grazing reflexion from a single mirror.

The number of perceptible bands increases *pari passu* with the approach of the light to homogeneity. For this purpose there are two methods that may be used.

Light originally homogeneous. We may employ light, such as that from the soda flame, which possesses *ab initio* a high degree of homogeneity. If the range of wave-length included be $\frac{1}{50000}$, a corresponding number of interference fringes may be made visible. The above is the number obtained by Fizeau, and Michelson has recently gone as far as 200,000. The narrowness of the bright line of light seen in the spectroscope, and the possibility of a large number of Fresnel's bands, depend upon precisely the same conditions; the one is in truth as much an interference phenomenon as the other.

Spectroscopic method. In the second method the original light may be highly composite, and homogeneity is brought about with the aid of a spectroscope. The analogy with the first method is closest if we use the spectroscope to give us a line of homogeneous light in simple substitution for the artificial flame. Or, following Foucault and Fizeau, we may allow the white light to pass, and subsequently analyse the mixture transmitted by a narrow slit in the screen upon which the interference bands are thrown. In the latter case we observe a channelled spectrum, with maxima of brightness corresponding to the wave-lengths $bu/(nD)$. In either case the number of bands observable is limited solely by the resolving power of the spectroscope (§ 13), and proves nothing with respect to the regularity, or otherwise, of the vibrations of the original light.

Achromatic bands. The truth of this remark is strikingly illustrated by the possible formation, with white light, of a large number of achromatic bands. The unequal widths of the bands for the various colours, and consequent overlapping and obliteration, met with in the usual form of the experiment, depend upon the constancy of b (the mutual distance of the two sources) while λ varies. It is obvious that, if b were proportional to λ, the widths of the bands would be independent of λ, and that the various systems would fit together perfectly. To carry out the idea in its entirety, it would be necessary to use a diffraction spectrum as a source, and to duplicate this by Lloyd's method with a single reflector placed so that $b=0$ when $\lambda=0$. In practice a sufficiently good result could doubtless be obtained with a prismatic spectrum (especially if the red and violet were removed by absorbing agents) under the condition that $d(b/\lambda)=0$ in the yellow-green. It is remarkable that, in spite of the achromatic character of the bands, their possible number is limited still by the resolving power of the instrument used to form the spectrum.

Airy's theory of the white centre. If a system of Fresnel's bands be examined through a prism, the central white band undergoes an abnormal displacement, which has been supposed to be inconsistent with theory. The explanation has been shown by Airy[2] to depend upon the peculiar manner in which the white band is in general formed.

"Any one of the kinds of homogeneous light composing the incident heterogeneous light will produce a series of bright and dark bars, unlimited in number as far as the mixture of light from the two pencils extends, and undistinguishable in quality. The consideration, therefore, of homogeneous light will never enable us to determine which is the point that the eye immediately turns to as the centre of the fringes. What then is the physical circumstance that determines the centre of the fringes?

"The answer is very easy. For different colours the bars have different breadths. If then the bars of all colours coincide at one part of the mixture of light, they will not coincide at any other part; but at equal distances on both sides from that place of coincidence they will be equally far from a state of coincidence. If then we can find where the bars of all colours coincide, that point is the centre of the fringes.

"It appears then that the centre of the fringes is *not* necessarily the point where the two pencils of light have described equal paths, but is determined by considerations of a perfectly different kind. . . . . The distinction is important in this and in other experiments."

The effect in question depends upon the dispersive power of the prism. If v be the linear shifting due to the prism of the originally central band, v must be regarded as a function of λ. Measured from the original centre, the position of the nth bar is now

$$v+n\lambda D/b.$$

The coincidence of the various bright bands occurs when this quantity is as independent as possible of λ, that is, when n is the nearest integer to

$$n=-\frac{b}{D}\frac{dv}{d\lambda} \quad . \quad . \quad . \quad . \quad . \quad . \quad . \quad (3);$$

or, as Airy expresses it in terms of the width of a band (h), $n=-dv/dh$.

The apparent displacement of the white band is thus not v simply, but

$$v-h\frac{dv}{dh} \quad . \quad . \quad . \quad . \quad . \quad . \quad . \quad . \quad (4).$$

The signs of dv and dh being opposite, the abnormal displacement is in addition to the normal effect of the prism. But, since dv/dh,

[2] "Remarks on Mr Potter's Experiment on Interference," *Phil. Mag.*, ii. p 161, 1833.

or $dv/d\lambda$, is not constant, the achromatism of the white band is less perfect than when no prism is used.

If a grating were substituted for the prism, v would vary as h, and (4) would vanish, so that in all orders of spectra the white band would be seen undisplaced.

The theoretical error, dependent upon the dispersive power, involved in the method of determining the refractive index of a plate by means of the displacement of a system of interference fringes (LIGHT, vol. xiv. p. 607) has been discussed by Stokes.[1] In the absence of dispersion the retardation R due to the plate would be independent of λ, and therefore completely compensated at the point determined by $u = \mathrm{DR}/b$; but when there is dispersion it is accompanied by a fictitious displacement of the fringes on the principle explained by Airy.

More recently the matter has engaged the attention of Cornu,[2] who thus formulates the general principle :—"*Dans un système de franges d'interférences produites à l'aide d'une lumière hétérogène ayant un spectre continu, il existe toujours une frange achromatique qui joue le rôle de frange centrale et qui se trouve au point de champ où les radiations les plus intenses présentent une différence de phase maximum ou minimum.*"

In Fresnel's experiment, if the retardation of phase due to an interposed plate, or to any other cause, be $\mathrm{F}(\lambda)$, the whole relative retardation of the two pencils at the point u is

$$\phi = \mathrm{F}(\lambda) + \frac{bu}{\lambda \mathrm{D}} \quad . \quad . \quad . \quad . \quad . \quad . \quad . \quad (5);$$

and the situation of the central, or achromatic, band is determined, not by $\phi = 0$, but by $d\phi/d\lambda = 0$, or

$$u = \lambda^2 \mathrm{DF}'(\lambda)/b \quad . \quad . \quad . \quad . \quad . \quad . \quad . \quad (6).$$

Limits to the width of the source of light.

In the theoretical statement we have supposed the source of light to be limited to a mathematical point, or to be extended only in the vertical direction (parallel to the bands). Such a vertical extension, while it increases illumination, has no prejudicial effect upon distinctness, the various systems due to different points of the luminous line being sensibly superposed. On the other hand, the horizontal dimension of the source must be confined within narrow limits, the condition obviously being that the displacement of the centre of the system incurred by using in succession the two edges only of the slit should be small in comparison with the width of an interference band.

Diffraction and Fresnel's bands.

Before quitting this subject it is proper to remark that Fresnel's bands are more influenced by diffraction than their discoverer supposed. On this account the fringes are often unequally broad and undergo fluctuations of brightness. A more precise calculation has been given by H. F. Weber[3] and by H. Struve,[4] but the matter is too complicated to be further considered here. The observations of Struve appear to agree well with the corrected theory.

§ 8. *Colours of Thin Plates.*

When plane waves of homogeneous light (λ) fall upon a parallel plate of index μ, the resultant reflected wave is made up of an infinite number of components, of which the most important are the first, reflected at the upper surface of the plate, and the second, transmitted at the upper surface, reflected at the under surface, and then transmitted at the upper surface. It is readily proved (LIGHT, vol. xiv. p. 608) that so far as it depends upon the distances to be travelled in the plate and in air the retardation (δ) of the second wave relatively to the first is given by

$$\delta = 2\mu t \cos \alpha' \quad . \quad . \quad . \quad . \quad . \quad . \quad . \quad (1),$$

where t denotes the thickness of the plate, and α' the angle of refraction corresponding to the first entrance. If we represent all the vibrations by complex quantities, from which finally the imaginary parts are to be rejected, the retardation δ may be expressed by the introduction of the factor $\epsilon^{-i\kappa\delta}$, where $i = \sqrt{(-1)}$, and $\kappa = 2\pi/\lambda$.

Summation of partial waves.

At each reflexion or refraction the amplitude of the incident wave must be supposed to be altered by a certain factor. When the light proceeds from the surrounding medium to the plate, the factor for reflexion will be supposed to be b, and for refraction c; the corresponding quantities when the progress is from the plate to the surrounding medium will be denoted by e, f. Denoting the incident vibration by unity, we have then for the first component of the reflected wave b, for the second $cef\epsilon^{-i\kappa\delta}$, for the third $ce^3f\epsilon^{-2i\kappa\delta}$, and so on. Adding these together, and summing the geometric series, we find

$$b + \frac{cef\epsilon^{-i\kappa\delta}}{1 - e^2\epsilon^{-i\kappa\delta}} \quad . \quad . \quad . \quad . \quad . \quad . \quad . \quad (2).$$

In like manner for the wave transmitted through the plate we get

$$\frac{cf}{1 - e^2\epsilon^{-i\kappa\delta}} \quad . \quad . \quad . \quad . \quad . \quad . \quad . \quad (3).$$

The quantities b, c, e, f are not independent. The simplest way to find the relations between them is to trace the consequences of supposing $\delta = 0$ in (2) and (3). For it is evident *a priori* that with a plate of vanishing thickness there must be a vanishing reflexion, and a total transmission. Accordingly,

$$b + e = 0, \qquad cf = 1 - e^2 \quad . \quad . \quad . \quad . \quad . \quad (4),$$

the first of which embodies Arago's law of the equality of reflexions, as well as the famous "loss of half an undulation." Using these we find for the reflected vibration,

$$-\frac{e(1 - \epsilon^{-i\kappa\delta})}{1 - e^2\epsilon^{-i\kappa\delta}} \quad . \quad . \quad . \quad . \quad . \quad . \quad . \quad (5),$$

and for the transmitted vibration

$$\frac{1 - e^2}{1 - e^2\epsilon^{-i\kappa\delta}} \quad . \quad . \quad . \quad . \quad . \quad . \quad . \quad (6).$$

Intensities.

The intensities of the reflected and transmitted lights are the squares of the moduli of these expressions. Thus

$$\text{Intensity of reflected light} = e^2 \frac{(1 - \cos \kappa\delta)^2 + \sin^2 \kappa\delta}{(1 - e^2 \cos \kappa\delta)^2 + e^4 \sin^2 \kappa\delta}$$

$$= \frac{4e^2 \sin^2(\tfrac{1}{2}\kappa\delta)}{1 - 2e^2 \cos \kappa\delta + e^4} \quad . \quad . \quad . \quad (7);$$

$$\text{Intensity of transmitted light} = \frac{(1 - e^2)^2}{1 - 2e^2 \cos \kappa\delta + e^4} \quad . \quad . \quad . \quad (8),$$

the sum of the two expressions being unity.

Zero reflexion at certain thicknesses.

According to (7) not only does the reflected light vanish completely when $\delta = 0$, but also whenever $\tfrac{1}{2}k\delta = n\pi$, n being an integer, that is, whenever $\delta = n\lambda$. When the first and third medium are the same, as we have here supposed, the central spot in the system of Newton's rings is *black*, even though the original light contain a mixture of all wave lengths. The general explanation of the colours of Newton's rings is given under LIGHT, to which reference must be made. If the light reflected from a plate of any thickness be examined with a spectroscope of sufficient resolving power (§ 13), the spectrum will be traversed by dark bands, of which the centre corresponds to those wave lengths which the plate is incompetent to reflect. It is obvious that there is no limit to the fineness of the bands which may be thus impressed upon a spectrum, whatever may be the character of the original mixed light.

Principle of reversibility.

The relations between the factors b, c, e, f have been proved, independently of the theory of thin plates, in a general manner by Stokes,[5] who called to his aid the general mechanical principle of *reversibility*. If the motions constituting the reflected and refracted rays to which an incident ray gives rise be supposed to be reversed, they will reconstitute a reversed incident ray. This gives one relation; and another is obtained from the consideration that there is no ray in the second medium, such as would be generated by the operation alone of either the reversed reflected or refracted rays. Space does not allow of the reproduction of the argument at length, but a few words may perhaps give the reader an idea of how the conclusions are arrived at. The incident ray (IA) being 1, the reflected (AR) and refracted (AF) rays are denoted by b and c. When b is reversed, it gives rise to a reflected ray b^2 along AI, and a refracted ray bc along AG (say). When c is reversed, it gives rise to cf along AI, and ce along AG. Hence $bc + ce = 0$, $b^2 + cf = 1$, which agree with (4).

Fig. 1.

It is here assumed that there is no change of phase in the act of reflexion or refraction, except such as can be represented by a change of sign. Professor Stokes has, however, pushed the application of his method to the case where changes of phase are admitted, and arrives at the conclusion that "the sum of the accelerations of phase at the two reflexions is equal to the sum of the accelerations at the two refractions, and the accelerations of the two refractions are equal to each other." The accelerations are supposed to be so measured as to give like signs to c and f, and unlike to b and e. The same relations as before obtain between the factors b, c, e, f, expressing the ratios of amplitudes.[6]

Thin plate in contact with a perfect reflector.

When the third medium differs from the first, the theory of thin plates is more complicated, and need not here be discussed. One particular case, however, may be mentioned. When a thin trans-

[1] *Brit. Ass. Rep.*, 1850.

[2] *Jour. de Physique*, i. p. 293, 1882.

[3] *Wied. Ann.*, viii. p. 407.

[4] *Wied. Ann.*, xv. p. 49.

[5] "On the Perfect Blackness of the Central Spot in Newton's Rings, and on the Verification of Fresnel's Formulæ for the Intensities of Reflected and Refracted Rays," *Camb. and Dub. Math. Jour.*, vol. iv. p. 1, 1849; reprint vol. ii. p. 89.

[6] It would appear, however, that these laws cannot be properly applied to the calculation of reflexion from a thin plate. This is sufficiently proved by the fact that the resultant expression for the intensity founded upon them does not vanish with the thickness. The truth is that the method of deducing the aggregate reflexion from the consideration of the successive partial reflexions and refractions is applicable only when the disturbance in the interior of the plate is fully represented by the transverse waves considered in the argument, whereas the occurrence of a change of phase is probably connected with the existence of additional superficial waves (§ 27). The existence of these superficial waves may be ignored when the reflected and refracted waves are to be considered only at distances from the surface exceeding a few wave-lengths, but in the application to thin plates this limitation is violated. If indeed the method of calculating the aggregate reflexion from a thin plate were sound when a change of phase occurs, we could still use the expressions (2) and (3), merely understanding by b, c, e, f, factors which may be complex; and the same formal relations (4) would still hold good. These do not agree with those found by Stokes by the method of reversion; and the discrepancy indicates that, when there are changes of phase, the action of a thin plate cannot be calculated in the usual way.

parent film is backed by a perfect reflector, no colours should be visible, all the light being ultimately reflected, whatever the wave length may be. The experiment may be tried with a thin layer of gelatin on a polished silver plate. In other cases where a different result is observed, the inference is that either the metal does not reflect perfectly, or else that the material of which the film is composed is not sufficiently transparent.

Colours of ancient glass.

Theory and observation alike show that the transmitted colours of a thin plate, *e.g.*, a soap film or a layer of air, are very inferior to those reflected. Specimens of ancient glass, which have undergone superficial decomposition, on the other hand, sometimes show transmitted colours of remarkable brilliancy. The probable explanation, suggested by Brewster, is that we have here to deal not merely with one, but with a series of thin plates of not very different thicknesses. It is evident that with such a series the transmitted colours would be much purer, and the reflected much brighter, than usual. If the thicknesses are strictly equal, certain wave-lengths must still be absolutely missing in the reflected light; while on the other hand a constancy of the interval between the plates will in general lead to a special preponderance of light of some other wave-length for which all the component parts as they ultimately emerge are in agreement as to phase.[1]

Colours of Newton's scale.

All that can be expected from a physical theory is the determination of the composition of the light reflected from or transmitted by a thin plate in terms of the composition of the incident light. The further question of the chromatic character of the mixtures thus obtained belongs rather to physiological optics, and cannot be answered without a complete knowledge of the chromatic relations of the spectral colours themselves. Experiments upon this subject have been made by various observers, and especially by Maxwell,[2] who has exhibited his results on a colour diagram as used by Newton. A calculation of the colours of thin plates, based upon Maxwell's data, and accompanied by a drawing showing the curve representative of the entire series up to the fifth order, has recently been published;[3] and to this the reader who desires further information must be referred, with the remark that the true colours are not seen in the usual manner of operating with a plate of air enclosed between glass surfaces, on account of the contamination with white light reflected at the other surfaces of the glasses. This objection is avoided when a soap film is employed, to the manifest advantage of the darker colours, such as the red of the first order. The colours of Newton's scale are met with also in the light transmitted by a somewhat thin plate of doubly-refracting material, such as mica, the plane of analysis being perpendicular to that of primitive polarization.

The same series of colours occur also in other optical experiments, *e.g.*, at the centre of the illuminated area when light issuing from a point passes through a small round aperture in an otherwise opaque screen (§ 10).

Bands approximately achromatic.

The colours of which we have been speaking are those formed at nearly perpendicular incidence, so that the retardation (reckoned as a distance), viz., $2\mu t\cos\alpha'$, is sensibly independent of λ. This state of things may be greatly departed from when the thin plate is rarer than its surroundings, and the incidence is such that α' is nearly equal to 90°, for then, in consequence of the powerful dispersion, $\cos\alpha'$ may vary greatly as we pass from one colour to another. Under these circumstances the series of colours entirely alters its character, and the bands (corresponding to a graduated thickness) may even lose their coloration, becoming sensibly black and white through many alternations.[4] The general explanation of this remarkable phenomenon was suggested by Newton, but it does not appear to have been followed out in accordance with the wave theory.

Let us suppose that plane waves of white light travelling in glass are incident at angle α upon a plate of air, which is bounded again on the other side by glass. If μ be the index of the *glass*, α' the angle of refraction, then $\sin\alpha'=\mu\sin\alpha$; and the retardation, expressed by the equivalent distance in air, is

$$2t\sec\alpha' - \mu\,.\,2t\tan\alpha'\sin\alpha = 2t\cos\alpha'\,;$$

and the retardation in *phase* is $2t\cos\alpha'/\lambda$, λ being as usual the wave-length in air.

The first thing to be noticed is that, when α approaches the critical angle, $\cos\alpha'$ becomes as small as we please, and that consequently the retardation corresponding to a given thickness is very much less than at perpendicular incidence. Hence the glass surfaces need not be so close as usual.

A second feature is the increased brilliancy of the light. According to (7) the intensity of the reflected light when at a maximum ($\sin\frac{1}{2}\kappa\delta=1$) is $4e^2/(1+e^2)^2$. At perpendicular incidence e is about $\frac{1}{5}$, and the intensity is somewhat small; but, as $\cos\alpha'$ approaches zero, e approaches unity (§ 26), and the brilliancy is much increased.

But the peculiarity which most demands attention is the lessened influence of a variation in λ upon the phase-retardation. A diminution of λ of itself increases the retardation of phase, but, since waves of shorter wave-length are more refrangible, this effect may be more or less perfectly compensated by the greater obliquity, and consequent diminution in the value of $\cos\alpha'$. We will investigate the conditions under which the retardation of phase is stationary in spite of a variation of λ.

In order that $\lambda^{-1}\cos\alpha'$ may be stationary, we must have

$$\lambda\sin\alpha'd\alpha' + \cos\alpha'd\lambda = 0\,,$$

where (α being constant)

$$\cos\alpha'd\alpha' = \sin\alpha\, d\mu\,.$$

Thus

$$\cot^2\alpha' = -\frac{\lambda}{\mu}\frac{d\mu}{d\lambda} \quad . \quad . \quad . \quad . \quad . \quad . \quad . \quad (9),$$

giving α' when the relation between μ and λ is known.

According to Cauchy's formula, which represents the facts very well throughout most of the visible spectrum,

$$\mu = A + B\lambda^{-2} \quad . \quad . \quad . \quad . \quad . \quad . \quad . \quad . \quad (10),$$

so that

$$\cot^2\alpha' = \frac{2B}{\lambda^2\mu} = \frac{2(\mu - A)}{\mu} \quad . \quad . \quad . \quad . \quad . \quad (11).$$

If we take, as for Chance's "extra-dense flint," $B = \cdot984\times10^{-10}$, and, as for the soda lines, $\mu=1\cdot65$, $\lambda=5\cdot89\times10^{-5}$, we get

$$\alpha' = 79°\ 30'.$$

At this angle of refraction, and with this kind of glass, the retardation of phase is accordingly nearly independent of wave-length, and therefore the bands formed, as the thickness varies, are approximately achromatic. Perfect achromatism would be possible only under a law of dispersion

$$\mu^2 = A' - B'\lambda^2.$$

If the source of light be distant and very small, the black bands are wonderfully fine and numerous. The experiment is best made (after Newton) with a right-angled prism, whose hypothenusal surface may be brought into approximate contact with a plate of black glass. The bands should be observed with a convex lens, of about 8 inches focus. If the eye be at twice this distance from the prism, and the lens be held midway between, the advantages are combined of a large field and of maximum distinctness.

Effect of a prism.

If Newton's rings are examined through a prism, some very remarkable phenomena are exhibited, described in his twenty-fourth observation.[5] "When the two object-glasses are laid upon one another, so as to make the rings of the colours appear, though with my naked eye I could not discern above eight or nine of those rings, yet by viewing them through a prism I could see a far greater multitude, insomuch that I could number more than forty. . . . . And I believe that the experiment may be improved to the discovery of far greater numbers. . . . . But it was on but one side of these rings, namely, that towards which the refraction was made, which by the refraction was rendered distinct, and the other side became more confused than when viewed with the naked eye. . . . .

"I have sometimes so laid one object-glass upon the other that to the naked eye they have all over seemed uniformly white, without the least appearance of any of the coloured rings; and yet by viewing them through a prism great multitudes of those rings have discovered themselves."

Newton was evidently much struck with these "so odd circumstances;" and he explains the occurrence of the rings at unusual thicknesses as due to the dispersing power of the prism. The blue system being more refracted than the red, it is possible under certain conditions that the nth blue ring may be so much displaced relatively to the corresponding red ring as *at one part of the circumference* to compensate for the different diameters. A white stripe may thus be formed in a situation where without the prism the mixture of colours would be complete, so far as could be judged by the eye.

The simplest case that can be considered is when the "thin plate" is bounded by plane surfaces inclined to one another at a small angle. By drawing back the prism (whose edge is parallel to the intersection of the above-mentioned planes) it will always be possible so to adjust the effective dispersing power as to bring the nth bars to coincidence for any two assigned colours, and therefore approximately for the entire spectrum. The formation of the achromatic band, or rather central black band, depends indeed upon the same principles as the fictitious shifting of the centre of a system of Fresnel's bands when viewed through a prism.

Condition of achromatism.

But neither Newton nor, as would appear, any of his successors has explained why the bands should be more numerous than usual, and under certain conditions sensibly achromatic for a large number of alternations. It is evident that, in the particular case of the wedge-shaped plate above specified, such a result would not occur. The width of the bands for any colour would be proportional to λ, as well after the displacement by the prism as before; and the succession of colours formed in white light and the number of perceptible bands would be much as usual.

[1] The analytical investigations and formulæ given by Stokes for a pile of plates (*Proc. Roy. Soc.*, xi. p. 545, 1860) may be applied to this question, provided that we understand the quantities r, t, ϕ, ψ, &c., to be complex, so as to express the luminous displacement in phase as well as in amplitude, instead of real quantities relating merely to *intensities*.

[2] Maxwell, "Theory of Compound Colours," *Phil. Trans.*, 1860.

[3] *Edin. Trans.*, 1887.

[4] Newton's *Optics*, bk. ii.; Fox Talbot, *Phil. Mag.*, ix. p. 401, 1836.

[5] Newton's *Optics*. See also Place, *Pogg. Ann.*, cxiv. p. 504, 1861.

The peculiarity to be explained appears to depend upon the *curvature* of the surfaces bounding the plate. For simplicity suppose that the lower surface is plane ($y=0$), and that the approximate equation of the upper surface is $y=a+bx^2$, a being thus the least distance between the plates. The black of the nth order for wave-length λ occurs when

$$\tfrac{1}{2}n\lambda = a + bx^2 \quad . \quad . \quad . \quad . \quad . \quad . \quad . \quad . \quad (12);$$

and thus the width (δx) at this place of the band is given by

$$\tfrac{1}{2}\lambda = 2bx\delta x \quad . \quad . \quad . \quad . \quad . \quad . \quad . \quad . \quad (13),$$

or

$$\delta x = \frac{\lambda}{4bx} = \frac{\lambda}{4\sqrt{b}\,.\,\sqrt{(\frac{1}{2}n\lambda - a)}} \quad . \quad . \quad . \quad . \quad . \quad (14).$$

If the glasses be in contact, as is usually supposed in the theory of Newton's rings, $a=0$, and $\delta x \propto \lambda^{\frac{1}{2}}$, or the width of the band of the nth order varies as the square root of the wave-length, instead of as the first power. Even in this case the overlapping and subsequent obliteration of the bands is greatly retarded by the use of the prism, but the full development of the phenomenon requires that a should be finite. Let us inquire what is the condition in order that the width of the band of the nth order may be stationary, as λ varies. By (14) it is necessary that the variation of $\lambda^2/(\frac{1}{2}n\lambda - a)$ should vanish. Hence $a = \frac{1}{4}n\lambda$, so that the interval between the surfaces at the place where the nth band is formed should be half due to curvature and half to imperfect contact at the place of closest approach. If this condition be satisfied, the achromatism of the nth band, effected by the prism, carries with it the achromatism of a large number of neighbouring bands, and thus gives rise to the remarkable effects described by Newton.

§ 9. *Newton's Diffusion Rings.*

In the fourth part of the second book of his *Optics* Newton investigates another series of rings, usually (though not very appropriately) known as the colours of thick plates. The fundamental experiment is as follows. At the centre of curvature of a concave looking-glass, quicksilvered behind, is placed an opaque card, perforated by a small hole through which sunlight is admitted. The main body of the light returns through the aperture ; but a series of concentric rings are seen upon the card, the formation of which was proved by Newton to require the co-operation of the two surfaces of the mirror. Thus the diameters of the rings depend upon the thickness of the glass, and none are formed when the glass is replaced by a metallic speculum. The brilliancy of the rings depends upon imperfect polish of the anterior surface of the glass, and may be augmented by a coat of diluted milk, a device used by the Duc de Chaulnes. The rings may also be well observed without a screen in the manner recommended by Stokes. For this purpose all that is required is to place a *small* flame at the centre of curvature of the prepared glass, so as to concide with its image. The rings are then seen surrounding the flame and occupying a definite position in space.

The explanation of the rings, suggested by Young, and developed by Herschel, refers them to interference between one portion of light scattered or diffracted by a particle of dust, and then regularly refracted and reflected, and another portion first regularly refracted and reflected and then diffracted at emergence by the same particle. It has been shown by Stokes[1] that no regular interference is to be expected between portions of light diffracted by different particles of dust.

Stokes's principle.

In the memoir of Stokes will be found a very complete discussion of the whole subject, and to this the reader must be referred who desires a fuller knowledge. Our limits will not allow us to do more than touch upon one or two points. The condition of fixity of the rings when observed in air, and of distinctness when a screen is used, is that the systems due to all parts of the diffusing surface should coincide; and it is fulfilled only when, as in Newton's experiments, the source and screen are in the plane passing through the centre of curvature of the glass.

Plane mirror and lens.

As the simplest for actual calculation, we will consider a little further the case where the glass is plane and parallel, of thickness t and index μ, and is supplemented by a lens at whose focus the source of light is placed. This lens acts both as collimator and as object-glass, so that the combination of lens and plane mirror replaces the concave mirror of Newton's experiment. The retardation is calculated in the same way as for thin plates. In fig. 2 the diffracting particle is situated at B, and we have to find the relative retardation of the two rays which emerge finally at inclination θ, the one diffracted at emergence following the path ABDBIE, and the other diffracted at entrance and following the path ABFGH. The retardation of the former from B to I is $2\mu t + \text{BI}$, and of the latter from B to the equivalent place G is $2\mu\text{BF}$. Now $\text{FB} = t\sec\theta'$, θ' being the angle of refraction ; $\text{BI} = 2t\tan\theta'\sin\theta$; so that the relative retardation R is given by

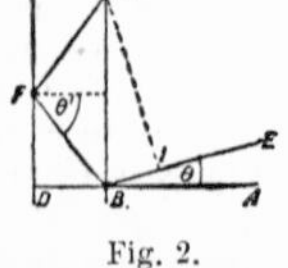

Fig. 2.

$$\text{R} = 2\mu t\left\{1 + \mu^{-1}\tan\theta'\sin\theta - \sec\theta'\right\} = 2\mu t(1 - \cos\theta').$$

If θ, θ' be small, we may take

$$\text{R} = 2t\theta^2/\mu \quad . \quad . \quad . \quad . \quad . \quad . \quad . \quad . \quad . \quad (1)$$

as sufficiently approximate.

The condition of distinctness is here satisfied, since R is the same for every ray emergent parallel to a given one. The rays of one parallel system are collected by the lens to a focus at a definite point in the neighbourhood of the original source.

The formula (1) was discussed by Herschel, and shown to agree with Newton's measures. The law of formation of the rings follows immediately from the expression for the retardation, the radius of the ring of nth order being proportional to n and to the square root of the wave-length.

§ 10. *Huygens's Principle. Theory of Shadows.*

The objection most frequently brought against the undulatory theory in its infancy was the difficulty of explaining in accordance with it the existence of shadows. Thanks to Fresnel and his followers, this department of optics is now precisely the one in which the theory has secured its greatest triumphs.

Huygens's principle.

The principle employed in these investigations is due to Huygens, and may be thus formulated. If round the origin of waves an ideal closed surface be drawn, the whole action of the waves in the region beyond may be regarded as due to the motion continually propagated across the various elements of this surface. The wave motion due to any element of the surface is called a *secondary* wave, and in estimating the total effect regard must be paid to the phases as well as the amplitudes of the components. It is usually convenient to choose as the surface of resolution a *wave-front, i.e.,* a surface at which the primary vibrations are in one phase.

Any obscurity that may hang over Huygens's principle is due mainly to the indefiniteness of thought and expression which we must be content to put up with if we wish to avoid pledging ourselves as to the character of the vibrations. In the application to sound, where we know what we are dealing with, the matter is simple enough in principle, although mathematical difficulties would often stand in the way of the calculations we might wish to make. The ideal surface of resolution may be there regarded as a flexible lamina; and we know that, if by forces locally applied every element of the lamina be made to move normally to itself exactly as the air at that place does, the external aerial motion is fully determined. By the principle of superposition the whole effect may be found by integration of the partial effects due to each element of the surface, the other elements remaining at rest.

Plane primary wave.

Huygens's zones.

We will now consider in detail the important case in which uniform plane waves are resolved at a surface coincident with a wave-front (OQ). We imagine the wave-front divided into elementary rings or zones, called Huygens's zones, by spheres described round P (the point at which the aggregate effect is to be estimated), the first sphere, touching the plane at O, with a radius equal to PO, and the succeeding spheres with radii increasing at each step by $\frac{1}{2}\lambda$. There are thus marked out a series of circles, whose radii x are given by $x^2 + r^2 = (r + \frac{1}{2}n\lambda)^2$, or $x^2 = n\lambda r$ nearly; so that the rings are at first of nearly equal area. Now the effect upon P of each element of the plane is proportional to its area; but it depends also upon the distance from P, and possibly upon the inclination of the secondary ray to the direction of vibration and to the wave-front. These questions will be further considered in connexion with the dynamical theory ; but under all ordinary circumstances the result is independent of the precise answer that may be given. All that it is necessary to assume is that the effects of the successive zones gradually diminish, whether from the increasing obliquity of the secondary ray or because (on account of the limitation of the region of integration) the zones become at last more and more incomplete. The component vibrations at P due to the successive zones are thus nearly equal in amplitude and opposite in phase (the phase of each corresponding to that of the infinitesimal circle midway between the boundaries), and the series which we have to sum is one in which the terms are alternately opposite in sign and, while at first nearly constant in numerical magnitude, gradually diminish to zero. In such a series each term may be regarded as very nearly indeed destroyed by the halves of its immediate neighbours, and thus the sum of the whole series is represented by half the first term, which stands over uncompensated. The question is thus reduced to that of finding the effect of the first zone, or central circle, of which the area is $\pi\lambda r$.

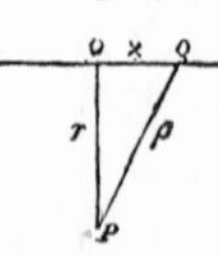

Fig. 3.

We have seen that the problem before us is independent of the law of the secondary wave as regards obliquity; but the result of the integration necessarily involves the law of the intensity and phase of a secondary wave as a function of r, the distance from the origin. And we may in fact, as was done by A. Smith,[2] determine

[1] *Camb. Trans.*, ix. p. 147, 1851.

[2] *Camb. Math. Jour.*, iii. p. 46, 1843.

the law of the secondary wave, by comparing the result of the integration with that obtained by supposing the primary wave to pass on to P without resolution.

Initial phase of secondary waves.

Now as to the phase of the secondary wave, it might appear natural to suppose that it starts from any point Q with the phase of the primary wave, so that on arrival at P it is retarded by the amount corresponding to QP. But a little consideration will prove that in that case the series of secondary waves could not reconstitute the primary wave. For the aggregate effect of the secondary waves is the half of that of the first Huygens zone, and it is the central element only of that zone for which the distance to be travelled is equal to r. Let us conceive the zone in question to be divided into infinitesimal rings of equal area. The effects due to each of these rings are equal in amplitude and of phase ranging uniformly over half a complete period. The phase of the resultant is midway between those of the extreme elements, that is to say, a quarter of a period behind that due to the element at the centre of the circle. It is accordingly necessary to suppose that the secondary waves start with a phase one-quarter of a period in advance of that of the primary wave at the surface of resolution.

Factor for secondary wave.

Further, it is evident that account must be taken of the variation of phase in estimating the magnitude of the effect at P of the first zone. The middle element alone contributes without deduction; the effect of every other must be found by introduction of a resolving factor, equal to $\cos\theta$, if θ represent the difference of phase between this element and the resultant. Accordingly, the amplitude of the resultant will be less than if all its components had the same phase, in the ratio

$$\int_{-\frac{1}{2}\pi}^{+\frac{1}{2}\pi} \cos\theta \, d\theta : \pi,$$

or $2:\pi$. Now 2 area $/\pi = 2\lambda r$; so that, in order to reconcile the amplitude of the primary wave (taken as unity) with the half effect of the first zone, the amplitude, at distance r, of the secondary wave emitted from the element of area dS must be taken to be

$$\frac{dS}{\lambda r} \quad . \quad . \quad . \quad . \quad . \quad . \quad . \quad . \quad . \quad (1).$$

By this expression, in conjunction with the quarter-period acceleration of phase, the law of the secondary wave is determined.

That the amplitude of the secondary wave should vary as r^{-1} was to be expected from considerations respecting energy; but the occurrence of the factor λ^{-1}, and the acceleration of phase, have sometimes been regarded as mysterious. It may be well therefore to remember that precisely these laws apply to a secondary wave of sound, which can be investigated upon the strictest mechanical principles.

Analytical investigation.

The recomposition of the secondary waves may also be treated analytically. If the primary wave at O be $\cos \kappa at$, the effect of the secondary wave proceeding from the element dS at Q is

$$\frac{dS}{\lambda\rho}\cos\kappa(at-\rho+\tfrac{1}{4}\lambda) = -\frac{dS}{\lambda\rho}\sin\kappa(at-\rho).$$

If $dS = 2\pi x dx$, we have for the whole effect

$$-\frac{2\pi}{\lambda}\int_0^\infty \frac{\sin\kappa(at-\rho)\, x dx}{\rho},$$

or, since $x dx = \rho d\rho$, $\kappa = 2\pi/\lambda$,

$$-\kappa\int_r^\infty \sin\kappa(at-\rho)\, d\rho = \Big[-\cos\kappa(at-\rho)\Big]_r^\infty .$$

In order to obtain the effect of the primary wave, as retarded by traversing the distance r, viz., $\cos\kappa\,(at-r)$, it is necessary to suppose that the integrated term vanishes at the upper limit. And it is important to notice that without some further understanding the integral is really ambiguous. According to the assumed law of the secondary wave, the result must actually depend upon the precise radius of the outer boundary of the region of integration, supposed to be exactly circular. This case is, however, at most very special and exceptional. We may usually suppose that a large number of the outer rings are incomplete, so that the integrated term at the upper limit may properly be taken to vanish. If a formal proof be desired, it may be obtained by introducing into the integral a factor such as $e^{-h\rho}$, in which h is ultimately made to diminish without limit.

Primary wave curved.

When the primary wave is plane, the area of the first Huygens zone is $\pi\lambda r$, and, since the secondary waves vary as r^{-1}, the intensity is independent of r, as of course it should be. If, however, the primary wave be spherical, and of radius a at the wave-front of resolution, then we know that at a distance r further on the amplitude of the primary wave will be diminished in the ratio $a:(r+a)$. This may be regarded as a consequence of the altered area of the first Huygens zone. For, if x be its radius, we have

$$\sqrt{\{(r+\tfrac{1}{2}\lambda)^2 - x^2\}} + \sqrt{\{a^2-x^2\}} = r+a,$$

so that

$$x^2 = \frac{\lambda a r}{a+r} \text{ nearly}.$$

Since the distance to be travelled by the secondary waves is still r, we see how the effect of the first zone, and therefore of the whole series is proportional to $a/(a+r)$. In like manner may be treated other cases, such as that of a primary wave-front of unequal principal curvatures.

Shadows.

The general explanation of the formation of shadows may also be conveniently based upon Huygens's zones. If the point under consideration be so far away from the geometrical shadow that a large number of the earlier zones are complete, then the illumination, determined sensibly by the first zone, is the same as if there were no obstruction at all. If, on the other hand, the point be well immersed in the geometrical shadow, the earlier zones are altogether missing, and, instead of a series of terms beginning with finite numerical magnitude and gradually diminishing to zero, we have now to deal with one of which the terms diminish to zero *at both ends*. The sum of such a series is very approximately zero, each term being neutralized by the halves of its immediate neighbours, which are of the opposite sign. The question of light or darkness then depends upon whether the series begins or ends abruptly. With few exceptions, abruptness can occur only in the presence of the first term, viz., when the secondary wave of least retardation is unobstructed, or when a *ray* passes through the point under consideration. According to the undulatory theory the light cannot be regarded strictly as travelling along a ray; but the existence of an unobstructed ray implies that the system of Huygens's zones can be commenced, and, if a large number of these zones are fully developed and do not terminate abruptly, the illumination is unaffected by the neighbourhood of obstacles. Intermediate cases in which a few zones only are formed belong especially to the province of diffraction.

Poisson's problem.

An interesting exception to the general rule that full brightness requires the existence of the first zone occurs when the obstacle assumes the form of a small circular disk parallel to the plane of the incident waves. In the earlier half of the 18th century[1] Delisle found that the centre of the circular shadow was occupied by a bright point of light, but the observation passed into oblivion until Poisson brought forward as an objection to Fresnel's theory that it required at the centre of a circular shadow a point as bright as if no obstacle were intervening. If we conceive the primary wave to be broken up at the plane of the disk, a system of Huygens's zones can be constructed which begin from the circumference; and the first zone external to the disk plays the part ordinarily taken by the centre of the entire system. The whole effect is the half of that of the first existing zone, and this is sensibly the same as if there were no obstruction.

Circular or annular aperture.

When light passes through a small circular or annular aperture, the illumination at any point along the axis depends upon the precise relation between the aperture and the distance from it at which the point is taken. If, as in the last paragraph, we imagine a system of zones to be drawn commencing from the inner circular boundary of the aperture, the question turns upon the manner in which the series terminates at the outer boundary. If the aperture be such as to fit exactly an integral number of zones, the aggregate effect may be regarded as the half of those due to the first and last zones. If the number of zones be even, the action of the first and last zones are antagonistic, and there is complete darkness at the point. If on the other hand the number of zones be odd, the effects conspire; and the illumination (proportional to the square of the amplitude) is four times as great as if there were no obstruction at all.

Soret's experiment.

The process of augmenting the resultant illumination at a particular point by stopping some of the secondary rays may be carried much further.[2] By the aid of photography it is easy to prepare a plate, transparent where the zones of odd order fall, and opaque where those of even order fall. Such a plate has the power of a condensing lens, and gives an illumination out of all proportion to what could be obtained without it. An even greater effect (fourfold) would be attained if it were possible to provide that the stoppage of the light from the alternate zones were replaced by a phase-reversal without loss of amplitude.

Degree of accuracy required.

In such experiments the narrowness of the zones renders necessary a pretty close approximation to the geometrical conditions. Thus in the case of the circular disk, equidistant (r) from the source of light and from the screen upon which the shadow is observed, the width of the first exterior zone is given by

$$dx = \frac{\lambda(2r)}{4(2x)},$$

$2x$ being the diameter of the disk. If $2r = 1000$ cm., $2x = 1$ cm., $\lambda = 6\times10^{-5}$ cm., then $dx = \cdot0015$ cm. Hence, in order that this zone may be perfectly formed, there should be no error in the circumference of the order of $\cdot001$ cm.[3] The experiment succeeds in a dark room of the length above mentioned, with a threepenny bit (supported by three threads) as obstacle, the origin of light being a small needle hole in a plate of tin, through which the sun's rays shine horizontally after reflexion from an external mirror. In the absence of a heliostat it is more convenient to obtain a point of light with the aid of a lens of short focus.

---

[1] Verdet, *Leçons d'Optique Physique*, i. § 66. [2] Soret, *Pogg. Ann.*, clvi. p. 99, 1875.

[3] It is easy to see that the radius of the bright spot is of the same order of magnitude.

Analytical expression.

The amplitude of the light at any point in the axis, when plane waves are incident perpendicularly upon an annular aperture, is, as above,

$$\cos\kappa(at-r_1)-\cos\kappa(at-r_2)=2\sin\kappa at\,.\,\sin\kappa(r_1-r_2),$$

r_2, r_1 being the distances of the outer and inner boundaries from the point in question. It is scarcely necessary to remark that in all such cases the calculation applies in the first instance to homogeneous light, and that, in accordance with Fourier's theorem, each homogeneous component of a mixture may be treated separately. When the original light is white, the presence of some components and the absence of others will usually give rise to coloured effects, variable with the precise circumstances of the case.

Uncertainty in the application of Huygens's principle.

Although what we have to say upon the subject is better postponed until we consider the dynamical theory, it is proper to point out at once that there is an element of assumption in the application of Huygens's principle to the calculation of the effects produced by opaque screens of limited extent. Properly applied, the principle could not fail; but, as may readily be proved in the case of sonorous waves, it is not in strictness sufficient to assume the expression for a secondary wave suitable when the primary wave is undisturbed, with mere limitation of the integration to the transparent parts of the screen. But, except perhaps in the case of very fine gratings, it is probable that the error thus caused is insignificant; for the incorrect estimation of the secondary waves will be limited to distances of a few wave-lengths only from the boundary of opaque and transparent parts.

§ 11. *Fraunhofer's Diffraction Phenomena.*

A very general problem in diffraction is the investigation of the distribution of light over a screen upon which impinge divergent or convergent spherical waves after passage through various diffracting apertures. When the waves are convergent and the recipient screen is placed so as to contain the centre of convergency—the image of the original radiant point, the calculation assumes a less complicated form. This class of phenomena was investigated by Fraunhofer (upon principles laid down by Fresnel), and are sometimes called after his name. We may conveniently commence with them on account of their simplicity and great importance in respect to the theory of optical instruments.

If f be the radius of the spherical wave at the place of resolution, where the vibration is represented by $\cos\kappa at$, then at any point M (fig. 4) in the recipient screen the vibration due to an element dS of the wave-front is (§ 9)

Fig. 4.

$$-\frac{dS}{\lambda\rho}\sin\kappa(at-\rho)\,,$$

ρ being the distance between M and the element dS.

Taking coordinates in the plane of the screen with the centre of the wave as origin, let us represent M by ξ, η, and P (where dS is situated) by x, y, z.

Then

$$\rho^2=(x-\xi)^2+(y-\eta)^2+z^2,\quad f^2=x^2+y^2+z^2\,;$$

so that

$$\rho^2=f^2-2x\xi-2y\eta+\xi^2+\eta^2.$$

In the applications with which we are concerned, ξ, η are very small quantities; and we may take

$$\rho=f\left\{1-\frac{x\xi+y\eta}{f^2}\right\}.$$

At the same time dS may be identified with $dxdy$, and in the denominator ρ may be treated as constant and equal to f. Thus the expression for the vibration at M becomes

$$-\frac{1}{\lambda f}\iint\sin\kappa\left\{at-f+\frac{x\xi+y\eta}{f}\right\}dx\,dy \quad . \quad . \quad . \quad (1);$$

Expression for intensity.

and for the intensity, represented by the square of the amplitude,

$$\mathrm{I}^2=\frac{1}{\lambda^2f^2}\left[\iint\sin\kappa\frac{x\xi+y\eta}{f}dxdy\right]^2$$
$$+\frac{1}{\lambda^2f^2}\left[\iint\cos\kappa\frac{x\xi+y\eta}{f}dxdy\right]^2 \quad . \quad . \quad . \quad . \quad (2).$$

This expression for the intensity becomes rigorously applicable when f is indefinitely great, so that ordinary optical aberration disappears. The incident waves are thus plane, and are limited to a plane aperture coincident with a wave-front. The integrals are then properly functions of the *direction* in which the light is to be estimated.

In experiment under ordinary circumstances it makes no difference whether the collecting lens is in front of or behind the diffracting aperture. It is usually most convenient to employ a telescope focused upon the radiant point, and to place the diffracting apertures immediately in front of the object-glass. What is seen through the eye-piece in any case is the same as would be depicted upon a screen in the focal plane.

Theorems of Bridge.

Before proceeding to special cases it may be well to call attention to some general properties of the solution expressed by (2).[1]

If, when the aperture is given, the wave-length (proportional to κ^{-1}) varies, the composition of the integrals is unaltered, provided ξ and η are taken universely proportional to λ. A diminution of λ thus leads to a simple proportional shrinkage of the diffraction pattern, attended by an augmentation of brilliancy in proportion to λ^{-2}.

If the wave-length remains unchanged, similar effects are produced by an increase in the scale of the aperture. The linear dimension of the diffraction pattern is inversely as that of the aperture, and the brightness at corresponding points is as the *square* of the area of aperture.

If the aperture and wave-length increase in the same proportion, the size and shape of the diffraction pattern undergo no change.

Rectangular aperture.

We will now apply the integrals (2) to the case of a rectangular aperture of width a parallel to x and of width b parallel to y. The limits of integration for x may thus be taken to be $-\frac{1}{2}a$ and $+\frac{1}{2}a$, and for y to be $-\frac{1}{2}b$, $+\frac{1}{2}b$. We readily find (with substitution for κ of $2\pi/\lambda$)

$$\mathrm{I}^2=\frac{a^2b^2}{f^2\lambda^2}\cdot\frac{\sin^2\dfrac{\pi a\xi}{f\lambda}}{\dfrac{\pi^2a^2\xi^2}{f^2\lambda^2}}\cdot\frac{\sin^2\dfrac{\pi b\eta}{f\lambda}}{\dfrac{\pi^2b^2\eta^2}{f^2\lambda^2}} \quad . \quad . \quad . \quad . \quad . \quad (3),$$

as representing the distribution of light in the image of a mathematical point when the aperture is rectangular, as is often the case in spectroscopes.

The second and third factors of (3) being each of the form $\sin^2u/u^2$, we have to examine the character of this function. It vanishes when $u=m\pi$, m being any whole number other than zero. When $u=0$, it takes the value unity. The maxima occur when

$$u=\tan u\,, \quad . \quad . \quad . \quad . \quad . \quad . \quad . \quad . \quad (4),$$

and then

$$\sin^2u/u^2=\cos^2u \quad . \quad . \quad . \quad . \quad . \quad . \quad . \quad (5).$$

To calculate the roots of (5) we may assume

$$u=(m+\tfrac{1}{2})\pi-y=\mathrm{U}-y\,,$$

where y is a positive quantity which is small when u is large Substituting this, we find $\cot y=\mathrm{U}-y$, whence

$$y=\frac{1}{\mathrm{U}}\left(1+\frac{y}{\mathrm{U}}+\frac{y^2}{\mathrm{U}^2}+\ldots\right)-\frac{y^3}{3}-\frac{2y^5}{15}-\frac{17y^7}{315}\,.$$

This equation is to be solved by successive approximation. It will readily be found that

$$u=\mathrm{U}-y=\mathrm{U}-\mathrm{U}^{-1}-\frac{2}{3}\mathrm{U}^{-3}-\frac{13}{15}\mathrm{U}^{-5}-\frac{146}{105}\mathrm{U}^{-7}-\,. \quad . \quad (6).$$

In the first quadrant there is no root after zero, since $\tan u>u$, and in the second quadrant there is none because the signs of u and $\tan u$ are opposite. The first root after zero is thus in the third quadrant, corresponding to $m=1$. Even in this case the series converges sufficiently to give the value of the root with considerable accuracy, while for higher values of m it is all that could be desired. The actual values of u/π (calculated in another manner by Schwerd) are 1·4303, 2·4590, 3·4709, 4·4747, 5·4818, 6·4844, &c.

Since the maxima occur when $u=(m+\frac{1}{2})\pi$ nearly, the successive values are not very different from

$$\frac{4}{9\pi^2}\,,\ \frac{4}{25\pi^2}\,,\ \frac{4}{49\pi^2}\,,\ \&c.$$

Diffraction pattern.

The application of these results to (3) shows that the field is brightest at the centre $\xi=0,\eta=0$, viz., at the geometrical image. It is traversed by dark lines whose equations are

$$\xi=mf\lambda/a\,,\quad \eta=mf\lambda/b\,.$$

Within the rectangle formed by pairs of consecutive dark lines, and not far from its centre, the brightness rises to a maximum; but these subsequent maxima are in all cases much inferior to the brightness at the centre of the entire pattern ($\xi=0,\eta=0$).

Total illumination.

By the principle of energy the illumination over the entire focal plane must be equal to that over the diffracting area; and thus, in accordance with the suppositions by which (3) was obtained, its value when integrated from $\xi=-\infty$ to $\xi=+\infty$, and from $\eta=-\infty$ to $\eta=+\infty$ should be equal to ab. This integration, employed originally by Kelland[2] to determine the absolute intensity of a secondary wave, may be at once effected by means of the known formula

$$\int_{-\infty}^{+\infty}\frac{\sin^2u}{u^2}du=\int_{-\infty}^{+\infty}\frac{\sin u}{u}du=\pi\,.$$

It will be observed that, while the total intensity is proportional to ab, the intensity at the focal point is proportional to a^2b^2. If the aperture be increased, not only is the total brightness over the focal plane increased with it, but there is also a concentration of the diffraction pattern. The form of (3) shows immediately that, if a and b be altered, the coordinates of any characteristic point in the pattern vary as a^{-1} and b^{-1}.

Diffusion of images due to finite wave-length.

The contraction of the diffraction pattern with increase of aperture is of fundamental importance with reference to the resolving power of optical instruments. According to common optics, where images are absolute, the diffraction pattern is sup-

[1] Bridge, *Phil. Mag.*, Nov. 1858.

[2] *Ed. Trans.*, xv. 315.

posed to be infinitely small, and two radiant points, however near together, form separated images. This is tantamount to an assumption that λ is infinitely small. The actual finiteness of λ imposes a limit upon the separating or resolving power of an optical instrument.

This indefiniteness of images is sometimes said to be due to diffraction by the edge of the aperture, and proposals have even been made for curing it by causing the transition between the interrupted and transmitted parts of the primary wave to be less abrupt. Such a view of the matter is altogether misleading. What requires explanation is not the imperfection of actual images so much as the possibility of their being as good as we find them.

At the focal point ($\xi=0, \eta=0$) all the secondary waves agree in phase, and the intensity is easily expressed, whatever be the form of the aperture. From the general formula (2), if A be the *area* of aperture,

$$I_0^2 = A^2/\lambda^2 f^2 \quad . \quad . \quad . \quad . \quad . \quad . \quad . \quad . \quad (7).$$

The formation of a sharp image of the radiant point requires that the illumination become insignificant when ξ, η attain small values, and this insignificance can only arise as a consequence of discrepancies of phase among the secondary waves from various parts of the aperture. So long as there is no sensible discrepancy of phase there can be no sensible diminution of brightness as compared with that to be found at the focal point itself. We may go further, and lay it down that there can be no considerable loss of brightness until the difference of phase of the waves proceeding from the nearest and furthest parts of the aperture amounts to $\frac{1}{4}\lambda$.

When the difference of phase amounts to λ, we may expect the resultant illumination to be very much reduced. In the particular case of a rectangular aperture the course of things can be readily followed, especially if we conceive f to be infinite. In the direction (suppose horizontal) for which $\eta=0$, $\xi/f=\sin\theta$, the phases of the secondary waves range over a complete period when $\sin\theta=\lambda/a$, and, since all parts of the horizontal aperture are equally effective, there is in this direction a complete compensation and consequent absence of illumination. When $\sin\theta=\frac{3}{2}\lambda/a$, the phases range one and a half periods, and there is revival of illumination. We may compare the brightness with that in the direction $\theta=0$. The phase of the resultant amplitude is the same as that due to the central secondary wave, and the discrepancies of phase among the components reduce the amplitude in the proportion

$$\frac{1}{3\pi}\int_{-\frac{3\pi}{2}}^{+\frac{3\pi}{2}} \cos\phi \, d\phi : 1,$$

or $-\frac{2}{3\pi} : 1$; so that the brightness in this direction is $\frac{4}{9\pi^2}$ of the maximum at $\theta=0$. In like manner we may find the illumination in any other direction, and it is obvious that it vanishes when $\sin\theta$ is any multiple of λ/a.

The reason of the augmentation of resolving power with aperture will now be evident. The larger the aperture the smaller are the angles through which it is necessary to deviate from the principal direction in order to bring in specified discrepancies of phase—the more concentrated is the image.

Luminous line.

In many cases the subject of examination is a luminous line of uniform intensity, the various points of which are to be treated as independent sources of light. If the image of the line be $\xi=0$, the intensity at any point ξ, η of the diffraction pattern may be represented by

$$\int_{-\infty}^{+\infty} I^2 d\eta = \frac{a^2 b}{\lambda f} \frac{\sin^2 \frac{\pi a \xi}{\lambda f}}{\frac{\pi^2 a^2 \xi^2}{\lambda^2 f^2}} \quad . \quad . \quad . \quad . \quad . \quad (8),$$

the same law as obtains for a luminous point when horizontal directions are alone considered. The definition of a fine vertical line, and consequently the resolving power for contiguous vertical lines, is thus *independent of the vertical aperture of the instrument*, a law of great importance in the theory of the spectroscope.

The distribution of illumination in the image of a luminous line is shown by the curve ABC (fig. 5), representing the value of the function $\sin^2 u/u^2$ from $u=0$ to $u=2\pi$. The part corresponding to negative values of u is similar, OA being a line of symmetry.

Double line.

Let us now consider the distribution of brightness in the image of a double line whose components are of equal strength, and at such an angular interval that the central line in the image of one coincides with the first zero of brightness in the image of the other. In fig. 5 the curve of brightness for one component is ABC, and for the other OA′C′; and the curve representing half the combined brightnesses is E′BE. The brightness (corresponding to B) midway between the two central points AA′ is ·8106 of the brightness at the central points themselves. We may consider this to be about the limit of closeness at which there could be any decided appearance of resolution, though doubtless an observer accustomed to his instrument would recognize the duplicity with certainty. The obliquity, corresponding to $u=\pi$, is such that the phases of the secondary waves range over a complete period, *i.e.*, such that the projection of the horizontal aperture upon this direction is one wave-length. We conclude that *a double line cannot be fairly resolved unless its components subtend an angle exceeding that subtended by the wave-length of light at a distance equal to the horizontal aperture.* This rule is convenient on account of its simplicity; and it is sufficiently accurate in view of the necessary uncertainty as to what exactly is meant by resolution.

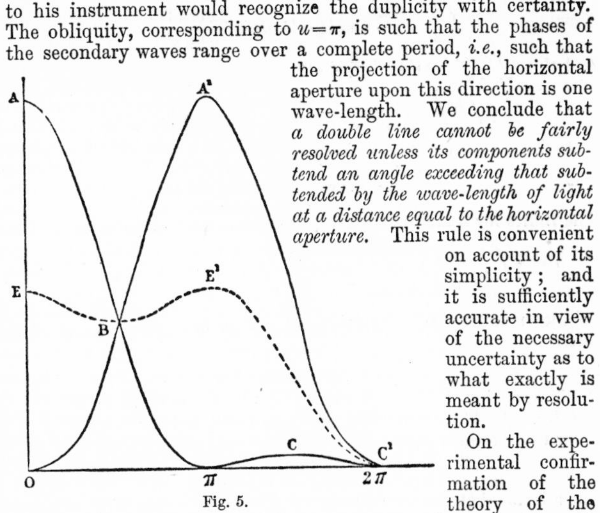

Fig. 5.

On the experimental confirmation of the theory of the resolving power of rectangular apertures, see OPTICS, vol. xvii. p. 807.

If the angular interval between the components of a double line be half as great again as that supposed in the figure, the brightness midway between is ·1802 as against 1·0450 at the central lines of each image. Such a falling off in the middle must be more than sufficient for resolution. If the angle subtended by the components of a double line be twice that subtended by the wave-length at a distance equal to the horizontal aperture, the central bands are just clear of one another, and there is a line of absolute blackness in the middle of the combined images.

Central stops.

Since the limitation of the width of the central band in the image of a luminous line depends upon discrepancies of phase among the secondary waves, and since the discrepancy is greatest for the waves which come from the edges of the aperture, the question arises how far the operation of the central parts of the aperture is advantageous. If we imagine the aperture reduced to two equal narrow slits bordering its edges, compensation will evidently be complete when the projection on an oblique direction is equal to $\frac{1}{2}\lambda$, instead of λ as for the complete aperture. By this procedure the width of the central band in the diffraction pattern is halved, and so far an advantage is attained. But, as will be evident, the bright bands bordering the central band are now not inferior to it in brightness; in fact, a band similar to the central band is reproduced an indefinite number of times, so long as there is no sensible discrepancy of phase in the secondary waves proceeding from the various parts of the *same* slit. Under these circumstances the narrowing of the band is paid for at a ruinous price, and the arrangement must be condemned altogether.

A more moderate suppression of the central parts is, however, sometimes advantageous. Theory and experiment alike prove that a double line, of which the components are equally strong, is better resolved when, for example, one-sixth of the horizontal aperture is blocked off by a central screen; or the rays quite at the centre may be allowed to pass, while others a little further removed are blocked off. Stops, each occupying one-eighth of the width, and with centres situated at the points of trisection, answer well the required purpose.

Total intensity proportional to aperture.

It has already been suggested that the principle of energy requires that the general expression for I^2 in (2) when integrated over the whole of the plane ξ, η should be equal to A, where A is the area of the aperture. A general analytical verification has been given by Stokes.[1] The expression for I^2 may be written in the form

$$I^2 = \frac{1}{\lambda^2 f^2} \iiiint \cos\frac{\kappa}{f}\left\{\xi(x'-x)+\eta(y'-y)\right\} dx\,dy\,dx'\,dy' . \quad (9),$$

the integrations with respect to x', y' as well as those with respect to x, y being over the area of the aperture; and for the present purpose this is to be integrated again with respect to ξ, η over the whole of the focal plane.

In changing the order of integration so as to take first that with respect to ξ, η, it is proper, in order to avoid ambiguity, to introduce under the integral sign the factor $e^{\mp\alpha\xi\mp\beta\eta}$, the + or − being chosen so as to make the elements of the integral vanish at infinity. After the operations have been performed, α and β are to be supposed to vanish.

Thus $\iint I^2 d\xi\, d\eta =$ Limit of

$$\frac{1}{\lambda^2 f^2}\iiiiiint e^{\mp\alpha\xi\mp\beta\eta}\cos\frac{\kappa}{f}\left\{\xi(x'-x)+\eta(y'-y)\right\} dx\,dy\,dx'\,dy'\,d\xi\,d\eta.$$

[1] *Ed. Trans.*, xx. p. 317, 1853.

Now $$\int_{-\infty}^{+\infty} e^{\mp\alpha\xi}\cos(h\xi-\text{H})\,d\xi=\frac{2\alpha\cos\text{H}}{\alpha^2+h^2}\,;$$

and thus $\iint_{-\infty}^{+\infty}\text{I}^2 d\xi\,d\eta$ = Limit of

$$\frac{1}{\lambda^2 f^2}\iiiint\frac{4\alpha\beta\,dx\,dy\,dx'\,dy'}{\left\{\alpha^2+\frac{\kappa^2(x'-x)^2}{f^2}\right\}\left\{\beta^2+\frac{\kappa^2(y'-y)^2}{f^2}\right\}}.$$

Let $$\frac{\kappa(x'-x)}{f}=\alpha u,\qquad dx'=\frac{f\alpha}{\kappa}du.$$

The limits for u are ultimately $-\infty$ and $+\infty$, and we have

$$\text{Limit}\int\frac{2\alpha\,dx'}{\left\{\alpha^2+\frac{\kappa^2(x'-x)^2}{f^2}\right\}}=\frac{2f}{\kappa}\int_{-\infty}^{+\infty}\frac{du}{1+u^2}=\frac{2f}{\kappa}\cdot\pi=f\lambda\,.$$

In like manner the integration for y' may be performed; and we find

$$\iint_{-\infty}^{+\infty}\text{I}^2 d\xi\,d\eta=\iint dx\,dy=\text{A}\quad.\quad.\quad.\quad.\quad(10).$$[1]

We saw that I_0^2 (the intensity at the focal point) was equal to $\text{A}^2/\lambda^2 f^2$. If A′ be the area over which the intensity must be I_0^2 in order to give the actual total intensity in accordance with

$$\text{A}'\text{I}_0'^2=\iint_{-\infty}^{+\infty}\text{I}^2\,d\xi\,d\eta\,,$$

the relation between A and A′ is $\text{AA}'=\lambda^2 f^2$. Since A′ is in some sense the area of the diffraction pattern, it may be considered to be a rough criterion of the definition, and we infer that the definition of a point depends principally upon the *area* of the aperture, and only in a very secondary degree upon the shape when the area is maintained constant.

§ 12. *Theory of Circular Aperture.*

We will now consider the important case where the form of the aperture is circular. Writing for brevity

$$\kappa\xi/f=p,\quad \kappa\eta/f=q\,,\quad.\quad.\quad.\quad.\quad.\quad.\quad.\quad(1),$$

we have for the general expression (§ 11) of the intensity

$$\lambda^2 f^2\text{I}^2=\text{S}^2+\text{C}^2\quad.\quad.\quad.\quad.\quad.\quad.\quad.\quad(2),$$

where
$$\text{S}=\iint\sin(px+qy)\,dx\,dy\,,\quad.\quad.\quad.\quad.\quad.\quad(3),$$
$$\text{C}=\iint\cos(px+qy)\,dx\,dy\,,\quad.\quad.\quad.\quad.\quad.\quad(4).$$

When, as in the application to rectangular or circular apertures, the form is symmetrical with respect to the axes both of x and y, S=0, and C reduces to

$$\text{C}=\iint\cos px\cos qy\,dx\,dy\,,\quad.\quad.\quad.\quad.\quad.\quad(5).$$

In the case of the circular aperture the distribution of light is of course symmetrical with respect to the focal point $p=0$, $q=0$; and C is a function of p and q only through $\sqrt{(p^2+q^2)}$. It is thus sufficient to determine the intensity along the axis of p. Putting $q=0$, we get

$$\text{C}=\iint\cos px\,dx\,dy=2\int_{-\text{R}}^{+\text{R}}\cos px\sqrt{(\text{R}^2-x^2)}\,dx\,,$$

R being the radius of the aperture. This integral is the Bessel's function of order unity, defined by

$$\text{J}_1(z)=\frac{z}{\pi}\int_0^{\pi}\cos(z\cos\phi)\sin^2\phi\,d\phi\quad.\quad.\quad.\quad.\quad(6).$$

Thus, if $x=\text{R}\cos\phi$,

$$\text{C}=\pi\text{R}^2\frac{2\text{J}_1(p\text{R})}{p\text{R}}\quad.\quad.\quad.\quad.\quad.\quad.\quad(7);$$

and the illumination at distance r from the focal point is

$$\text{I}^2=\frac{\pi^2\text{R}^4}{\lambda^2 f^2}\cdot\frac{4\text{J}_1^2\left(\frac{2\pi\text{R}r}{f\lambda}\right)}{\left(\frac{2\pi\text{R}r}{f\lambda}\right)^2}\quad.\quad.\quad.\quad.\quad.\quad.\quad(8).$$

The ascending series for $\text{J}_1(z)$, used by Airy[2] in his original investigation of the diffraction of a circular object-glass, and readily obtained from (6), is

$$\text{J}_1(z)=\frac{z}{2}-\frac{z^3}{2^2.4}+\frac{z^5}{2^2.4^2.6}-\frac{z^7}{2^2.4^2.6^2.8}+\ .\ .\ .\quad(9).$$

When z is great, we may employ the semi-convergent series

$$\text{J}_1(z)=\sqrt{\left(\frac{2}{\pi z}\right)}\sin\left(z-\tfrac{1}{4}\pi\right)\left\{1+\frac{3.5.1}{8.16}\left(\frac{1}{z}\right)^2-\frac{3.5.7.9.1.3.5}{8.16.24.32}\left(\frac{1}{z}\right)^4+\ .\ .\ .\right\}$$
$$+\sqrt{\left(\frac{2}{\pi z}\right)}\cos\left(z-\tfrac{1}{4}\pi\right)\left\{\frac{3}{8}\cdot\frac{1}{z}-\frac{3.5.7.1.3}{8.16.24}\left(\frac{1}{z}\right)^3+\frac{3.5.7.9.11.1.3.5.7}{8.16.24.32.40}\left(\frac{1}{z}\right)^5-\ .\ .\ .\right\}.\quad.\quad.\quad(10).$$

[1] It is easy to show that this conclusion is not disturbed by the introduction at every point of an arbitrary retardation ρ, a function of x, y. The terms $(\rho'-\rho)$ are then to be added under the cosine in (9); but they are ultimately without effect, since the only elements which contribute are those for which in the limit $x'=x$, $y'=y$, and therefore $\rho'=\rho$.

[2] "On the Diffraction of an Object-Glass with Circular Aperture," *Camb. Trans.*, 1834.

A table of the values of $2z^{-1}\text{J}_1(z)$ has been given by Lommel,[3] to whom is due the first systematic application of Bessel's functions to the diffraction integrals.

The illumination vanishes in correspondence with the roots of the equation $\text{J}_1(z)=0$. If these be called $z_1, z_2, z_3, \ldots$ the radii of the dark rings in the diffraction pattern are

$$\frac{f\lambda z_1}{2\pi\text{R}},\ \frac{f\lambda z_2}{2\pi\text{R}},\ \ldots$$

being thus *inversely* proportional to R.

The integrations may also be effected by means of polar coordinates, taking first the integration with respect to ϕ so as to obtain the result for an infinitely thin annular aperture. Thus, if

$$x=\rho\cos\phi\,,\quad y=\rho\sin\phi\,,$$
$$\text{C}=\iint\cos px\,dx\,dy=\int_0^{\text{R}}\int_0^{2\pi}\cos(p\rho\cos\theta)\,\rho\,d\rho\,d\theta\,.$$

Now by definition

$$\text{J}_0(z)=\frac{2}{\pi}\int_0^{\frac{1}{2}\pi}\cos(z\cos\theta)\,d\theta=1-\frac{z^2}{2^2}+\frac{z^4}{2^2.4^2}-\frac{z^6}{2^2.4^2.6^2}+\ .\ .\ .\quad(11).$$

The value of C for an annular aperture of radius r and width dr is thus

$$d\text{C}=2\pi\text{J}_0(p\rho)\rho\,d\rho\,,\quad.\quad.\quad.\quad.\quad.\quad.\quad(12).$$

For the complete circle,

$$\text{C}=\frac{2\pi}{p^2}\int_0^{p\text{R}}\text{J}_0(z)z\,dz$$
$$=\frac{2\pi}{p^2}\left\{\frac{p^2\text{R}^2}{2}-\frac{p^4\text{R}^4}{2^2.4}+\frac{p^6\text{R}^6}{2^2.4^2.6}-\ .\ .\ .\right\}$$
$$=\pi\text{R}^2\cdot\frac{2\text{J}_1(p\text{R})}{p\text{R}}\,,$$

as before.

In these expressions we are to replace p by $k\xi/f$, or rather, since the diffraction pattern is symmetrical, by kr/f, where r is the distance of any point in the focal plane from the centre of the system.

The roots of $\text{J}_0(z)$ after the first may be found from

$$\frac{z}{\pi}=i-\cdot25+\frac{\cdot050661}{4i-1}-\frac{\cdot053041}{(4i-1)^3}+\frac{\cdot262051}{(4i-1)^5}\quad.\quad.\quad(13),$$

and those of $\text{J}_1(z)$ from

$$\frac{z}{\pi}=i+\cdot25-\frac{\cdot151982}{4i+1}+\frac{\cdot015399}{(4i+1)^3}-\frac{\cdot245835}{(4i+1)^5}\quad.\quad.\quad(14),$$

formulæ derived by Stokes[4] from the descending series.[5] The following table gives the actual values:—

i	$\frac{z}{\pi}$ for $\text{J}_0(z)=0$	$\frac{z}{\pi}$ for $\text{J}_1(z)=0$	i	$\frac{z}{\pi}$ for $\text{J}_0(z)=0$	$\frac{z}{\pi}$ for $\text{J}_1(z)=0$
1	·7655	1·2197	6	5·7522	6·2439
2	1·7571	2·2330	7	6·7519	7·2448
3	2·7546	3·2383	8	7·7516	8·2454
4	3·7534	4·2411	9	8·7514	9·2459
5	4·7527	5·2428	10	9·7513	10·2463

In both cases the image of a mathematical point is thus a symmetrical ring system. The greatest brightness is at the centre, where

$$d\text{C}=2\pi\rho\,d\rho\,,\quad \text{C}=\pi\text{R}^2.$$

For a certain distance outwards this remains sensibly unimpaired, and then gradually diminishes to zero, as the secondary waves become discrepant in phase. The subsequent revivals of brightness forming the bright rings are necessarily of inferior brilliancy as compared with the central disk.

The first dark ring in the diffraction pattern of the complete circular aperture occurs when

$$r/f=1\cdot2197\times\lambda/2\text{R}\quad.\quad.\quad.\quad.\quad.\quad.\quad(15).$$

We may compare this with the corresponding result for a rectangular aperture of width a,

$$\xi/f=\lambda/a\,;$$

and it appears that in consequence of the preponderance of the central parts, the compensation in the case of the circle does not set in at so small an obliquity as when the circle is replaced by a rectangular aperture, whose side is equal to the diameter of the circle.

Again, if we compare the complete circle with a narrow annular aperture of the same radius, we see that in the latter case the first dark ring occurs at a much smaller obliquity, viz.,

$$r/f=\cdot7655\times\lambda/2\text{R}.$$

Central stop.

It has been found by Herschel and others that the definition of a telescope is often improved by stopping off a part of the central area of the object-glass; but the advantage to be obtained in this way is in no case great, and anything like a reduction of the aperture to a narrow annulus is attended by a development of the

[3] *Schlömilch*, xv. p. 166, 1870.

[4] *Camb. Trans.*, vol. ix., 1850.

[5] The descending series for $\text{J}_0(z)$ appears to have been first given by Sir W. Hamilton in a memoir on "Fluctuating Functions," *Roy. Irish Trans.*, 1840.

external luminous rings sufficient to outweigh any improvement due to the diminished diameter of the central area.[1]

Maximum of brightness. The maximum brightnesses and the places at which they occur are easily determined with the aid of certain properties of the Bessel's functions. It is known[2] that

$$J_0'(z) = -J_1(z)\,, \quad . \quad . \quad . \quad . \quad . \quad . \quad . \quad (16);$$

$$J_2(z) = \frac{1}{z}J_1(z) - J_1'(z) \quad . \quad . \quad . \quad . \quad . \quad (17);$$

$$J_0(z) + J_2(z) = \frac{2}{z}J_1(z) \quad . \quad . \quad . \quad . \quad . \quad (18).$$

The maxima of C occur when

$$\frac{d}{dz}\left(\frac{J_1(z)}{z}\right) = \frac{J_1'(z)}{z} - \frac{J_1(z)}{z^2} = 0\,;$$

or by (17) when $J_2(z) = 0$. When z has one of the values thus determined,

$$\frac{2}{z}J_1(z) = J_0(z)\,.$$

The accompanying table is given by Lommel,[3] in which the first column gives the roots of $J_2(z) = 0$, and the second and third columns the corresponding values of the functions specified. It appears that the maximum brightness in the first ring is only about $\frac{1}{57}$ of the brightness at the centre.

z	$2z^{-1}J_1(z)$	$4z^{-2}J_1^2(z)$
·000000	+1·000000	1·000000
5·135630	− ·132279	·017498
8·417236	+ ·064482	·004158
11·619857	− ·040008	·001601
14·795938	+ ·027919	·000779
17·959820	− ·020905	·000437

Integrated intensity. We will now investigate the total illumination distributed over the area of the circle of radius r. We have

$$I^2 = \frac{\pi^2 R^4}{\lambda^2 f^2}\cdot\frac{4J_1^2(z)}{z^2} \quad . \quad . \quad . \quad . \quad . \quad . \quad (19),$$

where

$$z = 2\pi R r/\lambda f\,. \quad . \quad . \quad . \quad . \quad . \quad . \quad . \quad (20).$$

Thus

$$2\pi\int I^2 r\,dr = \frac{\lambda^2 f^2}{2\pi R^2}\int I^2 z\,dz = \pi R^2 . \, 2\int z^{-1}J_1^2(z)\,dz\,.$$

Now by (17), (18)

$$z^{-1}J_1(z) = J_0(z) - J_1'(z)\,;$$

so that

$$z^{-1}J_1^2(z) = -\tfrac{1}{2}\frac{d}{dz}J_0^2(z) - \tfrac{1}{2}\frac{d}{dz}J_1^2(z)\,,$$

and

$$2\int_0^z z^{-1}J_1^2(z)\,dz = 1 - J_0^2(z) - J_1^2(z) \quad . \quad . \quad . \quad . \quad (21).$$

If r, or z, be infinite, $J_0(z)$, $J_1(z)$ vanish, and the whole illumination is expressed by πR^2, in accordance with the general principle. In any case the proportion of the whole illumination to be found outside the circle of radius r is given by

$$J_0^2(z) + J_1^2(z)\,.$$

For the dark rings $J_1(z) = 0$; so that the fraction of illumination outside any dark ring is simply $J_0^2(z)$. Thus for the first, second, third, and fourth dark rings we get respectively ·161, ·090, ·062, ·047, showing that more than $\frac{9}{10}$ths of the whole light is concentrated within the area of the second dark ring.[4]

When z is great, the descending series (10) gives

$$\frac{2J_1(z)}{z} = \frac{2}{z}\sqrt{\left(\frac{2}{\pi z}\right)}\sin\left(z - \tfrac{1}{4}\pi\right) \quad . \quad . \quad . \quad . \quad (22);$$

so that the places of maxima and minima occur at equal intervals.

The mean brightness varies as z^{-3} (or as r^{-3}), and the integral found by multiplying it by $z\,dz$ and integrating between 0 and ∞ converges.

It may be instructive to contrast this with the case of an infinitely narrow annular aperture, where the brightness is proportional to $J_0^2(z)$. When z is great,

$$J_0(z) = \sqrt{\left(\frac{2}{\pi z}\right)}\cos\left(z - \tfrac{1}{4}\pi\right).$$

The mean brightness varies as z^{-1}; and the integral $\int_0^\infty J_0^2(z)\,z\,dz$ is not convergent.

Resolving power of telescopes. The efficiency of a telescope is of course intimately connected with the size of the disk by which it represents a mathematical point. The resolving power upon double stars of telescopes of various apertures has been investigated by Dawes and others (OPTICS, vol. xvii. p. 807), with results that agree fairly well with theory.

Luminous line. If we integrate the expression (8) for I^2 with respect to η, we shall obtain a result applicable to a linear luminous source of which the various parts are supposed to act independently.

From (19), (20)

$$d\xi\int_{-\infty}^{+\infty} I^2\,d\eta = \frac{2\pi^2 R^4}{\lambda^2 f^2}\,d\xi\int_0^\infty 4z^{-2}J_1^2(z)\,d\eta = 2R^2\,d\xi\int\frac{J_1^2(z)\,dz}{z\,.\,\eta}\,,$$

since $\eta^2 = r^2 - \xi^2$.

If we write

$$\zeta = 2\pi R\xi/\lambda f \quad . \quad . \quad . \quad . \quad . \quad . \quad . \quad (23),$$

we get

$$d\xi\,.\int_{-\infty}^{+\infty} I^2\,d\eta = 2R^2\,d\zeta\,.\int_\zeta^\infty \frac{J_1^2(z)\,dz}{z\sqrt{(z^2-\zeta^2)}} \quad . \quad . \quad (24).$$

This integral has been investigated by H. Struve,[5] who, calling to his aid various properties of Bessel's functions, shows that

$$\int_\zeta^\infty \frac{J_1^2(z)\,dz}{z\sqrt{(z^2-\zeta^2)}} = \frac{2}{\pi}\frac{1}{\zeta}\int_0^{\frac{1}{2}\pi}\sin\left(2\zeta\sin\beta\right)\cos^2\beta\,d\beta \quad . \quad (25),$$

of which the right-hand member is readily expanded in powers of ζ. By means of (24) we may verify that

$$\int_{-\infty}^{+\infty}d\xi\int_{-\infty}^{+\infty} I^2\,d\eta = \pi R^2.$$

Contrary to what would naturally be expected, the subject is more easily treated without using the results of the integration with respect to x and y, by taking first of all, as in the investigation of Stokes (§ 11), the integration with respect to η. Thus

$$\lambda^2 f^2\int_{-\infty}^{+\infty} I^2\,d\eta = \text{Limit of}$$

$$\iiiint\!\!\int e^{\mp\beta\eta}\cos\frac{\kappa}{f}\left\{\xi(x'-x) + \eta(y'-y)\right\}dx\,dy\,dx'\,dy'\,d\eta \quad . \quad (26);$$

and

$$\int_{-\infty}^{+\infty} e^{\mp\beta\eta}\cos\frac{\kappa}{f}\left\{\xi(x'-x) + \eta(y'-y)\right\}d\eta$$

$$= \frac{2\beta\cos\frac{\kappa\xi}{f}(x'-x)}{\beta^2 + \frac{\kappa^2(y'-y)^2}{f^2}} \quad . \quad . \quad . \quad . \quad . \quad . \quad (27).$$

We have now to consider

$$\iint\frac{2\beta\,dy\,dy'}{\beta^2 + \kappa^2(y'-y)^2/f^2} \quad . \quad . \quad . \quad . \quad . \quad . \quad (28).$$

In the integration with respect to y' every element vanishes in the limit ($\beta = 0$), unless $y' = y$. If the range of integration for y' includes the value y, then

$$\text{Limit}\int\frac{2\beta\,dy'}{\beta^2 + \kappa^2(y'-y)^2/f^2} = f\lambda\,;$$

otherwise it vanishes.

The limit of (28) may thus be denoted by $\lambda f Y$, where Y is the *common part* of the ranges of integration for y' and y corresponding to any values of x' and x. Hence

$$\int_{-\infty}^{+\infty} I^2\,d\eta = \lambda^{-1}f^{-1}\iint Y\cos\frac{\kappa\xi}{f}(x'-x)\,dx\,dx'$$

$$= \lambda^{-1}f^{-1}\iint Y\cos\frac{\kappa\xi x}{f}\cos\frac{\kappa\xi x'}{f}\,dx\,dx' \quad . \quad . \quad . \quad (29),$$

if, as for the present purpose, the aperture is symmetrical with respect to the axis of y.

In the application to the circle we may write

$$\int_{-\infty}^{+\infty} I^2\,d\eta = 4\lambda^{-1}f^{-1}\int_0^R\int_0^R Y\cos\frac{\kappa\xi x}{f}\cos\frac{\kappa\xi x'}{f}\,dx\,dx',$$

where Y is the smaller of the two quantities

$$2\sqrt{(R^2 - x'^2)},\ 2\sqrt{(R^2 - x^2)},$$

i.e., corresponds to the *larger* of the two abscissæ x', x. If we take $Y = 2\sqrt{(R^2 - x^2)}$, and limit the integration to those values of x' which are less than x, we should obtain exactly the half of the required result. Thus

$$\int_{-\infty}^{+\infty} I^2\,d\eta = 16\lambda^{-1}f^{-1}\int_0^R\int_0^x\sqrt{(R^2-x^2)}\cos\frac{\kappa\xi x}{f}\cos\frac{\kappa\xi x'}{f}\,dx\,dx'$$

$$= \frac{4}{\pi\xi}\int_0^R\sqrt{(R^2-x^2)}\sin\frac{2\kappa\xi x}{f}\,dx$$

$$= \frac{4R^2}{\pi\xi}\int_0^{\frac{1}{2}\pi}\cos^2\beta\sin\frac{2\kappa\xi R\sin\beta}{f}\,d\beta\,.$$

Hence, writing as before $\zeta = \frac{2\pi R\xi}{\lambda f}$, we get

$$d\xi\int_{-\infty}^{+\infty} I^2\,d\eta = \frac{4R^2}{\pi}\cdot\frac{d\xi}{\xi}\cdot\int_0^{\frac{1}{2}\pi}\cos^2\beta\sin(2\zeta\beta)\,d\beta \quad . \quad . \quad (30),$$

in which we may replace $d\xi/\xi$ by $d\zeta/\zeta$, in agreement with the result obtained by Struve.

The integral in (30) may be written in another form. We have

$$\int\zeta\sin(2\zeta\beta)\cos^2\beta\,d\beta$$

$$= -\tfrac{1}{2}\cos\beta\cos(2\zeta\sin\beta) - \tfrac{1}{2}\int\cos(2\zeta\sin\beta)\sin\beta\,d\beta\,;$$

and thus

$$\int_0^{\frac{1}{2}\pi}\zeta\sin(2\zeta\beta)\cos^2\beta\,d\beta = \tfrac{1}{2}\int_0^{\frac{1}{2}\pi}\left\{1 - \cos(2\zeta\sin\beta)\right\}\sin\beta\,d\beta$$

$$= \int_0^{\frac{1}{2}\pi}\sin^2(\zeta\sin\beta)\sin\beta\,d\beta \quad . \quad . \quad . \quad . \quad . \quad (31).$$

[1] Airy, *loc. cit.* "Thus the magnitude of the central spot is diminished, and the brightness of the rings increased, by covering the central parts of the object-glass."

[2] Todhunter's *Laplace's Functions*, ch. xxxi.

[3] *Loc. cit.*

[4] *Phil. Mag.*, March 1881.

[5] *Wied. Ann.*, xvii. 1008, 1882.

The integral is thus expressible by means of the function K_1,[1] and we have

$$d\xi\int_{-\infty}^{+\infty} I^2 d\eta = \tfrac{1}{2}R^2\zeta^{-3}d\zeta\, K_1(2\zeta) \quad . \quad . \quad . \quad (32).$$

The ascending series for $K_1(z)$ is

$$K_1(z) = \frac{2}{\pi}\left\{\frac{z^3}{1^2.3} - \frac{z^5}{1^2.3^2.5} + \frac{z^7}{1^2.3^2.5^2.7} - \dots\right\} \quad . \quad . \quad (33);$$

and this is always convergent. The descending semi-convergent series is

$$K_1(z) = \frac{2}{\pi}\left\{z + z^{-1} - 3.z^{-3} + 1^2.3^2.5.z^{-5} - 1^2.3^2.5^2.7.z^{-7} + \dots\right\}$$
$$- \sqrt{\left(\frac{2z}{\pi}\right)}.\cos(z - \tfrac{1}{4}\pi)\left\{1 - \frac{(1^2-4)(3^2-4)}{1.2.(8z)^2} + \dots\right\}$$
$$- \sqrt{\left(\frac{2z}{\pi}\right)}.\sin(z - \tfrac{1}{4}\pi)\left\{\frac{1^2-4}{1.8z} - \frac{(1^2-4)(3^2-4)(5^2-4)}{1.2.3.(8z)^3} + \dots\right\} \quad (34),$$

the series within braces being the same as those which occur in the expression of the function $J_1(z)$.

When ζ (or ξ) is very great,

$$d\xi\int_{-\infty}^{+\infty} I^2 d\eta = \frac{2R^2}{\pi}\zeta^{-2}d\zeta,$$

so that the intensity of the image of a luminous line is ultimately inversely as the square of the distance from the central axis, or geometrical image.

As is evident from its composition, the intensity remains finite for all values of ζ; it is, however, subject to fluctuations presenting maxima and minima, which have been calculated by Ch. André,[2] using apparently the method of quadratures.

	ζ	Intensity.
On the axis itself..	0·00	1
First minimum.....	3·55	$\frac{1}{34}$
First maximum....	4·65	$\frac{1}{24}$
Second minimum..	6·80	$\frac{1}{115}$
Second maximum.	8·00	$\frac{1}{80}$
Third minimum....	9·60	$\frac{1}{419}$
Third maximum...	11·00	$\frac{1}{208}$
Fourth minimum.	13 20	$\frac{1}{10000}$

The results are also exhibited by M. André in the form of a curve, of which fig. 6 is a copy.

It will be seen that the distribution of brightness does not differ greatly from that due to a rectangular aperture whose width (perpendicular to the luminous line) is equal to the diameter of the circular aperture. It will be instructive to examine the image of a double line, whose components present an interval corresponding to $\zeta = \pi$, and to compare the result with that already found for a rectangular aperture (§ 11). We may consider the brightness at distance ζ proportional to

Double line.

$$L(\zeta) = \frac{1}{1^2.3} - \frac{2^2\zeta^2}{1^2.3^2.5} + \frac{2^4\zeta^4}{1^2.3^2.5^2.7} - \quad . \quad . \quad . \quad (35).$$

In the compound image the illumination at the geometrical focus of one of the luminous lines is represented by

$$L(0) + L(\pi);$$

and the illumination midway between the geometrical images of the two lines is

$$2L(\tfrac{1}{2}\pi).$$

Fig. 6.

We find by actual calculation from the series, $L(\pi) = ·0164$, $L(\tfrac{1}{2}\pi) = ·1671$, $L(0) = ·3333$, so that

$$L(0) + L(\pi) = ·3497, \quad 2L(\tfrac{1}{2}\pi) = ·3342,$$

and
$$\frac{2L(\tfrac{1}{2}\pi)}{L(0) + L(\pi)} = ·955.$$

Comparison with rectangular aperture.

The corresponding number for the rectangular aperture was ·811; so that, as might have been expected, the resolving power of the circular aperture is distinctly less than that of the rectangular aperture of equal width. Hence a telescope will not resolve a double line unless the angular interval between them decidedly exceeds that subtended by the wave-length of light at a distance equal to the diameter of the object-glass. Experiment shows that resolution begins when the angular interval is about a tenth part greater than that mentioned.

Uniform field of light terminated by straight edge.

If we integrate (30) with respect to ξ between the limits $-\infty$ and $+\infty$ we obtain πR^2, as has already been remarked. This represents the whole illumination over the focal plane due to a radiant point whose image is at O, or, reciprocally, the illumination at O (the same as at any other point) due to an infinitely extended luminous area. If we take the integration from ξ (supposed positive) to ∞ we get the illumination at O due to a uniform luminous area extending over this region, that is to say, the illumination at a point situated at distance ξ outside the border of the geometrical image of a large uniform area. If the point is supposed to be inside the geometrical image and at a distance ζ from its edge, we are to take the integration from $-\infty$ to ξ. Thus, if we choose the scale of intensities so that the full intensity is unity, then the intensity at a distance corresponding to $+\zeta$ (outside the geometrical image) may be represented by $\mathfrak{I}(+\zeta)$, and that at a distance $-\zeta$ by $\mathfrak{I}(-\zeta)$, where

$$\mathfrak{I}(+\zeta) + \mathfrak{I}(-\zeta) = 1,$$

and

$$\mathfrak{I}(\zeta) = \frac{1}{2\pi}\int_\zeta^\infty \zeta^{-3}d\zeta\, K_1(2\zeta) = \tfrac{1}{2} - \frac{1}{2\pi}\int_0^\zeta \zeta^{-3}d\zeta\, K_1(2\zeta) \quad . \quad . \quad (36).$$

Struve's results.

This is the result obtained by Struve, who gives the following series for $\mathfrak{I}(\zeta)$.

The ascending series, obtained at once by integration from (33), is

$$\mathfrak{I}(\zeta) = \tfrac{1}{2} - \frac{2}{\pi^2}\sum_{n=1}^{n=\infty}(-1)^{n-1}\frac{2n+1}{2n-1}\frac{2^{2n}\zeta^{2n-1}}{1^2.3^2.5^2\dots(2n+1)^2} \quad . \quad . \quad (37).$$

When ζ is great, we have approximately from the descending series

$$\mathfrak{I}(\zeta) = \frac{2}{\pi^2}\left(\frac{1}{\zeta} + \frac{1}{12\zeta^2}\right) - \frac{1}{2\pi^{3/2}}\frac{\cos(2\zeta + \tfrac{1}{4}\pi)}{\zeta^{5/2}}.$$

Thus "at great distances from the edge of the geometrical image the intensity is inversely proportional to the distance, and to the radius of the object-glass."

The following table, abbreviated from that given by Struve, will serve to calculate the enlargement of an image due to diffraction in any case that may arise.

$$\zeta = 2\pi R\xi/\lambda f.$$
$$\mathfrak{I}(-\zeta) = 1 - \mathfrak{I}(+\zeta).$$

ζ	$\mathfrak{I}(\zeta)$	ζ	$\mathfrak{I}(\zeta)$	ζ	$\mathfrak{I}(\zeta)$
0·0	·5000	2·5	·0765	7·0	·0293
0·5	·3678	3·0	·0630	9·0	·0222
1·0	·2521	4·0	·0528	11·0	·0186
1·5	·1642	5·0	·0410	15·0	·0135
2·0	·1073	6·0	·0328		

Integration of intensity further considered.

It may perhaps have struck the reader that there is some want of rigour in our treatment of (30) when we integrate it over the whole focal plane of ξ, η, inasmuch as in the proof of the formulæ ξ and η are supposed to be small. The inconsistency becomes very apparent when we observe that according to the formulæ there is no limit to the relative retardation of secondary waves coming from various parts of the aperture, whereas in reality this retardation could never exceed the longest line capable of being drawn within the aperture. It will be worth while to consider this point a little further, although our limits forbid an extended treatment.

The formula becomes rigorous if we regard it as giving the illumination on the surface of a sphere of very large radius f, in a direction such that

$$\xi = f\sin\theta\cos\phi, \quad \eta = f\sin\theta\sin\phi;$$

it may then be written

$$I^2 = \lambda^{-2}f^{-2}\iiiint \cos\kappa\left\{(x'-x)\sin\theta\cos\phi\right.$$
$$\left.+ (y'-y)\sin\theta\sin\phi\right\}dx\,dy\,dx'\,dy'.$$

The whole intensity over the infinite hemisphere is given by

$$\mathfrak{I} = f^2\int_0^{\frac{1}{2}\pi}\int_0^{2\pi} I^2\sin\theta\, d\theta\, d\phi \quad . \quad . \quad . \quad . \quad . \quad (38).$$

According to the plan formerly adopted, we postpone the integration with respect to x, y, x', y', and take first that with respect to θ and ϕ. Thus for a single pair of elements of area $dx\,dy$, $dx'\,dy'$ we have to consider

$$\iint \cos\kappa\left\{(x'-x)\sin\theta\cos\phi + (y'-y)\sin\theta\sin\phi\right\}\sin\theta\, d\theta\, d\phi,$$

or, if we write

$$x' - x = r\cos\alpha, \quad y' - y = r\sin\alpha,$$

$$\int_0^{\frac{1}{2}\pi}\int_0^{2\pi}\cos(\kappa r\sin\theta\cos\phi)\sin\theta\, d\theta\, d\phi.$$

Now it may be proved (*e.g.*, by expansion in powers of κr) that

$$\int_0^{\frac{1}{2}\pi}\int_0^{2\pi}\cos(\kappa r\sin\theta\cos\phi)\sin\theta\, d\theta\, d\phi = 2\pi\frac{\sin\kappa r}{\kappa r} \quad . \quad . \quad (39);$$

and thus

$$\mathfrak{I} = \frac{2\pi}{\lambda^2}\iiiint\frac{\sin\kappa r}{\kappa r}dx\,dy\,dx'\,dy' \quad . \quad . \quad . \quad . \quad (40),$$

r being the distance between the two elements of area $dx\,dy$, $dx'dy'$.

In the case of a circular area of radius R, we have[3]

$$\iiiint\frac{\sin\kappa r}{\kappa r}dx\,dy\,dx'\,dy' = \frac{2\pi R^2}{\kappa^2}\left\{1 - \frac{J_1(2\kappa R)}{\kappa R}\right\},$$

and thus

$$\mathfrak{I} = \pi R^2\left\{1 - \frac{J_1(2\kappa R)}{\kappa R}\right\} \quad . \quad . \quad . \quad . \quad . \quad (41).$$

When $\kappa R = \infty$,

$$\mathfrak{I} = \pi R^2, \text{ as before.}$$

[1] *Theory of Sound*, § 302.

[2] *Ann. d. l'École Normale*, v. p. 310, 1876.

[3] *Theory of Sound*, § 302.

It appears therefore that according to the assumed law of the secondary wave the total illumination is proportional to the area of aperture, only under the restriction that the linear dimensions of the aperture are very large in comparison with the wave-length.

A word as to the significance of (39) may not be out of place. We know that

$$\psi=\cos\kappa\{\sin\theta\cos\phi x+\sin\theta\sin\phi y+\cos\theta z\} \quad . \quad . \quad . \quad (42)$$

satisfies Laplace's extended equation $(\nabla^2+\kappa^2)\psi=0$, being of the form $\cos\kappa x'$, where x' is drawn in an oblique direction; and it follows that $\iint\psi\sin\theta\, d\theta\, d\phi$ satisfies the same equation. Now this, if the integration be taken over the hemisphere $\theta=0$ to $\theta=\frac{1}{2}\pi$, must become a function of r, or $\sqrt{(x^2+y^2+z^2)}$, only.

Hence, putting $x=r$, $y=0$, $z=0$, we get

$$\iint\psi\sin\theta\, d\theta\, d\phi=\int_0^{\frac{1}{2}\pi}\int_0^{2\pi}\cos(\kappa r\sin\theta\cos\phi)\sin\theta\, d\theta\, d\phi\,.$$

But the only function of r which satisfies Laplace's equation continuously through the origin is $\mathrm{A}\sin\kappa r/(\kappa r)$; and that $\mathrm{A}=2\pi$ is proved at once by putting $r=0$. The truth of the formula may also be established independently of the differential equation by equating the values of $\int_0^{\frac{1}{2}\pi}\int_0^{2\pi}\psi\sin\theta\, d\theta\, d\phi$, when $x=r$, $y=0$, $z=0$, and when $x=0$, $y=0$, $z=r$. Thus

$$\int_0^{\frac{1}{2}\pi}\int_0^{2\pi}\cos(\kappa r\sin\theta\cos\phi)\sin\theta\, d\theta\, d\phi$$

$$=\int_0^{\frac{1}{2}\pi}\int_0^{2\pi}\cos(\kappa r\cos\theta)\sin\theta\, d\theta\, d\phi=2\pi\frac{\sin\kappa r}{\kappa r}\,.$$

The formula itself may also be written

$$\int_0^{\frac{1}{2}\pi}\mathrm{J}_0(\kappa r\sin\theta)\sin\theta\, d\theta=\frac{\sin\kappa r}{\kappa r} \quad . \quad . \quad . \quad . \quad (43).$$

Coronas or glories.

The results of the preceding theory of circular apertures admit of an interesting application to *coronas*, such as are often seen encircling the sun and moon. They are due to the interposition of small spherules of water, which act the part of diffracting obstacles. In order to the formation of a well-defined corona it is essential that the particles be exclusively, or preponderatingly, of one size.

If the origin of light be treated as infinitely small, and be seen in focus, whether with the naked eye or with the aid of a telescope, the whole of the light in the absence of obstacles would be concentrated in the immediate neighbourhood of the focus. At other parts of the field the effect is the same, by Babinet's principle, whether the imaginary screen in front of the object-glass is generally transparent but studded with a number of opaque circular disks, or is generally opaque but perforated with corresponding apertures. Consider now the light diffracted in a direction many times more oblique than any with which we should be concerned, were the whole aperture uninterrupted, and take first the effect of a single small aperture. The light in the proposed direction is that determined by the size of the small aperture in accordance with the laws already investigated, and its phase depends upon the position of the aperture. If we take a direction such that the light (of given wave-length) from a single aperture vanishes, the evanescence continues even when the whole series of apertures is brought into contemplation. Hence, whatever else may happen, there must be a system of dark rings formed, the same as from a single small aperture. In directions other than these it is a more delicate question how the partial effects should be compounded. If we make the extreme suppositions of an infinitely small source and absolutely homogeneous light, there is no escape from the conclusion that the light in a definite direction is arbitrary, that is, dependent upon the chance distribution of apertures. If, however, as in practice, the light be heterogeneous, the source of finite area, the obstacles in motion, and the discrimination of different directions imperfect, we are concerned merely with the mean brightness found by varying the arbitrary phase-relations, and this is obtained by simply multiplying the brightness due to a single aperture by the number of apertures (n).[1] The diffraction pattern is therefore that due to a single aperture, merely brightened n times.

In his experiments upon this subject Fraunhofer employed plates of glass dusted over with lycopodium, or studded with small metallic disks of uniform size; and he found that the diameters of the rings were proportional to the length of the waves and inversely as the diameter of the disks.

In another respect the observations of Fraunhofer appear at first sight to be in disaccord with theory; for his measures of the diameters of the red rings, visible when white light was employed, correspond with the law applicable to dark rings, and not to the different law applicable to the luminous maxima. Verdet has, however, pointed out that the observation in this form is essentially different from that in which homogeneous red light is employed, and that the position of the red rings would correspond to the *absence* of blue-green light rather than to the greatest abundance of red light. Verdet's own observations, conducted with great care, fully confirm this view, and exhibit a complete agreement with theory.

By measurements of coronas it is possible to infer the size of the particles to which they are due, an application of considerable interest in the case of natural corona—the general rule being the larger the corona the smaller the water spherules. Young employed this method not only to determine the diameters of cloud particles (*e.g.*, $\frac{1}{1000}$ inch), but also those of fibrous material, for which the theory is analogous. His instrument was called the *eriometer*.[2]

§ 13. *Influence of Aberration. Optical Power of Instruments.*

Optical errors.

Our investigations and estimates of resolving power have thus far proceeded upon the supposition that there are no optical imperfections, whether of the nature of a regular aberration or dependent upon irregularities of material and workmanship. In practice there will always be a certain aberration or error of phase, which we may also regard as the deviation of the actual wave-surface from its intended position. In general, we may say that aberration is unimportant, when it nowhere (or at any rate over a relatively small area only) exceeds a small fraction of the wave-length (λ). Thus in estimating the intensity at a focal point, where, in the absence of aberration, all the secondary waves would have exactly the same phase, we see that an aberration nowhere exceeding $\frac{1}{4}\lambda$ can have but little effect.

Unsymmetrical aberration.

The only case in which the influence of small aberration upon the entire image has been calculated[3] is that of a rectangular aperture, traversed by a cylindrical wave with aberration equal to cx^3. The aberration is here unsymmetrical, the wave being in advance of its proper place in one half of the aperture, but behind in the other half. No terms in x or x^2 need be considered. The first would correspond to a general turning of the beam; and the second would imply imperfect focusing of the central parts. The effect of aberration may be considered in two ways. We may suppose the aperture (a) constant, and inquire into the operation of an increasing aberration; or we may take a given value of c (*i.e.*, a given wave-surface) and examine the effect of a varying aperture. The results in the second case show that an increase of aperture up to that corresponding to an extreme aberration of half a period has no ill effect upon the central band (§ 11), but it increases unduly the intensity of one of the neighbouring lateral bands; and the practical conclusion is that the best results will be obtained from an aperture giving an extreme aberration of from a quarter to half a period, and that with an increased aperture aberration is not so much a direct cause of deterioration as an obstacle to the attainment of that improved definition which should accompany the increase of aperture.

If, on the other hand, we suppose the aperture given, we find that aberration begins to be distinctly mischievous when it amounts to about a quarter period, *i.e.*, when the wave-surface deviates at each end by a quarter wave-length from the true plane.

Circular aperture. Symmetrical aberration.

For the focal point itself the calculations are much simpler. We will consider the case of a circular object-glass with a symmetrical aberration proportional to $h\rho^4$. The vibration will be represented by

$$2\int_0^1\cos(nt-h\rho^4)\,\rho\, d\rho\,,$$

in which the radius of the aperture is supposed to be unity. The intensity is thus expressed by

$$\mathrm{I}_0^2=\left[2\int_0^1\cos(h\rho^4)\,\rho\, d\rho\right]^2+\left[2\int_0^1\sin(h\rho^4)\,\rho\, d\rho\right]^2 . . . \quad (1),$$

the scale being such that the intensity is unity when there is no aberration ($h=0$).

By integration by parts it can be shown that

$$2\int_0^1 e^{ih\rho^4}\rho\, d\rho=e^{ih}\left\{1-\frac{4ih}{6}+\frac{(4ih)^2}{6.10}-\frac{(4ih)^3}{6.10.14}+\ldots\right\};$$

so that

$$2\int_0^1\cos(h\rho^4)\,\rho\, d\rho=\cos h\left\{1-\frac{(4h)^2}{6.10}+\frac{(4h)^4}{6.10.14.18}-\ldots\right\}$$
$$+\sin h\left\{\frac{4h}{6}-\frac{(4h)^3}{6.10.14}+\ldots\right\} \quad . \quad . \quad . \quad . \quad (2),$$

$$2\int_0^1\sin(h\rho^4)\,\rho\, d\rho=\sin h\left\{1-\frac{(4h)^2}{6.10}+\frac{(4h)^4}{6.10.14.18}-\ldots\right\}$$
$$-\cos h\left\{\frac{4h}{6}-\frac{(4h)^3}{6.10.14}+\ldots\right\} \quad . \quad . \quad . \quad . \quad . \quad (3).$$

Hence, when $h=\frac{1}{4}\pi$,

$$2\int_0^1\cos(\tfrac{1}{4}\pi\rho^4)\,\rho\, d\rho=1\cdot32945/\sqrt{2},$$

$$2\int_0^1\sin(\tfrac{1}{4}\pi\rho^4)\,\rho\, d\rho=\cdot35424/\sqrt{2},$$

$$\mathrm{I}_0^2=\cdot9464\,.$$

Similarly, when $h=\frac{1}{2}\pi$,

$$\mathrm{I}_0^2=\cdot8003\,;$$

and when $h=\pi$,

$$\mathrm{I}_0^2=\cdot3947\,.$$

1 See § 4.

2 "Chromatics," in vol. iii. of Supp. to *Ency. Brit.*, 1817

3 "Investigations in Optics," *Phil. Mag.*, Nov. 1879.

These numbers represent the influence of aberration upon the intensity at the central point, upon the understanding that the focusing is that adapted to a small aperture, for which h might be neglected. If a readjustment of focus be permitted, the numbers will be sensibly raised. The general conclusion is that an aberration between the centre and circumference of a quarter period has but little effect upon the intensity at the central point of the image.

Disturbance due to variation of temperature. As an application of this result, let us investigate what amount of temperature disturbance in the tube of a telescope may be expected to impair definition. According to Biot and Arago, the index μ for air at $t°$ C. and at atmospheric pressure is given by

$$\mu - 1 = \frac{\cdot 00029}{1 + \cdot 0037\, t}.$$

If we take 0° C. as standard temperature,

$$\delta\mu = -1\cdot 1\, t \times 10^{-6}.$$

Thus, on the supposition that the irregularity of temperature t extends through a length l, and produces an acceleration of a quarter of a wave-length,

$$\tfrac{1}{4}\lambda = 1\cdot 1\, lt \times 10^{-6};$$

or, if we take $\lambda = 5\cdot 3 \times 10^{-5}$,

$$lt = 12,$$

the unit of length being the centimetre.

We may infer that, in the case of a telescope tube 12 cm. long, a stratum of air heated 1° C. lying along the top of the tube, and occupying a moderate fraction of the whole volume, would produce a not insensible effect. If the change of temperature progressed uniformly from one side to the other, the result would be a lateral displacement of the image without loss of definition; but in general both effects would be observable. In longer tubes a similar disturbance would be caused by a proportionally less difference of temperature.

Images by simple apertures. We will now consider the application of the principle to the formation of images, unassisted by reflexion or refraction.[1] The function of a lens in forming an image is to compensate by its variable thickness the differences of phase which would otherwise exist between secondary waves arriving at the focal point from various parts of the aperture (OPTICS, vol. xvii. p. 802). If we suppose the diameter of the lens to be given (2R), and its focal length f gradually to increase, the original differences of phase at the image of an infinitely distant luminous point diminish without limit. When f attains a certain value, say f_1, the extreme error of phase to be compensated falls to $\frac{1}{4}\lambda$. But, as we have seen, such an error of phase causes no sensible deterioration in the definition; so that from this point onwards the lens is useless, as only improving an image already sensibly as perfect as the aperture admits of. Throughout the operation of increasing the focal length, the resolving power of the instrument, which depends only upon the aperture, remains unchanged; and we thus arrive at the rather startling conclusion that a telescope of any degree of resolving power might be constructed without an object-glass, if only there were no limit to the admissible focal length. This last proviso, however, as we shall see, takes away almost all practical importance from the proposition.

To get an idea of the magnitudes of the quantities involved, let us take the case of an aperture of $\frac{1}{5}$ inch, about that of the pupil of the eye. The distance f_1, which the actual focal length must exceed, is given by

$$\sqrt{(f_1^2 + R^2)} - f_1 = \tfrac{1}{4}\lambda;$$

so that

$$f_1 = 2R^2/\lambda \quad . \quad . \quad . \quad . \quad . \quad . \quad . \quad . \quad (4).$$

Thus, if $\lambda = \frac{1}{40000}$, $R = \frac{1}{10}$, we find

$$f_1 = 800 \text{ inches}.$$

The image of the sun thrown upon a screen at a distance exceeding 66 feet, through a hole $\frac{1}{5}$ inch in diameter, is therefore at least as well defined as that seen direct.

As the minimum focal length increases with the square of the aperture, a quite impracticable distance would be required to rival the resolving power of a modern telescope. Even for an aperture of 4 inches, f_1 would have to be 5 miles.

Simple *versus* achromatic lens. A similar argument may be applied to find at what point an achromatic lens becomes sensibly superior to a single one. The question is whether, when the adjustment of focus is correct for the central rays of the spectrum, the error of phase for the most extreme rays (which it is necessary to consider) amounts to a quarter of a wave-length. If not, the substitution of an achromatic lens will be of no advantage. Calculation shows that, if the aperture be $\frac{1}{5}$ inch, an achromatic lens has no sensible advantage if the focal length be greater than about 11 inches. If we suppose the focal length to be 66 feet, a single lens is practically perfect up to an aperture of 1·7 inch.

Some estimates of the admissible *aberration* in a spherical lens have already been given under OPTICS, vol. xvii. p. 807. In a similar manner we may estimate the least visible displacement of the eye-piece of a telescope focused upon a distant object, a question of interest in connexion with range-finders. **Accuracy of focusing.** It appears[2] that a displacement δf from the true focus will not sensibly impair definition, provided

$$\delta f < f^2\lambda/R^2, \quad . \quad . \quad . \quad . \quad . \quad . \quad . \quad . \quad (5),$$

2R being the diameter of aperture. The linear accuracy required is thus a function of the *ratio* of aperture to focal length. The formula agrees well with experiment.

Delicacy of mirror reading. The principle gives an instantaneous solution of the question of the ultimate optical efficiency in the method of "mirror-reading," as commonly practised in various physical observations. A rotation by which one edge of the mirror advances $\frac{1}{4}\lambda$ (while the other edge retreats to a like amount) introduces a phase-discrepancy of a whole period where before the rotation there was complete agreement. A rotation of this amount should therefore be easily visible, but the limits of resolving power are being approached; and the conclusion is independent of the focal length of the mirror, and of the employment of a telescope, provided of course that the reflected image is seen in focus, and that the full width of the mirror is utilized.

Comparison with material pointer. A comparison with the method of a material pointer, attached to the parts whose rotation is under observation, and viewed through a microscope, is of interest. The limiting efficiency of the microscope is attained when the angular aperture amounts to 180° (MICROSCOPE, vol. xvi. p. 267; OPTICS, vol. xvii. p. 807); and it is evident that a lateral displacement of the point under observation through $\frac{1}{2}\lambda$ entails (at the old image) a phase-discrepancy of a whole period, one extreme ray being accelerated and the other retarded by half that amount. We may infer that the limits of efficiency in the two methods are the same when the length of the pointer is equal to the width of the mirror.

Admissible errors of optical surfaces. An important practical question is the amount of error admissible in optical surfaces. In the case of a mirror, reflecting at nearly perpendicular incidence, there should be no deviation from truth (over any appreciable area) of more than $\frac{1}{8}\lambda$. For glass, $\mu - 1 = \frac{1}{2}$ nearly; and hence the admissible error in a refracting surface of that material is four times as great.

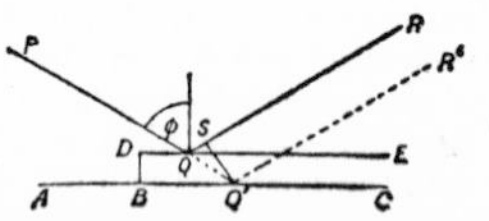

Fig. 7.

In the case of oblique reflexion at an angle ϕ, the error of retardation due to an elevation BD (fig. 7) is

$$QQ' - QS = BD\sec\phi(1 - \cos SQQ') = BD\sec\phi(1 + \cos 2\phi) = 2BD\cos\phi;$$

from which it follows that an error of given magnitude in the figure of a surface is less important in oblique than in perpendicular reflexion. It must, however, be borne in mind that errors can sometimes be compensated by altering adjustments. If a surface intended to be flat is affected with a slight general curvature, a remedy may be found in an alteration of focus, and the remedy is the less complete as the reflexion is more oblique.

Optical power of prisms. The formula expressing the optical power of prismatic spectroscopes is given with examples under OPTICS, vol. xvii. p. 807, and may readily be investigated upon the principles of the wave theory. Let A_0B_0 (fig. 8) be a plane wave-surface of the light before it falls upon the prisms, AB the corresponding wave-surface for a particular part of the spectrum after the light has passed the prisms, or after it has passed the eye-piece of the observing telescope. The path of a ray from the wave-surface A_0B_0 to A or B is determined by the condition that the optical distance, $\int \mu\, ds$, is a minimum (OPTICS, vol. xvii. p. 798); and, as AB is by supposition a wave-surface, this optical distance is the same for both points. Thus

Fig. 8.

$$\int \mu\, ds \,(\text{for A}) = \int \mu\, ds \,(\text{for B}) \quad . \quad . \quad . \quad . \quad . \quad (6).$$

We have now to consider the behaviour of light belonging to a neighbouring part of the spectrum. The path of a ray from the wave-surface A_0B_0 to the point A is changed; but in virtue of the minimum property the change may be neglected in calculating the optical distance, as it influences the result by quantities of the second order only in the changes of refrangibility. Accordingly, the optical distance from A_0B_0 to A is represented by $\int(\mu + \delta\mu)ds$, the integration being along the original path $A_0 \ldots A$; and similarly the optical distance between A_0B_0 and B is represented by $\int(\mu + \delta\mu)ds$, the integration being along $B_0 \ldots B$. In virtue of (6) the difference of the optical distances to A and B is

$$\int \delta\mu\, ds \quad (\text{along } B_0 \ldots B) - \int \delta\mu\, ds \quad (\text{along } A_0 \ldots A) \quad . \quad (7).$$

The new wave-surface is formed in such a position that the optical distance is constant; and therefore the *dispersion*, or the angle through which the wave surface is turned by the change of refrangibility, is found simply by dividing (7) by the distance AB. If, as in common flint-glass spectroscopes, there is only one dispersing substance, $\int \delta\mu\, ds = \delta\mu . s$, where s is simply the thickness traversed by the ray. If t_2 and t_1 be the thicknesses traversed by the

[1] *Phil. Mag.*, March 1881.

[2] *Phil. Mag.*, xx. p. 354, 1885.

extreme rays, and a denote the width of the emergent beam, the dispersion θ is given by

$$\theta = \delta\mu(t_2 - t_1)/a\ ,$$

or, if t_1 be negligible,

$$\theta = \delta\mu t/a \quad . \quad . \quad . \quad . \quad . \quad . \quad . \quad . \quad (8).$$

The condition of resolution of a double line whose components subtend an angle θ is that θ must exceed λ/a. Hence, in order that a double line may be resolved whose components have indices μ and $\mu + \delta\mu$, it is necessary that t should exceed the value given by the following equation:—

$$t = \lambda/\delta\mu \quad . \quad . \quad . \quad . \quad . \quad . \quad . \quad . \quad (9).$$

For applications of these results, see SPECTROSCOPE.

§ 14. *Theory of Gratings.*

The general explanation of the mode of action of gratings has been given under LIGHT (vol. xiv. p. 607). If the grating be composed of alternate transparent and opaque parts, the question may be treated by means of the general integrals (§ 11) by merely limiting the integration to the transparent parts of the aperture. For an investigation upon these lines the reader is referred to Airy's *Tracts* and to Verdet's *Leçons*. If, however, we assume the theory of a simple rectangular aperture (§ 11), the results of the ruling can be inferred by elementary methods, which are perhaps more instructive.

Apart from the ruling, we know that the image of a mathematical line will be a series of narrow bands, of which the central one is by far the brightest. At the middle of this band there is complete agreement of phase among the secondary waves. The dark lines which separate the bands are the places at which the phases of the secondary wave range over an integral number of periods. If now we suppose the aperture AB to be covered by a great number of opaque strips or bars of width d, separated by transparent intervals of width a, the condition of things in the directions just spoken of is not materially changed. At the central point there is still complete agreement of phase; but the amplitude is diminished in the ratio of $a : a+d$. In another direction, making a small angle with the last, such that the projection of AB upon it amounts to a few wave-lengths, it is easy to see that the mode of interference is the same as if there were no ruling. For example, when the direction is such that the projection of AB upon it amounts to one wave-length, the elementary components neutralize one another, because their phases are distributed symmetrically, though discontinuously, round the entire period. The only effect of the ruling is to diminish the amplitude in the ratio $a : a+d$; and, except for the difference in illumination, the appearance of a line of light is the same as if the aperture were perfectly free.

The lateral (spectral) images occur in such directions that the projection of the element $(a+d)$ of the grating upon them is an exact multiple of λ. The effect of each of the n elements of the grating is then the same; and, unless this vanishes on account of a particular adjustment of the ratio $a : d$, the resultant amplitude becomes comparatively very great. These directions, in which the retardation between A and B is exactly $mn\lambda$, may be called the principal directions. On either side of any one of them the illumination is distributed according to the same law as for the central image ($m=0$), vanishing, for example, when the retardation amounts to $(mn \pm 1)\lambda$. In considering the relative brightnesses of the different spectra, it is therefore sufficient to attend merely to the principal directions, provided that the whole deviation be not so great that its cosine differs considerably from unity.

Brightness.

We have now to consider the amplitude due to a single element, which we may conveniently regard as composed of a transparent part a bounded by two opaque parts of width $\frac{1}{2}d$. The phase of the resultant effect is by symmetry that of the component which comes from the middle of a. The fact that the other components have phases differing from this by amounts ranging between $\pm am\pi/(a+d)$ causes the resultant amplitude to be less than for the central image (where there is complete phase agreement). If B_m denote the brightness of the mth lateral image, and B_0 that of the central image, we have

$$B_m : B_0 = \left[\int_{-\frac{am\pi}{a+d}}^{+\frac{am\pi}{a+d}} \cos x\, dx \div \frac{2am\pi}{a+d}\right]^2 = \left(\frac{a+d}{am\pi}\right)^2 \sin^2 \frac{am\pi}{a+d} \quad . \quad (1).$$

If B denote the brightness of the central image when the whole of the space occupied by the grating is transparent, we have

$$B_0 : B = a^2 : (a+d)^2\ ,$$

and thus

$$B_m : B = \frac{1}{m^2\pi^2} \sin^2 \frac{am\pi}{a+d} \quad . \quad . \quad . \quad . \quad . \quad . \quad (2).$$

The sine of an angle can never be greater than unity; and consequently under the most favourable circumstances only $1/m^2\pi^2$ of the original light can be obtained in the mth spectrum. We conclude that, with a grating composed of transparent and opaque parts, the utmost light obtainable in any one spectrum is in the first, and there amounts to $1/\pi^2$, or about $\frac{1}{10}$, and that for this purpose a and d must be equal. When $d=a$, the general formula becomes

Equal opaque and transparent parts.

$$B_m : B = \frac{\sin^2 \frac{1}{2}m\pi}{m^2\pi^2} \quad . \quad . \quad . \quad . \quad . \quad . \quad . \quad (3),$$

showing that, when m is even, B_m vanishes, and that, when m is odd,

$$B_m : B = 1/m^2\pi^2\ .$$

The third spectrum has thus only $\frac{1}{9}$ of the brilliancy of the first.

Transparent parts small.

Another particular case of interest is obtained by supposing a small relatively to $(a+d)$. Unless the spectrum be of very high order, we have simply

$$B_m : B = \{a/(a+d)\}^2 \quad . \quad . \quad . \quad . \quad . \quad . \quad (4);$$

so that the brightnesses of all the spectra are the same.

The light stopped by the opaque parts of the grating, together with that distributed in the central image and lateral spectra, ought to make up the brightness that would be found in the central image, were all the apertures transparent. Thus, if $a=d$, we should have

$$1 = \frac{1}{2} + \frac{1}{4} + \frac{2}{\pi^2}\left(1 + \frac{1}{9} + \frac{1}{25} + \ldots\right),$$

which is true by a known theorem. In the general case

$$\frac{a}{a+d} = \left(\frac{a}{a+d}\right)^2 + \frac{2}{\pi^2} \sum_{m=1}^{m=\infty} \frac{1}{m^2} \sin^2\left(\frac{m\pi a}{a+d}\right),$$

a formula which may be verified by Fourier's theorem.

Babinet's principle.

According to a general principle formulated by Babinet, the brightness of a lateral spectrum is not affected by an interchange of the transparent and opaque parts of the grating. The vibrations corresponding to the two parts are precisely antagonistic, since if both were operative the resultant would be zero. So far as the application to gratings is concerned, the same conclusion may be derived from (2).

Gratings acting by retardation.

From the value of $B_m : B_0$ we see that no lateral spectrum can surpass the central image in brightness; but this result depends upon the hypothesis that the ruling acts by opacity, which is generally very far from being the case in practice. In an engraved glass grating there is no opaque material present by which light could be absorbed, and the effect depends upon a difference of retardation in passing the alternate parts. It is possible to prepare gratings which give a lateral spectrum brighter than the central image, and the explanation is easy. For if the alternate parts were equal and alike transparent, but so constituted as to give a relative retardation of $\frac{1}{2}\lambda$, it is evident that the central image would be entirely extinguished, while the first spectrum would be four times as bright as if the alternate parts were opaque. If it were possible to introduce at every part of the aperture of the grating an arbitrary retardation, all the light might be concentrated in any desired spectrum. By supposing the retardation to vary uniformly and continuously we fall upon the case of an ordinary prism; but there is then no diffraction spectrum in the usual sense. To obtain such it would be necessary that the retardation should gradually alter by a wave-length in passing over any element of the grating, and then fall back to its previous value, thus springing suddenly over a wave-length. It is not likely that such a result will ever be fully attained in practice; but the case is worth stating, in order to show that there is no theoretical limit to the concentration of light of assigned wave-length in one spectrum, and as illustrating the frequently observed unsymmetrical character of the spectra on the two sides of the central image.[1]

The whole light in one spectrum.

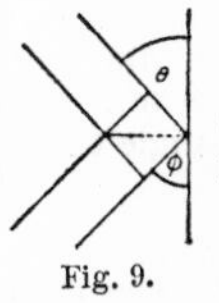

Oblique incidence.

We have hitherto supposed that the light is incident perpendicularly upon the grating; but the theory is easily extended. If the incident rays make an angle θ with the normal (fig. 9), and the diffracted rays make an angle ϕ (upon the same side), the relative retardation from each element of width $(a+d)$ to the next is $(a+d)$ $(\sin\theta + \sin\phi)$; and this is the quantity which is to be equated to $m\lambda$. Thus

Fig. 9.

$$\sin\theta + \sin\phi = 2\sin\tfrac{1}{2}(\theta+\phi) . \cos\tfrac{1}{2}(\theta-\phi) = m\lambda/(a+d) \quad . \quad (5).$$

The "deviation" is $(\theta+\phi)$, and is therefore a minimum when $\theta=\phi$, *i.e.*, when the grating is so situated that the angles of incidence and diffraction are equal.

Reflecting grating.

In the case of a reflexion grating the same method applies. If θ and ϕ denote the angles with the normal made by the incident and diffracted rays, the formula (5) still holds, and, if the deviation be reckoned from the direction of the regularly reflected rays, it is expressed as before by $(\theta+\phi)$, and is a minimum when $\theta=\phi$, that is, when the diffracted rays return upon the course of the incident rays.

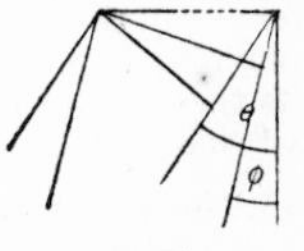

Fig. 10.

In either case (as also with a prism) the position of minimum deviation leaves the width of the beam unaltered, *i.e.*, neither magnifies nor diminishes the angular width of the object under view.

Grating interval less than λ.

From (5) we see that, when the light falls perpendicularly upon a grating ($\theta=0$), there is no spectrum formed (the image corre-

[1] *Phil. Mag.*, xlvii. 193, 1874.

sponding to $m=0$ not being counted as a spectrum), if the grating interval σ or $(a+d)$ is less than λ. Under these circumstances, if the material of the grating be completely transparent, the whole of the light must appear in the direct image, and the ruling is not perceptible. From the absence of spectra Fraunhofer argued that there must be a microscopic limit represented by λ; and the inference is plausible, to say the least.[1] Fraunhofer should, however, have fixed the microscopic limit at $\frac{1}{2}\lambda$, as appears from (5), when we suppose $\theta=\frac{1}{2}\pi$, $\phi=\frac{1}{2}\pi$.

Resolving power.

We will now consider the important subject of the resolving power of gratings, as dependent upon the number of lines (n) and the order of the spectrum observed (m). Let BP (fig. 11) be the direction of the principal maximum (middle of central band) for the wave-length λ in the mth spectrum. Then the relative retardation of the extreme rays (corresponding to the edges A, B of the grating) is $mn\lambda$. If BQ be the direction for the first minimum (the darkness between the central and first lateral band), the relative retardation of the extreme rays is $(mn+1)\lambda$. Suppose now that $\lambda+\delta\lambda$ is the wave-length for which BQ gives the principal maximum, then

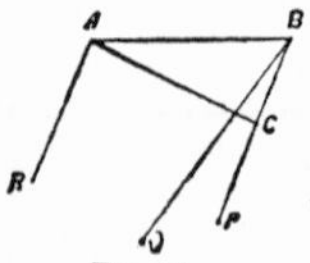

Fig. 11

$$(mn+1)\lambda=mn(\lambda+\delta\lambda);$$

whence

$$\delta\lambda/\lambda = 1/mn \quad . \quad . \quad . \quad . \quad . \quad . \quad . \quad (6).$$

According to our former standard, this gives the smallest difference of wave-lengths in a double line which can be just resolved; and we conclude that the resolving power of a grating depends only upon the total number of lines, and upon the order of the spectrum, without regard to any other considerations. It is here of course assumed that the n lines are really utilized.

In the case of the D-lines the value of $\delta\lambda/\lambda$ is about 1/1000; so that to resolve this double line in the first spectrum requires 1000 lines, in the second spectrum 500, and so on.

It is especially to be noticed that the resolving power does not depend directly upon the closeness of the ruling. Let us take the case of a grating 1 inch broad, and containing 1000 lines, and consider the effect of interpolating an additional 1000 lines, so as to bisect the former intervals. There will be destruction by interference of the first, third, and odd spectra generally; while the advantage gained in the spectra of even order is not in dispersion, nor in resolving power, but simply in brilliancy, which is increased four times. If we now suppose half the grating cut away, so as to leave 1000 lines in half an inch, the dispersion will not be altered, while the brightness and resolving power are halved.

No theoretical limit.

There is clearly no theoretical limit to the resolving power of gratings, even in spectra of given order. But it is possible that, as suggested by Rowland,[2] the structure of natural spectra may be too coarse to give opportunity for resolving powers much higher than those now in use. However this may be, it would always be possible, with the aid of a grating of given resolving power, to construct artificially from white light mixtures of slightly different wave-length whose resolution or otherwise would discriminate between powers inferior and superior to the given one.[3]

Expression for "dispersion."

If we define as the "dispersion" in a particular part of the spectrum the ratio of the angular interval $d\theta$ to the corresponding increment of wave-length $d\lambda$, we may express it by a very simple formula. For the alteration of wave-length entails, at the two limits of a diffracted wave-front, a relative retardation equal to $mnd\lambda$. Hence, if a be the width of the diffracted beam, and $d\theta$ the angle through which the wave-front is turned,

$$a\,d\theta=mn\,d\lambda,$$

or

$$\text{dispersion}=mn/a \quad . \quad . \quad . \quad . \quad . \quad . \quad . \quad (7).$$

The resolving power and the width of the emergent beam fix the optical character of the instrument. The latter element must eventually be decreased until less than the diameter of the pupil of the eye. Hence a wide beam demands treatment with further apparatus (usually a telescope) of high magnifying power.

Accuracy of ruling.

In the above discussion it has been supposed that the ruling is accurate, and we have seen that by increase of m a high resolving power is attainable with a moderate number of lines. But this procedure (apart from the question of illumination) is open to the objection that it makes excessive demands upon accuracy. According to the principle already laid down, it can make but little difference in the principal direction corresponding to the first spectrum, provided each line lie within a quarter of an interval $(a+d)$ from its theoretical position. But, to obtain an equally good result in the mth spectrum, the error must be less than $1/m$ of the above amount.[4]

There are certain errors of a systematic character which demand special consideration. The spacing is usually effected by means of a screw, to each revolution of which corresponds a large number (*e.g.*, one hundred) of lines. In this way it may happen that, although there is almost perfect periodicity with each revolution of the screw after (say) 100 lines, yet the 100 lines themselves are not equally spaced. The "ghosts" thus arising were first described by Quincke,[5] and have been elaborately investigated by Peirce,[6] both theoretically and experimentally. The general nature of the effects to be expected in such a case may be made clear by means of an illustration already employed for another purpose. Suppose two similar and accurately ruled transparent gratings to be superposed in such a manner that the lines are parallel. If the one set of lines exactly bisect the intervals between the others, the grating interval is practically halved, and the previously existing spectra of odd order vanish. But a very slight relative displacement will cause the apparition of the odd spectra. In this case there is approximate periodicity in the half interval, but complete periodicity only after the whole interval. The advantage of approximate bisection lies in the superior brilliancy of the surviving spectra; but in any case the compound grating may be considered to be perfect in the longer interval, and the definition is as good as if the bisection were accurate.

Approximate periodicity.

Gradually increasing interval.

The effect of a gradual increase in the interval (fig. 12) as we pass across the grating has been investigated by Cornu,[7] who thus explains an anomaly observed by Mascart. The latter found that certain gratings exercised a converging power upon the spectra formed upon one side, and a corresponding diverging power upon the spectra on the other side. Let us suppose that the light is incident perpendicularly, and that the grating interval increases from the centre towards that edge which lies nearest to the spectrum under observation, and decreases towards the hinder edge.

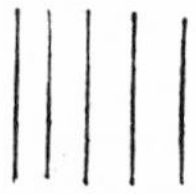

Fig. 12.—x^2.  Fig. 13.—y^2.  Fig. 14.—x^3.  Fig. 15.—xy^2.

It is evident that the waves from *both* halves of the grating are accelerated in an increasing degree, as we pass from the centre outwards, as compared with the phase they would possess were the central value of the grating interval maintained throughout. The irregularity of spacing has thus the effect of a convex lens, which accelerates the marginal relatively to the central rays. On the other side the effect is reversed. This kind of irregularity may clearly be present in a degree surpassing the usual limits, without loss of definition, when the telescope is focused so as to secure the best effect.

Fig. 16.—xy.  Fig. 17.—x^2y.  Fig. 18.—y^3.

It may be worth while to examine further the other variations from correct ruling which correspond to the various terms expressing the deviation of the wave-surface from a perfect plane. If x and y be coordinates in the plane of the wave-surface, the axis of y being parallel to the lines of the grating, and the origin corresponding to the centre of the beam, we have as an approximate equation to the wave-surface (§ 6)

$$z=\frac{x^2}{2\rho}+\beta xy+\frac{y^2}{2\rho'}+\alpha x^3+\beta x^2y+\gamma xy^2+\delta y^3+\ . \quad . \quad (8);$$

Curvature.

and, as we have just seen, the term in x^2 corresponds to a linear error in the spacing. In like manner, the term in y^2 corresponds to a general *curvature* of the lines (fig. 13), and does not influence the definition at the (primary) focus, although it may introduce astigmatism.[8] If we suppose that everything is symmetrical on the two sides of the primary plane $y=0$, the coefficients B, β, δ vanish. In spite of any inequality between ρ and ρ', the definition will be good to this order of approximation, provided α and γ vanish. The former measures the *thickness* of the primary focal line, and the latter measures its *curvature*. The error of ruling giving rise to α is one in which the intervals increase or decrease in *both* directions from the centre outwards (fig. 14), and it may often be compensated by a slight rotation in azimuth of the object-glass of the observing telescope. The term in γ corresponds to a *variation* of curvature in crossing the grating (fig. 15).

Other errors.

When the plane zx is not a plane of symmetry, we have to consider the terms in xy, x^2y, and y^3. The first of these corresponds

[1] "Notes on Some Fundamental Propositions in Optics," *Phil. Mag.*, June 1886.

[2] Compare also Lippich, *Pogg. Ann.*, cxxxix. p. 465, 1870; Rayleigh, *Nature*, Oct. 2, 1873.

[3] The power of a grating to construct light of nearly definite wave-length is well illustrated by Young's comparison with the production of a musical note by reflexion of a sudden sound from a row of palings. The objection raised by Herschel (*Light*, § 703) to this comparison depends on a misconception.

[4] It must not be supposed that errors of this order of magnitude are unobjectionable in all cases. The position of the middle of the bright band representative of a mathematical line can be fixed with a spider-line micrometer within a small fraction of the width of the band, just as the accuracy of astronomical observations far transcends the separating power of the instrument.

[5] *Pogg. Ann.*, cxlvi. p. 1, 1872.

[6] *Ann. Jour. Math.*, vol. ii. p. 330, 1879.

[7] *C. R.*, lxxx. p. 645, 1875.

[8] "In the same way we may conclude that in flat gratings any departure from a straight line has the effect of causing the dust in the slit and the spectrum to have different foci—a fact sometimes observed" (Rowland, "On Concave Gratings for Optical Purposes," *Phil. Mag.*, September 1883).

to a deviation from parallelism, causing the interval to alter gradually as we pass *along* the lines (fig. 16). The error thus arising may be compensated by a rotation of the object-glass about one of the diameters $y=\pm x$. The term in x^2y corresponds to a deviation from parallelism in the same direction on both sides of the central line (fig. 17); and that in y^3 would be caused by a curvature such that there is a point of inflexion at the middle of each line (fig. 18).

All the errors, except that depending on α, and especially those depending on γ and δ, can be diminished, without loss of resolving power, by contracting the *vertical* aperture. A linear error in the spacing, and a general curvature of the lines, are eliminated in the ordinary use of a grating.

The explanation of the difference of focus upon the two sides as due to unequal spacing was verified by Cornu upon gratings purposely constructed with an increasing interval. He has also shown how to rule a plane surface with lines so disposed that the grating shall of itself give well-focused spectra.[1]

Rowland's concave gratings.

A similar idea appears to have guided Rowland to his brilliant invention of concave gratings, by which spectra can be photographed without any further optical appliance. In these instruments the lines are ruled upon a spherical surface of speculum metal, and mark the intersections of the surface by a system of parallel and equidistant planes, of which the middle member passes through the centre of the sphere. If we consider for the present only the primary plane of symmetry, the figure is reduced to two dimensions. Let AP (fig. 19) represent the surface of the grating, O being the centre of the circle. Then, if Q be any radiant point and Q′ its image (primary focus) in the spherical mirror AP, we have

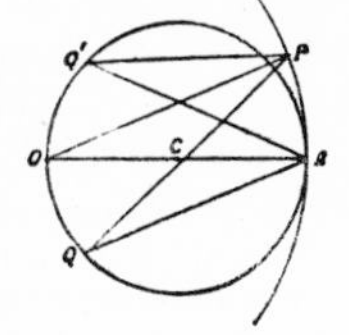

Fig. 19.

$$\frac{1}{v_1}+\frac{1}{u}=\frac{2\cos\phi}{a},$$

where $v_1=\text{AQ}'$, $u=\text{AQ}$, $a=\text{OA}$, $\phi=$ angle of incidence QAO, equal to the angle of reflexion Q′AO.[2] If Q be on the circle described upon OA as diameter, so that $u=a\cos\phi$, then Q′ lies also upon the same circle; and in this case it follows from the symmetry that the unsymmetrical aberration (depending upon α) vanishes.

This disposition is adopted in Rowland's instrument; only, in addition to the central image formed at the angle $\phi'=\phi$, there are a series of spectra with various values of ϕ', but all disposed upon the same circle. Rowland's investigation is contained in the paper already referred to; but the following account of the theory is in the form adopted by Glazebrook.[3]

In order to find the difference of optical distances between the courses QAQ′, QPQ′, we have to express QP − QA, PQ′ − AQ′. To find the former, we have, if $\text{OAQ}=\phi$, $\text{AOP}=\omega$,

$$\begin{aligned}\text{QP}^2&=u^2+4a^2\sin^2\tfrac{1}{2}\omega-4au\sin\tfrac{1}{2}\omega\sin(\tfrac{1}{2}\omega-\phi)\\&=(u+a\sin\phi\sin\omega)^2-a^2\sin^2\phi\sin^2\omega+4a\sin^2\tfrac{1}{2}\omega\,(a-u\cos\phi).\end{aligned}$$

Now as far as ω^4

$$4\sin^2\tfrac{1}{2}\omega=\sin^2\omega+\tfrac{1}{4}\sin^4\omega,$$

and thus to the same order

$$\begin{aligned}\text{QP}^2&=(u+a\sin\phi\sin\omega)^2\\&-a\cos\phi\,(u-a\cos\phi)\sin^2\omega+\tfrac{1}{4}a\,(a-u\cos\phi)\sin^4\omega.\end{aligned}$$

But if we now suppose that Q lies on the circle $u=a\cos\phi$, the middle term vanishes, and we get, correct as far as ω^4,

$$\text{QP}=(u+a\sin\phi\sin\omega)\sqrt{\left\{1+\frac{a^2\sin^2\phi\sin^4\omega}{4u}\right\}};$$

so that

$$\text{QP}-u=a\sin\phi\sin\omega+\tfrac{1}{8}a\sin\phi\tan\phi\sin^4\omega \quad . \quad . \quad . \quad (9),$$

in which it is to be noticed that the adjustment necessary to secure the disappearance of $\sin^2\omega$ is sufficient also to destroy the term in $\sin^3\omega$.

A similar expression can be found for Q′P − Q′A; and thus, if $\text{Q'A}=v$, $\text{Q'AO}=\phi'$, where $v=a\cos\phi'$, we get

$$\begin{aligned}\text{QP}+\text{PQ}'-\text{QA}-\text{AQ}'&=a\sin\omega(\sin\phi-\sin\phi')\\&+\tfrac{1}{8}a\sin^4\omega(\sin\phi\tan\phi+\sin\phi'\tan\phi') \quad . \quad . \quad . \quad (10).\end{aligned}$$

If $\phi'=\phi$, the term of the first order vanishes, and the reduction of the difference of path *via* P and *via* A to a term of the fourth order proves not only that Q and Q′ are conjugate foci, but also that the foci are exempt from the most important term in the aberration. In the present application ϕ' is not necessarily equal to ϕ; but if P correspond to a line upon the grating, the difference of retardations for consecutive positions of P, so far as expressed by the term of the first order, will be equal to $\mp m\lambda$ (m integral), and therefore without influence, provided

$$\sigma(\sin\phi-\sin\phi')=\mp m\lambda \quad . \quad . \quad . \quad . \quad . \quad . \quad (11),$$

where σ denotes the constant interval between the planes containing the lines. This is the ordinary formula for a reflecting plane grating, and it shows that the spectra are formed in the usual directions. They are here focused (so far as the rays in the primary plane are concerned) upon the circle OQ′A, and the outstanding aberration is of the fourth order.

In order that a large part of the field of view may be in focus at once, it is desirable that the locus of the focused spectrum should be nearly perpendicular to the line of vision. For this purpose Rowland places the eye-piece at O, so that $\phi=0$, and then by (11) the value of ϕ' in the mth spectrum is

$$\sigma\sin\phi'=\pm m\lambda \quad . \quad . \quad . \quad . \quad . \quad . \quad . \quad (12).$$

Aberration.

If ω now relate to the edge of the grating, on which there are altogether n lines,

$$n\sigma=2a\sin\omega,$$

and the value of the last term in (10) becomes

$$\tfrac{1}{16}n\sigma\sin^3\omega\sin\phi'\tan\phi',$$

or

$$\tfrac{1}{16}mn\lambda\sin^3\omega\tan\phi' \quad . \quad . \quad . \quad . \quad . \quad . \quad (13).$$

This expresses the retardation of the extreme relatively to the central ray, and is to be reckoned positive, whatever may be the signs of ω and ϕ'. If the semi-angular aperture (ω) be $\frac{1}{100}$, and $\tan\phi'=1$, mn might be as great as four millions before the error of phase would reach $\frac{1}{4}\lambda$. If it were desired to use an angular aperture so large that the aberration according to (13) would be injurious, Rowland points out that on his machine there would be no difficulty in applying a remedy by making σ slightly variable towards the edges. Or, retaining σ constant, we might attain compensation by so polishing the surface as to bring the circumference slightly forward in comparison with the position it would occupy upon a true sphere.

It may be remarked that these calculations apply to the rays in the primary plane only. The image is greatly affected with astigmatism; but this is of little consequence, if γ in (8) be small enough. Curvature of the primary focal line having a very injurious effect upon definition, it may be inferred from the excellent performance of these gratings that γ is in fact small. Its value does not appear to have been calculated. The other coefficients in (8) vanish in virtue of the symmetry.

Rowland's mechanical arrangements.

The mechanical arrangements for maintaining the focus are of great simplicity. The grating at A and the eye-piece at O are rigidly attached to a bar AO, whose ends rest on carriages, moving on rails OQ, AQ at right angles to each other. A tie between C and Q can be used if thought desirable.

The absence of chromatic aberration gives a great advantage in the comparison of overlapping spectra, which Rowland has turned to excellent account in his determinations of the relative wave-lengths of lines in the solar spectrum.[4]

Absolute measurements.

For absolute determinations of wave-lengths plane gratings are used. It is found [5] that the angular measurements present less difficulty than the comparison of the grating interval with the standard metre. There is also some uncertainty as to the actual temperature of the grating when in use. In order to minimize the heating action of the light, it might be submitted to a preliminary prismatic analysis before it reaches the slit of the spectrometer, after the manner of Von Helmholtz (OPTICS, vol. xvii. p. 802).

Bell found further that it is necessary to submit the gratings to calibration, and not to rest satisfied with a knowledge of the number of lines and of the total width. It not unfrequently happens that near the beginning of the ruling the interval is anomalous. If the width of this region be small, it has scarcely any effect upon the angular measurements, and should be left out of account in estimating the effective interval.

§ 15. *Theory of Corrugated Waves.*

The theory of gratings is usually given in a form applicable only to the case where the alternate parts are transparent and opaque. Even then it is very improbable that the process of simply including the transparent parts and excluding the opaque parts in the integrations of § 11 gives an accurate result. The condition of things in actual gratings is much more complicated, and all that can with confidence be asserted is the approximate periodicity in the interval σ. The problem thus presents itself—to determine the course of events on the further side of the plane $z=0$ when the amplitude and phase over that plane are periodic functions of x; and the first step in the solution would naturally be to determine the effect corresponding to the infinitesimal strip $y\,dx$ over which the amplitude and phase are constant. In fig. 20 QQ′ represents the strip in question, of which the effect is to be estimated at $\text{P}(0,0,z)$; $\text{QR}=y$, $\text{RP}=r$, $\text{QP}=\rho$.

Wave diverging in two dimensions.

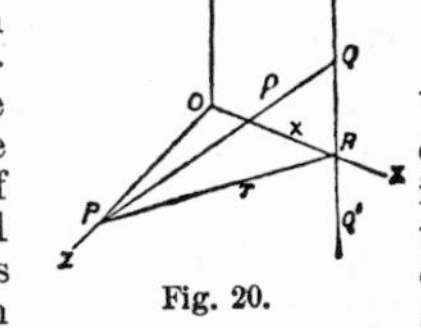

Fig. 20.

If we assume the law of secondary wave determined in § 10 so

[1] The ruling required is evidently that which would be marked out by interference bands, supposing sources of light of the prescribed wave-length to be situated at the radiant point and at the desired image.

[2] This formula may be obtained as in OPTICS, vol. xvii. p. 800, equation (3), and may indeed be derived from that equation by writing $\phi'=\phi$, $\mu=-1$.

[3] *Phil. Mag.*, June 1883, Nov. 1883.

[4] *Phil. Mag.*, March 1887.

[5] Bell, *Phil. Mag.*, March 1887.

as to suit the resolution of an infinite uniform primary wave, we have, as the effect of QQ′,

$$2\,dx\int_0^\infty \frac{dy}{\lambda\rho}\cos\kappa(at-\rho+\tfrac{1}{4}\lambda)$$

$$=-\frac{2\,dx}{\lambda}\int_r^\infty \frac{d\rho}{\sqrt{(\rho^2-r^2)}}\sin\kappa(at-\rho) \quad . \quad (1).$$

The development of this expression for the operation of a linear source would take us too far.[1] We must content ourselves with the limiting form assumed when κr is great, as it would almost always be in optics. Under these circumstances the denominator may be simplified by writing

$$\sqrt{(\rho^2-r^2)}=\sqrt{(2r)}.\sqrt{(\rho-r)},$$

so that (1) becomes

$$-\frac{2\,dx}{\lambda\sqrt{(2r)}}\int_0^\infty \frac{d(\rho-r)}{\sqrt{(\rho-r)}}\sin\kappa\,\{at-r-(\rho-r)\}.$$

Now

$$\int_0^\infty \frac{\sin\kappa u\,du}{\sqrt{u}}=\int_0^\infty \frac{\cos\kappa u\,du}{\sqrt{u}}=\sqrt{\left(\frac{\pi}{2\kappa}\right)}=\tfrac{1}{2}\sqrt{\lambda},$$

and thus we obtain

$$-\frac{dx}{\sqrt{(2\lambda r)}}\{\sin\kappa(at-r)-\cos\kappa(at-r)\}$$

$$=-\frac{dx}{\sqrt{(\lambda r)}}\sin\kappa(at-r-\tfrac{1}{8}\lambda) \quad . \quad . \quad . \quad . \quad . \quad (2),$$

which gives the effect of a linear source at a great distance. The occurrence of the factor $r^{-\frac{1}{2}}$ is a consequence of the cylindrical expansion of the waves. The whole effect is retarded *one-eighth* of a period in comparison with that of the central element, instead of one-quarter of a period as in the case of a uniform wave extending over the whole plane.

Plane uniform wave.

The effect of the uniform plane wave can be recovered by integrating (2) with respect to x from $-\infty$ to $+\infty$, on the supposition that κr is great. We have

$$\frac{dx}{\sqrt{r}}=\frac{r\,dr}{\sqrt{r}.x}=\frac{\sqrt{r}.d(r-z)}{\sqrt{(r+z)}.\sqrt{(r-z)}};$$

and in this, since the only elements which contribute sensibly to the integral are those for which $(r-z)$ is small, we may write

$$\frac{\sqrt{r}}{\sqrt{(r+z)}}=\frac{1}{\sqrt{2}}.$$

The integral can then be evaluated by the same formula as before, and we get finally $\cos\kappa\,(at-z)$, the same as if the primary wave were supposed to advance without resolution. The recomposition of the primary wave by integration with rectangular coordinates is thus verified, but only under the limitation, not really required by the nature of the case, that the point at which the effect is to be estimated is distant by a very great number of wave-lengths from the plane of resolution.

Variable amplitude and phase.

We will now suppose that the amplitude and phase of the primary wave at the plane of resolution $z=0$ are no longer constants, but periodic functions of x. Instead of $\cos\kappa at$ simply, we should have to take in general

$$\mathrm{A}\cos(px+f)\cos\kappa at+\mathrm{B}\cos(px+g)\sin\kappa at;$$

but it will be sufficient for our purpose to consider the first term only, in which we may further put for simplicity $\mathrm{A}=1$, $f=0$. The effect of the linear element at x, 0, upon a point at ξ, z, will be, according to (2),

$$-\frac{dx}{\sqrt{(\lambda r)}}\cos px\,\sin\kappa(at-r-\tfrac{1}{8}\lambda),$$

where r is the distance, expressed by $r^2=z^2+(x-\xi)^2$. Thus, if we write $x=\xi+\alpha$, the whole effect is

$$-\int_{-\infty}^{+\infty}\frac{d\alpha}{2\sqrt{(\lambda r)}}\{\sin(\kappa at+p\xi-\tfrac{1}{4}\pi-\kappa r+p\alpha)$$

$$+\sin(\kappa at-p\xi-\tfrac{1}{4}\pi-\kappa r-p\alpha)\} \quad . \quad . \quad (3),$$

where $r^2=z^2+\alpha^2$.

In the two terms of this integral the elements are in general of rapidly fluctuating sign; and the only important part of the range of integration in (for example) the first term is in the neighbourhood of the place where $p\alpha-\kappa r$ is stationary in value, or where

$$p\,d\alpha-\kappa\,dr=0 \quad . \quad . \quad . \quad . \quad . \quad . \quad . \quad . \quad (4).$$

In general $\alpha\,d\alpha-r\,dr=0$, so that if the values of α and r corresponding to (4) be called α_0, r_0, we have

$$\frac{\alpha_0}{p}=\frac{r_0}{\kappa}=\frac{z}{\sqrt{(\kappa^2-p^2)}} \quad . \quad . \quad . \quad . \quad . \quad . \quad (5).$$

Now, in the neighbourhood of these values, if $\alpha=\alpha_0+\alpha_1$,

$$p\alpha-\kappa r=p\alpha_0-\kappa r_0+\alpha_1\left(p-\kappa\frac{\alpha_0}{r_0}\right)-\frac{\kappa\alpha_1^2}{2r_0}\left(1-\frac{p^2}{\kappa^2}\right),$$

in which by (5) the term of the first order vanishes. Using this in (3), we get for the first term

$$-\int_{-\infty}^{+\infty}\frac{d\alpha_1}{2\sqrt{(\lambda r_0)}}\{\sin(\kappa at+p\xi-\tfrac{1}{4}\pi-\kappa r_0+p\alpha_0)\cos h\alpha_1^2$$

$$-\cos(\kappa at+p\xi-\tfrac{1}{4}\pi-\kappa r_0+p\alpha_0)\sin h\alpha_1^2\},$$

where for brevity h is written for

$$\frac{\kappa}{2r_0}\left(1-\frac{p^2}{\kappa^2}\right).$$

The integration is effected by means of the formula

$$\int_{-\infty}^{+\infty}\cos hu^2du=\int_{-\infty}^{+\infty}\sin hu^2du=\sqrt{\left(\frac{\pi}{2h}\right)};$$

and we find

$$\frac{\kappa}{2\sqrt{(\kappa^2-p^2)}}\cos(\kappa at+p\xi-\kappa r_0+p\alpha_0).$$

The other term in (3) gives in like manner

$$\frac{\kappa}{2\sqrt{(\kappa^2-p^2)}}\cos(\kappa at-p\xi-\kappa r_0+p\alpha_0);$$

so that the complete value is

$$\frac{\kappa\cos p\xi}{\sqrt{(\kappa^2-p^2)}}\cos\{\kappa at-\sqrt{(\kappa^2-p^2)}.z\} \quad . \quad . \quad . \quad . \quad (6).$$

When $p=0$, we fall back on the uniform plane wave travelling with velocity a. In general the velocity is not a, but

Velocity of propagation.

$$\kappa a/\sqrt{(\kappa^2-p^2)} \quad . \quad . \quad . \quad . \quad . \quad . \quad . \quad . \quad (7).$$

The wave represented by (6) is one in which the amplitude at various points of a wave-front is proportional to $\cos p\xi$, or $\cos px$; and, beyond the reversals of phase herein implied, the phase is constant, so that the wave-surfaces are given by $z=$ constant. The wave thus described moves forward at the velocity given by (7), and with type unchanged.

The above investigation may be regarded as applicable to gratings which give spectra of the first order only. Although κ vary, there is no separation of colours. Such a separation requires either a limitation in the width of the grating (here supposed to be infinite), or the use of a focusing lens.

It is important to remark that p has been assumed to be less than κ, or σ greater than λ; otherwise no part of the range of integration in (3) is exempt from rapid fluctuation of sign, and the result must be considered to be zero. The principle that irregularities in a wave-front of periods less than λ cannot be propagated is of great consequence. Further light will be thrown upon it by a different investigation to be given presently.

The possibility of the wave represented by (6) is perhaps sufficiently established by the preceding method, but the occurrence of the factor $\kappa/\sqrt{(\kappa^2-p^2)}$ shows that the laws of the secondary wave (determined originally from a consideration of uniform plane waves) was not rightly assumed.

Corrected law of secondary wave.

The correct law applicable in any case may be investigated as follows. Let us assume that the expression for the wave of given periodic time is

$$\psi=e^{i\kappa at}\iint\rho^{-1}e^{-i\kappa\rho}\,\mathrm{F}(x,y)\,dx\,dy\,; \quad . \quad . \quad . \quad (8),$$

and let us inquire what the value of $\mathrm{F}(x,y)$ must be in order that the application of Huygens's principle may give a correct result. From (8)

$$\frac{d\psi}{dz}=e^{i\kappa at}\iint\frac{z}{\rho}\frac{d}{d\rho}\left(\frac{e^{-i\kappa\rho}}{\rho}\right)\mathrm{F}(x,y)\,dx\,dy,$$

and

$$\frac{d}{d\rho}\left(\frac{e^{-i\kappa\rho}}{\rho}\right)=-\frac{e^{-i\kappa\rho}(1+\kappa\rho)}{\rho^2}.$$

We propose now to find the limiting value of $d\psi/dz$ when z is very small. The value of the integral will depend upon those elements only for which x and y are very small, so that we replace $\mathrm{F}(x,y)$ in the limit by $\mathrm{F}(0,0)$. Also, in the limit,

$$\iint\frac{z}{\rho}\frac{d}{d\rho}\left(\frac{e^{-i\kappa\rho}}{\rho}\right)dx\,dy=\iint\frac{-z}{\rho^3}\,dx\,dy=-2\pi\,;$$

so that

$$\text{Limit}\ \frac{d\psi}{dz}=-2\pi\,e^{i\kappa at}\,\mathrm{F}(0,0).$$

The proper value of $e^{i\kappa at}\mathrm{F}(x,y)$ is therefore that of $-d\psi/dz$ at the same point $(x, y, 0)$ divided by 2π, and we have in general

$$\psi=\frac{-1}{2\pi}\iint\left(\frac{d\psi}{dz}\right)\frac{e^{-i\kappa\rho}}{\rho}dx\,dy \quad . \quad . \quad . \quad . \quad (9).$$

In the case of the uniform plane wave,

$$\psi=e^{i\kappa(at-z)}, \quad d\psi/dz=-i\kappa e^{i\kappa(at-z)};$$

so that

$$\psi=\frac{ie^{i\kappa at}}{\lambda}\iint\frac{e^{-i\kappa\rho}}{\rho}dx\,dy=\iint\frac{e^{i\kappa(at-\rho+\frac{1}{4}\lambda)}}{\lambda\rho}dx\,dy,$$

agreeing with what we have already found for the secondary wave in this case.

[1] *Theory of Sound*, § 341.

But, if $\psi=\cos px \,.\, e^{i[\kappa at-\sqrt{(\kappa^2-p^2)}\,.\,z]}$,

$$\frac{d\psi}{dz}(z=0)=-i\sqrt{(\kappa^2-p^2)}\cos px\, e^{i\kappa at},$$

and

$$\psi=\frac{\sqrt{(\kappa^2-p^2)}}{2\pi}\iint\frac{e^{i\kappa(at-\rho+\frac{1}{4}\lambda)}}{\rho}\cos px\,dx\,dy\,.$$

The occurrence of the anomalous factor in (6) is thus explained.

It must be admitted that the present process of investigation is rather artificial; and the cause lies in the attempt to dispense with the differential equation satisfied by ψ, viz.,

$$\frac{d^2\psi}{dx^2}+\frac{d^2\psi}{dy^2}+\frac{d^2\psi}{dz^2}+\kappa^2\psi=0 \quad . \quad . \quad . \quad . \quad . \quad (10),$$

on which in the case of sound the whole theory is based. It is in fact easy to verify that any value of ψ included under (8), where

$$\rho^2=(\xi-x)^2+(\eta-y)^2+\zeta^2,$$

satisfies the equation

$$\frac{d^2\psi}{d\xi^2}+\frac{d^2\psi}{d\eta^2}+\frac{d^2\psi}{d\zeta^2}+\kappa^2\psi=0\,.$$

When there is no question of resolution by Huygens's principle, the distinction between ξ, η and x, y may be dropped.

Starting from the differential equation, we may recover previous results very simply. If ψ be proportional to $\cos px \cos qy$, we have

$$\frac{d^2\psi}{dz^2}+(\kappa^2-p^2-q^2)\psi=0 \quad . \quad . \quad . \quad . \quad . \quad (11).$$

If $\kappa^2-p^2-q^2=\mu^2$, μ being real, the solution of (11) is

$$\psi=\mathrm{A}e^{i\mu z}+\mathrm{B}e^{-i\mu z},$$

where A and B are independent of z. Restoring the factors involving t, x, y, we may write

$$\psi=\cos px\cos qy\{\mathrm{A}\,e^{i(\kappa at+\mu z)}+\mathrm{B}\,e^{i(\kappa at-\mu z)}\} \quad . \quad . \quad (12),$$

of which the first term may be dropped when we contemplate waves travelling in the positive direction only. The corresponding realized solution is of the type

$$\psi=\cos px\cos qy\cos\{\kappa at-\sqrt{(\kappa^2-p^2-q^2)}.z\} \quad . \quad . \quad (13).$$

When $\kappa^2>(p^2+q^2)$, the wave travels without change of type and with velocity

$$\mathrm{V}=\frac{\kappa a}{\sqrt{(\kappa^2-p^2-q^2)}} \quad . \quad . \quad . \quad . \quad . \quad . \quad (14).$$

We have now to consider what occurs when $\kappa^2<(p^2+q^2)$. If we write $\kappa^2-p^2-q^2=-\mu^2$, we have in place of (12)

$$\psi=\cos px\cos qy\{\mathrm{A}\,e^{i\kappa at+\mu z}+\mathrm{B}\,e^{i\kappa at-\mu z}\}. \quad . \quad . \quad (15);$$

and for the realized solution corresponding to (13)

$$\psi=\cos px\cos qy\,e^{-\mu z}\cos\kappa at\,. \quad . \quad . \quad . \quad . \quad (16).$$

We conclude that under these circumstances the motion rapidly diminishes as z increases, and that no wave in the usual sense can be propagated at all.

Corrugations of period less than λ die out.

It follows that corrugations of a reflecting surface (no matter how deep) will not disturb the regularity of a perpendicularly reflected wave, provided the wave-length of the corrugation do not exceed that of the vibration. And, whatever the former wave-length may be in relation to the latter, regular reflexion will occur when the incidence is sufficiently oblique.

Shadow of a grating.

The first form of solution may be applied to give an explanation of the appearances observed when a plane wave traverses a parallel coarse grating and then impinges upon a screen held at varying distances behind.[1] As the general expression of the wave periodic with respect to x in distance σ we may take

$$\mathrm{A}_0\cos(\kappa at-\kappa z)+\mathrm{A}_1\cos(px+f_1)\cos(\kappa at-\mu_1 z)$$
$$+\mathrm{B}_1\cos(px+g_1)\sin(\kappa at-\mu_1 z)+\mathrm{A}_2\cos(2px+f_2)\cos\kappa(at-\mu_2 z)+\ldots,$$

where

$$p=2\pi/\sigma\,,\ \kappa=2\pi/\lambda\,,\ \text{and}\ \mu_1{}^2=\kappa^2-p^2\,,\ \mu_2{}^2=\kappa^2-4p^2\,,\ \ldots,$$

the series being continued as long as μ is real. We shall here, however, limit ourselves to the first three terms, and in them suppose A_1 and B_1 to be small relatively to A_0. The intensity may then be represented by

$$\mathrm{A}_0{}^2+2\mathrm{A}_0\mathrm{A}_1\cos(px+f)\cos(\kappa z-\mu_1 z)$$
$$+2\mathrm{A}_0\mathrm{B}_1\cos(px+g)\sin(\kappa z-\mu_1 z) \quad . \quad . \quad . \quad . \quad (17).$$

The stripes thrown upon the screen in various positions are thus periodic functions of z, and the period is

$$z=\frac{2\pi}{\kappa-\sqrt{(\kappa^2-p^2)}}=\frac{2\sigma^2}{\lambda} \quad . \quad . \quad . \quad . \quad . \quad (18),$$

if λ be supposed small in comparison with σ. It may be noticed that, if the position of the screen be altered by the half of this amount, the effect is equivalent to a shifting parallel to x through the distance $\frac{1}{2}\sigma$. Hence, if the grating consists of alternate transparent and opaque parts of width $\frac{1}{2}\sigma$, the stripes seen upon the screen are *reversed* when the latter is drawn back through the distance σ^2/λ. In this case we may suppose B_1 to vanish, and (17) then shows that the field is uniform when the screen occupies positions midway between those which give the most distinct patterns. These results are of interest in connexion with the photographic reproduction of gratings.

[1] *Phil. Mag.*, March 1881, "On Copying Diffraction Gratings and on Some Phenomena Connected Therewith."

§ 16. *Talbot's Bands.*

These very remarkable bands are seen under certain conditions when a tolerably pure spectrum is regarded with the naked eye, or with a telescope, *half the aperture being covered by a thin plate, e.g., of glass or mica.* The view of the matter taken by the discoverer[2] was that any ray which suffered in traversing the plate a retardation of an odd number of half wave-lengths would be extinguished, and that thus the spectrum would be seen interrupted by a number of dark bars. But this explanation cannot be accepted as it stands, being open to the same objection as Arago's theory of stellar scintillation.[3] It is as far as possible from being true that a body emitting homogeneous light would disappear on merely covering half the aperture of vision with a half-wave plate. Such a conclusion would be in the face of the principle of energy, which teaches plainly that the retardation in question leaves the aggregate brightness unaltered. The actual formation of the bands comes about in a very curious way, as is shown by a circumstance first observed by Brewster. When the retarding plate is held on the side towards the red of the spectrum, *the bands are not seen.* Even in the contrary case, the thickness of the plate must not exceed a certain limit, however pure the spectrum may be. A satisfactory explanation of these bands was first given by Airy,[4] but we shall here follow the investigation of Stokes,[5] limiting ourselves, however, to the case where the retarded and unretarded beams are contiguous and of equal width. The aperture of the unretarded beam may thus be taken to be limited by $x=-h$, $x=0$, $y=-l$, $y=+l$; and that of the beam retarded by R to be given by $x=0$, $x=h$, $y=-l$, $y=+l$. For the former (1) § 11 gives

Brewster's observations.

$$-\frac{1}{\lambda f}\int_{-h}^{0}\int_{-l}^{+l}\sin\kappa\left\{at-f+\frac{x\xi+y\eta}{f}\right\}dx\,dy$$
$$=-\frac{2lh}{\lambda f}\cdot\frac{f}{\kappa\eta l}\sin\frac{\kappa\eta l}{f}\cdot\frac{2f}{\kappa\xi h}\sin\frac{\kappa\xi h}{2f}\cdot\sin\kappa\left\{at-f-\frac{\xi h}{2f}\right\} \quad . \quad (1),$$

on integration and reduction.

For the retarded stream the only difference is that we must subtract R from at, and that the limits of x are 0 and $+h$. We thus get for the disturbance at ξ, η due to this stream

$$-\frac{2lh}{\lambda f}\cdot\frac{f}{\kappa\eta l}\sin\frac{\kappa\eta l}{f}\cdot\frac{2f}{\kappa\xi h}\sin\frac{\kappa\xi h}{2f}\cdot\sin\kappa\left\{at-f-\mathrm{R}+\frac{\xi h}{2f}\right\} \quad . \quad (2).$$

If we put for shortness τ for the quantity under the last circular function in (1), the expressions (1), (2) may be put under the forms $u\sin\tau, v\sin(\tau-a)$ respectively; and, if I be the intensity, I will be measured by the sum of the squares of the coefficients of $\sin\tau$ and $\cos\tau$ in the expression

$$u\sin\tau+v\sin(\tau-a),$$

so that

$$\mathrm{I}=u^2+v^2+2uv\cos a\,,$$

which becomes on putting for u, v, and a their values, and putting

$$\left\{\frac{f}{\kappa\eta l}\sin\frac{\kappa\eta l}{f}\right\}^2=\mathrm{Q}\,. \quad . \quad . \quad . \quad . \quad . \quad . \quad (3),$$

$$\mathrm{I}=\mathrm{Q}\cdot\frac{4l^2}{\pi^2\xi^2}\sin^2\frac{\pi\xi h}{\lambda f}\left\{2+2\cos\left(\frac{2\pi\mathrm{R}}{\lambda}-\frac{2\pi\xi h}{\lambda f}\right)\right\} \quad . \quad . \quad (4).$$

If the subject of examination be a luminous line parallel to η, we shall obtain what we require by integrating (4) with respect to η from $-\infty$ to $+\infty$. The constant multiplier is of no especial interest, so that we may take as applicable to the image of a line

$$\mathrm{I}=\frac{2}{\xi^2}\sin^2\frac{\pi\xi h}{\lambda f}\left\{1+\cos\left(\frac{2\pi\mathrm{R}}{\lambda}-\frac{2\pi\xi h}{\lambda f}\right)\right\} \quad . \quad . \quad . \quad (5).$$

If $\mathrm{R}=\frac{1}{2}\lambda$, I vanishes at $\xi=0$; but the whole illumination, represented by $\int_{-\infty}^{+\infty}\mathrm{I}\,d\xi$, is independent of the value of R. If $\mathrm{R}=0$, $\mathrm{I}=\frac{1}{\xi^2}\sin^2\frac{2\pi\xi h}{\lambda f}$, in agreement with § 11, where a has the meaning here attached to $2h$.

The expression (5) gives the illumination at ξ due to that part of the complete image whose geometrical focus is at $\xi=0$, the retardation for this component being R. Since we have now to integrate for the whole illumination at a particular point O due to all the components which have their foci in its neighbourhood, we

[2] *Phil. Mag.*, x. p. 364, 1837.

[3] On account of inequalities in the atmosphere giving a variable refraction, the light from a star would be irregularly distributed over a screen. The experiment is easily made on a laboratory scale, with a small source of light, the rays from which, in their course towards a rather distant screen, are disturbed by the neighbourhood of a heated body. At a moment when the eye, or object-glass of a telescope, occupies a dark position, the star vanishes. A fraction of a second later the aperture occupies a bright place, and the star reappears. According to this view the chromatic effects depend entirely upon atmospheric dispersion.

[4] *Phil. Trans.*, 1840, p. 225; 1841, p. 1. [5] *Phil. Trans.*, 1848, p. 227.

may conveniently regard O as origin. ξ is then the coordinate relatively to O of any focal point O′ for which the retardation is R; and the required result is obtained by simply integrating (5) with respect to ξ from $-\infty$ to $+\infty$. To each value of ξ corresponds a different value of λ, and (in consequence of the dispersing power of the plate) of R. The variation of λ may, however, be neglected in the integration, except in $2\pi R/\lambda$, where a small variation of λ entails a comparatively large alteration of phase. If we write

$$\rho = 2\pi R/\lambda \quad . \quad . \quad . \quad . \quad . \quad . \quad . \quad (6),$$

we must regard ρ as a function of ξ, and we may take with sufficient approximation under any ordinary circumstances

$$\rho = \rho' + \varpi\xi \quad . \quad . \quad . \quad . \quad . \quad . \quad . \quad . \quad (7),$$

where ρ' denotes the value of ρ at O, and ϖ is a constant, which is positive when the retarding plate is held at the side on which the blue of the spectrum *is seen*. The possibility of dark bands depends upon ϖ being positive. Only in this case can

$$\cos\{\rho' + (\varpi - 2\pi h/\lambda f)\xi\}$$

retain the constant value -1 throughout the integration, and then only when

$$\varpi = 2\pi h/\lambda f \quad . \quad . \quad . \quad . \quad . \quad . \quad . \quad (8),$$

and

$$\cos\rho' = -1 \quad . \quad . \quad . \quad . \quad . \quad . \quad . \quad . \quad (9).$$

The first of these equations is the condition for the formation of dark bands, and the second marks their situation, which is the same as that determined by the imperfect theory.

The integration can be effected without much difficulty. For the first term in (5) the evaluation is effected at once by a known formula. In the second term if we observe that

$$\cos\{\rho' + (\varpi - 2\pi h/\lambda f)\xi\} = \cos\{\rho' - g_1\xi\}$$
$$= \cos\rho'\cos g_1\xi + \sin\rho'\sin g_1\xi\,,$$

we see that the second part vanishes when integrated, and that the remaining integral is of the form

$$w = \int_{-\infty}^{+\infty} \sin^2 h_1\xi \cos g_1\xi \,\frac{d\xi}{\xi^2}\,,$$

where

$$h_1 = \pi h/\lambda f, \quad g_1 = \varpi - 2\pi h/\lambda f \quad . \quad . \quad . \quad . \quad (10).$$

By differentiation with respect to g_1 it may be proved that

$w = 0$ from $g_1 = -\infty$ to $g_1 = -2h_1$,
$w = \frac{1}{2}\pi(2h_1 + g_1)$ from $g_1 = -2h_1$ to $g_1 = 0$,
$w = \frac{1}{2}\pi(2h_1 - g_1)$ from $g_1 = 0$ to $g_1 = 2h_1$,
$w = 0$ from $g_1 = 2h_1$ to $g_1 = \infty$.

The integrated intensity, I′, or

$$2\pi h_1 + 2\cos\rho\, w\,,$$

is thus

$$I' = 2\pi h_1 \quad . \quad . \quad . \quad . \quad . \quad . \quad . \quad (11),$$

when g_1 numerically exceeds $2h_1$; and, when g_1 lies between $\pm 2h_1$,

$$I = \pi\{2h_1 + (2h_1 - \sqrt{g_1^2})\cos\rho'\} \quad . \quad . \quad . \quad . \quad (12).$$

Best thickness.

It appears therefore that there are no bands at all unless ϖ lies between 0 and $+4h_1$, and that within these limits the best bands are formed at the middle of the range when $\varpi = 2h_1$. The formation of bands thus requires that the retarding plate be held upon the side already specified, so that ϖ be positive; and that the thickness of the plate (to which ϖ is proportional) do not exceed a certain limit, which we may call $2T_0$. At the best thickness T_0 the bands are black, and not otherwise.

The linear width of the band (e) is the increment of ξ which alters ρ by 2π, so that

$$e = 2\pi/\varpi \quad . \quad . \quad . \quad . \quad . \quad . \quad . \quad . \quad (13).$$

With the best thickness

$$\varpi = 2\pi h/\lambda f \quad . \quad . \quad . \quad . \quad . \quad . \quad . \quad (14),$$

so that in this case

$$e = \lambda f/h \quad . \quad . \quad . \quad . \quad . \quad . \quad . \quad . \quad (15).$$

Width of bands.

The bands are thus of the same width as those due to two infinitely narrow apertures coincident with the central lines of the retarded and unretarded streams, the subject of examination being itself a fine luminous line.

Experimental conditions.

If it be desired to see a given number of bands in the whole or in any part of the spectrum, the thickness of the retarding plate is thereby determined, independently of all other considerations. But in order that the bands may be really visible, and still more in order that they may be black, another condition must be satisfied. It is necessary that the aperture of the pupil be accommodated to the angular extent of the spectrum, or reciprocally. Black bands will be too fine to be well seen unless the aperture ($2h$) of the pupil be somewhat contracted. One-twentieth to one-fiftieth of an inch is suitable. The aperture and the number of bands being both fixed, the condition of blackness determines the angular magnitude of a band and of the spectrum. The use of a grating is very convenient, for not only are there several spectra in view at the same time, but the dispersion can be varied continuously by sloping the grating. The slits may be cut out of tin-plate, and half covered by mica or "microscopic glass," held in position by a little cement.

Use of telescope.

If a telescope be employed there is a distinction to be observed, according as the half-covered aperture is between the eye and the ocular, or in front of the object-glass. In the former case the function of the telescope is simply to increase the dispersion, and the formation of the bands is of course independent of the particular manner in which the dispersion arises. If, however, the half-covered aperture be in front of the object-glass, the phenomenon is magnified as a whole, and the desirable relation between the (unmagnified) dispersion and the aperture is the same as without the telescope. There appears to be no further advantage in the use of a telescope than the increased facility of accommodation, and for this of course a very low power suffices.

More general investigation of Stokes.

The original investigation of Stokes, here briefly sketched, extends also to the case where the streams are of unequal width h, k, and are separated by an interval $2g$. In the case of unequal width the bands cannot be black; but if $h = k$, the finiteness of $2g$ does not preclude the formation of black bands.

The theory of Talbot's bands with a half-covered *circular* aperture has been treated by H. Struve.[1]

§ 17. *Diffraction when the Source of Light is not Seen in Focus.*

The phenomena to be considered under this head are of less importance than those investigated by Fraunhofer, and will be treated in less detail; but, in view of their historical interest and of the ease with which many of the experiments may be tried, some account of their theory could not be excluded from such a work as the present. One or two examples have already attracted our attention when considering Huygens's zones, viz., the shadow of a circular disk, and of a screen circularly perforated; but the most famous problem of this class—first solved by Fresnel—relates to the shadow of a screen bounded by a straight edge.

In theoretical investigations these problems are usually treated as of two dimensions only, everything being referred to the plane passing through the luminous point and perpendicular to the diffracting edges, supposed to be straight and parallel. In strictness this idea is appropriate only when the source is a luminous line, emitting cylindrical waves, such as might be obtained from a luminous point with the aid of a cylindrical lens. When, in order to apply Huygens's principle, the wave is supposed to be broken up, the phase is the same at every element of the surface of resolution which lies upon a line perpendicular to the plane of reference, and thus the effect of the whole line, or rather infinitesimal strip, is related in a constant manner (§ 15) to that of the element which lies in the plane of reference, and may be considered to be represented thereby. The same method of representation is applicable to spherical waves, issuing from a *point*, if the radius of curvature be large; for, although there is variation of phase along the length of the infinitesimal strip, the whole effect depends practically upon that of the central parts where the phase is sensibly constant.[2]

Fig. 21.

Fresnel's integrals.

In fig. 21 APQ is the arc of the circle representative of the wave-front of resolution, the centre being at O, and the radius OA being equal to a. B is the point at which the effect is required, distant $a+b$ from O, so that $AB = b$; $AP = s$, $PQ = ds$.

Taking as the standard phase that of the secondary wave from A, we may represent the effect of PQ by

$$\cos 2\pi\left(\frac{t}{\tau} - \frac{\delta}{\lambda}\right).ds\,,$$

where $\delta = BP - AP$ is the retardation at B of the wave from P relatively to that from A.

Now

$$\delta = (a+b)s^2/2ab \quad . \quad . \quad . \quad . \quad . \quad . \quad . \quad . \quad (1),$$

so that, if we write

$$\frac{2\pi\delta}{\lambda} = \frac{\pi(a+b)s^2}{ab\lambda} = \frac{\pi}{2}v^2 \quad . \quad . \quad . \quad . \quad . \quad . \quad (2),$$

the effect at B is

$$\left\{\frac{ab\lambda}{2(a+b)}\right\}^{\frac{1}{2}}\left\{\cos\frac{2\pi t}{\tau}\int\cos\tfrac{1}{2}\pi v^2.dv + \sin\frac{2\pi t}{\tau}\int\sin\tfrac{1}{2}\pi v^2.dv\right\} \quad (3),$$

the limits of integration depending upon the disposition of the diffracting edges. When a, b, λ are regarded as constant, the first factor may be omitted,—as indeed should be done for consistency's sake, inasmuch as other factors of the same nature have been omitted already.

The intensity I^2, the quantity with which we are principally concerned, may thus be expressed

$$I^2 = \left\{\int\cos\tfrac{1}{2}\pi v^2.dv\right\}^2 + \left\{\int\sin\tfrac{1}{2}\pi v^2.dv\right\}^2 \quad . \quad . \quad . \quad (4).$$

[1] *St Petersburg Trans.*, xxxi., No. 1, 1883.

[2] In experiment a line of light is sometimes substituted for a point in order to increase the illumination. The various parts of the line are here *independent* sources, and should be treated accordingly. To assume a cylindrical form of primary wave would be justifiable only when there is synchronism among the secondary waves issuing from the various centres.

These integrals, taken from $v=0$, are known as Fresnel's integrals; we will denote them by C and S, so that

$$C=\int_0^v \cos\tfrac{1}{2}\pi v^2.dv,\quad S=\int_0^v \sin\tfrac{1}{2}\pi v^2.dv \quad . \quad . \quad . \quad (5).$$

When the upper limit is infinity, so that the limits correspond to the inclusion of half the primary wave, C and S are both equal to $\frac{1}{2}$, by a known formula; and on account of the rapid fluctuation of sign the parts of the range beyond very moderate values of v contribute but little to the result.

Knockenhauer's series. Ascending series for C and S were given by Knockenhauer, and are readily investigated. Integrating by parts, we find

$$C+iS=\int_0^v e^{i.\frac{1}{2}\pi v^2}dv=e^{i.\frac{1}{2}\pi v^2}.v-\tfrac{1}{3}i\pi\int_0^v e^{i.\frac{1}{2}\pi v^2}dv^3;$$

and, by continuing this process,

$$C+iS=e^{i.\frac{1}{2}\pi v^2}\left\{v-\frac{i\pi}{3}v^3+\frac{i\pi}{3}\frac{i\pi}{5}v^5-\frac{i\pi}{3}\frac{i\pi}{5}\frac{i\pi}{7}v^7+\dots\right\}.$$

By separation of real and imaginary parts,

$$\left.\begin{array}{l}C=M\cos\frac{1}{2}\pi v^2+N\sin\frac{1}{2}\pi v^2\\ S=M\sin\frac{1}{2}\pi v^2-N\cos\frac{1}{2}\pi v^2\end{array}\right\}\quad . \quad . \quad . \quad . \quad (6),$$

where

$$M=\frac{v}{1}-\frac{\pi^2v^5}{3.5}+\frac{\pi^4v^9}{3.5.7.9}-\quad . \quad . \quad . \quad . \quad . \quad . \quad . \quad . \quad (7),$$

$$N=\frac{\pi v^3}{1.3}-\frac{\pi^3v^7}{1.3.5.7}+\frac{\pi^5v^{11}}{1.3.5.7.9.11}\quad . \quad . \quad . \quad . \quad (8).$$

These series are convergent for all values of v, but are practically useful only when v is small.

Gilbert's integrals. Expressions suitable for discussion when v is large were obtained by Gilbert.[1] Taking

$$\tfrac{1}{2}\pi v^2=u \quad . \quad . \quad . \quad . \quad . \quad . \quad . \quad . \quad . \quad (9),$$

we may write

$$C+iS=\frac{1}{\sqrt{(2\pi)}}\int_0^u\frac{e^{iu}du}{\sqrt{u}}\quad . \quad . \quad . \quad . \quad . \quad (10).$$

Again, by a known formula,

$$\frac{1}{\sqrt{u}}=\frac{1}{\sqrt{\pi}}\int_0^\infty\frac{e^{-ux}dx}{\sqrt{x}}\quad . \quad . \quad . \quad . \quad . \quad (11).$$

Substituting this in (10), and inverting the order of integration, we get

$$C+iS=\frac{1}{\pi\sqrt{2}}\int_0^\infty\frac{dx}{\sqrt{x}}\int_0^u e^{u(i-x)}dx$$

$$=\frac{1}{\pi\sqrt{2}}\int_0^\infty\frac{dx}{\sqrt{x}}\frac{e^{u(i-x)}-1}{i-x}\quad . \quad . \quad . \quad . \quad . \quad (12).$$

Thus, if we take

$$G=\frac{1}{\pi\sqrt{2}}\int_0^\infty\frac{e^{-ux}\sqrt{x}.dx}{1+x^2},\quad H=\frac{1}{\pi\sqrt{2}}\int_0^\infty\frac{e^{-ux}dx}{\sqrt{x}.(1+x^2)}\quad . \quad (13),$$

$$C=\tfrac{1}{2}-G\cos u+H\sin u,\quad S=\tfrac{1}{2}-G\sin u-H\cos u\quad . \quad (14).$$

The constant parts in (14), viz. $\frac{1}{2}$, may be determined by direct integration of (12), or from the observation that by their constitution G and H vanish when $u=\infty$, coupled with the fact that C and S then assume the value $\frac{1}{2}$.

Comparing the expressions for C, S in terms of M, N, and in terms of G, H, we find that

$$G=\tfrac{1}{2}(\cos u+\sin u)-M,\quad H=\tfrac{1}{2}(\cos u-\sin u)+N\quad . \quad (15),$$

formulæ which may be utilized for the calculation of G, H when u (or v) is small. For example, when $u=0$, $M=0$, $N=0$, and consequently $G=H=\frac{1}{2}$.

Cauchy's series. Descending series of the semi-convergent class, available for numerical calculation when u is moderately large, can be obtained from (12) by writing $x=uy$, and expanding the denominator in powers of y. The integration of the several terms may then be effected by the formula

$$\int_0^\infty e^{-y}y^{q-\frac{1}{2}}dy=\Gamma(q+\tfrac{1}{2})=(q-\tfrac{1}{2})(q-\tfrac{3}{2})\dots\tfrac{1}{2}\sqrt{\pi};$$

and we get in terms of v

$$G=\frac{1}{\pi^2v^3}-\frac{1.3.5}{\pi^4v^7}+\frac{1.3.5.7.9}{\pi^6v^{11}}-\quad . \quad . \quad . \quad . \quad (16),$$

$$H=\frac{1}{\pi v}-\frac{1.3}{\pi^3v^5}+\frac{1.3.5.7}{\pi^5v^9}-\quad . \quad . \quad . \quad . \quad . \quad . \quad (17).$$

The corresponding values of C and S were originally derived by Cauchy, without the use of Gilbert's integrals, by direct integration by parts.

From the series for G and H just obtained it is easy to verify that

$$\frac{dH}{dv}=-\pi vG,\quad \frac{dG}{dv}=\pi vH-1\quad . \quad . \quad . \quad . \quad (18).$$

Straight edge. We now proceed to consider more particularly the distribution of light upon a screen PBQ near the shadow of a straight edge A. At a point P within the geometrical shadow of the obstacle, the half of the wave to the right of C (fig. 22), the nearest point on the wave-front, is wholly intercepted, and on the left the integration is to be taken from $s=$ CA to $s=\infty$. If V be the value of v corresponding to CA, viz.,

$$V=\sqrt{\left\{\frac{2(a+b)}{ab\lambda}\right\}}.CA,\quad . \quad . \quad . \quad . \quad . \quad (19),$$

we may write

$$I^2=\left(\int_V^\infty\cos\tfrac{1}{2}\pi v^2.dv\right)^2+\left(\int_V^\infty\sin\tfrac{1}{2}\pi v^2.dv\right)^2\quad . \quad . \quad (20),$$

or, according to our previous notation,

$$I^2=(\tfrac{1}{2}-C_V)^2+(\tfrac{1}{2}-S_V)^2=G^2+H^2\quad . \quad . \quad . \quad . \quad (21).$$

No bands inside shadow. Now in the integrals represented by G and H every element diminishes as V increases from zero. Hence, as CA increases, viz., as the point P is more and more deeply immersed in the shadow, the illumination *continuously* decreases, and that without limit. It has long been known from observation that there are no bands on the interior side of the shadow of the edge.

Fig. 22.

The law of diminution when V is moderately large is easily expressed with the aid of the series (16), (17) for G, H. We have ultimately $G=0$, $H=(\pi V)^{-1}$, so that

$$I^2=1/\pi^2V^2,$$

or the illumination is inversely as the square of the distance from the shadow of the edge.

For a point Q outside the shadow the integration extends over *more* than half the primary wave. The intensity may be expressed by

$$I^2=(\tfrac{1}{2}+C_V)^2+(\tfrac{1}{2}+S_V)^2\quad . \quad . \quad . \quad . \quad . \quad (22);$$

and the maxima and minima occur when

$$(\tfrac{1}{2}+C_V)\frac{dC}{dV}+(\tfrac{1}{2}+S_V)\frac{dS}{dV}=0,$$

whence

$$\sin\tfrac{1}{2}\pi V^2+\cos\tfrac{1}{2}\pi V^2=G\quad . \quad . \quad . \quad . \quad . \quad (23).$$

Position of exterior bands. When $V=0$, viz., at the edge of the shadow, $I^2=\frac{1}{2}$; when $V=\infty$, $I^2=2$, on the scale adopted. The latter is the intensity due to the uninterrupted wave. The quadrupling of the intensity in passing outwards from the edge of the shadow is, however, accompanied by fluctuations giving rise to bright and dark bands. The position of these bands determined by (23) may be very simply expressed when V is large, for then sensibly $G=0$, and

$$\tfrac{1}{2}\pi V^2=\tfrac{3}{4}\pi+n\pi\quad . \quad . \quad . \quad . \quad . \quad . \quad . \quad (24),$$

n being an integer. In terms of δ, we have from (2)

$$\delta=(\tfrac{3}{8}+\tfrac{1}{2}n)\lambda\quad . \quad . \quad . \quad . \quad . \quad . \quad . \quad (25).$$

The first maximum in fact occurs when $\delta=\frac{3}{8}\lambda-·0046\lambda$, and the first minimum when $\delta=\frac{7}{8}\lambda-·0016\lambda$,[2] the corrections being readily obtainable from a table of G by substitution of the approximate value of V.

Hyperbolic propagation of bands. The position of Q corresponding to a given value of V, that is, to a band of given order, is by (19)

$$BQ=\frac{a+b}{a}AD=V\sqrt{\left\{\frac{b\lambda(a+b)}{2a}\right\}}\quad . \quad . \quad . \quad (26).$$

By means of this expression we may trace the locus of a band of given order as b varies. With sufficient approximation we may regard BQ and b as rectangular coordinates of Q. Denoting them by x, y, so that AB is axis of y and a perpendicular through A the axis of x, and rationalizing (26), we have

$$2ax^2-V^2\lambda y^2-V^2a\lambda y=0,$$

which represents a hyperbola with vertices at O and A.

From (24), (26) we see that the width of the bands is of the order $\sqrt{\{b\lambda(a+b)/a\}}$. From this we may infer the limitation upon the width of the source of light, in order that the bands may be properly formed. If ω be the apparent magnitude of the source seen from A, ωb should be much smaller than the above quantity, or

$$\omega<\sqrt{\{\lambda(a+b)/ab\}}\quad . \quad . \quad . \quad . \quad . \quad . \quad (27),$$

If a be very great in relation to b, the condition becomes

$$\omega<\sqrt{(\lambda/b)}\quad . \quad . \quad . \quad . \quad . \quad . \quad . \quad (28),$$

so that if b is to be moderately great (1 metre), the apparent magnitude of the sun must be greatly reduced before it can be used as a source.

Fresnel's table. The values of V for the maxima and minima of intensity, and the magnitudes of the latter, were calculated by Fresnel. An extract from his results is given in the accompanying table.

	V	I^2
First maximum....	1·2172	2·7413
First minimum....	1·8726	1·5570
Second maximum..	2·3449	2·3990
Second minimum..	2·7592	1·6867
Third maximum...	3·0820	2·3022
Third minimum....	3·3913	1·7440

A very thorough investigation of this and other related questions, accompanied by fully worked-out tables of the functions concerned, will be found in a recent paper by Lommel.[3]

[1] *Mém. couronnés de l'Acad. de Bruxelles*, xxxi. 1. See also Verdet, *Leçons*, § 86.

[2] Verdet, *Leçons*, § 90.

[3] "Die Beugungserscheinungen geradlinig begrenzter Schirme," *Abh. bayer. Akad. der Wiss.*, ii. Cl., xv. Bd., iii. Abth., 1886.

Cornu's method.

When the functions C and S have once been calculated, the discussion of various diffraction problems is much facilitated by the idea, due to Cornu,[1] of exhibiting as a curve the relationship between C and S, considered as the rectangular coordinates (x, y) of a point. Such a curve is shown in fig. 23, where, according to the definition (5) of C, S,

$$x=\int_0^v \cos \tfrac{1}{2}\pi v^2.dv\,,\quad y=\int_0^v \sin \tfrac{1}{2}\pi v^2.dv \quad . \quad . \quad . \quad (29).$$

The origin of coordinates O corresponds to $v=0$; and the asymptotic points J, J′, round which the curve revolves in an ever-closing spiral, correspond to $v=\pm\infty$.

The intrinsic equation, expressing the relation between the arc σ (measured from O) and the inclination ϕ of the tangent at any point to the axis of x, assumes a very simple form. For

$$dx=\cos \tfrac{1}{2}\pi v^2.dv\,,\quad dy=\sin \tfrac{1}{2}\pi v^2.dv\,;$$

so that

$$\sigma=\int \surd(dx^2+dy)=v\,, \quad . \quad . \quad . \quad . \quad . \quad (30),$$

$$\phi=\tan^{-1}\frac{dy}{dx}=\tfrac{1}{2}\pi v^2 \quad . \quad . \quad . \quad . \quad . \quad . \quad (31).$$

Accordingly,

$$\phi=\tfrac{1}{2}\pi\sigma^2 \quad . \quad . \quad . \quad . \quad . \quad . \quad . \quad (32);$$

and for the curvature,

$$\frac{d\phi}{d\sigma}=\pi\sigma \quad . \quad . \quad . \quad . \quad . \quad . \quad . \quad (33).$$

Cornu remarks that this equation suffices to determine the general character of the curve. For the osculating circle at any point includes the whole of the curve which lies beyond; and the successive convolutions envelop one another without intersection.

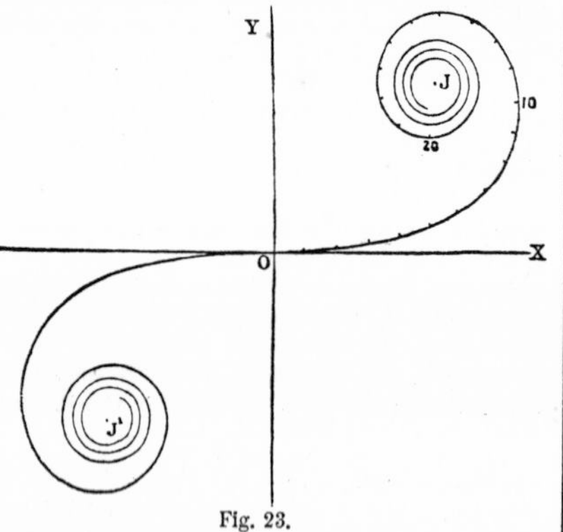

Fig. 23.

The utility of the curve depends upon the fact that the elements of arc represent, in amplitude and phase, the component vibrations due to the corresponding portions of the primary wave-front. For by (30) $d\sigma=dv$, and by (2) dv is proportional to ds. Moreover by (2) and (31) the retardation of phase of the elementary vibration from PQ (fig. 21) is $2\pi\delta/\lambda$, or ϕ. Hence, in accordance with the rule for compounding vector quantities, the resultant vibration at B, due to any finite part of the primary wave, is represented in amplitude and phase by the chord joining the extremities of the corresponding arc $(\sigma_2-\sigma_1)$.

In applying the curve in special cases of diffraction to exhibit the effect at any point P (fig. 22) the centre of the curve O is to be considered to correspond to that point C of the primary wave-front which lies nearest to P. The operative part, or parts, of the curve are of course those which represent the unobstructed portions of the primary wave.

Let us reconsider, following Cornu, the diffraction of a screen unlimited on one side, and on the other terminated by a straight edge. On the illuminated side, at a distance from the shadow, the vibration is represented by JJ′. The coordinates of J, J′ being $(\tfrac{1}{2}, \tfrac{1}{2})$, $(-\tfrac{1}{2}, -\tfrac{1}{2})$, I^2 is 2; and the phase is $\tfrac{1}{8}$ period in arrear of that of the element at O. As the point under contemplation is supposed to approach the shadow, the vibration is represented by the chord drawn from J to a point on the other half of the curve, which travels inwards from J′ towards O. The amplitude is thus subject to fluctuations, which increase as the shadow is approached. At the point O the intensity is one-quarter of that of the entire wave, and after this point is passed, that is, when we have entered the geometrical shadow, the intensity falls off gradually to zero, *without fluctuations*. The whole progress of the phenomenon is thus exhibited to the eye in a very instructive manner.

Diffraction through a slit.

We will next suppose that the light is transmitted by a slit, and inquire what is the effect of varying the width of the slit upon the illumination at the projection of its centre. Under these circumstances the arc to be considered is bisected at O, and its length is proportional to the width of the slit. It is easy to see that the length of the chord (which passes in all cases through O) increases to a maximum near the place where the phase-retardation is $\tfrac{3}{8}$ of a period, then diminishes to a minimum when the retardation is about $\tfrac{7}{8}$ of a period, and so on.

If the slit is of constant width and we require the illumination at various points on the screen behind it, we must regard the arc of the curve as of *constant length*. The intensity is then, as always, represented by the square of the length of the chord. If the slit be narrow, so that the arc is short, the intensity is constant over a wide range, and does not fall off to an important extent until the discrepancy of the extreme phases reaches about a quarter of a period.

Silvery lining of an obstacle.

We have hitherto supposed that the shadow of a diffracting obstacle is received upon a diffusing screen, or, which comes to nearly the same thing, is observed with an eye-piece. If the eye, provided if necessary with a perforated plate in order to reduce the aperture, be situated inside the shadow at a place where the illumination is still sensible, and be focused upon the diffracting edge, the light which it receives will appear to come from the neighbourhood of the edge, and will present the effect of a silver lining. This is doubtless the explanation of a "pretty optical phenomenon, seen in Switzerland, when the sun rises from behind distant trees standing on the summit of a mountain."[2]

§ 18. *Diffraction Symmetrical about an Axis.*

The general problem of the diffraction pattern due to a source of light concentrated in a point, when the system is symmetrical about an axis, has been ably investigated by Lommel.[3] We must content ourselves here with a very slight sketch of some of his results.

Spherical waves, centred upon the axis, of radius a fall upon the diffracting screen; and the illumination is required on a second screen, like the first perpendicular to the axis, at a distance $(a+b)$ from the source. We have first to express the distance (d) between an element dS of the wave-front and a point M in the plane of the second screen. Let ζ denote the distance of M from the axis of symmetry; then, if we take an axis of x to pass through M, the coordinates of M are $(\zeta, 0, 0)$. On the same system the coordinates of dS are

$$a\sin\theta\cos\phi\,,\quad a\sin\theta\sin\phi\,,\quad a(1-\cos\theta)+b\,;$$

and the distance is given by

$$d^2=b^2+\zeta^2-2a\zeta\sin\theta\cos\phi+4a(a+b)\sin^2\tfrac{1}{2}\theta\,.$$

In this expression ζ and θ are to be treated as small quantities. Writing ρ for $a\sin\theta$, we get approximately

$$d=b+\frac{\zeta^2}{2b}-\frac{\zeta\cos\phi}{b}\rho+\frac{a+b}{2ab}\rho^2 \quad . \quad . \quad . \quad . \quad . \quad (1).$$

The vibration at the wave-front of resolution being denoted by

$$a^{-1}\cos 2\pi t/\tau\,,$$

the integral expressive of the resultant of the secondary waves is (§ 17)

$$\frac{-1}{ab\lambda}\iint \sin 2\pi\left(\frac{t}{\tau}-\frac{d}{\lambda}\right)dS \quad . \quad . \quad . \quad . \quad . \quad (2).$$

Substituting $\rho\,d\rho\,d\phi$ for dS, and for d its value from (1), we obtain as the expression for the intensity at the point ζ,

$$I^2=\frac{1}{a^2b^2\lambda^2}(C^2+S^2) \quad . \quad . \quad . \quad . \quad . \quad . \quad (3),$$

where

$$C=\iint\cos(\tfrac{1}{2}\kappa\rho^2-l\rho\cos\phi).\rho\,d\rho\,d\phi\,, \quad . \quad . \quad . \quad . \quad (4),$$

$$^4\,S=\iint\sin(\tfrac{1}{2}\kappa\rho^2-l\rho\cos\phi).\rho\,d\rho\,d\phi \quad . \quad . \quad . \quad . \quad (5),$$

and the following abbreviations have been introduced

$$\frac{2\pi}{\lambda}\frac{a+b}{2ab}=\tfrac{1}{2}\kappa\,,\quad \frac{2\pi\zeta}{\lambda b}=l \quad . \quad . \quad . \quad . \quad . \quad . \quad (6).$$

The range of integration is for ϕ from 0 to 2π. The limits for ρ depend upon the particular problem in hand; but for the sake of definiteness we will suppose that in the analytical definitions of C and S the limits are 0 and r, so as to apply immediately to the problem of a circular aperture of radius r. If we introduce the notation of Bessel's functions, we have

$$C=2\pi\int_0^r J_0(l\rho)\cos(\tfrac{1}{2}\kappa\rho^2).\rho\,d\rho \quad . \quad . \quad . \quad . \quad (7).$$

$$S=2\pi\int_0^r J_0(l\rho)\sin(\tfrac{1}{2}\kappa\rho^2).\rho\,d\rho \quad . \quad . \quad . \quad . \quad (8).$$

Lommel's series.

By integration by parts of these expressions Lommel develops series suitable for calculation. Setting

$$\kappa r^2=y\,,\quad lr=z \quad . \quad . \quad . \quad . \quad . \quad . \quad . \quad (9),$$

he finds in the first place

$$C=\pi r^2\left\{\frac{\cos\frac{1}{2}y}{\frac{1}{2}y}U_1+\frac{\sin\frac{1}{2}y}{\frac{1}{2}y}U_2\right\} \quad . \quad . \quad . \quad . \quad (10),$$

$$S=\pi r^2\left\{\frac{\sin\frac{1}{2}y}{\frac{1}{2}y}U_1-\frac{\cos\frac{1}{2}y}{\frac{1}{2}y}U_2\right\} \quad . \quad . \quad . \quad . \quad (11),$$

[1] *Journal de Physique*, iii. p. 1, 1874. A similar suggestion has recently been made independently by Fitzgerald.

[2] Necker, *Phil. Mag.*, Nov. 1832; Fox Talbot, *Phil. Mag.*, June 1833. "When the sun is about to emerge . . . . every branch and leaf is lighted up with a silvery lustre of indescribable beauty. . . . . The birds, as Mr Necker very truly describes, appear like flying brilliant sparks." Talbot ascribes the appearance to diffraction; and he recommends the use of a telescope.

[3] *Abh. der bayer. Akad. der Wiss.*, ii. Cl., xv. Bd., ii. Abth.

[4] Used now in an altered sense.

where

$$U_1=\frac{y}{z}J_1(z)-\frac{y^3}{z^3}J_3(z)+\frac{y^5}{z^5}J_5(z)-\ \ldots\ \ldots \quad (12),$$

$$U_2=\frac{y^2}{z^2}J_2(z)-\frac{y^4}{z^4}J_4(z)+\ \ldots\ \ldots \quad (13).$$

These series are convenient when y is less than z.

The second set of expressions are

$$C=\pi r^2\left\{\frac{2}{y}\sin\frac{z^2}{2y}+\frac{\sin\frac{1}{2}y}{\frac{1}{2}y}V_0-\frac{\cos\frac{1}{2}y}{\frac{1}{2}y}V_1\right\} \quad \ldots \quad (14),$$

$$S=\pi r^2\left\{\frac{2}{y}\cos\frac{z^2}{2y}-\frac{\cos\frac{1}{2}y}{\frac{1}{2}y}V_0-\frac{\sin\frac{1}{2}y}{\frac{1}{2}y}V_1\right\} \quad \ldots \quad (15),$$

where

$$V_0=J_0(z)-\frac{z^2}{y^2}J_2(z)+\frac{z^4}{y^4}J_4(z)-\ \ldots\ \ldots \quad (16),$$

$$V_1=\frac{z}{y}J_1(z)-\frac{z^3}{y^3}J_3(z)+\ \ldots\ \ldots \quad (17).$$

These series are suitable when z/y is small.

When the primary wave is complete, $r=\infty$, and we have at once from the second set of expressions

$$C_\infty=\frac{2\pi}{\kappa}\sin\frac{l^2}{2\kappa},\quad S_\infty=\frac{2\pi}{\kappa}\cos\frac{l^2}{2\kappa} \quad \ldots \quad (18),$$

so that

$$I^2=\frac{C_\infty{}^2+S_\infty{}^2}{a^2b^2\lambda^2}=\frac{1}{(a+b)^2} \quad \ldots \quad (19),$$

as we know it should be.

Shadow of circular disk. In the application to the problem of the shadow of a circular disk the limits of integration are from r to ∞. If these integrals be denoted by C′, S′, we have

$$C'=C_\infty-C=\pi r^2\left\{-\frac{\sin\frac{1}{2}y}{\frac{1}{2}y}V_0+\frac{\cos\frac{1}{2}y}{\frac{1}{2}y}V_1\right\} \quad \ldots \quad (20),$$

$$S'=S_\infty-S=\pi r^2\left\{\frac{\cos\frac{1}{2}y}{\frac{1}{2}y}V_0+\frac{\sin\frac{1}{2}y}{\frac{1}{2}y}V_1\right\} \quad \ldots \quad (21);$$

and

$$C'^2+S'^2=\frac{4\pi^2}{\kappa^2}(V_0{}^2+V_1{}^2) \quad \ldots \quad (22),$$

$$I^2=\frac{V_0{}^2+V_1{}^2}{(a+b)^2} \quad \ldots \quad (23).$$

When the point where the illumination is required is situated upon the axis, ζ, l, z are zero. Hence $V_0=1, V_1=0$, and

$$I^2=\frac{1}{(a+b)^2},$$

the same as if the primary wave had come on unbroken. This is Poisson's theorem, already found (§ 10) by a much simpler method, in which attention is limited from the first to points upon the axis. The distribution of light at other points upon the screen is to be found from (23) by means of the series (16), (17) for V_0 and V_1. Lommel gives curves for the intensity when $y=\pi$, 2π, 3π, . . . 6π. The bright central spot is accompanied by rings of varying intensity.

The limit of the geometrical shadow $[\zeta/(a+b)=r/a]$ corresponds to $y=z$. In this case

$$V_0=J_0(z)-J_2(z)+J_4(z)-\ \ldots=\tfrac{1}{2}\{J_0(z)+\cos z\} \quad \ldots \quad (24),$$

$$V_1=J_1(z)-J_3(z)+J_5(z)-\ \ldots=\tfrac{1}{2}\sin z \quad \ldots \quad (25).$$

Condition of mathematical similarity. The numbers computed for special values of y and z apply to a whole class of problems. Since

$$y=\frac{2\pi}{\lambda}\frac{a+b}{ab}\cdot r^2,\quad z=\frac{2\pi}{\lambda}\frac{\zeta}{b}\cdot r,$$

both y and z remain unchanged, even when λ is constant, if we suppose

$$b\propto a,\quad r\propto\zeta\propto\sqrt{a} \quad \ldots \quad (26).$$

We may fall back upon Fraunhofer's phenomena by supposing $a=b=\infty$, or more generally $b=-a$, so that $y=0$.

Under these circumstances

$$C=\pi r^2\frac{J_1(z)}{z},\quad S=0.$$

But it is unnecessary to add anything further under this head.

§ 19. *Polarization.*

A ray of ordinary light is symmetrical with respect to the direction of propagation. If, for example, this direction be vertical, there is nothing that can be said concerning the north and south sides of the ray that is not equally true concerning the east and west sides. In polarized light this symmetry is lost. Huygens showed that when a ray of such light falls upon a crystal of Iceland spar, which is made to revolve about the ray as an axis, the phenomena vary in a manner not to be represented as a mere revolution with the spar. In Newton's language, the ray itself has *sides*, or is polarized.

Brewster's law. Malus discovered that ordinary light may be polarized by reflexion as well as by double refraction; and Brewster proved that the effect is nearly complete when the tangent of the angle of incidence is equal to the refractive index, or (which comes to the same) when the reflected and refracted rays are perpendicular to one another. The light thus obtained is said to be polarized in the plane of reflexion.

Reciprocally, the character of a polarized ray may be revealed by submitting it to the test of reflexion at the appropriate angle. As the normal to the reflecting surface revolves (in a cone) about the ray, there are two azimuths of the plane of incidence, distant 180°, at which the reflexion is a maximum, and two others, distant 90° from the former, at which the reflexion (nearly) vanishes. In the latter case the plane of incidence is perpendicular to that in which the light must be supposed to have been reflected in order to acquire its polarization.

Double refraction. The full statement of the law of double refraction is somewhat complicated, and scarcely to be made intelligible except in terms of the wave theory; but, in order merely to show the relation of double refraction in a uniaxal crystal, such as Iceland spar, to polarized light, we may take the case of a prism so cut that the refracting edge is parallel to the optic axis. By traversing such a prism, in a plane perpendicular to the edge, a ray of ordinary light is divided into two, of equal intensity, each of which is refracted according to the ordinary law of Snell. Whatever may be the angle and setting of the prism, the phenomenon may be represented by supposing half the light to be refracted with one index (1·65), and the other half with the different index (1·48). The rays thus arising are polarized,—the one more refracted in the plane of refraction, and the other in the perpendicular plane. If these rays are now allowed to fall upon a second similar prism, held so that its edge is parallel to that of the first prism, there is no further duplication. The ray first refracted with index 1·65 is refracted again in like manner, and similarly the ray first refracted with index 1·48 is again so refracted. But the case is altered if the second prism be caused to rotate about the incident ray. If the rotation be through an angle of 90°, each ray is indeed refracted singly; but the indices are exchanged. The ray that suffered most refraction at the first prism now suffers least at the second, and *vice versa.* At intermediate rotations the double refraction reasserts itself, each ray being divided into two, refracted with the above-mentioned indices, and of intensity dependent upon the amount of rotation, but always such that no light is lost (or gained) on the whole by the separation.

Law of Malus. The law governing the intensity was formulated by Malus, and has been verified by the measures of Arago and other workers. If θ be the angle of rotation from the position in which one of the rays is at a maximum, while the other vanishes, the intensities are proportional to $\cos^2\theta$ and $\sin^2\theta$. On the same scale, if we neglect the loss by reflexion and absorption, the intensity of the incident light is represented by unity.

A similar law applies to the intensity with which a polarized ray is reflected from a glass surface at the Brewsterian angle. If θ be reckoned from the azimuth of maximum reflexion, the intensity at other angles may be represented by $\cos^2\theta$, vanishing when $\theta=90°$.

Transverse vibrations. The phenomena here briefly sketched force upon us the view that the vibrations of light are transverse to the direction of propagation. In ordinary light the vibrations are as much in one transverse direction as in another; and when such light falls upon a doubly refracting, or reflecting, medium, the vibrations are *resolved* into two definite directions, constituting two rays polarized in perpendicular planes, and differently influenced by the medium. In this case the two rays are necessarily of equal intensity.

Consider, for example, the application of this idea to the reflexion of a ray of ordinary light at the Brewsterian, or polarizing, angle. The incident light may be resolved into two, of equal intensity, and polarized respectively in and perpendicular to the plane of incidence. Now we know that a ray polarized in the plane perpendicular to that of incidence will not be reflected, will in fact be entirely transmitted; and the necessary consequence is that all the light reflected at this angle will be polarized in the plane of incidence. The operation of the plate is thus purely selective, the polarized component, which is missing in the reflected light, being represented in undue proportion in the transmitted light.

If the incident light be polarized, suppose at an angle θ with the plane of incidence, the incident vibration may be resolved into $\cos\theta$ in the one plane and $\sin\theta$ in the other. The latter polarized component is not reflected. The reflected light is thus in all cases polarized in the plane of reflexion; and its *intensity*, proportional to the square of the vibration, is represented by $h\cos^2\theta$, if h be the intensity in which light is reflected when polarized in the plane of reflexion. The law of Malus is thus a necessary consequence of the principle of resolution.

Elastic solid theory. The idea of transverse vibrations was admitted with reluctance, even by Young and Fresnel themselves. A perfect fluid, such as the ethereal medium was then supposed to be, is essentially incapable of transverse vibrations. But there seems to be no reason *a priori* for preferring one kind of vibration to another; and the phenomena of polarization prove conclusively that, if luminous vibrations are analogous to those of a material medium, it is to solids, and not to fluids, that we must look. An isotropic solid is capable of propagating two distinct kinds of waves,—the first dependent upon *rigidity*, or the force by which shear is resisted, and the second analogous to waves of sound and dependent upon *compressibility*. In the former the vibrations are transverse to the direction of propagation, that is, they may take place in any direction parallel to the wave front, and they are thus suitable representatives of the vibrations of light. In this theory the luminiferous ether is distinctly assimilated to an elastic solid, and the velocity of light depends upon the *rigidity* and *density* assigned to the medium.

Medium incompressible. The possibility of longitudinal waves, in which the displacement is perpendicular to the wave-front, is an objection to the elastic solid theory of light, for there is nothing known in optics corresponding thereto. If, however, we suppose with Green that the medium is incompressible, the velocity of longitudinal waves becomes infinite, and the objection is in great degree obviated. Such a supposition is hardly a departure from the original idea, inasmuch as, so far as we know, there is nothing to prevent a solid material possessing these properties, and an approximation is actually presented by such bodies as jelly, for which the velocity of longitudinal vibrations is a large multiple of that of transverse vibrations.

§ 20. *Interference of Polarized Light.*

The conditions of interference of polarized light are most easily deduced from the phenomena of the colours of crystalline plates, if we once admit Young's view that the origin of the colours is to be sought in the interference of the differently refracted rays. Independently of any hypothesis of this kind, the subject was directly investigated by Fresnel and Arago,[1] who summarized their conclusions thus:—

Laws of interference. (1) Under the same conditions in which two rays of ordinary light appear to destroy one another, two rays polarized in contrary (viz., perpendicular) directions are without mutual influence.

(2) Two rays of light polarized in the same direction act upon one another like ordinary rays; so that, with these two kinds of light, the phenomena of interference are identical.

(3) Two rays *originally polarized in opposite directions* may afterwards be brought to the same plane of polarization, *without thereby acquiring the power to influence one another.*

(4) *Two rays polarized in opposite directions, and afterwards brought to similar polarizations,* react in the same manner as natural rays, *if they are derived from a beam originally polarized in one direction.*

The fact that oppositely polarized rays cannot be made to interfere may of itself be regarded as a proof that the vibrations are transverse; and the principle, once admitted, gives an intelligible account of all the varied phenomena in this field of optics. The only points on which any difficulty arises are as to the nature of ordinary unpolarized light, and the rules according to which *intensity* is to be calculated. It will be proper to consider these questions somewhat fully.

Plane polarization. In ordinary (plane) polarized light the vibrations are supposed to be in one direction only. If x and y be rectangular coordinates in the plane of the wave, we may take, as representing a regular vibration of plane-polarized light,

$$x = a\cos(\phi - \alpha) \quad . \quad . \quad . \quad . \quad . \quad . \quad . \quad (1),$$

where $\phi = 2\pi t/\tau$, and a, α denote constants. It must be remembered, however, that in optics a regular vibration of this kind never presents itself. In the simplest case of approximately monochromatic light, the amplitude and phase must be regarded (§ 4) as liable to incessant variation, and all that we are able to appreciate is the *mean* intensity, represented by $\mathrm{M}(a^2)$. If a number of these irregular streams of light are combined, the intensity of the mixture cannot be calculated from a mere knowledge of the separate intensities, unless we have assurance that the streams are *independent*, that is, without mutual phase-relations of a durable character. For instance, two thoroughly similar streams combine into one of *four-fold* intensity, if the phases are the same; while, if the phases are opposed, the intensity falls to zero. It is only when the streams are independent, so that the phase-relation is arbitrary and variable from moment to moment, that the apparent resultant intensity is necessarily the double of the separate intensities.

If any number of independent vibrations of type (1) be superposed, the resultant is

$$[\Sigma a_1 \cos\alpha_1]\cos\phi + [\Sigma a_1 \sin\alpha_1]\sin\phi,$$

and the momentary intensity is

$$[\Sigma a_1 \cos\alpha_1]^2 + [\Sigma a_1 \sin\alpha_1]^2,$$

or

$$a_1^2 + a_2^2 + \ldots + 2a_1a_2\cos(\alpha_1 - \alpha_2) + \ldots$$

The phase-relations being unknown, this quantity is quite indeterminate. But, since each cosine varies from moment to moment, and on the whole is as much positive as negative, the *mean* intensity is

$$\mathrm{M}(a_1^2) + \mathrm{M}(a_2^2) + \ldots,$$

that is to say, is to be found by simple addition of the separate intensities.

Elliptic polarization. Let us now dispense with the restriction to one direction of vibration, and consider in the first place the character of a *regular* vibration, of given frequency. The general expression will be

$$x = a\cos(\phi - \alpha), \qquad y = b\cos(\phi - \beta) \quad . \quad . \quad . \quad (2),$$

where a, α, b, β are constants. If $\beta = \alpha$, the vibrations are executed entirely in the plane $x/y = a/b$, or the light is plane-polarized. Or if $\beta = \pi - \alpha$, the light is again plane-polarized, the plane of vibration being $x/y = -a/b$. In other cases the vibrations are not confined to one plane, so that the light is not plane-polarized, but, in conformity with the path denoted by (2), it is said to be *elliptically-polarized*. If one of the constituents of elliptically-polarized light be suitably accelerated or retarded relatively to the other, it may be converted into plane-polarized light, and so identified by the usual tests. Or, conversely, plane-polarized light may be converted into elliptically-polarized by a similar operation. The relative acceleration in question is readily effected by a plate of doubly refracting crystal cut parallel to the axis.

If $\beta = \alpha \pm \frac{1}{2}\pi$, whether in the first instance or after the action of a crystalline plate,

$$x = a\cos(\phi - \alpha), \qquad y = \pm b\sin(\phi - \alpha) \quad . \quad . \quad (3).$$

The maxima and minima values of the one coordinate here occur synchronously with the evanescence of the other, and the coordinate axes are the *principal* axes of the elliptic path.

Circular polarization. An important particular case arises when further $b = a$. The path is then a circle, and the light is said to be *circularly*-polarized. According to the sign adopted in the second equation (3), the circle is described in the one direction or in the other.

Circularly-polarized light can be resolved into plane-polarized components in *any* two rectangular directions, which are such that the intensities are equal and the phases different by a quarter period. If a crystalline plate be of such thickness that it retards one component by a quarter of a wave-length (or indeed by any odd multiple thereof) relatively to the other, it will convert plane-polarized light into circularly-polarized, and conversely,—in the latter case without regard to the azimuth in which it is held.

The property of circularly-polarized light whereby it is capable of resolution into oppositely plane-polarized components of equal intensities is possessed also by natural unpolarized light; but the discrimination may be effected experimentally with the aid of the quarter-wave plate. By this agency the circularly-polarized ray is converted into plane-polarized, while the natural light remains apparently unaltered. The difficulty which remains is rather to explain the physical character of natural light. To this we shall presently return; but in the meantime it is obvious that the constitution of natural light is essentially irregular, for we have seen that absolutely regular, *i.e.*, absolutely homogeneous, light *is necessarily (elliptically) polarized.*

In discussing the vibration represented by (2), we have considered the amplitudes and phases to be constant; but in nature this is no more attainable than in the case of plane-polarized light. In order that the elliptic polarization may be of a definite character, it is only necessary that the *ratio* of amplitudes and the *difference* of phases should be absolute constants, and this of course is consistent with the same degree of irregularity as was admitted for plane vibrations.

The intensity of elliptically-polarized light is the sum of the intensities of its rectangular components. This we may consider to be an experimental fact, as well as a consequence of the theory of transverse vibrations. In whatever form such a theory may be adopted, the energy propagated will certainly conform to this law. When the constants in (2) are regarded as subject to variation, the apparent intensity is represented by

$$\mathrm{M}(a^2) + \mathrm{M}(b^2) \quad . \quad . \quad . \quad . \quad . \quad . \quad . \quad (4).$$

Unpolarized light. We are now in a position to examine the constitution which must be ascribed to natural light. The conditions to be satisfied are that when resolved in any plane the mean intensity of the vibrations shall be independent of the orientation of the plane, and, further, that this property shall be unaffected by any previous relative retardation of the rectangular components into which it may have been resolved. The original vibration being represented by

$$x = a\cos(\phi - \alpha), \qquad y = b\cos(\phi - \beta),$$

or, as we may write it, since we are concerned only with phase *differences*,

$$x = a\cos\phi, \qquad y = b\cos(\phi - \delta) \quad . \quad . \quad . \quad (5),$$

let us suppose that the second component is subjected to a retardation ϵ. Thus

$$x = a\cos\phi, \qquad y = b\cos(\phi - \delta - \epsilon) \quad . \quad . \quad . \quad (6),$$

in which a, b, δ will be regarded as subject to rapid variation,

[1] Fresnel's *Works*, vol. i. p. 521.

while ϵ remains constant. If the vibration represented by (6) be now resolved in a direction x', making an angle ω with x, we have

$$x' = a\cos\phi\cos\omega + b\cos(\phi-\delta-\epsilon)\sin\omega$$
$$= [a\cos\omega + b\sin\omega\cos(\delta+\epsilon)]\cos\phi + b\sin\omega\sin(\delta+\epsilon)\sin\phi\ ;$$

and the intensity is

$$a^2\cos^2\omega + b^2\sin^2\omega + 2ab\cos\omega\sin\omega\cos(\delta+\epsilon)\quad . \quad . \quad (7).$$

Of this expression we take the mean, ω and ϵ remaining constant. Thus the apparent intensity may be written

$$M(x'^2) = M(a^2)\cos^2\omega + M(b^2)\sin^2\omega + 2M[ab\cos(\delta+\epsilon)]\cos\omega\sin\omega\ (8).$$

Necessary conditions.

In order now that the stream may satisfy the conditions laid down as necessary for natural light, (8) must be independent of ω and ϵ; so that

$$M(a^2) = M(b^2)\quad . \quad . \quad . \quad . \quad . \quad . \quad . \quad . \quad (9),$$
$$M(ab\cos\delta) = M(ab\sin\delta) = 0\quad . \quad . \quad . \quad . \quad . \quad (10).[1]$$

In these equations a^2 and b^2 represent simply the intensities, or squares of amplitudes, of the x and y vibrations; and the other two quantities admit also of a simple interpretation. The value of y may be written

$$y = b\cos\delta\cos\phi + b\sin\delta\sin\phi\quad . \quad . \quad . \quad . \quad (11);$$

from which we see that $b\cos\delta$ is the coefficient of that part of the y vibration which has the same phase as the x vibration. Thus $ab\cos\delta$ may be interpreted as the product of the coefficients of the parts of the x and y vibrations which have the same phase. Next suppose the phase of y accelerated by writing $\frac{1}{2}\pi + \phi$ in place of ϕ. We should thus have

$$y = -b\cos\delta\sin\phi + b\sin\delta\cos\phi,$$

and $ab\sin\delta$ represents the product of the coefficients of the parts which are now in the same phase, or (which is the same) the product of the coefficients of the x vibration and of that part of the y vibration which was 90° behind in phase. In general, if

$$x = h\cos\phi + h'\sin\phi, \qquad y = k\cos\phi + k'\sin\phi\quad . \quad (12),$$

the first product is $hk + h'k'$ and the second is $hk' - h'k$.

Let us next examine how the quantities which we have been considering are affected by a transformation of coordinates in accordance with the formulæ

$$x' = x\cos\omega + y\sin\omega, \qquad y' = -x\sin\omega + y\cos\omega\quad . \quad (13).$$

We find

$$x' = \cos\phi\{a\cos\omega + b\sin\omega\cos\delta\} + \sin\phi\,.\,b\sin\delta\sin\omega\quad . \quad (14),$$
$$y' = \cos\phi\{-a\sin\omega + b\cos\omega\cos\delta\} + \sin\phi\,.\,b\sin\delta\cos\omega\ . \quad (15);$$

whence

$$\text{amp.}^2 \text{ of } x' = a^2\cos^2\omega + b^2\sin^2\omega + 2ab\cos\delta\sin\omega\cos\omega\quad . \quad (16),$$
$$\text{amp.}^2 \text{ of } y' = a^2\sin^2\omega + b^2\cos^2\omega - 2ab\cos\delta\sin\omega\cos\omega\quad . \quad (17).$$

In like manner

$$\text{First product} = (b^2 - a^2)\sin\omega\cos\omega + ab\cos\delta(\cos^2\omega - \sin^2\omega)\quad (18),$$
$$\text{Second product} = ab\sin\delta\quad . \quad . \quad . \quad . \quad . \quad . \quad . \quad . \quad . \quad . \quad . \quad . \quad (19).$$

The second product, representing the circulating part of the motion, is thus unaltered by the transformation.

Let us pass on to the consideration of the mean quantities which occur in (9), (10), writing for brevity

$$M(a^2) = A, \qquad M(b^2) = B, \qquad M(ab\cos\delta) = C, \qquad M(ab\sin\delta) = D.$$

From (16), (17), (18), (19), if A', B', C', D' denote the corresponding quantities after transformation,

$$A' = A\cos^2\omega + B\sin^2\omega + 2C\cos\omega\sin\omega\quad . \quad . \quad . \quad . \quad (20),$$
$$B' = A\sin^2\omega + B\cos^2\omega - 2C\cos\omega\sin\omega\quad . \quad . \quad . \quad . \quad (21),$$
$$C' = C(\cos^2\omega - \sin^2\omega) + (B - A)\cos\omega\sin\omega\quad . \quad . \quad . \quad (22),$$
$$D' = D\quad . \quad . \quad . \quad . \quad . \quad . \quad . \quad . \quad . \quad . \quad . \quad . \quad . \quad . \quad (23).$$

These formulæ prove that, if the conditions (9), (10), shown to be necessary in order that the light may behave as natural light, be satisfied for one set of axes, they are equally satisfied with any other. It is thus a matter of indifference with respect to what axes the retardation ϵ is supposed to be introduced, and the conditions (9), (10) are sufficient, as well as necessary, to characterize natural light.

Reverting to (8), we see that, whether the light be natural or not, its character, so far as experimental tests can show, is determined by the values of A, B, C, D. The effect of a change of axes is given by (20), &c., and it is evident that the new axes may always be so chosen that $C' = 0$. For this purpose it is only necessary to take ω such that

$$\tan 2\omega = 2C/(A - B).$$

If we choose these new axes as fundamental axes, the values of the constants for any others inclined to them at angle ω will be of the form

$$\left.\begin{aligned} A &= A_1\cos^2\omega + B_1\sin^2\omega \\ B &= A_1\sin^2\omega + B_1\cos^2\omega \\ C &= (B_1 - A_1)\cos\omega\sin\omega \end{aligned}\right\}\quad . \quad . \quad . \quad . \quad . \quad (24).$$

If A_1 and B_1 are here equal, then $C = 0$, $A = B$ for all values of ω. In this case, the light cannot be distinguished from natural light by mere resolution; but if D be finite, the difference may be made apparent with the aid of a retarding plate.

If A_1 and B_1 are unequal, they represent the maximum and minimum values of A and B. The intensity is then a function of the plane of resolution, and the light may be recognized as partially polarized by the usual tests. If either A_1 or B_1 vanishes, the light is plane-polarized.[2]

When several independent streams of light are combined, the values, not only of A and B, but also of C and D, for the mixture, are to be found by simple addition. It must here be distinctly understood that there are no permanent phase-relations between one component and another. Suppose, for example, that there are two streams of light, each of which satisfies the relations $A = B$, $C = 0$, but makes the value of D finite. If the two values of D are equal and opposite, and the streams are independent, the mixture constitutes natural light. A particular case arises when each component is circularly-polarized ($D = \pm A = \pm B$), one in the right-handed and the other in the left-handed direction. The intensities being equal, the mixture is equivalent to natural light, but only under the restriction that the streams are without phase-relation. If, on the contrary, the second stream be similar to the first, affected merely with a constant retardation, the resultant is not natural, but completely (plane) polarized light.

Analysis of general case.

We will now prove that the most general mixture of light may be regarded as compounded of one stream of light elliptically-polarized in a definite manner, and of an independent stream of natural light. The theorem is due to Stokes,[3] but the method that we shall follow is that of Verdet.[4]

In the first place, it is necessary to observe that the values of the fundamental quantities A, B, C, D are not free from restriction. It will be shown that in no case can $C^2 + D^2$ exceed AB.

In equations (2), expressing the vibration at any moment, let a_1, b_1, α_1, β_1, be the values of a, b, α, β during an interval of time proportional to m_1, and in like manner let the suffixes 2, 3, ... correspond to times proportional to m_2, m_3, ... Then

$$AB = m_1{}^2a_1{}^2b_1{}^2 + m_2{}^2a_2{}^2b_2{}^2 + \ldots + m_1m_2(a_1{}^2b_2{}^2 + a_2{}^2b_1{}^2) + \ldots$$

Again, by (12),

$$C = m_1a_1b_1(\cos\alpha_1\cos\beta_1 + \sin\alpha_1\sin\beta_1) + \ldots$$
$$= m_1a_1b_1\cos\delta_1 + m_2a_2b_2\cos\delta_2 + \ldots,$$
$$D = m_1a_1b_1\sin\delta_1 + m_2a_2b_2\sin\delta_2 + \ldots;$$

where, as before,

$$\delta_1 = \beta_1 - \alpha_1, \quad \delta_2 = \beta_2 - \alpha_2, \quad \ldots.$$

Thus,

$$C^2 + D^2 = m_1{}^2a_1{}^2b_1{}^2 + m_2{}^2a_2{}^2b_2{}^2 + \ldots + m_1m_2a_1b_1a_2b_2\cos(\delta_2 - \delta_1) + \ldots$$

From these equations we see that $AB - C^2 - D^2$ reduces itself to a sum of terms of the form

$$m_1m_2[a_1{}^2b_2{}^2 + a_2{}^2b_1{}^2 - 2a_1b_1a_2b_2\cos(\delta_2 - \delta_1)],$$

each of which is essentially positive.

The only case in which the sum can vanish is when

$$\delta_1 = \delta_2 = \delta_3 = \ldots,$$

and further $\qquad b_1 : a_1 = b_2 : a_2 = b_3 : a_3 = \ldots$

Under these conditions the light is reduced to be of a definite elliptic character, although the amplitude and phase of the system *as a whole* may be subject to rapid variation. The elliptic constants are given by

$$b^2/a^2 = B/A, \qquad \tan\delta = D/C\quad . \quad . \quad . \quad . \quad (25).$$

In general AB exceeds $(C^2 + D^2)$; but it will always be possible to find a positive quantity H, which when subtracted from A and B (themselves necessarily positive) shall reduce the product to equality with $C^2 + D^2$, in accordance with

$$(A - H)(B - H) = C^2 + D^2\quad . \quad . \quad . \quad . \quad . \quad . \quad (26).$$

The original light may thus be resolved into two groups. For the first group the constants are H, H, 0, 0; and for the second $A - H$, $B - H$, C, D. Each of these is of a simple character; for the first represents natural light, and the second light elliptically polarized.

Stokes's theorem.

It is thus proved that in general a stream of light may be regarded as composed of one stream of natural light and of another elliptically-polarized. The intensity of the natural light is 2H, where from (26)

$$H = \tfrac{1}{2}(A + B) - \tfrac{1}{2}\sqrt{\{(A - B)^2 + 4(C^2 + D^2)\}}\quad . \quad . \quad (27).$$

The elliptic constants of the second component are given by

$$b^2/a^2 = (B - H)/(A - H), \qquad \tan\delta = D/C\quad . \quad . \quad (28),$$

and

$$M(a^2) = A - H\quad . \quad . \quad . \quad . \quad . \quad . \quad . \quad . \quad (29).$$

If $D = 0$, and therefore by (28) $\delta = 0$, the second component is plane-polarized. This is regarded as a particular case of elliptic polarization. Again, if $A = B$, $C = 0$, the polarization is circular.

The laws of interference of polarized light, discovered by Fresnel and Arago, are exactly what the theory of transverse vibrations would lead us to expect, when once we have cleared up the idea of unpolarized light. Ordinary sources, such as the sun, emit unpolarized light. If this be resolved in two opposite directions, the

[1] Verdet, *Leçons d'Optique Physique*, vol. ii. p. 83.

[2] In this case D_1 necessarily vanishes.

[3] "On the Composition and Resolution of Streams of Light from Different Sources," *Camb. Phil. Trans.*, 1852.

[4] *Loc. cit.*, p. 94.

polarized components are not only each irregular, but there is no permanent phase-relation between them. No light derived from one can therefore ever interfere regularly with light derived from the other. If, however, we commence with plane-polarized light, we have only one series of irregularities to deal with. When resolved in two rectangular directions, the components cannot then interfere, but only on account of the perpendicularity. If brought back by resolution to the same plane of polarization, interference becomes possible, because the same series of irregularities are to be found in both components.

§ 21. *Double Refraction.*

The construction by which Huygens explained the ordinary and extraordinary refraction of Iceland spar has already been given (LIGHT, vol. xiv. p. 610). The wave-surface is in two sheets, composed of a sphere and of an ellipsoid of revolution, in contact with one another at the extremities of the polar axis. In biaxal crystals the wave-surface is of a more complicated character, including that of Huygens as a particular case.

Wave-surface.

It is not unimportant to remark that the essential problem of double refraction is to determine the two velocities with which plane waves are propagated, when the direction of the normal to the wave-front is assigned. When this problem has been solved, the determination of the wave-surface is a mere matter of geometry, not absolutely necessary for the explanation of the leading phenomena, but convenient as affording a concise summary of the principal laws. In all cases the wave-surface is to be regarded as the envelope at any subsequent time of all the plane wave-fronts which at a given instant may be supposed to be passing through a particular point.

Direction of ray.

In singly refracting media, where the velocity of a wave is the same in all directions, the wave-normal coincides with the *ray*. In doubly refracting crystals this law no longer holds good. The principles by which the conception of a ray is justified (§ 10), when applied to this case, show that the centre of the zone system is not in general to be found at the foot of the perpendicular upon the primary wave-front. The surface whose contact with the primary wave-front determines the element from which the secondary disturbance arrives with least retardation is now not a sphere, but whatever wave-surface is appropriate to the medium. The direction of the ray, corresponding to any tangent plane of the wave-surface, is thus not the normal, but the radius vector drawn from the centre to the point of contact.

The velocity of propagation (reckoned always perpendicularly to the wave-front) may be conceived to depend upon the direction of the wave-front, or wave-normal, and upon what we may call (at any rate figuratively) the direction of vibration. If the velocity depended exclusively upon the wave-normal, there could be no *double*, though there might be *extraordinary*, refraction, *i.e.*, refraction deviating from the law of Snell; but of this nothing is known in nature. The fact that there are in general two velocities for one wave-front proves that the velocity depends upon the direction of vibration.

Fresnel's views.

According to the Huygenian law, confirmed to a high degree of accuracy by the observations of Brewster and Swan,[1] a ray polarized in a principal plane (*i.e.*, a plane passing through the axis) of a uniaxal crystal suffers ordinary refraction only, that is, propagates itself with the same velocity in all directions. The interpretation which Fresnel put upon this is that the vibrations (understood now in a literal sense) are perpendicular to the plane of polarization, and that the velocity is constant because the direction of vibration is in all cases similarly related (perpendicular) to the axis. The development of this idea in the fertile brain of Fresnel led him to the remarkable discovery of the law of refraction in biaxal crystals.

The hypotheses upon which Fresnel based his attempt at a mechanical theory are thus summarized by Verdet:—

(1) The vibrations of polarized light are perpendicular to the plane of polarization;

(2) The elastic forces called into play during the propagation of a system of plane waves (of rectilinear transverse vibrations) differ from the elastic forces developed by the parallel displacement of a single molecule only by a constant factor, independent of the particular direction of the plane of the wave;

(3) When a plane wave propagates itself in any homogeneous medium, the components parallel to the wave-front of the elastic forces called into play by the vibrations of the wave are alone operative;

(4) The velocity of a plane wave which propagates itself with type unchanged in any homogeneous medium is proportional to the square root of the effective component of the elastic force developed by the vibrations.

Fresnel himself was perfectly aware that his theory was deficient in rigour, and indeed there is little to be said in defence of his second hypothesis. Nevertheless, the great historical interest of this theory, and the support that experiment gives to Fresnel's conclusion as to the actual form of the wave-surface in biaxal crystals, render some account of his work in this field imperative.

[1] *Edinb. Trans.*, vol. xvi. p. 375.

Energy of displacement.

The potential energy of displacement of a single molecule from its position of equilibrium is ultimately a quadratic function of the three components reckoned parallel to any set of rectangular axes. These axes may be so chosen as to reduce the quadratic function to a sum of squares, so that the energy may be expressed,

$$V=\tfrac{1}{2}a^2\xi^2+\tfrac{1}{2}b^2\eta^2+\tfrac{1}{2}c^2\zeta^2 \quad . \quad . \quad . \quad . \quad . \quad . \quad (1),$$

where ξ, η, ζ are the three component displacements. The corresponding forces of restitution, obtained at once by differentiation, are

$$X=a^2\xi, \qquad Y=b^2\eta, \qquad Z=c^2\zeta \quad . \quad . \quad . \quad (2).$$

The force of restitution is thus in general inclined to the direction of displacement. The relation between the two directions X, Y, Z and ξ, η, ζ is the same as that between the normal to a tangent plane and the radius vector ρ to the point of contact in the ellipsoid

$$a^2\xi^2+b^2\eta^2+c^2\zeta^2=1 \quad . \quad . \quad . \quad . \quad . \quad . \quad (3).$$

If a^2, b^2, c^2 are unequal, the directions of the coordinate axes are the only ones in which a displacement calls into operation a parallel force of restitution. If two of the quantities a^2, b^2, c^2 are equal, the ellipsoid (3) is of revolution, and every direction in the plane of the equal axes possesses the property in question. This is the case of a uniaxal crystal. If the three quantities a^2, b^2, c^2 are all equal, the medium is isotropic.

If we resolve the force of restitution in the direction of displacement, we obtain a quantity dependent upon this direction in a manner readily expressible by means of the ellipsoid of elasticity (3). For, when the total displacement is given, this quantity is proportional to

$$\frac{a^2\xi^2+b^2\eta^2+c^2\zeta^2}{\xi^2+\eta^2+\zeta^2},$$

that is to say, to the inverse square of the radius vector ρ in (3).

Directions of vibration.

We have now to inquire in what directions, limited to a particular plane, a displacement may be so made that the *projection* of the force of restitution upon the plane may be parallel to the displacement. The answer follows at once from the property of the ellipsoid of elasticity. For, if in any section of the ellipsoid we have a radius vector such that the plane containing it and the normal to the corresponding tangent plane is perpendicular to the plane of the section, the tangent line to the section must be perpendicular to the radius vector, that is, the radius vector must be a principal axis of the section. There are therefore two, and in general only two, directions in any plane satisfying the proposed condition, and these are perpendicular to one another. If, however, the plane be one of those of circular section, every line of displacement is such that the component of the force, resolved parallel to the plane, coincides with it.

According to the principles laid down by Fresnel, we have now complete data for the solution of the problem of double refraction. If the direction of the wave-front be given, there are (in general) only two directions of vibration such that a single wave is propagated. If the actual displacements do not conform to this condition, they will be resolved into two of the required character, and the components will in general be propagated with different velocities. The two directions are the principal axes of the section of (3) made by the wave-front, and the velocities of propagation are inversely proportional to the lengths of these axes.

The law connecting the lengths of the axes with the direction (l, m, n) of the plane is a question of geometry;[2] and indeed the whole investigation of the wave-surface may be elegantly carried through geometrically with the aid of certain theorems of MacCullagh respecting *apsidal* surfaces (Salmon, ch. xiv.). For this, however, we have not space, and must content ourselves with a sketch of the analytical method of treatment.

If v be the velocity of propagation in direction l, m, n, the wave-surface is the envelope of planes

$$lx+my+nz=v \quad . \quad . \quad . \quad . \quad . \quad . \quad . \quad (4),$$

where v is a function of l, m, n, whose form is to be determined. If (λ, μ, ν) be the corresponding direction of vibration, then

$$l\lambda+m\mu+n\nu=0 \quad . \quad . \quad . \quad . \quad . \quad . \quad . \quad (5).$$

According to the principles laid down by Fresnel, we see at once that the force of restitution $(a^2\lambda, b^2\mu, c^2\nu)$, corresponding to a displacement unity, is equivalent to a force v^2 along (λ, μ, ν), together with some force (P) along (l, m, n). Resolving parallel to the coordinate axes, we get

$$lP=a^2\lambda-v^2\lambda, \qquad mP=b^2\mu-v^2\mu, \qquad nP=c^2\nu-v^2\nu,$$

or

$$\lambda=\frac{lP}{a^2-v^2}, \qquad \mu=\frac{mP}{b^2-v^2}, \qquad \nu=\frac{nP}{c^2-v^2} \quad . \quad . \quad . \quad (6).$$

Law of velocity.

Multiplying these by l, m, n respectively, and taking account of (5), we see that

$$\frac{l^2}{a^2-v^2}+\frac{m^2}{b^2-v^2}+\frac{n^2}{c^2-v^2}=0 \quad . \quad . \quad . \quad . \quad . \quad . \quad (7)$$

is the relation sought for between v and (l, m, n). In this equation b, c are the velocities when the direction of propagation is

[2] See Salmon's *Analytical Geometry of Three Dimensions*, Dublin, 1882, § 102.

along x, the former being applicable when the vibration is parallel to y, and the latter when it is parallel to x.

The directions of vibration are determined by (5) and by the consideration that (l, m, n), (λ, μ, ν), and $(a^2\lambda, b^2\mu, c^2\nu)$ lie in a plane, or (as we may put it) are all perpendicular to one direction (f, g, h).

Thus
$$\left.\begin{array}{l} lf+\ mg+nh\ =0 \\ \lambda f+\ \mu g+\nu h\ =0 \\ a^2\lambda f+b^2\mu g+c^2\nu h=0 \end{array}\right\} \quad . \quad . \quad . \quad . \quad . \quad . \quad (8).$$

The determinant expressing the result of the elimination of $f:g:h$ may be put into the form
$$\frac{l}{\lambda}(b^2-c^2)+\frac{m}{\mu}(c^2-a^2)+\frac{n}{\nu}(a^2-b^2)=0 \quad . \quad . \quad . \quad . \quad (9),$$
which with (5) suffices to determine (λ, μ, ν) as a function of (l, m, n).

The fact that the system of equations (5), (8) is symmetrical as between (λ, μ, ν) and (f, g, h) proves that the two directions of vibration corresponding to a given (l, m, n) are perpendicular to one another.

The direct investigation of the wave-surface from (4) and (7) was first effected by Ampère, but his analytical process was very laborious. Fresnel had indeed been forced to content himself with an indirect method of verification. But in the following investigation of A. Smith[1] the eliminations are effected with comparatively little trouble.

A. Smith's investigation.

In addition to (4) and (7), we know that
$$l^2+m^2+n^2=1 \quad . \quad . \quad . \quad . \quad . \quad . \quad . \quad . \quad (10).$$

To find the equation to the envelope, we have to differentiate these equations, making l, m, n, v vary. Eliminating the differentials by the method of multipliers, we obtain the following:—
$$x=\mathrm{A}l\ +\mathrm{B}l/(v^2-a^2) \quad . \quad . \quad . \quad . \quad . \quad . \quad (11),$$
$$y=\mathrm{A}m+\mathrm{B}m/(v^2-b^2) \quad . \quad . \quad . \quad . \quad . \quad (12),$$
$$z=\mathrm{A}n\ +\mathrm{B}n/(v^2-c^2) \quad . \quad . \quad . \quad . \quad . \quad . \quad (13);$$
and
$$1=\mathrm{B}v\left\{\frac{l^2}{(v^2-a^2)^2}+\frac{m^2}{(v^2-b^2)^2}+\frac{n^2}{(v^2-c^2)^2}\right\} \quad . \quad . \quad . \quad (14).$$

The equations (11), (12), (13) multiplied by l, m, n respectively and added, give
$$v=\mathrm{A} \quad . \quad . \quad . \quad . \quad . \quad . \quad . \quad . \quad . \quad (15).$$

The same equations, squared and added, give
$$x^2+y^2+z^2=\mathrm{A}^2+\mathrm{B}/v.$$

If we put r^2 for $x^2+y^2+z^2$, and for A the value just found, we obtain
$$\mathrm{B}=v(r^2-v^2) \quad . \quad . \quad . \quad . \quad . \quad . \quad . \quad . \quad (16).$$

If these values of A and B be substituted in (11),
$$x=lv\left\{1+\frac{r^2-v^2}{v^2-a^2}\right\}=lv\frac{r^2-a^2}{v^2-a^2},$$
or
$$l=\frac{v^2-a^2}{r^2-a^2}\frac{x}{v} \quad . \quad . \quad . \quad . \quad . \quad . \quad . \quad . \quad (17).$$

If we substitute this value of l, and the corresponding values of m, n in (4), we get
$$\frac{(v^2-a^2)x^2}{r^2-a^2}+\frac{(v^2-b^2)y^2}{r^2-b^2}+\frac{(v^2-c^2)z^2}{r^2-c^2}=v^2=\frac{v^2x^2}{r^2}+\frac{v^2y^2}{r^2}+\frac{v^2z^2}{r^2},$$
whence

Fresnel's wave-surface.

$$\frac{x^2a^2}{r^2-a^2}+\frac{y^2b^2}{r^2-b^2}+\frac{z^2c^2}{r^2-c^2}=0 \quad . \quad . \quad . \quad . \quad . \quad . \quad (18),$$
as the equation of the wave-surface.

By (6) equation (11) may be written
$$x=\mathrm{A}l+\mathrm{BP}^{-1}\lambda,$$
from which and the corresponding equations we see that the direction (x, y, z) lies in the same plane as (l, m, n) and (λ, μ, ν). Hence in any tangent plane of the wave-surface the direction of vibration is that of the line joining the foot of the perpendicular and the point of contact (x, y, z).

The equation (18) leads to another geometrical definition of Fresnel's wave-surface. If through the centre of the ellipsoid reciprocal to the ellipsoid of elasticity (3), viz.,
$$x^2/a^2+y^2/b^2+z^2/c^2=1 \quad . \quad . \quad . \quad . \quad . \quad (19),$$
a plane be drawn, and on the normal to this plane two lengths be marked off proportional to the axes of the elliptic section determined by the plane, the locus of the points thus obtained, the apsidal surface of (19), is the wave-surface (18).

Fully developed in integral powers of the coordinates, (18) takes the form
$$(x^2+y^2+z^2)(a^2x^2+b^2y^2+c^2z^2)-a^2(b^2+c^2)x^2$$
$$-b^2(c^2+a^2)y^2-c^2(a^2+b^2)z^2+a^2b^2c^2=0 \quad . \quad . \quad . \quad (20).$$

Principal sections.

The section of (20) by the coordinate plane $y=0$ is
$$(x^2+z^2-b^2)(a^2x^2+c^2z^2-a^2c^2)=0 \quad . \quad . \quad . \quad . \quad (21),$$
representing a circle and an ellipse (fig. 24). That the sections by each of the principal planes would be a circle and an ellipse might have been foreseen independently of a general solution of the envelope problem. The forms of the sections prescribed in (21) and the two similar equations are sufficient to determine the character of the wave-surface, if we assume that it is of the *fourth degree*, and involves only the even powers of the coordinates. It was somewhat in this way that the equation was first obtained by Fresnel.

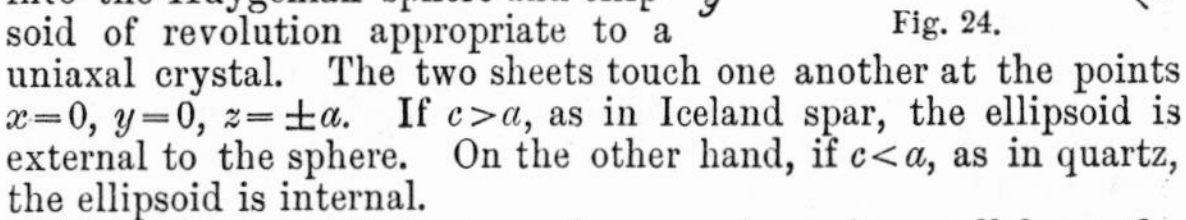

Fig. 24.

Uniaxal crystals.

If two of the principal velocities, *e.g.*, a and b, are equal, (20) becomes
$$(x^2+y^2+z^2-a^2)(a^2x^2+a^2y^2+c^2z^2-a^2c^2)=0 \quad . \quad (22),$$
so that the wave-surface degenerates into the Huygenian sphere and ellipsoid of revolution appropriate to a uniaxal crystal. The two sheets touch one another at the points $x=0$, $y=0$, $z=\pm a$. If $c>a$, as in Iceland spar, the ellipsoid is external to the sphere. On the other hand, if $c<a$, as in quartz, the ellipsoid is internal.

We have seen that when the wave-front is parallel to the circular sections of (3), the two wave velocities coincide. Thus in (7), if a^2, b^2, c^2 be in descending order of magnitude, we have $m=0$, $v=b$; so that
$$\frac{l^2}{a^2-b^2}=\frac{n^2}{b^2-c^2}=\frac{1}{a^2-c^2} \quad . \quad . \quad . \quad . \quad . \quad (23).$$

Optic axes.

In general, if θ, θ' be the angles which the normal to the actual wave-front makes with the optic axes, it may be proved that the difference of the squares of the two roots of (7) is given by
$$v_2{}^2-v_1{}^2=(a^2-c^2)\sin\theta\sin\theta' \quad . \quad . \quad . \quad . \quad (24).$$

In a uniaxal crystal the optic axes coincide with the axis of symmetry, and there is no distinction between θ' and θ.

Since waves in a biaxal crystal propagated along either optic axis have but one velocity, it follows that tangent planes to the wave-surface, perpendicular to these directions, touch both sheets of the surface. It may be proved further that each plane touches the surface not merely at two, but at an infinite number of points, which lie upon a circle.

The directions of the optic axes, and the angle included between them, are found frequently to vary with the colour of the light. Such a variation is to be expected, in view of dispersion, which renders a^2, b^2, c^2 functions of the wave-length.

Huygens's construction.

A knowledge of the form of the wave-surface determines in all cases the law of refraction according to the construction of Huygens. We will suppose for simplicity that the first medium is air, and that the surface of separation between the media is plane. The incident wave-front at any moment of time cuts the surface of separation in a straight line. On this line take any point, and with it as centre construct the wave-surface in the second medium corresponding to a certain interval of time. At the end of this interval the trace of the incident wave-front upon the surface will have advanced to a new position, parallel to the former. Planes drawn through this line so as to touch the wave-surface give the positions of the refracted wave-fronts. None other could satisfy the two conditions—(1) that the refracted wave-front should move within the crystal with the normal velocity suitable to its direction, and (2) that the traces of the incident and refracted waves upon the surface of separation should move together. The normal to a refracted wave lies necessarily in the plane of incidence, but the refracted *ray*, coinciding with the radius vector of the wave-surface, in general deviates from it. In most cases it is sufficient to attend to the wave normal.

Total reflexion.

As in total reflexion by simply refracting media, it may happen that no tangent planes can be drawn to satisfy the prescribed conditions, or that but one such can be drawn.

When the crystal is uniaxal, one wave is refracted according to the ordinary law of Snell. The accuracy of both the sphere and the ellipsoid of the Huygenian construction has been fully verified by modern observations.[2]

The simplest case of uniaxal refraction is when the axis of the crystal is perpendicular to the plane of incidence, with respect to which every thing then becomes symmetrical. The section of the wave-surface with which we have to deal reduces to two concentric circles; so that *both* waves are refracted according to the ordinary law, though of course with different indices.

In biaxal crystals one wave follows the ordinary law of refraction, if the plane of incidence coincide with a principal plane of the crystal. This consequence of his theory was verified by Fresnel himself, and subsequently by Rudberg and others. But the most remarkable phenomena of biaxal refraction are undoubtedly

[1] *Camb. Trans.*, vi., 1835.

[2] Stokes, *Proc. Roy. Soc.*, vol. xx. p. 443, 1872; Glazebrook, *Phil. Trans.*, 1880, p. 421; Hastings, *Amer. Jour.*, Jan. 1888.

those discovered by Hamilton and Lloyd, generally known as conical refraction.

Conical refraction.

In general there are two refracted rays, corresponding to two distinct waves. But the refracted waves coalesce when they are perpendicular to either optic axis, and (as we have seen) this wave touches the wave-surface along a circle. Thus corresponding to one wave direction there are an infinite number of rays, lying upon a cone. The division of a single incident ray into a cone of refracted rays is called internal conical refraction. If the second face of the crystal is parallel to the first, each refracted ray resumes on emergence its original direction, so that the emergent bundle forms a hollow cylinder.

External conical refraction depends upon the singular points in the principal plane of zx, where the two sheets of the surface cross one another (fig. 24). At such a point (P) an infinite number of tangent planes may be drawn to the surface, and each of the perpendiculars from O represents a wave direction, corresponding to the single *ray* OP. On emergence these waves will be differently refracted; and thus corresponding to a single internal ray there are an infinite number of external rays, lying upon a cone.

It has already been admitted that the dynamical foundations of Fresnel's theory are unsound; and it must be added that the rigorous theory of crystalline solids investigated by Cauchy and Green does not readily lend itself to the explanation of Fresnel's laws of double refraction. On this subject the reader should consult Prof. Stokes's Report. Sir W. Thomson has recently shown[1] that an originally isotropic medium, pressed unequally in different directions, may be so constituted as to vibrate in accordance with Fresnel's laws.

It may perhaps be worth while to remark that the equations, analogous to (2) § (24), which lead to these laws are

$$\frac{d^2\xi}{dt^2}=\frac{dp}{dx}+a^2\nabla^2\xi\,,\quad \frac{d^2\eta}{dt^2}=\frac{dp}{dy}+b^2\nabla^2\eta\,,\ \&c. \quad . \quad . \quad . \quad (25),$$

where a, b, c are the principal wave velocities. If we here assume

$$\xi=\lambda\theta\,,\quad \eta=\mu\theta\,,\quad \zeta=\nu\theta\,,$$
$$\theta/\theta_0=p/p_0=e^{ik(lx+my+nz-\mathrm{V}t)},$$

and substitute in (25), the condition of transversality leads at once to the desired results. But the equations (25) are not applicable to the vibrations of a crystalline solid.

Electromagnetic theory.

In the electromagnetic theory double refraction is attributed to æolotropic inductive capacity, and appears to offer no particular difficulty.

If the present position of the theory of double refraction is still somewhat unsatisfactory, it must be remembered that the uncertainty does not affect the general principle. Almost any form of wave theory involving transverse vibrations will explain the leading phenomenon, viz., the bifurcation of the ray. It is safe to predict that when ordinary refraction is well understood there will be little further trouble over double refraction.

Double absorption.

The wave-velocity is not the only property of light rendered unsymmetrical by crystalline structure. In many cases the two polarized rays are subject to a different rate of *absorption*. Tourmalines and other crystals may be prepared in plates of such thickness that one ray is sensibly stopped and the other sensibly transmitted, and will then serve as polarizing (or analysing) apparatus. Although for practical purposes Nicol's prisms (LIGHT, vol. xiv. p. 612) are usually to be preferred, the phenomenon of double absorption is of great theoretical interest. The explanation is doubtless closely connected with that of double refraction.

§ 22. *Colours of Crystalline Plates.*

When polarized light is transmitted through a moderately thin plate of doubly refracting crystal, and is then analysed, *e.g.*, with a Nicol, brilliant colours are often exhibited, analogous in their character to the tints of Newton's scale. With his usual acuteness, Young at once attributed these colours to interference between the ordinary and extraordinary waves, and showed that the thickness of crystal required to develop a given tint, inversely proportional to the doubly refracting power, was in agreement with this view. But the complete explanation, demanding a fuller knowledge of the laws of interference of polarized light, was reserved for Fresnel and Arago. The subject is one which admits of great development;[2] but the interest turns principally upon the beauty of the effects, and upon the facility with which many of them may be obtained in experiment. We must limit ourselves to a brief treatment of one or two of the simpler cases.

The incident vibration being plane-polarized, we will suppose that its plane makes an angle α with the principal plane of the crystal. On entering the crystal it is accordingly resolved into the two components represented by

$$\cos\alpha\cos\phi,\qquad \sin\alpha\cos\phi,\qquad \text{where } \phi=2\pi t/\tau.$$

[1] "On Cauchy's and Green's Doctrine of Extraneous Force to explain dynamically Fresnel's Kinematics of Double Refraction," *Phil. Mag.*, Feb. 1888.

[2] See Verdet's *Leçons*, vol. ii.

In traversing the crystal both waves are retarded, but we are concerned only with the difference of the retardations. Denoting the difference by ρ, we may take as the expressions of the waves on emergence

$$\cos\alpha\cos\phi\,,\qquad \sin\alpha\cos(\phi-\rho).$$

It may be remarked that, in the absence of *dispersion*, ρ would be inversely proportional to λ; but in fact there are many cases where it deviates greatly from this law.

Now let the plane of analysation be inclined at the angle β to that of primitive polarization (fig. 25). Then for the sum of the two resolved components we have

$$\cos\alpha\cos(\alpha-\beta)\cos\phi+\sin\alpha\sin(\alpha-\beta)\cos(\phi-\rho)\,,$$

of which the intensity is

$$\{\cos\alpha\cos(\alpha-\beta)+\sin\alpha\sin(\alpha-\beta)\cos\rho\}^2+\sin^2\alpha\sin^2(\alpha-\beta)\sin^2\beta$$
$$=\cos^2\beta-\sin 2\alpha\sin 2(\alpha-\beta)\sin^2\tfrac{1}{2}\rho \quad . \quad . \quad . \quad . \quad (1).$$

If in (1) we write $\beta+\frac{1}{2}\pi$ in place of β, we get

$$\sin^2\beta+\sin 2\alpha\sin 2(\alpha-\beta)\sin^2\tfrac{1}{2}\rho \quad . \quad . \quad . \quad . \quad (2);$$

and we notice that the sum of (1) and (2) is unity under all circumstances. The effect of rotating the analyser through 90° is thus always to transform the tint into its complementary. The two complementary tints may be seen at the same time if we employ a double image prism. In the absence of an analyser we may regard the two images as superposed, and there is no colour.

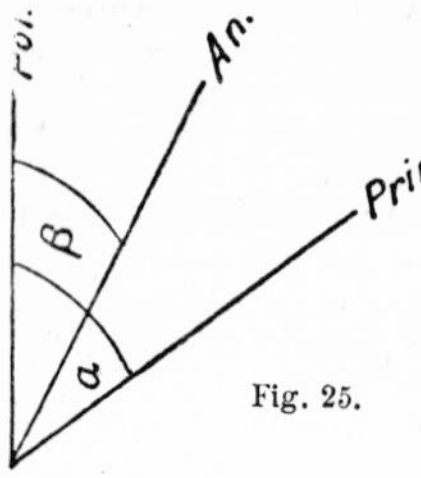

Fig. 25.

Colours of mica and selenite.

These expressions may be applied at once to the explanation of the colours of thin plates of mica or selenite. In this case the retardation ρ is proportional to the thickness, and approximately independent of the precise direction of the light, supposed to be nearly perpendicular to the plate, viz., nearly parallel to a principal axis of the crystal.

The most important cases are when $\beta=0$, $\beta=\frac{1}{2}\pi$. In the latter the field would be dark were the plate removed; and the actual intensity is

$$\sin^2 2\alpha\sin^2\tfrac{1}{2}\rho \quad . \quad . \quad . \quad . \quad . \quad . \quad . \quad (3).$$

The composition of the light is thus independent of the azimuth of the plate (α); but the *intensity* varies greatly, vanishing four times during the complete revolution. The greatest brightness occurs when the principal plane bisects the angle between the planes of polarization and analysis. If $\beta=0$, the light is complementary to that represented by (3).

If two plates be superposed, the retardations are added if the azimuths correspond; but they are subtracted if one plate be rotated relatively to the other through 90°. It is thus possible to obtain colour by the superposition of two nearly similar plates, although they may be too thick to answer the purpose separately.

If dispersion be neglected, the law of the colours in (3) is the same as that of the reflected tints of Newton's scale. The thicknesses of the plates of mica (acting by double refraction) and of air required to give the same colour are as 400 : 1. When a plate is too thick to show colour, its action may be analysed with the aid of a spectroscope.

Rings from uniaxal crystals.

Still thicker plates may be caused to exhibit colour, if the direction of the light within them makes but a small angle with an optic axis. Let us suppose that a plate of Iceland spar, or other uniaxal crystal (except quartz), cut perpendicularly to the axis, is interposed between the polarizing and analysing apparatus, and that the latter is so turned that the field is originally dark. The ray which passes perpendicularly is not doubly refracted, so that the centre of the field remains dark. At small angles to the optic axis the relative retardation is evidently proportional to the square of the inclination, so that the colours are disposed in concentric rings. But the intensity is not the same at the various parts of the circumference. In the plane of polarization and in the perpendicular plane there is no double refraction, or rather one of the refracted rays vanishes. Along the corresponding lines in the field of view there is no revival of light, and the ring system is seen to be traversed by a black cross.

In many crystals the influence of dispersion is sufficient to sensibly modify the proportionality of ρ to λ. In one variety of uniaxal apophyllite Herschel found the rings nearly achromatic, indicating that ρ was almost independent of λ. Under these circumstances a much larger number of rings than usual became visible.

In biaxal crystals, cut so that the surfaces are equally inclined to the optic axes, the rings take the form of lemniscates.

Double refraction due to strain.

A medium originally isotropic may acquire the doubly refracting property under the influence of strain; and, if the strain be *homogeneous*, the conditions are optically identical with those found in a natural crystal. The principal axes of the wave-surface coincide with those of strain. If the strain be symmetrical, the medium is optically uniaxal. In general, if P, Q, R be the principal stresses, the difference of velocities for waves propagated parallel to R is evidently proportional to (P – Q), and so on.

More often it happens that the strain is not homogeneous. Even then the small parts may be compared to crystals, but the optical constants vary from point to point. The comparatively feeble doubly refracting power thus developed in glass may best be made evident by the production of the colours of polarized light. Thus, in an experiment due to Brewster, a somewhat stout slab of glass, polished on the edges, is interposed between crossed Nicols. When the slab is bent in a plane perpendicular to that of vision, a revival of light takes place along the edges, where the elongation and contraction is greatest. If the width (in the direction of vision) be sufficient, the effect may be increased until the various colours of Newton's scale are seen. These colours vary from point to point of the thickness in the plane of bending, the "neutral axis" remaining dark. The optic axis, being everywhere coincident with the direction of elongation (or contraction), is parallel to the length of the slab. To this direction the plane of polarization should be inclined at about 45°.

Effects of heat.

The condition of internal strain is not necessarily due to forces applied from without. Thus, if glass originally free from strain be unequally heated, the accompanying expansions give rise to internal strains which manifest themselves in polarized light. If the heating be moderate, so as not to approach the softening point, the state of ease is recovered upon cooling, and the double refraction disappears. But if the local temperature be raised further, the hot parts may relieve themselves of the temporary strain, and then upon cooling they and other parts may be left in a condition of permanent strain. Sudden cooling of glass heated to the softening point leads to a similar result. The outer parts harden while the interior is still at a higher temperature, so that, when the whole is cooled down, the outside, being as it were too large for the inside, is in a condition of radial tension and circumferential compression. An examination in polarized light shows that the strains thus occasioned are often very severe. If any small part be relieved by fracture from the constraint exercised upon it by the remainder, the doubly refracting property almost or wholly disappears. In this respect unannealed glass differs essentially from a crystal, all parts of which are similar and independent. It may be remarked that it is difficult to find large pieces of glass so free from internal strain as to show no revival of light when examined between crossed Nicols.

§ 23. *Rotatory Polarization.*

Rotation by quartz.

In general a polarized ray travelling along the axis of a uniaxal crystal undergoes no change; but it was observed by Arago that, if quartz be used in this experiment, the plane of polarization is found to be rotated through an angle proportional to the thickness of crystal traversed. The subject was further studied by Biot, who ascertained that the rotation due to a given thickness is inversely as the square of the wave-length of the light, thus varying very rapidly with the colour. In some specimens of quartz (called in consequence right-handed) the rotation is to the right, while in others it is to the left. Equal thicknesses of right- and left-handed quartz may thus compensate one another.

Fresnel has shown that the rotation of the plane may be interpreted as indicating a different velocity of propagation of the two circularly-polarized components into which plane-polarized light may always be resolved. In ordinary media the right- and left-handed circularly-polarized rays travel at the same speed, and at any stage of their progress recompound a ray rectilinearly-polarized in a fixed direction. But it is otherwise if the velocities of propagation of the circular components be even slightly different.

The first circularly-polarized wave may be expressed by

$$\xi_1 = r\cos(nt - k_1 z), \qquad \eta_1 = r\sin(nt - k_1 z) \quad . \quad . \quad . \quad (1);$$

and the second (of equal amplitude) by

$$\xi_2 = r\cos(nt - k_2 z), \qquad \eta_2 = -r\sin(nt - k_2 z) \quad . \quad . \quad (2).$$

The resultant of (1) and (2) is

$$\xi = \xi_1 + \xi_2 = 2r\cos\tfrac{1}{2}(k_2 - k_1)z\cos\left\{nt - \tfrac{1}{2}(k_1 + k_2)z\right\},$$

$$\eta = \eta_1 + \eta_2 = 2r\sin\tfrac{1}{2}(k_2 - k_1)z\cos\left\{nt - \tfrac{1}{2}(k_1 + k_1)z\right\};$$

so that

$$\eta/\xi = \tan\tfrac{1}{2}(k_2 - k_1)z \quad . \quad . \quad . \quad . \quad . \quad . \quad . \quad (3),$$

which shows that for any fixed value of z the light is plane-polarized. The direction of this plane, however, varies with z. Thus, if $\eta/\xi = \tan\theta$, so that θ gives the angular position of the plane in reference to ξ, we have

$$\theta = \tfrac{1}{2}(k_2 - k_1)z \quad . \quad . \quad . \quad . \quad . \quad . \quad . \quad (4),$$

indicating a rotation proportional to z. The quantities k_1, k_2 are inversely as the wave-lengths of the two circular components for the same periodic time. When the relative retardation amounts to an entire period, $(k_2 - k_1)z = 2\pi$, and then, by (4), $\theta = \pi$. The revolution of the plane through two right angles restores the original state of polarization. In quartz the rotation is very rapid, amounting in the case of yellow light to about 24° for each millimetre traversed.

Delicacy of test.

It is interesting to observe with what a high degree of accuracy the comparison of the velocities of the two waves can be effected. If the plane of polarization be determined to one minute of angle, a relative retardation of $\lambda/10800$ is made manifest. If l be the thickness traversed, v and $v + \delta v$ the two velocities, the relative retardation is $l\delta v/v$. To take an example, suppose that $l = 20$ inches, $\lambda = \frac{1}{40000}$ inch; so that if $\delta v/v$ exceed 10^{-8}, the fact might be detected.

In quartz the rotation of the plane depends upon the crystalline structure, but there are many liquids, *e.g.*, oil of turpentine and common syrup, which exhibit a like effect. In such cases the rotation is of course independent of the direction of the light; it must be due to some peculiarity in the constitution of the molecules.

Right- and left-handed varieties.

A remarkable connexion has been observed between the rotatory property and the crystalline form. Thus Herschel found that in many specimens the right-handed and left-handed varieties of quartz could be distinguished by the disposition of certain subordinate faces. The crystals of opposite kinds are symmetrical in a certain sense, but are yet not *superposable.* The difference is like that between otherwise similar right- and left-handed screws. The researches of Pasteur upon the rotatory properties of tartaric acid have opened up a new and most interesting field of chemistry. At that time two isomeric varieties were known,—ordinary tartaric acid, which rotates to the right, and racemic acid, which is optically inactive, properties of the acids shared also by the salts. Pasteur found that the crystals of tartaric acid and of the tartrates possessed a right-handed structure, and endeavoured to discover corresponding bodies with a left-handed structure. After many trials crystallizations of the double racemate of soda and ammonia were obtained, including crystals of opposite kinds. A selection of the right-handed specimens yielded ordinary dextro-tartaric acid, while a similar selection of the left-handed crystals gave a new variety—lævo-tartaric acid, rotating the plane of polarization to the left in the same degree as ordinary tartaric acid rotates it to the right. A mixture in equal proportions of the two kinds of tartaric acid, which differ scarcely at all in their chemical properties,[1] reconstitutes racemic acid.

Magnetic rotation.

The possibility of inducing the rotatory property in bodies otherwise free from it was one of the finest of Faraday's discoveries. He found that, if heavy glass, bisulphide of carbon, &c., are placed in a magnetic field, a ray of polarized light, propagated along the lines of magnetic force, suffers rotation. The laws of the phenomenon were carefully studied by Verdet, whose conclusions may be summed up by saying that in a given medium the rotation of the plane for a ray proceeding in any direction is proportional to the difference of magnetic potential at the initial and final points. In bisulphide of carbon, at 18° and for a difference of potential equal to unity C. G. S., the rotation of the plane of polarization of a ray of soda light is ·0402 minute of angle.[2]

A very important distinction should be noted between the magnetic rotation and that natural to quartz, syrup, &c. In the latter the rotation is always right-handed or always left-handed with respect to the direction of the ray. Hence when the ray is reversed the absolute direction of rotation is reversed also. A ray which traverses a plate of quartz in one direction, and then after reflexion traverses the same thickness again in the opposite direction, recovers its original plane of polarization. It is quite otherwise with the rotation under magnetic force. In this case the rotation is in the same absolute direction even though the ray be reversed. Hence, if a ray be reflected backwards and forwards any number of times along a line of magnetic force, the rotations due to the several passages are all accumulated. The non-reversibility of light in a magnetized medium proves the case to be of a very exceptional character, and (as was argued by Thomson) indicates that the magnetized medium is itself in rotatory motion independently of the propagation of light through it.[3]

Polarimetry.

The importance of polarimetric determinations has led to the contrivance of various forms of apparatus adapted to the special requirements of the case. If the light be bright enough, fairly accurate measurements may be made by merely rotating a Nicol until the field appears dark. Probably the best form of analyser, when white light is used and the plane is the same for all the coloured components, is the Jellet,[4] formed by the combination of two portions of Iceland spar. By this instrument the field of view is duplicated, and the setting is effected by turning it until the two portions of the field, much reduced in brightness, appear *equally* dark. A similar result is attained in the Laurent, which, however, is only applicable to homogeneous light. In this apparatus, advantage is taken of the action of a half-wave plate. In passing such a plate the plane of polarization is as it were *reflected* by the principal section, that is, rotated until it makes the same angle with the principal section as at first, but upon the further side. The plate covers only half of the field of view, and the eye is focused upon the

Laurent analyser.

[1] It would seem that the two varieties could be chemically distinguished only by their relations with bodies themselves right-handed or left-handed.

[2] *Phil. Trans.*, 1885, p. 343.

[3] Maxwell's *Electricity and Magnetism*, vol. ii. chap. xxi.

[4] A description is given in Glazebrook's *Physical Optics*, London, 1883.

dividing edge. The planes of polarization of the two halves of the field are different, unless the original plane be parallel (or perpendicular) to the principal section. In the Laurent analyser the half-wave plate is rigidly combined with a Nicol in such a position that the principal section of the latter makes a small but finite angle with that of the plate. The consequence is that the two halves of the field of view cannot be blackened simultaneously, but are rendered equally dark when the instrument is so turned that the principal section of the plate is parallel to the plane of original polarization, which is also that of the uncovered half of the field. A slight rotation in either direction darkens one half of the field and brightens the other half.

In another form of "half-shade" polarimeter, invented by Poynting, the half-wave plate of the Laurent is dispensed with, a small rotation of one half of the field with respect to the other half being obtained by quartz (cut perpendicularly to the axis) or by syrup. In the simplest construction the syrup is contained in a small cell with parallel glass sides, and the division into two parts is effected by the insertion of a small piece of plate glass about $\frac{3}{16}$ inch thick, a straight edge of which forms the dividing line. If the syrup be strong, the difference of thickness of $\frac{3}{16}$ inch gives a relative rotation of about 2°. In this arrangement the sugar cell is a fixture, and only the Nicol rotates. The reading of the divided circle corresponds to the mean of the planes for the two halves of the field, and this of course differs from the original position of the plane before entering the sugar. This circumstance is usually of no importance, the object being to determine the *rotation* of the plane of polarization when some of the conditions are altered.

A discussion of the accuracy obtainable in polarimetry will be found in a recent paper by Lippich.[1]

Soleil's apparatus.

In Soleil's apparatus, designed for practical use in the estimation of the strength of sugar solutions, the rotation due to the sugar is compensated by a wedge of quartz. Two wedges, one of right-handed and the other of left-handed quartz, may be fitted together, so that a movement of the combination in either direction increases the thickness of one variety traversed and diminishes that of the other. The linear movement required to compensate the introduction of a tube of syrup measures the quantity of sugar present.

§ 24. *Dynamical Theory of Diffraction.*

The explanation of diffraction phenomena given by Fresnel and his followers is independent of special views as to the nature of the ether, at least in its main features; for in the absence of a more complete foundation it is impossible to treat rigorously the mode of action of a solid obstacle such as a screen. The full solution of problems of this kind is scarcely to be expected. Even in the much simpler case of sound, where we know what we have to deal with, the mathematical difficulties are formidable; and we are not able to solve even such an apparently elementary question as the transmission of sound past a rigid infinitely thin plane screen, bounded by a straight edge, or perforated with a circular aperture. But, without entering upon matters of this kind, we may inquire in what manner a primary wave may be resolved into elementary secondary waves, and in particular as to the law of intensity and polarization in a secondary wave as dependent upon its direction of propagation, and upon the character as regards polarization of the primary wave. This question is treated by Stokes in his "Dynamical Theory of Diffraction"[2] on the basis of the elastic solid theory.

Equations for elastic solid.

Let x, y, z be the coordinates of any particle of the medium in its natural state, and ξ, η, ζ the displacements of the same particle at the end of time t, measured in the directions of the three axes respectively. Then the first of the equations of motion may be put under the form

$$\frac{d^2\xi}{dt^2}=b^2\left(\frac{d^2\xi}{dx^2}+\frac{d^2\xi}{dy^2}+\frac{d^2\xi}{dz^2}\right)+(a^2-b^2)\frac{d}{dx}\left(\frac{d\xi}{dx}+\frac{d\eta}{dy}+\frac{d\zeta}{dz}\right),$$

where a^2 and b^2 denote the two arbitrary constants. Put for shortness

$$\frac{d\xi}{dx}+\frac{d\eta}{dy}+\frac{d\zeta}{dz}=\delta \quad . \quad . \quad . \quad . \quad . \quad . \quad . \quad . \quad (1),$$

and represent by $\nabla^2\xi$ the quantity multiplied by b^2. According to this notation, the three equations of motion are

$$\left.\begin{aligned}\frac{d^2\xi}{dt^2}&=b^2\nabla^2\xi+(a^2-b^2)\frac{d\delta}{dx}\\ \frac{d^2\eta}{dt^2}&=b^2\nabla^2\eta+(a^2-b^2)\frac{d\delta}{dy}\\ \frac{d^2\zeta}{dt^2}&=b^2\nabla^2\zeta+(a^2-b^2)\frac{d\delta}{dz}\end{aligned}\right\} \quad . \quad . \quad . \quad . \quad . \quad (2).$$

It is to be observed that δ denotes the dilatation of volume of the element situated at (x, y, z). In the limiting case in which the medium is regarded as absolutely incompressible δ vanishes; but, in order that equations (2) may preserve their generality, we must suppose a at the same time to become infinite, and replace $a^2\delta$ by a new function of the coordinates.

Plane waves.

These equations simplify very much in their application to plane waves. If the ray be parallel to OX, and the direction of vibration parallel to OZ, we have $\xi=0$, $\eta=0$, while ζ is a function of x and t only. Equation (1) and the first pair of equations (2) are thus satisfied identically. The third equation gives

$$\frac{d^2\zeta}{dt^2}=b^2\frac{d^2\zeta}{dx^2} \quad . \quad . \quad . \quad . \quad . \quad . \quad . \quad . \quad (3),$$

of which the solution is

$$\zeta=f(bt-x) \quad . \quad . \quad . \quad . \quad . \quad . \quad . \quad . \quad (4)$$

where f is an arbitrary function.

Stokes's law of secondary wave.

The question as to the law of the secondary waves is thus answered by Stokes. "Let $\xi=0$, $\eta=0$, $\zeta=f(bt-x)$ be the displacements corresponding to the incident light; let O_1 be any point in the plane P (of the wave-front), dS an element of that plane adjacent to O_1; and consider the disturbance due to that portion only of the incident disturbance which passes continually across dS. Let O be any point in the medium situated at a distance from the point O_1 which is large in comparison with the length of a wave; let $O_1O=r$, and let this line make an angle θ with the direction of propagation of the incident light, or the axis of x, and ϕ with the direction of vibration, or axis of z. Then the displacement at O will take place in a direction perpendicular to O_1O, and lying in the plane ZO_1O; and, if ζ' be the displacement at O, reckoned positive in the direction nearest to that in which the incident vibrations are reckoned positive,

$$\zeta'=\frac{dS}{4\pi r}(1+\cos\theta)\sin\phi f'(bt-r).$$

In particular, if

$$f(bt-x)=c\sin\frac{2\pi}{\lambda}(bt-x) \quad . \quad . \quad . \quad . \quad . \quad (5),$$

we shall have

$$\zeta'=\frac{c\,dS}{2\lambda r}(1+\cos\theta)\sin\phi\cos\frac{2\pi}{\lambda}(bt-r). \quad . \quad . \quad (6)."$$

It is then verified that, after integration with respect to dS, (6) gives the same disturbance as if the primary wave had been supposed to pass on unbroken.

The occurrence of $\sin\phi$ as a factor in (6) shows that the relative intensities of the primary light and of that diffracted in the direction θ depend upon the condition of the former as regards polarization. If the direction of primary vibration be perpendicular to the plane of diffraction (containing both primary and secondary rays), $\sin\phi=1$; but, if the primary vibration be in the plane of diffraction, $\sin\phi=\cos\theta$. This result was employed by Stokes as a criterion of the direction of vibration; and his experiments, conducted with gratings, led him to the conclusion that the vibrations of polarized light are executed in a direction *perpendicular* to the plane of polarization.

The factor $(1+\cos\theta)$ shows in what manner the secondary disturbance depends upon the direction in which it is propagated with respect to the front of the primary wave.

Analogy of sound.

If, as suffices for all practical purposes, we limit the application of the formulæ to points in advance of the plane at which the wave is supposed to be broken up, we may use simpler methods of resolution than that above considered. It appears indeed that the purely mathematical question has no definite answer. In illustration of this the analogous problem for sound may be referred to. Imagine a flexible lamina to be introduced so as to coincide with the plane at which resolution is to be effected. The introduction of the lamina (supposed to be devoid of inertia) will make no difference to the propagation of plane parallel sonorous waves through the position which it occupies. At every point the motion of the lamina will be the same as would have occurred in its absence, the pressure of the waves impinging from behind being just what is required to generate the waves in front. Now it is evident that the aerial motion in front of the lamina is determined by what happens at the lamina without regard to the cause of the motion there existing. Whether the necessary forces are due to aerial pressures acting on the rear, or to forces directly impressed from without, is a matter of indifference. The conception of the lamina leads immediately to two schemes, according to which a primary wave may be supposed to be broken up. In the first of these the element dS, the effect of which is to be estimated, is supposed to execute its actual motion, while every other element of the plane lamina is maintained at rest. The resulting aerial motion in front is readily calculated;[3] it is symmetrical with respect to the origin, *i.e.*, independent of θ. When the secondary disturbance thus obtained is integrated with respect to dS over the entire plane of the lamina, the result is necessarily the same as would have been obtained had the primary wave been supposed to pass on without resolution, for this is precisely the motion generated when every element of the lamina vibrates with a common motion, equal to that attributed to dS. The only assumption here involved is the evidently legitimate one that, when two systems of variously distri-

[1] *Wien. Ber.*, lxxxv., 9th Feb. 1882. See also *Phil. Trans.*, 1885, p. 360.
[2] *Camb. Phil. Trans.*, vol. ix. p. 1; reprint, vol. ii. p. 243.
[3] *Theory of Sound*, § 278.

buted motion at the lamina are superposed, the corresponding motions in front are superposed also.

Various methods of resolution.

The method of resolution just described is the simplest, but it is only one of an indefinite number that might be proposed, and which are all equally legitimate, so long as the question is regarded as a merely mathematical one, without reference to the physical properties of actual screens. If, instead of supposing the *motion* at dS to be that of the primary wave, and to be zero elsewhere, we suppose the *force* operative over the element dS of the lamina to be that corresponding to the primary wave, and to vanish elsewhere, we obtain a secondary wave following quite a different law.[1] In this case the motion in different directions varies as $\cos\theta$, vanishing at right angles to the direction of propagation of the primary wave. Here again, on integration over the entire lamina, the aggregate effect of the secondary waves is necessarily the same as that of the primary.

Impressed force.

In order to apply these ideas to the investigation of the secondary wave of light, we require the solution of a problem, first treated by Stokes,[2] viz., the determination of the motion in an infinitely extended elastic solid due to a locally applied periodic force. If we suppose that the force impressed upon the element of mass $D\,dx\,dy\,dz$ is

$$DZ\,dx\,dy\,dz\,,$$

being everywhere parallel to the axis of Z, the only change required in our equations (1), (2) is the addition of the term Z to the second member of the third equation (2). In the forced vibration, now under consideration, Z, and the quantities ξ, η, ζ, δ expressing the resulting motion, are to be supposed proportional to e^{int}, where $i=\sqrt{(-1)}$, and $n=2\pi/\tau$, τ being the periodic time. Under these circumstances the double differentiation with respect to t of any quantity is equivalent to multiplication by the factor $-n^2$, and thus our equations take the form

$$\left.\begin{array}{l}(b^2\nabla^2+n^2)\xi+(a^2-b^2)\dfrac{d\delta}{dx}=0\\[2ex](b^2\nabla^2+n^2)\eta+(a^2-b^2)\dfrac{d\delta}{dy}=0\\[2ex](b^2\nabla^2+n^2)\zeta+(a^2-b^2)\dfrac{d\delta}{dz}=-Z\end{array}\right\}\quad\ldots\quad(7).$$

It will now be convenient to introduce the quantities ϖ_1, ϖ_2, ϖ_3, which express the *rotations* of the elements of the medium round axes parallel to those of coordinates, in accordance with the equations

$$\varpi_3=\frac{d\xi}{dy}-\frac{d\eta}{dx},\quad \varpi_1=\frac{d\eta}{dz}-\frac{d\zeta}{dy},\quad \varpi_2=\frac{d\zeta}{dx}-\frac{d\xi}{dz}\quad\ldots\quad(8).$$

In terms of these we obtain from (7), by differentiation and subtraction,

$$\left.\begin{array}{l}(b^2\nabla^2+n^2)\varpi_3=0\\(b^2\nabla^2+n^2)\varpi_1=dZ/dy\\(b^2\nabla^2+n^2)\varpi_2=-dZ/dx\end{array}\right\}\quad\ldots\quad(9).$$

The first of equations (9) gives

$$\varpi_3=0\quad\ldots\quad(10).$$

For ϖ_1 we have

$$\varpi_1=-\frac{1}{4\pi b^2}\iiint\frac{dZ}{dy}\frac{e^{-ikr}}{r}\,dx\,dy\,dz\quad\ldots\quad(11),^3$$

where r is the distance between the element $dx\,dy\,dz$ and the point where ϖ_1 is estimated, and

$$k=n/b=2\pi/\lambda\quad\ldots\quad(12),$$

λ being the wave length.

Force locally applied.

We will now introduce the supposition that the force Z acts only within a small space of volume T, situated at (x, y, z), and for simplicity suppose that it is at the origin of coordinates that the rotations are to be estimated. Integrating by parts in (11), we get

$$\int\frac{e^{-ikr}}{r}\frac{dZ}{dy}dy=\left[Z\frac{e^{-ikr}}{r}\right]-\int Z\frac{d}{dy}\left(\frac{e^{-ikr}}{r}\right)dy\,,$$

in which the integrated terms at the limits vanish, Z being finite only within the region T. Thus

$$\varpi_1=\frac{1}{4\pi b^2}\iiint Z\frac{d}{dy}\left(\frac{e^{-ikr}}{r}\right)dx\,dy\,dz.$$

Since the dimensions of T are supposed to be very small in comparison with λ, the factor $\dfrac{d}{dy}\left(\dfrac{e^{-ikr}}{r}\right)$ is sensibly constant; so that, if Z stand for the mean value of Z over the volume T, we may write

$$\varpi_1=\frac{TZ}{4\pi b^2}\cdot\frac{y}{r}\cdot\frac{d}{dr}\left(\frac{e^{-ikr}}{r}\right)\quad\ldots\quad(13).$$

In like manner we find

$$\varpi_2=-\frac{TZ}{4\pi b^2}\cdot\frac{x}{r}\cdot\frac{d}{dr}\left(\frac{e^{-ikr}}{r}\right)\quad\ldots\quad(14).$$

From (10), (13), (14) we see that, as might have been expected, the rotation at any point is about an axis perpendicular both to the direction of the force and to the line joining the point to the source of disturbance. If the resultant rotation be ϖ, we have

$$\varpi=\frac{TZ}{4\pi b^2}\cdot\frac{\sqrt{(x^2+y^2)}}{r}\cdot\frac{d}{dr}\left(\frac{e^{-ikr}}{r}\right)=\frac{TZ\sin\phi}{4\pi b^2}\frac{d}{dr}\left(\frac{e^{-ikr}}{r}\right),$$

ϕ denoting the angle between r and z. In differentiating e^{-ikr}/r with respect to r, we may neglect the term divided by r^2 as altogether insensible, kr being an exceedingly great quantity at any moderate distance from the origin of disturbance. Thus

$$\varpi=\frac{-ik\,.\,TZ\sin\phi}{4\pi b^2}\cdot\frac{e^{-ikr}}{r}\quad\ldots\quad(15),$$

which completely determines the rotation at any point. For a disturbing force of given integral magnitude it is seen to be everywhere about an axis perpendicular to r and the direction of the force, and in magnitude dependent only upon the angle (ϕ) between these two directions and upon the distance (r).

The intensity of light is, however, more usually expressed in terms of the actual displacement in the plane of the wave. This displacement, which we may denote by ζ', is in the plane containing z and r, and perpendicular to the latter. Its connexion with ϖ is expressed by $\varpi=d\zeta'/dr$; so that

$$\zeta'=\frac{TZ\sin\phi}{4\pi b^2}\cdot\frac{e^{i(nt-kr)}}{r}\quad\ldots\quad(16),$$

where the factor e^{int} is restored.

Retaining only the real part of (16), we find, as the result of a local application of force equal to

$$DTZ\cos nt\quad\ldots\quad(17),$$

the disturbance expressed by

Resulting disturbance.

$$\zeta'=\frac{TZ\sin\phi}{4\pi b^2}\cdot\frac{\cos(nt-kr)}{r}\quad\ldots\quad(18).$$

The occurrence of $\sin\phi$ shows that there is no disturbance radiated in the direction of the force, a feature which might have been anticipated from considerations of symmetry.

We will now apply (18) to the investigation of a law of secondary disturbance, when a primary wave

$$\zeta=\sin(nt-kx)\quad\ldots\quad(19)$$

is supposed to be broken up in passing the plane $x=0$. The first step is to calculate the force which represents the reaction between the parts of the medium separated by $x=0$. The force operative upon the positive half is parallel to OZ, and of amount per unit of area equal to

$$-b^2D\,d\zeta/dx=b^2kD\cos nt\,;$$

and to this force acting over the whole of the plane the actual motion on the positive side may be conceived to be due. The secondary disturbance corresponding to the element dS of the plane may be supposed to be that caused by a force of the above magnitude acting over dS and vanishing elsewhere; and it only remains to examine what the result of such a force would be.

Law of secondary wave.

Now it is evident that the force in question, supposed to act upon the positive half only of the medium, produces just double of the effect that would be caused by the same force if the medium were undivided, and on the latter supposition (being also localized at a point) it comes under the head already considered. According to (18), the effect of the force acting at dS parallel to OZ, and of amount equal to

$$2b^2kD\,dS\cos nt\,,$$

will be a disturbance

$$\zeta'=\frac{dS\sin\phi}{\lambda r}\cos(nt-kr)\quad\ldots\quad(20),$$

regard being had to (12). This therefore expresses the secondary disturbance at a distance r and in a direction making an angle ϕ with OZ (the direction of primary vibration) due to the element dS of the wave-front.

Comparison with Stokes's law.

The proportionality of the secondary disturbance to $\sin\phi$ is common to the present law and to that given by Stokes, but here there is no dependence upon the angle θ between the primary and secondary rays. The occurrence of the factor $(\lambda r)^{-1}$, and the necessity of supposing the phase of the secondary wave accelerated by a quarter of an undulation, were first established by Archibald Smith, as the result of a comparison between the primary wave, supposed to pass on without resolution, and the integrated effect of all the secondary waves (§ 10). The occurrence of factors such as $\sin\phi$, or $\frac{1}{2}(1+\cos\theta)$, in the expression of the secondary wave has no influence upon the result of the integration, the effects of all the elements for which the factors differ appreciably from unity being destroyed by mutual interference.

The choice between various methods of resolution, all mathematically admissible, would be guided by physical considerations respecting the mode of action of obstacles. Thus, to refer again to the acoustical analogue in which plane waves are incident upon a perforated rigid screen, the circumstances of the case are best represented by the first method of resolution, leading to symmetrical secondary waves, in which the normal motion is supposed to

[1] *Loc. cit.*, equation (10). [2] *Loc. cit.*, §§ 27–30.

[3] This solution may be verified in the same manner as Poisson's theorem, in which $k=0$.

be zero over the unperforated parts. Indeed, if the aperture is very small, this method gives the correct result, save as to a constant factor. In like manner our present law (20) would apply to the kind of obstruction that would be caused by an actual physical division of the elastic medium, extending over the whole of the area supposed to be occupied by the intercepting screen, but of course not extending to the parts supposed to be perforated. In the present state of our ignorance this law seems to be at least as plausible as any other.

§ 25. *The Diffraction of Light by Small Particles.*

The theory of the diffraction, dispersion, or scattering of light by small particles, as it has variously been called, is of importance, not only from its bearings upon fundamental optical hypotheses, but on account of its application to explain the origin and nature of the light from the sky. The view, suggested by Newton and advocated in more recent times by such authorities as Herschel[1] and Clausius,[2] that the light of the sky is a blue of the first order reflected from aqueous particles, was connected with the then prevalent notion that the suspended moisture of clouds and mists was in the form of vesicles or bubbles. Experiments such as those of Brücke[3] pointed to a different conclusion. When a weak alcoholic solution of mastic is agitated with water, the precipitated gum scatters a blue light, obviously similar in character to that from the sky. Not only would it be unreasonable to attribute a vesicular structure to the mastic, but (as Brücke remarked) the dispersed light is much richer in quality than the blue of the first order. Another point of great importance is well brought out in the experiments of Tyndall[4] upon clouds precipitated by the chemical action of light. Whenever the particles are sufficiently fine, the light emitted laterally is blue in colour, and, in a direction perpendicular to the incident beam, is *completely polarized.*

About the colour there can be no *prima facie* difficulty; for, as soon as the question is raised, it is seen that the standard of linear dimension, with reference to which the particles are called small, is the wave-length of light, and that a given set of particles would (on any conceivable view as to their mode of action) produce a continually increasing disturbance as we pass along the spectrum towards the more refrangible end.

On the other hand, that the direction of complete polarization should be independent of the refracting power of the matter composing the cloud has been considered mysterious. Of course, on the theory of thin plates, this direction would be determined by Brewster's law; but, if the particles of foreign matter are small in all their dimensions, the circumstances are materially different from those under which Brewster's law is applicable.

The investigation of this question upon the elastic solid theory will depend upon how we suppose the solid to vary from one optical medium to another. The slower propagation of light in glass or water than in air or vacuum may be attributed to a greater density, or to a less rigidity, in the former case; or we may adopt the more complicated supposition that both these quantities vary, subject only to the condition which restricts the ratio of velocities to equality with the known refractive index. It will presently appear that the original hypothesis of Fresnel, that the rigidity remains the same in both media, is the only one that can be reconciled with the facts; and we will therefore investigate upon this basis the nature of the secondary waves dispersed by small particles.

Conceive a beam of plane polarized light to move among a number of particles, all small compared with any of the wave-lengths. According to our hypothesis, the foreign matter may be supposed to *load* the æther, so as to increase its *inertia* without altering its resistance to distortion. If the particles were away, the wave would pass on unbroken and no light would be emitted laterally. Even with the particles retarding the motion of the æther, the same will be true if, to counterbalance the increased inertia, suitable forces are caused to act on the æther at all points where the inertia is altered. These forces have the same period and direction as the undisturbed luminous vibrations themselves. The light actually emitted laterally is thus the same as would be caused by forces exactly the opposite of these acting on the medium otherwise free from disturbance, and it only remains to see what the effect of such force would be.

On account of the smallness of the particles, the forces acting throughout the volume of any individual particle are all of the same intensity and direction, and may be considered as a whole. The determination of the motion in the æther, due to the action of a periodic force at a given point, is a problem with which we have recently been occupied (§ 24). But, before applying the solution to a mathematical investigation of the present question, it may be well to consider the matter for a few moments from a more general point of view.

Polarization of diffracted light.

In the first place, there is necessarily a complete symmetry round the direction of the force. The disturbance, consisting of transverse vibrations, is propagated outwards in all directions from the centre; and, in consequence of the symmetry, the direction of vibration in any ray lies in the plane containing the ray and the axis of symmetry; that is to say, the direction of vibration in the scattered or diffracted ray makes with the direction of vibration in the incident or primary ray the least possible angle. The symmetry also requires that the intensity of the scattered light should vanish for the ray which would be propagated along the axis; for there is nothing to distinguish one direction transverse to the ray from another. The application of this is obvious. Suppose, for distinctness of statement, that the primary ray is vertical, and that the plane of vibration is that of the meridian. The intensity of the light scattered by a small particle is constant, and a maximum, for rays which lie in the vertical plane running east and west, while there is *no scattered ray along the north and south line.* If the primary ray is unpolarized, the light scattered north and south is entirely due to that component which vibrates east and west, and is therefore *perfectly polarized,* the direction of its vibration being also east and west. Similarly any other ray scattered horizontally is perfectly polarized, and the vibration is performed in the horizontal plane. In other directions the polarization becomes less and less complete as we approach the vertical.

The observed facts as to polarization are thus readily explained, and the general law connecting the intensity of the scattered light with the wave-length follows almost as easily from considerations of *dimensions.*

Method of dimensions.

The object is to compare the intensities of the incident and scattered light, for these will clearly be proportional. The number (i) expressing the ratio of the two amplitudes is a function of the following quantities:—(T) the volume of the disturbing particle; (r) the distance of the point under consideration from it; (λ) the wave-length; (b) the velocity of propagation of light; (D) and (D′) the original and altered densities: of which the first three depend only upon space, the fourth on space and time, while the fifth and sixth introduce the consideration of mass. Other elements of the problem there are none, except mere numbers and angles, which do not depend upon the fundamental measurements of space, time, and mass. Since the ratio (i), whose expression we seek, is of no dimensions in mass, it follows at once that D and D′ occur only under the form D : D′, which is a simple number and may therefore be disregarded. It remains to find how i varies with T, r, λ, b.

Now, of these quantities, b is the only one depending on time; and therefore, as i is of no dimensions in time, b cannot occur in its expression.

Moreover, since the same amount of energy is propagated across all spheres concentric with the particle, we recognize that i varies as r. It is equally evident that i varies as T, and therefore that it must be proportional to $T/\lambda r$, T being of three dimensions in space. In passing from one part of the spectrum to another, λ is the only quantity which varies, and we have the important law:—

Law of intensities.

When light is scattered by particles which are very small compared with any of the wave-lengths, the ratio of the amplitudes of the vibrations of the scattered and incident lights varies inversely as the square of the wave-length, and the ratio of *intensities* as the inverse fourth power.

The light scattered from small particles is of a much richer blue than the blue of the first order as reflected from a very thin plate. From the general theory (§ 8), or by the method of dimensions, it is easy to prove that in the latter case the intensity varies as λ^{-2}, instead of λ^{-4}.

Intensity of transmitted light.

The principle of energy makes it clear that the light emitted laterally is not a new creation, but only diverted from the main stream. If I represent the intensity of the primary light after traversing a thickness x of the turbid medium, we have

$$dI = -hI\lambda^{-4}dx,$$

where h is a constant independent of λ. On integration,

$$\log(I/I_0) = -h\lambda^{-4}x \quad . \quad . \quad . \quad . \quad . \quad . \quad (1),$$

if I_0 correspond to $x=0$,—a law altogether similar to that of absorption, and showing how the light tends to become yellow and finally red as the thickness of the medium increases.[5]

Captain Abney has found that the above law agrees remarkably well with his observations on the transmission of light through water in which particles of mastic are suspended.[6]

Mathematical investigation.

We may now investigate the mathematical expression for the disturbance propagated in any direction from a small particle upon which a beam of light strikes. Let the particle be at the origin of coordinates, and let the expression for the primary vibration be

$$\zeta = \sin(nt - kx) \quad . \quad . \quad . \quad . \quad . \quad . \quad . \quad (2).$$

The acceleration of the element at the origin is $-n^2 \sin nt$; so that the force which would have to be applied to the parts where the density is D′ (instead of D), in order that the waves might pass on undisturbed, is per unit of volume,

$$-(D' - D)n^2 \sin nt.$$

[1] Article "Light," *Enc. Metrop.*, 1830, § 1143.
[2] *Pogg. Ann.*, vols. lxxii., lxxvi., lxxxviii.; Crelle, vols. xxxiv., xxxvi.
[3] *Pogg. Ann.*, vol. lxxxiii.
[4] *Phil. Mag.* [4], vol. cxxxvii. p. 388.
[5] "On the Light from the Sky, its Polarization and Colour," *Phil. Mag.*, Feb. 1871.
[6] *Proc. Roy. Soc.*, May 1886.

To obtain the total force which must be supposed to act, the factor T (representing the volume of the particle) must be introduced. The opposite of this, conceived to act at O, would give the same disturbance as is actually caused by the presence of the particle. Thus by (18) (§ 24) the secondary disturbance is expressed by

$$\zeta' = \frac{D'-D}{D}\frac{n^2 T \sin\phi}{4\pi b^2}\frac{\sin(nt-kr)}{r}$$

$$= \frac{D'-D}{D}\frac{\pi T \sin\phi}{\lambda^2 r}\sin(nt-kr) \quad . \quad . \quad . \quad . \quad . \quad (3).^1$$

The preceding investigation is based upon the assumption that in passing from one medium to another the rigidity of the æther does not change. If we forego this assumption, the question is necessarily more complicated; but, on the supposition that the changes of rigidity (ΔN) and of density (ΔD) are relatively small, the results are fairly simple. If the primary wave be represented by

$$\zeta = e^{-ikx} \quad . \quad . \quad . \quad . \quad . \quad . \quad . \quad . \quad (4),$$

General expressions.

the component rotations in the secondary wave are

$$\left.\begin{aligned} \varpi_3 &= P\left(-\frac{\Delta N}{N}\frac{yz}{r^2}\right), \\ \varpi_1 &= P\left(\frac{\Delta D}{D}\frac{y}{r} + \frac{\Delta N}{N}\frac{xy}{r^2}\right), \\ \varpi_2 &= P\left(-\frac{\Delta D}{D}\frac{x}{r} + \frac{\Delta N}{N}\frac{z^2-x^2}{r^2}\right) \end{aligned}\right\} \quad . \quad . \quad . \quad . \quad (5),$$

where

$$P = \frac{ik^3 T}{4\pi}\frac{e^{-ikr}}{r} \quad . \quad . \quad . \quad . \quad . \quad . \quad . \quad (6).$$

The expression for the resultant rotation in the general case would be rather complicated, and is not needed for our purpose. It is easily seen to be about an axis perpendicular to the scattered ray (x, y, z), inasmuch as

$$x\varpi_1 + y\varpi_2 + z\varpi_3 = 0.$$

Either ΔN or ΔD vanishes.

Let us consider the more special case of a ray scattered normally to the incident ray, so that $x=0$. We have

$$\varpi^2 = \varpi_1^2 + \varpi_2^2 + \varpi_3^2 = P^2\left(\frac{\Delta N}{N}\right)^2\frac{z^2}{r^2} + P^2\left(\frac{\Delta D}{D}\right)^2\frac{y^2}{r^2} \quad . \quad . \quad (7).$$

If ΔN, ΔD be both finite, we learn from (7) that there is no direction perpendicular to the primary (polarized) ray in which the secondary light vanishes. Now experiment tells us plainly that there is such a direction, and therefore we are driven to the conclusion that either ΔN or ΔD must vanish.

The consequences of supposing ΔN to be zero have already been traced. They agree very well with experiment, and require us to suppose that the vibrations are perpendicular to the plane of polarization. So far as (7) is concerned the alternative supposition that ΔD vanishes would answer equally well, if we suppose the vibrations to be executed in the plane of polarization; but let us now revert to (5), which gives

$$\varpi_3 = -\frac{P\Delta N}{N}\frac{yz}{r^2}, \quad \varpi_1 = +\frac{P\Delta N}{N}\frac{xy}{r^2}, \quad \varpi_2 = +\frac{P\Delta N}{N}\frac{z^2-x^2}{r^2} \quad . \quad (8).$$

According to these equations there would be, in all, six directions from O along which there is no scattered light,—two along the axis of y normal to the original ray, and four ($y=0$, $z=\pm x$) at angles of 45° with that ray. So long as the particles are small no such vanishing of light in oblique directions is observed, and we are thus led to the conclusion that the hypothesis of a finite ΔN and of vibrations in the plane of polarization cannot be reconciled with the facts. No form of the elastic solid theory is admissible except that in which the vibrations are supposed to be perpendicular to the plane of polarization, and the difference between one medium and another to be a difference of density only.[2]

ΔN must vanish.

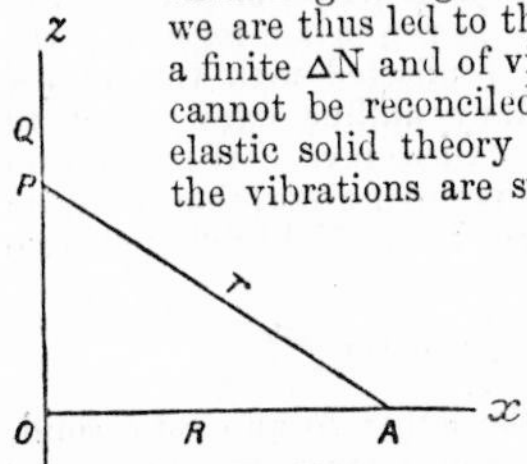

Fig. 26.

Cylindrical obstruction.

Before leaving this subject it may be instructive to show the application of a method, similar to that used for small particles, to the case of an obstructing *cylinder*, whose axis is parallel to the fronts of the primary waves. We will suppose (1) that the variation of optical properties depends upon a difference of density (D′−D), and is small in amount; (2) that the diameter of the cylinder is very small in comparison with the wave-length of light.

Let the axis of the cylinder be the axis of z (fig. 26), and (as before) let the incident light be parallel to x. The original vibration is thus, in the principal cases, parallel to either z or y. We will take first the former case, where the disturbance due to the cylinder must evidently be symmetrical round OZ and parallel to it. The element of the disturbance at A, due to PQ(dz), will be proportional to dz in amplitude, and will be retarded in phase by an amount corresponding to the distance r. In calculating the effect of the whole bar we have to consider the integral

$$\int_0^\infty \frac{dz}{r}\sin(nt-kr) = \int_R^\infty \frac{dr\sin(nt-kr)}{\sqrt{(r^2-R^2)}}.$$

The integral on the left may be treated as in § 15, and we find

$$\int_{-\infty}^{\infty} r^{-1}\sin(nt-kr)dz = \sqrt{(\lambda/R)}\sin(nt-kR-\tfrac{1}{4}\pi),$$

showing that the total effect is retarded $\frac{1}{8}\lambda$ behind that due to the central element at O. We have seen (3) that, if σ be the sectional area, the effect of the element PQ is

$$\frac{D'-D}{D}\frac{\pi\sigma dz\sin\phi}{\lambda^2 r}\sin(nt-kr),$$

where ϕ is the angle OPA. In strictness this should be reckoned perpendicular to PA, and therefore, considered as a contribution to the resultant at A, should be multiplied by $\sin\phi$. But the factor $\sin^2\phi$, being sensibly equal to unity for the only parts which are really operative, may be omitted without influencing the result. In this way we find, for the disturbance at A,

$$\frac{D'-D}{D}\frac{\pi\sigma}{\lambda^{\frac{3}{2}}R^{\frac{1}{2}}}\sin(nt-kR-\tfrac{1}{4}\pi) \quad . \quad . \quad . \quad . \quad (9),$$

corresponding to the incident wave $\sin(nt-kx)$.

When the original vibration is parallel to y, the disturbance due to the cylinder will no longer be symmetrical about OZ. If a be the angle between OX and the scattered ray, which is of course always perpendicular to OZ, it is only necessary to introduce the factor $\cos a$ in order to make the previous expression (9) applicable.

The investigation shows that the light diffracted by an ideal wire-grating would, according to the principles of Fresnel, follow the law of polarization enunciated by Stokes. On the other hand, this law would be departed from were we to suppose that there is any difference of rigidity between the cylinder and the surrounding medium.

§ 26. *Reflexion and Refraction.*

So far as the directions of the rays are concerned, the laws of reflexion and refraction were satisfactorily explained by Huygens on the principles of the wave theory. The question of the *amount* of light reflected, as dependent upon the characters of the media and upon the angle of incidence, is a much more difficult one, and cannot be dealt with *a priori* without special hypotheses as to the nature of the luminous vibrations, and as to the cause of the difference between various media. By a train of reasoning, not strictly dynamical, but of great ingenuity, Fresnel was led to certain formulæ, since known by his name, expressing the ratio of the reflected to the incident vibration in terms of one constant (μ). If θ be the angle of incidence and θ_1 the angle of refraction, Fresnel's expression for light polarized in the plane of incidence is

Fresnel's formulæ.

$$\frac{\sin(\theta-\theta_1)}{\sin(\theta+\theta_1)} \quad . \quad . \quad . \quad . \quad . \quad . \quad . \quad . \quad (1),$$

where the relation between the angles θ, θ_1, and μ (the relative refractive index) is, as usual,

$$\sin\theta = \mu\sin\theta_1 \quad . \quad . \quad . \quad . \quad . \quad . \quad . \quad (2).$$

In like manner, for light polarized perpendicularly to the plane of incidence, Fresnel found

$$\frac{\tan(\theta-\theta_1)}{\tan(\theta+\theta_1)} \quad . \quad . \quad . \quad . \quad . \quad . \quad . \quad . \quad (3).$$

In the particular case of perpendicular incidence, both formulæ coincide with one previously given by Young, viz.,

$$(\mu-1)/(\mu+1) \quad . \quad . \quad . \quad . \quad . \quad . \quad . \quad (4).$$

Since these formulæ agree fairly well with observation, and are at any rate the simplest that can at all represent the facts, it may be advisable to consider their significance a little in detail. As θ increases from 0 to $\frac{1}{2}\pi$, the sine-formula increases from Young's value to unity. We may see this most easily with the aid of a slight transformation:—

$$\frac{\sin(\theta-\theta_1)}{\sin(\theta+\theta_1)} = \frac{1-\tan\theta_1/\tan\theta}{1+\tan\theta_1/\tan\theta} = \frac{\mu-\cos\theta/\cos\theta_1}{\mu+\cos\theta/\cos\theta_1}.$$

Now, writing $\cos\theta/\cos\theta_1$ in the form

$$\sqrt{\left\{\frac{1-\sin^2\theta}{1-\mu^{-2}\sin^2\theta}\right\}},$$

we recognize that, as θ increases from 0 to $\frac{1}{2}\pi$, $\cos\theta/\cos\theta_1$ diminishes continuously from 1 to 0, and therefore (1) increases from $(\mu-1)/(\mu+1)$ to unity.

It is quite otherwise with the tangent-formula. Commencing at Young's value, it diminishes, as θ increases, until it attains zero, when $\theta+\theta_1=\frac{1}{2}\pi$, or $\sin\theta_1=\cos\theta$; or by (2) $\tan\theta=\mu$. This is the polarizing angle defined by Brewster. It presents itself here as the

---

[1] In strictness the force must be supposed to act upon the medium in its actual condition, whereas in (18) the medium is supposed to be absolutely uniform. It is not difficult to prove that (3) remains unaltered, when this circumstance is taken into account; and it is evident in any case that a correction would depend upon the square of (D′−D).

[2] See a paper, "On the Scattering of Light by Small Particles," *Phil. Mag.*, June 1871.

angle of incidence for which there is no reflexion of the polarized light under consideration. As the angle of incidence passes through the polarizing angle, the reflected vibration changes sign, and increases in numerical value until it attains unity at a grazing incidence ($\theta=\frac{1}{2}\pi$).

We have hitherto supposed that the second medium (into which the light enters at the refracting surface) is the denser. In the contrary case, total reflexion sets in as soon as $\sin\theta=\mu^{-1}$, at which point θ_1 becomes imaginary. We shall be able to follow this better in connexion with a mechanical theory.

If light falls upon the first surface of a parallel plate at the polarizing angle, the refracted ray also meets the second surface of the plate at the appropriate polarizing angle. For if μ be the index of the second medium relatively to the first, the tangent of the angle of incidence, which is also the cotangent of the angle of refraction, is equal to μ. At the second surface (the third medium being the same as the first) the angles of incidence and refraction are interchanged, and therefore the condition for the polarizing angle is satisfied, since the index for the second refraction is μ^{-1}.

Oblique polarization.

The principal formulæ apply to light polarized in, and perpendicular to, the plane of incidence. If the plane of polarization make an angle α with that of incidence, the original vibration may be resolved into two,—$\cos\alpha$ polarized in the plane of incidence, and $\sin\alpha$ polarized in the perpendicular plane. These components are reflected according to the laws already considered, and reconstitute plane-polarized light, of intensity

$$\cos^2\alpha\frac{\sin^2(\theta-\theta_1)}{\sin^2(\theta+\theta_1)}+\sin^2\alpha\frac{\tan^2(\theta-\theta_1)}{\tan^2(\theta+\theta_1)} \quad . \quad . \quad . \quad (5).$$

If the incident light be polarized in a plane making 45° with the plane of incidence, or be circularly-polarized (§ 20), or be unpolarized, (5) applies to the reflected light, with substitution of $\frac{1}{2}$ for $\cos^2\alpha$ and $\sin^2\alpha$. If β denote in the general case the angle between the plane of incidence and that in which the reflected light is polarized,

$$\tan\beta=\tan\alpha\frac{\cos(\theta+\theta_1)}{\cos(\theta-\theta_1)} \quad . \quad . \quad . \quad . \quad . \quad . \quad (6),$$

a result the approximate truth of which has been verified by Fresnel and Brewster.

Reflected rays.

The formulæ for the intensities of the refracted light follow immediately from the corresponding formulæ relative to the reflected light in virtue of the principle of energy. The simplest way to regard the matter is to suppose the refracted light to emerge from the second medium into a third medium similar to the first without undergoing loss from a second reflexion, a supposition which would be realized if the transition between the two media were very gradual instead of abrupt. The intensities of the different lights may then be measured in the same way; and the supposition that no loss of energy is incurred when the incident light gives rise to the reflected and refracted lights requires that the sum of the squares of the vibrations representing the latter shall be equal to the square of the vibration representing the former, viz., unity. We thus obtain, in the two cases corresponding to (1) and (3),

$$1-\frac{\sin^2(\theta-\theta_1)}{\sin^2(\theta+\theta_1)}=\frac{\sin 2\theta\sin 2\theta_1}{\sin^2(\theta+\theta_1)} \quad . \quad . \quad . \quad . \quad . \quad . \quad (7),$$

$$1-\frac{\tan^2(\theta-\theta_1)}{\tan^2(\theta+\theta_1)}=\frac{\sin 2\theta\sin 2\theta_1}{\sin^2(\theta+\theta_1)\cos^2(\theta-\theta_1)} \quad . \quad . \quad . \quad (8).$$

A plate of glass, or a pile of parallel plates, is often convenient as a polarizer, when it is not necessary that the polarization be quite complete. At the precise angle of incidence ($\tan^{-1}\mu$) there would be, according to Fresnel's formulæ, only one kind of polarized light reflected, even when the incident light is unpolarized. The polarization of the transmitted light, on the other hand, is imperfect; but it improves as the number of plates is increased.

Reflexion by a plate.

If we suppose that there is no regular interference, the intensity (r) of the light reflected from a plate is readily calculated by a geometric series when the intensity (ρ) of the light reflected from a single surface is known. The light reflected from the first surface is ρ. That transmitted by the first surface, reflected at the second, and then transmitted at the first, is $\rho(1-\rho)^2$. The next component, reflected three times and transmitted twice, is $\rho^3(1-\rho)^2$, and so on. Hence

$$r=\rho+(1-\rho)^2\{\rho+\rho^3+\rho^5+\ldots\}=\frac{2\rho}{1+\rho} \quad . \quad . \quad . \quad (9).$$

Pile of plates.

The intensity of the light reflected from a pile of plates has been investigated by Provostaye and Desains.[1] If $\phi(m)$ be the reflexion from m plates, we may find as above for the reflexion from $(m+1)$ plates,

$$\phi(m+1)=r+(1-r)^2\phi(m)\{1+r\phi(m)+r^2[\phi(m)]^2+r^3[\phi(m)]^3+\ldots\}$$
$$=\frac{r+(1-2r)\phi(m)}{1-r\phi(m)}$$

By means of this expression we may obtain in succession the values of $\phi(2)$, $\phi(3)$, &c., in terms of $\phi(1)$, viz., r. The general value is

$$\phi(m)=\frac{mr}{1+(m-1)r} \quad . \quad . \quad . \quad . \quad . \quad . \quad (10),$$

as may easily be verified by substitution.

The corresponding expression for the light *transmitted* by a pile of m plates is

$$\psi(m)=1-\phi(m)=\frac{1-r}{1+(m-1)r} \quad . \quad . \quad . \quad . \quad (11).$$

The investigation has been extended by Stokes so as to cover the case in which the plates exercise an absorbing influence.[2]

The verification of Fresnel's formulæ by direct photometric measurement is a matter of some difficulty. The proportion of perpendicularly incident light transmitted by a glass plate has been investigated by Rood;[3] but the deficiency may have been partly due to absorption. If we attempt to deal directly with the reflected light, the experimental difficulties are much increased; but the evidence is in favour of the approximate correctness of Fresnel's formulæ when light is reflected nearly perpendicularly from a recently polished glass surface. When the surface is old, even though carefully cleaned, there may be a considerable falling off of reflecting power.[4]

We have seen that according to Fresnel's tangent-formula there would be absolutely no reflexion of light polarized perpendicularly to the plane of incidence, when the angle of incidence is $\tan^{-1}\mu$, or, which comes to the same thing, common light reflected at this angle could be perfectly extinguished with a Nicol's prism.

It was first observed by Airy that in the case of the diamond and other highly refracting media this law is only approximately in accordance with the facts. It is readily proved by experiment that, whatever be the angle of incidence, sunlight reflected from a plate of black glass is incapable of being quenched by a Nicol, and is therefore imperfectly plane-polarized.

Jamin's observations.

This subject has been studied by Jamin. The character of the reflected vibration can be represented, as regards both amplitude and phase, by the situation in a plane of a point P relatively to the origin of coordinates O. The length of the line OP represents the amplitude, while the inclination of OP to the axis of x represents the phase. According to Fresnel's formula appropriate to light polarized perpendicularly to the plane of incidence, P is situated throughout on the axis of x, passing through O when the angle of incidence is $\tan^{-1}\mu$. Jamin found, however, that in general P does not pass through O, but above or below it. When P is on the axis of y, the amplitude is a minimum, and the phase is midway between the extreme phases. For one class of bodies the phase is in arrear of that corresponding to perpendicular incidence, and for another class of bodies in advance. In a few intermediate cases P passes sensibly through O; and then the change of phase is sudden, and the minimum amplitude is zero.

Metallic reflexion.

In the case of metals the polarization produced by reflexion is still more incomplete. Light polarized perpendicularly to the plane of incidence is reflected at all angles, the amount, however, decreasing as the angle of incidence increases from 0° to about 75°, and then again increasing up to a grazing incidence. The most marked effect is the relative retardation of one polarized component with respect to the other. At an angle of about 75° this retardation amounts to a quarter period.

The intensity of reflexion from metals is often very high. From silver, even at perpendicular incidence, as much as 95 per cent. of the incident light is reflected. There is reason for regarding the high reflecting power of metals as connected with the intense absorption which they exercise. Many aniline dyes reflect in abnormal proportion from their surface those rays of the spectrum to which they are most opaque. The peculiar absorption spectrum of permanganate of potash is reproduced in the light reflected from a surface of a crystal.[5]

§ 27. *Reflexion on the Elastic Solid Theory.*

On the theory which assimilates the æther to an elastic solid, the investigation of reflexion and refraction presents no very serious difficulties, but the results do not harmonize very well with optical observation. It is, however, of some importance to understand that reflexion and refraction can be explained, at least in their principal features, on a perfectly definite and intelligible theory, which, if not strictly applicable to the æther, has at any rate a distinct mechanical significance. The refracting surface and the wave-fronts may for this purpose be supposed to be plane.

Vibrations perpendicular to plane of incidence.

When the vibrations are perpendicular to the plane of incidence ($z=0$), the solution of the problem is very simple. We suppose that the refracting surface is $x=0$, the rigidity and density in the first medium being N, D, and in the second N_1, D_1. The displace-

[1] *Ann. d. Chim.* xxx. p. 159, 1850.

[2] *Proc. Roy. Soc.*, xi. p. 545, 1862.

[3] *Am. Jour.*, vol. l., July 1870.

[4] "On the Intensity of Light reflected from Certain Surfaces at nearly Perpendicular Incidence," *Proc. Roy. Soc.*, 1886.

[5] Stokes, "On the Metallic Reflection exhibited by Certain Non-Metallic Substances," *Phil. Mag.*, Dec. 1853.

ments in the two media are in general denoted by $\xi, \eta, \zeta; \xi_1, \eta_1, \zeta_1$; but in the present case ξ, η, ξ_1, η_1 all vanish. Moreover ζ, ζ_1 are independent of z. The equations to be satisfied in the interior of the media are accordingly (§ 24)

$$\frac{d^2\zeta}{dt^2}=\frac{N}{D}\left(\frac{d^2\zeta}{dx^2}+\frac{d^2\zeta}{dy^2}\right) \quad \ldots \quad (1),$$

$$\frac{d^2\zeta_1}{dt^2}=\frac{N_1}{D_1}\left(\frac{d^2\zeta_1}{dx^2}+\frac{d^2\zeta_1}{dy^2}\right) \quad \ldots \quad (2).$$

At the boundary the conditions to be satisfied are the continuity of displacement and of stress; so that, when $x=0$,

$$\zeta=\zeta_1, \quad N\frac{d\zeta}{dx}=N_1\frac{d\zeta_1}{dx} \quad \ldots \quad (3).$$

The incident waves may be represented by

$$\zeta=e^{i(ax+by+ct)}$$

where

$$Dc^2=N(a^2+b^2) \quad \ldots \quad (4);$$

and $ax+by=$const. gives the equation of the wave-fronts. The reflected and refracted waves may be represented by

$$\zeta=\zeta' e^{i(-ax+by+ct)} \quad \ldots \quad (5),$$

$$\zeta_1=\zeta_1' e^{i(a_1x+by+ct)} \quad \ldots \quad (6).$$

The coefficient of t is necessarily the same in all three waves on account of the periodicity, and the coefficient of y must be the same since the traces of all the waves upon the plane of separation must move together. With regard to the coefficient of x, it appears by substitution in the differential equations that its sign is changed in passing from the incident to the reflected wave; in fact

$$c^2=V^2\{(\pm a)^2+b^2\}=V_1^2\{a_1^2+b^2\} \quad \ldots \quad (7),$$

where V, V_1 are the velocities of propagation in the two media given by

$$V^2=N/D, \quad V_1^2=N_1/D_1 \quad \ldots \quad (8).$$

Now $b/\sqrt{(a^2+b^2)}$ is the sine of the angle included between the axis of x and the normal to the plane of waves—in optical language, the sine of the angle of incidence—and $b/\sqrt{(a_1^2+b^2)}$ is in like manner the sine of the angle of refraction. If these angles be denoted (as before) by θ, θ_1, (7) asserts that $\sin\theta : \sin\theta_1$ is equal to the constant ratio $V : V_1$, the well-known law of sines. The laws of reflexion and refraction follow simply from the fact that the velocity of propagation normal to the wave-fronts is constant in each medium, that is to say, independent of the *direction* of the wave-front, taken in connexion with the equal velocities of the traces of all the waves on the plane of separation ($V/\sin\theta = V_1/\sin\theta_1$).

The boundary conditions (3) now give

$$1+\zeta'=\zeta_1', \quad Na(1-\zeta')=N_1a_1\zeta_1' \quad \ldots \quad (9),$$

whence

$$\zeta'=\frac{Na-N_1a_1}{Na+N_1a_1} \quad \ldots \quad (10),$$

Realized expressions. a formula giving the reflected wave in terms of the incident wave (supposed to be unity). This completes the symbolical solution. If a_1 (and θ_1) be real, we see that, if the incident wave be

$$\zeta=\cos(ax+by+ct),$$

or in terms of V, λ, and θ,

$$\zeta=\cos\frac{2\pi}{\lambda}(x\cos\theta+y\sin\theta+Vt) \quad \ldots \quad (11),$$

the reflected wave is

$$\zeta=\frac{N\cot\theta-N_1\cot\theta_1}{N\cot\theta+N_1\cot\theta_1}\cos\frac{2\pi}{\lambda}(-x\cos\theta+y\sin\theta+Vt) \quad . \quad (12).$$

The formula for intensity of the reflected wave is here obtained on the supposition that the waves are of harmonic type; but, since it does not involve λ and there is no change of phase, it may be extended by Fourier's theorem to waves of any type whatever. It may be remarked that when the first and second media are interchanged the coefficient in (12) simply changes sign, retaining its numerical value.

Alternative suppositions. The amplitude of the reflected wave, given in general by (12), assumes special forms when we introduce more particular suppositions as to the nature of the difference between media of diverse refracting power. According to Fresnel and Green the rigidity does not vary, or $N=N_1$. In this case

$$\frac{N\cot\theta-N_1\cot\theta_1}{N\cot\theta+N_1\cot\theta}=\frac{\cot\theta-\cot\theta_1}{\cot\theta+\cot\theta_1}=\frac{\sin(\theta_1-\theta)}{\sin(\theta_1+\theta)}.$$

If, on the other hand, the density is the same in various media,

$$N_1 : N = V_1^2 : V^2 = \sin^2\theta_1 : \sin^2\theta,$$

and then

$$\frac{N\cot\theta-N_1\cot\theta_1}{N\cot\theta+N_1\cot\theta_1}=\frac{\tan(\theta_1-\theta)}{\tan(\theta_1+\theta)}.$$

If we assume the complete accuracy of Fresnel's expressions, either alternative agrees with observation; only, if $N=N_1$, light must be supposed to vibrate normally to the plane of polarization; while, if $D=D_1$, the vibrations are parallel to that plane.

An intermediate supposition, according to which the refraction is regarded as due partly to a difference of density and partly to a difference of rigidity, could scarcely be reconciled with observation, unless one variation were very subordinate to the other. But the most satisfactory argument against the joint variation is that derived from the theory of the diffraction of light by small particles (§ 25).

Total reflexion. We will now, limiting ourselves for simplicity to Fresnel's supposition ($N_1=N$), inquire into the character of the solution when total reflexion sets in. The symbolical expressions for the reflected and refracted waves are

$$\zeta=\frac{a-a_1}{a+a_1}e^{i(-ax+by+ct)} \quad \ldots \quad (13),$$

$$\zeta_1=\frac{2a}{a+a_1}e^{i(a_1x+by+ct)} \quad \ldots \quad (14),$$

and so long as a_1 is real they may be intrepreted to indicate

$$\zeta=\frac{a-a_1}{a+a_1}\cos(-ax+by+ct) \quad \ldots \quad (15),$$

$$\zeta_1=\frac{2a}{a+a_1}\cos(a_1x+by+ct) \quad \ldots \quad (16),$$

corresponding to the incident wave

$$\zeta=\cos(ax+by+ct) \quad \ldots \quad (17).$$

In this case there is a refracted wave of the ordinary kind, conveying away a part of the original energy. When, however, the second medium is the rarer ($V_1>V$), and the angle of incidence exceeds the so-called critical angle [$\sin^{-1}(V/V_1)$], there can be no refracted wave of the ordinary kind. In whatever direction it may be supposed to lie, its trace must necessarily outrun the trace of the incident wave upon the separating surface. The quantity a_1, as defined by our equations, is then imaginary, so that (13) and (14) no longer express the real parts of the symbolical expressions (5) and (6).

If $-ia_1'$ be written in place of a_1, the symbolical equations are

$$\zeta=\frac{a+ia_1'}{a-ia_1'}e^{i(-ax+by+ct)}, \quad \zeta_1=\frac{2a}{a-ia_1'}e^{i(-ia_1'x+by+ct)};$$

from which, by discarding the imaginary parts, we obtain

$$\zeta=\cos(-ax+by+ct+2\epsilon) \quad \ldots \quad (18),$$

$$\zeta_1=\frac{2a}{\sqrt{(a^2+a_1'^2)}}e^{a_1'x}\cos(by+ct+\epsilon) \quad \ldots \quad (19),$$

where

$$\tan\epsilon=a_1'/a \quad \ldots \quad (20).$$

Since x is supposed to be negative in the second medium, we see that the disturbance is there confined to a small distance (a few wave-lengths) from the surface, and no energy is propagated into the interior. The whole of the energy of the incident waves is to be found in the reflected waves, or the reflexion is *total*. There is, however, a change of phase of 2ϵ, given by (20), or in terms of V, V_1, and θ

$$\tan\epsilon=\sqrt{\{\tan^2\theta-\sec^2\theta(V^2/V_1^2)\}} \quad \ldots \quad (21).$$

Fresnel's interpretation. The principal application of the formulæ being to reflexions when the second medium is air, it will be convenient to denote by μ the index of the *first* medium *relatively to the second*, so that $\mu=V_1/V$. Thus

$$\tan\epsilon=\sqrt{\{\tan^2\theta-\sec^2\theta/\mu^2\}} \quad \ldots \quad (22).$$

The above interpretation of his formula $\sin(\theta_1-\theta)/\sin(\theta_1+\theta)$, in the case where θ_1 becomes imaginary, is due to the sagacity of Fresnel. His argument was perhaps not set forth with full rigour, but of its substantial validity there can be no question. By a similar process Fresnel deduced from his tangent-formula for the change of phase ($2\epsilon'$) accompanying total reflexion when the vibrations are executed in the plane of incidence,

$$\tan\epsilon'=\mu\sqrt{\{\mu^2\tan^2\theta-\sec^2\theta\}} \quad \ldots \quad (23).$$

The phase-differences represented by 2ϵ and $2\epsilon'$ cannot be investigated experimentally, but the *difference* $(2\epsilon'-2\epsilon)$ is rendered evident when the incident light is polarized obliquely so as to contribute components in both the principal planes. If in the act of reflexion one component is retarded more or less than the other, the resultant light is no longer plane but elliptically polarized.

From (22) and (23) we have

$$\tan(\epsilon'-\epsilon)=\cos\theta\sqrt{\{1-\mu^{-2}\operatorname{cosec}^2\theta\}},$$

whence

$$\cos(2\epsilon'-2\epsilon)=\frac{2\mu^2\sin^4\theta-(1+\mu^2)\sin^2\theta+1}{(1+\mu^2)\sin^2\theta-1} \quad \ldots \quad (24).$$

Difference of phases. The most interesting case occurs when the difference of phase amounts to a quarter of a period, corresponding to light circularly polarized. If, however, we put $\cos(2\epsilon'-2\epsilon)=0$, we find

$$4\mu^2\sin^2\theta=1+\mu^2\pm\sqrt{\{(1+\mu^2)^2-8\mu^2\}},$$

from which it appears that, in order that $\sin\theta$ may be real, μ^2 must exceed $3+\sqrt{8}$. So large a value of μ^2 not being available, the conversion of plane-polarized into circularly-polarized light by one reflexion is impracticable.

The desired object may, however, be attained by two successive reflexions. The angle of incidence may be so accommodated to the index that the alteration of phase amounts to $\frac{1}{8}$ period, in which case a second reflexion under the same conditions will give rise to light circularly polarized. Putting $(2\epsilon - 2\epsilon') = \frac{1}{4}\pi$, we get

$$2\mu^2 \sin^4\theta = (1+\sqrt{\tfrac{1}{2}})\{(1+\mu^2)\sin^2\theta + 1\} \quad . \quad . \quad . \quad (25),$$

an equation by which θ is determined when μ is given.

It appears that, when $\mu = 1{\cdot}51$, $\theta = 48^\circ\ 37'$ or $54^\circ\ 37'$.

Fresnel's rhomb.

These results were verified by Fresnel by means of the rhomb shown in fig. 27.

Vibrations in the plane of incidence.

The problem of reflexion upon the elastic solid theory, when the vibrations are executed in the plane of incidence, is more complicated, on account of the tendency to form waves of dilatation. In order to get rid of these, to which no optical phenomena correspond, it is necessary to follow Green in supposing that the velocity of such waves is infinite, or that the media are incompressible.[1] Even then we have to introduce in the neighbourhood of the interface waves variously called longitudinal, pressural, or surface waves; otherwise it is impossible to satisfy the conditions of continuity of strain and stress. These waves, analogous in this respect to those occurring in the second medium when total reflexion is in progress (19), extend to a depth of a few wave-lengths only, and they are so constituted that there is neither dilatation nor rotation. On account of them the final formulæ are less simple than those of Fresnel. If we suppose the densities to be the same in the two media, there is no correspondence whatever between theory and observation. In this case, as we have seen, vibrations perpendicular to the plane of incidence are reflected according to Fresnel's tangent-formula; and thus vibrations in the plane of incidence should follow the sine-formula. The actual result of theory is, however, quite different. In the case where the relative index does not differ greatly from unity, polarizing angles of $22\frac{1}{2}^\circ$ and $67\frac{1}{2}^\circ$ are indicated, a result totally at variance with observation. As in the case of diffraction by small particles, an elastic solid theory, in which the densities in various media are supposed to be equal, is inadmissible. If, on the other hand, following Green, we regard the rigidities as equal, we get results in better agreement with observation. To a first approximation indeed (when the refraction is small) Green's formula coincides with Fresnel's tangent-formula; so that light vibrating in the plane of incidence is reflected according to this law, and light vibrating in the perpendicular plane according to the sine-formula. The vibrations are accordingly perpendicular to the plane of polarization.

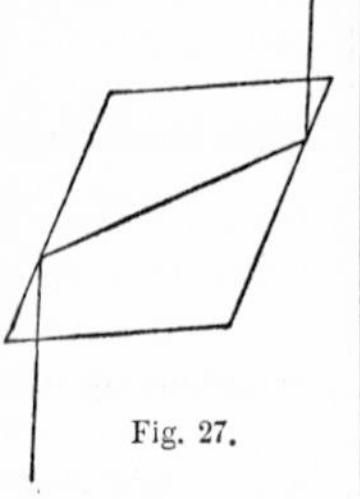

Fig. 27.

Green's formula.

The deviations from the tangent-formula, indicated by theory when the refraction is not very small, are of the same general character as those observed by Jamin, but of much larger amount. The minimum reflexion at the surface of glass ($\mu = \frac{3}{2}$) would be $\frac{1}{49}$,[2] nearly the half of that which takes place at perpendicular incidence, and very much in excess of the truth. This theory cannot therefore be considered satisfactory as it stands, and various suggestions have been made for its improvement. The only variations from Green's suppositions admissible in strict harmony with an elastic solid theory is to suppose that the transition from one medium to the other is gradual instead of abrupt, that is, that the transitional layer is of thickness comparable with the wave-length. This modification would be of more service to a theory which gave Fresnel's tangent-formula as the result of a sudden transition than to one in which the deviations from that formula are already too great.

Reflexion dependent upon discontinuity.

It seems doubtful whether there is much to be gained by further discussion upon this subject, in view of the failure of the elastic solid theory to deal with double refraction. The deviations from Fresnel's formulæ for reflexion are comparatively small; and the whole problem of reflexion is so much concerned with the condition of things at the interface of two media, about which we know little, that valuable guidance can hardly be expected from this quarter. It is desirable to bear constantly in mind that reflexion depends entirely upon an approach to discontinuity in the properties of the medium. If the thickness of the transitional layer amounted to a few wave-lengths, there would be no sensible reflexion at all.

Another point may here be mentioned. Our theories of reflexion take no account of the fact that one at least of the media is dispersive. The example of a stretched string, executing transverse vibrations, and composed of two parts, one of which in virtue of stiffness possesses in some degree the dispersive property, shows that the boundary conditions upon which reflexion depends are thereby modified. We may thus expect a finite reflexion at the interface of two media, if the dispersive powers are different, even though the indices be absolutely the same for the waves under consideration, in which case there is no refraction. But a knowledge of the dispersive properties of the media is not sufficient to determine the reflexion without recourse to hypothesis.[3]

[1] The supposition that the velocity is zero, favoured by some writers, is inadmissible. Even dilatational waves involve a shearing of the medium, and must therefore be propagated at a finite rate, unless the resistance to compression were *negative*. But in that case the equilibrium would be unstable.

[2] Green's *Papers*, by Ferrers, p. 333.

§ 28. *The Velocity of Light.*

No dispersion *in vacuo*.

According to the principles of the wave theory, the dispersion of refraction can only be explained as due to a variation of velocity with wave-length or period. In aerial vibrations, and in those propagated through an elastic solid, there is no such variation; and so the existence of dispersion was at one time considered to be a serious objection to the wave theory. Dispersion *in vacuo* would indeed present some difficulty, or at least force upon us views which at present seem unlikely as to the constitution of free æther. The weight of the evidence is, however, against the existence of dispersion *in vacuo*. "Were there a difference of one hour in the times of the blue and red rays reaching us from Algol, this star would show a well-marked coloration in its phases of increase and decrease. No trace of coloration having been noticed, the difference of times cannot exceed a fraction of an hour. It is not at all probable that the parallax of this star amounts to one-tenth of a second, so that its distance, probably, exceeds two million radii of the earth's orbit, and the time which is required for its light to reach us probably exceeds thirty years, or a quarter of a million hours. It is therefore difficult to see how there can be a difference as great as four parts in a million between the velocities of light coming from near the two ends of the bright part of the spectrum."[4]

Table of velocities.

For the velocity of light *in vacuo*, as determined in kilometres per second by terrestrial methods (LIGHT, vol xiv. p. 585), Newcomb gives the following tabular statement:—

Michelson, at Naval Academy, in 1879	299,910
Michelson, at Cleveland, 1882	299,853
Newcomb at Washington, 1882, using only results supposed to be nearly free from constant errors	299,860
Newcomb, including all determinations	299,810

To these may be added, for reference—

Foucault, at Paris, in 1862	298,000
Cornu, at Paris, in 1874	298,500
Cornu, at Paris, in 1878	300,400
This last result, as discussed by Listing	299,990
Young and Forbes, 1880–1881	301,382

Newcomb concludes, as the most probable result—

Velocity of light *in vacuo* $= 299{,}860 \pm 30$ kilometres.

It should be mentioned that Young and Forbes inferred from their observations a difference of velocities of blue and red light amounting to about 2 per cent., but that neither Michelson nor Newcomb, using Foucault's method, could detect any trace of such a difference.

When we come to consider the propagation of light through ponderable media, there seems to be little reason for expecting to find the velocity independent of wave-length. The interaction of matter and æther may well give rise to such a degree of complication that the differential equation expressing the vibrations shall contain more than one constant. The law of constant velocity is a special property of certain very simple media. Even in the case of a stretched string, vibrating transversely, the velocity becomes a function of wave-length as soon as we admit the existence of finite stiffness.

Formula for dispersion.

As regards the law of dispersion, a formula, derived by Cauchy from theoretical considerations, was at one time generally accepted. According to this,

$$\mu = A + B\lambda^{-2} + C\lambda^{-4} + \quad . \quad . \quad . \quad . \quad . \quad . \quad (1);$$

and there is no doubt that even the first two terms give a good representation of the truth in media not very dispersive, and over the more luminous portion of the spectrum. A formula of this kind treats dispersion as due to the smallness of wave-lengths, giving a definite limit to refraction (A) when the wave-length is very large. Recent investigations by Langley on the law of dispersion for rock-salt in the ultra red region of the spectrum are not very favourable to this idea. The phenomena of abnormal disper-

[3] The reader who desires to pursue this subject may consult Green, "On the Laws of Reflexion and Refraction of Light at the Common Surface of Two Non-Crystallized Media," *Camb. Trans.*, 1838 (Green's *Works*, London, 1871, pp. 242, 283); Lorenz, "Ueber die Reflexion des Lichts an der Gränzfläche zweier isotropen, durchsichtigen Mittel," *Pogg. Ann.*, cxi. p. 460 (1860), and "Bestimmung der Schwingungsrichtung des Lichtæthers durch die Reflexion und Brechung des Lichtes," *ibid.*, cxiv. p. 238 (1861); Strutt (Rayleigh), "On the Reflection of Light from Transparent Matter," *Phil. Mag.*, [4] xiii. (1871); Von der Mühll, "Ueber die Reflexion und Brechung des Lichtes an der Grenze unkrystallinischen Medien," *Math. Ann.*, v. 470 (1872), and "Ueber Greens Theorie der Reflexion und Brechung des Lichtes," *Math. Ann.*, xxvii. 506 (1886); Thomson, *Baltimore Lectures*; Glazebrook, "Report on Optical Theories," *Brit. Ass. Rep.*, 1886; Rayleigh, "On Reflection of Vibrations at the Confines of Two Media between which the Transition is gradual," *Proc. Math. Soc.*, xi.; and Walker, "An Account of Cauchy's Theory of Reflection and Refraction of Light," *Phil. Mag.*, 151 (1887). References to recent German writers, Ketteler, Lommel, Voigt, &c., will be found in Glazebrook's Report.

[4] Newcomb, *Astron. Papers*, vol. ii. parts iii. and iv., Washington, 1885.

sion indicate a close connexion between refraction and absorption, and Helmholtz has formulated a general theory of dispersion based upon the hypothesis that it may be connected with an absorbing influence operative upon invisible portions of the spectrum. Upon this subject, which is as yet little understood, the reader may consult Glazebrook's "Report on Optical Theories."[1]

chel- ı's re- ırches.

The limits of this article do not permit the consideration of the more speculative parts of our subject. We will conclude by calling attention to two recent experimental researches by Michelson, the results of which cannot fail to give valuable guidance to optical theorists. The first of these[2] was a repetition under improved conditions of a remarkable experiment of Fizeau, by which it is proved that when light is propagated through water, itself in rapid movement in the direction of the ray, the velocity is indeed influenced, but not to the full extent of the velocity of the water (v). Within the limits of experimental error, the velocity agrees with a formula suggested by Fizeau on the basis of certain views of Fresnel, viz.,

$$V = V_0 \pm \frac{\mu^2 - 1}{\mu^2} v \quad . \quad . \quad . \quad . \quad . \quad . \quad . \quad (2),$$

V_0 being the velocity when the medium is stationary. In the case of water, $(\mu^2-1)/\mu^2 = \cdot 437$. Conformably with (2), a similar experiment upon air, moving at a velocity of 25 metres per second, gave no distinct effect.

From the result of the experiments upon water we should be tempted to infer that at the surface of the earth, moving through space, the æther still retains what must be coarsely called relative motion. Nevertheless, the second research above alluded to[3] appears to negative this conclusion, and to prove that, at any rate within the walls of a building, the æther must be regarded as fully partaking in the motion of material bodies. (R.)

WAX is a solid fatty substance of animal and vegetable origin, allied both in sources and constitution to the fixed oils and fats. From fats or solid oils wax differs principally in its greater hardness and higher melting-point; but in the strictly chemical sense, while oils and fats are glycerides, a true wax contains no glycerin, but is a combination of fatty acids with certain solid monatomic alcohols. Of wax from animal sources there are in commerce beeswax, which forms wax *par excellence*, Chinese insect wax, and spermaceti. The more important vegetable waxes are Japanese wax, myrtle-berry wax, carnauba wax, and palm wax.

Beeswax is secreted by all honey bees, and by them formed into the cell walls, &c., of their comb. It is separated by draining the honey, melting the drained comb in boiling water, and collecting the wax which solidifies on the top as the water cools. In this state it is formed into cakes of raw or yellow wax, good examples of which are of a light yellow colour, translucent, with a faint pleasant odour of honey. At ordinary temperatures it breaks with a granular fracture; and in thin flakes or pellets it softens with the heat of the hand, and can be kneaded between the fingers. Its specific gravity is 0·960; it melts at about 62° C., and solidifies just under its melting-point without evolution of heat. It is soluble in hot ether, essential and fixed oils, benzol, bisulphide of carbon, and chloroform, and to some extent in boiling alcohol, but it is unaffected by water and cold alcohol. In chemical constitution it contains 10 per cent. of cerin, an ether of cerotic acid and ceryl alcohol, $\left.\begin{matrix} C_{27}H_{53}O \\ C_{27}H_{55} \end{matrix}\right\} O$, and 90 per cent. of myricin—ether of palmitic acid and myricyl alcohol, $\left.\begin{matrix} C_{16}H_{31}O \\ C_{30}H_{61} \end{matrix}\right\} O$. Yellow wax, on account of the colouring matter and other contaminations it contains, is unfit for many uses. The chief of these is candle-making. To remove soluble matter it is first melted over boiling water; and for bleaching it is formed into thin shreds and strips so as to expose the greatest possible surface. So prepared, it is spread out and frequently watered and turned in the direct sunlight, a slow but effective process. To hasten the bleaching action the wax may be mixed with about one-sixth of pure spirit of turpentine; and this preparation, on exposure, by its copious production of ozone, effects in four or five days a bleaching which otherwise would occupy three or four weeks. When the bleaching is complete all trace of turpentine oil will have disappeared. Bleaching may also be effected by chlorine, permanganate of potash, and other chemicals, but these injuriously affect the wax, in some cases forming substitution products which cannot be removed, and which in burning give off deleterious fumes. Wax is obtained in all parts of the world where there is vegetation sufficient to support bees; but it is most largely forthcoming from tropical and subtropical regions. It is subject to extensive adulteration from powdered mineral substances, flour, cheaper waxes, paraffin, &c. Its uses are multifarious; but it is most largely consumed in making candles for the religious services of Roman Catholic and Orthodox Greek Christians, and for wax figures and models (see WAX FIGURES).

Chinese Insect Wax, or *Pe La*, is a secretion deposited by an insect, *Coccus ceriferus*, Fabr., in the twigs of a species of ash, *Fraxinus chinensis*, Roxb. The wax is, in its origin and the functions it performs in the insect economy, closely related to the lac produced by the allied species of *Coccus* (see LAC, vol. xiv. p. 181). When separated from the twigs which it encrusts, and purified, it is a hard translucent white crystalline body, similar to spermaceti. It melts at from 82° to 86° C., and in composition consists of cerin, one of the constituents of beeswax. It is little known in European commerce, but forms a highly important article of trade in China and Japan, where it is largely used for candle-making and for medicinal purposes.

For SPERMACETI, see vol. xxii. p. 395.

Japanese Wax is a hard wax-like fat which now forms an important export from Japan, principally to London. It is obtained from the small stone fruits of several species of *Rhus* cultivated in Japan. For the extraction of the wax, which is present to the extent of about 20 per cent., the fruits are ground and treated by either of three methods—(1) heating and pressure, (2) boiling in water, and (3) maceration with ether or bisulphide of carbon. The wax is subsequently bleached, and as it comes into the market consists of yellowish hard cakes, covered often with a fine white powdery efflorescence. It has a resinous unpleasant rancid odour. It melts at about 54° C., and solidifies from melting at 41° C. with evolution of heat which raises the temperature about 5° C. Japanese wax becomes translucent about 12° C. under its melting-point, and when it has newly solidified from melting it can again be liquefied at 42° C., from which the melting-point rises by slow degrees with the lapse of time till it reaches the normal. It is not a true wax, but consists principally of the glyceride palmitin with small proportions of stearin and disseminated crystals of free palmitic acid. It is largely mixed with and used as a substitute for beeswax, excepting for uses where its rancidity renders it objectionable.

Myrtle-Berry Wax is obtained from the fruit of several species of *Myrica* in the United States, New Granada, Venezuela, the Cape of Good Hope, and other regions. It is a hard greenish substance, with a pleasant balsamic odour. Its melting-point is about 45° C., and it consists principally of free palmitic acid with a little stearic acid and myristic acid,—a very small proportion of these being combined as glycerides. It is consumed principally in the United States in combination with beeswax for candles; and it is said the Hottentots eat it like cheese.

Carnauba Wax is an exudation on the surface of the growing leaves of the carnauba palm, *Corypha cerifera*, L., which flourishes in tropical South America. The wax is obtained by cutting off and drying the young leaves, from which it is then shaken as fine dust, and caked by melting either over an open fire or in boiling water. It is a true wax, consisting of ethers of myricyl alcohol and ceryl alcohol with cerotic acid, and its melting-point ranges from 85° to 90° C. Carnauba wax is a substance of considerable commercial importance in Brazil, whence large quantities are sent to Europe for use in the candle-trade and otherwise as a substitute for beeswax.

Palm-Tree Wax is an exudation formed on the stems of two South American palms, *Ceroxylon andicola*, H. and K., and *Klop-*

[1] *Brit. Ass. Rep.*, 1886. In this matter, as in most others, the advantage lies with the lectromagnetic theory. See J. W. Gibbs, *Amer. Jour.*, xxiii., 1882.

[2] "Influence of Motion of the Medium on the Velocity of Light," by A. Michelson and E. W. Morley, *Amer. Jour.*, xxxi., May 1886.

[3] "On the Relative Motion of the Earth and the Luminiferous Æther," by Michelson and Morley, *Phil. Mag.*, Dec. 1887.

stockia cerifera, Kars. As scraped from the trees and compacted by melting it is a mixture of resin and wax, having a melting-point as high as 102° to 105° C. The pure wax may be separated by digesting with boiling spirit, when it is obtained with a melting-point of 72° C. and a composition analogous to carnauba wax, like which it is used for candles. Palm-tree wax is little seen in European commerce.

For the compound called SEALING WAX, see vol. xxi. p. 586.

WAX FIGURES. Beeswax is possessed of properties which render it a most convenient medium for preparing figures and models, either by modelling or by casting in moulds. At ordinary temperatures it can be cut and shaped with facility; it melts to a limpid fluid at a low heat; it mixes with any colouring matter, and takes surface tints well; and its texture and consistency may be modified by the addition of earthy matters and oils or fats. When molten, it takes the minutest impressions of a mould, and it sets and hardens at such a temperature that no ordinary climatic influences affect the form it assumes, even when it is cast in thin laminæ. The facilities which wax offers for modelling have been taken advantage of from the remotest times. Figures in wax of their deities were used in the funeral rites of the ancient Egyptians, and deposited among other offerings in their graves; many of these are now preserved in museums. That the Egyptians also modelled fruits can be learned from numerous allusions in early literature. Among the Greeks during their best art period, wax figures were largely used as dolls for children; statuettes of deities were modelled for votive offerings and for religious ceremonies, and wax images to which magical properties were attributed were treasured by the people. Wax figures and models held a still more important place among the ancient Romans. The masks (*effigies* or *imagines*) of ancestors, modelled in wax, were preserved by patrician families, this *jus imaginum* being one of the privileges of the nobles, and these masks were exposed to view on ceremonial occasions, and carried in their funeral processions. The closing days of the Saturnalia were known as *Sigillaria* on account of the custom of making, towards the end of the festival, presents of wax models of fruits and waxen statuettes which were fashioned by the *Sigillarii* or manufacturers of small figures in wax and other media. The practice of wax modelling can be traced through the Middle Ages, when votive offerings of wax figures were made to churches, and the memory and lineaments of monarchs and great personages were preserved by means of wax masks as in the days of Roman patricians. In these ages malice and superstition found expression in the formation of wax images of hated persons, into the bodies of which long pins were thrust, in the confident expectation that thereby deadly injury would be induced to the person represented; and this belief and practice continued till the 17th century. Indeed the superstition still holds a place in the Highlands of Scotland, where within the last few years a clay model of an enemy was found in a stream, having been placed there in the belief that, as the clay was washed away, so would the health of the hated one decline. With the renaissance of art in Italy, modelling in wax took a position of high importance, and it was practised by some of the greatest of the early masters. The bronze medallions of Pisano and the other famous medallists owe their value to the art qualities of wax models from which they were cast by the *cire perdue* process; and indeed all early bronzes and metal work were cast from wax models. The *Tête de cire* in the Wicar collection at Lille, the work of a Florentine artist of the 15th century, is one of the most lovely creations of that fertile era. From that period till towards the close of the 18th century modelling of medallion portraits and of relief groups, the latter frequently polychromatic, was in considerable vogue throughout Europe. About the end of the 18th century Flaxman executed in wax many portraits and other relief figures which Josiah Wedgwood translated into pottery for his jasper ware. The modelling of the soft parts of dissections, &c., for teaching illustrations of anatomy was first practised at Florence, and is now very common. Such preparations formed part of a show at Hamburg in 1721, and from that time wax-works, on a plane lower than art, have been popular attractions. These exhibitions consist principally of images of historical or notorious personages, made up of waxen masks on lay figures in which sometimes mechanism is fitted to give motion to the figure. Such an exhibition of wax-works with mechanical motions was shown in Germany early in the 18th century, and is described by Steele in the *Tatler*. The most famous modern wax-work exhibition is that of Madame Tussaud in London. This collection was originated in Paris, during the Revolution, by that lady, who, having modelled Charlotte Corday, Marat, and other well-known persons of that bloody period, settled in London with her collection early in the present century.

WAXWING, a bird first so-called apparently by Selby in 1825 (*Illustr. Brit. Ornithology*, p. 87), having been before known as the "Silk-tail" (*Philos. Transactions*, 1685, p. 1161)—a literal rendering of the German *Seidenschwanz*—or "Chatterer"—the prefix "German," "Bohemian," or "Waxen" being often also applied. Selby's convenient name has now been generally adopted, since the bird is readily distinguished from almost all others by the curious expansion of the shaft of some of its wing-feathers at the tip into a flake that looks like scarlet sealing-wax, while its exceedingly silent habit makes the name "Chatterer" wholly inappropriate, and indeed this last arose from a misinterpretation of the specific term *garrulus*, meaning a Jay (from the general resemblance in colour of the two birds), and not referring to any garrulous quality. It is the *Ampelis garrulus* of Linnæus and of more recent ornithologists.[1]

The Waxwing is a bird that for many years excited vast interest. An irregular winter-visitant, sometimes in countless hordes, to the whole of the central and some parts of southern Europe, it was of old time looked upon as the harbinger of war, plague, or death, and, while its harmonious coloration and the grace of its form were attractive, the curiosity with which its irregular appearances were regarded was enhanced by the mystery which enshrouded its birth-place, and until the summer of 1856 defied the searching of any explorer. In that year, however, all doubt was dispelled, through the successful search in Lapland, organized by the late John Wolley, as briefly described by him to the Zoological Society (*Proceedings*, 1857, pp. 55, 56, pl. cxxii.).[2] In 1858 Mr Dresser found a small settlement of the species on an island in the Baltic near Uleåborg, and with his own hands took a nest. It is now pretty evident that the Waxwing, though doubtless breeding yearly in some parts of northern Europe, is as irregular in the choice of its summer-quarters as in that of its winter-retreats. Moreover, the species exhibits the same irregular habits in America. Mr Drexler on one occasion, in Nebraska, saw it in "millions." In 1861 Kennicott found it breeding on the Yukon, and later Mr MacFarlane had the like good fortune on the Anderson River.

Beautiful as is the bird with its drooping crest, its cinnamon-

[1] Some writers, ignoring historical facts, have taken a South-American form (now known to belong to a wholly distinct Suborder of Birds) as the "type" of the Linnæan genus *Ampelis*. Linnæus had, as is well known, no conception of what is meant by the modern idea of a "type"; but none can doubt that, if such a notion had been entertained by him, he would have declared his type-species to be that to which the name was first applied, viz., the present, and hence those systematists are wrong who would remove this to a genus variously called *Bombycilla*, *Bombiciphora*, or, most absurd of all, *Bombicivora*. The birds which ought to be removed from *Ampelis* are those which are now generally recognized as forming a Family *Cotingidæ*, allied to the *Pipridæ* (*cf.* MANAKIN), and like them peculiar to the Neotropical Region, in the fauna of which they constitute, according to the investigations of Garrod and Forbes (ORNITHOLOGY, vol. xviii. pp. 41, 47), the natural group *Oligomyodæ*.

[2] A fuller account of his discovery, illustrated by Hewitson, is given in *The Ibis* (1861, pp. 92–106, pl. iv.).

brown plumage passing in parts into grey or chestnut, and relieved by black, white, and yellow—all of the purest tint—the external feature which has invited most attention is the "sealing-wax" (already mentioned) which tips some of the secondary or radial quills, and occasionally those of the tail.[1] This is nearly as much exhibited by the kindred species, *A. cedrorum*—the well-known Cedar-bird of the English in North America—which is easily distinguished by its smaller size, less black chin-spot, the yellower tinge of the lower parts, and the want of white on the wings. In the *A. phœnicopterus* of south-eastern Siberia and Japan, the remiges and rectrices are tipped with red in the ordinary way without dilatation of the shaft of the feathers.

Both the Waxwing and Cedar-bird seem to live chiefly on insects in summer, but are marvellously addicted to berries during the rest of the year, and will gorge themselves if opportunity allow. Hence they are not pleasant cage-birds, though quickly becoming tame. The erratic habits of the Waxwing are probably due chiefly to the supplies of food it may require, prompted also by the number of mouths to be fed, for there is some reason to think that this varies greatly from one year to another, according to season. The flocks which visit Britain and other countries outside the breeding range of the species naturally contain a very large proportion of young birds.

The systematic position of the genus *Ampelis* is very doubtful. It can hardly be said to have any near ally, for neither of the Neotropical and Antillean genera, *Ptilogonys* and *Myiodectes* (often erroneously spelt *Myiadestes*), can as yet be safely declared of kin to it, as has been alleged. (A. N.)

WEALTH. The most commonly accepted definition of wealth is that it consists of all useful and agreeable things which possess exchange value, and this again is generally regarded as coextensive with all desirable things except those which do not involve labour or sacrifice for their acquisition in the quantity desired. On analysis it will be evident that this definition implies, directly, preliminary conceptions of utility and value, and, indirectly, of sacrifice and labour, and these terms, familiar though they may appear, are by no means simple and obvious in their meaning. Utility, for the purposes of economic reasoning, is usually held to mean the capacity to satisfy a desire or serve a purpose (J. S. Mill), and in this sense is clearly a much wider term than wealth. Sunshine and fresh air, good temper and pleasant manners, and all the infinite variety of means of gratification, material and immaterial, are covered by utility as thus defined. Wealth is thus a species of utility, and in order to separate it from other species some *differentia* must be found. This, according to the general definition, is exchange value, but a little reflexion will show that in some cases it is necessary rather to contrast value with wealth. "Value," says Ricardo, expanding a thought of Adam Smith, "essentially differs from riches, for value depends not on abundance but on the difficulty or facility of production." According to the well-known tables ascribed to Gregory King, a deficiency of a small amount in the annual supply of corn will raise its value far more than in proportion, but it would be paradoxical to argue that this rise in value indicated an increase in an important item of national wealth. Again, as the mines of a country are exhausted and its natural resources otherwise impaired, a rise in the value of the remainder may take place, and as the free gifts of nature are appropriated they become valuable for exchange, but the country can hardly be said to be so much the wealthier in consequence. And these difficulties are rather increased then diminished if we substitute for value the more familiar concrete term "money-price,"—for the contrast between the quantity of wealth and its nominal value becomes more sharply marked. Suppose, for example, that in the total money value of the national inventory a decline were observed to be in progress, whilst at the same time, as is quite possible, an increase was noticed in the quantity of all the important items and an improvement in their quality, it would be in accordance with common-sense to say that the wealth of the country was increasing and not decreasing.

So great are these difficulties that some economists (*e.g.*, Ricardo) have proposed to take utility as the direct measure of wealth, and, as Mr Sidgwick has pointed out, if double the quantity meant double the utility this would be an easy and natural procedure. But even to the same individual the increase in utility is by no means simply proportioned to the increase in quantity, and the utility of different commodities to different individuals, and *a fortiori* of different amounts, is proverbial. The very same things may to the same individual be productive of more utility simply owing to a change in his tastes or habits, and a different distribution of the very same things, which make up the wealth of a nation, might indefinitely change the quantity of utility, but it would be paradoxical to say that the wealth had increased because it was put to better uses.

We thus seem thrown back on value as the essential characteristic, allowance being made for any change in the standard of value; but there are still difficulties to be overcome. Some things that undoubtedly possess value or that can command a price are immaterial, *e.g.*, the advice of a lawyer or physician or the song of a *prima donna*, and, although perhaps the skill of a workman (in any grade of the social scale) might be considered as attached to the man, as a coal mine is attached to a place, it is more in accordance with popular usage to consider skill as immaterial, whilst at the same time it seems equally natural *prima facie* to confine the term wealth to material things in the common sense. Again, the credit system of a country is a product of great labour and sacrifice, it is most closely connected with the production of its material wealth in the narrowest sense, and it certainly commands a pecuniary value, and yet credit is more generally held to be a representative rather than a part of wealth, owing apparently to its insubstantial character. Apart from the question of materiality some writers have insisted on relative permanence and possibility of accumulation as essential attributes of wealth, and have thus still further narrowed the scope of the definition.

There can be no doubt that it is on many grounds desirable in economics to use terms as far as possible in their popular acceptations; but this rule must always be subordinate to the primary object in view. In nearly every department of knowledge in which popular terms have been retained it has been found necessary either constantly to use qualifying adjectives where the context is not a sufficient guide, and in some cases, when analysis discloses very different elements, to make a selection. Sometimes it has been found convenient to use a term with some variation in the definition according to the branch of the subject in hand.[2] Applying these rules to the definition of wealth, perhaps the best solution is that which is generally connected with German economists (*e.g.*, Held). Wealth consists of utilities, and in the first great department of economics—the *consumption* of wealth—it is utility with which we are principally concerned,—the idea of value, for example, being overshadowed. The most general law of the consumption of wealth is that successive portions of any stock give a diminishing amount of utility when consumed. Then in the department of the *production* of wealth the most important characteristics are the labour and sacrifice necessary to put the utilities

[1] The structure of these appendages has been carefully described by Herr Andersen (*Œfvers. K. Vet.-Ak. Förhandlingar*, 1859, pp. 219–231, pl. ii.). Their development seems chiefly due to age, though, as Wolley shewed, they are perceptible in the nestling plumage. Mr Turner states (*Contr. Nat. Hist. Alaska*, p. 177) that the Eskimo name of the Waxwing means a "killer of small birds," these appendages being held to be "the clotted blood of its victims"!

[2] On the uses and difficulties of definitions in political economy compare Mr Sidgwick's *Principles*, bk. i. ch. ii., and Cairnes's *Logical Method of Political Economy*

desired into the things and to place the things where they are wanted. The idea of value is again secondary and subordinate. We can readily see the part played by nature, labour, and capital respectively in the production of any commodity without considering the *effects* on its value of the various factors; we can understand the principles of division of labour and of the relative productiveness of large and small industries without entering into questions of value except in the most general manner. In the department of the *distribution* of wealth the fundamental conception is the right of appropriation; and accordingly J. S. Mill very properly commences this part of his subject by an account of the relative advantages of the socialistic and individual systems of property. It is quite possible under the former to conceive of all the distribution being made without any exchange and with reference simply to the wants or the deserts of the members of the society. Thus it is not until we arrive at the department of the *exchange* of wealth that the characteristic of value becomes predominant, although of course value is closely connected with utility and labour and sacrifice.

Usually, however, it will be found that in most cases anything which can fairly be classed as wealth in one department is also wealth in the others, and thus the definition is reached that wealth in general consists of all "consumable utilities which require labour for their production and can be appropriated and exchanged." It only remains to add that "utilities" may be divided into "inner" and "outer" (to translate the German literally),—the "inner" being such as are simply sources of personal gratification to their possessor, *e.g.*, a good ear for music; the "outer" utilities again may be divided into "free" and "economic," the former, as a rule, *e.g.*, sunlight, not being the result of labour and not capable of appropriation or exchange, and the latter as a rule possessing each of these marks. It is these "economic utilities" which constitute wealth in the specific sense of the term, although its use may be extended by analogy to include almost all utilities. (J. S. N†.)

WEASEL. The smallest species of the group of animals of which the polecat and stoat are well-known members (see MAMMALIA, vol. xv. p. 440). It is *Mustela vulgaris* of Linnæus, but belongs to the section (*Putorius*) of the genus which has but three premolar teeth on each side above and below, instead of four as in the martens (to which *Mustela* is commonly restricted) and hence is now called *Putorius vulgaris*. The dentition is $i\ \frac{3}{3}$, $c\ \frac{1}{1}$, $p\ \frac{3}{3}$, $m\ \frac{1}{2} = \frac{8}{9}$; total 34.

The weasel is an extremely elegant little animal, with elongated slender body, the back generally much arched, the head small and flattened, ears short and rounded, neck long and flexible, limbs very short, five toes on each foot, all with sharp, compressed, curved claws, tail rather short, slender, cylindrical, and pointed at the tip, fur short and close. The upper parts, outside of limbs and tail, are a uniform reddish-brown, the under parts pure white. In very cold regions, both in Europe and America, it turns completely white in winter, but less regularly and at a lower temperature than its near ally the stoat or ermine, from which it is easily distinguished by its smaller size, and by its wanting the black end of the tail. The length of the head and body of the male is usually about 8 inches, that of the tail $2\frac{1}{2}$ inches; the female is smaller. The common weasel is pretty generally distributed throughout Europe, Northern and Central Asia, British North America, and the northern portions of the United States. It possesses in a full degree all the active, courageous, and bloodthirsty disposition of the rest of the genus, but its diminutive size prevents it attacking and destroying any but the smaller mammals and birds. Mice, rats, voles, and moles, as well as frogs, constitute its principal food. It is generally found on or near the surface of the ground, but it can not only pursue its prey through very small holes and crevices of rocks and under dense tangled herbage,

Weasel.

but follow it up the stems and branches of trees, or even into the water, swimming with perfect ease.

It constructs a nest of dried leaves and herbage, placed in a hole in the ground or a bank or hollow tree, in which it brings up its litter of four to six (usually five) young ones. The mother will defend her young with the utmost desperation against any assailant, having been often known to sacrifice her own life rather than desert them.

WEAVER-BIRD, the name[1] by which a group of between 200 and 300 species are now usually called, from the elaborately interwoven nests that many of them build, some of the structures being of the most marvellous kind. By the older systematists such of these birds as were then known were distributed among the genera *Oriolus*, *Loxia*, *Emberiza*, and *Fringilla*; and it was Cuvier who in 1817 first brought together these dissevered forms, comprising them in a genus *Ploceus*. Since his time others have been referred to its neighbourhood, and especially the genus *Vidua* with its allies, so as to make of them a Subfamily *Ploceinæ*, which in 1847 was raised by Prof. Cabanis to the rank of a Family *Ploceidæ*,—a step the propriety of which has since been generally admitted, though the grounds for taking it—far too technical to be here criticized—are very slight, and such as could not be held valid in any other Order than that of *Passeres*.

Where so many forms are concerned, only a few of the most important can now be mentioned. The type of Cuvier's genus is certainly the *Loxia philippina* of Linnæus, so termed from the islands it inhabits. But the typical Weaver-bird of Latham (not that he had the name in that precise form) is the *Hyphantornis cucullata* or *textor* of modern writers, an African species, and it is to the Ethiopian Region that by far the greatest number of these birds belong, and in it they seem to attain their maximum of development. They are all small, with, generally speaking, a Sparrow-like build; but in richness of colouring the males of some are very conspicuous—glowing in crimson, scarlet or golden-yellow, set off by jet-black, while the females are usually dull in hue. Some species build nests that are not very remarkable, except in

[1] First bestowed in this form apparently by Stephens in 1826 (*Gen. Zoology*, xiv. pt. i. p. 34); but in 1782 Latham (*Synopsis*, i. p. 435) had called the "*Troupiale du Sénégal*" of Buffon the "Weever Oriole," from its habit of entwining the wires of the cage in which it was kept with such vegetable fibres as it could get, and hence in 1788 Gmelin named it *Oriolus textor*. In 1800 Daudin used the term "*Tisserin*" for several species of the Linnæan genus *Loxia*, and this was adopted some years later by Cuvier as the equivalent of his *Ploceus*, as mentioned in the text.

being almost invariably domed—others (such as the Philippine Weaver-bird, *Ploceus philippinus*, just named) fabricate singular structures[1] of closely and uniformly interwoven tendrils or fine roots, that often hang from the bough of a tree over water, and, starting with a solidly wrought rope, open out into a globular chamber, and then contract into a tube several inches in length, through which the birds effect their exit and entrance. But the most wonderful nests of all, and indeed the most wonderful built by birds, are those of the so-called Sociable Grosbeak, *Philhetærus socius*, of Africa. These are composed wholly of grass, and are joined together to the number of 100 or 200—indeed 320 are said to have been found in one of these aggregated masses, which usually take the form of a gigantic mushroom,[2] affording a home and nursery to many pairs of the birds which have been at the trouble of building it. These nests, however, have been so often described and figured by South-African travellers that there is no need here to dilate longer on their marvels. It may be added that this species of Weaver-bird, known to French writers as the *Républicain*, is of exceptionally dull plumage.

The group of Widow-birds,[3] *Viduinæ*, is remarkable for the extraordinary growth of the tail-feathers in the males at the breeding-season. In the largest species, *Vidua* (sometimes called *Chera*) *progne*, the cock-bird, which, with the exception of a scarlet and buff bar on the upper wing-coverts, is wholly black, there is simply a great elongation of the rectrices; but in *V. paradisea* the form of the tail is quite unique. The middle pair of feathers have the webs greatly widened, and through the twisting of the shafts their inferior surfaces are vertically opposed. These feathers are comparatively short, and end in a hair-like filament. The next pair are produced to the length of about a foot—the bird not being so big as a Sparrow—and droop gracefully in the form of a sickle. But this is not all: each has attached to its base a hair-like filament of the same length as the feather, and this filament originally adhered to and ran along the margin of the outer web, only becoming detached when the feather is full grown.[4] In another species, *V. principalis*, the two middle pairs of rectrices are equally elongated, but their webs are convex, and the outer pair contains the inner, so that when the margins of the two pairs are applied a sort of cylinder is formed.[5] The females of all the Widow-birds differ greatly in appearance from the males, and are generally clothed in a plumage of mottled brown.

Usually classed with the Weaver-birds is a vast group of small seed-eating forms, often called *Spermestinæ*, but for which *Estreldinæ* would seem to be a more fitting name. These comprehend the numerous species so commonly seen in cages, and known as Amadavats, *Estrelda amandava*, Nutmeg-birds, *Munia punctularia*, Waxbills, *Pytelia melba* and *phœnicoptera*, Cutthroats, *Amadina fasciata*, the Java Sparrow, *Padda oryzivora*, and many more than we can name. Many of these genera are common to Africa and India, and some also to Australia, but the last has several genera peculiar to itself, such as *Donacicola* and *Poophila*, there known as Grass-finches. The true affinity of these seems to require further investigation.[6] (A. N.)

WEAVING is the art of forming cloth by the interlacing of yarn or other filaments in a loom. In weaving two kinds or sets of yarn are used, the warp and the weft. The warp consists of the threads of yarn which extend generally but not always in parallel lines from end to end the whole length of the web; the weft yarn crosses and intersects the warp at right angles, and fills up the breadth of the web. The warp is mounted on the loom for weaving, and into it the weft is thrown by means of a shuttle. Weaving is thus distinct from knitting, netting, looping, and plaiting, by all of which methods cloth may be made from yarns. Cloth also is prepared by felting, but in that operation the fibres are simply matted together without either spinning or intertwisting.

To appearance the varieties of woven cloth are endless; but these differences are only in part due to the method of weaving. The textile materials employed, the methods used in spinning and preparing yarns, the dye colours resorted to, and the finishing processes may vary indefinitely and so contribute to give variety of character to the resultant product. The complexities of the art of weaving itself are reducible to a few fundamental operations, which do not of necessity demand the most intricate mechanism. The gorgeous mediæval textiles of which numerous examples remain were made in looms of primitive construction. For producing the Indian muslins of the present day with their marvellous delicacy of texture, and for the elaborate and sumptuous shawls of Kashmir, the weavers have only rude and simple looms. But patient and tedious handiwork in these instances is devoted to produce effects which, with the application of modern machinery, can be automatically secured with as great rapidity as in the case of the plainest fabric.

The series of inventions which have led up to the marvellously ingenious looms of the present day began with the invention of the fly shuttle, so called because of the rapidity of its motion, by John Kay of Bury in 1733. Previous to Kay's time the shuttle was thrown by the weaver's hand across and through the warp threads from side to side of the web. His invention brought the plain hand-loom practically into the form in which it continues at present; and, as it forms the basis of all modern machinery, a description of its parts and working, and of the operations connected with plain weaving, may here be given. In accordance with the definition already laid down, plain cloth, such as an ordinary piece of calico or linen, will, on examination, be found to consist of two sets of threads, the one intersecting the other at right angles, with each single thread passing alternately over one and under the next. Such a web is produced by passing the weft thread over and under each alternate warp thread in the breadth of the loom, the warp threads under one shot of weft being above the next. To do this, and to beat or close up each successive weft thread so as to make an even and sufficiently close cloth, necessitates a series of operations of which the following is an outline.

Warping.—The number of longitudinal threads which go to form the web will vary, of course, according to its breadth and to the closeness with which they lie together; for fine webs several thousand warp threads, of sufficient length to form a web of many yards, may have to be laid parallel to each other. This is done in the warping frame, which consists of a large reel, set vertically, on which separate threads drawn from a range of bobbins are wound together in a spiral manner to the required length of the web. The yarns coming from the bobbins are brought together in a heck, which is made to slide up and down a guide post as the reel or warping frame revolves, and thus it delivers to the reel a band of thread which winds up and down the reel spirally by the rise and fall of the heck. Supposing 100 "ends" or warp threads are being reeled from bobbins, and 1000 ends of warp are required in the web, then the full lengths wound on the reel must be repeated upward and downward ten times. At each end of the warp the threads are, by a mechanical device in the heck, made to intersect alternately, forming leashes which are, when taken from the reel, separately tied up, and thus aid in maintaining the parallelism of the ends when they are bundled up. Such a bundle of warp when required for weaving is taken in hand by the beamer, whose duty is to spread the threads evenly and wind them on the warp beam, spreading the ends in the order in which they are to appear in the woven fabric, and giving them about the breadth of the web. Cotton warps are wound direct from the bobbins on the beam, there being a mechanical arrangement in the warping machine which stops its motion when any thread breaks, or when a bobbin

[1] These differ from those built by some of the ORIOLES (*q.v.*) and other birds, whose nests may be compared to pensile pockets, while those of these Weaver-birds can best be likened to a stocking hung up by the "toe," with the "heel" enlarged to receive the eggs, while access and exit are obtained through the "leg."

[2] But at a distance they may often be mistaken for a native hut, with its grass-roof.

[3] It has been ingeniously suggested that this name should be more correctly written Whydah bird—from the place on the West Coast of Africa so named; but Edwards, who in 1745 figured one of the species, states that he was informed that "the Portuguese call this bird the Widow, from its Colour and long Train" (*Nat. Hist. Birds*, i. p. 86).

[4] This curious structure was long ago described by Brisson (*Ornithologie*, iii. p. 123), and more recently by Strickland (*Contr. Ornithology*, 1850, pp. 88 and 149, pl. 59).

[5] Both these species seem to have been first described and figured in 1600 by Aldrovandus (lib. xv. cap. 22, 23) from pictures sent to him by Ferdinando de' Medici, duke of Tuscany.

[6] An illustrated *Monograph of the Weaver-Birds* by Mr Edward Bartlett is now in course of publication.

is exhausted. The contents of several beams filled from bobbins may be required to be rewound together on a single beam to supply the requisite quantity of ends for a web.

Plain Weaving.—The warp beam thus filled is laid in the loom (fig. 1), and the ends of warp are then separately drafted or drawn through a pair of heddles or healds. The essential features of the

FIG. 1.—Diagram of Hand-Loom.

heddle are the eyes, loops, or mails through which the warp is threaded, one end of warp only passing through any mail. This eye or mail is placed in the heddle half-way between an upper and a lower wooden sheaf, over which pass the heald threads or between which extend the wires on which such mails are supported. The distance between the mails and the lathes at each end must be sufficient to allow of that opening or "shedding" of the warp which it is the function of the heddle to secure. Through the mails of one heddle each alternate end of warp is drafted, and the remaining ends are passed similarly through the other. Thus each heddle receives every alternate thread across the whole breadth of the warp. From the heddles the ends are carried through the reed (fig. 2), which is the ultimate distributor of the warp, and the instrument by which the weft is beaten up and closed in weaving. It consists

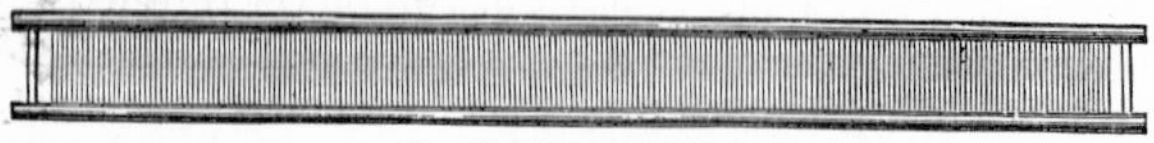

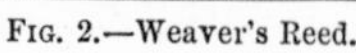

FIG. 2.—Weaver's Reed.

of an oblong narrow frame filled with fine strips of cane or of flattened brass or steel wire, these strips being placed in fine comb-like order more or less closely together, up to as many as 120 strips or "dents," or even more, per inch; two or more ends are passed through each slit of the reed, which is fixed in a "lay" or "batten," a suspended frame for moving the reed backward and forward in beating up the weft. On the lower part of the batten a ledge projects, which forms the "shuttle race" for carrying the shuttle in "picking" from and to the shuttle boxes at each end of the lay. From the reed the ends are carried forward and fastened to the cloth beam, and now the warp is ready for the weaving operation.

The three essential movements in weaving are (1) the "shedding" or dividing of the warp threads to permit of the passage between them of the shuttle containing the weft; (2) the "picking" or shooting of the weft; and (3) the "battening" or beating up of the weft. The shedding motion depends upon the heddles, which are corded or attached to a pair of treadles worked by the weaver's feet. Each treadle is connected with the heddles above and below by a system of levers or pulleys, so that the depression of one treadle while it raises one heddle depresses the other, and thus the opening or shed is made in the warp, one-half—consisting of alternate threads—being raised, the corresponding half pulled down. The weaver then with the left hand pushes the lay or batten back towards the heddles, till a sufficient portion of the shed is brought in front of the reed, and the depressed ends lie just over the shuttle race. A clear way is thus provided for picking or shooting the shuttle, which is done with a whipping jerk of the picking stick held in the right hand. This pulls the cord attached to the picker and projects the shuttle from one shuttle box into that at the opposite end of the lay. The lay is now drawn forward with the left hand, and the reed combs and beats up the weft thread. Treadle number two is next depressed and thereby a new shed is formed, the last made pick or shoot being enwrapped between the intersecting warp sheds; the lay is again thrown back, the pick of weft is shot and beaten up, and so on in regular succession (see fig. 3).

In plain weaving it is possible to produce stripes by the use of bands of coloured warp, and checks where both warp and weft are particoloured. In the latter case shuttles, or at least cops, equal in number to the different colours of weft required, must be provided. It is obvious that the repeated changing of shuttles, and

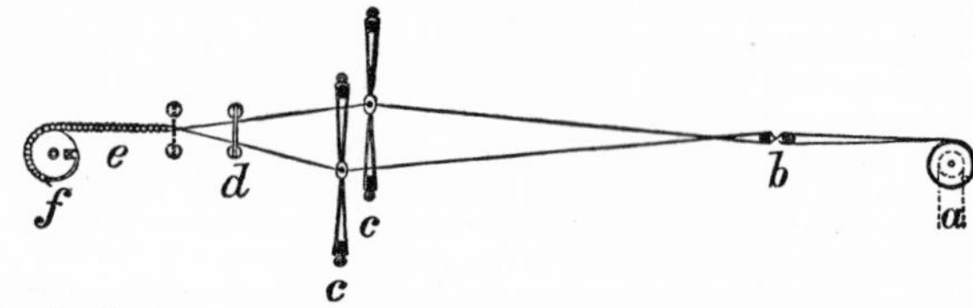

FIG. 3.—Section of plain web in process of weaving on the loom: *a*, warp beam; *b*, leash rods where the warp is divided and crossed; *c*, *c*, heddles; *d*, reed; *e*, the woven cloth; *f*, the cloth beam.

still more the withdrawing and replacing of cops in weaving with frequently changing weft, would occasion great loss of time. To avoid that, and to provide for the use of different coloured wefts, or of wefts of various counts, the drop box was invented, a device by which two or more shuttles can be successively used in any order desired. The drop box, and its numerous subsequent modifications of circular and other change boxes, consists of a series of compartments or divisions in the shuttle box, each made to hold a separate shuttle. These several compartments are by mechanical agency brought in line with the shuttle race in the order in which the changes of weft picks are necessary.

Twill Weaving.—So long as only two sets or leaves of treadles are used in a loom very little in the form of a pattern can be produced, seeing no variation can be effected in the alternate raising of each heddle. To a limited extent a corded surface may be produced by passing two or three warp ends through each mail, and by throwing two or three picks of weft between each shed. But for effective figure-weaving there must be numerous possible variations of shed; and that is secured first by increasing the number of heddles in the loom. Thus with three heddles alone it is possible to effect six combinations of shedding, and as the number of heddles is added to the variations of possible shedding increase in geometrical ratio. But the number of treadles which can be corded up to separate heddles is in practice limited, and therefore only simple twill patterns are for the most part woven with treadles and heddles. A twill is a cloth in which the warp and weft do not intersect alternately, but where the warp predominates on the one side and the weft on the other. The simplest of all is the three-leaf twill, in which the warp passes over two and under one weft thread, and *vice versa*, in regular succession, giving the appearance of a succession of diagonal lines on the surface. Regular twills of from four to eight leaves are woven in the same manner, the weft rising over each fourth to eighth warp thread as the case may be. Many variations and combinations are possible in connexion with these regular twills. For example, they may be combined with plain weaving: a cashmere twill may be made,—that is, a four-leaf combination, in which the weft passes alternately over and under two warp ends, and two picks are shot for each shed. Further, zig-zags, lozenges, squares, and other geometrical designs can be produced by reversing the order of the treading, and thereby causing the twill to run in different directions. The diagrams, figs. 4 and 5, show two arrangements of a four-leaf twill, the first being a regular twill and the second a dimity, the dark squares representing the point at which the weft rises to the surfaces.

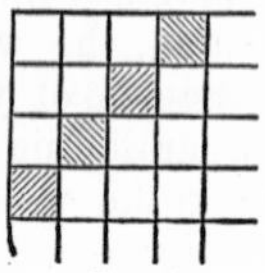

Fig. 4.

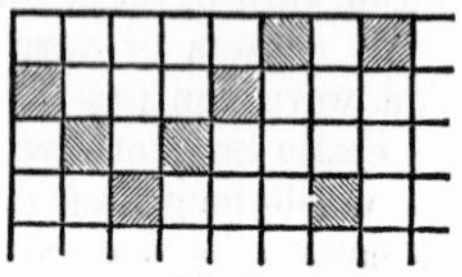

Fig. 5.

Satin or broken twills are those in which the warp threads are not intersected by the weft in regular succession, but only at intervals, and thereby the smooth continuous surface characteristic of satin and damask is secured. Common satin and double damask are eight-leaf twills, the order in which the weft rises being shown in the diagram, fig. 6. Rich satins may consist of sixteen to twenty leaf twills, the weft intersecting and binding down the warp at every sixteenth to twentieth pick as the case may be. Satins are usually woven with the face of the cloth downwards, because in weaving, say a sixteen-leaf satin, it would be necessary were the surface upwards to keep fifteen heddles raised and one down, whereas, with the face of the cloth under, only one heddle has to be raised at a time.

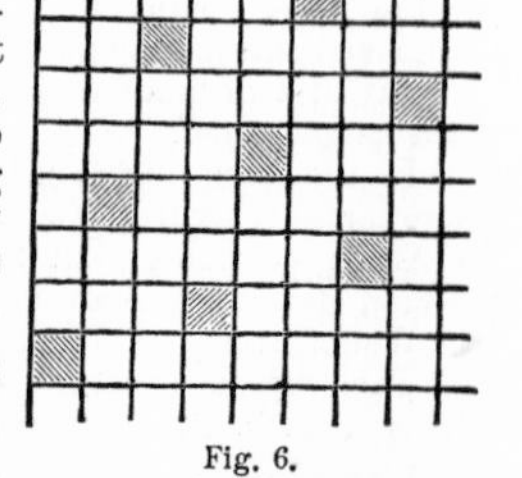

Fig. 6.

Figure Weaving.—Only a limited number of heddles can in actual working be attached each to a separate treadle to be under the control of the feet of the weaver. But to produce a complicated and irregular pattern a large number of different sheds of warp must be provided, and to secure with promptitude and certainty such manifold and complicated sheddings many of the most elegant and ingenious devices ever applied to mechanism have been invented. Before invention culminated in the Jacquard apparatus the draw loom or draw-boy loom was the machine employed for making figured patterns such as damasks. In it each separate heddle shaft was fastened to a cord, which passed over a pulley, and coming down by the side of the loom these cords were arranged in a board in the order in which the heddles required to be drawn. The drawing of the cords and consequent formation of the shed was originally the work of a boy assistant, whence the name draw-boy loom; but it was found possible, by various mechanical attachments worked from the treadles, to dispense with extra aid to the weaver. But even with this arrangement the number of heddles which can be hung in any loom is limited, though, by using thin shafts and arranging them in tiers, as many as eighty or ninety may be accommodated. Since as many as a thousand separate sheds may be required to form a complete pattern, a device other than shafts or leaves of heddles becomes necessary; and the solution of the difficulty is found in hanging the individual heddle mails, not in shafts, but independently, each with a small lead weight called a lingo attached to it. Thus in effect a separate heddle is provided for each thread of warp, and it becomes possible to effect any combination of shed by cording together such leashes or mails as carry the warp threads to be raised. This tying together of the separate leashes, called "tying the harness" in the case of elaborate designs, is a tedious and difficult operation, requiring the exercise of considerable skill and patience. The successive sheds of a pattern being tied up, it is only necessary to have the cords arranged in the order in which they are to be drawn and attached to the mechanical device for pulling them, and forming the sheds in proper succession.

The Jacquard Loom.—The Jacquard apparatus is the most important and ingenious appliance which has ever been adapted to weaving, since by its agency it has become possible to produce the most intricate and extended patterns with the same certainty and with almost as much rapidity as plain cloth. The credit of introducing and making the machine a practical success—if not the whole honour of the invention—is due to Joseph Marie Jacquard of Lyons (see vol. xiii. p. 539). Attention was first directed to this ingenious artisan by a model of a net-making machine invented by him, which was deposited in the Conservatoire des Arts et Métiers. He was requested in 1801 by Napoleon to examine and improve on a complicated loom, and thereupon he undertook to produce a simple appliance to supplant the involved mechanism. The germs of the idea which he perfected had been, early in the eighteenth century, conceived by Bouchon and Falcon, and in 1745 it was further developed and improved by Jacques de Vaucanson. Indeed, had Vaucanson been acquainted with the fly shuttle which was then known and used at least in England, it is probable he would have come to be regarded as the real inventor at once of the power-loom and of the apparatus which bears Jacquard's name.

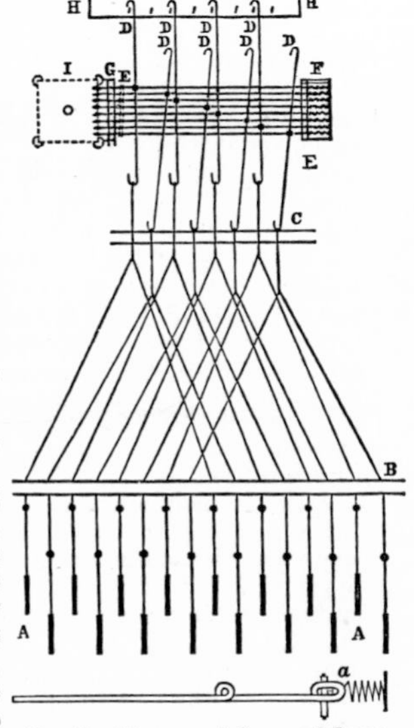

Fig. 7.—Diagram of Jacquard Loom.

The fundamental principle of the Jacquard apparatus is simple, although in its working fine mechanical details are essential. Its object is to effect the raising of any number of separate leashes, corded leashes, or heddles, in any order and succession without special tying of harness. How the apparatus works will be made plain by the diagram, fig. 7. Here A, A represent the separate leashes through which the warp threads are drafted. It will be observed that these leashes are tied in pairs, but they might equally well be single, many together, or shafts of heddles. The cord from each separate leash passes through a finely perforated board B, called the comber-board, between which and C, the bottom board, the pairs are tied to a cord. These cords pass up through the bottom board, and are caught in the lower hooks of a range of double-hooked long wires D, D. These hooked wires are supported and kept in position by being passed through loops or eyes in a range of cross-wires E, E. The head of each cross-wire is formed into an oblong eye as at *a* (an enlarged representation of a single cross-wire), through which a pin is passed for securing it in the spring-box F, in which each separate cross-wire presses against a small helical spring. The oblong eye permits a certain amount of play in the cross-wire, so that it can be pressed back against the helical spring when a force is applied at the opposite end. The points of the cross-wires pass through a perforated board G, called the needle-board, projecting about a quarter of an inch beyond its outer surface. The upper hooks of the upright wires threaded through these cross-wires are attached to a board H, called the griffe. The whole function of the apparatus is to liberate these hooks in the order and to the extent necessary for the successive sheds. The hooks are dislocated thus. At the side of the projecting points of the cross-wires there is a quadrangular frame I, called the cylinder. This cylinder can be drawn back, and turned so that each face may in succession be presented to and pressed against the face from which the cross-wires protrude. The cylinder alone does not affect the wires, but its function is to carry on its rotating faces a succession of pasteboard cards which are punctured with holes in a definite order. The wires connected with hooks which are not to be disturbed pass through the punctured holes and remain unaffected, while those supporting the hooks to be displaced are pressed back by the cardboard surface, and this motion of the cross-wire lifts the hook of the upright wire off the griffe. The griffe now rises, carrying with it the undisturbed hooks, making a shed of the warp threads attached to their cords. The weft is then shot, the griffe descends, and the next punctured card is by a quarter revolution of the cylinder brought into contact with the cross-wires, and so the work goes on, successive Jacquard cards being presented, new combinations of shed effected, and the weft shot till the pattern is completed. Hooks to any desired number may be arranged in a Jacquard apparatus, and when a separate hook is applied to each individual leash the most complete control and variety of shed may be secured. But in practice this is not necessary. Each repeat of a pattern across a web may be corded up to one series of hooks, and in many ways it is practicable to limit the number of hooks required in weaving and thus to simplify the apparatus itself, and the system of punctured cards by which its operation is governed. If the Jacquard apparatus, for example, is controlling only a few leaves of heddles, then only a corresponding number of hooks are called into use. Usually the machines are provided with 300, 400, 600, 900, and sometimes more hooks, and when intricate and extensive patterns are being woven two or more machines may be simultaneously brought to bear on the same loom.

The Power-Loom.—The first loom in which all the motions in weaving were connected and controlled by one motive power was the ribbon loom, known also as the Dutch or Dutch engine loom. A machine in which four to six pieces could be woven simultaneously is recorded to have been in existence in Dantzic in the last quarter of the sixteenth century (see Ribbons, vol. xx. p. 531). In 1745 John Kay, inventor of the fly shuttle, and Joseph Stell patented improvements on the Dutch engine loom, which they said "may go or be worked by hands, water, or any other force." The ribbon loom may be regarded as a series of distinct looms mounted within one frame, each having its own warp and cloth beams, heddles, and shuttle, but all worked by one set of treadles and with a single batten. The shuttles are thrown across the narrow web by a rack-and-pinion arrangement; they are simultaneously shot, and each occupies the place of its next neighbour to the right or left alternately. The Jacquard apparatus and the drop-box arrangement for changing shuttles with change of weft are applied to the ribbon loom.

The application of power to the weaving of ordinary webs has developed along a different line, and the common power-loom has nothing to do with the ribbon loom. So early as 1678 there was figured and described in the French *Journal des Sçavans* a machine "for making linen cloth without the aid of a workman," the invention of De Gennes, a French naval officer. The loom made in 1745 by Vaucanson, which also foreshadowed the Jacquard apparatus, embodied many improvements on the conception of De Gennes, and presented some of the important features of the modern power-loom. The practical realization of automatic weaving was, however, deferred for forty years, and the world owes it to a clergyman of the Church of England, the Rev. Dr Edmund Cartwright. His own graphic account of the history of his invention has already been given under COTTON (see vol. vi. p. 500). Dr Cartwright's original loom was but an imperfect machine, although his patent was minute and detailed. Both he and others devoted much labour to its improvement; and in bringing the invention to a successful issue he spent from £30,000 to £40,000, while in return he received only a gift of £10,000 in 1809 from the Government. The power-loom fought its way to supremacy but slowly, for an imperfect power-loom is no better than a hand-loom; and it was only after the minor adaptations and adjustments which frequently make the difference between success and failure were brought into operation that the real advantages of power-loom weaving became obvious. Even yet for many purposes the power-loom has not succeeded in supplanting hand-loom weaving.

The power-loom (fig. 8) differs much in appearance from the hand-loom, and is altogether more compact, from the fact that the lay, which is suspended from above in the latter, is in the power-loom centred below. The three principal motions, shedding, picking, and beating up, are of course the same in both. Motion is communicated to the working parts of the power-loom by the main

FIG. 8.—Power-Loom.

or crank shaft, so called because it is provided with the two cranks which give oscillating motion to the lay. By toothed wheels the crank shaft controls the motion of the tappet shaft which carries on it the cams or tappets (1) for the picking motion called the picking tappets, and (2) for the treadles called the shedding tappets. The picking tappets have always a direct relation to the motion of the crank shaft, because for every beat of the lay there must be a corresponding pick. As there are two picking tappets the shaft is therefore geared to make half a revolution for each revolution of the crank shaft. The relation of the shedding tappets is not so regular, their rotation being dependent on the number of heddles or sheds of warp they control, and it is only in plain weaving that they correspond in motion with the picking tappets.

For the successful working of a power-loom several adjustments are necessary which are not required in the case of the hand-loom. The hand-loom weaver winds up his web on the cloth beam from time to time as the work progresses, and he moves forward the temples by which the woven fabric is kept extended to its proper breadth. In the power-loom these must be accomplished automatically, and the motions must be self-adjusting with the progress of weaving. More important still, a self-acting appliance must be provided to stop the motion of the loom in case of the weft thread becoming exhausted or being broken. This is secured by a delicate and ingenious contrivance called the "fork-and-grid stop motion," which depends for its action on the lightly balanced prongs of a fork. These prongs come in contact with the weft thread between the selvedge of the web and the shuttle box each time the shuttle is shot to the side at which the apparatus is fixed. If the prongs meet no thread they are not thrown up, and being unmoved a connexion is formed to the moving lay, and by a system of levers the loom is immediately thrown out of gear and stopped. Equally essential is it to provide means to stop the loom should the shuttle stick in the warp or otherwise fail to be carried from side to side of the lay. It is clear that, should the lay beat up with the shuttle sticking in the weft, there would ensue complete wreck of the warp. There are two ways of dealing with such a contingency. The first, invented in 1796 by Miller of Glasgow, is the "stop-rod motion," the action of which depends on the shuttle raising, as it enters the shuttle-box, a catch which if left down would strike against a frog or stop, and so throw the loom out of gear. The second device is the loose reed, in which there is an appliance for liberating the lower part of the reed when any obstruction is met in the warp, and thereby preventing a blow being given by the beating-up motion.

Double Cloth.—For many purposes the weaving of double cloth is important. It permits of the formation of a ground of inferior material with a surface of finer texture; and it affords great scope for the formation of coloured patterns, allowing of the production of double-faced textures, which may or may not correspond in pattern according to pleasure. It moreover increases the thickness and weight of woven fabrics, and it is the basis of tubular weaving, such as is practised for making hose, tubes, seamless sacking, &c. There are three classes of double textures. The first consists of double warp surfaces with the weft in the centre; in the second it is the reverse—a warp centre and two weft faces; and in both these classes the two sides may be of different colours if two colours of warp and weft respectively are employed. In the third case the cloth may consist of distinct warps and wefts throughout, and practically be two separate cloths. These, if bound at the selvedges, would become woven tubes, and if at regular intervals over the surface a thread of warp or weft passes from the one into the other they are united as one texture. The intersection of double warps and wefts gives the opportunity of producing great diversity of colour and pattern in any fabric without waste of material, and the manner in which patterns may pass from side to side is illustrated in the sectional diagram, fig. 9. The diagram, fig. 10, illustrates

FIG. 9.—Section of Double Cloth.

the method of producing a plain double cloth with the use of four heddles. Heddles 1 and 2 shed the upper cloth, 3 and 4 the lower. When a pick is being put in through the upper warp heddle 1 is up and all the others are down; and when the shuttle is passed through the lower web heddles 1 2, 3 are raised and heddle 4 is depressed.

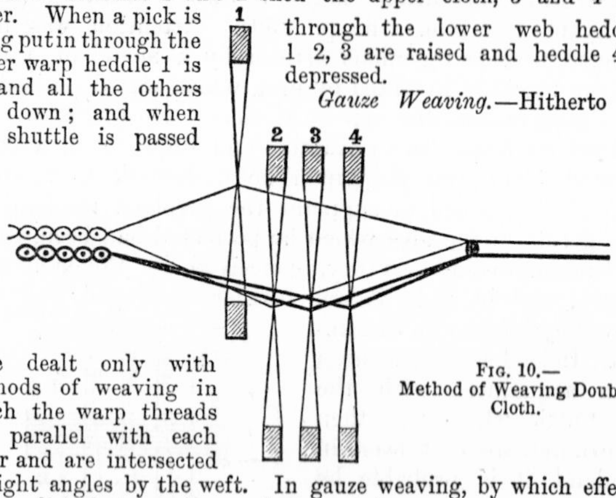

FIG. 10.—Method of Weaving Double Cloth.

Gauze Weaving.—Hitherto we have dealt only with methods of weaving in which the warp threads run parallel with each other and are intersected at right angles by the weft. In gauze weaving, by which effects intermediate between lace and plain cloth are produced, the warp threads are made to intertwist more or less among themselves, thereby favouring the production of light open textures, in which many ornamental lace-like combinations can be effected. Plain gauze is a thin open texture, in which two contiguous threads of warp make each a half twist around the other at every pick, the cloth having in section the appearance shown in fig. 11. A leno consists of a kind of muslin in which the crossing or whip warp intertwists with its neighbour only at every fourth pick. In fancy gauzes the crossing or whip warp may cross and entwine several ordinary warp threads at once, and in numerous other ways the simple principle of intertwisting may be used for ornamental effect. The mutual entwining of warp threads is accomplished by an extra heddle called a "doup," placed in front of the common heddles. The doup consists of a half heddle threaded through the eye of a plain heddle, of which it forms a part. The cross or whip warps are drafted first through one of the ordinary heddles and then passed under the thread or threads they are intended to entwine, and drafted through the doup heddle, as seen in the diagram, fig. 12, which shows the drafting of a plain gauze. The whole of the warp yarns which are to be entwined must with the whip

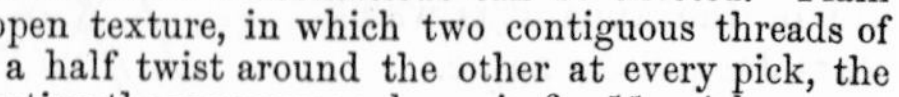

FIG. 11.—Section of ordinary Gauze.

warp be passed through a single split of the reed, except when the doups are placed in front of the reed, which is done in the case of complicated gauze weaving.

Piled fabrics are textures woven with a looped or otherwise raised surface. Looped pile is any fabric in which the woven loops remain uncut, as in Brussels and tapestry carpets and terry velvets. When these loops are cut in the finished texture then the material is a cut pile, such as ordinary velvet, fustian, imitation sealskin, and other imitation furs. For ordinary loop and cut pile fabrics two warps are required, the regular beam warp and the "pole" or pile warp. The latter, being raised into loops, is worked up more rapidly than the ordinary warp, and it has consequently to be of greater length and wound on a separate beam. The ground or foundation may be either a plain or a twilled texture, and after every third pick of weft a wire is introduced into the shed and beaten up and woven into the cloth. In this way, by the stretching of the pile warp over the wire, a row of loops is formed across the web, the size of the loops being regulated by the size of the wire. If a looped pile is being woven then it only remains to pull out the wires from behind and again weave them in in front as the work proceeds. But if cut pile is being made, then either the loops must be cut along the top before the wire is withdrawn, or the wire may at one end be provided with a knife edge which itself cuts the loops as it is being pulled out. For velvets, &c., the wires are provided with a groove on their upper face, and along this groove a cutting knife called a trivet is run to cut the loops. In fig. 13 the structure of a looped and cut velvet is illustrated. Fustian is a cut pile fabric in which the weft material, floated over the surface, forms the substance of the pile. It is not woven over wires, and the pile is cut by hand after the web leaves the loom. A third method of weaving pile fabrics consists of making a double web, the pile warp passing from the one to the other and binding them together, as shown in fig. 14. When the connecting threads are cut they form a pile surface for each separate cloth. The great difficulty which has been encountered in perfecting this method of pile weaving has been to keep the connecting pile equal in length throughout, and to cut it so as to produce uniform level surfaces. The success which has been attained in plush weaving with double cloth is largely due to the patient and well-directed efforts of Mr S. C. Lister, of Manningham Mills, Bradford.

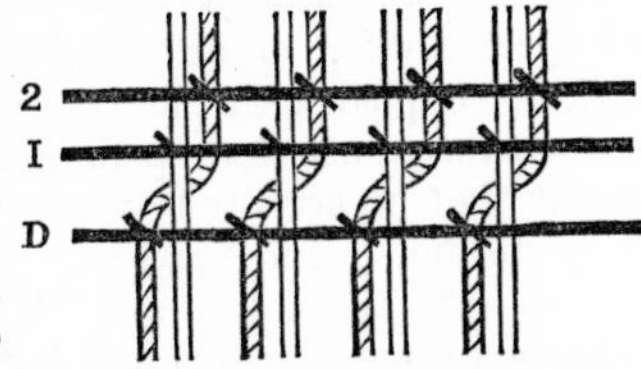

Fig. 12.—Drafting of Gauze Web. 1 and 2 ordinary heddles; D, doup heddle.

Fig. 13.—Section of Looped Pile Fabric.

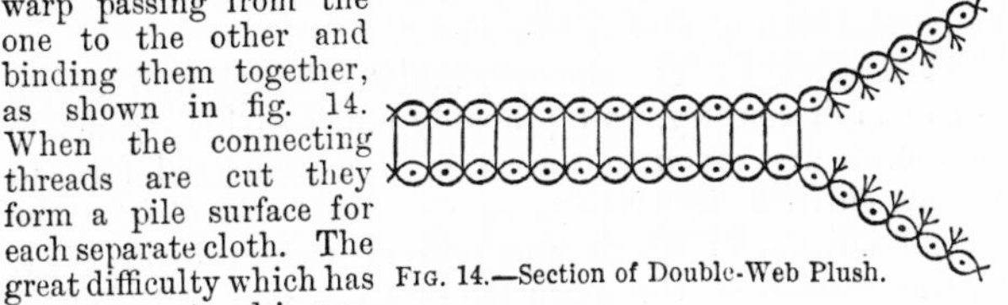
Fig. 14.—Section of Double-Web Plush.

There are many subsidiary but highly important and most ingenious features of the art of weaving. specially in connexion with the production of ornamental surfaces, for notice of which it has been impossible to find room in the preceding summary. The extent and complexity of the whole subject renders the presentation of a satisfactory outline of the art a matter of unusual difficulty; but those who wish to pursue the subject in detail, in addition to copious information to be gleaned from technical journals, may consult Darlow's *History and Principles of Weaving* (London, 1878), Ashenhurst's *Weaving and Designing of Textile Fabrics* (Bradford, 1879), and Brown's *Practical Treatise on the Art of Weaving* (4th ed., Dundee, 1883). To the two works first named we have to acknowledge our indebtedness for the suggestions of several diagrams. (J. PA.)

WEBER, Carl Maria Friedrich Ernst von (1786–1826), musical composer and creator of "romantic opera," was born at Eutin, near Lübeck, December 18, 1786, of a family that had long been devoted to art. His father, Baron Franz Anton von Weber, a military officer in the service of the palgrave Karl Theodor, was an excellent violinist, and his mother once sang on the stage. His cousins, Josepha, Aloysia, Constanze, and Sophie, daughters of Franz Anton's brother Fridolin, attained a high reputation as vocalists. Mozart, after having been cruelly deceived by Aloysia, made Constanze his wife, and thus became Franz Anton's nephew by marriage. Fridolin played the violin nearly as well as his brother; and the whole family displayed exceptional talent for music.

Franz Anton von Weber was a man of thriftless habits and culpable eccentricity. Having been wounded at Rosbach, he quitted the army, and in 1758 he was appointed financial councillor to Clement August, elector of Cologne, who for nine years overlooked his incorrigible neglect of duty. But the elector's successor dismissed him in 1768; and for many years after this he lived in idleness at Hildesheim, squandering the property of his wife, Anna de' Fumetti, and doing nothing for the support of his children until 1778, when he was appointed director of the opera at Lübeck. In 1779 the prince bishop of Eutin made him his kapellmeister, and not long afterwards his wife died of a broken heart. Five years later he went to Vienna, placed two of his sons under Michael Haydn, and in 1785 married the young Viennese singer Genovefa von Brenner, who in the following year gave birth, at Eutin, to the subject of the present article—a delicate child, afflicted with congenital disease of the hip-joint.

On his return from Vienna, Franz Anton, finding that a new kapellmeister had been chosen in his place, accepted the humbler position of "Stadt Musikant." This, however, he soon relinquished; and for some years he wandered from town to town, giving dramatic performances, in conjunction with the children of his first wife, wherever he could collect an audience. The effect of this restless life upon the little Carl Maria's health and education was deplorable; but, as he accompanied his father everywhere, he became familiarized with the stage from his earliest infancy, and thus gained an amount of dramatic experience that indisputably laid the foundation of his future greatness. Franz Anton hoped to see him develop into an infant prodigy, like his cousin Mozart, whose marvellous career was then rapidly approaching its close. In furtherance of this scheme, the child was taught to sing and place his fingers upon the pianoforte almost as soon as he could speak, though he was unable to walk until he was four years old. Happily his power of observation and aptitude for general learning were so precocious that he seems, in spite of all these disadvantages, to have instinctively educated himself as became a gentleman. His first music-master was Keuschler, who gave him instruction at Weimar in 1796. In 1798 Michael Haydn taught him gratuitously at Salzburg. In the March of that year his mother died, like her predecessor, of chagrin. In April the family visited Vienna, removing in the autumn to Munich. Here the child's first composition—a set of "Six Fughettas"—was published, with a pompous dedication to his half-brother Edmund; and here also he took lessons in singing from Valesi, and in composition from Kalcher, under whom he made rapid progress. Soon after this he began to play successfully in public, and his father compelled him to write incessantly. Among the compositions of this period were a mass and an opera—*Die Macht der Liebe und des Weins*—now destroyed. A set of "Variations for the Pianoforte," composed a little later, and dedicated to Kalcher, was lithographed by Carl Maria himself, under the guidance of Senefelder, the inventor of the process, in which both the father and the child took great interest.

In 1800 the family removed to Freiberg, where the Ritter von Steinsberg gave Carl Maria the libretto of an opera called *Das Waldmädchen*, which the boy, though not yet fourteen years old, at once set to music, and produced in November at the Freiberg theatre. The performance was by no means successful, and the composer himself was accustomed to speak of the work as "a very immature production"; yet it was afterwards reproduced at Chemnitz, and even at Vienna.

Carl Maria returned with his father to Salzburg in 1801, resuming his studies under Michael Haydn, and forming a close friendship with the Chevalier Neukomm. Here also he composed his second opera, *Peter Schmoll und seine Nachbarn*, which was unsuccessfully produced at Nuremberg in 1803. In that year he again visited Vienna, where, though the veterans Haydn and Albrechtsberger were both receiving pupils, his father preferred placing him under the Abbé Vogler, a man of kind and sympathetic nature, but quite unfit to train so great a genius. Through Vogler's instrumentality Carl Maria was appointed conductor of the opera at Breslau, before he had completed his eighteenth year. In this capacity he greatly enlarged his experience of the stage; but he lived a sadly irregular life, contracted debts which his slender salary was insufficient to defray, and lost his beautiful voice through accidentally drinking a poisonous liquid used in lithography,—a mishap that nearly cost him his life. These hindrances, however, did not prevent him from beginning a new opera called *Rübezahl*, the libretto of which was based upon a well-known legend of the Riesengebirge. The plot of the piece was "romantic" to the last degree, and Weber worked at it enthusiastically, but it was never completed, and little of it has been preserved beyond a quintett and the masterly overture, which, re-written in 1811 under the title of *Der Beherrscher der Geister*, now ranks among its author's finest instrumental compositions.

Quitting Breslau in 1806, Weber removed in the following year to Stuttgart, where he had been offered the post of private secretary to Duke Ludwig, brother of Frederick, king of Würtemberg. The appointment was a disastrous one. The stipend attached to it was insufficient to meet the twofold demands of the young man's new social position and the thriftlessness of his father, who was entirely dependent upon him for support. Court life at Stuttgart was uncongenial to him, though he yielded to its temptations. The king hated him. He fell hopelessly into debt, and, worse than all, became involved in a fatal intimacy with Margarethe Lang, a singer at the opera. Notwithstanding these distractions he worked hard, and in 1809 re-modelled *Das Waldmädchen*, under the title of *Sylvana*,[1] and prepared to produce it at the court theatre. But a dreadful calamity prevented its performance. Franz Anton had misappropriated a large sum of money placed in the young secretary's hands for the purpose of clearing a mortgage upon one of the duke's estates.[2] Both father and son were charged with embezzlement, and, on February 9, 1810, they were arrested at the theatre, during a rehearsal of *Sylvana*, and thrown by the king's order into prison. No one doubted Weber's innocence, but after a summary trial he and his father were ordered to quit the country, and on February 27 they began a new life at Mannheim.

Having provided a comfortable home for his father, and begun the composition of a new comic opera, in one act, called *Abu Hassan*, Weber removed to Darmstadt in order to be near his old master the Abbé Vogler, and his fellow-pupils Meyerbeer and Gänsbacher, with whom he lived on terms of the closest intimacy. On September 16, 1810, he reproduced *Sylvana* under its new title at Frankfort, but with very doubtful success. *Abu Hassan* was completed at Darmstadt in January 1811, after many interruptions, one of which exercised a memorable influence upon his later career. While reading with his friend, Alexander von Dusch, George Apel's then recently published *Gespensterbuch*, he was so much struck with the story of *Der Freischütz* that he at once began to meditate upon its transformation into an opera, and the two friends actually set to work upon it then and there. But it was not until many years afterwards that the idea was carried out in a practical form.

Weber started in February 1811 on an extended artistic tour, during the course of which he made many influential friends, and on June 4 brought out *Abu Hassan* with marked success at Munich. His father died at Mannheim in 1812, and after this he had no settled home, until in 1813 his wanderings were brought to an end by the unexpected offer of an appointment as kapellmeister at Prague, coupled with the duty of entirely remodelling the performances at the opera-house. The terms were so liberal that he accepted at once, engaged a new company of performers, and governed them with uninterrupted success until the autumn of 1816. During this period he composed no new operas, but he had already written much of his best pianoforte music, and played it with never-failing success, while the disturbed state of Europe inspired him with some of the finest patriotic melodies in existence. First among these stand ten songs from Körner's *Leyer und Schwerdt*, including "Vater, ich rufe dich," and "Lützow's wilde Jagd"; and in no respect inferior to these are the splendid choruses in his cantata *Kampf und Sieg*, which was first performed at Prague, December 22, 1815.

Weber resigned his office at Prague, September 30, 1816, and on December 21 Frederick Augustus, king of Saxony, appointed him kapellmeister at the German opera at Dresden. The Italian operas performed at the court theatre were superintended by Morlacchi, whose jealous and intriguing disposition produced an endless amount of trouble and annoyance. The king, however, placed the two kapellmeisters on an exact equality both of title and salary, and Weber found ample opportunity for the exercise of his remarkable power of organization and control. And now he once more gave his attention to the story of *Der Freischütz*, which, with the assistance of Friedrich Kind, he developed into an admirable libretto, under the title of *Des Jägers Braut*.

The legend of "The Seventh Bullet," though well known in the 17th century, and probably much earlier, seems to have been first given to the world in a connected form in a work entitled *Unterredungen vom Reiche der Geister*, the second edition of which was printed at Leipsic in 1731. In this version of the story the scene is laid in Bohemia, and the action referred to the year 1710. Apel reproduced the legend, under the title of "Der Freischütz," in the first volume of his *Gespensterbuch*, in 1810. Since then the story has been repeated in many varying forms, but it was Apel's version that first attracted Weber's attention, and it was from this that he and Kind together made their first sketch of the libretto, on February 21, 1817, though they found it necessary to increase the interest of the drama by the introduction of some accessory characters, and to substitute a happy ending for the fatal catastrophe of the original story. No subject could have been better fitted than this to serve as a vehicle for the new art-form which, under Weber's skilful management, developed into what is now universally recognized as the prototype of the true "romantic opera." He had dealt with the supernatural in *Rübezahl*, and in *Sylvana* with the pomp and circumstance of chivalry, but in neither case with the unquestioning faith which alone can invest the treatment of such subjects with befitting dignity. The shadowy impersonations in *Rübezahl* are scarcely less human than the heroine who invokes them; and the music of *Sylvana* might easily have been adapted to a story of the 19th century. But in the master's later operas all this is changed. We cannot choose but shudder at the fiend in *Der Freischütz*, for the infernal apparition comes straight to us from the nether world. Every note in *Euryanthe* breathes the spirit of mediæval romance; and the fairies in *Oberon* have a real existence, quite distinct from the tinsel of the stage. And this it is,—this uncompromising reality, even in face of the

[1] As the MS. of *Das Waldmädchen* has been lost, it is impossible now to determine its exact relation to the later work.

[2] Spitta gives a different account of the occurrence, and attributes the robbery to a servant.

unreal,—that forms the strongest characteristic of the pure "romantic school," as Weber understood and created it. It is true to nature even when dealing with the supernatural, for it treats its wildest subjects in earnest, and without a doubt as to the reality of the scenes it ventures to depict, or the truthfulness of their dramatic interpretation.

Weber and Kind sketched the *scenario* of the new opera in February 1817. On March 1 the poet placed the complete libretto in the hands of the composer, who wrote the first note of the music on July 2—beginning with the duet which opens the second act. But so numerous were the interruptions caused by Morlacchi's intrigues, the insolence of unfriendly courtiers, and the attacks of jealous critics that nearly three years elapsed before the piece was completed. In the meantime the performances at the opera-house were no less successfully remodelled at Dresden than they had already been at Prague, though the work of reformation was far more difficult; for the new kapellmeister was surrounded by enemies who openly subjected him to every possible annoyance, and even the king himself was at one time strongly prejudiced against him. Happily, he no longer stood alone in the world. Having, after much difficulty, broken off his miserable intimacy with Margarethe Lang, he married the well-known vocalist, Carolina Brandt, a noble-minded woman and consummate artiste, whose advice, even on subjects connected with the new opera, was extremely valuable. The great work was completed May 13, 1820, on which day Weber wrote the last note of the overture,—a portion of the design which, for obvious reasons, it was his custom to postpone until the rest of the music was finished. There is abundant evidence to prove that he was well satisfied with the result of his labours; but he gave himself no rest. He had engaged to compose the music to Wolff's Gipsy drama, *Preciosa*. Two months later this also was finished, and both pieces ready for the stage.

In consequence of the unsatisfactory state of affairs at Dresden, it had been arranged that both *Preciosa* and *Der Freischütz*—no longer known by its original title, *Des Jägers Braut*—should be produced at Berlin. In February 1821 Sir Julius Benedict was accepted by Weber as a pupil; and to his pen we owe a delightful account of the rehearsals and first performance of his master's *chef d'œuvre*. *Preciosa* was produced with great success at the old Berlin opera-house on June 14, 1821. On June 18, the anniversary of the battle of Waterloo, the opening of the new "Schauspielhaus" was celebrated by the production of *Der Freischütz*. Much anxiety was caused by unforeseen difficulties at the rehearsals; yet, so calm was Weber's mind that he devoted his leisure time to the composition of his *Concertstück* in F minor—one of his finest pianoforte pieces. Until the last moment his friends were anxious; the author was not; and the result justified his confidence in his own powers. The success of the piece was triumphant. The work was received with equal enthusiasm at Vienna on October 3, and at Dresden on January 26, 1822. Yet Weber's position as kapellmeister was not much improved by his success, though, in order to remain faithful to his engagements, he had refused tempting offers at Berlin and Cassel, and, at the last-named place, had installed Ludwig Spohr in a position much more advantageous than his own.

For his next opera Weber accepted a libretto based, by Frau Wilhelmine von Chezy, on the story of *Euryanthe*, as originally told in the 13th century, in Gilbert de Montreuil's *Roman de la Violette*, and repeated with alterations in the *Decamerone*, in Shakespeare's *Cymbeline*, and in several later forms. In place of the ghostly horrors of *Der Freischütz*, the romantic element was here supplied by the chivalric pomp of the Middle Ages. The libretto, though soundly abused by shallow critics, is really an exceptionally good one—in one respect superior to that of *Der Freischütz*, inasmuch as it substitutes elaborate recitative for the spoken dialogue peculiar to the German "Schauspiel" and French "opéra comique." It is, in fact, a "grand opera" in every sense of the words,—the prototype of the "musical drama" perfected fifty years later by Wagner. The overture—as usual, written last—presents a feature that has never been imitated. During its performance the curtain temporarily rises, to exhibit, in a *tableau vivant*, the scene in the sepulchral vault upon which the whole story turns. This episode is now rarely presented; but Weber himself well knew how much the interest of the piece depended on it. The work was produced at the Kärntnerthor theatre in Vienna, October 25, 1823, and received with enthusiasm. Being of a less popular character than *Der Freischütz*, it is not so frequently performed; but it still retains its place upon the stage, and ranks among the finest "romantic operas" that have ever been written.

Weber's third and last dramatic masterpiece was an English opera, written for Covent Garden theatre, upon a libretto adapted by Planché from Wieland's *Oberon*. Destined for the English stage sixty years ago, this was necessarily disfigured by the spoken dialogue abandoned in *Euryanthe*; but in musical beauty it is quite equal to it, while its fairies and mermaids are as vividly real as the spectres in *Der Freischütz*. Though already far gone in consumption, Weber began to compose the music on January 23, 1825. Charles Kemble had offered him £1000 for the work, and he could not afford to rest. He finished the overture in London, at the house of Sir George Smart, soon after his arrival, in March 1826; and on April 12 the work was produced with triumphant success. But it cost the composer his life. Wearied out with rehearsals and performances of the opera, and concerts at which he was received with rapturous applause, he grew daily perceptibly weaker; and, notwithstanding the care of his kind host, Sir George Smart, and his family, he was found dead in his bed on the morning of June 5, 1826. For eighteen years his remains rested in a temporary grave in Moorfields chapel; but in 1844 they were removed and placed in the family vault at Dresden.

Besides his three great dramatic masterpieces and the other works already mentioned, Weber wrote two masses, two symphonies, eight cantatas, and a vast amount of songs, orchestral and pianoforte pieces, and music of other kinds, amounting altogether to more than 250 compositions. (W. S. R.)

WEBER'S LAW is the principal generalization of that branch of scientific investigation which has come to be known as "psycho-physics." According to Fechner, who has done most to prosecute these inquiries and to consolidate them under a separate name, "psycho-physics is an exact doctrine of the relation of function or dependence between body and soul." In other words, it is throughout an attempt to submit to definite measurement the relation of physical stimuli to the resulting psychical or mental facts, and forms an important department of experimental psychology. It deals with the quantitative aspects of mental facts—their intensity or quantity proper and their duration. Physical science enables us, at least in the case of some of the senses, to measure with accuracy the objective amount of the stimulus, and introspection enables us to state the nature of the subjective result. Thus we are able to say whether a stimulus produces *any* psychical result, and can fix in that way the *minimum sensibile* or "threshold of consciousness" for each of the senses. In like manner (though with less accuracy, owing to the disturbing nature of the conditions) we can fix the sensational maximum, or upper limit of sensibility, in the different senses, that is to say, the point beyond which no increase of stimulus produces any appreciable increase of sensation. We thus determine, as Wundt puts it, the limit-values between which changes of intensity in the stimulus are accompanied by changes in sensation. But the central inquiry of psycho-physics remains behind. Between the quantitative minimum and the quantitative maximum thus fixed can we discover any definite relation between changes in the objective intensity of the stimuli and changes in the intensity of the sensations as estimated by consciousness? The answer of psycho-physics to this inquiry is given in the generalization variously known as "Weber's law," "Fechner's law," or the "psycho-physical law," which professes to formulate with exactitude the relations which exist between change of stimulus and change of sensation.

As we have no means of subjectively measuring the absolute intensity of our sensations, it is necessary to depend upon the mental estimate or comparison of two or more sensations. Comparison enables us to say whether they are equal in intensity, or if unequal which is the greater and which is the less. But as they approach equality in this respect it becomes more and more difficult to detect the difference. By a series of experiments, therefore, it will be possible, in the case of any particular individual, to determine the least observable difference in intensity between two sensations of any particular sense. This least observable difference is called by Fechner the "Unterschiedsschwelle," or "difference-threshold," that is to say, the limit of the discriminative sensibility of the sense in question. That such a "threshold," or least observable difference, exists is plain from very simple examples. Very small increases may be made in the objective amount of light, sound, or pressure—that is, in the physical stimuli applied to these senses—without the subject on whom the experiment is made detecting any change. It is further evident that, by means of this "Unterschiedsschwelle," it is possible to compare the discriminative sensibility of different individuals, or of different senses, or (as in the case of the skin) of different parts of the same sense organ: the smaller the difference observable the finer the discriminative sensibility. Thus the discrimination of the muscular sense is much more delicate than that of the sense of touch or pressure, and the discriminative sensibility of the skin and the retina varies very much according to the parts of the surface affected. Various methods have been adopted with a view to determine these *minima* of discriminative sensibility with an approach to scientific precision. The first is that employed by Weber himself, and has been named the method of just observable differences. It consists either in gradually adding to a given stimulus small amounts which at first cause no perceptible difference in sensation but at a certain point do cause a difference to emerge in consciousness, or, *vice versa*, in gradually decreasing the amount of additional stimulus, till the difference originally perceived becomes imperceptible. By taking the average of a number of such results, the minimum may be determined with tolerable accuracy. The second method is called by Fechner the method of correct and incorrect instances. When two stimuli are very nearly equal the subject will often fail to recognize which is the greater, saying sometimes that A is greater, sometimes that B is greater. When in a large number of trials the right and wrong guesses exactly balance one another we may conclude that the difference between the two stimuli is not appreciable by the sense. On the other hand, as soon as the number of correct guesses definitely exceeds half of the total number of cases, it may be inferred that there is a certain subjective appreciation of difference. This method was first employed by Vierordt. The third method, that of average errors, is very similar to the one just explained. Here a certain weight (to take a concrete example) is laid upon the hand of the person experimented upon, and he is asked, by the aid of subjective impression alone, to fix upon a second weight exactly equal to the first. It is found that the second weight sometimes slightly exceeds the first, sometimes slightly falls below it. Whether above or below is of no consequence to the method, which depends solely on the amount of the error. After a number of experiments, the different errors are added together, and the result being divided by the number of experiments gives us the average error which the subject may be calculated upon to make. This marks the amount of stimulus which is just below the difference-threshold for him. This method was first employed by Fechner and Volkmann. The different methods were first named, and the theory of their application developed by Fechner, in his *Elemente der Psychophysik* (1860).

These methods have been chiefly applied to determine the relation of the difference-threshold to the absolute magnitude of the stimuli employed. For a very little reflexion tells us that the smallest perceivable difference is not an amount whose absolute intensity is constant even within the same sense. It varies with the intensity of the stimuli employed. We are unable, for example, to recognize slight differences in weight when the weights compared are heavy, though we should be perfectly able to make the distinction if the weights compared were both light. Ordinary observation would lead us, therefore, to the conclusion that the greater the intensity of the original stimulus at work the greater must be the increase of stimulus in order that there may be a perceptible difference in the resulting sensation. E. H. Weber (1795–1878) was the first (after a prolonged series of experiments on the sensations of sight, hearing, and touch) to clothe this generality with scientific precision by formulating the law which has since gone by his name. The purport of the law is that, in order that the sensational difference may remain unchanged, the increase of stimulus must maintain the same proportion to the intensity of the preceding stimulus. The smallest perceptible difference is therefore not absolutely the same, but it remains relatively the same, that is, it remains the same fraction of the preceding stimulus. For example, if we can distinguish 16 oz. and 17 oz., we shall be able to distinguish 32 oz. and 34 oz. but not 32 oz. and 33 oz., the addition being in each case $\frac{1}{16}$ of the preceding stimulus. This fraction (supposing it to be the difference-threshold of the muscular sense) remains a constant, however light or however heavy the weights compared. The law may be formulated thus:—The difference between any two stimuli is experienced as of equal magnitude, in case the mathematical relation of these stimuli remains unaltered. Or, otherwise expressed, In order that the intensity of a sensation may increase in arithmetical progression, the stimulus must increase in geometrical progression. It is also expressed by Fechner in the form—The sensation increases as the logarithm of the stimulus.

The law has been variously interpreted. Fechner himself designated it the psycho-physical law, and treated it as the fundamental formula of the relation between body and mind, thus assigning to it an ontological dignity and significance. But in this "psycho-physical" interpretation of his results he has not had a numerous following. Wundt interprets the law in a purely "psychological" sense, making it a special instance of the general law of relativity which governs our mental states. Introspection can give us no information as to the absolute intensity of the stimulus; for a stimulus is known in consciousness only through its sensational resultant. Hence, he argues, we can only compare one psychical state with another, and our standard of measurement is therefore necessarily a relative one; it depends directly upon the preceding state with which we compare the present. Others have attempted to give the law a purely physical or "physiological" explanation. Instead of holding with Fechner that the law expresses a recondite relation between the material and the spiritual world, they prefer to regard the quantitative relation between the last physical antecedent in the brain and the resultant mental change as *prima facie* one of simple proportion, and to treat Weber's law as holding between the initial physical stimulus and the final action of the nerve-centres. According to this interpretation, the law would be altogether due to the nature of nervous action. As a nerve, says Sully, after a temporary degree of stimulation temporarily loses its sensibility, so the greater the previous stimulation of a nerve the greater is the additional stimulus required to produce an appreciable amount of sensation.

Weber's law, it must be added, holds only within certain limits. In the "chemical" senses of taste and smell experiments are almost impossible. It is not practicable to limit the amount of the stimulus with the necessary exactitude, and the results are further vitiated by the long continuance of the physiological effects. The same considerations apply with still more force to the organic sensations, and the results in the case of temperature sensations are completely uncertain. The law is approximately true in the case of sight, hearing, pressure, and the muscular sense,—most exactly in the case of sound. As this is the sense which affords the greatest facilities for measuring the precise amount of the stimulus, it may perhaps be inferred that, if we could attain the same exactitude in the other senses, with the elimination of the numerous disturbing extraneous influences at work, the law would vindicate itself with the same exactitude and certainty. It is further to be noted, however, that even in those senses in which it has been approximately verified, the law holds with stringency only within certain limits. The results are most exact in the middle regions of the sensory scale; on the contrary, when we approach the upper or lower limit of sensibility, they become quite uncertain.

Literature.—Weber's investigations were given to the public in his articles in Wagner's *Handwörterbuch der Physiologie.* Fechner's *Elemente der Psycho-physik*, referred to above, was published in 1860, and contains an elaborate exposition of the whole subject. He replied to his critics in two later works, *In Sachen der Psychophysik* (1877) and *Revision der Hauptpunkte der Psycho-physik* (1882). Delbœuf's *Étude psychophysique* (1873), and G. E. Müller's *Zur Grundlegung der Psycho-physik*, are also important documents; and the subject is fully treated in Wundt's *Physiologische Psychologie* and in Ladd's *Physiological Psychology*, which is based upon Wundt. Two English monographs may be referred to as containing important criticisms of the law,—the paper of Messrs Dewar and M'Kendrick in the *Transactions of the Royal Society of Edinburgh* for 1873, and Mr James Ward's "Attempt to Interpret Fechner's Law," in *Mind*, i. 452 *sq.* (A. SE.)

WEBSTER, Daniel (1782-1852), American statesman, was born at Salisbury, New Hampshire, January 18, 1782. His family can be traced back without difficulty to Thomas Webster, of Scottish ancestry, who settled in New Hampshire in 1636, but no further. Ebenezer Webster, the father of Daniel, rose to the rank of captain in the "French and Indian War." From him his sons Ezekiel and Daniel inherited great physical force; their mother, Abigail Eastman, gave them their intellectual powers. Daniel always insisted on considering his elder brother, who became a leading lawyer in his native State, as really his superior in intellect, and the correspondence between them was close and confidential until Ezekiel's death in 1829. Living on the frontier, Daniel was compelled to depend for early education on his mother and on the scanty schooling customary in winter; and for much of this he was indebted to the fact that he was physically the weakest of his family. It is a little odd, however, that he failed utterly in that with which his final reputation was so closely connected. In his own words: "There was one thing I could not do: I could not make a declamation; I could not speak before the school." When he was fifteen years old a family council decided to send him to college, a step involving severe abstinence and additional struggle on the part of his immediate relatives. After an imperfect preparation, he graduated at Dartmouth College in 1801, studied law, and was admitted to the bar in Boston in 1805, from the office of Christopher Gore.

Regard for his father made Webster begin practice in the town of Boscawen, near his early home; but his father died within a year, and he removed to Portsmouth, the largest town of the State. Here he took a leading place at the bar, having but one rival. In May 1813 he entered Congress as a representative from New Hampshire, being placed at once on the committee of foreign affairs. As a moderate Federalist, he held that attacks on Canada should cease, and that the war should be confined to the ocean. His first speech showed that the raw New Hampshire boy of a dozen years before had developed new powers. "If the war must continue, go to the ocean. If you are seriously contending for maritime rights, go to the theatre where alone those rights can be defended. Thither every indication of your fortune points you. There the united wishes and exertions of the nation will go with you. Even our party divisions, acrimonious as they are, cease at the water's edge." The position of any Federalist in Congress, however, was not a wide sphere of influence; and Webster, removing to Boston in 1816, gave up political life for some years.

At the Massachusetts bar Webster soon gained a place as prominent as he had held in New Hampshire, and within three years his reputation as a lawyer had become national. His national standing was gained by his argument in the "Dartmouth College case," practically endorsed by the Supreme Court. Dartmouth College had been chartered by the king in 1769. In 1816 the New Hampshire legislature undertook to alter the charter and reorganize the corporation; and the State courts sustained the legislature in a suit brought by the old trustees against the new. On appeal to the Supreme Court of the United States in 1818, Webster contended that the College was an eleemosynary corporation, over which the legislature had no more power than the king who chartered it; that the king had no power to void such a charter, and the New Hampshire legislature no such sovereign powers as parliament; that the legislature's action came within the Federal constitution's prohibition of State legislation altering contracts; that "the charter of 1769 is a contract;" that "the acts in question impair this contract;" and that they were therefore unconstitutional and void. The Supreme Court upheld Webster's view, and it was soon seen that he had worked a serious change in the relations of the States to corporations, as they had thus far been understood. The States endeavoured to meet the new rule by inserting in their charters clauses retaining the right to alter them; but the spirit of the "Dartmouth College case," which has always had its opponents among American lawyers, has had its influence upon judges everywhere, in every variety of cognate cases. From this time Webster was recognized as the leading lawyer of the country, and his services were in constant demand.

His cases are quite beyond statement within the space here available. Some of his leading constitutional cases were those of Gibbons *v.* Ogden, in 1824, in which he overthrew the action of the New York legislature, in granting to Ogden, assignee of Fulton and Livingstone, a monopoly of steam navigation in New York waters, as an interference with the right of Congress to regulate commerce; Ogden *v.* Saunders, in 1827, in which he attacked the right of a State to pass bankruptcy laws; the Girard College case, in 1844, in which he maintained that Christianity was an essential part of the common law; and the case of Luther *v.* Borden, commonly known as the Rhode Island case, in 1848, in which he laid the foundation for the subsequent definition of the "guarantee clause" of the constitution, and stated the meaning of the "republican government" of a State. Like other American lawyers, he made no distinction in his practice between kinds of cases, and was often retained in criminal causes. The most celebrated of these were the trials of Goodridge and Knapp; in the latter (6 Webster's *Works*, 53) is the passage on the power of conscience, which has been declaimed by countless American schoolboys.

Webster's reputation as an orator began with his address at Plymouth in 1820, on the 200th anniversary of the landing of the Pilgrims. It was increased by his address at the laying of the corner-stone of the Bunker Hill monument in 1825, on the 50th anniversary of the battle, and by that which commemorated in 1826 the 50th anniversary of the Declaration of Independence and the coincident deaths of Jefferson and John Adams. On every great public occasion thereafter, if Webster was obtainable, he was held to be the natural speaker to be chosen. His finest subsequent speeches were made on the completion of the Bunker Hill monument in 1843, and at the laying of the corner-stone of the addition to the Capitol at Washington in 1851.

In December 1823 Webster returned to Congress as a representative from Massachusetts, and his first speech, in January 1824, in support of a resolution to send a commissioner to Greece, then in insurrection, made him the first of Congressional speakers. During his service in the house the tariff of 1824 came up for discussion. Representing a commercial district, Webster's speech has always been a source of gratification to American opponents of protection. He repudiated the name of "American system," claimed by Clay for the system of protection which he was introducing. He cited with cordial approval the expressed belief of English statesmen that English manufactures had prospered in spite of protection, not because of it, and their desire for "unrestricted trade." He attacked the "old notion" of the balance of trade with such vigour that he felt compelled to apologize "for speaking irreverently of the dead." He stated the manner in which, under unrestricted trade, the American production in cotton, woollens, and iron had already come to rival that of England, protected for hundreds of years, and the loss in labour which would come from an attempt, by legal protection, to "support a business that cannot support itself." The whole speech would be a very striking free-trade argument even at the present day. When the tariff of 1828, which was still more protective, came up for discussion, Webster had ceased to oppose protection; but his speech does not attempt to argue in favour of it. It states that his people, after giving warning in 1824 that they would consider protection as the policy of the Government, had gone into protected manufactures, and that he now asked that that policy be not reversed to the injury of his constituents. It can hardly escape notice that, in his published *Works*, Webster has but two subsequent speeches in Congress on the tariff, both defending protection rather as a policy under which industries had been called into being than as an advisable policy, if the stage had been clear for the adoption of a new policy.

In 1827 Webster was sent to the senate, in which he remained until his death, with the exception of his service in the cabinet in Tyler's administration. In January 1830 came the crowning event of his political life. A debate on public lands, under a resolution offered by Senator Foot, thence known as "Foot's resolution," had wandered off into all possible fields. In course of it, Hayne, of South Carolina, attacked New England for having pursued a selfish policy as to western lands. Webster replied. During Hayne's answer Webster drew from him the first distinct and public statement of the new doctrine of nullification, of the constitutional right of a State to forbid the execution within its jurisdiction of Acts of Congress which it considered unconstitutional. This had been the product of Calhoun's intellect, which was generally taken to be the source of Hayne's inspiration. Webster's reply is his famous "second speech on Foot's resolution." He began by a defence of Massachusetts, which has been severely criticized, and is perhaps open to criticism. But if effect is to be taken as a test, it is above criticism. The remainder of the speech was of intense interest, not merely to New England, but to the whole North and West, and to all the progressive elements of the country. He stated the anarchistic doctrine of nullification in its nakedness, extorted from Hayne an unwilling half-admission of the exactness of his statement, and then went on to trample on it with such an exhibition of logic, sarcasm, and elephantine humour as has never been heard in the senate before or since. It is on this speech that Webster's fame was built. Southern men had taken the lead so long that it was a new sensation to the North and West to see a Southern leader completely overmatched by their champion; and "Black Dan Webster," a popular name, due to his dark complexion, beetling brows, and heavy cast of features, was for twenty years the representative of Northern sentiment as to the nature of the Union.

Calhoun took Hayne's place in the senate in 1833, introduced and defended resolutions endorsing the right of nullification, and was still more fully answered by Webster. For the next seventeen years the records of the senate are full of constitutional arguments between the two. Webster's oratory made him an invaluable member of the Whig party, and his addresses at political meetings are so numerous as to defy special mention. A leader so distinguished had a fair right to think of the presidency, but it always remained just beyond his reach. In the general Whig confusion of 1836 he received the fourteen electoral votes of Massachusetts. In 1840 the candidature of Harrison left him no chance. In 1844 Webster's retention of his position under Tyler gave Clay an overwhelming advantage with his party. In 1848 the nomination of Taylor, which Webster declared to be "one not fit to be made," was a fatal blow to the prospects of the Massachusetts leader. His final failure to obtain the Whig nomination in 1852 put an end to his political career.

When the Whig party came into power in 1841, Webster was appointed secretary of state (foreign affairs), and he retained his post under Tyler, after his colleagues had broken with the new president and resigned. There was good reason for his action. When he entered office war with Great Britain was a probable event of the near future. The M'Leod case, in which the State of New York insisted on trying a British subject, with whose trial the Federal Government had no power to interfere, while the British Government had declared that it would consider conviction and execution a *casus belli*; the exercise of the right of search by British vessels on the coast of Africa, of which Americans had a deep-seated detestation, quite apart from any feeling about the slave-trade; the Maine boundary, as to which the action of a State might at any time bring the federal Government into armed collision with Great Britain,—all these at once met the new secretary, and he felt that he had no right to abandon his work for party reasons. With the special commissioner from Great Britain, Lord Ashburton, he concluded the treaty of 1842, which settled all these questions satisfactorily to both parties. At the same time Webster took the opportunity to end the long controversy as to the right of impressment. Sixteen years afterwards the British Government admitted at last the correctness of the American position.

The treaty of 1842 also introduced the principle of extradition into the connexion between the two countries. It had been admitted once before, in Jay's treaty of 1794, but only as to murder and forgery, and only until 1806.

Leaving the cabinet in 1843, Webster was returned to the senate in 1845 and spent the remainder of his life there. He opposed the annexation of Texas and the Mexican War, and was, as before, the recognized spokesman of his party. As the growing intensity of the quarrel over the organization of the territory acquired from Mexico revealed the depth of the chasm which now yawned between the sections, Webster's standing-ground in American politics disappeared. His 7th of March speech, in 1850, which stamped him, in the opinion of many of his former Northern worshippers, as a recreant bidding for Southern votes for the presidency, was really little different from his former words. It was the country that had changed. He was still for the Union as the one controlling consideration, with an equal dislike for the abolitionist and the secessionist, who endangered the Union. But the North and the South were already so far apart that not even Webster could stand with one foot in one and the other foot in the other section; and his fate was parallel with that of John Dickinson, who essayed a similar rôle during the revolution. Angered at the spirit with which his speech was received, Webster threw all his influence towards driving through the Whig Convention of 1852 an endorsement of the compromise of 1850 "in all its parts," including, of course, the Fugitive Slave Act. The result was his own failure to receive the Whig nomination for the presidency, and the downfall of his party. Just before the election he died at his home, Marshfield, Massachusetts, October 1852.

Webster was twice married—to Grace Fletcher, of New Hampshire, in 1808, and two years after her death to Catherine Bayard le Roy, of New York, in 1829. One of his sons, Edward, lost his life in the Mexican War; his only surviving child, Fletcher Webster, colonel of a Massachusetts regiment, was killed at Bull Run. In marked contrast to Webster's wonderfully able treatment of public financial affairs, his management of his private finances was notoriously shiftless,—so much so that, in his later years, the care of them was assumed by a voluntary committee of Boston business men. Like other men of his time, he was neither careful nor temperate in table enjoyment. Washington people still tell of the enthusiasm with which, after dinner, he once insisted on standing up in a theatre-box, to join in the chorus of the American national hymn. He was a devoted angler, and intensely interested in scientific agriculture; much of his *Private Correspondence* is connected with the latter subject.

Webster named as his literary executors Edward Everett, C. C. Felton, George Ticknor, and George Ticknor Curtis. By this arrangement the standard edition of his *Works*, in six volumes, appeared (1851). In the first volume is a Life by Everett. See also Webster's *Private Correspondence*, Knapp's *Life of Webster* (1835), March's *Reminiscences of Congress* (1850), Lanman's *Private Life of Webster* (1856), Curtis's *Life of Webster* (1869), Harvey's *Reminiscences of Webster* (1877), Lodge's *Life of Webster* (1883). (A. J.)

WEBSTER, JOHN, the greatest of Shakespeare's contemporaries or successors, was a writer for the stage in the year 1601, and published in 1624 the city pageant for that year, "invented and written by John Webster, merchant-tailor." In the same year a tragedy by Ford and Webster was licensed for the stage; it is one of the numberless treasures now lost to us through the carelessness of genius or the malignity of chance. Beyond the period included between these two dates there are no traces to be found of his existence; nor is anything known of it with any certainty during that period, except that seven plays appeared with his name on the title page, three of them only the work of his unassisted hand. His first noteworthy appearance in print, as far as we know, was as the author of certain additions to Marston's tragicomedy of *The Malcontent*; these probably do not extend beyond the induction, a curious and vivacious prelude to a powerful and irregular work of somewhat morbid and sardonic genius. Three years later, in 1607, two comedies and a tragedy, "written by Thomas Dekker and John Webster," were given to the press. The comedies are lively and humorous, full of movement and incident; but the beautiful interlude of poetry which distinguishes the second scene of the fourth act of *Westward Ho!* is unmistakably and unquestionably the work of Dekker; while the companion comedy of *Northward Ho!* is composed throughout of homespun and coarse-grained prose. *The Famous History of Sir Thomas Wyatt* is apparently a most awkward and injurious abridgment of a historical play in two parts on a pathetic but undramatic subject, the fate of Lady Jane Grey. In this lost play of *Lady Jane* Heywood, Chettle, and Smith had also taken part; so that even in its original form it can hardly have been other than a rough piece of patchwork. There are some touches of simple eloquence and rude dramatic ability in the mangled and corrupt residue which is all that survives of it; but on the whole this "history" is crude, meagre, and unimpressive. In 1612 John Webster stood revealed to the then somewhat narrow world of readers as a tragic poet and dramatist of the very foremost rank in the very highest class. *The White Devil*, also known as *Vittoria Corombona*, is a tragedy based on events then comparatively recent—on a chronicle of crime and retribution in which the leading circumstances were altered and adapted with the most delicate art and the most consummate judgment from the incompleteness of incomposite reality to the requisites of the stage of Shakespeare. By him alone among English poets have the finest scenes and passages of this tragedy been ever surpassed or equalled in the crowning qualities of tragic or dramatic poetry,—in pathos and passion, in subtlety and strength, in harmonious variety of art and infallible fidelity to nature. Eleven years had elapsed when the twin masterpiece of its author —if not indeed a still greater or more absolute masterpiece —was published by the poet who had given it to the stage seven years before. *The Duchess of Malfy* (an Anglicized version of Amalfi, corresponding to such designations as Florence, Venice, and Naples) was probably brought on the stage about the time of the death of Shakespeare; it was first printed in the memorable year which witnessed the first publication of his collected plays. This tragedy stands out among its compeers as one of the imperishable and ineradicable landmarks of literature. All the great qualities apparent in *The White Devil* reappear in *The Duchess of Malfy*, combined with a yet more perfect execution, and utilized with a yet more consummate skill. No poet has ever so long and so successfully sustained at their utmost height and intensity the expressed emotions and the united effects of terror and pity. The transcendent imagination and the impassioned sympathy which inspire this most tragic of all tragedies save *King Lear* are fused together in the fourth act into a creation which has hardly been excelled for unflagging energy of impression and of pathos in all the dramatic or poetic literature of the world. Its wild and fearful sublimity of invention is not more exceptional than the exquisite justice and tenderness and subtlety of its expression. Some of these executive merits may be found in an ill-constructed and ill-conditioned tragi-comedy which was printed in the same year; but few readers will care to remember much more of *The Devil's Law-Case* than the admirable scenes and passages which found favour in the unerring and untiring sight of Webster's first and final interpreter or commentator, Charles Lamb. Thirty-one years later the noble tragedy of *Appius and Virginia* was given to the world,—a work which would alone have sufficed to perpetuate the memory of its author among all competent lovers of English poetry at its best. Seven years afterwards an unprincipled and ignorant bookseller published, under the title of *A Cure for a Cuckold*, a play of which he assigned the authorship to John Webster and William Rowley. This attribution may or may not be accurate; the play is a mixture of coarsely realistic farce and gracefully romantic comedy. An elegy on Henry, prince of Wales, and a few slight occasional verses, compose the rest of Webster's remaining works.

Webster's claims to a place among the chief writers of his country were ignored for upwards of two centuries. In 1830 the Rev. Alexander Dyce first collected and edited the works of a poet who had found his first adequate recognition twenty-two years earlier at the pious and fortunate hands of Lamb. But we cannot imagine that a presentiment or even a foreknowledge of this long delay in the payment of a debt so long due from his countrymen to the memory of so great a poet would seriously have disturbed or distressed the mind of the man who has given us the clue to his nature in a single and an imperishable sentence—"I rest silent in my own work." (A. C. S.)

WEBSTER, NOAH (1758–1843), American lexicographer, was descended on the father's side from John Webster of Warwickshire, England, one of the original settlers at Hartford, and for a time governor of Connecticut, and on the mother's side from William Bradford, second governor of Plymouth and one of the founders of that colony. He was the son of a farmer, and was born in West Hartford, Connecticut, 16th October 1758. In his early years he was engaged in agricultural work, but attended a district school in the winter, and when fourteen years of age began the study of the classics under the Rev. Nathan Perkins, D.D. He entered the freshman's class at Yale College in 1774, and while in his junior year there he took part as a volunteer in the expedition against General Burgoyne. After graduating in 1778 he supported himself by teaching while prosecuting the study of law. Having begun at this time to note down every word whose meaning he did not properly understand, he was first led to conceive the scheme of a new dictionary from his frequent inability to find proper definitions of words in those in current use. His experience as a teacher soon convinced him also of the need of better instruction books in English, and this he endeavoured to supply by his *Grammatical Institute of the English Language*, the first part of which appeared in 1783, and a second and third part in the following years. It comprehended a spelling-book, English grammar, and compilation of English reading, and very soon found a place in most of the schools of the United States. In 1785 he prepared a course of lectures on the English language, which he delivered in the principal American cities, and published in 1789 under the title *Dissertations on the English Language*. Meanwhile he also continued to take a deep interest in all prominent political questions. In his *Sketches of American Policy* (1784) he made the first distinct proposal for a new constitution for the United States, and when the work of the commissioners was completed in 1787 he was asked by them to recommend the new constitution to the American people, which he did in an *Examination of the Leading Principles of the Federal Constitution*. After his marriage in 1789 he established himself in the practice of law at Hartford. In 1793 he was induced to found at New York a paper called *Minerva*, with which was connected the *Herald*, a semi-weekly; the titles of the papers were subsequently altered respectively to the *Commercial Advertiser* and the *New York Spectator*. In 1795 he contributed to his paper several articles, under the signature of Curtius, in vindication of Jay's treaty with Great Britain, which were reprinted and had considerable effect in allaying opposition to it. In 1798 he removed to New Haven, which town he was chosen soon afterwards to represent in the general assembly of Connecticut. In 1802 appeared his well-known treatise on *The Rights of Neutrals*. Having removed in 1812 to Amherst, he took there a leading part in the establishment of the academy and then of the college, of which he was chosen the first president. He also represented Amherst in the court of Massachusetts. In 1822 he returned to New Haven. Meanwhile his lexicographical studies, though much interrupted by his professional and political duties, had never been entirely suspended. In 1806 he published his *Compendious Dictionary of the English Language*, but this was only preparatory to a larger work. In 1824 he sailed for Europe to complete his researches, and after spending some time in Paris continued his labours in the library at Cambridge, where he finished the dictionary. It was published in 1828, and a second edition with many additions appeared in 1841. He also completed the revision of an appendix a few days before his death, which took place 20th May 1843.

In 1833 Webster published an edition of the Bible, "with amendments of the language," and again in 1839 an edition of the New Testament. In early life he wrote a *History of the United States*, of which a revised edition appeared in 1839. He was also the author of *Historical Notices of Banking Institutions and Insurance Companies* (1802), and a *Collection of Papers on Political and Literary Subjects* (1843). Since his death several revised and enlarged editions of the *Dictionary* have appeared. It was the result of much labour and research, and on this account, as well as for the clearness and carefulness of its definitions, it still holds a leading place among dictionaries of the English language, especially in America. A biography of Webster, by C. A. Goodrich, D.D., is prefixed to the quarto editions of the *Dictionary*.

WEBSTER, THOMAS (1800–1886), figure painter, was born at Ranelagh Street, Pimlico, London, on March 20, 1800. His father was a member of the household of George III.; and the son, having shown an aptitude for music, became a chorister in the Chapel Royal, St James's. He, however, developed a still stronger love for painting, and in 1821 he was admitted student of the Royal Academy, to whose exhibition he contributed, in 1824, portraits of Mrs Robinson and Family. In the following year he gained the first medal in the school of painting. Till 1879 he continued to exhibit in the Royal Academy work of a genial and gently humorous character, dealing commonly with subjects of familiar incident, and especially of child life. Many of these were exceedingly popular, particularly his Punch (1840), which procured in 1841 his election as A.R.A., followed five years later by full membership. He became an honorary retired academician in 1877, and died at Cranbrook, Kent, on September 23, 1886. His Going into School, or the Truant (1836), and his Dame's School (1845) are in the National Gallery, and five of his works are in the South Kensington Museum. Many of his paintings have been transcribed by Lumb Stocks, A.R.A., and other of the best engravers of the time.

WEDDERBURN, Alexander (1733–1805), Baron Loughborough in 1780, earl of Rosslyn in 1801, lord high chancellor of Great Britain, was the eldest son of Peter Wedderburn (a lord of session as Lord Chesterhall), and was born in East Lothian on 13th February 1733. He acquired the rudiments of his education at Dalkeith, and in his fourteenth year was sent to the university of Edinburgh, where he matriculated on 18th March 1746. It was from the first his desire to practise at the English bar, though in deference to his father's wishes he qualified as an advocate at Edinburgh on 29th June 1754, and he did not neglect to enter himself at the Inner Temple on 8th May 1753, so that he might keep the Easter and Trinity terms in that year. His father was called to the bench in 1755, and for the next three years Wedderburn stuck to his practice in Edinburgh, during which period he zealously, with an eye to the main chance, employed his oratorical powers in the General Assembly of the Church of Scotland, and passed his evenings in the social and argumentative clubs which abound in its capital. In 1755 a short-lived precursor of the more famous *Edinburgh Review* of a later generation was started in Edinburgh, and it is chiefly remembered now from the circumstance that in its pages Adam Smith criticized the dictionary of Dr Johnson, and that the contents of its two numbers were edited by Wedderburn. The dean of faculty at this time, Lockhart, afterwards Lord Covington, a lawyer notorious for his harsh demeanour, in the autumn of 1757 assailed Wedderburn with more than ordinary insolence. His victim retorted with extraordinary powers of invective, and on being rebuked by the bench declined to retract or apologize, but placed his gown upon the table, and with a low bow left the court for ever. It was long supposed that this step was unpremeditated, but it is now believed that the altercation only made him act upon his previous decision of quitting the Scottish for the English courts. Through his prudence in having taken the preliminary steps some years previously he was called to the English bar at the Inner Temple on 25th November 1757. In his new position he acted with characteristic energy. To shake off his native accent and to acquire the graces of oratorical action, he engaged the services of Sheridan and Macklin. To secure business and to conduct his cases with adequate knowledge, he diligently studied the forms of English law, he solicited Strahan, the printer, "to get him employed in city causes," and he entered into social intercourse (as is noted in Alexander Carlyle's autobiography) with busy London solicitors, such as the brothers Dagge. His local connexions and the incidents of his previous career introduced him to the notice of his countrymen Lords Bute and Mansfield. When Bute was prime minister this legal satellite used, says Dr Johnson, to go on errands for him, and it is to Wedderburn's credit that he first suggested to the premier the propriety of granting Johnson a pension. Through the favour of the royal favourite he was returned to parliament (28th December 1761) for the Ayr burghs, and in consequence of the same patronage he was introduced into Churchill's *Rosciad* as "a pert prim prater," conspicuous for "guilt in his heart and famine in his face." In 1763 he became king's counsel and bencher of Lincoln's Inn, and for a short time went the northern circuits, but was more successful in obtaining business in the Court of Chancery. He obtained a considerable addition to his resources (Carlyle puts the amount at £10,000) on his marriage (31st December 1767) to Betty Anne, sole child and heiress of John Dawson of Marly in Yorkshire. When George Grenville, whose principles leaned to Toryism, quarrelled with the court, Wedderburn affected to regard him as his leader in politics. At the dissolution in the spring of 1768 he was returned by Sir Lawrence Dundas for Richmond as a Tory, but in the struggles over Wilkes he took the popular side of "Wilkes and liberty," and resigned his seat (May 1769). In the opinion of the people he was now regarded as the embodiment of all legal virtue; his health was toasted at the dinners of the Whigs amid rounds of applause, and, in recompense for the loss of his seat in parliament, he was returned by Lord Clive for his pocket-borough of Bishop's Castle, in Shropshire (January 1770). During the next session he acted vigorously in opposition, but his conduct was always viewed with distrust by his new associates, and his attacks on the ministry of Lord North grew less and less animated in proportion to its apparent fixity of tenure. In January 1771 he was offered and accepted the prize of solicitor-general. The high road to the woolsack was now open to his steps, but his defection from his former path has stamped his character with general infamy. Junius wrote of him—"As for Mr Wedderburn, there is something about him which even treachery cannot trust," and Colonel Barré attacked him in the House of Commons. The new law officer defended his conduct with the assertion that his alliance in politics had been with Mr George Grenville, and that the connexion had been severed on his death. In his new position his services were warmly appreciated. He was cool and ready in debate, and when his advice was sought for the deliberation of the cabinet it was given with promptness and energy. The expression of Gibbon that Lord North "was upholden on either hand by the majestic sense of Thurlow and the skilful eloquence of Wedderburn" was not overstrained. All through the lengthened folly of the American War his declamation was consistently employed against the cause of the colonies, but one incident in his conduct is indelibly written in history. Dr Franklin obtained in 1773, by means of some unknown member of parliament, certain letters from crown officials in Massachusetts, written before the outbreak of hostilities, and recommending the employment of a military force for the suppression of the discontent which prevailed in America. These letters he sent to the speaker of the house of assembly, and that body thereupon prayed for the recall of the officials. The application came before a committee of the privy council, when Wedderburn, amid the unrestrained applause of the majority of the judges, denounced Franklin in unmeasured terms, comparing "the coolness and apathy of the wily New Englander" with the "revengeful temper of the negro Zanga" in Dr Young's play of the *Revenge*. His victim preserved an impassive demeanour, but was cut to the quick. Years afterwards, on the termination of the war, when articles of peace were signed at Versailles—this is the usually accepted version of a story on which some doubt has been cast—Franklin wore the same clothes which he had worn when exposed to this invective. In June 1778 Wedderburn was promoted to the post of attorney-general, and in the same year he refused the dignity of chief baron of the exchequer because the offer was not accompanied by the promise of a peerage. At the dissolution in 1774 he had been returned for Okehampton in Devonshire, and for Castle Rising in Norfolk, and selected the former constituency; on his promotion as leading law officer of the crown he returned to his old love of Bishop's Castle. The coveted peerage was not long delayed. In June 1780 he was created chief justice of the Court of Common Pleas, and he was at the same time gratified by the title of Baron Loughborough. For thirteen years he presided over this court, and, although his knowledge of the principles and precedents of law was always deficient, his skill in marshalling his facts and his clearness of diction made his appointment generally acceptable.

During the existence of the coalition ministry of North and Fox, the great seal was in commission (April to December 1783), and Lord Loughborough held the leading place among the commissioners. For some time after its fall he was considered as the leader of the Whig party in the House of Lords, and, had the illness of the king brought about the return of the Whigs to power, the great seal would have been placed in his hands. The king's restoration to health secured Pitt's continuance in office, and disappointed the expectations of the Whigs. In 1792, during the period of the French Revolution, Lord Loughborough seceded from Fox, and on the 28th January 1793 he received the great seal in the Tory cabinet of Pitt. In legal knowledge he was exceeded by many of his predecessors, but his judgments were always remarkable for their perspicuity, and in the appeal cases to the House of Lords, where it was his function to criticize and elucidate the opinions of others, he shone pre-eminent. All the political acts of the administration in which he served met with his zealous support, and he remained faithful to his leader until the question of Catholic emancipation became of urgent importance, when he is supposed to have influenced by unfair means the mind of his sovereign. It was probably through his advice that George III. refused his assent to Pitt's proposals, and that the removal of the disabilities under which the Catholics groaned was delayed for another quarter of a century. When the prime minister found that he could not carry out his compact with his Catholic fellow-subjects he resigned, and Addington succeeded to his place. Much to Lord Loughborough's surprise, no place was found for him in Addington's cabinet, and he was obliged to resign his post of lord chancellor (14th April 1801). His first wife died 15th February 1781 without leaving issue, and he married in the following year (12th September) Charlotte, youngest daughter of William, Viscount Courtenay, but her only son died in childhood. Lord Loughborough accordingly obtained in 1795 a re-grant of his barony with remainder to his nephew, Sir James St Clair Erskine. His fall in 1801 was softened by the grant of an earldom (he was created earl of Rosslyn 21st April 1801, with remainder to his nephew), and by a pension of £4000 per annum. After this date he rarely appeared in public, but he was a constant figure at all the royal festivities. He attended one of those gatherings at Frogmore, 31st December 1804. On the following day he was seized with an attack of gout in the stomach, and on 2d January 1805 he died at his seat, Baylis, near Salt Hill, Windsor. His remains were buried in St Paul's Cathedral on the 11th January.

At the bar Wedderburn was the most elegant speaker of his time, but in legal erudition he was excelled by many of his contemporaries, and he is said to have been markedly afraid of Dunning's forensic powers. For cool and sustained declamation he stood unrivalled in parliament, and his readiness in debate was universally acknowledged. In social life, in the company of the wits and writers of his day, his faculties seemed to desert him. He was not only dull but the cause of dulness in others, and even Alexander Carlyle confesses that in conversation his illustrious countryman was "stiff and pompous." In Wedderburn's character ambition banished all rectitude of principle, but the love of money for money's sake was not among his faults. (W. P. C.)

WEDGWOOD, Josiah (1730–1795), the most distinguished of English manufacturers of pottery. Many members of the Wedgwood family had been established as potters in Staffordshire throughout the 17th century, but their productions were in no way remarkable. Josiah, born in 1730, was the youngest child of Thomas Wedgwood, who owned a thriving pottery in Burslem. At a very early age he distinguished himself by keen powers of observation and love for all that was curious and beautiful. Soon after the death of his father in 1739, Josiah, then scarcely ten years of age, was taken away from school and set to learn the art of moulding or "throwing" clay pottery, at which he soon became extraordinarily skilful. In 1744 he was apprenticed to his eldest brother, who had succeeded to the management of his father's pottery; and in 1751, when the term of his apprenticeship had expired, Josiah Wedgwood became manager of the neighbouring Alder pottery, with a very moderate salary. In 1759 he started as an independent potter at the Ivy-House works in Burslem, and soon introduced many improvements among the simple classes of pottery which were then made in Staffordshire. Soon, however, Wedgwood's tastes were turned in an archæological direction by the increasing interest then taken in Greek or (as they were then called) Etruscan vases. His enthusiasm was specially aroused by the illustrations in Comte de Caylus's *Recueil d'Antiquités* (1752–67); aided by this work he began to attempt to copy Greek designs, and in later years he was further assisted by loans of vases from the fine collection of Greek pottery possessed by Sir William Hamilton. In 1769 Wedgwood opened new potteries on a larger scale at Etruria in Staffordshire, having entered into partnership with Thomas Bentley of Liverpool, a man of great taste and culture, and in all respects a kindred spirit. Many able artists, and among them the young Flaxman, were engaged to design and model reliefs, busts, and other designs for the Wedgwood and Bentley pottery; and in a short time the productions of their kilns were widely sold and highly esteemed in all the chief countries of Europe. After Bentley's death in 1780, Wedgwood became sole owner of the Etruria pottery till 1790, when he took some of his sons into partnership. His chief artistic feat was perhaps the production of an accurate copy in clay of the celebrated glass Portland vase; reproductions of this were sold at £50 a piece, and about 50 copies—not all of equal merit—were produced during Wedgwood's lifetime. In 1764 Josiah married his cousin Sarah Wedgwood. He died on January 3, 1795, in the 65th year of his age, leaving to his children a well-earned fortune of more than half a million.

Josiah Wedgwood was a man of the highest moral worth, and skilled in many branches of knowledge. He was the intimate friend of Dr Erasmus Darwin and other distinguished men of science. For the chief characteristics of the Wedgwood pottery the reader is referred to the article Pottery, vol. xix. p. 632. See also Jewitt, *Life of Wedgwood*, 1865; and Eliza Meteyard, *Life of Wedgwood*, 1st ed., 1865-66.

WEDNESBURY, a market-town and parliamentary borough of Staffordshire, England, is situated near the source of the Tame, on the Great Western and London and North-Western railway lines, 8 miles north-west of Birmingham, and 136½ miles north-west of London. The church of St Bartholomew, a fine building in the Perpendicular style, is supposed to occupy the site of a heathen temple to Woden, and some remains of the ancient castle adjoin it. The church was erected probably in the 11th century, and from 1301 the advowson, tithes, &c., belonged to the abbot of Halesowen until 1535. It was partially rebuilt towards the close of the 15th century, and restored in 1766, in 1827, in 1878, and in 1885. Among other public buildings are the town-hall (1871–72), the free library in the Gothic style (1878), containing about 9000 volumes, the Liberal club (1875), the assembly rooms, the public baths, and the temperance hall. The neighbourhood of Wednesbury has been long celebrated for its iron and coal mines, the coal being unequalled as fuel for the smith's forge. A special kind of iron ore is obtained which is manufactured into axes and other edge-tools. The town possesses large steel and iron works, the more important manufactures being those of the large kind of iron work used by railway companies (such as bridges, cranes, switches, roofs, wheels, axletrees, boiler-plates, and rails), water, steam, and gas pipes, and various kinds of wrought-iron work. The population of the urban sanitary district (area 2124 acres), which is identical with the township, in 1871 was 25,030, and in 1881 it was 24,566. In 1811 the population was only 5372. Until 1885 the parliamentary borough had an area of 11,340 acres, with a population in 1871 of 116,809 and in 1881 of 124,437. West Bromwich, formerly included in it, has been erected into a separate borough, leaving in Wednesbury an area which in 1881 had a population of 68,142.

At Wednesbury (Wodensborough), Ethelfleda, widow of Ethelred of Mercia, in 916 constructed a castle. The place is not mentioned in Domesday, but appears to have belonged to the barony of Dudley. After the Conquest it became a demesne of the crown, and it was bestowed by Henry II. on the Heronvilles. It first received parliamentary representation in 1867.

WEEK. See CALENDAR and SABBATH.

WEEVER. The weevers (*Trachinus*) are small marine fishes which are common on the coasts of Europe, and which have attained notoriety from the painful and sometimes dangerous wounds they are able to inflict upon those who incautiously handle them. They belong to a family of spiny-rayed fishes (*Trachinidæ*), and are distinguished by a long low body with two dorsal fins, the anterior of which is composed of six or seven spines only, the posterior being long and many-rayed; their anal resembles in form and composition the second dorsal fin. The ventral fins are placed in advance of the pectorals, and consist of a spine and five rays. The caudal fin has the hind margin not excised. The body is covered with very small scales, sunk in and firmly adherent to the skin, but the upper surface of the head is bony, without integument. The head, like the body, is compressed, with the eyes of moderate size and placed on the side of the head; the mouth is wide, oblique, and armed with bands of very small teeth.

Several species of weevers are known, but two only occur on the British coasts, viz., the Greater Weever (*Trachinus draco*) and the Lesser Weever (*T. vipera*); the former is frequently found of a length of 12 inches, and possesses some thirty rays in the second dorsal fin, whilst the latter grows only to about half that length, and has about ten rays less in the dorsal. The coloration of both is plain, but the short first dorsal fin is always of a deep black colour. The weevers are bottom fish, burying and hiding themselves in the sand or between shingle,—the lesser species living close inshore and the greater preferring deeper water, and being found sometimes floating on the surface at a distance of several miles from the shore. Although weevers, especially the lesser, are in the habit of burying themselves in the sand, and are abundant in some localities much resorted to by bathers, accidents from stepping upon them are much more rare than from incautiously handling them after capture. They probably make their escape on perceiving the approach of a person. The wounds are inflicted by the dorsal and opercular spines, are very painful, and sometimes cause violent local inflammation. In the absence of any special poison organ it is most probable that the mucous secretion in the vicinity of the spines has poisonous properties. The spines are deeply grooved, the poisonous fluid which is lodged in the grooves being thus introduced into the punctured wound.

WEEVIL, a very old Anglo-Saxon term, now commonly applied to the members of a group of *Coleoptera* termed the *Rhyncophora* (see vol. vi. p. 133). This group is characterized by the prolongation of the head into a rostrum or proboscis, at the end of which the mouth, with its appendages, is placed. The antennæ are short, usually elbowed, and often end in a club-shaped swelling. The basal portion of the antennæ frequently lies in a depression at the side of the rostrum, and this gives the antennæ the appearance of emerging half-way along the rostrum. The mouth appendages are small; the mandibles, however, are stout. The palps are very short and conical as a rule. The body is usually small; in shape it varies very much. The elytra are very hard, and in some cases fused with one another, rendering flight impossible. The larvæ are white, fleshy, apodal grubs, with a series of tubercles along each side of the body; the head is round, and bears strong jaws, and sometimes rudimentary ocelli. They are exclusively phytophagous. The *Rhyncophora* embrace three families,—(1) the *Curculionidæ*, or true weevils, (2) the *Brenthidæ*, and (3) the *Bruchidæ*.

The *Curculionidæ* form one of the largest families amongst the *Coleoptera*, the number of species described exceeding 10,000, arranged in 1150 genera. The antennæ are elbowed, and clavate, with the basal portion inserted in a groove. The third tarsal joint is generally bilobed. Over 400 species exist in Great Britain, few of which exceed half an inch in length. The genera *Phyllobius* and *Polydrosus* include some of the most beautiful insects found in Britain,—their brilliancy, like that of the *Lepidoptera*, being due to the presence of microscopic scales. The diamond beetle of South America, *Entimus imperialis*, is another singularly beautiful weevil; its colour is black, studded with spangles of golden green. The immense family of the *Curculionidæ* includes members which differ greatly from one another in size, colour, and appearance; even the rostrum, the most striking common characteristic, varies greatly. The form of the body is very various: some are rounded or oval, others elongated, almost linear; some are covered with warty protuberances, whilst others are smooth and shining, often with a metallic lustre.

One of the commonest members of this family in Great Britain is the Nut Weevil, *Balaninus nucum*. It is of a brownish colour, varied with yellow, the legs reddish. Its rostrum is unusually long, being five-sixths of the body length in the female, and slightly shorter in the male. The antennæ are 7-jointed. The first three joints are much longer than thick; the four following are shorter, and the seventh not longer than thick. The larva is very common in hazel nuts and filberts. When the nuts are about half-grown, the female bores, with its rostrum, a minute hole in the still comparatively soft nut shell, and deposits an egg within the nut. The egg is said to be pushed in by means of the long rostrum. As the nut grows the slight puncture becomes almost obliterated, so that it is unnoticed by all but the most observant eye. The larva is a thick white grub with a brownish head, bearing fleshy tubercles along its side. It feeds upon the substance of the nut. The nuts which are infested by this insect are usually the first to fall to the ground; the larva then bores a round hole through the nut shell, by means of its jaws, and creeps out. It hides itself in the ground during the winter, and in the spring it passes into the pupa stage, from which it emerges about August as the full-grown insect. A nearly allied form, *Balaninus glandium*, attacks both hazel nuts and acorns.

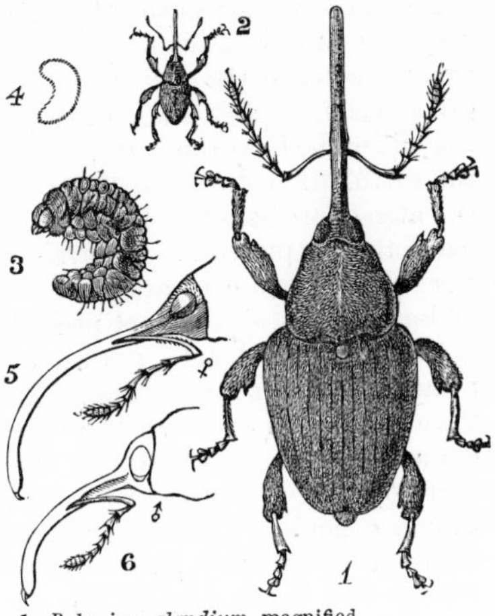

1. *Balaninus glandium*, magnified.
2. The same, natural size.
3. The larva, magnified.
4. The same, natural size.
5. Head and snout of the female, magnified.
6. The same parts of the male, magnified, to show arrangement of antennæ.

In an unobtrusive way weevils do immense harm to vegetation. This is effected not so much by their numbers and their powers of consumption, as amongst caterpillars, but by their habits of attacking the essential parts of a plant, and causing by their injuries the death of the plant affected. They destroy the young buds, shoots, and fruits, and attack the young plants in their most delicate organs. Many of them devour seed, as the Corn Weevils, *Calandra granaria* (see WHEAT) and *C. oryzæ*, and in this way vegetation is severely injured, and its spread seriously checked. Others cause much damage in forests, by boring under the bark and through the wood of trees, whilst some even burrow in the tissue of the leaves.

The *Brenthidæ* are by some authorities included in the family *Curculionidæ*. They include some 275 species, and are almost exclusively tropical. Their antennæ are 11-jointed, not elbowed. The rostrum is straight and very long. The shape of the body is very long and narrow, the first and second abdominal segment being very long. Allied to these is the sub-family *Attelabides*.

The *Bruchidæ* form a somewhat larger family than the foregoing, containing over 400 species. The antennæ are straight, and inserted upon the head just in front of the eyes; they are 11-jointed, and serrated or toothed in the inside. The rostrum is short. *Bruchus pisi* causes considerable damage to pease; during the spring the beetle lays its eggs in the young pea, which is devoured by the larva which hatches out in it. (A. E. S.)

WEIGHING MACHINES. See BALANCE; also MECHANICS (vol. xv. p. 771) and MINT (vol. xvi. p. 490)

WEIGHTS AND MEASURES

THIS subject may be best divided for convenience of reference into three parts:—I. SCIENTIFIC, including the facts and data usually needed for scientific reference; II. HISTORICAL, including the principles of research and results in ancient metrology; and III. COMMERCIAL, including the weights and measures of modern countries as used in commerce.

I. SCIENTIFIC.

A unit of length is the distance between two points defined by some natural or artificial standard, or a multiple of that. For instance, in Britain the unit of the yard is defined by the distance between two parallel lines on gold studs sunk in a bar of bronze, when at 62° F., which bar is preserved in the Standards Office. There are other units, such as the inch, foot, mile, &c.; but, as these are aliquot parts or multiples of the yard, there is no separate standard provided for them. A unit is an abstract quantity, represented by a certain standard, and more or less perfectly by copies of the standard.

A unit of mass is the matter of a standard of mass, or a multiple of that. For instance, in Britain the unit of the pound is defined by a piece of platinum preserved in the Standards Office.

A unit of weight is the attractive force exerted between a unit of mass and some given body at a fixed distance,—this force being the weight of the unit in relation to the given body, or any other body of equal mass.[1] Usually the given body is the earth, and the distance a radius of the earth. For instance, the unit of weight in Britain is the attraction between the earth and the standard pound when that is placed at sea-level at London, in a vacuum. For astronomical comparisons the unit of mass is the sun, and a unit of weight is not needed.

Standards of length are all defined on metal bars at present in civilized countries. Various natural standards have been proposed, such as the length of the polar diameter of the earth (inch), the circumference of the earth (metre) in a given longitude, a pendulum vibrating in one second at a fixed distance from the earth, a wave of light emitted by an incandescent gas, &c. But the difficulty of ascertaining the exact value of these lengths prevents any material standard being based upon them with the amount of accuracy that actual measurements, to be taken from the standard, require. A natural standard is therefore only a matter of sentiment.

Standards of length are of two types, the defining points being either at a certain part of two parallel lines engraven in one plane (a line-standard), or else points on two parallel surfaces, which can only be observed by contact (an end-standard). The first type is always used for accurate purposes. Units of surface are always directly related to standards of length, without any separate standards. Volume is either determined by the lineal dimensions of a space or a solid, or, for accurate purposes, by the mass of water contained in a volume at a given temperature, which again is measured either by liquid measure, or, more accurately, by weight. The standard of volume in Britain is a hollow cylinder of bronze, with a plate glass cover, when at 62° (gallon), legally defined as 277·274 cubic inches, or containing 10 pounds of water at 62° F.

Comparisons.—Lengths nearly equal are compared accurately by fixing two micrometer microscopes with their axes parallel, and at the required distance apart, on a massive support which will not quickly vary with temperature; then the two lengths to be compared, *e.g.*, the standard yard and another, are alternately placed beneath the microscopes, and their lengths observed several times. The error of a single observation in the Standards Department is stated to be a 100,000th of an inch. For fractional lengths a divided bar is required, the accuracy of which is ascertained by a shorter measure, which can be compared with successive sections of the whole length by micrometers. For ordinary purposes, where not less than ·001 inch is to be observed, measures may be placed in contact if one is divided on the edge, and the comparison made with a magnifier. In large field-work the ends of a measure are transferred vertically to the ground by a small transit instrument or theodolite. End-measures between surfaces are read by means of a pair of contact pieces bearing line marks, the value of which is ascertained separately, or by a second end-measure; if both measures bear a line for observation, reversals then give the value of each measure.

Volumes are always most accurately defined by their weight of water, as weighing can be more accurately done than measuring. If the volume is hollow, it may be filled with water and closed with a sheet of plate glass, or if solid the body may be weighed in water and out, the difference giving the weight of its volume of water. Unfortunately the relation between water-weight and absolute volume is not yet accurately known. Volumes of liquid are similarly ascertained by their weight. Volumes of gas are measured in a graduated glass vessel inverted over a liquid, or for commercial purposes by some form of registering flow-meter.

Masses are compared by the BALANCE (*q.v.*), which may be made to indicate a 100,000,000th of the mass. They may also be estimated, not by their attractive force being balanced by an equal mass, but by the elasticity of a spring; this, which is the only true weighing-machine showing weight and not mass, is useful for rough purposes, owing to its quick indication; the most accurate form probably is that with angular readings.[2]

Temperature and the Atmosphere.—All the serious difficulties of weighing and measuring result from these causes, the effects of which and their corrections we will briefly notice. In measurement, since all bodies expand by heat, the temperature at which any measure or standard bar represents the abstract unit requires to be accurately stated and observed, the accuracy of optical observation being about equal to $\frac{1}{100}$ of a degree F. of expansion in a standard. Great accuracy is therefore needed in the manufacture and reading of thermometers, and care that the standard and the thermometer shall be at the same temperature. Another method is to attach a parallel bar of very expansible metal to one end of the standard, and read its length on the standard at the other end; this ensures a more thorough uniformity of mean temperature between the standard and the heat-measurer. The most accurate method is by immersing the measures in a liquid, of which the temperature is read by several thermometers; but this is scarcely needful unless high or low temperatures are required to ascertain the rate of expansion. A room with thick walls, double windows, and the temperature regulated by a gas stove is practically sufficiently equable for comparisons.

The temperature adopted for the standards is not the

[1] The word weight has in common use two meanings,—(1) the force exerted between the earth and a body, and (2) a mass which is weighed against other bodies. In scientific use, however, weight means only a property of matter by which it is most convenient to compare the relative amounts of masses.

[2] See *Nature*, xxx. 205.

same in different countries. In Britain 62° F. has been adopted since the revision of the standards in 1822, as being a convenient average temperature for work; but, as it is purely a temperature of convenience, the rather higher point of 68° F. would be better. In any case an aliquot part of the thermal unit from freezing to boiling of water should be adopted; 62° is $\frac{1}{6}$ and 68° is $\frac{1}{5}$ of this interval. Whether a much higher temperature would not be more conducive to accuracy is a question; 92°, or $\frac{1}{3}$ of the thermal unit, would be so near the temperature of the observer's skin and breath that measures and balances could be approached with less production of error; and such a heat does not at all hinder accurate observing. The French temperature of 32° F. for standards has abandoned all other considerations in favour of readily fixing the temperature in practice by melting ice. This is a ready means of regulation, but a point so far from ordinary working temperatures has two great disadvantages: the observer's warmth produces more error, and the corrections for all observations not iced are so large that the rates of expansion require to be known very accurately for every substance employed. For water their standard temperature is 39°·2 F., when it is at its maximum density; this has the advantage that the density varies less with temperature than at any other point, but it is very doubtful if this is much used for actual work.

No substance expands uniformly with temperature, most materials expanding more rapidly at higher temperatures. The expansion of rods of the following metals, of 100 inches long, is given in decimals of an inch for the 90° from 32° to 122° F. (0 to 50° C.), and from 122° to 212° F. (50° to 100° C.):[1]—

	Platinum.	Platino-iridium.	Steel.	Iron.	Bronze.	Brass.	Zinc.
32° to 122°	·0445	·0435	·0536	·0591	·0876	·0915	·1469
122° to 212°	·0471	·0454	·0574	·0637	·0927	·0964	·1437

But variations of 3 or 4 per cent. may easily be found in the rates of different specimens apparently alike; hence the individual expansion of every important measure needs to be ascertained.

Weighing is complicated by being done in a dense and variable atmosphere, unless—as in the most refined work—the whole balance is placed in a vacuum. When in the air all bodies placed in the balance must, for accurate purposes, have their volume known; and the weight of an equal volume of such air as they are weighed in must be added to their apparent weight to get their true weight. The weight of air displaced by a pound of the following materials is given in grains, at temperature 62° F., barometer 30 inches,—also with barometer 29 inches (temperature 62°), and with temperature 32° (barometer 30 inches), to illustrate the variation[2] (allowing for contraction of the material as well):—

	Platinum.	Brass.	Gilt Bronze.	Iron, with Lead Adjustment.	Quartz.	Glass.	Water.
Sp. Gr.	21·157	8·143	8·283	7·127	2·650	2·518	1·000
62°, 30	·403	1·047	1·029	1·196	3·217	3·385	8·523
62°, 29	·390	1·012	·995	1·156	3·110	3·272	8·240
32°, 30	·429	1·112	1·093	1·271	3·422	3·600	9·056

The above is for London at sea-level; but where the force of gravity is less 30 inches height of mercury will weigh less, and will therefore balance a less weight of air; the air allowance must therefore be less for 30 inches of mercury barometer in lower latitudes and greater heights over sea-level. The change, for instance, in the allowance of air equal to the brass pound will make it, instead of 1·047 grains, become 1·046 when 15,000 feet above the sea, or 10° S. of London. Hence this reduction need rarely be noticed. The composition of the air also varies, and most seriously in the amount of aqueous vapour; the above is ordinary air, but if quite dry the 1·047 grains would become 1·052 grains; the change in carbonic acid is quite immaterial, unless in very close rooms, so that it may be concluded that the moisture of the air is the main point to be noted, after its temperature and pressure,—small errors in any of these three data making far more difference than any other compensation that can be made in the weight of air.

The more complex allowances for the expansion of water in glass, brass, or other vessels we need not enter on here; the principles are simple, but the data require to be accurately determined for the material in question. The expansion of water is, however, so often in question, especially for taking specific gravities, that it is here given. A constant volume which contains or displaces 10,000 grains of water at 62° will contain[3]—

At 32° F. (0° C.), 10,009·84 grains.	At 62° F. (16⅔° C.), 10,000·00 grains.
,, 39°·2 F. (4° C.), 10,011·20 ,,	,, 68° F. (20° C.), 9,993·76 ,,
,, 50° F. (10° C.), 10,008·89 ,,	,, 86° F. (30° C.), 9,968·76 ,,

Hence if a specific gravity is observed at any of these temperatures it must be × the corresponding weight ÷ 10,000 to reduce it to a comparison with water at 62°; the expansion of the body observed is another question altogether, and must be compensated also.

The weight of a cubic inch, or other linearly measured volume, of water is not yet very accurately known. The observations have been made by weighing closed hollow metal cases in and out of water (thus obtaining the weight of an equal volume of water), and then gauging the size of the case with exactitude. Cubes, cylinders, and spheres have been employed. The results are:[4]—

		Cubic Inch at 62° F.	Cubic Foot at 62° F.	Cubic Decimetre at 4° C.
		Grains.	Ounces.	Grammes.
1795	In France, by Lefevre-Gineau (legal French)	252·603	997·70	1000·000
1797 1821	In England, by Shuckburgh and Kater (legal British)	252·724	998·18	1000·480
1825	In Sweden, by Berzelius, Svanberg, and Akermann	252·678	998·00	1000·296
1830	In Austria, by Stampfer	252·515	997·35	999·653
1841	In Russia, by Kupffer	252·600	997·69	999·989

National Standards and Copies.—Having now noticed the principles and constants involved, we will consider the British and metric standards, the only ones now used in scientific work.

The imperial standard yard is a bronze bar 38 inches long, 1 inch square; the defining lines, 36 inches apart, are cut on gold studs, sunk in holes, so that their surface passes through the axis of the bar. Thus flexure does not tend to tip the engraved surfaces nearer or farther apart. This bar when in use rests on a lever frame, which supports it at 8 points, 4·78 inches apart, on rollers which divide the pressure exactly equally.[5] This standard is in actual use for all important comparisons at the Standards Office. Four copies, which are all equal to it, within $\frac{1}{6}$° of temperature, are deposited in other places in case of injury or loss of the standard. The standard pound is a thick disk of platinum about 1$\frac{1}{6}$ inches across, and 1 inch high, with a shallow groove around it near the top. Four copies are deposited with the above copies of the yard. For public use there are a series of end-standards exposed on the outer wall of Greenwich observatory; and a length of 100 feet, and another of 66 feet (1 chain), marked on brass

[1] Computed from Fizeau, *Ann. Bur. Long.*, 1878.

[2] Computed from Chisholm, *Weighing and Measuring*, 1877, p. 162; also see p. 158.

[3] Computed from *Report* of Standards Department, 1883.

[4] Computed from Chisholm, *op. cit.*, p. 112.

[5] See Chisholm, *op. cit.*, pp. 188, 189. For less refined purposes measuring bars should be supported on two points, 21 per cent. of the whole length from the ends. This equalizes the strains in the curves, and makes a minimum distortion.

plates let into the granite step along the back of Trafalgar Square. As this is a practically invariable earth-fast standard, and most convenient for reference, it is important to know the minute errors of it, as determined by the Standards Department.[1] Starting from 0 the errors are in inches—

at	0	10	20	30	40	50	60	70	80	90	100 feet.
error	0	−·007	−·019	−·022	−·015	−·008	−·007	+·011	+·021	+0·17	−·008 inches.

The mean uncertainty in these values is ·003, and the greatest uncertainty ·01. The total length of the chain standard is − ·019 inch from the truth. There is also a public balance provided at Greenwich observatory, which shows the accuracy of any pound weight placed upon it. For important scientific standards comparisons are made gratuitously, as a matter of courtesy, by the officials of the Standards Office, 7 Old Palace Yard, Westminster. The most delicate weighings are all performed in a vacuum case with glass sides, which is so constructed that the weights can be exchanged from one arm to the other without opening the case, so as to obtain double weighings.

The toleration of error in copies for scientific purposes, by the Standards Department, is ·0005 inch on the yard or lesser lengths, about equal to 15 divisions of the micrometer; on the pound ·0025 grain, about $\frac{1}{2}$ a division of the official balances; on the ounce ·001 grain; on the gallon 1 grain; and on the cubic foot 4 grains. The toleration for commercial copies is ·005 on the yard, ·001 on the foot and under, and ·1 grain on weights of 1 ounce to 1 pound.[2] The Standards Commission of 1851 recommended a limit of 1 in 20,000.

For practical work of moderate accuracy the most convenient forms of measures are—for lengths under a foot, feather-edge metal scales divided to $\frac{1}{50}$ inch (finer divisions are only confusing, and $\frac{1}{1000}$ of an inch can be safely read by estimation); for lengths of 1 to 10 feet, metal tubes or deep bars bearing line-divisions, and with permanent feet attached at 21 per cent. from either end, so that the deformation by flexure is always the same; for long distances a steel tape with fine divisions scratched across it and numbered by etching. The most accurate way of using such a tape is not to prepare a flat bed for it, but to support it at points not more than 50 feet apart; then by observing the distances and levels of these points, and knowing the weight of the tape, the correction for the sloping distance between the points and the difference of the catenary length of the tape from the straight distance can be precisely calculated; the corrections for stretching of the tape (best done by a lever arm with fixed weight), and for temperature, are all that are needful besides.

The first French standard metre (of 1799) is a platinum bar end-standard of about 1 inch wide and $\frac{1}{7}$ inch thick; the new standard of the International Metric Commission is a line-standard of platino-iridium, 40 inches long and ·8 inches square, grooved out on all four sides so that its section is between × and H form; this provides the greatest rigidity, and also a surface in the axis of the bar to bear the lines of the standard. The new standard kilogramme, like the old one, is a cylinder of platinum of equal diameter and height. These new standards are preserved in the International Metric Bureau at Paris, to which seventeen nations contribute in support and direction, and in which the most refined methods of comparison are adopted. For lineal comparisons the alternate substitution of the measures on a sliding bed beneath fixed micrometer microscopes is provided as in the British office, and a bath for the heating of one measure in a liquid to ascertain its expansion. For weighing four balances are provided, each with mechanism for the transposition of the weights, and the lowering of the balance into play on its bearings, so that weighings can be performed at 13 feet distance from the balance, thus avoiding the disturbance caused by the warmth of the observer. The readings of the balance scale are made by a fixed telescope, the motion being observed by the reflexion of a fixed scale from a mirror attached to the beam of the balance. In this bureau are also an equally fine hydrostatic balance for taking specific gravities by water weighing, a standard barometer, and an air thermometer, with all subsidiary apparatus. The special work of the bureau is the construction and comparison of metric standards for all the countries supporting it, and for scientific work of all kinds.

The legal theory of the British system of weights and measures is—(A) the standard yard, with all lineal measures and their squares and cubes based upon that; (B) the standard pound of 7000 grains, with all weights based upon that, with the troy pound of 5760 grains for trade purposes; (C) the standard gallon (and multiples and fractions of it), declared to contain 10 ℔ of water at 62° F., being in volume 277·274 cubic inches, which contain each 252·724 grains of water in a vacuum at 62°, or 252·458 grains of water weighed with brass weights in air of 62° with the barometer at 30 inches.

The legal theory of the metric system of weights and measures is—(A) the standard metre, with decimal fractions and multiples thereof; (B) the standard kilogramme, with decimal fractions and multiples thereof; (C) the litre (with decimal fractions and multiples), declared to be a cube of $\frac{1}{10}$ metre, and to contain a kilogramme of water at 4° C. in a vacuum. No standard litre exists, all liquid measures being legally fixed by weight. The metre was supposed, when established in 1799, to be a ten-millionth of the quadrant of the earth through Paris; it differs from this theoretical amount by about 1 in 4000.

The legal equivalents between the British and French systems are—metre = 39·37079 inches; kilogramme = 15432·34874 grains. By the more exact comparisons of Captain Clarke (1866) the metre (at 0° C., 32° F.) is equal to 39·37043196 inches of the yard at 62° F.; but Rogers in 1882 compared the metre as 39·37027. It must always be remembered that a French metre of perfect legal exactitude will, by expanding from 32° to 62° F., become equal to a greater number of inches when the two measures are placed together; thus a brass metre is equal to 39·382 inches when compared with British measures at the same temperature, and this is its true commercial equivalent. The kilogramme determination above is that of Professor Miller (1844), against the kilogramme des Archives, but in 1884 the international kilogramme yielded 15432·35639.

For further details, see H. W. Chisholm, *Weighing and Measuring* (Nature series), 1877, and *Reports* of the Warden of the Standards, subsequently of the Standards Department (all in British Museum Newspaper Room), for all practical details,—especially reports on metre (1868–9), errors of grain weights (1872), principles of measuring (long paper of German Standards Commission, translated 1872), Trafalgar Square standards (1876), density of water (1883), toleration of error, British and international (1883), standard wire and plate gauges in inches (1883), besides numerous practical tables, mainly in the earlier numbers before the wardenship was merged in the Board of Trade.

II. Historical.

Though no line can be drawn between ancient and modern metrology, yet, owing to neglect, and partly to the scarcity of materials, there is a gap of more than a thousand years over which the connexion of units[3] of

[1] *Report* of Warden of the Standards, 1875.

[2] *Report* of Warden, 1868, see also 1872.

[3] In the absence of the actual standards of ancient times the units of measure and of weight have to be inferred from the other remains; hence unit in this division is used for any more or less closely defined amount of length or weight in terms of which matter was measured.

measure is mostly guess-work. Hence, except in a few cases, we shall not here consider any units of the Middle Ages. A constant difficulty in studying works on metrology is the need of distinguishing the absolute facts of the case from the web of theory into which each writer has woven them,—often the names used, and sometimes the very existence of the units in question, being entirely an assumption of the writer. Therefore we shall here take the more pains to show what the actual authority is for each conclusion. Again, each writer has his own leaning: Böckh, to the study of water-volumes and weights, even deriving linear measures therefrom; Queipo, to the connexion with Arabic and Spanish measures; Brandis, to the basis of Assyrian standards; Mommsen, to coin weights; and Bortolotti to Egyptian units; but Hultsch is more general, and appears to give a more equal representation of all sides than do other authors. In this article the tendency will be to trust far more to actual measures and weights than to the statements of ancient writers; and this position seems to be justified by the great increase in materials, and the more accurate means of study of late. The usual arrangement by countries has been mainly abandoned in favour of following out each unit as a whole, without recurring to it separately for every locality.

The materials for study are of three kinds. (1) *Literary*, both in direct statements in works on measures (*e.g.*, Elias of Nisibis), medicine (Galen), and cosmetics (Cleopatra), in ready-reckoners (Didymus), clerk's (kátib's) guides, and like handbooks, and in indirect explanations of the equivalents of measures mentioned by authors (*e.g.*, Josephus). But all such sources are liable to the most confounding errors, and some passages relied on have in any case to submit to conjectural emendation. These authors are of great value for connecting the monumental information, but must yield more and more to the increasing evidence of actual weights and measures. Besides this, all their evidence is but approximate, often only stating quantities to a half or quarter of the amount, and seldom nearer than 5 or 10 per cent.; hence they are entirely worthless for all the closer questions of the approximation or original identity of standards in different countries; and it is just in this line that the imagination of writers has led them into the greatest speculations, unchecked by accurate evidence of the original standards. (2) *Weights and measures actually remaining.* These are the prime sources, and, as they increase and are more fully studied, so the subject will be cleared and obtain a fixed basis. A difficulty has been in the paucity of examples, more due to the neglect of collectors than the rarity of specimens. The number of published weights did not exceed 600 of all standards a short time ago; but the collections in the last three years from Naucratis (28),[1] Defenneh (29), and Memphis (44) have supplied over six times this quantity, and of an earlier age than most other examples, while existing collections have been more thoroughly examined; hence there is need for a general revision of the whole subject. It is above all desirable to make allowances for the changes which weights have undergone; and, as this has only been done for the above Egyptian collections and that of the British Museum, conclusions as to the accurate values of different standards will here be drawn from these rather than Continental sources. (3) *Objects which have been made by measure or weight*, and from which the unit of construction can be deduced. Buildings will generally yield up their builder's foot or cubit when examined (*Inductive Metrology*, p. 9). Vases may also be found bearing such relations to one another as to show their unit of volume. And coins have long been recognized as one of the great sources of metrology,—valuable for their wide and detailed range of information, though most unsatisfactory on account of the constant temptation to diminish their weight, a weakness which seldom allows us to reckon them as of the full standard Another defect in the evidence of coins is that, when one variety of the unit of weight was once fixed on for the coinage, there was (barring the depreciation) no departure from it, because of the need of a fixed value, and hence coins do not show the range and character of the real variations of units as do buildings, or vases, or the actual commercial weights.

[1] These figures refer to the list of publications at the end of the present section, p. 489.

PRINCIPLES OF STUDY.—(1) *Limits of Variation in Different Copies, Places, and Times.*—Unfortunately, so very little is known of the ages of weights and measures that this datum—most essential in considering their history—has been scarcely considered. In measure, Egyptians of Dynasty IV. at Gizeh on an average varied 1 in 350 between different buildings (27). Buildings at Persepolis, all of nearly the same age, vary in unit 1 in 450 (25). Including a greater range of time and place, the Roman foot in Italy varied during two or three centuries on an average $\frac{1}{400}$ from the mean. Covering a longer time, we find an average variation of $\frac{1}{200}$ in the Attic foot (25), $\frac{1}{150}$ in the English foot (25), $\frac{1}{170}$ in the English itinerary foot (25). So we may say that an average variation of $\frac{1}{400}$ by toleration, extending to double that by change of place and time, is usual in ancient measures. In weights of the same place and age there is a far wider range; at Defenneh (29), within a century probably, the average variation of different units is $\frac{1}{36}$, $\frac{1}{60}$, and $\frac{1}{67}$, the range being just the same as in all times and places taken together. Even in a set of weights all found together, the average variation is only reduced to $\frac{1}{60}$, in place of $\frac{1}{36}$ (29). Taking a wider range of place and time, the Roman libra has an average variation of $\frac{1}{50}$ in the examples of better period (43), and in those of Byzantine age $\frac{1}{35}$ (44). Altogether, we see that weights have descended from original varieties with so little intercomparison that no rectification of their values has been made, and hence there is as much variety in any one place and time as in all together. Average variation may be said to range from $\frac{1}{40}$ to $\frac{1}{70}$ in different units, doubtless greatly due to defective balances.

2. *Rate of Variation.*—Though large differences may exist, the rate of general variation is but slow,—excluding, of course, all monetary standards. In Egypt the cubit lengthened $\frac{1}{170}$ in some thousands of years (25, 44). The Italian mile has lengthened $\frac{1}{100}$ since Roman times (2); the English mile lengthened about $\frac{1}{300}$ in four centuries (31). The English foot has not appreciably varied in several centuries (25). Of weights there are scarce any dated, excepting coins, which nearly all decrease; the Attic tetradrachm, however, increased $\frac{1}{50}$ in three centuries (28), owing probably to its being below the average trade weight to begin with. Roughly dividing the Roman weights, there appears a decrease of $\frac{1}{40}$ from imperial to Byzantine times (43).

3. *Tendency of Variation.*—This is, in the above cases of lengths, to an increase in course of time. The Roman foot is also probably $\frac{1}{300}$ larger than the earlier form of it, and the later form in Britain and Africa perhaps another $\frac{1}{300}$ larger (25). Probably measures tend to increase and weights to decrease in transmission from time to time or place to place; but far more data are needed to study this.

4. *Details of Variation.*—Having noticed variation in the gross, we must next observe its details. The only way of examining these is by drawing curves (28, 29), representing the frequency of occurrence of all the variations of a unit; for instance, in the Egyptian unit—the kat—counting in a large number how many occur between 140

and 141 grains, 141 and 142, and so on; such numbers represented by curves show at once where any particular varieties of the unit lie (see *Naukratis*, i. p. 83). This method is only applicable where there is a large number of examples; but there is no other way of studying the details. The results from such a study—of the Egyptian kat, for example—show that there are several distinct families or types of a unit, which originated in early times, have been perpetuated by copying, and reappear alike in each locality (see *Tanis*, ii. pl. l.). Hence we see that if one unit is derived from another it may be possible, by the similarity or difference of the forms of the curves, to discern whether it was derived by general consent and recognition from a standard in the same condition of distribution as that in which we know it, or whether it was derived from it in earlier times before it became so varied, or by some one action forming it from an individual example of the other standard without any variation being transmitted. As our knowledge of the age and locality of weights increases these criteria in curves will prove of greater value; but even now no consideration of the connexion of different units should be made without a graphic representation to compare their relative extent and nature of variation.

5. *Transfer of Units.*—The transfer of units from one people to another takes place almost always by trade. Hence the value of such evidence in pointing out the ancient course of trade, and commercial connexions (17). The great spread of the Phœnician weight on the Mediterranean, of the Persian in Asia Minor, and of the Assyrian in Egypt are evident cases; and that the decimal weights of the laws of Manu (43) are decidedly not Assyrian or Persian, but on exactly the Phœnician standard, is a curious evidence of trade by water and not overland. If, as seems probable, units of length may be traced in prehistoric remains, they are of great value; at Stonehenge, for instance, the earlier parts are laid out by the Phœnician foot, and the later by the Pelasgo-Roman foot (26). The earlier foot is continually to be traced in other megalithic remains, whereas the later very seldom occurs (25). This bears strongly on the Phœnician origin of our prehistoric civilization. Again, the Belgic foot of the Tungri is the basis of the present English land measures, which we thus see are neither Roman nor British in origin, but Belgic. Generally a unit is transferred from a higher to a less civilized people; but the near resemblance of measures in different countries should always be corroborated by historical considerations of a probable connexion by commerce or origin (Head, *Historia Numorum*, xxxvii.). It should be borne in mind that in early times the larger values, such as minæ, would be transmitted by commerce, while after the introduction of coinage the lesser values of shekels and drachmæ would be the units; and this needs notice, because usually a borrowed unit was multiplied or divided according to the ideas of the borrowers, and strange modifications thus arose.

6. *Connexions of Lengths, Volumes, and Weights.*—This is the most difficult branch of metrology, owing to the variety of connexions which can be suggested, to the vague information we have, especially on volumes, and to the liability of writers to rationalize connexions which were never intended. To illustrate how easy it is to go astray in this line, observe the continual reference in modern handbooks to the cubic foot as 1000 ounces of water; also the cubic inch is very nearly 250 grains, while the gallon has actually been fixed at 10 ℔ of water; the first two are certainly mere coincidences, as may very probably be the last also, and yet they offer quite as tempting a base for theorizing as any connexions in ancient metrology. No such theories can be counted as more than coincidences which have been adopted, unless we find a very exact connexion, or some positive statement of origination. The idea of connecting volume and weight has received an immense impetus through the metric system, but it is not very prominent in ancient times. The Egyptians report the weight of a measure of various articles, amongst others water (6), but lay no special stress on it; and the fact that there is no measure of water equal to a direct decimal multiple of the weight-unit, except very high in the scale, does not seem as if the volume was directly based upon weight. Again, there are many theories of the equivalence of different cubic cubits of water with various multiples of talents (2, 3, 18, 24, 33); but connexion by lesser units would be far more probable, as the primary use of weights is not to weigh large cubical vessels of liquid, but rather small portions of precious metals. The Roman amphora being equal to the cubic foot, and containing 80 libræ of water, is one of the strongest cases of such relations, being often mentioned by ancient writers. Yet it appears to be only an approximate relation, and therefore probably accidental, as the volume by the examples is too large to agree to the cube of the length or to the weight, differing $\frac{1}{20}$, or sometimes even $\frac{1}{12}$. All that can be said therefore to the many theories connecting weight and measure is that they are possible, but our knowledge at present does not admit of proving or disproving their exactitude. Certainly vastly more evidence is needed before we would, with Böckh (2), derive fundamental measures through the intermediary of the cube roots of volumes. Soutzo wisely remarks on the intrinsic improbability of refined relations of this kind (*Étalons Ponderaux Primitifs*, note, p. 4).

Another idea which has haunted the older metrologists, but is still less likely, is the connexion of various measures with degrees on the earth's surface. The lameness of the Greeks in angular measurement would alone show that they could not derive itinerary measures from long and accurately determined distances on the earth.

7. *Connexions with Coinage.*—From the 7th century B.C. onward, the relations of units of weight have been complicated by the need of the interrelations of gold, silver, and copper coinage; and various standards have been derived theoretically from others through the weight of one metal equal in value to a unit of another. That this mode of originating standards was greatly promoted, if not started, by the use of coinage we may see by the rarity of the Persian silver weight (derived from the Assyrian standard), soon after the introduction of coinage, as shown in the weights of Defenneh (29). The relative value of gold and silver (17, 21) in Asia is agreed generally to have been 13⅓ to 1 in the early ages of coinage; at Athens in 434 B.C. it was 14 : 1; in Macedon, 350 B.C., 12½ : 1; in Sicily, 400 B.C., 15 : 1, and 300 B.C., 12 : 1; in Italy, in 1st century, it was 12 : 1, in the later empire 13·9 : 1, under Justinian 14·4 : 1, and in modern times 15·5 : 1, but at present 23 : 1,—the fluctuations depending mainly on the opening of large mines. Silver stood to copper in Egypt as 80 : 1 (Brugsch), or 120 : 1 (Revillout); in early Italy and Sicily as 250 : 1 (Mommsen), or 120 : 1 (Soutzo), under the empire 120 : 1, under Justinian 100 : 1; at present it is 150 : 1. The distinction of the use of standards for trade in general, or for silver or gold in particular, should be noted. The early observance of the relative values may be inferred from Num. vii. 13, 14, where silver offerings are 13 and 7 times the weight of the gold, or of equal value and one-half value.

8. *Legal Regulation of Measures.*—Most states have preserved official standards, usually in temples under priestly custody. The Hebrew "shekel of the sanctuary"

is familiar; the standard volume of the apet was secured in the dromus of Anubis at Memphis (35); in Athens, besides the standard weight, twelve copies for public comparison were kept in the city; also standard volume measures in several places (2); at Pompeii the block with standard volumes cut in it was found in the portico of the forum (33); other such standards are known in Greek cities (Gythium, Panidum, and Trajanopolis) (11, 33); at Rome the standards were kept in the Capitol, and weights also in the temple of Hercules (2); the standard cubit of the Nilometer was before Constantine in the Serapæum, but was removed by him to the church (2). In England the Saxon standards were kept at Winchester before 950 A.D., and copies were legally compared and stamped; the Normans removed them to Westminster to the custody of the king's chamberlains at the exchequer; and they were preserved in the crypt of Edward the Confessor, while remaining royal property (9). The oldest English standards remaining are those of Henry VII. Many weights have been found in the temenos of Demeter at Cnidus, the temple of Artemis at Ephesus, and in a temple of Aphrodite at Byblus (44); and the making or sale of weights may have been a business of the custodians of the temple standards.

9. *Names of Units.*—It is needful to observe that most names of measures are generic and not specific, and cover a great variety of units. Thus foot, digit, palm, cubit, stadium, mile, talent, mina, stater, drachm, obol, pound, ounce, grain, metretes, medimnus, modius, hin, and many others mean nothing exact unless qualified by the name of their country or city. Also, it should be noted that some ethnic qualifications have been applied to different systems, and such names as Babylonian and Euboic are ambiguous; the normal value of a standard will therefore be used here rather than its name, in order to avoid confusion, unless specific names exist, such as *kat* and *uten*.

All quantities stated in this article without distinguishing names are in British units of inch, cubic inch, or grain.

STANDARDS OF LENGTH.—Most ancient measures have been derived from one of two great systems, that of the cubit of 20·63 inches, or the digit of ·729 inch; and both these systems are found in the earliest remains.

20·63 ins.—First known in Dynasty IV. in Egypt, most accurately 20·620 in the Great Pyramid, varying 20·51 to 20·71 in Dyn. IV. to VI. (27). Divided decimally in 100ths; but usually marked in Egypt into 7 palms or 28 digits, approximately; a mere juxtaposition (for convenience) of two incommensurate systems (25, 27). The average of several cubit rods remaining is 20·65, age in general about 1000 B.C. (33). At Philæ, &c., in Roman times 20·76 on the Nilometers (44). This unit is also recorded by cubit lengths scratched on a tomb at Beni Hasan (44), and by dimensions of the tomb of Ramessu IV. and of Edfu temple (5) in papyri. From this cubit, *mahi*, was formed the *xylon* of 3 cubits, the usual length of a walking-staff; fathom, *nent*, of 4 cubits, and the *khet* of 40 cubits (18); also the *schœnus* of 12,000 cubits, actually found marked on the Memphis-Faium road (44).

Babylonia had this unit nearly as early as Egypt. The divided plotting scales lying on the drawing boards of the statues of Gudea (*Nature*, xxviii. 341) are of ½ 20·89, or a span of 10·44, which is divided in 16 digits of ·653, a fraction of the cubit also found in Egypt. Buildings in Assyria and Babylonia show 20·5 to 20·6. The Babylonian system was sexagesimal, thus (18)—

uban,	5=qat,	6=ammat,	6=qanu,	60=sos,	30=parasang,	2=kaspu.
·69 inch	3·44	20·6	124	7430	223,000	446,000

Asia Minor had this unit in early times,—in the temples of Ephesus 20·55, Samos 20·62; Hultsch also claims Priene 20·90, and the stadia of Aphrodisias 20·67, and Laodicea 20·94. Ten buildings in all give 20·63 mean (18, 25); but in Armenia it rose to 20·76 in late Roman times, like the late rise in Egypt (25). It was specially divided into ⅙th, the foot of ⅗ths being as important as the cubit.

12·45 ins. ⅗ of 20·75. This was especially the Greek derivative of the 20·63 cubit. It originated in Babylonia as the foot of that system (24), in accordance with the sexary system applied to the early decimal division of the cubit. In Greece it is the most usual unit, occurring in the Propylæa at Athens 12·44, temple at Ægina 12·40, Miletus 12·51, the Olympic course 12·62, &c. (18); thirteen buildings giving an average of 12·45, mean variation ·06 (25), = ⅗ of 20·75, m. var. ·10. The digit = ¼ palæste, = $\frac{1}{16}$ foot of 12·4; then the system is

foot,	1½=cubit,	4=orguia		100=	
	10		=acæna,	10=plethron,	6= stadion.
12·4 inch	18·7	74·7	124·5	1245	7470

In Etruria it probably appears in tombs as 12·45 (25); perhaps in Roman Britain; and in mediæval England as 12·47 (25).

13·8 ins. ⅔ of 20·7. This foot is scarcely known monumentally. On three Egyptian cubits there is a prominent mark at the 19th digit or 14 inches, which shows the existence of such a measure (33). It became prominent when adopted by Philetærus about 280 B.C. as the standard of Pergamum (42), and probably it had been shortly before adopted by the Ptolemies for Egypt. From that time it is one of the principal units in the literature (Didymus, &c.), and is said to occur in the temple of Augustus at Pergamum as 13·8 (18). Fixed by the Romans at 16 digits (13⅓ = Roman foot), or its cubit at 1⅘ Roman feet, it was legally = 13·94 at 123 B.C. (42); and 7½ Philetærean stadia were = Roman mile (18). The multiples of the 20·63 cubit are in late times generally reckoned in these feet of ⅔ cubit. The name "Babylonian foot" used by Böckh (2) is only a theory of his, from which to derive volumes and weights; and no evidence for this name, or connexion with Babylon, is to be found. Much has been written (2, 3, 33) on supposed cubits of about 17–18 inches derived from 20·63,—mainly, in endeavouring to get a basis for the Greek and Roman feet, but these are really connected with the digit system; and the monumental or literary evidence for such a division of 20·63 will not bear examination. There is, however, fair evidence for

17·30 ⅚ of 20·76. units of 17·30 and 1·730 or $\frac{1}{12}$ of 20·76 in Persian buildings (25); and the same is found in Asia Minor as 17·25 or ⅚ of 20·70. On the Egyptian cubits a small cubit is marked as about 17 inches, which may well be this unit, as ⅚ of 20·6 is 17·2; and, as these marks are placed *before* the 23rd digit or 17·0, they cannot refer to 6 palms, or 17·7, which is the 24th digit, though they are usually attributed to that (33).

We now turn to the second great family based on the digit. This has been so usually confounded with the 20·63 family, owing to the juxtaposition of 28 digits with that cubit in Egypt, that it should be observed how the difficulty of their incommensurability has been felt. For instance, Lepsius (3) supposed two primitive cubits of 13·2 and 20·63, to account for 28 digits being only 20·4 when free from the cubit of 20·63,—the first 24 digits being in some cases made shorter on the cubits to agree with the true digit standard, while the remaining 4 are lengthened to fill up to 20·6. In the

·727 ins. Dynasties IV. and V. in Egypt the digit is found in tomb sculptures as ·727 (27); while from a dozen examples in the later remains we find the mean ·728 (25). A length of 10 digits is marked on all the inscribed Egyptian cubits as the "lesser span" (33). In Assyria the same digit appears as ·730, particularly at Nimrud (25); and in Persia buildings show the 10-digit length of 7·34 (25). In Syria it was about ·728, but variable; in eastern Asia Minor more like the Persian, being ·732 (25). In these cases the digit itself, or decimal multiples, seem to have been used.

18·23 25 × ·729. The pre-Greek examples of this cubit in Egypt, mentioned by Böckh (2), give 18·23 as a mean, which is 25 digits of ·729, and has no relation to the 20·63 cubit. This cubit, or one nearly equal, was used in Judæa in the times of the kings, as the Siloam inscription names a distance of 1758 feet as roundly 1200 cubits, showing a cubit of about 17·6 inches. This is also evidently the Olympic cubit; and, in pursuance of the decimal multiple of the digit found in Egypt and Persia, the cubit of 25 digits was ¼ of the orguia of 100 digits, the series being

old digit,	25=cubit,	4=	orguia,	10=amma,	10=stadion.
	100	=			
·729 inch	18·2		72·9	729	7296

Then, taking ⅔ of the cubit, or ⅙ of the orguia, as a foot, the Greeks arrived at their foot of 12·14; this, though very well known in literature, is but rarely found, and then generally in the form of the cubit, in monumental measures. The Parthenon step, celebrated as 100 feet wide, and apparently 225 feet long, gives by Stuart 12·137, by Penrose 12·165, by Paccard 12·148, differences due to scale and not to slips in measuring. Probably 12·16 is the nearest value. There are but few buildings wrought on this foot in Asia Minor, Greece, or Roman remains. The Greek system, however, adopted this foot as a basis for decimal multiplication, forming

foot,	10=acæna,	10=plethron,
12·16 inches	121·6	1216

which stand as ⅙th of the other decimal series based on the digit. This is the agrarian system, in contrast to the orguia system, which was the itinerary series (33).

Then a further modification took place, to avoid the inconvenience of dividing the foot in 16⅔ digits, and a new digit was formed —longer than any value of the old digit—of $\frac{1}{16}$ of the foot, or ·760, so that the series ran

digit, { 10 = lichas / 96............ = orguia, 10 = amma, 10 = stadion.
·76 inch 7·6 72·9 729 7296

This formation of the Greek system (25) is only an inference from the facts yet known, for we have not sufficient information to prove it, though it seems much the simplest and most likely history.

11·62 16 × ·726. Seeing the good reasons for this digit having been exported to the West from Egypt—from the presence of the 18·23 cubit in Egypt, and from the ·729 digit being the decimal base of the Greek long measures—it is not surprising to find it in use in Italy as a digit, and multiplied by 16 as a foot. The more so, as the half of this foot, or 8 digits, is marked off as a measure on the Egyptian cubit rods (33). Though Queipo has opposed this connexion (not noticing the Greek link of the digit), he agrees that it is supported by the Egyptian square measure of the plethron, being equal to the Roman actus (33). The foot of 11·6 appears probably first in the prehistoric and early Greek remains, and is certainly found in Etrurian tomb dimensions as 11·59 (25). Dörpfeld considers this as the Attic foot, and states the foot of the Greek metrological relief at Oxford as 11·65 (or 11·61, Hultsch). Hence we see that it probably passed from the East through Greece to Etruria, and thence became the standard foot of Rome; there, though divided by the Italian duodecimal system into 12 unciæ, it always maintained its original 16 digits, which are found marked on some of the foot-measures. The well-known ratio of 25 : 24 between the 12·16 foot and this we see to have arisen through one being $\frac{1}{6}$ of 100 and the other 16 digits,—$16\frac{2}{3}$: 16 being as 25 : 24, the legal ratio. The mean of a dozen foot-measures (1) gives 11·616 ± ·008, and of long lengths and buildings 11·607 ± ·01. In Britain and Africa, however, the Romans used a rather longer form (25) of about 11·68, or a digit of ·730. Their series of measures was

digitus, 4 = palmus, 4 = pes, 5 = passus, 125 = stadium, 8 = milliare;
·726 inch 2·90 11·62 58·1 7262 58,100

also

uncia ·968 = $\frac{1}{12}$ pes, palmipes 14·52 = 5 palmi, cubitus 17·43 = 6 palmi.

Either from its Pelasgic or Etrurian use or from Romans, this foot appears to have come into prehistoric remains, as the circle of Stonehenge (26) is 100 feet of 11·68 across, and the same is found in one or two other cases. 11·60 also appears as the foot of some mediæval English buildings (25).

We now pass to units between which we cannot state any connexion.

25·1.—The earliest sign of this cubit is in a chamber at Abydos (44) about 1400 B.C.; there, below the sculptures, the plain wall is marked out by red designing lines in spaces of 25·13 ± ·03 inches, which have no relation to the size of the chamber or to the sculpture. They must therefore have been marked by a workman using a cubit of 25·13. Apart from mediæval and other very uncertain data, such as the Sabbath day's journey being 2000 middling paces for 2000 cubits, it appears that Josephus, using the Greek or Roman cubit, gives half as many more to each dimension of the temple than does the Talmud; this shows the cubit used in the Talmud for temple measures to be certainly not under 25 inches. Evidence of the early period is given, moreover, by the statement in 1 Kings (vii. 26) that the brazen sea held 2000 baths; the bath being about 2300 cubic inches, this would show a cubit of 25 inches. The corrupt text in Chronicles of 3000 baths would need a still longer cubit; and, if a lesser cubit of 21·6 or 18 inches be taken, the result for the size of the bath would be impossibly small. For other Jewish cubits see 18·2 and 21·6. Oppert (24) concludes from inscriptions that there was in Assyria a royal cubit of $\frac{7}{6}$ the U cubit, or 25·20; and four monuments show (25) a cubit averaging 25·28. For Persia Queipo (33) relies on, and develops, an Arab statement that the Arab *hashama* cubit was the royal Persian, thus fixing it at about 25 inches; and the Persian guerze at present is 25, the royal guerze being $1\frac{1}{2}$ times this, or $37\frac{1}{2}$ inches. As a unit of 1·013, decimally multiplied, is most commonly to be deduced from the ancient Persian buildings, we may take 25·34 as the nearest approach to the ancient Persian unit.

21·6.—The circuit of the city wall of Khorsabad (24) is minutely stated on a tablet as 24,740 feet (U), and from the actual size the U is therefore 10·806 inches. Hence the recorded series of measures on the Senkereh tablet are valued (Oppert) as—

susi, { 20 = (palm), 3 = U, 6 = qanu, 2 = sa, 5 = (*n*), 12 = us, 30 = kasbu. / 60 .... = U, 60 .... = (*n*).
·18 inch 3·6 10·80 64·8 129·6 648 7,776 223,280

Other units are the suklum or $\frac{1}{2}$U = 5·4, and cubit of 2U = 21·6, which are not named in this tablet. In Persia (24) the series on the same base was—

vitasti, 2 = arasni 360 = asparasa, 30 = parathañha, 2 = gāv;
10·7 inches 21·4 7704 231,120 462,240

probably

yava, 6 = angusta, 10 = vitasti; and gama = $\frac{3}{5}$ arasni; also bāzu = 2 arasni.
·18 inch 1·07 10·7 12·8 21·4 42·8 21·4

The values here given are from some Persian buildings (25), which indicate 21·4, or slightly less; Oppert's value, on less certain data, is 21·52. The Egyptian cubits have an arm at 15 digits or about 10·9 marked on them, which seems like this same unit (33).

This cubit was also much used by the Jews (33), and is so often referred to that it has eclipsed the 25·1 cubit in most writers. The Gemara names 3 Jewish cubits (2) of 5, 6, and 7 palms; and, as Oppert (24) shows that 25·2 was reckoned 7 palms, 21·6 being 6 palms, we may reasonably apply this scale to the Gemara list, and read it as 18, 21·6, and 25·2 inches. There is also a great amount of mediæval and other data showing this cubit of 21·6 to have been familiar to the Jews after their captivity; but there is no evidence for its earlier date, as there is for the 25-inch cubit (from the brazen sea) and for the 18-inch cubit from the Siloam inscription.

From Assyria also it passed into Asia Minor, being found on the city standard of Ushak in Phrygia (33), engraved as 21·8, divided into the Assyrian foot of 10·8, and half and quarter, 5·4 and 2·7. Apparently the same unit is found (18) at Heraclea in Lucania, 21·86; and, as the general foot of the South Italians, or Oscan foot (18), best defined by the 100 feet square being $\frac{3}{10}$ of the jugerum, and therefore = 10·80 or half of 21·60. A cubit of 21·5 seems certainly to be indicated in prehistoric remains in Britain, and also in early Christian buildings in Ireland (25).

22·2.—Another unit not far different, but yet distinct, is found apparently in Punic remains at Carthage (25), about 11·16 (22·32), and probably also in Sardinia as 11·07 (22·14), where it would naturally be of Punic origin. In the Hauran 22·16 is shown by a basalt door (British Museum), and perhaps elsewhere in Syria (25). It is of some value to trace this measure, since it is indicated by some prehistoric English remains as 22·4.

20·0.—This unit may be that of the pre-Semitic Mesopotamians, as it is found at the early temple of Muḳayyir (Ur); and, with a few other cases (25), it averages 19·97. It is described by Oppert (24), from literary sources, as the great U of 222 susi or 39·96, double of 19·98; from which was formed a reed of 4 great U or 159·8. The same measure decimally divided is also indicated by buildings in Asia Minor and Syria (25).

19·2.—In Persia some buildings at Persepolis and other places (25) are constructed on a foot of 9·6, or cubit of 19·2; while the modern Persian arish is 38·27 or 2 × 19·13. The same is found very clearly in Asia Minor (25), averaging 19·3; and it is known in literature as the Pythic foot (18, 33) of 9·75, or $\frac{1}{2}$ of 19·5, if Censorinus is rightly understood. It may be shown by a mark (33) on the 26th digit of Sharpe's Egyptian cubit = 19·2 inches.

13·3.—This measure does not seem to belong to very early times, and it may probably have originated in Asia Minor. It is found there as 13·35 in buildings. Hultsch gives it rather less, at 13·1, as the "small Asiatic foot." Thence it passed to Greece, where it is found (25) as 13·36. In Romano-African remains it is often found, rather higher, or 13·45 average (25). It lasted in Asia apparently till the building of the palace at Mashita (620 A.D.), where it is 13·22, according to the rough measures we have (25). And it may well be the origin of the dirá Stambuli of 26·6, twice 13·3. Found in Asia Minor and northern Greece, it does not appear unreasonable to connect it, as Hultsch does, with the Belgic foot of the Tungri, which was legalized (or perhaps introduced) by Drusus when governor, as $\frac{1}{8}$ longer than the Roman foot, or 13·07; this statement was evidently an approximation by an increase of 2 digits, so that the small difference from 13·3 is not worth notice. Further the pertica was 12 feet of 18 digits, *i.e.*, Drusian feet.

Turning now to England, we find (25) the commonest building foot up to the 15th century averaged 13·22. Here we see the Belgic foot passed over to England, and we can fill the gap to a considerable extent from the itinerary measures. It has been shown (31) that the old English mile, at least as far back as the 13th century, was of 10 and not 8 furlongs. It was therefore equal to 79,200 inches, and divided decimally into 10 furlongs, 100 chains, or 1000 fathoms. For the existence of this fathom (half the Belgic pertica) we have the proof of its half, or yard, needing to be suppressed by statute (9) in 1439, as "the yard and full hand," or about 40 inches,—evidently the yard of the most usual old English foot of 13·22, which would be 39·66. We can restore then the old English system of long measure from the buildings, the statute-prohibition, the surviving chain and furlong, and the old English mile shown by maps and itineraries, thus:—

foot, 3 = yard, 2 = fathom, 10 = chain, 10 = furlong, 10 = mile.
13·22 39·66 79·32 793 7932 79,320

Such a regular and extensive system could not have been put into use throughout the whole country suddenly in 1250, especially as it must have had to resist the legal foot now in use, which was enforced (9) as early as 950. We cannot suppose that such a system would be invented and become general in face of the laws enforcing the 12-inch foot. Therefore it must be dated some time before the 10th century, and this brings it as near as we can now hope to the Belgic foot, which lasted certainly to the 3d or 4th century, and is exactly in the line of migration of the Belgic tribes into Britain. It is remarkable how near this early decimal system of Germany and Britain is the double of the modern decimal metric system. Had it not been unhappily driven out by the 12-inch foot, and repressed by statutes both against its yard and mile, we should need but a small change to place our measures in accord with the metre.

The Gallic leuga, or league, is a different unit, being 1·59 British miles by the very concordant itinerary of the Bordeaux pilgrim. This appears to be the great Celtic measure, as opposed to the old English, or Germanic, mile. In the north-west of England and in Wales this mile lasted as 1·56 British miles till 1500; and the perch of those parts was correspondingly longer till this century (31). The "old London mile" was 5000 feet, and probably this was the mile which was modified to 5280 feet, or 8 furlongs, and so became the British statute mile.

STANDARDS OF AREA.—We cannot here describe these in detail. Usually they were formed in each country on the squares of the long measures. The Greek system was—

foot,	36=hexapodes	100=..............acæna,	25=aroura,	4=plethron.
1·027 sq. ft.	36·96	102·68	2567	10,268

The Roman system was—

pes,	100=decempeda,	36=clima,	4=actus,	2=jugerum,
·94 sq. ft.	94	3384	13,536	27,072

jugerum,	2=heredium,	100=centuria,	4=saltus.
·6205 acre	1·241	124·1	496·4

STANDARDS OF VOLUME.—There is great uncertainty as to the exact values of all ancient standards of volume,—the only precise data being those resulting from the theories of volumes derived from the cubes of feet and cubits. Such theories, as we have noticed, are extremely likely to be only approximations in ancient times, even if recognized then; and our data are quite inadequate for clearing the subject. If certain equivalences between volumes in different countries are stated here, it must be plainly understood that they are only known to be approximate results, and not to give a certain basis for any theories of derivation. All the actual monumental data that we have are alluded to here, with their amounts. The impossibility of safe correlation of units necessitates a division by countries.

Egypt.—The hon was the usual small standard; by 8 vases which have contents stated in hons (8, 12, 20, 22, 33, 40) the mean is 29·2 cubic inches ±·6; by 9 unmarked pottery measures (30) 29·1±·16, and divided by 20; by 18 vases, supposed multiples of hon (1), 32·1±·2. These last are probably only rough, and we may take 29·2 cubic inches ±·5. This was reckoned (6) to hold 5 utens of water (uten ∴ 1470 grains), which agrees well to the weight; but this was probably an approximation, and not derivative, as there is (14) a weight called shet of 4·70 or 4·95 uten, and this was perhaps the actual weight of a hon. The variations of hon and uten, however, cover one another completely. From ratios stated before Greek times (35) the series of multiples was

ro,	8=hon,	4=honnu,	10=apet or besha	4=tama	...........10=(Theban),	10=sa.
3·65 cub. in.	29·2	116·8	1168	4672	11,680	116,800

(Theban) is the "great Theban measure."

In Ptolemaic times the artaba (2336·), modified from the Persian, was general in Egypt, a working equivalent to the Attic metretes,—value 2 apet or $\frac{1}{2}$ tama; medimnus=tama or 2 artabas, and fractions down to $\frac{1}{400}$ artaba (35). In Roman times the artaba remained (Didymus), but $\frac{1}{6}$ was the usual unit (name unknown), and this was divided down to $\frac{1}{24}$ or $\frac{1}{144}$ artaba (35),—thus producing, by $\frac{1}{72}$ artaba a working equivalent to the xestes and sextarius (35). Also a new Roman artaba (Didymus) of 1540· was brought in. Beside the equivalence of the hon to 5 utens weight of water, the mathematical papyrus (35) gives 5 besha=$\frac{2}{3}$ cubic cubit (Revillout's interpretation of this as 1 cubit^3 is impossible geometrically, see *Rev. Eg.*, 1881, for data); this is very concordant, but it is very unlikely for 3 to be introduced in an Egyptian derivation, and probably therefore only a working equivalent. The other ratio of Revillout and Hultsch, 320 hons=cubit^3 is certainly approximate.

Syria, Palestine, and Babylonia.—Here there are no monumental data known; and the literary information does not distinguish the closely connected, perhaps identical, units of these lands. Moreover, none of the writers are before the Roman period, and many relied on are mediæval rabbis. A large number of their statements are rough (2, 18, 33), being based on the working equivalence of the bath or epha with the Attic metretes, from which are sometimes drawn fractional statements which seem more accurate than they are. This, however, shows the bath to be about 2500 cubic inches. There are two better data (2) of Epiphanius and Theodoret,—Attic medimnus=$1\frac{1}{2}$ baths, and saton ($\frac{1}{3}$ bath)=$1\frac{5}{8}$ modii; these give about 2240 and 2260 cubic inches. The best datum is in Josephus (*Ant.*, iii. 15, 3), where 10 baths=41 Attic or 31 Sicilian medimni, for which it is agreed we must read modii (33); hence the bath=2300 cubic inches. Thus these three different reckonings agree closely, but all equally depend on the Greek and Roman standards, which are not well fixed. The Sicilian modius here is $\frac{10}{31}$, or slightly under $\frac{1}{3}$, of the bath, and so probably a Punic variant of the $\frac{1}{3}$ bath or saton of Phœnicia. One close datum, if trustworthy, would be log of water=Assyrian mina ∴ bath about 2200 cubic inches. The rabbinical statement of cubic cubit of 21·5 holding 320 logs puts the bath at about 2250 cubic inches; their log-measure, holding six hen's eggs, shows it to be over rather than under this amount; but their reckoning of bath=$\frac{1}{2}$ cubit cubed is but approximate; by 21·5 it is 1240, by 25·1 it is 1990 cubic inches. The earliest Hebrew system was—

(log,	4=kab)............3=hin,	'issarón............	6 hin / 10 'issarón = bath, or epha,	10=homer—wet. or kor—dry.
32 cub. in.	128 / 230	283	2300	23,000

'Issarón ("tenth-deal") is also called gomer. The log and kab are not found till the later writings; but the ratio of hin to 'issarón is practically fixed in early times by the proportions in Num. xv. 4–9. Epiphanius stating great hin=18 xestes, and holy hin=9, must refer to Syrian xestes, equal to 24 and 12 Roman; this makes holy hin as above, and great hin a double hin, *i.e.*, seah or saton. His other statements of saton=56 or 50 sextaria remain unexplained, unless this be an error for bath=56 or 50 Syr. sext. and ∴=2290 or 2560 cubic inches. The wholesale theory of Revillout (35) that all Hebrew and Syrian measures were doubled by the Ptolemaic revision, while retaining the same names, rests entirely on the resemblance of the names apet and epha, and of log to the Coptic and late measure lok. But there are other reasons against accepting this, besides the improbability of such a change.

The Phœnician and old Carthaginian system was (18)—

log,	4=kab,	6=saton,	30=corus,
31 cub. in.	123	740	22,200

valuing them by 31 Sicilian=41 Attic modii (Josephus, above).

The old Syrian system was (18)—

cotyle,	2=Syr. xestes,	18=sabitha or saton,	$1\frac{1}{2}$=collathon,	2=bath-artaba;
21 cub. in.	41	740	1110	2220

also

Syr. xestes,	45=maris,	2=metretes or artaba.
41	1850	3700

The later or Seleucidan system was (18)—

cotyle,	2=Syr. xestes,	90=Syr. metretes,
22	44	4000

the Syrian being $1\frac{1}{3}$ Roman sextarii.

The Babylonian system was very similar (18)—

($\frac{1}{4}$), 4=capitha,	15=maris	18=.........epha,	10=homer,	6=achane.
33 cub. in. / 132	1980	2380	23,800	142,800

The approximate value from capitha=2 Attic chœnices (Xenophon) warrants us in taking the achane as fixed in the following system, which places it closely in accord with the preceding.

In Persia Hultsch states—

capetis..............48=artaba,	maris..................	40 artaba / 72 maris =achane,
74·4 cub. in. / 1983	3570	142,800

the absolute values being fixed by artaba =51 Attic chœnices (Herod., i. 192). The maris of the Pontic system is $\frac{1}{2}$ of the above, and the Macedonian and Naxian maris $\frac{1}{10}$ of the Pontic (18). By the theory of maris=$\frac{1}{5}$ of 20·6^3 it is 1755·; by maris=Assyrian talent, 1850, in place of 1850 or 1980 stated above; hence the more likely theory of weight, rather than cubit, connexion is nearer to the facts.

Æginetan System.—This is so called from according with the Æginetan weight. The absolute data are all dependent on the Attic and Roman systems, as there are no monumental data. The series of names is the same as in the Attic system (18). The values are $1\frac{1}{2}$×the Attic (Athenæus, Theophrastus, &c.) (2, 18), or more closely 11 to 12 times $\frac{1}{8}$ of Attic. Hence, the Attic cotyle being 17·5 cubic inches, the Æginetan is about 25·7. The Bœotian system (18) included the achane; if this=Persian, then cotyle=24·7. Or, separately through the Roman system, the mnasis of Cyprus (18)=170 sextarii; then the cotyle=24·8. By the theory of the metretes being $1\frac{1}{2}$ talents Æginetan, the cotyle would be 23·3 to 24·7 cubic inches by the actual weights, which have tended to decrease. Probably then 25·0 is the best approximation. By the theory (18) of 2 metretes=cube of the 18·67 cubit from the 12·45 foot, the cotyle would be about 25·4, within ·4; but then such a cubit is unknown among measures, and not likely to be formed, as 12·4 is $\frac{3}{5}$ of 20·6. The Æginetan system then was—

cotyle,	4=chœnix,	3=chous / 8=.........hecteus,	4=metretes,	16 chous / $1\frac{1}{2}$ metretes =medimnus.
25 cub. in.	100	300 / 800	3200	4800

This was the system of Sparta, of Bœotia (where the aporryma =4 chœnices, the cophinus=6 chœnices, and saites or saton or hecteus=2 aporrymæ, while 30 medimni=achane, evidently Asiatic connexions throughout), and of Cyprus (where 2 choes= Cyprian medimnus, of which 5=medimnus of Salamis, of which 2 =mnasis) (18).

Attic or Usual Greek System.—The absolute value of this system is far from certain. The best data are three stone slabs, each with several standard volumes cut in them (11, 18), and two named vases. The value of the cotyle from the Naxian slab is 15·4 (best, others 14·6–19·6); from a vase about 16·6; from the Panidum slab 17·1 (var. 16·2–18·2); from a Capuan vase 17·8; from the Ganus slab 17·8 (var. 17·–18·). From these we may take 17·5 as a fair approximation. It is supposed that the Panathenaic vases were intended as metretes; this would show a cotyle of 14·4–17·1. The theories of connexion give, for the value of the cotyle, metretes= Æginetan talent, ∴ 15·4–16·6; metretes $\frac{3}{4}$ of 12·16 cubed, ∴ 16·6;

metretes = $\frac{27}{20}$ of 12·16 cubed, ∴ 16·8; medimnus = 2 Attic talents, hecteus = 20 minæ, chœnix = $2\frac{1}{2}$ minæ, ∴ 16·75; metretes = 3 cubic spithami ($\frac{1}{2}$ cubit = 9·12), ∴ 17·5; 6 metretes = 2 feet of 12·45 cubed, ∴ 17·8 cubic inches for cotyle. But probably as good theories could be found for any other amount; and certainly the facts should not be set aside, as almost every author has done, in favour of some one of half a dozen theories. The system of multiples was for liquids—

cyathus,	$1\frac{1}{2}$ = oxybaphon,	4 = cotyle,	12 = chous,	12 = metretes,
2·9 cub. in.	4·4	17·5	210	2520

with the tetarton (8·8), 2 = cotyle, 2 = xestes (35·), introduced from the Roman system. For dry measure—

cyathus,	6 = cotyle,	4 = chœnix,	8 = hecteus,	6 = medimnus,
2·9 cub. in.	17·5	70	560	3360

with the xestes, and amphoreus (1680) = $\frac{1}{2}$ medimnus, from the Roman system. The various late provincial systems of division are beyond our present scope (18).

System of Gythium.—A system differing widely both in units and names from the preceding is found on the standard slab of Gythium in the southern Peloponnesus (*Rev. Arch.*, 1872). Writers have unified it with the Attic, but it is decidedly larger in its unit, giving 19·4 (var. 19·1–19·8) for the supposed cotyle. Its system is—

cotyle,	4 = hemihecton,	4 = chous,	3 = (*n*).
58 cub. in.	232	932	2796

And with this agrees a pottery cylindrical vessel, with official stamp on it (ΔΗΜΟΣΙΟΝ, &c.), and having a fine black line traced round the inside, near the top, to show its limit; this seems to be probably very accurate, and contains 58·5 cubic inches, closely agreeing with the cotyle of Gythium. It has been described (*Rev. Arch.*, 1872) as an Attic chœnix. Gythium being the southern port of Greece, it seems not too far to connect this 58 cubic inches with the double of the Egyptian hon = 58·4, as it is different from every other Greek system.

Roman System.—The celebrated Farnesian standard congius of bronze of Vespasian, "mensurae exactae in Capitolio P. X.," contains 206·7 cubic inches (2), and hence the amphora 1654. By the sextarius of Dresden (2) the amphora is 1695; by the congius of Ste Geneviève (2) 1700 cubic inches; and by the ponderarium measures at Pompeii (33) 1540 to 1840, or about 1620 for a mean. So the Farnesian congius, or about 1650, may best be adopted. The system for liquid was—

quartarius,	4 = sextarius,	6 = congius,	4 = urna,	2 = amphora;
8·6 cub. ins.	34·4	206	825	1650

for dry measure 16 sextarii = modius, 550 cubic inches; and to both systems were added from the Attic the cyathus (2·87), acetabulum (4·3), and hemina (17·2 cubic inches). The Roman theory of the amphora being the cubic foot makes it 1569 cubic inches, or decidedly less than the actual measures; the other theory of its containing 80 libræ of water would make it 1575 by the commercial or 1605 by the monetary libra,—again too low for the measures. Both of these theories therefore are rather working equivalents than original derivations; or at least the interrelation was allowed to become far from exact.

Indian and Chinese Systems.—On the ancient Indian system see *Numismata Orientalia*, new ed., i. 24; on the ancient Chinese, *Nature*, xxx. 565, and xxxv. 318.

STANDARDS OF WEIGHT.—For these we have far more complete data than for volumes or even lengths, and can ascertain in many cases the nature of the variations, and their type in each place. The main series on which we shall rely here are those—(1) from Assyria (38) about 800 B.C.; (2) from the eastern Delta of Egypt (29) (Defenneh); (3) from western Delta (28) (Naucratis); (4) from Memphis (44),—all these about the 6th century B.C., and therefore before much interference from the decreasing coin standards; (5) from Cnidus; (6) from Athens; (7) from Corfu; and (8) from Italy (British Museum) (44). As other collections are but a fraction of the whole of these, and are much less completely examined, little if any good would be done by including them in the combined results, though for special types or inscriptions they will be mentioned.

146 grains.—The Egyptian unit was the kat, which varied between 138 and 155 grains (28, 29). There were several families or varieties within this range, at least in the Delta, probably five or six in all (29). The original places and dates of these cannot yet be fixed, except for the lowest type of 138–140 grains; this belonged to Heliopolis (7), as two weights (35) inscribed of "the treasury of An" show 139·9 and 140·4, while a plain one from there gives 138·8; the variety 147–149 may belong to Hermopolis (35), according to an inscribed weight. The names of the kat and tema are fixed by being found on weights, the uten by inscriptions; the series was—

(*n*),	10 = kat,	10 = uten,	10 = tema.
14·6 grs.	146	1460	14,600

The tema is the same name as the large wheat measure (35), which was worth 30,000 to 19,000 grains of copper, according to Ptolemaic receipts and accounts (*Rev. Eg.*, 1881, 150), and therefore very likely worth 10 utens of copper in earlier times when metals were scarcer. The kat was regularly divided into 10; but another division, for the sake of interrelation with another system, was in $\frac{1}{3}$ and $\frac{1}{6}$, scarcely found except in the eastern Delta, where it is common (29); and it is known from a papyrus (38) to be a Syrian weight. The uten is found ÷ 6 = 245, in Upper Egypt (rare) (44). Another division (in a papyrus) (38) is a silver weight of $\frac{6}{10}$ kat = about 88,—perhaps the Babylonian siglus of 86. The uten was also binarily divided into 128 peks of gold in Ethiopia; this may refer to another standard (see 129) (33). The Ptolemaic copper coinage is on two bases,—the uten, binarily divided, and the Ptolemaic five shekels (1050), also binarily divided. (This result is from a larger number than other students have used, and study by diagrams.) The theory (3) of the derivation of the uten from $\frac{1}{1500}$ cubic cubit of water would fix it at 1472, which is accordant; but there seems no authority either in volumes or weights for taking 1500 utens. Another theory (3) derives the uten from $\frac{1}{1000}$ of the cubic cubit of 24 digits, or better $\frac{6}{7}$ of 20·63; that, however, will only fit the very lowest variety of the uten, while there is no evidence of the existence of such a cubit. The kat is not unusual in Syria (44), and among the hæmatite weights of Troy (44) are nine examples, average 144, but not of extreme varieties.

129 grs.; **258** grs. 7750; 15,500; 465,000. The great standard of Babylonia became the parent of several other systems; and itself and its derivatives became more widely spread than any other standard. It was known in two forms,—one system (24) of—

um,	60 = sikhir,	6 = shekel,	10 = stone,	6 = maneh,	60 = talent;
·36 grs.	21·5	129	1290	7750	465,000

and the other system double of this in each stage except the talent. These two systems are distinctly named on the weights, and are known now as the light and heavy Assyrian systems (19, 24). (It is better to avoid the name Babylonian, as it has other meanings also.) There are no weights dated before the Assyrian bronze lion weights (9, 17, 19, 38) of the 11th to 8th centuries B.C. Thirteen of this class average 127·2 for the shekel; 9 hæmatite barrel-shaped weights (38) give 128·2; 16 stone duck-weights (38), 126·5. A heavier value is shown by the precious metals,—the gold plates from Khorsabad (18) giving 129, and the gold daric coinage (21, 35) of Persia 129·2. Nine weights from Syria (44) average 128·8. This is the system of the "Babylonian" talent, by Herodotus = 70 minæ Euboic, by Pollux = 70 minæ Attic, by Ælian = 72 minæ Attic, and therefore about 470,000 grains. In Egypt this is found largely at Naucratis (28, 29), and less commonly at Defenneh (29). In both places the distribution, a high type of 129 and a lower of 127, is like the monetary and trade varieties above noticed; while a smaller number of examples are found, fewer and fewer, down to 118 grains. At Memphis (44) the shekel is scarcely known, and a $\frac{1}{2}$ mina weight was there converted into another standard (of 200). A few barrel weights are found at Karnak, and several egg-shaped shekel weights at Gebelen (44); also two cuboid weights from there (44) of 1 and 10 utens are marked as 6 and 60, which can hardly refer to any unit but the heavy shekel, giving 245. Hultsch refers to Egyptian gold rings of Dynasty XVIII. of 125 grains. That this unit penetrated far to the south in early times is shown by the tribute of Kush (34) in Dynasty XVIII.; this is of 801, 1443, and 23,741 kats, or 15 and 27 manehs and $7\frac{1}{2}$ talents when reduced to this system. And the later Ethiopic gold unit of the pek (7), or $\frac{1}{128}$ of the uten, was 10·8 or more, and may therefore be the $\frac{1}{2}$ sikhir or obolos of 21·5. But the fraction $\frac{1}{128}$, or a continued binary division repeated seven times, is such a likely mode of rude subdivision that little stress can be laid on this. In later times in Egypt a class of large glass scarabs for funerary purposes seem to be adjusted to the shekel (30). Whether this system or the Phœnician on 224 grains was that of the Hebrews is uncertain. There is no doubt but that in the Maccabean times and onward 218 was the shekel; but the use of the word darkemôn by Ezra and Nehemiah, and the probabilities of their case, point to the darag-maneh, $\frac{1}{60}$ maneh, or shekel of Assyria; and the mention of $\frac{1}{3}$ shekel by Nehemiah as poll tax nearly proves that the 129 and not 218 grains is intended, as 218 was never ÷ 3. But the Maccabean use of 218 may have been a reversion to the older shekel; and this is strongly shown by the fraction $\frac{1}{4}$ shekel (1 Sam. ix. 8), the continual mention of large decimal numbers of shekels in the earlier books, and the certain fact of 100 shekels being = mina. This would all be against the 129 or 258 shekel, and for the 218 or 224. There is, however, one good datum if it can be trusted: 300 talents of silver (2 Kings xviii. 14) are 800 talents on Sennacherib's cylinder (34), while the 30 talents of gold is the same in both accounts. Eight hundred talents on the Assyrian silver standard would be 267—or roundly 300—talents on the heavy trade or gold system, which is therefore probably the Hebrew. Probably the 129 and 224 systems coexisted in the country; but on the whole it seems more likely that 129 or rather 258 grains was the Hebrew shekel before the Ptolemaic times,—especially as the 100 shekels to the mina is parallelled by the following Persian system (Hultsch)—

shekel,	{ 50 = mina		60 = talent of gold	
	{ 60 = ...	mina		60 = talent of trade,
129 grs.	6450	7750	387,000	465,000

the Hebrew system being

gerah,	20 = shekel,	100 = maneh,	30 = talent,
12·9 grs.	258?	25,800	774,000

and, considering that the two Hebrew cubits are the Babylonian and Persian units, and the volumes are also Babylonian, it is the more likely that the weights should have come with these. From the east this unit passed to Asia Minor; and six multiples of 2 to 20 shekels (av. 127) are found among the hæmatite weights of Troy (44), including the oldest of them. On the Ægean coast it often occurs in early coinage (17),—at Lampsacus 131–129, Phocæa 256–4, Cyzicus 252–247, Methymna 124·6, &c. In later times it was a main unit of North Syria, and also on the Euxine, leaden weights of Antioch (3), Callatia, and Tomis being known (38). The mean of these eastern weights is 7700 for the mina, or 128. But the leaden weights of the west (44) from Corfu, &c., average 7580, or 126·3; this standard was kept up at Cyzicus in trade long after it was lost in coinage. At Corinth the unit was evidently the Assyrian and not the Attic, being 129·6 at the earliest (17) (though modified to double Attic, or 133, later) and being ÷ 3, and not into 2 drachms. And this agrees with the mina being repeatedly found at Corcyra, and with the same standard passing to the Italian coinage (17) similar in weight, and in division into $\frac{1}{3}$,—the heaviest coinages (17) down to 400 B.C. (Terina, Velia, Sybaris, Posidonia, Metapontum, Tarentum, &c.) being none over 126, while later on many were adjusted to the Attic, and rose to 134. Six disk weights from Carthage (44) show 126. It is usually the case that a unit lasts later in trade than in coinage; and the prominence of this standard in Italy may show how it is that this mina (18 unciæ = 7400) was known as the "Italic" in the days of Galen and Dioscorides (2).

126 grs. 6300. A variation on the main system was made by forming a mina of 50 shekels. This is one of the Persian series (gold), and the $\frac{1}{4}$ of the Hebrew series noted above. But it is most striking when it is found in the mina form which distinguishes it. Eleven weights from Syria and Cnidus (44) (of the curious type with two breasts on a rectangular block) show a mina of 6250 (125·0); and it is singular that this class is exactly like weights of the 224 system found with it, but yet quite distinct in standard. The same passed into Italy and Corfu (44), averaging 6000,—divided in Italy into unciæ ($\frac{1}{12}$), and scripulæ ($\frac{1}{288}$), and called litra (in Corfu?). It is known in the coinage of Hatria (18) as 6320. And a strange division of the shekel in 10 (probably therefore connected with this decimal mina) is shown by a series of bronze weights (44) with four curved sides and marked with circles (British Museum, place unknown), which may be Romano-Gallic, averaging 125 ÷ 10. This whole class seems to cling to sites of Phœnician trade, and to keep clear of Greece and the north,—perhaps a Phœnician form of the 129 system, avoiding the sexagesimal multiples.

If this unit have any connexion with the kat, it is that a kat of gold is worth 15 shekels or $\frac{1}{4}$ mina of silver; this agrees well with the range of both units, only it must be remembered that 129 was used as gold unit, and another silver unit deduced from it. More likely then the 147 and 129 units originated independently in Egypt and Babylonia.

86 grs. 8600; 516,000. From 129 grains of gold was adopted an equal value of silver = 1720, on the proportion of 1 : 13$\frac{1}{3}$, and this was divided in 10 = 172,—which was used either in this form, or its half, 86, best known as the siglus (17). Such a proportion is indicated in Num. vii., where the gold spoon of 10 shekels is equal in value to the bowl of 130 shekels, or double that of 70, *i.e.*, the silver vessels were 200 and 100 sigli. The silver plates at Khorsabad (18) we find to be 80 sigli of 84·6. The Persian silver coinage shows about 86·0; the danak was $\frac{1}{3}$ of this, or 28·7. Xenophon and others state it at about 84. As a monetary weight it seems to have spread, perhaps entirely, in consequence of the Persian dominion; it varies from 174· downwards, usually 167, in Aradus, Cilicia, and on to the Ægean coast, in Lydia and in Macedonia (17). The silver bars found at Troy averaging 2744, or $\frac{1}{3}$ mina of 8232, have been attributed to this unit (17); but no division of the mina in $\frac{1}{3}$ is to be expected, and the average is rather low. Two hæmatite weights from Troy (44) show 86 and 87·2. The mean from leaden weights of Chios, Tenedos (44), &c., is 8430. A duck-weight of Camirus, probably early, gives 8480; the same passed on to Greece and Italy (17), averaging 8610; but in Italy it was divided, like all other units, into unciæ and scripulæ (44). It is perhaps found in Etrurian coinage as 175–172 (17). By the Romans it was used on the Danube (18), two weights of the first legion there showing 8610; and this is the mina of 20 unciæ (8400) named by Roman writers. The system was—

obol,	6 = siglus,	100 = mina,	60 = talent.
14·3 grs.	86	8600	516,000

A derivation from this was the $\frac{1}{3}$ of 172, or 57·3, the so-called Phocæan drachma, equal in silver value to the $\frac{1}{60}$ of the gold 258 grains. It was used at Phocæa as 58·5, and passed to the colonies of Posidonia and Velia as 59 or 118. The colony of Massilia brought it into Gaul as 58·2–54·9.

224 grs. 11,200; 672,000. That this unit (commonly called Phœnician) is derived from the 129 system can hardly be doubted, both being so intimately associated in Syria and Asia Minor. The relation is 258 : 229 : : 9 : 8; but the exact form in which the descent took place is not settled: $\frac{1}{60}$ of 129 of gold is worth 57 of silver or a drachm, $\frac{1}{4}$ of 230 (or by trade weights 127 and 226); otherwise, deriving it from the silver weight of 86 already formed, the drachm is $\frac{1}{3}$ of the stater, 172, or double of the Persian danak of 28·7, and the sacred unit of Didyma in Ionia was this half drachm, 27; or thirdly, what is indicated by the Lydian coinage (17), 86 of gold was equal to 1150 of silver, 5 shekels, or $\frac{1}{10}$ mina. Other proposed derivations from the kat or pek are not satisfactory. In actual use this unit varied greatly: at Naucratis (29) there are groups of it at 231, 223, and others down to 208; this is the earliest form in which we can study it, and the corresponding values to these are 130 and 126, or the gold and trade varieties of the Babylonian, while the lower tail down to 208 corresponds to the shekel down to 118, which is just what is found. Hence the 224 unit seems to have been formed from the 129, after the main families or types of that had arisen. It is scarcer at Defenneh (29) and rare at Memphis (44). Under the Ptolemies, however, it became the great unit of Egypt, and is very prominent in the later literature in consequence (18, 35). The average of coins (21) of Ptolemy I. gives 219·6, and thence they gradually diminish to 210, the average (33) of the whole series of Ptolemies being 218. The "argenteus" (as Revillout transcribes a sign in the papyri) (35) was of 5 shekels, or 1090; it arose about 440 B.C., and became after 160 B.C. a weight unit for copper. In Syria, as early as the 15th century B.C., the tribute of the Rutennu, of Naharaina, Megiddo, Anaukasa, &c. (34), is on a basis of 454–484 kats, or 300 shekels ($\frac{1}{10}$ talent) of 226 grains. The commonest weight at Troy (44) is the shekel, averaging 224. In coinage it is one of the commonest units in early times; from Phœnicia, round the coast to Macedonia, it is predominant (17); at a maximum of 230 (Ialysus), it is in Macedonia 224, but seldom exceeds 220 elsewhere, the earliest Lydian of the 7th century being 219, and the general average of coins 218. The system was—

($\frac{1}{8}$),	8 = drachm,	4 = shekel,	25 = mina,	120 = talent.
7 grs.	56	224	5600	672,000

From the Phœnician coinage it was adopted for the Maccabean. It is needless to give the continual evidences of this being the later Jewish shekel, both from coins (max. 223) and writers (2, 18, 33); the question of the early shekel we have noticed already under 129. In Phœnicia and Asia Minor the mina was specially made in the form with two breasts (44), 19 such weights averaging 5600 (= 224); and thence it passed into Greece, more in a double value of 11,200 (= 224). From Phœnicia this naturally became the main Punic unit; a bronze weight from Iol (18), marked 100, gives a drachma of 56 or 57 (224–228); and a Punic inscription (18) names 28 drachmæ = 25 Attic, and ∴ 57 to 59 grains (228–236); while a probably later series of 8 marble disks from Carthage (44) show 208, but vary from 197 to 234. In Spain it was 236 to 216 in different series (17), and it is a question whether the Massiliote drachmæ of 58–55 are not Phœnician rather than Phocaic. In Italy this mina became naturalized, and formed the "Italic mina" of Hero, Priscian, &c.; also its double, the mina of 26 unciæ or 10,800, = 50 shekels of 216; the average of 42 weights gives 5390 (= 215·6), and it was divided both into 100 drachmæ, and also in the Italic mode of 12 unciæ and 288 scripulæ (44). The talent was of 120 minæ of 5400, or 3000 shekels, shown by the talent from Herculaneum, TA, 660,000 and by the weight inscribed PONDO CXXV. (*i.e.*, 125 libræ) TALENTUM SICLORVM. iii., *i.e.*, talent of 3000 shekels (2) (the M being omitted; just as Epiphanius describes this talent as 125 libræ, or θ (= 9) nomismata, for 9000). This gives the same approximate ratio 96 : 100 to the libra as the usual drachma reckoning. The Alexandrian talent of Festus, 12,000 denarii, is the same talent again. It is believed that this mina ÷ 12 unciæ by the Romans is the origin of the Arabic ratl of 12 úkíyas, or 5500 grains (33), which is said to have been sent by Harun al-Rashid to Charlemagne, and so to have originated the French monetary pound of 5666 grains. But, as this is probably the same as the English monetary pound, or tower pound of 5400, which was in use earlier (see Saxon coins), it seems more likely that this pound (which is common in Roman weights) was directly inherited from the Roman civilization.

80 grs. 4000; 400,000. Another unit, which has scarcely been recognized in metrology hitherto, is prominent in the weights from Egypt,—some 50 weights from Naucratis and 15 from Defenneh plainly agreeing on this and on no other basis. Its value varies between 76·5 and 81·5,—mean 79 at Naucratis (29) or 81 at Defenneh (29). It has been connected theoretically with a binary division of the 10 shekels or "stone" of the Assyrian systems (28), 1290 ÷ 16 being 80·6; this is suggested by the most usual multiples being 40 and 80 = 25 and 50 shekels of 129; it is thus akin to the mina of 50 shekels previously noticed. The tribute of the Asi,

Rutennu, Khita, Assaru, &c., to Thothmes III. (34), though in uneven numbers of kats, comes out in round thousands of units when reduced to this standard. That this unit is quite distinct from the Persian 86 grains is clear in the Egyptian weights, which maintain a wide gap between the two systems. Next, in Syria three inscribed weights of Antioch and Berytus (18) show a mina of about 16,400, or 200 × 82. Then at Abydus, or more probably from Babylonia, there is the large bronze lion-weight, stated to have been originally 400,500 grains; this has been continually ÷ 60 by different writers, regardless of the fact (*Rev. Arch.*, 1862, 30) that it bears the numeral 100; this therefore is certainly a talent of 100 minæ of 4005; and as the mina is generally 50 shekels in Greek systems it points to a weight of 80·1. Farther west the same unit occurs in several Greek weights (44) which show a mina of 7800 to 8310, mean 8050 ÷ 100 = 80·5. Turning to coinage, we find this often, but usually overlooked as a degraded form of the Persian 86 grains siglos. But the earliest coinage in Cilicia, before the general Persian coinage (17) about 380 B.C., is Tarsus, 164 grains; Soli, 169, 163, 158; Nagidus, 158, 161–153 later; Issus, 166; Mallus, 163–154,—all of which can only by straining be classed as Persian; but they agree to this standard, which, as we have seen, was used in Syria in earlier times by the Khita, &c. The Milesian or "native" system of Asia Minor (18) is fixed by Hultsch at 163 and 81·6 grains,—the coins of Miletus (17) showing 160, 80, and 39. Coming down to literary evidence, this is abundant. Böckh decides that the "Alexandrian drachma" was $\frac{6}{5}$ of the Solonic 67, or = 80·5, and shows that it was not Ptolemaic, or Rhodian, or Æginetan, being distinguished from these in inscriptions (2). Then the "Alexandrian mina" of Dioscorides and Galen (2) is 20 unciæ = 8250; in the "Analecta" (2) it is 150 or 158 drachmæ = 8100. Then Attic: Euboic or Æginetan : : 18 : 25 in the metrologists (2), and the Euboic talent = 7000 "Alexandrian" drachmæ; the drachma therefore is 80·0. The "Alexandrian" wood talent : Attic talent : : 6 : 5 (Hero, Didymus), and ∴ 480,000, which is 60 minæ of 8000. Pliny states the Egyptian talent at 80 libræ = 396,000; evidently = the Abydus lion talent, which is ÷ 100, and the mina is ∴ 3960, or 50 × 79·2. The largest weight is the "wood" talent of Syria (18) = 6 Roman talents, or 1,860,000, evidently 120 Antioch minæ of 15,500 or 2 × 7750. This evidence is too distinct to be set aside; and, exactly confirming as it does the Egyptian weights and coin weights, and agreeing with the early Asiatic tribute, it cannot be overlooked in future. The system was

drachm,	2 = stater,	50 = mina,	50 = talent.	60 = Greek talent.
80 grs.	160	8000	400,000	480,000

207 grs. to **190**
9650;
579,000.

This system, the Æginetan, one of the most important to the Greek world, has been thought to be a degradation of the Phœnician (17, 21), supposing 220 grains to have been reduced in primitive Greek usage to 194. But we are now able to prove that it was an independent system—(1) by its not ranging usually over 200 grains in Egypt before it passed to Greece; (2) by its earliest example, perhaps before the 224 unit existed, not being over 208; and (3) by there being no intermediate linking on of this to the Phœnician unit in the large number of Egyptian weights, nor in the Ptolemaic coinage, in which both standards are used. The first example (30) is one with the name of Amenhotep I. (17th century B.C.) marked as "gold 5," which is 5 × 207·6. Two other marked weights are from Memphis (44), showing 201·8 and 196·4, and another Egyptian 191·4. The range of the (34) Naucratis weights is 186 to 199, divided in two groups averaging 190 and 196, equal to the Greek monetary and trade varieties. Ptolemy I. and II. also struck a series of coins (32) averaging 199. In Syria hæmatite weights are found (30) averaging 198·5, divided into 99·2, 49·6, and 24·8; and the same division is shown by gold rings from Egypt (38) of 24·9. In the medical papyrus (38) a weight of $\frac{2}{3}$ kat is used, which is thought to be Syrian; now $\frac{2}{3}$ kat = 92 to 101 grains, or just this weight which we have found in Syria; and the weights of $\frac{2}{3}$ and $\frac{1}{3}$ kat are very rare in Egypt except at Defenneh (29), on the Syrian road, where they abound. So we have thus a weight of 207–191 in Egypt on marked weights, joining therefore completely with the Æginetan unit in Egypt of 199 to 186, and coinage of 199, and strongly connected with Syria, where a double mina of Sidon (18) is 10,460 or 50 × 209·2. Probably before any Greek coinage we find this among the hæmatite weights of Troy (44), ranging from 208 to 193·2 (or 104–96·6), *i.e.*, just covering the range from the earliest Egyptian down to the early Æginetan coinage. Turning now to the early coinage, we see the fuller weight kept up (17) at Samos (202), Miletus (201), Calymna (100, 50), Methymna and Scepsis (99, 49),[1] Ionia (197); while the coinage of Ægina (17, 12), which by its wide diffusion made this unit best known, though a few of its earliest staters go up even to 207, yet is characteristically on the lower of the two groups which we recognize in Egypt, and thus started what has been considered the standard value of 194, or usually 190, decreasing afterwards to 184. In later times, in Asia, however, the fuller weight, or higher Egyptian group, which we have just noticed in the coinage, was kept up (17) into the series of cistophori (196–191), as in the Ptolemaic series of 199. At Athens the old mina was fixed by Solon at 150 of his drachmæ (18) or 9800 grains, according to the earliest drachmæ, showing a stater of 196; and this continued to be the trade mina in Athens, at least until 160 B.C., but in a reduced form, in which it equalled only 138 Attic drachmæ, or 9200. The Greek mina weights show (44), on an average of 37, 9650 (= stater of 193), varying from 186 to 199. In the Hellenic coinage it varies (18) from a maximum of 200 at Pharæ to 192, usual full weight; this unit occupied (17) all central Greece, Peloponnesus, and most of the islands. The system was—

obol,	6 = drachm,	2 = stater,	50 = mina,	60 = talent.
16 grs.	96	192	9600	576,000

It also passed into Italy, but in a smaller multiple of 25 drachmæ, or $\frac{1}{4}$ of the Greek mina; 12 Italian weights (44) bearing value marks (which cannot therefore be differently attributed) show a libra of 2400 or $\frac{1}{4}$ of 9600, which was divided in unciæ and sextulæ, and the full-sized mina is known as the 24 uncia mina, or talent of 120 libræ of Vitruvius and Isidore (18) = 9900. Hultsch states this to be the old Etruscan pound.

412
4950 grs.

With the trade mina of 9650 in Greece, and recognized in Italy, we can hardly doubt that the Roman libra is the half of this mina. At Athens it was 2 × 4900, and on the average of all the Greek weights it is 2 × 4825, so that 4950—the libra—is as close as we need expect. The division by 12 does not affect the question, as every standard that came into Italy was similarly divided. In the libra, as in most other standards, the value which happened to be first at hand for the coinage was not the mean of the whole of the weights in the country; the Phœnician coin weight is below the trade average, the Assyrian is above, however, the Æginetan is below, but the Roman coinage is above the average of trade weights, or the mean standard. Rejecting all weights of the lower empire, the average (44) of about 100 is 4956; while 42 later Greek weights (nomisma, &c.) average 4857, and 16 later Latin ones (solidus, &c.) show 4819. The coinage standard, however, was always higher (18); the oldest gold shows 5056, the Campanian Roman 5054, the consular gold 5037, the aurei 5037, the Constantine solidi 5053, and the Justinian gold 4996. Thus, though it fell in the later empire, like the trade weight, yet it was always above that. Though it has no exact relation to the congius or amphora, yet it is closely = 4977 grains, the $\frac{1}{80}$ of the cubic foot of water. If, however, the weight in a degraded form, and the foot in an undegraded form, come from the East, it is needless to look for an exact relation between them, but rather for a mere working equivalent, like the 1000 ounces to the cubic foot in England. Böckh has remarked the great diversity between weights of the same age,—those marked "Ad Augusti Temp" ranging 4971 to 5535, those tested by the fussy præfect Q. Junius Rusticus vary 4362 to 5625, and a set in the British Museum (44) belonging together vary 4700 to 5168. The series was—

siliqua,	6 = scripulum,	4 = sextula,	6 = uncia,	12 = libra,
2·87 grs.	17·2	68·7	412	4950

the greater weight being the centumpondium of 495,000. Other weights were added to these from the Greek system—

obolus,	6 = drachma,	2 = sicilicus,	4 = uncia;
8·6 grs.	51·5	103	412

and the sextula after Constantine had the name of solidus as a coin weight, or nomisma in Greek, marked N on the weights. A beautiful set of multiples of the scripulum was found near Lyons (38), from 1 to 10 × 17·28 grains, showing a libra of 4976. In Byzantine times in Egypt glass was used for coin-weights (30), averaging 68·0 for the solidus = 4896 for the libra. The Saxon and Norman ounce is said to average 416·5 (*Num. Chron.*, 1871, 42), apparently the Roman uncia inherited.

67 grs.
6700;
402,000.

The system which is perhaps the best known, through its adoption by Solon in Athens, and is thence called Attic or Solonic, is nevertheless far older than its introduction into Greece, being found in full vigour in Egypt in the 6th century B.C. It has been usually reckoned as a rather heavier form of the 129 shekel, increased to 134 on its adoption by Solon. But the Egyptian weights render this view impossible. Among them (29) the two contiguous groups can be discriminated by the 129 being multiplied by 30 and 60, while the 67 or 134 is differently × 25, 40, 50, and 100. Hence, although the two groups overlap owing to their nearness, it is impossible to regard them as all one unit. The 129 range is up to 131·8, while the Attic range is 130 to 138 (65–69). Hultsch reckons on a ratio of 24 : 25 between them, and this is very near the true values; the full Attic being 67·3, the Assyrian should be 129·2, and this is just the full gold coinage weight. We may perhaps see the sense of this ratio through another system. The 80 grain system, as we have seen, was probably formed by binarily dividing the 10 shekels, or "stone"; and it had a talent (Abydus lion) of 5000 drachmæ; this is practically identical with the talent of 6000 Attic drachmæ. So the talent of

[1] That this unit was used for gold in Egypt, one thousand years before becoming a silver coin weight in Asia Minor, need not be dwelt on, when we see in the coinage of Lydia (17) gold pieces and silver on the same standard, which was expressly formed for silver alone, *i.e.*, 84 grains. The Attic and Assyrian standards were used indifferently for either gold or silver.

the 80 grain system was sexagesimally divided for the mina which was afterwards adopted by Solon. Such seems the most likely history of it, and this is in exact accord with the full original weight of each system. In Egypt the mean value at Naucratis (29) was 66·7, while at Defenneh (29) and Memphis (44)—probably rather earlier—it was 67·0. The type of the grouping is not alike in different places, showing that no distinct families had arisen before the diffusion of this unit in Egypt; but the usual range is 65·5 to 69·0. Next it is found at Troy (44) in three cases, all high examples of 68·2 to 68·7; and these are very important, since they cannot be dissociated from the Greek Attic unit, and yet they are of a variety as far removed as may be from the half of the Assyrian, which ranges there from 123·5 to 131; thus the difference of unit between Assyrian and Attic in these earliest of all Greek weights is very strongly marked. At Athens a low variety of the unit was adopted for the coinage, true to the object of Solon in depreciating debts; and the first coinage is of only 65·2, or scarcely within the range of the trade weights (28); this seems to have been felt, as, contrary to all other states, Athens slowly increased its coin weight up to 66·6, or but little under the trade average. It gradually supplanted the Æginetan standard in Greece and Italy as the power of Athens rose; and it was adopted by Philip and Alexander (17) for their great gold coinage of 133 and 66·5. This system is often known as the "Euboic," owing to its early use in Eubœa, and its diffusion by trade from thence. The series was—

chalcous,	8=obolus,	6=drachma,	100=mina,	60=talanton.
1·4 grs.	11·17	67	6700	402,000

Turning now to its usual trade values in Greece (44), the mean of 113 gives 67·15; but they vary more than the Egyptian examples, having a sub-variety both above and below the main body, which itself exactly coincides with the Egyptian weights. The greater part of those weights which bear names indicate a mina of double the usual reckoning, so that there was a light and a heavy system, a mina of the drachma and a mina of the stater, as in the Phœnician and Assyrian weights. In trade both the minæ were divided in $\frac{1}{2}$, $\frac{1}{4}$, $\frac{1}{8}$, $\frac{1}{3}$, and $\frac{1}{6}$, regardless of the drachmæ. This unit passed also into Italy, the libra of Picenum and the double of the Etrurian and Sicilian libra (17); it was there divided in unciæ and scripulæ (44), the mean of 6 from Italy and Sicily being 6600; one weight (bought in Smyrna) has the name "Leitra" on it. In literature it is constantly referred to; but we may notice the "general mina" (Cleopatra), in Egypt, 16 unciæ=6600; the Ptolemaic talent, equal to the Attic in weight and divisions (Hero, Didymus); the Antiochian talent, equal to the Attic (Hero); the treaty of the Romans with Antiochus, naming talents of 80 libræ, *i.e.*, mina of 16 unciæ; the Roman mina in Egypt, of 15 unciæ, probably the same diminished; and the Italic mina of 16 unciæ. It seems even to have lasted in Egypt till the Middle Ages, as Jabarti and the "kátíb's guide" both name the raṭl misri (of Cairo) as 144 dirhems =6760.

We have now ended our outline of ancient metrology, omitting all details that were not really necessary to a fair judgment on the subject, but trying to make as plain as possible the actual bases of information, to trust to no opinions apart from facts, and to leave what is stated as free as possible from the influence of theories. Theoretical values have nowhere been adopted here as the standards, contrary to the general practice of metrologists; but in each case the standard value is stated solely from the evidence in hand, quite regardless of how it will agree with the theoretical deduction from other weights or measures. Great refinement in statements of values is needless, looking to the uncertainties which beset us. There are innumerable theories unnoticed here; only those are explained which seem to have a reasonable likelihood, and others are only mentioned where it is needful to show that they have not been overlooked. In many cases fuller detail is given of less important points, when they have not been published before, and no other information can be referred to elsewhere; when any point is abundantly proved and known, it has been passed with a mere mention. Finally, to indicate where further information on different matters may be found reference is frequently made by a number to the list of works given below, some early and other works being omitted, of which all the data will be found in later books.

For historical reference we may state the following units legally abolished.

English Weights and Measures Abolished.—The yard and handful, or 40 inch ell, abolished in 1439. The yard and inch, or 37 inch ell (cloth measure), abolished after 1553; known later as the Scotch ell=37·06. Cloth ell of 45 inches, used till 1600. The yard of Henry VII. =35·963 inches. Saxon moneyers pound, or Tower pound, 5400 grains, abolished in 1527. Mark, $\frac{2}{3}$ pound= 3600 grains. Troy pound in use in 1415, established as monetary pound 1527, now restricted to gold, silver, and jewels, excepting diamonds and pearls. Merchant's pound, in 1270 established for all except gold, silver, and medicines=6750 grains, generally superseded by avoirdupois in 1303. Merchant's pound of 7200 grains, from France and Germany, also superseded. ("Avoirdepois" occurs in 1336, and has been thence continued: the Elizabethan standard was probably 7002 grains.) Ale gallon of 1601=282 cubic inches, and wine gallon of 1707=231 cubic inches, both abolished in 1824. Winchester corn bushel of 8×268·8 cubic inches and gallon of 274$\frac{1}{4}$ are the oldest examples known (Henry VII.), gradually modified until fixed in 1826 at 277·274, or 10 pounds of water.

French Weights and Measures Abolished.—Often needed in reading older works.

ligne,	12=pouce,	12=pied,	6=toise,	2000=lieue de poste.
·08883 in.	1·0658	12·7892	76·735	2·42219 miles.
grain,	72=gros,	8=once,	8=marc,	2=poids de marc.
·8197 gr.	59·021	472·17	3777·33	1·0792 lb.

Rhineland foot, much used in Germany, =12·357 inches=the foot of the Scotch or English cloth ell of 37·06 inches, or 3×12·353.

(1) A. Aurès, *Métrologie Égyptienne*, 1880; (2) A. Böckh, *Metrologische Untersuchungen*, 1838 (general); (3) P. Bortolotti, *Del Primitivo Cubito Egizio*, 1883; (4) J. Brandis, *Münz-, Mass-, und Gewicht-Wesen*, 1866 (specially Assyrian); (5) H. Brugsch, in *Zeits. Aeg. Sp.*, 1870 (Edfu); (6) M. F. Chabas, *Détermination Métrique*, 1867 (Egyptian volumes); (7) Id., *Recherches sur les Poids, Mesures, et Monnaies des anciens Égyptiens*; (8) Id., *Ztschr. f. Aegypt. Sprache*, 1867, p. 57, 1870, p. 122 (Egyptian volumes); (9) H. W. Chisholm, *Weighing and Measuring*, 1877 (history of English measures); (10) Id., *Ninth Rep. of Warden of Standards*, 1875 (Assyrian); (11) A. Dumont, *Mission en Thrace* (Greek volumes); (12) Eisenlohr, *Ztschr. Aeg. Sp.*, 1875 (Egyptian hon); (13) W. Golénischeff, in *Rev. Égypt.*, 1881, 177 (Egyptian weights); (14) C. W. Goodwin, in *Ztschr. Aeg. Sp.*, 1873, p. 16 (shet); (15) B. V. Head, in *Num. Chron.*, 1875; (16) Id., *Jour. Inst. of Bankers*, 1879 (systems of weight); (17) Id., *Historia Numorum*, 1887 (essential for coin weights and history of systems); (18) F. Hultsch, *Griechische und Römische Metrologie*, 1882 (essential for literary and monumental facts); (19) Ledrain, in *Rev. Égypt.*, 1881, p. 173 (Assyrian); (20) Leemans, *Monumens Égyptiens*, 1838 (Egyptian hon); (21) T. Mommsen, *Histoire de la Monnaie Romaine*; (22) Id., *Monuments Divers* (Egyptian weights); (23) Sir Isaac Newton, *Dissertation upon the Sacred Cubit*, 1737; (24) J. Oppert, *Étalon des Mesures Assyriennes*, 1875; (25) W. M. F. Petrie, *Inductive Metrology*, 1877 (principles and tentative results); (26) Id., *Stonehenge*, 1880; (27) Id., *Pyramids and Temples of Gizeh*, 1883; (28) Id., *Naukratis*, i., 1886 (principles, lists, and curves of weights); (29) Id., *Tanis*, ii., 1887 (lists and curves); (30) Id., *Arch. Jour.*, 1883, 419 (weights, Egyptian, &c.); (31) Id., *Proc. Roy. Soc. Edin.*, 1883–84, 254 (mile); (32) R. S. Poole, *Brit. Mus. Cat. of Coins, Egypt*; (33) Vazquez Queipo, *Essai sur les Systèmes Métriques*, 1859 (general, and specially Arab and coins); (34) *Records of the Past*, vols. i., ii., vi. (Egyptian tributes, &c.); (35) E. Revillout, in *Rev. Ég.*, 1881 (many papers on Egyptian weights, measures, and coins); (36) E. T. Rogers, *Num. Chron.*, 1873 (Arab glass weights); (37) M. H. Sauvaire, in *Jour. As. Soc.*, 1877, translation of Elias of Nisibis, with notes (remarkable for history of balance); Schillbach (lists of weights, all in next); (38) M. C. Soutzo, *Étalons Pondéraux Primitifs*, 1884 (lists of all weights published to date); (39) Id., *Systèmes Monétaires Primitifs*, 1884 (derivation of units); (40) G. Smith, in *Zeits. Aeg. Sp.*, 1875; (41) L. Stern, in *Rev. Ég.*, 1881, 171 (Egyptian weights); (42) P. Tannery, *Rev. Arch.*, xli., 152; (43) E. Thomas, *Numismata Orientalia*, pt. i. (Indian weights). Many isolated papers in *Revue Archéologique*, *Hellenic Journal*, &c., are not specified above; and (44) a great amount of material is yet unpublished of weighings of weights of Troy (supplied through Dr Schliemann's kindness), Memphis, at the British Museum, Turin, &c., which may probably appear before long, and which has been utilized in this article.

III. Commercial.

In this section we shall only refer to such measures as are in actual use at the present time; the various systems of the Continental towns have been superseded by the metric system now in force, and are therefore not needed now except for historical purposes.

English weights and measures.

Great Britain.—

Length:—

inch,	12=foot,	3=yard,	5½=pole,	4=chain,	10=furlong,	8=mile.
1 in.	12	36	198	792	7920	63360

Hand, 4 inches; fathom, 2 yards; knot or geographical mile = 1′= 1·1507 miles. The chain is divided in 100 links for land measure; link=7·92 inches.

Terms of square measure are squares of the long measures.

Volume: dry:—

	pint,	2=quart,	4=gallon,	2=peck,	4=bushel,	8=quarter.
cub. in.	34·659	69·318	277·274	554·548	2218·19	17745·6

Gill=$\frac{1}{4}$ pint; pottle=2 quarts; 5 quarters=wey or load; 2 weys= last.

Volume: wet:—

Pint and quart as above.	gallon,	9=firkin,	4=barrel or hogshead,	2=pipe, butt, or puncheon.
cub. ins.	277·274	2495·5	9981·9	19963·8

Avoirdupois weight, for everything not excepted below:—

drachm,	16=ounce,	16=pound,	14=stone,	2=quarter,	4=hundred,	20=ton.
27·3 grains.	437·5	7000	98,000	196,000 grs.	112 lb	2240 lb.

Troy weight (gold, silver, platinum, and jewels, except diamonds and pearls):—

grain,	24=pennyweight,	20=ounce,	12=pound.
1 grain	24	480	5760

Diamond and pearl weight:—

grain,	4=carat,	150=ounce Troy.
·8 grain	3·2	480

Apothecaries' dispensing weight, for prescriptions only:—

grain,	20=scruple,	3=drachm,	8=ounce,	12=pound.
1 grain	20	60	480	5760

Apothecaries' fluid measure:—

minim,	60=drachm,	8=ounce,	20=pint,	8=gallon.
·91 gr., water	54·7	437·5	8,750	70,000
·036 cub. in.	·216	1·733	34·659	277·274

Metric system

Metric System.—The report to the French National Assembly proposing this system was presented 17th March 1791, the meridian measurements finished and adopted 22d June 1799, an intermediate system of division and names tolerated 28th May 1812, abolished and pure decimal system enforced 1st January 1840. Since then Netherlands, Spain (1850), Italy, Greece, Austria (legalized 1876), Germany, Norway and Sweden (1878), Switzerland, Portugal, Mexico, Venezuela, Argentine Republic, Hayti, New Grenada, Mauritius, Congo Free State, and other states have adopted this system. The use of it is permissive in Great Britain, India, Canada, Chili, &c. The theory of the system is that the metre is a 10,000,000th of a quadrant of the earth through Paris; the litre is a cube of $\frac{1}{10}$ metre; the gramme is $\frac{1}{1000}$ of the litre filled with water at 4° C.; the franc weighs 5 grammes. The multiples are as follows:—

British.	France.	Netherlands.	Other Names.
·039 inch	millimetre	streep	strich
·394 ,,	centimetre	duim	zentimeter
3·937 ,,	decimetre	palm	...
39·370 ,,	METRE	elle or aune	metre, stab
·62138 mile	kilometre	mijle	kilometer, stadion
·176 pint	decilitre	maatje	...
1·761 ,,	LITRE	kop	liter or kanne
17·608 ,,	decalitre	schepel	...
88·038 ,,	(50 litres)	...	scheffel
176·077 ,,	hectolitre	mudde	hektoliter, fasse, kilot
·015 grain	milligramme	...	...
15·43 ,,	GRAMME	wigtije	drom
154·32 ,,	decagramme	lood	loth
1543·23 ,,	hectogramme	ons	...
7716·17 ,,	(500 grammes)	...	pfund, livre
15432·35 ,,	kilogramme	pond	...
110·23 lb	(50 kilogr.)	...	zentner, zollcentner
220·46 ,,	100 kilogr.	...	centner métrique, quintal
2204·62 ,,	1000 kilogr.	...	tonne, tonneau

In land measure the unit is the are (10 metres square)=119·60 square yards; and the hectare=2·4736 acres. Other multiples of the units are merely nominal and not practically used.

Table for Conversion of British and Metric Units.

Inches.	Millimetres.	Metres.	Feet.	Cubic Inches.	Cubic Centimetres.	Cubic Metres.	Cubic Feet.
1	25·399	1	3·2809	1	16·386	1	35·316
2	50·799	2	6·5618	2	32·772	2	70·633
3	76·199	3	9·8427	3	49·168	3	105·950
4	101·598	4	13·1236	4	85·545	4	141·266
5	126·998	5	16·4045	5	81·931	5	176·583
6	152·397	6	19·6854	6	98·317	6	211·899
7	177·797	7	22·9663	7	114·703	7	247·216
8	203·196	8	26·2472	8	131·089	8	282·533
9	228·596	9	29·5281	9	147·476	9	317·849
Pints.	**Litres.**	**Litres.**	**Gallons.**	**Grains.**	**Grammes.**	**Kilos.**	**Pounds.**
1	·56755	1	·22024	1	·064799	1	2·6792
2	1·13510	2	·44049	2	·129598	2	5·3584
3	1·70265	3	·66073	3	·194397	3	8·0377
4	2·27020	4	·88098	4	·259196	4	10·7169
5	2·83775	5	1·10122	5	·323994	5	13·3961
6	3·40530	6	1·32146	6	·388794	6	16·0754
7	3·97286	7	1·54171	7	·453593	7	18·7546
8	4·54041	8	1·76195	8	·518392	8	21·4338
9	5·10796	9	1·98220	9	·583190	9	24·1130

For approximate conversion either way use the following ratios:—8 metres=315 inches (to $\frac{1}{10000}$); 8 kilometres=5 miles (to $\frac{1}{170}$); 4 litres=7 pints (to $\frac{1}{150}$); 7 grammes=108 grains (to $\frac{1}{4000}$).

Burmah.—Paulgaut 1 inch, taim 18 inches, saundaung 22 inches, dha 154 inches, dain 2·43 miles. Kait 251 grains, vis 3·59 lb, sait 14·36, ten 57·36, candy 533 lb.

Candia.—Pic 25·11 inches, carga (corn) 4·19 bushels, rottolo 1·165 lb, cantaro 116·5 lb, okka 2·65 lb.

Ceylon.—Seer 1·86 pints; 10 parrahs, 1 amomam, 5·6 bushels.

China.—Fau ·141 inches, tsun 1·41, chik 14·1, cheung 141, yan 1410=117·5 feet. Other chiks—itinerary 12·17, imperial 12·61, surveyor's 12·70, Peking 13·12, Canton 14·70 inches. Li=1800 chiks of 12·17, 13·12, or 14·1. Kop 3·3 cubic inches; 10=shing tsong ·96 pint, tau 9·6 (12 catties of water), hwuh 96 pints. Tael 580·3 grains; 16=catty, 9328 grains or 1·333 lb; picul 133·3 lb.

Denmark.—Tomme 1·03 inches, fod 12·357, aln 24·714; mül 4·6807 miles. Pott ·2126 gallons; 2=kande, 2=stübchen, 2=viertel 1·7008 gallons; anker 8·2914 gallons. Pot ·02657 bushel, skieppe ·47835, fjerding ·9567, tonne 3·8268, last 84·188 bushels. Ort 15·1 grains, quintin 60·3, lod 241·2, unze 482·5, mark 3860, pund 7720=1·103 lb=½ kilogramme. Lispund 17·646 lb, skippund 3·151 cwt. Tönde (land) 1·25 acres, (coal) 4·6775 bushels.

Egypt.—Dirá' of Nilometer 21·3 inches, dirá' beledi 22·7, dirá' handasi 25·13, pic or dirá Stambuli 26·65 inches; pic of land, 29·53, kasab 139·8 inches. Feddán $1\frac{1}{20}$ acre. Rub'a 6·6 pints or quarts, wébe 6·6 gallons, ardeb 39·6 or 46·4 gallons. Dirhem 60·65 grains, ratl 1·0131 lb, okka 2·7274 lb, kantár 101·31 lb.

India.—Bengal—gaz=yard. Bombay—gaz 27 inches, háth 18 inches. Madras—covid 18·6 inches. Bengal—cottah (katthá) 80 square yards; 20=biggah, 1600 square yards. Madras—24 mauris =cawri, 6400 square yards. Seer, 40=maund, 20=candy. Equivalents of Indian and other weights are as follows:—

Commercial Weights, &c.	Avoirdupois.			Bengal Factory.			Madras.			Bombay.		
	lb	oz.	dr.	mds.	s.	ch.	mds.	vis.	pol.	mds.	s.	pice.
Acheen bahar of 200 catties of 2·117 lb.....	423	6	13	5	26	13	16	7	19	15	4	27
Acheen guncha of 10 nelly.....................	220	0	0	2	37	13·7	8	6	16	7	34	8·6
Anjengo candy of 20 maunds..................	560	0	0	7	20	0	22	3	8	20	0	0
Bencoolen bahar...........	560	0	0	7	20	0	22	3	8	20	0	0
Bengal factory maund....	74	10	10·7	1	0	0	2	7	35·7	2	26	20
Bengal bazaar maund.....	82	2	2·1	1	4	0	3	2	11·3	2	37	10
Bombay candy of 20 maunds.................	560	0	0	7	20	0	22	3	8	20	0	0
Bussorah maund of 76 vakias..................	90	4	0	1	8	5·6	3	4	35·2	3	8	27·9
Bussorah maund of 24 vakias..................	28	8	0	0	15	4·3	1	1	4·8	1	0	21·4
Calicut maund of 100 pools....................	30	0	0	0	16	1·1	1	1	24	1	2	25·7
Cochin candy of 20 maunds.................	543	8	0	7	11	2·6	21	5	36·8	19	16	12·9
Gombroon bazaar candy.	7	8	0	0	4	0	0	2	16	0	10	21·4
Goa candy of 20 maunds	495	0	0	6	25	2·9	19	6	16	17	27	4·3
Jonkceylon bahar of 8 capins..................	485	5	5·3	6	20	0	19	3	12	17	13	10
Madras candy of 20 maunds.................	500	0	0	6	28	0	20	0	0	17	34	8·6
Mocha bahar of 15 frazils	450	0	0	6	0	1	18	0	0	16	2	25·7
Muscat custom-house maund..................	8	12	0	0	4	11	0	2	32	0	12	15
Mysore candy of 7 morahs	560	0	0	7	20	0	22	3	8	20	0	0
Pegu candy of 150 vis.....	500	0	0	6	28	0	20	0	0	17	34	8·6
Penang pecul of 100 catties..................	133	5	5·3	1	31	6	5	2	26	4	30	14·3
Surat maund of 40 seers..	37	5	5·3	0	20	0	1	3	37·9	1	13	10
Surat pucca maund.......	74	10	10·7	1	0	0	2	7	35·7	2	26	20
Tillycherry candy of 20 maunds.............	600	0	0	8	0	2	24	0	0	21	17	4·3

Bengal bazaar weights are $\frac{1}{10}$ greater than factory weights. Grain and native liquids are usually weighed.

Japan.—Boo, 10=sun, 10=shaku (11·948 inches=$\frac{10}{33}$ metre), 6=ken, 60=cho, 39=ri (2·647 miles). Go (11·1 cubic inches), 10=sho, 10=to, 10=koku (5·011 bushels). Momme 57·97 grains, 160=kin or catty (1·325 lb), 1000 momme=kuamme (8·281 lb).

Java.—Ell 27¾ inches. Kanne ·3282 gallon; rand, 396=leaguer of arrack, 133⅓ gallons; 360 rands=leaguer of wine. Rice—sack, 2=picul 135⅝ lb, 5=timbang; coyang 3581 lb.

Malacca.—Covid 18⅛ inches; buncal 832 grains (gold and silver); kip 41 lb (tin); 100 catties=picul, 135 lb; 3 piculs=bahar; 40 piculs=coyau of salt or rice; 500 gantons=50 measures=1 last, nearly 29 cwts.; chupah=2¼ lb; gautang (=ganton?), 9 lb of water at 62°.

Malta.—Palmo 10·3 inches, foot 7·2 and 11·17 inches, canna 82·4 inches; 16 tumoli=salma, 4·44 acres. Caffiso (oil) 4·58 gallons; barile (wine) 9·16 gallons; salma (corn) 7·9 bushels. Ounce 407·2 grains; rottolo 1·745 lb; cantaro 174·5 lb.

Mexico.—Vara 32·97 inches. Fanega 1·50 bushels. Libra 1·0142 lb.

Morocco.—Canna 21 inches: commercial rottolo 1·19 lb, 100=quintal; market rottolo 1·785 lb.

Persia.—Gaz (gueze), 6 handbreadths or 25 inches. Royal gaz 37½ inches. Arash 38·27 inches. Parasang or farsakh 3 geographical miles (an hour's walk for a horse). Sextario (21 cubic inches), 4=chenica, 2=capicha (2·4 quarts), 25=artaba (1·9 bushels). (These, as the native names show, are not native measures. As Chardin remarks, there are no true measures of capacity; even liquids are sold by weight.) Dirhem, 143 (Bussora), 147·8 (Tabriz), or 150 grs. Mescal, 2=dirhem, 50=ratl (7300 grains), 6=man or batman.

Russia.—Vershok (1·75 inches), 16=archine, 3=sagene (7 feet British, legally), 500=verst (·663 mile); 2400 square sagenes=deciatine (2·7 acres). Tcharkey (·216 pint), 100=vedro, 3=anker, 40 vedros=sarakovaia (324·6 gallons). Garnietz 2=tchetverka, 4=tchetverik, 2=paiak, 2=osmin, 2=tchetvert (5·77 bushels). Dola (·68578 grains); 96=zolotnic; 8=lana; 12=funt (6319·7279 grains); 40=pud (36·112 lb); 10=berkovitz; 3=packen. Also 3 zolotnices=1 loth.

Siam.—Nin, 12=küb (10 inches), 2=sok, 4=wa (79·999 inches on silver bar at 85° Fahr.). Thangsat, 10×10×20 nin, actual standard 1159·8477 cubic inches at 85°=2·08 pecks. Thanan, 5×5×4 nin, standard 57·8800 at 85°=1·67 pints. Tical or bat (234·04 grains), 4=tael, 4=catty or chang, 50=picul or hap (133·738 lb).

Turkey.—Pic 26·8 or 27·06 inches; larger pic 27·9. Almud 1·15 gallons (of oil=8 okas); 4 killows=fortin of 3·7 bushels (killow of rice=10 okas). Dram (49·5 grains), 100=chequi, 4=oka (2·8286 ℔); dram (49·5 grains), 180=rotl, 100=kintal or kantar (127·29 ℔).

United States.—Inch=1·000049 British inch, and other measures in proportion. Gallon=·83292 British gallon. Bushel=·96946 British bushel. Weight, as Great Britain.

See Kelly's *Universal Cambist*; Doursther's *Dictionnaire Universelle des Poids et Mesures*; Woolhouse, *Weights and Measures*; recent *Reports* of Board of Trade and Standards Department.

As weights of grain are often needed we add pounds weight in cubic feet.

	Wheat, Usual.	Pease, American.	Indian Corn.	Oats, Russian.	Beans, Egyptian.	Barley, English.	Rice.
Loose......	49	50	44	28	46	39	} 56
Close......	53½	54	47	33	50	44	

See *Report of Standards Department*, 1884. (W. M. F. P.)

WEIMAR, the capital of the grand-duchy of Saxe-Weimar-Eisenach, the largest of the Thuringian states, is situated in a pleasant valley on the Ilm, 50 miles south-west of Leipsic and 136 miles south-west of Berlin. Containing no very imposing edifices, and plainly and irregularly built, the town presents at first a somewhat unpretending and even dull appearance; but there is an air of elegance in its quiet and clean streets, which recalls the fact that it is the residence of a grand-duke and his court, and it still retains an indescribable atmosphere of refinement, dating from its golden age, when it won the titles of "poets' city" and "the German Athens." Weimar has now no actual importance, though it will always remain a literary Mecca. It is a peaceful little German town, abounding in excellent educational, literary, artistic, and benevolent institutions; its society is cultured, though perhaps a little narrow; while the even tenour of its existence is undisturbed by any great commercial or manufacturing activity. The population in 1885 was 21,565; in 1782, six years after Goethe's arrival, it was about 7000; and in 1834, two years after his death, it was 10,638.

The reign of Goethe's friend and patron, the grand-duke Charles Augustus (1775–1828), represents accurately enough the golden age of Weimar; though even during the duke's minority, his mother, the duchess Amalia, had begun to make the little court a focus of light and leading in Germany. The most striking building in Weimar is the extensive palace, erected for Charles Augustus under the superintendence of Goethe in 1789–1803, in place of one burned down in 1770. This building, with the associations of its erection, and its "poets' rooms," dedicated to Goethe, Schiller, Herder, and Wieland, epitomizes the characteristics of the town. The main interest of Weimar centres in these men and their more or less illustrious contemporaries; and, above all, Goethe, whose altar to the "genius hujus loci" still stands in the ducal park, is himself the genius of the place, just as Shakespeare is of Stratford-on-Avon, or Luther of Wittenberg. Goethe's residence from 1782 to 1832 (now opened as a "Goethe museum," with his collections and other reminiscences), the simple "garden-house" in the park, where he spent many summers, Schiller's humble abode, where he lived from 1802 till his death in 1805, and the grand-ducal burial vault, where the two poets rest side by side, are among the most frequented pilgrim resorts in Germany. Rietschel's bronze group of Goethe and Schiller (unveiled in 1857) stands appropriately in front of the theatre (much altered in 1868) which attained such distinction under their combined auspices. Not far off is the large and clumsy parish church, built about 1400, of which Herder became pastor in 1776; close to the church is his statue, and his house is still the parsonage. Within the church are the tombs of Herder and of Duke Bernhard of Weimar, the hero of the Thirty Years' War. The altar-piece—a Crucifixion—is said to be the masterpiece of Lucas Cranach, whose house is pointed out in the market-place. Wieland, who came to Weimar in 1772 as the duke's tutor, is also commemorated by a statue, and his house is indicated by a tablet. Among the other prominent buildings in Weimar are the library, containing 200,000 volumes and a valuable collection of portraits, busts, and literary and other curiosities; the museum, built in 1863–68 in the Renaissance style; the ancient church of St James, with the tombs of Lucas Cranach and Musæus; and the town-house, built in 1841. Various points in the environs of Weimar are also interesting from their associations. Separated from the town by the park, laid out in the so-called English style by Goethe, is the chateau of Belvedere, built in 1724. To the north-east is Tiefurt, often the scene of al-fresco plays, in which the courtiers were the actors and the rocks and trees the scenery; and to the north-west is the chateau of Ettersburg, another favourite resort of Charles Augustus and his court.

Plan of Weimar.

The history of Weimar, apart from its brilliant record at the end of the 18th and the beginning of the 19th century, is of comparatively little interest. The town is said to have existed in the 9th century, and in the 10th to have belonged to a collateral branch of the family of the counts of Orlamünde. About 1376 it fell to the landgraves of Thuringia, and in 1440 it passed to the electors of Saxony. In 1806 it was visited by Napoleon, whose half-formed intention of abolishing the duchy was only averted by the tact and address of the duchess Luise. The Muses have never left Weimar. Since 1860 it has been the seat of a good school of painting, represented by the landscape painters Preller, Kalckreuth, and Max Schmidt, and the historical painters Pauwels, Heumann, and Verlat. The frequent residence here also of the Abbé Liszt, from 1848 till his death in 1886, has preserved for Weimar quite an important place in the musical world.

WEISSENFELS, an industrial town in the province of Saxony, Prussia, is situated on the Saale, 18½ miles south-west of Leipsic and 19 miles south of Halle. It contains three churches, a spacious market-place, and various educational and benevolent institutions. The former palace, called the Augustusburg, built in 1664–90, occupies a site on a sandstone eminence near the town; this spacious edifice is now used as a military school. Weissenfels manufactures machinery, sugar, pasteboard, paper, leather goods, pottery, and gold and silver wares. It contains also an iron-foundry, and carries on trade in timber and grain. In the neighbourhood are large deposits of sandstone and lignite. Weissenfels is a place of considerable antiquity, and from 1657 till 1746 it was the capital of the dukes of Saxe-Weissenfels, a branch of the electoral house of Saxony. The body of Gustavus Adolphus was embalmed at Weissenfels after the battle of Lützen. The population of the town in 1885 was 21,766.

WEKA, or WEEKA. See OCYDROME.

WELLESLEY, RICHARD WESLEY (or WELLESLEY), MARQUIS OF (1760–1842), eldest son of the first earl of Mornington, an Irish peer, and eldest brother of the duke of Wellington, was born June 20, 1760. He was sent to Eton, where he was distinguished as an excellent classical scholar, and to Christ Church, Oxford. By his father's death in 1781 he became earl of Mornington, taking his seat in the Irish House of Peers. In 1784 he entered the English House of Commons as member for Beeralston. Soon afterwards he was appointed a lord of the treasury by Pitt, with whom he rapidly grew in favour. In 1793 he became a member of the board of control over Indian affairs; and, although he was best known to the public by his speeches in defence of Pitt's foreign policy, he was now gaining the acquaintance with Oriental affairs which made his rule over India so wonderfully effective from the moment when, in 1797, he accepted the office of governor-general. Wellesley seems in a peculiar manner to have caught Pitt's own large political spirit during the years of his intercourse with him from 1793 to 1797. With equally profound conviction of the antagonism between the French republic and the interests of Great Britain all over the world, he had gained the same habit of dealing with political affairs in vast combinations and on the broadest survey. That Pitt and Wellesley had consciously formed the design of acquiring a great empire in India to compensate for the loss of the American colonies has not been proved ; but the rivalry with France, which in Europe placed England at the head of coalition after coalition against the French republic and empire, made Wellesley's rule in India an epoch of enormous and rapid extension of English power. On the journey outwards he formed, after a discussion at the Cape with officials and soldiers returning home, the design of annihilating French influence in the Deccan. Soon after his landing, in April 1798, he learnt that an alliance had actually been formed between Tippoo Saib and the French republic. Wellesley resolved to anticipate the action of the enemy, and ordered preparations for war. The invasion of Mysore followed in February 1799, and the campaign was brought to a rapid close by the capture of Seringapatam (see INDIA and WELLINGTON). In 1803 the restoration of the peshwa was taken in hand, which proved the prelude to the great Mahratta war against Sindhia and the raja of Berar. The result of these wars and of the treaties which followed them was that French influence in India was extinguished, that forty millions of population and ten millions of revenue were added to the British dominions, and that the powers of the Mahratta and all other princes were so reduced that England became the really dominant authority over all India. Nor was Wellesley's rule distinguished only by conquest. He was an excellent administrator, and sought to provide, by the foundation of the college of Fort William, for the training of a class of men adequate to the great work of governing India. In connexion with this college he established the governor-general's office, to which civilians who had shown great talent at the college were transferred, in order that they might learn something of the highest statesmanship in the immediate service of their chief. A free-trader, like Pitt, he endeavoured to remove some of the restrictions on the trade between England and India. Both the commercial policy of Wellesley and his educational projects brought him into hostility with the court of directors, and he more than once tendered his resignation, which, however, public necessities led him to postpone till the autumn of 1805. He reached England just in time to see Pitt before his death. On the fall of the coalition ministry in 1807 Wellesley (an English peer from 1797 and marquis in the peerage of Ireland from 1799) was invited by George III. to join the duke of Portland's cabinet, but he declined, pending the discussion in parliament of certain charges brought against him in respect of his Indian administration. Resolutions condemning him for the abuse of power were moved both in the Lords and Commons, but defeated by large majorities. In 1809 Wellesley was appointed ambassador to Spain. He landed at Cadiz just after the battle of Talavera, and endeavoured, but without success, to bring the Spanish Government into effective co-operation with his brother, who, through the failure of his allies, was compelled to retreat into Portugal. A few months later, after the duel between Canning and Castlereagh and the resignation of both, Wellesley accepted the post of foreign secretary in Perceval's cabinet. He held this office until February 1812, when he retired, partly from dissatisfaction at the inadequate support given to Wellington by the ministry, but also because he had become convinced that the question of Catholic emancipation could no longer be kept in the background. From early life Wellesley had, unlike his brother, been an advocate of Catholic emancipation, and with the claim of the Irish Catholics to justice he henceforward identified himself. On Perceval's assassination he refused to join Lord Liverpool's administration, and he remained out of office till 1821, criticizing with severity the proceedings of the congress of Vienna and the European settlement of 1814, which, while it reduced France to its ancient limits, left to the other great powers the territory that they had acquired by the partition of Poland and the destruction of Venice. He was one of the peers who signed the protest against the enactment of the Corn Laws in 1815. In 1821 he was appointed to the lord-lieutenancy of Ireland. Catholic emancipation had now become an open question in the cabinet, and Wellesley's acceptance of the viceroyalty was believed in Ireland to herald the immediate settlement of the Catholic claims. The Orange faction were incensed by the firmness with which their excesses were now repressed, and Wellesley was on one occasion mobbed and insulted. But the hopes of the Catholics still remained unfulfilled. Lord Liverpool died without having grappled with the problem. Canning in turn passed away ; and on the assumption of office by Wellington, who was opposed to Catholic emancipation, his brother resigned the lord-lieutenancy. He had, however, the satisfaction of seeing the Catholic claims settled in the next year by the very statesmen who had declared against them. In 1833 he resumed the office of lord-lieutenant under Earl Grey, but the ministry fell a few months later, and, with one short exception, Wellesley did not further take part in official life. His old age, which was vigorous and animated to the last, was occupied with literary and classical pursuits. He died on September 26, 1842. He had no successor in the marquisate, but the earldom of Mornington and minor honours devolved on his brother William, Lord Maryborough, on the failure of whose issue in 1863 they fell to the second duke of Wellington.

WELLINGBOROUGH, a market-town of Northamptonshire, England, is situated on the declivity of a hill near the junction of the Ise with the Nen, and on the London and North-Western and Midland railway lines, 63½ miles north-north-west of London, and 10½ east-north-east of Northampton. The church of St Luke contains some Norman and Early English portions, with later work of various periods, and a Decorated western tower and spire. The grammar-schools, founded in 1594 and endowed with the revenues of a suppressed guild, include a school of the second and a school of the third grade, the former a building of red brick in the Renaissance style erected in 1880 at a cost of £6000, and the latter an old Elizabethan structure. Another educational endowment is Freeman's school, founded by John Freeman in 1711. There are also several charities. The market-place, situated in the centre of the town, was founded in 1874. The principal public buildings include the corn exchange (erected in 1861 at a cost of £4000), and the "Priory," an old residence now used for Sunday school and other parochial purposes. Formerly the town was famed for the chalybeate springs to which it owes its name. It is now of some importance as a centre of agricultural trade; but the staple industry is leather. A great impulse to the prosperity of the town was given by the introduction of the boot and shoe trade, especially the manufacture of uppers. Smelting, brewing, and iron-founding are also carried on, as well as the manufacture of portable steam-engines. A coal depôt of the

Midland Railway is also situated in the town. The population of the township and urban sanitary district (area 3992 acres) in 1871 was 9385 and in 1881 it was 13,794.

In 948 Edred gave the church at Wellingborough to Croyland abbey, and the grant was confirmed by King Edgar in 966. In the reign of Edward II. the abbot was lord in full. It received the grant of a market in the 2d year of King John. In 1621 it was visited by Charles I. and his queen, who resided in tents during a whole season that they might drink the waters. It was after its almost total destruction by fire in 1738 that the town was built on its present site on the hill.

WELLINGTON, a town of Shropshire, England, on the Great Western and London and North-Western railway lines, and on the Shropshire Union Canal, 151¼ miles north-west of London, 11 east of Shrewsbury, and 31 north-west of Birmingham. The neighbourhood is picturesque, the Wrekin, about 1½ miles from the town, rising to a height of 1320 feet. The church of All Saints, built in 1790, was restored in 1876, and again in 1883. There are a number of charities. The manufacture of agricultural implements, iron and brass founding, and malting are carried on. The population of the urban sanitary district (area 352 acres) in 1871 was 5926, and in 1881 it was 6217.

Wellington, which is situated near the old Roman Watling Street, is referred to in Domesday as held by Earl Roger. It was granted by King John to Thomas de Erdinton for services rendered at Rome at the time of the interdict. It was held by Earl Edwin, but by the rebellion of Robert de Belesme was forfeited to the king. The church of Wellington was given by Earl Roger to Shrewsbury abbey. Wellington was the first rendezvous of Charles I., who on 19th September 1642 mustered his forces near the town.

WELLINGTON, a market-town of Somerset, England, is situated on a gentle elevation at the foot of the Blackdowns near the river Tone, and on the Great Western Railway, 170 miles south-south-west of London, and 7 south-west of Taunton. The church of St John, a handsome structure, with one of the characteristic Somersetshire towers, is of the Perpendicular style of architecture, except the nave, which is Early English. The church contains a monument to Sir J. Popham, lord justice of England in the time of Elizabeth and James I. Among other public buildings are the market-house or town-hall (1833), the West Somerset county school (1880), and the Popham hospital for aged men and women, founded by Sir John Popham in 1606 and rebuilt in 1833. On the highest summit of the Blackdowns, 2½ miles south of the town, is a triangular stone tower erected in honour of the duke of Wellington, who took his title from the town. The staple industry is the woollen manufacture; iron-founding and brick and tile making are also carried on. The population of the township and urban sanitary district (area 5195 acres) in 1871 was 6286, and in 1881 it was 6360.

King Alfred gave Wellington, with other two neighbouring manors, to Asser, who was afterwards raised to the see of Sherborne, and died in 883. Subsequently it was conferred on Aldhelm, the first bishop of Wells. In Domesday it occurs as Wallintone, and is valued at £25. In the 2d of Edward VI. the manor was granted by Bishop Barlow, together with the borough of Wellington, to Edward, duke of Somerset. On the duke's attainder it came to the crown, with whom it remained till the 22d of James I.

WELLINGTON, the chief town of Hutt county, New Zealand, and the seat of the colonial Government, is situated in the south-west of North Island, on the shores of Port Nicholson, in 41° 16′ 25″ S. lat. and 174° 47′ 25″ E. long., 80 miles east of Nelson, 160 south of New Plymouth, and 1200 south-east of Sydney. The immediate surroundings of Wellington were originally very uninviting, as it is walled in by high ranges unsuitable for tillage, but great enterprise has been shown in the construction of roads to the more fertile regions. Railways are being gradually extended towards both the north and the north-east. Owing to the prevalence of earthquakes the city is built chiefly of wood, but within recent years there has been an increasing tendency to make use of concrete and brick. Among the principal public buildings are the Government house, the houses of legislature, the Government buildings, the new postal and telegraph office, Wellington college, St Patrick's Catholic college, the oddfellows' hall, the freemasons' hall, the hospital, and the lunatic asylum. The city also possesses a colonial museum, an athenæum and mechanics' institute, a lyceum, and three theatres. The botanical gardens have an area of 100 acres. There is also a public park called the Town Belt. To supplement the water supply from two large reservoirs at Polhill's Gully, an aqueduct has lately been constructed from the Wainuiomata river, 16 miles distant, at an expense of £130,000.

Wellington was the first settlement of the New Zealand colonists. It owes its commercial prosperity and its selection as the capital to its convenient and central position. It is the seat of both a Protestant and a Catholic see. The harbour, which has lately been extended and improved, is one of the best and safest in New Zealand. There is a lighthouse at the eastern entrance, on Pincarrow Head, opposite which is the pilot station. There are two large wharves, and in Evans Bay there is a patent slip capable of receiving vessels of 2000 tons. As a shipping port Wellington ranks next to Auckland and Lyttelton. It possesses foundries, shipbuilding yards, boot factories, soap and candle works, tanneries, woollen, coffee, flour, and saw mills, breweries, aerated water works, coach factories, brick and tile works, and a very extensive meat-preserving establishment, which exports large supplies to Europe. The area of the municipal borough is 1100 acres, and from 4176 in 1861 the population increased to 13,488 in 1871 and 20,563 in 1881, while in 1886 the city and suburbs had 27,833 inhabitants.

WELLINGTON, ARTHUR WELLESLEY, DUKE OF (1769–1852), was the fourth son of Garrett, earl of Mornington, now remembered only as a musician. He was descended from the family of Colley or Cowley, which had been settled in Ireland for some centuries. The duke's grandfather assumed the name of Wesley on succeeding to the estates of Mr Garrett Wesley, a kinsman of the famous divine; the affinity between the families of Colley and Wesley rests, however, on nothing nearer than a common ancestor in the 15th century. In the duke's early letters the family name is spelt Wesley; the change to Wellesley seems to have been made about 1790. Arthur (born in Ireland in the spring of 1769[1]) was sent to Eton, and subsequently to the military college at Angers. He entered the army as ensign of the 73d regiment in 1787, passed rapidly through the subaltern grades, became major of the 33d, and purchased the lieutenant-colonelcy of that regiment in 1793 with money advanced to him by his eldest brother. Before reaching full age he was returned to the Irish parliament by the family borough of Trim. Little is known of his history during these years; but neither in boyhood nor early youth does he appear to have made any mark among his contemporaries. His first experience of active service was in the disastrous campaign of 1794–95, when the British force under the duke of York was driven out of Holland by Pichegru.

Indian service.

In 1796 he was sent with his regiment to India. Three years more passed before Wellesley became known to the world, but we have his own testimony that it was during these years of obscurity that he qualified himself in one direction for the great military career before him. As colonel commanding a regiment he gained the most minute and accurate acquaintance with every detail of the soldier's life, learned the precise amount of food

[1] In Merrion Street, Dublin, or at Dungan Castle, Meath, towards the end of April or on 1st May; but both place and date are uncertain.

required for every mouth, the exact weight that could be carried, the distances that could be traversed without exhaustion, the whole body of conditions in short which govern the activity both in peace and war of man and beast. It was to this absolutely complete knowledge of practical details that Wellington ascribed in great part his own success in the highest commands. It is probable, moreover, that he at this time made a serious study of the science and history of warfare. His training at the college of Angers is not sufficient to account for his great technical knowledge; no record, however, exists of the stages by which this was acquired. In 1798 Colonel Wellesley's eldest brother, Lord Mornington, afterwards marquis of Wellesley, arrived in India as governor-general. The war with Tippoo Saib followed. The 33d regiment was attached to the subsidiary force furnished by the nizam, and Colonel Wellesley was entrusted with the command of this division, under the orders of General Harris. In a preliminary attack upon the works of Seringapatam Wellesley met with a repulse; in the successful assault upon the town he commanded the reserve. Though his military services in this short campaign were not of a striking character, he was appointed by his brother to the supreme military and political command in Mysore. His great faculties now for the first time found opportunity for their exercise. In the settlement and administration of the conquered territory Wellesley rapidly acquired the habits and experience of a statesman. Nor, in the midst of his work of peaceful reorganization, was it possible for him to abandon the life of the soldier. The frontiers of Mysore were harassed by independent chieftains or marauders, especially by one Doondiah, an energetic leader, who had assumed the title of "the king of two worlds." Wellesley's operations against Doondiah were conducted with extraordinary energy; his marches in pursuit were prodigious, and his final success complete. More important, however, than the military side of these operations was their political character. When pressed in Mysore, Doondiah moved into Mahratta territory, and into this territory it was necessary for Wellesley to follow him. Here, negotiating and bargaining with the Mahratta chiefs, Wellesley acquired a knowledge of their affairs and an influence over them such as no other Englishman possessed. Simple and honourable himself, he was shrewd and penetrating in his judgment of Orientals; and, unlike his great predecessor Clive, he rigidly adhered to the rule of good faith in his own actions, however depraved and however exasperating the conduct of those with whom he had to deal. The result of Wellesley's singular personal ascendency among the Mahrattas came into full view when the Mahratta war broke out. In the meantime, however, his Indian career seemed likely to be sacrificed to the calls of warfare in another quarter. Wellesley was ordered by the governor-general, in December 1800, to take command of a body of troops collected for foreign service at Trincomalee, in Ceylon. It was at first intended that these troops should act against Java or Mauritius; their destination was, however, altered to Egypt, and a notification was made to Wellesley that in consequence of this change General Baird would be placed in command above him. Though deeply offended at the loss of the command, Wellesley so completely sank all personal grievance in his devotion to the public cause that, in opposition to his instructions, and at the risk of incurring severe censure, he moved the troops on his own responsibility from Trincomalee to Bombay, from the conviction that, if they were to be of any use in Egypt, it was absolutely necessary that they should provision at Bombay without delay. The documents in which Wellesley justified this step prove his singularly clear and profound acquaintance with the conditions of a successful invasion of Egypt from India. At Bombay Wellesley was attacked by fever, and prevented from going on to Egypt. He returned with great satisfaction to his government in Mysore, where he remained until the Mahratta war broke out. The power of the peshwa, nominally supreme in the Mahratta territory, had been overthrown by his rivals Holkar and others, and he had himself fled from Poona to Bassein on the coast. By the treaty of Bassein, made in December 1802, the Indian Government entered into an alliance with this potentate, and pledged itself to restore his authority. Wellesley was placed in command of the army charged with this task. Starting from Seringapatam, he crossed the frontier on March 12, 1803, and moved through the southern Mahratta territory on Poona. The march was one unbroken success. Wellesley's own arrangements, which displayed the utmost forethought and sagacity in dealing with the physical conditions to be encountered on the march, would no doubt have secured his victory had resistance been encountered; but his personal and diplomatic ascendency among the chieftains of the district worked even more powerfully than the fear of his arms. No hand was raised against him, and a march of six hundred miles was conducted without even a skirmish. "The confidence and respect of every class in the provinces south of the Kistna," wrote Major Malcolm, the political agent who accompanied the march, "is in a very great degree personal to Major-General Wellesley. To the admiration which the Mahratta chiefs entertain for that officer's military character, and the firm reliance which the inhabitants place on his justice and protection, the extraordinary success which has hitherto attended the progress of the march must be principally attributed." Wellesley had intended to reach Poona on the 23d of April. On the night of the 18th, when 60 miles distant from Poona, he received intelligence that Amrut Rao, a rival of the peshwa's, intended to burn the city at the approach of the English. Counting no moment to be lost, Wellesley pressed on with the cavalry, accomplished the march of 60 miles in thirty-two hours, and entered Poona on the afternoon of the 20th, in time to save the city from destruction. The peshwa was now restored to power, and entered into various military obligations with Wellesley, which he very imperfectly fulfilled.

Mahratta war.

In the meantime Sindhia and Holkar, with the raja of Berar, maintained a doubtful but threatening aspect farther north. It was uncertain whether or not a confederacy of the northern Mahrattas had been formed against the British Government. In these critical circumstances, while peace and war hung in the balance, Wellesley was charged with "the general direction and control of all the military and political affairs of the British Government in the territories of the nizam, of the peshwa, and of the Mahratta states and chiefs." Acting in execution of these powers, he required Sindhia, as a proof of good faith, to withdraw to the north of the Nerbudda. Sindhia not doing so, war was declared on August 6, 1803. Wellesley marched northwards, captured Ahmadnagar on August 11, crossed the Godavery ten days later, and moved against the combined forces of Sindhia and the rajah of Berar. Colonel Stevenson was meanwhile approaching with a second division from the east, and it was intended that the two corps should unite in an attack on the enemy. On the 23d of September Wellesley supposed himself to be still some miles from the Mahratta headquarters; he suddenly found that the entire forces of Sindhia and the rajah of Berar were close in front of him at Assaye. Weighing the dangers of delay, of retreat, and of an attack with his own unsupported division, Wellesley convinced himself that an immediate attack, though against greatly superior forces in a strong position, was the wisest course. He threw himself upon the Mahratta host, and ultimately gained a complete victory, though with the loss of 2500 men out of a total probably not much exceeding 7000. In comparison with the battle of Assaye, all fighting that had hitherto taken place in India was child's play. The enemy's artillery was of the most formidable character, and worked with deadly effect. A hundred cannon were taken by the conqueror, who now, uniting with Stevenson's division, followed up the pursuit, and brought the war to a close by a second victory at Argaum on November 29. The treaties with Sindhia and the raja of Berar which followed the overthrow of their arms, and which marked the downfall of the Mahratta power, were negotiated and signed by Wellesley in the course of the following month. Not yet thirty-five years old, Wellesley had proved himself as thorough a master in the sphere of Indian statesmanship and diplomacy as on the field of battle. Had his career ended at this time, his despatches on the negotiations with the Mahrattas and on the general conduct of Indian policy would have proved him to have been one of the wisest and strongest heads that have ever served England in the East.

In the spring of 1805 Wellesley, now Sir Arthur, quitted India and returned home. He was immediately sent on the expedition to Hanover which was rendered abortive by the battle of Austerlitz. In 1806 he was elected member of parliament for the borough of Rye, and in the following year was appointed Irish secretary. After serving in this office for a few months he was employed in the expedition against Copenhagen, where little glory was to be gained. In the summer of 1808 he took command of a body of troops destined to operate against the French in Spain or Portugal. Finding that the junta of Corunna wished for no foreign soldiery, he proceeded to fulfil his instructions by acting against Junot at Lisbon. He landed at Mondego Bay in the first week of August, and moved southwards, driving in the enemy's posts at Roliça on August 17. On the 21st the battle of Vimiero was fought and won. In the midst of this engagement, however, Sir Harry Burrard landed, and superseded Wellesley in the command. Wellesley in vain called upon this general to follow up the pursuit when the victory was gained. The consequence was that Junot's army, which would have been captured or annihilated if Wellesley's advice had been executed, escaped into a position which secured it the means of retreat if favourable terms of capitulation were refused. The convention of Cintra provided for the evacuation of Portugal by the French, but it gave Junot and all his troops a free return to France. So great was the public displeasure in England at the escape of the enemy that a court of inquiry was held into all the circumstances attending the convention of Cintra. At this inquiry the rejection of Wellesley's counsels by his superior officer at the close of the battle of Vimiero was fully proved.

Service in the Peninsula.

After the failure of Sir John Moore's campaign in the winter of 1808–9, Wellesley, who had in the meantime resumed his duties as Irish secretary, returned to the Peninsula as chief in command. His first move was against Soult, who had captured Oporto. He drove the French out of this city by a singularly bold and fortunate attack, and then prepared to march against Madrid by the valley of the Tagus. Some appearance of additional strength was given him by the support of a Spanish army under General Cuesta; but his movements were delayed by the neglect and bad faith of the Spanish Government, and time was given to Soult to collect a large force at Salamanca, with which he intended to fall upon the English line of communications. Wellesley, unconscious of Soult's presence in force on his flank, advanced against Madrid, and finally drew up at Talavera to meet the attack of Victor, who had defeated Cuesta and driven him back on the English. The battle was begun on the 27th and continued on the 28th of July. Wellesley gained a complete victory, and decisively proved the superiority of English troops under his command over those of the enemy. But within the next few days Soult's approach on the line of communication was discovered. It was impossible for Wellesley to follow up his advantages. The victory of Talavera had brought prestige but nothing else. Superiority of numbers had made the French the real winners of the campaign, and Wellesley, disgusted with his Spanish allies, had no choice but to withdraw into Portugal and there stand upon the defensive. A peerage, with the title of Viscount Wellington, was conferred upon him for his victory at Talavera.

Battle of Talavera.

Up to this time Napoleon, with the bulk of his armies, had been occupied with the war against Austria. The peace of Vienna, concluded in October 1809, made him free to throw an almost unlimited force into the Spanish Peninsula. Wellington, foreseeing that Portugal would now be invaded by a very powerful army, began the fortification of the celebrated lines of Torres Vedras, which followed the mountain-bastion on the north of Lisbon, and left no single point open between the Tagus and the sea. The English army in the meantime wintered in the neighbourhood of Almeida. As summer approached Wellington's anticipations were realized. Masséna, who had distinguished himself above every other general in the Austrian war of 1809, arrived in Spain, and moved against Portugal with an army of 70,000 men. Wellington was unable to prevent Ciudad Rodrigo from falling into the hands of the French. He retreated down the valley of the Mondego, devastating the country, and at length halted at Busaco, and gave battle. The French attack was repelled, but other roads were open to the invader, and Wellington continued his retreat. Masséna followed, and heard for the first time of the fortifications of Torres Vedras when he was within five days' march of them. On approaching the mountain-barrier the French general sought in vain for an unprotected point. It was with the utmost difficulty, while waiting for reinforcements, that he could keep his army from starving. At length, when the country was utterly exhausted, he commenced his retreat. Wellington descended from the heights, but his marching-force was too weak to risk a pitched battle. Masséna was in consequence able to maintain himself at Santarem for the winter. But in the spring of 1811 Wellington received reinforcements from England. He now moved against the enemy. Masséna retreated northwards, devastating the country with unsparing severity in order to check the pursuit. Such were the sufferings of his army, both in the invasion and in the retreat, that, although only one battle was fought during the campaign, the French, when they re-entered Spain, had lost 30,000 men.

Lines of Torres Vedras.

In the meantime Soult, who was besieging Cadiz, had received orders from Napoleon to move to the support of Masséna. Leaving part of his force in front of Cadiz, he marched northwards and captured Badajoz. Here, however, he learnt that Masséna was in full retreat, and also that his own army besieging Cadiz had been attacked and beaten. He in consequence returned and resumed the blockade. Wellington, freed from pressure on the south, and believing Masséna to be thoroughly disabled, considered that the time had come for an advance into Spain. The fortresses of Almeida, Ciudad Rodrigo, and Badajoz had to be recaptured from the French. Leaving a small force to besiege Almeida, Wellington went southwards to arrange with Beresford for the siege of Badajoz. During his absence Masséna again took the field, and marched to the relief of Almeida. Wellington returned in time to defeat him at Fuentes d'Onoro, and Almeida passed into the hands of the British. In the south Soult advanced to the relief of Badajoz. He was overthrown by Beresford at Albuera; but the junction of the two French armies compelled the English to raise the siege, and Wellington had to retire within the Portuguese frontier. Moving northwards with the view of laying siege to Ciudad Rodrigo, he was again outnumbered by the French, and forced to withdraw to cantonments on the Coa.

Wellington had from the first seen that, whatever number of men Napoleon might send against Portugal, it was impossible, owing to the poverty of the country, that any great mass of troops could long be held together. The French generals, by combining their armies, might for a while be superior to him, but the want of provisions would inevitably lead to their separation after a longer or shorter interval. This was verified at the end of 1811. Soult's division had to move southwards for support, and the English were again more than a match for the enemy in front of them. Wellington resumed the offensive, and on the 19th of January 1812 Ciudad Rodrigo was taken by storm. The road into Spain was now open; it only remained to secure Portugal itself and the line of communication by the capture of Badajoz. Wellington crossed the Tagus and completed the investment of this fortress by the middle of March. It was necessary at whatever cost to anticipate the arrival of Soult with a relieving army, and on the 6th of April Wellington ordered the assault. The fearful slaughter which took place before the British were masters of the defences caused Wellington to be charged with indifference to the loss of human life; but, whatever faults may have been made in the actual operations, a postponement of the attack would merely have resulted in more battles against Soult, in which a greater number of men would have perished. Of all generals Wellington was the last to throw away a single life needlessly.

Badajoz captured.

Advance into Spain.

The advance into Spain against the French line of communication between Madrid and the Pyrenees was now begun. Marmont, who had succeeded Masséna in the command, fell back and allowed Wellington to occupy Salamanca; but on reaching the Douro he turned upon his assailant, and, by superior swiftness in marching, threatened to cut the English off from Portugal. Wellington now retreated as far as Salamanca, and there extricated himself from his peril by one of the most brilliant victories which he ever gained (July 22). The French fell back on Burgos. Instead of immediately following them, which from a military point of view would have been the better course, Wellington thought it wise to advance upon the Spanish capital. King Joseph retired southwards and the English entered Madrid in triumph. The political effect of this act was very great, but the delay gave the French northern army time to rally. On marching against them Wellington was checked by the obstinate defence of Burgos. Moreover, in consequence of the loss of the capital, Soult was now ordered to raise the siege of Cadiz, and to move to the support of King Joseph. Gathering his forces, and uniting them with the French army of the centre, he pressed on towards Madrid. It was impossible for Wellington to maintain his position, and he was compelled once more to retire into Portugal, while Madrid passed back into the hands of the French. During this his last retreat the demoralization and misconduct of the British army surpassed anything that their chief had ever witnessed. The effect of the campaign was, however, that Cadiz was free, and that the southern provinces were finally cleared of the invader.

Battle of Salamanca.

Wellington was now invested by the cortes with the supreme command of the Spanish armies. He visited Cadiz in December 1812, and offered counsels of moderation to the democratic assembly, which were not followed. During the succeeding months he was occupied with plans and preparations for a great combined attack, and at length, in May 1813, the hour for his final and victorious advance arrived. The disasters of the Russian campaign had compelled Napoleon to withdraw some of his best regiments from the Peninsula. Against a weakened and discouraged adversary Wellington took the field with greatly increased numbers, and with the utmost confidence of victory. His design was to throw himself directly upon the French line of communication, keeping his left pushed forward in advance of his centre, so as to threaten the envelopment of the fortified posts held by the enemy. Napoleon had foreseen that this would be the strategy of the English commander, and had ordered King Joseph to neglect every point to the centre and east, and to concentrate at Valladolid. This order had been but imperfectly obeyed. The advance of the allied army was irresistible. Position after position was evacuated by the French, until Wellington, driving everything before him, came up with the retreating enemy at Vitoria, now encumbered with an enormous train of fugitives, and with the spoils of five years' occupation of Spain. His victory, won on the 21st of June, was overwhelming. All the artillery and almost all the treasure and stores of the French army fell into the hands of the conquerors. It only remained for Napoleon to commit to Marshal Soult, as his lieutenant, the task of defending the Pyrenees, and of delivering, if possible, the fortresses of St Sebastian and Pamplona, which Wellington now besieged. Soult's combats in the Pyrenees, and the desperate resistance of St Sebastian, prolonged the struggle through the autumn of 1813, and cost the English torrents of blood. But at length the frontier was passed, and after a succession of encounters on French soil Soult was forced back into his entrenched camp at Bayonne. Both armies now rested for some weeks, during which interval Wellington gained the confidence of the inhabitants of the district by his unsparing repression of marauding, his business-like payment for supplies, and the excellent discipline which he maintained among his soldiers. In February 1814 the advance was renewed. The Adour was crossed, and Soult, leaving a garrison in Bayonne, fell back on Orthes. At Orthes he was attacked and defeated. Bordeaux now declared in favour of the Bourbons and admitted the English. Soult's last move was upon Toulouse. Here, after the allies had entered Paris, but before the abdication of Napoleon had become known, the last battle of the war was fought. Peace being proclaimed, Wellington took leave of his army at Bordeaux, and returned to England, where he was received with extraordinary honours.

Battle of Vitoria.

Return to England.

After the treaty of Paris (May 30) Wellington was appointed British ambassador at the French capital. During the autumn and winter of 1814 he witnessed and reported the mistakes of the restored Bourbon dynasty, and warned his Government of the growing danger from conspiracies and from the army, which was visibly hostile to the Bourbons. "The truth is," he wrote, "that the king of France without the army is no king." His insight, however, did not extend beyond the circumstances immediately before and around him, and he entirely failed to apprehend the fact that the great mass of the French nation was still with Napoleon at heart. He remained in France until February 1815, when, in consequence of the return of Lord Castlereagh to England to meet the House of Commons, he took that minister's place at the congress of Vienna. All the great questions of the congress had already been settled, and Wellington's diplomatic work here was not of importance. His im-

Ambassador at Paris.

perfect acquaintance with French feeling was strikingly proved in the despatch which he sent home on learning of Napoleon's escape from Elba. "He has acted," he wrote, "upon false or no information, and the king (Louis XVIII.) will destroy him without difficulty and in a short time." Almost before Wellington's unfortunate prediction could reach London, Louis had fled beyond the frontier, and France was at Napoleon's feet. The ban of the congress, however, went out against the common enemy of mankind, and the presence of Wellington at Vienna enabled the allies at once to decide upon their plans for the campaign. To Wellington and Blücher was committed the invasion of France from the north, while the Russians and Austrians entered it from the east. Preparations were pushed forward, and it was supposed that the war would be opened by an attack upon Alsace about the middle of June. Wellington, with 35,000 English troops and about 60,000 Dutch, Germans, and Belgians, took his post in the Netherlands, guarding the country west of the Charleroi road. Blücher, with 120,000 Prussians, lay between Charleroi, Namur, and Liége. In the meantime Napoleon had outstripped the preparations of his adversaries, and by the 13th of June had concentrated 130,000 men on the northern frontier about Philippeville. It now became known to the allied leaders that large French forces were near at hand, but Wellington believed that Napoleon himself was still in Paris, and still expected that the war would be opened by a forward movement of Schwarzenberg into Alsace. He was, moreover, strongly of opinion that, if Napoleon did take up the offensive on the north, he would throw himself upon the west of the English line and endeavour to cut the English off from the sea. Persuaded that the danger lay rather towards the coast than at the centre of the Anglo-Prussian line, he kept his forces farther westward than he would have done if he had known Napoleon's real intentions. Although the French advance on the centre became evident at the front on the morning of the 14th, it was unknown to Wellington till the afternoon of the 15th (after the Prussians had been driven out of Charleroi) that the French had made any movement whatever. How it was that the advance remained unknown to Wellington for twenty-four hours has not been explained; had he learnt of it at once, he would probably have been able to reach Ligny with sufficient force to turn the Prussian defeat into a victory and to end the war at one blow. Commencing his concentration eastwards twenty-four hours too late, he was unable to fulfil his design of assisting Blücher. Ney, getting a start on the Brussels road, kept the English occupied at Quatre Bras during the 16th, while Napoleon was dealing with the Prussians at Ligny,—though the ultimate defeat of the French at Quatre Bras, and Napoleon's own failure to follow up his victory at Ligny by a rapid pursuit, rendered it possible for the allies to effect two days later the combination which they had failed to effect at Ligny. On the morning of Sunday, June 18, Wellington, assured of Blücher's assistance, awaited Napoleon's attack on the memorable plain of Waterloo. How, at the head of 30,000 English and 40,000 mixed troops, he withstood the onslaught of the French army, and ultimately, in union with Blücher, swept them from the field, needs not to be recounted here.

The Hundred Days.

Waterloo.

Ending his military career with one of the greatest achievements in history, Wellington suddenly became, from the peculiar circumstances of the moment, the most influential politician in Europe. The czar and the emperor of Austria were still at Nancy when Paris surrendered. Wellington had reason to believe that Alexander bore so hostile a feeling towards Louis XVIII. that, if matters were not settled before the arrival of the czar at Paris, the Bourbon dynasty might not be restored at all. He therefore took affairs into his own hands, and concluded an arrangement whereby the regicide Fouché, at that moment the most powerful man in Paris, was accepted as the minister of Louis XVIII. The difficulties which might otherwise have been thrown in the way of this monarch's return to the Tuileries by the troops or by the populace of Paris were thus removed; and when Alexander arrived he found Louis XVIII. already in possession. The negotiation with Fouché was not a dignified episode in Wellington's life; he stooped, however, to a somewhat humiliating expedient in order to avert substantial mischief. The next manifestation of his personal ascendency was of a finer kind. The conditions of peace with France had to be determined by the allies; and, while the czar urged that France should be left with undiminished territory, Prussia demanded, as a guarantee against renewed aggression, the annexation of Alsace and Lorraine. The British cabinet at first inclined to the Prussian view. Wellington, however, argued strongly for the opposite policy. He urged that the Bourbon dynasty would be hopelessly discredited if its second restoration were accompanied by the loss of the border provinces; that the allies had in their proclamations distinguished between the cause of Napoleon and the cause of the French people; and that the French people, by refraining from offering any general resistance, had shown their practical acceptance of this distinction and so entitled themselves to the advantages held out in it. Wellington's arguments brought the English Government round to his own view, and so turned the balance in favour of the czar's policy of forbearance and against the annexations demanded by Prussia. The policy which he thus successfully advocated has naturally been condemned by most German statesmen and historians; but its justification is to be found in the long continuance of the peace of 1815, a continuance which would hardly have been possible if the recovery of Alsace and Lorraine had been added to the other motives which, during the next thirty years, repeatedly brought France to the verge of war.

Restoration of the Bourbons.

Conditions of peace.

Peace being concluded, Wellington was appointed commander-in-chief of the joint army of occupation, by which it was stipulated that France should be watched for the next five years. The administrative duties attaching to this post, and the reconstruction of the military frontier of the Netherlands, were, however, but a small part of the work now imposed upon him. In conjunction, and sometimes in rivalry, with the representatives of the other powers, he observed the course of French politics, counselling King Louis XVIII., checking to the best of his ability the extravagances of the count of Artois and the ultra-royalist party, and advancing the financial negotiations with Messrs Baring which enabled the French Government to pay the indemnities due from it, and thus rendered it possible for the powers to reduce the period of occupation from five to three years. When this reduction was first proposed, Wellington had not been confident of its wisdom; he subsequently became convinced that it might be granted with safety, and at the congress of Aix-la-Chapelle in 1818 he supported the proposal for the immediate evacuation of France, though this cut short by two years his own tenure of an office of almost unparalleled influence and emolument. Returning to England, he sank into the comparative insignificance of master-general of the ordnance, with a seat in the cabinet. For the next three years he was little before the world; but in 1822, on the death of Castlereagh, he was sent in the place of this minister to represent Great Britain at the congress of Verona. The main question before the congress was the policy to be adopted with regard to

Congress of Verona.

the Spanish movement, whether called revolutionary or constitutional, by which the absolute monarchy of King Ferdinand had been overthrown. It was the settled policy of the British Government to oppose any joint intervention of the powers in Spain; it was not, however, known at London before Wellington set out that the project of intervention yet existed anywhere in a definite form. In passing through Paris the duke discovered the danger to be more imminent than had been supposed; he also learnt that, whatever might be the intentions of the French Government with regard to intervention in Spain by its own army, it was determined under no circumstances to give Russian troops a passage through France. No sooner had Wellington arrived at Verona than he found that the czar was bent upon obtaining a joint declaration of all the powers condemning the Spanish constitution, and committing to the Russian army, as the mandatory of Europe, the task of overthrowing it. In pursuance of his instructions, Wellington now stated that Great Britain would rather sever itself from the European alliance cemented at Aix-la-Chapelle than consent to any such joint declaration; and the information which he had privately acquired at Paris enabled him to inform the czar that his project of employing Russian troops in Spain would certainly be thwarted by France. Armed with these two powerful arguments—the one public and official, the other personal and private—Wellington had no great difficulty in preventing the summary framing of a decree against Spain like that which had been issued two years before by the congress of Troppau against the constitution of Naples. In this respect the British Government had gained its point; but its success was apparent rather than real. Although the congress of Verona published no declaration of joint European action against the Spanish constitution, it was not in Wellington's power to prevent the negotiations which followed between the French representative and the three Eastern courts. Out of these negotiations arose the French attack upon Spain in 1823, accompanied by diplomatic action on the part of the Eastern powers which rendered the restoration of Spanish absolutism more complete and more unqualified than it would have been if France had entered upon the work entirely alone.

In the cabinet of Lord Liverpool the influence of Canning had, since Castlereagh's death, been predominant on all matters of foreign policy. Though Wellington disliked the tone of defiance frequently used by Canning towards the autocratic courts, he was sincerely at one with Canning's Spanish policy; he did not oppose his recognition of the independence of the South-American republics; and, when Canning, abandoning his position of passive neutrality between the Turkish Government and insurgent Greece, proposed to attempt joint diplomatic action with Russia in hope of terminating the struggle, the duke was willing to co-operate in this policy within certain limits. Canning, while really anxious to assist the Greeks, based his new policy officially on the need of preventing Russia from acting alone. With the duke, the design of putting a check upon Russia was the sole active motive. He cared nothing whatever for the Greeks, but he did feel anxious to prevent Russia from making their cause a pretext of war with the Porte. He therefore consented, on the coronation of the czar Nicholas in 1826, to carry proposals to St Petersburg for the diplomatic co-operation of Russia and England in bringing about a settlement of the Greek question. On the 4th of April 1827 the protocol of St Petersburg was signed, by which the two powers agreed that the mediation of England should be offered to the Porte, on terms that Greece should be granted local autonomy, but remain part of the Ottoman empire and tributary to the sultan. No provision was made for further action in case the Porte should not accept England's mediation on these terms, nor was employment of force even alluded to. Scarcely had this protocol been signed when the accession of Canning to the premiership caused Wellington to withdraw from the Government. He was willing to serve with Canning under a common leader, but would not serve under him. The effect of his withdrawal was momentous in its bearing upon Eastern affairs. Canning, freed from Wellington's restraint, carried his intervention on behalf of Greece a step further, and concluded, on the 27th of July, the treaty of London, whereby France, England, and Russia bound themselves to put an end to the conflict in the East and to enforce the conditions of the St Petersburg protocol upon the belligerents. Against this treaty Wellington protested, on the ground that it "specified means of compulsion which were neither more nor less than measures of war." His apprehensions were fulfilled by the battle of Navarino.

Negotiations at St Petersburg.

Canning died in August 1827, and on the fall of Lord Goderich's cabinet five months later Wellington became prime minister. He had declared some time before that it would be an act of madness for him to take this post; but the sense of public duty led him to accept it when it was pressed upon him by the king. His cabinet included at the first Huskisson, Palmerston, and other followers of Canning. The repeal of the Test and Corporation Acts having been carried in the House of Commons in the session of 1828, Wellington, to the great disappointment of Tories like Lord Eldon, recommended the House of Lords not to offer further resistance, and the measure was accordingly carried through. Soon afterwards a quarrel between the duke and Huskisson led to the retirement from the ministry of all its more liberal members. It was now hoped by the so-called Protestant party that Wellington, at the head of a more united cabinet, would offer a steady resistance to Catholic emancipation. Never were men more bitterly disappointed. The Clare election and the progress of the Catholic Association convinced both Wellington and Peel that the time had come when Catholic emancipation must be granted; and, submitting when further resistance would have led to civil war, the ministry itself brought in at the beginning of the session of 1829 a bill for the relief of the Catholics. Wellington, who had hitherto always opposed Catholic emancipation, explained and justified his change of front in simple and impressive language. His undoubted seriousness and his immense personal reputation did not, however, save him from the excesses of calumny and misinterpretation; and in order to impose some moderation upon his aspersers the duke thought it necessary to send a challenge to one of the most violent of these, the earl of Winchelsea. No mischief resulted from the encounter.

Prime minister.

Catholic emancipation.

Catholic emancipation was the great act of Wellington's ministry; in other respects his tenure of office was not marked by much success. The imagination and the breadth of view necessary to a statesman of the highest order were not part of his endowment, nor had he the power of working harmoniously with his subordinates. His Eastern policy was singularly short-sighted. There might have been good reason, from Wellington's point of view, for condemning Canning's treaty of London; but when, in consequence of this treaty, the battle of Navarino had been fought, the Turkish fleet sunk, and the independence of Greece practically established, it was the weakest of all possible courses to withdraw England from its active intervention, and to leave to Russia the gains of a private and isolated war. This, however, was Wellington's policy; and, having permitted Russia to go

Eastern policy.

to war alone in 1828, nothing remained for him but to treat Greece as a pawn in Russia's hands, and to cut down the territory of the Greek kingdom to the narrowest possible limits, as if the restoration to the sultan of an inaccessible mountain-tract, inhabited by the bitterest of his enemies, could permanently add to the strength of the Ottoman empire. The result was the renunciation of the Greek crown by Prince Leopold; and, although, after the fall of Wellington's ministry, a somewhat better frontier was given to Greece, it was then too late to establish this kingdom in adequate strength, and to make it, as it might have been made, a counterpoise to Russia's influence in the Levant. Nor was the indulgence shown by the cabinet towards Dom Miguel and the absolutists of Portugal quite worthy of England. That Wellington actively assisted despotic Governments against the constitutional movements of the time is not true. He had indeed none of the sympathy with national causes which began to influence British policy under Canning, and which became so powerful under Palmerston; but the rule which he followed in foreign affairs, so far as he considered it possible, was that of non-intervention.

Agitation for reform.

As soon as Catholic emancipation was carried, the demand for a reform of parliament agitated Great Britain from end to end. The duke was ill-informed as to the real spirit of the nation. He conceived the agitation for reform to be a purely fictitious one, worked up by partisans and men of disorder in their own interest, and expressing no real want on the part of the public at large. Met with a firm resistance, it would, he believed, vanish away, with no worse result than the possible plunder of a few houses by the city mobs. Thus wholly unaware of the strength of the forces which he was provoking, the duke, at the opening of the parliament which met after the death of George IV., declared against any parliamentary reform whatever. This declaration led to the immediate fall of his Government. Lord Grey, the chief of the new ministry, brought in the Reform Bill, which was resisted by Wellington as long as anything was to be gained by resistance. When the creation of new peers was known to be imminent, Wellington was among those who counselled the abandonment of a hopeless struggle. His opposition to reform made him for a while unpopular. He was hooted by the mob on the anniversary of Waterloo, and considered it necessary to protect the windows of Apsley House with iron shutters.

Fall of Wellington ministry.

Later life.

For the next two years the duke was in opposition. On the removal of Lord Althorp to the House of Lords in 1834, King William IV. unexpectedly dismissed the Whig ministry and requested Wellington to form a cabinet. The duke, however, recommended that Peel should be at the head of the Government, and served under him, during the few months that his ministry lasted, as foreign secretary. On Peel's later return to power in 1841 Wellington was again in the cabinet, but without departmental office beyond that of commander-in-chief. He supported Peel in his Corn-Law legislation, and throughout all this later period of his life, whether in office or in opposition, gained the admiration of discerning men, and excited the wonder of zealots, by his habitual subordination of party spirit and party connexion to whatever appeared to him the real interest of the nation. On Peel's defeat in 1846, the duke retired from active public life. He was now nearly eighty. His organization of the military force in London against the Chartists in April 1848, and his letter to Sir John Burgoyne on the defences of the country, proved that the old man had still something of his youth about him. But the general character of Wellington's last years was rather that of the old age of a great man idealized. To the unbroken splendours of his military career, to his honourable and conscientious labours as a parliamentary statesman, life unusually prolonged added an evening of impressive beauty and calm. The passions excited during the stormy epoch of the Reform Bill had long passed away. Venerated and beloved by the greatest and the lowliest, the old hero entered, as it were, into the immortality of his fame while still among his countrymen. Death came to him at last in its gentlest form. He passed away on the 14th of September 1852, and was buried under the dome of St Paul's, in a manner worthy both of the nation and of the man. His monument, a mere fraction of the work originally designed, stands in the chapel at the south-western end of the cathedral.

Authorities.—The *Wellington Despatches*, edited by Gurwood; *Supplementary Despatches*; and *Wellington Despatches, New Series*, edited by the second duke of Wellington. Unlike Napoleon's despatches and correspondence, everything from Wellington's pen is absolutely trustworthy: not a word is written for effect, and no fact is misrepresented. Almost all the political memoirs of the period 1830–1850 contain more or less about Wellington in his later life. Those of Greville and Croker have perhaps most of interest. (C. A. F.)

WELLS, a municipal borough in the county of Somerset, England, at the foot of the Mendip Hills, 135 miles west of London. At present it is a place of little importance, except for its cathedral, markets, and assizes. The population of the city (726 acres) in 1881 was 4634.

The city of Wells is said to have derived its name from some springs called St Andrew's Wells, which during the Middle Ages were thought to have valuable curative properties. The municipality, consisting of a mayor, seven aldermen, and sixteen chief burgesses, was incorporated by a charter granted by King John in 1202. During Saxon times Wells was one of the most important towns of Wessex, and in 905 it was made the seat of a bishopric by King Edward the Elder. About the year 1091–92 Bishop John de Villula removed the see to Bath; and for some years Wells ceased to be an episcopal city. After many struggles between the secular clergy of Wells and the regulars of Bath, it was finally arranged in 1139 that the bishop should take the title of "bishop of Bath and Wells," and should for the future be elected by delegates appointed partly by the monks of Bath and partly by the canons of Wells. The foundation attached to the cathedral church of Wells consisted of a college of secular canons of St Augustine, governed by a dean, sub-dean, chancellor, and other officials.

The existing cathedral, one of the most magnificent of all the secular churches of England, was begun by Bishop Joceline soon after his election to the episcopate in 1220; and the greater part of the building was completed before his death in 1244. According to the usual mediæval practice, the eastern part of the church was begun first, and the choir was consecrated for use long before the completion of the nave, the western part of which, with the magnificent series of statues on the façade, was carried out during the second half of the 13th century, and probably finished about the year 1300. The upper half of the two western towers has never been built. The very noble and well-designed central tower, 160 feet high, was built early in the 14th century; the beautiful octagonal chapter-house on the north side, and the lady chapel at the extreme east, were the next important additions in the same century. The whole church is a building of very exceptional splendour and beauty; it is covered throughout with stone groining of various dates, from the Early English of the choir to the fan vaulting of the central tower. Its plan consists of a nave and aisles, with two short transepts, each with a western aisle and two eastern chapels. The choir and its aisles are of unusual length, and behind the high altar are two smaller transepts, beyond which is the very rich Decorated lady chapel, with an eastern semi-octagonal apse. The main tower is at the crossing. On the north of the choir is the octagonal chapter-house, the vaulting of which springs from a slender central shaft; as the church belonged to secular clergy, it was not necessary to place it in its usual position by the cloister. The cloister, 160 by 150 feet, extends along the whole southern wall of the nave. The extreme length of the church from east to west is 371 feet. The oak stalls and bishop's throne in the choir are magnificent examples of 15th-century woodwork, still well preserved.

The great glory of the church, and that which makes it unique among the many splendid buildings of mediæval England, is the wonderful series of sculptured figures which decorate the exterior of the west front,—the work of English sculptors of the latter part of the 13th century,—a series which shows that at that time England was, as far as the plastic art is concerned, in no degree inferior to Germany and France, or even Italy, if we except the work done by Niccola, the sculptor of the wonderful baptistery pulpit at Pisa. The whole of the façade, 147 feet wide, including the two western towers, is completely covered with this magnificent series; there are nine tiers of single figures under canopies, over 600 in number, mostly large life size, with some as much as 8 feet in height, and other smaller statues; these represent angels, saints, prophets, kings and queens of the Saxon, Norman, and Plantagenet dynasties, and bishops and others who had been benefactors to the see. There are also forty-eight reliefs with subjects from Bible history, and immense representations of the Last Judgment and the Resurrection, the latter alone containing about 150 figures. The whole composition is devised so as to present a comprehensive scheme of theology and history, evidently thought out with much care and ingenuity. As works of art, these statues and reliefs are of very high merit; the faces are noble in type, the folds of the drapery very gracefully treated with true sculpturesque simplicity, and the pose of the figures remarkable for dignity. The main lines of the sculpture throughout are carefully arranged in a severely architectonic manner, so as to emphasize and harmonize with the chief features of the structure. Complete self-restraint is shown in the subordination of each part to the general effect of the whole—one of the great merits of English sculpture down to the 16th century. Of course a great variety of hands and much diversity of workmanship can be traced in this mass of sculpture, but in very few cases does the work fall conspicuously below the general level of excellence, and some of the best figures show the very flower and crown of English plastic art, which was reaching its highest point about the time that the west front of Wells was completed.[1]

The interior of the central tower presents an interesting example of the very skilful way in which the mediæval builders could turn an unexpected constructional necessity into a novel and beautiful architectural feature. While it was being built the four piers of the great tower arches showed signs of failure, and therefore, in order to strengthen them, a second lower arch was built below each main arch of the tower; and on this a third inverted arch was added. Thus the piers received a steady support along their whole height from top to bottom, and yet the opening of each archway was blocked up in the smallest possible degree. The contrasting lines of these three adjacent arches on each side of the tower have a very striking and graceful effect; nothing similar exists elsewhere.

On the south side of the cathedral stands the bishop's palace, a stately moated building, originally built in the form of a quadrangle by Bishop Joceline (1205–1244), and surrounded by a lofty circuit wall. The hall and chapel are very beautiful structures, of rather later date, mostly of the 14th century.

The vicars' college was a secular foundation for two principals and twelve vicars; fine remains of this, dating from the 15th century, and other residences of the clergy stand within and near the cathedral close; some of these are among the most beautiful examples of mediæval domestic architecture which exist anywhere in England.

The church of St Cuthbert in Wells is one of the finest of the many fine parochial churches in Somersetshire, with a very noble tower and spire at the west end. It was originally an Early English cruciform building, but the central tower fell in during the 16th century, and the whole building was much altered during the Perpendicular period. Though much damaged, a very interesting reredos exists behind the high altar; erected in 1470, it consists of a "Jesse tree" sculptured in relief. Another very beautiful reredos was discovered in 1848, hidden in the plaster on the east wall of the lady chapel, which is on the north side. (J. H. M.)

[1] See Cockerell, *Iconography of Wells Cath.*, 1851; Reynolds, *Wells Cath.*, 1881; and Britton, *Wells Cath.*, 1821. The stone used for this sculpture is from the neighbouring Doulting quarry; it was once decorated with gold and colour, applied on a ground of fine *gesso* in the usual way.

WELSHPOOL, or POOL, a market-town and municipal and parliamentary borough in Montgomeryshire, North Wales, is situated in the upper Severn valley not far from the river, on the Shropshire Union Canal, and on the Cambrian Railway, 207 miles north-west of London, 8 north of Montgomery, and 18 west of Shrewsbury. The church of St Mary's, a Gothic structure, restored by Street at a cost of £4000, is a building of some antiquity; Christ Church, in Powis Park, in the Norman style, was erected in 1839. The town-hall, erected in 1873 at a cost of £6000, includes a corn and general market-house, assize courts, and assembly rooms. The Powysland Museum, containing a collection of local fossils and antiquities and a library, was in 1887 vested in the corporation as a free public library and museum. A mile south-west of the town is Powis Castle, the fine old baronial residence of the earl of Powis, and about the same distance to the east is Leighton Hall. The site of an old moated mound is now occupied by a bowling green. The flannel manufacture has now ceased, but there is a large manufactory of tweeds and woollen shawls. The population of the municipal borough (area 19,549 acres) in 1871 was 7370 and in 1881 it was 7107. The population of the parliamentary borough (area 6761 acres) in 1881 was 5211.

About 1109 a castle was begun at Welshpool by Cadwygan ap Bleddyn ap Cynvyn, and completed by Gwenwynwyn. In 1191 it was besieged by Hubert, archbishop of Canterbury, and after being undermined surrendered, but it was retaken by Gwenwynwyn in 1197. It was dismantled in 1233 by Llewelyn, prince of North Wales, and for several generations it remained in the hands of the lords of Powis. During the civil war Lord Powis declared for the royal cause, but he was taken prisoner, and the castle was subsequently demolished. The town was incorporated about 1279 by the lords of Powis. In 1406 its boundaries were enlarged to the present enormous dimensions, and in 1615 it received a charter from James I., which was confirmed and enlarged by Charles II. From the 27th of Henry VIII. it has been included in the Montgomery district of boroughs, which returns one member to parliament. The Welsh name of the town is Trallwns or Trallwm.

WENCESLAUS (1361–1419), German king, was the eldest son of the emperor Charles IV., of the house of Luxemburg. He was born in 1361, and when three years of age was crowned as his father's successor in Bohemia. In 1376 he was elected king of the Romans, and in 1378, on the death of Charles IV., he mounted the Bohemian and German thrones. He repeatedly thought of going to Rome to receive the imperial crown, but this intention was never fulfilled. During his reign there was great confusion both in church and state, and he was wholly powerless to cope with the forces of disorder. Although not without a rude sense of justice, he was of a rough and violent temper, and too fond of pleasure to devote much attention to serious duty. The cities of Germany, in which were some of the best elements of the national life, had been gradually learning how to defend themselves by combining with one another against princes and robber knights; and a wise king or emperor might with their aid have succeeded in re-establishing the authority of the crown. Wenceslaus, however, never understood the importance of the cities, and missed every opportunity of winning their friendship. At a diet in Nuremberg in 1383 an attempt was made to secure the public peace, but the cities, knowing that their liberties were threatened, gave no heed to the measures adopted by the diet. In 1381 the Rhenish cities had formed a confederation, and notwithstanding the threats of Wenceslaus had united with the Swabian League, which was regarded with fear and hatred by most of the southern princes. The battle of Sempach, in which the Swiss confederates gained a decisive victory over the house of Hapsburg, greatly encouraged the cities, but in 1388 a powerful coalition was formed against them, and at the battle of Döffingen their troops suffered so crushing a defeat that they were rendered incapable of further resistance. At a diet held in Eger in 1389 public peace was therefore proclaimed, and the cities of Swabia, the Rhine country, Alsace, the Wetterau, Franconia, and Bavaria were ordered, on pain of the king's displeasure, to dissolve their alliances. This really meant that the princes had both the king and the towns at their mercy. Wenceslaus was not more successful in his native kingdom Bohemia than in Germany. In 1393, in the course of a struggle with the archbishop of Prague, he shocked both friends and enemies by the murder of the vicar-general John of Pomuk, who, after being subjected to torture, was bound and thrown into the river Moldau. With all his faults, Wenceslaus was sincerely anxious to check the violence of the Bohemian nobles. They accordingly plotted against him, and in Jobst of Moravia, to whom Brandenburg had been given in pledge by Sigismund, the brother of Wenceslaus, they found a powerful friend and leader. Wenceslaus was taken prisoner in 1394, and kept for some months in close confinement, and he was set free only when the German princes threatened that if he were detained the conspirators would be treated as enemies of the empire. He was unable to recover more than the appearance of power, and in 1395 he made himself an object of general contempt by selling to John Galeazzo Visconti, of Milan, the dignity of a duke of Lombardy. After the defeat of his brother Sigismund, king of Hungary, at Nicopolis, Wenceslaus came to an understanding with Jobst, to whom he gave Brandenburg in fief; and he afterwards tried to assert authority in Germany by summoning a diet at Frankfort, where, early in 1398, public peace was once more proclaimed. But Wenceslaus could not now undo the results of his indolence and incapacity, and when, in association with the king of France, he supported a plan for the deposition of Popes Boniface IX. and Benedict XIII., and for the assembling of a general council, the spiritual electors and Rupert, elector of the Palatinate, resolved that he himself should be deposed. These electors met at Oberlahnstein, and on the 20th August 1400 a decree depriving Wenceslaus of the German crown was read by the elector of Mainz as chancellor of the empire. The decree was informal, but Wenceslaus was not in a position to set it aside, and Rupert of the Palatinate was elected king in his stead. Fresh troubles had overtaken him in Bohemia, and in 1402 he was made prisoner by his brother Sigismund, who kept him in confinement for nineteen months. After his release he was not less arbitrary than before, and he caused much discontent by encouraging the disciples of Huss, whom he supported, not apparently because he cared for their doctrines, but because he found it convenient to use them as an instrument against the clergy. On the death of Rupert in 1410 Wenceslaus, while retaining the title of king of the Romans, resigned his claims to the imperial dignity in favour of Sigismund, who was elected to the German throne. Wenceslaus died of a stroke of apoplexy on the 16th August 1419.

See Pelzel, *Lebensgeschichte des römischen und böhmischen Königs Wenzel* (1788–90); Weizsäcker, *Deutsche Reichstagsacten unter König Wenzel* (1868–74); Lindner, *Geschichte des Deutschen Reichs unter König Wenzel* (1875).

WENDS. See SAXONY, vol. xxi. p. 353, and SLAVS.

WENLOCK, or MUCH WENLOCK, a market-town and municipal borough of Shropshire, England, is situated on a branch of the Great Western Railway, 163½ miles north-west of London, 11 south of Wellington, and 12 south-east of Shrewsbury. There are some beautiful remains of the old priory church, including the southern half of the west front, three bays of the south aisle, and three sides of the south transept. The priory was originally founded as a nunnery by St Milburg, granddaughter of Penda, about 680, and after being destroyed by the Danes was refounded by Leofric in 1017. Afterwards it was remodelled by Roger de Montgomery as a house for Cluniac monks, and rose to great magnificence. The church of Holy Trinity is Norman and Early English, with portions of Decorated and Perpendicular. The other principal public buildings are the guild-hall, a quaint old timbered structure, the market-hall adjoining (erected in 1879 to harmonize with the old building), the corn exchange (1852), and the museum, occupying the site of the hospital of St John. The town is chiefly dependent on its agricultural trade. There are limestone quarries in the neigbourhood. The population of the municipal borough (the area of which is about 33,000 acres and embraces 17 parishes) in 1871 was 19,401 and in 1881 it was 18,442. In addition to the municipal authority the town itself is under the government of a local board. The population of the urban sanitary district (area 9737 acres) in 1871 was 2531 and in 1881 it was 2321.

Wenlock is said to date from the pre-Roman period, but owed its rise to importance to the religious foundation of St Milburg. It received the grant of a market from Henry III. in 1224. It was incorporated by Edward IV. in 1448, when it also received the privilege of returning members to parliament, but in 1885 it ceased to have separate representation.

WENTWORTH, THOMAS. See STRAFFORD.

WENZEL, KARL FRIEDRICH (1740–1793), German metallurgist, was born at Dresden in 1740. His father was a bookbinder, and Wenzel began to learn the same trade; but finding it monotonous he quietly left home and went to Holland at the age of fifteen. In Amsterdam he took lessons in surgery and chemistry, and then entered the Dutch navy as a surgeon. After some years a sea life lost its charm for him, and he resigned, returning to his native land in 1766 to complete his chemical studies at Leipsic. Wenzel now devoted his attention to metallurgy and assaying, working for a time with great success in the town of his birth. He received a prize for the best solution of a problem in working metals from the Copenhagen Society of Sciences. He also made some very careful chemical experiments, particularly on the mixture of solutions of various salts, and wrote several books on chemical subjects; his claim for remembrance rests on one of these, *Vorlesungen über die chemische Verwandtschaft der Körper*. It was published in 1777; a second edition appeared in 1782, and a third with additions in 1800. In 1780 Wenzel received the appointment of director of mines at Freiberg from the elector of Saxony, and in 1786 that of chemist in the porcelain works at Meissen. He died at Freiberg on February 26, 1793.

The discovery of the law of reciprocal proportions in chemistry (see CHEMISTRY, vol. v. p. 463) has been claimed for Wenzel as the result of his researches on the affinities of bodies; and, on the ground of his work being prior to that of Richter, and much more accurate than the earlier experiments of Bergmann on the same subject, he has been regarded as Dalton's precursor in laying the foundation of the atomic theory. It was pointed out by Hess in 1840 that this was a mistake, since Wenzel's researches led him to no definite conclusions as to invariable and reciprocal proportions in the combination of acids and bases, but rather pointed in the opposite direction. Kopp overlooked this criticism in writing his great *Geschichte der Chemie* (1844–1847), which has deservedly taken the highest place as an authority on chemical history; and, although in the supplementary work published in 1873 he acknowledges his mistake as to Wenzel and confirms Hess's statement, the writers of text-books continue in many cases to give currency to the erroneous view.

WERDAU, a manufacturing town of Saxony, is situated on the Pleisse, in the industrial district of Zwickau, about 40 miles south of Leipsic. Its chief industries are cotton and wool-spinning and the weaving of cloth; but machinery of various kinds, paper, and a few other articles are also manufactured. In addition to the usual schools, Werdau contains a weaving-school. The town is mentioned as early as 1304, and in 1398 it was purchased by the margrave of Meissen, who afterwards became elector of Saxony. The population, 4994 in 1834, was 14,638 in 1885. The adjoining village of Leubnitz, with 2400 inhabitants, is now practically a part of Werdau.

WEREWOLF. See LYCANTHROPY.

WERGELAND, HENRIK ARNOLD (1808–1845), Norwegian poet and prose writer. See vol. xvii. p. 590.

WERNER, ABRAHAM GOTTLOB (1750–1817), the father of German geology, was born in Oberlausitz, Saxony, 25th September 1750. The family to which he belonged had been engaged for several hundred years in mining pursuits. His father was inspector of Count Solm's iron-works at Mehrau and Lorzendorf, and from young Werner's infancy cultivated in him a taste for minerals and rocks. The boy showed early promise of distinction. In his fourth year he had learnt to read; in his fifth he could write and cipher; and by the time he was six or seven years old he had grown to be a great reader. Already, when only three years of age, he had begun to collect specimens of stones, and, when he could read, one of his favourite employments was to pore over the pages of a dictionary of mining. At the age of nine he was sent to school at Bunzlau in Silesia, where he remained until 1764, when he joined his father, with the idea of ultimately succeeding him in the post which the latter held there. In his eighteenth year ill-health compelled him to seek the mineral waters of Carlsbad. In journeying thither by way of Freiberg he showed such enthusiasm and knowledge in an excursion in that neighbourhood as to attract the notice of the officials there, who invited him to attend their mining school which had been established two years previously. This was the turning point in Werner's career. He came to Freiberg in 1769 when he was nineteen years of age, and found the school in its merest infancy. He soon distinguished himself by his industry and by the large amount of practical knowledge of mineralogy which he acquired. In 1771 he repaired to the university of Leipsic and went through the usual curriculum of study, but continued to devote himself with the greatest ardour to mineralogical pursuits. While still a student he wrote his first work on the external characters of minerals (*Ueber die äussern Kennzeichen der Fossilien*, Leipsic, 1764), which at once gave him a name among the mineralogists of the day. His friends in Freiberg, who had watched his progress with much gratification, called him at the close of his college life to be inspector in the mining school and teacher of mineralogy there. To the development of that school and to the cultivation of mineralogy and geognosy he thenceforth devoted the whole of his active and indefatigable industry. From a mere provincial institution the Freiberg academy under his care rose to be one of the great centres of scientific light in Europe, to which students from all parts of the world flocked to listen to his eloquent teaching. He wrote but little, and though he elaborated a complete system of geognosy and mineralogy he never could be induced to publish it. From the notes of his pupils, however, the general purport of his teaching was well known, and it widely influenced the science of his time. He had the art of infusing into those who listened to him some of his own ardent enthusiasm. His disciples accordingly left his rooms with the determination to preach his doctrine everywhere. They became ardent partisans, and carried on an active propaganda in most countries of Europe. He died at Freiberg on June 30, 1817.

One of the distinguishing features of Werner's teaching was the care with which he taught the succession of geological formations. He showed that the rocks of the earth are not disposed at random, but follow each other in a certain definite order. Unfortunately he had never enlarged his experience by travel, and the sequence of rock-masses which he had recognized in Saxony was believed by him to be of universal application all over the globe. He taught that the rocks were the precipitates of a primeval ocean, and followed each other in successive deposits of world-wide extent. Volcanoes were regarded by him as abnormal phenomena, probably due to the combustion of subterranean beds of coal. Basalt and similar rocks, which even then were recognized by other observers as of igneous origin, were believed by him to be water-formed accumulations of the same ancient ocean. Hence arose one of the great historical controversies of geology. Werner's followers preached the doctrine of the aqueous origin of rocks, and were known as Neptunists; their opponents, who recognized the important part taken in the construction of the earth's crust by subterranean heat, were styled Vulcanists. Though much of Werner's theoretical work was erroneous, science is indebted to him for so clearly demonstrating the chronological succession of rocks, for the enthusiastic zeal which he infused into his pupils, and for the impulse which he thereby gave to the study of geology.

See S. G. Frisch, *Lebensbeschreibung A. G. Werners*, Leipsic, 1825; Cuvier, *Éloge de Werner*; and Lyell, *Principles of Geology*.

WERNER, FRIEDRICH LUDWIG ZACHARIAS, German poet, was born at Königsberg on November 18, 1768, and died at Vienna on January 17, 1823. After an irregular life he joined the Church of Rome in 1809, was consecrated priest in 1814, and in his later years was well known as a preacher. As a dramatist he is remembered as the originator of the so-called "fate tragedies"; see GERMANY, vol. x. p. 543.

WERNIGERODE, a town of Prussian Saxony, about 12 miles to the south-west of Halberstadt, is picturesquely situated on the Holzemme, on the north slopes of the Harz Mountains. It contains several interesting Gothic buildings, including the fine town-house dating from the 14th century. Some of the quaint old houses which have escaped the numerous fires that have visited the town are elaborately adorned with wood-carving. The gymnasium, occupying a modern Gothic building, is the successor of an ancient grammar-school, which existed until 1825. Wooden articles, cigars, and dye-stuffs are among the manufactures of the place. Above the town rises the chateau of the count of Stolberg-Wernigerode. A pavilion in the park contains the library of 96,000 volumes, the chief feature in which is the collection of over 3000 Bibles and over 3600 volumes on hymnology. The population of Wernigerode in 1885 was 9083; including the immediately adjoining villages of Nöscherode and Hasserode, it was 13,804.

Wernigerode is the chief town of the county (grafschaft) of Stolberg-Wernigerode, which still retains a few shreds of nominal independence, though really an integral part of Prussia since the congress of Vienna. It was originally a free and independent imperial fief, and retains its peculiar national colours. The county has an extent of 107 square miles, with 26,484 inhabitants, and includes the Brocken within its limits.

WESEL, a strongly fortified industrial town in Westphalia, Prussia, is situated at the confluence of the Rhine and the Lippe, 46 miles south-west of Münster, and 35 miles south-east of Nimeguen in Holland. The Rhine is here crossed by a large railway bridge and by a bridge of boats. The island of Büderich in mid-stream is fortified, and the town is further protected by detached forts, one of which serves as a *tête-de-pont* on the left bank of the Rhine. Wesel contains some quaint old houses with high-pitched roofs, and a town-house, dating from 1396, with an elaborate façade. The large church of St Willibrord, a handsome late-Gothic edifice, was consecrated in 1181, though its present form dates from 1521. Since 1883 it has been undergoing a much-needed restoration. St Matthew's church dates from 1472–77. The two Roman Catholic churches, the commandant's house (built in 1417), the Berlin gateway (1722), and the modern gymnasium and military hospital are among the other chief buildings. Wesel carries on a considerable trade both by railway and its two rivers; wood and fish are perhaps the main exports. It has manufactures of wire, leaden pipes, and other metal goods, pianofortes, sugar, &c. The population, more than half Roman Catholic, was 20,677 in 1885.

Wesel, formerly known as Lippemünde, was one of the points from which Charlemagne directed his operations against the heathen Saxons. The present name is said to be derived from the numerous weasels (Germ., *Wiesel*) at one time found in the neighbourhood. In the Middle Ages it was a flourishing commercial town, and a member of the Hanseatic League, and as late as 1495 a free imperial city. A monument outside the town commemorates eleven of Schill's officers who were shot here in 1809 after their unsuccessful attempt at Stralsund. Wesel is occasionally spoken of as Unterwesel, to distinguish it from Oberwesel, a small town also on the Rhine (18 miles south-south-east of Coblentz), and also at one time a free imperial town.

WESEL, JOHN KUCHRATH, of Oberwesel (see above), was born in the early years of the 15th century, and died under sentence of imprisonment for life on a charge of heresy in the Augustinian convent in Mainz in 1481. He appears to have been one of the leaders of the humanist movement in Germany, and to have had some intercourse and sympathy with the leaders of the Hussites in Bohemia. Erfurt was then the headquarters of a humanism which was at the same time devout and opposed to the realist metaphysic and the Thomist theology which prevailed in the Rhenish universities at Cologne and at Heidelberg. Wesel was one of the professors at Erfurt between 1445 and 1456, and was vice-rector in 1458. In 1460 he was called to be a preacher either at Worms or at Mainz, and in 1479, when an old and worn-out man (he was led into the room by two Franciscans, and was obliged to support himself on a staff), he was brought before the Dominican inquisitor Gerhard Elten of Cologne. The charges brought against him were chiefly based on a treatise, *De Indulgentiis*, which he had composed while at Erfurt twenty-five years before.

It is somewhat difficult to determine the exact theological position of Wesel. Ullmann claims him as a "reformer before the Reformation," but it is more than doubtful that he had that experimental view of the doctrines of grace which lay at the basis of Reformation theology. He held that Christ is our righteousness in so far as we are guided by the Holy Ghost and the love towards God is shed abroad in our hearts, which clearly shows that he held the mediæval idea that justification is an habitual grace implanted in men by the gracious act of God. He seems, however, to have protested against certain mediæval ecclesiastical ideas which he held to be excrescences erroneously grafted on Christian faith and practice. He objected to the whole system of indulgences; he denied the infallibility of the church, on the ground that the church contains within it sinners as well as saints; he insisted that papal authority could be upheld only when the pope remained true to the evangel; and he held that a sharp distinction ought to be drawn between ecclesiastical sentences and punishments and the judgments of God.

The best account of Wesel is to be found in Ullmann's *Reformers before the Reformation*. His tract on *Indulgences* has been published in Walch's *Monumenta Medii Ævi*, vol. i., while a report of his trial is given in Ortuin Gratius's *Fasciculus Rerum Expetendarum et Fugiendarum* (ed. by Browne, London, 1690).

WESER (O. Germ. *Visuracha*, *Wisura*; Lat. *Visurgis*), one of the chief rivers of Germany, formed by the union of the Werra and the Fulda at Münden, in the Prussian province of Hanover, flows to the north and north-north-west, and enters the North Sea below Bremerhafen, to the east of the Jade Bay. The mouth is 170 miles from Münden, but the winding course of the river is 279 miles long; if the measurement be made from the source of the Werra, in Thuringia, the total length of the stream is 439 miles. At Münden the river surface is 380 feet above sea-level; the most rapid fall in its course is between Carlshafen and Minden in Westphalia, where it descends 70 feet in 20 miles. Nearly the entire course of the Weser lies in Prussia, but it also touches part of Brunswick and Lippe, and after flowing through Bremen expands into an estuary separating the duchy of Oldenburg from the Prussian province of Hanover. Between Münden and Minden its course lies through a series of picturesque valleys flanked by the irregular and disjointed mountain system known as the Weser Hills; but after it emerges from these mountains by the narrow pass called the "Porta Westphalica," to the north of Minden, its banks become flat and uninteresting. The breadth of the river varies from 110 yards at Münden to 220 yards at Minden, 250 yards at Bremen, $1\frac{1}{4}$ miles at Elsfleth, and $7\frac{1}{2}$ miles at its entrance into the sea. The Weser on the whole is shallow; and navigation on the upper Weser, *i.e.*, above Bremen, is sometimes interrupted for months by drought. Sea-going ships may ascend to Elsfleth, though Bremerhafen is the chief port for large vessels; smaller craft may reach Vegesack, and barges of 200 tons make their way to Münden. The stream discharges itself into the sea amid sandbanks, which leave only a single narrow fairway, 19–22 feet deep at high water and 12 feet at low water; on the upper Weser the navigation of the only available narrow channel, which is interrupted by occasional rapids, is assisted by locks and weirs. The Weser drains a basin estimated at 18,360 square miles. Its principal tributaries on the right are the Aller, Wümme, Drepte, Lune, and Geeste, and on the left the Diemel, Nethe, Emmer, Werre, Aue, and Hunte. The Werra and Fulda are both navigable when they unite to form the Weser; the Aller, Wümme, Geeste, and Hunte are also navigable. Beyond the junction of the Hunte the Weser, hitherto a single stream, is divided into several channels by islands.

The navigation of the Weser was long hampered by the various and vexatious claims and rights of the different states through whose territories it ran. Before 1866 the joint stream, including the Werra and the Fulda, changed its ruler no less than thirty-five times on its way to the sea. In 1823, however, a treaty was made establishing a fixed toll and a uniform system of management; this was further improved in 1856 and 1865; and when Prussia took possession of Hanover and Hesse-Nassau in 1866 the chief difficulties in the way of organizing the river-trade disappeared. The principal town on the Weser is Bremen (population in 1885, 118,043). Other towns past which it flows betwixt Münden and the sea are Carlshafen, Höxter, Holzminden, Bodenwerder, Hameln, Rinteln, Vlotho, Minden, Nienburg, Vegesack, Elsfleth, Braake, Blexen, Geestemünde, and Bremerhafen. The Weser gave name to a department in the short-lived kingdom of Westphalia; the chief town was Osnabrück. A canal between the Wümme and the Oste, and another between the Geeste and the mouth of the Elbe, connect the Weser system with that of the Elbe. A canal is also being constructed from the Hunte to a tributary of the Ems.

WESLEY, an English family of special ecclesiastical distinction, claims descent from the ancient De Wellesleys, one of whom, Guy, was made a thane by Athelstan about 938, the family seat being at Welswe, near Wells, in Somerset. Two brothers, John and Bartholomew, were among the ministers ejected for nonconformity in 1662.

SAMUEL (1662–1735), son of the above John, was born 17th December 1662. He was educated at an academy at Stepney, London, and in August 1683 entered Exeter College, Oxford, as a *pauper scholaris*, shortly after which he joined the Church of England, a step which so deeply offended his family that they left him henceforth to his own resources. While still an undergraduate he published *Maggots, or Poems on Several Subjects never before Handled*, 1685. He graduated B.A. 1688, was ordained priest 24th February 1689, and the following year was presented to the living of South Ormsby, Lincolnshire. In 1697 he removed to Epworth, Lincolnshire, where he died 25th April 1735. Among other works he was the author of *Life of Christ* (1693), *Elegies on Queen Mary and Archbishop Tillotson* (1695), *History of the Old and New Testaments in Verse* (1704), *Pious Communicant Rightly Prepared* (1700), and *Latin Commentary on the Book of Job* (1733). After the battle of Blenheim he published (1705) a long poem on *Marlborough, or the Fate of Europe*, for which Marlborough made him chaplain of a regiment. He had nineteen children, of whom three sons, Samuel, John, and Charles, acquired eminence.

SAMUEL (1690–1739) was born in London 10th February 1690, and educated at Westminster school, where he was nominated king's scholar. In 1711 he entered Christ Church, Oxford, and on taking his M.A. degree returned to Westminster as tutor. He lived on intimate terms with Harley, earl of Oxford, Pope, Swift, and Prior, and wrote somewhat clever squibs against Sir Robert Walpole, the Whigs, and the Low Church divines. They were collected and published 1736, reached a second edition 1743, and were reprinted, with notes by James Nicholls and life by W. Nicholls, in 1862. Wesley became master of Tiverton grammar-school in 1732, and died there 6th November 1739.

JOHN (1703–1791), brother of the preceding and founder of Methodism, was born, probably at Epworth, 17th June (O.S., 28th N.S.) 1703. There was a tradition in the family that he was christened John Benjamin, but he never made use of the second name. When his father's rectory was burnt down in 1709 he was for a time left in the building, and narrowly escaped death. He entered Charterhouse in 1714, whence in 1720 he was elected to Christ Church, Oxford. In 1726 he became fellow of Lincoln, and in 1727 graduated M.A. After acting for some time as his father's curate he settled in November 1729 at Oxford, and began to take pupils. About the same time, along with his brother Charles and others, he commenced that systematic course of religious life which led to their being termed by the Oxonians Methodists. A full record of the religious labours of Wesley is given under METHODISM (vol. xvi. pp. 185–189). In the organization of Methodism he displayed not only extraordinary energy and capacity for work but remarkable administrative powers. His oratory was colloquial, terse, and homely, but never vulgar, while his expressive and refined features and intense yet reasoned earnestness enabled him to acquire among his followers a personal influence of an unrivalled kind. Although from overwork or exposure he had one or two serious illnesses, he generally enjoyed robust health, an experience probably partly accounted for by his constant journeys on horseback. In 1790 he said, "I do not remember to have felt lowness of spirits for a quarter of an hour since I was born." He preached usually at 5 o'clock in the morning, and frequently twice again in the same day, the number of sermons he delivered in a year being over 800. He continued his labours almost to the last, but wrote, 1st January 1790, "I am now an old man decayed from head to foot." He died 2d March 1791. Wesley translated several hymns from the German for the collections edited by him and his brother Charles, but is not known to have been the author of any original hymns (see HYMNS, vol. xii. p. 594). The first collection of *Psalms and Hymns* edited by the brothers appeared anonymously in 1738, and a *Collection of Moral and Sacred Poems, from the Most Celebrated Authors*, in 1744. Wesley has no claims to rank as a thinker or even as a theologian, but within certain narrow limits was a skilful controversialist. He was the author of *Primitive Physic* (1747), *Explanatory Notes on the New Testament* (1755), *Notes on the Old and New Testaments* (1764), *Doctrine of Original Sin* (1757), *Survey of the Wisdom of God in Creation* (1763), *Preservative against Unsettled Notions in Religion* (1770), and *A Calm Address to our American Colonies* (1775). He also edited the *Christian Library*, in fifty volumes. His *Works* appeared in 1818, and an eleventh edition, with life by J. Beecham and preface by T. Jackson, was published in 15 vols., 1856–57.

CHARLES (1708–1788), brother of the preceding, was born prematurely at Epworth, 18th December 1708. He entered Westminster school in 1716, was admitted a king's scholar in 1721, and entered Christ Church, Oxford, in 1726. He accompanied his brother John to Georgia in 1735 as secretary to the managing committee, having been ordained priest a few days before leaving England; but on account of a strong feeling of opposition manifested against him in the religious communities of Frederica he left Georgia for England five months after landing. To a serious illness which happened to him in February 1738 he attributed a moral change which he associated with conversion and a conscious sense of pardon. He seconded his brother in his evangelizing labours in England with unceasing diligence, and, although not possessing his brother's gifts of oratory and personal magnetism, contributed by his hymns an element of success to the movement of prime and permanent importance. He published no fewer than 4100 hymns of his own composition, and left about 2000 in manuscript. Numerous editions both of the special and general collections of his hymns have been published. Both as regards the number of his compositions and their various excellences, he is entitled to the chief place among Methodist hymn writers (see HYMNS, *ut supra*). He died 29th March 1788. His *Sermons*, with memoir, appeared in 1816; a *Life*, by Rev. Thomas Jackson, in 1841; and his *Journal*, with notes by Rev. Thomas Jackson, 1849.

Two sons of Charles Wesley attained eminence as musicians:—CHARLES (1757–1815), organist of St George's, Hanover Square, London, who in 1778 published *Six Concertos for the Organ and Harp*; and SAMUEL (1766–1837), organist of the Chapel Royal, noticed below.

See, in addition to the authorities already mentioned, the *Lives* by Hampson (1791), Coke and Moore (1792), Whitehead (1793–96), Southey (1820), Moore (1824), Watson (1831), Miss Wedgwood (1870), and Tyerman (exhaustive and complete) (1870); J. Dove, *Biographical History of the Wesleys* (1833); and G. J. Stevenson, *Memorials of the Wesley Family* (1876).

WESLEY, SAMUEL (1766–1837), musical composer, son of Charles Wesley (see above), was born at Bristol, February 24, 1766, and developed so precocious a talent for music that at three years old he played the organ and at eight composed an oratorio entitled *Ruth*—a fact which is duly chronicled on a curious portrait, painted in 1774, and afterwards engraved, wherein he is represented in the childish costume of the period. Though suffering for many years from an accidental injury to the brain, Wesley was long regarded as the most brilliant organist and the most accomplished extempore fugue-player in England. He may indeed be regarded as the father of our present style of organ-playing, for he it was who, aided by his friends Benjamin Jacob and C. F. Horn, first introduced the works of Sebastian Bach to English organists, not only by his superb playing, but by editing with Horn, in 1810, the first copy of *Das wohltemperirte Clavier* ever printed in England. Wesley's last performance took place, September 12, 1837, at Christ Church, Newgate Street, London, where, after hearing the wonderful performances of Mendelssohn, he was himself induced to play an extempore fugue. He died, October 11, 1837, leaving a vast number of MS. and printed compositions.

His brother Charles (1757–1815) was also an accomplished organist, and still more famous was his son, Samuel Sebastian, (1810–1876), Mus. Doc., and organist of Gloucester cathedral.

WESSEL. WESSELUS GANSFORTIUS[1] was born at Groningen in 1400 (Hardenberg), in 1419 (Suffridus Petri), or in 1421, and on the death of his parents was adopted by a noble lady, Oda Clantes, who sent him along with her only son to the famous school at Deventer, which was under the supervision of the Brothers of Common Life, and was in close connexion with the convent of Mount St Agnes at Zwolle, where then lived Thomas a Kempis,

[1] The surname is from Gansfort or Gösevort, a Westphalian village from which his family came; the Christian name is the equivalent of the Greek Basilius.

the author of the *Imitatio Christi*. At Deventer, where the best traditions of the 14th-century mysticism were still cultivated, Wessel imbibed that earnest devotional mysticism which was the basis of his theology and which drew him irresistibly, after a busy life, to spend his last days among the Friends of God in the Low Countries. From Deventer he went to Cologne to be taught the Thomist theology, which was fondly cherished in that famous Dominican school; and there he learnt realism, which, although he afterwards became a nominalist in metaphysics, always coloured his theology. At Cologne too he came in contact with humanism. He learnt Greek and Hebrew from monks who, it is said, had been driven out of Greece. The Thomist theology sent him to study Augustine, and his Greek reading led him to Plato, and from both of these great thinkers he learnt much that went to enrich his own theological system. The echoes of the din raised in Paris by the disputes between the realists and the nominalists reached Wessel in Cologne, and a desire to mingle in the fray, or perhaps to learn on which side truth was, induced him to go to Paris, where he remained sixteen years, scholar and teacher. There he eventually took the nominalist side, prompted as much by his mystical anti-ecclesiastical tendencies as from any metaphysical insight; for the nominalists were then the anti-papal party. A desire to know more about humanism sent him to Rome, where we find him in 1470 the intimate friend of Italian scholars and under the protection of Cardinals Bessarion and Della Rovere (afterwards Pope Sixtus IV.). It is said that Sixtus would have gladly made Wessel a bishop, but that he had no desire for any ecclesiastical preferment. From Rome he returned to Paris, and speedily became a famous teacher, gathering round him a band of enthusiastic young students, among whom was Reuchlin. As old age approached he came to have a growing dislike to the wordy theological strife which surrounded him, and turned away from that university discipline, "non studia sacrarum literarum sed studiorum commixtæ corruptiones." After thirty years of academic life he went back to his native Groningen, and spent the rest of his life partly as director in a nuns' cloister there and partly in the convent of St Agnes at Zwolle. He was welcomed as the most renowned scholar of his time, and it was fabled that he had travelled through all lands, Egypt as well as Greece, gathering everywhere the fruits of all sciences—"a man of rare erudition," says the title page of the first edition of his collected works, "who in the shadow of papal darkness was called the light of the world." His remaining years were spent amid a circle of warm admirers, friends, and disciples, to whom he imparted the mystical theology, the devotion to higher learning, and the deep devotional spirit which characterized his own life. He died on October 4, 1489, with the confession on his lips, "I know only Jesus the crucified." He is buried in the middle of the choir of the church of the "Geestlichen Maegden," whose director he had been.

Wessel has been called one of the "reformers before the Reformation," and the title is a true one if by it is meant a man of deeply spiritual life, who protested against the growing paganizing of the papacy, the superstitious and magical uses of the sacraments, the authority of ecclesiastical tradition, and that tendency in later scholastic theology to lay greater stress in a doctrine of justification upon the instrumentality of the human will than on the objective work of Christ for man's salvation. His own theology was, however, essentially mediæval in type, and he never grasped that experimental thought of justification on which Reformation theology rests.

See *Vita Wesseli Groningensis*, by Albert Hardenberg, published in an incomplete form in the preface to Wessel's collected works, Amsterdam, 1614 (this preface also contains extracts from the works of several writers who have given facts about the life of Wessel); Muurling, *Com. Hist. Theol. de Wesseli Gansfortii Vita, &c.*, 1831; Ullmann, *Reformers before the Reformation* (the second volume of the German edition is a second and enlarged edition of a previous work, entitled *Johann Wessel, ein Vorgänger Luther's*, 1834); Friedrich, *Johann Wessel, ein Bild aus der Kirchengeschichte des 15ten Jahrhunderts*, 1862; Ritschl, *History of the Christian Doctrine of Justification and Reconciliation* (Edin., 1872). Wessel's two most important writings are his Treatise on Prayer (*De Oratione*) and his *Scala Meditationis*.

WESSEX. See England, vol. viii. pp. 270, 282 *sq.*, and Plate II. of same volume.

WEST, Benjamin (1738–1820), history and portrait painter, was born in 1738, at Springfield, in Pennsylvania, coming of an old Quaker family who had emigrated from Buckinghamshire. When a boy of seven he began to show his inclinations to art. According to the well-known story, he was sitting by the cradle of his sister's child, watching its sleep, when the infant happened to smile in its dreams, and, struck with its beauty, young Benjamin got some paper, and drew its portrait. The career thus begun was prosecuted amid many difficulties; but his perseverance overcame every obstacle, and at the age of eighteen he settled in Philadelphia as a portrait-painter. After a short time he removed to New York, where he practised his profession with considerable success. In 1760, through the assistance of some friends, he was enabled to complete his artistic education by a visit to Italy, where he remained nearly three years. Here he acquired reputation, and was elected a member of the principal academies of Italy. On the expiry of his Italian visit he settled in London as an historical painter. His success was not long doubtful. George III. took him under his special patronage; and commissions flowed in upon him from all quarters. In 1768 he was one of the four artists who submitted to the king the plan for a royal academy, of which he was one of the earliest members; and in 1772 he was appointed His Majesty's historical painter. He devoted his attention mainly to the painting of large pictures on historical and religious subjects, conceived, as he believed, in the style of the old masters, and executed with great care and much taste. So high did he stand in public favour that on the death of Sir Joshua Reynolds, in 1792, he was elected his successor as president of the Royal Academy, an office which he held for twenty-eight years. In 1802 he took advantage of the opportunity afforded by the peace of Amiens to visit Paris, and inspect the magnificent collection of the masterpieces of art, pillaged from the gallery of almost every capital in Europe, which then adorned the Louvre. On his return to London he devoted himself anew to the labours of his profession, which were, however, somewhat broken in upon by quarrels with some of the members of the Royal Academy. In 1804 he resigned his office, but an all but unanimous request that he should return to the chair induced him to recall his resignation. Time did not at all weaken the energy with which he laboured at his easel. When sixty-five he painted one of his largest works, Christ Healing the Sick. This was originally designed to be presented to the Quakers in Philadelphia, to assist in erecting a hospital. On its completion it was exhibited in London to immense crowds, and was purchased by the British Institution for 3000 guineas, West sending a replica to Philadelphia. His subsequent works were nearly all on the same grand scale with the picture which had been so successful, but for obvious reasons they did not meet with very ready sale. He died in 1820, in his eighty-second year, and was buried in St Paul's.

Since his death West's reputation has seriously declined. His works, which fond criticism ranked during his life with the great productions of the old masters, are now considered as in general formal, tame, wanting that freedom of nature and that life which genius alone can breathe into the canvas. His Death of Wolfe is interesting as introducing modern costume instead of the classical draperies which had been previously universal in similar subjects by English artists; and his Battle of La Hogue is entitled to an honourable place among British historical paintings. An account of West's life was published by Galt (*The Progress of*

Genius, 1816); and biographies of him occur in Cunningham's *Lives of Eminent British Painters* and Redgrave's *Century of Painters of the English School*.

WESTALL, RICHARD (1765–1836), subject painter, was born in Hertford in 1765, of a Norwich family. In 1779 he went to London, and was apprenticed to an engraver on silver, and in 1785 he began to study in the schools of the Royal Academy. He painted Esau Seeking Jacob's Blessing, Mary Queen of Scots Going to Execution, and other historical subjects in water-colour, and some good portraits in the same medium, but he is mainly known as a book-illustrator. He produced five subjects for the Shakespeare Gallery, illustrated an edition of Milton, executed a very popular series of illustrations to the Bible and the prayer-book, and designed plates for numerous other works. In 1808 he published a poem, *A Day in Spring*, illustrated by his own pencil. His designs are rather tame, mannered, and effeminate. He became an associate of the Royal Academy in 1792, and a full member in 1794; and during his later years he was a pensioner of the Academy. His last employment was to give art instruction to the Princess Victoria. He died on December 4, 1836. His brother, William Westall, A.R.A. (1781–1850), landscape painter, is mainly known by his illustrations to works of travel.

WEST BAY CITY, a city of Bay county, Michigan, United States, is situated on the Saginaw river, near its mouth, opposite Bay City. The city lies in one of the largest lumber districts of the United States, and its industries consist mainly in manufacturing and shipping lumber. It had a population of 9492 in 1885.

WEST BROMWICH, a municipal and parliamentary borough of Staffordshire, England, is situated near the river Tame, and on the Great Western Railway, 6 miles north-west of Birmingham, and 133¾ miles from London. It consists chiefly of one main street, the High Street, upwards of 1½ miles in length. The parish church (All Saints, formerly St Clement's) is of very early origin, and was given by Henry I. to the convent of Worcester, which subsequently gave it to the priory of Sandwell. The present church, a handsome structure in the Decorated style, was built in 1871–72. The principal other public buildings are the West Bromwich district hospital (erected in 1867 at a cost of £9000, and enlarged in 1882 at a cost of £4000), the town-hall and municipal offices (1875), the market-hall, the free library (1874), and the Liberal club (1884). There are two public charities—the Stanley (1613) and the Whorwood (1614). Since 1880 the town has manufactured its own gas, but the water is supplied by the South Staffordshire Waterworks Company. There re several large foundries, smelting-furnaces, and forges, ut the staple manufactures are the various kinds of mplements of wrought-iron used for household, agricultural, or mechanical purposes. The town also possesses brass foundries, maltings, limekilns, and brickyards. There are large collieries in the neighbourhood. The area of the municipal and parliamentary borough and urban sanitary district is 5719 acres, with a population in 1871 of 47,918 and in 1881 of 56,295.

In 1230 the manor of West Bromwich was vested in the barons of Dudley, and in 1293 it descended to Walter de Evereus; in 1448 it passed to the Stanleys, from whom it was purchased by Sir Richard Skelton, solicitor-general to Charles I.; and in 1626 it came into the possession of Sir Samuel Clarke, by whose descendants, who subsequently assumed the name of Clarke-Jervoise, it was sold in 1823 to the earl of Dartmouth. West Bromwich was incorporated 13th September 1882. By the Act of 1885 its parliamentary representation was separated from that of Wednesbury, and it was erected into a parliamentary borough returning one member.

WESTBURY, RICHARD BETHELL, BARON (1800–1873), was the son of Dr Richard Bethell, and was born at Bradford, Wilts. He was placed in the first class in classics and the second in mathematics at Oxford in 1818, and was elected a fellow of Wadham College. In 1823 he was called to the bar at the Middle Temple. On attaining the dignity of queen's counsel in 1840 he rapidly took the foremost place at the Chancery bar, and was appointed vice-chancellor of the county palatine of Lancaster in 1851. His most important public service was the reform of the then existing mode of legal education, a reform which ensured that students before call to the bar should have at least some acquaintance with the elements of the subject which they were to profess. In 1851 he obtained a seat in the House of Commons, where he continued to sit, first as member for Aylesbury, then as member for Wolverhampton, until he was raised to the peerage. Attaching himself to the Liberals, he became solicitor-general in 1852 and attorney-general in 1856 and again in 1859. On June 26, 1861, on the death of Lord Campbell, he was created lord high chancellor of Great Britain, with the title of Baron Westbury of Westbury, county Wilts. The object of his life was to set on foot the compilation of a digest of the whole law, but for various reasons this became impracticable. The conclusion of his tenure of the chancellorship was unfortunately marked by events which, although they did not render personal corruption imputable to him, made it evident that he had acted with laxity of practice and want of caution. Owing to the reception by parliament of reports of committees nominated to consider the circumstances of the acceptance by him of the resignations of Mr Wilde, the bankruptcy registrar at Leeds, and Mr Leonard Edmunds, a clerk in the patent office, and clerk of the parliaments, the lord chancellor felt it incumbent upon him to resign his office, which he accordingly did on July 5, 1865, and was succeeded by Lord Cranworth. After his resignation he continued to take part in the judicial sittings of the House of Lords and the privy council until his death. In 1872 he was appointed arbitrator under the European Assurance Society Act, 1872, and his judgments in that capacity have been collected and published by Mr F. S. Reilly. As a writer on law he made no mark, and few of his decisions take the highest judicial rank. Perhaps the best known is the judgment delivering the opinion of the judicial committee of the privy council in 1863 against the heretical character of certain extracts from the well-known publication *Essays and Reviews*. His principal legislative achievements were the passing of the Divorce Act, 1857, and of the Land Registry Act, 1862 (generally known as Lord Westbury's Act), the latter of which in practice proved a failure. What chiefly distinguished Lord Westbury was the possession of a certain sarcastic humour; and numerous are the stories, authentic and apocryphal, of its exercise. In fact, he and Mr Justice Maule fill a position analogous to that of Sydney Smith, convenient names to whom "good things" may be attributed. Lord Westbury died on July 20, 1873, within a day of the time of the death of Bishop Wilberforce, his special antagonist in debate.

A *Life* of Lord Westbury by T. A. Nash is now (1888) in the press.

WEST CHESTER, a borough and the county seat of Chester county, Pennsylvania, United States, is situated 27 miles west of Philadelphia, in a thickly settled farming region, devoted principally to market gardening and the dairy industry. Its population in 1880 was 7046, of whom 1164 were coloured and 517 of foreign birth.

WEST DERBY, a township in Lancashire, England, now virtually a suburb of Liverpool, about 4 miles north-east of Liverpool Exchange. It is chiefly composed of houses inhabited by the wealthier merchants of Liverpool. The parish church of St Mary was re-erected in 1856 in

WESTERN AUSTRALIA

English Miles

100 50 0 100

Railways

Long. East 125 of Greenw.

W.&A.K. Johnston.

the Early English style from the designs of Sir Gilbert Scott, and has a massive central tower with four pinnacles. The site of the former church is marked by a cross. Attached to the church of St James, also a modern structure in the Early English style, there is a library of 1800 volumes. In the centre of the old village there is an old court-house, erected in 1662, now belonging to the marquis of Salisbury as lord of the manor. Croxteth Hall, the seat of the earl of Sefton, is in the immediate vicinity. The population of the urban sanitary district (area 5561 acres) was 27,292 in 1871 and 33,614 in 1881.

In Saxon times West Derby gave its name to a hundred. Edward the Confessor had a castle there, the site of which is still called the Castle Hill. In 1266 the manor was bestowed on Edmund, earl of Lancaster. When Henry de Bolingbroke, duke of Lancaster, became king, this and other manors reverted to the crown. In the 4th of Charles I. it was granted to various citizens of London, who resold it in 1639 to James, Lord Stanley and Strange. The property of the Stanleys was afterwards partly sequestrated and partly alienated.

Plate IX. WESTERN AUSTRALIA. This British colony, the portion of Australia that lies to the west of 129° E. long., forming considerably more than one-third of the whole, has an area of 1,060,000 square miles, is 1400 miles in length and 850 in breadth, and has a coast-line of 3500 miles. It is divided into five districts—Central, Central Eastern, South-Eastern, North, and Kimberley. The Central or settled district, in the south-west, is divided into twenty-six counties. Apart from the coast lands, the map presents almost a blank, as the major portion is practically a dry waste of stone and sand, relieved by a few shallow salt lakes. The rivers of the south are small,—the Blackwood being the most considerable. To the north of this are the Murray, the well-known Swan, the Moore, the Greenough, and the Murchison. The last is 400 miles long. Sharks Bay receives the Gascoigne (200 miles long), with its tributary the Lyons. Still farther north, where the coast trends eastward, the principal rivers are the Ashburton, the Fortescue, and the De Grey. Kimberley district to the north-east has some fine streams,—the Fitzroy and Ord and their tributaries, on some of which (the Mary, Elvira, &c.) are the gold-fields, 250 miles south of Cambridge Gulf. The Darling mountain range is in the south-west, Mount William reaching 3000 feet; in the same quarter are Toolbrunup (3341 feet), Ellen's Peak (3420), and the Stirling and Victoria ranges. Gardner and Moresby are flat-topped ranges. Mount Elizabeth rises behind Perth. Hampton tableland overlooks the Bight. In the north-west are Mount Bruce (4000 feet), Augustus (3580), Dalgeranger (2100), Barlee, Pyrton, and the Capricorn range. Kimberley has the Leopold, M'Clintock, Albert Edward, Hardman, Geikie, Napier, Lubbock, Oscar, Mueller, and St George ranges. The lake district of the interior is in the Gibson and Victoria deserts from 24° to 32° S. The lakes receive the trifling drainage of that low region. Almost all of them are salt from the presence of saline marl.

Climate.—With little or no cold anywhere, the heat of summer over the whole area is considerable. Western Australia differs from the country to the east in having no extensive ranges to collect vapour, while the trade winds blow off the dry land instead of from the ocean; for these two reasons the climate is very dry. Thunderstorms often supply almost the only rainfall in the interior. The south-western corner, the seat of settlements, is the only portion where rains can be depended on for cultivation; but even there few places have a rainfall of 40 inches. As one goes northward the moisture lessens. The north-west and all the coast along to Kimberley, with most of that district, suffer much from dryness. The north-east comes in summer within the sphere of the north-west monsoons, though just over the low coast-range few showers are known. The south coast, exposed to polar breezes, with uninterrupted sea, has to endure lengthened droughts. In the Swan river quarter the rainfall is in winter, being brought by north-west winds, and summer days have little moisture. While the south wind cools the settled region, it comes over the parched interior to the northern lands. The hot wind of Swan river is from the east and north-east; but it is from the south in summer to Kimberley and the north-west. In one season the land breeze is hot, in another cool, but always dry. In the year 1885 Perth had a rainfall of 29 inches with an evaporation of 66. The temperature ranged from 34° to 109° in the shade. In 1885 there fell 32$\frac{3}{5}$ inches on 100 days, while Albany had 32 on 138 days, Augusta 46 on 122 days, and York less than 18 on 81 days. Geraldton port received the same as York, but on 63 days, while Cossack, the pearl port of the north-west, had but 9$\frac{1}{2}$ on 18 days throughout the year. Northampton showed 21$\frac{3}{4}$, Beverley 14$\frac{3}{4}$, and Eucla 9$\frac{9}{10}$ inches.

Geology.—The base of Western Australia is of granite and its kindred formations, which underlie Silurian or more ancient rocks. Not only are the principal elevations so composed, but throughout the vast extent of bare and sterile land eastward and inland granite is most prominent, rising through recent deposits in knobs and tables onward into South Australia. It is the rock of the Australian desert. The great lake district is a depression, with a granite floor permeated with igneous veins, surrounded by isolated hills and ranges of the Primary and metamorphic rocks. King George's Sound and the mountains around are granite, as also are disjointed ranges northward to Sharks Bay. The streams in the north-west, as well as the Lyons and Gascoigne, take their rise among the old igneous and Palæozoic formations. Kimberley is full of similar rocks. The upper Irwin has garnetiferous granite. Granite, both on the south and western shores, supports the recent deposits of calcareous and arenaceous material. The horizontal sandstone of the interior and the flat-topped hills of sandstone rest upon the granite. The arid region around Sharks Bay, glistening with limestone and sand, has the ancient stone for a foundation, upon which coralline forms built their reefs. All sorts of metamorphic rocks prevail in the Leopold, Weld, and other ranges of Kimberley. Quartz veins are common in the hills. Cambridge Gulf is lined with quartzose grit embodying rock crystal, and the Blackwood river with gneiss. Porphyry appears at York, on the Murchison, and elsewhere. Blue slate occurs on the Canning at Champion Bay, and on Hampton Plains. Carboniferous rocks are present near the Irwin, Canning, Fitzroy, and Murchison. Mr Hardman traced them north-east over 1500 square miles, bearing coal plants. Secondary formations are rare: a deposit of Oolite 400 feet thick is reported from the Murchison. Tertiary beds of limestone are more plentiful, generally seen near the coast; others of a coralline nature are more recent. Arenaceous limestone cliffs rise two to four hundred feet along the southern shore for hundreds of miles, and similar stone is seen at the junction of the Fitzroy and the Margaret. The spiriferous sandstone on the Denison Plains of Kimberley, like that of the Moresby range, is doubtless Palæozoic. The desert sandstone, so easily decomposed to furnish moving sand-dunes, is regarded as Miocene by Prof. Tate. Freemantle stands upon a recent calcareous sandstone. Roeburne is similarly situated. The south-west abounds in calcareous accretions. Cape Arid stops with its granite the progress of Tertiary beds. Tertiary agates and jaspers occur on the Ord and the Ashburton. Three terraces lead from the calcareous mud of the north-west shore to the granite of Mount Bruce. Nuyt's Land is probably Pliocene. Volcanic rocks of various ages have burst through other formations, from Kimberley down to King George's Sound. Basalt runs under the limestone of Bunbury, and even rises in pillars; it is in scoriaceous dykes at King Sound. Columnar greenstone occurs about Cape Leeuwin and Cape Naturaliste, while greenstone dykes yield copper in the Champion Bay district. There is a sort of Giant's Causeway at Géographe Bay. Dampier Archipelago, Nickol Bay, the sources of the Fortescue and the De Grey, Glenelg river, Camden harbour, Mount Waterloo, Fitzroy river, and the gold field all show traces of volcanic action. Of the geology of three-fourths of the colony, however, we know scarcely anything. The presence of a new carbonaceous mineral called cliftonite has been recently determined by Mr L. Fletcher in a meteorite brought by the Rev. Mr Nicholai from Western Australia.

Minerals.—The earliest mines were of lead and copper in Victoria district, the ore being sent to Geraldton, the port of Champion Bay, 30 miles from the Northampton mines of silver, lead, and copper. Berkshire valley has in addition plumbago, the Irwin antimony, and Woongong silver. The Geraldine lead and silver ores were first worked in 1845, and produced £43,000 in 1878. Wheal Fortune and Tortura mines are of silver-lead; Gelira, Wheel Alpha, and Narra Narra of copper. Iron ores are abundant; they are magnetic at Mount Magnet. Coal has not yet been found in any quantity. Carboniferous rocks are seen in several places, and fair specimens of coal have been obtained. A semi-bituminous mineral near the Swan and the Murray yields a pale oil, which would serve to varnish wood. Gold, long looked for, has been found in Kimberley; and diggers rushed to the country about the Margaret, Mary, and Elvira rivers. The majority did not find returns equal to expenditure; but auriferous quartz of great richness has been reported recently. The proclaimed gold-field lies between 16° and 19$\frac{1}{2}$° S., 126° and 129° E. Building stone is found of many varieties.

Agriculture.—This was once confined to the Swan river quarter, but is rapidly extending northward in Victoria district, where the land is free of timber, though the rainfall is very light. In Kimberley tropical produce, especially sugar, cotton, spices, and rice, can be readily raised. The south-west is essentially a farming country, but the soil is generally sandy. In 1886 86,248 acres were in crop (hay 25,718; wheat, 24,043; barley, 5185; oats, 1766; maize, 171; potatoes, 356; green forage, 1075; vines, 649). No settlement has a finer variety of fruits, and both wine and raisins are being exported. The cottage homesteads are surrounded with pleasant gardens, vineyards, and orchards.

Live Stock.—Timber was too thick in the old settlement for flocks and herds; the squatting districts are eastward of the dividing range and north of the Swan. The want of water both eastward and northward stops progress, but sheep stations are established in oases of reputed eastern deserts. The north-west, in spite of drought, is a favourite locality for squatters; but the better-watered Kimberley is regarded as the most hopeful. At the beginning of 1887 129,219,079 acres of the available country were leased by 6469 persons, at the rental of £73,863, averaging a little over half a farthing an acre. The horses numbered 38,360; cattle, 88,254; sheep, 1,809,071; pigs, 24,655; goats, 5301. Some parts, chiefly in the south-west, are troubled with poison plants. Borings in ill-watered places, as the southern and central districts, furnish water for stock. The Angora goat has been a success there. Rabbits already begin to trouble squatters. In proportion to inhabitants, Western Australia has advanced in pastoral pursuits beyond its neighbours, excepting in the quality of stock and the get-up of wool. Of 678,400,220 acres in the colony only 1,851,742 are alienated, though 130,000,000 are leased out by Government. The land laws are liberal. Lessees have pre-emptive rights over parts of runs at 5s. per acre, within a certain period. Inferior land is much cheaper. Kimberley leases are for not less than 50,000 acres at 10s. rent per 1000 acres,—this being the best pastoral country. A certain limited amount of stock is required according to acreage and district. Poisoned land can be leased for twenty-one years at £1 rent per 1000 acres, when the area is granted free if it be fenced and the poison plants eradicated; a licence, for that term, of such land, costs one-eighth of that rent. The break-up of the extensive original grants is still essential to further progress.

Flora.—Judged by its vegetable forms, Western Australia would seem to be older than eastern Australia, South Australia being of intermediate age. Indian relations appear on the northern side, and South African on the western. There are fewer Antarctic and Polynesian representatives than in the eastern colonies. European forms are extremely scarce. Compared with the other side of Australia, a third of the genera on the south-west are almost wanting in the south-east. In the latter, 55, having more than ten species each, have 1260 species; but the former has as many in 55 of its 80 genera. Of those 55, 36 are wanting in the south-east, and 17 are absolutely peculiar. There are fewer natural orders and genera westward, but more species. Baron Von Mueller declared that "nearly half of the whole vegetation of the Australian continent has been traced to within the boundaries of the Western Australian territory." He includes 9 *Malvaceæ*, 6 *Euphorbiaceæ*, 2 *Rubiaceæ*, 9 *Proteaceæ*, 47 *Leguminosæ*, 10 *Myrtaceæ*, 12 *Compositæ*, 5 *Labiatæ*, 6 *Cyperaceæ*, 13 *Convolvulaceæ*, 16 *Gramineæ*, 3 *Filices*, 10 *Amaranthaceæ*. Yet over 500 of its tropical species are identified with those of India or Indian islands. While seven-tenths of the orders reach their maximum south-west, three-tenths do so south-east. Cypress pines abound in the north, and ordinary pines in Rottnest Island. Sandalwood (*Santalum cygnorum*) is exported. The gouty stem baobab (*Adansonia*) is in the tropics. *Xanthorrhœa*, the grass tree, abounds in sandy districts. Mangrove bark yields a purple tan. Palms and zamias begin in the north-west. The *Melaleuca Leucadendron* is the paperbark tree of settlers. The rigid-leafed *Banksia* is known as the honeysuckle. *Casuarinæ* are the he and she oaks of colonists, and the *Exocarpus* is their cherry tree. Beautiful flowering shrubs distinguish the south-west; and the deserts are all ablaze with flowers after a fall of rain. Poison plants are generally showy *Leguminosæ*, *Sida*, and the *Gastrolobium*.

The timber trees of the south-west are almost unequalled. Of the Eucalypts, the jarrah or mahogany, *E. marginata*, is first for value. It runs over five degrees of latitude, and its wood resists the teredo and the ant. Sir Malcolm Fraser assigns 14,000 square miles to the jarrah, 10,000 to *E. viminalis*, 2300 to the karri (*E. colossea* or *E. diversicolor*), 2400 to York gum (*E. loxophleba*), 800 to the red gum (*E. calophylla*), and 500 to tuart or native pear (*E. gomphocephala*). Not much good wood is got within 20 miles of the coast. The coachbuilder's coorup rises over 300 feet. Morrel furnishes good timber and rich oil. An ever-increasing trade is done in the timber of the south-western forests.

Fauna.—Among the mammals are the *Macropus giganteus*, *M. irma*, *M. dama*, *M. brachyurus*, *Lagorchestes fasciatus*, *Bettongia penicillata*, *Phalangista vulpecula*, *Pseudochirus cooki*, *Dasyurus geoffroyi*. *Tarsipes rostratus*, *Antechinus apicalis*, *Perameles obesula*, *Perameles myosurus*, *Myrmecobius fasciatus*. Fossil forms partake of the existing marsupial character, *Diprotodon* being allied to the wombat and kangaroo. Nail-bearing kangaroos are in the north-west; the banded one, size of a rabbit, is on Sharks Bay. Nocturnal phalangers live in holes of trees or in the ground. Carnivorous *Phascogalæ* are found in south-west. There are three kinds of wombat. The rock-loving marsupial *Osphranter* is only in the north-east, and *Perameles bougainvillei* at Sharks Bay. The dalgyte or *Petrogale lagotis* is at Swan river and *Hypsiprymnus* in the south. The colony has only two species of wallabies to five in New South Wales. The *Halmaturus* of the Abrolhos is a sort of wallaby; a very elegant species is 18 inches long. The pretty *Dromicia*, 6 inches long, lives on stamens and nectar, like the *Tarsipes*, having a brush at the tip of its tongue; its tail is prehensile. The hare-like *Lagorchestes fasciatus* is a great leaper. The *Hapalotis* of the interior has nests in trees. Beaver rats and other small rodents are troublesome, and bats are numerous. The dingo is the wild dog. The platypus (*Ornithorhynchus*) and the *Echidna* are the only forms of the *Monotremata*. The seal, whale, and dugong occur in the adjacent seas.

The west is not so rich as the east of Australia in birds. Many forms are absent and others but poorly represented, though some are peculiar to the west. The timbered south-west has the greatest variety of birds, which are scarce enough in the dry and treeless interior. Of lizards the west has 12 genera not found in eastern Australia. Of snakes there are but 15 species to 3 in Tasmania and 31 in New South Wales. While the poisonous sorts are 2 to 1 in the east, they are 3 to 1 in the west. The turtle is obtained as an article of food. The freshwater fishes are not all like those of the east. They include the mullet, snapper, ring fish, guard fish, bonita, rock cod, shark, saw fish, parrot fish, and cobbler. Under the head of fisheries may be mentioned the pearl oyster, which is dived for by natives at Sharks Bay; the trepang or bêche-de-mer is also met with in the north. Insects are well represented, especially *Coleoptera*, *Lepidoptera*, *Hymenoptera*, *Hemiptera*, and *Diptera*.

Trade and Commerce.—Safe harbours are few, and hundreds of miles of the coast-line are without shelter for a vessel. The coasting traffic, until recently, was confined to the south-west, from the Sound to Victoria district; but wool is now shipped at the north-west, as well as pearls, while wool, pearl shells, hides, tallow, and gold are claiming attention in the tropical north-east. The imports for 1886 amounted to £758,011, of which £347,915 came from the United Kingdom, and £396,871 from other British possessions, principally the neighbouring colonies and India. The exports reached £630,392,—the main items being wool (£322,578), shells (£104,964), guano, timber, sandalwood, pearls, lead, copper, manna gum, and gold. Of these exports, £505,331 went to Great Britain, and £92,716 to other British ports.

Industries.—The pastoral industry occupies the first place. Fisheries are taking an important position (pearl shell, bêche-de-mer, and preserved or tinned fish). Mandurah, at the mouth of the Murray, and Freemantle have preserving sheds for mullet and snapper. Guano beds are worked to much advantage at the Lacepede Isles. Salt is produced largely at Rottnest Island. Raisins are dried, and the oil of castor trees is expressed. The mulberry tree succeeds well, and sericulture is making progress. Dugong oil is got from Sharks Bay. Honey and wax are becoming valuable exports; from the abundance of flowers the hives can be emptied twice a year. Manna and gums of various kinds are among the resources of the country. Among the wines made are the Riesling, Burgundy, Sweetwater, Hock, and Fontainebleau.

Roads and Railways.—Excellent roads were made during the period of convict labour. The northern railway from Northampton mines to Port Geraldton is 35 miles long. The eastern line is from Freemantle through Perth to Guildford (20 miles) and to Beverley (90 miles). A concession of 12,000 acres per mile is bringing the rail from York northward to Victoria district, and from Beverley southward to Albany on King George's Sound. Communication between the several ports is conducted by steamers, which have been aided by a state subsidy.

Administration.—Western Australia is a crown colony, administered by a governor, his executive council, and a legislative council partly nominated by the governor. The colonial revenue for 1887 amounted to £461,322, the expenditure to £456,897.

Education.—As in other colonies, the denominational system formerly prevailed; but lately an effort has been made to have public schools on a broader basis. The state in 1886 granted £7505 for 3169 scholars in the public schools, and £1415 for 1339, principally Roman Catholics, in the assisted schools. The Perth *Inquirer* was the first newspaper; there are now 11 in the colony.

Population.—Of the 42,000 inhabitants 7000 are in Perth, the capital, 5000 in Freemantle, 1000 at Albany, 900 at York. Some trouble from the aborigines was experienced by settlers at first, but now many of them are useful upon stations, making good shepherds. A successful mission for natives has been conducted for many years at New Norcia, about 80 miles north of Perth, by Spanish monks.

WEST INDIES

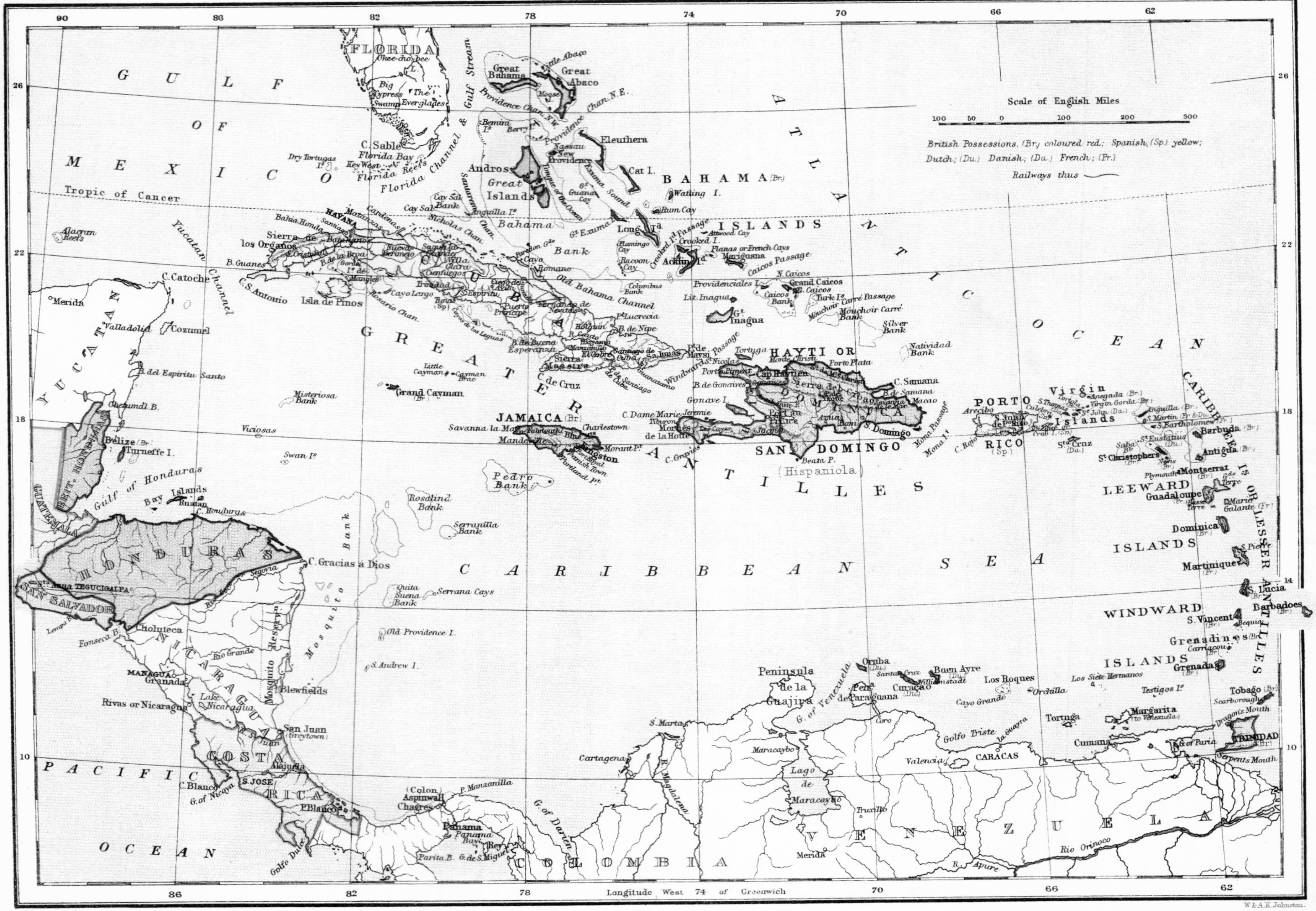

Scale of English Miles
100 50 0 100 200 300

British Possessions, (Br.) coloured red; Spanish, (Sp.) yellow;
Dutch; (Du.) Danish; (Da.) French; (Fr.)
Railways thus

GULF OF MEXICO
Tropic of Cancer
ATLANTIC OCEAN
BAHAMA ISLANDS (Br.)
GREATER ANTILLES
CARIBBEAN SEA
CARIBBEE Is. OR LESSER ANTILLES
LEEWARD ISLANDS
WINDWARD ISLANDS
PACIFIC OCEAN

FLORIDA
Okee-cho-bee L.
Big Cypress Swamp
The Everglades
C. Sable
Florida Bay
Key West
Florida Reefs
Dry Tortugas Is.
Florida Channel
Gulf Stream
Great Bahama
Little Abaco
Great Abaco
Providence Chan. N.E.
Providence Chan. N.W.
Bemini Is.
Berry Is.
Nassau
New Providence
Eleuthera
Andros
Great Islands
Tongue of the Ocean
Exuma Sound
Gt. Guana Cay
Cat I.
Watling I.
Rum Cay
Long I.
Gt. Exuma
Cay Sal Bank
Santaren Chan.
Nicholas Chan.
Anguilla Is.
Bahama Bank
Crooked I. Passage
Crooked I.
Attwood Cay
Acklin I.
Flamingo Cay
Racoon Cay
Planas or French Cays
Mariguana
Caicos Passage
N. Caicos
Grand Caicos
S. Caicos
Turk Is.
Caicos Bank
Providenciales I.
Lit. Inagua
Gt. Inagua
Mouchoir Carré Passage
Mouchoir Carré Bank
Silver Bank
Natividad Bank
Columbus Bank
Old Bahama Channel
Romano
Cayo
Paredon Gde.

CUBA
HAVANA
Matanzas
Cardenas
Bahia Honda
Santiago
Sierra de los Organos
B. Guanes
C. S. Antonio
Isla de Pinos
Cienfuegos
Villa Clara
Trinidad
Sancti Espiritu
Puerto Principe
Manzanillo
Holguin
B. de Nipe
Pt. Lucrecia
Sierra Maestra
Santiago de Cuba
C. de Cruz
Cayo Largo
Rosario Chan.
Cayos de las Leguas
Guantanamo
C. Maysi
Windward Passage
Tortuga

HAYTI OR SAN DOMINGO (Hispaniola)
Monte Christi
Porto Plata
Cap Haytien
Port Piment
B. de Gonaives
Gonave I.
Port au Prince
C. Dame Marie
Jeremie
Tiburon
Les Cayes
C. Gravois
Jacmel
Beata P.
Azua
Bani
S. Domingo
C. Samana
B. de Samana
Macao
Mona Passage
Mona I.
Sierra del Cibao

JAMAICA (Br.)
Savanna la Mar
Falmouth
Mandeville
Charlestown
Kingston
Spanish Town
Morant Pt.
Portland Pt.
Pedro Bank
Little Cayman
Cayman Brac
Grand Cayman (Br.)
Misteriosa Bank
Swan Is.
Viciosas
Rosalind Bank
Serranilla Bank
Quita Sueña Bank
Serrana Cays
Old Providence I.
S. Andrew I.

PORTO RICO (Sp.)
Arecibo
S. Juan de Pto. Rico
Culebra
Virgin Islands
S. Thomas
Tortola
Anegada (Br.)
Virgin Gorda (Br.)
S. John (Da.)
St. Croix (Da.)
Anguilla (Br.)
S. Martin (Fr. & Du.)
S. Bartholomew (Fr.)
Barbuda (Br.)
Saba
St. Eustatius (Du.)
St. Christophers
Antigua (Br.)
Montserrat (Br.)
Plymouth
Guadaloupe
Basse Terre
Marie Galante (Fr.)
Desirade
Dominica (Br.)
Martinique (Fr.)
S. Pierre
S. Lucia (Br.)
Barbadoes (Br.)
S. Vincent (Br.)
Bequia
Grenadines (Br.)
Carriacou
Grenada (Br.)
Tobago (Br.)
Scarborough
TRINIDAD (Br.)
Dragon's Mouth
Serpent's Mouth
G. of Paria
Testigos Is.
Margarita (to Venezuela)
Los Siete Hermanos
Orchilla
Los Roques
Tortuga
Cayo Grande
Buen Ayre (Du.)
Curaçao (Du.)
Williamstadt
Santa Cruz
Oruba (Du.)

YUCATAN
C. Catoche
Merida
Valladolid
Cozumel
B. del Espiritu Santo
Chetumal B.
Alacran Reefs
Yucatan Channel
BRIT. HONDURAS
Belize (Br.)
Turneffe I.
Gulf of Honduras
Bay Islands
Ruatan
C. Honduras
GUATEMALA
HONDURAS
TEGUCIGALPA
SAN SALVADOR
Fonseca B.
Choluteca
Segovia
C. Gracias a Dios
Mosquito Bank
Mosquito Reserve
Rio Grande
Blewfields
NICARAGUA
MANAGUA
Granada
Lake Nicaragua
Rivas or Nicaragua
San Juan (Greytown)
S. Juan
COSTA RICA
Alajuela
S. JOSE
C. Blanco
G. of Nicoya
P. Blanco
Golfo Dulce
(Colon) Aspinwall
Chagres
P. Manzanilla
Panama
Panama Bay
Rey
Parita B.
G. de S. Miguel
G. of Darien
COLOMBIA
Cartagena
S. Marta
R. Magdalena
Peninsula de la Guajira
G. of Venezuela
Pen. de Paraguana
Coro
Maracaybo
Lago de Maracaybo
Truxillo
Merida
VENEZUELA
Golfo Triste
La Guayra
Valencia
CARACAS
Cumana
R. Apure
Rio Orinoco

Longitude West 74 of Greenwich

W. & A. K. Johnston.

History.—Both the western and northern coasts of the colony are pretty accurately laid down on maps said to date from 1540 to 1550, where the western side of the continent terminates at Cape Leeuwen. The discovery of the coast may be attributed to Portuguese and Spanish navigators, who were in the seas northward of Australia as early as 1520. The next visitors, nearly a century later, were the Dutch. Edel explored northward in 1619, and De Witt in 1628. The "Gulde Zeepaard" in 1627 sailed along the south coast for 1000 miles, the territory being named Nuyt's Land. Tasman made a survey of the north shore in 1644, but did not advance far on the western border. Dampier was off the north-west in 1688 and 1696, naming Sharks Bay. Vancouver entered King George's Sound in 1791. The French, under D'Entrecasteaux, were off Western Australia in 1792; and their commodore Baudin, of the "Géographe" and "Naturaliste," in 1801 and 1802 made important discoveries along the western and north-western shores. Captain Flinders about the same time paid a visit to the Sound, and traced Nuyt's Land to beyond the South Australian boundary. Freycinet went thither in 1818. Captain King surveyed the northern waters between 1818 and 1822.

The earliest settlement was made from Port Jackson, at the end of 1825. Owing to a fear that the French might occupy King George's Sound, Major Lockyer carried thither a party of convicts and soldiers, seventy-five in all, and took formal British possession, though Vancouver had previously done so. Yet the Dutch had long before declared New Holland, which then meant only the western portion of Australia, to be Dutch property. This convict establishment returned to Sydney in 1829. In 1827 Captain Stirling was sent to report upon the Swan river, and his narrative excited such interest in England as to lead to an actual free settlement at the Swan river. Captain Freemantle, R.N., in 1827 took official possession of the whole country. Stirling's account stimulated the emigration ardour of Sir F. Vincent, and Messrs Peel, Macqueen, &c., who formed an association, securing from the British Government permission to occupy land in Western Australia proportionate to the capital invested, and the number of emigrants they despatched thither. In this way Mr Peel had a grant of 250,000 acres, and Colonel Latour of 103,000. Captain (afterwards Sir James) Stirling was appointed lieutenant-governor, arriving June 1, 1829. The people were scattered on large grants. The land was poor, and the forests heavy; provisions were at famine prices; and many left for Sydney or Hobart Town. The others struggled on, finding a healthful climate, and a soil favouring fruits and vegetables, whilst their stock grazed in the more open but distant quarters. The overland journey of Eyre from Adelaide to King George's Sound in 1839–40, through a waterless waste, discouraged settlers; but Grey's overland walk in 1838 from Sharks Bay to Perth revealed fine rivers and good land in Victoria district, subsequently occupied by farmers, graziers, and miners. Commanders Wickham and Stokes about that time made discoveries on the northern coast. Roe was an active explorer, and Austin in 1854 investigated the country to the eastward. F. H. Gregory traced the Gascoigne in 1857, and made known superior land to the north-west about Nickol Bay four years later. Austin in 1864 saw a good future for the Glenelg district, previously described by Grey. A. Gregory was at the north-east in 1856, and J. Forrest in 1870 proved the way along the south coast to be no hopeless desert. Giles crossed from the east. Major Warburton in 1873 had severe trials with his camels before reaching De Grey river from the east. The Messrs Forrest suffered much in another attempt to penetrate the eastern barren country. A. Forrest had a successful tour in 1877 through the Kimberley province; two years later he made the connexion between Kimberley and the north-west. The difficulties of the settlers had compelled them to seek help from the British treasury, in the offer to accept convicts. These came in 1850; but transportation ceased in 1868, in consequence of loud protests from the other colonies. Seeking responsible government, the settlers were told in 1888 that, if this were granted for the southern part, the north would still be retained as a crown colony. The discoveries of lead and copper, and lately of gold, must increase the working community; while the newly opened pastures have brought in a great accession of stockholders. Settlers are arriving from South Australia and other colonies, so that the prospects of Western Australia are brightening. (J. BO.)

WEST HAM, an eastern suburb of London, in the county of Essex, which gives its name to an extensive parish, urban sanitary district, and parliamentary borough stretching north and south from Wanstead and Leyton to the Thames, and east and west from Little Ilford and East Ham to the river Lea. West Ham proper is situated on the main road between Stratford and Plaistow, three-quarters of a mile south-east of the Stratford station on the Great Eastern Railway, but the original village is now completely absorbed in the new buildings which have sprung up around it. The church of All Saints has an Early English nave and a good Perpendicular tower, but the architecture of the remainder of the building is nondescript and incongruous. Some mural paintings have within recent years been laid bare, and there are a number of old monuments. Among other public buildings are the West Ham, Stratford, and South Essex dispensary (1878), and the conference hall for public meetings. There are a considerable number of charities. West Ham park, 80 acres in extent, was opened 20th July 1874 at a cost of £25,000. A large public cemetery was consecrated in 1857, and there is a Jews' cemetery. The northern main sewer of the metropolitan main drainage system traverses the parish, the chief pumping station being at Abbey Mills. In 1762 West Ham had 700 houses. Morant, in his *History of Essex*, 1768, describes it as the "residence of considerable merchants, dealers, and industrious artists." Since then its character has completely changed, and it is now a busy industrial district, its prosperity being in a large degree traceable to the formation of the Victoria and Albert docks at Plaistow. It possesses large chemical works, match works, candle factories, manure works, flour-mills, cocoa-nut fibre factories, patent leather cloth factories, smelting works, and copper works. The population of the parish, urban sanitary district, and parliamentary borough (area about 5390 acres) in 1871 was 62,919, and in 1881 it was 128,953.

At the time of the Conquest West Ham belonged to Alestan and Leured, two freemen, and at Domesday to Ralph Gernon and Ralph Peverel. West Ham village was included in the part which descended to the Gernons, who took the name of Montfichet. It received the grant of a market and annual fair in 1253, but these have not been kept for many years. The lordship was given to the abbey of Stratford, and, passing to the crown at the dissolution, it formed part of the dowry of Catherine of Portugal, and was therefore called the Queen's Manor. In 1885 the urban sanitary district was erected into a parliamentary borough, returning two members for the Northern and Southern Divisions respectively.

WEST HOUGHTON, a township of Lancashire, England, on the Lancashire and Yorkshire Railway, 5 miles west-south-west of Bolton, 15 north-west of Manchester, and 5 east-north-east of Wigan. The church of St Bartholomew was rebuilt in 1870 in the Gothic style at a cost of £6000. There are coal-mines in the neighbourhood, and the town possesses a silk factory, print-works, and cotton-mills. The population of the urban sanitary district (area 4341 acres) in 1871 was 6609 and in 1881 it was 9197.

West Houghton before the time of Richard II. was a manor belonging to the abbey of Cockersand. It was confiscated at the Reformation, and since then has been vested in the crown. It is now held by the representatives of the late Colonel Wilbraham. The army of Prince Rupert assembled on West Houghton moor before the attack on Bolton.

WEST INDIES. This important archipelago received the name of the West Indies from Columbus, who hoped that, through the islands, he had found a new route to India. It is also sometimes known as the Antilles (a name, however, more properly applied to a part than to the whole), as Columbus, on his arrival here, was supposed to have reached Antilla, a fabled country, said to lie far to the westward of the Azores, which found a vague and uncertain place on the maps and charts of many geographers before that time. Columbus first landed on St Salvador, or Watling Island, named by the natives Guanahani, and several voyages to this new land were made in rapid succession by the great discoverer, resulting in the finding of most of the larger islands, and a more intimate knowledge of those already known. The importance of its latest possession was at once recognized by the court of Spain, and, as a first move towards turning the

Plates X XI.

West Indies to profitable account, numbers of the natives, for the most part a harmless and gentle people, were shipped beyond seas and sold into slavery, others being employed in forced labour in the mines which the Spaniards had opened throughout the archipelago, and from which large returns were expected. Thus early in its history began that traffic in humanity with which the West-India plantations are so widely associated, and which endured for so long a time. Goaded to madness by the wrongs inflicted upon them, the aborigines at last took arms against their masters, but with the result which might have been expected—their almost utter extirpation. Many of the survivors sought release from their sufferings in suicide, and numbers of others perished in the mines, so that the native race soon almost ceased to exist. Spain was not long allowed to retain an undisputed hold upon the islands: British and Dutch seamen soon sought the new region, accounts concerning the fabulous wealth and treasure of which stirred all Europe, and a desultory warfare began to be waged amongst the various voyagers who flocked to this El Dorado, in consequence of which the Spaniards found themselves gradually but surely forced from many of their vantage grounds, and compelled very materially to reduce the area over which they had held unchecked sway. The first care of the English settlers was to find out the real agricultural capabilities of the islands, and they diligently set about planting tobacco, cotton, and indigo. A French West India Company was incorporated in 1625, and a settlement established on the island of St Christopher, where a small English colony was already engaged in clearing and cultivating the ground; these were driven out by the Spaniards in 1630, but only to return and again assume possession. About this time, also, the celebrated buccaneers, Dutch smugglers, and British and French pirates began to infest the neighbouring seas, doing much damage to legitimate traders, and causing commerce to be carried on only under force of arms, and with much difficulty and danger. Indeed, it was not till the beginning of last century—some time after Spain had, in 1670, given up her claim to the exclusive possession of the archipelago—that these rovers were rendered comparatively harmless; and piracy yet lingered off the coasts down to the early years of the present century. In 1640 sugar-cane began to be systematically planted, and the marvellous prosperity of the West Indies commenced; it was not from the gold and precious stones, to which the Spaniards had looked for wealth and power, but from the cane that the fortunes of the West Indies were to spring. The successful propagation of this plant drew to the islands crowds of adventurers, many of them men of considerable wealth. In Barbados alone, it is said that 50,000 British subjects arrived in one year about this period. The West Indies were for many years used by the English Government as penal settlements, the prisoners working on the plantations as slaves. In 1655 a British force made an unsuccessful attack on Hayti, but a sudden descent on Jamaica was more fortunate in its result, and that rich and beautiful island has since remained in the possession of Great Britain. The Portuguese were the first to import Negroes as slaves, and their example was followed by other nations having West-Indian colonies, the traffic existing for about 300 years. In 1660 a division of the islands was arranged between England and France, the remaining aborigines being driven to specified localities, but this treaty did not produce the benefits expected from it, and as wars raged in Europe the islands frequently changed hands. Hayti, now divided into two republics, has suffered much from internal broils and revolutions.

The West Indies are situated in about 20° N. lat. and 75° W. long., and form a broken, but upon the whole, continuous barrier, shutting out as it were the Atlantic Ocean, with its contents of 34,804,000 cubic miles of water, and its mean depth of 2135 fathoms, from the lesser basins of the Caribbean Sea and Gulf of Mexico, containing respectively 1,675,000 cubic miles and 628,000 cubic miles, and with mean depths of 1269 fathoms and 772 fathoms. These two seas are separated by the island of Cuba and the isthmus of Yucatan, with the great Campeche Bank surrounding three sides of the latter. Spring tides do not rise above 4 feet, nor neaps above 2½ feet. Complicated currents and dangerous shoals, especially in the neighbourhood of the Bahamas, necessitate the exercise of considerable skill and care when navigating this region. The equatorial current sweeps around Trinidad and the Antilles into the Caribbean Sea, and the Gulf Stream passes from the Gulf of Mexico by way of the Florida Channel. The well-known Sargasso Sea lies to the north-east of the islands.

The physical features of the region are clearly shown on the accompanying map (Plate XI.), the orographical and bathymetrical data being reproduced from a yet unpublished chart intended to illustrate one of the "Challenger" Reports, and inserted here by permission of Dr Murray, Director of the "Challenger" Expedition Commission. In the Gulf of Mexico and Caribbean Sea there are 394,850 square miles covered by depths of 100 fathoms and less, 363,950 square miles with from 100 to 500 fathoms, 263,250 square miles by from 500 to 1000 fathoms, 572,950 square miles by from 1000 to 2000 fathoms, 274,850 square miles by from 2000 to 3000 fathoms, and 7750 square miles by over 3000 fathoms. The average surface temperature of the sea in the neighbourhood of the islands is from 75° to 78° F. in February, from 79° to 80° in May, and from 82° to 84° in August. The mean annual temperature of the Gulf Stream in the Florida Channel is 80° F.

The various groups which go to form the West Indies have in some cases more than one name, but the following classification is that usually adopted. To the north lie the Bahamas, situated upon the Great Bahama Bank, south from which is Cuba; Jamaica, again, lies to the south of the latter, and to the east of Jamaica are Hayti and Porto Rico. Still farther to the east lie the Virgin Islands, south of which are the Caribbee Islands, or Antilles proper, divided by mariners into the Leeward and Windward groups. Trinidad lies close to the coast of South America. Thus the whole archipelago stretches, in the form of a rude arc, from Florida and Yucatan in North America to Venezuela in South America.

Area and Population of the Islands according to the latest Returns.

	Square Miles.	Population.		Square Miles.	Population.
SPANISH	49,479	2,275,997	INDEPENDENT	29,000	1,150,000
Cuba	45,883	1,521,684	Hayti	9,000	800,000
Porto Rico	3,596	754,313	San Domingo	20,000	350,000
BRITISH	12,031	1,213,144	FRENCH	1,103	352,400
Bahamas	4,466	43,521	Guadeloupe, &c.	714	180,800
Turks and Caicos	169	4,732	St Bartholomew	8	2,370
Jamaica	4,193	580,804	Martinique	381	169,230
Windward Islands.			DUTCH	434	44,734
St Lucia	238	38,551	Curaçoa	212	25,686
St Vincent	133	40,548	Bonaire	129	4,008
Barbados	166	171,860	Aruba	62	6,407
Grenada, &c.	133	42,403	St Eustatius	8	2,286
Tobago	114	18,051	St Martin and Saba	23	6,347
Leeward Islands			DANISH	223	33,763
Virgin Islands	57	5,287	Santa Cruz	135	18,430
St Christopher	65	29,137	St Thomas	53	14,389
Nevis	50	11,864	St John	35	944
Antigua, &c.	170	34,964			
Montserrat	32	10,083			
Dominica	291	28,211	Total	92,270	5,070,038
Trinidad	1,754	153,128			

The principal rivers are the Cauto, the Sagua la Grande, and the Sagua le Chica in Cuba, the Rio Grande and Plantain Garden in Jamaica, and the Gran Yacui, the

WEST INDIES

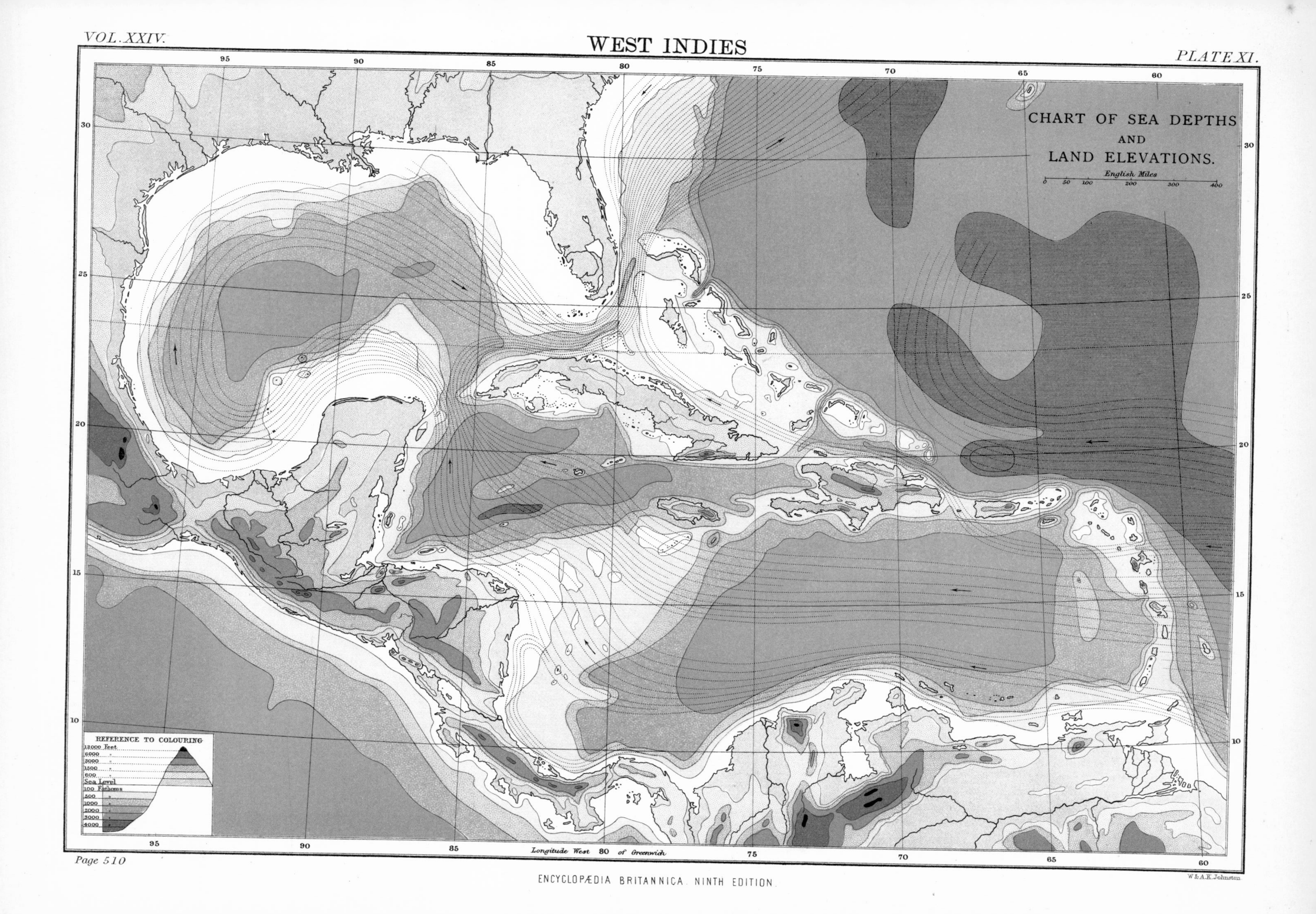

ENCYCLOPÆDIA BRITANNICA. NINTH EDITION.

W & A. K. Johnston

Neiba, and Yuna in Hayti. All have, necessarily, short courses, and none of them are of much importance.

The population is almost entirely of European, Negro, or East-Asiatic origin. The Negroes far outnumber the others, but the Asiatics are rapidly increasing in numbers.

As in most tropical countries where considerable heights are met with—and here over 15,500 square miles lie at an elevation of more than 1500 feet above sea-level—the climate of the West Indies (in so far at least as heat and cold are concerned) varies at different altitudes, and on the higher parts of many of the islands a marked degree of coolness may generally be found. With the exception of part of the Bahamas, all the islands lie between the isotherms of 77° and 82° F. The extreme heat, however, is greatly tempered by the sea breezes, and by long, cool, refreshing nights. Frost is occasionally formed in the cold season when hail falls, but snow is unknown. The seasons may be divided as follows. The short wet season, or spring, begins in April and lasts from two to six weeks, and is succeeded by the short dry season, when the thermometer remains almost stationary at about 80° F. In July the heat increases to an extent well nigh unbearable, and thunder is heard to rumble in the distance. No change need now be looked for till after a period varying from the end of July to the beginning of October, when the great rainfall of the year commences, accompanied by those tremendous and destructive hurricanes, so intimately and truly associated with popular ideas regarding this region, on which the annual rainfall averages 63 inches—an amount of precipitation calculated to represent a mass of water of 12,465,437,000,000 cubic feet. This season is locally known as the "hurricane months." Out of a total of 355 hurricanes, or, more properly, cyclones, recorded during the last three hundred years, 42 have occurred in July, 96 in August, 80 in September, and 69 in October. These storms commence in the Atlantic and towards the east. For a day or two they follow a westerly course, inclining, at the same time, one or two points towards the north, the polar tendency becoming gradually more marked as the distance from the equator increases. When the hurricanes reach latitude 25° N., they curve to the north-east, and almost invariably wheel round on arriving at the northern portion of the Gulf of Mexico, after which they follow the coast line of North America. Their rate of speed varies considerably, but may be said to average 300 miles per day among the islands. The usual signs of the approach of the cyclones are an ugly and threatening appearance of the weather, sharp and frequent puffs of wind increasing in force with each blast, accompanied with a long heavy swell and confused choppy sea, coming from the direction of the approaching storm. But the barometer is the true guide, which should always be consulted when a cyclone is expected. If a sudden fall of the barometer is observed, or even if a marked irregularity of its diurnal variations takes place, a storm may be confidently looked for. In some of these hurricanes the barometer has been found to stand 2 inches lower in the centre of the disturbance than it did outside the limits of the storm field. December marks the commencement of the long dry season, which, accompanied by fresh winds and occasional hail showers, lasts till April. The average temperature of the air at Barbados, which may be taken as a favourable average, is, throughout the year, 80° F. in the forenoon, and about 82° in the afternoon. The maximum is 87°, and the minimum 75°.

The geological features of the West Indies are interesting. A calcareous formation, often assuming the shape of marbles, is most common, and indeed preponderates above all the other rocks to a remarkable degree. The Bahamas, which are low, are composed wholly of limestone formed from coral and shells, crushed into a concretionary mass, hard on the surface, but soft where not exposed to atmospheric action, full of holes and indentations, and disposed in nearly level beds. The lower parts of the Antilles present a like formation where the land does not rise above 230 feet. Cuba shows two distinct compact limestones, one a clayey sandstone and the other a gypsum. These are confined to the central and western parts of the island, which has also syenitic rocks, with some serpentine from which petroleum is obtained. Four-fifths of Jamaica consists of limestone overlying granite and other igneous rocks. Hayti has much metamorphic strata, generally greatly uptilted, and often exhibiting marked folding. These rocks appear to have been limestones, shales, sandstones, and conglomerates. Auriferous quartz veins occur in slates, where these are found near eruptive masses; there is also some syenite, and both active and extinct craters are upon this island. The western Antilles are entirely of volcanic origin, and coral reefs occur along their shores; coral reefs are also presented on the coasts of many of the other islands, but are most irregular in their mode of occurrence, sometimes forming complete belts surrounding the land on all sides, but oftener appearing in the shape of unconnected masses. The fossils of the West Indies are important, as from many of them clear evidence is obtained to show that at no very remote geological period the islands formed part of the adjoining continents. The remains of the megatherium, mylodon, and cabylara, essentially South-American, are also found in North America, but only along the seaboards of Georgia and Carolina. As these are also found in some of the West India islands, as well as in South America, it is thus perfectly clear that at one time the archipelago formed a land passage between the two great divisions of the New World. These remains have also been found in conjunction with the fossil human skeletons of Guadeloupe and the rude weapons associated with them. We may therefore fairly conclude that in Pleistocene times the West Indies formed the connecting link between the two Americas. The occurrence of tree stumps *in situ* several feet below high-water mark also points to a comparatively late sinking of the land in some areas.

The mineral wealth of the islands is not remarkable. Gold, silver, iron, copper, tin, platinum, lead, coal of a poor quality, cobalt, mercury, arsenic, antimony, manganese, and rock salt either have been or are worked. Of late years asphalt has been worked to considerable advantage among the pitch lakes of Trinidad. Opal and chalcedony are the principal precious stones.

The fauna of the region is Neotropical, belonging to that region which includes South and part of Central America, although great numbers of birds from the North-American portion of the Holarctic realm migrate to the islands. The resident birds, however, eighteen genera of which are certainly Neotropical, show beyond doubt to which faunal region the islands properly belong. Mammals are, as in most island groups, rare. The agouti abounds, and wild pigs and dogs are sufficiently numerous to afford good sport to the hunter, as well as smaller game, in the shape of armadillos, opossums, musk-rats, and raccoons. The non-migrating birds include trogons, sugar-birds, chatterers, and many parrots and humming birds. Waterfowl and various kinds of pigeons are in abundance. Reptiles are numerous: snakes—both the boa and adder—are innumerable, while lizards, scorpions, tarantulas, and centipedes are everywhere. Insects are in great numbers, and are often very annoying. Among domestic animals mules are largely reared, and where the country affords suitable pasture and forage cattle-breeding is extensively engaged in. Much attention is not bestowed on horse-breeding, except in regard to the comparatively small numbers required for use in driving and riding by the officials and planters. Goats abound, and large flocks of sheep are kept for the sake of their flesh alone, as the climate is not adapted for wool-growing.

The flora of the islands is of great variety and richness, as plants have been introduced from most parts of the globe, and flourish either in a wild state or under cultivation; grain, vegetables, and fruits, generally common in cool climates, may be seen growing in luxuriance within a short distance of like plants which only attain perfection under the influence of extreme heat, nothing being here required for the successful propagation of both but a difference in the height of the lands upon which they grow. The forests, which are numerous and wide-spreading, produce the most valuable woods and delicious fruits. Palms are in great variety, and there are several species of gum-producing trees. Some locust trees have been estimated to have attained an age of 4000 years, and are of immense height and bulk. *Piptadenia* is, on account of its almost imperishable character when in the ground, universally used as a material for house-building. *Xanthoxylon*, the admired and valuable satin-wood of commerce, is common; *Sapindus* finds a ready market on account of its toughness; crab-wood yields a useful oil and affords reliable timber; and tree ferns of various species are common. Pimento is peculiar to Jamaica. But it is to the agricultural resources of the islands that the greatest importance attaches. For centuries almost the whole care of the planters was bestowed upon the cultivation of the sugar-cane and tobacco plant, but since the emancipation of the slaves and the fall in the price of sugar attention has been turned to the production of other and more varying crops. Perhaps this change has been most marked in the trade which has now sprung up in fruit, which is very large, and annually increasing. Sugar, however, is still the staple product, and has for some time been grown in considerable quantities on the small holdings of the Negroes and other labourers. Crops of tobacco, beans, pease, maize, and Guinea corn are also becoming popular, and a species of rice, which requires no flooding for its successful propagation, is largely produced. *Hymenachne striatum* covers many of the plains, and affords food for numerous herds of cattle.

For further particulars see CUBA, JAMAICA, HAYTI, and other articles on separate islands. Interesting information regarding the state of the islands immediately after the abolition of slavery may be found in *Extracts from Papers Printed by Order of the House of Commons, 1839, Relative to the West Indies*; and notices of the earlier British settlers are contained in Hotten's *Original Lists of Emigrants*, &c. (J. GU.)

WESTMACOTT, SIR RICHARD (1775–1856), one of the principal English sculptors of the classical revival, was born in London in 1775, and while yet a boy learned the rudiments of the plastic art in the studio of his father, who was then a sculptor of some reputation. In 1793, at the age of eighteen, he went to Rome and became a pupil of the Venetian Canova, who was then at the height of his fame. Under the prevailing influences of Italy, at that time Westmacott devoted all his energies to the study of classical sculpture, and throughout his life his real sympathies were with pagan rather than Christian art. Within a year of his arrival in Rome he won the first prize for sculpture offered by the Florentine academy of arts, and in the following year (1795) he gained the papal gold medal awarded by the Roman Academy of St Luke. On his return to London Westmacott began to exhibit his works yearly at the Royal Academy, and soon became the most popular of English sculptors. In 1805 he was elected an associate, and in 1811 a full member of the Royal Academy; in 1827 he was appointed to succeed Flaxman as Royal Academy professor of sculpture, and in 1837 he was knighted. A very large number of important public monuments were executed by him, including many portrait statues; but, like most sculptors of the pseudo-classic revival, he was not successful with this class of draped figure. Little can be said in praise of such works as the statue on the duke of York's column, the portrait of Fox in Bloomsbury Square, or that of the duke of Bedford in Russell Square. Much admiration was expressed at the time for Westmacott's monuments to Collingwood and Sir Ralph Abercromby in St Paul's Cathedral, and that of Mrs Warren in Westminster Abbey; but subjects like these were far less congenial to him than sculpture of a more classical type, such as the pedimental figures over the portico of the British Museum, and his colossal nude statue of Achilles in bronze, set up in Hyde Park in honour of the duke of Wellington; this last statue, though possessing little originality of design, is not without grandeur, and shows a skilful treatment of the nude. Originality was not Westmacott's strong point, but he was highly trained, and, in spite of his artistically degraded time, possessed a strong natural good taste, which preserved him from reproducing the meretricious feebleness of his master Canova. Westmacott wrote the article SCULPTURE for the 8th edition of the *Encyclopædia Britannica*. He died September 1, 1856, after about fifteen years of retirement from active work.

WESTMEATH, an inland county of Ireland, in the province of Leinster, is bounded N.W. by Longford, N. by Cavan, N.E. and E. by Meath, S. by King's County, and W. by Roscommon. Its greatest length from east to west is about 40 miles, and its greatest breadth from north to south about 35 miles. The total area is 453,453 acres, or about 708 square miles. Westmeath is included within the great central limestone plain of Ireland, but at Moat-a-Genogue and near Ballymahon the sandstone rises above the limestone bed and forms isolated protuberances. The general average height of the surface of the county is over 250 feet above sea-level. Being diversified with hill, valley, lake, and river it is highly picturesque, but in no part can it be termed mountainous, the highest summits being Knocklayde (795 feet), Hill of Ben (710 feet), and Knockayon (707 feet). Good limestone is obtainable for building or agricultural purposes, but in some cases the limestone is difficult to calcine. Copper, lead, coal, and marble have been dug, but are not found in sufficient quantities to make the speculation profitable. In some parts there are numerous eskers of calcareous gravel. A large surface is occupied by bog. A special feature of Westmeath is the number of large loughs, which have a combined area of nearly 17,000 acres. In the north, on the borders of Cavan, is Lough Sheelin, with a length of 5 miles and an average breadth of between 2 and 3 miles, and adjoining it is the smaller Lough Kinale. In the centre of the county there is a group of large loughs, of which Lough Dereveragh has an area of 2555 acres. To the north of it are Loughs Lene, Glore, Bawn, and others, and to the south Loughs Iron and Owel. Farther south is Lough Ennell or Belvidere, and in the south-west Lough Ree, forming part of the boundary with Roscommon. The river Inny, which rises in Cavan, enters Westmeath from Lough Sheelin, and, forming for parts of its course the boundary with Longford, falls into Lough Ree. The Inny has as one of its tributaries the Glore, flowing from Lough Lene through Lough Glore, a considerable part of its course being underground. From Lough Lene the Dale also flows southwards to the Irish Sea, and thus this lake sends its waters to the opposite shores of the island. The Brosna flows from Lough Ennell southwards by King's County into the Shannon.

WESTMORLAND

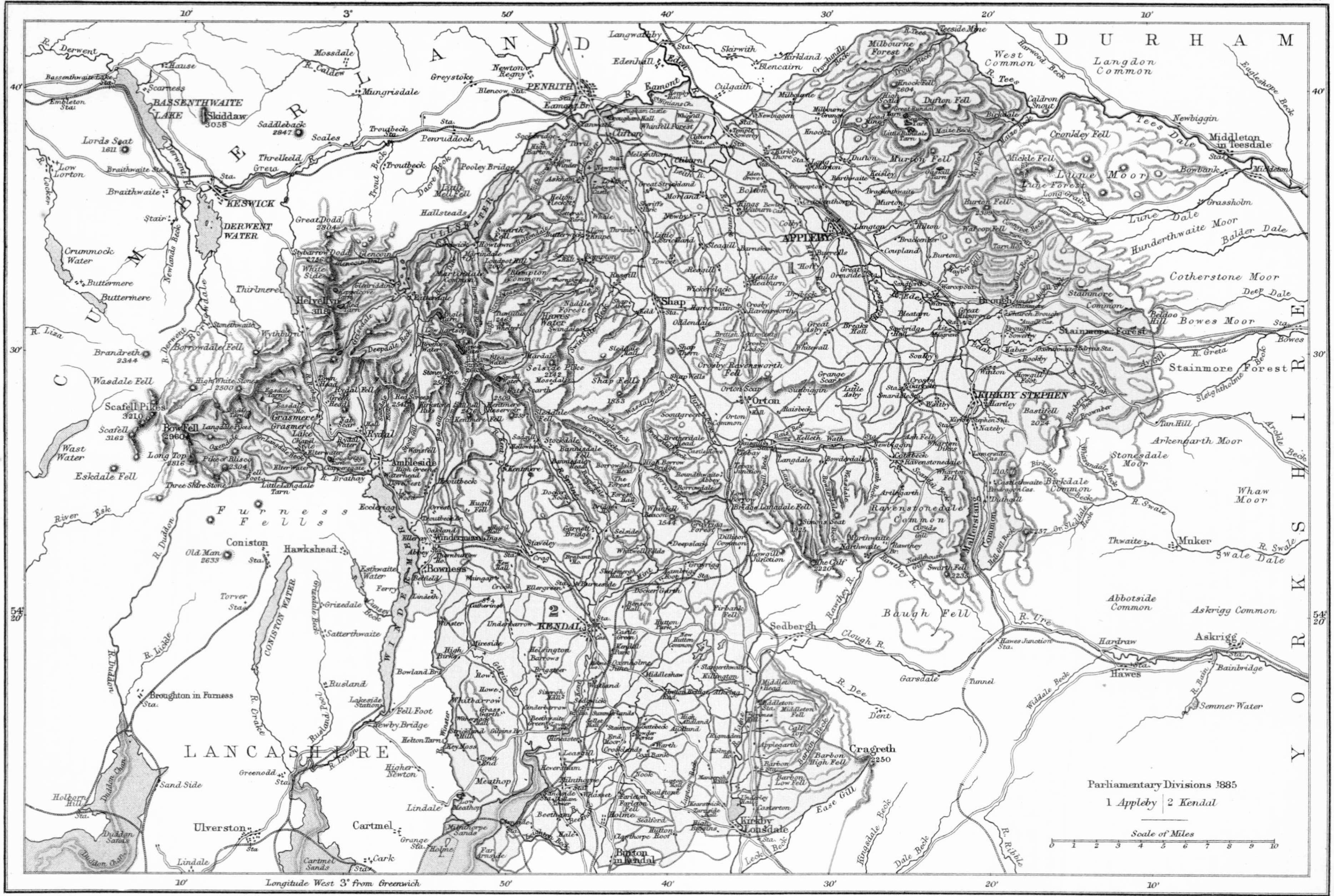

DURHAM
CUMBERLAND
YORKSHIRE
LANCASHIRE
PENRITH
APPLEBY
KIRKBY STEPHEN
KENDAL
KESWICK
DERWENT WATER
BASSENTHWAITE LAKE
ULLSWATER
WINDERMERE
CONISTON WATER
Furness Fells
Parliamentary Divisions 1885
1 Appleby | 2 Kendal
Scale of Miles
0 1 2 3 4 5 6 7 8 9 10
Longitude West 3° from Greenwich

W.&A.K. Johnston.

Agriculture.—According to the *Return of Owners of Land*, 1876, Westmeath was divided among 668 proprietors possessing 430,003 acres, at an annual value of £301,696, or about 14s. an acre. There were also 4262 acres of common or waste lands. Of the proprietors only 111 possessed less than one acre. The following possessed over 8000 acres:—earl of Longford, 15,014; John Malone, 12,555; Lord Castlemaine, 11,445; Lord Greville, 9784; Captain Thomas Smyth, 9779; Patrick Edward Murphy, 9694; Sir Benjamin Chapman, Bart., 9517; G. A. Rochfort-Boyd, 9431; Charles Brinsley Marley, 9060; and Sir John Ennis, Bart., 8775. The soil is generally a rich loam of great depth resting on limestone, and is well adapted both for tillage and pasturage. Even the hills when not under tillage are clothed with a rich pasturage to their summits. In 1886 22·2 per cent. of the entire area was under crops, 62·3 per cent. under grass, ·1 per cent. fallow, 1·8 per cent. woods and plantations, 9·4 per cent. bog and marsh, ·1 per cent. barren mountain land, and 4·1 per cent. water, roads, &c. The total number of holdings in 1886 was 10,992, of which 42 were above 500 acres in extent, 281 between 200 and 500 acres, 535 between 100 and 200 acres, 1094 between 50 and 100 acres, 3589 between 15 and 50 acres, 2466 between 5 and 15 acres, 1698 between 1 and 5 acres, and 1287 not exceeding 1 acre. Within about the last forty years the area under crops has diminished nearly a third. In 1849 it was 130,913 acres, and in 1859 it was 122,684. Between 1876 and 1886 it has been fluctuating rather than decreasing; in the former year it was 98,959, and in the latter 96,287. Only in the area under meadow and clover has there been an increase: in 1849 it was 35,359 acres, and by 1859 it had increased to 41,535, by 1876 to 51,262, and by 1886 to 56,619. The decline in the area under green crops has not been marked: in 1876 the area was 21,369 acres, and in 1886 it was 19,292; but since 1849, when it was 76,173 acres, the area under corn crops has declined more than two-thirds, and the decline has been continuous, the area in 1876 being 26,305 acres, and in 1886 only 20,375. More than half the area under green crops is occupied by potatoes (11,948 acres in 1876, and 11,106 acres in 1886), turnips occupying in these years respectively 6155 acres and 5362 acres, mangel-wurzel, &c., 1232 and 1129, and other green crops 2534 and 1695. The bulk of the area under corn crops has always been occupied by oats, but their area has declined from 59,424 acres in 1849 to 25,709 in 1876, and 19,969 in 1886. The areas under other corn crops are inconsiderable. The number of horses in 1886 was 13,014, of which 883 were kept for amusement and recreation. Mules numbered 659, and asses 4391. Cattle numbered 102,878, 15,806 of them milch cows, and 45,915 other cattle above two years of age. The number of sheep was 118,401, of which 44,265 were under one year old. Pigs numbered only 17,303, goats 6811, and poultry 265,759, including 21,014 turkeys and 36,908 geese.

Manufactures.—The occupations are almost wholly agricultural, dairy farming predominating. Flour and meal are largely made. The only textile manufactures are those of friezes, flannels, and coarse linens for home use. The only mineral of any value is limestone.

Administration and Population.—De Burgo in 1760 placed the population at 50,340; in the parliamentary census of 1812 it was given as 112,000; in 1821 it amounted to 128,819, in 1841 to 141,300, in 1861 to 90,879, and in 1881 to 71,798 (males 36,478, females 35,320). Between 1841 and 1881 the decrease has thus been 49·18 per cent. Roman Catholics in 1881 numbered 92·2 per cent. of the population, and Protestant Episcopalians 6·9. In 1881 54 per cent. of the population could read and write, 14·7 per cent. could read but could not write, and 31·3 per cent. could neither read nor write,—14·8 per cent. being under seven years of age. There were none who could speak Irish only; 828 could speak Irish and English. By the Act of 1885 Westmeath, which formerly returned two members to Parliament, was formed into two parliamentary divisions, North and South, each returning one member; and, Athlone having been disfranchised, that part of the borough within the county was included in the South Division. The principal towns are Athlone, of which about half (3072 inhabitants out of 6755) is within the county, the remainder being in Roscommon, and Mullingar (4787), the county town, a Catholic cathedral city, and an important railway junction. The county is divided into 12 baronies, and contains 63 parishes and 1356 townlands. It is in the home circuit, and assizes are held at Mullingar, and quarter sessions at Mullingar and Moate. There are 16 petty session districts. The county is within the Dublin military district, and forms part of No. 67 sub-district, the brigade depôt of which is at Birr. There is a barrack station at Mullingar.

History and Antiquities.—Westmeath was included in the kingdom of Meath formed by Tuathal, overlord of the Scoti (*ob. cir.* 160 A.D.), to serve as his mensal land. The district suffered much in the 10th and 11th centuries from the Danes, who burnt the town and abbey of Fore. In 1153 the northern region was the scene of a bloody battle under the leadership of the two sons of Dermod O'Brien, after which Turlough, having obtained the victory, put out his brother's eyes. On the settlement of the English in Leinster it formed part of the palatinate of Hugh de Lacy, who received about 800,000 acres from the king, and allotted large tracts to his followers. In the reign of Henry VIII. the palatinate was divided into two parts, the western of which was distinguished by the name of Westmeath. In the latter division a portion of Longford was included until this district was formed into a separate county by Elizabeth. The plan for the insurrection of 1641 was concerted in the abbey of Multifarnham, and both in the wars of this period and those of 1688 the gentry of the county were so deeply implicated that the majority of the estates were confiscated. There are a considerable number of old raths: one at Rathconrath is of great extent; another at Ballymore, originally a Danish fort, was fortified during the wars of the Cromwellian period and those of 1688, and afterwards was the headquarters of General Ginckell, when preparing to besiege Athlone; and there is a third of considerable size near Lough Lene. The ruins of the Franciscan abbey of Multifarnham, founded in 1236 by William Delaware, picturesquely situated near Lough Dereveragh, include a tower 93 feet in height. Others of less importance are at Fore, Kilmocahill, and Kilbeggan.

WESTMINSTER. See London.

WESTMORLAND, a northern inland county of England, adjoins Cumberland on the north-west, Lancashire on the south-west and south, Yorkshire on the east, and a small part of Durham on the extreme north-east. In form it may be regarded as an irregular polygon, with two large re-entering angles on the south-west and south-east. Its length from N.E. to S.W. is 42 miles, while from east to west it measures 40 miles. The total area is 505,864 acres, whereof 4958 acres are foreshore, and 8519 are water. No part of the county touches the sea, unless the estuary of the Kent be regarded as such.

Plate XII.

Physically the county may be roughly divided into four areas. (1) The great upland tract in the north-eastern part, bordering on the western margin of Yorkshire and part of Durham, consists mainly of a wild moorland area, rising to elevations of 2780 feet in Dun Fell, 2803 in Dufton Fell, 2591 feet in Mickle Fell, 2008 Nine Standards, 2328 High Seat, 2323 Wilbert Fell, and Swarth Fell 2235 feet above the sea. (2) The second area comprises about a third of the massif of the Lake District proper, with its eastward continuation, the Langdale and Ravenstonedale Fells, and also the fells of Middleton and Barbon farther south. These include Helvellyn (3118 feet), Bow Fell (2959), Pika Blisca (2304), Langdale Pike (2300), High Street (2663), Fairfield (2950), the Calf (2220), besides others of considerable elevation. All but the lower parts of the valleys within these two areas lie at or above 1000 feet above Ordnance datum; and more than half the remainder lies between that elevation and 1750 feet, the main mass of high land lying in the area first mentioned. (3) The third area includes the comparatively low country between the northern slopes of that just described and the edge of the uplands to the north-east thereof. This includes the so-called Vale of Eden. About three-fifths of this area lies between the 500 and the 1000 feet contour. (4) The Kendal area consists mainly of undulating lowlands, varied by hills ranging in only a few cases up to 1000 feet. More than half this area lies below the 500-feet contour. Westmorland may thus be said to be divided in the middle by uplands ranging in a general south-easterly direction, and to be bordered all along its eastern side by the elevated moorlands of the Pennine chain. The principal rivers are—in the northern area the higher part of the Tees, the Eden with its main tributaries, the Lowther and the Eamont, and in the southern area the Lune and the Kent, with their numerous tributary becks and gills. The lakes include Ullswater (the greater part), Windermere (the whole), Grasmere, Hawes Water, and numerous smaller lakes and tarns, which are chiefly confined to the north-western parts of the county. Amongst the other physical features of more or less interest are numerous crags and scars, chiefly in the neighbourhood of the lakes; others are Mallerstang Edge, Helbeck, above

Brough; Haikable, or High Cup Gill, near Appleby; Orton Scars; and the limestone crags west of Kirkby Lonsdale. Amongst the waterfalls are Caldron Snout, on the northern confines of the county, flowing over the Whin Sill, and Stock Gill Force, Rydal Force, Colwith Force, and Dungeon Gill Force, all situated amongst the volcanic rocks in the west. Hell Gill, near the head of the Eden, and Stenkrith, near Kirkby Stephen, are conspicuous examples of natural arches eroded by the streams flowing through them. Amongst the more striking hills outside the massif of the Lake District are Wilbert Fell, Roman Fell, Murton Pike (1949 feet), Dufton Pike (1578 feet), and Knock Pike (1306 feet).

Geology.—The geological formations represented in Westmorland are:—(A) (1) recent deposits, and (2) glacial drift; (B) New Red rocks—(1) Upper New Red, and (2) Lower New Red or Permian; (C) Carboniferous rocks—(1) Coal-Measures and Millstone Grit, (2) Yoredale Rocks and Mountain Limestone, including the Roman Fell beds, Calciferous Sandstones, and the Lower Limestone Shale, and (3) the Upper Old Red; (D) Siluro-Cambrian rocks—(1) Silurian rocks proper, (2) Upper Cambrian, Ordovician or Lower Silurian rocks, and (3) Cambrian rocks; (E) Metamorphic rocks of different ages; and (F) various Plutonic rocks.

Alluvium in some form or another occurs as marginal deposits alongside streams, or as deltas where streams enter lakes, or where they spread at the foot of a hill-side. Peat forms a mantle of varying thickness on the damper or the more shady parts of nearly all the uplands, ranging locally up to a thickness of 10 feet, and occurs on the sites of old tarns or of old swamps. Screes of rock waste are of general occurrence about the lower parts of nearly all the crags, and as such they play an important part in the scenery of the district. Glacial deposits, in the form of boulder clay, of sand and gravel, or of boulders, are extensively distributed over the lowlands, and to a variable distance up the hill-sides also. They seldom much exceed 100 feet in thickness; but their occurrence is of considerable importance in relation to the scenery, and still more so to the character of the subsoil. Boulders of various kinds are scattered far and wide over nearly all but the highest parts of the county.

Between the period represented by the boulder clay and the next older deposit in Westmorland a great hiatus exists, which is elsewhere represented by several very important geological formations. Here the newest rock next in the series is the St Bees Sandstone and the gypseous shales at its base, which together probably represent the Bunter series. These soft red sandstones, flags, and marls with gypsum are all confined to the northern part of the county, where they form much of the low ground extending along the foot of the Cross Fell escarpment from the county boundary east of Penrith south-eastward to Kirkby Stephen. Some of the prettiest scenery of these parts (Crowdundle Beck; Mill Beck, Dufton; and Podgill, Kirkby Stephen) owes its character to these rocks. The stone is used extensively for building. Gypsum occurs in workable quantities in the shales near the base. Where fully developed these rocks are not less than 2000 feet in thickness. The next formations in descending order consist of the Magnesian Limestone (0–30 feet), the Helton Plant Beds (0–40 feet), the Penrith Sandstone and its horizontal equivalents the Brockrams (0–1200 feet). All these are older than the rocks previously mentioned, but belong to the same series. They occur in the same tract of country.

The highest rocks of the Carboniferous age in Westmorland are represented by a tiny patch of true Coal-Measures, let down, and so preserved from denudation, by one of the great Pennine faults, between Brough and Barras, in north-eastern Westmorland. These rocks consist of several thick and valuable seams of coal, and of beds of fireclay equally valuable, interbedded with several hundred feet of the usual sandstones and shales.[1] True Coal-Measures are not yet known to occur elsewhere in Westmorland. Millstone Grit of the ordinary type underlies these Coal-Measures, and is seen to perhaps a thickness of nearly 2000 feet. Except a small patch exposed near Appleby, and also another near Kirkby Lonsdale, the remainder of the Millstone Grit is confined to the higher parts of the wild moorlands along the eastern border of the county. The highest member of the second subdivision of the Carboniferous is the Yoredale Rocks, which form the chief mass of the hills forming the Westmorland part of the great central watershed of northern England. Most of the Cross Fell escarpment, of Stainmoor, and of the higher parts of the valley of the Eden consist of these rocks, as do also much of the lowlands. They consist essentially of a series of thin beds of limestone, parted by variable thicknesses of sandstone and shales, with here and there a thin coal-seam. Their thickness ranges from 1500 to 2500 feet. The Borradale coal-seam, and the Tan Hill seam, in these rocks, have long been worked for local purposes. Below the Yoredale Rocks limestone preponderates, and the grey limestones of this series form very conspicuous and striking features in the landscape around Kendal, Beetham, and Farleton; Kirkby Stephen, Orton, and Shap; Brough, Helgill, and Murton, and thence north-westward. Near Kirkby Stephen is nearly 2000 feet of this limestone, locally almost undivided. Near Kendal, at Barbon, between Ravenstonedale and Shap Wells, and near Helton occur masses of red gravelly conglomerate and red sandstones belonging to the Upper Old Red. The materials of the conglomerate largely consist of rocks foreign to the district. For a period of immense length preceding the deposition of the Upper Old Red the older rocks of Westmorland seem to have been exposed to a complicated series of disturbances and denudations, with, as a result, the removal from some areas of a thickness of strata above (rather than below) 5 miles in thickness. It was across the upturned and denuded ends of this vast pile of rock that the Upper Old Red was laid down. The older strata, grouped under D above, are therefore separated from the Upper Old Red by an unconformity representing the removal from this area, and the accumulation in some unknown area elsewhere, of a pile of rock 5 miles in thickness. This is one of the greatest breaks yet made known in the whole of the geological record.

The Siluro-Cambrian rocks are perhaps more fully developed in Westmorland and Cumberland than they are anywhere else,—the aggregate thickness of strata referable to one or other of the horizons in this group being at least 6 miles. The highest member of this series is the Kirkby Moor Flags, which consist of a considerable thickness of mudstones and sandstones, much disturbed and contorted in places, and form the whole of the low hill country on the east side of the turnpike road between Kendal and Kirkby Lonsdale, and extending thence eastward to a little beyond the Lune. Lithologically and palæontologically these rocks agree in a general way with the Ludlow rocks of Shropshire. Their highest beds are unconformable to the Upper Old Red, sometimes violently so. These rocks graduate downward into the Bannisdale Slates, 5200 feet of close alternations of flaggy grits and rudely cleaved sandy mudstones. These rocks occupy a large area around Kendal, and to the south-west of that town. They also form a large part of the Howgill Fells. These in turn graduate downward into the Coniston Grits and Flags, which consist of 7000 feet of alternations of tough micaceous grits and rudely-cleaved mudstones,—the whole mass tending near its base to pass into finely-striped and cleaved mudstones, the Coniston Flags. The tough and durable nature of the harder beds of this series gives rise to a series of mammillated hills. All the rocks of the series here referred to give rise to a type of scenery different in many essential respects from that resulting from the waste of any other rocks in Westmorland, so that the hill scenery south of a line joining Ambleside and Shap Wells is distinctly different from that to the north of that line. Near their base the argillaceous members of the series graduate downwards into a few hundred feet of pale grey-green mudstone, with a peculiar porcellanous texture; and these, in their turn, graduate downwards into a small thickness of pitch-black mudstones, with much the general character of indurated fuller's earth, and usually crowded with graptolites having the general facies of those elsewhere found in the Llandeilo rocks. The pale grey beds are the Stockdale Beds, or "pale slates." The Graptolitic Mudstones locally have at their base a conglomerate, which consists of rolled fragments of rocks from various horizons in the older series. In general terms these two groups of rocks may be described as occurring along a narrow outcrop extending from near Ambleside to Shap Wells. They reappear also near Dufton and at Cautla. In Westmorland the Llandovery beds of Wales appear to be absent, as the rocks next older than the Graptolitic Mudstones consist of rocks characterized by fossils of an unmistakably Bala type. The Westmorland type of these rocks consists of a mass of alternations of volcanic tuffs and lavas, with the marine equivalents of these, and with limestones and shales, the whole series thinning as it is traced toward the centre of the Lake District near the head of Windermere. The Coniston Limestone is the best known member of this series. The series as a whole, however, finds its best and most fully-developed representatives outside the area of old subaerial volcanic cones and craters on whose surface the Coniston Limestone lies. The calcareous members of this series are usually replete with well-preserved fossils in great variety. The series under notice forms some conspicuous features along the foot of the Cross Fell escarpment. Rising from beneath these series just mentioned comes the vast pile of old volcanic ejectamenta, largely subaerial in the typical district, which is known as the Borradale Volcanic Series (see CUMBERLAND). Outside the massif of the Lake District we meet with the submarine equivalents of these subaerial accumulations. These are well seen at Milburn. They consist of many thousands of feet of alternations of submarine tuffs, with shales and mudstones, seemingly identical in character with the Skiddaw Slates, which in the centre of the Lake District mainly lie at the base of the volcanic rocks. The next type may be described as a

[1] These will be found described in detail in the *Trans. Cumb. and West. Assoc.*, part vii. pp. 163–177.

vast pile of old marine sedimentary accumulations, ten or more thousand feet in total thickness, and mainly consisting of alternations of indurated shales, mudstones, and flags, with subordinate beds of grit. This is the Skiddaw Slate, which may be conveniently examined on and around Murton Pike, near Appleby. The same general type of strata prevails over a very wide area. The bottom of these rocks has never been reached. The principal areas of metamorphic rocks in Westmorland are situated in the volcanic area. Rocks more or less altered by deep-seated action occur also around the Shap Granite. The alteration of the volcanic rocks here takes the form of an approach to the mineral characters of granite; but there is no passage from the one to the other. The sedimentary rocks are altered also, more or less, but in a different way: the calcareous beds are developed into idocrase rocks, the cleavage in the Coniston Flags is sealed or welded up anew, while the grits are rendered more or less quartzitic.

Amongst the plutonic rocks the chief is the well-known granitic porphyry, fragments of which occur in the Upper Old Red near Shap. There are many intrudes of diorite, gabbro, felsite, mica trap, and the like,—all Post-Silurian and Pre-Carboniferous in age. Another well-known plutonic rock, of later date than the Carboniferous period, is the Whin Sill, an intrusive sheet of dolerite, which has eaten its way into the Carboniferous rocks over hundreds of square miles in the north of England. It forms the most characteristic feature of the sombre and gloomy fell-side recess known as "High Cup Gill," or Haikable, near Appleby; and it also forms the waterfall known as Caldron Snout. It is the newest intrusive rock known in Westmorland.

The whole county is traversed in many directions by great numbers of faults. One set, the Pennine faults, call for a brief notice here. Two lines of disturbance continued northward from the Craven faults enter the county east of Kirkby Lonsdale. One ranges north-north-eastwards, on the east of the Barbon Fells, and lets in the Carboniferous rocks forming Gragreth, throwing down about 2000 feet on the east; it ranges by Dent, and east of Sedbergh, entering the county again in the valley between Clouds and the Ravenstonedale Fells. Here its effects are as strikingly exhibited as at Gragreth, as the Millstone Grit summit of Wilbert Fell on one side of the fault is let down to the same level as the summits of the Silurian hills on the other. The second set of faults referred to throws down in the opposite direction, letting down the Millstone Grit, the Yoredale Rocks, the Mountain Limestone, and finally, as its throw diminishes, the Old Red, against the foot of the Silurian massif of the Barbon Fells. This fault ranges parallel to the general course of the Lune nearly as far northward as Sedbergh, where it is joined by another set ranging east-north-east, which joins the set first described as ranging north-north-east to Ravenstonedale at a point near the county boundary north of Cautla. Thence the conjoined faults run northward in a very complex manner, producing some important effects upon the scenery about the foot of Mallerstang. Near Kirkby Stephen its throw changes from a downthrow to the east to one in the opposite direction, which throw increases rapidly in amount as the faults trend northwards, until at the foot of Stainmoor, below Barras, its throw amounts to quite 6000 feet down to the west; and we find the important patch of Coal-Measures above noticed let down in consequence. At this point it changes in direction, running north-westerly, with many complications, past Brough, Helton, Dufton, and Milburn, out of the county at the foot of Cross Fell. Along this line it throws down to the south-west several thousands of feet; and it is to the complicated disturbances accompanying this great dislocation that nearly the whole of the more striking physical features of North Westmorland owe their origin. It is in connexion with the same important sets of disturbances also that the existence of most of the mineral veins of the district is due.

Climate.—The rainfall is exceptionally heavy. The largest quantity recorded appears to be that in the mountains along the county boundary west of Grasmere, where the mean amounts to as much as 140 inches. At Sty Head the rainfall in 1872 amounted to 243·98 inches. The area of greatest rainfall forms a rude ellipsoid around these two places, lying with its longest dimensions towards the south-east, nearly coinciding with the distribution of land above 1500 feet. The heaviest precipitation takes place in the months of January, September, and October, and the smallest in July. At Grasmere, well in the heart of the mountains, but farther east, and at a much lower elevation, the mean rainfall for the past twenty years has been 80 inches, rain of ·01 inch or more falling on about 210 days of the year. Between Grasmere and Shap the rainfall diminishes somewhat in the mountain areas. But in the lower ground still farther east the rainfall steadily but more rapidly diminishes, until at Milburn (644 feet) the mean for the last ten years has been about 33 inches on 175 days in the year. At Kendal the mean appears to be about 50 inches, and the number of wet days about 190 in the year; at Kirkby Lonsdale it is rather less, and at Kirkby Stephen less again. The mean temperature for January is between 38° and 39° F., February 40°–41°, March 41°–42°, April 46°–47°, May 51°, June 58°, July 60°–61°, August 60°, September 56°, October 49°, November 42°, and December 38°–40°. The principal characteristic of the climate is the preponderance of cloudy, wet, and cold days, especially in the spring and the autumn,—combining to retard the growth of vegetation. The late stay of cold winds in the spring has much to do with the same, especially in the lowlands extending along the foot of the Cross Fell escarpment from Brough north-westwards. Here, for weeks at a time, prevails a kind of cyclone revolving on a horizontal axis parallel to the escarpment,—the "helm-wind." The remarkable feature connected with it is that, when the wind is rushing furiously from the slopes of the escarpment in the direction of the low grounds, little movement of the air can be detected on the summit.

Flora and Fauna.—Among the denizens of the mountains are several plants distinctly alpine in character; and others, more or less boreal in their principal stations, are here found at nearly their southernmost point of distribution. Bog plants are also conspicuous in their variety, and include several forms of some rarity. The lichens, mosses, and ferns are well represented. Of trees the oak and the common elm do not seem quite at home anywhere except in the more sheltered nooks, and in parks and other cultivated places. But the place of the common elm is well supplied by the wych elm, which grows to great perfection. In place of the oak the sycamore is seen almost everywhere in the lower lands; and there are probably few parts of England where the ash thrives so well, or attains to so large dimensions. On the higher lands, up to the upper limit of woodland growth, the birch, the hazel, and the mountain ash, and, in limestone districts especially, the yew are the prevailing trees. The alder is abundant, and willows of various kinds occur. The upland character of the region affects also its fauna. The badger, the polecat, and perhaps even the wild cat are still met with in Westmorland. The lineal descendants of the wild red deer range over a carefully-preserved remnant of the primeval forest in more than one place. The raven, the peregrine, and the buzzard may still be seen, and the moors sustain a considerable variety of birds other than grouse. The whistle of the golden plover and the note of the curlew are intimately associated with the scenery of the moory uplands. In the lowlands the avifauna is characterized rather by the absence of many forms common in the south than by the presence of birds elsewhere rare. The ornithologist cannot, however, help being struck with the comparative abundance of the redstart, the woodwren, and the grasshopper warbler, none of them very common in other parts of England.

Minerals.—Coal, the most important mineral product, occurs in connexion with the Carboniferous rocks, but most of the seams are thin and their quality is inferior, so that they have long ceased to have the industrial importance they once possessed. Fireclays of excellent quality and of unusual thickness occur with the coals at Argill, but have not hitherto been turned to industrial account. Amongst the building-stones those of the New Red certainly deserve the first rank. The warm-tinted, easily-worked, and durable Penrith Sandstone furnishes one of the finest building-stones in the kingdom; while the associated Brockrams are in their own way hardly less valuable; and the same may be said of the St Bees Sandstone, whence the materials used on so many of the larger public buildings of the northern part of the county have been derived. The Carboniferous rocks nearly everywhere furnish durable freestones and good flags. The Silurian rocks likewise yield building-stones, but somewhat difficult to work. Some of the thinner beds of Carboniferous sandstone are occasionally quarried for roofing purposes. The Coniston Flags are quarried at several places on the south side of the county; while in the north-western parts cleaved beds of volcanic ash, belonging to the Borradale Series, have long furnished an ample supply of the well-known "green slates." Amongst stones available for ornamental purposes the Shap granite-porphyry is undoubtedly the finest, as its choice for decorative purposes in our large cities has shown abundantly. In the way of marbles there are the bituminous limestones at the base of the Yoredale Rocks, and the encrinital limestones nearer their top, both much appreciated; while among limestones of different character there are the mottled and variegated limestones of several places in the neighbourhood of Kendal in the southern and of Asby in the northern parts of the county. Well-chosen specimens of Brockram have a pleasing effect when polished. Gypsum is worked extensively in the New Red rocks in the neighbourhood of Kirkby Thore and Temple Sowerby. Amongst the ores of the useful metals those of lead are of prime importance. The rich lodes of Greenside mines were until lately reckoned amongst the finest of their kind in the United Kingdom, and they have also supplied considerable quantities of silver, which has been extracted from the lead. These were worked in the volcanic rocks. Copper and zinc ores also occur in small quantities. Hæmatite has been discovered here and there at many points, especially where calcareous strata have been affected by infiltration from the New Red rocks.[1]

[1] For other minerals of Westmorland, the interest of which is chiefly scientific, see *Trans. Cumb. and West. Assoc.*, Nos. 7, 8, and 9.

Agriculture.—According to the Agricultural Returns for 1887 the total extent of green crops was 10,232 acres; of corn crops, 19,124, whereof 17,320 were of oats, and only 469 of wheat, and 118 of rye; seed-grasses, 14,951; and 207,017 acres of permanent pasture. The total number of horses is given as 8547; of cows and heifers in milk or in calf, 24,097; of other cattle, 39,225; of sheep, 334,978; and of pigs, 4731. There were 59 holdings of less than an acre; 495 of from 1 to 5 acres; 792 of from 5 to 20; 819 of from 20 to 50; 790 of from 50 to 100; 641 from 100 to 300; 64 from 300 to 500; 31 from 500 to 1000; and 3 holdings of above 1000 acres. The total number of owners is stated in the *Return of Owners of Land*, 1873, as 4376; the extent of lands held by them was 335,160 acres, with a gross estimated rental of £442,320, while 114,282 acres were commons or waste land. Seven proprietors then owned more than 5000 acres each:—earl of Lonsdale, 39,229; Sir H. J. Tufton, 16,094; marquis of Headfort, 12,851; Hon. Mary Howard, 8868; W. Wilson, 8690; G. E. Wilson, 7630; W. H. Wakefield, 5584. A large part of Westmorland was formerly in the hands of what are called "statesmen," whose holdings were usually of small extent, but were sufficient, with careful management, for the respectable maintenance of themselves and their families. The proportion of landowners of this class is now, however, comparatively small. The meadow-land yields grass of first-rate quality. Grass of inferior value characterizes the pasture-lands; while on the fell (or unenclosed) land, except in limestone areas, the herbage consists chiefly of the coarser kinds of grass, bents, and heather. These, however, furnish nourishment for the hardier breeds of sheep, which are pastured there in large numbers. It is from the sale of these, of their stock cattle, horses, and pigs, and of their dairy produce that the staple of the farmers' income is derived.

Manufactures.—The manufacturing industries, owing to the absence of any large supplies of native fuel, are not numerous. The principal is woollen manufacture in one form or another, and this is chiefly confined to the low country in and near Kendal. Bobbin-making, fulling, snuff-grinding, and several small industries are carried on at a profit, owing to the water-power available at so many points. Paper-making is also carried on.

Administration.—There are five lieutenancy subdivisions, and two police divisions. There are 109 civil parishes in the county. It is in the diocese of Carlisle, is in the York military district, and forms part of the northern circuit. There is one court of quarter sessions for the county, and five petty sessional divisions. The assizes are now held at Carlisle. The principal town is Kendal, which had in 1881 a population of 13,696. Other towns, all much less important as regards both size and population, are Appleby, Kirkby Lonsdale, Bowness, Kirkby Stephen, Ambleside, Shap, and Orton. The county sends two members to parliament, representing the Northern (or Appleby) and the Southern (or Kendal) Divisions respectively.

Population.—According to the census of 1881 there were 64,191 inhabitants (31,515 males, 32,676 females), the decrease since 1871 being 819. The proportion of population to acreage is 1 person to 7·80 acres. The people of Westmorland may be described as a prevalently tall, wiry, long-armed, big-handed, dark-grey-eyed, fresh-coloured race. In disposition they are a cautious, reserved, staid, matter-of-fact, sober-minded, unemotional race, somewhat slow-witted, but not by any means dull, and are thrifty beyond measure. The general character of the dialects of Westmorland is that of a basis of Anglian speech, influenced to a certain extent by the speech current amongst the non-Anglian peoples of Strathclyde. This is overlain to a much greater though variable extent by the more decidedly Scandinavian forms of speech introduced at various periods between the 10th and the 12th centuries. Three well-marked dialects can be made out.

Antiquities and History.—Amongst the oldest monuments of Westmorland are the circular earthworks called King Arthur's Round Table and Maybrough, both close to Penrith. Barrows and tumuli are common in the wilder parts of the county, more especially along the limestone hills near Orton. Traces of earthworks, regarded as Celtic, occur near Crosby Ravensworth, and at a few other places. Rude stone circles and other structures of the same nature exist at several places between Ravenstonedale and Shap. Stone implements of the Neolithic type and implements of bronze have been found all over the county. Cup-marked stones have been noticed near Penrith. At Brough church was found a slab bearing an inscription variously regarded as Greek, or Celtic, or Scandinavian. Well-marked traces of the occupation of the county by the Romans exist in their roads, their camps, their altars, and their coins. Monuments of later date, prior to the reign of Rufus, are exceedingly rare, and are chiefly confined to objects of an ecclesiastical character, which mostly owe their preservation to their having been worked up as building material in some of the older churches. Good examples are to be found at Kirkby Stephen, Long Marton, Bongate, and other churches. Vestiges of late Norman work, rarely earlier than 12th century, are preserved in several of the churches, and in a few of the castles. In the case of the castles especially it is evident that their sites had been used as strongholds through a long succession of periods, extending in some cases far back into prehistoric times. From the 12th century downward each period of the history of Westmorland may be said to be fairly well represented. (J. G. G.*)

WESTON-SUPER-MARE, a watering-place of Somerset, England, is situated at the northern extremity of Uphill Bay, a recess of the Bristol Channel, and on a branch of the Great Western Railway, 138½ miles from London, 20 south-west of Bristol, and 20 north-west of Wells. It is built partly on level ground near the shore, and partly on the slopes of Worlebury Hill, which aids in sheltering it from the north and east. On this account, as well as from its bracing and dry air, it has won considerable favour both as a winter residence and as a summer resort. Many villas have been built in it by persons engaged in business in Bristol. An esplanade about 3 miles in length has been constructed at a cost of £30,000. The pier, which altogether is 1040 feet in length, and includes the rocky island of Birnbeck, is north from the town at the extreme end of Worlebury Hill, where also are the Prince Consort promenade gardens. The church of St John, built in 1824, mostly on the site of the old one, contains some old monuments. The other principal public buildings are the town-hall in the Venetian style, the assembly rooms, the market-house, the Weston county club, the church institute, the hospital and dispensary, and the West of England sanatorium, which since its enlargement in 1882 contains 100 beds. The town has been long famed for its potteries. The population of the urban sanitary district (area 2770 acres) in 1871 was 10,568, and in 1881 it was 12,884.

The town was included in an ancient British settlement, of which Worlebury Hill was the citadel. The ramparts of this fortress still remain, including a number of hut circles, beneath which skeletons and Celtic remains have been found. In Domesday Westone is described as held by the bishop. In the time of Edward the Confessor it was held by Algar. In 1696 it was purchased by the Pigotts, the present lords of the manor. The growth of the town is entirely modern. About the beginning of the century it consisted of about twenty-four cottages inhabited by fishermen. A hotel for the reception of visitors was erected in 1805, and an esplanade begun in 1825, since which time it has made rapid progress.

WESTPHALIA (Germ. *Westfalen*), a province in the west of Prussia, is bounded on the N. by the province of Hanover, on the E. by the province of Hanover, the principalities of Lippe-Detmold and Schaumburg-Lippe, the duchy of Brunswick, the province of Hesse, and the principality of Waldeck, on the S.W. by Rhenish Prussia, and on the N.W. by Holland. Its greatest length from north to south is 110 miles, its greatest breadth is 124 miles, and its total area is 7800 square miles.

The Lippe, an affluent of the Rhine, flowing from east to west across the province, divides it into two parts, dissimilar in their character. The northern portion, a continuation of the plain of the Netherlands, is flat, with the exception of the east, which is occupied by the Weser Hills. South of the Lippe, on the other hand, the province is occupied by numerous small chains and groups of hills, enclosing many beautiful valleys. Between the parallel courses of the Lippe and Ruhr stretches the low chain of the Haar or Haarstrang (850–1050 feet), which is steep on its southern face, but slopes gradually down on the north to the valley of the Lippe, known as the Hellweg. The rugged mountain district south of the Ruhr is known as the Sauerland, and its eastern portion, the plateau of Winterberg, is the highest part of the province. The culminating point is the Astenberg (2760 feet). This plateau is connected with the Westerwald on the south-west border by the Rothhaar or Rothlagergebirge. Westphalia is divided between the basins of the Rhine, Ems, and Weser. The Rhine itself does not touch Westphalia, but its affluents, the Lippe and Ruhr, are the leading

WEST VIRGINIA

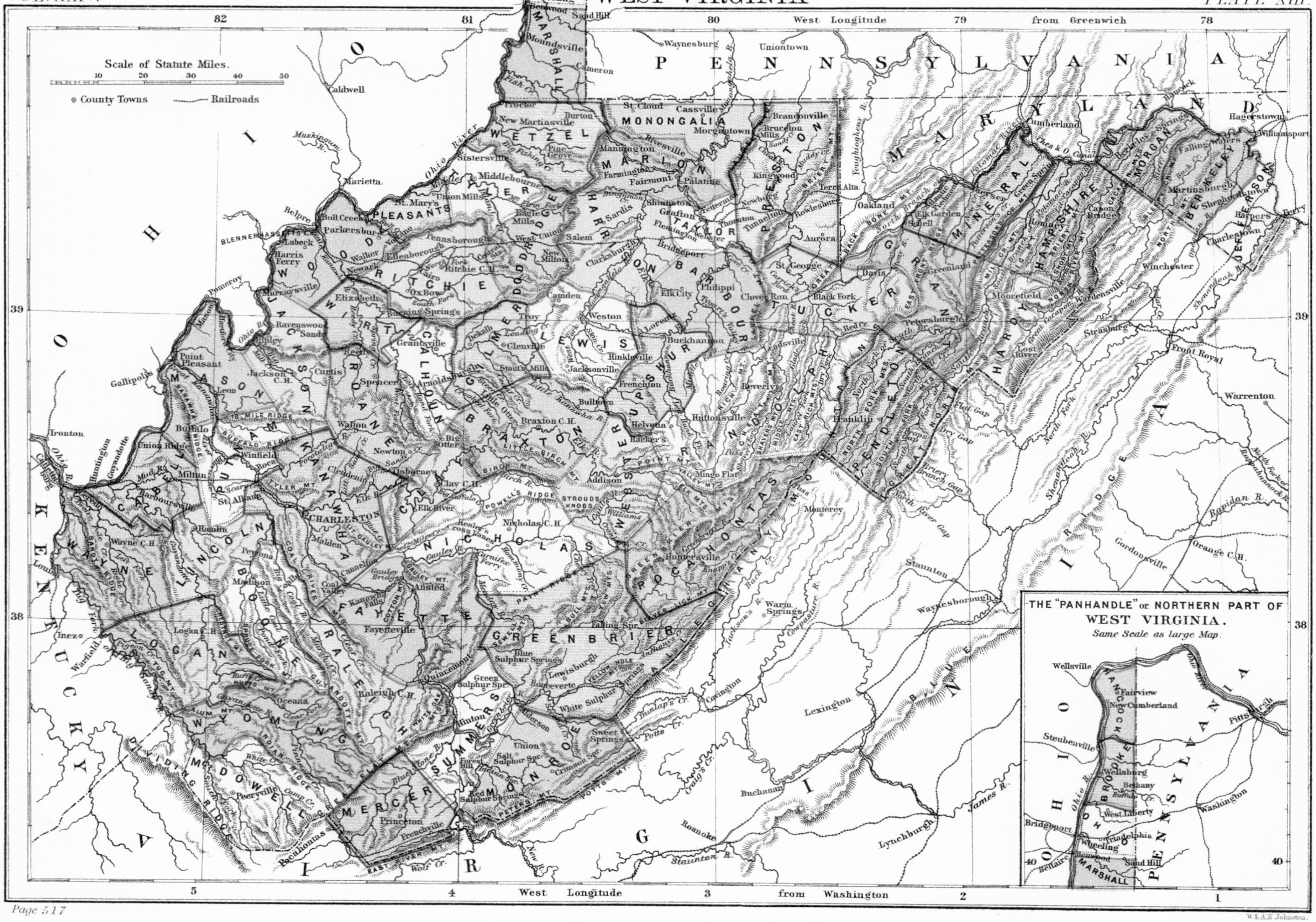

82 81 80 West Longitude 79 from Greenwich 78

Scale of Statute Miles.
10 20 30 40 50

◎ County Towns —— Railroads

O H I O

P E N N S Y L V A N I A

M A R Y L A N D

V I R G I N I A

K E N T U C K Y

MARSHALL
WETZEL
MONONGALIA
PRESTON
MARION
TAYLOR
TYLER
PLEASANTS
DODDRIDGE
HARRISON
BARBOUR
TUCKER
WOOD
RITCHIE
WIRT
JACKSON
MASON
ROANE
CALHOUN
GILMER
LEWIS
UPSHUR
RANDOLPH
BRAXTON
PUTNAM
KANAWHA
CLAY
NICHOLAS
WEBSTER
POCAHONTAS
CABELL
WAYNE
LINCOLN
BOONE
FAYETTE
GREENBRIER
LOGAN
RALEIGH
WYOMING
McDOWELL
MERCER
SUMMERS
MONROE
MINERAL
HAMPSHIRE
HARDY
GRANT
PENDLETON
MORGAN
BERKELEY
JEFFERSON

Wheeling
Moundsville
Parkersburg
Charleston
Point Pleasant
Huntington
Morgantown
Fairmont
Clarksburg
Grafton
Martinsburg
Charlestown
Romney
Moorefield
Franklin
Beverly
Lewisburg
Union
Princeton
Fayetteville
Logan C.H.
Wayne C.H.

39 38

THE "PANHANDLE" or NORTHERN PART OF
WEST VIRGINIA.
Same Scale as large Map.

HANCOCK
BROOKE
OHIO
MARSHALL
Wellsville
Fairview
New Cumberland
Steubenville
Wellsburg
Bethany
West Liberty
Bridgeport
Wheeling
Triadelphia
Benwood
Sand Hill
Bellaire
Pittsburgh
Washington
PENNSYLVANIA
OHIO
40

5 4 West Longitude 3 from Washington 2 1

W. & A.K. Johnston.

streams in the province. The Ems, entering Westphalia from Lippe, flows north-west and enters Hanover. The Weser crosses the north-east of the province, piercing the Weser Hills by means of the narrow pass known as the Porta Westphalica or Westphalian Gate. All these streams are navigable for barges and small vessels. There are no lakes in the province. The climate is on the whole temperate, though sometimes the winters are severe among the mountains.

About 42 per cent. of the surface is given up to agriculture, 25 per cent. to pastures and moors; 28 per cent. is under wood; and the remainder is unproductive. The fertility of the soil varies; it is most unfertile in the north and north-east. A great proportion of the land is in the hands of small farmers and peasant proprietors, who as a class are well-to-do, though their system of farming is in some respects antiquated. Grain of various kinds is grown, though not in sufficient quantity to meet the demands of the province; potatoes, pease and beans, fruit, and tobacco are also produced; but perhaps the most important crops are hemp and flax, which places Westphalia among the leading flax-producing districts of Germany. The forests are chiefly on the mountains of the Sauerland, and in the south generally. Considerable numbers of cattle and pigs are reared, the latter yielding the well-known Westphalian hams; goats are also numerous in some districts; and Government pays some attention to the breeding of horses in this province. Sheep are comparatively few. (Compare the agricultural statistics under PRUSSIA.)

In virtue of its abundant coal and iron Westphalia is one of the busiest industrial quarters of Germany. There are coal-fields in the north and in other districts, and the great coal-field of the Ruhr extends into the province. The district of Arnsberg, occupying the south of the province, is the centre of the mineral industry. Dortmund gives name to one of the five mining districts into which Prussia is officially divided. Westphalia produces more iron ore than any other province in Prussia except the Rhine province and Silesia; next to Silesia it produces the most zinc, and next to Saxony the most copper; and it yields more sulphur than any other province. Argentiferous lead, antimony, limestone, gypsum, marble, and slates are also worked. There are seven salt-works and numerous mineral springs.

The mineral wealth of the province encourages an extensive manufacturing industry, the leading branches of which are linen-weaving and iron-working. The linen industry is very ancient, and since the 14th century has flourished in this province between the Lippe and Weser. Its chief centre is now Bielefeld, which also manufactures jute. The cotton factories of Münster are important. Woollens, stockings, and ribbons are also manufactured to some extent. The principal seats of the metallic industries are Iserlohn, Lüdenscheid, Altena, Hagen, and the "Enneper Strasse," a valley 7 miles long and three quarters of a mile wide, lying along the Ennepe and containing as its chief towns Haspe (7318 inhabitants) and Gevelsberg (7055). Cast and wrought iron, steel, rails, wire, blades and tools, machinery and small iron and steel goods, bronze, brass, and plated articles are among the leading products. Vitriol, glass, and paper are also made. An active trade is carried on in the manufactured goods, and in timber, hams, and sausages. The leading commercial towns are Bielefeld, Iserlohn, and Dortmund. Minden has a port on the Weser; Beverungen is the centre of the corn trade; and Paderborn is the chief wool-market. The roads are good, and the railways numerous and convenient.

The population in 1885 was 2,202,726, or 282 per square mile. About 52 per cent. are Roman Catholics, most of whom are found in the southern district of Arnsberg. About 46½ per cent. are Protestants, the remainder are Jews and others. Education is well attended to. The seat of government is at Münster; and the province is divided into the three districts of Minden, Münster, and Arnsberg. It has thirty-one members in the Prussian parliament, and seventeen in the imperial diet.

Westphalia was the name given to the western portion of the early duchy of SAXONY (vol. xxi. p. 351). When Henry the Lion fell under the ban of the empire his Saxon domains were distributed by the emperor. The Sauerland and some other parts of Westphalia fell to the archbishops of Cologne, who afterwards received from Frederick Barbarossa the title of dukes of Westphalia and Angria. The northern portion of the original Westphalia became the nucleus of the circle of Westphalia in Maximilian's administrative organization of the empire, while the duchy of Westphalia, as an apanage of Cologne, was included in the scattered circle of the Lower Rhine. The circle of Westphalia embraced, roughly speaking, what is now Oldenburg, Hanover to the west of the Weser, the districts of Münster and Minden, and a few other territories, an area of about 27,000 square miles, which in Maximilian's time was divided among four bishoprics and innumerable small secular states with an aggregate population of about 3,000,000. The peace of Lunéville in 1801 transferred all parts of this circle west of the Rhine to France, while in 1803 the duchy of Westphalia was granted to the duke of Hesse-Nassau as compensation for his former possessions to the west of the Rhine, which had also been added to France.

In 1807 Napoleon constituted the kingdom of Westphalia and gave it to his youngest brother Jerome. It comprised all the Prussian provinces as far east as the Elbe, and extended south to Fulda and the Thuringian states, embracing an area of about 14,880 square miles, with a population of 2,000,000. Nearly the whole of Hanover was added to this kingdom in 1810; but next year Napoleon again took away the greater part, as well as other territories, leaving, however, 17,740 square miles, with 2,057,000 inhabitants. This kingdom was intended to take the lead in the Confederation of the Rhine. After the battle of Leipsic in 1813 the kingdom of Westphalia was abolished, and things reverted to their previous order until the congress of Vienna rearranged the map of Europe, when Westphalia as we now understand the term was assigned to Prussia.

The peace of Westphalia, concluded in 1648 at Osnabrück and Münster, put an end to the Thirty Years' War (see GERMANY, vol. x. p. 501).

WEST POINT, the seat of the United States military academy, on the Hudson, in Orange county, New York. See ARMY, vol. ii. p. 619.

WEST TROY, a village of Albany county, New York, United States, is situated in the bottom-land on the west bank of the Hudson, opposite Troy, with which it is connected by an iron bridge, and 5 miles north of Albany. It is at the termini of the Erie and Champlain Canals, and is on a railroad line of the Delaware and Hudson Canal Company. The village is well laid out, has water and gas, is provided with street cars, and has extensive manufactures of a varied character, but particularly of iron. The Watervliet (United States) arsenal is situated here. The population, 10,693 in 1870, was 8820 (2427 of foreign birth) in 1880.

WEST VIRGINIA, one of the North-Eastern Central States of the American Union, lying between 37° 6′ and 40° 38′ N. lat., is bounded on the N. by Pennsylvania and Maryland, on the E. and S. by Virginia, and on the W. by Kentucky and Ohio, and has an area of 24,780 square miles.

The form of the State is extremely irregular. It may be roughly likened to an ellipse, the greatest diameter of which lies nearly north-east and south-west. Its boundary upon the east and south is made up of the irregular line which limited the counties which were set off from Virginia for the formation of this State. Upon the west the boundary is low-water upon the further shore of the Big Sandy and Ohio rivers. A long narrow strip, known as the "Panhandle," projects northward some sixty miles along the Ohio,—the boundary being the continuation of the straight line which separates Ohio and Pennsylvania. To the east of this the northern boundary follows Mason and Dixon's line; then, dropping in a due south direction to the "Fairfax Stone," it follows thence easterly the course of the Potomac to its junction with the Shenandoah.

The entire State is mountainous or hilly, being comprised within the region known as the Cumberland or Alleghany plateau. The highest land in the State is upon the eastern and southern boundary, where the plateau in many places reaches elevations exceeding 4000 feet. Thence the country has a general slope to the north-west, and is lowest along the Ohio, where the elevation is but 600 to 800 feet. This plateau has been subjected to stream erosion until it has become a network of narrow crooked ridges with deep gorges or narrow valleys. The height of the ridges and the depth of the valleys, together with the ruggedness of the country, diminish towards the north-west, until near the Ohio the hills become rounded and softened in outline, and the valleys are broad and fertile.

The drainage system of the State is in some respects peculiar. Although the general slope is towards the north-west, the Potomac, which flows south-easterly to the Atlantic Ocean, has cut its way far back into the plateau, and drains, by means of numerous long branches, the north-eastern quarter of the State. The remainder of the State is drained to the Ohio by means of several large branches which flow in a general north-westerly direction. Heading in the south-west is the Big Sandy, forming a portion of the State boundary. Fourteen miles above its mouth enters the Guyandotte, and 50 miles above the Guyandotte comes the Great Kanawha, one of the principal branches of the Ohio. This large and powerful stream has cut its way back beyond the crest-line of the plateau, tapping numerous streams in south-west Virginia and western North Carolina, so that its sources are now against the Blue Ridge in the latter State. It is known in North Carolina and Virginia, and in West Virginia to the Great Falls, by the name of New River. In West Virginia it has numerous large tributaries—the Big and Little Coal rivers, Piney, and Bluestone from the south, and the Pocotaligo, Elk, Gauley, and Greenbrier from the north. The next branch of the Ohio, proceeding northward, is the Little Kanawha, which empties into the Ohio at Parkersburg. The north-western part of the State is drained by the Monongahela, one of the two head branches of the Ohio, and its tributaries, the principal of which are the Tygart's Valley, Cheat, and Buckhannon rivers. Of these streams the Ohio is navigable for river steamers at nearly all stages of water. The same may be said of the Kanawha to a point near the Kanawha Falls, while the Big Sandy, the Guyandotte, and the Monongahela are navigable for flat boats for long distances, and these, as well as numerous other streams, are largely used for the floating of lumber. All the streams of the State, and especially the smaller ones, have a rapid fall, but their enormous water-power has as yet been utilized only to a trifling extent.

Climate. The climate is nowhere severe, although, owing to the range in elevation within the State, there is a considerable range in temperature. The mean annual temperature ranges from 54° to 55° F., being highest in the neighbourhood of the Ohio, in the western part of the State, and lowest upon the high mountains in the eastern and north-eastern portion. The maximum is rarely above 95° in any portion of the State, while the minimum occasionally reaches 10° in the more mountainous section. The rainfall may be given broadly at between 40 and 50 inches annually. It also varies with the elevation, being less in the lower portions and greatest upon the high mountains.

Fauna. The fauna of the State is that common to the whole southern Appalachian region. Much of the area being as yet in a state of nature, deer of the white-tailed species are still abundant, and black bear are not unfrequently met with in the more rugged and remote portions. Wild turkeys are still found in some localities, and the mountains have long been a popular resort for hunters, while the streams, abounding in trout, afford an equally attractive field for the angler.

Timber. The timber resources of the State are enormous, and a small proportion of its area, amounting to only about 25 per cent., has been cleared. The remainder is covered with virgin forest. This consists mainly of broad-leafed trees of the most valuable sorts for lumber, such as chestnut, black walnut, cherry, ash, poplar, hickory, locust, maple, oak, &c. Considerable areas of white pine are found in the highest portions of the plateau, being practically the only original forests of this wood left in the United States. Besides these there are considerable quantities of yellow pine, hemlock, spruce, and cedar scattered through the State.

Minerals. Viewed broadly, the geological structure of West Virginia is extremely simple. Practically the entire State is overlaid by nearly horizontal beds of the Carboniferous formation. The coal of West Virginia forms its principal mineral wealth. It is estimated that of its entire area not less than 16,000 square miles are underlaid by workable beds of coal. The *Report* of the United States Geological Survey upon mineral resources defines the general boundaries of the coal fields of the State as follows :—"The eastern boundary begins at the south on the mountain range just east of the Bluestone River, and proceeds east to Little Sewell Mountain ; . . . . . thence with the common boundary of Nicholas and Greenbrier and of Webster and Pocahontas counties to Rich Mountain in Randolph county; following this last-named ridge to Laurel Mountain, the dividing line between Upshur county on the west and Randolph and Barbour counties on the east, and thence with the Briery Mountain into Preston county, and so on to the Pennsylvania State line." All the area to the west of this line is underlain by coal. To the east of it there are small outlying patches, as in Greenbrier, Meadow Mountain, and possibly in Pocahontas, Tucker, Grant, and Mineral counties, but these are unimportant as compared with the vast areas in the west. In the gorge of every large stream flowing through this area are seen outcropping beds of coal, easily accessible to the miner, and requiring only facilities of transportation to render the mineral of commercial value. In the matter of coal production the State is rapidly acquiring prominence. From a production in 1873 of 600,000 tons, it reached in 1886 a production of over 4,000,000 tons, being exceeded by only four of the States, viz., Pennsylvania, Illinois, Ohio, and Iowa. The production is limited only by the demand, as the supply is almost inexhaustible. The coals of the State are of every variety except anthracite, and are noted for their purity for coking, steam, and gas purposes and for domestic fuel.

Iron ore is abundant in various portions of the State, but is worked only to a comparatively limited extent.

Mineral springs. Salt springs are found in the valley of the Kanawha and in that of the Ohio, and there are extensive evaporating works in both these localities. The production, however, has been retarded by the competition of those in Michigan, owing to the greater cheapness of fuel and better facilities for transportation in the latter locality. The production of salt in West Virginia in 1886 amounted to 250,000 barrels. West Virginia contains numerous valuable mineral springs, among the best known of which are the Greenbrier White Sulphur springs in Greenbrier county, Capon springs in Hampshire county, Irondale springs in Preston county, and Red Sulphur springs and Salt Sulphur springs both in Monroe county. These are well-known and popular summer resorts in the mountains, and the waters from them are shipped to all parts of the United States.

Agriculture. While the entire State may be said to be either mountainous or hilly, it contains a large extent of arable land. Nearly all of the lower hill country can be cultivated, while in the mountainous region there are numerous broad valleys of excellent soil, and everywhere the hill and mountain sides can be cultivated if the slope is not excessively steep. The tenth census (1880) reported an area of 10,193,779 acres of land in farms, of which 3,792,327 acres, or about one-fourth the area of the State, was improved land, this being mainly in the lower and less mountainous portion. The average size of farms was 163 acres, showing as compared with the average 10 years earlier, viz., 214 acres, a decided decrease. The value of farms and farming implements was very nearly $136,000,000. The numbers of live stock upon farms, as distinguished from animals owned for business purposes in cities, consisted in January 1888 of 138,231 horses, 6475 mules, 474,933 sheep, 432,778 hogs, 171,273 milch cows, and 780,892 other cattle,—showing that the live-stock interests of the State are very large. The estimated value of all farm products sold, consumed, or on hand, as returned in 1880, was $19,360,049. The principal agricultural products are wheat, Indian corn, hay, tobacco, oats, and garden vegetables. The cereal products for 1887 consisted of 12,516,000 bushels of corn, 2,840,000 of wheat, and 2,531,000 of oats.

Manufactures. The manufactures, which are not extensive, are concentrated mainly at Wheeling, the largest city, on the Ohio, in the northern part of the State ; they consist mainly of manufactures of iron and steel, glass, flouring and grist mill products, lumber, and leather. There were in 1880 2375 manufacturing establishments, employing a capital of $13,883,390 and 14,351 persons. The value of manufactured products was $22,867,126.

Railways. There are 1200 miles of completed railroads, with several branches and one trunk line in process of construction. The Baltimore and Ohio Railroad traverses the State from Parkersburg and Bellaire on the Ohio, the two branches meeting at Grafton, and running thence eastward to Washington, Baltimore, and New York. The Newport News and Mississippi Valley Railroad runs across the State from the mouth of the Big Sandy on the west to the Alleghanies near White Sulphur springs, and thence extends to Richmond and Newport News. The Ohio River line runs from Wheeling to Huntington on the Ohio. The West Virginia Central extends from Piedmont on the Baltimore and Ohio line to a point in Randolph county, and is now in process of construction south-westward to intersect the Newport News and Mississippi Valley line. The Clarksburg and Weston, intersecting the Baltimore and Ohio at Clarksburg, extends to Weston in Lewis county, and this has two branches, one to Glenville in Gilmer county, and the other to Buckhannon in Upshur county. The Grafton and Greenbrier Railroad, intersecting the Baltimore and Ohio at Grafton, extends up the Valley river to Belington in Barbour county. The Norfolk and Western Railroad, one of the main trunk lines of the Atlantic States, has a part of its lines in the southern portion of

West Virginia. Railway construction is exceedingly active in all parts of the State, several new lines and numerous branches of existing lines being under construction and in contemplation.

Education. The State early in its history (December 1863) adopted a liberal system of free schools. The plan is known as the township or district system,—the magisterial district or subdivison of each county being taken as the unit for taxation, and the general control of all the school interests of the district being placed in the hands of a district board of education elected by the people, and authorized among other duties to levy taxes, to determine the number of months of school and the number of sub-districts, to plant and build schoolhouses, and to manage the financial and other school interests of the districts. There is likewise in each county a superintendent, and in the State a general superintendent. This system has since been maintained and strengthened by legislative enactment till from 133 schoolhouses and 431 public schools of all grades in 1865 there were in 1887 4587 schoolhouses in the State. In 1865 the amount expended in support of free schools was $7722; this gradually increased till in 1887 the amount was $1,087,674. The number of teachers employed by public appropriation was 387 in 1865; in 1887 it was 5106. The estimated value of schoolhouses in the State, 140,000 in 1865, was 2,000,000 in 1887. The average attendance in 1865 was 44 days; in 1887 it was 108. The school system of the State is made permanent by the constitutional enactment referred to, which requires that the legislature shall provide by general law for a thorough and efficient system of free schools. The general school system involves the education of teachers, and with this object from 1867 to 1872 the legislature provided for the establishment of six normal schools, which are in successful operation. In these schools tuition is free to all who desire to prepare themselves for teaching. They are popular among the people, and have done much to elevate the general standard of education. They prescribe courses of three years; nearly all of them have preparatory courses; four of them give collegiate training, and in all of them the study of ancient and modern languages is optional. The school system involves also what is known as the irreducible school fund. The principal, which now amounts to $600,000, is permanently invested. This fund is constantly augmented from sources provided by law and by voluntary contributions.

Public institutions. The United States Government has erected public buildings for its judicial, postal, and revenue departments within the State at Wheeling, Clarksburg, Parkersburg, and Charleston, the capital of the State. While WHEELING (*q.v.*) was temporarily the capital, a building was erected by its citizens for the uses of the State, which is now used for city purposes. The six normal schools already referred to have suitable buildings at Fairmont, Glenville, Huntington, Concord, Shepherdstown, and West Liberty. The hospital for the insane at Weston in Lewis county and a branch asylum in course of construction at Spencer in Roane county, a deaf-mute and blind asylum at Romney in Hampshire county, a penitentiary at Moundsville in Marshall county, and a university supported by the State at Morgantown in Monongalia county may be mentioned among the other public institutions of West Virginia.

Value of property. The assessed valuation of real estate in 1887 amounted to $118,753,342, and that of personal property to $43,710,175; that of railroad property in 1880 was $4,497,030, and in 1887 $22,797,984. The State tax is 30 cents on each hundred dollars of valuation.

Liquor laws. An amendment to the constitution is now pending, by which it is proposed to prohibit the sale or manufacture of intoxicating liquors. At present the laws of the State—and they have been enforced with more or less of modification almost since its foundation —involve the high licence system. The granting of the licence is based in all cases on good character, and is subject to the discretion of the county commissioners. Under the operation of these laws, and by virtue of local sentiment in its enforcement, no licence has been granted (and hence in effect the traffic has been prohibited) in as many as 38 of the 54 counties. The licence is subject to a tax fixed by the State law, and where sales are to be made in incorporated villages it is subject to an additional tax, which is fixed by the authorities of the incorporation.

Population. In 1880 the population of the State was 618,457. That of the principal cities was—Wheeling, 30,737; Parkersburg, 6582; Martinsburg, 6335; Charleston (the State capital), 4192; Grafton, 3030; and Charlestown, 2016. The coloured population numbered 25,886, the foreign-born population 18,265. The increase in population from 1870 to 1880 was 39·9 per cent. The proportion of native whites was 93 per cent. of the whole number of whites, which is larger than that of any other State in the Union. The popular vote at late elections indicates a population of 800,000, and that of Wheeling, Charleston, and Parkersburg is shown by local investigation to have very largely increased.

Administration. The executive power is vested in a governor elected by the people for a term of four years, and ineligible under the constitution for re-election. There are also an auditor, a treasurer, an attorney-general, a secretary of state and State superintendent of free schools, who with the governor constitute a board of public works, and are likewise elected by the people for terms of four years, except the secretary of state and a librarian (who is *ex officio* adjutant-general), who are appointed by the governor. The legislative power is vested in a senate and house of delegates. The senate embraces 26 members, half of whom are elected every alternate two years, for a term of four years. The house of delegates consists of 66 members, who are elected every two years. The legislature meets biennially, and may be convened in extraordinary session by the governor, or by the concurrence of three-fifths of its members. The veto power is vested in the governor, but a majority concurring in each house of the legislature overrides it. The judiciary consists of a supreme court of appeals, with four judges, who in case of their equal division affirm the judgment of the lower court, and of circuit courts, with one judge each, exercising general original power and appellate jurisdiction over magistrates or justices of the peace, and of magistrates and justices of the peace, whose jurisdiction in civil cases is limited to $300, and who exercise criminal jurisdiction in petty offences, and may issue warrants of arrest and make preliminary examination and commit for trial in the circuit court in cases of crime. The fiscal regulations of the counties are confided to a board, consisting of three county commissioners. The county organization consists of these commissioners, a sheriff, deputy sheriffs, a circuit court clerk, a county clerk, who is recorder of deeds, wills, &c., board of education, school trustees, overseers of roads, a commissioner of school lands, an overseer of the poor, and a commissioner of accounts. All these except the deputy sheriffs, commissioner of accounts, commissioner of school lands, and overseer of the poor are elected by the people.

History.—The establishment of West Virginia as a State was consummated on 20th June 1863. Its creation and admission were due to conditions which existed prior to the civil war of 1861–65, to popular sentiment which those conditions developed when the war was precipitated, and to the exigencies of the war itself. The Alleghany Mountains had divided the State of Virginia politically and commercially, and in the sentiment relating to her systems of taxation, revenue, and public expenditure into a Virginia and a "Western" Virginia, long before the civil conflict gave permanent result and fixed an official definition to the line of demarcation between them. Even after the war and the formation of the new State the title to two counties, Jefferson and Berkeley, "lying east of the mountains," was the subject of legislation and contention before the courts. They were in 1870 judicially declared by the supreme court of the United States to be a part of the State of West Virginia. The western part of Virginia was sparsely peopled, its great forests undeveloped, its vast mineral resources only partially realized, and its slave interests comparatively small. The eastern section contained the larger population, owned the great bulk of slave property, and exercised controlling power over State affairs. The Alleghanies, dividing the two sections, in the absence of transverse railroad facilities naturally sent the citizens of one side with the flow of their navigable waters to western and southern markets, while those of the other, moved by similar natural causes, turned to the seaboard for their commercial and business intercourse. The basis of taxation, the basis of representation, and the relation of the slave interests to these, with the measure and distribution of public funds for works of internal improvement and other questions of local concern, constituted elements of continual controversy, and served to detract largely from the homogeneity of the population. Early in January 1861 the legislature of Virginia, in extra session, passed a bill calling a convention of the people to meet in the following month. At the same election the people were to vote on the question whether the separation of Virginia from the Union should be determined by the convention or be submitted by the convention to the people for ratification or rejection. The majority at the election in favour of submitting the question of secession to the people was overwhelming, and was construed as indicating the loyal sentiment of the people of north-western Virginia. On the 17th of April, after the bombardment of Fort Sumter, the convention passed an ordinance of secession, and on the 24th a schedule submitting it to the people. The ordinance of secession was adopted by the people of Virginia, but the majority against it in the north-western part of the State was very large. A convention of the unionist counties, which met at Wheeling in June, adopted an ordinance for the reorganization of the State government, and in August adopted an ordinance providing for the formation of a new State, to be named "Kanawha," comprising thirty-nine specified counties, and to include other counties also named, provided their vote should indicate such desire. Under this provision a number of counties were afterwards added to the original thirty-nine. At the time of the vote upon the proposition to form a new State war was raging throughout its proposed borders, and many of its counties had been the scene of violence and blooodshed. Many citizens were in the field as soldiers on the respective sides, and this fact, coupled with the general conditions, caused a small vote to be polled. Of this comparatively small vote, however, a large majority was for the new State, and members were elected to a constitutional convention. This convention met at Wheeling in November, and formed a constitution for the proposed new State, and designated it the State of West Virginia. This constitution was submitted to the people, and adopted by an overwhelming majority in April 1862. In May the legislature of the "reorganized Government" of Virginia passed a bill to authorize the formation of the new State out of the territory of the old State of Virginia, as indicated by the recently ratified constitution, and in the same month this Act of the Legislature, accompanied by its memorial and a certified copy of the constitution and proceedings by which it had been adopted, was presented to Congress. The subject led to grave discussion in that body, but ultimately the proposed constitution was carried, with but one modification affecting the freedom of children of slaves thereafter to be born within the limits of the new State. A new constitution was adopted in 1872. The State of West Virginia being the result of a double revolution—that of the State of Virginia against the Federal Union and that of her north-western counties against the seceding State of Virginia—its people are conservative and strikingly homogeneous. Even in the throes of revolution declaring separation from the mother State provision was made for the assumption of a just share of the old State debt, though its adjustment has never yet been reached. West Virginia has no other debt. Falling naturally, as did most of the border States, immediately after the war, into violent proscriptions of the returning Confederate element, West Virginia was one of the first of the States to modify and repeal these enactments. By the election of 1870 they were abrogated for ever, and since that time the issues and consequences of war have so far disappeared as to leave no perceptible trace behind. (J. E. K.)

WETSTEIN, JOHN JACOB (1693–1754), New Testament critic, was born at Basel, March 5, 1693. His father, John Rudolph Wetstein, was pastor of St Leonard's in that city, and belonged to a learned family with wide ramifications. John Jacob studied the classics, Hebrew, and mathematics under distinguished professors, amongst whom was one of the Buxtorfs. Theology he studied under Samuel Werenfels, an influential anticipator of modern scientific theology and exegesis. While still a student he began to direct his attention to the special pursuit of his life—the text of the Greek New Testament. A relative, John Wetstein, who was the university librarian, gave him permission to examine and collate the principal MSS. of the New Testament in the library, and he copied the various readings which they contained into his copy of Gerard of Maestricht's edition of the Greek text. In 1713 in his public examination he defended a dissertation entitled *De Variis Novi Testamenti Lectionibus*, and sought to show that variety of readings did not detract from the authority of Sacred Scripture. Wetstein paid great attention also to Syriac and Talmudic Hebrew. In the spring of 1714 he undertook a learned tour, which led him to Paris and England, the great object of his inquiry everywhere being manuscripts of the New Testament. In Paris he examined the *Codex Ephraemi*, and on arriving in England in August 1715 the *Codex Alexandrinus* and the *Codex Bezæ* with many others. Early the next year he made the acquaintance of Bentley at Cambridge, who took great interest in his textual inquiries. The great scholar induced him to return to Paris to collate for him more carefully the *Codex Ephraemi*, Bentley having then in view a critical edition of the New Testament. In July 1717 Wetstein returned to Basel to take the office of a curate at large in his native city, a post which he held for three years, at the expiration of which he exchanged it to become his father's assistant in the parish of St Leonard's. At the same time he pursued his favourite study, and lectured also in the university on New Testament exegesis. It was then that he formed the resolution to prepare a critical edition of the Greek New Testament. He had in the meantime broken with Bentley, whose famous *Proposals* appeared in 1720. Wetstein was not permitted, however, to pursue his purpose without molestation. The rumour got abroad that his projected text would take the Socinian side in the case of such passages as 1 Timothy iii. 16, and in other ways he gave occasion for the suspicion of heresy. At length in 1729 the charge of projecting an edition of the Greek Testament savouring of Socinianism was formally laid against him. The end of the long and unedifying trial was his dismissal, May 13, 1730, from his office of curate of St Leonard's. He then removed from Basel to Amsterdam, where a relative, John Henry Wetstein, had an important printing and publishing business, from whose office excellent editions of the classics were issued, and also Gerard of Maestricht's edition of the Greek Testament. Previous to his removal from Basel Wetstein had commenced printing in this office an edition of the Greek Testament, which was suddenly stopped for some unknown reason. At his trial the first sheets of this edition were brought into court against him, though the new readings which had been adopted in his text were simply those which are now universally accepted. As soon as he reached Amsterdam he published anonymously the *Prolegomena*, which he had proposed should accompany his Greek Testament, and which was republished by him, with additions, as part of his great work, 1751. The next year (1731) the Remonstrants offered him the chair of philosophy in their college at Amsterdam, vacated by the illness of John Le Clerc, on condition that he should clear himself of the suspicion of heresy. He thereupon returned to Basel, and procured a reversal (March 22, 1732) of the previous decision, and readmission to all his clerical offices. But, on his becoming a candidate for the Hebrew chair at Basel, his orthodox opponents procured his defeat and his retirement to Amsterdam. Here the Remonstrants permitted him to hold lectures in their college, which led, however, to renewed opposition on the part of the Calvinistic party. At length, after much painful contention, he was allowed to instruct the Remonstrant students in philosophy and Hebrew on certain somewhat humiliating conditions. For the rest of his life he continued professor in the Remonstrant college, declining in 1744 the Greek chair at Basel. In 1746 he once more visited England, and collated Syriac MSS. for his great work. At last this appeared in 1751–52, in two folio volumes, under the title *Novum Testamentum Græcum Editionis Receptæ cum Lectionibus Variantibus Codicum MSS.*, &c. He did not venture to put new readings in the body of his page, but consigned those of them which he recommended to a place between the text and the full list of various readings. Beneath the latter he gave a commentary, consisting principally of a mass of invaluable illustrations and parallels drawn from classical and rabbinical literature, which has formed a storehouse for all later commentators. In his *Prolegomena* he gave an admirable methodical account of the MSS., the versions, and the readings of the fathers, as well as the troubled story of the difficulties with which he had had to contend in the prosecution of the work of his life. He did not long survive the completion of this work. He died at Amsterdam, March 9, 1754.

Wetstein's New Testament has never been republished entire. The London printer Bowyer published, in 1763, a text in which he introduced the readings recommended by Wetstein; Semler republished the *Prolegomena* and appendix, 1764; A. Lotze commenced a new edition of the work, but the *Prolegomena* only appeared (Rotterdam, 1831), and this "castigated." It is generally allowed that Wetstein rendered invaluable service to textual criticism by his collection of various readings and his methodical account of the MSS. and other sources, and that his work was rendered less valuable through his prejudice against the Latin version and the principle of grouping MSS. in families which had been recommended by Bentley and Bengel.

See Wetstein's account of his labours and trials in his *Nov. Test.*, i.; articles in Illgen's *Ztschr. für histor. Theol.* by C. R. Hagenbach (1839), by Van Rhyn in 1843, and again by Böttger in 1870; Tregelles, *Account of the Printed Text of the New Testament*; Scrivener's *Introduction to the Criticism of the New Testament*; Gass, *Protestantische Dogmatik*, vol. iii.; Bertheau's art. in *Herzog's Real-Encyklopädie*, 2d ed., 1886.

WETTE, DE. See DE WETTE.

WEXFORD, a maritime county of Ireland, in the province of Leinster, is bounded N. by Wicklow, E. and S. by St George's Channel, and W. by Waterford, Kilkenny, and Carlow. Its greatest length from its north-eastern extremity at Kilmichael Point to Hookhead Point at Waterford Harbour is upwards of 60 miles, and its greatest breadth from east to west 34 miles. The area is 576,588 acres, or about 901 square miles.

The coast-line does not present any striking features, and owing to the number of sandbanks navigation is dangerous near the shore. The only inlet of importance on the east coast and the only safe harbour is Wexford Harbour, which owing to a bar is not accessible to large vessels at ebb-tide. On the south coast are the fishing harbours of Crossfarnogue and Fethard. Several islets adjoin the coast. South from Crossfarnogue Point are the Saltee Islands, and Coningmore and Coningbeg, beyond the latter of which is the Saltee lightship. South-east from Greenore Point is the Tuskar Rock.

The basis of the county is clay-slate, and the surface is chiefly a series of verdant low hills, except towards the northern and western boundaries. The clay-slate formation is interrupted by patches of quartz rock near Gorey, one south of Enniscorthy, and another south of Wexford. To the north of Gorey there is a protrusion of greenstone trap. The elevated ridge on the north-western boundary forms the termination of the granitic range in Wicklow, and in Croghan Kinshela, on the borders of Wicklow, rises to a height of 1985 feet. On the western border, a granitic range, situated chiefly in Carlow, extends from the valley of the Slaney at Newtonbarry to the confluence of the Barrow with the Nore at New Ross. In the southern district, a hilly region, reaching in Forth Mountain a height of 725 feet, forms with Wexford Harbour the northern boundaries of the baronies of Forth and Bargy, a peninsula of flat and fertile land. Carboniferous limestone crops to the surface on the southern shore of Wexford Harbour, and forms also the extremity of Hookhead Point. Marble is quarried on the right bank of the Barrow, and ochres are dug on the coast districts. The river Slaney enters the county at its north-western extremity, and flows south-east to Wexford Harbour. Its chief tributary is the Bann, which flows south-westwards from the borders of Wicklow. The Barrow forms the western boundary of the county from the Blackstairs range of mountains till its confluence with the Suir at Waterford Harbour.

Agriculture.—The soil for the most part is a cold and stiff clay resting on clay-slate. The interior and western districts have it much inferior to those round the coasts. In the south-eastern peninsula of Forth and Bargy the soil is a rich alluvial mould mixed with coralline sandstone and limestone. The peninsula of Hookhead, owing to the limestone formation, is specially fruitful. In the western districts of the county there are large tracts of turf and peat-moss. In 1876, according to the *Return of Owners of Land*, Wexford was divided among 1757 proprietors possessing 573,052 acres at an annual value of £374,517, or about 13s. an acre all over. Of these proprietors 581 possessed less than 1 acre. There were about 4500 acres of waste or common land. The following proprietors possessed upwards of 8000 acres:—Lord Carew, 17,831; Lady Adelaide Forbes, 15,216; marquis of Ely, 14,023; Viscount Powerscourt, 11,730; Lord Templemore, 11,327; William Orme Foster, 9724; Hon. Mrs Deane Morgan, 9413; Anne Colclough, 9328; Sir James Power, 8599; F. A. Leigh, 8281; and representatives of J. H. R. Rowe, 8003. Out of a total area of 575,700 acres in 1886, there were 202,543 acres, or 35·2 per cent., under crops, including meadow and clover, 303,788 or 52·8 per cent. under grass, 431 acres fallow, 10,583 woods and plantations, 15,090 bog and marsh, 19,082 barren mountain land, and 24,183 water, roads, fences, &c. The total number of holdings in 1886 was 16,074, of which only 16 were above 500 acres in extent, 1045 between 100 and 500 acres, 2429 between 50 and 100, 2703 between 30 and 50, 3019 between 15 and 30, 3081 between 5 and 15, 2161 between 1 and 5, and 1620 not exceeding 1 acre. The decline in the area under crops between 1849 and 1886 has been much below the average for Ireland—from 245,514 acres to 202,543. In 1876 the area was 221,018 acres, so that there has been a large decline within the last ten years. In the area under meadow and clover there has been an increase from 39,343 in 1849 to 61,327 in 1876 and 64,064 in 1886, but within the last ten years the area has been fluctuating. There has been no marked change in the area under green crops, which was 44,735 acres in 1849, 50,498 in 1876, and 45,958 in 1886. The area under corn crops has, however, declined nearly a half, being in 1849 163,321 acres, in 1876 109,193 acres, and in 1886 only 92,512 acres. Of green crops there has been since 1849 a great increase in the area under turnips, and a corresponding decrease in the area under potatoes: in 1849 they were respectively 9763 and 32,017 acres, and by 1876 they had changed to 19,704 and 23,974 acres, and by 1886 to 21,857 and 18,888 acres. There were also in 1886 2848 acres under mangel-wurzel and beetroot, and 3365 under other green crops. Of the corn crops the area under wheat has declined from 44,592 acres in 1849 to 6948 in 1876 and 4541 in 1886, the area under oats from 80,166 acres to 47,065 in 1876 and 50,381 in 1886, while that under barley and bere increased from 36,563 acres in 1849 to 51,321 acres in 1876, but since then has declined to 35,036 acres. The number of horses in 1886 was 27,878, of which 942 were used for recreation. Mules numbered 1767, and asses 8031. Cattle numbered 126,410, of which 37,936 were milch cows. The number of sheep was 122,373, of which 48,243 were one year old and upwards. Pigs numbered 67,478, goats 6369, and poultry 571,107, of which 34,293 were turkeys and 60,414 geese.

Communications.—The Dublin, Wicklow, and Wexford Railway intersects the county; and from Wexford a branch of the Great Southern and Western passes north-westwards joining the lines to Kilkenny and Kildare. The river Slaney is navigable for barges to Enniscorthy, and the Barrow for large vessels to New Ross.

Manufactures.—Except in the town of Wexford the manufactures and trade are of small importance. There are important fisheries at Wexford, and one or two fishing villages along the south coast. The fishing grounds are good.

Administration and Population.—According to the calculation of De Burgo the population in 1760 was 66,804; the parliamentary census of 1812 places it at 112,000; in 1821 it amounted to 170,806, in 1841 to 202,033, in 1861 to 143,954, in 1871 to 132,666, and in 1881 to 123,854 (60,928 males and 62,926 females). Roman Catholics in 1881 formed 91·1 per cent. of the population, and Protestant Episcopalians 8·2 per cent. In 1881 the number of persons who could read and write amounted to 51·5 per cent. of the population, 15·3 per cent. could read but not write, and 33·2 per cent. could neither read nor write,—14·7 per cent. being under seven years of age. All could speak English, and 512 could speak English and Irish. By the Act of 1885 Wexford, which formerly returned two members to parliament, was divided into two parliamentary divisions, North and South, each returning one member, the borough of Wexford, which formerly returned one member, and the portion of the borough of New Ross within the county, being merged in the South Division. The principal towns are Wexford (12,163), New Ross (of which a portion containing 6375 is in this county, the other portion containing 295 inhabitants being in Kilkenny), Enniscorthy (5666), and Gorey (2450). The county is divided into ten baronies, and contains 144 parishes and 1600 town-lands. Episcopally it is in Ferns diocese, except a small portion, which is in Dublin. Judicially it is in the Leinster circuit, and assizes are held at Wexford, and quarter sessions at Enniscorthy, Gorey, New Ross, and Wexford. There are eleven petty sessions districts, and parts of two others. Wexford includes the poor law unions of Gorey and Wexford, and parts of Enniscorthy, New Ross, and Shillelagh. It is within the Cork military district, and along with Kilkenny, Tipperary, and Waterford forms No. 69 sub-district, the brigade depôt of which is at Clonmel. There are barrack stations at Wexford, Duncannon Fort, and New Ross.

History and Antiquities.—The peninsula of Hookhead is the ancient *Sacrum Promontorium.* The northern portion of Wexford was included in *Hy Kinselagh,* the peculiar territory of the Macmorroughs, overlords of Leinster, who had their chief residence at Ferns. Dermod Macmorrough, having been deposed from the kingdom of Leinster, asked help of Henry II., king of England, who authorized him to raise forces in England for the assertion of his claim. He secured the aid of Strongbow by promising him the hand of Eva, and in addition obtained assistance from Robert Fitzstephen and Maurice Fitzgerald of Wales. On the 1st May 1169 Fitzstephen landed at Bagenbon on the south side of Fethard, and after four days' siege captured the town of Wexford from its Danish inhabitants. After this Dermod granted the territory of Wexford to Fitzstephen and Fitzgerald and their heirs for ever. Macmorrough having died in 1172, Strongbow became lord of Leinster. At first Henry II. retained Wexford in his own possession, but in 1174 he committed it to Strongbow. The barony of Forth is almost entirely peopled by the descendants of those who accompanied these English expeditions. Wexford was one of the twelve counties into which the conquered territory in Ireland was divided by King John in 1210, and formed part of the possessions of William Mareschal, earl of Pembroke, who had married Strongbow's daughter. Through the female line it ultimately passed to John Talbot, earl of Shrewsbury, who in 1446 was made earl of Waterford and baron of Dungarvan. In 1474 George Talbot was seneschal of the liberty of Wexford. The district was actively concerned in the rebellion of 1641; and during the Cromwellian campaign the town of Wexford was on 9th October 1649 carried by storm, and a week later the garrison at New Ross surrendered,—a "seasonable mercy," according to Cromwell, as giving him an "opportunity towards Munster." Wexford was the chief seat of the rebellion of 1798, the leaders there being the priests. Evidences of the Danish occupation are seen in the numerous raths, especially at Dunbrody, Enniscorthy, and New Ross. Among the monastic ruins special mention may be made of Dunbrody abbey, of great extent, founded in 1182 for Cistercian monks by Henry de Montmorency, marshal of Henry II.; Tintern abbey, founded in 1200 by William Mareschal, earl of Pembroke, and peopled by monks from Tintern abbey in Monmouthshire; the abbey of St Sepulchre, Wexford, founded shortly after the invasion by the Roches, lords of Fermoy; Ferns abbey, founded by Dermod Macmorrough; and the abbey of New Ross, founded by St Alban in the 6th century. There are a considerable number of old castles, including Ferns, dismantled by the Parliamentary forces under Sir Charles Coote in 1641, and occupying the site of the old palace of the Macmorroughs; the massive pile of Enniscorthy, founded by Raymond le Gros; Carrick Castle, near Wexford, the first built by the English; and the fort of Duncannon, which has been garrisoned since the time of the Spanish Armada, and caused some trouble to Cromwell when in Wexford.

WEXFORD, a seaport, market-town, and municipal borough, and the chief town of the above county, is finely situated on the south side of the Slaney, where it discharges into Wexford Harbour, on the Dublin, Wicklow, and Wexford Railway and a branch line of the Great Southern and Western, 82 miles south of Dublin and 15 south-east of Enniscorthy. Wexford Harbour, formed by the estuary of the Slaney, is about 3 miles from north to south and about 4 from east to west, and has an area of about 1300 acres. A fine bridge of wood and iron 1500 feet in length crosses a narrow part of the estuary. The harbour affords splendid accommodation for shipping, but its advantages have been in great part lost by a bar at its mouth preventing the entrance of vessels drawing more than 12 feet. The construction of a pier at Rosslare connected with Wexford by a railway has, however, proved of great benefit. The town consists of the quay, about 1000 feet in length, with two narrow streets running parallel with it, and other smaller ones branching off at intervals. Some remains of the old walls and flanking towers still exist. The Protestant Episcopal church, near the ruins of the ancient abbey of St Sepulchre, is said to occupy the spot where the treaty was signed between the Irish and their English invaders in 1169. The principal modern buildings are the town-hall, the theatre, the court-house, the barracks, occupying the site of the ancient castle, St Peter's College for the education of Catholic clergy, the county infirmary, the union workhouse, and a number of convents. The port has communication by steamer with Liverpool and Bristol. In 1886 the number of vessels that entered the port was 847 of 85,004 tons, the number that cleared 836 of 84,065 tons. The principal exports are agricultural produce, live stock, and whisky. Shipbuilding is carried on, and also tanning, malting, brewing, iron-founding, distilling, and the manufacture of artificial manure, flour, agricultural implements, and rope and twine. The population of the town in 1871 was 12,077, and in 1881 it was 12,163.

Wexford was one of the earliest colonies of the English, having been taken by Fitzstephen. It was the second town that Cromwell besieged in 1649. It was garrisoned for William III. in 1690. In 1798 it was made the headquarters of the rebels, who, however, surrendered it on the 21st June. In 1318 the town received a charter from Aldomar de Valence, which was extended by Henry IV. in 1411, and confirmed by Elizabeth in 1558. By James I. it was in 1608 made a free borough corporate, by the title of "the town and free borough corporate of Wexford." It returned two members to parliament from 1374 till the Union, when they were reduced to one. In 1885 it was included in the South Division of the county.

WEYMOUTH AND MELCOMBE REGIS, a seaport, watering-place, market-town, and municipal borough of Dorset, England, is situated at the mouth of the small river Wey, on Weymouth Bay, opposite the Isle of Portland, and on the London and South-Western Railway and a branch of the Great Western, 7½ miles south of Dorchester, 27¼ west-south-west of Poole Junction, and 145½ from London. It is formed of Weymouth, a fishing town and seaport on the south-west of the Wey, and Melcombe Regis on the north-east of the river, the two towns being connected by a bridge reconstructed in 1881. An esplanade about a mile in length fronts the sea. To the south of the esplanade is a pier of stone on wooden piles 1050 feet in length, erected in 1859 at a cost of £12,000. The harbour lies between the pier on the north and the spur of land called the Nothe on the south, and is protected by a concrete wall extending 500 feet northward from the Nothe. The principal buildings are the old town-hall, the market-house, the guild-hall, the masonic hall, the royal Dorset yacht clubhouse, the theatre, the Royal Victoria Jubilee Hall, the Weymouth and Dorset eye infirmary, the Weymouth royal hospital and dispensary, the Weymouth sanatorium for women and children, and the infantry barracks. Opposite the Royal Terrace is an equestrian statue of George III., erected in 1809 in commemoration of his jubilee. A marble statue was also erected to Sir H. Edwards in 1885. A mile south-west of Weymouth is Sandsfoot Castle, a fort erected by Henry VIII. for the protection of the shipping. There are a number of almshouses and other charities. Weymouth has steam connexion with the Channel Islands, France, and various ports on the English coast. In 1886 903 vessels of 105,824 tons entered the port, and 905 of 98,964 tons cleared. The principal exports are Portland stone, bricks and tiles, and provisions, and the imports are coal, timber, garden and dairy produce, and wine. Ship and boat building, rope and sail making, and brewing are carried on. The population of the municipal borough of Weymouth and Melcombe Regis (area 763 acres) in 1871 was 13,259, and in 1881 it was 13,715.

Both Weymouth and Melcombe Regis are very ancient. The port is supposed to have traded with Tyrian merchants before the arrival of the Romans. Various Roman remains, including pavements and coins, have been found. Weymouth was the scene of Athelstan's vengeance on his half-brother Prince Edwin. It received a charter from Ethelred, which is preserved in Winchester cathedral. In the time of Edward the Confessor Weymouth and Melcombe were the property of the abbey of Cerne. In 1280 they formed a royal demesne and part of the dowry of Eleanor of Castile. Both Weymouth and Melcombe first returned members to parliament in the reign of Edward II. In 1347 they sent 20 ships and 264 men for the siege of Calais. Queen Margaret of Anjou landed at Weymouth 17th April 1471, and in 1506 Philip of Castile and his queen were driven into the port by stress of weather. In 1571 Weymouth and Melcombe Regis were united in one borough, under the title of "mayor, aldermen, bailiffs, burgesses, and commonalty of the borough and town of Weymouth and Melcombe Regis." The town was the scene of repeated conflicts during the Civil War, having been taken by the Royalists 9th August 1641, and retaken in 1644 by the Parliamentary forces, who stoutly defended it against an attack of nine days' duration in February of the following year. Originally the united borough sent four members to parliament (the only other place returning the same number being the city of London), but in 1832 these were reduced to two, and in 1885 it ceased to be separately represented. Its importance as a watering-place dates from the time that George III. selected it as his favourite resort in the summer season. On 6th December 1881 Weymouth was constituted a port, the limits to commence at St Alban's Head, the limit of the port of Poole, and to extend in a western direction along the coast to the western bank of the river Char, being the eastern limit of the port of Exeter, and to include the island of Portland. Among the representatives of the boroughs in parliament are Sir William Penn, father of the founder of Pennsylvania, and Sir Christopher Wren.

WHALE,[1] a name applied rather loosely to various animals of the order *Cetacea*, the general characters and classification of which have been described in the article MAMMALIA (vol. xv. p. 391). All the members of the sub-order *Mystacoceti*, or *Cetacea* with whalebone, are called "whales." But of the *Odontoceti*, or *Cetacea* with teeth, only certain of the larger ones are so termed, the smaller species being popularly spoken of as "bottlenoses," "dolphins," and "porpoises"; yet so indefinitely has the word been applied that a true dolphin (*Delphinus tursio*), not exceeding 8 feet in length, is described in some works as the "smaller bottlenosed whale."

Although by their mode of life so far removed from close observation that it is impossible to become as familiar with them in their natural condition as with many other animals, whales are in many respects the most interesting and wonderful of all creatures; and there is much in their structure and habits which is well worthy of study, much that is difficult to understand, and much that leads to great generalizations and throws light upon far-reaching philosophical speculations. One of the first lessons which a study of these animals affords is that, in the endeavour to discover what a creature really is, from what others it is descended, and to what it is related, the general outward appearance affords little clue, and we must go deep below the surface to find out the essential characteristics of its nature. There was once, and may be still in many places, a common idea that a whale is a fish. To realize the fallacy of this notion we have only to consider what a fish really is, what under all the diversities of form, size, and colour known among fishes there is common to them all, and we see that in everything which characterizes a true fish and separates it from other classes, as reptiles, birds, and mammals, the whale resembles the last-named and differs from the fish. It is as essentially a mammal as a cow or a horse, and simply resembles a fish externally because it is adapted to inhabit the same element; but it is no more on that account a fish than is a bat, because adapted to pass a great part of its existence on the wing in the air, nearly related to a bird. The whole structure of a whale is a most instructive instance of a type of organization which is common to and characteristic of the class *Mammalia*, only specially modified or adapted to a peculiar mode of life. We see in every part the result of two great principles acting and reacting upon each other,—on the one hand, adherence to type, or rather to fundamental inherited structural conditions, and, on the other, adaptation to the peculiar circumstances under which it lives, and to which in all probability it has become gradually more and more fitted. The external fish-like form is perfectly suited for swimming through the water; the tail, however, is not placed vertically as in fishes, but horizontally, a position which accords better with the constant necessity for rising to the surface for the purpose of breathing. The hairy covering characteristic of all mammals, which if present might interfere with rapidity of movement through the water, is reduced to the merest rudiments,—a few short bristles about the chin or upper lip,—which are often only present in very young animals. The function of keeping the body warm is supplied by a thick layer of non-conducting material, the "blubber," a peculiarly dense kind of fat placed immediately beneath the skin. The fore-limbs, though functionally reduced to mere paddles, with no power of motion except at the shoulder-joint, have beneath their smooth and continuous external covering all the bones, joints, and even most of the muscles, nerves, and arteries, of the human arm and hand; and rudiments even of hind legs are found buried deep in the interior of the animal, apparently subserving no useful purpose, but pointing an instructive lesson to those who are able to read it.

In what follows a more detailed account is given of the best known of those species of *Cetacea* to which the name "whale" is popularly applied, especially those frequenting British waters, than could be given under MAMMALIA.

I. Sub-order **MYSTACOCETI** or Whalebone Whales.

Greenland right whale. *Genus* **Balæna.**—The Greenland, or more properly Arctic, right whale (*Balæna mysticetus*) attains, when full-grown, a length of from 45 to 50 feet. Its external form is shown in fig. 1, from a careful drawing by Mr Robert Gray. In this species all the peculiarities which distinguish the head and mouth of the whales from those of other mammals have attained their greatest development. The head is of enormous size, exceeding one-third of the whole length of the creature. The cavity of the mouth is actually larger than that of the body, thorax, and abdomen together. The upper jaw is very narrow, but greatly arched from before backwards, to increase the height of the cavity and allow for the great length of the baleen or "whalebone" blades; the enormous rami of the mandible are widely separated posteriorly, and have a still further outward sweep before they meet at the symphysis in front, giving the floor of the mouth the shape of an immense spoon. The baleen blades attain the number of 380 or more on each side, and those in the middle of the series have a length of 10 or sometimes 12 feet. They are black in colour, fine and highly elastic in texture, and fray out at the inner edge and ends into long, delicate, soft, almost silky, but very tough, hairs. The remarkable development of the mouth and of the structures in connexion with it, which distinguishes the right whale among all its allies, is entirely in relation to the nature of its food. It is by this apparatus that it is enabled to avail itself of the minute but highly nutritious crustaceans and pteropods which swarm in immense shoals in the seas it frequents. The large mouth enables it to take in at one time a sufficient quantity of water filled with these small organisms, and the length and delicate structure of the baleen provide an efficient strainer or hair-sieve by which the water can be drained off. If the baleen were rigid, and only as long as is the aperture between the upper and lower jaws when the mouth is shut, a space would be left beneath it when the jaws were separated, through which the water and the minute particles of food would escape together. But instead of this the long, slender, brush-like, elastic ends of the whalebone blades fold back when the mouth is closed, the front ones passing below the hinder ones in a channel lying between the tongue and the lower jaw. When the mouth is opened, their elasticity causes them to straighten out like a bow unbent, so that at whatever distance the jaws are separated the strainer remains in perfect action, filling the whole of the interval. The mechanical perfection of the arrangement is completed by the great development of the lower lip, which rises stiffly above the jaw-bone and prevents the long, slender, flexible ends of the baleen from being carried outwards by the rush of water from the mouth, when its cavity is being diminished by the closure of the jaws and raising of the tongue.

FIG. 1.—Greenland or Arctic right whale (*Balæna mysticetus*).

If, as appears highly probable, the "bowhead" of the Okhotsk Sea and Behring Strait belongs to this species, its range is circumpolar. Though found in the seas on both sides of Greenland, and passing freely from one to the other, it is never seen so far south as Cape Farewell; but on the Labrador coast, where a cold stream sets down from the north, its range is somewhat farther. In the Behring Sea, according to Scammon, "it is seldom seen south of the fifty-fifth parallel, which is about the farthest southern extent of the winter ice, while in the Sea of Okhotsk its southern limit is about the latitude of 54°." As has been abundantly shown by Eschricht and Reinhardt in the case of the Greenland seas, "everything tends to prove," Scammon says, "that the *Balæna mysticetus* is truly an 'ice whale,' for among the scattered floes, or about the

[1] Icel., *hvalr*; Dan. and Swed., *hval*; Anglo-Saxon, *hwæl*; Germ., *wal, walfisch*. The meaning apparently is "roller," the word being closely allied to "wheel" (Skeat).

borders of the ice-fields or barriers, is its home and feeding-ground. It is true that these animals are pursued in the open water during the summer months, but in no instance have we learned of their being captured south of where winter ice-fields are occasionally met with." The occurrence of this species, therefore, on the British or any European coast is exceedingly unlikely, as when alive and in health the southern limit of its range in the North Sea has been ascertained to be from the east coast of Greenland at 64° N. lat. along the north of Iceland towards Spitzbergen, and a glance at a physical chart will show that there are no currents setting southwards which could bear a disabled animal or a floating carcase to British shores. To this *a priori* improbability may be added the fact that no authentic instance has been recorded of the capture or stranding of this species upon any European coast, for the cases of its having been reported as seen in British waters may be explained by the supposition of one of the other species of the genus being mistaken for it. Still, as two other Arctic cetaceans, the narwhal and the beluga, have in a few undoubted instances found their way to British shores, it would be rash absolutely to deny the possibility of the Greenland right whale doing the same. Further details of the migrations and habits of this species are given under "Whale Fisheries" (see p. 526 below).

Southern right whale. The southern right whale (*B. australis*) resembles the last in the absence of dorsal fin and of longitudinal furrows in the skin of the throat and chest, but differs in that it possesses a smaller head in proportion to its body, shorter baleen, a different-shaped contour of the upper margin of the lower lip, and a greater number of vertebræ. The genus inhabits the temperate seas of both northern and southern hemispheres and is divided into several species according to their geographical distribution:—*B. biscayensis* of the North Atlantic, *B. japonica* of the North Pacific, *B. australis* of the South Atlantic, and *B. antipodarum* and *B. novæ-zelandiæ* of the South Pacific. But the differential characters by which they have been separated, external as well as anatomical, are slight and subject to individual variation; and the number of specimens available for comparison in museums is not yet sufficient to afford the necessary data to determine whether these characters can be regarded as specific or not. The most interesting of these is the right whale, which was formerly abundant in the North Atlantic, but is now so scarce as to appear verging on extinction. This was the whale the pursuit of which gave occupation to a numerous population on the shores of the Basque provinces of France and Spain in the Middle Ages. From the 10th to the 16th centuries Bayonne, Biarritz, St Jean de Luz, and San Sebastian, as well as numerous other towns on the north coast of Spain, were the centres of an active whale "fishery," which supplied Europe with oil and whalebone. In later times the whales were pursued as far as the coast of Newfoundland. They were, however, already getting scarce when the voyages undertaken towards the close of the 16th century for the discovery of the north-eastern route to China and the East Indies opened out the seas around Spitzbergen; then for the first time the existence of the Greenland whale became known, and henceforth the energies of the European whale-fishers became concentrated upon that animal. It is a singular fact that the existence of the Atlantic right whale was quite overlooked by naturalists till lately, all accounts referring to it being attributed to the Greenland whale, supposed once to have had a wider distribution than now, and to have been driven by the persecution of man to its present circumpolar haunts. To the two Danish cetologists Eschricht and Reinhardt is due the credit of having proved its existence as a distinct species, from a careful collation of numerous historical notices of its structure, distribution, and habits; and their restoration of the animal, founded upon these documents, has been abundantly confirmed by the capture of various specimens in recent times, showing that it still lingers in some of the localities where it formerly was so abundant. The only known instances of its occurrence on the coasts of Europe in modern times are in the harbour of San Sebastian in January 1854, in the Gulf of Taranto, in the Mediterranean, in February 1877, and on the Spanish coast between Guetaria and Zarauz (Guipuzcoa) in February 1878. The skeletons of these three whales are preserved in the museums of Copenhagen, Naples, and San Sebastian respectively. On the coast of the United States several of these whales have been taken within the last few years. In the North Pacific a very similar if not identical species is regularly hunted by the Japanese, who tow the carcases ashore for the purposes of flensing and extracting the whalebone. In the tropical seas, however, according to Captain Maury's whale charts, right whales are never or rarely seen; but the southern temperate ocean, especially the neighbourhood of the Cape of Good Hope, Kerguelen's Island, Australia, and New Zealand, is inhabited by "black whales," once abundant, but now nearly exterminated through the wanton destruction of the females as they visit the bays and inlets round the coast, their constant habit in the breeding time. The range of these whales southward has not been accurately determined; but no species corresponding with the Arctic right whale has as yet been met with in the Antarctic icy seas.

Fig. 2.—Southern right whale (*B. australis*).

Humpback whale. *Genus* **Megaptera**.—The whale commonly called "humpback" (*Megaptera boops*) by whalers, perhaps on account of the low hump-like form of the dorsal fin, is very distinctly characterized from all others of the group, especially by the immense length of the pectoral fins or flippers, which are indented or scalloped along their margins, and are, except at their base, of a white colour, nearly all the rest of the body being black. It differs from the right whale and resembles the rorqual in having the skin of the throat and chest marked with deep longitudinal furrows. The baleen plates are short and broad and of a deep black colour. Though common in the North Atlantic between Norway and Greenland, this whale does not frequently appear on the coasts of the British Isles. One came ashore at Newcastle in 1839; another, a young one, was taken in the estuary of the Dee in 1863 and its skeleton is preserved in the Liverpool museum; and a nearly full-grown animal was captured in the mouth of the Tay in the winter of 1883-84. The usual length of the adult ranges from 45 to 50 feet. Whales of the genus *Megaptera* are found in the South Atlantic and in both the North and the South Pacific. They resemble those of British seas so closely that it is doubtful whether the differences which have been observed, and upon which several species have been founded, may not have been individual peculiarities; but zoologists have not yet had the opportunity of examining and comparing such a series of specimens of different ages and sexes from different localities as would be necessary to determine these points satisfactorily.

Fig. 3.—Humpbacked whale (*Megaptera boops*).

Rorqual or fin whale. *Genus* **Balænoptera**.—The rorquals or fin whales have the plicated skin of the throat like that of *Megaptera*, the furrows being more numerous and close-set; but the pectoral fin is comparatively small and the dorsal fin distinct and falcate. The head is comparatively small and flat, and pointed in front, the baleen short and coarse, the body long and slender, and the tail very much compressed before it expands into the "flukes." The rorquals are perhaps the most abundant and widely distributed of all the whales, being found in some of their modifications in all seas, except the extreme Arctic, and probably Antarctic, regions. Owing to the small quantity and inferior quality of their whalebone, the comparatively limited amount of blubber or subcutaneous fat, and their great activity and the difficulty of capturing them by the old methods, these whales were not until recently an object of pursuit by whale-fishers; but, since the introduction of steam-vessels, and especially of explosive harpoons fired from guns, in the place of those hurled by the human hand, a regular fishery has been established on the coast of Finmark (see p. 528 below). There are four distinct species of this genus in British seas. (1) *Balænoptera sibbaldii*, the "blue whale," the largest of all known animals, attains a length of 80 or even sometimes 85 feet. Its colour is dark bluish grey, with small whitish spots on the breast; the baleen is black; the flippers are larger proportionally than in other rorquals, measuring one-seventh of the total length of the body; and the dorsal fin is small and placed very far back. This whale has usually 64 vertebræ, of which 16 bear ribs. Like the others of the genus, this species seems to pass the winter in the open seas, and approaches the coast of Norway at the end of April or beginning of May. At this time its sole food is a small crustacean (*Euphausia inermis*), which swarms in the fjords. Several specimens have been taken on the British coasts, two fine skeletons from the Firth of Forth being preserved in the Edinburgh museums. (2) *Balænoptera musculus*, the common rorqual, has a length of 65 to 70 feet, is of a greyish slate colour above and white underneath, and the baleen is slate colour, variegated with yellow or brown.

It has usually 62 vertebræ, of which 15 bear ribs. This is the commonest of all the large whales on the British coasts; scarcely a winter passes without the body of one being somewhere washed

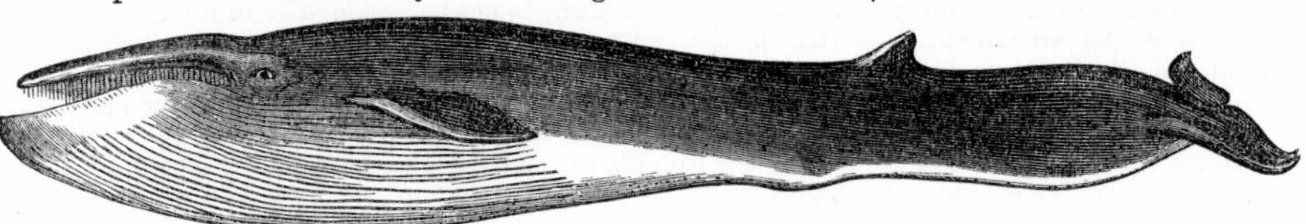

FIG. 4.—Common rorqual (*Balænoptera musculus*).

ashore, usually after stormy weather, and more frequently on the south coast, as this species has a more southern range than the last, and frequently enters the Mediterranean. It feeds largely on fish, and is frequently seen feasting among shoals of herrings. (3) *Balænoptera borealis*, often called Rudolphi's whale from its first describer, is a smaller species, scarcely attaining a length of 50 feet. It is bluish black above, with oblong light-coloured spots, whilst the under parts are more or less white; the whole of the tail and both sides of the flippers are black; the baleen is black, and the bristly ends fine, curling, and white; the flippers are very small, measuring one-eleventh of the total length of the body. There are 56 vertebræ, with 14 pairs of ribs. This species, according to Collett, feeds chiefly on minute crustaceans, mainly *Calanus finmarchicus* and *Euphausia inermis*, and not on fish. Until lately it was considered the rarest of the whales of European seas, and was only known to science from a few individuals stranded on the coasts of northern Europe at long intervals, the skeletons of which have been preserved in museums. The most southern point at which it has been met with hitherto is Biarritz in France. Since the establishment of the whaling station near the North Cape it has been shown to be a regular summer visitor, and in 1885 771 individuals were captured on the coast of Finmark. (4) *Balænoptera rostrata*, the lesser fin whale or rorqual, is the smallest species found in the northern seas, rarely exceeding 30 feet in length. Its colour is greyish black above, whilst the under side is white, including the whole of the lower side of the tail; the inner side of the flippers is white; and there is a broad white band across the outer side, which is a very characteristic mark of the species; the baleen is yellowish white. The dorsal fin in this and the last species is comparatively high, and placed far forwards on the body. This whale has usually 48 vertebræ, of which 11 bear ribs. It is common in summer in the fjords of Norway, and is often seen around the British Isles. It has been taken, though rarely, in the Mediterranean, and it ranges as far north as Davis Strait. Rorquals are met with in almost all seas throughout the world, but further and more accurate observations are required before their specific characters and geographical distribution can be made out. Nearly all the individuals hitherto examined with any care, whether from the North Pacific, the Australian seas, or the Indian Ocean, come very near in structure to one or the other of the Atlantic forms described above, so much so that some zoologists have been induced to believe that there are but four species, each of which has a wide, almost cosmopolitan range, while others have described and named almost every individual specimen captured as belonging to a different species.

Two totally distinct forms of whalebone whales, *Rachianectes glaucus*, the grey whale of the North Pacific (California and Japan), and *Neobalæna marginata* of New Zealand, have never been found in the British seas (see vol. xv. p. 395).

II. **ODONTOCETI** or Toothed Whales.

Sperm whale. Only one member of this group, the sperm whale or cachalot (*Physeter macrocephalus*), rivals the large whalebone whales in size, its length and bulk being about equal to, or somewhat exceeding,

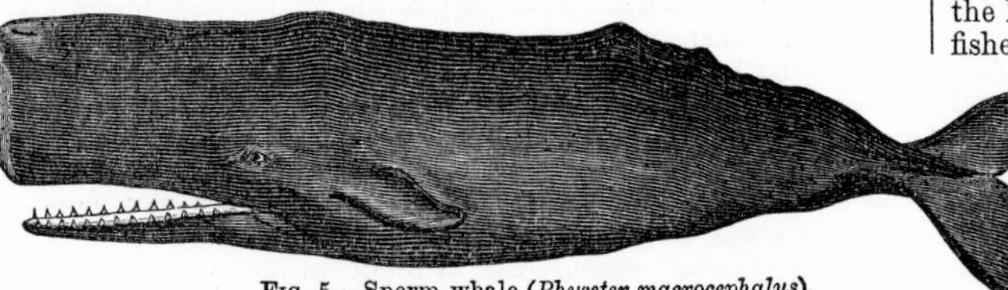

FIG. 5.—Sperm whale (*Physeter macrocephalus*).

the Arctic right whale, from which, however, it is very different in outward appearance and in structure. The head is about one-third of the length of the body, very massive, high and truncated in front, owing its huge size and remarkable form mainly to the great accumulation of a peculiarly modified form of fatty tissue, filling the large hollow on the upper surface of the skull. The oil contained in cells in this great cavity, when refined, yields spermaceti, and the thick covering of blubber, which everywhere envelopes the body, produces the valuable sperm-oil of commerce. The single blowhole is a longitudinal slit, placed at the upper and anterior extremity of the head to the left side of the middle line. The opening of the mouth is on the under side of the head, considerably behind the end of the snout. The lower jaw is extremely narrow, and has on each side from twenty to twenty-five stout conical teeth, which furnish ivory of good quality, though not in sufficient bulk for most of the purposes for which that article is required. The upper teeth are quite rudimentary and buried in the gum. The pectoral fin or flipper is short, broad, and truncated, and the dorsal fin a mere low protuberance. The general colour of the surface is black above and grey below, the colours gradually shading into each other. The only known species of sperm whale is one of the most widely distributed of animals, being met with, usually in herds or "schools," in almost all tropical and subtropical seas, but not occurring, except accidentally, in the Polar regions. Not unfrequently specimens appear on the coasts of Great Britain, but only as solitary stragglers, or as dead carcases, floated northwards by the Gulf Stream. It is remarkable that every case of which we have an accurate record has been an old male. The food of the sperm whale consists mainly of various species of cephalopods (squid and cuttlefish), but they also eat fish of considerable size. The substance called "ambergris," formerly used in medicine and now in perfumery, is a concretion formed in the intestine of this whale, and is found floating on the surface of the seas it inhabits. Its genuineness is proved by the presence of the horny beaks of the cephalopods on which the whale feeds.

Bottlenose whale. The remaining *Odontoceti* are all animals of much smaller size than the sperm whale, but to several of them the name of "whale" is commonly applied. The hyperoodon, sometimes called "bottlenose," a name also vaguely given to several species of dolphin, is a regular inhabitant of the North Atlantic, passing the summer in the Spitzbergen seas and going farther south in winter. It is allied to the sperm whale, and resembles it in possessing a large store of oil in the upper part of the head, which yields spermaceti when refined; on this account, and also for the sake of the blubber, which supplies an oil almost indistinguishable from sperm oil, this whale has been the object of a regular chase in recent years. It is stated in the article MAMMALIA (vol. xv. p. 396) that there are two species of this genus, *Hyperoodon rostratus*, the common hyperoodon, and *H. latifrons*, attaining when adult, respectively, the length of 24 and 30 feet; but recent investigations have shown that the latter is the male and the former the female of the same species. They feed exclusively on cephalopods, and are practically toothless; the only teeth which exist in the adult,—namely, a small pair at the front of the lower jaw,—are concealed beneath the gum during life. Smaller allied species, belonging to the genera *Ziphius* and *Mesoplodon*, occasionally find their way into British seas, but their proper habitat appears to be the South Seas.

Ca'ing or pilot whale. It frequently happens that large herds or "schools" of whales are captured in bays or inlets on the rocky coasts of Scotland, or the Orkney or Shetland Islands. These are the so-called ca'ing or pilot whale (*Globicephalus melas*), the grindhval of the Faroe Islanders and Norwegians. They attain the length of 20 feet, and are of a nearly uniform black colour, except a line down the middle of the under surface, which is grey. They are characterized by the round or globose form of the fore-part of the head, occasioned by the great development of a cushion of fat placed over the rostrum of the skull in front of the blowhole, and by the great length and narrowness of the pectoral fin. Their destruction in large numbers, amounting sometimes to hundreds at a time, arises from their eminently sociable character and their habit, when attacked, of rushing together and blindly following the leaders of the herd. When they are seen in the neighbourhood of land, the fishermen endeavour to get to seaward of them in their boats, and with shouting and firing of guns to drive them into a bay or fjord, pursuing them until they run themselves on shore in their alarm.

Beluga or white whale. The beluga (*Delphinapterus leucas*) is often called the "white whale," though scarcely exceeding the length of 12 feet. Its colour is almost pure white, and it has no dorsal fin, but a low ridge in its place. It is an inhabitant of the Arctic seas, extending on the American coast as far south as the river St Lawrence, which it ascends for a considerable distance. Several instances of its occurrence on the coast of Scotland are recorded, and it has been kept for some time in captivity in America, and even in London. Its external characters are represented in vol. xv. p. 399, fig. 50.

The other cetaceans of this group are generally distinguished as narwhals, grampuses, killers, bottlenoses, dolphins, and porpoises, and are not usually called whales.

Fossil species. We have no certain knowledge of the existence of whalebone whales before the latter part of the Eocene period. The earliest known forms were allied to the existing *Balænopteræ*. Right whales (*Balæna*), as might be expected in the case of such a highly specialized form, have not been found older than the Pliocene; and it is interesting to note that, instead of the individuals diminishing in bulk as we approach the times we live in, as with many other groups of animals, the contrary has been the case, no known extinct species of whale equalling in size those that are now to be met with in the ocean. The size of whales, as of all other things whose most striking attribute is magnitude, has been greatly exaggerated; but, when reduced to the limits of sober fact, the Greenland right whale of 50 feet long, the sperm whale of 60, and the great northern rorqual (*Balænoptera sibbaldii*) of 80 exceed all other organic structures known, past or present. Instead of living in an age of degeneracy of physical growth, we are in an age of giants, but, it may be, at the end of that age. Through countless ages of time whales have been gradually shaped into their present wonderful form and gigantic size; but the very perfection of their structure and their magnitude combined, the rich supply of oil protecting their internal parts from cold, the beautiful apparatus of whalebone by which their nutrition is provided for, have been fatal gifts, which, under the sudden revolution produced on the surface of the globe by the development of the wants and arts of civilized man, cannot but lead to their extinction in the not far future. (W. H. F.)

WHALE FISHERIES.

Commercially these may be conveniently classified under three heads,—the British, the American, and the Norwegian. The implements used, and the mode of capture of the different kinds of whales, being for the most part the same in all cases, the detailed account given below may be held to be of general application, unless the contrary is expressly stated.

Whaler. The *whaler* is a vessel of from 400 to 500 tons gross register, rigged either as a ship or a barque, and provided with auxiliary engines of some 75 horse-power. Built after the strongest fashion, she is protected along the water-line by an additional planking of iron bark, an Australian wood of great hardness; the bows are strengthened inside by beams and knees and outside by plates of iron. Underneath the hold-beams about 50 iron tanks are fitted, each capable of containing 200 to 250 tons of oil; above the hold-beams a deck is laid, engine and boiler space being reserved in the stern. A vessel of this description carries 8 whale-boats, and is manned by 50 to 60 hands all told. Her working expenses at sea, exclusive of insurance and interest on capital, are about £500 per month, and her cost as she leaves the builder's hands, supplied with all appurtenances, but exclusive of sea stores, is about £17,500.

Whale-boat. The *whale-boat* is 27 feet in length and 6 feet in breadth, with a depth amidships of 2 feet 6 inches. The bow is covered in for the distance of a few feet, forming a sort of platform, through which there project two wooden posts, that farthest forward being called the "gun-bollard head," on which the harpoon gun is mounted, while round the other, farther aft, the whale-line is run. At the stem, between the "head boards," a pulley is sunk, over which the whale-line glides. On the port bow, beside the gun-bollard head, a small tub is fitted, into which is coiled that part of the whale-line known as the "foregoer." The after-part of the boat, as well as a part amidships, is fitted up for the reception of the whale-line. The whale-boat is manned by five oarsmen and a boat-steerer. The bow oar acts as harpooner and has charge of the boat; the stroke oar is "line-manager" and watches the whale-line while it is running.

Harpoon gun. The *harpoon gun*, now almost universally used, measures 4 feet 6 inches in length and weighs 75 ℔; the barrel is 3 feet long with $1\frac{1}{2}$ inches bore and is mounted in a wooden stock, tapering behind into a pistol handle. The weapon is fired by means of percussion caps, doghead, and trigger-line, the nipples being protected from sea spray by a movable brass cover. Mounted in a swivel on the gun-bollard head, the harpoon gun from its elevated position commands both bows as well as right ahead; and with a charge of 11 drachms of powder it projects the harpoon with force and precision to a distance of 25 yards.

Harpoons. *Harpoons* are of two kinds, known respectively as gun and hand harpoons; the former are used as weapons of attack, the latter to assist in securing a whale that is already harpooned. The *gun harpoon* measures 4 feet in length and weighs 12 ℔. The "shank," or that part which enters the gun, is perforated throughout its length by an elongated slit, so as to allow the "shackle" connecting the harpoon with the line to remain outside the mouth of the gun when the shank is inserted in the barrel. When the gun is fired, the shackle travels along the slit until it is brought up by the butt, where the two rods of which the shank is composed unite, and after that the line is drawn out by the harpoon. The head of the harpoon is triangular and flattened, the two sides being continued backwards to form the barbs, which may be movable or fixed. When movable, they are attached to the head by steel pins, and previous to being fired fold backwards and lie parallel to the shank; the weapon having pierced a whale, and the strain on the whale-line causing it to retract, the barbs spread out and assume a transverse position, so as greatly to impede the withdrawal of the instrument. The *hand harpoon* is a light and efficient weapon which was introduced by the Americans, by whom it is known as a "toggle iron." It consists of a head and shank of iron, and is mounted on a wooden stock, by which it is darted. The head, a flattened piece of steel, somewhat triangular in form, is connected with the extremity of the shank by a steel pin, on which it pivots and moves freely. Previous to use the head folds back along the shank, in which position it is retained by a wooden pin. After the weapon has been darted into a whale, the strain on the line breaks the wooden pin, and the head assumes a position at right angles to the shank, somewhat in the form of the letter T, and becomes transfixed in the fibrous tissue under the blubber. The shank is a rod of $\frac{1}{2}$-inch iron, 2 feet 6 inches long, expanding at its upper extremity to form a socket to receive the wooden stock. The hand harpoon measures 8 feet in length, and, exclusive of the line, weighs 10 ℔. Expert harpooners can dart the weapon about 5 yards with considerable force and accuracy.

Whale-line. *Whale-line* is three-stranded rope, $2\frac{3}{4}$ inches in circumference, composed of the finest hemp, 32 yarns per strand; 600 fathoms are coiled into each whale-boat. The line is joined to the harpoon by the "foregoer," a piece of rope somewhat lighter and more pliable than whale-line. The foregoer being the only part of the line drawn out by the harpoon while in flight, its length, usually from 10 to 12 fathoms, regulates the distance the harpoon may be fired.

Whale-lance. The *whale-lance* consists of a simple rod of $\frac{1}{2}$-inch iron, 6 feet long, one end flattened to form a small lance-shaped point with cutting edges, the other expanding to form a socket to receive a short wooden handle. Gun lances, bomb lances, and exploding harpoons of various forms and devices have from time to time been introduced; but, mainly from the fact that in recent years the difficulty in securing a cargo lies not so much in effecting the capture of the animal as in discovering its whereabouts, and in approaching sufficiently near to permit the use of the harpoon, they have never come into general use.

Whale-hunting. Whether the ship is cruising amongst loose ice under canvas or lying "made fast" to a floe, a careful look-out is kept on board from the crow's nest (a barrel lashed to the main-top-gallant mast-head) as well as from the deck. Immediately on a whale being seen, boats are manned and sent in pursuit. If the animal is feeding, which it generally does when near the surface by swimming backwards and forwards horizontally round an ellipse, great caution is necessary to prevent its becoming aware of the approach of the boats. On the other hand, if the whale is "spanning," *i.e.*, swimming in a decided direction and appearing at the surface at intervals more or less regular, less caution is observed. In either case as well as under less usual circumstances the whale-boat, endeavouring to keep out of the angle of vision of the animal, approaches it from behind, swiftly but quietly; the harpooner rises to his gun and points it at the animal's back, withholding his fire, however, until within as short a distance as possible. On being harpooned the Greenland right whale usually dives perpendicularly, remaining under water about forty minutes and drawing out some 600 to 700 fathoms of line before it returns to the surface. Whales descend with such velocity that they have been known to break their upper jaw by coming into violent contact with the bottom even in 400 fathoms of water. Before the animal has returned to the surface other boats have arrived upon the scene, and, on the reappearance of the whale, give chase and attach more harpoons. Again the whale dives, but soon returns to the surface, still more exhausted. Whenever its motions become sufficiently slow to permit the approach of the boats, the lance is used, a few thrusts in the region of the heart or lungs being speedily fatal. Quantities of blood are thrown up by the spiracles; the animal lashes the water with its fins, and, after rushing violently through the water in its dying agony, rolls over on its side and lies stiff and rigid at the surface. Under favourable circumstances the capture of a full-grown whale from the time of first harpooning until its death occupies from one to one and a half hours. The operation of flensing is next performed. The body of the whale is lashed lengthwise alongside the ship with its under surface above water; the "cant-purchase," a powerful tackle, is then attached to the commencement of a transverse slip of blubber cut at the neck, known as the "cant-piece." By means of the cant-purchase the body is caused to rotate, whilst the fat is removed from the different parts as they appear above water in large "slips" or "blanket-pieces," each a ton or more in weight. After being received on deck, the blubber is cut into pieces about a foot square and stowed into the "'tween-decks." The whalebone is removed from each side of the upper jaw as it appears above water *en bloc*. The process of "cutting-in" occupies the ship's company about three hours. The only subsequent operations are the cutting up of the blubber into small pieces and its stowage in the oil tanks. The removal of the gum from the whalebone, the separation of the plates, and their stowage in the 'tween decks are operations performed subsequently.

British Fisheries.

Greenland fishing. *Greenland Right Whale.*—The Greenland right whale (*Balæna mysticetus*) is found amongst, or in the near vicinity of, the Polar ice. Its habitat, however, is materially reduced in extent by the shallowness of many parts of the Arctic Ocean—*e.g.*, of the Barents and Kara Seas and the sea to the north of Siberia—localities where the species is quite unknown. The fishing is prosecuted off Greenland and in Davis Strait by the British, and at Behring Strait by the Americans.

Sailing either directly from the home ports in April or proceeding thither after prosecuting the sealing, the British whale ships arrive at the north Greenland whaling-grounds off the west coast of Spitzbergen early in May. If it is a "close" season, *i.e.*, if the ice of the Barents Sea comes west round the south end of Spitzbergen, and effects a junction with the Greenland ice, so as to form a south-east pack, the ships have sometimes to force their way through several hundred miles of ice before reaching the grounds. On the other hand, if it is an "open" season, as more usually occurs, the barrier ice in lat. 80° may be reached without hindrance. In cruising for whales certain indications are sought which the whalemen know by experience to be favourable to the appearance of the animal. The first of these is "whaling ice," or moderately loose ice with close pack or floes in the neighbourhood. The second is abundance of food. The presence of this condition may be ascertained by a surface net, or it may be inferred from the colour of the water, which varies from the barrenness of clear cold cerulean to the richness of opaque and warm olive green. The crustacean *Calanus finmarchicus*, the pteropod *Clione limacina*, and the gasteropod *Limacina helicina* are amongst the most abundant forms, the first-mentioned contributing perhaps nine-tenths of the whale's food. Yet very little is known positively as to the food of the Greenland right whale. According to whalemen (and the idea has hitherto been generally accepted by naturalists), the animal lives upon various invertebrate forms, such as *Actiniæ*, *Schiæ*, *Cliones*, *Medusæ*, *Cancri*, and *Helices*. Scoresby states that some of these genera are always to be seen wherever whales are found stationary and feeding. Dr John Murray, however, is of opinion that whales also resort for food to the larger forms of pelagic fauna which exist in the immediate vicinity of the bottom of the ocean, and the presence of which was ascertained during the course of the "Challenger" investigations. The third condition is abundance of the higher forms of life, such as birds, especially guillemots (*Uria grylla*) and looms (*Alca arra*), also narwhals (*Monodon monoceros*), seals, bears, &c. The whales make their appearance amongst the ice near the sea edge about 15th May, but only remain in the locality until the opening of the barrier ice permits them to resume their northward journey, for usually about the middle of June they suddenly disappear from these grounds, and are last seen going north-west. The north Greenland whale-fishing is then over for the season. If unsuccessful in obtaining a cargo at the northern grounds, the whale ships next proceed southwards as far as lat. 75°; then, if the sea is sufficiently open, they penetrate westwards until the coast of Greenland is visible. There they cruise amongst the ice until August, when the darkness of the nights puts an end to the fishing.

Davis Strait fishing.

If the south-west fishing is first prosecuted, the vessels arrive at the ice edge near Resolution Island in April. Here, although numbers of large whales are usually seen, yet, owing to the boisterous weather and the compact nature of the ice, the fishing is seldom very successful, so that the majority of the vessels, after prosecuting the "saddle" sealing at Newfoundland or Greenland, proceed direct to Disco, where they usually arrive early in May. The whales make their appearance at South-East Bay about 15th May, and here, where once a great fishing was carried on, a few whales may be killed. The dangerous passage of Melville Bay is next performed and the whale ships, entering the north water in June, push on towards the sounds. If there is a "land-floe across," *i.e.*, if the land-ice of the west side is continuous across the entrance of Ponds Bay and Lancaster Sound, whales will be seen in considerable numbers and good cargoes may be obtained; but immediately the land-floe breaks up the whales depart to the westward. When there is no land-floe across, the whales proceed at once into the secluded waters of Eclipse Sound and Prince Regent Inlet, where they resort during the summer months. At this season of the year most of the vessels cruise in the sounds, while a few search the middle ice, until the darkness of the August nights compels them to seek an anchorage in some of the harbours of the west side, where they await the return of the whales south. This migration takes place on the formation of young ice in the sounds, usually in the latter part of September. Only the larger individuals, however, and the great majority of these males, come close down along the land of the west side. These the ships send their boats out to intercept, and this forms the inshore fishing or "rock-nosing", which is continued until the formation of young ice drives the vessels out of their harbours, usually early in October.

Hudson's Bay fishing.

A few vessels, American as well as British, occasionally enter Hudson's Bay and prosecute the fishing in the neighbourhood of Southampton Island, and even enter Fox Channel. There are whaling-stations in Cumberland Inlet, and a few vessels usually remain all winter, ready to take advantage of the opening of the ice in the following spring. Here the young as well as the old whales make their appearance in May; the former have migrated south during the previous autumn amongst the archipelago of islands forming the west side into Fox Channel, thence by Hudson's Strait to the pack-ice off Resolution Island, where, together with the old whales, they probably winter. Early in May the whalemen drag their boats over the ice to the open water at the floe edge, and the whales are seen amongst the pack-ice in the offing, the younger whales being nearest the land-floe. Encampments are formed along the floe edge, and the fishing is continued until the whales migrate north in June.

Produce of Greenland whale-fishing.

The average full-grown Greenland right whale yields about 15 tons of oil and 15 cwts. of whalebone, although individuals are occasionally killed which yield nearly 30 tons of oil and 30 cwts. of whalebone. The whalebone consists of about 590 slips, the longest measuring 10 feet 6 inches and weighing 5¼ lb in an average animal, 12 feet 6 inches and 9½ lb in a very large one. The following table shows the returns of these fisheries from 1860 to 1886 inclusive, in so far as British vessels were concerned. It will be seen that a constant decrease has taken place both in the number of whales killed and in the total value of the produce. The price to which oil has fallen little more than pays the expense and trouble attending its being taken on board and its subsequent preparation for the market, and there can be little doubt that, but for the high price which whalebone commands, the fishing would long ere this have been abandoned as unremunerative.

	Whales Killed.			Produce.		Value		
Year.	Off Greenland.	In Davis Strait.	Total.	Tons of Oil.	Cwts. of Whalebone.	Of Oil per cwt.	Of Whalebone[1] per cwt.	Of Total Produce.
						£ s. d.	£ s. d.	£
1860	8	76	84	1291	1539	1 12 6	20 10 0	70,828
1861	3	190	193	1947	2178	1 19 0	18 0 0	112,305
1862	1	97	98	940	1051	2 7 0	26 0 0	69,185
1863	15	25	40	618	679	2 10 0	27 0 0	48,627
1864	3	65	68	762	903	2 4 0	26 10 0	54,818
1865	8	58	66	742	869	2 9 0	26 0 0	57,039
1866	35	46	81	868	933	2 9 0	24 15 0	63,563
1867	7	17	24	228	240	2 3 0	20 0 0	12,366
1868	4	130	134	1228	1357	1 16 0	22 0 0	71,529
1869	4	17	21	266	207	2 2 0	23 15 0	15,960
1870	1	85	86	962	1111	1 18 0	18 5 0	54,871
1871	4	148	152	1348	1544	1 14 6	18 10 0	72,647
1872	25	113	138	1392	1486	1 19 0	24 10 0	87,601
1873	2	170	172	1429	1475	1 19 6	24 10 0	89,508
1874	1	208	209	1662	1680	1 18 0	26 0 0	103,130
1875	2	96	98	925	970	1 16 0	31 0 0	60,770
1876	13	70	83	987	1118	1 16 0	42 10 0	79,009
1877	2	95	97	867	935	1 13 0	60 0 0	79,892
1878	19	10	29	360	400	1 11 0	70 0 0	36,780
1879	6	72	78	755	829	1 7 9	50 0 0	58,892
1880	5	127	132	1000	1074	1 7 0	37 10 0	63,858
1881	23	58	81	709	696	1 11 0	35 0 0	44,268
1882	..	79	79	660	582	1 11 0	50 0 0	47,011
1883	1	17	18	200	216	1 12 0	110 0 0	28,150
1884	11	79	90	912	932	1 5 0	72 10 0	84,132
1885	12	29	41	430	435	1 1 9	60 0 0	33,233
1886	15	19	34	320	370	1 1 0	82 10 0	34,652

History of Greenland whale fishing.

History.—As already stated (see above, p. 524) a right whale fishery of great importance was prosecuted in the temperate waters of the Atlantic at a very early period, more especially by the hardy seamen of the Basque provinces from the 10th to the 16th century. Authorities are now agreed that the whale pursued was *Balæna biscayensis*, which differs from *B. mysticetus* in its smaller size, its greater activity, and its more southern distribution. The Greenland right whale fishery owes its origin to Henry Hudson's first voyage to Greenland and Spitzbergen in 1607. His glowing accounts of the great numbers of whales and morses led to the despatch of Jonas Poole to the Greenland Sea by the Muscovy Company, and the success of his four voyages (1609-1612) speedily attracted the vessels of other nations. For a time the English endeavoured to obtain a monopoly of the fishing; but, the other nations resisting, hostilities were engaged in, which resulted in the discomfiture of the English by a Dutch fleet in 1618. Thereafter it was agreed that different parts of the Spitzbergen coast should be allotted to different nationalities. The English interest in the industry, however, declined, and the fishing fell mainly into the hands of the Dutch, who until 1640 also carried on an important fishing in the seas surrounding the island of Jan Mayen. Meanwhile they did not neglect the Spitzbergen fishery, in which 10,019 whales were taken by them in the ten years 1679-1688. About 1680, when their fishing was probably at its most prosperous stage, they had 260 vessels and 14,000 seamen employed. Their fishery continued to flourish on almost as extensive a scale until 1770, when it began

[1] The figures given are the values of "size-bone," *i.e.*, slips of whalebone exceeding 6 feet in length, which is twice the value of whalebone under that length, so that before the exact value of the produce could be arrived at it has been found necessary to compute 17 per cent. of the whalebone at half the figure given, being the proportion of whalebone under size in an average whale.

to decline, and finally, owing to the war, came to a close before the end of the century. At the same time the Germans prosecuted the fishing to a very considerable extent: 79 vessels from Hamburg and Bremen were employed in 1721, and during the fifty years 1670-1719 an average of 45 vessels sailed yearly from Hamburg alone. German vessels continued to engage in the fishing until 1873. The Spaniards, although they took part in the pursuit at an early date, and appear at first to have supplied the skilled portion of the crews of the English and Dutch vessels, never seem to have engaged largely in the northern fishery; 20 of their vessels were employed in it in 1721, but before the end of the century they had entirely abandoned the occupation. The Danes, although likewise early appearing on the Spitzbergen fishing-grounds, never pursued the industry on a large scale until after the commencement of the Davis Strait fishing in 1721, in which year they had 90 sail engaged; in 1803 the number had fallen to 35. As for the English fishing, although sundry attempts had been made to revive it, notably in 1673 and in 1725 (the latter year by the South Sea Company), it was not until a bounty of 20s. per ton on the burden of the ships employed, granted in 1733, had been increased to 40s. in 1749 that the industry began to revive; in the same year vessels sailed from Scotland for the first time. Notwithstanding the reduction of the bounty to 30s. the number of ships sailing from British ports in 1787 amounted to 255. In 1814 the value of the gross freights of the Greenland and Davis Strait fleets amounted to £700,000, and in the same year the "Resolution" of Peterhead, Captain Souter, returned from Greenland with 44 whales, producing 299 tons of oil, the largest cargo ever brought into Great Britain. In 1824 the bounty was finally withdrawn. Since that time, owing to the scarcity of whales, and still more to their increasing shyness, caused in a great measure by the injudicious use of steam, the returns of the fishery have been gradually decreasing and the vessels employed have become fewer.

Sperm whale fishing.

Sperm Whale.—Since 1853 British vessels have ceased to prosecute this fishing. Begun in 1775, the British sperm whale fishing soon increased and by 1791 had assumed considerable importance, when the vessels engaged numbered 75, all hailing from London. It was British sperm whalemen who opened up the whaling-grounds of the Pacific and Indian Oceans.

American Fisheries.

The American whale fisheries embrace the Behring's Strait or Arctic fishery and the sperm whale or southern fishery.

Behring Strait fishery.

Greenland Right Whale.—As already mentioned above, the object of this fishery is the capture of *Balæna mysticetus.* In this case, however, the whales are mostly sought, not among the ice, but in open water, the vessels used being less adapted to ice navigation than those of the British, and nearly all are propelled by sail power alone. The hand harpoon is preferred and bomb lances are used to kill the whales. The vessels sail mostly from San Francisco in March, and arrive at the ice edge off Cape Navarin, where the fishing is first prosecuted, in May. The whales disappear during summer, but return in the autumn, when the "fall" fishing is carried on in the neighbourhood of Point Barrow; between seasons the vessels go south and prosecute the sperm whaling. The Behring Strait fishery was commenced in 1848, and in the three following years 250 ships obtained cargoes. In 1871 34 vessels were abandoned in the ice off Cape Belcher, the crews making good their escape to other vessels; again in 1876 12 vessels experienced a similar fate.

Sperm whale fishing.

Sperm Whale.—The capture of the sperm whale (*Physeter macrocephalus*) is prosecuted throughout the tropical seas of the globe. The distribution of the animal being, however, restricted to deep water, the fishing is usually carried on at a distance from land. The vessels used are generally barques of about 300 tons, carrying five boats and manned by a crew of thirty hands all told. The vessels have no particular time for sailing or arriving in port; the duration of a voyage is generally three years. The sperm whale is killed in the same manner as the Greenland right whale; the use of the hand harpoon is, however, preferred; and the whale-boats, which are not required to withstand contact with ice, are less strongly built, and much lighter and swifter than those used in the northern fisheries. The ordinary sperm whale yields about 60 barrels of oil (=10 tons), although large males are occasionally killed which yield a greater quantity. The oil is boiled at sea; hence its freedom from smell and the consequent high price which it commands as compared with that of the bottlenose whale.

Sperm whale fishing seems to have commenced early in the 18th century, the whaling community of Nantucket embarking in the industry about 1712; and in 1774, before the commencement of the War of Independence, a fleet of 360 vessels was engaged in it. This fishery perhaps reached its climax in 1846, when it occupied a total of 735 vessels, having an aggregate capacity of 233,199 tons. During the period 1877 to 1886 inclusive the average annual number of vessels employed was 159, their average annual aggregate burden being 35,713 tons. The average annual imports into the United States of whaling produce were as follows:—of sperm oil 31,824 barrels (=5304 tons), of whale oil 29,180 barrels (=4863 tons), of whalebone 325,559 lb (=145 tons). New Bedford and San Francisco are the principal whaling-ports.

Norwegian Fisheries.

The Norwegian fisheries include that of the fin whale and that of the bottle-nose whale.

Fin whale fishery

Fin Whale.—Associated with this fishery is the name of Svend Foyn, the seaman who first invented apparatus to attack successfully the large and active fin whales which abound in northern seas, and at certain seasons frequent the fjords of the north coast of Norway. The principal feature of the whaling gear is the use of an exploding harpoon, which virtually kills the animal immediately it is struck. Owing to its weight, a gun of large size is required to throw the harpoon, and in turn a craft of considerable burden is required to carry the gun. The harpoon bears a shell containing $\frac{3}{4}$ lb powder and weighs 123 lb; the gun, $4\frac{1}{2}$ inches thick at the muzzle, with 3 inches bore, requires a charge of 1 lb powder, and weighs about 15 cwts.; the vessel answering the purpose of a whale-boat is a steamer of about 80 tons burden and 30 horse-power. It is used not only for carrying the gun and pursuing the whales but also for towing the bodies of the animals when dead to the "factory" on shore, where the operation of flensing is performed. The whales hunted (in the order of their size and relative value) are (1) the blue whale (*Balænoptera sibbaldii*), (2) the humpback (*Megaptera longimana*), (3) the common rorqual (*Balænoptera musculus*), (4) Rudolphi's rorqual (*B. borealis*), and (5) the lesser rorqual (*B. rostrata*). All are killed for their oil, which is much inferior in quality to that of the Greenland right whale, for their whalebone, which is short and brittle, and for their bones and flesh, which are converted into manure. The whalers hail from the south of Norway (Sandefjord, Tönsberg, &c.), and have their whaling stations or "factories" on the fjords along the coast of Finmark. The fishing is prosecuted only in summer. In 1884 450 fin whales were killed, in 1885 1398, and in 1886 954.

Bottle-nose whale fishery.

Bottlenose Whale.—The bottlenose whale (*Hyperoodon rostratus*) abounds during summer in the northern seas adjacent to the ice edge, from the Labrador coast on the west to Nova Zembla on the east, but more particularly in the neighbourhood of Jan Mayen and Iceland, where the fishing is usually prosecuted during May, June, and July. Previous to May the weather is generally too stormy, and about the middle of July the whales, although hitherto numerous, suddenly disappear. The average-sized bottlenose whale yields 22 cwts. of oil, 5 per cent. of which is spermaceti; the oil is superior even to sperm as a lubricant. Although the whale-ships had frequented the northern seas for centuries, and sailed over the haunts of these animals season after season, it was not until recent years that they were discovered to exist there in immense numbers. The fishing may be said to date from the capture of 203 of these animals by the "Eclipse," Captain David Gray, of Peterhead in 1882. In the following year a number of British vessels took up the fishing, and at the same time the Norwegians embarked in it to such an extent that the market was soon glutted with oil, and the price fell from £55 per ton to £18, which no longer renders the industry remunerative to British vessels. A fleet of about thirty small sailing vessels annually leaves the Norwegian ports to prosecute this fishing. In 1885 they killed over 1300 whales and in 1886 about 1700.

Literature.—On British whale fisheries, see Scoresby, *Arctic Regions, Voyage to the Greenland Sea in 1822*; M'Culloch, *Dict. of Commerce*; Markham, *Whaling Cruise*; Southwell, "Notes on the Seal and Whale Fisheries," in *Zoologist*, 1884, &c.; F. D. Bennett, *Whaling Voyage round the Globe, 1833-36*; and Beale, *The Sperm Whale and its Captors*, 1839. On American whale fisheries the following works may be consulted:—Starbuck, *Hist. of Amer. Whale Fishery from its Earliest Inception to 1876*; *Report of U. S. Comm. of Fisheries*, 1875, vol. iv.; *Whalemen's Shipping List and Merchants' Transcript* (New Bedford); and Scammon, *Mammalia of North-Western America*, 1874. On the Norwegian whale fisheries there are various papers in the *Zoologist*, by A. H. Cocks, 1884 and succeeding years. (R. GR.)

WHALEBONE is the inaccurate name under which the baleen plates of the right whale are popularly known; and the trade-name of whale-fin, which the substance receives in commerce, is equally misleading. Three kinds of whalebone are recognized by traders—the Greenland, yielded by the Greenland whale, *Balæna mysticetus*; the South Sea, the produce of the Antarctic black whale, *B. australis*; and the Pacific or American, which is obtained from *B. japonica*. Of these the Greenland whalebone is the most valuable. It formed the only staple known in earlier times, when the northern whale fishery was a great and productive industry. This whalebone usually comes into the market trimmed and clean, with the hairy fringe which edges the plates removed. To prepare whalebone for its economic applications, the blades or plates are boiled for about twelve hours, till the substance is quite soft, in which state it is cut either into narrow strips or into small bristle-like filaments, according to the use to which it is to be devoted.

Whalebone possesses a unique combination of properties which render it peculiarly and almost exclusively suitable for several purposes. It is light, flexible, tough, and fibrous, and its fibres run parallel to each other without intertwisting. It has been found practicable to employ flexible steel for several purposes to which whalebone was formerly applied, especially in the umbrella and corset industries, in which steel is now almost exclusively used. Whalebone is, however, still in large demand among dressmakers and milliners; but it is principally used in the brush trade. In cases where bristles are too soft and weak, and where the available vegetable fibres possess insufficient elasticity and durability, whalebone offers the great advantage of being procurable in strips or filaments, long or short, thick or thin, according to requirement. Hence it is principally used for making brushes for mechanical purposes, such as machines for road-sweeping, chimney-sweeping, boiler-flue cleaning, the cleaning of ships' bottoms, and for stable use, &c. The use of whalebone in brush-making was originally patented by Samuel Crackles in 1808, and various special machines have been adapted for cutting the material into filaments. When whalebone came into the English market in the 17th century it cost at first about £700 per ton. In the 18th century its price ranged from £350 to £500 per ton, but early in the 19th century it fell as low as £25. Later it varied from £200 to £250; but with the decrease in whaling the article has become very scarce, and upwards of £1500 per ton is now paid for Greenland whalebone.

WHALE OILS. The whale or train (Germ., *Thran*) oil of commerce may be obtained from the blubber of any species of whale or dolphin (see WHALE FISHERIES, above). The only whale oil that is otherwise commercially distinguished is sperm or spermaceti oil, yielded by the sperm whales. Whale oil varies in colour from a bright honey yellow to a dark brown, according to the condition of the blubber from which it has been extracted. At best it has a rank fishy odour, and the darker the colour the more disagreeable the smell. Train oil consists of a glyceride of physetoleic acid (also found in earth-nut oil), together with stearin, palmitin, &c. With lowering of the temperature stearin, accompanied with a small proportion of spermaceti, separates from the oil, and a little under the freezing-point nearly the whole of these constituents may be crystallized out. When separated and pressed, this deposit is known as whale tallow, and the oil from which it is removed is distinguished as pressed whale oil; this, owing to its limpidity, is sometimes passed as sperm oil. Whale oil is principally used in oiling wools for combing, in batching flax and other vegetable fibres, in currying and chamois leather-making, and as a lubricant for machinery. Sperm oil is obtained from the enormous cavity in the head of the sperm whale, and from several smaller receptacles throughout the body of the animal. During the life of the whale the contents of these cavities are in a fluid condition, but no sooner is the "head matter" removed than the solid wax spermaceti separates in white crystalline flakes, leaving the oil a clear yellow fluid having a fishy odour. The oil, which has an acid reaction, is purified by treatment with a solution of potash, which precipitates impurities held by the acid of the oil. Refined sperm oil is a most valuable lubricant for small and delicate machinery.

WHARTON, MARQUIS OF. Two noblemen with this title, father and son, hold a certain place in English literary history as subjects of satiric portraiture.

THOMAS WHARTON (1640-1715), a prominent Whig politician at the Revolution, is reputed by Dr Percy to have been the author of the famous political ballad *Lilliburlero*, which "sang James II. out of three kingdoms." Wharton was lord-lieutenant of Ireland in Anne's reign, and incurred the wrath of Swift, who attacked him as Verres in the *Examiner* (No. 14), and drew a separate "character" of him, which is one of Swift's masterpieces. He was a man of great wit and versatile cleverness, and cynically ostentatious in his immorality, having the reputation of being the greatest rake and the truest Whig of his time. Addison dedicated to him the fifth volume of the *Spectator*, giving him a very different "character" from Swift's.

PHILIP WHARTON (1699-1731), the son of Thomas, succeeded to title and fortune at the age of sixteen, and quickly earned for himself, by his wild and profligate frolics and reckless playing at politics, Pope's satire of him as "the scorn and wonder of our days" (*Moral Essays*, i. 179). He spent his large estates in a few years, then went abroad and gave eccentric support to the Old Pretender. There is a lively picture of his appearance at Madrid in 1726 in a letter from the British consul, quoted in Stanhope's *History of England* (ii. p. 140).

The elder Wharton is described at length by Macaulay as one of the four chiefs of the Whigs after the Revolution (*History*, chap. 20). He was created earl of Wharton in 1706, and marquis in 1714, immediately after the arrival of George I. in England. The younger Wharton succeeded to the marquisate in 1715 on his father's death, and was created duke on coming of age in 1720.

WHATELY, RICHARD (1787-1863), archbishop of Dublin, was born in London on 1st February 1787. He was the youngest of the nine children of the Rev. Joseph Whately of Nonsuch Park, Surrey. After attending a private school near Bristol (where his father was prebendary), he went to Oxford in 1805 and entered Oriel College, then the most distinguished in the university. Copleston, afterwards bishop of Llandaff, was a college tutor when Whately entered, and had a marked influence upon the younger man. In their long walks together round Oxford they discussed and worked out much that was afterwards embodied in Whately's *Logic*. Whately took a double second-class in honours in 1808, afterwards gaining the prize for the English essay, and in 1811 he was elected fellow of Oriel. He continued to reside at Oxford as a private tutor, and in 1814 took holy orders. The Oriel common-room at that time was full of intellectual life, destined to discharge itself in very varied channels. Besides Copleston and Whately, Davison, Arnold, Keble, and Hawkins were among the fellows, and Newman and Pusey were added about the time of Whately's leaving Oxford. Newman has put on record in his *Apologia* his indebtedness to Whately, who, he says, opened his mind and taught him to think and to use his reason. They soon became separated; but between Arnold and Whately there was a warm friendship till the death of the former. It was at this time that Whately wrote his celebrated tract, *Historic Doubts relative to Napoleon Bonaparte*, a very clever *jeu d'esprit* directed against excessive scepticism as applied to the Gospel history. In 1820 Whately made the acquaintance of Elizabeth Pope, to whom he was married in July of the following year. After his marriage he first settled in Oxford, where he continued to take pupils, and in 1822 he was appointed Bampton lecturer. The lectures, *On the Use and Abuse of Party Spirit in Matters of Religion*, were published in the same year, and were followed by a volume of *Sermons* in 1823. In August 1823 he removed to Halesworth in Suffolk, a country living to which he had been presented. Here two years were spent in vigorous parish work; but the damp climate nearly proved fatal to Mrs Whately, and, when he was appointed in 1825 to the principalship of St Alban Hall, he returned with his family to Oxford. In the same year he took the degree of doctor of divinity. At St Alban Hall Whately found much to reform, and he left it a different place. In 1825 he published a series of *Essays on Some of the Peculiarities of the Christian Religion*, followed in 1828 by a second series *On Some of the Difficulties in the Writings of St Paul*, and in 1830 by a third *On the Errors of Romanism traced to their Origin in Human Nature*. He also published in 1829 a volume of his Halesworth sermons, under the title *A View of the Scripture Revelations concerning a Future*

State. It was while he was at St Alban Hall (1826) that the work appeared which is perhaps most closely associated with his name,—his treatise on *Logic*, originally contributed to the *Encyclopædia Metropolitana*. By this work, which gave a great impetus to the study of logic not only in Oxford but throughout Great Britain, Whately has been known to generation after generation of students; and, though it is no longer so much in use, the qualities of the book make much of it as admirable now as when it was written. Whately swept the webs of scholasticism from the subject, and raised the study to a new level. A similar treatise on *Rhetoric*, also contributed to the *Encyclopædia*, appeared in 1828. In 1829 Whately was elected to the professorship of political economy at Oxford in succession to Senior. In writing to a friend he gives the following characteristic reason for accepting the appointment: "It seems to me that before long political economists of some sort will govern the world. Now the anti-Christians are striving hard to have this science to themselves, and to interweave it with their notions; and, if these efforts are not met, the rising generation will be at the mercy of these men." It was a subject admirably suited to his lucid, practical intellect; but his tenure of office was cut short by his appointment to the archbishopric of Dublin in 1831. He published only one course of *Introductory Lectures* (1831), in which he sought to establish the true scope of the science; but one of his first acts on going to Dublin was to endow a chair of political economy in Trinity College out of his private purse. Whately's appointment by Lord Grey to the see of Dublin came as a great surprise to everybody, for though a decided Liberal Whately had from the beginning stood aloof from all political parties, and ecclesiastically his position was that of an Ishmaelite fighting for his own hand. The Evangelicals regarded him as a dangerous latitudinarian on the ground of his views on Catholic emancipation, the Sabbath question, the doctrine of election, and certain quasi-Sabellian opinions he was supposed to hold about the character and attributes of Christ, while his view of the church was diametrically opposed to that of the High Church party, and from the beginning he was the determined opponent of what was afterwards called the Tractarian movement. The appointment was challenged in the House of Lords, but without success. In Ireland it was immensely unpopular among the Protestants, both for the reasons just mentioned and as being the appointment of an Englishman and a Whig. Whately's blunt outspokenness and his "want of conciliating manners," which even his friends admit, prevented him from ever completely eradicating these prejudices; and the amount of opposition he met with from his own clergy would have daunted a man less resolute than the new archbishop in the performance of what he conceived to be his duty. He ran counter to their most cherished prejudices from the first by connecting himself prominently with the attempt to establish a national and unsectarian system of education. He enforced strict discipline in his diocese, where it had been long unknown; and he published an unanswerable, and all the more unpalatable, statement of his views on the Sabbath (*Thoughts on the Sabbath*, 1832). The archbishopric of Dublin at that time—just after the passing of the Catholic Emancipation Act, and in the midst of a general refusal to pay tithes—was anything but a bed of roses. Whately spoke of his appointment as "a call to the helm of a crazy ship in a storm," and one which nothing but an overpowering sense of duty could have induced him to accept. He took a small country place at Redesdale, four miles out of Dublin, where he could enjoy his favourite relaxation of gardening. Here his life was one of indefatigable industry. Questions of tithes, reform of the Irish Church, reform of the Irish Poor Laws, and, in particular, the organization of national education occupied much of his time. But he found leisure for the discussion of other public questions, for example, the subject of transportation and the general question of secondary punishments, in which he was strongly interested and on which he repeatedly published. In 1837 he wrote his well-known handbook of *Christian Evidences*, which was translated during his lifetime into more than a dozen languages. At a later period he also wrote, in a similar form, *Easy Lessons on Reasoning*, on *Morals*, on *Mind*, and on the *British Constitution*. He attached much importance himself to these unpretending but useful books. Among other works may be mentioned *Charges and Tracts* (1836), *Essays on some of the Dangers to Christian Faith* (1839), *The Kingdom of Christ* (1841). He also edited Bacon's *Essays*, Paley's *Evidences*, and Paley's *Moral Philosophy*. His cherished scheme of unsectarian religious instruction for Protestants and Catholics alike was carried out for a number of years with a measure of success, a selection of Scripture lessons and of Christian evidences by the archbishop himself being actually used in the model schools. But in 1852 the scheme broke down through the opposition of the new Catholic archbishop of Dublin, and Whately felt himself constrained to withdraw from the Education Board. This was felt by him as a grievous disappointment. From the beginning Whately was a keen-sighted observer of the condition of Ireland question, and gave much offence by openly supporting the state endowment of the Catholic clergy as a measure of justice. During the terrible years of 1846 and 1847 the archbishop and his family were unwearied in their efforts to alleviate the miseries of the people. Whately's private beneficence was not confined, however, to this period. Though so rigid a political economist that he could boast of never having given a penny to a beggar, his charities were princely, and oftenest bestowed without the knowledge of his nearest friends. From 1856 onwards symptoms of decline began to manifest themselves in a paralytic affection of the left side, which kept his arm in a constant tremor. In 1860 he lost his wife and a much-loved daughter. Still he continued the active discharge of his public duties till the summer of 1863, when he was prostrated by an ulcer in the leg, and after several months of acute suffering he died on 8th October 1863. In the following year his daughter published *Miscellaneous Remains* from his commonplace book and in 1866 his *Life and Correspondence* in two volumes. The loosely compiled *Anecdotal Memoirs of Archbishop Whately*, by W. J. Fitzpatrick (1864), may be used (with discretion) as enlivening Miss Whately's picture of her father.

Few eminent men have had more anecdotes and witty sayings attributed to them than Whately. He was a great talker, much addicted in early life to argument, in which he used others as instruments on which to hammer out his own views, and as he advanced in life much given to didactic monologue. But this didactic tendency was accompanied almost to the last by an intensely youthful delight in logic-chopping. At his monthly dinners to his clergy the archbishop would indulge even to an undignified extent in a species of logical horse-play. To this were added a keen wit, whose sharp edge often inflicted wounds never deliberately intended by the speaker, and a wholly uncontrollable love of punning. Whately often offended people by the extreme unconventionality of his manners. When at Oxford his white hat, rough white coat, and huge white dog earned for him the sobriquet of the White Bear, and he outraged the conventions of the place by exhibiting the exploits of his climbing dog in Christchurch Meadow. This free and easy manner clung to him in later life and accompanied him into the Dublin drawing-rooms, where it was often exaggerated by absence of mind. His fondness for dogs and animals generally was a passion through life, and he was also very fond of children, who, with their usual discrimination, gave him their confidence in return. He was an adept in various savage sports more especially in throwing the boomerang.

Whately was a man loved and reverenced by a narrow circle, hated, or at least distrusted, by a much larger number. This was largely owing to his own intellectual characteristics; for, with a remarkably fair and lucid mind, his sympathies were narrow, and by his blunt outspokenness on points of difference he alienated many. With no mystical fibre in his own constitution, the Tractarian movement was incomprehensible to him, and was the object of his bitter dislike and contempt. The doctrines of the Low Church party seemed to him to be almost equally tinged with superstition. In short, it is admitted even by his admirers that he had a tendency to depreciate those minds which could not rest content with his own "common-sense" view of Christianity. Seeing so clearly himself, he could not believe that there might be things which he could not see. Though a great logician, there was nothing philosophical or speculative about his mind, and he took a practical, almost business-like view of Christianity, which seemed to High Churchmen and Evangelicals alike little better than Rationalism. In this they did Whately less than justice, for his belief in Christianity as understood by himself was thoroughly genuine, and his religion was to him a real thing. But he may be said to have continued into our own times the typical Christianity of the 18th century—the Christianity of the theologians who went out to fight the Rationalists with their own weapons. It is to Whately essentially a belief in certain matters of fact, to be accepted or rejected after an examination of "evidences." Hence his endeavour always is to convince the logical faculty, and his Christianity inevitably appears as a thing of the intellect rather than of the heart. Whately himself was well aware that he was out of harmony with the general tendency of his time, and even Broad Church theology has in general proceeded since upon other lines than his. Nevertheless, though in no sense a fruitful or suggestive mind, his clear and massive intellect inspired general respect, and his books well repay reading by the shrewdness of their observation, the acuteness of the reasoning, the faculty of telling illustration, and the uniform excellence of style. Whately's qualities are exhibited at their best in his *Logic*, which is, as it were, the quintessence of the views which he afterwards applied to different subjects. He has written nothing better than the luminous Appendix to this work on "Ambiguous Terms." (A. SE.)

Structure of wheat plant.

WHEAT (*Triticum*), the most important and the most generally diffused of cereal grasses, is an annual plant, with hollow, erect, knotted stems, and produces, in addition to the direct developments from the seedling plant, secondary roots and secondary shoots (tillers) from the base. Its leaves have each a long sheath encircling the stem, and at the junction of the blade or "flag" with the sheath a small whitish outgrowth or "ligula." The inflorescence or ear consists of a central stalk bent zigzag, now to the one side, now to the other, thus forming a series of notches (see fig. 1), and bearing a number of flattened spikelets, one of which grows out of each notch and has its inner or upper face pressed up against it. At the base of each spikelet are two empty boat-shaped glumes or "chaff-scales," one to the right, the other to the left, and then a series of flowers, 2 to 8 in number, closely crowded together; the uppermost are abortive or sterile,—indeed, in some varieties only one or two of the flowers are fertile. Each flower consists of an outer or lower glume, called the flowering glume, of the same shape as the empty glume and terminating in a long, or it may be in a short, awn or "beard" On the other side of the flower and at a slightly higher level is the "palea," of thinner texture than the other glumes, with infolded margins and with two ribs or veins. These several glumes are closely applied one to the other so as to conceal and protect the ovary, and they only separate to allow of the passage of the empty anthers after fertilization. Within the pale are two minute, ovate, pointed, white membranous scales called "lodicles." These contain three stamens with thread-like filaments and oblong, two-lobed anthers. The stamens are placed round the base of the ovary, which is a rounded or oblong body, much smaller than the glumes, covered with down, and surmounted by two short styles, extending into feathery brush-like stigmas. The ripe fruit or grain, sometimes called the "berry," the matured state of the ovary and its contents, is oblong or ovoid, with a longitudinal furrow on one side. The ovary adheres firmly to the seed in the interior, so that on examining a longitudinal section of the grain by the microscope the outer layer is seen to consist of epidermal cells, of which the uppermost are prolonged into short hairs to cover the apex of the grain. Two or three layers of cells inside the epidermis constitute the tissue of the ovary, and overlie somewhat similar layers which form the coats of the seed. Within these last is a layer of square cells larger and more regular in form than those on each side; these contain the gluten or nitrogenous matter upon which so much of the nutritive value of the seed depends. This thin layer of gluten cells contains the albumen or perisperm, which constitutes the great mass of the seed, being composed of numerous cells of irregular form and size filled with starch grains. These layers of cells become more or less dry and inseparable one from another, forming the substance known as "bran." At the lower end of the albumen, and placed obliquely, is the minute embryo-plant, which derives its nourishment in the first instance from the albumen; this is destined to form the future plant.

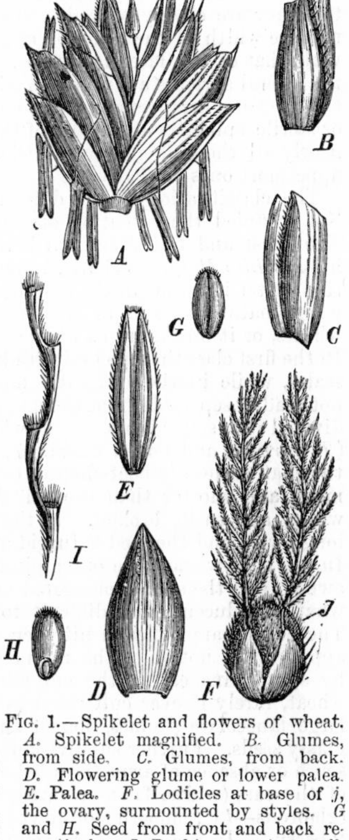

Fig. 1.—Spikelet and flowers of wheat. *A.* Spikelet magnified. *B.* Glumes, from side. *C.* Glumes, from back. *D.* Flowering glume or lower palea. *E.* Palea. *F.* Lodicles at base of *j*, the ovary, surmounted by styles. *G* and *H.* Seed from front and back respectively. *I.* Rachis, or central stalk of ear, spikelets removed.

Origin and species.

Such in brief is the general structure of the wheat plant as we now know it. Of its principal variations mention will be made below. What was its origin is not known; and opinion has differed as to whether more than one species is involved or whether all the varieties now known may not have been originally derived from one. The prevalent opinion among botanists is that the wheat plant is nowhere found in a wild condition. Recently, however, M. Frédéric Houssay is alleged to have discovered the plant wild in the mountains to the east of Kurdistan; but the statement requires confirmation. Some of the species of the genus *Ægilops* (now referred to *Triticum* by Bentham and Hooker and by Haeckel) may possibly have been the sources of our cultivated forms, as they cross freely with wheats. Haeckel, the latest monographer of the genus, considers that there are three species. (1) *Triticum mono*

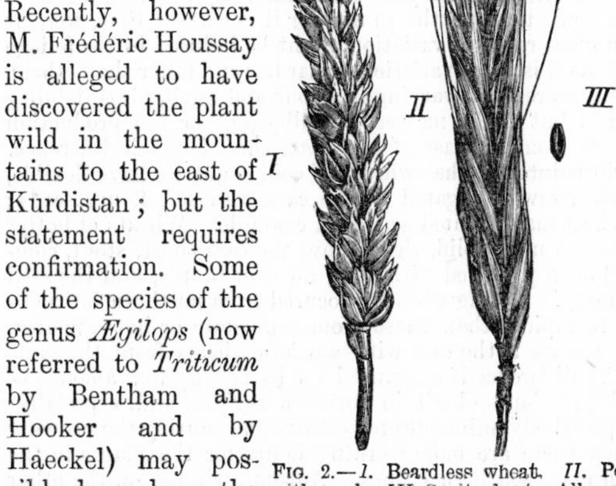

Fig. 2.—*I.* Beardless wheat. *II.* Polish wheat, with seed. *III.* Spelt wheat. All much reduced.

coccum, which undoubtedly grows wild in Greece and Mesopotamia, is cultivated in Spain and elsewhere, and was also cultivated by the aboriginal Swiss lake-dwellers, as well as at Hissarlik, as is shown by the grain[1] found in those localities. (2) *T. sativum* is the ordinary cultivated wheat, of which Haeckel recognizes three principal races, *spelta*, *dicoccum*, and *tenax*. Spelt wheats (see fig. 2) were cultivated by the aboriginal Swiss, by the ancient Egyptians, and throughout the Roman empire. The variety *dicoccum* was also cultivated in prehistoric times, and is still grown in southern Europe as a summer wheat and one suitable for starch-making. Other sub-varieties of *T. tenax* are *compactum*, *turgidum*, and *durum* (see below). (3) The third species, *T. polonicum*, or Polish wheat, is a very distinct-looking form, with long leafy glumes; its origin is not known. As these varieties intercross with each other, the presumption is that they, like the species of *Ægilops*, which also intercross with wheat, may have all originated from one common stock.

Home and distribution. Basing his conclusions upon philological data, such as the names of wheat in the oldest known languages, the writings of the most ancient historians, and the observations of botanical travellers, De Candolle infers that the original home of the wheat plant was in Mesopotamia, and that from thence its cultivation extended in very early times to the Canaries on the west and to China on the east. In the western hemisphere wheat was not known till the 16th century. Humboldt mentions that it was accidentally introduced into Mexico with rice brought from Spain by a negro slave belonging to Cortes, and the same writer saw at Quito the earthen vase in which a Flemish monk had introduced from Ghent the first wheat grown in South America.

Principal variations. As might be anticipated from the cultivation of the plant from time immemorial and from its wide diffusion throughout the eastern hemisphere, the varieties of wheat—that is, of *T. sativum*—are very numerous and of every grade of intensity. Those cases in which the variation is most extreme some botanists would prefer to consider as forming distinct species; but others, as De Vilmorin, having regard to the general facts of the case and to the numerous intermediate gradations, look upon all the forms as derivatives from one. In illustration of this latter point it may be mentioned that not only do the several varieties run one into the other, but their chemical composition varies likewise according to climate and season. According to Prof. Church,[2] even in the produce of a single ear there may be 3 to 4 per cent. more of albuminoid matters in some grains than in others; but on the average the proportion of gluten to starch is as 9·11 to 100. From the point of view of agriculture (see vol. i. p. 354) it is generally of no great moment what rank be assigned to the various forms. It is only important to take cognizance of them for purposes of cultivation under varying circumstances. Hence we only allude to some of the principal variations and to those characteristics which are found to be unstable. (1) Setting aside differences of constitution, such as hardihood, size, and the like, there is relatively little variation in the form of the organs of vegetation. This indicates that less attention has been paid to the straw than to the grain, for it is certain that, were it desirable, a great range of variation might be induced in the foliage and straw. As it is, some varieties are hardier and taller than others, and the straw more solid, varying in colour and having less liability to be "laid"; but in the matter of "tillering," or the production of side-shoots from the base of the stem, there is much difference. De Vilmorin points out that wheats of cold countries have flexible, thin, hollow straw, elongated fragile ears, and soft floury seeds; Hunter's wheat may be cited as a good example. Wheats of hotter countries have a more solid, rigid straw, the ears short, stout, compact, the glumes provided with long awns or beards, and the seed hard and horny. Spring wheats procured from northern latitudes mature more rapidly than those from temperate or hot climates, whilst the reverse is the case with autumn wheats from the same source. The difference is accounted for by the greater amount of light which the plants obtain in northern regions, and, especially, by its comparatively uninterrupted continuance during the growing period, when there are more working hours for the plants in the day than in more southern climes. Autumn wheats, on the other hand, are subjected to an enforced rest for a period of several months, and even when grown in milder climates remain quiescent for a longer period, and start into growth later in spring,—much later than varieties of southern origin. These latter, accustomed to the mild winters of those latitudes, begin to grow early in spring, and are in consequence liable to injury from spring frosts. Wheats of dry countries and of those exposed to severe winds have, says De Vilmorin, narrow leaves, pliant straw, bearded ears, and velvety chaff,—characteristics which enable them to resist wind and drought. Wheats of moist climates, on the other hand, have broader leaves, to admit of more rapid transpiration. No doubt careful microscopic scrutiny of the minute anatomy of the leaves of plants grown under various conditions would reveal further adaptations of structure to external conditions of climate. At any rate, it is certain that, as a general rule, the hard wheats are almost exclusively cultivated in hot, dry countries, the spelt wheats in mountainous districts and on poor soil, turgid wheats, like the Egyptian, in plains or in ill-drained valleys,—the best races of wheat being found on rich alluvial plains and in fertile valleys. The wheat used in the neighbourhood of Florence for straw-plaiting is a variety with very slender stalks. The seed is sown very thickly at the beginning of winter and pulled, not cut, about the end of May, before the ear is ripe. In the United Kingdom ordinary wheat, such as old red Lammas and Chiddam's white, is used for straw-plaiting, the straw being cut some time before the berry ripens. The propensity to "tiller" is of the greatest importance, as it multiplies the resources of the farmer. An instance of this is given in the *Philosophical Transactions* (1768), where it is stated that one seedling plant in the Cambridge botanic garden was divided into eighteen parts, each of which was replanted and subsequently again divided, till it produced sixty-seven plants in one season. In March and April of the following year these were again divided and produced 500 plants, which in due time yielded 21,109 ears. (2) The variations in root-development have not been much attended to, although it would be well to study them in order to ascertain the degree of adaptability to various depths and conditions of soil. (3) A most important difference is observable in the liability to attacks of rust (*Puccinia*), some varieties being almost invariably free from it, while others are in particular localities so subject to it as to be not worth cultivating. (4) Velvet-chaffed wheats do best in poor soil, and bearded wheats are usually hardiest. (5) The ears vary, not only in size, but also in form, this latter characteristic being dependent on the degree of closeness with which the spikelets are set on. In such varieties as Talavera the spikelets are loose, while in the club and square-headed varieties they are closely packed. The form of the ear depends on the relative width of the anterior and posterior surfaces as compared with that of the lateral surfaces. In the square-headed varieties the lateral surfaces are nearly as wide as the median ones, owing to the form and arrangement of the spikelets. The number of abortive or sterile spikelets at the top of the ear also varies: in some cases nearly all the spikelets are fertile, while in others several of the uppermost ones are barren.

Classification of cultivated wheats. The classification of the different varieties of cultivated wheat has occupied the attention of many botanists and agriculturists. The latest and fullest account is that of M. Henry de Vilmorin in his *Les Blés Meilleurs* (Paris, 1881). The classification adopted by this writer is based, in the first instance, on the nature of the ear: when mature its axis or stem remains unbroken, as in the true wheats, or it breaks into a number of joints, as in the spelt wheats. In the first class the ripe grain readily detaches itself from the chaff-scales, while in the spelts it is more or less adherent to them, or not readily separable from them. The true wheats are further subdivided into soft wheats, turgid wheats (*T. turgidum*), hard wheats (*T. durum*), and Polish wheats (*T. polonicum*). In the soft wheats the chaff-scales are boat-shaped, ovoid, of the consistence of parchment, and shorter than the spikelet; the seed is floury, opaque, white, and easily broken. In the turgid wheats the glumes have long awns, and the seed is turgid and floury, as in the soft wheats. In the hard wheats the outer glumes are keeled, sharply pointed, awned, and the seed is elongated and of hard glassy texture, somewhat translucent, and difficult to break owing to its toughness. These seeds are richer in nitrogen than the soft wheats, so that an approximate notion of the richness in albuminoids may be gained by simply inspecting the cut surface of the seed. The Polish wheat, rarely if ever cultivated in the United Kingdom, has very large lanceolate glumes, longer than the spikelet, and elongated glassy seeds. Further subdivisions are made, according to the presence or absence of awns (bearded and beardless wheats), the colour of the ears (white, fawn-coloured, or red), the texture of the ears (glabrous—*i.e.*, smooth—or downy), and the colour of the seed or "berry." In the jointed or spelt wheats the distinctions lie in the presence of awns, the direction of the points of the glumes (straight, bent outwards, or turned inwards), the form of the ear as revealed on a cross section, and the entire or cleft palea. As illustrating the fact of the occasional instability of these variations, Prof. Church mentions that a single grain will be sometimes horny and partly

[1] See drawings made to scale by Mr Worthington Smith in the *Gardener's Chronicle*, 25th December 1886.

[2] *Food Grains of India*, p. 94.

opaque and soft, in which case its composition will correspond with its aspect. The division into spring wheat and winter wheat is an agricultural one solely. Any variety may be a spring or a winter wheat according to the time at which it is sown. In the summer wheats it may often be observed that the median florets do not fill out so fully as in the autumn wheats. Among the turgid wheats there is a frequent tendency in the spike to branch or become compound, — a tendency which is manifested to a less degree in other forms. The Egyptian, or so-called "mummy" wheat is of this character, the lower part of the spike branching out into several subdivisions. This multiplication of the seed-bearing branches might at first sight be considered advantageous; but in practice the quality of the grain is found to be inferior, as if the force that should have been devoted to the maturation of the grain were, in a measure, diverted and expended in the production of additional branches to the spike.

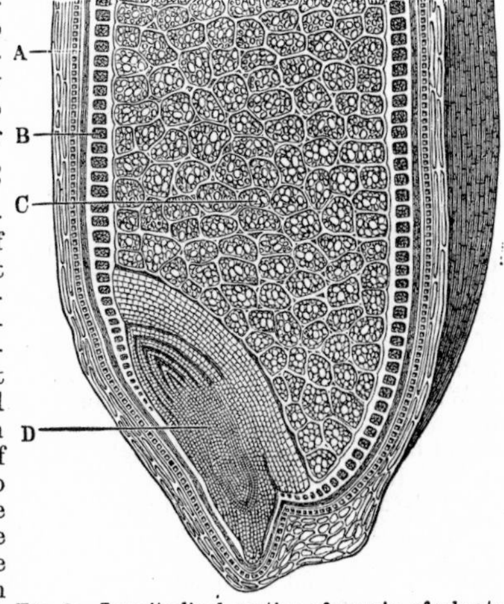

Fig. 3.—Longitudinal section of a grain of wheat; highly magnified. A. Epidermal cells. B. Cells containing gluten. C. Cells of perisperm or albumen, filled with starch. D. Embryo cut through the middle, root-end pointing downwards.

With regard to the chemical composition of the ripe grain, the Rothamsted experiments reveal a singular uniformity, even under very varied conditions of manuring, and even where much diversity was apparent in the constitution of the straw. A high or low percentage of nitrogen in the grain was also shown to depend more directly on the degree of ripening, as influenced by the character of the season, than on difference in manure; but it depends more upon the variety than upon soil or nutrition.

Adaptability to soil and locality.

Apart from the botanical interest of these diversities, as indications of the faculty of variation in plants, and possibly as clues to the genealogy and origin of the cultivated plant, their practical importance is very great. Some varieties are suited to hot, others to cold countries; some will flourish on one description of soil, others on another. Hence the paramount importance of ascertaining by experiment, not only what are the best varieties, but which are the best adapted for particular localities and particular climatic conditions. Porion and Dehérain have shown [1] the "infinite superiority" over the ordinary wheats of a particular square-headed variety grown on rich soil in the north of France. A good selection of seed, according to the nature of the soil, demands, says De Vilmorin, intelligence and accurate knowledge on the part of the farmer. If a good variety be grown in poor soil, the result will be unprofitable, while, if bad wheat be grown on good soil, the result may be nil. In botanical collections there exist, it is stated, herbarium specimens or other evidences of plants grown in Norway as far north as lat. 65° (Schubeler), in Switzerland at an elevation of 1200 feet above the valley of Zermatt (or 6500 feet above the sea), near the straits of Magellan, as well as in Teneriffe, the Cape of Good Hope, Abyssinia, Rodriguez, the Philippine Islands, and the Malay Archipelago. These widely-separated localities show the great area over which the culture is possible, and illustrate the powers of adaptation of the plant. The requirements of the consumer have also to be considered: for some purposes the soft wheats, with their large relative proportion of starch, are the best, for others the hard wheats, with their larger quantity of gluten. With the modern processes of milling, the hard wheats are preferred, for they make the best flour; and in North America the spring wheats are, as a rule, harder than the winter wheats. The soft wheats are those which are most general in European cultivation, and, as a rule, the beardless varieties, though more tender, are preferred. The bearded varieties are supposed to be hardier; at any rate they defy the ravages of predatory birds more completely than the unarmed varieties, and they are preferable in countries liable to storms of wind, as less likely to have their seeds detached. Hard wheats are specially employed in Italy for the fabrication of macaroni. Polish wheat is used for similar purposes. Spelt wheats are grown in the colder mountainous districts of Europe; their flour is very fine, and is used especially for pastry-making; but, owing to the construction of the grain, it requires special machinery for grinding (see Flour).

The following passage, reproduced from a German source in *Agricultural Science* (January 1887), may serve still further to illustrate the fitness of particular varieties for special purposes.

"Innumerable experiments have shown that the value of wheat for seed increases with the size of the grain: the larger kernel yields a stronger plant, and this will bear a heavier crop; the smaller grain contains the larger proportion of gluten, yields a better flour, and brings a higher price; but with the smaller yield per acre the profit may be less. The 'volume-weight' is dependent more on the well-rounded form of the grain than on its size; when about alike in respect to shape, the market value of the grain is closely proportionate to its weight per bushel. Grain of a higher specific gravity is usually richer in gluten. Richness in this constituent is of the greatest importance, as affecting the market value of the grain; it gives better baking qualities to the flour, besides a higher nutritive value, and is accompanied with greater richness in phosphate, also an important constituent of animal food. The proportion of gluten in wheat is determined largely by the climate, and especially by the proximity of the sea. Insular England produces a wheat grain with high absolute weight, but as a rule with less gluten than the wheat of eastern Europe. English wheat, and wheat in general grown in an ocean climate, seldom contains over ten per cent. of gluten, while in eastern Europe and in the western United States the proportion rises to twenty per cent. and above. Vigorous English seed wheat sown in eastern Europe yields larger crops than the native seed, and a grain richer in gluten than the parent, though not so rich as wheat from native seed." [2]

It is, however, to be observed that proximity to the sea does not produce soft wheat poor in gluten in Italy, Algeria, and other warm and tropical regions, where the plant is cultivated quite as much under the influence of the sea as in England. The soft wheat of Great Britain is to be explained rather by the mildness of the climate and the relative constancy of the temperature.

Wheat begins to grow at a temperature of 5° C. (41° Fahr.); and, when the aggregate temperature, as represented by the sum of the daily means, has mounted up to 185° Fahr., the germ begins to escape from the husk, if the seed be not deeply buried; but if it is deeply buried, an amount of heat is required greater in proportion to the depth. If the seed lies at a depth lower than a foot from the surface, it rarely germinates. The seedling plant ceases to grow if the mean temperature of the day remains below 42° Fahr. When the young plants have been influenced by an aggregate temperature amounting to 1896° Fahr. from the period when sown, or 1715° from the period of germination, branching or "tillering" goes on freely, and the young ears are formed. Under the influence of a mean temperature of 55°, or a little above, the flowers are produced. A still higher daily mean is required for the full development and ripening of the grain. The figures here cited are given by Risler and are calculated for the climate of Paris; but, of course, the same principles apply in the case of other countries. The amount of light and of moisture has also to be taken into account. The fact that the wheat plant requires less water than other cereals, and therefore does not suffer so much from drought, is one of great importance to the cultivator, and furnishes one reason for the greater proportionate culture of wheat in the eastern than in the western counties of England.

As for the soil requirements, see Agriculture, vol. i. p. 357. The following figures, cited by De Vilmorin from Joulie, will give an idea of the nature and amount of the demands made upon the soil by a wheat crop: in order to yield a crop of $44\frac{1}{2}$ bushels of wheat to the acre, the soil must supply to the crop during its growth in round numbers—202 lb of nitrogen, 81 lb of phosphoric acid, 55 lb of lime, 26 lb of magnesia, and 255 lb of potash.

Production of varieties.

The numerous varieties of wheat now in cultivation have been obtained either by selection or by cross-breeding. In any wheat-field there may be observed on close inspection plants differing in character from the majority. If seeds of these "sporting" plants be taken and grown in another season, they may (or may not) reproduce the particular variation. If they do, and the same process of selection be continued, the variation becomes in time "fixed," though it is always more or less liable to revert to its original condition. By continuously and systematically selecting the best grains from the best ears, Major Hallett has succeeded in introducing "pedigree wheats" of fine quality. But even greater results may be expected from cross-breeding, or the fertilization of the flowers of one description of wheat by the pollen of another. This has been attempted by Shireff, Le Couteur, Maund, and others in the past, and more recently by H. de Vilmorin and Messrs Carter. Under natural circumstances wheat is self-fertilized: that is to say, the pollen of any given flower impregnates the stigma and ovule of the same flower, the glumes and coverings of the flower being tightly pressed round the stamens and stigmas in such a way as to prevent the access of insects and to ensure the deposit of the pollen upon the stigmas of the same flower. This process of self-fertilization is the usual method, and no doubt keeps the variety true or unmixed; but the occasional presence of varieties in a wheat-field shows that cross-fertilization is sometimes secured. The stamens of the wheat plant may frequently be seen protruding beyond the glumes, and their position might lead to the inference that cross-fertilization was the rule; but on closer examination it will be found that the anthers are empty or nearly so, and that they are not protruded till after they have deposited the pollen upon the stigma. The separation of the glumes, which occurs at the time of fertilization,

[1] *Ann. Agronom.*, January 1888, p. 33.

[2] See Ritthausen, *Die Eiweisskörper d. Getreidearten, Hülsenfrüchte, und Oelsamen*, Bonn, 1872.

and which permits the egress of the useless stamens after that operation, is stated to occur only under certain conditions of temperature, when the heat, in fact, is sufficient to cause the lodicles of the flower to become turgid and thus to press apart the glumes. A temperature of about 75° Fahr. is found by Messrs Carter to be the most favourable. From what has been said it will be evident that the artificial fertilization of wheat is a very delicate operation. The glumes have to be separated and the anthers cut away before the pollen is fully formed, care being taken at the same time not to injure the stigma, and specially not to introduce, on the scissors or otherwise, any pollen except that of the variety desired. De Vilmorin's experiments have shown that all the varieties will intercross, and that even such a distinct form as the Polish is no exception. From this he concludes that all the forms have originated from one stock and are to be comprised within one species. In the progeny of these crossed wheats, especially in the second generation, much variation and difference of character is observable,—a phenomenon commonly noticed in the descendants from crosses and hybrids and styled by Naudin "irregular variation." Sometimes characteristics appear in the crossed wheats which are not found in the parent varieties, although they occur in other wheats. Thus, De Vilmorin records the presence of turgid wheats among seedlings raised from a soft wheat fertilized with the pollen of a hard variety, and spelt wheats among the descendants of a soft crossed with a turgid wheat. Other of De Vilmorin's experiments were made with the practical object of obtaining improved varieties or forms specially suitable to particular localities. Among those he has raised is one named "Dattel," which is highly esteemed; it was got from the red Chiddam, a valuable variety, but one in which the straw is defective. By crossing the red Chiddam with the pollen of Prince Albert a new variety has been produced which is stated to be early, very productive, and of good quality, as far as both grain and straw are concerned. Among many varieties raised by Messrs Carter some are very interesting: in one case the seed-parent was a short-strawed, downy-chaffed, awnless variety, the pollen-parent a large bearded American wheat. The offspring exceeded the seed-parent in stature by a foot, and had a smooth chaff and stout thickset ears with minute awns. Some of the crosses were made with the view to secure denser production of awns and thus to render the ears "bird-proof"; others were devised with a view of securing an early ripening variety, which was effected by crossing with the Talavera, a known early variety. The progeny was ready for cutting (in the neighbourhood of London) on 21st July 1886.

Yield of different varieties.

To show how considerable may be the variations in the produce yielded by different varieties, the following figures, taken from the "memoranda sheet" of the Rothamsted experiments, may be cited. For twelve successive years (1871-1882) Sir John Lawes cultivated 26 varieties of wheat, each variety each year in a different field and under different conditions of manuring. From various circumstances satisfactory averages were obtained during only eight years (1871-1878). The mean produce of all the varieties taken together during that period was 43½ bushels (dressed corn) per acre; the lowest average produce was 36½ bushels per acre, furnished by Hallett's original red; and the highest produce was 53⅝ bushels per acre, yielded by Rivett's red. As to manuring, the highest mean produce (51¾ bushels per acre) from 25 varieties taken together was obtained in 1878 on a field where all the 25 varieties were manured with 2 cwts. of nitrate of soda, the previous crop having been turnips, for which farmyard dung was applied, the turnips being partly consumed on the land, partly removed. Here again Rivett's red furnished the best crop (66⅛ bushels per acre). This variety in almost—but not in all—cases gave the highest produce. The lowest mean produce from all the varieties taken together was 21¼ bushels per acre in 1879,—a most disastrous season. In that year even Rivett's red furnished no more than 16 bushels per acre, among the lowest on the record, but nearly twice as much as red Rostock, which in the same year yielded only 8½ bushels per acre, the manuring consisting of 2 cwts. of nitrate of soda after clover, partly cut, partly "fed." This same variety in another year and under a different condition of manuring yielded 57 bushels per acre. The disastrous effect of the season of 1879 was manifested not only in diminished produce but in lessened germinative power; in the season following white wheats appear to have been the worst, the most satisfactory crop in 1880 being yielded by Webb's "challenge," seeds of which were received direct from Stourbridge and not grown on the Rothamsted farm, as in the case of the other varieties. As to the weight per bushel of the grains of the different varieties at Rothamsted, there was a more limited range than in the case of the absolute weight, the highest mean (63⅛ lb per bushel) being yielded by the "red nursery" variety, the lowest by Rivett's red (58¾), the general average of all the varieties amounting to 61¼ lb per bushel. The effect of the bad season of 1879 was also shown here: the general average in that year was only 53½ lb per bushel, while in 1876 it was 63½ for the same varieties. The greatest weight per bushel does not therefore correspond in all cases with the absolute amount of crop per acre, for a small crop often yields grain of relatively heavy weight. Nor does the same condition of manuring that brings an abundant crop necessarily yield a proportionate return calculated in weight per bushel. The greatest weight per bushel (63½ lb in 1876) was secured on the same plot which in the same year yielded less than an average crop, 42½ bushels per acre, very little difference being observable in the different varieties in point of quality, though much in quantity. The lowest average weight per bushel (56¾ lb), however, corresponded with a very low total produce, 23⅛ bushels per acre in 1880, on a poorly manured plot. These figures, added to those representing the cost for rent and taxes, manure, labour, and expenses of production generally, and considered in connexion with the enormous supplies imported from abroad, will show how great are the risks attendant upon wheat cultivation in the United Kingdom under existing circumstances; but of course they are of little value as regards the growth of wheat in India and the colonies.

The production of wheat, with the use of wheat bread, has increased enormously since the extension of railways has made possible the transportation of grain for great distances by land. The annual crop of the world is now estimated at nearly two thousand millions of bushels. Of late years the increase of production has been most notable in southern Russia, Australia, India, and North America.[1]

Wheat for fodder.

Wheat is sometimes grown as a forage crop. A variety has been introduced from Japan by Messrs Sutton which seems to be very useful for this purpose. Although it takes a longer time to mature its seed, it flowers a fortnight earlier than other varieties. It seems also to be a hardy plant, having withstood successfully eight degrees of frost. From a crop sown on 27th August a sample was cut on the following 13th October, with a stem more than 2 feet in length and very thick and succulent, and the autumn was not very genial. This variety tillers well, so that it makes a complete mass of green stuff, which is very serviceable either for feeding sheep or for "soiling." (M. T. M.)

Insects, &c., injurious to Wheat.

It will be convenient to arrange the insects injurious to wheat under the natural orders to which they belong, and afterwards to describe one or two other forms of animal life, such as the myriapod, *Polydesmus*, and the nematode worm which causes the ear-cockle, for, although these are not insects, they must be taken into account in any description of the animal pests of the wheat crop.

The order *Orthoptera* contains the mole cricket, *Gryllotalpa vulgaris*, one of the largest insects found in Great Britain. It is 2 inches or a little more in length, of a brownish colour, and covered over by velvety hairs; it is easily recognized by the peculiar character of its anterior legs, which are very strong and short and laterally compressed. These insects lead a subterranean life, burrowing through loose sandy soil by means of their fore limbs, which are structurally well adapted for digging. The sexes pair about the middle of June, and the female lays from 200 to 400 eggs in an oval chamber excavated some inches below the level of the ground. After laying her eggs, she does not, as is very generally the case amongst insects, die, but lives to keep guard over the eggs and the young larvæ, which appear in about three weeks; many of the latter, however, she eats. The young larvæ at first resemble black ants; they are very voracious and feed upon the young tender rootlets of corn and other plants. The adults prefer an animal diet, but do great damage by cutting through any roots which they encounter in their subterranean burrowings, and as these are winding and extensive considerable injury is caused to the crops. One of the natural enemies of mole crickets is the mole, which devours them readily; they are also eaten by those birds which scratch the soil for worms. They appear to be very sensitive to smell, and a dressing of a quart of paraffin oil to 1 cwt. of ashes or mould, or watering with solutions of quassia and soft soap, will often rid the field of them.

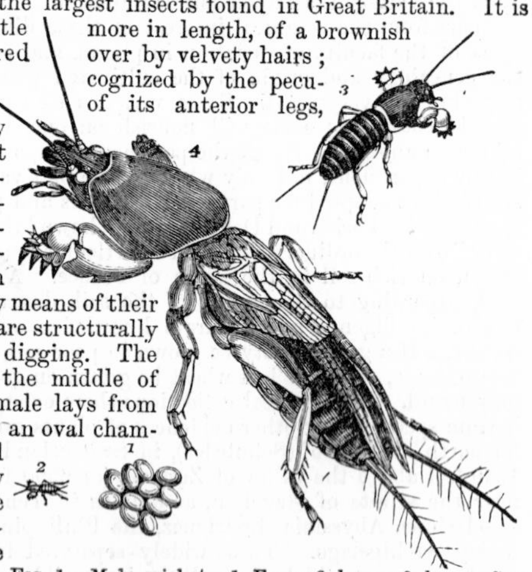

Fig. 1.—Mole cricket. 1, Eggs; 2, larva; 3, larva after first moult; 4, adult. Natural size.

The corn thrips, *Thrips cerealium*, is a member of the order *Thysanoptera*, which is by some authorities associated with the

[1] For a discussion of the methods of production followed in the United States, as well as in Canada, and for the chemical composition, trade, milling, and statistics of wheat, see Brewer, "Production of Cereals," in *Report* to tenth census of United States. vol. iii

Orthoptera. It is a minute insect about 2 mm. long, with a black and brown coloration. The male is wingless; the female bears four long narrow wings fringed with long hairs. The antennæ are eight-jointed. The legs terminate in characteristic swellings; there are no claws. The insects are very active. The larvæ are whitish yellow, with bright red eyes, and acquire their wings after the fourth casting of the skin. The damage done to corn crops by these minute insects is often very serious; they secrete themselves under the paleæ surrounding the seed, and feed upon the soft juices of the latter. In addition to this, they sometimes cause injury to the plant by attacking the stalk whilst it is soft and full of sap. Owing to their very small size it is exceedingly difficult to devise means for getting rid of them; much may be done, however, to prevent their appearance by keeping the land clean and free from weeds, which harbour them, and by destroying all refuse in which they may breed, and ploughing in the stubble to a considerable depth.

Fig. 2.—Corn thrips (*Thrips cerealium*), female; magnified.

The most injurious form amongst the *Hemiptera* is *Siphonophora granaria* (*Aphis granaria*, Kirby); it attacks wheat chiefly in England, but is also found upon oats, barley, and rye. The young *Aphides* attack the leaf blades whilst young and tender, and when the ear begins to appear it is covered with numbers of these insects in every stage of development, from the young larva

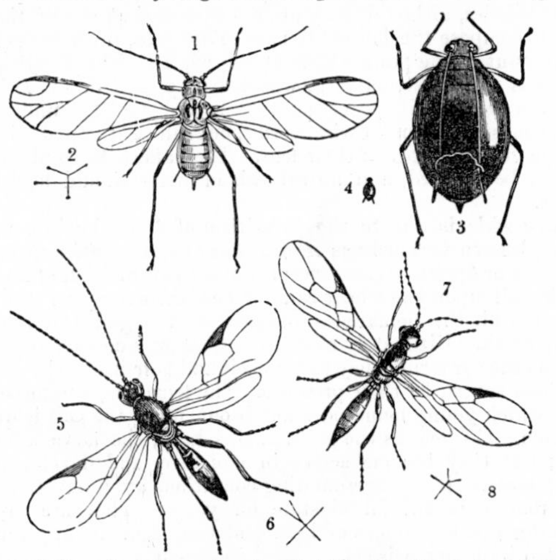

Fig. 3.—1, *Siphonophora granaria*, winged *Aphis*; 2, natural size of same; 3, wingless form; 4, natural size of same; 5, *Aphidius avenæ*; 6, natural size of same; 7, *Ephedrus plagiator*; 8, natural size of same.

to the perfect insect. The larvæ are of a green or dark green colour, with brown antennæ and yellow and black legs. The female, which produces the young viviparously, has a green abdomen, bearing two horns posteriorly; the rest of the body is brownish green, the legs black and yellow, the eyes red. The winged females, which appear late in the season, lay eggs; but whether these eggs serve to carry the species over the winter or whether this is done by hibernating larvæ is not definitely known. Both larvæ and females producing them have been found amongst the roots of the wheat plant during the winter. This *Aphis* is known to occur upon several of the common grasses of England; hence any grasses growing in a wheat field should be destroyed as much as possible when the pest is in the neighbourhood. Deep ploughing and rotation of crops may also be recommended. In cases where the insects are noticed at an early stage, a dressing of soot or gas lime will serve to check them. Their numbers are kept down by lady-birds (*Coccinella*), which should never be killed, and also by two species of ichneumons (*Aphidius avenæ* and *Ephedrus plagiator*), which lay their eggs in the body of the *Aphides.*

The order *Diptera* includes several insects which are very harmful to corn crops. The frit fly, *Oscinis vastator*, is a very active small fly, with a greenish black metallic lustre, about 2 to 3 mm. in length. The larvæ are yellow or light brown, pointed anteriorly. The flies emerge from the chrysalis about April, and the female deposits her little red eggs upon the under surface of the leaf of the wheat; the larva when it is hatched creeps down and bores its way into the terminal bud of the plant, thus arresting all growth of the ear. The larva assumes the chrysalis state inside one of the outermost leaf sheaths. There are believed to be two broods each year. If, as seems probable, the pupæ pass the winter amongst the stubble or grass weeds, it is important that these should either be burnt or ploughed deeply in.

Two closely allied species of flies also attack corn crops; they are *Chlorops tæniopus* and *Chlorops lineata.* The former is of a light straw colour, with three longitudinal dark stripes, and a greenish black abdomen; the antennæ are black, the eyes greenish; and the dark feet have a stripe of lighter colour. It is about 3 to 4 mm. long. The injury to the crops is caused by the fly laying its eggs between the leaves of the young plant; the larvæ which hatch out from these bore their way down the stem from the base of the ear to the first joint, and there they form swellings known to the farmer as the "gout." The ear is aborted or misformed. The dampest part of the field is most subject to attack. *Ch. lineata* is about 2 mm. long; the antennæ have their two proximal joints yellow, whilst the third is black on its outer side; in its habits this insect resembles *Ch. tæniopus*, but attacks chiefly barley crops.

The daddy long-legs, *Tipula oleracea*, causes great damage to corn and other crops by the larvæ gnawing the young plants whilst they are still below the level of the ground. The female deposits her eggs in the ground, or near it in some grass, &c., choosing as damp a place as possible. The larva is provided with a very tough skin and may measure 1½ inches in length. It is apodal, and bores its way beneath the surface of the earth by alternately contracting and expanding. It assumes the pupal condition during the later half of the summer. The pupæ are provided with backwardly directed spines, by means of which they raise themselves above the level of the ground. As a means of preservation against this pest, ditches and other damp places should be cleaned out. Rooks, which devour the larvæ at a great rate, should be encouraged; and deep ploughing to bury the eggs and the larvæ should be practised, and the land dressed with some such poisonous substance as gas lime before breaking up.

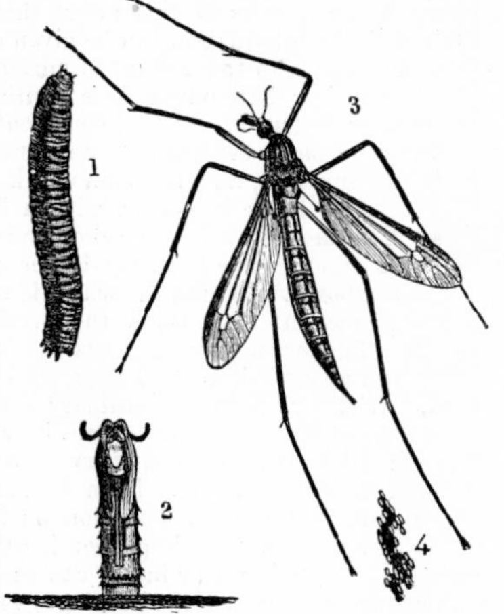

Fig. 4.—Daddy long-legs (*Tipula oleracea*). 1, Larva; 2, pupa case; 3, insect, natural size; 4, eggs.

Two species of *Cecidomyia* are most destructive to wheat. *Cecidomyia tritici*, the wheat midge, has been known in Great Britain for over a century. This fly is a little over 2 mm. in length, of an orange yellow colour, with black eyes; the female is provided with a long ovipositor, by means of which it deposits ten or more eggs in the ears of wheat. The larvæ hatch out in about ten days. They are at first transparent, but become yellow, and their colour gradually deepens. Most of the larvæ fall off the plant and bury themselves in the ground, where they change into pupæ; some, however, remain in the ear and are found in some numbers in chaff. The perfect insect emerges from the pupa in the spring. It is probable that more than one brood is produced during the season. The damage caused to the crop is due to the larva feeding upon the soft tissue of the ear and thus causing the seed to be imperfect; some authorities state that it also devours the pollen. Since the larvæ exist in chaff, great care must be taken that this does not prove a source of infection, and land which has been badly affected must be ploughed deep, in order to bury them. *C. destructor* is well known under the name of the Hessian fly. It was first noticed in Great Britain during the summer of 1886, in Hertfordshire, and within a few months its presence was reported throughout the eastern half of England and Scotland,—a circumstance which led some authorities to believe that it had existed in Great Britain for some little time; there has been, however, no definite proof of this. The fly has been known in North America since 1776, where it has done very extensive damage, especially during warm moist summers. It is known to occur throughout central Europe; in 1879 it made its appearance in Russia, and in four years had spread over the greater part of that country. The female fly is about 3 mm. long, brownish in colour, but becoming black in the thorax and head. The wings are fringed, rounded at their ends, and the third nerve is branched. The antennæ are also fringed and consist of two globular basal joints,

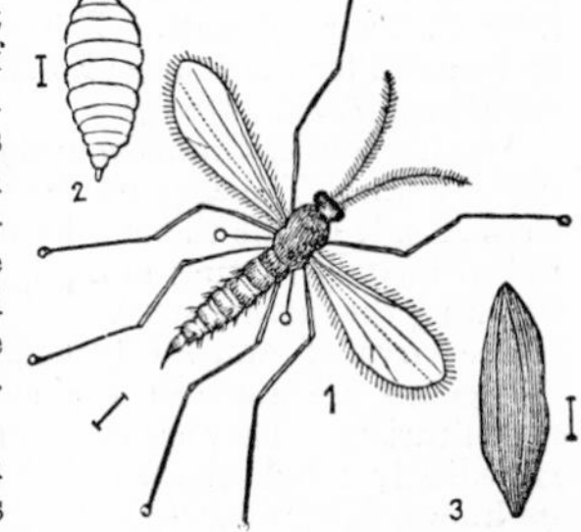

Fig. 5.—Hessian fly (*Cecidomyia destructor*). 1, Insect; 2, larva; 3, pupa or "flax seed." All magnified.

and 14 to 16 smaller joints, which diminish in length towards the ends. The male fly is smaller than the female; the abdomen terminates in two claspers. The female lays in the spring 40 or more eggs upon the leaves of the corn plants,—wheat, barley, and rye; oats are not affected. The larvæ are hatched in about 5 or 6 days, and make their way down to the axils of the leaves, feeding upon the sap which is passing up the stem. After a few weeks they are transformed into the "flax seed" pupæ, which are usually found just above the second joint of the stem. From these pupæ the autumn brood of flies emerge; these lay eggs, and their larvæ tide over the winter in the pupal condition. Sometimes only one brood is produced in the year. The injury done to the plant by the larvæ living upon the sap usually causes the infected plants to bend over just above the second joint; this renders them easily distinguishable from the healthy plants. The numbers of this most injurious insect are fortunately kept down to a considerable extent by parasites. Five species of *Chalcididæ* are known to be parasitic on *C. destructor* in America and six in Russia. Fortunately these are not absent in Great Britain. When a crop has been infected by this pest, the corn should be reaped above the second joint, and the stubble carefully ploughed in. A sharp look-out should be kept for the appearance of the "flax seed" both in the plant and in samples of corn, especially if the latter has been badly cleaned. Some species of wheat seem to have a greater power of resisting the attacks of this insect than others, but as yet very little definite information can be given on this point. These two pests do damage to the amount of millions of pounds every year in North America; but none of those mentioned before them are either common or destructive on that continent.

Cephus pygmæus belongs to that destructive group of the *Hymenoptera*, the saw-flies, and is commonly known as the corn saw-fly. The insect is black in colour, with a large head and prominent eyes. The mouth parts are yellow, and in the male the legs are the same colour. The female is darker and has its black ovipositor slightly exposed. Whilst the wheat is still young and tender, the female pierces the stalk below the forming ear and there deposits an egg. The larva, which hatches out in about ten days, is when full-grown about half an inch long, whitish in colour, with a brown head. It differs from the ordinary saw-fly larva in having but three pairs of legs. This larva bores its way down the stem, cutting through the knots, and about harvest time it cuts the stem nearly through at its base. The larva assumes the pupal stage in the lowest part of the stem and remains in this condition till the following spring, when the perfect insect emerges. Plants which have been affected by this insect can easily be recognized by their thin empty ears. Since the insect passes the winter in the stubble, every effort should be made to destroy this wherever the disease has been prevalent.

The caterpillars of some species of *Lepidoptera* do considerable damage to corn crops. On the Continent the larvæ of *Agrotis clavis* (*segetum*) devour the roots of wheat and are especially destructive to autumn-sown crops. *Tinea granella*, a member of the family *Tineidæ*, causes much harm to grain in store. This small moth, of a dusky white colour, lays one or two minute eggs upon each grain; as soon as they are hatched, the caterpillars bore their way into the grain, and by means of a web bind several grains together. Through these it bores minute passages and lives in them, devouring the substance of the grain. The larvæ ultimately withdraw to the angles and corners of the granary; hence, wherever this pest is prevalent, care must be taken to keep the building free from dust, cobwebs, &c. There is a member of the *Coleoptera* which is frequently mistaken for the above-mentioned pest. This beetle is known as *Trogosita mauritanica*; it is supposed to have been introduced from Africa. The larva is $\frac{3}{4}$ inch long, with a whitish body, bearing tufts of hairs and a brown head. It gnaws the corn grains and lives on their contents. The beetle is carnivorous, and is said to compensate for the damage its larva causes by devouring the above-mentioned *Tinea granella*.

Another beetle, *Calandra granaria*, the corn weevil, also attacks stored grain. The eggs are deposited in the grains of corn and the larva spends its life therein, living upon the substance of the grain, and ultimately turning to a pupa. It leaves the grain first upon attaining the mature state.

The larvæ of *Elater* (*Agriotes*) *lineatus* and of other species of this genus are amongst the most destructive insects known to agriculturists. They are commonly known as wire-worms from the exceedingly tough character of their skins. The mature beetles are known as skip-jacks, from the power they possess of regaining their normal position when placed on their back by means of a loose articulation between the pro-thorax and the meso-thorax. This when put in action causes the beetle to jump into the air, and they usually fall on their feet. The wire-worms have a rather flattened body, yellowish brown in colour; it consists of twelve segments, and bears three pairs of legs. The larvæ live for several years, and then, burying themselves deep in the earth, emerge as the perfect insect in about a fortnight. The beetles pair in June, and the female deposits her eggs upon blades of grass or the sheathing leaves of corn. The best preventative for this pest is clean farming and scarifying the land after harvest, so as to kill all roots which might serve as food for the wire-worms. When a crop is badly attacked, soot or gas lime may be applied and the land well rolled to compress the earth. The numbers of the larvæ are to some extent kept down by moles and insectivorous birds.

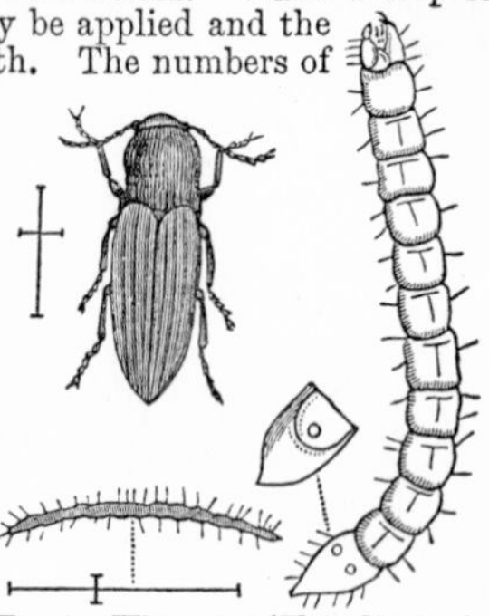

Fig. 6.—Wire-worm (*Elater lineatus*), showing insect and larva.

The cockchafer, *Melolontha vulgaris*, is injurious to corn crops, in both its mature and its larval condition. During the former state it devours the leaves of wheat and of most other grasses, trees, and shrubs. The larva, which is very voracious, lives upon roots. This larva is very thick and fleshy, of a whitish hue, with three pairs of legs; it usually lies in a curled-up position. The larval condition lasts several years; but ultimately the larvæ become pupæ, and in this condition live through the winter. Much may be done to prevent the spread of this pest by shaking the cockchafers from the trees, amongst the leaves of which they hang, and destroying them. They are eagerly eaten by pigs and poultry.

An allied but much smaller species of beetle, *Anisoplia horticola*, with much the same habits as the above, also occurs in England, and attacks wheat and grass crops.

Millepedes, although they are not insects, but one of the groups which compose the larger division *Tracheata*, must be included in an account of the pests which attack wheat. The English species which is most destructive to wheat, barley, and oats is *Polydesmus complanatus*. Millepedes pass their life underground, and are sometimes mistaken for wire-worms, but can be at once distinguished by the great number of their legs. They affect damp places, which should be drained, and no rubbish or litter should be left lying about.

Ear-cockle is due to the parasitism of a small white nematoid worm, known variously as *Anguillula* (*Vibrio*) *tritici* or *Tylenchus scandens* or *tritici*. These worms cause the formation of a brownish black gall upon the wheat ear. When the ear ripens and falls to the ground, the nematodes escape from the gall and live in the damp earth. Ultimately they make their way on to a young plant, and, as the ear forms, they pass into it and pair inside the gall which has been caused by their presence. The female lays numerous eggs, from which young nematodes hatch out, until the gall is quite full of them. As long as the gall remains hard, the larvæ are motionless; but they become active in moisture, and develop into the adult state. If the surrounding conditions are unfavourable they will remain in the larval state for years. They are capable of resisting great extremes of heat and cold, and are apparently unaffected by many poisons. Allied species affect the roots of wheat, grasses, and other plants.

For fungoid diseases, see FUNGUS, vol. ix. p. 831, and MILDEW, vol. xvi. p. 293. (A. E. S.)

WHEATEAR, as a bird's name perhaps of doubtful meaning,[1] though Taylor, the "water poet" (d. 1654), in whose writings it seems first to occur, and Willughby explain it (in the words of Ray, the latter's translator) as given "because [in] the time of wheat harvest they wax very fat." It would seem also from this author to have been originally the local name for the species in Sussex, on the South Downs of which county its capture in a very simple kind of trap has been the occupation of many generations of shepherds, who thereby have made an excellent trade, since Wheatears in their proper season, from the end of July till towards the end of September, are justly esteemed for the table and fetch a price that for many years has been continually rising owing to the failing supply, which is chiefly due to the bringing under tillage of so much of the sheep-walk, heath, down, and other open country that was formerly in a natural condition.

The Wheatear, the *Saxicola œnanthe* of ornithologists, is one of the earliest migrants of its kind to return to its home, often reaching

[1] The vulgar supposition of its being an euphemism of an Anglo-Saxon name (*cf.* Bennett's ed. of White's *Nat. Hist. Selborne*, p. 69, note) must be rejected until evidence that such a name ever existed be adduced. It is true that "Whittaile" (*cf.* Dutch *Witstaart* and French *Culblanc*) is given by Cotgrave in 1611; but the older names, according to Turner, in 1544, of "Clotburd" (= Clod-bird) and Smatch (= Chat) do not favour the usual derivation. "Fallow-chat" is another old name still locally in use, as is "Coney-chuck."

England at the end of February and almost always by the middle of March. The cock bird, with his bluish grey back and light buff breast, set off by black ear-coverts, wings, and part of the tail, is rendered still more conspicuous by his white rump as he takes short flights in front of those who disturb him, while his sprightly actions and gay song harmonize so well with his delicately-tinted plumage as to render him a welcome object to all who delight in free and open country. When alarmed both sexes have a sharp monosyllabic note that sounds like *chat*; and this has not only entered into some of the local names of this species and of its allies, but has caused all to be frequently spoken of as "Chats." The nest is constantly placed under ground; the bird takes advantage of the hole of some other animal, or the shelter of a clod in a fallow-field, or a recess beneath a rock. A large amount of soft materials is therein collected, and on them from 5 to 8 pale blue eggs are laid. The Wheatear has a very wide range throughout the Old World, extending in summer far within the Arctic Circle, from Norway to the Lena and Yana valleys, while it winters in Africa beyond the Equator, and in India. But it also breeds regularly in Greenland and some parts of North America. Its reaching the former and the eastern coast of the latter, as well as the Bermudas, may possibly be explained by the drifting of individuals from Iceland; but far more interesting is the fact of its continued seasonal appearance in Alaska without ever showing itself in British Columbia or California, and without ever having been observed in Kamchatka, Japan, or China, though it is a summer resident in the Tchuktchi peninsula. Hence it would seem as though its annual flights across Bering's Strait must be in connexion with a migratory movement that passes to the north and west of the Stanovoi range of mountains, for Mr Nelson's suggestion (*Cruise of the Corwen*, pp. 59, 60) of a north-west passage from Boothia Felix, where Ross observed it, is less likely.[1]

More than 60 other species more or less allied to the Wheatear have been described,[2] but probably so many do not really exist. Some 8 are included in the European fauna; but the majority are inhabitants of Africa. Several of them are birds of the desert; and here it may be remarked that, while most of these exhibit the sand-coloured tints so commonly found in animals of like habitat, a few assume a black plumage, which, as explained by Canon Tristram, is equally protective, since it assimilates them to the deep shadows cast by projecting stones and other inequalities of the surface.

Of other genera closely allied to, and by some writers included in, *Saxicola* there is only need here to mention *Pratincola*, which comprises among others two well-known British birds, the Stone-chat and Whinchat, *P. rubicola* and *P. rubetra*, the latter a summer-migrant, while the former is resident as a species, and the black head, ruddy breast, and white collar and wing-spot of the cock render him a conspicuous object on almost every furze-grown common or heath in the British Islands, as he sits on a projecting twig or flits from bush to bush. This bird has a wide range in Europe, and several other species, more or less resembling it, inhabit South Africa, Madagascar, Réunion, and Asia, from some of the islands of the Indian Archipelago to Japan. The Whinchat, on the other hand, much more affects enclosed lands, and with a wide range has no very near ally.

Placed near these forms by nearly all systematists is the group containing the Australian genus *Petrœca*, containing about a dozen species,—the "Robins," so called of the colonists, some of them remarkable for their bright plumage; and possibly allied to them, as indeed is generally thought, with 5 or 6 species peculiar to New Zealand, are the genera *Miro* and *Myiomoira*. But Prof. Parker has seen in the osteology of the first inferior characters which appear to him to separate them from their presumed colleagues, and, as stated before (ORNITHOLOGY, vol. xviii. p. 48), he terms them "Struthious Warblers." Like so many other forms from the same countries, they probably preserve the more generalized structure of earlier and lower types, and should possibly be distinguished as a separate sub-family *Petrœcinæ*.

All the birds mentioned in this article form the group *Saxicolinæ* of most authors. Some, however, have raised them to the rank of a distinct Family *Saxicolidæ* (*cf.* WARBLER); and Mr Sharpe (*Cat. Birds Brit. Mus.*, iv. pp. 164-199) has placed *Petrœca* and *Pratincola* in the Family *Muscicapidæ*. (A. N.)

WHEATLEY, FRANCIS (1747-1801), English portrait and landscape painter, was born in 1747 at Wild Court, Covent Garden, London. He studied at Shipley's drawing-school and the Royal Academy, and won several prizes from the Society of Arts. He assisted in the decoration of Vauxhall, and aided Mortimer in painting a ceiling for Lord Melbourne at Brocket Hall (Hertfordshire). In youth his life was irregular and dissipated. He eloped to Ireland with the wife of Gresse, a brother artist, and established himself in Dublin as a portrait-painter, executing, among other works, an interior of the Irish House of Commons. His scene from the London Riots of 1780 was admirably engraved by Heath. He painted several subjects for Boydell's *Shakespeare Gallery*, designed illustrations to Bell's edition of the poets, and practised to some small extent as an etcher and mezzotint-engraver. It is, however, as a painter, in both oil and water-colour, of landscapes and rustic subjects that Wheatley will be most favourably remembered. His work in these departments is graceful and pleasing, but lacks force and the impress of reality. He was elected an associate of the Royal Academy in 1790, and an academician in the following year. He died on 28th June 1801. His wife, afterwards Mrs Pope, was known as a painter of flowers and portraits.

WHEATON, HENRY (1785-1848), American lawyer and diplomatist, was born at Providence, Rhode Island, on 27th November 1785. He graduated at Brown university in 1802, was admitted to the bar in 1805, and, after two years' study abroad, practised law at Providence (1807-12) and at New York City (1812-25). He was a justice of the Marine Court of the city of New York from 1815 to 1819, and reporter of the United States Supreme Court from 1816 to 1827, aiding in 1825 in the revision of the laws of New York. His diplomatic career began in 1825, with an appointment to Denmark as chargé d'affaires, followed by that of minister to Prussia, 1835 to 1845. During this period he had published a *Digest of the Law of Maritime Captures* (1815); twelve volumes of *Supreme Court Reports*, and a *Digest*; a great number of historical articles, and some collected works; *Elements of International Law* (1836); *Histoire du Progrès du Droit des Gens en Europe* (1841), translated in 1845 by William B. Lawrence as a *History of the Law of Nations in Europe and America*; and the *Right of Visitation and Search* (1842). The *History* took at once the rank which it has always held, that of the leading work on the subject of which it treats.[3] Wheaton's general theory is that international law consists of "those rules of conduct which reason deduces, as consonant to justice, from the nature of the society existing among independent nations, with such definitions and modifications as may be established by general consent." The publication of a second translation by Dana in 1866 led to a prolonged lawsuit between him and Lawrence. In 1846 Wheaton, who was more than sixty years of age, was requested to resign by the new president, Polk, who needed his place for another appointment. The request provoked general condemnation; but Wheaton resigned and returned to the United States. He was called at once to Harvard College as lecturer on international law; but he died at Dorchester, Massachusetts, on 11th March 1848.

WHEATSTONE, SIR CHARLES (1802-1875), the practical founder of modern telegraphy, was born at Gloucester in February 1802, his father being a music-seller in that city. In 1806 the family removed to London. Wheatstone's education was carried on in several private schools, at which he appears to have displayed no remarkable attainments, being mainly characterized by a morbid shyness and sensitiveness that prevented him from making friends. About 1816 he was sent to his uncle, a musical instrument maker in the Strand, to learn the trade; but with his father's countenance he spent more time in read-

[1] On this subject see also Dr Stejneger's observations in his "Ornithological Exploration of Kamtschatka," in *Bull. U.S. Nat. Museum*, No. 29, pp. 349-351, and those of Prof. Palmén, *Vega-Exped. Vetenskapl. Iakttagelser*, v. pp. 260-262.

[2] *Cf.* the monograph of Messrs Blanford and Dresser, in *Proc. Zool. Society*, 1874, pp. 213-241.

[3] See Davis's *Outlines of International Law*, 26, and Woolsey's *International Law* (Index, under Wheaton).

ing books of all kinds than at work. For some years he continued making experiments in acoustics, following out his own ideas and devising many beautiful and ingenious arrangements. Of these the "acoucryptophone" was one of the most elegant—a light box, shaped like an ancient lyre and suspended by a metallic wire from a piano in the room above. When the instrument was played, the vibrations were transmitted silently, and became audible in the lyre, which thus appeared to play of itself. On the death of his uncle in 1823 Wheatstone and his brother took up the business; but Charles never seems to have taken a very active part in it, and he virtually retired after six years, devoting himself to experimental research, at first chiefly with regard to sound. In 1823 he published his first paper, "New Experiments on Sound," in Thomson's *Annals of Philosophy*, and was greatly encouraged by the appreciative translations which appeared in several Continental journals. Wheatstone's shyness still clung to him; for, although he occasionally read a paper to scientific societies when a young man, he never could become a lecturer. Hence many of his investigations were first described by Faraday in his Friday evening discourses at the Royal Institution. By 1834 Wheatstone's originality and resource in experiment were fully recognized, and he was appointed professor of experimental philosophy at King's College, London, in that year. This appointment was inaugurated by two events,—a course of eight lectures on sound, which proved no success and was not repeated, and the determination by means of a revolving mirror of the speed of electric discharge in conductors, a piece of work leading to enormously important results. The great velocity of electrical transmission suggested the possibility of utilizing it for sending messages; and, after many experiments and the practical advice and business-like co-operation of Cooke, a patent for an electric telegraph was taken out in their joint names in 1837. Wheatstone's early training in making musical instruments now bore rich fruit in the continuous designing of new instruments and pieces of mechanism. His life was uneventful except in so far as the variety of his work lent it colour. He became a fellow of the Royal Society in 1837; in 1847 he married; and in 1868, after the completion of his masterpiece, the automatic telegraph, he was knighted. While in Paris perfecting a receiving instrument for submarine cables, Sir Charles Wheatstone caught cold, and died on 19th October 1875.

Wheatstone was enthusiastic in his work; and, in spite of the invincible repugnance to public speaking, he could explain his machines and describe results to his friends with animation and remarkable clearness. Owing to the cast of his mind he could only undertake work with some distinct end or definite application in view; hence he applied himself chiefly to the useful embodiment of scientific principles, and to researches designed to throw light on such subjects as the interference of mental impressions with the evidence of the senses. As a natural consequence of the nervous enthusiasm which possessed him, several researches which had been commenced, and sometimes carried to a considerable distance, were relinquished as new sources of interest presented themselves, and remained unfinished at his death. Many of his ideas were expanded and appropriated by other workers, more persevering, if less original, who carried them into effect. Wheatstone's physical investigations are described in more than thirty-six papers in various scientific journals, the more important being in the *Philosophical Transactions*, the *Proceedings of the Royal Society*, the *Comptes Rendus*, and the British Association *Reports*. They naturally divide themselves into researches on sound, light, and electricity, but extend into other branches of physics as well. But his best work by far was in the invention of complicated and delicate mechanism for various purposes, in the construction of which he employed a staff of workmen trained to the highest degree of excellence. For his insight into mechanism and his power over it he was unequalled, except perhaps by Babbage. A cryptographic machine, which changed the cipher automatically and printed a message, entirely unintelligible until translated by a duplicate instrument, was one of the most perfect examples of this. Cryptography had a great fascination for Wheatstone; he studied it deeply at one time, and deciphered many of the MSS. in the British Museum which had defied all other interpreters. In acoustics his principal work was a research on the transmission of sound through solids (see TELEPHONE), the explanation of Chladni's figures of vibrating solids, various investigations of the principles of acoustics and the mechanism of hearing, and the invention of new musical instruments, *e.g.*, the concertina. The kaleidophone, intended to present visibly the movements of a sonorous body, consisted of a vibrating wire, which could be varied in length, carrying a silvered bead reflecting a point of light. The motion of the bead was thus shown by persistence of the successive images on the retina, and mazy lines of light traced out its successive positions. A photometer was constructed on the same principle. In light there are a series of papers on the eye, on the physiology of vision, on binocular vision, including the invention of one of the most popular of scientific toys, the STEREOSCOPE (*q.v.*), and on colour. The polar clock, devised for use in place of a sun-dial, applies the fact that the plane of polarization of sky light is always 90° from the position of the sun; hence by measuring the azimuthal angle of the plane, even when the sun is below the horizon, correct apparent solar time may be obtained. In 1835, in a paper on "The Prismatic Decomposition of Electrical Light," he proved that sparks from different metals give distinctive spectra, which could be used as a means of detecting them. This is the fundamental experiment of chemical analysis by spark spectra. But it is by his electrical work that Wheatstone will best be remembered. Much of this, such as the famous "bridge" for measuring resistances that bears his name, will be found described under ELECTRICITY (vol. viii. p. 44). He not only guided the growth of scientific telegraphy on land wires, but made the earliest experiments with submarine cables, foreseeing the practicability of this means of communication as early as 1840. For short descriptions of the "A, B, C" telegraph instrument—so popular before the introduction of the telephone—and of the automatic transmitter, by which messages may be sent at the rate of 500 words a minute, see TELEGRAPH. He also devised printing telegraph receivers of various forms, electrical chronoscopes, and many forms of electrical recording apparatus,—amongst others two sets of registering meteorological instruments, of which the earlier, described in 1842, was afterwards developed by Secchi and Van Rysselberghe (see THERMOMETER, vol. xxiii. p. 293), but the later, put forward in 1867, included metallic thermometers and was less successful.

Wheatstone's *Scientific Papers* were collected and published by the Physical Society of London in 1879. The best biographical notices of him will be found in *Min. Proc. Inst. C.E.*, vol. xlvii. p. 283, and *Proc. Roy. Soc.*, vol. xxiv. p. xvi. For Wheatstone's connexion with the growth of telegraphy, see *Nature*, xi. p. 510, and xii. p. 30 *sq.*

WHEELING, a city of Ohio county, West Virginia, U.S., the largest and most important in the State, stands on the eastern bank of the Ohio and on an island in the river, in what is popularly known as the "Pan-Handle." The main portion of the city lies in the bottom land, 40 to 50 feet above low water in the river, and, on an average, about 650 feet above the sea. Immediately east of it the bluffs rise to a height of 400 feet above the river. The island portion is connected with the mainland by a fine suspension bridge, 1010 feet long. The surrounding country is quite open and well cultivated, being timbered only on the hillsides; cereals and tobacco are the principal crops, and wool is largely grown. Wheeling has railway connexions eastward by the Baltimore and Ohio line to Baltimore and Washington; westward by the same line and by the Pittsburg, Cincinnati and St Louis; northward by the Cleveland and Pittsburg; and southward by the Ohio River Railroad. The Ohio, which is navigable to Pittsburgh, furnishes another means of communication. The depth of water in front of the city ranges from 20 inches at the lowest stage to 30 or 40 feet during floods, while the width of the river varies from 100 to 1000 feet. The principal manufacturing industries are those of iron and steel, which employ some 2600 persons or about one-twelfth of the population. Wheeling is popularly known as the "nail city" from the large quantity of cut nails made in its workshops. It has also manufactories of glass and queensware, wine (from home-grown grapes), cigars and tobacco, lanterns, and leather, as well as breweries. The city has a large market for ginseng, which is exported almost exclusively to China. The population of Wheeling in 1880 amounted to 30,737, of whom one-fifth were foreign-born.

The first settlement (Fort Fincastle) on the present site of Wheeling was made in 1769. In 1776 its name was changed to Fort Henry; it was twice besieged by the British and Indians, in 1777 and 1782. It was incorporated as a village under its present name in 1806, and in 1836 it received a city charter. Upon the formation of the State of West Virginia in 1863 Wheeling was made the capital. In 1870 this dignity was conferred upon Charleston; in 1875 it was restored to Wheeling, but lost again in 1885 to Charleston. The following figures illustrate the growth of Wheeling:—population in 1810, 914; in 1820, 1567; in 1840, 7385; in 1860, 14,083; in 1870, 19,280; and in 1880, 30,737.

WHEWELL, William (1794-1866), philosopher and historian of science, was born on 24th May 1794 at Lancaster, where his father was a house-carpenter. He was educated at the blue school and the grammar school of Lancaster, and afterwards at Heversham grammar school, where he obtained the exhibition which enabled him to enter Trinity College, Cambridge, in October 1812. For the remainder of his life his home was within the walls of Trinity. He graduated as second wrangler in 1816, was elected fellow in 1817, appointed a mathematical lecturer in the following year, and in due course became one of the college tutors. From 1828 to 1832 he held the professorship of mineralogy and from 1838 to 1855 that of moral philosophy, or (as it was then called) moral theology and casuistical divinity. In 1841 he was appointed master of the college on the resignation of Dr Wordsworth. He died on 6th March 1866 from the effects of a fall from his horse.

Soon after taking his degree Whewell began to lay the foundation of his reputation by great and varied activity as an author, as well as by the prominent part he took in all matters educational and constitutional concerning the college and university. His first work, *An Elementary Treatise on Mechanics* (1819), was influential—along with the works of Peacock and Herschel—in reforming the traditional method of mathematical teaching in Cambridge; and it was also largely due to him that, at a later period (1856), the circle of Cambridge studies was widened by the admission of the moral and natural sciences to an academic position. On the other hand, his attitude with respect to questions of university and college reform was (especially in later life) conservative. Claiming to be a reformer, he had yet no sympathy with the constitutional changes proposed at the time, and since commonly accepted as desirable and necessary. He upheld strenuously the tutorial system, while endeavouring to improve its efficiency; he opposed the admission of Dissenters to the university in a controversy with Thirlwall (1834); he defended the system of clerical fellowships, the custom which admitted a privileged class of students under the name of "fellow-commoners," and the large powers which the "caput" or head of a college then possessed in university government. The appointment of the University Commission in 1850 encountered his opposition, and the proposed reform of the university in 1855 called forth from him two pamphlets of hostile *Remarks*. The reform really wanted was, he contended, to encourage scientific and professorial work, and to utilize the college funds, not to put elections in the hands of the members of senate.

In the summer of 1826, and again in 1828, Whewell was engaged along with Airy in conducting experiments in Dolcoath mine, Cornwall, in order to determine the density of the earth. Their united labours were unsuccessful, and Whewell did little more in the way of experimental science. He was the author, however, of an *Essay on Mineralogical Classification*, published in 1828, and contributed various memoirs on the tides to the *Philosophical Transactions* of the Royal Society between 1833 and 1850. But it is on his *History* and *Philosophy of the Sciences* that his claim to an enduring reputation mainly rests. The *History of the Inductive Sciences, from the Earliest to the Present Time* appeared originally in 1837. Whewell's wide acquaintance with various branches of science—though he cannot be said to have been a specialist in any department—enabled him to write a comprehensive account of their development, which has not yet been superseded, although it may want the thoroughness, and even in many respects the accuracy, of various subsequent histories of the special sciences. In his own opinion, moreover, the *History* was to be regarded as an introduction to the *Philosophy of the Inductive Sciences* (1840). The latter treatise[1] analyses the method exemplified in the formation of ideas, in the new inductions of science, and in the applications and systematization of these inductions, all exhibited by the *History* in the process of development.

The *Philosophy* is described by the author as "an application of the plan of Bacon's *Novum Organum* to the present condition of physical science," and as an attempt "to extract from the actual past progress of science the elements of a more effectual and substantial method of discovery" than Bacon's. The *Philosophy* is divided into two parts, treating respectively of ideas and of knowledge. The first part begins with an investigation of ideas in general, analysing the fundamental nature of scientific truths, the grounds of our knowledge of them, and the mental processes by which they are ascertained, and then applies these general principles to the philosophy of each of the subdivisions of science adopted in the *History*. The second part discusses knowledge or the construction of science, the processes by which our conceptions are brought to bear on facts, binding them together into ideal combinations. By the "explication of conceptions" the ideas appropriate to particular classes of facts are brought forward and explained; and by the "colligation of facts" the conceptions involving those ideas are united to the facts for the construction of science. But no art of discovery, such as Bacon anticipated, follows from the analysis of the method of scientific discovery; for the elements of "invention, sagacity, genius," are needed at each forward step in scientific progress. At the same time Whewell claimed that the methods exhibited in his analysis were, not only the methods by which discoveries had actually been made, but also as definite and practical as any that had been put forward. The process of induction (or colligation of ascertained facts into general propositions) is analysed into three steps,—(1) the selection of the (fundamental) idea, such as space, number, cause, or likeness; (2) the formation of the conception, or more special modification of those ideas, as a circle, a uniform force, &c.; and (3) the determination of magnitudes. Upon these follow special methods of induction applicable to quantity, viz., the method of curves, the method of means, the method of least squares, and the method of residues, and special methods depending on resemblance (to which the transition is made through the law of continuity), viz., the method of gradation and the method of natural classification.

Whewell's philosophy of science, as well as his ethical doctrine, was conditioned by opposition to the empirical tendency then prevalent amongst English thinkers. In this he was influenced by the results of the Kantian philosophy. He maintained the distinction between necessary and contingent truths,—the former involved in the innate constitution of the mind, the latter coming from experience. It is on this reference to the mind of what the current English philosophy attempted to derive from impressions of sense that the leading positions of his philosophy depend, and on it hinges the controversy between himself and J. S. Mill. He defended the *a priori* necessity of axioms attacked by the latter, and in his inductive theory attributed more importance to the function of the mental idea in the colligation of facts than Mill did, while he would have dispensed with the inductive methods of Mill by his rules for the construction of conceptions.

Between 1835 and 1861 Whewell was the author of various works on the philosophy of morals and politics, the chief of which, *Elements of Morality, including Polity*, was published in 1845. The peculiarity of this work—written, of course, from what is known as the intuitional point of view—is its fivefold division of the springs of action and of their objects, of the primary and universal rights of man (personal security, property, contrast, family rights, and government), and of the cardinal virtues (benevolence, justice, truth, purity, and order). Among Whewell's other works—too numerous to mention—reference must be made to writings popular in their day, such as the Bridgewater Treatise on *Astronomy* (1833), and the essay, *Of the Plurality of Worlds* (1854), in which he argued

[1] Afterwards broken up into three parts published separately: (1) the *History of Scientific Ideas* (1858), substantially a reproduction of the first part of the *Philosophy*; (2) the *Novum Organum Renovatum* (1858), containing the second part of the same work, but without the historical review of opinions, which was issued with large additions as (3) the *Philosophy of Discovery* (1860).

against the probability of planetary life, and also to the *Platonic Dialogues for English Readers* (1859-61), to the *Lectures on the History of Moral Philosophy in England* (1852), to the essay, *Of a Liberal Education in General, with particular reference to the Leading Studies of the University of Cambridge* (1845), to the important edition and abridged translation of Grotius, *De Jure Belli et Pacis* (1853), and to the edition of the *Mathematical Works* of Isaac Barrow (1860).

Full bibliographical details are given by Isaac Todhunter, *W. Whewell: an Account of his Writings*, 2 vols. (1876). The *Life of W. Whewell* has been written by Mrs Stair Douglas (1881).

WHIG AND TORY. Parliamentary parties came into existence in England as soon as parliament achieved or aimed at predominance in the state. In 1641, shortly after the meeting of the Long Parliament, they were divided on the question of church reform, passing, as soon as political questions were involved, into Cavaliers and Roundheads. After the expulsion of the Cavaliers in 1642 and 1643 the Houses were divided into a peace party and a war party, and these in 1643 took the shape of Presbyterians and Independents. After the Restoration there was a country party and a court party, and to these the names of Whig and Tory were applied in 1679, in the heat of the struggle which preceded the meeting of the first short parliament of Charles II. The words were nicknames given by the opponents of each party. To call a man a Whig was to compare him with the Presbyterian rebels of the west of Scotland. To call a man a Tory was to compare him with the Papist outlaws of Ireland. In fact, at this time the Whigs were maintainers of parliamentary power over the crown and of toleration for Dissenters, the Tories maintainers of the hereditary indefeasible rights of the wearer of the crown and of the refusal of toleration to Dissenters. The relation between the parties was further qualified by the fact that the heir to the crown was a Roman Catholic, whose claim to succeed was defended by the Tories and assailed by the Whigs.

The persistency of the names of the two parties is mainly owing to their unmeaningness. As new questions arose, the names of the old parties were retained, though the objects of contention were no longer the same. The Revolution of 1688-89 made it impossible for the Tories to retain their old attitude of attachment to the hereditary right of the occupant of the throne, with the exception of the extreme wing of the party, which remained Jacobite. They still, however, continued, though accepting the Toleration Act, to oppose the offering of further favours to Dissenters. In Anne's reign, after the war with France had gone on for some time, they supported a peace policy, whilst the Whigs advocated a continuance of the war. On the whole, during the last years of the 17th and the first years of the 18th century the Whigs may be regarded as the party of the great landowners, and of the merchants and tradesmen, the Tories as the party of the smaller landowners and the country clergy. The Whigs established, through their hold upon the boroughs under the influence of the great landowners, a firm government, which could keep in check, and at last practically set aside, the power of the crown. The Tories, distrusting the authority of the ministerial Government, and fearing a new despotism based on parliamentary corruption, became, especially after Bolingbroke's return from exile, almost democratic in their views and in their demands for the purification of the existing system.

With the accession of George III. Toryism took a new form. The struggle about the Dissenters was now a thing of the past, and the king was accepted as a leader in carrying on the attack against the power of the great Whig families. The attack was the easier because the Whig families had split into factions. For some time the dividing line between Whigs and Tories was this: the Tories asserted that the king had a right to choose his ministers and control their policy, subject to the necessity of securing a majority of the House of Commons, whilst the Whigs thought that the choice should lie with leading members of parliament, and that the king should have no controlling power. The Whig view appears to resemble that subsequently adopted; but in the middle of the 18th century the corruption which prevailed rendered the analogy worthless, and the real conflict was between the corrupt influence of the crown and the influence of a clique of great landowners resting on their possession of electoral power through the rotten boroughs. In 1770 the king had his way and established Lord North at the treasury as his nominee. The Whigs, deprived of power, improved their position by the loss of one great instrument of corruption; but they were weakened by the establishment of two distinct currents of opinion in their own ranks. The main body under Rockingham was influenced by Burke to demand practical reforms, but set its face against any popular changes in the constitution. The Whigs who followed Chatham wished to place parliament on a more popular basis by the reform of the House of Commons. When in 1783 Chatham's son Pitt became prime minister, the Tory party took a new start. It retained the Tory principle of reliance on the crown, and joined to it Chatham's principle of reliance on the people as opposed to the great Whig families. It also supported Pitt in practical reforms.

All this was changed by the French Revolution. In opposition to the new democracy, the Tories coalesced with a section of the Whig families, the representatives of which entered the ministry in 1794. From this time till 1822 Toryism was synonymous with a desire to retain the existing state of things, however full of abuses it might be. When Canning and Peel entered the ministry in 1822, a gradual change took place, and a tendency to practical reform manifested itself. The refusal of Wellington to listen to any proposal for altering the constitution of the House of Commons threw power once more into the hands of the Whigs in 1830. Shortly afterwards the name Tory gave place to that of Conservative, though of late years there has been an attempt to revert to it by those Conservatives who wish to assert their power of originating a definite policy, and who do not like to be branded with a purely negative appellation. The name of Whig on the other hand was replaced by that of Liberal, being assigned for some time to the less progressive portion of the party, and thus, by becoming a term of reproach, threatening entirely to disappear.

WHIRLPOOL, a hollow in running water, caused or accompanied by a whirling motion which attracts and engulfs floating objects. The popular conception of a whirlpool was probably based on the ancient accounts of that of Charybdis, strengthened by exaggerated rumours of the Mälström in the Lofoten Islands, and, in Great Britain at least, largely consolidated by the legends of Corrievreckan. The various reports of travellers and descriptions of poetical "philosophers" as to the appearance of the Mälström were faithfully collated and thrown into stereoscopic relief by Edgar Allan Poe in his celebrated story. He describes how, with the rise of the tide, "the current acquired a monstrous velocity. . . . The vast bed of the waters, seamed and scarred into a thousand conflicting channels, burst suddenly into frenzied convulsions—heaving, boiling, hissing—gyrating in gigantic and innumerable vortices, and all whirling and plunging on to the eastward with a rapidity water never elsewhere assumes, except in precipitous descents. In a few minutes more there came over the scene another radical alteration. . . . The gyratory motions of the subsided vortices seemed to form the germ of another more vast. Suddenly—very suddenly—this assumed a distinct and definite existence, in a circle of over a mile in diameter. The edge of the whirl was represented by a broad belt of gleaming spray; but no particle of this slipped into the mouth of the terrific funnel, whose interior, as far as the eye could fathom it, was a smooth, shining, and jet-black wall of water, inclined to the horizon at an angle of some 45°, speeding dizzily round and round with a swaying and sweltering motion, and sending forth to the winds an appalling voice, half shriek, half roar, such as not even the mighty cataract of Niagara ever lifts up in its agony to heaven." Nothing could escape the violence of such a vortex. Whales caught in it were swallowed down, and the largest ship was engulfed as easily as the smallest boat. After an hour or two the funnel slowly filled, and the fragments of the vessels which it had sucked down were thrown up, dashed to pieces against rocks at an unknown depth. Bearing such a reputation, whirlpools were naturally avoided by the mariner; and their real nature long remained unknown.

It was supposed that every whirlpool formed round a central rock; under it opened a great cavern or gulf, down which the waters rushed, and so the whirling was produced as in a basin emptying through a central hole. This notion was developed by Athanasius Kircher (1602-80). In his theory whirlpools marked the entrances to subterranean channels connecting different seas, and the phenomena of tides were produced by the alternate flow of water in opposite directions. Kircher gives a curious diagram of the Mälström or "umbilicus maris," illustrating his supposition that the water, after pouring into the vast funnel, flowed along a channel under the Scandinavian peninsula and rose in the Gulf of Bothnia. When the level of this gulf had been raised to a sufficient height, he thought that the current was reversed, and, aided by a stream pouring through a subterranean tunnel from the White Sea, raised the tide on the coast of Norway. Carrying his theory a degree farther to account for the Gulf Stream and the Antarctic drift, Kircher, with great ingenuity, placed a grand vortex at the North pole, down which all the water of the ocean tumbled, and, passing through the earth's axis, emerged at the South pole, thus keeping up "a circulation like that of the blood in the human body."

The facts which gave rise to the wild theories of mediæval geographers and the extravagant descriptions of early voyagers are impressive enough in themselves to rank amongst the grandest phenomena of nature. No one who has seen the tide-streams racing through the Pentland Firth at 12 miles an hour, now swirling along with a smooth dimpled surface, like molten glass, now meeting the counter-current and leaping high into the air in columns of water and spray, or who has heard the roar of Corrievreckan as the Atlantic tide rushes between Scarba and Jura against an easterly gale, will be disposed to deny the terrible danger to small open vessels or to wonder that horror strengthened imagination to the confusion and exaggeration of fact.

The formation of whirlpools is a natural result of water flowing rapidly in an irregular channel (see HYDROMECHANICS, vol. xii. pp. 468, 510); it takes place in all rivers and in every tide-race of the sea, the depth, diameter, and velocity depending on accidental causes. The form of the surface of an ordinary whirlpool is given by Prof. J. Thomson[1] as that generated by the revolution of a curve whose formula is $y = c^3/x^2$, where y is the depth of any point on the curve below the general level remote from the whirl, x the distance of the point from the axis of revolution, and c a constant. Every point on the surface moves with the velocity a heavy body would attain in falling from the general level of the water surface to that point, and any point in the interior of the revolving mass has a velocity equal to that of the point on the surface immediately above itself. Prof. Thomson applied his researches on the motion of whirlpools to the construction of a particularly effective form of turbine.[2]

All the famous whirlpools are situated in channels essentially similar in configuration and in tidal phenomena: their vortices are produced at certain phases of the tide or with certain directions of the wind; and they are all dangerous to navigation, but the danger is due to the cause which produces the whirlpools—the tidal race—not to the "roaring wells" themselves. Whirlpools in a tidal stream are not stationary, but travel along with the current, filling up and again forming in irregular succession. Small boats have repeatedly been drawn into these vortices in the northern fjords and capsized; and trading steamers in passing through a tideway are violently deflected from their course. It is on record that a seventy-four gun ship has been whirled right round in the vortices of the Straits of Messina. The fishermen of the Norwegian fjords and of the northern island groups,—Lofoten, Faroe, Shetland, and Orkney,—still believe that, if they can throw a heavy or bulky object into a whirlpool, it will close up without harming their boats. Lithgow in his *Travels*, speaking of the Pentland Firth, says, "I denote this credibly, in a part of the north-west end of this gulf there is a certain place of sea where these distracted tides make their rencountering rendezvous, that whirleth ever about, cutting in the middle circle a sloping hole, with which, if either ship or boat shall happen to encroach, they must quickly either throw over something into it, as a barrel, a piece of timber, and such like, or that fatal euripus shall then suddenly become their swallowing sepulchre." This custom, it has been supposed, is sacrificial in its origin. Its continued practice, however, suggests what is probably the case, that the bulky object splashing into the whirl breaks the continuity of the surface and causes a collapse or filling-up. In windy weather, when there is a broken sea, vortices are not formed. The tidal stream passing through the irregular channels between islands gives rise to a complicated series of eddies and counter-currents, which, according to the British Admiralty's *Sailing Directions*, make navigation dangerous, except when guided by local knowledge and aided by fair wind and a favourable tide. The general effect appears to be that, as the tide rises, the strength of the stream increases; and the counter-currents set up along the shore, as well as the overfalls produced by inequalities of the bottom, thoroughly mix the water to a depth of from 50 to 100 fathoms. This has been proved by observations of temperature amongst the tidal currents off the Mull of Cantyre, where at all times of the year there is no difference between the surface and bottom temperature. At high water a state of rest ensues; and ebb tide usually reverses the order of phenomena, the main stream, counter-currents, and eddies running in the opposite direction, but with nearly equal strength, until low tide brings another pause.

Charybdis, a whirlpool famous in classical literature, is situated in the Straits of Messina. The rise of tide at Messina does not exceed one foot, but the current may attain the velocity of nearly 6 miles an hour. Where the north-going flood tide meets the south-running counter-current, and where the southerly ebb meets its induced northerly stream, great eddies or *garofola* are formed, one of which is Charybdis. These depend very much on the wind for the intensity of their phenomena.

In ancient maps of the united Aral-Caspian Sea two whirlpools are represented. Near the position laid down there are in the river Amu-Daria two whirlpools at the junction of several channels. These have been recently examined[3] and found to arise from the river flowing over two conical hollows in its bed, respectively 120 and 60 feet deep; these do not appear to have been formed by running water, but closely resemble craters of mud volcanoes.

The most violent tidal current is said to be that of Salten Fjord to the south of Bodö on the north-west coast of Norway.

[1] *Brit. Assoc. Rep.*, 1852, Sections, p. 130.

[2] *Brit. Assoc. Rep.*, 1852, Report, p. 317.

[3] Wood, in *Journ. Roy. Geogr. Soc.* (1875), xlv. p. 372.

known by the name of the Saltenström, and dreaded on account of its turbulence and its numerous vortices. Opposite Salten Fjord, on the western side of Vest Fjord, the wild jagged range of the Lofoten Islands runs like a row of shark's teeth from south to north. Between two of the southernmost of the group, Moskenæs and Mosken, runs the Moskenström, a tidal current which after low water commences to flow towards the north-east, then gradually changes its direction to east, to south, and at high water to south-west; after half an hour's cessation the ebb begins to flow towards the south-west, at half ebb due west, and then gradually turns through north to north-east at low water. The current thus rotates round Mosken once in 12 hours. It runs with a velocity of 7 miles an hour when a strong wind blows in the same direction, and, as the sea-bed is very irregular and rises abruptly from 200 fathoms seaward of Mosken to 20 fathoms in the channel and Vest Fjord, the flow is very turbulent, with occasional whirlpools and opposing currents set up along the shore, giving it a character very similar to that of the Strait of Messina. This is the place of the Mälström.

In the Faroe Islands several dangerous tide-races exist in which are dreaded whirlpools, the two worst being the Quærne off Sand Island and one round the rock of Sumboe-musk off Süder Island.

The Shetland and Orkney Islands are traversed by a system of formidable tideways called *roosts*, dangerous to fishing boats and very frequently forming whirlpools. It is sufficient to refer to the swiths or wells of Swona in Orkney, to the whirlpool of the Swelchie off Stroma, and the Merry Men of Mey, also in the Pentland Firth. The channel of Jura Sound in the Hebrides, which contains Corrievreckan whirlpool, resembles that of Mosken and Messina in being narrow and of very irregular configuration. The sea to the west is about 70 fathoms deep; a trough over 50 fathoms in depth and quarter of a mile wide runs through towards the east, deepening about the centre to 105 and 120 fathoms in consecutive holes. The channel is less than a mile in width, and the water is shallow (15 to 20 fathoms) from the shore out to the central trough, where the deepening is abrupt. To this fact, and not to the supposed existence of "a submerged rock of pyramidal form shooting up from a depth of 100 fathoms," are due, in all probability, the tidal stream, running sometimes at 9 miles an hour, and the great vortices which are occasionally formed, as well as the dangerous counter-currents and overfalls.

Folklore.—Many marvellous stories are told of the dwellers in whirlpools. Fish are supposed to be more abundant there than anywhere else. Whales have from earliest times been associated, if not confounded, with these gulfs; and all manner of sea-beings,—krakens, trows (trolls), and mermaids,—claim sanctuary beneath the turmoil. Ramus, two centuries ago, tried by dint of misapplied philological ingenuity to identify Charybdis with the Mälström, alleging that the fact of Ulysses's voyage to northern seas was plainly recorded in the names of islands and headlands. For the myth of Charybdis, see SCYLLA AND CHARYBDIS. Whirlpools have been brought forward to explain the origin of the tides; but a well-known Norse folk-tale in one of its forms gives to a particular vortex—the Swelchie—an additional and more important office, that of maintaining the salinity of the ocean. "Mälström" (mill-stream) probably refers to the rapid current resembling a mill-race. The Quærne in the Faroe Islands suggests the same idea from its name. A mist of poetical romance has always played over the roaring surges of Corrievreckan, and this finds expression in many poems and tales. Horrible sea-monsters made the gulf their home in the earliest times; but they gave place to the seductive mermaid who captivated a Macphail of Colonsay, and entertained him in her coral caves and fairy palaces beneath the sea for many years. Scott in his *Border Minstrelsy* gives another version of this story, in which Macphail outwits the mermaid and remains faithful to the maid of Colonsay. The name of the whirlpool is sometimes derived from *coire bhreacan*, "the speckled cauldron," referring to the foam that usually variegates its surface; but the legend makes it the corry or gulf of Vrekan, a prince of Norway, who, having come there to woo a Hebridean chieftain's daughter, was swept into the whirlpool, and drawn down from sight for ever. George Macdonald has embodied this legend in a highly dramatic poem.

Literature.—References to whirlpools occur incidentally in many places. See A. Kircher's *Mundus Subterraneus*, vol. i., Amsterdam, 1664; Pontoppidan's *Natural History of Norway*, 1755 (this work cites the opinions of earlier writers, Ramus, Arraboe, &c.). For a good description of Charybdis, see *Nicholson's Journal*, vol. i. (1798) p. 12; of Corrievreckan, *Athenæum*, 3d September 1864. Full and trustworthy details of the actual state and dangers of special whirlpools will be found in the *Sailing Directions* or *Coast Pilots* of the British Admiralty for the various seas. (H. R. M.)

WHIRLWIND. See METEOROLOGY, vol. xvi. p. 129 *sq.*

WHISKY, or WHISKEY, a spirit distilled for drinking, which originated, at least so far as regards the name,[1] with the Celtic inhabitants of Ireland and Scotland; and its manufacture and use still continue to be closely associated with these two countries. Distilled spirit first became popularly known as aqua vitæ, and it was originally used only as a powerful medicinal agent. It was not till about the middle of the 17th century that it came into use in Scotland as an intoxicating beverage. In August 1655 the town council of Glasgow issued regulations for persons who should "brew, sell, and tap ail and acquavitæ," and in 1656 the town treasurer was indemnified for "aquavytie sent to ane friend." In 1660 an excise duty was first imposed on "acquavitæ" consumed in England; but not till the year 1684 was any record kept of the quantities on which duty was charged. In that year duty was paid on the considerable quantity of 527,492 gallons. The consumption thereafter rose with great rapidity, reaching one million gallons at the end of the century, and in 1743 the enormous quantity of 8,200,000 gallons was consumed. Meantime the evils of the traffic had induced the legislature to pass, in 1736, the Gin Act (see GIN) with the view of checking the demoralization attendant on the drinking habits of the people. It was principally in the form of gin that distilled spirits were consumed in England; but gin is nothing else than a rectified and specially flavoured variety of whisky. In Scotland and Ireland the attempts of the excise authorities to control the distillation of whisky, and to derive revenue from it, led to unlimited smuggling and open evasion of the law, and it was not till well into the 19th century that efficient regulations and energetic supervision brought the traffic in these countries under public control. Indeed illicit distillation is still extensively practised in Ireland, where the detections average more than eight hundred yearly.

It is not easy at the present day to define whisky. Originally it was made from malted barley, the fermented wort from which was distilled in the common pot-still (see DISTILLATION, vol. vii. p. 264); but with the introduction of the Coffey and other continuous stills, which yield a "silent" or flavourless spirit, it has become possible to prepare alcoholic liquor, which is sold as whisky, from any cereal grain, malted or unmalted, and from potato starch, grape sugar, and numerous other starch and sugar yielding substances. As a rule, however, whisky is made from grain, and by preference from barley, malted or raw. The bulk of the whisky made in the United Kingdom can be separated into three classes. (1) Malt whisky is the product of malted barley alone, distilled in the ordinary pot-still. Its flavour is partly due to the circumstance that the malt is dried over a peat fire; and a spirit so prepared constitutes the pure Highland malt whisky of Scotland. (2) Grain whisky, under which heading comes the bulk of the Irish whisky of commerce, is made in the pot-still, principally from raw barley, with only a small proportion of malted barley to favour the transformation of starch into sugar in the preparation of the wort. (3) Plain spirit is produced from barley, rice, and other cereals distilled in the Coffey patent still. Plain spirit forms the basis from which gin, British brandy, and other rectifier's drinks are prepared; and it is used for blending with other flavoured pot-still spirits, to produce a certain character of potable spirit sold by wholesale dealers and known by special blend names. It is only the finer qualities of matured malt and grain whisky that can be used as single or unblended spirit. In the United States whisky is distilled chiefly from corn and rye, wheat and barley malt being used, though only to a limited extent. When spirit is distilled as whisky, it retains the natural principles which impart an agreeable flavour to the beverage; for the fusel oil, which is contained in alcohol, and is acrid to the taste and stupefying in its effects, is to a great extent extracted. Whisky is greatly improved by age; it is not mellow, nor its flavour agreeable, until it is several years old. In its original state it is almost colourless, but it derives a reddish hue from the wood of the barrels into which it is drawn, the inner surfaces of which are usually charred to facilitate the colouring.

In the financial year ending 31st March 1886 there were in England 10 distilleries, in Scotland 127, and in Ireland 27. The quantity of spirits distilled in that year in the United Kingdom was 38,961,842 gallons; the number of gallons consumed as beverage was 26,342,851 (England 15,290,816, Scotland 6,297,365, Ireland 4,754,670); the quantity exported was 2,808,198 gallons; and the stock held in bonded stores at the end of 1885 was 64,405,817 gallons. The total excise revenue from the manufacture, sale, and consumption of British spirits was £13,140,695, a considerable decrease on previous years; and distilled spirits are now a steadily declining source of public income.

[1] Celtic *uisge* (water); the term in its present use is probably an abbreviation of "usquebaugh" (*uisge-beatha*, "water of life"). *Cf.* Skeat, *Etym. Dict.*, s.v.

Distilled spirits in the United States are the principal, and an increasing, source of internal revenue. In the fiscal year ending 30th June 1887 there were in the United States 969 grain distilleries; and the quantity of spirits distilled in that year (including whisky, alcohol, high-wines, and cologne or neutral spirits, and excluding fruit-brandy) was 77,831,599 gallons. The stock of spirits remaining in bonded warehouse on 30th June 1887 was 65,145,269 gallons. The total revenue from the manufacture and sale of distilled spirits for the fiscal year ending 30th June 1887 was $65,829,322. This includes the tax upon whisky, fruit-brandy, alcohol, high-wines, cologne spirits, and rum. The revenue from the manufacture of whisky alone was $2,263,718,070.

WHIST, a game at cards. The etymology of the name is disputed; probably it is of imitative origin, from "whist" (hist, hush, silence), the game being so named because of the silence required to play it attentively.

Triumph or trump.

In the 16th century a card game called *triumph* or *trump* (corrupted from "triumph") was commonly played in England. A game called *trionfi* is mentioned as early as 1526, and *triumphus Hispanicus* in 1541. *La triomphe* occurs in the list of games played by Gargantua (Rabelais, first half of 16th century). In Florio's *Worlde of Wordes* (1598) *trionfo* is defined as "the play called trump or ruff." It is probable that the game referred to by the writers quoted is *la triomphe* of the early editions of the *Académie des Jeux*. It is important to note that this game, called by Cotton "French ruff," is similar to écarté. "English ruff-and-honours," also described by Cotton, is similar to whist. If we admit that ruff and trump are convertible terms, of which there is scarcely a doubt, the game of trump was the precursor of whist. A purely English origin may, therefore, be claimed for trump (not *la triomphe*). No record is known to exist of the invention of this game, nor of the mode of its growth into ruff-and-honours, and finally into whist. The earliest reference to trump in English is believed to occur in a sermon by Latimer, "On the Card," preached at Cambridge, in Advent, about the year 1529. He says, "The game that we play at shall be the triumph. . . . Now turn up your trump, . . . and cast your trump, your heart, on this card." The game of trump is frequently mentioned in the second half of the 16th century. In *Gammer Gurton's Needle* (1575) Dame Chat says, "We be fast set at trumpe." Eliot (*Fruits for the French*, 1593) calls trump "a verie common ale-house game." Rice (*Invective against Vices*, printed before 1600) observes that "renouncing the trompe and comming in againe" (*i.e.*, revoking intentionally) is a common sharper's trick. Decker (*Belman of London*, 1608) speaks of the deceits practised at "tromp and such like games." Trump also occurs in *Antony and Cleopatra* (written about 1607), with other punning allusions to card-playing—

> "She, Eros, has
> Packed cards with Cæsar, and false-played my glory
> Unto an enemy's triumph."—Act iv. sc. 12.

Ruff-and honours.

Ruff-and-honours, if not the same game as trump, was probably the same with the addition of a score for the four highest cards of the trump suit. A description of the game is first met with in *The Compleat Gamester* (1674) by Charles Cotton. He states that ruff-and-honours (*alias* slamm) and whist are games very commonly known in England. It was played by four players with partners, and it was compulsory to follow suit when able. The cards ranked as at whist, and honours were scored as now. Twelve cards were dealt to each player, four being left in the stock. The top card of the stock was turned up for trumps. The holder of the ace of trumps was allowed to *ruff*, *i.e.*, to take in the stock and to put out four cards from his hand. The game was played nine up; and at the point of eight honours could be called, as at long whist. Cotton adds that at whist there was no stock. The deuces were put out and the bottom card was turned up for trumps.

Whisk or whist.

It is believed that the earliest mention of whist is by Taylor, the Water Poet (*Motto*, 1621). He spells the word "whisk." The earliest known use of the present spelling is in *Hudibras, the Second Part* (spurious), 1663. The word is then spelt indifferently whisk or whist for about half a century. Cotton (1674) spells it both ways. Seymour (*Court Gamester*, 1734) has "whist, vulgarly called whisk." While whist was undergoing this change of name, there was associated with it the additional title of *swabbers* (probably allied to sweep, or sweepstakes). Fielding (*History of Mr Jonathan Wild*) says that whisk-and-swabbers was "the game then [1682] in chief vogue." Grose (*Dictionary of the Vulgar Tongue*, 1785) states that swabbers are "the ace of hearts, knave of clubs, ace and duce of trumps at whist." The true function of the swabbers is not positively known; it is probable that the holders of these cards were entitled to receive a certain stake from the other players. Swabbers dropped out of general use during the 18th century. The points of the game rose from nine to ten ("nine in all," Cotton, 1725; "ten in all," Seymour, 1734, "rectified according to the present standard of play"). Simultaneously with this alteration, or closely following it, the entire pack of fifty-two cards was used, the deuces being no longer discarded. This improvement introduces the odd trick, an element of great interest in modern whist. Early in the 18th century whist was not a fashionable game. The Hon. Daines Barrington (*Archæologia*, vol. viii.) says it was the game of the servants' hall. Contemporary writers refer to it in a disparaging way, as being only fit for hunting men and country squires, and not for fine ladies or people of quality. According to Barrington, whist was first played on scientific principles by a party of gentlemen who frequented the Crown Coffee House in Bedford Row, London, about 1728. They laid down the following rules:—"Lead from the strong suit; study your partner's hand; and attend to the score." Shortly after the celebrated Edmond HOYLE (*q.v.*) published his *Short Treatise* (1742). It has been surmised by some that Hoyle belonged to the Crown Coffee House party. This, however, is only a conjecture. There is abundant evidence to show that, in the middle of the 18th century, whist was regularly played at the coffee houses of London and in fashionable society. And it is notorious that, ever since the time of Hoyle, the game has continued to increase in public estimation.

Crown Coffee House party.

Cotton.

It will be of interest to mark the successive stages through which whist has passed from the time of Cotton to the present day. The only suggestions as to play in Cotton are that, "though you have but mean cards in your own hand, yet you may play them so suitable to those in your partner's hand that he may either trump them or play the best of that suit;" also that "you ought to have a special eye to what cards are play'd out, that you may know by that means either what to play if you lead or how to trump securely and advantagiously." It appears from this that the main ideas were to make trumps by ruffing, to make winning cards, and to watch the fall of the cards with these objects. In the rules laid down by the Crown Coffee House school a distinct advance is to be noticed. Their first rule, "Lead from the strong suit," shows a knowledge of the game only to be acquired by careful study, together with a long train of reasoning. The arguments in favour of the original strong-suit lead would be out of place here; they are to be found in any modern manual. Their second rule, "Study your partner's hand," though sound, is rather vague, and savours somewhat of a repetition of Cotton. Their third rule, "Attend to the score," if amended into "Play to the score," is most valuable.

Hoyle.

From the Crown Coffee House school to Hoyle is rather a wide jump; but there is no intervening record. Whether or not Hoyle derived at least a part of his inspiration from that school, certain it is that in his *Short Treatise* he endorsed and illustrated their rules. He also brought the doctrine of probabilities to bear on the game, and gave a number of cases which show a remarkable insight into the play. Two examples will suffice. He distinguishes between the lead of king from king, queen, knave, and one small card and of knave from king, queen, knave, and more than one small card. He also directs the third hand holding queen, ten, nine, and a small card to play the nine, not the small one, to his partner's lead of ace. This whist is so good, and so advanced, that even now, a hundred and fifty years later, only the very best players can be depended on to observe and profit by it.

Payne.

About 1770 was published Payne's *Maxims for Playing the Game of Whist.* The advance in this book is decided. Leading from five trumps, in the hope of bringing in your own or your partner's long suit, is made into a general rule. And here, for the first time, the rule with respect to returned leads is printed, viz., "In returning your partner's lead play the best you have, when you hold but three originally." This rule, of all elementary ones, is, according to Clay, "the most important for the observance of whist-players." Hoyle does not give any such rule for returned leads, whence it may be inferred that no settled practice prevailed in his day. Matthews's *Advice to the Young Whist-Player* (anon., 1804) repeats the "maxims of the old school," with "observations on those he thinks erroneous" and "with several new ones." Matthews's book was a valuable contribution to whist literature, but some of the maxims which he thinks erroneous are now generally allowed to be correct. Thus, he prefers leading a single card to opening a long weak suit, the modern practice being just the contrary. He rejects leads from suits of three cards, except when the leader has reason to think it is his partner's suit; then he should "play off the highest, though the king or queen," and he adds, "*N.B.*—This is contrary to the general practice, but undoubtedly right." Assuming his statement to be true, the general practice was evidently wrong. Matthews is sometimes credited with the discovery of the modern principle with regard to discarding. The old rule was always to discard from the weakest suit. The modern rule is to discard from the best protected suit when the opponents have the command of trumps. What Matthews does say is, "If weak in trumps, keep guard to your adversaries' suits; if strong, throw away from them." This advice, though good, does not amount to anything like a principle of play.

Matthews.

Short whist.

Soon after Matthews wrote, the points of the game were cut down from ten to five. Clay's account of this change is that, about the beginning of the 19th century, Lord Peterborough having lost a large sum of money, the players proposed to make the game five up, in order to give the loser a chance of recovering his loss. The new game, short whist, was found to be so lively that it soon became general, and eventually superseded the long game. This produced in 1835 *Short Whist* by "Major A." "Major A." is only Matthews done into short whist by a literary hack, who substituted "five" for "ten," and so on throughout. The book would not call for notice here, but that Major A. was regarded as the authority on whist for a considerable time, probably because it was erroneously supposed that the author was the well-known Major Aubrey, one of the best players of his day. Similarly "Cœlebs" (*Laws and Practice of Whist*, 1851), who mainly repeats former writers, only calls for mention because he first printed in his second edition (1856) an explanation of the call for trumps. Calling for trumps was first recognized as part of the game by the players at Graham's Club about 1840. Long whist may be said to have died about the same time that Major A.'s book was published. The new game necessarily caused a change in the style of play, as recorded by James Clay in *The Laws of Short Whist, and a Treatise on the Game* (1864). That distinguished player says that, when he first remembered whist, its celebrities were for the most part those who had been educated at long whist. In his judgment the old school was very accurate and careful, but was wanting in the dash and brilliancy of the best modern players, and sinned by playing what is now called a backward game.

Clay.

French whist.

Whist then travelled, and about 1830 some of the best French whist-players, with Deschapelles at their head, modified and improved the old-fashioned system. They were but little influenced by the traditions of long whist, and were not content merely to imitate the English. The French game was the scorn and horror of the old school, who vehemently condemned its rash trump leads. Those who adopted the practice of the new school were, however, found to be winning players. By way of example, the English player of the old school never thought of playing to win the game before it was saved; the French player never thought of saving the game until he saw he could not win it. As between the two systems, Clay preferred the rash attack to the cautious defence, and recommended a middle course, leaning more to the new than to the old doctrine.

Dr Pole (*Philosophy of Whist*, 1883) remarks that the long experience of adepts had led to the introduction of many improvements in detail since the time of Hoyle, but that nothing had been done to reduce the various rules of the game to a systematic form until between 1850 and 1860, when a knot of young men proceeded to a thorough investigation of whist, and in 1862 one of the members of this "little whist school" brought out a work, under the pseudonym of "Cavendish," which "gave for the first time the rules which constitute the art of whist-playing according to the most modern form of the game." The little school was first brought prominently into notice by an article on whist in the *Quarterly Review* of January 1871. On the appearance of this article it was fiercely debated by the press whether the "little school" did anything extraordinary, whether they elaborated anything, or compassed anything, or advanced a science, or whether they drew their inspiration from external sources, and merely gave a systematic arrangement to what was well known and procurable before. It was finally allowed that the little school did originate something, as they were the first to give, logically and completely, the reasoning on which the principles of play are based. Whist had previously been treated as though the "art" of the game depended on the practice of a number of arbitrary conventions. But the fact is that all rules of whist-play depend upon and are referable to general principles. Hence, as soon as these general principles were stated, and the reasons for their adoption were argued, players began to discuss and to propose innovations on the previously established rules of play.

Cavendish.

Discarding.

A critical examination of the more important proposals made since 1862 may here be appropriately introduced. The older authorities laid down the rule, Discard from the weakest suit. It was shrewdly noticed that, when command of trumps was shown by the adversaries, the rule was more honoured in the breach than in the observance, the reason being that, when the attack was adverse, the instinct of the player prompted him to guard his weak suits. Hence the rule was modified, and it became the practice to discard from the best protected suit when the command of trumps is with the opponents. There can be no doubt as to the soundness of this modern rule of play, and it has been generally accepted. It was suddenly discovered that Matthews advanced a similar doctrine.

Echo of call for trumps.

His pretensions to this distinction have already been examined. Soon after this (1872) followed the echo of the call for trumps. Calling for trumps, as all whist-players know, is effected by throwing away an unnecessarily high card. When the lower card is subsequently played, a royal invitation is given to the partner to abandon his own game and to lead trumps, there being great strength in the caller's hand. In practice it was found for various reasons (for which manuals must be consulted) to be highly advantageous for the caller's partner to be able to indicate whether he also had numerical strength in trumps (*i.e.*, a minimum of four). The rule was eventually adopted that the caller's partner with at least four trumps should, if he had an opportunity, call in response, or *echo*, by also throwing away an unnecessarily high card; of course, if he had the opportunity, and refrained from echoing, he had less than four trumps. This rule of play was not appreciated at the time; but now (1888) it has the adherence of all thoughtful players.

Lead from penultimate card.

Contemporaneously with the echo, the lead of the penultimate card from suits of five or more cards was strenuously advocated in some quarters, and as strenuously opposed in others. Up to this date it had been the general practice, when leading a low card from a strong suit, to prefer the lowest card of the suit, irrespective of the number held. But some acute players departed from this rule when they held an intermediate sequence of three cards. Thus, with king, ten, nine, eight, two (intermediate sequence of ten, nine, eight), they would lead the eight in preference to the two, as a card of protection, in case the partner should happen to be very weak in the suit, when the eight must force an honour, whereas the two might enable the opponent to win the first trick with a six or a seven. Equally acute partners soon observed that, when a strong-suit player began with, say, an eight, and afterwards played a small card, the card must have been from a suit of at least five cards. As soon as this inference was established, the acute leader argued that, if he could show number in his strong suit (an important exhibition in modern whist), he need not confine this exhibition to those suits only in which he held an intermediate sequence. He contended that the right play is to lead the lowest but one (or the penultimate) from all suits containing five or more cards, with which the less advanced player would begin by leading the lowest. Then ensued the grand battle of the penultimate. The old players regarded it with the same "horror" as they had formerly displayed with respect to the French school, and even went so far as to stigmatize it as a private understanding and as cheating. The next stock objection raised was that it was an innovation. These feeble arguments were soon disposed of. The method was accessible to every one through the medium of the press; and, as Clay (*Short Whist*, 1864) rightly observes, "It is fair to give your partner any intimation which could be given, if the cards were placed on the table, each exactly in the same manner as the others, by a machine, the players being out of sight and hearing each of the others." The more genuine strictures were that penultimate leads complicate the game, that they give no advantage to the players, and that they simulate leads from weak suits (from which the highest is led). It is very doubtful whether penultimate leads do complicate the game. But, admitting for the sake of argument that they do, it is no objection to an intellectual pastime that it exercises the brains of the players. The question whether those who practise penultimate leads reap any advantage therefrom is one which can only be determined by experience. The best test is the habit of those who play for a stake. They all hope to win; they are not likely to persist obstinately in a practice by which they find they gain nothing; and at the present moment (1888) there is scarcely a player of any ability who deliberately rejects the penultimate lead when he has a partner capable of understanding it. Hence it may be inferred that the experience of some sixteen years has resulted in a decided feeling that penultimate leads are on the whole advantageous to those who practise them. The simulation of a lead from a weak suit has no *locus standi* if it is borne in mind that original leads are contemplated, and that the original lead of all good players is from a strong suit. James Clay, the greatest player of his day, was at first opposed to penultimate leads. When he had considered the full arguments for and against them, he "put them to the test of his individual experience, acknowledged their value, and did not hesitate to give his adhesion to them."[1]

Antepenultimate lead.

The consideration of the proper card to lead from five-card suits naturally led to that of the correct lead from more than five cards, in the case of suits opened with a small card. General Drayson (*Art of Practical Whist*, 1879) was the first to lay down that six of a suit can be shown by leading the antepenultimate card. Thus, from queen, nine, seven, four, three, two of a suit he advised the lead of the four. General Drayson's proposal did not find favour with many players, though it distinctly follows where the penultimate from five is admitted.

Meanwhile, leads from high cards, having regard to the number held in the suit, had not escaped attention. Thus, from suits headed by ace, queen, knave it had always been the custom to lead ace, then queen, irrespective of number. The third hand, holding king and small ones, was expected to pass the queen. But, if the lead was from five cards or more, and the third hand held king and two small ones, this play often resulted in blocking the leader's strong suit. It was therefore held, after some discussion and tentative play, that with more than four of the suit the leader should proceed with knave after ace, in order to invite his partner to put on king, if it remained singly guarded. From this it follows that a similar distinction should be drawn as to the second lead from queen, knave, ten, according to the number of accompanying small cards. If the lead is from four cards only, queen should be led, then knave; if from more than four, queen, then ten. These innovations were introduced about 1874-75. It will be observed that the original idea in choosing a penultimate or antepenultimate card was to protect the suit, and that the original idea in choosing the higher or lower of two high indifferent cards was to give the partner the option of unblocking. Behind this there was seen to lie the collateral advantage of showing number. Hence these rules of play were frequently resorted to merely for the purpose of telling whether four or more than four cards of the suit selected to lead from were present in the hand of the original leader.

American leads.

So far the indicated method, sound enough in itself, amounted only to the enunciation of modified rules of play. It yet remained for some one to propound a constant method of treating all leads, and to classify the isolated rules so as to render it possible to lay down general principles. This was accomplished in 1883-84 by Nicholas Browse Trist of New Orleans, U.S.A.; and hence the method of leading reduced to form by him is known by the name of *American leads*. American leads propose a systematic course of play when opening and continuing the lead from the strong suit. First, with regard to a low card led. When you open a strong suit with a low card, lead your fourth best. When opening a four-card suit with a low card, the lowest, which is the fourth best, is the card selected. When opening a five-card suit with

[1] Preface by the editors to Clay's *Short Whist*, 1881.

a low card, the penultimate card is selected. Instead of calling it the penultimate, call it the fourth best. So with a six-card suit; but, instead of antepenultimate, say fourth best. And so on with suits of more than six cards: disregard all the small cards and lead the fourth best. Secondly, with regard to a high card led, followed by a low card. When you open a strong suit with a high card and next lead a low card, lead your original fourth best. The former rule was to proceed with the lowest. Thus, from ace, knave, nine, eight, seven, two the leader was expected to open with the ace, and then to lead the two. An American leader would lead ace, then eight. Thirdly, with regard to a high card led, followed by a high card. When you remain with two high indifferent cards, lead the higher if you opened a suit of four, the lower if you opened a suit of five or more. Examples have already been given of the cases of ace, queen, knave, &c., and of queen, knave, ten, &c. On the promulgation of these general principles another pitched battle followed, which raged with great fury. The objections urged against American leads are much the same as those against the penultimate, viz.,—(1) that they complicate the game, (2) that they seldom affect the result, (3) that the information afforded may be of more use to the opponents than to the leader's partner. The complication argument has but little foundation in fact. All an American leader asks his partner to observe is that, when he originally leads a low card, he holds exactly three cards higher than the one led; when he originally leads a high card, and next a low one, he still holds exactly two cards higher than the second card led; and when he originally leads a high card, and follows it with a high card, he indicates in many cases, to those who know the analysis of leads (as laid down in whist books), whether the strong suit consisted originally of four or of more than four cards. It cannot be denied that moderate players may lack the quick perception which will enable them to take full advantage of the information afforded; but that is no reason why better players should be deprived of the advantage, and it is no reason why the moderate player should not learn to speak the language of whist intelligibly, for the benefit of partners who do understand it. The answer to the effect-on-the-result argument is that American leads add but little which is new to the game. They only aim at consolidating the received practice, and at extending a law of uniformity to cases not previously provided for. The who-gets-the-best-of-the-information argument is more difficult to meet. Under other whist conditions experience tells that it is advantageous in the long run to convey information of strength, notwithstanding its publication to the whole table. It is most improbable, therefore, that a player will be at a disadvantage by publishing too much and too precise information as to his strength. But it must be admitted that this is not necessarily a *sequitur*; long experience can only decide on which side the balance of advantage lies. Five years' experience is hardly enough. But it may be remarked that no instances are known of players who, having once adopted these leads, have voluntarily relinquished them.

Play of second and third hands.

The introduction of American leads rendered it necessary thoroughly to overhaul the received play of the second and third hands,—of the second hand, in consequence of the information given, as to when he should cover or pass the card led; of the third hand, for the same reason, when he should play to unblock his partner's long suit. A discussion of these refinements would be out of place here. It is to be found in *Whist Developments*, by "Cavendish" (1885).

Laws of whist.

A printed existence was first given to the laws of whist by Hoyle in 1743. The fourteen laws then issued were subsequently increased to twenty-four. These laws were the authority until 1760, when the members of White's and Saunders's Chocolate Houses revised them. The revised laws (nearly all Hoyle) were accepted by whist players for over a century, notwithstanding that they were very incomplete. In 1863 the Turf Club undertook to frame a more comprehensive code, and to solicit the co-operation of the Portland Club. The laws of short whist, approved by these two clubs, were brought out in 1864. They were at once adopted by numerous other clubs, and are now (1888) the standard by which all disputed points are decided.

Laws of Whist.[1]

Rubber.

The Rubber.—1. The rubber is the best of three games. If the first two games be won by the same players, the third game is not played.

Scoring.

Scoring.—2. A game consists of five points. Each trick, above six, counts one point.

3. Honours—*i.e.*, ace, king, queen, and knave of trumps—are thus reckoned: if a player and his partner, either separately or conjointly, hold—(i.) the four honours, they score four points; (ii.) any three honours, they score two points; (iii.) only two honours, they do not score.

4. Those players who, at the commencement of a deal, are at the score of four, cannot score honours.

5. The penalty for a revoke takes precedence of all other scores; tricks score next; honours last.

6. Honours, unless claimed before the trump card of the following deal is turned up, cannot be scored.

7. To score honours is not sufficient: they must be called at the end of the hand; if so called, they may be scored at any time during the game.

8. The winners gain—(i.) a treble, or game of three points, when their adversaries have not scored; (ii.) a double, or game of two points, when their adversaries have scored less than three; (iii.) a single, or game of one point, when their adversaries have scored three or four.

9. The winners of the rubber gain two points (commonly called the rubber points), in addition to the value of their games.

10. Should the rubber have consisted of three games, the value of the losers' game is deducted from the gross number of points gained by their opponents.

11. If an erroneous score be proved, such mistake can be corrected prior to the conclusion of the game in which it occurred, and such game is not concluded until the trump card of the following deal has been turned up.

12. If an erroneous score, affecting the amount of the rubber, be proved, such mistake can be rectified at any time during the rubber.

Cutting.

Cutting.—13. The ace is the lowest card.

14. In all cases every one must cut from the same pack.

15. Should a player expose more than one card, he must cut again.

Formation of table, &c.

Formation of Table.—16. If there are more than four candidates, the players are selected by cutting, those first in the room having the preference. The four who cut the lowest cards play first, and again cut to decide on partners. The two lowest play against the two highest; the lowest is the dealer, who has choice of cards and seats, and, having once made his selection, must abide by it.

17. When there are more than six candidates, those who cut the two next lowest cards belong to the table, which is complete with six players. On the retirement of one of those six players, the candidate who cut the next lowest card has a prior right to any after-comer to enter the table.

Cutting Cards of Equal Value.—18. Two players cutting cards of equal value, unless such cards are the two highest, cut again; should they be the two lowest, a fresh cut is necessary to decide which of those two deals.

19. Three players cutting cards of equal value cut again. Should the fourth (or remaining) card be the highest, the two lowest of the new cut are partners, the lower of those two the dealer. Should the fourth card be the lowest, the two highest are partners, the original lowest the dealer.

Cutting Out.—20. At the end of a rubber, should admission be claimed by any one or by two candidates, he who has, or they who have, played a greater number of consecutive rubbers than the others is, or are, out. But, when all have played the same number, they must cut to decide upon the out-goers; the highest are out.

Entry and Re-entry.—21. A candidate wishing to enter a table must declare such intention prior to any of the players having cut a card, either for the purpose of commencing a fresh rubber or of cutting out.

22. In the formation of fresh tables those candidates who have neither belonged to, nor played at, any other table have the prior right of entry; the others decide their right of admission by cutting.

23. Any one quitting a table prior to the conclusion of a rubber may, with consent of the other three players, appoint a substitute in his absence during that rubber.

24. A player cutting into one table whilst belonging to another loses his right of re-entry into that latter, and takes his chance of cutting in as if he were a fresh candidate.

25. If any one break up a table, the remaining players have the prior right to him of entry into any other; and, should there not be sufficient vacancies at such other table to admit all those candidates, they settle their precedence by cutting.

Shuffling.

Shuffling.—26. The pack must neither be shuffled below the table nor so that the face of any card be seen.

27. The pack must not be shuffled during the play of the hand.

28. A pack, having been played with, must neither be shuffled by dealing it into packets nor across the table.

29. Each player has a right to shuffle, once only, except as provided by rule 32, prior to a deal, after a false cut, or when a new deal has occurred.

30. The dealer's partner must collect the cards for the ensuing deal, and has the first right to shuffle that pack.

31. Each player after shuffling must place the cards, properly collected and face downwards, to the left of the player about to deal.

32. The dealer has always the right to shuffle last; but, should a card or cards be seen during his shuffling or whilst giving the pack to be cut, he may be compelled to re-shuffle.

Deal.

The Deal.—33. Each player deals in his turn. The right of dealing goes to the left.

34. The player on the dealer's right cuts the pack, and in dividing it must not leave fewer than four cards in either packet. If in cutting or in replacing one of the two packets on the other a card be exposed, or if there be any confusion of the cards, or a doubt as to the exact place in which the pack was divided, there must be a fresh cut.

35. When a player, whose duty it is to cut, has once separated the pack, he cannot alter his intention: he can neither re-shuffle nor re-cut the cards.

36. When the pack is cut, should the dealer shuffle the cards, he loses his deal.

[1] From the club code, edited by J. L. Baldwin, by permission of Messrs. De La Rue and Co.

A New Deal.—37. There must be a new deal—(i.) if during a deal or during the play of a hand the pack be proved incorrect or imperfect; (ii.) if any card, excepting the last, be faced in the pack.

38. If whilst dealing a card be exposed by the dealer or his partner, should neither of the adversaries have touched the cards, the latter can claim a new deal. A card exposed by either adversary gives that claim to the dealer, provided that his partner has not touched a card. If a new deal does not take place, the exposed card cannot be called.

39. If during dealing a player touch any of his cards, the adversaries may do the same, without losing their privilege of claiming a new deal, should chance give them such option.

40. If in dealing one of the last cards be exposed, and the dealer turn up the trump before there is reasonable time for his adversaries to decide as to a fresh deal, they do not thereby lose their privilege.

41. If a player whilst dealing look at the trump card, his adversaries have a right to see it, and may exact a new deal.

42. If a player take into the hand dealt to him a card belonging to the other pack, the adversaries, on discovery of the error, may decide whether they will have a fresh deal or not.

Misdeal.

A Misdeal.—43. A misdeal loses the deal.

44. It is a misdeal—(i.) unless the cards are dealt into four packets, one at a time in regular rotation, beginning with the player to the dealer's left; (ii.) should the dealer place the last (*i.e.*, the trump) card face downwards on his own or any other pack; (iii.) should the trump card not come in its regular order to the dealer; but he does not lose his deal if the pack be proved imperfect; (iv.) should a player have fourteen cards and either of the other three less than thirteen; (v.) should the dealer, under an impression that he has made a mistake, count either the cards on the table or the remainder of the pack; (vi.) should the dealer deal two cards at once or two cards to the same hand, and then deal a third; but if, prior to dealing that third card, the dealer can, by altering the position of one card only, rectify such error, he may do so, except as provided by the second paragraph of this law; (vii.) should the dealer omit to have the pack cut to him, and the adversaries discover the error prior to the trump card being turned up, and before looking at their cards, but not after having done so.

45. A misdeal does not lose the deal if during the dealing either of the adversaries touch the cards prior to the dealer's partner having done so; but, should the latter have first interfered with the cards, notwithstanding [that] either or both of the adversaries have subsequently done the same, the deal is lost.

46. Should three players have their right number of cards, the fourth have less than thirteen, and not discover such deficiency until he has played any of his cards, the deal stands good. Should he have played, he is as answerable for any revoke he may have made as if the missing card or cards had been in his hand; he may search the other pack for it or them.

47. If a pack during or after a rubber be proved incorrect or imperfect, such proof does not alter any past score, game, or rubber. That hand in which the imperfection was detected is null and void. The dealer deals again.

48. Any one dealing out of turn, or with the adversary's cards, may be stopped before the trump card is turned up, after which the game must proceed as if no mistake had been made.

49. A player can neither shuffle, cut, nor deal for his partner, without the permission of his opponents.

50. If the adversaries interrupt a dealer whilst dealing, either by questioning the score or asserting that it is not his deal, and fail to establish such claim, should a misdeal occur, he may deal again.

51. Should a player take his partner's deal and misdeal, the latter is liable to the usual penalty, and the adversary next in rotation to the player who ought to have dealt then deals.

Trump card.

The Trump Card.—52. The dealer, when it is his turn to play to the first trick, should take the trump card into his hand. If left on the table after the first trick be turned and quitted, it is liable to be called. His partner may at any time remind him of the liability.

53. After the dealer has taken the trump card into his hand it cannot be asked for. A player naming it at any time during the play of that hand is liable to have his highest or lowest trump called.

54. If the dealer take the trump card into his hand before it is his turn to play, he may be desired to lay it on the table. Should he show a wrong card, this card may be called, as also a second, a third, &c., until the trump card be produced.

55. If the dealer declare himself unable to recollect the trump card, his highest or lowest trump may be called at any time during that hand, and, unless it cause him to revoke, must be played. The call may be repeated, but not changed, *i.e.*, from highest to lowest, or *vice versa*, until such card is played.

Cards liable to be called.

Cards Liable to be Called.—56. All exposed cards are liable to be called, and must be left on the table; but a card is not an exposed card when dropped on the floor, or elsewhere below the table. The following are exposed cards:—(i.) two or more cards played at once; (ii.) any card dropped with its face upwards, or in any way exposed on or above the table, even though snatched up so quickly that no one can name it.

57. If any one play to an imperfect trick the best card on the table, or lead one which is a winning card as against his adversaries, and then lead again, or play several such winning cards one after the other, without waiting for his partner to play, the latter may be called on to win, if he can, the first or any other of those tricks, and the other cards thus improperly played are exposed cards.

58. If a player or players, under the impression that the game is lost or won, or for other reasons, throw his or their cards on the table face upwards, such cards are exposed, and liable to be called, each player's by the adversary; but, should one player alone retain his hand, he cannot be forced to abandon it.

59. If all four players throw their cards on the table face upwards, the hands are abandoned, and no one can again take up his cards. Should this general exhibition show that the game might have been saved, or won, neither claim can be entertained, unless a revoke be established. The revoking players are then liable to the following penalties: they cannot under any circumstances win the game by the result of that hand, and the adversaries may add three to their score, or deduct three from that of the revoking players.

60. A card detached from the rest of the hand so as to be named is liable to be called; but, should the adversary name a wrong card, he is liable to have a suit called when he or his partner have the lead.

61. If a player, who has rendered himself liable to have the highest or lowest of a suit called, fail to play as desired, or if, when called on to lead one suit, [he] lead another, having in his hand one or more cards of that suit demanded, he incurs the penalty of a revoke.

62. If any player lead out of turn, his adversaries may either call the card erroneously led, or may call a suit from him or his partner when it is next the turn of either of them to lead.

63. If any player lead out of turn, and the other three have followed him, the trick is complete, and the error cannot be rectified. But, if only the second or the second and third have played to the false lead, their cards, on discovery of the mistake, are taken back; there is no penalty against any one, excepting the original offender, whose card may be called, or he or his partner, when either of them has next the lead, may be compelled to play any suit demanded by the adversaries.

64. In no case can a player be compelled to play a card which would oblige him to revoke.

65. The call of a card may be repeated until such card has been played.

66. If a player called on to lead a suit have none of it, the penalty is paid.

Cards played in error.

Cards Played in Error, or not Played to a Trick.—67. If the third hand play before the second, the fourth hand may play before his partner.

68. Should the third hand not have played, and the fourth play before his partner, the latter may be called on to win or not to win the trick.

69. If any one omit playing to a former trick, and such error be not discovered until he has played to the next, the adversaries may claim a new deal. Should they decide that the deal stand good, the surplus card at the end of the hand is considered to have been played to the imperfect trick, but does not constitute a revoke therein.

70. If any one play two cards to the same trick, or mix his trump, or other card, with a trick to which it does not properly belong, and the mistake be not discovered until the hand is played out, he is answerable for all consequent revokes he may have made. If during the play of the hand the error be detected, the tricks may be counted face downwards, in order to ascertain whether there be among them a card too many. Should this be the case, they may be searched, and the card restored; the player is, however, liable for all revokes which he may have meanwhile made.

Revoke.

The Revoke.—71. [This] is when a player, holding one or more cards of the suit led, plays a card of a different suit.

72. The penalty for a revoke—(i.) is at the option of the adversaries, who at the end of the hand may either take three tricks from the revoking player, or deduct three points from his score, or add three to their own score; (ii.) can be claimed for as many revokes as occur during the hand; (iii.) is applicable only to the score of the game in which it occurs; (iv.) cannot be divided, *i.e.*, a player cannot add one or two to his own score and deduct one or two from the revoking player; (v.) takes precedence of every other score, *e.g.*,—the claimants two, their opponents nothing—the former add three to their score, and thereby win a treble game, even should the latter have made thirteen tricks and held four honours.

73. A revoke is established, if the trick in which it occur be turned and quitted, *i.e.*, the hand removed from that trick after it has been turned face downwards on the table, or if either the revoking player or his partner, whether in his right turn or otherwise, lead or play to the following trick.

74. A player may ask his partner whether he has not a card of the suit which he has renounced. Should the question be asked before the trick is turned and quitted, subsequent turning and quitting does not establish the revoke, and the error may be corrected, unless the question be answered in the negative, or unless the revoking player or his partner have led or played to the following trick.

75. At the end of the hand, the claimants of a revoke may search all the tricks.

76. If a player discover his mistake in time to save a revoke, the adversaries, whenever they think fit, may call the card thus played in error, or may require him to play his highest or lowest card to that trick in which he has renounced. Any player or players who have played after him may withdraw their cards and substitute others. The cards withdrawn are not liable to be called.

77. If a revoke be claimed, and the accused player or his partner mix the cards before they have been sufficiently examined by the adversaries, the revoke is established. The mixing of the cards only renders the proof of a revoke difficult, but does not prevent the claim, and possible establishment, of the penalty.

78. A revoke cannot be claimed after the cards have been cut for the following deal.

79. The revoking player and his partner may, under all circumstances, require the hand in which the revoke has been detected to be played out.

80. If a revoke occur, be claimed, and proved, bets on the odd trick or on amount of score must be decided by the actual state of the latter after the penalty is paid.

81. Should the players on both sides subject themselves to the penalty of one or more revokes, neither can win the game; each is punished at the discretion of his adversary.

82. In whatever way the penalty be enforced, under no circumstances can a player win the game by the result of the hand during which he has revoked; he cannot score more than four. (*Vide* rule 61.)

Calling for New Cards.—83. Any player (on paying for them) before, but not after, the pack be cut for the deal may call for fresh cards. He must call for two new packs, of which the dealer takes his choice.

General rules.

General Rules.—84. Where a player and his partner have an option of exacting from their adversaries one of two penalties, they should agree who is to make the election, but must not consult with one another which of the two penalties it is advisable to exact. If they do so consult, they lose their right; and if either of them, with or without consent of his partner, demand a penalty to which he is entitled, such decision is final. This rule does not apply in exacting the penalties for a revoke; partners have then a right to consult.

85. Any one during the play of a trick, or after the four cards are played, and before, but not after, they are touched for the purpose of gathering them together, may demand that the cards be placed before their respective players.

86. If any one, prior to his partner playing, should call attention to the trick—either by saying that it is his, or by naming his card, or, without being required so to do, by drawing it towards him—the adversaries may require that opponent's partner to play the highest or lowest of the suit then led, or to win or lose the trick.

87. In all cases where a penalty has been incurred, the offender is bound to give reasonable time for the decision of his adversaries.

88. If a bystander make any remark which calls the attention of a player or players to an oversight affecting the score, he is liable to be called on, by the players only, to pay the stakes and all bets on that game or rubber.

89. A bystander by agreement among the players may decide any question.

90. A card or cards torn or marked must be either replaced by agreement, or new cards called at the expense of the table.

91. Any player may demand to see the last trick turned, and no more. Under no circumstances can more than eight cards be seen during the play of the hand, viz., the four cards on the table which have not been turned and quitted, and the last trick turned.

Etiquette of Whist.

Etiquette of whist.

The following rules belong to the established etiquette of whist. They are not called laws, as it is difficult, in some cases impossible, to apply any penalty to their infraction, and the only remedy is to cease to play with players who habitually disregard them.

Two packs of cards are invariably used at clubs; if possible this should be adhered to.

Any one having the lead, and several winning cards to play, should not draw a second card out of his hand until his partner has played to the first trick, such act being a distinct intimation that the former has played a winning card.

No intimation whatever by word or gesture should be given by a player as to the state of his hand or of the game.

A player who desires the cards to be placed, or who demands to see the last trick, should do it for his own information only, and not in order to invite the attention of his partner.

No player should object to refer to a bystander who professes himself uninterested in the game, and able to decide any disputed question of facts,—as to who played any particular card, whether honours were claimed though not scored, or *vice versa*, &c.

It is unfair to revoke purposely: having made a revoke, a player is not justified in making a second in order to conceal the first.

Until the players have made such bets as they wish, bets should not be made with bystanders.

Bystanders should make no remark, neither should they by word or gesture give any intimation of the state of the game until concluded and scored, nor should they walk round the table to look at the different hands.

No one should look over the hand of a player against whom he is betting.

DUMMY.

Dummy. Dummy is played by three players. One hand, called dummy's, lies exposed on the table. The laws are the same as those of whist, with the following exceptions:—(i.) dummy deals at the commencement of each rubber; (ii.) dummy is not liable to the penalty for a revoke, as his adversaries see his cards; should he revoke and the error not be discovered until the trick is turned and quitted, it stands good; (iii.) dummy being blind and deaf, his partner is not liable to any penalty for an error whence he can gain no advantage: thus, he may expose some or all of his cards, or may declare that he has the game or trick, &c., without incurring any penalty; if, however, he lead from dummy's hand when he should lead from his own, or *vice versa*, a suit may be called from the hand which ought to have led.

Double Dummy.—[This] is played by two players, each having a dummy or exposed hand for his partner. The laws of the game do not differ from dummy whist, except in the following special law:—there is no misdeal, as the deal is a disadvantage. (H. J.)

WHISTON, WILLIAM (1667-1752), English divine and mathematician, was born on 9th December 1667 at Norton in Leicestershire, of which village his father was rector. He was educated privately, partly on account of the delicacy of his health and partly that he might act as amanuensis to his father, who had lost his sight. He afterwards entered at Clare College, Cambridge, where he applied himself with extraordinary diligence to mathematical study, and obtained a fellowship in 1693. He next became chaplain to Moore, the learned bishop of Norwich, from whom he received the living of Lowestoft in 1698. He had already given several proofs of his noble but over-scrupulous conscientiousness, and at the same time of the propensity to paradox and the pragmatical and wayward temper which almost destroyed the usefulness of the fine example of disinterestedness which he gave to a lax and lukewarm age. His *Theory of the Earth* (1696), although destitute of sound scientific foundation, obtained the praise of both Newton and Locke, the latter of whom justly classed the author among those who, if not adding much to our knowledge, "at least bring some new things to our thoughts." In 1701 he resigned his living, where his conduct had been most exemplary, to become deputy at Cambridge to Sir Isaac Newton, whom he shortly afterwards succeeded as Lucasian professor of mathematics. For several years Whiston continued to write and preach both on mathematical and theological subjects with considerable success; but his study of the *Apostolical Constitutions* had convinced him that Arianism was the creed of the primitive church; and with him to form an opinion and to publish it were things almost simultaneous. His heterodoxy soon became notorious, and in 1710 he was deprived of his professorship and expelled the university. The rest of his life was spent in incessant controversy,—theological, mathematical, chronological, and miscellaneous. He vindicated his estimate of the *Apostolical Constitutions* and the Arian views he had derived from them in his *Primitive Christianity*, published in 1711. In 1713 he produced a reformed liturgy, and in 1730 one of the most valuable of his books, the *Life of Samuel Clarke*. While heretical on so many points, he was a firm believer in supernatural Christianity, and frequently took the field in defence of prophecy and miracle, including anointing the sick and touching for the king's evil. His dislike to rationalism in religion also made him one of the numerous opponents of Hoadly's *Plain Account of the Lord's Supper*. He proved to his own satisfaction that Canticles was apocryphal and that Baruch was not. He was ever pressing his views of ecclesiastical government and discipline, derived from the *Apostolical Constitutions*, on the rulers of the church, and was lost in sincere astonishment that they could not see the matter in the same light as himself. He assailed the memory of Athanasius with a virulence at least equal to that with which orthodox divines had treated Arius. He attacked Sir Isaac Newton's chronological system with success; but he himself lost not only time but money in an endeavour to discover the longitude. Of all his singular opinions the best known is his advocacy of clerical monogamy, immortalized in the *Vicar of Wakefield*. Of all his labours the most useful is his translation of Josephus, with valuable notes and dissertations, which continues to be reprinted to this day. This appeared in 1736. His last "famous discovery, or rather revival of Dr Giles Fletcher's," which he mentions in his autobiography with infinite complacency, was the identification of the Tartars with the lost tribes of Israel. About the same time (1747) he finally left the communion of the Church of England for the Baptist, leaving the church literally as well as figuratively by quitting it as the clergyman began to read the Athanasian creed. He died in London, at the house of his son-in-law, on 22d August 1752, leaving an autobiography, which deserves more attention than it has received, both for its characteristic individuality and as a storehouse of curious anecdotes and illustrations of the religious and moral tendencies of the age. It does not, however, contain any account of the proceedings taken against him at Cambridge, these having been published separately at the time.

Whiston is a striking example of a not unfrequent phenomenon, the association of an entirely paradoxical bent of mind with proficiency in the exact sciences. He is still more interesting as exemplifying a less ordinary observation, the possibility of arriving at rationalistic conclusions in theology without the slightest tincture of the rationalistic temper. His conclusions were in many respects those of the latitudinarian divines of his day; but anything more unlike the processes by which they attained these, or the spirit in which they supported them, would be difficult to imagine. He was not only paradoxical to the verge of craziness, but intolerant to the verge of bigotry. "I had a mind," he says, "to hear Dr Gill preach. But, being informed that he had written a folio book on the Canticles, I declined to go to hear him." This moral and intellectual unreason effectually destroyed the weight otherwise due to his erudition and acuteness, and left nothing recommendable for imitation in his conduct as a whole, except his passion for truth and his heroic disinterestedness,—virtues in which few have rivalled him, though some may have exhibited them less ostentatiously. When not engaged in controversy he was not devoid of good sense. He often saw men and things very clearly, and some of his bon-mots are admirable.

WHITBY, a seaport and watering-place in the North Riding of Yorkshire, England, is picturesquely situated on both banks of the Esk, at its entrance into the North Sea, and on the North-Eastern Railway, 247½ miles north of London and 56 north-east of York. The river is crossed by a bridge which opens in the centre to permit the passage of vessels. The old parts of the town present a very antique and picturesque appearance, with narrow, steep, and irregular streets and plain old-fashioned houses, while the modern portion, included chiefly in West Cliff, possesses the usual characteristics of a fashionable watering-place. Of the old abbey all that now remains are the ruins of the church, occupying the site of the old Saxon building, but exhibiting no traces of remains earlier than the 12th century. The oldest portion is the choir, which is Early English; the transept also is Early English but of later date; and the nave is rich Decorated. The west side of the nave fell in 1763 and the tower in 1830. On the south side are foundations of cloisters and domestic buildings. Adjoining the abbey is Whitby Hall, built by Sir Francis Cholmley about 1580 from the materials of the monastic buildings, enlarged and fortified by Sir Hugh Cholmley about 1635, and restored within recent years. A little below the abbey is the parish church of St Mary, at first Norman, which still retains some portions of the original building, but owing to a variety of alterations and reconstructions at different periods presents a very incongruous appearance. The principal public buildings are the town-hall, the museum, the public baths, St Hilda's Hall, the temperance hall, and the sea-side home. Previous to 1632 the piers of the harbour were constructed of wood, but in that year a west pier of stone was constructed by Sir Hugh Cholmley. Under an Act of Parliament obtained in 1702 the west pier was reconstructed and the east pier greatly improved. Lately further improvements have been in progress, including the dredging of the river and the extension of the quay to permit the landing of fish close to the railway station. In 1886 the number of vessels that entered the port was 384 of 48,439 tons, the number that cleared 371 of 48,504 tons. The chief exports are jet ornaments and iron, but the shipping trade is on the decline; in fact the town is being gradually transformed into a fashionable watering-place. The manufacture of alum, by which in the reign of Elizabeth the foundations of its prosperity were laid, is now discontinued. The introduction of iron ship-building has also affected an industry (the building of wooden ships) for which Whitby was at one time famous: it was here that the ships for Captain Cook's voyages were built. In 1886 the number of vessels built at the port was 3 of 1356 tons. Whale-fishing, established in 1753, began to decline in 1823, and was abandoned in 1837. The only manufacture that maintains its importance is that of jet ornaments, peculiar to the town, and made from time immemorial from a variety of petrified wood found towards the bottom of the Upper Lias. The fishing industry, owing to improved railway communications, has been progressive within late years. In 1886 it employed 231 boats of 1830 tons. Whitby is an important herring fishing station. The population of the urban sanitary district (area 2008 acres) was 12,460 in 1871 and 14,086 in 1881.

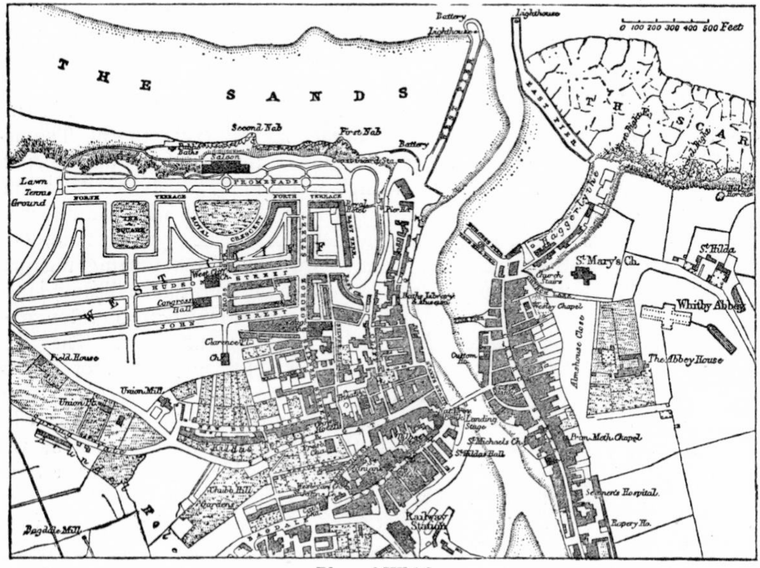

Plan of Whitby.

Whitby was called by the Saxons *Streonshalh*, but in Domesday the name occurs as Whitteby or the "white town." It owes its origin to the foundation of a monastery by Oswy, king of Northumbria, in 658, in fulfilment of a vow for a victory gained over King Penda. The monastery embraced an establishment both for nuns and for monks of the Benedictine order, and under Hilda, a grand-niece of Edwin, a former king of Northumbria, acquired high celebrity. In 664 it was the meeting-place of a synod held under the presidency of Oswy to determine the time of keeping Easter and the shape of the religious tonsure. In 867 the town and abbey were destroyed by the Danes, after which they lay waste for upwards of 200 years. At the Conquest they belonged to Gospatric, earl of Northumberland, whose lands were confiscated by William and given to Hugh, earl of Chester, who sold them to William de Percy. In 1074 the restoration of the abbey was begun by Reinfrid, who had been a soldier in the Conqueror's army. In 1539 the abbey and lands were surrendered to the crown, and in 1555 were purchased by Sir Richard Cholmley. Whitby obtained the grant of a market from Henry II., and of a fair from Henry VI. It was created a parliamentary borough in 1832, but in 1885 it was included in the Whitby division of the North Riding.

WHITE, Gilbert (1720-1793), the natural historian of Selborne, was born on 18th July 1720 in the little Hampshire village which his writings have rendered so familiar to all lovers of either books or nature. He was educated at Basingstoke under Warton, father of the poet, and subsequently at Oriel College, Oxford, where he obtained a fellowship (1744). Entering upon a country curacy in 1753, he returned to Selborne in 1755, where he seems soon to have discontinued his ministrations. He obtained a sinecure living from his college in 1758; but after his father's death in the same year he became curate of the neighbouring parish of Faringdon, and repeatedly declined valuable livings elsewhere, until 1784, when he returned to the curacy of Selborne, and there ministered until his death on 26th June 1793. He was never married.

His daily life was practically unbroken by any great changes or incidents; for nearly half a century his pastoral duties, his watchful country walks, the assiduous care of his garden, and the scrupulous posting of his calendar of observations made up the essentials of a full and delightful life, but hardly of a biography. At most we can only fill up the portrait by reference to the tinge of simple old-fashioned scholarship, which on its historic side made him an eager searcher for antiquities and among old records, and on its poetic occasionally stirred him to an excursion as far as that gentlest slope of Parnassus inhabited by the descriptive muse. Hence we are thrown back upon that correspondence with brother naturalists which has raised his life and its influence so far beyond the commonplace. His strong naturalist tendencies are not, however, properly to be realized without a glance at the history of his younger brothers. The eldest, Thomas, retired from trade to devote himself to natural and physical science, and contributed many papers to the Royal Society, of which he was a fellow. The next, Benjamin, became the publisher of most of the leading works of natural history which appeared during his lifetime, including that of his brother. The third, John, became vicar of Gibraltar, where he accumulated much material for a work on the natural history of the rock and its neighbourhood, and carried on a scientific correspondence, not only with his eldest brother, but with Linnæus. The youngest, Henry, who died soon after entering the church, is mentioned as having engaged in meteorological observations. The sister's son, Samuel Barker, also became in time one of White's most valued correspondents. With other naturalists, too, he had intimate relations: with Pennant and Daines Barrington he was in constant correspondence, often too with the botanist Lightfoot, and sometimes with Sir Joseph Banks and others, while Chandler and other antiquaries kept alive his historic zeal. At first he was content to furnish information from which the works of Pennant and Barrington largely profited; but gradually the ambition of separate authorship developed from a suggestion thrown out by the latter of these writers in 1770. The next year White sketched to Pennant the project of "a natural history of my native parish, an *annus historico-naturalis*, comprising a journal for a whole year, and illustrated with large notes and observations. Such a beginning might induce more able naturalists to write the history of various districts and might in time occasion the production of a work so much to be wished for, a full and complete natural history of these kingdoms." Yet the famous *Natural History of Selborne* did not appear until 1789. It was well received from the beginning.

To be a typical parish natural history so far as completeness or order is concerned, it has of course no pretensions; batches of letters, an essay on antiquities, a naturalist's calendar, and miscellaneous jottings of all kinds are but the unsystematized material of the work proper, which was never written. Yet it is largely to this very piecemeal character that its popularity has been due. The style has the simple, yet fresh and graphic, directness of all good letter writing, and there is no lack of passages of keen observation, and even shrewd interpretation. White not only notes the homes and ways, the times and seasons, of plants and animals,—comparing, for instance, the different ways in which the squirrel, the field-mouse, and the nuthatch eat their hazel-nuts,—or watches the migrations of birds, which were then only beginning to be properly recorded or understood, but he knows more than any other observer until Darwin about the habits and the usefulness of the earthworms, and is as certain as the latest physicists that plants distil dew and do not merely condense it. The book is also interesting as having appeared on the borderland between the mediæval and the modern school of natural history, avoiding the uncritical blundering of the old Encyclopædists, without entering on the technical and analytic character of the opening age of separate monographs. Moreover, as the first book which raised natural history into the region of literature, much as the *Compleat Angler* did for that gentle art, we must affiliate to it the more finished products of later writers like Thoreau or Jefferies. Yet, while these are essential merits of the book, its endearing charm lies deeper, in the sweet and kindly personality of the author, who on his rambles gathers no spoil, but watches the birds and field-mice without disturbing them from their nests, and quietly plants an acorn where he thinks an oak is wanted, or sows beech-nuts in what is now a stately row. He overflows with anecdotes, seldom indeed gets beyond the anecdotal stage, yet from this all study of nature must begin; and he sees everywhere intelligence and beauty, love and sociality, where a later view of nature insists primarily on mere adaptation of interests or purely competitive struggles. The encyclopædic interest in nature, although in White's day culminating in the monumental synthesis of Buffon, was also disappearing before the analytic specialism inaugurated by Linnæus; yet the catholic interests of the simple naturalist of Selborne fully reappear a century later in the greater naturalist of Down.

WHITE, Joseph Blanco (1775-1841), author, was born at Seville on 11th July 1775. He was educated for the Roman Catholic priesthood; but after his ordination doubts as to the principles of Catholicism led him to escape from Spain to England (1810), where he ultimately entered the Established Church, having studied theology at Oxford and made the friendship of Arnold, Newman, and Whately. He became tutor in the family of the last-named when he was made archbishop of Dublin (1831). While in this position he embraced Unitarian views; and he found an asylum amongst the Unitarians of Liverpool, where he died on 20th May 1841.

His principal writings are *Doblado's Letters from Spain*, 1822; *Evidence against Catholicism*, 1825; *Second Travels of an Irish Gentleman in Search of a Religion*, 1834; *Observations on Heresy and Orthodoxy*, 1835. They all show literary ability, and were extensively read in their day. It is probable that his name will be longest known in the world of letters by his sonnet addressed *To Night* ("Mysterious night! when our first parent knew"), which has found its way into almost all the recent anthologies, and was spoken of by his contemporaries, Hunt and Coleridge, as one of the finest in English or indeed in any language.

See *Life of the Rev. Joseph Blanco White, written by himself, with portions of his Correspondence*, edited by John Hamilton Thom, London, 1845.

WHITE, Robert (1645-1704), engraver and draughtsman, was born in London in 1645. He studied engraving under David Loggan, for whom he executed many architectural subjects; his early works also include landscapes and engraved title-pages for books. He acquired great skill in portraiture, his works of this class being commonly drawn with the black-lead pencil upon vellum, and afterwards excellently engraved in line. Portraits executed in this manner he marked "ad vivum," and they are prized by collectors for their artistic merit and their authenticity. Virtue catalogued 275 portrait engravings by White, including the likenesses of many of the most celebrated personages of his day; and nine portraits engraved in mezzotint are assigned to him by J. Chaloner Smith. White died at Bloomsbury, London, in 1704.

His son, George White, who was born about 1671 and died about 1734, is also known as an engraver and portrait-painter.

WHITEBAIT, the vernacular name of a small Clupeoid fish which appears in large shoals in the estuary of the Thames during the summer months, and is held in great esteem as a delicacy for the table. As to whether or not it is a distinct form, the opinions of naturalists have been divided ever since their attention was directed to the question. Pennant and Shaw believed it tc be some kind of Cyprinoid fish, similar to the bleak, whilst Donovan, in his *Natural History of British Fishes* (1802-8), misled by specimens sent to him as whitebait, declared it to be the young of the shad. In 1820 Yarrell proved conclusively that Donovan's opinion was founded upon an error; unfortunately he contented himself with comparing whitebait with the shad only, and in the end adopted the opinion of the Thames fishermen, whose interest it was to represent it as a distinct adult form; thus the whitebait is introduced into Yarrell's *History of British Fishes* (1836) as *Clupea alba*. The French ichthyologist Valenciennes went a step further, declaring it to be not only specifically but also generically distinct from all other Clupeoids. On examining the specimens of *Clupea alba* which passed from Yarrell's collection into the British Museum, the present writer found them to be the young of the common herring (*Catal. Fish. Brit. Mus.*, vii. p. 416, 1868); and this conclusion was fully borne out by visits to the Thames boats and by an examination of their captures on the spot. The bulk of the whitebait caught consists, in May and June, chiefly of the fry of herring, mixed with a number of shrimps, gobies, sticklebacks, pipe-fishes, young flounders, and an occasional sprat. But, the Thames being unequal to the supply of the large demand for this delicacy, large quantities of whitebait are now brought to London and other markets from many parts of the coast. They frequently consist of a much greater proportion of young sprats than the fish obtained from the Thames; and they sometimes prove a valuable mine for the collector, who may find mixed with them pelagic animals (such as the smaller kinds of Cephalopods) which are not at all, or but rarely, met with at the mouth of the Thames or on the south coast generally. In times past whitebait were considered to be peculiar to the estuary of the Thames; and, even after the specific identification of Thames whitebait with the young of the herring from other localities, it was still thought that there was a distinctive superiority in the condition and flavour of the former. It is possible that the young herrings find in the estuary of the Thames a larger amount of suitable food than on other parts of the coast, where the water may be of greater purity, but possesses less abundance of the minute animal life on which whitebait thrive. Indeed, Thames whitebait which have been compared with young herrings from the mouth of the Exe, the Cornish coast, Menai Strait, and the Firth of Forth seemed to be better fed; but, of course, the specific characteristics of the herring,—into which we need not enter here,—were nowise modified.

The fry of fishes is used as an article of diet in almost every country: in Germany the young of various species of Cyprinoids, in Italy and Japan the young of nearly every fish capable of being readily captured in sufficient numbers, in the South Sea Islands the fry of *Teuthis*, in New Zealand young *Galaxias* are consumed at certain seasons in large quantities; and, like whitebait, these fry bear distinct names, different from those of the adult fish.

Whitebait fishing in the Thames lasts from the end of March to September. The majority of the fish caught at the beginning of spring are about two inches long; as the season advances the proportion of larger specimens becomes greater, although very small ones occur abundantly throughout the season,—thus apparently confirming the opinion of those who maintain that the herring is in its spawning not bound to any particular month. Whitebait are caught on the flood-tide from boats moored in from 3 to 5 fathoms of water. The net used is a bag some 20 feet long, narrow and small-meshed towards the tail-end, the mouth being kept open in the direction of the advancing tide by a framework 3 or 4 feet square. It is placed alongside the boat and sunk to a depth of 4 feet below the surface; from time to time the end of the bag is lifted into the boat, to empty it of its contents. The "schools" of whitebait, advancing and retiring with the tide for days and probably for weeks, have to run the gauntlet of a dozen of these nets, and therefore get very much thinned in number by the end of the season. When the view commenced to gain ground that whitebait were young herring, the question arose whether or not the immense destruction of the young brood caused by this mode of fishing injuriously affected the fishery of the mature herring. This undoubtedly it does; but, since it has been ascertained that the herring is much more restricted in its migrations than was formerly believed, and that it merely moves from the feeding-grounds in the depth of the ocean to the shallower spawning-grounds of the neighbouring coast, the injury, such as it is, must be local and limited to the particular district in which the fishing for whitebait is methodically practised.

WHITEFIELD, or STAND, a large manufacturing village of Lancashire, England, in the township of Pilkington, is situated a short distance from the Radcliffe Bridge station on the Lancashire and Yorkshire Railway, 5½ miles north of Manchester and 196 from London. It possesses a number of fine villas inhabited by Manchester merchants. The church of All Saints, commonly called Stand church, was erected in 1826 from the designs of Sir Charles Barry. There is a school founded and endowed by Henry Siddal in 1688. Whitefield has risen into importance since 1829. There are coal mines in the neighbourhood, and cotton-spinning and hand and power loom weaving are carried on. The population of the urban sanitary district (area 2048 acres) was 9054 in 1871 and 9516 in 1881.

A family of the name of Pilkington was settled at Pilkington Tower or Stand soon after the Conquest, Leonard Pilkington being mentioned as lord of the manor in the tenth year of Henry I. The manor of Pilkington was granted to the earl of Derby by Henry VII. after the battle of Bosworth. The old hall of the Pilkington family, called Stand Hall, existed as recently as 1848. On the foundation stone was the date 1580.

WHITEFIELD, GEORGE (1714-1770), one of the most eloquent of pulpit orators, was born on 16th December 1714 at the Bell Inn, Gloucester, of which his father was landlord. At about twelve years of age he was sent to the school of St Mary de Crypt, Gloucester, where on account of his skill in elocution he was chosen to perform in a piece acted before the corporation of the school. He also became very fond of reading plays, a circumstance which probably had considerable influence on his subsequent career, for his eloquence was essentially dramatic in its character. At the age of fifteen he was taken from school to assist his mother in the public-house, and for a year and a half was a common drawer. He then again returned to school to prepare for the university, and in 1733 entered as a servitor at Pembroke College, Oxford. There he came under the influence of the Methodists (see WESLEY), and entered so enthusiastically into their practices and habits that he was attacked by a severe illness, which compelled him to return to his native town. His sincere and enthusiastic piety attracted the notice of Dr Benson, bishop of Gloucester, who ordained him deacon on 20th June 1736. Having in the following week returned to Oxford and taken his degree, he began an evangelizing tour in Bath, Bristol, and other towns, his eloquence at once attracting immense multitudes. In 1736 he was invited by Wesley to go out as a missionary to Georgia, and went to London to wait on the trustees. Before setting sail he preached in some of the principal London churches, and so rapidly did the fame of his eloquence spread that crowds began to assemble at the church doors long before daybreak. Several of the sermons which he then preached were published "at the request of the hearers." On 28th December 1737 he embarked for Georgia, which he reached on 7th May 1738. After three months' residence there he returned to England to receive priest's orders, and to raise contributions for the support of an orphanage. He was, however, coldly received by the clergy generally, and began to preach in the open air. At Bristol his addresses to the colliers soon attracted crowds, which were latterly estimated to exceed 20,000 persons. Whitefield's voice was so powerful that it penetrated to the utmost limits of the crowd. His fervour and dramatic action held them spell-bound, and his homely pathos soon broke down all barriers of resistance. "The first discovery of their being affected," he says, "was by seeing the white gutters made by their tears, which plentifully fell down their black cheeks." In 1738 an account of Whitefield's voyage from London to Georgia was published without his knowledge. In 1739 he published his *Journal* from his arrival in Savannah to his return to London, and also his *Journal* from his arrival in London to his departure thence on his way to Georgia. As his embarkation was further delayed for ten weeks he published *A Continuation of the Rev. Mr Whitefield's Journal during the time he was delayed in England by the Embargo.* His unfavourable reception in England by the clergy led him to make reprisals. To Dr Trapp's attack on the Methodists he published in 1739 *A Preservative against Unsettled Notions*, in which the clergy of the Church of England were rather bitterly denounced; he also published shortly afterwards *The Spirit and Doctrine and Lives of our Modern Clergy*, and a reply to a pastoral letter of the bishop of London in which he had been attacked. In the same year appeared *Sermons on Various Subjects* (2 vols.), the *Church Companion, or Sermons on Several Subjects*, and a recommendatory epistle to the *Life of Thomas Halyburton.* He again embarked for America in August 1739, and remained there two years, preaching in all the principal towns. While there he published *Three Letters from Mr Whitefield*, in which he referred to the "mystery of iniquity" in Tillotson, and asserted that that divine knew no more of Christ than Mohammed did.

During his absence from England Whitefield found that a divergence of doctrine from Calvinism had been introduced by Wesley; and notwithstanding Wesley's exhortations to brotherly kindness and forbearance he withdrew from the Wesleyan communion. Thereupon his friends built for him near Wesley's church a wooden structure, which was named the Tabernacle. In 1741, on the invitation of Ralph and Ebenezer Erskine, he paid a visit to Scotland, commencing his labours in the Secession meeting-house, Dunfermline. But, as he refused to limit his ministrations to one sect, the Seceders and he parted company, and without their countenance he made a tour through the principal towns of Scotland, the authorities of which in most instances presented him with the freedom of the burgh, in token of their estimate of the benefits to the community resulting from his preaching. From Scotland he went to Wales, where on 14th November he married Mrs James, a widow. The marriage was not a happy one. On his return to London he preached to the crowds in Moorfields during the Whitsun holidays with such effect as to attract nearly all the people from the shows. After a second visit to Scotland, June to October 1742, and a tour through England and Wales, 1742-44, he embarked in August 1744 for America, where he remained till June 1748. On his return to London he found his congregation at the Tabernacle dispersed; and his circumstances were so depressed that he was obliged to sell his household furniture to pay his orphan-house debts. Having, however, made the acquaintance of the countess of Huntingdon, he soon found his pecuniary affairs on a better footing. The countess appointed him one of her chaplains, built and endowed Calvinistic Methodist chapels in various parts of the country, and erected a college for the training of candidates for the ministry. The remainder of Whitefield's life was spent chiefly in evangelizing tours in Great Britain, Ireland, and America. It has been stated that "in the compass of a single week, and that for years, he spoke in general forty hours, and in very many sixty, and that to thousands." On his return from America to England for the last time the change in his appearance forcibly impressed Wesley, who wrote in his *Journal*: "He seemed to be an old man, being fairly worn out in his Master's service, though he had hardly seen fifty years." When health was failing him he placed himself on what he called "short allowance," preaching only once every week day and thrice on Sunday. In 1769 he returned to America for the seventh and last time. He was now affected by a severe asthmatic complaint; but to those who advised him to take some rest, he answered, "I had rather *wear* out than *rust* out." He died on the 30th September 1770 at Newbury, New England, where he had arrived on the previous evening with the intention of preaching next day. In accordance with his own desire he was buried before the pulpit in the Presbyterian church of the town where he died.

Whitefield, says Lecky, "was chiefly a creature of impulse and emotion. He had very little logical skill, no depth or range of knowlege, not much self-restraint." He possessed neither Wesley's organizing power, nor his personal authority and influence. His one talent was his gift of popular oratory, the secret of which was his command of clear and direct English, his remarkable elocutionary and dramatic skill, and his passionate fervour and simple pathos. His printed works convey a totally inadequate idea of his oratorical powers, and are all in fact below mediocrity. They appeared in a collected form in 1771-72 in seven volumes, the last containing *Memoirs of his Life*, by Dr John Gillies. His *Letters*, 1734-70, were comprised in vols. i., ii., and iii. of his *Works* and were also published separately. His *Select Works*, with memoir by J. Smith, appeared in 1850.

See also Philip's *Whitefield's Life and Times*, 1837; Tyerman's *Life of Whitefield*, 1876-77; and Lecky's *History of England*, vol. ii. (T. F. H.)

WHITEFISH is a collective name applied in different countries to very different kinds of freshwater fishes, which, however, have this in common, that their body is covered with regularly arranged silvery scales, without spots or ornamental colours. Thus the numerous European species of the Cyprinoid genus *Leuciscus* are frequently comprised under the name of "Whitefish," whilst in North America this term is in general use for the various species of the Salmonoid genus *Coregonus*, which abound in every lake and river of Canada and the northern parts of the United States.

WHITEHAVEN, a parliamentary borough of England and the principal seaport of Cumberland, is situated at the extremity of the Solway Firth, facing the Irish Sea, 41 miles south-west of Carlisle and 304 north-west of London. It is connected by a branch line with the London and North Western Railway. The town is built chiefly in a valley overlooked by high grounds on the north and south. The streets are spacious, with handsome shops. The principal public buildings are the town-hall, court-room, custom-house, police office, theatre, baths, free library, infirmary, and dispensary. The harbour is protected by two stone piers; the west pier (erected 1824-39) is 965 feet long, and the north pier (1837-41) 918 feet. There is daily communication with Liverpool, Glasgow, Belfast, Dublin, and the Isle of Man. The town has an import trade from America, the Baltic ports, France, Spain and Portugal, and the Mediterranean. The principal exports are coal, pig iron, lime, freestone, and grain. The number of vessels that entered the port in 1886 was 2377, of 269,811 tons, the number that cleared 2297, of 257,025 tons. Iron ship-building is carried on, but the number of vessels built in 1886 was only 2 of 2406 tons. The other principal industries are engineering, brass-founding, boiler-making, brick and earthenware manufacturing, and dyeing. There are two large collieries, one extending about 1½ miles under the sea. Fishing is carried on to a small extent, the number of boats engaged in 1886 being 18 of 441 tons. The population of the urban sanitary district (area 679 acres) was 18,243 in 1871 and 19,295 in 1881.

Whitehaven owes its name to the light colour of the rocks adjoining it. In the reign of Henry I. the manor formed part of the monastery of St Mary's at York, to which the priory of St Bees belonged. In 1599 the manor of St Bees was purchased from Sir Thomas Chaloner by General Lowther and Thomas Wybergh, and the whole in 1644 came into the possession of Sir John Lowther, under whose auspices the town advanced with great rapidity. From Charles II. the Lowthers obtained an additional grant of 150 acres, now partly included in the town, soon after which means were taken greatly to improve the harbour. By Acts passed in the 7th and 11th years of Queen Anne's reign the town is governed by twenty-two trustees elected triennially. The earl of Lonsdale, whose castle adjoins the town, is lord of the manor. Whitehaven has returned one member to parliament since 1832.

WHITELOCKE, BULSTRODE (1605-1675), son of Sir James Whitelocke, a justice of the King's Bench, was born at London, on 2d August 1605. He was educated at Eton and afterwards at Merchant Taylors' School, London. In 1620 he entered St John's College, Oxford. In preparing for the bar he became acquainted with Selden, who aided him in his studies and gave him the use of his library. Whitelocke sat for Stafford in the parliament of 1626, and in the course of that year was called to the bar. In 1630 he married a daughter of Alderman Bennett. During the years that followed he was in the favour of Laud. He was not a man likely to raise disturbances in church and state; and he took an active part in the preparation of the law of Court Masque after Prynne's condemnation in 1634, not long after which his wife died. Before the year was out he made a runaway match with the sister of Lord Willoughby of Parham.

When the troubles began Whitelocke's cautious nature led him to distrust Laud, though he kept himself from all communication with the Scots. In the Long Parliament he represented Great Marlow, and took part in the impeachment of Strafford. Later on he did his best to avert a civil war, but prudently remained at Westminster instead of joining the king. When the Royalists advanced after Edgehill, his house, Fawley Court, was pillaged by the soldiers. When attempts were subsequently made to open negotiations with the king, he became a leading member of the peace party, though, as he tells us himself, he "kept fair with the other leading men of the House, as Mr Pym, Hampden, and the rest, and would not entirely engage in any party, which made him the more courted by all." He was one of the commissioners appointed to carry the terms of the Parliament to Oxford in May, and drew on himself suspicions of too close intercourse with the king. Having at the close of 1644 taken part in a conference between some of the Scots and the English Presbyterians, his advice did much to frustrate a proposal for a parliamentary accusation of Cromwell. On the other hand, he spoke in the Commons against the Self-Denying Ordinance. He was again a commissioner in the negotiation with the king at Uxbridge early in 1645. Whitelocke was present at the siege of Oxford in 1646, and was on excellent terms with Fairfax and Cromwell. Later in the year he opposed an ordinance for punishing heretics. His common-sense seems to have rallied him to the tolerationists, and he took their side in opposing the divine right of presbytery and in getting rid of the Scottish army. In 1647 he tried to moderate the opposition of the Presbyterians to the army, but as usual he did not throw himself violently on either side. In 1648 he was named a commissioner of the great seal. He was much troubled at the attack on the House of Commons by Pride's "purge," but he did not resign his post. He refused to have anything to do with the king's trial; but he accepted a commissionership of the new great seal of the commonwealth after the king's execution. Both before the trial and afterwards he was on intimate terms with Cromwell. In May 1649 his second wife died. In January 1650 he proposed to Lady Hungerford, but, being refused by her, he was married in the following August to the widow of Alderman Wilson. Whitelocke was now a member of the council of state, striving to keep on good terms with all parties. After Cromwell's return from the Scottish war in 1651 Whitelocke was much consulted by him; but he gave offence by suggesting a restoration of the young king. After the dissolution of the Long Parliament in 1653 he was sent as ambassador to Sweden, as he thought, merely to get him out of the way. Returning in July 1654, he was chosen member of the first parliament of the Protectorate by the county of Buckingham, and he again became a commissioner of the great seal. In May 1655, after the dissolution of that parliament, he refused to execute an ordinance made by the Protector and council only for the reform of Chancery, and was consequently dismissed in June, but was soon afterwards appointed commissioner of the treasury. He again sat for Buckinghamshire in the second Protectorate parliament in 1657, and took an active part in forwarding the Humble Petition and Advice. In December he was appointed one of Cromwell's lords.

After Cromwell's death Whitelocke rallied to his son, and in January 1659 was again a commissioner of the great seal. After Richard's fall he sat in the council of state, and when the Rump was turned out by the soldiers he accepted an appointment to the army's committee of safety. On 1st November he became keeper of the great seal; but on the return of the Rump he thought it prudent to go into hiding. Monk's arrival delivered him from his fears; but, when the Convention Parliament was chosen, he, characteristically "foreseeing what would come to pass, did not think fit to labour to be a Parliament man." Of course he accepted the Restoration and was included in the Act of Oblivion. He died at his seat at Chilton in Wiltshire in 1675.

WHITETHROAT, a name commonly given to two species of little birds, one of which, the *Motacilla sylvia* of Linnæus and *Sylvia rufa*[1] or *S. cinerea* of some recent authors, is regarded as the type, not only of the genus *Sylvia*, but of the so-called Family *Sylviidæ* (*cf.* WARBLER).

Very widely spread over Great Britain, in some places tolerably common, and by its gesticulations and song rather conspicuous, it is one of those birds which has gained a familiar nickname, and "Peggy Whitethroat" is the anthropomorphic appellation of schoolboys and milkmaids, though it shares "Nettle-creeper" and other homely names with perhaps more than one congener, while to the writers and readers of books it is by way of distinction the Greater Whitethroat. The song of this bird, except by association with the season at which it is uttered, can scarcely be called agreeable, some of its notes being very harsh; but the performer may be seen to be always in earnest, erecting the feathers of his crown, puffing out those of his throat, shaking his wings, and making other rapid movements expressive of his feelings. Occasionally he will deliver his song as he flies up in a peculiar fashion, describing small circles in the air, stopping with a jerk, and then returning to the spot whence he arose.

The Lesser Whitethroat, *Sylvia curruca*,[2] is both in habits and plumage a much less sightly bird: the predominant reddish brown of the upper surface, and especially the rufous edging of the wing-feathers, that are so distinctive of its larger congener, are wanting, and the whole plumage above is of a smoky-grey, while the bird in its movements is never obtrusive, and it rather shuns than courts observation, generally keeping among the thickest foliage, whence its rather monotonous song, uttered especially in sultry weather, may be continually heard without a glimpse of the vocalist being presented. The nests of each of these species are very pretty works of art, firmly built of bents or other plant-stalks, and usually lined with horsehair; but the sides and bottom are often so finely woven as to be like open basket-work, and the eggs, splashed, spotted, or streaked with olive-brown, are frequently visible from beneath through the interstices of the fabric. This style of nest-building seems to be common to all the species of the genus *Sylvia*, as now restricted, and in many districts has obtained for the builders the name of "Hay-Jack," quite without reference to the kind of bird which puts the nests together, and thus is also applied to the Blackcap, *S. atricapilla*, and the Garden-Warbler—this last being merely a book-name—*S. salicaria* (*S. hortensis* of some writers).[3] The former of these deserves mention as one of the sweetest songsters of Great Britain, and fortunately it is very generally distributed in summer. To quote the praise bestowed upon it, in more than one passage, by Gilbert White would here be superfluous. The name Blackcap is applicable only to the cock bird, who further differs from his brown-capped mate by the purity of his ashy-grey upper plumage; but, notwithstanding the marked sexual difference in appearance, he takes on himself a considerable share of the duties of incubation, and has been declared by more than one writer to sing while so employed—a statement that seems hardly credible. All these four birds, as a rule, leave Great Britain at the end of summer to winter in the south.[4] Two other species, one certainly belonging to the same genus, *S. orphea*, and the other, *S. nisoria*, a somewhat aberrant form, have occurred two or three times in Great Britain. The rest, numbering perhaps a dozen, must be passed over.

Nearly allied to *Sylvia*, if indeed it can be properly separated, is *Melizophilus*, which consists of two species, one of them the curious Dartford Warbler of English writers, *M. undatus* or *provincialis*. This is on many accounts a very interesting bird, for it is one of the few of its family that winter in England,—a fact the more remarkable when it is known to be migratory in most parts of the Continent. Its distribution in England is very local, and chiefly confined to the southern counties, where through causes very insufficiently known it has of late years become so scarce that its extermination seems probable. It is a pretty little dark-coloured bird, which here and there may be seen on furze-grown heaths from Kent to Cornwall. In spasmodic gesticulations the cock surpasses the Whitethroat; but these feats are almost confined to the pairing-season, and at other times of the year the bird's habits are retiring. For a species with wings so feebly formed it has a wide range, inhabiting nearly all the countries of the Mediterranean seaboard, from Palestine to the Strait of Gibraltar, and thence along the west coast of Europe to the English Channel; but everywhere else it seems to be very local.

This may be the most convenient place for noticing the small group of Warblers belonging to the well-marked genus *Hypolais*, which, though in general appearance and certain habits resembling the *Phylloscopi* (*cf.* [Willow] WREN), would seem usually to have little to do with those birds, and to be rather allied to the *Sylviinæ*, if not to the *Acrocephalinæ* (*cf.* WARBLER). They have a remarkably loud song, and in consequence are highly valued on the continent of Europe, where two species at least spend the summer. One of them, *H. icterina*, has occurred more than once in the British Islands, and their absence as regular visitors is to be regretted. Among the minor characteristics of this little group is one afforded by their eggs, which are of a deeper or paler brownish pink, spotted with purplish black. Their nests are beautiful structures, combining warmth with lightness in a way that cannot be fully appreciated by any description.

A great number of other more or less allied forms, interesting as they are in various ways, cannot for want of space be here mentioned. (A. N.)

WHITFIELD, JOHN CLARKE (1770-1836), organist and composer, was born at Gloucester, 13th December 1770, and educated at Oxford under Dr Philip Hayes. In 1789 he was appointed organist of the parish church at Ludlow. Four years later he took the degree of Mus. Bac. at Cambridge, and in 1795 he was chosen organist of Armagh cathedral, whence he removed in the same year to Dublin, with the appointments of organist and master of the children at St Patrick's cathedral and Christchurch. Driven from Ireland by the rebellion of 1798, he accepted the post of organist at Trinity and St John's Colleges, Cambridge, and about the same time assumed the surname of Whitfield, in addition to that of Clarke, by which he had been previously known. He took the degree of Mus. Doc. at Cambridge in 1799, and in 1810 proceeded to the same grade at Oxford. In 1820 he was elected organist and master of the choristers at Hereford cathedral; and on the death of Dr Haig he was appointed professor of

[1] This specific term has been very constantly but most inaccurately, not to say absurdly, used for a very different bird, the Chiffchaff (*cf.* [Willow] WREN). Its only proper application is to the Whitethroat.

[2] Of course this is not the *curruca* of ancient writers, that being almost certainly the Hedge-Sparrow (see SPARROW), the ordinary dupe of the Cuckow.

[3] This bird, if it has any true English name at all, should perhaps be called the "Pettichaps," that being applied to it, though not exclusively, in Lancashire and Yorkshire, but not, it would seem, in Northamptonshire or Hampshire (*cf.* Yarrell's *Br. Birds*, 4th ed. pp. 415, 416).

[4] The Blackcap is recorded as having occurred several times in England in winter; but its tarrying was doubtless involuntary.

music at Cambridge. Three years afterwards he resigned these appointments in consequence of an attack of paralysis. He died at Hereford, 22d February 1836.

Whitfield's compositions were very numerous. Among the best of them are four volumes of anthems, published in 1805. He also composed a great number of songs, one of which—*Bird of the Wilderness*, written to some well-known verses by James Hogg, the "Ettrick Shepherd"—attained a high degree of popularity. But the great work of his life was the publication, in a popular and eminently useful form, of the oratorios of Handel, which he was the first to present to the public with a complete pianoforte accompaniment. Before his time these works could only be obtained either in full score or with a plain-figured bass, in which forms they were absolutely useless to the unlearned musician. But so great was the success of his experiment that at the present day the form he originated is the only one with which the general public is familiar. His own volumes, indeed, have been long out of print, and are not now very easy to obtain; but every one of the great oratorios, arranged on a similar plan, may be bought at a price within the reach of the poorest student of art.

WHITGIFT, JOHN (1530 or 1533-1604), archbishop of Canterbury, was descended from a middle-class family, the elder branch of which had been long settled in Yorkshire. He was the eldest son of Henry Whitgift, merchant of Great Grimsby, Lincolnshire, where he was born, according to one account in 1533, but according to a calculation founded on a statement of his own in 1530. At an early age his education was entrusted to his uncle, Robert Whitgift, abbot of the neighbouring monastery of Wellow, by whose advice he was afterwards sent to St Anthony's school, London. There he lodged with his aunt, wife of the verger of St Paul's cathedral; but, having through his uncle's teaching imbibed so much of the Reformation doctrine that he declined to attend mass in the cathedral, he quarrelled with his aunt and had to return home. In 1549 he matriculated at Queen's College, Cambridge, and in May 1550 he migrated to Pembroke Hall, where he had the martyr John Bradford for a tutor. On 31st May 1555 he became a fellow of Peterhouse. Having taken holy orders in 1560, he became in the same year chaplain to Dr Cox, bishop of Ely, who collated him to the rectory of Teversham, Cambridgeshire. In 1563 he was appointed Lady Margaret professor of divinity at Cambridge, and his lectures gave such satisfaction to the authorities that on 5th July 1566 they considerably augmented his stipend. The following year he was appointed regius professor of divinity, and also became master of Trinity. He had a principal share in compiling the statutes of the university, which passed the great seal on 25th September 1570, and in November following he was chosen vice-chancellor. Macaulay's description of Whitgift, as "a narrow, mean, tyrannical priest, who gained power by servility and adulation," is tinged with rhetorical exaggeration; but undoubtedly Whitgift's extreme High Church notions led him to treat the Puritans with exceptional intolerance. In a pulpit controversy with Cartwright, regarding the constitutions and customs of the Church of England, he showed himself Cartwright's inferior in oratorical effectiveness, but the balance was redressed by the exercise of arbitrary authority. Whitgift, with other heads of the university, deprived Cartwright in 1570 of his professorship, and in September 1571 he exercised his prerogative as master of Trinity to deprive him of his fellowship. In June of the same year Whitgift was nominated dean of Lincoln. In the following year he published *An Answere to a Certain Libel intituled an Admonition to the Parliament*. To this Cartwright replied by a *Second Admonition to the Parliament*; and in 1573 Whitgift published a third edition of his *Answere*, with additions bearing on Cartwright's *Admonition*. Cartwright thereupon rejoined by a *Replye to an Answere made of M. Doctor Whitegifte*; and in 1574 Whitgift published *Defence of the Answere to the Admonition against the Replye of T. C.* On 24th March 1577 he was appointed bishop of Worcester, and during the absence of Sir Henry Sidney in Ireland he for two and a half years acted as vice-president of Wales. In August 1583 he was nominated archbishop of Canterbury, and thus was largely instrumental in giving its special complexion to the church of the Reformation. Although he wrote a letter to Queen Elizabeth remonstrating against the alienation of church property, Whitgift always retained her special confidence. In his policy against the Puritans, and in his vigorous enforcement of the subscription test, he was only obeying her behests. His course of action gave rise to the Mar-prelate tracts, in which the bishops and clergy were bitterly attacked. Through Whitgift's vigilance the printers of the tracts were, however, discovered and punished; and in order more effectually to check the publication of such opinions he got a law passed in 1593 making Puritanism an offence against the statute law. In the controversy between Travers and Hooker he interposed by prohibiting the preaching of the former; and he moreover presented Hooker with the rectory of Boscombe in Wiltshire, in order to afford him more leisure to complete his *Ecclesiastical Polity*, a work which, however, cannot be said to represent either Whitgift's theological or his ecclesiastical standpoint. Towards the close of his episcopate he, in conjunction with the bishop of London and other prelates, drew up the Calvinistic instrument known as the Lambeth Articles. They were, however, not accepted by the church. Whitgift attended Elizabeth on her deathbed, and crowned James I. He was present at the Hampton Court Conference in January 1604, and died at Lambeth on the 29th of the following February. He was buried in the church of Croydon, and his monument there with his recumbent effigy was in great part destroyed in the fire by which the church was burnt down in 1867.

Whitgift is described by his biographer, Sir G. Paule, as of "middle stature, strong and well shaped, of a grave countenance and brown complexion, black hair and eyes, his beard neither long nor thick." He was noted for his hospitality, and was somewhat ostentatious in his habits, sometimes visiting Canterbury and other towns attended by a retinue of 800 horsemen. He left several unpublished works, which are included among the MSS. *Angliæ*. Many of his letters, articles, injunctions, &c., are calendared in the published volumes of the State Paper series of the reign of Elizabeth. His *Collected Works*, edited for the Parker Society by Rev. John Ayre, 3 vols., Cambridge, 1851-53, include, besides the controversial tracts already alluded to, two sermons published during his lifetime, a selection from his letters to Cecil and others, and some portions of his unpublished MSS.

A *Life* of Whitgift by Sir G. Paule appeared in 1612, 2d ed. 1649. It has been embodied by Strype in his *Life and Acts of Whitgift*, 1718. There is also a life in Wordsworth's *Ecclesiastical Biography*, Hook's *Archbishops of Canterbury*, and vol. i. of Whitgift's *Collected Works*. See also Cooper's *Athenæ Cantabrigienses*.

WHITING, a marine fish (*Gadus merlangus*), abundant on the shores of the German Ocean and all round the coasts of the British Islands. It is distinguished from the other species of the genus *Gadus* or Cod-fish by having from thirty-three to thirty-five rays in the first anal fin, and by lacking the barbel on the chin (which is so well developed in the common cod-fish, whiting-pout, &c.) entirely, or possessing only a minute rudiment of it. The snout is long, and the upper jaw longer than the lower. A black spot at the root of the pectoral fin is also very characteristic of this species, and but rarely absent. The whiting is one of the most valuable food fishes of northern Europe, and is caught throughout the year by hook and line and by the trawl. It is in better condition at the beginning of winter than after the spawning season, which falls in the months of February and March. Its usual size is from 1 to 1½ pound, but it may attain to twice that weight. In the south of Europe it is replaced by an allied species, *Gadus euxini*, which, however, seems to be limited to the cold waters of the Adriatic and Black Seas.

WHITLOW is a name applied loosely to any inflammation involving the pulp of the finger, attended by swelling and throbbing pain. In the simplest form, apt to occur in sickly children, the inflammation results in a whitish vesicle of the skin, containing watery or bloody fluid. In all such cases, where the deeper structures are not implicated, no radical local treatment is needed, although the illness is an indication for constitutional treatment. The affection is not usually spoken of as whitlow unless it involves the deeper structures of the last joint of the finger. These are in a peculiarly close relation to the surface; hence the liability to deep-seated formations of matter, from some slight scratch or prick (poisoned or otherwise) of the skin over the pulp of the finger, or even when there is no obvious external provocation. The intimate connexion of the surface with the deep structures is near the finger-tip; in that region there are certain regular bundles of strong fibres passing from the under layers of the skin, through the fat of the finger pulp, down to the free end of the bone, which is roughened and expanded in a very peculiar manner for their insertion. These fibres, which are proper to adults, serve to convey an inflammatory infection from the skin down to the bone, or to the periosteum or covering of the bone, and to the tendon (of the deep flexor muscle of the finger) inserted into that part of the last joint of the finger next to the hand. The peculiar danger of a whitlow is that, if it be not opened in time by a deep cut down to the bone along the middle line of the phalanx, the inflammation will attack the covering of the bone, and so produce mortification or necrosis of the latter, and then attack the insertion of the tendon, causing sloughing of it also. In this way a whitlow, which has been neglected or treated by temporizing and ineffective methods, often leads to a loss of the bony tip of the last finger-joint, or even of the whole of the joint, and to a proportionate shortening and deformity of the finger. In another class of cases, which are fortunately less common, the deep-seated inflammation travels along the various structures of the finger towards the palm of the hand. The inflammation extends inside the dense fibrous tunnel or sheath which contains and binds down both tendons upon the middle and proximal joints of the finger. In that confined space the inflammation becomes peculiarly virulent: the tension of the part gives the pain a bursting character; the redness and swelling extend all round the fingers and to the back of the hand and wrist; and the result of all this suppuration and sloughing may be rigidity and contraction of the fingers and hand. Whenever matter burrows in this way, the treatment must be by free incisions. In all cases of whitlow the general disturbance of health is excessive.

The general treatment of all whitlow inflammations consists at the outset in relief of a congested state of the system, where such exists, by a purge and by a restricted diet, in applying poultices or hot compresses to the affected finger, and in carrying the arm in a sling. The presence of matter will not be obvious by the ordinary signs of a gathering; attempts to let out the matter by anything short of a free and deep incision are likely to fail and to cause the loss of more or less of the bone.

Whitlows have sometimes been observed to occur among a number of persons together, in a sort of epidemic, especially where the individuals are all subject to the same conditions of living, as among troops in garrison. These epidemics usually occur at a season (probably the spring) when erysipelas, carbuncles, and boils are prevalent.

WHITSTABLE, a watering-place and seaport of Kent, England, is situated on the south side of the Thames estuary and on the South Eastern and the London, Chatham, and Dover Railway lines, 6 miles north-north-west of Canterbury and 62 south-south-east of London. It consists chiefly of one main street, about a mile in length, and two narrower streets parallel with it, built on an embankment. The church of All Saints, in the Decorated and Perpendicular styles, possesses some old brasses; it was restored in 1875. The other principal buildings are the institute for literature, science, and art (in connexion with which there are a library, museum, and aquarium), the assembly rooms, the foresters' hall, and the Wynn Ellis almshouses. The "Street," a low narrow ledge of shingle running for three quarters of a mile towards the sea, forms a natural pier and promenade. Whitstable has been famous for its oyster beds from time immemorial. The oysters raised there greatly excel all others in delicacy of flavour, and to economize space spat from other beds is brought to Whitstable to mature. The lands are held by a company of dredgers incorporated by Act of Parliament in 1793, the affairs being administered by a foreman, deputy foreman, and jury of twelve men. The less extensive Seasalter and Ham oyster fishery adjoins. Of late years the productiveness of the beds has been declining, owing, it is said, to the emptying of refuse and rubbish into the Thames. There is a considerable coasting trade in coal in conjunction with the South Eastern Railway Company, who are the owners of the harbour. The population of the township and parish (3601 acres) in 1871 was 4881 and 4882 in 1881. A portion of Seasalter is included in Whitstable.

Whitstable and Seasalter embrace what was formerly known as the "borough of Harwich," but its boundaries are not now recognizable. Some Roman remains have been discovered. At Domesday the manor of Whitstable was held by Odo, bishop of Bayeux. Subsequently it came by female descent to the earls of Athole, and afterwards was several times in the hands of the crown, before it came to St John, Viscount Bolingbroke. In modern times it was held by Wynn Ellis, who left a valuable collection of paintings to the nation.

WHITSUNDAY, or PENTECOST (πεντηκοστή), the fiftieth day after Easter Sunday, one of the principal feasts of the Christian Church, is enumerated among these along with Easter Sunday, Good Friday, and the Sundays throughout the year by Origen (*Cont. Cels.*, viii. 392), and is thus enjoined in the *Apostolical Constitutions* (v. 20): "After ten days from the Ascension, which from the first Lord's Day is the fiftieth day, do ye keep a great festival on the day the Lord Jesus sent on us the gift of the Holy Ghost." The origin of the Anglo-Saxon name of White Sunday, which also occurs in Icelandic, is somewhat obscure, for in the Roman Church the Dominica in Albis (Low Sunday), so called from the white robes then worn by candidates for baptism, has always been the Sunday immediately following Easter. A very probable suggestion is that in northern countries the colder climate made it desirable to postpone the great baptismal festival to a time when the spring season was further advanced.

WHITTINGTON, a town of Derbyshire, England, is situated on the Chesterfield Canal and on the Midland Railway, 9½ miles south-east of Sheffield and 153 north-north-west of London. The church of St Bartholomew, in the Early English style, was erected in 1863 near the site of an older one; it contains the old font and also a mural monument to the antiquary, Dr Pegge (died 1796). The principal works are large iron factories. The manufacture of stone bottles and coarse earthenware is also carried on. Whittington was placed under the government of a local board in 1873. The population of the urban sanitary district (area 1581 acres) was 5578 in 1871 and 7271 in 1881.

WHITTINGTON, SIR RICHARD (died 1423), was the son of Sir William de Whittington of Pauntley, Gloucestershire, who died an outlaw in 1360. His mother was Joan, daughter of William Mansell, who was high-sheriff of Gloucestershire in 1308. Richard Whittington makes his first appearance in 1379, when he contributed five marks to a city loan. In 1392 he was elected alderman and sheriff of London, being at that time a member of the

Mercers' Company. He was appointed or elected mayor in 1397, 1398, 1406, and 1419; and in 1416 he was chosen member of parliament for London. In April 1402 he supplied cloth of gold for the marriage of the king's daughter Blanche with Louis, son of the emperor Rupert, and four years later (July 1406) for that of Philippa and Erik VII. of Denmark. In March 1413 the king repaid him a loan of £1000, and in September 1415 he was granted a lien on the customs of Boston, Kingston-on-Hull, and London, in discharge of 700 marks lent to Henry V. (by whom he seems to have been knighted). He died in March 1423. Among his chief benefactions by will were the rebuilding of St Michael's church, in connexion with which he founded a college, and of Newgate. He is said to have also restored St Bartholomew's hospital, London.

All that is known about Whittington has been carefully collected in the Rev. Samuel Lysons's *Model Merchant of the Middle Ages* (London, 1860), from which the above account is taken. Lysons argues very strongly in favour of the famous story of "Whittington and his Cat," and rejects the rationalization which explains the legend by supposing Whittington's fortunes to have been made in the voyages of a mediæval *cat* or merchant-vessel. He is, however, only able to trace back the actual quadruped to a picture which is inscribed "R Whittington 1536." Even this picture he had never seen; and he has to admit that it bore marks of having been altered from its original size, and that the inscription is later than the alteration. The story, however, was evidently current by the end of the 16th century. Moreover, it is said that the figure of a cat was represented at the feet of the statue of Liberty on the gate of Newgate previous to the great fire of 1666; or, according to another account, Whittington's own "statue with the cat remained in a niche to its final demolition on the rebuilding of the present prison." In repairing a house which once belonged to the Whittington family at Gloucester in 1862, a stone of 15th-century workmanship was discovered and on it appeared in bas-relief the figure of a boy nursing a cat in his arms. All this, however, cannot be said to go very far towards proving the veracity of the old legend. Clouston (*Popular Tales and Fictions*, London, 1887, ii. 65-78) traces the main features of the story in the folk-lore of Denmark, Russia, Norway, Brittany, and even Persia. It was current in Italy during the 15th century; but its earliest appearance seems to be in Abdullah's *History of Persia*, written towards the close of the 13th century. This writer ascribes the occurrences he tells of to the first half of the 11th century. Even this, in Clouston's opinion, is not the original form of the story, which from one or two of its details he suspects to be of Buddhist origin.

WHITWORTH, a manufacturing village of Lancashire, England, is situated on the river Spodden and on the Rochdale and Bacup branch of the Lancashire and Yorkshire Railway, 3 miles north of Rochdale. It possesses the usual characteristics of the cotton-manufacturing districts. Coal-mining is also carried on in the neighbourhood. The church of St Bartholomew is in the Early English style. The manor of Whitworth was granted to the abbey of Stanilaw in the reign of John. A local board of twelve members was formed in 1874. The urban sanitary district, which includes the villages of Hallfold, Facit, and Leavingreave, had an area of 8000 acres, with a population of 11,892, in 1881.

WHOOPING-COUGH. See HOOPING-COUGH.

WHORTLEBERRY, a vernacular name corrupted from the Latin *myrtillus*, under which appellation, according to Prior, the berries of the common myrtle were employed in the Middle Ages for culinary purposes. In more modern times the term has been applied to various species of *Vaccinium*, particularly to *V. Myrtillus*, also known as the bilberry. The berries of this plant have a considerable similarity to those of the myrtle. Several species of *Vaccinium* occur on moorlands throughout the northern hemisphere. They are low shrubs allied to heaths, usually with evergreen leaves and with small bell-shaped or urn-shaped flowers, which have an inferior ovary surmounted by five calyx lobes. The stamens, though in a single row, are double the number of the corolla lobes. The anthers have usually two horns at the back and are generally prolonged at the top into two longish tubes, each with a hole at the extremity, through which the pollen escapes. The fruit is a globular or ovoid, many-seeded berry. *V. Myrtillus* and *V. uliginosum* have blue berries; *V. Vitis idæa*, the cowberry, has red fruits. A hybrid between *V. Myrtillus* and *V. Vitis idæa*, called *V. intermedium*, occurs in Shropshire and Staffordshire. The cranberry (*Oxycoccus*) is very closely allied to the whortleberry.

WHYDAH. See DAHOMEY, vol. vi. p. 765.

WICHITA, a city of the United States, the county seat of Sedgwick county, Kansas, is situated on the east bank of the Arkansas river, in the midst of an extremely fertile region. It is entered by six lines of railway, thus being one of the most important railway centres of the State. Its growth has been remarkable, even in this region of rapid development. In 1870 its site was without inhabitants; in 1880 it contained 4911 persons, while in 1886 it had a population of 20,129, making it the fourth city of the State.

WICK, a royal and parliamentary burgh and seaport of Scotland, the county town of Caithness, is situated on the German Ocean at the head of Wick Bay and at the eastern terminus of the Sutherland and Caithness section of the Highland Railway, 374 miles north of Edinburgh by rail and 18½ south of John O'Groat's House. It consists of the old burgh of Wick on the north bank of the river, Louisburgh, a northern continuation of Wick, and Pultneytown, the chief seat of commerce and trade, on the south side of the river. Pultneytown, laid out in 1805 by the British Fishery Society, is built on a regular plan; and Wick proper consists chiefly of the narrow and irregular High Street, off which is the temperance hall, with Bridge Street, somewhat more regularly built, and containing the town-hall and the county buildings. In Pultneytown there are an academy, a chamber of commerce, a naval reserve station, and a fish exchange. The port consists of two harbours of fair size; but the entrance is dangerous in stormy weather. Several expensive schemes for constructing a breakwater have resulted in disastrous failure. In 1886 the number of vessels that entered the port was 1128 of 109,142 tons, the number that cleared 1094 of 103,162 tons. The average value of the exports for the five years ending 1887 was about £150,000; but in 1886 it was only £89,641. The chief exports are fish, cattle, and agricultural produce, and the imports include coal, wood, and provisions. Steamers from Granton and Aberdeen to Thurso, the Orkneys, and the Shetlands call at Wick going and returning. It is, however, chiefly to its fisheries that the town owes its prosperity. For many years it was the chief seat of the herring-fishing on the east coast of Scotland; but its insufficient harbour accommodation has greatly hampered its progress, and both Peterhead and Fraserburgh more than rival it as fishing ports. The number of boats belonging to the port in 1885 was 807; the value of the herrings cured was £117,754 and of cod, ling, and skate, £61,928. Shipbuilding, formerly prosecuted, has now been discontinued; but boat-building and net-making are extensively carried on. There are also cooperages, flour-mills, steam saw-mills, a rope and a woollen manufactory, and a distillery. Wick forms one of a group of parliamentary burghs called the Wick burghs. The population of the parliamentary burgh, which includes the royal burgh of Wick, Pultneytown, and Louisburgh, was 8145 in 1871 and 8053 in 1881. In the last year the population of the royal burgh was only 1420. In 1883 the royal burgh was extended by the inclusion of Louisburgh. The population of this extended area in 1881 was 2954.

Wick (Vik or "bay") is mentioned as early as 1140. It was constituted a royal burgh by James VI. in 1589, its superior being then George, earl of Caithness. By a parliamentary bounty in 1768 some impetus was given to the herring-fishery, but its real importance dates from the construction of a harbour in 1808. It has sent one member to parliament since 1832.

WICKLIFFE. See WYCLIFFE.

WICKLOW, a maritime county of Ireland, in the province of Leinster, is bounded on the E. by St George's Channel, N. by the county of Dublin, S. by Wexford, and W. by Carlow and detached portions of Kildare. The area is 500,178 acres or about 781 square miles.

Physical Features.—The coast is precipitous and picturesque, but very dangerous of approach owing to sandbanks. There are no inlets that can be properly termed bays. The harbour at Wicklow has lately been improved; but that of Arklow is suitable only for small vessels. To the north of the town of Wicklow there is a remarkable shingle beach, partly piled up by the waves and currents. The central portion of the county is occupied by a granite mountain range, forming one of the four principal mountain groups of Ireland. The direction of the range is from north-east to south-west, and the highest elevations are generally attained along the central line. The range consists of long sweeping moorlands, rising occasionally by precipitous escarpments into culminating points, the highest summits being Kippure (2473 feet), Duff Hill (2369), Douce Hill (2384), and Lugnaquilla (3039). The range rises from the north by a succession of ridges intersected by deep glens, and subsides towards the borders of Wexford and Carlow. Though the range is metamorphic, it is also in part intrusive, and its formation has been accompanied by a considerable elevation of Silurian rocks, beyond which it does not penetrate, notwithstanding that the Cambrian rocks occupy a large tract along the sea coast. In the valleys there are many instances of old river terraces, the more remarkable being those at the lower end of Glenmalure and the lower end of Glendalough. It is in its deep glens that much of the peculiar charm of Wicklow scenery is to be found, the frequently rugged natural features contrasting finely with the rich and luxuriant foliage of the extensive woods which line their banks. Among the more famous of these glens are the Dargle, Glencree, Glen of the Downs, Devil's Glen, Glenmalure, Glen of Ismail, and the beautiful vale of Ovoca. The eastern districts of the county are occupied by clay slate or quartzite, the latter of which presents frequently a smooth polished surface and shows indications of Glacial erosion. Evidences of Glacial action also appear in the moraines of Glenmalure and Glendalough. The principal rivers are the Liffey, on the north-western border; the Vartry, which passes through Devil's Glen to the sea north of Wicklow Head; the Avonmore and the Avonbeg, which unite at the "meeting of the waters" to form the Ovoca, which is afterwards joined by the Aughrim and falls into the sea at Arklow; and the Slaney, in the west of the county, passing southwards into Carlow. There are a number of small but romantic lakes in the valleys, the principal being Loughs Dan, Bray, and Tay or Luggelaw, and the loughs of Glendalough.

Minerals.—Lead is raised at Lugganure (near Rathdrum), the principal lead mine in Ireland. In 1796 gold was discovered near Croghan Kinshela, but not in quantities to render working remunerative. Auriferous silver occurs in the slaty strata. There are important copper mines at Ovoca, where sulphur and iron are also dug. Slates for roofing are quarried at Dunganstown and elsewhere. Limestone, limestone gravel, and marl are obtained near the sea and in the river valleys.

Agriculture.—According to the latest landowners' return, Wicklow was divided among 1041 proprietors, possessing 497,656 acres, at an annual valuation of £254,800, or about 10s. 2¾d. per acre. There were also about 2500 acres of waste land. Of the proprietors 534, or rather more than a half, possessed less than 1 acre each. The following possessed over 8000 acres each:—William Kemmis, 8042; J. S. Moore, 8731; R. A. G. Cunninghame, 10,479; earl of Meath, 14,718; marquis of Downshire, 15,766; earl of Carysfort, 16,292; J. Mandeville Hugo, 17,937; earl of Wicklow, 22,104; marquis of Waterford, 26,035; Viscount Powerscourt, 36,693; and earl Fitzwilliam, 89,891. The climate near the sea is remarkably mild, and permits the myrtle and arbutus to grow. The land in the lower grounds is fertile; and, although the greater part of the higher districts is covered with heath and turf, it affords good pasturage for sheep. There is a considerable extent of natural timber, as well as artificial plantations. Out of a total area of 499,894 acres in 1886 105,642 or 21·1 per cent. were under crops, 234,890 or 47 per cent. under grass, 175 acres fallow, 19,479 or 3·9 per cent. woods and plantations, 29,028 or 5·8 per cent. bog and marsh, 94,347 or 18·9 per cent. barren mountain land, and 16,333 or 3·3 per cent. water, roads, fences, &c. The total number of holdings in 1886 was only 8072 and their size is much above the average for Ireland, 70 being above 500 acres in extent, 973 between 100 and 500 acres, 2615 between 30 and 100 acres, 2646 between 5 and 30 acres, 855 between 1 and 5 acres, and 913 not exceeding 1 acre each. Between 1849 and 1886 the area under crops decreased from 126,251 to 105,642 acres; but within the last ten years the decrease was not so marked, the area in 1876 being 111,488 acres. The area under meadow and clover has been gradually increasing: in 1849 it was 50,793 acres, and, while in 1876 it was 60,086 acres, in 1886 it was 60,390. The area under green crops shows very slight fluctuations: in 1849 it was 18,837 and in 1886 it was 18,114. Potatoes and turnips, which occupied respectively 10,847 and 5304 acres in 1886, have not perceptibly altered in the proportions of the areas. The decrease in the area under corn crops has, on the other hand, been remarkable; from 56,616 acres in 1849 it fell to 31,361 in 1876 and to 27,129 in 1886. The area under wheat in 1849 was 7817 acres, but between 1876 and 1886 it decreased from 3639 to 814 acres. The area under oats has decreased from 44,527 acres in 1849 to 26,920 in 1876 and 25,344 in 1886; the area under barley, bere, and other corn crops being in these years 4272, 1480, and 971 acres respectively. The number of horses in 1886 was 11,300 (of which 7206 were used for agricultural purposes), asses 3465, mules 351, cattle 81,577 (of which 24,523 were milch cows), sheep 169,334, pigs 22,329, and goats 6278.

Communication.—The Dublin, Wicklow, and Wexford Railway skirts the coast from Bray to the town of Wicklow, after which it bends westward to Rathdrum, and then passes by the vale of Ovoca to Arklow. At Wooden Bridge a branch goes off south-westwards to Shillelagh.

Manufactures and Trade.—Except in the Ovoca district, where the mining industry is of some importance, the occupations are chiefly agricultural. The manufacture of flannel, which formerly gave employment to a considerable number of people, is now in a very depressed condition. Herring and round fish are caught off the coast, but these fisheries are much neglected. There is, however, a rather prosperous oyster fishery at Arklow. Of late years the harbour at Wicklow has been improved, the bed of the river deepened, and a steam-packet pier erected.

Administration and Population.—According to De Burgo's estimate, the population of Wicklow in 1760 amounted to 43,872; the parliamentary census of 1812 placed it at 83,109; by 1821 it had increased to 110,767, and by 1841 to 126,143, but by 1861 it had diminished to 86,451, by 1871 to 78,697, and by 1881 to 70,386 (males 35,101, females 35,285). Roman Catholics in 1881 numbered 79·9 per cent. of the population, Protestant Episcopalians 18·3 (an unusually large proportion for the south of Ireland), Presbyterians 0·4, Methodists 1·0, and other denominations 0·4. The number of persons who could read and write numbered 57·4 of the population, able to read only 12·8 per cent., illiterate 29·8. There were none who could speak Irish only, and the number who could speak Irish and English was 243. Wicklow, which formerly returned two members to parliament, was in 1885 formed into two parliamentary divisions, an eastern and a western, each returning one member. The principal towns are part of Bray (4387), a fashionable watering-place, the other part (2148) being in Dublin; Wicklow (3391), the county town; and Arklow (4777), a fishing-station of some importance. The county is divided into eight baronies and contains fifty-nine parishes. According to the Protestant Episcopal arrangements, it is in the dioceses of Dublin and Glendalough, with portions in those of Leighlin and Ferns. It is in the home or Leinster circuit; and assizes are held at Wicklow and quarter-sessions at Bray, Baltinglass, Tinahely, Arklow, and Wicklow. There are ten petty sessions districts within the county, and portions of four others. It includes two poor-law unions and portions of the unions of Naas, Rathdown, and Shillelagh. It is in the Dublin military district.

History and Antiquities.—On the division of the district of the Pale by King John into twelve counties Wicklow was included in Dublin county. It was made a separate county by James I. in 1605. It sided with the royal cause during the Cromwellian wars, but on Cromwell's advance submitted to him without striking a blow. During the rebellion of 1798 some of the insurgents took refuge within its mountain fastnesses. An engagement took place between them and General Holt near Aughrim, which was speedily decided in Holt's favour ; a second was fought at Arklow between them and General Needham with a similar result. Of the ancient cromlechs there are three of some interest, one near Enniskerry, another on the summit of Lugnaquilla, and a third, with a druidical circle, at Donoughmore. There are comparatively unimportant monastic remains at Rathdrum, Baltinglass, and Wicklow. The ruins in the vale of Glendalough, known as the "seven churches," are, with the doubtful exception of Clonmacnoise, the most remarkable ecclesiastical remains in Ireland. They owe their origin to St Kevin, who lived in the vale as a hermit, and is reputed to have died on 3d June 618. On the site of St Kevin's cell an extensive monastic establishment was founded, and around it a town sprang up, which was long famed as a seat of learning. The buildings which constitute the "seven churches" are the round tower, one of the finest in Ireland, 110 feet in height and 51 in circumference ; St Kevin's kitchen or church, of which the nave, 25 feet by 15, with a curious high-pitched roof and a round belfry (supposed to be the earliest example of a round belfry springing from the roof or gable), still remains ; a structure within the cemetery called the cathedral, in a state of great dilapidation, but from its position and dimensions seemingly well entitled to its name ; the lady chapel, chiefly remarkable for its doorway of wrought granite, in a style of architecture allied to the Greek ; Trinity church, consisting of nave (29 feet 6 inches by 17 feet 6 inches), chancel (13 feet 6 inches by 9 feet), and a basement story, and presenting some of the finest characteristics of the ancient architecture of Ireland, including a very beautiful specimen of the square-headed doorway ; the monastery, or St Saviour's abbey, with peculiar ornamental sculpture, and supposed to contain the tomb of St Kevin ; and the Refeart or cemetery church. In the cemetery and all along the valley there are a large number of monuments and stone crosses of various size and style. The cave known as St Kevin's bed shows evidence of having been artificially constructed, but is probably only an enlarged natural cavity. Of the old fortalices or strongholds associated with the early wars those of special interest are Black Castle, near Wicklow, originally founded by the Norse invaders, but taken by the Irish in 1301, and afterwards rebuilt by William FitzWilliam ; the scattered remains of Castle Kevin, the ancient stronghold of the O'Tooles, by whom it was probably originally built in the 12th century ; and the ruins of the old castle of the Ormondes at Arklow, founded by Theobald FitzWalter (died 1285), the scene of frequent conflicts up to the time of Cromwell, by whom it was demolished in 1649, and now containing within the interior of its ruined walls a constabulary barrack. The fine mansion of Powerscourt occupies the site of an old fortalice founded by De la Poer, one of the knights who landed with Strongbow ; in the reign of Henry VIII. it was taken by the O'Tooles and O'Brynes. (T. F. H.)

WIDDIN, or WIDIN, a fortified town of Bulgaria, within 20 miles of the Servian frontier and about 130 miles south-east of Belgrade, in 44° N. lat. and 22° 50′ E. long. It occupies a strong position on the right bank of the Danube over against the Roumanian town of Kalafat, with which it is connected by a bridge of boats over a mile long. Owing to its low situation, the soil is marshy and the city is liable to inundation (six floods having occurred since 1839). Its population in 1888 amounted to 13,435, including 6929 Bulgarians, 3387 Turks, and 1304 Jews. The citadel, always a formidable stronghold, has recently been strengthened and enlarged with a double line of ramparts reaching to the water's edge, while on the land side the approaches are naturally protected by the extensive marshy tracts formed here by a sharp bend of the Danube from the east to the south. The old town within these lines was formerly inhabited exclusively by Mohammedans, and still presents an Oriental aspect, with its mosques, minarets, and over 1700 stalls lining the bazaar or main thoroughfare of Plevna Ulica. There are a few local industries, such as the making of gold and silver filigree work, saddlery, beer, flour, and cutlery, besides a brisk riverine trade, mainly in the hands of the Jews and Bulgarians. The fisheries in the Danube are of some importance (£20,000 annually).

Widdin stands on the site of the Roman town of *Bononia* in Mœsia Superior, not to be confounded with the Pannonian Bononia, which stood higher up the Danube to the north of Sirmium. Its name figures conspicuously in the military annals of mediæval and recent times ; and it is specially memorable for the overthrow of the Turks by the imperial forces in 1689 and for the crushing defeat of the hospodar Michael Sustos by Pasvan Oglu in 1801. It was again the scene of stirring events during the Russo-Turkish wars of 1854-55 and 1877-78, and successfully resisted the assaults of the Servians in the Servo-Bulgarian War of 1886-87.

WIDNES, a manufacturing town of Lancashire, England, is situated on the Mersey, where it is joined by the Sankey Brook Navigation, and on the London and North-Western Railway, 13 miles south-east of Liverpool and 188 from London. Capacious private docks were constructed in 1866 and extended in 1884. The Mersey is crossed by a wrought-iron bridge, 1000 feet long and 95 in height, completed in 1868, and having two lines of railway and a footpath. The church of St Mary was erected in 1856, that of St Ambrose in 1880, and that of St Paul in 1884. Widnes is one of the principal seats of the alkali and soap manufacture, and has also grease-works for locomotives and waggons, copper-works, iron-foundries, oil and paint works, and sail-cloth manufactories. It is governed by a local board of fifteen members. Until comparatively recent years it was a small township, dependent chiefly on agriculture. In 1851 the population was under 2000, but by 1861 the numbers had more than trebled. In 1871 the population of the urban sanitary district (area 3339 acres) was 14,359, and 24,935 in 1881 ; in 1888 it was estimated to exceed 30,000.

The barony of Widnes came from the Lacy family to the dukes of Lancaster and thence to the crown. In 1554-55 it was declared to be part of the duchy of Lancaster.

WIELAND, CHRISTOPHER MARTIN (1733-1813), German man of letters, was born on the 5th September 1733 at Oberholzheim, a Swabian village near Biberach, then an imperial city. He was carefully educated by his father, who was a clergyman at Oberholzheim ; and at a very early age he gave evidence of a strong literary impulse. In his fourteenth year he was sent to the school of Klosterbergen, near Magdeburg, where he attracted a good deal of attention, not only by his knowledge of the classics and of French and English literature, but by his power of lucid and graceful expression. When he was about sixteen he left school and went to live with a relative at Erfurt, who undertook to prepare him for the university by reading with him the writings of the philosopher Wolff. Having spent a year and a half with this relative, he went for some time to Biberach, whither his father had been transferred from Oberholzheim. At Biberach he met a young kinswoman, Sophie Gutermann, with whom he fell in love, and who exercised a powerful influence upon the development of his intellect and imagination. While talking with her, after they had heard his father preach a sermon on the text "God is Love," he conceived the scheme of his first poem, *Die Natur der Dinge*. In 1750 he went to the university of Tübingen, nominally for the purpose of studying law; but in reality he devoted his attention wholly to literature. At Tübingen he wrote his poem on the *Nature of Things*, and in 1752 it was published anonymously. Here also he wrote *Anti-Ovid*, *Lobgesang auf den Frühling*, *Moralische Briefe*, and *Moralische Erzählungen*. At home Wieland had been strictly brought up, and his home training had been confirmed at the Klosterbergen school, the head-master of which was a member of the straitest sect of the Pietists. In his early writings, therefore, Wieland appears as a youth of a deeply serious disposition, with an ardent enthusiasm for what he conceives to be the highest ideas of theology and ethics.

Bodmer, the Swiss critic and poet, strongly attracted by this new literary force, cordially invited Wieland to visit him at Zurich. Wieland accepted the invitation, and lived for many months in Bodmer's house. In 1754 the two friends parted; for, although they had apparently the same aims and motives, they were in reality very unlike one another, and Bodmer was apt to play rather too ostentatiously the part of a guide and patron. Wieland continued to reside in Switzerland, remaining in Zurich about five years and in Bern about a year, and supporting himself by working as a tutor. During the early part of his residence in Switzerland Wieland maintained the serious tone that had marked his first writings. In his *Briefe von Verstorbenen an hinterlassene Freunde*, *Sympathien*, *Empfindungen eines Christen*, and other works of this period he sought to give expression to the loftiest spiritual aspirations; and in the letter in which he dedicated the *Empfindungen* to the court preacher Sack, in Berlin, he went out of his way to rebuke the frivolity of certain Anacreontic poets, whom he denounced as "a band of epicurean pagans." But Wieland's mystical and ascetic doctrines did not at all correspond to his real impulses, and soon after he left Bodmer's house he began to feel that he had misunderstood his own character. His piety became less enthusiastic, and he learned to have a keen appreciation of pleasures which he had formerly condemned as incompatible with any high or worthy conception of the ends of human life. This change led to a kind of literary activity wholly different from that by which he had made his reputation. He wrote two dramas, *Johanna Grey* (in which he made free use of Rowe's play *Lady Jane Grey*) and *Clementina von Poretta*; and he chose as the subject of an epic poem the career of Cyrus, who was to be presented as a hero closely resembling Frederick the Great. *Cyrus* he never finished; but he completed *Araspes und Panthea*, a poem in which he developed an episode from the *Cyropædia* of Xenophon.

In 1760 he settled at Biberach as director of the chancery. The appointment was a poor one, and for a time Wieland found life at Biberach extremely dull and tiresome. By and by, however, he made the acquaintance of Count Stadion, an experienced man of the world, at whose house Wieland became a constant visitor; there he met, among many other persons whose society he liked, his first love, Sophie, who had married Von Laroche, the count's confidential friend and "factotum." Under these new influences the change of tone which had been begun in Switzerland was soon completed; and in *Don Sylvio von Rosalva* (1764), a romance, intended to be taken as an imitation of *Don Quixote*, he gave himself the pleasure of laughing at principles and sentiments which he had formerly held to be sacred. This work was followed by *Komische Erzählungen* (1766), the cynical grossness of which far surpassed that of any contemporary German writer. Wieland himself seems to have felt that in these tales he had gone too far, for, although in his next work, *Agathon* (1766-67), the hero of which is a disciple of Plato, he sometimes treads on slippery ground, his ultimate aim is to show that the true rule of life is to hold the balance even between the spiritual and the physical impulses of man. His unfinished *Idris und Zenide* (1768) has a less worthy motive; but in the didactic poem *Musarion* (1768) he returned to the idea of *Agathon*, that fanaticism and sensuality are equally opposed to enduring happiness, and that he is most to be envied who knows how to gratify all legitimate impulses without allowing any of them to become unduly powerful. To Wieland, when his mind and character were fully developed, this law of conduct seemed to be the highest to which man can attain, and he was never tired of indirectly expounding it in his later writings. At Biberach he devoted much time to the study of Shakespeare, and in 1762-66 he published, in eight volumes, translations of twenty-two of Shakespeare's plays.

In 1765 Wieland had married a lady of Augsburg, to whom he was warmly attached. Four years afterwards he was made professor of philosophy at Erfurt, where he remained until 1772. During his stay at Erfurt he wrote *Dialogen des Diogenes von Sinope*; *Beiträge zur geheimen Geschichte des menschlichen Verstandes und Herzens, aus den Archiven der Natur*; *Der goldene Spiegel*; *Die Grazien*, a didactic poem; *Combabus*, a disagreeable tale in verse; and *Der neue Amadis*, a comic poem in eighteen cantos.

In 1772 Wieland settled for life at Weimar, his position at first being that of a tutor to the two sons of the duchess Anna Amalia. Here he founded the monthly periodical, *Der Deutsche Mercur*, which he edited until 1796. For this periodical he wrote constantly, and, considering the immense number of his productions, it is surprising that he was able to maintain, on the whole, so high a level of excellence. By far the best of his works is the poem *Oberon*, the only work by him which has still a wide circle of readers in Germany. It was published in 1780. Among other original writings produced in Weimar may be named a comic romance, *Die Geschichte der Abderiten* (1774), *Der verklagte Amor* (1774), *Das Wintermärchen* (1776), and *Das Sommermärchen* (1777). In 1782 and 1786 appeared translations of the *Epistles* and *Satires* of Horace; and in 1788 and 1789 he issued a translation of Lucian, his study of whom led to his writing *Neue Göttergespräche* (1791), *Geheime Geschichte des Philosophen Peregrinus Proteus* (1791), and *Agathodämon* (1799). From 1793 to 1802 he was engaged in issuing a revised edition of his writings; but in 1796 he found time to establish a new periodical, *Das Attische Museum*, in which he printed, among other things, translations of some of the comedies of Aristophanes. In 1797 Wieland bought Osmannstädt, an estate near Weimar; and there he lived for some years with his large family. At Osmannstädt he wrote his last important romance, *Aristipp und einige seiner Zeitgenossen* (1800-2). In 1801 his wife died, and two years afterwards he sold his estate and returned to Weimar, where he spent his last years in translating and annotating the *Letters* of Cicero. He died on 20th January 1813.

Wieland was a man of many moods, and his friends, when talking with him, could never be quite sure that they would not unintentionally offend him. But, although vain and over-sensitive, he often gave evidence of an essentially humane and generous spirit. As a writer he lacked force of imagination and depth of feeling; and even at his best he had too narrow a range of vision to be a great moral teacher. Nevertheless, he has an important place in the history of German literature. He was the founder in Germany of the psychological romance, and few of his successors in this kind have surpassed his delicate and subtle analyses of complicated motives. Both in prose and in verse he was a master of the art of composition, and most of the younger writers of his day learned something from the clearness, ease, and grace of his style. To him belongs the merit of having first suggested to his countrymen that it might be worth their while to study their native literature as well as that of France, England, and Italy.

Wieland's *Collected Works*, edited by Gruber, were issued in 53 vols. in 1818-1828 and in 36 vols. in 1851-56. There are biographies of him by Gruber (1827-28), Loebell (1858), and Ofterdingen (1877). Much light is thrown on his character by his letters; see *Ausgewählte Briefe* (1815-16) and *Briefe an Sophie Laroche* (1820). (J. SI.)

WIENER NEUSTADT. See NEUSTADT.

WIESBADEN, capital of the former duchy of Nassau and now the chief town of a district in the province of Hesse-Nassau in Prussia, disputes with Baden-Baden the title to be considered the most frequented and most fashionable watering-place in Germany. It is situated in a small and fertile valley on the south-west slopes of Mount Taunus, 5 miles to the north of Mainz and 3 miles from the Rhine (see the subjoined plan). The town is neat and well-built, with broad and regular streets. Its prosperity is entirely owing to its hot springs; and the general character and appearance of the place, with its numerous hotels, lodging-houses, villas, bath-houses, promenades, and places of entertainment, are dictated by the requirements of the visitors, who number annually about 60,000. The principal buildings are the palace, built in 1837-42 and restored in 1882; the Cursaal, a large and handsomely fitted up establishment, built in 1810, and adjoined by a beautiful and shady park; the Protestant church, built of polished bricks in 1852-60, with five tall towers, in the Gothic style; the Roman Catholic church; the new synagogue in the Moorish style; the museum, with a picture gallery, a collection of antiquities, and a library of 70,000 volumes; the theatre; the Berg church; and the Russian chapel, erected on the Neroberg in 1855. Wiesbaden contains numerous scientific societies and educational institutions, including a well-known chemical laboratory. The thermal springs contain only ½ per cent. of salt, and very little carbonic acid; and a good deal of their efficacy is due to their high temperature, which varies from 156° to 142° Fahr. The water is generally cooled to 93° Fahr. for bathing. The principal spring is the Kochbrunnen (156° Fahr.), the water of which is drunk by sufferers from gout, chronic dyspepsia, obesity, &c. There are twenty-eight other springs used for bathing, and efficacious in cases of rheumatism, gout, scrofula, and nervous ailments. The town lies 320 feet above the sea-level. Its climate is mild and warm, so that even in winter it is frequented by from 5000 to 6000 visiters. The population in 1885 was 55,457; in 1816 it was 4608; in 1867, 30,085.

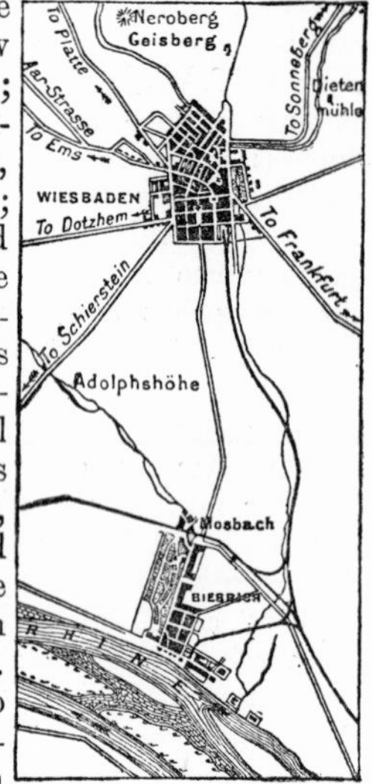

Environs of Wiesbaden.

Plan of Wiesbaden.

Wiesbaden is one of the oldest watering-places in Germany, and may be regarded as the capital of the Taunus spas. The springs, mentioned by Pliny as *Fontes Mattiaci*, were known to the Romans, who appear to have fortified the place. Under the Carolingian monarchs it was the site of a palace. Otho I. made it a town. The name Wisibada appears in 830. Though the springs never passed out of knowledge, they did not attain their greatest repute until the close of the 18th century. From 1771 till 1873 Wiesbaden was a notorious gambling resort; but in the latter year public gambling was suppressed by the Prussian Government.

See *Geschichte und historiche Topographie der Stadt Wiesbaden*, by F. W. C. Roth, and *Balneologische Studien über Wiesbaden*, ed. by Dr Pfeiffer, both published at Wiesbaden in 1883, and both containing copious bibliographical lists.

WIFE. See HUSBAND AND WIFE, and WOMEN.

WIG.[1] Artificial hair appears to have been worn from very ancient times, as is testified by well-made wigs recovered from Egyptian mummy figures. The full and flowing locks which adorn the sculptured reliefs of human figures found at Nineveh also suggest that wigs were not unknown among the ancient Assyrians. In the 16th century the fashion of wearing false hair became prevalent among ladies in Europe. At one period Elizabeth of England was possessed of no fewer than eighty attires of false hair. Mary of Scotland throughout her life was also in the habit of varying the attires of hair she wore; and much of the confusion which has arisen in connexion with her portraits is traceable to this circumstance.[2] The periwig of the 16th century was, however, merely false hair worn like, and sometimes with, the real hair, as an adornment or to supply the defects of nature. It was not till the 17th century that the peruke was worn as a distinctive feature of costume; as such it was first employed by Louis XIII. when his hair failed. His successor, Louis XIV., did not adopt it till 1673. In the meantime it had been freely donned by courtiers and gallants of the era. Charles I. of England, while in Paris on his way to Spain, "shadowed himself the most he could under a burly perruque, which none in former days but bald-headed people used." The wearing of the peruke became general in the days of Charles II. Pepys records that he parted with his own hair, and "paid £3 for a periwigg"; and on going to church in one he says, "it did not prove so strange as I was afraid it would." About this time the peruke is described as "a counterfeit hair which men wear instead of their own, a thing much used in our days by the generality of our men, contrary to their forefathers." The wig obtained its maximum development during the reign of Queen Anne, who was patroness of the full-bottomed wig,—a huge head-dress which covered the back and shoulders and floated down over the chest. In 1724 the peruke-makers advertised "full-bottom tyes, full bobs, minister's bobs, naturals, half naturals, Grecian flyes, curley roys, airey levants, qu perukes, and bagg wiggs" among the variety of artificial head-gear which they supplied. Early in the reign of George III. the general fashion of wearing wigs began to wane and gradually died out; but among professional men the practice continued to hold its place, and it was by slow degrees that military officers and clergymen gave up the habit. The wig of the 17th century now holds its place only on the judicial bench, and with the speaker of the English House of Commons, barristers, and advocates; but even on the bench its use is being threatened. Wigs of course continue to be worn by many to make up for natural deficiencies; and on the stage the wig is, as in all times, an indispensable adjunct. Many of the modern stage wigs are made of jute, a fibre which lends itself to marvellously perfect imitations of human hair.

WIGAN, a municipal and parliamentary borough and market-town of Lancashire, England, is situated on the river Douglas and on the main line of the London and North Western Railway, 18 miles west-north-west of Manchester, 18 north-east of Liverpool, and 195 north-west of London. The Douglas is spanned by several bridges, and is connected with the Leeds and Liverpool Canal. There is also a branch canal by Leigh and Worsley to Manchester. The older portions of the town occupy the north bank of the river, the modern additions being chiefly on the south bank. The church of All Saints, Late Perpendicular, con-

[1] Shortened from *periwig*, a lengthened form (through the Dutch) of *peruke*. This word is extant in all the Romance languages (Ital. *parrucca*, or, in Sardinian, *pilucca*; Span. *peluca*; Portug. *peruca*; Fr. *perruque*; Walloon *perik*) and is derived from *pelo* (*pilus*).

[2] Whilst a prisoner in Lochleven Castle she received "plusieurs perruques et aultres choses y servant"; and there was sent after her to Carlisle "ung paqué de perruques de cheveux." Her maid, Mary Seton, was a skilled busker, and, according to Sir F. Knollys, "she did set such a curled hair upon the queen that was said to be a perwyke, that shewed very delicately, and every other day she hath a new device of hair dressing." Even on the scaffold, according to an eye-witness, she wore "borrowed heire aburne," her own hair being "polled very short."

sisting of chancel with aisles and two chapels, was restored in 1630 and again in 1847 There are six other ecclesiastical parishes. The principal public buildings are the Royal Albert Edward Infirmary and Dispensary (1873, enlarged 1884), the public hall (1853), the borough courts and offices (1866), the arcade (1872), the market-hall (1877), the free public library (1878), the public baths (1882), and the county justices courts and offices (1888). The educational institutions include the free grammar school (founded by James Leigh in 1619 and rebuilt in 1876), the mining and mechanical school, and the mechanics' institution. The charities are numerous but of small individual importance, their aggregate annual value amounting to about £2500. A public park of 27 acres was opened in 1878. The town owes much of its prosperity to its coal mines, which afford employment to a large proportion of the inhabitants and supply fuel for the factory furnaces. Mills for making hats were established at Wigan in 1482; and subsequently bell-founding and pottery-making were of some importance. The chief industry is now the maufacture of cotton fabrics; the town also possesses iron forges, iron and brass foundries, oil and grease works, railway waggon factories, and bolt, screw, and nail works. The population of the municipal and parliamentary borough (area 2188 acres) was 20,774 in 1831; by 1861 it had increased to 37,658, by 1871 to 39,110, and by 1881 to 48,194 (23,508 males and 24,686 females); in 1888 it was estimated at 55,000.

Wigan is situated at the junction of three Roman roads, and there was a ford across the river where Millgate now stands. Many Roman coins have been found in the neighbourhood; hence it is supposed that Wigan was an important Roman station. Numerous Danish barrows also exist in the neighbourhood. After the Conquest Newton (in which Wigan is situated) was bestowed on Roger de Poictou, but on account of his rebellion was forfeited to the crown. The rectory of Wigan existed before 1243, and the rector as lord of the manor received a charter for the town in the 30th year of Henry III. Wigan was a city of refuge for runaway slaves during the Middle Ages. It was one of the 120 boroughs selected to send members to parliament in 1306; but the privilege lay dormant until 1547. From the charter it received in the 24th year of Edward III., confirming its liberties, it is evident that it was already an important market town, while its fairs were on a large scale and regulated by special laws. It also received charters from Richard II. and Charles II. Leland refers to it as a paved town "as bigge as Warrington, and better builded." Camden describes it as "neat and plentiful." Wigan contributed £50 of ship-money to Charles I. in 1636. On the outbreak of the Civil War in 1642 it was occupied by the earl of Derby, and formed the central garrison for the king in Lancashire; but the entrenchments were taken by Sir John Seaton in 1643 after a desperate battle. It was again repossessed by the earl of Derby, but was retaken by Colonel Ashton in March, when the outworks and fortifications were demolished. On 25th August 1651 the earl of Derby was defeated at Wigan by Colonel Lilburne, when Sir Thomas Tyldesley was slain. A memorial pillar to Tyldesley was erected in 1679 and restored in 1882. The town was governed by a mayor, recorder, 12 aldermen, and 2 bailiffs till the charter of 2d William IV. Under the Municipal Act it was divided into five wards, and is governed by a mayor, recorder, 10 aldermen, and 30 councillors. It has a commission of the peace and a separate court of quarter sessions. In 1885 the number of its parliamentary representatives was reduced to one.

See Sinclair's *History of Wigan*, 1882.

WIGEON (French *Vigeon*, from the Latin *Vipio*),[1] also called locally "Whewer" and "Whew" (names imitative of the whistling call-note of the male), the *Anas penelope* of Linnæus and *Mareca penelope* of many modern ornithologists, one of the most abundant species of Ducks throughout the greater part of Europe and northern Asia, reaching northern Africa and India in winter. A good many pairs breed in the north of Scotland; but the nurseries of the vast numbers which resort in autumn to the waters of temperate Europe are in Lapland or farther to the eastward. Comparatively few breed in Iceland.

Intermediate in size between the Teal and the Mallard, and less showy in plumage than either, the drake Wigeon is a beautiful bird, with the greater part of his bill blue, his forehead cream-colour, his head and neck chestnut,[2] passing into pinkish grey below and above into lavender-grey, which last, produced by the transverse undulations of fine black and white lines, extends over the back and upper surface of the wings, except some of the coverts, which are conspicuously white, and shows itself again on the flanks. The wings are further ornamented by a glossy green speculum between two black bars; the tail is pointed and dark; the rest of the lower parts is white. The female has the inconspicuous coloration characteristic of her sex among most of the Duck tribe. In habits the Wigeon differs not a little from most of the *Anatinæ*. It greatly affects tidal waters during the season of its southern stay, and becomes the object of slaughter to hundreds of gunners on the coasts of Britain and Holland; but, when it resorts to inland localities, as it also does to some extent, it passes much of its time in grazing, especially by day, on the pastures which surround the lakes or moors that it selects.

The Wigeon occurs occasionally on the eastern coast of North America, and not uncommonly, it would seem, on the Pribyloff Islands in the Pacific. But the New World has two allied species of its own. One of them, *M. americana* (a freshly killed example of which was once found in a London market), inhabiting the northern part of that continent, and in winter reaching Central America and the West Indian islands as far as Trinidad, wholly resembles its Old-World congener in habits and much in appearance. But in it the pale frontlet and the rich chestnut are mingled into, as it were, a compromise of light warm brown, the white wing-coverts are wanting, and nearly all the plumage is subdued in tone. The other species, *M. sibilatrix* or *chiloensis*, inhabits the southern portion of South America and its islands, from Chili on the west to the Falklands on the east, and is easily recognized by its nearly white head, nape glossy with purple and green, and other differences. (A. N.)

WIGHT, Isle of, a small island in the English Channel, situated off the coast of Hampshire, between 50° 35′ and 50° 46′ N. lat. and 1° 34′ and 1° 5′ W. long. (see vol. xi. Pl. VII.). It forms a portion of the county of Hampshire, and is separated from the mainland by a narrow strait, the Solent and Spithead. The island is, roughly speaking, diamond-shaped, the shorter diameter, from north to south, measuring 13 miles, and the longer, from east to west, 23 miles. The area is 92,931 acres, or about 145 square miles. The most prominent feature in its physical geography is a range of high chalk downs running from east to west across the centre of the island, and terminating in the Culver and Freshwater cliffs respectively. This range is broken through in the centre by the valley of the Medina, which flows due north and is the only river of consequence in the island; it is navigable up to Newport. A second smaller range of chalk downs occurs in the south near Ventnor. Along the south coast, extending from St Catherine Point to Ventnor, there is the remarkable district known as the Undercliff, celebrated for its wild and romantic beauty and for its mild climate. It is sheltered from the north by a line of high cliffs. North of the central chalk range the country is for the most part flat and well-wooded. Parkhurst Forest, where timber is grown for the use of the British navy, is 3000 acres in extent. The geology of the island affords within a small area abundant opportunities for studying many different formations. The uppermost of the strata represented in the island is the Eocene, and the lowest the Wealden. All the strata between these two may be studied in good sections, and very numerous and interesting fossils may be collected. The various Eocene beds are exhibited along

[1] Just as Pigeon (*q.v.*) is from *Pipio*. Other French names, more or less local, are, according to M. Rolland, *Vignon*, *Vingeon*, *Wagne*, *Woinge*, *Wignet*, *Wuiot*, *Vioux*, and *Digeon*. In some parts of England the small teasing flies, generally called midges, are known as "wigeons."

[2] Hence come the additional local names "Bald-pate" and "Red-head."

the north coast, and may also be studied to great advantage in White Cliff and Alum Bays. In the neighbourhood of Gurnet Bay there is a very remarkable bed, containing beautifully-preserved remains of insects and spiders. In Alum Bay, in the extreme west, the strata are vertically disposed, and consist of a very curious series of coloured sands and clays. Here also the junction between the Eocene and the underlying Chalk is admirably shown. The central range of chalk downs is part of the northern slope, and the downs behind the Undercliff are part of the southern slope of a lesser anticlinal axis, the upper portion of the Chalk strata having been denuded in such a way as to expose the underlying Greensand, of which the greater portion of the southern half of the island is composed. The Greensand formation may best be studied in the cliff section from Atherfield Point to Rocken End. Beneath the Greensand the Wealden is exposed in the section from Brook to Atherfield, and also, to a much less extent, in Sandown Bay. The Wealden strata have yielded abundant fossil remains of extinct reptiles (*Iguanodon*), especially in the neighbourhood of Brook and Cowleaze Chines; and at Brook Point an extensive fossil forest exists, being the remains of a great raft of timber floated down and deposited in estuarine mud at the mouth of a great river. At Brook also the characteristic Wealden mollusk, *Unio valdensis*, occurs abundantly.

The climate is mild and relaxing, and enjoys the reputation of being peculiarly salubrious. In winter and spring, however, the east winds are very trying, and in summer the heat is at times very great. The climate of the Undercliff is especially mild, and a large consumption hospital (the Royal National Hospital for Consumption and Diseases of the Chest), arranged on the cottage principle, has been established here. Partly owing to the mildness of the climate, and partly to the beauty of the scenery, the island has long been a favourite resort of tourists, and within recent years several fashionable watering-places have sprung up. Of these the principal are Cowes, at the mouth of the Medina, the headquarters of the Royal Yacht Squadron, Ryde (11,461 inhabitants in 1881), Bembridge, Sandown, Ventnor (5739), Shanklin (1780), Freshwater (2809), and Yarmouth (787). Newport (9357), on the Medina, is the capital of the island, but is comparatively little frequented by visiters. Hitherto many parts of the island have been more or less inaccessible owing to the deficiency of railways; but it is being rapidly opened up, and a railway is now in course of construction between Newport, Carisbrooke, Yarmouth, and Freshwater. There are few industries in the island. The population is chiefly agricultural, a large proportion of the land being devoted to sheep-grazing. Fishing is also carried on to a considerable extent on the south coast,—lobsters, crabs, and prawns being plentiful. Oyster cultivation has been attempted in the Medina, in Brading Harbour, and in the Newtown river. At Cowes shipbuilding is carried on, and on the Medina there are cement-works. In the towns, however, the chief occupation of the inhabitants consists in providing for the wants of the summer visiters; in winter very little business is done. The island is divided into two liberties, East and West Medina, excluding the two boroughs of Newport and Ryde; and it forms one petty and special sessional division of the county. Until 1885 there was one member of parliament for the island and one for the borough of Newport; now, however, there is only one member for the whole island. Episcopally the island has for many centuries belonged to the see of Winchester. In 1881 the population was 73,633, as against 66,219 in 1871.

History.—The Isle of Wight (Roman *Vectis*) was originally inhabited by Celts, and was conquered for the emperor Claudius by Vespasian in 43. The Romans remained in possession for four centuries. In 530 it was conquered by Cerdic and Cymric and added to the kingdom of Wessex. Later on it again became free from the control of Wessex and remained independent until the inhabitants of their own accord submitted to Edward, the son of Alfred. William the Conqueror gave the island as an independent lordship to William Fitz-Osborne, but it was again forfeited to the crown on the rebellion of his son, the earl of Hereford. Henry I. gave the lordship to Richard de Redvers, in whose family it remained until 1293, when Isabella de Fortibus, the lady of the island, sold it to Edward I. Richard II. again appointed a lord of the island, and the office continued until the reign of Henry VII., when it was finally abolished. From that date onwards the government has been vested in a captain or governor, whose office is now honorary. Charles I. was confined in Carisbrooke Castle for some time in 1649. The antiquities include the British pit villages near Rowborough, the Celtic tumuli on several of the chalk downs, the long stone at Mottistone, the Roman villas near Brading and Carisbrooke, the ruins of Quarr Abbey, and numerous ancient churches. Carisbrooke Castle, almost in the centre of the island, is a fine old ruin built upon the site of an ancient British stronghold. The British fortifications were probably occupied as a camp by the Romans under Vespasian, and they were subsequently held by the Saxons, who made the high mound known as the keep. The inner walls of the castle were erected in the 11th century, and the outer defences were constructed in the reign of Elizabeth. The Roman villa near Brading contains some beautiful and well-preserved examples of tesselated pavements; that at Carisbrooke is smaller and not so interesting.

WIGTOWN, or WIGTON, a maritime county in the south-west corner of Scotland, forming the western division of the old district of Galloway, is bounded N. by the Irish Channel and Ayrshire, E. by Kirkcudbright and Wigtown Bay, S. by the Irish Sea, and W. by the Irish Channel. It is of very irregular form. Its greatest breadth, east and west, is about 33 miles and its greatest length, north and south, about 26 miles. The area is 310,742 acres or 485½ square miles.

Physical Features.—The coast-line has a total length of about 120 miles. On the eastern boundary the estuary of the Cree expands into Wigtown Bay. Between Wigtown and Luce Bays is the peninsula of the Machers, of which Burrow Head is the southern extremity. Luce Bay has a length of about 15 miles and an average breadth of 12. By its indentation on the south and that of Loch Ryan (about 9 miles long and nearly 3 broad) on the north the two-pronged peninsula of the Rinns is formed, of which the Mull of Galloway, the most southerly point in Scotland, is the southern extremity, and Kirkcolm Point the northern. The coast is more or less precipitous, with many small inlets, few of which, on account of dangerous hidden rocks, afford suitable landing-places for vessels. Loch Ryan forms, however, a splendid natural harbour, of which Stranraer is the port. Portpatrick on the Irish Channel is the nearest port in Great Britain to Ireland, and 7 miles to the south is Port Logan. With the exception of Port William on its eastern shore, Luce Bay is destitute of harbours. Wigtown Bay includes on the Wigtown side the small harbours of the Isle of Whithorn, Garliestown, Wigtown, and Carty, but the upper portions of the bay are not navigable at low water. The county is occupied almost solely by Silurian strata, its characteristic feature being a series of rocky hills, which extend more or less over the whole county, attaining their highest elevation in the north, on the borders of Ayrshire. A considerable number range between 400 and 800 feet in altitude, the highest summits being Miltonish (970 feet), on the northern border, and Craigairie Fell (1000 feet) in Kirkcowan parish. A great part of the county has a wild and bleak appearance, the hills being covered with heath and whins, while in the lower parts there are long stretches of bog and moss. The Silurian rocks are in some parts interpenetrated by small areas of granite; and immense granite boulders are occasionally scattered over the lower grounds, doubtless the result of the Glacial action of the Kirkcudbrightshire ice bed. Along the western edge of Loch Ryan there is a narrow band of Carboniferous strata, consisting of sandstones which have been classed as calciferous. They rest unconformably on a narrow belt of Permian strata separating them from the Silurian rocks. In the Carboniferous strata various plant impressions are met with. Between Luce Bay and Loch Ryan, and on the upper shores of Wigtown Bay, there are raised beaches. Galena, copper pyrites, and barytes have been found in small quantities; grey shales for roofing slates and flags for pavement are dug at Cairn Ryan on the eastern shores of Loch Ryan, where sandstone is also quarried for building purposes; from the clays in the neighbourhood of

Stranraer bricks are manufactured. Owing to the irregular hilly character of the county the streams, though numerous, are generally small. The Cree, forming the boundary with Kirkcudbrightshire, flows past Newton Stewart and Carty into Wigtown Bay; the Bladenoch, from Loch Maberry on the Ayrshire border, falls into Wigtown Bay at the town of Wigtown, after having received the Tarf, the Malzie, and the Black Burn; and the Luce, formed by the junction of the Main Water and the Cross Water at New Luce, flows south into Luce Bay. There are a very large number of lochs, but none of them very extensive, the principal being the beautiful one in Inch parish included in the grounds of Castle Kennedy, Lochs Maberry and Dornal on the Ayrshire border, Loch Connel in Kirkcolm parish, Loch Ronald in Kirkcowan parish, and Castle Loch and the four lochs of Mochrum in Mochrum parish. Dowalton Loch, at the junction of Kirkinner, Sorbie, and Glasserton parishes, was drained in 1862.

Agriculture.—Although the rainfall exceeds the average in Scotland, the climate is not specially unfavourable for the ripening of crops, and frosts are not generally of long continuance. A considerable portion of Wigtownshire consists of stony moors, which have insufficient soil to render reclamation possible. Along the shores there is some extent of gravelly soil, which, however, requires heavy manuring to render it fruitful. Where the higher districts are arable a rocky soil prevails, better adapted for grass and green crops than for corn crops. A large extent of the county is black top reclaimed from moors; in other districts loam and clay prevail. The most common method of cropping is a six years' shift of oats, green crops, corn crop, and three years' grass. According to the *Agricultural Returns* for 1887, the arable area was 147,063 acres or about 46 per cent. of the whole, considerably above the average for even the lowland counties of Scotland. The area under corn crops was 37,392 acres, of which 35,511 were under oats. The latter area has not materially changed within the last thirty years, the chief diminution having been in wheat, which in 1855 occupied 7343 acres and in 1887 only 736. Barley and bere in 1887 occupied 796 acres, rye 38, and beans 310. The bulk of the green crops consists of turnips and swedes, occupying in 1887 15,678 acres, whilst 1902 acres were potatoes, 229 mangold, 100 carrots, 153 cabbage, &c., and 135 vetches. There were 69,326 acres under clover and rotation grasses and 21,883 under permanent pasture. In 1881 (the latest return) there were over 8009 acres under woods, and in 1887 there were 40 under nursery grounds, 6 under market gardens, and 7 under orchards. The large area under grass and turnips is owing to the general prevalence of dairy farming. In 1887 the number of cattle was 42,062, of which 21,197 were milch cows, a number exceeded in only four other counties in Scotland, although in the number of its cattle it is surpassed by ten counties. The Galloway cattle, a black polled breed, are now chiefly confined to the eastern districts, the Ayrshire being found a much more suitable breed for dairy purposes. In some cases Galloway bulls are kept for breeding with Ayrshire cows. Many dairy farms send milk to Glasgow and the neighbouring towns; but the manufacture of cheese has greatly increased within late years, large cheese factories having been established. Dunlop is now almost wholly superseded by Cheddar cheese. Horses, chiefly Clydesdale, for which breed Wigtownshire has acquired some fame, numbered 5699 in 1887; sheep, chiefly blackfaced on the hilly farms, and in other districts crosses with Leicesters and other long-woolled breeds, numbered 116,264; and pigs 10,380. From 1345 returns obtained from occupiers of land in 1887, out of 147,104 acres 142,266 were rented and occupied and 4838 owned and occupied. The following table gives a classification of agricultural holdings according to size in 1880 and 1885:—

Year.	50 acres and under.		50 to 100 acres.		100 to 200 acres.		200 to 500 acres.		500 to 1000 acres.		Above 1000 acres.		Total.	
	No.	Acres.	No.	Acres.	No.	Acres.	No.	Acres.	No.	Acres.	No.	Acres.	No.	Acres.
1880	608	9241	208	16,090	422	74,576	88	32,638	20	12,271	1	1,210	1347	146,026
1885	597	8778	216	15,851	421	75,837	91	34,426	18	11,186	1	1,220	1344	147,298

According to the latest landowners' *Return*, the county was divided among 1820 proprietors, possessing 309,087 acres at an annual value of £230,589, or about 14s. 11d. per acre. Of the proprietors 1674 possessed less than one acre each. The following owned over 5000 acres each:—earl of Stair, 79,174; E. J. S. Blair, 37,268; earl of Galloway, 23,203; marquis of Bute, 20,157; Sir W. Maxwell, 16,877; James M'Douall, 16,290; Sir Andrew Agnew, 12,962; D. Hunter Blair, 8255; William Maitland, 7848; Sir J. Dalrymple Hay, 7400; R. Vans Agnew, 6777; W. C. S. Hamilton, 6300; Mrs S. O. M'Taggart, 5998; Lieut.-Col. Sir W. T. F. Agnew Wallace, 5785; and R. H. J. Stewart, 5552.[1]

Communication.—The Portpatrick Railway crosses the county from Newton Stewart by Kirkcowan, Glenluce, and Stranraer to Portpatrick. From Newton Stewart the Wigtownshire Railway passes south by Wigtown and Garliestown to Whithorn. The Girvan and Portpatrick Railway branches off from the Portpatrick line at East Challoch near Dunragit and passes northwards by New Luce. There is a line of steamers to Ireland by Portpatrick.

Manufactures and Trade.—Although agriculture is the main industry, there is a variety of small manufactures in the towns, including a woollen factory at Kirkcowan, engineering and locomotive works at Stranraer, hand-loom weaving in various places, distilling, tanning, and currying. The fishing industry is of almost no account. There is, however, an oyster fishery in Loch Ryan, and herrings are caught in Loch Ryan and the Bay of Luce. The value of the salmon fisheries, including those of the rivers, is less than £1000 a year.

Administration and Population.—From 22,918 in 1801 the population had by 1821 increased to 33,240 and by 1851 to 43,389; but it declined to 42,095 in 1861, to 38,830 in 1871, and to 38,611 (males 18,143, females 20,468) in 1881. In point of density Wigtown stands twenty-first among the counties of Scotland, the number of persons to the square mile being 79. The proportion of females to every 100 males was 112·82, the largest proportion of any county with the exceptions of Orkney and Shetland and Forfar. The number of persons who could speak Gaelic was only twenty-eight. The town population in 1881 numbered 9060, the village 8574, and the rural 20,977. The county has three royal burghs—Wigtown (1789), Stranraer (3455), and Whithorn (1643). The last two are also police burghs (Stranraer, 6342). Part (2645) of the police burgh of Newton Stewart is within the county, the remainder being in Kirkcudbrightshire. Newton Stewart is also a burgh of barony, as are likewise Glenluce (901) and Portpatrick (591). The county returns one member to parliament. Formerly Wigtown, Stranraer, and Whithorn formed with New Galloway a group of burghs returning one member, but by the Act of 1885 they were merged in the county. The county includes seventeen parishes. Wigtownshire is in the same sheriffdom as the counties of Kirkcudbright and Dumfries. Sheriff courts are held during certain periods at Wigtown and Stranraer, and quarter sessions are held at Wigtown and Glenluce.

History and Antiquities.—The portion of Galloway now forming Wigtownshire was in early times occupied chiefly by the Novantæ. When the district was overrun by the Romans under Agricola in 82, they fixed their headquarters at Whithorn (*Leucophibia*), and one of their principal stations, *Rerigonium*, was on the eastern shore of Loch Ryan. The Devil's dyke, a defensive work of the Romans, extended from Loch Ryan to the upper part of the Solway Firth. A sketch of the early history of Galloway, including Wigtownshire, is given under KIRKCUDBRIGHT (vol. xiv. p. 98). The district was the scene of the labours of the Christian missionary St NINIAN (*q.v.*), who arrived at Whithorn (*Candida Casa*) towards the close of the 4th century. Whithorn was a bishop's see from 727 till the Reformation. In addition to the caves on the sea coast, which, like those of Kirkcudbrightshire, are associated with early human occupation, the ancient inhabitants have left traces of themselves in cairns, standing stones, hut circles, and remains of ancient villages. Numerous early relics have also been dug up, including flint and other stone implements, as well as a great variety of ancient bronze implements and ornaments.[2] The Dowalton crannogs were the first lake dwellings discovered in Scotland, and are among the most remarkable in the country.[3] Among the ancient fortalices may be mentioned the sea towers of Carghidown and Castle Feather, south of Whithorn; the ruins of Baldoon, south of Wigtown, associated with events which suggested to Scott the tale of the *Bride of Lammermoor*; the tower of Corsewall near the west shore of Loch Ryan; the foundations of a Norse stronghold in Cruggleton Bay; Dunskey at the head of Castle Bay, built in the 16th century, but occupying the site of an ancient fortress; the fragments of Long Castle at Dowalton Loch, the ancient seat of the M'Doualls; the castle of Mochrum and Myrtoun Castle, the seat of the Maccullochs, in Mochrum parish; and the ruined tower of Sorbie, the ancient keep of the Hannays. Of the Cistercian abbey of Glenluce, founded in 1190 by Roland, lord of Galloway, the principal remains are the chapter house in the Decorated style, the walls of the cloister, and a small portion of the church in the Early English

1 For further particulars regarding the agriculture, see a paper by W. H. Ralstone, in *Trans. Royal and Highland Agric. Soc.*, vol. xvii., new ser. (1885).

2 For lists with illustrations, see papers by Rev. G. Wilson and Sir Herbert Maxwell in *Ayr and Wigton Archæological Collections*, vols. i., ii., and v.

3 See CRANNOGS, vol. vi. 552; and for descriptions of these and other lake dwellings in Wigtownshire, consult a paper by Robert Munro, in *Ayr and Wigton Arch. Coll.*, vol. v., and "Notes on Crannogs and Lake Dwellings of Wigtonshire," by Rev. G. Wilson, in *Proceedings Soc. Antiq. Scot.*, vol. ix. pp. 368-378 and x. 737-739.

style. The ancient cathedral of Whithorn, though in a dilapidated condition, forms a picturesque ruin, and near it are some slight remains of the ancient priory founded by St Ninian. The Dominican priory of Wigtown, founded in 1267, has, like the ancient castle, entirely disappeared; and only some slight mounds remain of Saulseat abbey, founded for Premonstratensians by Fergus, lord of Galloway, in 1148. Wigtown was probably created a sheriffdom in the 13th century. In 1341 the earldom of Wigton, which included the whole of the county, with the jurisdiction of a regality, was bestowed upon Sir Malcolm Fleming. In 1372 the earldom was purchased by Archibald Douglas, who the same year was created lord of Galloway. In the reign of James I. William Douglas of Leswalt was sheriff of Wigtown and keeper of the castle of Lochnaw; but in 1426 the constableship of Lochnaw, with the sheriffdom of Wigtown, was acquired by Andrew Agnew. These dignities continued to be held by the Agnew family till 1682, when Sir Andrew Agnew refused to take the test and was superseded by Graham of Claverhouse. At the Restoration in 1688 the office of sheriff was restored to the Agnew family, and they held it till the abolition of hereditary jurisdictions in 1747. The principal modern mansions are Galloway House, built in 1740, the seat of the earls of Galloway; Castle Kennedy, built by the first earl of Stair after the destruction of the old castle by fire in 1716; the baronial castle of Lochnaw, including, with large modern additions, the battlemented tower of the ancient building; and Barnbarroch House, the seat of R. Vans Agnew.

See Symson, *Description of Galloway*, 1823; Murray, *Literary History of Galloway*, 1882; Sir Andrew Agnew, *Hereditary Sheriffs of Galloway*, 1864; *Histories of Galloway*, by Mackenzie, 1841, and P. H. Mackerlie, 1870-78. (T. F. H.)

WILBERFORCE, SAMUEL (1805-1873), bishop of Oxford and afterwards of Winchester, was the third son of William WILBERFORCE (see below), and was born at Clapham Common near London on 7th September 1805. Until he entered Oriel College, Oxford, in 1823 he was educated privately. In the "United Debating Society," which afterwards developed into the "Union," Wilberforce distinguished himself as a zealous advocate of liberalism. The set of friends with whom he chiefly associated at Oxford were sometimes named, on account of their exceptionally decorous conduct, the "Bethel Union"; but he was by no means averse to amusements, and specially delighted in hurdle jumping and hunting. He graduated in 1826; and the summer and autumn of 1827 were spent in a Continental tour. After his marriage on 11th June 1828 to Emily Sargent, he was in December ordained and appointed curate-in-charge at Checkenden near Henley-on-Thames. In 1830 he was presented by Bishop Sumner of Winchester to the rectory of Brightstone in the Isle of Wight. In this comparatively retired sphere he soon found scope for that manifold activity which so prominently characterized his subsequent career. In 1831 he published a tract on tithes, "to correct the prejudices of the lower order of farmers," and in the following year a collection of hymns for use in his parish, which had a large general circulation; a small volume of stories entitled the *Note Book of a Country Clergyman*; and a sermon, *The Apostolical Ministry*. He now began to be sought for as a preacher and declined several offers of appointments. In February 1836 he was made a rural dean. At the close of 1837 he published the *Letters and Journals* of Henry Martyn. Although a High Churchman Wilberforce held aloof from the Oxford movement, and in 1838 his divergence from the "Tract" writers became so marked that J. H. Newman declined further contributions from him to the *British Critic*, not deeming it advisable that they should longer "co-operate very closely." In 1838 Wilberforce published, with his elder brother Robert, the *Life* of his father and two years later his father's *Correspondence*. In 1839 he also published *Eucharistica* (from the old English divines), to which he wrote an introduction, *Agathos and other Sunday Stories*, and a volume of *University Sermons*, and in the following year *Rocky Island and other Parables*. In November 1839 he was installed archdeacon of Surrey, in August 1840 collated canon of Winchester, and in October he accepted the rectory of Alverstoke. In 1841 he was chosen Bampton lecturer, and shortly afterwards made chaplain to the Prince Consort, an appointment he owed to the impression produced by a speech at an anti-slavery meeting some months previously. In October 1843 he was appointed by the archbishop of York to be sub-almoner to the queen. In 1844 appeared his *History of the American Church*. In March of the following year he accepted the deanery of Westminster, and in October the bishopric of Oxford.

The bishop in 1847 became involved in the Hampden controversy, and signed the remonstrance of the thirteen bishops to Lord John Russell against Dr Hampden's appointment to the bishopric of Hereford. He also endeavoured to obtain satisfactory assurances from Dr Hampden; but, though unsuccessful in this, he withdrew from the suit against him. The publication of a papal bull in 1850 establishing a Roman hierarchy in England brought the High Church party, of whom Wilberforce was the most prominent member, into temporary disrepute. The secession to the Church of Rome of his brother-in-law, Archdeacon (now Cardinal) Manning, and afterwards of his two brothers, brought him under further suspicion, and his revival of the powers of convocation lessened his influence at court; but his unfailing tact and wide sympathies, his marvellous energy in church organization, the magnetism of his personality, and his eloquence, both on the platform and in the pulpit, gradually won for him recognition as without a rival on the episcopal bench. In the House of Lords he took a prominent part in the discussion of social and ecclesiastical questions. He has been styled the "bishop of society"; but society occupied only a fraction of his time. The great bent of his energies was ceaselessly directed to the better organization of his diocese and to the furtherance of schemes for increasing the influence and efficiency of the church. In 1854 he opened a theological college at Cuddesdon, which was afterwards the subject of some controversy on account of its alleged Romanist tendencies. His attitude towards *Essays and Reviews* in 1861, against which he wrote an article in the *Quarterly*, won him the special gratitude of the Low Church party, and latterly he enjoyed the full confidence and esteem of all except the extreme men of either side and party. On the publication of Colenso's *Commentary on the Romans* in 1861 Wilberforce endeavoured to induce the author to hold a private conference with him; but after the publication of the first two parts of the *Pentateuch Critically Examined* he drew up the address of the bishops which called on Colenso to resign his bishopric. In 1867 he framed the first *Report* of the Ritualistic Commission, in which coercive measures against ritualism were discountenanced by the use of the word "restrain" instead of "abolish" or "prohibit." He also endeavoured to take the sting out of some resolutions of the second Ritualistic Commission in 1868, and was one of the four who signed the *Report* with qualifications. Though strongly opposed to the disestablishment of the Irish Church, yet, when the constituencies decided for it, he prudently advised that no opposition should be made to it by the House of Lords. After twenty-four years' labour in the diocese of Oxford, he was named by Mr Gladstone for the bishopric of Winchester. His unremitting labours had, however, seriously told on his constitution, and the change to a new diocese, entailing a repetition of the work of organization which he had completed in the old one, proved too much for his health. The result was a severe affection of the heart, which on more than one occasion threatened to prove fatal. He was killed on 19th July 1873 by the shock of a fall from his horse near Dorking, Surrey.

Besides the works already mentioned, Wilberforce wrote *Heroes of Hebrew History* (1870), originally contributed to *Good Words*, and several volumes of sermons. See *Life of Samuel Wilberforce, with*

Selections from his Diary and Correspondence, vol. i., ed. by Ashwell, and vols. ii. and iii., ed. by his son Reginald G. Wilberforce.

WILBERFORCE, WILLIAM (1759-1833), whose name is chiefly associated with the abolition of the slave trade, was descended from a Yorkshire family which possessed the manor of Wilberfoss in the East Riding from the time of Henry II. till the middle of the 18th century. He was the only son of Robert Wilberforce, member of a commercial house at Hull, by his wife Elizabeth, daughter of Thomas Bird of Barton, Oxon, and was born at Hull on 24th August 1759. It was from his mother that he inherited both his feeble frame and his many rich mental endowments. He was not a diligent scholar, but at the grammar school of Hull his skill in elocution attracted the attention of the master. Before he had completed his tenth year he lost his father and was transferred to the care of a paternal uncle in London; but in his twelfth year he returned to Hull, and soon afterwards was placed under the care of the master of the endowed school of Pocklington. Here his love of social pleasure made him neglectful of his studies; but he entered St John's College, Cambridge, in October 1766. Left by the death of his grandfather and uncle the possessor of an independent fortune under his mother's sole guardianship, he was somewhat idle at the university, though he acquitted himself in the examinations with credit; but in his serious years he "could not look back without unfeigned remorse" on the opportunities he had then neglected. In 1780 he was elected to the House of Commons for his native town, his success being due to his personal popularity and his lavish expenditure. He soon found his way into the fast political society of London, and at the club at Goosetrees renewed an acquaintance begun at Cambridge with Pitt, which ripened into a friendship of the closest kind. In the autumn of 1783 he set out with Pitt on a tour in France; and after his return his eloquence proved of great assistance to Pitt in his struggle against the majority of the House of Commons. In 1784 Wilberforce was elected for both Hull and Yorkshire, and took his seat for the latter constituency.

A journey to Nice in the autumn of the same year with Dr Isaac Milner led to his conversion to Evangelical Christianity and the adoption of more serious views of life. The change had a marked effect on his public conduct. In the beginning of 1787 he busied himself with the establishment of a society for the reformation of manners. About the same time he made the acquaintance of Thomas Clarkson, and began the agitation against the slave trade. Pitt entered heartily into their plans, and recommended Wilberforce to undertake the guidance of the project as a subject suited to his character and talents. While Clarkson conducted the agitation throughout the country, Wilberforce took every opportunity in the House of Commons of exposing the evils and horrors of the trade. In 1788, however, a failure of his digestive powers compelled him to retire for some months from public life, and the introduction of the subject in parliament therefore devolved on Pitt, whose representations were so far successful that an Act was passed providing that the number of slaves carried in ships should be in proportion to the tonnage. On 12th May of the following year Wilberforce, in co-operation with Pitt, brought the subject of abolition again before the House of Commons; but the friends of the planters succeeded in getting the matter deferred. On 27th January following Wilberforce carried a motion for referring to a special committee the further examination of witnesses, but after full inquiry the motion for abolition in May 1791 was lost by 163 votes to 88. In the following April he carried a motion for gradual abolition by 238 to 85 votes; but in the House of Lords the discussion was finally postponed till the following session. Notwithstanding his unremitting labours in educating public opinion and annual motions in the House of Commons, it was not till 1807, the year following Pitt's death, that the first great step towards the abolition of slavery was accomplished. When the anti-slavery society was formed in 1823, Wilberforce and Clarkson became vice-presidents; but before their aim was accomplished Wilberforce had retired from public life, and the Emancipation Bill was not passed till August 1833, a month after his death.

In 1797 Wilberforce published *A Practical View of the Prevailing Religious System of Professed Christians in the Higher and Middle Classes of this Country Contrasted with Real Christianity*, which within half a year went through five editions and was afterwards translated into French, Italian, Dutch, and German. Shortly after the appearance of this work he occupied himself with a plan for a religious periodical which should admit "a moderate degree of political and common intelligence," the result being the appearance in January 1801 of the *Christian Observer*. He also interested himself in a variety of schemes for the advancement of the social and religious welfare of the community, including the establishment of the Association for the Better Observance of Sunday, the foundation, with Hannah MORE (*q.v.*), of schools at Cheddar, Somersetshire, a project for opening a school in every parish for the religious instruction of children, a plan for the education of the children of the lower classes, a bill for securing better salaries to curates, and a method for disseminating, by Government help, Christianity in India. In parliament he was a supporter of parliamentary reform and of Catholic emancipation. In 1812, on account of failing health, he exchanged the representation of Yorkshire for that of a constituency which would make less demands on his time, and was returned for Bramber. In 1825 he retired from the House of Commons, and the following year settled at Highwood Hill, "just beyond the disk of the metropolis." He died at London on 29th July 1833, and was buried in Westminster Abbey close to Pitt, Fox, and Canning. In Westminster Abbey a statue was erected to his memory, and in Yorkshire a county asylum for the blind was founded in his honour. A column was also erected to him by his townsmen of Hull.

See *Life of William Wilberforce*, by his sons, 1838, 5 vols.; *Correspondence*, 2 vols., 1840.

WILDBAD, a watering-place in the north-west of Würtemberg, is picturesquely situated in the romantic pine-clad gorge of the Enz, 28 miles west of Stuttgart and 14 east of Baden-Baden. Its thermal alkaline springs have a temperature of 90°-100° Fahr., and are used for bathing in cases of rheumatism, gout, neuralgia, and similar ailments (see MINERAL WATERS, vol. xvi. p. 433). The fact that the springs rise within the baths, and are thus used at the fountain-head, is considered to contribute materially to their curative influence. The system of bathing in common is customary at Wildbad, although of course separate baths may be obtained. The water is applied internally for affections of the stomach and digestive organs, and of the kidneys, bladder, &c. Wildbad possesses all the usual arrangements for the comfort and amusement of the visiters (over 6000 annually), including large and well-appointed hotels, a curhaus, a trink-halle, and promenades. The neighbourhood is picturesque, the most attractive spot being the Wildsee, of which many legends are told. The population of the town in 1885 was 3514.

WILFRID (*c.* 634-709), archbishop of York from 665 till 709, was born of good parentage in Northumbria, *c.* 634. When nearly fourteen years of age he was sent away from a harsh stepmother to serve in King Oswy's court, where he attracted the notice of the queen, Eanfled,

She, fostering his inclination for a religious life, placed him under the care of an old noble, Cudda, who had betaken himself to a monastic life at Lindisfarne. Later on Eanfled enabled him to visit Rome under the protection of Benedict Biscop, the son of a Northumbrian, or rather Anglian, noble. At Lyons Wilfrid's pleasing features and quick intelligence made Dalfinus, or Aunemund, the archbishop, desire to adopt him and marry him to his niece. Resisting his offers, the youth went on to Rome, received the papal benediction, and then, in accordance with his promise, returned to Lyons, where he stayed for three years, till the murder of his patron (?656), whose fate he would have shared had not his beauty stayed the hand of the executioners. On his return home, Oswy's son Alchfrid gave him a monastery at Ripon, and before long Bishop Agilbert of Paris ordained him priest. He was probably already regarded as the leading exponent of the Roman discipline in England when his speech at the council of Whitby determined the overthrow of the Celtic party (664). About a year later he was consecrated to the see of York (not in England, where perhaps he could not find the fitting number of orthodox prelates, but at Compiègne). On his return journey he narrowly escaped the pagan wreckers of Sussex, and only reached his own country to find he had been supplanted in his see. The rest of his life is a record of wandering and misfortune. For three years (665-668) he ruled his monastery at Ripon in peace, occasionally, however, exercising his episcopal functions in Mercia and Kent. On Archbishop Theodore's arrival (668) he was restored to his see, but only to be driven out through the anger of King Egfrid's queen (677). Theodore now divided Wilfrid's large diocese into three; and the aggrieved prelate went to lay his case before the bishop of Rome. On his way he narrowly escaped murder at the hands of foreign princes, whom his own countrymen had stirred up against him. A synod held at Rome under Agatho (?679) ordained his restitution; but even a papal decision could not prevent his being cast into prison on his return home. When released he wandered first to Mercia, whence Egfrid once more drove him forth to Sussex. Here he rescued the pagan folk from an impending famine, and established a bishop's see at Selsea. After Egfrid's death (20th May 685) Wilfrid was restored to York and Ripon (686-687). He was once more driven out in 691-692, and after appealing to Rome in person obtained another decision in his favour (703-704). Despite the intercession of Berghtwald, archbishop of Canterbury, Egbert's brother Aldfrid refused to admit the aged prelate into his kingdom till his last illness (705). This year or the next a council was held near the river Nidd, the papal letters were read, and, despite the opposition of the bishops, Wilfrid once more received the abbeys of Ripon and Hexham. Not long after he died at Oundle (Northamptonshire) as he was going on a visit to Ceolred, king of Mercia (709). He was buried at Ripon, whence, according to Eadmer, his bones were afterwards removed to Canterbury.

Wilfrid's is a memorable name in English history, not only because of the large part he played in supplanting the Celtic discipline and in establishing a precedent of appeal to papal authority, but also by reason of his services to architecture and learning. At York he renewed Paulinus's old church, roofing it with lead and furnishing it with glass windows; at Ripon he built an entirely new basilica with columns and porches; at Hexham in honour of St Andrew he reared a still nobler church, over which Eddius grows eloquent. In the early days of his bishopric he used to travel about his diocese attended by a little troop of skilled masons. He seems to have also reformed the method of conducting the divine services by the aid of his skilled chanters, Ædde and Æonan, and to have established or renewed the rule of St Benedict in the monasteries. On each visit to Rome it was his delight to collect relics for his native land; and to his favourite basilica at Ripon he gave a bookcase wrought in gold and precious stones, besides a splendid copy of the Gospels. As a missionary his success was extraordinary, and even on his way to Rome in 679 he found time to convert the Frisian king, Aldgislus, though the latter had been bribed to slay him by the offer of "a measure of gold solidi." Later in life he ordained Suidbert as the first bishop of Frisia. In earlier years his influence was so great that he supplied the Franks with one of their later Merovingian kings, Dagobert II.

Wilfrid's life was written shortly after his death by Eddius at the request of Acca, his successor at Hexham, and Tatbert, abbot of Ripon,—both intimate friends of the great bishop. Other lives were written by Frithegode in the 10th, by Folcard in the 11th, and by Eadmer early in the 12th century. The dates have to be supplied mainly from Bede's *Hist. Eccl.*, iii. c. 25, &c., 13, &c., v. 19, &c. All the lives are printed in Raine's *Historians of the Church of York*, vol. i. (Rolls Series).

WILHELMSHAVEN, or WILHELMSHAFEN, the chief naval station and war harbour of Germany on the North Sea, is situated on the east side of the Jahde, a large basin united with the sea by a channel 3 miles long. The ground on which it stands was purchased by Prussia from the duke of Oldenburg in 1853, and though reckoned a part of the province of Hanover is completely surrounded on the landward side by Oldenburg territory. The town is laid out on a regular and ample scale, and the streets are wide and shaded with trees. A statue has been erected to Admiral Prince Adalbert of Prussia (d. 1873). Most of the inhabitants, who numbered 13,972 in 1885, including 1326 Roman Catholics, are connected with the dockyard and fleet; and there is an additional colony of dockyard employés at Bant (3000 inhabitants), on Oldenburg soil.

The original harbour, constructed in 1855-69, consists of an inner and outer basin. To the south-east of the inner harbour, which is used by war-vessels not in active service, a large new harbour has recently been constructed for war-vessels in commission and for commercial purposes. The entrance to both the old and the new harbour is sheltered by long and massive moles. A torpedo harbour has also been formed. The inner harbour and the adjacent docks, building-slips, machine-shops, &c., form the Government dockyard, which is enclosed by a lofty wall with fourteen iron gates. The whole establishment is defended by strong fortifications.

WILKES, JOHN (1727-1797), the champion of the right of free representation by British constituencies, was descended from a family long connected with Leighton-Buzzard in Bedfordshire, but he himself was born at Clerkenwell, London, on 17th October 1727. His father, Israel Wilkes, was a rich distiller, and the owner, through his wife Sarah, daughter of John Heaton of Hoxton, of considerable house property in its north-eastern suburbs. After some training under private tuition John Wilkes was sent to the university of Leyden, matriculating there on 8th September 1744. Several young men of talent from Scotland and England were studying in this Dutch university at that period, and a lively picture of their life, in which Wilkes displays the gaiety of temper which remained faithful to him all his days, is presented to us by "Jupiter" Carlyle. With this training he acquired an intimate knowledge of classical literature, and he enlarged his mind by travelling through Holland, Flanders, and part of Germany. At the close of 1748 he returned to his native land, and in a few months (October 1749) was drawn by his relations into marrying Mary, sole daughter and heiress of John Mead, citizen and grocer of London, who was ten years his senior. The ill-assorted pair,—for she was grave and staid, while he rioted in exuberant spirits and love of society,—lived together in the country for some months, when, to make matters worse, they returned to town to dwell with the wife's mother. One child, a daughter, was born to them, when Wilkes left his wife and removed to Westminster, where he kept open house for many young men about town possessing more wit than morals. To this unfortunate marriage should in justice be attributed some of his errors in life. In 1754 he contested the constituency of Berwick-upon-Tweed, but failed to gain the seat. Wilkes was now a well-known figure in the life of the West End, and among his associates were Thomas Potter, the son of the archbishop of Canterbury, Sir Francis Dashwood, afterwards Lord le Despencer, and Lord Sandwich, the last of whom in after years showed great animosity towards his old companion in revelry. In July 1757, by a triangular arrangement in which Potter and the first William Pitt played the other parts, Wilkes was elected for Aylesbury, and for this constituency he was again returned at the general election in March 1761. Pitt was his leader in politics; but to Pitt he applied in vain for a seat at the board of trade; nor was he successful in his other applications for office. Stung by these disappointments, Wilkes threw himself into bitter opposition to Bute, and to make his antagonism more effective established a paper called *The North Briton*, in which he from the first attacked the Scotch prime minister with exceeding bitterness, and grew bolder as it proceeded in its course. One of its articles ridiculed Lord Talbot, the steward of the royal household, and a duel was the result. When Bute resigned, the issue of the journal was suspended; but, when the royal speech framed by George Grenville's ministry showed that the change was one of men only, not of measures, a supplementary number, No. 45, was published, 23d April 1763, containing a caustic criticism of the king's message to his parliament. Lord Halifax, the leading secretary of state, issued a general warrant "to search for authors, printers, and publishers," and to bring them before him for examination. Charles Churchill, the poet and a coadjutor in this newspaper enterprise, escaped through the good offices of Wilkes; but the chief offender was arrested and thrown into the Tower. A week later, however, he was released by order of the Court of Common Pleas on the ground that his privilege as a member of parliament afforded him immunity from arrest. General warrants were afterwards declared illegal, and Halifax himself after a series of discreditable shifts was cast in heavy sums, on actions brought against him by the persons whom he had injured,—the total expenses incurred by the ministry in these lawless proceedings amounting to at least £100,000. So far Wilkes had triumphed over his enemies, but he gave them cause for rejoicing by an indiscreet reprint of the obnoxious No. 45, and by striking off at his private press thirteen copies of an obscene *Essay on Woman*, written by his friend Potter, in parody of Pope's *Essay on Man*, one of which got into the hands of Lord Sandwich. Immediately on the meeting of the House of Commons (15th November 1763) proceedings were taken against him. Lord North moved that No. 45 was "a false, scandalous, and seditious libel," and, as the motion was of course carried, the paper was publicly burnt in Cheapside on 4th December. The *Essay on Woman* was brought before the Upper House by Lord Sandwich, and, on account of the improper use which had been made of Bishop Warburton's name as the author of some coarse notes, the work was voted a breach of privilege, and Wilkes was ordered to be prosecuted in the Court of King's Bench for printing and publishing an impious libel. He was expelled from the House of Commons on 19th January 1764; and on 21st February he was found guilty in the King's Bench of reprinting No. 45 and of printing and publishing the *Essay on Woman*. Wilkes was on these dates absent from England. Some strong expressions applied to him by Samuel Martin, an ex-secretary of the treasury, had provoked a duel (16th November 1763), in which Wilkes was severely wounded in the stomach. He withdrew to Paris, and as he did not return to England to receive his sentence in the law courts was pronounced an outlaw.

For several years Wilkes remained abroad, receiving £1000 a year from the leading Whigs, and in the course of his travels he visited many parts of Italy. In March 1768 he returned to London and sued the king for pardon, but in vain. His next step was to offer himself as a candidate for the representation of the City of London, when he was the lowest at the poll. Undaunted by this defeat, he solicited the freeholders of Middlesex to return him as their champion, and they placed him at the head of all competitors. He appeared before the King's Bench, and on a technical point procured a reversal of his outlawry; but the original verdict was maintained, and he was sentenced to imprisonment for twenty-two months as well as to a fine of £1000, and he was further ordered to produce securities for good behaviour for seven years after his liberation. His conduct was brought before the House of Commons, with the result that he was expelled from the House on 3d February 1769, and with this proceeding there began a series of contests between the ministry and the electors of Middlesex without parallel in English history. They promptly re-elected him (16th February), only to find him pronounced incapable of sitting and his election void. Again they returned him (16th March) and again he was rejected. A fourth election then followed, when Colonel Henry Lawes Luttrell, with all the influence of the court and the Fox family in his favour, obtained but 296 votes to 1143 given for Wilkes, whereupon the House declared that Luttrell had been duly elected. Through these audacious proceedings a storm of fury broke out throughout the country. In the cause of "Wilkes and liberty" high and low enlisted themselves. His prison cell was thronged daily by the chief of the Whigs, and large sums of money were subscribed for his support. So great was the popular sympathy in his favour that a keen judge of contemporary politics declared that, had George III. possessed a bad and Wilkes a good character, the king would have been an outcast from his dominions. At the height of the combat in January 1769 Wilkes was elected an alderman for the City of London; in 1771 he served as sheriff for London and Middlesex, and as alderman he took an active part in the struggle between the corporation and the House of Commons by which freedom of publication of the parliamentary debates was obtained. His admirers endeavoured in 1772 to procure his election as lord mayor of London, but he was set aside by the aldermen, some of whom were allied with the ministry of Lord North, while others, as Oliver and Townshend, leant to the Liberalism of Lord Shelburne. In 1774, however, he obtained that dignity, and he retained his seat for Middlesex from the dissolution in 1774 until 1790. He moved in 1776 for leave to bring in a bill "for a just and equal representation of the people of England in parliament"; but attempts at parliamentary reform were premature by at least half a century. After several failures better fortune attended his efforts in another direction, for in 1782 all the declarations and orders against him for his elections in Middlesex were ordered to be expunged from the journals of the House. In 1779 Wilkes was elected chamberlain of the city by a large majority, and the office became his freehold for life. He died at his house in Grosvenor Square, London, on 20th December 1797.

Wilkes printed editions of Catullus and Theophrastus, and at the time of his death had made considerable progress with a translation of Anacreon. His conversation was often sullied by obscenity and profanity; but he knew how to suit his conversation to his company, and his well-known assertion that, ugly as he was, with the start of a quarter of an hour he could get the better of any man, however good-looking, in the graces of any lady, shows his confidence in his powers of fascination. The king was obliged to own that he had never met so well-bred a lord mayor, and Dr Johnson, who made his acquaintance at the house of Dilly, the bookseller in the Poultry, confessed that "Jack has great variety of talk, Jack is a scholar, and Jack has the manners of a gentleman." It is doubtful how far he himself believed in the justice of the principles which he espoused. To George III. he remarked of his devoted friend and legal adviser, Serjeant Glynn, "Ah sir! he was a Wilkite, which I never was." His writings were marked by great power of sarcasm. Two collections of his letters were published, one of *Letters to his Daughter*, in four volumes in 1804, the other *Corre-*

spondence with his Friends, in five volumes in 1805. A *Life* by Fitzgerald has quite recently been published. (W. P. C.)

WILKESBARRE, a city of the United States, the county seat of Luzerne county, Pennsylvania, is situated on the right bank of the north branch of the Susquehanna river in the Wyoming valley, 98 miles north-north-west from Philadelphia. The business portion lies in the bottom lands, while the residence portions have extended into the adjacent hilly country. It is entered by four railways,—the Central of New Jersey, that of the Delaware and Hudson Canal Company, the Lehigh Valley, and the Pennsylvania. The city is irregularly laid out. The population in 1880 was 23,339; in 1870 it was 10,174. Wilkesbarre is in an anthracite mining district, and its industries, while relating in general to this product, include also important manufactories of lace, wire, and cutlery, and numerous machine-shops.

After several attempts, which were rendered futile by Indian hostilities, a settlement was finally effected upon the site of Wilkesbarre in 1770. Eight years later the whole region was depopulated by the Wyoming massacre, and the infant town, with many others, was sacked and burned. In the same year a fort was erected upon the site of the ruined village, around which the town was rebuilt. Up to 1855 its growth was very slow and uncertain. The discovery of means of using the anthracite coal, which is found in abundance in the neighbourhood, gave an immense impetus to the growth and prosperity of the city.

WILKIE, SIR DAVID (1785-1841), Scottish subject-painter, was born on 18th November 1785, the son of the parish minister of Cults in Fifeshire. He very early developed an extraordinary love for art: he was accustomed to say that he could draw before he could read and paint before he could spell, and at school he used to barter his sketches and portraits for slate-pencils and marbles. He was also noted for his keen and constant observation of the village life around him; and a friend has recorded that he "liked better to stand and look at his companions at their games than to join in their play." In 1799, after he had attended school at Pitlessie, Kettle, and Cupar, his father reluctantly yielded to his desire to become a painter; and through the influence of the earl of Leven Wilkie was admitted to the Trustees' Academy in Edinburgh, and began the study of art under John Graham, the able teacher of the school. From William Allan (afterwards Sir William Allan and president of the Royal Scottish Academy) and John Burnet, the engraver of Wilkie's works, we have an interesting account of his early studies, of his indomitable perseverance and power of close application, of his habit of haunting fairs and market-places, and transferring to his sketch-book all that struck him as characteristic and telling in figure or incident, and of his admiration for the works of Carse and David Allan, two Scottish painters of scenes from humble life. Among his pictures of this period are mentioned a subject from Macbeth, Ceres in Search of Proserpine, and Diana and Calisto, which in 1803 gained a premium of ten guineas at the Trustees' Academy, while his pencil portraits of himself and his mother, dated that year, and now in the possession of the duke of Buccleuch, prove that he had already attained considerable certainty of touch and power of rendering character. A scene from Allan Ramsay, and a sketch from Macneill's ballad of *Scotland's Skaith*, afterwards developed into the well-known Village Politicians, were the first subjects in which his true artistic individuality began to assert itself.

In 1804 Wilkie returned to Cults, established himself in the manse, and commenced his first important subject-picture, Pitlessie Fair, which includes about 140 figures, and in which he introduced portraits of his neighbours and of several members of his family circle. This work, which was purchased by Kinnear of Kinloch for £25, is rather hot and unpleasant in tone and colouring; but it is a picture of the greatest interest and promise, so full of incident and character as to justify its painter's remark, when he saw it twelve years afterwards, that it contains "more subject and entertainment than any other three pictures which I have since produced." In addition to this elaborate figure-piece, Wilkie was much employed at the time upon portraits, both at home and in Kinghorn, St Andrews, and Aberdeen.

In the spring of 1805 he left Scotland for London, carrying with him his Bounty-Money, or the Village Recruit, which he soon disposed of for £6, and began to study in the schools of the Royal Academy. One of his first patrons in London was Stodart, a pianoforte maker, a distant connexion of the Wilkie family, who commissioned his portrait and other works and introduced the young artist to the dowager countess of Mansfield. This lady's son was the purchaser of the Village Politicians, which attracted great attention when it was exhibited in the Royal Academy of 1806, where it was followed in the succeeding year by the Blind Fiddler, a commission from the painter's lifelong friend Sir George Beaumont. Wilkie now turned aside into the paths of historical art, and painted his Alfred in the Neatherd's Cottage, for the gallery illustrative of English history which was being formed by Alexander Davison. The picture was executed with the most conscientious care, and subjected to many alterations, but in the end it proved far from a success. It bears no vivid impress of reality; the figure of the king is wanting in dignity and character; indeed the subject was one for which the artist had no essential sympathy, and into which he was unable to project his imagination effectively. After its completion he wisely returned to genre-painting, producing the Card-Players and the admirable picture of the Rent Day, which was composed during recovery from a fever contracted in 1807 while on a visit to his native village. His next great work was the Ale-House Door, afterwards entitled the Village Festival (now in the National Gallery), which was purchased by J. J. Angerstein for 800 guineas. It has been styled by Leslie "the most artificial of Wilkie's earlier productions." Its figures seem rather small for the extent of canvas; but the separate groups are excellent, and in its handling, in the exquisite delicacy and refinement of touch, and in the variety and beauty of its broken tints it bears marks of the most distinct progress. It was followed in 1813 by the well-known Blind Man's Buff, a commission from the prince regent, to which a companion picture, the Penny Wedding, was added in 1818.

Meanwhile Wilkie's eminent success in art had been rewarded by professional honours. In November 1809 he was elected an associate of the Royal Academy, when he had hardly attained the age prescribed by its laws, and in February 1811 he became a full academician. In 1812 he opened an exhibition of his collected works in Pall Mall, but the experiment was unsuccessful, entailing pecuniary loss upon the artist. In 1814 he executed the Letter of Introduction, one of the most delicately finished and perfect of his cabinet pictures. In the same year he made his first visit to the Continent, and at Paris entered upon a profitable and delighted study of the works of art collected in the Louvre. Interesting particulars of the time are preserved in his own matter-of-fact diary, and in the more sprightly and flowing pages of the journal of Haydon, his fellow-traveller. On his return he began Distraining for Rent, one of the most popular and dramatic of his works. In 1816 he made a tour through Holland and Belgium in company with Raimbach, the engraver of many of his paintings. The Sir Walter Scott and his Family, a cabinet-sized picture with small full-length figures in the dress of Scottish peasants, was the result of a visit to Abbotsford in 1818. Reading a Will, a commission from the king of Bavaria, now in the New Pinakothek at Munich, was completed in 1820; and two years later the great picture of Chelsea Pensioners Reading the Gazette of the Battle of Waterloo, commissioned by the duke of Wellington in 1816, at a cost of 1200 guineas, was exhibited at the Royal Academy. The subject was a particularly happy one, and was carried out with the greatest fulness of incident and variety of character; it appealed powerfully to the popular sentiment of the time, while the accomplished and masterly technique of the work won the admiration of the artistic portion of the public.

In 1822 Wilkie visited Edinburgh, in order to select from the royal progress of George IV. a fitting subject for a picture. The Reception of the King at the Entrance of Holyrood Palace was the incident ultimately chosen; and in the following year, when the artist, upon the death of Raeburn, had been appointed royal limner for Scotland, he received sittings from the monarch, and began to work diligently upon the subject. But several years elapsed before its completion; for, like all such ceremonial works, it proved a harassing commission, uncongenial to the painter while in progress and unsatisfactory when finished. His health suffered from the strain to which he was subjected, and his condition was aggravated by heavy domestic trials and responsibilities. In 1825 he sought relief in foreign travel: after visiting Paris, he passed into Italy, where, at Rome, he received the news of fresh disasters through the failure of his publishers. A residence at Töplitz and Carlsbad was tried in 1826, with little good result, and then Wilkie returned to Italy, to Venice and Florence. The summer of 1827 was spent in Geneva, where he had sufficiently recovered to paint his Princess Doria Washing the Pilgrims' Feet, a work which, like several small pictures executed at Rome, was strongly influenced by the Italian art by which the painter had been surrounded. In October he passed into Spain, whence he returned to England in June 1828.

It is impossible to over-estimate the influence upon Wilkie's art of these three years of foreign travel. It amounts to nothing short of a complete change of style. Up to the period of his leaving England he had been mainly influenced by the Dutch genre-painters, whose technique he had carefully studied, whose works he frequently kept beside him in his studio for reference as he painted, and whose method he applied to the rendering of those scenes of English and Scottish life of which he was so close and faithful an observer. Teniers, in particular, appears to have been his chief master; and in his earlier productions we find the sharp, precise, spirited touch, the rather subdued colouring, and the clear, silvery grey tone which distinguish this master; while in his subjects of a slightly later period,—those, such as the Chelsea Pensioners, the Highland Whisky Still, and the Rabbit on the Wall, executed in what Burnet styles his second manner, which, however, may be regarded as only the development and maturity of his first,—he begins to unite to the qualities of Teniers that greater richness and fulness of effect which are characteristic of Ostade. But now he experienced the spell of the Italian masters, and of Velazquez and the great Spaniards. His change of feeling is accurately marked in an entry in his journal during his last visit to The Hague. "One feels wearied," he writes, "with the perfections of the minor Dutch paintings, and finds relief in contemplating even the imperfect sketches and incomplete thoughts of those great Italians. My friend Woodburn used to say when we were in Italy that 'all collectors begin with Dutch pictures but end with Italian.'"

In the works which Wilkie produced in his final period he exchanged the detailed handling, the delicate finish, and the reticent hues of his earlier works for a style distinguished by breadth of touch, largeness of effect, richness of tone, and full force of melting and powerful colour. His subjects, too, were no longer the homely things of the genre-painter: with his broader method he attempted the portrayal of scenes from history, suggested for the most part by the associations of his foreign travel. His change of style and change of subject were severely criticized at the time; to some extent he lost his hold upon the public, who regretted the familiar subjects and the interest and pathos of his earlier productions, and were less ready to follow him into the historic scenes towards which this final phase of his art sought to lead them. The popular verdict had in it a basis of truth: Wilkie was indeed greatest as a genre-painter. He possessed the keenest instinct for the portrayal of what was around him, the truest insight for the effective selection, the artistic and telling combination, of the things that met his every-day sight, and were dear to him through life-long nearness; but he was destitute of that higher and more recondite kind of imagination which "bodies forth the form of things unseen," and gives life and reality to its re-creations of the past. It is, however, undoubtedly true that on technical grounds his change of style was criticized with undue severity. While his later works are admittedly more frequently faulty in form and draughtsmanship than those of his earlier period, some of them at least (the Bride's Toilet, 1837, for instance) show a true gain and development in power of handling, and in mastery over complex and forcible colour harmonies. Most of Wilkie's foreign subjects,—the Pifferari, Princess Doria, the Maid of Saragossa, the Spanish Podado, a Guerilla Council of War, the Guerilla Taking Leave of his Family, and the Guerilla's Return to his Family,—passed into the English royal collection; but the dramatic Two Spanish Monks of Toledo, also entitled the Confessor Confessing, became the property of the marquis of Lansdowne. On his return to England Wilkie completed the Reception of the King at the Entrance of Holyrood Palace,—a curious example of a union of his earlier and later styles, a "mixture" which was very justly pronounced by Haydon to be "like oil and water." His Preaching of John Knox before the Lords of the Congregation had also been begun before he left for abroad; but it was painted throughout in the later style, and consequently presents a more satisfactory unity and harmony of treatment and handling. It was one of the most successful pictures of the artist's later period.

In the beginning of 1830 Sir Thomas Lawrence died, and Wilkie was appointed to succeed him as painter in ordinary to the king, and in 1836 he received the honour of knighthood. The main figure-pictures which occupied him until the end were Columbus in the Convent at La Rabida, 1835; Napoleon and Pius VII. at Fontainebleau, 1836; Sir David Baird Discovering the Body of Tippoo Sahib, 1838; the Empress Josephine and the Fortune-Teller, 1838; and Queen Victoria Presiding at her First Council, 1838. His time was also much occupied with portraiture, many of his works of this class being royal commissions. His portraits are pictorial and excellent in general distribution, but the faces are frequently wanting in drawing and character. He seldom succeeded in showing his sitters at their best, and his female portraits, in particular, rarely gave satisfaction. A favourable example of his cabinet-sized portraits is that of Sir Robert Liston; his likeness of W. Esdaile is an admirable three-quarter length; and one of his finest full-lengths is the gallery portrait of Lord Kellie, now in the town-hall of Cupar.

In the autumn of 1840 Wilkie resolved on a voyage to the East. In a letter to Sir Robert Peel he states that his object was "to judge, not whether I can, but whether those that are younger, or with far higher attainments and powers, may not in future be required, in the advance and spread of our knowledge, to refer at once to the localities of Scripture events, when the great work is to be essayed of representing Scripture history,"—a sentence which foreshadows the new direction and aims of Mr Holman Hunt and other modern realists. Passing through Holland and Germany, he reached Constantinople, where, while detained by the war in Syria, he painted a portrait of the young sultan. He then sailed for Smyrna and travelled to Jerusalem, where he remained for some five busy weeks. The last work of all upon which he was engaged was a portrait of Mehemet Ali, done at Alexandria. On his return voyage he suffered from an attack of illness at Malta, and died at sea off Gibraltar on the morning of 1st June 1841. His body was consigned to the deep in the Bay of Gibraltar.

An elaborate *Life of Sir David Wilkie*, by Allan Cunningham, containing the painter's journals and his observant and well-considered "Critical Remarks on Works of Art," was published in 1843. Redgrave's *Century of Painters of the English School* and John Burnet's *Practical Essays on the Fine Arts* may also be referred to for a critical estimate of his works. A list of the exceptionally numerous and excellent engravings from his pictures will be found in the *Art Union Journal* for January 1840. Apart from his skill as a painter Wilkie was an admirable etcher. The best of his plates, such as the Gentleman at his Desk (Laing, VII.), the Pope examining a Censer (Laing, VIII.), and the Seat of Hands (Laing, IV.), are worthy to rank with the work of the greatest figure-etchers. During his lifetime he issued a portfolio of seven plates, and in 1875 Dr David Laing catalogued and published the complete series of his etchings and dry-points, supplying the place of a few copper-plates that had been lost by reproductions, in his *Etchings of David Wilkie and Andrew Geddes*. (J. M. G.)

WILL, or TESTAMENT, is an instrument by which a person regulates the rights of others over his property or family after his death. For the devolution of property not disposed of by will, see INHERITANCE, INTESTACY. In strictness "will" is a general term, whilst "testament" applies only to dispositions of personalty; but this distinction is seldom observed. The conception of freedom of disposition by will, familiar as it is in modern England, is by no means universal. In fact, complete freedom is the exception rather than the rule. Legal systems which are based upon Roman law, such as those of Scotland and France, allow the whole property to be alienated only where the deceased leaves no widow or near relatives. In France this restriction has met with condemnation from eminent legal and economical authorities. M. Troplong, for instance, holds that "un peuple n'est pas libre, s'il n'a pas le droit de tester, et la liberté du testament est la plus grande preuve de la liberté civile."[1]

Roman law.

History.—The will, if not purely Roman in origin, at least owes to Roman law its complete development,—a development which in most European countries was greatly aided at a later period by ecclesiastics versed in Roman law. In India, according to the better opinion, it was unknown before the English conquest; in the Mosaic law and in ancient Athens the will, if it existed at all, was of a very rudimentary character. The same is the case with the *Leges Barbarorum*, where they are unaffected by Roman law. The will is, on the other hand, recognized by Rabbinical and Mohammedan law. The early Roman will, as Sir H. Maine shows,[2] differed from the modern will in most important respects. It was at first effectual during the lifetime of the person who made it; it was made in public; and it was irrevocable. Its original object, like that of adoption, was to secure the perpetuation of the family. This was done by securing the due vesting of the *hereditas* in a person who could be relied upon to keep up the family rites. There is much probability in the conjecture that a will was only allowed to be made when the testator had no *gentiles* discoverable, or when the *gentiles* had waived their rights. It is certain from the text of Gaius[3] that the earliest forms of will were those made in the *comitia calata*, and those made *in procinctu*, or on the eve of battle. The former were published before the *comitia*, as representative of the patrician *gentes*, and were originally a legislative act. These wills were the peculiar privilege of patricians. At a later time grew up a form of plebeian will (*testamentum per æs et libram*), and the law of succession under testament was further modified by the influence of the prætor, especially in the direction of recognition of *fideicommissa* (see TRUST). *Codicilli*, or informal wills, also came into use, and were sufficient for almost every purpose but the appointment of an heir. In the time of Justinian a will founded partly on the *jus civile*, partly on the edict of the prætor, partly on imperial constitutions and so called *testamentum tripartitum*, was generally in use. The main points essential to its validity were that the testator should possess testamentary capacity, and that the will should be signed or acknowledged by the testator in the presence of seven witnesses, or published orally in open court. The witnesses must be *idonei*, or free from legal disability. For instance, women and slaves were not good witnesses. The whole property of the testator could not be alienated. The rights of heirs and descendants were protected by enactments which secured to them a legal minimum. The age at which testamentary capacity began was fourteen in the case of males, twelve in the case of females. Up to 439 A.D. a will must have been in Latin; after that date Greek was allowed. Certain persons, especially soldiers, were privileged from observing the ordinary forms. The liability of the heir to the debts of the testator varied at different periods. At first it was practically unlimited. Then the law was gradually modified in his favour, until in the time of Justinian the heir who duly made an inventory of the property of the deceased was liable only to the amount of the property to which he had succeeded. This limitation of liability is generally termed by the civilians *beneficium inventarii*. Closely connected with the will was the *donatio mortis causa*, the rules of which have been as a whole adopted in England (see below). An immense space in the *Corpus Juris* is occupied with testamentary law. The whole of part v. of the *Digest* (books xxviii.-xxxvi.) deals with the subject, and so do a large number of constitutions in the *Code* and *Novels*.[4]

The effect of Christianity upon the will was very marked. For instance, the duty of bequeathing to the church was inculcated as early as Constantine, and heretics and monks were placed under a disability to make a will or take gifts left by will. A will was often deposited in a church. The canon law follows the Roman law with a still greater leaning to the advantage of the church. No church property could be bequeathed. Manifest usurers were added to the list of those under disability. For the validity of a will it was generally necessary that it should be made in the presence of a priest and two witnesses, unless where it was made *in pias causas*. The witnesses, as in Roman law, must be *idonei*. Gifts to the church were not subject to the deductions in favour of the heir and the children necessary in ordinary cases.[5] In England the church succeeded in holding in its own hands for centuries jurisdiction in testamentary matters.

The Roman law of wills has had considerable effect upon English law. In the words of Sir H. Maine, "The

[1] *Traité des donations entre-vifs et des testaments* (1855), preface.
[2] *Ancient Law*, chap. vi.
[3] ii. 101.
[4] For further information as to the history of the Roman will, see ROMAN LAW, especially pp. 674, 691, 702, 706, 713.
[5] Most of the law is contained in *Decretals*, iii. 26, "De Testamentis."

Roman and English law contrasted.

English law of testamentary succession to personalty has become a modified form of the dispensation under which the inheritances of Roman citizens were administered."[1] At the same time there are some broad and striking differences which should be borne in mind. The following among others may be noticed. (1) A Roman testator could not, unless a soldier, die partly testate and partly intestate. The will must stand or fall as a whole. This is not the case in England. (2) There is no one in English law to whom the *universitas juris* of the testator descends as it did to the Roman *heres*, whose appointment was essential to the validity of a formal will, and who partook of the nature of the English heir, executor, administrator, devisee, and legatee. (3) The disabilities of testators differed in the two systems. The disability of a slave or a heretic is peculiar to Roman law, of a youth between fourteen and twenty-one to English law. (4) The whole property may be disposed of in England; but it was not so at Rome, where, except by the wills of soldiers, children could not be disinherited unless for specified acts of misconduct. During the greater part of the period of Roman law the heir must also have had his fourth in order to induce him to accept the inheritance. (5) In English law all wills must conform to certain statutory requirements; the Romans recognized from the time of Augustus an informal will called *codicilli*. The English codicil has little in common with this but the name. It is not an informal will, but an addition to a will, read as a part of it, and needing the same formalities of execution. (6) There is a striking difference, unknown to Roman law, between wills of realty and wills of personalty. Probate is necessary for the latter but not for the former. The Roman *legatum* applied to both movables and immovables; in England a legacy or bequest is a gift of personalty only, a gift of real estate being called a devise.[2] (7) The Roman will spoke from the time of making; the English speaks from the time of death. This difference becomes very important in case of alteration in the position of the testator between the making of the will and his death. As a rule the Roman will could not, the English can, pass after-acquired property.

Liberty of alienation by will is found at an early period in England. To judge from the words of a law of Canute, intestacy appears to have been the exception at that time.[3] How far the liberty extended is uncertain: it is the opinion of some authorities that complete disposition of land and goods was allowed, of others that limited rights of wife and children were recognized. However this may be, after the Conquest a distinction, the result of feudalism, to use a convenient if inaccurate term, arose between real and personal property. It will be convenient to treat the history of the two kinds of will separately.

Real estate in England.

It became the law after the Conquest, according to Sir E. Coke,[4] that no estate greater than for a term of years could be disposed of by will, unless in Kent, where the custom of GAVELKIND (*q.v.*) prevailed, and in some manors and boroughs (especially the City of London), where the pre-Conquest law was preserved by special indulgence. The reason why devise of land was not acknowledged by law was, no doubt, partly to discourage death-bed gifts in mortmain, partly because the testator could not give the devisee that SEISIN (*q.v.*) which was the principal element in a feudal conveyance. By means of the doctrine of uses, however, the devise of land was secured by a circuitous method, generally by conveyance to feoffees to uses in the lifetime of the feoffer to such uses as he should appoint by his will (see TRUST).[5] On the passing of the Statute of Uses lands again became non-devisable, with a saving in the statute for the validity of wills made before the 1st of May 1536. The inconvenience of this state of things soon began to be felt, and was probably aggravated by the large amount of land thrown into the market after the dissolution of the monasteries. As a remedy the Act of 32 Hen. VIII. c. 1 was passed in 1540, and was afterwards explained by 34 and 35 Hen. VIII. c. 5. The effect of these Acts was to make lands held in fee simple devisable by will in writing, to the extent of two-thirds where the tenure was by knight service, and the whole where it was in socage. Corporations were incapacitated to receive, and married women, infants, idiots, and lunatics to devise. The Act 12 Car. II. c. 24, by abolishing tenure by knight service, made all lands devisable. In the same reign the Statute of Frauds (29 Car. II. c. 3) dealt with the formalities of execution. Up to this time simple notes, even in the handwriting of another person, constituted a sufficient will, if published by the testator as such. The Statute of Frauds required, *inter alia*, that all devises should be in writing, signed by the testator or by some person for him in his presence and by his direction, and should also be subscribed by three credible witnesses. The strict interpretation by the courts of the credibility of witnesses led to the passing of 26 Geo. II. c. 6, making interested witnesses sufficient for the due execution of the will, but declaring gifts to them void. The will of a man was revoked by marriage and the birth of a child, of a woman by marriage only. A will was also revoked by an alteration in circumstances, and even by a void conveyance *inter vivos* of land devised by the will made subsequently to the date of the will, which was presumed to be an attempt by the grantor to give legal effect to a change of intention. As in Roman law, a will spoke from the time of the making, so that it could not avail to pass after-acquired property without republication, which was equivalent to making a new will. Copyholds were not devisable before 1815, but were usually surrendered to the use of the will of the copyhold tenant; 55 Geo. III. c. 192 made them devisable simply. Devises of lands have gradually been made liable to the claims of creditors by a series of statutes beginning with 3 and 4 W. and M. c. 14.

Personalty.

The history of wills of personalty was considerably different, but to some extent followed parallel lines. In both cases partial preceded complete power of disposition. The general opinion of the best authorities is that by the common law of England a man could only dispose of his whole personal property if he left no wife or children; if he left either wife or children he could only dispose of one-half, and one-third if he left both wife and children. The shares of wife and children were called their *pars rationabilis*. This *pars rationabilis* is expressly recognized in Magna Charta. At what period the right of disposition of the whole personalty superseded the old law is uncertain. That it did so is certain, and the places where the old rule still existed,—the province of York, Wales, and the City of London,—were regarded as exceptions. The right of bequest in these places was not assimilated to the general law until comparatively recent times by Acts passed between 1693 and 1726. A good will of personalty could be made by a male at fourteen, by a female at twelve. The formalities in the case of wills of personalty were not as numerous as in the case of wills of land. Up to 1838 a nuncupative or oral will was sufficient, subject, where the gift was of £30 or more, to the restrictions contained in the Statute of Frauds. The witnesses to a written will need not be

[1] *Ancient Law*, chap. vi.

[2] The distinction between bequest and devise did not always exist. For instance, the Assize of Northampton, c. 4, speaks of a devise (*divisa*) of chattels.

[3] *Secular Laws*, c. 68.

[4] 2 *Inst.*, 7.

[5] Many instances of such conveyances occur in Sir Harris Nicolas's *Testamenta Vetusta* and in *Fifty Earliest English Wills* (1387-1439), edited by Mr F. J. Furnivall in 1882.

"credible," and it was specially enacted by 4 and 5 Anne c. 3 that anyone who could give evidence in a court of law was a good witness to a will of personalty. A will entirely in the testator's handwriting, called a holograph will, was valid without signature. At one time the executor was entitled to the residue in default of a residuary legatee. But 11 Geo. IV. and 1 Will. IV. c. 40 made him in such an event trustee for the next of kin.

Jurisdiction of courts.

Jurisdiction over wills of personalty was till 1858 in the ecclesiastical courts, probate being granted by the diocesan court[1] if the goods of the deceased lay in the same diocese, in the provincial court of Canterbury or York (the Prerogative Court) if the deceased had *bona notabilia*, that is, goods to the value of £5 in two dioceses. The ecclesiastical jurisdiction was of very ancient origin. It was fully established under Henry II., as it is mentioned by Glanvill. In the City of London wills were enrolled in the Court of Hustings from 1258 to 1688 after having been proved before the ordinary. Contested cases before 1858 were tried in the Prerogative Court with an appeal originally to the Court of Delegates, later to the judicial committee of the privy council. There were also a few special local jurisdictions, probably for the most part survivals of the pre-Conquest period, when wills seem to have been published in the county court. The ecclesiastical courts had no jurisdiction over wills of land, and the common law courts were careful to keep the ecclesiastical courts within their limits by means of PROHIBITION (*q.v.*). No probate of a will of land was necessary, and title to real estate by will might be made by production of the will as a document of title. This is still the law in ordinary cases; but the Act of 1857 has introduced probate of will of land as an exceptional proceeding. The liability of the executor and legatee for the debts of the testator has been gradually established by legislation. In general it is limited to the amount of the succession. Personal liability of the executor beyond this can by the Statute of Frauds only be established by contract in writing.

Existing law.

Such were the principal stages in the history of the law as it affected wills made before 1838 or proved before 1858. The principal Acts now in force are the Wills Act, 1837 (7 Will. IV. and 1 Vict. c. 26), the Court of Probate Act, 1857 (20 and 21 Vict. c. 77), and the Judicature Acts. Some of the earlier Acts are still law, though of little importance since the more modern and comprehensive enactments. The earliest on the statute roll is 20 Hen. III. c. 2, enabling a widow to bequeath the crops of her lands. Before the Wills Act uniformity in the law had been urgently recommended by the Real Property Commissioners in 1833. It appears from their report[2] that at the time of its appearance there were ten different ways in which a will might be made under different circumstances.

Making of wills.

The Act of 1837 affected both the making and the interpretation of wills.[3] Excluding the latter for the present, its main provisions were these. All property, real and personal, and of whatever tenure, may be disposed of by will. If customary freeholds or copyholds be devised, the will must be entered on the court rolls. No will made by any person under the age of twenty-one is valid. Every will is to be in writing, signed at the foot or end thereof by the testator or by some person in his presence and by his direction, and such signature is to be made or acknowledged by the testator in the presence of two or more witnesses present at the same time, who are to subscribe the will in the presence of the testator. Publication is not necessary. A will is not void on account of the incompetency of a witness. Gifts to a witness or the husband or wife of a witness are void. A creditor or executor may attest. A will is revoked (except where made in exercise of a power of appointment of a certain kind) by a later will, or by destruction with the intention of revoking, but not by presumption arising from an alteration in circumstances. Alterations in a will must be executed and attested as a will. A will speaks from the death of the testator, unless a contrary intention appear. The Act of 1857 transferred the jurisdiction, both voluntary and contentious, of all ecclesiastical, royal peculiar, peculiar, and manorial courts to the Court of Probate constituted by the Act, created a judge and registrars of that court, abolished the old exclusive rights in testamentary matters of the advocates of Doctors' Commons, and laid down rules of procedure. Contentious jurisdiction was given to county courts where the personal estate of the deceased was under £200 in value. The Judicature Act, 1873, merged the old Court of Probate in the Probate, Divorce, and Admiralty Division of the High Court of Justice. The division now consists of the president and one other judge. The practice of the division is mainly regulated by the Rules of the Supreme Court, 1883. Appeals lie to the Court of Appeal and thence to the House of Lords. Before the Judicature Act they lay directly to the House of Lords. The principal rules now obtaining as to probate are these. Probate is confined as a rule to wills of personalty or of mixed personalty and realty, and is either in common form, where no opposition to the grant is made, or in solemn form, generally after opposition, when the witnesses appear in court. The Act of 1857 introduced proof of wills of realty in solemn form after citation of the heir-at-law and devisees. Probate may be granted either in the principal or in a district registry, and should be obtained within six months after the testator's death. Where no executor is named in a will, the will is not now invalid, as was once the case, but administration *cum testamento annexo* is granted. The same course is pursued where the executor renounces or dies intestate before administering the estate of the deceased. After probate the probate (as the official copy of the will is called) itself becomes evidence, the original will being deposited in the principal registry at Somerset House, London. On grant of probate a duty, denoted by a stamp on the probate, is payable. It varies according to the amount at which the personalty is fixed by the oath of the executor. Other Acts dealing with the practice in wills and probate may be shortly stated. 15 and 16 Vict. c. 24 removed some of the difficulties which had arisen on the clause of the Wills Act that the signature was to be at the foot or end. 44 Vict. c. 12 enabled any officer of inland revenue to grant probate where the personal estate does not exceed £300. The main duty of an executor is to pay the debts of the deceased in a certain order of priority, to administer the estate, to pay probate and legacy duties, and in general to carry out the intention of the testator. There are numerous Acts, especially the Conveyancing Act, 1881, dealing with the rights and liabilities of executors, the general effect of which is to discharge an executor from liability for *bona fide* payment of debts, for distribution of assets after public notice to persons interested, &c. (see EXECUTORS).

Interpretation of wills.

Rules of interpretation or construction depend chiefly on decisions of the courts, to a smaller extent on statutory enactment. The law was gradually brought into its present condition through precedents extending back for centuries, especially decisions of the Court of Chancery, the court *par excellence* of construction, as distinguished from the Court of Probate. The Court of Probate did not deal unless incidentally with the meaning of the will; its jurisdiction was confined to seeing that it was duly executed. The present state of the law of interpretation is highly technical. Some phrases have obtained a conventional meaning which the testators who used them probably did not dream of. Many of the judicial doctrines which had gradually become established were altered by the Wills Act. These provisions of the Act have since that time themselves become the subject of judicial decision. Among other provisions are these, most of them to take effect only in the absence of a contrary intention. A residuary devise is to include estates comprised in lapsed and void devises. A general gift of the testator's lands is to include copyholds and leaseholds. A general gift of real or personal estate is to include real or personal estate over which the testator had a general power of appointment. A devise without words of limitation is to pass the fee simple. The words "die without issue" or similar words are to mean die without issue living at the time of the death of the person whose issue was named. Trustees under an unlimited devise are to take the fee simple. Devises of estates tail are not to lapse if the devisee, though he predeceased the testator, left issue inheritable under the entail. Gifts to children or other issue leaving issue living at the testator's death are not to lapse. Rules of interpretation founded on principles of equity independent of statute are very numerous, and for them the works devoted to the subject must be consulted. Some of the more important, stated in as general a form as possible, are these. The intention of the testator is to be observed. This rule is called by Sir E. Coke the pole star to guide the judges. There is a presumption against intestacy, against double portions, against constructing merely precatory words to import a trust, &c. One part of the will is to be expounded by another. Interlineations and alterations are presumed to have been made after, not as in deeds before, execution. Words are supposed to be used in their strict and primary sense. Many words and phrases, however, such as "money," "residue," and "issue" and other words of relationship, have become invested with a technical meaning. Evidence is admissible in certain cases to explain latent ambiguity, and parol evidence of the terms of a lost will may be given.

[1] The testamentary jurisdiction of the archdeacon's court is alluded to by Chaucer in the "Friar's Tale," but it was afterwards completely superseded by the bishop's court.

[2] *Fourth Report*, p. 12.

[3] By sect. 1 of the Act the word "will" includes codicil.

Invalidation of wills.

A will may be void, in whole or in part, for many reasons, which may be divided into two great classes, those arising from external circumstances and those arising from the will itself. The main examples of the former class are revocation by burning, tearing, &c., by a later will, or by marriage of the testator, incapacity of the testator from insanity, infancy, or legal disability (such as being a convict), undue influence, and fraud, any one of which is ground for the court to refuse or revoke probate of a will good on the face of it, or declare a will of lands void. Undue influence is a ground upon which frequent attempts are made to set aside wills. Its nature is well explained in a judgment of Lord Penzance's: "Pressure of whatever character, whether acting on the fears or the hopes, if so exerted as to overpower the volition without convincing the judgment, is a species of restraint under which no valid will can be made."[1] The circumstances appearing on the face of the will which make it open to objection may either avoid it altogether or create a partial intestacy, the will remaining good as a whole. Where the will is not duly executed, *e.g.*, if it is a forgery or if it is not signed by the testator or the proper number of witnesses, the will is not admitted to probate at all. Where it contains devises or bequests bad in law, as in general restraint of marriage, or tending to create perpetuities, or contrary to public policy, or to some particular enactment, only the illegal part is void. A remarkable instance is a well-known case in which a condition subsequent in a devise was held void as against public policy, being a gift over of the estate devised in case the first devisee, the eldest son of an earl, did not before his death obtain the lapsed title of duke of Bridgewater.[2]

Wills of exceptional character.

There are some wills of an exceptional kind which demand special notice. *King.*—It was resolved in parliament in the 16th Ric. II. that the king, his heirs and successors, might lawfully make their testaments.[3] In some later cases parliamentary authority has been given to royal wills, in others not. The executors of Henry IV. were confirmed in their office by letters patent of Henry V., those of Henry V. by parliament. The largest testamentary powers ever conferred on an English king were given to Henry VIII. by 25 Hen. VIII. c. 7, empowering him to limit and appoint the succession to the crown by will, in default of children by Jane Seymour or any future wife. By 39 and 40 Geo. III. c. 88 the king and his successor may devise or bequeath their private property.[4] No court, however, has jurisdiction to grant probate of the will of a king. *Guardianship.*—As a general rule wills deal with property, but even at common law a will simply appointing a guardian was good. The common law was superseded by 12 Car. II. c. 24, under which a father may dispose of the custody of his unmarried infant children by will. The Guardianship of Infants Act, 1886, extended such powers in certain cases to the mother. *Married Woman.*—At common law a married woman could not (with a few exceptions) make a will without her husband's licence and consent, and this disability was specially preserved by the Wills Acts of Henry VIII. and of 1837. A common mode of avoiding this difficulty was for the husband to contract before marriage to permit the wife to make an appointment disposing of personalty to a certain value. Courts of equity from an early time allowed her, under certain restrictions, to make a will of property held for her separate use. In some cases her husband could dispose of her property by will, in others not. The law as it existed previously to 1882 is now practically obsolete, the Married Women's Property Act of that year enabling a married woman to dispose by will of any real or personal property as her separate property as a *feme sole* without the intervention of any trustee. The Act also enables a married woman who is executrix of a will to act as if she were a *feme sole*. *Alien.*—Before 1870 an alien enemy resident in England could only dispose of property by will with the king's licence. The Naturalization Act, 1870, enables him to do so as fully as a natural-born British subject. *Soldier and Sailor.*—Wills of soldiers in actual military service, and of sailors, are subject to special legislation, and are excepted from the operation of the Wills Act. The privilege only applies to wills of personal estate. Wills of soldiers on an expedition may be made by unattested writing or by nuncupative testament before two witnesses. Wills of petty officers and seamen in the navy, and of marines, as far as relates to their pay or prize-money, must be attested by an officer, and wills made by a seaman in the merchant service must, if made at sea, be attested by the master or mate, if made on land by a superintendent of a mercantile marine office, a clergyman, justice of the peace, or consular or customs officer. The wills of prisoners of war are subject to special regulations, and the Admiralty may at its discretion waive the due execution of wills in other instances. The effects of seamen, marines, and soldiers, killed or dying in the service, are exempt from probate duty. Pay, wages, prize money, and pensions due to persons employed in the navy may be paid out without probate where the whole assets do not exceed £32. The Board of Trade may at its discretion dispense with probate of the will of a merchant seaman whose effects do not exceed £50 in value. By an Act passed in 1868 the existing exemptions are extended to the sum of £100 in the case of civil service pay or annuities, of civil or military allowances chargeable to the army votes, and of army prize money. *Will made under power.*—A will made under a power of appointment is not revoked by marriage when the real or personal estate thereby appointed would not in default of appointment pass to the testator's executor or administrator or to the next of kin. Before the Wills Act a will exercising a power of appointment had to conform to any special requisitions in the power, but since the Act the power is duly exercised if executed and attested like an ordinary will. *Registration.*—In the register counties memorials of wills affecting lands in those counties must be registered (see REGISTRATION).

Criminal law relating to wills.

At common law there could be no larceny of a will of lands. But now by the Larceny Act of 1861 stealing, injuring, or concealing a will, whether of real or personal estate, is punishable with penal servitude for life. Forgery of a will (at one time a capital crime) renders the offender liable to the same penalty. Fraudulent concealment of a will material to the title by a vendor or mortgagor of land or chattels is by 22 and 23 Vict. c. 35 a misdemeanour punishable by fine or imprisonment or both.

Donatio mortis causa.

Connected with the subject of this article, though not falling directly under it, is the *donatio mortis causa*, depending for the most part upon rules adopted from Roman law. Unlike a bequest under a will, such a gift passes without probate and does not need the presence of any statutory number of witnesses. It is, however, liable to legacy duty and is part of the assets of the deceased. For its validity two elements are essential: the gift must be conditional on the donor's dying from his existing illness, and therefore revocable, and there must be delivery. Money, jewels, or other chattels may be the subjects of a *donatio mortis causa*; so may negotiable instruments passing by delivery, but not cheques signed by the giver, as his authority to draw is revoked by his death. If presented before his death, the gift, being unconditional, is wanting in one of the elements of a good *donatio mortis causa*.[1]

Ireland.

Ireland.—The Act of 1837 applies to Ireland. In 1857 an Act on lines similar to the English Act was passed for Ireland, 21 and 22 Vict. c. 79. Under the Irish Judicature Act of 1877 the then existing Court of Probate was merged in the High Court of Justice.

Scotland.

Scotland.—Up to 1868 wills of immovables were not allowed in Scotland. The usual means of obtaining disposition of heritage after death was a trust disposition and settlement by deed *de præsenti*, under which the truster disponed the property to trustees according to the trusts of the settlement, reserving a life interest. Thus something very similar to a testamentary disposition was secured by means resembling those employed in England before the Wills Act of Henry VIII. The main disadvantage of the trust disposition was that it was liable to be overthrown by the heir, who could reduce *ex capite lecti* all voluntary deeds made to his prejudice within sixty days of the death of his ancestor. In 1868 the Titles to Land Consolidation Act made it competent to any owner of lands to settle the succession to the same in the event of death by testamentary or *mortis causa* deeds or writings. In 1871 reduction *ex capite lecti* was abolished by 34 and 35 Vict. c. 81. A will of immovables must be executed with the formalities of a deed and registered to give title (see REGISTRATION). The disability of a woman as a witness was removed by the Titles to Land Consolidation Act. As to wills of movables, there are several important points in which they differ from corresponding wills in England, the influence of Roman law being more marked. Males may make a will at fourteen, females at twelve. A nuncupative legacy is good to the amount of £100 Scots (£8, 6s. 8d.), and a holograph testament is good without witnesses, but it must be signed by the testator, differing in this from the old English holograph. By the Conveyancing Act, 1874, such a will is presumed to have been executed on the date which it bears. Not all movables can be left, as in England. The movable property of the deceased is subject to *jus relictæ*, or widow's right to half if there be no child or children, one-third if there be a child or children, and the *legitim*, or bairn's part, of half if there be no widow, one-third if there be a widow. Only the remainder is disponible as dead's part. Legitim depends upon survivance and is not transmissible on predecease of a person prospectively entitled to it. Both jus relictæ and legitim may be excluded by discharge or satisfaction, as by provision in the contract of marriage. Executor in Scotch law is a more extensive term than in English. He is either nominate or dative, the latter appointed by the court and corresponding in most respects to the English administrator. Caution is required from the latter, but not from the former. Confirmation includes both the probate and letters of administration of English procedure. Without confirmation by the court interference by the executor becomes a vitious

---

1 Hall *v.* Hall, *Law Rep.*, 1 Probate, 481.

2 Egerton *v.* Earl Brownlow, 4 *House of Lords Cases*, 210.

3 4 *Inst.*, 335.

4 See the *Collection of Royal Wills* printed for the Society of Antiquaries by J. Nichols (1780).

1 The principal authorities for the English law are, for the formalities, Williams, *Executors*; for the construction, the works of Sir James Wigram and of Messrs Jarman, F. V. Hawkins, and Theobald. Precedents will be found in Hayes and Jarman's *Concise Forms of Wills* and in ordinary collections of precedents in conveyancing.

intromission. Originally confirmation of testaments of movables fell, as in England, under the cognizance of the church courts. Such jurisdiction certainly existed at the time of *regiam majestatem*. This ecclesiastical right continued through the Commissary Court at Edinburgh (constituted by Queen Mary in 1563) and the local commissaries until modern times, when the jurisdiction of these courts was at first transferred and then abolished by a series of enactments from 4 Geo. IV. c. 97 to the Sheriff Courts Act, 1876. The Act of George IV. placed the commissary jurisdiction in the sheriff courts; by the Act of 1876 the sheriffs sit as sheriffs in testamentary matters, no longer as commissaries. Confirmation of wills where the whole estate is under £300 is regulated by 44 Vict. c. 12 and other Acts. An eik is an addition to a confirmation made on discovery of additional effects of the deceased after confirmation. By the common law doctrine of passive representation the heir or executor was liable to be sued for implement of the deceased's obligations. The Roman principle of *beneficium inventarii* was first introduced by an Act of 1695. As the law at present stands, the heir or executor is liable only to the value of the succession, except where there has been vitious intromission in movables, and in *gestio pro herede* and some other cases in heritables. The present inventory duty on succession to movables depends upon 44 Vict. c. 12. In England the executor is bound to pay the debts of the deceased in a certain order; in Scotland they all rank *pari passu*, except privileged debts.[1] (See PRIVILEGE.)

The *will of a summons* is the conclusion of a writ containing the will of the sovereign or judge, charging the executive officer to cite the party whose attendance is required. It is regulated by several Acts, *e.g.*, 1 and 2 Vict. c. 114, 31 and 32 Vict. c. 100. (See SUMMONS, WARRANT, WRIT.)

United States.

United States.—By the constitutions of many States laws giving effect to informal or invalid wills are forbidden. The age of testamentary capacity varies very much. Eighteen is a common one. Full liberty of disposition is not universal. Homesteads generally, and dower estates frequently, are not devisable. In some States only a disposable portion of the property can be left, so that children cannot be disinherited without good cause, and in some children omitted in a will may still take their share. It is frequently provided that a certain amount must be left to the widow. Louisiana follows French law, by which the testator can under no circumstances alienate by will more than half his property if he leave issue or ascendants. In some States a married woman may not leave more than half her property away from her husband. Some require the husband's consent and subscription to make the will of a married woman valid. Nuncupative and holograph wills are in use. The former are confined to personalty and must generally be reduced to writing within a short time after the words are spoken. In Louisiana there is a special form of will, borrowed from Roman law, called the mystic or sealed will, in which the testator declares a sealed packet to be his will before witnesses. The number of witnesses necessary for the validity of a will of any kind is usually two, sometimes three. Wills of soldiers and sailors are privileged, as in England. Probate is granted sometimes by the ordinary chancery or common law courts, more frequently by courts of special jurisdiction, such as the Prerogative Court in New Jersey, the Surrogate's Court in New York.[2]

International law.

International Law.—There are three main directions which the opinion of jurists and the practice of courts have taken. (1) The whole property of the testator may be subjected to the law of his domicil. To this effect is the opinion of Savigny and the German practice. (2) The property may be subjected to the law of the place where it happens to be at the time of the testator's death. (3) The movable property may be subjected to the law of the domicil, the immovable to the law of the place where it is situate, the *lex loci rei sitæ*. England and the United States follow this rule. Testamentary capacity is generally governed by the law of the testator's domicil, the form of the instrument in most countries either by the law of his domicil or the law of the place where the will was made, at his option. The old rule of English law was to allow the former alternative only. The law was altered for the United Kingdom in 1861 by Lord Kingsdown's Act (24 and 25 Vict. c. 114), by which a will made out of the United Kingdom by a British subject is, as far as regards personal estate, good if made according to the forms required by the law of the place where it was made, or by the law of the testator's domicil at the time of making it, or by the law of the place of his domicil of origin. Subsequent change of domicil does not avoid such a will. Another Act passed on the same day (24 and 25 Vict. c. 121) enacted that by convention with any foreign Government foreign domicil could not be acquired by a testator without a year's residence and a written declaration of intention to become domiciled. In the United States some States have adopted the narrow policy of enacting by statute the old common law rule, and providing that no will is valid unless made in the form required by the law of the State of the testator's domicil. The construction of a will is governed by the law of the domicil of the testator, as he must be supposed to have used language in consonance with that law, unless indeed he express himself in technical language of another country. The persons who are to take under a will are decided by different rules according as the property is movable or immovable, the former being governed by the law of the domicil, the latter by the *lex loci rei sitæ*. It was held recently by the Court of Appeal in England that, under the will of an Englishman domiciled in Holland, leaving personal property to children, children legitimated *per subsequens matrimonium* could take, as they were legitimate by the law of Holland, though not by the law of England.[3] Such children could not, however, have succeeded simply under that designation to real property in England devised by the will. A will duly executed abroad is generally required to be clothed with the authority of a court of the country where any property affected by the will is situate. As far as regards the different kingdoms composing the United Kingdom, 21 and 22 Vict. c. 56 enables an English or Irish probate, or a Scotch confirmation, to be sealed as of course in the proper court of one of the other kingdoms. (J. Wt.)

[1] See M'Laren, *Wills and Succession*. Styles of wills will be found both in that work and in *Juridical Styles*.

[2] See Stimson, *American Statute Law*, §§ 2600-2844.

WILLENHALL, a township of Staffordshire, England, in the parish of Wolverhampton, is situated on a branch of the Birmingham Canal and on the Midland and the London and North Western Railways, 3 miles east of Wolverhampton, 12 north-west of Birmingham, and 124 north-west of London. The township includes seven hamlets. The church of St Giles, originally erected in 1350, was rebuilt in 1867 in the Decorated style. There are three other churches in connexion with the Established Church, all of modern origin, and a Roman Catholic church. Willenhall possesses a literary institute, a free library, and a higher grade board school, erected in 1883. The waterworks became in 1868 the property of the Wolverhampton corporation. Willenhall is situated in the neighbourhood of extensive coal and iron mines, and possesses brass and iron foundries, and manufactories of various kinds of ironware, including door locks and padlocks, ironmongery for doors and gates, ferules, files, gridirons, steel traps, screws, and currycombs. There are also varnishing works and maltings. The population of the urban sanitary district (area 1368 acres) was 15,902 in 1871 and 16,067 in 1881.

The village began to be of importance in the reign of Elizabeth, when the coal and iron were first wrought.

WILLESDEN, a suburb and parish of London, about 4 miles north-west from Hyde Park Corner, is situated on a number of railway lines affording very convenient access to the City. It consists of a number of houses grouped round the parish church of St Mary, Queenstown, a district inhabited chiefly by the working classes; Willesden Green and the outlying hamlets of Brondesbury, Harlesden, Neasdon, Dollis Hill, Stroud Green, and Stonebridge Park are now largely occupied by villas. The church of St Mary, dating probably from the early part of the 14th century, contains some remains of Early English, with a Perpendicular chancel and tower. It was enlarged in 1851 and again in 1872. At Queenstown there are a working-men's institute, a workmen's hall, and a Good Templars' orphanage. In Willesden Lane there is a Jewish cemetery. The population of the urban sanitary district (area 4383 acres) was 15,869 in 1871 and 27,453 in 1881.

At Domesday the manor of Willesden and Harlesden was held by the canons of St Paul's. In the 12th century it was formed into eight distinct manors, seven of which are held by the same number of prebendaries. The district is associated with the exploits of Jack Sheppard.

WILLIAM I. (1027 or 1028-1087), king of England, surnamed the CONQUEROR, was born in 1027 or 1028. He was the bastard son of Robert, duke of Normandy, and Herleva, daughter of Fulbert, a tanner of Falaise. When he was about seven years old his father, intending to go on pilgrimage and having no legitimate sons, proposed him as his heir. The great men of the duchy did homage to the child, and a year later (1035) his father's death left

[3] "*Re* Goodman's Trusts," *Law Rep.*, 17 Chancery Div., 266.

him to make good his claim. Anarchy was the natural result of a minority. William's life was on more than one occasion in danger and several of his guardians perished in his service. At the earliest possible age he received knighthood from the hands of Henry I. of France, and speedily began to show signs of his capacity for government. In 1042 he insisted that the "truce of God" should be proclaimed and observed in Normandy. When he was about twenty years old, his authority was threatened by a general conspiracy, which spread through the western half of his duchy. An attempt was made to seize him at Valognes, and he only escaped by riding hard all night to his own castle at Falaise. Bessin and Cotentin, the most Norman parts of Normandy, rose in rebellion. William sought and obtained aid from King Henry, and completely defeated the rebels at Val-es-Dunes near Caen (1047). The battle was but a combat of horse, but it decided the fate of the war and left William master of his duchy. The debt which he owed to Henry was repaid next year. War broke out between Geoffrey, count of Anjou, and Henry (1048), and William came to his suzerain's assistance. Alençon, one of the chief border fortresses between Normandy and Maine, which had received an Angevin garrison, was captured by the duke. The inhabitants had taunted him with his birth, and William, who had dealt leniently with the rebels after Val-es-Dunes, took a cruel revenge. Soon afterwards Domfront, another important border fortress, fell into his hands.

In 1051 William visited England (see vol. viii. p. 289). Two years later he married Matilda, daughter of Baldwin, earl of Flanders, and a descendant of Alfred. The marriage had been forbidden by a council at Rheims as uncanonical, and was opposed by Lanfranc, prior of Bec. This produced a quarrel between Lanfranc and William, who ravaged the lands of the abbey and ordered the banishment of its prior. Lanfranc, however, soon came to terms with the duke, and engaged to obtain a dispensation from Rome, which, however, was not granted till 1059. Strengthened by this alliance with Flanders, William showed himself more than a match for all his enemies. Henry, who had hitherto been for the most part friendly, now turned against him. After the suppression of some isolated revolts, William was threatened in 1054 by a great confederacy. His dominions were invaded by the forces of the French king, in combination with those of Geoffrey of Anjou, Theobald of Blois, and others. William remained at first on the defensive; then, falling suddenly on one of the French armies at Mortemer, in the north-eastern corner of his duchy, he cut it to pieces. This blow put an end to the war; Henry made peace (1055) and William took the opportunity of extending his dominions in a southerly direction. He built fresh fortresses and exacted homage from Count Geoffrey of Mayenne. In 1058 Henry and Count Geoffrey made a final effort to crush their dangerous neighbour; but the effort failed, like those which preceded it. William again allowed the allies to enter and ravage his territory; but, while the French army was crossing the Dive at Varaville, he attacked and completely destroyed their rear-guard, which was cut off from the van by the advancing tide. Henry again made peace, and soon afterwards died (1060). The death of Geoffrey of Anjou in the same year relieved William of his most formidable rival for the possession of Maine. Herbert Wake-Dog, the lawful ruler of that territory, who had been dispossessed by Geoffrey, recovered his dominions on the latter's death. He at once "commended" himself to William, thus making the duke his heir. On his death in 1063 William took possession of Le Mans and the county of which it was the capital,—an acquisition which extended his southern frontier nearly to the Loire, almost severed Brittany from the rest of France, and paved the way for the subsequent junction with Anjou.

It was apparently soon after this event, in the year 1064, that Harold, then earl of Wessex, visited Normandy. For the relations between him and William which grew out of this visit, see ENGLAND, vol. viii. pp. 290-291. When Harold was elected and crowned king of England (1066), William's first step was to send an embassy to him demanding the fulfilment of his promise. The purport of the demand is as uncertain as that of the pledge; but, whatever it was, Harold rejected it. The duke thereupon summoned a council of his supporters, who advised him to call together an assembly representing the whole duchy. This assembly, a typical feudal parliament, met at Lillebonne. While acting together it appears to have opposed the scheme for the conquest of England which William laid before it, but its members were won over singly. He then made a compact with Tostig, the banished brother of Harold; he came to terms with the emperor Henry; he conciliated Philip, king of France, by offering to hold England as his vassal; and—most important of all—he obtained the sanction of Rome. Pope Alexander II. not only issued a bull declaring William to be the rightful heir to the throne, but sent him a ring and a banner as symbols that the blessing of heaven was on his claim. Embarking at St Valéry, William landed on 28th September at Pevensey. The battle of Senlac or Hastings (14th October 1066) was a decisive victory for the duke of Normandy; but it took five years more to complete the conquest of England.

Early in 1067 William made a progress through the eastern and central parts of his new dominions. All that had as yet submitted to him was comprised in the old kingdoms of Wessex and East Anglia, and a small portion of Mercia. He at once secured his hold over these districts by the erection of fortresses in London, Norwich, and elsewhere. He received homage from the great men; he confiscated the lands of those who had resisted him; and, while keeping a large number of manors for himself, he granted others to his followers. Even those who had not resisted were regarded as having legally forfeited their title and had to submit to a re-grant on less advantageous terms. In March 1067 William returned to Normandy, taking with him as hostages the earls Eadwine, Morkere, and Waltheof. The revolts which broke out in the north and south-west compelled him to return to England in December. Early in 1068 he marched on Exeter, as the centre of the western revolt. He took the town and built a castle, after which he subdued Cornwall, and then marching northward forced Bristol to submit. In the summer of 1068 there was a general rising of the north, of which Eadgar was the nominal head; but Eadwine and Morkere were the moving spirits. The insurgents were aided by Malcolm, king of Scotland. William had, however, only to show himself in order to put down the insurrection. He journeyed northward, by way of Warwick and Nottingham, to York, received the submission of Eadwine, Morkere, and Malcolm, and returned by way of Lincoln and Cambridge. His march was accompanied by heavy confiscations, and great castles, rising in places of vantage, rendered the Norman power at once visible and secure. In the spring of 1069 a fresh revolt broke out. Robert of Comines, the newly appointed earl of Northumberland, was slain at Durham; a Danish fleet entered the Humber, and a Danish army, joined by Eadgar and Waltheof, seized and burned York. The sons of Harold attacked Devon, while other isolated outbreaks took place in the west. These were speedily put down by William's lieutenants; and in the autumn the king himself, going northward a second time, recovered York and harried Northumberland with ruthless deliberation. Returning to keep Christmas at York, he set out again in January 1070 to oppose Malcolm, who had crossed the border in aid of the insurgents. He forced Waltheof to submit, and drove the Scottish king back into his own country; then, marching over pathless fells in the depth of winter, he reached Chester, took the town, and founded another castle. Northumbria, exhausted and ruined, gave up the struggle, and the omission of the northern counties from the Domesday survey throws a grim light on the completeness of the Conquest. In one district only, the fens of Cambridgeshire, where Hereward still held out, the spirit of resistance survived. In April 1071 William arrived at Cambridge and commenced a regular blockade. Advancing cautiously by means of a causeway through the fens, he entered Ely in October, and therewith the last flicker of independence died out. The conquest of England was completed. To guard against any fresh incitements to rebellion from Scotland, William in 1072 invaded that country and forced Malcolm to do him homage,—an event which had an important effect on the subsequent relations of the two countries.

Henceforward such trouble as William met with came, not from the English, but from his Norman vassals or his own family. In 1073 the citizens of Le Mans took advantage of his absence to set up a "commune," and invited Fulk of Anjou to protect them. William was soon in the field, this time assisted by English troops. He harried the country, recovered Le Mans, and made an advantageous peace with the count. By a skilful compromise he recognized Fulk as overlord of Maine, but kept actual possession of the district, for which his son Robert did homage. A year later a formidable revolt broke out in England. Two of William's great vassals, Ralph, earl of Norfolk, and Roger, earl of Hereford, rebelled, and a Danish fleet, probably in alliance with them, appeared in the Humber. William returned at once to England and put down the insurrection. A great meeting of the witan was summoned to try Roger and Waltheof, for the latter, though he took no part in the rebellion, had undoubtedly been privy to it. Roger was imprisoned for life and Waltheof was condemned to death. This was the last instance of opposition to William in England; but the remaining ten years of his life were occupied with almost continuous troubles on the Continent. In 1076 he was engaged in a war with Brittany, which the interference of Philip of France forced him to bring to an unsuccessful conclusion. Next year he quarrelled with his son Robert. Matilda took the young man's side against her husband, and Philip lent him his assistance. In 1080 William was at open war with his son. While besieging him at Gerberoi he received a wound and was forced to raise the siege. A temporary reconciliation followed, soon to give way to another and a final quarrel. Three years later Matilda died, and troubles thickened upon William. A rebellious vassal, Hubert of Beaumont, seems to have held him at bay for nearly three years. Rival claims to Vexin, a district on the eastern frontier of Normandy, involved him in another war with France. He was growing old and weary, and, as he lay sick at Rouen in the summer of 1087, the French army harried his territories with impunity. When he had recovered sufficiently to take the field, he invaded Vexin and burned the town of Mantes. But his horse, plunging in the burning cinders, inflicted on him an internal injury which proved his death-wound. He was carried to St Gervais, where, on 9th September 1087, he died. His body was conveyed to Caen and buried in the great minster which he had built.

The career of William as a warrior and conqueror occupies of necessity the largest space in his life; but his fame as a statesman and administrator is not less than that which he won on the battlefield. This is not the place to discuss the results of the Conquest, but the policy of the Conqueror in regard to church and state cannot be overlooked. An orthodox churchman, a supporter of union under the successor of Peter against the schismatic tendencies of the English Church, he nevertheless repelled any claim on the part of Rome to interference with his political sovereignty. He allowed Peter's pence to be collected, but refused to pay tribute to the pope. While recognizing him as head of the church, he declined to hold his kingdom as his vassal, nor would he permit papal bulls to enter England or excommunications to be issued against any of his subjects without his leave. He controlled all appointments to important ecclesiastical dignities; he made laws for the church; he dealt justice to ecclesiastics, high and low, in his own courts. At the same time he had no desire to humiliate the church; on the contrary, he sought to elevate it to a higher position in the state, to make it a more potent agent of civilization. A weaker statesman might have seen his own advantage in encouraging the rivalry between Canterbury and York; William strengthened the church by forcing the younger to give way to the elder see. With the same object, that of increasing the efficiency of ecclesiastical organization, he severed the temporal and spiritual jurisdictions and furthered the enforcement of clerical celibacy. Finally, the trust which he reposed in Lanfranc from the time of his appointment to the see of Canterbury in 1070 shows not only his insight into character but his respect for the head of the English Church.

In regard to temporal affairs William was rather an administrator than a lawgiver. His reign is not marked by a series of legislative acts like those of Henry II. or Edward I.; but his work was the indispensable preliminary to theirs, for a strong monarchy was the first requisite of the state. To establish the power of the crown was William's principal care. The disintegrating tendencies of feudalism had already been visible under the Anglo-Saxon kings. William, while he established fully developed feudalism as a social, territorial, and military system in his new dominions, took measures to prevent it from undermining his own authority. He scattered the estates of his great vassals, so as to hinder them from building up provincial principalities; he maintained the higher popular courts against the encroachments of manorial jurisdictions; he prevented the claims of feudal lordship from standing between himself and the mass of his subjects by exacting an oath from every landholder at the meeting on Salisbury plain; finally, by the great survey which resulted in Domesday Book he not only asserted his right to make a general inquisition into property, but laid the firm basis of knowledge which was indispensable to centralized government and taxation. The care which he took to maintain English laws and institutions is part of the same policy. He balanced the two nationalities over which he ruled, and obliged each to depend upon him as its leader or protector against the other. He ruled as an English king; his feudal council was the witenagemot with a new qualification; but at the same time he was lord of the land as no king had been before him, and he enjoyed not only all the income of his predecessors but in addition all the dues which came to him as feudal sovereign. He was thus perhaps the strongest and most absolute monarch that has ever sat upon the English throne.

In character William was stern, self-reliant, and imperious in a high degree. He was not naturally cruel; but he was ruthless if it served his purpose, and could take pitiless vengeance for an insult or a wrong. He was too strong to prefer deceit when force would serve as well, but his diplomacy was subtle and guileful, and no scruple turned him aside from his aim. His temper, originally forgiving, was soured by opposition towards the end of his life, and his tyrannical tendencies were strengthened by the long exercise of uncontrolled power. His passionate devotion to the chase is only too clearly shown in the harshness of his forest laws. In private life he displayed domestic virtues, and his fidelity to his wife was exceptional in the annals of his house and time.

Authorities.—William of Jumiéges, *Hist. Norman.*, and William of Poitiers, *Gesta Willelmi* (both in Duchesne's *Hist. Norm. Script.*); Wace, *Roman de Rou*; Ordericus Vitalis, *Hist. Eccl.*; the *Anglo-Saxon Chronicle*; the Bayeux tapestry; Freeman, *Hist. of Norman Conquest.* (G. W. P.)

GENEALOGICAL TABLE OF NORMAN KINGS OF ENGLAND.

WILLIAM I. = Matilda.

Robert, duke of Normandy.	Richard.	WILLIAM II.	HENRY I. = Matilda, daughter of Malcolm and Margaret.	Adela = Stephen, count of Blois.
			William. ; Matilda = Geoffrey, count of Anjou.	STEPHEN.
			HENRY II.	

WILLIAM II. (1056-1100), king of England, surnamed RUFUS, third son of William I. and Matilda, was born in 1056. Little is known of his youth, except that in the quarrel between the Conqueror and Robert he remained loyal to his father. When the Conqueror was on his deathbed he sent William to England with a letter to Lanfranc, requesting the archbishop to secure his election to the throne. Accordingly on 26th September 1087 William was elected and crowned at Westminster. His brother Robert, to whom the Conqueror had bequeathed the duchy, was not likely to give up his claim to the larger part of his father's dominions without a struggle. A general revolt in his favour broke out in the summer of 1088. Roger Bigod rose in Norfolk, Roger, earl of Shrewsbury, and Robert of Mowbray on the western border, while Odo of Bayeux, the king's uncle, whom he had reinstated against his father's advice in the earldom of Kent, occupied Rochester. But there was little combination among the rebels. After being foiled in attacks on Ilchester and Worcester, the rebellion in the west seems to have died away. William won over the earl of Shrewsbury, and summoned his English subjects to his aid. He promised good government, the repeal of the forest laws, and the reduction of taxes. Thus conciliated, the *fyrd*, or national levy, flocked to his standard. It was the beginning of that alliance between the monarchy and the people which, fostered by Henry I. and Henry II. and confirmed by the great Edward, secured victory for the crown in its struggle with the feudal aristocracy. With the aid of his English troops William took castle after castle, repelled an attempted landing of the Norman fleet, and forced Odo to surrender his stronghold of Rochester. The rebellion being thus suppressed, he held a great council, at which, although the rebels in general were leniently treated, many confiscations and sentences of banishment were pronounced. A later meeting at Salisbury (November 1088) was notable for the trial of William of Saint-Calais, bishop of Durham, who had been one of the chief promoters of the rebellion. The bishop denied the jurisdiction of the king's court and appealed to Rome. It was the first instance of such an appeal. The court, however, acting under the advice of Lanfranc, refused to allow the plea, and the bishop, condemned to lose the temporalities of his see, retired to Normandy.

Two years later William sent an army to Normandy (Easter 1090), which under the misgovernment of Robert had lapsed into a state of anarchy. The re-conquest of the duchy by England was begun by the capture of St Valéry; but there was not much fighting, place after place yielding to William's lieutenants or to English gold. Robert called King Philip to his aid, but William bribed him to retire. In Rouen itself a popular movement took place for the surrender of the town; but Henry, the duke's youngest brother, put a stop to it by killing its leader, Conan, with his own hands. In February 1091 William himself crossed the Channel, and at once received homage from many of his brother's subjects. Unable to resist, Robert consented to a disgraceful peace. By the treaty of Caen William engaged to pay Robert a sum of money, in return for which he received some of the most important districts of eastern Normandy, as well as Cherbourg and other places in the west. It was agreed, among other stipulations, that whichever brother died first the other should succeed to his dominions. Later in the same year William marched against Malcolm III., who had invaded Northumberland, and, penetrating as far as the Firth of Forth, obliged the Scottish king to do him homage. Whether it was for the whole of Scotland or for Lothian only, history does not say; but the latter is most probable. For an account of the subsequent relations between Malcolm and William, see SCOTLAND, vol. xxi. p. 481. Meanwhile war had broken out again with Normandy. At Christmas 1093 Robert sent a challenge to his brother, reproaching him with violations of the treaty. Accordingly in March 1094 William invaded Normandy a second time. On this occasion fortune turned against him. Philip assisted the duke, and William, who had exhausted his supplies, was unable to buy him off as before. In this predicament his justiciar, Ralph Flambard, assembled an English army on the pretext of an expedition to Normandy, took from each man the money which had been provided for his expenses, and then dismissed the soldiers to their homes. With the money so obtained William bribed the French king, and then returned to England. Next year the first crusade was being preached, and Robert took the cross. A peace was made between the brothers through papal mediation, William supplying Robert with funds, for the repayment of which the latter pledged his duchy. When, in September 1096, Robert set off for the crusade, William took possession of Normandy, where he soon put an end to the anarchy which had resulted from Robert's misrule; and he held the country till his death. Shortly before the acquisition of Normandy William had subdued a second rebellion in England. Robert of Mowbray was again one of the chief conspirators, and he was joined by William of Saint-Calais, whom the king, in accordance with the treaty of Caen, had restored to his bishopric, and by others. Mowbray refused to obey a summons to the king's court, whereupon William marched against him, captured his castles of Bamborough and Tynemouth, and took him prisoner (1095). As on the suppression of the earlier rebellion, William called a great assembly, this time consisting of all his tenants-in-chief, and by their judgment the rebels were condemned. During the next two years he made a serious attempt at the conquest of Wales. The southern portion of the principality had been to a great extent reduced, first by Harold, afterwards by the Norman border lords. William's efforts were mainly directed against the northern districts. He made three invasions, and penetrated to Snowdon, but seeming victories were immediately followed by revolts, and in the end little ground was actually won.

The last three years of the 11th century were much occupied by tedious wars with France and efforts to recover Maine. In 1097 he quarrelled with Philip about Vexin, and crossed the Channel to make good his claim to that district; but the French king was able to hold his own. Next year William set about the recovery of Maine. That territory had been allowed by Robert to slip out of his hands, and had been governed since 1091 by Helias de la Flèche. William's vassal, Robert of Bellême, attacked Helias, and, having succeeded in taking him prisoner, handed over his prize to the king. William thereupon marched into Maine, and a desultory war of forays, sieges, and skirmishes followed. Fulk of Anjou opposed the Norman claim; but in August 1098 a treaty was made, by which William's rights over the country were recognized, and Helias was at the same time set free. William now turned again to France. Strengthened by an alliance with the duke of Aquitaine, he invaded the French territory and advanced as far as Pontoise. But, tiring of the fruitless war, he made a truce with Philip and returned to England early in 1099. He had only been there a few months when he heard that Helias de la Flèche was attacking his castles in Maine and had won back Le Mans. He crossed the Channel with great speed, and a last campaign replaced him in possession of the coveted borderland. But he took no pains to secure his hold, and the Norman power in Maine fell to pieces immediately on his death.

William II.'s relations with Anselm form perhaps the most important episode of his reign. Lanfranc died in 1089. The worst features of William's character began at once to show themselves. At the instigation or with the assistance of Ralph Flambard, he applied to the possessions of the church all the principles of feudal law developed in the interest of the monarchy. He treated vacant benefices as if they had been lay fiefs and bishops as tenants-in-chief, while he made simony the rule and degraded the heads of the church into servile courtiers. He had kept the see of Canterbury vacant for nearly four years, when a severe illness aroused him to a sense of his enormities. Sending for Anselm, at that time abbot of Bec, he forced the crozier into his unwilling hands (1093). Anselm insisted on three conditions,—that the temporalities of the see should be fully restored, that William should act in ecclesiastical affairs by his counsel, and that he should be allowed to recognize Urban II. as pope. After some hesitation William yielded the first demand, and Anselm did homage for the temporalities. The other two demands remained unsettled. In December 1093 Anselm was consecrated archbishop of Canterbury. On the outbreak of war against Normandy in 1094 Anselm offered William a contribution of £500. William declared the sum insufficient and angrily rejected the gift. Anselm refused to offer more, lest he should seem, even by a gift after his appointment, to be guilty of simony. Other grounds of quarrel were found in the reproofs which the archbishop levelled against the vices of the court, and his demand for ecclesiastical reform. In 1095 a more serious dispute arose. Anselm asked leave to go to Rome in order to obtain his *pallium* from the pope. As this involved a recognition of Urban, and William wished to secure his independence by acknowledging no pope, the permission was refused. The archbishop demanded that the question should be discussed at a great council. Accordingly an assembly was held at Rockingham (March 1095), in which Anselm was treated by the king as if he had been on trial for contumacy. The bishops sided with the king; the laity took part mostly with the primate. Anselm refused to renounce allegiance to the pope, but denied that this was incompatible with obedience to the king. The assembly broke up without coming to a decision. William now tried to win over the pope and received a legate who brought with him the pall. In the hope of getting the legate to suspend Anselm, he consented to recognize Urban. But, when he found that the pope had no intention of throwing over the archbishop, he reconciled himself with Anselm and allowed him to take the pall from the altar at Canterbury. But it was not long before he found an opportunity of taking his revenge. A contingent of knights sent by the primate to aid the king in his Welsh war (1097) was declared to be worthless, and Anselm was summoned to explain his conduct at court. Tired of the persecution and despairing of reform, Anselm again asked leave to go to Rome. William, believing, whether rightly or not, that Anselm intended to appeal against him, refused his request. Twice repeated, it met with the same answer. Anselm was charged with having broken his oath to observe the laws of the kingdom in threatening to leave England without the king's permission. He answered that he had only sworn to the laws subject to his duty to God and the verdict of his conscience. This answer alienated many who had supported him on the previous occasion. He was asked to swear that he would not appeal against the king, and on his refusal was ordered to leave the country. In October 1097 Anselm left England. William at once seized the archbishopric and kept possession of it till his death.

The unscrupulous tyranny which Rufus displayed in his quarrel with Anselm was equally characteristic of his temporal government. The feudal customs of aids, reliefs, escheats, &c., were developed into a great system of extortion. The townsfolk and the cultivators of the soil were weighed down by heavy taxes. The forest laws were carried out with ruthless severity. On the other hand, order was maintained, and the tyranny was to a certain extent veiled or limited by the frequent use which William made of his great councils, in the trials of great men like Odo, in the declaration of war, in the settlement of disputes such as that with Anselm. It is clear that the national assembly was neither extinct nor inefficient during this reign. It was in this period too that the office of justiciar became permanent in the person of William's chief minister, Ralph Flambard, although in his hands its powers were used merely in support of despotism.

In his private character William was as vicious as in his public capacity he was tyrannical. He was harsh and violent, extravagant and lustful, regardless of God and pitiless to man. He had a strong vein of mockery and sarcasm, and no little of the grim Norman humour. Almost the only redeeming feature of his character is his chivalrous observation of his plighted word; but for ordinary promises or obligations he had no respect. He died under mysterious circumstances in the New Forest, Hampshire, on 2d August 1100. William II. was not married; he was succeeded by his brother Henry.

Authorities.—Ordericus Vitalis, *Historia Ecclesiastica*; Geoffrey Gaimar, *Histoire des Angles*; Eadmer, *Historia Novorum*; the *Anglo-Saxon Chronicle*; Freeman, *Reign of William Rufus*. (G. W. P.)

WILLIAM III. (1650-1702), king of England and prince of Orange,[1] was the son of William II., stadtholder of the United Netherlands, and Mary, daughter of Charles I. of England. He was born on 14th November 1650. His father died eight days before his birth, whereupon the states-general abolished the office of stadtholder. As he grew up, William became the head of the party, at once democratic and monarchical, which was attached to the house of Orange. But all power was concentrated in the hands of John de Witt and other leaders of the rival or aristocratic republican party. Hence William learned caution, reserve, insight into character, and the art of biding his time.

When, however, France and England declared war upon the Netherlands in the spring of 1672, the rapid success of the French arms, and the rejection by Louis of the terms offered by the Dutch Government, produced a revolution in favour of William. A popular rising obliged De Witt to repeal the perpetual edict (which ratified the suppression of the stadtholdership in 1667), and on 8th July 1672 the prince of Orange was declared by the states-general stadtholder, captain-general, and admiral for life. The revolution was followed by a riot in which John and Cornelius de Witt lost their lives. There appears no evidence connecting William with the attack on the De Witts; but he made no attempt to punish it: on the contrary, he rewarded the leaders. Then, rejecting the outrageous terms offered by the allies, he placed his private fortune and the revenues of his offices at the disposal of the state, and declared himself ready to die in the last ditch. In order to check the French advance the sluices were opened and vast tracts of country placed under water. The Dutch fleet prevented an English landing. An alliance was made with the elector of Brandenburg, whose forces effected a useful diversion on the eastern frontier. Next year (1673) William lost Maestricht, but he more than balanced this disaster by treaties with Spain and the empire. The war now began to turn in his favour. Early in 1674 the French troops evacuated Holland, and in February of the same year peace was made with England in the treaty of Westminster. As the tide turned, William's allies became more active in his behalf. The league of The Hague, the first of those great coalitions by which he sought to set a limit to the aggressions of Louis XIV., was joined by the elector of Brandenburg, who had been obliged a year

[1] For some account of this family, see HOLLAND, vol. xii. pp. 74 and 79 *sq*.

before to come to terms with France, and by several other German princes. In Flanders William himself opposed Condé and fought the indecisive battle of Seneffe (August 1674). For the next two years the war dragged on without very important results. William, although he had saved Holland, could not prevent France from winning places at the expense of the empire and Spain. In April 1677 he was decisively beaten by the duke of Orleans near St Omer. A great part of the Spanish Netherlands as well as Franche Comté was now in the hands of France. These advances caused much alarm in England; and the prince of Orange linked himself closer to that country by marrying Mary, elder daughter of James, duke of York, in November 1677. Early next year William signed a treaty of alliance with England, the object of which was to compel Louis to come to terms. The duplicity of Charles and the attitude of the country party in England, anxious for war with France but unwilling to put an army into the king's hands, prevented this arrangement from taking effect. A fresh treaty was, however, made between the two powers (July), and the pressure thus brought to bear upon Louis led to the peace of Nimeguen (August 1678). Four days after the peace was signed William attacked the French army under the duke of Luxembourg in its entrenchments round Mons. A sanguinary but resultless battle ensued. William attempted to justify this bloodshed by the insufficient and incredible plea that he was not aware that the peace had been signed. He can hardly have wished to prolong the war; but it is not surprising if he was dissatisfied with a peace which gave Franche Comté and many places in the Spanish Netherlands to France.

During the years which immediately followed the peace of Nimeguen, Louis's aggressive proceedings provoked a general uneasiness, of which the prince of Orange made skilful use. The French king had seized on William's ancestral principality of Orange in the south of France. William declared publicly that he would make Louis repent the outrage, and when called on to withdraw his words refused to do so. Personal affront was thus added to the national grounds of his hostility. The second of his coalitions against France began by a treaty between the Netherlands and Sweden (October 1681) for the maintenance of the peace of Nimeguen, which was soon joined by the empire and Spain, and by several of the German states. When, however, Louis declared war on Spain, invaded the Spanish Netherlands, and even took Luxemburg (1683-84), William could not persuade the states-general to raise an army, and the allied powers acquiesced in the truce of Ratisbon, which left the French king in possession of all that he had won (1685). Certain claims on the Palatinate which Louis urged on behalf of his sister-in-law, the duchess of Orleans, gave William an occasion for organizing a further combination against him. In July 1686 the emperor, with the kings of Spain and Sweden, acting as members of the empire, and the most important German princes entered into the league of Augsburg, which, however, William did not himself join.

Meanwhile, as heir presumptive to the English throne, he paid close attention to what was passing in England. He sought to win Charles by sheltering the duke of Monmouth during the exile to which his father had unwillingly condemned him. The same motives led him to dismiss the duke when James II. succeeded his brother, and to discourage the attempt which Monmouth made to win the crown. He also endeavoured to stop Argyll and his friends when they were setting out for England; and he tried to dissuade Monmouth from his rash expedition, and to induce him to take service against the Turks in Hungary, and, when this failed, he sought, with as little success, to prevent his crossing to England. Throughout the whole crisis he showed a scrupulous regard for the interests of his father-in-law, which fortunately coincided with his own; but at the same time he astutely avoided any step which would have alienated from him the constitutional party. When, however, James II. began to show himself in his true colours, William became the head of the opposition in England. As such, he strongly disapproved of the first Declaration of Indulgence (1686) and remonstrated with James on the unconstitutional nature of his act. When the king requested him, a year later, to place Papists instead of Protestants in command of the English regiments then in the service of Holland, he declined to do so, and rejected with equal firmness a demand from James that he should send the troops back to England. Nevertheless he refused to listen to Mordaunt's premature suggestion that he should undertake an invasion in 1686, and, even when Edward Russell visited him at The Hague (May 1688), he was unwilling to move till he was assured that the majority of the nation would be with him. The letter, signed by seven leaders of the two great English parties, which Admiral Herbert carried to Holland (June 30) set his scruples at rest.

On 30th September he issued a declaration in which he recapitulated James's unconstitutional acts, and stated that he was coming to England in order to secure the assembling of a free parliament, by whose decision he was resolved to abide. On 2d November he sailed from Holland, and three days later landed at Torbay. At first only few persons joined him, but presently the gentry began to come in. James, who had massed his troops at Salisbury, was compelled by William's advance and by the desertion of Churchill and others to fall back upon London. Here he attempted to treat with the invader. William, anxious to avoid all appearance of conquest, consented to negotiate, and it was agreed that a parliament should be summoned, both armies meanwhile holding aloof. James, however, attempted to leave the country, but was stopped and returned to Whitehall. For a moment he seemed to contemplate resistance, but William now insisted on his retiring from London. His final flight relieved the prince of a great difficulty. On 19th December William arrived in London, and at once called a meeting of peers and others who had sat in the parliaments of Charles II.'s reign. By their advice he summoned a convention, which met on 22d January 1689 and settled the crown on William and Mary, who, after accepting the Declaration of Rights, were on 13th February proclaimed king and queen.

The revolution had so far succeeded beyond expectation; but William's difficulties had only begun. His primary object was to bring England into the field against France. But he had first to secure his own throne, which was still endangered by resistance in Scotland and Ireland; in order to do it with effect he had to gain the good will of the English parliament and to harmonize or control its two great factions, which, momentarily united by the imminence of despotism, were again almost on the verge of civil war. He wished to be superior to party, which he could only become by being independent of parliament, and this the revolution had rendered impossible. The revolution was due mainly to the Whigs, who were therefore William's natural allies; but the political principles of the Whigs led them to curtail the power of the sovereign. The principles of the Tories were much more to his taste; but the Tories were disinclined to apply their principles on behalf of a sovereign whose title they could not conscientiously acknowledge. In selecting his first ministry William endeavoured to conciliate both sides and to hold the balance even. He eventually saw that such a policy was impracticable, and that, the nation having arrived at its majority, ministers must represent the party which was strongest in parliament. His natural reluctance to recognize this change, or to give up any of the powers which his predecessors had possessed, led to not unfrequent collisions with parliament and exposed him to some humiliation, while the struggle between the two parties at times reduced him to despair, and constantly hampered his action on the Continent.

For nearly a year and a half after William's acceptance of the crown he was occupied in forming the coalition against Louis XIV. known as the Grand Alliance. As stadtholder of the United Netherlands, William had already entered into an alliance with the emperor. In December he joined the league as king of England, and in 1690 the coalition was completed by the adhesion of Spain, Brandenburg, and Savoy. William had thus gained his first great object: he had united Europe against the Bourbon. Meanwhile, however, his arms had made little progress in Scotland and Ireland. James had landed in Ireland in March 1689 and nearly the whole island was in his hands. The relief of Londonderry (July) and the battle of Newtown Butler (August) saved the north for William, but elsewhere Schomberg could make no way. In Scotland the convention had offered the crown to William and Mary; but in the battle of Killiecrankie (July) the clans under Dundee had routed William's army. The convention, which shortly after his accession had been turned into a parliament, met for its second session in the autumn of 1689, and the two parties quarrelled so violently over the Corporation and Indemnity Bills that William threatened to leave the country. He was induced by Nottingham and Shrewsbury to give up this intention, but in January 1690 he dissolved the parliament. William put an end to the quarrel about the indemnity by issuing an Act of Grace, which gave an almost complete amnesty; and, after placing the government in the hands of the queen and a council of nine persons, he left for Ireland. The defeat of the English and Dutch fleets off Beachy Head and the repulse of the allied forces at Fleurus (June and July 1690) were severe blows to William's hopes; but the former led to no important results and the latter was more than balanced by the victory which William won at the battle of the Boyne (1st July 1690). James fled from the country, and William entered Dublin in triumph. In September he returned to England, leaving Marlborough to conquer the south of Ireland in a short but brilliant campaign. Meanwhile the resistance in Scotland had collapsed, and Mackay reduced the Highlands to tranquillity. In 1691 William was able to go abroad and to take the command in Flanders, where, however, his efforts were unsuccessful.

The next year (1692) opened with the massacre of Glencoe. It is improbable that, in signing an order for the "extirpation" of the Macdonalds, he intended that the order should be literally executed. Nevertheless, the order came from him, and he cannot be acquitted of all blame. About the same time the insecurity of his position was shown by the discovery of Marlborough's treachery; and Marlborough did not stand alone. While many whom William trusted or appeared to trust were intriguing with James, an invasion of England was being organized by the French Government. Fortunately, and in great measure owing to the politic conduct of Mary, the commanders of the fleet were induced to stand firm, and the great victory of La Hogue (19th May 1692) put a stop to the projected invasion. But the fortune of war went against William on the Continent. He could not save Namur from the French, and he was severely defeated in an attempt to surprise the duke of Luxembourg at Steenkerke (4th August 1692). Next year he was again beaten by the same commander at Neerwinden (19th July). The battle of La Hogue had not given England the command of the seas, and French privateers inflicted great damage on English trade. In June 1693 the Smyrna fleet was almost entirely destroyed off Cape St Vincent.

In spite of these reverses William struggled on with indomitable courage, and he was well supported by the country. Parliament, under the skilful guidance of Montague, adopted various important financial measures to meet the expenses of the war. The land-tax was re-assessed, the national debt created, the Bank of England established, and the coinage renewed (1693-95). In 1694 William confirmed the parliamentary system by giving his consent, though an unwilling consent, to the Triennial Act, and he recognized the principles of ministerial government by modifying the ministry, until in 1696 it was in thorough harmony with the parliamentary majority. In 1695 William won his first important success on the Continent by recovering Namur, and, though no advance was made by the allies next year, the exhaustion of France was becoming more and more evident. At length, in March 1697, a congress met at Ryswick, and in September peace was made. Louis was obliged to give up all (with the exception of Strasburg) that he had added to his dominions since 1678, and he recognized William as king of England. With the conclusion of the war the dread of a standing army revived in England, and, much to William's disgust, a vote of parliament reduced the military force to 10,000 men, although the question of the Spanish succession (see vol. ix. p. 580) was pending. The new parliament which met early in 1699 reduced the army still further and resolved that it should consist solely of English troops, thus compelling William to dismiss his favourite Dutch guards. They went on to institute an inquiry into the manner in which the forfeited estates in Ireland had been disposed of, and in their second session (November 1699) they passed a bill for the "resumption" of these estates. William died on 8th March 1702 from the consequences of a fall from his horse on 20th February.

Authorities.—Burnet, *History of his own Times*; Voltaire, *Siècle de Louis XIV.*; *Negotiations of the Count d'Avaux* (London, 1754); *Négociations relatives à la Succession d'Espagne*, &c., collected by Mignet (Paris, 1835); *Lettres et Mémoires de Marie, Reine d'Angleterre*, &c. (The Hague, 1880); Harris, *History of the Life and Reign of William III.* (Dublin, 1749); Mackintosh, *History of the Revolution in England*; Macaulay, *History of England*; Ranke, *English History*. (G. W. P.)

WILLIAM IV. (1765-1837), king of England, was the third son of George III. He was born at Windsor, 21st August 1765. When he was fourteen years old he was sent to sea as a midshipman under Admiral Digby. Next year he sailed under Rodney and took part in the action off Cape St Vincent (16th January 1780). During the rest of the war the young prince saw plenty of service, for which he imbibed a strong liking, and so laid the foundation of his popularity. On the conclusion of the war he travelled in Germany, visiting Hanover and Berlin, where he was entertained by Frederick the Great. In 1785 he passed for lieutenant; next year he was made captain and stationed in the West Indies. Shortly after 1787, being tired of his station, he sailed home without orders, and was punished for his insubordination by being obliged to stay at Plymouth till his ship was refitted, when he again sailed for the West Indies.

In 1789 he was made duke of Clarence. When war was declared against the French republic in 1793, he strongly supported it and was anxious for active employment; but, though he was made rear-admiral of the red, he could obtain no command. Thus condemned to inactivity, he amused or revenged himself by joining the prince of Wales and the duke of York in their opposition to the king. He threw himself into the dissipations of society, and his hearty geniality and bluff, sailor-like manners gained him popularity, though they did not secure him respect. He took his seat in the House of Lords, where he defended the extravagancies of the prince of Wales, spoke on the Divorce Bill, vehemently opposed the emancipation of slaves, and defended slavery on the ground of his experience in the West Indies. Meanwhile he formed a connexion with Mrs Jordan, the actress, with whom he lived on terms of mutual affection and fidelity for nearly twenty years, and the union was only broken off eventually for political reasons. During all this period the prince had lived in comparative obscurity. The death of Princess Charlotte in 1817 brought him forward as in the line of succession to the crown. In 1818 he married Adelaide of Saxe-Meiningen, a lady half his age, without special attractions, but of a strong, self-willed nature, which enabled her subsequently to obtain great influence over her husband. On the death of the duke of York in 1827 the duke of Clarence became heir to the throne, and in the same year he was appointed lord high admiral. In discharging the functions of that office he endeavoured to assume independent control of naval affairs, although his patent precluded him from acting without the advice of two members of his council. This involved him in a quarrel with Sir George Cockburn, in which he had to give way. As he still continued to act in defiance of rules, the king was at length obliged to call upon him to resign.

On 28th June 1830 the death of George IV. placed him on the throne. During the first two years of his reign England underwent an agitation more violent than any from which it had suffered since 1688. William IV. was well-meaning and conscientious; but his timidity and irresolution drove ministers to despair, while his anxiety to avoid extremes and his want of insight into affairs prolonged a dangerous crisis and brought the country to the verge of revolution. Immediately after his accession the revolution of July broke out in France and gave a great impulse to the reform movement in England. The king, though he called himself an "old Whig," did not dismiss the Tory ministry which had governed the country during the last two years of his brother's reign; but the elections for the new parliament placed them in a minority. Within a fortnight of the opening of parliament they were beaten on a motion for the reform of the civil list, and resigned. Lord Grey undertook to form a ministry, with the avowed intention of bringing in a large measure of reform. This was not in itself displeasing to the king, who had liberal tendencies, and a few years before had supported Catholic emancipation. But, when the struggle in parliament began, his disinclination to take up a decided attitude soon exposed the Government to difficulties. The first Reform Bill was introduced on 1st March 1831; the second reading was carried on 21st March by a majority of one. Shortly afterwards the Government were beaten in committee, and offered to resign. The king declined to accept their resignation, but at the same time was unwilling to dissolve, although it was obvious that in the existing parliament a ministry pledged to reform could not retain office. From this dilemma William was rescued by the conduct of the opposition, which, anxious to bring on a change of ministry, moved an address against dissolution. Regarding this as an attack on his prerogative, William at once dissolved parliament (April 1831). The elections gave the ministry an overwhelming majority. The second Reform Bill was brought in in June, and passed its third reading (21st September) by a majority of 109. A fortnight later (8th October) the Lords threw out the Bill by a majority of 41. For an account of the subsequent stages of the struggle, see GREY, vol. xi. pp. 191-192.

During the rest of his reign William IV. had not much opportunity of active political interference, but on one other occasion he made an unjustifiable use of his prerogative. Two years after the passing of the Reform Bill the ministry of Lord Grey had become unpopular. In July 1834 Lord Grey himself retired and Lord Melbourne took the lead. There were divergences of opinion in the cabinet, and the king strongly objected to the ministerial policy respecting the Irish Church. On the shallow pretext that Lord Althorp's removal to the Upper House would weaken the ministry in the House of Commons, where, however, they still had a majority, he suddenly dismissed them and summoned Sir Robert Peel (14th November). Peel's ministry, containing many members who had been in the government on the king's accession, was called from its short duration "the ministry of the hundred days." Its formation clearly indicated that the Whig proclivities of the king, which had never been more than partial or lukewarm, had wholly disappeared. The step was regarded with general disapprobation. It was immediately followed by a dissolution, and the ministry soon found themselves in a minority. Beaten on Lord John Russell's motion respecting the Irish Church (3d April 1835), Peel resigned and Melbourne again came into power. Under him the Whigs retained the lead during the remainder of the reign. This *coup d'état* of November 1834 was the last occasion on which the English sovereign has attempted to impose an unpopular ministry on the majority in parliament.

In May 1837 the king began to show signs of debility, and died from an affection of the heart on the 20th of June, leaving behind him the memory of a genial, frank, warm-hearted man, but a blundering, though well-intentioned prince. He was succeeded by his niece Victoria.

Authorities.—Correspondence of Earl Grey with William IV. and Sir Herbert Taylor, London, 1867; Fitzgerald's *Life and Times of William IV.*; Greville's *Memoirs*; *Memoirs* of Sir Robert Peel; *Civil Correspondence of the Duke of Wellington*; Walpole's *History of England*; Martineau's *History of the Peace*; Molesworth's *History of England*. (G. W. P.)

WILLIAM, surnamed the LION, king of Scotland from 1165 to 1214. See SCOTLAND, vol. xxi. p. 484.

WILLIAM I. (1797-1888), king of Prussia and German emperor, was the second son of Frederick William III. of Prussia and Louisa, a princess of Mecklenburg-Strelitz. He was born at Berlin on 22d March 1797, and received the names of Wilhelm Friedrich Ludwig. He was a delicate child and had to be carefully nurtured. His constitution, however, was sound, and he became one of the most vigorous men in Germany. After the battle of Jena he spent three years at Königsberg and Memel. Meanwhile he had given evidence of sterling honesty, a strict love of order, and an almost passionate interest in everything relating to war. On 1st January 1807 he received an officer's patent, and on 30th October 1813 was appointed a captain. William accompanied his father in the campaign of 1814, and early in the following year received the iron cross for personal bravery shown at Bar-sur-Aube. He took part in the entry into Paris on 31st March 1814, and afterwards visited London. He joined the Prussian army in the final campaign of the Napoleonic wars, and again entered Paris. The prince was made a colonel and a member of the permanent military commission immediately after his twentieth birthday, and at the age of twenty-one became a major-general. In 1820 he received the command of a division; and during the following nine years he not only made himself master of the military system of his own country but studied closely those of the other European states. In 1825 he was promoted to the rank of lieutenant-general, and obtained the command of the corps of guards. On 11th June 1829 he married Augusta of Saxe-Weimar.

On the death of his father in 1840—the new king, Frederick William IV., being childless—Prince William, as heir presumptive to the throne, received the title of prince of Prussia. He was also made lieutenant-governor of Pomerania and appointed a general of infantry. In politics he was decidedly Conservative; but at the outbreak of the revolutionary movement of 1848 he saw that some concessions to the popular demand for liberal forms of government were necessary. He urged, however, that order should be restored before the establishment of a constitutional system. At this time he was the best-hated man in Germany, the mass of the Prussian people believing him to be a vehement supporter of an absolutist and reactionary policy. He was even held responsible for the blood shed in Berlin on 18th March, although he had been relieved nine days before of his command of the guards. So bitter was the feeling against him that the king entreated him to leave the country for some time, and accordingly he went to London, where he formed intimate personal relations with Prince Albert, Sir Robert Peel, Lord John Russell, Lord Palmerston, and other English statesmen. On 8th June he was back at Berlin, and on the same day he took his seat as member for Wirsitz in the Prussian national assembly, and delivered a speech in which he expressed belief in constitutional principles. In 1849, when the revolutionary party in the grand-duchy of Baden became dangerous, he accepted the command of "the army of operation in Baden and the Palatinate," and his plans were so judiciously formed and so skilfully executed that in the course of a few days the rebellion was crushed. At the beginning of the campaign an unsuccessful attempt was made on his life. In October 1849 he was appointed military governor of the Rhineland and Westphalia, and took up his residence at Coblentz. In 1854 the prince was raised to the rank of a field-marshal and made governor of the confederate fortress of Mainz. When the king was attacked with a disease of the brain, Prince William assumed the regency (7th October 1858).

On 2d January 1861 Frederick William IV. died, and his brother succeeded him as William I. For the internal conflict between the king and the house of representatives on the question of military reorganization, which filled up the first years of his reign, see GERMANY (vol. x. p. 510) and PRUSSIA (vol. xx. p. 12). The events and results of the war with Denmark, and of that with Austria which arose out of the Schleswig-Holstein question, belong to the history of Austria and of Prussia, and have been already described under those articles. The brilliant achievements of the army in this last contest finally convinced the king's subjects that his aims had been wise. On his return to Berlin he was received with unbounded enthusiasm, and from this time he was looked up to as a father rather than as a sovereign. On the outbreak of the war with France in 1870 all Germans rallied round the king of Prussia, and, when on 31st July he quitted Berlin to join his army, he knew that he had the support of a united nation. He crossed the French frontier on the 11th of August, and personally commanded at the battles of Gravelotte and Sedan. It was during the siege of Paris, at his headquarters in Versailles, that he was proclaimed German emperor on 18th January 1871. On 3d March 1871 he signed the preliminaries of peace which had been accepted by the French assembly; and on 21st March he opened the first imperial parliament of Germany. On 16th June he triumphantly entered Berlin at the head of his troops.

After that period the emperor left the destinies of Germany almost entirely in the hands of Bismarck, who held the office of imperial chancellor (see PRUSSIA). In his personal history the most notable events were two attempts upon his life in 1878,—one by a working lad called Hödel, another by an educated man, Karl Nobiling. On the first occasion the emperor escaped without injury, but on the second he was seriously wounded. These attacks grew out of the socialist agitation; and a new reichstag, elected for the purpose, passed a severe anti-socialist law, which was afterwards from time to time renewed. The socialists, however, far from being crushed, again and again gave proof of their power by returning a considerable number of deputies to parliament. In the hope of alienating from them the mass of the working class, Bismarck introduced, with the cordial approval of the emperor, a series of measures for the benefit of the poorer members of the community. Until within a few days of his death the emperor's health was remarkably robust; he died at Berlin on 9th March 1888.

The reign of William I. marked an era of vast importance in the history of Germany. In his time Prussia became the first power in Germany and Germany the first power in Europe. These momentous changes were due in a less degree to him than to Bismarck and Moltke; but to him belongs the credit of having recognized the genius of these men, and of having trusted them absolutely. Personally William was a man of a singularly noble and attractive character. His supreme wish was to discharge loyally the duties which had been imposed upon him, and he never shrank from any personal sacrifice that seemed to be demanded in the interests of his people. The best traditions of the Hohenzollerns were maintained, not only by the splendour of the achievements with which his name will always be intimately associated, but by the simplicity, manliness, and uprightness of his daily life.

WILLIAM IV. (1532-1592), landgrave of Hesse, well known as an astronomer, son of Philip the Magnanimous, was born at Cassel on 14th June 1532. During his father's captivity after the battle of Mühlberg (1547) he carried on the government in his name for five years, and succeeded him on his death in 1567. At an early age he became interested in astronomy; and in 1561 he built an observatory at Cassel, where observations were regularly made, first by himself, afterwards by Rothmann and Bürgi. The last-named was not only a very skilful mechanic (it seems probable that he applied the pendulum to clocks long before Huygens did) but an original mathematician, who independently invented logarithms. William died on 25th August 1592.

Most of the mechanical contrivances which made Tycho Brahe's instruments so superior to those of his contemporaries were adopted at Cassel about 1584, and from that time the observations made there seem to have been about as accurate as Tycho's; but the resulting longitudes were 6′ too great in consequence of the adopted solar parallax of 3′. The principal fruit of the observations was a catalogue of about a thousand stars, the places of which were determined by the methods usually employed in the 16th century, connecting a fundamental star by means of Venus with the sun, and thus finding its longitude and latitude, while other stars could at any time he referred to the fundamental star. It should be noticed that clocks (on which Tycho Brahe depended very little) were used at Cassel for finding the difference of right ascension between Venus and the sun before sunset; Tycho preferred observing the angular distance between the sun and Venus when the latter was visible in the day time. The Hessian star catalogue was published in Lucius Barettus's *Historia Cœlestis* (Augsburg, 1668), and a number of other observations are to be found in *Cœli et Siderum in eo Errantium Observationes Hassiacæ*, Leyden, 1618, edited by SNELLIUS (*q.v.*). R. Wolf, in his "Astronomische Mittheilungen," No. 45 (*Vierteljahrsschrift d. naturforschenden Gesellschaft in Zürich*, 1878), has given a résumé of the manuscripts still preserved at Cassel, which throw much light on the methods adopted in the observations and reductions.

WILLIAM (1533-1584), surnamed the SILENT, prince of Orange, count of Nassau, was born at the castle of Dillenburg in Nassau on 16th April 1533. He was the eldest son of William of Nassau (died 1559) and his second wife, Juliana of Stolberg, a woman of remarkable piety and discretion, who devoted much thought and care to the training of her children. In 1544 he inherited from his cousin René or Renatus the principality of Orange and the great estates belonging to his family in the Netherlands (see HOLLAND, vol. xii. p. 74 *sq.*). He was educated at the court of Brussels in the Roman Catholic faith. Having attracted the attention of Charles V., he was invested by the emperor at the age of twenty-two with the command of the army on the French frontier; and it was on his shoulder that Charles V. leaned when in 1555, in the presence of a great assembly at Brussels, he transferred to his son Philip the sovereignty of the Netherlands. Orange was also selected to carry the insignia of the empire to Ferdinand, king of the Romans, when Charles resigned the imperial crown. He took part in Philip II.'s first war with France, and negotiated the preliminary arrangements for the treaty of Cateau-Cambrésis (1559). He was one of the hostages sent to France for the due execution of the treaty, and during his stay in that country Henry II., who entirely misunderstood his character, revealed to him a plan for the massacre of all Protestants in France and the Netherlands. The prince was horrified by this disclosure, but said nothing; and it was on account of his extraordinary discretion on this occasion that he received the surname of "the Silent." The epithet is apt to convey a mistaken impression as to his general character. He was of a frank, open, and generous nature, without a touch of moroseness in the ordinary intercourse of life.

The persecution of the Protestants in the Netherlands, carried on with such reckless ferocity by Cardinal Granvella, led Orange, Egmont, and Horn, the most prominent of the great nobles, to protest against the violence of the Government; and in 1563 they wrote to Philip urging him to withdraw Granvella, and ceased to attend the state council. In the following year Granvella was displaced, whereupon they resumed their seats at the council; yet shortly afterwards it was decided by Philip that the canons of the Council of Trent, the edicts, and the Inquisition should be immediately promulgated in every town and village of the provinces, and that the process should be repeated every six months. At the meeting of the state council at which this was formally decided Orange disclaimed any responsibility for the consequences, and he whispered to his neighbour that now the most extraordinary tragedy the world had ever seen was about to begin. The proceedings of the Gueux or reforming party so alarmed the regent, Margaret of Parma, that she was persuaded to sign an accord, declaring the abolition of the Inquisition and granting liberty of worship in all places where the new forms of religion had been already accepted. In consequence of these concessions the great nobles undertook to restore order, the prince of Orange especially distinguishing himself at Antwerp. But Philip, who had been longing for an excuse to crush the independent spirits of the Netherlanders, now resolved to send the duke of Alva into the country, with a Spanish force. Orange, since he could not count upon the hearty support of Egmont or Horn, had no alternative but to resign his offices and withdraw from the Netherlands (1567), taking up his residence at Dillenburg. He was warmly attached to Egmont, and before his departure, at an interview at Willebroeck, urged him to seek refuge in some foreign land; but Egmont was not to be persuaded, and the two friends parted never to see one another again.

Orange was repeatedly summoned to Brussels; but he declined to appear before the Council of Disturbances, on the ground that it had no jurisdiction over an independent prince and a knight of the order of the Fleece. The havoc wrought by Alva filled him with grief and anger; and in 1568 he contrived to collect two forces, one of which, commanded by his brothers Louis and Adolphus, gained a victory in Groningen, where Adolphus fell. Alva, having ordered the execution of Egmont and Horn, advanced against Louis and defeated him in East Friesland. Orange then invaded Brabant, but could neither bring Alva to a decisive engagement nor induce the people to rise against him. The army had therefore to be disbanded, and its disappointed leader joined Wolfgang of Zweibrücken in an attempt to aid the Huguenots. Acting on the advice of Coligny, Orange issued letters of mark to seamen against the Spaniards; and for years the "sea beggars" harassed the enemy along the coast, and often did no little harm to their own countrymen. In 1572 the revolt against Spain was so far successful that Orange resumed the functions of stadtholder of Holland and Zealand, a position to which he had been appointed in 1559; but he professed to rule in the name of the king, for as yet the people had no wish to throw off their allegiance to the Spanish crown. Orange had won their confidence not only by acting as their champion but by accepting the Protestant faith. He had never been an enthusiastic Catholic, and as a Protestant he was distinguished among the eminent men of his time by his mastery of the true principles of toleration. Meanwhile he had been using the utmost diligence in bringing together an army, and his brother Louis, by a brilliant stroke, had captured the city of Mons. On 15th July 1572 the estates of Holland met at Dort, and, recognizing Orange as the legal stadtholder of Holland, Zealand, Friesland, and Utrecht, voted the sums necessary for the prosecution of the war. In August he crossed the Meuse at the head of an army, trusting mainly to the promised co-operation of France. All his hopes, however, were shattered by the massacre of St Bartholomew. He was obliged to disband his troops, and Mons was re-taken by the Spaniards. On 14th April 1574, at the village of Mook, near Nimeguen, the patriots were again routed, and Orange's brothers, Louis and Henry, slain. But many fortified places held out, and on 3d October Orange, who had ordered the country to be inundated, was able to relieve Leyden, which had for months been defended with splendid bravery and self-sacrifice. At length the brutality and despotism of the Spaniards were so fiercely and generally resented that Orange was able to enter upon a series of negotiations, which resulted on 8th November 1576 in the pacification of Ghent, signed on behalf of nearly all the provinces. By this treaty the provinces bound themselves to drive the Spaniards from the Netherlands, to convoke the states-general, and to establish freedom of worship both for Roman Catholics and for Protestants.

Don John of Austria, Spanish regent of the Netherlands (1576-78), granted all the demands of the states; but Orange was suspicious of the intentions of the Government, and in no way relaxed his vigilance. Troubles soon broke out, and Orange was called to Brussels to the aid of the states, being elected *ruwaard* (governor) of Brabant. When the archduke Matthias (afterwards emperor) was invited by the Catholic nobles to accept the position of governor-general, Orange prudently refrained from resisting the scheme; and he acted with equal discretion in regard to the duke of Alençon, who came nominally as the protector of the liberties of the Netherlands. Orange, however, retained in his own hands complete control over the movement in the seven northern provinces, which by the Union of Utrecht, signed on behalf of five of the provinces on 23d January 1579, laid the foundations of the commonwealth of the United Netherlands. Orange's relation to the new federal republic was somewhat vaguely defined; but in his lifetime it was not felt that there was any very urgent need for an exact delimitation of the relative functions of the executive and the legislative authorities. Negotiations for the conclusion of peace with Spain were carried on for some time in vain; and in 1580 Philip issued a ban against the prince, and set a price of 25,000 gold crowns upon his head. Orange published a vigorous "apology," and on 26th July 1581 the estates of the United Provinces formally renounced their allegiance to the Spanish crown. An unsuccessful attempt on the life of Orange was made in 1582. But on 10th July 1584 he was shot dead in his house at Delft by Balthazar Gerard, who seems to have been actuated in part by fanaticism, in part by the hope of gain.

William of Orange was tall and well-formed, of a dark complexion, with brown hair and eyes. He was a man of a singularly upright and noble character. He has been charged with excessive ambition; but his ruling motive was undoubtedly a love of justice, for the sake of which he often risked his life and willingly sacrificed his wealth and leisure. He was a born statesman, capable of forming wise and far-reaching plans, and of modifying them to suit the changing circumstances in which it was necessary to execute them. In moments of difficulty he displayed splendid resource and courage, and he had a will of iron, which misfortunes were never able either to bend or to break. To him chiefly belongs the honour of having permanently crippled the tyrannical power of Spain, and of having founded the independence and greatness of the United Provinces.

He was married four times. His wives were (1) Anne of Egmont (died 1558), by whom he had a daughter and a son, Philip William, who was seized by Alva in 1567 and sent to the court at Madrid, where he was educated; (2) Anne of Saxony (divorced in 1575, died in 1577), the mother of several daughters and of Maurice of Orange (see HOLLAND, vol. xii. p. 77); (3) Charlotte of Bourbon (died 1582), who had six daughters; (4) Louisa, Coligny's daughter, the mother of Frederick Henry of Orange (*loc. cit.*, p. 79), who represented the family after the death of his two elder brothers, and succeeded Maurice as stadtholder.

See Schiller, *Geschichte des Abfalls der Vereinigten Niederlande*; Klose, *Wilhelm I. von Oranien*; Gachard, *Correspondance de Guillaume le Taciturne* and *Correspondance de Philippe II. sur les Affaires des Pays-Bas*; Groen van Prinsterer, *Archives ou Correspondance Inédite de la Maison d'Orange-Nassau*; Juste, *Guillaume le Taciturne d'après sa Correspondance et les Papiers d'État*; Motley, *The Rise of the Dutch Republic*. (J. SI.)

WILLIAM of Holland, second count of the name, was born about 1227, succeeded his brother Floris IV. in 1235, and was chosen king of the Romans by the papal party in 1247. See GERMANY, vol. x. p. 491, and HOLLAND, vol. xii. p. 71. He died on 28th January 1256.

WILLIAM I., king of the Netherlands from 1815 to 1840, was born at The Hague on 24th August 1772, and died at Berlin on 7th November 1843. His son, WILLIAM II. (1792-1849), reigned from 1840, and was in turn succeeded by his son, WILLIAM III. (born 1817). See HOLLAND, vol. xii. p. 83.

WILLIAM, archbishop of Tyre, was doubtless a native of the Holy Land. He was perhaps born about 1137; but this is a mere inference from his own statement that he was still pursuing his studies "across the seas" when Amalric came to the throne (17th February 1163), and did not return till late in 1166 or early in 1167. As a child he had seen Ralph, the patriarch of Antioch, who died about 1141-42; he remembered the fall of Edessa (December 1144); and he seems to call himself a contemporary historian from the accession of Baldwin III., an event which he dates 10th November 1142 (*Hist. Rer. Transmarin.*, xvi., pref., and xix. 4, 12). Unfortunately the chapter (xix. 12) which relates to his own early life has been excised or omitted from every MS. of his great work now extant,—a remark which holds good, not only for the original Latin, but also for the 13th-century French translation. William was appointed archdeacon of Tyre at the request of Amalric on 31st August 1167. Next summer he was despatched on an embassy to the emperor Manuel. At the time of the disastrous campaign against Damietta (October–December 1169) he had to take refuge at Rome from the "unmerited anger" of his archbishop. About 1170 he was appointed tutor to Amalric's son Baldwin, afterwards Baldwin IV. A very few months after Baldwin's accession William was made chancellor of the kingdom (*c.* October 1174), and less than a year later (13th June 1175) was consecrated archbishop of Tyre. The former office he still held in 1182. He belonged to the commission which negotiated with Philip of Flanders in 1177; and in the following October (1178) he was one of six bishops sent to represent the Latin Church of the East at the Lateran Council (19th March 1179). He returned home by way of Constantinople, where he stayed seven months (October 1179–April 1180) with Manuel. This is his last authentic appearance in history; but we know from his own works that he was writing his *History* in 1182 (xix. 20), and that it breaks off abruptly at the end of 1183 or the beginning of 1184. Some fifty years later his first continuator accused Heraclius, patriarch of Jerusalem, of having procured William's death at Rome. This story, however, seems to be pure legend; nor perhaps is much more credit to be attached to the theory that identifies him with the archbishop of Tyre sent over to Europe to preach a new crusade in 1188. It is true that Matthew Paris speaks of Henry II.'s receiving the cross from the hands of "Willelmus episcopus Tyrensis"; but more contemporary writers omit the Christian name, while others write it Josce or Joscius.

If not the greatest, William of Tyre is at least among the greatest, of mediæval historians. His *Historia Rerum in Partibus Transmarinis Gestarum* is the main authority for the Latin kingdom of the East between 1127, where Fulcher of Chartres leaves off, and 1184, where Ernoul takes up the narrative. It was translated into French in the 13th century, or possibly before the end of the 12th. A little later it was united to Ernoul's chronicle or that of Bernard the Treasurer, and continued in more than one form to 1249, 1261, or 1275. In this shape the combined histories form the *Livre d'Outremer* quoted by Joinville (cxvii. § 77),—the standard mediæval account of the exploits of the Frankish warriors in the East. William's own work consists of twenty-two books and a fragment (one chapter and a preface) of book xxiii. It extends from the preaching of the first crusade by Peter the Hermit and Urban II. to the end of 1183 or the beginning of 1184. Like William's other work, the *Historia de Orientalibus Principibus*, it was undertaken at the request of Amalric, who was himself a lover of history and supplied the author with Arabic MSS.; but, whereas the latter book (now unfortunately lost) was mainly based upon the writings of a certain "Seith, the son of Patrick (*Patricii*), patriarch of Alexandria," of the *Historia Transmarina* its author remarks, "In this work we have had no guide, whether Greek or Arab, but have had recourse to traditions only, save as regards a few things that we have ourselves seen." The "traditions" here spoken of must be taken to include the *Gesta Francorum* of Tudebode, Raymund of Agiles, Fulcher of Chartres, and, above all, Albert of Aix. It is only with the accession of Baldwin I., even if so early as this, that William's claim to originality can fairly be sustained; and even here his narrative, till towards the close of book xiii., is based upon that of Fulcher. From this point William of Tyre is indebted to no other historian. Of the remaining books two are devoted to the reign of Fulk (xiv.-xv.), three to that of Baldwin III. (xvi.-xviii.), two to that of Amalric, and the rest to that of Baldwin IV.

No mediæval writer, except perhaps Giraldus Cambrensis, possesses William's power of delineating the physical and mental features of his heroes. Again, very few had his instinctive insight into what would be of real value to future ages: genealogy, topography, archæology, social life (political and ecclesiastical), military matters and naval, all find a due exposition in his pages. It is hardly too much to say that from his work alone a fairly detailed map of the Levant, as it was in the 12th century, might be constructed; and it is impossible to praise too highly the scrupulous fidelity with which he defines nearly all the technical terms (whether relating to land or sea) of which he makes use. His chief fault is in the matter of chronology, where indeed he is not unfrequently at discord with himself. In the later books his information, even as regards what was taking place beyond the Nile or the Euphrates, as well as in Europe, is singularly exact. Nor did he consider any trouble too severe if by its means he might attain to the truth. Though a man of great learning and almost certainly acquainted with Arabic and Greek, he is as ready to enliven his pages with a country proverb as to embellish them with quotations from Cicero, Virgil, Ovid, or Plato. He was a prelate of pious character, inclined to see the judgment of God on the iniquities of his fellow-countrymen in every disaster that overtook his native land and every Saracen success.

WILLIAM OF CHAMPEAUX. See SCHOLASTICISM, vol. xxi. pp. 422-423.

WILLIAM OF LORRIS, the first author of the *Roman de la Rose*, derives his surname from a small town about equidistant from Montargis and Gien, in the old district of the Gâtinais, and in the present department of Loiret. This and the fact of his authorship may be said to be the only things positively known about him. The rubric of the poem, where his own part finishes, attributes Jean de Meung's continuation to a period forty years later than William's death and the consequent interruption of the romance. Arguing backwards, this death used to be put at about 1260; but Jean de Meung's own work has recently been dated earlier, and so the composition of the first part has been thrown back to a period before 1240. The author represents himself as having dreamed the dream which furnished the substance of the poem in his twentieth year, and as having set to work to "rhyme it" five years later. The general characteristics of the *Roman* will be found noticed under France (see vol. ix. p. 643). It may be added here that, though the later and longer part shows signs of greater intellectual vigour and wider knowledge than the earlier and shorter, William of Lorris has more poetry than his continuator, made a much greater impression on the spirit of his own and following ages, and is to all appearance more original. The great features of his four or five thousand lines are, in the first place, the extraordinary vividness and beauty of his word-pictures, in which for colour, freshness, and individuality he has not many rivals except in the greatest masters, and, secondly, the fashion of allegorical presentation, which, hackneyed and wearisome as it afterwards became, was evidently in his time new and striking. There are of course traces of it before, as in some romances, such as those of Raoul de Houdenc, in the troubadours, and in other writers; but it was unquestionably William of Lorris who fixed the style. And to have fixed a style which captivated Europe for at least two centuries, if not three, does not happen to many of the personages of literary history.

The most convenient edition of the *Roman de la Rose* is that of F. Michel (2 vols., Paris, 1864).

WILLIAM of Malmesbury. See Malmesbury, William of.

WILLIAM of Newburgh, born about 1136, was a canon of Newburgh in the North Riding of Yorkshire, and author of a valuable chronicle of English affairs from the Norman Conquest to 1197. He calls himself Gulielmus Parvus, and is frequently referred to as William Petyt or Little. His work (*Gulielmi Neubrigensis Rerum Anglicarum Libri V.*) was edited by Silvius at Antwerp in 1567 and by Hearne at Oxford in 1719 (3 vols. 8vo); the latest edition is that by H. C. Hamilton for the English Historical Society (*Historia Rerum Anglicarum Willelmi Parvi, S.T.D.*, Ordinis Sancti Augustini Canonici Regularis in Cœnobio B. Mariæ de Novoburgo in Agro Eboracensi, 2 vols., 1856).

WILLIAM of Occam. See Occam.

WILLIAM of Wykeham (1324-1404), bishop of Winchester and chancellor of England, was born in 1324 at Wickham in Hampshire. His father was a yeoman; his mother is said to have been of noble descent. He was educated at the priory school, Winchester, at the cost of Sir John Scures, lord of the manor of Wickham and governor of Winchester Castle, who afterwards took him into his service. When he was twenty-two years old he passed into the service of Edingdon, bishop of Winchester. In 1347 the bishop introduced him to the king as a young man likely to be useful from his skill in architecture. Edward III., who was then completing the Round Tower at Windsor, made him his chaplain. But his employment for some time was mainly secular: he acted as guardian of several of the king's manors and as clerk of the works at Henley and elsewhere. In 1356 he was appointed surveyor of the works at Windsor, and a little later surveyor and warden of several other castles. In 1359 he began the building of the great quadrangle to the east of the keep at Windsor, a work which occupied ten years. This building established his fame as an architect. Two years after its completion he was employed to build Queenborough Castle (Kent). Meanwhile he was also gaining experience in affairs of state. In 1360 he must have been a member of the king's council, for he appears as a witness to the ratification of the treaty of Brétigny. In 1364 he became keeper of the privy seal. In 1365 he was one of the commissioners to treat for peace with Scotland. And, although he was not yet in holy orders, he was loaded by the king with preferments, one of which, the living of Pulham in Norfolk, involved him (about 1360) in a dispute with the pope. In fact he had attained to such eminence that Froissart says, "At this time there reigned in England a priest called Sir William de Wican, so much in favour with the king that by him everything was done."

Early in life William had received the tonsure; but it was not till 1362 that he was ordained deacon and priest. In 1363 he became archdeacon of Northampton, and provost and prebendary of Wells. Although at this time he possessed a number of prebends, it appears, from a return which he made in 1366 on account of a papal bull against pluralities, that he only held one benefice with cure of souls. On the translation of Bishop Edingdon in this year from Winchester to Canterbury William was nominated by the king to the vacant bishopric; but the pope withheld his confirmation for some time, and it was not till October 1367 that William was consecrated bishop of Winchester. A month previously he had been made chancellor of England. During his first chancellorship the war with France was renewed and went against the English. The blame for this fell in great measure on the ministry, and in 1371 William resigned the great seal. But in 1373 he was one of a committee of the Lords appointed to confer with the Commons on the question of an aid. About this time he fell out with John of Gaunt, with whom he had previously been on good terms. Since the overthrow of the clerical ministry in 1371 John of Gaunt had been practically head of the government, but the conduct of his supporters caused general discontent. In the "Good Parliament" of 1376 Lord Latimer was impeached, and the bishop was active in promoting his trial and punishment. This was a great blow to John of Gaunt. The death of the Black Prince in June 1376 enabled him to take his revenge. The bishop was attacked in the council on the ground of malversation and misconduct of public affairs during his chancellorship, condemned to pay an enormous fine, and deprived of the temporalities of his see. The other bishops took his side and regarded his punishment as an insult to their order. It was not, however, till after the accession of Richard II. (1377) that William recovered his position. He then received a full pardon, and was reconciled to John of Gaunt.

During the next ten years he became more and more clearly identified with the constitutional or Lancastrian party. In 1380 and 1381 he was named on commissions for the reform of the king's household. In 1382 he took part in a conference with the Commons. Next year he successfully opposed a demand from the lords of the Scottish marches for a share in the public funds in order to defray the expense of guarding the border, a duty on the performance of which rested their title to their lands. In 1386 he became one of the commission appointed to examine into the Exchequer and to act as a sort of council of regency. It was before this commission that the five "lords appellant" impeached Richard II.'s favourites, who next year were condemned by the "Merciless Parliament." A year later (1389) the king suddenly resumed the reins of power. In order, apparently, to conciliate the clergy, Richard at once offered the great seal to the bishop of Winchester, who after some hesitation accepted the charge. His second chancellorship lasted for two years, and was marked by efforts on his part to reform the government and place it on a more constitutional basis. After he had held office for a year he and his colleagues in the ministry resigned their appointments, and challenged a public inquiry into their conduct. This being pronounced satisfactory, they resumed their offices. The chancellor drew up rules for the conduct of business in the council; and from this time minutes of the proceedings were regularly kept. In 1391 he resigned the great seal, and thenceforward retired from public life.

It is, however, as the founder of two great colleges that William is principally known to fame. Immediately after his promotion to the bishopric of Winchester he appears to have begun to carry out his educational schemes. Between 1369 and 1379 he bought the land enclosed in the north-eastern corner of the city walls at Oxford on which New College now stands (see OXFORD, vol. xviii. p. 97). Meanwhile he was taking steps to establish the sister foundation at Winchester. In 1378 he obtained a licence from the pope to found a college there, which was confirmed by the king four years later. The ground on which Winchester College stands belonged partly to the bishop and partly to other proprietors, from whom he bought it. In 1387 he began to build, and the buildings were occupied by his scholars in 1393, though they do not appear to have been finished till 1395. When his two colleges were established and endowed, he provided them with statutes, which after several revisions took their final form in 1400. Nor does he appear to have neglected his duties as a bishop. He visited and reformed the hospital of St Cross near Winchester; he corrected the abuses which had crept into the priory of St Swithin; and he rebuilt or transformed the nave of Winchester cathedral. He kept a strict watch on the clergy under his charge, endeavouring to ensure their efficiency by frequently moving them from one living to another, and he promoted the material prosperity of his diocese by repairs of bridges and roads. In the relations between England and the papacy William of Wykeham strongly supported the nationalist policy of Edward III. The Statutes of Provisors and Præmunire met with his full approval. So far he was in accord with Wycliffe, but he showed no sympathy with the doctrinal opinions of the reformer. Bishop Courtenay, who headed the attack on Wycliffe, was a life-long friend of the bishop of Winchester, who published in 1382 the interdict condemning Wycliffe's heresies, and in 1392 sat on an episcopal commission to try his follower Henry Crumpe. William of Wykeham died at Waltham on 27th September 1404, and was buried in the cathedral of Winchester.

Authorities.—The episcopal register of William of Wykeham (preserved at Winchester); Walsingham, *Historia Anglicana*; Lowth, *Life of William of Wykeham*, London, 1758; Walcott, *William of Wykeham and his Colleges*, 1852; Moberly, *Life of William of Wykeham*, Winchester, 1887. (G. W. P.)

WILLIAMS, JOHN (1796-1839), English missionary, was born at Tottenham near London, on 29th June 1796. He was trained as an ironmonger, and acquired while young considerable experience in mechanical work. Having offered himself to the London Missionary Society, he was sent, after some training, in 1816 to the South Sea Islands as a missionary. He was first stationed at Eimeo, in the Society Islands, where he rapidly acquired a knowledge of the native language. After staying there for a short time, he finally settled at Raiatea, which became his permanent headquarters. His success as a missionary here and elsewhere was remarkable. The people rapidly became Christianized and adopted many of the habits of civilization. Williams was fairly liberal for his age, and the results of his labours among the Pacific Islands were essentially beneficial. He travelled unceasingly among the various island groups, planting stations and settling native missionaries whom he himself had trained. From the Society Islands he visited the Hervey group, where he discovered, and stayed for a considerable time on, the island of Rarotonga. Most of the inhabitants of the group were converted in a remarkably short time, and Williams's influence over them, as over the people of other groups, was very great. Besides establishing Christianity and civilization among them, he also, at their own request, helped them to draw up a code of laws for civil administration upon the basis of the new religion. While at Rarotonga he, with the help of the natives, built himself a ship, within about four months; with this he returned to Raiatea, and made voyages among other island groups, including Samoa and the neighbouring islands. Williams returned to England in 1834 (having previously visited New South Wales in 1821); and during his four years' stay at home he had the New Testament, which he had translated into Rarotongan, printed. Returning in 1838 to the Pacific, he visited the stations already established by him, as well as several fresh groups. He went as far west as the New Hebrides, and, while visiting Erromango, one of the group, for the first time, was murdered by the natives, 20th November 1839.

Williams was probably on the whole one of the most successful of Christian missionaries, both as regards the extent and the permanence of the work he accomplished. His *Narrative of Missionary Enterprises in the South Sea Islands* was published in 1837, and formed an important contribution to our knowledge of the islands with which Williams was acquainted. See *Memoir of John Williams*, by Rev. Ebenezer Prout, London, 1843.

WILLIAMS, ROGER (*c.* 1600–*c.* 1684), one of the founders of the colony of Rhode Island, North America, was born either of Welsh or Cornish parents, but this as well as the date of his birth has been the subject of dispute. In early life he went to London, where his skill as a reporter commended him to the notice of Sir Edward Coke, who sent him to Sutton's Hospital (Charterhouse school). From Charterhouse he went to one of the universities, but whether to Oxford or Cambridge there is no direct evidence to show. The register of Jesus College, Oxford, has the following entry under date 30th April 1624: "Rodericus Williams, filius Gulielmi Williams, de Conwelgaio Pleb., an. Nat. 18." If this entry refers to the founder of Rhode Island he was of Welsh parentage and born about 1606. As Coke was a Cambridge student, the probability is, however, that Williams was sent there; and a Roger Williams matriculated at Pembroke College of that university on 1st July 1625, and took his B.A. degree in January 1627. This Roger Williams was the second son of William Williams, and was baptized at Gwinsea, Cornwall, on 24th July 1600, a date which corresponds with a statement regarding his age made by Williams himself. After leaving the university he entered on the study of law; but, soon forsaking it for theology, he was admitted into holy orders and is said to have had a parochial charge. On account of his Puritan beliefs he left England for Massachusetts Bay, where he arrived in the beginning of 1631. He accepted an invitation to become pastor of a church at Salem, on 12th April 1631, the same day that the magistrates were assembled at Boston to express disapproval of the scheme. To escape persecution he went to Plymouth, beyond the jurisdiction of Massachusetts Bay, and became assistant pastor there, but in the autumn of 1633 he returned to Salem as assistant pastor, succeeding in the following year as sole pastor. Chiefly on account of his pronounced opinions regarding the restricted sphere of the civil magistrate in religious matters, he came into conflict with the court of Massachusetts, and, being banished from the colony, left with a few sympathizers in January 1636 for Narragansett Bay. At first they received a grant of land from an Indian chief, which is now included in Seekonk, Massachusetts, and began to build houses, but in June following he and five others embarked in a canoe for Rhode Island, and founded a settlement to which Williams, in remembrance "of God's providence to him in his distress," gave the name of Providence. In 1639 he was publicly immersed and became pastor of the first Baptist church of Providence. As Massachusetts now began to claim jurisdiction over Narragansett Bay, Williams proceeded in June 1643 to England, and through the mediation of his friend Sir Henry Vane, whose acquaintance he had made at Massachusetts, obtained an independent charter, 14th March 1644. In 1649 he was chosen deputy president. He again visited England in 1651 to obtain a more explicit charter, and remained there till 1654, enjoying the friendship of Milton, Cromwell, and other prominent Puritans. On his return to the colony in 1654 he was chosen president or governor, and remained in office till 1658. He lived to the age of eighty-four, but the exact date of his death is uncertain.

Williams was the author of a *Key into the Language of the Indians of America* (written at sea on his first voyage to England; London, 1643, reprinted in vol. i. of *Collections* of Rhode Island Historical Society, 1827); *Mr Cotton's Letter Examined and Answered*, 1644; *The Bloody Tenent of Persecution for the Cause of Conscience*, 1644; *Queries of Highest Consideration*, 1644; *The Bloody Tenent yet more Bloody*, 1652; *The Hireling Ministry None of Christ's*, 1652; *Experiments of Spiritual Life and Health*, 1652; and *George Fox Digged out of his Burrows*, 1676. A complete collection of all his letters that have been recovered forms vol. vi. of the *Publications* of the Narragansett Club. See *Lives* by Knowles (1833), Gammell (1846), and Elton (1852); Spark's *Library of American Biography*; Savage's *Genealogical Dictionary of New England Settlers*; *Biographical Cyclopedia of Representative Men of Rhode Island*, 1883; Guild's *Account of the Writings of Roger Williams*, 1862; and Dexter's *As to Roger Williams and his Banishment from Massachusetts Bay*, 1876.

WILLIAMSPORT, a city of the United States, the county seat of Lycoming county, Pennsylvania, is situated in the valley of the west branch of the Susquehanna river, amid the hills of the Alleghany plateau, and is entered by four railway lines,—the Northern Central, the Philadelphia and Erie, the Philadelphia and Reading, and the Corning, Cowanesque, and Antrim. The city is somewhat irregularly laid out, and the streets are mainly unpaved. The population in 1880 was 18,934; in 1870 it was 16,030. Williamsport owes its importance chiefly to its large lumber industry. The healthfulness of its climate and the beauty of the surrounding scenery have made it a popular summer resort in recent years.

WILLIBRORD, St, the apostle of the Frisians, was born about 657. His father, Wilgils, an Angle or, as Alcuin styles him, a Saxon, of Northumbria, withdrew from the world and constructed for himself a little oratory dedicated to St Andrew. The king and nobles of the district endowed him with estates till he was at last able to build a church, over which Alcuin afterwards ruled. Willibrord, almost as soon as he was weaned, was sent to be brought up at Ripon, where he must doubtless have come under the influence of Wilfrid. About the age of twenty the desire of increasing his stock of knowledge (*c.* 679) drew him to Ireland, which had so long been the headquarters of learning in western Europe. Here he stayed for twelve years, enjoying the society of Egbert and Wictbert, from the former of whom he doubtless received his first impulse to missionary work among the North-German tribes. In his thirty-third year (*c.* 690) he started with twelve companions for the mouth of the Rhine. These districts were then occupied by the Frisians under their king Rabbod or Radbod. After a time he found in Pippin, the mayor of the palace, a strong supporter, who sent him to Rome, where he was consecrated bishop by Pope Sergius on St Cecilia's Day 696. Bede says that when he returned to Frisia his see was fixed in Utrecht. He now seems to have spent several years in founding churches and the work of conversion, till his success tempted him to pass into those parts of the land which did not own the Frankish sway. Being kindly received by Radbod, but failing to convert him, he passed on to Denmark, whence he carried away thirty boys to be brought up among the Franks. On his return he was wrecked on the holy island of Fosite (Heligoland), where his disregard of the pagan superstition nearly cost him his life. When Pippin died, Willibrord found a supporter in his son Charles Martel, who, according to Alcuin's version of the story, established the bishop in Utrecht upon Radbod's death (719). At this time he was assisted for three years in his missionary work by St Boniface (719-722). Of the later years of his life we have no special chronological details. He passed throughout his diocese on horseback, working petty miracles and prophetically anticipating the future glory of Charles's son Pippin at his baptism. He was still living when Bede wrote in 731. A passage in one of Boniface's letters to Stephen III. speaks of his preaching to the Frisians for fifty years, apparently reckoning from the time of his consecration. This would fix the date of his death in 738; and, as Alcuin tells us he was eighty-one years old when he died, it may be inferred that he was born in 657,—a theory on which all the dates given above are based, though it must be added that they are substantially confirmed by the incidental notices of Bede. The day of his death was 6th November, and his body was buried in the monastery of Epternac, which he had himself founded. Even in Alcuin's time miracles were reported to be still wrought at his tomb.

The chief authorities for Willibrord's life are Alcuin's *Vita Willibrordi*, both in prose and in verse, and Bede's *Hist. Eccl.*, v. cc. 9-11. See also Eddius's *Vita Wilfridii*.

WILLIMANTIC, a borough in the town of Windham, Windham county, Connecticut, United States, is situated in a broken hilly country, on the Westfield river and on three railway lines,—the New York and New England, the New York, New Haven, and Hartford, and the Central Vermont. The population in 1880 was 6608. The industries consist chiefly of cotton manufactures, in which the town has acquired great prominence, owing to the fine water power afforded by the Westfield river.

WILLIS, Nathaniel Parker (1806-1867), American author, was descended from George Willis, described as a "Puritan of considerable distinction," who arrived in New England about 1630 and settled in Cambridge, Mass. Nathaniel Parker was the eldest son and second child of Nathaniel Willis, a newspaper proprietor in Boston, and was born in Portland, Maine, 20th January 1806. After attending Boston grammar school and the academy at Andover, he entered Yale College in October 1823. Although he did not specially distinguish himself as a student, university life had considerable influence in the development of his character, and furnished him with much of his literary material. Immediately after leaving Yale he published in 1827 a volume of *Poetical Sketches*, which attracted some attention, although the critics found in his verses more to blame than to praise. It was followed by *Fugitive Poetry* (1829) and *Poems* (1831). He also contributed frequently to magazines and periodicals. In 1829 he started the *American Monthly Magazine*, which was continued from April of that year to August 1831, but failed to achieve success. On its discontinuance he went to Europe as foreign editor and correspondent of the *New York Mirror*. To this journal he contributed a series of letters, which, under the title *Pencillings by the Way*, were published at London in 1835 (3 vols.; Philadelphia, 1836, 2 vols.; and first complete edition, New York, 1841). Their vivid and rapid sketches of scenes and modes of life in the Old World at once gained them a wide popularity; but he was censured by some critics for indiscretion in reporting conversations in private gatherings. Notwithstanding, however, the small affectations and fopperies which were his besetting weaknesses as a man as well as an author, the grace, ease, and artistic finish of his style won general recognition. His *Slingsby Papers*, containing descriptions of American life and adventure, republished in 1836 under the title *Inklings of Adventure*, were as successful in England as were his *Pencillings by the Way* in America. He also published while in England *Melaine and Other Poems* (London, 1835; New York, 1837), which was introduced by a preface by Barry Cornwall. After his marriage to Mary Stace, daughter of General Stace of Woolwich, he returned to America, and settled at a small estate on Oswego Creek, just above its junction with the Susquehanna. Here he lived off and on from 1837 to 1842 and wrote *Letters from Under a Bridge* (1840), the most charming of all his works. During a short visit to England in 1839-40 he published *Two Ways of Dying for a Husband*. Returning to New York, he established, along with George P. Morris, a newspaper entitled the *Evening Mirror*. On the death of his wife in 1845 he again visited England. Returning to America in the spring of 1846, he again married, and established the *National Press*, afterwards named the *Home Journal*. In 1845 he published *Dashes at Life*, in 1846 a collected edition of his *Prose and Poetical Works*, in 1849 *Rural Letters*, and in 1850 *Life Here and There*. In the last-mentioned year he settled at Idlewild, and on account of failing health spent the remainder of his life chiefly in retirement. Among his later works were *Hurrygraphs*, 1851; *Outdoors at Idlewild*, 1854; *Ragbag*, 1855; *Pearl Fane*, 1856; and the *Convalescent*, 1859. He died 20th July 1867, and was buried in Mount Auburn, Boston.

His *Poems*, with memoir, appeared in 1867, an English edition of his *Poems* in 1868, and a *Selection from his Prose Writings*, edited by Henry A. Beers, New York, 1885. His *Life*, by Henry A. Beers, appeared in the series of *American Men of Letters* the same year.

WILLIS, Thomas (1621-1675), English physician, was born at Great Bedwin, Wiltshire, on 27th January 1621. He studied at Christ Church, Oxford; and when that city was garrisoned for the king he bore arms for the Royalists. He took the degree of bachelor of medicine in 1646, and after the surrender of the garrison applied himself to the practice of his profession. In 1660, shortly after the Restoration, he became Sedleian professor of natural philosophy in place of Dr Joshua Cross, who was ejected, and the same year he took the degree of doctor of physic. In 1664 he discovered the medicinal spring at Astrop, near Brackley in Northamptonshire. He was one of the first members of the Royal Society, and was elected an honorary fellow of the Royal College of Physicians in 1664. In 1666, after the fire of London, he removed to Westminster, on the invitation of Dr Sheldon, archbishop of Canterbury. There he rapidly acquired an extensive practice, his reputation and skill marking him out as one of the first physicians of his time. He died at St Martin's on 11th November 1675 and was buried in Westminster Abbey.

Willis was admired for his piety and charity, for his deep insight into natural and experimental philosophy, anatomy, and chemistry, and for the elegance and purity of his Latin style. He wrote in English *A Plain and Easy Method for Preserving those that are Well from the Infection of the Plague, and for Curing such as are Infected*. His Latin works were printed in two vols. 4to at Geneva in 1676, and at Amsterdam in 1682. His grandson, Browne Willis, was the author of several antiquarian works.

See Munk, *Roll of the Royal College of Physicians, London* (2d ed., vol. i., London, 1878).

WILLMORE, James Tibbitts (1800-1863), English line engraver, was born at Bristnall's End, Handsworth, near Birmingham, on 15th September 1800. At the age of fourteen he was apprenticed to William Radcliffe, a Birmingham engraver, and in 1823 he went to London and was employed for three years by Charles Heath. He was afterwards engaged upon the plates of Brockedon's *Passes of the Alps* and Turner's *England and Wales*. He engraved after Chalon, Leitch, Stanfield, Landseer, Eastlake, Creswick, and Ansdell, and especially after Turner, from whose Alnwick Castle by Moonlight, the Old Téméraire, Mercury and Argus, Ancient Rome, and the subjects of the Rivers of France he executed many admirable plates. He was elected an associate engraver of the Royal Academy in 1843. He died on 12th March 1863.

WILLOW (*Salix*), a very well marked genus of plants constituting, with the Poplar (*Populus*), the order *Salicaceæ*. Willows are trees or shrubs, varying in stature from a few inches to a hundred feet, and occurring most abundantly in cold or temperate climates in both hemispheres, and generally in moist situations. They are not unrepresented in the tropics, but have hitherto not been discovered in Australia or the South Sea Islands. Their leaves are deciduous, alternate, simple, generally much more long than broad, whence the term willow-leaved has become proverbial. At their base they are provided with stipules, which are also modified to form the scales investing the winter buds. The flowers are borne in catkins or amenta, which are on one tree male only, on another female. Each

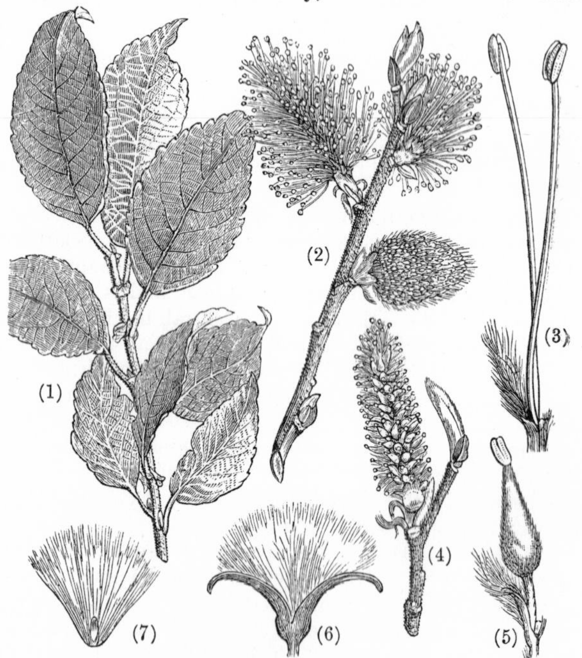

Willow. (1) Leaf shoot; (2) male catkin; (3) male flower; (4) female catkin; (5) female flower; (6) capsule, opened; (7) seed.

male flower consists of a small scale or bract, in whose axil are usually two, sometimes three, rarely five stamens, and still more rarely a larger number. In addition there is a small glandular disk, which assumes different shapes in different species. The female flowers are equally simple, consisting of a bract, from whose axil arises usually a very short stalk, surmounted by two carpels adherent one to the other for their whole length, except that the upper ends of the styles are separated into two stigmas. When ripe the two carpels separate in the form of two valves and liberate a large number of seeds, each provided at the base with a tuft of silky hairs, and containing a straight embryo without any investing perisperm or albumen. Fertilization is effected by insects, especially by bees, which are directed in their search by the colour and fragrance of the flowers

Some pollen must also be transported by the wind to the female flowers. The tuft of hairs at the base of the seed doubtless facilitates rapid dispersion of the seed, early germination of which is rendered desirable owing to its tenuity and the absence of any perisperm. Although the limitations of the genus are well marked, and its recognition in consequence easy, it is otherwise with regard to the species. The greatest difference of opinion exists among botanists as to their number and the bounds to be assigned to each. The cross-fertilization that takes place between the species of course intensifies the difficulty. Andersson, a Swede, spent nearly a quarter of a century in their investigation, and ultimately published a monograph which is the standard authority on the subject. He admits about a hundred species. Some botanists have enumerated eighty species from Great Britain alone, while others count only a dozen or fifteen. To illustrate the great perplexity surrounding the subject, we may mention that to one species, *S. nigricans*, one hundred and twenty synonyms have been attached. Some of these are doubtless such as no botanist, with adequate material for forming an opinion, would accept; but, after making the necessary deductions for actual mistakes and misstatements, there still remains a large number upon which legitimate differences of opinion prevail. Andersson says that he has rarely seen two specimens of this species which were alike in the collective characters offered by the stature, foliage, and catkins. No better example could be found of the almost limitless variation in so-called species, so that the attempt to define the indefinable can at best result only in an arbitrary grouping.

Few genera have greater claims to notice from an economic point of view. As timber trees many of the species are valuable from their rapidity of growth and for the production of light durable wood, serviceable for many purposes. Among the best trees of this kind are *S. fragilis*, especially the variety known as *S. fragilis*, var. *Russelliana*, and *S. alba*, the white or Huntingdon willow. These trees are usually found growing by rivers' banks or in other moist situations, and are generally pollarded for the purpose of securing a crop of straight poles. This plan is, however, objectionable, as inducing decay in the centre of the trunk. Where poles are required, it is better to treat the trees as coppice and to cut the trunk level with the soil. *S. Capræa*, a hedgerow tree, generally grows in drier situations. It is a useful timber tree, and its wood, like that of *S. alba*, is prized in the manufacture of charcoal. Its catkins are collected in England in celebration of Palm Sunday, the gaily-coloured flowers being available in early spring when other decorations of the kind are scarce. Certain sorts of willow are largely used for basket-making and wicker-work. The species employed for this purpose are mostly of shrubby habit, and are known under the collective name of osiers. The best for planting, according to Mr Scaling, is the bitter osier, *S. purpurea*; planted on rich, well-drained soil, subject to occasional immersion, this willow may be grown profitably for basket-work. It is also well adapted for forming wind-breaks or screens, or for holding the banks of streams and preventing the removal of the soil by the current. *S. viminalis* is one of the best of the green osiers, suitable for hoops and valuable for retaining the soil on sloping embankments. *S. vitellina* yields the yellow osiers. Osiers are largely imported into England from Belgium and France, but might with advantage be much more abundantly grown in the United Kingdom than they are. They are easily propagated by truncheons or cuttings, inserted in a slanting direction into the soil for a depth of 8 to 10 inches. Mr Scaling recommends that they be planted 18 inches apart, thus employing about 20,000 cuttings per acre, the whole cost of planting being estimated at £25 the acre. A crop is obtained the third year after planting, and one may be expected annually for the succeeding ten years. The average yield is cited at 6 to 7½ tons, ranging in price from £2, 10s. to £3, 10s. a ton (unpeeled). Land unsuitable for root or grain crops can be utilized for the growth of osiers; but, as in the case of all other plants, good cultivation, including the selection of sorts appropriate to the locality, drainage, manure, &c., ensures the best return. *S. acuminata* and other species do well by the seaside, and are serviceable as wind-screens, nurse-trees, and hedges. *S. daphnoides*, *S. repens*, and other dwarf kinds are useful for binding heathy or sandy soil. In addition to their use for timber or basket-making, willows contain a large quantity of tannin in their bark. A bitter principle named SALICIN (*q.v.*) is also extracted from the bark. As ornamental trees some willows also take a high rank. The white willow is a great favourite, while the drooping habit of the weeping willow renders it very attractive. Though named *S. babylonica*, it is really a native of China, the willow of the Euphrates (Ps. cxxxvii.) being in all probability *Populus euphratica*. *S. babylonica* is sometimes spoken of as Pope's willow, having been cultivated by that poet, or as Napoleon's willow, because his tomb at St Helena is overshadowed by a tree of this species, from which many offsets exist or are reputed to exist in modern gardens. *S. regalis* has very white, silvery leaves. *S. rosmarinifolia* is remarkable for its very narrow leaves, —purplish above, silvery beneath.

WILLUGHBY, FRANCIS (1635-1672), English ornithologist and ichthyologist, who is memorable as the pupil, friend, and patron as well as the active and original co-worker of John RAY (*q.v.*), and hence to be reckoned as one of the most important precursors of Linnæus. He was the son of Sir Francis Willughby, and was born in 1635. His connexion with Ray dated from his studies at Cambridge (1653-59); and, after concluding his academic life by a brief sojourn at Oxford, and acquiring considerable experience of travel in England, he made an extensive Continental tour in his company. The specimens, figures, and notes thus accumulated were in great part elaborated on his return into his *Ornithologia*, which, however, he did not live to publish, having injured a naturally delicate constitution by alternate exposure and over-study. This work was published in 1676, and translated by Ray as the *Ornithology of Fr. Willughby* (London, 1678, fol.); the same friend published his *Historia Piscium* (1686, fol.). Willughby died on 3d July 1672.

In Ray's preface to the former work he gives Willughby much of the credit usually assigned to himself, both as critic and systematist. Thus, while founding on Gesner and Aldrovandus, he omitted their irrelevancies, being careful to exclude "hieroglyphics, emblems, morals, fables, presages, or ought else pertaining to divinity, ethics, grammar, or any sort of humane learning, and present him [the reader] with what properly belongs only to natural history." Again, he not only devised artificial keys to his species and genera, but, "that he might clear up all these obscurities [of former writers] and render the knowledge and distinction of species facile to all that should come after, he bent his endeavours mainly to find out certain characteristic notes of each kind," while finally, in apologizing for his engravings, he yet not unjustly claims that "they are best and truest of any hitherto graven in brass." See further ORNITHOLOGY, vol. xviii. p. 4.

WILMINGTON, the largest city of the State of Delaware, United States, and the county seat of New Castle county, is situated between Brandywine and Christiana creeks and on the Delaware river. The site is low, but with sufficient slope to afford suitable drainage. The surrounding country is fertile and well cultivated. Wilmington is a railway centre of considerable importance, being entered by the Philadelphia, Wilmington, and Baltimore, the Baltimore and Ohio, and the Wilmington and Northern Railways. The Brandywine and Christiana creeks are navigable for large vessels. The city is laid out quite regularly. The population, which in 1870 was 30,841, in 1880 was 42,478. The manufactures in 1880 gave occupation to 7852 persons, the principal branches being the manufacture of paper, iron and steel, shipbuilding, and the making of waggons and carriages, steam-engines, bricks, morocco leather, glass, cotton, gunpowder and other explosives, matches, and flour.

Wilmington was settled by Swedes in 1638. The settlement was conquered by the Dutch, who in turn handed it over to the English. It was chartered as a city in 1832, and since the middle of the century has grown rapidly.

WILMINGTON, the county seat of New Hanover county, North Carolina, United States, the principal seaport and the largest city of the State, is situated on the east bank of Cape Fear river, 30 miles from the ocean. It has railroad communication to the north, south, and west, and this, together with its maritime position, makes it an important shipping point. The principal objects of trade are lumber (southern pine), naval stores, and cotton. The manufactures include fertilizers, creosote, and carpets (made from pine leaves). The value of its exports, principally cotton, turpentine, and rosin, is about $7,000,000 annually. The city, which is in the main regularly laid out, had in 1870 a population of 13,446, and in 1880 of 17,350, of whom 60 per cent. were Negroes.

The site of Wilmington was originally occupied by a town named Newton, laid out in 1730. The name was changed to Wilmington nine years later. The place was incorporated as a city in 1866. During the Civil War it was the principal port of entry for the Confederate blockade-runners.

WILMOT, JOHN. See ROCHESTER, EARL OF.

WILNO. See VILNA.

WILSON, ALEXANDER (1766-1813), "the American ornithologist," was born in Paisley, Scotland, on 6th July 1766. His father, a handloom weaver, soon removed to the country, and there combined weaving with agriculture, distilling, and smuggling,—conditions which no doubt helped to develop in the boy that love of rural pursuits and adventure which was to determine his career. At first he was placed with a tutor and destined for the church; but his father's circumstances soon compelled him to apprentice the boy to his own trade. The lad's real life, however, was spent in reverie and versification, and in long woodland rambles, in the course of which he combined his poetic musings with the keen observation of a naturalist, supplemented by the woodcraft of an accomplished poacher. As these tastes developed, he decided to exchange the loom for the pedlar's pack, and then spent a year or two in travelling through Scotland, recording in his journal every matter of natural history or antiquarian interest, like another Sibbald or White of Selborne. Having incurred a short imprisonment for lampooning the master-weavers in a trade dispute, he emigrated to America in 1794. After a few years of weaving, peddling, and desultory observation, he became a village schoolmaster, and in 1800 obtained an appointment near Philadelphia, where he formed the acquaintance of Bartram the naturalist, from whom he received much instruction and encouragement. Under his influence Wilson commenced to draw birds, having conceived the idea of illustrating the ornithology of the United States; and thenceforward he steadily accumulated materials and made many expeditions. In 1806 he obtained the assistant-editorship of *Rees's Encyclopædia*, and thus acquired more means and leisure for his great work, the first volume of which appeared in the autumn of 1808, after which he spent the winter in a journey "in search of birds and subscribers." By the spring of 1813 seven volumes had appeared; but the arduous expedition of that summer, in search of the marine waterfowl to which the remaining volume was to be devoted, gave a shock to his already impaired health, and soon after he succumbed to dysentery after a short illness, dying at Philadelphia on 23d August 1813.

Of his poems, not excepting the *Foresters* (Philadelphia, 1805), nothing need now be said, save that they no doubt served to develop his descriptive powers. His *American Ornithology*, however, remains a fundamental classic. In the words of Jardine, "He was the first who studied the birds of North America in their natural abodes and from real observation; and his work will remain an ever to be admired testimony of enthusiasm and perseverance, one certainly unrivalled in description; and, if some plates and illustrations may vie with it in finer workmanship or pictorial splendour, few indeed can rival it in fidelity and truth of delineation." The eighth and ninth volumes were edited after his decease by his friend Ord, and the work was continued by Lucien Bonaparte (4 vols., Philadelphia, 1828-33). The *American Ornithology* was also republished by Sir William Jardine (3 vols., London, 1832), and an edition of his entire works has been edited by Rev. A. B. Grosart (Paisley, 1876). A statue was also erected to him at Paisley in 1876.

WILSON, FLORENCE. See VOLUSENUS.

WILSON, HENRY (1812-1875), vice-president of the United States from 1873 to 1875, was born at Farmington, N.H., on 16th February 1812. His proper name was Jeremiah J. Colbath. His parents were day-labourers and very poor. At ten years of age he went to work as a farm-labourer. The boy was greedy for reading, and before the end of his apprenticeship had read more than a thousand volumes. At the age of twenty-one, for some unstated reason, he had his name changed by Act of the Legislature to that of Henry Wilson. Walking to Natick, Mass., he learned the trade of shoemaker, and by it supported himself through the Concord academy. After successfully establishing himself as a shoe manufacturer, he became a noted public speaker in support of Harrison during the presidential election of 1840. For the next ten years he was regularly returned to the State legislature. In 1848 he left the Whig party and became a "Free Soiler." The Free Soil party nominated him for governor of the State in 1853, but he was defeated. In 1855 he was sent to the United States Senate by the Free Soil and Democratic parties, and remained there by re-elections until 1873. When the Civil War broke out he found a severe test awaiting him. He had been deeply interested from 1840 until 1850 in the militia of his State, and had risen through its grades of service to that of brigadier-general. He was now made chairman of the military committee, and in this position performed most laborious and important work for the four years of the war. The position offered boundless and safe opportunities for becoming wealthy. But so far was Wilson from using them that he died poor, owing to his necessary neglect of his private affairs. Sumner says that in 1873 Wilson was obliged to borrow a hundred dollars from him to meet the expenses of his inauguration as vice-president. The Republicans nominated Wilson for the vice-presidency in 1872, and he was elected; but he died, before completing his term of service, at Washington on 22d November 1875. He left two small but useful works, *Anti-Slavery Measures in Congress* (Boston, 1864) and *Military Measures in Congress* (Hartford, 1868), and a larger work in three volumes, *The Rise and Fall of the Slave Power in America* (Boston, 1871-76). His *Life* has been written by E. Nason and by J. B. Mann.

WILSON, HORACE HAYMAN (1786-1860), one of the most distinguished Orientalists of England, was born in London on 26th September 1786. He was educated for the medical profession, and on completing his studies went out to India in 1808 as an assistant-surgeon on the Bengal establishment of the East India Company. Instead of entering the regular medical service, however, his knowledge of chemistry and the practical analysis of metals caused him to be attached to the mint at Calcutta, where he was for a time associated with John Leyden, the Scottish poet and Orientalist. It was not long before he himself became deeply interested in the ancient language and literature of India, and attracted the attention of Henry T. Colebrooke, the famous Sanskrit scholar, on whose recommendation he was in 1811 appointed secretary to the Asiatic Society of Bengal. In 1813 he published the Sanskrit text—with a graceful, if somewhat free, translation in English rhymed verse—of Kālidāsa's charming lyrical poem, the *Meghadūta*, or *Cloud-Messenger* (2d ed. 1843, 3d ed. 1867). He then undertook the arduous task of preparing the first *Sanskrit-English Dictionary* from materials compiled by native scholars for the college of Fort William, supplemented by his own researches. The work appeared in 1819, prefaced with an excellent general survey of Sanskrit lexicology. A second, much enlarged, edition, but without the introduction, was published in 1832, and has recently been reprinted at Calcutta. The appearance of the *Dictionary* at once placed Wilson in the first rank of Sanskrit scholars; and, while patiently pursuing his study of the writings and institutions of ancient India, he became one of the most valuable contributors to the *Asiatic Researches* and the *Calcutta Quarterly*. Among his more important contributions to these journals may be mentioned essays on the "Medical and Surgical Sciences of the Hindus" (1823); the "Hindu History of Kashmir" (1824); "Hindu Fiction" (1825); and his masterly "Account of the Religious Sects of the Hindus, their History, Doctrines, and Practices" (1828-32). In 1827 he published *Select Specimens of the Theatre of the Hindus*, in 3 vols., in which, besides a very full and highly appreciative survey of Indian dramaturgy, which still remains the standard authority on the subject, he offered elegant translations of six complete plays and short accounts of twenty-three others. This work was reprinted in London in 1835, in 2 vols., and again in Wilson's *Collected Works* (vols. xi. and xii.). Of considerable importance, alike to Sanskrit and vernacular students, and to Eastern antiquarians generally, was his next publication, the *Mackenzie Collection* (2 vols., 1828; 2d ed. in one vol., 1882), being a descriptive catalogue of the extensive collection of Oriental, especially South Indian, MSS. and antiquities made by Col. Colin Mackenzie, and purchased from his widow by the Indian Government, now deposited partly in the India Office, London, and partly at Madras. Neither his extensive literary researches, however, nor the official duties of an assay master and mint secretary, at any time prevented Wilson from taking a prominent part in all social amusements of the Anglo-Indian community of Calcutta, especially in musical and theatrical entertainments. His interest in political and economic affairs in India is shown by his *Historical Sketch of the First Burmese War, with Documents, Political and Geographical* (1827, reprinted in London), and his *Review of the External Commerce of Bengal from 1813 to 1828* (1830), as well as by his *History of British India from 1805 to 1835*, in continuation of Mill's *History*, 3 vols. (1844-48), and largely based on his personal impressions and recollections. He also acted for many years as secretary to the committee of public instruction. As such, he not only organized and superintended the studies of the Hindu College from the time of its establishment, but took a leading part in the promotion of public education among the natives, and the introduction of the English language and European science, although, as one of the staunchest opponents, on grounds of expediency and feasibleness, of the proposal that English should be made the sole medium of instruction in native schools, he became for a time the object of bitter attacks. Long, however, before this controversy came to an end he had been called away to a different sphere of scholarly activity. In 1832 the university of Oxford, in recognition of his services to Oriental scholarship, selected Dr Wilson to be the first occupant of the newly founded Boden chair of Sanskrit. Shortly after his return to England he was also appointed librarian to the East India Company. He now found himself in a position singularly favourable to learned research and literary pursuits; and the long record of his subsequent work shows that he made the best of his opportunities. He immediately joined the Royal Asiatic Society, and, succeeding Colebrooke as director (in 1837), he was the very soul of the society up to the time of his death, scarcely a number of its journal appearing without some interesting contribution from his pen. His death took place at London on 8th May 1860.

Of these contributions we need only mention here his "Historical Sketch of the Kingdom of Pāndya" (1836), based on documents contained in the Mackenzie collection; the continuation of his "Analysis of the Purānas" (1836), begun in the *Bengal Society's Journal* (1832); "Civil and Religious Institutions of the Sikhs" and "Religious Festivals of the Hindus" (1848); "Analysis and Revised Translation of the Rock Inscriptions of Kapur di Giri" (1850); and his popular lecture "On the Present State of the Cultivation of Oriental Literature" (1852). Hardly less numerous, and certainly not less valuable, are his separate publications during this period, by which important light was thrown on many departments of Eastern inquiry. The most noteworthy of these works are the text of, and commentary on, the Sānkhyakārikā (1837), being a very popular summary of the Sānkhya philosophy, with a translation (of the text by Colebrooke, and the commentary by Wilson); translation of the *Vishnu Purāna* (1840, 2d annotated ed. by F. E. Hall; *Works*, vols. vi.-x.); *Ariana Antiqua, Antiquities and Coins of Afghanistan* (1841); edition of *Dasakumāracharita* (1846); *Glossary of Indian Revenue, Judicial, &c., Terms* (1855); *Translation of the First Four Ashṭakas* (rather more than one-half) *of the Sacred Hymns of the Rigveda*, 3 vols., 1850-57; *Grammar of the Sanskrit Language*, in several editions; and two lectures on the *Religious Practices and Opinions of the Hindus*, delivered at Oxford in 1840. In the *Collected Works* (12 vols.) the more valuable of his papers and lectures form three volumes of essays on *Sanskrit Literature* and two volumes of essays on *The Religion of the Hindus*, edited by Dr R. Rost. While in point of accurate scholarship Wilson was perhaps scarcely the equal of Colebrooke, any deficiency in this respect is far more than counterbalanced by the many-sidedness of his genius, by literary powers of a very high order, by his admirable artistic taste, and by broad human sympathies, which enabled him fully to appreciate and enjoy the merits and beauties of the ancient Indian literature. A considerable number of Sanskrit MSS. (540 vols.) collected by Wilson in India are now in the Bodleian.

WILSON, JOHN (1785-1854), better known as CHRISTOPHER NORTH (the pen-name which he used in his contributions to *Blackwood's Magazine*), was born at Paisley on 18th May 1785. His father, who bore the same name with himself, was a wealthy gauze manufacturer of no particular family or education. His mother, Margaret Sym, was of gentler blood, possessing also beauty and talents. John was the fourth child, but the eldest son, and he had nine brothers and sisters.[1] He appears, like many Scotchmen of genius, to have been rather irregularly educated in his earlier days,—the best of his physical and sporting, if not of his scholastic, training being received at the manse of the village of Mearns, of which constant notices appear in the *Essays*. He was only twelve when he was first entered at the university of Glasgow, and he continued to attend various classes in that university for six years, being for the most part domiciled with and under the tutorship of Prof. Jardine. His father's death had immediately preceded his first entry at Glasgow. In these six years Wilson "made himself" in all ways, acquiring not inconsiderable scholarship, perfecting himself in all sports and exercises, and falling in love with a certain "Margaret," who was the object of his affections for several years. The most curious literary memorial of these early years is a letter to Wordsworth, written in 1802 without any personal acquaintance or introduction, and betraying not a little priggishness, as we should now count it, but in that respect only showing the difference of contemporary manners, and interesting as being the first evidence of what was nearly a lifelong connexion of admiring though sometimes recalcitrant criticism.

In June 1803 Wilson was entered as a gentleman commoner at Magdalen College, Oxford. Men have seldom felt more than Wilson the charm which Oxford exercises on all but a very few, and generally (with some noteworthy exceptions, such as Gibbon and Jeffrey) very worthless, sons; and in much of his later work, notably in the essay called "Old North and Young North," he has expressed his feeling. But it does not appear that his Magdalen days were altogether happy, though he perfected himself in "bruising," pedestrianism, and other sports, and read so as to obtain a brilliant first class. His love affairs with "Margaret" did not go happily, and he seems to have made no intimate friends at his own college and few in the university. He took his degree in 1807 and found himself at twenty-two his own master; and he had a good

[1] The youngest brother was James Wilson "of Woodville" (1795-1856), who became a zoologist of some repute. He contributed to *Blackwood's Magazine* and to the *North British* and *Quarterly Reviews*, and wrote most of the articles on natural history ("Entomology," "Helminthology," "Mammalia," "Ornithology," "Reptiles," &c.) in the seventh edition of the *Encyclopædia Britannica*.

income, no father or guardian to control him, no property requiring management, and apparently was not under the influence of the etiquette which in similar circumstances generally makes it necessary for a young man to adopt some profession, if only in name. His profession was an estate on Windermere called Elleray, and ever since imperishably connected with his name. Here he built, boated, wrestled, shot, fished, walked (he was always an astonishing pedestrian), and otherwise diverted himself for four years, besides composing or collecting from previous compositions a considerable volume of poems. But Wilson was too genuine a man to be happy without a wife, and in 1810 the place of "Margaret" was taken by Jane Penny, a Liverpool girl of some family and fortune, whom he married on 11th May 1811. *The Isle of Palms*, his first published volume, consisting of poems, was issued not long after this. Four years of married life at Elleray succeeded, which, except as being happier and therefore less historied, do not seem to have differed much from the earlier four. Then came the event which definitely made a working man of letters of Wilson, and without which he would probably have produced a few volumes of verse and nothing more. His whole fortune, or at least the major part of it, was lost by the dishonest speculation of an uncle in whose hands, with no doubt rather culpable carelessness, Wilson had left it. At the same time this hard fate was by no means unqualified in its hardness. His mother had a house in Edinburgh, in which she was able and willing to receive her son and his family; nor had he even to give up Elleray, though henceforward he was not able constantly to reside in it. He read law and was called to the Scotch bar, taking plentiful sporting and pedestrian excursions, on some of which his wife accompanied him, publishing in 1816 a second volume of poems (*The City of the Plague*), and generally leading a very pleasant life, if not such an entirely independent one as formerly. The year 1817 was the turning point in Wilson's life. The famous Cevallos article, which resulted in the secession of Scott and other Tories from the *Edinburgh Review* and the establishment of the *Quarterly*, was years earlier; but there had still been no formal declaration that the "Blue and Yellow" was for Whigs only. Wilson was a Tory and the son of Tories ("If you turn Whig, John," said his mother to him, "this house will not hold you and me"), but he was glad to accept Jeffrey's invitation to contribute. Almost at the same time, however, a far more suitable chance appeared. Wilson was not patient of being edited, and his reckless humour as well as his political bias would in the long run have pretty certainly disqualified him for the *Edinburgh*. The growth of *Blackwood's Magazine*, and its sudden transformation from a colourless or Whiggish monthly rival to Constable's *Review* into an organ at once of the most red-hot Toryism in politics and of the wildest irreverence towards received notions in literature and other matters, took place in the same year. The petard of the "Chaldee Manuscript," nominally due to Hogg, but with most of the gunpowder put in by Wilson and Lockhart, determined the character of the new periodical, and Wilson's career was fixed. He was never exactly editor, for the powers of "Christopher North" in that respect were a fantastic imagination; and we have definite and authoritative assertions, not only that he never received any stipend for editing, but that the publishers always retained a certain supervision even over Wilson's own contributions. The famous series of the *Noctes Ambrosianæ* is said to have been of Maginn's invention, and for nearly ten years was so very partially representative of Wilson's own work and thought that none of its numbers during that time have been included by his son-in-law in the authorized, but by no means complete, edition. Lockhart, a somewhat less genial but far more concentrated and deliberate writer, was, until his departure for London to take charge of the *Quarterly*, at least as potent in the management as Wilson; and, although the facts are not known with absolute certainty, there is no doubt that it was a daring "alarum and excursion" of Lockhart's, under the alias (one of many) of Baron von Lauerwinkel, which caused Jeffrey, nominally because of an attack on Prof. Playfair, but obviously for other reasons, to inform Wilson, almost in so many words, that his further contributions were not desired for the *Edinburgh*. Wilson had also some share—though, if internal evidence may be trusted, not much—in Lockhart's *Peter's Letters*, which, harmless as they seem nowadays, infuriated the Whig society of the Scottish capital.

The first result of this new business on Wilson's general mode of life was that he left his mother's house and established himself (1819) in Ann Street, Edinburgh, on his own account with his wife and family of five children. The second was much more unlooked for: it was his candidature for and election to the chair of moral philosophy in the university of Edinburgh (1820). To speak honestly, his qualifications for the post were almost *nil*, even if the fact that the best qualified man in Great Britain, Sir William Hamilton, was also a candidate, be left out of the question. But, luckily for Wilson and for letters, the matter was made a political one; the Tories still had a majority in the town council; he was powerfully backed up by friends, Scott at their head; and his adversaries played into his hands by attacking, not his competence (which, as has been said, was very vulnerable), but his moral character, which was not open to any fair reproach. Yet he made a very excellent professor, never perhaps attaining to any great scientific knowledge in his subject or power of expounding it, but acting on generation after generation of students with a stimulating force that is far more valuable than the most exhaustive knowledge of a particular topic. His duties left him plenty of time for magazine work, and for many years his contributions to *Blackwood* were extraordinarily voluminous. Most of the best and best-known of them appeared between 1825 and 1835, that is, between the departure of Lockhart for London in the former year and the death of Blackwood the publisher and of Mrs Wilson in the latter.

The domestic events of Wilson's life in the last thirty years of it may be very briefly told. He oscillated between Edinburgh and Elleray, with plentiful excursions and summer residences elsewhere, a sea trip on board the Experimental Squadron in the Channel during the summer of 1832, and a few other unimportant diversions. The death of his wife was an exceedingly severe blow to him, especially as it coincided very nearly with that of his friend Blackwood. For many years after it (though he never up to the date of his death gave up writing) his literary work was intermittent, and, with some exceptions, not up to the level of the earlier. Late in 1850 his health showed definite signs of breaking up; and in the next year a civil list pension of £300 a year was conferred on him. He died at Edinburgh on 3d April 1854.

But a very small part of Wilson's extensive work was published in a collected and generally accessible form during his lifetime, the chief and almost sole exceptions being the two volumes of poems above referred to, the *Lights and Shadows of Scottish Life* (prose tales and sketches), and the *Recreations of Christopher North*, a selection, mostly limited to sporting and descriptive pieces, of his magazine articles. These volumes, with a selected edition of the *Noctes Ambrosianæ* in four volumes, and of further essays, critical and imaginative, also in four volumes, were collected and re-issued uniformly after his death by his son-in-law, Prof. Ferrier. The collection is very far from exhaustive; and, though it undoubtedly contains most of his best work and comparatively little that is not good, it has been complained, with some justice, that the characteristic, if rather immature, productions of his first eight years on *Blackwood* are almost entirely omitted, that the *Noctes* are

WILTSHIRE

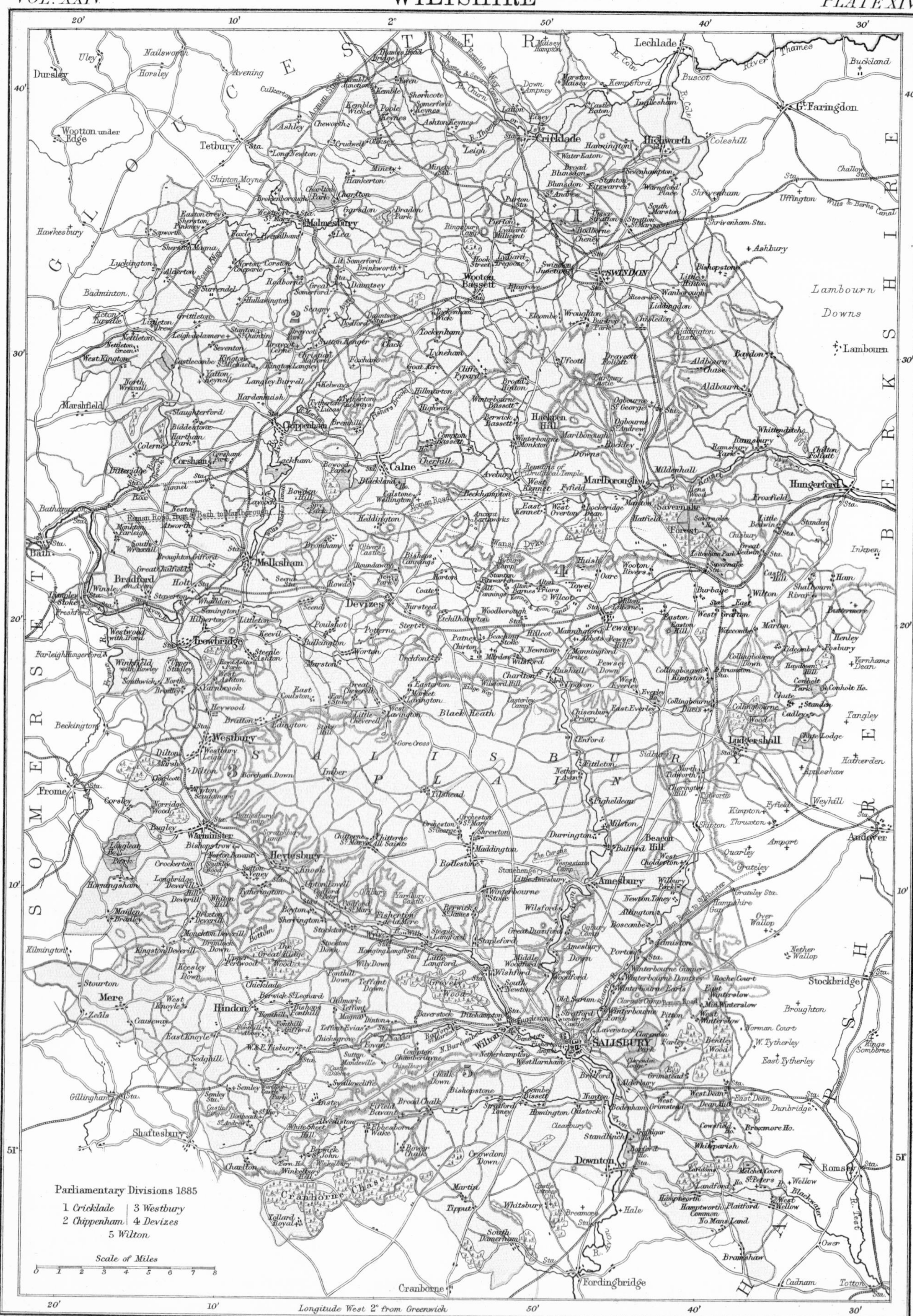

W. & A. K. Johnston

given but in part, if in their best part, and that at least three long, important, and interesting series of papers, less desultory than is his wont, on "Spenser," on "British Critics," and the set called "Dies Boreales," have been left out altogether. Wilson's characteristics are, however, uniform enough, and the standard edition exhibits them sufficiently, if not exhaustively. His poems may be dismissed at once as little more than interesting. They would probably not have been written at all if he had not been a young man in the time of the full flood of influence of Coleridge, Wordsworth, Byron, and Scott. His prose tales have in some estimates stood higher, but will hardly survive the tests of universal criticism. It is as an essayist and critic of the most abounding geniality, if not genius, of great acuteness, of extraordinary eloquence, and of a fervid and manifold sympathy, in which he has hardly an equal, that "Christopher North" lives and will live. The *Noctes Ambrosianæ*, a series of convivial table-talk, giving occasion to wonderfully various digressions of criticism, description, and miscellaneous writing, have been of late years ranked far below their real value. From their origin it necessarily followed that there was much that is ephemeral, a certain amount that is purely local, and something that is purely trivial in them. But their dramatic force, their incessant flashes of happy thought and happy expression, their almost incomparable fulness of life, and their magnificent humour give them all but the highest place among genial and recreative literature. It is often thought, and sometimes said, that no one but a Scotchman can relish them—an utter mistake, against which it is desirable most energetically to testify in the name of lovers of them who have not a drop of Scottish blood in their veins. The same qualities, together with a greater share of purely literary and critical power (to the display of which the form of the *Noctes* was inimical), and of a sometimes abused but very admirable faculty of word-painting, appear in the miscellaneous essays. Wilson's defects lay in the directions of measure and of taste properly so called, that is to say, of the modification of capricious likes and dislikes by reason and principle. He is constantly exaggerated, boisterous, wanting in refinement. But these are the almost necessary defects of his qualities of enthusiasm, eloquence, and generous feeling. The well-known adaptation of phrase in which he not recanted but made up for numerous earlier attacks on Leigh Hunt, "the Animosities are mortal, but the Humanities live for ever," shows him as a writer at his very best, but not without a little characteristic touch of grandiosity and emphasis. As a literary critic, as a sportsman, as a lover of nature, and as a convivial humorist, he is not to be shown at equal advantage in miniature; but almost any volume of his miscellaneous works will exhibit him at full length in either capacity or in all.

The chief, if not the sole, authentic source of information for Wilson's life is the memoir by his daughter, Mrs Gordon (Edinburgh, 1862). (G. SA.)

WILSON, Richard (1714-1782), English landscape painter, was born at Penegoes, Montgomeryshire, where his father was a clergyman, on 1st August 1714. His early taste for art was observed by a relative of his mother, Sir George Wynne, who in 1729 sent him to London to study under Thomas Wright, a little-known portrait painter of the time, by whom he was instructed for six years. He then started on his own account, and was soon in a good practice. Among his commissions was a full-length of the prince of Wales and the duke of York, painted for their tutor, the bishop of Norwich. Examples of his portraits may be studied in Greenwich Hospital, in the Garrick Club, and in various private collections. In 1749 Wilson visited Italy, where he spent six years. He had previously executed some landscapes, but it was now that the advice of Zuccarelli and Joseph Vernet decided him to adopt this department of art exclusively. He studied Claude and Poussin, but retained his own individuality, and produced some admirable views of Rome and the Campagna. In 1755 he returned to England, and became one of the first of English landscape painters. Niobe, one of his most powerful works, was exhibited at the Society of Artists in 1760. On the establishment of the Royal Academy in 1768 he was appointed one of the original members, and he was a regular contributor to its exhibitions till 1780. He frequently executed replicas of his more important subjects, repeating some of them several times; in the figures which he introduced in his landscapes he was occasionally assisted by Mortimer and Hayman. During his lifetime his landscapes were never widely popular; his temper was consequently embittered by neglect, and so impoverished was he that he was obliged to seclude himself in an obscure, half-furnished room in Tottenham Court Road, London. In 1776, however, he obtained the post of librarian to the Academy; and by the death of a brother he acquired a small property near Llanferras, Denbighshire, to which he retired to spend his last days, and where he died suddenly in May 1782. After his death his fame increased, and in 1814 about seventy of his works were exhibited in the British Institution. The National Gallery, London, contains nine of his landscapes.

The works of Wilson are skilled and learned compositions rather than direct transcripts from nature. His landscapes are treated with great breadth, and with a power of generalization which occasionally led to a disregard of detail. They are full of classical feeling and poetic sentiment; they possess noble qualities of colour, and of delicate silvern tone; and their handling is vigorous and easy, the work of a painter who was thoroughly master of his materials.

See *Studies and Designs by Richard Wilson, done at Rome in the year 1752* (Oxford, 1811); T. Wright, *Some Account of the Life of Richard Wilson* (London, 1824); Thomas Hastings, *Etchings from the Works of Richard Wilson, with some Memoirs of his Life* (London, 1825). Many of Wilson's best works were reproduced by Woollett and other engravers of the time.

WILTS, a south-western county of England, is bounded N.W. and N. by Gloucestershire, E. by Berks and Hants, S. by Hants and Dorset, and W. by Somerset. It is of an irregular oval form, its greatest length from north to south being 54 miles and its greatest breadth from east to west 37. The area is 866,677 acres, or about 1354 square miles.

Plate XIV.

Geology. About two-thirds of the surface of Wilts is occupied by a great Chalk upland, embracing the greater part of the wild wooded tract of Cranborne Chase, the undulating elevation of Salisbury Plain, and the hilly district of the Marlborough Downs, with Savernake Forest. In some cases the Chalk rises into steep escarpments; and the scenery of the north-western region, bordering on the lower ground, is varied and picturesque. A large portion of the Chalk region is over 600 feet above sea-level, and several summits have an elevation of over 900 feet, the highest being Inkpen Beacon (1011 feet) at the junction of Wilts, Hants, and Berks. Scattered over the surface of the northern downs are huge blocks of silicious Tertiary grits, called sarsen stones or grey wethers, which have been used in the formation of the Druidical circles of Stonehenge and Avebury. The underlying Greensand is exposed in the deep valleys of the Chalk, especially in the broad vale of Pewsey, separating the Marlborough Downs from Salisbury Plain. It also appears as a narrow fringe between the Chalk and Oolite formations on the north and west, and in Alfred's Tower near Stourton on the Somersetshire border reaches an elevation of 800 feet. Outliers of the London Clay cap some of the hills in the neighbourhood of Great and Little Bedwin and Savernake Forest; and the clays and sands of the Woolwich and Reading beds appear in the south-eastern extremity of the county. About a third of the surface of the county, to the north-west of the Chalk, including a portion of the White Horse Vale, consists mainly of Oolite limestones and clays resting chiefly on the Greensand. The Lower, Middle, and Upper varieties are all represented. At one time the fuller's earth of the Lower Oolite was dug for use in the cloth-mills. In the Coral Rag of the Middle Oolite a useful bed of iron is wrought near Westbury, the annual output of ore varying in value from £12,000 to £20,000. The valuable Portland stone of the Upper Oolite is quarried for building purposes at Chilmark, Tisbury, and Swindon, and the famous Bath stone of the Great Oolite is obtained at Corsham and Box on the Somersetshire border. The Oolite yields a variety of interesting fossils: the pear encrinite (*Apiocrinites rotundus*) is found in the Bradford clay; many fine corals are obtained in the Coral Rag; and *Isastræa oblonga* is very plentiful at Tisbury.

Rivers.

One of the most charming features of Wilts is its rich and finely wooded valleys. The three principal rivers are the Kennet, the Lower or Bristol Avon, and the Southern or Christchurch Avon. The Kennet, rising in the Marlborough Downs, winds eastwards past Marlborough and Hungerford into Berkshire, to join the Thames at Reading. The Lower Avon, which rises in Gloucestershire, flows southwards by Malmesbury, Chippenham, Melksham, and Bradford, where it bends north-westwards into Somersetshire. Besides several smaller streams, it receives from the south the Frome, which forms for a short distance the boundary between Wilts and Somersetshire. The Southern Avon, which rises near Bishop's Cannings in the centre of the county, flows southwards by Amesbury and Salisbury into Hants. At Salisbury it receives from the west the Nadder, after its junction with the Wily at Wilton, and from the north-east the Bourne. The Thames skirts the north-eastern border of the county.

Agriculture.

Agriculture.—According to returns made on 4th June 1887, the total area of land occupied was 759,538 acres, of which 646,653 were rented and 112,885 owned and occupied; 759,412 acres, or about seven-eighths of the whole area, were under cultivation. Of this area 395,010 acres were permanent pasture, a great portion consisting of sheep-runs on the Chalk downs. In some places, especially in Salisbury Plain, tillage was in former years extensively introduced in the Chalk districts, but much of this has again reverted to pasture. There were 174,876 acres under corn crops, 99,388 under green crops, 79,049 under rotation grasses, and 11,086 under fallow. In north-west Wilts the prevailing soil is a reddish chalky clay resting on a subsoil of broken stones, whilst on the Chalk formation the arable land is of a lighter character. There are also extensive tracts of richer soil well adapted for wheat and beans. In 1887 wheat occupied 67,357 acres, barley 50,928, oats 44,047, rye 1728, beans 7274, and pease 3542. The bulk of the green crops are grown for the feeding of cattle and sheep, potatoes occupying only 3339 acres and carrots 237, while 54,869 acres were under turnips and swedes, 5673 mangold, 10,473 cabbage, rape, &c., and 24,527 vetches, &c. The total area under nursery grounds in 1887 was 91 acres, while market gardens occupied 3525, and orchards 3346. Woods in 1881 occupied 45,270 acres, a great part being comprised in the ancient forests, including Cranborne Chase and Savernake Forest, which contain some remarkable old oaks and beeches. The number of horses in 1887 was 23,616, of which 18,980 were used solely for purposes of agriculture. Cattle numbered 106,020, 60,113 being cows and heifers in milk or in calf. Dairy farming is the leading industry in the north-western districts, Wiltshire being famous for its cheese. Of the cattle 15,505 were two years and above, and 30,402 under two years, an indication that comparatively few cattle are kept for purposes of feeding. Sheep in 1887 numbered 643,125, and pigs 66,422.

According to the latest landowners' *Return*, Wiltshire was divided among 14,013 owners, possessing 828,949 acres at an annual valuation of £1,599,239, or about £1, 18s. 7d. per acre. There were 9635 owners possessing less than one acre each, 1519 acres being divided amongst them. The estimated extent of commons or waste lands was 1931 acres. The following proprietors owned over 7000 acres each:—earl of Pembroke, 39,601 acres; marquis of Ailesbury, 37,994; marquis of Bath, 19,978; earl of Radnor, 17,173; Simon W. Taylor, 14,960; R. P. Long, 13,618; Sir John Neeld, 13,113; trustees of Sir H. Meux, 11,896; marquis of Lansdowne, 11,146; earl of Suffolk, 11,098; earl of Normanton, 9812; Lord Ashburton, 9592; Sir E. Antrobus, 8374; Sir Francis D. Astley, 7888; Sir M. E. Hicks Beach, 7200; and T Fraser Grove, 7179.

Communication.

Communication.—A considerable amount of traffic is carried on in the northern districts by means of canals. The Thames and Severn Canal crosses the north-west corner of the county. Between Cricklade and Swindon it is joined by a branch canal to the Wilts and Berks Canal. This last has a semicircular course southwestwards by Swindon, Wootton Basset, and Melksham, 2 miles beyond which it is joined by the Kennet and Avon Canal, which crosses the centre of the county by Hungerford, Devizes, and Bradford. The railway communication is supplied chiefly by the Great Western and the London and South Western lines.

Manufactures and trade.

Manufactures and Trade.—Wiltshire has long been celebrated for its cloths, the chief seats of the industry being Bradford and Trowbridge, while among other places Melksham and Chippenham are perhaps the most important. Wilton is still celebrated for its carpets. Haircloth weaving and the manufacture of cocoa-nut fibres are carried on at Melksham, and there are silk works at Chippenham, Malmesbury, Mere, and Warminster. Iron-smelting from the mines of the neighbourhood is carried on at Westbury; portable engines are made at Devizes; and at Swindon are the engineering works of the Great Western Railway. Various towns are associated with different branches of the agricultural trade: Salisbury and Devizes have important corn markets; Chippenham, besides a trade in cheese, has a condensed milk manufactory; Wilton has a large sheep fair; and Calne is the centre of the Wiltshire bacon trade.

Population, &c.

Administration and Population.—Wiltshire comprises 29 hundreds, the city of Salisbury or New Sarum (population 14,792 in 1881), and the municipal boroughs of Calne (2474), Chippenham (1352), Devizes (6645), and Marlborough (3343). The county has one court of quarter sessions and is divided into fifteen petty sessional divisions. The city of Salisbury and the borough of Devizes have commissions of the peace and separate courts of quarter sessions, and the borough of Marlborough has a commission of the peace. Previous to the Act of 1885 the county was divided for parliamentary purposes into North and South Wilts, each returning two members, and included the following parliamentary boroughs—Calne, Chippenham, part of Cricklade, Devizes, Malmesbury, Marlborough, Salisbury city, part of Shaftesbury, Westbury, and Wilton. All these returned one member each, with the exception of Salisbury, which returned two; by the Act of 1885 they were all merged in the county divisions, with the exception of Salisbury, which was deprived of one member. The county was reformed into five parliamentary divisions, each returning one member,—north (Cricklade), into which the Wiltshire portion of Cricklade is merged; north-west (Chippenham), into which Chippenham and Malmesbury are merged; south (Wilton), into which Wilton is merged; east (Devizes), into which Devizes and Marlborough are merged; and west (Westbury), into which Westbury is merged. The county contains 340 civil parishes, with parts of seven others. It is mostly in the diocese of Salisbury. From 183,820 in 1801 the population by 1821 had increased to 219,574, and by 1841 to 256,280, and, although by 1861 it had diminished to 249,311, by 1871 it had again increased to 257,177; in 1881 it was 258,965, of whom 128,114 were males and 130,851 females. The number of persons to an acre is 0·30 and of acres to a person 3·35.

History and antiquities.

History and Antiquities.—In the importance of its early archæological remains Wilts takes a foremost place among the counties of England. In the river gravel-beds near Salisbury and elsewhere several specimens of flint implements of the Palæolithic age have been dug up, and the numerous barrows of the Chalk downs have yielded a great variety of stone implements of the Neolithic age, as well as of a later period. The ancient British boundary, the Wans Dyke, passed westwards across the county from Great Bedwin; west of Marlborough it still remains for many miles in a perfect condition. Traces of several other boundaries of a somewhat similar character are met with in other parts of the county. The British "ridgeway" runs north-eastwards from Avebury, near the tumulus of Silbury Hill, to the ancient forts of Barbury and Badbury; other ancient British trackways have been converted into Roman roads. Among the principal ancient defensive works are Battlesbury and Scratchbury near Warminster; the entrenchments of Barbury and Badbury; Bratton, near Westbury, defended by double ramparts, in some places 36 feet in height, to which Guthrum the Dane is said to have retreated after his defeat by King Alfred; Casterly, on a ridgeway about 7 miles south-east of Devizes, described by Sir R. C. Hoare as "one of the most original and unaltered works of the British era which our country can produce"; Figbury Ring, 3 miles north-east of Salisbury, sometimes called Chlorus's camp, from the tradition that it was made by the British general Constantine Chlorus; Sidbury, 3 miles south-west of Collingbourne, probably an ancient British town; Vespasian's camp, between Amesbury and Stonehenge; and Yarnbury camp, in very perfect preservation, to the north of Wily. Ogbury camp, 6 miles north of Salisbury, is an undoubted British entrenchment, but probably a sheep-fold. The stone circles of Avebury and Stonehenge are the most remarkable megalithic structures in the kingdom; but their origin and date are the subject of much dispute. Durrington "walls," north of Amesbury, are probably the remains of a British village; there are also traces of others at several places on the slopes of the Marlborough Downs and Salisbury Plain.

Ancient British roads and fortifications.

Roman roads.

There are no records of the Roman invasion, though many evidences of Roman occupation remain. The ancient Fosse Way crossed the north-west corner of the county from Bath to Cirencester. From this last town another road passed southwards to *Cunetro* (Folly Farm near Marlborough), joining the *Via Julia*, which crossed the county from Bath to Silchester. From Salisbury one went north-east to Silchester, another east to Winchester, and another north-west to Bath. On the line of these roads remains of Roman villages have been found at different places.

History.

After the departure of the Romans Wilts was the scene of frequent contests, first between the Britons and the Saxons and afterwards between the Saxons and the Danes. Badbury is the reputed *Mons Badonicus* where King Arthur defeated Cerdic in 520. In 552 Cynric inflicted a severe defeat on a large army of Britons at Old Sarum, and in 556, after a great victory over them at Barbury Hill, he incorporated the country of the Wilsaetas in the kingdom of Wessex. In 823 Egbert, king of the West Saxons, gained a victory over Beornwulf, king of Mercia, at Ellandune near Wilton. Wilton itself was the scene of Alfred's defeat by the Danes in 871. In 878 the Danes plundered Chippenham, where Alfred had one of his residences, and made the town their headquarters; but afterwards Alfred inflicted on Guthrum such a severe defeat at Ethandune (supposed to be Edington near Westbury) that the Danes came to terms with him, the south-western part of Mercia being henceforth held by the Saxons and the north-eastern by the Danes. During the Danish invasions at the close of the 10th and the beginning of the 11th century the district was overrun by Sweyn, who pillaged and burned Wilton, as well as Old Sarum. At the latter town Canute died in 1036. During the conflict between Stephen and Matilda the strongholds of Sarum, Devizes, and Malmesbury were held by Bishop Roger for Matilda, until he was compelled to surrender them. During the Civil War Wiltshire sided chiefly with the Parliament. In 1643 Wardour Castle near Tisbury was bravely defended by Lady Blanche Arundell against Sir Edward Hungerford, and, although she was forced to capitulate, the castle was again taken by her son in 1645. In 1643 Essex was routed by Charles I. and Rupert at Aldbourn, and the same year Waller was defeated by Wilmot at Roundaway near Devizes. After the storming of Devizes Castle by Cromwell in September 1645 the Cavaliers were wholly driven from the county.

Ancient edifices, &c.

The church of St Lawrence, Bradford, converted at one time into cottages, is one of the most perfect specimens of ancient Saxon architecture existing; and there is also Saxon work in the churches of Britford (north and south door), Burcombe (east end of the chancel), Manningford Bruce, and a few other places. There is a large amount of Roman work in the church of Malmesbury abbey, much of it, however, being Transition; the church of St John's, Devizes, retains its original Norman tower and exhibits Norman vaulting in the chancel; the chancel of St Mary's in the same town is also Norman, and its porch has characteristic Norman mouldings; the churches of Preshute and Corsham contain interesting examples of the same style. Salisbury cathedral is the finest and most perfect example of Early English existing; and there is much good architecture of the same style in the churches of Amesbury, Bishop's Cannings, Cricklade, Collingbourne-Kingston, Downton, Edington, and Purton. The prevailing architecture is, however, Perpendicular, of which there are numerous fine examples, especially in the districts where good building stone is found; but in the Chalk districts, where the churches are constructed of flint, the architecture is generally inferior. There are numerous interesting examples of domestic architecture of the 14th, 15th, and 16th centuries. The only monastic remains of importance within the county are the abbey church of Malmesbury; the picturesque ruins of Lacock or Laycock abbey (3 miles south of Chippenham), founded in 1232 by Ella, countess of Salisbury; the walls of Bradenstoke priory (north-east of Chippenham), founded in 1142 by Walter d'Evreux for Augustinian canons, now converted into a farmhouse; and slight remains of the Cluniac priory of Monkton-Farleigh, founded in 1125. The fortress of Old Sarum is almost completely demolished, but the outlines of the defences remain; Devizes retains a few fragments, "built up again," according to Freeman, as "meaningless ornaments in the midst of the most fearful piece of modern gimcrack that human eyes ever beheld"; and the mound of Marlborough has been made into a "hill of pleasure." Trowbridge Castle, which was held for Matilda by Humphrey de Bohun, has completely disappeared, its site being occupied by modern buildings; and only a few small fragments remain of Ludgershall, which Matilda occupied on her escape from Winchester.

Distinguished persons.

Wilts has an unusually long roll of illustrious persons. Among divines, Hugh Latimer was rector of West Kington; Richard Hooker was rector of Boscombe; George Crabbe was for eighteen years rector of Trowbridge, and was buried in the chancel of the church; Dr Henry Sacheverell was the son of a Marlborough clergyman; George Herbert and Archdeacon William Coxe were both rectors of Bemerton (near Salisbury); and Dr Joshua Marshman, the Indian missionary, was born at Westbury. Of persons who have distinguished themselves in some form of literature we may mention Thomas Chubb, the Deist, who was a native of Harnham; Hobbes of Malmesbury; Philip Massinger, who was born at Salisbury; Joseph Addison, the son of the rector of Milston; Bryan Edwards, the historian; Aubrey and Britton, the antiquaries; Edmund Ludlow, author of the *Memoirs* of the Restoration period; and Sir R. Colt Hoare, the historian of Wilts. Statesmen are represented by "Orator" Hunt, Sir John Davies, Bolingbroke, Hyde first earl of Clarendon, Harris first earl of Malmesbury, Fox first Lord Holland, Protector Somerset, and Henry Fawcett. Other persons of special distinction are Sir Christopher Wren, Sir B. Collins Brodie, and Thomas Willis, one of the founders of the Royal Society.

See Sir H. C. Hoare's *Ancient Wiltshire*, 1812-21, and *Modern Wiltshire*, 1822-1844; Aubrey and Jackson's *Topographical Collections for Wilts*, 1864; Britton's *Beauties*, 1801; Kite's *Monumental Brasses of Wilts*, 1860; Jackson's *Ancient Chapels of Wilts*, 1867; Jones's *Early Annals*, 1871; Saint George's *Visitation of Wilts 1623*, 1882; Stratford's *Wiltshire and its Worthies*, 1882; and A. C. Smith's *British and Roman Antiquities in North Wilts*, 1884-85. (T. F. H.)

WIMBLEDON, a suburb of London, in the county of Surrey, is situated on the London and South Western Railway, 7¼ miles south-west of London. The old village of Wimbledon has been greatly extended of late years, the district being now a favourite residence for the London middle classes. Wimbledon Common, to the north-west of the village, was the meeting-place of the Rifle Association from its foundation in 1860 till 1888. At its south-western extremity are the outlines of a British earthwork, called Cæsar's camp, having an extreme diameter of 950 feet and a diameter within the vallum of 750 feet. At Coombe's Hill and elsewhere British relics have been found. The parish church of St Mary is supposed to date from Saxon times; but, after it had undergone various restorations and reconstructions, it was rebuilt in 1833 in the Perpendicular style. There are various other churches and chapels, all modern. A free library was established in 1887. The benevolent institutions include nine almshouses (1838), a cottage hospital (1867), a convalescent hospital (1867), and a hospital for infectious diseases (1877). The population of the urban sanitary district (area 3220 acres) was 9087 in 1871 and 15,950 in 1881.

Wimbledon (Wibbandune) is supposed to have been the scene of a battle in 568 between Ceawlin, king of Wessex, and Ethelbert, king of Kent, in which the latter was defeated. At Domesday it formed part of the manor of Mortlake, held by the archbishops of Canterbury. Afterwards the name was sometimes used interchangeably with Mortlake, and in 1327 it is described as a grange or farm belonging to Mortlake. On the impeachment of Arundel, archbishop of Canterbury, in 1398, it was confiscated. In the reign of Henry VIII. Cromwell, earl of Essex, held the manor of Wimbledon, with Bristow Park as an appendage. On the confiscation of Cromwell's estates in 1540 it again fell to the crown, and by Henry VIII. it was settled on Catherine Parr for life. By Queen Mary it was granted to Cardinal Pole. In 1574 Elizabeth bestowed the manor house, while retaining the manor, on Sir Christopher Hatton, who sold it the same year to Sir Thomas Cecil. In 1588 Elizabeth transferred the manor to his son Sir Edward Cecil, in exchange for an estate in Lincolnshire. At the time of the Civil War the manor was sold to Adam Baynes, who shortly afterwards sold it to General Lambert; and at the Restoration it was granted to the queen dowager, Henrietta Maria, who sold it in 1661 to George Digby, earl of Bristol. On his death in 1676 it was sold by his widow to the lord-treasurer Danby. Some years after Danby's death it was purchased by Sarah, duchess of Marlborough, who demised it to her grandson, John Spencer. It was sold by the fifth Earl Spencer in 1877. Wimbledon House, built by Sir Thomas Cecil in 1588, was destroyed by fire in 1785, and a new house, called Wimbledon Park House, was erected about 1801.

WIMBORNE MINSTER, a market town of Dorset, England, is situated on a gentle slope above the river Allen, near its confluence with the Stour, and on the Great Western Railway, 6 miles north of Poole and 114 west-south-west of London. The feature of the town is the ancient minster. As it now stands, it is a fine cruciform structure of various styles from Early Norman to Perpendicular, and consists of a central lantern tower, nave and choir with aisles, transepts without aisles, western or bell tower, north and south porches, crypt, and vestry or sacristy, with the library over it. Its maximum length is 182 feet, and its maximum breadth 102. The interior was restored in 1856-57. It contains a large number of interesting monuments, including a brass with the date 873 (supposed to mark the resting-place of Ethelred, third son of Ethelwulf), an orrery of the 14th century, and an octagonal Norman font of Purbeck marble. A new church, dedicated to St John the Evangelist, was built and partly endowed in 1876. The free grammar-school, established in 1497, was refounded by Elizabeth, a portion of the revenues of the monastery being devoted to this purpose. New school buildings in the Elizabethan style were erected in 1851. There are two hospitals, St Margaret's and Courtenay's. Near Wimborne is Canford Hall, the seat of Lord Wimborne, a mansion in the Tudor style, built by

Blore in 1826, and improved from designs of Sir Charles Barry. The town depends chiefly on agriculture; but the manufacture of hose is carried on to a small extent, and there are also coachbuilding works. The population of the parish of Wimborne Minster (area 11,966 acres) was 5019 in 1871 and 5390 in 1881.

Wimborne (Saxon *Vinburnan*) is supposed to have been the *Vindogladia* or *Ventagladia* of the Romans. A nunnery was founded here in 712 by St Cuthberga, sister of Ina, king of the West Saxons. It was destroyed by the Danes about 900, and subsequently became a house of secular canons, when the church became collegiate. The establishment existed till 1547. Wimborne is supposed to have been the scene of a battle between the earl of Devon and the Danes in 851, in which the latter were defeated. It was taken possession of by Ethelwold in 901. The duke of Monmouth was apprehended near Wimborne after his escape from Sedgemoor. The town claims to have been the birthplace of Matthew Prior, the poet.

WINCHESTER, a city, and a parliamentary and municipal borough, of Hampshire, England, is situated on the river Itchen, 66 miles south-west of London by the London and South Western Railway. The *Caer Gwent* (White City) of the Britons and *Venta Belgarum* of the Romans, Winchester was a town of much importance in early times, mainly on account of its central position on the Roman high roads in the south of England.[1] Temples to Apollo and Concord stood within the precincts of the present cathedral close; but in the 3d century the place is said to have become one of the chief centres of the early Celtic Christians. The Saxon invaders at the end of the 5th century treated the Roman name Venta as if it were a feminine substantive, and, transforming it into "Winte," called the town *Winte-ceaster*, "the City of the Winte;" hence the modern name Winchester. Throughout the Saxon period the city was one of the highest importance: early in the 6th century it became the capital of Wessex; and the kings of Wessex were crowned and usually buried in the cathedral. Even after the formation of the united kingdom of Anglia by Egbert, the great witan was still held in Winchester. It was also one of the chief centres for the coining of money under the pre-Norman kings: in the time of Athelstan it contained six mints, while London possessed only three. Even after the Norman Conquest many sovereigns were crowned and many parliaments held here; the celebrated Statutes of Winchester were passed in a parliament held in 1285. The city continued to be a favourite royal residence, and Henry II. rebuilt the palace on a larger scale.[2] This same king gave it its first regular charter of incorporation (1184). In the Middle Ages Winchester was famed for its wool trade and textile fabrics; in the 14th century it was the chief wool mart of England and had an extensive trade with France, Belgium, and Holland. In the 15th century its prosperity began to decline. In Cromwell's time the city suffered severely from a siege, during which Winchester Castle was dismantled. Charles II. began to build a palace on the site of this fortress, after designs by Sir Christopher Wren, but the death of the king prevented the work from being completed.[3]

The first Christian church at Winchester is said to have been destroyed during the persecution of Aurelian, and rebuilt in 293. It was again burned by the Saxons in 495. St Swithun held the episcopate from 852 to 862, and enlarged the cathedral. The foundations of the adjacent abbey church of Hyde, in which some of the Saxon kings were buried, were discovered in 1886 close to the north side of the cathedral nave. The cathedral church was at one time associated with a priory of secular canons, but St Ethelwold, bishop from 963 to 984, suppressed the secular foundation and built a Benedictine abbey in its place.[4] A wholly new cathedral was begun by Bishop Walkelin (1070-98), and in 1093 the eastern portion was consecrated jointly to St Peter, St Paul, and St Swithun. The two Norman transepts and the low central tower still exist, as does also the very curious early crypt, east of the crossing. This is a low vaulted structure partly supported by a central row of columns; it has an apsidal termination, and is surrounded by an ambulatory, out of which a second smaller apse extends eastwards,—apparently a survival of the "confessio" of the earlier cathedral. The whole of the Norman nave was pulled down and rebuilt on a more magnificent scale by William of Wykeham at the end of the 14th century; the work was completed after his death by means of a large bequest. The choir was also remodelled in the 14th century and again much altered by Bishop Fox (1501-28).

In plan Winchester cathedral consists of a nave, two transepts, choir, and retro-choir, all with aisles. A large lady chapel extends still further eastwards. The length of the whole building is no less than 546 feet, thus being greater than that of any other church in England, with the exception of St Albans, which measures about the same length. One of its chief beauties is the magnificent reredos behind the high altar; this consists of a lofty wall, the full width of the choir, pierced by two processional doors, and covered with tiers of rich canopied niches, which once contained colossal statues. A cross of plain ashlar stone in the centre shows where an immense silver crucifix was once attached; and a plain rectangular recess above the altar once contained a massive silver-gilt retable, covered with cast and repoussé statuettes and reliefs, an elaborate work of the most costly magnificence. A second stone screen, placed at the interval of one bay behind the great reredos, served to enclose the small chapel in which stood the magnificent gold shrine, studded with jewels, the gift of King Edgar,[5] which contained the body of St Swithun. In the choir is the plain tomb of William II., and under many of the arches of the nave and choir are a number of very elaborate chantry chapels, each containing the tomb of its founder. Some of these have fine recumbent effigies, noble examples of English mediæval sculpture; the most notable are the monuments of Bishops Edingdon, Wykeham, Waynflete, Cardinal Beaufort, Langton, and Fox. The font of black marble is an interesting example of 11th-century art; its sides are covered with curious reliefs representing scenes from the life of St Nicholas. A good deal of very magnificent 14th-century stained glass still exists at Winchester.

Winchester College was built from 1387 to 1393 by WILLIAM OF WYKEHAM (*q.v.*). The foundation of the school consisted of a warden, ten fellows, three chaplains, seventy scholars, and sixteen choristers. Its fine chapel, hall, cloister, and other buildings still exist in good preservation. About a mile distant from the town stands the hospital of St Cross, founded in 1136 by Henry de Blois, bishop of Winchester, to provide board and lodging for 13 poor men and a daily dinner for 100 others. It was enlarged and mostly rebuilt by Cardinal Beaufort, 1405-47. The buildings are still in a good state of preservation, including the simple but very stately cruciform chapel, built about the year 1180, which in plan resembles a fine parochial church.[6] The whole place has been much injured by so-called "restoration."

Winchester suffered greatly in the plague of 1666, and its population was much reduced. At present its prosperity chiefly depends on the presence of the cathedral, the college, and its barracks, which accommodate about 2000 men. The city has several good schools and the usual public and charitable institutions. From the 23d year of Edward I. it returned two members to parliament until

[1] See Milner, *History of Winchester*, and Smirke, "Consuetudinary of Winchester," in *Arch. Jour.*, vol. ix.

[2] The hall of this palace still exists; it is illustrated by Turner in *Domestic Architecture*, London, 1851, vol. i. p. 176.

[3] Evelyn in his *Diary* (16th Sept. 1685) speaks of this as a "stately fabric" which had been "brought almost to the covering."

[4] See Britton, *Winchester Cathedral*, London, 1817.

[5] Great treasures of gold and jewels were presented to this cathedral by many of the early kings of England, especially by Canute, who gave his gold gem-studded crown to be hung over the great crucifix above the high altar.

[6] See a valuable account of St Cross in the Winchester volume of the *Archæological Institute*, by E. A. Freeman.

1885, when it lost one member. The population of the municipal and parliamentary borough (area 1032 acres) was 16,366 in 1871 and 17,780 in 1881. (J. H. M.)

WINCHESTER, a city and the county seat of Frederick county, Virginia, United States, is situated in the Shenandoah valley, about 700 feet above sea-level, and on a branch of the Baltimore and Ohio Railroad. It lies about 67 miles west-north-west of Washington. The surrounding country is rich and fertile, devoted to agriculture and cattle-raising, for which Winchester serves as a centre of supply and distribution. The city has manufactories of shoes, furniture, gloves, &c., and some iron foundries and tanneries. The population in 1880 was 4958 (1517 coloured). In 1888 it was estimated at over 5000.

Winchester was laid out as a town in 1752 and incorporated in 1779. It has had a very slow growth, and during the Civil War it suffered severely from the armies of both combatants.

WINCKELMANN, Johann Joachim (1717-1768), historian of ancient art and the founder of scientific archæology, was born at Stendal in the Altmark (Prussia) on 9th December 1717. His father was a poor shoemaker, and in his early years Winckelmann had to contend with great difficulties. With a passion for knowledge, however, he combined a resolute will; and by acting for some time as amanuensis to an old and blind rector he contrived to pass through the necessary courses of instruction at school. In 1737 he attended a gymnasium at Berlin and the school at Salzwedel, and in the following year he went as a student of theology to the university of Halle. He took little real interest in theology, and such interest as he had was quenched partly by the influence of the philosophy of Wolff, partly by the unfavourable impression made upon him by the Pietists. Through his connexion with the chancellor Von Ludewig he was led to enter upon the study of German history; he devoted himself also with great enthusiasm to the study of Greek literature. He thought of becoming a physician, and began to attend medical classes at Jena; but the accomplishment of this scheme was beyond his means, and he was obliged to accept a tutorship near Magdeburg. In 1743 he was made associate-rector of a school at Seehausen in the Altmark, and this appointment he held for five years. He then went to Dresden, where he acted as librarian and general assistant to Count Henry Von Bünau, for whose history of the Holy Roman empire he collected materials. The treasures in the Dresden gallery awakened in his mind an intense interest in art, which was deepened by association with various artists, and especially with Oeser, who afterwards exercised so powerful an influence over Goethe when Goethe was a young student at Leipsic. Winckelmann's study of ancient literature had inspired him with a strong desire to visit Rome, and now he sought, through the papal nuncio Archinto, to obtain the appointment of librarian to Cardinal Passionei. Nothing could be done for him, however, unless he joined the Roman Catholic Church; this condition, after long hesitation, he ultimately decided to comply with.

In 1755 Winckelmann gave the first indication of his genius by the publication of his *Gedanken über die Nachahmung der griechischen Werke in Malerei und Bildhauerkunst*. This was followed by a pretended attack on the work, and a defence of its principles, nominally by an impartial critic. In the *Gedanken* Winckelmann suggested most of the doctrines he afterwards developed; and the book was warmly admired not only for the new ideas it contained but for the power and charm of its style. One good result of the impression it produced was that Augustus III., elector of Saxony and king of Poland, was induced to grant him a pension of 200 thalers, that he might have an opportunity of prosecuting his studies in Rome. He arrived in Rome in November 1755, and, with the exception of some brief intervals, remained there during the rest of his life. He became librarian to Cardinal Archinto, and also received much kindness from Cardinal Passionei; and after their death he was received as librarian and as a friend into the house of Cardinal Albani, who was forming his magnificent collection in his villa at Porta Salara. In 1763, while retaining this position, Winckelmann was made prefect of antiquities.

From the time of his arrival in Rome he devoted himself earnestly, at first with the aid of his friend Raphael Mengs, to the study of Roman antiquities, and he gradually acquired what was then an unrivalled knowledge of ancient art. In 1760 appeared his *Description des Pierres Gravées du Feu Baron de Stosch*, embodying the results of much work at Florence, where he had spent nine months in cataloguing the engraved gems collected by his friend Baron von Stosch. He published in 1762 *Anmerkungen über die Baukunst der Alten*, including an account of the temples at Pæstum. In 1758 and 1762 Winckelmann visited Naples for the purpose of studying the treasures excavated at Pompeii and Herculaneum; and from his *Sendschreiben von den herculanischen Entdeckungen* (1762) and his *Nachricht von den neuesten herculanischen Entdeckungen* (1764) scholars obtained their first authentic information about those groups of antiquities. Winckelmann again visited Naples in 1765 and 1767, and wrote for the use of the electoral prince and princess of Saxony his *Briefe an Bianconi*, which were published, eleven years after his death, in the *Antologia Romana*. For several years his energies were devoted chiefly to the preparation of his masterpiece, the *Geschichte der Kunst des Alterthums*, which was issued in 1764. It at once commanded attention and was soon recognized as a book that would take a permanent place in the literature not only of Germany but of Europe. In this great work Winckelmann sets forth both the history of Greek art and the principles on which it seemed to him to be based. He also presents a glowing picture of the conditions, political, social, and intellectual, which tended to foster creative activity in ancient Greece. The fundamental idea of his theory is that the end of art is beauty, and that this end can be attained only when individual and characteristic features are strictly subordinated to the artist's general scheme. According to Winckelmann, the true artist, selecting from nature the phenomena fitted for his purpose, and combining them through the imagination, creates an ideal type marked in action by "noble simplicity and calm greatness,"—an ideal type in which normal proportions are maintained, particular parts, such as muscles and veins, not being permitted to break the harmony of the general outlines. In the historical part he used not only the works of art he himself had studied but the scattered notices on the subject to be found in ancient writers; and his wide knowledge and active imagination enabled him to offer many fruitful suggestions as to periods about which he had little direct information. The materials for the study of Greek art which have been recovered since Winckelmann's time have compelled archæologists to reject some of his conclusions, to modify others, and to present the subject as a whole in a somewhat different light; but the writer was penetrated by so fine an enthusiasm, his style is at once so strong, so graceful, and so animated, and his descriptions of particular works of art are so vivid and true, that his book can never wholly lose its freshness. It marked an epoch by indicating the spirit in which the study of Greek art should be approached, and the methods by which investigators might hope to attain to solid results. To Winckelmann's contemporaries the work came as a revelation, and it exercised a profound influence on the best minds of the age. Goethe studied it eagerly, and it was read with intense interest by Lessing, who had found in a statement in the earliest of Winckelmann's works the starting-point for his *Laocoon*.

Winckelmann contributed various admirable essays to the *Bibliothek der Schönen Wissenschaften*; and in 1766 he published his *Versuch einer Allegorie*, which, although containing the results of much thought and reading, is not conceived in a thoroughly critical spirit. Of far greater importance was the splendid work entited *Monumenti Antichi Inediti* (1767-68), prefaced by a *Trattato Preliminare*, presenting a general sketch of the history of art. The plates in this work are representations of objects which had either been falsely explained or not explained at all. Winckelmann's explanations were of the highest service to archæology, by showing that in the case of many works of art which had been supposed to be connected with Roman history the ultimate sources of inspiration were to be found in Homer.

In 1768 Winckelmann left Rome with the Italian sculptor Cavaceppi, intending to visit Germany. But he went no farther than to Vienna, where he was received with honour by Maria Theresa. At Trieste on his way back to Italy he made the acquaintance of a man called Arcangeli, to whom he showed some gold coins that had been given to him by the empress; Arcangeli's cupidity was excited, and during the night he entered Winckelmann's room, and, after having tried to throttle him, stabbed him five times. Winckelmann died of his wounds on 8th June 1768. His murderer was caught and executed.

Winckelmann ranks among the foremost writers of the 18th century, and it is hardly possible to overrate the services rendered by him to archæology and the study of ancient art. With wide learning and an extraordinary power of accurate observation he combined imagination and feeling, and through him the modern world obtained for the first time something like a true conception not only of particular works of Greek art but of the general intellectual movement from which they sprang. If many of his ideas have now been abandoned, that is to a large extent due to the fact that scholars and thinkers were put upon the right track by his researches. His character as a man corresponded to his greatness as a writer. No difficulty was formidable enough to deter him from working out his vast schemes; and in relation to his friends and in general social intercourse he was distinguished by a noble generosity of spirit and thorough honesty of purpose.

An edition of his works was begun by Fernow in 1808 and completed by Meyer and Schulze (1808-20). There is an admirable study of his character and work in Goethe's *Winckelmann und sein Jahrhundert* (1805), to which contributions were made by Meyer and Wolf. The best biography of Winckelmann is the one by Justi, 2 vols., Leipsic, 1866-72. (J. SI.)

WIND. See METEOROLOGY, vol. xvi. pp. 124, 143, 154.

WINDHAM, WILLIAM (1750-1810), English politician, came from an ancient family long resident at Felbrigg near Cromer in Norfolk. His father, Colonel William Windham, was an adventurous soldier with a taste for languages, both ancient and modern; William Windham, the statesman, was born in Golden Square, London, on 3d May 1750. At the age of seven he went to Eton, which he quitted in 1766 for the university of Glasgow, and under the care of Dr Simson he acquired the taste for mathematics which always distinguished him. In 1767 he matriculated as gentleman commoner at University College, Oxford, where he remained until 1771. He never took the degree of B.A., but qualified as M.A. on 7th October 1782, and received the degree of D.C.L. on 3d July 1793. He made a tour in Norway in 1773 and visited Switzerland and Italy between 1778 and 1780. His maiden speech on the political platform was delivered at Norwich on 28th January 1778, when he vehemently opposed the prosecution of the American War. On his return to England in 1780 he contested the representation of the city of Norwich, but was not successful. His entrance into public life took place in April 1783, when he went to Ireland as chief secretary to Lord Northington, the lord-lieutenant under the coalition ministry of Fox and Lord North. Windham was his own keenest critic, his distrust in his own powers and his disappointment at his own achievements being conspicuous on every page of his *Diary*. Sickness compelled his return to England early in July 1783; but change of scene and constant exercise restored him to health before the end of that year. In April 1784 he again contested Norwich and was returned by a majority of 64 votes, thus scoring one of the few triumphs attained by the adherents of the coalition cabinet. This seat he retained until 1802, when he was beaten by William Smith, one of the leaders of the Nonconformists. Though he strenuously opposed all proposals for parliamentary reform, to which most of the Whigs were deeply committed, Windham remained in alliance with that party until after the outbreak of the French Revolution, when he and several of his chief allies joined Pitt. The place of secretary-at-war was conferred upon him in July 1794, and he was at the same time created a privy councillor and admitted to a seat in the cabinet. Windham discharged the duties of his office with unflagging zeal, his efforts being particularly directed towards ameliorating the condition of the inferior grades of the army. In the autumn of 1794 he was despatched to the duke of York's camp in Flanders with the views of his ministerial colleagues, but their advice could not counteract the military incapacity of the royal duke. When Pitt was frustrated in his intention of freeing the Catholics from their political disabilities, Windham, who in religious matters always inclined to liberal opinions, took his place among the ministers who retired from office (February 1801). He was a constant opponent of all negotiations for peace with France, preferring to prosecute the campaign at whatever cost until some decisive victory had been gained, and the temporary peace of Amiens, which was carried through under Addington's administration, did not meet with his approval. When he was ousted from the representation of Norwich (July 1802), a seat for the pocket borough of St Mawes in Cornwall was found for him by its patron, the marquis of Buckingham, whose opinions coincided with Windham's on the leading political questions of the day. He declined a place in Pitt's new cabinet (May 1802) on the ground that the exclusion of Fox, who had joined with them in opposition to the weak ministry of Addington, prevented the formation of an administration sufficiently strong in parliament and the country to cope with the dangers which threatened the safety of the nation, and he offered a general opposition to the measures which the prime minister proposed. On Pitt's death in January 1806 the ministry of "All the Talents" was formed under the leadership of Lord Grenville, and Windham accepted the seals as secretary of state for war and the colonies. Fox's death necessitated several official changes; and a peerage was proposed for Windham, but he declined the proffered honour, and remained in office as long as the ministry existed. A general election took place in October 1806 and Windham was elected for the county of Norfolk; but the election was declared void on petition, and he was compelled to sit for the Treasury borough of New Romney, for which he had also been elected. In 1807, when the House was dissolved under the influence of the "No Popery" cry of Spencer Perceval, a seat was found for Windham by Lord Fitzwilliam in his close constituency of Higham Ferrers. Liberty of religious opinion he uniformly supported at all periods of his life, and with equal consistency he opposed all outbreaks of religious fanaticism; hence with these convictions in his mind few of the domestic measures of the new ministers met with his approbation. Moreover, he disapproved of the expedition to the Scheldt, and thought the charges brought against the duke of York, as commander-in-chief, required his retirement from office. At the same time he actively opposed the bill of Sir Samuel Romilly, his colleague on most political questions, for reducing the number of offences visited with the punishment of death. In July 1809 he received a blow on the hip whilst rendering assistance at a fire, which he thought little of at the time; but a tumour subsequently formed on the spot and an operation became necessary. This brought on a fever, and Windham rapidly sank. He died on 4th June 1810, and was buried in the family vault at Felbrigg.

Windham was tall and well-proportioned; and the impressiveness of his speeches was heightened by the excellence of his address. Exercise of all kinds had charms for him. He attended all the celebrated prize-fights of his day, and he more than once spoke in the House of Commons against the prevention of bull-baiting. Nor did he neglect the pleasures of literature and science. His speeches were published in three volumes in 1806, with a memoir by Thomas Amyot, his private secretary while he was in office in 1806, and his *Diary* was edited by Mrs Henry Baring in 1866. The passages in the latter work relative to Dr Johnson's declining days have been of considerable use to the later editors of Boswell.

WINDMILL. The date when windmills were first erected is unknown; but they were certainly used in Europe in the 12th century. Of late they have generally been replaced by steam engines in Great Britain; but they are still extensively employed in Holland in draining the polders and grinding trass. In America they are largely used; Wolff states that in some cities in the United States over 5000 windmills are manufactured annually. In spite of the competition of more powerful and tractable motors, windmills may often be used with success and economy, especially in new countries where fuel is scarce, and for work which can be done intermittently. The Indian Government recently made inquiries with a view to using windmills for irrigation, and a good deal of information will be found in a report by Colonel Brownlow in the *Professional Papers on Indian Engineering*, vol. viii. A windmill is not a very powerful motor, and in its employment its power is variable and intermittent. In good situations it will generally work for about eight hours out of the twenty-four on an average. Small windmills are useful on farms for working machines and pumping, in brickfields for pumping, and on ships for clearing out bilge water. They are employed for drainage purposes in Holland and Norfolk, and for mining purposes in some new countries. In America they are used to pump water at railway stations. Sir W. Thomson has proposed to utilize them in charging electric accumulators. As an auxiliary to a steam engine they are sometimes useful; thus at Faversham a 15-horse-power windmill raised in ten months 21,000,000 gallons of water from a depth of 109 feet, saving 100 tons of coal.

European Windmills.—In all the older windmills a shaft, called the wind shaft, carried four to six arms or whips on which long rectangular narrow sails were spread. The wind shaft was placed at an inclination of 10° or 15° with the horizontal, to enable the sails to clear the lower part of the mill. The whip carrying the sail was often 30 to 40 feet in length, so that the tips of the sails described a circle 60 to 80 feet in diameter. The sails were rectangular, 5 to 6 feet wide, and occupying five-sixths of the length of the whip. A triangular leading sail was sometimes added. Sometimes the sails consisted of a sail-cloth spread on a framework; at other times narrow boards were used. The oldest mill was no doubt the *post* mill, the whole structure being carried on a post; to bring the sails to face the wind, the structure was turned round by a long lever. The post mill was succeeded by the *tower*, *smock*, or *frock* mill, in which the mill itself consisted of a stationary tower, and the wind shaft and sails were carried in a revolving cap rotating on the top of the tower. Meikle introduced in 1750 an auxiliary windmill or fan, placed at right angles to the principal sails, for automatically turning the mill face to the wind. If the wind shifts, the small fan begins to revolve and, acting through gearing, rotates the cap of the mill. Mills are exposed to great danger if the sails are not reefed or furled in high winds, and the reefing serves also to prevent the speed of the mill becoming excessive. In 1807 Sir W. Cubitt introduced automatic reefing arrangements. The sails were made of thin boards held up to the wind by a weight. As the strength of the wind increased, the boards were pressed back and exposed less surface.

American Windmills.—American windmills generally have the sails arranged in an annulus or disk. The sails consist of narrow boards or slats arranged radially, each board inclined at a constant angle of weather (see below); and the impulse of the wind on these inclined surfaces drives the mill. An American mill presents a larger surface for a given length of sail, and consequently the construction is lighter. To turn the mill face to the wind, a simple large rudder or fish-tail is used, projecting backwards in a plane at right angles to the plane of rotation of the sails. There are a great variety of mills in America, but those most commonly used are of two types. (1) In those which have side-vane governor wheels the action equivalent to reefing the sails is effected by turning the whole wheel formed by the sails oblique to the wind, so as to diminish the wind's action. A side vane projects in the plane of rotation of the wheel, and the pressure of the wind on this tends to turn the wheel edgeways to the wind. This turning force is counterbalanced by a weight. Hence for moderate winds the wheel is held up face to the wind; for stronger winds it is turned obliquely. (2) In centrifugal governor mills the slats forming the wheel are connected together in sets of six or eight, each set being fixed on a bar at about the middle of its length. By rotating this bar, the boards or slats are brought end on to the wind, the action being analogous to shutting an umbrella. The boards are held up to the wind by a weight, and are also connected to a centrifugal governor. If the speed of the governor increases, the balls fly out and lift the weight; at the same time the sails are partially furled.

Warner's Annular Sail Windmill.—Messrs Warner of Cripplegate (London) make a windmill somewhat similar to American mills. The shutters or vanes consist of a frame covered with canvas, and these are pivoted between two angle-iron rings so as to form an annular sail. The vanes are connected with spiral springs, which keep them up to the best angle of weather for light winds. If the strength of the wind increases, the vanes give to the wind, forcing back the springs, and thus the area on which the wind acts diminishes. In addition, there are a striking lever and tackle for setting the vanes edgeways to the wind when the mill is stopped or a storm is expected. The wheel is kept face to the wind by a rudder in small mills; in large mills a subsidiary fan and gear are used. Fig. 1 shows a large mill of this kind, erected in a similar manner to a tower mill. The tower is a framework of iron, and carries a revolving cap, on which the wind shaft is fixed. Behind is the subsi-

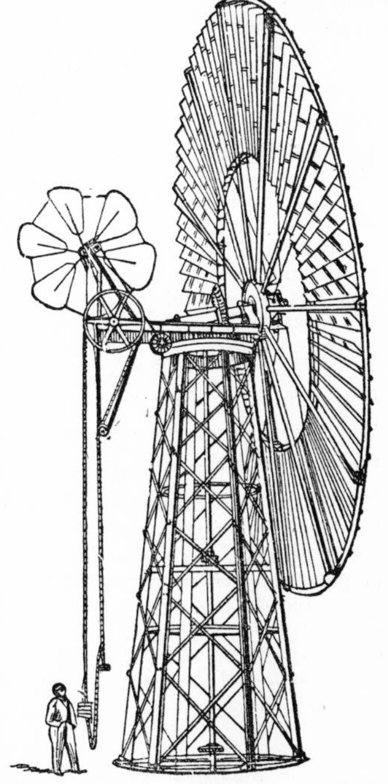

Fig. 1.—Warner's annular sail windmill.

diary fan with its gearing, acting on a toothed wheel fixed to the cap.

Relation between the Velocity of the Wind and its Pressure on Surfaces.—When a flat thin plate is exposed normally to the wind, the pressure on its front surface is increased and that on its back surface somewhat diminished. The resultant total pressure per square foot in the direction of the wind is given approximately by the equation

$$p = \cdot005\ v^2 \ldots\ldots\ldots\ldots(1)$$

if v is in miles per hour, or

$$p = \cdot0023\ v^2 \ldots\ldots\ldots\ldots(1a)$$

if v is in feet per second. Thus, winds at velocities of 5, 10, and 20 miles per hour would give a pressure of $\frac{1}{8}$ ℔, $\frac{1}{2}$ ℔, and 2 ℔ respectively on each square foot of a surface normal to the wind, and these may be considered ordinary working velocities for windmills. In storms the velocity of the wind may reach a much greater value. Pressures of 28 or 30 ℔ per square foot have been frequently registered by anemometers, and at exceptionally exposed stations pressures of 50, 80, and even 90 ℔ per square foot have been recorded. These pressures, which are useless for working the windmill, must, nevertheless, be reckoned with in deciding on its structural strength.

Pressure on Surfaces Oblique to the Wind.—The variation of pressure with inclination of surface is only known experimentally. Let R be the direction of the wind, making an angle θ with the normal to the surface, supposed to be at rest. Then, if p is the pressure per square foot of surface when the wind is normal to the surface, the resultant normal pressure on the oblique surface is

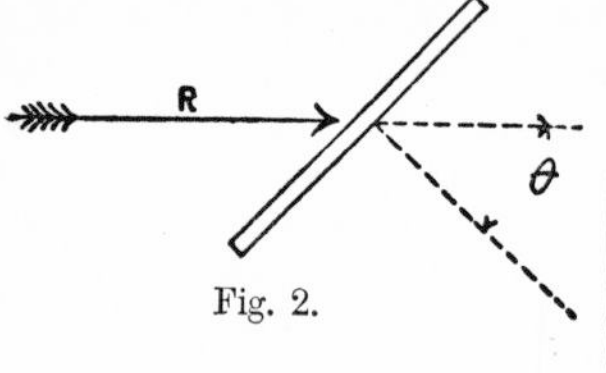

Fig. 2.

$$n = p\frac{2\cos\theta}{1+\cos^2\theta} \text{ ℔ per square foot} \ldots\ldots\ldots(2).$$

But the windmill sail moves in a direction perpendicular to the wind. Hence, if v is the velocity of the wind and u that of the sail, the relative velocity is $\sqrt{u^2+v^2}$, and the direction of relative motion can be found as follows. Let aa be the plane of rotation of the sail. The inclination θ of the sail to the plane of rotation is called the *angle of weather*, and is the same as the angle the wind makes with the normal to the sail. Set off $ob=v$, $bc=u$, then oc is the relative velocity, and this makes an angle $\phi=\tan^{-1}\frac{u}{v}$ with the direction of the wind and an angle $\theta+\phi$ with the normal to the sail. Hence for the moving sail

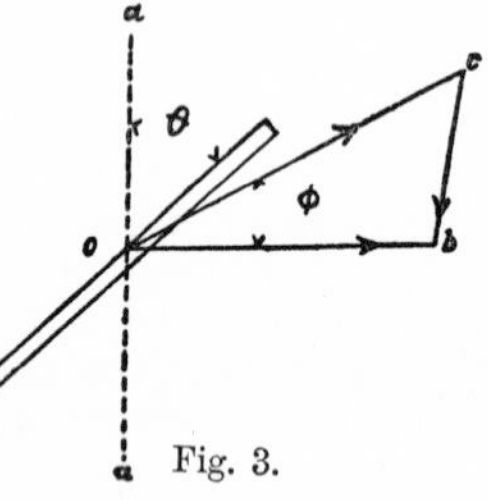

Fig. 3.

$$n = p\frac{2\cos(\theta+\phi)}{1+\cos^2(\phi+\theta)} \ldots\ldots\ldots(3).$$

Before replacing p by its value in (1) another consideration requires attention. The sail generally moves faster than the wind; it is not a thin-edged plane, but presents a not inconsiderable surface at right angles to its direction of motion, and thus creates resistance. Of the whole pressure of the wind a part only is effective, the rest being used to overcome the resistance of the sail. It will be assumed that the effective pressure driving the sails is only, for v in feet per second, $p = \cdot001\ v^2$ ℔ per square foot, and, therefore, the effective normal pressure on the sails is, for the relative velocity $\sqrt{v^2+u^2}$, $n = \cdot001(v^2+u^2)\frac{\cos(\theta+\phi)}{1+\cos^2(\theta+\phi)}$. The component of this in the direction of motion of the sail is $n \sin\theta$. Consequently the useful work of the sail expressed in foot-pounds per square foot is $nu\sin\theta = \cdot001(v^2+u^2)u\frac{\sin\theta}{\sec(\theta+\phi)+\cos(\theta+\phi)}$. By dividing the sail into strips and introducing the known values of u, v, and θ the work done is easily found.

Best Angle of Weather.—The best angle of weather is that which makes $\frac{\sin\theta}{\sec(\theta+\phi)+\cos(\theta+\phi)}$ a maximum. This gives the very simple rule $\theta = 67\frac{1}{2}° - \frac{3}{4}\phi$. Given the velocity of the wind and that of the tips of the sails, the value of ϕ is easily found for any point of the sail, and thence θ. Thus, for

$\frac{u}{v}$ = 3·0	2·5	2·0	1·5	1·0	0·5,
ϕ = 72°	68°	64°	57°	45°	27°,
θ = 13½°	16½°	19½°	24½°	33½°	47½°.

Horse-Power of Windmills.—For the older kinds of windmills the following rule derived from some experiments by Coulomb may be used. Let n = no. of sails, A area of each sail in square feet, v velocity of wind in feet per second; then the horse-power of the mill is $\frac{nAv^3}{1{,}660{,}000}$; this assumes the speed of the tips of the sails to be about $2\frac{1}{2}$ to 3 times the wind velocity. For American wheels Wolff gives the horse-power which may be expected for an average of 8 hours per day as follows:—

Diameter of Wheel in Feet.	Velocity of Wind in Miles per Hour.	Horse-Power of Mill.	Revolutions of Wheel per Minute.
8½	16	0·04	70–75
10	16	0·12	60–65
12	16	0·21	55–60
14	16	0·28	50–55
16	16	0·41	45–50
18	16	0·61	40–45
20	16	0·78	35–40
25	16	1·34	30–35

Further information will be found in Rankine, *The Steam Engine and other Prime Movers*; Weisbach, *The Mechanics of Engineering*; and Wolff, *The Windmill as a Prime Mover*. (W. C. U.)

WINDSOR,[1] a parliamentary and municipal borough of Berkshire, England, 21 miles from London by the Great Western Railway, situated on the right bank of the Thames, is chiefly remarkable for its royal castle. The town itself[2] is of no special interest, in spite of its great antiquity. In 1276 Edward I. made Windsor a free borough. In 1302 it began to send representatives to parliament, though at irregular intervals, and from the time of Henry VI. it returned two members till 1867, when they were reduced to one. The town is presided over by a mayor, aldermen, and councillors, who were incorporated by a charter of Edward IV. The town-hall was built in 1686 by Sir Christopher Wren, but was much altered in 1852. The Thames is crossed here by a bridge resting on three granite piers (1823). The parish church of St John the Baptist was rebuilt in 1822; the other two churches are also modern. The town was formerly celebrated for the number of its inns, of which "The Garter" and "The White Hart" were the chief. The former was the favourite inn of Shakespeare's Sir John Falstaff, and is frequently mentioned in the *Merry Wives of Windsor*. In 1650 the town contained 70 inns, many of which were very picturesque half-timbered buildings; but none of these now exist. In

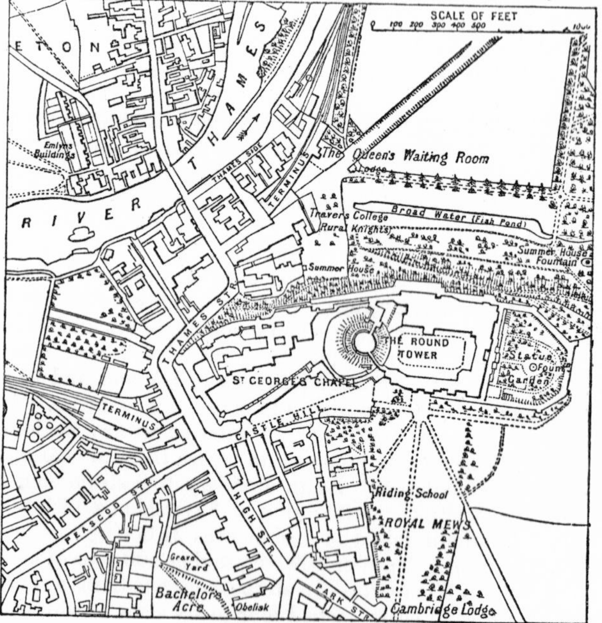

Plan of Windsor.

[1] The name is said to be derived from *Windelsora* (A.S. *windel*, "to wind," and *or*, a "shore," from the winding course of the Thames).

[2] In official documents the town is called New Windsor, to distinguish it from its parent settlement Old Windsor, which is now a village prettily situated about two miles to the south-east of Windsor Castle.

1871 the population of the municipal borough was 11,769 and in 1881 12,273; that of the parliamentary borough (area 3253 acres) in the same years was 17,281 and 19,082 respectively. Of this last total 3464 were in Buckinghamshire, into which county the parliamentary borough of Windsor extends.

Windsor Castle, from its commanding position, its stately group of ancient buildings, and its long list of historical associations, is one of the most magnificent and interesting of royal palaces. It has for many centuries been the chief residence of the English sovereigns.[1] As early as the time of the Heptarchy a stronghold of some importance existed at Windsor; the chief part of this still remains, and forms the great circular mound, about 125 feet in diameter, on which the Round Tower now stands. This great earthwork was once surrounded by the fosse, agger, and vallum which were usually constructed to defend both Roman and Saxon strongholds. The primitive wooden enclosure was replaced by a stone circuit-wall in the time of William the Conqueror; and the first complete Round Tower was built by Henry III. about 1272, but was wholly reconstructed on a more massive scale by Edward III., who in 1344 designed the new tower to form a meeting-place for his newly-established order of the Knights of the Garter. Edward selected this spot because, according to a popular legend (quoted by Froissart), it was on the summit of the circular mound that King Arthur used to sit surrounded by his knights of the Round Table. The main bulk of the present Round Tower is of this date; but its walls were heightened, and the tall flag-turret was added by the court architect, Sir Jeffrey Wyatville, in the reign of George IV. In addition to the Round Tower, Henry III. constructed long lines of circuit-walls, crowned at intervals with many smaller towers, one of which, named after him, still exists in good preservation. He also built a great hall, kitchen, and other apartments, together with a chapel, which was afterwards pulled down to make room for the present chapel of St George. The beautiful little chapel cloister which Henry III. built still exists, and on its walls are traces of contemporary paintings in distemper. Another chapel was built by Henry III. and dedicated to his favourite saint, Edward the Confessor. This graceful building, with an eastern apse, is now called the Albert Memorial Chapel; a good deal of Henry III.'s work still exists in the lower part of its walls, but the upper part was rebuilt in 1501-3 by Henry VII. Some years later the unfinished chapel was given by Henry VIII. to Cardinal Wolsey, and for long after it was known as "Wolsey's tomb-house." Wolsey engaged a Florentine sculptor named Benedetto[2] to make him a very magnificent and costly tomb of marble and gilt bronze, with a recumbent effigy at the top, probably very similar in design to Torrigiano's tomb of Henry VII. at Westminster. The rich bronze work of Wolsey's tomb was torn off and melted by order of the Commonwealth in 1642, and the mere metal was sold for the then large sum of £600. In 1805 the black marble sarcophagus, stripped of its bronze ornaments, was moved from Windsor and used as a monument over Nelson's grave in the crypt of St Paul's. Though Wolsey's tomb-house was roofed in and used for mass by James II., the stone vaulting was not completed till recent times, when the whole place was fitted up by Sir Gilbert Scott as a memorial to the Prince Consort. Its internal walls were then lined with rich marbles, and decorated with reliefs by Baron Triqueti, in a style somewhat tawdry and discordant with the old building.

The magnificent chapel of St George ranks next to Westminster Abbey as a royal mausoleum, though no king was buried there before Edward IV., who left directions in his will that a very splendid tomb was to be erected with an effigy of himself in silver. Nothing now remains of this, except part of the wrought iron grille which surrounded the tomb—one of the most elaborate and skilfully wrought pieces of iron-work in the world. This grille has recently been moved from the north aisle to the north side of the sanctuary. The next sovereign buried here was Henry VIII., who directed that his body should be laid beside that of Jane Seymour, in a magnificent bronze and marble tomb. The tomb was never completed, and what existed of its metal-work was probably melted down by the Commonwealth. No trace of it now remains. The chapel itself is one of the finest examples of Perpendicular architecture in England, and is on the whole finer in design than the other two royal chapels, those of King's College at Cambridge and that of Henry VII. at Westminster, which were a little later in date. The existing building was begun by Edward IV., who in 1473 pulled down almost the whole of the earlier chapel, which had been completed and filled with stained glass by Edward III. in 1363. The nave of St George's was vaulted about the year 1490, but the choir groining was not finished till 1507; the hanging pendants from the fan vaulting of the choir mark a later development of style, which contrasts strongly with the simpler lines of the earlier nave vault. In 1516 the lantern and the rood-screen were completed, but the stalls and other fittings were not finished till after 1519.

The present private apartments of the sovereign at Windsor were mostly rebuilt or remodelled by Sir Jeffrey Wyatville, but some of the rooms, and especially the library, contain fine mantelpieces and ceilings of the 16th and 17th centuries. Among the many treasures preserved in the royal library is a fine collection of drawings by the chief Italian painters, together with three volumes of MSS. in the autograph of Leonardo da Vinci, illustrated with many drawings by his hand.[3] The library also contains a magnificent series of portraits by Holbein, eighty-seven in number, highly finished in sepia and chalk, representing the chief personages of Henry VIII.'s court—all of them works of the highest beauty and marvels of iconic vigour. The foundation attached to the royal chapel, which possesses the privileges of a "royal peculiar," consists of a dean, who is exempt from any episcopal jurisdiction, and a college of canons.

The royal forest of Windsor is one of the finest in the country, though it has been much reduced in size even since 1790, when it contained about 60,000 acres; many of its oaks are of great size and antiquity. (J. H. M.)

WINDWARD ISLANDS. See West Indies.

WINE

THE word "wine" in its widest sense includes all alcoholic beverages derived from sacchariferous vegetable juices by spontaneous fermentation; in the narrower sense of its ordinary acceptance it designates the fermented product of grape juice, with which alone the present article proposes to deal.

Part I.—Chemistry.

Vinous fermentation, phenomenally and chemically, is

[1] See Loftie, *Windsor*, reprinted with etchings from *The Portfolio*, London, 1885; Tighe and Davis, *Annals of Windsor*, 1860: and Ashton, *Illustrations of Windsor Castle*, 1841.

[2] Probably a son or nephew of the Florentine sculptor Benedetto da Maiano, who died in 1497; another member of the same family was employed by Wolsey at Hampton Court.

[3] These have recently been printed with an English translation by Dr Richter, London, 1883. See also Dr Waagen, *Treasures of Art in Britain*, London, 1854, vol. ii.

Vinous fermentation.

fully explained under FERMENTATION (vol. ix. p. 92 *sq.*). From what is said there it will be readily understood that wine-making is an easy art where there is a sufficient supply of perfectly ripe grapes. In Italy, Spain, Greece, and other countries of southern Europe nature takes care of this; in the more northern of the wine-producing districts of France, and especially on the Rhine in Germany, the culture of the vine means hard work from one end of the year to the other, which only exceptionally finds its full reward. And yet it is in those naturally less favoured districts that the most generous wines are produced. Southern wines excel in body and strength; but even the best of them lack the beautiful aroma (*Blume* or *bouquet*) characteristic of high-class Rhine wine. The large proportion of sugar in southern grape juice would appear to be inimical to the development of that superior flavour. Yet in Missouri, for instance, where wine is produced in pretty much the Rhenish way, from Rhenish kinds of grapes, which there ripen far more readily than they do at home, no wine equal in flavour to real Rhine wine has as yet been made. It seems that the hard struggle for existence which the vine-plant has to fight on the Rhine is essential for the development of the peculiar flavour of the wine.

Processes for maturing wine.

To secure the highest attainable degree of maturity in the grapes, the vintage on the Rhine is postponed until the grapes almost begin to wither, and the white grapes on the sunny side of the bunches exhibit a yellowish brown (instead of a green) colour and show signs of flaccidity. In the best vineyards (where it is worth the trouble) the bunches are carefully sorted, the ripest being put aside and pressed by themselves. In some places even the individual bunches are analysed and the best berries cut out with a pair of scissors, to be used by themselves. The processes concerned in the extraction of the juice are described below (p. 605). If the production of red wine is intended, the juice is allowed to ferment over the stalks and skins until enough of alcohol has been produced to enable the juice to extract the pigment from the skins. After that juice and residue are separated. The alcohol, however, extracts other things besides the pigment, especially tannin, which imparts to red wines their characteristic astringency. The must (or magma of crushed grapes) is immediately conveyed to a cool cellar, the temperature of which should lie between 9° and 12° C., and is placed in large tubs or vats or open casks, and is then left to itself. Although no yeast is added from without, vinous fermentation sets in sooner or later, and after some four to five days is in full swing. On the seventh day, as a rule, the process has passed its climax, and after ten to fourteen days the yeast-scum on the surface disappears and the liquid clears up. It now constitutes what is called *Jungwein*, which still contains a considerable remnant of unfermented sugar. This young wine is drawn off into large casks and placed in cellars having a temperature of 9° to 12° C.; there it is left for some months, generally until the following March. The casks are filled almost to the bung-hole and kept full by the occasional addition of wine, the small bung-hole being covered so as to provide an outlet for the carbonic acid, without giving any greater access to the air than is absolutely unavoidable, to prevent acetous fermentation. During this period the small remnant of sugar in the young wine gradually ferments away, while the percentage of alcohol undergoes a corresponding gradual increase. As this after-fermentation progresses very slowly, there is no perceptible increase of temperature in the liquid, and even the newly-formed yeast cells remain deposited at the bottom as a precipitate. On it certain components of the must, being less soluble in (alcoholic) wine than in the must, separate out, as, for instance, the albumenoids and, most markedly, the bitartrate of potash; this last separates out conjointly with tartrate of lime and colouring-matters, as a coherent crust known as *argol*. The finished young wine is drawn off clear into smaller casks, bunged up, and allowed to mature. It is during this period that the "bloom" of the wine develops, probably through the very slow formation of ethers from the alcohol and the acids previously produced, or from traces of higher alcohols by oxidation. How long a wine should be allowed to mature depends on its richness. With relatively poor wines a year's maturing may be amply sufficient; rich wines continue improving for years.

To give an idea of the composition of grape juice, we quote two analyses of high-class musts of 1868, by Neubauer:—

	Neroberg Riesling.	Steinberger Auslese.
Sugar	18·06	24·24
Free acid	0·42	0·43
Albumenoids	0·22	0·18
Combined organic acids and extracts	4·11	3·92
Mineral matter	0·47	0·45
Total solids	23·28	29·22
Water (by diff.)	76·72	70·78
	100	100

Supposing such musts to ferment, the albumenoids are partly precipitated as components of the yeast or otherwise, or decomposed, with formation of ammonia salt; part of the phosphates go into the yeast likewise; the greater part of the bitartrate of potash of the juice is precipitated as argol; and the greater part, if not all, of the sugar is decomposed, with formation from every 100 parts of sugar destroyed of alcohol 48·5, carbonic acid 46·9, succinic acid 0·7, glycerin 3·0, matter passing into the yeast 0·9 as principal products.

Minor fermentations.

Besides the predominating process of vinous fermentation proper, certain minor fermentations and other bye-reactions take place, which lead to the formation of free acetic and other fatty acids, ethers, and traces of higher alcohols. Of these last, however, which play such an important part in whisky-brewing, only very little is formed in grape-juice fermentation. Of the bye-products the ethers are undoubtedly the most important, because it is they that constitute the bloom; but our knowledge regarding them is very limited. The flavour of a wine is due to two sets of volatile bodies, namely—(i.) œnanthic ether (see ŒNANTHIC ACID, vol. xvii. p. 731), to which is due the smell common to all wines (which remains in an empty wine cask after the bloom proper has gone), and (ii.) a set of ethers (are they ethers?) which constitute the *Blume*. Geiger distilled a bottle of good wine and then re-mixed residue and distillate. But the mixture was not drinkable; yet, after having been bottled up for a long time, it gradually regained its original virtues. These remarks apply only to white Rhenish wines. Red wines, in addition to the components named, contain chiefly colouring and astringent matters. The wines of Hungary, France, &c., as is well known, have a different character from those of the Rhine region; but the scientific analysis of the relations is of comparatively little importance.

In all rich musts part of the sugar escapes fermentation and imparts to the wine a higher or lower degree of sweetness; southern wines (port, sherry, &c.), even in their natural condition, contain relatively large percentages of sugar. In their case it is chiefly this sugar, in Rhine wine the glycerin and what there may be of unchanged sugar, which constitute the "body" of the wine. Spanish and Portuguese wines, however, especially those intended for exportation into Great Britain, are habitually doctored by the addition of cane sugar and cognac.

Wine-brewing.

Wine-Brewing.—One mode of assisting nature in wine-making is the process of "gallisizing," so called from its inventor (Gall), which is largely practised on the Rhine. In a given vineyard the must produced in a good year is characterized by certain percentages of free acid and of sugar. In bad years the latter decreases and the former increases. But this, according to Gall, can be easily remedied by adding sugar and water in sufficient quantity to establish the percentages of free acid and sugar which are characteristic of the best years, and then allowing the mixture to ferment. The sugar is added sometimes in the form of cane sugar (which is no doubt the best substitute for natural grape sugar obtainable), but more frequently in the form of what is known in commerce as "grape sugar," which is in reality more or less impure dextrose produced from potatoes or maize starch (see SUGAR, vol. xxii. p. 623). Scientifically speaking, Gall's method appears to be unobjectionable; but that it does so is really owing to our ignorance of the intricacies of the actual process of grape-juice fermentation. In any case, grape juice is one thing and dextrose plus so much pump-water is another; and the sale of gallisized as "natural" wine must be pronounced a fraud. Science affords a means of distinguishing a gallisized from a natural wine, if the added sugar consisted of dextrose. The sugar of normal grape juice is half dextrose and half lævulose; a similar mixture is produced from added cane sugar. In the process of fermentation the dextrose is the first to disappear; the rest of the lævulose then follows. Hence a finished natural wine, if it turns the plane of polarized light at all, will turn it to the left; but, if the wine was doctored with dextrose, certain dextro-rotatory impurities survive to the end and the wine turns the plane of polarization to the right (Neubauer). A commission of experts who met in Berlin in 1884 declared gallisizing to be a legitimate practice as long as the water added does not amount to more than twice the weight of the added sugar. Liebig long ago recommended the addition of a concentrated solution of neutral tartrate of potash to ready-made wine, as a means for reducing its acidity. If the free acid is tartaric, it combines with the tartrate into cream of tartar, which gradually separates out and can be removed by decantation or filtration. Long before Gall, Chaptal showed that bad must may be improved by adding the calculated weight of (cane) sugar and neutralizing the excessive acid by means of powdered marble. The principal feature in Chaptal's, as compared with Gall's method, is that it discards the resources of the pump.

Plastering wine.

In Spain, Portugal, and France it is a very common practice to dust over the grapes with plaster of Paris or to add the plaster to the must. The intention is, in the former case, to prevent putrefaction of the berries, in the latter to add to the chemical stability of the wine. According to experience, a plastered wine is ready for bottling sooner than it would be in its natural condition. The chemical process involved consists in this: the sulphate of lime, $CaSO_4$, decomposes the bitartrate of potash, $(C_4H_4O_6)KH$, of the must, with the formation of insoluble tartrate of lime, $(C_4H_4O_6)Ca$, and soluble acid sulphate of potash, $KHSO_4$. The latter takes up potash from, chiefly, the phosphate present and becomes normal salt, K_2SO_4, with the formation of free acid (*e.g.*, phosphoric acid). A plastered wine is relatively rich in potash and in sulphuric acid. Amongst German wine-analysts it is customary to report all the sulphuric acid found as sulphate of potash, K_2SO_4. If the calculated sulphate amounts to less than 2 grammes per litre, the wine is passed as being at any rate not excessively plastered. But the interpretation of a sulphuric acid determination, in the case of German wines more especially, is rendered very uncertain owing to the widely spread practice that prevails of disinfecting wine-casks with sulphurous acid (by burning sulphur within them) before they are used.

Want of space will not allow of the treatment of wine analysis generally; but sufficient has been said to show how far the genuineness of a wine can be proved by chemical analysis. Against the most important and frequently occurring fraud, namely, the substitution of a genuine, but inferior, for a high class wine of a similar kind, chemical analysis is at present absolutely powerless.

Injurious ferments, &c.

It sometimes happens that wine becomes viscous and forms threads when poured from the bottle. This mischief, which is caused by the development of a foreign ferment, can be cured by the judicious addition of a solution of tannin, which precipitates the "gum." From a similar cause comes acetous fermentation, which always takes place in a moderate degree, but may assume undue dimensions. Red wines are liable to develop a foreign substance which imparts to them a bitter taste. A wine kept in a mouldy cask assumes of course a mouldy taste and smell. Sometimes a wine will "capsize": the alcohol and the acid disappear and what was wine becomes an insipid undrinkable liquid. Most of the injurious effects caused in wine by foreign ferments can be prevented by a process introduced by Pasteur. The wine is kept for a sufficient time at a temperature of 70° C. in the absence of air, and then transferred to a germ-free cask, without allowing it to come in contact with more air than can be helped. The only objection to Pasteur's precautionary method is that it renders the wine slightly flat through the removal of part of its carbonic acid. No doubt these deleterious consequences might be prevented to a very great extent if the fermentation were conducted from the first in casks which communicated with the air only through a (wide enough) tube full of cotton wool, which medium is known to filter off all germs (see FERMENTATION, vol. ix. p. 95).

Sparkling wines.

Effervescing or Sparkling Wines.—These wines are largely impregnated with carbonic acid engendered by an after-fermentation in the closed bottle by means of added sugar. The art originated in Champagne, where the best sparkling wines are produced, and whence it has spread to the Rhine, the Moselle, and other districts. The natural wine of Champagne is not of a very high order; yet it produces the best champagne. For champagne-making blue grapes are preferred. In eliminating the juice excessive pressure is avoided, so as to keep the must clear of particles of skin. The processes of fermentation and clearing, as well as those connected with the making of champagne generally, are described in detail below (p. 606). Champagne-makers distinguish three grades of effervescence. In *mousseux* the pressure in the bottle amounts to from 4 to 4½ atmospheres; in *grand mousseux* it reaches 5 atmospheres; and less than 4 atmospheres' pressure constitutes *cremant* (from *la crème*, "cream"), a wine which throws up a froth but does not give off carbonic acid violently. A champagne which contains relatively little sugar is called "dry"; it is chiefly this kind which is imported into Great Britain, where champagne is used habitually as a dinner wine. In France a sweet wine is preferred. The intensely sweet substance called "saccharine" (see SUGAR, vol. xxii. p. 623) has been utilized for producing a sparkling wine which is both sweet and dry. Cheap champagnes may be (and we believe are) produced by simply adding sugar and some flavouring matter to wine, and then pumping in carbonic acid in the soda-water fashion. The following extract from a table by August Dupré will show the chemical composition of the wines most popular in Great Britain. The numbers may be read as grammes per litre or as ounces per 1000 fluid ounces.

	Alcohol.	Free Acid, fixed.	Volatile Acid.	Total Dry Matter.	Glucose.
Hock at 30s. a dozen	96	3·5	0·6	18·6	nil
,, at 120s. ,,	104	4·3	0·9	20·6	1·1
Claret at 15s. ,,	85	4·2	1·5	21·4	4·3
,, at 66s. ,,	85	3·2	1·8	18	1·0
Sherry at 22s. ,,	172	2·7	1·5	42	26
,, high price	184	2·8	1·6	56	35
Port at 32s. a dozen ...	186	3·1	0·8	75	43
,, high price	182	2·7	1·1	31	10

(W. D.)

Part II.—Industry and Trade.

At the present day wine is practically a European product, although a certain quantity is made in the United States, at the Cape of Good Hope, and in Australia. The principal countries in Europe where the vine is grown to any extent are France, Spain, Portugal, Austria-Hungary, Italy, Germany, and the southern portions of Russia and Greece; but in the first six alone is wine an article of much commercial importance.

Historical sketch. In the lands of the Levant the use of wine is as old as the earliest memory of civilization, and we find its introduction ascribed to gods (Dionysus in Greece, Osiris in Egypt), or, in the case of the Hebrews, to the patriarch Noah, the second father of mankind. Corn, wine, and oil appear together (as in the Old Testament) as the main gifts of the soil, the material bases of life and comfort. The cultivation of the vine was the highest achievement of ancient husbandry, impossible to semi-nomadic peoples, who might grow a corn crop, but did not remain long enough in one spot to form vineyards. Thus the vine and the olive are in antiquity the marks and almost the symbols of settled and cultured life. Starting perhaps from Armenia and eastern Pontus, viticulture gradually made its way through the lands of ancient civilization, rejected only by a race like the Nabatæans (*q.v.*), whose laws were directed to prevent the transition from nomadic to settled life (cp. the Old Testament Rechabites). Of Asiatic wines the most famous was that of Chalybon (Helbon) near Damascus, which was an article of Phœnician commerce in the time of Ezekiel (xxvii. 18) and at a later date furnished the tables of the Persian kings. Of Greek wines the most famous came from the islands (as Chios, Lesbos, Cos) or from points on the Asiatic coast (Strabo, xiv. p. 637). The vine reached Spain through the Phœnicians, and Italy and southern Gaul (Marseilles) from Greece; it had no place in the oldest Roman husbandry, nor was wine used in the oldest Roman ritual. But in time Italy became a great wine country, and Cato regards viticulture as the most profitable branch of husbandry. It was indeed artificially fostered by the Roman republic, which prohibited the import of foreign growths into Italy and stimulated exports by restrictions on wine-growing in the provinces, especially in southern Gaul, which thus became a great market for Italian wines. These restrictions were not wholly removed till the time of Probus (*q.v.*), when the reins of empire were no longer in Italian hands. In the first century of our era Spanish and Gaulish as well as Greek wines were drunk at Rome (Pliny), but in Gaul the production seems to have been limited to the districts of the Allobroges and Bituriges on the Rhone and the Gironde. It was after Probus's time that viticulture seems to have been established on the Seine and the Moselle, and Julian when in Gaul still found occasion to discharge an epigram against the false Dionysus of Celtic beer. The northward spread of the vine was doubtless also retarded by difficulties of acclimatization, which were only gradually overcome. In the Middle Ages, when transport was difficult, wine was produced in the south of England and in several parts of Germany where there is now no motive for urging a precarious husbandry.[1] The exact mode of vine-culture and wine-making amongst the ancients is somewhat obscure; but there is reason to believe that the latter, although in a somewhat cruder form, closely resembled the system in use at the present day. As far as viticulture is concerned, we find from Pliny and others that the Romans encouraged the upward growth of the vine upon trees and palisades in preference to the dwarf system now followed in the more northern regions, such as France,—a fact doubtless attributable to the almost tropical luxuriance which the vine attains in Italy. Little comparative information can be obtained as to the style of wine made by the ancients; but from the few facts we do know it may be presumed that, apart from alcoholic qualities, the wines of Greece and Rome had not the high properties possessed by those of the present day.

[1] On the history of viticulture, see especially Hehn, *Culturpflanzen*, &c., 3d ed., p. 63 *sq.*, and Mommsen, *Röm. Gesch.*, v. 98 *sq.* In accordance with the history of the plant, the names wine, *vinum*, &c., are traced by philologists to οἶνος. The further history of the name is obscure; but it seems to be Indo-European; the Hebrew *yayin* is almost certainly a loan-word.

The introduction of resinous flavours or of salt, then usually resorted to, would hardly suit the present high rearing of vinous products. The vintage in the more favoured districts began towards the end of September and in the less favoured during the following month. Grapes were not gathered until they had attained their fullest maturity, and in many instances they were allowed to dry three or four days in the sun after gathering in order to obtain further sweetness and body. The grapes were trodden and then submitted to the press, much after the custom still prevalent in Burgundy and Portugal. When, however, the juice was deemed too thin and watery for the production of good wine, it was boiled down to a greater consistency, whilst a small portion of gypsum was added to it. The original receptacles for wine appear to have been the skins of animals, rendered impervious by oil or resinous substances, but later on the principal vessels were made of earthenware (amphoræ and the like) or, in certain districts, though less frequently, of wood, after the style of modern casks. In modern as compared with ancient times the wine-growing industry has considerably changed its locality. Although Italy and (in a very minor degree) Greece still produce a considerable quantity of wine, yet France, Spain, and Portugal must now be recognized as the chief homes of viticulture. France is the country whose modern agricultural history and export trade are most connected with wine production; and, although, in consequence of the *Phylloxera* and mildew, the yield has fallen off of late years, it still holds the premier position for quantity, variety, and general excellence of quality.

France.

France. It was only by degrees, owing partly to its soil and partly to the aptitude of its inhabitants, that France developed the position which it now holds as a wine-producing country. Geographically and meteorologically speaking, it is in every way eminently fitted for this. The winters are not too cold, nor, on the other hand, have the summers the intense heat and drought which are often so prejudicial to the vine in southern climates. The country is throughout of that gently undulating character which is so important for the proper exposure and ripening of the grape, whilst the calcareous properties of the soil are especially favourable to the growth of the plant. The habits of the people, moreover, and the system of small holdings have also undoubtedly done much in developing the industry; for there is, perhaps, no branch of agriculture which requires more minute attention, or for which such a system of land tenure is more suitable, than vine culture. At present throughout all France there are only ten departments in which wine is not produced,—Calvados, Côtes-du-Nord, Finistère, Manche, Nord, Oise, Orne, Pas-de-Calais, Seine-Inférieure, and Somme; and in 1887 the total production amounted to 24,333,284 hectolitres, or some 535,332,250 gallons, which, however, is considerably less than the average for the previous ten years, owing to the immense injury caused by the *Phylloxera*. In 1875, the *annus mirabilis* of wine-production in France, the yield amounted to 83,632,391 hectolitres, or nearly three and a half times that of twelve years later.

Médoc. As France is the home of wine-growing, so must the Médoc district in its turn be considered the very heart of that industry in France, for nowhere have such elegance, *finesse*, and distinct variety been obtained as on the banks of the Gironde. Unlike the products of the different vineyards of most other districts, which are purchased by the merchant and vatted to supply a general wine of commerce, the yields of the principal estates of Médoc are kept distinct, and reach the consumer as the product of the particular growth and the particular year. This practice is, almost without exception, resorted to with what are known as the classed growths and the superior bourgeois, whilst in seasons in which the wines are of good quality it is continued down to the lower grades. The area of the department of Gironde is about 2,407,000 acres, of which some 500,000 acres are under the vine. There are six descriptions of soil:—(1) that of the valleys, chiefly alluvial, the vines on which produce wines of considerable colour and vinosity, but wanting in *finesse*; (2) the strong lands, which require frequent working and the assistance of lighter earths and manures, although, when of a ferruginous colour, this soil is very favourable to the vine; (3) the marshy lands, which are of considerable extent, and which, when gravel enters into their composition, are extremely fertile; (4) lands formed at the surface of gravel, quartz, and heavy sand, with clay subsoil, over which are grown most of the finest vines of the Médoc; (5) the silicious or flinty soils, covering about one-half of the department, of which some portions, when worked with clay and calcareous elements, are suitable for vine cultivation; (6) the intermediate lands, between the strong soil and the last-named, which are chiefly available for the growth of the commoner descriptions of white wines. The principal vines used in the Médoc are, for red wines, the Cabernets (2), the Merlot, and the Malbec, and for white wines, the Semillon, the Sauvignon, and the Muscatelle. The vines of the Cabernet species, although producing excellent grapes, are especially susceptible to damage from weather at flowering time, and consequently are not so greatly used as the Merlot, which is very productive, and not so liable to attacks from *Oidium* as other descriptions. The grapes of this vine, however, have to be gathered with promptitude, as they ripen very quickly and if subjected to rain soon become rotten. The vine most generally selected, however, is the Malbec, which is a remarkably early bearer, its chief disadvantage being that it is very susceptible to frost. Of the various vine diseases and pests the chief is undoubtedly the *Phylloxera* (see VINE, p. 238 above), which was first seen in Médoc in 1869. The amount of damage caused by this insect during the past fifteen years is almost incredible, and at one time it was feared that the vineyards would be wholly destroyed. Of late, however, considerable success has been met with in checking its inroads, the area now under vine cultivation being larger than was the case when its ravages first began to make themselves severely felt. Another evil which has occasionally been very virulent is the *Oidium*, a species of fungus, which first made its appearance in France in 1851, about which time it also devastated the vineyards of Madeira. Another cause from which an enormous amount of damage has been done of recent years is the mildew, which not only destroys the leaves and fruit, but further leaves its taint on wines made from grapes affected by it. It is believed, however, that a complete cure or prevention for this pest has been found in a solution of sulphate of copper. In addition to these enemies, the vine-grower has to take account of hail, frost, and *coulure*—this last caused by too great humidity of the soil, which leads to large quantities of flowers falling from the branches before turning into grapes, and also to the grapes themselves falling. The vintage in Médoc usually commences between the middle and end of September and lasts from two to three weeks. The process is a very simple one. The grapes are gathered and brought on bullock drays to the press-house; here they are separated from the stalks and placed in vats, where they are allowed to ferment for a period of from seven to fifteen days. As soon as the wine is sufficiently made, it is drawn off into hogsheads and removed to light and airy stores. The first month the bung is put lightly in and the cask filled up every three or four days; the second month it is put in more firmly and the cask filled every eight days. In March, the lees having fallen, the first *soutirage* or drawing-off takes place. A second is made in June and a third in November, after which the hogsheads are turned on their side and the fillings-up cease. In the second and following years, after the wine has been removed to dark cellars, two drawings-off suffice, one in spring and the other in autumn. After this, if the wine ferments, it is drawn off in a sulphured cask, and if necessary fined with eggs and again drawn off in a fortnight.

The great variety of qualities that the wines of Médoc possess has necessitated their classification, by which they have been divided into paysan, artisan, bourgeois, and fine growths, the last-named being subdivided into five categories, and known as the "classed growths." This classification is the result of years of observation and study, going back to the 18th century, its present form being the result of a conference of brokers in 1855. Subjoined is a list of the red wines of Médoc (the English "claret"), with the names of the cantons to which they belong.

FIRST GROWTHS.

Château Lafitte, Pauillac.	Château Latour, Pauillac.
,, Margaux, Margaux.	,, Haut-Brion, Pessac.

SECOND GROWTHS.

Château Mouton-Rothschild, Pauillac.	Château Gruaud-Larose, St Julien.
,, Rauzan-Ségla, Margaux.	,, Branne-Cantenac, Cantenac.
,, Rauzan-Gassies, ,,	,, Pichon-Longueville, Pauillac.
,, Léoville-Lascases, St Julien.	,, Pichon-Longueville-Lalande, Pauillac.
,, Léoville-Poyferré, ,,	,, Ducru-Beaucaillou, St Julien.
,, Léoville-Barton, ,,	Cos d'Estournel, St Estèphe.
,, Durfort-Vivens, Margaux.	Château Montrose, ,,
,, Lascombes, ,,	
,, Gruaud-Larose-Sarget, St Julien.	

THIRD GROWTHS.

Château Kirwan, Cantenac.	Château Palmer, Cantenac.
,, D'Issan, Cantenac.	,, La Lagune, Ludon.
,, Lagrange, St Julien.	,, Desmirail, Margaux.
,, Langoa, ,,	,, Calon-Ségur, St Estèphe.
,, Giscours, Labarde.	,, Ferrière, Margaux.
,, Malescot, Margaux.	,, Becker, ,,
,, Brown Cantenac, Cantenac.	

FOURTH GROWTHS.

Château Saint-Pierre, St Julien.	Château La Tour Carnet, St Laurent.
,, Branaire-Duluc, ,,	,, Rochet, St Estèphe.
,, Talbot, ,,	,, Beychevelle, St Julien.
,, Duhart-Milon, Pauillac.	Le Prieuré, Cantenac.
,, Poujet, Cantenac.	Marquis de Therme, Margaux.

FIFTH GROWTHS.

Château Pontet-Canet, Pauillac.	Château Le Tertre, Arsac.
,, Batailley, ,,	,, Haut-Bages, Pauillac.
Grand-Puy-Lacoste, ,,	,, Pedesclaux, ,,
Ducasse-Grand-Puy, ,,	,, Belgrave, St Laurent.
Château Lynch-Bages, ,,	,, Camensac, ,,
,, Lynch-Moussas, ,,	Cos-Labory, St Estèphe.
,, Dauzac, Labarde.	Château Clerc-Milon, Pauillac.
,, Mouton-d'Armailhacq, Pauillac.	,, Croizet-Bages ,,
	,, Cantemerle, Macau.

The average yield of the Gironde during the ten years 1876-1886 amounted to 1,435,863 hectolitres, or about 31,589,000 gallons, an average which has been placed considerably lower than that of the preceding decade by the small yields of 1881, 1882, 1884, and 1885. In each of the prolific years of 1874 and 1875 the production of the Gironde exceeded 5,000,000 hectolitres, and in 1869 it reached 4,500,000. The principal claret vintages of the 19th century are considered to have been those of 1815, '25, '28, '31, '34, '41, '47, '48, '58, '64, '69, '70, '74, and '75. From 1875 to 1882 nothing exceptional was produced. Of the vintages since 1882 it is still too early to speak, although it is probable that some of the 1884's, where they have escaped the mildew, and the 1887's will turn out well.

Sauterne.

Sauterne, or what is known as the white-wine-producing district of Médoc, lies to the south of Bordeaux; and to those who are only familiar with the Médoc vineyards it gives the impression of being quite a distinct country, having more the appearance of the Rhine provinces than of the south of France. The vintage in the Sauterne district is frequently as late as the end of October, and in some cases does not take place until November. The method followed differs from that of Médoc, the grapes being gathered almost one by one, and not until they have almost assumed the appearance of rottenness, or extreme ripeness, so that in fact fermentation has commenced before the fruit is taken from the plant. The Sauterne grapes are white and of medium size, and yield a must which does not lose the whole of the sugar during fermentation, but remains sweet without the addition of spirit. In gathering the grapes, it is customary for women to cut off with scissors the berries as they ripen, the vintage thus lasting over a considerable time. The grapes, moreover, are not put into vats, but are carefully pressed and the juice put into hogsheads, while the fermentation completes itself. The first result is a very sweet luscious wine, known as the *tête*, which is chiefly sent to Russia, where it makes enormous prices. Following this a second wine, of a drier character, called *millieu*, is made from the less saccharine grapes, this being the class of wine generally known as Sauterne. There is also a third process, in which all the remaining grapes are mixed together and pressed, the result being called the *queue*. In the preparation of the better class wines for the English market the three varieties are usually mixed in certain proportions, so that the wine sent to the United Kingdom is very different from the oily liqueur-like article which is in such favour in the colder climate of Russia. As a rule all the finer descriptions are put into bottle before shipment, the corks bearing the name of the château and the vintage, as is the case with the château-bottled red wine. The character of Sauterne may be best described as being, in good years, very luscious and yet very delicate, and possessing a special *sève*, or, in other words, having that special taste which, while it remains in the mouth, leaves the palate perfectly fresh. The Sauterne district comprises the communes of Sauternes, Bommes, and Barsac, with part of those of Preignac, Saint-Pierre-de-Mons, and Fargues. The finer growths, like the red wines of Médoc, are arranged in classes, in the following order:—

GRAND FIRST GROWTH.

Château Yquem, Sauternes.

FIRST GROWTHS.

Château La Tour Blanche, Bommes.	Château Climens, Barsac.
,, Peyraguey, ,,	,, Bayle (Guiraud), Sauternes.
,, Vigneau, ,,	,, Rieussec, Fargues.
,, Suduiraut, Preignac.	,, Rabaut, Bommes.
,, Coutet, Barsac.	

SECOND GROWTHS.

Château Myrat, Barsac.	Château Caillou, Barsac.
,, Doisy, ,,	,, Suau, ,,
,, Peyxotto, Bommes.	,, Malle, Preignac.
,, D'Arche, Sauternes.	,, Romer, ,,
,, Filhot, ,,	,, Lamothe, Sauternes.
,, Bronstet-Nérac, Barsac.	

The prices of the "grand" Sauterne wines vary enormously according to the year, the quality of which is also very various. Between 1870 and 1885 the first growths have ranged from £8 to £60 per hogshead. Château Yquem in the ordinary way fetches from one-fifth to one-fourth more than the other first growths, whilst a rather greater difference rules between the first and second growths. There is, however, no positive rule in this respect; for if, as occasionally happens, a first growth is vintaged a little too late and does not succeed so well as some second growths, the latter will fetch quite as high, if not higher, prices.

Champagne.

Champagne takes its name from the old province which is now represented by the departments of Marne, Haute-Marne, Aube, and Ardennes. It is from the first two that the greater portion of this description of wine is derived, the best qualities being produced in Marne. The vineyards are situated on the banks of the river in the neighbourhood of Épernay, and extend from the right bank over the mountains of Rheims to the vicinity of that city and from the left bank to the small town of Vertus. Of those near the river the principal are at Ay, Dizy, Hautvillers, and Mareuil on the right bank, and at Pierry and Moussy on the left, whilst in the district reaching to the south of these are those of Avize, Cramant, and Vertus. The vineyards of the mountain include those of Verzenay, Sillery, Rilly-en-Montagne, and Bouzy. The sparkling champagnes are made from both white and red grapes, carefully pressed, and the wine is of an amber colour, more or less deep according to vintage and to the proportion of black grapes used. The grapes are pressed in a large *pressoir*, the first pressing yielding the best quality, whilst the second and third are proportionately inferior. The wine from the first pressing is about equal in quantity to that of the other two combined. The vintage usually takes place in the first week in October, the young wines being left to ferment in the cask until the winter, when the first racking takes place, which operation is repeated a month later, when the wines are fined previously to being put in bottle. The wines of the various growths are mixed in the proportions desired, and a certain quantity of old wine (preserved in cask) is added. The amount of saccharine in the wine is also ascertained, and if deficient the requisite quantity in the form of refined candied sugar is added to bring it to the necessary degree for producing fermentation in the bottle. The bottles, which are carefully selected,—those showing the least flaw being rejected,—have sloping shoulders, in order that the sediment may not adhere to the sides in the after-process. The wine, after being corked, is secured by an iron clip, and the bottles are arranged in piles in a horizontal position, in which they remain throughout the summer months. During this time the carbonic acid gas is generated, as is also a sediment, which falls to the side of the bottle. The wines are then stacked away in cellars until required for shipment. Previous to the wine being prepared for this purpose, the bottles are placed in a slanting position, neck downwards, in cranks made in the shape of the letter A, and are daily shaken very slightly, so that by degrees the sediment falls into the cork. This operation is very delicate, the slightest twist being disastrous. The incline is gradually increased, so that at last the bottle is almost perpendicular,—a process which generally takes from three to six weeks. With the sediment thus on the cork, the iron clip is removed, when the force of the wine sends out the cork together with the sediment. The wine is now subjected to *dosage* or liqueuring, the amount of which depends upon the sweetness required; the bottles are then filled up with wine, corked, and wired ready for shipment. The liqueur used is made from the finest wine, candied sugar, and cognac, the usual amount of which for wine sent to the United Kingdom is from one to four per cent. For colder countries the percentage of liqueur is much greater, in some cases exceeding twenty per cent. The liqueuring is regulated by a machine, by which the quantity is measured to a nicety; but in some establishments it is still measured by hand with a small ladle. The principal centres of the champagne trade are Rheims and Epernay, although important establishments exist at Ay, Avize, Châlons, and Dizy. The total production of Marne averages about a million hectolitres annually. A large proportion of this, however, is unsuited for making champagne. At the same time the supply is still considerably in excess of the demand, the stock in merchants' cellars in the district having amounted in May 1887 to upwards of 82,000,000 bottles, whilst at least half that quantity existed in cask, the total stock thus equalling nearly six years' requirements.

Saumur.

Another district of France which produces large quantities of sparkling white wine is that of Saumur, in the department of Maine-et-Loire. These wines have been known for centuries, but up to 1834 were only used as still wines. At that date a successful attempt was made to convert them into sparkling wines, after which they were principally used to supplement the deficient vintages in Champagne. In 1874 sparkling Saumur was introduced into the United Kingdom in its own name, and has since made considerable advance in the English market, owing mainly to its good quality and its moderate price. It has a great resemblance to the wines of Champagne, and is very fine and wholesome; and, although it lacks the body and *finesse* of the best growths of Marne, it compares very favourably with the lower grades of these wines, and is also much lower in price, the best descriptions being obtainable by the English consumer at little more than three shillings a bottle. The judges of taste and analysis at the Paris exhibition in 1878 gave the following award: "The wine does not differ from Champagne in respect of sweetness and lightness; it is equally white, clear, and sparkling. It contains in nearly the same proportion the same substances as the wines of Champagne." The town of Saumur is situated on the banks of the Loire and at the foot of a commanding range of hills, to which latter fact the country in a great measure owes its success as a producer of sparkling wines, as the hills furnish, at a trifling cost and in excellent quality, mile upon mile of the excellent cellarage which is indispensable to their preparation. These cellars are excavations in the hills from which the limestone has been taken, and possess the advantages of easy access and even temperature. The best wines of the district are made from black grapes pressed *en blanc*, as in Champagne, the usual variety of vine being the Breton. The white grapes employed are the *Pineau blanc*, which are vintaged a full fortnight later than the red grapes. According to the system of manufacturing sparkling Saumur, one-half of each year's must is put into barrels by itself to ferment and become wine, and is kept to be mixed with one-half of the next year's must. In the following May the mixture is put into bottles to undergo its second fermentation, which is induced in the same manner as in champagne, the wine being treated in precisely the same manner. The sediment is also worked into the neck in a similar way, and is thrown off by the system of disgorgement. The average yield of Maine-et-Loire for the ten years ended 1887 was about 11,990,000 gallons.

Burgundy.

Next to those of Médoc, the wines of Burgundy are the best French red wines known in England. This district comprises the departments of Côte-d'Or, Yonne, and Saône-et-Loire, known in former days as Upper and Lower Burgundy. By far the finest qualities are grown in Côte-d'Or, in the two communes of Nuits and Beaune. The former lies in the neighbourhood of Dijon, and comprises some of the choicest growths, merging into Beaune in the south, which in its turn adjoins the Mâcon district, in the department of Saône-et-Loire. The wines of Côte-d'Or are grown on the slopes of a range of hills which traverses the department, the best vineyards lying about half-way up the side, where they get the full rays of the sun, the vine apparently deteriorating as it is planted above or below this altitude. As in the case of Médoc wines, the best growths are kept distinct and have a high reputation. The usual classification is as follows:—

Red Wines.

Class I.—Romanée-Conti, Chambertin, Clos Vougeot, Richebourg, La Tâche.
Class II.—Musigny, Romanée-St-Vivant, Le Clos Saint-Georges, Le Corton, Les Bonnes Mares, Le Clos du Tart.
Class III.—Arvelets, Rugiens, Beaumont, Cailles, Cras-Murge, Boudots, Porrets, Pruliers, Thaurey, Vaucrains, Cailleret, Champans, Clavoillon, Clos Margeot, Clos Tavannes, Noyer, Bart, part of Corton, Echezaux, Fêves, Grèves, Ferrière, Sautenot.

White Wines.

Class I.—Montrachet.
Class II.—Chevalier Montrachet, Bâtard Montrachet, Charmes, Combettes, Genevrières, Goutte d'Or, Charlemagne.

The wines of Côte-d'Or are full-bodied and of excellent colour; they are of great reputation on the Continent, especially in Belgium, although till recently not so well known in England, owing to the difficulty experienced in keeping them. But this drawback has now been removed by increased care in their treatment, and by a system of freezing in the young wines, by which a quantity of the natural water is removed and the alcoholic strength of the remainder thereby increased. One of the principal features of the Côte-d'Or is the Hospice de Beaune, a celebrated charitable institution and hospital, the revenues of which are principally derived from certain vineyards in Beaune, Corton, Volnay, and Pommard. The wines of these vineyards are sold every year by auction on the first Sunday in November, and the prices they make serve as standards for the various growths of Burgundy. In Yonne, lying to the north-west of Côte-d'Or, a considerable quantity of wine is made, both red and white. The former has good colour and body, with a fair bouquet, but is much inferior to the wines of Burgundy proper. The latter, grown mostly in the commune of Chablis, is of fair quality and is generally known by the name of this district. Saône-et-Loire, which lies to the south of Beaune, produces the wine known as Mâcon, grown in the neighbourhood of that town, the best growths being those of Théorine. The wines of Mâcon have most of the Burgundy characteristics, but are lighter in colour and body, and lack much of their bouquet and flavour.

Chablis.

Mâcon.

Hermitage.

Red and white wines are produced in the arrondissement of Valence in the department of Drôme. These wines are of excellent quality and improve greatly in bottle, in which state they will keep for many years. The white wines are especially choice, and have a far greater reputation than the red. They are soft and rich, and are said to have no analogy to any other white wine known.

Charente.

The departments of Charente and Charente-Inférieure, although their wines are unknown in the United Kingdom, are celebrated on account of the brandy distilled from them. This industry has suffered enormously of late years from the ravages of the *Phylloxera*, which has destroyed many of the best vineyards in the neighbourhood of Cognac. The wines of the district are in themselves common and of little use but for the still, for which purpose they cannot be approached by those of any other department. But the proportion of wine required to make brandy is so high that, unless it can be produced at a moderate price, the cost of the spirit becomes enormous; hence the proprietors have been unable to obtain a sufficiently high price for their wines to make it worth their while to incur the cost of resisting the plague, and consequently a large quantity of vine-land has gone out of cultivation. In 1874 the produce of the two departments amounted to over 250,000,000 gallons, whereas that of 1887 was little over 14,000,000 gallons. During the last two or three years re-planting has been diligently carried on.

The above constitute the principal varieties of French wines known in the United Kingdom; they form, however, but a small fraction of the entire production of the country. Enormous quantities are produced in the southern provinces, but they are of a commoner description and are reserved for home consumption. Thus in 1887 the two departments of Aude and Hérault yielded between them 5,643,832 hectolitres, or about 124,160,000 gallons, which was considerably in excess of the total produce of the districts previously alluded to. In the department of Pyrénées-Orientales, in the old province of Roussillon, a full-bodied and deep-coloured wine is produced, a small portion of which is sent to Great Britain and is of a better quality than most southern growths. This wine is known by the old name of the province and is of considerable value for blending light thin wines. There are also some very fair wines made in the department of Jura and in the district lying east of Burgundy.

Algeria.

Algeria.—Owing to the devastation caused by the *Phylloxera* in France much attention has of recent years been bestowed on vine culture in Algeria. The result of the first experiments has been very encouraging. M. Bouchardat in a recent report to the Medical Society of Paris wrote—"In the not very distant future by means of the vine we may look for the definite conquest of Algeria. Through its cultivation new colonists will be brought into the country and the habit of labour and its accompaniment, wealth, will result both for them and for the natives. It is through the cultivation of the vine also that we may hope to remove the greatest present obstacle to progress in Algeria, viz., the unhealthiness of the marshlands; for in reality on all the soils where the vine is cultivated we soon see those conditions disappear to which intermittent fevers owe their origin." Algeria undoubtedly possesses soil and climate suitable to vine culture; in fact, the vine seems almost to grow at will and is productive in the third year after being planted. The laying out of vineyards is consequently proceeding very rapidly, and considerable improvement by means of skilled labour is becoming noticeable in the making of the wines. The wines of Algeria resemble that of Roussillon in general character, being full-bodied, with good colour and alcoholic strength. The greatest quantity is produced in the province of Algiers, although there is a considerable yield in the provinces of Constantine and Oran, the latter being cultivated principally by Spaniards.

Spain.

Spain is second only in reputation to France among wine-growing countries. Its white wine, known as sherry, first brought it into prominence; and the red wines of Tarragona and Rioja have of late years formed a great feature in the commerce of the Peninsula. The reduced yield of the French vineyards, especially of those producing the cheapest wines, owing to the ravages of the *Phylloxera*, combined with an increased home consumption, has compelled that country to import large quantities of wine for its own use, and Spain has taken a foremost place in supplying the demand which has thus sprung up. In addition to this, a considerable quantity is exported to other countries, Great Britain amongst the number, in the shape of Spanish claret and port, which are perhaps of as good an intrinsic value as any that reach the United Kingdom. The wines of Andalusia naturally claim a priority in description.

Sherry.

Sherry, so called from the town of Jerez (Xeres) de la Frontera, the headquarters of this industry, is produced in Andalusia in the area included between San Lucar in the north, Port St Mary in the south, and Jerez in the east. This tract of country contains in all about 25,000 acres of vine-growing soil. The system of preparing sherry is different from that followed in the case of most other wines. In France every small grower can make his few hogsheads of wine, and when these have been made the process is complete. In Jerez, on the contrary, the immense establishments, many of them owned by Englishmen, purchase the grape juice or fruit and make their own must. The wines, which are stored in *bodegas* or sheds above ground, are reared for a number of years as *soleras*. These *soleras* consist of vats of various characters of sherry, the style of which is unvaryingly kept up, and whenever a quantity is drawn off they are filled up with wines of the same description. Certain quantities taken from various *soleras* are blended in order to make up the regular marks, by which means the style of different shipments is maintained. There are several different varieties of sherry known in the United Kingdom, which may be divided into the Amontillado and the Manzanilla classes. The Amontillado class may be again subdivided into Fino and Oloroso, the former being the more delicate; frequently the two descriptions are different developments of exactly the same wine. The Manzanilla wines are very much lighter and drier, and are the produce of vines grown on the coast. In making up the marks for the different markets several varieties of sweetness and colour are required. These are obtained by the addition of *vino dulce* made from grapes which are allowed to grow dead-ripe, and of colouring matters made from wine boiled down almost to a liqueur. A certain amount of grape spirit is added to check the tendency to re-fermentation. This system applies only to the Amontillado class. The Manzanillas are mostly shipped in their natural state, with spirit added in small quantities only where it is feared that the wines will otherwise not be able to stand the journey. This description of wine, however, has not hitherto been in great demand in Great Britain. In addition to Manzanilla, there is another description of somewhat similar wine, but with less characteristic taste and somewhat more body, known as Montilla; it is grown in the province of Cordova. Yet another description of wine grown in the vicinity, on the right bank of the Guadalquivir, is that known as Moguer, which resembles a cheap sherry, and is only used for blending with the commonest qualities. Of late a large quantity of this wine has found its way to France to assist in making a cheap wine for the French consumers. Other districts in the south of Spain well known for the production of wine are those of Malaga and Rota. The former yields a sweet description, principally made from Muscat grapes, although a coarse drier wine of the sherry type is also produced. The Rota district is known principally for a sweet red wine, known in England as "tent" (*tinto*), mainly used for ecclesiastical purposes.

Montilla, Moguer, &c.

Val de Peñas.

The central districts of Spain also produce some good red wines suitable for exportation, such as Val de Peñas, which have moderate colour and considerable strength, and are said to be the produce of vines brought from Burgundy. The name Val de Peñas, however, is often given also to wines grown in the neighbouring districts. The system of storing these wines is very similar to that mentioned by Horace in connexion with Falernian, and is still practised at Montilla. The wines are placed in large earthen jars (*tinajas*) like Roman amphoræ, which are prepared inside with a kind of varnish with a view to the preservation of the wine.

Rioja and Tarragona.

Leon and Old Castile in the northern and central parts of Spain furnish about one-half of the wine grown in the entire country. On the border of this region is the rich and fertile district of Rioja (Logroño), which has a climate admirably suited to the production of wines of moderate strength. The wines of Navarre are more full-bodied and have more colour and alcoholic strength, but owing to want of care in their production are less suitable for exportation. In Catalonia there is a much more important wine industry, the district producing what is known in England as Tarragona or Spanish red. The best quality produced is the wine of the Priorato district (about 15 miles inland from Tarragona), which is very rich and full-bodied, and keeps well. Unfortunately this particular area, which is chiefly mountainous, is limited. The next description to this is the wine of Huesca, which is also fine-coloured and full-flavoured. The wines of Aragon are also good, but require special care owing to their liability to a second fermentation. The best growth is that of Cariñena (Zaragoza). The greater part of the Spanish wines imported into France are supplied from Catalonia and Aragon. A French authority on the subject states that "of all the towns in Catalonia which supply wines to France Manresa is in reality the one which, for several years, has sent the largest quantity. This region enjoys a climate more temperate than that of Roussillon, and from hence are derived three-quarters of the wine shipped to France from Barcelona. Hence may be found all types of wines, including dry white and natural red."

Canary wine.

The only islands of the Canary group on which vine culture is now carried on on a commercial scale are those of Gran Canaria (Grand Canary) and Teneriffe, for although a certain amount is produced at Palma it is all used for local purposes. On the two first-named islands the industry has fallen away of late, owing to the attacks of *Oidium*, which destroyed the vines at about the same period as in Madeira. Since then the islands have been chiefly devoted to the production of cochineal, until the recent discovery of aniline dyes, which has, to a great extent, ruined the industry, and again led the inhabitants to turn their attention to vine culture. This has been especially the case in Gran Canaria, where a considerable area of ground is now planted with vines, and a fair return of wine is obtained. These are being treated similarly to those of Madeira, which they greatly resemble in character. In Teneriffe a wine known as Vidonia, which is of a somewhat similar type, is produced, and is exported in small quantities. Vine-growers in this island adhere more to the methods in vogue in Spain.

Portugal.

Port.

The generous, full-flavoured wines known as port are the produce of the district of Alto Douro in the north-east of Portugal, which begins at a point on the river Douro some 60 miles above Oporto, whence these wines are shipped. The whole of the port-wine district, comprising a region between 30 and 40 miles in length with a maximum breadth of about 12, is rugged and mountainous, necessitating the construction of terraces supported by walls, without which protection the soil would inevitably be washed away by the winter rains. The climate of Alto Douro is very cold in winter and extremely hot in summer (frequently 108° Fahr. in the shade). It is owing to this intense heat combined with the peculiar richness of the soil, which is of argillaceous schist formation, that port wines attain to such perfection of colour, body, and ripeness. Till quite recently the means of communication between Oporto and Alto Douro were extremely limited. Roads in the district itself there were none, or very few, and the only way of getting the produce to the port of shipment was by the river, the navigation of which, at all times difficult and even dangerous, on account of the numerous rocks and rapids which obstruct its course, is often rendered impossible by freshets. The Douro railway, however, now traverses the whole length of the wine country along the river bank from Oporto, and other lateral railways are in course of construction which will open up several fine wine-producing districts hitherto unavailable owing to want of roads.

Cultivation of the vine for port.

The method of cultivating the vine in Alto Douro differs considerably from those employed in various other parts of the country, where the vines are either trained over pollarded trees or treillaged at a certain height from the ground, or where they are planted in rows and grown like bushes. The method is as follows. In November or December trenches are dug, 3 feet to 3 feet 6 inches deep, according as the soil is heavy or light, and 2 feet broad, in which vine cuttings are placed at a distance of 3 feet to 4 feet 6 inches apart from each other. The trenches are then partly filled in, in order that the vines may get all the benefit of the rain-water collecting in them. During the first year of planting great care is taken to keep down all weeds whilst the vines are shooting. At the end of two years the young vines, if they have come on well, can be grafted, the best time for performing this operation being October or February; in this way the period of production is hastened, and the vineyard will yield in four instead of five years' time. Should some of the vines die, their places are usually supplied by the process called *mergulho* or layering: that is, a trench is dug in the direction of the space left bare and in it the stock of the nearest vine is turned down. The trench is then partly filled in, leaving two or three shoots of the buried vine visible to the extent of a couple of "eyes" above the surface, which shoots are to take the place of the missing vines. There is also the system of planting from nurseries, which are made with either Portuguese or American varieties. The plot of ground used for the nursery must be kept well clear of weeds and, if in a dry situation, well watered. In two years' time and during the month of February the young vines can be transplanted, and the year after grafted, when the vineyard is planted. The first of the regular operations in the course of cultivation is to clear away the soil from the feet of the stocks, which takes place directly the vintage is over. At the same time manure may be given, and, if the vines are strong enough to bear the application, sulphate of carbon may be injected, on account of the prevalence of *Phylloxera*. After this the vines are pruned. In March the first annual turning of the soil takes place; then the branches of the vines are tied to stakes or canes, in which process considerable skill is brought to bear so as to make the vine shoot in the required direction. Immediately after or about the time they blossom the vines are sulphured, to keep off the *Oidium*, which disease is still active in Portugal; and lastly in June the soil is hoed over to destroy the weeds. The turning of the soil, which is effected with an implement resembling a two-pronged hoe, and the cultivation of the vineyards generally, are to a great extent performed by labourers (*Gallegos*) from Galicia in Spain, but at vintage time *serranos* from the neighbouring *serras* also flock in to work.

Vintage in Alto Douro.

The vintage in Alto Douro generally commences late in September. The grapes are cut by women and children, and are conveyed in large baskets—twenty-two of which full of grapes will yield a pipe of wine—by Gallegos to the place where the wine is to be made. Here they are emptied into large stone tanks, 2 feet to 2 feet 6 inches in depth, each holding from seven to thirty pipes of wine. Each tank is fitted with a beam press, except where the modern screw press has taken its place. As the grapes come in, the stalks are removed, either with a kind of rake or, as in the best managed establishments, with machines called *desingaçadores*, made for the purpose. The white grapes are separated from the red, the "white port" being made from the former; this wine was formerly much appreciated in England, but now finds its chief market on the Continent. When the tank is full, a number of men, and sometimes even women, begin the process of treading, which is continued for about forty-eight hours; after that the must is left to ferment by itself. When the weather has been cold or the year a very ripe one, it has sometimes been found necessary to give as much as seventy-two hours' treading; nowadays, however, there is seldom need for so much work. When the must has sufficiently fermented, it is drawn off into huge vats, holding as a rule about twenty-five pipes each; at the same time sufficient alcohol is added to prevent acetous fermentation and retain part of the sweetness of the grape. Formerly the drawing-off of the must from the tank was determined simply by taste or judgment, but of late years the saccharometer is employed to decide when the must has reached the requisite degree of sweetness. The wines are left untouched in the vats till the cold weather causes them to deposit the lees, when they are racked, and at the same time another small addition of brandy is made. The brandy used is with hardly any exception simply distilled wine, and is of very fine quality. About March or April the wines are again racked from their lees into casks, and are sent down either by boat or rail to Oporto, where they are stored, in most cases for a considerable number of years previous to being shipped. The cheaper wines are an exception, being as a rule shipped when young, also those of the so-called "vintage" class, which are the finest wines of a good year kept separate and shipped as the produce of that particular year. The following is a list of the most famous "vintages" of the 19th century—1809, '12, '15, '20, '27, '34, '40, '47, '51, '63, '68, '70, '73, '78, '81, the last year when the wine was shipped as a vintage being 1884. The stores or lodges where the wines are warehoused are chiefly situated on the Villa Nova side of the river, facing Oporto, and generally speaking comprise a series of long one-storied stone buildings, with thick partition walls and heavy tiled roofs. The wines are kept in casks ranged in rows of two or three tiers; in some establishments large vats, holding from 10 to 110 pipes, are also used, being especially serviceable for blending purposes. The amount of wine contained at the present day in these lodges is calculated at something like 80,000 pipes, the gross value of which cannot be less than two and a half or three million pounds sterling, by far the greater part of this sum representing English capital.

Port-wine trade.

The chief market for port wine is, as it always has been, England. Its introduction into England, which was the beginning of the trade in these wines, dates from the end of the 17th century. At first the exportation was small, the annual average for the first ten years being just over 600 pipes. The consumption, however, gradually increased till 1753, when, owing to adulterations and various other causes, port wine fell into disrepute, and the shipments receded to a very low figure. The prices of new wine to the farmer at this time varied between £2 and £3 per pipe, whilst the shipping prices for old wine did not exceed £9. To remedy this state of things the Old Wine Company was established in 1756 by the marquis of Pombal. The first act of the company was to make an arbitrary circumscription of what they considered the viticultural region of Alto Douro, outside of which no vines could be planted. The territory within the limits of the demarcation was then divided into three districts,—(1) that producing the factory wines, *i.e.*, those set apart for England, (2) that whence the supplies for the Brazils were drawn, and (3) that the produce of which was reserved for tavern use or distillation. For all the wine allowed to be exported permits were issued, without which not a single cask could be sent down to Oporto for shipment. Later on, however, these permits were openly sold in the market, fetching as a rule about £3. The inconvenience and damage to the trade resulting from these absurd regulations led to the abolition of the company in 1833. But in 1843 the creditors of the Old Wine Company, whose lodges, with their valuable contents, had been destroyed at the raising of the siege of Oporto by the retreating Miguelites, induced the Government, as an indemnity for their losses, to re-establish the former company's monopoly. The new company had no authority to prevent the planting of vines; but their powers as to the classification and exportation of port wine were the same as those possessed by the old company. For instance, in 1848 over 11,000 pipes were produced, but only 7000 were approved for exportation to England. At this time the export duty on wine destined for England was £3 per pipe—in reality £6, if the £3 permit is taken into consideration, whilst that on wine destined for countries out of Europe was only 6d. per pipe. The consequence was that considerable quantities of wine were shipped to America and thence to England, the difference in the duty just paying expenses with a slight profit to the shipper. This state of things lasted till 1853, when the company was finally "exonerated from its official duties" and the export duty equalized on wine to all countries. Since that time the port-wine trade has been entirely unrestricted.

Ravages of Phylloxera and Oidium.

Besides the curse of monopolies, Alto Douro has suffered severely from the *Oidium* and *Phylloxera*. The former appeared about 1848, but it was not till 1853 that the disease assumed serious proportions. The climax was reached in 1856, when only 15,000 pipes were vintaged, about one-sixth of the usual quantity. At one time it seemed as if the whole trade would collapse, as the exportation dropped from 41,621 pipes in 1856 to 16,696 pipes in 1858. Fortunately, however, the sulphur remedy was discovered and applied in time, and since then the *Oidium*, though not entirely got rid of, has at any rate been effectually prevented from doing much harm. The same, as yet, cannot be said of the *Phylloxera*, the ravages of which have been much more serious. Its presence in Alto Douro was suspected as early as 1868; but for years hardly any attempt was made to save the vines, owing to the incredulity of the large farmers, who considered the cause of the withering of their vines to be the continuous drought of successive dry seasons. More energetic efforts are now being made to cope with the disease; but in the meantime the yield has been getting less year by year, and at the present time is little more than half what it used to be during the three years previous to the appearance of the *Oidium*, when the average was over 100,000 pipes. The excess of exportation over production for the last few years is owing, in the first place, to the enormous increase in the Brazilian trade, which is largely made up of wines from the Minho and Beira districts, and, secondly, to the new trade in common country wines with France. The shipments of wine of all kinds from Oporto to the Brazils amounted during

1887 to over 25,000 pipes, whilst those to France exceeded 10,000. According to the latest accounts, the *Phylloxera* still continues to extend the area of its attacks, although, on the other hand, many of the abandoned vineyards are again being brought under cultivation; also the number and extent of the new plantations are steadily increasing.

Statistics of port-wine trade.

Exportation of wine from Oporto from 1678 to 1756, when the Wine Company monopoly was established:—1678-87, average 632 pipes per annum; 1688-97, 7668; 1698-1707, 7188; 1708-17, 9644; 1718-27, 17,692; 1728-37, 19,234; 1738-47, 18,556; 1748-56, 16,354. Total, 953,362 pipes. Total exportation of wine from Oporto from 1757 to 1833, or during the existence of the Wine Company monopoly, 2,564,096 pipes. Average to Great Britain, 27,938 pipes; to rest of the world, 5362. Total, 33,300 pipes. Total exportation of wine from Oporto from 1834 to 1842 during the absence of restrictions—to Great Britain, 233,469 pipes; to continent of Europe, 11,980; to rest of the world, 41,600; total, 287,049 pipes. Average to Great Britain, 25,941 pipes per annum; to continent of Europe, 1331; to rest of the world, 4622. Total exportation of wine from Oporto from 1843 to 1853 during the existence of the New Wine Company monopoly—to Great Britain, 272,799 pipes; to continent of Europe, 47,271; to the rest of the world, 75,197; total, 395,267 pipes. Average to Great Britain, 24,800 pipes per annum; to continent of Europe, 4297½; to rest of the world, 6836.

Exportation of Wine from Oporto from 1854 to 1887, during the absence of restrictions and equalized rate of export duties to all parts.

Year.	To Great Britain.	Rest of the world.	Total.	Year.	To Great Britain.	Rest of the world.	Total.
	Pipes.	Pipes.	Pipes.		Pipes.	Pipes.	Pipes.
1854	33,831	5,421	39,252	1885	29,656	35,071	64,727
1864	29,942	5,677	35,619	1886	31,467	43,362	74,829
1874	35,753	20,778	56,531	1887	32,052	39,459	71,511
1884	30,281	31,741	62,022				
				Total	992,436	569,365	1,561,801

Lisbon wines.

In addition to port, a large quantity of wine is produced in other districts of Portugal, notably in the neighbourhood of Lisbon. Of these the principal are Torres Vedras, to the north of the city, where a large quantity of red wine of a coarse claret type is grown; Collares, the vineyards of which lie beyond Cintra, and where a higher class is produced; Carcavellos, at the mouth of the Tagus; and Bucellas, in which a white wine is produced from the Riesling grape, known in the United Kingdom as Bucellas hock. Carcavellos yields a fuller-bodied description, which savours more of the Madeira type.

Madeira.

There is every reason to believe that vines were introduced into Madeira soon after the discovery of the island. But it was not till some 200 years later, after the marriage of the infanta Catherine of Portugal with Charles II. of England, that British merchants established themselves at Funchal, from which point the wine trade of Madeira commenced. The system of cultivation is somewhat peculiar. The vines are trained over a lattice-work of cane, about 4 feet from the ground, supported on stakes, thus giving room for the vine-dresser to pass underneath and keep the ground clear from weeds. This system of keeping the ground clear and moist has much to do with the excellent character of the wine produced. An English acre can yield about seven pipes (644 gallons), but the average is considerably below this quantity. The vintage commences as a rule about the last week in August, and the grapes are all pressed before the October rains set in. This latter operation is still carried out in the primitive fashion, the fruit being thrown into large presses and trodden with the naked feet. Madeira wine improves much with age, and is occasionally to be met with from fifty to a hundred years old. The choicest descriptions are Malmsey, Sercial, Bual, and Tinta. The Jesuits at one time contrived to hold the monopoly of the Malmsey wine, and were owners of the vineyards at Cama de Lobos, in which it was produced. Of the other wines the choicest are found on the south side of the island; but here as the elevation above the sea increases the quality falls off. The grapes from which Malmsey is made are not gathered till a month later than those for other wines of a drier character. Sercial is also a much-esteemed wine; it is said to combine all the attributes of a perfect wine, being full-bodied and having a rich aromatic flavour peculiar to itself. The grape from which it is produced is of the Riesling variety, and is supposed to have been transplanted from the banks of the Rhine. Bual is a very luscious wine, the produce of a white grape. Tinta, on the other hand, is obtained from a red grape, and has somewhat of the character and appearance of the wines of Burgundy, whence the vines are said to have been derived.

Trade in Madeira.

Madeira wine became well known in England about the middle of the 18th century, when it became fashionable, owing to the strong recommendation of officers who had served in the West Indies and America. The great demand at the beginning of the 19th century caused the culture of the vine on the island to be greatly increased. The annual production must ultimately have reached over 30,000 pipes, larger quantities of the commoner sorts being consumed on the island or turned into brandy. So much of the land indeed was under the vine that nearly all bread-stuffs had to be imported, the corn grown on the island being at that time only equal to three months' consumption, whereas now, owing to the decreased number of the vineyards, it grows an amount equal to nine months' requirements. In evidence of the importance which at one time attached to the Madeira wine trade, it may be mentioned that in 1799 a fleet of ninety-six ships was convoyed from Portsmouth to the port of Funchal by three men-of-war. This fleet took on to the West Indies 3041½ pipes of Madeira, partly for the supply of the West Indian colonies and partly shipped for the voyage there and back to England. For many years this practice of sending wine for a voyage to the East or West Indies and back has existed amongst the Madeira merchants. The voyage matures the wine, and at the same time gives it a peculiar bouquet and flavour, derived most probably from the intense heat of the ship's hold and the continual motion to which it is subjected. There is, however, a marked difference between wines shipped to the East and those sent to the West Indies, the only reason assignable being the difference in the length of the voyage. A custom prevails of submitting the wine, shortly after its manufacture, to a high temperature in buildings especially designed for the purpose, the result of which is the earlier development and mellowing of the wine, and the prevention of re-fermentation. The exact temperature to which the wines are thus subjected and the length of time depend on individual judgment, although the temperature never exceeds 130° to 140° Fahr. for inferior and 100° to 120° for better class wines. It is this process which gives Madeira its characteristic flavour, to which again its popularity in Great Britain is due. The large stone buildings, two stories high, in which this process is carried on are divided into compartments and heated by flues with hot air from stoves below. On the wines being removed after a lapse of three, four, or six months, as the case may be, they are fined and racked, a second proportion of brandy being added if necessary, and they are then left to themselves, except for an occasional fining and racking, until they are shipped, which scarcely ever takes place before the second or third year.

As long ago as 1785 the quantity of Madeira shipped to England was 120,000 gallons, which gradually increased up to 1820, when it reached 520,000 gallons. After 1852, however, this amount was greatly reduced, and, although it has again improved of late years, the quantity imported in 1885 was only 108,771 gallons. With reference to the wine trade of Madeira with all parts of the world, it appears that in 1646 as many as 2000 pipes were exported. About this time English and other foreign houses established themselves in Funchal, and it is without doubt owing to them that the culture of the vine was increased and an export trade of some importance commenced. It was not, however, until the latter half of the 18th century that, in consequence of the wars between France and England and the closing of the French ports, the Madeira trade increased to large proportions. In 1774 some 7000 pipes were shipped, which by 1780 had increased to over 16,000. In 1813 it is said some 22,000 pipes of Madeira were exported, at an average price of 300 dollars per pipe. After the war the large convoys to the East and West Indies ceased, but the Indiamen still called at Madeira on their outward voyage. Nearly all the regimental messes in the East Indies were supplied with Madeira wine, whilst large shipments were also made to America, Russia, and Germany. The taste for Madeira has of late very much died away, the cause of which must be traced to the appearance, in the spring of 1852, of the *Oidium Tuckeri*, which devastated the vineyards of the island. Vines were rooted up and sugar-canes planted in their stead, whilst, with production practically at a standstill, holders refused to part with their wines except at enormous figures. In consequence of these high prices Madeira was soon placed beyond the reach of all but the wealthiest classes. When in the course of time a cessation of the disease came about, the Madeira vineyards began to be re-planted, so that the production of the island has again reached some 5000 to 6000 pipes annually, and brought about a corresponding reduction in price, genuine wine being now obtainable at considerably less than £20 per pipe. Popular prejudice is in consequence being removed, and a gradual although slow revival in the Madeira trade is taking place.

Italy.

Italian wines.

In point of quantity of production, though far inferior in quality, Italy ranks ahead of France. The estimated area under the vine is in excess of that of France. The annual yield is some 660,000,000 gallons, valued at about £100,000,000. Whereas in France and Spain the acreage under the vine is devoted exclusively to that plant, the vine in Italy is grown simultaneously with the olive, corn, &c. The vines are simply trained on wires at some distance from the ground, and are frequently allowed to run from tree to tree, mingling in the general vegetation, nature doing so much for the vine-grower that he, in most instances, does but little to assist her. The vintage usually takes place in September and October, and, except in Sicily and some of the southern provinces, the system employed is somewhat rude in comparison with those of other nations. Yet considerable improvement has taken place during the last few years. Greater attention is being paid to the selection of suitable plants, whilst on the larger estates modern wine-presses and utensils are coming into use, and the necessity of care and cleanliness for the production of good wine is beginning to be better understood. Amongst the chief faults still noticeable, but remediable with cultivation and care, are a strong flavour peculiar to the soil and a disposition on the part of the proprietors to over-alcoholize wines destined for exportation. In many instances also the grapes are gathered indiscriminately, often before they are ripe, whilst the quality is also frequently further damaged by want of attention and cleanliness in treatment. There can be no doubt that with proper treatment the wines of Italy would hold a much higher position than they do at present, the exports being, so far, trifling compared with the amount of production, and consisting to a great extent of Sicilian wines. Of the wines of northern Italy the best known descriptions are perhaps those of Montferrat and Asti. These are mostly light in colour, hard, and somewhat difficult to keep. Some of the white wines of this district are very good. A large quantity of sparkling wine is also produced. The general nature of the soil is extremely fertile and the climate moderate, so that everything points to northern Italy as very suitable for wine production. In central Italy the best wines are those of Montepulciano, Chianti, Pomino, Montalcino, and Carmignano. The greater proportion of the wine made here is from the province of Tuscany, which is also a very suitable one for the vine. These wines have considerable alcoholic strength, and are fit for consumption in about six to twelve months after the vintage, attaining perfection in two years. The price usually varies from 11d. to 2s. 11d. per gallon, according to growth. The wines of Montepulciano have a brilliant purple colour and a luscious flavour, although not cloying to the palate, their sweetness being generally tempered with an agreeable sharpness and astringency. The rocky hills of Chianti near Siena furnish another description of red wine, which is also sweet, but less aromatic. An excellent wine of the claret type is produced at Artimino. But perhaps the choicest wines grown in Italy are those of the Neapolitan district. Of these the best known are the Lacryma Christi a red wine of good bouquet and an elegant taste, several descriptions of good class Muscat wine, and also a description of Malvoisie. These three sorts are the produce of vines grown on the slopes of Mount Vesuvius nearest the sea. Of the Lacryma Christi only a small quantity is made, but many of the second-rate wines of the neighbourhood take the name and pass in common for the growth.

Until recently the greater portion of the wines exported by Italy to other countries were for blending purposes. Lately, however, there has been a marked improvement in this respect, and a considerable quantity of wine is now exported in bottle. A trade of some importance is being developed with the United States, the imports in 1887 having amounted to 26,340 dozen bottles and 71,020 gallons in bulk.

Sicilian.

The principal wine produced in Sicily is that grown in the neighbourhood of Marsala, from which town it takes its name. The character of the wine is somewhat after the style of Madeira, it having good bouquet and improving with age. It is the result of a mixture of various kinds of grapes carefully selected, amongst which are included the usual Madeira varieties. Thanks to the care bestowed upon its production, Marsala has of late years acquired considerable reputation. The vintage usually takes place about the third week in September, which, although somewhat late for so southern a latitude, allows the grapes to mature thoroughly, whilst all the rotten ones are carefully picked out before the fruit is put into the press. The shippers usually arrange to purchase the vintage from the growers, subject to the condition that the wine is made in a certain manner. The must is collected in large casks capable of holding about 250 gallons each, in which it is allowed to ferment. The system pursued in the preparation of Marsala, as in the case of other strong wines, consists in the addition of a certain quantity of spirit, according as the wine is intended for shipment to England or for consumption in Italy, the former being generally brought up to a strength of 33° to 35°, or about 5° more than that reserved for home consumption, the extra strength being to enable the wine to stand the sea voyage. Taken generally, there is very little difference between the qualities of the different growths of Marsala; in fact, where the system of fortifying and sweetening is properly carried out and the best description of finings used to reduce the reddish tint found in most of the wines, it is almost impossible when the wines are two or three years old to detect any great variation, whilst such a thing as bad Marsala can scarcely be said to exist. Formerly all Marsala wines judged not sufficiently good for consumption as such were made into spirit for fortifying the better description; but, since the Italian Government have raised the duty on alcohol, a different system is adopted. The inferior class of must is not now fermented, but is reduced by evaporation to about two-thirds of its original bulk, thus forming a sort of essence. This essence is added to the wine intended for consumption in the proportion of from 5 to 10 per cent. at the commencement of the fermentation. Within about two months of the first drawing-off of the wine the contents of each cask are carefully examined, and all which may be considered not sufficiently good for Marsala is set aside; and this operation is repeated in March or April. Immediately after the next vintage it is examined for the third time, after which it is fined and drawn off into large vats capable of holding up to 18,000 gallons each. These vats, like the Spanish soleras, are never entirely emptied, a certain quantity of old wine being allowed to remain in them, which gives the new wines the bouquet and character peculiar to true Marsala.

Austria-Hungary.

Hungarian.

Of the Austrian-Hungarian empire Hungary, from a viticultural point of view, forms by far the most important part. The quantity of wine produced in that country has assumed of late years considerable proportions, the white wines being both greater in quantity and of better description than the red. Inclusive of Croatia and Slavonia, it is estimated that there are in Hungary upwards of 1,000,000 acres of vineland, producing annually some 250,000,000 gallons of wine, the value of which is estimated at over £16,000,000. The wines of central Hungary are strong, and include white varieties varying in colour from a light to a deep yellow tinge, as well as wines of considerable depth of colour. Those of the south of Croatia are as a rule less strong, but are for the most part of a deep colour and are generally known as black wines. The produce of Transylvania ranks extremely high, and is for the most part white, although some excellent red wines are grown. The strength of Hungarian wines is moderate, that of Tokay being from about 20 to 25 per cent. of proof spirit, whilst Carlowitz averages from 24 to 25. The other descriptions generally have a less alcoholic strength. Foremost among the wines of Hungary is the sweet Tokay, grown in the submontane district around the town of Tokay, which covers a space of about 20 square miles. Throughout the whole of this district it is the custom to collect the grapes only when they have become dry and sweet, almost like raisins. The fruit is gathered separately and the best wine made from selected grapes. The grapes are first put together in a cask, in the bottom of which holes are bored to let that portion of the juice escape which will run away without pressure. This forms the highest quality. The grapes are then squeezed for the ordinary wine. In abundant years the yield of Tokay reaches nearly 2,000,000 gallons, of which about 15 per cent. are of really superior quality, and of this about one-fifth is classified as extra fine. The three classes of Tokay are known as *essentia*, *ausbruch*, and *máslás*, the first-named being the yield of the juice taken without pressure. It is, however, so scarce that it never appears in the market. The vineyards of Menes (in the county of Arad) produce a sweet red wine. Carlowitz is produced farther south, on the banks of the Danube, some 40 miles north-west of Belgrade. It has somewhat of the character of port wine, although more astringent and lacking in fruitiness. Many of the Hungarian vineyards also produce Muscat-flavoured wines which are highly appreciated. The vintage in Hungary lasts from the commencement of October to the end of November, and for the most part is conducted on an imperfect principle, although great improvements have been introduced of late years. The grapes are crushed by the feet in some places, whilst in others a kind of mill is used, and in others again they are pressed in sacks. The wine is usually prepared in wooden utensils, generally made on the spot, the trade of the cooper being but little known. The system of carrying on the fermentation in closed barrels is not always adopted, and the wine is frequently spoilt by not being drawn off in time.

Dalmatian.

Next to Hungary the principal vine-growing district of the empire is Dalmatia, in which the vine culture has of late increased to an enormous extent. Fifty years ago the vine was scarcely grown, except in the islands and on the sea-coast; but it has now penetrated into the interior, and occupies about one-twentieth part of the soil under cultivation. The Dalmatian wines, which are almost entirely red, have generally full colour and contain a high degree of alcohol, whilst they also possess a good body and bouquet, resembling in a great measure the wines of Burgundy. The average annual production is 22,000,000 gallons, of which only about 4,000,000 are exported; but this branch of the trade is gradually increasing. Defective cellarage, imperfect fermentation, and general ignorance as to manipulation prevented the development of the wine trade of Dalmatia for many years; but these defects have of late been in a great manner remedied by the action of the Austrian Government in educating the proprietors in this respect. The best wines produced in the province are Moscato Roso, Vino Taitaro, Prosecco Vugova, Maraschino, and Malvasia.

Germany.

Rhine wines.

German wines, generically spoken of as Hock and Moselle, are the products of the most northern latitude of successful vine-culture in Europe. To this circumstance must be attributed the fact that a greater inequality exists in the different vintages than is known in connexion with the wines of any other country. In a successful season, when the grapes have been able to mature thoroughly, perhaps no class of wine shows more elegance and quality than do those of the Rhine provinces, while, on the other hand, there are none on which the adverse influence of cold and wet is more apparent. The principal wine-producing districts of Germany are Alsace-Lorraine, Baden, Würtemberg, the Hessian and Bavarian Palatinates, and the Rheingau, the total annual production of which is about 80,000,000 gallons. Of these the first three give half the aggregate yield; but their wines are chiefly light and poor, and are only used for home consumption. The best wines of Germany are grown on the banks of the Rhine in the neighbourhood of Mainz: the Rheingau, in which the choicest descriptions are grown, lies on the right bank of the river, whilst the vineyards of Hesse lie on the left. The wines produced on the left bank are full-bodied and with good flavour, the best growths being Liebfraumilch, Nierstein, Scharlachberg, and Forst, which are considered nearly equal to the Rheingau wines. Amongst the latter are the wines of Johannisberg and Steinberg; the first-named is looked upon as the king of German wines. In the same neighbourhood are also the celebrated vineyards of Rüdesheim, Gräfenberg, and Rauenthal. The vineyard of Johannisberg is said to have been planted about the year 1009, under the direction of Ruthard, archbishop of Mainz. During the Thirty Years' War these vineyards were destroyed, but in 1722 the abbot of Fulda built a château on the site of the old convent and re-planted the vineyards. Hochheimer is the produce of a comparatively small district situated on the banks of the Main, several miles above its junction with the Rhine. The name (whence Hock) has been known in England for upwards of two hundred years, and no doubt originally included and denoted the general body of Rhine wines. The wines of the Moselle, many of which are shipped as sparkling wines, occupy only a secondary position, although in favourable seasons they are characterized by a light pleasant flavour with a marked aroma. The wines of Germany, at least of the descriptions exported, are mostly white, although a small quantity of red is grown in the Palatinate, notably at Assmannshausen, which resembles Burgundy. The yield, however, is comparatively trifling. Amongst the leading descriptions of vine plants in German vineyards the Riesling stands out pre-eminent. It is generally planted on the rocky mountain slopes, and the bunches of white grapes which it produces only ripen perfectly in years of high temperature. When this is the case, however, they yield a wine of high quality, the characteristics of which develop as the wine grows older. On the lower lands the species known as the Kleinberger and Oestreicher are planted, the grapes of which ripen more easily and produce more freely than the Pineau Riesling grape. The French vines, the Pineau and Gros Blanc, are also cultivated in Germany. But one-half of the vines growing on the banks of the Rhine are Riesling plants, which are probably indigenous to the valley, as, although planted elsewhere, they have never been found to yield fruit of such quality as in the Rheingau. Great care is bestowed upon the process of vintage, which usually takes place at as late a date as possible, as a rule not before the end of October or beginning of November, in order to allow the grapes to ripen as thoroughly as may be. The wine is allowed to ferment in casks instead of in vats, as in most other countries, owing to which circumstance considerable difference in quality and price is apt to exist in the produce of the same growth and vintage. After the grapes are gathered, they are pressed as they attain ripeness; and, after the fermentation is duly effected, the wine is fined and racked into vats, which are constantly filled up so that the wine improves with age. The time for racking varies with different proprietors, some taking the wine off the lees in the February following the vintage, whilst others allow the lees to remain a year in the wine, a process which gives it a fuller and sweeter taste. Several years are required to get the wine fit for bottling, as there is no fixed period at which it will finish its fermentation, in fact the finer the wine the longer the time requisite to get it in condition. During this period it receives the greatest attention and is frequently tested, condition being perhaps the greatest difficulty in connexion with German wines.

Moselle wines.

Russia and Greece.

Russia and Greece.

A certain quantity of wine is made in the southern portions of Russia and in Greece; but the quality is mostly coarse and common, and the produce is almost entirely used for home consumption.

United States.

United States.

The cultivation of the vine has made rapid progress of late years in the United States, and American wines are steadily taking the place of the foreign product. The soil and climate of the Pacific coast seem best adapted to the growth of the vine, and wine-making appears likely to become one of the leading industries of California, where the vine was first introduced by the Franciscan fathers about the year 1769. The variety of grape first planted in that region was known as the "Mission" grape, and is generally supposed to have been imported from Mexico. Subsequently the principal varieties of French, German, and Spanish vines were introduced into that State and have all been tried with more or less success. The result is that several descriptions of wine are now made in California resembling, to a certain extent, the leading European types, although, as a rule, of a coarser style,—a defect, however, which is disappearing with the spread of technical knowledge. Although California is by far the largest grape-growing State in the Union, producing nearly one-half of the wines made in the United States, yet the rate of increase of the product during the past five years has been greatest in other States. In Ohio, upon the shores of Lake Erie and along the Ohio river, the vine is extensively cultivated. The champagnes and clarets made in the neighbourhood of Sandusky and Cleveland, and the "sparkling Catawba," made originally by Nicholas Longworth of Cincinnati, are produced in considerable quantities. New York, Missouri, Illinois, and Pennsylvania are likewise large wine-producing States, the largest wine-manufacturing establishment being in New York State, in Steuben county. The annual yield in each of these States ranges now (1888) from 2,000,000 to 4,000,000 gallons. Wines of inferior quality are made in small quantities in nearly all the States. In the eastern and middle States the principal grapes are the Catawba and Ives seedling, while in the south the Virginia seedling and the Scuppernong grapes are the favourites. The wine-grapes in these regions resemble the grapes of Germany and France, containing more acid and flavour, while those grown on the Pacific coast are of a milder and sweeter character, resembling the wines of Spain. The principal obstacles in the way of the cultivation of the vine in the United States are mildew and blight, which sometimes destroy the entire foliage of the vine, and the grape-rot, which in some localities has baffled the grower and caused the abandonment of grape-culture. The ravages of the *Phylloxera* are likewise encountered in certain localities, but these are not so extensive in the United States as in France, and, indeed, certain varieties of vine are entirely free from them. The exports of American wines, though still small, are rapidly increasing. The imports of foreign wines have steadily decreased during the past fifteen years. The total annual production of wine in the United States now amounts to about 35,000,000 gallons.

Cape of Good Hope.

Cape of Good Hope.

Previous to the alteration of the wine duties in 1860, which placed foreign and colonial wines on a similar basis, a considerable business was developing in the United Kingdom in favour of Cape wines, especially of those descriptions most resembling the traditional port and sherry. The Cape of Good Hope in its geographical and climatic elements greatly resembles the vine-growing countries of Europe, and, notwithstanding certain earthy characteristics (due in the main to imperfect cultivation) which were inseparable from its wines, bade fair at one time to rival the best of its competitors north of the equator. The equalization of duty, however, has considerably checked the trade in Great Britain, notwithstanding the great improvement which has since taken place in wine-making at the Cape.

Australia.

Australia.

Wine-producing has been prosecuted as an industry for many years in the Australian colonies, and in some instances with considerable energy. But it has not hitherto developed to any great extent, owing to the absence of differential duties to favour the growers and the cost of freight, although from the quality of their production they have no reason to dread competition with the wine-growers of Europe. The Australian colonies (Victoria, South Australia, New South Wales) have suffered much from want of technical knowledge both in vine selection and wine preparation, though in both of these branches considerable progress has been made during the last few years. According to Mr J. P. Stow, in his *History of South Australia*, the tentative stage of vine culture in that colony has now passed. Good markets for its vintages may be expected in Europe as soon as wines of certain qualities are made in sufficient quantities to allow of heavy stocks being kept. As with the growths of Médoc, attempts are being made to keep the yields of the various vineyards distinct, those of Highercombe, Auldana, Tintara, &c., in South Australia being well known in Great Britain. In their principal characteristics these wines resemble those of France, the red wines being intermediate between claret and Burgundy, while the white wines, although the fuller descriptions come near Sauterne and Chablis, as a rule take more after those of the Rhine. The quantity imported into England during 1887 amounted to 168,188 gallons.

Asia.

Asia.

Although holding a position of little importance in wine-growing, as compared with Europe, Asia yields a certain quantity for home consumption. Chief amongst these are the wines of Caucasia and Armenia, which, according to Thudicum, are more notable for their alcoholic strength than for their colour. Wines are also made in Persia, especially in the district of Shiraz; these, however, rarely find their way into the market. (H. J. N.)

WINKELRIED, Arnold von. The incident with which this name is connected is, after the feat of Tell, the best known and most popular in the early history of the Swiss Confederation. We are told how, at a critical moment in the great battle of Sempach, when the Swiss had failed to break the serried ranks of the Austrian knights, a man of Unterwalden, Arnold von Winkelried by name, came to the rescue. Commending his wife and children to the care of his comrades, he rushed towards the Austrians, gathered a number of their spears together against his breast, and fell pierced through and through, having opened a way into the hostile ranks for his fellow-countrymen, though at the price of his own life. But the Tell and Winkelried stories stand in a very different position when looked at in the dry light of history, for, while in the former case imaginary and impossible men (bearing now and then a real historical name) do imaginary and impossible deeds at a very uncertain period, in the latter we have some solid ground to rest on, and Winkelried's act might very well have been performed, though, as yet, the amount of genuine and early evidence in support of it is very far from being sufficient.

The Winkelrieds of Stanz[1] were a knightly family when we first hear of them, though towards the end of the 14th century they seem to have been but simple men without the honours of knighthood, and not always using their prefix "von." Among its members we find an Erni Winkelried acting as a witness to a contract of sale on May 1, 1367, while the same man, or perhaps another member of the family, Erni von Winkelried, is plaintiff in a suit at Stanz on September 29, 1389, and in 1417 is the landamman (or head man) of Unterwalden, being then called Arnold Winkelriet. We have, therefore, a real man named Arnold Winkelried living at Stanz about the time of the battle of Sempach. The question is thus narrowed to the points, Was he present at the battle, and did he then perform the deed commonly attributed to him? involving a minute investigation of the history of that battle, to ascertain if there are any authentic traces of this incident, or any opportunity for it to have taken place.

(1) *Evidence of Chronicles.*—The earliest known mention of the incident is found in a Zurich chronicle (discovered in 1862 by Herr G. von Wyss), which is a copy, made in 1476, of a chronicle written in or at any rate not earlier than 1438, though it is wanting in the 16th-century transcript of another chronicle written in 1466, which up to 1389 closely agrees with the former. It appears in the well-known form, but the hero is stated to be "ein getrüwer man under den Eidgenozen," no name being given, and it seems clear that his death did not take place at that time. No other mention has been found in any of the numerous Swiss or Austrian chronicles till we come to the book *De Helvetiæ Origine*, written in 1538 by Rudolph Gwalther (Zwingli's son-in-law), when the hero is still nameless, being compared to Decius or Codrus, but is said to have been killed by his brave act. Finally, we read the full story in the original draft of Giles Tschudi's chronicle, where the hero is described as "a man of Unterwalden, of the Winkelried family," this being expanded in the final recension of the chronicle (1564) into "a man of Unterwalden, Arnold von Winckelried by name, a brave knight," while he is entered (in the same book, on the authority of the "Anniversary Book" of Stanz, now lost) on the list of those who fell at Sempach at the head of the Nidwald (or Stanz) men as "Herr Arnold von Winckelriet, ritter," this being in the first draft "Arnold Winckelriet."

(2) *Ballads.*—There are several war songs on the battle of Sempach which have come down to us, but in one only is there mention of Winkelried and his deed. This is a long ballad of 67 four-line stanzas, part of which (including the Winkelried section) is found in the additions made between 1531 and 1545 to Etterlin's chronicle by H. Berlinger of Basel, and the whole in Werner Steiner's chronicle (written 1532). It is agreed on all sides that the last stanza, attributing the authorship to Halbsuter of Lucerne, "as he came back from the battle," is a very late addition. Many authorities regard it as made up of three distinct songs (one of which refers to the battle and Winkelried), possibly put together by the younger Halbsuter (citizen of Lucerne in 1435, died between 1470 and 1480), though others contend that the Sempach-Winkelried section bears clear traces of having been composed after the Reformation began, that is, about 1520 or 1530. Some recent discoveries have proved that certain statements in the song usually regarded as anachronisms are quite accurate; but no nearer approach has been made towards fixing its exact date, or that of any of the three bits into which it has been cut up. In this song the story appears in its full-blown shape, the name of Winckelriet being given.

(3) *Lists of Those who Fell at Sempach.*—We find in the "Anniversary Book" of Emmetten in Unterwalden (drawn up in 1560) the name of "der Winkelriedt" at the head of the Nidwald men; and in a book by Horolanus, a pastor at Lucerne (about 1563), that of "Erni Winckelried" occurs some way down the list of Unterwalden men.

(4) *Pictures and Drawings.*—In the MS. of the chronicle of Diebold Schilling of Bern (*c.* 1480) there is in the picture of the battle of Sempach a warrior pierced with spears falling to the ground, which may possibly be meant for Winkelried; while in that of Diebold Schilling of Lucerne (1511), though in the text no allusion is made to any such incident, there is a similar picture of a man who has accomplished Winkelried's feat, but he is dressed in the colours of Lucerne. Then there is an engraving in Stumpf's chronicle (1548), and, finally, the celebrated one by Hans Rudolph Manuel (1551), which follows the chronicle of 1476 rather than the ballad.

The story seems to have been first questioned about 1850 by Moritz von Stürler of Bern, but the public discussion of the subject originated with a lecture by Prof. O. Lorenz on "Leopold III. und die Schweizer Bünde," which he delivered in Vienna on March 21, 1860. This began the lively paper war humorously called "the second war of Sempach," in which the Swiss (with but rare exceptions) maintained the historical character of the feat against various foreigners—Austrians and others.

Most of the arguments against the genuineness of the story have been already more or less directly indicated. (1) There is the total silence of all the old Swiss and Austrian chroniclers until 1538, with the solitary exception of the Zurich chronicle of 1476 (and this while they nearly all describe the battle in more or less detail). The tale, as told in the 1476 chronicle, is clearly an interpolation, for it comes immediately after a distinct statement that "God had helped the Confederates, and that with great labour they had defeated the knights and Duke Leopold," while the passage immediately following joins on to the former quite naturally if we strike out the episode of the "true man," who is not even called Winkelried. (2) The date of the ballad is extremely uncertain, but cannot be placed earlier than at least 60 or 70 years after the battle, possibly 130 or 140, so that its claims to be regarded as embodying an oral contemporary tradition are of the slightest. (3) Similar feats have been frequently recorded, but in each case they are supported by authentic evidence which is lacking in this case. Five cases at least are known: a follower of the count of Hapsburg, in a skirmish with the Bernese in 1271; Stülinger of Ratisbon in 1332, in the war of the count of Kyburg against the men of Bern and Solothurn; Conrad Royt of Lucerne, at Nancy in 1477; Herni Wolleben, at Frastenz in 1499, in the course of the Swabian war; and a man at the battle of Kappel in 1531. (4) It is argued that the course of the battle was such that there was little or no chance of such an act being performed, or, if performed, of having turned the day. This argument rests on the careful critical narrative of the fight constructed by Herr Kleissner and Herr Hartmann from the contemporary accounts which have come down to us, in which the pride of the knights, their heavy armour, the heat of the July sun, the panic which befell a sudden part of the Austrian army, added to the valour of the Swiss, fully explain the complete rout. Herr Hartmann, too, points out that, even if the knights (on foot) had been ranged in serried ranks, there must have been sufficient space left between them to allow them to move their arms, and therefore that no man, however gigantic he might have been, could have seized hold of more than half a dozen spears at once.

Herr K. Bürkli (*Der Wahre Winkelried,—die Taktik der alten Urschweizer*, Zurich, 1886) has put forth a theory of the battle which is, he allows, opposed to all modern accounts, but entirely agrees, he strongly maintains, with the contemporary authorities. According to this the fight was not a pitched battle but a surprise, the Austrians not having had time to form up into ranks. Assuming this, and rejecting the evidence of the 1476 chronicle as an interpolation and full of mistakes, and that of the song as not proved to have been in existence before 1531, Herr Bürkli comes to the startling conclusion that the phalanx formation of the Austrians, as well as the name and act of Winkelried, have been transferred to Sempach from the fight of Bicocca, near Milan (April 27, 1522), where a real leader of the Swiss mercenaries in the pay of France, Arnold Winkelried, really met his death in very much the way

[1] Their history from 1248 to 1534 has been minutely worked out from the documents by Herr Hermann von Liebenau, in a paper published in 1854, and reprinted at Aarau in 1862, with much other matter, in his book, *Arnold von Winkelried, seine Zeit und seine That.*

that his namesake perished according to the story. Herr Bürkli confines his criticism to the first struggle, in which alone mention is made of the driving back of the Swiss, pointing out also that the chronicle of 1476 and other later accounts attribute to the Austrians the manner of attack and the long spears which were the special characteristics of *Swiss* warriors, and that if Winkelried were a knight (as is asserted by Tschudi) he would have been clad in a coat of mail, or at least had a breastplate, neither of which could have been pierced by hostile lances.

Whatever may be thought of this daring theory, it seems clear that, while there is some doubt as to whether such an act as Winkelried's was possible at Sempach, taking into account the known details of the battle, there can be none as to the utter lack of any early and trustworthy evidence in support of his having performed that act in that battle. It is quite conceivable that such evidence may later come to light; for the present it is wanting.

Authorities.—See in particular Theodor von Liebenau's *Die Schlacht bei Sempach—Gedenkbuch zur fünften Säcularfeier* (1886), published at the expense of the Government of Lucerne. This contains every mention or description of the battle or of anything relating to it, published or unpublished, in prose or in verse, composed within 300 years after the battle, and is a most marvellous and invaluable collection of original materials, in which all the evidence for Winkelried's deed has been brought together in a handy shape. Besides the works mentioned in the text, the following are the most noteworthy pamphlets relating to this controversy. In support of Winkelried's act: G. v. Wyss, *Ueber eine Zürcher-Chronik aus dem 15ten Jahrhundert*, Zurich, 1862; A. Daguet, "La Question de Winkelried," in *Musée Neuchâtelois* for Dec. 1883; G. H. Ochsenbein, "Die Winkelriedfrage," in *Sonntagsblatt* of the *Bund* newspaper for Jan. and Feb. 1879; A. Bernouilli, *Winkelrieds That bei Sempach*, Basel, 1886; W. Oechsli, *Zur Sempacher Schlachtfeier*, Zurich, 1886; E. Secretan, *Sempach et Winkelried*, Lausanne, 1886; and the summary in K. Dändliker's larger *Geschichte der Schweiz*, i. 510–525, Zurich, 1884. Against Winkelried's claims we have the remarkable study of O. Kleissner, *Die Quellen zur Sempacher Schlacht und die Winkelriedsage*, Göttingen, 1873; O. Hartmann, *Die Schlacht bei Sempach*, Frauenfeld, 1886; and the concise summary of the evidence given by M. v. Stürler (the first to suspect the story) in the *Anzeiger für Schweiz. Geschichte*, 1881, 392–394. (W. A. B. C.)

WINNIPEG, capital of the province of Manitoba, in the Dominion of Canada, stands at the confluence of the Red River and the Assiniboine, in 49° 56′ N. lat. and 97° 7′ W. long., and 764 feet above the sea. Its name is taken from Lake Winnipeg (Ojibway, *Win*, "muddy," and *Nipi*, "water"). The waters of the Red River reach the lake 45 miles north of the city. For some five miles north of "the Forks," as the junction of the rivers was formerly called, lay the old Red River colony of Lord Selkirk, founded in 1812 (see vol. xx. p. 315). Five fur traders' or colonists' forts have stood within the city limits:—(1) Fort Rouge (1736), of the French voyageurs; (2) Fort Gibraltar (1804–15), built by the north-west traders of Montreal; (3) Fort Douglas (1813–35), Lord Selkirk's fort; (4) old Fort Garry (1821–35), of Hudson's Bay Company; and (5) new Fort Garry (1835–82). The transfer of Rupert's Land to Canada in 1870 led to the formation of the province of Manitoba. Then, too, Winnipeg was begun as a village, half a mile north of Fort Garry. The city is built on the prairie; a part of the site was swampy, but is being well drained. The city includes both sides of the Assiniboine, but on the east side of the Red River there is an independent corporation, the town of St Boniface, which is virtually a suburb. St Boniface, with 1449 inhabitants, was first settled by Lord Selkirk's German De Meuron soldiers in 1817. The growth of Winnipeg has been remarkable. Living on its site in 1871 there were but 241 souls. As Canadian immigration increased the village grew, and in 1873 it was incorporated as a city, in the face of strenuous opposition by the Hudson's Bay Company. The census of 1881 gave the city 7985 inhabitants. In the following year Winnipeg, as being the central point of the Canadian Pacific Railway, which connects the Atlantic and Pacific Oceans, became a place of great prospective importance. An enormous rise in values took place. The population of the city doubled in a few months, and the wildest speculation took place. This inflation, locally known as "the boom," caused much damage, and in the following year the collapse brought down almost all the business men of the city. The population diminished very rapidly, but has risen again, and is now increasing. The census of 1886 gave Winnipeg 20,238 inhabitants. The city has water, gas, electricity, and ample fire protection, and architecturally presents a fine appearance. Main Street, which is 132 feet wide and block-paved for a mile, is stated to be one of the best streets in Canada. Being on the eastern edge of the prairies, which run for a thousand miles to the Rocky Mountains, and standing to the west of the great Laurentian formation extending from Montreal, Winnipeg is an important railway centre. The first railway to reach the city was the Pembina branch of the Canadian Pacific Railway, which connects with the railway system of the United States. This took place in December 1878. The Canadian Pacific Railway has not only its main line now running through the city, but five other branches radiating from this centre. Forty miles of the Hudson's Bay Railway, to run from Winnipeg to York Factory, are already completed, and the Government of Manitoba is constructing (1888) an independent line to connect with the American railway system, to be known as the Red River Valley Railway. The total valuation of property for the city for 1887 was $19,392,410, while the exports of the port of Winnipeg for the year were of the value of $816,260, with $1,929,120 of imports. There are seven chartered banks, and many branches of Canadian and English life assurance and loan associations are in operation. In education Winnipeg is the centre of the Canadian North-West. The Winnipeg public and secondary schools compare favourably with those of other Canadian cities, and employ 50 teachers, male and female. At Winnipeg is situated the provincial university, to which are affiliated four colleges,—St Boniface (Roman Catholic), St John's (Church of England), Manitoba (Presbyterian), and Manitoba medical college. The university has been voted 150,000 acres of wild land by the Dominion Government, and has received $85,000 of a legacy from a native of Rupert's Land. There are 24 church buildings in the city and neighbourhood. The census of 1886 gives the religion of the population as follows:—Church of England, 5962; Presbyterians, 5271; Methodists, 3217; Roman Catholics, 2244. The societies are the historical and scientific society, and St Andrew's, St George's, St Patrick's, St Jean Baptiste, Scandinavian, and Hebrew national societies. Masonic, oddfellows', and temperance organizations are strong. There are two hospitals, besides a children's home and maternity hospital. The finer buildings and erections are the city hall, post-office, parliament buildings, governor's residence, court-house, college buildings, Hudson's Bay Company warehouse, Westminster block, Cauchon block, and the volunteer monument of 1886 on the City Square.

WINONA, a city and the county seat of Winona county, Minnesota, United States, is situated upon the west bank of the Mississippi, on a terrace slightly elevated above the river. This terrace is in the bottom-land, which is here 5 to 7 miles in width between the bluffs, which rise 400 to 500 feet above it. The surrounding country is fertile and well settled, being devoted principally to the culture of the cereals. There are ample railroad communications, and the Mississippi is navigable for 160 miles above the city. Lumber and flour are manufactured largely. The population in 1885 was 15,664; in 1880 it was 10,208, one-third being foreign-born. The coloured element was inconsiderable.

The town was laid out in 1852, and five years later a city government was organized. In 1860 a large part of the city was destroyed by fire, but the losses were speedily repaired, and since that time the growth of Winona has been rapid.

WINSLOW, EDWARD (1595–1655), was born in Worcestershire, England, October 19, 1595. He became a member of Robinson's church at Leyden, and in 1620 joined the "Mayflower" company of pilgrims with his wife and brother, being one of the party which discovered Plymouth Harbour. His wife died soon after their arrival, and his marriage with Mrs Susanna White was the first marriage in Plymouth colony. He was chosen a magistrate in 1624, and governor in 1633, 1636, and 1644, when Bradford, the usual governor, "by importunity got off." He made several voyages to England as the colony's agent. Returning to England in 1649, he remained until 1655, when Cromwell sent him on a mission to the West Indies. He died on the voyage, May 8, 1655.

Winslow's portrait is in the gallery of the Pilgrim Society at Plymouth. Winsor (*Narrative and Critical History of the United States*, 277, and autograph at page 268) gives a copy of it as "the only authentic likeness of any of the 'Mayflower' pilgrims." The list of his writings is given in the same volume. See also Allen's *American Biography*, and Belknap's *American Biography*.

WINTER, PETER (1754–1825), dramatic composer, was born at Mannheim in 1754 (or, according to other accounts, in 1758). He received some instruction from the abbé Vogler, but so little that he may be almost considered as self-taught. After playing in the "kapelle" of the elector Karl Theodor, at Munich, he became in 1776 director of the court theatre. When Mozart produced his *Idomeneo* at Munich in 1781, Winter, annoyed at his success, conceived a violent hatred towards him; yet his own popularity was both brilliant and lasting, and of more than thirty operas written by him between 1778 and 1820 very few were unsuccessful, though, through lack of dramatic power, none have survived him. His most popular work, *Das unterbrochene Opferfest*, was produced in 1796 at Vienna, where in 1797–98 he composed *Die Pyramiden von Babylon* and *Das Labyrinth*, both written for him by Schickaneder in continuation of the story of Mozart's *Zauberflöte*. While in Vienna Winter gratified his spite against Mozart by propagating scandalous and utterly baseless reports concerning his private life. He returned to Munich in 1798. Five years later he visited London, where he produced *Calypso* in 1803, *Proserpina* in 1804, and *Zaïra* in 1805, with great success. His last opera, *Sänger und Schneider*, was produced in 1820 at Munich, where he died October 17, 1825. Besides his dramatic works he composed some effective sacred music, including twenty-six masses.

WINTERTHUR, a flourishing industrial town in the Töss valley, canton of Zurich, Switzerland. It is 1450 feet above sea-level, and has a rapidly increasing population (in 1870, 9404; in 1880, 13,595; in 1887, 15,516), all German-speaking and nearly all Protestants. It is the point of junction of eight lines of railway, and is therefore of considerable commercial importance. Its main industries are cambric-weaving, cotton-printing, the manufacture of machinery, and wine-growing, Stadtberg being the best variety of wine grown in the neighbourhood of the town. It is a modern well-built town with a fine town-hall and well-arranged school buildings. It was formerly very wealthy and thriving, but has suffered severely from the disastrous financial enterprise of the National Railway of Switzerland which it promoted. In 1878 it had to sell its property in that line, and from 1881 to 1885 it was in great difficulties in the matter of a loan of nine million francs guaranteed in 1874 by the town, together with three others in Aargau, to that ill-fated railway. As the three co-guarantor towns were unable to pay their share, the whole burden fell on Winterthur, which has struggled valiantly to meet its liabilities, and has been helped by large loans from the cantonal and federal Governments.

The Roman settlement of *Vitudurum* (Celtic *dur*, water) was a little north-east of the present town, at the place now known as Ober-Winterthur. It was there that in 919 Burkhard II., duke of Alemannia, defeated Rudolph II., king of Transjurane Burgundy. It was practically refounded in the valley in 1180 by the counts of Kyburg, who granted it great liberty and privileges, making it the seat of their district court for the Thurgau. In 1260 the townsmen, in their zeal for additional power, overthrew the castle of the counts. In 1264 the town passed with the rest of the Kyburg inheritance to the Hapsburgs, who showed very great favour to it, and thus secured its unswerving loyalty. In 1292 the men of Zurich were beaten back in an attempt to take the town. For a short time after the outlawry of Duke Frederick of Austria, it became a free imperial city (1415-42); but after the conquest of the Thurgau by the Swiss confederates (1460–61) Winterthur, which had gallantly stood a nine weeks' siege, was isolated in the midst of non-Austrian territory. Hence it was sold by the duke to the town of Zurich in 1467, its rights and liberties being reserved, and its history since then has been that of the other lands ruled by Zurich. In 1717–26 Zurich tried hard by means of heavy dues to crush the rival silk and cotton industries at Winterthur, which, however, on the whole very successfully maintained its ancient rights and liberties against the encroachments of Zurich.

J. C. Troll, *Gesch. d. Stadt Winterthur*, 1840.

WINTHROP, JOHN (1587–1649), was born at Groton, Suffolk, England, January 12, 1587. He graduated at Trinity College, Cambridge, about 1605, and was bred to the law. He became a Puritan, and in 1629 was made governor of the Massachusetts Bay Company. The next year he headed the great emigration to Massachusetts, landing at Salem and settling at Boston. The remainder of his life was closely identified with the history of his colony. He was re-elected governor until 1634, and afterwards in 1637–40, 1641–43, and 1646–49. He died at Boston, March 26, 1649.

The tenderness and gentleness of Winthrop's nature are beyond dispute; even such political opponents as Vane retained their personal friendship for him. These qualities, however, were supplemented by a decided antipathy to democracy in every form, which made him the best of civil leaders for the supporters of the ecclesiastical system of early Massachusetts. A vigorous, perhaps captious, statement of this side of his influence will be found in Brooks Adams's *Emancipation of Massachusetts*. His *Life and Letters* have been edited by his descendant, R. C. Winthrop. His *Journal* has been edited by James Savage, who has given it the more appropriate and exact title of *The History of New England, 1630-1649*. *The Winthrop Papers* are in the *Collections* of the Massachusetts Historical Society. Winthrop's descendants have been numerous, and have included an unusual number of men and women of marked ability; see Whitmore's *Notes on the Winthrop Family*. One of them, Theodore Winthrop (1828–1861), of New Haven, was one of the earliest victims of the civil war.

WINTHROP, JOHN (1606–1676), son of the preceding, was born at Groton, England, February 12, 1606. He graduated at Trinity College, Dublin, studied law at the Inner Temple, London, and then travelled on the Continent, seeing some military and diplomatic service. In 1631 he followed his father to Massachusetts, being made a magistrate in 1633. Returning to England, he obtained a commission as governor of Connecticut under the Say and Sele patent, and sent out the party which put up the fort at Saybrook, at the mouth of the Connecticut river. In 1645 he obtained a title to lands in south-eastern Connecticut, and founded there the present city of New London. Connecticut made him a magistrate in 1651, and elected him governor annually from 1657 until his death. He was the agent who obtained for the colony the charter of 1662. He died at Boston, April 5, 1676.

All of the father's fine qualities, and more, came out in the son. The father has had a few unfavourable critics; the son has always been looked upon as the flower of American Puritanism. Even the son, however, was only the representative, in obtaining the charter, of a knot of able and determined men, who had clearer notions of the commonwealth life at which they were aiming; and the governor does not seem to have approved all of their somewhat vigorous proceedings in putting it into effect. Physical science had strong attractions for Winthrop. He was one of the first members of the Royal Society, and was constantly interested in mines and mining in New England. The authorities for his life are those given in the preceding sketch.

WINTON, or WYNTOUN, ANDREW OF. See WYNTOUN.

WIRE. The physical properties requisite to make useful wire are possessed by only a limited number of metals and metallic alloys. The metals must in the first place be ductile; and, further, the wire when drawn out must possess a certain amount of tenacity, the quality on which the utility of wire principally depends. The metals suitable for wire, possessing almost equal ductility, are platinum, silver, iron, copper, and gold; and it is only from these and certain of their alloys with other metals, principally brass and bronze, that wire is prepared. By careful treatment wire of excessive tenuity can be produced. Dr Wollaston first succeeded in drawing a platinum wire $\frac{1}{30000}$ inch in diameter by encasing a fine platinum wire within silver to ten times its diameter. The cored wire he then reduced to $\frac{1}{3000}$ inch, and by dissolving away the silver coating the platinum wire $\frac{1}{30000}$ inch thick only remained. By continued treatment in this way wires of platinum used for spider-lines of telescopes are now obtained of such extreme tenuity that a mile length of the wire weighs not more than a grain; and it is said that platinum wire has been made which measures not more than $\frac{1}{2000}$ mm., equal to less than the fifty-thousandth part of an inch. The accompanying table shows the comparative tenacity of the wire of metals and metallic alloys.

	Diameter.	Strain.
Gold	·0162 inches.	5·61– 5·42 lb
Platinum	·0161 „	6·70– 6·59 „
Silver	·0157 „	7·86– 7·78 „
Copper	·0177 „	10·11–10·20 „
Iron	·0169 „	11·12–10·89 „
Copper	·0605 „	233 lb
Brass	·0640 „	203 „
Steel	·0600 „	342 „
Phosphor Bronze	·0630 „	394 „

Wire was originally made by beating the metal out into plates, which were then cut into continuous strips, and afterwards rounded by beating. The art of wire-drawing does not appear to have been known till the 14th century, and it was not introduced into England before the second half of the 17th century. Wire is usually drawn of cylindrical form; but it may be made of any desired section by varying the outline of the holes in the draw-plate through which it is passed in the process of manufacture. The draw-plate is a disk of hard steel pierced with a series of holes corresponding in aperture with the size and section of the wire to be made. The holes are funnel-shaped, being widest at the side where the metal enters, and tapering to their small diameter at the face where the wire is drawn away. The excessive friction, which is partly relieved by lubricants, causes a rapid enlargement of the holes; and where great uniformity of size is required, as in the case of fine gold, silver, and platinum wire, perforated rubies or similar hard stones are fitted in the draw-plate. The draw-plate is mounted in the draw-bench, which is provided with a reel on which the wire is wound, and in drawing down to smaller dimensions it passes through successive smaller holes in the draw-plate—one at a time—and is wound on another reel or frame on the bench. During the drawing the wire requires to be annealed more or less frequently according to the nature of the metal under treatment. The ductility of the metal and the diameter of the wire operated on determine the rapidity with which the wire can be drawn: iron and brass travel at rates varying from 12 to 45 inches per second, while gold and silver wires of fine section may be drawn through at 60 to 70 inches per second. Stout iron wire down to a section of $\frac{1}{4}$ inch or thereby is made by rolling bars of fine fibrous metal in a rolling mill, in the same way as nail rods, small bars, and angles are rolled. The thinner wires are drawn from these stout wires by the ordinary process of drawing. Iron requires repeated annealing in the process of attenuation, and to preserve it from oxidation it is treated with a scour-bath, consisting of dilute sulphuric acid and a proportion of sulphate of copper. The minute film of copper thus deposited on the wire not only prevents oxidation, but also favours the drawing by lessening the friction in passing through the draw-plate. Much of the iron wire which is to be used in exposed situations is further protected from oxidation by a covering of zinc in the so-called galvanizing process.

In commerce the sizes of wire are estimated by certain more or less recognized standard wire gauges. The most commonly quoted is the Birmingham wire gauge. It gives forty measurements, which bear no definite relation to each other, ranging from the largest No. 0000 = ·454 inch to No. 36 = ·004 inch. Sir Joseph Whitworth in 1857 proposed a standard wire gauge which is coming to be generally recognized. His measurements range from half an inch to one-thousandth of an inch by regular gradations of one-thousandth. Beginning at the smallest, No. 1 is ·001 inch, 2 = ·002 inch, 10 = ·010 inch, and so on, larger breaks being made in the scale as the size increases, but the number and ratio continuing the same till it ends at No. 500 = ·500 inch. In America a standard wire gauge, proposed in 1864 by Messrs Brown and Sharpe, of Providence, R.I., is now extensively recognized. In it the gradations are uniform, increasing in geometric ratio, so that the size of each successive number is found by multiplying the preceding by 1·123. The standard is calculated from wire No. 36, which in the American gauge represents a diameter of ·005, while in the Birmingham gauge No. 36 is equal to ·004 inch.

It must be obvious that the uses of wire are multifarious and diverse beyond all enumeration. It forms the raw material of important manufactures, such as the wire-net industry, wire-cloth making, and wire-rope spinning, in which it occupies a place analogous to a textile fibre. Wire-cloth of all degrees of strength and fineness of mesh is used for sifting and screening machinery, for draining paper pulp, for window screens, and for many other purposes. Vast quantities of copper and iron wire are employed for telegraph and telephone wires and cables, and as conductors in electric lighting. It is in no less demand for fencing, and much is consumed in the construction of suspension bridges, and cages, &c. In the manufacture of stringed musical instruments and philosophical apparatus wire is again largely used. Among its other sources of consumption it is sufficient to mention pin and hair-pin making, the needle and fish-hook industries, nail, peg, and rivet making, and carding machinery; but indeed there are few industries into which wire does not more or less enter.

WIRE ROPE. See Rope, vol. xx. p. 846.

WISBECH, or Wisbeach, a municipal borough, market-town, and seaport of Cambridge, England, in the Isle of Ely, is situated on the river Nene, on the Wisbech Canal, by which there is connexion by the Ouse with Hertford, and on branches of the Great Eastern and Midland Railways, 40 miles north of Cambridge, 21 east-north-east of Peterborough, and about 90 from London. It possesses a spacious market-place, a handsome crescent, and several good streets. There is a public park, 18 acres in extent. The greater part of the town is situated on the south side the river, which is crossed by an iron bridge. The church of St Peter and St Paul is very singularly constructed, having two parallel naves, two aisles, and two chancels, with a large square tower at the west end, originally dating from the 12th century, but almost entirely reconstructed about the close of the 15th century. The church contains some semicircular Saxon arches as well as some traces of Early Norman. Among the other public buildings are the corn exchange (re-erected 1811), the public hall, the custom-house, the new cattle market, the working men's club and institute, and the museum and literary institute, with a library of 12,000 volumes and a fine collection of Roman remains and other antiquities. Besides the Cambridgeshire Hospital (1873) and the twelve corporation almshouses there are a large number of other charities. A grammar-school was established in the middle of the 16th century, and provision was made in the charter of Edward VI. for its continuance. A Gothic monument was erected here to Thomas Clarkson, the anti-slavery orator, in 1881. Vessels of 500 tons burden can enter the port, and extensive wharfage has been erected at a cost of £60,000. The number of vessels that entered the port in 1886 was 294, of 50,721 tons, and the number that cleared 286, of 50,812 tons. The chief imports are corn, potatoes, wool, timber, and iron, and the exports agricultural produce and salt. In the neighbourhood immense quantities of fruit are grown, including apples, pears, plums, gooseberries, and strawberries. Potatoes, asparagus, and other vegetables are also largely grown for the London market. The town possesses agricultural implement works, coach-building works, breweries, ropeworks, planing and sawing mills, and corn and oil-cake mills, many of them driven by water, and others by steam. The town is divided into two wards, and is governed by a mayor, six aldermen, and eighteen councillors. It has a separate commission of the peace. The corporation act as the urban sanitary authority. Water is obtained from chalk springs near Norfolk. The population of the municipal borough in 1871 was 9362 and in 1881 it was 9249.

Wisbech was most probably a fort of the Romans, who it is supposed constructed the river banks in the neighbourhood. It takes its name from the river Ouse (Wyse). It is first noticed in 664, in a charter of Wulfhere, son of Penda. In the early part of the

11th century it was given by Oswy and Leoflede to the convent of Ely, on the admission of their son Alwyn into that monastery. After the subjugation of the Isle of Ely William erected a strong castle at Wisbech to hold the district in subjection. At Domesday the manor was held by the abbot of Ely, and possessed extensive fisheries, especially of eels. In 1190 Richard I. granted to the tenants of the manor exemption from tolls at all fairs and markets in England, a privilege confirmed by King John, who in 1216 visited the town. In 1236 the town and a great part of the castle was destroyed by an inundation, and the castle lay in ruins till the 15th century, when Morton, bishop of Ely, erected a new building of brick for an episcopal residence. In the reign of Elizabeth it was appropriated to the confinement of state prisoners, among others of Robert Catesby. During the Protectorate it was purchased by Thurloe, afterwards secretary of state, who in 1660 erected an entirely new one from designs of Inigo Jones, when some Roman bricks were discovered. On the Restoration it again came into the possession of the bishops of Ely, who sold it in 1793, and all remains of it have now disappeared. Anciently the town possessed eight guilds in addition to that of the Holy Trinity, to which they were subordinate. This guild received royal sanction from Richard II. in 1393, and held its last meeting in 1557. The town received a charter of incorporation from Edward VI. in 1549, which was renewed by James I. in 1611, and confirmed by Charles II. in 1669, remaining in force till the passing of the Municipal Act.

See Watson's *Historical Account of Wisbech*, 1827; *History of Wisbech*, 1833; and "Wisbech Castle," in *Journal of Brit. Arch. Assoc.*, 1879.

WISBY, a picturesque old town on the west coast of the Swedish island of Gotland. It has a considerable trade, but does not occupy half the space enclosed within its old walls, which, with their towers, still survive. These walls, which were built partly on the site of older structures, date from the thirteenth century. The vacant spaces of the town are used as gardens, in some of which are fine ruined churches. The church of St Mary (built 1190–1225) is used as the cathedral. Of the ten ruined churches the most interesting is that of St Nicholas, partly in the Romanesque partly in the Gothic style. In 1880 the population of the town was 6924.

In the Middle Ages Wisby was a port of the Hanseatic League, and a great centre of trade. Its wealth was so celebrated that in an old ballad the people were said to play with the choicest jewels, and the women to spin with golden distaffs. All the principal nations of Europe had representatives at Wisby, and some of its beautiful churches were built by foreign residents. In 1361 it was attacked and plundered by King Waldemar III. (Atterdag) of Denmark. It never recovered from this blow, and when, in 1645, Gotland was finally united to Sweden by the treaty of Brömsebro Wisby had altogether lost its importance.

Plate XV. WISCONSIN, one of the North-Eastern Central States of the American Union, has the parallel of 42° 30′ N. lat. for its southern limit, Lake Michigan for its border on the E., Lake Superior on the N., and the Mississippi on the W. Michigan on the E., Minnesota and Iowa on the W., and Illinois on the S. are its neighbour States. Its area, exclusive of water surface, is estimated at 54,450 square miles. Its length from north to south is 300 miles, its breadth 250 miles; its lake shore-line exceeds 500 miles. Its surface contours are gentle and pleasing. The lower parts of the State lie about 600 feet above the sea, the highest summits about 1800 feet. Few peaks rise more than 400 feet above their bases, and abrupt elevations of more than 200 or 300 feet are not common except along the Mississippi. The State is merely a swell of land between three notable depressions,—the basins of Lake Michigan, Lake Superior, and the Mississippi. The summit of the swell lies within 30 miles of Lake Superior, whence there is a rapid descent northward, with gentler declines to the south-east and south-west, separated by a low swell extending from the summit southward into Illinois. This is traversed in the south-central portion of the State by a remarkable diagonal valley, occupied by Green Bay and the Fox and Wisconsin rivers, cutting it down to within about 200 feet of the lake levels. The easterly slope is traversed longitudinally by a ridge of Niagara limestone, running nearly parallel to the shore of Lake Michigan, at an average distance of about 30 miles.

The greatest topographical interest—and it is very considerable—lies in the minor surface features. The ice of the Glacial period invaded in force the eastern and northern parts of the State, while an area of 10,000 square miles in the south-western portion was left untouched. Flowing but very irregular contours, accented by morainic peaks and ridges, by gravel knolls, and by domes of drift, mark the former area; while deep dendritic valleys, erosion cliffs, and castellated outliers give more striking relief to the latter. About 2000 minor lakes dot the eastern and northern portions, all lying within the glaciated area, and caused by the irregular heaping of the drift, or by the erosion of the glaciers. Numerous waterfalls occur in this portion, likewise due to the disturbance of the river-courses by the ice incursion. None occur in the unglaciated area.

Geology.—The geological structure of the State is unusually symmetrical (see general geological map in Plate XV.). It has for its nucleus a great mass of the most ancient crystalline rocks (Archæan). This nucleus occupies the north-central portion of the State, and about it are wrapped successive layers of later-formed rocks, lying concentrically upon each other, and occupying all the rest of the State. The ancient nucleus consists of granites, gneisses, syenites, and various highly crystalline schists. These are warped, contorted, and twisted among themselves in the most intricate fashion, and, since their original upheaval, have been extensively cut away, exhibiting what was formerly the interior of a much distorted mass. Whether this was originally sedimentary or igneous is undetermined, so great are the vicissitudes it has suffered since its original formation. It is extensively traversed by dykes and veins. As yet it has not proved to be productive in minerals of notable commercial value, but affords a wealth of the finest of building material. This formation is confidently referred to the Laurentian age, and ranks among the earliest known formations. Around the borders of this nucleus, though not skirting it continuously at the surface, are tracts of Huronian rocks. For the greater part these lie in highly inclined beds, and exhibit evidence of much disturbance since their original formation. Where they come in contact with the Laurentian nucleus, they show, by their unconformity to it, and the erosion of the strata at the contact, that a vast but unknown interval of time separated the two formations. The Huronian rocks are chiefly quartzites, with which are associated quartz-porphyries and various slates and schists, together with layers of igneous rock, either formed at the same time with other members of the series, or subsequently intruded. They embrace also, especially in the north-eastern and northern portions of the State, and extending into the upper peninsula of Michigan, valuable beds of iron-ore, as well as beds of carbonaceous material. The amount of carbon contained is large, but unfortunately impure and in the graphitic condition. Limestone also occurs, among the most ancient of its kind. The quartzites of Barron county embrace deposits of pipestone, which also occurs in the Baraboo quartzite, but less notably. Several isolated knobs of quartz-porphyry in central Wisconsin are referred to this formation, and are being extensively utilized for building material, paving, and macadamizing. Apart from the igneous beds, the members of this series were originally sediments, and even now show clearly their fragmental origin. The thickness of the Huronian beds reaches at least 13,000 feet. Overlying the Huronian rocks in the north-western part of the State is an immense series of igneous beds, sandwiched between which, and also overlying which, are layers of sandstone, shale, and conglomerate, the whole constituting the great copper-bearing (Keweenaw) formation of Lake Superior. This crosses the entire north-western corner of the State. The strata are bowed downwards, forming a great trough, the axis of which stretches from near the mouth of the Montreal river to the St Croix. The igneous beds were formed by great outwellings of molten matter, which spread widely over the surface, following each other at longer or shorter intervals, as shown by the presence or absence of intervening deposits or by erosion. The copper of the formation appears to have been brought up by these igneous ejections, and to have been subsequently concentrated by percolating water in the vesicular portions of the old lavas, or in the intervening sandstones or conglomerates, or in fissures traversing the beds,—all these forms being present. The formation in Wisconsin has not yet proved sufficiently rich to pay the expense of mining. The thickness of this formation is truly stupendous, estimates ranging from 25,000 to 45,000 feet.

The preceding formations are found tilted at various angles; those which follow lie nearly flat. The Potsdam sandstone, next in order, rests upon all of these at points, coming in contact with different ones in different places. The wear which they had suffered before it was placed upon them indicates a long interval of time. The thickness of the Potsdam is very irregular, owing to the un-

ENCYCLOPÆDIA BRITANNICA, NINTH EDITION

even worn surface of these underlying formations. In places it is upwards of 1000 feet deep. Being an open-textured water-bearing formation, dipping south-eastward and south-westward from the central axis of the State, and embracing and being overlaid by impervious beds, it furnishes many fine-flowing wells to the districts bordering Lake Michigan and the Mississippi. Some of its beds supply excellent building material, though in general it is not sufficiently firm. The Potsdam sandstone forms a broad irregular crescentic belt, sweeping around the southern border of the Archæan nucleus. It also skirts the northern side in the Lake Superior basin. Overlying the Potsdam sandstone is a stratum of impure Magnesian Limestone, ranging from 50 to 250 feet in thickness. It forms the surface rock in an irregular ragged belt, stretching from the St Croix southward along the Mississippi, and south-easterly to the south-central part of the State, and thence north-easterly to the upper peninsula of Michigan. Small quantities of the ores of lead, iron, and copper are found in it, and certain portions furnish an excellent building stone. Overlying this, the Lower Magnesian Limestone, is an irregular stratum of nearly pure sandstone (St Peter's), ranging from a few feet to upwards of 200 feet in thickness. It is composed of nearly pure grains of quartz, and from the absence of cementing material generally crumbles with ease, though in exceptional places it is sufficiently hard to be used as a building-stone. Being porous and gently dipping between impervious beds, it supplies some of the finest artesian fountains in the State. Its purer portions afford sand.

Upon the St Peter's sandstone rests a series of limestone beds, the lower part of which is known as Trenton, the upper as Galena. Their united thickness varies considerably, averaging about 250 feet. In the south-western part of the State they have yielded large quantities of lead and zinc ores, and some copper. The formation occupies a small area in the north-west of the State, a large area in the south-west, and a belt stretching from south to north through the valleys of Rock river and Green Bay.

Overlying the above limestones is a stratum of about 200 feet in thickness, composed of clay, earthy, and calcareous shales (Hudson River). This is a soft formation and easily eroded, and hence occupies little area at the surface. It forms a narrow north-and-south belt on the eastern margin of the Green Bay and Rock river valley. It has little economic value. At a few points on the surface of these shales there are accumulations of a peculiar Oolitic iron ore (Clinton), popularly known as "seed" or "shot ore," from its concretionary structure. Its highest development is at Iron Ridge in Dodge county, where its thickness ranges from 15 to 25 feet. It is a soft ore, lying in regular horizontal beds, is quarried with great ease, and yields about 45 per cent. of metallic iron.

The next formation is a thick limestone stratum (Niagara), ranging from 400 to 800 feet. The different portions vary greatly in texture and purity, some being very fine-grained, others of admirable granular texture, and others uneven, cavernous, or full of chert nodules. It furnishes excellent building rock, and quicklime of high quality. The formation occupies a broad tract adjacent to Lake Michigan, reaching from the southern line of the State to the head of the Green Bay peninsula. It also caps the elevated mounds in the south-west of the State. The Lower Helderberg limestone, which attains great thickness farther east, is barely (indeed, somewhat doubtfully) represented in the State by some thin shaly beds of limestone found north of Milwaukee. The remainder of the normal Silurian beds and the Lower Devonian formations are not represented in the State, but just north of Milwaukee is a small area of limestone which represents the Hamilton period (Middle Devonian), a portion of which possesses hydraulic properties of a high degree of excellence, and is the basis of an important industry.

From the middle of the Devonian age until the ice incursion of the Glacial period, Wisconsin appears to have been a land surface, subjected to erosion, which developed the hills and valleys that diversify its surface, except as they were modified by the invading ice. As previously indicated, the ice of the Glacial period overrode the northern and eastern portions of the State, while it left about one-fifth of the State in the south-west untouched. The paths of the invading ice were determined by the great valleys of Lake Superior, Lake Michigan, and Green Bay, aided by the diverting influence of the intervening heights. There appear to have been two important invasions,—the earlier covering the larger area, while the later exhibited the more forceful action. There were also minor episodes of glacial advance and retreat. Both spread out an irregular sheet of mixed rock debris, partly derived from the old decomposed surface, and partly produced by the grinding action of the glaciers themselves. The underlying rock was smoothed, scratched, and polished, and in some moderate measure filed down by the overriding ice. A remarkable chain of hills formed about the edge of the ice (the Kettle moraine) constitutes an interesting feature topographically and geologically. It forms a part of an extensive series of terminal moraines that stretch from the Atlantic to the Saskatchewan.

Soils.—The soils of the State are varied. Those of the drift-bearing region are derived from the heterogeneous mixture of pre-glacial soils and glacial grindings, and constitute for the greater part loamy clays and sandy loams of a high degree of fertility and permanence. In the south-west a considerable portion of the soils are derived from the decomposition of the underlying limestone, and are highly fertile and easily tilled. In the central portion there is a considerable area underlaid by the Potsdam sandstone, from which sandy soils, of relatively low fertility, have been derived.

Vegetation.—The greater part of the State was originally covered by forest, but in the south and west considerable areas of prairies were found interspersed with woodlands. The prevalent trees of this region are the oaks, poplars, hickories, and their usual associates. Along the eastern border of the State, except at the very south, is an extensive tract of heavy timber, in which maple, elm, ash, and their usual associates predominate. Towards the north the pines, hemlocks, and spruces come in. The north part of the State was originally covered by an almost unbroken forest, composed of groves of pine, of hard wood, and of a promiscuous mixture of species embracing both conifers and deciduous trees. This constitutes the great lumber region of Wisconsin.

Climate.—Lying between $42\frac{1}{2}°$ and 47° N. lat., and near the centre of the continent, Wisconsin has a typical temperate continental climate. Its summers are warm, and diversified by short rains and clear skies; its winters are somewhat severe but relatively dry and stimulating, and are less chilly than more humid atmospheres at similar or even higher temperatures. The average rainfall is about 30 inches. The mean summer temperature varies from about 70° in the south to about 60° in the north; the mean winter temperature varies from about 25° in the south to about 15° in the extreme north. The great lakes produce a marked effect on the seasonal temperature of the State, elevating it in winter and depressing it in summer, so that the summer isotherms run from the north-west to south-east, forced south by the cooling influence of the lakes; while those of the winter run from south-west to north-east, forced north by their warming influence. As a result, productions requiring a high summer temperature flourish in the south-western and central portions of the State, but are precarious in the vicinity of the lakes, while fruits and crops requiring milder winters and more equable temperatures can be produced near the lakes, but are uncertain away from them. (T. C. C.)

Population.—In 1840 Wisconsin Territory had a population of 30,945. The accompanying table exhibits the population from 1850 to 1880. The State census of 1885 gives the number as 1,563,423. The Federal census of 1880 showed 1,309,618 whites, 2702 coloured, and 3161 Indians. The foreign-born population numbered 405,425, or 30·81 per cent. of the whole, of whom 184,328 came from the German empire, 66,284 from the Scandinavian countries, and 78,057 from Great Britain and Ireland.

	Population.			Density per Square Mile.
	Total.	Males.	Females.	
1850	305,391	164,716	140,675	5·61
1860	775,881	407,449	368,432	14·25
1870	1,054,670	544,886	509,784	19·37
1880	1,315,497	680,069	635,428	24·16

Cities.—In 1885 Milwaukee had a population of 158,509; Oshkosh, 22,064; La Crosse, 21,740; Eau Claire, 21,668; Racine, 19,636; Fond du Lac, 12,726; Madison (the State capital), 12,064; Sheboygan, 11,727; Appleton, 10,927; and Janesville, 9941.

Agriculture.—By the United States census of 1880 Wisconsin had 134,322 farms, embracing 15,353,118 acres, of which 9,162,528 acres were improved land. Of these farms 122,163 were cultivated by the owners and 12,159 were rented. The State census of 1885 estimates the total number of persons engaged in agriculture at 332,500, and the value of farms and agricultural products at $568,187,288. The produce is estimated approximately as follows:—wheat, 21,000,000 bushels; Indian corn, 37,700,000; oats, 43,000,000; barley, 11,500,000; rye, 2,100,000; potatoes, 11,700,000; hay, 2,300,000 tons; sorghum, 599,000 gallons; apples, 1,671,000 bushels; berries, 71,000 bushels. 29,500 acres of tobacco produced nearly 29,595,000 ℔ (this is in demand for cigar wrappers). Of cheese nearly 33,480,000 ℔ were produced, and of butter 36,240,000 ℔. There were in 1886 about 389,000 horses, 1,256,000 cattle, 6700 mules and asses, 917,000 sheep and lambs, and 777,000 swine.

Manufactures, &c.—Large water-powers are found, chiefly on the Fox, Wisconsin, and Chippewa rivers. In 1885 the value of real estate and machinery used in manufacturing was over $38,000,000; stock and fixtures over $24,000,000; value of manufacturing establishments and their products, $193,700,000. There were about 58,500 men employed. The lumber, shingles, and lath manufactured amounted to $27,113,000; milling (including all flour manufactured from cereals), $19,870,000; wooden articles, $13,719,000; iron products and manufactured articles of iron, $10,300,000; beer, more than 1,445,000 barrels, valued at $9,081,000 (over 75 per cent. of this coming from the great brewing city of Milwaukee); manufactured articles of leather, $8,629,000; waggons, carriages, and sleighs, $4,678,000; paper, $2,804,000; woollen fabrics, $613,000; cotton fabrics, $556,000. The census of 1880 valued the slaughtering and meat-packing product at about $6,534,000 and agricultural implements at $3,742,000.

Lumbering.—The proximity of Wisconsin to the prairie States renders its lumbering interests especially important. In 1886 the total forest area of the State was 17,000,000 acres, or 48·8 per cent. of the whole area. According to the census of 1880, Wisconsin was exceeded only by Michigan and Pennsylvania in the value of its lumber product. Operations are chiefly carried on along the Menomonee, Peshtigo, Oconto, Wolf, Wisconsin, Yellow, Black, Chippewa, Red Cedar, and St Croix rivers; but the rapid increase in railroads has opened the northern forests very generally. The lumber, shingles, and lath manufactured amounted to about 3,323,390,000 feet in 1885.

Mines and Quarries.—In 1880 Wisconsin ranked sixth among the iron-producing States, but since then its importance has increased. The most extensive iron deposits occur in the Huronian formation in the Menominee region, and along the Montreal river. In 1882 the total product of the Menominee region was 276,017 tons; the Montreal range, divided between Wisconsin and Michigan, about a dozen miles south of Lake Superior, has just been opened up, and there is a rich deposit of Bessemer ore. In 1886 the product of the whole range was about 800,000 tons. The lead and zinc region lies in the south-west of the State; production had been declining, but recently new discoveries have revived it. There is a rich supply of building-stone; limestone quarries are most numerous, but the red-brown sandstone of Bayfield county and the granite of Marquette county are especially valued.

Fisheries.—The white fish and lake-trout fishing industries of Lake Michigan and Lake Superior are extensive, and the inland lakes[1] and streams abound in bass, pike, pickerel, sturgeon, and brook-trout. A State fisheries commission annually stocks the waters with brook-trout, white fish, and pike.

Railways and Canals.—There were in Wisconsin in June 1886 4576 miles of railway. The leading lines are the Chicago, Milwaukee, and St Paul; the Chicago and North-Western; the Chicago, Minneapolis, St Paul, and Omaha; the Milwaukee, Lake Shore, and Western; and the Wisconsin Central. A canal connects the Fox and Wisconsin rivers at Portage, and the Sturgeon Bay Canal unites Green Bay and Lake Michigan.

Administration, &c.—The State, which is divided into sixty-eight counties, is represented in the Congress of the United States by two senators and nine representatives. The supreme court is composed of a chief justice and four associate justices; there are fourteen judicial circuits, each with a judge; and besides these are county and municipal judges and justices of the peace. The State legislature, composed of the senate (33 members) and the assembly (100 members), meets bienially.

Finances.—The value of all taxable property of the State for the year 1886, as determined by the State board of assessment, was as follows:—personal property, $114,922,900; city and village lots, $110,564,625; lands, $271,019,627; total assessed value of all property, $496,507,152. Taxes were as follows:—State tax, $241,137; county taxes, $2,590,375; town, city, and village taxes, $7,835,385. The total indebtedness of the towns, cities, villages, and school districts in 1885 was $6,848,123; total indebtedness of counties, $1,569,444; bonded debt of the State, $2,252,000.

Charitable, Reformatory, and Penal Institutions.—The State supports two hospitals for the insane, containing together 1141 inmates in 1885, while there are 1240 insane in county asylums, jails, and poorhouses. The school for the deaf has an attendance of 205, school for the blind, 62; industrial school for boys, 292; industrial school for girls, 268; State prison school, 443; a school for dependent children has just been established. The whole number of prisoners in all places of confinement during 1885 was 19,829, and in reformatories 771. The State board of control and the board of charities and reforms have charge of these institutions.

Education.—The State makes liberal provision for its public schools; it sets apart as a permanent fund the Federal grant of section 16 in each township, with 500,000 acres of land, and 5 per cent. of the proceeds of the sale of public lands in the State, together with less important items. In 1886 there were still 103,130 acres unsold, and the amount of the fund at interest was nearly $3,000,000. This school-fund income, which in 1887 was $341,289, is supplemented by a State tax of one mill on the dollar, which amounted to $896,138; the combined amount is annually apportioned among the counties, towns, villages, and cities in proportion to the number of children in each of from four to twenty years of age; in their turn the counties must levy upon each town, city, and village a tax equal to their proportion of the combined school fund and State mill tax. The total receipts from all sources for school purposes in 1886 was $4,192,962, and the disbursements $3,184,958. In the same year there were 556,093 persons of school age. Of these 59·4 per cent. were enrolled in the public schools. The enrolments in normal schools and university (2481), in colleges, seminaries, and academies (1131), and in private schools (14,164) made the total enrolment over 350,000. In 1879 attendance at a public or private school for at least twelve weeks each year was made compulsory on all children between the ages of seven and fifteen years. Women are eligible to all school offices, except that of State superintendent of public instruction. In 1888 there are 137 free high schools, receiving special aid from the State. Provision is made for the education of teachers by the five normal schools. The leading denominational colleges are Beloit, Ripon, Milton, Racine, and Lawrence university. The public school system is crowned by the State university at Madison, organized in 1848. It derives its support chiefly from an annual State tax of one-eighth of a mill on the dollar. The total regular income of the university in 1886 was $105,000; the attendance in 1887 was 600. Connected with the university are a teachers' institute lectureship and farmers' institutes held in different portions of the State, as well as over sixty accredited high schools.

The State historical society at Madison, the capital, has a reference library of 125,000 volumes and pamphlets, and is the richest in the nation upon the history of the Mississippi basin; the State law library there has 19,000 volumes, the university library 14,500, and the city library 9000. Milwaukee has a public library of 35,000 volumes.

Antiquities and History.—The State is noted for its exceptionally large number of animal mounds, the work of the "mound-builders." They are found along rivers and lake banks, and are from 2 to 6 feet high, sometimes 200 feet long; remains of prehistoric circumvallations, with brick baked *in situ*, have been found, and the largest collection of prehistoric copper implements has been made in this State. Wisconsin was the meeting ground of the Algonkin and Dakota Indian tribes. Its water system connecting the Great Lakes and the Mississippi made it the keystone of the French possessions in Canada and Louisiana. The genesis of Wisconsin was from the fur trade. French explorers, ascending the Ottawa, crossed to Lake Huron, whence they easily passed through the Straits of Mackinaw to Green Bay, thence up the Fox to the portage between it and the Wisconsin, and on to the Mississippi. In 1634 an agent of Champlain, Jean Nicolet, first of recorded white men to reach Wisconsin soil, ascended the Fox a considerable distance. In 1658–59 Radisson and Groscilliers, two fur traders who afterwards induced England to enter the Hudson Bay region, passing along the south shore of Lake Superior, struck southward to the tributaries of the Mississippi. Radisson's journal describes a great river visited by him, which was probably the Mississippi. In 1665 Father Claude Allouez founded a Jesuit mission at La Pointe, and in 1669 the mission of St Francis Xavier on the shores of Green Bay. Louis Joliet, leaving Quebec under orders to discover the South Sea, in 1673, took with him Father Marquette from Mackinaw, and reached the Mississippi by the diagonal waterway of the Fox and Wisconsin rivers. In 1679 La Salle, accompanied by Father Hennepin, passed along the western shore of Lake Michigan to the Illinois, and in the next year Hennepin, ascending the Mississippi, met Du Luth, who had reached it by way of the western extremity of Lake Superior. Thus were traced out the bounds and principal river-courses of Wisconsin. The epoch of the fur trade followed, during which stockade posts were erected at various key-points on the trading routes; they became dependencies of Mackinaw, long the emporium of the fur trade. In the French and Indian war of 1755–60 Wisconsin savages served under Charles de Langlade against the English at Braddock's defeat and elsewhere. Near the middle of the 18th century De Langlade and his father had established a trading post at Green Bay, which afterwards became a fixed settlement; at the close of the revolutionary war Prairie du Chien, at the mouth of the Wisconsin, grew into a like settlement; and towards the close of the century Milwaukee, La Pointe, and Portage became permanent trading posts. The British garrison that was sent in 1761 to hold Green Bay left at the outbreak of Pontiac's war, and did not return. In the revolutionary war Wisconsin Indians under De Langlade supported the British. England having retained Mackinaw despite the treaty of 1783, American domination was not practically felt by the Wisconsin traders until after the war of 1812. In this war they favoured Great Britain, and in 1814 the latter wrested Prairie du Chien from an American detachment. But the formation of Astor's American Fur Company to deal in this region was followed by a United States law excluding English traders, which resulted in an increase of American influence. At the close of the war the United States placed forts at Green Bay and Prairie du Chien. By the ordinance of 1787 Wisconsin had been a part of the territory north-west of the river Ohio; in 1800 it was included in Indiana Territory, whence in 1809 it passed to Illinois Territory, and in 1818 to Michigan Territory. In 1825 the lead-mines in south-western Wisconsin, which had been known from the earliest days of French exploration, and had been worked by the Sacs and Foxes and by Winnebagoes, attracted a considerable mining population. Hostilities with the Winnebagoes followed, resulting in the cession by the latter of the lead region, and the erection of Fort Winnebago in 1828 at Portage. In 1832 occurred Black Hawk's War, occasioned

[1] There are about 3000 square miles of clear-water lakes.

by the refusal of a Sac band to remove beyond the Mississippi from Illinois, in accordance with treaty stipulations. Pursued by regulars and Illinois militia to the head-waters of Rock river, the band fled across south-western Wisconsin to the Mississippi, where they were nearly exterminated. This expedition disclosed the rich farming lands of the region. In 1836 Wisconsin Territory was formed. Before this the fur trade and lead-mining had been the chief factors in development, but a wave of land speculation and immigration reached here at this period. In 1840 there was a population of 30,945, more than double that of four years before. On August 9, 1846, Congress authorized Wisconsin to form a State government. The constitution framed in 1846 being rejected by the people, a second one was ratified in 1848, and Wisconsin became a State on May 29 of that year.

At an early period the State adopted the policy of attracting immigration by cheap lands, a work in which the railroads have greatly aided, with the result that Wisconsin has the remarkable proportion of persons of foreign parentage indicated above. There are whole communities of the same foreign nationality,—such as the German groups along the shore of Lake Michigan, the Scandinavian in various localities, the Swiss colony of New Glarus, the Belgians in Door county, and many others. The recent development of lumbering has rapidly built up northern Wisconsin, a process now being accelerated by the mining interests on the Montreal range. Wisconsin furnished to the Union armies in the civil war over 91,000 men, the famous Iron Brigade being chiefly from that State. (F. J. T.)

WISHAW, a police burgh of Lanarkshire, Scotland, and an important mining and iron town, is situated on the face of a hill, a short distance south of the South Calder water, and on the Caledonian Railway, 12 miles east-south-east of Glasgow. It is rather irregularly built, but contains some spacious streets, although the majority of the houses are inhabited by the working classes. It has numerous churches belonging to the different denominations, and a public library. Wishaw has risen to importance since the development of the coal and iron industry within recent years. The coal-pits of the district are among the most extensive in Scotland, and in the town there are iron and steel works, malleable-iron works, fireclay works, and a distillery. Wishaw was created a police burgh in 1855, and in 1874 the limits of the burgh were extended so as to include the villages of Cambusnethan and Craigneuk. The population of Wishaw according to its old limits was 8812 in 1871 and 8953 in 1881, that of the extended area in 1881 being 13,112, of which 1829 belonged to Cambusnethan and 2330 to Craigneuk. The town has borne in succession the following names:—New Town of Cambusnethan, New Town of Wishaw, Wishawtown, and Wishaw.

WISMAR, the second commercial town and seaport of Mecklenburg-Schwerin, Germany, is situated on the Bay of Wismar, one of the best harbours on the Baltic, 18 miles almost due north of Schwerin. The town is well and regularly built, with broad and straight streets, and contains numerous handsome and quaint buildings in the northern Gothic style. The church of St Mary, a Gothic edifice of 1353, with a tower 260 feet high, and the church of St Nicholas (1381–1460), with very lofty vaulting, are regarded as good examples of the influence exercised in these northern provinces by the large church of St Mary in Lübeck. The elegant cruciform church of St George dates from the 14th and 15th centuries. The Fürstenhof, at one time a ducal residence but now occupied by the municipal authorities, is a richly decorated specimen of German Renaissance. Built in 1554, it was restored in 1877–79. The "Old School," dating from about 1300, has been restored, and is now occupied as a museum. The chief manufactures of Wismar are iron, chicory, cigars, roofing-felt, asphalt, &c. Fishing and agriculture are carried on by the inhabitants, but their main industry is connected with shipping and trade. The leading exports are grain, oil-seeds, butter, and cattle; the imports are coal, timber, iron, stoneware, and lime. The harbour is deep enough to admit vessels of 16-feet draught. In 1886 the port owned 35 ships (2 steamers), of 8302 tons burden; in 1875, however, it had 46 ships, with a total burden of 10,447 tons. The population, 6009 in 1810 and 14,462 in 1875, was 16,011 in 1885.

Wismar is said to have received town-rights in 1229. In the 13th and 14th centuries it was a flourishing Hanse town, with important woollen factories. Though a plague carried off 10,000 of the inhabitants in 1376, the town seems to have remained tolerably prosperous until the 16th century. By the peace of Westphalia in 1649 it passed to Sweden, along with a barony to which it gives name. In 1803 Sweden pledged both town and barony to Mecklenburg for a sum of money, reserving, however, the right of redemption after 100 years. In view of this contingent right of Sweden, Wismar is not represented in the diet of Mecklenburg; but it still enjoys some of its ancient rights and privileges as a free town.

WITCHCRAFT. This subject has already been considered in its general aspects under ASTROLOGY, DEMONOLOGY, DIVINATION, MAGIC, and SPIRITUALISM. In this place what will be mainly attempted will be to illustrate the position assumed by the law towards a crime which was regarded for centuries not only as possible but also as specially noxious. It is a long interval from the Twelve Tables to the Bill of Rights, but the lawyers of the latter age accepted the existence of witchcraft with a faith almost as unquestioning as those of the former, and comparatively few were they, whether lawyers or laymen, who in the interval dared to raise their voices against the prevailing superstition. The writings of Shakespeare and the other Elizabethan dramatists are sufficient of themselves to show the universal prevalence of the belief in England. For the purposes of this article witchcraft may be taken to include any claim of a power to produce effects by other than natural causes. By whatever name such a power might be called in a particular case, whether witchcraft, conjuration, sorcery, incantation, divination, or any similar name, the legal effects attaching to its supposed exercise were usually the same. Witchcraft was the most comprehensive English name, *sortilegium* the most comprehensive in ecclesiastical Latin.

In Roman law it was provided by the Twelve Tables that no one should remove his neighbour's crops to another field by incantation or conjure away his corn. At a later date the *Lex Cornelia de Sicariis et Veneficis* was extended by decree of the senate to cases of offering sacrifice to injure a neighbour.[1] Exercise of magical and diabolical arts rendered the magicians themselves liable to be burned alive, and those who consulted them to crucifixion. Even the possession of magical books was criminal. To administer a love potion, even though harmless, was punished by labour in the mines, or relegation and fine in the case of persons of rank.[2] One title of the *Code* of Justinian is entirely taken up with the subject.[3] Astrologers (*mathematici*) seem to have been specially objectionable to both the pagan and Christian emperors. Sorcery was punished by Constantine with banishment, or death by burning; and an accusation of witchcraft, as of treason, rendered every one, whatever his rank, liable to torture. To teach or to learn magic art was equally criminal. The only exceptions allowed (and these were afterwards removed by Leo[4]) were magic remedies for disease and for drought, storms, and other natural phenomena injurious to agriculture. A constitution of Honorius and Theodosius in 409 rendered *mathematici* liable to banishment unless they gave up their books to be burned in the presence of a bishop.[5] The trial of APULEIUS (*q.v.*) for magic in 150 A.D. is the most familiar instance occurring under Roman law.

The church followed and amplified Roman law. The

[1] *Dig.*, xlviii. 8, 13.
[2] Paulus, *Sententiæ*, v. 21, 23
[3] *Cod.*, ix. 18 (*De Maleficis et Mathematicis*).
[4] *Const.*, 65.
[5] *Cod.*, i. 4. 10.

graver forms of witchcraft constituted HERESY (*q.v.*), and jurisdiction over such offences was claimed by the church courts to a comparatively late date.[1] This authorization of belief in witchcraft was based partly on well-known texts of the Mosaic law—especially Exodus xxii. 18,—partly on peculiar constructions of other parts of Scripture, such as 1 Cor. xi. 10, where the words "because of the angels" were supposed to prove the reality of the class of demons called *incubi*.[2] What kinds of witchcraft were heresy was a question learnedly discussed by Farinaccius and other writers on criminal law. The practical effect of this mode of regarding witchcraft was that, although according to the better opinion the offence was in itself the subject of both secular and ecclesiastical cognizance, in fact it was on the continent of Europe seldom punished by the secular power, except as the mere executive of ecclesiastical sentences. The earliest ecclesiastical decree appears to have been that of Ancyra, 315 A.D., condemning soothsayers to five years' penance. In canon law the *Decretum* subjected them to excommunication as idolaters and enemies of Christ, and the bishop was to take all means in his power to put down the practice of divination.[3] The *Decretals* contained, among others, the provision that a priest seeking to recover stolen goods by inspection of an astrolabe might be suspended from his office and benefice.[4] In the 14th century John XXII. published a bull against witchcraft. In the 15th a vigorous crusade was begun by the bull "Summis desiderantes affectibus" of Innocent VIII. in 1484. Under the authority of this bull Sprenger and Krämer (Latinized into "Institor") were appointed inquisitors, and five years later they published the famous work *Malleus Maleficarum* or *Hexenhammer*, the great text-book on procedure in witchcraft cases, especially in Germany.[5] The third part of the work deals with the practice at length. One or two of the more interesting points of practice deserve a brief notice. Witnesses incompetent in ordinary cases were on account of the gravity of the offence admissible on a charge of witchcraft against but not for the accused. An alleged witch was to be conjured by the tears of our Saviour and of our Lady and the saints to weep, which she could not do if she were guilty. The authors explain that witchcraft is more natural to women than to men, on account of the inherent wickedness of their hearts. In the Roman and Greek Churches the form of EXORCISM (*q.v.*) still survives,[6] and was acknowledged by the Church of England as lately as 1603. The 72d canon of that year forbade attempts by the clergy at casting out devils by fasting and prayer unless by special licence from the bishop. No such canon appears among the Irish canons of 1634. On one occasion in 1612 punishment of the exorcised demons was attempted. The bishop of Beauvais, in a document which Garinet has preserved, pronounced sentence of excommunication against five such demons.[7]

England.—As in other countries, ecclesiastical law claimed cognizance of witchcraft as a crime against God. The *Penitentials* of Archbishops Theodore and Egbert and the *Confessional* of Egbert are full of condemnations of magic divinations, diabolical incantations, love-philtres, &c. An exception is made in favour of incantation by a priest by means of the Lord's prayer or the creed. The practice of magic by women is set out in the same document with minute and disgusting detail. After the Conquest, commissions were from time to time issued empowering bishops to search for sorcerers. A form of such a commission to the bishop of Lincoln in 1406 is given by Rymer.[8] The ecclesiastical courts punished by penance and fine up to 1542.[9] For graver punishments the secular power acted as executive. Many persons guilty of sorcery were, according to Sir Edward Coke,[10] burned by the king's writ *de hæretico comburendo* after condemnation in the ecclesiastical courts. The secular courts dealt with witchcraft from a very early period. It was an indictable offence at common law and later by statute, though apparently not a felony until the Act of Henry VIII. The earliest trial recorded in England was in a secular court. In 1324 several persons were appealed before the coroners of the king's household, and the record, certifying acquittal by a jury, was then brought up by writ of *certiorari*.[11]

In proceedings against a woman the doctrine of coercion by the husband (see WOMEN) did not apply. A distinction, more curious than important, was drawn between conjurers, witches, and sorcerers. Conjurers by force of magic words endeavoured to raise the devil and compel him to execute their commands. Witches by way of friendly conference bargained with an evil spirit that he should do what they desired of him. Sorcerers or charmers, by the use of superstitious forms of words or by means of images or other representations of persons or things, produced strange effects above the ordinary course of nature. Legislation on the subject began in the pre-Conquest codes. Thus the laws of Ethelred banished witches, soothsayers, and magicians. The laws of Canute included love-witchcraft under heathendom. It was evidently regarded as a survival of paganism. The first Act after the Conquest was passed in 1541 (33 Hen. VIII. c. 8), which dealt with a somewhat remarkable mixture of offences. It declared felony without benefit of clergy various kinds of sorceries, discovery of hidden treasure, destruction of a neighbour's person or goods, making images and pictures of men, women, children, angels, devils, beasts, and fowls, and pulling down crosses. The Act having been repealed at the accession of Edward VI., another Act on similar lines but distinguishing different grades of witchcraft was passed in 1562. By this Act, 5 Eliz. c. 16, conjuration and invocation of evil spirits, and the practice of sorceries, enchantments, charms, and witchcrafts, whereby death ensued, were made felonies without benefit of clergy and punishable with death. If only bodily harm ensued, the punishment for a first offence was a year's imprisonment and the pillory, and for a second death. If the practice was to discover hidden treasure or to provoke to unlawful love, the punishment for a first offence was the same as in the last case, for a second imprisonment for life and forfeiture of goods. At the accession of James I., perhaps in compliment to the king's position as an expert and specialist in the matter, was passed 1 Jac. I. c. 12, which continued law for more than a century. The strange verbiage of the most important section of the Act is worth quoting in full. "If any person or persons shall use, practise, or exercise any

[1] The name of one form of heresy (*vauderie*) came in time to denote a particular kind of witchcraft.

[2] A reference to the *incubus* as a matter of common knowledge occurs in the prologue to Chaucer's *Wife of Bath's Tale*.

[3] Pt. ii. caus. xxvi. qu. 5.

[4] Bk. v. c. 21 (*De Sortilegiis*).

[5] The practice was also regulated by instructions promulgated by the Inquisition. A code of such instructions framed in 1657 will be found in the later editions of *Cautio Criminalis* (see below).

[6] The extraordinary minuteness of detail by which the practice of exorcism was regulated, even in the last century, appears from a curious little Portuguese book by Brognolo, *Methodo de exorcizar expelindo Demonios* (Coimbra, 1727).

[7] For the Roman and ancient church law, see Smith's *Dict. of Antiquities*, s.vv. "Magica," "Mathematici," and *Dict. of Chr. Antiq.*, s.v. "Magic."

[8] *Fœdera*, vol. vii. p. 427.

[9] See Hale, *Ecclesiastical Precedents*, cited in Stephen, *Hist. of the Criminal Law*, vol. ii. p. 410.

[10] 3 *Inst.*, 44.

[11] *Parliamentary Writs* (Record Commission edition), vol. ii. div. i. p. 403.

invocation or conjuration of any evil and wicked spirit, or shall consult, covenant with, entertain, employ, feed, or reward any evil and wicked spirit to or for any intent or purpose, or take up any dead man, woman, or child out of his, her, or their grave or any other place where the dead body resteth, or the skin, bone, or any part of any dead person, to be employed or used in any manner of witchcraft, sorcery, charm, or enchantment, or shall use, practise, or exercise any witchcraft, enchantment, charm, or sorcery, whereby any person shall be killed, destroyed, wasted, consumed, pined, or lamed in his or her body or any part thereof," every such offender is a felon without benefit of clergy. The Act further punished with imprisonment for a first offence, and for a second made it felony without benefit of clergy, to declare by witchcraft where treasure was, to provoke to unlawful love, or to attempt to hurt cattle, goods, or persons. This Act was repealed in 1736 by 9 Geo. II. c. 5. It will be noticed that in all the Acts it was necessary (except in the case of love-philtres) that injury should have been caused or intended or gain made. There were statutes which, although not directly concerned with witchcraft, aimed at the suppression of analogous offences. Thus multiplication of gold and silver (by means of the philosopher's stone) was made felony in 1403 by 5 Hen. IV. c. 4. This was repealed by 1 Will. and M. c. 30,—it is said, by the influence of Robert Boyle. Numerous Acts dealing with the practice of palmistry and fortune-telling by Egyptians or Gipsies were passed at different times, beginning in 1530 with 22 Hen. VIII. c. 10. They are now superseded by the provisions of the Vagrant Act of 1824.

Trials for witchcraft in England do not seem to have been proportionately as numerous or to have been accompanied with such circumstances of cruelty as those in most other countries. This may be accounted for partly by the diminishing authority of the church courts, partly by the absence of TORTURE (*q.v.*) as a recognized means of procedure, though no doubt it was too often used in an informal manner. The pricking of the body of an alleged witch by Hopkins the witch-finder and similar wretches in order to find the insensible spot or devil's mark, the proof by water (a popular survival of the old water ordeal), and similar proceedings, if not judicial torture, at least caused as much pain to the victims. Charges of witchcraft seem to have been made with great frequency against persons of rank during the Wars of the Roses for political purposes. The cases of the duchess of Gloucester and Jane Shore will at once occur to the mind, and neither Edward IV. nor his queen were exempt. The duke of Clarence was accused of imputing witchcraft to the former; and the latter and her mother, the duchess of Bedford, were charged with having obtained the promise of marriage from the king by magical means. Trials in England were most numerous in the 17th century. In the case of the Lancashire witches in 1634 seventeen persons were condemned on the evidence of one boy. In the period from 1645 to 1647 between two and three hundred are said to have been indicted in Suffolk and Essex alone, of whom more than half were convicted.[1] The *State Trials* contain several instances of such trials, viz., those of Anne Turner in 1615,[2] and the countess of Somerset in 1616 [3] (where a charge of witchcraft was joined with the charge of poisoning Sir Thomas Overbury), Mary Smith in 1616,[4] the Essex witches in 1645,[5] the Suffolk witches in 1665,[6] and the Devon witches in 1682.[7] The most interesting trial is that of the Suffolk witches, because Sir Matthew Hale was the judge and Sir Thomas Browne was the medical expert witness.[8] In many of these trials the accused confessed before execution. The reasons which urged them to confess not only impossibilities, but impossibilities of the most revolting kind, are not very easy to discover. In some cases, no doubt, the object was to escape the misery of life as a reputed witch. The theory of witchcraft, too, was universal and well known, and the revolting details of worship of the devil and of the witches' sabbath must have been familiar to all. Torture, as the Milan case shows (see TORTURE), might force from the accused confession of an impossible crime, and even without torture instances have been known in modern times where women have charged themselves with offences in which they were the only believers.[9] These considerations may partially, if not fully, solve a difficulty which has been felt ever since the time of Cardan.

Towards the end of the 17th century the feeling towards witchcraft began to change. The case of Hathaway in 1702 no doubt accelerated the decay of the old belief. He was convicted of cheating and assault by falsely pretending to be bewitched and by making an attack on an alleged witch.[10] The last trial in England was that of Jane Wenham in 1712, convicted at Hertford, but not executed. A case said to have occurred in 1716 does not rest on good authority. This change of feeling was no doubt caused to a great extent by the works of writers, few in number but strong in argument, who from the time of Reginald SCOT (*q.v.*) struck at the very foundations of the popular belief. One of the most interesting but least-known writers is George Gifford, whose views are in the nature of a compromise. His point is that the devil may deceive not only witches but their accusers.[11] The jury who convict may sometimes be right, but it must be very seldom. As lately as 1718 Dr Hutchinson, bishop of Down and Connor, thought it worth while to argue against witchcraft, but rather from the popular than the scientific point of view.[12] Legal writers did little to shake the prevailing opinion. Coke, Bacon, and Hale certainly admitted the possibility of witchcraft; Selden at least

1 2 *State Trials*, 1052 n.
2 *Ibid.*, 930.
3 *Ibid.*, 951.
4 *Ibid.*, 1050.
5 4 *Ibid.*, 817.
6 6 *Ibid.*, 647.
7 8 *Ibid.*, 1017.

8 In this case, tried at the assizes at Bury St Edmunds on March 16, 1664–65, two widows named Rose Cullender and Annie Duny were accused of bewitching young children. The main points of the evidence were these. There had been a quarrel between the accused and the parents of the children, and the accused had uttered threats against them. The children fell into fits and vomited crooked pins, and once one of them vomited a twopenny nail with a broad head; they cried out the names of the accused in their fits; they could not pronounce the words "Lord," "Jesus," or "Christ" in reading, but when they came to "Satan" or "devil" they cried, "This bites, but makes me speak it right well." One of the children fell into a swoon after being suckled by one of the accused, and out of the child's blanket fell a great toad which exploded in the fire like gunpowder, and immediately afterwards the alleged witch was seen sitting at home maimed and scorched. Evidence of finding the witch's mark was given, and then evidence of reputation, viz., that the accused, besides being themselves accounted witches, had had some of their kindred condemned as such. A farmer swore that once when his cart had touched Cullender's house it overturned continually and they could not get it home. Sir Thomas Browne testified that the swooning fits were natural, heightened to great excess by the subtlety of the devil co-operating with the witches. Experiments upon the children were then made in court by bringing them into contact with the witches and others. These were of so unsatisfactory a nature that many present openly declared that they thought the children impostors. The chief baron in his summing up said that there were such creatures as witches was undoubted, for the Scriptures affirmed it and the wisdom of nations had provided laws against such persons. The report alleges that after conviction of the accused the children immediately recovered.

9 A remarkable instance is a case of Robinson *v.* Robinson and Lane (to be found in the Divorce Court Reports in 1859), where purely imaginary acts of adultery were recorded by the respondent in her diary.

10 14 *St. Tr.*, 643.

11 *A Discourse of the Subtle Practices of the Devil by Witches* (1587), and *A Dialogue concerning Witches and Witchcraft* (1603). John Webster's *Displaying of Supposed Witchcraft* (1677) takes a similar line.

12 *Historical Essay concerning Witchcraft*, 1st ed., 1718.

approved the statutory provisions on the subject; and Blackstone in guarded language said that its exclusion from the list of crimes was not to be understood as implying a denial of the possibility of such an offence, though, following Addison, he would not give credit to any particular modern instance.

In the present state of the law pretended supernatural powers may be such as to bring those professing them under the criminal law, or to make void a transfer of property caused by belief in their existence. The Act of 1736 enacted that any person pretending to use witchcraft, tell fortunes, or discover stolen goods by skill in any occult or crafty science, was to be imprisoned for a year, to stand in the pillory, and to find sureties for good behaviour. This is still law, except as to the pillory. By the Vagrant Act of 1824, 5 Geo. IV. c. 83, s. 4, any person pretending or professing to tell fortunes, or using any subtle craft, means, or device, by palmistry or otherwise, to deceive and impose on any of Her Majesty's subjects, is to be deemed a rogue and vagabond. Under this Act a person may be convicted for attempting to deceive by falsely pretending to have the supernatural faculty of obtaining from invisible agents and the spirits of the dead answers, messages, and manifestations of power, viz., noises, raps, and the winding up of a musical box.[1] So may one who issues an advertisement professing to forecast the future, though no money is received, and the future of a particular person is not told.[2] A false pretence of witchcraft is also punishable under the Larceny Act of 1861, 24 and 25 Vict. c. 96. It has been held that a false pretence that the defendant had the power to bring back the husband of the prosecutrix over hedges and ditches was within the statute.[3] In a case in Chancery in 1868 a widow lady, aged seventy-five, was induced by the defendant, a spiritual medium, to transfer a large sum of money to him, under the belief that such was the wish of her deceased husband as declared in spiritualistic manifestations. The court held that his claim of supernatural power constituted undue influence, and that the gift must be set aside.[4]

See, in addition to the authorities cited, Sir Walter Scott's *Letters on Demonology and Witchcraft*; Stephen, *Hist. of the Criminal Law*, vol. ii. ch. xxv.; Pike, *Hist. of Crime in England*, esp. vol. ii. p. 131 *sq.*; Dr Nicholson's Introduction to Reginald Scot's *Discovery of Witchcraft*; Spalding, *Elizabethan Demonology*, ch. iii.; also reports of particular cases, such as the trial of the Suffolk witches, published in a separate form in 1682, and the indictment of the astrologer Lilly for advising to recover stolen goods (when the grand jury threw out the bill), to be found in his autobiography.

Scotland.—The principal Act of the Scottish parliament was 1563, c. 73 (ratified and confirmed in 1649), making it a capital offence to use witchcraft, sorcery, or necromancy, or to pretend to such knowledge, or to seek help from witches. It was repealed by 9 Geo. II. c. 5. Trials were either before the ordinary courts or, more frequently, before special tribunals erected by the authority of commissions from time to time issued by the privy council, often on the petition of a presbytery or the General Assembly. Boxes were placed in the churches to receive accusations. The frequency of cases is shown by an order of parliament in 1661 that justices depute should go once a week at least to Musselburgh and Dalkeith to try persons accused of witchcraft. In these trials evidence of the wildest description was admitted. Anything was relevant, especially if sworn to by a professed witch-finder or witch-pricker, a position in which one Kincaid, like Hopkins in England, attained special eminence. Torture was used in most cases, and in an aggravated form, as it was supposed that the devil protected his votaries from the effects of ordinary torture. A special form of iron collar and gag called "the witch's bridle" was generally used. The details of the trials in Pitcairn's *Criminal Trials* are utterly revolting, especially those of Bessie Dunlop in 1576 and of Dr Fian in 1590. One of the charges in the former case is very remarkable, and the accused herself confessed it, that she acted under the guidance of the spirit of Thome Reid who had been killed at Pinkie in 1547. In some cases a charge of witchcraft was joined with a charge of another crime, as of murder in the master of Orkney's case, of treason in Dr Fian's, accused of raising a storm at sea when the king was on a voyage.[5] James VI. was frequently present in person at trials for witchcraft, and the most horrible cases recorded are those which occurred in his reign. The full pleadings in a charge are given in the case of Margaret Wallace.[6] It is noticeable that the articles of dittay began by resting the criminality of sorcery upon the divine law as contained in the 20th chapter of Leviticus and the 18th chapter of Deuteronomy. The punishment was generally burning. The last execution took place in 1722, after conviction before the sheriff of Sutherland. As to pretended powers, the Act of 1736 applies to Scotland, and at common law obtaining money by pretending to tell fortunes or recover property by enchantment is punishable as falsehood, fraud, and wilful imposition.

See, further, Sir Walter Scott's *Letters*; appendix vii. to Pitcairn; the *Register of the Privy Council of Scotland, passim*; Buckle, *Hist. of Civilization*, vol. ii. p. 190.

Ireland.—The earliest recorded case is in the same year as the earliest in England, 1324, but in an ecclesiastical and not as in England in a secular tribunal. It was a proceeding against Dame Alice Kyteler and others in the bishop of Ossory's court, which led to a considerable conflict between the church and the civil power.[7] The English statute of Elizabeth was adopted almost word for word by 28 Eliz. c. 2 (I.). The only other Act of the Irish parliament bearing on the question was 10 Car. I., sess. 2, c. 19 (I.), enacting that if a person bewitched in one county died in another the person guilty of causing his death might be tried in the county where the death happened. It is remarkable that this Act is based upon an English Act, 2 and 3 Edw. VI. c. 24, dealing with the venue in criminal trials, but the English Act does not mention witchcraft. 28 Eliz. c. 2 was not repealed until 1821 by 1 and 2 Geo. IV. c. 18, so that Ireland appears to be distinguished as the last country in which penalties against witchcraft were retained in statute law.

United States.—The earliest execution in New England is said to have been in 1648. In the abstract of the laws of New England printed in 1655 appear these articles:—"III. Witchcraft, which is fellowship by covenant with a familiar spirit, to be punished with death. IV. Consulters with witches not to be tolerated, but either to be cut off by death or banishment or other suitable punishment."[8] The fanatical outbreak at Salem in 1691–92 is one of the most striking incidents in the history of New England. Nineteen persons were executed for witchcraft, among whom was Giles Cory, the only person who ever perished by the *peine forte et dure* in America (see TORTURE). In 1692 fifty were tried, but only three convicted, and they received the governor's pardon. For these proceedings the writing and preaching of Cotton Mather were largely responsible. The States have now their own legislation against pretended supernatural powers. Provisions similar to those of the English Vagrant Act are common.

A full account of the proceedings at Salem will be found in Hutchinson's *Hist. of Massachusetts Bay* (vol. ii. ch. 1), in Bancroft's *Hist. of the Colonization of the United States* (iii. 84), and in Cotton Mather's *Memorable Providences* (Boston, 1689) and *Wonders of the Invisible World* (Boston, 1693).

Continental States.—The law against witchcraft was minutely treated by Continental jurists of the 16th and 17th centuries, especially by those who, like Farinaccius and Julius Clarus, were either churchmen or laymen holding ecclesiastical appointments. The extent to which legal refinement could go is well illustrated by the treatise on criminal law by Sinistrari de Ameno,[9] an Italian writer of the 17th century, whose belief in sorcery is strikingly shown by his strange work on the subject called *Dæmonialitas.*[10] He defines *sortilegium* as "actus humanus quo per media inutilia aut vetita aliquis effectus procuratur ad damnum aut utilitatem propriam aut alienam." Six species, it appears, were recognized, called *amatorium, defensorium, revelatorium, lucratorium, malefactorium, divinatorium.* There were eleven distinct modes of profession to the service of the devil. Some of the *indicia* on which torture might be inflicted were absence of the accused from bed during the night, drawing cabalistic signs on the ground, threats of injury, anointing the body. The text of Roman law was sometimes distorted in an extraordinary way: *e.g.*, it was a maxim that a contract with a demon was not binding, and this was expressed in the language of Roman law in the formula "in dæmonem cadere non potest obligatio." In Germany the ecclesiastical courts generally acted, though the crime was sometimes the subject of secular legislation, especially in the *Constitutio Criminalis* of

[1] Monck *v.* Hilton, *Law Rep.*, 2 Exch. Div., 268.

[2] Penny *v.* Hanson, 16 *Cox Crim. Cas.*, 173.

[3] Reg. *v.* Giles, *Leigh and Cave's Rep.*, 502.

[4] Lyon *v.* Home, *Law Rep.*, 6 Equity, 655. A very similar case occurs among the *plaidoyers* of D'Aguesseau, *Œuvres*, vol. v. p. 514.

[5] All these cases will be found in vol. i. of Pitcairn. In one case (noted at p. 216), a jury having acquitted an accused woman who had confessed under torture, the king had them tried for wilful error.

[6] Pitcairn, vol. iii. p. 508.

[7] The case, edited by Mr Thomas Wright, forms vol. xxiv. of the Camden Society's publications.

[8] Cited in 6 *State Trials*, 647, where an account of the Salem trials will be found.

[9] *De Delictis et Pœnis Tractatus Absolutissimus*, Rome, 1754.

[10] Published at Paris with an English translation in 1879.

Charles V. (the *Carolina*).[1] The number of victims perhaps exceeded that in any other country. It was in Germany too that the last execution for witchcraft in Europe took place, at Posen in 1793. In France prosecutions for *vauderie* occurred in the 13th and 14th centuries. In the 15th century Joan of Arc was condemned on a charge of witchcraft.[2] Henry III., like Edward IV. of England, was accused by his enemies of practising sorcery. The most numerous prosecutions were set on foot in the 17th century, and as in other countries they met with the firmest support from some literary men, among whom P. de l'Ancre is conspicuous for his orthodoxy.[3] A royal edict of 1682 revived all previous ordinances against the practice of sorcery and divination, and punished with corporal punishment any persons consulting sorcerers, with death those who exercised magic themselves. The "Chambre Ardente" tried some cases, and the last case ever brought before such a tribunal resulted in the condemnation in 1680 of a woman named Voisin for sorcery and poisoning in connexion with the Marquise de Brinvilliers. The law against sorcery held its place in French legal works till at least the middle of the last century. It was treated at length both by the Sieur de Lamarre[4] and by Muyart de Vouglans.[5] The latter distinguishes white from black magic, the black only being criminal as a part of the larger offence of *lèse-majesté divine*, which included also heresy, blasphemy, and perjury. Burning was the usual punishment. Among the more remarkable of the *indicia* upon which torture might be inflicted was the finding on the premises of the accused instruments of magic, as wax figures transfixed with needles, feathers in the form of a circle, or a written pact with the devil. Pretended exercise of magic is now punished by the *Code Pénal*. A very curious case of slander is mentioned by Merlin.[6] It was tried in 1811 in the department of Yonne. The slander consisted in an allegation by the defendant that the complainants had danced around the devil, who was seated on a gilded arm-chair as president of the dance. The tribunal of police thought the matter more a subject of ridicule than of injury and dismissed it, but this judgment was quashed by the court of cassation on the ground that the charge was one which might trouble the public peace. In Spain and Italy there is a considerable body of legislation on the subject of witchcraft. For instance, the code of the *Siete Partidas*[7] in Spain punished with death those who acted as diviners or witches, especially in love matters. A distinction was drawn between divination by astronomy, which was legitimate, and that by augury from birds or by incantation over water or a mirror. On the Continent, as in England, there was during two centuries a steady flow of literary attack on the reasonableness of belief in witchcraft. The earliest attack was made in Germany, the country which had distinguished itself by the vigour of its prosecutions of the crime. Cornelius Agrippa, in his *De Occulta Philosophia*, was not entirely orthodox on the subject; and it was more directly treated in the *De Præstigiis Dæmonum* of Johann Wier or Weier in 1563, twenty-one years earlier than Reginald Scot's work. Wier was followed in the next century by Father Frederick Spee[8] in Germany, and by B. BEKKER (*q.v.*) in the Netherlands. The work of Spee, originally published anonymously, appears to have caused a great sensation at the time and to have caused a relaxation of prosecutions in order to give opportunity for further inquiry. The work takes the form of fifty-two doubts, the first of which is "An Sagæ Striges seu Malefici revera existant?" The general conclusion is that, although witches exist in general, the question of their operation in particular cases is open to so much doubt that it would be well to suspend proceedings for a time. The writer did not profess entire disbelief, as did Bekker. The main idea of *De Betooverde Wereld* of the latter is that good and evil spirits could have no effect or influence on earthly affairs, for spirit could not act on matter. All prosecutions for witchcraft were therefore unjust, and against the honour of God and the advantage of man. During the same period other writers both lay and legal treated the question incidentally. Montaigne was sceptical; Montesquieu, while not actually intimating disbelief, enjoined the greatest care in trying accusations. As in England, the current of literary feeling was not uniformly opposed to popular belief, for Wier was answered by Bodin, and Luther and other eminent writers no doubt had full faith in the existence of witchcraft.

See Lecky, *Hist. of Rationalism in Europe*, vol. i. ch. i., where an immense number of authorities are cited; works on magic, such as those by Delrio and Garinet; Scheltema, *Geschiedenis der Heksenprocessen*, Haarlem, 1828; Soldan, *Geschichte der Hexenprocesse*, Stuttgart, 1843; and various reports of particular trials, *e.g.*, the proceedings against fifty-three magicians at Logroño in Castile in 1610, by P. de l'Ancre (Paris, 1612), the trials in Sweden in 1669 and 1670, by Dr Anthony Horneck (London, 1700), the proceedings against G. Köbbing at Coesfeld in 1632, by Niesert (Coesfeld, 1827), and *Les Procédures de Sorcellerie à Neuchâtel*, by Lardy (Neuchâtel, 1866). (J. W†.)

[1] Art. 44 gives the *indicia* which suffice to put to the torture. Art 52 gives the questions which are to be asked by the judge.

[2] The numerous allusions to Joan of Arc's witchcraft in the First Part of Shakespeare's *Henry VI.* will be familiar.

[3] *L'Incredulité et Mescréance du Sortilége Plainement Convaincue*, Paris, 1622.

[4] *Traité sur la Magie, Sortilége, Possessions, Obsessions, et Maléfices*, Paris, 1737.

[5] *Institutes au Droit Criminel*, Paris, 1757.

[6] *Répertoire de Jurisprudence*, s.v. "Sortilége."

[7] Partida vii. tit. 23.

[8] *Cautio Criminalis, seu de Processibus Contra Sagas*, the first edition (Frankfort, 1632) being anonymous, "auctore incerto theologo Romano," while later ones bear the name of the author. A full account of an ordinary trial for witchcraft will be found in the work. One of the most shameful parts of it, the stripping and shaving of an alleged witch, meets with the author's strongest reprobation.

WITENAGEMOT. See ENGLAND, vol. viii. p. 276.

WITHER, GEORGE (1588–1667), appears in the *Dunciad* as "sleeping among the dull of ancient days, safe where no critics damn." The once ardent poet's slumbers were disturbed towards the close of the 18th century by George Ellis, who in his *Specimens* resuscitated some of Wither's poetry, not to condemn but to praise. Thereafter he was speedily released from Pope's limbo. Wordsworth prefixed a dozen of Wither's most exquisite lines to his own poem *To the Daisy*; Southey quoted him eulogistically; Brydges republished a selection of his poems, and searched out the facts of his life; Park made a list of his voluminous writings, over 100 in number, for *The British Bibliographer*; and, most fortunate stroke of all for Wither's memory, Charles Lamb wrote upon him one of his most delightful essays, re-creating and immortalizing the old poet's poetic spirit.[9] Wither's life was full of adventure. Born June 11, 1588, the son of a Hampshire gentleman, educated at Magdalen College, Oxford, he entered at Lincoln's Inn, conceived an ardent passion for poetry, put forward as a satirist in 1613 with *Abuses Stript and Whipt*, and was promptly lodged in the Marshalsea. It was the year of the Essex divorce case, when so plain a satirist, though he whipt abuses in the abstract, might easily have given offence. In prison he wrote *The Shepherd's Hunting*, the fourth eclogue of which contains his memorable praise of poetry. Wither's *Motto* was published in 1618; *Fair Virtue, or The Mistress of Philarete*, the longest, freshest, and most captivating lover's panegyric in the language, in 1622. When the civil war broke out, Wither took the side of the Parliament, sold his estate in Hampshire and raised a troop of horse, was taken prisoner and saved from death at the intercession of Denham, backed by a timely jest, was promoted and enriched by Cromwell, was stript of his possessions at the Restoration and thrown into prison, but released under bond for good behaviour. Besides the poems above mentioned, which are the basis of Lamb's admiration, and his curious *Emblems*, published in 1635, Wither, a man of most radiant energy and eloquence, wrote a host of satirical and polemical tracts, for which readers may be referred to the *Bibliographer*. The famous song "Shall I, wasting in despair," occurs in *The Mistress of Philarete*. He died in London May 2, 1667.

WITHINGTON, a township of Lancashire, England, 4 miles south of Manchester, of which it is practically a suburb. It is chiefly occupied by better-class mansions and villas. The township is within the old parish of Manchester, but was formed into a separate ecclesiastical parish in 1854. The urban sanitary district includes part of the parish of Withington and three other parishes (area 5728 acres), the population being 10,099 in 1871 and 17,109 in 1881. The population of the Withington portion (area 2229 acres) in 1871 was 4863, and in 1881 it was 9328.

WITNESS, in law, is a person who gives or might give evidence in a court of justice. The law of witnesses is on the one hand a branch of the law of EVIDENCE (*q.v.*), and on the other is closely connected with the JURY (*q.v.*), for the jurors were originally chosen for their knowledge or presumed knowledge of the facts in dispute. The part of the Scotch juror's oath "and no truth conceal" is an

[9] The marginal notes forming the original MS. of this essay have recently been reproduced by Mr Swinburne, *Miscellanies*, p. 157.

obvious survival of the time when the juror was a witness. It is only by gradual steps that the law has reached its present stage in the United Kingdom and the United States. At present the disabilities of witnesses are few; almost every one is a capable witness, and the main question has become one of credibility rather than of capability. It was far otherwise in Roman and ecclesiastical law and in the older law of England and Scotland. A reference to TORTURE will show that in Roman and mediæval law the testimony of many persons was not admissible without the application of torture. At the same time a large body of possible witnesses was excluded for reasons which have now ceased to be considered expedient, and was subject to rules which have long become obsolete. In Roman law witnesses must be *idonei*, or duly qualified. Minors, certain heretics, infamous persons (such as women convicted of adultery), and those interested in the result of the trial were inadmissible. Parents and children could not testify against one another, nor could slaves against their masters, or those at enmity with the party against whom their evidence was offered. Women and slaves were under a disability to be witnesses to a will. The canon law extended the disability to testify to an excommunicated person, and to a layman in a criminal charge against a clerk, unless he were actually the prosecutor. In the days of trial by battle a party could render a witness against him incompetent by challenging and defeating him in the judicial combat. A policy similar to that of Roman law was followed for centuries in England by excluding the testimony of parties or persons interested, of witnesses for a prisoner, and of infamous persons, such as those who had been attainted, or had been vanquished in the trial by battle, or had stood in the pillory. All these were said *vocem non habere.* Many systems of law excluded witnesses from policy of a local or temporary nature. WOMEN (*q.v.*) were generally regarded as wholly or partially incompetent. The evidence of Jews was frequently rejected in Spain and other countries during the 14th and 15th centuries. In the United States, while slavery was lawful, the evidence of slaves (and in some States that of free persons of colour) was not received for or against whites. There were in Roman law some hard and fast rules as to number. Seven witnesses were necessary for a will, five for a *mancipatio* or manumission or to determine the question whether a person were free or a slave. Five was also the number necessary under the *Liber Feudorum* for proving ingratitude to the lord. Two were generally necessary, as in the Mosaic law, as a minimum number to prove any fact. *Unius responsio testis omnino non audiatur* are the words of a constitution of Constantine. The evidence of a single witness was simply *semiplena probatio*, to be supplemented, in default of a second witness, by torture or by reference to oath. In the canon law the evidence of a notary was generally equivalent to that of two ordinary witnesses. The evidence of the pope and that of a witness who simply proved baptism or heresy (according to some authorities) are perhaps the only other cases in which canon law dispensed with confirmatory evidence. In England one witness is as a rule sufficient. But in certain cases two or more are necessary. Two must attest a marriage or a will,[1] and two are necessary for a conviction of perjury, treason, and some other crimes, such as offences against the Act of Supremacy of Elizabeth. In the United States the number necessary for the attestation of a marriage or will is not uniform in all the States. Sometimes a special number has been fixed in England by statute in exceptional cases. A curious Act of Richard II., passed in 1383 (6 Ric. II. st. 2, c. 5), fixed the number of compurgators necessary to free an accused person from complicity in the peasant revolt at three or four. Corroborative evidence —not necessarily the evidence of another witness, but corroboration in a material particular—must in England be given to entitle the complainant or plaintiff to succeed in an affiliation summons or in an action for breach of promise of marriage. The evidence of an accomplice also needs confirmation, if not in strict law, at least in practice. The number of witnesses had in one instance in old Scotch law the curious effect of determining the punishment. By the assizes of King William, the ordeal of water was undergone by the accused on the oaths of three witnesses; if to them the oaths of three *seniores* were added, the penalty was immediate hanging. Witnesses need not now in English law be *idonei* or credible, except in the case of witnesses to bills of sale under the Bills of Sale Act, 1882. The "credible" of the Statute of Frauds has not been repeated in the Wills Act (see WILL). In the case of dishonour of a foreign bill of exchange the evidence of a notary is required, and a solicitor must attest a warrant of attorney, as was also required for a bill of sale from 1878 to 1882.

The modern law of witnesses has been already treated to a considerable extent under EVIDENCE. It should be noticed that since the date of that article a new rule of great importance has received statutory sanction. The rules of the Supreme Court, 1883 (Ord. xxxvi., r. 38), enable the judge in all cases to disallow any questions put in cross-examination of any party or other witness which may appear to him to be vexatious and not relevant to any matter proper to be inquired into in the cause or matter. It will suffice here to give a brief statement of the law as it at present stands, rather by way of supplement to what has been already said than as an exhaustive notice. Witnesses may be either sworn or unsworn, either judicial or non-judicial, the unsworn and non-judicial almost coinciding. The evidence of judicial witnesses may be given *viva voce* or by deposition or affidavit, the latter being the more usual course in chancery and bankruptcy proceedings. Where evidence is taken on commission, the usual course where the witness is out of the jurisdiction, the questions and the witness's answers are produced in writing to the court which issued the commission, it being a delegation of the authority of the court. As a rule all witnesses coming before a court of justice, whether to give evidence as to a fact or a professional opinion, must be sworn (see OATHS).[2] To this rule certain exceptions exist at common law and have been introduced by statute, the one of the most importance being the law by which persons objecting to take an oath may affirm. Another exception was introduced by the Criminal Law Amendment Act, 1885, the Act allowing the evidence of a child of tender years to be received without oath. But to ensure a conviction such evidence must be corroborated. At common law a person merely producing documentary evidence need not as a rule be sworn. A witness, too, may be examined unsworn on the *voir dire*, as it is called, to decide the preliminary question of his competency. Non-judicial witnesses are those who attest an act of unusual importance, for the due execution of which evidence may afterwards be required. They are either made necessary by law, as the witnesses to marriages and wills, or used by general custom, as the witnesses to deeds. In some cases the attestation has become a mere form, such as the attestation of the lord chancellor to a writ of summons (see WRIT). Those witnesses whose evidence is not received may be divided into incompetent and privileged,—classes which must be carefully distinguished. The evidence of the former is wholly inadmissible; that of the latter is admissible if they waive their privilege. Among the incompetent witnesses are those of too tender years to understand the nature of an oath, idiots and lunatics, those convicted of perjury under an Act of Elizabeth (see PERJURY),[3] and accused persons or their husbands or wives (except where the trial is for treason or for personal injuries inflicted by one spouse against the other). The exclusion of the latter class has led to much dis-

[1] The absence of two witnesses does not, however, avoid a marriage as it does a will. The section of 4 Geo. IV. c. 76 providing for the presence of witnesses at a marriage has been held to be merely directory.

[2] The giving of evidence unsworn appears to have been at one time regarded as a privilege. The men of Ripon, for instance, were by a charter of Athelstan to be believed on their yea and nay in all disputes.

[3] A person convicted of perjury at common law is not on that account incompetent in England; his evidence may be given for what it is worth. It is otherwise in the United States, see Revised Statutes, § 5392. In France disability to be a witness may be inflicted as part of the punishment on conviction for certain crimes (see *Code Pénal*, § 42).

cussion among English lawyers. In 1878 the Criminal Code Commission recommended that prisoners should be allowed to give evidence on their own behalf on oath. Several recent Acts have modified in some degree the rigour of the common law. The accused, or the husband or wife of the accused, may give evidence on oath in certain proceedings, nominally criminal, substantially of a civil nature, such as indictments for nuisance or non-repair of a highway (40 Vict. and 41 Vict. c. 14). The same is the case under the Merchant Shipping, Licensing, and Customs Acts, the Married Women's Property Act, 1882, the Criminal Law Amendment Act, 1885, the Merchandise Marks Act, 1887, and other Acts. Up to 1702 the prisoner was under the further disability of not being able to have his witnesses examined on oath. This harsh rule, borrowed from Roman law, was not abrogated in Ireland until 1711, in Scotland until 1735. Where a witness is competent, he is also compellable, except the king. The only privileged witnesses practically now recognized in England are high officers of state, executive or judicial, and members of the legal profession, who need not divulge what has been disclosed to them in professional confidence. Clergy and medical men are not privileged, though attempts have sometimes been made to protect disclosures to them, especially to priests in the confessional. Any witness is privileged from answering questions the answers to which might expose him to penalty or forfeiture or to a charge of adultery. Lists of witnesses intended to be called by the crown must be supplied to the accused in charges of TREASON (*q.v.*), and are generally on the back of the indictment in ordinary cases, though the prosecution is not bound to call them. In Scotland lists of the witnesses are supplied in all cases, and in the United States in capital charges.

The mode of securing the attendance of a witness is by subpœna (see WRIT) in civil actions in the High Court, by subpœna or RECOGNIZANCE (*q.v.*) before an assize court, by SUMMONS (*q.v.*) in a county court or court of summary jurisdiction. In exceptional cases attendance may be secured by writ of *habeas corpus ad testificandum* or by WARRANT (*q.v.*) of a secretary of state. In Scotland attendance is generally secured by citation. Disobedience to a subpœna is punishable as CONTEMPT OF COURT (*q.v.*).[1] False evidence renders the offender liable to the penalties of perjury. Various Acts of Parliament deal with compelling appearance before committees of parliament, courts of martial, and other tribunals of a special nature. A witness is protected from any action for slander for words spoken in the witness box. He is also protected from arrest *eundo, morando, et redeundo.* The scale of allowances to witnesses depends upon orders of court made with the approval of the Treasury. It is graduated according to the social position of the witnesses. (J. Wt.)

WITSIUS, HERMANN (1636–1708), Dutch theologian, was born February 12, 1636, at Enckhuysen, North Holland, studied at Utrecht, Leyden, and Groningen, and was ordained to the ministry in 1657. In 1675 he became professor of divinity at Franeker, and in 1680 he was translated to a corresponding chair at Utrecht. In 1685 he acted as chaplain to the Dutch embassy sent to London to congratulate James II. on his accession. In 1698 he succeeded Spanheim at Leyden, where he died on October 22, 1708.

Subjoined is a list of his more important works. *Judæus Christianizans,—circa Principia Fidei et SS. Trinitatem*, Utrecht, 1661; *De Œconomia Fœderum Dei cum Hominibus*, 1677 (often reprinted, both in Latin and in English, and still regarded as one of the clearest and most suggestive expositions of the so-called "federal" theology); *Diatribe de Septem Epistolarum Apocalypticarum Sensu Historico ac Prophetico*, Franeker, 1678; *Exercitationes Sacræ in Symbolum quod Apostolorum dicitur et in Orationem Dominicam*, Franeker, 1681; *Miscellanea Sacra*, Utrecht, 1692–1700 (2 vols. 4to).

WITT. See DE WITT.

WITTEN, a rapidly growing town of Westphalia, Prussia, is favourably situated among the coalfields of the Ruhr, 14 miles east of Essen and 15 miles north-east of Elberfeld. The coal-mines in the neighbourhood provide abundant fuel for large cast-steel works, iron-foundries, railway workshops, machinery and boiler works, glass-works, distilleries, and other industrial establishments. In 1843 the population was 3444; in 1885 it was 23,903.

WITTENBFRG, now an unimportant manufacturing town in the province of Saxony, Prussia, is situated 55 miles to the south-west of Berlin, on the Elbe, which is here spanned by a stone bridge 300 yards long, and by an iron railway bridge 320 yards long. The three suburbs which adjoin the town are not older than 1817. Wittenberg is interesting chiefly on account of its close connexion with Luther and the dawn of the Reformation; and several of its buildings are associated with the events of that time. Part of the Augustinian monastery in which Luther dwelt, at first as a monk and in later life as owner with his wife and family, is still preserved, and has been fitted up as a "Luther museum." The Augusteum, built in 1564–83 on the site of the monastery, is now a clerical seminary. The Schlosskirche, to the doors of which Luther nailed his famous ninety-five theses in 1517, dated originally from 1490–99; it was, however, seriously damaged by fire during the bombardment of 1760, and has practically been re-built. The old wooden doors, burnt in 1760, are replaced by bronze doors, bearing the Latin text of the theses. In the interior of the church are the tombs of Luther, Melanchthon, and the electors Frederick the Wise and John the Constant. The parish church, in which Luther often preached, was built in the 14th century, but has been much altered since Luther's time. The present infantry barracks were at one time occupied by the university of Wittenberg, founded in 1502, but incorporated with the university of Halle in 1817. Luther was appointed professor of philosophy here in 1508; and the new university rapidly acquired a considerable reputation from its connexion with the early Reformers. Shakespeare makes Hamlet and Horatio study at Wittenberg. The ancient electoral palace is another of the buildings that suffered severely in 1760; it now contains archives. Melanchthon's house and the house of Lucas Cranach the Elder (1472–1553), who was burgomaster of Wittenberg, are also pointed out. Statues of Luther and Melanchthon embellish the town. The spot, outside the Elster Gate, where Luther publicly burned the papal bull in 1520 is marked by an oak tree. Woollen and linen-weaving, stocking-making, leather-working, distilling, and brewing are carried on in Wittenberg. The formerly considerable manufacture of the heavier kinds of cloth has died out. The population in 1885 was 13,856; in 1816 it was 6206.

Wittenberg is mentioned as early as 1180. It was the capital of the little duchy of Saxe-Wittenberg (vol. xxi. p. 352), the rulers of which afterwards became electors of Saxony; and it continued to be the chief town of Saxony under the Ernestine electors. The capitulation of Wittenberg (1547) is the name given to the treaty by which John Frederick the Magnanimous was compelled to resign the electoral dignity and most of his territory to the Albertine branch of the Saxon family. In 1760 the town was bombarded by the Austrians. In 1813 it was refortified by command of Napoleon; but in 1814 it was stormed by the Prussians under Tauentzien, who received the title of "Von Wittenberg" as a reward. Wittenberg continued to be a fortress of the third class until the reorganization of the German defences after the foundation of the new empire in 1871 led to its being dismantled.

WŁOCŁAWEK, or VLOTSLAVSK, a district town of the government of Warsaw, on the left bank of the Vistula, which is crossed by an iron bridge, 118 miles by rail to the N.W. of Warsaw. It was founded about 1139, and became known under the name of Vladislavia, or Old Ladislaus, as a centre for trade of some importance. Later on it fell into decay; but, owing to its position on the great water highway of Poland and on the railway connecting Warsaw with Berlin and Dantzic, its population has rapidly increased of late, and now amounts to 22,600. Its merchants carry on an active trade in grain. It has a fine cathedral, dating from the 14th century.

WOBURN, a town of Middlesex county, Massachusetts, United States, lies about 10 miles somewhat west of north from Boston; it comprises within its limits four villages of greater or less size, besides a small rural population. The town contains 75 miles of streets. The population in 1885 was 11,750, about three-tenths of foreign birth. The

[1] In the ecclesiastical courts it was formerly punished by EXCOMMUNICATION (*q.v.*).

industries, which are largely manufacturing, are connected chiefly with the tanning of leather and the making of boots and shoes.

Woburn is one of the older towns of Massachusetts, having been settled in 1642. Its growth, however, was slow, and it is only in recent years that it has attained to importance.

WOELFL, Joseph (1772–1812), pianist and composer, was born in 1772 at Salzburg, where he studied music under Leopold Mozart and Michael Haydn. After a short residence at Warsaw he produced his first opera, *Der Höllenberg*, with some success at Vienna, where it was soon followed by *Das schöne Milchmädchen* and some other dramatic pieces. These, however, have been long forgotten, and his fame now rests upon his compositions for the pianoforte, and the skill with which he is said to have met their formidable demands upon his power as an executant. The perfection of his *technique* was immeasurably enhanced by the enormous stretch of his fingers; and to the wide grasp of the key-board this placed at his command he owed a facility of execution which he turned to excellent account, especially in his extempore performances. So remarkable were these that even the youthful Beethoven did not disdain to play in company with him at the house of Count Wetzlar, and in memory of this exhibition of good-humoured rivalry he dedicated to Beethoven his Three Sonatas, *Op.* 6. Quitting Vienna in 1798 Woelfl exhibited his skill in most of the great European capitals, and, after spending some years in Paris, made his first appearance in London, May 27, 1805. Here he enjoyed a long term of popularity, crowned about 1808 by the publication of his Sonata, *Op.* 41, containing some variations on "Life let us cherish." This, on account of its technical difficulty, he entitled *Non Plus Ultra*; and, in reply to the challenge, Dussek's London publishers reprinted a sonata by that composer, originally called *Le Retour à Paris*, with the title *Plus Ultra*, and an ironical dedication to *Non Plus Ultra*. Woelfl died in Great Marylebone Street, London, May 21, 1812. Some stories once current concerning his ruin by a card-sharper and death upon a heap of straw are proved to have been utterly without foundation.

WÖHLER, Friedrich (1800–1882), chemist, was born on July 31, 1800, in Eschersheim, near Frankfort-on-the Main. While attending the village school of Rödelheim, he received valuable additional instruction from his father, a man of more than ordinary acquirements. In 1812 the family removed to Frankfort, where he entered the gymnasium, and by the kindness of a scientific friend, Dr Buch, was introduced to the study of mineralogy, chemistry, and physics. He afterwards studied medicine at Marburg and Heidelberg, graduating in that faculty at the latter university. Having, on the advice of Leopold Gmelin, decided upon devoting himself henceforth to chemistry, he completed his chemical education at Stockholm, under Berzelius, in whose laboratory he worked for a considerable time, and with whom, during his subsequent life, he maintained the most friendly relations. While in Sweden he took part in a scientific expedition through Norway, which made him acquainted with the brothers Brongniart and with Humphrey Davy.

After his return from Sweden in 1825, he accepted a call to Berlin as teacher of chemistry in the then newly-erected "gewerbschule," and remained there until 1832, when family affairs caused him to take up his abode in Cassel. In 1836 Wöhler became professor of chemistry in the medical faculty of the university of Göttingen, which office, in his case, was combined with that of inspector-general of pharmacy for Hanover. He held his chair till his death, which occurred, after a short illness, on the 23rd September 1882.

Wöhler's career as a chemist extends over two generations. Some sixty years ago, when the elementary nature of chlorine had just been established, and the isolation of cyanogen was still a novelty, young Wöhler already worked as an investigator, the same Wöhler who rejoiced with the chemists of to-day over the synthesis of indigo. Of the world of chemical discoveries that lie between he *magna pars fuit*. Within the limits of the present article, however, it is impossible to do more than indicate briefly the nature of some of his greater achievements. Amongst these his discovery of cyanic acid, and what it led him to, occupy a prominent place. From these investigations of his the science of organic chemistry may be said to date.

When, in 1828, Wöhler prepared the ammonia salt of his acid, he was astonished to find that the salt, although made by what appeared to be a straightforward double decomposition, did not exhibit the character of an ammonia salt at all, but turned out to be identical with urea, a substance which heretofore had been known only as one of the *organic* components of urine. Prior to this discovery a wide and impassable gulf had in the minds of chemists separated the mineral from the organic kingdom. Inorganic bodies all appeared to be derivable from their elements by a succession of acts of binary combination; the full analysis of such a body contained in itself the full instruction for its synthetical production in the laboratory. Organic substances, on the other hand, were supposed to be things of an entirely different order; in them the few elements which they all consist of were assumed to be united with one another, each with each, in a mysterious manner, which could be brought about only by the agency of "vital force." Vital force, it was now seen, had nothing to do with the formation of urea at any rate. The gulf was bridged over, and a great and new morning full of the highest promise dawned over chemistry. If the promise was more than fulfilled, if organic chemistry from a mere possibility developed into a reality, we owe this chiefly to the great researches which were carried out conjointly by Wöhler and Liebig.

One of the first, if not the first, of these was an investigation on the oxygenated acids of cyanogen, which they published in 1830. In their research they proved, both analytically and synthetically, that cyanic and cyanuric acid, although distinct bodies, have the same elementary composition, and that the former, when simply kept in a sealed-up tube, gradually passes wholly into a porcelain-like neutral solid, cyamelide, which is widely different from either. By these discoveries, and by Wöhler's synthesis of urea, the fact of isomerism was firmly established. Compared with this great conquest their joint work on mellitic acid (1830) and on sulphovinic acid (1831) appears small; it sinks into insignificance when viewed in the light of their immortal researches on bitter-almond oil and on uric acid.

In 1832 bitter-almond oil was supposed to be to bitter almonds what a hundred and one other essential oils are to their vegetable sources. Of its chemistry nothing was known except the fact that it contains loosely combined prussic acid, and that, when kept for a long time, it is liable to deposit a crystalline solid, as various other essential oils do. Liebig and Wöhler, being struck by the absence from even powdered bitter almonds of the intense smell characteristic of the oil, set about tracing the latter to its origin, and soon solved the question. In 1830 Robiquet and Boutron-Charlard had succeeded in extracting from bitter almonds a crystalline nitrogenous solid, soluble without decomposition in alcohol and in water, which they called amygdaline. What Liebig and Wöhler found was that, when bitter-almond meal is mashed up with water, this amygdaline, by the action of the water and a ferment (common to both sweet and bitter almonds), breaks up into sugar, prussic acid, and bitter-almond oil. They also succeeded in separating the prussic acid from the distilled oil, and found the thus purified oil to be a non-poisonous liquid of the composition C_7H_6O. This liquid, when exposed to the air, readily takes up oxygen and assumes the form of a solid, which is identical at the same time with the quasi-stearoptene of the oil and with Scheele's benzoic acid, $C_7H_6O_2$. When treated with chlorine, the purified oil yields a chloride, $C_7H_5O.Cl$,—the chlorine of which, by treatment with the respective potassium compounds, is displaced by its equivalent in bromine, iodine, sulphur, cyanogen, and, on treatment with ammonia, by the group NH_2. Water converts it into hydrochloric and benzoic acids. In all these reactions the group C_7H_5O holds together; it moves forwards and backwards as if it were a compound element,—a common-place enough fact in the eyes of the chemical student of 1882, but a most wonderful revelation to the chemist of 1832. Berzelius, who certainly was not much given to dealing in superlatives, greeted the discovery in his *Jahresbericht* as opening up a new era in organic chemistry, and, rejecting the prosaic name of benzoyl which Wöhler and Liebig had given to their radical, proposed to name it proine, from πρωΐ, early in the day, or orthrine, from ὄρθρος, the dawn.

Equally important in a scientific sense, but greater as a piece of experimental work, was their joint research on Uric Acid (*q.v.*). After their uric acid research the ways of Wöhler and Liebig diverged. The latter continued to prosecute organic research; the former turned his attention more to inorganic subjects,—not exclusively, however, as the well-known research on narcotine (which was carried out in his laboratory, partly by himself partly by Blyth, and published in 1848) is alone sufficient to prove.

Amongst Wöhler's inorganic publications, a short notice on the improvements in the preparation of potassium is significant as forming the small beginning of a brilliant series of researches on the isolation of elementary substances and on their properties, a subject for which he evidently had a great love, as he always comes back to it in the intervals of other work. In 1827 he for the first time succeeded in isolating aluminium, the metal of clay, by means of a method which was soon found to be more generally applicable. Alumina, like many other metallic oxides, is not reducible by electrolysis or by the action of charcoal at any temperature. But, when heated with charcoal in chlorine gas, it passes into the state of a volatile chloride. What Wöhler found was that this chloride, when heated with potassium or sodium, readily gives up its chlorine and assumes the elementary form. The aluminium which Wöhler thus obtained was a grey powder; but in 1845 he succeeded in producing the metal in the shape of well-fused, fully metallic globules. Wöhler, on this second occasion, correctly ascertained all the properties which everybody now knows to be characteristic of this metal; and it is as well to add that where Wöhler's aluminium differed from what now occurs in commerce under this name it differed to its own advantage. That Wöhler should not have seen the practical importance of his discovery is not to be credited; if he never suggested an attempt to manufacture the metal industrially, that is only the natural consequence of the circumstances in which he was placed.

The earlier aluminium research was followed in 1828 by the isolation of beryllium and yttrium. These earlier metal reductions fall into the Berlin period. While in Cassel he worked out processes for the manfacture of nickel free from arsenic, and this laid the foundation for what is now a flourishing chemical industry in Germany. The several methods for the analysis of nickel and cobalt ores which he describes in his *Mineral-Analyse* appear to be an incidental outcome of this work. This subject was one of his favourite topics; as late as 1877 we see him coming back to it in the publication of a short process for the separation of nickel and cobalt from arsenic and iron.

In 1849 metallic titanium arrested his attention. Since the days of Wollaston those beautiful copper-like cubes which are occasionally met with in blown-out blast furnaces had been supposed to be metallic titanium pure and simple. Wöhler observed that the reputed metal, when fused with caustic alkali, emitted torrents of ammonia, and on further inquiry ascertained the crystals to be a ternary compound, containing the elements of a nitride and of a cyanide of the metal. In pursuance of this research Wöhler taught us how to prepare real titanium and really pure titanic acid.

In 1854 Deville's energetic attempts to produce aluminium industrially caused Wöhler to turn his attention again to this early and almost forgotten child of his genius. His first incentive, no doubt, was the natural and just desire to claim his right as the real discoverer of what Deville, in his ignorance of foreign scientific work, quite honestly thought he had been the first to find out. This dispute came to a very satisfactory issue: Deville, after a little pardonable hesitation, fully acknowledged Wöhler's priority, and the two henceforth were friends, and worked together.

The first fruit of this happy union was a memorable joint research (published in 1856 and 1857), which led to their discovery of an adamantine and of a graphitoidal (in addition to the long known amorphous) modification of boron. This graphitoidal species subsequently, in their own hands, proved to be a mistake; but the adamantine modification lives to this day as a true analogue of ordinary (carbon) diamond.

From boron to silicon is an easy transition, so we need not wonder at finding Wöhler, in 1857, engaged (conjointly with the physicist Buff) in a research on new compounds of silicon. On electrolysing a solution of common salt with silicon-containing aluminium as a positive electrode, they obtained a self-inflammable gas which they recognized as hydrogen contaminated with the previously unknown hydride of silicon, SiH_4, which body Wöhler subsequently, with the co-operation of Martius, obtained in a state of greater purity. Wöhler and Buff also obtained, though in an impure state, what were subsequently recognized by Friedel and Ladenburg as silicon-chloroform and as silicon-formic anhydride.

Space does not allow of more than a mere reference to Wöhler's researches on metallic or semimetallic nitrides. What we know of this as yet little understood class of bodies, with barely an exception, came out of his laboratory, if it was not done by himself in the strict sense of the word. And only a reference can be made to the numerous processes which Wöhler, in the course of his long laboratory practice, has worked out for the preparation of pure chemicals, and for the execution of exact analytical separations. He had better work to do than to take up analytical problems for their own sake; but what he did in this direction incidentally amounts to a great deal. The analysis of meteorites was one of his favourite specialties,—one of his results being the discovery of organic matter in a meteorite which he examined in 1864.

As a teacher Wöhler ranks with Liebig and Berzelius. In a sense he was the greatest of the three. Berzelius never had the opportunity to teach large numbers of students in his laboratory; and Liebig lacked the many-sidedness so characteristic of the Göttingen laboratory as long as it really was under Wöhler's personal direction. One student might wish to work on organic chemistry, another on minerals, a third on metallurgy, a fourth on rare elements; let them all go to Wöhler, and all, as well as the fifth or sixth, would find themselves in the right place. That Wöhler in these circumstances was able to do much literary work is truly marvellous. His *Grundriss der Chemie*, which he published anonymously at first, has passed through many editions, and been translated into various foreign languages,—never, unfortunately, into English. A more valuable teaching book still, and more unique in its character, is his excellent *Practische Uebungen in der chemischen Analyse* (entitled in the second edition *Mineral-Analyse in Beispielen*), of which we have two English translations. To a man like him the compilation of either book probably gave little trouble; what must have taken up a very large portion of his valuable time are his translations of Berzelius's *Lehrbuch der Chemie*, and of all the successive volumes of Berzelius's *Jahresbericht*, which only thus became really available to the scientific world at large. From 1838, too, Wöhler was one of the editors of Liebig's *Annalen*.

Wöhler's last publication (1880) treats of a new kind of galvanic element in which the one metal aluminium serves for either pole.

A very excellent biography of Wöhler by Hofmann is published in the *Berichte der deutschen chemischen Gesellschaft* for 1882. (W. D.)

WOHLGEMUTH, MICHAEL (1434–1519), an able painter of the school of Franconia, of which Nuremberg, where he was born in 1434, was the chief artistic centre. Little is known of his private life beyond the fact that in 1472 he married the widow of the painter Hans Pleydenwurff, whose son Wilhelm worked as an assistant to his stepfather. The importance of Wohlgemuth as an artist rests, not only on his own individual paintings, but also on the fact that he was the head of a large workshop, in which many different branches of the fine arts were carried on by a great number of pupil-assistants, including Albert Dürer (see vol. vii. pp. 555–56). In this *atelier* not only large altar-pieces and other sacred paintings were executed, but also elaborate retables in carved wood, consisting of crowded subjects in high relief, richly decorated with gold and colour, such as pleased the rather doubtful Teutonic taste of that time (see p. 648 *infra*). Wood-engraving was also carried on in the same workshop, the blocks being cut from Wohlgemuth's designs, many of which are remarkable for their vigour and clever adaptation to the special necessities of the technique of woodcutting. Two large and copiously illustrated books have woodcuts supplied by Wohlgemuth and his stepson Wilhelm Pleydenwurff. The first is the *Schatzkammer der wahren Reichthümer des Heils*, printed by Koberger in 1491; the other is the *Historia Mundi*, by Schedel, 1493–94, a sort of encyclopædia, usually known as the *Nuremberg Chronicle*, which attained a very high degree of popularity at the time, and is now highly valued, not for the text, but for its remarkable collection of spirited engravings.

Among the paintings ascribed to Wohlgemuth a large number are clearly the work of less able assistants, but those by the hand of the master himself possess merit of a very high order, in their rich colour, powerful drawing, and refined delicacy of finish. The earliest known work by Wohlgemuth is a retable consisting of four panels, dated 1465, now in the Munich gallery, a decorative work of much beauty. In 1479 he painted the retable of the high altar in the church of St Mary at Zwickau, which still exists, receiving for it the large sum of 1400 gulden. One of his finest and largest works is the great retable painted for the church of the Austin friars at Nuremberg, now moved into the museum; it consists of a great many panels, with figures of those saints whose worship was specially popular at Nuremberg. In 1501 Wohlgemuth was employed to decorate the town-hall at Goslar with a large series of paintings; some on the ceiling are on panel, and others on the walls are painted thinly in tempera on canvas. As a portrait-painter he enjoyed much repute, and some of his works of this class are very admirable for their realistic vigour and minute finish. Outside Germany Wohlgemuth's paintings are scarce: the Royal Institution at Liverpool possesses two good examples,—Pilate Washing his Hands, and the Deposition from the Cross, parts probably of a large altarpiece. During the last ten years of his life Wohlgemuth appears to have produced little by his own hand. One of his latest paintings is the retable at Schwabach, executed in 1508, the contract for which still exists. He died at Nuremberg in 1519.

WOLCOT, JOHN (1738–1819), painter and satirist under the pseudonym of PETER PINDAR, was son of Alexander Wolcot, surgeon at Dodbrooke, adjoining Kingsbridge, in Devonshire, and was baptized there 9th May 1738. He was educated at Kingsbridge free school under John Morris, at the Bodmin grammar school, and in France, and as the result of this training was well acquainted with Greek and Latin, and spoke French with facility. For seven years he was apprenticed to his uncle, John Wolcot, a surgeon at Fowey, and it was intended that he should in due course succeed to the practice. Among his uncle's patients were Sir William Trelawny and his household, at Trelawne, near Fowey, and when Trelawny went to Jamaica as governor in 1769 he was accompanied by Wolcot, who had now qualified as M.D. of the university of Aberdeen (8th September 1767). Considerable ecclesiastical patronage was in the gift of the governor of Jamaica, and, to render himself eligible for any desirable living which might fall vacant, Wolcot returned to England, and was ordained deacon on 24th June 1769 and priest on the following day. With these qualifications he once more repaired to the West Indies, and in 1772 became incumbent of Vere, Jamaica, but on the death of his patron (11th December 1772) he bade adieu to the colony, and on his arrival in England settled as a physician at Truro. Party politics ran high in that borough, and Wolcot threw himself into the fray, making an especial butt of an influential merchant, afterwards the representative of Truro in parliament. In consequence of those indiscretions he left in 1779, and in 1781 he fixed his permanent abode in London. He brought with him the young Cornish artist John Opie, whose talents in painting received the enthusiastic admiration of the doctor. Wolcot exerted himself energetically in spreading the fame of his young protegé by puffs in the papers and by introductions to the leaders of fashion.[1] From this date he dropped the profession of medicine, as he had previously thrown off his clerical orders, and earned the means of subsistence by his satirical productions. Wolcot had long dabbled in poetry. His first effusion, on the recovery of the elder Pitt from gout, is said to have appeared in *Martin's Magazine*, about 1756, when he was resident at Fowey, and he dictated verses until within a few days of his death. Many of his serious pieces were marked by taste and feeling, and his translation of Thomas Warton's Latin epigram on sleep dwells in the memory through its happy simplicity. After his settlement in London he threw off with marvellous rapidity a succession of pungent satires. George III. was his favourite subject of ridicule, and his peculiarities were described or distorted in *The Lousiad, Peeps at St James's, The Royal Visit to Exeter*. Two of Wolcot's happiest satires on the "farmer king" depicted the royal survey of Whitbread's brewery and the king's wonder how the apples got into the apple dumplings. The most entertaining biography which the English language has yet produced was ridiculed in *An Epistle to James Boswell*, and in a piece on the rival biographers, happily called *Bozzy and Piozzi*. The leading man of science and the adventurous traveller fell under his lash,—the former in *Sir Joseph Banks and the Emperor of Morocco*, and the latter in a *Complimentary Epistle to James Bruce*. When Wolcot came to London with his rough artistic genius from the west his hand was directed against the painters of the day who had already established their reputation, and his *Lyric Odes to the Academicians* often turned their modes of painting into a jest with marvellous effect. Wolcot was himself no mean artist, and in 1797 there was published *Six Picturesque Views from Paintings by Peter Pindar, engraved by Alken*. His knowledge of the art of painting lent force to his strictures on the academicians of the age. In 1795 he disposed of his works to the booksellers for an annuity of £250 a year, which he lived to enjoy for many more years than the purchasers expected or desired. His various pieces were published in 1796 in four octavo volumes, and they were often reprinted. His satires are said to have exercised such an effect on public opinion that the ministers pressed upon him a Government pension, on condition that he refrained from any further attacks on the king's peculiarities; but it is also asserted that he speedily declined to accept it any longer, and that he even returned the moneys which he had received. Like many another ridiculer of the idiosyncracies of others he was himself very susceptible to criticism, and for some attacks made on him by Gifford, the editor of the *Quarterly Review*, he attempted to belabour his satirical opponent in Wright's shop in Piccadilly, but Gifford was too quick for him, and Wolcot was soundly thrashed. He died at Latham Place, Somer's Town, London, on 14th January 1819, and seven days later was buried near Samuel Butler, the author of *Hudibras*, in the vestry vault in the churchyard of St Paul's, Covent Garden.

Polwhele, the Cornish historian, was well acquainted with Wolcot in his early life, and the best account of his residence in the west is found in vol. i. of Polwhele's *Traditions* and in Polwhele's *Biographical Sketches*, vol. ii. Cyrus Redding was a frequent visitor at the old man's house, and has described Wolcot's later days in his *Past Celebrities*, vol. i., and his *Fifty Years' Recollections*, vols. i. and ii. John Taylor, "everybody's Taylor," lived "on the most friendly footing with the doctor," who figures in the *Records of my Life*. Wolcot's humour was broad, and he cared little whether he hit above or below the belt, but he had a keen eye for the ridiculous, and was endowed with a wondrous facility of diction.

WOLF. The zoological position and general characters of the wolf (*Canis lupus*) are described in the article MAMMALIA (vol. xv. p. 438), where the difficulties that naturalists meet with in separating and defining the numerous variations of the animals called wolves, dogs, jackals, and foxes are shown. The true wolves are (excluding some varieties of the domestic dog) the largest members of the genus, and have a wide geographical range, extending over nearly the whole of Europe and Asia, and North America from Greenland to Mexico, but they are not found in South America or Africa, being replaced in both of these continents by various species of jackals and foxes. As might be expected from this extensive range, and the varied character of the climatic conditions of the countries they inhabit, they present great diversities of size, length and thickness of fur, and coloration, although resembling each other in all important structural characters. These differences have given rise to a supposed multiplicity of species, expressed by the names of *C. lupus*, *C. lycaon* (Central Europe), *C. laniger* and *C. niger* (Tibet), *C. pallipes* (India), *C. occidentalis*, *C. nubilis*, *C. mexicanus*, &c., of North America, but it is very doubtful whether these ought to be distinguished as other than local varieties. In North America there is a second distinct smaller species, called the coyote or prairie wolf (*Canis latrans*), and perhaps the Japanese wolf (*C.

[1] See *Opie and his Works*, by J. Jope Rogers.

hodophylax) may also be distinct, although, except for its smaller size and shorter legs, it is scarcely distinguishable from the common species. Though generally distributed throughout the Indian peninsula, the wolf is not found in Ceylon nor in Burmah and Siam. The ordinary colour of the wolf is a yellowish or fulvous grey, but specimens have been met with almost pure white and others entirely black. In northern countries the fur is longer and thicker, and the animal generally larger and more powerful than in the southern portion of its range. Its habits are similar everywhere, and it is still, and has been from time immemorial, especially known to man in all the countries it inhabits as the devastator of his flocks of sheep. Wolves do not catch their prey by lying in ambush, or stealing up close to it, and making a sudden spring as the cat tribe do, but by fairly running it down in open chase, which their speed and remarkable endurance enable them to do, and usually, except during summer, when the young families of cubs are being separately provided for by their parents, they assemble in troops or packs, and by their combined and persevering efforts are able to overpower and kill even such great animals as the American bison. It is singular that such closely allied species as the domestic dog and the Arctic fox are among the favourite prey of wolves, and, as is well known, children and even full-grown people are not unfrequently the objects of their attack when pressed by hunger. Notwithstanding the proverbial ferocity of the wolf in a wild state, many instances are recorded of animals taken when quite young becoming perfectly tame and attached to the person who has brought them up, when they exhibit many of the ways of a dog. They can, however, rarely be trusted by strangers.

The history of the wolf in the British Isles, and its gradual extirpation, has been thoroughly investigated by Harting in his work on *Extinct British Animals*, from which the following account is abridged. To judge by the osteological remains which the researches of geologists have brought to light, there was perhaps scarcely a county in England or Wales in which, at one time or another, wolves did not abound, while in Scotland and Ireland they must have been still more numerous. The fossil remains which have been discovered in Britain are not larger than, nor in any way to be distinguished from, those of European wolves of the present day. Wolf-hunting was a favourite pursuit of the ancient Britons as well as of the Anglo-Saxons. In Athelstan's reign these animals abounded to such an extent in Yorkshire that a retreat was built by one Acehorn, at Flixton, near Filey, wherein travellers might seek refuge if attacked by them. As is well known, great efforts were made by King Edgar to reduce the number of wolves in the country, but, notwithstanding the annual tribute of 300 skins paid to him during several years by the king of Wales, he was not altogether so successful as has been commonly imagined. In the reign of Henry III. wolves were sufficiently numerous in some parts of the country to induce the king to make grants of land to various individuals upon the express condition of their taking measures to destroy these animals wherever they could be found. In Edward II.'s time, the king's forest of the Peak, in Derbyshire, is especially mentioned as infested with wolves, and it was not until the reign of Henry VII. (1485–1509) that wolves appear to have become finally extinct in England. This, however, is rather a matter of inference from the cessation of all mention of them in local records than from any definite evidence of their extirpation. Their last retreat was probably in the desolate wolds of Yorkshire. In Scotland, as might be supposed from the nature of the country, the wolf maintained its hold for a much longer period. There is a well-known story of the last of the race being killed by Sir Ewen Cameron of Lochiel in 1680, but there is evidence of wolves having survived in Sutherlandshire and other parts into the following century (perhaps as late as 1743), though the date of their final extinction cannot be accurately fixed. In Ireland, in Cromwell's time, wolves were particularly troublesome, and said to be increasing in numbers, so that special measures were taken for their destruction, such as the offering of large rewards for their heads, and the prohibition (in 1652) of the exportation of "wolf-dogs," the large dogs used for hunting the wolves. The active measures taken then and later reduced their numbers greatly, so that towards the end of the century they became scarce, but, as in the case of the sister island, the date of their final disappearance cannot now be ascertained. It has been placed, upon the evidence of somewhat doubtful traditions, as [illegible] as 1766.

It is entirely owing to their insular position that the British Islands have been able to clear themselves of these formidable and destructive animals, for the neighbouring country of France, with no natural barriers to prevent their incursions from the vast continent to the east, is still liable every winter to visits from numbers of them, as the following figures indicate. Government rewards were paid in 1883 for 1316 wolves destroyed, in 1884 for 1035, in 1885 for 900, and in 1886 for 760. The increase of the reward just before the first-named date seems thus to have had some effect in lessening the number. (W. H. F.)

WOLF, Friedrich August (1759–1824), was born in 1759 at Hainrode, a little village not far from Nordhausen, in the province of Hanover. His father, who was village schoolmaster and organist, was in his way an enthusiast in education, and gave his son whatever advantage is to be gained by the earliest possible cultivation. In time the family removed to Nordhausen, and there young Wolf went to the grammar school, where he soon acquired all the Latin and Greek that the masters could teach him, besides learning French, Italian, Spanish, and music. This, however, was in the earlier and (as he himself regarded it) the idler part of his schooltime. He presently took his education into his own hands, devoted himself entirely to classics, borrowed books wherever he could, and rapidly stored his young and powerful memory with their contents. The precocity of his attainments was only equalled by the force of will and confidence in his own powers which characterized him throughout life.

After two years of solitary study, at the age of eighteen, Wolf went to the university of Göttingen. His first act there was a prophecy—one of those prophecies which spring from the conscious power to bring about their fulfilment. He had to choose his "faculty," and chose one which then existed only in his own mind, the faculty of "philology." What is even more remarkable, the omen was accepted. He carried his point, and was enrolled as he desired.

Wolf's relations with Heyne, who was then the chief ornament of Göttingen, form an unpleasant chapter, which may well be passed over here. Heyne was a scholar of little force or originality, but he was one of those who, by their power of assimilating and transmitting the thoughts of others, often rise to the highest reputation. Wolf soon left him, and fell back upon the university library, from which he borrowed with his old avidity.

During the years 1779–83 Wolf was a schoolmaster, first at Ilfeld, then at Osterode. His success as a teacher was striking, and he found time to publish an edition of the *Symposium*, which excited notice, and led to his promotion to a chair in the Prussian university of Halle.

The moment was a critical one in the history of education. The literary impulse of the Renaissance was almost spent; scholarship had become dry and trivial. A new school, that of Locke and Rousseau, sought to make teaching more modern and more human, but at the sacrifice of mental discipline and scientific aim. Wolf was eager to throw himself into the contest on the side of antiquity. In Halle (1783–1807), by the force of his will and the enlightened aid of the ministers of Frederick the Great, he was able to carry out his long-cherished ideas, and found the science of philology. By one of England's insular aberrations, the word "philology" threatens to be confined to the study of the forms of language. Wolf defined it to be "knowledge of human nature as exhibited in antiquity." The matter of such a science, he held, must be sought in the history and education of some highly cultivated nation, to be studied in written remains, works of art, and whatever else bears the stamp of national thought or skill. It has therefore to do with both history and language, but primarily as a science of *interpretation*, in which historical facts and linguistic facts take their place in an organic whole. Such was the ideal which Wolf had in his mind when he established the philological *seminarium* at Halle.

Wolf's writings make little show in a library, and were always subordinate to his teaching. During his time at Halle he published his commentary on the *Leptines* (1789)—which suggested to his pupil, Aug. Boeckh, the *Public Economy of Athens*—and a little later the *Prolegomena* to Homer (1795). This book, the work with which his name is chiefly associated, was thrown off in comparative haste to meet an immediate need. It has all the merits of a great piece of oral teaching—command of method, suggestiveness, breadth of view. The reader does not feel that he has to do with a theory, but with great ideas, which are left to bear fruit in his mind (see HOMER).

The Halle professorship ended tragically, and with it the happy and productive period of Wolf's life. He was swept away, and his university with him, by the deluge of the French invasion. A painful gloom oppressed his remaining years (1807-24), which he spent at Berlin. He became so fractious and intolerant as to alienate some of his warmest friends. He gained a place in the department of education, through the exertions of W. von Humboldt. When this became unendurable, he once more took a professorship. But he no longer taught with his old success; and he wrote very little. His most finished work, the *Darstellung der Alterthumswissenschaft*, though published at Berlin (1807), belongs essentially to the Halle time. At length his health gave way. He was advised to try the south of France. He got as far as Marseilles, and was laid in the classic soil of that ancient Hellenic city.

The chief source of this sketch has been the admirable article by Mr Mark Pattison in the *North British Review* of June 1865, soon (we believe) to be reprinted by the Clarendon Press. Since the date of that article Wolf's *Kleine Schriften* have been edited by G. Bernhardy (Halle, 1869). The works not included in that collection are the *Prolegomena*, the *Letters to Heyne* (Berlin, 1797), the commentary on the *Leptines* (Halle, 1789), and a translation of the *Clouds* of Aristophanes (Berlin, 1811). To these must be added the *Vorlesungen* on *Iliad* i.-iv., taken from the notes of a pupil, and edited by Usteri (Bern, 1830). (D. B. M.)

WOLFE, CHARLES (1791-1823), author of *The Burial of Sir John Moore*, born in Dublin in 1791, was an Irish clergyman, curate of Ballyclog, in Tyrone, and afterwards of Donoughmore. The poem seems to have been written when Wolfe was still a student in Trinity College, Dublin, and it originally appeared in an Irish newspaper (the *Newry Telegraph*) in 1817. The initials C. W. were affixed to it at first, but as it was quoted from newspaper to newspaper these were dropped, and, eventually finding its way into the *Edinburgh Annual Register*, it was claimed for and by as many people as *Punch's* famous advice to those about to marry. Wolfe's Trinity College friends came to the rescue, and one of them (Archdeacon Russell) wrote a memoir which, in spite of its being one of the dullest memoirs ever written, went through at least eight editions—a curious testimony to the popularity of the poem. Wolfe died of consumption at Cork in 1823, at the early age of thirty-two.

WOLFE, JAMES (1727-1759), the hero of Quebec, was the son of Lieutenant-General Edward Wolfe, and was born in the vicarage of Westerham, Kent, on January 2, 1727. At an early age he evinced a keen interest in the adventures and achievements of war, and at thirteen accompanied his father to Cartagena. Obtaining a commission as ensign in the 12th regiment of foot in 1741, he embarked for Flanders on the 10th May of the following year, and during the campaign of 1743, in which he acted as adjutant, he was present at the battle of Dettingen. Having exhibited, in addition to high courage, a rare talent for command, he received while yet a youth a commission, on 3d June 1744, as captain in the 4th or king's regiment of foot, and shortly afterwards was made brigade-major. In this capacity he took part in the suppression of the rebellion of 1745, being present both at Falkirk and at Culloden. In January 1747 he sailed for the Continent, and for his valour at the battle of Lawfeldt on the 2d July he received the public thanks of the commander-in-chief, the duke of Cumberland. On 5th January 1749 he was gazetted major of the 20th regiment, and in the following year he became lieutenant-colonel. In this position he began to manifest those great qualities as a commander which were the secret of his success, and, while introducing into the regiment that perfect discipline necessary to the highest proficiency, secured the personal affection of almost every soldier. In the luckless Rochefort expedition he was quartermaster-general, and by his dashing gallantry attracted the special notice of Pitt. When therefore it was decided in 1758 to send an expedition to Cape Breton under Amherst, Wolfe was appointed by Pitt brigadier-general. Under the eye of Amherst and Admiral Boscawen he conducted the landing at Louisburg through a heavy surf and in face of the well-directed fire of the enemy. He himself was the first to land, and forming his division into compact order attacked and carried with the bayonet the nearest French battery, after which he formed the camp. Chiefly through his ardent energy the siege operations were brought to a successful issue after an investment of six months. Wolfe then eagerly urged an attack on Quebec, expressing his determination to leave the service if nothing further was to be done. Pitt not only acted on his advice, but selected him as the leader of the difficult and almost chimerical enterprise. Quebec, besides being strongly fortified, was occupied by forces which greatly outnumbered those placed at Wolfe's disposal. Moreover, Montcalm the French commander had an open country behind him for supplies, and was only called upon to protract the defence behind his ramparts till the resources of the besiegers were exhausted. It was incumbent on Wolfe to force Montcalm to give battle, and this could only be effected by manœuvres of the most daring kind. After bombarding the city from the heights of Point Levi, Wolfe made an attempt, 29th June 1759, to attack Montcalm's camp in front, but his instructions were not carried out with sufficient accuracy, and foreseeing that irretrievable disaster was imminent he found it necessary after the attack had begun to recall his troops and retire. As the enemy were now on their guard against a second attack of a similar kind, Wolfe saw that the problem must be solved by some other method, and after some time spent in careful consideration he hit upon a still more daring plan. In the evening of the 12th September with 5000 men he silently descended the St Lawrence in boats, and, scaling the heights of Abraham in the darkness, drew up his forces on the plains so as to cut off Montcalm's supplies. The audacity of the movement was too much for Montcalm's patience. On his attention being called to it he exclaimed "Oui, je les vois où ils ne doivent pas être; je vais les écraser." But the genius of Wolfe was equal to the occasion. With calm self-possession he forbade a single shot to be fired till the enemy were within thirty yards. The crushing volleys with which they were then met, followed by an impetuous attack with the bayonet, was decisive of the action. While leading a charge at the head of the Louisburg grenadiers, Wolfe had one of his wrists shattered by a shot, but wrapping a handkerchief round it he kept on. Another shot struck him, and he still advanced, when a third lodged in his breast. While he was lying in a swoon some one near him exclaimed, "They run; see how they run!" "Who run?" demanded Wolfe, like one roused from sleep. "The enemy," was the answer; "they give way everywhere." Wolfe then signified that a regiment should be sent down to Charles river to cut off their retreat, and on learning that his orders had been obeyed he turned on his side, and murmured as his last words, "Now God be praised, I will die in peace." Montcalm, the French commander, was mortally wounded in the same action, and died soon afterwards. By the surrender of Quebec Canada was lost to the French.

See Wright, *Life of Major-General James Wolfe* (1864), and Parkman, *Montcalm and Wolfe* (2 vols., 1884).

WOLFENBÜTTEL, a small town in the duchy of Brunswick, is situated on both banks of the Oker, 7 miles to the south of Brunswick. It contains various minor tribunals, some schools, and a small garrison; and it carries on a few unimportant manufactures (machinery, copper goods, linen, cork, preserves, &c.). Wolfenbüttel, in fact, may be accepted as tolerably representative of the average dull German provincial town, clinging more or less faithfully to the traditions of the period when it was the residence of the ducal family. It owes its chief interest to its connexion with Lessing, who was ducal librarian there from 1770 till his death in 1781. The old library building, designed in 1723 in imitation of the Pantheon at Rome, contains a marble statue of the poet. The library, including 300,000 printed books and 7000 MSS., has, however, been transferred to a large new Renaissance edifice, opened in October 1887. It is especially rich in copies of the Bible and in books of the early Reformation period. Opposite the old library is the palace, occupied since 1835 by a theatre, a law court, and a seminary. The ducal burial-vault is in the church of St Mary. There are two other Evangelical churches and a Roman Catholic church in Wolfenbüttel, and perhaps the only other noteworthy building is the large prison. The ancient fortifications have been converted into promenades, once a favourite resort of Lessing. In 1885 the population of Wolfenbüttel, including the suburbs of Auguststadt and Juliusstadt, was 13,455. The "Wolfenbüttel Fragments" are alluded to under LESSING, vol. xiv. p. 481; see also REIMARUS.

A castle is said to have been founded on the site of Wolfenbüttel by a margrave of Meissen about 1046. When this began in 1267 to be the residence of the early Brunswick or Wolfenbüttel line of counts, a town gradually grew up around it. In 1542 it was taken by the Saxons and Hessians, who however evacuated it five years later after the battle of Mühlberg. In the Thirty Years' War, in June 1641, the Swedish, under Wrangel and Königsmark, defeated the Austrians under the archduke Leopold at Wolfenbüttel. The town passed wholly into the possession of the Brunswick-Wolfenbüttel family in 1671, and for nearly one hundred years enjoyed the distinction of being the ducal capital. In 1754, however, Duke Charles transferred the ducal residence to Brunswick, a blow from which Wolfenbüttel has never recovered.

WOLFF, CASPAR FRIEDRICH (1733-1794), who is justly reckoned the founder of modern embryology, was born at Berlin in 1733, and studied anatomy and physiology under Meckel, and later at Halle, where he graduated in medicine in 1759, his thesis being his famous *Theoria Generationis*. After serving as a surgeon in the Seven Years' War, he wished to lecture on anatomy and physiology in Berlin; but being refused permission he accepted a call from the empress Catherine to become professor of those subjects at the academy of St Petersburg, and acted in this capacity until his death in 1794.

While the theory of "evolution" in the crude sense of a simple growth in size and unfolding of organs all previously existent in the germ was in possession of the field, his researches on the development of the alimentary canal in the chick first clearly established the converse view, that of *epigenesis, i.e.*, of progressive formation and differentiation of organs from a germ primitively homogeneous (see EMBRYOLOGY, vol. viii. p. 165). He also largely anticipated the modern conception of embryonic layers, and is said even to have foreshadowed the cell theory. It is certain that he discerned, long before Goethe, the leafy homology of the parts of flowers.

WOLFF, CHRISTIAN (1679-1754), is an important figure in the history of philosophy, and his life has more dramatic interest than is usually the case with an academic teacher. He was the son of a tanner, and was born at Breslau on the 24th January 1679. His father had dedicated him before his birth to a life of learning, having been disappointed himself in similar aspirations, and Wolff accordingly received a gymnasium training in Breslau, whence he proceeded in 1699 to the university of Jena. Mathematics and physics formed at first his chief attraction, to which he soon added philosophy. He studied the Cartesian philosophy as well as the works of Grotius and Pufendorf, but was chiefly influenced by Tschirnhausen's *Medicina Mentis*. In 1703 he qualified as privat-docent in the university of Leipsic, where he lectured till 1706, when he was called as professor of mathematics to Halle. Before this time he had made the acquaintance of Leibnitz, of whose philosophy his own system is a modification. In Halle Wolff limited himself at first to mathematics, but on the departure of a colleague he annexed physics, and presently included in his lectures all the main philosophical disciplines. He followed the example of Thomasius in lecturing in German instead of Latin. This fact, and the remarkable clearness of his exposition, caused his class-rooms to be crowded. He also became known as a writer to a wider circle, and was made member of the Royal Society of London and the Academy of Berlin. But the claims which Wolff advanced on behalf of the philosophic reason appeared impious to his theological colleagues. Halle was the headquarters of Pietism, which, after a long struggle against the rigidity of the older Lutheran dogmatism, had itself assumed the characteristics of a new orthodoxy. This orthodoxy, represented by Joachim Lange and A. H. Francke, considered the cause of supernaturalism endangered by a philosophy which professed by the unassisted reason to present the whole universe as a rational and necessarily determined system. Wolff's professed ideal was to base theological truths on evidence of mathematical certitude. Personal grounds accentuated the bitterness. Strife broke out openly in 1721, when Wolff, on the occasion of laying down the office of pro-rector, delivered an oration "On the Moral Philosophy of the Chinese," in which he praised the purity of the moral precepts of Confucius, pointing to them as an evidence of the power of human reason to attain by its own efforts to moral truth. The attacks and accusations in connexion with this address were unsuccessful at the time, but Wolff continued to give offence to his colleagues, and to Lange in particular, by his action in the filling up of university chairs, and in 1723 a disappointed pupil, a docent in the same university, published a hostile criticism upon Wolff's system, at the instigation, it is said, of Lange. This was contrary to university etiquette and statute, and Wolff somewhat injudiciously appealed to the Government for an interdict upon such attacks. He succeeded in obtaining this, but his enemies retaliated by sending to court a united representation of the dangerous character of his views. Through a worthless courtier, they gained the ear of the king, Frederick William I., by a concrete example, which touched him most nearly. If one of His Majesty's famous grenadiers at Potsdam should desert, the king would have no right, it was represented, upon the principles of Wolff, to punish the man, seeing that he only did what it was necessarily predetermined that he should do. The result of this representation was swifter and more drastic than Wolff's bitterest enemies had calculated on. On the 13th November 1723 a cabinet order arrived in Halle deposing Wolff from his office, and commanding him to leave Halle and quit Prussian territory within forty-eight hours on pain of a halter. The same day Wolff passed into Saxony, and presently proceeded to Marburg, to which university he had received a call before this crisis. The landgrave of

Hesse received him with every mark of distinction, and the circumstances of his expulsion drew universal attention to his philosophy. It was everywhere discussed, and over two hundred books and pamphlets appeared for or against it before 1737, not reckoning the systematic treatises of Wolff and his followers. The seventeen years which Wolff spent at Marburg witnessed the publication of his chief works, and the rise of his philosophy to almost undisputed sway throughout Germany. His earlier treatises were, like his lectures, composed in German:—a treatise on logic, called *Vernünftige Gedanken von den Kräften des menschlichen Verstandes* (1712); a metaphysic, *Vernünftige Gedanken von Gott, der Welt, und der Seele des Menschen, auch aller Dinge überhaupt* (1719); treatises on ethics and politics with similar titles (1721); three on the philosophy of nature (1723–4–5), followed by an encyclopædic review of his system in 1726. From that time he began to go over the same ground more fully and methodically in a series of Latin works. The logic, ontology, cosmology, and empirical psychology appeared between 1728 and 1732, followed by the rational psychology and natural theology in 1734. Meanwhile, after some years the king of Prussia made overtures to Wolff to return, and in 1739, by the irony of events, a cabinet order prescribed the study of the Wolffian philosophy to all candidates for ecclesiastical preferment. In 1740 Frederick William died suddenly, and one of the first acts of his successor, Frederick the Great, was to recall Wolff to Halle on the most flattering and advantageous terms. His entry into Halle on the 6th of December 1740 partook of the nature of a triumphal procession. In 1743 he became chancellor of the university, and in 1745 he received the title of "freiherr" from the elector of Bavaria. But, though he was thus loaded with honours, and his philosophy everywhere triumphant, he found that he had outlived his power of attracting the academic youth. His matter was no longer fresh, nor were his own powers what they had been when he left Halle seventeen years before, and he had the bitter experience of lecturing to empty class-rooms. He died on the 9th April 1754, in the seventy-sixth year of his age, fourteen years after his return to Halle.

The Wolffian philosophy held almost undisputed sway in Germany till it was displaced by the Kantian revolution. It is essentially a common-sense adaptation or watering-down of the Leibnitian system; or, as we can hardly speak of a system in connexion with Leibnitz, Wolff may be said to have methodized and reduced to dogmatic form the thoughts of his great predecessor, which often, however, lose the greater part of their suggestiveness in the process. Since his philosophy disappeared before the influx of new ideas and the appearance of more speculative minds, it has been customary to dwell almost exclusively on its defects—the want of depth or freshness of insight, and the aridity of its neo-scholastic formalism, which tends to relapse into verbose platitudes. But this is to do injustice to Wolff's real merits. These are mainly his comprehensive view of philosophy, as embracing in its survey the whole field of human knowledge, his insistence everywhere on clear and methodic exposition, and his confidence in the power of reason to reduce all subjects to this form. To these must be added that he was practically the first to "teach philosophy to speak German." It will be seen that these merits concern the form rather than the matter of philosophy, the latter being mainly derived from Leibnitz, with some modifications in the sense of the older scholastic Aristotelianism. The Wolffian system retains the determinism and optimism of Leibnitz, but the monadology recedes into the background, the monads falling asunder into souls or conscious beings on the one hand and mere atoms on the other. The doctrine of the pre-established harmony also loses its metaphysical significance, and the principle of sufficient reason introduced by Leibnitz is once more discarded in favour of the principle of contradiction which Wolff seeks to make the fundamental principle of philosophy. Philosophy is defined by him as the science of the possible, and divided, according to the two faculties of the human individual, into a theoretical and a practical part. Logic, sometimes called *philosophia rationalis*, forms the introduction or propædeutic to both. Theoretical philosophy has for its parts ontology or *philosophia prima*, cosmology, rational psychology, and natural theology; ontology treats of the existent in general, psychology of the soul as a simple non-extended substance, cosmology of the world as a whole, and rational theology of the existence and attributes of God. These are best known to philosophical students by Kant's treatment of them in the *Critique of Pure Reason*. Practical philosophy is subdivided into ethics, economics, and politics. Wolff's moral principle is the realization of human perfection. (A. SE.)

WOLF-FISH. See SEA-WOLF.

WOLFRAM VON ESCHENBACH, mediæval German poet, lived in the latter part of the 12th and the early part of the 13th century. Little is known about the facts of his life, and such knowledge as we possess is derived wholly from his own writings. He belonged to a poor but noble family. He speaks of himself as a Bavarian, and refers to the count of Wertheim as his feudal lord. His home was the castle of Eschenbach (near Ansbach), and in the churchyard at Eschenbach what was said to be his grave was shown as late as the beginning of the 17th century. He spent some time at the court of Hermann, landgrave of Thuringia, where he met Walther von der Vogelweide, to whom he makes two references in his works. Wolfram survived Hermann, who died in 1216. His residence at the Thuringian court led to his being included among the poets who were afterwards said to have taken part in a great competition for poetic supremacy at the Wartburg. Wolfram seems to have been happily married, and to have had children. In politics he was a supporter of the emperor Otho IV. He understood French, but could neither read nor write.

His greatest work is *Parzival*, an epic poem completed between 1205 and 1215. It combines the story of the Holy Grail with incidents from the legends of southern France about the old princes of Anjou and from the legendary history of Arthur and the Knights of the Round Table. To Wolfram's contemporary, Gottfried of Strasburg, the style of this poem seemed abstract and obscure; and *Parzival* certainly lacks the lightness and grace of Gottfried's masterpiece *Tristan*. It has, however, high imaginative qualities, and, regarded as a whole, is the most splendid achievement in the literature of Germany during the period of Middle High German. Even in Wolfram's day the poem produced a profound impression, and in the 15th century it was still so warmly appreciated that it was one of the earliest works made accessible to the public through the invention of printing. The principal authority used by Wolfram seems to have been the *Conte del Gral* of Chrestien de Troyes. He mentions, besides this work, a poem by Kiot, a Provençal poet; but nothing is known of Kiot, and it may be that he never really existed. Whatever may have been the sources of *Parzival*, Wolfram gave to everything he borrowed from others a wholly new character, impressing upon it strongly the mark of his own great ideal spirit. Besides his chief work and various lyrics he composed two epic fragments, *Titurel* and *Willehalm*, the former before *Parzival*, the latter after. *Titurel*, a love-tale, belongs to the same cycle of legends as the story of *Parzival*, and, so far as form is concerned, it is the brightest and most artistic of Wolfram's works. *Willehalm* presents the legendary history of St William of Orange, a contemporary of Charlemagne. The so-called third part of this poem was continued by Ulrich von Türheim about 1250, the first part by Ulrich von dem Türlin between 1252 and 1278.

A complete edition of Wolfram's works was issued by Lachmann in 1833. Bartsch afterwards published, with notes, an edition of *Parzival* and *Titurel*. There are renderings into modern German by San-Marte and Simrock. See San-Marte's *Parzival-Studien*, and essays by Bartsch, Pfeiffer, Rochat, and Zingerle in Pfeiffer's *Germania*.

WOLLASTON, WILLIAM (1659–1724), English philosophical writer, was born at Coton-Clanford in Staffordshire, March 1659. He was educated under disadvantages both at school and at the university, but left his college (Sidney, Cambridge) with a high reputation for his acquirements, in September 1681. He then became assistant-master of the Birmingham grammar school, and in that position took holy orders. In 1688 an uncle unexpectedly left him an ample fortune, on which he retired, moving to London, where he married a lady of fortune, and devoted himself to his domestic duties and the pursuit of learning and philosophy. In his studies he occupied himself more especially with the foundation of the common doctrines of "natural religion," which were in those years so universally discussed. The substance of his thinking on these doctrines he embodied, towards the end of his life, in the one book by which he is now remembered, *The Religion of Nature Delineated*, the first edition of which was privately printed in 1722, and the second, revised, in 1724. He died in October of the same year.

Wollaston's *Religion of Nature*, which falls between Clarke's *Discourse of the Unchangeable Obligations of Natural Religion* and Butler's *Sermons*, was one of the popular philosophical books of its day. More than 10,000 copies of it were sold in a few years. It was highly valued by Bishop Butler and a favourite book of Queen Caroline, the wife of George II., and she ordered the numerous quotations from Latin, Greek, and Hebrew in the notes to be translated into English for her use. To the 8th edition (1750) was added a life of the author. Though the book is now remembered chiefly for the theory of the nature of moral good and evil advocated in it, it was rather its defence of natural religion, and its bold, sometimes original, penetrating, and often eloquent discussion of great ethical religious problems which secured for it "deserved reputation." It was designed to be an answer to the two questions—Is there such a thing as natural religion? and If there is, what is it? Wollaston starts with the assumption that religion and morality are identical, and labours to show that religion is "the pursuit of happiness by the practice of *truth* and reason." The moral theory on which he values himself as propounding a view met with nowhere else is that moral evil is the practical denial of a true proposition and moral good the affirmation of it. To steal is wrong because it is to deny that the thing stolen is what it is—the property of another. In Wollaston's view "happiness" occupies a large place. He makes pain an evil and pleasure a good. Happiness is a duty and an end to be aimed at by every intelligent being. He makes the production of happiness also the test of the rightness or wrongness of all social regulations. But he admits that in this world happiness and virtue only *tend* to coincide, and derives from their defective coincidence his argument for a state of future rewards and punishments.

In addition to this work Wollaston published anonymously a small book *On the Design of the Book of Ecclesiastes, or the Unreasonableness of Men's Restless Contention for the Present Enjoyments, represented in an English Poem*, London, 1691. The subject of the book is sufficiently indicated in its title, and was in form and argument so worthless that its author consulted his reputation by immediately suppressing it. It is now very scarce. The university library of Cambridge possesses a copy.

See Wollaston's life prefixed to the 8th ed. of his *Religion of Nature*; John Clarke, *Examination of the notion of Moral Good and Evil advanced in a late book entitled The Religion of Nature Delineated*, London, 1725; Drechsler, *Ueber Wollaston's Moral-Philosophie*, Erlangen, 1802; Leslie Stephen's *History of English Thought in the Eighteenth Century*, London, 1876, ch. iii. and ch. ix.; H. Sidgwick's *History of Ethics*, 1886, p. 194 *sq.* A French translation of his book, *Ébauche de la Religion Naturelle*, appeared at The Hague in 1726.

WOLLASTON, WILLIAM HYDE (1766–1828), chemist and natural philosopher, was born at East Dereham, in Norfolk, on August 6, 1766, the second of seventeen children. His father, the Rev. Francis Wollaston, rector of Chislehurst, grandson of William Wollaston noticed above, was an enthusiastic astronomer. Wollaston studied at Caius College, Cambridge, of which he remained a fellow until his death. He took the degree of M.B. in 1787, and that of M.D. six years later, and commenced to practise medicine in 1789 at Bury St Edmunds. Failing to make headway he removed to London, where he was equally unsuccessful. He applied for a vacant physicianship at St George's Hospital, but was not appointed; and he never got over the feeling of irritation, which indeed led him to abandon medicine altogether. Wollaston betook himself to original research, and for a time ranged pretty impartially over the sciences. He is said to have accumulated a fortune by the manufacture of platinum and of various optical and mechanical inventions. He devoted much attention to the affairs of the Royal Society, of which he was elected a fellow in 1793 and made secretary in 1806. For many years he was a vice-president, but did not care to enter on competition with Sir Humphry Davy when the latter was elected president in 1820. Beyond appearing at the meetings of learned societies Wollaston took little part in public affairs; he lived alone, conducting his investigations in a deliberate and very exhaustive manner, but in the most rigid seclusion, no person being admitted to his laboratory on any pretext. Towards the close of 1828 he felt the approach of the fatal malady—a tumour in the brain—and devoted his last days to a careful revisal of his unpublished researches and industrial processes, dictating several papers on these subjects, which were afterwards published in the *Philosophical Transactions*. On December 22, 1828, he died, as he had lived, self-possessed, stern, and silent.

Wollaston's character presents a very remarkable analogy with that of Henry Cavendish: both studied all branches of science; both were highly respected by their contemporaries for intellectual power and achievements in research; both were reserved and distant, making few friends, never acting from impulse, but occasionally displaying unexpected generosity. Wollaston's character can only be partially divined from his public actions and relations with other scientific men, and unfortunately no other data are available. A dispute as to priority in discovering electromagnetic rotation is referred to under FARADAY, vol. ix. p. 29; and suggestions as to the prior invention of his process of manufacturing platinum are to be found in the article PLATINUM (vol. xix. p. 190). The incidents associated with the discovery of the metal palladium were more serious than either of these. Wollaston detected this element, extracted a considerable quantity, and exposed it for sale in an instrument-maker's shop, calling attention to it by an anonymous advertisement. A chemist, Chenevix, purchased some of the metal, and concluded from a few hasty experiments that it was an amalgam of platinum. He submitted a paper to the Royal Society, which Wollaston as secretary read, after, it is said, vainly advising Chenevix to withdraw it. A controversy, supported by elaborate series of experiments, took place, and was only terminated when Wollaston acknowledged that he was the discoverer, and described the process of extraction from the ores of platinum. Chenevix was disgusted, and deserted chemistry. Yet Wollaston was a most thorough and conscientious worker: it was his extreme caution in coming to conclusions until the facts were irresistible that occasionally led him to the unfortunate method of tentative anonymous publication; but the same quality ensured a solidity and trustworthiness in his Royal Society memoirs which make them models to subsequent investigators.

Most of Wollaston's papers deal more or less directly with chemistry, but they diverge beyond that science on all sides into optics, physiology, botany, acoustics, astronomy, and even touch on art. He discovered the metals palladium and rhodium, and proved the identity of columbium with titanium. The minute scale on which his analytical processes were carried out was rendered possible by his extraordinary keenness of sight and neatness in manipulation.

The Royal Society awarded him a royal medal for his process of manufacturing platinum,—a work which, in its immediate effects, it is almost impossible to over-estimate. Wollaston was the first to produce the metal in a state fit to manufacture, and in quantity sufficient to make platinum crucibles generally available, thus supplying analytical chemistry with its most powerful instrument of advance. In optics his most important theoretical observation, to which, however, he gave little attention, was the discovery in 1802 of dark lines in the solar spectrum (see LIGHT, vol. xiv. p. 593), but practically the reflecting GONIOMETER and CAMERA LUCIDA (*qq.v.*) were of greatest value, the former supplying the crystallographer with his chief data, the latter indispensable in the development of modern microscopical research. Amongst his other papers may be mentioned those dealing with the physiology of vision, the apparent direction of the eyes in a portrait, a comparison of the light of the sun with that of the moon and fixed stars, a slide-rule for calculating chemical equivalents, sounds inaudible to certain ears, and a theory of the formation of fairy-rings.

An appreciative essay on the "Life of Wollaston" will be found in George Wilson's *Religio Chemici* (1862).

WOLLIN, an island belonging to Prussia, is the more easterly of the islands at the mouth of the Oder, which separate the Stettiner Haff from the Baltic Sea (vol. xvii. p. 724). It is divided from the mainland on the E. by the Dievenow, and from Usedom on the W. by the Swine. It is roughly triangular in shape, and has an area of 90 square miles. Heath and sand alternate with swamps, lakes, and forest on its surface, which is quite flat, except towards the south-west, where the low hills of Lebbin rise. The coast is fenced with dunes and shifting sand-hills. Cattle-rearing and fishing are the chief resources of the inhabitants, who number about 14,000. Misdroy, on the north-west coast, is a favourite sea-bathing resort, and some of the other villages, as Ostswine, opposite Swinemünde, Pritter, famous for its eels, and Lebbin, are also visited in summer.

WOLLIN, the only town, is situated on the Dievenow, and is connected with the mainland by three bridges. It carries on the industries of a small seaport and fishing-town, and has (1885) a population of 5241. Near the site of the present town once stood the ancient and opulent Baltic capital of the Slavs, called Wolin by the Wends, Julin by the Danes, and Winetha or Vineta by the Germans. Jomsburg, Hynnisborg, and Waltzborg, names or epithets occurring in several of the northern sagas, are said by Schafarik also to refer to this town. In the 10th and 11th centuries Wolin was the centre of an active and extensive trade. Adam of Bremen (d. 1076) extols its size and wealth; he mentions that "Greeks" and other foreigners frequented it, and that "Saxons" were permitted to settle there on equal terms with the Wends, so long as they did not obtrude the fact of their Christianity. In 1125, however, Wolin itself became the seat of a Christian bishopric, which was removed to Cammin in 1170. A colony of Scandinavian vikings, often mentioned in the sagas, flourished in this neighbourhood from about 970 till their stronghold of Jomsburg was destroyed in 1083 by Magnus of Norway and Denmark. In 1183 Wolin itself was burned by Canute VI. of Denmark. Within modern times Wollin was captured by the Swedish in 1630 and 1759, and by the Brandenburgers in 1659 and 1675. A tradition long reigned, though now proved to be baseless, that the Wendish Vineta had been overwhelmed by the sea, and some submarine granite blocks near Damerow, in Usedom, were popularly recognized as its ruins. These are still pointed out as such to strangers.

WOLLSTONECRAFT, MARY. See GODWIN, MARY W., and SHELLEY, MARY W.

WOLSEY, THOMAS (*c.* 1471–1530), cardinal, was born at Ipswich, and seems to have been the eldest son, as perhaps he was the eldest of all the four known children, of Robert Wolsey and his wife Joan. The name Wolsey, spelt Wulcy by both Robert and Thomas, is a diminutive of Wulf, that is, Wolf, and clearly proves their descent from those Teutonic folk who gave names to two English counties, to the southern one of which the Wolseys belonged. Simple repetition has made it commonly believed that Robert Wolsey was to trade a butcher. The assertion was first set afloat by enemies of the great cardinal, and was intended to be disparaging. The probability, however, seems to be that he was really a grazier, and perhaps also a wool merchant. He certainly belonged to the better class of merchants, was connected with wealthy people, and himself died possessed of lands and property in and about Ipswich. Fairly trustworthy tradition points to a house in St Nicholas Street there as occupying the site of his own dwelling. According to Fiddes, supported as to the year by Cavendish, Wolsey's birth happened in March 1471, though contemporary evidence would place it some years later. His education began doubtless at the grammar school of his native town, where he showed himself an apt scholar. That reputation was fully sustained when he passed to Magdalen College, Oxford, for he took his B.A. degree at the early age of fifteen, whence he was known as "the boy bachelor." He became M.A. with such credit and distinction that he had conferred upon him a fellowship and the mastership of the grammar school attached to his college, of which last in 1498 we find him bursar. The whole course of college training was scholastic; it strengthened and trained the intellect for actual life. Wolsey is said to have been deeply versed in the subtleties of Aquinism; certain it is he remained wholly unaffected by the Greek revival of the Renaissance, and looked but indifferently upon its followers. From arts he went on to the study of divinity, in which the unfriendly Polydore Virgil is compelled to admit he was "not unlearned," but of which he did not become bachelor till 1510. That there was in fact, from whatever cause, some delay in Wolsey's taking orders is evidenced by his father's will, made on the last day of September 1496, probably just before his death. That instrument appointed Joan sole legatee, and directed "that if Thomas my son be a priest within a year next after my decease" he, or, failing him, another priest, should be paid ten marks, equal to about £60 present money, for a year's singing of masses "for me and my friends."

Among Wolsey's pupils at Magdalen school were three sons of the marquis of Dorset. So well was the marquis satisfied with the progress of his children that he invited Wolsey to spend with him the Christmas holidays of what must have been the year 1499. When Wolsey returned to Oxford it was with the presentation to the quiet Somerset parish of Lymington. In the October following he was inducted. He had not been long placed when a neighbouring squire, Sir Amias Paulet, put him in the stocks. The cause of this indignity is not clear; but it was remembered and resented with all the keenness attaching to an injustice suffered. Fifteen years after, as soon as he became lord chancellor, Wolsey summoned Paulet before him, administered a severe rebuke, and ordered him not to leave London without licence. From then till 1523 Paulet's name disappears from the state papers, where previously its occurrence had been frequent. In September 1501 Dorset died, and that event finally decided Wolsey to quit Lymington. Paulet's proceeding had not affected Wolsey's character, for he now became one of the private chaplains of Henry Dean, archbishop of Canterbury. But any hopes he may have founded on this appointment were soon blighted by the death of Dean in February 1503. Dean's executors, of whom the chief was the favoured servant of Henry VII., Sir Reginald Bray, deputed the carrying out of his instructions respecting his funeral to Wolsey and another chaplain. Through Bray, probably, Wolsey next obtained a chaplaincy with another favourite agent of Henry's, Sir Richard Nanfan, deputy-lieutenant of Calais. Nanfan was an old man; and so excellent did Wolsey's business capacity prove that the knight soon entrusted to him the whole work of the deputyship. In 1505 Nanfan resigned and returned to England to pass his latter days in peace; but so thoroughly had his chaplain gained his esteem that, "through his instant labour and especial favour," Wolsey became chaplain to Henry VII. himself, and when in 1506 Sir Richard died Wolsey was one of his executors.

Henry was a cold master, and did not offer much opportunity for making way in his favour, but Wolsey immediately set himself to win the approval of the leading privy councillors, Bishop Fox and Sir Thomas Lovell. As usual he succeeded. And he retained their friendship to the last,—his relations with Fox being perhaps the most beautiful episode in all Wolsey's life. Through their recommendation he began his political life by a mission, probably in 1507 and to the emperor Maximilian. According to Cavendish, who gives Wolsey himself as his authority, not only was the embassy performed in the extraordinarily short space of about eighty hours, but Wolsey took upon him to add to his instructions some items which he afterwards found the king had sent after him. The expedition and bold intelligence displayed established him in the king's good opinion. Other missions ensued, one of them to Scotland in the spring of 1508, all executed to the royal satisfaction. Under Henry high ecclesiastical promotion came by political service. On the 2d February 1509 Wolsey, who by this time held several minor preferments, was collated to the deanery of Lincoln. Within three months Henry died and his son came to the throne. Already had Wolsey ingratiated himself with the young Henry, and almost at once commenced his unprecedentedly rapid rise to power. Lymington having been resigned by July, he in October received a grant of The Parsonage, part of the forfeited property of Sir Richard Empson; and another month brought him the office and title by which he was chiefly known for the next four years, that of king's almoner. From that time forward his history becomes entwined with the annals of his country, where all that concerns the statesman must be sought.

On the 20th November 1511 his signature as a privy councillor first occurs. The council was composed of two parties,—the old officials, chiefly ecclesiastics and headed by Fox, who favoured peace, and the old nobility, led by Surrey, who advocated a spirited policy, even at the risk of war. Friendship and his cloth naturally attached Wolsey to the former, thereby giving rise to that family hatred of the Howards which pursued him to the end of his life. Fox had long been anxious to withdraw from political life, and he now gradually shifted his state duties on to the willing, able, and younger shoulders of Wolsey. Nor was Wolsey's opportunity of distinguishing himself long in coming. An expedition against Guienne in 1512 had effected nothing and returned in disgrace. This only roused Henry's pride and persistence, and he resolved to invade France from the north in the following year. The organization of the necessary force he committed to Wolsey. Churchman though he was, Wolsey succeeded to admiration. The royal army crossed the Channel, fought what French wit styled the Battle of Spurs, and took Thérouanne and Tournai, while at home Surrey won the bloody battle of Flodden. Success had crowned Wolsey's labours and covered his royal master with glory. Wolsey's favour with Henry was confirmed. Rewards came thick and fast. On the capture of Tournai, Henry named Wolsey to the bishopric of that see, which just then fell vacant; but the English nomination was never ratified by the pope, who in the end issued bulls promoting the French nominee Guillard. Despite this miscarriage Wolsey was not long in being a bishop. In the succeeding January (1514) the see of Lincoln lost its episcopal head, and next month the new pope Leo X. confirmed Wolsey's appointment to it. The preferment proved but temporary; for in July Cardinal Bainbridge, archbishop of York, was poisoned at Rome, and on the 5th August Wolsey was raised to his place.

Two days later Wolsey brought to a triumphant termination his first great effort in diplomacy, and made with Louis XII. of France a treaty which really undid the notorious league of Cambrai, defeated Ferdinand of Spain with his own weapons, and left England, for the moment, the first power in Europe. Wolsey thereby began a new era in English politics. Since its origin with the Norman Conquest English foreign policy had been bounded by the horizon of France. It had been dynastic and insular. Wolsey made it European by taking the empire, Italy, and Spain into his calculations. He deliberately set himself to preserve the balance of power in Europe as a means of raising his country from a third to a first rate state. And that end he accomplished solely by diplomacy founded on the successes of 1513, which impressed on Continental statesmen a sense of England's power and thus gave to Wolsey's succeeding diplomacy a weight it would not otherwise have commanded and which it never afterwards lost. The character of the policy accounts for its fluctuations: as the scales turned, so was Wolsey compelled to vary his pressure.

The year 1515 brought him two new honours. For years Warham, archbishop of Canterbury, had desired to be released from the lord chancellorship, and Henry had repeatedly urged Wolsey to accept it. Wolsey naturally shrank from adding to his already arduous duties; but both Warham and the king became so urgent that he at last yielded. By patent dated 21st December he assumed the post, and at once threw himself into its work with his accustomed vigour, dispensing justice and introducing reforms with fearless impartiality. The second dignity, the cardinalate, was obtained through the active intervention of Henry himself, and only by the most threatening arguments did the king overcome the fears and reluctance of Leo. On the 10th September Wolsey was elected cardinal sole. The bearer of the red hat and ring arrived in London in November, and on Sunday the 18th Wolsey was installed amidst all the ceremonial magnificence which he valued not only for his own sake but for his king's. By similar strong measures was wrung from Leo the legateship, an office Wolsey sought in order to carry out ecclesiastical reforms. In 1518 Leo, ostensibly on account of a crusade, sent legates to the four chief courts of Europe. Campeggio, the legate to England, was allowed to reach Calais, where his further progress was stopped till the pope had joined Wolsey with him. Next year Wolsey was appointed sole legate for a year, and, finally, in 1524, following several extensions, he became legate for life, after receiving unusual powers. In virtue of this commission he erected a court and instituted reformations by which he incurred much odium. In 1518 he received the see of Bath and Wells *in commendam*, which in 1523 he resigned for Durham, replaced in turn by Fox's bishopric of Winchester in 1529. At the conclusion of the Calais conference in 1521, Henry recompensed him with the rich abbacy of St Albans, held, like the episcopates, *in commendam*. From these and other sources he received immense revenues, which were almost entirely devoted to state purposes or national objects. He was prime minister of Henry, and in his income as in his master's there was no distinction between public and private money. Vast sums were used in founding his college at Ipswich and Cardinal College at Oxford, now known as Christ Church, which formed but part of a splendid scheme of national education, a scheme ultimately ruined by the greed of the king. Even what was expended on his own resplendent establishment redounded to the honour of his king and country. His was an age when power and pomp were more closely connected than they are now, and Wolsey's power was extraordinary. "He is in great repute," reported the unfriendly Venetian ambassador Giustinian; "seven times more so than if he were pope." No wonder, then, that he cared but little to fill the papal chair. When, in 1522, and again in 1523, his candidature for the papacy came to nothing, he was not disappointed. And, if in 1529, on the illness of Clement VII., he showed himself seriously anxious on the subject, it was in all likelihood that he might compass Henry's will respecting divorce from Catherine, and prevent that rupture with the apostolic see which he foresaw would result from papal opposition.

Wolsey's favour with the king had been founded on success, and it fell by failure. In the region of politics one diplomatic victory had followed another. The balance had been firmly held between Francis I. and the emperor Charles V., an enterprise rendered memorable by the splendours of the Field of the Cloth of Gold (1520), planned and directed by Wolsey, and amidst which the Middle Ages passed away. Suddenly across his minister's diplomatics Henry dragged the question of the divorce, and everything had to be sacrificed to its accomplishment. Seeing too clearly how much, both personal and national, depended on attaining Henry's desire, Wolsey strove his very uttermost to further a design to which he was himself opposed, stooping to the most discreditable and unworthy means. But the decision lay with Pope Clement, who was in the power of Charles V., Catherine's nephew, and all Wolsey's efforts were in vain. Vain, too, were all attempts to intimidate Catherine herself. A collusive suit was begun before Wolsey by which she was to be condemned unheard; she got word of it and thwarted the plan by demanding counsel. A commission was obtained from the pope for Campeggio and Wolsey to try the cause in England (1529); she appeared before the legatine court at Blackfriars only to appeal to Rome, and thither under imperial pressure Clement revoked the case. It was plain Wolsey had failed, and all Henry's wrath burst out against his too faithful servant. He pointedly employed a secretary, and Wolsey's occupation was gone. Wolsey's foreign policy and domestic reforms had united against him every party and class in the nation, while at the same time he bore the blame of Henry's mistakes and extravagance. So long, however, as his royal master remained true to him he could defy all hostility. But now that the king, too, had turned against him his sole support had given way, and the hungry pack of enemies was unloosed. On the 20th September Henry parted from Wolsey without any sign of displeasure, but they parted for the last time. Anne Boleyn and her uncle Norfolk were Wolsey's bitter foes. By Anne's sway over Henry Wolsey was kept from the royal presence while Norfolk plotted his ruin. On the 17th October, at the king's command, Wolsey delivered up the great seal to Norfolk and the base ungrateful Suffolk. He was deprived of his dignities, his goods were confiscated, and, surrendering York Place, he retired to Esher. The Court of King's Bench found him guilty in a præmunire, and sentenced him to imprisonment, while a bill precluding his restoration to power or dignities reached the Commons. The bill was dropped, but not till February 1530 did Henry grant him a full pardon and restore him to the archbishopric of York, on condition that he resigned Winchester and St Albans. Dreading his proximity to the king, his enemies procured his banishment into his diocese. Thither he went in April, and won the hearts of the people by his simplicity of life and graciousness of manner. His foes were alarmed; his death alone could quiet their fears. He was preparing to be installed archbishop on Monday, 7th November, when on the 4th he was arrested at Cawood Castle by the earl of Northumberland for high treason. On the way south, at Sheffield Park, Nottinghamshire, he was met by Sir William Kingston, keeper of the Tower, and at last Wolsey knew his doom. Long years of toil, anxiety, and the ceaseless vexations of his cruel enemies had shattered his health, and some pears sufficed to bring on dysentery, which was unskilfully treated, and aggravated by Kingston's appearance. Nevertheless he set out, and by three stages reached Leicester abbey on Saturday the 26th. "Father abbot," he said, as the convent with its head came out to receive him, "I am come hither to leave my bones among you." He felt that he was dying. Kingston assisted him upstairs, and he at once went to bed. Vomiting and faintings came on, and he rapidly sank, yet his last moments were spent in speaking to Kingston of the objects of his life's best energies, his king and country. At eight o'clock on the morning of the 29th he died; and within twenty-four hours was buried in a rude coffin all that remained of the genius who made possible the glories of Elizabeth and the British empire of to-day. He left two children, born before he became a bishop, of "one Larke's daughter,"—a son who went by the name of Thomas Winter and was an ecclesiastic, and a daughter who passed as Dorothy Clansey and was a nun.

See *Lives* of Wolsey by Cavendish, Fiddes, and Grove, and J. S. Brewer's *Reign of Henry VIII., 1509-30*. There is no complete correct account of his life up to 1509, in connexion with which see Pinkerton's *History of Scotland*, ii., app. 445-50, along with J. Gairdner's *Letters and Papers, &c., of Richard III. and Henry VII.*, M. R. Series, pref.; and *Letters*, &c., pref. and i., app. B, 426-52. An excellent short view of Wolsey as a statesman will be found in Prof. M. Creighton's *Thomas Wolsey*. (T. W. C.)

WOLVERHAMPTON, a municipal and parliamentary borough and market-town of Staffordshire, England, one of the principal seats of the hardware manufacture in the Midlands, is situated on an eminence commanding an extensive view towards Wales, on the Birmingham and Liverpool, the Staffordshire and Worcestershire, and the Wyrley and Essington Canals, and on the London and North-Western, the Midland, and the Great Western Railways, 13 miles north-west of Birmingham, 16 south of Stafford, and 126 from London. The principal streets diverge from Queen Square, and are for the most part regular and well built, with numerous handsome shops. Towards the west there are pleasant suburbs of villas, the country being rich and well wooded. The old church of Wolverhampton, founded by Wulfruna in 996 and dedicated to the Virgin, was in the reign of Henry III. rededicated to St Peter. It has undergone frequent alterations, and in 1862-65 underwent extensive restoration. It is now a fine cruciform building, with south porch and central tower. Internally the church consists of a long and lofty nave with side aisles and north and south transepts, and terminating in a chancel with apsidal ending. The lower portion of the tower, south transept, &c., belong to the 13th century; the nave, clerestory, upper part of the tower, and north transept were erected in the 15th century; and the chancel is wholly modern, having been rebuilt in 1865. Wolverhampton was formerly a deanery, and on its abolition in 1846 the township was divided into ecclesiastical parishes, the number of which is now thirteen. At the old free grammar school, founded in 1515 by Sir Stephen Jenyns, a native of the town and an alderman of London, Sir W. Congreve and Dr Abernethy received their education. New buildings for the school were erected in 1876 in the western part of the town at a cost of £22,000. There is also a blue-coat school, founded in 1710. The other principal public buildings are the town-hall (1871), the corn exchange (1851, £15,000), the market-hall (1853, £10,500), the agricultural hall (1863, £6000), the public baths (1850), the post-office (1873), the art gallery, museum, and school of art (1884-85), and the free library. There is a cattle market about 5 acres in extent, and also a large pig market. The theatre royal (1844) is a handsome building in the Doric style. The benevolent institutions include a general hospital, the eye infirmary, the orphan asylum, and the institute of the society for outdoor blind. In Queen Square there is an equestrian statue of the late Prince Consort, unveiled by the queen in 1866, and on Snow Hill a statue in Sicilian marble (1879) of the Right Honourable Charles Pelham Villiers, who has represented the borough from 1835 to the present time (1888). Street improvements have been carried out on a large scale within recent years. Main drainage works on a thorough method have also been completed, and a large farm purchased for the utilization of the sewage. The water-works, opened in 1847, belong to the corporation. The water is supplied from springs in the Red Sandstone by wells sunk to a great depth. The old racecourse, 50 acres in extent, has been laid out as a public park; and a new racecourse was opened in 1887. The population of the municipal borough and urban sanitary district (area 3396 acres) in 1871 was 68,291, and in 1881 it was 75,766 (males 37,827, females 37,939); while that of the parliamentary borough (18,888 acres) was 156,978 in 1871, and 164,332 (males 82,657, females 81,675) in 1881.

Situated in a district abounding in coal and ironstone, Wolverhampton has become famous for the manufacture both of the heavier and the smaller kinds of iron-wares, although in the finer class of metal manufactures for which the neighbouring town of Birmingham is famous it has little or no share. It possesses large smelting furnaces, and iron and brass foundries, but is specially occupied in the manufacture of all kinds of iron implements, tools, and domestic requisites, including locks and fastenings, hinges and nails, kitchen furniture, gardeners', wrights', and smiths' tools and implements, tinplate goods, and every variety of japanned ware, of which it may be regarded as the principal seat. There are also extensive clay-retort works, chemical works, grease works, dye-works, varnish works, coach works, corn and saw mills, cooperages, ropewalks, maltings, and breweries.

The place was originally called Hanton or Hamtune, but on the foundation of a college for a dean and secular canons in 996 by Wulfruna, sister of Ethelred II. and widow of Anthelm, duke of Northumberland, it was named Wulfrunahamton. By William Rufus the church was placed under the care of Sampson, bishop of Worcester, who settled it on a prior and convent of his own cathedral. In the reign of Stephen it was taken possession of by Roger, bishop of Salisbury, and subsequently it came into the hands of the secular canons, who held it until Dean Peter of Blois resigned it to Hubert, archbishop of Canterbury, that he might build an abbey of Cistercian monks. The church was accounted one of the king's free chapels, and was annexed by Edward IV. to the deanery of Windsor. The college and prebends were granted to the duke of Northumberland in the reign of Edward VI., and on his attainder they came again to the crown. The deanery and prebends were refounded by Queen Mary, and this was confirmed by James I. The town received the grant of a market and fair from Henry III. in 1258. It suffered severely from fire in 1590, the conflagration lasting five days. During the Civil War its sympathies were Royalist, and it was visited by Charles I., accompanied by his sons Charles and James. In 1645 it was for a time the headquarters of Prince Rupert. Its importance as a seat of manufactures is entirely of modern date and due to the rise of the iron industry. Although it received the privilege of returning members to parliament in 1832, it was not incorporated as a municipal borough till 1848. It is divided into eight wards, and is governed by a mayor, 12 aldermen, and 36 councillors. It has separate commissions of the peace and quarter sessions. In 1885 the number of its parliamentary representatives was increased to three, the borough being separated into three parliamentary divisions—East, South, and West.

WOMBAT. The animals which have received this name belong to the Marsupial family *Phascolomyidæ* (see MAMMALIA, vol. xv. p. 383). They have the following dental formula: $i\,\frac{1}{1}$, $c\,\frac{0}{0}$, $p\,\frac{1}{1}$, $m\,\frac{4}{4} = \frac{6}{6}$; total 24. All the teeth are of continuous growth, having persistent pulps. The incisors are large and scalpriform, much as in Rodents. The body is broad and depressed, the neck short, the head large and flat, the eyes small. The tail is rudimentary, hidden in the fur. The limbs are equal, stout, and short. The feet have broad, naked, tuberculated soles; the fore-feet

Common Wombat (*Phascolomys ursinus*).

with five distinct toes, each furnished with a long, strong, and slightly curved nail, the first and fifth considerably shorter than the other three. The hind feet have a very short nailless hallux; the second, third, and fourth toes partially united by integument, of nearly equal length; the fifth distinct and rather shorter; these four are provided with long and curved nails.

There are two distinct forms of wombat:—

(1) *Phascolomys* proper. Fur rough and coarse. Ears short and rounded. Muffle naked. Post-orbital process of the frontal bone obsolete. Ribs fifteen pairs. Vertebræ: C 7, D 15, L 4, S 4, C 10–12. The wombat of Tasmania and the islands of Bass's Straits (*P. ursinus*) and the closely similar but larger animal of the southern portion of the mainland of Australia (*P. platyrhinus*) belong to this form.

(2) *Lasiorhinus.* Fur smooth and silky. Ears large and more pointed. Muffle hairy. Frontal region of skull broader than in the other section, with well-marked post-orbital processes. Ribs thirteen. Vertebræ: C 7, D 13, L 6, S 4, C 15–16. One species, *P. latifrons*, the Hairy-Nosed Wombat of Southern Australia.

In their general form and actions the wombats resemble small bears, having a somewhat similar shuffling manner of walking, but they are still shorter in the legs, and have broader flatter backs than bears. They live entirely on the ground, or in burrows or holes among rocks, never climbing trees, and they feed entirely on grass, roots, and other vegetable substances. They sleep during the day, and wander forth at night in search of food, and are shy and gentle in their habits generally, though they can bite strongly when provoked. The only noise the common wombat makes is a low kind of hissing, but the hairy-nosed wombat is said to emit a short quick grunt when annoyed. The prevailing colour of the last-named species, as well as *P. ursinus* of Tasmania, is a brownish grey. The large wombat of the mainland is very variable in colour, some individuals being found of a pale yellowish brown, others dark grey, and some quite black. The length of head and body is about three feet. Fossil remains of wombats, some of larger size than any now existing, have been found in caves and post-Pliocene deposits in Australia, but in no other part of the world. (W. H. F.)

WOMBWELL, a township of England, in the West Riding of Yorkshire, on the Manchester, Sheffield, and Lincolnshire Railway, 4½ miles south-east of Barnsley, 7 north-west of Rotherham, and 184 from London by rail. The church of St Mary is an ancient structure, enlarged and altered in 1835. The inhabitants are chiefly employed in the extensive collieries. The population of the urban sanitary district (area 3851 acres) in 1871 was 5009, and in 1881 it was 8451.

WOMEN, LAW RELATING TO. The law as it relates to women has been gradual in its operation, but its tendency has been almost uniformly in one direction. Disabilities of women, married or unmarried, have been one after another removed, until at the present day, in most civilized countries, the legal position of women differs little from that of men as far as regards private rights. Politically and professionally the sexes are still not upon an equality, but even in this aspect women have considerably greater rights than they once possessed, and the old theory of their intellectual and moral inferiority is virtually exploded. Those who defend their exclusion must now do so on other grounds. Much of the law relating to married women has been already dealt with under the heads of ADULTERY, BIGAMY, DIVORCE, MARRIAGE, HUSBAND AND WIFE, and SETTLEMENT, the last two especially dealing with their rights of property.

The dependent position of women in early law is proved by the evidence of most ancient systems which have in whole or in part descended to us. In the Mosaic law divorce was a privilege of the husband only,[1] the vow of a woman might be disallowed by her father or husband,[2] and daughters could inherit only in the absence of sons, and then they must marry in their tribe.[3] The guilt or innocence of a wife accused of adultery might be tried by the ordeal of the bitter water.[4] Besides these instances,

[1] Deut. xxiv. 1.
[2] Numb. xxx. 3.
[3] Numb. xxvii., xxxvi.
[4] Numb. v. 11.

which illustrate the subordination of women, there was much legislation dealing with, *inter alia*, offences against chastity, and marriage of a man with a captive heathen woman or with a purchased slave. So far from second marriages being restrained, as they were by Christian legislation, it was the duty of a childless widow to marry her deceased husband's brother. In India subjection was a cardinal principle. "Day and night must women be held by their protectors in a state of dependence," says Manu.[1] The rule of inheritance was agnatic, that is, descent traced through males to the exclusion of females.[2] The gradual growth of *stridhana*, or property of a woman given by the husband before or after marriage, or by the wife's family, was probably what led to the suttee, for both the family of the widow and the Brahmans had an interest in getting the life estate of a woman out of the way.[3] Women in Hindu law had only limited rights of inheritance, and were disqualified as witnesses. In Roman law a woman was even in historic times completely dependent. If married she and her property passed into the power of her husband; if unmarried she was (unless a vestal virgin) under the perpetual tutelage of her father during his life, and after his death of her agnates, that is, those of her kinsmen by blood or adoption who would have been under the power of the common ancestor had he lived. Failing agnates, the tutelage probably passed to the *gens*. The wife was the purchased property of her husband, and, like a slave, acquired only for his benefit. A woman could not exercise any civil or public office. In the words of Ulpian, "feminæ ab omnibus officiis civilibus vel publicis remotæ sunt."[4] A woman could not continue a family, for she was "caput et finis familiæ suæ,"[5] could not be a witness, surety, tutor, or curator; she could not adopt or be adopted, or make a will or contract. She could not succeed *ab intestato* as an agnate, if further removed than a sister. A daughter might be disinherited by a general clause, a son only by name. On the other hand, a woman was privileged in some matters, but rather from a feeling of pity for her bodily weakness and presumed mental incapacity[6] than for any more worthy reason. Thus she could plead ignorance of law as a ground for dissolving an obligation, which a man could not as a rule do; she could accuse only in cases of treason and witchcraft; and she was in certain cases exempt from torture. In succession *ab intestato* to immovable property Roman law did not, as does English, recognize any privilege of males over females. Legal disabilities were gradually mitigated by the influence of fictions, the prætorian equity, and legislation. An example of the first was the mode by which a woman freed herself from the authority of her tutor by fictitious cession into the authority of a tutor nominated by herself, or by sale of herself into the power of a nominal husband on the understanding that he was at once to emancipate her to another person, who then manumitted her. The action of equity is illustrated by the recognition by the prætor of cognatic or natural as distinguished from agnatic or artificial relationship, and of a widow's claim to succeed on the death of her husband intestate and without relations. Legislation, beginning as early as the Twelve Tables, which forbade excessive mourning for the dead by female mourners, did not progress uniformly towards enfranchisement of women. For instance, the Lex Voconia (about 169 B.C.), called by St Augustine the most unjust of all laws, provided that a woman could not be instituted heir to a man who was registered as owner of a fortune of 100,000 asses.[7] A constitution of Valentinian I. forbade bequests by women to ecclesiastics. But the tendency of legislation was undoubtedly in the direction indicated. Adoption of women was allowed by Diocletian and Maximian in 291. The tutelage of women of full age was removed by Claudius, and, though afterwards in part revived, has disappeared by the time of Justinian. This implied full testamentary and contractual liberty. In regard to the separate property of the married woman, the period of *dos* had by the time of Justinian long superseded the period of *manus* (see SETTLEMENT). The result was that, in spite of a few remaining disabilities, such as the general incapacity to be surety or witness to a will or contract, of a wife to make a gift to her husband, of a widow to marry within a year of her husband's death, the position of women had become, in the words of Sir H. Maine, "one of great personal and proprietary independence."[8] For this improvement in their position they were largely indebted to the legislation of the Christian emperors, especially of Justinian, who prided himself on being a protector of women. The following are a few of the matters in which Christianity appears to have made alterations, generally but perhaps not always improvements, in the law. As a rule the influence of the church was exercised in favour of the abolition of the disabilities imposed by the older law upon celibacy and childlessness, of increased facilities for entering a professed religious life,[9] and of due provision for the wife. The church also supported the political power of those who were her best friends. The government of Pulcheria or Irene would hardly have been endured in the days of the pagan empire. Other cases in which Christianity probably exercised influence may be briefly stated. (1) All differences in the law of succession *ab intestato* of males and females were abolished by Justinian. (2) The appointment of mothers and grandmothers as tutors was sanctioned by the same emperor. (3) He extended to all cases the principle established by the Senatus Consultum Tertullianum (158), enabling the mother of three (if a freed woman four) children to succeed to the property of her children who died intestate, and gave increased rights of succession to a widow. (4) The restrictions on the marriage of senators and other men of high rank with women of low rank were extended by Constantine, but almost entirely removed by Justinian. (5) Second marriages were discouraged (especially by making it legal to impose a condition that a widow's right to property should cease on re-marriage), and the Leonine Constitutions at the end of the 9th century made third marriages punishable. (6) The same constitutions made the benediction of a priest a necessary part of the ceremony of marriage.[10] The criminal law in its relation to women presents some points of interest. Adultery was punished with death by Constantine, but the penalty was reduced by Justinian to relegation to a convent. A woman condemned for adultery could not re-marry. A marriage between a Christian and a Jew

[1] Ch. ix. § 2 (Sir W. Jones's translation).

[2] Whether this was the oldest rule of inheritance has been much debated. See FAMILY. That birth of a child gave the mother certain legal rights in a primitive stage of society is the view of many writers. See especially *Das Mutterrecht* of J. J. Bachoffen (Stuttgart, 1861).

[3] Maine, *Early History of Institutions*, lect. xi.

[4] *Dig.*, i. 16, 195.

[5] *Ibid.*

[6] *Imbecillitas* is the term used more than once in the texts of Roman law.

[7] The way in which this law was evaded was by non-enrolment of the testator in the census (see Montesquieu, *Esprit des Lois*, bk. xxvii.). Another way was by leaving her the inheritance by *fideicommissum* (see TRUST).

[8] *Ancient Law*, ch. v. Hence the necessity of such laws as the Lex Oppia (see SUMPTUARY LAWS).

[9] A remarkable example of this tendency was the provision that an actress might leave the stage and break her contract of service with impunity in order to become a nun (see THEATRE). Even under the pagan emperors a constitution of Diocletian and Maximian in 285 had enacted that no one was to be compelled to marry (*Cod.*, v. 4, 14).

[10] See Troplong, *De l'Influence du Christianisme sur le Droit Civil.*

rendered the parties guilty of adultery. Severe laws were enacted against offences of unchastity, especially procurement and incest. It was a capital crime to carry off or offer violence to a nun. A wife could not commit *furtum* of her husband's goods, but he had a special action *rerum amotarum* against her. By several sumptuary constitutions, contained in the *Code*, bk. xi., women as well as men were subject to penalties for wearing dress or ornaments (except rings) imitating those reserved for the emperor and his family. Actresses and women of bad fame were not to wear the dress of virgins dedicated to Heaven. If a consul had a wife or mother living with him, he was allowed to incur greater expense than if he lived alone. The interests of working women were protected by enactments for the regulation of the *gynæcia*, or workshops for spinning, dyeing, &c.

The canon law, looking with disfavour on the female independence prevailing in the later Roman law, tended rather in the opposite direction. The *Decretum* specially inculcated subjection of the wife to the husband, and obedience to his will in all things.[1] The chief differences between canon and Roman law were in the law of marriage, especially in the introduction of publicity and of the formalities of the ring and the kiss. The benediction of a priest was made a necessary part of the ceremony, as indeed it had been made by the civil power, as has been already stated, in the post-Justinian period of Roman law. But in practice this rule appears to have fallen into disuse until it was again revived by the council of Trent. It was, however, the rule of the English common law after the Reformation. The ceremony was not to be performed during Lent. The woman was to be veiled during the ceremony. A promise of marriage was so sacred that it made a subsequent marriage with another person void. Spiritual cognation was a bar to marriage. The sentence of the church was made necessary for divorce. As to women in general the law does not say very much. Women, even relatives, were not to live with priests unless in case of necessity. They were not to approach the altar or fill any public office of the church; nor might they lend money on usury. Baptism might be valid although administered by a woman. Women who had professed religion could not be forced to give evidence as witnesses. In some cases the evidence of women was not receivable (see WITNESS).[2]

The early law of the northern parts of Europe is interesting from the different ways in which it treated women. In the words of Sir H. Maine[3]—"The position of women in these barbarous systems of inheritance varies very greatly. Sometimes they inherit, either as individuals or as classes, only when males of the same generation have failed. Sometimes they do not inherit, but transmit a right of inheritance to their male issue. Sometimes they succeed to one kind of property, for the most part movable property, which they probably took a great share in producing by their household labour; for example, in the real Salic law (not in the imaginary code) there is a set of rules of succession which, in my opinion, clearly admit women and their descendants to a share in the inheritance of movable property, but confine land exclusively to males and the descendants of males. . . . The idea is that the proper mode of providing for a woman is by giving her a marriage portion; but, when she is once married into a separate community consisting of strangers in blood, neither she nor her children are deemed to have any further claim on the parent group." Among the Scandinavian races women were under perpetual tutelage, whether married or unmarried. The first to obtain freedom were the widows.[4] As late as the code of Christian V., at the end of the 17th century, it was enacted that if a woman married without the consent of her tutor he might have, if he wished, administration and usufruct of her goods during her life.[5] The provision made by the Scandinavian laws under the name of morning-gift was perhaps the parent of the modern settled property.[6] The Brehon law of Ireland excepted women from the ordinary course of the law. They could distrain or contract only in certain named cases, and distress upon their property was regulated by special rules. In the pre-Conquest codes in England severe laws were denounced against unchastity, and by a law of Canute a woman was to lose nose and ears for adultery. The laws of Athelstan contained the peculiarly brutal provision for the punishment of a female slave convicted of theft by her being burned alive by eighty other female slaves. Other laws were directed against the practice of WITCHCRAFT (*q.v.*) by women. Monogamy was enforced both by the civil and ecclesiastical law; and second and third marriages involved penance. A glimpse of cruelty in the household is afforded by the provision, occurring no less than three times in the ecclesiastical legislation, that if a woman scourged her female slave to death she must do penance. Traces of wife-purchase are seen in the law of Ethelbert, enacting that if a man carry off a freeman's wife he must at his own expense procure the husband another wife. The codes contain few provisions as to the property of married women, but those few appear to prove that she was in a better position than at a later period. The laws of Ine gave her a third of her husband's property; the laws of Edmund as to betrothal allowed this to be increased to half by antenuptial contract, to the whole if she had children and did not re-marry after her husband's death. No doubt the dower *ad ostium ecclesiæ* favoured by the church generally superseded the legal rights where the property was large—in fact this is specially provided by Magna Charta, c. 7—just as at present rights under a marriage settlement take the place of those given by statute. "Provisio hominis tollit provisionem legis." The legal rights of a married woman apart from contract were gradually limited, until by the time of Glanvill her person and property had become during her husband's lifetime entirely at his disposal, and after his death limited to her dower and her *pars rationabilis* (see WILL).

A few of the more interesting matters in which the old common and statute law of England placed women in a special position may be noticed. A woman was exempt from legal duties more particularly attaching to men and not performable by deputy. She could apparently originally not hold a proper feud, *i.e.*, one of which the tenure was by military service.[7] The same principle appears in the rule that she could not be endowed of a castle maintained for the defence of the realm and not for the private use of the owner. She could receive homage, but not render it in the form used by men, and she was privileged from suit and service at the sheriff's tourn. She was not sworn to the law by the oath of allegiance in the leet or

[1] Pt. ii. caus. xxxiii. qu. v. ch. 16.

[2] On this branch of the subject Manssen's *Het Christendom en de Vrouw* (Leyden, 1877) may be consulted with advantage.

[3] *Early Law and Custom*, ch. v.

[4] See Stiernhöök, *De Jure Sveonum* (Stockholm, 1672), bk. ii. ch. i.; Messenius, *Leges Svecorum* (Stockholm, 1714).

[5] Bk. iii. ch. xvi. §§ 1, 2.

[6] The development of the bride-price no doubt was in the same direction. Its original meaning was, however, different. It was the sum paid by the husband to the wife's family for the purchase of part of the family property, while the morning-gift was paid as *pretium virginitatis* to the bride herself. In its English form morning-gift occurs in the laws of Canute; in its Latinized form of *morgangiva* it occurs in the *Leges Henrici Primi*.

[7] It is remarkable that the great fiefs of France except the Isle of France, the special apanage of the crown, all became in time female fiefs. This is shown by the table at the end of Laboulaye's *Recherches*.

tourn, and so could not be outlawed (see OUTLAW), but was said to be waived. She could be constable, either of a castle or a vill, but not sheriff, unless in the one case of Westmorland, an hereditary office, exercised in person in the 17th century by the famous Anne, countess of Dorset, Pembroke, and Montgomery. In certain cases a woman could transmit rights which she could not enjoy. On such a power of transmission, as Sir H. Maine shows,[1] rested the claim of Edward III. to the crown of France. The claim *through* a woman was not a breach of the French constitutional law, which rejected the claim *of* a woman. The jealousy of a woman's political influence is strikingly shown by the case of Alice Perrers, the mistress of Edward III. She was accused of breaking an ordinance by which women had been forbidden to do business for hire and by way of maintenance in the king's court.[2]

By Magna Charta a woman could not appeal any one for murder except that of her husband. This disability no doubt arose from the fact that in trial by battle she naturally did not appear in person but by a champion. She was not admitted as a witness to prove the status of a man on the question arising whether he were free or a villein. She could not appoint a testamentary guardian, and could only be a guardian even of her own children to a limited extent. Her will was revoked by marriage, that of a man only by marriage and the subsequent birth of a child (see WILL). By 31 Hen. VI. c. 9 the king's writ out of chancery was granted to a woman alleging that she had become bound by an obligation through force or fraud. By 39 Hen. VI. c. 2 a woman might have livery of land as heiress at fourteen. Benefit of clergy was first allowed to women partially by 21 Jac. I. c. 6, fully by 3 Will. and M. c. 9 and 4 and 5 Will. and M. c. 24. Public whipping was not abolished until 57 Geo. III. c. 75, whipping in all cases until 1 Geo. IV. c. 57. Burning was the punishment specially appropriated to women convicted of treason or witchcraft. A case of sentence to execution by burning for petit treason occurred as lately as 1784. In some old statutes very curious sumptuary regulations as to women's dress occur. By the sumptuary laws of Edward III. in 1363 (37 Edw. III. cc. 8–14) women were in general to be dressed according to the position of their fathers or husbands. Wives and daughters of servants were not to wear veils above twelve pence in value. Handicraftsmen's and yeomen's wives were not to wear silk veils. The use of fur was confined to the ladies of knights with a rental above 200 marks a year. Careful observance of difference of rank in the dress was also inculcated by 3 Edw. IV. c. 5. The wife or daughter of a knight was not to wear cloth of gold or sable fur, of a knight-bachelor not velvet, of an esquire or gentleman not velvet, satin, or ermine, of a labourer not clothes beyond a certain price or a girdle garnished with silver. By 22 Edw. IV. c. 1, cloth of gold and purple silk were confined to women of the royal family. It is worthy of notice that at the times of passing these sumptuary laws the trade interests of women were protected by the legislature. By 37 Edw. III. c. 6, handicraftsmen were to use only one mystery, but women might work as they had been accustomed. 3 Edw. IV. c. 3 forbade importation of silk and lace by Lombards and other alien strangers, imagining to destroy the craft of the silk spinsters and all such virtuous occupations for women. In some cases the wives and daughters of tradesmen were allowed to assist in the trades of their husbands and fathers; see, for instance, the Act concerning tanners, 1 Jac. I. c. 22. Some trading corporations, such as the East India Company, recognized no distinction of sex in their members. The disabilities imposed on women by substantive law are sometimes traceable in the early law of procedure. For instance, by the Statute of Essoins (12 Edw. II. st. 2), essoin *de servitio regis* did not lie where the party was a woman; that is, a woman (with a few exceptions) could not excuse her absence from court by alleging that she was on public duty. The influence of the church is very clearly traceable in some of the earlier criminal legislation. Thus by 13 Edw. I. st. 1, c. 34, it was punishable with three years' imprisonment to carry away a nun, even with her consent. The Six Articles, 31 Hen. VIII. c. 14, forbade marriage and concubinage of priests and sanctioned vows of chastity by women.

English law.

The present position of women in English law may be treated, for purposes of convenience, under several heads. Sex alone, as will appear, does not determine the law: sex and marriage together must often be taken into consideration.

Political rights.

Political Rights.—This branch of the law is full of singular anomalies. A woman may fill some of the highest positions in the state. She may be a queen, a regent, or a peeress in her own right.[3] A queen regnant has, by 1 Mary, sess. 3, c. 1, as full rights as a king. A peeress is entitled, by 20 Hen. VI. c. 9, to be tried like a peer by the House of Lords or the court of the lord high steward (see TRIAL), and has a seat in the House of Lords, but no right of speaking or voting. Other public offices which a woman can fill are those of overseer, guardian of the poor, churchwarden, and sexton. She may also, if married, be one of a jury of matrons empanelled to determine the question of pregnancy of a widow on a writ *de ventre inspiciendo* or of a female prisoner, but she cannot serve on an ordinary jury. If unmarried or a widow she can vote in municipal, school board, local government, poor law, and other elections of a local character (such as polls of ratepayers under the Free Libraries and Borough Funds Acts), and can be a member (whether married or not) of a school board, but apparently not an overseer or guardian if married and living with her husband. She cannot be registered as a voter or vote at a parliamentary election or be elected a member of parliament. It was decided in 1868 that the words of Lord Brougham's Act (13 and 14 Vict. c. 21, § 4), by which in all Acts words importing the masculine gender are to be taken to include females unless the contrary is expressly provided, did not bring a woman within the word "man" in the Representation of the People Act, 1867.[4] The same would no doubt be held, if the point were raised, under the Representation of the People Act, 1884. The question of granting the parliamentary franchise to women was first brought before the House of Commons by John Stuart Mill in 1867, as an amendment to the Representation of the People Bill of that year, and has uniformly been rejected on that and several subsequent occasions. At present the Isle of Man is the only part of the United Kingdom where such a right exists. It was there conceded in 1882 to unmarried women with sufficient property qualification. For the precedence of women, see PRECEDENCE. The national status of married women and widows is provided for by the Naturalization Act, 1870.

Professions and trades.

Professions and Trades.—The only one of the learned professions open to women is the medical. Such rights as may be possessed by the Society of Apothecaries and the College of Surgeons to admit women to their respective qualifications are specially saved by 37 and 38 Vict. c. 34 and 38 and 39 Vict. c. 43. By an Act of 1876 (39 and 40 Vict. c. 41) medical qualifications may be granted, irrespective of sex, by any body empowered to grant such qualifications. As a matter of fact the College of Surgeons does not at present allow women to qualify, but the Society of Apothecaries and the College of Surgeons of Ireland and the King's and Queen's College of Physicians in Ireland follow the more liberal course. Admission to degrees, medical and others, in the universities is only allowed to a limited extent. Oxford and Cambridge admit women to examinations, but not to degrees. London, under its supplemental charter of 1878, admits to all degrees. The University Education (Ireland) Act, 1879, contains a section empowering the Royal University of Ireland to examine women for degrees and certificates of proficiency. The Endowed Schools Act, 1869, provides for extending to girls the benefits of educational endowments. A similar provision is included in the City of London Parochial Charities Act, 1883. Under the powers of these Acts, as well as by private munificence, a considerable sum of money has been during the last few years provided for the purposes of female education. Special regulations are made by the Factories and Mines Acts as to the employment of women and girls in factories and mines. Under no circumstances is a woman allowed to work underground. The Shop Hours Regulation Act, 1886 (a temporary provision), forbids the employment in shops of girls under eighteen for more than

[1] *Early Law and Custom*, ch. v.

[2] *Rot. Parl.*, vol. iii. p. 12.

[3] Most peeresses are those who have succeeded to ancient peerages by writ. Modern peerages are almost always limited to heirs-male.

[4] Chorlton *v.* Lings, *Law Rep.*, 4 Common Pleas, 374.

seventy-four hours in a week. Women have recently been employed to a greater extent than formerly in Government departments, especially in the post-office. A married woman may, since the Married Women's Property Act, 1882, carry on a trade separately from her husband, and in such a case is liable to be made a bankrupt. She may apparently be a partner of her husband, and may lend him money, but in this case her claim to a dividend on his bankruptcy is postponed to that of other creditors.

Family rights.

Family Rights.—The age at which a girl can contract a valid marriage is, following Roman law, twelve; she is thus two years in advance of a boy, who must be fourteen. Under the Infants Settlement Act (see SETTLEMENT) a valid settlement can be made by a woman at seventeen with the approval of the court, the age for a man being twenty. An unmarried woman is liable for the support of illegitimate children till they attain the age of sixteen. She is generally assisted, in the absence of agreement, by an affiliation order granted by magistrates. A married woman having separate property is, under the Married Women's Property Act, liable for the support of her husband, children, and grandchildren becoming chargeable to any union or parish. At common law the father was entitled as against the mother to the custody of a legitimate child up to the age of sixteen, and could only forfeit such right by misconduct. But the Court of Chancery, wherever there was trust property and the infant could be made a ward of court, took a less rigid view of the paternal rights and looked more to the interest of the child, and consequently in some cases to the extension of the mother's rights at common law. Legislation has tended in the same direction. By 36 Vict. c. 12 the Court of Chancery was empowered to enforce a provision in a separation deed, giving up the custody or control of a child to the mother. The Judicature Act, 1873, § 25 (10), enacted that in questions relating to the custody and education of infants the rules of equity should prevail. The Guardianship of Infants Act, 1886, largely extended the mother's powers of appointing and acting as a guardian, and gave the court a discretion to regard the mother's wishes as to the custody of the children. The children of women convicted of crime or frequenting the company of prostitutes may be sent to an industrial school. The principal disabilities under which women are now placed may perhaps be classed under the head of family rights, viz., exclusion of female heirs from intestate succession to real estate, unless in absence of a male heir (see INHERITANCE, PRIMOGENITURE), and the obtaining of DIVORCE (*q.v.*) by a husband for the adultery of his wife, while the wife can only obtain it for adultery coupled with some further cause, such as cruelty or desertion.

Rights of property.

Rights of Property.—Unmarried women and widows have practically equal rights with men. Since the date of the article HUSBAND AND WIFE the Married Women's Property Act, 1882, has extended the change in the law attempted to a limited degree by the previous Acts of 1870 and 1874. The most important provisions of the Act (45 and 46 Vict. c. 75) falling under this head are the following. A married woman is capable of acquiring, holding, and disposing by will or otherwise of any real and personal property as her separate property, in the same manner as if she were a *feme sole*, without the intervention of any trustee. Every contract entered into by a married woman is to be deemed to bind her separate property, unless the contrary be shown. Property of a woman married after the commencement of the Act, whether belonging to her at the time of marriage or acquired after marriage, is to be held by her as a *feme sole*. The same is the case with property acquired after the commencement of the Act by a woman married before the Act. After marriage a woman remains liable for antenuptial debts and liabilities, and as between her and her husband, in the absence of contract to the contrary, her separate property is to be deemed primarily liable. The husband is only liable to the extent of property acquired from or through his wife. The Act also contains provisions as to stock, investment, insurance, evidence (see WITNESS), and other matters. The effect of the Act is to render obsolete the old law as to what creates a separate use or a reduction into possession of choses in action (see PERSONAL ESTATE), as to equity to a settlement, as to fraud on the husband's marital rights,[1] and as to the inability of one of two married persons to give a gift to the other. Also, in the case of a gift to a husband and wife in terms which would make them joint-tenants if unmarried, they no longer take as one person but as two. The construction of the Act by the courts has been in one or two cases perhaps somewhat narrow; still there is no doubt that it has affected the proprietary rights of married women to an immense extent. Its effect has been principally to improve the position of wives of the humbler class unprotected by marriage settlement. There is a special saving in the Act of existing and future settlement. A settlement is still necessary where it is desired to secure only the enjoyment of the income to the wife and to provide for children. The Act by itself would enable the wife, without regard to family claims, instantly to part with the whole of any property which might come to her. Restraint on anticipation, a means of protecting a married woman's property from her husband's influence, is also preserved by the Act, subject to the liability of such property for antenuptial debts, and to the power given to the court by the Conveyancing Act, 1881, to bind a married woman's interest notwithstanding a clause of restraint. This possibility of being restrained from anticipation is now one of the principal points of difference between the proprietary rights of men and women. Formerly remaining unmarried could be attached as a condition of the enjoyment of property by a widow only, but it has been recently decided that such a condition may be imposed upon a widower as well. In one case, however, the widow has still an advantage over the widower. Limitations contained in her marriage settlement in favour of her children by a former marriage are not treated as voluntary, while similar limitations in the settlement of a widower are regarded as voluntary, and therefore void as against a subsequent mortgagee of the settled property.[2] By Magna Charta, c. 7, a widow is to have her QUARANTINE (*q.v.*), and is not to be forced to re-marry.

Procedure.

Procedure.—An action for breach of promise of marriage[3] and an affiliation summons under the Bastardy Acts are, the former practically, the latter entirely, confined to women. An action of SEDUCTION (*q.v.*), though not brought in England by the woman herself, is for injury suffered by her. The Rules of the Supreme Court and the Married Women's Property Act contain various provisions for the bringing and defending of actions by married women. The main provision is § 1 (2) of the Act, enabling a married woman to sue and be sued, either in contract or in tort or otherwise, in all respects as if she were a *feme sole*. Her position, however, is not, owing to the judicial interpretation of the Act, as completely independent as the words of the Act would at first sight appear to imply. It has been held, for instance, that she cannot since the Act, any more than before it, be next friend or guardian *ad litem* of an infant. The husband and wife too may still be sued jointly for a tort committed by the wife after marriage. Apart from proceedings for divorce or judicial separation, a husband cannot sue his wife for a tort committed during the coverture, nor a wife her husband, unless for the protection and security of her separate property. She can, however, cause him to be bound over in recognizances to keep the peace towards her in case of violence on his part. The Married Women's Property Act contains a useful section enabling questions between husband and wife as to property to be decided in a summary way. A judgment against a married woman under the Act is limited to execution against her separate property; she cannot like an ordinary debtor be committed to prison under the Debtors Act for default in payment.

Criminal law.

Criminal Law.—There are some offences which can be committed only by women, others which can be committed only against them. Among the former are concealment of birth (in ninety-nine cases out of a hundred), the now obsolete offence of being a common scold, and prostitution and kindred offences. Many offences of the latter kind were up to a recent date dealt with under the Contagious Diseases Acts, which were repealed in 1886. Where a married woman commits a crime in company with her husband, she is generally presumed to have acted by his coercion, and so to be entitled to acquittal. This presumption, however, was never made in witchcraft cases, and is not now made in cases of treason, murder, and other grave crimes, or in crimes in which the principal part must necessarily be taken by the wife, such as keeping a brothel. In fact, the exceptions to the old presumption are now perhaps more numerous than those falling within it. The doctrine of coercion and the practice of separate acknowledgment of deeds by married women (necessary before the Married Women's Property Act) seem to be vestiges of the period when women, besides being chattels, were treated as chattels.[4] Formerly a wife could not steal her husband's property, but since the Married Women's Property Act this has become possible. The evidence of a wife is not usually receivable for or against her husband (see WITNESS). She does not become an accessory after the fact by receiving and harbouring her husband after he has committed a felony; the husband, however, is not equally privileged if the offence be committed by the wife. Adultery is now no crime, England being almost the only country where such is the case. It was punished by fine in the ecclesiastical courts up to the 17th century, and was made criminal for a short

[1] This was a rule of law, confirmed, though not for the first time established, by the well-known decision of Lord Thurlow in Countess of Strathmore *v.* Bowes, in 1789, to the effect that a secret conveyance by a woman during her engagement to her future husband might be set aside by him after marriage A legal relation was in this case created by engagement or betrothal. The only other instance in English law in which betrothal gives any rights appears to be the action for breach of promise of marriage. In the Mosaic law betrothal was, for the purposes of punishment of adultery, equivalent to marriage (see Deut. xxii. 23). In some modern systems betrothal is a matter of more importance than it is in England. In Germany, for instance, it is publicly advertised.

[2] See *Re* Cameron and Wells, *Law Rep.*, 37 Chancery Div., 32.

[3] A brief sketch of the law relating to this branch of the subject has been added by way of appendix to this article.

[4] It was certainly laid down by the Court of Chancery, in more than one case, that the reason for enforcing acknowledgment of deeds by a married woman apart from her husband was the presumption that in matters of property she was sure to be coerced by him. If such were the truth, the separate acknowledgment—a matter of a few minutes' conversation—was but a poor safeguard. The doctrine of coercion in felonies is attributed by Mr Justice Stephen to the wish to give women, while they had not benefit of clergy, the same chance of escape as men (see his *Digest of the Criminal Law*, App., note 1).

time by an ordinance of the Long Parliament. The offences which can be committed only against women are chiefly those against decency, such as rape, procurement, and similar crimes, in which a considerable change in the law in the direction of increased protection to women was made by the Criminal Law Amendment Act, 1885. Another offence is abduction, which needs to be separately mentioned, as it appears in law to be an offence partly against the person, partly against property, for a difference is made between the abduction of a woman with property and of one without property. As to offences committed against a wife, recent legislation has made some considerable changes. By the Matrimonial Causes Act, 1878, if a husband be convicted of an aggravated assault upon his wife, the court before which he is tried may order (subject to an appeal to the Probate, Divorce, and Admiralty Division of the High Court) that the wife be no longer bound to cohabit with him, such order to have the effect of a judicial separation on the ground of cruelty. The order may also provide for payment of a weekly allowance by the husband to the wife and for the custody of the children of the marriage. That of the children under ten may be given to the wife. The Married Women's Property Act gives a married woman criminal remedies against all persons (including her husband) for the protection of her separate property, with a proviso that no such criminal proceeding shall be taken against a husband while they are living together, nor while they are living apart, concerning any act done while they were living together, unless the wife's property have been wrongfully taken by the husband on desertion of his wife. The section just cited extends the common law, under which the wife's redress for injuries committed by her husband was confined to injuries to the person. But it extends it only to injuries to the separate property, and it has recently been held that a wife cannot, under the terms of the section, proceed against her husband criminally for a libel.[1] The Married Women (Maintenance in Case of Desertion) Act, 1886, enables a wife to summon her husband before a court of summary jurisdiction for desertion, and the court may make an order for her support. Before the Act the wife's only course was to become chargeable to the parish, allowing the guardians to seek to recover from the husband the cost of her maintenance. The punishment of a woman may still be different from that of a man in TREASON (*q.v.*). Where whipping is allowed after conviction for robbery, or of juvenile offenders for larceny, it cannot be inflicted on females. Chastisement of a wife by a husband, possibly at one time lawful to a reasonable extent, would now certainly constitute an assault. The husband's rights are limited to restraining the wife's liberty in case of her misconduct.

Scottish law.

Scotland.—As early as *Regiam Majestatem* (12th century) women were the object of special legal regulation. In that work the *mercheta mulieris* (probably a tax paid to the lord on the marriage of his tenant's daughter) was fixed at a sum differing according to the rank of the woman. Numerous ancient laws dealt with trade and sumptuary matters. By the *Leges Quatuor Burgorum* female brewsters making bad ale were to forfeit eightpence and be put on the cucking-stool, and were to set an ale-wand outside their houses under a penalty of fourpence. The same laws also provided that a married woman committing a trespass without her husband's knowledge might be chastised like a child under age. The *Statuta Gilde* of the 13th century enacted that a married woman might not buy wool in the streets or buy more than a limited amount of oats. The same code also ensured a provision for the daughter of one of the guild-brethren unable to provide for herself through poverty, either by marrying her or putting her in a convent. By the Act 1429, c. 9, wives were to be arrayed after the estate of their husbands. By 1457, c. 13, no woman was to go to church with her face covered so that she could not be known. 1581, c. 18, was conceived in a more liberal spirit, and allowed women to wear any head-dress to which they had been accustomed. 1621, c. 25, permitted servants to wear their mistress's cast-off clothes. 1681, c. 80, contained the remarkable provision that not more than two changes of raiment were to be made by a bride at her wedding. In its more modern aspect the law is in most respects similar to that of England. A woman may be queen or a peeress of Scotland.[2] In the old law she could not do homage, but only fealty, and she could not be arbiter, cautioner, or witness. A married woman could be warrantor of heritables only where her husband was under age and she was of full age. All disabilities of women as witnesses were removed by 31 and 32 Vict. c. 101, § 139. A woman is still not receivable as cautioner for an executor-dative. Nor can she be tutor-at-law, but she may be appointed tutor by testament or by the court. While tests existed women were exempt from the test oath (see TEST ACTS). The Court of Session decided in 1868 that the parliamentary suffrage was confined to males.[3] But, as in England, women possess votes in elections to school boards and to municipal and local bodies, the latter specially conferred by the Municipal Elections Amendment Act, 1881, and the General Police and Improvement Act, 1882. The right of married women to vote at school-board elections under the Education Act, 1872, appears to have caused some difficulty, and to have been differently decided in different counties. Women are not admitted to degrees by the Scottish universities, though several attempts have been made to confer upon them this privilege. At one time, indeed, they seem to have practised medicine without qualification, for in 1641, in a ratification of the privileges of the Edinburgh chirurgeons, a complaint was recited that women practised chirurgy without having learned the art. In 1873 the Court of Session decided that female students could not graduate in medicine at Edinburgh.[4] A bill to enable the universities to grant degrees to women was rejected in 1875. St Andrews grants them not the ordinary degree but a special title of L. L. A.[5] The powers given by the Act of 1876 (39 and 40 Vict. c. 41) have recently been exercised in favour of women by the Colleges of Physicians and of Surgeons of Edinburgh and the Faculty of Physicians and Surgeons of Glasgow. By the Educational Endowments Act, 1882, the benefits of endowments are to be extended as far as possible to both sexes. In 1881 the Married Women's Property Act (44 and 45 Vict. c. 21) made important extensions of the rights given to married women by the Act of 1877, for which see HUSBAND AND WIFE. A wife married after the date of the Act has a separate estate in movable and heritable property. A husband has the same rights in the movable estate of his deceased wife as a widow had before the Act in the estate of her deceased husband. Children have a right of legitim in their mother's movable estate. The criminal law differs slightly from that of England. At one time drowning was a punishment specially reserved for women. Incest or an attempt to commit incest is still punishable as a crime, and has been so punished within the last few years. Adultery and fornication are still nominally crimes under old Acts, but criminal proceedings in these cases have fallen into desuetude. The age of testamentary capacity is still twelve, not twenty-one, as in England.

Law in United States.

United States.—The Acts of Congress contain little affecting the subject. Any woman married to a citizen of the United States who might herself be lawfully naturalized is to be deemed a citizen. Women are allowed as clerks in Government departments, and may be employed as nurses and hospital matrons in the army. The right of voting for Congress or for the State legislatures is still denied in the country as a whole, in spite of the strong attempts which have been made by the advocates of female suffrage. The right, however, exists to a limited extent. In the Territories of Washington, Wyoming, and Utah women vote, and in the constitutions of some States, such as Colorado and Wisconsin, it is provided that the right of suffrage may be extended to women by a majority of electors at a general election. The constitutions of most States confine the parliamentary franchise to male electors. The admission of women to the school franchise is, however, largely increasing, and had in 1887 been adopted by fourteen States. In a limited number of States the professions (except the military) are open to women. Where the legal profession is not so open, a refusal by a State court to grant a licence to practise law is no breach of the Federal constitution (see PRIVILEGE). In most States the policy adopted in England by the Married Women's Property Act is the rule, and there is in general no distinction of sex in succession to real estate. For the testamentary rights of married women see WILL. In some of the State universities women are admitted to full privileges of instruction and graduation. In others, such as the university of Pennsylvania, they are admitted to instruction and examination, but not to graduation. The law in some cases gives women remedies for tort which are unknown in England. For instance, by the law of some States a woman may bring an action of SEDUCTION (*q.v.*) in her own name, and may recover damages for slander imputing unchastity, without proof of special damage, which cannot be done in England. The criminal law is also more extensive. In the New England and some of the other States mere fornication is punishable as a crime. Adultery is criminal by the law of most States.

Literature.—Besides those already cited, the following authorities may be consulted. For the general law Montesquieu, *Esprit des Lois*, bk. vii.; Laboulaye, *Recherches sur la Condition Civile et Politique des Femmes*, 1843; Thos. Wright, *Womankind in Western Europe*, 1869; Sheldon Amos, *Difference of Sex as a Topic of Jurisprudence and Legislation*, 1870; Paul Gide, *Étude sur la Condition Privée de la Femme*, 1885; Ernest Naville, "La Condition Sociale des Femmes," in the *Bibliothèque Universelle et Revue Suisse*, for Oct., Nov., and Dec., 1887. For old English law, *The Law's Resolutions of Women's Rights*, 1632; *The Lady's Law*, 1737; *The Laws Respecting Women*, 1777 (these three works are anonymous); C. S. Kenny, *Hist. of the Law of England as to the Effects of Marriage on Property and on the Wife's Legal Capacity*, 1879. For modern English law, T. Barrett-Lennard, *The Position in Law of Women*, 1883; R. Thicknesse, *Digest of the Law of Husband and Wife*, 1884; Wolstenholme and Turner, *Conveyancing Acts* (4th ed.), 1885; W. P. Eversley, *Law of the Domestic Relations*, 1885; Félix Remo, *L'Égalité des Sexes en Angleterre*, 1886.

[1] Reg. *v.* Lord Mayor of London, *Law Rep.*, 16 Queen's Bench Div., 772.

[2] The rule of succession to Scottish peerages is different from that regulating the succession to English peerages by writ. In case of the death of a peer leaving several daughters and no son, the English peerage would fall into abeyance among the daughters, but the eldest daughter would succeed to the Scottish peerage. In the peerage law of Scotland there was no presumption that a peerage was limited to males, and the more ancient peerages were often held by females or their husbands in their right.

[3] Brown *v.* Ingram, 7 *Court of Sess. Cases*, 3d ser., 281.

[4] Jex-Blake *v.* Edinburgh Univ., 11 *Court of Sess. Cases*, 3d ser., 784.

[5] Lady Literate in Arts.

Breach of promise.

Breach of Promise of Marriage.—The action for breach of promise of marriage is in some of its incidents peculiar to English law. In Roman law, betrothal (*sponsalia*) imposed a duty on the betrothed to become husband and wife within a reasonable time, subject to the termination of the obligation by death, repudiation by the words *conditione tua non utor*, or lapse of time, the time fixed being two years. No action lay for breach of promise to marry unless *arrhæ sponsalitiæ* had been given, *i.e.*, earnest of the bargain, to be forfeited by the party refusing to carry it out. The *arrha* might also be given by a parent, and was equally liable to forfeiture. A provincial governor, or one of his relations or household, could not recover any *arrha* that might have been given, it being supposed that he was in a position of authority and able to exercise influence in forcing consent to a betrothal.

In the canon law breach of the promise made by the *sponsalia*, whether *de præsenti* or *de futuro*, a division unknown to Roman law, does not without more appear to have sufficed to found an action for its breach, except so far as it fell under ecclesiastical cognizance as *læsio fidei*, but it had the more serious legal effect of avoiding as a canonical disability the subsequent marriage, while the original *sponsalia* continued, of a betrothed person to any other than the one to whom he or she was originally betrothed. The *sponsalia* became inoperative, either by mutual consent or by certain supervening impediments, such as ordination or a vow of chastity. The canonical disability of pre-contract was removed in England by 32 Hen. VIII. c. 38, re-established in the reign of Edward VI., and finally abolished in 1753.

In England the duty of the parties is the same as in Roman law, viz., to carry out the contract within a reasonable time, if no time be specially fixed. Formerly a contract to marry could be specifically enforced by the ecclesiastical court compelling a celebration of the marriage *in facie ecclesiæ*. The last instance of a suit for this purpose was in 1752, and the right to bring it was abolished in 1753 by Lord Hardwicke's Act (26 Geo. II. c. 33). The action for breach of promise may be brought by a man or a woman, though the former case has been of rare occurrence, and a male plaintiff has still more rarely been rewarded with anything more than nominal damages. It may be brought by but not against an infant, and not against an adult if he or she has merely ratified a promise made during infancy; it may be brought against but not by a married man or woman (in spite of the inherent incapacity of such a person to have married the plaintiff), and neither by nor against the personal representatives of a deceased party to the promise (unless where special damage has accrued to the personal estate of the deceased). The promise need not be in writing. The parties to an action are by 32 and 33 Vict. c. 68 competent witnesses; the plaintiff cannot, however, recover a verdict without his or her testimony being corroborated by other material evidence. The measure of damages is to a greater extent than in most actions at the discretion of the jury; they may take into consideration the injury to the plaintiff's feelings, especially if the breach of promise be aggravated by seduction. Either party has a right to trial by jury under the rules of the Supreme Court, 1883. The action cannot be tried in a county court, unless by consent, or unless remitted for trial there by the High Court. Unchastity of the plaintiff unknown to the defendant when the promise was made and dissolution of the contract by mutual consent are the principal defences which are usually raised to the action. Bodily infirmity of the defendant is no defence to the action, though it may justify the other party in refusing to marry the person thus affected. Where the betrothed are within prohibited degrees of consanguinity or affinity, there can be no valid promise at all, and so no action for its breach.

In Scotland a promise in the nature of *sponsalia de futuro* not followed by consummation may be resiled from, subject to the liability of the party in fault to an action for the breach, which by 6 Geo. IV. c. 120, s. 28, is a proper cause for trial by jury. If, however, the *sponsalia* be *de præsenti*, and, according to the more probable opinion, if they be *de futuro* followed by consummation, a pre-contract is constituted, giving a right to a decree of declarator of marriage and equivalent to marriage, unless declared void during the lifetime of the parties.

In the United States the law is in general accordance with that of England. The statute law of California and Dakota provides that the unchastity of one party of which the other is ignorant is a good defence, but it is no defence if both participate therein. (J. W†.)

WOOD. See BOTANY, vol. iv. p. 100; BUILDING, FORESTS, STRENGTH OF MATERIALS; also FIR, OAK, PINE, TEAK, &c.

WOOD, ANTHONY À[1] (1632–1695), antiquary, was the fourth son of Thomas Wood (1580–1643), B.C.L. of Oxford, where Anthony was born 17th December 1632. He was sent to New College school in that city in 1641, and at the age of twelve was removed to the free grammar school at Thame, where his studies were interrupted by civil war skirmishes. He was then placed under the tuition of his brother Edward (1627–55), of Trinity College; "while he continued in this condition his mother would alwaies be soliciting him to be an apprentice which he could never endure to heare of" (*Life*, 1848, p. 33). He was entered at Merton College in 1647, and made postmaster. In 1652 "he began to exercise his natural and insatiable genie he had to musick" (*ibid.*, 53), and was examined for the degree of B.A. He engaged a music-master, and obtained permission to use the Bodleian, "which he took to be the happiness of his life." He was admitted M.A. in 1655, and in the following year published a volume of sermons of his late brother Edward. Dugdale's *Warwickshire* came into his hands, and he describes how "his tender affections and insatiable desire of knowledge were ravished and melted downe by the reading of that book. What by musick and rare books that he found in the public library, his life, at this time and after, was a perfect Elysium" (*ibid.*, p. 68). He now began systematically to copy monumental inscriptions and to search for antiquities in the city and neighbourhood. He went through the Christ Church registers, "at this time being resolved to set himself to the study of antiquities." Dr John Wallis, the keeper, allowed him free access to the university registers in 1660; "here he layd the foundation of that book which fourteen years afterwards he published, viz., *Hist. et Antiq. Univ. Oxon.*" He steadily investigated the muniments of all the colleges, and in 1667 made his first journey to London, where he visited Dugdale, who introduced him into the Cottonian library, and Prynne showed him the same civility for the Tower records. On October 22, 1669, he was sent for by the delegates of the press, "that whereas he had taken a great deal of paines in writing the *Hist. and Antiq. of the Universitie of Oxon*, they would for his paines give him an 100 *li.* for his copie, conditionally, that he would suffer the book to be translated into Latine" (*ibid.*, 167). He accepted the offer and set to work to prepare his English MS. for the translators, Richard Peers and Richard Reeve, both appointed by Dr Fell, dean of Christ Church, who undertook the expense of printing. The translation was supervised by Fell, with whom and the translators Wood has endless quarrels about alterations of his text. In 1674 appeared *Historia et Antiquitates Universitatis Oxoniensis*, handsomely printed "e Theatro Sheldoniano," in two folio volumes, the first devoted to the university in general and the second to the colleges. Copies were widely distributed, and university and author received much praise. On the other hand, Bishop Barlow told a correspondent that "not only the Latine but the history itself is in many things ridiculously false" (*Genuine Remains*, 1693, p. 183). In 1678 the university registers which had been in his custody for eighteen years were removed, as it was feared that he would be implicated in the Popish Plot. To relieve himself from suspicion he took the oaths of supremacy and allegiance. During this time he had been gradually completing his great work, which was produced by a London publisher in 1691–92, 2 vols. folio, *Athenæ Oxonienses: an Exact History of all the Writers and Bishops who have had their Education in the University of Oxford from 1500 to 1690, to which are added the Fasti, or Annals for the said time.* On 29th July 1693 he was condemned in the vice-chancellor's court for certain libels against the late earl of Clarendon, fined, banished from the university until he recanted, and the book burnt. The proceedings were printed in a volume of *Miscellanies*

[1] In the *Life* he speaks of himself and his family as Wood and not à Wood, a pedantic return to old usage adopted by himself. A pedigree is given in Bliss's edition, 1848, p. 357.

published by Curll in 1714. Wood was attacked by Bishop Burnet in a *Letter to the Bishop of Lichfield and Coventry*, 1693, 4to, and defended by his nephew Dr Thomas Wood, in a *Vindication of the Historiographer, to which is added the Historiographer's Answer*, 1693, 4to, reproduced in the subsequent editions of the *Athenæ*. The nephew also defended his uncle in *An Appendix to the Life of Bishop Seth Ward*, 1697, 8vo. On 9th October 1695 Wood had an interview with the earl of Clarendon, but was not able to get his fine remitted. After a short illness he died 28th November 1695, in his sixty-third year, and was buried in the ante-chapel of St John Baptist (Merton College), in Oxford, where he superintended the digging of his own grave but a few days before.

He is described as "a very strong lusty man," of uncouth manners and appearance, not so deaf as he pretended, of reserved and temperate habits, not avaricious, and a despiser of honours. He received neither office nor reward from the university which owed so much to his labours. He never married, and led a life of self-denial, entirely devoted to antiquarian research. Bell-ringing and music were his chief relaxations. His literary style is poor, and his taste and judgment are frequently warped by prejudice, but his two great works and unpublished collections form a priceless source of information on Oxford and her worthies. He was always suspected of being a Roman Catholic, and invariably treated Jacobites and Papists better than Dissenters in the *Athenæ*, but he died in communion with the Church of England.

Wood's original manuscript (purchased by the Bodleian in 1846), was first published by John Gutch, as *The History and Antiquities of the Colleges and Halls in the University of Oxford, with a continuation*, 1786–90, 2 vols. 4to, and *The History and Antiquities of the University of Oxford*, 1792–96, 3 vols. 4to, with portrait of Wood. To these should be added *The Antient and Present State of the City of Oxford, chiefly collected by A. à Wood, with additions by Sir J. Peshall*, 1773, 4to. A new edition is in preparation by the Oxford Historical Society. *Modius Salium, a Collection of Pieces of Humour*, chiefly ill-natured personal stories, was published at Oxford in 1751, 12mo. Some letters between Aubrey and Wood were given in the *Gentleman's Magazine* (3d ser., ix., x., xi.). Wood consulted Dr Hudson about getting a third volume of the *Athenæ* printed in Holland, saying, "When this volume comes out I'll make you laugh" (*Reliq. Hearnianæ*, i, 59). This was included in a second edition of the *Athenæ* published by Tonson in 1721, 2 vols. folio, "very much corrected and enlarged, with the addition of above 500 new lives." The third appeared as "a new edition, with additions, and a continuation by Philip Bliss," 1813–20, 4 vols. 4to. The Ecclesiastical History Society proposed to bring out a fourth edition, which stopped at the *Life*, ed. by Bliss, 1848, 8vo (see *Gent. Mag.*, N.S., xxix. 135, 268). Dr Bliss's interleaved copy is in the Bodleian, and Dr Griffiths announced in 1859 that a new edition was contemplated by the Press, and asked for additional matter (see *Notes and Queries*, 2d ser., vii. 514, and 6th ser., vi. 5, 51). Wood bequeathed his library (127 MSS. and 970 printed books) to the Ashmolean Museum, and the keeper, William Huddesford, printed a catalogue of the MSS. in 1761. In 1860 the whole collection was transferred to the Bodleian, where 25 volumes of Wood's MSS. had been since 1690. Many of the original papers from which the *Athenæ* was written, as well as several large volumes of Wood's correspondence and all his diaries, are in the Bodleian.

The chief authority is the *Life* of Wood written by himself, and first published by Hearne in the appendix to T. Caii *Vindiciæ*, 1730; the memoirs after 1672 were compiled by Rawlinson from the original diaries, and printed by Huddesford with the *Lives* of Leland and Hearne, 1772, 2 vols. 8vo. A new edition was issued by Bliss, 1848. See also *Reliquiæ Hearnianæ*, ed. Bliss, 2d ed., 1869, 3 vols. 12mo; Hearne's *Remarks and Collections* (Oxford Hist. Soc., 1885, &c.); Macray's *Annals of the Bodleian Library*, 1868; Nichols's *Literary Anecdotes*, i., iv., v., viii.; Noble's *Biogr. History of England*, i. (H. R. T.)

WOOD, Mrs Henry (1814–1887), novelist, was born on the 17th January 1814. Her maiden name was Ellen Price; her father was a glove manufacturer in Worcester—the original of the cathedral city which, with its church dignitaries and schools, is the scene of so many of her tales. From certain vague memoirs published by her son in the *Argosy*[1] (of which her novels were the mainstay for the last twenty years of her life) it appears that the industrial distress described in *Mildred Arkell* is a reminiscence of the collapse of the glove trade in Worcester, consequent on Huskisson's tariff reforms in 1823, from which her father suffered along with other English glove manufacturers. She married young, it is said, and after her marriage lived for the most part in France, her husband being "at the head of a large shipping and banking firm abroad." She first came before the public in her own name as the author of a temperance tale (*Danesbury House*), which had gained the prize of £100 offered by the Scottish Temperance League. This was in 1860; but it appears from the memoirs already referred to that "for many years" before this she had been a regular contributor of stories anonymously, month after month, to Mr Harrison Ainsworth's magazines, Bentley's *Miscellany*, and Colburn's *New Monthly*. *Danesbury House* was very favourably reviewed, her genuine gifts as a story-teller making themselves apparent in spite of the didactic purpose of the tale; but Mrs Wood's first great success was made in the following year with *East Lynne*, one of the most popular novels of the century. A long review in the *Times*, in which a place was claimed for her in the foremost rank of novelists, was the loudest note in a general chorus of praise, and fairly established her position. The praise of the critics continued throughout the next half-dozen of her novels, which followed one another with great rapidity: *The Channings* and *Mrs Halliburton's Troubles*, in 1862; *Verner's Pride* and *The Shadow of Ashlydyat*, in 1863; *Lord Oakburn's Daughters*, *Oswald Cray*, and *Trevlyn Hold*, in 1864. These works were held to confirm the promise of *East Lynne*, and *The Shadow of Ashlydyat* was pronounced to be (as it is still generally considered) the best of them all. Complaints of sameness,—almost inevitable, considering the rate of production, —of commonplaceness of sentiment and material, and of a certain narrowness and insufficiency in her conceptions of poetical justice first began to be heard in connexion with *Mildred Arkell* (1865), and became louder as the fertile novelist continued to pour forth her stories with inexhaustible fluency. She became owner of the *Argosy* in 1867, and her stories quickly raised it to an enormous circulation. She had a certain triumph over her critics with the *Johnny Ludlow* tales, an imitation of Miss Mitford's *Tales of Our Village*. Mrs Wood's name was not put to them as they appeared in the *Argosy*, and when the first series was collected and published separately in 1874 they excited among reviewers an approach to the enthusiasm with which her first efforts had been welcomed. Undoubtedly Mrs Wood possessed many of the qualities of a first-rate story-teller,—great simplicity of style, unfailing fluency, a lively interest in prominent traits of character, abundant circumstantiality, skill in exciting curiosity and keeping up suspense, and withal a wonderful clearness of method. Amidst her crowd of characters and incidents you are never puzzled or perplexed, and she very rarely lapses into tediousness. If ever she is tedious, it is from repeating herself. Her "criticism of life" is not very broad or very profound, though it is generally for moral edification; she is simply an excellent story-teller out of the ordinary materials of the craft. In private life Mrs Wood seems to have been a most amiable person: her son gives a very lovable picture of her. Her death took place on 10th February 1887, at the age of seventy-three. She was active in her work till the very last, and left several completed stories, short and long, ready for publication.

WOOD-CARVING. In most countries, during the early development of the plastic art, sculpture in wood took a very important position, and was much used for statues on a large scale, as well as for small works decorated with surface carving. On the whole, wood is much more suitable for carving in slight relief than for sculpture in the round, and its special structure, with bundles of long fibres, strong in one direction and weak in

[1] See "Mrs Henry Wood, *In Memoriam*," *Argosy*, vol. xliii., 1887.

another, make it very necessary for the carver to suit his design to the exigencies of the material. Large curves should be avoided, on account of their tendency to split across with the grain, and deep under-cutting is objectionable for the same reason. A tough fibrous substance like wood obviously calls for a very different treatment from that which is suitable to a homogeneous substance like stone or marble. This adaptation of the design to the material is very conspicuous in the wood-carving of the finest kinds, such as the Scandinavian doorways of the 9th to the 12th centuries, the Perpendicular roofs and screens of England in the 15th century, and the richly carved panelling of Moslem countries throughout the Middle Ages.

Some woods, such as pear, lime, and more especially box, are comparatively free from any distinct grain, and may be carved almost like marble, but these woods are only to be had in small pieces, and from their want of fibre are structurally weak, and are therefore only available for decorative purposes on a small scale. It is this absence of grain which makes boxwood the material selected for engraving on wood, a form of wood-carving in which the artist needs to be as little as possible hampered by the structure of his material. In ancient times cedar wood was specially used for decorative carving, and in the East various perfumed woods, such as that of the sandal-tree, have always been favourites with the carver. In Europe the oak, the chestnut,[1] the fir, and the walnut have been chiefly used, and for sculpture in the round or high relief the sycamore and the plane-tree, as well as the oak.

One objection to using wood for life-sized or colossal sculpture is that large blocks are very liable to crack and split from end to end, owing to the fact that the parts near the surface dry and shrink more rapidly than the core. For this reason the mediæval carvers usually hollowed out their wooden statues from the back, so as to equalize the shrinkage and prevent splitting. In all cases wood for carving should be very well seasoned, and it is especially necessary to get rid of the natural sap, which causes rot if it is not dried out. It is useful to soak newly cut timber in running water, so that the sap may be washed away; it is then comparatively easy to dry out the water which has soaked into the pores of the wood and taken the place of the sap.

Egyptian.—One of the most remarkable examples of ancient Egyptian art, dating probably from nearly 4000 years B.C., is a life-sized portrait statue of a stout elderly man, now in the Boulak museum. This is carved out of a solid block of sycamore wood, except that the right arm is worked separately and attached by a mortice and tenon; the eyes are formed by inlaid bits of shell and crystal, and the whole is a most wonderful piece of life-like realism (see fig. 1). Although dating from so remote a period, this statue bears witness to an amount of technical skill and artistic knowledge which shows that long centuries of experience and artistic development must have preceded its production,—a period of which we have no remains, this statue being one of the earliest works of art which even Egypt has preserved for us. In the same museum are also some very remarkable wooden panels from the tomb of Hosi, about four feet high, carved in low relief with standing figures of men and hieroglyphs. These large slabs of wood formed part of the wall lining of the tomb. The reliefs are executed with the utmost spirit and extreme delicacy of treatment, and are highly decorative in style; they show, moreover, a keen sense of the special treatment suitable to the material in which they are carved. These also date from nearly 4000 B.C. After the early dynasties in Egypt wood does not seem to have been used for sculpture on a large scale, although it was very commonly employed for mummy cases or coffins, one end carved with a human face and the rest almost plain, except for its elaborate painted ornaments in gold and colours, applied on a thin coat of stucco laid evenly over the wood. A large number of smaller examples of Egyptian wood-carving exist in various museums, such as furniture, boxes, implements for the toilet, and the like, frequently decorated with slight surface reliefs of animals or plants, and graceful patterns formed of the lotus or papyrus flower treated with great decorative skill.

Fig. 1.—Life-sized Portrait Statue from a Tomb of the Fourth Dynasty.

Greek.—Owing to the perishable nature of the material, almost the only ancient examples of wood-carving which have survived to our time are those from the tombs of Egypt.[2] The many important pieces of wooden sculpture which once existed in Greece and other ancient countries are only known to us by the descriptions of Pausanias and various classical writers. It is probable that the earliest examples of the plastic art among the Hellenic race were the rude wooden images of the gods (ξόανα), of which many examples were preserved down to late historic times. The art of sculpture, and especially sculpture in wood, is probably older than that of painting, as it requires less artistic knowledge to rudely fashion a log of wood into a rough body with rounded head, two holes for the eyes and slits for the mouth and nose, than to conceive mentally and set down on a plane surface any attempt even at the rudest outline drawing,—a process which requires a distinct act of abstraction and some notion of treating the subject in a conventionally symbolic way. Real things have of course no enclosing line, and the representation of an object in outline conveys little or no idea to the mind of a man who is yet in a very early stage of culture. The Palladium, or sacred figure of Pallas, which was guarded by the vestal virgins in Rome, and which was fabled to have been brought by Æneas from the burning Troy, was one of these wooden ξόανα (see Vesta). A wooden figure of the Armed Aphrodite at Cythera is mentioned by Pausanias, iii. 23, 1. Of the same kind was the wooden statue of Hermes in the shrine of Athene Polias on the Acropolis of Athens, said to have been the offering of Cecrops (Pausan., i. 27, 1); and the figure of Athene Polias itself was an ancient wooden ξόανον. Another very ancient statue, carved out of cedar wood, was the statue of Apollo in his temple, dedicated 428 B.C., in the Campus Martius of Rome; this statue was called Apollo

[1] In many cases it is almost impossible to distinguish between chestnut and oak, especially in the mediæval roofs of England.

[2] Acacia and sycamore wood were chiefly used for the larger wood sculpture of Egypt. A wooden coffin, covered with fine Greek paintings of *c.* 300 B.C., was discovered in a tomb at Panticapæum (Kertch), and is now in the museum at St Petersburg.

Sosianus, from Sosius the præfect of Syria, who presented it to the temple (Pliny, *H. N.*, xiii. 5 and xxxvi. 4). Pausanias (ii. 24) mentions another early wooden statue at Argos,—that of Zeus Larissæus, which was remarkable for having three eyes. A very elaborate example of cedar-wood carving enriched with gold and ivory is described by Pausanias (v. 17 to 19). This was a coffer dedicated at Olympia by the children of Cypselus, tyrant of Corinth in the 7th century B.C. It was decorated with bands in relief, with scenes from the lives of various gods and heroes. A cedar box, with two carved dogs attached to it, was found at Mycenæ by Dr Schliemann, and is now in the museum at Athens. During the most flourishing period of Greek art wood was sometimes used for important plastic purposes, as, for example, the colossal statue of Athene at Platæa, carved by Phidias. The figure was of gilt or plated wood, with the exception of the nude parts,—the face, hands, and feet,—which were of Pentelic marble.

Roman.—Of the wood-carving of the Roman period almost no important examples now exist; but the carved panels of the main doors of S. Sabina on the Aventine Hill are very interesting specimens of wooden relief-sculpture of early Christian times, dating, as the costumes show, from the 5th century. The doors are made up of a large number of small square panels, each minutely carved with a scene from the Old or New Testament; the whole feeling of these reliefs is thoroughly classical, though of course in a very debased form.

Mediæval.—The most remarkable examples of early mediæval wood-carving are the doorways of wooden churches of Scandinavia and Denmark, dating from the 9th to the 13th centuries. These are framed with great planks or slabs of pine wood, the whole surface of which is covered with rich and intricate patterns of interlacing scroll-work, mixed with figures of dragons and serpents, designed with extraordinary wealth of invention, and of the highest decorative value. The relief is very low, except where occasionally a monster's head projects from the general level; and yet the utmost vigour of effect is gained by the grand sweeping curves of the leading lines. These are masterpieces of wood-carving, designed and executed with the most perfect sense of the necessities of the material. Fig. 2 shows part of the architrave of a door from Aal church, Norway, dating from the 12th century. Unhappily almost the last of these interesting wooden churches have been destroyed in recent years, and merely the wrecks of their grand wooden sculpture have been occasionally preserved in some museum; some very valuable casts of these are in the South Kensington Museum.

English.—For various ecclesiastical purposes a large amount of important sculpture in wood was produced in Britain throughout the Middle Ages. At the time of the Reformation every church had its rood-screen, surmounted by a large crucifix between two standing figures of St Mary and St John. These were of wood, except perhaps in some of the richest cathedral or abbey churches, which occasionally had the rood made of silver. A very large number of churches also had retables over the various altars, with reliefs carved in wood and decorated with gold and colours. Many examples of this class still exist in Germany and Spain, but almost all the English examples perished under the iconoclasm of the Reformation.[1]

Another important class of wood-carving was that of large recumbent effigies from tombs, of which a good many examples still exist. One of the earliest is that of Robert, duke of Normandy, in Gloucester cathedral, illustrated in SCULPTURE, fig. 5 (vol. xxi. p. 558). It is a work of the 12th century, but was broken to pieces, and is now much restored. Like most wooden sculpture in England, it is carved out of oak. The finest example of English wood sculpture is a life-sized effigy in the south choir aisle of Abergavenny church, that of the young knight George de Cantelupe (d. 1273). The face is a portrait of very high plastic merit, and the whole treatment of the figure, with the graceful drapery of its tunic, and its carefully carved armour, is very remarkable as an example of the very high level of excellence that was reached by the English contemporaries of Niccola Pisano. The usual treatment of these wooden figures was to cover the whole surface with a thin coating of *gesso* or fine stucco, in which various details or ornaments were modelled or stamped in relief, and then richly decorated with gold and colour. A similar treatment was adopted for all the wooden sculpture of the mediæval period throughout Europe.

FIG. 2.—Part of the Carved Architrave of a Door from Aal Church.

The church at Abergavenny, already referred to, also contains part of what once must have been a very large and magnificent example of wooden sculpture. This is a colossal recumbent figure of Jesse, and formed the lower part of what was called a "Jesse tree." Out of the recumbent figure grew a great tree, on the branches of which were figures of the illustrious descendants of Jesse's line. Merely the stump of this tree now remains, springing from the side of Jesse, but when complete the whole tree must have reached high up towards the roof, with its network of branches forming a sort of screen behind the high altar—very rich and magnificent in effect, when the whole was perfect with its brilliant coloured decoration, and the stained glass of the large east window seen dimly through the open branches of the tree. The existing figure of Jesse, which is 10 feet long, is cut out of a solid block of oak; a figure of an angel at the head is worked out of the same piece of wood.[2]

Another very important application of wood-carving was for the decoration of the church stalls, screens, and

[1] Only three English examples of the figure of Christ on the rood are now known to exist. One of these was recently found built up in the rood-staircase of a small church in Wales. It is a work of the 14th century, carved roughly, but with much spirit.

[2] See a valuable monograph on the church of Abergavenny by Octavius Morgan, published by the Cambrian Archæological Society. For an account of other wooden effigies, see *Arch. Jour.*, xi. p. 149; and on existing rood figures, a paper by J. T. Micklethwaite in the *Proc. Soc. Ant.* for 1886, p. 127.

roofs, which in the 15th century in England reached so high a pitch of splendour. The development of architectural wood-carving was much slower than that of sculpture in stone. During the "Early English" period wood-work was rather heavy in style and coarse in detail; in "Decorated" times wood-work of much beauty and richness was produced, but forms more suitable to stone were still used, and it was not till the later "Perpendicular" period in the 15th century that the wood-carvers of England learnt to perfectly adapt their designs to the nature of their material. Very beautiful roofs, for example, were produced in the 14th century, such as that at Adderbury,[1] but the principals are frequently constructed with large arched braces, richly moulded and very graceful in effect but constructionally weak, and very wasteful of the material. Enormous balks of oak were required to enable the large curves of the braces to be cut out of the solid. The builders of the 15th century corrected these defects, and designed their sumptuous screens, stall-canopies, and open roofs with straight lines for the leading framework,—only using curves on a smaller scale, and in places where much strain does not fall upon them. Nothing can exceed the beauty, in its own class, of the 15th and early 16th century wood-work in England; the many fine examples that still exist give us some notion of the wealth of the country in this branch of art at a time when every church was obliged by canon law to have its rood-screen, and almost always also possessed carved oak stalls and many other fittings, such as statues and retables, in the same material.[2]

The rich oak work of England was no exception to the universal application of coloured decoration, and nearly every screen, roof, or choir-stall was covered with minute painting in gold and colours. The modern notion that oak should be left unpainted was quite unknown to our mediæval forefathers; and they, as a rule, preferred even a simple coating of white, red, or other colour to the natural tint of the oak, which would have looked very dull and heavy in tone when surrounded by the polychromatic brilliance of the floor, the walls, and the windows. In most cases, however, the wood-work was not left with its uniform ground of paint; delicate and graceful patterns of diapers or sprigs of foliage were added on to all the main lines of the work, and covered the chief members of all the mouldings, in exactly the same way as was done with the sculpture in stone. Many of the Norfolk screens still have much of their painted ornament in good preservation[3]; and additional richness was gained by the groundwork of delicately moulded stucco with which the whole surface of the wood was covered before the colouring and gilding were applied. Modern "restorers" have in most cases scraped off all that remained of this brilliant decoration, and frequently no signs are now visible of this universal system of decoration. The very rich and graceful "watching gallery"[4] in the abbey church of St Albans is now bare of any colouring, though it was once a very brilliant example of polychromatic decoration.

Great richness of carving is lavished on the church roofs especially of Norfolk and Suffolk. Carved bosses cover the intersections of the moulded timbers, some with bunches of delicate foliage, others carved into figures of angels with outspread wings. Other statuettes of angels often cover the ends of the hammer-beams, and the whole cornice frequently has running foliage inserted in a hollow of the moulding. All this wood-carving is usually of very high artistic merit, and combines delicacy of detail with strength of decorative effect in a way that has never been surpassed by the mediæval artists of any country of the Continent. These magnificent roofs, which are peculiar to England, and even to certain districts such as East Anglia, are among the most perfect artistic productions of the Middle Ages.[5]

Norfolk, Suffolk, Devonshire, and other counties are still rich in elaborate chancel screens, carved with delicate foliage, especially in the hollows of the cornice, and light open cresting or "brattishing" along the top. The tracery which fills in the upper part of these screens is of wonderful beauty, and executed with the most minute finish and delicate moulding. The ends of the 15th-century stalls were often richly decorated with carving, and are crowned with finials or "poppy-heads" of the most elaborate and spirited design. The underside of the "misericords"[6] of the monastic stalls were specially selected for minute enrichment, in spite of their very inconspicuous position. The utmost wealth of fancy and minuteness of workmanship is often lavished upon these, and their reliefs are frequently works of art of a very high order. In some cases the carver took his design from contemporary engravings by some distinguished German or Flemish artist, such as Schongauer or Albert Dürer. One of these in the chapel of Henry VII. at Westminster, representing "The Golden Age," is a work of wonderful beauty and delicacy of touch. Genre and satirical subjects are often selected: the regulars are made fun of in the churches of the secular clergy, and the vices of the secular priests are satirized on the stalls of the monastic churches. This satire is often carried to the verge of indecency, especially in the scenes frequently selected by clerical carvers to set forth the miseries of the married state.

In England during the 16th and 17th centuries little wood-carving of much merit was produced; the oak panelling, furniture, and other fittings of the Elizabethan and Jacobean periods were largely enriched with surface reliefs, coarse in execution, but often decorative in effect, and chiefly remarkable for their showy appearance produced with the minimum of labour,[7] a great contrast to the rich detail and exquisite finish of the pre-Reformation work. Towards the end of the 17th century a very realistic style of wood-carving came into use, in which great technical skill was displayed but little real artistic feeling. Grinling Gibbons (1648–1721) and his pupils produced the most elaborate works of this class, such as wreaths, scrolls, and friezes carved in high relief, or in the round, with fruit and flowers, modelled and carved with wonderful imitative skill, but weak in true decorative effect. These clever groups of foliage and fruit were carved in pear or lime wood, and fastened on to the surface of wall-panels, mantelpieces, and other wooden fittings. The stalls and screens in St Paul's Cathedral are some of Gibbons's best works, and a great deal of his realistic carving still exists at Oxford in Trinity College, at Trinity College, Cambridge, at Chatsworth, at Petworth, and in many of the great country houses of that time. Since then wood-carving has not taken an important position among the lesser arts of the country.

[1] The roof of Westminster Hall, of the early part of the 15th century, is in size and richness of detail the most magnificent open timber roof in the world; it has curved braces of very wide span, cut out of enormous balks of oak or chestnut.

[2] It should be noted that in Old English the word "picture" was often used for a statue or a relief,—partly no doubt from the fact that all sculpture was decorated with painting.

[3] See Talbot Bury, *Ecclesiastical Wood-Work*, London, 1847.

[4] So called because from it a guardian used constantly to watch, day and night, the great gold shrine of St Alban, with its treasure of precious offerings all round it.

[5] A number of fine examples are well illustrated by Brandon, *Open Timber Roofs*, London, 1856.

[6] Often wrongly called "misereres."

[7] See Sanders, *Woodwork of the 16th and 17th Centuries*, London, 1883; and Small, *Scottish Wood-Work of the 16th and 17th Centuries*, Edinburgh, 1878.

Italian.—During the mediæval period wood was often used by the greatest sculptors of Italy, especially for crucifixes and statues of saints for ecclesiastical purposes. Fig. 3 shows a magnificent example of the school of Nino Pisano, dating from about the middle of the 14th century. It is a colossal figure of the Angel of the Annunciation, said to have once belonged to Pisa cathedral, and now one of the chief treasures of the South Kensington Museum. It is very remarkable for the delicate beauty of the face, and for the sculpturesque simplicity of the folds of the drapery. The original wings were probably much larger than the present ones, which are restorations.

Fig. 3.—Colossal Statue of an Angel in the South Kensington Museum.

Many fine roods or crucifixes of life size still exist in the churches of Italy. One attributed to Donatello is preserved at Florence, in the church of S. Croce; another by Brunelleschi still exists. Nothing like the magnificent oak open roofs and choir screens of England were made in Italy. The latter were usually of marble or of metal, and the roofs were of the plain king-post construction, usually concealed by vaulted or panelled ceilings. Towards the end of the 15th century, and especially in the first half of the 16th, wood-carving of the most elaborate and magnificent sort was largely used to decorate church stalls, wall-panelling, doors, and the like. A very important school of this branch of art was founded by Raphael, whose designs were used or adapted by a large number of very skilful wood-carvers. The shutters of "Raphael's Stanze" in the Vatican and the choir stalls of the church of S. Pietro de' Cassinesi at Perugia are among the most beautiful examples of this class of carving.[1] The work is in slight relief, carved in walnut with the graceful arabesque patterns which Raphael developed out of the newly discovered remains of ancient Roman wall-painting from the palace of Nero and other places.[2] Fig. 4 shows a panel with carving of this school, which is always remarkable for its high finish and delicate cameo-like execution.

Fig. 4.—Example of a Carved Walnut-Wood Panel; school of Raphael.

Spanish.—Spain during the 15th and 16th centuries was specially remarkable for the production of large and elaborate retables, carved with statues and reliefs, very like those of contemporary Germany. Alonso Cano and other sculptors frequently used wood for large statuary, which was painted in a very realistic way with the most startling life-like effect.

Danish.—Denmark also possessed a school of able wood-carvers, who imitated the great altarpieces of Germany. A very large and well-carved example still exists in the metropolitan cathedral of Röskilde.

French.—In France during the mediæval period wooden sculpture was produced which was very similar in character to that of England, and was decorated with similar colouring. Many of the French cathedral and abbey choir stalls are works of the utmost magnificence. Those at Amiens are specially remarkable. Fig. 5 shows an example of the delicate tracery work of the 15th century. In the 16th century many wood-carvers in France imitated the rich and delicate work of the Raphaelesque school in Italy, and much wood-work of great refinement was produced, very different from the coarsely effective work of Elizabethan and Jacobean England.[3] In the 18th century large sums were spent on elaborate wooden panelling for rooms, the walls being divided into series of spaces with rococo framing, formed by applied scroll-work, made up of many fantastic and incongruous bits of curved mouldings, which were usually gilt. The general effect was very inartistic, and was unredeemed by any beauty of detail. The intermediate spaces were sometimes filled with tapestry or paintings designed by Watteau, Boucher, or other popular artists.

Fig. 5.—Traceried Panel in Oak; French work of the 15th century.

German.—In Germany, during the 15th century, wood was used for the most important sculpturesque purposes, such as large triptychs or retables made up of many reliefs, with sacred subjects, and statues of saints,—the whole framed and canopied with rich Gothic "tabernacle work." See SCULPTURE, vol. xxi. p. 565. Fig. 6 shows a fine example of one of these retables, said to be the work of Veit Stoss, now in the South Kensington Museum. As in England the whole of the wood was covered with fine *gesso*, and then richly gilt and painted with vivid colours. Nothing could exceed the decorative effect of these great retables, rich with minute sculpture and carved foliage, and shining with gold and brilliant colours, some of which were mixed with a transparent varnish medium, and applied over a ground of gold leaf, so that the metallic lustre shone through the transparent pigments over it. Stall ends and panels were enriched with carving of the highest order of merit; life-sized human figures are often introduced at the ends of the book-rests, and large surfaces

[1] Bergamo, *Ornati del Coro di S. Pietro dei Cassinesi*, Rome, 1845.
[2] See Finochietti, *Scultura in Legno*, Florence, 1873.
[3] See Roumier, *Sculpture en Bois . . . . l'Église des Pères Jacobins*, Paris, n.d. (17th cent.); and Pascal, *Boiseries sculptées de Notre-Dame de Paris*, 1855.

are covered with grand scroll-work, with the most graceful lines and extreme decorative vigour. Fig. 7 shows a fine example of the treatment of a large panel in the front of the stalls at Ulm cathedral, carved in unusually high relief

Fig. 6.—The Centre of a Wooden Triptych, attributed to Veit Stoss, now in the South Kensington Museum.

with bold conventional foliage, full of spirit and vigorous beauty. These splendid stalls were executed in 1468 by Jörg Syrlin. During this period the wood-carving of Germany occupied a foremost position in the world, and

Fig. 7.—Carved Panel from the Front of the Stalls in Ulm Cathedral.

in many places, such as Nuremberg and parts of Bavaria, great technical skill has survived down to the present time.

Switzerland and Tyrol have also been for long celebrated for delicate wood-carving on a small scale. The cleverly executed figures of peasants and of animals, especially the chamois, are widely popular, and their production gives occupation to a large class of able artisans, who, however, rarely rise to the level of original artists, though they attain a fairly high average of excellence.

Mohammedan.—Nothing can exceed the skill with which the Moslem wood-carvers of Persia, Syria, Egypt, and Spain designed and executed the richest panelling and other decorations for wall-lining, ceilings, pulpits, and all kinds of fittings and furniture. The mosques and private houses of Cairo, Damascus, and other Oriental cities are full of the most elaborate and minutely delicate wood-work. A favourite style of ornament was to cover the surface with very intricate interlacing patterns, formed by delicately moulded ribs; the various geometrical spaces between the ribs were then filled in with small pieces of wood with carved foliage in slight relief. The use of different woods, such as ebony or box, inlaid so as to emphasize the design, combined with the ingenious richness of the patterns, give this class of wood-work an almost unrivalled splendour of effect. Carved ivory is also often used for the filling in of the flat spaces. Fig. 8 shows a fine example of this sort of work, dating from the 14th century,—part of a wall-lining in the Alhambra; special

Fig. 8.—Example of Moslem Wood-Panelling, with inlay of different woods.

skill is shown by the way in which the Moslem carver has adapted his design to his material—avoiding curved lines, and utilizing woods which he could only get in small pieces. Another very elaborate class of Oriental wood-work is the rich ceilings and domes built up of small pieces of wood into the ingeniously intricate "stalactite" patterns, which were then covered with stucco and decorated with rich painting in gold and colours.

In the early mediæval period very elaborate wood-work for screens and other fittings was produced for the Coptic churches of Egypt by native Christian workmen; some of these had small panels carved in a hard dark wood, with saints and Bible subjects in low relief, very Byzantine in style. The British Museum possesses some fine examples of this carved work from a church in Old Cairo. These early wood fittings are now rapidly disappearing.[1]

Asiatic.—In India wood-carving of the most magnificent kind has been constantly produced for many centuries. The ancient Hindu temples were decorated with doors, ceilings, and other fittings, carved in sandal and other

[1] See Butler, *Coptic Churches of Egypt*, Oxford, 1884.

woods, with patterns of extreme richness and minute elaboration. The doors of the temple at Somnauth, on the north-west coast of India, were especially famed for their magnificence, and were very highly valued as sacred relics. In 1024 they were carried off to Ghuznee by the Moslem conqueror Sultan Mahmoud, and are now lying in the fort at Agra. The gates which still exist are very fine specimens of ancient wood-carving, but they are probably only copies of the original very early doors.[1]

In many parts of India wood-carving of the most beautiful kind is largely used for architectural purposes, especially for the enrichment of the wooden framework of houses, and for forming delicate open lattices for windows. In the main, however, the native carvers of India excel rather in richness of effect and minute delicacy of workmanship than in general gracefulness of line and purity of design. In these respects the wood-work of Moslem carvers in India is very far superior to that of the Hindus.

In China and Japan the wood-carvers are absolutely unrivalled in technical skill; grotesque and imitative work of the most wonderful perfection is produced, and some of the wood-carvings of these countries are really beautiful as works of art, especially when the carver copies the lotus lily or other aquatic plants. In many cases, however, as in the other arts of Japan and China, extreme ugliness of design is combined with the most perfect execution and exquisite finish, and the carvers have very little notion of the really decorative treatment of surface reliefs. The extensive use of wood or bamboo for architectural purposes creates a wide field for the wood-carver, whose very limited sense of true beauty is to some extent made up for by his wealth of grotesque fancy and extreme deftness of hand, which are the main characteristics of the workmen of China and Japan in all branches of art.

Wood-Carving of Savage Races.—Many savage races, such as the Maoris and Polynesians, are very skilful in the decorative treatment of wood in slight relief. Intricate geometrical designs of much beauty and suitability to the material are used to decorate canoes, paddles, and the beams of huts. Great richness of effect is often produced by the smallest possible amount of cutting into the surface of the wood. The wooden architecture of the Maoris is sometimes decorated in the most lavish way. The main uprights of the walls are carved into grotesque semi-human monsters, enriched with painting and inlay of iridescent shell, which show much imaginative power. Other beams are carved with series of spirals, bearing much resemblance to the very early sculptured ornaments of Mycenæ, Tiryns, and other Hellenic cities,—one of the many examples which show that very similar stages of artistic development are passed through by men of the most different races and age. In many cases the freshness of invention and freedom of hand shown in the carved ornament of savage races give a more really artistic value to their work than is usually found in the modern laboured and mechanical carving of highly civilized people.

In modern Europe decorative wood-carving shares the general low level of the lesser arts. The commercial spirit of the age, and the general desire to produce the utmost display with the smallest cost and labour, have reduced the art of wood-carving to a very low state.

See Williams, *History of the Art of Sculpture in Wood*, London, 1835; for practical information see Bemrose and Jewitt, *Manual of Wood-Carving*, London, 1862; Rogers, *Art of Wood-Carving*, London, 1867; and Lacombe, *Manuel de la Sculpture sur Bois*, Paris, 1868. (J. H. M.)

WOODCOCK (A.-S., *Wude-cocc*, *Wudu-coc*, and *Wudu-snite*), a bird as much extolled for the table, on account of its flavour, as by the sportsman, who, from its relative scarcity in regard to other kinds of winged game,[2] the uncertainty of its occurrence, as well as the suddenness of its appearance and the irregularity of its flight, thinks himself lucky when he has laid one low. Yet, under favourable conditions, large bags of Woodcocks are made in many parts of Great Britain, and still larger in Ireland, though the numbers are trifling compared with those that have fallen to the gun in various parts of the European Continent, and especially in Albania and Epirus. In England of old time Woodcocks were taken in nets and springes, and, though the former method of capture seems to have been disused for many years, the latter was practised in some places until nearly the middle of the present century (*cf.* Knox, *Game-birds and Wild Fowl*, pp. 148–151) or even later.

The Woodcock is the *Scolopax rusticula*[3] of ornithology, and is well enough known to need no minute description. Its long bill, short legs, and large eyes—suggestive of its nocturnal or crepuscular habits—have over and over again been the subject of remark, while its mottled plumage of black, chestnut- and umber-brown, ashy-grey, buff, and shining white—the last being confined to the tip of the lower side of the tail-quills, but the rest intermixed for the most part in beautiful combination—could not be adequately described within the present allotted space. Setting aside the many extreme aberrations from the normal colouring which examples of this species occasionally present (and some of them are extremely curious, not to say beautiful), there is much variation to be almost constantly observed in the plumage of individuals, in some of which the richer tints prevail while others exhibit a greyer coloration. This variation is often, but not always accompanied by a variation in size or at least in weight.[4] The paler birds are generally the larger, but the difference, whether in bulk or tint, cannot be attributed to age, sex, season, or, so far as can be ascertained, to locality. It is, notwithstanding, a very common belief among sportsmen that there are two "species" of Woodcock, and many persons of experience will have it that, beside the differences just named, the "little red Woodcock" invariably flies more sharply than the other. However, a sluggish behaviour is not really associated with colour, though it may possibly be correlated with weight—for it is quite conceivable that a fat bird will rise more slowly, when flushed, than one which is in poor condition. It may suffice here to say that ornithologists, some of whom have taken a vast amount of trouble about the matter, are practically unanimous in declaring against the existence of two "species" or even "races," and moreover in agreeing that the sex of the bird cannot be determined from its plumage, though there are a few who believe that the young of the year can be discriminated from the adults by having the outer web of the first quill-feather in the wing marked with angular notches of a light colour, while the old birds have no trace of this "vandyke" ornament. Careful dissections, weighings, and measurings seem to shew that the male varies most in size; on an average he is slightly heavier than the female, yet some of the lightest birds have proved to be cocks.[5]

Though there are probably few if any counties in the United Kingdom in which the Woodcock does not almost yearly breed, especially since a "close time" has been afforded by the legislature for the protection of the species, there can be no doubt that by far the greater number of those shot in the British Islands have come from abroad,—mostly, it is presumed, from Scandinavia. These arrive on the east coast in autumn—generally about the middle of October—often in an exhausted and impoverished state. Most of them seem to cross the sea by night, and at that season it is a brutal practice for men to sally forth and slaughter the helpless and almost starving wanderers, who are often found seeking refuge in any shelter that may present itself. If unmolested, however, they are soon rested, pass inland, and, as would appear, in a marvellously short time recover their condition. Their future destination seems to be greatly influenced by the state of the weather. If cold or frost stop their supply of food on the eastern side of Great Britain

[1] See art. ELLENBOROUGH for an account of the recent history of these celebrated doors. They are illustrated in *Archæologia*, xxx. p. 174.

[2] In the legal sense of the word, however, Woodcocks are not "game," though Acts of Parliament require a "game licence" from those who would shoot them.

[3] By Linnæus, and many others after him, misspelt *rusticola*. The correct form of Pliny and the older writers seems to have been first restored in 1816 by Oken (*Zoologie*, ii. p. 589).

[4] The difference in weight is very great, though this seems to have been exaggerated by some writers. A friend who has had much experience tells us that the heaviest bird he ever knew weighed 16¼ oz., and the lightest 9 oz. and a fraction.

[5] *Cf.* Dr Hoffmann's monograph *Die Waldschnepfe*, ed. 2, p. 35, published at Stuttgart in 1887.

they press onward and, letting alone Ireland, into which the immigrant stream is pretty constant, often crowd into the extreme south-west, as Devonshire and Cornwall, and to the Isles of Scilly, while not a few betake themselves to the unknown ocean, finding there doubtless a watery grave, though instances are on record of examples having successfully crossed the Atlantic and reaching Newfoundland, New Jersey, and Virginia. To return, however, to the Woodcocks which breed in Britain, whose habits have been much more frequently observed since the folly and cruelty of killing them in spring has been recognized, and it may be hoped abandoned. Pairing takes place very early in February and the eggs are laid often before the middle of March. These are four in number, of a yellowish cream-colour blotched and spotted with reddish-brown, and seldom take the pyriform shape so common among those of Limicoline birds. The nest—always made on the ground amid trees or underwood, and usually near water or at least in a damp locality—is at first little more than a slight hollow in the soil, but as incubation proceeds dead leaves are collected around its margin until a considerable mass is accumulated. During this season the male Woodcock performs at twilight flights of a remarkable kind (*cf.* BIRDS, vol. iii. p. 771), repeating evening after evening (and it is believed at dawn also) precisely the same course, which generally describes a triangle, the sides of which may be a quarter of a mile or more long. On these occasions the bird's appearance on the wing is quite unlike that which it presents when hurriedly flying after being flushed, and though its speed is great the beats of the wings are steady and slow. At intervals an extraordinary sound is produced, whether from the throat of the bird, as is commonly averred, or from the plumage is uncertain. To the present writer the sound seems to defy description, though some hearers have tried to syllable it. This characteristic flight is in some parts of England called "roading," and the track taken by the bird a "cock-road."[1] In England in former times advantage was taken of this habit to catch the simple performer in nets called "cock-shutts," which were hung between trees across the open glades or rides of a wood, and in many parts of the Continent it still is, or was till very lately, the disgraceful habit of persons calling themselves sportsmen to lie in wait and shoot the bird as he indulges in his measured love-flight. A still more interesting matter in relation to the breeding of Woodcocks is the fact, asserted by several ancient writers, but for long doubted if not disbelieved, and yet finally established on good evidence, that the old birds transport their newly-hatched offspring, presumably to places where food is more accessible. The young are clasped between the thighs of the parent, whose legs hang down during the operation, while the bill is to some extent, possibly only at starting, brought into operation to assist in adjusting the load if not in bearing it through the air.[2]

The Woodcock inhabits suitable localities across the northern part of the Old World, from Ireland to Japan, migrating southward towards autumn. As a species it is said to be resident in the Azores and other Atlantic Islands; but it is not known to penetrate very far into Africa during the winter, though in many parts of India it is abundant during the cold weather, and reaches even Ceylon and Tenasserim. The popular belief that Woodcocks live "by suction" is perhaps hardly yet exploded; but those who have observed them in confinement know that they have an almost insatiable appetite for earthworms, which the birds seek by probing soft ground with their highly sensitive and flexible bill.[3] This fact seems to have been first placed on record by Bowles,[4] who noticed it in the royal aviary at San Ildefonso in Spain, and it has been corroborated by other observers, and especially by Montagu, who discovered that bread and milk made an excellent substitute for their ordinary food.

The eastern part of North America possesses a Woodcock, much smaller than though generally (and especially in habits) similar to that of the Old continent. It is the *Scolopax minor* of most authors; but, chiefly on account of its having the outer three primaries remarkably attenuated, it has been placed in a separate genus, *Philohela*. In Java is found a distinct and curiously coloured species, described and figured many years ago by Horsfield (*Trans. Linn. Society*, xiii. p. 191, and *Zoolog. Researches*, pl.) as *S. saturata*. To this Mr Seebohm[5] has lately referred the *S. rosenbergi* of Schlegel (*Nederl. Tijds. v. d. Dierkunde*, iv. p. 54) from New Guinea; but, as the culpable destruction of the type-specimen of the former (during its transfer from the old museum of the East India Company to the British Museum) has made a comparison of the two impossible, the identification can scarcely be said to be free from doubt. Another species is *S. rochusseni* from the Moluccas, but this last, though resembling the other Woodcocks in most of the characters which distinguish them from the SNIPES (*q.v.*), has like the latter the lower part of the tibia bare of feathers. (A. N.)

WOOD-ENGRAVING. See ENGRAVING.

WOODPECKER, a bird that pecks or picks holes in wood, and from this habit is commonly reputed to have its name; but since it is in some parts of England also known as "Woodspeight" (erroneously written "Woodspite")—the latter syllable being cognate with the German *Specht* and the French *Épeiche*, to say nothing possibly of the Latin *Picus*—the vulgar explanation seems open to doubt.[6] More than 300 species of Woodpecker have been described, and they have been very variously grouped by systematists; but all admit that they form a very natural Family *Picidæ*, which according to the view taken in this series of articles belongs to the Order *Picariæ*. Prof. Huxley (*Proc. Zool. Society*, 1867, p. 467) would separate the Woodpeckers still more under the name of *Celeomorphæ*, and Prof. Parker (*Trans. R. Microsc. Society*, 1872, p. 219) would raise them still higher as *Saurognathæ*. They are generally of bright particoloured plumage, in which black, white, brown, olive, green, yellow, orange, or scarlet—the last commonly visible on some part of the head—mingled in varying proportions, and most often strongly contrasted with one another, appear; while the less conspicuous markings take the form of bars, spangles, tear-drops, arrow-heads, or scales. Woodpeckers inhabit most parts of the world, with the exception of Madagascar and the Australian Region, save Celebes and Flores; but it may be worth stating that no member of the group is known to have occurred in Egypt.

Of the three British species, the Green Woodpecker, *Gecinus* or *Picus viridis*, though almost unknown in Scotland or Ireland, is the commonest, frequenting wooded districts, and more often heard than seen, its laughing cry (whence the name "Yaffil" or "Yaffle," by which it is in many parts known), and undulating flight afford equally good means of recognition, even when it is not near enough for its colours to be discerned. About the size of a Jay, its scarlet crown and bright yellow rump, added to its prevailing grass-green plumage, make it a sightly bird, and hence it often suffers at the hands of those who wish to keep its stuffed skin as an ornament. Besides the scarlet crown, the cock bird has a patch of the same colour running backward from the base of

[1] The etymology and consequently the correct spelling of these expressions seem to be very uncertain. Some would derive the word from the French *rôder*, to rove or wander, but others connect it with the Scandinavian *rode*, an open space in a wood (see *Notes and Queries*, ser. 5, ix. p. 214, and ser. 6, viii. pp. 523, 524). Looking to the regular routine followed by the bird, the natural supposition would be that it is simply an application of the English word *road*; but of course natural suppositions are often wrong, and they always require the support of evidence before acceptance.

[2] *Cf.* J. E. Harting, *Zoologist*, 1879, pp. 433–440, and Mr. Wolf's excellent illustration. Sir R. Payne-Gallwey, in the "Badminton Library" (*Shooting*, ii. p. 118, note), states that he himself has witnessed the performance.

[3] The pair of muscles said by Loche (*Expl. Scient. de l'Algérie*, ii. p. 293) to exist in the maxilla, and presumably to direct the movement of the bill, do not seem to have as yet been precisely described.

[4] *Introduccion a la Historia Natural y a la Geografia fisica de España*, pp. 454. 455 (Madrid, 1775).

[5] *Geographical Distribution of the Family* Charadriidæ, p. 506, pl. This work will be found of much interest to those who would speculate on the causes which have led to the distribution of existing Limicoline birds.

[6] The number of English names, ancient and modern, by which these birds are known is very great, and even a bare list of them could not be here given. The Anglo-Saxon was *Higera* or *Higere*, and to this may plausibly be traced "Hickwall," now-a-days used in some parts of the country, and the older "Hickway," corrupted first into "Highhaw," and, after its original meaning was lost, into "Hewhole," which in North America has been still further corrupted into "Highhole" and more recently into "High-holder." Another set of names includes "Whetile" and "Woodwale," which, different as they look, have a common derivation perceptible in the intermediate form "Witwale." The Anglo-Saxon *Wodake* (=Woodhack) is another name apparently identical in meaning with that commonly applied to Woodpecker.

the lower mandible, a patch that in the hen is black.[1] Woodpeckers in general are very shy birds, and to observe the habits of the species is not easy. Its ways, however, are well worth watching, since the ease with which it mounts, almost always spirally, the vertical trunks and oblique arms of trees as it searches the interstices of the bark for its food, flying off when it reaches the smaller or upper branches—either to return to the base of the same tree and renew its course on a fresh line, or to begin upon another tree near by—and the care it shews in its close examination, will repay a patient observer. The nest almost always consists of a hole, chiselled by the birds' strong beak, impelled by very powerful muscles, in the upright trunk or arm of a tree, the opening being quite circular, and continued as a horizontal passage that reaches to the core, whence it is pierced downward for nearly a foot. There a chamber is hollowed out in which the eggs, often to the number of six, white, translucent, and glossy, are laid with no bedding but a few chips that may have not been thrown out.[2] The young are not only hatched entirely naked, but seem to become fledged without any of the downy growth common to most birds. Their first plumage is dull in colour, and much marked beneath with bars, crescents, and arrowheads.

Of generally similar habits are the two other Woodpeckers which inhabit Britain—the Pied or Greater Spotted, and the Barred or Lesser Spotted Woodpecker—*Dendrocopus major* and *D. minor*—each of great beauty, from the contrasted white, blue-black, and scarlet that enter into its plumage. Both of these birds have an extraordinary habit of causing by quickly-repeated blows of their beak on a branch, or even on a small bough, a vibrating noise, louder than that of a watchman's rattle, and enough to excite the attention of the most incurious. Though the Pied Woodpecker is a resident in Britain, its numbers receive a considerable accession nearly every autumn.

The three species just mentioned are the only Woodpeckers that inhabit Britain, though several others are mistakenly recorded as occurring in the country—and especially the Great Black Woodpecker, the *Picus martius* of Linnæus, which must be regarded as the type of that genus.[3] This fine species considerably exceeds the Green Woodpecker in size, and except for its red cap is wholly black. It is chiefly an inhabitant of the fir forests of the Old World, from Lapland to Galicia, and across Siberia to Japan.[4] In North America this species is replaced by *Picus pileatus*, there generally known as the Logcock, an equally fine species, but variegated with white; and further to the southward occur two that are finer still, *P. principalis*, the Ivory-billed Woodpecker, and *P. imperialis*. The *Picinæ* indeed flourish in the New World, nearly one-half of the described species being American, but out of the large number that inhabit Canada and the United States there is here room to mention only a few.

First of these is the Californian Woodpecker, *Melanerpes formicivorus*, which has been said to display an amount of providence beyond almost any other bird in the number of acorns which it collects and, as shewn in the accompanying figure, fixes tightly in holes which it purposely makes in the bark of trees, and thus "a large pine forty or fifty feet high will present the appearance of being closely studded with brass nails, the heads only being visible." An extraordinary thing is that this is not done to furnish food in winter, for the species migrates, and after journeying a thousand miles or more only returns in spring to the forests where its supplies are laid up. It has been asserted that the acorns thus stored are always those which contain a maggot, and, being fitted into the sockets prepared for them cup-end foremost, the enclosed insects are unable to escape, as they otherwise would, and are thus ready for consumption by the birds on their return from the south. But this statement has again been contradicted, and moreover it is alleged that these Woodpeckers follow their instinct so blindly that "they do not distinguish between an acorn and a pebble," so that they "fill up the holes they have drilled with so much labor, not only with acorns but occasionally with stones" (*cf.* Baird, Brewer, and Ridgway, *North American Birds*, ii. pp. 569–571).

Californian Woodpecker (*Melanerpes formicivorus*).

The next North-American form deserving notice is the genus *Colaptes*, represented in the north and east by *C. auratus*, the Golden-winged Woodpecker or Flicker, in most parts of the country a familiar bird, but in the south and west replaced by the allied *C. mexicanus*, easily distinguishable among other characteristics by having the shafts of its quills red instead of yellow. It is curious, however, that, in the valleys of the upper Missouri and Yellowstone rivers, where the range of the two kinds overlaps, birds are found presenting an extraordinary mixture of the otherwise distinctive features of each, and these birds have been described as hybrids. It would be premature to say whether this view be correct or not, and in regard to it Dr Coues has well remarked (*Birds of the Northwest*, p. 294), "that it is only in virtue of missing links we are enabled to predicate species in any case," thereby indicating the possibility (not entertained for the first time) that these supposed hybrids are examples of the more generalized form of *Colaptes*, which becomes differentiated further to the north and south into the specialized *C. auratus* and *C. mexicanus*. Thus the subject is one highly interesting to the student of evolution.[5]

Some other Woodpeckers deserve especial notice,—among them the *Colaptes* or *Soroplex campestris*, which inhabits the treeless plains of Paraguay and La Plata, and had become fully adapted to a territorial mode of life, as long ago observed by Azara and Darwin, but yet has readily returned, since the opportunity has been afforded, to the arboreal habits of its relatives, as remarked by Mr Hudson (*Proc. Zool. Society*, 1870, pp. 158–160). A similar provision of habit and haunt obtains in a South-African Woodpecker, *Geocolaptes olivaceus*, which lives almost entirely on the ground or rocks, and picks a hole for its nest in the bank of a stream (*Zoologist*, 1882, p. 208).

The *Picidæ* offer a fruitful ground for taxonomical speculation. At least three Subfamilies are admitted by all modern systematists—the Woodpeckers proper, *Picinæ*; the Piculets, *Picumninæ*, which are small birds wanting the stiff rectrices of the former; and the WRYNECKS (*q.v.*). Sundevall (*Conspectus Avium Picinarum*, Stockholm, 1866) gave up the attempt to establish genera in the first of these, though he separated the 254 species which he admitted into 4 Series and 30 Tribes, thereby differing from the method of Malherbe, who, in his great monograph of the Family,[6] recognized 277 species and 19 genera, as well as from Prof. Cabanis, who (*Mus. Heineanum*, iv. part 2) strove to establish 48 genera in about three-fourths of the whole Family, and from G. R. Gray, who in his *Hand List* recognized 4 Subfamilies, 19 genera, 74 subgenera, and 312 species. It seems obvious that until

[1] A patch of conspicuous colour, generally red, on this part is characteristic of very many Woodpeckers, and careless writers often call it "mystacial," or some more barbarously "moustachial." Considering that moustaches spring from above the mouth, and have nothing to do with the mandible or lower jaw, no term could be more misleading.

[2] It often happens that, just as the Woodpecker's labours are over, a pair of STARLINGS (*q.v.*) will take possession of the newly-bored hole, and, by conveying into it some nesting-furniture, render it unfit for the rightful tenants, who thereby suffer ejectment, and have to begin all their trouble again. It has been stated of this and other Woodpeckers that the chips made in cutting the hole are carefully removed by the birds to guard against their leading to the discovery of the nest. The present writer has had ample opportunity of observing the contrary as regards this species and, to some extent, the Pied Woodpecker next to be mentioned. Indeed there is no surer way of finding the nest of the Green Woodpecker than by scanning the ground in the presumed locality, for the tree which holds the nest is always recognizable by the chips scattered at its foot.

[3] The expression *Picus martius* was by old writers used in a very general sense for all birds that climbed trees, not only Woodpeckers, but for the NUTHATCH and TREE-CREEPER (*qq.v.*) as well. The adjective *martius* loses all its significance if it be removed from *Picus*, as some even respectable authorities have separated it.

[4] The persistency with which many writers on British birds have for years included this species among them is a marvellous instance of the durability of error, for not a case of its asserted occurrence in this country is on record that will bear strict investigation, and the origin of the mistake has been more than once shewn.

[5] When more is known it will very likely be found that a somewhat similar state of things exists in the Palæarctic area in regard to the various local races of, or "species" allied to, *Dendrocopus major* and *D. minor* respectively. At present the only cases that seem to be strictly parallel are those furnished by the genera *Coracias* (*cf.* ROLLER) and *Euplocamus* (*cf.* PHEASANT).

[6] *Monographie des Picidées*, 4 vols. folio, Metz, 1859–62.

the aid of the anatomist is invoked no satisfactory arrangement can be supplied, and it is not certain that even then will the desired end be reached, for Macgillivray, who furnished Audubon with elaborate descriptions of parts of the structure of several North-American forms, found considerable differences to exist between species which can hardly be but nearly allied. Some of the most striking of these differences often lie in the form and development of the hyoid bones, and of the muscles which work the extensile tongue. Unhappily the subject does not seem to have been pursued by any other investigator; but it may be mentioned that some limited researches on the *pterylosis*, conducted by Kessler (*Bull. Soc. Nat. Moscou*, xvi. p. 285), in addition to those of Nitzsch, indicate that as being also a promising line of inquiry, though one that has scarcely been attempted by any other workers.[1] (A. N.)

WOODSTOCK, an ancient corporate market-town of Oxfordshire, England, is situated on a stream formerly called the Ennis and now the Glyme, which separates Old and New Woodstock, about 8 miles north-west of Oxford. The church of St Mary Magdalene, in New Woodstock, is of Norman date, but has been greatly altered by restoration, and now has Decorated chancel with Perpendicular additions, clerestoried nave, Decorated north aisle and Early English south aisle retaining a portion of the Norman doorway, Perpendicular west porch, and Perpendicular west tower. The church contains many interesting monuments. The town-hall, erected in 1766 after the designs of Sir William Chambers, includes a market-place and the fire brigade station, with public hall and council-chamber above. Almshouses were erected in 1798 by Caroline, duchess of Marlborough, and endowed with £3500, which has been increased by bequest at different periods. The town is dependent chiefly on agriculture, but the manufacture of leather gloves has been carried on from an early period. By the Municipal Corporations Act, 1882, the borough (area about 30 acres), formerly governed by a charter of Charles II., was placed under a corporation. The population of the parliamentary borough (area 20,804 acres), which had been extended in 1832 and ceased to be separately represented in 1885, was 7033 in 1881.

The old manor house of Woodstock, which is supposed to have been built upon the site of a Roman villa, was at an early period a royal residence. Here Alfred the Great is said to have resided while translating Boetius. At a witenagemot held at Woodstock by King Ethelred a code of laws was published for the government of the Anglo-Saxon kingdom. Henry I. made Woodstock a favourite residence, and formed a zoological garden there. Woodstock was the scene of Henry II.'s courtship of Rosamond Clifford, and his frequent visits to the place led to the building of the nucleus of the town of New Woodstock. A first assize was held at Woodstock in 1184. It sent representatives to parliament from 1301–2 till 1885. It was incorporated by Henry VI. in 1453, and the charter was confirmed and extended by successive monarchs, that granted by Charles II. remaining the governing charter till 1882. Queen Elizabeth was a prisoner at Woodstock from May 1554 till May 1555, and after her accession to the throne visited it in 1566 and again in 1575. In 1576 she made the town a staple of wool and yarn. Woodstock was visited by James I. and by Arabella Stuart. During the Civil War it was the scene of frequent military operations, and after a siege it surrendered to the parliament 20th April 1646. After the battle of Blenheim the manor of Woodstock was by Act 3 and 4 of Queen Anne, chap. 4, bestowed in perpetuity on John duke of Marlborough. Blenheim palace, built by the duke from the designs of Sir John Vanbrugh, was completed in 1715. In 1723 the old manor house was destroyed and the site levelled.

See Marshall's *Early History of Woodstock Manor*, 1873.

WOODSTOCK, a town, port of entry, and the capital of Oxford county, province of Ontario, Canada, is situated on the river Thames and Cedar Creek, and on the Great Western Railway, 80 miles south-west of Toronto. The trade is of growing importance. There is good water-power, and the town possesses several corn-mills and a woollen factory. Its healthy situation and the beauty of the neighbouring scenery attract a number of summer visitors. The population in 1881 was 5373.

WOOD-WORK. See BUILDING, vol. iv. pp. 476–500.

WOOL AND WOOLLEN MANUFACTURES. Wool is a modified form of hair, distinguished by its slender, soft, and wavy or curly structure, and by the highly imbricated or serrated surface of its filaments. The numerous varieties of the sheep are the most characteristic, as they are also by far the most important, producers of wool; but the sheep is by no means the only animal which yields wool employed for industrial purposes. The alpaca and other allied fibres obtained from the alpaca and its congeners in South America (see ALPACA, vol. i. p. 597, and LLAMA, vol. xiv. p. 738), the mohair yielded by the Angora goat (MOHAIR, vol. xvi. p. 544), and the soft woolly hair of the camel are all wools of much industrial importance, while the most costly wool in the world is that yielded by the Cashmere goat of the Himalayan Mountains. At what point indeed it can be said that an animal fibre ceases to be hair and becomes wool it is impossible to determine, because in every characteristic the one class by imperceptible gradations merges into the other, so that a continuous chain can be formed from the finest and softest merino to the rigid bristles of the wild boar.

Early History.

Next to cotton, wool is the most important of all textile fibres used by mankind. From the ease with which it may be made into thread, and owing to the comfort derived from clothing of woollen texture, it naturally would be the textile first used by mankind for clothing. The testimony of all ancient records goes to prove the high antiquity of woollen textures and the early importance of the sheep. The different kinds of wool and the cloth made from them in antiquity are described by Pliny (*H. N.*, viii. 73, 74, 190 *sq.*).

Wool in Britain.

Among the arts of civilized life which the British Isles owe to the Romans not the least important was the spinning and weaving of wool. The sheep certainly was a domestic animal in England long before the period of the Roman occupation; and it is most probable that such use was made of sheep skins and of wool as was common among uncivilized races. But the Romans established a woollen factory whence the occupying army was supplied with clothing, and the value of the manufacture was soon recognized by the Britons, of whom Tacitus remarks, "Inde etiam habitus nostri honor et frequens toga" (*Agric.*, c. 21). The product of the Winchester looms, and the wool whence it was made, soon established a reputation abroad, it being remarked that "the wool of Britain is often spun so fine that it is in a manner comparable to the spider's thread." The reputation which English wool at this early period established was maintained throughout mediæval times; and the fibre was in great demand in the Low Countries and other Continental centres where skill in manufacture was highly developed. There are many allusions to woollen manufactures in England in early times; but altogether the native industry could not rival the products of the Continent, although the troubles in various industrial centres, from time to time, caused skilled workers in wool to seek an asylum in England. In the time of William the Conqueror Flemish weavers settled under the protection of the queen at Carlisle, but subsequently they were removed to Pembrokeshire. At various periods in the reigns of succeeding monarchs further immigrations of skilled Flemish weavers occurred, and they were planted at different places throughout the

[1] Mr Hargitt, author of many papers in *The Ibis* on birds of this Family, has undertaken a catalogue of the specimens belonging to it contained in the British Museum.

country. The cloth fair in the church yard of the priory of St Bartholomew was instituted by Henry II.; guilds of weavers were established; and the exclusive privilege of exporting woollen cloth was granted to the city of London. Edward III. made special efforts to encourage woollen industries according to the manner in which it was supposed in mediæval times that trade could be best encouraged. He brought weavers, dyers, and fullers from Flanders; he himself wore Flemish cloth; and to stimulate native industry he prohibited under pain of life and limb the exportation of English wool. Previous to the time of Edward III. English wool had been in larger demand on the Continent, where it had a reputation exceeded only by the wool of Spain, which for ages provided Europe with the best material for cloth-making. The customs duties levied on the export of wool were an important source of the royal revenue, and Edward III.'s attempt to stop the trade appears to have been an honest though misguided attempt to foster native manufactures. His prohibitory law was, however, found to be unworkable, and the utmost that both he and his successors were able to effect was to hamper the export trade by vexatious restrictions and to encourage much "running" or smuggling of wool. Thus while Edward III. limited the right of exporting to merchant strangers, we find that Edward IV. decreed that no alien should export wool and that denizens should export it only to Calais. Legislation of this kind prevailed till the reign of Elizabeth, when the free exportation of English wool was permitted; and Smith, in his *Memoirs of Wool*, points out that it was during this reign that the manufacture made the most rapid progress in the country. In 1660 the absolute prohibition of the export of wool was again decreed, and it was not till 1825 that this prohibitory law was finally repealed. The prohibition appears to have been based on the mistaken notion that England possessed a monopoly of the finest kinds of wool, and that by withholding it from foreign competitors the home manufacturers would command the markets of the world. The results of the prohibitory law were exceedingly detrimental: the production of wool far exceeded the consumption; the price of the raw material fell; wool "running" or smuggling became an organized traffic; and the whole industry became disarranged. Extraordinary expedients were resorted to for stimulating the demand for woollen manufactures, among which was an Act passed in the reign of Charles II. decreeing that all dead bodies should be buried in woollen shrouds,—an enactment which remained in the Statute Book, if not in force, for a period of 120 years. On the opening up of the colonies, every effort was made to encourage the use of English cloth, and the manufacture was discouraged and even prohibited in Ireland.

It was not without reason that the attention of monarchs and legislators was so frequently directed to the woollen industries. Wool was indeed "the flower and strength and revenue and blood of England," and till the development of the cotton trade, towards the end of the 18th century, the woollen industries were, beyond comparison, the most important sources of wealth in the country. What the actual value of the trade at any early period was it is impossible to ascertain, and the estimates of wool production and the value of the manufactures in the 17th and 18th centuries vary widely. Towards the close of the 17th century the wool produced in England was estimated to be worth £2,000,000 yearly, furnishing £8,000,000 worth of manufactured goods, of which there was exported about £2,000,000 in value. In 1700 the official value of woollen goods exported was about £3,000,000, and in the third quarter of the century the exports had increased in value by about £500,000 only. In 1774 Dr Campbell (*Political Survey of Great Britain*) estimated the number of sheep in England at 10,000,000 or 12,000,000, the value of the wool produced yearly at £3,000,000, the manufactured products at £12,000,000, and the exports at £3,000,000 to £4,000,000. He also reckoned that the industry then gave employment to 1,000,000 persons. These figures, in the light of the dimensions of present day industries, may appear small, but they bore a predominant relationship to the other great sources of employment and trade of the period. In 1800 the native crop of wool was estimated to amount to 96,000,000 ℔; and, import duty not being imposed till 1802, the quantity brought from abroad was 8,600,000 ℔, 6,000,000 ℔ of which came from Spain. In 1825 the importation of colonial wool became free, the duty leviable having been for several previous years as high as 6d. per ℔, and in 1844 the duty was finally remitted on foreign wool also.

Wool in America.

Sheep were introduced at Jamestown in Virginia in 1609, and in 1633 the animals were first brought to Boston. Ten years later a fulling mill was erected at Rowley, Mass., "by Mr Rowley's people, who were the first that set upon making cloth in this western world." The factory woollen industry was, however, not established till the close of the 18th century, and it is recorded that the first carding machine put in operation in the United States was constructed in 1794 under the supervision of John and Arthur Schofield.

The sheep

The prevailing colour of sheep's wool is white, but it must not be forgotten that there are races with black, brown, fawn, yellow, and grey shades of wool. For manufacturing purposes generally white wool is, of course, most valuable, but for the homespuns, which in earlier times absorbed the bulk of wool, natural colours were in many cases desirable and used with good effect. In domestic spinning, knitting, and weaving, natural colours are still largely taken advantage of, as in the cases of rough yarns, Shetland knitted shawls, Highland tweeds, &c.

Characteristics of wool.

As has already been indicated, the distinction between wool and hair lies chiefly in the great fineness, softness, and waved delicacy of woollen fibre, combined with a highly serrated surface. These peculiarities are precisely the characters which give wool its distinctive value as a textile fibre, and most distinctive of all is the serrated structure which specially belongs to wool and gives it the important property of felting, upon which many of its applications depend. The serrations of wool and the wavy structure it assumes are closely connected, those wools which have the greatest number of serrations being also most finely waved in structure. The appearance presented by wool under the microscope, as compared with the aspect of certain other animal fibres, is shown in fig. 1 (compare vol. ix. p. 133). The imbrications all lie in one direction,—from the root, their growing point, upwards to the apex of the fibre,—so that, while a lock of wool drawn between the finger and thumb from the root end outwards slips quite smoothly, if drawn in the contrary direction from point to root it offers a distinct resistance, and the fibre feels harsh and rough. Under the influence of moisture and pressure, tangled masses of wool thoroughly interlock and mat together, by the mutual clutching of the serrations of the fibres, and it is thus that the shrinking and thickening of woollen textures under washing is accounted for, and the capacity of cloth for felting or fulling is due to this condition of the fibre. The serrations are most numerous, acute, pointed, and distinct in fine merino wools, as many as 2800 per inch being counted in specimens of the finest Saxony wools. In the Leicester wool of England, on the other hand, which is a long bright staple, the serratures are not only much fewer in number, counting about 1800, but they are also less pronounced in character, so that the fibre presents a smoother, less waved character. In some inferior wools the serrations are not so many as 500 per inch. A similar difference may be noted in the fineness of the fibres. Saxony lambs' wool has a diameter of from $\frac{1}{1500}$ to $\frac{1}{1800}$ inch, whilst coarse Algerian wools may rise to a maximum diameter of about $\frac{1}{275}$ inch.

Other distinguishing qualities of good wool consist in uniformity and strength of fibre with freedom from tender or weak portions in its length, a condition which not unfrequently arises from ill health in the sheep. In ill-bred wool there may also be found intermingled "kemps" or dead hairs,—straight coarse shining fibres which show conspicuously among the wool, and become even more prominent in the manufactured and dyed goods. Wool also possesses a softness of touch and an elasticity both in the raw and manufactured condition which distinguish it from all other fibres. In length of staple it varies very much, attaining in combing wools to a length of as much as 15 to 20 inches. As a rule the fine felting wools are short in staple, these constituting carding or woollen yarn wools; and the longer are lustrous and comparatively straight, and thus most suitable for combing or worsted wools. The latter wools approach mohair and alpaca in their characters, and they are prepared and spun by the same class of machinery.

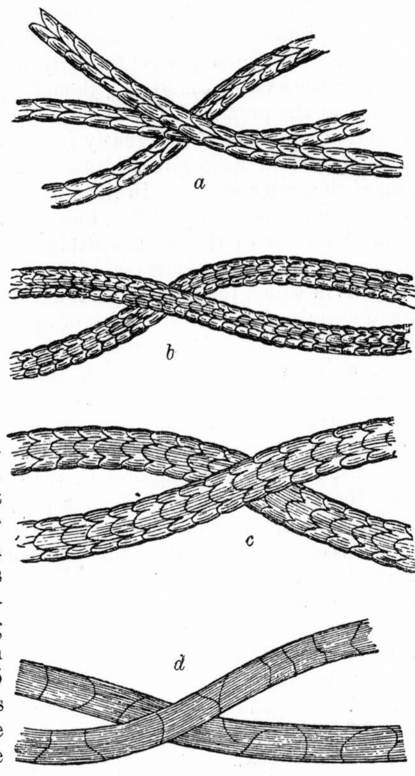

FIG. 1.—Microscopic Structure of Wool. *a*, merino; *b*, Southdown: *c*, Leicester: *d*, mohair.

The bulk of the wool of commerce comes into the market in the form of fleece wool, the product of a single year's growth, cut from the body of the living animal. The first and finest clip, called lambs' wool, may be taken from the young sheep at about the age of eight months. When the animal is not shorn till it attains the age of twelve or fourteen months the wool is known as hogg or hogget, and it, like lambs' wool, is fine and tapers into long thin ends. All subsequently cut fleeces are known as wether wool, and possess relatively somewhat less value than the first clip. Fleece wool as it comes into the market is either "in the grease," that is, unwashed, and with all the dirt which gathers to the surface of the greasy wool present; or it is received as "washed" wool, the washing being done as a preliminary to the sheep-shearing. Skin wool is that which is obtained from sheep which either die or are killed. Such wool is always of inferior value and much impregnated with lime from the steeping pits in the tan-yards in which the skins are first treated to soften and swell the skin for facilitating the easy separation of the wool from it.

The wool market is supplied from almost every quarter of the globe, and the qualities and varieties of the article are exceedingly numerous. The range of woollen and worsted manufactures is also very wide, and the raw material suitable for one section of the trade is not at all fitted to supply other sections. Much more than is the case in any other textile industry we have in the woollen trades practically a series of separate and distinct industries, each with its own appropriate class of raw materials. The main distinctions are—(1) carding wools, in which felting properties are desirable; (2) combing wools, requiring length of staple and brightness of fibre, for hard-spun non-felting worsteds; and (3) carpet and knitting wools, in which long and strong if somewhat coarse staple are the essential qualities. Breeding, climate, and food are the main factors in developing and rearing special races of sheep in which the qualities essential for producing the raw materials of any of these sections of industry are secured.

Merino wool. For centuries the finer wools used for cloth-making throughout Europe were obtained from Spain, which was the home of the famous merino breed developed from races of sheep originally introduced into the Peninsula by the Romans. Till early in the present century the superiority of Spanish merinos remained unchallenged, but the Peninsular War and its attendant evils produced a depreciation of quality concurrently with the introduction of Saxon and Silesian wools, which suddenly supplanted the product of Spain, and hold the first place down to the present day. The Spanish merino sheep was introduced into Saxony by the elector in 1765, and by judicious crossing with the best native race developed the famous electoral breed. Merinos were carried to Hungary in 1775, and to France in 1776, and in 1786 Daubenton brought them to Rambouillet, whence a famous race developed. In 1802 the first merinos known to have left pure descendants were taken to the United States, and in 1809–10 an importation (4000) of merino sheep was made. The introduction of merino blood has also largely modified certain of the breeds of English sheep, and from them, crossed with the English breeds, Southdowns and Leicesters, have sprung the vast flocks of sheep in the various Australasian colonies, which now bid fair to supply the whole world with wools of the merino class, and of the very highest quality.

Colonial wool. Of colonial wools, which are now by a long way the most important supplied to the British market, the best qualities come from Port Phillip, Sydney, and Adelaide, the first of these being excelled in quality as a cloth-making wool by the merinos of Saxony and Silesia alone. New Zealand also yields a very large annual crop of wool of high quality, and the wool of Tasmania is generally of fine colour, sound and uniform in staple. The Cape of Good Hope is the source of a large supply of wool, much of which, however, is unequal in strength and somewhat kempy in character. A great proportion of the wool which comes from South America is seriously deteriorated by burrs, and it is of a character which fits it for the worsted manufacture alone.

British wool. The wools grown in the United Kingdom may be separated into three classes—(1) short or carding wool; (2) long or combing wool; and (3) blanket, carpet, and knitting wool. Of short wools Southdown may be taken as the type and best example. It is a staple of excellent quality, milling well, and suitable either for the woollen or worsted trade. The long wools of greatest importance are obtained from the Lincoln and Leicester sheep. These breeds yield a long fleece of remarkable lustre, and it was the possession of this class of wool which gave England its high reputation in former times as a wool-producing country. A similar quality of wool is also obtained from the East Riding Yorkshire breed of sheep. Cheviot wool approaches the Leicester class in some qualities, but is destitute of the latter's peculiar lustre, and is shorter in staple, though strong in fibre, with good milling qualities, which render it valuable for the tweed manufacture. Intermediate between the long and short there are several British breeds, which have been established either by crosses or local conditions and treatment, the most important of these being found in Shropshire, Staffordshire, and Norfolk. The carpet wools are yielded by sheep of the type of the Blackface of the mountainous regions of Scotland, from which is obtained a fleece of long staple but somewhat unequal qualities. Much of the Highland wool is "laid," that is, impregnated with tar, from the practice of the stock-masters of smearing the animals with a mixture of tar and fat immediately after shearing, with a view of protecting them from the rigours of the climate. Of wools of a special character there may be noted Welsh wool, which possesses properties fitting it pre-eminently for the making of the famed Welsh flannels, and Shetland wool, which being very fine and soft in its nature is almost entirely worked up into delicate yarns for knitting the well-known Shetland shawls and other knitted work.

The weight of a fleece of wool of the various breeds of sheep ranges from under 2 ℔ in the case of the small Shetland breeds up to 8 or 9 ℔ for the large merinos and other heavy races, and in exceptional cases a heavy ram's fleece may reach so much as 15 ℔; but, taken all over, sheep may be reckoned to yield on an average 5 ℔ of wool in a year.

Sheep washing.

Where there is abundance of water and other conveniences it is the practice to wash or half-wash sheep previous to shearing, and such wool comes into the market as washed or half-washed fleece. The surface of a fleece has usually a thick coating of dirt adhering to it, and in the cases of merino breeds the fleece surface is firmly caked together into large solid masses, from the adhesion of dirt to the wool constantly moist with the exudation from the skin of the greasy yolk or "suint," so that in an unwashed fleece nearly 30 per cent. of weight may represent dirt, and about 40 per cent. the greasy suint which lubricates the wool, while the pure wool is not more than one-third part of the whole. The yolk forms a protective covering to the sheep, rendering the fleece impervious to moisture, and while left in the wool also preserves it soft, pliant, and silky to touch. It forms a kind of natural soap, consisting principally of potash salts with animal oil, almost entirely soluble in cold water. The following analyses of German merino wool—the variety in which suint is most largely developed—illustrate the difference which may result in the composition of the fibre from the simple washing of the fleece on the sheep's back:—

	Unwashed Merino.		Washed Merino.	
Mineral matter	6·3	16·8	0·94	1·3
Suint and fatty matter	44·3	44·7	21·00	40·0
Pure wool	38·8	28·5	72·00	56·0
Moisture	11·4	7·0	6·06	2·7

Wool, however, which is merely washed in the rough-and-ready manner described below still retains great and variable quantities of suint, &c. Where running streams exist, the sheep are penned by the side of the water, and taken one by one and held in the stream while they are washed, one man holding and the other washing. The operation is objectionable in many ways, as it pollutes the stream, and it dissipates no mean amount of potash salts, valuable for manure or for other chemical purposes. Sheep washing appliances are now largely employed, the arrangement consisting of a pen into which the sheep are driven and subjected to a strong spray of water either hot or cold, which soaks the fleece and softens the dirt. This done, they are caused to swim along a tank which narrows towards the exit, and just as they pass out of the pen they are caught and subjected to a strong douche of pure water. After a few days the wool of a washed sheep is sufficiently dry for shearing or clipping, which is thereupon done.

Sheep shearing.

A skilful shepherd will clip the fleece from a sheep in one unbroken continuous sheet, retaining the form and relative positions of the mass almost as if the creature had been skinned. In this unbroken condition each fleece is rolled up by itself, which greatly facilitates the sorting or stapling which all wool undergoes for the separation of the several qualities which make up the fleece.

Wool stapling.

Sorting or stapling was formerly a distinct industry, and to some extent it is so still, though frequently the work is done in the premises of the spinners. Carding wools are separated and classed differently from combing wools, and in dealing with fleeces from different races the classification of the sorter varies. In the woollen trade short-staple wool is separated into qualities, known, in descending series from the finest to the most worthless, as picklock, prime, choice, super, head, seconds, abb, and breech, and the proportions in which the higher and lower qualities are present are determined by the qualities of the fleece or the race yielding the wool. In the worsted trade the classification goes, also in descending series, from fine, blue, neat, brown, breech, downright, seconds, to abb. The last three are short and not commonly used in the worsted trade. The greater proportion of good English long wool will be classified as blue, neat, and brown; it is only in exceptional cases that more than from 5 to 8 per cent. is "fine" on the one hand, or of lower quality than breech on the other Generally speaking, the best portion of a fleece is from the shoulders and side of the animal (1 in fig. 2). The wool from 2 is irregular in growth, and often filled with burrs, &c.; from the loin 3 it is shorter of staple and coarser, characters which become increasingly pronounced as we approach the tail and hind quarter 4. The belly wool 5 is short, worn, and dirty, as is also the front of the throat 6, while on the head and shins 7 the product is short, stiff, and straight, more like hair than wool.

Fig. 2.—Qualities of Fleece.

The sorter works at a table or frame covered with wire netting through which dust and dirt fall as he handles the wool. Fleeces which have been hard packed in bales, especially if unwashed, go into dense hard masses, which must be heated till the softening of the yolk and the swelling of the fibres make them pliable and easily opened up. When the fleece is spread out the stapler first divides it into two equal sides; then he picks away all straws, large burrs, and tarry fragments which are visible; and then with marvellous precision and certainty he picks out his separate qualities, throwing each lot into its allotted receptacle. Sorting is very far removed from being a mere mechanical process of selecting and separating the wool from certain regions of the fleece, because in each individual fleece qualities and proportions differ, and it is only by long experience that a stapler is enabled, almost as it were by instinct, rightly to divide up his lots, so as to produce even qualities of raw material.

Scouring.

The washing which a fleece receives on the live sheep

is not sufficient for the ordinary purposes of the manufacturer. The scouring process is thus the first link in the long chain of manufacturing processes through which wool passes. On the careful and complete manner in which scouring is effected much depends. The qualities of the fibre may be seriously injured by injudicious treatment, while, if the wool is imperfectly cleansed, it will take on dye colours unevenly, and all the subsequent manufacturing operations will be more or less unsatisfactory. The water used should be soft and pure, both to save soap and still more because the insoluble lime soap formed in dissolving soap in hard water is deposited on the woollen fibres and becomes so entangled that its removal is a matter of extreme difficulty. Wool washed with hard water is always harsh to the touch, and takes on dye colours but unevenly, owing to the interference of unremoved lime soap. In former times stale urine was a favourite medium in which to scour wool; but that is now disused, and a specially prepared potash soap is the detergent principally relied on. Excess of alkali has to be guarded against, since uncombined caustic acts energetically on the wool fibre, and is indeed a solvent of it. On this account a soap solution of too great strength leaves the wool harsh and brittle, and the same detrimental result arises when the soapy solution is applied too hot.

In former days, when the method of hand-scouring prevailed, the wool to be washed was placed with hot soapsud in a large scouring "bowl" or vat, and two men with long poles kept stirring it gently about till the detergent loosened and separated the dirt and dissolved the grease. The wool was then lifted out and drained, after which it was rinsed in a current of clean water to remove the "scour," and then dried. These operations are now performed by mechanical agencies; and, to save soap, it is the practice to first steep the wool in steepers,—tubs having a perforated false bottom in which steam is blown through the wool steeped in pure water. The process removes much mechanically mixed dirt, and softens the other impurities, expanding the fibres themselves, and thus rendering the scouring operation easier and more expeditious. In machine scouring the object aimed at is to bring all the wool equally under the influence of the soapy solution, and to prevent it from matting into lumps in its progress through the washing bowls. Usually the wool passes through two sets of bowls, the soap solution being stronger in the first set. The wool is fed into one extremity of the bowl, which is an oblong vat, by an endless apron from which it passes to an immersed plate which sinks it into the hot soapy solution, where the whole is thoroughly soaked. It is then carried to the opposite end of the bowl, either by a series of forks or rakes with reciprocating motion, or by sets of iron prongs fixed at a uniform distance on a frame to which reciprocating action is communicated by eccentric mounting. These carry the wool forward by gentle progression, so as not to ball it, till at the upper end it is caught and squeezed between rollers to wring out part of the water from the fibres, and then passed on for further drying.

Drying.

The more gently and uniformly the drying can be effected the better is the result attained, and over-drying of wool has to be specially guarded against. By some manufacturers the wool from the squeezing rollers is whizzed in a hydro-extractor, which drives out so much of the moisture that the further drying is easily effected. The commonest way, however, of drying is to spread the wool as uniformly as possible over a framework of wire netting, under which are a range of steam-heated pipes, the sides being enclosed in a framing of wood. A fan blast blows air over these hot pipes, and the heated air passes up and is forced through the layer of wool which rests on the netting. Unless the wool is spread with great evenness it gets unequally dried, and at points where the hot air escapes freely it may be much over-dried. A more rapid and uniform result is obtained by the use of Petrie's wool drier, which consists of a close chamber divided into five horizontal compartments, the floors of which consist of alternate fixed and movable bars. Under the chamber are a tubular heating apparatus and a fan by which a powerful current of heated air is blown up the side of the chamber, and through all the shelves or compartments successively, passing in the path over which the wool slowly travels. The wool is entered by continuous feed at one side of the chamber; the strength of the blast carries it up and deposits it on the upper shelf, and by the action of the movable bars, which are worked by cranks, it is carried forward to the opposite end, whence it drops to the next lower shelf, and so on it travels till at the extremity of the lower shelf it passes out by the delivery lattice well and equally dried. Moore's drier is a simpler and less expensive form of drying apparatus, intermittent in its action. It consists of a case enclosed except as regards the top, where there are openings to allow the escape of moist air. It contains two tiers of steam-heated pipes, and directly over the top of each tier there is a row of iron rollers of small diameter set close together. At one end of the machine is a door for feeding wool into it, and at the opposite extremity is a spiked drum geared to rotate at a high speed. A fixed quantity of wool is fed into the machine at one time and placed on the lower series of rollers. These in their rotation carry the wool forward exposed to the heat of the pipes both above and below, till it reaches the drum, which, revolving rapidly, lifts it to the higher range of rollers. Over these the wool is carried back, till at the other end it again falls to the lower range, and so it circulates through the machine till the drying is completed. To withdraw the dried wool it is only necessary to raise the outlet door over the revolving drum, when it throws out the contents of the machine as fast as the wool comes within its range.

Teazing.

The dried wool, notwithstanding the several manipulations to which it has been subjected, is still in the condition of matted locks, which have to be opened up and the whole material brought into a uniformly free and loose condition. This is effected in the Willey or teazing machine, which consists of a large drum and three small cylinders mounted in an enclosed frame. The drum is armed with ranges of powerful hooked teeth or spikes, and is geared to rotate with great rapidity, making about 500 revolutions per minute. The smaller cylinders, called workers, are also provided with strong spikes; they are mounted over the drum and revolve more slowly in a direction contrary to the drum, the spikes of which just clear those of the workers. The wool is fed into the drum, which carries it round with great velocity; but, as it passes on, the locks are caught by the spikes of the workers, and in the contest for possessing the wool the matted locks are torn asunder till the whole wool is delivered in a light, free, and disentangled condition.

Burring.

For certain classes of dirty wool, notably such as that which comes from Buenos Ayres, still another preparing operation is essential at this stage—that is, the removal of burrs or small persistently adherent seeds and other fragments of vegetable matter which remain in the wool. Two methods of effecting this—one chemical, the other mechanical—may be pursued. The chemical treatment consists in steeping the wool in a dilute solution of sulphuric acid, draining off the dilute acid by means of the hydro-extractor, and then immediately exposing the wool to further rapid drying in a heat of about 250° F. The acid leaves the wool itself uninjured, but is retained by the more absorbent vegetable matter, and the high heat causes it to combine so energetically with the water left in the burrs that the vegetable matter becomes completely carbonized. The wool is thereupon washed in water rendered sufficiently alkaline to neutralize any free acid which may remain, and dried. The same burr-removing effect is obtained by the use of a solution of chloride of aluminium, a method said to be safer for the wool and less hurtful to the attendant workmen than is the sulphuric acid process. For mechanical removing of burrs, a machine something like the Willey in appearance is employed. The main feature of this apparatus is a large drum or swift armed with fine short spikes curved slightly in the direction in which it rotates. By a series of beaters and circular brushes the wool is carried to and fed on these short spikes, and in its rotation the burrs, owing to their weight, hang out from the swift. The swift as it travels round is met by a series of three burring rollers rotating in an opposite direction, the projecting rails of which knock the burrs off the wool. The burrs fall on a grating and are ejected, with, of course, a good deal of wool adhering to them, by another rotating cylinder.

Oiling. There remains yet another preliminary operation through which wool generally has to pass previous to the spinning processes. As delivered from the drying apparatus the wool is bright and clean, but somewhat harsh and wiry to the touch owing to the removal of the yolk which is its natural lubricant. To render it properly soft and elastic, and to improve its spinning qualities, the fibre is sprinkled with a percentage of oil, comparatively small quantities —by some spinners none—being used for worsted wools, but a larger amount being applied in the oiling of wool for woollen manufactures. The oil further has the advantage of producing a certain adhesiveness of the fibre in the spinning process, and thus it enables the spinner to get a more level and finer yarn, and it prevents loss from the flying off of separate fibres. As the oil is a costly item, it is of consequence that it should be equally distributed and used in a thrifty manner, for which end various forms of oiling apparatus have been devised, which sprinkle the oil in a very fine spray over thinly distributed wool carried by an endless cloth under the sprinkler. Gallipoli olive oil is the best medium for oiling combing wool; and for carding wool the liquid olein expressed from tallow and lard in the preparation of stearin is employed with advantage.

Blending. The raw material is now ready for the various spinning and other processes by which it is worked into useful forms; but pure wool of one quality alone is not generally used in the production of woven fabrics. For many reasons—among which cheapness figures prominently—wools are blended, and to no inconsiderable extent the added material consists of shoddy, mungo, or extract wools (see below). Blending with cotton is also practised, and for some purposes silk and wool are mixed. The question of colour as well as quality also determines blending operations, natural coloured wools being frequently intermixed to obtain particular shades for tweeds, knitting yarns, &c. The various materials to be intermixed are bedded in due proportion in separate layers over each other, and passed through a teazer, from which they issue so intimately intermixed that they present a uniform appearance.

Woollen manufactures. The processes hitherto described—although woollen manufacture has been specially kept in view—are more or less essential to wool for all purposes to which it is applied. But from this point the manufacturing operations diverge into three main channels, which may be regarded as almost distinct textile industries. First and simplest we have the felt manufacture, in which cloth is made without either spinning or weaving; second is the woollen yarn and cloth manufacture, embracing the preparation of carded yarns and of cloth which is so milled or felted as to have the appearance of felt; and, thirdly, in the worsted yarn and cloth industry combed yarn is prepared and cloth showing the yarn and pattern is woven. These definitions must be taken to be accurate only in the broad general acceptation.

Felt. Felt is a kind of cloth made without spinning or weaving, but simply by the mutual adhesion of the imbricated fibres. The peculiar property is most distinctly developed in the short or carding wools, but all wool, in common with mohair, alpaca, vicugna, and camel's hair, possesses it. Felting properties are also found in the hair of other animals; the rabbit, especially, supplies the finer felts used for hat-making, while the beaver hat, which is the ancestor of the modern dress hat, was a felt of beaver hair. Felted cloth is made by the combined influence of heat, moisture, and pressure or rubbing on a uniformly spread-out mass of woollen fibres. The wool is scribbled or carded out into a uniform lap of extreme thinness, but of a length and breadth sufficient for the size of the cloth to be made. A series of these carded laps are superimposed on each other till the requisite thickness of material is attained, and generally the two external laps are made of material superior to the body. The lap so prepared is passed on between a series of pairs of rollers, which press against each other partly immersed in a trough of water, the upper rollers being solid and heavy while those under are hollow and heated by steam. To the upper rollers a gentle reciprocating motion is communicated, so that the material is felted as it passes on. When duly condensed, the cloth, of leathery consistence, is dyed, printed, dressed, and finished, when required, like ordinary woollen cloths. Felt has extensive applications, there being made from it druggets, carpets, table-covers, horse-cloths, &c.; the coarser varieties are used for boiler-covering and other mechanical purposes.

Woollens and worsteds. It becomes necessary here to indicate the specific distinction of woollen and worsted yarns and cloth. In a general way it may be said that woollen yarns are those made from short wools possessed of high felting qualities, which are prepared by a process of carding, whereby the fibres are as far as possible crossed and interlocked with each other, and that these cardings, though hard spun on the mule frame, form a light fluffy yarn, which suits the material when woven into cloth for being brought into the semi-felted condition by milling which is the distinguishing characteristic of woollen cloth. On the other hand, worsted yarns are generally made from the long lustrous varieties of wool; the fibres are so combed as to bring them as far as possible to lie parallel to each other; the spinning is done on the throstle frame, and the yarn is spun into a compact, smooth, and level thread, which, when woven into cloth, is not milled or felted. At all points, however, woollen and worsted yarns as thus defined overlap each other, some woollens being made from longer wool than certain worsteds, and worsteds being, when made from short staple wool, also carded as well as combed; and occasionally worsted yarn is spun on the mule frame, while milling or felting is a process done in all degrees,—woollen being sometimes not at all milled, while to some worsteds a certain milling finish is given. The fundamental distinction between the classes rests in the crossing and interlacing of the fibres in preparing woollen yarn,—an operation confined to this alone among all textiles, while for worsted yarn the fibres are treated, as in the case of all other textile materials, by processes designed to bring them into a smooth parallel relationship to each other.

Carding. Woollen yarns, as above explained, are exclusively made by the process of carding. The simple apparatus—the hand-cards—with which carding was done before the introduction of machinery and factory-work consisted of square or oblong pieces of board with handles, one face of the board being covered with card leather, which was closely studded with fine elastic steel teeth, pointed in one direction and bent as in fig. 3. These teeth were strong or fine according to the nature, length, and strength of the fibre to be carded, but the finer the teeth the more closely were they studded together. A quantity of teased and oiled wool was placed on the surface of one card, which, taken in the left hand, was held teeth upward on the lap of the operator, while the other card, held in the right hand teeth downward, and consequently pointed in an opposite direction, was drawn from end to end over it, each card thus taking up a share of the wool which became entangled in its teeth. In this way, by drawing the one card over the other repeatedly, the whole of the wool was ultimately separated and equally distributed over the pair of cards. The wool was then stripped out of the cards by drawing the teeth of one through those of the other in the direction of their inclination. The carded wool thus lifted out was condensed into a loose but uniform round pipe or "carding" by rolling on the back of the card, and these cardings were then ready for spinning on the wheel.

Fig. 3.—Card Teeth.

For the apparently simple operation of carding, the factory machinery is complex, delicate, and very expensive. Ordinarily it consists of three carding-engines, called respectively the scribbler, the intermediate, and the finisher, but sometimes the intermediate is omitted. In each of these there is a complicated series of card-covered cylinders of different diameters running at different rates of speed, sometimes in a contrary and sometimes in the same direction, which are engaged in contending with each other for the

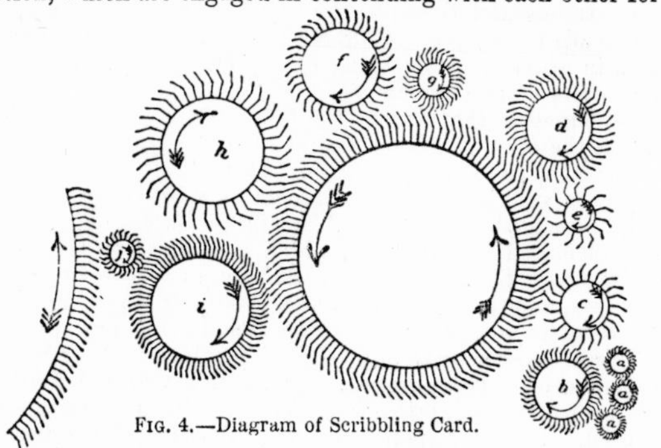

FIG. 4.—Diagram of Scribbling Card.

wool supplied to the machine, in abstracting it altogether from their neighbours, and passing it on to be again contended for and teased in the operation, and finally passed clean out of the machine. A sectional illustration (fig. 4) of the first portion of a "scribbler" will serve as an illustration of the whole operation from beginning to end. The wool is entered to the apparatus by a travelling lattice, the supply being equalized and carefully distributed by a mechanical feed. It is caught between the lower two of a range of three feed-rollers *a*, revolving immediately behind which is the "licker-in" roller *b*, which immediately takes possession of the portion of the feed which has fallen to the share of the lower or No. 1 feed-roller. The remainder of the feed is carried upward on the middle feed-roller, from which it is taken by the uppermost of the three rollers *a*, and from it the wool is delivered to the "licker-in." In this way a certain amount of preliminary blending and intermixing is accomplished. Against the licker-in revolves the "angle stripper" *c*, the function of which is to remove the wool from the former and deliver it over to the great breast cylinder, which revolves at a high speed (surface-velocity about $\frac{1}{7}$ mile per minute). By the cylinder it is carried on till it comes against a small roller revolving slowly in the opposite direction, called "worker No. 1" *d*, which abstracts part of the wool, and carrying it round gives it up to the somewhat smaller roller, the "stripper" *e*, which again delivers it to the breast cylinder. Passing on it carries the wool partly to

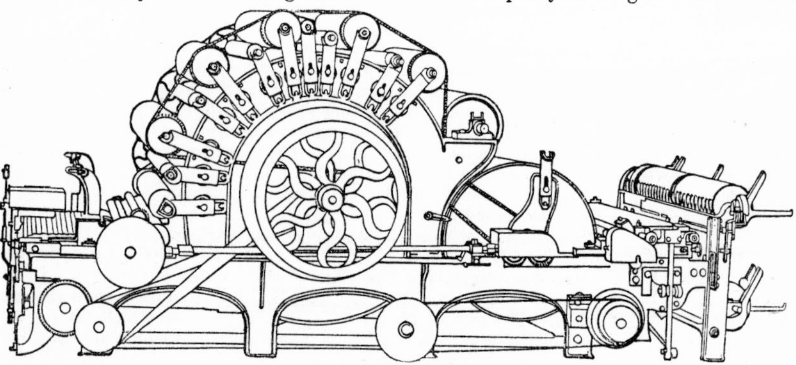
FIG. 5.—Single-Cylinder Carding Engine.

the second worker *f*, and stripper *g*, when the same operation is repeated. Continuing its progress, the cylinder with its covering of wool next comes in contact with the "fancy" *h*, the teeth of which are set so as to pass a little way into those of the cylinder. Its effect is to throw the wool partly out of its teeth and prepare it for being entirely removed by the "doffer" *i*, which is the next roller met by the cylinder, and which, like the "fancy," revolves in a contrary direction to the breast cylinder. The angle stripper *j* passes the wool from the doffer to the next cylinder, which is called a "swift," and which has the same workers, strippers, fancy and doffer rollers as the breast cylinders. The scribbler contains three such sets of cylinders and rollers over which the wool passes till it is delivered. The intermediate carding-engine has two swifts, with relative workers, &c., and the finisher has also two swifts and a condenser. In some carding-engines the swifts are provided with more than two sets of workers and strippers. This is particularly the case in a class of carding-engines provided with only one swift or cylinder of very large diameter, around which there are five sets of workers and strippers (fig. 5).

Condensing. The carded wool, as it leaves the last swift of the finisher card, is in the form of a continuous equally-distributed lap. To prepare it for spinning, this lap must now be divided into a series of equal strips or ribbons, and these then condensed into a rounded carding or sliver sufficiently compact to bear winding on a bobbin. The condenser for doing this is attached to the finisher card, and consists of rings or bands of card-cloth the width of the strips to be made, placed on one or on two cylinders, which rings doff the portion of the lap against which they revolve and yield it up to a stripper. These strips as they pass out are acted on by a pair of rubbers which, by a partly oscillating motion, rub the strip into the form of a carding of rounded loose untwisted fibres, which in the subsequent operation of spinning is easily drawn out to the degree of tenuity required in the yarn to be made.

Mule spinning. The mule-frame employed for spinning woollen yarns is the same in principle as, but in some respects modified in action from, the spinning-mule used for fine counts of cotton yarn. The mule (fig. 6) consists of a stationary frame on which the bobbins of sliver are placed, and of a carriage which travels back and forward a distance of in all about 2 yards from the stationary frame. The carriage contains in a horizontal row the spindles which give twist to the yarn and wind it on the bobbins or paper tubes fixed on them;

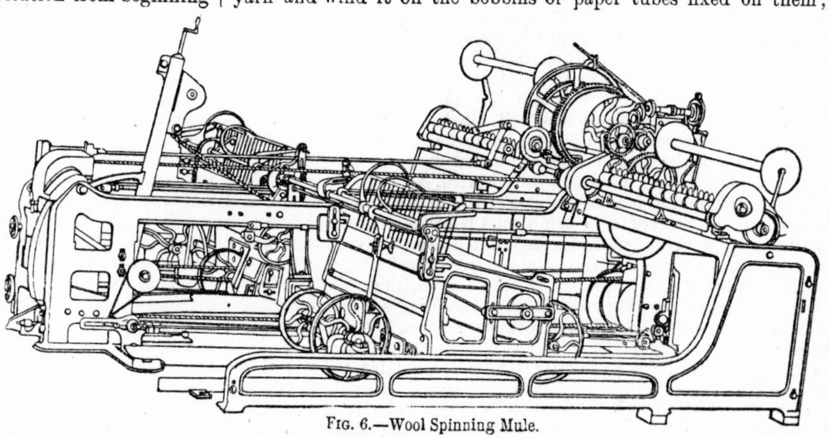
FIG. 6.—Wool Spinning Mule.

and the complicated motions of the whole machine are regulated by gearing and belting from head-stocks on the stationary frame. The carriage being close up to the stationary frame, the ends of the slivers are passed through a pair of small giving-off rollers and attached to the bobbins or tubes in the carriage. The carriage then begins to travel back on its rails, the slivers being simultaneously delivered to it through the rollers, at the same rate at which it travels, till, say, a yard length is given out, and as the carriage has been moving back the spindles have been revolving slowly so as to communicate some twist to the sliver; but up to this point there has been no drawing out or drafting. But now the rollers cease to give out sliver, the carriage continues travelling back, and the spindles revolve at a greatly increased rate, simultaneously drawing out the sliver and giving it the requisite twist, till, when it comes to the end of the rails over which it runs, the yard of original sliver is drawn out to 2 yards of yarn and twisted almost enough. The full twist is given while the carriage remains standing at the end; then the spindles are reversed two or three times to unwind a small proportion of yarn which the twisting operation leaves near the point of the bobbin; and lastly the carriage is run in to the stationary frame while the spindles wind the now finished yarn on the bobbins or tubes, an automatic arrangement securing due tension and the proper winding of the yarn.

Woollen yarn. Yarn, as delivered from the mule in woollen-spinning, or from the throstle in the case of worsteds, is in the condition known as singles. For twisting the singles into yarn of two or more ply it is wound on bobbins; sometimes the bobbins from the spinning-frame are used direct, and placed on pegs in the twisting-frame, which is a mechanism like the throstle, but without the arrangement for drafting. The twist is given in the reverse direction from that in which the singles are spun, and thereby the single is to some extent untwisted. Yarns of two-, three-, and five-ply and upwards are made; these are sometimes redoubled or again twisted together. The yarn may be made up of precisely the same singles; sometimes different counts or sizes of singles are twisted together; in other cases the colours may be different; and yet again yarns may be made of distinct fibres, such as wool and cotton, or wool and silk, &c. Numerous variations of the method of twisting are employed to produce loops, knots, and other irregularities in the yarn, for convenience in weaving and knitting fancy textures.

Worsted yarn.

If we adhere to the definition of worsted yarn which distinguishes it as being made from wool fibres brought as far as possible into a level parallel condition, we shall have to do only with two methods of manufacture,—(1) of yarn from long wool by the method of drawing, gilling, and combing, and (2) of yarn from medium and short staple wools, which are first carded and afterwards combed. But there is commonly added a third class of worsted yarns, worsted only in the sense that they are not meant for felting. These are carpet yarns and lightly twisted knitting yarns, which, being meant to be full and open in structure, are prepared for spinning by carding alone, precisely as in making woollen yarns.

Combing.

The primitive method of wool-combing, and the simple implements employed till comparatively recent days, when the ingenious machinery now used was invented, will serve to illustrate the problem of preparing long wool for spinning. The hand combs employed were studded with two—sometimes three—rows of long, smooth, rounded, and sharp-pointed steel spikes. The operative was provided with a pair of these combs. He had a comb-post to which he could attach them, and a comb-pot or small stove in which he heated the teeth of his combs and the wool which he worked. The teeth of one comb being duly heated he fixed it in the comb-post, and taking a quantity of wool previously oiled he dashed it in portions into the teeth of the comb and drew it through, leaving a portion locked in the spikes, and this operation he continued till the comb was well filled with wool. Then he placed it in the comb-pot to heat up, while he similarly proceeded to fill the teeth of the second comb, which in the meantime had been heating. With both filled and duly heated, he took one comb in his left hand, laying it in his lap teeth upwards, and with the other in his right he proceeded to comb out the locks, beginning first at the tips and working gradually in as the fibres were smoothed and opened out. In the end the combs were worked with teeth close up to each other and through the entire mass, the noils or short fibre being thus entirely combed out, excepting a small quantity left in the teeth which could not be reached by the opposing combs.

The typical modern process in worsted-yarn fabrication is that in which the preparation consists in gilling and subsequent combing, as practised when long wool is the staple to be treated. The object of gilling is to bring all the fibres level and parallel to each other, and to prepare a uniform sliver for the subsequent combing operation. The gilling-machine or gill-box (fig. 7) in its essential features consists first of a pair of rollers to which the wool is

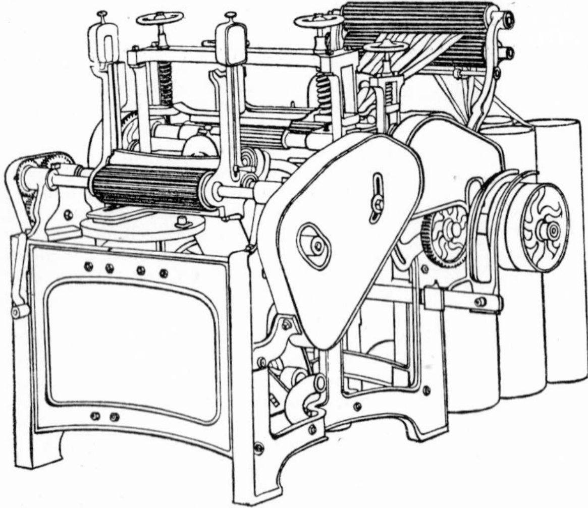

Fig. 7.—Screw Gilling Machine.

fed. Beyond these it is caught by rows of steel pins fixed in heavy steel bars, termed fallers, which rise in close and constant succession immediately behind the feed-rollers, penetrate the wool presented to them, and travel forward with it towards a second pair of rollers which catch the fibre and draw it away. The spike-covered fallers are so called because they travel from one to the other pair of rollers, carried forward by endless screws into which they are threaded, then, falling down, are returned by the action of similar screws operating in the opposite direction, till just under the feed-rollers they rise again to catch the feed of wool, and so continue to circulate. There is thus a continuous line of fallers travelling between feed-rollers and back rollers, but as the back rollers revolve much more quickly than the front rollers, and also draw the wool through them more rapidly than it is presented to them by the fallers, there is a constant and steady drawing of wool away from the front rollers and through the teeth of the fallers, and this draught tends to cause all the fibres to arrange themselves in the direction in which they are being gently dragged. A set of gill-boxes consists of five or six machines constructed on the same principle, but with the pins of the fallers finer and more closely studded as the fibre travels on and as the orderly and symmetrical arrangement of the sliver increases. From the first two or three machines the wool is generally delivered as a broad lap, and it is similarly presented to the next, but in the later boxes the product is condensed into a sliver, which is received in large cylindrical tin cans. Six of these cans are brought to the front of the next gill-box, and the six slivers are, in passing through, drawn into and delivered as one, and, such an operation being repeated three times, it will be seen that any original portion of sliver must be distributed over a great length, and in this way the fibres are brought even with each other and a very level and uniform strand is produced. In the original form of gill-box the fallers travelled from front to back at a uniform speed, and thus all the draughting was done by the rapid rotation of the back rollers. Now, by a graduated pitch in the screws which carry the fallers forward, they travel at a steadily accelerated rate, beginning slow, and reaching their greatest rapidity just as they deliver the wool to the back rollers, which revolve still more rapidly. Thus there is steady draughting throughout the whole range of the machine, and the wool is at once more gently treated and more uniformly drawn out than in the old forms of the machine.

It will be obvious that the gill-boxes through which long wool passes, while possessing the power of bringing the fibres into a smooth, equal, and regular condition, do nothing in the way of selecting and separating out the long and straight from the short and curly fibres which are always intermixed. To obtain an even and smooth worsted yarn it is necessary to effect this separation, and it is the function of the various forms of combing machine now in use to separate the "top" or long fibre from the "noil" or short and broken wool, and to deliver the former as a continuous sliver of uniform size. The invention of a successful combing machine has been the great triumph of the modern worsted industry, and the introduction of the apparatus led, as is commonly the case with all great inventions, to a vast amount of dispute and litigation, and many conflicting claims of merit. About 1840 at least three investigators were separately at work on the problem —Mr S. C. Lister of Bradford, Mr Donisthorpe of Leicester, and M. Heilmann of Alsace. Messrs Lister and Donisthorpe conjointly secured a patent for a combing machine, in connexion with which they entered into partnership, but their patent rights were successfully disputed by Heilmann under a patent granted to him in 1847, and they were obliged to buy up his invention for £30,000. Since that time much attention has been given to combing machinery, not for wool alone, but also for spun silk and cotton; and now there are many varieties of apparatus in the market for doing what not very long ago was pronounced to be utterly impracticable. The three principal classes of machine at present used for wool-combing are—(1) the Lister or nip machine, which is most suitable for long combing wools, mohair, and alpaca; (2) the Noble or circular comb, principally useful for combing shorter staple or intermediate wools; and (3) the Holden or square-motion comb, which is applicable for short staple wools. It is impossible here to convey a full conception of the delicate almost intelligent manner in which these machines work. A principal feature of them is a large ring or circle studded with rows of fine steel pins, which is made to revolve horizontally within the machine. By various devices the wool is fed into the teeth of the ring in a continuous series of tufts with its ends overlapping the edge of the ring as it revolves. In the case of the nip machine the wool is fed in by fallers as in the gill-box. The end of the sliver is caught by a nip which tears a tuft through the pins of the fallers, and thus partly combs it out. This tuft the nip places on the teeth of the revolving circle, by which it is carried on till it comes to a pair of upright rollers revolving close to the edge of the circle. These rollers catch between them the ends of the long fibre and draw it out of the teeth of the circle in a continuous sliver as it revolves. The Noble or circular comb is provided with three pin-studded rings, one large and two small, the latter being so centred within the larger ring that in rotating their outer edges just meet the inner edge of the large ring which rotates around them. The tufts of wool are dabbed down over the pins of the larger and smaller circles at the points where they meet, and of course as they rotate the teeth immediately begin to draw apart, and the wool is divided, the long fibres hanging over the edge of each circle. These fibres are caught between upright rollers, which thus deliver four continuous slivers of top, and leave the noil to be otherwise lifted out of the teeth.

Drawing. The sliver as delivered from the combing machine is made up into a ball by a balling gill-box, behind the back rollers of which instead of a can there is a large bobbin for receiving the sliver, which is wound on it in a diagonal manner from the oscillating rotation given to the bobbin. Such balls of sliver then undergo the operation of drawing, the purpose of which is still further to equalize the strand of fibre, and to bring it into a sufficiently attenuated form for spinning. The principle of drawing or draughting consists in presenting the sliver to a pair of receiving rollers which pass it on to a pair of delivery rollers, which rotate proportionately faster than the receivers, and to that extent draw out and attenuate the sliver. Supposing the wool to pass through six such drawing frames, six slivers may be fed into the first and drawn out to the dimensions of one; the same may be repeated in the second, five slivers may be reduced to one in the third, four to one in the fourth and fifth frames; and in the roving frame, in which a little twist is given to the sliver before it is wound on a bobbin, two slivers may be elongated into one. Thus we have any length of sliver drawn out $6 \times 6 \times 5 \times 4 \times 4 \times 2 = 5760$ times its original extension, and with increase of frames this extension multiplies enormously. Treating the slivers in nine drawing frames, we may have $8 \times 6 \times 5 \times 5 \times 5 \times 4 \times 3 \times 2 \times 2 = 288,000$ of extension.

Carded worsted. Short and medium staple wools are carded before being gilled and combed. The preliminary operations differ in no way from those employed for woollen yarns. After carding the wool is generally washed, previous to gilling in a back washer. The machine consists of two sud bowls or vats provided with immersers and squeezing rollers through which the cardings are passed; then they are carried round two copper cylinders internally heated by steam, from which they are passed on and delivered by the fallers of a gilling apparatus.

Throstle spinning. The bobbins of elongated and slightly twisted rovings are now ready for spinning on the throstle spinning-frame, on which it is simultaneously drawn out to its ultimate tenuity, twisted, and wound on a bobbin. The drawing out is done practically by the same device as the drafting of sliver in the drawing-frame. The bobbins of rove are placed on pegs on the frame slightly canted forward, so that the roving as drawn off comes away at right angles from the bobbin. The rovings pass first between a pair of rollers, and are carried on and supported by small carrier rollers till they reach a front pair of rollers, the upper of which is covered with leather and the lower grooved or furrowed. The space between the back and front pairs of rollers, termed the ratch, is that in which the final drawing is effected, and the amount of attenuation effected is dependent on the relatively faster rate at which the front rollers rotate as compared with the back pair. Immediately the slender cord has passed the front pair of rollers, twist is imparted to it by the spindle working either on the old flyer principle, on the cup principle, or with the more recent ring and traveller. See also YARN. The doubling and subsequent treatment of worsted singles are the same as in the case of woollen yarn singles from the mule frame.

Shoddy and mungo. The term shoddy was formerly one of some opprobrium in connexion with woollen manufactures, but the substance is now frankly recognized as a material of great utility for many purposes when body and warmth are more essential than toughness or elasticity. Shoddy consists of rags and shreds of stockings, flannels, and other soft worsted fabrics torn and reduced to such fragments of the original fibre as can be made by the operation. Mungo is a similar preparation made from rags, and from shreds and clippings of milled woollen cloths, being divided into new mungo made from tailor's waste, and old mungo from rags of all degrees of degradation. Extract wool is that which is recovered from rags of various cloths in which cotton and wool are variously woven together. The wool is freed from the cotton by the same chemical or carboning process which is employed in freeing dirty wool from burrs, viz., by treating the union fabric with a solution of sulphuric acid and heating it in a stove, when the acid energetically attacks and chars the vegetable fibre, leaving the wool unharmed. Shoddy and mungo are prepared by dusting the rags and fragments, classifying them according to colour and quality, picking out seams, oiling the material, and then passing it into a machine significantly called the "devil," which literally rends the rags, &c., to fragments, which look more like dust than fibres, by the exceedingly rapid rotation of a swift or large cylinder armed with powerful iron spikes, with equally strong toothed rollers revolving in an opposite direction. Into the same category with these come the flocks formed in the various processes of finishing cloth, which are, of course, even shorter than the others. Indeed the shoddy manufacturers hold that "anything long enough to have two ends" is sufficient for manufacturing purposes. The shoddy trade was begun in Batley, Yorkshire, by Mr Benjamin Law in 1813, and, notwithstanding the disfavour with which it was long viewed, it prospered and developed till the shoddy district of Batley, Dewsbury, and their surroundings became the centre of a great and prosperous branch of the woollen trade entirely dependent on these disintegrated materials. It is said that as much as 125,000,000 lb of shoddy material is now yearly worked up into cloth in England alone. Shoddy, &c., cannot be used without a due proportion of natural-length wool, usually one-third of pure wool being employed in spinning shoddy yarn; but sometimes as much as 80 per cent. of the finished cloth consists of shoddy. It finds its way into a very large proportion of woollen goods, but its use is detrimental where tenacity and wear are required. For linings, rugs, wraps, and heavy friezes, pilots, druggets, blankets, &c., in which bulk and warmth more than wear-resisting qualities are required, it is suitable, and it also makes into good light milled cloth for ladies' jackets. Shoddy is practically a new source of textile material; its employment is a utilization of waste, and furnishes cheap serviceable textures.

Cloth finishing. For the dyeing and weaving of woollen and worsted fabrics the reader is referred to the separate articles relating to these processes. But a piece of cloth—woollen cloth especially—as it comes from the loom is very far from being a finished product. Indeed the most characteristic operations in woollen-cloth manufacture are subsequent to the weaving stage. Woollen cloth from the loom, called "roughers," has an irregular, slack aspect, very different from the same web when it comes to be sold as, say, broad-cloth. The web as it leaves the loom is still saturated with the oil with which it was sprinkled before spinning, and impregnated with the size applied to the yarn to give it tenacity and consistency in weaving. To remove these it is scoured with hot soap-sud in a trough having a convex bottom, and fitted with wooden mallets which are made to fall obliquely against the cloth. After being scoured in this way, it is stretched in a frame for burling or perching, an operation which consists in going carefully over the whole web, picking out all burrs and knots in the texture, and darning up holes and open spots which it may show.

Fulling. Fulling is the one process which is specially distinctive of woollen textures,—its results being shown in the highest degree in broad-cloths, doeskins, and other like goods. Every one knows how flannels, blankets, and hosiery tend to contract with frequent washing, gaining in thickness and solidity what they lose in extension and elasticity; such shrinking is greatly accelerated when woollen articles are much rubbed in very hot water. This shrinking or fulling is, as already explained, the result of the serrated wavy structure of wool. The operation of fulling or milling is performed in the fulling stocks, or in the more modern milling-machine; but, by whatever agency carried out, the effect is always the same. The old method of fulling by the stocks is wasteful of power, and the blows the stocks give tend sometimes to tear the cloth, drawbacks from which the milling-machine is comparatively free. The cloth to be fulled is well saturated with hot soap and water, and either worked under the falling weight of the stocks or pressed and rubbed between rollers in the milling-machine while so heated and soaped. The more prolonged the operation the more does the material shrink up and thicken, and a piece of cloth may even be milled till it is reduced to half its original length and breadth. The degree of fulling is a distinctive feature of many different varieties of cloth. In the treatment of broad-cloth, doeskins, meltons, and all nap-finished cloth, the milling is carried so far that the fibres become densely matted, obliterating the appearance of weave, and giving the piece more the aspect of felt than of cloth. Fabrics such as Venetian cloths, and diagonals, &c., to which no pile-finish is given, are milled only to the extent of solidifying and increasing the substance and strength of the texture, and tweeds are only very slightly felted to give them a dressed surface. On the conclusion of the fulling operation the goods are scoured to free them from soap, which is very simply done by gradually supplanting the soap-sud with pure water, which is tepid at first but is gradually cooled by additions till in the end the cloth is being worked in pure cold water.

Teasling. The cloth that is taken from the fulling-machine must immediately be stretched uniformly in all directions by hooks on a frame, so that it may dry evenly without wrinkle or curl. The frame may be placed in a hot-air chamber to hasten the drying, or the cloth may be allowed to dry under ordinary atmospheric conditions. In this operation a pile or nap is raised on the surface of milled cloth. The raising of the pile is effected by the agency of the flower-head of the teasle (*Dipsacus fullonum*), which forms a cone-like spike covered with imbricated scales. These scales end in sharp, recurved hooks, possessed of high elasticity, combined with just sufficient stiffness for the work they have to do. The use of these hooked teasles is to scratch the surface of the milled cloths, and getting entangled with minute surface fibres break these or pull out their ends, and so raise over the whole surface a fine but unequal nap. Formerly the teasles were set together in a flat frame, and by hand the workmen brushed them in a uniform manner over the whole surface of the tightly stretched cloth. But this laborious handicraft has long been superseded by the use of the gig-mill or dressing-machine. This apparatus consists of a cylinder made to rotate at a high rate of speed. The surface of the cloth to be raised is, in a state of uniform tension, brought in contact with the revolving cylinder. An automatic arrangement in the machine regulates the lightness or closeness of contact of cloth and teasles. The myriads of elastic hooks scratch the entire surface, disengaging and opening up short fibres, and thus covering the whole with a nap. There are, however, several varieties of pile desired in dressing woollen cloths, and a pile may be raised in a certain class of fabrics for a purpose quite the opposite of that for which other piles are formed. Thus in cloth dressing the object is to get a glossy and smooth nap which quite covers and conceals the underlying structure, while tweeds and similar goods are teasled with the view of ultimately removing all pile from the surface and leaving the pattern of the cloth well defined and free from all hairiness. Pile-dressed fabrics are raised by the wet method: that is, the cloth to be operated upon in the dressing-machine is first damped, and the nap so produced lies smooth, flat, and level in one direction, covering the surface in much the same way as short hairs cover the skin of an animal. Cloth raised dry, on the other hand, throws its fibre ends straight out from the cloth, the action indeed being a kind of combing-up of all the more loose and open surface fibres so as to prepare them for being entirely cropped or shorn off in order to leave the fabric with a clean, bare surface. Metallic teasles have frequently been suggested and to some extent employed as a substitute for the vegetable product, but hitherto such devices have not proved quite satisfactory.

Cropping.

The operation of cropping was also formerly a handicraft, the worker using a huge pair of shears, and the employment demanded much dexterity and skill to produce a uniform smooth pile or a well-cleaned surface. It is now done with equal rapidity and certainty by a machine which in principle is the same as the lawn-mower. It consists of a cylinder armed with a series of helical knives or cutters, the cylinder revolving with great velocity against the smooth stretched surface of the cloth, partly cutting away and partly tearing off the tips of the projecting fibres which come within the range of its ledger-blades. Four hundred years before the practical introduction of this helical cropping machine, it was invented and proposed for modern use by Leonardo da Vinci.

Pressing.

With the view of giving lustre to the finished cloth, it is, when taken from the cropping machine and brushed on the brushing machine to remove the flocks produced in shearing, wound tightly round a huge drum, and boiled, or rather immersed in water heated to from 160° to 180° F., for three or four hours. It is then unwound, the ends are reversed, winding first on the roller the end which was on the outside in the previous boiling, and again boiled. Finally it is pressed in an hydraulic press, in which the cloth is heated either by the introduction of hot iron-plates between the folds or by forcing steam through it in the press, this last process adding to the solidity and smoothness of the cloth and developing the lustre characteristic of a well-finished fabric.

Manufactures in wool.

The range and variety of cloths and other textures made from wool are exceedingly great. Under the heading of cloth manufactures, there may be enumerated, of piled cloths, broad-cloth, doeskins, cassimeres, meltons, beavers, and friezes. Of cloths milled and cropped bare there are venetians, sataras, and diagonals, which differ in the arrangements of warp and weft in the weaving. Tweeds, which form an important item, are cloths only slightly felted, raised dry, cropped, and pressed. The variety of worsted cloths is still greater, embracing says, serges, sateens, repps, merinos, mousselaines-de-laine, tartans, camlets, Russell cords, coburgs, lastings, delaines, and Orleans cloth. Hosiery forms a manufacture apart, as do also the processes of making carpets, blankets, flannels, shawls, rugs, and wrappers, curtain-cloths, and alpaca and mohair textures.

As an illustration of the advantages which have resulted from the application of machinery to the many and complicated processes of cloth manufacture, it has been calculated by M. Alcan that, whereas in the 17th century the labour of more than 10,000 men was needed to produce in one day a ton of cloth from a ton of wool, that amount of work now can be done in one day by about 1900.

Trade.

Wherever civilized mankind dwell there is found wool production, with more or less of woollen manufacture. This fact notwithstanding, the cultivation of wool tends to become increasingly associated with special localities, and from age to age different regions enter into competition as sources of wool, and the great sources of supply correspondingly change their position. Neglecting the produce of Britain, which probably has not varied to any notable extent during the century, though its movement as an article of export has developed greatly in that interval, we may briefly note the vast developments which have taken place in some sources of supply. In 1800 most of the wool, other than that from native sources, used in England came from Spain. In 1810 167 ℔ was imported from the Australian colonies, and now the imports from these colonies reach 400,000,000 ℔ yearly, and the imports from Spain have dwindled to 1,700,000 ℔. Similarly the quantity brought from the Cape of Good Hope has grown from about 30,000 ℔ in 1820 to 61,250,000 ℔ in 1886. The growth and fluctuation in the imports from these and other regions are exhibited in the following table:—

Imports of wool.

Imports of Wool into the United Kingdom from the Principal Countries, Foreign and Colonial (given in thousands of lbs.).

	Spain.	Germany.	Australia.	South Africa.	East Indies.	Total from all Countries.
1800	6,062	412	...	...	...	8,609
1810	5,592	778	167	...	...	10,914
1820	3,536	5,113	99	30	...	9,775
1830	1,643	26,073	1,967	33	...	32,305
1840	1,266	21,812	9,721	751	2,441	49,436
1850	440	9,166	39,018	5,709	3,473	74,326
1860	1,000	9,954	59,166	16,574	20,214	151,218
1870	25	4,406	175,081	32,785	11,143	263,250
1880	1,580	7,174	300,627	51,386	29,190	463,309
1886	1,710	3,281	401,426	61,257	34,597	615,998

Exports of wool.

The exports of raw wool have risen in fairly steady proportion to the imports, springing up from 92,542,384 ℔ in 1870 to 311,902,741 ℔ in 1886, the average excess of the imports over the exports each year being from 200,000,000 to 230,000,000 ℔.

Factory employment.

The following table exhibits the relative position and progress of the principal textile manufactures in the United Kingdom at various periods:—

Description of Factories.	Persons Employed.				Power Looms.			
	1838.	1856.	1870.	1878.	1836.	1856.	1870.	1878.
Cotton......	259,104	379,213	450,087	482,903	108,751	298,847	440,676	514,911
Woollen....	54,808	79,091	125,130	134,344	2,150	14,453	48,140	56,944
Worsted....	31,628	87,794	109,587	130,925	2,969	38,956	64,654	87,393
Flax.........	43,557	80,262	129,772	108,806	1,714	9,260	35,300	40,448
Silk..........	34,303	56,137	48,124	40,985	209	7,689	12,378	12,546
Totals.......	423,400	682,497	862,700	897,963	115,793	369,205	601,148	712,242

Export of manufactures.

The growth of the export trade from the United Kingdom in woollen and worsted manufactures from 1820 is exhibited in the subjoined table (in thousands of pounds sterling):—

	Manufactured Goods.	Woollen and Worsted Yarns.	Total Woollen and Worsted Exports.		Manufactured Goods.	Woollen and Worsted Yarns.	Total Woollen and Worsted Exports.
1820	5,586	...	5,586	1857	10,703	2,943	13,646
1830	4,728	122	4,851	1865	20,141	5,100	25,241
1840	5,327	452	5,780	1870	21,665	4,994	26,659
1850	8,588	1,451	10,040	1880	17,265	3,345	20,610

The following is the detailed statement of exports from the United Kingdom from the Board of Trade Returns for 1887:—

	Quantities.	Value.
Woollen and worsted yarns..........	40,165,100 ℔.	£3,970,205
Coatings, all wool....................................	17,175,900 yds.	3,843,872
Do., mingled with other materials....	29,057,500 yds.	3,682,913
Woollen stuffs..	49,582,300 yds.	2,311,107
Worsted coatings......................................	10,038,800 yds.	1,832,072
Worsted stuffs..	151,362,000 yds.	5,113,191
Flannels..	10,925,000 yds.	416,307
Carpets..	12,980,300 yds.	1,310,241
Blankets...	1,578,912 pairs.	545,576
Hosiery..	...	734,691
Small wares and unenumerated..............	...	794,539
Total....................................	...	£24,554,714
Alpaca and mohair yarn.........................	12,196,100 ℔.	£1,081,971

Centres of industry.

Particular districts have attained a predominant hold on certain branches of the manufacture, and with great tenacity the industries have clung for long periods to the districts which have succeeded in establishing a reputation for the branches they cultivated. In this way the manufacture of superfine broad-cloths has been long associated with the West of England, specially with Wiltshire and Gloucestershire, and in that district the trade in fine cloth is still chiefly centred. In point of quantities produced, however, and of persons employed, the West Riding of Yorkshire woollen cloth districts far outstrip the West of England, and are the true centres of all industries connected with wool. Of woollen cloths of all kinds the towns of Leeds and Huddersfield are the most important producers. The shoddy trade has been specially developed at Batley and Dewsbury, and the numerous manufactures of worsted have their principal centre in Bradford and the populous district surrounding it. Norwich, at one time the capital of worsted manufactures, and a large producer of shawls, thanks to the immigration of Flemings, has entirely lost its supremacy, probably owing to the superior coal facilities of Yorkshire, but it is yet the seat of no inconsiderable worsted manufacture. The hosiery trade is developed chiefly in and around Leicester, and at Kilmarnock the allied knitting of bonnets is a specialty. Flannels and blankets are associated with Wales; the carpet trade belongs principally to Kidderminster, Halifax, Glasgow, and Kilmarnock. Shawls are made in Paisley, Alva, and Alloa in Scotland, knitting-yarns being a largely developed industry in the two last-mentioned towns. Tweeds are the special industry of Hawick, Galashiels, Dumfries, and Aberdeen, and also form an important part of the manufactures of Leeds.

(J. PA.)

WOOLLETT, William (1735–1785), engraver, was born at Maidstone, of a family which came originally from Holland, on August 15, 1735. He was apprenticed to John Tinney, an engraver in Fleet Street, London, and he also studied in the St Martin's Lane academy. His first important plate was from the Niobe of Richard Wilson, published by Boydell in 1761, which was followed in 1763 by a companion engraving from the Phaethon of the same painter. After West he engraved his fine plate of the Battle of La Hogue (1781), and the Death of General Wolfe (1776), which is usually considered Woollett's masterpiece. In 1775 he was appointed engraver-in-ordinary to George III.; and he was a member of the Incorporated Society of Artists, of which for several years he acted as secretary. He died in London May 23, 1785.

In his plates, which unite work with the etching-needle, the dry-point, and the graver, Woollett shows the greatest richness and variety of execution. In his landscapes the foregrounds are distinguished by depth and vigour, the distances by the utmost tenderness; and his rendering of water is particularly excellent. In his portraits and historical subjects the textures are varied and well discriminated, and the rendering of flesh is characterized by great softness and delicacy. His works rank among the great productions of the English school of engraving. Louis Fagan, in his *Catalogue Raisonné of the Engraved Works of William Woollett* (1885), has enumerated 123 plates by this engraver.

WOOLSORTER'S DISEASE (Anthrax, Anthracæmia, Charbon, or Malignant Pustule) is the term applied to a virulent acute malady occasionally occurring in workers in the wool or hair, as well as in those handling the carcases, of animals, chiefly sheep and oxen, which had been affected with splenic fever. The disease, as it is seen in animals, has been described in the article Murrain (*q.v.*). The present notice refers only to the malady in man.

For many years cases of sudden death had been observed to occur from time to time among healthy men engaged in woollen manufactories, particularly in the work of sorting or combing wool. In some instances death appeared to be due to the direct inoculation of some poisonous material into the body, for a form of malignant pustule was observed upon the skin; but, on the other hand, in not a few cases without any external manifestation, symptoms of blood-poisoning, often proving rapidly fatal, suggested the probability of other channels for the introduction of the disease.

In 1880 the occurrence of several such cases among woolsorters at Bradford, reported by Dr Bell of that town, led to an official inquiry by the Local Government Board, and an elaborate investigation into the pathology of the disease was at the same time conducted at the Brown Institution, London, by Professor Greenfield.

Among the results of this inquiry it was ascertained—(1) that the disease appeared to be identical with that known by the name of splenic fever or anthrax occurring among sheep and cattle; (2) that in the blood and tissues of the body was found in abundance, as in the disease in animals, the *bacillus anthracis*, which is held to be the infecting agent in communicating the malady; and (3) that the skins, hair, wool, &c., of animals dying of splenic fever retain this infecting organism, which, under certain conditions, finds ready access to the bodies of the workers.

Two well-marked forms of this disease are recognized, external anthrax and internal anthrax. In external anthrax the infecting agent is accidentally inoculated into some portion of skin, the seat of a slight abrasion, often the hand, arm, or face. A minute swelling soon appears at the part, and develops into a vesicle containing serum or bloody matter, and varying in size, but seldom larger than a shilling. This vesicle speedily bursts, and leaves an ulcerated or sloughing surface, round about which are numerous smaller vesicles which undergo similar changes, and the whole affected part becomes hard and tender, while the surrounding surface participates in the inflammatory action, and the neighbouring lymphatic glands are also inflamed. This condition, termed malignant pustule, is frequently accompanied with severe constitutional disturbance, in the form of fever, delirium, perspirations, together with great prostration and a tendency to death from septicæmia, although on the other hand recovery is not uncommon. It was repeatedly found that the matter taken from the vesicle during the progress of the disease, as well as the blood in the body after death, contained the *bacillus anthracis*, and when inoculated into small animals produced rapid death, with all the symptoms and post-mortem appearances characteristic of splenic fever.

In internal anthrax there is no visible local manifestation of the disease, and the infecting material appears to gain access to the system from the air charged with it, as in rooms where the contaminated wool or hair is unpacked, or again during the process of sorting. The symptoms usually observed are those of rapid physical prostration, with a small pulse, somewhat lowered temperature (rarely fever), and quickened breathing. Examination of the chest reveals inflammation of the lungs and pleura. In some cases death takes place by collapse in less than one day, while in others the fatal issue is postponed for three or four days, and is preceded by symptoms of blood-poisoning, including rigors, perspirations, extreme exhaustion, &c. In some cases of internal anthrax the symptoms are more intestinal than pulmonary, and consist in severe exhausting diarrhœa, with vomiting and rapid sinking. Recovery from the internal variety, although not unknown, is more rare than from the external, and its most striking phenomena are its sudden onset in the midst of apparent health, the rapid development of physical prostration, and its tendency to a fatal termination despite treatment. The post-mortem appearances in internal anthrax are such as are usually observed in septicæmia, but in addition evidence of extensive inflammation of the lungs, pleura, and bronchial glands has in most cases been met with. The blood and other fluids and the diseased tissues are found loaded with the *bacillus anthracis*, and inoculation experiments, such as those already referred to, produced similar results.

Treatment in this disease appears to be of but little avail, except as regards the external form, where the malignant pustule may be dealt with early by strong caustics to destroy the affected textures. For the relief of the general constitutional symptoms, quinine, stimulants, and strong nourishment appear to be the only available means. As preventive measures in woollen manufactories, the disinfection of suspicious material, or the wetting of it before handling, is recommended as lessening the risk to the workers.

WOOLSTON, Thomas (1669–1731), English deist, born at Northampton in 1669, was the son of a "reputable tradesman," entered Sidney College, Cambridge, in 1685, studied theology, and was made a fellow of his college. Whiston states that he "was in his younger days a clergyman of very good reputation, a scholar, and well esteemed as a preacher, charitable to the poor, and beloved by all good men that knew him." After a time, by the study of Origen, he became possessed, to fanaticism bordering on insanity, with the notion of the importance of an allegorical interpretation of Scripture, and advocated its use in the defence of Christianity both in his sermons and in his first book, *The Old Apology for the Truth of the Christian Religion against the Jews and Gentiles Revived* (1705). For many years he published nothing, and was left to pursue his allegorical fancies in peace. But in 1720–21 the publication of letters and pamphlets in advocacy of his notions, with open challenges to the clergy to refute them, brought him into trouble. It was reported that his mind was disordered, and Whiston states that his college allowed him his fellowship, though not in residence, on account of his illness, but that when he appeared at college to prove that he was well he was ordered to go into residence. On his refusing to do this his fellowship was taken from him (1721). Whiston interceded for him in vain, "the clamour against him running so high." In the "Life" prefixed to the collected edition of his works, his non-residence is described as only "a pretence for depriving him." From 1721 he lived for the most part in London, on an allowance of £30 a year from his brother and other presents. He continued to publish bitter and scurrilous pamphlets against the clergy and the advocates of the literal sense of Scripture. His influence on the course of the deistical controversy commenced with his book, *The Moderator between an Infidel and an Apostate, or the Controversy between the Author of the Discourse of the Grounds and Reasons of the Christian Religion and his Reverend Ecclesiastical Opponents Set in a Clear Light* (1725, 3d ed. 1729). The "infidel" intended was Anthony Collins, who had maintained in his book alluded to that the New Testament is based on the Old, and that not the literal but only the allegorical sense of the prophecies can be quoted in proof of the Messiahship of Jesus. Woolston interposed as umpire in the controversy thus started, and, passing from the evidence from prophecy, which alone he allowed, opened the great debate on the evidential value of the miracles of Christ. He denied absolutely the proof from miracles, called in question the fact of the resurrection of Christ and other miracles of the New Testament, and maintained that they must be interpreted allegorically, or as types of spiritual things. Two years later he commenced a series of *Discourses* on the same subject, in which he applied the principles of his *Moderator* to the miracles of the Gospels in detail. The *Discourses*, 30,000 copies of which were said to have been sold, were six in number, the first appearing in 1727, the next five 1728–29, with two *Defences* in 1729–30. The publication of the *Moderator* drew upon him a prosecution by the attorney-general in 1726 for blasphemy and profaneness, which was suspended in consequence of Whiston's intercession. But the appearance of the first four of his *Discourses* caused the renewal of the prosecution, and on March 4, 1729, the trial ended in his being found guilty of the alleged crime. He was sentenced (Nov. 28) to pay a fine of £25 for each of the first four *Discourses*, with imprisonment till paid, and also to a year's imprisonment and to give security for his good behaviour during life, namely, to be bound himself in a recognizance of £2000 and two securities of £1000 each, or four of £500 each. He failed to find this security, and remained in confinement until his death, though he mitigated its severity by purchasing the liberty of the rules of the King's Bench. Dr Samuel Clarke solicited at court for his release, but Woolston's death anticipated any results of his efforts. He died in prison January 21, 1731.

In his attack on the miracles Woolston does not raise the general philosophical question of their possibility, but confines himself to the task of seeking to prove that the accounts of them as given in the Gospels are, when taken literally, full of contradictions, absurdities, and incredibilities, and that they must therefore be interpreted as allegory, and emblems of Christ's more mysterious work. In his view, however, that work of Christ appears to be nothing more than to teach the mystical sense of the Old Testament, the best part of which is the "simple golden religion of nature." He evidently had formed to himself no clear theory of the origin of the accounts of the miracles, sometimes ascribing them to the fancy of the writers, sometimes to deliberate invention, and he does not seek to harmonize any such view of them with their emblematic character, of which he is such a fanatical advocate. Whiston remarks, probably with truth, "When Woolston died he hardly knew himself whether he believed the Christian religion or not." Though it cannot be denied that he anticipated, in some of his criticisms of the details of the miraculous narratives, many points since urged by Reimarus, Strauss, and others, he nowhere exhibits the least soundness of judgment, historical sense, or consistency of thought, while his language and illustrations are coarse and offensive in the extreme.

Upwards of sixty more or less weighty pamphlets appeared in the next few years in reply to his *Moderator* and *Discourses*. As amongst the abler and most popular of them may be mentioned Dr Z. Pearce's *The Miracles of Jesus Vindicated*, 1729; Sherlock's *The Tryal of the Witnesses of the Resurrection of Jesus*, 1729, 13th ed. 1755; and Lardner's *Vindication of Three of Our Saviour's Miracles*, 1729, Lardner being one of those who did not approve of the prosecution of Woolston (see Lardner's Life by Kippis, in Lardner's *Works*, vol. i.).

See Life of Woolston prefixed to his *Works* in five volumes, London, 1733; *Memoirs of Life and Writings of William Whiston*, London, 1749, pp. 231–35; Appendix to *A Vindication of the Miracles of our Saviour, &c.*, by J. Ray, 2d ed. 1731; Lechler's *Geschichte des Englischen Deismus*, 1841; Leland's *View of the Principal Deistical Writers*, 1734; Leslie Stephen's *History of English Thought in 18th Century*, ch. iv.; Cairns's *Unbelief in the Eighteenth Century*, 1880; Sayons's *Les Déistes Anglais*, 1882.

WOOLWICH, a parliamentary borough and garrison town of Kent, England, is situated chiefly on the south bank of the Thames, on the declivity of Shooter's Hill, which slopes downwards to the river, 10 miles from Charing Cross by rail and 12 by steamer. The town is irregularly built, with narrow streets, and for the most part mean-looking houses. The spacious level at the summit of the hill is known as Woolwich Common. The feature of Woolwich is the Royal Arsenal, at which the number of men usually employed is about 10,000. It occupies an area of 333 acres, and includes four departments:—the royal gun factories, employed in the manufacture of rifled wrought-iron and steel ordnance, the principal divisions being the rolling and puddling furnaces, the coiling mills, the boring mills, the tanneries, and the steam-hammers, including one of 40 tons; the royal carriage department, for the manufacture of gun carriages, pontoon trains, baggage and store waggons, and ambulances for the sick and wounded; the royal laboratory department, for the manufacture of shot and shell, caps, fuzes, &c.; and the ordnance store department of the army, for the supply of every kind of military equipment. Separated from the other portions of the arsenal are the laboratories for the manufacture of rockets and cannon cartridges. The Royal Artillery Barracks, facing the Common, originally erected in 1775, has been greatly extended at different times, and now consists of six ranges of brick building, each over 400 feet in length. It includes a church in the Italian Gothic style erected in 1863, a theatre, and a library of 40,000 volumes in connexion with the officers' mess room. Opposite the barracks is the memorial to the officers and men of the royal artillery who fell in the Crimean War, a bronze figure of Victory cast out of cannon captured in the Crimea. Near the barracks is the Royal Artillery Institution, with a fine museum and a lecture hall. On the western side of the barrack field is the Royal Military Repository, where all officers of artillery pass a term of instruction. Within the Repository enclosure is the Rotunda, originally erected in St James's Park for the reception of the allied sovereigns in 1814, and shortly afterwards transferred to its present site. It contains models of the principal dockyards and fortifications of the British empire, naval models of all dates, and numerous specimens of weapons of war from the remotest times to the present day. On the Common is the Royal Military Academy, where cadets are trained for the artillery and engineering services, erected in the castellated style from the design of Sir J. Wyatville in 1801. Within the grounds is a memorial erected to the prince imperial of France, for two years a student in the academy; while near the Rotunda is a monument erected in 1882 to the memory

WORCESTER

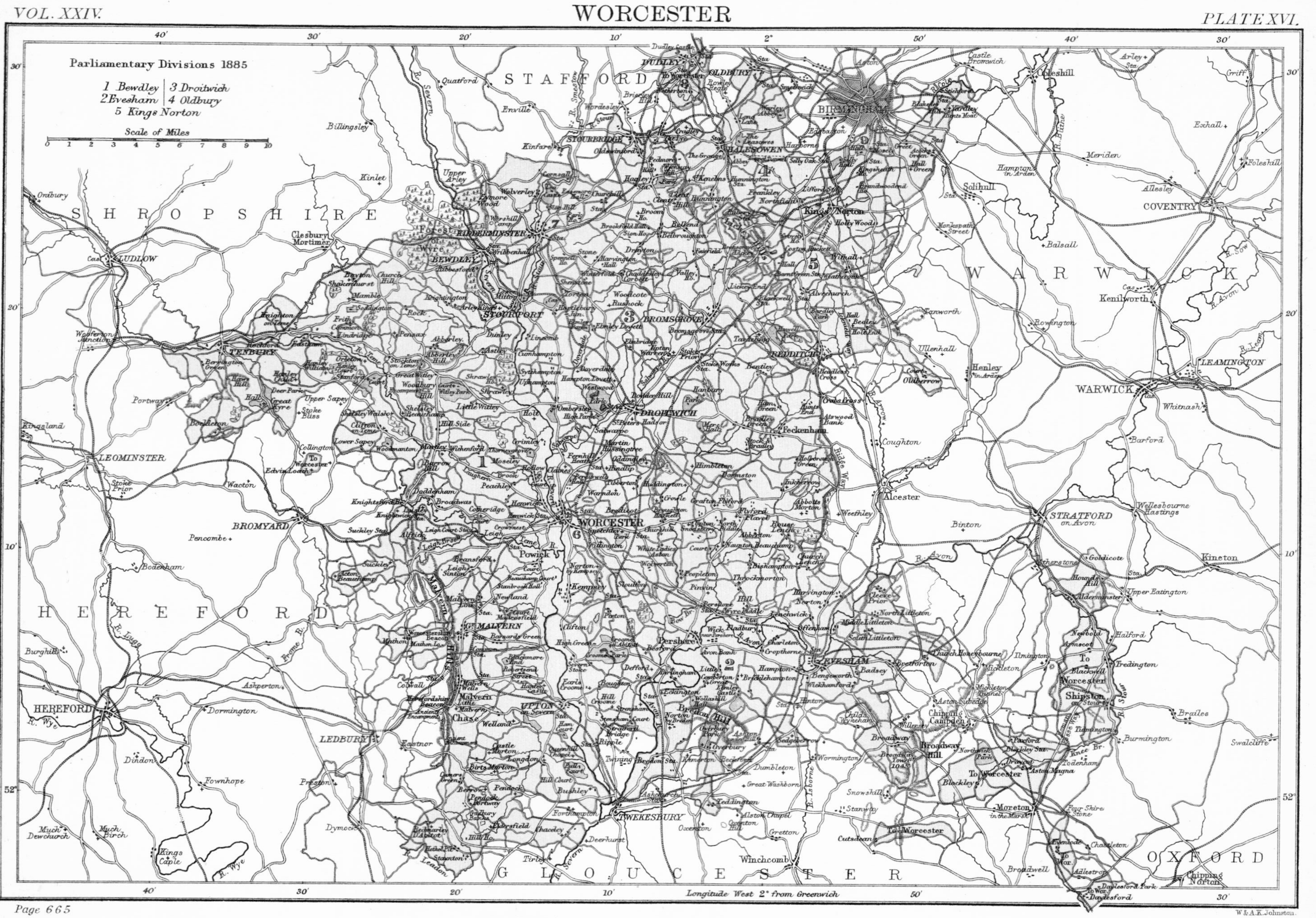

W. & A. K. Johnston.

ENCYCLOPÆDIA BRITANNICA. NINTH EDITION.

of the members of the royal artillery who fell in the Zulu and Afghan wars of 1879. In addition to the great barracks of the royal artillery there are a number of other barracks, and a permanent camp of huts. At the south-east extremity of the Common is the Herbert military hospital. The parish church of St Mary Magdalene was rebuilt, in 1726–29, near the site of the old one dating from before the 12th century. The other parishes are Holy Trinity, St John the Evangelist, and St Michael's and All Angels. The Goldsmiths' almshouses, originally founded by Sir Martin Bowes, who was lord mayor of London in 1545, and rebuilt in 1771 by the Goldsmiths' Company, are (1888), on the appropriation of the charity to pensions, to be purchased by the trustees of the present parochial almshouses, built by private benevolence. Behind the Royal Military Academy is a mineral well, "the Shooter's Hill waters" of Evelyn. Near Woolwich Common there are brick and tile kilns and sand and chalk pits. In the neighbourhood are extensive market-gardens. The town is governed by a local board of health, and is within the jurisdiction of the central criminal court and the metropolitan police. The population of the entire parish of Woolwich (area 1126 acres) in 1871 was 35,557 and in 1881 it was 36,665. The population of the district now included in the parliamentary borough, which comprises the parishes of Woolwich, Eltham, and Plumstead, was 74,963 in 1881.

Woolwich (Wulewich) is mentioned in a grant of land by King Edward in 964 to the abbey of St Peter at Ghent. In Domesday, where the manor is mentioned as consisting of 63 acres of land, it is named Hulviz. The Roman Watling Street crossed Shooter's Hill, and a Roman cemetery is supposed to have occupied the site of the Royal Arsenal, numerous Roman urns and fragments of Roman pottery having been dug up in the neighbourhood. Woolwich seems to have been a small fishing village until in the beginning of the 16th century it rose into prominence as a dockyard and naval station. There is evidence that ships were built at Woolwich in the reign of Henry VII., but it was with the purchase by Henry VIII. of two parcels of land in the manor of Woolwich, called Boughton's Docks, that the foundation of the town's prosperity was laid, the launching of the "Harry Grâce de Dieu," of 1000 tons burden, making an epoch in its history. Woolwich remained the chief dockyard of the English navy until the introduction of iron ship building, but the dockyard was finally closed in 1870. The town has been the headquarters of the royal artillery since the establishment of a separate branch of this service in the reign of George I. An arsenal existed at Woolwich in the reign of Henry VII., and the laboratory is mentioned in 1695. On account of an explosion at Moorfields, the gun foundry was removed to Woolwich in 1716, but the establishment was of minor importance until the commencement of the Napoleonic wars. In 1860 the arsenal was greatly extended. Formerly Woolwich was included in the parliamentary borough of Greenwich, but in 1885 it was made a separate borough returning one member.

WOONSOCKET, a town of Providence county, Rhode Island, United States, on the Blackstone river, 16 miles from Providence and 37 from Boston. The surrounding country, which is fertile, is devoted to market-gardening and dairying. There are 64 miles of streets. The population (11,527 in 1870) was 16,050 in 1880, being nearly half of foreign birth, a fact explained by its extensive manufactures. The principal industries are the manufacture of cotton and woollen goods; of the latter Woonsocket produces more than any other city in the United States, while in the former industry it is excelled by few. Its importance as a manufacturing town is due to the magnificent water-power within its limits.

Plate XVI.

WORCESTER, a midland county of England, of a very irregular shape, and of curious arrangement. Some of its parishes are detached from the county, while portions of other counties extend within its boundaries. It is bounded on the N. by Staffordshire, E. by Warwickshire, S. by Gloucestershire, W. by Herefordshire, and N.W. by Shropshire. The greatest length from north to south is 34 miles, and its breadth 30 miles. The area is 472,453 acres, or about 738 square miles.

Surface and Geology.—The surface consists of very fine and picturesque hills and well-watered and fruitful valleys, and the county is certainly one of the fairest and most picturesque in England. Its finest hills are the well-known Malvern Hills on its south-west border, the Abberley Hills running north from them, the Lickey and Clent Hills in the east, and in the south the Bredon Hills, which are a continuation of the Cotswolds. The principal rivers are the Severn, which is navigable, and runs through the county from north to south; the Stour, which joins the Severn at Stourport; the Teme, which enters the county at Tenbury, receives the Kyre and the Leigh, and falls into the Severn below Worcester; and the Warwickshire Avon, which joins the Severn at Tewkesbury. The valley of the Severn is appropriately named the Vale of Worcester, and that of the Avon the Vale of Evesham,—the latter being generally considered one of the loveliest valleys in England. The rivers are well stocked with fish,—salmon, trout, grayling, shad, and lampreys being found in most of them.

The chief geological formation of the county is the Triassic, and a line running north and south through the Malvern Hills and the Forest of Wyre coalfield would divide the hard and ancient Palæozoic strata from the softer and more recent Mesozoic. Black shales, of about 1000 feet thick, rest upon the Hollybush sandstone near Bransill Castle; and the Silurian formation extends west of the Malverns as far as Abberley. The sandstone known as May Hill exists in the south-west, reaching the Herefordshire Beacon; fossils are often found in it. To the west of Raggedston and Midsummer Hills the Cambrian formation extends; this also is fairly rich in fossils. There is but little of the Old Red Sandstone in the county, but the Carboniferous formation extends from the Forest of Wyre coalfield to the Abberley Hills, and from Bewdley to the western limits of the county. The Permian formation is found near Martley, Abberley, Bewdley, and the Clent Hills, while red marls and sandstones of the Triassic period constitute about three-fourths of the county. At Droitwich and in the Vale of Evesham limestones and a bluish clay exist; and in the gravels deposited by the Severn and the Avon the remains of extinct mammals have been found.

Climate and Agriculture.—The climate is generally equable and healthy, and is very favourable to the cultivation of fruit, vegetables, and hops, for which Worcestershire has long held a high reputation, the red marls and the rich loams which are so prevalent being good both for market gardens and tillage. Its agricultural production consists principally of wheat, barley, beans, fruit, and hops, in the cultivation of which great care and skill are employed. The large and well-stocked orchards, the picturesque hop fields, and the wonderfully productive market gardens are the pride of the county, and one of the most attractive objects to all visitors. According to the agricultural returns for 1887, the area under cultivation was 401,936 acres, distributed as follows:—corn crops, 90,735; green crops, 32,709; clover and rotation grasses, 31,519; permanent pasture, 232,998; flax, 2; hops, 2828; and fallow, 11,145. The area under orchards was 18,687 acres; market gardens, 3525; and nursery grounds, 386. In 1881—the latest return—there were 18,871 acres under woods and plantations. The number of horses in 1887 was 20,249, of which 14,155 were used solely for agriculture; cows in milk or calf, 27,808; other cattle, 38,472; sheep, 174,371, of which 75,065 were under one year; pigs, 33,695.

According to the landowners' return of 1872–3, the total number of proprietors in the county was 21,804, possessing 441,060 acres, with a gross annual estimated rental of £1,685,736. Of the owners, only 5796 possessed one acre or upwards. There were also 3415 acres of waste land. The following are the names of the larger landowners:—earl of Dudley, 14,699 acres; earl of Coventry, 13,021; Earl Beauchamp, 10,624; Lord Windsor, 8519; Harry F. Vernon, 7448; Earl Somers, 6265; Lord Lyttelton, 5908; the Ecclesiastical Commissioners, 5213; R. Berkeley, 4812; Duc D'Aumale, 4604; Sir John Pakington, 4868; Lord Northwick, 4215; and Sir F. Winnington, 4196.

Industries.—Agriculture in its various branches is the principal industry of the county. Its mineral wealth consists of coal, iron, and salt; and a considerable number of people find employment in the quarries of limestone around Pershore and Evesham, and at other quarries of freestone and flagstone. There is not much mining in the county; the largest number of artisans are employed in the various hardware trades, as the making of nails, at Halesowen and the neighbouring villages, and of needles at Redditch, Astwood Bank, and elsewhere. Glass is largely produced at Dudley and Stourbridge. Worcester is famous for its porcelain, its gloves, and its coach-building, and Kidderminster for its carpets. The salt works at Droitwich are as old as the Roman occupation, and there are others at Stoke. There are a large variety of other trades, including crate making, coke burning, alkali, vinegar, and vitriol works, button making, leather staining, paper making, and tanning.

Communication.—The county is well provided with railways and canals. The roads are good, and the means of intercourse and communication are excellent.

Administration and Population.—Worcestershire comprises five hundreds (Halfshire, Doddingtree, Oswaldslow, Pershore, and Blackenhurst), the city of Worcester, and the municipal boroughs of Bewdley, Droitwich, Dudley, Evesham, and Kidderminster. There are eleven market towns. The city of Worcester has a separate court of quarter sessions, and a commission of the peace, and all the boroughs have commissions of the peace. It is in the Oxford circuit; the assizes as well as quarter sessions are held at Worcester. There is one court of quarter sessions in the whole county, and there are sixteen petty sessional divisions. The shire contains 243 civil parishes, and is mostly in the diocese of Worcester but partly in that of Hereford. The principal places besides the city of Worcester are Bewdley (population 3088 in 1881), Bromsgrove (12,813), Droitwich (3761), Dudley (46,252), Evesham (5112), Halesowen (7763), Kidderminster (24,270), Oldbury (18,841), Redditch (9961), Stourbridge (9757), and Tenbury (2083).

By the Redistribution Act of 1885, the county was divided into three parliamentary boroughs and five county divisions. The boroughs, each returning one member, are Dudley, Kidderminster, and Worcester; the county divisions are West (Bewdley), East, South (Evesham), Mid (Droitwich), and North (Oldbury). The population in 1861 was 307,397; in 1871, 338,837; and in 1881, 380,283 (males 184,205, females 196,078). The number of persons to an acre was 0·80, and of acres to a person 1·24.

History.—Worcestershire was not a district of much importance in the days of the Roman occupation of Britain. By occupying Gloucester the Romans held the valley of the lower Severn, and thence their roads ran to Hereford, and not till *Uriconium* (Wroxeter) on the side of the Wrekin did they regard the Severn valley as again habitable. This was due to the fact that the greater part of the district now contained in Worcestershire was forest and jungle, not inviting occupation to the colonist. Here and there the Romans held a military outpost, as at Worcester, keeping on the east side of the river; but the west side was left to the Britons, who found a home on the summits of the Malvern Hills. It was long before the English invaders thought the Severn valley worthy of their arms; but in the beginning of the 7th century the tribe of the Hwiccas was in possession of the lands now contained in Warwickshire, Worcestershire, and Gloucestershire. The Hwiccas formed part of the Mercian kingdom, and when Archbishop Theodore undertook the ecclesiastical organization of England he set up at Worcester a bishop of the Hwiccas, and the diocese of Worcester continued to mark the limits of the Hwiccan territory till Henry VIII. founded the separate see of Gloucester.

The church was the main instrument of civilization in Worcestershire. The abbey of Evesham was the centre of agricultural life along the valley of the Avon; the priory of Malvern began the clearing of the forest which reached from the hills to the Severn. Many other religious houses were spread over the county. There were no great barons, as much of the land was given in early times to the church, and much consisted of forest which was only slowly cleared. The bishop of Worcester was the undoubted head of the district, and provided for its defence. The chief historical event connected with the county in the Middle Ages, the battle of Evesham, was owing to the fact that Walter de Cantilupe, bishop of Worcester, was a firm friend and adherent of Simon de Montfort in his opposition to the misgovernment of Henry III. When Earl Simon had seized the king's person in the battle of Lewes, the chief opposition to his government was raised by the lords marchers on the Welsh borders. Simon went to Hereford for the purpose of reducing them to submission; but Edward's escape from captivity gave them a leader, and awakened the hopes of the royalists. Simon sent for reinforcements, but his son was surprised and cut off at Kenilworth. Ignorant of the fact, but afraid to wait any longer lest the passage of the Severn should be closed against him, Simon withdrew to the friendly territory of the bishop of Worcester, and took up his abode in the abbey of Evesham. There in 1265 he was surprised by Edward, and died fighting a hopeless fight.

As Wales became more settled, Worcester developed its trade slowly. From early times the salt mines at Droitwich were worked, and a "salt-way" was made for the carriage of their produce. A trade with Wales and Bristol was established, and clothiers sent their wares from Bewdley and Worcester down the Severn. The dissolution of the monasteries affected very seriously a district which was so closely connected with the church, and it was some time before it recovered from the shock which its social life then received. In the great civil war Worcestershire, in common with the west of England, was Royalist, and suffered considerably from the Parliamentary forces. In 1651 Charles II. with the Scottish army marched to Worcester, where he was welcomed by the citizens. Cromwell followed, and took up his position on the Red Hill just outside the city gates. Lambert succeeded in passing the Severn at Upton, and drove back the Royalist troops to the neighbourhood of Worcester, on the other side of the Severn. Charles determined to take advantage of this division of the Parliamentary army on the two sides of the river, and made an attack on Cromwell's camp. At first he was successful, but Cromwell was reinforced by Lambert's troops from the other side in time to drive back Charles's foot, who were not supported by the Scottish horse. Their rout was complete; Charles managed to escape into the city, where he escaped in disguise, and began his adventurous journey to Boscobel. Since that time Worcestershire has pursued a course of peaceful development.

See Nash, *History of Worcestershire* (2 vols. fol., 1799); Chambers, *Biographical Illustrations of Worcestershire* (1820); Turberville, *Worcestershire in the 19th Century* (1852); Allies, *Antiquities and Folk-Lore of Worcestershire* (1852), and Noake, *Guide to Worcestershire* (1868).

WORCESTER, an episcopal city, municipal and parliamentary borough, the capital of the above county, and a county of itself, is situated on the eastern bank of the Severn, 120 miles from London by rail, and a little over 26 from Birmingham.

The principal building and chief glory of the city is the cathedral. The see was founded by the advice of Archbishop Theodore in 673, though, owing to opposition on the part of the bishop of Lichfield, it was not finally established

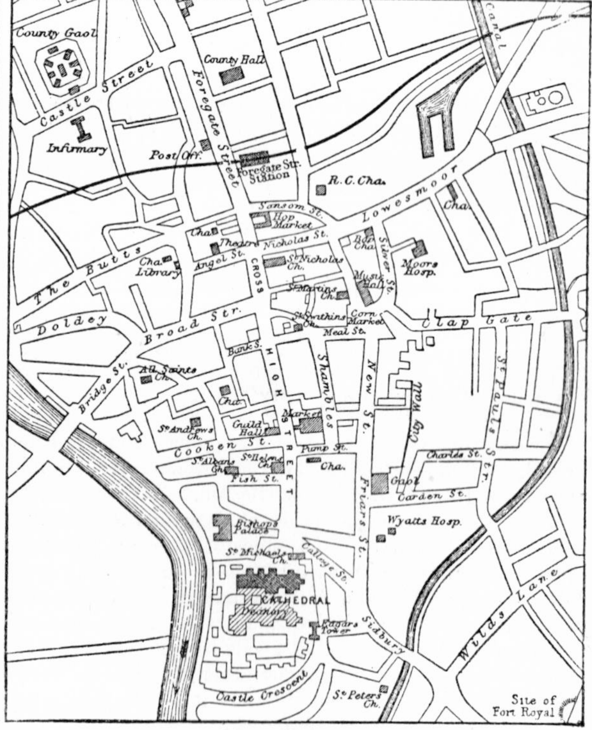

Plan of Worcester.

till 780. In its formation the tribal division was followed, and it contained the people of the Hwiccas. The bishop's church of St Peter's, with its secular canons, was absorbed by Bishop Oswald into the monastery of St Mary. The canons became monks, and in 983 Oswald finished the building of a new monastic cathedral. After the Norman Conquest the saintly bishop of Worcester, Wulfstan, was the only English prelate who was left in possession of his see. He so far adopted Norman customs as to undertake the building of a great church of stone according to the Norman pattern. In 1088 an incursion of the Welsh stopped his labours for a time, but in 1094 he held a synod in the crypt. Of the work of Wulfstan, the outer walls of the nave, aisles, a part of the walls of the transepts, some shafts, and the crypt remain. The crypt is apsidal, a style of which there are only four examples in England—Winchester, 1079; Worcester, 1084; Gloucester, 1089; and Canterbury, 1096. Wulfstan's building seems to have extended no farther than the transepts, but the nave was continued, though much of it was destroyed by the fall of the central tower in 1175. In 1203 Wulfstan was canonized, and the monks, growing richer by the offerings at his shrine, finished the cathedral in 1216. Soon after this date they built a lady chapel at the east end, extending the building by 50 feet; then they were so satisfied with their new work that the choir was rebuilt to match in the Early English style. The nave was similarly remodelled in the 14th century, the north side in the Decorated, the south side in the Perpendicular style. The building is cruciform, and is without transept aisles, but has secondary transepts to the choir. The tower is in the centre, and is 162 feet high. There is an interesting chapter house of Late Norman architecture, a round building with its stone roof supported on a central pillar. The refectory is a fine room of Decorated architecture, and the cloisters are Perpendicular. The cathedral was very much out of repair in 1857, when the restoration was undertaken by the cathedral architect, Mr Perkins, in which most of the work of previous generations was wholly swept away, and in some important particulars replaced by conjectural work of Early English style. The cost was about £100,000, raised principally by public subscription, though for four years the dean and chapter had provided the funds required.

In the cathedral are several good monuments and monumental effigies. That of King John, in the choir, is the earliest sepulchral effigy of an English king in the country. There is an altar tomb, in a chantry chapel, of Arthur, prince of Wales, son of Henry VII., who died in 1503. There are also monuments of John Gauden, the bishop who wrote *Icon Basilike*, so often attributed to Charles I., of Bishop Hough by Roubillac, and of Mrs Digby by Chantrey. There are many other monuments; and in the north alley of the cloister is a stone on which is cut the sad and significant word "Miserrimus," and nothing more—a tragedy in a single word.

There are eleven parish churches in the city:—St Helen's, the oldest, was rebuilt in 1820; St Albans, ancient, partially restored in 1850; All Saints, built in 1740, which contains a peal of ten bells; St Andrew's, repewed in 1850; St Nicholas, begun in 1728 and finished in 1730; St Martin's, erected in 1772; St Swithin's, in 1736; St Peter's, dating from 1686, which has annexed to it the chapelry of Whittington; St Michael's, in Bedwardine, modern; St John's, Bedwardine, made a parish church in 1371; and St Clement's, built in 1823. In 1874 a parish was formed out of Claines, named the Tything, and in 1876 the church (St Mary Magdalene) was built; St Paul's was built in 1837, and constituted a separate parish in 1844; St George's, built by subscription in 1830, was made a parish out of Claines, in 1862; Holy Trinity, erected in 1865, was formed a parish in 1866. There are also a Roman Catholic chapel and places of worship for all descriptions of Dissenters.

There are no remains of the old castle of Worcester; it adjoined the monastery so closely that King John gave its yard to the monks, and after that time it ceased to be a stronghold. The Commandery, founded by St Wulfstan in 1095, is one of the "rarest specimens of early house architecture in existence." The hall contains an open timber roof of the time of Henry VII., "a good bay window, a fine door, the projecting canopy of the dais, a music-screen and gallery, and some fragments of stained glass." The cathedral grammar school, founded by Henry VIII. in 1541, occupies the refectory of the old monastery, which has just been restored by Mr Christian, and has many interesting architectural features.

The guild-hall, built in 1723, is an admirable building in the Italian style; it contains a portrait of George III., painted by Sir Joshua Reynolds, and presented by the king to commemorate his visit to the city at the triennial musical festival in 1788. The corporation possess some very interesting old charters and manuscripts, and good municipal regalia. The shire-hall, erected in 1835 at a cost of £35,000, is a fine stone building in the Ionic style, with a portico supported by six fluted columns. The county jail, built in 1809 at a cost of £19,000, was entirely reconstructed on the separate principle in 1860, at a further cost of £24,000. The infirmary was built in 1770, the dispensary in 1822, and the ophthalmic institution in 1866. There is a museum of natural history; and a free library was opened in 1881. Worcester has long been famous for several important branches of industry. The Clothiers' Company possess a charter granted by Queen Elizabeth; but the great industries are now the manufacture of gloves and of porcelain. A company of glovers was incorporated in 1661; it is principally occupied with the making of skin gloves, in which the skins of deer, sheep, lambs, goats, and kids are used. The manufacture of porcelain was introduced by Dr Wall, a Worcester physician, in 1751 (see vol. xix. p. 642). The materials employed are china clay and china stone from Cornwall, felspar from Sweden, fire-clay from Stourbridge and Broseley, marl, flint, and calcined bones. Pickles and sauces are among the notable productions of the city: and among its other trades are those of carriage making, rope and twine spinning, boat and barge building, tanning, and the production of chemical manures and of cider and perry.

The charities of Worcester are numerous, and include St Oswald's hospital, Nash's almshouses, Wyatt's almshouses, the Berkeley hospital, Goulding hospital, Shewring's hospital, Inglethorpe's almshouses, Waldgrave's almshouses, Moore's blue-coat school, Queen Elizabeth's charity, and others, which produce an annual income of more than £10,000. The population of the city and municipal borough (area 1263 acres) in 1871 was 33,226 and in 1881 it was 33,956. The population of the parliamentary borough (area 3266 acres) in 1871 was 38,116 and in 1881 it was 40,354.

Among the charters still preserved in the guild-hall is one of Richard I. dated November 12, 1189, which grants to the burgesses to hold of the king and his heirs the town of Worcester at a yearly rental of £24. In the reign of Philip and Mary the town was raised to the dignity of a city, and this with other privileges was confirmed by Elizabeth in 1558; and in 1622 James I. granted a charter ordaining that the city shall be a free city of itself, and a county separate from all other counties. From the time of Edward I. until 1885 Worcester returned two members to parliament, but the number was then reduced to one. Municipally the city is divided into five wards. The county assizes are held in the city, as are also the quarter sessions, the county court, the borough court, town and county petty sessions, and the ecclesiastical and probate court.

The Romans found a British settlement and held it as a military station, to which they gave the name *Vigorna*. By the Saxons it was called Wigorna-ceaster, whence we have the present name of Worcester. It was more than once burnt and pillaged by the Danes, but at the date of the Conquest it was of sufficient importance to have a mint. From its proximity to Wales, it frequently suffered from the inroads of the Welsh. It was taken by the empress Maud, and retaken by Stephen, after severe contests. The king kept the Easter week there in 1139,—as it is recorded, with "great pomp"; and in 1234 Henry III. held the Whitsuntide festival in the city. Queen Elizabeth rested there in one of her progresses; in 1687 James II. came, and touched for the king's evil. He attended mass in the Catholic chapel; but the mayor and the corporation, though accompanying him to the chapel door, firmly and patriotically declined to enter.

For the part this city took in the great civil war see p. 666.

WORCESTER, a city and the county seat of Worcester county, Massachusetts, United States, is situated in a region of Glacial hills, lakes, and ponds, which form varied and pleasing landscapes, 39 miles west of Boston. Besides the closely-built portion, the city includes a large suburban district, which contains fourteen villages of various sizes. The closely-built portion is very irregularly laid out, conforming in some degree to the slope of the ground. There are 197 miles of streets, very little of which is paved. The public parks have an aggregate area of 35 acres. The population in 1885 was 68,389 (20,182, or 29·51 per cent. of foreign birth). The proportion of coloured people was very small. The manufacturing industries are very large and varied; prominent among them are the manufactures of iron and steel, foundry and machine shop products and tools, and second to these the manufacture of boots and shoes.

The settlement of Worcester began in 1713. Earlier attempts had been made, but the incursions of Indians had frustrated them. It was incorporated as a town in 1722, but made very slow progress in growth until the completion of the Boston and Worcester (now Boston and Albany) Railroad in 1835. Since that date, with the extension of its railroad connexions, it has developed rapidly. In 1848 it received a city charter, and at present it is the third city of the State in population and wealth. The population, which in 1765 was 1478 and in 1790 was 2095, rose to 4173 in 1830, 7497 in 1840, 17,049 in 1850, 41,105 in 1870, and 58,291 in 1880.

WORCESTER, Florence of. See vol. ix. p. 337.

WORDSWORTH, William (1770–1850), the poet, was born at Cockermouth, on the Derwent, in Cumberland, on the 7th of April 1770. His parentage offers a curious parallel to Scott's: he was the son of an attorney, law-agent to the earl of Lonsdale, a prosperous man in his profession, descended from an old Yorkshire family of landed gentry. On the mother's side also Wordsworth was connected with the middle territorial class: his mother, Anne Cookson, was the daughter of a well-to-do mercer in Penrith, but her mother was a Crackanthorpe, whose ancestors had been lords of the manor of Newbiggin, near Penrith, from the time of Edward III. He was thus, as Scott put it in his own case, come of "gentle" kin, and like Scott he was proud of it, and dictated the fact in his short fragment of prose autobiography. The country squires and farmers whose blood flowed in Wordsworth's veins were not far enough above local life to be out of sympathy with it, and the poet's interest in the common scenes and common folk of the North country hills and dales had a traceable hereditary bias.

Though his parents were of sturdy stock, both died prematurely, his mother when he was five years old, his father when he was thirteen, the ultimate cause of death in his mother's case being exposure to cold in "a best bedroom" in London, in his father's exposure on a Cumberland hill, where he had been befogged and lost his way. At the age of eight Wordsworth was sent to school at Hawkshead, in the Esthwaite valley in Lancashire. His father died while he was there, and at the age of seventeen he was sent by his uncle to St John's College, Cambridge. He did not distinguish himself in the studies of the university, and for some time after taking his degree of B.A., which he did in January 1791, he showed what seemed to his relatives a most perverse reluctance to adopt any regular profession. His mother had noted his "stiff, moody, and violent temper" in childhood, and it seemed as if this family judgment was to be confirmed in his manhood. After taking his degree, he was pressed to take holy orders, but would not; he had no taste for the law; he idled a few months aimlessly in London, a few months more with a Welsh college friend, with whom he had made a pedestrian tour in France and Switzerland during his last Cambridge vacation; then in the November of 1791 he crossed to France, ostensibly to learn the language, made the acquaintance of revolutionaries, sympathized with them vehemently, and was within an ace of throwing in his lot with the Brissotins to give them the steady direction that they needed. When it came to this, his relatives cut off his supplies, and he was obliged to return to London towards the close of 1792. But still he resisted all pressure to enter any of the regular professions, published *An Evening Walk* and *Descriptive Sketches* in 1793, and in 1794, still moving about to all appearance in stubborn aimlessness among his friends and relatives, had no more rational purpose of livelihood than drawing up the prospectus of a periodical of strictly republican principles to be called "The Philanthropist." At this stage, at the age of twenty-four, Wordsworth seemed to his friends a very hopeless and impracticable young man.

But all the time from his boyhood upwards a great purpose had been growing and maturing in his mind. *The Prelude* expounds in lofty impassioned strain, treating of simple facts in diction that would be "poetic" beyond the worst extravagances of the panegyrical school but for the genuine emotion that inspires its amplitude of phrase, how his sensibility for nature was "augmented and sustained," and how it never, except for a brief interval, ceased to be "creative" in the special sense of his subsequent theory. But it is with his feelings towards nature that *The Prelude* mainly deals; it says little regarding the history of his ambition to express those feelings in verse. It is the autobiography, not of the poet of nature, but of the worshipper and priest. The salient incidents in the history of the poet he communicated in prose notes and in familiar discourses. And it appears that, while he was still a schoolboy of fourteen, the delight that he took in contemplating and moralizing from nature was mingled with the enthusiasm of a poet's ambition and joy in the discovery of a fresh imperfectly worked field. Commenting on the couplet in the *Evening Walk*—

"And, fronting the bright west, yon oak entwines
Its darkening boughs and leaves in stronger lines—"

he said:

"This is feebly and imperfectly exprest; but I recollect distinctly the very spot where this first struck me. It was on the way between Hawkshead and Ambleside, and gave me extreme pleasure. The moment was important in my poetical history; for I date from it my consciousness of the infinite variety of natural appearances which had been unnoticed by the poets of any age or country, so far as I was acquainted with them; *and I made a resolution to supply in some degree the deficiency.* I could not at that time have been above fourteen years of age."

About the same time he wrote, as a school task at Hawkshead, verses that show considerable acquaintance with the poets of his own country at least, as well as some previous practice in the art of verse-making.[1] The fragment that stands at the beginning of his collected works, recording a resolution to end his life among his

[1] *Memoirs of William Wordsworth*, by Canon Wordsworth, vol. i. pp. 10, 11. According to his own statement in the memoranda dictated to his biographer, it was the success of this exercise that "put it into his head to compose verses from the impulse of his own mind." The resolution to supply the deficiencies of poetry in the exact description of natural appearances was probably formed while he was in this state of boyish ecstasy at the accidental revelation of his own powers. The date of his beginnings as a poet is confirmed by the lines in *The Idiot Boy*, written in 1798—

"I to the Muses have been bound
These fourteen years by strong indentures."

native hills, was the conclusion of a long poem written while he was still at school. And, undistinguished as he was at Cambridge in the contest for academic honours, the *Evening Walk*, his first publication, was written during his vacations.[1] He published it in 1793, to show, as he said, that he could do something, although he had not distinguished himself in university work. It is significant of his persistency of purpose that in this poem, as well as in the *Descriptive Sketches* founded on his tour abroad during his last vacation, he is seen to be steadily fulfilling his resolution to supply defects in the minute description of nature. There are touches here and there of the bent of imagination that became dominant in him soon afterwards, notably in the moral aspiration that accompanies his *Remembrance of Collins* on the Thames:—

> "O glide, fair stream! for ever so
> Thy quiet soul on all bestowing,
> Till all our minds for ever flow
> As thy deep waters now are flowing."

But in the main this first publication represents the poet in the stage described in the twelfth book of *The Prelude*:—

> "Bent overmuch on superficial things,
> Pampering myself with meagre novelties
> Of colour and proportion; to the moods
> Of time and season, to the moral power,
> The affections, and the spirit of the place
> Insensible."

Nature was little more than a picture-gallery to him; the pleasures of the eye had all but absolute dominion; and he

> "Roamed from hill to hill, from rock to rock,
> Still craving combinations of new forms,
> New pleasures, wider empire for the sight,
> Proud of her own endowments, and rejoiced
> To lay the inner faculties asleep."

But, though he had not yet found his distinctive aim as a poet, he was inwardly bent, all the time that his relatives saw in him only a wayward and unpromising aversion to work in any regular line, upon poetry as "his office upon earth."

In this determination he was strengthened by his sister Dorothy, who with rare devotion consecrated her life henceforward to his service. A timely legacy enabled them to carry their purpose into effect. A friend of his, whom he had nursed in a last illness, Raisley Calvert, son of the steward of the duke of Norfolk, who had large estates in Cumberland, died early in 1795, leaving him a legacy of £900. And here it may be well to notice how opportunely, as De Quincey half-ruefully remarked, money always fell in to Wordsworth, enabling him to pursue his poetic career without distraction. Calvert's bequest came to him when he was on the point of concluding an engagement as a journalist in London. On it and other small resources he and his sister, thanks to her frugal management, contrived to live for nearly eight years. By the end of that time Lord Lonsdale, who owed Wordsworth's father a large sum for professional services, and had steadily refused to pay it, died, and his successor paid the debt with interest. His wife, Mary Hutchinson, whom he married in 1802, brought him some fortune; and in 1813, when in spite of his plain living his family began to press upon his income, he was appointed stamp-distributor for Westmorland, with an income of £500, afterwards nearly doubled by the increase of his district. By this succession of timely godsends, Wordsworth, though he did not escape some periods of sharp anxiety, was saved from the necessity of turning aside from his vocation.

To return, however, to the course of his life from the time when he resolved to labour with all his powers in the office of poet. The first two years, during which he lived with his self-sacrificing sister at Racedown, in Dorset, were spent in half-hearted and very imperfectly successful experiments, satires in imitation of Juvenal, the tragedy of *The Borderers*,[2] and a poem in the Spenserian stanza, the poem now entitled *Guilt and Sorrow*. How much longer this time of doubtful self-distrustful endeavour might have continued is a subject for curious speculation; an end was put to it by a fortunate incident, a visit from Coleridge, who had read his first publication, and seen in it, what none of the public critics had discerned, the advent of "an original poetic genius." It would be impossible to exaggerate the importance for Wordsworth of the arrival of this enthusiastic Columbus. Under his sister's genial influence[3] he was groping his way doubtfully out of the labyrinth of poetic conventions, beginning to see a new pathos and sublimity in human life, but not yet convinced except by fits and starts of the rightness of his own vision. Stubborn and independent as Wordsworth was, he needed some friendly voice from the outer world to give him confidence in himself. Coleridge rendered him this indispensable service. He had begun to seek his themes in

> "Sorrow, that is not sorrow, but delight;
> And miserable love, that is not pain
> To hear of, for the glory that redounds
> Therefrom to human kind, and what we are."

He read to his visitor one of these experiments, the story of the ruined cottage, afterwards introduced into the first book of *The Excursion*.[4] Coleridge, who had already seen original poetic genius in the poems published before, was enthusiastic in his praise of them as having "a character, by books not hitherto reflected," and his praise gave new heart and hope to the poet hitherto hesitating and uncertain.

June 1797 was the date of this memorable visit. So pleasant was the companionship on both sides that, when Coleridge returned to Nether Stowey in Somerset, Wordsworth at his instance changed his quarters to Alfoxden, within a mile and a half of Coleridge's temporary residence, and the two poets lived in almost daily intercourse for the next twelve months. During that period Wordsworth's powers rapidly expanded and matured; ideas that had been gathering in his mind for years, and lying there in dim confusion, felt the stir of a new life, and ranged themselves in clearer shapes under the fresh quickening breath of Coleridge's swift and discursive

[1] In *The Prelude*, book iv., he speaks of himself during his first vacation as "harassed with the toil of verse, much pains and little progress." To the same time belongs an incident recorded later in the same book, when he was returning in early morning from a dance—

> "My heart was full: I made no vows, but vows
> Were then made for me; bond unknown to me
> Was given, that I should be, else sinning greatly,
> A dedicated spirit."

[2] Not published till 1842. For the history of this tragedy see *Memoirs*, vol. i. p. 113; for a sound, if severe, criticism of it, Mr Swinburne's *Miscellanies*, p. 118. And yet it was of the blank verse of *The Borderers* that Coleridge spoke when he wrote to Cottle that "he felt a little man by the side of his friend."

[3] The character of Dorothy Wordsworth is shown in the extracts from her Journal printed in the *Memoirs*, and in her *Recollections of a Tour in Scotland*, edited by the late Principal Shairp, 1874. The poet's acknowledgments of obligation to her were not mere grateful words thrown out at random—

> "She gave me eyes, she gave me ears,
> And humble cares, and delicate fears;
> A heart, the fountain of sweet tears,
> And love, and faith, and joy."

The fourteenth book of *The Prelude* especially enables us to understand the full meaning of this eulogium, every word of which has been carefully weighed. This book contains a complete picture of the state of mind in which Coleridge found the poet, when he "seemed to gain clear sight of a new world—a world, too, that was fit to be transmitted and made visible to other eyes."

[4] The version read to Coleridge, however, must have been in Spenserian stanzas, if Coleridge was right in his recollection that it was in the same metre with *The Female Vagrant*, the original title of *Guilt and Sorrow*.

dialectic. The radiant restless vitality of the more variously gifted man stirred the stiffer and more sluggish nature of the recluse to its depths, and Coleridge's quick and generous appreciation of his power gave him precisely the encouragement that he needed.

The *Lyrical Ballads* were the poetic fruits of their companionship. Out of their frequent discussions of the relative value of common life and supernatural incidents as themes for imaginative treatment grew the idea of writing a volume together, composed of poems of the two kinds. Coleridge was to take the supernatural; and, as his industry was not equal to his friend's, this kind was represented by the *Ancient Mariner* alone. Among Wordsworth's contributions were *The Female Vagrant*, *We are Seven*, *Complaint of a Forsaken Indian Woman*, *The Last of the Flock*, *The Idiot Boy*, *The Mad Mother* ("Her eyes are wild"), *The Thorn*, *Goody Blake and Harry Gill*, *The Reverie of Poor Susan*, *Simon Lee*, *Expostulation and Reply*, *The Tables Turned*, *Lines left upon a Yew-tree Seat*, *An Old Man Travelling* ("Animal Tranquillity and Decay"), *Lines above Tintern Abbey*. The volume was published by Cottle of Bristol in September, 1798.

It is necessary to enumerate the contents of this volume in fairness to the contemporaries of Wordsworth, whom it is the fashion to reproach for their cold or scoffing reception of his first distinctive work. Those Wordsworthians who give up *The Idiot Boy*, *Goody Blake*, and *The Thorn* as mistaken experiments have no right to triumph over the first derisive critics of the *Lyrical Ballads*, or to wonder at the dulness that failed to see at once in this humble issue from an obscure provincial press the advent of a great master in literature. The poems that have not yet won general acceptance even among the most devoted Wordsworthians formed a large part of the whole revelation, and attention was specially drawn to them by the title. While the taste for *The Idiot Boy* is still uncreated, still far from general, while critics of authority can still so completely miss the poet's intention as to suggest that the poem might have been enjoyable if Betty Foy's imbecile son had been described as beautiful and the word "idiot" had not been left to convey uncorrected its repulsive associations, while intimate disciples acknowledge themselves unable to understand the "glee" with which Wordsworth told the simple story, and wonder whether he intended it as a "comic poem,"[1] it may be doubted whether now, after nearly a century of discipleship and exposition, the *Lyrical Ballads* would receive a much more cordial or much wider welcome than they did in 1798. It is true that *Tintern Abbey* was in the volume, and that all the highest qualities of Wordsworth's imagination and of his verse could be illustrated now from the lyrical ballads proper in this first publication; but before we accuse our predecessors of purblindness, corrupt taste, and critical malignity, as is the sweet and reasonable custom of too many professing Wordsworthians,[2] we should remember that clear vision is easier for us than it was for them when the revelation was fragmentary and incomplete.

Although Wordsworth was not received at first with the respect to which we now see that he was entitled, his power was not entirely without recognition. There is a curious commercial evidence of this, which ought to be noted, because a perversion of the fact is sometimes used to exaggerate the supposed neglect of Wordsworth at the outset of his career. When the Longmans took over Cottle's publishing business in 1799, the value of the copyright of the *Lyrical Ballads*, for which Cottle had paid thirty guineas, was assessed at *nil*. Cottle therefore begged that it might be excluded altogether from the bargain, and presented it to the authors. But in 1800, when the first edition was exhausted, the Longmans offered Wordsworth £100 for two issues of a new edition with an additional volume and an explanatory preface. The sum was small compared with what Scott and Byron soon afterwards received, but it shows that the public neglect was not quite so complete as is sometimes represented. Another edition was called for in 1802, and a fourth in 1805. The new volume in the 1800 edition was made up of poems composed during his residence at Goslar in the winter of 1798–99, and after his settlement at Grasmere in December 1799. It contained a large portion of poems now universally accepted:—*Ruth*, *Nutting*, *Three Years She Grew*, *A Poet's Epitaph*, *Hartleap Well*, *Lucy Gray*, *The Brothers*, *Michael*, *The Old Cumberland Beggar*, *Poems on the Naming of Places*. But it contained also the famous Preface, in which he infuriated critics by presuming to defend his eccentricities in an elaborate theory of poetry and poetic diction.

Comparatively few in the present day have actually read and studied this famous document, although it is constantly referred to as a sort of revolutionary proclamation against the established taste of the eighteenth century. For one that has read Wordsworth's original, hundreds have read Coleridge's brilliant criticism, and the fixed conception of the doctrines actually put forth by Wordsworth is taken from this. Now, although the Preface and the extensive and bitter discussion provoked by it had not a tithe of the influence on poetry ascribed to it by a natural liking for sudden changes and simple personal agencies, although the result on literary practice was little more than the banishment of a few overdriven phrases and figures of speech from poetic diction,[3] it is desirable, considering the celebrity of the affair, that Wordsworth's exact position should be made clear. To do this is to contradict several "vulgar errors" on the subject, probably too vulgar and deeply rooted to be affected by any exposure. Coleridge's criticism of his friend's theory proceeded avowedly "on the assumption that his words had been rightly interpreted, as purporting that the proper diction for poetry in general consists altogether in a language taken, with due exceptions, from the mouths of men in real life, a language which actually constitutes the natural conversation of men under the influence of natural feelings." Coleridge assumed further that, when Wordsworth spoke of there being "no essential difference between the language of prose and metrical composition," he meant by language not the mere words but the style, the structure, and the order of the sentences; on this assumption he argued as if Wordsworth had held that the metrical order should always be the same as the prose order. Given these assumptions, which formed the popular interpretation of the theory

[1] The defect of *The Idiot Boy* is really rhetorical, rather than poetic. Wordsworth himself said that "he never wrote anything with so much glee," and, once the source of his glee is felt in the nobly affectionate relations between the two half-witted irrational old women and the glorious imbecile, the work is seen to be executed with a harmony that should satisfy the most exacting criticism. The poet not only felt but gave complete expression to the most exquisitely tender humour in telling the story of the simple incident. Poetically, therefore, the poem is a success; not a note is out of tune, with the exception perhaps of the boisterous ridicule of the romantic ballad in his speculations as to the employment of the lost horseman; otherwise, as a work of art in a rare vein of humorous tenderness elevated by the moral dignity of the subject, *The Idiot Boy* is as perfect as anything that Wordsworth wrote. But rhetorically this particular attempt to "breathe grandeur upon the very humblest face of human life" must be pronounced a failure, inasmuch as the writer did not use sufficiently forcible means to disabuse his readers of vulgar prepossessions.

[2] Herein curiously, if not ridiculously, inconsistent, as their master was not, with his tranquillizing creed.

[3] Sir Henry Taylor, one of the most acute and judicious of Wordsworth's champions, came to this conclusion in 1834.

by its opponents, it was easy to demonstrate its absurdity, and Coleridge is very generally supposed to have given Wordsworth's theory in its bare and naked extravagance the *coup de grâce*. But the truth is that neither of the two assumptions is warranted; not only so, but both were expressly disclaimed by Wordsworth in the Preface itself. There is not a single qualification introduced by Coleridge in correction of the theory that was not made by Wordsworth himself in the original statement.[1] In the first place, it was not put forward as a theory of poetry in general, though from the vigour with which he carried the war into the enemy's country it was naturally enough for polemic purposes taken as such; it was a statement and defence of the principles on which his own poems of humbler life were composed, undertaken at the instance of friends interested in "a class of poetry well adapted to interest mankind permanently, and not unimportant in the quality and in the multiplicity of its moral relations." He assailed the public taste as "depraved," first and mainly in so far as it was adverse to simple incidents simply treated, being accustomed to "gross and violent stimulants," "craving after extraordinary incident," possessed with a "degrading thirst after outrageous stimulation," "frantic novels, sickly and stupid German tragedies, and deluges of idle and extravagant stories in verse." This, and not adherence to the classical rule of Pope, which had really suffered deposition a good half century before, was the first count in Wordsworth's defensive indictment of the taste of his age. To make it perfectly clear that he was pleading only for his own maligned and misunderstood poems, he repeated at the close of the Preface that, "if his purpose were fulfilled, a species of poetry would be produced which is genuine poetry, in its nature well adapted to interest mankind, &c." It is true that he said also that, "in order entirely to enjoy the poetry which I am recommending, it would be necessary to give up much of what is ordinarily enjoyed"; but the context makes it plain that in so saying he referred to startling incident and gaudy ornament, his own purpose being to make "the feeling give importance to the action and situation, not the action and situation to the feeling," and to use language as near as possible to the language of real life. In the second place, as regards this language of real life, and the "poetic diction," the liking for which was the second count in his indictment of the public taste, it is most explicitly clear that, when he said that there was no essential difference between the language of poetry and the language of prose, he meant words, plain and figurative, and not structure and order, or, as Coleridge otherwise puts it, the "ordonnance" of composition. Coleridge says that if he meant this he was only uttering a truism, which nobody that knew Wordsworth would suspect him of doing; but, strange to say, it is as a truism, nominally acknowledged by everybody, that Wordsworth does advance his doctrine on this point. Only he adds—"if in what I am about to say it shall appear to some that my labour is unnecessary, and that I am like a man fighting a battle without enemies, such persons may be reminded that, whatever be the language outwardly holden by men, a practical faith in the opinions which I am wishing to establish is almost unknown"; and what he wished to establish, as may be seen by any person of average intelligence who grapples honestly with his stiff and condensed exposition, and interprets it with reference to the controversy in which it was an incident, was the simple truth that what is false, unreal, affected, bombastic, or nonsensical in prose is not less so in verse. There was no greater heresy than this in Wordsworth's theory of poetic diction. The form in which he expresses the theory was conditioned by the circumstances of the polemic, and readers were put on a false scent by his purely incidental and collateral and very much overstrained defence of the language of rustics, as being less conventional and more permanent, and therefore better fitted to afford materials for the poet's selection. But this was a side issue, a paradoxical retort on his critics, seized upon by them in turn and made prominent as a matter for easy ridicule; all that he says on this head might be cut out of the Preface without affecting in the least his main thesis. The drift of this is fairly apparent all through, but stands out in unmistakable clearness in his criticism of the passages from Johnson and Cowper.

"But the sound of the church-going bell
These valleys and rocks never heard,
Ne'er sighed at the sound of a knell
Or smiled when a Sabbath appeared."

The epithet "church-going" offends him as a puritan in grammar; whether his objection is well founded or ill founded, it applies equally to prose and verse. Poetic licence does not justify bad grammar. Whether this is strictly defensible or not, all the same it illustrates his contention. To represent the valleys and rocks as sighing and smiling in the circumstances would appear feeble and absurd in prose composition, and is not less so in metrical composition; "the occasion does not justify such violent expressions." These are examples of all that Wordsworth meant by saying that "there is no essential difference between the language of prose and metrical composition"; and it is mere pedantry to detach this phrase from the context, and hold him bound by the precise scholastic sense of the word essential to a meaning that he expressly repudiates. So far is Wordsworth from contending that the metrical order should always be the same with the prose order, that part of the preface is devoted to a subtle analysis of the peculiar effect of metrical arrangement, assigning the pleasure proper to this as his reason for writing in verse rather than in prose, and repeating again and again such phrases as "fitting to metrical arrangement a selection of the real language of men in a state of vivid sensation," and "language closely resembling that of real life, and yet in the circumstance of metre differing from it so widely."[2] What he objects to is not departure from the structure of prose, but the assumption, which seemed to him to underlie the criticisms of his ballads, that a writer of verse is not a poet unless he uses artificially ornamental language, not justified by the strength of the emotion expressed. The farthest that he went in defence of prose structure in poetry was to maintain that, if the words in a verse happened to be in the order of prose, it did not follow that they were prosaic in the sense of being unpoetic,—a side-stroke at critics who complained of his prosaisms for no better reason than that the words stood in the order of prose composition.

[1] Although Coleridge makes the qualifications more prominent than they were in the original statement, the two theories are at bottom so closely the same that one is sometimes inclined to suspect that parts, at least, of the original emanated from the fertile mind of Coleridge himself. The two poets certainly discussed the subject together in Somerset when the first ballads were written, and Coleridge was at Grasmere when the Preface was prepared in 1800. The diction of the Preface is curiously Hartleian, and, when they first met, Coleridge was a devoted disciple of Hartley, naming his first son after the philosopher, while Wordsworth detested analytic psychology. If Coleridge did contribute to the original theory in 1798 or 1800, he was likely enough to have forgotten the fact by 1814. At any rate he evidently wrote his criticism without making a close study of the Preface, and what he did in effect was to restate the original theory against popular misconceptions of it.

[2] He expressly admitted also that, in the expression of passion, owing to "the tendency of metre to divest language to a certain degree of its reality," a strength of language might be used in verse that good taste would not tolerate in prose.

Wordsworth was far from repudiating elevation of style in poetry. "If," he said, "the poet's subject be judiciously chosen, it will naturally, and upon fit occasion, lead him to passions the language of which, if selected truly and judiciously, must necessarily be dignified and variegated, and alive with metaphors and figures." But no "foreign splendours" should be interwoven with what "the passion naturally suggests," and "where the passions are of a milder character the style also should be subdued and temperate."

Such was Wordsworth's theory of poetic diction. Nothing could be more grossly mistaken than the current notion, which has been repeated by so many critics of authority that it has become an established belief, that the greater part of Wordsworth's poetry was composed in defiance of his own theory, and that he succeeded best when he set his own theory most at defiance. All commentators on Wordsworth who feel tempted to repeat this pretty paradox should pause and read his own statement of his theory before giving further currency to a misconception which they will see is absurdly unwarrantable. It is traceable to the authority of Coleridge. His just, sympathetic, and penetrating criticism on Wordsworth's work as a poet did immense service in securing for him a wider recognition; but his proved friendship and brilliant style have done sad injustice to the poet as a theorist. It was natural to assume that Coleridge, if anybody, must have known what his friend's theory was; and it was natural also that readers under the charm of his lucid and melodious prose should gladly grant themselves a dispensation from the trouble of verifying his facts in the harsh and cumbrous exposition of the theorist himself.[1] After all, the theory is a minor affair. It is the work that counts; only it is hardly fair to Wordsworth that he should go down as a stupid genius who did right against his own reasoned principles, or an arrogant person who knew himself to be wrong but refused to admit it.

The question of diction made most noise, but it was far from being the most important point of poetic doctrine set forth in the Preface. If in this he merely enunciated a truism, generally admitted in words but too generally ignored in practice, there was real novelty in his plea for humble subjects, and in his theory of poetic composition. We might, indeed, easily exaggerate to ourselves the amount of innovation in mere abstract theory; this might have been insignificant enough but for the turn that was given to it by the poet's individuality. But in view of all that was most distinctive and influential in Wordsworth's own work, his remarks on poetry in general, on the supreme function of the imagination in dignifying humble and commonplace incidents, and on the need of active exercise of imagination in the reader as well as in the poet—passiveness in this particular not being recommended as wise—his remarks on these points are immeasurably more important than his theory of poetic diction. It is much to be regretted that Coleridge's genius for luminous and brilliant exposition was not applied to the development of the few stiff phrases in which Wordsworth sought to generalize his own practice. Such sayings as that poetry "takes its origin from emotion recollected in tranquillity," or that it is the business of a poet to trace "how men associate ideas in a state of excitement," are, like the detached parts of a Chinese puzzle, meaningless till they are pieced together with views of the poet's art expressed and illustrated elsewhere. They are significant of Words worth's endeavour to lay the foundations of his art in an independent study of the feelings and faculties of men in real life, unbiassed as far as possible by poetic custom and convention. If this had meant, as many might suppose from the bare statement of the idea, that the new poet was to turn his back on his predecessors and never look behind him to what they had done, was to reject absolutely as valueless for him the accumulating tradition of thought and expression, was to write in short as if nobody before him had ever written a line, even going to common speech for his diction, a more foolish and unfruitful, silly and presumptuous, ambition could not be conceived. But Wordsworth was guilty of no such extravagance. He was from boyhood upwards a diligent student of poetry, and was not insensible of his obligations to the past. His purpose was only to use real life as a touchstone of poetic substance. Imagination operates in all men for the increase or the abatement of emotion. Incidents that have lodged in the memory are not allowed to lie there unchanged; joy is sustained by the instinctive activity of the imagination in assembling kindred ideas round the original incident, and under the instinctive operation of the same faculty pain is relieved by the suggestion of ideas that console and tranquillize. Now the poet, in Wordsworth's conception, is distinctively a man in whom this beneficent energy of imagination, operative as a blind instinct more or less in all men, is stronger than in others, and is voluntarily and rationally exercised for the benefit of all in its proper work of increase and consolation. If the poet is to discharge this mission profitably, he must study how the imagination works in real life, that is to say, "how men associate ideas in a state of excitement." Not every image that the excited mind conjures up in real life is necessarily poetical. Joy may be chilled and pain exaggerated by morbid imaginative activity. It is the business of the poet to select and modify for his special purpose of producing immediate pleasure. "Nor," says the ardent theorist, "let this necessity of producing immediate pleasure be considered as a degradation of the poet's art. It is far otherwise. It is an acknowledgment of the beauty of the universe, an acknowledgment the more sincere because it is not formal but indirect; it is a task light and easy to him who looks at the world in the spirit of love; further, it is a homage paid to the native and naked dignity of man, to the grand elementary principle of pleasure, by which he knows and feels and moves."

All this is elementary enough as Hartleian psychology. The formal recognition of it will not make a man a poet. But there were several respects in which the formal

[1] So deeply rooted is the misconception that even Mr Myers, after quoting the Preface itself, and the famous stanza "Perhaps some dungeon hears thee groan," &c., from *The Affliction of Margaret*, comments as follows:—"These lines, supposed to be spoken by 'a poor widow at Penrith,' afford a fair illustration of what Wordsworth calls 'the language really spoken by men,' with 'metre superadded.' 'What other distinction from prose,' he asks, 'would we have?' We may answer that we would have what he has actually given us, viz., an appropriate and attractive music, lying both in the rhythm and the actual sound of the words used." But in the theory this is covered by the phrases *metrical arrangement* and *selection of* the real language of men *in a state of vivid sensation, dignified and variegated and alive with metaphors and figures.* Wordsworth was not an adroit expositor in prose, and he did not make his qualifications sufficiently prominent, but the theory of diction taken with those qualifications left him free without inconsistency to use any language that was not contrary to "true taste and feeling." He acknowledged that he might occasionally have substituted "particular for general associations," and that thus language charged with poetic feeling to himself might appear trivial and ridiculous to others, as in *The Idiot Boy* and *Goody Blake*; he even went so far as to withdraw *Alice Fell*, first published in 1807, from several subsequent editions; but he argued that it was dangerous for a poet to make alterations on the simple authority of a few individuals or even classes of men, because if he did not follow his own judgment and feelings his mind would infallibly be debilitated

recognition of these elementary principles of poetic evolution powerfully affected Wordsworth's practice. One of these may be indicated, though not fully expressed, by saying that he endeavoured always to work out an emotional motive from within. Instead of choosing a striking theme and working at it like a decorative painter, embellishing, enriching, dressing to advantage, standing back from it and studying effects, his plan was to take incidents that had set his own imagination spontaneously to work, and to study and reproduce with artistic judgment the modification of the initial feeling, the emotional motive, within himself. There is room for an endless amount of subtle discussion, which would be out of place here, as to the exact difference between the methods thus broadly stated. It is obvious that they tend to approximate, inasmuch as all poets must work to some extent from within and all to some extent from without. The mere fact of using words, the medium of communication between man and man, implies a reference, unconscious or deliberate, to the effect produced on others. But undoubtedly in Wordsworth's case the reference to others was of deliberate purpose as much as possible suppressed. Probably from natural stiffness of temper, he could not make it easily, and found the effort, as it must always be when it is an effort and not a happy instinct, embarrassing and chilling. At any rate, if an association, to use his own terminology, gave pleasure to himself, he did not pause long to consider the probable effect on others. If he did reflect upon it when the act of composition was over, he was often able to satisfy himself that, if an association which seemed to him just, reasonable, and humane, was not acceptable to general sentiment, the general sentiment was corrupt. To this, as he himself with his habits of self-criticism was fully aware, was owing much of his strength and much of his unpopularity. By keeping his eye on the object, as spontaneously modified by his own imaginative energy, he was able to give full and undistracted scope to all his powers in poetic coinage of the wealth that his imagination brought. On the other hand, readers whose nature or education was different from his own, were repelled or left cold and indifferent, or obliged to make the sympathetic effort to see with his eyes, which he refused to make in order that he might see with theirs.

> "He is retired as noontide dew
> Or fountain in a noon-day grove,
> And you must love him ere to you
> He will seem worthy of your love."

From this habit of taking the processes of his own mind as the standard of the way in which "men associate ideas in a state of excitement," and language familiar to himself as the standard of the language of "real men," arises a superficial anomaly in Wordsworth's poetry, an apparent contradiction between his practice and his theory. His own imagination, judged by ordinary standards, was easily excited, excited by emotional motives that have little force with ordinary men. Most of his poems start from humbler, slighter, less generally striking themes than those of any other poet of high rank. But his poetry is not correspondingly simple. On the contrary, much of it, much of the best of it—for example, the *Ode to Duty*, and that on the *Intimations of Immortality*—is as intricate, elaborate, and abstruse, as remote from the ordinary paths of thought, as is to be found in literature. The emotional motive is simple; the passion has almost always a simple origin, and often is of no great intensity; but the imaginative structure is generally elaborate, and, when the poet is at his best, supremely splendid and gorgeous. No poet has built such magnificent palaces of rare material for the ordinary everyday homely human affections. It is because he has invested our ordinary everyday principles of conduct, which are so apt to become threadbare, with such imperishable robes of finest texture and richest design that Wordsworth holds so high a place among the great moralists, the greatest of moralists in verse. And yet he attained this end in his most effectively moral poems, though not by any means in all his poems, without in the least confusing the boundaries between poetry and preaching, his conception of the end of poetry as immediate pleasure serving him as a load-star.

His practice was influenced also, and not always for good, by his theory that poetry "takes its origin from emotion recollected in tranquillity." This was a somewhat doubtful corollary from his general theory of poetic evolution. A poem is complete in itself; there must be no sting in it to disturb the reader's content with the whole; through whatever agitations it progresses, to whatever elevations it soars, to this end it must come, otherwise it is imperfect as a poem. Now the imagination in ordinary men, though the process is not expressed in verse, and the poet's special art has thus no share in producing the effect, reaches the poetic end when it has so transfigured a disturbing experience, whether of joy or grief, that this rests tranquilly in the memory, can be recalled without disquietude, and dwelt upon with some mode and degree of pleasure, more or less keen, more or less pure or mixed with pain. True to his idea of imitating real life, Wordsworth made it a rule for himself not to write on any theme till his imagination had operated upon it for some time involuntarily; it was not in his view ripe for poetic treatment till this transforming agency had subdued the original emotion to a state of tranquillity.[1] Out of this tranquillity arises the favourable moment for poetic composition, some day when, as he contemplates the subject, the tranquillity disappears, an emotion kindred to the original emotion is reinstated, and the poet retraces and supplements with all his art the previous involuntary and perhaps unconscious imaginative chemistry.

When we study the moments that Wordsworth found favourable for successful composition, a very curious law reveals itself, somewhat at variance with the common conception of him as a poet who derived all his strength from solitary communion with nature. We find that the recluse's best poems were written under the excitement of some break in the monotony of his quiet life—change of scene, change of companionship, change of occupation. The law holds from the beginning to the end of his poetic career. We have already noticed the immense stimulus given to his powers by his first contact with Coleridge after two years of solitary and abortive effort. *Above Tintern Abbey* was composed during a four days' ramble with his sister; he began it on leaving Tintern, and concluded it as he was entering Bristol. His residence amidst strange scenes and "unknown men" at Goslar was particularly fruitful: *She Dwelt among the Untrodden Ways*, *Ruth*, *Nutting*, *There was a Boy*, *Wisdom and Spirit of the Universe*, all belong to those few months of unfamiliar environment. The breeze that met him as he issued from the city gates on his homeward journey brought him the first thought of *The Prelude*. The second year of his residence at Grasmere was unproductive; he was "hard at work" then on *The Excursion*; but the excitement of his tour on the Continent in the autumn of 1802, combined perhaps with a happy change in his pecuniary circumstances and the near prospect of marriage, roused him to one of his happiest fits of activity. His first great sonnet,

[1] *The Prelude* contains a record of his practice, after the opening lines of the first book—

> "Thus far, O friend! did I, not used to make
> A present joy the matter of a song,
> Pour forth, &c."

the *Lines on Westminster Bridge*, was composed on the roof of the Dover coach; the first of the splendid series "dedicated to national independence and liberty," the most generally impressive and universally intelligible of his poems, *Fair Star of Evening*, *Once did she Hold the Gorgeous East in Fee*, *Toussaint*, *Milton, thou shouldst be Living at this Hour*, *It is not to be Thought of that the Flood*, *When I have Borne in Memory what has Tamed*, were all written in the course of the tour, or in London in the month after his return. A tour in Scotland in the following year, 1803, yielded the *Highland Girl* and *The Solitary Reaper*. Soon after his return he resumed *The Prelude*; and *The Affliction of Margaret* and the *Ode to Duty*, his greatest poems in two different veins, were coincident with the exaltation of spirit due to the triumphant and successful prosecution of the long-delayed work. The *Character of the Happy Warrior*, which he described to Miss Martineau as "a chain of extremely *valooable* thoughts," though it did not fulfil "poetic conditions,"[1] was the product of a calmer period. The excitement of preparing for publication always had a rousing effect upon him; the preparation for the edition of 1807 resulted in the completion of the ode on the *Intimations of Immortality*, the sonnets *The World is too much with us*, *Methought I saw the Footsteps of a Throne*, *Two Voices are there*, and *Lady, the Songs of Spring were in the Grove*, and the *Song at the Feast of Brougham Castle*. After 1807 there is a marked falling off in the quality, though not in the quantity, of Wordsworth's poetic work. It is significant of the comparatively sober and laborious spirit in which he wrote *The Excursion* that its progress was accompanied by none of those casual sallies of exulting and exuberant power that mark the period of the happier *Prelude*. The completion of *The Excursion* was signalized by the production of *Laodamia*. The chorus of adverse criticism with which it was received inspired him in the noble sonnet to Haydon —*High is our Calling, Friend*. He rarely or never again touched the same lofty height.

It is interesting to compare with what he actually accomplished the plan of life-work with which Wordsworth settled at Grasmere in the last month of the eighteenth century.[2] The plan was definitely conceived as he left the German town of Goslar in the spring of 1799. Tired of the wandering unsettled life that he had led hitherto, dissatisfied also with the fragmentary occasional and disconnected character of his lyrical poems, he longed for a permanent home among his native hills, where he might, as one called and consecrated to the task, devote his powers continuously to the composition of a great philosophical poem on "Man, Nature, and Society." The poem was to be called *The Recluse*, "as having for its principal subject the sensations and opinions of a poet living in retirement." He communicated the design to Coleridge, who gave him enthusiastic encouragement to proceed. In the first transport of the conception he felt as if he needed only solitude and leisure for the continuous execution of it. But, though he had still before him fifty years of peaceful life amidst his beloved scenery, the work in the projected form at least was destined to remain incomplete. Doubts and misgivings soon arose, and favourable moments of felt inspiration delayed their coming. To sustain him in his resolution he thought of writing as an introduction, or, as he put it, an antechapel to the church which he proposed to build, a history of his own mind up to the time when he recognized the great mission of his life. One of the many laughs at his expense by unsympathetic critics has been directed against his saying that he wrote this *Prelude* of fourteen books about himself out of diffidence. But in truth the original motive was none other than distrust of his own powers. He began this review of his early life to reassure himself from misgivings whether nature and education had fitted him for his proposed task, partly by elevating his mind to a confidence in nature's special destination, and partly by making practical trial of his powers in a simpler work. He turned aside from *The Prelude* to prepare the second volume of the *Lyrical Ballads* and write the explanatory Preface, which as a statement of his aims in poetry had partly the same purpose of strengthening his self-confidence. From his sister's *Journal* we learn that in the winter of 1801-2 he was "hard at work on *The Pedlar*"— the original title of *The Excursion*. But this experiment on the larger work was also soon abandoned. It appears from a letter to his friend Sir George Beaumont that his health was far from robust, and in particular that he could not write without intolerable physical uneasiness. We should probably not be wrong in connecting his physical weakness with his rule of waiting for favourable moments. His next start with *The Prelude*, in the spring of 1804, was more prosperous; he dropped it for several months, but, resuming again in the spring of 1805, he completed it in the summer of that year. But still the composition of the great work to which it was intended to be a portico proceeded by fits and starts. It was not till 1814 that the second of the three divisions of *The Recluse*, ultimately named *The Excursion*, was ready for publication; and he went no further in the execution of his great design. It is possible that he had his own unfinished project in mind when he wrote the sonnet on Malham Cove.—

> "'Mid the wreck of Is and Was,
> Things incomplete and purposes betrayed
> Make sadder transits o'er thought's optic glass
> Than noblest objects utterly decayed."

We shall speak presently of the reception of *The Excursion*. Meantime we must look elsewhere for the virtual accomplishment of the great design of *The Recluse*. The purpose was not after all betrayed; it was really fulfilled, though not in the form intended, in his various occasional poems. In relation to the edifice that he aspired to construct, he likened these poems to little cells, oratories, and sepulchral recesses; they are really the completed work, much more firmly united by their common purpose than by any formal and visible nexus of words. Formally disconnected, they really, as we read and feel them, range themselves to spiritual music as the component parts of a great poetic temple, finding a rendezvous amidst the scenery of the district where the poet had his local habitation. The Lake District, as transfigured by Wordsworth's imagination, is the fulfilment of his ambition after an enduring memorial. The *Poems* collected and published in 1807 compose in effect "a philosophical poem on man, nature, and society," the title of which might fitly have been *The Recluse*, "as having for its principal subject the sensations and opinions of a poet living in retirement." As a realization of the idea of *The Recluse*, these poems are from every poetical point of view infinitely superior to the kind of thing that he projected and failed to complete.

The derisive fury with which *The Excursion* was assailed upon its first appearance has long been a stock example of critical blindness, conceit, and malignity. And yet, if we look at the position claimed for the *Excursion* now by competent authorities, the error of the first critics is seen to lie not in their indictment of faults, but in the prominence they gave to the faults and their generally dis-

[1] This casual estimate of his own work is not merely amusing but also instructive, as showing—what is sometimes denied—that Wordsworth himself knew well enough the difference between "poetry" and such "valuable thoughts" as he propounded in *The Excursion*.

[2] Wordsworth's residences in the Lake District were Townend, Grasmere, from December 1799 till the spring of 1808; Allan Bank, from 1808 to 1811; the parsonage at Grasmere, from 1811 to 1813; Rydal Mount, for the rest of his life.

respectful tone towards a poet of Wordsworth's greatness. Jeffrey's petulant "This will never do," uttered, professedly at least, more in sorrow than in anger, because the poet would persist in spite of all friendly counsel in misapplying his powers,[1] has become a byword of ridiculous critical cocksureness. But the curious thing is that *The Excursion* has not "done," and that the Wordsworthians who laugh at Jeffrey are in the habit of repeating the substance of his criticism, though in more temperate and becoming language. Thus Dean Church, in a criticism at once sympathetic and judicious, after the usual fling at Jeffrey's "insolence," goes on to say—

> "In *The Excursion* and *The Prelude* there are passages as magnificent as perhaps poet ever wrote; but they are not specimens of the context in which they are embedded, and which in spite of them does not carry along with it the reader's honest enjoyment. We read on because we must."[2]

This is the very substance of Jeffrey's criticism, which was far from being unreservedly damnatory, as the following will show:—

> "Besides those more extended passages of interest or beauty which we have quoted and omitted to quote, there are scattered up and down the book, and in the midst of its most repulsive portions, a very great number of single lines and images that sparkle like gems in the desert and startle us by an intimation of the great poetic powers that lie buried in the rubbish that has been heaped around them."

Jeffrey, it will be seen, was not blind to the occasional felicities and unforgetable lines celebrated by Coleridge, and his general judgment on *The Excursion* has been abundantly ratified.[3] It is not upon *The Excursion* that Wordsworth's reputation as a poet can ever rest, whatever defence may be made for it as "a chain of extremely valuable thoughts," varied by passages of lofty or quietly beautiful description, invigorating exhortation, and gentle pathos. The two "books" entitled *The Churchyard among the Mountains* are the only parts of the poem that derive much force from the scenic setting; if they had been published separately, they would probably have obtained at once a reception very different from that given to *The Excursion* as a whole. The dramatic setting is merely dead weight, not because the chief speaker is a pedlar—Wordsworth fairly justifies this selection—but because the pedlar, as a personality to be known, and loved, and respected, and listened to with interest, is not completely created. We know Uncle Toby better than Sterne, but we do not know the Wanderer so well as Wordsworth, and consequently we are more easily bored by him than by the poet speaking in his own person as he does in *The Prelude*. His cheerfulness after reciting the tale of Margaret at the ruined cottage is almost offensive; the assigned motive for it in the beauty of nature that remains though the poor broken-hearted woman is gone is hardly higher than the dropsical scullion's philosophy in *Tristram Shandy*. "'He is dead. He is certainly dead,' said Obadiah. 'So am not I,' said the foolish scullion."[4]

There can be little doubt that adverse criticism had a depressing influence on Wordsworth's poetical powers, notwithstanding his nobly expressed defiance of it and his determination to hold on in his own path undisturbed. Its effect in retarding the sale of his poems and thus depriving him of the legitimate fruits of his industry was a favourite topic with him in his later years;[5] but the absence of general appreciation, and the ridicule of what he considered his best and most distinctive work, contributed in all probability to a still more unfortunate result—the premature depression and deadening of his powers. He schooled himself to stoical endurance, but he was not superhuman, and in the absence of sympathy not only was any possibility of development checked but he ceased to write with the spontaneity and rapture of his earlier verse. The common theory that the marked stiffening of his powers after 1807 was the effect of age only may be true; but the coincidence of this falling off with the failure of the strenuous effort made in that year to conquer the hostility of critics and the indifference of the public makes the theory extremely doubtful as a whole truth. Wordsworth's true nature is often misjudged under the fallacy that the preacher of high and serene fortitude in the face of failure and misfortune must himself be imperturbable. On the contrary the most eloquent advocate of this heroic virtue is the man who most feels the need of it in the frailty of his own temper. It is on record that Wordsworth, with all his philosophy of consolation, did not easily recover serenity after domestic bereavements, and we go very far wrong when we confound his proud and self-reliant defiance of criticism with insensibility to it or power to rise at will above its disheartening and benumbing influence.

For five years after the condemnation of *The Excursion* Wordsworth published almost nothing that had not been composed before. The chief exception is the *Thanksgiving Ode* of 1816. He was occupied mainly in the task of putting his work and his aims more fully before the world, maintaining his position with dignity and unflinching courage, so far unmoved by criticism that he would not alter his course one jot for the sake of public favour. In 1815 he published a new edition of his poems, in the arrangement according to faculties and feelings in which they have since stood; and he sought to explain his

[1] The lively lawyer, to whom reviewing was a recreation, obviously enjoyed the process of "slating" more than is quite consistent with his strong protestations of sorrow over the poet's waywardness; but it should not be overlooked that he did make ample acknowledgment, when he had sated himself with denunciations of the Wanderer's verbosity, of the power and beauty of isolated passages. In the second part of his article, indeed, he quoted so much that was admirable that he confessed himself disposed to rescind his severe judgment, but re-perusal of the Wanderer's arguments convinced him that it could not be rescinded. Jeffrey's criticisms in their entirety are dead and buried, except for the professional student, but even critics have their humble rights, and it is time that his four opening words should receive the privilege of interment also, if they are not to be fairly interpreted. His criticism of *The White Doe* is valueless enough, because the sentiment of that poem is more abstruse, less palpable to the running reader; but what he said of *The Excursion* has simply been repeated in duller language by the Wordsworthians who have denounced his arrogance in daring to say it.

[2] Ward's *English Poets*, vol. iv. p. 13. Mr Myers and Mrs Oliphant might be quoted to the same effect.

[3] In joining *The Prelude* with *The Excursion* in the same condemnation, Dean Church goes farther than Jeffrey. As a poem *The Prelude* is infinitely superior; its autobiographical character gives it a certain unity, and it contains a greater number of lofty passages in Wordsworth's best vein.

[4] Charles Lamb's review of *The Excursion* in the *Quarterly* (Oct. 1814), in spite of the editor Gifford's modifications, remains the most sympathetic of competent criticisms of the poem. In one point there is an oversight, significant of the indefiniteness of Wordsworth's exposition; Lamb supposes the conversion of the Solitary to be accomplished within *The Excursion*. It was really reserved for the third part of *The Recluse*. It was the poet's intention, as expressed in his conversations with Miss Fenwick, to effect this conversion not by argument, but by carrying the sceptic back to his native Scotland, making him witness of a sacrament service, and making early associations thereupon reassert themselves. This would have been in accordance with his theory of the value of early associations. What makes the position of the Solitary a little difficult to grasp at first is that Wordsworth, on principle, does not present this character in marked contrast to the other characters in the poem, but rather lays stress on what he has in common with them, tender-heartedness towards suffering and intense enthusiasm for nature; hence it arises that the reader cannot see without some study what it is that the other interlocutors find lacking in him, and aim at supplying to him.

[5] Mr Matthew Arnold heard him say that "for he knew not how many years his poetry had never brought him in enough to buy his shoe-strings" (preface to *Selection*, p. v.). The literal facts are that he received £100 from the Longmans in 1800, and nothing more till he was sixty-five, when Moxon bought the copyright of his writings for £1000 (*Prose Works*, iii. 437).

purposes more completely than before in an essay on "Poetry as a Study." In the same year he was persuaded to publish the *The White Doe of Rylstone*, written mainly eight years before. In purely poetic charm the *White Doe* ought to be ranked among the most perfect of Wordsworth's poems, the most completely successful exhibition of his finest qualities; nowhere is the peculiar music of his verse more happily sustained or more perfectly in harmony with the noble and tender feeling which here springs as if from infinite depths, to flow round and subdue the tragic agony of the incidents. But Jeffrey, who was much too busy a man to enter into a vein of poetry so remote from common romantic sentiment, would have none of the *White Doe*: he pronounced it "the very worst poem ever written," and the public too readily endorsed his judgment. Two other poems, with which Wordsworth made another appeal, were not more successful. *Peter Bell*, written in 1798, was published in 1819; and at the instigation of Charles Lamb it was followed by *The Waggoner*, written in 1805. Both were mercilessly ridiculed and parodied. These tales from humble life are written in Wordsworth's most unconventional style, and with them emphatically "not to sympathize is not to understand," but when they are read sympathetically they are felt to be written with the spontaneity and freedom of the poet's most inspired moments, although they are not in his high serious vein.

Meantime, the great design of *The Recluse* languished. The neglect of what Wordsworth himself conceived to be his best and most characteristic work was not encouraging; and there was another reason why the philosophical poem on man, nature, and society did not make progress. Again and again in his poetry Wordsworth celebrates the value of constraint, and the disadvantage of "too much liberty," of "unchartered freedom."[1] This thought was impressed upon him by his own experience. There was "too much liberty" in his vague scheme of a philosophical poem. He needed more of the constraint of a definite form to stimulate his working powers to prosperous vigour. The formlessness of the scheme prevented his working at it continuously. Hence his "philosophy" was expressed in casual disconnected sonnets, or in sonnets and other short poems connected by the simplest of all links, sequence in time or place. He stumbled upon three or four such serial ideas in the latter part of his life, and thus found beginning and end for chains of considerable length, which may be regarded as fragments of the project which he had not sufficient energy of constructive power to execute. The *Sonnets on the River Duddon*, written in 1820, follow the river from its source to the sea, and form a partial embodiment of his philosophy of nature. The *Ecclesiastical Sonnets*, written in 1820–21, trace the history of the church from the Druids onwards, following one of the great streams of human affairs, and exhibit part of his philosophy of society. A tour on the Continent in 1820, a tour in Scotland in 1831, a tour on the west coast in 1833, a tour in Italy in 1837, furnished him with other serial forms, serving to connect miscellaneous reflections on man, nature, and society; and his views on the punishment of death were strung together in still another series in 1840. He sought relief from "the weight of too much liberty" in this voluntary subjection to serial form, taking upon himself that

> "Constraint
> Whence oft invigorating transports flow
> That choice lacked courage to bestow."

His resolute industry was productive of many wise, impressive, and charitable reflexions, and many casual felicities of diction, but the poet very seldom reached the highest level of his earlier inspirations.

[1] See the Sonnet, *Nuns fret not*, &c., *The Pass of Kirkstone*, and the *Ode to Duty*.

Wordsworth was appointed poet-laureate on the death of Southey in 1843. His only official composition was an ode on the installation of the Prince Consort as chancellor of Cambridge university in 1847. This was his last writing in verse. He died at Rydal Mount after a short illness, on the 23d of April 1850, and was buried in Grasmere churchyard.

It was Wordsworth's own desire that there should be no elaborate criticism of his poetry. This desire has not been respected. We have already referred to Lamb's severely edited review of *The Excursion* (1814), and to Coleridge's criticism in the *Biographia Literaria* (1817). This last, together with the enthusiastic and unreserved championship of Wilson in *Blackwood's Magazine* in a series of articles between 1819 and 1822 (see *Recreations of Christopher North*), formed the turning point in Wordsworth's reputation. From 1820 to 1830 De Quincey says it was militant, from 1830 to 1840 triumphant. By 1850 there were signs of reaction, but, though the language of criticism has become more judicial, there has been no falling off in veneration for Wordsworth's character or appreciation of his best work. Among critics that are specially interesting for various reasons we may mention De Quincey (*Works*, vols. ii. and v.), Sir Henry Taylor (*Works*, vol. v.), George Brimley (*Essays*), Matthew Arnold (preface to *Selection*), Mr Swinburne (*Miscellanies*), Mr F. W. H. Myers ("Men of Letters" series), and Mr Leslie Stephen (*Hours in a Library*, 3d series, "Wordsworth's Ethics").

Wordsworth's writings in prose have been collected by Mr Grosart (London, 1876). This collection contains the previously unpublished *Apology for a French Revolution*, written in 1793, besides the scarce tract on the *Convention of Cintra* (1809) and the political addresses *To the Freeholders of Westmoreland* (1818). The bulk of three volumes is made up by including letters, notes, prefaces, &c. Wordsworth's *Guide to the Lakes* originally appeared in 1810 as an introduction to Wilkinson's *Select Views*, and was first published separately in 1822.

The standard editions of Wordsworth are Moxon's six-volume edition originally settled by the poet himself in 1836–7, and Moxon's single-volume double-column edition sanctioned by the poet in 1845. A carefully annotated edition in nine large volumes, by Prof. Knight, is in course of publication. It contains a useful chronological table of the poems; and the hitherto unpublished part of *The Recluse* is promised for the ninth volume. Prof. Knight's book on *The English Lake District* is also useful to minute students of Wordsworth. (W. M.)

WORKINGTON, a seaport and market-town of Cumberland, England, on the south bank of the Derwent, where it enters the Solway Firth, and on several branch railway lines, 34 miles south-west of Carlisle and 311 miles from London by rail. The Derwent is crossed by a stone bridge of three arches erected in 1841. In the more ancient portions of the town the streets are narrow and irregular, but there are now many spacious streets with handsome houses and shops. The ancient parish church of St Michael was rebuilt in 1770, and, this building having been destroyed by fire in 1887, another is now (1888) in course of erection. The other public buildings are the jubilee hall, the assembly-rooms, the temperance hall, the mechanics' institute, the infirmary, the new covered market, the custom-house, and the bonded warehouses. Near the town is Workington Hall, the seat of the ancient lords of the manor, a quadrilateral castellated structure in great part modern, but still retaining some of the ancient rooms, including that in which Mary queen of Scots is said to have slept when she escaped to England after the battle of Langside in May 1568. The harbour is remarkably safe, and has been improved by the construction of a breakwater 600 feet in length. The Lonsdale dock, 4½ acres in extent, was opened in 1862. In 1886 37 vessels in the foreign and colonial trade (19,806 tons) entered the port, and 24 cleared (10,495 tons); 1687 in the coasting-trade entered (197,487 tons), and 1682 cleared (206,404 tons). The value of the exports of the produce of the United Kingdom in 1882 was £181,012, but in 1885 it was only £13,845, and in 1886 it was £38,468. The chief exports are pig-iron, lime, coal, steel rails, and steel plates. The value of the imports of foreign and colonial merchandise in 1882 was £57,512, but since then it has declined, and was only £18,282 in 1885, and £27,448 in 1886. A considerable proportion of the imports are, however, from the ports of the United Kingdom, the principal items being iron-ore and moulding-sand. In the neighbourhood there are large collieries, but the chief industry is the manufacture of iron and steel by the Bessemer and Siemens process. There are large blast-furnaces, engineering works, and bolt and rivet and tinplate works. Iron shipbuilding is also carried on: 2 vessels were built in 1886, of 3986 tons. The population of the urban sanitary district (area 641 acres) in 1871 was 7979, which by 1881 had increased to 13,308. In 1882 the area was extended to embrace 3463 acres, the population of that area in 1871 being 8413, which by 1881 had increased to 14,371. The town is about to be incorporated (1888).

WORKSOP, a market-town of Nottinghamshire, England, is situated on the Chesterfield Canal, and on the Manchester, Sheffield, and Lincoln Railway and the Midland Railway, 16 miles east-south-east of Sheffield and 146½ from London. It is a well-built and pleasant country town, with considerable traces of antiquity. The church of St Mary and St Cuthbert is an old priory church, once divided internally into two buildings, the eastern dedicated to St Mary being for the use of the canons, and the western dedicated to St Cuthbert for the parishioners. When the priory was demolished at the Reformation only the western portion of the church was spared, and for many years it was in a dilapidated condition until it was restored with Perpendicular additions. Behind it are the ruins of the lady chapel, containing some fine Early English work. The priory gatehouse, chiefly in the Decorated style, now forms the entrance to the precincts of the church. It is supposed to have been built early in the 14th century by the third Lord Furnival, when the market was established. Of the priory itself the only remains are a wall at the north-west corner of the church which includes the cloister gateway. There was a Norman keep on the castle hill, but no remains of the building are now left. The magnificent manor-house, built by Gilbert, first earl of Shrewsbury, and occasionally occupied by Mary queen of Scots during her captivity under the sixth earl, was in great part destroyed by fire in 1761, while being restored at great expense by the duke of Norfolk, and when the estate came into the possession of the duke of Newcastle in 1840 the ruined portion of the mansion remaining was removed and a smaller mansion built near it. The ecclesiastical parish of St John's was formed in 1867. There is a corn exchange, erected in 1854, in the Venetian style, and a mechanics' institute, erected in 1852. Formerly liquorice was extensively grown, but malting is now the principal industry. A large corn market and a cattle and horse fair are held. The town also possesses brass and iron foundries, agricultural implement works, saw-mills, and chemical works. The population of the urban sanitary district (18,220 acres) was 10,409 in 1871, and 11,625 in 1881.

Worksop occurs in Domesday as Withercope. By William the Conqueror the manor was bestowed on Roger de Busli. It subsequently passed to William de Lovitot, who in 1103 founded a priory for Augustinian canons dedicated to St Mary. From the De Lovitots it passed successively to the Furnivals, the Nevilles, the Talbots, earls of Shrewsbury, and the Howards, earls of Arundel and afterwards dukes of Norfolk. By the duke of Norfolk it was sold in 1840 to the duke of Newcastle, whose country mansion, Clumber, is in the parish. In December 1460 an engagement took place at Worksop between the forces of the duke of York and those of the duke of Somerset.

See White's *Worksop*, 1875; and Sissons, *Guide to Worksop*, 1888.

WORM. This word has no definite significance in modern zoological classification; it is constantly applied to several phyla of the animal kingdom which have for the most part no special relations to each other. By Linnæus the Latin equivalent "Vermes" was applied to the modern divisions of MOLLUSCA, CŒLENTERA, PROTOZOA, TUNICATA, ECHINODERMATA (*qq.v.*), as well as to those animals which are in many current text-books of zoology grouped together under the same name.[1] The group *Vermes* as used, for example, by Claus includes several distinct phyla, viz., NEMATOIDEA (*q.v.*), *Platyhelminthes* (see PLANARIANS, TAPE-WORMS, and TREMATODA), NEMERTINES (*q.v.*), *Chætognatha* (see SAGITTA), *Gephyrea* (see ANNELIDA), ROTIFERA (*q.v.*), *Discophora* (see LEECH), *Chætopoda*.

The *Chætopoda* are divided into *Oligochæta* and *Polychæta*, which have been shortly treated of, together with *Discophora* and *Gephyrea*, in the article ANNELIDA (*q.v.*). The leech and its kindred (*Discophora*) have been more fully described in another article (LEECH, *q.v.*). The present article will treat of the earthworm and its immediate allies. The earthworm belongs to the order *Oligochæta*, which also includes a number of freshwater forms; these latter *Oligochæta* have been distinguished as "*Limicolæ*" from the earthworms or "*Terricolæ*." There are, however,, no structural peculiarities of any importance which absolutely distinguish the terrestrial from the aquatic forms. Earthworms are, it is true, characterized by the simplicity of their setæ, by the absence of cilia upon the body, by the thickness of the body-wall, which implies an increased thickness of the muscular layers, and by the thickness of the intersegmental septa, particularly in the anterior region of the body. All these structural modifications, however, are so obviously connected with the density of the medium in which they live that they cannot be held to be of primary importance. On the other hand, there is no deep-seated anatomical character which distinguishes earthworms from the freshwater *Oligochæta*. An article on earthworms must therefore necessarily include an account of the aquatic and mud-inhabiting *Oligochæta*.

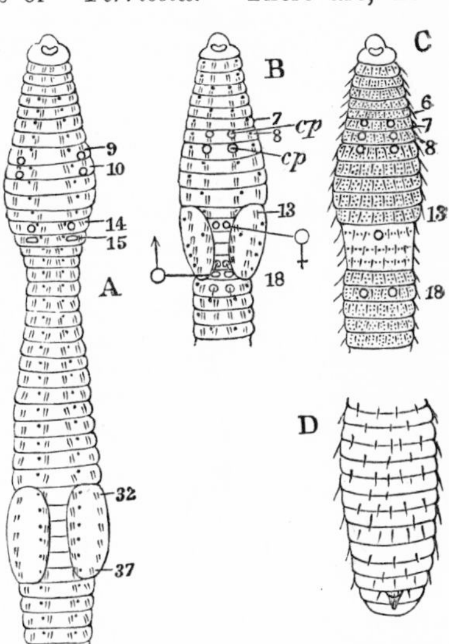

FIG. 1.—Diagrams of Various Earthworms, to illustrate external characters. A, B, C, anterior segments from the ventral surface; D, hinder end of body of *Urochæta*. A. *Lumbricus*: 9, 10, segments containing spermathecæ, the orifices of which are indicated; 14, segment bearing oviducal pores; 15, segment bearing male pores; 32, 37, first and last segments of clitellum. B, *Acanthodrilus*: *cp*, orifices of spermathecæ; ♀, oviducal pores; ♂, male pores; on 17th and 19th segments are the apertures of the atria. C, *Perichæta*: the spermathecal pores are between segments 6 and 7, 7 and 8, 8 and 9, the oviducal pores upon the 14th and the male pores upon the 18th segment. In all the figures the nephridial pores are indicated by dots and the setæ by strokes.

The *Oligochæta* range in size from a few lines to several feet in length; the large earthworm from the Cape Colony (*Microchæta rappi*) measures 5 or 6 feet in length when fully extended. On the whole the terrestrial forms (earthworms) are larger than the aquatic forms. The *Oligochæta* are found all over the globe, but at present no details of value can be given as to their distributional

[1] Gegenbaur, *Elements of Comp. Anat.*, Eng. trans., 1878; Claus, *Text-Book of Zoology*, Eng. trans., 1884.

areas.[1] As might be imagined from their soft perishable bodies, nothing is known respecting the distribution of the *Oligochæta* in past time.

The most prominent characteristic of the *Oligochæta*, as of the *Chætopoda* generally, is the segmentation of the body: the body is divided into a series of segments or metameres, which resemble each other most closely in the lowest forms. This metamerism is seen externally in the presence of transverse furrows, corresponding with the internal divisions of the body cavity, and in the disposition of the setæ. The mouth opens into the first segment, which is usually unprovided with setæ; in front of the mouth is a preoral lobe; this latter is aborted in some *Oligochæta* (*Urochæta*, *Thamnodrilus*).

Body-wall.

Body-Wall.—In all *Oligochæta* three layers can be distinguished in the body-wall—(1) an outer epidermis, which secretes a delicate cuticle, (2) a circular muscle layer, (3) a longitudinal muscle layer. Within the last-named is the peritoneal lining of the cœlom.

Clitellum.—During sexual maturity certain of the segments of the body in *Lumbricus* and other earthworms undergo a change in appearance which is caused by the development of several layers of unicellular glands beneath the epidermis. Among the "*Limicolæ*" (*e.g.*, in *Limnodrilus*, *Rhynchelmis*, *Enchytræidæ*) the clitellum is, on the contrary, furnished with an epidermal layer only one cell thick; some of these cells become large and glandular. In these points *Criodrilus* agrees with earthworms. The secretion of these glands may form the cocoon in which the eggs are deposited, but it appears to be also used to attach individuals together during copulation. The clitellum is universal among the *Oligochæta*. *Moniligaster* and *Criodrilus* were for some time considered as an exception to this rule, but a clitellum has recently been demonstrated in these two genera by Bourne (17)[2] and Benham (7). The clitellum in earthworms never occupies less than two segments, and in *Trigaster* it extends over twenty-seven.

Setæ.—These are universally found in the *Oligochæta*, but differ in their shape, as well as in their number and arrangement, in different families. In the majority of forms the setæ are disposed in four longitudinal rows; the setæ in each of these rows may be comparatively numerous (*Naidomorpha*), or may be limited to two

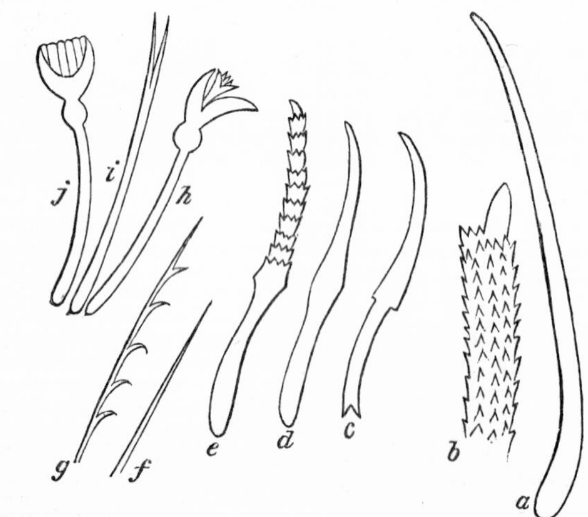

FIG. 2.—Setæ of *Oligochæta*. *a*, penial seta of *Perichæta ceylonica*; *b*, extremity of penial seta of *Acanthodrilus* (after Horst); *c*, seta of *Urochæta* (Perier); *d*, seta of *Lumbricus*; *e*, seta of *Criodrilus*; *f*, *g*, setæ of *Bohemilla comata*; *h*, *i*, *j*, setæ of *Psammoryctes barbatus* (*f* to *j* after Vejdovsky).

Lumbriculidæ and many earthworms). In *Acanthodrilus multiporus* and other earthworms the eight setæ are no longer in pairs, but separated by nearly equivalent intervals. In *Urochæta* (fig. 1, D) and *Diachæta* each segment has also eight setæ, but these are disposed more or less alternately in successive segments. In the former of these two genera, as also in *Eudrilus*, peculiar structures of a chitinous nature exist between the individual setæ of a segment; these are similar to certain structures described in *Anachæta* by Vejdovsky (15) as abortive setæ; their presence in *Urochæta* and *Eudrilus* may indicate that the number of setæ in these worms has been reduced from a continuous circle round each segment, such as exists in the family *Perichætidæ* (fig. 1, C). Among the *Naidomorpha* there are delicate hair-like setæ which pass by numerous intermediate forms into setæ with a bifurcate extremity; in many limicolous forms, as in earthworms, the setæ are simple in form, ending in a slightly curved extremity. The setæ are developed in the interior of cells of ectodermic origin; special muscles effect their movements.

Cœlom.

Cœlom.—The *Oligochæta*, like other Annelids, have a cœlom which is formed by the excavation of paired mesoblastic somites; the intersegmental septa represent the walls of each two adjacent somites; the dorsal and ventral mesenteries, which in the *Archiannelida* suspend the gut from the body-wall, are largely absent in the *Oligochæta*, the cavities of each pair of somites becoming continuous. Traces of the dorsal mesentery are met with in some forms; in almost all the ventral mesentery persists to a great extent in a sheet which suspends the ventral blood-vessel from the intestine.

The cœlom communicates with the exterior by the nephridia and ducts of the reproductive organs and by certain dorsally-placed pores. These latter are sometimes present only on the head segment (*Criodrilus* and many aquatic genera), sometimes on the body segments also (*Enchytræida*); in the majority of earthworms they appear to exist only on the body segments, and the first one does not usually appear before the third and fourth segment. In *Pontodrilus* and a few other species the dorsal pores are entirely absent. The cœlom is lined with a peritoneum, the cells of which exhibit different characters in different parts of the body. The intestine is covered with a layer of large cells containing numerous granules; this cellular investment was originally described as hepatic, but it is now known to have no relation to the alimentary tract. The investigations of Kükenthal (16) show that these cells are concerned with the excretory function.

Nervous system.

Nervous System.—This consists of (1) a pair of cerebral ganglia connected by a circumœsophageal ring with a chain of ventral ganglia arranged in pairs—a pair to each segment; (2) a system of small ganglia and nerves arising from the cerebral ganglia and innervating the anterior part of the alimentary tract; and (3) two lateral ganglionated cords, which have a special interest for those who believe that the segmented worms are the Invertebrate group from which the *Chordata* (including the *Vertebrata*) have sprung. The discovery of Eisig ("Die Capitelliden," *Naples Monographs*), that this lateral cord is on both sides connected with segmentally arranged sense-organs in the *Capitellidæ*, is an additional argument for considering this lateral system as the homologue of the lateral line in fishes.

The nervous system of *Æolosoma* is probably degenerate; it consists merely of a pair of cerebral ganglia, which are situated in the procephalic lobe in connexion with the epidermis. In *Ctenodrilus* the nervous system, like that of the *Archiannelida* (see below), is imbedded in the epidermis throughout its whole extent. In the higher forms, in fact in all the remaining *Oligochæta*, the central nervous system has lost its primitive connexion with the epidermis. Moreover, in these forms the cerebral ganglia, originally developed in the procephalic lobe, have moved back, and may lie as far back as in the fourth segment.

Vascular system.

Vascular System.—All the *Oligochæta* possess, in addition to the corpusculated fluid of the cœlom, a system of closed vessels which in the higher forms attains to a very highly developed condition. This vascular system contains in nearly all the *Oligochæta*, as in the *Polychæta* and *Hirudinea*, a red-coloured fluid, which has been proved to owe its coloration to hæmoglobin, and in which are suspended corpuscles. *Æolosoma* has a colourless pseudhæmal fluid. In the lower forms the walls of the blood-vessels are excessively delicate, and contain no muscles; in the higher forms (*e.g.*, *Lumbricus*) the blood-vessels are furnished with muscular tissue as well as with an epithelial lining. The cells of the latter give rise to the corpuscles of the blood, which consist of little more than the nucleus.

The simplest form of vascular system occurs in *Æolosoma* and *Ctenodrilus*. The alimentary tract is surrounded with a network of blood capillaries, which in the œsophageal region unite to form a dorsal vessel; this passes along the œsophagus, but is situated between the walls of the intestine and its covering of peritoneal cells; beneath the cerebral ganglia the dorsal vessel gives off a branch on either side; these unite with a ventral vessel, which passes beneath the intestine, and gives off branches to it, which are regularly arranged in pairs. In the *Enchytræidæ* the dorsal vessel is also restricted to the anterior segments of the body, and originates from a blood sinus in the walls of the alimentary tract. The dorsal vessel gives off anteriorly two branches which unite to form the ventral vessel; three pairs of slender vessels, a pair to each segment, originate from the dorsal vessel, and are connected with these two branches. In all the higher *Oligochæta* there is reticulum of blood capillaries developed in the walls of the alimen-

[1] The genus *Acanthodrilus* is almost entirely Antarctic in its range. It occurs in Patagonia, S. Georgia, Kerguelen's Land, New Zealand, Cape of Good Hope and other parts of Africa, Madagascar, and New Caledonia. *Perichæta* is characteristic of the Old and New World tropics, particularly of the former; in the Old World it ranges from India to China and Japan, and through the Indian Islands to Australia and New Zealand. Australia has the peculiar genera *Megascolides*, *Notoscolex*, and *Cryptodrilus*, but the greatest number of peculiar genera are found in the Neotropical region. In Europe the most characteristic genera are *Lumbricus* and *Allolobophora*; these are found in most other parts of the world, but it is possible that they have been accidentally imported.

[2] These figures refer to the "Literature," p. 684.

tary canal, but the dorsal vessel, although connected with this network, does not originate from it, but passes from end to end of the body. The dorsal vessel is also connected with the ventral vessel by paired trunks, which are segmentally disposed, *i.e.*, a pair to each segment. In the *Naidomorpha* and *Lumbriculidæ*, the vascular system consists only of these parts, together with some few branches which penetrate the layers of the body-wall and reach to the epidermis. Among earthworms the vascular system is more complex; our knowledge of the details of the circulation in certain tropical genera (*Urochæta, Pontodrilus*) is due to Perrier, and but little of importance has been added to his descriptions. The circulation of *Lumbricus* is known principally from the investigations of D'Udekem, Claparède, and recently of Horst. In *Lumbricus* there are three longitudinal trunks (fig. 3) which run from end to end of the body—(1) dorsal, (2) supranervian, (3) subnervian. The dorsal vessel is connected with the supranervian by seven

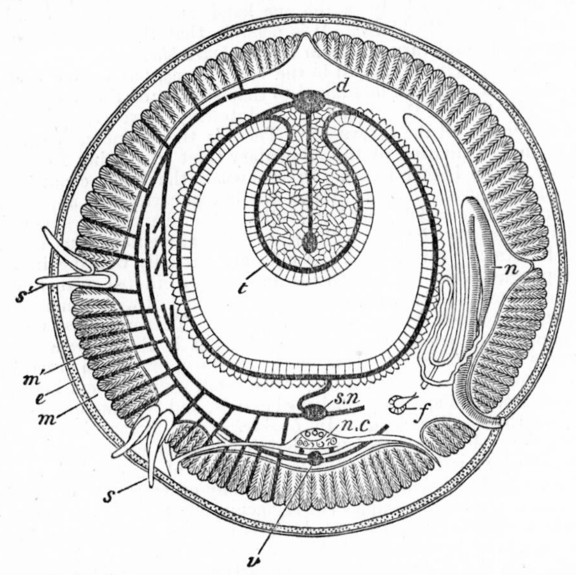

Fig. 3.—Diagrammatic Transverse Section through one of the Posterior Segments of *Lumbricus* (partly after Marshall and Hurst). *n*, nephridium; *f*, funnel of nephridium; *n.c*, nerve cord; *e*, epidermis; *m*, transverse muscles; *m'*, longitudinal muscles; *s*, *s'*, ventral and dorsal pairs of setæ; *t*, typhlosole; *d*, dorsal blood-vessel, connected by a vertical branch with typhlosole and by branches with intestinal blood-plexus; *s.n*, supranervian vessel; *v*, infranervian vessel. On the left side are indicated the chief vessels given off from the main trunk to the body-wall and nephridium.

pairs of stout trunks in the outer part of the body; from the dorsal vessel in front of the last of these originates on either side a lateral longitudinal vessel which passes along the sides of the œsophagus and gives off branches to it. In the intestinal region the dorsal vessel is connected by branches with the capillary network of the intestine, and also directly by lateral branches with the subnervian vessel; the latter gives off branches to the body-walls. The majority of earthworms possess in addition a small vessel running above the alimentary canal, but below the dorsal vessel; this is especially concerned with the blood supply of the alimentary tract, and in the intestinal region it runs in the interior of the typhlosole; the presence of this supra-intestinal trunk was first noted by Perrier, who also discovered that more or fewer of the large contractile "hearts" of the anterior segments are connected with this vessel as well as with the dorsal vessel. The subnervian vessel is absent in *Pontodrilus* and other genera. The immense development of the integumental capillary system is characteristic of earthworms, and is no doubt to be explained by the much greater thickness of the body-wall; it has been already stated that among the lower *Oligochæta* the integumental capillary system is present though feebly developed. In some genera of earthworms the capillaries penetrate the epidermic layer, as in some of the aquatic genera and in many leeches. It has been recently stated by Sarasin that these epidermic capillaries open by pores on to the exterior. That the vascular system of *Æolosoma* represents a primitive condition is shown by the investigations of Vejdovsky (15) into the development of *Rhynchelmis*. In this worm the dorsal vessel is at first only visible in the anterior region of the body, where it lies upon the œsophagus below the peritoneal covering of the latter; posteriorly it communicates with a blood sinus surrounding the intestine; this stage exactly corresponds to the adult *Æolosoma*, and the blood is also colourless; subsequently the dorsal vessel becomes connected with the ventral by a few lateral trunks; this stage is retained in the *Enchytræidæ*. Moreover, in the *Chloræmidæ* a similar condition exists (Horst, *Zool. Anzeig.*, viii. p. 12), and in the larval *Terebella*.

Excretory organs.

Excretory Organs.—It has been recently shown by Vejdovsky (15) that the *Oligochæta*, like *Polygordius*, many *Polychæta*, *Gephyrea*, and *Hirudinea*, possess temporary larval excretory tubules as well as the definitive nephridia. These organs have been found in *Rhynchelmis*, *Nais*, *Chætogaster*, and *Æolosoma*. In the first mentioned type they appear as a pair of fine tubes with a ciliated lumen, without any apparent internal aperture; they run on either side of the pharynx, and each opens by a pore placed at the side of the mouth. In the young asexually produced individual of *Nais*, *Chætogaster*, and *Æolosoma* similar organs are to be seen. The permanent excretory organs consist in the majority of *Oligochæta* of three parts:—(1) a funnel-shaped expansion furnished with cilia, opening into the body cavity; (2) a coiled glandular tube; and (3) a terminal vesicle furnished with muscular layers, and opening on to the exterior of the body. The latter section may be absent, and in the relative proportions of the different parts as well as in certain details of their structure there are great differences. As a general rule, the funnel lies in a segment anterior to that which bears the external pore; but in *Plutellus* Perrier states that the whole organ lies in one segment. In the majority of forms there are not more than a single pair of nephridia to each segment (except in *Perichæta*, &c.). In the limicolous *Oligochæta* nephridia are generally wanting in the anterior segments of the body, and disappear in those which contain the generative ducts when the latter are developed; in the terricolous forms, on the other hand, the nephridia usually commence in the second or third segment. *Ctenodrilus* is remarkable for the fact that it only possesses a single pair of nephridia, the funnel of which is situated on the anterior side of the first dissepiment; but in no form are these organs entirely wanting. The glandular part of the organ consists, as in the *Hirudinea* and most Platyhelminths, of a row of cells placed end to end, which are perforated by the lumen; the lumen of the tubule is therefore, as was first discovered by Claparède, *intra*-cellular; in this particular the nephridia of the *Oligochæta* differ from those of the *Polychæta*, where the walls of the duct are made up of rows of cells, the lumen therefore being *inter*-cellular.[1] While in the greater number of *Oligochæta* the lumen of the tubule is simple and unbranched, in *Chætogaster* fine branches are given off, which ramify in the substance of the cells; this is an important point of resemblance to the nephridia of the *Hirudinea*, where Vejdovsky and Bourne (*Q. J. M. S.*, 1884) have described a similar branching of the duct. The glandular part of the nephridium is often, as in *Lumbricus*, differentiated into two parts; the anterior section is composed of more delicate cells, the posterior of larger and more glandular cells; the lumen is furnished with cilia. The external surface of the organ is frequently covered with rounded cells of a glandular appearance, which are to be looked upon as modified peritoneal cells; in certain cases (*e.g.*, *Pontodrilus* and many "*Limicolæ*") those cells form a solid mass in the interior of which are concealed the windings of the excretory tubule. Special dilatations of the tubule are occasionally met with, as in *Rhynchelmis*; and, among leeches, *Clepsine*, *Pontobdella*, &c., show a similar dilatation, which, as in *Rhynchelmis*, comes immediately after the funnel. The terminal section of the nephridium, the "contractile" vesicle, is more marked among earthworms than in the "*Limicolæ*"; it is lined by a delicate layer of cells and furnished with muscular fibres; in *Urobenus* (Benham, 7), as well as in many other species, this region of the nephridium is very largely developed, and is furnished with a long sac-like diverticulum. The differences in structure between the various parts of the nephridium are due to their different origin: the funnel is formed independently of the glandular tubule, though both take their origin from the mesoblast; the contractile vesicle is invaginated from the ectoderm.

In *Acanthodrilus multiporus* Beddard found that the number of nephridial pores in the anterior region of the body to each segment was more than 100. In *Typhæus* an almost identical arrangement exists, and in *Perichæta* (Beddard, 4). In the last-named genus, as well as in an Australian form, *Megascolides* (Spencer, 12), the nephridial system forms a continuous network of tubules, uninterrupted by the septa. In *Acanthodrilus* the network of each segment is independent. In this genus, as in *Perichæta*, there are numerous ciliated funnels in each segment.

The relation of the nephridia of the *Chætopoda* to those of the Platyhelminths, on the one hand, and to those of the *Hirudinea* and *Gephyrea* are variously interpreted. It has been proved that in *Polygordius*, many *Chætopoda*, and many *Hirudinea* and *Gephyrea*, the larvæ, like those of the *Oligochæta*, possess excretory organs, which are constructed on the type of the nephridia in Platyhelminths. This is at any rate the case with *Polygordius*, the Chætopod larva, and the larva of *Echiurus*; in all these types the nephridia are paired branched tubes, which open separately on to the exterior; they have, however, no internal openings, the flagellate cells of the Platyhelminth, with their single flagellum and funnel-shaped per-

[1] Nussbaum has lately (*Arch. Slav. de Biol.*, i.) found that in the leech a number of cells fuse to form a single drain-pipe cell. This would tend to prove that the intercellular lumen preceded the intracellular.

foration, being absent. The larval excretory organs of the *Hirudinea*, like these of the *Oligochæta* referred to above, are to be looked upon as in a more rudimentary condition; they are unbranched, and are sometimes without an external orifice. Moreover, essentially similar organs are found in the larval mollusc. In many of the above-cited examples it is certain that the larval excretory organs have no connexion with the permanent excretory organs; they atrophy before the latter appear. Hatchek, however, has stated that there is a connexion between the larval and permanent excretory organs in *Polygordius*; doubts have been thrown upon this observation by some who believe that the facts already cited showed (1) that the excretory system of *Annelida* and *Hirudinea* is a new formation, while (2) the excretory system of their Platyhelminth ancestors is represented by the transitory excretory system of the *Annelida*, which has therefore naturally no connexion with the permanent excretory system. This view has the merit of explaining the presence of apparently similar structures (*i.e.*, the larval nephridia) in such diverse types as *Mollusca*, *Hirudinea*, and *Gephyrea*, and is perhaps further supported by the high development of the larval excretory organ in the active larvæ of *Polygordius*, *Echiurus*, and the *Chætopoda*, and its rudimentary character in the embryo *Oligochæta*. It follows from this that the permanent nephridia of the *Chætopoda* are new structures, unless the views of Bergh (18) be accepted, who would derive these organs from the generative ducts of the Platyhelminths.

Against this hypothesis may be urged (1) the unlikelihood of a new formation of excretory organs in Annelids, and the probability of these organs being really homologous with those of their Platyhelminth ancestors, and (2) the fact that the larval excretory organs of *Polygordius*, *Polychæta*, and *Oligochæta* and *Hirudinea* are connected with the permanent system or at least are not in any way replaced by the permanent excretory system; in the *Oligochæta* the larval excretory organs appear comparatively late, and the segment occupied by them never gives rise to a pair of permanent nephridia.

The following facts lead to another hypothesis, which is in many respects more acceptable.

A connexion between the nephridia of consecutive segments has been recently stated by Wilson to occur in the embryo *Lumbricus*. Meyer and Cunningham have observed the same in *Terebella*. Vejdvosky (15) has recorded in *Anachæta bohemica* a connexion between the nephridia of the 21st and 22d segments, and moreover the first pair of nephridia has two internal funnels. In the leech *Pontobdella* the nephridia (Bourne, *Q. J. Min. Sci.*, 1884) form a network, the internal funnels and external apertures alone being arranged metamerically. The presence of numerous external pores to each segment in certain earthworms, and the continuity of nephridia of adjacent segments are facts to be referred to the same category. Eisig's discovery of the presence of many nephridia in each of the segments of the *Capitellidæ*, which are connected together, is also, like the other facts referred to, in harmony with the supposition that the excretory system of the *Annelida* has been directly derived from that of the Platyhelminths somewhat as follows. The excretory system is at first, as in the Platyhelminth, a continuous system, opening by numerous apertures into the body cavity by a single orifice or a pair of orifices on to the exterior. Secondary external apertures are then formed, which are irregular in their disposition (these actually occur in certain Platyhelminths), and more or less numerous; this condition is largely retained in *Acanthodrilus* and *Perichæta*; the secondary external apertures as well as the internal apertures then become reduced in number and metamerically arranged; this condition occurs in *Pontobdella* and *Terebella*, and to a very limited extent in *Anachæta*. The connexion between the nephridial system of succession segments then disappears, and the characteristic Annelid excretory system is arrived at.

Alimentary tract.

Alimentary Tract.—The alimentary canal of all the *Oligochæta* is a straight tube running from mouth to anus, but even in the lowest forms is specialized into different regions. A pharynx, œsophagus, and intestine can be recognized universally; the pharynx is formed by the stomodæal invagination of the epiblast, while the terminal section of the intestine is formed by the proctodæal invagination; the rest of the alimentary canal is hypoblastic. In *Æolosoma* the pharynx is restricted to the first segment of the body, a condition which is seen in the embryonic stages of other *Oligochæta*, but also in the adult *Polygordius* (see below). This is followed by the narrow œsophagus, which leads, in the fourth segment, into the intestine; the intestine is at first wide, but afterwards becomes narrower; the whole alimentary canal is ciliated. In the higher types the pharynx occupies several segments, and is preceded by a buccal cavity, the epithelium of which is not ciliated; in many *Oligochæta* (*e.g.*, *Enchytræus*) the pharynx is protrusible. It is frequently furnished with glands, which are of two kinds, and probably not morphologically comparable. In many *Enchytræidæ* and *Naidomorpha* certain of the anterior segments contain glands attached to the anterior faces of the intersegmental septa; these have been termed septal glands. In *Anachæta* there are only two pairs of these glands, but four in *Pachydrilus*; the glands of each side of the body are connected by a continuous longitudinal duct which opens into the pharynx. Similar glands appear to occur in most *Lumbricidæ* in the form of unicellular glands attached to the pharynx.

Another series of glandular structures are connected with the pharynx, which have been termed by Vejdovsky salivary glands; these are found in the *Enchytræidæ*, and consist of simple or branched tubes, which open into the hinder end of the pharynx at each side by a single duct; since these glands agree in their minute structure with nephridia, which are not found in the segments which contain the glands, it is probable that they represent slightly metamorphosed nephridia (Vejdovsky). Among earthworms *Urochæta*, *Diachæta*, and *Acanthodrilus multiporus* possess a pair of glands at the anterior end of the body (glandes à mucosité, Perrier), which are larger and more complicated than the nephridia, though their structure is the same; in *Acanthodrilus* these glands open into the buccal cavity; in *Urochæta* they are branched and open on to the surface of the body on the one hand, and into the cœlom by several funnels (Beddard). It is possible that they are the homologues of the salivary glands in the *Enchytræidæ*.

The œsophagus is ciliated in the lower forms, but among earthworms cilia appear to be limited to that section of the œsophagus which lies behind the gizzard. The intestine, however, appears to be ciliated in all the *Oligochæta*. There is thus a gradual diminution in the ciliation of the alimentary tract in passing from the lower to the higher forms. In *Æolosoma* the whole canal from mouth to anus is ciliated. When the buccal cavity first appears it is lined with a cuticle, and has no cilia. The pharynx loses its cilia in the *Enchytræidæ*, while the rest of the alimentary tract is ciliated. Among earthworms the cilia are partially wanting in the œsophagus, while the intestine is lined with a ciliated epithelium.

In some *Oligochæta* the œsophagus is furnished with a muscular dilatation, which is usually termed gizzard. This organ first makes its appearance among the *Naidomorpha*, but is absent from other genera of "*Limicolæ*." It is, on the contrary, present in nearly all earthworms; the gizzard is lined with a tall columnar epithelium, which secretes a specially thickened cuticle, and the muscular layers are enormously increased. In *Lumbricus* the gizzard lies at the posterior end of the œsophagus, but in all other earthworms it is succeeded as well as preceded by a section of œsophagus, as in *Nais*. In *Lumbricus*, as well as in many other genera of earthworms, the gizzard occupies two segments, and the septum dividing these segments has disappeared, or is at most represented by a few bands of muscle, which bind down the gizzard to the body-wall. On the other hand, in some earthworms as well as in the *Naidomorpha* the gizzard only occupies one segment. In *Digaster* and *Trigaster* there are, as the names of these genera imply, two or three separate gizzards, while in *Moniligaster* there are four or five. In *Trigaster* and *Moniligaster* each gizzard only occupies a single segment; it is possible that the single gizzard of *Lumbricus*, &c., which occupies two segments, is due to the fusion of two separate gizzards lying in as many consecutive segments.

The œsophagus in most earthworms is furnished with from one to six pairs of glandular diverticula, which are known as "calciferous glands" or "glands of Morren." Those glands produce a calcareous secretion.[1]

The intestine is wider than the œsophagus, but has much the same structure; in *Æolosoma* the walls of the intestine consist of little more than a single layer of ciliated cells, but in the higher forms this is surrounded by a layer of circular and longitudinal muscular fibres. A remarkable peculiarity distinguishes the intestine of the majority of earthworms; this is a longitudinal fold on the dorsal side which projects into the lumen of the intestine, and which is known as the "typhlosole" (fig. 3, *t*). A typhlosole does not exist in *Pontodrilus* nor in any known limicolous form. In *Perichæta* the intestine is furnished with one or more pairs of short cæca; in *Megascolex* and other genera there are series of compact glands opening into the intestine.

Reproductive organs.

Reproductive Organs.—The *Oligochæta* are, so far as is known, invariably hermaphrodite; in this particular they differ from the *Polychæta*, where as a rule the testes and ovaries are found in distinct individuals. Among the *Polychæta*, however, *Protula* and other *Serpulidæ* are hermaphrodite. The reproductive organs consist of testes and ovaries, with their ducts, and spermathecæ, which are filled with spermatozoa during copulation. The reproductive glands are developed as a proliferation of the peritoneal epithelium, but are restricted to one or two segments; these organs moreover have a definite form, and are commonly surrounded by a layer of cells of different nature from the sexual cells which make up the substance of the gland.

(1) *Male Reproductive Organs*—(*a*) *Testes.*—In *Lumbricus* these organs consist of two minute pairs of solid cellular masses attached close to the median ventral line upon the posterior face of the septa which divide segments 9–10 and 10–11 (fig. 4). These organs were first discovered by Hering. In the majority of earthworms (*Acantho-*

[1] For an account of the function of these glands, as well as of the part which earthworms play as geological agents, see Darwin, *Formation of Vegetable Mould*, &c.

drilus, *Eudrilus*, *Perichæta*, &c.) there is an identical number of testes occupying the same segments. It is probable but not yet proved that in *Urochæta* and *Moniligaster*, where there is only a single seminal reservoir and vas deferens on each side, there is but one pair of testes; at any rate, in *Typhæus*, where the seminal reservoirs and vasa deferentia are single, there is but one testis on each side placed in the 10th segment.

Among the "*Limicolæ*" there is rarely (*Phreoryctes*) more than a single pair of testes, which may be in the 5th (*Naidomorpha*), 9th (*Lumbriculidæ*), 10th (*Tubifex*), or 11th (*Enchytræus*, &c.) segment.

(*b*) *Seminal Reservoirs*.—The spermatozoa are not, however, developed within the testes, but in special receptacles, the seminal reservoirs (seminal vesicles, vesiculæ seminales). These structures frequently enclose the testes, with which they have been confounded by many writers. By the earlier writers the seminal reservoirs were regarded as ovaries; this opinion was due to the numerous parasitic Gregarines which these organs contain; the encysted parasites were mistaken for ova. In *Lumbricus terrestris*, &c. (Bergh), there is a single median reservoir, which encloses the testes, the funnels of the vasa deferentia, and the nerve cord in each of segments 9 and 10; with these are connected three pairs of lateral outgrowths situated respectively in segments 8, 10, and 11. In *Allolobophora fœtida* there are four pairs of isolated seminal reservoirs in segments 8, 9, 10, and 11; there is no median unpaired portion; and the testes as well as the vasa deferentia lie freely in the body cavity; the first two pairs lie on the posterior septa of their segments, and open by an aperture into the cavity of the segment behind; the last two pairs lie upon the anterior septa of their segments, and open into the cavity of the segment in front. In all cases the seminal reservoirs are formed as outgrowths of the septa. The cavity of the seminal reservoirs is broken up by anastomosing trabeculæ, in the interstices of which the spermatozoa undergo their development. There is very great variety among earthworms in the number and arrangement of the seminal reservoirs, but there is no form known in which they are absent. In *Urochæta*, *Typhæus*, *Titanus*, and *Diachæta* there appear to be only a single pair, which are of great length. In *Diachæta* (Benham) they occupy 26 segments.

In many of the "*Limicolæ*," as was first proved by Lankester in *Tubifex*, seminal reservoirs are found; and where their development has been traced they appear to originate as outgrowths of the septa. In some of the simpler forms, *e.g.*, *Chætogaster*, seminal reservoirs are not developed, but the testicular products float freely in the perivisceral cavity, where they undergo their development.

(*c*) *Vasa Deferentia*.—It is a rule without any exceptions among the *Oligochæta* that the spermatozoa are carried out of the body by special ducts, which perform only this function. In this respect the *Oligochæta* are in marked contrast to the *Polychæta*, where the ripe spermatozoa are either set free by a rupture of the body-wall, or are conveyed to the exterior by means of the nephridia, which, however, may be slightly modified in relation to this function. These ducts are termed vasa deferentia; they invariably open freely into the body cavity, and only sometimes (*e.g.*, *Lumbricus*) acquire a secondary relation with the testes by way of the seminal reservoirs; they are developed independently of the testes. In the *Hirudinea* and Platyhelminths, on the other hand, the efferent ducts are *continuous with the testes*, of which they appear to be mere outgrowths; Nussbaum has, however, recently (*Zool. Anzeiger*, viii. p. 181) stated that in *Clepsine* the vasa deferentia are developed independently of the testes.

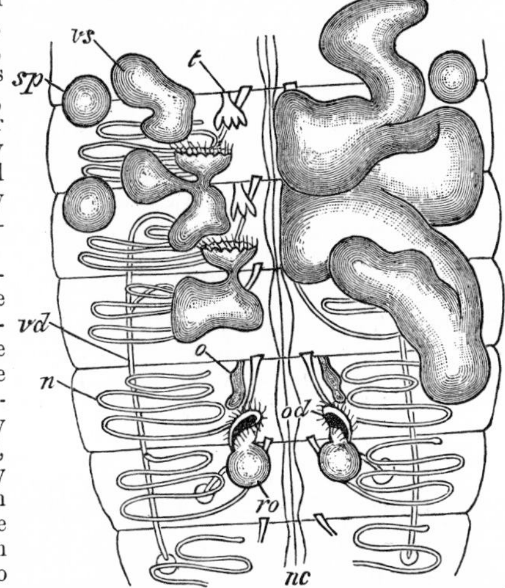

Fig. 4.—Genital Segments of *Lumbricus* (slightly altered from Howes, *Biological Atlas*). The left side represents the immature, the right the mature condition, so far as the male reproductive organs are concerned. *t*, anterior pair of testes (the second pair are in the next segment); *vs*, seminal vesicles; *sp*, spermathecæ; *vd*, vas deferens; *o*, ovary; *od*, oviduct; *ro*, receptaculum ovorum; *n*, nephridia; *nc*, nerve cord.

In their simplest form (in many *Enchytræidæ*) the vasa deferentia consist of a single pair of convoluted tubes, which open by a wide funnel-shaped aperture into one segment, while the external aperture is situated in the following segment. Very generally in those *Oligochæta* the funnel-shaped expansion is continued into a wide cylindrical tube, which narrows abruptly on passing through the intersegmental septum into a slender tube; the walls of both sections of the vas deferens are formed of cylindrical ciliated cells; the external aperture is often surrounded by several rows of large glandular cells. Among a large number of the lower *Oligochæta* there is a single pair of vasa deferentia, which occupy in the same way two segments; the internal funnel-shaped aperture opens into one segment, while the greater part of the tube and the external orifice are situated in the following segment. A further complication is, however, introduced in the form of a glandular terminal organ, which opens on to the exterior by one extremity, and communicates with the vas deferens at the other. In *Stylaria lacustris* this organ is pear-shaped, narrowing towards the external aperture; it is lined by a layer of cylindrical glandular cells, outside of which is a layer of muscular fibres; the whole organ is covered by large peritoneal cells of a glandular appearance. This organ is termed the *atrium*; the vas deferens, which is short, only curved (not convoluted), opens by one end into the broad extremity of the atrium, and terminates in a ciliated funnel, which has this peculiarity that it does not lie in the segment in front, but in the same segment (in the 6th) as the atrium; it is, however, closely applied to the intersegmental septum of segments 5–6.

This condition of the vasa deferentia is exactly repeated in the earthworm *Moniligaster barwelli*; the seminal reservoirs (Beddard) lie partly in the 8th and partly in the 9th segment; the vas deferens, which is much coiled, lies in the same segment; it is continuous at one end with the seminal reservoir, and at the other with a glandular body opening between segments 9–10, which has a structure apparently identical with that of the atrium of *Stylaria*. *Chætogaster diaphanus* (Vejdovsky, 15) has the same general disposition of the vasa deferentia, but the atrium is divided into a glandular "vesicula seminalis," into which opens the vas deferens, and a distal non-glandular portion, which can be everted during copulation.

The reproductive ducts of the *Tubificidæ* are still further complicated in their structure. In *Tubifex rivulorum* the structure of the atrium at an early stage is like that of *Stylaria*; a simple globular or pear-shaped atrium is formed as an invagination of the integument; later this is differentiated into two parts, as in *Chætogaster*; an additional structure is, however, developed in

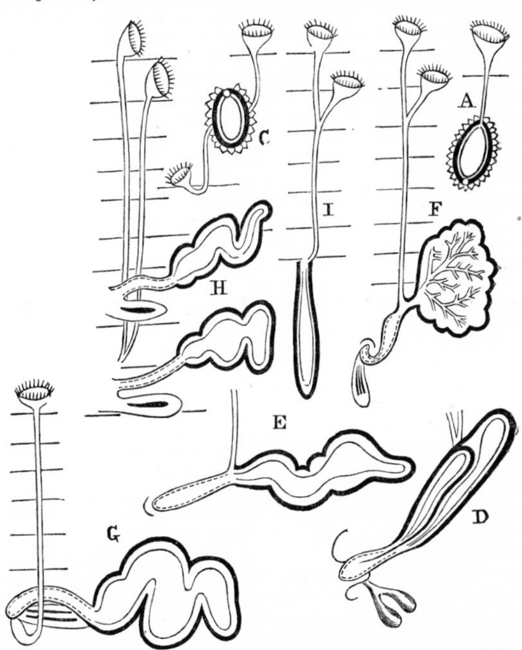

Fig. 5.—Male Genital Ducts of Various *Oligochæta*. In most cases the whole length of the vasa deferentia is shown; the transverse lines indicate the boundaries of the segments through which they pass. The thick black lines indicate the atria, the dotted lines the muscular part of the atria. In F, G, H the penial setæ are shown lying in a sac opening in common with the atria. A, *Moniligaster barwelli* (outside the atrium in A and C is a layer of glandular tissue); C, *Phreatothrix pragensis* (after Vejdovsky); D, *Eudrilus silvicola*; E, *Pontodrilus marionis*; F, *Perichæta armata*; G, *Typhæus gammii*; H, *Acanthodrilus novæ-zelandiæ*; I, *Ocnerodrilus* (after Eisen).

the form of a group of unicellular glands, collectively termed the prostate, which open into the glandular distal region of the atrium; in the adult *Tubifex* the proximal section of the atrium is developed into a protrusible penis; this is surrounded by a second invagination of the integument, which forms a penis sheath and part of the penis proper. The glandular part of the atrium (vesicula seminalis) is ciliated, but cilia are wanting in the penis. In *Telmatodrilus*

(Eisen) the prostates are very numerous, and arranged in pairs; in *Psammoryctes* (Vejdovsky) and in *Hemitubifex* (Eisen) the upper part of the vesicula seminalis, into which open the vas deferens and the prostate, forms a globular chamber distinct from the remainder of the atrium.

Another type of efferent apparatus is found in the *Lumbriculidæ*. In *Stylodrilus* there is a single pair of atria, which have much the same structure as in *Stylaria*, but the proximal end of the organ is less glandular and can be everted as a penis. With each atrium, however, are connected two vasa deferentia; one of these opens by a funnel-like expansion into the segment in front, the other passes back into the segment behind that which contains the atrium, and after again perforating the septum opens by a funnel-shaped expansion into the atrial segment. Among earthworms *Moniligaster*, as already stated, is furnished with an efferent apparatus exactly comparable to that of the lower "*Limicolæ*." In other genera the same divisions can be recognized in the efferent apparatus, which may also be single or double. In all earthworms, however, with the exception of *Moniligaster*, the internal funnels are situated several segments in front of the external pore, instead of being placed in the next segment. This is the case also with *Ocnerodrilus* (Eisen), a form usually referred to the "*Limicolæ*." *Urochæta* and *Typhæus* are the only genera known, besides *Moniligaster*, in which there is a single vas deferens on each side. In all others there are a pair of vasa deferentia on each side, which open by separate funnels into two consecutive segments (10th and 11th); the vasa deferentia open on to the exterior by a common pore; they may become united into a single tube in the segment behind that which contains the posterior funnel (*Lumbricus, Perichæta*), or one or two segments farther back (*Microchæta*), or, finally, as in *Eudrilus*, they may unite in the terminal apparatus.

The structure of the vasa deferentia and the funnels corresponds to that of the lower *Oligochæta*, except that the funnels are usually much plicated. In *Lumbricus, Urochæta*, &c., the vasa deferentia open directly on to the exterior; in other types, however, an atrium can be recognized. The most primitive form of these organs (in some respects) is seen in the genus *Eudrilus* (Beddard, 3); the two vasa deferentia open into the interior of a glandular organ, which is probably the homologue of the atrium; this organ is divided into two parts by a longitudinal septum, but is covered by continuous layers of muscles; it communicates with two muscular tubes, also covered by a continuous layer of muscle, which unite into a single muscular penis, which is probably eversible. The penis, like the atrium, is lined by a single layer of non-ciliate cells; the cells of the glandular portion are non-ciliate, and are arranged in two layers; the penis projects into the interior of a cavity open to the exterior; this corresponds to the penis sheath of the *Naidomorpha*. With the penis sheath ("bursa copulatrix," Perrier) is also connected a small rigid diverticulum with muscular walls.

It is not certain whether the partial longitudinal division of the atrium and vesicula represents the partial fusion of the primitively distinct atria or the commencing separation into two parts of a single atrium; the latter alternative, on the whole, is the more probable.

In *Perichæta, Acanthodrilus*, &c., certain glandular bodies are connected with the termination of the vas deferens, which have been termed "prostates." These glands are of two kinds: (1) in *Acanthodrilus, Pontodrilus*, &c., they consist of a single somewhat convoluted tube of uniform diameter; (2) in *Perichæta*, &c., they have a racemose lobulated appearance. It is probable that these structures are homologous. The prostates of *Perichæta* (fig. 5, F) are made up of numerous ductules, which are connected with groups of cells that have the character of unicellular glands; each cell is connected by a long stalk with the termination of the ductule; in *Acanthodrilus*, &c., the prostate is lined by a double layer of cells which surround a central lumen; the innermost layer of cells are narrow and columnar, the outer layer are large pear-shaped glandular cells. The difference between the two organs is this: in *Perichæta* the glandular cells have become segregated into groups, while the lumen of the gland is branched. In at least one species of *Perichæta* both these differences from *Acanthodrilus* are less marked.

The so-called prostates of *Acanthodrilus* and *Pontodrilus* agree in their minute structure with the vesicula seminalis of *Eudrilus*, and they open on to the exterior, like the corresponding structures in *Perichæta*, by a thick-walled muscular tube; the vas deferens, however, is connected in *Pontodrilus* with the muscular part of the atrium, and not with the vesicula; the condition of the efferent apparatus is therefore a more modified one. In *Typhæus* this modification is carried still further: the vas deferens enters the body-wall independently of the vesicula and atrium, and only joins the latter below the epidermis just before its opening on to the exterior. If Vejdovsky be right in interpreting the so-called receptaculum seminis of *Ocnerodrilus* (Eisen) as the atrium, the relations of the several parts of the efferent system in this worm are much the same as in *Typhæus*. In *Acanthodrilus* (fig. 5, H) the two pairs of atria open on to the 17th and 19th segments respectively; the vasa deferentia open on to the 18th independently of them.

(*d*) *Genital Setæ*.—It is commonly the case among the *Oligochæta* that the setæ upon the clitellum, in the neighbourhood of the spermathecæ and the male sexual apertures, undergo a certain amount of modification. Thus in *Lumbricus* the setæ in these regions of the body are longer and more slender than the setæ elsewhere (Hering); in *Urochæta* and *Thamnodrilus* the setæ upon the clitellum are ridged. Analogous modifications are found in *Nais* and other "*Limicolæ*." The function of these setæ is probably, as Lankester has suggested, to assist in attaching the worms together during copulation. Before the individual is mature these setæ are absent, and the ordinary setæ occupy their place; when the clitellum is developed the ordinary setæ drop out, and are replaced by the genital setæ (Vejdovsky).

In *Acanthodrilus, Typhæus*, and some species of *Perichæta* the apertures of the atria are furnished with a thin-walled muscular diverticulum in which are found a bundle of extraordinarily long setæ; these can be protruded through the sexual orifice and may possibly serve to assist in the transference of the sperm to the spermathecæ of another individual. These setæ may be termed "penial" setæ (Lankester) (fig. 2, *a*, *b*).

(2) *Female Reproductive Apparatus*—(*a*) *Ovaries*.—The ovaries of *Lumbricus* were first discovered by D'Udekem; they consist of a pair of minute pear-shaped bodies attached to the anterior septum of the 13th segment (fig. 4, *o*); their position exactly corresponds to that of the testes, and like those organs they are covered by a delicate layer of flattened peritoneal cells. In *Perichæta* and *Acanthodrilus*, where the testes are prolonged into numerous digitate processes, the ovaries have an identical form; finally, the contents of the young ovaries and testes consist of entirely similar germinal cells (Bergh); these facts all tend to prove the serial homology of the ovaries and testes. With the exception of *Euclipidrilus* and *Phreoryctes*, the *Oligochæta* possess but a single pair of ovaries, which appear to be invariably[1] placed behind the testes.

(*b*) *Receptaculum Ovorum*.—Corresponding to the seminal reservoirs are a pair of outgrowths from the posterior side of the septum which separates segments 13–14; the ripe or nearly ripe ova are stored in these receptacles. Their presence in *Lumbricus* was first discovered by Hering. They have the same structure as the seminal reservoirs; their cavity is similarly divided by anastomosing trabeculæ; and they have been proved by Bergh (19) to originate in the same way. In *Moniligaster* (Horst) these bodies are of large size, and therefore resemble more closely the seminal reservoirs. They are generally present in earthworms. Among the *Naidomorpha* organs are met with which appear to resemble the receptacula. In *Stylaria lacustris* a pair of delicate sacs are developed in the same segment as that which contains the ovaries; in these the ova undergo their development; the extremity of the sac encircles the ovary, so that the ova can readily find their way into it. This organ is, however, compared by Vejdovsky (15) to the delicate peritoneal covering of the ovary in *Lumbricus*, and more particularly to a tube-like projection of this peritoneal covering at the free extremity of the ovary where the ripe ova are found.

(*c*) *Oviduct*.—The oviducts in *Lumbricus* are two minute trumpet-shaped bodies composed of a single layer of ciliated cells; the funnel-shaped expansion opens into the 13th segment; the tube perforates the mesentery, and opens on to the exterior in the 14th segment. The mouth of the oviduct is in close relation with the aperture of the receptaculum ovorum into the same segment. In most earthworms a pair of oviducts of similar structure have been recognized; in *Perichæta* the two oviducts open by a common pore situated in the median ventral line of the 14th segment. The apertures of the oviducts are, with the exception of *Moniligaster* (Horst) and *Allurus* (Beddard, 5), invariably placed in front of the male generative pores. Among the "limicolous" forms oviducts have been described in *Rhynchelmis, Phreoryctes*, and *Phreatothrix*; in these genera, however, the oviducts consist of little more than the funnel which is sessile on the ventral body-wall of the 11th segment, and opens on to the exterior in the groove between this and the following segment; in *Phreoryctes*, Beddard (6), there are two pairs of oviducts entirely contained in one segment. It is important to note that in *Rhynchelmis* and *Phreatothrix* the female pore is behind the male pore, while in earthworms (except *Moniligaster, Allurus*) it is in front. Among the lower *Oligochæta* oviducts are absent; their place is taken in the *Enchytræidæ* and others by a pair of slit-like orifices placed on the clitellar segment behind the apertures of the vasa deferentia. That these pores represent the external orifices of the oviducts in the higher forms is shown by the following considerations: (1) their position behind the male pores; (2) the probability urged by Vejdovsky that the clitellar segment really represents three fused segments, in which case the oviducal pores are really one segment behind the male efferent pores; (3) the remarkable analogy with the *Cyclostomata* among fishes, where the abdominal pores act as oviduct (Weber, *Zeitsch. f. wiss. Zool.*, 1887).

The ovaries and oviducts of *Eudrilus* (Beddard, Horst), differ in many particulars from those of other *Oligochæta*. The ovaries (fig. 6) are two solid bodies situated on the anterior septum of segment

[1] *Plutellus* is, according to Perrier, an exception; the ovaries are in front of the testes.

14. They are surrounded by layers of muscles, and the interior is divided by trabeculæ into numerous compartments; directly continuous with each ovary is a contorted tube which passes through the septum into the 13th segment, and then again passes through the septum, and opens on to the exterior in the 14th segment, in common with a large spermathecal pouch and a small glandular body. The oviduct opens by a wide mouth into the interior of the ovary, and is lined throughout with a ciliated epithelium; it is covered by layers of muscular fibres, which are continuous with those of the ovary. The continuity of the ovary and its duct is unknown in any other *Oligochæta*, but is analogous to the condition of the ovaries and their ducts in the leeches. It is possible that the muscular wall of the ovary is to be regarded as an hypertrophy of the peritoneal covering of the ovary in *Lumbricus*, &c., and that this has involved the oviduct; or the muscular coat of the ovary may be regarded as the receptaculum ovorum, which, as in *Stylaria*, is developed in the same segment as the ovary; this supposition is strengthened by the fact that the oviduct traverses the septum between the 13th and 14th segments.

Fig. 6.—Female Reproductive Apparatus of *Eudrilus*. On the right side the spermatheca has been cut away to show the contorted oviduct *ov*. *o*, ovary; *sp*, spermatheca; *gl*, gland opening into conjoined duct of spermatheca and oviduct.

Spermathecæ.—Of these organs there are from one to eight pairs; they consist of spherical or pear-shaped vesicles, often furnished with accessory diverticula. They receive the semen during copulation and by their epithelium is fabricated the generally chitinous spermatophore in which the spermatozoa are enveloped, and in which they are conveyed to the neighbourhood of the clitellum of another individual.

The genital ducts have been compared with nephridia by many writers; there is not only a considerable anatomical resemblance, but a developmental similarity; the vasa deferentia (and the oviducts ?), like the nephridia, consist of a funnel, of a more or less elongated tubule, and of a distal vesicular part. The *intra*cellular duct of the nephridium and the *inter*cellular duct of the vas deferens may be explained by the different functions which the organs perform.[1] The spermathecæ, on the other hand, are comparable to the vesicle of the nephridium, which is formed in both cases by an ectodermic ingrowth. The fact that the funnel and the tubule in both cases are developed independently, but both from the mesoblast, is a striking point of similarity between the vasa deferentia and oviducts and the nephridia. The belief of Claparède that in the "*Limicolæ*" the genital ducts were the homologues of nephridia, but not in the "*Terricolæ*," was based upon the erroneous assumption that nephridia are absent in the genital segments of the former. This has been shown by Vejdovsky to be an error: nephridia are present at first in the genital segments, but degenerate and disappear when the genital ducts are formed. Moreover, enough has been already said to prove the extreme unlikelihood of a non-homology between the generative ducts in earthworms and those in the "limicolous" forms. Lankester put forward the theory that there were primitively two pairs of nephridia in each segment, each series being connected with one of the pairs of setæ; the genital ducts were supposed to be the remains of one series which had aborted, except in the genital segments. This theory was at first espoused by Perrier, who found that the nephridia were sometimes connected with one series of setæ and sometimes with the other, and sometimes (*Plutellus*) alternated from segment to segment, opening in one segment by the ventral and in another by the dorsal setæ; these facts appeared to show that one or other of the two series of nephridia was partially or entirely retained in different genera. In his later publications Perrier was not inclined to attach much weight to this hypothesis, inasmuch as it did not satisfactorily refer the genital ducts to one or other of the presumed double series of nephridia; the apertures of the genital ducts and nephridia were found occasionally to coincide at the same pair of setæ.

The discovery that each segment of a worm may contain numerous nephridial pores disposes of any *a priori* difficulties as to the homology between nephridia and genital ducts, though the question is far from being settled.

Classification.

Classification and Affinities.—It has already been stated that the *Oligochæta* form a group which cannot be subdivided into *Limicolæ* and *Terricolæ* as was proposed by Claparède. The genera of *Oligochæta* have been arranged in families by Vejdovsky (14), to whom the reader is referred for a classification, which is satisfactory as regards the "limicolous" forms, and some of the families (*e.g.*, *Lumbricidæ* and *Perichætidæ*) of earthworms. Since that time, however, a large number of new genera and species of earthworms have been described, which cannot at present be satisfactorily arranged. Perrier divided earthworms into three groups:—(1) *Preclitellians* (*e.g.*, *Lumbricus*), where the male pores are situated in front of the clitellum; (2) *Intraclitellians* (*e.g.*, *Eudrilus*), where the male pores are within the clitellum; and (3) *Postclitellians* (*e.g.*, *Perichæta*), where the male pores open behind the clitellum. Advancing knowledge has shown this classification to be untenable, for two principal reasons: first, because it separates some species of *Acanthodrilus* which are postclitellian from others which are intraclitellian, and it separates the intraclitellian *Megascolex* from the postclitellian *Perichæta*, between which genera there are numerous points of affinity; and, secondly, because this classification is based on the assumption that earthworms can be considered as a group apart from other *Oligochæta*, whereas it is now impossible to draw any line of division between any two such groups.

The simplest forms of *Oligochæta* are the genera *Æolosoma* and *Ctenodrilus*. *Æolosoma* has a "head," consisting of one segment which contains the pharynx. The nervous system consists of cerebral ganglia, which are placed in the first segment, and retain connexion with the epiblast; the apparent absence of a ventral nervous cord is in all probability to be looked upon as evidence of degeneration. The body possesses considerable traces of the primitively continuous ciliation; upon the head are a pair of ciliated pits. In all these particulars, as well as in the characters of the vascular system, *Æolosoma* agrees with *Ctenodrilus*; the latter form has, however, a ventral nerve cord, which, like the cerebral ganglia, is lodged in the epidermis. In most of these points *Æolosoma* and *Ctenodrilus* resemble larval forms of the higher *Oligochæta*. The reproductive organs of *Ctenodrilus* are not known, but those of *Æolosoma* are constituted on the Oligochætous plan. These two genera are also closely allied to the *Archiannelida*, of which a short description is appended, as they are not treated elsewhere in this work.

Æolosoma therefore retains certain Archiannelid characters, but is to be referred to the *Oligochæta* on account of—(1) the limitation of the reproductive glands to two segments and the presence of special efferent testicular ducts; (2) the paired arrangement of the setæ bundles, which agree in their structure with those of other *Oligochæta*; and (3) the relative complication of the nephridia, as compared with *Archiannelida*.

The affinities of *Ctenodrilus* are not so plain; but, in the absence of any knowledge respecting the generative organs, it is impossible to refer them definitely to the *Oligochæta* or to the *Polychæta*.

Archiannelida.

Archiannelida.—This subclass includes certain small marine worms which were formerly placed among the *Polychæta*. Hatchek originally created the group for the reception of *Polygordius* and *Protodrilus*; and recently Föttinger has placed *Histriodrilus*[2] (an animal formerly referred to the *Discophora*) in the same group. The name *Archiannelida* implies that these forms stand at the base of the *Annelida*, and that they represent most nearly the common ancestral form from which both the *Polychæta* and *Oligochæta* have been derived. Their structure, which bears out this supposition, suggested the name.

Polygordius is found on the northern and southern coasts of Europe; it is a small slender worm, varying in length (according to the species) from 30 m. to 1 decim. The segmentation is hardly marked externally. The head segment is divided as in the *Chætopoda* generally into a prostomium and a peristomial ring; the prostomium gives rise to two tentacles. On either side of the prostomium is a ciliated pit, which is of special interest, as it occurs on the one hand among the Nemertines (*q.v.*), and on the other among certain *Polychæta* (*e.g.*, *Ophelidæ*), and in the lowly organized Oligochæt *Æolosoma*. Cilia are found in certain species in the neighbourhood of the mouth and on the anal segment.

The ciliation of the body is more marked in *Protodrilus*, where there is a continuous ventral groove lined by cilia; there are rings of cilia also on each segment. The partial ciliation of *Polygordius* is to be derived from this by reduction. Certain *Oligochæta* retain traces of the primitive ciliation of the body (*e.g.*, *Æolosoma*).

There are no traces of setæ in *Polygordius* or its allies. The segmentation of the body, although hardly marked externally, is very clearly marked internally; the body-cavity is divided by successive septa into a series of segments; there is no such fusion of the anterior segments as is met with among the *Polychæta* and *Oligochæta*, and the segments are less differentiated among themselves than is usually the case in the higher *Chætopoda*. The head segment contains the pharynx, which is limited to this segment; the nephridia, which consist of simple tubes (probably but not certainly formed of a chain of "drain-pipe" cells, as in *Oligochæta*) are found in all the segments except the first and last. The nephridia do not lie freely within the cœlom, but in the thickness of the parietal peritoneum; the funnel only just opens into the cavity of the segment preceding that which bears the external pore; that is to say, it is chiefly contained within the thickness of the septum.

---

1 The difference between the nephridia and genital ducts in this respect cannot be regarded as being of importance; the nephridia of *Polychæta* differ from those of *Oligochæta* in having an intercellular lumen. Lang, moreover, has shown ("Die Polycladen," *Naples Monographs*) that in some Planarians the reproductive ducts, like the nephridia, may have an *intra*cellular lumen.

2 The correct name of this worm is *Histriobdella*. The altered termination is to express the change in the view regarding its affinities.

In having the form of simple sinuous (not coiled) tubes, and in lying within the peritoneum, the nephridia are in a very archaic condition; the same thing occurs in the *Capitellidæ*; in the higher Annelids the nephridia lie within the cœlom, and are usually much coiled and complicated in structure.

The vascular system consists of a dorsal and a ventral trunk, which traverse the thickness of the dorsal and ventral mesenteries. The development of these vessels shows that their cavity is continuous with the blastocœle, and is not a secondary canalization of a solid chain of mesoblast cells, as is so commonly the case in the *Annelida*. The two trunks communicate in every segment except the last two or three by two lateral vessels, one on each side; each of these latter gives off a cæcal tube running backwards along the somatic peritoneum. Thus the vascular system undergoes but little modification in different segments. In *Protodrilus* the blood-vessels have no walls, and therefore permanently retain a condition which is found in the young *Polygordius* before the adjacent mesoblast cells have become differentiated into an extremely delicate membrane. The condition of the vascular channels in *Polygordius* represents that of the larval *Polychæta* and *Oligochæta* before the special muscular walls have been formed. *Æolosoma*, however, is identical with the adult *Polygordius* in these particulars.

The digestive tube consists of only a single layer of ciliated cells covered by a single layer of peritoneal cells, and is therefore in an embryonic condition as compared with the *Chætopoda* and *Oligochæta*. It is, however, specialized into a pharynx, œsophagus, and intestine. The nervous system is extremely simple, and lies in the thickness of the epidermis, thus presenting an embryonic character, which is, however, met with in certain *Polychæta*.

In *Polygordius* the cerebral mass is situated in the prostomium, and communicates by a circumœsophageal commissure with a ventral cord which is single and median, and shows no trace of ganglionic enlargements. In *Protodrilus* there are two ventral cords, while in *Histriodrilus* there are a series of ganglionic swellings. A nervous plexus also exists in the thickness of the longitudinal muscles.

Polygordius is of separate sexes; *Protodrilus* is hermaphrodite. The sexual products are developed in all except the first few and last few segments from the lining of the cœlom; the ova and spermatozoa are apparently liberated by the rupture of the body-wall. *Histriodrilus* has special efferent ducts for the ovaries and testes (found in different individuals), the nature of which is not yet settled.

Polygordius leaves the egg as an active larva, first discovered by Loven. This larva is shaped like a humming-top, and has a preoral circlet of cilia; immediately behind this on one side is the mouth, which leads into an alimentary canal opening at the posterior end of the body; at the apical region is an ectodermic thickening.

Literature.—(1) Beddard, "On the Nephridia of *Acanthodrilus*," *Proc. Roy. Soc.*, 1885; *Ann. Sci. Nat.*, 1886; (2) Id., "On the Atrium in Earthworm," *Zool. Anz.*, 1888; (3) Id., "Structure of *Eudrilus*," *Proc. Zool. Soc.*, 1886; (4) Id., "Nephridia of *Perichæta*," *Q. J. M. S.*, 1888; (5) Id., "*Allurus*," *ibid.*; (6) Id., "*Phreoryctes*," *Ann. Nat. Hist.*, 1888; (7) Benham, "Studies in Earthworms," Nos. i., ii., iii., *Q. J. M. S.*, 1886–7; (8) Id., "*Brachydrilus*," *Zool. Anz.*, 1887; (9) Horst, "Notes on Earthworms," *Notes from Leyden Museum*, 1886–7; (10) Rosa, "*Criodrilus*," *Atti R. Acad. Sci. Torino*, 1886; (11) Id., "*Hormogaster*," *ibid.*, 1888; (12) Spencer, "Nephridia of Earthworms," *Nature*, June 28, 1888; (13) Scharff, "*Ctenodrilus*," *Q. J. M. S.*, 1887; (14) Fletcher, "Australian Earthworms," *Proc. L. S. N. S. W.*, 1886; (15) Vejdovsky, *System u. Morphol. d. Oligochäten*;[1] (16) Kükenthal, "Lymphoidzellen d. Anneliden," *Jen. Zeitsch.*, 1885; (17) Bourne, "Indian Earthworms," *Proc. Zool. Soc.*, 1886; (18) Bergh, "Excretionsorgane d. Würmer," *Kosmos*, 1885; (19) Id., "Geschlechtsorgane d. Regenwürmer," *Zeitsch. f. wiss. Zool.*, 1886. On *Archiannelida* see Fraipont, "*Polygordius*," *Fauna und Flora des Golfen v. Neapel* (complete references to previous papers).

(F. E. B.)

WORMS, one of the oldest, and from an historical point of view one of the most interesting, cities in Germany, is situated on the left bank of the Rhine, in the grand-duchy of Hesse-Darmstadt, 25 miles south of Mainz and 20 miles north-west of Heidelberg. The town is irregularly built, and some of the old walls and towers still remain, but its general aspect is modern and commercial. The chief squares are the market-place and the Dom-Platz. Worms formerly contained many ecclesiastical buildings, now represented by eight churches, two of which, however, are no longer used for divine service. The principal church and chief building is the spacious Romanesque cathedral, which ranks beside the cathedrals of Spires and Mainz among the famous ecclesiastical edifices of the Rhine. This magnificent building, with four round towers, two large domes, and a choir at each end, has a specially imposing exterior, though the impression produced by the interior is also one of great dignity and simplicity, heightened by the natural colour of the red sandstone of which it is built. In this last particular it differs from the cathedrals of Mainz and Spires, where the natural colour of the stone no longer appears in the interior. Only the lower part of the western towers belongs to the original building consecrated in 1110; the remainder dates from 1181, with the exception of the west choir and the vaulting, which were built in the 13th century, and the elaborate south portal, which was added in the 14th century. The ornamentation of the older parts is simple to the verge of rudeness; and even the more elaborate later forms show no high development of workmanship. The church is 485 feet long and 114 feet wide; the transepts, which are at the west end, are about 120 feet long (inside measurement), and the choir is 160 feet high. The cathedral belongs to the Roman Catholic community, who possess also the church of St Martin and the Liebfrauenkirche, a handsome Gothic edifice outside the town, finished in 1467. The principal Protestant place of worship is Trinity church, built in 1726. Second in interest to the cathedral is the church of St Paul, also in the Romanesque style, and dating from 1102–16, with a choir of the early 13th century. It is adjoined by the remains of an abbey and cloisters of various epochs. Since 1881 this church has contained an interesting museum of national antiquities. The late Romanesque St Andrew's church is also used for secular purposes. The synagogue, an unassuming building erected in the 11th century and restored in the 13th, is now completely modernized. The Jewish community of Worms (about 1400 in number) claims to be the most ancient in Germany, and to have existed continuously since before the Christian era, though the earliest authentic mention of it occurs in 588. A curious tradition, illustrating the efforts of the dispersed people to conciliate their oppressors, asserts that the Jews of Worms gave their voice against the crucifixion, but that their messenger did not arrive at Jerusalem until after the event.

The town-house of Worms was restored in 1884. The Bischofshof, in which the most famous diet of Worms (1521) was held, is now replaced by a handsome modern residence. The Luginsland is an old watch-tower of the 13th century. Worms also contains numerous schools and a richly endowed hospital. In the Luther-Platz rises the imposing Luther monument (unveiled in 1868), consisting of a series of twelve statues on a platform 16 feet square. In the centre the colossal statue of Luther rises, on a pedestal at the base of which are sitting figures of Peter Waldus, Wycliffe, Huss, and Savonarola, the heralds of the Reformation; at the corners of the platform, on lower pedestals, are statues of Luther's contemporaries, Melanchthon, Reuchlin, Philip of Hesse, and Frederick the Wise of Saxony, between which are allegorical figures of Magdeburg (mourning), Spires (protesting), and Augsburg (confessing). The greater part of the work, which took nine years to execute, was designed by Rietschel, and carried out after his death in 1861 by Kietz, Dondorf, and Schelling.

The trade and industry of Worms are not unimportant. The leading resource of the inhabitants is wine-growing, the most famous vintage being known as Liebfrauenmilch, grown on vineyards near the Liebfrauenkirche. Luginlander and Katterlocher are also well-known varieties. The manufacture of patent leather employs 3000 hands. Machinery, chicory, slates, &c., are also produced. Worms possesses a river-harbour, and carries on some trade by water. The population in 1885 was 21,903, of whom about one-third were Roman Catholic. In its prosperous days Worms is estimated to have had from 40,000 to 70,000 inhabitants.

[1] This work is a general summary of investigation into anatomy of *Oligochæta* up to 1884, with complete list of literature. For this reason the present bibliography refers only to more important papers published since that date.

Borbetomagus, the name by which Worms was known in Roman times, seems to indicate a Celtic origin for the town. The modern name is usually connected with Wurm or Lindwurm, the German word for a dragon. Drusus is said to have erected a fort on the site of the town in 14 B.C. As a settlement of the Germanic tribe of the Vangiones, it existed under Roman protection till about the middle of the 5th century. The Burgundians then took it and made it their capital, and its name appears in many of the heroic legends of that people. King Gunther and Brunhilde held their court at Worms; and here Sigfried wooed the fair Chriemhild. The "Rosengarten," often mentioned in these legends, lay on the opposite bank of the Rhine. Under the Franconians this town was also important; and it was a frequent residence of Charlemagne and his successors. The scene of the graceful though unhistorical romance of Eginhard and Emma, the daughter of Charlemagne, is laid at Worms. The first bishop of Worms of whom anything authentic is known was Erembert (670), though an "episcopus Vangionum" is said to have attended a council at Cologne in 347. Worms seems to have thriven under the bishops, but the citizens invariably espoused the cause of the emperors against them, and were rewarded by privileges which fostered the trade of the town and eventually led to its recognition as a free imperial city. Worms was frequently visited by the imperial court, and won the proud title of "Mother of Diets." The most famous diet was that held in 1521, at which Luther appeared to defend his doctrines before Charles V. Four years later the town formally embraced Protestantism. Worms preserved a tolerable prosperity even through the hardships of the Thirty Years' War; but in 1689 it was laid in ashes by the French, a blow from which it has never thoroughly recovered. The peace of Lunéville annexed it in 1801 to France; but in 1815 it passed to Hesse-Darmstadt, being then an unimportant town with 6250 inhabitants.

WORSBROUGH, a township in the West Riding of Yorkshire, is situated on a branch of the Dearne and Dove Canal, and near several branch lines of the Manchester, Sheffield, and Lincolnshire Railway, 9 miles north-west of Rotherham and 3 south of Barnsley. The church of St Mary, an interesting structure with remains of Norman work, but chiefly in the Transition Early English style, underwent restoration in 1864. It contains some old monuments and brasses. There are extensive collieries and gunpowder mills in the neighbourhood, and the township possesses iron and steel works and corn-mills. A short distance to the west is Wentworth Castle, built in 1730 by Thomas, earl of Strafford, on the site of an ancient fortress, and containing a large number of portraits of historical interest. The population of the urban sanitary district (3779 acres) was 6030 in 1871, and 8443 in 1881.

WORSTED. See Wool.

WORTHING, a watering-place of Sussex, is situated on the London, Brighton, and South Coast Railway, 61 miles south of London and 10½ west of Brighton. On account of its sheltered situation at the foot of the South Downs it has some reputation as a health-resort for pulmonary complaints. As a general sea-side resort it is increasing in favour, especially with the wealthier classes. There is a marine parade 1¼ mile in length, a long range of firm sands, and an iron promenade pier, 960 feet in length, constructed in 1882. A public park, 21 acres in extent, was opened in 1881. The churches and chapels are all modern. The other principal buildings are the town-hall (1834), a quadrangular structure with square clock tower, Montague hall, the literary institute, the workmen's institute, the infirmary and dispensary (1882), the Thomas Banting memorial convalescent home, the public baths, erected in 1886, Humphrey's almshouses, and Queen Elizabeth's almshouses. The mother parish of Worthing is Broadwater, the church of which, three-quarters of a mile north of Worthing, a cruciform building in the Transition style, has some old monuments and brasses. The population of the urban sanitary district (979 acres) was 7401 in 1871, and 10,976 in 1881.

Pottery and other Roman remains have been found at Worthing. In Domesday the manor appears under the name of Ordinges, and consisted of eleven hides, or about 110 acres. In the reign of Edward I. it was valued at 100 shillings. It formed part of the endowment of the priory of Easebourne, near Midhurst, and at the Reformation was granted with other possessions to Henry Fitzwilliam, earl of Southampton. It afterwards passed through several hands to the earl of Warwick. It was of some importance in the reign of Edward III., who granted it the privilege of a market, but it declined to a poor fishing hamlet. Its rise as a watering place began about 1760, and after a visit of the Princess Amelia in 1797 it made rapid progress.

WOTTON, SIR HENRY (1568–1639), an accomplished literary amateur, was one of the favourite diplomatists of James I. of England, although, following the quietistic habit of his family, he never would undertake employments of the greatest weight and difficulty. The seat of the family, which was founded in the 14th century by a lord mayor of London, was Bocton or Boughton Malherbe in Kent. It was, as described by Izaak Walton in his *Life* of Sir Henry, a typical English family of wealthy landed gentry, keeping up a connexion with the court, but avoiding the risks of factious ambition, often holding offices of high trust, but always prudently declining the highest. Henry, the youngest of four sons, was sent to school at Winchester, and thence to Oxford (New College and afterwards Queen's). At the age of twenty-two, with a high academic reputation for wit and scholarship, he was sent abroad to complete his education, and spent eight years in France, Spain, and Germany, making acquaintance with men of learning as well as courtiers, a general favourite. Returning to England at the age of thirty, he sought political employment, and became one of the secretaries of Essex. On the fall of Essex he made his escape from England and took refuge at Florence, where he employed his leisure in writing a sketch of "the state of Christendom." While he was at Florence the grand-duke discovered a plot against King James, and Wotton was sent to Scotland with the information and a casket of antidotes. King James was so charmed with the emissary that on his accession to the English throne he at once offered Wotton ambassadorial employment. He might have had the embassy to Spain, but this he prudently declined, and chose instead the easier duty of managing relations with Venice and the German states. After twenty years of diplomatic service he craved and obtained the post of provost of Eton in 1624. He had studied and written not a little at odd times during his active life, and when he settled at Eton he intended to write a life of Luther; but in this and other large literary projects he never got beyond the stage of collecting materials. In his fifteen years' provostship he set an example of careful, dignified, and gracious supervision; and his wit, wisdom, courtesy, and benignity are well represented in the *Reliquiæ Wottonianæ*, published with Walton's *Life* in 1651. Two of his witticisms are immortal,—his definition of an ambassador as "an honest man sent to lie abroad for the good of his country,"[1] and his advice to a young diplomatist to tell the truth, and so puzzle and confound his adversaries. He died in 1639.

WOTTON, WILLIAM (1666–1726), is now remembered chiefly for his part in the famous "Battle of the Books," but to his own generation his *Reflections upon Ancient and Modern Learning* was only one of many proofs of his extraordinary amount and variety of scholarship. Born in 1666, the son of an English clergyman, rector of Wrentham, in Suffolk, he was one of the wonders of his age in precocity. He could translate from several languages at the age of five. He was under ten when he was sent to Cambridge, and he took the degree of B.A. at the age of twelve years and five months, having already created such a sensation by his linguistic attainments that Latin poems were addressed to him as a prodigy. In the Battle of the Books he took a judicious middle course between the extreme champions, Fontenelle

[1] The full story of this witticism is given in Walton's *Life*.

and Temple, making a succinct, elaborate, and careful comparison between ancients and moderns in oratory, poetry, mathematics, philosophy, astronomy, anatomy, botany, and other arts and sciences. His *Reflections*, the first edition of which appeared in 1694, show that his prodigious memory was not confined to languages, and that he possessed also strong judgment and argumentative power. The treatise may still be read with interest, as a survey of the state of various sciences at the close of the 17th century. Wotton, who was made D.D. in 1707, wrote also on subjects so diverse as fossils and Welsh laws, besides producing various historical works. He was engaged on his translation of the Welsh laws at the time of his death, which took place in 1726.

WOUWERMAN, PHILIP (1619-1668), a Dutch painter of battle and hunting scenes, was born at Haarlem in May 1619. He received the elements of his art instruction from his father, Paul Joosten Wouwerman, an historical painter of moderate ability, and he then studied under Jan Wynants, and for a short time under Evert Decker. Returning to Haarlem, he became a member of its guild of painters in 1640. In that city he seems to have led the rest of his singularly productive life, and there he died in May 1668. About seven or eight hundred pictures are enumerated in Smith's *Catalogue Raisonné* as the work of Philip Wouwerman, but probably many of these are the productions of his brothers Peter and Jan, and of his many other imitators. His authentic works are distinguished by great spirit and animation, and are infinitely varied and full of incident, though dealing recurrently with cavalry battle-pieces, military encampments, scenes of cavalcades, and hunting or hawking parties. He is equally excellent in his vivacious treatment of figures, in his skilful animal painting, and in his admirable and appropriate introduction of landscape backgrounds. Three different styles have been observed as characteristic of the various periods of his art. His earlier works are marked by the prevalence of a foxy-brown colouring, and by a tendency to an angular form in the draughtsmanship; the productions of his middle period have greater purity and brilliancy; and his latest and greatest pictures possess more of force and breadth, and are full of a delicate silvery-grey tone.

WRASSE. This name is applied to the fishes of the family *Labridæ* generally, and more especially to certain members of the family to be mentioned hereafter. They are without exception inhabitants of the sea, very abundant in the tropical zone, less so in the temperate, and disappearing altogether on the confines of the Arctic and Antarctic Circles. Their body is generally compressed, like that of a carp, covered with smooth (cycloid) scales; they possess one dorsal fin only, the anterior portion of which consists of numerous spines. Many wrasses are readily recognized by their thick lips, the inside of which is sometimes curiously folded, a peculiarity which has given to them the German name of "lip-fishes." The dentition of their jaws consists of strong conical teeth, of which some in front, and often one at the hinder end of the upper jaw, are larger than the others. But the principal organs with which they crush shell-fish, crustaceans, and other hard substances are the solid and strongly-toothed pharyngeal bones, of which the lower are coalesced into a single flat triangular plate. The majority of wrasses are beautifully coloured, exhibiting extraordinarily varied patterns of permanent pigmentary colours, as well as evanescent reflexions of the scales. All of them are surface fishes, living close to the shore or coral-banks. Rocky parts of the coast overgrown with seaweed are their favourite haunts in the temperate, and coral-reefs in the tropical seas. Some 450 species of wrasses (including Parrot-Wrasses) are known, chiefly from the tropics; some grow to a large size and are esteemed as food, whilst others, like the British species, are small and but rarely eaten.

Lips of *Labrus festivus*.

Of the British wrasses the Ballan Wrasse (*Labrus maculatus*) and the Striped or Red Wrasse or Cook (*Labrus mixtus*) are the most common. Both belong to the genus *Labrus*, in which the teeth stand in a single series, and which has a smooth edge of the præoperculum and only three spines in the anal fin. The ballan wrasse is the larger, attaining to a length of 18 inches, and, it is said, to a weight of 8 lb; its colours are singularly variegated, green or brownish, with red and blue lines and spots; the dorsal spines are twenty in number. The cook wrasse offers an instance of well-marked secondary sexual difference,—the male being ornamented with blue streaks or a blackish band along the side of the body, whilst the female has two or three large black spots across the back of the tail. This species possesses only from sixteen to eighteen spines in the dorsal fin. The Goldsinny or Corkwing (*Crenilabrus melops*) is much more frequent on the southern coasts of England and Ireland than farther north, and rarely exceeds a length of 10 inches. As in other wrasses, its colours are beautiful, but variable; but it may be readily distinguished from the two preceding species by the toothed edge of the præoperculum. The three other British wrasses are much scarcer and more local, viz., Jago's Goldsinny (*Ctenolabrus rupestris*), with a large black spot on the anterior dorsal spines, and another on the base of the upper caudal rays; *Acantholabrus palloni*, which is so rarely captured that it lacks a vernacular name, but may be easily recognized by its five anal spines and by the teeth in the jaws forming a band; and the Rock-Cook (*Centrolabrus exoletus*), which also has five anal spines, but has the jaws armed with a single series of teeth.

On the Atlantic coasts of the Northern States of North America the wrasses are represented by the genus *Tautoga*, which is distinct from the European forms. The only species of this genus, known by the names of Tautog or Blackfish, is a fish of considerable economic value, being much esteemed as food. It is caught in great numbers, and generally sold of a weight of about 2 lb.

WRECK (in Low Latin *wreccum* or *warectum maris*) is a ship or goods cast on land by the sea in tidal waters. While still at sea such ship or goods do not constitute wreck but derelict, which includes flotsam, jetsam, and lagan (see FLOTSAM). In Roman law wreck was restored to the owner if he claimed it before a judicial tribunal within a year and a day, the *fiscus* waiving its claim after a constitution attributed to either Marcus Aurelius or Constantine. Theft from a wreck was regarded as aggravated by the helpless position of the owner, and the thief was liable for fourfold the loss if an action was brought against him within a year, after that time for the loss simply. Plunderers of wreck and exhibitors of false lights were also punished criminally. Most of the Roman law on the subject is contained in *Digest* xlvii. 9, *Code* xi. 5. The Leonine Constitutions, c. 64, made a concealer of wreck liable to the fourfold penalty. In France it was provided by the laws of Oléron (see SEA LAWS) that succour was to be afforded to shipwrecked persons, and their property returned to them. Wreck afterwards became a right of the crown (a right limited to one-third of the value by an ordinance of Francis I.), but was often granted to feudal seigneurs under the name of *droit de bris.* In England the rule seems in the time of Bracton (the reign of Henry III.) to have been the same as that of the Roman law, that wreck only belonged to the king if no claimant appeared within a year and a day. It would perhaps be more accurate to say that it vested in the crown, subject to be divested on proof of ownership within the period limited. The reason for this rule of law appears to be the necessity of enabling persons in authority to protect wreck from the pillage which it was otherwise certain to have undergone at a time when wreck was looked upon as legitimate prey of the wrecker. In Bracton (120, 5) it is said that even if a dog escaped, or if any certain mark were put upon the goods, it was no wreck. The Statute of Westminster the First (3 Edw. I. c. 4) is merely declaratory of the common law as it is found in Bracton. It enacts that, where a man, a dog, or a cat escaped alive out of a ship, such ship should not be adjudged wreck, but the goods should be saved and kept by view of the sheriff, coroner, or king's bailiff, and delivered into the hands of such as were of the town where the goods were found, so that if any sued for the goods, and proved that they were his or perished in his keeping within a year and a day, they should be restored to him without delay; if not, they should remain to the king, and where wreck belonged to another than the king he should have it in like manner. In both Bracton and the statute the escape of a living thing appears to be used rather as an example of a means of proof than as the sole means of proof. The latter, however, became the doctrine of the courts for centuries; it was wreck unless a living thing escaped, and as such part of the hereditary revenue of the crown, and expressly recognized by the Statute *De Prærogativa Regis* (see PREROGATIVE). To hold inquests of wreck was by the Statute *De Officio Coronatoris* (4 Edw. I. c. 2) one of the duties of the coroner, of which he has only recently been relieved by the Coroners Act, 1887, repealing the Act of Edward I. In 1771 a return was made by Lord Mansfield to the older and more reasonable view of the common law as it stood in Bracton. That distinguished judge considered that the rule that it was wreck unless a living thing came to shore was contrary to principles of law, justice, and humanity, and that the escape of an animal was simply a medium of proof. It was the proof and not the escape that was the important fact.[1] Claims to wreck were, by Ric. II. c. 3, not cognizable in the Admiralty Court as was derelict, for that was in and upon the sea, while wreck must have touched the land before it became wreck. Unclaimed derelict was, like unclaimed wreck, a right of the crown, but in a different way. It was not a direct right *jure coronæ*, but claimed by the king in his office of Admiralty as an admiralty droit. As wreck in the last resort became crown property, it was never subject to forfeiture as a DEODAND (*q.v.*) where lives were lost. Wreck was frequently granted to subjects as a franchise, *e.g.*, to lords of manors and to various maritime cities and boroughs, among others to the Cinque Ports. Within the Cinque Ports the serjeants of the Admiralty of the Cinque Ports still act as receivers of wreck (17 and 18 Vict. c. 120).

So stood the common law as affected by early legislation. It is now of comparatively small importance, as the law now depends chiefly on the Merchant Shipping Act, 1854, part viii., and the amendments introduced by later Acts.

The definition of wreck for the purposes of the Merchant Shipping Acts (which is in effect for all practical purposes) is considerably extended beyond its common law meaning. By s. 2 of the Act of 1854, it includes jetsam, flotsam, lagan, and derelict. By the Sea Fisheries Act, 1883, it is still further extended to include all fishing boats, all their small boats, all rigging gear or other appurtenances of fishing boats, all nets, lines, buoys, floats, or other fishing implements whatsoever found or picked up at sea whether marked or unmarked. The principal provisions of the Act of 1854 are as follows. The general superintendence throughout the United Kingdom of all matters relating to wreck is committed to the Board of Trade. No person exercising Admiralty jurisdiction is to interfere with wreck. Whenever any ship or boat is stranded or in distress at any place on the shore of the sea, or of any tidal water, the receiver of wreck of the district is to proceed thither and take command, and issue such directions as he may think fit with a view to the preservation of the ship. All cargo and other articles washed ashore, or lost or taken from the ship, are to be delivered to the receiver. In the absence of the receiver, customs officers, justices of the peace, and others have the power of the receiver. The receiver is as soon as possible to examine on oath any person who may be able to give any account of a ship in distress or her cargo or stores, and forward the result of his examination to the Board of Trade (where it is deposited in the wreck register) and to Lloyd's. On proof of title of a lord of the manor or other person entitled to unclaimed wreck, the receiver is to hold it on behalf of such person. The receiver is aided and protected by numerous provisions making it punishable to refuse men or vehicles on his demand, to secrete or fail to give notice of wreck, to obstruct the receiver or any other person on his way to the wreck, &c. In case of suspected concealment of wreck, he may obtain a search warrant (see WARRANT) from a justice of the peace. Whenever any wreck is saved by any person other than a receiver, SALVAGE (*q.v.*) is payable. In case of no claim being made within a year by the owner, and in the absence of any private right of a lord of a manor or other person, the receiver is to sell the wreck, and pay the proceeds, after deducting expenses and salvage, to the exchequer, to become part of the consolidated fund. The Admiralty Division of the High Court of Justice has jurisdiction to decide upon all claims of salvage, whether the wreck is found at sea or cast upon the land, or partly in the sea and partly on land. Wreck, if foreign goods, is liable to customs duties. Goods saved from a ship wrecked on its homeward voyage are to be forwarded to the port of its original destination. A seaman is entitled to wages up to the time of a vessel being wrecked, unless he has not exerted himself to the utmost to save the ship, cargo, and stores. Receivers' districts under the Act of 1854 were formed by a Board of Trade order of October 7, 1856. The Merchant Shipping Act, 1862, provides, *inter alia*, that the receiver may appoint a valuer in salvage cases, that the delivery of wreck by the receiver to any person is not to prejudice the right of third parties, and that the payment of proceeds of wreck claimed by the crown is to be made to the consolidated fund or the revenues of the duchies of Cornwall or Lancaster according to circumstances. Instructions to receivers were issued by the Board of Trade in 1865 and 1886. In 1876 a new tribunal for the investigation of shipping casualties was created by the Merchant Shipping Act, 1876, which has in most cases superseded the procedure provided by the Act of 1854. The Act enabled the lord chancellor to appoint a wreck commissioner, or wreck commissioners not exceeding three, and gave the commissioner or commissioners power to act with or without skilled assessors, and in certain cases which were not within the purview of the Act of 1854, viz., where a ship on the coast of the United Kingdom or a British ship elsewhere has been stranded or damaged and any witness is found at any place in the United Kingdom, and where a British ship has been lost or is supposed to have been lost, and any evidence can be obtained in the United Kingdom as to the circumstances under which she proceeded to sea or was last heard of. In addition to the Acts mentioned, there are several others which affect the subject of wreck more or less directly. By 6 Geo. IV. c. 87 consuls in foreign ports are to have credit for disbursements on behalf of shipwrecked persons. Where a foreign ship is wrecked, the consul-general or other consular officer is by 18 and 19 Vict. c. 91 to be deemed the owner. Removal of wrecks is provided for in dockyards by 28 and 29 Vict. c. 125, in most other cases by the Harbours Clauses Act, 1847, and the Removal of Wrecks Act, 1877, giving powers of removal to the harbour or general lighthouse authorities. Provision is made by special Acts for raising wreck in the Thames, Mersey, Humber, Clyde, and other rivers. Burial of bodies washed ashore from wrecks is regulated by 48 Geo. III. c. 75 and 49 Vict. c. 20. The criminal law relating to wreck has been the subject of a considerable mass of legislation. The protection of the receiver in his duties by the Act of 1854 has been already mentioned. The Act further provides against wrongfully carrying off or removing wreck, impeding or hindering the saving of wreck, and secreting wreck or obliterating or defacing any marks thereon. Taking wreck into a foreign port and there disposing of it is made felony, punishable with ten years' penal servitude. Other provisions are made by the Criminal Law Consolidation Acts of 1861. To plunder or steal any part of a wrecked ship or vessel, or any goods belonging to such vessel, is a felony, punishable with fourteeen years' penal servitude. Any person in possession of such goods, and not giving a satisfactory account of how he came by them, may be committed to prison on summary

[1] Hamilton *v.* Davis, 5 Burrow's *Rep.*, 2733.

conviction, and such goods, if exposed for sale, may be seized and carried before a justice of the peace, and the vendor called upon to satisfy the justice that he came lawfully by them, 24 and 25 Vict. c. 96, ss. 64–66. Destruction of and injury to ships or wrecks, and masking, alteration, or removal of lights or exhibition of false lights, and injury to or concealment of buoys and other marks of navigation, are all punishable by 24 and 25 Vict. c. 97, ss. 42–49, penal servitude for life being the maximum penalty. To impede a shipwrecked person or any person in his endeavour to save him, and to assault any magistrate, officer, or other person in the exercise of his duty in the preservation of wreck, are crimes by 24 and 25 Vict. c. 100, ss. 17, 37. In the case of plunder, damage, or destruction of any ship or boat stranded or in distress on the shore of the sea or tidal water, or of any part of its cargo or apparel, by persons riotously and tumultuously assembled, either ashore or afloat, the owner has a right to compensation against the police authority of the district under the Riot (Damages) Act, 1886.

Scotland.—As in England, unclaimed wreck was a right of the crown, often granted to subjects, generally under the style of "wrak, waith, and ware," the last two words signifying derelict and seaweed. It was so granted to the earl of Orkney in 1581. It was occasionally dealt with by the Scottish Parliament. Thus by 1426, c. 15, ships wrecked on the coast of Scotland were to be escheat to the king if they belonged to a country observing a similar law, otherwise to have the favour shown to ships of Scotland. Compensation for destruction of wreck by a riotous assembly is to be made by the inhabitants of the nearest county, city, or borough under the Riot Act of George I. (see RIOT), the Act of 1886 not applying to Scotland.

United States.—The State legislation as to disposition of wrecked property is generally in favour of the owner on his claim being made within a limited time. As to the Acts of Congress on the subject, the secretary of the treasury is empowered to make contracts and provisions for the preservation, sale, or collection of wrecked property, *Revised Statutes*, § 3755, and may issue a register for a foreign vessel wrecked in the United States and purchased and repaired by a citizen of the United States, § 4136. Special provisions are made as to wreck in Florida, §§ 4239–4241. Plundering wreck, or impeding the escape of a shipwrecked person, or showing false or extinguishing true lights in order to cause wreck are punishable offences, § 5358. Wreck is not confined as in England to loss on tidal waters, but extends to that happening on the great freshwater lakes and rivers. Wreck commissioners and wreck masters are generally appointed, with powers and duties similar to those of the receiver in the United Kingdom. (J. Wт.)

WREN (Anglo-Saxon *Wrænna* and *Wrenne*, Icelandic *Rindill*), the well-known little brown bird—with its short tail, cocked on high—inquisitive and familiar, that braves the winter of the British Islands and even that of the European continent, and, except in the hardest of frosts, will daily sing its spirit-stirring strain. It is the *Motacilla* or *Sylvia troglodytes* of the earlier systematists, and the *Troglodytes parvulus*, *europæus*, or *vulgaris* of most later writers, save a few who (ignoring not only common sense but also the accepted rules of scientific nomenclature), by an utterly mistaken view of Vieillot's intention in establishing the genus *Troglodytes*, reserve that term for some American species—which can hardly be generically separated from the European form—and have attempted to fix on the latter the generic term *Anorthura*, which is its strict equivalent and was proposed by Rennie on grounds that are wholly inadmissible.

The interest taken in this bird throughout all European countries is scarcely exceeded by that taken in any other, and, though in Britain comparatively few vernacular names have been applied to it, two of them—"Jenny" or "Kitty-Wren"—are terms of endearment. M. Rolland records no fewer than 139 local names for it in France; and Italy, Germany, and other lands are only less prolific. Many of these carry on the old belief that the Wren was the King of Birds, a belief connected with the fable that on one occasion the fowls of the air in general assembly resolved to choose for their leader that one of them which should mount highest. This the Eagle seemed to do, and all were ready to accept his rule, when a loud burst of song was heard, and perched upon him was seen the exultant Wren, which unseen and unfelt had been borne aloft by the giant. The curious association of this bird with the Feast of the Three Kings, on which day in South Wales, or, in Ireland and in the south of France, on or about Christmas Day, it was customary for men and boys to "hunt the Wren," addressing it in a song as "the King of Birds," is very remarkable, and has never yet been explained.

The Wren hardly needs description here, and its domed nest, apparently so needlessly large for the size of the bird, is a well-known object, for it is built with uncommon care, and often (though certainly not always) in such a fashion as to assimilate its exterior to its surroundings and so to escape observation. Very curious too is the equally unaccountable fact, that near any occupied nest may generally be found another nest, or more than one, of imperfect construction. The widespread belief concerning these unfinished fabrics is implied by their common name of "cocks' nests," but evidence to that effect is not forthcoming. The breeding-habits of the Wren were most closely studied and accurately reported by Mr Weir to Macgillivray (*Brit. Birds*, iii. pp. 23–30) in a way that leads every ornithologist to wish that the same care might be bestowed on other kinds of birds.

The range of the Wren in Europe[1] is very extensive, though it seems to stop short of the Arctic Circle; but it occurs in Algeria, Madeira, and, according to Bolle, in the Canaries. It also inhabits Palestine. Further to the eastward its limits are difficult to trace, because they inosculate with those of a considerable number of local races or species. As might be expected, the form inhabiting Japan, *T. fumigatus*, seems to be justifiably deemed a species. In North America, *T. alascensis* occurs in the extreme north-west, and is replaced further to the southward by *T. pacificus*. Eastward of the Rocky Mountains, the form is *T. hyemalis*—the well-known Winter-Wren of Canada and the United States. The number of species of Wrens inhabiting North America is, however, very considerable; but authorities are by no means agreed as to how many should be reckoned valid, and they have been segregated into six or seven genera. Here the House-Wren, *T. domesticus* or *aedon*, can alone be mentioned. It is a very common summer-visitant to most parts of the Eastern States, and where it occurs is of a very familiar disposition, entering into the closest relations with those that cultivate its acquaintance. It is represented in the West by *T. parkmanni*.

The *Troglodytidæ*, if they are to be regarded as forming a distinct Family, predominate in the New World, no fewer than 60 species being enumerated in the *Nomenclator* of Messrs Sclater and Salvin as belonging to the Neotropical Region. But the *Troglodytidæ* by no means contain all the birds to which the name "Wren" is applied. Several of the *Sylviidæ* (*cf.* WARBLER) bear it, especially the beautiful little Golden-crested Wren (*cf.* KINGLET) and the group commonly known in Britain as "Willow-Wrens"—forming the genus *Phylloscopus*. Three of these are habitual summer-visitants, which differ much more in their manners than in their look. The largest, usually called the Wood-Wren, *P. sibilatrix*, is more abundant in the north than in the south of England, and chiefly frequents woods of oak or beech. It has a loud and very peculiar song, like the word *twēē*, sounded very long, and repeated several times in succession—at first slowly, but afterwards more quickly, and near the end accompanied by a peculiar quivering of the wings, while at uncertain intervals comes another note, which has been syllabled as *chea*, uttered about three times in succession. The Willow-Wren proper, *P. trochilus*, is in many parts of Great Britain the commonest summer-bird, and is the most generally dispersed. In spring its joyous burst of song is repeated time after time, until all around thrills with the loud and merry chorus, and yet never tires the ear. The restless but graceful activity of the bird, as it flits from twig to twig, adds to the charm of its appearance, which Hewitson so well appreciated. The third species, *P. collybita* or *minor* (frequently but most wrongly called *Sylvia rufa* or *P. rufus*), commonly known as the Chiffchaff, from the peculiarity of its constantly repeated two-noted cry, is very numerous in the southern and western part of England, but seems to be scarcer northward. These three species make their nest upon or very close to the

[1] Much interest has lately attached to the discovery, announced by Mr Seebohm (*Zoologist*, 1884, p. 333), that the Wren, for 200 years and upwards, known to inhabit St Kilda differed in hue from that of the other British Islands and of the continent of Europe, and it has by him been described as a distinct species, *T. hirtensis*. It had for more than twenty years been known that the Wren of the Færoes and Iceland deserved separation from the ordinary *T. parvulus*, by being larger, and especially by having larger and stouter feet. It is the *T. borealis* of Fischer (*Journ. für Ornithologie*, 1861, p. 14, pl. i.).

ground, and the building is always domed. Hence they are commonly called "Oven-birds,"[1] and occasionally, from the grass used in their structure, "Hay-jacks," a name common to the WHITE-THROAT (*q.v.*) and its allies.

To return, however, to the *Troglodytidæ* or true Wrens. If it cannot be said that they form a peculiar Family, it would be rather to the *Sylviidæ* that they and the *Certhiidæ* (*cf.* TREE-CREEPER) should be assigned, and they seem to be very unfitly placed among the *Timeliidæ*, as has lately been done (*Cat. B. Brit. Museum*, vi. p. 1). These last, so far as any definition can be given of them, belong to the Ethiopian and Indian Regions, while the predominance of the *Troglodytidæ* in the Neotropical Region, as already remarked, is very obvious. (A. N.)

WREN, SIR CHRISTOPHER (1631–1723), the son of a clergyman, was born at East Knoyle, Wiltshire, in 1631; he entered at Wadham College, Oxford, in 1646, took his degree in 1650, and in 1653 was made a fellow of All Souls. While at Oxford Wren distinguished himself in geometry and applied mathematics;[2] in 1657 he became professor of astronomy at Gresham College, and in 1660 was elected Savilian professor of astronomy at Oxford. It is, however, as an architect that Wren is best known, and the great fire of London, by its destruction of the cathedral and nearly all the city churches, gave Wren a scope for his talent such as probably no architect has ever had to the same extent. Just before the fire Wren was asked by Charles II. to prepare a scheme for the restoration of the old St Paul's. In May 1666 Wren submitted his report and designs[3] for this work; the old cathedral was in a very ruinous state, and Wren proposed to remodel the greater part, as he said, "after a good Roman manner," and not "to follow the Gothick Rudeness of the old Design." According to this scheme, only the old choir was left; the nave and transepts were to be rebuilt after the classical style, with a lofty dome at the crossing—not unlike the plan which was eventually carried out.

In September of the same year (1666) the fire occurred, and the old St Paul's was completely gutted, though the greater part of its walls still remained standing. From 1668 to 1670 attempts were being made by the chapter to restore the ruined building; but Dean Sancroft was anxious to have the cathedral wholly rebuilt, and in 1668 he had asked Wren to prepare a design for a wholly new church. This first design, the model for which is preserved in the South Kensington Museum, is very inferior to what Wren afterwards devised. In plan it is an immense rotunda surrounded by a wide aisle, and approached by a double portico; the rotunda is covered with a dome taken from that of the Pantheon in Rome; on this a second dome stands, set on a lofty drum, and this second dome is crowned by a tall spire. This plan was devised as being specially suitable to the needs of a Protestant church, but the dean and chapter objected to the absence of a structural choir, nave, and aisles, and wished to follow the mediæval cathedral arrangement, at least as far as concerned the plan. Thus, in spite of its having been approved by the king, this design was happily abandoned—much to Wren's disgust; and he prepared another scheme with a similar treatment of a dome crowned by a spire, which in 1675 was ordered to be carried out. Wren had, however, been much hampered by ignorant interference, and apparently did not himself approve of this second design, for he got the king to give him permission to alter it as much as he liked, without showing models or drawings to any one. Wren fully availed himself of this permission, and the actual building bears little resemblance to the approved design, to which it is very superior in almost every possible point. Wren's earlier designs have the exterior of the church arranged with one order of columns; the division of the whole height into two orders was an immense gain in increasing the apparent scale of the whole, and makes the exterior of St Paul's very superior to that of St Peter's in Rome, which is utterly dwarfed by the colossal size of the columns and pilasters of its single order.[4] The present very graceful dome and the drum on which it stands, masterpieces of graceful line and harmonious proportion, were very important alterations from the earlier scheme. As a scientific engineer and practical architect Wren was perhaps more remarkable than as an artistic designer. The construction of the wooden external dome, and the support of the stone lantern by an inner cone of brickwork, quite independent of either the external or internal dome, are wonderful examples of Wren's constructive ingenuity. The first stone of the new St Paul's was laid on June 21, 1675; the choir was opened for use December 2, 1697; and the last stone of the cathedral was set in 1710. The stone used is from the Portland quarries; the wooden dome is covered with lead, not copper as was at first proposed. The fine oak stalls were carved by Grinling Gibbons, who received £1333, 7s. 5d. for them. The whole cost of the cathedral was £1,167,474,—of which £810,181 was provided by the London import duty on coal.[5]

After the destruction of the city of London Wren was employed to make designs for rebuilding its fifty burnt churches, and he also prepared a scheme for laying out the whole city on a new plan, with a series of wide streets radiating from a central space. Difficulties arising from the various ownerships of the ground prevented the accomplishment of this scheme.

Among Wren's city churches the most noteworthy are St Michael's, Cornhill; St Bride's and St Mary le Bow, Fleet Street, the latter remarkable for its graceful spire; and St Stephen's, Walbrook, with a plain exterior, but very elaborate and graceful interior. In the design of spires Wren showed much taste and wonderful power of invention. He was also very judicious in the way in which he expended the limited money at his command; he did not fritter it away in an attempt to make the whole of a building remarkable, but devoted it chiefly to one part or feature, such as a spire or a rich scheme of internal decoration. Thus he was in some cases, as in that of St James's, Piccadilly, content to make the exterior of an almost barn-like plainness.

The other buildings designed by Wren were very numerous. Only a few of the principal ones can be mentioned:—the custom house, the royal exchange, Marlborough House, Buckingham House, and the Hall of the College of Physicians—now destroyed; others which exist are—at Oxford, the Sheldonian theatre, the Ashmolean museum, the Tom Tower of Christ Church, and Queen's College chapel; at Cambridge, the library of Trinity College and

[1] By ornithologists this name is given to a wholly distinct group—not even belonging to the *Oscines*—the *Furnariidæ* of Garrod, consisting of about 8 genera of Tracheophonine Birds, some of which build marvellous nests of mud spherical in form. For their habits see Darwin (*Jour. of Researches*, chap. v.) and Mr Hudson's account (*Argentine Ornithology*, i. pp. 167–170).

[2] Newton, in his *Principia*, p. 19, ed. of 1713, speaks very highly of Wren's work as a geometrician.

[3] Wren's drawing for this exists in the All Souls collection.

[4] Proportionally the apparently greater size of St Paul's is very remarkable; it is very difficult to realize that the top of the dome of St Paul's is only as high as the springing of that of St Peter's. In actual fact the one looks about as high as the other.

[5] Wren also designed a colonnade to enclose a large piazza forming a clear space round the church, somewhat after the fashion of Bernini's colonnade in front of St Peter's, but space in the city was too valuable to admit of this. Wren was an enthusiastic admirer of Bernini's designs, and visited Paris in 1665 in order to see him and his proposed scheme for the rebuilding of the Louvre. Bernini showed his design to Wren, but would not let him copy it, though, as he said, he "would have given his skin" to be allowed to do so.

the chapel of Pembroke, the latter at the cost of Bishop Matthew Wren, his uncle. The western towers of Westminster Abbey are usually attributed to Wren, but they were not carried out till 1735–45, many years after Wren's death, and there is no reason to think that his design was used. Wren (D.C.L. from 1660) was knighted in 1673, and was elected president of the Royal Society in 1681.[1] He was in parliament for many years, representing Plympton from 1685, Windsor from 1689, and Weymouth from 1700. He occupied the post of surveyor of the royal works for fifty years, but by a shameful cabal was dismissed from this office a few years before his death. He died in 1723, and is buried under the choir of St Paul's; on a tablet over the inner north doorway is the well-known epitaph—"Si monumentum requiris, circumspice."

Wren's genius as an artist is very difficult to estimate; he lived at a most unhappy time, when architecture had sunk almost to its lowest point of degradation. If, however, we bear this in mind we must admit that he was an artist of very remarkable ability; his inventive genius no one can dispute.

For further information the reader should consult the *Parentalia*, published by Wren's grandson in 1750, an account of the Wren family and especially of Sir Christopher and his works; also the two biographies of Wren by Elmes and Miss Phillimore; Milman, *Annals of St Paul's*, 1868; and Longman, *Three Cathedrals dedicated to St Paul in London*, 1873, pp. 77 *sq.* See also Clayton, *Churches of Sir C. Wren*, 1848–49; Taylor, *Towers and Steeples of Wren*, London, 1881; and Niven, *City Churches*, London, 1887, illustrated with fine etchings. In the library of All Souls at Oxford are preserved a large number of drawings by Wren, including the designs for almost all his chief works, and a fine series showing his various schemes for St Paul's Cathedral. (J. H. M.)

WRESTLING AND BOXING. Wrestling is the art of forcing an antagonist to the ground without resorting to blows or kicks. It is a trial of strength and skill between two opponents standing face to face, who strive to throw one another. As a gymnastic exercise it was greatly encouraged among the ancient Greeks, and the highest honours and rewards were bestowed on the victors at the Olympic, Isthmian, Nemean, and other games (see GAMES). It was also cultivated by the Romans, though their tastes inclined to more savage and brutalizing exhibitions than that of wrestling. It was not unknown in Egypt and at Nineveh, as may be seen from the sculptures in the British Museum. At the same time it differed very much in its ancient form from the wrestling of to-day, the wrestlers of old being wont to compete almost if not quite nude, their bodies besmeared with oil or some other kind of grease by way of making their muscles supple; but, as this practice rendered it very difficult to get fair hold of one another, the wrestlers were accustomed to use sand on their hands, or even to roll in the dust of the arena as a corrective. In their contests they took hold of each other by the arms, drew forward, pushed backward, used many contortions of the body, interlocked their limbs, seized one another by the neck, throttled, lifted each other off the ground, and butted like rams, though the chief point of their art was to become master of their opponent's legs, when a fall was the immediate result. In England the pastime has been popular from an early period, more especially in the Middle Ages, for in 1222, in Henry III.'s reign, it is on record that a wrestling match took place between the men of Westminster and the citizens of London in St Giles Fields, the latter winning easily. The return match was held at Westminster on Lammas day following, but was interrupted by the bailiff of Westminster and his associates, who maltreated the Londoners and drove them into the city. At a later period Clerkenwell was the usual trysting place. At one of the matches there in 1453 another riot occurred, and the lord mayor, who usually attended these athletic carnivals, was again routed and driven within the city boundary. In those days the prize was sometimes a ram and sometimes a cock.

[1] The Royal Society possesses a good portrait of Wren by Kneller.

The four English systems of wrestling include those of (1) Cornwall and Devon, (2) Lancashire, (3) Catch hold, first down to lose, and (4) Cumberland and Westmorland. The Cornwall and Devon men compete in strong loose linen jackets, catching hold above the waist or of any portion of the jacket. Kicking, which used to be a prominent feature of the west-country style, is now forbidden, and the men wrestle in their stockinged feet. In order to be fairly thrown, two shoulders and one hip must be on the ground, or two hips and one shoulder, and a man must be thrown flat on his back before any other portion of his body touches the earth ere a decision can be given against him. Formerly each county wrestled under different rules, but the systems are now amalgamated and are classed as one and the same. In Lancashire the wrestlers compete in their stockinged feet, but are allowed to catch hold of any portion of the body. This is the most barbarous of all the English systems, and includes the objectionable battling on the ground which is the fatal characteristic of the French method. Tripping, however, is not forbidden, and a fall is sometimes secured without a resort to scrambling tactics, which is impossible under French rules. The "catch hold, first down to lose" style of wrestling is of recent origin and promises to become popular. The utmost simplicity distinguishes it. Ordinary wrestling attire is worn, such as jersey, drawers or knickerbockers, and stockings. The men on closing must not grip lower than the waist, and the competitor who touches the ground first by any part of his body is the loser. This system is perhaps the fairest for all parties, as the competitors set to work on equal terms without that delay in getting into holds so frequent in north-country wrestling. The Cumberland and Westmorland system is probably the best and most scientific of all. On taking hold, the wrestlers stand up chest to chest, each placing his chin on his opponent's right shoulder and grasping him round the body, the right arm of each being under the left arm of the other, and each joins his hands behind his opponent. When both have got hold the play commences. Kicking is forbidden, and if one competitor lets go his hold before the other the decision is given against him. If both fall on the ground—an undecided or dogfall, as it is termed—they wrestle over again, but if one falls before the other his defeat is registered at once. This kind of wrestling is free from danger, and the German style much resembles it, but in the latter a competitor's hands are not required to remain locked behind his adversary's back, as is the practice in the north of England. No catching hold of legs, thighs, or arms is allowed, but each man tries to throw his adversary by using the "buttock," which consists of facing to the right, twisting so as to place the left hip under an opponent's middle, pulling him close, stooping forwards and lifting him off the ground, and throwing him; or the "crossbuttock," facing to the right about to such an extent as to turn the back to the adversary, and then proceeding as before; or the "back-hank," which consists in commencing as in the "buttock," and then passing the left leg from inside round an antagonist's left leg, when by keeping a tight hold with the arms and pulling backwards the leverage supplied by the leg being inside usually secures the fall; or the "back heel," which consists in pulling an opponent towards one, putting the left heel behind his right heel, forcing his leg up forwards, and throwing him bodily backwards; or the "left leg hipe," which consists in lifting and swinging him round to the right, then striking the inside of his right thigh with the outside of the left thigh, by which he gets off his balance and falls; the "right leg hipe" is the same action *mutatis mutandis*. There is also the "left leg stroke," which consists in striking an antagonist's right leg with one's left leg, swinging him round to the left and off his balance; the "right leg stroke" is the same thing with the right leg. Of course there is an umpire to see that no competitor takes an unfair advantage or plays foul, and to determine disputed points according to the rules in force.

Boxing.—This, though perhaps hardly as popular as wrestling, is closely identified with it in the gymnasium, if not outside it. In the United Kingdom prize fighting is an illegal sport, but it is hardly likely that glove boxing will ever fall into the same disrepute. Its present comparative popularity is principally due to the efforts of the late Mr John G. Chambers, who in 1866 founded the Amateur Athletic Club, and in conjunction with the marquis of Queensberry drew up a code of rules (known as the Queensberry rules), which regulate the principal glove contests throughout the kingdom, as follows:—

Challenge Cups (Open to Gentlemen Amateurs).—1. That the entries be drawn to contend by lots. 2. That the entrance fee be 10s. 3. Heavy weights to be over 11 stone 4 lb; middle weights not to exceed 11 stone 4 lb; light weights not to exceed 10 stone. 4. That there be three judges appointed by the committee. 5. That the boxing take place in a 24 feet ring. 6. That no wrestling, roughing, or hugging on the ropes be allowed. 7. That each heat consist of three rounds, with one minute interval between; the duration of each round to be at the discretion of the judges, but not to exceed five minutes. 8. Any competitor not coming up to time shall be deemed to have lost. 9. That no shoes or boots with spikes or spriggs be allowed. 10. Competitors to wear jerseys. 11. Gloves to be provided by the club. 12. The cups to be boxed for once in each year; the winner to receive a silver medal.

Definition of Gentleman Amateur.—Any gentleman who has never competed in an open competition, or for public money, or for admission money, or with professionals for a prize, public money, or admission money, and who has never at any period of his life taught, pursued, or assisted in the pursuit of athletic exercises as a means of livelihood. The committee reserve the right of requiring a reference or of refusing an entry.

Contests for Endurance.—To be a fair stand-up boxing match, in a 24 feet ring, or as near that size as practicable; no wrestling or hugging allowed; the rounds to be of three minutes' duration and one minute time; if either man fall through weakness or otherwise he must get up unassisted; ten seconds to be allowed him to do so; the other man meanwhile to retire to his corner, and when the fallen man is on his legs the round is to be resumed and continued until the three minutes have expired, and, if one man fails to come to the scratch in the ten seconds allowed, it shall be in the power of the referee to give his award in favour of the other man; a man hanging on the ropes in a helpless state, with his toes off the ground, shall be considered down; no seconds or any other person to be allowed in the ring during the rounds; should the contest be stopped by any unavoidable interference, the referee to name time and place for finishing the contest as soon as possible, so that the match must be won or lost, unless the backers of both men agree to draw the stakes. The gloves to be fair-sized boxing gloves of the best quality, and new; should a glove burst or come off, it must be replaced to the referee's satisfaction. A man on one knee is considered down, and if struck is entitled to the stakes. No shoes or boots with spriggs allowed. (E. D. B.)

WREXHAM, a market-town and municipal and parliamentary borough of Denbighshire, North Wales, 11 miles south-south-west of Chester and 201 miles from London by rail. It was characterized by the poet Churchyard in the 16th century as "Trim Wricksam towne, a pearle of Denbighshiere," and the description is not altogether inapplicable at the present day, the streets being spacious, with many handsome houses. Wrexham church, dedicated to St Giles, contains 14th and 15th century work, but was in great part reconstructed at the beginning of the 16th century. The tower, erected between 1506 and 1520, has been styled "one of the seven wonders of Wales." It is 135 feet in height, and consists of several successive stages panelled throughout, and decorated with numerous statues of saints placed in niches of the buttresses. It is surmounted by an open-work balustrade, from which spring four lantern-shaped turrets of pierced open-work. The church was restored in 1867. It contains a large number of monuments. The bells, ten in number, are the most famous in the principality. In 1647 the church was used as a prison by Cromwell. The other principal public buildings are the guild-hall (formerly the old grammar school); the public and corn exchange (formerly the Union Hall), opened in 1873, after alteration, at a cost of £4900; the infirmary; and the infantry barracks of the Royal Welsh Fusiliers. In the neighbourhood there are a racecourse and training-ground. The town is situated on the edge of the Denbighshire coalfield, in the vicinity of coal, iron, and lead mines. It has long been celebrated for its ales, and possesses also corn and paper mills and tanneries. The surrounding country is very fertile, and the agricultural trade is of some importance. The parliamentary borough unites with Denbigh, Ruthin, and Holt in returning a member to parliament. The town has a special commission of the peace and a petty sessions court. The population of the municipal borough and urban sanitary district (1306 acres) was 8576 in 1871, and 10,978 in 1881. The population of the parliamentary borough (1791 acres) in 1881 was 12,333.

Although Wrexham was situated on the eastern side of Offa's Dyke, it was reckoned one of the towns of Mercia. In the Saxon Chronicle the name occurs as Wrightesham. Edward I. granted the town with the lordship of Bromfield and Yale to John Earl Warren. The township of Wrexham Regis within the borough and the township of Stansty without constitute ancient manors. Formerly the township of Wrexham Abbot was ecclesiastical property, and an appendage to the abbey of Valle Crucis, near Llangollen. During the civil war the town was occupied by the Parliamentary troops. Wrexham town was constituted a parliamentary borough in 1832, and incorporated as a municipal borough in 1857.

See A. N. Palmer's *Wrexham* and *History of the Parish Church of Wrexham.*

WRIGHT, Joseph (1734–1797), styled Wright of Derby, subject, landscape, and portrait painter, was born at Derby on September 3, 1734, the son of an attorney of the place, who was afterwards town-clerk. During his early years he manifested an aptitude for mechanical pursuits, and also for music, but he finally resolved to become a painter, and in 1751 he went to London and for two years studied under Thomas Hudson, the master of Reynolds. Returning to Derby he practised portrait-painting; but feeling the need for further instruction he again placed himself for fifteen months under his former master. He then settled in Derby, and varied his work in portraiture by the productions of the subjects seen under artificial light with which his name is chiefly associated, and by landscape painting. He married in 1773, and in the end of that year he visited Italy, where he remained till 1775. While at Naples he witnessed an eruption of Vesuvius, which under various treatment formed the subject of many of his subsequent pictures. On his return from Italy he established himself at Bath as a portrait-painter; but meeting with little encouragement he returned to Derby, where he spent the rest of his life. He was a frequent contributor to the exhibitions of the Society of Artists, and to those of the Royal Academy, of which he was elected an associate in 1781 and a full member in 1784. He, however, declined the latter honour on account of a slight which he believed that he had received, and severed his official connexion with the Academy, though he continued to contribute to the exhibitions from 1783 till 1794. He died at Derby on August 29, 1797.

There has been a tendency in recent criticism to over-estimate the works of Joseph Wright. His portraits are frequently defective in drawing, and without quality or variety of handling, while their flesh tints are often hard, and unpleasant in their purple-grey shadows. He is seen at his best in his subjects of artificial light, of which the Orrery (1766), the property of the corporation of Derby, and the Air-pump (1768), in the National Gallery, are excellent examples. His Old Man and Death (1774) is also a striking and individual production. An exhibition of Wright's works was brought together at Derby in 1883, and twelve of his pictures were shown in the winter exhibition of the Royal Academy in 1886. A careful and elaborate biography of the artist, by William Bemrose, was published in 1885.

WRIGHT, SILAS (1795-1847), was born at Amherst, Massachusetts, May 24, 1795. He graduated at Middlebury College, Vermont, in 1815, was admitted to the bar in 1819, and began practice at Canton, in northern New York. From the first he showed those characteristics which finally made him a representative American Democratic leader. He had settled in what was almost a wilderness. His farm was a small one, and no hired labourer upon it worked harder than he. His manner of life was of the simplest. In his professional work he was a type of the lawyer of the old school,—shrewd, skilful, rigidly just, and controlled by the belief that his profession was a public trust, and that judicial qualities must mingle with those of the advocate. He seems never to have sought an office, and never to have felt at liberty to refuse one, even that of village postmaster, if he could possibly serve. He was appointed surrogate in 1820, and was elected successively to the State senate in 1823, to the house of representatives in 1827–29, comptroller of the State 1829–33, United States senator 1833–44, and governor of New York 1844–46. During his public life he had become a leader of the Democratic party of New York, Van Buren being his closest associate. When the national Democratic party in 1844 nominated and elected Polk to the presidency, instead of Van Buren, Wright and the State organization took an attitude of armed neutrality towards the new administration. Renominated for governor in 1846, Wright was defeated, and the result was ascribed to the hostility of the Polk administration. The death of the defeated candidate, at Canton, August 27, 1847, gave intense bitterness to New York politics for several years; and his faction, in 1848, succeeded in defeating their national party's candidates in the presidential election.

Wright was one of a class of politicians which has influenced American development largely, finding its most characteristic types in the State of New York. It may be traced clearly from about 1820, beginning with what was then known as "the Albany Regency," including Dix, Marcy, Wright, Seymour, Tilden, to Cleveland (president from 1885), and many of the new men who have come into the national administration with him. Absolutely and punctiliously honest, devoted to the public good, and believing intensely that the public good depended on the political principles of their party, they have been prone to consider politics as a warfare, and merciless exclusion of opponents from office as a legitimate war-weapon. One of their earliest leaders, Marcy, declared the rule of party struggle, that "the spoils (of office) belong to the victor"; the latest, President Cleveland, has been the first to recognize the merit system of appointment in practice, Tilden having already accepted it in theory. The sternness of Wright's integrity in office was illustrated in 1845, when the "anti-rent troubles" broke out again, and it seemed probable that the votes of the disaffected would decide the coming election. The governor asked and obtained from the legislature the power to suppress the disturbance by armed force, ordered the militia into the disturbed district, arrested the offenders, had them tried, convicted, and punished, and put an end to what was really an insurrection. His defeat in 1846 was a transition from the old to the new phase of American politics; but his name is still the representative of all that was best in the old.

Wright's *Life* has been written by Jenkins, who also has a sketch of him in his *Governors of New York*; but the best biography of him is that of Hammond.

WRIGHT, THOMAS (1810–1877), antiquary, was born at Ludlow, in Shropshire, 21st April 1810, and was descended from a Quaker family formerly living at Bradford, in Yorkshire. He was educated at the old grammar school at Ludlow, and afterwards at Trinity College, Cambridge, where he graduated in 1834. While at Cambridge he contributed to the *Gentleman's Magazine* and other periodicals, and in 1835 he came to London to devote himself to a literary career. His first separate work was *Early English Poetry in Black Letter, with Prefaces and Notes*, 1836, 4 vols. 12mo, which was followed during the next forty years by a very extensive series of publications, many of lasting value. He helped to found the British Archæological Association and the Percy, Camden, and Shakespeare societies. In 1842 he was elected corresponding member of the Académie des Inscriptions et Belles Lettres of Paris, and was a fellow of the Society of Antiquaries as well as member of many other learned British and foreign bodies. In 1859 he superintended the excavations of the Roman city of Uriconium, near Shrewsbury, of which he issued a description. He died at Chelsea, 23d December 1877, in his sixty-seventh year. A portrait of him is in the *Drawing Room Portrait Gallery* for October 1, 1859. His fertility was remarkable, and the list of seventy-eight articles in Allibone's *Dictionary* (1871, iii. pp. 2864–67) includes examples of almost every department of literature. He was a great scholar, but will be chiefly remembered as an industrious antiquary and the editor of many relics of the Middle Ages. In the British Museum catalogue are 121 references under his name.

His chief publications are—*Queen Elizabeth and Her Times, a Series of Original Letters*, 1838, 2 vols.; *Reliquiæ Antiquæ*, 1839–43, again 1845, 2 vols., edited with Mr J. O. Halliwell-Phillipps W. Mapes's *Latin Poems*, 1841, 4to, Camden Society; *Political Ballads* and *Carols*, published by the Percy Society, 1841; *Popular Treatises on Science*, 1841; *History of Ludlow*, 1841, &c., again 1852; *Collection of Latin Stories*, 1842, Percy Society; *The Vision and Creed of Piers Ploughman*, 1842, 2 vols., 2d ed. 1855; *Biographia Literaria*, vol i., Anglo-Saxon Period, 1842, vol. ii., Anglo-Norman Period, 1846; *The Chester Plays*, 1843–47, 2 vols., Shakespeare Society; *St Patrick's Purgatory*, 1844; *Anecdota Literaria*, 1844; *Archæological Album*, 1845, 4to; *Essays connected with England in the Middle Ages*, 1846, 2 vols.; Chaucer's *Canterbury Tales*, 1847–51, Percy Society, a new text with notes, reprinted in 1 vol., 1853 and 1867; *Early Travels in Palestine*, 1848, Bohn's Antiq. Lib.; *England under the House of Hanover*, 1848, 2 vols., several editions, reproduced in 1868 as *Caricature History of the Georges*; Mapes, *De Nugis Curialium*, 1850, 4to, Camden Society; Geoffrey Gaimar's *Metrical Chronicle*, 1850, Caxton Society; *Narratives of Sorcery and Magic*, 1851, 2 vols.; *The Celt, the Roman, and the Saxon*, 1852, 4th ed. 1885; *History of Fulke Fitz Warine*, 1855; Jo. de Garlandia, *De Triumphis Ecclesiæ*, 1856, 4to, Roxburghe Club; *Dictionary of Obsolete and Provincial English*, 1857; *A Volume of Vocabularies*, 1857, 2d ed. by R. P. Wülcker, 1884, 2 vols.; *Les Cent Nouvelles Nouvelles*, Paris, 1858, 2 vols.; Malory's *History of King Arthur*, 1858, 2 vols., revised 1865; *Political Poems and Songs from Edward III. to Richard III.*, 1859-61, 2 vols., Rolls Series; *Songs and Ballads of the Reign of Philip and Mary*, 1860, 4to, Roxburghe Club; *Essays on Archæological Subjects*, 1861, 2 vols.; *Domestic Manners and Sentiments in England in the Middle Ages*, 1862, 4to, reproduced in 1871 as *The Homes of other Days*; *Roll of Arms of Edward I.*, 1864, 4to; *Autobiography of Thomas Wright* (1736–97), his grandfather, 1864; *History of Caricature*, 1865, 4to; *Womankind in Western Europe*, 1869, 4to; *Anglo-Latin Satirical Poets of 12th Cent.*, 1872, 2 vols., Rolls Series.

WRIT, in law, is a formal commission from the crown or other supreme executive officer to an inferior executive officer or to a private person, enjoining some act or omission. The word represents the Latin *brevis* or *breve* (both forms are found, the latter more commonly), so called, according to Bracton, from its shortly expressing the intention of the framer, "quia breviter et paucis verbis intentionem proferentis exponit."[1] The *breve* can be traced back as far as the *Codex Theodosianus* (438 A.D.), where one of its meanings is that of an official report or letter. It bears a similar meaning in some of the capitularies of the Frankish kings. The *interdictum* of Roman law sometimes represents the writ of English law; *e.g.*, there is considerable likeness between the Roman *interdictum de libero homine exhibendo* and the English writs of *habeas corpus* and *de homine replegiando*. From Roman law the *breve* passed into the *Liber Feudorum* and the canon law, in

[1] It is perhaps doubtful whether *intentio* is here used in its ordinary sense or in the technical signification which it bore as a part of the Roman *formula* (see ROMAN LAW, vol. xx. p. 707–8).

both in a sense differing from that at present borne by the writ of English law. The *breve testatum* of the *Liber Feudorum* was an instrument in writing made on the land at the time of giving seisin by the lord to the tenant, and attested by the seals of the lord and the *pares curiæ* or other witnesses. In England such witnesses were part of the inquest, and joined in the verdict in case of disputed right until 12 Edw. II. st. 1, c. 2. The *breve testatum* in England developed into the Feoffment (*q.v.*), later into the deed of grant (see Real Estate); in Scotland into the charter, and later into the disposition. In canon law *breve* denoted a letter under the pope's seal. In old English ecclesiastical law a brief meant letters patent issued out of Chancery to churchwardens or other officers for the collection of money for church purposes. Such briefs were regulated by 4 Anne c. 14, but are now obsolete, although they are still to be found named in one of the rubrics in the communion service of the Book of Common Prayer. In English legal practice brief now denotes the written instructions put into the hands of counsel to form the basis of his case. It was probably so called from its at first being only a copy of the original writ. Such a brief is in Scotland called a memorial.

History of writ in English law.

The writ in English law still occupies a very important position, which can scarcely be understood without a sketch of its history. To a certain extent this history has already been given under Pleading, for the whole theory of pleading depends in the last resort upon the writ. Writ or *breve* was at first used in a less technical sense than that which it afterwards assumed: thus in the *Leges Henrici Primi* it simply means a letter from the king, and in the Assize of Clarendon (1166) *imbreviari* means to be registered. It became formalized by the reign of Henry II., and precedents are given by Glanvill. The writ process was at that date the foundation of all civil justice in the king's court, and of much in the lower courts, and was a profitable source of revenue to the exchequer. Every writ had to be purchased (*breve perquirere* was the technical term). This purchase developed in later times into the payment of a fine to the king where the damages were laid above £40. The usual scale was 6s. 8d. for every 100 marks claimed. In suing out a writ of covenant, the basis of the proceedings in levying a fine (see Entail), the king was entitled to his *primer fine*, *i.e.*, one-tenth of the annual value of the land concerned. The sale of writs was forbidden by Magna Charta and other statutes in certain cases, especially that of the writ *de odio et atia* in favour of the liberty of the subject. A solicitor was so called because his original duty was to solicit or sue out a writ and take the due proceedings by paying the proper fine. The costs of a writ purchased were first allowed to a successful demandant by the Statute of Gloucester, 6 Edw. I. c. 1. Through the Norman period the prerogative of issuing writs seems to have been undisputed. Glanvill's precedents did not exhaust all possible forms, for in the time of Bracton, in the 13th century, it was still possible to frame new writs at the pleasure of the crown. The Provisions of Oxford in 1258 put an end to this by enacting that the chancellor should not seal anything out of course (*i.e.*, any writ for which there was no precedent) by the will of the king, but that he should do it by the council. In 1285 the Statute of Westminster the Second, 13 Edw. I. st. 1, c. 24, re-established the power of the crown within certain limits, that is, in causes of action in a similar case falling under the same law (*in consimili casu cadente sub eodem jure*) as those for which precedents of writs already existed in the Chancery (see Trespass, Trover). These precedents were at an early date recorded in the *Registrum Brevium*, called by Sir Edward Coke the oldest book in the common law. Apart from the powers given by the statute, new writs could only be issued by the authority of parliament, and writs are sometimes found set out in statutes, especially in the *Statutum Walliæ*, 12 Edw. I. c. 7, where precedents of the most usual writs will be found. The Statute of Westminster the Second itself contained precedents of the writ of formedon and of many others. The original flexibility of the writ was thus limited within comparatively narrow bounds. The right to the issue of the writ determined the right of action. So essential was the writ that it was a legal axiom in Bracton that no one could sue at law without a writ, and it was called by Coke, in his introduction to Littleton, "the heartstrings of the common law." As such it occupied an important place in some of the leading statutes dealing with constitutional rights. The Statute of Marlbridge, 52 Hen. III. c. 22, forbade a lord to distrain his freeholders to answer for their freeholds, or for anything touching their freeholds, without the king's writ. By 25 Edw. III. st. 5, c. 4, it was accorded, asserted, and stablished that none should be taken by petition or suggestion made to the king or his council unless by indictment or presentment in due manner or by process made by writ original at the common law. 42 Edw. III. c. 3 provided that no man should be put to answer without presentment before justices, or matter of record, or by due process and writ original according to the old law of the land. Both these statutes were recited and the general principle confirmed by 16 Car. I. c. 10. Uniformity of procedure was secured by 27 Hen. VIII. c. 24, by which all writs were to be in the king's name in a county palatine or liberty, but tested by those who had the county palatine or liberty. It was not until 1731 that, by virtue of 4 Geo. II. c. 26, writs were framed in the English language. They had previously been in Latin; this accounts for the Latin names by which a large number are still known. The writ was issued from the common law side of the Chancery, and was in the special charge of the manager and petty bag offices. Though issuing from the king's Chancery, it did not necessarily direct the trial of the question in the king's court. In whatever court it was returnable, it called in the aid of the sheriff as executive officer. It was either addressed to him or, if addressed to the party alleged to be in default, it concluded with a threat of constraint by the sheriff in the event of disobedience, generally in those terms, "et, nisi feceris, vicecomes de N. faciat ne amplius clamorem audiam pro defectu justitiæ." If the writ was returnable in the county court or the lord's court, the sheriff or the lord sat as the deputy of the king, not by virtue of his inherent jurisdiction. The writ was not necessary for the initiation of proceedings in these courts or before the justices in eyre (who sat as judges of the county court),[1] but a custom seems to have grown up of suing out a writ from the king where the claim was above 40s. Cases were transferred from the lord's court to the county court by writ of *tolt* (so called because it removed, *tollit*, the case), from the latter to the king's court by writ of *pone* (so called from its first word). By Magna Charta the power of bringing a suit in the king's court in the first instance by writ of *præcipe* was taken away, and the writ was thenceforth only returnable in the king's court where the tenant held of the king *in capite*, or where the lord had no court or abandoned his right. Hence it became a common form in the writ of right to allege that the lord had renounced his court (*dominus remisit curiam*) so as to secure trial in the king's court. Besides being used for the trial of disputes, writs addressed to sheriffs, mayors, commissioners, or others were in constant use for financial

[1] The distinction between the royal and local courts was not perhaps at all times very strictly drawn. Thus in the *Leges Henrici Primi*, c. 31, the county court is called *curia regis*.

and political purposes, *e.g.*, for the collection of fifteenths, scutage, tallage, &c., for summons to the council and later to parliament, and for recalling a parliament, the last by means of the rarely occurring writ *de revocatione parliamenti.*

There were several divisions of writs (excluding those purely financial and political), the most important being that into original and judicial, the former (tested in the name of the king) issued to bring a suit before the proper court, the latter (tested in the name of a judge) issued during the progress of a suit or to enforce judgment. Original were either optional, *i.e.*, giving an option of doing a certain act or of showing cause why it was not done, beginning with the words *præcipe quod reddat*, the principal example being the writ on which proceedings in a common recovery (see ENTAIL) were based, or peremptory, *i.e.*, calling on a person to do a certain act, beginning with the words *si A fecerit te securum.* Original were also either *de cursu* or *magistralia*, the former those fixed in form and depending on precedent, the latter those framed by the masters in Chancery under the powers of the Statute of Westminster the Second. They were also either general or special, the latter setting forth the grounds of the demand with greater particularity than the former. By 5 Geo. II. c. 27 special writs were confined to causes of action amounting to £10 or upwards. There was also a division of writs into writs of right (*ex debito justitiæ*), such as *habeas corpus*, and prerogative writs (*ex gratia*), such as *mandamus* (see PREROGATIVE). Coke and other authorities mention numerous other divisions, but those which have been named appear to be the principal.

The most interesting form of writ from the historical point of view was the writ of right (*breve de recto*), called by Blackstone "the highest writ in the law," used at first for debt and other personal claims, afterwards confined to the recovery of real estate as the writ of right *par excellence.* It was so called from the words *plenum rectum* contained in it, and was the remedy for obtaining justice for ouster from or privation of the freehold. By it property as well as possession could be recovered. It generally lay in the king's court, as has been said, by virtue of a fictitious allegation. In that case it was addressed to the sheriff and was called a writ of right close. It was also a writ of right close where the lands in dispute were held in antient demesne. When addressed to the lord and tried in his court, it was generally a writ of right patent. After the appearance of the tenant the demandant in a writ of right counted, that is, claimed against the tenant according to the writ, but in more precise terms, the writ being as it were the embryo of the future count. The trial was originally by battle (see TRIAL), but in the reign of Henry II. an alternative procedure was introduced, interesting as the earliest example of the substitution of something like the JURY (*q.v.*) system for the judicial combat. A writ *de magna assisa eligenda* was directed to the sheriff commanding him to return four knights of the county and vicinage to the court, there to return twelve other knights of the vicinage to try upon oath the question contained in the writ of right (technically called the *mise*). This mode of trial was known as trial by the grand assize. Generally the whole of the sixteen knights were sworn, though twelve was a sufficient number. The last occasion of trial by the grand assize was in 1835. But long before that date possessory had from their greater convenience tended to supersede proprietary remedies, and in most cases the title was sufficiently determined by the assizes of other kinds, especially that of novel disseisin and later by proceedings in ejectment (see POSSESSION). The oath of the champion on proceedings in a writ of right where the alternative of the judicial combat was accepted was regulated by statute, 3 Edw. I. c. 41. The writ of right is also interesting as being the basis of the law of LIMITATION (*q.v.*). By the Statute of Merton, 20 Hen. III. c. 8, no seisin could be alleged by the demandant but from the time of Henry II. By 3 Edw. I. c. 39 the time was fixed at the reign of Richard I., by 32 Hen. VIII. c. 2 at sixty years at the most. There were other writs of right with special names, *e.g.*, the writ of right by the custom of London for land in London, the writ of right of advowson, brought by the patron to recover his right of presentation to a benefice, and the writs of right of dower and *de rationabili parte*, the latter brought by coparceners or brothers in gavelkind. There were also writs in the nature of a writ of right, *e.g.*, formedon, brought by a reversioner on discontinuance by a tenant in tail and given by the Statute *De Donis* (see ENTAIL); escheat, brought by the lord where the tenant died without an heir; *ne injuste vexes*, to prohibit the lord from exacting services or rents beyond his due; *de nativo habendo*, to recover the inheritance in a villein; and the little writ of right close according to the custom of the manor, to try in the lord's court the right of the king's tenants in antient demesne.

Up to 1832 an action was (except as against certain privileged persons, such as attorneys) commenced by original writ, and writ practically became the equivalent of action, and is so used in old books of practice, such as Booth on *Real Actions.* The law was gradually altered by legislation and still more by the introduction of fictitious proceedings in the common law courts, to be described later, by which the issue of the original writ was suspended, except in real actions, which were of comparatively rare occurrence. The original writ is no longer in use in civil procedure, an action being now in all cases commenced by the writ of summons, a judicial writ, a procedure first introduced in 1832 by 2 Will. IV. c. 39. In the following year an immense number of the old writs were abolished by 3 and 4 Will. IV. c. 27. An exception was made in favour of the writ of right of dower, writ of dower *unde nihil habet*, QUARE IMPEDIT (*q.v.*), and EJECTMENT (*q.v.*), and of the plaints for free bench and dower in the nature of writs of right. Ejectment was remodelled by the Common Law Procedure Act, 1852; the other writs and plaints remained up to the Common Law Procedure Act, 1860, by which they were abolished. Other writs which have been superseded by simpler proceedings, generally by ordinary actions, are those of the four assizes of novel disseisin, *juris utrum*, *mort d'auncester*, and *darrein presentment* (see ASSIZE), estrepement and waste (see WASTE), *monstrans de droit* (see PETITION), NUISANCE (*q.v.*), PARTITION (*q.v.*), *præmunire* (see TREASON), QUO WARRANTO (*q.v.*), SCIRE FACIAS (*q.v.*), *subpœna* (see TRUST), and *warrantia chartæ* (see WARRANTY). The number of writs was so large that any exhaustive list of them is almost impossible, but a few of those of more special interest which have become obsolete may be shortly mentioned.

Obsolete writs.

Admensuratio lay against persons usurping more than their share of property. It was either *dotis* or *pasturæ*, the latter, like the Scotch "souming and rouming," being the remedy for surcharge of common. *Alias* and *pluries* writs were issued when a previous writ had been disobeyed. *Attaint* lay to inquire by a jury of twenty-four whether a jury of twelve had given a false verdict. It was superseded in the 16th century by the practice of setting aside a verdict or granting a new trial, and was finally abolished by 6 Geo. IV. c. 50. *Audita querela* was a means of relieving a defendant by a matter of discharge occurring after judgment. After having been long practically superseded by stay of execution it was finally abolished by the rules made under the Judicature

Act, 1875. *Capias, latitat*, and *quominus* are interesting as showing the extraordinary mass of fictitious allegation in the old procedure of the common law courts before 1832. By *capias ad respondendum* followed by *alias* and *pluries* the Court of Common Pleas was enabled to take cognizance of an action without the actual issue of an original writ. The *capias* was a judicial writ issued to follow an original writ of trespass *quia clausum fregit*. The issue of the original writ and after a time the issue of the *capias* became mere fictions, and proceedings commenced with the issue of another writ called *capias testatum*. On return of the writ the plaintiff elected to proceed with a cause of action other than trespass, and the real merits of the case were eventually reached in this tortuous manner. After being served with the *capias* the defendant was bound to put in common or special bail, the former being sufficient in all but exceptional cases. Here again there was a fiction, for his common bail were John Doe and Richard Roe. The same fictitious pair also appeared on the side of the plaintiff as his pledges for the due prosecution of his action. By *latitat* and *quominus* the Courts of King's Bench and Exchequer respectively assumed jurisdiction by a further series of fictions over ordinary civil actions. The writ of *latitat*, following the bill of Middlesex, itself in later times generally a fiction, alleged that the defendant was in hiding out of Middlesex, after committing a trespass *quia clausum fregit*, for which he was in the custody of the king's marshal in the Marshalsea prison. The real cause of action was then stated in what was called the *ac etiam* clause. Writs filed in the King's Bench and Common Pleas were in the custody of an officer of each court called the *custos brevium*. The writ of *quominus* alleged that the plaintiff was the king's debtor and that through the defendant's default he was unable to discharge the debt. *Deceit* or *disceit* lay for the redress of anything done deceitfully in the name of another, but was especially used to reverse a judgment in a real action obtained by collusion. *Distraint of knighthood* was a mode of obtaining money for the crown by the exercise of the prerogative of forcing every one who held a knight's fee under the crown to be knighted or to pay a fine. The earliest extant writ was issued in 1278. It was abolished by 16 Car. I. c. 20. *Entry* was a possessory remedy against one alleged to hold land unlawfully. It was divided into a large number of kinds, and was the subject of much of the old real property learning. The ones most commonly occurring were the writs of entry in the *per* and in the *post*, the former alleging, the latter not, the title of the heir from the original disseisor. When writ had come to be equivalent in meaning to action, one of the divisions of possessory actions was into writs of entry and writs of assize. A special writ of entry for dower was given by 6 Edw. I. c. 7. *Excommunicato capiendo* was the authority for arresting an excommunicated person and detaining him until he was reconciled to the church, when he was liberated by the writ *de excommunicato deliberando*. These proceedings were abolished and the writ *de contumace capiendo* substituted by 57 Geo. III. c. 127 (see EXCOMMUNICATION). *Hæretico comburendo* was issued on certificate of conviction for heresy by the ecclesiastical court. A case of burning two Arians under this writ occurred as lately as the reign of James I. It was abolished by 29 Car. II. c. 9. *Homine replegiando*, mainprize, and *odio et atia* (or *bono et malo*) were all ancient means of securing the liberty of the subject, long superseded by the more effective procedure of *habeas corpus*. The last of the three enjoined the sheriff to inquire whether a committal on suspicion of murder was on just cause or from malice and ill-will. It was regulated by Magna Charta and the Statute of Westminster the Second, but, having been abused to the advantage of sheriffs, it was taken away by 28 Edw. III. c. 9. *Nisi prius* was given by the Statute of Westminster the Second, 13 Edw. I. c. 30. Its place is now taken by the commission of NISI PRIUS (*q.v.*). *Orando pro rege et regno*, before the present Book of Common Prayer, enjoined public prayers for the high court of parliament. *Privilege* commanded the release of a prisoner entitled to privilege of parliament. *Protection* was given for enabling a man to be quit of suits brought against him while absent beyond seas. It was dealt with by a large number of old statutes, but none has been issued since 1692. *Rebellion* was a means of enforcing obedience to the process of the Court of Chancery. In modern procedure attachment takes its place. *Rege inconsulto* commanded judges of a court not to proceed in a case which might prejudice the king until his pleasure should be known. *Replevin* was a survival of the most archaic law. The procedure consisted of writ on writ to an almost unlimited extent. It originally began by the issue of a writ of replevin or *replegiari facias*. The case might be removed from the county court to a superior court by writ of *recordari facias loquelam*. If the distrainor claimed a property in the goods distrained, the question of property or no property was determined by a writ *de proprietate probanda*, and, if decided in favour of the distrainor, the distress was to be returned to him by writ *de retorno habendo*. If the goods were removed or concealed, a writ of *capias in withernam* enabled the sheriff, after due issue of *alias* and *pluries* writs, to take a second distress in place of the one removed. It is said that the question whether goods taken in *withernam* could be replevied was the only one which the Admirable Crichton found himself unable to answer. For the modern practice, see DISTRESS, REPLEVIN. *Restitutione extracti ab ecclesia* lay for restoring a man to a sanctuary from which he had been wrongfully taken (see SANCTUARY). *Secta* lay for enforcing the duties of tenants to their lord's court, *e.g.*, *secta ad molendinum*, where the tenants were bound to have their corn ground at the lord's mill. *Seisina habenda* allowed delivery of lands of a felon to the lord after the king had had his year, day, and waste (see WASTE). *Vi laica removenda* is curiously illustrative of ancient manners. It lay where two parsons contended for a church, and one of them entered with a great number of laymen and kept out the other by force. As lately as 1867 an application for the issue of the writ was made to the Chancery Court of the Bermuda Islands, but refused on the ground that the writ was obsolete, and that the same relief could be obtained by injunction. On appeal this refusal was sustained by the privy council.

Writs now in use.

Of writs now in use, other than those for elections, all are judicial, or part of the PROCESS (*q.v.*)[1] of the court, except perhaps the writ of error in criminal cases. They are to be hereafter issued out of the central office of the Supreme Court, or the office of the clerk of the crown in Chancery, provision having been made by the Great Seal (Officers) Act, 1874, and the Judicature (Officers) Act, 1879, for the transfer on the next vacancy of the duties of the clerk of the petty bag to those officers. By the latter Act the record and writ clerks, previously officers of the Chancery Division, were abolished. By 40 and 41 Vict. c. 41 the wafer great seal or the wafer privy seal may be attached to writs instead of the impression of the great or privy seal. The judicial writs issue chiefly, if not entirely, from the central office, with which the old crown office was incorporated by the Act of 1879. The crown office had charge of writs occurring in crown practice, such as *quo warranto* and *certiorari*.

Judicial writs.

In local civil courts, other than county courts, writs are usually issued out of the office of the registrar, or an officer of similar jurisdiction. By 35 and 36 Vict. c. 86 writs of execution from such courts for sums under £20 may be stamped or sealed as of course by the registrar of a county court, and executed as if they had issued from the county court. In county court practice the

[1] It may be noticed that by the interpretation clause of the Sheriffs Act, 1887, the expression "writ" includes any process.

WARRANT (*q.v.*) corresponds generally to the writ of the Supreme Court. Most of the present law on the subject of writs is contained in the Rules of the Supreme Court, 1883, Ord. xlii.–xliv., and in the Crown Office Rules, 1886. Both sets of rules contain numerous precedents in their schedules. By Ord. ii. r. 8 of the rules of 1883 all writs (with certain exceptions) are to be tested in the name of the lord chancellor, or, if that office be vacant, in the name of the lord chief justice. The main exceptions are those which occur in crown practice, which are tested by the lord chief justice. The writ of error bears the tests of the king or queen, "witness ourselves." Before the issue of most writs a *præcipe*, or authority to the proper offices to issue the writ, is necessary. This is of course not to be confounded with the old original writ of *præcipe*. Writs affecting land must generally be registered in order to bind the land (see REGISTRATION). A writ cannot as a rule be served on Sunday (see SUNDAY). Some of the more important modern writs (other than those of an extrajudicial nature) may be shortly noticed. HABEAS CORPUS, MANDAMUS, and PROHIBITION (*qq.v.*) have been already treated. Writs are generally, unless where the contrary is stated, addressed to the sheriff. *Abatement* or *nocumento amovendo* enjoins the removal of a nuisance in pursuance of a judgment to that effect. *Ad quod damnum* is for the purpose of inquiring whether a proposed crown grant will be to the damage of the crown or others. It is still in use, and recent examples will be found in the *London Gazette*. If the inquiry be determined in favour of the subject, a reasonable fine is payable to the exchequer by 27 Edw. I. st. 2. *Attachment* is issued as a means of supporting the dignity of the court by punishment for contempt of its orders (see CONTEMPT OF COURT). Since the Judicature Acts a uniform practice has been followed in all the branches of the High Court, and a writ of attachment can now only be issued by leave of the court or a judge after notice to the party against whom it is to be issued. *Capias*: the old writs of *capias ad satisfaciendum* and *capias utligatum* may still be used, but their importance has been much diminished since the alterations made in the law by the Debtors Act, 1869, and the abolition of civil outlawry (see OUTLAW). *Certiorari* is a writ in very frequent use, by which the proceedings of an inferior court are brought up for review by the High Court. In general it lies for excess of jurisdiction as *mandamus* does for defect. The Summary Jurisdiction Act, 1879, makes the writ no longer necessary where a special case has been stated by a court of quarter sessions. *Delivery* enforces a judgment for the delivery of property without giving the defendant (unless at the option of the plaintiff) power to retain it on payment of the assessed value. *Distringas* lay to distrain a person for a crown debt or for his appearance on a certain day. Its operation has been much curtailed by the substitution of other proceedings by 28 and 29 Vict. c. 104, and the rules of the Supreme Court. It now seems to lie only against inhabitants for non-repair of a highway. *Distringas nuper vicecomitem* is a writ calling on an ex-sheriff to account for the proceeds of goods taken in execution. *Elegit* is founded on the Statute of Westminster the Second, and is so named from the words of the writ, that the plaintiff has chosen (*elegit*) this particular mode of satisfaction. It originally ordered the sheriff to seize a moiety of the debtor's land and all his goods, save his oxen and beasts of the plough. By 1 and 2 Vict. c. 110 the *elegit* was extended to include the whole of the lands, and copyholds as well as freeholds. By the Bankruptcy Act, 1883, an *elegit* no longer applies to goods. *Error*, the only example of an original writ remaining, was at one time largely used in both civil and criminal proceedings. It was abolished in civil procedure by the Common Law Procedure Act, 1852, and proceedings in error by the rules made under the Judicature Act, 1875. A writ of error to the Queen's Bench Division still lies in criminal cases, though it is rarely brought, for it only lies for mistakes appearing on the record, and recent legislation has given large powers of amending such mistakes. The fiat of the attorney-general is necessary before it can be sued out. *Exigent* (with *proclamation*) forms part of the process of outlawry now existing only against a criminal. It depends on several statutes, commencing in 1344, and is specially mentioned in the Statute of Provisors of Edward III., 25 Edw. III. st. 6. *Extent* is the writ of execution issued by the crown for a crown debt of record. The sale of chattels seized under an extent takes place under a writ of *venditioni exponas*. A crown debtor is entitled to an *extent in aid* against a person indebted to him. Where a crown debtor has died a writ reciting his death, and so called *diem clausit extremum*, issues against his property. *Fieri facias* is the ordinary writ of execution on a judgment commanding the sheriff to levy the sum, interest, and costs on the personal property of the party. Where the sheriff has not sold the goods, *venditioni exponas* issues to compel him to do so. Where the party is a beneficed clergyman, the writ is one of *fieri facias de bonis ecclesiasticis* or of *sequestrari facias* (addressed to the bishop). The latter writ also issues in other cases of an exceptional nature, as against a corporation and to seize a pension. It is addressed to commissioners, not to the sheriff. *Habere facias possessionem* is given to the owner of a tithe or rent charge, enabling him to have possession of the lands chargeable therewith until arrears due to him are paid (see TITHES). *Indicavit* is still nominally grantable under the Statute *De Conjunctim Feoffatis* of 34 Edw. I., and is a particular kind of prohibition granted to the patron of an advowson. *Inquiry* issues for the assessment of damages by the sheriff or his deputy. It represents to some extent the old writ of *justicies*, and the later writ of trial allowed by 3 and 4 Will. IV. c. 42, but is narrower in its operation, for under the last-named writs the whole case or issues under it could be tried. Before an inquiry the liability has been already established. *Levari facias* is the means of levying execution for forfeited recognizances (see RECOGNIZANCE). The Bankruptcy Act, 1883, abolished it in civil proceedings. *Ne exeat regno* was at one time issued by virtue of the prerogative to prevent any person from leaving the realm, a form of restraint of liberty recognized by parliament in 5 Ric. II. c. 2. It has now become a means of preventing a debtor from quitting the kingdom, and so withdrawing himself from the jurisdiction of the court without giving security for the debt. There is some doubt whether it has not been impliedly superseded by the powers given by Ord. lxix. of the Rules of the Supreme Court. *Non omittas* is for executing process by the sheriff in a liberty or franchise, where the proper officer has neglected to do so. It rested originally chiefly upon the Statute of Westminster the Second, c. 39, and is now regulated by the Sheriffs Act, 1887, which repeals the previous enactment. *Possession* (also called *assistance*) enjoins the sheriff to give possession of land to the party entitled thereto under a judgment for such possession. In admiralty, where the judgment is for possession of a ship, the writ is addressed to the marshal. *Procedendo* is the converse of prohibition. It directs the lower court to proceed with the case. It also lies to restore the authority of commissioners suspended by *supersedeas*. *Restitution* restores property, either real or personal, after the right to it has been judicially declared. Thus it lies on behalf of the owner of real property under the statutes of forcible entry and of personal property under the Larceny Act, 1861. *Significavit*, once a writ, appears since 57 Geo. III. c. 127 to be merely a notice. It is a part of the proceedings against a person disobeying the order of an ecclesiastical court, and consists in a notification to the crown in Chancery of the disobedience. Thereupon a writ *de contumace capiendo* issues for his arrest. On his subsequent obedience or satisfaction, a writ of *deliverance* is granted. Precedents of these writs are given in the Act named. *Subpœna* is the ordinary means of securing the presence of a witness in court, and is addressed to the person whose attendance is required. It is so called from its containing the words "and this you are not to omit under the penalty of £100," &c. The *subpœna* may be either *ad testificandum*, to give evidence, or *duces tecum*, to produce documents, &c., or both combined. By special order of a judge under 17 and 18 Vict. c. 23 a *subpœna* may be issued from any court in England, Scotland, or Ireland to compel the attendance of a witness out of the jurisdiction. *Summons* is the universal means of commencing an action in the High Court. It is addressed to the defendant, and may be either generally or specially indorsed with a statement of the nature of the claim made. The latter form of indorsement is allowed in certain cases of debt or liquidated demand, and gives the plaintiff the great advantage of entitling him to final judgment in default of appearance by the defendant, and even in spite of appearance unless the defendant can satisfy a judge that he has a defence or ought to be allowed to defend. No statement of claim is necessary in case of a specially indorsed writ, the indorsement being deemed to be the statement. The writ may be issued out of the central office or out of a district registry, and the plaintiff may name on his writ the division of the High Court in which he proposes to have the case tried. There are special rules governing the issue of writs in probate and admiralty actions. The writ remains in force for twelve months, but may be renewed for good cause after the expiration of that time. Service must be personal, unless where substituted service is allowed, and in special cases, such as actions to recover land and admiralty actions. Service out of the jurisdiction of a writ or notice of a writ is allowed only by leave of the court or a judge. Notice of the issue of a writ, and not the writ itself, is served on a defendant who is neither a British subject nor in British dominions. The law is contained in the Rules of the Supreme Court, especially Ord. ii.–xi. and xiv. *Supersedeas* commands the stay of proceedings on another writ. It is often combined with *procedendo*, where on a *certiorari* the High Court has decided in favour of the jurisdiction of the inferior court. It is also used for removing from the commission of the peace, and for putting an end to the authority of, any persons acting under commission from the crown. *Venire facias* is the first proceeding in outlawry, calling upon the party to appear. Under the old practice a *venire facias de novo* was the means of obtaining a new trial. *Ventre inspiciendo* appears still to be competent, and is a curious relic of antiquity. It issues on the application of an heir presumptive in order to determine by a jury of matrons whether the widow of a deceased owner of lands be with child or not. Almost exactly the same proceeding was known in Roman law under the name of *interdictum de inspiciendo ventre*, the prætor sending five women to make a report.

on-judicial writs.

The principal writs of a non-judicial nature relate to parliament or some of its constituent elements. Parliament is summoned by the king's writ issued out of Chancery by advice of the privy council. The period of forty days once necessary between the writ and the assembling is now by 15 and 16 Vict. c. 23 reduced to thirty-five days. Writs of summons are issued to the lords spiritual and temporal before every new parliament. Those to Irish representative peers are regulated by the Act of Union, those to archbishops and bishops by 10 and 11 Vict. c. 108. New peerages are no longer created by writ, but the eldest son of a peer is occasionally summoned to the House of Lords in the name of a barony of his father's. Earl Percy, the eldest son of the duke of Northumberland, was so summoned in 1887, and sits as Baron Lovaine (see PEERAGE). With respect to election of members of the House of Commons, the procedure differs as the election takes place after a dissolution or on a casual vacancy. After a dissolution the writ is issued, as already stated, by order of the crown in council. For a single election the warrant for a new writ is issued during the session by the speaker after an order of the house made upon motion; during the recess by the speaker's authority alone, under the powers given by 24 Geo. III. sess. 2, c. 26, 21 and 22 Vict. c. 110, and 26 Vict. c. 20. The warrant is addressed to the clerk of the crown in Chancery for Great Britain, to the clerk of the crown and hanaper of Ireland. A *supersedeas* to a writ has sometimes been ordered where the writ was improvidently issued. The time allowed to elapse between the receipt of the writ and the election is fixed by the Ballot Act, 1872, sched. 1, at nine days for a county or a district borough, four days for any other borough. The writ is to be returned by the returning officer to the clerk of the crown with the name of the member elected endorsed on the writ. Sched. 2 gives a form of the writ, which is tested, like the writ of error, by the queen herself. The returning officer is the sheriff in counties and counties of cities (such as Chester), generally the mayor in cities and boroughs, and the vice-chancellor in universities (see PARLIAMENT). Other writs for election are those for CONVOCATION (*q.v.*), which is by 25 Hen. VIII. c. 19 summoned by the archbishop of the province on receipt of the king's writ, and for election of coroners, verderers of royal forests, and some other officers whose office is of great antiquity. The writ *de coronatore eligendo*, addressed to the sheriff, is specially preserved by the Coroners Act, 1887.

Offences relating to writs are dealt with by the Criminal Law Consolidation Acts of 1861; larceny by 24 and 25 Vict. c. 96, s. 30; forgery by 24 and 25 Vict. c. 98, s. 27. The maximum penalty is seven years' penal servitude.

Scotland.

Scotland.—Writ is a more extensive term than in England. Writs are either judicial or extrajudicial, the latter including deeds and other instruments,—as, for instance, in 42 and 43 Vict. c. 44, and in the common use of the phrase "oath or writ" as a means of proof. In the narrower English sense both "writ" and "brieve" are used. The brieve was as indispensable a part of the old procedure as it was in England, and many forms are given in *Regiam Majestatem* and *Quoniam Attachiamenta*. It was a command issued in the king's name, addressed to a judge, and ordering trial of a question stated therein. Its conclusion was the will of the summons (see WILL, SUMMONS). In some cases proceedings which were by writ in England took another form in Scotland. For instance, the writ of attaint was not known in Scotland, but a similar end was reached by trial of the jury for wilful error.[1] The English writ of *ne exeat regno* is represented by the *meditatio fugæ* warrant. Most proceedings by brieve, being addressed to the sheriff, became obsolete after the institution of the Court of Session, when the sheriffs lost much of that judicial power which they had enjoyed to a greater extent than the English sheriff (see SHERIFF). The executive functions of the English sheriff are performed by the messengers-at-arms. An English writ of execution is represented in Scotland by diligence, chiefly by means by warrants to messengers-at-arms under the authority of signet letters in the name of the king. The brieve, however, has not wholly disappeared. Brieves of tutory, terce, and division are still competent, but not in use. Other kinds of brieve have been superseded by simpler procedure, *e.g.*, the brieve of service of heirs by 10 and 11 Vict. c. 47, for which a petition to the sheriff was substituted by that Act and 31 and 32 Vict. c. 101. The brieve of cognition of insane persons is now the only one of practical importance. The old brieves of furiosity and idiotcy were abolished, and this new form was introduced by the Act last named. Writs *eo nomine* have been the subject of much recent legislation. The writs of *capias*, *habeas*, *certiorari*, and extent were replaced by other proceedings by 19 and 20 Vict. c. 56. The writ of *clare constat* was introduced by 21 and 22 Vict. c. 76. It and the writs of resignation and confirmation (whether granted by the crown or a subject superior) were regulated by 31 and 32 Vict. c. 101. By the same Act crown writs are to be in the English language, and registered in the register of crown writs. They need not be sealed unless at the instance of the party against whom they are issued. Writs of progress (except crown writs, writs of *clare constat*, and writs of acknowledgment) were abolished by 37 and 38 Vict. c. 94. The *clare constat* writ is one granted by the crown or a subject superior for the purpose of completing title of a vassal's heirs to lands held by the deceased vassal. Where the lands are leasehold the writ of acknowledgment under 20 and 21 Vict. c. 26 is used for the same purpose. By 40 and 41 Vict. c. 40 the form of warrant of execution on certain extracts of registered writs is amended. Extracts of registered writs are to be equivalent to the registered writs themselves. Writs registered in the register of sasines for preservation only may afterwards be registered for preservation and execution. By 22 Geo. II. c. 48, passed for the purpose of assimilating the practice of outlawry for treason in Scotland to that in use in England, the court before which an indictment for treason or misprision of treason is found, is entitled on proper cause to issue writs of *capias*, proclamation, and *exigent*. Many writs are by the Stamp Act, 1870, chargeable with a duty of five shillings. In some respects the proceedings in parliamentary elections differ from those in use in England. Thus the writ in university elections is directed to the vice-chancellors of Edinburgh and Glasgow respectively, but not to those of St Andrews and Aberdeen, and there is an extension of the time for the return in elections for Orkney and Shetland, and for the Wick burghs. Representative peers of Scotland were by the Act of Union to be elected after writ issued to the privy council of Scotland. On the abolition of the privy council a proclamation under the great seal was substituted by 6 Anne, c. 23.

United States.

United States.—Writs in United States courts are by Act of Congress to be tested in the name of the chief justice of the United States. By State laws writs are generally bound to be in the name of the people of the State, in the English language, and tested in the name of a judge. Writs of error have been the subject of much legislation by the United States and by the States. In New York writs of error and of *ne exeat* have been abolished. Writs as parts of real actions have been generally superseded, but in Massachusetts a writ of entry on disseisin is still a mode of trying title. Writs of dower and of estrepement are still in use in some States. By the law of some States, *e.g.*, New Jersey, writs of election are issued to supply casually occurring vacancies in the legislature.

Authorities.—The importance of the writ in procedure led to the compilation of a great body of law and precedent at an early date. In addition to the *Registrum Brevium* there were, among other old works, the *Natura Brevium*, first published in 1525; Theloall, *Le Digest des Briefes Originales* (1579); Fitzherbert, *Le Nouvel Natura Brevium* (1588); *Officina Brevium* (1679). See too Coke upon Littleton, 158, 159, 2 Coke's *Institutes*, 39. Many precedents will also be found in the collection of Parliamentary Writs and in Stubbs's *Select Charters*. Old books of practice, such as Tidd's *Practice*, Corner's *Crown Practice*, and Booth *On Real Actions*, contained much law on the subject. For the history Spence's *Equitable Jurisdiction*, vol. i. bk. ii. ch. viii., Forsyth's *Hist. of Trial by Jury*, Stephen *On Pleading*, and Bigelow's *Hist. of Procedure*, ch. iv., may be consulted. There appears to be no book dealing with the writ in modern practice, but sufficient information is contained in the ordinary treatises on procedure. (J. Wt.)

WRITING MACHINES. Machines and appliances of various kinds are in common use to facilitate the process of writing, and to produce copies of writings already made with the pen. Such facsimile writings are obtained by numerous devices, all of which, however, come under the heads (1) of manifolding, (2) of processes analogous in principle to lithography, and (3) of stencilling. The simplest form of manifold writing is by sheets of paper prepared with lamp-black being interleaved between the sheets of white paper on which the impressions are to be taken, and writing over the whole with a style or other sharp-pointed instrument. By this means a considerable number of copies can be made at one time, and the method is in general use among newspaper writers and telegraphists in the production of what is technically known as "flimsy," where several copies of the same matter are required. Of processes analogous to lithography, the best known is the "hektograph" method, in which the writing is done in the first instance on paper with aniline ink, and then a transfer is made to a gelatine composition which gives off a considerable number of impressions. In principle the autocopyist is like the hektograph, but in this apparatus the writing is done with a special ink, which is transferred to a prepared and properly stretched sheet of parchment. From this parchment copies are obtained precisely as from a lithographic stone on which a transfer has been impressed. Of the apparatus worked in the stencil method, the cyclostyle has been most extensively

[1] An example occurring in the reign of James VI. will be found in Pitcairn's *Criminal Trials*, vol. i. p. 216.

adopted. This machine consists of a frame of sufficient size containing a plate of tin on which the paper from which the impression is to be taken is rested. The paper is prepared in a particular way, and the "pen" with which the writing is done consists of an ordinary wooden holder, at the end of which is fixed on a pivot a minute wheel. The edge of the wheel is studded with fine points, which, as it revolves and turns in the direction of the writing, pierce the paper, thus making a perfect stencil. The ink is passed over the top of this stencil by means of a roller, and the impression is left on a sheet of ordinary paper placed beneath.[1]

The principal substitute for the pen, however, is the machine now generally known as the type-writer, which in its present form dates only from 1873, but it has within that time come into extensive use, especially in America, the country of its origin. Numerous attempts to produce type-writing machines had been previously made both in England and America. So long ago as 1714 one Henry Mill took out a patent for a machine which he described as "an artificial machine or method for the impressing or transcribing of letters, singly or progressively, one after another as in writing, whereby all writings whatsoever may be engrossed in paper or parchment so neat and exact as not to be distinguished from print"; but his instrument is said to have been clumsy and useless, and led to no practical result. In 1867 the idea was taken up by Messrs C. Latham Sholes and Samuel W. Soulé, printers in Milwaukee, and Mr Carlos Glidden, and, after many experiments and failures, a practical working machine was elaborated in 1873, which, being originally made by Messrs E. Remington and Sons, of Ilion, N.Y., is known as the Remington standard type-writer. The success of this machine has induced many inventors to enter the field, and now three principal classes of type-writers are more or less in use. These are (1) type-bar machines, (2) cylinder machines, and (3) wheel machines. The Remington is the type and original of all type-bar machines, which are so called because the steel types are fixed at the extremity of a bar or rod of iron. These bars are in the Remington arranged in a circle around a common centre, and by striking the key of any particular letter, a lever is moved which raises the type-bar, and causes the type at its point to strike on an inked ribbon, and impresses the letter on the paper, which lies against an india-rubber roller. The type-bars are so hinged that all the types as they are struck hit precisely the same spot, so that were the paper to remain stationary the impressions of all the types struck would be superimposed on each other; but, by an automatic mechanism, the cylinder with the paper moves a space to the left after the impression of each type, and the depression of a wooden bar similarly moves the cylinder a space after each word without impressing any sign. In the recent forms of the Remington machine, each type bar carries two types, capital and lower case, or other duplicate signs, the one a little behind the other, and when a capital letter is to be printed the depression of a key shifts the position of the cylinder so as to bring the second type in contact with the ink ribbon. In this way from one set of keys two sets of type can be with facility acted upon. With practice, an average writing speed of forty words per minute can easily be attained on the Remington type-writer, and very expert writers have been able to keep up a speed of from sixty to seventy words for a short time. It is safe to say that type-writing can be ordinarily done at about three times the speed of ordinary handwriting. In the cylindrical machines the letters and signs are all upon a cylinder or "sleeve," and the striking of a key produces a combined lateral and rotary motion for bringing the proper type to the common printing point. Thus, for every separate impression the entire cylinder has ordinarily to make two movements of variable length, and the instrument is noisy in operation, and does not possess the rapid direct action of the type-bar machines. On the other hand, it is a variable spacer, giving more space to such wide letters as m and w than to the narrow letters i, t, and l, a distinct advantage over the type bar machines, where each letter, wide or narrow, occupies precisely the same space. Of such cylinder machines the newest form is the Crandall type-writer, an apparatus supplied with spare type cylinders or "sleeves," which are easily separated and attached, so that many kinds of type can be brought into actual use. Of wheel machines the Columbia may be taken as one of the most recent examples. It is a simple and cheap apparatus in which the letters and signs are placed on the periphery of a wheel by the rotation of which any desired type is brought into position for printing. The machine is furnished with a dial index and pointer to indicate the type which is in position. The wheel machine has the advantages of variable spacing, and wheels with type of different character can readily be placed on it; on the other hand, it is not capable of being run with a rapidity nearly so great as can be secured with type-bar machines.

[1] The trypograph is also a stencil-using device, in which a simple style is used for writing, but the paper is stretched over a fine and sharply corrugated metallic plate which punctures the paper as the style passes over it.

WRYNECK (Germ. *Wendehals*, Dutch *Draaihalzen*, French *Torcol*), a bird so called from its wonderful way of writhing its head and neck, especially when captured, as it may easily be, on its nest in a hollow tree. The *Iynx*[2] *torquilla* of ornithology, it is a regular summer-visitant to most parts of Europe, generally arriving a few days before the Cuckow, and it is in many countries known by some name associating it with that well-known bird—as in England "Cuckow's leader" and "Cuckow's mate"—but occasionally it is called "Snake-bird," not only from the undulatory motions just mentioned, but from the violent hissing with which it seeks to repel an intruder from its hole.[3]

The very unmistakable note of the Wryneck, without having any intrinsic merit, is always pleasant to hear as a harbinger of spring. It is merely a repetition of what may be syllabled *que, que, que*, many times in succession, rapidly uttered at first, but gradually slowing and in a continually falling key. This, however, is only heard during a few weeks, and for the rest of the bird's stay in Europe it seems to be mute. It feeds almost exclusively on insects, especially on ants, and may often be seen on the ground, busily engaged at their nests. Somewhat larger than a Sparrow, its plumage is not easily described, being beautifully variegated with black, brown, buff, and grey—the last produced by minute specks of blackish-brown on a light ground—the darker markings disposed in patches, vermiculated bars, freckles, streaks, or arrow-heads—and the whole blended most harmoniously, so as to recall the coloration of a GOATSUCKER (*q.v.*) or of a WOODCOCK (*q.v.*). The Wryneck builds no nest, but commonly lays its translucent white eggs on the bare wood of a hole in a tree, and it is one of the few wild birds that can be induced to go on laying by abstracting its eggs day after day, and thus upwards of forty have been taken from a single hole—but the proper complement is from six to ten. As regards Britain, the bird is most common in the south-east, its numbers decreasing rapidly towards the west and north, so that in Cornwall and Wales and beyond Cheshire and Yorkshire its occurrence is but rare, while it appears only by accident in Scotland and Ireland.

Some writers have been inclined to recognize five other

[2] Frequently misspelt, as by Linnæus in his later years, *Yunx*.

[3] The peculiarity was known to Aristotle, and possibly led to the cruel use of the bird as a love-charm, to which several classical writers refer, as Pindar (*Pyth.* iv. 214; *Nem.* iv. 35), Theocritus (iv. 17, 30), and Xenophon (*Memorabilia*, III. xi. 17, 18). In one part at least of China a name, *Shay-ling*, signifying "Snake's neck," is given to it (*Ibis*, 1875, p. 125).

species of the genus *Iynx*; but the so-called *I. japonica* is specifically indistinguishable from *I. torquilla*; while that designated, through a mistake in the locality assigned to it, *I. indica*, has been found to be identical with the *I. pectoralis* of South Africa. Near to this is *I. pulchricollis*, discovered by Emin Pasha in the east of the Bar-el-Djebel (*Ibis*, 1884, p. 28, pl. iii.). Another distinct African species is the *I. æquatorialis*, originally described from Abyssinia. The Wrynecks, as already stated (WOODPECKER, *supra*, p. 652), form a Subfamily *Iynginæ* of the *Picidæ*, from the more normal groups of which they differ but little in internal structure, but much in coloration and in having the tail-quills flexible, or at least not stiffened to serve as props as in the climbing *Picinæ*. (A. N.)

WUHU, or Woo-Hoo, a district city in the province of Gan-hwuy, China, is situated about a mile from the south bank of the Yang-tsze Keang river, with which it is connected by a straggling suburb. By the treaty of 1858 it was marked out as one of the treaty ports, but it was not opened to trade until 1877. At first its commercial progress was very slow, the neighbourhood of the older ports of Kew-keang and Chin-keang militating against its success; but of late years there has been a distinct improvement in the trade of the port, the gross value of which was £1,316,863 in 1885 and £2,011,327 in 1886. The principal exports are rice and silk piece goods, while next in importance come feathers, hides, nutgalls, and tea. For the production of feathers large quantities of ducks are reared in the surrounding districts. Of imports, opium is by far the most considerable item, amounting in 1886 to 779,728 lb, of the value of £652,223. In the same year £126,093 worth of cotton goods were imported, and £124,014 worth of sugar. Of the minor articles, matches, needles, sandalwood, and window glass form the largest items. During the same period 1088 vessels entered the port (691 British, 362 Chinese). The city, which is one of the largest of its rank in China, was laid desolate during the T'ai-p'ing rebellion, but it is gradually becoming repeopled.

WÚN, a British district in the chief commissionership of Berar, lying between 19° 46′ and 20° 42′ N. lat. and between 77° 26′ and 79° 10′ E. long., and containing an area of 3907 square miles. It is bounded on the N. and W. by Amraoti and Basim districts, on the S. by the Nizam's Dominions, and on the E. by Wardhá and Chándá districts of the Central Provinces. Wún is a wild hilly country intersected by offshoots from the Ajanta chain of mountains. For the most part the hills in the district are bare, or clothed only with dwarf teak or small jungle; but on the heights near Wún town the bamboo grows abundantly, and elsewhere small bamboos are found in the ravines. The Wardhá and Paingangá, which bound the district on the east and south, unite at its south-east corner. The Paingangá carries off nearly all the drainage of the district. Wún is rich in coal and iron ores. Of wild animals the tiger, leopard, and hyæna abound; bears, wolves, and jackals are also numerous; while small game is plentiful in all parts. There is a great want of means of communication; during the rains cart traffic is entirely suspended, the only means of transit at this time of the year being that afforded by water from the Wardhá for a short distance. The climate is enervating and unhealthy, and the average annual rainfall is about 41 inches.

Wún district forms part of the territory assigned by the nizam to the British Government under the treaties of 1853 and 1860. It was undisturbed during the mutiny of 1857. In 1886–87 the gross revenue amounted to £86,174, of which the land contributed £57,391. The population in 1881 was 392,102 (males 201,491, females 190,611); Hindus numbered 335,787, Mohammedans 17,031, Christians 127, and aboriginals 37,252. Wún, the chief town of the district (population 4207), has some fine temples.

WÜRTEMBERG,[1] or WÜRTTEMBERG, a European kingdom, forms a tolerably compact mass in the south-west angle of the German empire, of which it is the third factor in point of area and the fourth in point of population. In the south it is cleft by the long narrow territory of Hohenzollern, belonging to Prussia; and it encloses six small enclaves of Baden and Hohenzollern, while it owns seven small exclaves within the limits of these two states. It lies between 47° 34′ 48″ and 49° 35′ 17″ N. lat., and between 8° 15′ and 10° 30′ E. long. Its greatest length from north to south is 140 miles; its greatest breadth is 100 miles; its boundaries, almost entirely arbitrary, have a circuit of 1116 miles; and its total area is 7531 square miles, or about one twenty-eighth of the entire empire. It is bounded on the E. by Bavaria, and on the other three sides by Baden, with the exception of a short distance on the S., where it touches Hohenzollern and the Lake of Constance. For administrative purposes the country is divided into the four circles ("kreise") of the Neckar in the north-west, the Jagst in the north-east, the Black Forest in the south-west, and the Danube in the south-east.

See sketch map vol. iii. p. 224.

Würtemberg forms part of the South-German tableland, and is hilly rather than mountainous. In fact the undulating fertile terraces of Upper and Lower Swabia may be taken as the characteristic parts of this agricultural country. The usual estimates return one-fourth of the entire surface as "plain," less than one-third as "mountainous," and nearly one-half as "hilly." The average elevation above the sea-level is 1640 feet; the lowest point is at Böttingen (410 feet), where the Neckar quits the country; the highest is the Katzenkopf (3775 feet), on the Hornisgrinde, on the western border.

Mountains.

The chief mountains are the Black Forest on the west, the Swabian Jura or Rauhe Alb, stretching across the middle of the country from south-west to north-east, and the Adelegg Mountains in the extreme south-east, adjoining the Algau Alps in Bavaria. The Rauhe Alb or Alp slopes gradually down into the plateau on its south side, but on the north it is sometimes rugged and steep, and has its line broken by isolated projecting hills. The highest summits are in the south-west, viz., the Lemberg (3326 feet), Ober-Hohenberg (3312 feet), and Plettenberg (3293 feet). In a narrower sense the name Rauhe Alb is reserved for the eastern portion only of the Swabian Jura, lying between Hohenzollern and Bavaria; in the narrowest sense of all it is applied to a single group near Reutlingen. Most of the isolated summits above referred to (none of which are over 2630 feet) project from this eastern section; among them are the hills of Hohenstaufen, Teck, Mossingen, and Hohenzollern.

Black Forest.

The Black Forest (Germ. *Schwarzwald*), a mountain group or system deriving its name from the dark foliage of its pine forests, lies partly in Würtemberg and partly in Baden. Its general shape is that of a triangle, its base resting on the Rhine between the Lake of Constance and Basel, and its apex pointing north. It stretches along the east bank of the Rhine from Basel to Durlach, at a distance varying from 4 to 15 miles from the river, and parallel to the Vosges range on the west bank. The south, west, and north faces of the group are rugged and steep, but on the east it loses its mountainous character, and melts so gradually into the bounding plateau that it is difficult to assign it definite limits on that side. The total length of the Black Forest range is 93 miles, its breadth varies from 46 to 13 miles, and its area is 1913 square

[1] The origin of the name is disputed, though the once popular derivation from "Wirth am Berg" is universally rejected. Some authorities derive it from an old proper name Wirnto or Wirtino, others from a Celtic place-name Virodunum or Verdunum. Wirtenberc, Wirtenberg, Wirtemberc are early forms. Wirtemberg was long current, and in the latter half of the 16th century Würtemberg and Württemberg appear. The last was adopted in 1806 as the official spelling, though Würtemberg, the ordinary English spelling, is also common, and occurs sometimes in official documents and even on coins issued after that date.

miles. The average elevation decreases from south to north from 3280 feet to 2296 feet. The hills do not rise in peaks but in rounded summits and plateau-like masses and combs, separated from each other by the deep ravines of the streams.

The south part of the Black Forest was called *Mons Abnoba* by the Romans, and the whole was known to them from the 3rd century as *Silva Marciana*. The name *Silva Nigra* appears in mediæval Latin. This retired district, always somewhat overshadowed by the majestic beauties of the neighbouring Swiss Alps, was long unvisited and almost unheard of. Within comparatively recent years, however, it has become a favourite resort for summer visitors and tourists. Though not boasting any very striking mountain scenery, the Black Forest includes romantic and wild vales as well as smiling and picturesque valleys; and the beauty of its streams and waterfalls, its fragrant and shady forests, the quaintness of its sequestered villages, and the primitive simplicity of its inhabitants, who still retain their peculiar costume, are all objects of interest.

About two-thirds of the Black Forest belongs to Baden and the remaining third to Würtemberg; but it is convenient to disregard the political boundaries, and to consider it as formed of the Southern or Upper and the Northern or Lower Black Forest, separated from each other by the deep and romantic gorge of the Kinzig. The principal rocks are stratified gneiss and eruptive granite, though some of the summits are porphyritic. In the north and east those rocks are covered with a tolerably thick layer of variegated and red sandstone, which also appears, though not so abundantly, in the south and west. The kernel of the Southern Black Forest is the Feldberg (4803 feet), the highest point in the range, round which the other summits and masses are grouped. Among the chief summits are the Belchen (4640 feet), the Erzkasten (4218 feet), the Hochkopf (4150 feet), and the Kandelberg (4077 feet). The average height of the crest in this division of the forest is about 3300 feet. The chief streams are the Wutach, Alb, Wehra, Wiese, Neumagen, and Dreisam, all tributaries of the Rhine, and the Brege and Bregach, regarded as the head-waters of the Danube. On the eastern slopes lie the Feldsee, Titisee, Schuchsee, and numerous other small lakes, most of them in bleak and solitary situations among the extensive moors. The waterfall on the Gutach, at Triberg, is 170 feet high. The central height of the Northern Black Forest is the Hornisgrinde (3825 feet), on the border between Würtemberg and Baden. Other heights are the Hohe Ochenskopf (3460 feet), the Hohloh (3225 feet), and the Kniebishohen (3180 feet), with the Kniebis Pass. The average height of the crest is 2470 feet. The principal streams are the Kinzig and Murg, which join the Rhine, and the Glatt, Enz, and Nagold, which fall into the Neckar. The eastern slopes of this division also are sprinkled with lakes, the chief of which are the gloomy Mummelsee and the Wildesee.

As the name implies, the Schwarzwald is largely covered with forests, chiefly of pines and firs. Oaks, beeches, &c., also flourish, especially in the valleys and towards the west. The timber trade and its cognate industries are thus the chief resources of the inhabitants. The felled timber is floated in the form of rafts down the numerous streams to the Neckar or Rhine, where larger rafts are formed, sometimes requiring a crew of several hundred men, for the voyage to Holland, the principal market. The increase of railways has, however, considerably diminished the quantity of wood thus exported by water; and numerous sawmills within the limits of the forest are engaged in cutting timber into planks for export by rail. Perhaps, however, the most characteristic industry of the Black Forest is the manufacture of wooden clocks (often spoken of as "Dutch clocks"). This industry has long flourished in the district, and has recently been organized and extended, while considerable factories have been established at Furtwangen, Triberg, and other chief centres. Clocks to the value of about £2,000,000 are said to be annually produced, and 1400 persons are engaged in their manufacture. Musical-boxes are also extensively made here. Straw-plaiting occupies a large number of girls and women, especially in winter; and glass-blowing, charcoal-burning, and potash-boiling are also carried on. Agriculture is of no great importance, as the soil is poor, and the crops scanty. Cattle are kept in considerable numbers; they are driven up to the mountains in summer, and return to the valleys in autumn. The mining industry is quite insignificant; coal is worked to a small extent in and near Rotliegenden. In spite of their industrial resources, aided by the wealth introduced by tourists and visitors to the numerous mineral springs, the population of the Black Forest is too numerous to find support at home, and large numbers go abroad as pedlars, merchants, servants, &c.

The climate of the Schwarzwald is severe, but healthy. The forests cease at 4250 feet, and are succeeded by scanty grass and herbs. On many of the summits snow lies for ten months in the year, yet in some of the valleys vines, almonds, and chestnuts ripen. Wild boars, deer, hares, foxes, and various kinds of game are found. The carriage-roads follow the valleys, but innumerable footpaths lead in all directions through the magnificent woods. The Black Forest railway, opened in 1873, ascends the picturesque valleys of the Kinzig and Gutach by means of bridges, viaducts, and tunnels, often of the boldest construction.

To the south of the Rauhe Alb the plateau of Upper Swabia stretches to the Lake of Constance and eastwards across the Iller into Bavaria. Between the Alb and the Black Forest in the north-west are the fertile terraces of Lower Swabia, continued on the north-east by those of Franconia.

Rivers.

About 70 per cent. of Würtemberg belongs to the basin of the Rhine, and about 30 per cent. to that of the Danube. The principal river is the Neckar, which flows northward for 186 miles through the country to join the Rhine, and with its tributaries drains 57 per cent. of the kingdom. On the west it receives the Enz, swelled by the Nagold, and on the east the Fils, Rems, Murr, Kocher, and Jagst. The Danube flows from east to west across the south half of Würtemberg, a distance of 65 miles, a small section of which is in Hohenzollern. Just above Ulm it is joined by the Iller, which forms the boundary between Bavaria and Würtemberg for about 35 miles. The Tauber in the north-east joins the Main; the Argen and Schussen in the south enter the Lake of Constance. The lakes of Würtemberg, with the exception of those in the Black Forest, all lie south of the Danube. The largest is the Federsee (640 acres) near Buchau. About one-fifth of the Lake of Constance is reckoned to belong to Würtemberg. Mineral springs are abundant; the most famous spa is Wildbad, in the Black Forest.

Climate and soil.

The climate is temperate,—colder among the mountains in the south than in the north. The mean temperature varies at different points from 43° to 50° F. The abundant forests induce much rain, most of which falls in summer. The soil is on the whole fertile and well-cultivated; and for many centuries agriculture was almost the only resource of the inhabitants. Middle and Lower Swabia are the most fertile districts. The removal of burdens and restrictions in 1848 and 1849, and intelligent state-aid, combined with the formation of agricultural societies, have encouraged farming, but the practice of parcelling the land in minute patches among the members of the communities still retards progress. According to returns made in 1878, 45·2 per cent. of the land was under agriculture, 30·7 under forest, 19·4 in pasture, 1·2 in vineyards, and the remainder unproductive. Grain is produced in excess of the home demand.

Agriculture.

The following table shows the average annual extent (in acres) of the chief crops in 1878–1880, and the value:—

Crop	Acres	Value	Crop	Acres	Value
Spelt....	492,000	£3,001,410	Barley..	225,000	£1,288,200
Oats.....	334,400	1,475,470	Potatoes	194,900	718,600
Rye.....	96,800	493,475	Beetroot	49,242	340,200

Pease, maize, rape, hemp, flax, hops, and chicory are also produced in considerable quantity; tobacco is grown in the valley of the Neckar. Würtemberg is very rich in fruit trees of various kinds, and market-gardening flourishes near the larger towns and in the Remsthal. In 1880 there were 35,000 acres under vegetables. The cultivation of the vine is a highly important industry in the valleys of the Neckar and some of the other streams. In the period 1827–1882 the average annual area under vines was 63,327 acres, yielding 5,701,454 gallons of wine, worth £411,700. The best year was 1835, when 22,303,006 gallons were produced, the worst was 1854, with 1,696,376 gallons. Among the best Würtemberg wines are those known as Rothenberger, Türkheimer, Lämmler, Brodwasser, Käsberger, Elpinger, Schalksteiner, Weinsberger, Markelsheimer, Verrenberger, and Lindelberger. About one-third of the entire country is under forest, the greater proportion of which consist of deciduous trees (oaks, beeches, &c.). Coniferous trees are most numerous in the Black Forest, in Upper Swabia, and in the circle of Jagst. Most of the forests belong to the state or to public companies, and are carefully and skilfully managed. Large tracts in the Black Forest are in the hands of the "Schiffergesellschaft," a very ancient guild of timber merchants.

Live stock.

In 1883 Würtemberg contained 96,885 horses, 904,139 cattle, 550,104 sheep, 292,206 swine, and 54,876 goats. The breeding of horses commands a good deal of attention from Government, which maintains several stud-farms. Cattle, bred for export, are reared mainly in the Jagst and Danube divisions, sheep on and near the Alb.

erals.

Salt and iron are the only minerals of industrial importance found in Würtemberg, and both are worked almost entirely by Government. There are five Government salt-works (the chief of which are Friedrichshall and Wilhelmsglück), employing together 425 hands. In 1879–80 970,084 tons of salt were produced, two-thirds by mining. The salt industry only began to be of importance at the beginning of the present century. The iron industry on the other hand is of great antiquity, though it is much hampered by the entire absence of coal mines in Würtemberg. The chief fuel used in smelting the iron is wood or charcoal. Iron is mined at Neuenbürg, Freudenstetten, and, to a very limited extent, in the Black Forest. In 1877–80 15,546 tons of ore were raised by 110 miners, yielding about 33 per cent. of raw metal. Cement, gypsum, grindstones, millstones, building-stones, &c., are also found. The annual value of the minerals of all kinds raised in Würtemberg has been roughly estimated at about £350,000.

nu-
ures.

Until the close of the Napoleonic wars, Würtemberg was almost exclusively an agricultural and bucolic country; but since that period it has turned its attention to trade and manufactures, and perhaps now stands second only to Saxony among the German states in commercial and industrial activity. The want of coal is naturally a serious drawback, but it is to a certain extent compensated by the abundant water-power. The textile industry is carried on in most of its branches. Wool, from both domestic and foreign sources, is woven at Esslingen, Göppingen, and other towns in Lower Swabia; cotton is manufactured in Göppingen and Esslingen, and linen in Upper Swabia. Lace-making also flourishes in the last-named district, as a rural house-industry. The silk industry of Würtemberg, which employs about 1100 hands, though not very extensive in itself, is the most important silk industry in Germany. Ravensburg claims to have possessed the earliest paper-mill in Germany; paper-making is still important in that town and at Heidenheim, Heilbronn, Göppingen, and other places in Lower Swabia. Government owns six iron foundries and puddling works, the most important of which is at Wasseralfingen, where over 1000 hands are employed. The locomotive engines of Esslingen enjoy a wide reputation; and agricultural and other machinery, boilers, and tools of various kinds are also manufactured and exported by various towns. The organs of Ludwigsburg are well known; bell-founding is carried on at Stuttgart, Reutlingen, and Cannstatt; beetroot sugar and beer are considerable items in the list of annual produce;—wine has been already mentioned. The manufacture of chemicals at Stuttgart, Heilbronn, &c., is important.

de.

Trade has prospered since Würtemberg joined the North German Customs Union in 1834. The leading trading towns are Heilbronn, Stuttgart, Ulm, and Friedrichshafen. Cattle, horses, sheep, agricultural produce, timber, salt, and various manufactured goods are the chief exports; coal, hops, steel goods of various kinds, eggs, and poultry are among the chief imports. The book-trade of Stuttgart is very extensive; that town has been called the Leipsic of southern Germany.

mmu-
ation.

In 1887 991 miles of railway were open for traffic in Würtemberg. With the insignificant exception of two private lines, together no more than 31 miles long, all the railways are in the hands of the state. The Neckar, the Schussen, and the Lake of Constance are all navigable for boats; the Danube begins to be navigable at Ulm. The roads of Würtemberg are fairly good; the oldest are Roman. Würtemberg, like Bavaria, retained the control of its own postal and telegraph system on the foundation of the new German empire. In 1885 there were 1750 miles of telegraph wires in the kingdom.

pula-
n.

In 1885 the population of Würtemberg was 1,995,168, or one twenty-third of the total population of Germany on one twenty-eighth of its area. The average per square mile is 264·9. The following table shows the distribution of the population among the administrative districts, and their religion. The Neckar division contains most large towns.

Division.	Population.	Area in Square Miles.	Inhabitants per Square Mile.	Protestants in 1880.	Roman Catholics in 1880.
Neckar.......	639,470	1285	497·6	562,700	53,026
Black Forest	475,299	1843	257·8	351,144	119,750
Jagst..........	405,034	1984	204·1	280,374	122,987
Danube	475,365	2419	196·5	170,362	294,527

The people of the north-west belong to the Alemannic stock, those of the north-east to the Franconian, and those of the centre and south to the Swabian. According to the occupation census of 1882, the following were the numbers of those (including their families and dependants) engaged in the various departments of work:—in agriculture, forestry, &c., 942,924; in mining and industrial pursuits, 674,081; in trade and commerce, 143,258; in domestic and other service, 11,254; in professions, 95,712; "no returns," 90,240. In 1886 there were 3717 emigrants; in 1881 there were 11,470.

In 1885 there were 15 towns with more than 10,000 inhabitants, viz., Stuttgart (125,906), Ulm (33,610), Heilbronn (27,758), Esslingen (20,864), Cannstatt or Canstatt (18,031), Reutlingen (17,319), Ludwigsburg (16,201), Gmünd (15,321), Tübingen (12,551), Göppingen (12,102), and Ravensburg (11,482).

Religion.

About two-thirds of the population are Protestant. In 1880, when the total population was 1,971,118, there were 1,364,580 Protestants, 590,290 Roman Catholics, 13,331 Jews, 2817 of other Christian sects, and 98 "others." The Protestant church is controlled (under the minister of religion and education) by a consistory and a synod,—the latter being made up of the consistory and six general superintendents or "prelates" from six principal towns. But no laws are made or altered without the consent of a representative council, including both lay and clerical members. The Roman Catholic church is subject to the bishop of Rottenburg, in the archdiocese of Freiburg. Politically it is under a Roman Catholic council, appointed by Government. The Jews also since 1828 have been subject to a state-appointed council.

Educa-
tion.

Würtemberg is one of the best educated countries of Europe. School attendance is compulsory on children from seven to fourteen years of age, and young people from fourteen to eighteen must either attend the schools on Sunday or some other educational establishment. Every community of at least 30 families must have a school. The different churches attend to the schools of their own confession. There is a university at Tübingen, and a polytechnic school at Stuttgart. Technical schools of various kinds are established in many of the towns, in addition to a thorough equipment of gymnasia, commercial schools, seminaries, &c. The conservatory of music at Stuttgart enjoys a high reputation.

Consti-
tution.

Würtemberg is a constitutional monarchy and a member of the German empire, with 4 votes in the federal council and 17 in the imperial diet. The constitution rests on a law of 1819, amended in 1868 and 1874. The crown is hereditary, and conveys the simple title of king of Würtemberg. The king receives a civil list of £90,670, and the "apanages" of the crown amount to £14,900 more. The legislature is bi-cameral. The upper chamber (Standesherren) is composed of adult princes of the blood, heads of noble families from the rank of count (Graf) upwards, representatives of territories (Standesherrschaften) which possessed votes in the old German diet, and of life members nominated by the king. The number of this last class must not exceed one-third of the house. The lower house (Abgeordneten-Haus) has 93 members, viz., 13 noble landowners, elected by their peers (Ritterschaft), the 6 Protestant "prelates," the Roman Catholic bishop, and 2 other official Roman Catholic members, the chancellor of the university of Tübingen, 7 representatives from the chief towns, and 63 representatives from country districts. The king appoints the president of the upper chamber; since 1874 the lower chamber has elected its own chairman. Members are elected for six years by ballot; the suffrage is enjoyed by all male citizens. With the exception of the royal princes and the life-members of the upper house that reside in Stuttgart, the members of both houses receive a daily payment of 9m. 41pf. (9s. 5d.) each.

The highest executive is in the hands of a ministry of state (Staatsministerium), consisting of six ministers and the privy council, the members of which are nominated by the king. There are ministers of justice, war, finance, home affairs, religion and education, and foreign affairs, railways, and the royal household. The legal system is framed in imitation of that of the German empire. The judges of the supreme court for impeachments of ministers, &c., named the Staatsgerichtshof, are partly elected by the chambers and partly appointed by the king. The country is divided into four administrative "circles," subdivided into 64 "Oberämter," each of which is under an "Oberamtmann," assisted by an "Amtsversammlung" or local council. At the head of each of the four large divisions is a "Regierung."

Finance.

The official finance period of Würtemberg embraces two years. For 1885–87 the budget showed an annual income of £2,811,921, balanced by the expenditure, which included a payment of £2500 to a reserve fund. The chief sources of income were taxes (£1,392,893, including £691,773 of direct taxes), and public domains and monopolies (£1,095,336, including £662,385 from railways and £72,741 from post and telegraphs). The chief expenditure was on the interest (£875,525) and sinking fund (£122,873) of the public debt. This debt amounted in 1887 to £21,202,570, of which by far the greater proportion (£18,966,700) was incurred for constructing and buying railways. Most of it bears interest at 4 per cent.

Army.

In terms of the convention of 1870 the troops of Würtemberg form the 13th army corps in the imperial German army. They include 8 regiments of infantry, 4 of cavalry, and 2 of field artillery, &c. By the army law of March 11, 1887, the peace strength of the army was fixed at 773 officers, 18,815 men, and 64 cannon. The town of Ulm is one of the strongest fortresses in Germany.

History. The earliest known inhabitants of the country now called Würtemberg seem to have been Suevi. The Romans, who appeared first about 15 B.C., added the south part of the land to the province of Gaul in 84 A.D., and defended their positions there by a wall or rampart. About the beginning of the 3d century the Alemanni drove the Romans beyond the Rhine and the Danube; but they in their turn were conquered by the Franks under Clovis (496), and the land was divided between Rhenish Franconia and the duchy of Alemannia. The latter, however, disappears about 760, and its territories were administered for the Frankish monarchs by "grafs" or counts, until they were finally absorbed in the duchy of Swabia. The last duke of Swabia died in 1268, and a large share of his power and possessions fell into the hands of the "grafs" of Würtemberg, whose ancestral castle crowned a hill between Esslingen and Cannstatt. Tradition mentions a Conradus de Wirtemberc in 1090, but the earliest authentic count seems to have been Ulrich (1241–1265), who had large possessions in the valleys of the Neckar and the Rems. The power of this family grew steadily under successive counts; and in 1482 their possessions were declared indivisible. This early adoption of the principle of primogeniture saved Würtemberg from the wasting effects of those family feuds and jealousies which interfered so seriously with the development of some of the other German states. Eberhard V., surnamed "im Bart" (1482–1496), was one of the most energetic and illustrious rulers that Würtemberg ever had, and in 1495 his possessions were raised by the emperor to the dignity of an immediate imperial duchy. The reign of Ulrich I. (1498–1550), who succeeded to the duchy while still a child, was a most eventful period for the country, and many stories and traditions cluster round the name of this gifted and vigorous but unscrupulous and ambitious man. The extortions by which he sought to raise money for his extravagant pleasures excited a rising known as the "arme Konrad" (poor Conrad)—not unlike the rising of Wat Tyler in England; and by the treaty of Tübingen in 1514 his people undertook to pay his debts in exchange for various political privileges, which in effect laid the foundation of the constitutional liberties of the country. A few years later, however, Ulrich quarrelled with the Swabian league of imperial towns, and their army headed by the duke of Bavaria, who was incensed by Ulrich's ill-treatment of his wife, a Bavarian princess, invaded Würtemberg, expelled the duke, and in 1520 sold the duchy to Austria for 220,000 florins. Ulrich, however, found his opportunity in the discontent caused in Würtemberg by the military and religious oppression of Austria, and in the disturbed state of the empire during the Peasants' War, and the commotions excited by the Reformation. Aided by Philip of Hesse and other Protestant princes, he fought a victorious battle at Lauffen in 1534; and by the treaty of Kadan he was recognized once more as duke, though forced to acknowledge his duchy a fief of Austria. One of his first acts was to introduce the Reformation, and to endow Protestant churches and schools throughout his land. His connexion with the Schmalkaldian League once more cost him a temporary expulsion from his throne, but Charles V. reinstated him in 1547, though under severe conditions. Ulrich's son Christopher (1550–1568) introduced systems of law and church government (Grosse Kirchenordnung) which have endured in part to the present day. The establishment in this reign of a kind of standing committee to superintend the finances was the beginning of popular representation in the government, though its members belonged exclusively, of course, to the higher ranks. Frederick I. (1593–1608), an energetic and ambitious prince, induced the emperor Rudolph II. in 1599 to raise the duchy once more to the dignity of an immediate fief of the empire. In the reign of his successor, John Frederick (1608–1628), Würtemberg suffered severely from the Thirty Years' War, though the duke took no active share in that struggle. His son and successor, however, Eberhard III. (1628–1674), eagerly joined in it, but with disastrous effects. Würtemberg was occupied by imperial troops, the duke was driven into exile, and when the peace of Westphalia once more reinstated him he found but 50,000 subjects where he had left 400,000. In the reign of Eberhard IV. (1677–1733), who was but one year old when his father William died, Würtemberg made acquaintance with another destructive enemy. In 1688, 1692, 1703, and 1707 the French entered the country with fire and sword, annihilating whole villages in their ruthless brutality, and leaving deserts in their track. The depopulated country eagerly afforded a welcome and a home to the Waldensians, who had been driven from their valleys by the duke of Savoy in 1699. Charles Alexander, who became duke in 1733, had embraced the Roman Catholic faith when an officer in the Austrian service, while his favourite minister was the unscrupulous Jew Süss Oppenheimer. The duke, instigated by his minister, was believed to aim at the suppression of the diet, and at the introduction of the Romish faith, but Charles's sudden death in 1737 put an abrupt end to these plans. Süss Oppenheimer was hanged by the regent, before the next duke, Charles Eugene (1737–1793) came of age in 1744. The prince was gifted but vicious, and he soon fell into the hands of unworthy favourites. His whole reign was disturbed by dissensions betwixt the ruler and the ruled, in which the intervention of foreign powers (Prussia and England) was invoked, though in vain, by the unhappy people. Alarmed by the gathering discontent, Charles made a few concessions in his old age. Frederick Eugene (1795–1797), a brother of Charles Eugene, had been brought up at the court of Frederick the Great, whose niece he married. His children were, through this influence, educated as Protestants, and the royal family of Würtemberg have been Protestants since his death.

Frederick II. (1797–1816) resembled the first of his name in becoming embroiled with the diet. He declared war against France in defiance of the wishes of his people, and when the French invaded the country he retired to Erlangen, till after the peace of Lunéville (1801). By a private treaty at the same date, he exchanged Montbéliard (which had belonged to Würtemberg since 1418) and his Alsatian possessions for nine imperial towns and other territories, amounting in all to 850 square miles, with 124,000 inhabitants. He accepted also the title of elector from Napoleon. The newly acquired districts were not incorporated with his former possessions, but remained separate under the name "New Würtemberg." The new district had no diet. This was the first of a series of transactions with the national enemy, which swelled Frederick's territory, though they added but little to his credit. In 1805 Würtemberg took up arms on the side of France, and the elector was rewarded at the peace of Pressburg by various Austrian possessions in Swabia, and the title of king. On January 1, 1806, Frederick assumed the royal style, abrogated the constitution, and united old and new Würtemberg. He subsequently united church and state, and proclaimed religious equality. In 1806 King Frederick I. joined the Confederation of the Rhine, and received fresh territories, with 160,000 inhabitants; and the peace of Vienna brought 110,000 new subjects under his sceptre. But he had to perform his part of the bargain by joining Napoleon in his campaigns against Prussia, Austria, and Russia. Of 16,000 Würtembergers who marched to Moscow, only a few hundred returned. When fortune turned, Frederick with ready adroitness changed sides, and managed to preserve his royal title and most of his new-won lands by joining the allies immediately after the battle of Leipsic.

Würtemberg had been promised a constitution by Frederick before he died in 1816, but a good deal of discussion took place before it was granted in 1819 by William I. (1816–1864). A period of quiet now set in, and the educational condition of the kingdom, its agriculture, and its trade and manufactures began to receive earnest attention. The desire for political freedom had by no means been satisfied by the constitution of 1819, and a "liberal opposition" began to make itself felt about 1830. The agitation of 1848 did not leave Würtemberg undisturbed, though no scenes of actual violence took place in the kingdom. The conservative ministry granted freedom of the press and other privileges, too late, however, to avert their fall. The king was compelled to call the liberals to power in March 1848, and a new liberal constitution was granted. But as soon as the stress was over the "March ministry" was dismissed, and the reactionary party were again in the ascendant. By a high-handed interference with recently granted popular rights on the part of the king and his ministers a servile diet was assembled in 1851, which yielded up without hesitation all that had been gained since 1848. The constitution of 1819 was reinstituted, and it has remained, with only a few modifications, ever since. In 1864 Charles ascended the throne. In the duel between Prussia and Austria for supremacy in Germany, the sympathies of the rulers of Würtemberg were always on the side of the latter, although the country entered the Customs Union under Prussia's protection in 1864. In 1866 Würtemberg took up arms on behalf of Austria; but the Würtemberg troops were defeated at Tauberbischofsheim, three weeks after Sadowa, and its ministers sued for peace. Prussia exacted an indemnity of 8 million florins, and Würtemberg struck a secret offensive and defensive treaty with its conqueror. In 1870 this kingdom shared in the national enthusiasm which swept over Germany when France declared war; and its troops had a creditable share in the memorable campaign of 1870–71. Since the foundation of the present German empire, the separate history of Würtemberg has been of almost exclusively local interest. The tendency of legislation has been, on the whole, liberal.

A very full and minute description of Würtemberg, together with copious lists of authorities on all subjects connected with it, will be found in *Das Königreich Württemberg*, Stuttgart, 1882 *sq*, officially publi hed by the Königliches Statistisch-Topographisches Bureau. (F. MU.)

WURTZ, CHARLES ADOLPHE (1817–1884), chemist, was born at Strasburg on November 26, 1817. His father, Jean Jacques Wurtz, was then Lutheran pastor at the small village of Wolfisheim near Strasburg. His mother, Sophie Kreiss, was the sister of Theodore Kreiss, professor of Greek at the Protestant gymnasium of Strasburg, and of Adolphe Kreiss, a Lutheran pastor. When Wurtz was nine years old his father was translated to the church of St Pierre le Jeune in Strasburg, and died there in 1845. Madame Wurtz, after the death of her husband, remained at Strasburg with her brother Theodore, and after his death lived with her son Adolphe in Paris till her own death in 1878.

Wurtz was educated first at Wolfisheim and afterwards at the Protestant gymnasium of Strasburg. There he obtained several prizes, but seems rather to have disappointed his father, who said he would never turn out anything extraordinary. He took special interest in those studies which bore upon nature; in 1828 he took part in a botanical class with excursions, which developed his taste for natural science.

His education owed more perhaps to his home circle than to the school. His learned and pious father, his more generally cultured uncles, and the circle of friends attracted by them opened to him a wide view of what there is for a man to know. His holidays were mostly spent at the house of a grand-aunt at Rothau, where he learned to know the hills and woods of Alsace, and amused himself in the spinning, weaving, bleaching, and printing works in the neighbourhood. In 1834 he left the gymnasium with the degree of bachelier-ès-lettres. His father seems to have wished him to devote himself to the church. But he had already made his choice. For some time he had fitted up a sort of laboratory in the washing-house, and had there repeated the experiments he had seen performed in the class-rooms of the gymnasium. His father took no interest in science, but consented to his study of medicine as next best to theology. He went through his studies conscientiously, and passed all his examinations with credit, but of course devoted himself specially to the chemical side of his profession. In 1839 he was appointed superintendent of practical chemistry in the faculty of medicine under Professor Cailliot. He graduated as M.D. 13th August 1843, the title of his thesis being "On Albumin and Fibrin." He then went for a year to Giessen, to study under Liebig. There he made the acquaintance of Hofmann, Strecker, and Kopp. On leaving Giessen he went to Paris, where he worked in Dumas's private laboratory, and in 1845 was appointed assistant to Dumas in the École de Médecine. In 1847, on his presentation of a thesis "On Pyrogenic Bodies," he was appointed "professor aggrégé," and in 1849 he gave the lectures on organic chemistry in place of Dumas. His laboratory in the École Pratique de la Faculté de Médecine was very inconvenient and ill fitted up; he therefore, in 1850, along with Dollfus and Verdeil, who had just returned to Paris from Giessen, opened a private laboratory in the Rue Garancière. The adventure was successful in a scientific sense as long as it lasted; but unfortunately the three chemists had neglected to secure fixity of tenure, the house was sold, and they had to retire and sell their furnishings. The same year Wurtz was appointed professor of chemistry in the Institut Agronomique, then founded at Versailles. But here also the want of fixity was felt. Louis Napoleon abolished the Institut in 1852. In 1853 Dumas resigned the chair of organic chemistry in the faculty of medicine; at the same time the chair of mineral chemistry and toxicology became vacant by the death of Orfila; the two chairs were united, and Wurtz was appointed to the post thus constituted. In 1866 he was made dean of the faculty of medicine, and used his influence for the rearrangement and reconstruction of the buildings devoted to scientific teaching. In 1874 he persuaded the Government to found a chair of organic chemistry at the Sorbonne, and resigned his office of dean, retaining the title of honorary dean. At the Sorbonne he had a smaller but better prepared audience than at the École de Médecine. But he had great difficulty in persuading the Government to build him a suitable laboratory, and indeed did not live to see the new laboratory opened. He was appointed senator in 1881. He was one of the founders of the Chemical Society of Paris, of which he was the first secretary, and was three times president. He was elected member of the Academy of Sciences in 1867, in succession to Pelouze. He was vice-president in 1880 and president in the following year. He died, after a short illness, May 12, 1884. Wurtz was an honorary member of nearly every scientific society in Europe. In 1878 he gave the Faraday lecture of the Chemical Society of London, and in 1881 was awarded the Copley medal by the Royal Society of London. Through life he remained warmly attached to the church of his fathers, and took a practical interest in its affairs.

Wurtz's work is chiefly to be found in the *Annales de Chimie et de Physique*, in the *Comptes Rendus*, and in the *Bulletin de la Société Chimique*. The following is a short outline of his most important discoveries. First, with respect to the constitution of hypophosphorous and phosphorous acids, he showed that the salts of these acids all contain the elements of water, and proposed formulæ for them, in which the salt radical is represented as containing hydrogen. These formulæ, translated, of course, into the modern language, which Wurtz did so much to introduce, are still used as the best representations of the constitution of these salts. In the course of this investigation he discovered the curious and interesting compound cuprous hydride. He also discovered sulphophosphoric acid and the oxychloride of phosphorus. His next great work was on cyanuric acid. He discovered the cyanic ethers $(R-N=C=O)$, and from them obtained the mono-alkyl ureas. From the cyanic ethers he produced a class of substances which opened the way into a new field of organic chemistry. On treating these ethers with caustic potash he obtained potassium carbonate and an ammoniacal vapour. These vapours he soon recognized as ammonia, in which an equivalent of hydrogen had been replaced by methylium, CH_3, or ethylium, C_2H_5. By acting on the cyanic ethers with his new bases he obtained the dialkyl ureas. In 1855 he reviewed the various substances that had been obtained from glycerin, and came to the conclusion that glycerin is a body of alcoholic nature formed on the type of three molecules of water, as common alcohol is on that of one. This speculation led him in 1856 to the discovery of the glycols, alcoholic bodies similarly related to the type of two molecules of water. This discovery he worked out very thoroughly, in investigations on oxide of ethylene and the polyethylenic alcohols. The oxidation of the glycols led him to homologues of lactic acid, and to a discussion of the constitution of the latter. On this question a controversy arose with Kolbe, in the course of which many important facts were discovered, and valuable additions were made to chemical theory. In 1867 Wurtz obtained neurine synthetically, by the action of trimethylamine on glycol-chlorhydrine. In 1873 he discovered aldol, $CH_3-CH(OH)-CH_2-CHO$, and pointed out its double character as at once an alcohol and an aldehyde.

His investigations on the olefines had led him to the discovery of the peculiar behaviour of the substance called by him chlorhydrate of amylene and of its analogues, when the temperature of their vapour is raised. The gradual passage from a gas of approximately normal vapour density to one of half the normal density was used by him as a powerful argument in favour of the opinion that abnormal vapour densities, such as those of sal-ammoniac and pentachloride of phosphorus, are to be explained by dissociation. By experiments at low temperatures and pressures he obtained nearly the normal density in the case of the pentachloride of phosphorus, and showed how the dissociation depends on the temperature and pressure. He took an active part in the discussion as to the dissociation of the vapour of hydrate of chloral, in which H. Sainte-Claire Deville and M. Berthelot were his chief opponents. By well-chosen experiments he brought to light the facts involved, and stated the case for dissociation in a very clear and to most minds very convincing way.

Wurtz for twenty years, from 1852 to 1872, published in the *Annales de Chimie et de Physique* abstracts of chemical work done out of France. In 1868 he began, with the assistance of many French chemists, the publication of the *Dictionnaire de Chimie Pure et Appliquée*. This great work, many important articles in which were written by himself, was finished in 1878. (Two volumes of appendix have since been added.) In 1864 he published a book in two volumes entitled *Chimie Médicale*, and in 1867 *Leçons Élémentaires de Chimie Moderne*, an excellent little text-book which has gone through five editions in French, and has been translated into English by Prof. Greene. In 1879 appeared his *Théorie Atomique*, and in 1885 *Traité de Chimie Biologique*. This was his last work;

he corrected the last proof-sheets himself, and the last part of the book was published a few weeks after his death.

A full account of the life and work of Wurtz, with a list of his published books and papers, will be found in the obituary notice by M. Friedel in the *Bulletin de la Société Chimique*, vol. xliii., i.–lxxx., 1885. (A. C. B.)

WÜRZBURG, or WIRZBERG, the fourth largest town in Bavaria, and the chief town of the district of Lower Franconia in the north-west of that kingdom, is situated on both sides of the Main, 60 miles south-east of Frankfort. An ancient stone bridge (1474–1607), 650 feet long, and adorned with statues of saints, connects the two parts of the town. Würzburg is quaintly and irregularly built; many of the houses are interesting specimens of mediæval antiquity; and the numerous old churches recall the fact that it was long the capital of an ecclesiastical principality. The principal church is the imposing Romanesque cathedral, a basilica with transepts, begun in 1042 and consecrated in 1189. The four towers, however, date from 1240, the (rococo) façade from 1711–19, and the dome from 1731. The spacious transepts terminate in apses. The beautiful Marienkapelle, a Gothic edifice of 1377–1441, was restored in 1856; it is embellished with fourteen statues by Tilman Riemenschneider, who died at Würzburg in 1531. The Stifthaug church, with two towers and a lofty dome, was built in the Italian Renaissance style in 1670–91. The bones of St Kilian, patron saint of Würzburg, are preserved in the Neumünster church, which dates from the 11th century; Walther von der Vogelweide is buried in the adjoining cloisters. The church of St Burkard is externally one of the best preserved architectural monuments in the city. It was built in 1033–42, in the Romanesque style, and was restored in 1168. The Late Gothic choir dates from 1494–97. The Neubaukirche, or university church, curiously unites a Gothic exterior with a Classical interior. The Protestant church of St Stephen (1782–89) originally belonged to a Benedictine abbey. Of the secular buildings in Würzburg the most conspicuous is the royal (formerly episcopal) palace, a huge and magnificent edifice built in 1720–44 in imitation of Versailles. The Julius hospital, a large and richly endowed institution affording food and lodging to 600 persons daily, was founded in 1576 by Bishop Julius Echter von Mespelbrunn. The quaint town-house dates in part from 1456. Among the other chief buildings are the Government offices, the theatre, the Maxschule, the observatory, and the various university buildings. A university was founded at Würzburg in 1403, but only existed for a few years. The present university was founded by Bishop Julius in 1582. Owing to its connexion with the large hospital, its laboratories, and its rich anatomical collections, the medical faculty speedily became famous, and has remained the most important faculty at Würzburg ever since. The university library contains 200,000 volumes, and there are numerous scientific institutes connected with the main institution. In 1886 it was attended by 800 students (600 medical), and had a teaching staff of 70 professors and lecturers. The other educational establishments of Würzburg are numerous; among them is a music institute, which gives instruction gratis in vocal and instrumental music.

Würzburg is surrounded by vineyards, which yield some of the best wines in Germany; it also carries on the manufacture of beer, leather, tobacco, and railway carriages. The environs are highly picturesque as well as fertile; the most interesting point is the Leistenburg, on which stands the fortress of Marienburg, the residence of the bishops until 1720. This position was occupied by a Roman fort, and seems to have been fortified by Bishop Conrad, who died in 1203. The population of Würzburg in 1885 was 55,100, of whom 9000 were Protestants.

Würzburg is one of the most ancient and interesting towns of Germany, and as the capital of an immediate episcopal principality long played an important part in the history of the empire. The first bishop was Burkard, consecrated in 741, though the town seems to have existed in the previous century. The bishops soon acquired a considerable share of temporal power, and in the 15th century enjoyed the title of dukes of East Franconia. The citizens of Würzburg espoused the cause of Henry IV. against their bishop, and in 1086 the town was twice taken by the contending armies. Various imperial diets were held in Würzburg, the chief being those of 1180, when Henry the Lion was placed under the ban, and of 1209, when Otto IV. was betrothed. In 1525 the rebellious peasants under Götz von Berlichingen took the town, but were repulsed from the Marienburg, and were defeated with great slaughter by the Swabian forces. The bishopric, which at one time embraced an area of 190 square miles, with 250,000 inhabitants, was secularized at the peace of Lunéville, and passed to Bavaria in 1803. The peace of Pressburg (1805) transferred it, under the name of an electorate, to the grand-duke of Tuscany, who joined the Confederation of the Rhine, assuming the title grand-duke of Würzburg. The congress of Vienna restored it to Bavaria. Archduke Charles defeated Marshal Jourdan near Würzburg in 1796; and in 1866 the bombarding of the citadel was the last warlike act of the Prussian army of the Main. The Würzburg conference is the name given to the meeting of the representatives of the smaller German states in November 1859 to devise some means of mutual support in the imperial diet. *Wircebirgum* is the old Latin form of the name of the town; *Herbipolis* (herb-town; Wurz is the German for root or herb) appears in the 12th century.

WYANDOTTE, formerly a city and the county seat of Wyandotte county, Kansas, United States, had in 1886 a population of 13,840. In that year Armourdale (2634) and Kansas City, Kansas (4755), were consolidated with Wyandotte under the name of Kansas City, Kansas. The city is situated upon the west bank of the Missouri river and north bank of the Kansas river, in eastern Kansas, immediately adjoining the State line, and separated by it from Kansas City, Missouri. The surrounding country is a fertile and highly cultivated prairie. The city is intersected by several railroads, most of which are branches of the Missouri Pacific system. It is rather irregularly laid out, being an aggregation of independent settlements, and its municipal improvements are in a formative stage. The population in 1886 was 21,229 (about 16 per cent. of foreign birth and 20 per cent. coloured). Kansas City is the third in the State in point of population.

WYAT, SIR THOMAS (1503–1542), is an important figure historically in English literature, although his poetry does not rank very high in intrinsic value. He was undoubtedly the leader, the first in point of time, and the acknowledged master of "the company of courtly makers" who in the reign of Henry VIII., under Italian influence, transformed the character of English poetry. SURREY (*q.v.*) is usually associated with Wyat in this leadership, and his influence was probably greater, as his verse was superior in fluency, dexterity, and force. But the priority, the actual lead, undoubtedly belongs to Wyat, who was Surrey's senior by fourteen years, and was celebrated by the younger poet with all the homage of an enthusiastic disciple. That there should ever have been any doubt upon the point arises from the fact that their poems were not printed till several years after both were dead, that they were then printed together in the same collection (*Tottel's Miscellany*, 1557), and that Surrey's name was placed first on the title-page by the publisher, while his poems preceded Wyat's in the *Miscellany*. It is to Wyat that the praise rightfully belongs of being the first writer of sonnets in English. He is also our first writer of satires in the classical form. Apart from the question of their services as pioneers of new metres and a new vein of love sentiment, there is a wide difference in character between Surrey and Wyat. Their poetry strongly corroborates the evidence of their portraits by Holbein. Wyat is much less bright and radiant, of a grave, sedate cast, with a vein of humorous melancholy and satiric observation. It is not known for certain that Wyat ever travelled in Italy, but the probability that he did so is strong. Wyat's father, Sir Henry, the owner of Allington castle in Kent, was a prominent figure at the court of Henry VII., and a residence at one of the Italian courts was then a usual part of the education of a young man of rank. Wyat was born in 1503, and we have no record of him between his taking his bachelor's degree at Cambridge at the age of fifteen and his being sworn a member of the privy council at the age of thirty, except that he took part in the tournament at a great feast held by the king at Greenwich in 1525. He was knighted in 1536, and twice sent as ambassador to the emperor, a strong proof of his repute as a statesman and diplomatist. He died in 1542, in the course of a hurried journey to Falmouth to meet and convoy an ambassador from the emperor. Wyat is commonly known as Sir Thomas Wyat the elder, to distinguish him from his son of the same name, who headed an insurrection against Mary in 1554, and paid the penalty of failure.

WYATT, James (1743–1813), a popular architect, born in Staffordshire in 1743, who lived at a time when architectural taste was at its lowest ebb. He spent some time in Rome making measured drawings of the classical remains, and on his return to England became one of the most successful architects of his time, and eventually was elected president of the Royal Academy. On the death of Sir William Chambers in 1796, Wyatt was appointed surveyor to the Board of Works. His chief works were a number of buildings at Kew for George III., all in the worst taste, and Fonthill Abbey for the rich and eccentric Mr Beckford, author of *Vathek*. This enormous and costly mansion, a sort of theatrical parody of a Gothic abbey, was erected in an incredibly short space of time by relays of workmen labouring day and night. The massive and lofty tower collapsed soon after it was finished, and a great part of this extravagant architectural freak has since been pulled down. James Wyatt was killed by a fall from his carriage in 1813.

WYCHERLEY, William (*c.* 1640–1715), the typical "Restoration dramatist," and one of the greatest masters of the comedy of repartee, was born about 1640 at Clive, near Shrewsbury, where for several generations his family had been settled on a moderate estate of about £600 a year. Like Vanbrugh, Wycherley spent his early years in France, whither, at the age of fifteen, he was sent to be educated in the very heart of the "precious" circle who disported on the banks of the Charente. Wycherley's friend, Major Pack, tells us that his hero "improved, with the greatest refinements," the "extraordinary talents" for which he was "obliged to nature." Although the harmless affectations of the Rambouillets and Montausiers, among whom he was thrown, are certainly not chargeable with the "refinements" of Wycherley's comedies—comedies which caused even his great admirer Voltaire to say afterwards of them, "Il semble que les Anglais prennent trop de liberté et que les Françaises n'en prennent pas assez"—these same affectations seem to have been much more potent in regard to the "refinements" of Wycherley's religion.

Wycherley, though a man of far more intellectual power than is generally supposed, was a fine gentleman first, a responsible being afterwards. Hence under the manipulations of the heroine of the "Garland" he turned from the Protestantism of his fathers to Romanism—turned at once, and with the same easy alacrity as afterwards, at Oxford, he turned back to Protestantism under the manipulations of such an accomplished master in the art of turning as Bishop Barlow. And if, as Macaulay hints, Wycherley's turning back to Romanism once more had something to do with the patronage and unwonted liberality of James II., this merely proves that the deity he worshipped was the deity of the "polite world" of his time—gentility. Moreover, as a professional fine gentleman, at a period when, as the genial Major Pack says, "the amours of Britain would furnish as diverting memoirs, if well related, as those of France published by Rabutin, or those of Nero's court writ by Petronius," Wycherley was obliged to be a loose liver. But, for all that, Wycherley's sobriquet of "Manly Wycherley" seems to have been fairly earned by him, earned by that frank and straightforward way of confronting life which, according to Pope and Swift, characterized also his brilliant successor Vanbrugh.

That effort of Wycherley's to bring to Buckingham's notice the case of Samuel Butler (so shamefully neglected by the court Butler had served) shows that the writer of even such heartless plays as *The Country Wife* may be familiar with generous impulses, while his uncompromising lines in defence of Buckingham, when the duke in his turn fell into trouble, show that the inventor of so shameless a fraud as that which forms the pivot of *The Plain Dealer* may in actual life possess that passion for fairplay which is believed to be a specially English quality. But among the "ninety-nine" religions with which Voltaire accredited England there is one whose permanency has never been shaken—the worship of gentility. To this Wycherley remained as faithful to the day of his death as Congreve himself. And, if his relations to that "other world beyond this," which the Puritans had adopted, were liable to change with his environments, it was because that "other world" was really out of fashion altogether.

Wycherley's university career seems also to have been influenced by the same causes. Although Puritanism had certainly not contaminated the universities, yet English "quality and politeness" (to use Major Pack's words) have always, since the great rebellion, been rather ashamed of possessing too much learning. As a fellow-commoner of Queen's College, Oxford, Wycherley only lived (according to Wood) in the provost's lodgings, being entered in the public library under the title of "Philosophiæ Studiosus" in July 1660. And he does not seem to have matriculated or to have taken a degree.

Nor when, on quitting Oxford, he entered himself of the Middle Temple, did he give any more attention to the dry study of the law than was proper to one so warmly caressed "by the persons most eminent for their quality or politeness." Pleasure and the stage were alone open to him, and in 1672 was produced, at the Theatre Royal, *Love in a Wood*. With regard to this comedy Wycherley told Pope—told him "over and over" till Pope believed him—believed him, at least, until they quarrelled about Wycherley's verses—that he wrote it the year before he went to Oxford. But we need not believe him: the worst witness against a man is mostly himself. To pose as the wicked boy of genius has been the foolish ambition of many writers, but on inquiry it will generally be found that these inkhorn Lotharios are not nearly so wicked as they would have us believe. When Wycherley charges himself with having written, as a boy of nineteen, scenes so callous and so depraved that even Barbara Palmer's appetite for profligacy was, if not satisfied, appeased, there is, we repeat, no need to believe him. Indeed, there is every reason to disbelieve him,—not for the reasons advanced by Macaulay, however, who in challenging Wycherley's date does not go nearly deep enough. Macaulay points to the allusions in the play to gentlemen's periwigs, to guineas, to the vests which Charles ordered to be worn at court, to the great fire, &c., as showing that the comedy could not have been written the year before the author went to Oxford. We must remember, however, that even if the play had been written in that year, and delayed in its production till 1672, it is exactly this kind of allusion to recent events which any dramatist with an eye to freshness of colour would be certain to weave into his dialogue. It is not that "the whole air and spirit of the piece belong to a period subsequent to that mentioned by Wycherley," but that "the whole air and spirit of the piece" belong to a man,—an experienced and hardened young man of the world,—and not to a boy who would fain pose as an experienced and hardened young man of the world. The real defence of Wycherley against his foolish impeachment of himself is this, that *Love in a Wood*, howsoever inferior in structure and in all the artistic economies to *The Country Wife* and *The Plain Dealer*, contains scenes which no inexperienced boy could have written—scenes which, not for moral hardness merely, but often for real dramatic ripeness, are almost the strongest to be found amongst his four plays. With regard to dramatic ripeness, indeed, if we were asked to indicate the finest touch in all Wycherley, we should very likely select a speech in the third scene of the third act of this very play, where the vain, foolish, and boastful rake Dapperwit, having taken his friend to see his mistress for the express purpose of advertising his lordship over her, is coolly denied by her and insolently repulsed. "I think," says Dapperwit, "women take inconstancy from me worse than from any man breathing."

Now, does the subsequent development of Wycherley's dramatic genius lead us to believe that, at nineteen, he could have given this touch, worthy of the hand that drew Malvolio? Is there anything in his two masterpieces—*The Country Wife* or *The Plain Dealer*—that makes it credible that Wycherley, the boy, could have thus delineated by a single quiet touch vanity as a chain-armour which no shaft can pierce—vanity, that is to say, in its perfect development? However, Macaulay (forgetting that, among the myriad vanities of the writing fraternity, this of pretending to an early development of intellectual powers that ought not to be, even if they could be, developed early is at once the most comic and the most common) is rather too severe upon Wycherley's disingenuousness in regard to the dates of his plays. That the writer of a play far more daring than Etheredge's *She Would if She Could*—and far more brilliant too—should at once become the talk of Charles's court was inevitable; equally inevitable was it that the author of the song at the end of the first act, in praise of harlots and their offspring, should touch to its depths the soul of the duchess of Cleveland. Possibly Wycherley intended this famous song as a glorification of Her Grace and her profession, for he seems to have been more delighted than surprised when, as he passed in his coach through Pall Mall, he heard the duchess address him from her coach window as a "rascal," a "villain," and as a son of the very kind of lady his song had lauded. For his answer was perfect in its readiness: "Madam, you have been pleased to bestow a title on me which belongs only to the fortunate." Perceiving that Her Grace received the compliment in the spirit in which it was meant, he lost no time in calling upon her, and was from that moment the recipient of those "favours" to which he alludes with pride in the dedication of the play to her. Voltaire's story (in his *Letters on the English Nation*) that Her Grace used to go to Wycherley's chambers in the Temple disguised as a country wench, in a straw hat, with pattens on and a basket in her hand, may be apocryphal, —very likely it is,—for disguise was quite superfluous in the case of the mistress of Charles II. and Jacob Hall,—but it at least shows how general was the opinion that, under such patronage as this, Wycherley's fortune as poet and dramatist, "eminent for his quality and politeness," was now made.

Charles, who had determined to bring up his son, the duke of Richmond, like a prince, was desirous of securing for tutor a man so entirely qualified as was Wycherley to impart what was then recognized as the princely education, and it seems pretty clear that, but for the accident, to which we shall have to recur, of his meeting the countess of Drogheda at Bath and secretly marrying her, the education of the young man would actually have been entrusted by his father to Wycherley as a reward for the dramatist's having written *Love in a Wood*.

Whether Wycherley's experiences as a naval officer, which he alludes to in his lines "On a Sea Fight which the Author was in betwixt the English and the Dutch," occurred before or after the production of *Love in a Wood* is a point upon which opinions differ, but on the whole we are inclined to agree with Macaulay, against Leigh Hunt, that these experiences took place not only after the production of *Love in a Wood* but after the production of *The Gentleman Dancing Master*, in 1673. We also think, with Macaulay, that he went to sea simply because it was the "polite" thing to do so—simply because, as he himself in the epilogue to *The Gentleman Dancing Master* says, "all gentlemen must pack to sea."

This second comedy is inferior to *Love in a Wood*, and for the reasons already discussed in connexion with the works of another dramatist (see VANBRUGH). In *The Relapse*, however, the artistic mistake of blending comedy and farce damages a splendid play, but leaves it a splendid play still. In *The Gentleman Dancing Master* this mingling of discordant elements destroys a play that would never under any circumstances have been strong,—a play nevertheless which abounds in animal spirits, and is luminous here and there with true dramatic points.

It is, however, on his two last comedies—*The Country Wife* and *The Plain Dealer*—that must rest Wycherley's fame as a master of that comedy of repartee which, inaugurated by Etheredge, and afterwards brought to perfection by Congreve and Vanbrugh, supplanted the humoristic comedy of the Elizabethans. *The Country Wife*, produced in 1675, is so full of wit, ingenuity, animal spirits, and conventional humour that, had it not been for its motive—a motive which in any healthy state of society must always be as repulsive to the most lax as to the most moral reader—it would probably have survived as long as the acted drama remained a literary form in England. So strong, indeed, is the hand that could draw such a character as Marjory Pinchwife (the undoubted original not only of Congreve's Miss Prue but of Vanbrugh's Hoyden), such a character as Sparkish (the undoubted original of Congreve's Tattle), such a character as Horner (the undoubted original of all those cool impudent rakes with whom our stage has since been familiar), that Wycherley is certainly entitled to a place alongside Congreve and Vanbrugh. And, indeed, if priority of date is to have its fair and full weight, it seems difficult to challenge Prof. Spalding's dictum that Wycherley is "the most vigorous of the set."

In order to do justice to the life and brilliance of *The Country Wife* we have only to compare it with *The Country Girl*, afterwards made famous by the acting of Mrs Jordan, that Bowdlerized form of *The Country Wife* in which Garrick, with an object more praiseworthy than his success, endeavoured to free it of its load of unparalleled licentiousness by disturbing and sweetening the motive,—even as Voltaire afterwards (with an object also more praiseworthy than his success) endeavoured to disturb and sweeten the motive of *The Plain Dealer* in *La Prude*. While the two Bowdlerized forms of Garrick and Voltaire are as dull as the *Æsop* of Boursault, the texture of Wycherley's scandalous dialogue would seem to scintillate with the changing hues of shot silk or of the neck of a pigeon or of a shaken prism, were it not that the many-coloured lights rather suggest the miasmatic radiance of a foul ditch shimmering in the sun. It is easy to share Macaulay's indignation at Wycherley's satyr-like defilement of art, and yet, at the same time, to protest against that disparagement of their literary riches which nullifies the value of Macaulay's criticism. And scarcely inferior to *The Country Wife* is *The Plain Dealer*, produced in 1677,—a play of which Voltaire said, "Je ne connais point de comédie chez les anciens ni chez les moderns ou il y ait autant d'esprit." Strong language, no doubt; but Voltaire has prevented it from seeming too strong by turning the play into *La Prude*, and offering us in that a subject for comparison. No one has pointed out the immense influence of this comedy, as regards manipulation of dialogue, upon all our subsequent comedies of repartee, from those of Congreve and Vanbrugh to those of Douglas Jerrold and T. W. Robertson; and, as to characters, he who wants to trace the ancestry of Tony Lumpkin and Mrs Hardcastle has only to turn to Jerry Blackacre and his mother, while Manly (for whom Wycherley's early patron, the duke of Montausier, sat), though he is perhaps overdone, has dominated this kind of stage character ever since. If but few readers know how constantly the blunt sententious utterances of this character are reappearing, not on the stage alone, but in the novel and even in poetry, it is because a play whose motive is monstrous and intolerable can only live in a monstrous and intolerable state of society; it is because Wycherley's genius was followed by Nemesis, who always dogs the footsteps of the defiler of literary art. When Burns said—

> "The rank is but the guinea stamp
> The man 's the gowd for a' that,"

when Sterne, in *Tristram Shandy*, said, "Honours, like impressions upon coin, may give an ideal and local value to a bit of base metal, but gold and silver will pass all the world over without any other recommendation than their own weight," what did these writers do but adopt—adopt without improving—Manly's fine saying to Freeman, in the first act:—"I weigh the man, not his title; 'tis not the king's stamp can make the metal better or heavier"? And yet it is in the fourth and fifth acts that the coruscations of Wycherley's comic genius are the most dazzling; also, it is there that the licentiousness is the most astonishing. Not that the worst scenes in this play are really more wicked than the worst scenes in Vanbrugh's *Relapse*, but they are more seriously imagined. Being less humorous than Vanbrugh's scenes, they are more terribly and earnestly realistic; therefore they seem more wicked. They form indeed a striking instance of the folly of the artist who selects a story which cannot be actualized without hurting the finer instincts of human nature. When Menander declared that, having selected his plot, he looked upon his comedy as three parts finished, he touched upon a subject which all workers in drama—all workers in imaginative literature of every kind—would do well to consider. In all literatures—ancient and modern—an infinite wealth of material has been wasted upon subjects that are unworthy, or else incapable, of artistic realization; and yet Wycherley's case is, in our literature at least, without a parallel. No doubt it may be right to say, with Aristotle, that comedy is an imitation of bad characters, but this does not mean that in comedy art may imitate bad characters as earnestly as she may imitate good ones,—a fact which Thackeray forgot when he made Becky Sharp a murderess, thereby destroying at once what would otherwise have been the finest specimen of the comedy of convention in the world. And perhaps it was because Vanbrugh was conscious of this law of art that he blended comedy with farce. Perhaps he felt that the colossal depravity of intrigue in which the English comedians indulged needs to be not only warmed by a superabundance of humour but softened by the playful mockery of farce before a dramatic circle such as that of the Restoration drama can be really brought within human sympathy. Plutarch's impeachment of Aristophanes, which affirms that the master of the Old Comedy wrote less for honest men than for men sunk in baseness and debauchery, was no doubt unjust to the Greek poet, one side of whose humour, and one alone, could thus be impeached. But does it not touch all sides of a comedy like Wycherley's—a Comedy which strikes at the very root of the social compact upon which civilization is built? As to comparing such a Comedy as that of the Restoration with the Comedy of the Elizabethans, Jeremy Collier did but a poor service to the cause he undertook to advocate when he set the occasional coarseness of Shakespeare alongside the wickedness of Congreve and Vanbrugh. And yet, ever since Macaulay's essay, it has been the fashion to speak of Collier's attack as being levelled against the immorality of the "Restoration dramatists." It is nothing of the kind. It is (as was pointed out so long ago as 1699 by Dr Drake in his little-known vigorous reply to Collier) an attack upon the English drama generally, with a special reference to the case of Shakespeare. While dwelling upon that noxious and highly immoral play *Hamlet*, Collier actually leaves unscathed the author of *The Country Wife*, but fastens on Congreve and Vanbrugh, whose plays—profligate enough in all conscience—seem almost decent beside a comedy whose incredible *vis motrix* is "the modish distemper."

That a stage, indeed, upon which was given with applause *A Woman Killed with Kindness* (where a wife dies of a broken heart for doing what any one of Wycherley's married women would have gloried in doing) should, in seventy years, have given with applause *The Country Wife* shows that in historic and social evolution, as in the evolution of organisms, "change" and "progress" are very far from being convertible terms. For the barbarism of the society depicted in these plays was, in the true sense of the word, far deeper and more brutal than any barbarism that has ever existed in these islands within the historic period. If civilization has any meaning at all for the soul of man, the Englishmen of Chaucer's time, the Anglo-Saxons of the Heptarchy, nay, those half-naked heroes, who in the dawn of English history clustered along the southern coast to defend it from the invasion of Cæsar, were far more civilized than that "race gangrenée"—the treacherous rakes, mercenary slaves, and brazen strumpets of the court of Charles II., who did their best to substitute for the human passion of love (a passion which was known perhaps even to palæolithic man) the promiscuous intercourse of the beasts of the field. Yet Collier leaves Wycherley unassailed, and classes Vanbrugh and Congreve with Shakespeare!

It was after the success of *The Plain Dealer* that the turning-point came in Wycherley's career. The great dream of all the men about town in Charles's time, as Wycherley's plays all show, was to marry a widow, young and handsome, a peer's daughter if possible,—but in any event rich, and spend her money upon wine and women. While talking to a friend in a bookseller's shop at Tunbridge, Wycherley heard *The Plain Dealer* asked for by a lady who, in the person of the countess of Drogheda, answered all the requirements. An introduction ensued, then love-making, then marriage—a secret marriage, for, fearing to lose the king's patronage and the income therefrom, Wycherley still thought it politic to pass as a bachelor. He had not seen enough of life to learn that in the long run nothing is politic but "straightforwardness." Whether because his countenance wore a pensive and subdued expression, suggestive of a poet who had married a dowager countess and awakened to the situation, or whether because treacherous confidants divulged his secret, does not appear, but the news of his marriage oozed out, —it reached the royal ears, and deeply wounded the father anxious about the education of his son. Wycherley lost the appointment that was so nearly within his grasp, —lost indeed the royal favour for ever. He never had an opportunity of regaining it, for the countess seems to have really loved him, and *Love in a Wood* had proclaimed the writer to be the kind of husband whose virtue prospers best when closely guarded at the domestic hearth. Wherever he went the countess followed him, and when she did allow him to meet his boon companions it was in a tavern in Bow Street opposite to his own house, and even there under certain protective conditions. In summer or in winter he was obliged to sit with the window open and the blinds up, so that his wife might see that the party included no member of a sex for which her husband's plays had advertised his partiality. She died at last, however, and left him the whole of her fortune. But the title to the property was disputed; the costs of the litigation were heavy—so heavy that his father was unable (or else he was unwilling) to come to his aid; and the result of his marrying the rich, beautiful, and titled widow was that the poet was thrown into the Fleet prison. There he languished for seven years, being finally released by the liberality of James II.,—a liberality which, incredible as it seems, is too well authenticated to be challenged. James had been so much gratified by seeing *The Plain Dealer* acted that, finding a parallel between Manly's "manliness" and his own, such as no spectator had before discovered, he paid off Wycherley's execution creditor. Other debts still troubled Wycherley, however, and he never was released from his embarrassments, not even after succeeding to a life estate in the family property. In coming to Wycherley's death, we come to the worst allegation that has ever been made against him as a man and as a gentleman. At the age of seventy-five he married a young girl, and is said to have done so in order to spite his nephew, the next in succession, knowing that he himself must shortly die and that the jointure would impoverish the estate. No doubt it is true enough that he did marry the girl and did die eleven days afterwards; but, if we consider that the lady he married was young and an heiress (or was supposed to be an heiress), and if we further consider how difficult it was for an old gallant of Wycherley's extraordinary personal vanity to realize his true physical condition, we may well suppose that, even if he talked about "marrying to spite his nephew," he did so as a cloak for other impulses, such as senile desire or senile cupidity, or a blending of these impulses.

Wycherley wrote verses, and, when quite an old man, prepared them for the press by the aid of Alexander Pope, then not much more than a boy. But, notwithstanding all Pope's tinkering, they remain contemptible. He died in December 1715, and was buried in the vault of the church in Covent Garden. (T. W.)

WYCLIFFE,[1] or WYCLIF, JOHN (*c.* 1320–1384), was born, according to Leland,[2] our single authority on the point, at Ipreswel (evidently the place now called Hipswell), a mile from Richmond, in Yorkshire. The date may have been somewhere about 1320. Leland elsewhere mentions that he "drew his origin" from Wycliffe-on-Tees (*Collectanea*, ii. 329), so that his lineage was of the ancient family which is celebrated by Scott in *Marmion*. The Wycliffes had a natural connexion with the college at Oxford which had been founded in the latter part of the previous century by their neighbours, the Balliols of Barnard Castle; and to Balliol College, then distinctively an "arts" college,[3] John Wycliffe in due time proceeded. It has been generally believed, and was in fact believed not many years after his death, that he was a fellow of Merton College in 1356; but in all probability this identification rests upon a confusion with another and contemporary John Wycliffe. That the future reformer was a fellow of Balliol College is implied in the fact that some time after 1356, but before the summer of 1360, he was elected master of the college. This office he held but a short time. So soon as 1361 he accepted a college living, that of Fillingham in Lincolnshire, and probably left Oxford for some time. In 1363, however, he was back again, this time resident in Queen's College, where he seems to have rented rooms at various dates from this year onwards;[4] on the 13th April 1378 he obtained from his bishop leave of absence "insistendo literarum studio in universitate Oxon. per biennium," and in the following November he exchanged his benefice for one more conveniently situate, at Ludgarshall, in Buckinghamshire. A certain amount of residence at Oxford was necessary if he was now proceeding to a degree in divinity, and still more if, as is generally understood, he is the same person with the John Wycliffe who was appointed, December 1365, to the wardenship of Canterbury Hall, a house which Archbishop Islip had lately founded for a mixed body of monks and secular clergymen, and then, changing his mind, had filled exclusively with the latter. His successor Archbishop Langham in 1367 reversed the arrangement, expelled Wycliffe and his colleagues, and substituted monks. Wycliffe appealed to Rome and lost his case, 1370. There seems no reason to dispute the legality of the action either of Archbishop Langham or of the cardinal who tried the appeal at Viterbo; but Wycliffe no doubt felt himself hardly used, and (if he be rightly identified with the reformer) the experience may have confirmed him in some of the opinions which are characteristic of his subsequent career, and which have been attributed, but only on the authority of a bitter opponent, Thomas Netter of Walden, to disappointment at not receiving the bishopric of Worcester (perhaps at its voidance in 1368). But the doubt as to the identification in the one case, and the suspicion attaching to the evidence in the other, may disincline us to reason about the motives which directed Wycliffe on to the path of reform.

[1] A note is necessary as to the spelling of Wycliffe's name. Out of thirteen contemporary entries in *documents*, twelve give "y" in the first syllable; the seven entries in the Queen's College accounts show four with "y" to three with "i," but these do not certainly refer to the reformer. In not one of these is there a "ck" (though once a "kc") (see Mr F. D. Matthew, in the *Academy*, June 7, 1884). The chroniclers, &c., offer every imaginable variety of spelling, and it is possible that our favourite form in more recent times, "Wickliffe," derived its popularity from the old play on the name, "nequam vita," which we find in Gascoigne. Our choice must be decided by usage, and the spelling adopted in the present article is that of the village from which Wycliffe derived his name; it is also preferred by the editors of the Wycliffe Bible, by Milman, and by Bishop Stubbs. Among the rest "Wyclif" has the support of Shirley, of Mr T. Arnold, and of the Wyclif Society; while "Wiclif" is the popular form in Germany.

[2] *Itinerary*, Stow's transcript, Bodleian Library, Tanner MS., p. 464, f. 45 (Leland's original being mutilated at this place). Hearne misprinted the name "Spreswel," and thus set all Wycliffe's biographers on a search after a vox nihili.

[3] See a document of 1325 printed in the appendix to the *Fourth Report* of the Historical Manuscripts Commission, p. 442 *sq.* Provision for theological study was made by the benefaction of Sir Philip Somerville in 1340 (Lyte, *Hist. of the Univ. of Oxford*, p. 154, 1886).

[4] Hence arose the common mistake, which was repeated so lately as in Milman's *Hist. of Latin Christianity*, bk. xiii. ch. vi., that Wycliffe *began* his university career at Queen's College. It is indeed open to question whether this be not yet another John Wycliffe; see Mr H. T. Riley's remarks in the *Second Report* of the Historical Manuscripts Commission, appendix, p. 141 *sq.*

Some years indeed before this time he had thrown himself publicly into the defence of what had become the national resistance to the papacy at Avignon, closely associated as the latter was with the interests of France. He had entered the service of the royal court, and apparently as king's chaplain ("peculiaris regis clericus") had published a tract, *Determinatio quædam de Dominio*, in support of the action of parliament in 1366, when it repudiated the tribute due to the pope. The tract is of interest, not only because it contains the first trace of the writer's special doctrine of "dominium" or *lordship* (adjusting the spiritual relation to a feudal framework), but also because it shows the line of thought by which Wycliffe's position became determined in a sense hostile to the papal system. It was not at the outset dogmatic but political elements in it which provoked his censure. He disputed the right of the spiritual power to interfere in temporal matters, and was gradually led on to deny the lawfulness of any temporal possessions of the church, and thus to become the common enemy of the beneficed clergy and of the endowed monks; with the friars he was at present on friendly terms. Wycliffe thus drew from Richard Fitz-Ralph, archbishop of Armagh, whose instruction he may have personally followed in his youth,[1] his doctrine of "dominium," which the latter had employed against the friars and in favour of the endowed clergy; while at the same time he combined it with the doctrine of the excellence of "evangelical poverty" which he derived from William of Ockham and the tradition of the Spiritual Franciscans nearly half a century earlier. Wycliffe's position may appear paradoxical; but in truth he made a selection from the discordant views, and built up a consistent theory of his own, of which the salient principles were (1) that sin deprived a man of all right to possess anything; (2) that all property should be held in common; (3) that the spiritual power is entirely separate from the civil, and thus (4) that, should it overstep its bounds and come into contact with temporal concerns, it becomes thereby subject to civil jurisdiction; (5) that the church should hold no property; (6) that excommunication is of no effect unless justified by the sin of him against whom it is directed; and (7) that in no case should it be pronounced for any offence connected with temporal affairs. These views are expounded in Wycliffe's several treatises *De Dominio*, which were written some time before 1377 and probably not long after 1370, though their precise date has not yet been established.[2]

Plainly such a writer was likely to be useful to the court, where John of Gaunt was now supreme,—especially since Wycliffe enjoyed the reputation of an unmatched proficiency in the scholastic learning of his day. On the 7th April 1374 he was presented by the crown to the rectory of Lutterworth, in Leicestershire, which he held until his death; and on the following July 26th he was nominated one of the royal ambassadors to proceed to Bruges to confer with the papal representatives on the long-vexed question of "provisions." The rank he took is shown by the facts that his name stands second, next after that of the bishop of Bangor, on the commission, and that he received pay at the princely rate of twenty shillings per diem. The commission itself was appointed in consequence of urgent and repeated complaints on the part of the Commons, but the negotiations were practically fruitless; the king had an interest in keeping up the system of papal provisions and reservations, and it could hardly be expected that any concessions that might be gained by his commissioners would imply more than a temporary compromise or an illusory advantage. Yet it is possible that the real result of the negotiations is to be found, not in the formal stipulations, but in certain articles not then committed to writing which were laid before the English parliament in February 1377.

Some time after his return Wycliffe was given the prebend of Aust in the collegiate church of Westbury-on-Trim, which he held but a short time, the confirmation of his appointment (November 6, 1375) being followed within a fortnight by the grant of the benefice to another person. Henceforth he lived mainly at Lutterworth and Oxford, making, however, frequent and, as it seems, prolonged visits to London from time to time. He assumed the position of a popular preacher there, and delighted an audience already sufficiently disaffected towards the rich and powerful clergy. He was also closely allied with John of Gaunt, who welcomed him as an instrument towards his design of humbling the church. Wycliffe indeed expressly refused to affirm that it was in such a condition as to deserve spoliation; but when to this he added that the decision was the affair of statesmen, "politicorum qui intendunt praxi et statui regnorum" (*De Civili Dominio*, i. 37, p. 269), it is plain that his theory might readily commend itself to the duke, while the proviso could only increase the hostility towards him of the endowed clergy. For some years he was suffered to spread his doctrines without hindrance. The archbishop of Canterbury, Simon Sudbury, had no mind to proceed against him until at length the pressure of the bishops compelled him to summon the dangerous preacher to appear before the bishop of London and answer certain charges laid against him. The nature of these accusations is not stated, but their purport can hardly be doubtful. On the 19th February 1377 Wycliffe made his appearance at St Paul's. He was accompanied by the duke of Lancaster, by Lord Percy the marshal of England, and by four doctors of the four mendicant orders. The trial, however, came to nothing; for, before Wycliffe could open his mouth, the court was broken up by a rude brawl between his protectors and Bishop Courtenay, ending in a general riot of the citizens of London, who were so much enraged by the insult to their bishop in his own cathedral church—coming as this did at the same time as a serious attempt at an invasion by the duke in parliament of their civic liberties (*Chron. Angl.*, p. 120)—that they would have sacked his palace of the Savoy had not Courtenay himself intervened.

Wycliffe had escaped for the time, but his enemies did not rely solely on their own weapons. Probably before this they had set their case before the pope; and towards the end of May five bulls were issued by Gregory XI., who had just returned to Rome from Avignon, condemning eighteen (or in other copies nineteen) "conclusions" drawn from Wycliffe's writings. All the articles but one are taken from his first book *De Civili Dominio*, the recent publication of which shows the charges to be honestly made and the quotations to be entirely free from any

[1] Archbishop FitzRalph had been a fellow of Balliol College, and was vice-chancellor of the university in or about 1333 (A. à Wood, *Fasti Oxon.*, p. 21, ed. Gutch, 1790). His work, on which Wycliffe mainly based his theory, is entitled *De Pauperie Salvatoris*, and exists only in manuscript; but Mr R. L. Poole is preparing the greater part of it for publication. An old legend makes Wycliffe take part in the archbishop's controversy with the friars so early as 1360. It was suspected by Robert Vaughan, and then denied by Shirley. The further researches of Dr Lechler have placed the late date at which Wycliffe began his opposition to the friars on a sure foundation; and the fact has been confirmed decisively by the publication of the St Albans *Chronicon Angliæ*, by Mr E. M. Thompson, in 1874 (see pp. 116, 118), and more recently by that of the reformer's earlier Latin works.

[2] It is uniformly asserted that Wycliffe fell into heresy after his admission to the degree of doctor (*Fasc. Ziz.*, p. 2). The process about Canterbury Hall makes the warden B.D. in 1367 or 1368 (Lyte, p. 252, n. 5),—so that if he be the reformer we have an approximate *terminus a quo* for his inception.

suspicion of unfairness. The bulls truly stated Wycliffe's intellectual lineage; he was following in the error of Marsiglio of Padua; and the articles laid against him are concerned entirely with questions agitated between church and state—how far ecclesiastical censures could lawfully affect a man's civil position, and whether the church had a right to receive and hold temporal endowments. The bulls were addressed (May 22) to the archbishop of Canterbury and the bishop of London, the university of Oxford, and the king. The university was to take Wycliffe and send him to the prelates; the latter were then to examine the truth of the charges and to report to the pope, Wycliffe being meanwhile kept in confinement. The execution of the papal bulls was impeded by three separate causes,—the king's death on the 21st June; the tardy action of the bishops, who enjoined the university to make a report, instead of simply sending Wycliffe to them; and the unwillingness of the university to admit external authority, and, above all, the pope's right to order the imprisonment of any man in England. The convocation, indeed, as the St Albans chronicler[1] states with lamentation, made serious objections to receiving the bull at all; and in the end it merely directed Wycliffe to keep within his lodgings at Black Hall for a time.

If the university was disposed to favour the reformer, the Government was not less so. John of Gaunt was for the moment in retirement; but the mother of the young king appears to have adopted his policy in church affairs, and she naturally occupied a chief position in the new council. As soon as parliament met in the autumn of 1377 Wycliffe was consulted by it as to the lawfulness of prohibiting that treasure should pass out of the country in obedience to the pope's demand. Wycliffe's affirmative judgment is contained in a state paper still extant; and its tone is plain proof enough of his confidence that his views on the main question of church and state had the support of the nation.[2] Indeed he had laid before this same parliament his answer to the pope's bulls, with a defence of the soundness of his opinions. His university, moreover, confirmed his argument; his tenets, it said, were true (*i.e.*, orthodox), though their expression was such as to admit of an incorrect interpretation. But Wycliffe was still bound to clear himself before the prelates who had summoned him, and early in 1378 he appeared for this purpose in the chapel of Lambeth Palace. His written defence, expressed in some respects in more cautious language than he had previously used, was laid before the council; but its session was rudely interrupted, not only by an inroad of the London citizens with a crowd of the rabble, but also by a messenger from the princess of Wales enjoining them not to pass judgment against Wycliffe; and thus a second time he escaped, either without sentence, or at most with a gentle *request* that he would avoid discussing the matters in question. Meanwhile his "protestatio" was sent on to Rome.

In the autumn of this year Wycliffe was once more called upon to prove his loyalty to John of Gaunt. The duke had violated the sanctuary of Westminster by sending a band of armed men to seize two knights who had taken refuge there. They resisted, and one of them was killed. After a while the bishop of London excommunicated all concerned in the crime (excepting only the king, his mother, and his uncle), and preached against the culprits publicly at St Paul's Cross. The duke, fearing the anger of the Londoners, arranged that the ensuing parliament should be held at a safe distance, at Gloucester, and, it was rumoured, proposed to bring before it a sweeping scheme of spoliation of church property. Wycliffe was required to write an apology for the duke's actions at Westminster. His paper, which is still preserved, and forms part of the *De Ecclesia*, seeks, without excusing the homicide, to lay down the limits within which the privilege of asylum is permissible, and maintains that the duke was right in invading the sanctuary in order to bring escaped prisoners to justice. But the duke's whole behaviour seems to have been high-handed, and Wycliffe can with difficulty be excused from a charge of subserviency to his patron.

The year 1378 forms a turning point in Wycliffe's career. The schism in the papacy caused by the election in September of Clement VII. in opposition to Urban VI. slowly decided Wycliffe towards a more revolutionary attitude with respect to the Roman see, a power which he now convinced himself was at the root of the disorders of the church. He set on foot an active propaganda, choosing the two special means of sending forth his "poor" or "simple priests" to preach pure doctrine throughout the country, and of making the first complete English version of the Bible. This latter work was mainly executed by Wycliffe himself, but his friend Nicholas Hereford did part of the Old Testament. Afterwards the whole was revised by John Purvey, who assisted Wycliffe in his parish duty at Lutterworth, and finished his edition probably not long after the reformer's death. Most existing copies are of the latter redaction, which is printed in parallel columns with the older one in the great edition of the version edited by J. Forshall and Sir F. Madden (Oxford, 1851). Wycliffe's translation of the Bible, and still more his numerous English sermons and tracts, establish his now undisputed position as the founder of English prose writing.

Wycliffe's itinerant preachers were not necessarily intended to work as rivals to the beneficed clergy. The idea that underlay their mission was rather analogous to that which animated Wesley four centuries later. Wycliffe aimed at supplementing the services of the church by regular religious instruction in the vernacular; and his organization included a good number of men who held or had held respectable positions in their colleges at Oxford. The influence of their teaching was soon felt throughout the country. The common people were rejoiced by the plain and homely doctrine which dwelt chiefly on the simple "law" of the gospel, while they no doubt relished the denunciation of existing evils in the church which formed, as it were, the burthen of such discourses. The feeling of disaffection against the rich and careless clergy, monks, and friars was widespread but undefined. Wycliffe turned it into a definite channel (he was now persuaded that the friars were as bad as the monks); he insensibly passed from an assailant of the papal to an assailant of the sacerdotal power; and in this way he was led to reject the distinctive symbol of that power, the doctrine of transubstantiation. It was in the summer of 1381[3] that Wycliffe propounded at Oxford a set of theses, substituting for the accredited doctrine of the church one which

[1] When he says that the bull was only received at Oxford shortly before Christmas, he is apparently confounding it with the prelates' mandate, which is dated December 18 (Lewis, appendix xvii.)—*Chron. Angl.*, p. 173.

[2] In one text of this document a note is appended, to the effect that the council enjoined silence on the writer as touching the matter therein contained (*Fasciculi Zizaniorum*, p. 271). This, if true, was apparently a measure of precaution.

[3] This is the date given in the *Fasciculi Zizaniorum*. Wood, however, makes Berton chancellor in 1380 and 1382. But if Wycliffe's heresy was first put forth in the latter year there seems to be hardly time for the condemnation and then for the archbishop's summons to the London council in May. It is safest therefore to leave the date of the *Fasciculi Zizaniorum* undisturbed. The Peasants' Revolt in June 1381, and the murder of Archbishop Sudbury, may sufficiently account for the interval between the Oxford and the London proceedings.

allowed the real presence of Christ in the consecrated elements, but denied any change of substance, a doctrine practically undistinguishable (unless by its scholastic form) from the modern Lutheran doctrine. The theologians of the university were at once roused. The chancellor, William Berton, sat with twelve doctors (half of whom were friars), and solemnly condemned the theses; Wycliffe appealed to the king, and John of Gaunt hastily sent down a messenger enjoining the reformer to keep silence on the subject.

The condemnation at Oxford was almost immediately followed by the Peasants' Revolt, with which it has been supposed that Wycliffe had something to do. The only positive fact implicating him is the confession of one of its leaders, John Ball, that he learned his subversive doctrines from Wycliffe. But the confession of a condemned man can seldom be accepted without reserve; and we have not only the precise and repeated testimony of Knyghton that he was a "precursor" of Wycliffe, but also documentary evidence that he was excommunicated as early as 1366, long before Wycliffe exposed himself to ecclesiastical censure. Wycliffe in truth was always careful to state his communistic views in a theoretical way; they are confined to his Latin scholastic writings, and thus could not reach the people from him directly. At the same time it is very possible that his less scrupulous followers translated them in their popular discourses, and thus fed the flame that burst forth in the rebellion. Perhaps it was a consciousness of a share of responsibility for it that led them to cast the blame on the friars. In any case Wycliffe's advocates must regret that in all his known works there is only one trace of any reprobation of the excesses that accompanied the outbreak.

In the following spring his old enemy William Courtenay, now archbishop of Canterbury, resolved to take measures for stamping out Wycliffe's crowning heresy. He called a provincial council at the Blackfriars in London, which assembled on the 21st May 1382, and sat with intervals until July. The council was met by a hardly expected manifestation of university feeling on Wycliffe's side. The chancellor and both the proctors stood by him. They allowed a Wycliffite sermon to be preached before the university on Ascension Day. The archbishop's commissary complained that his life was not safe at Oxford. Still no steps were taken to bring Wycliffe to judgment. Twenty-four articles extracted from his works were condemned; some of his prominent adherents were imprisoned until they recanted; the university officers were soon brought to submission, but Wycliffe himself remained at large and unmolested. It is said indeed by Knyghton that at a council held by Courtenay at Oxford in the following November Wycliffe was brought forward and made a recantation; but our authority fortunately gives the text of the recantation, which proves to be nothing more nor less than a plain English statement of the condemned doctrine. It is therefore lawful to doubt whether Wycliffe appeared before the council at all, and even whether he was ever summoned before it. Probably after the overthrow of his party at Oxford by the action of the Blackfriars council Wycliffe found it advisable to withdraw permanently to Lutterworth. That his strength among the laity was undiminished is shown by the fact that an ordinance passed by the House of Lords alone, in May 1382, against the itinerant preachers was annulled on the petition of the Commons in the following autumn. In London, Leicester, and elsewhere there is abundant evidence of his popularity. The reformer, however, was growing old. There was work, he probably felt, for him to do, more lasting than personal controversy. So in his retirement he occupied himself, with restless activity, in writing numerous tracts, Latin and English, as well as one of his most important books, the *Trialogus*. In spite of a paralytic seizure which came upon him in 1382 or early in 1383, he continued his labours. In 1384 it is stated that he was cited by pope Urban VI. to appear before him at Rome; but to Rome he never went. On the 28th December of this year, while he was hearing mass in his own church, he received a final stroke, from the effects of which he died on the New Year's eve.[1] He was buried at Lutterworth; but by a decree of the council of Constance, May 4, 1415, his remains were ordered to be dug up and burned, an order which was carried out by Bishop Fleming in 1428.

At this distance of time Wycliffe's reputation is still a battle-ground of parties. By those who uphold the indefeasible sanctity of church property, the exemption of the church from all control or oversight on the part of the state, or yet more the apostolic prerogative of the Roman see, his political doctrine is judged as revolutionary, sacrilegious, and heretical. His denial of transubstantiation is conceived to imply a base hypocrisy in his continued discharge of priestly functions; but they who maintain this argument should bear in mind that the office of the mass is older than the doctrine of transubstantiation, and a man cannot be fairly accused of dishonesty in using words in a sense at all events nearer that in which they were originally written. A sober study of Wycliffe's life and works justifies a conviction of his complete sincerity and earnest striving after what he believed to be right. If he cannot be credited (as he has been by most of his biographers with all the Protestant virtues, he may at least claim to have discovered the secret of the immediate dependence of the individual Christian upon God, a relation which needs no mediation of any priest, and to which the very sacraments of the church, however desirable, are not essentially necessary. When he divorces the idea of the church from any connexion with its official or formal constitution, and conceives it as consisting exclusively of the righteous, he may seem to have gone the whole length of the most radical reformers of the 16th century. And yet, powerful as was his influence in England, it was but transient, and within forty years it was nearly extinct. His true tradition is to be found not in his own country but in Bohemia, where his works were eagerly read and multiplied, and where his disciple John Huss, with less originality but greater simplicity of character and greater spiritual force, raised Wycliffism to the dignity of national religion. To Huss, whose works are to a great extent a cento of extracts from Wycliffe, Luther owed much; and thus the spirit of the English teacher had its influence on the reformed churches of Europe.

The documentary materials for Wycliffe's biography are to be found in John Lewis's *Life and Sufferings of J. Wiclif* (new ed., Oxford, 1820), which contains a valuable appendix of illustrative papers and records; Foxe's *Acts and Monuments*, vol. iii., ed. 1855, with app.; Forshall and Madden's preface to the Wycliffe Bible, p. vii. note, Oxford, 1851; W. W. Shirley's edition of the *Fasciculi Zizaniorum* (probably the work of Thomas Netter of Walden), 1858; and H. T. Riley's notices in the appendices to the *Second* and *Fourth Reports* of the Historical Manuscripts Commission. Among contemporary records the recently discovered narrative of a monk of St Albans—a bitter opponent of John of Gaunt—is of conspicuous value; it was published under the title of *Chronicon Angliæ*, by Mr E. M. Thompson, 1874. Of this the account in Walsingham's *Historia Anglicana* (ed. H. T. Riley, 1863, 1864) is mainly a modified version. Knyghton, who wrote *De Eventibus Angliæ* at Leicester in the heart of what may be called the Wycliffe country, is very well informed as to certain passages in the reformer's history, though his chronology is extremely faulty (printed in Twysden's *Hist. Anglic. Scriptores Decem*, 1652). There are valuable notices also in the continuation of the *Eulogium Historiarum* (vol. iii., ed. F. S. Haydon, 1863), in the *Chronicle* of Adam of Usk (ed. E. M. Thompson, 1876), and in more than one of the continuations of Higden. For the study of Wycliffe's theology the controversial works of Wodeford and Walden are important, but must necessarily be used with caution.

Of modern biographies that by Dr G. V. Lechler (*Johann von Wiclif und die Vorgeschichte der Reformation*, 2 vols., Leipsic, 1873; partial Engl. trans., by P. Lorimer, 1878, 1881, and 1884) is by far the most comprehensive; it includes a detailed exposition of the reformer's system, based to a considerable extent on works which were then unpublished. Shirley's masterly introduction to the *Fasciculi Zizaniorum*, and Mr F. D. Matthew's to his edition of *English Works of Wyclif hitherto unprinted* (1880). as well as Mr Creighton's *History of the Papacy during the Period of the Reformation*, vol. i., 1882, and Mr H. C. Maxwell Lyte's account in his *History of the University of Oxford* (1886), add to or correct our stock of biographical materials, and contain much valuable criticism. Wycliffe's political doctrine is discussed by Mr R. L. Poole (*Illustrations of the History of Mediæval Thought*, 1884); and his relation to Huss is elaborately demonstrated by Dr J. Loserth (*Hus und Wiclif*, Prague, 1884; also Engl. trans.)

Wycliffe's works are enumerated in a *Catalogue* by Shirley (Oxford, 1865). The following are published:—*A. Latin.*—*De Officio Pastorali*, ed. G. V. Lechler, Leipsic, 1863; *Trialogus*, ed. G. V. Lechler, Oxford, 1869; portions of the *Summa in Theologia*, viz., *De Civili Dominio*, i., ed. R. L. Poole, 1885, and *De Ecclesia*, ed. J. Loserth, 1886; *De Benedicta Incarnatione*, ed. E. Harris, 1886; *Dialogus sive Speculum Ecclesiæ Militantis*, ed. A. W. Pollard, 1886; *Sermones*, ed. J. Loserth, 2 vols., 1887-88; *Polemical Tracts*, ed. R. Buddensieg, 2 vols., 1883; *De Compositione Hominis*, an early work, ed. R. Beer, 1884. All but the first two of these are issued by the Wyclif Society, which was founded in 1882 for the purpose of publishing all the reformer's unedited works.

[1] Of Wycliffe's personal appearance we know hardly more than that he was a spare man with frail health. None of the existing portraits of him is contemporary.

B. *English.*—*Select English Works*, ed. T. Arnold, 3 vols., 1869-71, and *English Works hitherto unprinted*, ed. F. D. Matthew, 1880, chiefly sermons and short tracts, of many of which the authenticity is uncertain. *The Wicket* (Nuremberg, 1546; reprinted Oxford, 1828) is not included in either of these collections. (R. L. P.)

WYCOMBE, HIGH WYCOMBE, or CHIPPING WYCOMBE, a municipal borough and market-town of Bucks, is situated in the valley of the Wyck and on a branch of the Great Western Railway, 29 miles west-north-west of London, 25 south-east of Oxford, and 10 north of Maidenhead. Notwithstanding many additions to the town within recent years, it still retains many evidences of antiquity, including several mediæval buildings. The parish church of All Saints, the largest in the county, was rebuilt in 1273 by the abbess and nuns of Godstowe, Oxfordshire, on the site of an earlier Norman structure, and underwent extensive reconstruction in the beginning of the 15th century. The present western tower, 108 feet in height, was completed in 1522, and adorned with pinnacles in 1753. The style of the building is now Early English with Decorated and Perpendicular additions. The interior underwent extensive restoration in 1874, under the direction of the late G. E. Street, and the restoration of the exterior is at present (1888) in progress. For the grammar school, founded in 1555 by the mayor and burgesses of Wycombe, and now under the direction of the charity commissioners, a handsome new building was erected in 1883. The remains of the Norman hall of St John the Baptist, incorporated in the old school building, with its chapel in the Early English style, adjoins the new building. The other principal public buildings are the guild-hall, originally erected by the earl of Shelburne in 1757, and altered and improved in 1859; the literary institute, 1854; the free library, permanently endowed by a subscription of the townspeople after the premises had been presented by J. O. Griffiths; the High Wycombe hospital, established in 1875; the shambles, erected in 1761 on the site of the old hog market; and the South Bucks auction mart, 1887. Some remains still exist of Desborough Castle, supposed to have been erected for defence against the Danes. There are a number of almshouses, including those of Queen Elizabeth, endowed in 1562 out of the revenues of the dissolved fraternity of St Mary. In 1797 a military college was established at Wycombe, which was transferred to Farnham and the junior department to Sandhurst in 1812 and 1813. The Frogmore gardens were presented to the town by J. O. Griffiths in 1877 as public pleasure-grounds. There is a common pasturage, 30 acres in extent, called the Rye. Formerly lace and strawplait making were the staple industries, but they have been superseded by chair-making, which of late years has greatly increased, the number of chairs made annually now amounting to over 1½ millions. The rise of the industry was due to the beech-woods in the neighbourhood; but, in addition to the cane and rush-bottomed chairs, for which these woods supply the frames, chairs of a finer kind are now also made from walnut, cherry, and other more valuable woods. There are also flour and paper mills. The borough, which is divided into three wards, is governed by a mayor, six aldermen, and eighteen councillors. The population of the municipal borough in 1871 (area then 122 acres) was 4811; in 1880 the area was extended to 400 acres, and the population in 1881 was 10,618. The population of the parliamentary borough (area 6395 acres), which existed till 1885, was 10,492 in 1871 and 13,154 in 1881.

From the character of Roman remains found at Wycombe it seems to have been an important Roman station. By the Saxons a fortress called Desborough castle was erected for its defence. At the Conquest it was a borough town, and was then held by Robert Doily or Doyley. In the 9th year of Edward I. it reverted to the crown. The incorporation of the borough is ascribed to Henry I. From the 28th of Edward I. it returned two members to parliament, but in 1867 the number was reduced to one, and in 1885 it was merged in the South or Wycombe Division of the county. Camden, writing in the beginning of the 17th century, says of it, "This town for largeness and beauty compares with the best in the county, and as it is governed by a mayor is justly preferred to the rest." During the Civil War it was the scene of a skirmish between Prince Rupert and the Parliamentarian forces, in which the latter were defeated.

See Parker's *Antiquities of Wycombe*, 1878.

WYNTOUN, ANDREW OF, a Scottish monk who flourished at the beginning of the 15th century, was the author of the *Orygynale Cronykil of Scotland.* The chronicle, which is in verse and has some historical value from the use made in it of the St Andrews registers, is called "original" because it begins with the beginning of the world, the second chapter giving an account of the creation of man. The history of Scotland is brought down to the death of Robert III. in 1406. Of the chronicler himself nothing is known except what he tells us in his prologue, namely, that he was a canon regular of St Andrews, and prior of Serf's Inch in Lochleven. The chronicle has been twice carefully edited and annotated,—by Macpherson in 1795, and by David Laing in 1872-79.

WYOMING, a Territory of the United States, is nearly rectangular in shape, having as its boundaries the 41st and 45th parallels of N. latitude and the 27th and 34th meridians west of Washington. South of it are Colorado and Utah; on the west, Utah, Idaho, and Montana; on the north, Montana; and on the east, Dakota and Nebraska. The area is 97,890 square miles.

Plate XVII.

Mountains.

The surface is greatly diversified. Its mean elevation is great, being probably not less than 6400 feet. The lowest portions of the Territory are along the northern and eastern borders, where in several places the surface is less than 5000 feet above sea-level, while its highest points exceed 13,000 feet. By far the greater part consists of high plains, which are broken by numerous mountain ranges and ridges, which form parts of the Rocky Mountain system. This system enters the Territory in the south-eastern part, and traverses it in a north-west direction. On the south it consists of three members, the Laramie range, which is crossed by the Union Pacific railroad at Sherman, and the Medicine Bow and Park ranges, which separate branches of the North Platte river. These ranges run out and fall down into the plain in the southern part of the Territory, leaving for 150 miles a broad flat plateau to represent the Rocky Mountain system. The ill-defined summit of this plateau forms the parting between the waters of the Missouri and Colorado. Eastward this plateau slopes to the Great Plains, and westward to the Green river basin. The Union Pacific Railroad traverses it, and therefore the traveller upon this road sees little of the Rocky Mountains except at a distance. Farther north the mountains rise again from this plateau in several ranges. The principal of these is that known as the Wind River range, which in a sense is continued northward beyond the northern boundary of the Territory by the Absaroka range. The former contains the most elevated land in the Territory, its highest peak being Frémont's, with an elevation of 13,790 feet. The latter range is in its southern part a great volcanic plateau, elevated 10,000 to 11,000 feet above the sea, while farther north it is eroded into very rugged mountain forms. About the point where these ranges join, there is a confused mass of mountains of great breadth and considerable height. In this elevated mass rise streams flowing to the Atlantic, the Gulf of California, and the Pacific. The highest peaks of these mountains are those known as the Three Tétons, the most elevated of which, Mount Hayden, has an altitude of 13,691 feet. East of the Wind River and Absaroka ranges, and separated from them by the valley of the Wind River and the Big Horn basin, is the range

WYOMING, IDAHO,

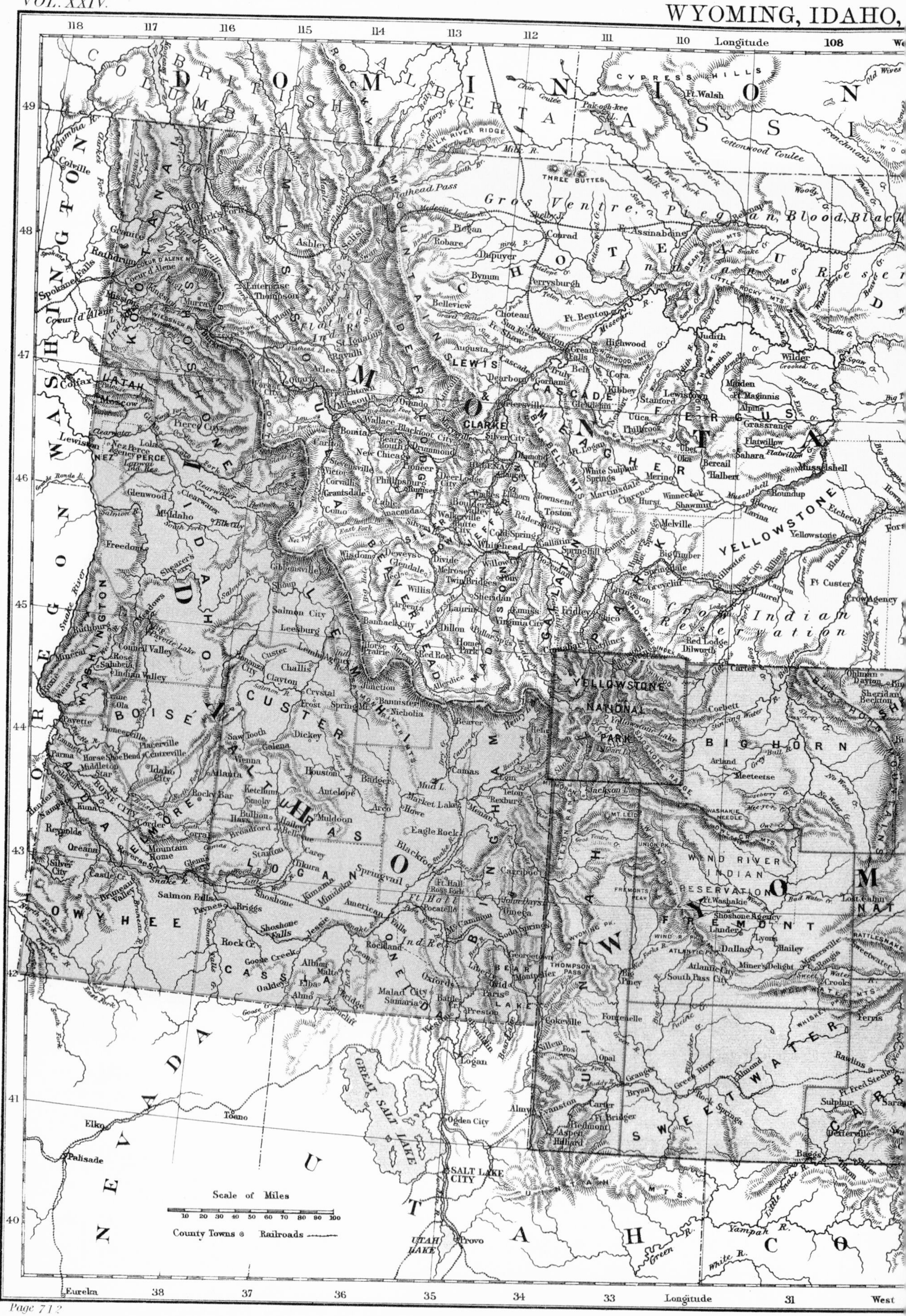

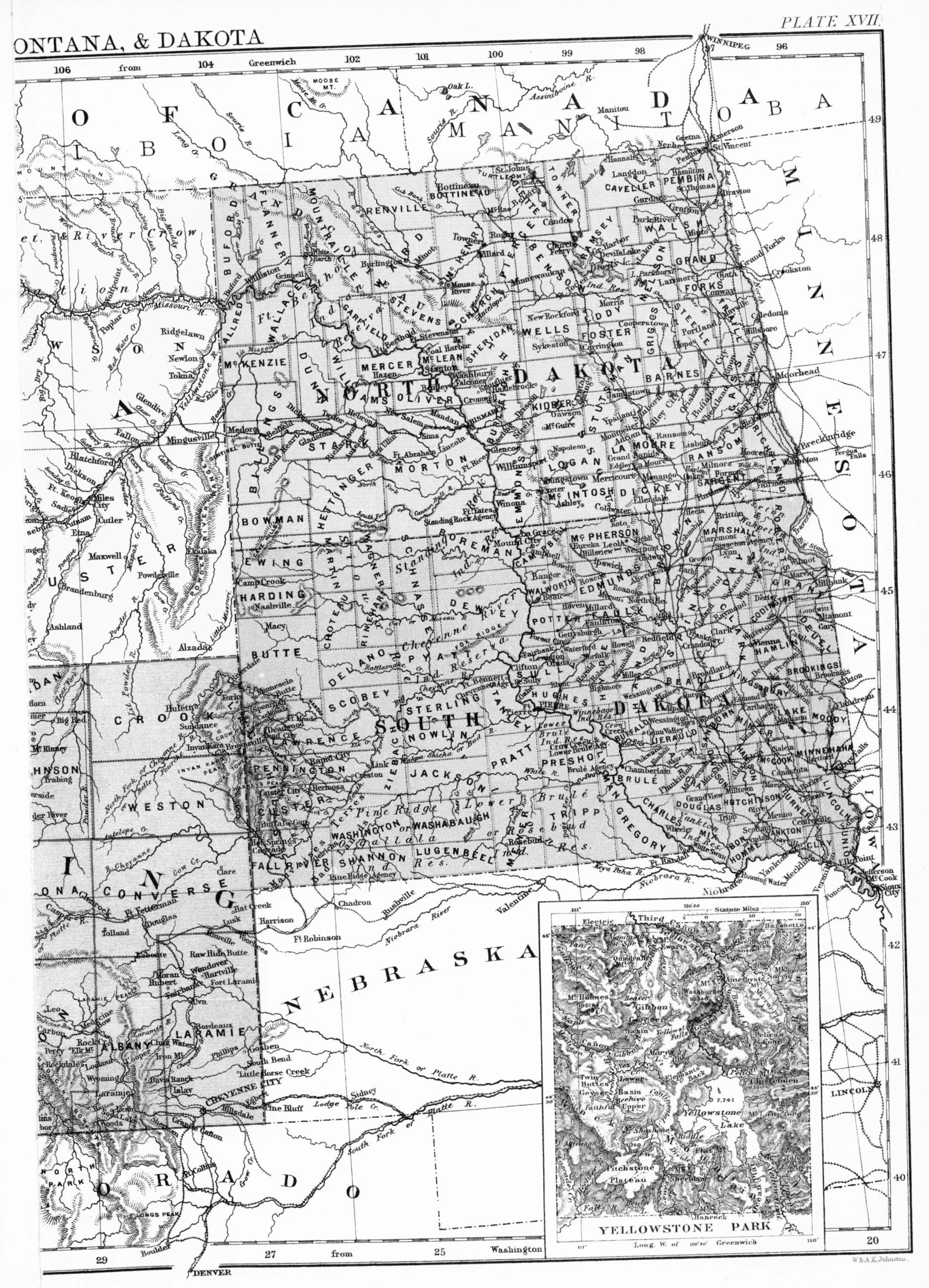
ONTANA, & DAKOTA
106
from
104
Greenwich
102
101
100
99
98
97
96
WINNIPEG
DOMINION OF CANADA
MANITOBA
MINNESOTA
IOWA
NEBRASKA
COLORADO
NORTH DAKOTA
SOUTH DAKOTA
BUFORD
FLANNERY
MOUNTRAIL
RENVILLE
BOTTINEAU
ROLETTE
TOWNER
CAVELIER
PEMBINA
WALSH
RAMSEY
GRAND FORKS
BENSON
NELSON
STEELE
TRAILL
GRIGGS
EDDY
FOSTER
WELLS
SHERIDAN
McLEAN
MERCER
McKENZIE
ALLRED
WALLACE
GARFIELD
STEVENS
DUNN
WILLIAMS
OLIVER
STARK
BILLINGS
HETTINGER
MORTON
EMMONS
LOGAN
KIDDER
STUTSMAN
BARNES
CASS
RANSOM
LA MOURE
DICKEY
McINTOSH
SARGENT
RICHLAND
BOWMAN
EWING
HARDING
BUTTE
MARTIN
SCHNASSE
BOREMAN
CAMPBELL
McPHERSON
EDMUNDS
WALWORTH
POTTER
FAULK
BROWN
MARSHALL
DAY
GRANT
ROBERTS
CODINGTON
DEUEL
HAMLIN
CLARK
SPINK
HAND
HYDE
SULLY
HUGHES
BEADLE
KINGSBURY
BROOKINGS
LAKE
MOODY
MINNEHAHA
McCOOK
TURNER
LINCOLN
UNION
CLAY
YANKTON
BON HOMME
HUTCHINSON
DOUGLAS
CHARLES MIX
AURORA
JERAULD
SANBORN
MINER
DAVISON
HANSON
BRULÉ
BUFFALO
PRESHO
LYMAN
GREGORY
TRIPP
PRATT
JACKSON
NOWLIN
STERLING
SCOBEY
DELANO
PYATT
DEWEY
ZIEBACH
STANLEY
PENNINGTON
CUSTER
FALL RIVER
SHANNON
WASHINGTON
WASHABAUGH
LUGENBEEL
MEYER
LAWRENCE
CROOK
WESTON
CONVERSE
LARAMIE
ALBANY
CUSTER
DAWSON
Bismarck
Fargo
Grand Forks
Jamestown
Mandan
Pierre
Sioux Falls
Yankton
Deadwood
Rapid City
Aberdeen
Watertown
Huron
Mitchell
Cheyenne City
Miles City
Glendive
Sioux City
Lincoln
Sidney
Denver
Boulder
Longs Peak
North Park
Missouri R.
Yellowstone R.
Cheyenne River
Niobrara R.
North Fork or Platte R.
Lodge Pole Cr.
Platte R.
South Fork of Platte R.
Standing Rock Ind. Res.
Lower Brulé Ind. Res.
Crow Creek Ind. Res.
Pine Ridge Agency
Yankton Ind. Res.
Fort Berthold Ind. Res.
49
48
47
46
45
44
43
42
41
40
29
27
from
25
Washington
20
YELLOWSTONE PARK
Statute Miles
Long. W. of 110°30' Greenwich
Yellowstone Lake
Pitchstone Plateau
Mt. Washburn
Gibbon
Mt. Holmes
Mt. Sheridan
Hancock
Electric
Third
W & A.K. Johnston.

known as the Big Horn Mountains, which is reputed to contain peaks having an altitude of 12,000 feet. These ranges form the backbone of the Territory. Eastward from the Big Horn and Laramie ranges stretch the plains in an almost unbroken expanse, gently sloping to the eastward from an altitude of about 6000 feet at the base of the mountains, while south-west of the Wind River range is spread the expanse of the Green river basin, through which flows the principal fork of the Colorado.

Rivers. The drainage system of Wyoming is somewhat complex. While the mountainous regions are well watered by numerous streams, the broad valleys and the plains are poorly supplied with streams. Many of those which flow full in the mountains during the entire year run dry in summer upon the plains. None of the streams are navigable. The eastern three-fourths of the Territory is drained by the tributaries of the Missouri to the Atlantic. Of this area the North Platte drains the southern portion of the Rocky Mountain system, together with a large part of the plains lying north and east of it. Farther northward and eastward the plains are drained by the Cheyenne river. The eastern face of the Big Horn mountains is drained by the Powder and Tongue rivers, while from its western slopes, and from the eastern slopes of the Wind River and Absaroka ranges, the Wind River, known lower down in its course as the Big Horn, collects the waters. The Yellowstone, heading in the confused mass of mountains about the north end of the Wind River range, flows northward through a beautiful lake, draining the west slope of the Absaroka range. The Snake, or "Mad" river of the early explorers, heading in the same mass of mountains, flows south-westward to seek an exit from them, while the Green, whose sources are in the same elevated country, drains the west slope of the Wind River range, and flows southward through the broad sage-covered expanse known as the Green river basin. In the south-west corner of the Territory is a small area drained by means of Bear river into Great Salt Lake.

Geology. The geological structure of Wyoming is even more complicated than its surface features. In the north-western corner is an area in which volcanic action, as represented in hot springs and geysers, is still alive, while the evidences of volcanic action upon a tremendous scale, in recent geological time, are seen in the form of sheets of lava and volcanic breccia, which are spread over the land, and from which mountain ranges have been carved. Most of this region is comprised in the YELLOWSTONE NATIONAL PARK (*q.v.*), which has been set apart from settlement by the general Government. Many of the mountain slopes show a succession of the stratified formations, from the Triassic downwards through the series. The plains region is mainly floored by Tertiary and Cretaceous formations, as is also the case with the higher plateaus and with the Green river basin.

Fauna. The native fauna of Wyoming resembles that of the other north-west Territories. The larger quadrupeds, which were formerly very abundant, and which are now not unfrequently to be met with, are the grizzly, black, and cinnamon bears, the North American panther, the elk, the moose, two or three species of deer, and the antelope. Upon the plains are seen the grey wolf and the coyote, the jack rabbit, the prairie dog, and the gopher. The buffalo, which was formerly extremely abundant upon the plains, is now practically extinct.

Flora. The eastern plains are mainly grass-covered, but as one goes westward the grass gradually disappears, and gives place to artemisia and greasewood. Forests are confined almost entirely to the mountains, although the high plains in the Yellowstone Park, in the north-western corner of the Territory, are covered with timber. The forests are composed of quaking aspen upon the lower slopes, succeeded at greater elevations by pines and spruces, the upper limit of timber in the Territory being about 10,000 feet above the sea.

Climate. Wyoming has, in common with most of the western States, an arid climate. In the arable regions the rainfall is nowhere sufficient for the needs of agriculture, and irrigation is universally practised. The rainfall ranges in this part of the Territory from 8 to 15 inches, being greater in the eastern part and diminishing westward. Upon the mountains it probably reaches, if it does not exceed, 30 inches annually.

The temperature ranges with the elevation. Upon the plains and plateaus and in the valleys (this comprising nearly all the habitable parts of Wyoming) the annual temperature is between 40° and 50° F. Upon the mountains it diminishes until at an altitude of 10,000 feet it reaches approximately the freezing point.

Population. At the last census (1880) the Territory contained 20,789 inhabitants. In 1870 there were only 9118, showing an increase of 128 per cent. The population is now (1888) estimated at not far from 40,000. As in all frontier communities, a large proportion consists of adult males. In 1880 there were 14,152 males to 6637 females. The proportion of the foreign born was large, there being 5850 of this class to 14,939 natives.

The Territory contains eight counties:—Albany (population 4626), Carbon (3438), Crook (239), Johnson (637), Laramie (6409), Sweetwater (2561), Uinta (2879), and Frémont (formed since 1880). The principal cities are Cheyenne, the capital, which is situated upon the plains, near the east base of the Laramie range (population in 1880, 3456); Laramie City, near the west base of the same range (2696); Rawlins, upon the high plateau forming the continental watershed (1451); and Evanston, in the south-west corner of the Territory (1277).

Cattle raising. The industries of Wyoming mainly relate to the raising of cattle and to mining. The former industry is in proportion to the number of inhabitants very large, and has been until recently extremely profitable. The raising of cattle is carried on at slight expense, the cattle being allowed to range freely over the plains, and little provision is made for feeding and shelter, even in winter, as the loss from exposure and starvation is not sufficiently great to warrant the additional expense. In 1880 the number of cattle was returned as 521 213, and sheep as 450,225. In 1887 the report of the governor states that the number of cattle has increased to 753,648, while that of sheep has slightly diminished, being 421,688.

Mining. Mines of gold and silver have been worked to a limited extent near the east base of the Wind River range and in the north-western part of the Territory, and also at the extreme south, in the Park range, but the production is insignificant. On the other hand, the coal mines of Wyoming are very valuable; they are mainly situated in the southern part of the Territory, at Carbon, Rock Spring, Almy, and Twin Creek, on or near the Union Pacific Railroad. The production in 1886 was 829,355 tons, valued at $2,488,065.

Government. As in other Territories, the government of Wyoming is under the immediate jurisdiction of the United States, the executive and judicial officers being appointed by the president. The treasurer is appointed by the governor. The Territory has a legislature consisting of two houses, the members of which are elected by the people.

History. The area of Wyoming was in the main included in the Territory of Louisiana, acquired by the United States by purchase from France. The western part was acquired by prior settlement, as was the case with Washington, Oregon, and Idaho. It was organized as a Territory in 1868. The progress of settlement has until recent years been very slow, owing to the inhospitable character of the country along its southern border, traversed by the Union Pacific railroad, and to the occupation by Indians of the more fertile districts. Latterly, as the Indians have been removed, settlement has progressed more rapidly. (H. G*.)

WYON, THOMAS (1792-1817), medallist, was born at Birmingham in 1792. He was apprenticed to his father, the chief engraver of His Majesty's seals, and studied in the schools of the Royal Academy, London, where he gained silver medals in both the antique and the life class; he also obtained a gold medal from the Society of Arts. He was appointed probationary engraver to the mint in 1811, and soon after engraved his medal commemorative of the peace, and his Manchester Pitt medal. In 1815 he was appointed chief engraver to the mint; but he sank into ill-health, and died at Hastings on September 22, 1817, at the age of twenty-five.

A memoir of Wyon, with a list of his works, appeared in the *Gentleman's Magazine* for February 1818. His younger brother, Benjamin Wyon (1802-1858), and his nephews, Joseph Shepherd Wyon (1836-1873) and Alfred Benjamin Wyon (1837-1884), were also well-known medallists. They successively held the appointment of chief engraver of Her Majesty's seals.

WYON, WILLIAM (1795-1851), medallist, cousin of Thomas Wyon, was born at Birmingham in 1795. In 1809 he was apprenticed to his father, a die-sinker. Removing to London, he studied the works of Flaxman, attended the schools of the Royal Academy, and gained a gold medal from the Society of Arts for a copy of the head of Ceres, and a second for an original group. In 1816 he was appointed assistant engraver to the mint, and in 1828 chief engraver; in 1831 he was elected associate and in 1838 full member of the Royal Academy. He executed coinages for George IV., William IV., and Queen Victoria, the Peninsular, Trafalgar, and Cabul medals, the William IV. coronation medal, and those of many learned societies. He died at Brighton on October 29, 1851. A memoir, with a list of his works, by Nicholas Carlisle, was privately issued in 1837.

WYTTENBACH, Daniel Albert (1746–1820), a famous classical scholar, was born at Bern, of a family whose nobility and distinction he loved to recall. In particular, he was proud of his descent from Thomas Wyttenbach, professor of theology in Basel at the end of the 15th and beginning of the 16th centuries, who numbered the Reformer Zwingli and other distinguished men among his pupils. Wyttenbach's own father was also a theological professor of considerable note, first at Bern, and then at Marburg. His removal to Marburg, which took place in 1756, was partly due to old associations, for the elder Wyttenbach had studied there under the famous Christian Wolff, and embodied the philosophical principles of his master in his own theological teaching. Soon after the Wyttenbachs settled in Germany the great war broke out, and the region around Marburg suffered severely, so that the scenes and excitement of military life must have powerfully affected the growth of the boy's somewhat sensitive character. After a careful preliminary education, partly in the schools of Bern and Marburg, partly by private tutors, and always under the eye of a severe but conscientious and affectionate father, young Wyttenbach entered at the age of fourteen the university of Marburg, and passed through a four years' course there. His parents intended that he should become a Lutheran pastor. The first two years were given up to general education, principally to mathematics, "philology," and history. The professor of mathematics, Spangenberg, acquired great influence over young Wyttenbach. He is said to have taught his subject with great clearness, and with equal seriousness and piety, often referring to God as the supreme mathematician, who had constructed all things by number, measure, and weight. "Philology" in the German universities of that age meant Hebrew and Greek. These two languages were generally handled by the same professor, and were taught almost solely to theological students. Wyttenbach's university course at Marburg was troubled about the middle of the time by mental unrest, due to the fascination exercised over him by Bunyan's *Pilgrim's Progress*. Like Bunyan himself, he believed that he was doomed to perdition, and that he had committed the inexpiable sin against the Holy Ghost. The disorder was cured by Spangenberg. The principal study of the third year was metaphysics, which took Wyttenbach entirely captive. The fourth and last year was to be devoted to theology and Christian dogma. Wyttenbach had hitherto submitted passively to his father's wishes concerning his career, in the hope that some unexpected occurrence might set him free. But he now turned away from theological lectures, and privately devoted his time to the task of deepening and extending his knowledge of Greek literature. His father was wise enough to leave him to follow his own bent. To use Wyttenbach's own words, he looked up to every Greek book as a temple of wisdom. But the struggle for knowledge was hard, and taxed all his powers. He possessed at the time, as he tells us, no more acquaintance with Greek than his own pupils at a later time could acquire from him during four months' study. He was almost entirely without equipment beyond the bare texts of the authors. Each author only yielded after a protracted siege. But Wyttenbach was undaunted, and four years' persistent study gave him a knowledge of Greek such as few Germans of that time possessed. His love for philosophy carried him towards the Greek philosophers, especially Plato. He describes himself as walking about the meadows near Marburg, conning portions of his text of Plato, which he had taken to pieces for easier carriage. During this period Ruhnken's notes on the Platonic lexicon of *Timæus* fell into his hands. Ruhnken was for him almost a superhuman being, whom he worshipped day and night, and with whom he imagined himself as holding converse in the spirit. Taking up the works of Julian, he emended them on the principles of Ruhnken. When Wyttenbach was twenty-two he determined to seek elsewhere the aids to study which Marburg could not afford. His father, fully realizing the strength of his son's pure passion for scholarship, permitted and even advised him to seek Heyne at Göttingen. From this teacher he received the utmost kindness and encouragement, and he was urged by him to dedicate to Ruhnken the first fruits of his scholarship. Wyttenbach therefore set to work on some notes to Julian, Eunapius, and Aristænetus, and Heyne wrote to Ruhnken to bespeak his favourable consideration for the work. Before it reached him Ruhnken wrote a kind letter to Wyttenbach, which the recipient "read, re-read, and kissed," and another on receipt of the tract, in which the great scholar declared that he had not looked to find in Germany such knowledge of Greek, such power of criticism, and such mature judgment, especially in one so young. Wyttenbach was now able with boldness to devote himself to the career of a scholar. He studied with ardour the works of the great scholars of the Netherlands, and in his morning and evening petitions prayed that it might be given him to see Valckenaer and Ruhnken in the flesh. By Heyne's advice, he now worked hard at Latin, which he knew far less thoroughly than Greek, and we soon find Heyne praising his progress in Latin style to both Ruhnken and Valckenaer. He now wrote to ask their advice about his scheme of coming to the Netherlands to follow the profession of a scholar. Ruhnken strongly exhorted Wyttenbach to follow his own example, for he too had been designed by his parents for the Christian ministry in Germany, but had settled at Leyden on the invitation of Hemsterhuis. Valckenaer's answer was to the same effect, but he added that Wyttenbach's letter would have been pleasanter to him had it been free from excessive compliments. These letters were forwarded to the elder Wyttenbach, with a strong recommendation from Heyne. The old man had been himself in Leyden in his youth, and entertained an admiration for the scholarship of the Netherlands; so his consent was easily won. Young Wyttenbach reached Leyden in 1770. According to his own description, he approached the gates of the city with a feeling of religious awe such as might have passed over an ancient visitant to Athens and the Acropolis. As he neared Ruhnken's door, the words of Homer "surely there is some god within" were in his mind. He was delighted to find the great man entirely free from the pomposity and assumption which had made many of the German professors disagreeable to him. A year was spent with great contentment, in learning the language of the people, in attending the lectures of the great "duumviri" of Leyden, and in collating MSS. of Plutarch. At the end of 1771 a professor was wanted at Amsterdam for the College of the Remonstrants. By the recommendation of Ruhnken, Wyttenbach obtained the chair, which he filled with great success for eight years. His lectures took a wide range. Those on Greek were repeated also to the students of the university of Amsterdam (the "Athenæum"). In 1775 a visit was made to Paris, which was fruitful both of new friendships and of progress in study. About this time, on the advice of Ruhnken, Wyttenbach began the issue of his *Bibliotheca Critica*, which appeared at intervals for the next thirty years. The object professed in the preface was to help in rescuing classical studies from the neglect into which they had fallen, by creating an interest in new works of merit, through critical notices, embodying the results of original research by the writer himself. It was in fact a kind of critical review written by one man. The methods of criticism employed were in the main those established by Hemsterhuis, and carried on by Valckenaer and Ruhnken, and the publication met with acceptance from the learned all over Europe. In 1777 the younger Burmann ("Burmannus Secundus") retired from his professorship at the Athenæum, and Wyttenbach hoped to succeed him. When another received the appointment, he was sorely discouraged. Only his regard for Ruhnken and for Dutch freedom (in his own words "Ruhnkeni et Batavæ libertatis cogitatio") kept him in Holland. For fear of losing him, the authorities at Amsterdam nominated him in 1779 professor of philosophy. Some of his lectures given in this capacity were worked up for publication; in particular a treatise on logic belongs to this period. In philosophy Wyttenbach never shook off the influence of Wolff, and the Kantians were irate because he failed to appreciate their master. In 1785 Toll, Burmann's successor, resigned, and Wyttenbach was at once appointed to succeed him. His full title was "professor of history and eloquence and Greek and Latin literature." He had hardly got to work in his new office when Valckenaer died, and he received a call to Leyden. Greatly to Ruhnken's disappointment, he declined to abandon the duties he had so recently undertaken. In 1787 began the internal commotions in Holland, afterwards to be aggravated by foreign interference. Scarcely during the remaining thirty-three years of Wyttenbach's life was there a moment of peace in the land. He held entirely aloof from factions, and yearned continually after quiet and reconciliation. About this time two requests were made to him for an edition of the *Moralia* of Plutarch, for which a recension of the tract "De sera numinis vindicta" had marked him out in the eyes of scholars. One request came from the famous "Societas Bipontina," the other from the delegates of the Clarendon Press at Oxford. Wyttenbach, influenced at once by the reputation of the university, and by the liberality of the Oxonians in tendering him assistance of different kinds, declined the offer of the Bipontine Society,—very fortunately, since their press was soon destroyed by the French. The fortunes of Wyttenbach's edition curiously illustrate the text "habent sua fata libelli." The first portion was safely conveyed to Oxford in 1794. Then war broke out between Holland and Great Britain. Randolph, Wyttenbach's Oxford correspondent, advised that the next portion should be sent through the British ambassador at Hamburg, and the MS. was duly consigned to him "in a little chest well protected by pitch." After sending Randolph a number of letters without getting any answer, Wyttenbach in disgust put all thought of the edition from him, and a shudder ran through his frame whenever Plutarch was mentioned. At last, after simultaneous letters had been despatched to a good many delegates of the Clarendon Press, the missing box was discovered in a forgotten corner at Hamburg, where it had lain for two years and a half. The work was finally completed in 1805. Meanwhile Wyttenbach received repeated invitations to leave Amsterdam, which were refused. One came from his native city Bern, another from Leyden, where vacancies had been created by the refusal of professors to swear allegiance to the new Dutch republic set up in 1795, in which Wyttenbach had acquiesced. But he only left Amsterdam in 1799, when on Ruhnken's death he succeeded him at Leyden. Even then his chief object in removing was to facilitate an arrangement by which the necessities of his old master's family might be relieved. His removal came too late in life, and he was never so happy at Leyden as he had been at Amsterdam. Before long appeared the ever-delightful *Life of David Ruhnken.* Though written in Latin, this biography deserves to rank high in the modern literature of its class. It is composed in a style that is lucid, flowing, and graceful, not imitated from any one ancient author, but (a few grammatical matters apart) such as we can imagine that some gifted Roman of the classical time might well have struck out for himself. One of Ruhnken's friends called it "a Milesian tale," partly from the fascination of the style, and partly because the book often took such a wide range that Ruhnken was lost amid extended observations springing out of his relation to the classical studies of his age. Of Wyttenbach's life at Leyden there is little to tell. The continual changes in state affairs greatly disorganized the universities of Holland, and Wyttenbach had to work in face of much detraction; still his success as a teacher was very great. In 1805 he narrowly escaped with his life from the great gunpowder explosion, which killed 150 people, among them the Greek scholar Luzac, Wyttenbach's colleague in the university. One of Wyttenbach's letters gives a vivid account of the disaster. During the last years of his life he suffered severely from illness and became nearly blind. After the conclusion of his edition of Plutarch's *Moralia* in 1805, the only important work he was able to publish was his well-known edition of Plato's *Phædo.* Many honours were conferred upon him both at home and abroad, and in particular he was made a member of the French Institute. Shortly before his death, he obtained the licence of the king of Holland to marry his sister's daughter, Johanna Gallien, who had for twenty years devoted herself to him as housekeeper, secretary, and aider in his studies. The sole object of the marriage was to secure for her a better provision after her husband's death, because as the widow of a professor she would be entitled to a pension. Johanna Gallien was a woman of remarkable culture and ability, and wrote works held in great repute at that time. On the festival of the tercentenary of the foundation of the university of Marburg, celebrated in 1827, the degree of doctor was conferred upon her. Wyttenbach died of apoplexy in 1820, and he was buried in the garden of his country house near Amsterdam, within sight, as he noted, of the dwellings of Descartes and Boerhaave.

Although his work can hardly be set on the same level as that of Hemsterhuis, Valckenaer, and Ruhnken, yet he was a very eminent exponent of the sound methods of criticism which they established. These four men, more than any others after Bentley, laid the foundations of Greek scholarship as it exists to-day. The precise study of grammar, syntax, and style, and the careful criticism of texts by the light of the best manuscript evidence, were upheld by these scholars in the Netherlands when they were almost entirely neglected elsewhere on the Continent, and were only pursued with partial success in England. Wyttenbach may fairly be regarded as closing a great period in the history of scholarship. He lived indeed to see the new birth of German classical learning, but his work was done, and he was unaffected by it. Wyttenbach's criticism was less rigorous, precise, and masterly, but perhaps more sensitive and sympathetic than that of his great predecessors in the Netherlands. In actual acquaintance with the philosophical writings of the ancients, he has probably never been surpassed. In character he was upright and simple-minded, but shy and retiring, and often failed to make himself appreciated. His life was not passed without strife, but his few friends were warmly attached to him, and his many pupils were for the most part his enthusiastic admirers. Wyttenbach's biography was written in a somewhat dry and lifeless manner by Mahne, one of his pupils, who also published some of his letters. His *Opuscula*, other than those published in the *Bibliotheca Critica*, were collected in two volumes (Leyden, 1823). (J. S. R.)

X

X represents the Phœnician letter Samekh, to which the old Ionian Ξ is singularly close in form. This form is familiar to Greek students, because it belongs to the alphabet that superseded the alphabet of the Eubœan type which was first in use at Athens. But the Eubœan form of the letter was + (see Roehl, *I.G.A.*, No. 372); and this form went with the Eubœan alphabet of Chalcis to the western Hellenic world, and passed in Italy into the form X, which survives with us. The history of the symbol in Italy is not, however, perfectly clear, because in the extremely archaic alphabets of Cære and Formello we find not only + but also a symbol ⊞, and this has the place of *Xι* in the Ionian alphabet, whereas + stands after U, instead of in its proper place, which has been thus usurped by this huge and otherwise unknown intruder. There would be no difficulty in supposing that + is only a curtailed portion of the fuller form, and that the two survived for a time side by side in the alphabet, perhaps with some differentiation of value, were it not that this is inconsistent with the ultimate derivation of the Italic alphabet from Chalcis, where the large form certainly does not appear. The name *Xι* (ksi) is clearly Greek, not, like the names of the letters in general, borrowed from the Phœnician. It is obviously modelled upon Psi, just as Psi was itself modelled upon Pi. The value of the sound in Phœnician was probably a strong sibilant, with a weak guttural preceding. In the old inscriptions of the Ægean Islands—Thera, Naxos, &c.—we find a double symbol **KM** (*i.e.*, *ks*); in Naxos we find also **XΣ** and **BΣ** (*i.e.*, *hs*), which indicates a guttural breathing before the *s*; and in old Attic inscriptions also we find **XΣ**.

But this same symbol X had another very different value in Greece from *ks*, and by this value, *i.e.*, a guttural aspirate, *kh* or *ch*, it is familiar to Greek students under the name Chi. This value is confined to alphabets of the Ionian type. In the islands we find **KB** or **KH**, also **ΦB** at Thera, digraphs being employed in the same manner as for *ks* and *ps*. This same guttural sound is represented in alphabets of the Eubœan type under the form **Y** or **Ψ**, which appears naturally in the Cære alphabet, but in the derived Italian alphabets was retained by the Etruscan only. In Greece it was found in Bœotia and the Peloponnesus: *e.g.*, it appears on the tripod at Delphi set up by the Lacedæmonians to commemorate the victory of Platææ. But in the Ionic alphabet alone this same symbol has a totally different value, to wit, *ps*, and to this value the Greeks gave the name Psi. It is noteworthy that the old Attic way of writing this double sound was **ΦΣ**. The origin of this second X and that of its companion **Y** is very uncertain. The Attic writings above mentioned, and the **ΦB** of Thera, give colour to the idea that X and Φ may be survivals of a ruder alphabet, superseded by the Phœnician, with the values *k* and *p*. On the other hand, it does not seem impossible that **Ψ**, with the value *ch*, may be a descendant of the useless **Ϙ** (koppa), obtained by opening out the circle (Taylor, *Alphabet*, ii. 93); but the same writer maintains that X is a variation of K, which seems very improbable. It is at least as credible that it is a variant of Samekh, in which the guttural element of the original complex sound superseded the sibilant.

There is nothing noteworthy in the history of *x* in English. In French, when medial, it has generally passed into *ss*, as in *laisser* (from *laxare*); and it has the same sound, even when written, as in *soixante*. It is frequently found at the end of words owing to a mis-writing, the contraction for final *us* having been confounded with it, as in plurals, *yeux*, *animaux*, &c., where the *u* has been added again, also in *époux* (esponsus), *faux* (falsus), *roux* (russus), &c. Not unnaturally the *x* has been substituted still further, as in *prix*; in other cases, like *croix*, we have probably a learned imitation of the Latin. Italian also substitutes *ss* for *x*, as in *massimo* for *maximus*, *lussuria*, &c. On *x* in Spanish, see vol. xxii. p. 350.

XALAPA. See JALAPA.

XANTHUS, an ancient city of LYCIA (*q.v.*), on the river Xanthus, about 8 miles above its mouth. It is chiefly memorable in history for its two sieges, and the desperate but unavailing resistance made on both occasions. The first siege was by the Persian general Harpagus (see vol. xviii. p. 566), when the acropolis was burned and the inhabitants, with all their possessions, perished (Herod., i. 176). The city was afterwards rebuilt; and in 42 B.C. it was besieged by the Romans under Brutus. It was taken by storm and set on fire; and the inhabitants, refusing to surrender, all perished in the flames. During its prosperity, Xanthus contained many fine temples and other buildings, extensive remains of which, in excellent preservation, were discovered by Sir C. Fellows (*Excursion in Asia Minor*, 1839). A large collection of marbles, chiefly sepulchral, from Xanthus is now in the British Museum.

XAVIER, FRANCISCO (1506-1552), surnamed the "Apostle of the Indies," was the youngest son of Juan de Jasso, privy councillor to Jean d'Albret, king of Navarre, and his wife Maria Azpilcueta Xavier, sole heiress of two noble Navarrese families. He was born at his mother's castle of Xavero or Xavier, at the foot of the Pyrenees and close to the little town of Sanguesa, on 7th April 1506, according to a family register, though his earlier biographers fix his birth in 1497. Following a Spanish custom of the time, which left the surname of either parent optional with children, he was called by his mother's family name, and grew up tall, strong, healthy, and active both in mind and body, with a lively, cheerful disposition. He showed no taste, however, for the career of arms, and early disclosed a preference for literary pursuits. His father accordingly strained his slender resources to send him, in 1524, to the university of Paris, then much frequented by Spaniards, where he entered the College of St Barbara, and made such rapid progress that he was appointed in 1528 lecturer in Aristotelian philosophy at the Collége de Beauvais. In 1530 he took his degree as master of arts. The same year which saw his nomination as lecturer at the university saw also the arrival there of the man who was to mould his destiny and that of his chamber-mate Pierre le Fèvre, namely, Ignatius Loyola, even then meditating the foundation of his celebrated institute (see JESUITS, vol. xiii. p. 652). Ignatius speedily recognized in Xavier the qualities which made him the first missionary of his time, —and set himself to win him as an associate in his vast enterprise. Xavier, after a protracted resistance, yielded to the spell, and was one of the little band of seven persons, including Loyola himself, who took the original Jesuit vows and founded the company, on 15th August 1534, in the crypt of Notre Dame de Montmartre. They continued in Paris for two years longer, though there is some uncertainty whether Xavier retained his chair; but on 15th November 1536 they started for Italy, to concert with Ignatius (then in Spain, but purposing to join them) plans for a mission to convert the Moslems of Palestine About Epiphany-tide 1537, after a journey attended with much fatigue and some danger, owing to the disturbed posture of political affairs, they arrived in Venice, where they found Ignatius awaiting them. As some months must needs elapse before they could sail for the Holy Land, Ignatius determined that the time should be spent partly in hospital work at Venice and later in the journey to Rome, there to obtain their credentials. Accordingly, Xavier devoted himself for nine weeks to the care of the patients in the hospital for incurables, at the end of which time he set out with eight companions for Rome, where Pope Paul III. received them favourably, sanctioned their enterprise, and gave them facilities for obtaining ordination. Returning to Venice, Xavier was ordained priest on Midsummer Day 1537; but the outbreak of war between Venice and Turkey put an end to the Palestine expedition. Hereupon the companions agreed to disperse for a twelvemonth's home mission work in the Italian cities, and Bobadilla and Xavier betook themselves, first to Monselice, thence to Bologna, where they remained till summoned to Rome by Ignatius at the close of 1538, to consider his plans for erecting the company into a religious order, with a formal constitution under papal sanction. The draft rules were signed by the whole number on 15th April 1539, though it was not till 1540 that the pope's confirmation was given, nor was it published till 1541. While the remaining members dispersed anew for work in various parts of Italy, Ignatius retained Xavier at Rome as secretary to the new institute. Meanwhile John III., king of Portugal, had resolved on sending a mission to his East Indian dominions, and, at the instance of his minister Govea, applied through his envoy Pedro de Mascarenhas to the pope for six Jesuits to undertake the task. Ignatius could spare but two, and chose Rodriguez and Bobadilla for the purpose; and the former set out at once for Lisbon to confer with the king. Bobadilla, sent for to Rome, arrived there just before Mascarenhas was about to depart, but fell too ill to respond to the call made on him. Hereupon Ignatius on 15th March 1540 told Xavier to leave Rome the next day with Mascarenhas, in order to join Rodriguez in the Indian mission. Xavier complied, merely waiting long enough to obtain the pope's benediction, and set out for Lisbon, where he was presented to the king, and soon won his entire confidence, attested notably by procuring for him from the pope four briefs, one of them appointing him papal nuncio in the Indies. On 7th April 1541, his thirty-fifth birthday, he sailed from Lisbon with Martin Alphonso de Souza, governor of India, and, refusing all accommodations for the voyage offered him, except a few books and some clothing, lived amongst the common sailors on board, ministering to their religious and temporal needs, especially during an outbreak of scurvy. After five months' voyage the ship reached Mozambique, where the captain resolved to winter, and Xavier was prostrated with a severe attack of fever. When the voyage was resumed, the ship touched at the Mohammedan town of Melinde, whose sultan told Xavier of the marked decline of Islam. But neither there nor at the island of Socotra, the next point of arrival, where Christianity was equally declining, was the missionary able to remain long enough to attempt any work; and he finally reached Goa on 6th May 1542. Exhibiting his brief to João d' Albuquerque, bishop of Goa, he asked his permission to officiate in the diocese, and at once began a mission, walking through the streets ringing a small bell, and telling all those attracted by its sound to come themselves, and send their children and servants, to the "Christian doctrine" or catechetical instruction in the principal church. He spent five months actively employed in Goa, where he is stated to have effected much reformation in morals, and then turned his attention to the fishery coast, extending from Cape Comorin to the Paumbum Pass, where he had heard that the Paravas, a tribe engaged in the pearl-fishery, had relapsed into heathenism after having professed Christianity. He laboured assiduously amongst them for fifteen months, and at the end of 1543 returned to Goa to procure colleagues for the mission. Travancore was his next field of action, and there he is said to have succeeded in founding no fewer than forty-five Christian settlements, each with numerous converts. It is to be noted that his own letters contain, both at this time and later on, express disproof of his possession of that miraculous gift of tongues with which he was credited even in his lifetime, and which is attributed to him in the *Breviary* office for his festival. Not only was he obliged to employ interpreters, but he relates that in their absence he was compelled to use signs only, and he never appears to have displayed any special aptitude for acquiring new languages. He sent a missionary to the isle of Manaar, and himself visited Ceylon, where he proved unsuccessful in an effort to invoke Portuguese interference in a dynastic dispute, and betook himself thence to Meliapur, the traditionary tomb of St Thomas the apostle, which he reached in April 1544, continuing there four months. His next sphere of active work was Malacca, which he reached on 25th September 1545, and where he remained another four months, but had comparatively little success, and abandoned it at last as wholly intractable. While there he addressed a letter to King John of Portugal, urging him to set up the Inquisition in Goa to repress Judaism, and was readily listened to, although the actual erection of the tribunal did not take place till 1560, some years after his own death. After a missionary expedition to Amboyna and other isles of the Molucca group, he returned to Malacca in July 1547, and found three Jesuit recruits from Europe awaiting him. An attack upon Malacca by the sultan of Acheen, which the governor was disinclined to punish, aroused the warlike temper which slumbered in Xavier's breast, and he compelled the organization of an expedition to chastise the invaders, which proved a triumph and much increased his local influence. While in Malacca he met one Han-Siro, a Japanese exile (known to the biographies as Anger), whose conversation fired him with zeal for the conversion of Japan. But he first paid a series of visits to the scenes of his former labours, and then, returning to Malacca, took ship for Japan, accompanied by Han-Siro, now known as Paul of the Holy Faith. After a perilous voyage they reached Kagoshima, at the south of Kiusiu, the southernmost of the larger Japanese islands, and in the territory of the daimio of Satsuma. Kagoshima was Han-Siro's birthplace, and he was himself heartily welcomed by his friends, whom he induced to extend their good-will to his companions. The daimio, who desired to secure the Portuguese trade, was friendly at first; but, finding that the merchant vessels preferred the safer anchorage of Firando (or Hirado) far to the north of his fief, he withdrew his permission to preach and threatened converts with the penalty of death. Xavier judged it well to move elsewhither, and travelled on foot to Firando, making some converts on the road, and proving far more successful at Firando itself than in Kagoshima. Thence he proceeded to the capital of the empire, the city then known as Miako, subsequently as Kioto, and now as Saikio or "western capital." But the mikados or emperors had been little more than puppets under the control of the shoguns or hereditary commanders-in-chief for some centuries before this time, so that Xavier judged that he could work more effectually at the courts of the great daimios than at that of their nominal sovereign. He also noticed that asceticism and poverty had no such attractive power in Japan as they had exercised in India, and determined to try the effect of some measure of pomp and display on his return from Miako. Making but a brief stay at Firando, he went to Amanguchi (Yamaguchi), capital of Suwo, and there presented himself to the daimio in some state, bringing him valuable presents. He was allowed to preach, and had some success, which encouraged him to proceed to Fucheo, capital of the fief of Bungo (Bugo), where his mission prospered more than anywhere else in Japan; and, feeling that he could now safely leave the work in other hands, he quitted that empire in 1551, intending to attempt next the conversion of China. On board the "Santa Cruz," the vessel in which he sailed to Malacca, he discussed this project with Diego Pereira, the captain, and devised the plan of persuading the viceroy of Portuguese India to despatch an embassy to China, in whose train he might enter, in despite of the law which then excluded foreigners from that empire. He reached Goa in February 1552, and after settling some disputes which had arisen in his absence obtained from the viceroy consent to the plan of a Chinese embassy and to the nomination of Pereira as envoy. Large sums for the necessary expenses were contributed by the treasury, by Pereira himself, and by subscriptions from private persons interested in the missionary part of the scheme. Xavier left India on 25th April 1552 and betook himself to Malacca, there to meet Pereira and to re-embark on the "Santa Cruz." But Alvaro d' Ataide, governor of Malacca, had a private grudge against Pereira, and besides desired the Chinese embassy for himself, and therefore threw difficulties in the way of the expedition, though Xavier, anticipating something of the kind, had procured for him the high office of captaincy of the neighbouring seas, and had also provided himself with stringent orders from the viceroy for the furtherance of his object, with threats of punishment for disobedience. Ataide, however, paid no attention to them, and laid an embargo on the "Santa Cruz." Xavier, who with characteristic modesty had kept his dignity as papal nuncio private (save for exhibiting the brief to the bishop at Goa on his first arrival in India), determined to avail himself of it now, and desired the vicar-general of Malacca to inform the governor, and to remind him that such as impeded a nuncio in the discharge of his office were subject to excommunication by the pope himself. Ataide paid no more regard to the papal brief than he had done to the viceroy's letter, and even charged Xavier with having forged it,—if not both documents,—while the people of Malacca sided with him against Xavier and Pereira. At last, however, he agreed to a compromise. The embassy was stopped and Pereira detained, while some of the governor's people were substituted for as many of the crew of the "Santa Cruz," in which Xavier and two companions were allowed to proceed. The vicar-general asked him to take formal leave of the governor; but he refused, saying that they would meet no more till the day of judgment, when Ataide must give account for his resistance to the spread of the gospel, and, shaking the dust of Malacca from his shoes, he embarked 16th July 1552. After a short stay at Singapore, whence he despatched several letters to India and Europe, the ship at the end of August 1552 reached San-chan (Chang-chuang), an island at no great distance from Canton, which served as port and rendezvous for Europeans, not then admitted to trade directly with China. Xavier was seized with fever soon after his arrival, and was, in addition, delayed by the failure of the interpreter he had engaged, as well as by the reluctance of the Portuguese to attempt the voyage to Canton for the purpose of landing him. He arranged for his passage in a Chinese junk and had made all other preparations for starting, when he was again attacked by fever, and died on 2d December 1552. He was buried close to the cabin where he had died, but his body was later transferred to Malacca, and thence to Goa, where it still lies. He was beatified by Paul V. in 1619 and canonized by Gregory XV. in 1621.

The chief authorities for the life of St Francis Xavier are *De Vita Sancti Francisci Xaverii Libri VI.*, by the Jesuit Torsellino (Tursellinus), Rome, 1596, of which there is a vigorous English version, Paris, 1632; another biography by Lucena, Lisbon, 1600; his *Letters*, published in seven books by the Jesuit Poussines (Possinus), Rome, 1667; a fuller collection of the *Letters* by another Jesuit, Menchacha, Bologna, 1795, translated into French by Léon Pagès, Paris, 1854; Faria y Souza, *Asia Portuguesa*, Lisbon, 1655; Bouhours, *Vie de St François Xavier*, Paris, 1684; Bartoli, *Asia*, part i., Rome, 1653; H. J. Coleridge, *Life and Letters of St Francis Xavier*, London, 1872; while a graphic sketch of the more striking episodes is to be found in Sir James Stephen's article on the "Founders of Jesuitism," reprinted in his *Essays in Ecclesiastical Biography*, London, 1849. (R. F. L.)

XENIA, a city of the United States, the county seat of Greene county, Ohio, is situated in the midst of a rich agricultural region, and on the Pittsburg, Cincinnati, and St Louis and the Dayton, Fort Wayne, and Chicago Railways. It is one of the oldest cities of Ohio, having been laid out in 1803. It is the seat of the Methodist Episcopal Xenia college (1850), a Presbyterian theological seminary (1794), and Wilberforce university (1863), this last designed for the education of coloured youth of both sexes. The population in 1880 was 7026.

XENOCRATES of Chalcedon, scholarch or rector of the Academy from 339 to 314 B.C., was born in 396. Removing to Athens in early youth, he became the pupil of the Socratic Æschines, but presently joined himself to Plato, whom he attended to Sicily in 361. Upon his master's death (347 B.C.), in company with Aristotle he paid a visit to Hermias at Atarneus. In 339, Aristotle being then in Macedonia, Xenocrates succeeded Speusippus in the presidency of the school, defeating his competitors Menedemus and Heracleides by a few votes. On three occasions he was member of an Athenian legation, once to Philip, twice to Antipater. Soon after the death of Demosthenes in 322, resenting the Macedonian influence then dominant at Athens, Xenocrates declined the citizenship offered to him at the instance of Phocion, and, being unable to pay the tax levied upon resident aliens, was, it is said, sold, or on the point of being sold, into slavery. He died in 314, and was succeeded as scholarch by Polemon, whom he had reclaimed from a life of profligacy. Besides Polemon, the statesman Phocion, Chæron tyrant of Pellene, the Academic Crantor, the Stoic Zeno, and Epicurus are alleged to have frequented his lectures.

Xenocrates's earnestness and strength of character won for him universal respect, and stories were remembered in proof of his purity, integrity, and benevolence. Wanting in quickness of apprehension and in native grace, he made up for these deficiencies by a conscientious love of truth and an untiring industry. Less original than Speusippus, he adhered more closely to the letter of Platonic doctrine, and is accounted the typical representative of the Old Academy. In his writings, which were numerous, he seems to have covered nearly the whole of the Academic programme; but metaphysics and ethics were the subjects which principally engaged his thoughts. He is said to have invented, or at least to have emphasized, the tripartition of philosophy under the heads of physic, dialectic, and ethic.

In his ontology Xenocrates built upon Plato's foundations: that is to say, with Plato he postulated ideas or numbers to be the causes of nature's organic products, and derived these ideas or numbers from unity (which is active) and plurality (which is passive). But he put upon this fundamental dogma a new interpretation. According to Plato, existence is mind pluralized: mind as a unity, *i.e.*, universal mind, apprehends its own plurality as eternal, immutable, intelligible ideas; and mind as a plurality, *i.e.*, particular mind, perceives its own plurality as transitory, mutable, sensible things. The idea, inasmuch as it is a law of universal mind, which in particular minds produces aggregates of sensations called things, is a "determinant" (πέρας ἔχον), and as such is styled "quantity" (ποσόν) and perhaps "number" (ἀριθμός); but the ideal numbers are distinct from arithmetical numbers, and the elements of ideal numbers from the elements of arithmetical numbers. Xenocrates, however, failing, as it would seem, to grasp the idealism which was the metaphysical foundation of Plato's theory of natural kinds, took for his principles arithmetical unity and plurality, and accordingly identified ideal numbers with arithmetical numbers. In thus reverting to the crudities of certain Pythagoreans he laid himself open to the criticisms of Aristotle, who, in his *Metaphysics*, recognizing amongst contemporary Platonists three principal groups—(1) those who, like Plato, distinguished mathematical and ideal numbers; (2) those who, like Xenocrates, identified them; and (3) those who, like Speusippus, postulated mathematical numbers only—has much to say against the Xenocratean interpretation of the theory, and in particular points out that, if the ideas are numbers made up of arithmetical units, they not only cease to be principles but also become subject to arithmetical operations. Xenocrates's theory of inorganic nature was substantially identical with the theory of the elements which is propounded in the *Timæus*, 53 C *sq.* Nevertheless, holding that every dimension has a principle of its own, he rejected the derivation of the elemental solids—pyramid, octahedron, icosahedron, and cube—from triangular surfaces, and in so far approximated to atomism. Moreover, to the tetrad of simple elements—namely, fire, air, water, earth—he added the πέμπτη οὐσία, ether.

His cosmology, which is drawn almost entirely from the *Timæus*, and, as he intimated, is not to be regarded as a cosmogony, should be studied in connexion with his psychology. Soul is a self-moving number, derived from the two fundamental principles, unity (ἕν) and plurality (δυὰς ἀόριστος), whence it obtains its powers of rest and motion. It is incorporeal, and may exist apart from body. The irrational soul, as well as the rational soul, is immortal. The universe, the heavenly bodies, man, animals, and presumably plants, are each of them endowed with a soul, which is more or less perfect according to the position which it occupies in the descending scale of creation. With this Platonic philosopheme Xenocrates combines the current theology, identifying the universe and the heavenly bodies with the greater gods, and reserving a place between them and mortals for the lesser divinities.

If the extant authorities are to be trusted, Xenocrates recognized three grades of cognition, each appropriated to a region of its own,—namely, knowledge, opinion, and sensation, having for their respective objects supra-celestials or ideas, celestials or stars, and infra-celestials or things. Even here the mythological tendency displays itself,—νοητά, δοξαστά, and αἰσθητά being severally committed to Atropos, Lachesis, and Clotho. Of Xenocrates's logic we know only that with Plato he distinguished τὸ καθ' αὑτό and τὸ πρός τι, rejecting the Aristotelian list of ten categories as a superfluity.

Valuing philosophy chiefly for its influence upon conduct, Xenocrates bestowed especial attention upon ethics. The catalogue of his works shows that he had written largely upon this subject; but the indications of doctrine which have survived are scanty, and may be summed up in a few sentences. Things are goods, ills, or neutrals. Goods are of three sorts—mental, bodily, external; but of all goods virtue is incomparably the greatest. Happiness consists in the practice of virtue, the requisite powers and opportunities being presupposed. Hence the virtuous man is always happy, though his happiness cannot be perfect unless he is adequately provided with personal and extraneous advantages. The virtuous man is pure, not in act only, but also in heart. To the attainment of virtue the best help is philosophy; for the philosopher does of his own accord what others do under the compulsion of law. Speculative wisdom and practical wisdom are to be distinguished. Meagre as these statements are, they suffice to show that in ethics, as elsewhere, Xenocrates worked upon Platonic lines, and that in his theory of the relations of external advantages to happiness, as well as in the technicalities of his exposition, he closely resembled Aristotle.

Xenocrates was not in any sense a great thinker. His metaphysic was a travesty rather than a reproduction of that of his master. His ethic had little which was distinctive. But his austere life and commanding personality made him an effective teacher, and his influence, kept alive by his pupils Polemon and Crates, ceased only when Arcesilaus, the founder of the so-called Second Academy, gave a new direction to the studies of the school.

Bibliography.—D. Van de Wynpersse, *De Xenocrate Chalcedonio*, Leyden, 1822; C. A. Brandis, *Gesch. d. Griechisch-Römischen Philosophie*, Berlin, 1853, ii. 2, 1, 19-37; E. Zeller, *Philosophie d. Griechen*, Leipsic, 1875, ii., 1, 840-842, 862-883; F. W. A. Mullach, *Fragmenta Philosophorum Græcorum*, Paris, 1881, iii. 100-130. (H. JA.)

XENOPHANES of Colophon, the reputed founder of the Eleatic school of philosophy, is supposed to have been born in the third or fourth decade of the 6th century B.C. An exile from his Ionian home, he resided for a time in Sicily, at Zancle and at Catana, and afterwards established himself in southern Italy, at Elea, a Phocæan colony founded in the sixty-first Olympiad (536-533). In one of the extant fragments he speaks of himself as having begun his wanderings sixty-seven years before, when he was twenty-five years of age, so that he was not less than ninety-two when he died. His teaching found expression in poems, which he recited rhapsodically in the course of his travels. In the more considerable of the elegiac fragments which have survived he ridicules the doctrine of the migration of souls (xviii.), asserts the claims of wisdom against the prevalent athleticism, which seemed to him to conduce neither to the good government of states nor to their material prosperity (xix.), reprobates the introduction of Lydian luxury into Colophon (xx.), and recommends the reasonable enjoyment of social pleasures (xxi.). Of the epic fragments the more important are those in which he attacks the "anthropomorphic and anthropopathic polytheism" of his contemporaries. According to Aristotle, "this first of Eleatic unitarians was not careful to say whether the unity which he postulated was finite or infinite, but, contemplating the whole firmament," (or perhaps "the whole world," for the word οὐρανός is ambiguous), "declared that the One is God." Whether Xenophanes was a monotheist, whose assertion of the unity of God *suggested* to Parmenides the doctrine of the unity of Being, or a pantheist, whose assertion of the unity of God was also a declaration of the unity of Being, so that he *anticipated* Parmenides,—in other words, whether Xenophanes's teaching was purely theological or had also a philosophical significance,—is a question about which authorities have differed and will probably continue to differ. The silence of the extant fragments, which have not one word about the unity of Being, favours the one view; the voice of antiquity, which proclaims Xenophanes the founder of Eleaticism, has been thought to favour the other.

Of Xenophanes's utterances about (1) God, (2) the world, (3) knowledge, the following survive. (1) "There is one God, greatest among gods and men, neither in shape nor in thought like unto mortals. . . . He is all sight, all mind, all ear (*i.e.*, not a composite organism). . . . Without an effort ruleth he all things by thought. . . . He abideth ever in the same place motionless, and it befitteth him not to wander hither and thither. . . . Yet men imagine gods to be born, and to have senses, and voice, and body, like themselves. . . . Even so the gods of the Ethiopians are swarthy and flat-nosed, the gods of the Thracians are fair-haired and blue-eyed. . . . Even so Homer and Hesiod attributed to the gods all that is a shame and a reproach among men—theft, adultery, deceit, and other lawless acts. . . . Even so lions and horses and oxen, if they had hands wherewith to grave images, would fashion gods after their own shapes and make them bodies like to their own. (2) From earth all things are and to earth all things return. . . . From earth and water come all of us. . . . The sea is the well whence water springeth. . . . Here at our feet is the end of the earth where it reacheth unto air, but, below, its foundations are without end. . . . The rainbow, which men call Iris, is a cloud that is purple and red and yellow. (3) No man hath certainly known, nor shall certainly know, aught of that which I say about the gods and about all things; for, be that which he saith ever so perfect, yet doth he not know it; all things are matters of opinion. . . . That which I say is opinion like unto truth. . . . The gods did not reveal all things to mortals in the beginning; long is the search ere man findeth that which is better."

There is very little secondary evidence to record. "The Eleatic school," says the Stranger in Plato's *Sophist*, 242 D, "beginning with Xenophanes, and even earlier, starts from the principle of the unity of all things." Aristotle, in a passage already cited, *Metaphysics*, A 5, speaks of Xenophanes as the first of the Eleatic unitarians, adding that his monotheism was reached through the contemplation of the οὐρανός. Theophrastus (in Simplicius's *Ad Physica*, 5) sums up Xenophanes's teaching in the propositions, "The All is One and the One is God." Timon (in Sext. Empir., *Pyrrh.*, i. 224), ignoring Xenophanes's theology, makes him resolve all things into one and the same unity. The demonstrations of the unity and the attributes of God, with which the treatise *De Melisso, Xenophane, et Gorgia* (now no longer ascribed to Aristotle or Theophrastus) accredits Xenophanes, are plainly framed on the model of Eleatic proofs of the unity and the attributes of the Ent, and must therefore be set aside. The epitomators of a later time add nothing to the testimonies already enumerated.

Thus, whereas in his writings, so far as they are known to us Xenophanes appears as a theologian protesting against an anthropomorphic polytheism, the ancients seem to have regarded him as a philosopher asserting the unity of Being. How are we to understand these conflicting, though not irreconcilable, testimonies? According to Zeller, the discrepancy is only apparent. The Greek gods being the powers of nature personified, pantheism lay nearer to hand than monotheism. Xenophanes was then a pantheist. Accordingly his assertion of the unity of God was at the same time a declaration of the unity of Being, and in virtue of this declaration he is entitled to rank as the founder of Eleaticism, inasmuch as the philosophy of Parmenides was his forerunner's pantheism divested of its theistic element. This reconciliation of the internal and the external evidence, countenanced as it is by Theophrastus, one of the best-informed of the ancient historians, and approved by Zeller, one of the most acute of the modern critics, is more than plausible; but there is something to be said on the contrary part. In the first place, it may be doubted whether to a Greek of the 6th century pantheism was nearer than monotheism. Secondly, the external evidence does not bear examination. The Platonic testimony, if it proved anything, would prove too much, namely, that the doctrine of the unity of Being originated, not with Xenophanes, but before him; and, in fact, the passage from the *Sophist* no more proves that Plato attributed to Xenophanes the philosophy of Parmenides than *Theætetus*, 160 D, proves that Plato attributed to Homer the philosophy of Heraclitus. Again, Aristotle's description of Xenophanes as the first of the Eleatic unitarians does not necessarily imply that the unity asserted by Xenophanes was the unity asserted by Parmenides; the phrase, "contemplating the firmament (or the world), he declared that the One is God," leaves it doubtful whether Aristotle attributed to Xenophanes any philosophical theory whatever; and the epithet ἀγροικότερος discourages the belief that Aristotle regarded Xenophanes as the author of a new and important departure. Thirdly, when Xenophanes himself says that his theories about gods and about things are not knowledge, that his utterances are not verities but verisimilitudes, and that, so far from learning things by revelation, man must laboriously seek a better opinion, he plainly renounces the "disinterested pursuit of truth." If then he was indifferent to the problem, he can hardly be credited with the Eleatic solution. In the judgment of the present writer, Xenophanes was neither a philosopher nor a sceptic. He was not a philosopher, for he despaired of knowledge. He was not a sceptic, if by "sceptic" is meant the misologist whose despair of knowledge is the consequence of disappointed endeavour, for he had never hoped. Rather he was a theologian who arrived at his theory of the unity of God by the rejection of the contemporary mythology. But, while he thus stood aloof from philosophy, Xenophanes influenced its development in two ways: first, his theological monism led the way to the philosophical monism of Parmenides and Zeno; secondly, his assertion that so-called knowledge was in reality no more than opinion taught his successors to distinguish knowledge and opinion, and to assign to each a separate province.

Apart from the old controversy about Xenophanes's relations to philosophy, doubts have recently arisen about his theological position. In fragments i., xiv., xvi., xxi., &c., he recognizes, thinks Freudenthal, a plurality of deities; whence it is inferred that, besides the One God, most high, perfect, eternal, who, as immanent intelligent cause, unifies the plurality of things, there were also lesser divinities, who govern portions of the universe, being themselves eternal parts of the one all-embracing Godhead. Whilst it can hardly be allowed that Xenophanes, so far from denying, actually affirms a plurality of gods, it must be conceded to Freudenthal that Xenophanes's polemic was directed against the anthropomorphic tendencies and the mythological details of the contemporary polytheism rather than against the polytheistic principle, and that, apart from the treatise *De Melisso, Xenophane, et Gorgia*, now generally discredited, there is no direct evidence to prove him a consistent monotheist. The wisdom of Xenophanes, like the wisdom of the Hebrew Preacher, showed itself, not in a theory of the universe, but in a sorrowful recognition of the nothingness of things and the futility of endeavour. His theism was a declaration not so much of the greatness of God as rather of the littleness of man. His cosmology was an assertion not so much of the immutability of the One as rather of the mutability of the Many. Like Socrates, he was not a philosopher, and did not pretend to be one; but, as the reasoned scepticism of Socrates cleared the way for the philosophy of Plato, so did Xenophanes's "abnormis sapientia" for the philosophy of Parmenides.

Bibliography.—S. Karsten, *Xenophanis Colophonii Carminum Reliquiæ*, Brussels, 1830; F. W. A. Mullach, *Frag. Phil. Græc.*, Paris, 1860, i. 99-108; G. Teichmüller, *Studien z. Gesch. d. Begriffe*, Berlin, 1874, pp. 589-623; E. Zeller, *Phil. d. Griechen*, Leipsic, 1877, i. 486-507; J. Freudenthal, *Ueber d. Theologie d. Xenophanes*, Breslau, 1886, and "Zur Lehre d. Xen.," in *Archiv f. Gesch. d. Philos.*, Berlin, 1888, i. 322-347. For a fuller bibliography, including the controversy about the *De Melisso, Xen., et Gorgia*, see Ueberweg, *Grundriss d. Gesch. d. Philos.*, Berlin, 1871, i. § 17. See also art. PARMENIDES. (H. JA.)

XENOPHON, Greek historian and essayist, was born at Athens about 430 B.C.[1] He was a citizen of good position, belonging to the order of the knights. Early in life he came under the influence of Socrates. In 401 B.C., being invited by his friend Proxenus to join the expedition of the younger Cyrus against his brother, Artaxerxes II. of Persia, he jumped at the offer, for he was a needy man, and his prospects at home may not have been very good, as the knights were at this time out of favour from having supported the Thirty Tyrants. At the suggestion of Socrates Xenophon went to Delphi to consult the oracle; but his mind was already made up, and he at once crossed to Asia, to Sardis, the place of rendezvous. He joined neither as officer nor as soldier: he went simply to see new countries and peoples out of a spirit of curiosity and love of excitement. Of the expedition itself he has given a full and detailed account in his *Anabasis*, or the "Up-Country March." (See PERSIA, vol. xviii. p. 577.) After the battle of Cunaxa the officers in command of the Greeks were treacherously murdered by the Persian satrap Tissaphernes, with whom they were negotiating an armistice with a view to a safe return. The army was now in the heart of an unknown country, more than a thousand miles from home and in the presence of a troublesome enemy. It was decided to march northwards up the Tigris valley and make for the shores of the Euxine, on which there were several Greek colonies. Xenophon became the leading spirit of the army; he was elected an officer, and he it was who mainly directed the retreat. To his skill, good temper, and firmness the Greeks seem to have largely owed their safety. He seems indeed to have been an Athenian of the best type, having tact and sympathy, with a singular readiness of resource and a straightforward businesslike eloquence which could both persuade and convince. All through the perils and hardships of the retreat he shared the men's privations. Part of the way lay through the wilds of Kurdistan, where they had to encounter the harassing guerilla attacks of savage mountain tribes, and part through the highlands of Armenia and Georgia. After a five months' march they reached Trapezus (Trebizond) on the Black Sea (February 400 B.C.), having given splendid proof of what Greek discipline and spirit could accomplish. When they reached the Euxine a tendency to demoralization began to show itself, and even Xenophon almost lost his control over the soldiery. At Cotyora he aspired to found a new colony; but the idea, not being unanimously accepted, was abandoned, and ultimately Xenophon with his Greeks arrived at Chrysopolis (Scutari) on the Bosphorus, opposite Byzantium. After a brief period of service under a Thracian chief, Seuthes, they were finally incorporated in a Lacedæmonian army which had crossed over into Asia to wage war against the Persian satraps Tissaphernes and Pharnabazus, Xenophon going with them. Near Pergamum he captured a wealthy Persian nobleman with his family, and the ransom paid for his recovery seems to have been sufficient to provide Xenophon with a fair competency.

On his return to Greece Xenophon served under Agesilaus, king of Sparta, which state was at this time at the head of the Greek world. With his native Athens and its general policy and institutions he was not in sympathy. At Coronea he fought with the Spartans against the Athenians and Thebans, for which his fellow-citizens decreed his banishment. The exile found a home at Scillus in Elis, about two miles from Olympia; there he settled down to indulge his tastes for sport and for literature. It was probably at Scillus that he wrote most of his books; there too he built and endowed a temple to Artemis, modelled on the great temple at Ephesus. After Sparta's great defeat at Leuctra in 371 B.C., which fatally shattered

[1] The story that he was present at the battle of Delium in 424 B.C., which would carry back the date of his birth to 444 or 443, is now generally rejected, as it is impossible to reconcile it with his own statements about himself in the *Anabasis*, implying that in 401 B.C. he was a comparatively young man,—we may fairly assume not over thirty years of age.

its ascendency, Xenophon was driven from his home by the people of Elis. Meantime Sparta and Athens had become allies, and the Athenians repealed the decree which had condemned Xenophon to exile. There is, however, no evidence that he ever returned to his native city. According to the not very trustworthy authority of his biographer (Diogenes Laertius), he made his home at Corinth. He was still living in 357 B.C.;[1] but how much longer he lived we have no means of knowing.

The *Anabasis* is a work of singular interest, and is brightly and pleasantly written. Xenophon, like Cæsar, tells the story in the third person, and there is a straightforward manliness about the style, with a distinct flavour of a cheerful lightheartedness, which at once enlists our sympathies. His description of places and of relative distances is very minute and painstaking. The researches of modern travellers attest his general accuracy.[2]

The *Cyropædia*, which describes the boyhood and training of Cyrus, hardly answers to its name, being for the most part an account of the beginnings of the Persian empire and of the victorious career of Cyrus its founder. But Xenophon had little or nothing to build on except the floating stories and traditions of the East that had gathered round the figure of the great Persian hero-king. The *Cyropædia* contains in fact the author's own ideas of training and education, as derived conjointly from the teachings of Socrates and his favourite Spartan institutions. A distinct moral purpose, to which literal truth is sacrificed, runs through the work.

The *Hellenica*, though by no means a first-class historical work, fills a gap by giving the events of the fifty years from 411 to 362 B.C. Thus it includes the downfall of the Athenian empire, the supremacy of Sparta, and the sudden collapse of that power after Leuctra in 371 B.C. It takes up Greek history at the point at which Thucydides's great work abruptly ends. His credit as an historian has been specially impugned, and it has been suggested that he was much more influenced by his political likes and dislikes than by a love of truth. However that may be, there are certainly serious omissions and defects in the work, which greatly detract from its value. At the time he probably wrote it he was no doubt a strong political partisan and a thorough believer in Sparta. But subsequently a change came over him; and, when he described the terrible reverse at Leuctra, he seems to have felt that Sparta's prestige had been deservedly destroyed, and that its downfall was heaven's vengeance on an ungracious and treacherous policy. He always clings to a belief in a divine overruling providence, though in the *Hellenica* there are unmistakable traces of a pettiness of mind and narrowness of view very far below the dignity of an historian.

The *Memorabilia*, or "Recollections of Socrates," is the tribute of an affectionate and admiring disciple who felt that the nobleness of his master's aims and life was his best defence. The work is not a literary masterpiece: it lacks coherence and unity, and the picture it gives of Socrates fails to do him justice. Still it is an honest piece of work and a labour of love, and, as far as it goes, we may well believe it faithfully describes the philosopher's manner of life and style of conversation. It was the moral and practical side of Socrates's teaching which most interested Xenophon; into his abstruse metaphysical speculations he seems to have made no attempt to enter; for these indeed he had neither taste nor genius. It was the philosophy which aims at "a sound mind in a sound body" which specially suited the robust and healthy mind of Xenophon. Moving within a limited range of ideas, he doubtless gives us "considerably less than the real Socrates, while Plato gives us something more."

Xenophon has left several minor works, some of which are very interesting and give us an insight into the home-life of the Greeks.

The *Œconomics*, which deals with the management of the house and of the farm, presents a pleasant and amusing picture of the Greek wife and of her home duties. She was to be thoroughly domestic, devoted to her household work, without any intellectual aspiration; she must keep up her good looks by healthy exercise, not by rouging or painting. There are some good practical remarks on matrimony and on the respective duties of husband and wife; in these it is assumed that providence has endowed each sex with capacities peculiar to itself and that the highest happiness is to be found in union and in well-organized cooperation. The true sphere of woman is in the faithful and diligent discharge of her home duties; this, above all things, will win her husband's respect and esteem.

In the essays on horsemanship (Ἱππική) and hunting (*Cynegeticus*), Xenophon deals with matters with which he had a thorough practical acquaintance. In the former he gives rules how to choose a horse, and then tells how it is to be groomed and ridden and generally managed. All this has still great interest for the modern reader. We gather from this little work that the ancient Greeks never used the stirrup, nor had they any idea of providing their horses with iron shoes. The book on hunting deals chiefly with the hare, though the author speaks also of boar-hunting and describes the hounds, tells how they are to be bred and trained, and gives specimens of suitable names for them. On all this he writes with the zest of an enthusiastic sportsman, and he observes that those nations will be most likely to be successful in war of which the upper classes have a taste for field-sports.

The *Hipparchicus* explains the duties of a cavalry officer; it is not, according to our ideas, a very scientific treatise, showing that the art of war was but very imperfectly developed and that the military operations of the Greeks were on a somewhat petty scale. He dwells at some length on the moral qualities which go to the making of a good cavalry officer, and hints very plainly that there must be strict attention to religious duties.

The *Agesilaus* is a eulogy of the Spartan king, who had two special merits in Xenophon's eyes: he was a rigid disciplinarian and he was particularly attentive to all religious observances. We have a summary of his virtues rather than a good and striking picture of the man himself.

The *Hiero* works out the line of thought indicated in the story of the Sword of Damocles. It is a protest against the notion that the "tyrant" is a man to be envied, as having more abundant means of happiness than a private person. This is one of the most pleasing of his minor works; it is cast into the form of a dialogue between Hiero, tyrant of Syracuse, and the lyric poet Simonides.

The *Symposium*, or "Banquet," is a brilliant little dialogue in which Socrates is the prominent figure. He is represented as "improving the occasion," which is that of a lively Athenian supper-party, at which there is much drinking, with flute-playing, and a dancing girl from Syracuse, who amuses the guests with the feats of a professional conjuror. Socrates's table-talk runs through a variety of topics, and winds up with a philosophical disquisition on the superiority of true heavenly love to its earthly or sensual counterfeit, and with an earnest exhortation to one of the party, who had just won a victory in the public games, to lead a noble life and do his duty to his country.

There are also two short essays on the political constitution of Sparta and Athens, written with a decided bias in favour of the former, which he praises without attempting to criticize. Sparta seems to have presented to Xenophon the best conceivable mixture of monarchy and aristocracy.

In the essay on the *Revenues of Athens*, he offers suggestions for making Athens less dependent on tribute received from its allies: first, more foreign settlers should be attracted to the city by holding out strong commercial inducements and from these a moderate capitation tax should be collected; secondly, more should be made of the silver mines of Laurium by leasing them out to private capitalists, who might work them by slaves purchased with public money and hired at a fixed rate by the lessees. But above all, he would have Athens use its influence for the maintenance of peace in the Greek world and for the settlement of questions by diplomacy, the temple at Delphi being for this purpose an independent centre and supplying a divine sanction.

The *Apology*, Socrates's defence before his judges, is rather a feeble production, and in the general opinion of modern critics not a genuine work of Xenophon.

The editions both of Xenophon's entire and of his separate works, especially of the *Anabasis*, are very numerous. A few of the best are enumerated below:—(1) *Anabasis*, text of L. Dindorf, with notes by J. S. Watson, 1868; (2) *Memorabilia*, edited, with short notes, by J. R. King, 1874 (Oxford); (3) *Hellenics*, text of C. G. Cobet, 1862; (4) *Cyropædia*, from the text of L. Dindorf, with notes by E. H. Barker, 1831. The minor works have been repeatedly edited. Useful editions of the *Hiero* (London, 1883) and *Œconomics* (London, 1884) have been issued by H. A. Holden. There is an English translation of the entire works by various hands, published in 1831; also a French translation, similarly executed, in 1845. To Sir A. Grant's monograph on Xenophon, in Blackwood's "Ancient Classics for English Readers," the present writer is considerably indebted. (W. J. B.)

XENOPHON OF EPHESUS. See ROMANCE, vol. xx. p. 635.

XERES. See JEREZ DE LA FRONTERA and WINE, p. 607 above.

XERXES (Old Persian *Khshayârshâ*; in the book of Esther, *Ahasuerus*), the name of two Achæmenian kings of Persia. Xerxes I., son of Darius Hystaspis and of Atossa, daughter of Cyrus, reigned from 485 to 464 B.C., and is famous for his unsuccessful expedition against Greece (480 B.C.); see PERSIA, vol. xviii. p. 572 *sq.* Xerxes II., the son of Artaxerxes I. and grandson of Xerxes I., came to the throne in 424 and was murdered by his brother Secydianus after a reign of a month and a half; *ibid.*, p. 575.

XIMENES See JIMENES.

[1] In the *Hellenics* (vi. 4, 37) he mentions Tisiphonus, who succeeded Alexander, tyrant of Pheræ, in 357 B.C.

[2] Major Milligan, in his *Wild Life among the Koords* says, "My researches have put beyond doubt the accuracy of his statements, and are of a nature to show the historical, geographical, and ethnological importance which is to be attached to the accounts handed down to posterity by that illustrious writer."

Y

Y. The history of this symbol has already been given under U. The three symbols U, V, Y are only differentiations of one original form.

The sound of *y* in Greek was that of French *u* in "lune" and German *ü* in "übel." In Bœotian and Laconian Greek the old *u*-sound was retained; but it was represented by *ου*, a digraph which had also the value of *u* in other dialects where it arose from phonetic change, *e.g.*, in τοὺς (for τόνς). The name ὖ ψιλόν was probably given to distinguish it from ὖ διὰ διφθόγγου,—that is, the same sound, but denoted by *οι*, which in the 2d century B.C. was beginning to have the value of *υ*; just so ἒ ψιλόν is opposed to *αι*, or ἒ διὰ διφθόγγου. The difference in sound between the full and the modified *u* is this: for the first the lips are rounded as much as possible, and the back part of the tongue is raised towards the palate; for the second the rounding of the lips is the same, but the tongue is in the position for *i*, so that in sounding *ü* we are sounding *i* with the lips rounded in addition. This explains the ease with which the *i*-sound is produced instead of *ü* by persons unfamiliar with the latter sound: when an Englishman pronouncing "Müller" says "Miller," he puts the tongue right for *i* but omits to round the lips as well. This change has been a regular one in our language. There is no doubt that *y* (*i.e.*, *ü*) was a sound of Early English (or Anglo-Saxon), as of the other Teutonic languages, in words like "fȳr" (fire), "synn" (sin); it was the "umlaut" of *u*, especially when followed in the next syllable by *i* or *e*; so "burg" has for gen. and dat. "byrig," orig. "burges," "burge." But in Middle English *y* passed into *i*: thus "fȳr" (sounded as fūr) came to be sounded as "fīr" (feer), and this (as in other cases where ī occurs) was diphthongized in comparatively modern times into "fire" (faiər). Thus in the middle of a word *y* lost its special value; on the other hand, at the beginning of a word it easily passed into the consonant *y*, the value which it has regularly in modern English. This explains the fact that the English language had no symbol for the sound of French *u* when this sound was re-introduced into England after the Norman Conquest. Accordingly the French symbol as well as the sound was taken: it is found in words like "muse," "lute," sounded as "myyz," "lyyte." The *yy* gradually developed into the *iu* sound with which we are familiar in "miūz," "liūt"; but the spelling remained unchanged. It must have been awkward to have the symbol *u* representing both the full (native) sound and the modified (French) sound; this was partially obviated by borrowing for the full *u*-sound the French writing *ou*: *e.g.*, "hūs" was written "house," without at first any change of sound; but this was not consistently carried out. Much later, at the end of the 16th century, the sound was diphthongized into "haus" (as now), but the spelling (*ou*) remained. The fact that *y* and *i* became indistinguishable led to the use of *y* at the end of a word instead of *i*: thus we write "day" instead of the older "dai."

In Early English we find the symbol ȝ (which is a modification of the Anglo-Saxon *g*) used initially with the value of *g*, and medially (chiefly before *t*) where modern English writes *gh*, as in *light*. This is due to French scribes, who used the French (*i.e.*, our modern) form of *g* for the *g*-sound, and then the ȝ for the sound which had been weakened in Anglo-Saxon from *g* to *y*, as in *ȝeard* (our *yard*) for original *gard* (Norse *garth*; in North English Aysgarth and Gatesgarth). About the 15th century this same symbol was mistaken for *z*, and as such it is still occasionally employed in cursive, when ȝ is written instead of *z*.

YACHOW-FU, a prefectural city in the Chinese province of Sze-ch'uen, is situated in 30° 4′ N. lat. and 103° 4′ E. long., and is a place of some antiquity and note, being first mentioned in history during the Chow dynasty (1122-255 B.C.). It is prettily placed in a valley surrounded by an amphitheatre of hills, on the banks of the river Ya. The town is large, populous, and busy, and owes its importance to the fact that it stands at the parting of the tea and tobacco trade route to Tibet *via* Tatsien-lu and the cotton trade route to western Yun-nan *via* Ningyuen-Fu. Yachow-Fu is the seat also of a considerable silk manufacture; and in its immediate neighbourhood there exist both coal and iron. The city wall measures 2 miles in circumference, and is pierced by four gates. The population is estimated at about 40,000.

YACHTING is the sport of racing in yachts [1] and boats with sails for money or plate, and also the pastime of cruising for pleasure in sailing or steam vessels. The history of yachting is the history of yacht-racing, inasmuch as competition improved yachts just as horse-racing improved horses. It dates from the beginning of the 19th century; for, although there were sailing yachts long before, they were but few, and belonged exclusively to princes and other illustrious personages. For instance, in the Anglo-Saxon period Athelstan had presented to him by the king of Norway a magnificent royal vessel, the sails of which were purple and the head and deck wrought with gold, apparently a kind of state barge. Elizabeth had one, and so has every English sovereign since. During her reign a pleasure ship was built (1588) at Cowes, so that the association of that place with the sport goes back three hundred years. In 1660 Charles II. was presented by the Dutch with a yacht named the "Mary," until which time the word "yacht" was unknown in England. The Merrie Monarch was fond of sailing, for he designed a yacht of 25 tons called the "Jamie," built at Lambeth in 1662, as well as several others later on. In that year the "Jamie" was matched for £100 against a small Dutch yacht, under the duke of York, from Greenwich to Gravesend and back, and beat her, the king steering part of the time—apparently the first record of a yacht match and of an amateur helmsman.

The first authentic record of a sailing club is in 1720, when the Cork Harbour Water Club, now known as the Royal Cork Yacht Club, was established in Ireland, but the yachts were small. Maitland, in his *History of London* (1739), mentions sailing and rowing on the Thames as among the amusements then indulged in; and Strutt, in his *Sports and Pastimes* (1801), says that the Cumberland Society, consisting of gentlemen partial to this pastime, gave yearly a silver cup to be sailed for in the vicinity of London. The boats usually started from Blackfriars Bridge, went up the Thames to Putney, and returned to Vauxhall, being, no doubt, mere sailing boats and not yachts or decked vessels. From the middle to the end of the 18th century yachting developed very slowly: although matches were sailed at Cowes as far back as 1780, very few yachts of any size, say 35 tons, existed in 1800 there or elsewhere. In 1812 the Royal Yacht Squadron was established by fifty yacht-owners at Cowes and was called the Yacht Club, altered to the Royal Yacht Club in 1820; but no regular regatta was held there until some years later. The yachts of the time were built of heavy materials, like the revenue cutters, full in the fore body and fine aft;

[1] The English word yacht is the Dutch *jacht*, *jagt*, from *jachten*, "to hurry," "to hunt."

but it was soon discovered that their timbers and scantlings were unnecessarily strong, and they were made much lighter. It was also found that the single-masted cutter was more weatherly than the brigs and schooners of the time, and the former rig was adopted for racing, and, as there was no time allowance for difference of size, they were all built of considerable dimensions. Among the earliest of which there is any record were the "Pearl," 95 tons, built by Sainty at Wivenhoe near Colchester in 1820, for the marquis of Anglesey, and the "Arrow," 84 tons, originally 61 feet 9½ inches long and 18 feet 5¼ inches beam, built by Joseph Weld in 1822, which is still extant as a racing yacht, having been rebuilt and altered several times, and again entirely rebuilt in 1887-88. The Thames soon followed the example of the Solent and established the Royal Thames Yacht Club in 1823, the Clyde founding the Royal Northern Yacht Club in 1824, and Plymouth the Royal Western in 1827. In this year the Royal Yacht Squadron passed a resolution disqualifying any member who should apply steam to his yacht,—the enactment being aimed at T. Assheton Smith, an enthusiastic yachtsman and fox-hunter, who was having a paddle-wheel steam yacht called the "Menai" built on the Clyde. In 1830 one of the largest cutters ever constructed was launched, viz., the "Alarm," built by Inman at Lymington for Joseph Weld of Lulworth Castle, from the lines of a famous smuggler captured off the Isle of Wight. She was 82 feet on the load line by 24 feet beam, and was reckoned of 193 tons, old measurement, in which length, breadth, and half-breadth (supposed to represent depth) were the factors for computation. Some yachtsmen at this time preferred still larger vessels and owned square-topsail schooners and brigs like the man-o'-war brigs of the day, such as the "Waterwitch," 381 tons, built by White of Cowes, in 1832, for Lord Belfast, and the "Brilliant," barque, 493 tons, belonging to J. Holland Ackers, who invented a scale of time allowance for competitive sailing. In 1834 the first royal cup was given by William IV. to the Royal Yacht Squadron—a gift which has been continued ever since (except in 1862, when it was dropped for one year, owing to the death of the Prince Consort), and in recent years supplemented by similar gifts to other clubs. In 1836 the Royal Eastern Yacht Club was founded at Granton near Edinburgh; in 1838 the Royal St George's at Kingstown and the Royal London; in 1843 the Royal Southern at Southampton and the Royal Harwich; in 1844 the Royal Mersey at Liverpool and the Royal Victoria at Ryde. The number of vessels kept pace with the clubs—the fifty yachts of 1812 increasing nearly tenfold before the middle of the century, which was the critical epoch of yacht-building.

In 1848, after J. Scott Russell had repeatedly drawn attention to the unwisdom of constructing sailing vessels on the "cod's head and mackerel tail" plan, and had enunciated his wave-line theory, Mare built at Blackwall an entirely new type of vessel, with a long hollow bow and a short after body of considerable fulness. This was the iron cutter "Mosquito," of 59 feet 2 inches water line, 15 feet 3 inches beam, and measuring 50 tons. Prejudice against the new type of yacht being as strong as against the introduction of steam, there were no vessels built like the "Mosquito," with the exception of the "Volante," 59 tons, by Harvey of Wivenhoe, until the eyes of English yachtsmen were opened by the Americans three years later. About this period yacht-racing had been gradually coming into favour in the United States, the first yacht club being founded at New York in 1844 by nine yacht-owners; and in 1846 the first match between yachts in the States was sailed, 25 miles to windward and back from Sandy Hook lightship, between J. C. Stevens's new centre-board sloop "Maria," 170 tons, 100 feet water line and 26 feet 8 inches beam, with a draught of 5 feet 3 inches of water, and the "Coquette," schooner, 74 tons, belonging to J. H. Perkins, the latter winning; but the appearance of the "Maria," which had a clipper or schooner bow, like that of the newest racing cutters of 1887-1888, did much for yachting in America. Stevens then commissioned George Steers of New York, builder of the crack pilot schooners, to construct a racing schooner to visit England in the year of the great exhibition, and the result was the "America" of 170 tons. Like the "Mosquito," she had a very long and hollow bow, with considerable fulness aft. She crossed the Atlantic in the summer of 1851, but failed to compete for the queen's cup at Cowes in August, although the club for that occasion threw the prize open to all the world, as her owner declined to concede the usual time allowance for difference of size. The members of the Yacht Squadron, not wishing to risk the reproach of denying the stranger a fair race, decided that their match for a cup given by the club, to be sailed round the Isle of Wight later on in the same month, should be without any time allowance. The "America," thus exceptionally treated, entered and competed against fifteen other vessels. The three most dangerous competitors being put out through accidents, the "America" passed the winning-post 18 minutes ahead of the 47-ton cutter "Aurora," and won the cup; but, even if the time allowance had not been waived, the American schooner yacht would still have won by fully a couple of minutes.

The prize was given to the New York Yacht Club and constituted a challenge cup, called the America cup, for the yachts of all nations, by the deed of gift of the owners of the winner. Not only was the "America" as great a departure from the conventional British type of yacht as the "Mosquito," but the set of her sails was a decided novelty. In England it had been the practice to make them baggy, whereas those of the "America" were flat, which told materially in working to windward. The revolution in yacht designing and canvassing was complete, and the bows of existing cutters were lengthened, that of the "Arrow" among others. The "Alarm" was also lengthened and turned into a schooner of 248 tons, and the "Wildfire," cutter, 59 tons, was likewise converted. Indeed there was a complete craze for schooners, the "Flying Cloud," "Gloriana," "Lalla Rookh," "Albertine," "Aline," "Egeria," "Pantomime," and others being built between 1852 and 1865, during which period the centre board, or sliding keel, was applied to schooners as well as sloops in America. The national or cutter rig was nevertheless not neglected in England, for Hatcher of Southampton built the 35-ton cutter "Glance"—the pioneer of the subsequent 40-tonners—in 1855, and the "Vampire"—the pioneer of the 20-tonners—in 1857, in which year Weld also had the "Lulworth," an 82-ton cutter of comparatively shallow draught, constructed at Lymington. At this time too there came into existence a group of cutters, called "flying fifties" from their tonnage, taking after the "Mosquito" as their pioneer; such were the "Extravaganza," "Audax," and "Vanguard." In 1866 a large cutter was constructed on the Clyde called the "Condor," 135 tons, followed by the still larger "Oimara," 163 tons, in 1867. In 1868 the "Cambria" schooner was built by Ratsey at Cowes for Ashbury of Brighton, and, having proved a successful match-sailer, was taken to the United States in 1870 to compete for the America cup, but was badly beaten, as also was the "Livonia" in 1871.

The decade between 1870 and 1880 may be termed the Golden Age of yachting, inasmuch as the racing fleet had some very notable additions made to it, of which it will suffice to mention the schooners "Gwendolin," "Cetonia"

"Corinne," "Miranda," and "Waterwitch;" the large cutters "Kriemhilda," "Vol au Vent," "Formosa," "Samæna," and "Vanduara;" the 40-tonners "Foxhound," "Myosotis," and "Norman;" the 20-tonners "Vanessa" (Hatcher's masterpiece), "Quickstep," "Enriqueta," "Louise," and "Freda;" and the yawls "Florinda," "Corisande," "Jullanar," and "Latona." Lead, the use of which commenced in 1846, was entirely used for ballast after 1870 and placed on the keel outside. Of races there was a plethora; indeed no less than 400 matches took place in 1876, as against 63 matches in 1856, with classes for schooners and yawls, for large cutters, for 40-tonners, 20-tonners, and 10-tonners. The sport too was better regulated, and was conducted on a uniform system: the Yacht-Racing Association, established in 1875, drew up a simple code of laws for the regulation of yacht races, which was accepted by the yacht clubs generally, though a previous attempt to introduce uniformity, made by the Royal Victoria Yacht Club in 1868, had failed. The Association adopted the rule for ascertaining the size or tonnage of yachts which had been for many years in force, known as the Thames rule; but in 1879 they altered the plan of reckoning length from that taken on deck to that taken at the load water line, and two years later they adopted an entirely new system of calculation. Subsequently to these repeated changes yacht-racing gradually waned, the new measurement exercising a prejudicial effect on the sport, as it enabled vessels of extreme length, depth, and narrowness, kept upright by enormous masses of lead on the outside of the keel, to compete on equal terms with vessels of greater width and less depth, in other words, smaller yachts carrying an inferior area of sail. Of this type are the yawls "Lorna" and "Wendur," the cutters "May," "Annasona," "Sleuth-hound," "Tara," and "Marjorie,"—the most extreme of all being perhaps the 40-tonner "Tara," which is six times as long as she is broad, and unusually deep, with a displacement of 75 tons, 38 tons of lead on her keel, and the sail spread of a 60-tonner like "Neva."

In 1884 two large 80-ton cutters of the above type were built for racing, viz., the "Genesta" on the Clyde and the "Irex" at Southampton. Having been successful in her first season, the former went to the United States in 1885 in quest of the America cup; but she was beaten by a new yacht, called the "Puritan," built for the purpose of defending it, with a moderate draught of 8 feet 3 inches of water, considerable beam, and a deep centre-board. The defeat of the "Genesta" is not surprising when it is recollected that she drew 13 feet of water, had a displacement or weight of 141, as against the "Puritan's" 106 tons, and a sail area of 7887 square feet to the American's 7982,—a greater mass with less driving power; but she did not leave the States empty-handed, as she won and brought back the Cape May and Brenton Reef challenge cups, though they were wrested from her by the "Irex" in the following year. The same thing happened to the "Galatea," which was beaten by the "Mayflower" in 1886. In 1887 a new cutter, called the "Thistle," was built on the Clyde to try to win back the America cup; but, although built very differently from the "Genesta" and "Galatea," *i.e.*, of a much greater width than modern English racing yachts generally, the "Thistle," when matched with the new centre-board "Volunteer," had no better fortune than her predecessors. These new American racing vessels are something very different from the old flat-bottomed sloop "Maria," with one head-sail and a trivial draught of water, inasmuch as they are lead-ballasted cutters with two head-sails and a draught of nearly 10 feet of water, with the additional advantage of a centre-board descending as much as 8 or 10 feet below the keel. In this connexion it is noteworthy that a prize won by a fixed-keel schooner should be defended by centre-board craft with a single mast.

From 1887 an entirely new system of measurement for competitive sailing has been adopted in the United Kingdom, the old plan of measuring the hull having given way to the more rational one of taking the length on the water-line and the sail area of the vessel as the factors for rating. This leaves naval architects free to adopt a long and narrow or a short and "beamy" hull.

Yacht-racing as at present conducted is simple and easily managed. A course is chosen by the committee of the club giving the prizes, averaging for first-class vessels 40 or 50 nautical miles in length, such as the old queen's course from Cowes eastward to the Nab lightship, back past Cowes to Lymington, and returning to the starting-post. The competitors, *i.e.*, cutters, yawls, and schooners,—cutters sailing at their full, yawls at four-fifths, and schooners at three-fourths of their tonnage or rating—cruise about under way in readiness for crossing an imaginary line between the club-house or committee vessel and a mark-boat, which forms the starting as well as winning place, on the signal being given. No time is allowed at the start, but only at the finish, and consequently there is a good deal of manœuvring to get across the line first and to windward. The yachts make the best of their way onwards, running if the wind is abaft them, reaching if it is on the beam, and close-hauled if it is foul, the greatest skill being shown in cross-tacking and getting the weather-gauge. When close-hauled and reaching, the ordinary fore-and-aft sail (see SAIL, SEAMANSHIP, and SHIPBUILDING) is used; but when going free a large racing sail called a spinnaker is set on a long boom projecting from the foot of the mast at right angles to the vessel. This sail, which is a triangular one, extends from the topmasthead to the deck, on the opposite side to that occupied by the main boom, though occasionally shifted to the bowsprit end. After leaving all the marks on the port or starboard hand, as may be directed in their instructions, the competing yachts arrive at the winning-place generally in single file, the moment at which each competitor passes the line being noted by a time-keeper. It is then ascertained whether any and which vessel has saved her time allowance, which varies according to the length of the course, and the first which has done so is declared to have won. The amount of prize money gained by the most successful vessel of the season—almost always a cutter—generally exceeds 1000 sovereigns, exclusive of cups or plate. The expense of racing is enormous; in the case of an 80 or 100-ton cutter it amounts to fully £2000 or £3000 a year. The cost of cruising is of course not so great, the wages of non-racing crews (which are much smaller in number) being less, and averages perhaps £10 a ton. There are not such frequent renewals of sails; there are not so many breakages of spars, no entrance fees, and no "winning money" to pay the crew, nor any of the thousand and one extras which go to swell the yearly account of the racing owner. Racing yachts make good cruisers if their spars are shortened and their wings clipped; and it is a very common practice to turn an ex-racing cutter into a yawl, by shortening her boom and adding a mizzen-mast and mizzen-sail to her counter. The yawl rig is comfortable for cruising, but not so successful for racing as the cutter. The speed of yachts varies according to their length, and this is one reason why an allowance in time should be given by a large yacht to a smaller one. As instances of pace it is on record that the "Arrow" in 1858 sailed 45 knots in 4 h. 19 m., and 50 knots in 1872 in 4 h. 40 m. In the latter year the "Kriemhilda" did 50 knots in 4 h. 37 m., while the "Marjorie" did the same distance in 4 h. 26 m., and the "Samæna" in 4 h. 15 m. in 1883; the "Lorna" (yawl) in 4 h. 14 m., and the "Irex" in 4 h. 7 min., both in 1885,—all these distances being sailed inside the Isle of Wight, irrespective of the state of the tide. A greater pace has been developed by schooners in bursts of speed with a fair tide and half a gale of wind behind them, but in racing inside the Isle of Wight the "Egeria" in 1870 did 50 knots in 4 h. 27 m., the "Olga" in 4 h. 25 m. in 1875, the "Enchantress" in 4 h. 18 m. in 1879, which is not so quick as the cutters.

As to the number of yachts now afloat, cruisers as well as racers, the British yacht fleet, which in 1850 consisted of 500 sailing and 3 steam vessels, now numbers 2209 sailing yachts, of 64,051 tons, and 700 screw steam yachts, of 68,667 tons, or a gross total of 2909 yachts, of 132,718 tons—in round numbers 3000 yachts, allowing for small craft not included in the above total. They are constructed of wood, iron, or steel—this last gradually coming to the front in the pleasure fleet as well as in the mercantile marine and royal navy. Next to Great Britain the United States possesses the largest number afloat, amounting to nearly if not quite 1200 yachts; and, if to the foregoing are added the yachts of other countries included in Lloyd's list, a grand total of upwards of 5000 is reached. While the taste for sailing vessels has made marked strides since 1850, that for steam yachts has made still more extraordinary progress, one noteworthy feature being the increase in their size, and another their enormous prime cost. More than thirty of those recently built exceed 500 tons, while double that number range from 300 to 500 tons; two or three even exceed 1000 tons each.

Admiralty warrants are granted to clubs and their members to fly the white, blue, or red ensign with device on it, such yachts being registered according to the provisions of the Merchant Shipping Acts. The white man-of-war or St George's ensign, used by British war-ships, is flown by the Royal Yacht Squadron alone of yacht clubs. The ordinary red ensign of the merchant navy may be flown by any English vessel without permission of Government, as it is the national flag. Yachts with Admiralty warrants are entitled to certain privileges, such as exemption from excise and some other dues; they may enter Government harbours without paying dues, and may make fast and lie to Government buoys when these are not required by any of H.M. ships; they need not have their names painted on their sterns, though it is better that they should; and their masters need not hold Board of Trade certificates.

Literature.—Vanderdecken, *Yachts and Yachting* (1862); H. C. Folkard, *The Sailing Boat* (1870); Stonehenge, *British Rural Sports* (1876); Dixon Kemp, *Yacht Architecture* (1885), *Yacht Designing* (1876), and *Yacht and Boat Sailing* (1878-86); *Yacht-Racing Calendar* (annual); *Lloyd's Yacht Register* (annual); and *Hunt's Yacht List* (annual). (E. D. B.)

YAK. This animal is the *Bos grunniens* of Linnæus and all subsequent zoologists, so called on account of the pig-like grunting sounds it makes. It is structurally more closely allied to the common ox than to the bison, with which group of the *Bovidæ* it has been sometimes erroneously associated. It is only found in the lofty plateau of Asia between the Altai Mountains and the Himalayas, and occurs both wild and as the ordinary domestic animal of the inhabitants of that region, supplying milk, food, and raiment, as well as being used as a beast of burden. The wild yaks inhabit the most inaccessible parts of the mountains, ranging up to an elevation of 20,000 feet,—higher it is said, than any other animal,—delighting in extreme cold, and finding their sustenance in the coarse, wiry grass which is almost the only vegetable production of those desolate regions. They cannot live to the south of the

Yak.

Himalayas beyond the immediate neighbourhood of the snow. Their size is that of a small ox. The horns are long, nearly cylindrical, smooth, and pointed at the ends, and with a peculiar and characteristic curve, being directed at first outwards, then upwards, forwards, and inwards, and finally a little backwards. Some of the domestic yaks are hornless. The most remarkable external character is the excessive growth and peculiar distribution of the hairy covering. The upper parts of the body and sides are clothed with a thick, soft, woolly hair, more fully developed along the middle of the back, especially on the shoulders, where it forms a great bunch; on the sides it is comparatively short. From the upper parts of the limbs and the whole of the lower surface of the body a thick growth of long, straight pendent hair descends, in old animals sweeping the ground and almost concealing the somewhat short legs. The tail is profusely covered with a thick mass of such hairs. The calves are at first covered only with a soft, shortish woolly hair, of nearly uniform length all over. Domestic yaks vary considerably in size and appearance according to their treatment and the purpose for which they are bred. The finest are those used for carrying the native chiefs. Those employed for ploughing are very inferior-looking animals. They vary also in colour. The wild animals are nearly uniformly black; the domestic yaks are often quite white. It is not uncommon to see the long hair on the ridge of the back, that on the tail, and the long flowing hair of the under parts white, whilst all the rest of the animal is black. The tails of the domestic yaks are used as ornamental standards by the Tartars, and are largely imported into India as chowries or fly-flaps.

YAKUTSK, a province of Eastern Siberia, which includes nearly the whole of the basin of the Lena, and covers an area of 1,517,127 square miles (nearly one-third of Siberia and almost one-fifth of the entire Russian empire). It has the Arctic Ocean on the N., Yeniseisk on the W., Irkutsk, Transbaikalia, and Amur on the S., and is separated from the Pacific (Sea of Okhotsk) only by the narrow Maritime Province (see vol. xxii. pl. I.).

Physical features.

The Vitim plateau, from 2500 to 3500 feet in altitude, and bordered on the south-east by the Stanovoi Mountains, occupies the south-eastern portion of the province. Its moist, elevated valleys, intersected by ranges of flat, dome-shaped hills, which rise nearly 1000 feet above the plateau, are unsuited for agriculture, and form an immense desert of forest and marsh, visited only by Tungus hunters, save in the south-west, where a few settlements of gold-miners have lately sprung up. The high border-ridge of the plateau (see SIBERIA) stretches from the South Muya Mountains towards the north-east, thus compelling the river Aldan to make its great bend in that direction. The ridge is almost entirely unknown, having been crossed by only two geographers at points more than 500 miles apart. The alpine country fringing the plateau all along its north-western border is better known in the south-west, where rich gold-mines are wrought in the spurs between the Vitim and the Lena; and farther north-east it has been crossed by several geographers (Middendorff, Erman, the Siberian expedition) on their way from Yakutsk to the Sea of Okhotsk. The Lena, in that part of its course where it flows north-east, waters the outer base of this alpine region. It is a wild land, traversed by several chains of mountains, all having a north-eastern direction and intersected by deep, narrow valleys, where wild mountain streams flow amidst immense boulders and steep cliffs. The whole is covered with dense forests, through which none but the Tunguses can find their way, and they only by means of marks made on the trees. The summits of the mountains, ranging from 4000 to 6000 feet, mostly rise above the limits of tree vegetation, but in no case pass the snow-line. Summits and slopes alike are strewn with crystalline rock débris, mostly hidden under thick layers of lichens, where only the larch, which sends out its roots horizontally, can find support and sustenance. Birch and aspen grow on the lower slopes; and where strips of alluvium have been deposited in the narrow bottoms of the valleys thickets of poplar and willow make their appearance, or a few patches of grassy soil are occasionally found. These last, however, are so rare that all of them are known to the gold-diggers for scores of miles around their settlements, and hay has to be brought at considerable cost from the lowlands. All necessaries of life for the gold-diggings have to be shipped from Irkutsk down the Lena, and deposited at entrepôts, whence they are transported in winter by means of reindeer to their destination. A line drawn south-west and north-east, from the mouth of the Vitim towards that of the Aldan, separates the mountain tracts from the elevated plains (from 1500 to 2000 feet) which fringe the highlands all the way from the upper Lena to Verkhne-Kolymsk, and probably to the mouth of the Kolyma. Immense and sometimes marshy meadows extend over those plains in the south-west; farther north mosses and lichens are the prevalent vegetation. The surface is much furrowed by rivers and diversified by several mountain-chains (Verkhoyansk, Tas-karyktakh, Kolymsk, and Alazeya). Little is known as to the real character of these mountains, although they are figured on maps as isolated ridges shooting north-west from the highlands, between the chief rivers which flow into the Arctic Ocean. Beyond the elevated plains vast tundras, covered with mosses and lichens, stretch to the shores of the ice-bound ocean; only a few trees succeed in the struggle for a miserable existence, though some isolated groups penetrate farther north along the courses of the Lena, the Indighirka, and the Kolyma, almost reaching in the first-named valley the seventy-second degree of north latitude.

Northern coast.

The Arctic coast is indented by several bays—Borkhaya and Yana to the east of the wide Lena delta, and Omulyakh, Kolyma, and Tchaunskaya still farther to the east. Islands have been explored as far as 78° N. lat. These fall into three groups,—the Lyakhovskiye, the Anjou or New Siberian, and the De Long Islands. The Medvyezhie (Bear) Islands off the Kolyma and the two Ayun Islands in Tchaunskaya Bay are merely littoral. Wrangel's Land seems to be the outer island of a great and as yet unknown archipelago. The entire coast of Yakutsk is full of memorials of the courageous explorations made in 1735-41 by Minin, Lapteff, and Prontchischeff in small boats, without any of the modern appliances for Arctic explorations, and Tchaunskaya Bay recalls the loss of Shalauroff's expedition. The prospects of regular navigation recently raised by Nordenskjöld's bold circumnavigation of Asia seem unlikely to be fully realized, the ice apparently having never again been in so favourable a condition as in 1878-79. Every year, however, a narrow passage close by the coast is left almost free of ice, enabling a ship or two to reach the estuary of the Yenisei, or even the delta of the Lena.

Rivers.

The great artery of Yakutsk, the Lena, rises on the western slope of the Baikal Mountains, its sources being separated only by a narrow ridge from the great Siberian lake. It soon issues from the mountain valleys, and flows over the elevated plains, where it has carved a deep channel between horizontal layers of Old Red Sandstone and further on of contorted beds of limestone. As far as Yakutsk it maintains its north-eastern direction, with but one great bend in 60° N. lat. and several small windings in its upper course. At Katchug—a lading-place 180 miles north-east from Irkutsk—it is still shallow, but soon becomes a mighty stream of much beauty, which is increased by the high crags and mountains amidst which it has dug its channel. Though thus picturesque, its valley can hardly be called hospitable: the narrow level stretches along the base of the mountains are often marshy, while the raw and wet climate renders agriculture most difficult; the villages are poverty-stricken, and in most of them goitre is endemic. About 60° N. lat. the Lena receives from the right its first great tributary, the Vitim (1400 miles in length), which after a very sinuous course leaves the great plateau below Lake Oron, by a narrow gorge which has not yet been visited by any geographer. It is navigable by steamers in its lower course. The next large tributary of the Lena is the Olekma (about 800 miles), which also rises on the plateau and crosses it from south to north; it is navigable only in the very lowest part of its course; higher up, its valley, which offers the greatest difficulties for the traveller, has been utilized as a route only by the Cossack conquerors of Siberia and by one of the members of the Siberian expedition. The next important tributary, also from the right, is the Aldan (nearly 1300 miles), which first flows parallel to the Lena and then turns north-westwards to join it, itself receiving on the left a large tributary, the Amga. It is navigated from Ust-Maya. The only large tributary of the Lena on the left is the Vilui (about 1300 miles), which has an immense drainage-area on the lower plains, and since 1887 has been navigated by a steamer. At Yakutsk the Lena becomes a magnificent stream of more than 4 miles in width, with numerous islands, and this character it maintains for the next 1200 miles of its course, sometimes reaching a width of 17 miles and a depth of 7 to 8 fathoms. It enters the Arctic Ocean by a wide delta, occupying more than 250 miles of the coast-line; here the river divides into seven or eight principal branches, the chief of which vary from 35 to 65 miles in length, the largest being more than 6 miles broad. The bar, however, has only 8 feet of water, and the Swedish steamer "Lena" had great difficulty in entering from the sea. The lower course of the river is subject to terrible inundations when the ice breaks up on its upper part, whilst at the same time the higher reaches of its lower course are still covered with ice several feet in thickness. Large portions of the banks are then torn away by the enormous masses of ice. The Olenek (1200 miles), which enters the Arctic Ocean to the west of the Lena, is also a considerable river; the Yana (1000 miles), Indighirka (950), and Kolyma (1000) to the east all rise in the mountain region between 61° and 62° N. lat. and flow north and north-east into the Arctic Ocean.

Geology and mineral

The granites, granitic syenites, and gneisses of the high plateau are surrounded by a variety of crystalline slates, Huronian and Laurentian; and vast layers of Silurian and Devonian limestones and sandstones extend over large areas. Farther north the Carboniferous, Chalk, and Jurassic formations are spread over a wide region, and the whole is covered with layers of Glacial deposits in the highlands and of post-Glacial elsewhere. The mineral wealth of Yakutsk is very great; but gold (262,200 oz. in 1884) and salt (obtained from springs to the amount of about 6000 cwts. annually) only are worked. Coal has been recently discovered on the Vilui close by its mouth, as also on the lower Lena.

Climate.

Though there are spots in the North-American archipelago and in northern Greenland where the cold is as intense as at Yakutsk, no region can be named which has such extremes of cold and heat or winter temperatures so low, so long continued, or spread over so immense an area. Verkhoyansk on the Yana (67° 34′ N. lat. and 134° 20′ E. long.) is, in respect of cold, the pole of the Old World; nowhere, even in Siberia, do we find such low winter temperatures: from whatever quarter the wind may blow it cannot fail to bring a warmer temperature to Verkhoyansk. Frosts of −76° Fahr. have been observed there, and the average temperature of the three winter months is −53°·1; even that of March is but little above the freezing-point of mercury (−37°·9). Neither Ust-Yansk (70° 55′ N. lat., but close to the sea coast), nor Yakutsk, nor even the polar station of Sagastyr at the mouth of the Lena (73° 23′ N. lat.), has a winter so cold and so protracted. And yet at Sagastyr temperatures of −63°·6 were measured in February 1883, and the average temperature of that month was only −43°·6. At Yakutsk the average temperature of the winter is −40°·2, and the soil is frozen to a depth of 600 feet (Middendorff). Even at a depth of 382 feet the temperature of the soil is 26°·4 Fahr. For further particulars, see SIBERIA, vol. xxii. p. 6. The Lena, both at Kirensk and at Yakutsk, is free from ice for only 161 days in the year, the Yana at Ust-Yansk for 105. While at Yakutsk only 145 days and at Verkhoyansk only 73 have no snow; the interval between the latest frosts of one season and the earliest frosts of the next is barely 37 days, and even less in the north.

Population.

In spite of the rigours of its climate, the province of Yakutsk had 243,450 inhabitants in 1883, and the population is supposed to be increasing notwithstanding the infectious diseases which sometimes sweep away whole villages. The Russians constitute but a trifling element in the population; and their villages, numbering scarcely twenty, are chiefly peopled by exiled Nonconformists, belonging to the sects reputed "dangerous." In 1879 there were 5400 exiles living in the towns or settled in the Yakut encampments, 5300 peasants (also formerly exiles), 1890 military, and 4100 artisans, merchants, and officials. The remainder were chiefly Yakuts (211,900), and partly Tunguses (10,400), with a few Yukaghirs, Lamuts, and Tchuktchis. The Yakuts belong to the Turkish stem (see vol. xxiii. p. 661), and speak a dialect of Turkish, with an admixture of Mongolian words. They call themselves Sokha (pl. Sokhalar), their present name having been borrowed by the Russians from the Tunguses, who call them Yeko or Yekot. Most probably they formerly inhabited southern Siberia, and especially the upper Yenisei, where a Tartar stem calling itself Sakha still remains in Minusinsk. They are middle-sized, have dark and rather narrow eyes, a broad flat nose, thick black hair, and almost no beard. On the whole they are healthy and reach an advanced age, are very laborious and enterprising, and display in schools much more intelligence than the Tunguses or Buriats. Their implements show a great degree of skill and some artistic taste. They live in log *yurtas* with small windows, into which plates of ice or pieces of skin are inserted instead of glass. A large fire is kept continually burning in the middle of the yurta, which always has a wooden chimney. The yurtas are usually at some distance from one another, but at the same time are grouped into villages or *naslegs*. During summer they abandon their wooden dwellings and encamp in conical tents, consisting of a few poles covered with prepared birch bark. Their food is chiefly flesh, and their drink koumiss. Though nearly all are nominally Christians, they retain much of their original Shamanism. Their settlements, which formerly were limited to the valleys of the Lena and its northern tributaries, are now steadily advancing southwards into the hunting domains of the Tunguses, who give way before the superior civilization of the Yakuts. Wherever they penetrate, even in the valleys at the base of the Vitim plateau (Muya, Tchara), they always cultivate some barley, and carry on some trade.[1]

Occupations.

Both the Russians and the Yakuts carry on some agriculture wherever possible in the southern parts of the province; it was estimated in 1879 that 40,000 quarters of barley, summer rye, wheat, and oats were cropped in Yakutsk (23,000 quarters by the Yakuts). But cattle-breeding is the chief means of support; in 1879 there were in Yakutsk 130,400 horses of an excellent small, but most hardy breed, 260,900 cattle, 49,000 reindeer, and several thousands of dogs, which are used for travelling purposes. The hunting of the wild reindeer affords the chief means of subsistence in the tundras; wealth or famine depends upon its success or failure. The herds are attacked on the routes they pursue during their migrations, especially where they have to cross a river. Farther north the pursuit of water-birds, which come in innumerable flocks to breed on the lakes of the tundras and the shores of the ocean, is a most important resource. Fishing also is carried on even in winter from beneath the ice. The mountains between the Lena and the Vitim have, during the last thirty years, become a most important centre of gold-washings, and, notwithstanding the difficulties of communication, and the necessity of bringing everything from Irkutsk or Transbaikalia, the population of the gold-mines of the Olekma and Vitim numbered more than 13,000 in 1882. Thousands of workmen go every spring down the Lena to work at the mines and return to their villages in autumn.

Communication and trade.

The principal channel of communication in Yakutsk is the Lena. As soon as the spring arrives, scores of boats are built at Katchug, Verkholensk, and Ust-Ilga, and the goods brought on sledges in winter from the capital of Eastern Siberia, including considerable amounts of corn and salt meat, are shipped down the river. Steamers ply all along its course, and enter its tributary, the Vitim, which is navigated almost to the gorges beneath Lake Oron. A few steamers descend to the delta of the Lena, and return with cargoes of fish and furs. There are very few overland routes. A new one, available for the transport of live stock from Transbaikalia to the gold-mines of Olekma, was opened in 1869, and cattle are brought every year from Transbaikalia, notwithstanding the hardships of the 700 miles' route across the plateau and the wild mountain tracts. Two other routes, also mere footpaths, on which travellers and goods are transported on horseback, radiate from Yakutsk to Ayan and to Okhotsk. Manufactured goods and groceries, chiefly tea, rice, and sugar, were imported to Yakutsk by the former route to the amount of some 1000 cwts. in 1883; these goods cross the Stanovoi Mountains and the plateau on sledges as far as the Maya, whence they are shipped to Yakutsk.

The province is divided into five districts, the chief towns of which are—YAKUTSK (see below), Sredne-Kołymsk (560), Olekminsk (500), Verkhoyansk (290), and Viluisk (390). Except Yakutsk, these "towns" are but miserable villages. (P. A. K.)

YAKUTSK, capital of the above province, situated in 62° 2′ N. lat. and 129° 44′ E. long., 1800 miles to the north-east of Irkutsk, was founded by Cossacks in 1622. It stands on a branch of the Lena, Khatystakh, between which and the main river, five miles distant, lie several low islands. During the break-up of the ice the water of the Khatystakh, finding no outlet into the Lena on account of the huge masses of ice, rises and floods the lower parts of the town, leaving after its subsidence great pools, which, as well as Lake Tałoye close by, become a source of infectious disease. The town is, however, protected to some extent by a wooden embankment. The old fort is now destroyed, but its five wooden towers, erected in the 17th century, are still standing. The streets are unpaved, and the wooden houses are built upon high basements to protect them from the inundations. The shops only are of stone. There are in Yakutsk a cathedral, three churches, a monastery, two gymnasia for boys and girls, and several elementary schools. It is the residence of the Russian governor and the provincial authorities, as well as of a few wealthy merchants, who carry on trade in furs, mammoth bone, and reindeer hides, which are exported to Russia, and in imported groceries and manufactured goods. The arrival of the latter gives occasion to a fair in July, which is frequented by natives from all parts of the province; the returns are estimated at about £450,000. The population was 5290 in 1885.

[1] Besides the older literature, the bibliography of which is given in Semenoff's *Geogr. Dictionary* (Russian), compare Radloff's *Aus Sibirien* (Leipsic, 1884); F. Müller's *Tungusen und Yakuten* (Leipsic, 1882); and Vambéry's *Das Türkenvolk* (Leipsic, 1885); and several interesting monographs in *Izvestia* of East Siberian Geogr. Soc.

YAM, a term usually applied to the tubers of various species of *Dioscorea*. These are plants with thick rootstocks, from which protrude long slender, climbing stems, bearing alternate or opposite, entire or lobed leaves and unisexual flowers in long clusters. The flowers are generally small and individually inconspicuous, though collectively showy. Each consists of a greenish bell-shaped or flat perianth of six pieces, enclosing six or fewer stamens in the case of the male flowers, and a three-celled, three-winged ovary in that of the female flowers. The ovary ripens into a membranous capsule, bursting by three valves to liberate numerous flattish or globose seeds. The species are natives of the warmer regions of both hemispheres, and many of them are important on account of the large amount of starch contained in their tubers. According to Prof. Church's analysis of the Chinese yam, it contains more nutritive or nitrogenous matter, but less starch, than potatoes: in 100 parts there are of water 82·6, starch 13·1, albumen 2·4, fat 0·2, woody fibre 0·4, and mineral matter 1·3 parts.

D. sativa and *D. alata* are the species most widely diffused in tropical and sub-tropical countries. *D. aculeata*, grown in India, Cochin China, and the South Sea Islands, is esteemed one of the best varieties. *D. japonica*, the Chinese yam, is hardy in Great Britain, but the great depth to which its enormous tubers descend renders its cultivation unprofitable; the tubers of *D. alata* sometimes attain a weight of 100 ℔. Most of the yams contain an acrid principle, which is dissipated in cooking.

The only European *Dioscorea* is that known as *D. pyrenaica*, found in 1845 in the Pyrenees, a remarkable instance of a species growing at a long distance from all its congeners. True yams must not be confounded with the sweet potato, *Convolvulus Batatas* (see vol. xix. p. 597), as they sometimes are in London markets. The common black briony (*Tamus communis*) of hedges in England is closely allied to the yams of the tropics, and has a similar rootstock, which is reputed to be poisonous.

YAMBO, or YEMBO, more properly YANBOʿ, a town of Arabia on the Red Sea, in 24° 4′ N. lat. Having the best harbour on this coast, it has taken the place of Al-Jâr (which lay to the south and is now ruined) as the port of Medina, and is visited by steamships in connexion with the pilgrim traffic and for the import of grain. The town is surrounded by dilapidated walls, and the fixed population probably does not exceed 4000 (Von Maltzan). The Johaina Arabs are the dominant element, though there is a Turkish officer and guard who maintain a certain authority within the walls. Six or seven hours' journey inland at the base of the mountains (Jebel Radwâ) is the fruitful valley of Yanboʿ al-Nakhl, with palm-groves, several hamlets of the Johaina, and country houses of the merchants of the port. This inland town, or group of villages, is the Yanboʿ of the old Arab geographers, and lies on the route of the Egyptian pilgrim caravan, one night's journey from the famous battlefield of Bedr. The port is sometimes distinguished as Yanboʿ al-Baḥr (Yanboʿ on the Sea).

YANAON, a French settlement in India, near the mouth of the Godavari on the Orissa coast, in the Godavari district, Madras presidency. It is situated in 16° 44′ 10″ N. lat. and 82° 12′ 5″ E. long., and has an area of 2258 acres and a population of 4473.

Yanaon was founded shortly before 1750, and its fortunes followed the vicissitudes of French history in southern India. With the other French possessions in India it was secured by the treaty of 1814-15.

YANG-CHOW FU, or HANG-CHOW FOO, a prefectural city in the Chinese province of Kiang-su, is situated on the Grand Canal in 32° 21′ N. lat. and 119° 15′ E. long. The walls are between three and four miles in circumference, and the streets both in the suburbs and in the city are well supplied with handsome shops. The temples, colleges, and other public buildings are fine and large, and there is generally a well-to-do look about the place. The flourishing trade of the town may be either the cause or the result of an almost Jewish predilection shown by the people for mercantile pursuits. Unlike Chinamen generally, they prefer trade to husbandry, and have earned for themselves pre-eminence as a community of shopkeepers. Another of their characteristics is their extreme superstition. Their observance of full moons and festivals exceeds in ritualistic display that which is commonly thought to be good enough for such occasions by their fellow-countrymen; and their jealousy for the honour of their gods has on more than one occasion led to religious outbreaks. The most violent of these fanatical ebullitions, so far as foreigners are concerned, occurred in 1868, when Mr Hudson Taylor first attempted to open a mission there. But Yang-chow Fu possesses an earlier historical connexion with foreigners. Marco Polo ruled over it for three years by appointment from Kublai Khan (? 1282-85). The great traveller speaks of it as "a noble city," "which has seven and twenty other wealthy cities under its administration. . . . The people," he adds, "are idolaters and use paper money." They "live by trade and manufactures, for a great amount of harness for knights and men-at-arms are made there." The population of the city and suburbs is estimated at about 360,000. In 1880 the value of foreign goods imported into the town amounted to about £96,956.

YANG-TSE KIANG, or YANG-TSZE KEANG. See CHINA, vol. v. p. 631.

YANINA. See JANINA.

YANKTON, one of the principal cities of the Territory of Dakota, United States, and until recently its capital, is the county seat of Yankton county, and is situated upon both banks of the James or Dakota river at its confluence with the Missouri, and on the Chicago and St Paul and the Chicago and North Western Railroads. It serves as a centre of supply and distribution for the adjacent fertile plains. The population in 1880 was 3431; in 1888 this had probably increased to 5000.

The city derives its name from the Yankton division of the Sioux Indians. A trading-post was first established on its site in 1859, and the city was incorporated ten years later.

YARKAND, or YARKEND, the chief town of the principal oasis of East Turkestan, is situated on the Yarkand-Daria, in 38° 25′ N. lat. and 77° 16′ E. long., at an altitude of about 4100 feet above sea-level. The settlements of the Yarkand oasis occupy the south-western corner of East Turkestan, and are scattered along the numerous rivers which issue from the steep slopes of the Pamir in the west, and the Karakorum and Kuen-Lun Mountains in the south. The oasis of Kashgar limits it in the north, and a tract of desert separates it from the oasis of Khotan in the south-east. The Yarkand-Daria and its numerous tributaries, which are fed by the glaciers of the mountain regions, as also many rivers which no longer reach the main stream but are lost in the steppe or amidst the irrigated fields, bring abundance of water to the desert; one of them is called Zerafshan ("gold-strewing"), as much on account of the fertility it brings to the desert as of the small amount of gold discovered in its auriferous sands. Numberless irrigation canals, some of them of considerable length, carry the water of the rivers to the fields, which occupy a broad zone of loess skirting the base of the mountains. Higher up, in the spurs of the mountains, there are rich pasturages, where large numbers of goats, yaks, camels, sheep, and cattle are reared. On the whole, the oasis of Yarkand is regarded as the richest of East Turkestan, and its population probably numbers about 200,000 inhabitants (32,000 households in 1873). Wheat, barley, rice, beans, and various oil-yielding plants are grown in the fields, and the gardens supply abundance of melons, grapes, apples, and other fruits. The cotton tree and the mulberry are cultivated in the warmer parts of the oasis. There is no lack of gold, lead, and precious stones in the mountains, though only the first-named is at present extracted. A variety of petty trades are carried on in the towns; Yarkand is renowned for its leather-ware and saddlery. The population consists of Persians, who have almost given up the use of their mother tongue and now speak Turkish, and of Turkish Sarts.

The town of Yarkand, which has a population of about 60,000 according to Forsyth (5000 houses in the city, and as many in Yanghishar and the suburbs), is very favourably situated on the river of the same name, five days' journey south-east from Kashgar. It is surrounded by a thick earthen wall, nearly four miles long, with towers in the Chinese style of architecture, and is well watered by numberless canals, which are drawn from the river and, after having irrigated the rich gardens of the city, lead to cisterns in which water is collected for the winter. The square fortress of Yanghishar, which was built by the Chinese, stands within four hundred yards of the walls of the town. The ten mosques and madrasas of Yarkand, although much poorer than those of Bokhara or Samarcand, enjoy a wide renown in the Moslem world. There is a brisk trade, especially in horses, cotton, leather-ware, and all kinds of imported manufactured goods.

Yarkand is surrounded by a number of smaller towns, the chief of which are—Yanghi-hissar, which has about 600 houses and is the centre of a populous district, Tash-kurgan on the Pamir, now reckoned as belonging to the Russians, Posgam (1600 houses), Kargałyk, at the junction of the routes leading to Ladak and Khotan (2000 houses), Sanju (2000), Tagarchi, Kartchum, Besh-taryk (1800), Guma (3000), and several smaller ones.

Yarkand was but very imperfectly known until the second half of the 19th century. Marco Polo visited it between 1271 and 1275, and Goes in 1603; but the continuous wars which marked the history of the oasis (see TURKESTAN, vol. xxiii. pp. 637-640) prevented Europeans from frequenting it, so that until 1863 the information borrowed from mediæval travellers and from Chinese sources, along with that supplied by the pandit Mir Isset Ullah in 1812, was all that was known about the Yarkand region. The first European who reached it in the 19th century was Adolph Schlagintweit, who passed by Yarkand in August 1857, but was killed a few days later at Kashgar. The pandit Mohammed Hamid visited it in 1863 and determined its geographical position and altitude. The best recent information is due to Robert Shaw[1] and G. W. Hayward, who stayed at Yarkand in 1869, and to Sir Douglas Forsyth, who first visited it in 1870. Three years later he visited it again with an expedition which had Gordon, Bellew, Chapman, Trotter, Biddulph, and Stoliczka as members, and afterwards published a detailed report upon the scientific results of the mission.[2] In 1886, after a remarkable journey through East Turkestan, A. D. Carey reached Yarkand and spent the winter there.

YARMOUTH, or GREAT YARMOUTH, a municipal and parliamentary borough, seaport, watering place, and important fishing station of England, chiefly in Norfolk, with a small portion (of the municipal borough only) in Suffolk, is situated on a long and narrow peninsula of sand, bounded on the west by the river Bure, the Breydon (formed by the Yare and the Waveney), and the estuary of these rivers. It stands on the Great Eastern and the Eastern and Midland Railway lines, 20 miles east of Norwich and 122

[1] R. Shaw, *Visits to High Tartary, Yarkand, and Kashgar*, London, 1871.

[2] *Report of a Mission to Yarkund in 1873*, Calcutta, 1875, with numerous photographs.

north-east of London. The old town of Great Yarmouth was built chiefly along the eastern bank of the Yare, but within recent years the town has extended beyond its ancient walls, of which some remains still exist, to the sea-shore, where there are a marine drive and three piers—two of them 700 feet long. The principal features of Yarmouth are the north and south quays, and the straight narrow lanes, 145 in number, called "rows," running at right angles to them. These rows were at one time inhabited by the wealthy burgesses, and many of the houses now tenanted by the poorer classes have curiously panelled rooms, with richly decorated ceilings. The market place of Yarmouth is one of the most spacious in the kingdom, its area being about three acres. The old town of Great Yarmouth is connected with Little Yarmouth by a bridge across the Yare of stone and iron, erected in 1854. The Bure is crossed by a suspension bridge. The church of St Nicholas, founded in 1101 by Herbert Losinga, the first bishop of Norwich (who removed the see from Thetford), and consecrated in 1119, is one of the largest parish churches in England. Originally it was in the form of a Latin cross, but only the tower of the ancient building remains; and by successive alterations the form of the church has been completely changed. The clerestoried nave in the Early English style, with columns alternately oct-angular and circular, was rebuilt in the reign of King John. A portion of the chancel is of the same date. About fifty years later the aisles were widened, so that the nave is now the narrowest part of the building. A grand west front with towers and pinnacles was constructed in 1330-38, but the building was interrupted by a visitation of the plague. Within the church there were at one time eighteen chapels, maintained by guilds or private families, but these were demolished by the Reformers, who sold the valuable utensils of the building and applied the money to the widening of the channel of the harbour. During the Commonwealth the Independents appropriated the chancel, the Presbyterians the north aisle, and the Episcopalians were allowed the remainder of the building. The brick walls erected at this time to separate the different portions of the building remained till 1847. In 1864 the tower was restored, and the east end of the chancel rebuilt; in 1869-70 the south aisle was rebuilt; and in 1884 the south transept, the west end of the nave, and the north aisle underwent restoration. The width of the nave is 26 feet, and its length to the tower 117, that of the tower 27 feet, and of the chancel 92,—total 236 feet. The Roman Catholic church is a handsome Gothic building erected in 1850. In 1551 a grammar school was founded, the great hall of the dissolved hospital, founded in the reign of Edward I. by Thomas Fastolfe, being appropriated as the building. The school was closed from 1757 to 1860, when it was re-established by the charity trustees; and in 1872 new buildings were erected. In the hospital school a number of boys and girls were formerly boarded and educated, but since 1850 the charity has been administered as a place of free education only. Among the other principal public buildings are the town-hall and public offices, of red brick and red sandstone in the Queen Anne style of architecture, with a tower 125 feet in height, erected in 1883; the aquarium, erected in 1877 and extended in 1882; the old toll-house, formerly the town-hall, a building of the 14th century, which has been carefully preserved as a relic of antiquity; and the assembly and reading rooms, the drill-hall, the custom-house, the barracks at Southtown, the bathhouse, the workhouse, the public library, and two theatres. A Doric column, 144 feet in height, was erected on the downs in 1817 to the memory of Nelson. Among the charitable and benevolent institutions are the royal naval lunatic asylum, originally founded as a lunatic hospital in 1811; the sailors' home (1859), the boys' home (1870), the Walrond memorial smack-boys' home (1875), the fishermen's hospital (1702), and Warne's and various minor charities.

Yarmouth Roads, except in east or north-east winds, afford excellent anchorage. The present channel to the quays was made in 1567 by Joost Jansen, a Netherlands engineer. It affords a depth of water at the bar of 12 feet, and at high water of 18 to 20 feet. The town owes its origin to the fisheries, and is now one of the chief fishing stations on the east coast of England, being specially famed for its herring and mackerel fisheries (see FISHERIES, vol. ix. pp. 251-252), while cod and other white fish are also caught in great quantities. The number of boats registered under the Fisheries Act in December 1886 was 439, employing from 4500 to 6100 men and boys. The boats engaged in fishing are mostly trawling smacks. The curing of fish is an important industry, Yarmouth bloaters being celebrated throughout the kingdom. A great stimulus was given to the fishing trade by the erection of a fish wharf in 1869, having a length of 2257 feet. There is a considerable inland trade on the rivers by means of lighters and wherries. In 1883 the value of the imports of foreign and colonial produce reached £285,742, and, although in 1886 it sank to £173,636, the average for the five years preceding 1888 was about £235,000. The value of the exports in 1882 was £3399 and in 1886 £14,706. The principal imports are coal, timber, and provisions. The trade is chiefly with the Baltic ports, France, Portugal, Spain, the Channel Islands, the United States, and British North America. The number of vessels engaged in the foreign and colonial trade that entered in 1886 was 191 of 38,134 tons, that cleared 99 of 18,299 tons. The number in the coasting trade was 1033 of 110,312 tons entered, and 1083 of 124,527 tons cleared. Steam-packets ply between London, Hull, and Newcastle. Ship-building and boat-building are carried on chiefly in connexion with the fisheries, the number built in 1886 being 11 of 781 tons. There are also rope, twine, and trawl-net manufactories, silk-crape works, and extensive maltings. Yarmouth is frequented in summer as a seaside resort. It is governed by a mayor, twelve aldermen, and thirty-six councillors. The corporation act as the urban sanitary authority. Water is obtained from one of the "broads" at Ormesby. The borough has a separate commission of the peace and court of quarter-sessions. The population of the municipal borough (area 3685 acres) was 41,819 in 1871 and 46,159 (9008 being in Gorleston in Suffolk) in 1881.

At the close of the 5th century Yarmouth is said to have been the landing-place of a Saxon invader Cerdic. At an early period it was resorted to by fishermen from the Cinque Ports and from the Continent for the herring-fishing, who dried their nets on the denes or downs, and also erected tents where they sold their fish to merchants from London and elsewhere. At Domesday the place is described as the king's demesne, and as having seventy burgesses. Henry I. appointed a provost as governor, and in the 9th year of John it received a charter of incorporation. It received another charter from Henry III., who permitted the inhabitants to enclose the borough with walls and moats. In 1338-39 the town suffered severely from the plague, during which 7000 persons are said to have died. In 1381 the rebels under Wat Tyler were defeated by the inhabitants of Yarmouth. The town also rendered considerable assistance when England was threatened by the Spanish Armada; in recognition of this Elizabeth empowered the "bailiffs, burgesses, and commonalty" to hold an admiralty court, and extended their liberties in other ways. In 1588 a castle was built in the centre of the town, and a mound called the south mound raised and crowned with heavy ordnance. The castle was demolished in 1621 and new fortifications thrown up, having a circuit of 2½ miles. On account of the hardship experienced by the town from the levying of ship-money by Charles I., it declared for the Parliament. At the close of the war the fortifications were demolished. From an early period the Cinque Ports had the power of sending bailiffs to Yarmouth to govern the town during the herring-fishing season, from Michaelmas to Martinmas, their jurisdiction being concurrent with that of the bailiffs of Yarmouth; but on account of the jealousies that were thus created the privilege was abolished in the reign of Charles II. Until the Act of William IV. the town was governed by a charter of Queen Anne. It sent two members to parliament from the reign of Edward I. till 1867, when it was disfranchised; but by the Act of 1885 it was again allowed to return one member. (T. F. H.)

YARN consists of any textile fibre prepared by the process of spinning for being woven into cloth. It is only in a few minor and exceptional cases, such as the weaving of hair-cloth or of wire, that there is any making of woven fabrics without the previous spinning of yarn. As weaving can be shown to be among the earliest and most universal of the industries of mankind, the process of spinning yarn, which of necessity accompanies or rather precedes weaving, can be claimed as one of the primal employments of the race. There is ample evidence obtainable, not only of the great antiquity, but also of the wide —almost universal—diffusion of the art of spinning. Remains of the implements employed are found wherever traces of prehistoric and early man make their appearance. It happens that the exceedingly simple apparatus which was used in the earliest ages continued to be the spinning implements of civilized communities till comparatively recent times, and it may therefore be said that there is no art which has been more widely diffused, more uniformly practised, and which remained so long fixed and unprogressive, as that of yarn-spinning. On the other hand, since human ingenuity bent itself to improve the art—and these efforts only began in earnest about the middle of the 18th century—there have not been developed in the whole range of mechanical industries implements of greater variety, complexity, delicacy of action, and manifold productive capacity than the varied machines now adapted for the production of yarn.

The primitive spinning implement consists of a spindle, a rod of wood, usually from 9 to 12 inches in length, rounded and tapering towards both extremities, as shown in the accompanying cut. At the upper extremity there

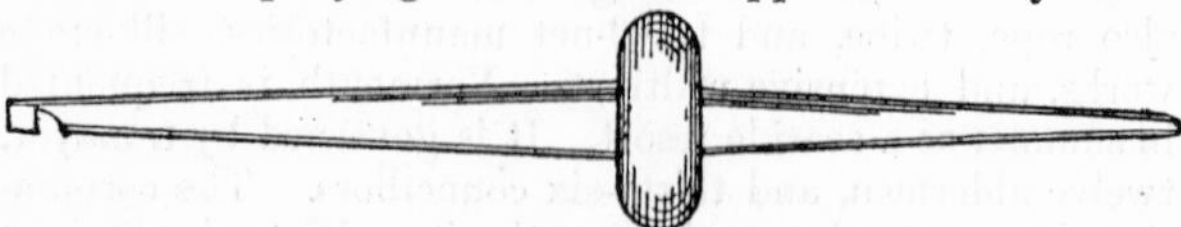

Primitive spindle.

is usually a notch, in which the yarn is caught while undergoing the operation of twisting, and to the spindle there is commonly added a whorl—a perforated disk of stone or other heavy material—the object of which is by its weight to give momentum and steadiness to the spindle when it is rotated by the hands of the spinner. The fibre to be spun is commonly attached loosely to a distaff or "rock" of wood, which is held under the left arm of the operator; but in the case of certain short fibres the material is made up in rolls or cardings. A rotatory motion is given to the spindle by twirling it between the fingers of the right hand; and the fibre to be spun is then drawn out in a uniform strand between the fingers of both hands and simultaneously twisted into yarn by the rotating spindle to which it is attached. The portion that is sufficiently twisted is wound on the body of the spindle, and the operation is continued till the spindle is filled with yarn of a smooth and equal calibre. The quantity thus rolled up gives the name to a now definite measure of yarn, "the spindle." Simple and primitive as is this apparatus, a dexterous and experienced spinner is able to produce yarn of an evenness, strength, and delicacy such as can scarcely be exceeded with the aid of the most complicated appliances and by the numerous processes of perfected modern spinning. The cotton yarns with which the famous Dacca muslins of India,—textures which from their extreme flimsy airiness receive such names as "woven air" and "evening dew,"—are spun with the aid only of these simple and rude appliances. The spindle used by the deft Hindu is a slender strip of bamboo not much bigger than a darning needle, lightly weighted with a pellet of clay; and, as the tender thread formed cannot even support the weight of so slight a spindle, the apparatus is rotated in a socket, which consists of a piece of hollow shell. The spindle as here described was the sole apparatus with which, so far as is known, the whole of the yarn woven into cloth by mankind till comparatively modern times was made, and even at the present day it is not wholly obsolete. Apart from its use in Eastern countries and among the untutored tribes of Central Africa, the spindle in its original form continues to be used in the remote districts of the Scottish Highlands and islands, and in many other regions of Europe.

Throughout all the changes and developments of modern yarn-spinning the rotating spindle continues to be the essential implement, and all the improvements which have been effected have had for their object,—(1) the providing of mechanical means of rotating the spindle, (2) an automatic method of drawing out and attenuating the fibre, and (3) devices for working a large group of spindles together.

The first improvement on the simple spindle consisted in mounting it horizontally in bearings, and giving it a rotatory motion by a band from a large wheel, passing round a small pulley or "wharve" fixed on the spindle itself. Such was the first spinning wheel which, in the form of the "charka," has long been known in the East Indies; and from a drawing in a 14th-century MS. in the British Museum it is obvious that it was not unknown, although certainly far from common, in Europe at that early date. A jewelled model hand-wheel of this description was formerly the property of Mary of Guise. This form of wheel came ultimately to be known in Scotland as the "muckle wheel," in contradistinction to one of later invention, and the method of working it is not yet an altogether forgotten art.

No strict record of the dates at which various developments of the art of spinning took place are to be found, and it is certain that many appliances were long known and to some extent used before their adoption became general. Thus it is quite clear that the flier, which is fitted around modern spindles for twisting the yarn before it is wound on the bobbin, was known to Leonardo da Vinci and probably invented by him. Among the numerous mechanical drawings left by that man of genius there is one which shows a spindle with flier and bobbin, with a device for moving the bobbin up and down on the spindle so as to effect an even distribution of the yarn. But the use of the flier does not seem to have been known in England till about the end of the 17th century. In a pamphlet issued in 1681 by Thomas Firmin, entitled *Some Proposals for the Employment of the Poor*, there is an illustration of an improved wheel, with two spindles provided with fliers, having on them hooks or pins for directing the yarn on different parts of the bobbin. The sketch also shows the spindle and flier driven by different bands, as was the case with the spinning-wheel which subsequently came into common use. In hand-spinning the further application of the treadle motion, with connecting-rod and crank-axle to drive the little wheel with the feet alone, was the final development. By this agency both hands of the spinner were free, continuous and uniform motion was secured, and the spinner could work two spindles simultaneously, the one with the right and the other with the left hand. It was in this condition that the most advanced form of yarn-making was carried on in the 18th century, when a great series of inventions revolutionized the entire range of textile industries and laid the foundation of the gigantic factory system of spinning and weaving which now prevails.

The problem which lay before inventors was to bring tangled masses of fibrous material into parallel order, and to draw out and twist these fibres into uniform strands by automatic means, without the continuous application of intelligent attention. The first stage in the evolution of mechanical spinning was effected under the patent of Louis Paul in 1738, in which there was clearly described and foreshadowed what is now one of the most important features of spinning machinery—the drawing rollers. In his specification he says:—

"One end of the mass, rope, thread, or sliver is put betwixt a pair of rowlers, cillinders, or cones, or some such movements, which, being turned round, by their motion draws in the raw mass of wool or cotton to be spun, in proportion to the velocity given to such rowlers, cillinders, or cones. As the prepared mass passes regularly through or betwixt these rowlers, cillinders, or cones, a succession of other rowlers, cillinders, or cones, moving proportionably faster than the first, draw the rope, thread, or sliver into any degree of fineness which may be required."

Next, to James Hargreaves of Blackburn is due the first conception of the famous spinning-jenny, which he devised about 1767 and patented in 1770. In his specification Hargreaves describes his invention as a machine or engine to be managed by one person only, and that the wheel or engine will spin, draw, and twist sixteen or more threads at one time by a turn or motion of one hand and a draw of the other. At the same time the humble barber of Preston, Richard Arkwright, was busily engaged in developing the important series of inventions and adaptations which resulted in the modern throstle spinning-frame. Arkwright's principal patents were secured in 1769 and 1775; and in the latter year Samuel Crompton of Bolton brought before the world his mule spinning-frame, in which the drawing rollers of Paul and Arkwright were with happy effect applied to the jenny of Hargreaves. These inventions are at the foundation of all modern systems of yarn-spinning; details regarding them are given under COTTON, LINEN, SILK, and WOOL.

The various methods by which the sizes or counts of yarn have been fixed in different countries have long been a source of much inconvenience in the international exchange of spun yarns. The methods of estimating sizes or weights of yarn are indeed complicated in the extreme, for not only has each country different standards, which may locally be disregarded, but for the yarn from each separate fibre there may be different lengths of hank and different methods of estimating sizes. Thus, taking English standards, we find that cotton yarns are made up into hanks of 560 "threads" of 1½ yards, giving 840 yards per hank, and the "counts" are the number of hanks which go to make 1lb weight of yarn. For linen yarns there are 2½ yards in a thread, and 120 threads or 300 yards in a lea, and the count is the number of leas per lb. In a hank of worsted or woollen yarn there are 560 yards, and the count similarly is the number of hanks per lb. In Continental countries the length of the hank or its equivalent is different; the weight by which the count is reckoned also varies; and, as the weights and measures of the several countries have only the most involved ratio to each other, to estimate comparative sizes complex calculated tables are necessary. Attempts have been made to establish an international standard of numbering yarns based on the French metric system, in which the count is the number of grams which a definite length of yarn—1000 metres—weighs. No progress, however, has been made in coming to an international agreement in the question. (J. PA.)

YAROSŁAVL, a government of central Russia, separated from Moscow by narrow strips of Vladimir and Tver on the S., and having Tver and Novgorod on the W., Vologda on the N., and Kostroma on the E., is one of the smallest, but at the same time one of the most populous and industrial governments of Great Russia. It has an area of 13,751 square miles, and the population was 1,118,130 in 1884. It consists of a broad and shallow depression, elongated from west to east, where the Volga flows at a level ranging from 260 to 230 feet above the sea, while the surrounding hills rise to altitudes of from 700 to 800 feet. In the west, especially between the Mołoga and the Sheksna, the country is covered with marshes and ponds, which become completely flooded when the water rises in the rivers. There is another region of low and marshy tracts in the south, about Rostoff. Gentle sloping hills appear in the north on the left bank of the Sheksna.

Jurassic clays, sandstones, and sands cover nearly the whole of Yarosłavl, but they are concealed almost everywhere by thick deposits of Glacial boulder clay, which is regarded by Russian geologists as the bottom moraine of the great ice-cap of the Glacial period. Triassic "variegated marls," widely diffused throughout the whole of the middle Volga region, undoubtedly underlie nearly all the Jurassic deposits of the government, but only a few patches come to the surface; many salt springs exist in these deposits. The Upper Carboniferous limestones come to the surface only in the north-west and towards the east.[1] The chief mineral products are bog-iron ores, sulphate of copper, and pottery clay. Peat occurs in thick beds. There are also several mineral springs. The soil is mostly a kind of loess of moderate fertility; sandy tracts are not uncommon; and wide areas are covered with marshes—relics of the great lakes of the Lacustrine period.

The chief river of the government is the Volga, which traverses it for 180 miles, making a great bend to the north. The chief towns—Rybinsk, Yarosłavl, Mołoga, Romanoff-Borisoglyebsk, Uglitch, and Myshkin—are situated on its banks, and a brisk traffic is carried on, both by the river itself and by two canals, Mariinsk and Tikhvinsk, which connect it with the Neva through its tributaries the Sheksna and the Mołoga. Another tributary received by the Volga within the government is the Kotorost, which has many manufactories on its banks and is navigated, especially in spring. The Kostroma flows along the eastern border and is a channel for the export of timber and fuel. Small lakes are numerous, the chief being Lake Nero or Rostoff. The forests, which consist chiefly of fir and Scotch pine, cover one-third of the aggregate area; but they are rapidly being destroyed. The flora of Yarosłavl, although similar to that of Moscow, bears a northern stamp owing to the presence of the dwarf birch, *Rubus arcticus*, and *Linnæa borealis*.

The climate is as continental as that of middle Russia generally. The average temperature at Yarosłavl is 36°·7 Fahr. (January 6°·5, July 61°·5); the prevailing south-western and western winds render it moister than in central Russia; and the average number of days with rain or snow is 114. The rivers remain frozen from 118 to 183 days every year.

The population is thoroughly Great Russian. The aboriginal Meryas have been completely Russified; and traces of the Karelians, who immigrated in the 17th century, can only be discovered in the names and features of some inhabitants on the Siti river. There are moreover some 1000 Tartars, 2100 Jews, and about 500 Gipsies. Leaving out of account some 2700 Catholics and Protestants, the population belongs to the Greek Orthodox Church or is *Raskolnik*.

Although Yarosłavl is one of the chief manufacturing governments of the empire, its inhabitants have by no means abandoned agriculture, 27 per cent. of the total area being under crops (36 per cent. under forests and 8 per cent. untillable); on the lands of the peasantry the percentage is still greater (from 46 to 58 per cent.). Rye, oats, and barley, with some wheat and pease, are the chief crops, and in good seasons Yarosłavl has even a surplus of corn, which is either sent to the distilleries or exported. The average crops of 1883-85 were 960,100 quarters of rye, 36,000 of wheat, 97,400 of barley, 1,097,100 of oats, 19,600 of other grain, and 6,992,800 bushels of potatoes. Nearly 40,000 cwts. of flax are cropped every year. Market-gardening is largely engaged in and the Yarosłavl gardeners have a wide repute throughout Russia. Chicory, sweet pease, cucumbers, apples, and berries are exported. Although there is no want of meadows, cattle-breeding is not greatly developed. In 1882-84 there were 178,370 horses, 260,000 cattle, 188,700 sheep, and 4700 pigs. One-third of the peasant households had no horses. Cheese-making on the co-operative principle has spread extensively of late, owing to the efforts of the *zemstvo*; 93 associations have a yearly production to the value of £12,700. Domestic trades are carried on in great variety in the villages, including the making of linen cloth, boots, gloves, sheepskins, knitted wares, clothes, felts, all kinds of wooden wares, pottery, and a variety of metallic goods. The total production is very considerable, although no details are available. The manufactures are growing rapidly, the yearly production of 1708 establishments being estimated at £2,210,000 in 1884. Cotton and linen are the chief items (nearly £1,000,000); flour-mills, distilleries, and tobacco works come next; and these are followed by chemical works and workshops for machinery, metallic wares, and so on, which are rapidly developing. The trade of the government is very active both on the Volga and on the two railway lines, one of which connects Rybinsk with the St Petersburg and Moscow line and the other connects Yarosłavl with Moscow and Vologda. Rybinsk and Yarosłavl are the chief commercial centres, but Rostoff, Mołoga, Romanoff, and Poshekhonie also carry on an active trade in corn, timber, and manufactured wares. The total merchandise shipped or discharged to and from the towns and villages of Yarosłavl is estimated at 1,600,000 tons annually, one-half by rail.

One of the most distinctive features of Yarosłavl is the large numbers of its male population who annually leave their homes in order to work all over Russia as locksmiths, masons, plasterers, waiters in restaurants, greengrocers, tailors, gardeners, carpenters, joiners, pilots, or boatmen. Many of these employments have been specialties of the population of Yarosłavl from a remote antiquity, and the native of this government can easily be distinguished by his enterprising spirit, keen air, and energetic and nervous temperament. In Moscow and St Petersburg together there are about 76,400 employed in the above capacities, and it may be estimated that as many as 100,000 persons annually leave their homes in this way.

The educational institutions were represented in 1884 by a lyceum (197 students), six gymnasia (569 boys and 1219 girls), a military school (492 boys), a seminary for teachers (81 students), and 745 elementary schools (25,780 boys, 10,140 girls).

Yarosłavl is divided into ten districts, the chief towns of which, with their population in 1884, are—YAROSŁAVL (see below), Daniloff (5780), Lubim (3180), Mołoga (6360), Myshkin (2390), Poshekhonie (5990), Romanoff-Borisoglyebsk (5300), Rostoff (12,450), Rybinsk (19,900), and Uglitch (11,930). Petrovsk (1760) has municipal institutions.

[1] *Geological Survey of Russia*, sheet 56, by Nikitin (Russian and German), St Petersburg, 1884.

History.—As early as the 9th century the Slavonians had become masters of the Yarosłavl territory, which was formerly occupied by the Finnish stems Vess and Merya, as also by Mordvinians, Muroms, and Tcheremisses in the south. Rostoff was already in existence; but Yarosłavl, Rybinsk, and Uglitch begin to be mentioned in the annals only in the 11th and 12th centuries. The independent principality of Rostoff was divided in the 13th century into three parts, but these were soon afterwards successively annexed to Moscow.

See the *Trudy* of the Yarosłavl Statistical Committee, 8 vols., and the *Vyestnik* of the Yarosłavl zemstvo, published since 1872. (P. A. K.)

YAROSŁAVL, capital of the above government, stands on the right bank of the Volga, at its junction with the Kotorost, 173 miles by rail to the north-east of Moscow, and had a population of 48,310 inhabitants in 1884; but this number is temporarily much increased during the period of navigation. The suburbs of the town occupy the left bank and are inundated at high water. A fine quay borders the Volga for nearly two miles. The cathedrals and several churches are very old. The Uspenskiy cathedral was begun in 1215 and rebuilt in 1648; the churches of the Preobrazhenskiy monastery, St John's, and Voskreseniye date from the 15th and 17th centuries, the second being a fine specimen of the architectural style exemplified in the Vasiliy Blazhennyi church of Moscow. Yarosłavl has a lyceum, founded by Demidoff, with a juridical faculty, three gymnasia (409 boys, 669 girls), and various primary schools. The manufactories, whose total production in 1862 barely reached the value of £200,000, now employ 5100 hands and yield an output valued at about £1,000,000 (one-half from one cotton-mill). The trade, especially that in corn, is very active and accounts for one-quarter of the whole traffic of the government. The Yarosłavl merchants also carry on a large import trade in manufactured goods and groceries.

The town of Yarosłavl was founded in 1026-1036 by Yarosłav Vladimirovitch, who caused a wooden fort to be erected at the confluence of the Kotorost with the Volga. It became the chief town of a principality in 1218 and remained so until 1471, when it fell under the dominion of Moscow. Even in the 13th century Yarosłavl was an important town, and, although it suffered during subsequent wars, it maintained its importance until the 19th century, when the trade on the Volga and its rising manufactures again gave it a position of predominance in the upper basin of the Volga.

YARRELL, William (1784-1856), one of the most popular of British naturalists, was born at Westminster in June 1784. His father was a newspaper agent, and he himself succeeded to the business on his father's death, and prosecuted it till within a few years of his own. He availed himself of any interval of relaxation to enjoy such sport as the neighbourhood of London afforded, acquired the reputation of being the best shot and the first angler in the metropolis, and soon also became an expert naturalist. In 1824 he became a fellow of the Linnean Society, and was a diligent contributor to their *Transactions*; and he was one of the earliest members of the Zoological Society. The greater part of his leisure towards the end of his life was devoted to his two great works, *The History of British Fishes* (2 vols., 1836) and *The History of British Birds* (2 vols., 1843). These works are compiled on the same plan; they contain accurate figures, with accompanying descriptions, of every British fish or bird; and they have from the first taken their position as standard authorities. Few books on natural history are more agreeable to the general reader: the style is pleasant, and the truth with which he describes the habits of the birds is such as might have been expected from a keen and observant sportsman. In 1856 he had an attack of paralysis, of which he died at Yarmouth on 1st September of the same year.

YAWS is the name in use in the British West Indies and on the West Coast of Africa for a peculiar disease of the skin in Negroes. The learned name, first applied by Sauvages (1761), is *framboesia*, from the likeness of the typical excrescences to a raspberry. For many years yaws was thought to be peculiar to the African Negro, either in his home (both west and east coasts) or in the West Indies and Brazil. But a disease the same in every respect has long been known in the East Indies (first mentioned by Bontius early in the 17th century), affecting the Malays rather than the Negroes, its chief seats being Amboyna, Ternate, Timor, Celebes, Java, and Sumatra. It has been identified more recently by De Rochas and other observers in New Caledonia and Fiji. The *parangi* of Ceylon has been shown by Kynsey to be the same as the West Indian yaws. Also in the Samoa group, to which there has been no Negro migration, an identical malady occurs. The closely allied *verrugas* of the Peruvian Andes (see Wart) is so different in its endemic circumstances that it is not usually classified as a form of yaws. The account that follows applies equally to all of the local forms, while it has more especial reference to yaws in the Negroes of the West Indies.

The general course of the disease is as follows. Previous to the eruption there may or may not be any disorder of health; in children (who form a large part of the subjects of yaws) there will probably be rheumatic pains in the limbs and joints, with languor, debility, and upset of the digestion; in adults of ordinary vigour the eruption is often the first sign, and it is attended with few or no constitutional troubles. The eruption begins as small pimples like a pin's head, smooth and nearly level with the surface; they have a little whitish speck on their tops, grow rapidly, and reach the size of a sixpence or a shilling. The pustules then break, and a thick viscid ichor exudes and dries upon them as a whitish slough, and around their base as a yellowish brown crust. Beneath the whitish slough is the raspberry excrescence or yaw proper, a reddish fungous growth with a nodular surface. The favourite seats of the eruption are the forehead, face, neck, armpits, groin, genitals, perinæum, and buttocks. Hairs at the seat of a yaw turn white. In young children or infants the corners of the mouth ulcerate, as in syphilis, and the perineal excrescences resemble condylomata. The pustules and excrescences do not all arise in one crop: some are found mature while others are only starting. If the patient be of sound constitution and good reaction, the yaws may reach the full size of a mulberry in a month, in which case they will probably be few; but in persons of poor health they may take three months to attain the size of a wood-strawberry, in which case they will be numerous inversely to their size. Often there is one yaw much larger than the rest, and longer in falling; it is called the "master yaw" or "mother yaw." On the soles of the feet (less often on the palms of the hands) the bursting yaws are as if imprisoned beneath the horny cuticle; they cause swelling and tenderness of the foot, until set free by paring the callous skin down to the quick; these yaws are called "crab yaws" or *tubbas*. Usually a yaw is painless unless when rubbed or irritated. The absence of pain is used as a diagnostic sign if there be any doubt as to the nature of the attack: a pustule is opened, and a little of the juice of capsicum dropped into it; if it be a yaw, no smarting will be felt. In some cases a few yaws will show themselves long after the primary attack is over; these are called "memba yaws" (from "remember"), the term being sometimes applied also to protracted cases with successive crops of eruption. Six weeks is the average time in a good case, from the first of the eruption to the fall of the excrescences; in such regular cases a scar remains, it may be for many months, darker than the rest of the (Negro) skin. But the disease is often a much more tedious affair, the more protracted type having become common in the West Indies of recent years. In such cases the eruption comes out by degrees and as if with difficulty, crop after crop; foul, excavating, and corroding ulcers may remain, or a limb may be in part seamed and mutilated by the scars of old ulceration. The scars after ulceration are not so dark as the skin around.

That yaws is a communicable disease is beyond question; but that it has always arisen by conveyance of yawey matter from a previous case is neither proved nor probable. Being to a great extent a disease of childhood, it is not usually conveyed after the manner of syphilis, but by contact in other ways (as in the epidemic syphilis of 1494-1520 and in recent circumscribed epidemics). An abrasion or wound of the surface, such as a chigoe bite or a cut of the foot, is a likely point of entrance for the virus. If the yawey matter finds access to a pre-existing sore or ulcer, it causes the latter to take on a foul and sloughing condition. No sore or yaw is induced at the point of infection, which will probably be healed long before the eruption appears. It is said, however, that the pustules appear earliest and in greatest numbers on the skin near the spot where the virus entered. They follow the infection at an interval of several weeks (incubation period). Cases of yaws by infection are not unknown in white persons of good position, both children and adults, in the West Indies and elsewhere.

The nature of the disease is obscure. It is alleged to be hereditary by some, and denied to be so by others; the fact seems to be that some constitutions are much more susceptible than others, and susceptible at some periods or states of health more than at others. As an epidemic, the disease in a locality has seasons of activity and quiet. One attack in childhood gives a large degree of immunity for the rest of life. Yaws used to break out in the slaves on board Guineamen. Both in Africa and among the slaves in the West Indies it was a custom to inoculate the yaws, so as to get the attack over (called "buying the yaws") or to get put upon the sick list.

As regards treatment, the malady in a person of good constitution runs its course and gets well in a few weeks. Whatever tends to check the eruption, such as exposure to chill, is to be avoided. A week's course of cream of tartar and sulphur (confection of sulphur) at the beginning of the illness is often resorted to, so as to bring the eruption well out. The patient should remain indoors, in a well-aired room, and take daily warm baths and diluent drinks. If the excrescences are flabby and unhealthy, it is an indication for generous diet. Mercurial treatment is no longer in vogue. As external applications, weak lotions of zinc or carbolic acid may be used, and, if the excrescences are irritable, a watery solution of opium. Tedious and unhealthy yaws should be dressed with a wash of sulphate of zinc or of copper; the same may be applied to a yaw ulcer. The crab yaws of the horny soles or palms, after they are let through by paring the cuticle, may be dusted with alum powder. The most intractable cases occur in badly nourished and anæmic subjects, and these will often go on for months in hospital without mending. Of late in the West Indies the disease has become largely a *morbus miseriæ*, and to that extent less amenable to treatment.

The date of the first appearance of yaws in the West Indies and Brazil is matter of dispute; the general belief is that it came in with the African Negro. After the emancipation in 1838 there was a marked decline in the prevalence of the disease in Jamaica and other colonies. In Jamaica it began to be seen again from 1854 to 1864, the cases being more of adult age than formerly. The worst recent centre of yaws has been Dominica, which is occupied by Negro communities unprovided with medical attendance. In 1871 the Government opened and maintained two special hospitals for yaws (under a board of commissioners), one at Morne Bruce near Roseau, and the other at Prince Rupert's. In Barbados and Antigua cases of yaws are rarely seen, the population being more creole than Negro. Trinidad has a good deal of the disease from time to time in the inland villages; bad cases are admitted to the leper asylum at Port of Spain. In Grenada, which has a special yaws hospital, and in St Vincent the immigration of Hindu coolies received a check owing to the ravages made by the disease among them. It prevails also in San Domingo, Guadeloupe, and others of the Antilles. At Berbice and Essequibo there were 23 fatal cases in one year (1870). The disease is common in all parts of Brazil. In western Africa cases are found along the whole coast from the Senegal to the Congo, and in the interior (Timbuktu and Bornu). On the East Coast it is found in Mozambique, Madagascar, and the Comoros. Its localities in the East Indies and islands of the Pacific have been already mentioned.

For the literature dealing with the subject, see Hirsch, *Geographical and Historical Pathology* (Engl. trans.), vol. ii., London, 1885 (New Sydenham Soc.).

YAZD, or YEZD, a city of Persia, capital of the district of Yazd, province of Farsistán, in 31° 50′ N. lat. and 54° 25′ E. long. Yazd stands on a flat sandy plain, about 50 miles broad and encircled by an amphitheatre of picturesque hills, on the high road between Ispahán and Karmán, 190 miles south-east of the former and 220 north-west of the latter place. The old and dilapidated walls enclose a very large space, which, however, is much encumbered with ruins, the population having fallen from about 100,000 at the beginning of the 19th century (Christie) to about 30,000 in 1868 (Smith). Since the famine of 1870 the place has recovered some of its former prosperity, and has at present (1888) an estimated population of 50,000, including 1000 Jews and about 4000 fire-worshippers, Yazd being the only town in Persia where these still form a separate community. There are fifty mosques, sixty-five public baths, eight public schools, but no building of any note except the chief mosque, a very old and decayed structure, which still presents a lofty and imposing frontage. With the exception of a fine new bazaar, which is well stocked with goods and much frequented the markets and other parts of the town are irregularly planned, with narrow dark streets and little life. Yazd is in fact a city of the wilderness, whose oasis, planted chiefly with mulberries and other fruit trees, is everywhere surrounded by the shifting sands, which at some points already threaten to encroach on the town itself (Macgregor). In this way was engulfed its predecessor, Old Yazd or Askizár, whose ruins are still visible 10 miles to the north-west on the road to Kashan. Nevertheless the local traders maintain their old reputation for intelligence and enterprise, and their agents still visit the distant markets of India, Java, and China. The trade with India formerly carried on through Shiráz now takes the more direct route through Karmán. The exports are chiefly sugar, silks, opium (4000 chests in a single year to China), cordage, cotton, felts, and copper; the imports wheat, rice, cotton goods, and henna. This henna, together with rang for dyeing the hair, is brought from the Mináb and Bandar-Abbás districts to be ground and prepared for the Persian market. From the neighbouring villages and the remote province of Ghilán comes the raw material for the silk-looms, which produce two kinds—*kasb* and *aluhí*—both of the very finest quality. Other noted products of the local industries are the felts, equal to the best in Karmán, and the candied sugars and sweetmeats, in the preparation of which the fire-worshippers excel. A great drawback to Yazd is the defective and irregular supply of water, which largely depends on the yearly snow and rainfall on the surrounding hills. The annual revenue averages £35,000 to £40,000, of which three-fifths go to the public treasury; the rest supports the local administration and household of the governor, who resides in a kind of citadel within the city walls

YEADON, a manufacturing town in the West Riding of Yorkshire, is situated on a hill north of Airedale, about 1½ miles from Guiseley station on the Midland Railway and 8½ miles north-west of Leeds. The streets are generally irregular and tortuous, but within recent years greater care has been taken in the arrangement of new buildings. The church of St John in the Pointed Gothic style, erected in 1843, consists of chancel and nave, with square tower surmounted by pinnacles. The town-hall and mechanics' institute, a handsome Gothic building erected in 1883, includes a large public hall, the rooms of the Liberal club and of the local board, and class and lecture rooms. Yeadon is chiefly of modern growth, although wool-combing and cloth manufacture were carried on to some extent before the establishment of the first woollen-mill in 1831. Since 1850 the town has made rapid progress, and now possesses several mills, in which woollen cloths are manufactured, especially materials for ladies' jackets, ulsters, mantles, &c. The township was formed out of Guiseley in 1845. The local board of health was established in 1863. The population of the urban sanitary district (area 1723 acres) was 5246 in 1871 and 6534 in 1881.

YEAR. See CALENDAR, vol. iv. p. 666.

YEAST, an insoluble substance forming an essential component of all sacchariferous juices when in the state of vinous fermentation. This subject is pretty fully dealt with under FERMENTATION (see vol. ix. pp. 92, 95, 97); one important application of yeast, however, viz., that which it finds in the baker's trade, is there only referred to. To produce a spongy loaf, the dough, before being made into loaves, is mixed with a ferment which, if allowed to act for a sufficient time before baking, produces alcohol and carbonic acid from a small portion of the actual or potential sugar present; and the carbonic acid, being liberated from within the dough, causes it to "rise." In former times leaven (see BAKING, vol. iii. p. 253) used to be employed exclusively. For higher classes of bakery yeast is now preferred. The yeast produced so abundantly in beer-brewing is available; but its bitter taste is an objection to it. Hence it has long been customary in Germany to produce yeast expressly for bakers' and cooks' purposes, which may, of course, be done in a variety of ways. A method frequently used is to produce a wort (see BREWING, vol. iv. p. 275) from barley, malt, and rye, and by the addition of a little ready-made yeast to let it ferment under conditions which favour the growth of yeast-cells, but restrict the proportion of alcohol produced to a minimum (comp. FERMENTATION, vol. ix. p. 97). During the most tumultuous period of the process the yeast is skimmed off from the surface, washed with water, and either "filter-pressed" or "centrifuged" to obtain it as a relatively dry paste; it is then mixed with a proportion of dry starch, to give it a higher degree of dryness. Such yeast goes into commerce as *presshefe* or *pfundhefe* (German yeast or barm). This industry used to be a monopoly of Germany; but quite lately the manufacture of German yeast has been taken up in Scotland.

YEDO. See TOKIO.

YEISK, a district town of the Russian province of Kuban (Caucasus), was founded in 1848 at the mouth of the Yeia, on a narrow sandbank which separates the shallow Bay of Yeisk from the Sea of Azoff, 108 miles to the south-west of Rostoff-on-the-Don. Notwithstanding its shallow roadstead, which has a depth of 14 feet only at 2 miles from the shore, Yeisk has grown with great rapidity, and in 1884 had 23,725 inhabitants. Corn, linseed, and wool are exported to a considerable extent (1,730,000 cwts. of corn and flax and 10,000 cwts. of wool in 1885), and the port was visited in 1886 by 69 ships (30,000 tons) engaged in foreign trade and by 697 (80,800 tons) engaged in the coasting trade. There are large wool-cleansing factories, oil-works, and tanneries.

YEKATERINBURG. For this and similar forms of Russian town-names, see EKATERINBURG, &c.

YELETS, a district town of the Russian government of Orel, 121 miles by rail to the east of Orel, stands on the great trunk railway which connects Riga with Tsaritsyn on the lower Volga; a branch line connects it also with the railway which runs from Tula to Samara and Orenburg. Owing to its advantageous position Yelets, which had been for a long time an important entrepôt for the corn trade, has rapidly grown of late, and in 1883 had 36,680 inhabitants. The Yelets merchants buy large quantities of grain in the fertile neighbouring provinces, and send their agents to southern and south-eastern Russia; nearly 150 flour-mills, many of them driven by steam, prepare flour, which is forwarded chiefly to Moscow and partly to Riga. The trade in cattle is also very important. Yelets has become of late a manufacturing centre, and has some important tanneries, foundries for cast-iron and copper, tallow-melting works, sieve manufactories, &c. The town has several educational institutions. Its cathedral and two monasteries contain venerated historic relics.

Yelets is first mentioned in 1147, when it was a fort of Ryazañ. The Polovtsys attacked it in the 12th century, and the Mongols destroyed it during their first invasion. The Tartars plundered it in 1415 and 1450; and it seems to have been completely abandoned in the latter half of the 15th century. Its development dates from the second half of the 17th century, when it became a centre for the trade with south Russia.

YELIZAVETGRAD. See ELIZABETHGRAD.

YELIZAVETPOL. See ELIZABETHPOL.

Type and circumstances.

YELLOW FEVER is a typhus-like fever of certain ports, or of ships hailing from them. It differs from all other existing types of fevers and infections in largely sparing the Negro. It resembles cholera in being endemic in some parts of the world (but only shipping places) and in being importable to others, in being an infection that issues from the soil or some medium equivalent thereto, and in being a virulent filth-disease; but it differs from cholera in having at the outset a violent febrile paroxysm lasting two or three days. As a fever it resembles typhus; but it differs from typhus in all those "exogenous" characters wherein it resembles cholera. The generic place and affinities of yellow fever are perhaps best provided for in the nosology of Cullen: the symptoms are within the sphere of the organic nervous system; they stand for excitement first and prostration afterwards; and they are an effect of human effluvia. Its differentia among the "nervous" fevers due to "human effluvia" would be its maritime or amphibious habitat, its association with tropical heat, the chief part played by the liver in its symptomatology (on the lines of acute yellow atrophy), and the singular immunity of the Negro race.

Characteristics.

An attack of yellow fever may follow definite exposure (such as landing at an endemic port) within a few hours, as in corresponding cases of cholera; but the outbreak of symptoms is more often delayed for a few days, the limit of "incubation" being about eight. The few hours' languor, chilliness, headache, and muscular pains, which might be the precursors of any febrile attack, are followed by a peculiar look of the eyes and face, which is characteristic: the face is flushed, and the eyes suffused at first and then congested or ferrety, the nostrils and lips red, and the tongue scarlet,—these being the most obvious signs of universal congestion of the skin, mucous membranes, and organs. Meanwhile the temperature has risen to fever heat, and may reach a very high figure (maximum of 110° Fahr., it is said); the pulse is quick, strong, and full, but may not keep up in these characters with the high temperature throughout. There are all the usual accompaniments of high fever, including hot skin, failure of appetite, thirst, nausea, restlessness, and delirium (which may or may not be violent); albumen will nearly always be found in the urine. The fever is a continued one so long as it lasts; but the febrile excitement comes to an end after two or three days. In a certain class of ambulatory or masked cases the febrile reaction may never come out, and the shock of the infection after a brief interval may lead unexpectedly and directly to prostration and death. The cessation of the paroxysm makes the *stadium*, or lull, characteristic of yellow fever. The hitherto militant or violent symptoms cease, and prostration or collapse ensues. The internal heat falls below the normal; the action of the heart (pulse) becomes slow and feeble, the skin cold and of a lemon-yellow tint, the act of vomiting effortless, like that of an infant, the first vomit being clear fluid, but afterwards black from an admixture of blood. It is at this period that the prospect of recovery or of a fatal issue declares itself. The prostration following the paroxysm of fever may be no more than the weakness of commencing recovery, with copious flow of urine, which even then is very dark-coloured from the presence of blood. The prostration will be all the more profound according to the height reached by the temperature during the acute paroxysm. Much blood in the vomit and in the stools, together with all other hæmorrhagic signs, is of evil omen. Constant hiccough, with loud cries or wailing, is a certain sign of death, which may also be ushered in by suppression of urine, coma, and convulsions, or by fainting from failure at the heart. The proportion of recoveries is usually less than one-half; but it has been now and then very large (as in the New Orleans epidemic of 1878). Convalescence is on the whole rapid; but, if some old disease, such as ague, have been lighted up, or abscesses induced, it may go on slowly for months. One attack of yellow fever confers a high degree of immunity from a second.

Treatment.

The treatment of yellow fever has been one of the classical subjects of controversy. In the Philadelphia epidemics of the end of the 18th century, Rush gained much credit for his incessant labours in bleeding the victims during the violence of the paroxysm. Although blood-letting to relieve the congestions has been given up, experience still favours the resort to vigorous measures at the outset. The following practice was adopted with much success by Dr Joseph Jones during the epidemic of 1878 at New Orleans,—an emetic of ipecacuanha, followed by a powder of calomel (10 to 20 grains), with as much quinine added (the latter ingredient of doubtful utility), and that again followed by a full dose of castor oil. Beyond that heroic medication at the outset of the febrile paroxysm, the treatment was directed to assisting the action of the skin and kidneys, by keeping the temperature of the room uniform, by mustard foot-baths, and by copious draughts of lemonade or other aerated water, or of barley water. The diet indicated is fever diet: *i.e.*, it should exclude solid food. For such symptoms as tenderness over the stomach a mustard poultice is applied; for diminished secretion of urine, dry cupping over the loins. When the lull occurs, the patient should on no account be allowed to get up, as sudden failure of the heart is apt to follow exertion. Iced champagne and beef-tea are found to be the best supports for this stage. The only thing to do when black vomit threatens is to give the patient ice to suck, or (more questionably) to place an ice-bag on the abdomen. When the stage of prostration assumes a "typhoid" character, an enema of ice-cold water, with a little turpentine in it, helps to get rid of the flatus and to stimulate the kidneys. Recovery is in all cases more probable where there is abundant cubic space and good ventilation.

tho-
gy.

Yellow fever is of the nature of typhus, in the language of older writers, a nervous or putrid fever. The two salient things about it are the internal hæmorrhages and the almost complete arrest of the function of the liver; of these the latter would seem to be primary and the former secondary. The state of the liver on examination after death from yellow fever is by far the most significant feature in the morbid anatomy: the bile-ducts and gall-bladder are empty, or contain only a clear albuminoid fluid; the organ is bloodless and of a golden yellow colour; and the hepatic cells are everywhere full of fatty granules or other molecular detritus. It shows, in fact, the morbid anatomy of acute yellow atrophy, or that state of the hepatic structure and functions which is due to total inhibition or arrest (see PATHOLOGY, vol. xviii. p. 386), whether the inhibiting influence be phosphorus poisoning, or emotional strain, or something in the pregnant state, or the infective influence of yellow fever. All the other phenomena of this fever are grouped around the liver derangement, as around a centre, namely, the yellow tint of the skin, the fatty degeneration of the heart favouring syncope, the hæmorrhages from the mucous membranes (including the black vomit), the degeneration of the renal epithelium with albuminuria, and the coma and convulsions. Yellow fever therefore may be styled a sudden or arbitrary infection imposed from without, the distinctive mark or "note" of which is the same peculiar group of symptoms that is found in the rare and sporadic cases of yellow atrophy. To reach the full and correct doctrine of yellow fever, we have to harmonize the clinical and pathological facts of the disease, as already given, with the historical, geographical, racial, and other associated circumstances now to be stated.

istory
nd geo-
aphical
stribu-
on.

The first authentic account of yellow fever comes from Bridgetown, Barbados, in 1647, where it was recognized as a "nova pestis," that was unaccountable in its origin, except that Ligon, the historian of the colony, who was then on the spot, connected it with the arrival of ships. It was the same new pestilence that Dutertre, writing in 1667, described as having occurred in the French colony of Guadeloupe in 1635 and 1640; it recurred at Guadeloupe in 1648, and broke out in a peculiarly disastrous form at St Kitt's the same year, and again in 1652; in 1655 it was at Port Royal, Jamaica; and from those years onwards it became familiar at many harbours in the West Indies and Spanish Main, and in the Atlantic ports of the British American colonies. It is a question whether it had not occurred at Porto Rico, San Domingo, and other places in the Spanish Antilles a good many years before; but the reports from the colonies of New Spain, both for that and subsequent periods, are highly defective as regards the data needed to distinguish yellow fever from the bilious remittent form of malarial fever, which is a non-infective sickness. The Mexican form of typhus, called "matlazahuatl," which has been an indigenous disease of the native population in the interior for several centuries, has no other connexion with yellow fever than that it belongs to the same family of typhus; its circumstances are quite different, especially in respect that it is a purely inland form of *febris pauperum*. In 1853 yellow fever appeared for the first time at Callao and Lima in Peru; and almost in the same months a severe epidemic prevailed among the plantation hands in the sierra region of the interior. The two forms were described as the same disease by Dr Archibald Smith; but the fever of the sierras was afterwards shown to be a form of typhus, analogous to the native Mexican form, and quite unconnected with the yellow fever of the coast.

In the harbours of the American colonies (United States) the history of yellow fever has been as follows. It begins to be heard of at Charleston in 1693, and at Philadelphia the same year. The South Carolina port has the fullest record of it, next in order in the earlier period being Philadelphia, New York, and Norfolk (Va.). Towards the end of the 18th century the ports of New England, as far north as New Hampshire, have visitations, and it begins to be quite common at Baltimore, Wilmington, Savannah, and New Orleans. At a still later period (within the 19th century) we find the centre of incidence shifting so as to include Mobile, Memphis, Natchez, St Francisville, and Baton Rouge; and in the most recent period outbreaks are recorded at Galveston and other ports of Texas, and at Pensacola, Vicksburg, and Key West. The Atlantic ports gradually lost it and the Gulf ports took up the inheritance, several of them keeping it still. Some of the epidemics were very disastrous, one of the Philadelphia outbreaks corresponding to the pestilence which figures in the last section of Longfellow's *Evangeline*: "Wealth had no power to bribe, nor beauty to charm the oppressor." In the New Orleans epidemic of 1878 the deaths numbered 4056. The American ports mentioned have been only its principal seats, many other smaller harbours having had outbreaks now and then, such as New Haven (Conn.), Providence (R.I.), Swedesborough (N.J.), Alexandria (Va.), Augusta (Ga.), St Augustine (Fla.), Opelousas (La.), and Houston (Tex.).

Along with the harbours and anchorages of the West Indies and Spanish Main, the three chief harbours of Guiana (Cayenne, Surinam, and Demerara) have had an equal share, and for almost the same period. But for Brazilian ports there is no record of yellow fever until 1849, when it appeared for the first time at Rio de Janeiro, Bahia, and other places. These ports became endemic seats of the infection from that year, and are now more distinctively the headquarters of the disease than its old West Indian and Mexican Gulf centres. Monte Video had a disastrous epidemic in 1857, and Buenos Ayres a visitation in 1858; but the shipping places of the river Plate are not in the same class of endemic foci as the harbours of Brazil.

There have been a few epidemics at trading places on the West Coast of Africa, most of them subsequent to 1820, and all of them confined generally to white residents.

During the great period of yellow fever (1793-1805), and for some years afterwards, the disease found its way time after time to various ports of Spain. Cadiz, indeed, suffered five epidemics in the 18th century, Malaga one, and Lisbon one; but from 1800 down to 1821 the disease assumed much more alarming proportions, Cadiz being still its chief seat, while Seville, Malaga, Cartagena, Barcelona, Palma, Gibraltar, and other shipping places suffered severely, as well as some of the country districts nearest to the ports. These Spanish outbreaks were clearly connected with the arrival of ships, but for the most part there had not been cases of yellow fever on board the ships. The last severe epidemic on Spanish soil was at Barcelona in the summer of 1821, when 5000 persons died. The most recent disastrous epidemic in Europe was at Lisbon in 1857, when upwards of 6000 died in a few weeks. The outbreaks at St Nazaire (1861), Leghorn, Swansea (1864), and Southampton have been carefully studied, but are otherwise of minor importance.

Special
local and
racial
circum-
stances.

Yellow fever is dependent upon high summer temperature for its epidemic development, and it requires a good deal of heat to continue even after it has once acquired epidemic intensity. In its endemic centres in the New World it clings peculiarly to the lower quarters of the seaports, to the alluvial foreshores, and to the anchorages; on many occasions it has been prevalent among the crews of men-of-war and of merchantmen at anchor, or moored in the harbour, or lying up in the *carénage*, when there has been none of it among the residents ashore. It is admitted that the endemic influence which causes it is effluvial or miasmatic from the harbour mud, or from the bilge-water of a ship that had lain in the harbour, or from the alluvial foundations of houses nearest to the beach. So far as prevalence on shore is concerned, it seems to follow the same laws as cholera and typhoid fever: that is to say, it is an exogenous or soil infection, a fermentation of filth in the ground, with a seasonal activity closely following the movements of the subsoil water. In like manner, when it has been imported to Spain, it has clung to alluvial soil and has spread after the fashion of a soil-borne infection rather than by personal contagion, although in Spanish ports, just as in Philadelphia, according to Rush's opinion, contagiousness has been found to be "contingent" to it under certain circumstances. To establish an epidemic in a distant port, it has been necessary that there should be carried thither a material quantity of the specifically poisonous harbour-filth in a ship's bilges, and that the conditions favourable to its increase and diffusion by fermentation should exist in the new soil.

The next most significant thing in the incidence of this fever is that new arrivals at an indigenous centre are peculiarly liable to take it, and most liable of all the sailors and others from northern latitudes, such as Sweden, Finland, Holland, and Germany. In fact an epidemic outburst in a yellow-fever port or endemic centre at the present day is commonly connected with an unusual influx of strangers. It is not to be supposed, however, that the residents acquire immunity by acclimatization: they have no greater immunity in that sense than have the Bengalis from cholera, or than those who permanently reside in unsanitary localities from typhoid fever or diphtheria. The only immunity is that of the Negro race, an immunity all the more striking that the Negroes in yellow-fever ports are mostly found living in the favourite haunts of the disease, and that their race is peculiarly liable to all other infections of the kind, including cholera, typhus, and typhoid. Although the protection of the Negro of pure blood is not absolute, it is nearly so. In ordinary circumstances Negroes become liable when of mixed blood, and almost exactly in proportion to the degree of white stock in their breeding. These racial peculiarities have been so often remarked and are so universally admitted in their broad significance that no detailed proofs need be adduced. It may be stated, however, that all African Negroes, whether fresh from Africa or long acclimatized to the New World, have the same natural protection; thus the Nubian regiment in the French service during the Mexican expedition did not lose a single man, and did not even have a single case, in the epidemic at Vera Cruz in 1866. The protection is profoundly racial, and not due to the Negroes being inured to yellow-fever localities. There is no other instance of the same racial immunity in the whole range of infective sickness.

Theory of the disease. Two things stand out prominently in the foregoing recital of facts,—(1) that yellow fever, in time and place, has dogged the steps of the African slave trade, and (2) that the African Negro has a very large racial immunity from yellow fever. The first of these facts was generalized by Audouard (Paris, 1825), but has been neglected and forgotten; the second fact, which no one seriously disputes, is the complement and confirmation of the historical and geographical induction. The circumstances in Peru, although apparently in contradiction, are really corroborative: a form of yellow fever established itself at certain ports of that country in the wake of a notorious Chinese coolie trade (see COOLIE, vol. vi. p. 334); but the Chinese themselves were exempt from the fever at the time, and would appear not to have suffered from it in the subsequent epidemics on the Peruvian coast. The question thus arises as to the particular connexion between the African slave trade (or the analogous Chinese coolie trade) and yellow fever. The first point is that the fever has not been a fever of the voyage but of the landing place, although there are several authentic instances (*e.g.*, cases of the "Regalia" and "La Pique") of yellow fever arising at sea from the exposure of white men to the stench of a shipful of Negroes. Again, the filthy condition of a Guineaman on her arrival from Africa was a notorious fact; and the filth of that kind was discharged into the creeks, *carénages*, and anchorages of slave ports in material quantity year after year for a long period. At Havana as many as a hundred slavers would arrive in one year. Steady accretions of the filth of slave-ships from the beginning of the traffic to America down to its abolition in 1808, and its final cessation previous to 1860, would account for a peculiarly pestiferous state of the harbour mud, of the beach, and even of the water; in fact, the water in the Bay of Havana was pestiferous and full of organic matter where it was several fathoms deep, and there was a standing order in the British navy against admitting it into ships. Wherever the harbours were most tideless, as around the Gulf of Mexico and in the West Indian Islands, and wherever the soil was most alluvial, and the movements of the ground-water most extensive, the specific putrefaction or fermentation thus introduced into the harbour would spread farthest on shore, being aided or encouraged always by the abundance of other organic matter which it met with at particular spots, such as the foundations of houses.

The next step is to consider the connexion between this wholesale befouling of slave ports and the particular type of endemic disease. One of the points most emphasized by Audouard was the fundamental physiological differences between the African Negro race and the white. The discharges of the Negro body might become by their effluvia specifically poisonous, he argued, to white men under special circumstances. A more direct factor in the ætiology was the very common, if not uniform, prevalence of dysentery and diarrhœa in the passage from the Guinea coast to the western shores of the Atlantic: the filth in a slave-ship's bilges was, in part at least, dysenteric in its source and properties. Now, there is much independent evidence, collected from times of war and famine, to prove a certain correlation or equivalence between dysentery and typhus; according to Blane's phrase, the one was vicarious to the other. Yellow fever is admittedly a form of typhus, a form distinguished by a hæmorrhagic tendency. Thus we find the connexion explained between dysenteric and other evacuations of the Negro race, carried to the mud and alluvial soil of ports under very peculiar circumstances, and a special form of endemic typhus, differing from the ordinary form in being earth-borne instead of air-borne. The remaining part of the synthesis concerns the differential type of yellow fever within the genus "typhus:" Whence did it obtain the "note" or distinctive mark, anatomical and clinical, of an acute yellow atrophy of the liver? The dysenteric filth that was imported into the harbours of the New World represented that almost unique unwholesomeness of life which is summed up in the phrase "horrors of the middle passage." Among such horrors nostalgia, despair, and the sense of wrong were not the least; and these are among the states of human feeling that have been known, now and then, in the ordinary way of life to assume that peculiar visceral embodiment, or to find that means of expression, which amounts to acute yellow atrophy of the liver, and stands, in fact, for a total arrest of the hepatic functions, biliary and other.

There is no other theory of yellow fever to contest the field with the slave-trade hypothesis; that alone satisfies all the conditions of a correct synthesis—historical, geographical, ethnological, physiological, and, some would say, even ethical. There have been various other theories put forward from time to time, all of them much too fragmentary, and therefore erroneous, such as the hypothesis of rotting timber (in wharves, ships' hulls, &c.), of sugar cargoes, of common foul bilge-water, of madrepores, and of bacilli. The bacillary or parasitic hypothesis is the fashionable one at present, but it is much too ambitious, as ordinarily held, and altogether wide of the mark. The part played by putrefactive organisms is a subordinate one. In the general grouping of factors they can only come in after we have found the specific integral of the yellow-fever soil in its endemic seats; they cannot elaborate the miasmatic poison of yellow fever without a definite pabulum, any more than the "lactic bacillus" can produce lactic fermentation without milk-sugar.

Sanitation. The sanitary or public health aspects of yellow fever have been discussed in great part under QUARANTINE (vol. xx. p. 156). In regard to its sanitation at the endemic seats in the West Indies, Guiana, Brazil, Central America, and the Gulf States of the American Union, the same principles apply as to other filth-diseases. The object is to secure a clean soil, and to that end drainage and sewerage serve best. In the sanitation of yellow fever the case is so far peculiar that the harbour bottom, the adjoining mudbanks and mangrove swamps, and even the seawater itself, are apt to retain the specific taint, especially where the cleansing action of the tides is slight. But there is good reason to think that the specific taint in the soil is everywhere slowly disappearing, now that it is no longer reinforced by fresh supplies year after year. It has practically vanished from the Atlantic ports of the United States, and has become almost rare in such harbours as Port Royal, Jamaica. Its headquarters are now the Brazilian ports, which were the last to develop it (in 1849).

Literature.—The chief work is that of La Roche, *Yellow Fever*, 2 vols., Philadelphia, 1855. A very full bibliography is given by Hirsch at the end of his section on "Yellow Fever," in *Historisch-Geographische Pathologie*, vol. i., Stuttgart, 1881 (Engl. transl. by Creighton, London, 1883). Recent experience, epidemiological and clinical, is given in the writings (2 vols.) of Dr Joseph Jones of New Orleans, 1887; see also Maclean's *Diseases of Tropical Climates*, London, 1886. Among the numerous monographs may be specially mentioned those of Pym (*Observations upon the Bulam Fever*, London, 1815), who showed that one attack gave immunity, and of Daniel Blair (*Some Account of the Last Yellow Fever Epidemic of British Guiana*, with plates, 3d ed., London, 1852). A popular exposition of the slave-trade hypothesis of Audouard (with additions by the writer of the present article) will be found in *North. Amer. Rev.*, October 1884. Audouard's three papers were collected under the title *Recueil de Mémoires sur le Typhus Nautique, ou Fièvre Jaune*, Paris, 1825. (C. C.)

YELLOW RIVER. See CHINA, vol. v. pp. 630-631.

YELLOWSTONE NATIONAL PARK, an area situated mainly in north-western Wyoming, United States, which has been withdrawn from settlement by the United States Government and dedicated to the purposes of a public park. It is a region of hot springs and geysers, mountains and cañons, lakes and waterfalls. While it is almost entirely comprised in Wyoming, a narrow strip 2 miles wide projects on the north into Montana, and on the west a strip about 5 miles in width projects into the same Territory and into Idaho. Its boundaries, which were defined at a time when the country was little known, are as follows. The northern boundary is a parallel of latitude running through the mouth of Gardiner river, a branch of the Yellowstone, 2 miles north of 45° N. The eastern boundary is a meridian 10 miles east of the most easterly point of Yellowstone Lake, which places it almost on the 110th meridian. The southern boundary is a parallel 10 miles south of the most southerly portion of the same body of water, in lat. 44° 10′ N. The western boundary is a meridian 15 miles west of the most westerly portion of Madison (now Shoshone) Lake, this meridian being approximately that of 111° 6′. The Park is therefore very nearly a rectangle in shape, its length north and south being 61·8 miles and its breadth 53·6. Its area is 3312 square miles.

See Plate XVII.

Its surface is mainly an undulating plateau, with a mean

elevation above the sea of about 8000 feet, upon the surface of which the minor streams flow, while the larger ones have cut cañons for themselves, several of them being of great depth. The eastern portion, however, is occupied by an extremely rugged mountain chain, known as the Absaroka Range, peaks of which rise to heights exceeding 11,000 feet. These mountains, which separate the waters of the Yellowstone from those of the Big Horn, are unsurpassed in the United States for sublimity and grandeur of scenery. The Gallatin Range, which separates the Yellowstone from the Gallatin river, enters the Park near the north-western corner and extends southwards some 20 miles within it. It reaches its culminating point in Electric Peak, 11,050 feet high, just within the Park boundary. Another group of mountains, in the form of a horseshoe, occurs near the middle of the Park, known as the Washburne Mountains, the highest summit of which, Mount Washburne, has an elevation of 10,346 feet. The Red Mountains are in the southern part, their culminating peak being Mount Sheridan, 10,385 feet in height. In this part of the Park the plateau is more elevated and broken, and just beyond its southern limits it rises into a confused maze of mountains.

The Park has an abundant rainfall, and its streams are numerous and bold. It contains many beautiful lakes and ponds. Within its area are the sources of the Yellowstone and the Madison, which go to make up the Missouri, and of the Snake, one of the forks of the Columbia. This last stream, which drains the south-western part, takes its rise in several branches, among them being Lewis Fork, which has its origin in the beautiful Shoshone Lake, and Heart river, which rises in Heart Lake, under the shadow of Mount Sheridan. The Yellowstone drains the eastern part. Rising just beyond its southern limits, it flows into and through Yellowstone Lake, a magnificent sheet of water, of very irregular shape, having an area of 150 square miles. A few miles below the lake, the river, after a succession of rapids, leaps over a cliff, making the Upper Fall, 112 feet in height. Half a mile lower down it rolls over the Lower Fall, which has a clear descent of 300 feet. The river at this point carries, at the average stage of water, about 1200 cubic feet per second. With this fall the river enters the Grand Cañon, which in many scenic effects has not its equal on the globe. Its depth is not great, at least as compared with the cañons upon the Colorado river system, ranging from 600 feet at its head to 1200 near the middle, where it passes the Washburne Mountains. Its length to the mouth of Lamar river is 24 miles. It is cut in a volcanic plateau, and its ragged broken walls, which are inclined at very steep angles, are of a barbaric richness of colouring that almost defies description. Reds, yellows, and purples predominate, and are set off very effectively against the dark green of the forests upon the plateau, and the white foam of the rushing river which fills the bottom of the chasm. Near the foot of the Grand Cañon, Tower creek, which drains the concavity of the horseshoe formed by the Washburne Mountains, enters the Yellowstone. Just above its mouth this stream makes a beautiful fall of 132 feet into the gorge in which it joins the river. A few miles farther down the Yellowstone is joined by an eastern branch, Lamar river, which drains a large part of the Absaroka Range. Then it enters the Third Cañon, from which it emerges at the mouth of Gardiner river. The latter stream drains an area of elevated land by means of its three forks, and upon each of them occurs a fine fall in its descent toward the Yellowstone. The Madison rises in the western part of the Park and flows in a generally northward and then westward course out of the Park. Its waters are mainly collected from the rainfall upon the plateaus, and from the hot springs and geysers, most of which are within its drainage area. Upon this river and its affluents are several fine falls. Indeed all the streams of this region show evidence, in the character of their courses, of a recent change of level in the surface of the country.

The climate is characterized by a considerable degree of humidity and a heavy rainfall, as compared with adjacent portions of the West. The temperature is that of a semi-arctic region. Frost may occur in midsummer and snow begins to fall in September.

The native fauna is abundant and varied. The policy of the Government, which protects game within this reservation, has induced it to take shelter here against the sportsman and pot-hunter, so that elk, deer, antelope, mountain sheep, bear, and numerous smaller game animals are very abundant and tame. The only herd of wild bisons left in the United States is upon this reservation; and in some parts moose are occasionally seen.

The flora is very varied. With the exception of a few limited areas in the northern part, the region is covered with forests, generally so dense that landmarks are invisible and the traveller is forced to guide himself by the sun or by compass. The trees are mainly the Douglas spruce and the yellow pine, and are not of large size or great commercial value.

The surface of the park is almost entirely covered with volcanic rocks. The Gallatin Range, however, in the north-western corner, is made up of stratified beds ranging from the Silurian system up to the Cretaceous. In a few localities also Tertiary lake beds and local drift are found. The plateaus generally are composed of rhyolite, while the mountain ranges are made up of later volcanic deposits, mainly conglomerates. In this region the ancient volcanic fires, which formerly extended far and wide, especially to the south and west, are still in existence, as is shown by the vast numbers of hot springs and geysers. The number of the former is by a close estimate not less than 3000, varying in size from a few inches in diameter to an area of many acres. The number of active geysers is 71. These phenomena are found in groups in numerous localities, the most important of which—for they contain most of the great geysers—are the Upper and the Lower Geyser basins near the head of the Madison, here known as the Firehole river. The former contains 26 geysers, several of which are of such power as to throw water to heights exceeding 200 feet, and the amount of water thrown out is so great as to raise the temperature of the river water many degrees. The Lower basin contains 16 geysers. The Norris basin, upon Gibbon river, a branch of the Madison, contains 9 geysers, and the Shoshone basin, upon the shore of Shoshone Lake, contains 8 active spouters. Others are found at Heart Lake, upon Pelican creek, in Hayden's valley, and in Monument basin. In all these localities the water holds silica in solution in considerable quantities, so that as it cools and evaporates it deposits siliceous matter, which has covered with a hard white floor many square miles of these valleys, and has built up craters around the springs and geysers of considerable size and great beauty of form. Besides silica, the water of many of the springs contains sulphur, iron, alum, and other materials in solution, which in places stain the pure white of the siliceous deposits with bright bands of colour. Upon Gardiner river, near the northern boundary of the Park, there is a large group of springs, known as the Mammoth Hot Springs, which differ from the others in holding carbonate of lime in solution. These springs have deposited so freely as to build up a hill 200 feet in height, from the top of which the springs boil out. The slopes of this mound have been built in the form of a succession of basins rising one above another, and the water from the springs overflows from one into another, growing gradually cooler as it descends. Upon the bank of Yellowstone river, between the falls and the lake, there was, when the region was first explored, a geyser which at intervals of about 4 hours threw up a column of mud to a height of 40 or 50 feet. In more recent times this geyser has ceased action. These phenomena have been under observation since 1871; and, while there have been changes in them, certain geysers having ceased and others having been formed, no evidence of a diminution of power has been observed.

The Park is accessible by means of the Northern Pacific Railroad, by a branch which extends up the valley of the Yellowstone within a few miles of the northern boundary; and with this a line of stage coaches is connected.

The most stringent laws have been enacted in regard to the killing of game, the starting of forest fires, and the removal of the deposits of the springs.

Although exploring parties had at various times passed on all sides of this strange region, its wonders remained undiscovered until so late a period as 1870. This fact is all the more remarkable because at that time the frontier of settlement was in the Gallatin valley, not a hundred miles from the great geyser region. Some rumours of hot springs and geysers, coming from stray trappers and Indians, had been received, however, and these were sufficient to start a party from the Montana settlements in 1870, to investigate the strange tales. The discoveries made by this, the Washburne party, induced Dr F. V. Hayden, then in charge of a Government survey, to turn his explorations in this direction. The reports brought back by him induced Congress to reserve this area from settlement, which was done in the spring of 1872. In that year further explorations were made, and in subsequent years army expeditions carried the work of exploration still farther. In 1878 a map of the Park, based upon triangulation, was drawn up by the Hayden survey, and in 1883-85 a more detailed map was made by the United States Geological Survey, and a systematic study of its geological phenomena was instituted. (H. G*.)

YELLOW-TAIL. This name is given by seafaring men to a variety of marine fishes, chiefly of the family of Horse-Mackerels, which have this in common, that they are edible and have a yellow caudal fin. As the latter peculiarity, which has found expression in the specific names of *chrysurus*, *xanthurus*, &c., of systematic ichthyology, is not confined to that family, very different kinds of fishes bear the same name: thus, for instance, the fishermen of the United States apply it to species of the Meagre family (*Sciænidæ*) and to others. Economically the most important kinds of these fishes, the yellow-tail of the South Atlantic and the southern Indo-Pacific Ocean, are species of the genera *Seriola*, *Seriolichthys*, and *Micropteryx*, some of which, like *Seriola lalandii* and *S. gigas*, attain to the size of a cod or a coal-fish, and are preserved in a similar manner, either salted or dried. They abound in many localities, and are valued as food fish everywhere. They form a large proportion of the dried fish which are exported from the Cape of Good Hope to Mauritius and Batavia, or are sold to the whalers visiting the Southern Ocean. They are equally abundant at St Helena, where, however, their value as an article of trade does not seem to be fully understood. On the coasts of South Australia and New Zealand they are likewise a staple article of food, but are chiefly eaten fresh, the most esteemed species being *Seriola lalandii*, also known to the colonists as the "king-fish."

YEMEN, in Arabia, literally the land "on the right hand" of one who faces east, meant originally all the land southwards from Syria (Shám). The Arabia Felix (εὐδαίμων) of Ptolemy and other ancients is a mistranslation, the right hand being taken to mean "lucky" (δεξιός, *dexter*). Arabia Felix included all Arabia except the peninsula of Sinai (Arabia Petræa) and the Syrian desert (Arabia Deserta): *i.e.*, it took in the Ḥijáz and Nejd as well as South Arabia. The Arabs use the term Yemen in various extensions. A tradition of the Prophet makes Yemen and Shám meet at Tabbák; but Abú ʿAbbás already confines the name to all Arabia south of Mecca. This usage, which excludes Nejd and Hijáz from Yemen, is not merely that of Moslem geographers, who take Mecca as their imaginary standpoint, but is found in the heathen poets. When Imraolḳais speaks of a Yemenite trader, Ṭarafa, of tanned ox-hides from Yemen, Labíd of a youth from Yemen who knew letters, or a poet of Hodhail of the excellent work of a Yemenite smith, they all mean by Yemen the southern region where trade, letters, and industry had their early home in the peninsula. The northern boundary of Yemen is variously laid down. Al-Asmaʿí makes it a line drawn obliquely from ʿOmán to Nejrán; but Hamdání rightly draws it farther north, from ʿOmán and Yebrín in the south of Yemáma by way of Al-Ḥujaira, Tathlíth, and Jorash to Kodommol (Kotumble of the Admiralty chart, in lat. 17° 52′). In its narrowest limitation Yemen comprises, not the whole south of the peninsula, but only the south-west as far as Ḥadramaut, which was viewed as a dependency of Yemen. The physical conformation of the south-western portion of the peninsula differs greatly from that of Arabia proper, being similar to that of Ethiopia. A range of mountains, which rises into peaks of considerable elevation, and descends with a steep slope towards the shore of the Red Sea, stretches from the southern extremity northwards as far as Ṭáif. This range is pierced by several streams and wadies, which flow into the Red Sea.[1] In old times the region cannot of course have been called "the Southland" by its own inhabitants.

Map of Yemen.

Sabæans.—The ancient name of the people of Yemen was Saba (Saba' with final *hemza*); and the oldest notices of them are in the Hebrew Scriptures. The list of the sons of Joktan in Gen. x. 26-29 contains in genealogical form a record of peoples of South Arabia which must rest on good information from Yemen itself. Many of these names are found on the inscriptions or in the Arabic geographers,—Sheba (Saba'), Hazarmaveth (Ḥadramaut), Abimael (Abimeʿathtar), Jobab (Yuhaibib, according to Halévy), Jerah (Waráḥ of the geographers), Joktan (Arab Ḳaḥtan; *waḳata* = *ḳaḥata*). On the other hand, the names of some famous nations mentioned on the inscriptions are lacking, from which it may be concluded that they did not rise to prominence till a later date. Saba' (Sheba) itself, which was in later times the chief name, has in Gen. x. 28 a subordinate place; it was perhaps only a collective name for the companies of merchants who conducted the South-Arabian export trade (the root *saba'* in the inscriptions meaning to make a trading journey), and in that case would be of such late origin as to hold one of the last places in a list that has genealogical form. Two other accounts in Genesis, originally independent, give supplementary information drawn from the Sabæan colonies, the stations and factories established to facilitate trade through the desert. The inscriptions of Al-ʿOla published by D. H. Müller show that there were Minæan colonies in North Arabia. Other South Arabs, and especially the Sabæans, doubtless also planted settlers on the northern trade routes, who in process of time united into one community with their North-Arab kinsmen and neighbours. Thus we can understand how in Gen. xxv. 2-3 Sheba and Dedan appear among the North-Arab "sons of Keturah." Again, the Sabæans had colonies in Africa and there mingled with the black Africans; and so in Gen. x. 7 Sheba and Dedan, the sons of Raamah (Raghma), appear in the genealogy of the Cushites. With the Ethiopians *Saba'* means "men," a clear indication of their Sabæan descent.

The queen of Sheba who visited Solomon may have come with a caravan trading to Gaza, to see the great king

[1] An excellent topographical description of Yemen is given in Hamdání's *Geogr. d. Arab. Halbinsel*, ed. D. H. Müller (1884).

whose ships plied on the Red Sea. The other Biblical books do not mention the Sabæans except incidentally, in allusion to their trade in incense and perfumes, gold and precious stones, ivory, ebony, and costly garments (Jer. vi. 20; Ezek. xxvii. 15, 20, 22 *sq.*; Isa. lx. 6; Job vi. 19). These passages attest the wealth and trading importance of Saba from the days of Solomon to those of Cyrus. When the prologue to Job speaks of plundering Sabæans (and Chaldæans) on the northern skirts of Arabia, these may be either colonists or caravans, which, like the old Phœnician and Greek traders, combined on occasion robbery with trade. The prologue may not be historical; but it is to be presumed that it deals with historical possibilities, and is good evidence thus far.

The Biblical picture of the Sabæan kingdom is confirmed and supplemented by the Assyrian inscriptions. Tiglath Pileser II. (733 B.C.) tells us that Teima, Saba', and Ḥaipá (=Ephah, Gen. xxv. 4 and Isa. lx. 6) paid him tribute of gold, silver, and much incense. Similarly Sargon (715 B.C.) in his *Annals* mentions the tribute of Shamsi, queen of Arabia, and of Itamara of the land of Saba',—gold and fragrant spices, horses and camels.

The earliest Greek accounts of the Sabæans and other South-Arabian peoples are of the 3d century B.C. Eratosthenes (276-194 B.C.) in Strabo (xv. 4, 2) says that the extreme south of Arabia, over against Ethiopia, is inhabited by four great nations,—the Minæans (Μειναῖοι, Μηναῖοι; Ma'ín of the inscriptions) on the Red Sea, whose chief city is Carna; next to them the Sabæans, whose capital is Mariaba (Mariab of the inscriptions); then the Catabanes (Katabán of the inscriptions), near the Straits of Báb-al-Mandeb, the seat of whose king is Tamna; fourthly, and farthest east, the people of Ḥadramaut (Chatramotitæ), with their city Sabota. The Catabanes produce frankincense and Ḥadramaut myrrh, and there is a trade in these and other spices with merchants who make the journey from Ælana (Elath, on the Gulf of 'Aḳaba) to Minæa in seventy days; the Gabæans (the Gaba'án of the inscriptions, Pliny's Gebanitæ) take forty days to go to Ḥadramaut. This short but important and well-informed notice is followed a little later by that of Agatharchides (120 B.C.), who speaks in glowing terms of the wealth and greatness of the Sabæans, but seems to have less exact information than Eratosthenes. He knows only the Sabæans and thinks that Saba is the name of their capital. He mentions, however, the "happy islands" beyond the straits, the station of the Indian trade (§ 103). Artemidorus (100 B.C.), quoted by Strabo, gives a similar account of the Sabæans and their capital Mariaba, of their wealth and trade, adding the characteristic feature that each tribe receives the wares and passes them on to its neighbours as far as Syria and Mesopotamia.

The accounts of the wealth of the Sabæans brought back by traders and travellers excited the cupidity of Rome, and Augustus entrusted Ælius Gallus with an expedition to South Arabia, of which we have an authentic account in Strabo (xvi. 4, 22). He hoped for assistance from the friendly NABATÆANS (*q.v.*); but, as they owed everything to their position as middlemen for the South-Arabian trade, which a direct communication between Rome and the Sabæans would have ruined, their viceroy Syllæus, who did not dare openly to refuse help, sought to frustrate the emperor's scheme by craft. Instead of showing the Romans the caravan route, he induced them to sail from Cleopatris to Leucocome, and then led them by a circuitous way through waterless regions, so that they reached South Arabia too much weakened to effect anything. But the expedition brought back a considerable knowledge of the country and its products, and the Roman leader seems to have perceived that the best entrance to South Arabia was from the havens on the coast. So at least we may conclude when, a hundred years later (77 A.D., as Dillmann has shown), in the *Periplus* of an anonymous contemporary of Pliny (§ 23) we read that Charibael of Ẓafar, "the legitimate sovereign of two nations, the Homerites and Sabæans," maintained friendly relations with Rome by frequent embassies and gifts. Pliny's account of Yemen, too, must be largely drawn from the expedition of Gallus, though he also used itineraries of travellers to India, like the *Periplus Maris Erythræi* just quoted.

Nautical improvements, and the discovery that the south-west monsoon (Hippalus) gave sure navigation at certain seasons, increased the connexion of the West with South Arabia, but also wrought such a change in the trade as involved a revolution in the state of that country. The hegemony of the Sabæans now yields to that of a new people, the Homerites or Ḥimyar, and the king henceforth bears the title "king of the Himyarites and Sabæans." Naval expeditions from Berenice and Myoshormus to the Arabian ports brought back the information on which Claudius Ptolemy constructed his map, which still surprises us by its wealth of geographical names.

Sabæan colonies in Africa have been already mentioned. That Abyssinia was peopled from South Arabia is proved by its language and writing; but the difference between the two languages is such as to imply that the settlement was very early and that there were many centuries of separation, during which the Abyssinians were exposed to foreign influences. New colonies, however, seem to have followed from time to time, and, according to the *Periplus* (§ 16), some parts of the African coast were under the suzerainty of the Sabæan kings as late as the Sabæo-Himyaritic period; the district of Azania was held for the Sabæan monarch by the governor of Maphoritis (Ma'áfir), and was exploited by a Sabæan company. Naturally difficulties would arise between Abyssinia and the Sabæan power. In the inscription of Adulis (2d century) the king of Ethiopia claims to have made war in Arabia from Leucocome to the land of the Sabæan king. And the Ethiopians were not without successes, for on the Greek inscription of Aksúm (*c.* the middle of the 4th century) King Æizanes calls himself "king of the Aksumites, the Homerites, and Raidán, and of the Ethiopians, Sabæans, and Silee." More serious was the conflict under Dhú-Nu'ás (Dhú-Nuwás of the Arab historians) in the beginning of the 6th century; it ended in the overthrow of the Himyarite king and the subjugation of Yemen, which was governed by a deputy of the Aksumite king, till (about 570) the conquerors were overthrown by a small band of Persian adventurers (see PERSIA, vol. xviii. p. 613).

With the exception of what the South-Arabian Hamdání relates of his own observation or from authentic tradition, the Mohammedan Arabic accounts of South Arabia and Sabæa are of little worth. The great event they dwell on is the bursting of the dam of Ma'rib, which led to the emigration northwards of the Yemenite tribes. We may be sure that this event was not the cause but the consequence of the decline of the country. When the inland trade fell away and the traffic of the coast towns took the sea route, the ancient metropolis and the numerous inland emporia came to ruin, while the many colonies in the north were broken up and their population dispersed. To this the Koran alludes in its oracular style, when it speaks (xxxiv. 17) of well-known cities which God appointed as trading stations between the Sabæans and the cities He had blessed (Egypt and Syria), and which He destroyed because of their sins.

Inscriptions.—This abstract of the history of Yemen from ancient sources can now be verified and supplemented from inscriptions. Doubts as to the greatness and importance of the Sabæan state, as attested by the ancients, and as to the existence of a special Sabæan writing, called "Musnad," of which the Arabs tell, were still current when Niebuhr, in the 18th century, brought to Europe the first account of the existence of ancient inscriptions (not seen by himself) in the neighbourhood of Yarím. Following this hint, Seetzen, in 1810, was able to send to Europe, from porphyry blocks near Yarím, the first copies of Sabæan inscriptions. They could not, however, be read. But the inscriptions found by Wellsted in 1834 at Ḥiṣn Ghoráb were deciphered by Gesenius and Rödiger. Soon after this the courageous explorer Arnaud discovered the ancient Mariab, the royal city of the Sabæans, and at great risk copied fifty-six inscriptions and took a plan of the walls, the dam, and the temple to the east of the city. These, with other inscriptions on stone and on bronze plates brought home by Englishmen, found a cautious and sound interpreter in Osiander. The historical and geographical researches of Kremer and Sprenger gave a fresh impulse to inquiry. Then Joseph Halévy made his remarkable journey through the Jauf, visiting districts and ruins which no European foot had trod since the expedition of Gallus, and returned with almost 800 inscriptions. Of more recent travellers S. Langer and E. Glaser have done most for epigraphy, while Manzoni is to be remembered for his excellent geographical work.

The *alphabet* of the Sabæan inscriptions is most closely akin to the Ethiopic, but is purely consonantal, without the modifications in the consonantal forms which Ethiopic has devised to express vowels. There are twenty-nine letters, one more than in Arabic, *Samech* and *Sin* being distinct forms, as in Hebrew. This alphabet, which is probably the parent of the South-Indian character, is undoubtedly derived from the so-called Phœnician alphabet, the connecting link being the forms of the Ṣafa inscriptions and of the Thamudæan inscriptions found by Doughty and Euting. Of the latter we can determine twenty-six characters, while a twenty-seventh probably corresponds to Arabic ẓ (ظ). A sign for ض also probably existed, but does not occur in the known inscriptions. In the Thamudæan and Sabæan alphabets the twenty-two original Phœnician characters are mostly similar, and so are the differentiated forms for غ and خ, while ث, ذ, and probably also ظ and ض, have been differentiated in different ways. This seems to imply that the two alphabets had a common history up to a certain point, but parted company before they were fully developed. The Thamudæan inscriptions are locally nearer to Phœnicia, and the letters are more like the Phœnician; this character therefore appears to be the link connecting Phœnician with Sabæan writing. It may be noticed that a Thamudæan legend has been found on a Babylonian cylinder of about 1000 B.C., and it is remarkable that the Sabæan *saṭara*, "write," seems to be borrowed from Assyrian *shaṭâru*.

The *language* of the inscriptions is South Semitic, forming a link between the North Arabic and the Ethiopic, but is much nearer the former than the latter. To the details already given in the article SEMITIC LANGUAGES (vol. xxi. p. 653 *sq.*) it may be added that of the two dialects commonly called Sabæan and Minæan the latter might be better called Hadramitic, inasmuch as it is the dialect of the inscriptions found in Ḥadramaut, and the Minæans seem undoubtedly to have entered the Jauf from Ḥadramaut.

The inscriptions not only give names of nations corresponding to those in the Bible and in classical authors but throw a good deal of fresh light on the political history of Yemen. The inscriptions and coins give the names of more than forty-five Sabæan kings. The chronology is still vague, since only a few very late inscriptions are dated by an era and the era itself is not certain. But the rulers named can be assigned to three periods, according as they bear the title "mukrab of Saba," "king of Saba," or "king of Saba and Raidán." The last, as we know from the Aksum inscriptions, are the latest, and those with the title "mukrab" must be the earliest. Four princes of the oldest period bear the name Yatha'amar, and one of these may, with the greatest probability, be held to be the "Itamara Sabai" who paid tribute to Sargon of Assyria. This helps us to the age of some buildings also. The famous dam of Ma'rib and its sluices were the work of this ancient prince—structures which Arnaud in the 19th century found in the same state in which Hamdání saw them a thousand years ago. The power of these old sovereigns extended far beyond Ma'rib, for their names are found on buildings and monuments in the Jauf.

We cannot tell when the kings took the place of the mukrab, but the Sabæo-Himyaritic period seems to begin with, or a little after, the expedition of Ælius Gallus. A fragmentary inscription of Ma'rib (Br. Mus., 33) was made by "Ilsharh Yaḥḍib and Ya'zil Bayyin, the two kings of Saba and Raidán, sons of Far'm Yanhab, king of Saba." If this Ilsharḥ is identical with the Ἰλάσσαρος of Strabo, king of Mariaba at the time of the Roman invasion, the inscription preserves a trace of the influence of that event on the union of the two kingdoms.

The inscriptions of the latest period present a series of dates—669, 640, 582, 573, 385—of an unknown era. Reinaud thought of the Seleucid era, which is not impossible; but Halévy observes that the fortress of Mawiyyat (now Ḥiṣn Ghoráb) bears the date 640, and is said to have been erected "when the Abyssinians overran the country and destroyed the king of Himyar and his princes." Referring this to the death of Dhú Nuwás (525 A.D.), Halévy fixes 115 B.C. as the epoch of the Sabæan era. This ingenious combination accords well with the circumstance that the oldest dated inscription, of the year 385 (270 A.D.), mentions 'Athtar, Shams, and other heathen deities, while the inscriptions of 582 (467 A.D.) and 573 (458 A.D.), so far as they can be read, contain no name of a heathen god, but do speak of a god Rahmánán—that is, the Hebrew Rahmán, "the compassionate" (Arabic, Al-Rahmán), agreeably with the fact that Jewish and Christian influences were powerful in Arabia in the 4th century. The only objections to Halévy's hypothesis are (1) that we know nothing of an epoch-making event in 115 B.C., and (2) that it is a little remarkable that the latest dated inscription, of the year 669 (554 A.D.), should be twenty-five years later than the Abyssinian conquest. An inscription found by Wrede at 'Obne is dated "in the year 120 of the Lion in Heaven," which we must leave the astronomers to explain.

The inscriptions throw considerable light not only on the Sabæans but on other South-Arabian nations. The Minæans, whose importance has been already indicated, appear in the inscriptions as only second to the Sabæans, and with details which have put an end to much guesswork, *e.g.*, to the idea that they are connected with Miná near Mecca. Their capital, Ma'ín, lay in the heart of the Sabæan country, forming a sort of enclave on the right hand of the road that leads northward from Ma'rib. South-west of Ma'ín, on the west of the mountain range, and commanding the road from San'a to the north, lies Barákish, anciently Yathil, which the inscriptions and Arabic geographers always mention with Ma'ín. The third Minæan fortress, probably identical with the Κάρνα of the Greeks, lies in the middle of the northern Jauf, and north of the other two. The three Minæan citadels lie nearly in this position (.·.), with old Sabæan settlements (Raiam) all round them, and even with some Sabæan places (*e.g.*, Nask and Kamná) within the triangle they form. The dialect of the Minæans is sharply distinguished from the Sabæans (see above). The inscriptions have yielded the names of twenty-seven Minæan kings, who were quite independent, and, as it would seem, not always friends of the Sabæans, for neither dynasty mentions the other on its inscriptions, while minor kings and kingdoms are freely mentioned by both, presumably when they stood under the protection of the one or the other respectively. The Minæans were evidently active rivals of the Sabæan influence, and a war between the two is once mentioned. In Ḥadramaut they disputed the hegemony with one another, the government there being at one time under a Minæan, at another under a Sabæan prince, while the language shows now the one and now the other influence. The religions also of the two powers present many points of agreement, with some notable differences. Thus, puzzling as the fact appears, it is clear that the Minæans formed a sort of political and linguistic island in the Sabæan country. The origin of the Minæans from Ḥadramaut is rendered probable by the predominance of their dialect in the inscriptions of that country (except in that of Ḥiṣn Ghoráb), by the rule, already mentioned, of a Minæan prince in Ḥadramaut, and by Pliny's statement (*H. N.*, xii. 63) that frankincense was collected at Sabota (the capital of Ḥadramaut; inscr. שבות), but exported only through the Gebanites, whose kings received custom dues on it, compared with xii. 69, where he speaks of Minæan myrrh "in qua et Atramitica est et Gebbanitica et Ausaritis Gebbanitarum regno," &c., implying that Minæan myrrh was really a Hadramite and Gebanite product. All this suggests a close connexion between the Minæans and Hadramaut; and from the Minæan inscriptions we know that the Gebanites were at one time a Minæan race, and stood in high favour with the queen of Ma'ín. Thus we are led to conclude that the Minæans were a Hadramite settlement in the Jauf, whose object was to secure the northern trade road for their products. We cannot but see that their fortified posts in the north of the Sabæan kingdom had a strategical purpose; and so Pliny (xii. 54) says, "Attingunt et Minæi, pagus alius, per quos evehitur *uno tramite angusto* [from Ḥadramaut]. Hi primi commercium turis fecere maximeque exercent, a quibus et Minæum dictum est." Besides this road, they had the sea-route, for, according to Pliny, their allies, the Gebanites, held the port of Ocelis. If the Minæans were later immigrants from Ḥadramaut, we can understand how they are not mentioned in Gen. x. In later times, as is proved by the Minæan colony in Al-'Olá, which Euting has revealed to us, they superseded the Sabæans in some parts of the north. In the 'Olá inscriptions we read the names of Minæan kings and gods. Notable also is the mention in 1 Chron. iv. 41 of the "Bedouin encampments (אהלים) and the Ma'ínim" smitten by the Simeonites, which may possibly refer to the destruction of a Minæan caravan protected by these Bedouins. The LXX. at least renders Ma'ínim by Μιναίους. It seems bold to conjecture that the Minæans were in accord with the Romans under Ælius Gallus, yet it is noteworthy that no Minæan town is named among the cities which that general destroyed, though ruin fell on Nask and Kamna, which lie inside the Minæan territory.

The inscriptions seem to indicate that the monarchies of South Arabia were hereditary, the son generally following the father, though not seldom the brother of the deceased came between, apparently on the principle of seniority, which we find also in North Arabia. Eratosthenes (in Strabo xvi. 4, 3) says that the first child born to one of the magnates after a king came to the throne was his designated successor; the wives of the magnates who were pregnant at the king's accession were carefully watched and the first child born was brought up as heir to the kingdom. There seems to be a mistake in the first part of this statement; what Eratosthenes will have said is that the oldest prince after the king was the designated successor. This law of succession explains how we repeatedly find two kings named together among the Sabæans, and almost always find two among the Minæans; the second king is the heir. The principle of seniority, as we know from North-Arabian history, gives rise to intrigues and palace revolutions, and was probably often violated in favour of the direct heir. On the other hand, it readily leads to a limited power of election by the magnates, and in fact good Arabian sources speak of seven electoral princes. Some inscriptions name, besides the king, an eponymus, whose office seems to have been priestly, his titles being *dhú ḳarif*, *eponymus*, and *rashúw*, "sacrificer." All royal inscriptions are signed by him at the beginning and the end, and he appears with the king on coins.

Religion.—In spite of the many ruins of temples and inscriptions, the religion of the Sabæans is obscure. Most of the many names of gods are mere names that appear and vanish again in particular districts and temples. Of the great national gods of the Sabæans and Minæans we know a little more. The worship of the heavenly bodies, for which there is Arabic evidence, had really a great place in Yemen. Sun-worship seems to have been peculiar to the Sabæans and Hamdanites; and, if the Sabis of Sabota (Pliny) was in fact the sun deity Shams, this must be ascribed to Sabæan influence. The Sabæan Shams was a goddess, while the chief divinity of the Minæans was the god ʽAthtar, a male figure, worshipped under several forms, of which the commonest are the Eastern ʽAthtar and ʽAthtar Dhú Kabḍ. Wadd and Nikrah, the gods of love and hate, are possibly only other forms of the two ʽAthtars. The Sabæans also recognize ʽAthtar; but with them he is superseded by Almakah, who, according to Hamdání, is the planet Venus, and therefore is identical with ʽAthtar. The moon-god Sín appears on an inscription of Shabwat; but, according to Hamdání, Haubas, "the drier," was the Sabæan moon-god. On the Shabwat inscription ʽAthtar is the father of Sín, and it is noteworthy that these two deities also appear as nearly related in the Babylonian legend of ʽIshtar's descent to Hades, where ʽIshtar is conversely the daughter of the god Sín. The mother of ʽAthtar on another inscription is probably the sun. We find also the common Semitic Il (El) and a Dhú Samai answering to the northern Baʽal Shamayim. Three gods of the inscriptions are named in the Koran,—Wadd, Yaghúth, and Nasr. In the god-name Ta'lab there may be an indication of tree-worship. The many minor deities may be passed over; but we must mention the sanctuary of Riyám, with its images of the sun and moon, and, according to tradition, an oracle. In conformity with old Semitic usage, pilgrimages were made at definite seasons to certain deities, and the Sabæan pilgrim month, Dhú Ḥijjatán, is the northern Dhú'l-Ḥijja. The outlines, and little more, of a few of the many temples can still be traced. Noteworthy are the elliptic form of the chief temples in Ma'rib and Ṣirwáḥ, and the castle of Naḳab-al-Ḥajar with its entrances north and south.

Sacrifices and incense were offered to the gods. The names for altar (*midhbaḥ*) and sacrifice (*dhibḥ*) are common Semitic words, and the altar of incense has among other names that of *miḳṭar*, as in Hebrew. A variety of spices—the wealth of the land—are named on these altars, as *rand*, *ladanum*, *costus*, *tarum*, &c. Frankincense appears as *lubán*, and there are other names not yet understood. The gods received tithes of the produce of trade and of the field, in kind or in ingots and golden statues, and these tributes, with freewill offerings, erected and maintained the temples. Temples and fortifications were often combined. The golden statues were votive offerings; thus a man and his wife offer four statues for the health of their four children and a man offers to Dhú Samai statues of a man and two camels, in prayer for his own health and the protection of his camels from disease of the joints.

Their commerce brought the Sabæans under Christian and Jewish influence; and, though the old gods were too closely connected with their life and trade to be readily abandoned, the great change in the trading policy, already spoken of, seems to have affected religion as well as the state. The inland gods lost importance with the failure of the overland trade, and Judaism and Christianity seem for a time to have contended for the mastery in South Arabia. Jewish influence appears in the name Raḥmán (see above), while efforts at Christianization seem to have gone forth from several places at various times. According to Philostorgius, the Homerites were converted under Constantius II. by the Indian Theophilus, who built churches in Ẓafar and Aden. Another account places their conversion in the reign of Anastasius (491-518). In Nejrán Syrian missionaries seem to have introduced Christianity (Nöldeke). But, as the religion of the hostile Ethiopians, Christianity found political obstacles to its adoption in Yemen; and, as heathenism had quite lost its power, it is intelligible that Dhú Nuwás, who was at war with Ethiopia before the last fatal struggle, became a Jew. His expedition against Christian Nejrán had therefore political as well as religious motives. The Ethiopian conquest rather hurt than helped Christianity. The famous *ḳalís* (ἐκκλησία) of Abraha in San'á seems to have been looked on as a sign of foreign dominion, and Islám found it easy to supersede Christianity in Yemen.

Coins.—In older times and in many districts coins were not used, and trade was carried on mainly by barter. Nor have there yet been many great finds of coins; indeed most of the pieces in European collections probably come from the same hoard. At the same time the coins throw a general light on the relations of ancient Yemen. The oldest known pieces are imitations of the Athenian mintage of the 4th century B.C., with the legend ΑΘΕ and the owl standing on an overturned amphora. The reverse has the head of Pallas with a Sabæan N. Of younger coins the first series has a king's head on the reverse, and the old obverse is enriched with two Sabæan monograms, which have been interpreted as meaning "majesty" and "eponymus" respectively. In a second series the Greek legend has disappeared, and, instead of the two Sabæan monograms, we have the names of the king and the eponymus. A third series shows Roman influence and must be later than the expedition of Gallus. As the standard of the coins of Attic type is not Attic but Babylonian, we must not think of direct Athenian influence. The type must have been introduced either from Persia or from Phœnicia (Gaza). One remarkable tetradrachm with the Sabæan legend Abyath'á is imitated from an Alexander of the 2d century B.C., the execution being quite artistic and the weight Attic. There are also coins struck at Raydán and Harib, which must be assigned to the Himyarite period (1st and 2d century A.D.). The inscriptions speak of "bright Hayyilí coins in high relief," but of these none have been found. They also speak of selaʽ pieces. The selaʽ in late Hebrew answers to the older shekel and the mention of it seems to point to Jewish or Christian influence.

Literature.—Fresnel, *Pièces rel. aux Inscrr. Himyarites déc. par M. Arnaud*, 1845; *Inscriptions in the Himyaritic Character in the British Museum*, London, 1863; Prætorius, *Beitr. zur Erklärung der himjar. Inschr.*, 3 parts, Halle, 1872-74; Kremer, *Südarabische Sage*, 1866; Sprenger, *Alte Geogr. Arabiens*, 1873; D. H. Müller, *Südarabische Studien*, Vienna, 1877; Id., *Die Burgen u. Schlösser Südarabiens*, 2 parts, Vienna, 1879-81 (especially for chronology and antiquities); Mordtmann and Müller, *Sabäische Denkmäler*, Vienna, 1883; Derenbourg, *Études sur l'Épigraphie du Yemen*, Paris, 1884; Id., *Nouv. Étud.*, 1885; Glaser, *Mittheilungen über . . . sab. Inschr.*, 1886; Hamdání, *Geogr. d. Arab. Halbinsel*, ed. D. H. Müller, vol. i., Leyden, 1884. See also papers by Osiander, *Z.D.M.G.*, xix.-xx. (1864-65); Halévy, *Journ. As.*, 1872-74; D. H. Müller, *Z.D.M.G.*, xxix.-xxxi., xxxvii.; Prideaux, *Tr. Soc. Bibl. Arch.*, 1873; Derenbourg, *Bab. and Or. Record*, London, 1887. In the press, D. H. Müller, *Epigraphische Denkmäler nach . . . Copien Eutings*. Further cp. the travels of Niebuhr, Seetzen, Wellsted, Wrede, Maltzan, Halévy, Manzoni, and Glaser. (D. H. M.)

YENISEI. See SIBERIA and YENISEISK.

YENISEISK, a province of Eastern Siberia, which extends from the Chinese frontier to the shores of the Arctic Ocean, with an area of 992,870 square miles—as large as one-half of European Russia—has Tobolsk and Tomsk on the W., Yakutsk and Irkutsk on the E., north-western Mongolia on the S., and the Arctic Ocean on the N. (see vol. xxii. pl. I.). Its southern extremity being in 51° 45′ N. lat. and its northern (Cape Tcheluskin) in 77° 38′, it combines a great variety of orographical types, from the Sayan alpine regions in the south to the *tundras* of the Arctic littoral.

Orography.

The border-ridge of the high plateau of north-western Mongolia, which is known under the general name of the Western Sayans, and reaches altitudes of from 7000 to 8000 feet, limits it in the south. This is girdled on the north-western slope by a zone, nearly 100 miles wide, of alpine tracts, characterized by narrow valleys separated by several parallel chains of mountains, which are built up of crystalline slates, from 6000 to 7000 feet high. Here in the impenetrable forests only a few Tungus families find a precarious living by hunting. Towards the south, in the basins of the tributaries of the Tuba, the Sisim, and the Yus, and in those of the Kan, the Agul, and the Biryusa, the valleys of the alpine tracts contain rich auriferous deposits, and numerous gold-washings have been established along the *taiga*. In 53° 10′ N. lat. the Yenisei emerges from the mountain tracts into the wide steppes of Abakan and Minusinsk, from 1500 to 2000 feet above sea-level, which extend along the base of the mountain region north-eastwards towards the upper Lena. A flattened ridge of mountains, hardly attaining more than 3000 to 3500 feet, shoots north-east from the Kuznetskiy Atatau (see TOMSK) and separates the dry steppes of Minusinsk and Abakan from the next terrace of plains, from 1200 to 1700 feet in height, which also stretches in a north-eastern direction from Barnaul in the Altai to Krasnoyarsk, and into the upper basin of the Vilui. Another system of mountains, known under the general name of the Yeniseisk Taiga, rises on the outer border of this terrace, in the space between the Upper Tunguska, or Angara, and the Podkamennaya Tunguska. This system consists of several parallel chains running south-west to north-east, from 2500 to 3500 feet in altitude, though they are much lower on the left bank of the Yenisei, and passing on north-eastwards into the basin of the Olenek. For many years past the Yeniseisk Taiga has been one of the richest auriferous regions of Siberia, not so much on account of the percentage of gold in its alluvial deposits (which are poor in comparison with those of Olekminsk) as on account of the facilities for supplying the gold-fields with articles of food produced in the steppes of Minusinsk.

Lowlands. Beyond the Yeniseisk Taiga begin the lowlands, which at no point rise more than a few hundred feet above the sea and which slope gently towards the Arctic Ocean. They are covered with lakes, thin forests, and marshes; and, as they approach the ocean, they assume more and more the characters of barren tundra, devoid of tree vegetation and covered with lichens. Beyond 70° N. lat. trees occur only along the courses of the rivers. Two ranges, however, break the monotony of the lowlands,—the Tungusskiy ridge, which stretches north-east between the Khatanga and Anabara rivers, and the Byrranga Mountains, which run along the north-western shore of the Taimyr peninsula.

Arctic shores. The shores of the Arctic Ocean are indented by deep estuaries, that of the Taz penetrating 600 miles into the interior of the continent, and that of the Yenisei 300 miles. Gyda Bay, between the estuaries of the Ob and the Yenisei, and Taimyr, Thaddeus, and Khatanga Bays, are wide and deep indentations, ice-bound almost all the year round. Taimyr peninsula, which protrudes as a massive block of land between the Yenisei and the Khatanga, is an utterly barren stony tundra.

Geology. In the south are the granites and granitic syenites of the border-ridge of the plateau. In the alpine region all varieties of crystalline slates—gneisses, diorite slates, talc and mica-schists, and clay slates—are found, the latter being auriferous, and the whole intersected with dykes and veins of protogene, diorites, porphyry, marble, and quartz. The same crystalline rocks are met with in the Kuznetskiy Atatau, the Yeniseisk Taiga, and the Byrranga Mountains. The plains are built up of Silurian, Devonian, Carboniferous, and Triassic limestones and sandstones, with extensive freshwater deposits of the Jurassic period. Chalk and Eocene deposits are met with farther north. The mountain region bears traces of extensive glaciation, and the lowlands of having been covered during the post-Glacial period with immense lakes and marshy tundras, where thousands of mammoths and rhinoceroses were buried, along with other (now fossil) representatives of extinct Tertiary and post-Tertiary mammals. All the country gives evidence of having been covered with numberless lakes during the Lacustrine period.

Minerals. Yeniseisk is exceedingly rich in all kinds of metals and minerals. Gold dust appears in three different regions,—the northern Yeniseisk Taiga, where 100,740 oz. of gold were extracted in 1884; the region of the Kuznetskiy Atatau and its spurs, with the basins of the Tuba, Sisim, and Black and White Yus (25,860 oz. in 1884); and the upper parts of the tributaries of the Kan and Agul (12,540 oz.), where the gold-washings merge into those of the Nijne-Udinsk district of Irkutsk. Silver ore is found at several places in the basin of the Abakan, but the mines have been abandoned. Iron ore occurs almost everywhere in south Yeniseisk, but there is only one iron-work on the Abakan (25,000 cwts. in 1884). Salt lakes are very common, and about 50,000 cwts. of salt are extracted every year.

Rivers. The whole of Yeniseisk is watered by the Yenisei and its affluents. The Yenisei rises in north-western Mongolia in several branches (Bei-khem, Ulu-khem, &c.), the chief of which, the Ulu-khem, has its source in marshes to the west of Lake Kossogol at a height of more than 5000 feet. As far as the Russian frontier its course crosses the plateau at an altitude of not less than 3000 feet; on entering Yeniseisk it pierces the great border-ridge and the series of parallel chains of the alpine region. At Sayansk (53° 10′ N. lat.) it emerges from the highlands and traverses the elevated steppes, receiving the Abakan on the left and the Tuba on the right. In 55° N. lat. it suddenly turns to the north-east, skirting the base of a low range of hills, on the northern slope of which flows the Tchulym, a tributary of the Ob, separated from the Yenisei by an isthmus only 6 miles in width. The possibility of connecting at this point the two great river-systems of Siberia has often been discussed; the difficulty is that the Tchulym valley is 440 feet higher than the other. A little below Krasnoyarsk the Yenisei is joined by a great tributary, the Kan, and farther north by the Angara or Upper Tunguska, which brings the waters of Lake Baikal[1] and is navigable from Irkutsk, notwithstanding a series of rapids in its middle course. The right-hand tributaries of the Ob,—the Ket, the Tym, and the Vakh,—approach the Yenisei so closely, and their sources are so thoroughly inosculated with those of the left-hand tributaries of the Yenisei, that the question of connecting the two systems by means of a canal has been more than once raised; indeed something has been done to connect the Great Kas, a tributary of the Yenisei, with the Ket,—a boat with some 150 cwts. of cargo having already passed from the one to the other.[2] A railway across the narrow isthmus between the Tchulym and the Yenisei is now regarded as the best solution of the question. In 61° N. lat. the Yenisei, already more than two miles broad, divides into several branches, which wind amidst many islands, and has several dangerous rapids. Then, before piercing a ridge of hills, it expands into a kind of lake, 10 miles across, just above its junction with the Podkamennaya Tunguska. Almost exactly at the Arctic Circle, opposite Turukhansk, it receives from the right another large tributary, the Lower Tunguska, which rises within a short distance of the upper Lena. The Yenisei, thus augmented, becomes more than 6 miles wide in lat. 68°. Its estuary begins at the village of Dudino, and has a breadth of 40 miles; it contains numberless islands. The great river narrows once more (12 miles) before entering the Arctic Ocean (Yenisei Bay), after a total course of more than 3000 miles. It is navigable on its middle and lower courses, steamers plying between Krasnoyarsk and Minusinsk, as also on the lower Yenisei. Its mouth has been visited almost every year of late by steamers from Norway or Great Britain; and it is expected that regular communication will be established between Dudino and European ports.

Climate. The climate, though very severe throughout, offers, as might be expected, great varieties. The Minusinsk steppes have a dry and relatively mild climate, so that they are sometimes called the Italy of Siberia. At Krasnoyarsk (55° 1′ N. lat.) the climate is more severe, and the winds are exceedingly disagreeable. The yearly fall of snow is so small that the winds blow it away in the neighbourhood of the town; hence a circuit has to be made by the convoys of sledges to avoid it, or the sledges changed for wheeled carriages. Yeniseisk (58° 27′ N. lat.) has an average temperature below freezing-point, and at Turukhansk the coldest month (February) has an average temperature of −24° Fahr. On the Taimyr peninsula the average summer temperature hardly reaches 45°. For additional particulars, see SIBERIA, vol. xxii. p. 6.

Flora. The highlands of Sayan and Atatau are thickly clothed with forests of cedar, pitch-pine, larch, elder, and birch, with a rich undergrowth of rhododendrons, *Berberis*, and *Ribes*; the Scotch fir appears only in the lower and drier parts of the valleys. The summits and slopes of the mountains are strewn with débris and boulders, and thickly sheeted with lichens and mosses; but there are also patches of meadow land covered with flowers, most of which are known in Europe. Still, the flora is poor as a rule, and Dr Martianoff, after several years' collecting, succeeded in gathering only 104 species of phanerogams.[3] On the other hand, the flora of the Minusinsk plains and of the steppes of the Abakan at once strikes the traveller by the variety and brilliancy of its forms. The meadows are covered with bright flowers scattered amid the common *Gramineæ*, and in June and July they are adorned and perfumed by the *Polygala*, *Dianthus*, *Medicago*, *Lathyrus*, yellow sweet-scented lily, and scores of other flowers, mostly familiar in Europe, but attaining in Yeniseisk a larger size and greater brilliancy of colour. The rich carpet of grass and flowers is overtopped by the tall white blossoms of *Archangelica* and *Spiræa Ulmaria*, and

[1] According to recent measurements, the Angara, where it issues from Lake Baikal, has a volume of 121,400 cubic feet per second (*Izvestia*, East Siberian Geogr. Soc., xvii., 1886).

[2] According to Baron Aminoff's measurements, Lake Bolshoye, through which the canal would have to pass, is 66 feet above the Ket at its junction with the Ozernaya, and 181 feet above the Yenisei at its junction with the Kas.

[3] N. Martianoff, "Materials for a Flora of the Minusinsk Region." in *Trudy* of the Kasan Society of Naturalists, xi. 3, 1882.

the blue masses of the tall *Veronica longifolia*. The meadows of the moister localities, surrounded by thickets of willow, poplar, wild cherry, and hawthorn, are still more attractive, on account of their wealth in anemones, violets, gentians, and so on, and the numerous creepers which festoon the trees and shrubs. M. Martianoff's lists enumerate a total of 760 flowering and 760 cryptogamic plants. Of the lower *Fungi* and parasitical *Myxomycetes* 1300 species were noted, and out of the 823 species hitherto described by specialists no less than 124 have proved to be new. Farther northward the flora of Yeniseisk is similar in character to that of the Siberian lowlands (see SIBERIA, vol. xxii. p. 7). In the Taimyr peninsula it is represented by only 124 species of flowering plants.

una. For the fauna of Yeniseisk, see SIBERIA, vol. xxii. p. 7.

opula- on. The steppes of the upper Yenisei have been inhabited from a very remote antiquity, and numberless *kurgans*, graves, rock inscriptions, and smelting furnaces of the successive inhabitants are scattered all over the prairies of Abakan and Minusinsk.[1] The present population exhibits traces of all these predecessors (see SIBERIA and TARTARS). Numerous survivals of Turkish and Samoyedic stems are found in the steppe land and in the Sayans; but some of them are greatly reduced in numbers (only a few hundreds). The Kaibals, the Katcha Tartars, the Sagais, the Kyzyl and Milet Tartars, and the Kamasins have settlements of their own, and maintain their national features; but the Karagasses, the Kotts, and the Arintses have almost entirely disappeared, and are represented only by a few families in the spurs of the Sayans.[2] The Tunguses are scattered in the least accessible tracts, and may number about 2000, or less. Several hundreds of Yakuts inhabit the Turukhansk district; and in the tundras between the Taz and the Yenisei there are a few hundred OSTIAKS (*q.v.*) and Yuraks of the Samoyedic stem. The remainder of the population, which numbered in all 447,076 in 1885, consists of Russians,—partly exiles, but mostly voluntary settlers. Nearly 50,000 belong to the unfortunate category of "settled" exiles. The "indigenes"—Tartars, Tunguses, Ostiaks, &c.—number about 50,000.

ccupa- ons. The chief occupation of the Russians is agriculture, which prospers in Minusinsk, the granary of the province; it is also carried on in west Kansk, Krasnoyarsk, and Atchinsk, and in a few villages of the Yeniseisk district, the total area of land under corn being reckoned at nearly 2,500,000 acres. Wheat, summer and winter rye, oats, barley, and buckwheat are the chief crops. Gardening is carried on in Minusinsk. Cattle-breeding is important, especially in Minusinsk. It has been estimated that there are in Yeniseisk about 270,000 horses, 240,000 cattle, 300,000 sheep, and 30,000 reindeer in Turukhansk. These figures, however, must be below the true ones. The cattle being kept throughout the winter in the steppes, the snow-storms of early spring prove disastrous, as also do the murrains, to which no fewer than 200,000 head succumbed in the Minusinsk district in 1881. Hunting and fishing are an important resource for most of the indigenes and for many of the Russians.

Ianu- actures. The manufactures of Yeniseisk are hardly worth mentioning, all capital being engaged in gold-washing or in commerce. The chief trade is in furs (exported), and in groceries and manufactured goods (imported). The gold-fields of the Yeniseisk Taiga are supplied with grain and cattle by river from the Minusinsk region, and with salt, spirits, and iron by the Angara. Attempts have recently been made to stimulate the trade in tea with north-west Mongolia.

'owns. Yeniseisk is divided into five districts, the chief towns of which are KRASNOYARSK (*q.v.*), the capital, which had 17,155 inhabitants in 1884; Atchinsk (7190) and Kansk (4050), two small towns on the great Siberian highway, of which the latter is an entrepôt for the gold-mines; Minusinsk (8270) on the Tuba, close by its junction with the Yenisei, which has now a small but excellent natural history and ethnographical museum; and Yeniseisk (7050), the chief entrepôt for the gold-mines, having a public library and a natural history museum, created of late by exiles. Turukhansk (139) is the chief town of a vast "region" (*krai*). (P. A. K.)

YEOLA, a municipal town of India, in the Násik district, Bombay presidency, with a population (1881) of 17,685 (males 8975, females 8710). It is situated in 20° 4′ 10″ N. lat. and 74° 30′ 30″ E. long., 44 miles east of Násik town, 13 miles south of Manwar station on the north-east line of the Great Indian Peninsular Railway, and nearly 12 miles from the frontier of the Nizam's dominions. Yeola is a flourishing commercial town, trading in silk and cotton goods, which it weaves, and in gold-twist, which it also manufactures.

At the time of its foundation Yeola was under the emperor of Delhi; it subsequently passed into the hands of the rajas of Satara and then the peshwás. Finally it was given in grant to Vithal, the ancestor of the present chief of Vinchur, who still enjoys the revenue from the lands attached to the town, though he has no authority within it.

[1] Besides the works of Radloff, and those mentioned in the bibliography of Semenoff's *Dictionary*, see N. Savenkoff's paper on recent explorations, in *Izvestia* of East Siberian Geogr. Soc., xvii., 1887, and the *Descriptive Catalogue of the Minusinsk Museum*, by D. Klementz.

[2] Radloff's *Aus Sibirien* (2 vols., Leipsic, 1880) contains full accounts of the various Turkish stems of Yeniseisk.

YEOMANRY CAVALRY. See VOLUNTEERS.

YEOVIL, a market town and municipal borough of Somerset, England, is situated on the river Yeo or Ivel, which here separates Somerset from Dorset, and on branch lines of the London and South Western and the Great Western Railways, 40 miles south of Bristol and 124 west-south-west of London. The streets are regular and spacious, with a number of handsome public buildings. A few of the houses are of considerable antiquity, but within recent years the town has undergone much alteration. The church of St John the Baptist, occupying a commanding site in the centre of the town, is a large and beautiful cruciform structure in the Perpendicular style, consisting of chancel, nave of seven bays, aisles, transepts, and lofty western tower. It is described by Mr Freeman as "a grand and harmonious whole, as truly the work of real artistic genius as Cologne or Winchester." There are two ecclesiastical parishes within the borough, Hendford and Yeovil Marsh. The principal secular public buildings are the town-hall in the Grecian style, erected in 1849, and the corn exchange. There are a reading room and a library in connexion with the young men's Christian association and mutual improvement society. The benevolent institutions include Woborne's almshouses for six men and six women, the portreeves' almshouses, and a few smaller charities. Water is obtained from Holywell, 8 miles distant, by works constructed by the corporation. Formerly the woollen manufacture was of some consequence, but this industry has now died out. The staple industry is the manufacture of gloves, for which the town has long been celebrated. Brewing and brick-making are also carried on. The agricultural trade of Yeovil is of some importance, large corn markets and cattle and horse fairs being held. The corporation consists of a mayor, four aldermen, and twelve councillors, who hold the manorial rights and also form the urban sanitary authority. The town has a commission of the peace, and petty sessions are held both by the county and the borough magistrates. The population of the municipal borough and urban sanitary district (area about 700 acres) in 1871 was 8527, and in 1881 it was 8479.

Yeovil was a borough by prescription. Anciently it was called the town, borough, lordship, and hundred of Yeovil, and was included in a district which soon after the Conquest was taken possession of by the crown. The manor of Yeovil included in this district was some time afterwards assigned to the rector of St John the Baptist church, and was incorporated under the name of the portreeve and burgesses of Yeovil. In 1418 it was resigned by the rector to Henry V., who gave the manor to the convent of the Virgin Mary and Saint Bridget. The grant was confirmed by Edward IV. After the dissolution of the monasteries the manor was settled by Henry VIII. on Catherine Parr, who held it till her death. In 1449 the town was visited by a fire, by which 117 houses were destroyed. In 1853 Yeovil was placed under the Municipal Act.

YEW. This tree (*Taxus*) belongs to a genus of *Coniferæ* in which the ordinarily woody cone is represented by a fleshy cup surrounding a single seed. Usually it forms a low-growing tree of very diverse habit, but generally with dense spreading branches, thickly covered with very dark green linear leaves, which are given off from all sides of the branch, but which, owing to a twist in the base of the leaf, become arranged in a single series on each side of it. The trees are usually diœcious: the male flowers are borne on one individual and the female on another, although instances occur in which flowers of both sexes are formed on the same tree. The male flowers are more or less globular and occur in the axils of the leaves. They consist of a number of overlapping brownish scales, gradually increasing in size from below upwards and surrounding a naked stalk that bears at its summit a head of anthers. Each anther has a flat five-lobed top, something like a shield; from its under surface five, six, or more pollen cases hang down, and

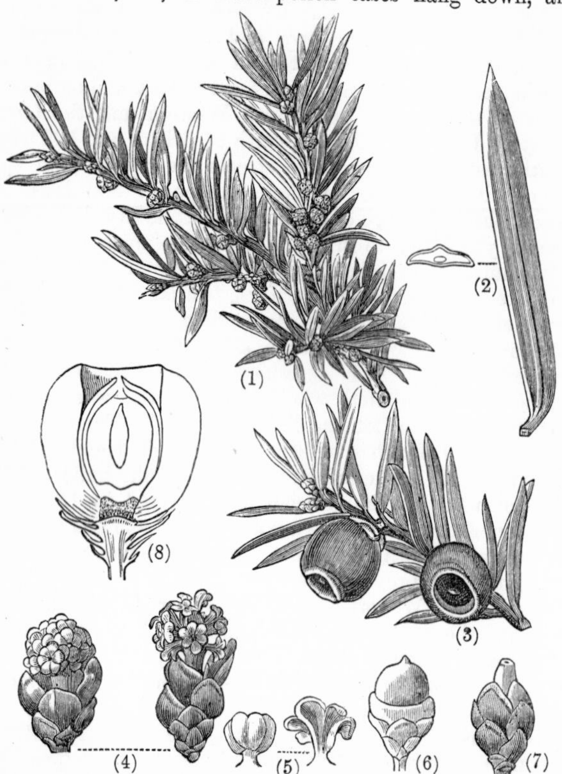

Yew. (1) Shoot with male flowers; (2) leaf and in section, magnified; (3) fruit; (4) male flowers; (5) stamens; (6), (7) female flower in different stages; (8) section of female flowers, magnified.

these open lengthwise to liberate the globose pollen-grains. Each flower thus consists of a number of monadelphous stamens; but, according to the older view of its structure, each stamen constitutes of itself a single flower, the whole mass being considered as an amentaceous inflorescence or catkin of numerous monandrous flowers. The female flowers are also placed each separately in the axil of a leaf, and consist of a number of overlapping scales, as in the male. These scales surround a cup which is at first shallow, green, and thin, but which subsequently becomes fleshy and red, while it increases so much in length as almost entirely to conceal the single straight seed. It is clear that the structure of the female flower differs from that of most conifers; but the structure of the wood and other characters forbid its being separated from them except as a subdivision (*Taxaceæ*).

The poisonous properties, referred to by classical writers such as Cæsar, Virgil, and Livy, reside chiefly if not entirely in the foliage. This, if eaten by horses or cattle, especially when it has been cut and thrown in heaps so as to undergo a process of fermentation, is very injurious. The leaves have also been used for various medicinal purposes, but are seldom employed now. The succulent portion of the yew berry is quite harmless; but it is probable that some noxious principle is contained in the seed. As, however, it is hard and disagreeable to the taste, the danger from this source is not great. As a timber tree it is used for cabinet-work, axle-trees, bows, and the like, where strength and durability are required.

The yew occurs wild over a very large area of the northern hemisphere. In north-eastern America and in Japan trees are found of a character so similar that by some botanists they are all ranged under one species. The varieties grown in the United Kingdom are very numerous, one of the most striking being that known as the Irish yew,—a shrub with the pyramidal or columnar habit of a cypress, in which the leaves spread from all sides of the branches, not being twisted, as they usually are, out of their original position. In the ordinary yew the main branches spread more or less horizontally, and the leaves are so arranged as to be conveniently exposed to the influence of the light; but in the variety in question the branches are mostly vertical, and the leaves assume a direction in accordance with the ascending direction of the branches.

The yew is a favourite evergreen tree, either for planting separately or for hedges, for which its dense foliage renders it well suited. The wood is very hard, close-grained, and of a deep red brown colour internally. Its younger branches, owing to their toughness, were formerly used for bows. The planting of the yew in churchyards was at one time supposed to have been done with a view to the supply of yew staves. But, while importation from abroad was fostered, there seems to have been no statute enforcing the cultivation of the yew in Great Britain; on the other hand, a statute of Edward I. (cited in *Gard. Chron.*, 6th March 1880) states that the trees were often planted in churchyards to defend the church from high winds. Be this as it may, yews of huge size and great antiquity still exist in various parts of the country in the vicinity of churches. Some of these are of historic interest; but it is hardly prudent to cite either the measurements or the allegations as to age, the circumstances under which the estimates were framed being different in each case. Accurate comparative measurements made on a uniform plan would be very serviceable. The Crowhurst yew, mentioned by Evelyn as 30 feet in circumference, was still in existence in 1876 (*Gard. Chron.*, 22d July 1876). The large yew at Ankerwyke near Staines, with a trunk 27⅝ feet in circumference, might well have been in existence in 1215, when Magna Charta was signed. Considerable interest also attaches to the fine yew in Buckland churchyard near Dover, which in 1880 was removed to a distance of 60 yards. The trunk had been split so that it had a direction nearly parallel with the soil. This huge tree was moved with a ball of soil round its roots, 16 feet 5 inches by 15 feet 8 inches, by 3 feet 6½ inches in depth, the weight of the entire mass being estimated at 56 tons. The dimensions of the tree in 1880 were as follows—"circumference of the main trunk, 22 feet; of the upright portion of the trunk, 6 feet 10 inches; second horizontal trunk, 10 feet 10 inches; do., south limb forking off at 9 feet from the main trunk, 7 feet 10 inches; do., west limb forking off at 9 feet from the main trunk, 8 feet 8 inches; extent of branches from centre of main trunk southwards, 30 feet 10 inches, and from north to south 48 feet; they extend from the main trunk westward 33 feet." The tree was replanted so that the horizontal portions were replaced in their original erect position and the natural symmetry restored (*Gard. Chron.*, 1st May 1880).

YEZD. See Yazd, p. 733 above.

YEZO. See Japan.

YOH-CHOW FU, a prefectural city in the Chinese province of Hoo-nan ("south of the lakes"), stands on high ground on the east side of the outlet of Tung-ting Lake, in 29° 18′ N. lat. and 113° 2′ E. long. The district in which Yoh-chow Fu stands is the ancient habitat of the aboriginal San Miao tribes, who were subsequently deported into north-western China, and who, judging from some of the non-Chinese festival customs of the people, would appear to have left traditions behind them. The present city, which was built in 1371, is about 3 miles in circumference and is entered by four gates. The walls are high and well built, but were not strong enough to keep out the Taiping rebels in 1853. Situated between Tung-ting Lake and the Yang-tze-kiang, Yoh-chow Fu forms a depôt for the native products of the province which are destined for export, and for foreign goods on their way inland. In 1885 foreign goods to the value of 28,228 taels were sent from Hankow to Yoh-chow Fu, the principal items being grey shirting, oil, and lead. The city is 4250 Chinese miles from Peking, and contains a population of about 60,000.

YOKOHAMA, situated in 35° 26′ 53″ N. lat. and 139° 38′ 39″ E. long. (see map in vol. xxiii. p. 433), is the most important of the five ports in Japan open by treaty to foreign commerce and residence, both on account of its proximity to Tokio, the capital, and of the extent of its trade. It stands on a plain, extending along the Bay of Tokio and shut in by hills, one of which, towards the south-east, terminates in a promontory called Honmoku-misaki. Its area extends over ·873 of a square mile, of which ·26 is occupied by the foreign settlement. The climate is variable, the range in temperature being from 95° to 43° Fahr., and the mean temperature 57°·7. The cold in winter is severe owing to the prevalence of northerly

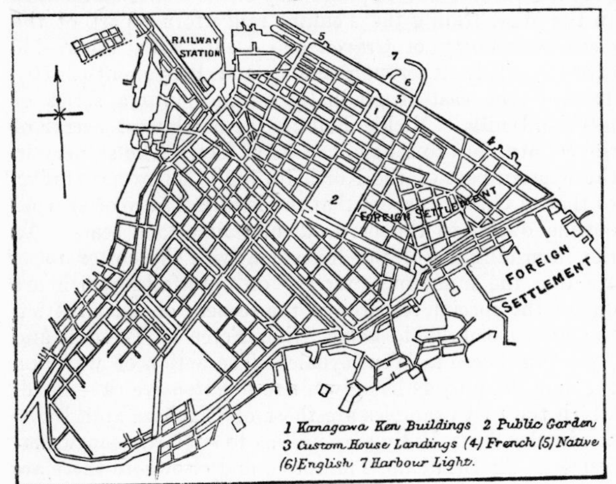

Plan of Yokohama.

winds, while the heat is great in summer, though it is tempered by sea breezes from the south-west. The rainfall is large—according to Dr Hepburn's observations (1863-1869) 69¼ inches annually. In 1859, when the neighbouring town of Kanagawa was opened to foreigners under the treaty with the United States, Yokohama was an insignificant fishing village; and notwithstanding the protests of the foreign representatives the Japanese Government shortly afterwards chose the latter place as the settlement instead of Kanagawa. The town has since increased so rapidly that in 1886 the population was 111,179 (3904 foreigners, including 2573 Chinese, 256 Americans, and 625 British). The Japanese Government has constructed various public buildings, a granite breakwater, and a causeway 2 miles long, connecting the town with Kanagawa. Waterworks on the most improved principle have been completed recently, the water being supplied from the Sagamigawa. The foreign settlement consists of well-constructed streets with business establishments. The wealthier portion of the foreigners reside, however, on a hilly locality to the south of the town, called the Bluff. The land occupied by foreigners has been leased to them by the Japanese Government, 20 per cent. of the annual rent being set aside for municipal expenses.

The harbour, which is a part of the Bay of Tokio, is good and commodious, extending from Honmoku-misaki (Treaty Point) to the mouth of the Tsurumi, a distance of about 5 miles. The average depth at high water is about 46 feet, with a fall of tide of about 8 feet, the entrance being marked by a lightship and two buoys. There are two landing-places, the English and the French "hatoba"; but, as there are no quays available for large vessels, goods have to be carried to the shore in junks. Steamers from San Francisco, Vancouver's Island, China, &c., call regularly. A railway about 18 miles long connects Yokohama with Tokio. This, the first railway in Japan, was constructed in 1872. Yokohama is the terminus of the Tokaido line, which will ultimately connect Yokohama with Kioto, the former capital.

The following table shows the value of the foreign trade of Yokohama from 1878 to 1886:—

	Exports.	Imports.
1878	£3,116,896	£5,077,769
1879	3,873,459	4,799,456
1880	3,792,991	5,378,385
1881	4,319,077	4,404,289
1882	5,451,803	4,155,628
1883	5,245,290	3,925,392
1884	4,381,026	3,967,644
1885	......	......
1886	6,502,466	4,116,842

The figures for the bullion trade in 1886 were—export (gold) £9291, (silver) £1,243,569; import (gold) £4776, (silver) £1,903,010. The revenue from custom duties, &c., in the same year was—export duties, £212,587; import duties, £198,866; warehouses, £1979; harbour dues, £1870.

YOKOSUKA, a seaport and naval station of Japan, is situated in the province of Sagami and on the Bay of Tokio, 12 miles south of Yokohama (see map in vol. xxiii. p. 433). The port is sheltered by hills and affords good anchorage. The site was occupied by a small fishing village until 1865, when the shogun's Government established a shipyard there. Since then it has grown rapidly and come into prominence. In 1868 the Japanese Government converted the shipyard into a naval dockyard, and subsequently carried out many improvements. In 1884 the port became a first-class naval station; and naval barracks, warehouses, offices, hospitals, &c., were established there. A large number of ships-of-war and of the mercantile marine are always found in the port, as well as an increasing number of foreign vessels, which come to be docked and repaired. The dockyard was first constructed by French engineers; but since 1875 the work has been entirely in the hands of Japanese engineers. The number of hands employed is about 2800. There are three dry docks and slips. The area occupied by the dockyard and other naval establishments is 7000 acres, and that of the town 270 acres. The population was 5800 in 1888.

YONKERS, a city of Westchester county, New York, United States, is situated upon the east bank of the Hudson river, about 18 miles from its mouth, and on the New York Central and Hudson River and the New York City and Northern Railroads. The site is very hilly, consisting of ridges forming terraces parallel to the river. The city had in 1880 a population of 18,892 (12,733 in 1870). Yonkers has important manufacturing industries, principally of carpets, hats, silk, brass goods, elevators (lifts), steam engines, and machinery; but it is chiefly as a residence suburb, being within an hour of the business centre of the metropolis, that it has acquired its population and importance.

Yonkers was settled by the Dutch of New Amsterdam about the middle of the 17th century, and was held as a manor until 1779. In 1788 it was organized as a township, and in 1872 it received a city charter.

YONNE, a department of central France, was formed in 1790 partly from the province of Champagne proper (with its dependencies, Sénonais and Tonnerrois), partly from Burgundy proper (with its dependencies, the county of Auxerre and Avallonnais), and partly from Gâtinais (Orléanais and Île-de-France). It lies between 47° 18′ and 48° 25′ N. lat. and 2° 50′ and 4° 20′ E. long., and is bounded by Aube on the N.E., Côte-d'Or on the E., Nièvre on the S., Loiret on the W., and Seine-et-Marne on the N.W. The highest elevation (2000 feet) of the department is in the granite mountains of Morvan, in the south-east, where other peaks range from 1300 to 1600 feet. These mountains are flanked by limestone plateaus, from 700 to 1200 feet in height, traversed by the Yonne and its tributaries. The department belongs wholly to the basin of the Seine, except a small district in the south-west, which belongs to that of the Loire. The river Yonne flows through it from south to north-north-west, receiving on the right bank the

Cure (with its tributary the Cousin), the Serein, the Armançon (the valley of which is traversed by the Burgundy Canal and by the railway from Paris to Lyons through Burgundy), and the Vanne (from which Paris is partly supplied by an aqueduct). To the west of the Yonne lie the sources of the Loing, another tributary of the Seine, and of its affluents, the Ouanne and the Lunain. The Yonne is navigable throughout the department, and is connected with the Loire by the Canal of Nivernais, which in turn is connected with that of Briare joining the Seine and the Loire. The climate of Yonne resembles that of Paris; but the extremes of heat and cold are greater on the plateaus. The annual rainfall is 27 inches at Auxerre and 32 in the east of the department. The prevailing winds are from the south-west and west.

Of a total area of 1,835,475 acres 1,125,412 acres are arable, 426,757 are under wood, 91,309 under vines, 79,366 under grass, and 39,316 are returned as occupied by heaths, pasture-lands, and marshes. The live stock in 1880 included 41,295 horses, 1280 mules, 8438 asses, 126,636 cattle, 238,522 sheep of native and 58,416 of superior breed (wool-clip in 1880 566 tons), 30,561 pigs, and 6516 goats. There were also 21,411 beehives (61 tons of honey). Oxen are fattened and the well-known St Florentin cheeses made. The wines of Tonnerre and Auxerrois are the finest red wines of Lower Burgundy, and those of Chablis are the finest white. The principal crops in 1884 were—wine 22,486,420 gallons (average of ten preceding years 28,607,370 gallons), wheat 5,500,000 bushels, meslin 192,600, rye 680,625, barley 948,750, oats 4,677,750, buckwheat 35,200, potatoes 3,410,088, beetroot for fodder 25,060 tons, hops 79 tons, colza seed 206, hemp seed 138, hemp 99, linseed 40, flax 22, tobacco 33, hay 386,650, clover 34,245, lucerne 30,189, and sainfoin 6297 tons. The forests consist of oak, beech, elm, hornbeam, ash, and birch, and re-plantations are being made with different kinds of pine and with larch; chestnut trees are not uncommon. In 1880 700 tons of peat were extracted; and there are fine quarries of Oolitic limestone, and of cement, ochre, fossil phosphates, china clay, and chalk. The chief industrial establishments are tanneries, forges (11,863 tons of iron in 1882), paper-mills, saw-mills, and breweries; files and other articles of steel, boots and shoes, hosiery, and champagne are also manufactured. Cereals, wines, firewood, charcoal, ochre, and bark are exported; southern wines and building materials are among the imports. There are 286 miles of railway, 318 of national and 6755 of other roads, and 205 of waterway. The population was 357,029 in 1881, and 355,364 in 1886. About 217,000 are engaged in agricultural pursuits. The department constitutes the archiepiscopal diocese of Sens, has its court of appeal at Paris, its academy at Dijon, and belongs to the district of Orleans army corps. It is divided for administrative purposes into five arrondissements. Places of note are the chef-lieu Auxerre (16,754 inhabitants in 1886), the picturesque Avallon (5768), Joigny (6189), famous for its wines, and Tonnerre (4650), for its wines and building stones.

Plate XVIII.

YORK, a northern county of England, is bounded E. by the North Sea, N. by Durham (the boundary line being formed by the Tees), S. by Lincoln, Nottingham, Derby, and Chester, and W. by Lancaster and Westmorland. It is much the largest county in England, being more than double the size of Lincolnshire, which ranks next to it. The area is 3,882,851 acres, or nearly 6067 square miles, almost one-eighth of the surface of England. Of the total area 750,828 acres or about 1173 square miles are in the East Riding, 1,361,664 acres or about 2127½ square miles in the North Riding, and 1,768,380 acres or about 2763 square miles in the West Riding. The city of York, which forms an administrative division separate from the Ridings, embraces an area of 1979 acres or about 3 square miles.

Geology.

The marked differences in the geological structure of Yorkshire are reflected in the great variety of its scenery. The stratification is for the most part regular, but owing to a great line of dislocation nearly coincident with the western boundary of the county the rocks dip towards the east, while the strike of the strata is from north to south. The bold and picturesque scenery of the western hills and dales is due to the effects of denudation among the harder rocks, which here come to the surface. A portion of the Pennine chain, stretching from Derbyshire to the Cheviots, runs north and south through Yorkshire, where it has an average breadth of about 30 miles. The strata here consist of (1) Silurian beds, occupying a small area in the north-west corner of the county; (2) the Carboniferous or Mountain Limestone, which has been subjected to great dislocations, the more important of which are known as the North and South Craven faults; (3) the Yoredale series, consisting of shales, flagstones, limestone, and thin seams of coal; and (4) the Millstone Grit, forming part of the hilly moorlands, and capping many of the loftier eminences. In the West Riding the Pennine range forms part of the elevated country of Craven and Dent, with Whernside (2384 feet), Ingleborough (2361), and Penyghent (2270). Towards the east it gradually declines into a series of moorland hills. Mickle Fell in the north-west corner of the county rises to a height of 2581 feet. The scenery in the western part of the North Riding is somewhat similar to that in Craven, except that the lower hills are of sharper outline owing to the perpendicular limestone scars. To the intermingling of the limestone with the softer rocks are due the numerous "forces" or waterfalls, which are one of the special features of the scenery of this district, the more remarkable being High Force in Teesdale and Aysgarth Force in Wensleydale. The action of water on the limestone rocks has given rise to extensive caverns, of which the best examples are those of Clapham and Ingleton in the West Riding, as well as to subterranean water-courses. At Brimham, Plumpton, and elsewhere there are curious fantastic masses of rock due to irregular weathering of the Millstone Grit. The Pennine region is bounded on the south-east by the Coal Measures, forming the northern portion of the Derbyshire, Nottingham, and Yorkshire coalfield, which in Yorkshire extends from Sheffield northwards to Leeds. To the east the Measures dip beneath the Permian beds, of which a narrow band crops up from Masham southwards. The Permian strata are overlain to the east by the Trias or New Red Sandstone, which is scarcely ever exposed, but having been partly worn away is covered with Glacial deposits of clay and gravel, forming the low-lying Vale of York, extending from the Tees south to Tadcaster and east beyond York to Market Weighton. Farther east the Triassic beds are overlain by Lias and Oolite. The Lias crops to the surface in a curve extending from Redcar to the Humber. In the Middle Lias there is a seam of valuable iron ore, the source of the prosperity of the Cleveland region. The moorlands extending from Scarborough and Whitby are formed of Liassic strata topped with beds of Lower Oolite, rising gradually to the north-east and attaining at Burton Head a height of 1489 feet, the greatest elevation of the Oolite formation in England. In the bottom bed there is a seam of ironstone, an immense nugget of which, in Rosedale, now nearly all removed, formed at one time a conspicuous cliff. In this district there are a number of picturesque eminences capped by Lower Oolites, and among the eastern slopes of the moorlands there are several charming and fertile valleys. Along the line of the Lower Oolites there is a series of low flat hills, which slope southwards under the clays of the Vale of Pickering. These clays are covered by the Chalk, forming the district of the Wolds, which again dips southwards below the clays and sands of Holderness.

Coast.

The coast is not deeply indented at any part, the inlets scarcely deserving the name of bays. Except in the Holderness region, the shore as far north as Saltburn is bold and rocky, and presents a great variety of picturesque cliff scenery, while below the cliffs there are in many cases long stretches of beautiful sands.

Rivers.

Yorkshire is famed for the beauty of its river scenery, in which respect it is scarcely surpassed by Scotland. The great majority of the rivers issue from the higher western regions and flow eastwards. The Tees, which rises on the

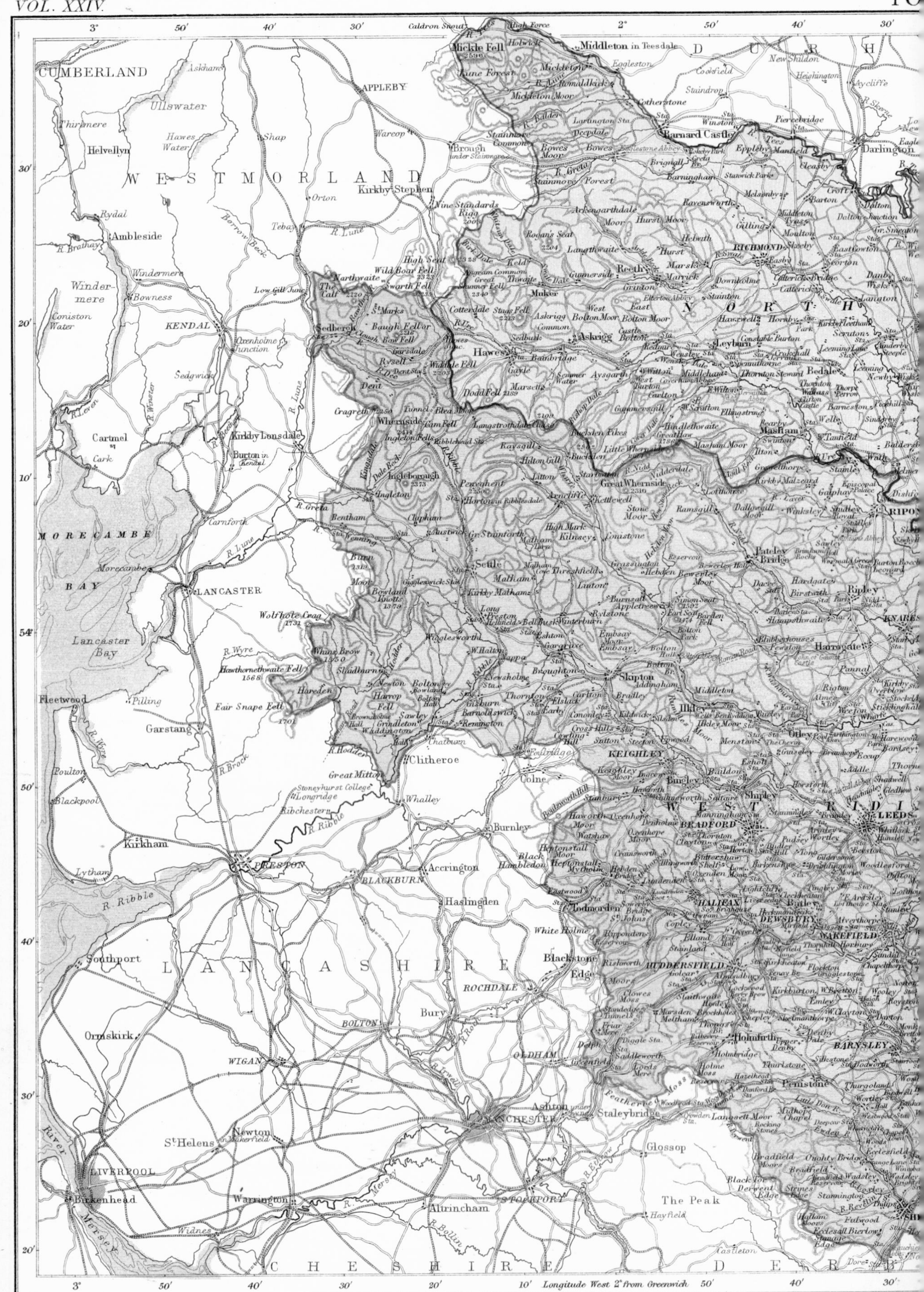
CUMBERLAND
WESTMORLAND
LANCASHIRE
CHESHIRE
DURHAM
NORTH
WEST RIDI
DERB
MORECAMBE BAY
Lancaster Bay
Ullswater
Thirlmere
Helvellyn
Hawes Water
Shap
APPLEBY
Askham
Warcop
Brough under Stainmore
Kirkby Stephen
Orton
Tebay
R. Lune
Borrow Beck
Rydal
Ambleside
R. Brathay
Windermere
Winder-mere
Bowness
Coniston Water
KENDAL
Oxenholme Junction
Sedgwick
R. Winster
R. Leven
Cartmel
Cark
Kirkby Lonsdale
Burton in Kendal
Carnforth
R. Greta
Morecambe
LANCASTER
Wolfhole Crag 1731
R. Wyre
Hawthornethwaite Fell 1568
Fleetwood
Pilling
Fair Snape Fell 1701
Garstang
R. Brock
Poulton
Blackpool
Kirkham
Lytham
PRESTON
R. Ribble
BLACKBURN
Accrington
Haslingden
Southport
Ormskirk
WIGAN
BOLTON
Bury
ROCHDALE
OLDHAM
St Helens
Newton in Makerfield
LIVERPOOL
Birkenhead
River Mersey
Warrington
Widnes
Altrincham
STOCKPORT
MANCHESTER
Ashton under Lyne
Staleybridge
Glossop
Hayfield
The Peak
Castleton
R. Bollin
R. Irwell
R. Roch
Sedbergh
Baugh Fell
Garsdale
Dent
Gragreth 2250
Whernside 2414
Ingleborough 2373
Ingleton
Bentham
Clapham
Austwick
Settle
Giggleswick
Malham
Kirkby Malham
Long Preston
Hellifield
Wigglesworth
Slaidburn
Whins Brow 1550
Hareden
Newton
Bolton by Bowland
Harrop Fell
Sawley
Grindleton
Waddington
Chatburn
Clitheroe
Great Mitton
Stoneyhurst College
Longridge
Ribchester
R. Hodder
Whalley
Burnley
Colne
Barnoldswick
Gisburn
Black Hambledon
Todmorden
Eastwood
White Holme
Blackstone Edge
Hawes
Bainbridge
Gayle
Dodd Fell 2189
Askrigg
Aysgarth
Semmer Water
Muker
Reeth
Keld
Great Shunner Fell 2340
Rogan's Seat 2204
Nine Standards Rigg 2006
High Seat 2328
Wild Boar Fell 2323
Swarth Fell 2235
Mickle Fell 2596
Holwick
High Force
Caldron Snout
Middleton in Teesdale
Mickleton
Romaldkirk
Lune Forest
Middleton Moor
Eggleston
Cotherstone
Barnard Castle
Bowes
Bowes Moor
Stainmore Forest
R. Greta
Staindrop
Cockfield
New Shildon
Heighington
Aycliffe
Piercebridge
Winston
Darlington
Gainford
Barningham
Brignall
Ravensworth
Melsonby
Gilling
Middleton Tyas
Croft
Barton
Dalton Junction
RICHMOND
Easby
Marske
Hurst
Hurst Moor
Arkengarthdale
Langthwaite
Gunnerside
Downholme
Catterick
Catterick Bridge
Scorton
Moulton
Langton
Danby Wiske
Hornby
Leyburn
Wensley
Middleham
Bedale
Masham
Leeming
Thornton Steward
Swinton
Ilton
Grewelthorpe
Kirkby Malzeard
RIPON
Galphay
Winksley
Dallowgill Moor
Ramsgill
Lofthouse
Great Whernside 2310
Buckden Pike
Kettlewell
Arncliffe
Litton
Kilnsey
Conistone
Grassington
Hebden
Threshfield
Linton
Burnsall
Appletreewick
Rylstone
Pateley Bridge
Hardgate
Birstwith
Ripley
Harrogate
Pannal
KNARES
Skipton
Embsay
Bolton Abbey
Addingham
Ilkley
Otley
Middleton
Carlton
Bradley
Cononley
Kildwick
Cowling Hill
Sutton
Steeton
Earby
Elslack
Thornton
Broughton
Gargrave
Hellifield
Bell Busk
Winterburn
KEIGHLEY
Keighley Moor
Bingley
Baildon
Shipley
Haworth
BRADFORD
LEEDS
Pudsey
Wortley
Beeston
Halifax
HALIFAX
Brighouse
Elland
Copley
Ripponden
Rishworth
Sowerby Bridge
Hebden Bridge
Heptonstall
Mytholm
HUDDERSFIELD
Almondbury
Kirkburton
Holmfirth
Marsden
Slaithwaite
Meltham
Honley
Saddleworth
Delph
Diggle Sta.
Greenfield
Holme Moss
Woodhead
Langsett Moor
Penistone
Thurlstone
Midhope Chapel
DEWSBURY
Mirfield
WAKEFIELD
Ossett
Horbury
Sandal
Crigglestone
BARNSLEY
Darton
Emley
Woolley
Silkstone
Hoyland
Thurgoland
Wortley
Oughtibridge
Bradfield
Ecclesfield
Stannington
Fulwood
Hallam Moors
Ecclesall Bierlow
Bradfield Moors
Derwent Edge
Black Tor
R. Derwent
Ringinglow
Longitude West 2° from Greenwich
3°
50'
40'
30'
20'
10'
2°
54°

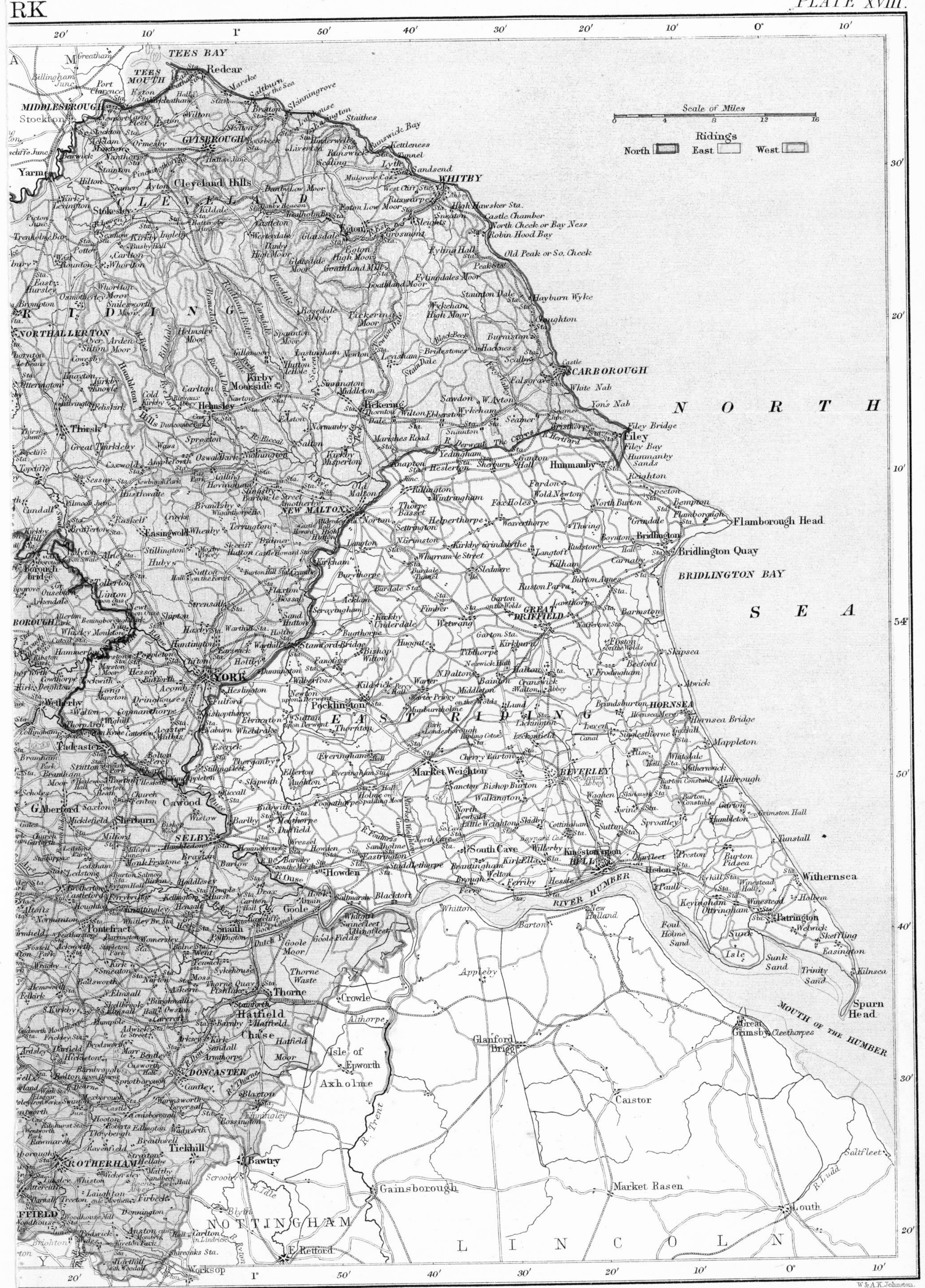
TEES BAY
Redcar
TEES MOUTH
MIDDLESBROUGH
Stockton
GUISBOROUGH
Cleveland Hills
C L E V E L A N D
Stokesley
Runswick Bay
WHITBY
Robin Hood Bay
Old Peak or So. Cheek
Hayburn Wyke
NORTHALLERTON
Kirby Moorside
Helmsley
Pickering
SCARBOROUGH
White Nab
Yon's Nab
Filey Bridge
Filey
Filey Bay
Thirsk
NEW MALTON
Flamborough Head
Bridlington
Bridlington Quay
BRIDLINGTON BAY
N O R T H
S E A
Easingwold
GREAT DRIFFIELD
Stamford Bridge
YORK
Wetherby
Tadcaster
Pocklington
E A S T   R I D I N G
HORNSEA
Hornsea Bridge
Mappleton
Market Weighton
BEVERLEY
Aldbrough
Cawood
Sherburn
SELBY
Howden
South Cave
HULL
Hedon
Withernsea
RIVER HUMBER
Patrington
Pontefract
Snaith
Goole
Thorne
Crowle
Hatfield Chase
Isle of Epworth
Axholme
Spurn Head
MOUTH OF THE HUMBER
Great Grimsby
Cleethorpes
Glanford Brigg
Caistor
DONCASTER
Tickhill
ROTHERHAM
Bawtry
Gainsborough
Market Rasen
Saltfleet
Louth
NOTTINGHAM
L I N C O L N
E. Retford
Worksop
Scale of Miles
0 4 8 12 16
Ridings
North
East
West
54°
W.&A.K. Johnston.

south-east borders of Cumberland, forms throughout almost its entire length the boundary between Yorkshire and Durham. The Swale rises on the confines of Westmorland, and after a semicircular course by Richmond joins the Ure a few miles below Boroughbridge. This latter river flows in a similar direction some miles south of the Swale through the beautiful Wensleydale, and then past Jervaulx Abbey, Masham, and Ripon. After its junction with the Swale it takes the name of the Ouse, and on being joined by the Nidd passes by York and Selby, beyond which it receives the Aire and the Trent, and finally it falls into the Humber. The Wharfe flows south-eastwards from the Pennine range past Bolton Abbey, Otley, Wetherby, and Tadcaster to the Ouse near Cawood. The Aire rises in full stream from the foot of Malham Cove in Craven, and, flowing past Skipton, Keighley, and Leeds, receives the Calder at Castleford, and falls into the Ouse near Goole. The Ribble flows southwards through the district of Craven into Lancashire. The Don rises in the Penistone moors, and flowing northwards by Sheffield and Doncaster falls into the Ouse near Goole. The Hull flows southwards through the East Riding to the Humber at Hull.

.kes. The county is almost destitute of lakes, the only sheets of water of size sufficient to lay claim to that title being Semmer Water at the upper end of Wensleydale, Malham Tarn at the head of Airedale, and Hornsea Mere near the sea-coast at Hornsea.

.nerals. One of the chief sources of the mineral wealth of Yorkshire is the coalfield in the West Riding, the most valuable seams being the Silkstone, which is bituminous and of the very highest reputation as a house coal, and the Barnsley thick coal, the great seam of the Yorkshire coalfield, which is of special value, on account of its semi-anthracitic quality, for use in iron-smelting and in engine furnaces. The average yearly production of the Yorkshire coalfield is nearly twenty million tons, the number of persons employed above and below ground at the coal-pits being over 60,000. Associated with the Upper Coal Measures there is a valuable iron ore, occurring in the form of nodules. Large quantities of fire-clay are also raised, as well as of gannister and oil-shale. In the Middle Lias of the Cleveland district there is a remarkable bed of iron ore, of which the annual production is over six million tons, the greater proportion of the ore being converted into pig-iron in Middlesbrough, by far the most important centre of pig-iron manufacture in the kingdom. Altogether the production of pig-iron in Yorkshire is nearly one-third of that produced in England, and nine-tenths of the produce of Yorkshire belongs to the Cleveland district. Lead ore is obtained in the Yoredale beds of the Pennine range in Wharfedale, Airedale, Niddesdale, Swaledale, Arkendale, and Wensleydale. Slates and flagstones are quarried in the Yoredale rocks. In the Millstone Grit there are several beds of good building stone, but that most largely quarried is the Magnesian Limestone of the Permian series, which, however, is of somewhat variable quality.

ineral rings. Yorkshire is noted for the number of its mineral springs, chiefly sulphureous and chalybeate, the principal, besides those at Harrogate, being Askern, Aldfield, Boston Spa, Croft, Filey, Guisbrough, Hovingham, and Scarborough.

gricul- re. *Agriculture.*—The hilly country in the west of Yorkshire, embracing the north-western corner of the North Riding and a great part of the West Riding, is chiefly pasture land, sheep being grazed on the higher grounds and cattle on the rich pastures where the limestone rock prevails. The Vale of York, with an area of about 1000 square miles, includes much fertile land occupied by all kinds of crops. The Chalk downs by careful cultivation now form one of the best soils for corn crops, the rotation being grasses, wheat, turnips, and barley. The till or boulder clay of Holderness is the richest soil in Yorkshire. A great part of the land in this district has been reclaimed from the sea, from 20,000 to 30,000 acres being protected by embankments. The Vale of Cleveland in the North Riding is well cultivated, the higher grounds in the district being chiefly pastoral. The smallest proportional area under cultivation is in the North Riding, 860,820 acres out of 1,361,664 in 1887, while in the East Riding there were 666,291 acres out of 804,798, and in the West Riding 1,210,639 acres out of 1,716,389. The proportion of permanent pasture is largest in the West Riding, 803,514 acres or about two-thirds of the area under cultivation, while in the North Riding it was 488,958 acres or rather more than one-half, and in the East Riding only 191,519 acres or considerably less than a third. On the other hand, the area under corn crops in the West Riding was 208,890 acres, in the North Riding 197,846 acres, and in the East Riding 254,162 acres. Wheat in 1887 occupied 66,341 acres in the East Riding, 38,437 in the North, and 58,659 in the West; barley 64,042 in the East, 61,367 in the North, and 54,592 in the West; and oats 101,410 in the East, 85,554 in the North, and 81,314 in the West. Rye, beans, and pease occupied comparatively small areas. Liquorice is grown in the neighbourhood of Pontefract. Flax is still grown, but occupies a comparatively small area, only 868 acres in 1887. Green crops in the East Riding occupied 110,806 acres (potatoes 12,956, turnips 75,590, mangold 5297, carrots 613, cabbage, &c., 7419, and vetches, &c., 8931), in the North Riding 78,689 (potatoes 11,246, turnips 58,121, mangold 2379, carrots 110, cabbage, &c., 3329, and vetches, &c., 3504), and in the West Riding 99,596 (potatoes 23,044, turnips 62,079, mangold 3331, carrots 250, cabbage, &c., 2219, and vetches, &c., 8673). Clover and rotation grasses occupied in the East, North, and West Ridings 92,982, 71,846, and 85,075 acres respectively, and fallow land 16,388, 23,460, and 13,141 acres respectively. The areas under orchards in 1887 were—in the East Riding 849 acres, in the North 1015, and in the West 1694, the areas under market gardens being 520, 369, and 2652 acres, under nursery grounds 104, 154, and 807 acres, and under woods (in 1881) 14,480, 49,106, and 66,014 acres respectively. Horses numbered 38,046 (23,508 used for agriculture, 14,538 unbroken horses and mares kept solely for breeding) in the East Riding, 40,384 (26,026 used for agriculture) in the North Riding, and 53,149 (35,180 used for agriculture) in the West Riding. These horses are only such as are returned by occupiers of land, and do not include the large number used for commercial purposes. The draught horses are generally of a somewhat mixed breed, but the county is famed for its breeds of hunters and of carriage and saddle horses. A breed known as Cleveland bays is much used in London carriages. Horse-racing is a favourite Yorkshire sport, the principal stables being at Malton, Beverley, Doncaster, and Middleham. Cattle in 1887 numbered 86,169 (26,211 cows and heifers) in the East Riding, 162,462 (54,111 cows and heifers) in the North Riding, 264,876 (122,457 cows and heifers) in the West Riding. The breeds of cattle are not much attended to, the custom in the hilly districts, in both the West and the North Riding, being to purchase lean cattle at the northern fairs to fatten for the Lancashire and Yorkshire butchers. The Teeswater breed is, however, on the increase in Yorkshire. In Holderness there is a short-horned breed, chiefly valuable for its milking qualities. Cheese-making is largely carried on in some districts. Sheep in 1887 numbered in the East Riding 429,252, in the North Riding 638,320, and in the West Riding 646,809. The Leicester, the Lincoln, and the South Down, and crosses between the Cheviot and Leicester, are perhaps the most common breeds. The old Wolds sheep have also been improved by crossing with Leicesters. The total number of pigs in the East Riding in 1887 was 46,332, in the North Riding 48,990, and in the West Riding 71,887. Though the large long-eared breed is still kept, the small breed is that chiefly in favour. Large numbers of pigs are kept at the dairy farms and fed mainly on whey. Yorkshire bacon is famed for its flavour.

According to the latest landowners' *Return*, 1873, the East Riding was divided among 19,576 proprietors, possessing 710,733 acres at an annual value of £2,032,195, or about £2, 17s. 2d. per acre. There were 15,012 who owned less than one acre each, and there were 4049 acres of common lands. The following possessed over 10,000 acres each:—Sir Tatton Sykes 34,010 acres, Lord Londesborough 33,006, Sir G. Cholmley 20,503, Lord Wenlock 19,453, Lord Hotham 18,683, W. H. H. Broadley 14,208, William F. Bethel 13,396, Lord Leconfield 13,247, Lord Middleton 12,295, Crown Property 12,230, Viscountess Downe 11,595, and T. A. C. Constable 10,981. The North Riding was divided among 16,313 proprietors, possessing 1,278,884 acres at an annual value of £1,841,945, or about £1, 8s. 9d. per acre. The following owned over 10,000 acres each:—John Bowes 48,887, Lord Feversham 39,312, marquis of Ailesbury 15,370, Lord Bolton 15,419, Viscount Downe 15,271, earl of Carlisle 13,030, Sir G. O. Wombwell 11,912, Lord Londesborough 11,884, Mrs D. Harcourt 11,442, Mrs J. T. D. Hutton 10,902. There were 10,115 proprietors who possessed less than one acre, and the area of common land was 247,409 acres. The West Riding was divided among 76,913 proprietors, possessing 1,632,259 acres at an annual value of £8,199,840, or about £5, 0s. 5½d. per acre, the large rental being due to the increased rent of land in towns. There were 59,496 proprietors who owned less than one acre each, and the estimated area of common land was 99,912 acres. The following proprietors owned over 10,000 acres each:—Charles Towneley 23,153, earl of Harewood 20,330, duke of Devonshire 19,333, Earl Fitzwilliam 19,165, Andrew Montagu 17,591, duke of Norfolk 15,270, George Lane Fox 15,018, earl of Dartmouth 14,723, Walter Morrison 14,118, Sir H. J. Tufton 12,202, T. W. S. Stanhope 11,357, Ayscough Fawkes 11,205, James Farrer 11,088, marquis of Ripon 10,908, Sir H. D. Ingilby 10,610, and duke of Leeds 10,034.

Communication.

Communication.—The county, especially in the manufacturing districts, is intersected with railways in all directions, the principal companies being the North Eastern, the Manchester, Sheffield, and Lincoln, the Lancashire and Yorkshire, the Midland, and the Great Northern. A considerable amount of traffic, especially in coal, is carried on by means of the canals.

Manufactures and trade.

Manufactures and Trade.—For many years an extensive district in the West Riding has been famed for its woollen and worsted manufactures. The early development of the industry was due partly to the abundance of water power supplied by the numerous streams in the valleys by which the district is indented; and in recent times the happy accident of the proximity of coal and iron has enabled the industry to keep pace with modern requirements. The West Riding is now the chief seat of the woollen manufacture in the United Kingdom, and has almost a monopoly in the manufacture of worsted cloths. In this industry nearly all the important towns in the Riding are engaged, Leeds having for its specialty almost every variety of woollen and worsted cloth, Bradford yarns and mixed worsted goods, Dewsbury, Batley, and the neighbouring districts shoddy, Huddersfield both plain goods and fancy trouserings and coatings, and Halifax, to the neighbourhood of which the cotton industry of Lancashire has also penetrated, worsted and carpets. Next to the woollen industry comes the manufacture of iron and steel machinery and implements of every variety, Leeds being one of the principal seats of all kinds of mechanical engineering, and Sheffield of iron work and cutlery. For the minor manufactures in the district, and for more specific details, reference must be made to the separate articles on the different towns. Until comparatively recently agriculture was the chief calling of the North Riding; but the discovery of iron ore in the Cleveland region has led to the formation of another great manufacturing centre, mainly devoted to the production of pig-iron, the manufacturing of steel by the basic process, and iron shipbuilding. The industrial activity of the East Riding is mostly centred in Hull, the chief port of the county, although the Lancashire ports must be regarded as the principal ports for the trade, especially of the West Riding. In the North Riding Middlesbrough is rising into importance as a shipping port, and Whitby, though not progressing as a port, has a considerable coasting trade. The fishing industry, which is of minor importance, is carried on at Hull, Filey, Whitby, and Scarborough, and a considerable number of villages.

Watering-places and spas.

Scarborough is by far the most attractive and thriving watering-place north of the Thames; and a number of others, such as Whitby, Bridlington, Filey, and Saltburn, are rising yearly in repute. Among others, chiefly of local celebrity, are Redcar, Hornsea, and Withernsea. There are a considerable number of inland spas frequented to some extent by persons from other parts of the county, but the only one of wide reputation is Harrogate.

Administration and population.

Administration and Population.—Yorkshire has from an early period been divided into three ridings, each of which has a lord lieutenant. The East Riding has a separate court of quarter sessions and a commission of the peace. The city of York within the municipal limits constitutes a separate division of the county. The municipal city and the ainsty are for parliamentary purposes included in the North Riding, for registration purposes in the East Riding, and for all other purposes in the West Riding. The parliamentary city of York, which formerly extended beyond the municipal limits, is partly in the North and partly in the East Riding. The following table gives the population of the county and of the three ridings in 1801, 1821, 1871, and 1881:—

	1801	1821	1871	1881
East Riding..........	139,433	190,449	268,466	315,460
North Riding (with the municipal city of York)..............	155,506	183,381	346,518	395,790
West Riding..........	363,953	799,357	1,821,371	2,175,314
Yorkshire............	658,892	1,173,187	2,436,355	2,886,564

The population has more than quadrupled since 1801, the increase having been much the greatest in the West Riding. Though in area much the largest, Yorkshire is in population third among English counties, being exceeded in this respect both by Lancashire and Middlesex. The number of males in 1881 was 1,420,001 and of females 1,466,563. The number of persons to an acre in the county was 0·74—East Riding 0·42, North Riding (not including the city of York) 0·25, and West Riding 1·23. The East Riding comprises 6 wapentakes and the municipal boroughs of Beverley (pop. 11,425), Kingston-upon-Hull (154,240), and Hedon (966). It is divided into 12 petty and special sessional divisions. The borough of Kingston-upon-Hull has a separate court of quarter sessions and a commission of the peace, and the borough of Beverley has a commission of the peace. The riding contains 352 civil parishes with part of one other, viz., Filey, which extends into the North Riding. It is entirely in the diocese of York. The North Riding comprises 11 wapentakes, the liberties of East and West Langbaurgh and of Whitby Strand, and the municipal boroughs of Middlesbrough (55,934), Richmond (4502), and Scarborough (30,504). It is divided into 19 petty and special sessional divisions. The boroughs of Richmond and Scarborough have separate courts of quarter sessions and commissions of the peace, and the borough of Middlesbrough has a commission of the peace. The riding contains 554 civil parishes and parts of five others. It is almost entirely in the diocese of York and Ripon. The West Riding comprises 9 wapentakes, the city of Ripon (7390), and the municipal boroughs of Barnsley (29,790), Batley (27,505), Bradford (183,032), Dewsbury (29,637), Doncaster (21,139), Halifax (73,630), Harrogate (9482), Huddersfield (81,841), Leeds (309,119), Pontefract (8798), Rotherham (34,782), Sheffield (284,508), Wakefield (30,854), and Keighley (12,085). The riding is divided into 25 petty and special sessional divisions. The city of York, the boroughs of Bradford, Doncaster, Leeds, Pontefract, and Sheffield, and the liberty of Ripon (including the city) have separate courts of quarter sessions and commissions of the peace, and the boroughs of Batley, Dewsbury, Halifax, Huddersfield, and Wakefield have commissions of the peace. The liberty and the borough of Ripon are not included in the West Riding for the purposes of the county rate, but are rated separately. The riding contains 724 civil parishes and parts of six others. It is mostly in the dioceses of York, Ripon, and Manchester. For parliamentary purposes the East Riding is formed into three divisions,—Buckrose, Holderness, and Howdenshire, each returning one member. It also includes the parliamentary borough of Kingston-upon-Hull, returning three members, with part of the borough of York city, which returns two members. The North Riding for parliamentary purposes is formed into four divisions,—Cleveland, Richmond, Thirsk, and Whitby, each returning one member. It also includes the boroughs of Middlesbrough and Scarborough, each returning one member, with portions of the boroughs of Stockton and York city. The West Riding for parliamentary purposes is formed into three divisions, which are again subdivided into districts each returning one member,—the north division into five districts, the south into eight, and the east into six. The riding also includes the following parliamentary boroughs:—Bradford returning three members, Dewsbury one, Halifax two, Huddersfield one, Leeds five, Pontefract one, Sheffield five, and Wakefield one.

History

History and Antiquities.—Traces of the old British inhabitants are numerous in the Wolds of the East Riding and the moors of the North Riding. Remains of the circular pit-dwellings of ancient Brigantian villages still exist at Egton Grange, Hole Pits, Killing Pits, Danby, and Roseberry Topping. A large number of implements, of both flint and bronze, have been discovered in the barrows on the Wolds and moors, and in the caves of the limestone district. Circles and other stone monuments are not uncommon, the most remarkable being the monolith, 29 feet in height, at Rudston, and the group of monoliths called the Devil's Arrows at Boroughbridge, 16½, 21½, and 22½ feet in height respectively. On the hill-sides there are numerous ancient earthworks and dykes, such as the fortification on Flamborough Head, incorrectly called the Danes' dyke. Yorkshire was included in the territory of the Brigantes at the time of its invasion by the Romans in 51; it did not, however, make formal submission till 79. It afterwards formed part of the district of *Maxima Cæsariensis*, of which the capital was *Eboracum* (York). The central districts of Yorkshire seem to have been densely peopled by the Romans. Watling Street entered the county near Bawtry, crossed the Don at *Danum* (Doncaster), the Aire at *Legeolium* (Castleford), and the Wharfe at *Calcaria* (Tadcaster). Thence it proceeded by *Eboracum* (York), *Isurium* (Aldborough), and *Cataractonium* (Catterick Bridge) to *Ad Tisam* (Pierce Bridge), where it crossed the Tees. Another road passed eastwards from York to Malton, and various branches traversed the county in different directions. A great variety of Roman remains have been discovered and traces of Roman camps are numerous, such as *Cataractonium*, the outlines of the station at Old Malton, the ancient wall with the multangular tower at York, and the remains of *Isurium*. After the departure of the Romans Yorkshire was overrun by the Picts. Subsequently it formed the Anglo-Saxon kingdom of Deira to the south of Bernicia (see vol. viii. p. 270). The two were included in Northumbria, which seems to have been under the rule sometimes of a single prince and sometimes of two separate princes in Bernicia and Deira, the northern boundary of the latter kingdom being probably the Tees and the southern always the Humber (see NORTHUMBERLAND, vol. xvii. p. 568 *sq.*, where the early history of the district, including a notice of the Danish invasions, is given). After the Conquest Yorkshire was divided among several Norman earls—including Alan of Brittany, who held Richmond Castle, Ilbert de Lacy, and William de Percy. The district was at this period frequently invaded by the Scots. In 1138 David of Scotland laid waste the country to the gates of York; but he was completely defeated by the English on 22d August of that year in the battle of the Standard at Northallerton. In 1312 Thomas Plantagenet, earl of Lancaster, raised an insurrection in Yorkshire against Gaveston, the favourite of Edward II., whom he captured in Scarborough and beheaded at Warwick on 19th June. The earl again in 1322 headed a party against the Despensers, but on 16th March was defeated and captured at Boroughbridge, and on 22d was beheaded at Pontefract. During the Wars of the Roses the county was the scene of frequent conflicts, including the battle of Wakefield (31st December 1460), in which Richard, duke of York, was defeated by Queen Margaret and slain, and the battle of Towton (29th March 1461), in which Edward IV. defeated Henry VI. In 1536 the county was the scene of the insurrection under Robert Aske, known as the "Pilgrimage of Grace," caused by the dissolution of the monasteries. In 1569 a rising took place in Yorkshire under the earls of Westmorland and Northumberland in behalf of Mary Queen of Scots. During the Civil War the county was chiefly Royalist, although some of the most famous Parliamentary officers were Yorkshiremen, the more noted being Fairfax and Lambert. Bradford, Hull, Scarborough, Pontefract, and York sustained long sieges; and on 2d July 1644 the great and decisive battle of the war occurred at Marston Moor. The annals of the county are destitute of further incidents of special historic importance.

Ancient castles.

Of ancient strongholds or castles Yorkshire has still many interesting examples in a more or less complete condition, including Barden Tower, built in the reign of Henry VII. by Henry Clifford, "the shepherd lord," which has been in ruins since 1774; Bolton Castle, pronounced by Leland "the fairest in Richmondshire," a square building with towers at the corners, erected in the reign of Richard II. by Richard Scrope, chancellor of England, occupied by Queen Mary while under the charge of Lord Scrope, besieged during the Civil War, and rendered untenable in 1647; the square tower or keep of Bowes Castle, supposed to have been built by Alan Niger, first earl of Richmond; the gateway tower (erected in the reign of Henry VI.) of Cawood Castle, said to have been originally built by King Athelstan in 920; the keep and various portions of the walls of the extensive fortress of Conisbrough, of uncertain origin, but probably dating from Saxon times; the remains of Danby Castle, said to have been built shortly after the Conquest by Robert de Bruce; Harewood, of great extent, originally founded soon after the Conquest, but now containing no portions earlier than the reign of Edward III.; the keep, in the Early English style, and other remains of Helmsley, built in the 12th century by Robert de Roos surnamed Fursan; detached portions, including the principal tower, of Knaresborough, probably dating originally from Norman times; the picturesque remains of the quadrangular fortress of Middleham, built soon after the Conquest by Robert FitzRanulph, afterwards possessed by the Nevilles, and rendered untenable by order of Parliament in 1647; the ruins of the ancient stronghold of Mulgrave, said to have been originally founded two centuries before the Conquest by a Saxon giant named Wade or Wada, dismantled after the Civil War; the extensive remains—including Rosamond's Tower, associated with the misfortunes of Fair Rosamond, the mistress of Henry II.—of Pickering Castle, of unknown date, dismantled after the Civil War; the ruins of Pontefract, formerly one of the most important fortresses of the kingdom, built by Ilbert de Lacy about 1080; a few remains of Ravensworth Castle, dating from before the Conquest; the keep and other remains of the great Norman fortress of Richmond, founded about 1070 by Alan Rufus of Brittany; the tower of Ripley, built in 1555 by Sir William Ingilby, included in the modern mansion; slight remains of the fortress of Sandal, erected in 1320 by John, eighth earl of Warren; the great tower, in the Roman style, and other remains of the extensive fortress of Scarborough, founded by William le Gros in 1136; the detached ruins of Sheriff Hutton, founded by Bertram de Bulmer in the reign of Stephen; slight remains of the ancient Skelton Castle; Skipton Castle, of various dates, but originally Norman; Slingsby Castle, originally built probably soon after the Conquest; the ruins of Spofforth, originally erected by Henry de Percy in 1309; the foundations of the keep and some fragments of the walls of Tickhill, built or enlarged by Roger de Busli in the 11th century; the remains of Whorlton, dating from the time of Richard II.; and one side of the great quadrangular castle of Wressell, built by Thomas Percy, earl of Worcester, in the reign of Richard II.

Ecclesiastical structures.

At the time of the dissolution of the monasteries Yorkshire possessed 28 abbeys, 26 priories, 23 nunneries, 30 friaries, 13 cells, 4 commanderies of Knights Hospitallers, and 4 preceptories of the Knights Templars. The principal monastic ruins still existing are St Mary's, York (see York); Bolton Priory, generally called Bolton Abbey, one of the most romantically situated ruins in the kingdom, originally founded at Embsay, two miles distant, by William de Meschines for Augustinian canons, removed to its present situation by his daughter Alice over against the spot where her only son perished in the Wharfe; the church and other ruins in the Early English style of Byland Abbey, founded for Cistercian monks in the 12th century; the picturesque ruins of Easby near Richmond, containing interesting examples of Norman and Early English, founded in 1152 for Præmonstratensians by Ronaldus, constable of Richmond Castle; Egglestone on the Tees, founded in the 12th century for Præmonstratensians; Fountains Abbey, one of the finest and most complete among the monastic ruins of the kingdom, exhibiting fine specimens of various styles of architecture from Norman to Perpendicular, founded in 1132 for certain monks of the Benedictine abbey of St Mary's, York, who had adopted the Cistercian rule; the eastern end of the church of Guisbrough Priory in the Pointed style, founded in 1119 by Robert de Bruce, the burial-place of many illustrious nobles; the picturesque ruins of Jervaulx, exhibiting examples of Norman and Early English, founded in 1156 for Cistercian monks by Conan, fifth earl of Richmond; the gateway and other remains of Kirkham, founded in 1121 by Walter l'Espec; the beautiful ruins of Kirkstall, exhibiting remarkably fine examples of Norman, founded in 1152 by Henry de Lacy for Cistercian monks from Fountains Abbey; the church, refectory, and other remains, in the Early English style with some traces of Norman, of Rievaulx Abbey, founded in 1131 by Walter l'Espec. There are other monastic remains of less importance at Bridlington, Coverham, Marrick, Meaux, Monk Bretton, Mount Grace, Old Malton, Roche, Rosedale, Sawley, Selby, Watton, and Whitby. In respect of church architecture Yorkshire excels any other county in the kingdom for variety of style, and the size and importance of many of the buildings. Space forbids entrance into minute details; but it may be mentioned here that, in addition to the cathedral churches of York, Ripon, and Beverley, there are several other churches on a very large scale, including St Mary's, Beverley, chiefly Perpendicular, very elaborate in style, originally built by Archbishop Thurstan in the 12th century; the parish church of Bradford, a very fine example of Decorated; the priory church of Bridlington, containing fine examples of Norman, Early English, and Perpendicular; Halifax parish church, chiefly of the 15th century; St Augustine's church, Hedon, Early English, Decorated, and Perpendicular, with some transition Norman; Howden, one of the finest in Yorkshire, chiefly 13th century with later additions; Holy Trinity, Hull, one of the largest parish churches in England, of the 13th century, chiefly Early English and Perpendicular; St Mary's, Masham, dating from Saxon times and having a fine Norman tower; St Patrick's, Patrington, in the Decorated style, with a remarkably graceful spire, 189 feet in height; All Saints, Rotherham, a beautiful cruciform building, described by Rickman as "one of the finest Perpendicular churches of the north"; the abbey church, Selby, containing fine specimens of Norman, Early English, and Decorated; the parish church, Sheffield, chiefly Perpendicular; St Mary's, Thirsk, said to have been built out of the ruins of the old castle, chiefly Perpendicular; and Wakefield parish church, chiefly of the latter part of the 15th century, with a spire 250 feet in height, rebuilt in 1860-61.

The bibliography of Yorkshire is very extensive. For histories of the several towns and districts reference may be made to Anderson's *English Topography*. The chief works relating to Yorkshire as a whole are Leland's *Itinerary*; Allen's *History of Yorkshire*, 3 vols., 1828-31; Baines's *Yorkshire Past and Present*, 4 vols., 1871-77; and Smith's *Old Yorkshire*, 5 vols., 1881-84. Among numerous works on the geology, reference may be made to Phillips's *Geology of the Yorkshire Coast*, 3d ed., 1875; Davis and Lees, *West Yorkshire*, 1878; Bird's *Sketch of the Geology of Yorkshire*, 1881; and Simpson's *Fossils of Yorkshire*, 1884. In the publications of the Surtees Society there are many volumes of genealogical or antiquarian interest relating to the county, and in *Journ. Yorks. Arch. Soc.* many valuable topographical and historical papers. See also Lefroy's *Ruined Abbeys of Yorks.*, 1883, and Bulmer's *Arch. Studies in Yorks.*, 1887. (T. F. H.)

YORK, a cathedral city and archbishop's see, the county town of Yorkshire, a county in itself, and a municipal and parliamentary borough, is situated on the river Ouse at its junction with the Foss, and on the main joint line of the North Eastern and Great Northern Railways, 188 miles north of London. The surrounding country is flat, but the plain of York is one of the richest and most fertile districts in England. While the special feature of York is the cathedral, the city generally has an antique appearance, with narrow picturesque streets, the remains of ancient walls, and many churches and other buildings of considerable architectural interest. The Ouse is crossed by three bridges for general traffic,—the Ouse bridge, of three elliptical arches, erected 1810-20 where a bridge had stood from time immemorial; Lendal bridge, opened in 1863, a handsome structure of iron, consisting of a single arch 175 feet in span; and Skeldergate bridge, 1880, constructed of iron resting on stone piers. The Foss is crossed by five bridges. Of the old Roman city there are some remains of the fortifications, including ten sides of a thirteen-sided building called the multangular tower, occupying one of the four angles of the ancient wall, with the lower part of the wall leading from this tower to Bootham Bar, the upper part of the wall being of later origin. The walls of the English city, enclosing a much wider area, though they have undergone reconstruction at various periods and were much battered during the siege of the city in 1644, are in remarkably good preservation, especially the portion to the west of the Ouse. They contain Norman and Early English architecture, but the bulk of the walls are in the Decorated style. There are four principal gates or "bars"—Micklegate Bar, at the southern entrance to the city, where the heads of traitors were formerly exposed, consisting of a square tower built over a circular arch, probably Norman, with embattled turrets at the angles; Bootham Bar, the main entrance from the north, having also a Norman arch; Monk Bar, on the Scarborough road, the most imposing of the four, probably belonging to the 14th century, formerly called Goodramgate, which after the Restoration was changed to Monk Bar in honour of General Monk; and Walmgate Bar, belonging to the time of Edward I. and retaining the barbican rebuilt in 1648. Of the Norman fortress built by William the Conqueror in 1068 some portions were probably incorporated in Clifford's Tower, which was partly destroyed by fire in

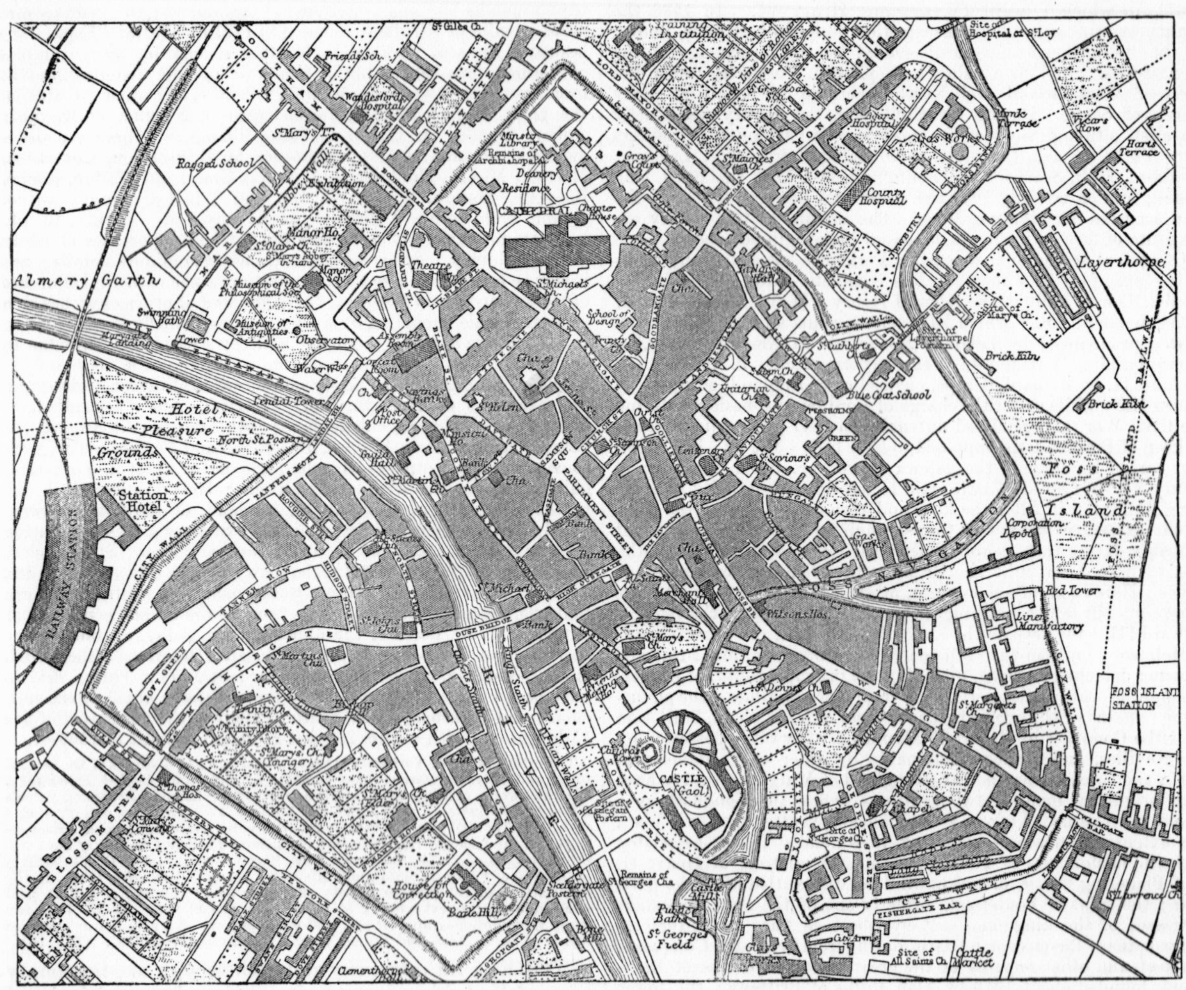

Plan of York.

1684. It formed the keep or donjon of the later fortress, which was dismantled at the Civil War and converted into a prison. The debtors' prison, erected in 1708, and the North and East Riding assize courts, erected in 1777, are also included within the castle wall, which was constructed in 1836.

The cathedral of St Peter, if surpassed by some other English cathedrals in certain special features, is as a whole the most striking and imposing specimen of ecclesiastical architecture in England. It is in the form of a Latin cross, consisting of nave with aisles, transepts, choir with aisles, a central tower, and two western towers. The extreme external length is 524 feet 6 inches, the breadth across the transepts 250 feet, the height of the central tower 213 feet, and the height of the western towers 202 feet. The material is magnesian limestone. The cathedral occupies the site of the wooden church in which King Edwin was baptized by Paulinus on Easter Day 627. After his baptism Edwin, according to Bede, began to construct "a large and more noble basilica of stone," but it was partly destroyed during the troubles which followed his death, and was repaired by Archbishop Wilfrid. The building suffered from fire in 741, and, after it had been repaired by Archbishop Albert, was described by Alcuin as "a most magnificent basilica." At the time of the Norman invasion the Saxon cathedral, along with the library of Archbishop Egbert, perished in the fire by which the greater part of the city was destroyed, the only relic of it now remaining being the central wall of the crypt. It was reconstructed by Archbishop Thomas of Bayeux (1070-1100); but of this building few portions now remain. The apsidal choir and crypt were reconstructed by Archbishop Roger (1154-91), the south transept by Archbishop Walter de Gray (1215-55), and the north transept and central tower by John Romanus, treasurer of the cathedral (1228-56). With the exception of the crypt, the transepts are the oldest portions of the building now remaining. They represent the Early English style at its best, and the view across the great transept is unsurpassed for architectural effect. The south transept is the richest and most elaborate in its details, one of its principal features being the magnificent rose window; and the north transept contains a series of beautiful lancet windows called the Five Sisters. The foundation of the new nave was laid by Archbishop Romanus (1285-96), son of the treasurer, the building of it being completed by Archbishop Melton about 1345. The chapter-house was built during the same period. The west front, consisting of a centre and two divisions corresponding with the nave and aisles, is one of the finest features of the whole building, and has been described as "more architecturally perfect as a composition and in its details than that of any other English cathedral," the great window above the door being, in the words of Mr Britton, "an unrivalled specimen of the leafy tracery that marks the style of the middle of the 14th century." In 1361 Archbishop Thoresby (1352-73) began the lady chapel and presbytery, both in the Early Perpendicular style. The rebuilding of the choir, begun about the same period, was not completed till about 1400. It is a very fine specimen of Late Perpendicular, the great east window being one of the finest in the world. With the rebuilding of the choir the whole of the ancient Norman edifice was removed, the only Norman architecture now remaining being the eastern portion of the crypt of the second period, built by Archbishop Roger (1154-91). To correspond with later alterations, the central tower was re-cased and changed into a Perpendicular lantern tower, the work being completed in 1444. The south-west tower was begun in 1432 during the treasurership of John de Bermingham, and the north-west tower in 1470. With the erection of this tower the church was completed as it now stands, and on 3d February 1472 it was re-consecrated by Archbishop Neville. On 2d February 1829 the woodwork of the choir was set on fire by Jonathan Martin, a madman. On 2d May 1840 a fire broke out in the south-west tower, reducing it to a mere shell. The cathedral within recent years has undergone extensive restoration.

Next to the cathedral the most interesting building in York is St Mary's Abbey, situated in Museum Gardens, founded for Benedictines by Alan, earl of Richmond, and latterly one of the most powerful ecclesiastical establishments in England, its head having the rank of a mitred abbot with a seat in parliament. The principal remains of the abbey are the north wall and the ruins of the church, in the Early English and Decorated style, and the principal gateway with a Norman arch. The hospitium, a curious building of wood, is now used as a museum of antiquities, and contains a fine collection of Roman remains discovered in the vicinity. A considerable portion of the abbey was employed for the erection of the king's manor, a palace for the lord president of the north, now occupied as a school for the blind. In the gardens is also situated the ambulatory of St Leonard's hospital, founded by King Athelstan and rebuilt by Stephen. Besides the cathedral, York possesses a large number of churches of special architectural interest, including All Saints, North Street, Decorated and Perpendicular, with a spire 120 feet in height; Christ Church, with south door in the Decorated style, supposed to occupy the site of the old Roman palace; Holy Trinity in Goodramgate, Decorated and Perpendicular with Perpendicular tower; Holy Trinity, Micklegate, in a dilapidated condition, with Roman masonry in its foundation walls; St Denis, Walmgate, with rich Norman doorway and Norman tower; St Helen's, St Helen's Square, chiefly Decorated; St John's, North Street, chiefly Perpendicular; St Lawrence, without the bar of Walmgate, with rich Norman doorway; St Margaret's, Walmgate, celebrated for its curiously sculptured Norman porch and doorway; St Mary the Elder, Bishophill, Early English and Decorated, with brick tower, rebuilt in 1659; St Mary the Younger, Bishophill, with a square tower in the Saxon style, rebuilt probably in the 13th century; St Mary, Castlegate, with Perpendicular tower and spire 154 feet in height; St Michael-le-Belfry, founded in 1066, but rebuilt in 1538 in the Late Perpendicular style; and St Olave, Marygate, Perpendicular, said to have been founded by Siward, earl of Northumberland. Among the principal secular buildings are the guild hall, with a fine old room in the Perpendicular style erected in 1446, and containing a number of stained-glass windows; the mansion-house, built in 1725 from designs by the earl of Burlington; the assembly rooms, erected in 1730, also from designs by the earl of Burlington, with the concert-room adjoining, built in 1823; the corn exchange; the infantry barracks; the cattle market; the theatre, founded by Tate Wilkinson in 1765, and lately re-faced in the Gothic style by the corporation, who own the property; the De Grey rooms for balls and concerts; the fine old merchant's hall; the merchant tailors' hall; and the masonic hall. The public institutions of a learned or educational character include the Yorkshire Philosophical Society, whose museum in the Grecian style was opened in February 1830; the subscription library, instituted 1784, and containing upwards of 20,000 volumes; the York institute of science and literature, established in 1827, and removed to the present premises in 1846; the Wilberforce school for the blind; the York fine art and industrial institution; and the Government school of art. The charities include the York county hospital, the union workhouse, the dispensary, Colton's hospital for 8 poor men, Harrison's hospital, Dorothy Wilson's hospital (founded in 1777) for 16 poor women, Sir Arthur Ingram's hospital (founded in 1640) for 10 poor widows, and the old maids' hospital for 10 poor spinsters. The principal schools are St Peter's cathedral grammar-school (originally endowed in 1557), Archbishop Holgate's grammar-school, the York and diocesan grammar-school, and the blue-coat school for boys (founded in 1705), with the associated grey-coat school for girls.

In modern times York has ceased to retain its commercial importance; but it possesses several iron foundries, railway engineering works, a large glass factory, breweries, flour-mills, tanneries, glove manufactories, and confectionery and other minor establishments. Within its municipal limits the city of York constitutes a separate division of the county of York; the municipal city and the ainsty are for parliamentary purposes included in the North Riding, for registration purposes in the East Riding, and for all other purposes in the West Riding. The parliamentary city of York, which formerly extended beyond the municipal limits, is partly in the North and partly in the East Riding. The corporation consists of a lord mayor, 12 aldermen, and 36 councillors. The city returns two members to parliament. In 1884 the boundaries of the city were extended to include the townships of Holgate and St Olave, and part of the townships of Clifton, Dringhouses, Fulford, Heworth, and Middlethorpe. The population of the municipal borough (area 1979 acres) was 43,796 in 1871 and 49,530 in 1881, and that of the parliamentary borough (area 2789 acres) 50,765 in 1871 and 60,343 in 1881. The new area is about 3553 acres, with a population estimated at over 70,000 in 1888.

York, the British name of which was Caer-Ebroc, was chosen by the Romans as an important depôt after the conquest of the Brigantes by Agricola in 79 and named *Eboracum*. Ultimately it became the military capital and centre of the Roman power in Britain. The original Roman city was rectangular in form, about 650 yards by 550, and built somewhat after the plan of ancient Rome on the east bank of the Ouse. In York the emperors sat in the prætorium, and a temple was erected there to Bellona. The first emperor to take up his residence in York was Hadrian, when he visited Britain in 120. Severus died at York in February 211, and his body is supposed to have been burnt at Severus's Hill, a short distance south of the city. Constantius Chlorus also died at York in July 306, and his son Constantine the Great was there inaugurated Roman emperor. Early in the 7th century the city, under the name of Eoforwic, became the capital of the Bretwaldas. Edwin after his conversion in 627 made it an archbishop's see. The province of York, of which Paulinus was the first bishop, formerly included a great part of Scotland, but is now confined to the ten northern dioceses of England. From the time of Archbishop Egbert (732-766) York became celebrated as a school of learning and under Alcuin was one of the most famous places of education in Europe. The city was one of the principal Danish settlements and seats of commerce, its population in 990 being estimated at 30,000. It was the capital of the Danish jarl; and Siward is stated to have died at York in 1055 and to have been buried in St Olave's church. After the death of Edward the Confessor York was captured by Harold Hardrada, who, however, was shortly afterwards defeated and slain at Stamford Bridge. It was captured by William I. in 1068 and to guard it he erected a tower; but it was re-taken and the whole Norman garrison put to death. In revenge for their slaughter William, on re-capturing the city after a siege of six months, devastated the country between York and Durham. In 1175 Henry II. held the first English parliament at York, when Malcolm of Scotland did homage for his kingdom. The city was frequently visited by subsequent monarchs, and was the scene of important conventions and parliaments. After the suppression of the rebellion known as the Pilgrimage of Grace in 1569, the Council of the North was established at York. The city was besieged during the Civil War by the Parliamentary troops, to whom it surrendered on 16th July 1644. York received its first charter of incorporation from Henry I.

See Drake's *Eboracum*, 1736; Sheahan and Whellan's *History of York*, 1855-56; Hargrove's *History of York*, 1818; Dixon's *Fasti Eboracenses*, 1863; Ornsby's *Diocesan History of York*, 1882; Raine's *Historians of the Church of York*, 1879-86; Davies's *Walks through York*, 1880; Twyford's *York and York Castle*, 1883; and Benson and Jefferson's *Picturesque York*, 1886. (T. F. H.)

YORK, a borough and the county seat of York county, Pennsylvania, United States, is situated upon Codorus Creek, a branch of the Susquehanna river, and upon three railway lines,—the Pennsylvania, the Northern Central, and the Peachbottom. The surrounding country is undulating and is devoted to agriculture. The city is regularly laid out, with streets running diagonally to the cardinal points. It contains some manufactories of agricultural implements, paper-mills, car-shops, &c. The population in 1880 was 13,940; in 1870 it was 11,003.

The settlement of York dates from 1741. For nearly a year (1777-78) it was the place of meeting of the Continental Congress. In 1787 York was incorporated as a borough.

YORK, House of. Richard, duke of York, who claimed the crown of England in opposition to Henry VI., though he never succeeded to the throne himself, was, nevertheless, the founder of a royal line. It may be said, indeed, that his claim, at the time it was advanced, was rightly barred by prescription, the House of Lancaster having then occupied the throne for three generations, and that it was really owing to the misgovernment of Margaret of Anjou and her favourites that it was advanced at all. Yet it was founded upon strict principles of lineal descent, and was certainly a strong one, if it could only be maintained that hereditary right did not suffer from interruption. For the duke was descended from Lionel, duke of Clarence, the third son of Edward III., while the House of Lancaster came of John of Gaunt, a younger brother of Lionel. The House of Lancaster, therefore, had been clearly in wrongful possession of the throne, and Richard, duke of York, claimed it as the true heir. One thing which might possibly have been considered an element of weakness in his claim was that it was derived through females,—an objection actually brought against it by Chief-Justice Fortescue. For Lionel, duke of Clarence, left only a daughter, Philippa, who married Edmund Mortimer, third earl of March; and the male line of the Mortimers also failed on the death of Edmund, the fifth earl, whose sister, and ultimately his sole heir, Anne, married Richard, earl of Cambridge, and became by him the duke of York's mother. But a succession through females could not reasonably have been objected to after Edward III.'s claim to the crown of France; and, apart from strict legality, the duke's claim was probably supported in the popular estimation by the fact that he was descended from Edward III. through his father no less than through his mother. For his father, Richard, earl of Cambridge, was the son of Edmund, duke of York, fifth son of Edward III.; and he himself was the direct lineal heir of this Edmund, just as much as he was of Lionel, duke of Clarence. His claim was also favoured by the accumulation of hereditary titles and estates. The earldom of Ulster, the old inheritance of the De Burghs, had descended to him from Lionel, duke of Clarence; the earldom of March came from the Mortimers, and the dukedom of York and the earldom of Cambridge from his paternal ancestry. And in addition to all this his own marriage with Cecily Neville, though she was but the youngest daughter of Ralph, first earl of Westmoreland, allied him to a powerful family in the north of England, to whose support both he and his son were greatly indebted.

The reasons why the claims of the line of Clarence had been so long forborne are not difficult to explain. Roger Mortimer, fourth earl of March, was actually designated by Richard II. as his successor; but he died the year before Richard was dethroned, and his son Edmund, the fifth earl, was but a child at Henry IV.'s usurpation. Henry took care to secure his person; but the claims of the family troubled the whole of his own and the beginning of his son's reign. It was an uncle of this Edmund who took part with Owen Glendower and the Percies; and for advocating the cause of Edmund Archbishop Scrope was put to death. And it was to put the crown on Edmund's head that his brother-in-law Richard, earl of Cambridge, conspired against Henry V. soon after his accession. But this was the last attempt made in favour of the family for a long time. The plot was detected, being revealed, it is said, by the earl of March himself, who does not appear to have given it any encouragement; the earl of Cambridge was beheaded. The popularity gained by Henry V. in his French campaigns secured the weak title of the House of Lancaster against further attack for forty years.

Richard, duke of York, seems to have taken warning by his father's fate; but, after seeking for many years to correct by other means the deplorable weakness of Henry VI.'s government, he first took up arms against the ill advisers who were his own personal enemies, and at length claimed the crown in parliament as his right. The Lords, or such of them as did not purposely stay away from the House, admitted that his claim was unimpeachable, but suggested as a compromise that Henry should retain the crown for life, and the duke and his heirs succeed after Henry's death. This was accepted by the duke and an Act to that effect received Henry's own assent. But the Act was repudiated by Margaret of Anjou and her followers, and the duke was slain at Wakefield fighting against them. In little more than two months, however, his son was proclaimed king at London by the title of Edward IV., and the bloody victory of Towton immediately after drove his enemies into exile and paved the way for his coronation.

We need not follow the vicissitudes of Edward's reign, of which a brief account will be found under Edward IV. (vol. vii. p. 684). After his recovery of the throne in 1471 he had little more to fear from the rivalry of the House of Lancaster. But the seeds of distrust had already been sown among the members of his own family, and in 1478 his brother Clarence was put to death—secretly indeed, within the Tower, but still by his authority and that of parliament—as a traitor. In 1483 Edward himself died; and his eldest son, Edward V., after a nominal reign of two months and a half, was put aside by his uncle, the duke of Gloucester, who became Richard III., and then caused him and his brother Richard, duke of York, to be murdered. But in little more than two years the usurper was defeated and slain at Bosworth by the earl of Richmond, who, being then proclaimed king as Henry VII., shortly afterwards fulfilled his pledge to marry the eldest daughter of Edward IV. and so unite the Houses of York and Lancaster.

Here the dynastic history of the House of York ends, for its claims were henceforth merged in those of the House of Tudor. But the family history has still much to do with the story of those reigns. For, although the union of the Roses ought to have extinguished controversy, a host of debatable questions and plausible pretexts for rebellion still remained. The legitimacy of Edward IV.'s children had been denied by Richard III. and his parliament, and, though the Act was denounced as scandalous, the slander might still be re-asserted. The duke of Clarence had left two children, a son and a daughter, and the attainder of their father could not be a greater bar to the crown than the attainder of Henry VII. himself. Seeing this, Henry had, immediately after his victory at Bosworth, secured the person of the son, who was named Edward, earl of Warwick, and kept him a prisoner in the Tower of London. Yet a formidable rebellion was raised in his behalf by means of Lambert Simnel, who, personating the prisoner in the Tower, professed to have escaped, went to Ireland, and, after being actually crowned as king in Christchurch cathedral, Dublin, came over with a host of Yorkist sympathizers into England, where he was defeated and taken prisoner at the battle of Stoke in 1487. The earl of Warwick lived for twelve years later in unjust confinement, and was ultimately put to death in 1499 because he had consented to a plot for his own liberation. As to his sister Margaret, she was married to one of Henry VII.'s Welsh followers, Sir Richard Pole (or Poole), and could give no trouble, so that, when Henry VIII. came to the throne, he thought it politic to treat her with kindness. He made her countess of Salisbury, reversed her brother's attainder, created her eldest son, Henry, Lord Montague, and caused one of her younger sons, Reginald, who displayed much taste for learning, to be very carefully educated. This, however, was the very thing which involved the whole family in ruin. For Henry looked to the learning and abilities of Reginald Pole to vindicate before Europe the justice of his divorce from Catherine of Aragon; and, when Pole not only was unable to comply but was conscientiously compelled to declare the very opposite, the king's indignation knew no bounds. Pole himself was safe, having secured some time before a retreat in Italy. He was even, for his great merits, made a cardinal by the pope. But this only made matters worse for his family at home: his brother, Lord Montague, and even his mother, the aged countess of Salisbury, were beheaded as traitors because they had continued to correspond with him. Cardinal Pole, however, came back to his own country with great honour in the reign of Queen Mary, and was made archbishop of Canterbury on the deprivation of Cranmer.

Two nephews of this cardinal, named Arthur and Edmund Poole, are the last members of the family whom it is needful here to mention. Early in the reign of Queen Elizabeth, being ardent young men, they conspired to go over to the duke of Guise in France, hoping to return with an army into Wales and so promote the claims of Mary Queen of Scots to the crown of England, for which service the elder, Arthur, expected to be restored to the dukedom of Clarence. The result was that they were condemned to death, but were only imprisoned for the rest of their days in the Tower, where they both carved inscriptions on the walls of their dungeon, which are still visible in the Beauchamp tower.

There was yet another branch of the House of York which might have given trouble to the Tudors, if they had not been very narrowly watched and ultimately extinguished. Of the sisters of Edward IV. the eldest, Anne, who married the duke of Exeter, left only one daughter by her second husband, Sir Thomas St Leger; but the second, Elizabeth, married John de la Pole, duke of Suffolk, and had several children of both sexes. Their eldest son was created earl of Lincoln during his father's life, and Richard III., after the death of his own son, had designated him as his successor. Disappointed of a kingdom by the success of Henry VII., he joined in Simnel's rebellion and was killed at the battle of Stoke. His brother Edmund thus became heir to his father; but in the reduced circumstances of the family he agreed to forbear the title of duke and take that of earl of Suffolk. He continued for some years in favour with the king, who made him a knight of the Garter; but, having killed a man in a passion, he fled abroad and was for some time entertained at the court of the emperor Maximilian and afterwards of Philip, king of Castile, when resident in the Low Countries, before his departure for Spain. But Philip, having been driven on the English coast when going to take possession of his Spanish kingdom, was entertained at Windsor by Henry VII., to whom he promised to deliver up the fugitive on condition that his life should be spared. Edmund de la Pole accordingly was brought back to his native country, to be lodged in the Tower for the remainder of his days. And, though the promise to spare his life was kept by the king who gave it, his son Henry VIII. caused him to be executed in 1513, when war broke out with France, apparently for treasonable correspondence with his brother Richard, then in the French service. After his death Richard de la Pole, remaining in exile, called himself earl of Suffolk, and was flattered occasionally by Francis I. with faint hopes of the crown of England. He was killed at the battle of Pavia in 1525. There were no more De la Poles who could advance even the most shadowy pretensions to disturb the Tudor dynasty.

GENEALOGICAL TABLE OF THE HOUSE OF YORK.

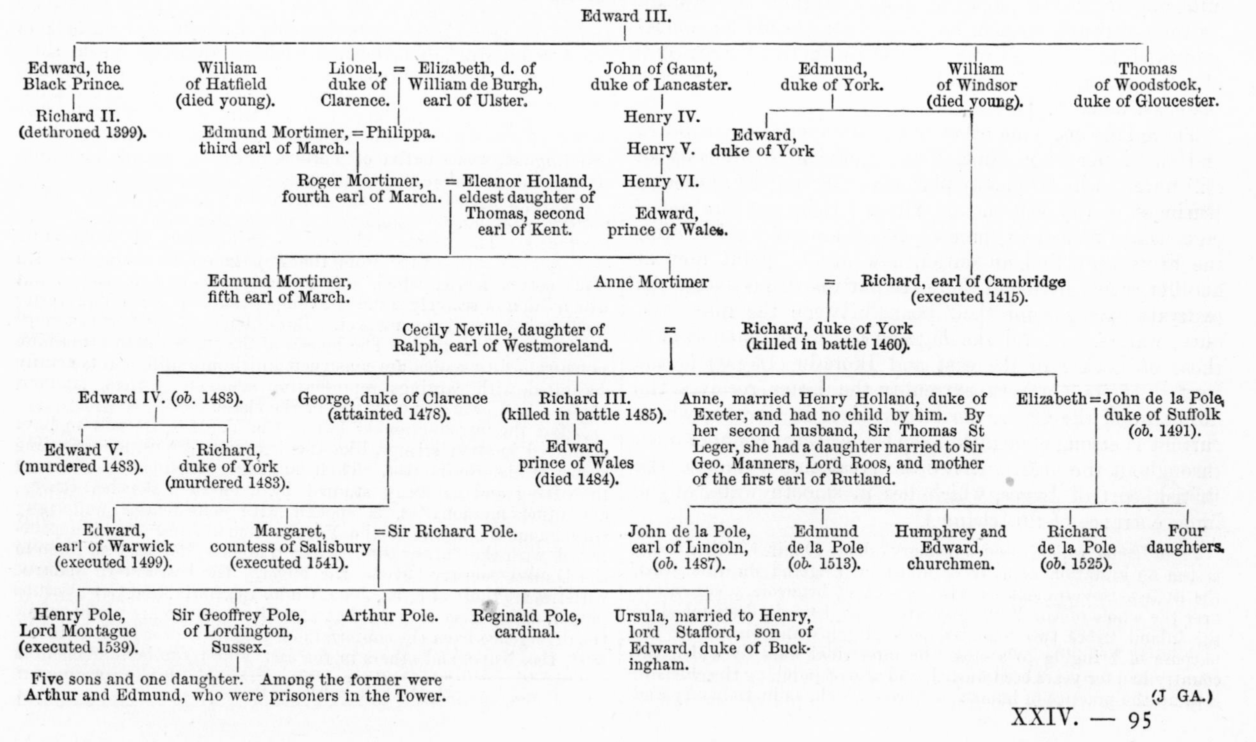

(J. GA.)

YORUBA, or YARIBA, a country of West Africa, occupying the eastern half of the Slave Coast region in 6°-9° N. lat. and 3°-7° E. long. Taken in its widest sense, so as to include the whole domain of the Yoruba race and speech, the Yoruba country stretches from the Bight of Benin northwards in the direction of the unexplored region of Borgu, and from the ill-defined eastern frontier of Dahomey to the Niger and its delta, which enclose it on the north-east, east, and south-east. Within these limits it covers an area of at least 40,000 square miles, with a population roughly estimated at over 2,000,000. But since 1820-21, when the old Yoruba empire was broken up by the Fulah invaders, the northern part, comprised between the Niger and the water-parting of the streams flowing north to that river and south to the Gulf of Guinea, has been included in the Fulah state of Gando. This water-parting, which constitutes the main physical feature of the land, is formed by the eastern continuation of the mountain range which in the Mahi country, north of Dahomey, appears to rise to over 6000 feet (Skertchley), but which in Yoruba gradually falls to considerably under 2000 feet. But towards the east, about the upper course of the river Oshun, the system again rises to what is described as "a very mountainous country" (Higgins and Smith). The city of Ilorin, near the northern slope of the divide, stands at an elevation of a little over 1300 feet, which is probably about the average height of the range in Yoruba. Gerhard Rohlfs, who in 1867 traversed the whole region from Rabba on the Niger to Lagos on the Gulf of Guinea, describes the section north of the water-parting as an open, gently sloping, and highly cultivated plain, to which the profusion of flowering plants gives the aspect of a vast garden. Here abundant crops of cereals, cotton, yams, ground-nuts, and kola nuts are raised. South of the divide the land, which is intersected by the nearly parallel courses of the rivers Ogun, Omi, Oshun, Oni, and Oluwa, falls in continuous undulations down to the coast, the open cultivated ground gradually giving place in the same direction to forest tracts, where the most characteristic tree is the oil-palm. Flowering trees and shrubs are here also plentiful, while the chief cultivated plants are corn, yams, plantains, bananas, tobacco, cotton, *okro*, ground-nuts, and *ata-ile* yielding a yellow dye (Higgins and Smith). As the sea is approached, the wooded tracts merge almost everywhere in a broad zone of dense primeval forest, completely separating the arable lands of the interior from the coast lagoons.

These lagoons, lying between the outer surf-beaten beach and the inner shore line, form a navigable highway of still waters, which in many places is several miles in extent. During the dry season the rivers discharging into the lagoons are unable to force a passage seawards; but after the rains they find an outlet, now at one point now at another, while here and there the natives themselves often excavate passages for their boats between the inner and outer waters. Of all the lagoons the most extensive are those of Leckie in the east and Ikoradu (Lagos) in the west. At its northern extremity the latter receives the discharge of the Ogun, the largest river in Yoruba, whose current is strong enough to keep the seaward channel open throughout the year. Hence the great importance of the British port of Lagos, which lies in smooth water at the inner entrance of this channel.

From Lagos, which, besides Badagry (about 40 miles farther west), is the only station actually occupied by England on this coast, the British Government exercises a sort of benevolent suzerainty over the whole of the Yoruba country. In 1886 it despatched to the inland tribes two commissioners (Higgins and Smith) for the purpose of bringing to a close the intertribal wars by which the country had for years been wasted, and also of inducing the chiefs to give up the practice of human sacrifices, which, as in Dahomey and Ashantee, though to a less degree, has always prevailed throughout this region. The commissioners obtained and embodied in their reports (*Blue Books*, 1887) a considerable amount of information regarding the present political and social condition of the Yoruba peoples. Since the dismemberment of their empire by the Fulahs (1820-21) the country has been divided into a number of semi-independent states, chieftaincies, or kingdoms, hanging loosely together, or rather constantly at war, and with a feeble sense of common nationality. The direct representative of the old Yoruba power is the "alafin" or king of the Yoruba country proper, occupying the northern and central parts of the whole region. Round about this central state are grouped the kingdoms of Ilorin, Ijesha, Ife, and Ondo in the east, Mahin and Jebu in the south, and Egba in the west. The alafin resides at Oyo, on a headstream of the Oshun, a place which as metropolis of the Yoruba nation has succeeded the older capitals, Bohu and Katunga, lying farther north and destroyed during the wars with the Fulahs. Oyo has an estimated population of 70,000 or 80,000; but it is greatly exceeded in size by several other places in Yoruba Land, where for mutual protection the inhabitants have mainly grouped themselves in large walled towns. Thus have sprung up the great cities of Abeokuta (200,000 ?), capital of Egba, on the Ogun, due north of Lagos; Ibádan (150,000), on a branch of the Omi, 30 miles south of Oyo; Ilorin (200,000 ?), one of the great markets of West Africa, capital of the Ilorin state; Ogbomosho (60,000), between Oyo and Ilorin; Ejigbo (40,000), Ilobu (60,000), and Ikirun (60,000), following successively nearly due east from Oyo; Ilesha (40,000), Oshogbo (60,000), and Ede (50,000), following each other due west in the Ilesha state; Ipetumodu (40,000), in Ife; Ode Ondo (60,000), capital of Ondo; Jebu Ode (60,000), Epe (40,000 ?), and Lagos (75,000), in the Jebu state and British protectorate. The constitution of some of these great urban groups is most remarkable. Thus Abeokuta, dating from 1825, owes its origin to the incessant inroads of the slave-hunters from Dahomey and Ibádan, which compelled the village populations scattered over the open country to take refuge in this rocky[1] stronghold against the common enemy. Here they constituted themselves a free confederacy of some sixty distinct tribal groups, each preserving the traditional customs, religious rites, systems of government, and even the very names, of their original villages. Yet this apparently incoherent aggregate has since held its ground successfully against the powerful armies often sent against the place both by the king of Dahomey from the west and by the people of Ibádan from the east. The different tribes are clearly distinguished by their several tattoo markings, usually some simple pattern of two or more parallel lines, disposed horizontally or vertically on both cheeks or other parts of the face.

Notwithstanding their political feuds, the Yoruba people are distinguished above all the surrounding races for their generally peaceful disposition, love of industry, friendliness, and hospitality towards strangers. Physically they resemble closely their Ewe and Dahomey neighbours, but are of somewhat lighter complexion, taller, and of less pronounced Negro features. Their superior intelligence is shown in their greater susceptibility to Christian and Mohammedan influences, their capacity for trade, and their remarkable progress in the industrial arts. Although the bulk of the nation is still pagan, Islam has made great advancement since the cessation of the Fulah wars, while Protestant and Roman Catholic missions have been at work for many years at Abeokuta, Oyo, Ibádan, and other large towns. Samuel Crowther, the first Negro bishop, who was distinguished as an explorer, geographer, and linguist, was a native of Yoruba, rescued by the English from slavery and educated at Sierra Leone.

Although agriculture is the chief industry, such useful arts as pottery, weaving, tanning, dyeing, and forging are practised in all the towns. The people make their own agricultural implements, extract a palatable wine from the *Raphia vinifera*, and weave a stout cotton fabric, which was formerly exported to Brazil, but which can now scarcely stand the competition of cheaper Manchester goods even in the home market. But as builders the Yorubas know no rivals in Negroland. The houses of the chiefs, often containing as many as fifty rooms, are constructed with rare skill, and tastefully decorated with carvings representing symbolic devices, fabulous animals, and even scenes of war or the chase.

Before the introduction of letters the Yorubas are said to have employed knotted strings, like the Peruvian quipus, for recording events of historic interest. Their language, which has been reduced to writing and carefully studied by Crowther, Bouché, Bowen, and other missionaries, is spoken with considerable uniformity throughout the whole of the Yoruba domain, and has even penetrated with the enterprising native traders as far east as Kano in the Haussa country beyond the Niger. The best-known dialectic varieties are those of Egba, Jebu, Ondo, Ife, Ilorin, and Oyo (Yoruba proper, called also Nago); but the discrepancies are slight, while the divergence from the conterminous linguistic groups (Ewe in the west, Ibo, Nupe, and others in the east) appears to be fundamental.

[1] Abeokuta = "under the rocks."

The most marked feature is a strong tendency towards monosyllabism, which has been produced by phonetic decay, and which, as in the Indo-Chinese family, has given rise to the principle of intonation, required to distinguish words originally different but reduced by corruption to the condition of homophones. Besides the tones, of which there are three,—high, low, and middle,—Yoruba has also developed a degree of vocalic harmony, in which, as in Ural-Altaic, the vowels of the affixes are assimilated to that of the root. Inflexion, as in Bantu, is effected chiefly by prefixes; and there is a remarkable power of word-formation by the fusion of several relational elements in a single compound term. The Bible and several eligious treatises have been translated into Yoruba, which as a medium of general intercourse in West Africa ranks in importance next to Haussa and Mandingan. (A. H. K.)

YOUGHAL, a seaport, borough, and market town in the county of Cork, Ireland, is situated on the west side of the estuary of the Blackwater, and on the Cork and Youghal branch of the Great Southern and Western Railway, 157 miles south-west of Dublin and 28 east of Cork. The fine collegiate church of St Mary, in the Later Decorated style, was originally erected in the 11th century, but rebuilt in the 13th, and since that time it has been frequently repaired. It contains a fine monument to the first earl of Cork. There are still a few fragments of the Dominican friary founded by Fitzgerald in 1269. Myrtle Grove, formerly the residence of Sir Water Raleigh, still remains. The harbour is safe and commodious, and there are several good quays. At the northern extremity of the harbour the river is crossed by a bridge resting on wooden piles. The principal exports are corn and other agricultural produce; the imports are coal, culm, timber, and slate. Coarse earthenware and bricks are manufactured. There is a salmon fishery in the Blackwater. Youghal is of some repute as a watering-place. The population of the town (area 345 acres) in 1871 was 6081, and in 1881 it was 5826.

Youghal is one of the most ancient towns in Ireland, and was incorporated by King John in 1209. The Franciscan monastery, founded at Youghal by Fitzgerald in 1224, was the earliest house of that order in Ireland. Sir Roger Mortimer landed at Youghal in 1317. The town was plundered by the earl of Desmond in 1579. In 1641 it was garrisoned and defended by the earl of Cork. In 1649 it declared for the Parliament. It sent two members to Parliament from 1374 till the union, after that only one down to 1885, when it was for parliamentary purposes merged in the East Division of the county.

YOUNG, Arthur (1741-1820), a writer on agriculture and social economy, the third son of Rev. Arthur Young, rector of Bedingfield, in Suffolk, was born on 7th September 1741. After having been for some time at a school at Lavenham, he was in 1758 placed in a mercantile house at Lynn, but showed no taste for commercial pursuits. He gave early evidence of literary inclinations by publishing, when only seventeen years old, a pamphlet *On the War in North America* and by beginning a periodical work, entitled *The Universal Museum*, which, however, was soon dropped by the advice of Dr Samuel Johnson.

After his father's death in 1759, his mother gave him the direction of Bradfield Hall; and in 1767 he undertook on his own account the management of a farm in Essex. Possessing no practical acquaintance with agriculture, but being active-minded and of an inquiring turn, he engaged in experiments of various kinds, and embodied the results of them in *A Course of Experimental Agriculture*, which appeared in 1770. Though Young's experiments were, in general, unsuccessful, he acquired in the process of making them a solid knowledge of agriculture; and, writing in a lively style, he was able to make his disquisitions on the subject interesting to the public. He had already commenced a series of journeys through different parts of England and Wales, and gave an account of his observations in books which appeared from 1768 to 1770—*A Six Weeks' Tour through the Southern Counties of England and Wales*, *A Six Months' Tour through the North of England*, and the *Farmer's Tour through the East of England*. He says that these books contained the only extant information relative to the rental, produce, and stock of England that was founded on actual examination. They were very favourably received at home and abroad, being translated into most Continental languages by 1792.

In 1768 he published the *Farmer's Letters to the People of England*, in 1771 the *Farmer's Calendar*, which has gone through a great number of editions, and in 1774 his *Political Arithmetic*, which was soon translated into several foreign languages. About this time Young acted as parliamentary reporter for the *Morning Post*. He made a tour in Ireland in 1776, and drew up the results, with copious observations on the state of that kingdom, in the years 1776-79, publishing a quarto volume on them in 1780. In 1784 he commenced the publication of the *Annals of Agriculture*, which was continued for 45 volumes; this work had contributions from many authors, among whom was George III., writing under the *nom de plume* of Ralph Robinson. Young's first visit to France was made in 1787. In May of that year he went to join Rochefoucauld-Liancourt at Paris, and accompanied by him and another gentleman travelled south to Bagnères de Luchon, making also an excursion into Spain. In November he was again in London; but in July 1788 he returned to France to study at leisure what he had before cursorily observed. He then saw the western part of the country, travelling alone on horseback, and came back a third time to see the east. The motive of these visits was "to make himself a master of their agriculture, that, if he found anything good and applicable to England, he might copy it." But he had an eye no less for political and social phenomena, and, traversing France in every direction just before and during the first movements of the Revolution, he has given us interesting and valuable notices of the condition of the people and the conduct of public affairs at that critical juncture. The *Travels in France* appeared in two vols. 4to in 1792. On his return home he was appointed secretary of the Board of Agriculture, then just formed under the presidency of Sir John Sinclair. In this capacity he gave the most valuable assistance in the collection and preparation of agricultural surveys of the English counties. In 1765 he had married a Miss Allen; but the union is said not to have been a very happy one, though he was of domestic habits and a most affectionate father. His sight failed, and he submitted to an operation for cataract, which proved unsuccessful. He suffered also in his last years from stone. He died in February 1820.

"To the works of Arthur Young," said Kirwan, "the world is more indebted for the diffusion of agricultural knowledge than to any writer who has yet appeared." To the same effect is the more recent testimony of Mr Hoskyns, who tells us that "the *Farmer's Letters* and *Calendar*, as well as the *Tours*, displayed the mind and pen of a master in his art, and went far towards laying the foundation of a practical agricultural literature." But it is as a social and political observer that Young is now best known to the reading public, and the books which have established his reputation in these departments—his *Tour in Ireland* and *Travels in France*—are still full of interest and instruction.

He found that Ireland had "flourished for the last thirty years to an uncommon degree, more," he believed, "than any country in Europe"; and he protested against the turbulence of the population and the outcries of the gentry at a time when Ireland had "experienced more favour from three sessions of a British parliament than from three centuries before." But he saw clearly and exposed unsparingly the causes which retarded the progress of the nation. He strongly urged the repeal of the penal laws which pressed upon the Catholics; he thought, however, that their disabilities should be removed, not by a single measure, but gradually. He protested against the harshness with which the labouring classes were treated by their superiors, and denounced the middlemen as being, not merely a useless class, but by their oppression and insolent manners the chief causes of popular discontent. He condemned the restrictions imposed by Great Britain on the commerce of Ireland, and also the perpetual interference of the Irish parliament with industry by prohibitions and bounties; of the latter he censured in specially strong terms the bounty on the inland carriage of corn to Dublin. He deplored the drain of rents and the neglect of their tenantry by absentee proprietors. The state of agriculture, generally low though improving, he found particularly unsatisfactory in Ulster, owing to the prevalence there of the linen manufacture, at that time carried on in the homes of the people, who were constantly divided between this occupation and the labours of the field. Emigration, he thought, was not sufficiently encouraged; indeed it scarcely existed at the period of his visit. It had previously been practised to a greater extent, and, besides relieving the population which remained, had been useful in removing restless spirits who would have been troublesome at home. He favoured a legislative union of Ireland with Great Britain, though he did not regard such a measure as absolutely necessary, many of its advantages being otherwise attainable, without incurring the risk of some possible inconveniences.

The soil of France he found in general superior to that of England, and its produce less. Agriculture was neither as well understood nor as much esteemed as in England. He severely censured the higher classes for their neglect of it. "Banishment (from court) alone will force the French nobility to execute what the English do for pleasure—reside upon and adorn their estates." Young saw the commencement of violence and outrage in the rural districts, being himself more than once in peril from popular suspicion. His sympathies began to take the side of the classes suffering from the excesses of the Revolution, and this change of attitude was distinctly shown by his publication in 1793 of a tract entitled *The Example of France a Warning to England.* Of the profounder significance of the French outbreak, as the commencement of a world-wide movement and a new era in social history, he seems to have had little idea, and thought the crisis would be sufficiently met by a constitutional adjustment in accordance with the English type. Yet he had much of the feeling which then inspired the Revolutionary actors, and, along with it, it may be added, something of the general sentimentalism of the period. Another enthusiasm he frequently exhibits—namely, for music, and especially for the Italian opera. But his master passion was the devotion to agriculture, which constantly showed itself. He strongly condemned the *métayer* system then widely prevalent in France, as "perpetuating poverty and excluding instruction," as, in fact, the curse and ruin of the country. Some of his phrases have been often quoted by the advocates of peasant proprietorship as favouring their view. "The magic of property turns sand to gold." "Give a man the secure possession of a bleak rock, and he will turn it into a garden; give him a nine years' lease of a garden, and he will convert it into a desert." But these sentences, in which the epigrammatic form exaggerates a truth, and which might seem to represent the possession of capital as of no importance in agriculture, must not be taken as conveying his approbation of the system of small properties in general. He approved it only when the subdivision was strictly limited, and even then with great reserves; and he remained to the end what J. S. Mill calls him, "the apostle of *la grande culture.*" The French acknowledge the valuable services which his criticisms and counsels rendered to their agriculture. The directory in 1801 ordered his writings on the art to be translated and published at Paris in 20 volumes under the title of *Le Cultivateur Anglais.* His *Travels in France* were translated in 1793-94 by Soulès; and a new version by M. Lesage, with an introduction by M. de Lavergne, appeared in 1856. An interesting review of the latter publication, under the title of *Arthur Young et la France de 1789*, will be found in M. Baudrillart's *Publicistes Modernes*, 2d ed., 1873. (J. K. I.)

YOUNG, Brigham (1801-1877), Mormon president, was born in Whitingham, Vermont, on 1st June 1801. His father was a farmer, and he himself learned the trade of a painter and glazier. He originally belonged to the Baptist Church, but joined the Mormons at Kirtland, Ohio, in 1832. In the same year he was ordained "elder;" in 1835 he was made an apostle; and in 1844 he succeeded Joseph Smith as president. He died at Salt Lake City, on 29th August 1877. See Mormons.

YOUNG, Edward (1681-1765), author of *Night Thoughts*, was born at Upham, near Winchester, in 1681. The minute facts of his life are to be found in the biography contributed to Johnson's *Lives of the Poets* by Herbert Croft. The son of the dean of Sarum, educated at Winchester and Oxford (New College and Corpus), Young obtained a law fellowship at All Souls in 1708, and proceeded to use it as a base of operations for gratifying his "ruling passion," the love of fame. There was at the time an open career for young men of talent who showed ability to recommend the policy and the persons of statesmen in their struggle for power, and Young, full of unbounded energy and eloquence, exuberant to eccentricity, joined in the race with a vigour that soon raised him to distinction. He seems to have been for a time in the family of the earl of Exeter as tutor; but the notorious marquis of Wharton (see Wharton) took a fancy to him, bribed him away from this post with liberal promises of maintenance and patronage, settled two annuities on him, and tried to get him into Parliament. Meantime Young began to publish and to dedicate, the poems and the dedications taken together (*The Last Day*, 1713, and *The Force of Religion*, 1714) showing the simple mixture of piety and worldliness that is one of the notes of his character. He essayed tragedy, writing at mid-day with closed shutters, by the light of a candle fixed in a human skull. *Busiris* was performed at Drury Lane in 1719, *The Revenge* in 1721. Far from gloomy in the company of Wharton and his friends, he had a decided bent for gloomy themes when alone, and a most copious and lofty—often extravagantly lofty—eloquence in the treatment of them; a paraphrase of the book of Job was one of his productions about this time. But he showed equal facility in dashing and effective satire: his first great literary success was made with the series of satires published between 1725 and 1728, and collected in the latter year under the title *Love of Fame, the Universal Passion.* These satires do not bear comparison with Pope's, to which they pointed the way, but they have a charm of exuberant vitality and power, an irregular abundance of wit and bold imagery, a frequent felicity of diction, that entitle them to Johnson's praise—"a very great performance"—and enable us to understand the impression produced by Young in conversation. One of the features in Young's character that disarms resentment of his fulsome adulation, and other extravagances and eccentricities, is his humorous Falstaffian consciousness of his own faults. "Who can write the true absurd like me?" he cries in one of his satires. He abundantly proved this in *Ocean: an Ode*, with which he hailed the accession of George II. Soon after, when nearly fifty, he took orders, was appointed a royal chaplain, and presented by his college to the rectory of Welwyn. He was disappointed in his desire of further promotion in the church; he had succeeded some time before in extracting a pension of £200 from Walpole, and this favour was cynically treated as a satisfaction in full of his claims on the Government. The *Night Thoughts* were published in separate "Nights" between 1742 and 1744. In the preface Young said that "the occasion of this poem was real, not fictitious, and that the facts mentioned did naturally force these moral reflexions on the mind of the writer." Croft has shown that this statement, though justifiable in the main, has to be taken with some qualifications, and that a common belief that Lorenzo was meant for the author's own son was undoubtedly a mistake. Still, it is true that Young's wife, her daughter, and her daughter's husband died in rapid succession, and the poem—a great work in spite of all its inequalities—was, like *In Memoriam*, the expression of a real sorrow and search for consolation. Young continued to write occasionally even after he had passed his eightieth year. His death took place on 12th April 1765.

Besides Croft's *Life*, there are interesting references to Young in Boswell's *Johnson* (see Birkbeck's ed., iv. 119, v. 270).

YOUNG, Thomas (1773-1829), one of the most remarkable figures alike in literature and science in the beginning of the 19th century in Great Britain. He belonged to a Quaker family of Milverton, Somerset, and was the youngest of ten children, having been born on 13th June 1773. His precocity, especially in the acquirement of languages, was remarkable, being little inferior to that of Sir W. Rowan Hamilton. But his thirst for knowledge was unlimited in its range. He was not content with languages, mathematics, and physical science: natural science, medicine, and even ancient philosophy were eagerly studied by him; and he was passionately devoted to athletic exercises. His medical studies were pursued successively in London, Edinburgh, Göttingen, and finally at Emmanuel College, Cambridge, where he took his doctor's degree. The death of a maternal uncle put him in a position of comfortable independence, and he did not heartily enter upon practice. He was secured in 1802 by the Royal Institution as a colleague of Davy and professor of natural philosophy. Here his special talents found ample occupation, and the chief result was the publication in 1807 of his celebrated *Course of Lectures on Natural Philosophy*, a work which is even now regarded as a valuable authority. Some years before he had made his remarkable discovery of the interference of light, and begun that wonderful series of researches which, as completed by Fresnel, secured the triumph of the undulatory theory. He was foreign secretary of the Royal Society for more than a quarter of a century; and it is curious to note that his reputation stood higher in foreign than in home scientific circles. He was one of the eight foreign associates of the Institute of France. He was one of the Commissioners of Weights and Measures, and secretary to the Board of Longitude, which in those days conducted the *Nautical Almanac*. A few years before his death he became interested in life assurance, with great benefit to the company whose scientific business he conducted. His death, on 10th May 1829, was probably hastened by the extraordinary amount and variety of the labours he undertook, and the self-sacrificing zeal with which he devoted himself to them.

His *Life*, by Dr Peacock, dean of Ely and a well-known mathematician, was published in 1855, along with a collection of his *Miscellaneous Works* and *Scientific Memoirs*. Young was a somewhat copious contributor to the 6th edition of this *Encyclopædia*, and some of the best of his smaller papers appeared in it for the first time. For a résumé of his contributions to the subject of hæmadynamics, see VASCULAR SYSTEM, p. 97 *supra*. Another of the multitudinous problems that claimed his attention was the decipherment of the Egyptian hieroglyphics, in which he had made some progress as early as 1814; see his *Account of some Recent Discoveries in Hieroglyphical Literature* (London, 1823).

YOUNGSTOWN, a city and the county seat of Mahoning county, Ohio, United States, is situated upon the Mahoning river, a tributary of the Ohio. The prevailing industries of the surrounding country are agriculture and coal-mining. Youngstown is directly connected with six railway lines. Owing to the contour of the site, the city is laid out very irregularly. The population in 1880 was 15,435 (8075 in 1870). The industries of Youngstown are connected chiefly with the manufacture of iron: there are several furnaces and rolling-mills, and manufactories of rails and stoves and of agricultural tools and machines.

Youngstown was laid out in 1797, being one of the first settlements made in that part of Ohio known as the Western Reserve. Since the rebellion it has grown with great rapidity.

YPRES (Flem. *Yperen*), a town of Belgium, capital of an arrondissement in the province of West Flanders, stands in a fertile plain on the Yperlee, 21 miles north-north-west of Lille. In the 14th century it is said to have contained 200,000 inhabitants; and it was long famous for its woollen and linen manufactures, though the once current derivation of the word "diaper" from the name of this town can no longer be maintained. Of the old fortifications some traces still remain, as well as a few picturesque dwelling-houses of the 14th and 15th centuries. The fine Gothic cloth hall (1201-1342), with a façade 462 feet in length, is pierced by two rows of pointed windows; there are two corner turrets; and in the centre rises a massive square clock tower. The forty-four statues of counts of Flanders and their consorts which formerly adorned it were restored in 1860. The town-hall (1730) contains some interesting frescos and sculptures of modern date. The finest parts of the Gothic cathedral of St Martin (1221-70) are the choir, and the portal and rose window of the south transept; in the interior is some good wood-carving; the old frescos were "restored" in 1826. In the cloister is the tomb of Cornelius JANSEN (*q.v.*). The town contains several other churches, as well as hospitals, a military school, a museum, and a public library. The chief manufactures are those of linen thread and lace and of woollen and linen cloth; dyeing, bleaching, and tanning are also carried on. The population in 1876 was 15,515.

YRIARTE. See IRIARTE.

YTTRIUM, the name of a rare element which in its character is closely allied to, and in nature is always associated with, cerium, lanthanum, didymium, and erbium (see LANTHANUM, vol. xiv. p. 291). For the preparation of yttrium compounds the best raw material is a rare Swedish mineral called gadolinite, which, according to König, consists of 22·61 per cent. of silica, 34·64 of yttria, Y_2O_3, and 42·75 of the oxides of erbium, cerium, didymium, lanthanum, iron, beryllium, calcium, magnesium, and sodium. Bunsen and Bahr, in 1866, elaborated a method for extracting the several rare oxides in the state of purity; but the method is too complicated to reproduce here.[1] Metallic yttrium is obtainable by reducing the chloride with potassium; but this operation has never been carried out with pure chloride. Yttria, Y_2O_3, is a yellowish white powder, which at high temperatures radiates out a most brilliant white light. It is soluble, slowly but completely, in mineral acids. It is recognized most surely by its very characteristic spark spectrum. Solutions of yttria salts in their behaviour to reagents are not unlike those of zirconia. The atomic weight of yttrium, according to the latest researches,[2] is 89·02, if $O=16$.

YUCATAN, a peninsular region of Central America, forming the south-eastern extremity of Mexico (see vol. xvi. pl. I.), of which, since 1861, it constitutes the two confederate states of Campeche (Campeachy) in the west and Yucatan in the east. At its neck the peninsula is conterminous on the south-east with British Honduras, on the south-west with the state of Tabasco (Mexico), and on the south with the republic of Guatemala, the boundaries towards these territories being largely of a purely conventional character. From this base the land projects in a compact rectangular mass between the Gulf of Mexico and the Caribbean Sea, west and east, for 280 miles northwards, across nearly four degrees of latitude (18° to 21° 40′ N.) and three of longitude (87° 30′ to 90° 30′ W.), to within 120 miles of Cuba, from which it is separated by the Yucatan Channel. It has a mean breadth of about 200 miles, a coast-line of 700 miles, and a total area of 55,400 square miles, with a population in 1882 of 393,000 (Yucatan, 29,570 square miles, population 302,500; Campeche, 25,830 square miles, population 90,500).[3]

Boundaries, area, &c.

The coast-line presents a uniform monotonous aspect, being fringed by no islands except Cozumel near the north-east point, and broken by no indentations except the shallow Lake Terminos on the west and the inlets of Ascension, Espiritu Santo, and Chetumal Bays on the east side. But the north coast is skirted by an almost continuous line of low dunes, nearly 200 miles long, enclosing a broad lagoon, which varies in length and depth with the

Physical features.

[1] See the handbooks of chemistry and the original memoir in Liebig's *Annalen*, vol. cxxxvii. p. 1.

[2] Cleve, *Jahresber. der Chemie*, 1882, p. 15.

[3] Previous estimates assigned 32,650 square miles to Yucatan and 26,100 to Campeche.

seasons. Behind the lagoon a bed of coralline and porous limestone rocks, composing nearly the whole tableland of Yucatan, rises continuously southwards in the direction of the Sierra Madre, which, beyond the frontier, traverses the whole of Guatemala and Central America. Geologically, Yucatan thus presents the character of a comparatively recent formation, built up by polypi in shallow waters, and gradually covered with a layer of thin dry soil by the slow weathering of the coral rocks. But the surface is not so uniformly level and monotonous as it appears on most maps; for, although there are scarcely any running streams, it is diversified here and there by a few lacustrine basins, of which Lakes Bacalar and Chicankanah are the largest, as well as by some low isolated hills and ridges in the west, and on the east side by the Sierra Alta, a range of moderate elevation, traversing the whole peninsula from Catoche Point southwards to the neighbourhood of Lake Peten in Guatemala.

Climate.

There are thus no elevations sufficiently high to intercept the moisture-bearing clouds from the Atlantic, while those from the Pacific are cut off by the Sierra Madre. Hence the climate is necessarily dry, with a deficient and uncertain rainfall, especially in the central and northern districts. Here also the tropical heats are intensified by the neighbourhood of the Gulf Stream, which in its passage through the Yucatan Channel flows much nearer to the coast of the peninsula than to that of Cuba. Still, the climate, although "hot of the hottest" (Ober), with a temperature ranging from 75° to 98° Fahr. in the shade, is comparatively healthy, owing to its great dryness and to the cool breezes which prevail night and day throughout a great part of the year. The atmosphere is also occasionally purified by the fierce *temporales* or "northers," which sweep across the Gulf freely over this open low-lying region. Yellow fever, however, periodically visits the Campeche coast, while ague is endemic in the undrained swampy districts towards the southern frontiers. Like most regions lying entirely within the tropics, Yucatan has two seasons only, which are determined by the alternations not so much of temperature as of atmospheric moisture. The dry season lasts from October to May, the wet season for the rest of the year; the hottest months appear to be March and April, when the heat is increased by the burning of the corn and henequen fields on the plateau.

Vegetable productions.

All the northern districts, as well as the greater part of the Sierra Alta, are destitute of large trees; but the coast-lands on both sides towards Tabasco and British Honduras enjoy a sufficient rainfall to support large forest growths, including the mahogany tree, several valuable cabinet woods, vanilla, logwood, and other dye-woods. Logwood forests fringe all the lagoons and many parts of the seaboard which are flooded during the rainy season. The chief cultivated plants are maize, the sugar-cane, tobacco, cotton, coffee, and especially henequen, the so-called Yucatan hemp or Sisal hemp, which, however, is not a hemp at all, but a true fibre. It is yielded by *Agave sisalensis*, which grows everywhere, and is used chiefly for the manufacture of coarse sackcloth, cordage, and hammocks. In 1880 as much as 40,000,000 ℔ of this article, valued at £350,000, was shipped at Progreso. The yearly maize crop is estimated to be worth over £1,000,000, and the whole of the agricultural produce about £2,000,000. But a comparatively small area is under tillage, owing largely to the prevailing system of vast haciendas (estates), which the owners have neither the necessary capital nor the energy to administer. Hence symptoms of decay are everywhere visible; the whole country is "mainly a wilderness" (Ober); and there is probably much less land under cultivation than at the time of the Spanish conquest.

Towns.

Of the state of Yucatan the capital is Merida (40,000 inhabitants in 1882), which is connected with its port of Progreso, on the north-west coast, by a railway 25 miles long, the only line in the country. The state of Campeche has for its capital the town and seaport of the same name (16,000), on the west coast. Other towns in the peninsula are Tikul, Ixmal, and Valladolid in Yucatan, and the port of El Carmen on an island in Lake Terminos in Campeche. According to the official returns, there are at present (1888) in Yucatan altogether 7 "cities," 13 towns, and 143 villages, besides 15 abandoned settlements and 333 haciendas. But scarcely any of these places have as many as 10,000 inhabitants, while the population of the great majority falls below 1000.

Condition at Spanish conquest.

The contrast is most striking between the picture conveyed by these returns, which also include 62 "ruined cities," and the state of the country at the time of the Spanish conquest, as revealed by the innumerable remains of towns, cities, temples, palaces, and other public buildings dotted over the plateau, being especially numerous round the now desolate northern and north-eastern shores of the peninsula. The whole of the northern section of Yucatan, which is now destitute alike of running waters, of dense vegetation, and almost of inhabitants, was at that time thickly peopled and full of populous cities remarkable for the great size, splendour, and artistic taste of their public monuments. For Maya, as the land was then called,[1] was the chief centre of the wide-spread Maya-Quiché power and culture, which rivalled, and in some respects excelled, those of the Peruvian Incas and of the Aztecs on the Anahuac plateau. Although the Maya nation had at that time already entered on a period of decadence, it was still strong and vigorous enough to resist the conquistadores for a period of fully twenty years (1527-47), the reduction of this barren region costing "the lives of more Spaniards than had been expended in wresting from the Incas and the Montezumas the wealthiest empires of the western world" (Bancroft).

Mayan irrigation works

Wonder has been expressed that such a bleak, arid, and almost streamless land could have ever become the seat of empire and the home of a flourishing civilization. But the absence of rivers on the plateau appears to be due not so much to the deficient rainfall as to the extremely porous nature of the calcareous soil, which absorbs the waters like a sponge and prevents the development of surface streams. Beneath the surface, however, the waters accumulate in such abundance that a sufficient supply may always be had by sinking wells in almost any part of the tableland. What the present inhabitants neglect to do was systematically practised by the former populations, whose aguadas or artificial lakes and underground reservoirs must be reckoned amongst the most remarkable monuments of Maya culture. "Intelligence, much skill in masonry, and much labour were required to construct them. They were paved with several courses of stone laid in cement, and in their bottoms wells or cavities were constructed. More than forty such wells were found in the bottom of one of these aguadas at Galal, which has been repaired and restored to use. In some places long subterranean passages lead down to pools of water, which are used in the dry season. One of these subterranean reservoirs is 450 feet below the surface of the ground, and the passage leading to it is about 1400 feet long" (Baldwin, p. 145). Thus the Mayan, like the Peruvian, the Egyptian, and the Babylonian culture, was based on a well-planned and carefully executed system of waterworks, specially adapted to the peculiar physical conditions of the country.

Ruined cities.

The monumental remains which must be assigned to the Maya-Quiché, as distinguished from other native civilizations, are spread over a great part of Central America, but are mainly comprised within the triangular space formed by connecting Mitla in Oajaca, Copan in Honduras, and the north coast of Yucatan above Tizimin by three straight lines. But of the "sixty-two ruined cities" of Yucatan proper the most important, or at least the best known and most fully described, are Izamal, Mayapan, Aké, Acanceh, Uxmal, Tikul, and Kabah, all centred in the north-west corner of the peninsula round about Merida, which itself stands on the ruins of Tihu; Chichen-Itza, about midway between Tikul and the east coast; and Labna, Nohbecan, and Potonchan in the Campeche district. Most of these places were described and illustrated by Stephens and Catherwood over forty years ago, and have recently been re-visited and re-described by M. Désiré Charnay. The structures especially of Uxmal, Aké, Kabah, and Chichen-Itza rival in magnitude and splendour those of Palenque in Chiapas, of Coban and Lorillard (the "Phantom City") in Guatemala, and of Copan in Honduras. There is nothing comparable to them on the Mexican tableland, and in the New World they are surpassed in architectural skill and artistic taste only by the beautiful edifices at Mitla in Oajaca and some of the monuments of Peruvian culture.

Mayapan.

Mayapan ("El Pendon de los Mayas," or "Banner City of the Maya Nation") was already in ruins at the time of the conquest, having been overthrown during a general revolt of the feudatory states about a century before that period.[2] Yet its ruins, overgrown with vegetation, still cover a considerable space, and include a huge artificial mound which from a distance looks like a wooded hill.

Uxmal.

But Uxmal stands altogether unrivalled for the magnitude of its buildings, the richness of its sculptured façades, and the almost classic beauty of its statuary. Conspicuous amongst its edifices are the so-called "nunnery" and the famous Casa del Gobernador or governor's palace, the latter with a wonderful frieze, 325 feet long, "having a row of colossal heads divided in panels, filled alternately with grecques in high relief" (Charnay). The nunnery, which contained eighty-eight compartments of all sizes, forms a vast quad-

[1] Yet the term *Yucatan* occurs in the very earliest Spanish records, although clearly originating in a misunderstanding, of which several versions are given by Bancroft (*Hist. Pacific States*, iv. p. 11). It appears even on the very oldest maps, on which, however, the country figures as an island, and is spoken of as such in conjunction with Cozumel ("the islands of Yucatan and Cozumel") in the commission (1526) granted to Francesco Montejo the elder to occupy and settle those lands (*op. cit.*, i. p. 154).

[2] Or, according to other interpretations of the confused national traditions, by the people of Chichen-Itza some three centuries before the arrival of the Spaniards.

rangle, with one front 280 feet long and enclosing a court 258 by 214 feet. Here Dr Le Plongeon discovered in 1881 a surprisingly beautiful statue, surpassing anything of the kind ever found in Central America. But this object he again carefully hid away to prevent it from falling into the hands of the Mexican authorities, who had seized another remarkable statue previously brought to light by this industrious explorer (Ober).

Aké. Conspicuous amongst the crumbling monuments of Aké, which lies ten leagues east of Merida, is a huge pyramid, with an immense flight of steps, presenting some extraordinary features different from anything elsewhere discovered in Yucatan. This strange monument is surmounted by thirty-six pillars (twenty-nine still standing), each 4 feet square and from 14 to 16 feet high, disposed in three parallel rows 10 feet apart, the whole supported by a platform 212 feet by 46 and approached by steps from 4½ to 6½ feet long and from 1 to 1½ feet high.

Izamal. At Izamal, a few miles east of Aké, stands another great pyramid, with a base of nearly 650 feet, besides three others, and a colossal head 13 feet high, not, however, a monolith, but built up of rough stones coated with mortar. But the gigantic face described and reproduced by Stephens had disappeared at the time of Charnay's visit to Izamal.

Chichen-Itza. To this explorer we are indebted for the first detailed account of the wonderful remains of Chichen-Itza, which include another nunnery, a tennis-court, several temples, and other buildings profusely embellished with rich friezes, statues, pillars, reliefs, and the like, the whole grouped round a central pyramid of great size, known as the Castillo, from the beautiful structure still standing on its summit. Chichen-Itza, which was certainly inhabited at the time of the conquest, was the capital of the Itzaes, one of the most powerful Maya nations, who appear to have afterwards migrated southwards to the neighbourhood of Lake Peten, where tribes of this name are still found. They constituted one of the eighteen semi-independent Maya states, whose incessant internecine wars at last brought about the dismemberment of the once potent theocratic empire of Xibalba (Palenque?) and the destruction of the Maya civilization.

Kabah. Scarcely less important than those of Chichen-Itza are the monuments of Kabah, which lies about 12 miles south of Uxmal. The two places were formerly connected by a plastered causeway, traces of which are still visible, and Kabah must have been a very large city, for its ruins are scattered over a considerable area. Amongst them are comprised lofty pyramids, vast terraces, and sumptuous palaces or temples, with elaborate ornamentation, sometimes almost completely disguising the architectural features of the edifices.[1] Charnay mentions "triumphal arches," but adds that he sought in vain for the unique specimen of this kind of monument in America which is mentioned and figured by Stephens, and which bears such a striking resemblance to the triumphal arches of the Roman type. Many other remains have either disappeared or crumbled away almost beyond recognition since they were first sketched by Catherwood.[2] But, on the other hand, numerous buried cities and monuments probably still remain concealed amid the rank tropical vegetation, especially in the almost unknown territory of the unreduced Lacandons and Itzaes towards the Guatemala frontier. But enough has already been surveyed fully to justify Maudslay's general remark, that Yucatan is thickly covered with the ruins of great buildings "even superior in some respects to those found in other parts of Central America."

Inscriptions. Like those of Palenque, Lorillard Town, Tikul, and Copan, many of these buildings are covered with inscriptions, the key to the deciphering of which has not yet been discovered. Notwithstanding certain divergences, seen especially at Lorillard, all belong obviously to the same writing system. But whether that system is purely ideographic, phonetic, or intermediate cannot be asserted with any certainty, although Holden, who has attacked the problem from a fresh standpoint, declares emphatically that they are not phonetic, "except in so far as their rebus character may make them in a sense phonetic." He claims by his system to have fixed the order in which the inscriptions are to be read (in lines left to right, in columns vertically downwards), and fancies he has determined the meaning of three characters representing Maya divinities. But Holden is ignorant of the Maya-Quiché language, of which a few manuscripts have been rescued from the fury of the early Spanish iconoclasts. One of these documents, the *Popol-Vuh*, written or copied about 1558 from an older Quiché book, has been edited and even translated by Brasseur de Bourbourg. This uncritical writer makes use of a so-called Maya-Quiché alphabet preserved by Diego de Landa, first bishop of Yucatan, in his *Relacion* or history of the Mayas. But the alphabet in question is admittedly extremely defective and inadequate to interpret the native writings, and has even been pronounced "a Spanish fabrication" by Dr Valentini,[3] a view which Holden appears to endorse. The puzzle thus remains still unsolved, and no safe inference can be drawn beyond the fact that the inscriptions and manuscripts are composed in a highly conventional form of writing, and probably in more than one Maya-Quiché dialect.

Origin and antiquity of Maya culture. Other difficult questions connected with the origin and antiquity of the Maya culture, and the nature of its relations to that of Mexico, will be found discussed under MEXICO (*q.v.*). But, since that article was written, fresh materials have been collected and published which help to throw some further light on these obscure subjects. Unfortunately M. Charnay, who since the time of Stephens and Catherwood has undoubtedly contributed most to our knowledge of the Central-American remains, has revived in an exaggerated form the old views of Morelet, Orozco y Berra, and others regarding the Toltec origin of all these monuments. This observer sees everywhere the clearest evidences, not merely of Toltec influences, which are obvious enough, but of the Toltec institutions themselves, of the Toltec religion, architecture, and civilization, to the exclusion of all others in Central America. He even boldly traces on the map the lines of a twofold Toltec migration, from Tula along the Atlantic and from Toluca along the Pacific side, to their junction at Copan in Honduras, some few centuries before the discovery of the New World. But our faith in the soundness of these views is greatly shaken when we find M. Charnay identifying the Toltecs themselves somewhat wildly with Malays, Indo-Chinese, and other Asiatic races. Some of the present populations of Yucatan are even pronounced to be "a cross between the Malay and the Chinese," and all the exploded theories are thus revived of an Asiatic origin of the civilized inhabitants of the New World and of their cultures. But, as Ober well remarks, the evidence is cumulative in favour of the independent evolution of these cultures. Late contact,—that is, contact since the remote Stone Age,—with the inhabitants of the eastern hemisphere has been either of the most casual nature or else as shadowy as the Atlantis itself, which is seriously referred to in this connexion by otherwise sane writers, but which was obviously as pure an invention of Plato as the Utopia was of Sir Thomas More.

An essential condition of the Toltec theory is the assumed recent, or comparatively recent, date of all the Central-American monuments, and Charnay has certainly dispelled the extravagant ideas at one time prevalent regarding the hoary antiquity of some of these remains. He has shown in particular that no argument in favour of great age can be drawn from the size of the trees by which many of them are overgrown. By actual experiment he has proved that the concentric circles of these trees correspond, not to so many years, as had been supposed, but rather to so many months, if not even to shorter periods of growth. Thus collapse the extravagant estimates of 2000 years (Waldeck) or 1700 (Lorainzar) assigned to the buildings on this assumption. At the same time some of the cities were already forgotten ruins at the time of the conquest, and many of the structures date evidently back to a period prior to the Toltec migrations southwards. The bas-reliefs of Kabah also clearly show that these Toltecs, probably of Nahua stock and closely related to the Aztecs, already found the land occupied by a civilized people, able to record on stone monuments their triumphs over the northern invaders. Some of these monuments themselves equal, if not surpass, in artistic taste and workmanship anything the Toltec builders are known to have produced on the Anahuac plateau. They also present many distinctive features, especially in their design and decorative parts, while the inscriptions are altogether different from those of the Aztecs as seen in extant manuscripts. The conclusion seems inevitable that the Maya-Quiché culture was an independent growth, brought in later times under Nahua influences, the relations being perhaps somewhat analogous to those existing between the Græco-Bactrian and Indian or the Moorish and Spanish in the Old World.

Classification of Maya-Quiché nation. At the time of the conquest a great part of Central America was found to be occupied, as it still is, by peoples related, at least in speech, to the Maya inhabitants of Yucatan. The numerous branches of this widespread family ranged from Tamaulipas (about the Tropic of Cancer) southwards to north Honduras and San Salvador (14° N. lat.). But the chief divisions were the Mayas of Yucatan and the Quichés of Guatemala, whence the compound term Maya-Quiché collectively applied to the whole race. Owing partly to the uncertainty of their mutual affinities, but mainly to the confusing and inconsistent nomenclature of the early Spanish and later writers, the classification of the various Maya-Quiché nations presents serious difficulties, some of which have not yet been overcome. In the subjoined scheme are embodied the results of the researches of De Bourbourg, Berendt, Stoll, and others in this intricate branch of ethnology:—

[1] On one of the palaces "two salient cornices form a frame to immense friezes which in their details would compare favourably with our proudest monuments" (Charnay). On others are sculptured some remarkable bas-reliefs, which represent Maya warriors receiving the swords of kneeling Aztec captives, the nationalities of the figures being clearly identified by their respective costumes. The significance of records of this sort has either been altogether overlooked or else strangely misinterpreted by most writers on Central-American antiquities.

[2] In 1841 Stephens was assured by the cura of Santa Cruz del Quiché that the palaces of that place, then in a dilapidated state, were quite perfect thirty years before, and that the now deserted city of Utatlan in the province of Vera Paz was then almost as perfect as when its inhabitants had abandoned it. He had himself walked in its silent streets amid its colossal buildings, which were as entire as those of Santa Cruz.

[3] In a paper read before the American Antiquarian Society, 28th April 1880.

Maya Group.—*Huasteca*, Vera Cruz and Tamaulipas; *Totonac* (?),[1] north part of Vera Cruz; *Maya proper*, throughout Yucatan; *Chol* (Cholti, Colchi), between the Salinas and Mondaguas rivers, Guatemala; *Mopan*, north of the Chols; *Chontal*, Tabasco, distinct from the Nicaraguan Chontales; *Tzental* (Cendal), Ocosingo district, Chiapas; *Tzotzil* (Zotzil, Zotzlem), San Cristobal, Chiapas; *Chañabal*, Comitan district, Chiapas.

Quiché Group.—*Cakchiquel* (Kacchikil), Tecpan to Sta Lucia and the Pacific; *Tzutujil* (Sotojil, Zutuhil), Aitlan district, Guatemala; *Quiché proper* (Kiché, Utatlica), Cunen and Rabinal districts, and thence south-west to the Pacific, Guatemala; *Uspanteca*, San Miguel Uspantan, Guatemala.

Poconchi Group.—*Poconchi proper* (Pokomchi, Pacomchi), Tactic district, Guatemala; *Quekchi* (Caechi, Aquacateca), Coban district, Guatemala; *Chorti* (Lenguaapay), Zacapa and Chichimula, and thence eastwards to Honduras; *Pokomam*, Jalapa, and thence to San Salvador.

Mame Group.—*Mame proper* (Mem, Zakloh-pakap), throughout south-western Guatemala; *Ixil*, Cotzal district, Guatemala; *Aguacatecas* (Sinca, Xinca), throughout south-eastern Guatemala; *Alagiulac* (?), San Cristobal, Chiapas.

Modern inhabitants.

Yucatan is still almost entirely inhabited by the same Maya race that was found in possession of the land at the time of the discovery. About five-sixths of the population are of nearly pure Maya stock and speech, the Spanish and mestizo elements being mostly confined to the large towns. The mestizos are said to be the handsomest on the continent, while the full-blood natives are perhaps the least characteristic of all the aboriginal populations. They have the coarse black and straight hair, the arched nose, and the reddish-brown complexion common to most of the primitive inhabitants of America. But they can be readily distinguished from all of them by their regular features, low cheek-bones, small mouth and ears, straight jaws, frank expression, and a certain air of refinement betraying descent from a highly cultured people. "It would be difficult," says Charnay, "to find among the rural classes of Europe men of a better build, or with more intelligent and open countenances." Although generally peaceful, patient under oppression, and even somewhat indolent, their history since the conquest (1547) has not been wholly uneventful. After more than two centuries of passive resistance, there was a general revolt in 1761, brought about by the intolerable misrule of the Spanish administration. The declaration of independence (1821) was followed in 1824 by the union with the Mexican confederacy, which continued without interruption till 1840. In that year an independent republic was set up in Yucatan, which, however, was suppressed in 1843. Then came the general uprising of the natives in 1846, when Mexico was engaged in a disastrous war with the United States. To quell the revolt, the ruling classes were obliged to call in the aid of the Mexicans (1847-53), whereby the peninsula again lost its autonomy, and was divided (1861) into the two federal states of Yucatan and Campeche. But the rebellion was not entirely suppressed, and many of the natives, withdrawing eastwards to the coast-lands beyond the Sierra Alta, have hitherto defied all the efforts of the authorities to reduce them.

Bibliography.—D. L. Cogolludo, *Historia de Yucathan*, Madrid, 1688; Diego de Landa, *Relacion de las Cosas de Yucatan*, ed. by Br. de Bourbourg, Paris, 1864; Brasseur de Bourbourg, *Hist. des Nations Civilisées du Mexique et de l'Amérique Centrale*, Paris, 1857-59, and *Études sur le Système Graphique et la Langue des Mayas*, Paris, 1869-70; Lord Kingsborough, *Antiquities of Mexico*, London, 1831-48 (vols. ii. and iii.); H. H. Bancroft, *Native Races of the Pacific States*, New York, 1875, and *Hist. of the Pacific States* (vols. iv. and v.), San Francisco and London, 1882-87; J. L. Stephens, *Incidents of Travel in Yucatan*, new edition, New York, 1858; E. G. Squier, *Travels in Central America*, New York, 1853, and *Notes on Central America*, New York, 1855; J. D. Baldwin, *Ancient America*, New York, 1872; Marquis de Nadaillac, *Prehistoric America*, London, 1885; Désiré Charnay, *The Ancient Cities of the New World*, London, 1887; F. A. Ober, *Travels in Mexico* (bk. i., Yucatan), Boston, 1884; A. P. Maudslay, "Exploration, &c., of Copan," in *Proc. Roy. Geogr. Soc*, September, 1886; E. S. Holden, "Studies in Central-American Picture-Writing," in *Annual Report* of Bureau of Ethnology, Washington, 1879-80. (A. H. K.)

YUCCA,[2] a genus of the order *Liliaceæ*, the species of which are remarkable for their stately appearance and generally magnificent inflorescence. They occur in greatest frequency in Mexico and the south-western States of the American Union, extending also into Central America, and occurring in such numbers in some places as to form "straggling forests." They have a woody or fibrous stem, sometimes short, and in other cases, even in the same species, attaining a height of 15 to 20 feet, and branching at the top into a series of forks. The leaves are crowded in tufts at the ends of the stem or branches and are generally stiff and sword-shaped, with a sharp point, sometimes flaccid and in other cases fibrous at the edges. The numerous flowers are usually white, bell-shaped, and pendulous, and are borne in much-branched terminal panicles. Each flower consists of a perianth of six regular pieces, as many hypogynous stamens, with dilated filaments, bearing relatively small anthers. The three-celled ovary is surmounted by a short thick style, dividing above into three stigmas, and ripens into a succulent berry in some of the species, and into a dry three-valved capsule in others. The flowers are fertilized by the agency of moths.

A coarse fibre is obtained by the Mexicans from the stem and foliage, which they utilize for cordage. The succulent fruits, which resemble small bananas, are cooked as an article of diet; and the roots contain a saponaceous matter used in place of soap.

Most of the species are hardy in Great Britain, and their striking appearance renders them attractive in gardens even when not in flower. Their rigid foliage, invested by thick epidermis, also enables them to resist the noxious air of towns better than most plants. A popular name for the plant is "Adam's needle." The species which split up at the margins of their leaves into filaments are called "Eve's thread."

YUN-NAN. See China, vol. v. p. 640.

YUN-NAN FU, the capital of the Chinese province of Yun-nan, is situated in 25° 6′ N. lat. and 102° 52′ E. long. Originally the district surrounding Yun-nan Fu was known as the "land of the southern barbarians." The city, which under different dynasties has borne different names, is situated on a plain, and is surrounded by well-fortified walls, 6½ miles in circuit. Marco Polo describes it, under the name of Yachi, as "a very great and noble city, in which are numerous merchants and craftsmen. The people are of sundry kinds, for there are not only Saracens and idolaters but also a few Nestorian Christians. They have wheat and rice in plenty. . . . Their money is . . . certain white porcelain shells that are found in the sea." For many years Mahommedans have been very numerous in the city and neighbourhood; and in 1855 a Mahommedan rising took place within the city. Yun-nan Fu has a prosperous and busy aspect: the shops are large and well supplied with native silken goods, saddlery, &c., while English cotton, Russian cloths, and raw cotton from Burmah constitute the main foreign merchandise. Employment for large numbers of workpeople is found in the copper factories. A local mint at Yun-nan Fu issued annually 101,000,000 cash before the outbreak of the rebellion in 1855. The population of the city is estimated at about 200,000.

YVETOT, a town of France, chef-lieu of an arrondissement in the department of Seine-Inférieure, stands on the plateau of Caux, 24 miles north-west of Rouen on the railway to Havre, and is chiefly known from Béranger's famous song. Calicoes, tickings, Siamese, *rouennerie* cotton, reps, and handkerchiefs are made here, as in most places in the department, and a trade is carried on in wool. The church is ugly, but contains a marble altar from the Carthusian monastery at Rouen, some fine woodwork from the abbey of St Wandrille, and an elegant pulpit. The remains of a Bernardine monastery are occupied in part by the court and jail. The hospital and seminary are both modern. The population was 7625 (commune 8397) in 1881 and 7333 (commune 7972) in 1886.

From the 15th till the middle of the 16th century the lords of Yvetot bore the title of king, and their lands were exempt from all service to the French crown. The town was occupied during the Hundred Years' War by Henry V. of England, and afterwards retaken by Charles VII. of France. On 8th May 1592 Henry IV. defeated here the troops of the League under the duke of Parma. A Bernardine monastery was founded at Yvetot in 1650, and suppressed in 1781. In 1658 part of the town was destroyed by fire.

[1] Although Totonac is grouped by Brinton and others in this family, Gatschet is inclined to regard it as an independent stock language (*Réplique à Mr D. G. Brinton*, Paris, 1888, p. 8).

[2] A Spanish word meaning "bayonet."

Z

Z, the last letter of our alphabet, has fallen away from its old place in the Phœnician and Greek alphabets. In these it stood seventh, probably with the value of *dz* or *zd*. In shape it was I in all the older writings both of the Ionian and the Eubœan type. Later it became Z, as we have it, by a natural and convenient change. But I is the older Italian as well as the Greek form; it remained so in Oscan; in Etruscan and Umbrian the cross strokes were brought near together, but the upright line remained. The Latin alphabet, however, dropped the symbol, having apparently no need of it; it appears on an old coin of Cosa (*Corpus*, i. 14), unless the letter there be only a modified *s*. Later, in the 1st century B.C., the letter in the form Z was re-introduced, where we have it, to represent more accurately the sound of *z* in words borrowed from the Greek, in which alone it appears; *ss* (or initial *s*) had previously been employed for this purpose. The original place of the letter had been occupied in the meantime by G, the Latin modified form of C (see under G), so Z had to take the lowest place together with Y, which had been also borrowed from Greece for a similar purpose.

The exact value of zeta in Greek has been much discussed (see Blass, *Aussprache des Griechischen*, p. 95). That it was a double sound—not French *z* (the voiced sibilant corresponding to the voiceless *s*)—seems clear from Aristotle's statement that ξ, ψ, and ζ were all *συμφώνιαι*, and from its power of lengthening a previous short vowel in scanning. The arguments, however, for the *dz* or the *zd* value are about evenly balanced, and it is not improbable that it may have had both. In Latin the value was doubtless that of the Greek *z*.

In Old English *z* hardly occurs; when it does it is in borrowed names with the value of *ts*, as in Betzaida, Zabulon. It was introduced in order to represent French *z* in words borrowed from France, as *zeal*, *zone* (see article S). But it is used in only a very small number of the words where the sound occurs: we still adhere to the usage of our forefathers and employ *s* for the *s*-sound and the *z*-sound alike, indeed rather inclining to use *s* for *z*, and to differentiate *s* by doubling the symbol: compare *his* (*i.e.*, hiz) and *hiss* (*i.e.*, his). In German *z* represents *ts*, the sound into which Teutonic *t* passed in High German—*e.g.*, in *herz*, our "heart." It was also used formerly, either alone or in combination with *s*, to denote the voiceless sibilant when final: thus the conjunction *dass*, which is nothing but the neuter pronoun *das*, was formerly written *daz*, and is sometimes even now written *dasz*. In French the Latin *z* became the voiced sibilant; and a similar process has taken place in modern Greek. In French, however, the final sound must once have been stronger—*e.g.*, in *fils* (filius), later *fiz*, and still later *fis* (as it is still pronounced), which passed into England in the form *Fitz* in proper names. Still plainer is the evidence of verbal forms like *avez* = avets = habetis.

For the history of the English variant ʒ for *z*, see article Y. (J. P.)

ZAANDAM, ZAANREDAM, or SAARDAM, a village of Holland, in the province of North Holland, 5 miles by rail to the north-west of Amsterdam, at the confluence of the Zaan with the Y. The houses are mostly of wood, painted white or green, and the place shares with the other villages of North Holland a high reputation for neatness and cleanliness. In the immediate neighbourhood are a very large number of windmills, including corn, paper, saw, coffee, snuff, and other mills. Peter the Great of Russia wrought at Zaandam as a ship-carpenter for a short time in 1697, and the hut in which he is said to have lived is still shown and much visited. Some shipbuilding is still carried on. The population in 1887 was 14,351.

ZACATECAS, a city of Mexico, capital of the state of the same name, lies 340 miles by rail north-west of Mexico, in 22° 46′ N. lat. and 102° W. long. Zacatecas, which had a population of 46,000 in 1886, is the centre of one of the oldest and most productive silver-mining districts in the republic, and the town itself stands on the rich vein discovered here by Juan de Tolosa in 1546. It lies on the great Mexican tableland, 7976 feet above the sea, in a narrow ravine surrounded by rolling hills, all containing almost inexhaustible deposits of the precious metal. Within half an hour's walk of the centre of the town are situated twelve mines, some of which have been worked with little interruption for over three hundred years. Owing to the irregular nature of the ground and the great value of the land, the city is laid out in narrow tortuous streets, which, unlike most other Mexican towns, are lined by high houses of three and four stories. Noteworthy amongst the public buildings are the cathedral, with a finely sculptured façade, the Government palace, the city hall, the theatre, and the mint; this last, during the period from 1772 to 1865, issued silver money to the value of £41,000,000, besides £110,000 in gold. The streets, although narrow, are well paved and partly lit by electricity. Since the completion of the Central Mexican Railway to this place in 1884 it has increased in population and prosperity. From the Bufa Hill, 500 feet high, lying to the north of the city, an extensive view is commanded of the surrounding district, which is of an extremely rugged character and almost destitute of vegetation. In the neighbourhood are nine small lakes, yielding an abundance of salt and carbonate of soda. Zacatecas, which received the title of city from Philip II. in 1585, is supplied with water by a large, well-constructed aqueduct.

The state of Zacatecas lies between Coahuila and Jalisco north and south respectively, and is elsewhere conterminous with Guanajuato, Durango, and San Luis Potosi. It has an area of 25,227 square miles and a population (1882) of 422,506, of whom a preponderating proportion are Indians or mestizos. It stands at a mean altitude of over 7000 feet above sea-level, and is traversed by the Mazapil, Norillos, Guadaloupe, and other metalliferous ranges, this state ranking among the first in the republic for mineral wealth. Next to the Veta Madre of Guanajuato and the famous Comstock lode, Nevada, the Veta Grande of Zacatecas is held to be the most remarkable silver vein in North America. The chief mining districts are Zacatecas, Espiritu Santo, Chapala, Los Arcos, Norias, Ipala, Santa Lucia, Naranjal, and Santo Martino; and in 1886 about 324 mines were open (21 gold, 67 gold and silver, 167 silver alone, 15 copper, 37 lead, and 16 quicksilver). Besides its minerals the state possesses considerable agricultural resources, the south-eastern parts especially being very fertile and well watered by the rivers Tlaltenango and Juchipila. Maize, wheat, fruits—such as peaches, apricots, grapes,—and all kinds of vegetables are extensively cultivated, the annual maize crop being valued at over £1,000,000, wheat at about £250,000, and the remaining crops at about £600,000. Even in the bleak and arid northern districts there are some extensive grazing-grounds, where cattle, horses, mules, sheep, and goats thrive well. Some of the slopes are well timbered, the chief species being the mountain cedar, oak, elm, ash, and cotton-wood. Besides the capital, the chief mining towns are Fresnillo (pop. 15,000), Garcia (8000), Villanueva (7000), Linos (7000), Sombrerete (6000), and Nieves (3000).

ZACH, FRANZ XAVER, BARON VON (1754-1832), astronomer, was born at Pesth in June 1754. He served for some time in the Austrian army, and afterwards lived in London from 1783 to 1786 as tutor in the house of the Saxon minister, Count Brühl. In 1786 he was appointed by Ernest II. of Saxe-Coburg-Gotha director of the new observatory on the Seeberg at Gotha, which was finished in 1791. From 1806 Zach accompanied the duke's widow on her travels in the south of Europe. He died in Paris on 2d September 1832.

Zach published *Tables of the Sun* (Gotha, 1792; new and improved edition, *ibid.*, 1804), and numerous papers on geographical subjects, particularly on the geographical positions of many towns and places, which he determined on his travels with a sextant. His principal importance is, however, as editor of three scientific journals of great value,—*Allgemeine Geographische Ephemeriden* (4 vols., Gotha, 1798-99), *Monatliche Correspondenz zur Beförderung der Erd- und Himmels-Kunde* (28 vols., Gotha, 1800-13, from 1807 edited by Lindenau), and *Correspondance Astronomique, Géographique, Hydrographique, et Statistique* (Genoa, 1818-26, 14 vols., and one number of the 15th suppressed at the instigation of the Jesuits).

ZACHARIAE VON LINGENTHAL, KARL SALOMO (1769-1843), German jurist, was born on 14th September 1769 at Meissen in Saxony. His family came from Austria. His father was a lawyer; his mother, a Hessian, was the daughter of a pastor. Of feeble health and long the only child of his parents, Karl did not go to school until the age of fifteen. He afterwards studied philosophy, history, mathematics, and philology at the university of Leipsic. In 1792 he went to Wittenberg as tutor to Count zur Lippe, and whilst there he began to study law. There he came greatly under the influence of Kant, traces of whose teaching remain even in his latest writings. In 1794 Zachariae became a privat-docent, lecturing on canon law, in 1798 extraordinary professor, and in 1802 ordinary professor of feudal law. From that time to his death in 1843, with the exception of a short period in which public affairs occupied him, he poured out a succession of works covering the whole field of jurisprudence and extending into other adjoining regions. He was also indefatigable in the labour of his chair, and he was the editor of, or a copious contributor to, more than one periodical. In 1807 he went to Heidelberg, then beginning its period of splendour as a school of law. There, resisting many calls to Göttingen, Berlin, and other universities, he remained until his death. In 1811 he married under romantic circumstances. His wife died in four years.

In 1820 he was elected representative of the university in the first Baden chamber, and four years later was made a member of the second. From 1825 to 1829 he devoted much time to political affairs and to the preparation of a code. He was a constitutional reformer, averse to great or violent changes. He loved to cite the saying of the Roman emperor to his adopted son,—"Imperaturus es hominibus qui nec totam servitutem pati possent nec totam libertatem,"—"a truth," he observes in one of his many brochures (*Die Souverainetätsrechte der Krone Würtemberg*, &c.), "which no Government and no people should ever forget." In 1842 he was ennobled with the title of Von Lingenthal. To the last days of his life he toiled with the ardour of a young student. His fame extended beyond Germany. The German universities then enjoyed by tacit consent a jurisdiction in regard to legal questions of international importance which had come down from the Middle Ages; and Zachariae was often consulted as to questions arising in Germany, France, and England. Elaborate "opinions," some of them forming veritable treatises,—*e.g.*, on Sir Augustus d'Este's claim to the dukedom of Sussex, Baron de Bode's claim as an English subject to a share in the French indemnity, the famous dispute as to the debts due to the elector of Hesse-Cassel, confiscated by Napoleon, and the constitutional position of the Mecklenburg landowners,—were composed by Zachariae. He died on 27th March 1843, leaving a son who has worthily continued his father's labours in jurisprudence.

Zachariae's true history is in his writings, which are extremely numerous and multifarious. They deal with almost every branch of jurisprudence; they are philosophical, historical, and practical; they relate to Roman, canon, German, and French law; and his curiosity extended to the writings of his contemporaries, Bentham and Austin. A work on Sulla, in whom he sees another Napoleon, and an unpublished translation of his favourite Tacitus were some of the fruits of his restless activity. The first book of much consequence which he published was *Die Einheit des Staats und der Kirche mit Rücksicht auf die Deutsche Reichsverfassung* (1797), one of the most original of his works, displaying the writer's power of analysis, his skill in making a complicated set of facts appear to be deductions from a few principles,—a study even now well worth reading. His theme is the relation of religion to the state. Zachariae undertakes to show that with Christianity three systems only are possible,—(1) what he calls the system of hierarchy, according to which the state is under the power of the church, the object of the former being subordinated to that of the latter; (2) the territorial system, according to which the church is subject to the power of the state; and (3) what he terms the collegiate system, according to which neither of the two societies is subject to the other, and both have different objects in view. The consequence of the adoption of these various systems—the principles of law which must be accepted according as one or the other of them is supreme—he deduces with much acumen. While much of his work has lost its interest, it remains a luminous example of the application of the deductive process to historical investigation, a proof that legal conceptions may often serve to give unity to the complex facts of history. In 1805 appeared *Versuch einer allgemeinen Hermeneutik des Rechts*. Neither in English nor in Scotch legal literature is there any book, so far as known to the present writer, covering the field to which it relates. It is an attempt to found on the rules of grammar and logic a system of interpretation applicable to all systems of law. The weak part of the book is that, like so many of Zachariae's works, it stops short at the point where the inquiry would be most fruitful. Illustrations are taken from Roman law; we miss any adequate treatment of the problems which the forms of modern legislation raise. In 1806 appeared *Die Wissenschaft der Gesetzgebung*, a fragment, which is a curious outcome of the French Revolution. Impressed by the overthrow or decay of the forces which had hitherto held society together, he looked about for a better substitute for them than *politique de circonstance* offered. Many of Zachariae's maxims seem fanciful; there are divisions which do not elucidate, and distinctions made apparently for their own sake. But the work is interesting; it shows that the author was groping after the principle of utility as the guide of the legislator; the study of very different facts had brought him independently to much the same conclusion as Bentham had reached. Zachariae's last work of importance was *Vierzig Bücher vom Staate*, published in 1839-42, with the motto *non omnis moriar*. This was his favourite work, and is the one to which his admirers point as his enduring monument. Undoubtedly it contains much erudition and, what is rarer, many original ideas as to the future of the state and of law. It has been compared to *L'Esprit des Lois*, and Zachariae, in spite of his pedantry, has some tincture of the discursive brilliancy of Montesquieu. It covers no small part of the field of Buckle's first volume of the *History of Civilisation*. The reader will, however, seek in vain for any order or system in some of the chapters of *Vierzig Bücher vom Staate*. He was recasting many of his ideas as he wrote, and the book ends before the process is completed. Among the most esteemed of the works of Zachariae is that on *Staatsrecht*, of the originality of which he was proud, and his treatise on the *Code Napoléon*, a marvellous work, considering it was composed by a German professor who did not much concern himself with this subject till somewhat late in life. There are no fewer than three French editions of his book, and it has been translated into Italian. Zachariae edited with Mittermaier the *Kritische Zeitschrift für Rechtswissenschaft und Gesetzgebung des Auslandes*, and the introduction which he wrote illustrates his wide reading and his constant desire for new light upon old problems.

Zachariae exhibits the best and the worst sides of German jurisprudence: there is the desire not to base generalizations or conclusions on the peculiarities of any one system, but to master the whole facts. He does not assume a distinction or classification of Roman law to be necessarily scientific. He seeks real reasons; he avoids the English lawyer's favourite fallacy of proving *idem per idem*, of seeking to show the reasonableness of anything by saying the same thing again in different language. Though a scholar, Zachariae has not the weakness of exaggerating the importance of whatever is rare or unpublished, and he has no delight in barren erudition. Himself a learned pandectist, he had cast aside his countrymen's proneness to find all things in the *Corpus Juris*. His books, however, have the failings of so many German works on law. They want actuality; they have little relation to the facts of life. They are leavened by metaphysics—often very bad metaphysics, and not always by the same system. Nor is he a clear thinker. We are never sure what is his notion of the province of jurisprudence; his favourite idea appears to be that law creates among men an order similar to that which exists in the physical world, and that it is a security for the freedom of man's will. The influence of Kant is observable in all his works. In his later that of Hegel also appears;

and his mental changes do not end there. He does not indeed say, "Back to Montesquieu; study facts, the simplest and primitive facts above all; adopt his method, and improve upon it;" but that is the wise spirit of some of his later works. Unfortunately he did not fulfil the promise which they contain. He had not learned to distinguish sharply between the science and the practical art of jurisprudence, and we are never certain in what capacity he speaks. He had not conceived clearly the truth that society forms one whole, that the phenomena of law at any given time or place are not accidents but the outcome of a long train of events, that, so regarded, they are as much susceptible of scientific treatment as the facts of language, and that a treatise on botany or, still more, one on comparative philology is a better guide to what jurisprudence may yet be than a volume of Hugo or even Austin. It was made a reproach to Zachariae that he changed his opinions. He did so; it was a sign of his single-mindedness and restless curiosity. It is also one of the reasons why his works are now little read. They opened paths, and they were superseded by others which could not have existed without them.

There is no adequate account of Zachariae and his works; the best are Robert von Mohl's *Geschichte u. Literatur der Staatswissenschaften* (1855-58) and Charles Brocher's *K. S. Zachariæ, sa Vie et ses Œuvres* (1870). (J. Mt.)

ZACHARIAS, St, pope from 741 to 752, was a Greek by birth, and appears to have been on intimate terms with Gregory III., whom he succeeded (November 741). Contemporary history dwells chiefly on his great personal influence with the Lombard king Luitprand, and with his successor Rachis; it was largely through his tact in dealing with these princes in a variety of emergencies that the exarchate of Ravenna was rescued from becoming part of the Lombard kingdom. A correspondence, of considerable extent and of great interest, between Zacharias and St Boniface, the apostle of Germany, is still extant, and shows how great was the influence of this pope on events then passing in France and Germany: he encouraged the deposition of Childeric, and it was with his sanction that Boniface crowned Pippin as king of the Franks at Soissons in 752. Zacharias is stated to have remonstrated with the emperor Constantine Copronymus on the part he had taken in the iconoclastic controversy. He died 14th March 752, and was succeeded by Stephen II.

ZAIRE,[1] or CONGO, designations of the river now generally known under the latter name (see vol. i. pl. II.) This river system occupies a large part of equatorial Africa,—1,540,000 square miles according to a probable estimate; and in the length of its course (some 2900 miles) and the volume of its discharge (1,500,000 or at least 1,200,000 cubic feet per second) the river ranks among the most important in the world.[2] The history of the exploration of the Congo basin is a matter of yesterday and to-day; and in several directions the exact limits, with the relations of the affluents to the system, have still to be determined. The mouth of the river lies on the west coast of the continent in 6° S. lat. and 12° 25′ E. long. The head-waters of its most eastern stream (Malagarazi) rise only 370 miles from the Indian Ocean. The course of the main river describes a vast bow, the central portion of which lies as far north as 2° N. lat.

To the north of the Lokinga or Mushinga Mountains, a range, reaching about 6000 feet in altitude, which sends its southward drainage to the Zambesi, lies Bangweolo (Bemba, Shuia, or Chama) Lake, at a height of 3700 feet above the sea according to Livingstone, or 4300 according to Giraud. It has a very irregular outline. Nowhere more than 18 or 20 feet deep, it is nevertheless fed by several large rivers, of which the Chambesi or Chasi ranks first. Livingstone, who discovered the Chambesi in 1867 in 10° 34′ S. lat., describes it as "flooded with clear water, not more than 40 yards wide, showing abundant animal life in its waters and on its banks." Its head-streams drain the country between the south end of Lake Tanganyika and the north end of Lake Nyassa.

From the south-west extremity of Lake Bangweolo issues the Luapula, which is generally regarded as the main head-stream of the Congo. It is about 20 feet deep and 200 yards wide. Our knowledge of its course is still imperfect, though from Giraud (1883) and Capello and Ivens (1884-85) we learn that it is interrupted by dangerous rapids (at Mambirima, &c.); and there is no doubt that it is gradually deflected northwards and is the main affluent of Lake Moero. This extensive basin is quite different from Lake Bangweolo: its southern end is situated in a low marshy plain and the difference between high and low water level is as much as the whole depth of Bangweolo. From north to south the total length is upwards of 90 miles, though during the rainy season vast additional tracts to the south are under water. Several considerable affluents fall into the lake from the east. The river has not been followed between Lake Moero and Lake Lanji; but near the latter it is known to receive the Kamirondo from the left and the Lukugu from the right.

The basin of the Tanganyika is a "vast chasm enclosed within mountain ranges or cliffs, often rising steeply from the shore and terminating in elevated plateaus," with depths of 300 or 350 fathoms. The total length is 380 miles; and, while the northern end narrows to about 10 miles, the width towards the centre is from 30 to 50 miles. The islands are few and unimportant, and, except at the great peninsula of Ubwari on the west coast, near the northern end of the lake, the shore line is remarkably regular. The water is perfectly fresh. Of the various settlements on Tanganyika the most important is Ujiji (4° 54′ S. lat. on the east coast), which formerly gave its name to the lake. "It is the terminus," in the words of Captain Hore, "of what for many years was the only safe and well-known route from the East Coast of Africa to the lake, and an important station upon a line of traffic, geographically suited and by common consent adopted as convenient, right across the continent." Another point of interest is Karema (in 6° 50′ S. lat., on the eastern shore), originally a station of the African International Association. A lighthouse has also been erected on Kavala Island.

The connexion of Tanganyika with the system of the Congo is one of the most curious points in Central African hydrography. When Livingstone and Stanley were at Ujiji in 1871 the level of the lake was low. Between that date and 1874 it appears to have risen greatly, as Commander Cameron found that the Lukuga (mouth in 5° 35′ S. lat.) was acting as an overflow pipe. In 1876 Stanley obtained further proof of the increase of the lake: three palm-trees which had stood in the market place of Ujiji in 1871 were then 100 feet in the lake, and the sand beach over which he had walked with Livingstone was over 200. But his careful examination of the Lukuga outlet showed (curiously enough) that there was no distinct outflow from the lake, though he thought it pretty certain that the Lukuga had at one time been an effluent and that it was about to resume its old function. In March 1879 Captain Hore placed a gauge on the shore at Ujiji. By the 27th of May he found the waters had fallen 2 feet, and in August 1880 they reached a point 10 feet 4½ inches below the original mark. They were still subsiding in 1886.

The Lukuga outlet seems to be a comparatively modern formation. The portion towards Tanganyika appears to have been originally a stream flowing into the lake, all its affluents still having a lake-ward direction, while the section towards the Congo was a minor tributary of that river. At what period and by what circumstances the affluent was turned into an emissary it is hard to determine. Stanley proposed the bold theory that Tanganyika at one time consisted of two divisions, one at a higher level than the other, and that the sudden destruction of the barrier caused the lower lake to rise with such violence as to force a passage up the Lukuga and across the ridges to the Congo. Captain Storms suggests instead that Lake Hikwa or Rikwa (discovered by Joseph Thomson in 1880), which lies 50 miles to the east of Tanganyika, was more probably the source of the inundation. A visit to the plain of Katawi convinced him that this must at one time have formed part of Lake Hikwa, then about three times its present size. About 12 leagues N.N.E. of Karema he says there is a gap in the chain which separates the basin of the smaller from that of the larger lake. Not improbably, however, no such cataclysm as that proposed by Stanley or Storms is really necessary to account for the Lukuga pheno-

[1] Zaire is a Portuguese corruption of a native word. It is doubtful whether Congo was first the name of the kingdom or of the river; according to Janko (*Petermann's Mitteilungen*, 1888), the word probably means originally a "spear." Stanley called the river the Livingstone; but this designation has not become popular.

[2] Dr Murray of the "Challenger" Expedition estimates the mean annual discharge of the Congo at 419·291 cubic miles, making it in this respect only second to the Amazons (*Scot. Geog. Mag.*, 1887). The annual rainfall of the basin he puts at 1213·344 cubic miles.

menon. The very fact that, in the short space of time during which the Tanganyika has been observed by Europeans, its level has undergone such considerable alteration seems to suggest that a series of unusually rainy seasons may have been the source of all the inundation that was requisite.[1]

Below Lake Lanji there is another portion of the stream still unexplored; but from the junction of the Luama, a river 400 yards wide at its mouth (about 5° S. lat.), the whole course of the Congo down to the Atlantic (1800 miles) is known. At Nyangwe the channel is about a mile wide, with (according to Stanley) a volume of 230,000 cubic feet per second. As it flows northward it receives the Elila, the Ulinde, the Lowa, and the Munduku Lilu, all of moderate importance. The first point of much interest is the series of cataracts known as the Stanley Falls, situated at the equator. The first cataract occurs just after the Congo has received the Black river and the Leopold river; about 6 miles farther down follow in somewhat rapid succession the second, third, fourth, and fifth; and then the river is divided into two by the large inhabited island of Asama. The sixth cataract, caused by a broad dyke of greenish shale, does not occur for upwards of 20 miles, and between the sixth and seventh there is a distance of 25 miles. At the last of these the Congo is about 1300 yards broad, of which width 40 yards is occupied by the right branch, 760 yards by the island of Wemya, and 500 yards by the main river. The fall is only about 10 feet; but the enormous mass of water, and the narrow limits to which it is suddenly contracted, make it much more imposing than many a far loftier cataract. After passing the falls the first great left-hand affluent is the Lubilash or Boloko, first ascended by Grenfell in 1884 to the neighbourhood of 1° 30′. Next we come to an important right-hand affluent, the Aruwimi, Arawhimi, or Biyerre, which is now recognized as identical with the Nepoko, discovered by Junker in the south of the Monbuttu territory. About 24° 30′ E. lat. this stream, which discharges 158,850 cubic feet per second, is interrupted by the Yambuga Falls; but above the falls Stanley in 1887 found it navigable for his steel boat. Another right-hand affluent of similar rank is the Itimbiri or Loika, ascended in 1884 by Grenfell for 100 miles, as far as the Lubi Falls. No other tributary of equal importance is known to exist till we come to the Lulongo, about 45 miles north of the equator, formed by the junction of the Lopuri and the Masinga, which drain the country to the south of the great bend of the river. The Lopuri is 500 yards wide at the confluence and has a depth of from 7 to 8 feet. The Lulongo is 500 yards wide at its mouth and higher up occupies a channel from one-half to three-quarters of a mile in width. According to Von François, it discharges 494,200 cubic feet per second. It was ascended in 1885 by Grenfell, who describes it as commercially the most important affluent of the Congo, on account of the value of its ivory and slave trade. Just to the north of the equator is the junction of the Juapa or Chuapa, which Grenfell has followed as far east as 23° E. long., a distance of 400 miles. This is Stanley's Black river. An unusual amount of geographical interest attaches to the next Congo tributary—the Ubangi or Mobangi; if the latest reports are to be trusted, it is the recipient of the waters of the Welle-Makua, the river discovered by Schweinfurth in 1870, which has ever since been one of the hydrographic problems of the time.[2] Grenfell ascended the Ubangi in 1885 for some distance above the rapids of Zongo, which are formed by the river striking athwart a line of hills running north-west and south-east, with peaks from 600 to 700 feet above the level of the stream. At this point the breadth is reduced to about 800 yards. In 1886 M. van Gèle failed in his attempt to surmount the Zongo rapids; but in 1888, according to the latest reports, he succeeded in advancing sufficiently far up the river (which turns eastward at the rapids) to prove its identity with the Welle-Makua. By this discovery the limits of the Congo basin are carried eastward as far as within 40 miles of the Nile at Wadelai—the Welle being mainly formed of the Kibali, a stream about 80 yards wide, whose head-waters rise in that neighbourhood.[3] Quite a multitude of secondary streams join the upper course of the Ubangi, and it continues to receive accessories from the north and west till it merges in the longer river, into which it is calculated to pour about 529,500 cubic feet per second. Its last right-hand tributary probably drains the Tukki swamp in 13 E. long. The Nghiri Muinda or Loij, a comparatively small river draining the peninsula between the Ubangi and the Congo, joins the former about 30′ N. lat., with a current 100 yards wide and from 15 to 20 feet deep. It was ascended by the "Henry Reed" in 1886 as far as Mikutu (1° 20′ N. lat.), where the stream, still 9 feet deep, was found to be formed of a number of small channels issuing from a swampy forest. The Ibangi, a right-hand tributary of the Ubangi, was also navigated for 60 miles, to a spot where the depth was still 10 feet; but the passage was obstructed by a barrier of tree trunks. The ascent of the Lobay, which is about 200 yards wide and 13 feet deep at its junction with the Ubangi in 3° 50′ N. lat., was interrupted at a distance of 40 miles by a three-foot fall.

A short distance below the confluence of the Ubangi and Congo there enters from the left the emissary of Mantumba Lake, a considerable basin discovered by Stanley in 1883 and since examined by W. H. Bentley in the missionary ship "Peace." When the Congo is in flood there is a back-flow into the lake, and, as the whole country is very flat, it is quite possible that there is a connexion both with the Uruki and Bussera, on the one hand, and with Lake Leopold II., on the other. This latter lake is much larger, and is certainly connected southward with the Lukinje or Lukatta, a tributary of the Kassai.

In its further course the Congo is joined by a number of moderate-sized streams from the west. Below Lukolela it spreads out into a kind of river lake 20 to 25 kil. (12½ to 15½ miles) wide, and along its left bank extends a swampy region, the chain of low wood-covered hills which has hitherto confined the valley retiring for a mile or two. In 3° 15′ S. lat. it receives its last great affluent—the Kassai or Kwa, which has recently been proved to be the most important of the southern or left-hand, as the Ubangi is the most important of the northern or right-hand, tributaries. The Kassai rises to the south of 12′ S. lat. and flows north through Muata Yamvo's kingdom. In its upper course it possibly receives an emissary from Lake Dilolo, which also sends a branch south to the Zambesi. As it advances northwards it is joined by a large number of streams, all generally flowing northward. The Kassai enters the Congo in 3° 10′ S. lat., with a depth of 25 to 80 feet and a breadth of 600 yards, at a height of 942 feet above the sea. The exploration of the system was carried out by Wissmann, Wolf, Von François, and Mueller in 1883-85. The Kassai itself has been ascended as far as the Wissmann Fall in 5° 40′ S. lat., and its course has been struck at Digundu in 10° S. lat. The Lulua, which joins it from the right, is known as high up as Kangombe Fall; it is there about 200 yards wide; but it does not become truly navigable till it is joined by the Luebo. The Sankuru, at one time supposed to flow directly into the Congo,

[1] See *Bull. Soc. Roy. Belge de Géog.*, 1886, or *Scot. Geog. Mag.*, 1886.

[2] For the discussion of the Welle problem, see *Mouvement Géographique*, 1886, Janko's resumé of theories in *Scot. Geogr. Mag.*, 1888, and Wills's criticism of the same.

[3] See map illustrating the journeys of Dr W. Junker, *Proc. Roy Geogr. Soc.*, 1887.

enters the Kassai by two arms, 820 feet and 200 feet in breadth, in 4° 17′ S. lat. and 20° 15′ E. long., its bright yellow waters forming a strong contrast with the brown of the larger stream. The Kuango, a fine stream, with its head-waters in the same district as those of the Kassai, flows in a wonderfully straight course north to join that river in 17° 30′ E. long. It was ascended by Mechow in 1880 as far as the rocky ledge at Kikamshi or Kinganshi; and, though it is only 3 feet high, the same barrier prevented the ascent of Grenfell's steamer in 1887.

For 87 miles after receiving the Kassai or Kwa the Congo flows in a deep gorge, between banks sometimes 700 feet high. In 4° 5′ S. lat. it enters Stanley Pool, an island-studded lake 1147 feet above the sea, expanding southward of the main course of the river. Its rim is "formed by sierras of peaked and picturesque mountains, ranging on the southern side from 1000 feet to 3000 feet in height." The banks offer considerable variety in character. A striking object on the north bank is the Dover Cliffs, so named by Stanley from their white and glistening appearance, produced, however, not by chalk but by silver sand, the subsidence of which into the water renders approach to the bank sometimes dangerous. Towards the lower end of the lake the country on both sides becomes comparatively low and flat, and at places swampy. On the south side, however, stands the great red cliff of Kallina Point (about 50 feet high), so named after an Austrian lieutenant drowned there in 1882. Round the point rushes a strong current 7½ knots an hour, difficult to stem even for a steamer. On the river, as it leaves the Pool, are situated (south side) Leopoldville, founded by Stanley in 1881, and Brazzaville, a station established by the French explorer De Brazza. Below Stanley Pool the Congo begins to break through the coast ranges, and forms a long series of rapids and falls, often enclosed between rocky shores, and even cliffs. Among the more important falls are those named Mahmey, Zinga, Ntambo, Uataka, Itunzima, Isangila, Ngoma, and Yellala. At Yellala, just above Vivi, the river escapes into the lowlands and is navigable for the rest of its journey to the sea (113 miles). Below Boma (5° 48′ S. lat.) it widens out and is interrupted by numerous islands; but it does not break up into several channels so as to form a delta, though there are various creeks that appear as if they might yet become deltaic outlets. Between Banana Point on the north and Shark Point on the south the mouth of the Congo has a width of 7 miles. At Banana Point (at which there is not a vestige of the plant whose name it bears) there is fair harbourage for sea-going vessels. Shark Point is also known as Padron Point, from the remains of a stone pillar (*padrão*) erected by the Portuguese explorer Diogo Cão (visited by Burton, 1863; by Daunett, 1887).

The exploration of the Congo system has been accompanied and followed by one of the most remarkable political movements of modern times. On 15th September 1876 the International African Association was constituted, under the presidency of Leopold II., king of the Belgians, for the purpose of devising the best means of opening up equatorial Africa to civilization. Later on (25th November 1878) was founded under the same auspices a Comité d'Études du Haut Congo, which afterwards became known as the International Association of the Congo. It was as an agent of this association that Mr Stanley undertook his epoch-making ascent of the river in 1879. In September the first permanent station of the association was founded at Vivi;[1] in December the second at Jangila; and in May 1881 the third at Manyanga. The association was recognized as an independent territorial government by the United States in April 1884 and by Germany in November of the same year. An international conference for the regulation of the relations of the new state and the various European Governments was held at Berlin under the presidency of Prince Bismarck (15th November 1884–26th February 1885). The permanent neutrality of the Congo State territory, freedom of commerce in the Congo basin, and the abolition of the slave trade were among the main points established by the plenipotentiaries. In the close of 1884 and the early part of 1885 the association was recognized by England (16th December 1884), Italy, Austria-Hungary, the Netherlands, France, &c. In April 1885 the Belgian chamber of representatives authorized King Leopold to become sovereign of the new state—the union between Belgium and the Congo to be purely personal. The total area of the Independent State of the Congo, as it is officially designated, is estimated at 807,125 square miles, and its population may be about 40,000,000. It has a very limited coast-line, being hemmed in by French territory on the north and by Portuguese territory on the south. The southern limit is a conventional line from Nokki (on the south bank of the river below Vivi) across the continent to Langi Lake; the northern limit follows the fourth parallel of N. lat. from 17° to 30° E. long. French territory occupies all the north bank of the river from Ngombi (15 E. long.) up to Lukolela. In 1888 the state maintained 146 white officials, and had a force of upwards of 1000 native soldiers (Zanzibaris, Haussas, and Bangalas). It has four steamers on the lower Congo and five on the upper. The value of the commerce is as yet only £560,000, the principal exports being india-rubber, ivory, coffee, palm nuts and oil, copal, and wax. As to the possibility of developing the country into a great consumer of European goods, there has been much and bitter discussion; at the present stage it is admitted that it has no native product of value in sufficient quantity to pay for a large importation. The river, however, has recently been proved navigable for sea-going vessels as far as the capital, Boma, and no serious difficulties have been met by the engineers engaged in surveying a railway from the lower Congo up to Stanley Pool.

See Stanley, *The Dark Continent* and *The Congo*; Johnson, *The Congo to Bolobo*; Thy, *Au Congo et au Kasai*, 1888; Coquithat, *Sur le Haut Congo*, 1888; Wissmann, Wolf, &c., *Im Innern Afrikas*, 1888.

[1] See list of stations—some of which have been since abandoned—in *Scot. Geogr. Mag.*, 1885.

ZALEUCUS. See Locri.

ZAMBESI, the most important river on the East Coast of Africa (see vol. i. pl. II.), and the fourth largest on the continent, drains during its course of about 1200 miles an area of 600,000 square miles. Its head-streams, which have not yet been fully explored, are the Leeambye or Iambaji, rising in Cazembe's country; the Lungebungo, which descends from the Mossamba Mountains; and the Leeba river, from the marshy Lake Dilolo (4740 feet), situated between 10° and 12° S. lat. and 22° and 23° E. long. These three rivers, reinforced by the Nhengo, unite to form the upper Zambesi (Leeambye), which flows at first southwards and slightly eastwards through the Barotse valley, then turns prominently to the east near its junction with the Chobe (Chuando or Linianti), and passes over the Victoria Falls. Thence, as the middle reach of the Zambesi, the river sweeps north-east towards Zumbo and the Kebrabassa rapids above Tete, and finally forms the lower Zambesi, which curves southwards until it reaches the Indian Ocean at 18° 50′ S. lat. Fed chiefly from the highland country which stretches from Lake Nyassa to inner Angola, its chief tributaries are the Loangwa and the Shiré, the last an important river draining out of Lake Nyassa, and which in the dry season contains probably as great a volume of water as the Zambesi, and is much more navigable. Except for an interruption of 70 miles at the Murchison cataracts, the Shiré is open throughout its entire length to the lake.

On the whole the Zambesi has a gentle current, and flows through a succession of wide fertile valleys and richly wooded plains; but, owing to the terrace-like structure of the continent, the course of the river is interrupted from point to point by cataracts and rapids. These form serious, and in some cases insurmountable, hindrances to navigation. Those on the lower Zambesi begin with its delta. The bar here was long held to be impassable, except to vessels of the shallowest draught; but the difficulty was exaggerated partly through ignorance and partly in the interests of the Portuguese settlement of Quilimane, which, before the merits of the Kongone entrance were understood, had been already established on the Qua-qua river, 60 miles to the north. The Zambesi is now known to have four mouths, the Milambe to the west, the Kongone, the Luabo, and the Timbwe. The best of these, the Kongone, has altered and the channel improved recently. There are at least 18 feet of water on the bar at high water neap tides; and steamers drawing 15 feet, and sailing vessels drawing 3 feet less, have no difficulty in entering. The deep water continues only a short distance; and, after Mazaro (60 miles) is reached, where the river has already dwindled to the breadth of a mile, the channel is precariously open in the dry season as far as Senna (120 miles from the mouth) for vessels drawing $4\frac{1}{2}$ feet. Up to this point navigation could only be successfully and continuously carried on by vessels of much lighter draught—stern-wheelers for preference with a draught of little more than 18 inches. About 90 miles from Senna the river enters the Lupata gorge, the impetuous current contracting between walls to a width of scarcely 200 yards. Passing Tete (240 miles from the mouth with a smooth course), the channel becomes dangerous at Kebrabassa, 90 miles farther on. From the Kebrabassa rapids upwards, and past the Victoria Falls, there are occasional stretches of navigable water extending for considerable distances, while the upper Zambesi with its confluents and their tributaries forms a really fine and extensive waterway. Like the Nile, the Zambesi is visited by annual inundations, during which the whole country is flooded and many of the minor falls and rapids are then obliterated.

The chief physical feature of the Zambesi is the Mosi-oa-tunya ("smoke sounds there") or Victoria Falls, admitted to be one of the noblest waterfalls in the world. The cataract is bounded on three sides by ridges 300 or 400 feet high, and these, along with the many islands dotted over the stream, are covered with sylvan vegetation. The falls, according to Livingstone, are caused by a stupendous crack or rent, with sharp and almost unbroken edges, stretching right across the river in the hard black basalt which here forms the bed. The cleft is 360 feet in sheer depth and close upon a mile in length. Into this chasm, of more than twice the depth of Niagara, the river rolls with a deafening roar, sending up vast columns of spray, which are visible for a distance of 20 miles. Unlike Niagara, the Mosi-oa-tunya does not terminate in an open gorge, the river immediately below the fall being blocked at 80 yards distance by the opposing side of the (supposed) cleft running parallel to the precipice which forms the waterfall. The only outlet is a narrow channel cut in this barrier at a point 1170 yards from the western end of the chasm and some 600 from its eastern, and through this the Zambesi, now only 20 or 30 yards wide, pours for 120 yards before emerging into the enormous zig-zag trough which conducts the river past the basalt plateau.

The region drained by the Zambesi may be represented as a vast broken-edged plateau 3000 or 4000 feet high, composed in the remote interior of metamorphic beds and fringed with the igneous rocks of the Victoria Falls. At Shupanga, on the lower Zambesi, thin strata of grey and yellow sandstones, with an occasional band of limestone, crop out on the bed of the river in the dry season, and these persist beyond Tete, where they are associated with extensive seams of coal. Gold is also known to occur in several places.

The higher regions of the Zambesi have only been visited by one or two explorers; and the lower, though nominally in possession of the Portuguese since the beginning of the 16th century, are also comparatively little known. The Barotse valley or valley of the upper Zambesi is a vast pastoral plain, 3300 feet above sea-level, about 189 miles in length and 30 to 35 broad. Though inundated in the rainy season, it is covered with villages and supports countless herds of cattle. The Luinas who inhabit it are clothed with skins, work neatly in ivory, and live upon milk, maize, and sweet potatoes. In the neighbourhood of the falls the tsetse fly abounds, so that the Batoka people who live there, and who are the only arboriculturists in the country, live upon the products of their gardens. Zumbo, on the north bank, and Chicova, opposite on the southern side (500 miles above the delta), were the farthest inland of the Portuguese East African settlements, and are well placed for commerce with the natives. Founded by Pereira, a native of Goa, these settlements were ultimately allowed to go to ruins; but Zumbo has been recently re-occupied. The once celebrated gold mines of Parda Pemba are in the vicinity. The only other Portuguese settlements on the Zambesi are Tete and Senna. Tete, formerly a large and important place, now nearly in ruins, still possesses a fort and several good tiled stone and mud houses. Thither Portuguese goods, chiefly wines and provisions, are carried by means of canoes. The exports, which include ivory, gold dust, wheat, and ground-nuts, are limited owing to the difficulty of transport; but this difficulty is not insurmountable, for Tete has been twice visited by small steam vessels. Senna, farther down the river, a neglected and unhealthy village, has suffered much from political mismanagement, and has ceaseless troubles with the Landeens or Zulus, who own the southern bank of the river and collect in force every year to exact a heavy tribute-money. The industrial possibilities of the lower Zambesi, and indeed of the whole river-system, are enormous. India-rubber, indigo, archil, beeswax, and calumba root are plentiful, and oil seeds and the sugar-cane could be produced in sufficient quantity to supply the whole of Europe.

The Zambesi region was known to the mediæval geographers as the empire of Monomotapa, and the course of the river, as well as the position of Lakes N'gami and Nyassa, was filled in with a rude approximation to accuracy in the earlier maps. These were probably constructed from Arab information. The first European to visit the upper Zambesi was Livingstone in his exploration from Bechuanaland between 1851 and 1853. Two or three years later he descended the Zambesi to its mouth and in the course of this journey discovered the Victoria Falls. In 1859, accompanied by Dr Kirk (now Sir John Kirk), Livingstone ascended the river as far as the falls, after tracing the course of its main tributary the Shiré and discovering Lake Nyassa. The mouths of the Zambesi were long claimed exclusively by the Portuguese, but in 1888 the British Government opened negotiations with Portugal to have the river declared free to all nations. (H. D.)

ZAMORA, an inland province of Spain, one of the three into which the former province of Leon has since 1833 been divided, is bounded on the W. by Tras-os-Montes (Portugal) and Orense, on the N. by Leon, on the E. by Valladolid, and on the S. by Salamanca; its area is 4135 square miles. It is traversed from east to west by the Douro, which receives within the province the Valderaduey and the Esla on the right and the Guareña on the left; the Tormes also skirts the south-western boundary for some 25 miles. Except in the north-west and west, where it is entered by spurs from the Cantabrian chain (Sierra de la Culebra and Sierra de Peña Negra), the province is flat; its lowest point is 1070 feet above sea-level. Its plains, especially the "tierra de campo" formed by the valley of the Esla, yield large quantities of grain and pulse; wine and flax are also produced; and on the higher grounds large numbers of merino sheep are fed. The industries of Zamora are unimportant. The province is traversed by no railway except that connecting its capital with Medina del Campo on the northern line. There are eight partidos judiciales and 300 ayuntamientos; besides ZAMORA (see below), the capital, there is only one town, the historic city of Toro (7754), with a population exceeding 5000. The total population of the province in 1877 was 250,000.

ZAMORA, capital of the above province, is situated 2000 feet above sea-level, on the right bank of the Douro (here crossed by a bridge of seventeen pointed arches) a little below its junction with the Valderaduey, 57 miles by rail west by north from Medina del Campo and 182 miles north-west from Madrid. The population in 1877 was 13,632. It has a small but fine Romanesque cathedral (completed about 1174) and an ancient castle, as well as several other interesting churches of the 12th century. It is the seat of a seminary and an academy of engineering, and has unimportant linen and woollen manufactures.

In the early period of the Christian re-conquest Zamora, from its position on the north of the Douro, was a place of considerable strategic importance. It was taken from the Arabs by Alonso the

Catholic in 748, but was again held by them for short periods in 813, 939, 963, 984, and 986. It was entirely repaired by Ferdinand I., who in 1061 gave it to his daughter Doña Urraca. After his death in 1065 Sancho disputed possession with his sister and laid siege to the town, but without success, although the famous Ruy Diaz de Bivar was among his warriors, and indeed at this time received his title of El Cid Campeador. The town became subject to Alphonso VI. in 1073.

ZANESVILLE, a city of the United States, the county seat of Muskingum county, Ohio, is situated on both banks of the Muskingum river, at the mouth of Licking river, 170 miles north-east of Cincinnati and 37 nearly due south of Cleveland. The surrounding country is thickly populated, the inhabitants being engaged in agriculture and in coal and iron mining. Zanesville has railway communication by several lines. The population in 1880 was 18,113, showing a gain of about 80 per cent. since 1870.

Zanesville was founded about the beginning of the 19th century, and in 1804 was made the county seat. From 1810 to 1812 the Ohio legislature met at Zanesville. It was incorporated as a city in 1855. Its growth prior to 1870 was slow.

ZANTE, the ancient ZACYNTHUS, an island of Greece, one of the Ionian group, in the Ionian Sea, in 37° 40′ N. lat. and 21° E. long., is 25 miles long, about 12 broad, and 64 miles round, with an area of 277 square miles, and a population in 1879 of 44,522, and estimated in 1887, at 48,000. Zante lies 8 miles south of Cephalonia, forming with it, Leucas, and Ithaca a crescent-shaped insular group, which represents the crests of a submerged limestone ridge facing the Gulf of Patras. At Ithaca, its northernmost member, the ridge almost touches the adjacent coast of Acarnania, with which it is geologically connected; and at Zante, its southernmost member, it recedes about 15 miles from the coast of Elis in Morea. Zante is of somewhat irregular oval shape, with its main axis disposed in the direction from north-west to south-east, and indented by a deep inlet at its southern extremity. The surface is mainly occupied by an extensive and highly productive central plain, skirted on the west side by a range of bare limestone hills from 1000 to 1200 feet high, which fall gently landwards, but present bold steep cliffs towards the sea, and which culminate northwards in Mount Skopos (1500 feet?), the highest point in the island. On the east side the plain is also limited by a low ridge, which still justifies the epithet of *nemorosa*, or the "wooded," applied by Virgil to Zacynthus. These hills are densely clothed to their summits with an exuberant growth of olives, figs, myrtles, laurels, oranges, aloes, vines, and other sub-tropical plants. Travellers sailing between this coast and the mainland describe in enthusiastic language the charming effect produced by these masses of evergreen vegetation rising in long terraces above the surrounding waters, and everywhere interspersed with pleasant homesteads and hamlets embowered in verdure. Nevertheless Zante, notwithstanding its Italian title of "Fior di Levante," is inferior in picturesque beauty to Corfu, owing to the less elevation of its hills and the somewhat monotonous character of the great central plain. This plain, however, is highly cultivated, forming an almost continuous stretch of gardens and vineyards, varied here and there with a few patches of cornfields and pasture lands. Here is grown a peculiar dwarf vine, whose fruit, the "currant" (from "Corinth") of commerce, forms the chief resource and staple export of Zante, as well as of the neighbouring mainland. In 1886 the currant crop for the whole of Greece was valued at £2,000,000, of which nearly one-fifth was raised in Zante, chiefly for the English market. The vine, which grows to a height of 3 feet, begins to yield in seven years and lasts for over a century. From the grape, which has a pleasant bitter-sweet taste, a wine is also extracted, which is said to excel all others in flavour, fire, and strength. Besides this species, there are nearly forty different kinds of vine and ten of the olive, including the *karudolia*, which yields the best edible olive berry. For size, vigorous growth, and productiveness the olive tree of Zante is rivalled only by that of Corfu.

The island enjoys a healthy climate; and, although there are no perennial streams, an abundant supply of good water is obtained from the numerous springs, occurring especially in the eastern and central districts. But earthquakes are frequent and at times disastrous. During recent times the most destructive were those of 1811, 1820, and 1840; and, although the prevailing geological formations are sedimentary, chiefly calcareous, there seems no doubt that these disturbances are of igneous origin. Other indications of volcanic agency are the oil springs occurring on the coast, and even in the bed of the sea near Cape Skinari on the north side, and especially the famous pitch or bituminous wells already mentioned by Herodotus (*Hist.*, bk. iv.). These have been productive throughout the historic period and still yield a considerable supply of pitch. They are situated in a swamp near the coast village of Chieri, and comprise two basins, with alternate layers of water and bitumen, the lower sheet of water apparently communicating with the sea.

Zante, capital of the island, is a considerable seaport on the east side, with a population of 16,250 (1879). It occupies the site of the ancient city of Zacynthus, said to have been founded by Zacynthus, son of a legendary Arcadian chief, Dardanus, to whom was also attributed the neighbouring citadel of Psophis. But of this, as well as of the temple of Diana that formerly crowned the summit of Mount Scopus, no vestiges can now be discovered.

Traditionally the island formed part of the territory of Ulysses, king of Ithaca, and at one time it appears to have also received a colony of Achæans from Peloponnesus. Later it joined the Athenian hegemony; but after the fall of Athens the democratic party was replaced by an oligarchy, which ruled in the interests of Sparta. Under the Romans Zacynthus was included in the province of Epirus, and passed in mediæval times successively from Byzantium to the Normans (11th century), the Orsini, counts of Cephalonia (after the 4th crusade), and the Tocco family, who held it with Cephalonia as vassals of the Neapolitan Angevine dynasty. In the 15th century it was occupied by the Venetians, and was held by them till the fall of the republic in 1797. Wrested in 1799 by the Russians from the French, it was soon after seized by the English, and in 1815 constituted with the other Ionian Islands a "septinsular republic" under British protection, till the union with Greece in 1864.

The long Venetian occupation is reflected in the appearance, character, and to some extent even the language and religion of the Zantiots. Nearly all the aristocracy claim Venetian descent; most of the upper classes are bilingual, speaking both Greek and Italian; and a considerable section of the population are Roman Catholics of the Latin rite. Even the bulk of the people, although mainly of Greek stock, form in their social usages a connecting link between the Hellenes, whose language they speak, and the Western nations by whom they were so long ruled. They have the reputation of being industrious and enterprising, but passionate and revengeful. But no more high-minded, enlightened, and courteous people can anywhere be found than in the circle of the Maddalenas, Terzettis, Mercatis, and other families of Venetian lineage.

See Balthazar Raimondini, *De Zacynthi Antiquitatibus*; C. Parrigopoulo, *Histoire de la Civilisation Hellénique*; S. de Nolhac, *La Dulmatie, les Îles Ioniennes*, &c., Paris, 1882.

ZANZIBAR, or, more correctly, ZANGUEBAR, a sultanate of east central Africa, which till recently comprised the four islands of Zanzibar, Pemba, Lamu, and Mafia (Monfia), together with the adjacent seaboard from about 3° N. to 10° S. lat., with undefined limits towards the interior. But by the Anglo-German convention, signed in London on 29th October 1886, the territory on the mainland was restricted to the strip of coastlands ten nautical miles broad, stretching from the mouth of the Miningani river at the bay of Tunghi, just south of Cape Delgado, northwards to Kipini at the mouth of the Tana, together with the isolated stations of Kisimayu (Kismayu), Brava, Merka, and Magdoshu (Magadoxo) on the Somal coast, each with a land circuit of ten nautical miles, and Warsheikh on the same coast, with a land circuit of five nautical miles. Since then, however, further changes have taken place. The sultan's officers have been replaced in the seaports of Dar-es-Salaam and Pangani on the Zanzibar coast proper by commissioners of the German East African Association, to whom the customs of those places have been farmed; the port of Tunghi below Cape Delgado has been claimed and forcibly occupied (1887) by the Portuguese; the island of Pemba appears to have been ceded (May 1888) to the recently chartered British East African Company; lastly, the station of Kisimayu on the Somal coast is claimed (June 1888) by Italy in reparation of an affront offered to the Italian consul at Zanzibar. But, as defined by the above-mentioned convention, the reduced dominions of the sultan have areas (in square miles) and estimated populations (1887) as under:—

	Area.	Population.
Island of Zanzibar	640	220,000
,, ,, Pemba	380	10,000
,, ,, Mafia	200	7,000
,, ,, Lamu	50	20,000
Zanzibar coastlands	6000	500,000
Stations on Somal coast	150	8,000
Total...	7420	765,000

The political and commercial, as well as the geographical, centre of the state is the fertile and densely peopled island of Zanzibar, which lies at a mean distance of 20 miles from the Swahili coast, between 5° 40′ and 6° 30′ S. lat. With the neighbouring Pemba (to the north) and the more distant Mafia (to the south) it forms an independent geological system, resting on a foundation of coralline reefs, and constituting a sort of outer coast-line, which almost everywhere presents a rocky barrier to the fury of the waves rolling in from the Indian Ocean. All three are disposed parallel to the adjacent seaboard, from which they are separated by shallow waters, mostly under thirty fathoms, and strewn with numerous reefs dangerous to navigation, especially in the Mafia channel opposite the Rufiji delta.

Mafia itself is low and fertile, and extensively planted with cocoa-nut palms. It is continued southwards by an extensive reef, on which stands the chief village, Chobe, the residence of the governor and of a few Arab and Hindu (Banyan) traders. Chobe stands on a shallow creek inaccessible to shipping.

Zanzibar, the Unguya of the natives, is not exclusively of coralline formation, but also presents several heights of a reddish ferruginous clay, rising in gentle slopes above the central plains. In the south these heights nowhere exceed 400 or 450 feet; but on the north-west coast they develop a chain of hills disposed parallel to the shore and attaining an elevation of a little over 1000 feet. The forests by which the island was formerly covered have mostly disappeared, and the greater part of the rich soil is carefully cultivated, yielding two annual crops of corn, and four of manioc, the staple food of the people. There are extensive cocoa-nut groves, and from India and Malaysia have been introduced the mangosteen, guava, durian, cinnamon, nutmeg, and cloves, all of which thrive well. The soil seems specially suited for the clove, which, although nearly destroyed by the terrific cyclone of 1872, has already recovered from that disaster, and the annual export of this spice now exceeds £10,000 in value. Although the fauna is almost exclusively continental, Zanzibar till recently possessed a distinct variety of *Colobus* (*C. kirkii*), which appears to be now extinct.[1] Some years ago a hippopotamus visited the island from the mainland; but no carnivora are now found larger than the serval and wild cat.

On the east side of the island there still survive a few groups of Wa-Hadimu Bantus, who represent the aboriginal stock. But elsewhere, and especially in the capital (for which, see below), the population is of an extremely heterogeneous character, including full-blood and half-caste Arabs, Indian "Canarians" (that is, half-caste Portuguese from Kanara on the Malabar Coast of India), Swahili of every shade, slaves or freedmen from all parts of East Africa, Europeans, and Americans. (See SWAHILI.)

[1] H. H. Johnston, *The Kilima-Njaro Expedition*, p. 38.

The neighbouring island of Pemba, intersected by 5° S. lat., is even more fertile, but much less cultivated, than Zanzibar. From the luxuriant vegetation which everywhere clothes the cliffs to their summits it takes the name of the "Green." The land is exclusively owned by great Arab proprietors, who work their plantations with scarcely disguised slave labour and export considerable quantities of cloves, which here also find a congenial home. The capital, Shaki-Shaki, which lies at the head of a shallow creek on the west side, is inaccessible to shipping. But at Kishi-Kashi, at the north-west extremity, there is a deep and well-sheltered harbour, though of somewhat difficult approach. Here resides the chief of the Arab landed aristocracy, who has hitherto been more of a vassal than a subject of the sultan, and whose allegiance has lately been transferred to the British East African Association.

Lamu also, the fourth member of the sultan's former insular possessions, has ceased to fly the Zanzibar flag. It is a small flat island lying close to the mainland above the mouth of the Ozi branch of the Tana delta, and appears to be now incorporated in the adjacent German territory of Vitu land. Lamu, its capital, with a reported population of 15,000, has a fine harbour, formed by a long deep channel separating it from the neighbouring island of Manda.

The Zanzibar seaboard (now more generally known as the Swahili coast) is a low-lying swampy and alluvial region, rising gently from the sea towards the first terraced escarpments of the continental plateau. Owing to the numerous streams reaching the coast along this seaboard —Rovuma, Ukeredi, Umbi-Kuru, Rufiji, Rufu, Wami, Umba, and others—a great part of the surface consists of rich alluvial soil, densely covered with a tropical vegetation. Here the warm currents setting landwards from the Indian Ocean bring both moisture and heat, so that this coast has a higher temperature and heavier rainfall than the Atlantic seaboard under the same parallels of latitude.[2] Thanks to these conditions, while the climate is oppressive and malarious, the vegetation is extremely luxuriant, assuming about the marshy deltas the aspect of an impenetrable jungle of mangroves, reeds, and tall grasses, growing to a height of 12 or 14 feet. A characteristic plant is the *msandarusi* or copal-tree of the lower Rufiji valley, which yields the best gum known to commerce. Other economic plants more or less extensively cultivated are rice, maize, millet, the cocoa-nut and oil palm, besides several European species already acclimatized at Bagamoyo and other stations. But nearly the whole of this region is well suited for raising tropical produce, such as sugar, coffee, cotton, indigo, cinnamon, cloves, and other spices.

Besides Dar-es-Salaam and Pangani, surrendered to the Germans (see above), the chief stations and seaports, going northwards, are Lindi, Kilwa (Quiloa), Bagamoyo, Mombasa (Mombas), and Malindi (Melinda). Of these Bagamoyo is at present the most important, as the starting-point of travellers and traders for the interior. Here are also the headquarters of the French Roman Catholic missions in east equatorial Africa, with training schools, extensive plantations, and gardens of acclimatization. Kilwa, Mombasa, and Malindi, great and flourishing emporiums under the Zenj empire, are now almost abandoned. This remark applies also to Magdoshu, the chief isolated station on the Somal coast belonging to Zanzibar.

From the earliest times of which there is any authentic record the whole of the seaboard from the Somal coast to an unknown distance southwards was comprised within the dominions of the Zenj (Zang) potentates, who for centuries claimed and vindicated the title of "sovereign of the sea." From them the seaboard

[2] Mean temperature of the West and East Coasts 72° and 80° Fahr. respectively; average annual rainfall at Zanzibar 60 inches; at Loanda (Atlantic side) 36 inches; rainfall at Zanzibar in 1859 (exceptional) 170 inches.

itself took the name of *zanguebar*,[1] the Bálíd-ez-Zenj, or "Land of the Zenj" of the Arabs, a term which thus corresponds to the Hindu-bar, or "land of the Hindu," formerly applied to the west coast of India on the opposite side of the intervening Arabian Sea. By Ibn Batuta and other Arab writers the Zenj people themselves are spoken of in a general way as Mohammedan Negroes; and they are no doubt still represented by the semi-civilized and highly intelligent Mohammedan Bantus now collectively known as the Swahili or "coast people." Their empire began to decline soon after the appearance of the Portuguese in the eastern waters towards the close of the 15th century. To them fell in rapid succession the great cities of Kilwa with its 300 mosques (1505), Mombasa the "Magnificent" (1505), and soon after Malindi and Magdoshu the "Immense" (Ibn Batuta). On the ruins of the Portuguese power in the 17th century was built up that of the imams of Muscat, who ruled over a great part of south Arabia and the whole of the Zanzibar coast for over a century and a half down to 1856. On the death of the imam, or rather the "sayyid," Said of Muscat in that year his dominions were divided between his two sons, the African section falling to Majid, who was succeeded in 1870 by his younger brother Bargash ibn Said, commonly known as sultan of Zanzibar. He lived long enough to witness the recent dismemberment of his dominions, and in March 1888 left to his son and successor, Sayyid Khalif, a mere fragment of the former powerful Mohammedan empire on the East-African seaboard. The administration of the "ten-mile zone" on the mainland, although reserved to the sultan by the Anglo-German convention of 1886, was practically surrendered to the Germans in August 1888 when the German East African Company hoisted their flag jointly with the sultan's at fourteen ports along this seaboard.

See J. L. Krapf, *Travels*, &c., London, 1830; Baron von der Decken, *Reisen in Ost-Afrika*, Leipsic, 1869; Captain R. F. Burton, *The Lake Regions of Central Africa*, London, 1860; Keith Johnston and A. H. Keane, *Africa* (Stanford series), London, 1878; H. M. Stanley, *Through the Dark Continent*, London, 1878; H. H. Johnston, *The Kilima-Njaro Expedition*, London, 1885; Joseph Thomson, *To the Central African Lakes*, &c., London, 1881. (A. H. K.)

ZANZIBAR, capital of the island and state of the same name, is the largest city on the African seaboard next to Alexandria and Tunis. It lies in sheltered waters, from 30 to 40 feet deep, on the west side of the island, in 6° 10′ S. lat., about 25 miles north-east of Bagamoyo, its port on the mainland. It comprises two distinct quarters,—Shangani, the centre of trade and residence of the sultan, and the eastern suburb occupied by the lowest classes (fishermen, porters, slaves, &c.), with a total joint population estimated in 1887 at about 100,000. Viewed from the sea, the place presents a pleasant prospect with its glittering mosques, palace, white houses, barracks, forts, and round towers. But the interior is a labyrinth of narrow filthy streets, winding through a dense mass of hovels, a "cesspool of wickedness Oriental in its appearance, Mohammedan in its religion, Arabian in its morals, . . . a fit capital for the Dark Continent."[2] Nevertheless Zanzibar, which is now regularly visited by several lines of ocean steamers, is the necessary centre of trade for the eastern seaboard, the focus of all exploring and missionary work for the interior, the portal through which civilizing influences have hitherto penetrated into the eastern section of equatorial Africa. The imports, chiefly raw and bleached cottons and European wares, were valued at £1,220,000 in 1883, the exports at £800,000, of which £215,000 represented ivory, £153,000 caoutchouc, £13,000 sesame seed, £10,600 cloves. In 1885 the port was visited by 124 vessels of 115,500 tons, of which 49 of 60,674 tons were British. There are several Protestant and Roman Catholic missions stationed in Zanzibar, the health of which has been much improved by a recently constructed aqueduct yielding a good supply of pure water.

ZARA (Slav. *Zadar*), an Austrian seaport, the capital of Dalmatia, and the seat of a Roman Catholic archbishop and of a Greek bishop, lies on the Adriatic, 130 miles south-east of Trieste, opposite the islands of Ugliano and Pasman, from which it is separated by the narrow Channel of Zara. The promontory on which it stands is separated from the mainland by a deep moat, practically making an island of the site of the city. Down to 1873 Zara was strongly fortified; but its ramparts have now been converted into elevated promenades, which command extensive views to seaward and to landward. Of its four old gates one, the Porta Marina, incorporates the relics of a Roman arch, and another, the Porta di Terraferma, was designed by Sanmichele. The general aspect of the town, which is oval in form, is thoroughly Venetian. The main streets, dividing it into four quarters, are straight and wide, but the side-streets are ill-paved and narrow. The chief interest of Zara lies in its churches, the most remarkable of which is the cathedral of St Anastasia, a fine Romanesque basilica, founded by Doge Enrico Dandolo after the capture of the town in 1202 and finished in 1205. The churches of St Chrysogonus and St Simeon are also in the Romanesque style, and St Mary's retains a fine Romanesque campanile of 1105. The old octagonal church of St Donatus, traditionally (but in all probability erroneously) said to have been erected in the 9th century on the site of a temple of Juno, has been converted to secular purposes. Most of the Roman remains were used up in the construction of the fortifications. But two squares are embellished with lofty marble columns; a Roman tower stands on the east side of the town; and some remains of a Roman aqueduct may be seen outside the ramparts. Among the other chief buildings are the Loggia del Comune, rebuilt in 1565, containing a public library of 34,000 volumes; the old palace of the priors, now the governor's residence; and the episcopal palace. The harbour, to the north-east of the town, is safe and spacious, and it is annually entered by about 1200 vessels, of 185,000 tons, mainly engaged in the coasting trade. The chief industry is the preparation of maraschino, made from the marasco, or wild cherry, which covers the hills of Dalmatia. About 340,000 bottles of this liqueur are exported annually. Glass-making and fishing are also carried on. The population of the town in 1881 was 11,861, of the commune 24,536. Almost all of these are of Italian descent, and Italian is practically the only language spoken in the town.

The foundation of Zara is ascribed by tradition to the Liburni. In the early days of the Roman empire it became a flourishing Roman colony under the name of *Jadera*, subsequently changed to *Diadora*. It remained united with the Eastern empire down to about the year 1000, when it sought the Venetian protection. For the next four centuries it was a bone of contention between Venice and Hungary, changing hands repeatedly. It was occupied by the Hungarians at the end of the 12th century, but was re-captured by the Venetians in 1202, with the aid of French crusaders on their way to the Holy Land. In 1409 it was finally purchased from Hungary by the island republic for 100,000 ducats. In 1792 it passed, with Venice, into the possession of Austria. From 1809 to 1813 it belonged to France.

About 15 miles to the south-east lies Zara Vecchia, or Old Zara, an insignificant village on the site of Biograd (White Town), formerly the residence of the Croatian kings, but destroyed during the Hungarian-Venetian wars.

Comp. *Zara, e suoi Dintorni* (Zara, 1878), and *Notize Storiche della Città di Zara* (Zara, 1883), both by Angelo Nani.

ZARAGOZA, or SARAGOSSA, an inland province of Spain, one of the three into which Aragon is now divided, is bounded on the N.E. and E. by Huesca, Lerida, and Tarragona, on the S. by Teruel and Guadalajara, and on the W. by Soria and Navarre; the area is 6607 square miles. It belongs wholly to the basin of the Ebro, by which river it is traversed from north-west to south-east. The main valley is bounded on the S.W. by the Sierra de Moncayo, which reaches a maximum elevation—the highest in the province—of 7700 feet, and is continued in a south-easterly direction by the lower sierras of La Virgen and Vicor; on the north-west are the spurs of the Pyrenees. The principal tributaries of the Ebro within the province are the Jalón, Huerva, and Aguas on the right and the Arva and Gállego on the left; the Aragon also, which flows principally through Navarre, has part of its course in the

[1] Mispronounced *Zanzibar* by the local Banyans and other Indian traders.

[2] Prof. H. Drummond, *Tropical Africa*, p. 5.

north of this province. At its lowest point, where the Ebro quits it, Zaragoza is only 105 feet above sea-level. The soil is in its level portions comparatively fertile, the chief productions being wheat, rye, barley, oats, hemp, flax, oil, and wine. Silkworms are bred; and on the higher grounds sheep are reared. There are considerable forests on the lower mountain slopes. Zaragoza has no manufactures of importance. The province is traversed by the Ebro Valley Railway, which connects Miranda on the northern line with Lerida, Barcelona, and Tarragona, and has a branch to Huesca; it also has communication with Madrid; and there are local lines to Cariñena (south-west from Zaragoza) and to Puebla de Hijar (along the right bank of the Ebro). The Aragon Canal, originally intended to connect the Mediterranean with the Atlantic, is open from Tudela (El Bocal) to a point below Zaragoza. There are 13 partidos judiciales and 312 ayuntamientos; of these only Calatayud (11,512) and ZARAGOZA (see below) have more than 10,000 inhabitants. The total population of the province in 1877 was 400,587.

ZARAGOZA, capital of the above province, formerly capital of the kingdom of Aragon, lies at a height of 600

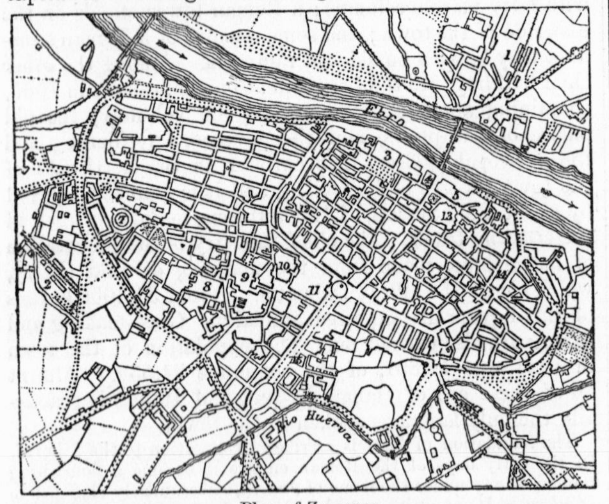

Plan of Zaragoza.

1, 2. Railway stations.
3. Cathedral del Pilar, or of the Pillar.
4. Municipal buildings.
5. Archbishop's palace.
6. Aljaferia.
7. Bull-ring.
8 Civil hospital.
9. Military hospital.
10. Academy of Fine Arts.
11. Government offices.
12. Church of St Philip and St James.
13. Cathedral of La Seo.
14. University.
15. Capitania general.
16. S. Engracia.

feet above sea-level, on a rich plain on the right bank of the Ebro, just above its confluence with the Huerva, 212 miles by rail to the north-east of Madrid. The river is here crossed by a fine stone bridge of seven arches, erected in 1437, and another bridge—of iron—much needed for the convenience of through railway traffic, is projected. Seen from a distance, the city with its numerous domes and towers has an imposing appearance, which it hardly maintains on a nearer approach. The older streets are narrow, gloomy, and ill paved; the massive buildings formerly inhabited by the Aragonese nobility are either in ruins or turned into wood-stores and granaries; and an air of poverty and decay pervades the whole town. By the river side there are public walks and avenues of poplar. The two most important buildings of Zaragoza are its cathedrals, in each of which the chapter resides alternately for six months. La Seo ("The See") is the older of the two, dating chiefly from the 14th century; its prevailing style is Gothic, but the oldest portion, the lower portion of the apse, is Byzantine, and the façade is of the Late Pseudo-Classical style, by which so many churches in Spain have been disfigured. The Iglesia Metropolitana del Pilar is the larger and more modern building, dating only from the latter half of the 17th century; it was built after designs by Herrera el Mozo, and owes its name to one of the most venerated objects in Spain, the "pillar" of jasper on which the Virgin is said to have alighted when she manifested herself to Santiago as he passed through Zaragoza. It has no architectural merit; externally its most conspicuous features are its domes, which are decorated with rows of green, yellow, and white glazed tiles. The church of San Pablo dates mainly from the 13th century. Adjoining the church of San Felipe is the Torre Nueva, an octangular clock tower in diapered brickwork, dating from 1504; it leans some 9 or 10 feet from the perpendicular, owing to faulty foundations. Among other conspicuous public buildings are the municipal buildings, the exchange (*Lonja*), and the civil and military hospitals, which are among the largest in Spain. The university was founded in 1474, but its history has not been brilliant. To the west of the town is the Aljaferia or old citadel, an irregular pile originally built as a palace by the Moors and also used as such by its Christian owners. It was afterwards assigned by Ferdinand and Isabella to the Inquisition, and has since been used as barracks, a military hospital, and a prison; it is now unoccupied and falling into decay. The chief manufactures of Zaragoza are silk, woollen cloth, leather, saltpetre, soap, and chocolate; and there is considerable trade in agricultural produce, and in wine and spirits. The population of the town in 1877 was 84,575.

Zaragoza, the Celtiberian *Salduba*, was colonized at the close of the Cantabrian War (25 B.C.) by Augustus, who gave it his own name, *Cæsarea Augusta*, or *Cæsaraugusta*. It was a colonia immunis and the seat of a conventus juridicus. No remains of the ancient city have been preserved. It was taken by the Goths about 466 and in 712 by the Moors. In 1118 it was recovered by Alonso el Batallador of Aragon after a siege of five years, during which the defenders were reduced by famine to the direst straits. In 1710 Stanhope defeated the French under Philip V. not far from the town. The most memorable recent events in the history of Zaragoza are those which took place during the Napoleonic invasion. In 1808 the citizens rose against the French, and, under the command of PALAFOX (*q.v.*), defended the town for two months. The first siege was raised on 15th August 1808; but the respite then gained was not made use of to strengthen the defences, and, when the enemy renewed their attack in greater force in December, the place was compelled to surrender (20th February 1809), after losing in all nearly 60,000 men.

ZARLINO, GIOSEFFE or GIUSEPPE (1517-1590),[1] musical theorist, surnamed from his birthplace, ZARLINUS CLODIENSIS, was born at Chioggia, Venetia, in 1517. Studying in his youth for the church, he was admitted to the minor orders in 1539 and ordained deacon in 1541 at Venice; but he soon devoted himself entirely to the study of music under the guidance of Adrian Willaert, then choir-master at St Mark's. Willaert, dying in 1562, was succeeded by Cipriano di Rore, on whose removal to Parma in 1565 Zarlino was elected choir-master. Though now remembered chiefly as a theorist, it is evident that he must have been famous both as a practical musician and as a composer; for, notwithstanding the limited number of his printed works, consisting of a volume entitled *Modulationes Sex Vocum* (Venice, 1566), and a few motets and madrigals scattered through the collections of Scotto and other contemporary publishers, he both produced and superintended the public performance of some important pieces in the service of the republic. First among these was the music written to celebrate the battle of Lepanto (7th October 1571). Again, when Henry III. of France passed through Venice on his return from Poland in 1574, Zarlino directed on board the "Bucentaur" the performance of an ode for which he himself had composed the music, to verses supplied by Rocco Benedetti and Cornelio Frangipani. The ode

[1] Burney and Hawkins place Zarlino's birth in 1540, and his death in 1590. Caffi gives the true dates. Zarlino himself tells us that he was ordained deacon in 1541.

was followed by a solemn service in St Mark's, in which Zarlino's music formed a prominent feature, and the festival concluded with the representation of a dramatic piece entitled *Orfeo* composed by Zarlino. When the church of S. Maria della Salute was founded in 1577 to commemorate the plague, he composed a solemn mass for the occasion. Not one of these works is now known to be in existence; the only example we possess of Zarlino's compositions on a grand scale is a MS. mass for four voices, in the library of the Philharmonic Lyceum at Bologna. He died at Venice on 14th February 1590.

Fortunately for the science of music, Zarlino's theoretical writings have all been preserved. Though he was by no means free from certain visionary ideas concerning the transcendental powers of music, in which the theorists of the 16th century delighted, Zarlino was, in practical knowledge and intelligent application of scientific truth to the development of art, immeasurably in advance of the age in which he lived. His clear insight into the mathematical foundation of the scale placed him in direct antagonism to the leaders of the school of the Renaissance, which, with Vincenzo Galilei at its head, blindly followed the mistaken reasoning of Boetius (see vol. xvii. p. 80), and adhered as a matter of principle to the Pythagorean section of the canon. This difference of opinion, occurring at a critical period in the development of art, made Zarlino many bitter enemies; but he steadily maintained his principles in temperate and unanswerable argument; and his theory is now accepted as the basis of modern art, while that of his opponents is utterly discarded.

Zarlino's first theoretical work was the *Istitutioni Armoniche* (Venice, 1558; reprinted 1562 and 1573). This was followed by the *Dimostrationi Armoniche* (Venice, 1571; reprinted 1573) and by the *Sopplimenti Musicali* (Venice, 1588). Finally, in a complete edition of his works published shortly before his death Zarlino reprinted these three treatises, accompanied by a *Tract on Patience*, a *Discourse on the True Date of the Crucifixion of Our Lord*, an essay on *The Origin of the Capuchins*, and the *Resolution of Some Doubts Concerning the Correction of the Julian Calendar* (Venice, 1589).[1]

The *Istitutioni* and *Dimostrationi Armoniche* deal, like most other theoretical works of the period, with the whole science of music as it was understood in the 16th century. The earlier chapters, treating chiefly of the arithmetical foundations of the science, differ but little in their line of argument from the principles laid down by Pietro Aron, Zacconi, and other early writers of the Boetian school; but in bk. ii. of the *Istitutioni* Zarlino boldly attacks the false system of tonality to which the proportions of the Pythagorean tetrachord, if strictly carried out in practice, must inevitably lead. The fact that, so far as can now be ascertained, they never were strictly carried out in the Italian mediæval schools, at least after the invention of counterpoint, in no wise diminishes the force of the reformer's argument. The point at issue was, that neither in the polyphonic school, in which Zarlino was educated, nor in the later monodic school, of which his recalcitrant pupil, Vincenzo Galilei, was the most redoubtable champion, could those proportions be tolerated in practice, however attractive they might be to the theorist in their mathematical aspect. So persistently does the human ear rebel against the division of the tetrachord into two greater tones and a leimma or hemitone, as represented by the fractions $\frac{8}{9}$, $\frac{8}{9}$, $\frac{243}{256}$, that, centuries before the possibility of reconciling the demands of the ear with those of exact science was satisfactorily demonstrated, the Aristoxenian school advocated the use of an empirical scale, sounding pleasant to the sense, in preference to an unpleasing tonality founded upon immutable proportions. Didymus, writing in the year 60, made the first step towards establishing this pleasant-sounding scale upon a mathematical basis, by the discovery of the lesser tone; but unhappily he placed it in a false position below the greater tone. Claudius Ptolemy (130) rectified this error, and in the so-called syntonous or intense diatonic scale reduced the proportions of his tetrachord to $\frac{8}{9}$, $\frac{9}{10}$, $\frac{15}{16}$,—*i.e.*, the greater tone, lesser tone, and diatonic semitone of modern music.[2] Ptolemy set forth this system as one of eight possible forms of the diatonic scale. But Zarlino uncompromisingly declared that the syntonous or intense diatonic scale was the only form that could reasonably be sung; and in proof of its perfection he exhibited the exact arrangement of its various diatonic intervals, to the fifth inclusive, in every part of the diapason or octave. The proportions are precisely those now universally accepted in the system called "just intonation." But this system is practicable only by the voice and instruments of the violin class. For keyed or fretted instruments a compromise is indispensable. To meet this exigency, Zarlino proposed that for the lute the octave should be divided into twelve equal semitones; and after centuries of discussion this system of "equal temperament" has, within the last thirty-five years, been universally adopted as the best attainable for keyed instruments of every description.[3]

Again, Zarlino was in advance of his age in his classification of the ecclesiastical modes. These scales were not, as is vulgarly supposed, wholly abolished in favour of our modern tonality in the 17th century. Eight of them, it is true, fell into disuse; but the mediæval Ionian and Hypo-ionian modes are absolutely identical with the modern natural scale of C; and the Æolian and Hypo-æolian modes differ from our minor scale, not in constitution, but in treatment only. Mediæval composers, however, regarded the Ionian mode as the least perfect of the series and placed it last in order. Zarlino thought differently and made it the first mode, changing all the others to accord with it. His numerical table, therefore, differs from all others made before or since, prophetically assigning the place of honour to the one ancient scale now recognized as the foundation of the modern tonal system.

These innovations were violently opposed by the apostles of the monodic school. Vincenzo Galilei led the attack in a tract entitled *Discorso Intorno alle Opere di Messer Gioseffe Zarlino*, and followed it up in his famous *Dialogo*, defending the Pythagorean system in very unmeasured language. It was in answer to these strictures that Zarlino published his *Sopplementi*.

ZEA. See CEOS.

ZEALAND, or SJAELLAND, the largest and most easterly island of DENMARK (*q.v.*), is separated from Fünen on the west by the Great Belt and from Sweden on the east by the Sound; its greatest length from north to south is 81 miles, its breadth 65, and its area 2636 square miles.[4] Its surface is for the most part undulating, but on the whole little above sea-level; the highest elevations are in the south-east, where Cretaceous hills (the oldest geological formation on the island) reach heights of upwards of 350 feet. The coast is indented by numerous deep bays and fjords: the Ise fjord in the north in particular, with its branches the Roeskilde fjord on the east and the Lamme fjord on the west, penetrates inland for about 40 miles. There are no rivers of importance; but several large lakes, the most considerable being Arre and Esrom, occur in the north-east. The soil is fertile and produces grain, especially rye and barley, in great abundance, as well as potatoes and other vegetables, and fruit. Agriculture and cattle-raising, along with some fishing, are the leading occupations of the inhabitants; linen is almost the only article of domestic industry. The population in 1880 was 610,000. The principal towns, besides COPENHAGEN (*q.v.*), the capital (234,850 inhabitants in 1880), are Roeskilde (5893), formerly the capital and still the see of the primate; Elsinore (8978); Slagelse (6076), a great agricultural centre; Sorö (1464), formerly the seat of a university and still educationally important; and Korsör (3954), the port for mail steamers to the mainland, connected by rail with Sorö, Roeskilde, and Copenhagen.

ZEALAND, the most westerly province of Holland, is bounded on the north by South Holland, on the east by North Brabant and Belgium, on the south-east and south by Belgium, and on the west by the North Sea. Its area is 689 square miles, the greater part of which consists of the islands Schouwen, Duiveland, St Philipsland, Tholen, North, South, and East Beveland, Wolfaartsdyk, and Walcheren. The greater part of the surface is below sea-level. The westward coasts of Schouwen and Walcheren are partly sheltered by dunes; but the province is mainly

---

[1] Ambros mentions an edition of the *Istitutioni* dated 1557, and one of the *Dimostrationi* dated 1562. The present writer has never met with either.

[2] We have given the fractions in the order in which they occur in the modern system. Ptolemy, following the invariable Greek method, placed them thus—$\frac{15}{16}$, $\frac{8}{9}$, $\frac{9}{10}$. This, however, made no difference in the actual proportions.

[3] It was first used in France, for the organ, in 1835; in England, for the pianoforte in 1846 and for the organ in 1854. Bach had advocated it in Germany a century earlier; but it was not generally adopted.

[4] The province of Zealand and Möen, which includes the island of Samsö as well as that of Möen, has an area of 2828 square miles and a population of 721,703; the "stift" or bishopric of Zealand includes also the island of Bornholm.

dependent for protection from the sea on its artificial dykes, which have a total length of 300 miles, and on the repair of which upwards of £80,000 is spent annually. The soil consists of a fertile sea clay (see vol. xii. p. 62), which specially favours the production of wheat; much rye is also cultivated, as well as barley (for malting), beans and pease, flax, and madder. Cattle and swine are reared, and dairy produce is largely exported; but the sheep of the province are small and their wool indifferent. The industries (linen, yarn-spinning, distilling, brewing, salt-refining, shipbuilding) are comparatively unimportant. The inhabitants, who still retain many quaint and archaic peculiarities of manner and dress, speak the variety of Dutch known as Low Frankish (see vol. xii. p. 84). The capital is Middelburg (population 16,378 in 1887), in Walcheren, where also is Flushing (12,005). The total population of the province in 1887 was 198,567.

ZEBRA. In the article HORSE (vol. xii. p. 175) the general zoological and anatomical characters of the genus *Equus*, and its relationship to other animals, were fully described. Among the existing species mention was made of certain forms distinguished from the rest by the peculiar coloration, being marked by conspicuous dark stripes on a lighter ground, and by their exclusively African habitat. These are the QUAGGA (see vol. xx. p. 146) and two, if not three, distinct species to which the name zebra is commonly applied. The animal of this group which was first known to Europeans, and was formerly considered the most common, is the True Zebra (*Equus zebra*, Linn.), sometimes called the Mountain Zebra. It inhabits the mountainous regions of the Cape Colony; but now, owing to the advances of civilized man into its somewhat restricted range, it has become very scarce, and is even, like its ally the quagga, threatened with extermination at no distant date. The second species, Burchell's Zebra (*Equus burchelli*, Gray), still roams in large herds over the plains to the north of the Orange river, but in yearly diminishing numbers. Both species are subject to considerable individual variations in marking, but the following are the principal characters by which they can be distinguished.

Equus zebra is the smaller of the two (about 4 feet high at the shoulders), and has longer ears, a tail more scantily clothed with

FIG. 1.—True or mountain zebra (*Equus zebra*).

hair, and a shorter mane. The general ground colour is white, and the stripes are black; the lower part of the face is bright brown. With the exception of the abdomen and the inside of the thighs, the whole of the surface is covered with stripes, the legs having narrow transverse bars reaching quite to the hoofs, and the base of the tail being also barred. The outsides of the ears have a white tip and a broad black mark occupying the greater part of the surface, but are white at the base. Perhaps the most constant and obvious distinction between this species and the next is the arrangement of the stripes on the hinder part of the back, where there are a number of short transverse bands reaching to the median longitudinal dorsal stripe, and unconnected with the uppermost of the broad stripes which pass obliquely across the haunch from the flanks towards the root of the tail. There is often a median longitudinal stripe under the chest.

Equus burchelli is a rather larger and more robust animal, with smaller ears, a longer mane, and fuller tail. The general ground colour of the body is pale yellowish brown, the limbs nearly white, the stripes dark brown or black. In the typical form they do not extend on to the limbs or the tail; but there is a great variation in this respect, even in animals of the same herd, some being striped quite down to the hoofs (this form has been named *E. chapmanni*).

FIG. 2.—Burchell's zebra (*E. burchelli*).

There is a strongly marked median longitudinal ventral black stripe, to which the lower ends of the transverse side stripes are usually united, but the dorsal stripe (also strongly marked) is completely isolated in its posterior half, and the uppermost of the broad haunch stripes runs nearly parallel to it. A much larger proportion of the ears is white than in the other species. In the middle of the wide intervals between the broad black stripes of the flanks and haunches fainter stripes are generally seen.

E. grevyi.—Under this name a zebra has lately been described which was sent in 1882 to Paris from the Galla country, lying to the south of Abyssinia, the most northern locality in which zebras have hitherto been met with. In most of its characters it resembles *E. zebra*, but the stripes are finer and more numerous than in the typical examples of that species, and it has a strong, black, and isolated dorsal stripe. Considering the great variations that are met with in the markings of animals of this group, it is doubtful whether the aberrant characters of this individual are sufficient to separate it specifically from the true zebra of South Africa. The question will be cleared up when any complete scientific examination has been made of other specimens, and also of the zebras which are known to exist in the neighbourhood of Lake Nyanza, and which are apparently of the same form. It is curious that the most northern and the most southern of the districts inhabited by zebras both contain identical or closely allied species, while the intermediate territory is occupied by a totally different form, *E. burchelli*. It should be mentioned that the last-named animal is generally spoken of as the "quagga" by colonists and hunters. Its flesh is relished by the natives as food, and its hide is very valuable for leather. Although the many attempts that have been made to break in and train zebras for riding or driving have sometimes been rewarded with partial success, the animal has never been domesticated in the true sense of the word. (W. H. F.)

ZEBULUN (זְבוּלֻן), one of the twelve tribes of Israel, derived, according to Gen. xxx. 20, from the sixth son of Leah. The verse offers two etymologies of the name, from the roots ZBD, "give," and ZBL, "inhabit." The form Ζαβουλων (LXX.), with ŏ in the last syllable, agrees with the vocalization of the adjective זְבוּלֹנִי, "Zebulonite." The country of Zebulun lay in the fertile hilly country to the north of the plain of Jezreel, which forms the first step towards the mountains of Asher and Naphtali, and included the goodly upland plain of Baṭṭauf. The description of its boundaries in Josh. xix. 10 *sq.* contains few names that can be identified with any certainty: Chisloth-tabor is apparently the modern Iksâl, a little to the west of Tabor, Daberath the modern Dabûrîya, at the foot of Tabor, Gath-hepher (A.V. Gittah-hepher) the village of Al-Meshhed, and Remmon Rummâna. Thus the eastern boundary laid down in Conder and Kitchener's reduced Ordnance Survey map comes too near the Lake of Tiberias. The west boundary is not defined in Josh. xix., but should agree with the somewhat vague east boundary of Asher in verse 27. At one period Zebulun must have reached the sea and bordered on Phœnician territory (Gen. xlix. 13, Deut. xxxiii. 18, 19). In the latter passage allusion is made to a feast upon a sacred mountain (Mount Tabor?) held by Zebulun and Issachar in common, and to the wealth these tribes derived from commerce by sea. Zebulun had a chief part in the war with Sisera (Jud. iv. 6); it furnished one of the judges, Elon the Zebulonite (Jud. xii. 11, 12); and the prophet Jonah, who foretold the victories of Jeroboam II., came from the town of Gath-hepher (2 Kings xiv. 25). The captivity of the northern tribes under Tiglath Pileser (2 Kings xv. 29) appears to have included Zebulun (Isa. ix. 1 [viii. 23]). Nazareth lay within the territory of Zebulun, but is not mentioned in the Old Testament.

ZECHARIAH, son of Berechiah, son of Iddo, or by contraction son of Iddo, appeared as a prophet in Jerusalem along with HAGGAI (*q.v.*), in the second year of Darius Hystaspes (520 B.C.), to warn and encourage the Jews to address themselves at length to the restoration of the temple, which, since their return from exile eighteen years before, had lain unaccomplished, less through want of zeal than through the pressure of unfavourable circumstances. Supported by the prophets, Zerubbabel and Joshua set about the work, and the elders of Judah built and the work went forward (Ezra v. 1 *sq.*, vi. 14). The first eight chapters of the book of Zechariah exactly fit into this historical setting. They are divided by precise chronological headings into three sections,—(*a*) chap. i. 1-6, in the eighth month of the second year of Darius; (*b*) chap. i. 7–vi. 15, on the twenty-fourth day of the eleventh month of the same year; (*c*) chap. vii.-viii., on the fourth day of the ninth month of the fourth year of Darius. The first section is a preface containing exhortation in general terms. The main section is the second, containing a series of night visions, the significant features of which are pointed out by an angel who stands by the prophet and answers his questions.

i. 7-17. The divine chariots and horses that make the round of the world by Jehovah's orders return to the heavenly palace and report that there is still no movement among the nations, no sign of the Messianic crisis. Seventy years have passed, and Zion and the cities of Judah still mourn. Sad news! but Jehovah gives a comfortable assurance of His gracious return to Jerusalem and the rebuilding of His temple.

i. 18-21 (Heb. ii. 1-4). Four horns, representing the hostile world-power that oppresses Israel and Jerusalem, are routed by four smiths.

ii. 1-13 (Heb. ii. 5-17). The new Jerusalem is laid out with the measuring line. It is to have no walls, that its population may not be limited, and it needs none, for Jehovah is its protection. The catastrophe of the nations is near to come; then the exiles of Zion shall stream back from all quarters, the converted heathen shall join them, Jehovah Himself will dwell in the midst of them, even now He stirs Himself from His holy habitation.

iii. 1-10. The high priest Joshua is accused before Jehovah by Satan, but is acquitted and given rule in Jehovah's house and courts, with the right of access to Jehovah in priestly intercession. The restoration of the temple and its service is a pledge of still higher things. The promised "branch" (or "shoot," צמח), the Messiah, will come: ***i.e.***, the Persian lordship has an end; the national kingdom is restored in its old splendour; and a time of general felicity dawns, when every man shall sit happy under his vine and under his fig tree. As by rights the Messianic kingdom should follow immediately on the exile, it is probable that the prophet designs to hint in a guarded way that Zerubbabel, who in all other places is mentioned along with Joshua, is on the point of ascending the throne of his ancestor David. The jewel with seven facets is already there, only the inscription has still to be engraved on it (iii. 9). The charges brought against the high priest consist simply in the obstacles that have hitherto impeded the restoration of the temple and its service; and in like manner the guilt of the land (iii. 9) is simply the still continuing domination of foreigners.

iv. 1-14. Beside a lighted golden candlestick of seven branches stand two olive trees—Zerubbabel and Joshua, the two anointed ones—specially watched over by Him whose seven eyes run through the whole earth. This explanation of the vision is separated from the description by an animated dialogue, not quite clear in its expression, in which it is said that the mountain of obstacles shall disappear before Zerubbabel, and that, having begun the building of the temple, he shall also bring it to an end in spite of those who now mock at the day of small beginnings.

v. 1-4. A written roll flies over the Holy Land; this is a concrete representation of the curse which in future will fall of itself on all crime, so that, *e.g.*, no man who has suffered theft will have occasion himself to pronounce a curse against the thief (*cf.* Jud. xvii. 2).

v. 5-11. Guilt, personified as a woman, is cast into an ephah-measure with a heavy lid and carried from Judah to Chaldæa, where it is to have its home for the future.

vi. 1-8. The divine teams, four in number, again traverse the world toward the four winds, to execute Jehovah's commands. That which goes northward is charged to wreak His anger on the north country. The series of visions has now reached its close, returning to its starting-point in i. 7 *sqq.*

An appendix follows (vi. 9-15). Jews from Babylon have brought gold and silver to Jerusalem; of these the prophet must make a crown designed for the "branch" who is to build Jehovah's house and sit king on the throne, but retain a good understanding with the high priest. Zerubbabel is certainly meant here, and, if the received text names Joshua instead of him (vi. 11), this is only a correction, made for reasons easy to understand, but which breaks the context and destroys the sense and the reference of "them both" in verse 13.

The third section (chaps. vii.-viii.), dated from the fourth year of Darius, contains an inquiry whether the fast days that arose in the captivity are still to be observed, with a comforting and encouraging reply of the prophet.

Thus throughout the first eight chapters the scene is Jerusalem in the early part of the reign of Darius. Zerubbabel and Joshua, the prince and the priest, are the leaders of the community. But, while the spiritual head is in office, the authority of the civil head is rather moral than official, and is not so much actual as hoped for. The great concern of the time and the chief practical theme of these chapters is the building of the temple; but its restoration is only the earnest of greater things to follow, viz., the glorious restoration of David's kingdom. The horizon of these prophecies is everywhere limited by the narrow conditions of the time, and their aim is clearly seen. The visions hardly veil the thought, and the mode of expression is usually simple, except in the Messianic passages, where the tortuousness and obscurity are perhaps intentional. Noteworthy is the affinity between some notions evidently not framed by the prophet himself and the prologue to Job,—the heavenly hosts that wander through the earth and bring back their report to Jehovah's throne, the figure of Satan, the idea that suffering and calamity are evidences of guilt and of accusations presented before God.

Passing from chaps. i.-viii. to chaps. ix. *sq.*, we at once feel ourselves transported into a different world.

Jehovah's word is accomplished on Syria-Phœnicia and Philistia; and then the Messianic kingdom begins in Zion, and the Israelites detained among the heathen, Judah and Ephraim combined, receive a part in it. The might of the sons of Javan is broken in battle against this kingdom (ch. ix.). After an intermezzo of three verses (x. 1-3: "Ask rain of Jehovah, not of the diviners") a second and quite analogous Messianic prophecy follows. The foreign tyrants fall; the lordship of Assyria and Egypt has an end; the autonomy and martial power of the nation are restored. The scattered exiles return as citizens of the new theocracy, all obstacles in their way parting asunder as when the waves of the Red Sea gave passage to Israel at the founding of the old theocracy (x. 3-12). Again there is an interlude of three verses (xi. 1-3): fire seizes the cedars of Lebanon and the oaks of Bashan, which the rabbins refer to the burning of the sanctuary of Jerusalem.[1] The difficult passage about the shepherds follows.

The shepherds (rulers) of the nation make their flock an article of trade and treat the sheep as sheep for the shambles. Therefore the inhabited world shall fall a sacrifice to the tyranny of its kings, while Israel is delivered to a shepherd who feeds the sheep for those who make a trade of the flock (כְּנַעֲנִיֵּי הַצֹּאן, xi. 7, 11 = "they that sell them," ver. 5) and enters on his office with two staves, "Favour" and "Union." He destroys "the three shepherds" in one month, but is soon weary of his flock and the flock of him. He breaks the staff "Favour," *i.e.*, the covenant of peace with the nations, and asks the traders for his hire. Receiving thirty pieces of silver, he casts it into the temple treasury and breaks the staff "Union" *i.e.*, the brotherhood between Judah and Israel. He is succeeded by a foolish shepherd, who neglects his flock and lets it go to ruin. At length Jehovah intervenes; the foolish shepherd falls by the sword; two-thirds of the people perish with him in the Messianic crisis, but the remnant of one-third forms the seed of the new theocracy (xi. 4-17 taken with xiii. 7-9, according to the necessary transposition proposed by Ewald). All this must be an allegory of past events, the time present to the author and his hopes for the future beginning only at xi. 17, xiii. 7-9. The general situation is clear: foreign kings govern Israel through native princes. The details cannot be explained in the absence of information as to the date and historical course of the events described by the prophet in allegorical form. But those who seek to escape this difficulty, by supposing that the word of the prophet was unintelligible to his contemporaries, and gained a true meaning only in its New Testament fulfilment,[2] must forget that in Zech. xi. 9 the shepherd wearies of his office and abandons the flock, while in the New Testament the shepherd gives his life for the sheep, and that in Zech. xi. 12, 13 the price is paid to the shepherd, but in the New Testament to the traitor.

Chap. xii. presents a third variation on the Messianic promise. All heathendom is gathered together against Jerusalem and perishes there. Jehovah first gives victory to the countryfolk of Judah and then they rescue the capital. After this triumph the noblest houses of Jerusalem hold, each by itself, a great lamentation over a martyr "whom they have pierced" (or "whom men have pierced"). In xii. 10 אֵלַי followed by עָלָיו cannot be right. If את be deleted, we may read אֵלֵי אשר, but not אליו אשר, which is not Hebrew. Yet it is very doubtful if the deletion of את is justifiable or sufficient. It is taken for granted that the readers will know who the martyr is, and the exegesis of the church applies the passage to our Lord. Chap. xiii. 1-6 is a continuation of chap. xii.; the dawn of the day of salvation is accompanied by a general purging away of idolatry and the enthusiasm of false prophets. Yet a fourth variation of the picture of the incoming of the Messianic deliverance is given in chap. xiv. The heathen gather against Jerusalem and take the city, but do not utterly destroy the inhabitants. Then Jehovah, at a time known only to Himself, shall appear with all His saints on Mount Olivet and destroy the heathen in battle, while the men of Jerusalem take refuge in their terror in the great cleft that opens where Jehovah sets His foot. Now the new era begins, and even the heathen do homage to Jehovah by bringing due tribute to the annual feast of tabernacles. All in Jerusalem is holy down to the bells on the horses and the cooking-pots.

There is a striking contrast between chaps. i.-viii. and chaps. ix.-xiv. The former prophecy is closely tied to the situation and wants of the community of Jerusalem in the second year of Darius I., and all that it aims at arises out of the necessities of the time, and is of a practical and possible kind—the restoration of the temple and perhaps the elevation of Zerubbabel to the throne of David. The latter chapters, on the other hand, soar far above the field of reality; the historical situation from which they start can hardly be recognized; and the future hope has very little connexion with the present. The fundamental difference between the two parts of the book lies, not in the subject but in the nature of the prophecy,—in the first part realistic and almost prosaic, in the second vague and fantastic. There are corresponding differences in style and speech; and it is particularly to be noted that, while the superscriptions in the first part name the author and give the date of each oracle with precision, those in the second part (ix. 1, xii. 1) are without name or date. That both parts do not belong to the same author must be admitted. But most recent critics make the second part the older. Chaps. ix.-xi. are ascribed to a contemporary of Amos and Hosea, about the middle of the 8th century B.C., because Ephraim is mentioned as well as Judah, and Assyria along with Egypt (x. 10), while the neighbours of Israel appear in ix. 1 *sq.* in the same way as in Amos i.-ii. That chaps. xii.-xiv. are also pre-exilic is held to appear especially in the attack on idolatry and lying prophecy (xiii. 1-6); but, as this prophecy speaks only of Judah and Jerusalem, it is dated after the fall of Samaria, and is assigned to the last days of the Judæan kingdom on the strength of xii. 11, where an allusion is seen to the mourning for King Josiah, slain in battle at Megiddo. Some suppose that the author of ix.-xi. is the Zechariah, son of Jeberechiah, of Isa. viii. 2, and Bunsen ascribes xii.-xiv. to the prophet Urijah, son of Shemaiah (Jer. xxvi. 20 *sq.*). It is more likely that chaps. ix.-xiv. go all together and are of much later date. These vague predictions have no real spiritual affinity either with the prophecy of Amos, Hosea, and Isaiah, or with that of Jeremiah, where we always feel the solid ground of present reality under our feet. It was only after the exile that prophecy lost its close connexion with history and ceased to be built on present realities. The kind of eschatology which we find in Zech. ix.-xiv. was first introduced by Ezekiel, who in particular is the author of the conception that the time of deliverance is to be preceded by a joint attack of all nations on Jerusalem, in which they come to final overthrow (Ezek. xxxviii. *sq.*; Isa. lxvi. 18-24; Joel). The importance attached to the temple service, even in Messianic times (Zech. xiv.), implies an author who lived in the ideas of the religious commonwealth of post-exile times. A future king is hoped for; but in the present there is no Davidic king, only a Davidic family standing on the same level with other noble families in Jerusalem (xii. 7, 12). The "bastard" (mixed race) of Ashdod reminds us of Neh. xiii. 23 *sqq.*; and the words of ix. 12 ("to-day, also, do I declare that I will render double unto thee") have no sense unless they refer back to the deliverance from Babylonian exile. But the decisive argument is that in ix. 13 the sons of Javan, *i.e.*, the Greeks, appear as the representatives of the heathen world-power. The prophecy, therefore, is later than Alexander; and indeed the hostility to the Jews implied in the passage just cited dates only from the time when Palestine passed from the hands of the Ptolemies to those of the Seleucids. Assyria and Egypt (x. 11) may well be the Ptolemaic and Seleucid kingdoms, which together made up for the Jews the empire of the sons of Javan. In ix. 1 *sq.* (imitated from Amos i.-ii.) Seleucid Syria is described as parcelled out into a number of small principalities, some of which were at the time nearly independent. That the Jews had reason enough to hate their neighbours, even in later times, appears, *e.g.*, in 1 Mac. v.; compare especially ix. 6, 7 with 1 Mac. v. 68. The reference in ix. 8 would fit well with the Egyptian campaigns of Antiochus IV. Epiphanes, when Jerusalem suffered so much on the outward march and still more on the return of his troops. That the victory of Judah over the heathens is to precede the deliverance of Jerusalem (xii. 5 *sqq.*) is a remarkable feature, hardly to be explained except by the history of the Maccabee wars. The complaint about idolatry also fits this period; and that a new kind of prophecy then came up, in an age where it no longer had a legitimate place, is far from unlikely.

If this date is assumed for chaps. ix.-xiv., we must hold that, by the copious use of phrases from older prophets and other means, the author sought to give his oracles an archaic garb. That this is no unfair assumption appears especially in xiv. 5, in the reference to the earthquake in the days of Uzziah, which is natural only if the author addressed

[1] See Wagenseil, *Sota*, p. 927; Lightfoot, on Matt. xxvi. 3.
[2] Matt. xxvii. 3-10; cp. *Jahrbb. f. D. Theol.*, 1878, p. 471 *sq.*

contemporaries of that catastrophe. This passage is indeed a stronger argument for a date in the Assyrian period than anything cited from chaps. ix.-xi. If, notwithstanding this, no commentator dates chap. xiv. less than 150 years after Uzziah, it is illegitimate to protest against the view that in chaps. ix. *sq.* Ephraim is an archaizing name for the Diaspora (1 Mac. v. 23, 45, 53).

How so late a piece was admitted among the prophetic writings, while Daniel, written about the same time, is placed only among the hagiographa, is a question not yet answered. We know too little about the history of the canon. A similar case is that of Isa. xxiv.-xxvii. But it is not less difficult to explain how a prophecy of the 8th century could have turned up in post-exile times and been appended to the book of Zechariah.

The literature of the book is cited by C. H. H. Wright, *Zechariah and his Prophecies*, 2d ed., London, 1879. See also Stade, "Deuterozacharja," in *Zeitschr. f. AT. Wiss.*, 1881, p. 1 *sq.*; 1882, pp. 151 *sq.*, 275 *sq.* (J. WE.)

ZEITZ, an ancient manufacturing town in the extreme south of the province of Saxony, Prussia, is pleasantly situated on a hill on the White Elster, 22 miles south-south-west of Leipsic and 29 south-south-east of Halle. The river is here crossed by two iron bridges, and one stone and one timber bridge. The Gothic abbey church dates from the 15th century, but its Romanesque crypt from the 12th. The old Franciscan monastery, now occupied by a seminary, contains a library of 20,000 volumes. Just outside the town rises the Moritzburg, built in 1564 by the dukes of Saxe-Zeitz, on the site of the bishop's palace; it is now a reformatory and poorhouse. Zeitz has manufactures of cottons and woollens, machinery, wax-cloth, musical instruments, vinegar, cigars, &c.; and wood-carving, dyeing, and calico-printing are carried on. In the neighbourhood there are considerable deposits of lignite, and mineral-oil works. In 1885 the population was 21,261 (18,265 in 1880); in 1816 it was 6640.

Zeitz is an ancient place of Slavonic origin. From 968 till 1028 it was the seat of a bishopric, afterwards removed to Naumburg, 15½ miles to the north-west, and styled Naumburg-Zeitz. In 1564 the last Roman Catholic bishop died, and his dominions were thenceforward administered by princes of Saxony. From 1653 till 1718 Zeitz was the capital of the dukes of Saxe-Zeitz or Sachsen-Zeitz. It thereafter remained in the possession of the electors of Saxony until 1815, when it passed to Prussia.

ZELLE, or more usually CELLE, an industrial and commercial town in the district of Lüneburg in Prussia, is situated on the left bank of the navigable Aller, near its junction with the Fuse and the Lachte, 23 miles to the north-east of Hanover. The town, with which three suburbs were incorporated in 1869, is well built. It is the legal and official centre of a "circle," and contains the usual tribunals and bureaux, besides several schools, benevolent institutions, and a prison. The library of the appeal court-house consists of 60,000 vols. The principal church contains a ducal burial vault, in which is buried Sophia Dorothea, first wife of the elector George of Hanover, afterwards George I. of England. The town-house dates from the 14th century. The most interesting building in Zelle is the former ducal castle, begun in 1485 in the Late Gothic style, but with extensive Renaissance additions of the close of the 17th century. Caroline Matilda, the divorced wife of Christian VII. of Denmark and sister of George III. of England, resided here from 1772 till her death in 1775; she is buried in the above-mentioned church, and a memorial tablet has been erected to her in the "French garden" outside the town. The industries of the place include the manufacture of woollen yarn, cigars, glue, printers' ink, philosophical instruments, stoves, bricks, &c.; and it carries on trade in wood, wool, honey, wax, cranberries, and other articles. Nursery-gardening flourishes in the fertile environs, where there are also a large paper-mill and a Government stud farm. The population in 1885 was 18,782, almost entirely Protestant.

Zelle received town-rights in 1292. From about 1369 it was the residence of the ducal family of Brunswick-Lüneburg-Zelle, which became extinct in 1705. In the 17th century Zelle was the most strongly-fortified town in Lüneburg. In 1757 it was besieged and partly laid in ashes by Richelieu. At the peace of Zelle (5th February 1679) Sweden gave in her adhesion to the peace of Nimeguen. Zelle is the birthplace of Thaer (1752-1828), the eminent agriculturist, and of Ernst K. F. Schulze (1789-1817), the poet.

ZEND-AVESTA, the original document of the religion of ZOROASTER (*q.v.*), and still used by the PARSEES (*q.v.*) as their bible and prayer book. The name "Zend-Avesta" has been current in Europe since the time of Anquetil Duperron (*c.* 1771), but the Parsees themselves call it simply *Avesta*,—*Zend* (*i.e.*, "interpretation") being specially employed to denote the translation and exposition of a great part of the Avesta which exists in PAHLAVI (*q.v.*). Text and translation are often spoken of together in Pahlavi books as *Avistâk va Zand* ("Avesta and Zend"), whence (through a misunderstanding) our word Zend-Avesta. The origin and meaning of the word "Avesta" (or in its older form *Avistâk*) are alike obscure; it cannot be traced further back than the Sasanian period. The language of the Avesta is still frequently called Zend; but, as already implied, this is a mistake. We possess no other document written in it, and on this account modern Parsee scholars, as well as the older Pahlavi books, speak of the language and the writing indifferently as Avesta. As the original home of the language can only be very doubtfully conjectured, we shall do well to follow the usage sanctioned by old custom and apply the word to both. Although the Avesta is a work of but moderate compass (comparable, say, to the *Iliad* and *Odyssey* taken together), there nevertheless exists no single MS. which gives it in its entirety. This circumstance alone is enough to reveal the true nature of the book: it is a composite whole, a collection of writings as the Old Testament is. It consists, as we shall afterwards see, of the last remains of the extensive sacred literature in which the Zoroastrian faith was formerly set forth.

Contents and Character.—As we now have it, the Avesta consists of four parts,—the Yasna, the Vispered, the Vendidad, and the Khordah Avesta.

1. The *Yasna*, the principal liturgical book of the Parsees, in 72 chapters (*hâiti*, *hâ*), contains the texts that are read by the priest at the solemn Yasna (Izeshne) ceremony. The arrangement of the chapters is purely liturgical, although their matter in many cases has nothing to do with the liturgical action. The kernel of the whole book, around which the remaining portions are grouped, consists of the *Gâthâs* or "hymns" of ZOROASTER (*q.v.*), the oldest and most sacred portion of the entire canon. The Yasna accordingly falls into three sections of about equal length. (*a*) The introduction (chaps. 1-27) for the most part is made up of long-winded, monotonous, reiterated invocations. (*b*) The Gâthâs (chs. 28-54) contain the discourses, exhortations, and revelations of the prophet, written in a metrical style and an archaic language, different in many respects from that ordinarily used in the Avesta. As to the authenticity of these hymns, see ZOROASTER. The Gâthâs proper, arranged according to the metres in which they are written, fall into five subdivisions (28-37, 43-46, 47-50, 51, 53). Between chap. 37 and chap. 43 is inserted the so-called Seven-Chapter Yasna (*haptanghâiti*), a number of small prose pieces not far behind the Gâthâs in antiquity. (*c*) The so-called Later Yasna (*Aparô Yasnô*) (chaps. 54-72) has contents of considerable variety, but consists mainly of invocations.

2. The *Vispered*, a minor liturgical work in 24 chapters (*karde*), is alike in form and substance completely dependent on the Yasna; it is based upon the arrangement of the Yasna in its present form, a circumstance proving its much later date as a whole. The name Vispered, meaning "all the chiefs" (*vispê ratavô*), has reference to the spiritual heads of the religion of Ormuzd, invocations to whom form the main contents of the book.

3. The *Vendidad* (*Vîdaêvô Dâtem*), *i.e.*, the law for the "enemies of the devil," contains in 22 chapters (*fargard*) a kind of dualistic account of creation (chap. 1), the legend of Yima and the golden age (chap. 2), the praises of agriculture (chap. 3), and in the bulk of the remaining chapters the circumstantial precepts of the religion

with reference to purification and ecclesiastical penance. It may with propriety be called the "priestly code" of the Parsees.

The Yasna, Vispered, and Vendidad together constitute the Avesta in the stricter sense of that word, and the reading of them appertains to the priest alone. For liturgical purposes the separate chapters of the Vendidad and the Vispered are sometimes inserted amongst those of the Yasna so as to form what is known as the Vendidad Sâde, which then, accompanied by certain liturgical actions, is publicly read in the Parsee worship. The reading of the Gâthâs and Vendidad in this case may, when viewed according to the original intention, be taken as corresponding in some sense to the sermon, while that of the Vispered and the rest of the Yasna may be taken as corresponding to the hymns and prayers of Christian worship.

4. In marked contrast to the three already mentioned is the *Khordah Avesta*, or Little Avesta, which is designed equally for priesthood and laity, and serves rather as a book of private devotion. Besides some short prayers, such as the Nyâishes, the favourite daily prayers of the Parsees, it contains the Yashts or songs of praise, twenty-one in number, addressed to the Yazatas (Izads), the deities and angels of the Ormuzd creed.

Over and above the four books just enumerated there are a considerable number of fragments from other books, as well as quotations, glosses, and glossaries.

In its present form, however, the Avesta is only a fragmentary remnant of the old priestly literature of Zoroastrianism, a fact confessed by the learned tradition of the Parsees themselves, according to which the number of Yashts was originally thirty. The truth is that we possess but a trifling portion of a very much larger original Avesta, if we are to believe native tradition, carrying us back to the Sasanian period, which tells of an original Avesta in twenty-one books called *nasks* or *nosks*, as to the names, contents, and chapters of which we have several more or less detailed accounts, particularly in the Pahlavi Dînkard and in the Rivayats. From the same sources we learn that even then a considerable portion of the original Avesta had been lost: we are told that of a number of nosks only a small portion was found to be extant "after Alexander." For example, of the seventh nosk, which "before Alexander" had as many as fifty chapters, there then remained only thirteen; and similar things are alleged about the eighth, ninth, tenth, and other nosks. But even of the remains of the original Avesta, as these lay before the authors referred to, only a small portion has survived to our time. Of all the nosks one only, the nineteenth, has come down to us unimpaired and intact,—the Vendidad. All the others, with the exception of slight traces, have disappeared in the course of centuries.

It would be rash to treat in an offhand way this old tradition about the twenty-one nosks as pure invention. The number twenty-one indeed points to an artificial arrangement of the material; for twenty-one is a sacred number, and the most sacred prayer of the Parsees, the so-called Ahunô Vairyô (Honovar) contains twenty-one words; and it is also true that in the enumeration of the nosks we miss the names of the books we know—Yasna, Vispered, as well as the Yashts and the Khordah Avesta. But either we must regard them as having been included among the nosks, though under other names, or, what is even more probable, we must assume that even at that early date special liturgical manuals—the Yasna especially—distinct from the nosks had already been compiled for the practical use of the priests. Further, the statements of the Dînkard and other writings leave on one a very distinct impression that the authors actually had before them the text of the nosks, or at all events of a large part of them. And, besides, in other directions there are numerous indications that such books had once really existed. In the Khordah Avesta as we now have it we find two Srôsh Yashts; with regard to the first, it is expressly stated in old MSS. that it was taken from the Hâdôkht nosk (the twentieth, according to the Dînkard). From the same nosk also a considerable fragment (*Yt.*, 21 and 22 in Westergaard) has been taken. So also the extensive quotations from Avesta texts in the *Niringistân*, a Pahlavi book, are probably the disjecta membra of the seventeenth (or Hûspâram) nosk. Lastly, the numerous other fragments, the quotations in the Pahlavi translation, the many references in the *Bundahish* to passages of this Avesta not now known to us, all presuppose the existence in the Sasanian period of a much more extensive Avesta literature than the mere prayer book now in our hands. The existence of an original Avesta is far from being a mere myth. But, even granting that a certain obscurity still hangs undispelled over the problem of the old Avesta, with its twenty-one nosks, we may well believe the Parsees themselves, when they tell us that their sacred literature has passed through successive stages of decay, the last of which is represented by the present Avesta. There is evidence of this in the patchwork and fragmentary character of some portions of the present Avesta; and, moreover, in the MS. evidence of recent centuries we are able to observe with our own eyes the actual process of abridgment gradually going on, and to trace the manner in which certain portions of the present Avesta slowly passed out of currency. This holds good, in particular, of the greater Yashts. The transcribers of the Khordah Avesta satisfied themselves for the most part with those prayers which were currently in use, such as the Nyâishes and one or two of the smaller and intermediate Yashts. The great Yashts are not of very frequent occurrence: some of them indeed are already met with but seldom, and MSS. containing all the Yashts are of great rarity. Of the fifteenth, seventeenth, and nineteenth Yashts we might even venture to predict that some centuries hence they may perhaps be found defying the tooth of time in not more than a single manuscript copy.

Origin and History.—While all that Herodotus (i. 132) has got to say is that the Magi sang "the theogony" at their sacrifices, Pausanias is able to add (v. 27, 3) that they read from a book. Hermippus in the 3d century B.C. affirmed that Zoroaster, the founder of the doctrine of the Magi, was the author of twenty books, each containing 100,000 verses. According to the Arab historian Tabari, these were written on 1200 cowhides, a statement confirmed by Masudi, who writes, "Zartusht gave to the Persians the book called Avesta. It consisted of twenty-one parts, each containing 200 leaves. This book, in the writing which Zartusht invented and which the Magi called the writing of religion, was written on 12,000 cowhides, bound together by golden bands. Its language was the Old Persian, which no one now understands." These statements sufficiently establish the existence and great bulk of the sacred writings. Parsee tradition adds a number of interesting statements as to their history. According to the *Arda-Viraf-Nâma*, stated to have been written during the Sasanian period, the religion revealed through Zoroaster had subsisted in its purity for 300 years when Iskander Rumi (Alexander the Great) invaded and devastated Iran, and burnt the Avesta which, written on cowhides with golden ink, was preserved in the archives at Persepolis. According to the Dînkard, there were two copies, of which one was burnt, while the second perished at the hands of the Greeks in some other way. The Rivayats have it that Alexander burnt the greater part of the twenty-one nosks, and go on to say that after his death the Zoroastrian priests met, gathered the scattered fragments which had escaped the ravages of war, and put together the present collection, which is but a small portion of the original book. With regard to this editing the Dînkard gives various details. It tells us that the collecting of the Avesta fragments, so far as these were still extant, whether in writing or in oral tradition, began under the last of the Arsacids at the command of King Vologeses. The first of the Sasanians,

Ardeshîr Bâbagân, and his son Shapûr I. resumed and continued the work, and proclaimed the new Avesta thus produced as canonical. Finally, under Shapûr II. (309-380) a new revision and final redaction were made by Adarbâd Mahraspand

It is possible enough for historical criticism to regard this tradition in many of its features as mere fiction, or as a perversion of facts made for the purpose of transferring the blame for the loss of a sacred literature to other shoulders than those really responsible for it. People may, if they choose, absolve Alexander from the charge of vandalism of which he is accused, but the fact nevertheless remains, that he suffered the palace at Persepolis to be burnt (Diod., xvii. 72; Curt., v. 7). Even the statement as to the one or two complete copies of the Avesta may be given up as the invention of a later day. Nevertheless the essential elements of the tradition remain unshaken, viz., that the original Avesta or old sacred literature, divided on account of its great bulk and heterogeneous contents into many portions and a variety of separate works, had an actual existence in numerous copies and also in the memories of priests, that, although gradually diminishing in bulk, it remained extant during the long period of foreign domination and ecclesiastical decay after the time of Alexander, and that it served as a basis for the redaction subsequently made. The kernel of this native tradition—the fact of a late collection of older fragments—appears indisputable. The character of the book is entirely that of a compilation.

In its outward form the Avesta as we now have it belongs to the Sasanian period, the last survival of the compilers' work already alluded to. And it need hardly be said that the collecting and arranging of the scattered fragments often rendered necessary, or at least desirable, certain additions by the redactors' own hands. But, broadly speaking, the materials out of which the compilers reared their building belonged originally to older structures and are of very various dates. Opinions differ greatly as to the precise age of the original texts brought together by subsequent redactors: according to some, they are pre-Achæmenian; according to Darmesteter, they were written in Media under the Achæmenian dynasty; according to Eduard Meyer, they are on the whole of Sasanian origin; according to some, their source must be sought in the east, according to others, in the west, of Iran. But to search for a precise time or exact locality is to deal with the question too narrowly; it is more correct to say that the Avesta was worked at from the time of Zoroaster down to the Sasanian period. Its oldest portions, the Gâthâs, proceed from Zoroaster himself. This conclusion is inevitable for everyone to whom Zoroaster is an historical personality, and who does not shun the labour of an unprejudiced research into the meaning of those difficult texts (comp. ZOROASTER). The rest of the Avesta, in spite of the opposite opinion of learned Parsees, does not even claim to come from Zoroaster. As the Gâthâs constitute the kernel of the Later Yasna, so they ultimately proved to be the first nucleus of a religious literature at large. The language in which Zoroaster taught, especially a later development of it,—an idiom indisputably belonging to eastern Iran,—remained as the standard with the followers of Zoroaster, and became the sacred language of the priesthood of the faith which he had founded; as such it became, so to speak, absolved from the ordinary conditions of time and space. Taught and acquired as an ecclesiastical language, it was enabled to live an artificial life long after it had become extinct as a vernacular,—in this respect comparable to the Latin of the Middle Ages or the Hebrew of the rabbinical schools. The various texts themselves enable us to trace its gradual paralysis, decay, and death. It is only from this point of view that the language can be used as a criterion for the relative chronology of these. Any more exact arrangement seems almost impossible; we have practically no other tests to apply. The priests by whom the texts were edited gave them the form intended to be valid once for all and refrained from any allusion to ephemeral relations. The following conclusions may be stated in a general way.

The language of the Avesta travelled with the Zoroastrian religion and with the main body of the priesthood, in all probability, that is to say, from east to west; within the limits of Iran it became international. The Avesta texts must have passed through a long process of development, which did not reach its close till at a comparatively late period. Many portions are the result of repeated redacting and compiling; older texts are removed from their original connexion, and worked into new ones or made use of in these. In these operations the revisers of the Sasanian epoch may be presumed to have had only the smallest share; the texts they had before them were already for the most part in a revised form. They were no longer in a position to give a relatively correct text; what they still had in their power to some extent to perform is approximately exhibited in such passages as *Yt.*, 1, 12 *sq.*; *Yt.*, 2, 11 *sq.*; *Yt.*, 10, 120 *sq.*,—perhaps in part translated back from the Pahlavi.

The great Yashts and the Vendidad are the most instructive portions for the history of the text. The original kernel of *Yashts* 5. 8, 15, 17, 19 consists of the Iranian mythology of gods and heroes which had its origin in the East, and there also was cast into a poetical form. Fragments of it were worked into the framework of the great Yashts at a much later date. The author of *Vend.*, 2 used in a fragmentary way a poetic version of the Yima legend. The redactor of *Vend.*, 3, judging from the monotonous and clumsy style of the opening sections, must have been prosaic enough; yet from the twenty-fourth paragraph onwards we have a bright and pleasant description of the blessings of agriculture, in a poetical form, that contrasts singularly with what immediately precedes it, and must certainly have been borrowed from an older source. In this way alone can we in other instances also account for the numerous verses with which the prose is often interspersed. Their function often was merely to set off and ornament the later prose. Of "genuine" and "spurious" there can be in this connexion no question, but only of "older" and "more recent." However vague and obscure the question may remain after all has been said, we can at least lay so much down as fundamentally fixed, namely, that all that is metrical in the Avesta bears the stamp of a higher antiquity than does the prose.

As has been already stated, the Avesta now in our hands is but a small portion of the book as edited under the Sasanians. The large part perished under the devastating wave of persecution which broke over Iran with the Mohammedan invasion, or under the still more fatal influences of the apathy and forgetfulness of its proper guardians. The understanding of the older Avesta texts was far from perfect even at the time when they were being edited and revised. The need for a translation and interpretation became evident; and under the later Sasanians the majority of the books, if not the whole of them, were rendered into the current Pahlavi. A thorough use of this translation will not be possible until we have it in good critical editions, and acquaintance with its language ceases to be the monopoly of a few privileged individuals. For the interpretation of the older texts it is of great value. The Parsee priest Neryosangh subsequently translated a portion of the Pahlavi version into Sanskrit.

The MSS. of the Avesta are comparatively speaking of recent date. The oldest is the Pahlavi Vispered in Copenhagen, of date

1258. Next come the four MSS. of the Herbad Mihirâpân Kaî Khusro at Cambay (1323 and 1324), two Vendidads with Pahlavi in London and Copenhagen, and two Yasnas with Pahlavi in Copenhagen and Bombay, in the possession of Dastur Jamaspji Minocheherji, who of all the Parsees is richest in old and good MSS. Generally speaking, the MSS. fall off in quality and carefulness in proportion to their lateness; an honourable exception must be made in favour of those proceeding from Kirman and Yazd in Persia, mostly dating from the 17th and 18th centuries.

The first European scholar to direct attention to the Avesta was Hyde of Oxford, in his *Historia Religionis Veterum Persarum eorumque Magorum* (1700), which, however, failed to awaken any lasting interest in the sacred writings of the Parsees. The merit of achieving this belongs to the enthusiastic Orientalist Anquetil Duperron, the fruit of whose prolonged stay in India (from 1754 to 1761) and his acquaintance with the Parsee priests was a translation (certainly very defective) of the Zend-Avesta. The foundation of a scientific exegesis was laid by Burnouf. The interpretation of the Avesta is one of the most difficult problems of Oriental philology. To this very day no kind of agreement has been reached by conflicting schools even upon some of the most important points. The most salient contributions are those of Westergaard, Spiegel, Darmesteter, Roth, and Bartholomae. Opinion is divided also as to the significance of the Avesta in the literature of the world. The exaggerated enthusiasm of Anquetil Duperron has been followed, especially since Spiegel's translation, by an excessive reaction. The future will doubtless be more just with regard to the importance of the book for the history of religion in general and even of Christianity.

Editions.—The first complete editions were that by Westergaard (Copenhagen, 1852-54) and that of the Avesta in the stricter sense, along with the Pahlavi translation, by Spiegel (Vienna, 1853-58). A new and complete edition by Geldner has been in course of publication since 1885. The best translation is that by Darmesteter and Mills in *Sacred Books of the East* (3 vols., Oxford, 1880 *sq.*, with an excellent introduction by the first-named).

Literature.—See Anquetil Duperron, *Zend-Avesta, Ouvrage de Zoroastre*, &c., (Paris, 1771); Haug, *Essays on the Sacred Language*, &c., *of the Parsis*, especially in the new edition by E. W. West (London, 1878); De Harlez, *Introduction à l'Étude de l'Avesta* (Paris, 1881); Max Duncker, *Geschichte des Alterthums*, vol. iv.; and Eduard Meyer, *Geschichte des Alterthums* (Stuttgart, 1884). (K. G.)

ZENO, emperor of the East from 474 to 491, was an Isaurian of noble birth, and originally bore the name of Trascalissæus, which he exchanged for that of Zeno on his marriage with Ariadne, daughter of Leo I., in 468. Of his early life nothing is known; after his marriage (which was designed by Leo to secure the Isaurian support against his ambitious minister Aspar) he became patrician and commander of the imperial guard and of the armies in the East. While on a campaign in Thrace he narrowly escaped assassination; and on his return to the capital he avenged himself by compassing the murder of Aspar, who had instigated the attempt. In 474 Leo I. died after appointing as his successor Leo the son of Zeno and Ariadne; Zeno, however, with the help of his mother-in-law Verina, succeeded in getting himself crowned also, and on the death of his son before the end of the year became sole emperor. In the following year, in consequence of a revolt fomented by Verina in favour of her brother Basiliscus, he was compelled to take refuge in Isauria, whither he was pursued by Illus and Trocundus, two of the usurper's generals, and where, after sustaining a defeat, he was compelled to shut himself up in a strong castle. Basiliscus, however, soon outstripped Zeno in avarice, cruelty, and self-indulgence, and the vicissitudes of war and intrigue ultimately enabled the latter to re-enter Constantinople unopposed (July 477), while his rival was banished to Phrygia, where he soon afterwards died. The remainder of Zeno's reign was disturbed by numerous other less formidable revolts, and it was to relieve himself of the pressure of one of these that in 487 he gave THEODORIC (*q.v.*) permission to invade Italy and dethrone Odoacer, which led to the establishment of the Ostrogothic kingdom in Italy. At an earlier period of his reign (476) Zeno had received the deputation from the Roman senate which announced the deposition of Romulus Augustulus. In ecclesiastical history the name of Zeno is associated with the *Henoticon* or instrument of union, promulgated by him and signed by all the Eastern bishops, with the design of terminating the Monophysite controversy. The document, which is given by Evagrius (*H.E.*, iii. 14), re-affirms the doctrine of the Nicæno-Constantinopolitan creed, and renews the condemnation of Nestorius pronounced by the council of Ephesus, but adroitly avoids the crucial point as to the unity or duality of natures in the Incarnate Word, treating this as an open question.

ZENO OF CITIUM. See STOICS.

ZENO OF ELEA, son of Teleutagoras, is supposed to have been born towards the beginning of the 5th century B.C. The pupil and the friend of Parmenides, he sought to recommend his master's doctrine of the existence of the One by controverting the popular belief in the existence of the Many. In virtue of this method of indirect argumentation he is regarded as the inventor of "dialectic," that is to say, disputation having for its end not victory but the discovery or the transmission of truth. He is said to have been concerned in a plot against a tyrant, and on its detection to have borne with exemplary constancy the tortures to which he was subjected; but authorities differ both as to the name and the residence of the tyrant and as to the circumstances and the issue of the enterprise.

In Plato's *Parmenides*, Socrates, "then very young," meets Parmenides, "an old man some sixty-five years of age," and Zeno, "a man of about forty, tall and personable," and engages them in philosophical discussion. But it may be doubted whether such a meeting was chronologically possible. Plato's account of Zeno's teaching (*Parmenides*, 128 *sq.*) is, however, presumably as accurate as it is precise. In reply to those who thought that Parmenides's theory of the existence of the One involved inconsistencies and absurdities, Zeno tried to show that the assumption of the existence of the Many carried with it inconsistencies and absurdities grosser and more numerous. In early youth he collected his arguments in a book, which, according to Plato, was put into circulation without his knowledge.

Of the paradoxes used by Zeno to discredit the belief in plurality and motion, eight survive in the writings of Aristotle and Simplicius. They are commonly stated as follows.[1] (1) If the Existent is Many, it must be at once infinitely small and infinitely great,—infinitely small, because the parts of which it consists must be indivisible and therefore without magnitude; infinitely great, because, that any part having magnitude may be separate from any other part, the intervention of a third part having magnitude is necessary, and that this third part may be separate from the other two the intervention of other parts having magnitude is necessary, and so on *ad infinitum*. (2) In like manner the Many must be numerically both finite and infinite,—numerically finite, because there are as many things as there are, neither more nor less; numerically infinite, because, that any two things may be separate, the intervention of a third thing is necessary, and so on *ad infinitum*. (3) If all that is is in space, space itself must be in space, and so on *ad infinitum*. (4) If a bushel of corn turned out upon the floor makes a noise, each grain and each part of each grain must make a noise likewise; but, in fact, it is not so. (5) Before a body in motion can reach a given point, it must first traverse the half of the distance; before it can traverse the half of the distance, it must first traverse the quarter; and so on *ad infinitum*. Hence, that a body may pass from one point to another, it must traverse an infinite number of divisions. But an infinite distance (which Zeno fails to distinguish from a finite distance infinitely divided) cannot be traversed in a finite time. Consequently, the goal can never be reached. (6) If the tortoise has the start of Achilles, Achilles can never come up with the tortoise; for, while Achilles traverses the distance from his starting-point to the starting-point of the tortoise, the tortoise advances a certain distance, and while Achilles traverses this distance the tortoise makes a further advance, and so on *ad infinitum*. Consequently, Achilles may run *ad infinitum* without overtaking the tortoise. [This paradox is virtually identical with (5), the only difference being that, whereas in (5) there is one body, in (6) there are two bodies, moving towards a limit. The "infinity" of the premise is an infinity of subdivisions of a distance which is finite; the "infinity" of the conclusion is an infinity of distance. Thus Zeno again confounds a finite distance infinitely divided with an infinite distance. If the tortoise has a start of 1000 feet, Achilles,

[1] See Zeller, *Die Philosophie d. Griechen*, I. 540 *sq.*; *Grundriss*, 54

on the supposition that his speed is ten times that of the tortoise, must traverse an infinite number of spaces,—1000 feet, 100 feet, 10 feet, &c.,—and the tortoise must traverse an infinite number of spaces,—100 feet, 10 feet, 1 foot, &c.,—before they reach the point, distant from their starting-points $1111\frac{1}{9}$ feet and $111\frac{1}{9}$ feet respectively, at which the tortoise is overtaken. In a word, 1000, 100, 10, &c., in (6) and $\frac{1}{2}$, $\frac{1}{4}$, $\frac{1}{8}$, &c., in (5) are convergent series, and $1111\frac{1}{9}$ and 1 are the limits to which they respectively approximate.] (7) So long as anything is in one and the same space, it is at rest. Hence an arrow is at rest during every moment of its flight, and therefore also during the whole of its flight. (8) Two bodies moving with equal speed traverse equal spaces in equal times. But, when two bodies move with equal speed in opposite directions, the one passes the other in half the time in which it passes it when at rest. These propositions appeared to Zeno to be irreconcilable.

In short, the ordinary belief in plurality and motion seemed to him to involve fatal inconsistencies, whence he inferred that Parmenides was justified in distinguishing the mutable movable Many from the immutable immovable One, which alone is really existent. In other words, Zeno re-affirmed the dogma, "The Ent is, the Non-ent is not." It may seem strange that a reasoner so acute should confound that which is infinitely divisible with that which is infinitely great, as in (1), (2), (5), and (6); that he should identify space and magnitude, as in (3); that he should neglect the imperfection of the organs of sense, as in (4); that he should resolve motion into a series of states of rest, and on the strength of this analysis deny the reality of motion, as in (7); and that he should ignore the relativity of speed, as in (8). But Zeno's perplexity was genuine, and his end was positive. He was neither an eristic seeking an argumentative victory, nor a sceptic despairing of truth, but an honest thinker, breaking ground in a new field with indifferent success.

Great as was the importance of these paradoxes of plurality and motion in stimulating speculation about space and time, their direct influence upon Greek thought was less considerable than that of another paradox,—strangely neglected by historians of philosophy,—the paradox of predication. We learn from Plato (*Parmenides*, 127 D) that "the first hypothesis of the first argument" of Zeno's book above mentioned ran as follows: "If existences are many, they must be both like and unlike [unlike, inasmuch as they are not one and the same, and like, inasmuch as they agree in not being one and the same, Proclus, *On the Parmenides*, ii. 143]. But this is impossible; for unlike things cannot be like, nor like things unlike. Therefore existences are not many." That is to say, not perceiving that the same thing may be at once like and unlike in different relations, Zeno regarded the attribution to the same thing of likeness and unlikeness as a violation of what was afterwards known as the principle of contradiction; and, finding that plurality entailed these attributions, he inferred its unreality. Now, when without qualification he affirmed that the unlike thing cannot be like, nor the like thing unlike, he was on the high road to the doctrine maintained three-quarters of a century later by the Cynics, that no predication which is not identical is legitimate. He was not indeed aware how deeply he had committed himself; otherwise he would have observed that his argument, if valid against the Many of the vulgar, was valid also against the One of Parmenides, with its plurality of attributes, as well as that, in the absence of a theory of predication, it was useless to speculate about knowledge and being. But others were not slow to draw the obvious conclusions; and it may be conjectured that Gorgias's sceptical development of the Zenonian logic contributed, not less than Protagoras's sceptical development of the Ionian physics, to the diversion of the intellectual energies of Greece from the pursuit of truth to the pursuit of culture.

For three-quarters of a century, then, philosophy was at a standstill; and, when in the second decade of the 4th century the pursuit of truth was resumed, it was plain that the difficulty raised by Zeno must be met before the problems which had occupied the earlier thinkers—the problem of knowledge and the problem of being—could be so much as attempted. Accordingly, in the seventh book of the *Republic*, where Plato propounds his scheme of Academic education, he directs the attention of studious youth primarily, if not exclusively, to the concurrence of inconsistent attributes; and in the *Phædo*, 102 B–103 A, taking as an instance the tallness and the shortness simultaneously discoverable in Simmias, he offers his own theory of the immanent idea as the solution of the paradox. Simmias, he says, has in him the ideas of tall and short. Again, when it presently appeared that the theory of the immanent idea was inconsistent with itself, and moreover inapplicable to explain predication except where the subject was a sensible thing, so that reconstruction became necessary, the Zenonian difficulty continued to demand and to receive Plato's best attention. Thus, in the *Parmenides*, with the paradox of likeness and unlikeness for his text, he inquires how far the current theories of being (his own included) are capable of providing, not only for knowledge, but also for predication, and in the concluding sentence he suggests that, as likeness and unlikeness, greatness and smallness, &c., are relations, the initial paradox is no longer paradoxical; while in the *Sophist*, Zeno's doctrine having been shown to be fatal to reason, thought, speech, and utterance, the principle which in the *Parmenides* is applied to αὐτὰ καθ' αὑτὰ εἴδη and to sensible particulars is extended to include the case of εἴδη which are not αὐτὰ καθ' αὑτά. It would seem then that, not to Antisthenes only, but to Plato also, Zeno's paradox of predication was a substantial difficulty; and we shall be disposed to give Zeno credit accordingly for his perception of its importance.

In all probability Zeno did not observe that in his controversial defence of Eleaticism he was interpreting Parmenides's teaching anew. But so it was. For, while Parmenides had recognized, together with the One, which is, and is the object of knowledge, a Many, which is not, and therefore is not known, but nevertheless becomes, and is the object of opinion, Zeno plainly affirmed that plurality, becoming, and opinion are one and all inconceivable. In a word, the fundamental dogma, "The Ent is, the Non-ent is not," which with Parmenides had been an assertion of the necessity of distinguishing between the Ent, which is, and the Non-ent, which is not, but becomes, was with Zeno a declaration of the Non-ent's absolute nullity. Thus, just as Empedocles developed Parmenides's theory of the Many to the neglect of his theory of the One, so Zeno developed the theory of the One to the neglect of the theory of the Many. With the severance of its two members Eleaticism proper, the Eleaticism of Parmenides, ceased to exist.

The first effect of Zeno's teaching was to complete the discomfiture of philosophy. For the paradox of predication, which he had used to disprove the existence of plurality, was virtually a denial of all speech and all thought, and thus led to a more comprehensive scepticism than that which sprang from the contemporary theories of sensation. Nevertheless, he left an enduring mark upon Greek speculation, inasmuch as he not only recognized the need of a logic, and grappled, however unsuccessfully, with one of the most obvious of logical problems, but also by the invention of dialectic provided a new and powerful instrument against the time when the One and the Many should be reunited in the philosophy of Plato.

Bibliography.—F. W. A. Mullach, *Fragmenta Philosophorum Græcorum*, Paris, 1860, i. 266 *sq.*; Zeller, *Die Philosophie d. Griechen*, Leipsic, 1876, i. 534-552; P. Tannery, *Pour l'Histoire de la Science Hellène*, Paris, 1887, pp. 247-261. Ignoring the philosophical aspect of Zeno's teaching, Tannery supposes him to have maintained in opposition to the Pythagoreans that body is not a sum of points, time not a sum of moments, and motion not a sum of passages from point to point. For histories of philosophy and other works upon Eleaticism, see PARMENIDES. (H. JA.)

ZENOBIA. See PALMYRA, vol. xviii. p. 201 *sq.*

ZENTA, a market town of Hungary, in the county of Bács-Bodrog, on the right bank of the river Theiss, 20 miles south of Szegedin, is historically known for the decisive victory won in its vicinity by Prince Eugene over the Turks in 1697. The population, which is purely agricultural, numbered 21,200 in 1880, and 16,000 in 1886.

ZEPHANIAH (*Sophonias*, Σοφονίας, Heb. צְפַנְיָה, "whom Jehovah hides" or "protects"; compare the Phœnician man's or woman's name צפנבעל, *C.I.S.*, No. 207, Euting, *Pun. Steine*, p. 16), son of Cushi, the ninth, according to the order of his book, among the twelve minor prophets, flourished in the reign of Josiah of Judah, and apparently before the great reformation in the eighteenth year of that king (621 B.C.). For various forms of idolatry put down in that year are spoken of by Zephaniah as still prevalent in Judah (chap. i. 4 *sq.*), and are specified in such a connexion as to imply that they were not the secret sins of individuals, but held the first place among the national backslidings that could, as the prophet teaches, be removed only by a sweeping judgment on the state. Of the person of Zephaniah nothing is known; but it has been conjectured that his great-great-grandfather Hezekiah (chap. i. 1) is the king of that name, and if so he belonged to the highest class of Judæan society.

The genuineness and integrity of the short prophecy ascribed to Zephaniah do not seem to be open to reasonable doubt. Stade (*Gesch. Isr.*, i. 644) raises a question about chap. iii., and if this were a distinct oracle there would be no cogent reason to ascribe it to the author of the two chapters that precede; for the book of the minor prophets is made up of a number of short pieces, some bearing a name and some anonymous, and it is only old usage that ascribes the anonymous pieces to the last preceding prophet whose name is prefixed to his prophecy. But, though the sequence of thought in the book of Zephaniah is not so smooth as a Western reader may desire, a single leading motive runs through the whole, and the first two chapters would be incomplete without the third, which moreover is certainly pre-exilic (verses 1-4), and presents specific points of contact with what precedes as well as a general agreement in style and idea.

The dominating motive of the whole is the approach of a sweeping and world-wide judgment, which the prophet announces as near at hand, and interprets, on the lines laid down by Isaiah in his prophecies about Israel and Assyria, as designed to destroy the wicked and prepare the way for the visible sovereignty of the righteous God of Israel. As regards Judah, which forms the subject of the first and third chapters, the effect of the judgment will be to sift out the idolaters, the men of violence and wrong, the false prophets and profane priests, the hardened men of the world to whom all religion is alike and who deem that the Lord will do neither good nor evil. The men who seek meekness and righteousness will be left, a poor and lowly people, trusting in the name of the Lord and eschewing falsehood. To them a future of gladness is reserved, a peaceful life under Jehovah's immediate kingship and loving protection. Such an ideal necessarily implies that they shall no longer be threatened by hostility from without, and this condition is satisfied by the prophet's view of the effect of the impending judgment on the ancient enemies of his nation. The destruction of the Philistines on the west and of Moab and Ammon on the east will enable the Hebrews to extend their settlements from the Mediterranean to the Syrian desert; and their remoter oppressors, the Ethiopians and Assyrians, shall also perish. That Ethiopia appears instead of Egypt is in accordance with the conditions of the time. It was with Ethiopic dynasts holding sway in Egypt that Assyria had to contend during the 7th century B.C., when the petty kingdoms of Palestine were so often crushed between the collision of the two great powers, and even Psammetichus, the contemporary of Josiah, and the restorer of a truly Egyptian kingdom, was nominally the heir of the great Ethiopian sovereigns.

These conceptions are closely modelled on the scheme of Jehovah's righteous purpose worked out by Isaiah a century before, when Judah first felt the weight of the Assyrian rod, and they afford the most conclusive evidence of the depth and permanence of that great prophet's influence. But in one point there is an important divergence. In Isaiah's view Assyria is the rod of God's anger; and, when the work of judgment is complete and Jehovah returns to the remnant of His people, the theodicea is completed by the fall of the unconscious instrument of the divine decrees before the inviolable walls of the holy mountain. Zephaniah in like manner looks to an all-conquering nation as the instrument of divine judgment on Judah and the rest of the known world. He represents the day of Jehovah, according to the old meaning of that phrase, as a day of battle (not an assize day); he speaks of the guests invited to Jehovah's sacrifice, *i.e.*, to a great slaughter, of alarm against fenced cities, of blood poured out as dust, of pillage and desolation at the hand of an enemy. But beyond this all is vague; we neither hear who the sword of Jehovah (ii. 12) is, nor what is to become of him when his work is completed. Isaiah's construction has in all its parts a definite reference to present political facts, and is worked out to a complete conclusion; Zephaniah borrows the ideas of his predecessor without attaining to his clearness of political conception, and so his picture is incomplete. The foreign conqueror, by whom Judah is to be chastised and Nineveh and Ethiopia destroyed, is brought on to the stage, but never taken off it. It is safe to conclude that the principal actor in the prophetic drama, who is thus strangely forgotten at the last, was not as real and prominent a figure in Zephaniah's political horizon as Assyria was in the horizon of Isaiah. At the same time it is reasonable to think that so complete a reproduction of Isaiah's ideas in the picture of a new world-judgment was not formed without some stimulus from without, and this stimulus has been sought in the Scythian invasion of western Asia, to which some of Jeremiah's earlier prophecies also appear to refer; see ISRAEL, vol. xiii. p. 415. But from the analysis given in the article SCYTHIA (vol. xxi. p. 577) it is doubtful whether the Scythians had appeared even on the distant horizon at the date of Zephaniah's prophecy,[1] while, on the other hand, the movements in the far East which preceded the first siege of Nineveh are chronologically suitable, and appear to afford quite sufficient basis for Zephaniah's undefined anticipation of a general political convulsion. How the danger that threatened Nineveh stirred the mind of the Hebrews appears also from the prophecy of Nahum.

Be this as it may, the comparison between Isaiah and Zephaniah affords an instructive example of the difference between original and reproductive prophecy. All the prophets have certain fundamental ideas in common, and each has learned something from his predecessors. If Zephaniah draws from Isaiah, Isaiah himself drew from Amos and Hosea. But Isaiah goes to his predecessors for general principles, and shapes the application of these principles to the conditions of his own time in a manner altogether fresh and independent. Zephaniah, on the other hand, goes to his predecessor for details; he does not clearly distinguish between the form and the substance of the prophetic ideas, and looks for a final consummation of the divine purpose, not only in accordance with the principles of Isaiah, but on the very lines which that prophet had laid down. But these lines were drawn on the assumption that the Assyrian judgment was final and would be directly followed by the reign of righteousness. This assumption was not justified by

[1] The Scythians appeared in Media about 619 B.C., and, if they were really Sacæ and came from the East, their appearance in Palestine would fall still later.

the event; the deliverance and reformation were incomplete; and the inbringing of the reign of righteousness was again deferred. Zephaniah sees this, but fails to draw the true inference. He postulates a new crisis in history similar to the Assyrian crisis of which Isaiah wrote, and assumes that it will run such a course as to fulfil Isaiah's unfulfilled predictions. But the movements of history do not repeat themselves; and the workings of God's righteous providence take fresh shape in each new scene of the world's life, so that a prediction not fulfilled under the conditions for which it was given can never again be fulfilled in detail. As it is an essential feature of prophecy that all ideas are not only presented but thought out in concrete form, and with reference to present historical conditions, the distinction between the temporary form and the permanent religious truth embodied in that form is also essential. The tendency to confound the two, to ascribe absolute truth to what is mere embodiment, and therefore to regard unfulfilled predictions as simply deferred, even where the form of the prediction is obviously dependent on mere temporary conditions of the prophet's own time, gained ground from the time of Zephaniah onwards, and culminated in the Apocalyptic literature. As it grew, the eternal ideas of the great prophets fell into the background, and were at length entirely lost in the crass Jewish conception of a Messianic age, which is little more than an apotheosis of national particularism and selfrighteousness. Zephaniah's eschatology is not open to this charge: with him, as with Isaiah, the doctrine of the salvation of the remnant of Israel is inspired by spiritual convictions and instinct with ethical force. The emphasis still lies on the moral idea of the remnant, not on the physical conception Israel. He does not yield to Amos or Isaiah in the courage with which he denounces sin in high places, and he is akin to Hosea in his firm hold of the principle that the divine governance is rooted not only in righteousness but in love, and that the triumph of love is the end of Jehovah's working. Yet even here we see the difference between the first and second generations of prophecy. The persuasion to which Hosea attains only through an intense inward struggle, which lends a peculiar pathos to his book, appears in Zephaniah, as it were, ready made. There is no mental conflict before he can pass through the anticipation of devastating judgment to the assurance of the victory of divine love, and the sharp transitions that characterize the book are not, as with Hosea, due to sudden revulsion of feeling, but only mark the passage to some new topic in the circle of received prophetic truth. The finest thing in the book—in spite of certain obscurities, which may be partly due to corruptions of the text—is the closing passage; but the description of the day of Jehovah, the *dies iræ dies illa* of chap. i. 15, which furnishes the text of the most striking of mediæval hymns, has perhaps taken firmer hold of the religious imagination. Least satisfactory is the treatment of the judgment on heathen nations, and of their subsequent conversion to Jehovah. In the scheme of Isaiah it is made clear that the fall of the power that shatters the nations cannot fail to be recognized as Jehovah's work, for Assyria falls *before Jerusalem* as soon as it seeks to go beyond the limits of the divine commission, and thus the doctrine "With *us* is God" is openly vindicated before the nations. But Zephaniah assumes that the convulsions of history are Jehovah's work, and specially designed for the instruction and amendment of Israel (iii. 6 *sq.*), and neglects to show how this conviction, which he himself derives from Isaiah, is to be brought home by the coming judgment to the heart of heathen nations. Their own gods indeed will prove helpless (ii. 11), but this is not enough to turn their eyes towards Jehovah. Here, therefore, there is in his eschatology a sensible lacuna, from which Isaiah's construction is free, and a commencement of the tendency to look at things from a merely Israelite standpoint, which is so notable a feature of the later Apocalyptic.

There is no important separate commentary on Zephaniah; the student must refer to the commentaries on the minor prophets (see HOSEA). The relative section in Duhm, *Theologie der Propheten*, deserves attention. An apocryphal prophecy ascribed to Zephaniah is quoted by Clement of Alexandria, *Stromata*, v. 11, § 78. (W. R. S.)

ZEPHYRINUS, ST, bishop of Rome from about 202 to 26th August 217, succeeded Victor I. He is described as a man of little intelligence or strength of character, and the somewhat important controversies on doctrine and discipline that marked his pontificate are more appropriately associated with the name of HIPPOLYTUS (*q.v.*) and of Calixtus, his principal adviser and afterwards his successor (see POPEDOM, vol. xix. p. 489).

ZEPHYRUS, the west wind, brother of Boreas, the north wind, was the son of the Titan Astræus and Eos, the dawn (Hes., *Theog.*, 579), and had his palace in Thrace (*Il.*, ix. 5; *Od.*, v. 295). He was married to Chloris, the goddess of flowers (Ov., *Fast.*, v. 195), by whom he had a son, Carpus; by the harpy Podarge he was also the father of Xanthus and Balius, the horses of Achilles (*Il.*, xvi. 150).

ZERAFSHAN, an independent "circle" or province of Russian Turkestan, includes the valley of the river Zerafshan from its sources to Katty-Kurgan, as well as the mountains which bound the valley to the north and south. It is the SOGDIANA (*q.v.*) of the ancients, famed for its fertility, which is due to the waters of the Polytimetus. The present Russian province of Zerafshan, which is densely peopled along the course of the river, has a length of nearly 250 miles from west to east, a width of from 50 to 100 miles, and an area of 19,665 square miles. It is bounded on the W. by Bokhara, on the N. by the Kizil-kum Desert of Syr-Daria and the Russian province of Ferghana, on the E. by the Alai plateau, and on the S. by the vassal khanates of Bokhara,—Karategin, Hissar, Shahr-i-Syabs, and Karshi. High chains of mountains enclose the province on three sides. To the north are the Turkestan Mountains, which separate the tributaries of the Syr from those of the Amu, rising to 22,000 feet in their highest snow-clad peaks, and crossed by but few passes, which themselves range from 10,000 to 13,000 feet. In the west the Turkestan Mountains are joined by the Nura-tau Mountains, which have a north-westerly direction (see TURKESTAN). In the south-east the valley of the Zerafshan is separated from that of the Surkhab by the grand snow-clad Hissar Range, which runs from north-east to south-west, and by several chains parallel to it, while farther west a series of mountains, partly running also towards the south-west and partly towards the north-west, separate it from the Bokhara plains of the Amu. The lowest passes across these chains have altitudes of not less than 7000 feet. But the valley of the Zerafshan lies broadly open towards the steppes in the west, and has supplied an easy route for the railway from the Caspian by Merv to Samarkand.

Granites and all kinds of crystalline slates are widely developed in the mountains which enclose Zerafshan. Carboniferous limestones are met with in the west; but the great bulk of the deposits which overlie the crystalline slates, and are raised to the greatest heights in the highlands, belong to a more recent geological time, namely, to the Secondary—chiefly Chalk—and Tertiary periods. The Zerafshan valley owes its fertility to the thick terraces of loess which surround the base of the mountains and sometimes reach a thickness of 100 feet.

The Zerafshan river, which owes its name ("gold-spreading") probably more to the fertility it brings than to the gold which is found in very small quantities in its sands, rises under the name of Matchi from a large glacier, fed by the high peaks which rise at the junction (improperly called Kok-su) of the Turkestan Mountains with the Alai Range. The altitude of the glacier is about 9000 feet, and thence the Zerafshan flows due west in a narrow valley, with a fall of not less than 40 feet per mile. Several villages are scattered over the slopes of the mountains; and some thirty bridges, made of poplar trees felled across the river and swaying under the weight of the foot passenger, furnish means of communication. After a course of nearly 100 miles in the mountains the Zerafshan receives from the left the Fan, with the Yagnob, which flows in a high longitudinal valley, separated from the main river by the lofty Zerafshan Range. About Pendjakent it enters on its middle course along a broad valley from 20 to 50 miles wide. Large *aryks*, or irrigation canals, one of which is 50 miles in length and has all the appearance of a river, distribute the waters of the Zerafshan over the valley, while the river itself divides into two great branches, 10 to 12 miles apart, forming a large island, the Miankal, which is the most fertile part of the province. A dam keeps up the water in the southern branch, Kara-Daria, close by which is situated SAMARKAND (*q.v.*), and five large *aryks* distribute its water over the fields. Numberless canals drain off its waters farther west in the neighbourhood of the city of Bokhara, so that, after carrying an insignificant volume of water to the small Lake Kara-kul, it stops its course there, some 30 miles from the Amu-Daria, of which it formerly was an affluent.

The population of Zerafshan was reckoned at 351,900 in 1883. The bulk of the inhabitants are Uzbegs and Tajiks, the remainder consisting of a few thousand Persians, Hindus, and Jews respectively; the Russians are mainly military, civil functionaries, merchants, and a few peasant settlers. Wheat, barley, rice, and other cereals, as also lucerne, are widely cultivated, and the gardens of Zerafshan are beautiful. A variety of petty trades are carried on in the towns and villages.

Zerafshan is divided into three districts, the chief towns of which are Samarkand (36,000 inhabitants), now connected by rail with Bokhara, Merv, and Mikhailovsk on Krasnovodsk Bay in the Caspian Sea; Katty-Kurgan (4425), close by the frontier of Bokhara; and Pendjakent (1880), chief town of the mountain district of the upper Zerafshan, known as Kohistan.

ZERBST, a manufacturing town in the duchy of Anhalt, Germany, is situated on the Nuthe, 11 miles north-west of Dessau and 21 south-east of Magdeburg. It contains five churches, one of which (St Nicholas), built in 1446-88, is a good example of the Late Gothic style as developed in Saxony, with its spacious proportions, groined vaulting, and bare simple pillars. The town-house dates from about 1480, but it was disfigured by additions in the beginning of the 17th century. The palace (1681-1750) has been used as a depository of archives since 1872. There are several quaint old houses, with high gables, in the market-place, in the middle of which stand a Roland column, of about 1445, and a bronze figure known as the "Butterjungfer" (butter-girl), of uncertain origin and meaning, but now regarded as the palladium of the town. The old Franciscan monastery, with fine cloisters, founded in 1250, contains the gymnasium; a nunnery of 1214 has been converted into barracks; and the Augustinian monastery of 1390 has been a hospital since 1525. The site of the old fortifications is occupied by pretty promenades. Gold and silver articles, silk, plush, cloth, leather, soap, starch, chemicals, and carriages are among the chief manufactures. Iron-founding is carried on; and several breweries are engaged in the preparation of Zerbster bitter beer, which enjoys considerable repute. Market-gardening is also a profitable industry at Zerbst. The population, almost entirely Protestant, was 15,069 in 1885; in 1849 it was 9350.

Zerbst is an ancient town, mentioned in 949. In 1307 it came into the possession of the Anhalt family, and from 1603 till 1793 was the capital of the collateral branch of Anhalt-Zerbst. In 1793 it passed to Anhalt-Dessau.

ZEUS, the chief deity of ancient Greek religion, bears a name which almost certainly means "sky." His title is identified by etymologists with the Sanskrit *Dyaus*, the "bright one," "sky," though his legend and place in religion are not closely akin to those of the Vedic deity. It seems nearly certain that the peoples who speak Aryan languages had at some remote time a common word for the sky, and nothing can be more probable than that they also worshipped the vault of heaven. In what sense the sky may have been an Aryan deity before the distant and obscure process called the Aryan dispersion, it is not possible with certainty to say. The followers of Mr Herbert Spencer might not inconsistently suppose that there was once an Aryan medicine-man or chief named Sky, and that on his death his ghost was worshipped and his cult finally blended with that of the actual natural phenomenon. Or, again, it might be argued that the sky was originally adored as a symbol of the Infinite, and that men, losing the original conception, and misled by the personal appearance of the name as other words for sky became more familiar, were deceived into the belief that "sky" was a personal deity. Or, once more, theorists might urge that Sky was first worshipped at a stage of early fancy, when all things in nature were looked on as personal and of human parts and passions, while later the sky sank back into the category of lifeless things, leaving Zeus as a distinct personal being and deity. Other hypotheses might, no doubt, be invented, but unhappily we have no means of proving their historical accuracy. It is a common thing among backward races, for example on the Gold Coast, to find Sky worshipped as a god, or regarded as the dwelling-place of gods. How and in what manner such conceptions were attained by the ancestors of the ancient Greeks we can never know as a matter of fact.

Coming to historical and documentary evidence, our earliest knowledge of Zeus is derived from the Homeric and Hesiodic poems. It is very probable that in the legend and ritual of remote towns and temples in Greece we have traces of a conception of Zeus much older than that which meets us in Homer. But Homer and Hesiod are the most ancient literary testimonies; next to these come the speculations of the early philosophers and the writings of the lyric poets, Pindar, Herodotus, and the tragedians. Finally, we have the Zeus of the philosophers of the central period,—Plato and Aristotle,—and the Zeus of the later philosophic periods down to the prevalence of Christianity.

By the time that Zeus meets us in Homer he has wandered far from the original conception of him. Whatever that may have been, Zeus cannot have been first imagined in an age of advanced society on the heroic system, that is, in an age of the fully developed monogamous family of city states each governed by a king, and of a general loose confederation, with a kind of upper and lower house,—the prince's council and the assembly of the people. It is, however, on the model of such a society that the Olympian consistory is organized in Homer, with Zeus for the bretwalda, the principal chief of the gods. Such a position Zeus holds in Homer. The poet represents him as anthropomorphic,—a powerful, humorous, amorous ruler, sometimes troubled by disputes among his younger brethren,—Hades and Poseidon,—his wife, and his children. His claim to supreme authority is based on primogeniture (*Il.*, xv. 187), whereas in Hesiod Zeus is the successful youngest son of Cronus. Both poets agree that he has overthrown the paternal dynasty, and established his own power after violent struggles. The legends in Hesiod are full of ugly and puerile fables and conceits, dating doubtless from remote and uncivilized antiquity. Though Zeus be so much of a magnified man in Homer, there are probably traces of the elemental conception, and his union with Hera (*Il.*, xiv. 152) on the crest of Ida may be a poetic memory of the old story of Heaven wedding Earth, though Hera cannot as a rule be regarded as a form of Gæa or of Demeter. While among the gods Zeus is a father, brother, and emperor, Homeric men sometimes use his name as we might use that of God, in a religious rather than in a mythological sense. Now regarded as subject to Fate, so that he cannot save even his own children from her decree, elsewhere he seems to hold the gifts of Fate in his own hand: from two vast jars he deals out good and evil to mankind. Where morals are concerned, he sanctions the oath (*Il.*, iii. 227) both in this world and the next, and he is the friend of strangers and suppliants, the patron of the hospitable hearth. In Homer Zeus does not assume the form of the lower animals, and in the strange passage where he recounts his loves, the Leporello of his own Don Juan, he says nothing of those well-known disguises. In Hesiod the old wild tales revive, and we learn, for example (*Theog.*, 886; compare the scholiast), that Zeus swallowed his own wife, Metis, after inducing her to take the shape of a fly, just as Puss-in-Boots got rid of the ogre who turned himself into a mouse. In Hesiod, too, we have the tale of Prometheus and Pandora, a tale which afforded such an admirable theme for moral handling by Æschylus. Zeus tempted Epimetheus by the aid of the woman Pandora; hence came death into the world and all our woe. Then Prometheus pitied and aided men, whom Zeus had intended to destroy, and the hero was fixed to a rock in Caucasus by order of the god. The myth may be allegorized in a dozen ways, and perhaps may be taken to mean that man does not increase happiness by increasing knowledge, science, and the arts of life. Without the gifts of Prometheus, carried to what Horace would have thought a profane pitch of perfection, we should not have reached modern industrialism and the horrors of modern war. In Hesiod Prometheus may stand for humanity vainly struggling to be powerful and happy against that inflexible and ruthless law which is Zeus And what shall the end be? How shall the ways of Zeus be justified to men, and man's rebellion be justified to Zeus? We no more know how Æschylus solved the problem mythically than we can discover the actual solution. The idea that another shall voluntarily take the place of Prometheus (Æsch., *Prom. Vinct.*, 1026) naturally recalls the theory of the Atonement. To such mysteries does the Greek mind attain, and in such ultimate perplexities is the conception of Zeus, the *Bon Dieu* of the Homeric Olympian festivals, involved.

At the opposite pole from the Hesiodic Zeus is the Zeus who practically means the unknown god, as Terpander sings,

Ζεῦ πάντων ἀρχὰ, πάντων ἀγήτωρ,

or, as the Orphic hymn (whatever its date) proclaims him,

Ζεὺς κεφαλή, Ζεὺς μέσσα, Διὸς δ' ἐκ πάντα τέτυκται.

Thus Zeus becomes a shorthand symbol for the pantheistic deity.

The Zeus of pure religion and of speculation is very different from the Zeus of ritual and of local myth. To ritual, and to the local myths treasured by priests, which often tried to explain the ritual, we owe the unbecoming anecdotes of Zeus as the god who, in the form of ant, snake, bull, eagle, and so forth, made love to the daughters of men. On this point reference may be made to the work of the present writer, *Myths, Ritual, and Religion* (ii. 189). The hypothesis there offered is that the Greeks in their early uncivilized state, dwelling in tribes and in scattered kraals or villages, retained traditions like the totemic and magical beliefs of Red Indians or Australians. When they became more united and more civilized, they did not drop wholly the faith that they were descended from animals, nor wholly forget such tales as the Indians tell of Manibozho and the Australians of Punjel, but they transferred the old anecdotes to Zeus. In place of saying, "We descend from a bull," they said, "We descend from Zeus, who for purposes of amorous disguise took the shape of a bull," or a swan, or an ant, as the case might be. Probably some foreign legends, Phœnician or African, were also borrowed and attached to Zeus. If this be a correct, as it seems a possible, hypothesis, then it will be well to be cautious in explaining the myths about Zeus as if they were all of elementary origin, and all expressed in images some natural process or series of natural phenomena. We must regard Zeus as an extremely difficult complex, in which elemental myths, myths of savage fancy, myths of perverted history, theories of early natural philosophy, and the ideas of pantheistic speculation are all confusedly mingled. He is the sum of the religious thought of Hellas, formed in the numberless ages between savagery and complete civilization. He received human sacrifices even after the Christian era; yet long before it he all but corresponded to the Unknown Substance of Spencerian philosophy. (See Plato, *Rep.*, viii. 565 D; Suidas, *s.v.* "Laphystius.") A summary of the Zeus myths will be found in Dr William Smith's *Dictionary of Classical Mythology*. For a comparison between the character and attributes of Jupiter and Zeus, see the article JUPITER.

Among modern works in which the character and legend of Zeus are discussed may be recommended Welcker's *Griechische Götterlehre* (Göttingen, 1857); Preller's *Griechische Mythologie* (Berlin, 1872); the *Selected Essays* of Mr Max Müller; *Le Sentiment Religieux en Grèce* of M. Jules Girard (3d ed., Paris, 1887); and C. O. Müller's *Introduction to a Scientific System of Mythology* (Eng. transl., London, 1844). The subject has not yet been reached (1888) in Roscher's great *Lexikon*. The authorities named will introduce the reader in turn to other authors, their researches and speculations. Heyne's *Apollodorus* (Göttingen, 1803) is also useful. (A. L.)

ZEUXIS, a Greek painter, who flourished about 420 390 B.C., and described himself as a native of Heraclea, meaning probably the town in Magna Græcia. To this neighbourhood seem to point the facts of his having painted a figure of Helena for a temple in Croton, of his presenting a picture of Alcmena to the people of Agrigentum, and of his having been, in one account, a pupil of Damophilus of Himera in Sicily, the other statement being that he was a pupil of Neseus of Thasos. Afterwards he appears to have resided in Ephesus. His known works are—

1. Zeus Surrounded by Deities.
2. Eros Crowned with Roses.
3. Marsyas Bound.
4. Pan.
5. Centaur Family.
6. Boreas or Triton.
7. Infant Hercules Strangling the Serpents in Presence of his Parents, Alcmena and Amphitryon.
8. Alcmena, possibly another name for 7.
9. Helena at Croton.
10. Penelope.
11. Menelaus.
12. Athlete.
13. An Old Woman.
14. Boy with Grapes.
15. Grapes.
16. Monochromes.
17. Plastic works in clay.

In ancient records we are told that Zeuxis, following the initiative of Apollodorus, had introduced into the art of painting a method of representing his figures in light and shadow, as opposed to the older method of outline, with large flat masses of colour for draperies, and other details, such as had been practised by Polygnotus and others of the great fresco painters. The new method led to smaller compositions, and often to pictures consisting of only a single figure, on which it was the more easy for the painter to demonstrate the combined effect of the various means by which he obtained perfect roundness of form. The effect would appear strongly realistic, as compared with the older method, and to this was probably due the origin of such stories as the contest in which Zeuxis painted a bunch of grapes so like reality that birds flew towards it, while Parrhasius painted a curtain which even Zeuxis mistook for real. The story reads in Pliny (*N. H.*, xxxv. 65) as if Parrhasius had brought forward a picture with an apparent curtain hung in front to protect the colours from the light, and that Zeuxis had tried to pull the curtain aside. It is perhaps a variation of this story when we are told (Pliny, *loc. cit.*) that Zeuxis also painted a boy holding grapes, towards which birds flew, the artist remarking that if the boy had been as well painted as the grapes the birds would have kept at a distance. But, if the method of Zeuxis led him to real roundness of form, to natural colouring, and to pictures consisting of single figures or nearly so, it was likely to lead him also to search for striking attitudes or motives, which by the obviousness of their meaning should emulate the plain intelligibility of the larger compositions of older times. Lucian, in his *Zeuxis*, speaks of him as carrying this search to a novel and strange degree, as illustrated in the group of a Female Centaur with her Young. When the picture was exhibited, the spectators admired its invention and overlooked the skill of the painter, to the vexation of Zeuxis. The pictures of Hercules Strangling the Serpents to the astonishment of his father and mother (7), Penelope (10), and Menelaus Weeping (11) are quoted as instances in which strong motives naturally presented themselves to him. But, in spite of the tendency towards realism inherent in the new method of Zeuxis, he is said to have retained the largeness of form which had characterized his predecessors. Of all his known works it would be expected that this quality would have appeared best in his famous picture of Helena, for this reason, that we cannot conceive any striking or effective incident for him in her career. In addition to this, however, Quintilian states (*Inst. Orat.*, xii. 10, 4) that in respect of largeness of form Zeuxis had followed Homer, while there is the fact that he had inscribed two verses of the *Iliad* (iii. 156 *sq.*) under his figure of Helena. As models for the picture he was allowed the presence of five of the most beautiful maidens of Croton at his own request, in order that he might be able to "transfer the truth of life to a mute image." Cicero (*De Invent.*, ii. 1, 1) assumed that Zeuxis had found distributed among these five the various elements that went to make up a figure of ideal beauty. It should not, however, be understood that the painter had made up his figure by the process of combining the good points of various models, but rather that he found among those models the points that answered to the ideal Helena in his own mind, and that he merely required the models to guide and correct himself by during the process of transferring his ideal to form and colour. This picture also is said to have been exhibited publicly, with the result that Zeuxis made much profit out of it. By this and other means, we are told, he became so rich as to rather give away his pictures than to sell them. He presented his Alcmena to the Agrigentines, his Pan to King Archelaus of Macedonia, whose palace he is also said to have decorated with paintings. According to Pliny (*N. H.*, xxxv. 62), he made an ostentatious display of his wealth at Olympia in having his name woven in letters of gold on his dress. But, as there would not be much ostentation in that, and as Pliny at times makes mistakes in translating from his Greek sources, it is possible that Zeuxis may merely have presented some piece of tapestry to a temple at Olympia with the customary inscription woven in letters of gold. Under his picture of an Athlete (12) he wrote that "It is easier to revile than to rival" (μωμήσεταί τις μᾶλλον ἢ μιμήσεται). A contemporary, Isocrates (*De Permut.*, 2), remarks that no one would say that Zeuxis and Parrhasius had the same profession as those persons who paint *pinakia*, which is equivalent to the vase-painters of the time. We possess many examples of the vase-painting of the period *circa* 400 B.C., and it is noticeable on them that there is great freedom and facility in drawing the human form, so as to suggest roundness and perspective. In the absence of fresco paintings of that date we have only these vases to fall back upon. Yet, with their limited resources of colour and perspective, they in a measure show the influence of Zeuxis, while, as would be expected, they retain perhaps more of the largeness of form of older times. It is said that he died of laughter at the quaintness of a picture he had painted of an Old Woman.

ZHITOMIR, or JITOMIR, a town of western Russia, capital of the government of Volhynia, is situated on the Tetereff river, 646 miles to the south-west of Moscow. The railway which connects Riga and Königsberg with Odessa, *via* Berditcheff, passes within 27 miles of the old Lithuanian city without sending a branch towards it; and the whole place, with its old abandoned mansions of the Polish nobility, has an air of decay. Nor is it rich in historical monuments of its troubled past, its churches and cathedral mostly dating from the 18th century. Its population, however, reached 54,830 in 1884,—Jews constituting more than one-third of the total. Two large printing offices in Zhitomir issue nearly one-half of all the Hebrew books printed in Russia. The Jewish merchants carry on a considerable export trade in the agricultural produce of the plains surrounding the city, as also in timber and wooden wares from the forests to the north.

Zhitomir is a very old city, tradition tracing its foundation as far back as the times of Askold and Dir. The annals, however, mention it chiefly in connexion with invasions of the Tartars, who plundered it in the 13th, 14th, and even the 17th century (1606), or in connexion with destructive conflagrations. It fell under Lithuanian rule in 1320, and during the 15th century was one of the fifteen chief cities of the kingdom. Later on it became part of Poland, and when the Cossacks rose under Khmelnitsky (1648) they sacked the town. It became annexed to Russia along with the rest of the Ukraine.

ZIMMERMANN, JOHANN GEORG, RITTER VON (1728-1795), a Swiss philosophical writer and physician, was born at Brugg, in the canton of Aargau, on 8th December 1728. He studied at Göttingen, where he took the degree of doctor of medicine. Afterwards he practised as a physician in his native place, and here he wrote *Ueber die Einsamkeit* (1755) and *Vom Nationalstolz* (1758). These books made a great impression in Germany, and were translated into almost every European language. They are now only of historical interest. In Zimmermann's character there was a strange combination of sentimentalism, melancholy, and enthusiasm; and it was by the free and eccentric expression of these qualities that he excited the interest of his contemporaries. Another book by him, written at Brugg, *Von der Erfahrung in der Arzneiwissenschaft* (1764), also attracted much attention. In 1768 he settled at Hanover as private physician of George III. with the title of Hofrath. Catherine II. invited him to the court of St Petersburg, but this invitation he declined. He attended Frederick the Great during that monarch's last illness, and afterwards issued various books about him, of which the chief were *Ueber Frederich den Grossen und meine Unterredung mit ihm kurz vor seinem Tode* (1788) and *Fragmente über Friedrich den Grossen* (1790). These writings display extraordinary personal vanity, and convey a wholly false impression of Frederick's character. Zimmermann died at Hanover on 7th October 1795.

See *Zimmermann's Briefe an einige seiner Freunde in der Schweiz* (1830) and Bodemann's *Johann Georg Zimmermann* (1878).

ZINC, the name both of an important useful metal and of the element of which the metal consists. Zinc as a component of brass had currency in metallurgy long before it became known as an individual metal. Aristotle refers to the alleged fact that the Mossinecians produced a bright and light-coloured χαλκός, not by addition of tin, but by fusing up with an earth. Pliny explicitly speaks of a mineral *cadmia* as serving for the conversion of copper into *aurichalcum*, and says further that the deposit (of ZnO) formed in the brass furnaces could be used instead of the mineral. The same process was used for centuries after Pliny, but its rationale was not understood. Stahl, as late as 1702, quoted the formation of brass as a case of the union of a metal with an earth into a metallic compound; but he subsequently adopted the view propounded by Kunkel in 1677, that cadmia is a metallic calx, and that it dyes the copper yellow by giving its metal up to it. In 1597 Libavius described a "peculiar kind of tin" which was prepared in India, and of which a friend had given him a quantity. From his account it is quite clear that that metal was zinc, but he did not recognize it as the metal of calamine. It is not known to whom the discovery of isolated zinc is due; but we do know that the art of zinc-smelting was practised in England from about 1730. The first Continental zinc-works were erected at Liége in 1807. The atomic weight of zinc is 65·37 (the mean of the results obtained by Marignac and Baubigny), O = 16.

Zinc Ores.—The following may be named as important.

(1) *Red Zinc Ore* (impure ZnO) occurs in quartz-like crystals, but more frequently presents itself in large-grained and lamellar masses. Sp. gr. 5·4 to 5·7. Colour, hyacinth-red to brown. Lustre, adamantine.

(2) *Franklinite* ($RO.M_2O_3$, where R stands for Zn, Fe, Mn; M for Fe, Mn). The zinc averages about 10 per cent. It crystallizes in regular octahedra, with rounded-off edges and angles. Sp. gr. 5·1. Colour, black; streak, reddish-brown. Lustre, sub-metallic. This and the preceding occur in association with each other and other things in New Jersey, U.S.

(3) *Calamine* ($ZnCO_3$). The pure mineral (zinc spar) forms well-

defined, though small, rhombohedra. The ordinary ore is massive, and is contaminated, often largely, with clay, silica, oxide of iron, and the like. Sp. gr. 4 to 4·5. Sometimes colourless, but as a rule light grey, yellow, or buff-coloured. Lustre, vitreous. It is found in association with silicates of zinc, zinc-blende, and lead ores, chiefly in limestone and dolomitic strata, at the Kelmisberg or Vieille Montagne in Belgium, in Derbyshire and Northumberland, and in Silesia; but these last deposits are well nigh exhausted. Irregular deposits occur near Santander and Cartagena in Spain, and in Sardinia. At Wiesloch in Baden a yellow variety is found, which contains as much as 3 per cent. of cadmium. Smaller percentages of cadmium are met with in many other zinc ores.

(4) *Electric Calamine*, the German *Kieselzinkerz* ($ZnOSiO_2+H_2O$), is also called *hemimorphite* on account of the marked hemimorphism in its (ortho-rhombic) crystals. Sp. gr. 3·35 to 3·5. Sometimes colourless, but more frequently grey, yellow, red, green, brown, blue,—always, however, light-coloured. Lustre, vitreous. The crystals, when heated, exhibit electric polarity; hence the name. As a rule they are small and united into cuneiform, spheroidal, or kidney-shaped masses; there are also granular, dense, and earthy varieties. It occurs with willemite and calamine at the Altenberg near Aix-la-Chapelle, with blende and lead ore at Raibel and Bleiberg in Carinthia, near Iserlohn in Westphalia, at Matlock in Derbyshire, near Tarnowitz in Silesia, at Olbucs, Rezbanya in Hungary, and Nertchinsk in Siberia. American sources are at Phœnixville and Friedensville in Pennsylvania and in the Austin mine in Virginia.

(5) *Willemite*, anhydrous $ZnOSiO_2$, occurs in New Jersey and elsewhere; it is a comparatively rare ore.

(6) *Zinc-Blende*, or shortly *Blende* (ZnS).—The five ores mentioned above, as indeed all oxidized zinc ores, having become scarce, most of the zinc which now occurs in commerce is derived from zinc-blende. This ore crystallizes in combinations of the two tetrahedra and other forms of the regular system. Sp. gr. 3·9 to 4·2. Colour, green, yellow, red, but mostly brown or black. Colourless crystals are scarce. Lustre, fatty or diamond-like. The ordinary ore forms crypto-crystalline or fibrous or granular masses, which sometimes present the form of kidneys, consisting of concentric layers. The finest crystals are found in Franklin, New Jersey, which are colourless and consist of pure ZnS, and in the Peñas de Europa, Asturias (Spain), in which liquid enclosures are often met with. The darker varieties, which always include more or less of foreign sulphides, are found in a great number of places. In Cornwall, Wales, Alston Moor in Cumberland, Teesdale in Yorkshire, Derbyshire, and the Isle of Man dark-coloured blende is found in the lead-mining districts with galena, quartz, and limestone. In Belgium and on the Rhine massive blende occurs with iron pyrites and galena; this requires much preparation for smelting. In Sweden blende is frequently found: at Ammeberg on Lake Wetter a vast deposit occurs in the gneiss. Blende is the English miners' "black Jack," the South American "chumbe." The principal American deposits are in Missouri, Illinois, and Wisconsin.

Metallurgy.—Oxide of zinc, like most heavy metallic oxides, is easily reduced to the metallic state by heating it to redness with charcoal; but, as zinc has the exceptional property of being readily volatile at the temperature of its reduction, the operation must be carried out in some kind of retort, and the zinc be recovered as a distillate. To pure red zinc ore the operation of distilling with charcoal might be applied quite directly; and the same might be done with pure calamine of any kind, because the carbonic acid of carbonate of zinc goes off below redness and the silica of silicate of zinc only retards, but does not prevent, the reducing action of the charcoal. Zinc-blende, however, being sulphide of zinc, is not directly reducible by charcoal; but it is easy to convert it into oxide by roasting: the sulphur goes off as sulphurous acid, whilst the zinc remains in the (infusible) form of oxide, ZnO. In practice, however, we never have to deal with pure zinc minerals, but with complex mixtures, which must first of all be subjected to mechanical operations, to remove at least part of the gangue, and if possible also of the heavy metallic impurities (see METALLURGY, vol. xvi. p. 59 *sq.*). And, supposing this to be done, the ore, even if it is not blende, must be roasted, in order to remove all volatile components as completely as possible, because these, if allowed to remain, would carry away a large proportion of the zinc vapour during the distillation. If the zinc is present as blende, this operation offers considerable difficulties, because in the roasting process the sulphide of zinc passes in the first instance into sulphate, which demands a high temperature for its conversion into oxide. Another point to be considered in this connexion is that the masses of sulphurous acid evolved, being destructive of vegetable life, are an intolerable nuisance to the neighbourhood in which the operations take place.

Hasenclever and Helbig have constructed a furnace by which some two-thirds of the sulphurous acid can be conducted into chambers and condensed into the useful form of oil of vitriol. Figs. 1, 2, and 3 show how the furnace is constructed. *k* is a Siemens gas furnace, *n* being the orifice for the introduction of the fuel; the gases go out at *m*, where they mix with air; the flame travels between the sole *g* and the bottom of the muffle *c*, and then goes along the top of the muffle to the flue *q*; it passes below the slanting canal *bb* and keeps it at a temperature above the fusing-point of antimony (432° C.). The ore is introduced through the funnel *a*; it slides down the slanting canal *bb*; the partition walls *d*, *d*, which follow each other at distances of half a metre, compel it to spread out evenly into a thin layer. The partition walls, as shown by fig. 3, are arranged so that the gases

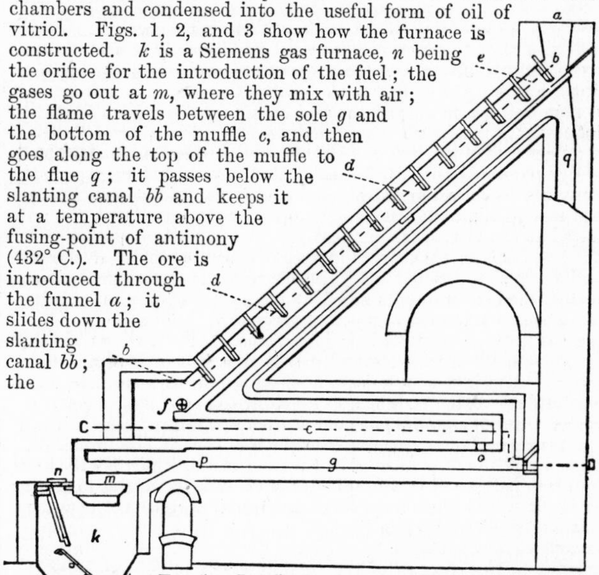

FIG. 1.—Longitudinal section along A B of fig. 2.

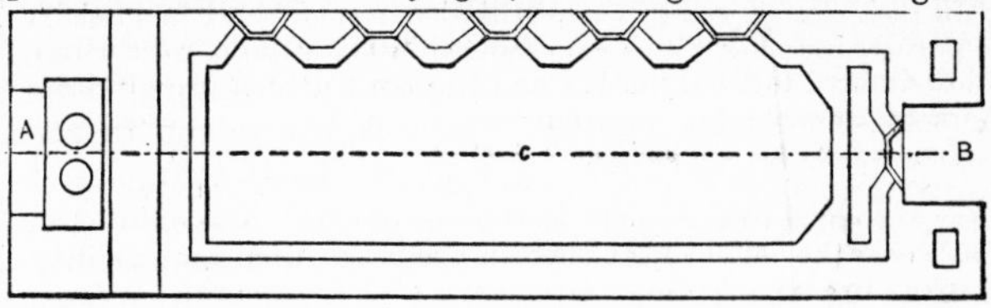

FIG. 2.—Horizontal section along C D of fig. 1.

coming from the muffle must travel along an undulating line and lick up as much as possible of the sulphur of the ore. From the last compartment *e* the gaseous product goes first to a cooling chamber, and thence to the vitriol chamber. The hollow cylinder *f*, which is cooled internally by air while made to revolve, conveys the ore in instalments from the bottom end of the canal to the muffle. At intervals of two hours it is spread evenly on the bottom of the muffle, and at last it is drawn out through *o* and transferred to the sole *g*, to be finally roasted ("todtgeröstet") there. The apparatus works very satisfactorily even with ores poor in sulphur. An ore containing 20 per cent. of sulphur contained at the end *f* of the inclined canal 10 per cent., at the end *o* of the muffle 6·4 per cent., and at last, when "todtgeröstet," only 1·2. About one-third of the sulphur is lost, *i.e.*, goes out through the chimney, as SO_2.

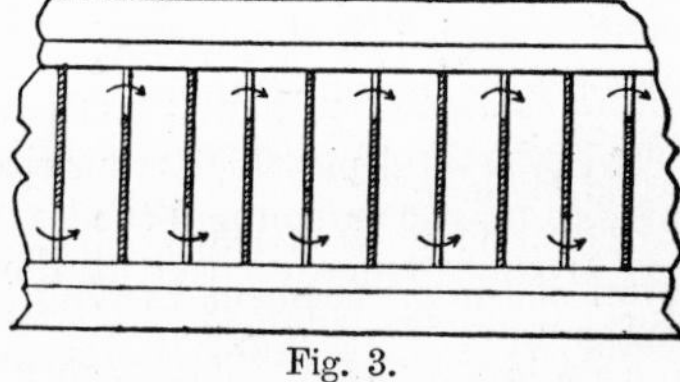
Fig. 3.

The distillation process in former times, especially in England, used to be carried out "per descensum." The bottom of a crucible is perforated by a pipe which projects into the crucible to about two-thirds of its height. The powdery mixture of ore and charcoal is put into the crucible around the pipe, the crucible closed by a luted-on lid, and placed in a furnace constructed so as to permit of the lower end of the pipe projecting into the ash-pit. The zinc vapour produced descends through the pipe and condenses into liquid zinc, which is collected in a ladle held under the outlet end of the pipe. For manufacturing purposes a furnace similar to that used for the making of glass was employed to heat a circular row of crucibles standing on a shelf along the wall of the furnace. This system, however, has long been abandoned; at present one or other of the following methods is used as a rule.

In the *Belgian process* the reduction and distillation are carried out in cylindrical retorts of fire-clay, about a metre long and 0·15 metre wide inside. Some forty-six or more retorts, arranged in eight parallel horizontal rows, are heated in one furnace. The furnaces are square and open in front, to allow the outlet ends of the retorts to project; they are grouped together by fours; and their several chimneys are within the same enclosure. Each retort is provided with two adapters, namely, a conical pipe of fire-clay, about 0·4 metre long, which fits into the retort end, and a conical tube of black sheet iron, which fits over the end of the fire-clay pipe, and which at its outlet end is only 2 centimetres wide. To start a new furnace, the front side is closed provisionally by a brick wall, a fire lighted inside, and the temperature raised very gradually to a white heat. After four days' heating the provisional front wall is removed piecemeal, and the retorts, after having been heated to redness, are inserted in corresponding sets. The charge of the retorts consists of a mixture of 1100 ℔ of roasted calamine and 550 ℔ of dry powdered coal per furnace. A newly-started furnace, however, is used for a time with smaller charges. Supposing the last of these preliminary distillations to have been completed, the residues left in the retorts are removed and the retorts, as they lie in the hot furnace, are charged by means of semi-cylindrical shovels, and their adapters put on. The charging operation being completed, the temperature is raised, and as a consequence an evolution of carbonic oxide soon begins, and becomes visible by the gas bursting out into the characteristic blue flame. After a time the flame becomes dazzling white, showing that zinc vapour is beginning to escape. The iron adapters are now slipped on without delay, and left on for two hours, when, as a matter of experience, a considerable amount of zinc has gone out of the retort, the greater part into the fire-clay adapter, the rest into the iron cone. The former contains a mixture of semi-solid and molten metal, which is raked out into iron ladles and cast into plates of 66 to 77 ℔ weight, to be sold as "spelter." The contents of the iron recipient consist of a powdery mixture of oxide and metal, which is added to the next charge, except what is put aside to be sold as "zinc dust." This dust may amount to 10 per cent. of the total production. As soon as the adapters have been cleared of their contents, they are replaced, and again left to themselves for two hours, to be once more emptied and replaced, &c. The complete exhaustion of the charge of a furnace takes about 11 hours.

In the *Silesian process* the distillation is conducted in specially constructed muffles, which are arranged in two parallel rows within a low-vaulted furnace, pretty much like the pots in a glass furnace. As a rule every furnace accommodates ten muffles. Through an orifice in the outlet pipe (which during the distillation is closed by a loose plug) a hot iron rod can be introduced from time to time to clear the canal of any solid zinc that may threaten to obstruct it. As soon as the outlet pipe has become sufficiently hot the zinc flows through it and collects in conveniently placed receptacles. About 6 or 8 hours after starting the distillation is in full swing, and in 24 hours it is completed. A fresh charge is then put in at once, the muffles being cleared only after three successive distillations. The distillate consists of a conglomerate of drops ("drop zinc"). It is fused up in iron basins lined with clay, and cast out into the customary form of cakes. In some modern works the muffles are heated by means of Siemens's regenerative gas furnace, by which a more uniform heat can be secured and maintained at a less cost.

Of the several metallic impurities in zinc ores iron is at once the most common and the least objectionable, because it is absolutely non-volatile at the temperature of a zinc retort; whenever commercial zinc contains iron, this comes from its having been re-fused in iron vessels after its distillation. Lead, though hardly volatile by itself at a red heat, if present in the ore, is, so to say, carried over by the zinc vapour and passes at least partly into the distillate. Cadmium and arsenic being more volatile than zinc itself, if present, accumulate in the first fractions of the distillate, but may pervade it in traces to the end. Zinc made from oxidized ores is usually free from arsenic; that derived from blende is almost sure to contain it. This in practice is equivalent to saying that, while in former times it was easy, it is now very difficult, to obtain in commerce zinc free from arsenic. Traces of arsenic do not, however, interfere with any of the technical applications of the metal. As for cadmium, it is not (metallurgically speaking) an impurity at all, but, like silver in lead, a rather desirable admixture which it may be worth while to extract.

No reliable method is known by which commercial zinc could be purified so as to render it fit for all the purposes of the analyst; the only way to obtain really pure zinc is to prepare it from pure oxide by distillation with charcoal in a non-metallic retort.

Properties of Pure Zinc.—Zinc, a bluish-white metal, fuses at 415° C. and under ordinary atmospheric pressure boils at 1040° C. (Deville and Troost). The molten metal on cooling deposits crystals, and at last freezes into a compact crystalline solid, which may be brittle or ductile according to circumstances. According to Bolley, if zinc be cast into a mould at a red heat, the ingot produced is laminar and brittle; if cast at just the fusing-point, it is granular and sufficiently ductile to be rolled into sheet at the ordinary temperature. According to some authorities, pure zinc always yields ductile ingots. A clue to the explanation of these anomalous facts is afforded by certain observations of Gustav Rose and others, from which it appears that zinc is dimorphous and may or may not crystallize in the regular system. Supposing a mass of molten zinc to freeze into, say, cubes, the ingot will be ductile; an ingot of, say, rhombohedra, on the other hand, is almost bound to be brittle, because the crystals are orientated in a lawless fashion, and, as they cannot be expected to contract at the same rate in all directions, we must be prepared for a brittle ingot. Commercial "spelter" always breaks under the hammer; but at 100° to 150° C. it is susceptible of being rolled out into even a very thin sheet. Such a sheet, if once produced, remains flexible when cold. At about 200° C., again, the metal becomes so brittle that it can be pounded in a mortar. The specific gravity of zinc cannot be expected to be perfectly constant; according to Karsten, that of pure ingot is 6·915, and rises to 7·191 after rolling. The coefficient of linear expansion is 0·002,905 for 100° from 0° upwards (Fizeau). The specific heat is 0·093,93 (Schüller and Wartha). Compact zinc is bluish white; it does not tarnish much in the air. It is pretty soft, and clogs the file. If zinc be heated up to near its boiling-point, it catches fire and burns with a brilliant light into its powdery white oxide, which forms a reek in the air (*lana philosophica*). Boiling water attacks it appreciably, but no more, with evolution of hydrogen and formation of hydroxide, $Zn(OH)_2$. A rod of perfectly pure zinc, when immersed in dilute sulphuric acid, is so very slowly attacked that there is no visible evolution of gas; but, if a piece of platinum or other less basilous metal is brought into contact with the zinc, it dissolves readily, with evolution of hydrogen and formation of sulphate. The ordinary impure metal dissolves at once, the more readily the less pure it is. Cold dilute nitric acid dissolves zinc as nitrate, with evolution of nitrous oxide, N_2O, and formation of nitrate of ammonia. At higher temperatures, or with stronger acid, nitric oxide, NO, is produced besides or instead of nitrous.

Oxide of Zinc, ZnO.—There is only this one oxide. It is prepared chiefly in two ways,—(1) by burning the metal, a method now being carried out industrially, the zinc vapour being sometimes produced *extempore* from a mixture of roasted ore and carbon, and (2) by heating the basic carbonate (see below). It is an infusible solid, which is intensely yellow at a red heat, but on cooling becomes white. This at least is true of the oxide produced from the metal by combustion; that produced from the carbonate, if once made yellow at a red heat, retains a yellow shade permanently. Oxide of zinc is insoluble in water, and does not combine directly with it; it dissolves readily in all aqueous acids, with formation of "zinc salts." It also dissolves in aqueous caustic alkalies, including ammonia, forming "zincates" (*e.g.*, ZnO.KHO). Oxide of zinc is used in the arts as a white pigment; it has not by any means the covering power of white lead, but offers the advantage of being non-poisonous and of not becoming discoloured in sulphuretted hydrogen. It is used also in medicine, chiefly externally.

The *hydrate*, $Zn(OH)_2$, is prepared by precipitating a solution of any zinc salt with caustic potash. The alkali must be free from carbonate and an excess of it must be avoided, otherwise the hydrate re-dissolves. It is a white powder, and is insoluble in water. To acids and to alkalies it behaves like the oxide, but dissolves more readily.

The *basic carbonate*, $ZnCO_3.xZn(OH)_2$, where x is variable, is prepared by precipitation of a solution of the sulphate or chloride with carbonate of soda. To obtain a product free of Cl or SO_4, there must be an excess of alkali and the zinc salt must be poured into the hot solution of the carbonate. The precipitate, even after exhaustive washing with hot water, still contains a trace of alkali; but from the oxide, prepared from it by ignition, the alkali can be washed away. The basic carbonate is, like the oxide, used as a pigment. Normal carbonate of zinc, $ZnCO_3$, has never been prepared artificially, but it exists in nature as zinc spar.

The *sulphate*, $ZnSO_4+7H_2O$, white vitriol, is prepared by dissolving the ordinary metal in dilute sulphuric acid. If care be taken to keep the zinc in excess, the solution will be free from all foreign metals except iron and perhaps manganese. Both are easily removed by passing chlorine through the cold solution, to produce ferric and manganic salt, and then digesting the liquid with a washed precipitate of basic carbonate, produced from a small portion of the solution by means of carbonate of soda. The iron and manganese are precipitated as hydrated sesquioxides, and are filtered off. The filtrate is acidified with a little sulphuric acid and evaporated to crystallization. The salt crystallizes out on cooling with 7 molecules of water, forming colourless ortho-rhombic prisms, usually small and needle-shaped. They are permanent in the air. According to Poggiale, 100 parts of water dissolve respectively of ($7H_2O$) salt

115·2, 138·2, 161·5, 263·8, 442·6, and 653·6 parts
at 0°, 10°, 20°, 50°, 80°, and 100° C.

At 100° C. the crystals lose 6 of their 7 H_2O's; the rest of the water goes off only at a higher temperature, which lies close to that at which the salt begins to decompose. The anhydrous salt, when exposed to a red heat, breaks up into oxide, sulphur dioxide, and oxygen. An impure form of the salt is prepared by roasting zinc-blende at a low temperature. Sulphate of zinc is used in medicine, chiefly externally. In the arts it is employed in the preparation of varnishes, and as a mordant for the production of colours on calico. A green pigment known as *Rinmann's green* is prepared by mixing 100 parts of zinc vitriol with 2·5 parts of nitrate of cobalt and heating the mixture to redness, to produce a compound of the two oxides. Sulphate of zinc, like sulphate of magnesia, unites with the sulphates of the potassium metals and of ammonium into crystalline double salts, $ZnSO_4.R_2SO_4+6H_2O$, isomorphous with one another and the magnesium salts.

The *chloride*, $ZnCl_2$, is produced by heating the metal in dry chlorine gas, when it distils over as a white translucent mass, easily fusible, and boiling sufficiently low to be distillable from out of a retort of hard Bohemian glass. Its vapour-density at 900° C. is 4·57, air=1, corresponding to $ZnCl_2$ (V. and C. Meyer). Chloride of zinc is extremely hygroscopic; it dissolves in a fraction of its weight of even cold water, forming a syrupy solution. A solution of chloride of zinc is easily produced from metal and hydrochloric acid, but it cannot be evaporated to dryness without considerable decomposition of the hydrated salt into oxy-chloride and hydrochloric acid. A concentrated solution of chloride of zinc converts starch, cellulose, and a great many other organic bodies into soluble compounds; hence the application of the fused salt as a caustic in surgery, and the impossibility of filtering a strong $ZnCl_2$ ley through paper. At a boiling heat chloride of zinc dissolves in any proportion of water, and highly concentrated solutions, of course, boil at high temperatures; hence they afford a convenient medium for the maintenance of high temperatures.

Oxide of zinc unites with the chloride in a great number of proportions, forming oxy-chlorides. A (mixed) compound of this order is used as a cement for stuffing teeth and other purposes. One part of extremely fine glass powder is mixed with three of finely powdered oxide of zinc free from carbonic acid. On the other hand, one part of borax is dissolved in the least sufficiency of hot water and added to fifty parts of solution of chloride of zinc of 1·5 to 1·6 sp. gr. Immediately before use the powder is made into a paste with the solution; it hardens in a few minutes, forming a stone-like mass.

For other zinc compounds, the reader is referred to the handbooks of chemistry.

Analysis.—From neutral solutions of its salts zinc is precipitated by sulphuretted hydrogen as sulphide, ZnS,—a white precipitate, soluble, but by no means readily, in dilute mineral acids, but insoluble in acetic acid. In the case of acetate the precipitation is quite complete; from a sulphate or chloride solution the greater part of the metal goes into the precipitate; in the presence of a sufficiency of free HCl the metal remains dissolved; sulphide of ammonium precipitates the metal completely, even in the presence of ammonia salts and free ammonia. The precipitate, when roasted at the end of an asbestos stick over a "bunsen," passes into oxide, which is yellow in the heat and white after cooling; and, if it be moistened with cobalt solution and re-heated, it exhibits a green colour after cooling. By these tests the precipitate is easily identified with certainty. For further information, see handbooks of analysis. (W. D.)

ZINCKEN, or ZINKEN, the German name of a family of wind instruments now obsolete, known in Italy as *cornetti*, in France as *cornets à bouquin*, and in England as "cornets," but differing entirely from the modern *cornets à pistons*; these last will also be noticed here, as bearing the same name.

The old cornets were of two kinds,—the straight and the curved. The straight (Germ. *gerade Zincken*, *stille Zincken*; Ital. *cornetti diritti*, *cornetti muti*) were usually made with the mouthpiece (a cupped mouthpiece analogous to that of the trumpet) forming part of the tube. The curved (Germ. *krumme Zincken*; Ital. *cornetti curvi*) are formed of two pieces of wood of different lengths, each having half the channel in which the column of air is to vibrate hollowed out, the diameter increasing from the mouthpiece towards the lower end. The two pieces of wood, when thus prepared, are joined together with glue; they are then finished off so as to form a pipe with eight sides, and are finally covered with leather. The mouthpieces are made of wood, horn, or ivory, and are fixed by a tenon to the upper extremity of the pipe. The primitive instrument was an animal's horn. Pipes of such small length give only, besides the first or fundamental, the second and sometimes the third note of the harmonic series. Thus, a pipe that has for its fundamental note A will, if the pressure of the lips be steadily increased, give the octave A and the twelfth E. To connect diatonically the first and second, the length of the pipe was progressively shortened, by making holes in its substance for the fingers to cover. The opening of these holes successively furnished the instrumentalist with the different intervals of the scale, six holes sufficing for this purpose: The fundamental was thus connected with its octave by all the degrees of a diatonic scale which could become chromatic by the help of cross fingerings and greater or less pressure of the lips within the mouthpiece. The fingering was completed by a seventh hole, which had for its object the production of the octave without the necessity of closing all the holes in order to produce the second note of the harmonic series. The first complete octave, thus obtained by a succession of fundamental notes, is easily octaved by a stronger pressure of the lips against the mouthpiece, and thus the ordinary limits of the compass of a zincke or cornet extend to a fifteenth. Whether straight or curved, it is pierced laterally with seven holes, six through the front and the seventh, that nearest to the mouthpiece, through the back. The first three holes were usually covered with the third, second, and first fingers of the right hand, the next four with the third, second, and first fingers and the thumb of the left hand. But some instrumentalists inverted the position of the hands. Virdung[1] shows a kind of zincke made of an animal's horn with only four holes, three at the back of the pipe and one in front. Such an instrument as this had naturally a very limited compass, since with the help of these four holes only the intermediate notes between the second and third proper tones of the harmonic scale could be produced, the lower octave comprised between the first and second remaining incomplete. At the beginning of the 17th century Prætorius[2] represents the zincken as a complete family arranged thus:—(1) the little zincke, of which the lowest note was that shown in (i.); (2) the ordinary zincke, with lowest note (ii.); and (3) the *cornon*, *corno torto*,

(i.) (ii.) (iii.)

[1] *Musica getutscht und auszgezogen*, Basel, 1511.

[2] *Syntagmatis Musici*, vol. ii.; *De Organographia*, Wolfenbüttel 1618.

or great zincke, with lowest note (iii.). In France the family was composed of the following instruments:—(1) the *dessus*, with lowest note (*a*); (2) the *haute-contre*, with lowest note (*b*); (3) the *taille*, with lowest note (*c*); and (4) the *basse*, with lowest note (*d*). Numbers (2), (3), and (4) in this last series were sometimes furnished with an open key, which, when the closed tube was lengthened, augmented the compass downwards by a note.

(a) (b) (c) (d)

During the Middle Ages these instruments were in such favour that an important part was given to them in all instrumental combinations. In Germany, in the 18th century, they were used with trombones in the churches to accompany the chorales. There are examples of this employment in the sacred cantatas of J. S. Bach. Monteverde made use of them in his opera *Orfeo* in 1608, as did Gluck in the opening chorus of his *Orfeo*, played at Vienna in 1762. The great vogue of the zincke is not to be accounted for by its musical qualities; for it has a hard, hoarse, piercing sound, and it failed utterly in truth of intonation; and these natural defects could only be modified with great difficulty. It is now hard to understand Mersenne's eulogium of the *dessus*, then more employed than the other cornets, "because it was used in vocal concerts and to make the treble with the organ, which is ravishing when one knows how to play it to perfection, like the Sieur Quiclet," and, farther on, "as to the property of its tone, it resembles the brilliancy of a sunbeam piercing the darkness, when it is heard among the voices in churches, cathedrals, or chapels."

The *serpent* is another instrument of the cornet family, though not usually classed with it. Its construction and its acoustic principle are the same as those of the old cornet. It is, properly speaking, an enlarged cornet with one hole less, that which is stopped with the thumb. The mouthpiece is fixed to the instrument by means of a long brass crook. A detailed account of the serpent and its congeners is given under OPHICLEIDE (vol. xvii. p. 778). The zincke or cornet has now entirely disappeared, and the rare specimens still met with are eagerly sought by collectors. The serpent has lasted longest, and even within the last twenty years has been used in many churches in the south of France.

CORNET, CORNET À PISTONS.

At present the names of cornet, cornet à pistons, and cornopean are given to an instrument that has no analogy whatever to the mediæval cornet. It is a transformation of the old post-horn, with a shorter tube than that of the trumpet, and improved to such a degree that its quality of tone is intermediate between the brightness of the trumpet and the softness of the flügel-horn bugle with pistons. The extent of the modern cornet without pistons is comprised within the second and eighth of the harmonic scale

2 3 4 5 6 8

The seventh, being too flat, owing to a well-known acoustic phenomenon, is rarely used. The cornet à pistons of the highest pitch is in B♭, and is used for a trumpet in that key. The notes written therefore sound a major second lower than the notation. It is furnished with three pistons, which lower the principal tube by a whole tone (1st piston), a half tone (2d piston), and a tone and a half (3d piston) respectively. It has already been explained under TROMBONE how the different pistons are combined to produce the entire chromatic compass of the instrument from the lowest limit to the highest. 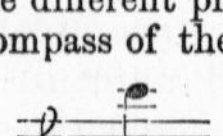 At first the cornet à pistons was supplied with a great many crooks. There were crooks for A, A♭, G, F, E, E♭, and D; but it is easy to understand that, if the additional tubes put in communication with the principal column of air by means of the pistons are adjusted for the key of B♭, the same additional tubes are too short to fulfil the same office for an instrument lowered to the extent of a minor sixth, as it would be for the key of D. Hence nearly all these crooks have disappeared, only those for B♭, A, and A♭ being retained. The invention of the modern cornet, or more exactly the application of pistons to the post-horn, is German, and dates from the first quarter of the 19th century, almost immediately after the invention of pistons by Stölzel and Blümel. It was introduced into Great Britain and France about 1830. There were at first only two pistons,—that of the whole tone and that of the half tone,—from which there naturally resulted gaps in the chromatic scale of the instrument. The history of the cornet is that of the improvement brought about by pistons apart from their successive transformations, and it has remained to the present time what it was when first invented. The great favour the cornet meets with is due to the facility with which it speaks, to the little fatigue it causes, and to the simplicity of its mechanism. We may, however, regret, from the point of view of art, that its success has been so great, and that it has ended by usurping in brass bands the place of the bugles, the quality of their tone being infinitely preferable as a foundation for an ensemble composed exclusively of brass instruments. Even the symphonic orchestra has not been secure from its intrusion. In fact, the cornet is taking the place of the trumpet nearly everywhere, and, if care is not taken, the latter will in a few years have completely disappeared, to the great detriment of orchestral tone colour; for the quality of tone of the cornet can never be an adequate substitute for the brilliant and majestic sonorousness so characteristic of the trumpet. (V. M.)

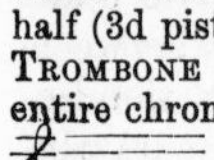

ZINZENDORF, NICOLAUS LUDWIG, COUNT OF ZINZENDORF AND POTTENDORF (1700-1760), religious reformer, descended from an ancient family belonging to Lower Austria, was born on 26th May 1700, at Dresden. His family had taken the Protestant side in the Reformation struggle, and in consequence his grandfather, Max Erasmus, had abandoned his Austrian estates to settle near Nuremberg. Max's second son, George Louis, was a member of the Saxon cabinet and a personal friend of the Pietist Spener. George's second wife, Charlotte Justine, the mother of Nicolaus, who was an only son, was a daughter of Nicolas and Catherine von Gersdorf, who were also Pietist. The boy was thus born into a Pietist circle; and Spener was his godfather. He never knew his father, who died six weeks after he was born. His mother married again when he was four years old, and he was educated under the charge of his pious and gifted grandmother,[1] Catherine von Gersdorf, to whom more than to any other he was indebted for the absorbing and enthusiastic piety which characterized him from childhood. His school days were spent at the pædagogium at Halle amidst Pietist surroundings, and in 1716 he went to the university of Wittenberg, to study law and fit himself for a diplomatic career. Three years later he was sent to travel in Holland, in France, and in various parts of Germany. These two years of wandering were employed by him in making the personal acquaintance of men distinguished for practical piety and belonging to a variety of churches. On his return he visited the branches of his family settled at Oberbirg and at Castell. During a lengthened visit at Castell he fell in love with his cousin Theodora; but the widowed countess, her mother, objected to the marriage, and the lady afterwards became the wife of Count Henry of Reuss. Zinzendorf seems to have considered this disappointment to be a call in providence to betake himself to some special work for God. He had previously, in deference to his family, who wished him to become a diplomatist, rejected the invitation of Francke to take Count Canstein's place in the Halle orphanage; and he now resolved to settle down as a Christian landowner, spending his life on behalf of a pious tenantry. He bought Berthelsdorf from his grandmother, and selected John Andrew Rothe for pastor and John George Heiz for factor; he married Erdmute Dorothea, sister of Count Henry of Reuss, and began living on his estate. His intention was to carry out into practice the Pietist ideas of Spener. He did not mean to found a new church or religious organization distinct from the Lutheranism of the land. He meant to create a Christian association, members of which by preaching, by tract

[1] A volume of *Spiritual Songs*, written by Zinzendorf's grandmother Catherine, was published in 1729 by Anton.

and book distribution, and by practical benevolence might awaken the somewhat torpid religion of the Lutheran Church. The "band of four brothers" (Rothe, pastor at Berthelsdorf; Schäffer, pastor at Görlitz; Francis von Wattewille, a friend from boyhood; and himself) set themselves by sermons, books, journeys, and correspondence to create a revival of religion, and by frequent meetings for prayer to preserve in their own hearts the warmth of personal trust in Christ. From the printing establishment at Ebersdorf large quantities of books and tracts, catechisms, collections of hymns, and cheap Bibles were issued; and a translation of Arndt's *True Christianity* was published for circulation in France. Dislike to the high and dry Lutheran orthodoxy of the period gave Zinzendorf some sympathy with that side of the growing rationalism which was attacking dogma, while he at the same time felt its lack of earnestness, and of a true and deep understanding of religion and of Christianity, and endeavoured to counteract its tendency by pointing men to the historical Christ, the revelation of the Father. It is also more than probable that he began to doubt the wisdom of Spener's plan of not separating from the Lutheran Church, and that he began to think that true Christianity could be best promoted by free association of Christians, who in course of time might grow into churches with no state connexion. These thoughts of his took a practical turn from his connexion with the Bohemian or Moravian Brethren. Zinzendorf offered an asylum to a number of persecuted wanderers from Moravia (see MORAVIAN BRETHREN), and built for them the village of Herrnhut on a corner of his estate of Berthelsdorf. The refugees who came to this asylum—the first detachment under Christian David in 1722—and continued coming from various regions where persecution raged, for a succession of years (till 1732), belonged to more than one Protestant organization. Persecution had made them cling pertinaciously to the small peculiarities of creed, organization, and worship, and they could scarcely be persuaded to live in peace with each other. Zinzendorf devoted himself to them. He, with his wife and children, lived in Herrnhut and brought Rothe with him. He had hard work to bring order out of the confusion. He had to satisfy the authorities that his religious community could be brought under the conditions of the peace of Augsburg; he had to quiet the suspicions of the Lutheran clergy; and, hardest of all, he had to rule in some fashion men made fanatical by persecution, who, in spite of his unwearied labours for them, on more than one occasion, it is said, combined in his own house to denounce him as the Beast of the Apocalypse, with Pastor Rothe as the False Prophet. Patience had at last its perfect work, and gradually Zinzendorf was able to organize his refugees into something like a *militia Christi*, based not on monastic but on family life. He was able to establish a common order of worship in 1727, and soon afterwards a common organization, which has been described in the article MORAVIAN BRETHREN. Zinzendorf took the deepest interest in the wonderful missionary enterprises of the Brethren, and saw with delight the spread of this Protestant family (not monastic) order in Germany, Denmark, Russia, and England. He travelled widely in its interests, visiting America in 1741-42 and spending a long time in London in 1750. Missionary colonies had by this time been settled in the West Indies (1732), in Greenland (1733), amongst the North American Indians (1735); and before Zinzendorf's death the Brethren had sent from Herrnhut missionary colonies to Livonia and the northern shores of the Baltic, to the slaves of North Carolina, to Surinam, to the Negro slaves in several parts of South America, to Travancore in the East Indies, to the Copts in Egypt, and to the west coast of South Africa. The community in Herrnhut, from which almost all these colonies had been sent out, had no money of its own, and its expenses had been almost exclusively furnished by Zinzendorf. His frequent journeyings from home made it almost impossible for him to look after his private affairs; he was compelled from time to time to raise money by loans, and about 1750 was almost reduced to bankruptcy. This led to the establishment of a financial board among the Brethren, on a plan furnished by a lawyer, John Frederick Köber, which worked well. In 1752 Zinzendorf lost his only son, Christian Renatus, whom he had hoped to make his successor; and four years later he lost his wife Erdmute, who had been his counsellor and confidante in all his work, and without whose wise guidance he could never have accomplished what he achieved. Zinzendorf remained a widower for one year, and then (June 1757) contracted a second marriage with Anna Nitschmann, on the ground that a man in his official position ought to be married. Three years later, overcome with his labours, he fell ill and died (on 9th May), leaving John de Wattewille, who had married his eldest daughter Benigna, to take his place at the head of the community.

See Spangenberg, *Leben des Grafen von Zinzendorf*, 1772-75; Schrautenbach, *Der Graf v. Zinzendorf*, 1871 (written in 1782, and interesting because it gives Zinzendorf's relations to such Pietist rationalists as Dippel); F. Bovet, *Le Comte de Zinzendorf*, 1860; Becker, *Zinzendorf im Verhältniss z. Philosophie u. Kirchenthum seiner Zeit*, 1886 (the best account; written by the author of the article "Zinzendorf" in Herzog-Plitt's *Encykl.*). See also the books mentioned under MORAVIAN BRETHREN. (T. M. L.)

ZION. See JERUSALEM and TEMPLE.

ZIRCONIUM, a rare element, closely allied to titanium. Klaproth in 1789 analysed zircon and found it to contain a new earth, which he called "zirconia." Zircon is essentially a silicate of zirconia, $ZrO_2.SiO_2$. For the extraction from it of zirconia the mineral is first of all heated and quenched in water to render it brittle, and then reduced to a fine powder, which is fused up with three to four parts of acid fluoride of potassium at a gentle heat in a platinum crucible. When the mass fuses tranquilly and all the water is expelled, the platinum crucible is placed in a Hessian crucible; the two crucibles are then covered and kept for two hours at the highest temperature producible by means of a wind-furnace. The porcelain-like fuse is powdered, boiled in water, and acidified with hydrofluoric acid, and the residual fluosilicate of potassium is filtered off. The filtrate on cooling deposits crystals of fluozirconate of potassium, ZrF_6K_2, which are purified by re-crystallization from hot water. The double fluoride is decomposed with hot concentrated sulphuric acid; the mixed sulphate is dissolved in water; and the zirconia is precipitated with ammonia in the cold. The precipitate, being difficult to wash, is (after a preliminary washing) re-dissolved in hydrochloric acid and re-precipitated with ammonia. Hydrated zirconia, $Zr(OH)_4$, as thus obtained, is quite appreciably soluble in water and easily in mineral acids, with formation of zirconic salts, *e.g.*, $ZrCl_4$, analogous to $SnCl_4$. But, if the hydrate is precipitated in the heat, it demands concentrated acids for its solution. The hydrate readily loses its water at a dull red heat and passes into anhydride with vivid incandescence. The anhydrous oxide, ZrO_2, is with difficulty soluble even in hydrofluoric acid; but a mixture of two parts of concentrated sulphuric acid and one of water dissolves it on continued heating as $Zr(SO_4)_2$. Zirconia, when heated to whiteness remains unfused, and radiates out abundance of white light. This property has been utilized for the construction of a new kind of gas lamp, in which a colourless flame, produced by the combustion of a mixture of gas and air, serves to heat a hollow cylinder of zirconia suspended over it by means of platinum gauze. Zirconia, like oxide of tin and oxide of titanium, unites not only with acids but also with basic oxides. For instance, if it be fused up with an excess of carbonate of soda, 2 of CO_2 are expelled by every ZrO_2, with formation of ortho-zirconate (analogous to ortho-silicate) of soda, $ZrO_2.2Na_2O$. On treating the fuse with water we obtain the salt $Na_2O.8ZrO_2+12H_2O$, which crystallizes in hexagonal plates.

Zirconic chloride, $ZrCl_4$, is prepared, by igniting a mixture of zirconia and charcoal in a current of chlorine, as a white sublimate. It has the exact vapour-density corresponding to the formula. It dissolves in water with evolution of heat; on evaporation a basic salt, $2ZrOCl_2+9H_2O$, separates out in star-shaped aggregates of needles.

Metallic zirconium is obtainable, by heating the double fluoride of zirconium and potassium with metallic potassium, as an iron-grey powder. Troost produced crystallized zirconium by fusing the double fluoride with aluminium in a graphite crucible at the temperature of melting iron, and extracting the aluminium from the fuse with hydrochloric acid. The crystals look like antimony and are brittle; their specific gravity is 4·15. The powdery metal burns readily in air; the crystalline metal requires to be heated in an oxyhydrogen flame if it is to catch fire. Mineral acids generally attack the crystallized metal very little even in the heat; aqua regia, however, dissolves it readily, and so does hydrofluoric acid. The spark spectrum of zirconium is characterized by five lines, whose wave-lengths are as follows:—6127 in the red, and 4815, 4771, 4738, 4709, and 4686 in the blue. The atomic weight is not known exactly; according to Marignac and Deville, it lies near 90, if $O=16$.

ZITTAU, the centre of the Saxon linen trade and the most populous town in the district of Bautzen, in the kingdom of Saxony, is situated on the left bank of the Mandau, near its confluence with the Neisse, 25 miles south-east of Bautzen and 48 east-south-east of Dresden. The town is built in a regular and modern style. The town-house dates from 1844, and contains a public library of 30,000 volumes. The church of St John was rebuilt in 1834-37; and the church of St Peter and St Paul, with its elegant tower, belonged to an old Franciscan monastery. The latter was restored in 1882 and part of it fitted up as an historical museum. There are five other churches in the town. Zittau is well equipped with schools, including a gymnasium (founded in 1586) and a commercial school, both accommodated in the Johanneum, and several technical institutions. The leading branch of industry is linen and damask weaving; but woollen stuffs, trimmings, &c., are also produced in the factories of the town, and in the surrounding weaving villages, 37 of which, with 70,000 inhabitants, are included in the municipal jurisdiction. The town, which is one of the best endowed in Saxony, also owns valuable forests on the mountains of Upper Lusatia. There are various steam-mills, iron-foundries, brick-fields, and potteries near the town, and extensive deposits of lignite, employing over 1000 hands. Zittau is situated near the border of Bohemia, with which it carries on some trade. In 1885 the population was 23,215, of whom less than one-fifth were Roman Catholics; in 1834 the population was 8508.

Zittau is of Wendish origin (Chytawa is its Wendish name), and was made a town by Ottocar II. of Bohemia. It was one of the six towns of the Lusatian league (1346), at which period it belonged to Bohemia. It suffered severely in the Hussite wars and in the Thirty Years' War, and was bombarded and burnt by the Austrians in 1757 during the Seven Years' War. The musical composer Marschner (1795-1861) was born at Zittau.

ZIZKA, or ZISKA, JOHN (*c.* 1360-1424), leader of the HUSSITES (*q.v.*) from 1419, was born at Trocznow in the neighbourhood of Budweis in Bohemia about the year 1360. He was of noble descent, and was brought up from an early age at Prague at the court of King Wenceslaus. In 1410 he fought as a volunteer, on the losing side, in the great battle of Grünwald, near Tannenberg in Prussia, in which the knights of the Teutonic Order were completely routed by the Lithuanians and Poles. He afterwards took part in the Hungarian wars against the Turks, and is also said to have fought on the English side in the battle of Agincourt. In the discontents which followed the martyrdom of Huss and Jerome in Bohemia he sided with the liberal party, and ultimately, on the outbreak of hostilities, became its leader. He soon organized a formidable body of infantry, and from his newly fortified stronghold of Tabor as a centre achieved various successes, of which the most signal was the victory over the imperial troops at Deutschbrod (8th January 1422). At an early period of the war,—at the siege of Raby in 1421,—Zizka, who from boyhood had been blind of an eye, completely lost his sight; but his strength of will enabled him almost wholly to overcome this formidable disadvantage, and his extraordinary presence of mind, fertility of resource, and keenness of mental vision, coupled with a zeal that was wholly sincere, though not always free from fanaticism, continued to mark him out as the leader in the cause he had espoused until his death, which was caused by an infectious disorder while he was besieging Przibislaw (11th October 1424).

See Millauer, *Diplomatisch-historische Aufsätze über Johann Ziska* (1824). Zizka's life has been made the subject of an epic by the German poet Meissner (1846; 10th edition 1867), and has also been related in prose by George Sand.

ZLATOUST, in the Russian government of Ufa, is one of the chief towns and iron-works of the Urals. It is situated on the Ai, a tributary of the Ufa, in a picturesque valley of the middle Urals, at a height of 1200 feet above sea-level. The 270 miles which stretch between Zlatoust and Ufa in the west will soon be covered by rail, while a branch line is projected to connect it with Ekaterinburg in the north. The town is well built, mostly of wood, has a first-class meteorological and magnetic observatory, and is the seat of the mining administration for the Zlatoust district, which includes, besides several iron-works, the rich gold-washings of the basin of the Mias. Its merchants carry on a brisk trade in agricultural produce and cattle, as well as in manufactured wares, imported for the use of the mining villages of the neighbourhood. The Ai and several ponds supply the crown iron-works with motive power, and in 1884 the iron furnaces of Zlatoust yielded 90,800 cwts. of pig-iron, which were used almost entirely for the manufacture of swords, bayonets, and artillery munition. The population of Zlatoust in 1884 was 19,000.

ZNAIM, or ZNAYM (Czech *Znojmo*), an interesting old town of Moravia, is picturesquely situated on the left bank of the Thaya, 45 miles north-north-west of Vienna. The town proper is adjoined by four suburbs, and it contains three fine open squares, while the site of the old fortifications is occupied by a pleasant promenade. The Räuberthurm is a relic of the old castle of the margraves of Moravia; the round castle-chapel, known as the heathen temple (Heiden-Tempel), in the Romanesque style of the 12th century, was at one time considered the most ancient building in Moravia. The Gothic church of St Nicholas was built about 1348 by the emperor Charles IV.; the town-house, with an elegant Gothic tower, 250 feet high, dates from about 1446. The ancient and once powerful Præmonstratensian abbey of Bruck, to the east of the town, is now occupied as barracks. The town is well equipped with technical and other schools, and carries on manufactures of earthenware, leather, chocolate, vinegar, and other articles. Large quantities of cucumbers, grain, and wine are produced in the fertile environs. In 1880 the population, chiefly of German origin, was 12,254.

The present town of Znaim was founded in 1226 by Ottocar I. of

Bohemia on the site of Znojmo, the ancient capital of the tributary margraves of Moravia, which had been destroyed in 1145. Znaim is best known to history for the armistice concluded here in 1809 after the battle of Wagram between Napoleon I. and the archduke Charles. In 1866 the Prussians occupied the town from July 13th till September 3d. The novelist Karl Postel (1793-1864), who wrote under the pseudonym of Charles Sealsfield, was born at Poppitz, 2½ miles to the south-west.

Definition.

ZODIAC (ὁ ζωδιακὸς κύκλος, from ζώδιον, "a little animal"), an imaginary zone of the heavens within which lie the paths of the sun, moon, and principal planets. It is bounded by two circles equidistant from the ecliptic, about eighteen degrees apart; and it is divided into twelve signs, and marked by twelve constellations. The signs—the Greek δωδεκατημόρια—are geometrical divisions thirty degrees in extent, counted from the spring equinox in the direction of the sun's progress through them. The whole series accordingly shifts westward through the effect of precession by about one degree in seventy-two years. At the moment of crossing the equator towards the north the sun is said to be at the first point of Aries; some thirty days later it enters Taurus, and so on through Gemini, Cancer, Leo, Virgo, Libra, Scorpio, Sagittarius, Capricornus, Aquarius, and Pisces (see ASTRONOMY, vol. ii. p. 771). The constellations bearing the same names coincided approximately in position, when Hipparchus observed them at Rhodes, with the divisions they designate. The discrepancy now, however, amounts to the entire breadth of a sign, the sun's path in Aries lying among the stars of Pisces, in Taurus among those of Aries, &c.

Signs and constellations.

Duodenary division.

The twelvefold division of the zodiac was evidently suggested by the occurrence of twelve full moons in successive parts of it in the course of each year. This approximate relation was first systematically developed by the early inhabitants of Mesopotamia, and formed the starting-point for all their divisions of time. As the year separated, as it were of itself, into twelve months, so the day was divided into twelve "double hours," and the great cosmical period of 43,200 years into twelve "sars." Each sar, month, and hour was represented at once visibly and symbolically by a twelfth part of the "furrow" drawn by the solar Bull across the heavens. The idea of tracing the sun's path among the stars was, when it occurred to Chaldæan astronomers, an original and, relatively to their means, a recondite one. We owe to its realization by them the constitution and nomenclature of the twelve signs of the zodiac. Assyrian cylinders and inscriptions indicate for the familiar series of our text-books an antiquity of some four thousand years. Ages before Asurbanipal reigned at Nineveh the eighth month (Marchesvan) was known as "the month of the star of the Scorpion," the tenth (Tebet) belonged to the "star of the Goat," the twelfth (Adar) to the "star of the Fish of Hea."[1] The motive underlying the choice of symbols is in a few cases obvious, but in most remains conjectural. The attributes of the deities appointed to preside over the months and signs were to some extent influential. Two of them, indeed, took direct possession of their respective portions of the sky. The zodiacal Virgo is held to represent the Assyrian Venus, Ishtar, the ruling divinity of the sixth month, and Sagittarius the archer-god Nergal, to whom the ninth month was dedicated. But no uniform system of selection was pursued; or rather perhaps the results of several, adopted at various epochs, and under the influence of varying currents of ideas, became amalgamated in the final series.

First sign.

This, there is reason to believe, was the upshot of a prehistoric reform. So far as positive records go, Aries was always the first sign. But the arrangement is, on the face of it, a comparatively modern one. None of the brighter stars of the constellation could be said even roughly to mark the equinox much before 1800 B.C.; during a long stretch of previous time the leading position belonged to the stars of Taurus.[2] Numerous indications accordingly point to a corresponding primitive zodiac. Setting aside as doubtful evidence derived from interpretations of cuneiform inscriptions, we meet, in connexion with Mithraic and Mylittic legends, reminiscences of a zodiac and religious calendar in which the Bull led the way.[3] Virgil's

> Candidus auratis aperit cum cornibus annum
> Taurus

perpetuates the tradition. And we shall see presently that the Pleiades, not only were originally, but continued to be until well within historical memory, the first asterism of the *lunar* zodiac.

In the Chaldæan signs fragments of several distinct strata of thought appear to be embedded. From one point of view, they shadow out the great epic of the destinies of the human race; again, the universal solar myth claims a share in them; hoary traditions were brought into *ex post facto* connexion with them; or they served to commemorate simple meteorological and astronomical facts.

Second sign.

The first Babylonian month Nisan, dedicated to Anu and Bel, was that of "sacrifice"; and its association with the Ram as the chief primitive object of sacrifice is thus intelligible.[4] According to an alternative explanation, however, the heavenly Ram, placed as leader in front of the flock of the stars, merely embodied a spontaneous figure of the popular imagination. An antique persuasion, that the grand cycle of creation opened under the first sign, has been transmitted to modern cognizance by Dante (*Inf.*, i. 38). The human race, on the other hand, was supposed to have come into being under Taurus. The solar interpretation of the sign goes back to the far-off time when the year began with Taurus, and the sun was conceived of as a bull entering upon the great furrow of heaven as he ploughed his way among the stars. In the third month and sign the building of the first city and the fratricidal brothers—the Romulus and Remus of Roman legend—were brought to mind. The appropriate symbol was at first indifferently a pile of bricks or two male children, always on early monuments placed feet to feet. The retrograde movement of a crab typified, by an easy association of ideas, the retreat of the sun from his farthest northern excursion, and Cancer was constituted the sign of the summer solstice. The Lion, as the symbol of fire, represented the culmination of the solar heat. In the sixth month, the descent of Ishtar to Hades in search of her lost husband Tammuz was celebrated, and the sign of the Virgin had thus a purely mythological signification.

Third to sixth sign.

Seventh and eighth signs.

The history of the seventh sign is somewhat complicated. The earlier Greek writers,—Eudoxus, Eratosthenes, Hipparchus,—knew of only eleven zodiacal symbols, but made one do double duty, extending the Scorpion across the seventh and eighth divisions. The Balance, obviously indicating the equality of day and night, is first mentioned as the sign of the autumnal equinox by Geminus and Varro, and obtained, through Sosigenes of Alexandria, official recognition in the Julian calendar. Nevertheless, Virgil (*Georg.*, i. 32) regarded the space it presided over as so much waste land, provisionally occupied by the "Claws" of the Scorpion, but readily available for the

[1] Lenormant, *Origines de l'Histoire*, vol. i. p. 236.

[2] The possibility should not, however, be overlooked that the "stars of the months" were determined by their heliacal risings (see Bosanquet and Sayce on Babylonian astronomy, in *Monthly Notices Roy. Astr. Soc.*, vol. xl. p. 117). This would give a further extension backwards of over 1000 years, during which the equinox might have occurred in the month of the Ram.

[3] Lajard, *Recherches sur le Culte de Mithra*, p. 605.

[4] Sayce, *Trans. Society of Biblical Archæology*, vol. iii. p. 162.

apotheosis of Augustus. Libra was not of Greek invention. Ptolemy, who himself chiefly used the "Claws" (Χηλαί), speaks of it as a distinctively Chaldæan sign;[1] and it occurs as an extra-zodiacal asterism in the Chinese sphere. An ancient Chinese law, moreover, prescribed the regularization of weights and measures at the *spring* equinox.[2] No representation of the seventh sign has yet been discovered on any Euphratean monument; but it is noticeable that the eighth is frequently doubled,[3] and it is difficult to avoid seeing in the pair of zodiacal scorpions carved on Assyrian cylinders the prototype of the Greek scorpion and claws. Both Libra and the sign it eventually superseded thus owned a Chaldæan birthplace. The struggle of rival systems of nomenclature, from which our zodiacal series resulted, is plainly visible in their alternations; and the claims of the competing signs were long sought to be conciliated by representing the Balance as held between the claws of the Scorpion.

Ninth to twelfth sign.

The definitive decline of the sun's power after the autumnal equinox was typified by placing a Scorpion as the symbol of darkness in the eighth sign. Sagittarius, figured later as a Centaur, stood for the Babylonian Mars. Capricornus, the sign of the winter solstice, is plausibly connected with the caprine nurse of the young solar god in Oriental legends, of which that of Zeus and Amalthea is a variant.[4] The fish-tailed Goat of the zodiac presents a close analogy with the Mexican calendar sign Cipactli, a kind of marine monster resembling a narwhal.[5] Aquarius is a still more exclusively meteorological sign than Leo. The eleventh month was known in Euphratean regions as that of "want and rain." The deluge was traditionally associated with it. It was represented in zodiacal symbolism by the god Ramman, crowned with a tiara and pouring water from a vase, or more generally by the vase and water without the god. The resumption of agricultural labours after the deluge was commemorated in the twelfth month, and a mystical association of the fishes, which were its sign, with the life after death is evident in a monument of Assyrian origin described by M. Clermont-Ganneau, showing a corpse guarded by a pair of fish-gods.[6] The doubling of the sign of Pisces still recalls, according to Mr Sayce,[7] the arrangement of the Babylonian calendar, in which a year of 360 days was supplemented once in six years by a thirteenth month, a second Adar. To the double month corresponded the double sign of the "Fishes of Hea."[8]

Cyclical meaning of the succession of signs.

The cyclical meaning of the succession of zodiacal signs, though now obscured by interpolations and substitutions, was probably once clear and entire. It is curiously reflected in the adventures of the Babylonian Hercules, the solar hero Izdubar.[9] They were recorded in the comparatively late surviving version of the 7th century B.C., on twelve tablets, with an obvious design of correlation with the twelve divisions of the sun's annual course. Izdubar's conquest of the winged bull Heabani was placed under Taurus; his slaying of the tyrant Houmbaba (the prototype of Geryon) in the fifth month typified the victory of light over darkness, represented in plastic art by the group of a lion killing a bull, which is the form ordinarily given to the sign Leo on Ninevite cylinders.[10] The wooing of Ishtar by the hero of the epic falls under Virgo, and his encounter with two scorpion men, guardians of the rising and the setting sun, under Scorpio. The eleventh tablet narrates the deluge; the twelfth associates the apotheosis of Heabani (the Babylonian Chiron) with the zodiacal emblems of the resurrection.

The constellations.

In the formation of the constellations of the zodiac very little regard was paid to stellar configurations. The Chaldæans chose three stars in each sign to be the "councillor gods" of the planets.[11] These were called by the Greeks "decans," because ten degrees of the ecliptic and ten days of the year were presided over by each. The college of the decans was conceived as moving, by their annual risings and settings, in an "eternal circuit" between the infernal and supernal regions. Our modern asterisms first appear in the *Phænomena* of Eudoxus about 370 B.C. But Eudoxus, there is reason to believe, consulted, not the heavens, but a celestial globe of an anterior epoch, on which the stars and the signs were forced into unnatural agreement. The representation thus handed down to us (in the verses of Aratus) has been thought to tally best with the state of the sky about 2000 B.C.;[12] and the mention of a pole-star, for which Eudoxus was rebuked by Hipparchus, seems, as Mr W. T. Lynn has pointed out,[13] to refer to the time when α Draconis stood near the pole. The data afforded by Eudoxus, however, are far too vague to serve as the basis of any chronological conclusion.

Egyptian zodiacal signs.

The Egyptians adopted from the Greeks, with considerable modifications of its attendant symbolism, the twelve-fold division of the zodiac. Aries became the Fleece; two Sprouting Plants, typifying equality or resemblance, stood for Gemini; Cancer was re-named Scarabæus; Leo was converted, from the axe-like configuration of its chief stars, into the Knife; Libra into the Mountain of the Sun, a reminiscence, apparently, of the Euphratean association of the seventh month with a "holy mound," designating the Biblical tower of Babel. A Serpent was the Egyptian equivalent of Scorpio; the Arrow only of Sagittarius was retained; Capricornus became "Life," or a Mirror as an image of life; Aquarius survived as Water; Taurus, Virgo, and Pisces remained unchanged.[14] The motive of some of the substitutions was to avoid the confusion which must have ensued from the duplication of previously existing native asterisms; thus, the Egyptian and Greek Lions were composed of totally different stars. Abstractions in other cases replaced concrete objects, with the general result of effacing the distinctive character of the Greek zodiac as a "circle of living things."

Spread of Greek system.

Early Zoroastrian writings, though impregnated with star-worship, show no traces of an attempt to organize the heavenly array. In the *Bundehish*, however (9th century), the twelve "Akhtârs," designated by the same names as our signs, lead the army of Ormuzd, while the seven "Awakhtârs" or planets (including a meteor and a comet) fight for Ahriman. The knowledge of the solar zodiac thus turned to account for dualistic purposes was undoubtedly derived from the Greeks. By them, too, it was introduced into Hindustan. Âryabhaṭa, about the beginning of our era, reckoned by the same signs as Hipparchus. They were transmitted from India by Buddhist missionaries to China, but remained in abeyance until the Jesuit reform of Chinese astronomy in the 17th century.

The native zodiacal system was of unexampled complexity. Besides divisions into twenty-eight and twenty-four

[1] In citing a Chaldæan observation of Mercury dating from 235 B.C. (*Almagest*, vol. ii. p. 170, ed. Halma).

[2] See *Uranographie Chinoise*, by Gustav Schlegel, who, however, claims an extravagant antiquity for the Chinese constellational system.

[3] Lenormant, *Origines*, vol. i. p. 267. [4] *Ibid.*, p. 259.

[5] Humboldt, *Vues des Cordillères*, 1810, p. 157.

[6] *Rev. Archéol.*, 1879, p. 344.

[7] *Trans. Soc. Bibl. Archæol.*, vol. iii. p. 166.

[8] The god Hea, the Oannes of Berosus, equivalent to the fish-god Dagon, came to the rescue of the protagonist in the Chaldæan drama of the deluge.

[9] Sir H. Rawlinson, *Athenæum*, 7th December 1872.

[10] Lenormant, *Origines*, vol. i. p. 240.

[11] Diod. Sic., *Hist.*, ii. 30, where, however, by an obvious mistake the number of "councillor gods" is stated at only thirty.

[12] R. Brown, *Babylonian Record*, No. 3, p. 34.

[13] *Babylonian Record*, No. 5, p. 79.

[14] Brugsch, *Z. D. M. G.*, vol. ix. p. 513.

Chinese series of signs.

parts, it included two distinct duodenary series. The *tse* or "stations" were referred by Biot to the date 1111 B.C. Measured from the winter solstice of that epoch, they corresponded, in conformity with the Chinese method of observation by intervals of what we now call right ascension, to equal portions of the celestial equator.[1] Projected upon the ecliptic, these were, of course, considerably unequal, and the *tse* accordingly differed essentially from the Chaldæan and Greek signs. Their use was chiefly astrological, and their highly figurative names—"Great Splendour," "Immense Void," "Fire of the Phœnix," &c. —had reference to no particular stars. They became virtually merged in the European series, stamped with official recognition upwards of two centuries ago. The twenty-four *tsieki* or demi-*tse* were probably invented to mark the course of weather changes throughout the year. Their appellations are purely meteorological.

The characteristic Chinese mode of dividing the "yellow road" of the sun was, however, by the twelve "cyclical animals,"—Rat, Ox, Tiger, Hare, Dragon or Crocodile, Serpent, Horse, Sheep, Monkey, Hen, Dog, Pig. The opening sign corresponds to our Aquarius, and it is remarkable that the rat is, in the far East, frequently used as an ideograph for "water." But here the agreement ceases. For the Chinese series has the strange peculiarity of proceeding in a retrograde direction or *against* the course of the sun. Thus, the second sign (of the Ox) occupies the position of Capricorn, the third that of Sagittarius, and so on. The explanation of this seeming anomaly is to be found in the primitive destination of the "animals" to the purposes of an "horary zodiac." Their succession, established to mark the hours of day and night, was not unnaturally associated with the diurnal revolution of the sphere from east to west.[2] They are unquestionably of native origin. Tradition ascribes their invention to Tajao, minister of the emperor Hwang-te, who reigned *c.* 2697 B.C., and it can scarcely be placed later than the 7th century B.C.[3]

The Chinese circle of the "animals" obtained early a wide diffusion. It was adopted by Tartars, Turks, and Mongols, in Tibet and Tong-king, Japan and Corea. It is denominated by Humboldt[4] the "zodiac of hunters and shepherds," and he adds that the presence in it of a tiger gives it an exclusively Asiatic character. It appears never to have been designed for astronomical employment. From the first it served to characterize the divisions of time. The nomenclature not only of the hours of the day and of their minutest intervals was supplied by it, but of the months of the year, of the years in the Oriental sixty-year cycle, and of the days in the "little cycle" of twelve days. Nor has it yet fallen into desuetude. Years "of the Rat," "of the Tiger," "of the Pig," still figure in the almanacs of Central Asia, Cochin China, and Japan.

Aztec signs.

A large detachment of the "cyclical animals" even found its way to the New World. Seven of the twenty days constituting the Aztec month bore names evidently borrowed from those of the Chinese horary signs. The Hare (or Rabbit), Monkey, Dog, and Serpent reappeared without change; for the Tiger, Crocodile, and Hen, unknown in America, the Ocelot, Lizard, and Eagle were substituted as analogous.[5] The Aztec calendar dated from the 7th century; but the zodiacal tradition embodied by it was doubtless much more ancient. Of the zodiac in its true sense of a partitioned belt of the sphere there was no aboriginal knowledge on the American continent. Mexican acquaintance with the signs related only to their secondary function as dies (so to speak) with which to stamp recurring intervals of time.

Lunar zodiac.

The *synodical* revolution of the moon laid down the lines of the solar, its *sidereal* revolution those of the lunar zodiac. The first was a circlet of "full moons"; the second marked the diurnal stages of the lunar progress round the sky, from and back again to any selected star. The moon was the earliest "measurer" both of time and space; but its services can scarcely have been rendered available until stellar "milestones" were established at suitable points along its path. Such were the Hindu *nakshatras*, a word originally signifying stars in general, but appropriated to designate certain small stellar groups marking the divisions of the lunar track. They exhibit in an exaggerated form the irregularities of distribution visible in our zodiacal constellations, and present the further anomaly of being frequently reckoned as twenty-eight in number, while the ecliptical arcs they characterize are invariably twenty-seven. Now, since the moon revolves round the earth in $27\frac{1}{3}$ days, hesitation between the two full numbers might easily arise; yet the real explanation of the difficulty appears to be different. The superfluous asterism, named *Abhijit*, included the bright star α Lyræ, under whose influence the gods had vanquished the Asuras. Its invocation with the other *nakshatras*, remoteness from the ecliptic notwithstanding, was thus due (according to Prof. Max Müller's plausible conjecture)[6] to its being regarded as of especially good omen. Acquaintance with foreign systems of twenty-eight lunar divisions tended doubtless to fix its position, which remained, nevertheless, always equivocal.[7] Alternately admitted into or rejected from the series, it was finally, some six or seven centuries ago, eliminated by the effects of precession in reversing the order of culmination of its limiting stars.

Hindu system of *nakshatras*.

The notion of a twenty-seven-fold division of the zodiac was deeply rooted in Hindu tradition. The number and the name were in early times almost synonymous. Thus a *nakshatra-mālā* denoted a necklace of twenty-seven pearls;[8] and the fundamental equality of the parts was figured in an ancient legend, by the compulsion laid upon King Soma (the Moon) to share his time impartially between all his wives, the twenty-seven daughters of Prajápati. Everything points to a native origin for the system of *nakshatras*. Some were named after exclusively Vedic deities; they formed the basis of the sacrificial calendar of the Brahmans; the old Indian names of the months were derived from them; their existence was presupposed in the entire structure of Hindu ritual and science.[9] They do not, however, obtain full recognition in Sanskrit literature until the Brāhmana period (7th or 8th century B.C.). The *Rig-Veda* contains only one allusion to them, where it is said that "Soma is placed in the lap of the *nakshatras*"; and this is in a part including later interpolations.

Positive proof of the high antiquity of the Hindu lunar zodiac is nevertheless afforded by the undoubted fact that the primitive series opened with Krittikā (the Pleiades) as the sign of the vernal equinox. The arrangement would have been correct about 2300 B.C.; it would scarcely have been possible after 1800 B.C.[10] We find nowhere else a well-authenticated zodiacal sequence corresponding to so early a date. The reform by which Krittikā, now relegated to the third place, was superseded as the head of the series by "Açvini"[11] was accomplished under Greek

[1] Biot, *Journ. des Savans*, 1839, p. 729, and 1840, p. 151; Gaubil, *Hist. de l'Astr. Chinoise*, p. 9.

[2] Humboldt, *Vues des Cordillères*, p. 168.

[3] G. Schlegel, *Ur. Chin.*, pp. 37, 561.

[4] *Op. cit.*, p. 219.

[5] *Ibid.*, p. 152; Prescott, *Conquest of Mexico*, vol. iii. p. 321 (ed. 1860).

[6] *Rig-Veda Samhita*, vol. iv., 1862, Preface, p. lxii.

[7] Whitney, *Journ. Am. Orient. Soc.*, vol. viii. p. 394.

[8] Max Müller, *op. cit.*, p. lxiv.

[9] *Ibid.*, p. 42.

[10] A. Weber, *Indische Studien*, vol. x. p. 241.

[11] Named from the Açvins, the Hindu Castor and Pollux. It is

influence somewhere near the beginning of our era. For purposes of ritual, however, the Pleiades, with Agni or "Fire" as their presiding deity, continued to be the first sign. Hindu astronomy received its first definite organization in the 6th century, with results embodied in the *Sūrya-Siddhānta*. Here the "signs" and the "constellations" of the lunar zodiac form two essentially distinct systems. The ecliptic is divided into twenty-seven equal parts, called *bhogas* or arcs, of 800′ each. But the *nakshatras* are twenty-eight, and are represented by as many "junction stars" (*yogātāra*), carefully determined by their spherical coordinates. The successive entries of the moon and planets into the *nakshatras* (the ascertainment of which was of great astrological importance) were fixed by means of their conjunctions with the *yogātāras*. These, however, soon ceased to be observed, and already in the 11th century Al-Bīrūnī could meet with no Hindu astronomer capable of pointing out to him the complete series. Their successful identification by Colebrooke[1] in 1807 had a purely archæological interest. The modern *nakshatras* are twenty-seven equal ecliptical divisions, the origin of which shifts, like that of the solar signs, with the vernal equinox. They are, in fact, the *bhogas* of the *Sūrya-Siddhānta*. The mean place of the moon in them, published in all Hindu almanacs, is found to serve unexceptionally the ends of astral vaticination.[2]

The system upon which it is founded is of great antiquity. Belief in the power of the *nakshatras* evidently inspired the invocations of them in the *Atharva-Veda*. In the Brāhmana period they were distinguished as "deva" and "yama," the fourteen lucky asterisms being probably associated with the waxing, the fourteen unlucky with the waning moon.[3] A special *nakshatra* was appropriated to every occurrence of life. One was propitious to marriage, another to entrance upon school-life, a third to the first ploughing, a fourth to laying the foundation of a house. Festivals for the dead were appointed to be held under those that included but one star. Propitiatory abstinences were recommended when the natal asterism was menaced by unfavourable planetary conjunctions. The various members of the body were parcelled out among the *nakshatras*, and a rotation of food was prescribed as a wholesome accompaniment of the moon's revolution among them.[4]

Nomenclature of Hindu signs.

The nomenclature of the Hindu signs of the zodiac, save as regards a few standard asterisms, such as Açvini and Krittikā, was far from uniform. Considerable discrepancies occur in the lists given by different authorities.[5] Hence it is not surprising to meet in them evidence of foreign communications. Reminiscences of the Greek signs of Gemini, Leo, Libra, Sagittarius, Capricornus, and Pisces are obvious severally in the Hindu Two Faces, Lion's Tail, Beam of a Balance, Arrow, Gazelle's Head (figured as a marine nondescript), and Fish. The correspondence does not, however, extend to the stars; and some coincidences adverted to by Humboldt between the *nakshatras* and the zodiacal animals of Central Asia are of the same nominal character.[6] Mexican loans are more remarkable. They were apparently direct as well as indirect. The Aztec calendar includes *nakshatra* titles borrowed, not only through the medium of the Tartar zodiac, but likewise straight from the Indian scheme, apart from any known intervention. The "three footprints of Vishnu," for example, unmistakably gave its name to the Mexican day Ollin, signifying the "track of the sun"; and both series further contain a "flint weapon," a "stick," and a "house."[7] Several houses and couches were ranged along the Hindu zodiac with the naive idea of providing resting-places for the wandering moon.

Connexion with other systems.

Relative antiquity of Hindu, Chinese, and Arabian systems.

Relationship of a more intimate kind connects the Hindu lunar mansions with those of the Arabs and Chinese. The resemblance between the three systems is indeed so close that it has been assumed, almost as axiomatic, that they must have been framed from a single model; and the question of their origin has been debated with all the resources of varied erudition by scholars such as Biot, Weber, Whitney, and Max Müller. As the upshot of the controversy it appears nevertheless to have become tolerably clear that the *nakshatras* were both native to India, and the *sieu* to China, but that the *manāzil* were mainly of Indian derivation. The assertion, paradoxical at first sight, that the twenty-eight "hostelries" of the Chinese sphere had nothing to do with the moon's daily motion seems to convey the actual fact. Their number, as a multiple of four, was prescribed by the quaternary partition of the heavens, fundamental in Chinese astronomy. It was considered by Biot to have been originally twenty-four, but to have been enlarged to twenty-eight about 1100 B.C., by the addition of determinants for the solstices and equinoxes of that period.[8] The essential difference, however, between the *nakshatras* and the *sieu* is that the latter were equatorial, not ecliptical, divisions. They were measured by the meridian-passages of the limiting stars, and varied in amplitude from 2° 42′ to 30° 24′.[9] The use of the specially observed stars constituting or representing the *sieu* was as points of reference for the movements of sun, moon, and planets. They served, in fact, and still serve (though with astrological ends in view), the precise purpose of "fundamental stars" in European astronomy. All that is certainly known about the antiquity of the *sieu* is that they were well established in the 3d century B.C. Their initial point at the autumnal equinox marked by Kio (Spica Virginis) suits a still later date; and there is no valid evidence that the modern series resulted from the rectification of an older superannuated arrangement, analogous to the Krittikā sequence of *nakshatras*. The Hindu zodiacal constellations belong then to an earlier epoch than the Chinese "stations," such as they have been transmitted to our acquaintance. Yet not only were the latter an independent invention, but it is almost demonstrable that the *nakshatras*, in their more recent organization, were, as far as possible, assimilated to them. The whole system of junction stars was doubtless an imitation of the *sieu*; the choice of them by the Hindu astronomers of the 6th century A.D. was plainly instigated by a consideration of the Chinese list, compiled with a widely different intent. Where they varied from it, some intelligible reason can generally be assigned for the change. Eight junction stars lie quite close to, seven others are actually identical with, Chinese determinants;[10] and many of these coincidences are between insignificant and, for the purposes of ecliptical division, inconveniently situated objects.

Chinese asterisms or stations.

Arabian mansions of the moon.

The small stellar groups characterizing the Arab "mansions of the moon" (*manāzil al-kamār*) were more equably distributed than either the Hindu or Chinese series. They presented, nevertheless, striking resemblances to both. Twenty-four out of twenty-eight were formed, at least in part, of *nakshatra* or *sieu* stars.[11] That the Arab was essentially a copy of the Hindu lunar zodiac can scarcely admit

composed of the stars in the head of Aries, and is figured by a horse's head.

1 *As. Res.*, vol. ix. p. 330.

2 J. B. Biot, *Études sur l'Astronomie Indienne*, p. 225.

3 A. Weber, "Die Vedischen Nachrichten von den Naxatra," in *Berliner Abhandlungen*, 1861, p. 309.

4 *Ibid.*, p. 322; H. Kern, *Die Yogatara des Varamihira*; Weber's *Ind. Stud.*, vol. xv. pp. 174-181.

5 Sir William Jones, *As. Res.*, vol. ii. pp. 294-5.

6 Humboldt, *Vues des Cordillères*, p. 154.

7 *Ibid.*, p. 152.

8 Biot, *Jour. des Savans*, 1845, p. 40.

9 G. Schlegel, *Ur. Chin.*, p. 77.

10 Biot, *Études*, p. 136.

11 Whitney, Notes to *Sûrya-Siddhânta*, p. 200.

of a doubt. They were divided on the same principle; each opened at the spring equinox; the first Arab sign Sharatān was strictly equivalent to the Hindu Açvini; and eighteen constellations in each were virtually coincident. The model of the *sieu* was, however, also regarded. Eighteen Chinese determinants were included in the Arab asterisms, and of these five or six were not *nakshatra* stars; consequently, they must have been taken directly from the Chinese series. Nor were the Greek signs without effect in determining the names of the *manāzil*,[1] the late appearance of which, in a complete form, removes all difficulty in accounting for the various foreign influences brought to bear upon them. They were first enumerated by Alfarghāni early in the 9th century, when the Arabs were in astronomy the avowed disciples of the Hindus. But, although they then received perhaps their earliest quasi-scientific organization, the mansions of the moon had for ages previously figured in the popular lore of the Bedouin. A set of twenty-eight rhymes associated their heliacal risings with the changes of season and the vicissitudes of nomad life; their settings were of meteorological and astrological import;[2] in the Koran (x. 5) they are regarded as indispensable for the reckoning of time. Yet even this intimate penetration into the modes of thought of the desert may be explained by prehistoric Indian communication. The alternative view, advocated by Weber, that the lunar zodiac was primitively Chaldæan, rests on a very shadowy foundation. It is true that a word radically identical with *manāzil* occurs twice in the Bible, under the forms *mazzaloth* and *mazzaroth* (2 Kings xxiii. 5; Job xxxviii. 32); but the heavenly halting-places which it seems to designate may be solar rather than lunar. Euphratean exploration has so far brought to light no traces of ecliptical partition by the moon's diurnal motion, unless, indeed, zodiacal associations be claimed for a set of twenty-eight deprecatory formulæ against evil spirits inscribed on a Ninevite tablet.[3]

The safest general conclusions regarding this disputed subject appear to be that the *sieu*, distinctively and unvaryingly Chinese, cannot properly be described as divisions of a lunar zodiac, that the *nakshatras*, though of purely Indian origin, became modified by the successive adoption of Greek and Chinese rectifications and supposed improvements; while the *manāzil* constituted a frankly eclectic system, in which elements from all quarters were combined. It was adopted by Turks, Tartars, and Persians, and forms part of the astronomical paraphernalia of the *Bundehish*. The *sieu*, on the other hand, were early naturalized in Japan.

The refined system of astrological prediction based upon the solar zodiac was invented in Chaldæa, obtained a second home and added elaborations in Egypt, and spread irresistibly westward about the beginning of our era. For genethliacal purposes the signs were divided into six solar and six lunar, the former counted onward from Leo, the "house" of the sun, the latter backward from the moon's domicile in Cancer. Each planet had two houses—a solar and a lunar—distributed according to the order of their revolutions. Thus Mercury, as the planet nearest the sun, obtained Virgo, the sign adjacent to Leo, with the corresponding lunar house in Gemini; Venus had Libra (solar) and Taurus (lunar); and so for the rest. A ram frequently stamped on coins of Antiochus, with head reverted towards the moon and a star (the planet Mars), signified Aries to be the lunar house of Mars. With the respective and relative positions in the zodiac of the sun, moon, and planets, the character of their action on human destiny varied indefinitely. The influence of the signs, though secondary, was hence overmastering: Julian called them θεῶν δυνάμεις,[4] and they were the objects of a corresponding veneration. Cities and kingdoms were allotted to their several patronage on a system fully expounded by Manilius:—

> Hos erit in fines orbis pontusque notandus,
> Quem Deus in partes per singula dividit astra,
> Ac sua cuique dedit tutelæ regna per orbem,
> Et proprias gentes atque urbes addidit altas,
> In quibus exercent præstantia sidera vires.[5]

Syria was assigned to Aries, and Syrian coins frequently bear the effigy of a ram; Scythia and Arabia fell to Taurus, India to Gemini. Palmyra, judging from numismatic evidence, claimed the favour of Libra, Zeugma that of Capricorn; Leo protected Miletus, Sagittarius Singara.[6] The "power of the signs" was similarly distributed among the parts of the human body:—

> Et quanquam communis eat tutela per omne
> Corpus, et in proprium divisis artubus exit:
> Namque aries capiti, taurus cervicibus hæret;
> Brachia sub geminis censentur, pectora cancro.[7]

Warnings were uttered against surgical treatment of a member through whose sign the moon happened to be passing;[8] and zodiacal anatomy was an indispensable branch of the healing art in the Middle Ages. Some curious memorials of the superstition have survived in rings and amulets, engraven with the various signs, and worn as a kind of astral defensive armour. Many such, of the 14th and 15th centuries, have been recovered from the Thames.[9] Individuals, too, adopted zodiacal emblems. Capricornus was impressed upon the coins of Augustus, Libra on those of Pythodoris, queen of Pontus; a sultan of Iconium displayed Leo as his "horoscope" and mark of sovereignty; Stephen of England chose the protection of Sagittarius.

Egyptian astrology.

In Egypt celestial influences were considered as emanating mainly from the thirty-six "decans" of the signs. They were called the "media of the whole circle of the zodiac;"[10] each ten-day period of the Egyptian year was consecrated to the decanal god whose section of the ecliptic rose at its commencement; the body was correspondingly apportioned, and disease was cured by invoking the zodiacal regent of the part affected.[11] As early as the 14th century B.C. a complete list of the decans was placed among the hieroglyphs adorning the tomb of Sethos I.; they figured again in the temple of Rameses II.,[12] and characterize every Egyptian astrological monument. Both the famous zodiacs of Dendera display their symbols, unmistakably identified by Lepsius. The late origin of these interesting representations was established by the detection upon them of the cartouches of Tiberius and Nero. As the date of inception of the circular one now at Paris the year 46 B.C. has, however, been suggested with high probability, from (among other indications) the position among the signs of the emblem of the planet Jupiter.[13] Its design was most likely to serve as a sort of *thema cœli* at the time of the birth of Cæsarion. The companion rectangular zodiac still *in situ* on the portico of the temple of Isis at Dendera suits, as to constellational arrangements, the date 29 A.D. It set forth, there is reason to believe, the natal scheme, not of the emperor Tiberius, as had been conjectured by Lauth,[14] but of the building it served to decorate. The Greek signs of the zodiac, including Libra, are obvious upon both these monuments, which have thrown some useful light upon the calendar system and method of stellar grouping of the ancient Egyptians.[15]

Planispheres

An Egypto-Greek planisphere, first described by Bianchini,[16] resembles in its general plan the circular zodiac of Dendera. The decans are ranged on the outermost of its five concentric zones; the planets and the Greek zodiac in duplicate occupy the next three; while the inner circle is unaccountably reserved for the Chinese cyclical animals. The relic was dug up on the Aventine in 1705, and is now in the Louvre. It dates from the 2d or 3d century of our era. The Tartar zodiac is not unfrequently found engraven on Chinese mirrors in polished bronze or steel of the 7th century, and figured on the "plateau of the twelve hours" in the treasury of the emperors of the Tang dynasty.[17]

Probably the most ancient zodiacal representation in existence is a fragment of a Chaldæan planisphere in the British Museum, once inscribed with the names of the twelve months and their governing signs. Two only now remain.[18] A zodiac on the "astrological altar of Gabies" in the Louvre illustrates the apportionment of the signs among the inmates of the Roman Pantheon;[19] and they occur

[1] Whitney, Notes to *Sûrya-Siddhânta*, p. 206.
[2] A. Sprenger, *Z. D. M. G.*, vol. xiii. p. 161; Bīrūnī, *Chronology*, trans. by Sachau (London, 1879), p. 336 *sq.*
[3] Lenormant, *Chaldean Magic*, p. 1.
[4] 'Orat. in Solem," *Op.*, vol. i. p. 148, ed. 1696.
[5] *Astr.*, bk. iv., ver. 696 *sq.*
[6] Eckhel, *Descriptio Nummorum Antiochiæ Syriæ*, pp. 18, 25.
[7] Manilius, *Astr.*, bk. iv. ver. 702-5.
[8] A. J. Peirce, *Science of the Stars*, p. 84.
[9] *Journ. Arch. Soc.*, xiii. pp. 254, 310, and xx. p. 80.
[10] In a fragment of *Hermes* translated by Th. Taylor at p. 362 of his version of Iamblichus.
[11] Pettigrew, *Superstitions Connected with Hist. of Medicine*, p. 30
[12] Lepsius, *Chronologie der Aegypter*, part i. p. 68.
[13] *Ibid.*, p. 102. [14] *Les Zodiaques de Denderah*, p. 78.
[15] See Riel's *Das feste Jahr von Denderah*, 1878.
[16] *Mém. de l'Acad.*, Paris, 1708, Hist., p. 110; see also Humboldt, *Vues des Cordillères*, p. 170; Lepsius, *op. cit.*, p. 83; Fröhner, *Sculpture du Louvre*, p. 17.
[17] Schlegel, *Ur. Chin.*, p. 561; Pettigrew, *Jour. Arch. Soc.*, vol. viii. p. 21. [18] Fox Talbot, *Trans. Soc. Bibl. Archæol.*, vol. iv. p. 260.
[19] Ménard, *La Mythologie dans l'Art*, p. 388.

Zodiacal symbols in architecture. as a classical reminiscence in the mosaic pavements of San Miniato and the baptistery at Florence, the cathedral of Lyons, and the crypt of San Savino at Piacenza.[1] Zodiacal symbolism became conspicuous in mediæval art. Nearly all the French cathedrals of the 12th and 13th centuries exhibit on their portals a species of rural calendar, in which each month and sign has its corresponding labour. The zodiac of Notre Dame of Paris, opening with Aquarius, is a noted instance.[2] A similar series, in which sculptured figures of Christ and the Apostles are associated with the signs, is to be seen in perfect preservation on the chief doorway of the abbey church at Vézelay. The cathedrals of Amiens, Sens, and Rheims are decorated in the same way. In Italy the signs and works survive fragmentarily in the baptistery at Parma, completely on the porch of the cathedral of Cremona and on the west doorway of St Mark's at Venice. They are less common in England; but St Margaret's, York, and the church of Iffley in Oxfordshire offer good specimens. In the zodiac of Merton College, Oxford, Libra is represented by a judge in his robes and Pisces by the dolphin of Fitzjames, warden of the college, 1482-1507.[3] The great rose-windows of the Early Gothic period were frequently painted with zodiacal emblems; and some frescos in the cathedral of Cologne contain the signs, each with an attendant angel, just as they were depicted on the vault of the church at Mount Athos. Giotto's zodiac at Padua was remarkable (in its undisturbed condition) for the arrangement of the signs so as to be struck in turns, during the corresponding months, by the sun's rays.[4] The "zodiac of labours" was replaced in French castles and hôtels by a "zodiac of pleasures," in which hunting, hawking, fishing, and dancing were substituted for hoeing, planting, reaping, and ploughing.[5]

It is curious to find the same sequence of symbols employed for the same decorative purposes in India as in Europe. A perfect set of signs was copied in 1764 from a pagoda at Verdapettah near Cape Comorin, and one equally complete existed at the same period on the ceiling of a temple near Mindurah.[6]

Zodiacal hieroglyphs. The hieroglyphs representing the signs of the zodiac in astronomical works are of late introduction. They are found in manuscripts of about the 10th century, but in carvings not until the 15th or 16th.[7] Their origin is unknown; but some, if not all of them, have antique associations. The hieroglyph of Leo, for instance, occurs among the symbols of the Mithraic worship.[8] (A. M. C.)

ZODIACAL LIGHT. The zodiacal light is usually described as a cone or lenticularly-shaped glow of nebulous light, seen after sunset or before sunrise, extending upwards from the position of the sun nearly in the direction of the ecliptic or of the sun's equator. This description, though fairly correct for the higher latitudes, does not represent accurately what is seen in the tropics, where the light is often a very conspicuous object. There, if an observer on a clear, moonless night watches the western sky from soon after sunset till the last trace of twilight has disappeared, he will notice that the twilight seems to linger longer near where the sun sank below the horizon, and that gradually a nebulous whitish band of light, broad towards the horizon and narrowing first rapidly and then more slowly upwards, begins to stand out clearly from the vanishing twilight, which spreads along a much wider and nearly horizontally-topped arc of the horizon. This is the zodiacal light. When seen on a perfectly clear night, it will be noticed that it fades imperceptibly on both borders and towards the vertex, and that its light is distinctly brighter towards the base than at greater altitudes. Its width and brightness, and the height of the vertex, differ very much from time to time, partly on account of actual variations, but much more from differences in the transparency of the atmosphere. In England it is seldom observed except in the months of March, April, and May shortly after sunset, or about October before sunrise. This is due to no change in the light itself, but simply to the circumstance that at other seasons the ecliptic makes so small an angle with the horizon that a light lying in or near it does not rise sufficiently high above the mists of the horizon to be seen after the twilight has vanished. In lower latitudes, where the angle made with the horizon is greater, while the duration of twilight is shorter, it can be easily seen at all seasons when there is a clear sky and no moon, except when Venus is an evening star, in which case the great brightness of that planet often almost completely obliterates the comparatively faint zodiacal light, at least in its neighbourhood. The zodiacal light has frequently been described as having a reddish yellow tint; but this seems to be erroneous, for, when seen under favourable conditions, it is distinctly white and very similar to that of the Milky Way. Any colour that may have been observed is doubtless due to atmospheric causes.

Among the Moslems, to whom it is important on ritual grounds to determine accurately the moment of daybreak, at which during Ramadan the daily fast begins, the morning zodiacal light appears to have been observed from an early period, and is known as the "false dawn" or the "wolf's tail" (Redhouse, in *Journ. R. A. S.*, July 1878). But in Christian Europe it seems to have been first observed by Kepler, who described its appearance with considerable accuracy and came to the conclusion that it was the atmosphere of the sun. Descartes wrote about it in 1630 and Childrey in 1659; but the attention of astronomers was first prominently called to it by Dominic Cassini, who first saw it on 18th March 1683. It is to him that it owes the name which it now bears. He explained it by supposing the existence of a flat, luminous ring encircling the sun, nearly in the plane of his equator, and accounted for its disappearance on the same principle as that which accounts for the vanishing of Saturn's ring. Mairan (1731), like Kepler, ascribed the light to the sun's atmosphere; and this explanation was generally accepted, till Laplace showed that it was untenable, since no real solar atmosphere could extend to anything like the distance from the sun which is reached by the zodiacal light. He further showed that, even if the solar atmosphere did extend far enough, it would not have the lenticular appearance ascribed by observers to the zodiacal light, since the polar axis would be at least two-thirds of the equatorial axis. Since then many observers have made a study of the subject, amongst whom may be mentioned Jones, Piazzi Smyth, Jacob, Brorsen, Schmidt, Backhouse, Liais, and Wright.

Extent.—The way in which the light fades off gradually towards the boundaries makes it extremely difficult to determine accurately the true position of the light or its extent. Various observations show that at times the base, at an elongation of about 20°, may have a width of from 25° to 30°, while at an elongation of 60° the breadth is frequently as much as 20°, but usually much less. The distance of the vertex from the sun frequently exceeds 90°, and Mr Liais and others have recorded cases when the light has been traced completely round from the western to the eastern horizon. This is very uncommon; but it is not at all rare to find the light stretching nearly to the meridian three hours after sunset, and several observers have recorded the existence of a bright patch of light almost opposite to the position of the sun. This is known as the *Gegenschein*, and though it has been seen comparatively seldom its existence must be accepted as proved; for its position has been determined by actual measurement by several astronomers, and their results agree with quite as great closeness as can be expected in the determination of the position of such an object. A lengthened series of observations was made on the zodiacal light by the Rev. G. Jones, chaplain of the United States steam frigate "Mississippi," in the China and Japan Seas in 1855. He charted the apparent position of the cone of light on a large number of nights and mornings, and came to the somewhat startling conclusion that his observations could be explained only by supposing the existence of a nebulous ring round the earth within the orbit of the moon. He recorded that twice near 23° 28′ N. lat., with the sun at the opposite solstice, he had seen "the extraordinary spectacle of the zodiacal light simultaneously at both the east and west horizons from 11 to 1

[1] Fowler, *Archæologia*, vol. xliv. p. 172.

[2] Viollet-le-Duc, *Dict. de l'Arch. Française*, vol. ix. p. 551; Le Gentil, *Mém. de l'Acad.*, Paris, 1785, p. 20.

[3] Fowler, *Archæologia*, vol. xliv. p. 150.

[4] *Ibid.*, p. 175.

[5] Viollet-le-Duc, *Dict. de l'Arch.*, vol. ix. p. 551.

[6] John Call, *Phil. Trans.*, vol. lxii. p. 353. Comp. Houzeau, *Bibliographie Astronomique*, vol. i. pt. i. p. 136, where a useful sketch of the general results of zodiacal research will be found.

[7] R. Brown, *Archæologia*, vol. xlvii. p. 341; Sayce, in *Nature*, vol. xxv. p. 525.

[8] See Lajard, *Culte de Mithra*, pl. xxvii. fig. 5, &c.

o'clock for several nights in succession." On reading this statement, Baron Humboldt communicated to the *Monatsberichte d. kön. preuss. Akad. d. Wiss.* some unpublished observations of his own on a similar phenomenon. These were to the effect that on the 17th and 18th of March the light was very bright in the west, and "we constantly perceived in the east (and this is beyond doubt a very striking phenomenon) a whitish light which was also of a pyramidal form. The latter augmented the brightness of the sky in a very striking manner." The light in the west was so conspicuous that "even the sailors were delighted with this double light." He noted, too, what is a very important fact, that the two lights set at the same time; and there is much to be said in defence of his view that the eastern light was the reflexion of the true zodiacal light in the west, just as the eastern sunset glows are the reflexion of those in the west. The chief obstacle in the way of accepting this view is that it is difficult to believe that a light so faint as the zodiacal light could have a reflexion bright enough to be seen, and even to be seen distinctly. On the other side must be set the circumstance that the simultaneous glow at both horizons seems never to have been observed from great altitudes. This is easily understood if the second glow is a mere reflexion; whereas, if it comes from another source of light, it ought to be more conspicuous at high than at low levels.

Position.—The exact position of the axis of the zodiacal light relatively to the ecliptic has not yet been satisfactorily fixed. The extreme haziness of outline and the excessive faintness of the light near the vertex make it quite impossible to use a telescope for measuring its limits. Most observers have tried to fix its position by tracing its outline on a star chart, while Prof. C. Piazzi Smyth employed two sights mounted equatorially. But even by these means no great accuracy can be attained, for the limits of the light can be traced only when the eye is quite unfatigued and when the light is looked at with averted vision. The difficulty experienced is well illustrated by the wide divergencies between the results of different observers—divergencies not only in the extent of the light, which would be quite natural, but even in the direction of the axis of the cone. Thus, Captain Jacob, who observed in Madras in 1856-57-58, found that his evening observations placed the vertex of the western cone in from 2° S. lat. to 6° N. lat., with an average of about 3° N. lat. His morning observations were less numerous and gave positions for the vertex of the eastern cone varying from ½° N. to 8° S., with an average of about 2° S. Mr Backhouse from 418 observations found a mean deviation from the ecliptic of 2°·06, while Captain Tupman, observing in the Mediterranean in August and September, found an inclination of no less than 20°. He also found that the plane of the light did not pass through the sun. His observations, however, differ somewhat widely from those of most other observers. Mr A. Searle has made a very careful study of all the best published records. In his first paper more than 650 observations by Jones, Heis, Schmidt, and others are discussed, and he concludes that apparent changes in latitude are mainly, if not entirely, produced by the effect of atmospheric absorption, which affects the lower boundary more than the upper and to an extent depending on the inclination of the axis of the light to the horizon. In a second paper he discusses Jones's observations alone and comes to the conclusion that, after making allowance for the effects of absorption, there is some evidence that the zodiacal light, as seen during the second half of the 19th century, has had a more northern latitude near 180° long. than near 0° long. It seems somewhat doubtful, however, whether the observations hitherto made are sufficiently accurate to justify this conclusion, and all that can be confidently asserted is that the observations made so far point to such a difference as being probable. Similar variations in the greatest elongation, the breadth, and the brightness have been asserted to exist. Thus Mr J. F. Julius Schmidt, as the result of several years' observations, finds a variation in the inclination of the axis of the cone of light to the ecliptic from 4° 18′ at the end of December to 0° towards the end of March, a similar variation in the greatest elongation from the sun from 120° in January to 70° in April, and a further similar variation in breadth at corresponding elongations, with a minimum for all three about 30th March. It may be pointed out that observations regarding the extent of the visible light are absolutely valueless unless accompanied by careful records of the clearness of the sky as evidenced by the visibility of faint objects, for all observers of the zodiacal light must have noticed that a thin film of mist, which hardly affects the colour of the sky or the visibility of the brighter stars, may almost completely obliterate the zodiacal light. No accurate photometric observations seem to have been made on the strength of the light and observers have differed widely in their estimates. Some assert that it is much brighter than the Milky Way, while others—and especially those who have observed in the tropics—say that it is seldom so bright as the brighter parts of the Milky Way. It is certainly often brighter than most of the Milky Way. Mr Searle deduces from Sir W. Herschel's and Celoria's observations that the Milky Way is about 2 magnitudes brighter than the mean brightness of the sky, and says that on this estimate the brighter parts of the zodiacal light would be commonly 3 or 4 magnitudes brighter than the surrounding sky. This is almost certainly an over-estimate. There seems to be very little doubt that the brightness undergoes periodic fluctuations, but no estimate can as yet be made of the length of the period. It is probable that the brightness has been below the average for the last few years, but is now increasing. Most observers have also reported rapid changes of brightness, or undulations, such as are seen in the aurora and in the tails of some comets; but, as was pointed out by Olbers in 1833, these undulations must be produced in the earth's atmosphere. In this connexion it may be mentioned that in observing the spectrum rapid flickerings, like waves moving along the spectrum, are often very marked.

The Moon's Zodiacal Light.—Several observers have recorded observations which appeared to show that the moon produced an appearance very similar to that of the zodiacal light. Piazzi Smyth, however, when observing on the Peak of Teneriffe, saw this appearance and showed by actual measurement that the glow seen before moonrise does not lie near the ecliptic, but is nearly vertical, and is due simply to refraction in the earth's atmosphere. This explanation will hardly account for an interesting observation made by Mr L. Trouvelot, which if repeated would require to be very carefully investigated. On a night when the zodiacal light was very bright and there were magnetic disturbances followed by an auroral display, but when no aurora was actually visible, he saw a conical light rising obliquely from the top of the roof of a building behind which the moon, then about 15° or 20° above the horizon, was concealed. The axis of the light coincided nearly with the ecliptic and the light could be traced on both sides of the moon, when the moon itself was concealed. The whole of the circumstances led Mr Trouvelot to conclude that this light and the zodiacal light were phenomena of the same order, while this and other observations, he considered, rendered it probable that there was some connexion between the zodiacal light and auroras.

Physical Constitution.—As has already been pointed out, it is impossible to see the zodiacal light through a telescope, and this, taken along with the extreme faintness of the light, renders it exceedingly difficult to examine it satisfactorily with either the polariscope or the spectroscope. Many attempts have been made to determine whether or not the light was to any extent polarized, but with questionable results until Prof. A. W. Wright attacked the problem, using a polariscope specially designed for studying very faint lights. With this he was enabled to determine with certainty that the light was partially polarized in a plane passing through the sun, and that the amount of polarization was most probably as much as 15 per cent., but less than 20 per cent. Many attempts have been made to observe the spectrum. In 1867 Ångström, observing at Upsala in March, obtained the bright aurora line (W. L. 5567), and concluded that in the zodiacal light there was the same material as is found in the aurora and in the solar corona, and probably through all space. Upsala, however, is a place where the aurora spectrum can often be observed in the sky even when no aurora is visible, and it has generally been believed that what Ångström really saw was an auroral and not a zodiacal light spectrum. Señor A. T. Acrimiz, observing at Cadiz, obtained a continuous but faint spectrum with two bright lines—a yellowish line, probably an aurora line, and a line in the blue, more refrangible than F, which he could not identify, but which in all probability was another auroral line. The fact that he saw this spectrum with a five-prism spectroscope attached to an equatorial seems conclusive evidence that it was not the zodiacal light spectrum that he was observing. The most satisfactory observations hitherto published seem to be those of Prof. Piazzi Smyth and Prof. A. W. Wright. Both used spectroscopes specially designed for the examination of faint lights, and their results agree completely with each other. Prof. Smyth made his observations at Palermo and found a faint continuous spectrum extending from about W. L. 5550 to W. L. 5000 (British inches scale), with a maximum brightness at about W. L. 5350. In fact, the light was almost exactly similar to that of faint diffused sunlight, such as is got in the last traces of twilight. Prof. Wright's conclusion was that the spectrum differs from that of sunlight only in intensity. Some recent unpublished observations made in the tropics indicate that, while the spectrum is usually that described by Prof. Smyth, there are times when a bright line is seen. Too much stress, however, must not be laid on this, as the observations are by no means conclusive, and the apparent line may in reality be only a part of the continuous spectrum which is brighter than usual.

The discussion of the real cause of the zodiacal light is rendered very difficult by the want of agreement in the observations that have been made upon it, and by the existence of a small number of apparently trustworthy observations of a very abnormal extension of the light, as detailed above; but certain conclusions may be safely arrived at. The theory that it is due to a ring of small bodies surrounding the earth seems to be entirely negatived, as pointed out by Proctor and others, by several of its features. The best observations leave no room for the parallactic displacement which would be observed if there were such a ring round the earth, and the absence of a large part of the luminous circle on ordinary occasions would be inexplicable on any such hypothesis. There can therefore be very little doubt that we must look for the cause of the light to the existence of a mass of small bodies moving in orbits round the sun, and that, as shown by the polarization and the spectrum, the light is chiefly, if not entirely, reflected sunlight. To account for all the observations, Proctor has shown that the bodies must travel in orbits of considerable eccentricity, carrying them far beyond the limits of what we may term the zodiacal disk. Under these conditions the constitution of the disk would become variable within exceedingly wide limits, and all the recorded variations might be fairly explained. The appearance of a complete arch, as seen by Liais and others, would indicate an extension far beyond the earth's orbit; but, at present at least, this must be looked on as very exceptional. The spectroscopic evidence, so far as it goes, confirms this theory, since it indicates that the light is mainly reflected sunlight; and, even if further observations should confirm the opinion that bright lines are sometimes present, this need in no way invalidate the conclusions that have been arrived at. Indeed, it seems highly probable—especially if Mr Lockyer's views regarding meteorites are confirmed—that bright lines should be seen in such a body of meteorites. Olbers long ago suggested that the corona was the brightest part of the zodiacal light, and there is nothing in recent observations to contradict this view, for all observations go to show that the outer corona has no definite boundary, but shades off imperceptibly and becomes invisible at a great distance from the sun. Dr Huggins, while holding that the corona is most probably due to the ceaseless outflow of extremely minute particles from the sun, thinks it not improbable that the zodiacal light may be in some way connected with this outflow. Dr Siemens, when discussing his theory of the conservation of solar energy, sought for an explanation of the zodiacal light in the dust which he supposed to be ejected from equatorial regions, rendered luminous partly by reflected sunlight, partly by phosphorescence, and partly by electrical action.

With the increasing number of observatories at high altitudes it may fairly be hoped that before long astronomers will be put in possession of such definite measurements as will enable some at least of the points still under discussion to be finally settled, and that far more accurate observations will soon be available on which to construct a satisfactory theory.

Bibliography.—Childrey, *Natural History of England* (1659) and *Britannia Baconica*, p. 183 (1661); Cassini (D.), *Nouv. Phénom. d'une lumière céleste* [zodiacale] (1683) and *Découverte de la lumière céleste qui paroist dans le zodiaque* (1685); Hooke (R.), *Explication of a Glade of Light*, &c. (1685); Mairan, *Observations de la lumière zodiacale*; Euler (L.), *Sur la cause de la lumière zodiacale* (1746); Mairan, *Sur la cause de la lumière zodiacale* (1747); Wolf (R.), *Beobachtungen des Zodiacallichtes* (1850-52); Brorsen, *Ueber den Gegenschein des Zodiacallichts* (1855) and in Schumacher, 998; Schmidt (J. F. J.), *Das Zodiacallicht*, Brunswick (1856), and in *Astron. Nachr.*, lxxiii. p. 199; Jacob, *Memoirs R.A.S.*, xxviii. p. 119; Jones (G.), in Gould, No. 84, in *Monthly Notices R.A.S.*, xvi. p. 18, and in *U. S. Exploring Expedition Narrative*, vol. iii. (1856); Humboldt, in *Monatsber. d. k. preuss Akad. d. Wiss.*, July 1855, also in *M. Not. R.A.S.*, xvi. p. 16; Smyth (C. P.), in *Trans. R.S.E.*, xx. p. 489 (1852), and in *M. Not. R.A.S.*, xvii. p. 204 and xxxii. p. 277; Backhouse (T. W.), in *M. Not. R.A.S.*, xxxvi. p. 1 and xli. p. 333; Tupman, in *M. Not. R.A.S.*, xxxii. p. 74; Liais, in *Comptes Rendus*, lxiv. p. 262 (January 1872); Wright (A. W.), in *Amer. Jour. of Science*, cvii. p. 451 and cviii. p. 39; Ångström, in *Pogg. Annal.*, cxxxvii. p. 162; Searle (Arthur), in *Proc. Amer. Acad.*, xix. p. 146 and vol. xi. p. 135; and Trouvelot, in *Proc. Amer. Acad.*, xiii. p. 183 (1877). (C. M. S.)

ZOHAR. See KABBALAH.

ZÖLLNER, JOHANN CARL FRIEDRICH (1834-1882), astronomer and physicist, was born at Berlin on 8th November 1834. From 1872 he held the chair of astrophysics at Leipsic university. He is the author of numerous papers on photometry and spectrum analysis in *Poggendorff's Annalen* and *Berichte der k. sächsischen Gesellschaft der Wissenschaften*, of two works on astronomical photometry (*Grundzüge einer allgemeinen Photometrie des Himmels*, Berlin, 1861, 4to, and *Photometrische Untersuchungen*, Leipsic, 1865, 8vo), and of a very strange book, *Ueber die Natur der Cometen* (Leipsic, 1872, 8vo). He died at Leipsic on 25th April 1882.

Zöllner's "astrophotometer" compares the light of a star as seen in a telescope with that of an artificial star produced by a paraffin lamp. From the latter the light passes through three Nicol's prisms, of which two can be turned so as to vary the intensity of the light, the latter being proportional to the square of the cosine of the angle through which the prisms are turned, which angle is read off on a small circle. In order to vary the colour of the artificial star, so as to make it resemble the natural star as much as possible, there is inserted between the first and second prisms a plate of left-handed quartz, cut perpendicular to the axis, the rotation of which is read off on another circle. This instrument has been used by Zöllner, Lindemann, Engelmann, J. T. Wolff, and others for photometric observations of stars and planets; but it labours under several defects, among which the difficulty of keeping the flame of the lamp at a constant height is the most serious.

ZOMBOR, a royal free city of Hungary, the capital of the county of Bács-Bodrog, lies about 120 miles south of Budapest in a fertile plain, on the Francis Canal that connects the Danube and the Theiss. The town has some fine streets and squares, and several handsome buildings, among which may be mentioned the county and town halls, the theatre, and the Roman Catholic and Greek churches. Zombor is a station on the Alföld-Fiume Railway and the centre of the corn and cattle trade of an extensive area. The population numbered 24,693 in 1880 and about 31,000 in 1886.

ZONARAS, JOANNES, historian and theologian, flourished at Constantinople in the 12th century. Under Alexius I. Comnenus he held the offices of commander of the bodyguard and private secretary to the emperor, but in the succeeding reign he retired to Mount Athos, where he spent the rest of his life in writing his books. He is said to have lived to the age of eighty-eight.

His most important work, the *Chronicon*, is in eighteen books, and extends from the creation of the world to the death of Alexius (1118). The earlier part is largely drawn from Josephus; for Roman history he chiefly followed Dion Cassius, whose first twenty books are only known to us through Zonaras. Of contemporary events which he himself witnessed he writes more briefly and meagrely than might have been expected. His history was continued by Nicetas Acominatus. Among the other works of Zonaras is an *Exposition of the Apostolical Canons*. The *Chronicon* or *Annals* was first printed at Basel in 1557; Du Cange next edited it in 1686; and it also forms part of the Bonn collection of Byzantine writers, having been edited by Pinder (2 vols.) in 1841-44. The latest edition is by Dindorf, with Du Cange's notes (6 vols. 8vo, Leipsic, 1868-75). The *Opera Omnia Historica, Canonica, Dogmatica*, were published by Migne in 2 vols. 4to, at Paris in 1865. A lexicon, also attributed to Zonaras, has been edited by Tittmann (Leipsic. 1808).

ZOOLOGY

THE branch of science to which the name zoology is strictly applicable may be defined as that portion of biology which relates to animals, as distinguished from that portion which is concerned with plants.

Relation of biology to other sciences.

The science of biology itself has been placed by Mr Herbert Spencer in the group of concrete sciences, the other groups recognized by that writer being the "abstract-concrete" and the "abstract." The abstract sciences are logic and mathematics, and treat of the blank forms in which phenomena occur in relation to time, space, and number. The abstract-concrete sciences are mechanics, physics, and chemistry. The title assigned to them is justified by the fact that, whilst their subject-matter is found in a consideration of varied concrete phenomena, they do not aim at the explanation of complex concrete phenomena as such, but at the determination of certain "abstract" quantitative relations and sequences known as the "laws" of mechanics, physics, and chemistry, which never are manifested in a pure form, but always are inferred by observation and experiment upon complex phenomena in which the abstract laws are disguised by their simultaneous interaction. The group of concrete sciences includes astronomy, geology, biology, and sociology. These sciences have for their aim to "explain" the concrete complex phenomena of (*a*) the sidereal system, (*b*) the earth as a whole, (*c*) the living matter on the earth's surface, (*d*) human society, by reference to the properties of matter set forth in the generalizations or laws of the abstract-concrete sciences, *i.e.*, of mechanics, physics, and chemistry.

The classification thus sketched exhibits, whatever its practical demerits, the most important fact with regard to biology, namely, that it is the aim or business of those occupied with that branch of science to assign living things, in all their variety of form and activity, to the one set of forces recognized by the physicist and chemist. Just as the astronomer accounts for the heavenly bodies and their movements by the laws of motion and the property of attraction, as the geologist explains the present state of the earth's crust by the long-continued action of the same forces which at this moment are studied and treated in the form of "laws" by physicists and chemists, so the biologist seeks to explain in all its details the long process of the evolution of the innumerable forms of life now existing, or which have existed in the past, as a necessary outcome, an automatic product, of these same forces.

Science may be defined as the knowledge of causes; and, so long as biology was not a conscious attempt to ascertain the causes of living things, it could not be rightly grouped with other branches of science. For a very long period the two parallel divisions of biology,—botany and zoology,—were actually limited to the accumulation of observations, which were noted, tabulated, and contemplated by the students of these subjects with wonder and delight, but only to a limited extent and in restricted classes of facts with any hope or intention of connecting the phenomena observed with the great nexus of physical sequence or causation. A vague desire to assign the forms and the activities of living things in all their variety to general causes has always been present to thoughtful observers from the earliest times of which we have record, but the earlier attempts in this direction were fantastic in the extreme; and it is the mere truth that, at the time when the phenomena of inorganic nature had been recognized as the outcome of uniform and constant properties capable of analysis and measurement, living things were still left hopelessly out of the domain of explanation, the earlier theories having been rejected and nothing as yet suggested in their place.

Scope of the history of zoology.

The history of zoology as a science is therefore the history of the great biological doctrine of the evolution of living things by the natural selection of varieties in the struggle for existence,—since that doctrine is the one medium whereby all the phenomena of life, whether of form or function, are rendered capable of explanation by the laws of physics and chemistry, and so made the subject-matter of a true science or study of causes. A history of zoology must take account of the growth of those various kinds of information with regard to animal life which have been arrived at in past ages through the labours of a long series of ardent lovers of nature, who in each succeeding period have more and more carefully and accurately tested, proved, arranged, and tabulated their knowledge, until at last the accumulated lore of centuries—almost without the consciousness of its latest heirs and cultivators—took the form of the doctrine of descent and the filiation of the animal series.

HISTORY.

There is something almost pathetic in the childish wonder and delight with which mankind in its earlier phases of civilization gathered up and treasured stories of strange animals from distant lands or deep seas, such as are recorded in the *Physiologus*, in Albertus Magnus, and even at the present day in the popular treatises of Japan and China. That omnivorous universally credulous stage, which may be called the "legendary," was succeeded by the age of collectors and travellers, when many of the strange stories believed in were actually demonstrated as true by the living or preserved trophies brought to Europe by adventurous navigators. The possibility of verification established verification as a habit; and the collecting of *things*, instead of the accumulating of *reports*, developed a new faculty of minute observation. The early collectors of natural curiosities were the founders of zoological science, and to this day the naturalist-traveller and his correlative, the museum curator and systematist, play a most important part in the progress of zoology. Indeed, the historical and present importance of this aspect or branch of zoological science is so great that the name "zoology" has until recently been associated entirely with it, to the exclusion of the study of minute anatomical structure and function which have been distinguished as anatomy and physiology. It is a curious result of the steps of the historical progress of the two divisions of biological science that, whilst the word "botany" has always been understood, and is at the present day understood, as embracing the study, not only of the external forms of plants, their systematic nomenclature and classification, and their geographical distribution, but also the study of their minute structure, their organs of nutrition and reproduction, and the mode of action of the mechanism furnished by those organs, the word "zoology" has been limited to such a knowledge of animals as the travelling sportsman could acquire in making his collections of skins of beasts and birds, of dried insects and molluscs' shells, and such a knowledge as the museum curator could acquire by the examination and classification of these portable objects. Anatomy and the study of animal mechanism, animal physics, and animal chemistry, all of which form part of a true zoology, have been excluded from the usual definition of the word by the mere accident that the zoologist of the last three centuries has had his museum but has not had his garden of living specimens as the botanist has had;[1] and, whilst the zoologist has thus

Era of collectors and travellers.

[1] The mediæval attitude towards both plants and animals had no

for a long time been deprived of the means of anatomical and physiological study—only supplied within the past century by the method of preserving animal bodies in alcohol—the demands of medicine for a knowledge of the structure of the human animal have in the meantime brought into existence a separate and special study of human anatomy and physiology.

Relation to anatomy and physiology. From these special studies of human structure the knowledge of the anatomy of animals has proceeded, the same investigator who had made himself acquainted with the structure of the human body desiring to compare with the standard given by human anatomy the structures of other animals. Thus comparative anatomy came into existence as a branch of inquiry apart from zoology, and it is only now, in the latter part of the 19th century, that the limitation of the word "zoology" to a knowledge of animals which expressly excludes the consideration of their internal structure has been rejected by the general consent of those concerned in the progress of science; it is now generally recognized that it is mere tautology to speak of zoology *and* comparative anatomy, and that our museum naturalists must give attention as well to the inside as to the outside of animals.

The anatomy and physiology of plants have never been excluded from the attention of botanists, because in contrast to the earlier zoologists they always were in possession of the whole living plant, raised from seed if need be in a hot-house, instead of having only a dried skin, skeleton, or shell. Consequently the study of vegetable anatomy and physiology has grown up naturally and in a healthy way in strict relation to the rest of botanical knowledge, whilst animal anatomy and physiology have been external to zoology in origin, the product of the medical profession and, as a consequence, subjected to a misleading anthropocentric method.

Restricted use of the term physiology. Whilst we may consider the day as gone by in which zoology could be regarded as connoting solely a special museum knowledge of animals (as twenty-five years ago was still the case), it is interesting to observe by the way the curious usurpation of the word "physiology," which, from having a wide connotation, indicated by its etymology,—the *physiologus* of the Middle Ages being nothing more nor less than the naturalist or student of nature,—has in these later days acquired a limitation which it is difficult to justify or explain. Physiology to-day means the study of the physical and chemical properties of the animal or vegetable body, and is even distinguished from the study of structure and strictly confined to the study of function. It would hardly be in place here to discuss at length the steps by which physiology became thus limited, any more than to trace those by which the words "physician" and "physicist" (which both mean one who occupies himself with nature) came to signify respectively a medical practitioner and a student of the laws of mechanics, heat, light, and electricity (but not of chemistry), whilst the word "naturalist" is very usually limited to a lover and student of living things, to the exclusion of the so-called physicist, the chemist, and the astronomer. It is probable that physiology acquired its present significance, viz., the study of the properties and functions of the tissues and organs of living things, by a process of external attraction and spoliation which gradually removed from the original *physiologus* all his belongings and assigned them to newly named and independently constituted sciences, leaving at last, as a *residuum* to which the word might still be applied, that medical aspect of life which is concerned with the workings of the living organism regarded as a piece of physico-chemical apparatus.

Rise of scientific zoology Whatever may be the history of the word "physiology," we find zoology, which really started in the 16th century with the awakening of the new spirit of observation and exploration, for a long time running a separate course uninfluenced by the progress of the medical studies of anatomy and physiology. The history of every branch of science involves a recognition of the history, not only of other branches of science, but of the progress of human society in every other relation. The century which destroyed the authority of the church, witnessed the discovery of the New World, and in England produced the writings of Francis Bacon is rightly regarded as the starting-point of the modern knowledge of natural causes or science. The true history of zoology as a science lies within the three last centuries; and, whilst the theories and fables which were current in earlier times in regard to animal life and the various kinds of animals form an important subject of study from the point of view of the history of the development of the human mind, they really have no bearing upon the history of scientific zoology. The great awakening of western Europe in the 16th century led to an active search for knowledge by means of observation and experiment, which found its natural home in the universities. Owing to the connexion of medicine with these seats of learning, it was natural that the study of the structure and functions of the human body and of the animals nearest to man should take root there; the spirit of inquiry which now for the first time became general showed itself in the anatomical schools of the Italian universities of the 16th century, and spread fifty years later to Oxford.

Influence of academies and societies. In the 17th century the lovers of the new philosophy, the investigators of nature by means of observation and experiment, banded themselves into academies or societies for mutual support and intercourse. It is difficult to exaggerate the importance of the influence which has been exercised by these associations upon the progress of all branches of science and of zoology especially. The essential importance of academies is to be found, as Laplace, the great French astronomer, has said, "in the philosophic spirit which develops itself in them and spreads itself from them as centres over an entire nation and all relations. The isolated man of science can give himself up to dogmatism without restraint; he hears contradictions only from afar. But in a learned society the enunciation of dogmatic views leads rapidly to their destruction, and the desire of each member to convince the others necessarily leads to the agreement to admit nothing excepting what is the result of observation or of mathematical calculation."

The first founded of surviving European academies, the Academia Naturæ Curiosorum (1651),[1] especially confined itself to the description and illustration of the structure of plants and animals; eleven years later (1662) the Royal Society of London was incorporated by royal charter, having existed without a name or fixed organization for seventeen years previously (from 1645). A little later the Academy of Sciences of Paris was established by Louis XIV. The influence of these great academies of the 17th century on the progress of zoology was precisely to effect that bringing together of the museum-men and the physicians or anatomists which was needed for further development. Whilst the race of collectors and systematizers culminated in the latter part of the 18th century

relation to real knowledge, but was part of a peculiar and in itself highly interesting mysticism. A fantastic and elaborate doctrine of symbolism existed which comprised all nature; witchcraft, alchemy, and medicine were its practical expressions. Animals as well as plants were regarded as "simples" and used in medicine, and a knowledge of them was valued from this point of view. Plants were collected and cultivated for medicinal use; hence the physic gardens and the botanist's advantage.

[1] The Academia Secretorum Naturæ was founded at Naples in 1560, but was suppressed by the ecclesiastical authorities.

in Linnæus, a new type of student made its appearance in such men as John Hunter and other anatomists, who, not satisfied with the superficial observations of the popular "zoologists," set themselves to work to examine anatomically the whole animal kingdom, and to classify its members by aid of the results of such profound study. From them we pass to the comparative anatomists of the 19th century and the introduction of the microscope as a serious instrument of accurate observation.

The influence of the scientific academies and the spirit in which they worked in the 17th century cannot be better illustrated than by an examination of the early records of the Royal Society of London. The spirit which animated the founders and leaders of that society is clearly indicated in its motto "Nullius in verba." Marvellous narrations were not permitted at the meetings of the society, but solely demonstrative experiments or the exhibition of actual specimens. Definite rules were laid down by the society for its guidance, designed to ensure the collection of solid facts and the testing of statements embodying novel or remarkable observations. Under the influence of the touchstone of strict inquiry set on foot by the Royal Society, the marvels of witchcraft, sympathetic powders, and other relics of mediæval superstition disappeared like a mist before the sun, whilst accurate observations and demonstrations of a host of new wonders accumulated, amongst which were numerous contributions to the anatomy of animals, and none perhaps more noteworthy than the observations, made by the aid of microscopes constructed by himself, of Leeuwenhoek, the Dutch naturalist (1683), some of whose instruments were presented by him to the society.

Results of use of the microscope.

It was not until the 19th century that the microscope, thus early applied by Leeuwenhoek, Malpighi, Hook, and Swammerdam to the study of animal structure, was perfected as an instrument, and accomplished for zoology its final and most important service. The earlier half of the 19th century is remarkable for the rise, growth, and full development of a new current of thought in relation to living things, expressed in the various doctrines of development which were promulgated, whether in relation to the origin of individual animals and plants or in relation to their origin from predecessors in past ages. The perfecting of the microscope led to a full comprehension of the great doctrine of cell-structure and the establishment of the facts—(1) that all organisms are either single corpuscles (so-called cells) of living material (microscopic animalcules, &c.) or are built up of an immense number of such units; (2) that all organisms begin their individual existence as a single unit or corpuscle of living substance, which multiplies by binary fission, the products growing in size and multiplying similarly by binary fission; and (3) that the life of a multicellular organism is the sum of the activities of the corpuscular units of which it consists, and that the processes of life must be studied in and their explanation obtained from an understanding of the chemical and physical changes which go on in each individual corpuscle or unit of living material or protoplasm (cell-theory of Schwann).

Ideas of development.

On the other hand, the astronomical theories of development of the solar system from a gaseous condition to its present form, put forward by Kant and by Laplace, had impressed men's minds with the conception of a general movement of spontaneous progress or development in all nature; and, though such ideas were not new but are to be found in some of the ancient Greek philosophers, yet now for the first time they could be considered with a sufficient knowledge and certainty as to the facts, due to the careful observation of the two preceding centuries. The science of geology came into existence, and the whole panorama of successive stages of the earth's history, each with its distinct population of strange animals and plants, unlike those of the present day and simpler in proportion as they recede into the past, was revealed by Cuvier, Agassiz, and others. The history of the crust of the earth was explained by Lyell as due to a process of slow development, in order to effect which he called in no cataclysmic agencies, no mysterious forces differing from those operating at the present day. Thus he carried on the narrative of orderly development from the point at which it was left by Kant and Laplace,—explaining by reference to the ascertained laws of physics and chemistry the configuration of the earth, its mountains and seas, its igneous and its stratified rocks, just as the astronomers had explained by those same laws the evolution of the sun and planets from diffused gaseous matter of high temperature.

The Natur-philosophen.

The suggestion that living things must also be included in this great development was obvious. They had been so included by poet-philosophers in past ages; they were so included by many a simple-minded student of nature who, watching the growth of the tree from the seed, formed a true but unverified inference in favour of a general process of growth and development of all things from simpler beginnings. The delay in the establishment of the doctrine of organic evolution was due, not to the ignorant and unobservant, but to the leaders of zoological and botanical science. Knowing as they did the almost endless complexity of organic structures, realizing as they did that man himself with all the mystery of his life and consciousness must be included in any explanation of the origin of living things, they preferred to regard living things as something apart from the rest of nature, specially cared for, specially created by a Divine Being, rather than to indulge in hypotheses which seemed to be beyond all possibility of proof, and were rather of the nature of poets' dreams than in accordance with the principles of that new philosophy of rigid adherence to fact and demonstration which had hitherto served as the mainsprings of scientific progress. Thus it was that the so-called "Natur-philosophen" of the last decade of the 18th century, and their successors in the first quarter of the 19th, found few adherents among the working zoologists and botanists. Lamarck, Treviranus, Erasmus Darwin, Goethe, and Saint-Hilaire preached to deaf ears, for they advanced the theory that living beings had developed by a slow process of transmutation in successive generations from simpler ancestors, and in the beginning from simplest formless matter, without being able to demonstrate any existing mechanical causes by which such development must necessarily be brought about. They were met in fact by the criticism that possibly such a development had taken place; but, as no one could show as a simple fact of observation that it *had* taken place, nor as a result of legitimate inference that it *must* have taken place, it was quite as likely that the past and present species of animals and plants had been separately created or individually brought into existence by unknown and inscrutable causes, and (it was held) the truly scientific man would refuse to occupy himself with such fancies, whilst ever continuing to concern himself with the observation and record of indisputable facts. The critics did well; for the "Natur-philosophen," though right in their main conception, were premature.

Darwin's doctrine of organic evolution.

It was reserved for Charles Darwin, in the year 1859, to place the whole theory of organic evolution on a new footing, and by his discovery of a mechanical cause actually existing and demonstrable by which organic evolution must be brought about to entirely change the attitude in regard to it of even the most rigid exponents of the scientific method. Since its first publication in 1859 the history of Darwin's theory has been one of continuous and decisive conquest, so that at the present day it is universally accepted as the central, all-embracing doctrine of zoological and botanical science.

Introduction of thremmatology.

Darwin succeeded in establishing the doctrine of organic evolution by the introduction into the web of the zoological and botanical sciences of a new science. The subject-matter of this new science, or branch of biological science, had been neglected: it did not form part of the studies of the collector and systematist, nor was it a branch of anatomy, nor of the physiology pursued by medical men, nor again was it included in the field of microscopy and the cell-theory. The area of biological knowledge which Darwin was the first to subject to scientific method and to render, as it were, contributory to the great stream formed by the union of the various branches, the outlines of which we have already traced, is that which relates to the breeding of animals and plants, their congenital variations, and the transmission and perpetuation of those variations. This branch of biological science may be called thremmatology (θρέμμα, "a thing bred"). Outside the scientific world an immense mass of observation and experiment had grown up in relation to this subject. From the earliest times the shepherd, the farmer, the horticulturist, and the "fancier" had for practical purposes made themselves acquainted with a number of biological laws, and successfully applied them without exciting more than an occasional notice from the academic students of biology. It is one of Darwin's great merits to have made use of these observations and to have formulated their results to a large extent as the laws of variation and heredity. As the breeder selects a congenital variation which suits his requirements, and by breeding from the animals (or plants) exhibiting that variation obtains a new breed specially characterized by that variation, so in nature is there a selection amongst all the congenital variations of each generation of a species. This selection depends on the fact that more young are born than the natural provision of food will support. In consequence of this excess of births there is a struggle for existence and a survival of the fittest, and consequently an ever-present necessarily-acting selection, which either maintains accurately the form of the species from generation to generation or leads to its modification in correspondence with changes in the surrounding circumstances which have relation to its fitness for success in the struggle for life.

New development of teleology.

Darwin's introduction of thremmatology into the domain of scientific biology was accompanied by a new and special development of a branch of study which had previously been known as teleology, the study of the adaptation of organic structures to the service of the organisms in which they occur. It cannot be said that previously to Darwin there had been any very profound study of teleology, but it had been the delight of a certain type of mind—that of the lovers of nature or naturalists *par excellence*, as they were sometimes termed—to watch the habits of living animals and plants, and to point out the remarkable ways in which the structure of each variety of organic life was adapted to the special circumstances of life of the variety or species. The astonishing colours and grotesque forms of some animals and plants which the museum zoologists gravely described without comment were shown by these observers of living nature to have their significance in the economy of the organism possessing them; and a general doctrine was recognized, to the effect that no part or structure of an organism is without definite use and adaptation, being *designed* by the Creator for the benefit of the creature to which it belongs, or else for the benefit, amusement, or instruction of his highest creature—man. Teleology in this form of the doctrine of design was never very deeply rooted amongst scientific anatomists and systematists. It was considered permissible to speculate somewhat vaguely on the subject of the utility of this or that startling variety of structure; but few attempts, though some of great importance, were made to systematically explain by observation and experiment the adaptation of organic structures to particular purposes in the case of the lower animals and plants. Teleology had, however, an important part in the development of what is called physiology, viz., the knowledge of the mechanism, the physical and chemical properties, of the parts of the body of man and the higher animals allied to him. The doctrine of organs and functions—the organ designed so as to execute the function, and the whole system of organs and functions building up a complex mechanism, the complete animal or plant—was teleological in origin (see PHYSIOLOGY), and led to brilliant discoveries in the hands of the physiologists of the last and the preceding century. As applied to lower and more obscure forms of life, teleology presented almost insurmountable difficulties; and consequently, in place of exact experiment and demonstration, the most reckless though ingenious assumptions were made as to the utility of the parts and organs of lower animals, which tended to bring so-called comparative physiology and teleology generally into disrepute. Darwin's theory had as one of its results the reformation and rehabilitation of teleology. According to that theory, every organ, every part, colour, and peculiarity of an organism, must either be of benefit to that organism itself or have been so to its ancestors: no peculiarity of structure or general conformation, no habit or instinct in any organism, can be supposed to exist for the benefit or amusement of another organism, not even for the delectation of man himself. Necessarily, according to the theory of natural selection, structures either are present because they are selected as useful or because they are still inherited from ancestors to whom they were useful, though no longer useful to the existing representatives of those ancestors.

The conception thus put forward entirely re-founded teleology. Structures previously inexplicable were explained as survivals from a past age, no longer useful though once of value. Every variety of form and colour was urgently and absolutely called upon to produce its title to existence either as an active useful agent or as a survival. Darwin himself spent a large part of the later years of his life in thus extending the new teleology. A beginning only has as yet been made in the new life of that branch of zoological and botanical study.

The old doctrine of types, which was used by the philosophically-minded zoologists (and botanists) of the first half of the century as a ready means of explaining the failures and difficulties of the doctrine of design, fell into its proper place under the new dispensation. The adherence to type, the favourite conception of the transcendental morphologist, was seen to be nothing more than the expression of one of the laws of thremmatology, the persistence of hereditary transmission of ancestral characters, even when they have ceased to be significant or valuable in the struggle for existence, whilst the so-called evidences of design which was supposed to modify the limitations of types assigned to Himself by the Creator were seen to be adaptations due to the selection and intensification by selective breeding of fortuitous congenital variations, which happened to prove more useful than the many thousand other variations which did not survive in the struggle for existence.

Effects of Darwin's theory upon zoology.

Thus not only did Darwin's theory give a new basis to the study of organic structure, but, whilst rendering the general theory of organic evolution equally acceptable and necessary, it explained the existence of low and simple forms of life as survivals of the earliest ancestry of more highly complex forms, and revealed the classifications of the systematist as unconscious attempts to construct the genealogical tree or pedigree of plants and animals. Finally, it brought the simplest living matter or formless protoplasm before the mental vision as the starting-point whence, by the operation of necessary mechanical causes, the highest forms have been evolved, and it rendered unavoidable the conclusion that this earliest living material was itself evolved by gradual processes, the result also of the known and recognized laws of physics and chemistry, from material which we should call not living. It abolished the conception of life as an entity above and beyond the common properties of matter, and led to the conviction that the marvellous and exceptional qualities of that which we call "living" matter are nothing more nor less than an exceptionally complicated development of those chemical and physical properties which we recognize in a gradually ascending scale of evolution in the carbon compounds, containing nitrogen as well as oxygen, sulphur, and hydrogen as constituent atoms of their enormous molecules. Thus mysticism was finally banished from the domain of biology, and zoology became one of the physical sciences, —the science which seeks to arrange and discuss the phenomena of animal life and form as the outcome of the operation of the laws of physics and chemistry.

Nature and Scope of Zoology.

Division into morphology and physiology inadequate.

The brief historical outline above given is sufficient to justify us in rejecting, for the purposes of an adequate appreciation of the history and scope of zoology, that simple division of the science into morphology and physiology which is a favourite one at the present day. No doubt the division is a logical one, based as it is upon the distinction of the study of form and structure in themselves (morphology) from the study of what are the activities and functions of the forms and structures (physiology). Such logical divisions are possible upon a variety of bases, but are not necessarily conducive to the ascertainment and remembrance of the historical progress and present significance of the science to which they are applied. As a matter of convenience and as the outcome of historical events it happens that in the universities of Europe, whilst botany in its entirety is usually represented by one chair, the animal side of biology is represented by a chair of so-called zoology, which is understood as the old-fashioned systematic zoology, a chair of human and comparative anatomy, and a chair of physiology (signifying the mechanics, physics, and chemistry of animals especially in relation to man). Fifty years ago the chairs of anatomy and physiology were united in one. No such distinction of mental activities as that involved in the division of the study of animal life into morphology and physiology has ever really existed: the investigator of animal forms has never entirely ignored the functions of the forms studied by him, and the experimental inquirer into the functions and properties of animal tissues and organs has always taken very careful account of the forms of those tissues and organs.

A subdivision based on historical progress.

A more instructive subdivision of the science of animal biology or zoology is one which shall correspond to the separate currents of thought and mental preoccupation which have been historically manifested in western Europe in the gradual evolution of what is to-day the great river of zoological doctrine to which they have all been rendered contributory. Such a subdivision of zoology, whilst it enables us to trace the history of thought, corresponds very closely with the actual varieties of mental attitude exhibited at the present day by the devotees of zoological study, though it must be remembered that the gathering together of all the separate currents by Darwin is certain sooner or later to entail new developments and branchings of the stream.

We accordingly recognize the following five branches of zoological study:—

1. *Morphography.*—The work of the collector and systematist: exemplified by Linnæus and his predecessors, by Cuvier, Agassiz, Haeckel.
2. *Bionomics.*—The lore of the farmer, gardener, sportsman, fancier, and field-naturalist, including thremmatology, or the science of breeding, and the allied teleology, or science of organic adaptations: exemplified by the patriarch Jacob, the poet Virgil, Sprengel, Kirby and Spence, Wallace, and Darwin.
3. *Zoo-Dynamics, Zoo-Physics, Zoo-Chemistry.*—The pursuit of the learned physician,—anatomy and physiology: exemplified by Harvey, Haller, Hunter, Johann Müller.
4. *Plasmology.*—The study of the ultimate corpuscles of living matter, their structure, development, and properties, by the aid of the microscope; exemplified by Malpighi, Hook, Schwann, Kowalewsky.
5. *Philosophical Zoology.*—General conceptions with regard to the relations of living things (especially animals) to the universe, to man, and to the Creator, their origin and significance: exemplified in the writings of the philosophers of classical antiquity, and of Linnæus, Goethe, Lamarck, Cuvier, Lyell, H. Spencer, and Darwin.

It is true that it is impossible to assign the great names of the present century to a single one of the subdivisions of the science thus recognized. With men of an earlier date such special assignment is possible, and there would be no difficulty about thus separating the minor specialists of modern times. But the fact is that as we approach Darwin's epoch we find the separate streams more and more freely connected with one another by anastomosing branches; and the men who have left their mark on the progress of science have been precisely those who have been instrumental in bringing about such confluence, and have distinguished themselves by the influence of their discoveries or generalizations upon several lines of work. At last, in Darwin we find a name which might appear in each of our subdivisions,—a zoologist to whose doctrine all are contributory, and by whose labours all are united and reformed.

We shall now briefly sketch the history of these streams of thought, premising that one has (so far as the last three centuries are concerned) but little start of another, and that sooner or later the influence of the progress of one branch makes itself felt in the progress of another.

Morphography.

Under this head we include the systematic exploration and tabulation of the facts involved in the recognition of all the recent and extinct kinds of animals and their distribution in space and time. (1) The museum-makers of old days and their modern representatives the curators and describers of zoological collections, (2) early explorers and modern naturalist-travellers and writers on zoo-geography, and (3) collectors of fossils and palæontologists are the chief varieties of zoological workers coming under this head. Gradually since the time of Hunter and Cuvier anatomical study has associated itself with the more superficial morphography until to-day no one considers a study of animal form of any value which does not include internal structure, histology, and embryology in its scope.

Edward Wotton.

The real dawn of zoology after the legendary period of the Middle Ages is connected with the name of an Englishman, Wotton, born at Oxford in 1492, who practised as a physician in London and died in 1555. He published a treatise *De Differentiis Animalium* at Paris in 1552. In many respects Wotton was simply an exponent of Aristotle, whose teaching, with various fanciful additions, constituted the real basis of zoological knowledge throughout the Middle Ages. It was Wotton's merit that he rejected the legendary and fantastic accretions, and returned to Aristotle and the observation of nature. The most ready means of noting the progress of zoology during the 16th, 17th, and 18th centuries is to compare the classificatory conceptions of successive naturalists with those which are to be found in the works of Aristotle himself.

Aristotle's classification.

Aristotle did not definitely and in tabular form propound a classification of animals, but from a study of his treatises *Historia Animalium*, *De Generatione Animalium*, and *De Partibus Animalium* the following classification can be arrived at:—

A. **Ἔναιμα,** blood-holding animals (=*Vertebrata*).
1. Ζωοτοκοῦντα ἐν αὑτοῖς, viviparous *Enæma* (=Mammals, including the Whale).
2. Ὄρνιθες (=Birds).
3. Τετράποδα ἢ ἄποδα ᾠοτοκοῦντα, four-footed or legless *Enæma* which lay eggs (=Reptiles and *Amphibia*).
4. Ἰχθύες (=Fishes).

B. **Ἄναιμα,** bloodless animals (=*Invertebrata*).
1. Μαλάκια, soft-bodied *Anæma* (=*Cephalopoda*).
2. Μαλακόστρακα, soft-shelled *Anæma* (=*Crustacea*).
3. Ἔντομα, insected *Anæma* or Insects (=*Arthropoda*, exclusive of *Crustacea*).
4. Ὀστρακοδέρματα, shell-bearing *Anæma* (=*Echini*, *Gastropoda*, and *Lamellibranchia*.)

Wotton's modifications.

Wotton follows Aristotle in the division of animals into the *Enæma* and the *Anæma*, and in fact in the recognition of all the groups above given, adding only one large group to those recognized by Aristotle under the *Anæma*, namely, the group of *Zoophyta*, in which Wotton includes the *Holothuriæ*, Star-Fishes, *Medusæ*, Sea-Anemones, and Sponges. Wotton divides the viviparous quadrupeds into the many-toed, double-hoofed, and single-hoofed. By the introduction of a method of classification which was due to the superficial Pliny,—viz., one depending, not on structure, but on the medium inhabited by an animal, whether earth, air, or water,—Wotton is led to associate Fishes and Whales as aquatic animals. But this is only a momentary lapse, for he broadly distinguishes the two kinds.

Gesner.

Conrad Gesner (1516-1565), who was a physician and held professorial chairs in various Swiss cities, is the most voluminous and instructive of these earliest writers on systematic zoology, and was so highly esteemed that his *Historia Animalium* was republished a hundred years after his death. His great work appeared in successive parts,—*e.g.*, *Vivipara*, *Ovipara*, *Aves*, *Pisces*, *Serpentes et Scorpio*,—and contains descriptions and illustrations of a large number of animal forms with reference to the lands inhabited by them. Gesner's work, like that of John Johnstone (*b.* 1603), who was of Scottish descent and studied at St Andrews, and like that of Ulysses Aldrovandi of Bologna (*b.* 1522), was essentially a compilation, more or less critical, of all such records, pictures, and relations concerning beasts, birds, reptiles, fishes, and monsters as could be gathered together by one reading in the great libraries of Europe, travelling from city to city, and frequenting the company of those who either had themselves passed into distant lands or possessed the letters written and sometimes the specimens brought home by adventurous persons.

Medical anatomists and microscopists.

The exploration of parts of the New World next brought to hand descriptions and specimens of many novel forms of animal life, and in the latter part of the 16th century and the beginning of the 17th that careful study by "specialists" of the structure and life-history of particular groups of animals was commenced which, directed at first to common and familiar kinds, was gradually extended until it formed a sufficient body of knowledge to serve as an anatomical basis for classification. This minuter study had two origins, one in the researches of the medical anatomists, such as Fabricius (1537-1619), Severinus (1580-1656), Harvey (1578-1657), and Tyson (1649-1708), the other in the careful work of the entomologists and first microscopists, such as Malpighi (1628-1694), Swammerdam (1637-1680), and Hook (1635-1702). The commencement of anatomical investigations deserves notice here as influencing the general accuracy and minuteness with which zoological work was prosecuted, but it was not until a late date that their full influence was brought to bear upon systematic zoology by Georges Cuvier (1769-1832).

John Ray.

The most prominent name between that of Gesner and Linnæus in the history of systematic zoology is that of John Ray (*q.v.*). Though not so extensive as that of Linnæus, his work is of the highest importance, and rendered the subsequent labours of the Swedish naturalist far easier than they would otherwise have been. A chief merit of Ray is to have limited the term "species" and to have assigned to it the significance which it has until the Darwinian era borne, whereas previously it was loosely and vaguely applied. He also made considerable use of anatomical characters in his definitions of larger groups, and may thus be considered as the father of modern zoology. Associated with Ray in his work, and more especially occupied with the study of the Worms and *Mollusca*, was Martin Lister (1638-1712), who is celebrated also as the author of the first geological map.

From Ray to Linnæus.

After Ray's death in London in 1705 the progress of anatomical knowledge, and of the discovery and illustration of new forms of animal life from distant lands, continued with increasing vigour. We note the names of Vallisnieri (1661-1730) and Alexander Monro (1697-1767); the travellers Tournefort (1656-1708) and Shaw (1692-1751); the collectors Rumphius (1637-1706) and Hans Sloane (1660-1753); the entomologist Réaumur (1683-1757); Lhwyd (1703) and Linck (1674-1734), the students of Star-Fishes; Peyssonel (b. 1694), the investigator of Polyps and the opponent of Marsigli and Réaumur, who held them to be plants; Woodward, the palæontologist (1665-1722),—not to speak of others of less importance.

Linnæus

Two years after Ray's death Carl Linnæus (*q.v.*) was born. Unlike Jacob Theodore Klein (1685-1759), whose careful treatises on various groups of plants and animals were published during the period between Ray and Linnæus, the latter had his career marked out for him in a university, that of Upsala, where he was first professor of medicine and subsequently of natural history. His lectures formed a new departure in the academic treatment of zoology and botany, which, in direct continuity from the Middle Ages, had hitherto been subjected to the traditions of the medical profession and regarded as mere branches of "materia medica." Linnæus taught zoology and botany as branches of knowledge to be studied for their own intrinsic interest. His great work, the *Systema Naturæ*, ran through twelve editions during his lifetime (1st ed. 1735, 12th 1768). Apart from his special discoveries in the anatomy of plants and animals, and his descriptions of new species, the great merit of Linnæus was his introduction of a method of enumeration and classification which may be said to have created systematic zoology and botany in their present form, and establishes his name for ever as the great organizer, the man who recognized a great practical want in the use of language and supplied it. Linnæus adopted Ray's conception of species, but he made species a practical reality by insisting that every species shall have a double Latin name,—the first half to be the name of the genus common to several species, and the second half to be the specific name. Previously to Linnæus long many-worded names had been used, sometimes with one additional adjective, sometimes with another, so that no true *names* were fixed and accepted. Linnæus by his binomial system made it possible to write and speak with accuracy of any given species of plant or animal. He was, in fact, the Adam of zoological science. He proceeded further to introduce into his enumeration of animals and plants a series of groups, viz., genus, order, class, which he compared to the subdivisions of an army or the subdivisions of a territory, the greater containing several of the less, as follows:—

Class.	Order.	Genus.	Species.	Variety.
Genus summum.	Genus intermedium.	Genus proximum.	Species.	Individuum.
Provincia.	Territorium.	Parœcia.	Pagus.	Domicilium.
Legio.	Cohors.	Manipulus.	Contubernium.	Miles.

Linnæus himself recognized the purely subjective character of his larger groups; for him species were, however, objective: "there are," he said, "just so many species as in the beginning the Infinite Being created." It was reserved for a philosophic zoologist of the 19th century (Agassiz, *Essay on Classification*, 1859) to maintain dogmatically that genus, order, and class were also objective facts capable of precise estimation and valuation. This climax was reached at the very moment when Darwin was publishing the *Origin of Species* (1859), by which universal opinion has been brought to the position that species, as well as genera, orders, and classes, are the subjective expressions of a vast ramifying pedigree in which the only objective existences are individuals, the apparent species as well as higher groups being marked out, not by any distributive law, but by the purely non-significant operation of human experience, which cannot transcend the results of death and decay.

Classification of Linnæus.

The classification of Linnæus (from *Syst. Nat.*, 12th ed., 1766) should be compared with that of Aristotle. It is as follows,—the complete list of Linnæan genera being here reproduced:—

Class I. MAMMALIA.
Order 1. *Primates.*
Genera: *Homo, Simia, Lemur, Vespertilio.*
,, 2. *Bruta.*
Genera: *Elephas, Trichecus, Bradypus, Myrmecophaga, Manis, Dasypus.*
,, 3. *Feræ.*
Genera: *Phoca, Canis, Felis, Viverra, Mustela, Ursus, Didelphys, Talpa, Sorex, Erinaceus.*
,, 4. *Glires.*
Genera: *Hystrix, Lepus, Castor, Mus, Sciurus, Noctilio.*
,, 5. *Pecora.*
Genera: *Camelus, Moschus, Cervus, Capra, Ovis, Bos.*
,, 6. *Belluæ.*
Genera: *Equus, Hippopotamus, Sus, Rhinoceros.*
,, 7. *Cete.*
Genera: *Monodon, Balæna, Physeter, Delphinus.*

Class II. AVES.
Order 1. *Accipitres.*
Genera: *Vultur, Falco, Strix, Lanius.*
,, 2. *Picæ.*
Genera: (*a*) *Trochilus, Certhia, Upupa, Buphaga, Sitta, Oriolus, Coracias, Gracula, Corvus, Paradisea*; (*b*) *Ramphastos, Trogon, Psittacus, Crotophaga, Picus, Yunx, Cuculus, Bucco*; (*c*) *Buceros, Alcedo, Merops, Todos.*
,, 3. *Anseres.*
Genera: (*a*) *Anas, Mergus, Phaethon, Plotus*; (*b*) *Rhyncops, Diomedea, Alca, Procellaria, Pelecanus, Larus, Sterna, Colymbus.*
,, 4. *Grallæ.*
Genera: (*a*) *Phœnicopterus, Platalea, Palamedea, Mycteria, Tantalus, Ardea, Recurvirostra, Scolopax, Tringa, Fulica, Parra, Rallus, Psophia, Cancroma*; (*b*) *Hematopus, Charadrius, Otis, Struthio.*
,, 5. *Gallinæ.*
Genera: *Didus, Pavo, Meleagris, Crax, Phasianus, Tetrao, Numida.*
Order 6. *Passeres.*
Genera: (*a*) *Loxia, Fringilla, Emberiza*; (*b*) *Caprimulgus, Hirundo, Pipra*; (*c*) *Turdus, Ampelis, Tanagra, Muscicapa*; (*d*) *Parus, Motacilla, Alauda, Sturnus, Columba.*

Class III. AMPHIBIA.
Order 1. *Reptilia.*
Genera: *Testudo, Draco, Lacerta, Rana.*
,, 2. *Serpentes.*
Genera: *Crotalus, Boa, Coluber, Anguis, Amphisbæna, Cæcilia.*
,, 3. *Nantes.*
Genera: *Petromyzon, Raja, Squalus, Chimæra, Lophius, Acipenser, Cyclopterus, Balistes, Ostracion, Tetrodon, Diodon, Centriscus, Syngnathus, Pegasus.*

Class IV. PISCES.
Order 1. *Apodes.*
Genera: *Muræna, Gymnotus, Trichiurus, Anarrhichas, Ammodytes, Ophidium, Stromateus, Xiphias.*
,, 2. *Jugulares.*
Genera: *Callionymus, Uranoscopus, Trachinus, Gadus, Blennius.*
,, 3. *Thoracici.*
Genera: *Cepola, Echeneis, Coryphæna, Gobius, Cottus, Scorpæna, Zeus, Pleuronectes, Chætodon, Sparus, Labrus, Sciæna, Perca, Gasterosteus, Scomber, Mullus, Trigla.*
,, 4. *Abdominales.*
Genera: *Cobitis, Amia, Silurus, Zeuthis, Loricaria, Salmo, Fistularia, Esox, Elops, Argentina, Atherina, Mugil, Mormyrus, Exocœtus, Polynemus, Clupea, Cyprinus.*

Class V. INSECTA.
Order 1. *Coleoptera.*
Genera: (*a*) *Scarabæus, Lucanus, Dermestes, Hister, Byrrhus, Gyrinus, Attelabus, Curculio, Silpha, Coccinella*; (*b*) *Bruchus, Cassida, Ptinus, Chrysomela, Hispa, Meloe, Tenebrio, Lampyris, Mordella, Staphylinus*; (*c*) *Cerambyx, Leptura, Cantharis, Elater, Cicindela, Buprestis, Dytiscus, Carabus, Necydalis, Forficula.*
,, 2. *Hemiptera.*
Genera: *Blatta, Mantis, Gryllus, Fulgora, Cicada, Notonecta, Nepa, Cimex, Aphis, Chermes, Coccus, Thrips.*
,, 3. *Lepidoptera.*
Genera: *Papilio, Sphinx, Phalæna.*
,, 4. *Neuroptera.*
Genera: *Libellula, Ephemera, Myrmeleon, Phryganea, Hemerobius, Panorpa, Raphidia.*
,, 5. *Hymenoptera.*
Genera: *Cynips, Tenthredo, Sirex, Ichneumon, Sphex, Chrysis, Vespa, Apis, Formica, Mutilla.*
,, 6. *Diptera.*
Genera: *Œstrus, Tipula, Musca, Tabanus, Culex, Empis, Conops, Asilus, Bombylius, Hippobosca.*
,, 7. *Aptera.*
Genera: (*a*) Pedibus sex; capite a thorace discreto: *Lepisma, Podura, Termes, Pediculus, Pulex.*
(*b*) Pedibus 8-14; capite thoraceque unitis: *Acarus, Phalangium, Aranea, Scorpio, Cancer, Monoculus, Oniscus.*
(*c*) Pedibus pluribus; capite a thorace discreto: *Scolopendra, Julus.*

Class VI. VERMES.
Order 1. *Intestina.*
Genera: (*a*) Pertusa laterali poro: *Lumbricus, Sipunculus, Fasciola.*
(*b*) Imperforata poro laterali nullo: *Gordius, Ascaris, Hirudo, Myxine.*
,, 2. *Mollusca.*
Genera: (*a*) Ore supero; basi se affigens: *Actinia, Ascidia.*
(*b*) Ore antico; corpore pertuso laterali foraminulo: *Limax, Aplysia, Doris, Tethis.*
(*c*) Ore antico; corpore tentaculis antice cincto: *Holothuria, Terebella.*
(*d*) Ore antico; corpore brachiato: *Triton, Sepia, Clio, Lernæa, Scyllæa.*
(*e*) Ore antico; corpore pedato: *Aphrodita, Nereis.*
(*f*) Ore infero centrali: *Medusa, Asteria, Echinus.*

Order 3. *Testacea.*
Genera: (*a*) Multivalvia: *Chiton, Lepas, Pholas.*
(*b*) Bivalvia (= *Conchæ*): *Mya, Solen, Tellina, Cardium, Mactra, Donax, Venus, Spondylus, Chama, Arca, Ostrea, Anomia, Mytilus, Pinna.*
(*c*) Univalvia spira regulari (= *Cochleæ*): *Argonauta, Nautilus, Conus, Cypræa, Bulla, Voluta, Buccinum, Strombus, Murex, Trochus, Turbo, Helix, Nerita, Haliotis.*
(*d*) Univalvia absque spira regulari: *Patella, Dentalium, Serpula, Teredo, Sabella.*
„ 4. *Lithophyta.*
Genera: *Tubipora, Madrepora, Millepora, Cellepora.*
„ 5. *Zoophyta.*
Genera: (*a*) Fixata: *Isis, Gorgonia, Alcyonium, Spongia, Flustra, Tubularia, Corallina, Sertularia, Vorticella.*
(*b*) Locomotiva: *Hydra, Pennatula, Tænia, Volvox, Furia, Chaos.*

The characters of the six classes are thus given by Linnæus:—

Cor biloculare, biauritum; Sanguine calido, rubro:	viviparis, *Mammalibus*; oviparis, *Avibus.*
Cor uniloculare, uniauritum;[1] Sanguine frigido, rubro:	pulmone arbitrario, *Amphibiis*; branchiis externis, *Piscibus.*
Cor uniloculare, inauritum; Sanie frigida, albida:	antennatis, *Insectis*; tentaculatis, *Vermibus.*

From Linnæus to Cuvier.

Between Linnæus and Cuvier there are no very great names; but under the stimulus given by the admirable method and system of Linnæus observation and description of new forms from all parts of the world, both recent and fossil, accumulated. We can only cite the names of Charles Bonnet (1720-1793), the entomologist, who described the reproduction of *Aphis*; Banks and Solander, who accompanied Captain Cook on his first voyage (1768-1771); Thomas Pennant (1726-1798), the describer of the English fauna; Peter Simon Pallas (1741-1811), who specially extended the knowledge of the Linnæan *Vermes*, and under the patronage of the empress Catherine explored Russia and Siberia; De Geer (1720-1778), the entomologist; Lyonnet (1707-1789), the author of the monograph of the anatomy of the caterpillar of *Cossus ligniperdus*; Cavolini (1756-1810), the Neapolitan marine zoologist and forerunner of Della Chiaje (fl. 1828); O. F. Müller (1730-1784), the describer of freshwater *Oligochæta*; Abraham Trembley (1700-1784), the student of *Hydra*; and Ledermüller (1719-1769), the inventor of the term *Infusoria*. The effect of the Linnæan system upon the general conceptions of zoologists was no less marked than were its results in the way of stimulating the accumulation of accurately observed details. The notion of a *scala naturæ*, which had since the days of classical antiquity been a part of the general philosophy of nature amongst those who occupied themselves with such conceptions, now took a more definite form in the minds of skilled zoologists. The species of Linnæus were supposed to represent a series of steps in a scale of ascending complexity, and it was thought possible thus to arrange the animal kingdom in a single series,—the orders within the classes succeeding one another in regular gradation, and the classes succeeding one another in a similar rectilinear progression. LAMARCK (*q.v.*) represents most completely, both by his development theory (to be further mentioned below) and by his scheme of classification, the high-water mark of the popular but fallacious conception of a *scala naturæ*. His classification (1801 to 1812) is as follows:—

Lamarck's classification.

Invertebrata.
1. *Apathetic Animals*
Class I. INFUSORIA.
Orders: *Nuda, Appendiculata.*
Class II. POLYPI.
Orders: *Ciliati* (*Rotifera*), *Denudati* (Hydroids), *Vaginati* (*Anthozoa* and *Polyzoa*), *Natantes* (Crinoids).
Class III. RADIARIA.
Orders: *Mollia* (*Acalephæ*), *Echinoderma* (including *Actiniæ*).
Class IV. TUNICATA.
Orders: *Bothryllaria, Ascidia.*
Class V. VERMES.
Orders: *Molles* (Tape-Worms and Flukes), *Rigiduli* (Nematoids), *Hispiduli* (*Nais*, &c.), *Epizoariæ* (Lernæans, &c.).
2. *Sensitive Animals.*
Class VI. INSECTA (*Hexapoda*).
Orders: *Aptera, Diptera, Hemiptera, Lepidoptera, Hymenoptera, Neuroptera, Orthoptera, Coleoptera.*
Class VII. ARACHNIDA.
Orders: *Antennato-Trachealia* (= *Thysanura* and *Myriapoda*), *Exantennato-Trachealia, Exantennato-Branchialia.*
Class VIII. CRUSTACEA.
Orders: *Heterobranchia* (*Branchiopoda, Isopoda, Amphipoda, Stomapoda*), *Homobranchia* (*Decapoda*).
Class IX. ANNELIDA.
Orders: *Apoda, Antennata, Sedentaria.*
Class X. CIRRIPEDIA.
Orders: *Sessilia, Pedunculata.*
Class XI. CONCHIFERA.
Orders: *Dimyaria, Monomyaria.*
Class XII. MOLLUSCA.
Orders: *Pteropoda, Gasteropoda, Trachelipoda, Cephalopoda, Heteropoda.*
Vertebrata.
3. *Intelligent Animals.*
Class XIII. FISHES. Class XV. BIRDS.
„ XIV. REPTILES. „ XVI. MAMMALS.

The enumeration of orders above given will enable the reader to form some conception of the progress of knowledge relating to the lower forms of life during the fifty years which intervened between Linnæus and Lamarck. The number of genera recognized by Lamarck is more than ten times as great as that recorded by Linnæus.

We have mentioned Lamarck before his great contemporary Cuvier because, in spite of his valuable philosophical doctrine of development, he was, as compared with Cuvier and estimated as a systematic zoologist, a mere enlargement and logical outcome of Linnæus.

Cuvier.

The distinctive merit of CUVIER (*q.v.*) is that he started a new view as to the relationships of animals, which he may be said in a large measure to have demonstrated as true by his own anatomical researches. He opposed the *scala naturæ* theory, and recognized four distinct and divergent branches or *embranchemens*, as he called them, in each of which he arranged a certain number of the Linnæan classes, or similar classes. The *embranchemens* were characterized each by a different type of anatomical structure. Cuvier thus laid the foundation of that branching tree-like arrangement of the classes and orders of animals which we now recognize as being the necessary result of attempts to represent what is practically a genealogical tree or pedigree. Apart from this, Cuvier was a keen-sighted and enthusiastic anatomist of great skill and industry. It is astonishing how many good observers it requires to dissect and draw and record over and over again the structure of an animal before an approximately correct account of it is obtained. Cuvier dissected many Molluscs and other animals which had not previously been anatomized; of others he gave more correct accounts than had been given by earlier writers. Skilful as he was his observations are very frequently erroneous. Great accuracy in work as well as great abundance of production has only distinguished one amongst all the great names of zoology—that of Johann Müller. It certainly did not

[1] The anatomical error in reference to the auricles of Reptiles and Batrachians on the part of Linnæus is extremely interesting, since it shows to what an extent the most patent facts may escape the observation of even the greatest observers, and what an amount of repeated dissection and unprejudiced attention has been necessary before the structure of the commonest animals has become known.

distinguish Cuvier. Another special distinction of Cuvier is his remarkable work in comparing extinct with recent organisms, his descriptions of the fossil *Mammalia* of the Paris basin, and his general application of the knowledge of recent animals to the reconstruction of extinct ones, as indicated by fragments only of their skeletons.

It was in 1812 that Cuvier communicated to the Academy of Sciences of Paris his views on the classification of animals. He says—

"Si l'on considère le règne animal d'après les principes que nous venons de poser, en se debarassant des préjugés établis sur les divisions anciennement admises, en n'ayant égard qu' à l'organisation et à la nature des animaux, et non pas à leur grandeur, à leur utilité, au plus ou moins de connaissance que nous en avons, ni à toutes les autres circonstances accessoires, on trouvera qu'il existe quatre formes principales, quatre plans généraux, si l'on peut s'exprimer ainsi, d'après lesquels tous les animaux semblent avoir été modelés et dont les divisions ultérieures, de quelque titre que les naturalistes les aient décorées, ne sont que des modifications assez légères, fondées sur le développement, ou l'addition de quelques parties qui ne changent rien à l'essence du plan."

Cuvier's classification.

His classification as finally elaborated in *Le Règne Animal* (Paris, 1829) is as follows:—

First Branch. **Animalia Vertebrata.**
- Class I. MAMMALIA.
  - Orders: *Bimana, Quadrumana, Carnivora, Marsupialia, Rodentia, Edentata, Pachydermata, Ruminantia, Cetacea.*
- Class II. BIRDS.
  - Orders: *Accipitres, Passeres, Scansores, Gallinæ, Grallæ, Palmipedes.*
- Class III. REPTILIA.
  - Orders: *Chelonia, Sauria, Ophidia, Batrachia.*
- Class IV. FISHES.
  - Orders: (*a*) *Acanthopterygii, Abdominales, Subbrachii, Apodes, Lophobranchii, Plectognathi*; (*b*) *Sturiones, Selachii, Cyclostomi.*

Second Branch. **Animalia Mollusca.**
- Class I. CEPHALOPODA.
- Class II. PTEROPODA.
- Class III. GASTROPODA.
  - Orders: *Pulmonata, Nudibranchia, Inferobranchia, Tectibranchia, Heteropoda, Pectinibranchia, Tubulibranchia, Scutibranchia, Cyclobranchia.*
- Class IV. ACEPHALA.
  - Orders: *Testacea, Tunicata.*
- Class V. BRACHIOPODA.
- Class VI. CIRRHOPODA.

Third Branch. **Animalia Articulata.**
- Class I. ANNELIDES.
  - Orders: *Tubicolæ, Dorsibranchiæ, Abranchiæ.*
- Class II. CRUSTACEA.
  - Orders: (*a*) Malacostraca: *Decapoda, Stomapoda, Amphipoda, Læmodipoda, Isopoda*; (*b*) Entomostraca: *Branchiopoda, Pœcilopoda, Trilobitæ.*
- Class III. ARACHNIDES.
  - Orders: *Pulmonariæ, Tracheariæ.*
- Class IV. INSECTS.
  - Orders: *Myriapoda, Thysanura, Parasita, Suctoria, Coleoptera, Orthoptera, Hemiptera, Neuroptera, Hymenoptera, Lepidoptera, Rhipiptera, Diptera.*

Fourth Branch. **Animalia Radiata.**
- Class I. ECHINODERMS.
  - Orders: *Pedicellata, Apoda.*
- Class II. INTESTINAL WORMS.
  - Orders: *Nematoidea, Parenchymatosa.*
- Class III. ACALEPHÆ.
  - Orders: *Simplices, Hydrostaticæ.*
- Class IV. POLYPI (including the *Cœlentera* of later authorities and the *Polyzoa*).
  - Orders: *Carnosi, Gelatinosi, Polypiarii.*
- Class V. INFUSORIA.
  - Orders: *Rotifera, Homogenea* (this includes the *Protozoa* of recent writers and some *Protophyta*).

Von Baer.

The leading idea of Cuvier, his four *embranchemens*, was confirmed by the Russo-German naturalist Von Baer (1792-1876), who adopted Cuvier's divisions, speaking of them as the peripheric, the longitudinal, the massive, and the vertebrate types of structure. Von Baer, however, has another place in the history of zoology, being the first and most striking figure in the introduction of embryology into the consideration of the relations of animals to one another.

The morphologists.

Cuvier may be regarded as *the* zoologist by whom anatomy was made the one important guide to the understanding of the relations of animals. But it should be noted that the belief, dating from Malpighi (1670), that there *is* a relationship to be discovered, and not merely a haphazard congregation of varieties of structure to be classified, had previously gained ground. Cuvier was familiar with the speculations of the "Natur-philosophen," and with the doctrine of transmutation and filiation by which they endeavoured to account for existing animal forms. The noble aim of F. W. J. Schelling, "das ganze System der Naturlehre von dem Gesetze der Schwere bis zu den Bildungstrieben der Organismus als ein organisches Ganze darzustellen," which has ultimately been realized through Darwin, was a general one among the scientific men of the year 1800. Lamarck accepted the development theory fully, and pushed his speculations far beyond the realm of fact. The more cautious Cuvier adopted a view of the relationships of animals which, whilst denying genetic connexion as the explanation, recognized an essential identity of structure throughout whole groups of animals. This identity was held to be due to an ultimate law of nature or the Creator's plan. The tracing out of this identity in diversity, whether regarded as evidence of blood-relationship or as a remarkable display of skill on the part of the Creator in varying the details whilst retaining the essential, became at this period a special pursuit, to which Goethe, the poet, who himself contributed importantly to it, gave the name "morphology." C. F. Wolff, Goethe, and Oken share the credit of having initiated these views, in regard especially to the structure of flowering plants and the Vertebrate skull. Cuvier's doctrine of four plans of structure was essentially a morphological one, and so was the single-scale doctrine of Buffon and Lamarck, to which it was opposed. Cuvier's morphological doctrine received its fullest development in the principle of the "correlation of parts," which he applied to palæontological investigation, namely, that every animal is a definite whole, and that no part can be varied without entailing correlated and law-abiding variations in other parts, so that from a fragment it should be possible, had we a full knowledge of the laws of animal structure or morphology, to reconstruct the whole. Here Cuvier was imperfectly formulating, without recognizing the real physical basis of the phenomena, the results of the laws of heredity, which were subsequently investigated and brought to bear on the problems of animal structure by Darwin.

R. Owen.

Richard Owen[1] may be regarded as the foremost of Cuvier's disciples. Owen not only occupied himself with the dissection of rare animals, such as the Pearly Nautilus, *Lingula, Limulus, Protopterus, Apteryx*, &c., and with the description and reconstruction of extinct Reptiles, Birds, and Mammals,—following the Cuvierian tradition,—but gave precision and currency to the morphological doctrines which had taken their rise in the beginning of the century by the introduction of two terms, "homology" and "analogy," which were defined so as to express two different kinds of agreement in animal structures, which, owing to the want of such "counters of thought," had been hitherto continually confused. *Analogous* structures in any two animals compared were by Owen defined as structures performing similar functions, but not necessarily derived from the modification of one and the same part in the "plan" or "archetype" according to which the two animals compared were supposed to be constructed. *Homologous* structures were such as, though greatly differing in appearance and detail from one another, and though performing widely different functions, yet were

Homology and analogy.

[1] Born in 1804 in Lancaster; conservator of the Hunterian Museum, London, 1830-56; superintendent Nat. Hist. Brit. Mus., 1856-84.

capable of being shown by adequate study of a series of intermediate forms to be derived from one and the same part or organ of the "plan-form" or "archetype." It is not easy to exaggerate the service rendered by Owen to the study of zoology by the introduction of this apparently small piece of verbal mechanism; it takes place with the classificatory terms of Linnæus. And, though the conceptions of "archetypal morphology," to which it had reference, are now abandoned in favour of a genetic morphology, yet we should remember, in estimating the value of this and of other speculations which have given place to new views in the history of science, the words of the great reformer himself. "Erroneous observations are in the highest degree injurious to the progress of science, since they often persist for a long time. But erroneous theories, when they are supported by facts, do little harm, since every one takes a healthy pleasure in proving their falsity" (Darwin). Owen's definition of analogous structures holds good at the present day. His homologous structures are now spoken of as "homogenetic" structures, the idea of community of representation in an archetype giving place to community of derivation from a single representative structure present in a common ancestor. Darwinian morphology has further rendered necessary the introduction of the terms "homoplasy" and "homoplastic"[1] to express that close agreement in *form* which may be attained in the course of evolutional changes by organs or parts in two animals which have been subjected to similar moulding conditions of the environment, but have no genetic community of origin, to account for their close similarity in form and structure.

Owen's classification.

The classification adopted by Owen in his lectures (1855) does not adequately illustrate the progress of zoological knowledge between Cuvier's death and that date, but, such as it is, it is worth citing here.

Province: **Vertebrata** (*Myelencephala*, Owen).
 Classes: MAMMALIA, AVES, REPTILIA, PISCES.
Province; **Articulata.**
 Classes: ARACHNIDA, INSECTA (including Sub-Classes *Myriapoda, Hexapoda*), CRUSTACEA (including Sub-Classes *Entomostraca, Malacostraca*), EPIZOA (Epizootic *Crustacea*), ANNELLATA (Chætopods and Leeches), CIRRIPEDIA.
Province: **Mollusca.**
 Classes: CEPHALOPODA, GASTEROPODA, PTEROPODA, LAMELLIBRANCHIATA, BRACHIOPODA, TUNICATA.
Province: **Radiata.**
 Sub-Province: **Radiaria.**
  Classes: ECHINODERMATA, BRYOZOA, ANTHOZOA, ACALEPHÆ, HYDROZOA.
 Sub-Province: **Entozoa.**
  Classes: CŒLELMINTHA, STERELMINTHA.
 Sub-Province: **Infusoria.**
  Classes: ROTIFERA, POLYGASTRIA (the *Protozoa* of recent authors).

The real centre of progress of systematic zoology was no longer in France nor with the disciples of Cuvier in England, but after his death moved to Germany. The wave of morphological speculation, with its outcome of new systems and new theories of classification, which were as numerous as the professors of zoological science,[2] was necessarily succeeded in the true progress of the science by a period of minuter study in which the microscope, the discovery of embryological histories, and the all-important cell-theory came to swell the stream of exact knowledge.

We have already mentioned Von Baer in this connexion, and given a passing reference to Johann MÜLLER (*q.v.*), the greatest of all investigators of animal structure in the present century. Müller (1801-1858) was in Germany the successor of Rathke (1793-1860) and of Meckel (1781-1833) as the leader of anatomical investigation; but his true greatness can only be estimated by a consideration of the fact that he was a great teacher not only of human and comparative anatomy and zoology but also of physiology, and that nearly all the most distinguished German zoologists and physiologists of the period 1850 to 1870 were his pupils and acknowledged his leadership. The most striking feature about Johann Müller's work, apart from the comprehensiveness of his point of view, in which he added to the anatomical and morphological ideas of Cuvier a consideration of physiology, embryology, and microscopic structure, was the extraordinary accuracy, facility, and completeness of his recorded observations. He could do more with a single specimen of a rare animal (*e.g.*, in his memoir on *Amphioxus*, Berlin, 1844) in the way of making out its complete structure than the ablest of his contemporaries or successors could do with a plethora. His power of rapid and exhaustive observation and of accurate pictorial reproduction was phenomenal. His most important memoirs, besides that just mentioned, are those on the anatomy and classification of Fishes, on the Cœcilians, and on the developmental history of the Echinoderms.

J. V. Thompson.

A name which is apt to be forgotten in the period between Cuvier and Darwin, because its possessor occupied an isolated position in England and was not borne up by any great school or university, is that of John Vaughan Thompson, who was an army surgeon, and when past the age of forty, being district medical inspector at Cork (1830), took to the study of marine *Invertebrata* by the aid of the microscope. Thompson made three great discoveries, which seem to have fallen in his way in the most natural and simple manner, but must be regarded really as the outcome of extraordinary genius. He showed that the organisms like *Flustra* are not hydroid Polyps, but of a more complex structure resembling Molluscs, and he gave them the name *Polyzoa*. He discovered the *Pentacrinus europæus*, and showed that it was the larval form of the Feather-Star *Antedon* (*Comatula*). He upset Cuvier's retention of the Cirripedes among *Mollusca*, and his subsequent treatment of them as an isolated class, by showing that they begin life as free-swimming *Crustacea* identical with the young forms of other *Crustacea*. Vaughan Thompson is a type of the marine zoologists, such as Dalyell, Michael Sars, P. J. Van Beneden, Claparède, and Allman, who during the present century have approached the study of the lower marine organisms in the same spirit as that in which Trembley and Schäffer in the last century, and Swammerdam in the 17th, gave themselves to the study of the minute freshwater forms of animal life.

It is impossible to enumerate or to give due consideration to all the names in the army of anatomical and embryological students of the middle third of this century whose labours bore fruit in the modification of zoological theories and in the building up of a true classification of animals. Their results are best summed up in the three schemes of classification which follow below—those of Rudolph Leuckart (b. 1823), Henri Milne-Edwards (1800-1884), and T. H. Huxley (b. 1825), all of whom individually contributed very greatly by their special discoveries and researches to the increase of exact knowledge.

Single-fact systems of classification.

Contemporaneous with these were various schemes of classification which were based, not on a consideration of the entire structure of each animal, but on the variations of a single organ, or on the really non-significant fact of the structure of the egg. All such single-fact systems have proved to be useless and in fact departures from the true line of growth of the zoological system which was shaping itself year by year—unknown to those who so shaped it—as a genealogical tree. They were attempts to arrive at a true knowledge of the relationships of animals by "royal roads"; their followers were landed in barren wastes.

[1] See Lankester, "On the Use of the Term Homology in Modern Zoology and the Distinction between Homogenetic and Homoplastic Agreements," *Ann. and Mag. Nat. Hist.*, 1870.

[2] See Agassiz, *Essay on Classification*, 1859, for an account of them.

Leuckart's classification.

R. Leuckart's[1] classification is as follows :—

Type 1. **Cœlenterata.**
Class I. POLYPI.
Orders : *Anthozoa* and *Cylicozoa.*
,, II. ACALEPHÆ.
Orders : *Discophoræ* and *Ctenophoræ.*
Type 2. **Echinodermata.**
Class I. PELMATOZOA.
Orders : *Cystidea* and *Crinoidea.*
,, II. ACTINOZOA.
Orders : *Echinida* and *Asterida.*
,, III. SCYTODERMATA.
Orders : *Holothuriæ* and *Sipunculida.*
Type 3. **Vermes.**
Class I. ANENTERÆTI.
Orders : *Cestodes* and *Acanthocephali.*
,, II. APODES.
Orders : *Nemertini, Turbellarii, Trematodes,* and *Hirudinei.*
,, III. CILIATI.
Orders : *Bryozoa* and *Rotifera.*
,, IV. ANNELIDES.
Orders : *Nematodes, Lumbricini,* and *Branchiati.*
Type 4. **Arthropoda.**
Class I. CRUSTACEA.
Orders : *Entomostraca* and *Malacostraca.*
,, II. INSECTA.
Orders : *Myriapoda, Arachnida* (*Acera,* Latr.), and *Hexapoda.*
Type 5. **Mollusca.**
Class I. TUNICATA.
Orders : *Ascidiæ* and *Salpæ.*
,, II. ACEPHALA.
Orders : *Lamellibranchiata* and *Brachiopoda.*
,, III. GASTEROPODA.
Orders : *Heterobranchia, Dermatobranchia, Heteropoda, Ctenobranchia, Pulmonata,* and *Cyclobranchia.*
,, IV. CEPHALOPODA.
Type 6. **Vertebrata.** (Not specially dealt with.)

Milne-Edwards's classification.

The classification given by Henri Milne-Edwards[2] is as follows :—

Branch I. **Osteozoaria** or **Vertebrata.**
Sub-Branch 1. **Allantoidians.**
Class I. MAMMALIA.
Orders : (*a*) Monodelphia : *Bimana, Quadrumana, Cheiroptera, Insectivora, Rodentia, Edentata, Carnivora, Amphibia, Pachydermata, Ruminantia, Cetacea* ; (*b*) Didelphia : *Marsupialia, Monotremata.*
,, II. BIRDS.
Orders : *Rapaces, Passeres, Scansores, Gallinæ, Grallæ, Palmipedes.*
,, III. REPTILES.
Orders : *Chelonia, Sauria, Ophidia.*
Sub-Branch 2. **Anallantoidians.**
Class I. BATRACHIANS.
Orders : *Anura, Urodela, Perennibranchia, Cœciliæ.*
,, II. FISHES.
Section 1. *Ossei.*
Orders : *Acanthopterygii, Abdominales, Subbrachii, Apodes, Lophobranchii, Plectognathi.*
Section 2. *Chondropterygii.*
Orders : *Sturiones, Selachii, Cyclostomi.*
Branch II. **Entomozoa** or **Annelata.**
Sub-Branch 1. **Arthropoda.**
Class I. INSECTA.
Orders : *Coleoptera, Orthoptera, Neuroptera, Hymenoptera, Lepidoptera, Hemiptera, Diptera, Rhipiptera, Anopleura, Thysanura.*
,, II. MYRIAPODA.
Orders : *Chilognatha* and *Chilopoda.*
,, III. ARACHNIDS.
Orders : *Pulmonaria* and *Trachearia.*
Class IV. CRUSTACEA.
Section 1. *Podophthalmia.*
Orders : *Decapoda* and *Stomopoda.*
Section 2. *Edriophthalmi.*
Orders : *Amphipoda, Læmodipoda,* and *Isopoda.*
Section 3. *Branchiopoda.*
Orders : *Ostracoda, Phyllopoda,* and *Trilobitæ.*
Section 4. *Entomostraca.*
Orders : *Copepoda, Cladocera, Siphonostoma, Lernæida, Cirripedia.*
Section 5. *Xiphosura.*
(The orders of the classes which follow are not given in the work quoted.)
Sub-Branch 2. **Vermes.**
Class I. ANNELIDS. Class IV. CESTOIDEA.
,, II. HELMINTHS. ,, V. ROTATORIA.
,, III. TURBELLARIA.
Branch III. **Malacozoaria** or **Mollusca.**
Sub-Branch 1. **Mollusca** proper.
Class I. CEPHALOPODA. Class III. GASTEROPODA.
,, II. PTEROPODA. ,, IV. ACEPHALA.
Sub-Branch 2. **Molluscoidea.**
Class I. TUNICATA. Class II. BRYOZOA.
Branch IV. **Zoophytes.**
Sub-Branch 1. **Radiaria.**
Class I. ECHINODERMS. Class III. CORALLARIA or POLYPI.
,, II. ACALEPHS.
Sub-Branch 2. **Sarcodaria.**
Class I. INFUSORIA. Class II. SPONGIARIA.

Huxley's classification.

In England T. H. Huxley adopted in his lectures (1869) a classification which was in many respects similar to both of the foregoing, but embodied improvements of his own. It is as follows :—

Sub-Kingdom I. **Protozoa.**
Classes : RHIZOPODA, GREGARINIDA, RADIOLARIA, SPONGIDA.
Sub-Kingdom II. **Infusoria.**
Sub-Kingdom III. **Cœlenterata.**
Classes : HYDROZOA, ACTINOZOA.
Sub-Kingdom IV. **Annuloida.**
Classes : SCOLECIDA, ECHINODERMATA.
Sub-Kingdom V. **Annulosa.**
Classes : CRUSTACEA, ARACHNIDA, MYRIAPODA, INSECTA, CHÆTOGNATHA, ANNELIDA.
Sub-Kingdom VI. **Molluscoida.**
Classes : POLYZOA, BRACHIOPODA, TUNICATA.
Sub-Kingdom VII. **Mollusca.**
Classes : LAMELLIBRANCHIATA, BRANCHIOGASTROPODA, PULMOGASTROPODA, PTEROPODA, CEPHALOPODA.
Sub-Kingdom VIII. **Vertebrata.**
Classes : PISCES, AMPHIBIA, REPTILIA, AVES, MAMMALIA.

We now arrive at the period when the doctrine of organic evolution was established by Darwin, and when naturalists, being convinced by him as they had not been by the transmutationists of fifty years' earlier date, were compelled to take an entirely new view of the significance of all attempts at framing a "natural" classification.

Classifications based on structure.

Many zoologists—prominent among them in Great Britain being Huxley—had been repelled by the airy fancies and assumptions of the "philosophical" morphologists. The efforts of the best minds in zoology had been directed for thirty years or more to ascertaining with increased accuracy and minuteness the structure, microscopic and gross, of all possible forms of animals, and not only of the adult structure but of the steps of development of that structure in the growth of each kind of organism from the egg to maturity. Putting aside fantastic theories, these observers endeavoured to give in their classifications a strictly objective representation of the facts of animal structure and of the structural relationships of animals to one another capable of demonstration. The groups within groups adopted for this purpose were necessarily wanting in symmetry: the whole system presented a strangely irregular character. From time to time efforts were made by those who believed that the Creator must have followed a symmetrical system in his production of animals to force one or other artificial, neatly balanced

[1] *Die Morphologie und die Verwandtschaftsverhältnisse der wirbellosen Thiere,* Brunswick, 1848. The *Protozoa,* recognized as a primary group by Siebold and Stannius (*Lehrbuch d. vergleich. Anatomie,* Berlin, 1845), are not included at all by Leuckart in his scheme. The name *Protozoa* was first used by Goldfuss (1809) to include microscopic animals and also the Polyps and *Medusæ,* and Siebold and Stannius first used it in its modern signification as comprising and limited to the *Infusoria* and *Rhizopoda.*

[2] *Cours Élémentaire d'Histoire Naturelle,* Paris, 1855.

L. Agassiz.

scheme of classification upon the zoological world. The last of these was that of Louis Agassiz (*Essay on Classification*, 1859), who, whilst surveying all previous classifications, propounded a scheme of his own, in which, as well as in the criticisms he applies to other systems, the leading notion is that sub-kingdoms, classes, orders, and families have a real existence, and that it is possible to ascertain and distinguish characters which are of class value, others which are only of ordinal value, and so on, so that the classes of one sub-kingdom should on paper, and in nature actually do, correspond in relative value to those of another sub-kingdom, and the orders of any one class similarly should be so taken as to be of equal value with those of another class, and have been actually so created.

Influence of Darwinian doctrine on taxonomy.

The whole position was changed by the acquiescence, which became universal, in the doctrine of Darwin. That doctrine took some few years to produce its effect, but it became evident at once to those who accepted Darwinism that *the* natural classification of animals, after which collectors and anatomists, morphologists, philosophers, and embryologists had been so long striving was nothing more nor less than a genealogical tree, with breaks and gaps of various extent in its record. The facts of the relationships of animals to one another, which had been treated as the outcome of an inscrutable law by most zoologists and glibly explained by the transcendental morphologists, were amongst the most powerful arguments in support of Darwin's theory, since they, together with all other vital phenomena, received a sufficient explanation through it. It is to be noted that, whilst the zoological system took the form of a genealogical tree, with main stem and numerous diverging branches, the actual form of that tree, its limitation to a certain number of branches corresponding to a limited number of divergencies in structure, came to be regarded as the necessary consequence of the operation of the physico-chemical laws of the universe, and it was recognized that the ultimate explanation of that limitation is to be found only in the constitution of matter itself.

Haeckel.

The first naturalist to put into practical form the consequences of the new theory, in so far as it affected zoological classification, was Ernst Haeckel of Jena (b. 1834), who in 1866, seven years after the publication of Darwin's *Origin of Species*, published his suggestive *Generelle Morphologie*. Haeckel introduced into classification a number of terms intended to indicate the branchings of a genealogical tree. The whole "system" or scheme of classification was termed a genealogical tree (*Stammbaum*); the main branches were termed "phyla," their branchings "sub-phyla"; the great branches of the sub-phyla were termed "cladi," and the "cladi" divided into "classes," these into sub-classes, these into legions, legions into orders, orders into sub-orders, sub-orders into tribes, tribes into families, families into genera, genera into species. Additional branchings could be indicated by similar terms where necessary. There was no attempt in Haeckel's use of these terms to make them exactly or more than approximately equal in significance; such attempts were clearly futile and unimportant where the purpose was the exhibition of lines of descent, and where no natural equality of groups was to be expected *ex hypothesi*. Haeckel's classification of 1866 was naturally enough only a first attempt. In the edition of the *Natürliche Schöpfungsgeschichte* published in 1868, he made a great advance in his genealogical classification, since he now introduced the results of the extraordinary activity in the study of embryology which followed on the publication of the *Origin of Species*.

Cellular embryology.

The pre-Darwinian systematists since the time of Von Baer had attached very great importance to embryological facts, holding that the stages in an animal's development were often more significant of its true affinities than its adult structure. Von Baer had gained unanimous support for his dictum, "Die Entwickelungsgeschichte ist der wahre Lichtträger für Untersuchungen über organische Körper." Thus J. Müller's studies on the larval forms of Echinoderms and the discoveries of Vaughan Thompson were appreciated. But it was only after Darwin that the cell-theory of Schwann was extended to the embryology of the animal kingdom generally, and that the knowledge of the development of an animal became a knowledge of the way in which the millions of cells of which its body is composed take their origin by fission from a smaller number of cells, and these at last from the single egg-cell. Kölliker (*Development of Cephalopods*, 1844), Remak (*Development of the Frog*, 1850), and others had laid the foundations of this knowledge in isolated examples; but it was Kowalewsky, by his accounts of the development of Ascidians and of *Amphioxus* (1866), who really made zoologists see that a strict and complete cellular embryology of animals was as necessary and feasible a factor in the comprehension of their relationships as at the beginning of the century the coarse anatomy had been shown to be by Cuvier. Kowalewsky's work appeared between the dates of the *Generelle Morphologie* and the *Schöpfungsgeschichte*. Haeckel himself, with his pupil Miklucho-Maclay, had in the meantime made studies on the growth from the egg of Sponges,—studies which resulted in the complete separation of the unicellular or equicellular *Protozoa* from the Sponges, hitherto confounded with them. It is this introduction of the consideration of cell-structure and cell-development which, subsequently to the establishment of Darwinism, has most profoundly modified the views of systematists, and led in conjunction with the genealogical doctrine to the greatest activity in research,—an activity which culminated in the work (1873-82) of F. M. Balfour, and produced the profoundest modifications in classification.

Haeckel's second arrangement.

Haeckel's earlier pedigree is worth comparing with his second effort, as showing the beginning of the influence just noted. The second pedigree is as follows:—

Phyla.	Clades.	Classes.
Protozoa.	OVULARIA.	*Archezoa.*
		Gregarinæ.
		Infusoria.
	BLASTULARIA.	*Planæada.*
		Gastræada.
Zoophyta.	SPONGIÆ.	*Porifera.*
	ACALEPHÆ.	*Coralla.*
		Hydromedusæ.
		Ctenophora.
Vermes.	ACŒLOMI.	*Platyhelminthes.*
	CŒLOMATI.	*Nemathelminthes*
		Bryozoa.
		Tunicata.
		Rhynchocœla.
		Gephyræa.
		Rotatoria.
		Annelida.
Mollusca.	ACEPHALA.	*Spirobranchia.*
		Lamellibranchia.
	EUCEPHALA.	*Cochlides.*
		Cephalopoda.
Echinoderma.	COLOBRACHIA.	*Asterida.*
		Crinoida.
	LIPOBRACHIA.	*Echinida.*
		Holothuriæ.
Arthropoda.	CARIDES.	*Crustacea.*
	TRACHEATA.	*Arachnida.*
		Myriapoda.
		Insecta.
Vertebrata.	ACRANIA.	*Leptocardia.*
	MONORRHINA.	*Cyclostoma.*
	ANAMNIA.	*Pisces.*
		Dipneusta.
		Halisauria.
		Amphibia.
	AMNIOTA.	*Reptilia.*
		Aves.
		Mammalia.

Dendriform distribution of animal kingdom.

In representing pictorially the groups of the animal kingdom as the branches of a tree, it becomes obvious that a distinction may be drawn, not merely between the individual main branches, but further as to the level at which they are given off from the main stem, so that one branch or set of branches may be marked off as belonging to an earlier or lower level than another set of branches; and the same plan may be adopted with regard to the clades, classes, and smaller branches. The term "grade" was introduced by Lankester[1] to indicate this giving off of branches at a higher or lower, *i.e.*, a later or earlier, level of a main stem. The mechanism for the statement of the genealogical relationships of the groups of the animal kingdom was thus completed. Renewed study of every group was the result of the acceptance of the genealogical idea and of the recognition of the importance of cellular embryology. On the one hand, the true method of arriving at a knowledge of the genealogical tree was recognized as lying chiefly in attacking the problem of the genealogical relationships of the smallest twigs of the tree, and proceeding from them to the larger branches. Special studies of small families or orders of animals with this object in view were taken in hand by many zoologists. On the other hand, a survey of the facts of cellular embryology which were accumulated in regard to a variety of classes within a few years of Kowalewsky's work led to a generalization, independently arrived at by Haeckel and Lankester, to the effect that a lower grade of animals may be distinguished, the *Protozoa* or *Plastidozoa*, which consist either of single cells or colonies of equiformal cells, and a higher grade, the *Metazoa* or *Enterozoa*, in which the egg-cell by "cell division" gives rise to two layers of cells, the endoderm and the ectoderm, surrounding a primitive digestive chamber, the archenteron. Of these latter, two grades were further distinguished by Lankester,—those which remain possessed of a single archenteric cavity and of two primary cell-layers (the *Cœlentera* or *Diploblastica*), and those which by nipping off the archenteron give rise to two cavities, the cœlom or body-cavity and the metenteron or gut (*Cœlomata* or *Triploblastica*). To the primitive two-cell-layered form, the hypothetical ancestor of all *Metazoa* or *Enterozoa*, Haeckel gave the name *Gastræa*; the embryonic form which represents in the individual growth from the egg this ancestral condition he called a "gastrula." The term "diblastula" has more recently been adopted in England for the gastrula of Haeckel. The tracing of the exact mode of development, cell by cell, of the diblastula, the cœlom, and the various tissues of examples of all classes of animals has been pursued during the last twenty years with immense activity and increasing instrumental facilities, and is still in progress.

Fritz Müller's recapitulation.

Two names in connexion with post-Darwinian taxonomy and the ideas connected with it require brief mention here. Fritz Müller, by his studies on *Crustacea* (*Für Darwin*, 1864), showed the way in which genealogical theory may be applied to the minute study of a limited group. He is also responsible for the formulation of an important principle, called by Haeckel "the biogenetic fundamental law," viz., that an animal in its growth from the egg to the adult condition tends to pass through a series of stages which are recapitulative of the stages through which its ancestry has passed in the historical development of the species from a primitive form; or, more shortly, that the development of the individual (ontogeny) is an epitome of the development of the race (phylogeny). Pre-Darwinian zoologists had been aware of the class of facts thus interpreted by Fritz Müller, but the authoritative view on the subject had been that there is a parallelism between (*a*) the series of forms which occur in individual development, (*b*) the series of existing forms from lower to higher, and (*c*) the series of forms which succeed one another in the strata of the earth's crust, whilst an explanation of this parallelism was either not attempted, or was illusively offered in the shape of a doctrine of harmony of plan in creation. It was the application of Fritz Müller's law of recapitulation which gave the chief stimulus to recent embryological investigations; and, though it is now recognized that "recapitulation" is vastly and bewilderingly modified by special adaptations in every case, yet the principle has served, and still serves, as a guide of great value.

Dohrn's doctrine of degeneration.

Another important factor in the present condition of zoological knowledge as represented by classification is the doctrine of degeneration propounded by Anton Dohrn. Lamarck believed in a single progressive series of forms, whilst Cuvier introduced the conception of branches. The first post-Darwinian systematists naturally and without reflexion accepted the idea that existing simpler forms represent stages in the gradual progress of development,—are in fact survivors from past ages which have retained the exact grade of development which their ancestors had reached in past ages. The assumption made was that (with the rare exception of parasites) all the change of structure through which the successive generations of animals have passed has been one of progressive elaboration. It is Dohrn's merit to have pointed out[1] that this assumption is not warranted, and that degeneration or progressive simplification of structure may have, and in many lines certainly has, taken place, as well as progressive elaboration and continuous maintenance of the *status quo*. The introduction of this conception necessarily has had a most important effect in the attempt to unravel the genealogical affinities of animals. It renders the task a more complicated one; at the same time it removes some serious difficulties and throws a flood of light on every group of the animal kingdom.

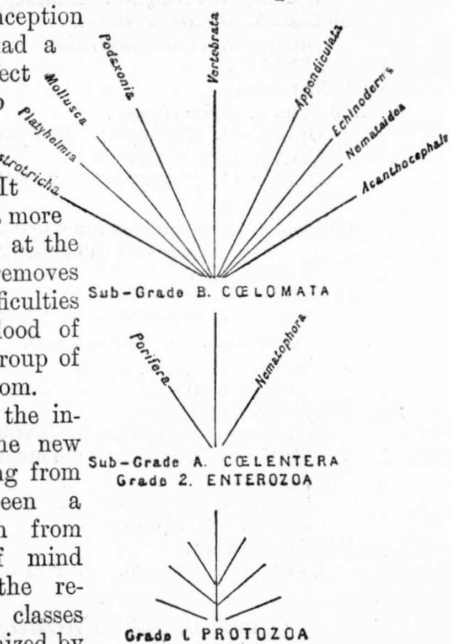

Genealogical tree of animal kingdom.

One result of the introduction of the new conceptions dating from Darwin has been a healthy reaction from that attitude of mind which led to the regarding of the classes and orders recognized by authoritative zoologists as sacred institutions which were beyond the criticism of ordinary men. That state of mind was due to the fact that the groupings so recognized did not profess to be simply the result of scientific reasoning, but were necessarily regarded as the expressions of the "insight" of some more or less gifted persons into a plan or system which had been arbitrarily chosen by the Creator. Consequently there was a tinge of theological dogmatism about the whole matter. To deny the Linnæan, or later the Cuvierian, classes was very much like denying the Mosaic cosmogony. At the present time systematic zoology is entirely free from any such prejudices, and the Linnæan taint which is apparent

[1] "Notes on Embryology and Classification," in *Quart. Journ. Micr. Sci.*, 1877.

[1] *Ursprung der Wirbelthiere*, Leipsic, 1875; and Lankester, *Degeneration*, London, 1880.

even in Haeckel and Gegenbaur may be considered as finally expunged.

Classification of Ray Lankester.

We give below the classification of Ray Lankester as an example of the most recent genealogical classification. It is represented by the above genealogical tree and the tabular statement which follows. The chief points in this classification are the inclusion of *Balanoglossus* and the *Tunicata* in the phylum *Vertebrata*, the association of the *Rotifera* and the *Chætopoda* with the *Arthropoda* in the phylum *Appendiculata*, the inclusion of *Limulus* and the *Eurypterina* in the class *Arachnida*, and the total abandoning of the indefinite and indefensible group of "*Vermes*."

Grade A. *PLASTIDOZOA* (*PROTOZOA*).

Grade *a*. *GYMNOMYXA*.
Class I. PROTEOMORPHA (no orders recognized).
,, II. MYCETOZOA.
Orders.—1. *Sorophora*. 2. *Endosporea*. 3. *Exosporea*.
,, III. LOBOSA.
Orders.—1. *Nuda*. 2. *Testacea*.
,, IV. LABYRINTHULIDEA (no orders).
,, V. HELIOZOA.
Orders.—1. *Aphrothoraca*. 2. *Chlamydophora*. 3. *Chalarothoraca*. 4. *Desmothoraca*.
,, VI. RETICULARIA.
Sub-Class *a*. *Imperforata*.
Orders.—1. *Gromiidea*. 2. *Astrorhizidea*. 3. *Miliolidea*. 4. *Lituolidea*.
Sub-Class *b*. *Perforata*.
Orders.—1. *Textularidea*. 2. *Chilostomellidea*. 3. *Lagenidea*. 4. *Globigerinidea*. 5. *Rotalidea*. 6. *Nummulinidea*.
,, VII. RADIOLARIA.
Sub-Class *a*. *Silicoskeleta*.
Orders.—1. *Peripylæa*. 2. *Monopylæa*. 3. *Phæodaria*.
Sub-Class *b*. *Acanthinoskeleta*.
Order.—1. *Acanthometridea*.

Grade *b*. *CORTICATA*.
Class I. SPOROZOA.
Sub-Class *a*. *Gregarinidea*.
Orders.—1. *Haplocyta*. 2. *Septata*.
Sub-Class *b*. *Coccidiidea*.
Orders.—1. *Monosporea*. 2. *Oligosporea*. 3. *Polysporea*.
Sub-Class *c*. *Myxosporidea* (no orders).
,, *d*. *Sarcocystidea* (no orders).
,, II. FLAGELLATA.
Sub-Class *a*. *Lissoflagellata*.
Orders.—1. *Monadidea*. 2. *Euglenoidea*. 3. *Heteromastigoda*. 4. *Isomastigoda*.
Sub-Class *b*. *Choanoflagellata*.
Orders.—1. *Nuda*. 2. *Loricata*. 3. *Gelatinigera*.
,, III. DINOFLAGELLATA.
Orders.—1. *Adinida*. 2. *Dinifera*.
,, IV. RHYNCHOFLAGELLATA (no orders).
,, V. CILIATA.
Orders.—1. *Peritricha*. 2. *Heterotricha*. 3. *Holotricha*. 4. *Hypotricha*.
,, VI. ACINETARIA.
Orders.—1. *Suctoria*. 2. *Non-Suctoria*.

Grade B. *ENTEROZOA*.

Sub-Grade A. *CŒLENTERA*.

Phylum 1. **NEMATOPHORA.**

Class I. HYDROMEDUSÆ.
Orders.—1. *Anthomedusæ* (*Gymnoblastœa*). 2. *Leptomedusæ* (*Calyptoblastœa*). 3. *Narcomedusæ*. 4. *Trachomedusæ*. 5. *Hydrocorallinæ*. 6. *Siphonophora*.
,, II. SCYPHOMEDUSÆ.
Sub-Class *a*. *Tetrameralia*.
Orders.—1. *Calycozoa*. 2. *Peromedusæ*. 3. *Cubomedusæ*.
Sub-Class *b*. *Octomeralia*.
Orders.—1. *Cannostomæ*. 2. *Semostomæ*. 3. *Rhizostomæ*.
,, III. ANTHOZOA.
Sub-Class *a*. *Actiniomorpha*.
Orders.—1. *Actiniaria*. 2. *Antipatharia*. 3. *Madreporaria*.
Sub-Class *b*. *Alcyoniomorpha*.
Orders.—1. *Protalcyonaria*. 2. *Stolonifera*. 3. *Alcyonaria*. 4. *Paragorgonaria*. 5. *Gorgonaria*. 6. *Pennatularia*. 7. *Helioporaria*.
Class IV. CTENOPHORA.
Orders.—1. *Saccata*. 2. *Eurystoma*. 3. *Tæniata*. 4. *Lobata*.

Phylum 2. **PORIFERA.**

Class I. CALCISPONGIÆ (=*Megamastictora*).
Orders.—1. *Homocœla*. 2. *Heterocœla*.
,, II. SILICOSPONGIÆ (=*Micromastictora*).
Sub-Class 1. *Hyalospongiæ*.
Order. *Hexactinellaria*.
Sub-Class 2. *Demospongiæ*.
Orders.—1. *Tetractinellaria*. 2. *Monaxonaria*. 3. *Halisarcaria*.

Sub-Grade B. *CŒLOMATA*.

Phylum 1. **VERTEBRATA.**

Branch A. **Hemichorda** (*Balanoglossus*).
,, B. **Urochorda.**
Grade I. **Larvalia** (no divisions recognized).
,, II. **Saccata.**
Class I. ASCIDIÆ.
Orders.—1. *Simplices*. 2. *Sociales*. 3. *Compositæ*. 4. *Pyrosomiidea*.
,, II. SALPIFORMIA.
Orders.—1. *Salpiidea*. 2. *Doliolidea*.
Branch C. **Cephalochorda** (*Amphioxus*).
,, D. **Craniata.**
Grade I. **Cyclostoma.**
Class I. MYXINOIDEA (no orders).
,, II. PETROMYZONTIA (no orders).
Grade II. **Gnathostoma.**
Sub-Grade *a*. **Branchiata Heterodactyla.**
Class I. PISCES.
Sub-Class 1. *Selachii*.
Orders.—1. *Squali*. 2. *Raii*.
Sub-Class 2. *Holocephali* (no orders).
,, 3. *Ganoidei*.
Orders.—1. *Chondrostei*. 2. *Polypterini*. 3. *Lepidosteini*. 4. *Amidini*. 5. *Cephalaspidini*. 6. *Placodermi*. 7. *Acanthodini*. 8. *Pycnodontini*. 9. *Cœlacanthini*. 10. *Dipterini*.
Sub-Class 4. *Teleostei*.
Orders.—1. *Physostomi*. 2. *Pharyngognathi*. 3. *Anacanthini*. 4. *Acanthopteri*. 5. *Plectognathi*. 6. *Lophobranchia*.
,, II. DIPNOI.
Orders.—1. *Monopneumones*. 2. *Dipneumones*.
Sub-Grade *b*. **Branchiata Pentadactyla.**
Class I. AMPHIBIA.
Sub-Class 1. *Urodela*.
Orders.—1. *Ichthyoidea*. 2. *Salamandrina*.
Sub-Class 2. *Gymnophiona* (*Cœcilia*, &c.).
,, 3. *Stegocephala* (*Labyrinthodon*, &c.).
,, 4. *Anura* (*Rana*, &c.).
Sub-Grade *c*. **Lipobranchia Pentadactyla.**
Branch *a*. *MONOCONDYLA*.
Class I. REPTILIA.
Sub-Class 1. *Chelonia* (orders not tabulated).
,, 2. *Lacertilia*.
Orders.—1. *Rhynchocephala*. 2. *Chamæleonina*. 3. *Lacertina*.
Sub-Class 3. *Ophidia*.
Orders.—1. *Opoterodonta*. 2. *Colubriformia*. 3. *Proteroglypha*. 4. *Solenoglypha*.
Sub-Class 4. *Crocodilia*.
Orders.—1. *Amphicœlia*. 2. *Opisthocœlia*. 3. *Procœlia*.
Sub-Class 5. *Pterosauria* (orders not tabulated).
,, 6. *Dinosauria*.
Orders.—1. *Sauropoda*. 2. *Stegosauria*. 3. *Ornithopoda*. 4. *Theriopoda*. 5. *Cœluria*. 6. *Compsognatha*. 7. *Hallopoda*.
Sub-Class 7. *Anomodontia* (*Dicynodon*, &c.).
,, 8. *Plesiosauria*.
,, 9. *Icthyosauria*.
,, II. AVES.
Grade *a*. **Phanerodactyla.**
Order. *Saururæ*.
Grade *b*. **Cryptodactyla.**
Orders.—1. *Ratitæ*. 2. *Carinatæ*.
Branch *b*. *AMPHICONDYLA*.
Class. MAMMALIA.
Grade 1. **Monotrema** (*Ornithorhynchus* and *Echidna*).

Grade 2. **Ditrema.**
Branch *a.* *Marsupialia.*
Orders.—1. *Barypoda.* 2. *Rhizophaga.* 3. *Macropoda.* 4. *Carpophaga.* 5. *Pedimana.* 6. *Cantharophaga.* 7. *Creophaga.* 8. *Edentula.*
Branch *b.* *Placentalia.*
Sub-Branch *a.* *Typidentata.*
Orders.—1. *Proinsectivora.* 2. *Insectivora.* 3. *Carnivora.* 4. *Cetacea.* 5. *Ungulata.* 6. *Amblypoda.* 7. *Sirenia.* 8. *Toxodontia.* 9. *Rodentia.* 10. *Proboscidea.* 11. *Hyracoidea.* 12. *Cheiroptera.* 13. *Prosimiæ.* 14. *Simiæ.*
Sub-Branch *b.* *Edentata.*
Orders.—1. *Bradypoda.* 2. *Effodientia.*

Phylum 2. **ECHINODERMA.**

Branch A. **Ambulacrata.**
Class I. HOLOTHURIDEA.
Orders.—1. *Elasipoda.* 2. *Pedata.* 3. *Apoda.*
,, II. ECHINOIDEA.
Grade *a.* **Palæechini** (*Melonites, Eocidaris*).
Grade *b.* **Autechini.**
Branch 1. *Desmosticha.*
Orders.—1. *Regularia.* 2. *Exocyclica.*
Branch 2. *Petalosticha.*
Orders.—1. *Clypeastrina.* 2. *Spatangina.*
,, III. ASTEROIDEA.
Orders.—1. *Colastra.* 2. *Brisingastra.*
,, IV. OPHIUROIDEA.
Orders.—1. *Ophiastra.* 2. *Phytastra.*

Branch B. **Tentaculata.**
Class I. CRINOIDEA.
Orders.—1. *Palæocrina.* 2. *Neocrina.*
,, II. CYSTOIDEA.
Orders.—1. *Agelacrina.* 2. *Echinencrina.*
,, III. BLASTOIDEA.
Orders.—1. *Elæacrina.* 2. *Eleutherocrina.*

Phylum 3. **PODAXONIA.**

Class I. GEPHYRÆA.
Sub-Class 1. *Echiuromorpha.*
Orders.—1. *Sternaspida.* 2. *Echiurina.*
Sub-Class 2. *Sipunculomorpha.*
Orders.—1. *Sipunculina.* 2. *Priapulina.*
,, II. POLYZOA.
Sub-Class 1. *Vermiformia.*
(Genus: *Phoronis.*)
,, 2. *Eupolyzoa.*
Branch *a.* **Ectoprocta.**
Orders.—1. *Phylactolæma.* 2. *Gymnolæma.*
Branch *b.* **Entoprocta.**
(*Loxosoma,* &c.)

[The sub-class *Pterobranchia* (*Rhabdopleura* and *Cephalodiscus*) hitherto referred to *Polyzoa* are probably related to the *Hemichorda* of the Vertebrate phylum.]

,, III. BRACHIOPODA.
Orders.—1. *Ecardines.* 2. *Cardinata.*

Phylum 4. **NEMATOIDEA.**

Class I. EUNEMATOIDEA (no orders).
,, II. CHÆTOSOMARIA.
(*Chætosoma, Rhabdogaster.*)
,, III. CHÆTOGNATHA.
(*Sagitta, Spadella.*)

Phylum 5. **ACANTHOCEPHALA.**
(Genus: *Echinorhynchus.*)

Phylum 6. **GASTROTRICHA.**
(Genera: *Chætonotus, Ichthydium,* &c.)

Phylum 7. **PLATYHELMIA.**

Branch A. **Ciliata.**
Class I. RHABDOCŒLA.
Orders.—1. *Acœla.* 2. *Orthocœla.* 3. *Allœocœla.*
,, II. DENDROCŒLA.
Orders.—1. *Triclada.* 2. *Polyclada.*
,, III. NEMERTINA.
Orders.—1. *Palæonemertina.* 2. *Schizonemertea.* 3. *Hoplonemertea.*

[The *Mesozoa* of Van Beneden may be classed here as a degenerate parasitic group including *Orthonectida* and *Rhombozoa.*]

Branch B. **Cotylophora.**
Class I. TREMATOIDEA.
Sub-Class *a.* *Monogenea.*
Orders.—1. *Tristoma.* 2. *Polystoma.*
Sub-Class *b.* *Digenea.*
Orders.—1. *Monostoma.* 2. *Distoma.* 3. *Gasterostoma.* 4. *Holostoma.*
Class II. CESTOIDEA.
Orders.—1. *Amphilinaria.* 2. *Caryophyllaria.* 3. *Ligularia.* 4. *Echinobothriaria.* 5. *Tetrarhyncharia.* 6. *Phyllobothriaria.* 7. *Tæniaria.*
,, III. HIRUDINEA.
Orders.—1. *Rhynchobdella.* 2. *Gnathobdella.*

Phylum 8. **APPENDICULATA.**

Branch A. **Rotifera.**
Class I. PARAPODIATA.
(Genus: *Pedalion.*)
,, II. LIPOPODA.
Orders.—1. *Ploima.* 2. *Bdelligrada.* 3. *Rhizota.*

Branch B. **Chætopoda.**
Class I. POLYCHÆTA.
Sub-Class 1. *Errantia* (orders not tabulated).
,, 2. *Sedentaria* (orders not tabulated).
,, II. OLIGOCHÆTA.
Orders.—1. *Lumbricomorpha.* 2. *Sænuridomorpha.* 3. *Naidomorpha.* 4. *Bdellomorpha.*
,, III. MYZOSTOMARIA.
(Genus: *Myzostomum.*)
,, IV. SACCOCIRRIDEA.
(Genus: *Saccocirrus.*)
,, V. HAPLOANNELIDA.
(Genera: *Polygordius, Protodrilus, Histriobdella*).

Branch C. **Arthropoda** (=*Gnathopoda*).
Grade 1. **Ceratophora.**
Class I. PERIPATIDEA.
(Genus: *Peripatus.*)
,, II. MYRIAPODA.
Orders.—1. *Diplopoda.* 2. *Chilopoda.*
,, III. HEXAPODA.
Orders.—1. *Orthoptera* (Sub-Orders: *Thysanura, Autorthoptera, Pseudoneuroptera*). 2. *Neuroptera* (Sub-Orders: *Planipennia, Trichoptera*). 3. *Strepsiptera.* 4. *Rhyncota* (Sub-Orders: *Pedicularia, Aphidaria, Cicadaria, Hemiptera*). 5. *Diptera* (Sub-Orders: *Brachycera, Nemocera, Aphaniptera*). 6. *Lepidoptera.* 7. *Coleoptera.* 8. *Hymenoptera.*
Grade 2. **Acerata.**
Class I. CRUSTACEA.
Grade 1. **Entomostraca.**
Orders.—1. *Phyllopoda.* 2. *Ostracoda.* 3. *Copepoda.* 4. *Cirripedia.*
Grade 2. **Leptostraca.**
(Genus: *Nebalia.*)
Grade 3. **Malacostraca.**
Branch *a.* *Arthrostraca.*
Orders.—1. *Amphipoda.* 2. *Isopoda.*
Branch *b.* *Thoracostraca.*
Orders.—1. *Cumacea.* 2. *Stomapoda.* 3. *Podophthalmia.*
,, II. ARACHNIDA.
Grade *a.* **Delobranchia.**
Orders.—1. *Eurypterina.* 2. *Xiphosura.* 3. *Trilobitæ.*
Grade *b.* **Embolobranchia.**
Orders.—1. *Scorpionina.* 2. *Thelyphonina.* 3. *Araneina.*
Grade *c.* **Lipobranchia.**
Orders.—1. *Galeodina.* 2. *Opilionina.* 3. *Pseudoscorpionina.* 4. *Acarina.*
,, III. PANTOPODA.
(Genera: *Pycnogonum,* &c.)
,, IV. TARDIGRADA.
(Genera: *Macrobiotus, Milnesium,* &c.)
,, V. LINGUATULINA.
(Genera: *Pentastoma,* &c.)

Phylum 9. **MOLLUSCA.**

Branch A. **Glossophora.**
Class I. GASTROPODA.
Grade 1. **Isopleura.**
Orders.—1. *Polyplacophora.* 2. *Neomeniaria.* 3. *Chætodermaria.*
Grade 2. **Anisopleura.**
Branch *a.* *Streptoneura.*
Orders.—1. *Zygobranchia.* 2. *Azygobranchia.*
Branch *b.* *Euthyneura.*
Orders.—1. *Opisthobranchia.* 2. *Pulmonata.*
,, II. SCAPHOPODA.
(Genus: *Dentalium.*)
,, III. CEPHALOPODA (=*Siphonopoda*).
Orders.—1. *Tetrabranchia.* 2. *Dibranchia.*

Branch B. **Lipocephala.**
Class. LAMELLIBRANCHIA.
Orders.—1. *Isomya.* 2. *Heteromya.* 3 *Monomya.*

We have now traced the history of the morphography of animals so as to show that increasingly in successive epochs independent branches of knowledge have been brought to bear on the consideration of the main problem, namely, the discrimination of the kinds and the relations to one another of animal forms. Before glancing at the history of the remaining branches of zoological science, which have had an independent history whilst ultimately contributory to taxonomy and morphography, it may be briefly pointed out that the accumulation of knowledge with regard to the distribution of animal forms on the earth's surface and in the seas has progressed simultaneously with the discrimination of the mere forms of the species themselves, as has also the knowledge derived from fossilized remains as to the characters of former inhabitants of the globe. Both these subdivisions of morphography have contributed to the establishment of Darwinism,—the one (palæontology) by direct evidence of organic evolution in time, the other (zoo-geography) in a more indirect way.

Development of new species.

Alfred Russel Wallace stands prominently forward as a naturalist-traveller who by his observations, chiefly on Lepidopterous Insects, in both South America and the Malay Archipelago, was led to the conclusion that a production of new species is actually going on, and that, too, by means of a process of natural selection of favourable variations. Wallace and Darwin, who each recognized cordially and fully the other's work, laid their views before the Linnean Society on the same day in 1859.

Geographical distribution of animals.

The facts of the geographical distribution of animals were systematized, and great zoo-geographical provinces first clearly recognized, by P. L. Sclater in 1857. The application of the Darwinian theory to the facts tabulated by Sclater, combined with a knowledge of the distribution of animals in past geological periods, has led to a full explanation of the migrations of terrestrial animals, and has furnished a striking corroboration of the sufficiency of the doctrine of organic evolution, as reformed by Darwin, to account for all the phenomena of zoology.

Study of marine fauna.

The study of the marine fauna by means of the dredge and trawl had been enthusiastically prosecuted by British, French, and Scandinavian naturalists in the two decades before Darwin's book; the collection of forms, the discovery of new species, and the recording of their bathymetrical and local distribution had produced a great mass of knowledge through the labours of E. Forbes, Gwyn-Jeffreys, Sars, Quatrefages, Norman, and others. The post-Darwinian developments of this line of inquiry have been two. In the first place, dredging and trawling have been extended by the aid of steamships of the Norwegian, British, American, French, and Italian navies into greater depths than were previously supposed to contain living things. New species and genera, and a vast extension of knowledge as to distribution, have been the outcome of these expeditions, connected with the names of G. O. Sars and Daniellsen in Norway, of Alex. Agassiz in America, and of Carpenter and Wyville Thomson in Great Britain. It is worthy of note that the practical demand for sounding the Atlantic in connexion with the laying of the first deep-sea telegraph-cable is what led to these explorations, the first recognition of life at these great depths in the ocean being due to Dr Wallich, who accompanied a sounding expedition in 1860 to the North Atlantic, and to Prof. Fleeming Jenkin, who in the same year acted as engineer in raising the submarine cable between Sardinia and Africa, upon which living corals were found. In the second place, the study of marine zoology has, since the publication of the *Origin of Species*, been found to require more complete arrangements in the form of laboratories and aquaria than the isolated vacation student could bring with him to the seaside. Seaside laboratories have come into existence: the first was founded in France by Coste (1859) at Concarneau (Brittany), again with a practical end in view, viz., the study of food-fishes with an aim to pisciculture. The demand for a knowledge of the embryology of all classes of animals, and for further facts as to the structure and life-history of the minuter microscopic or very delicate forms of marine life, is what has determined the multiplication of these marine "stations." The largest and best supported pecuniarily is that founded at Naples by Anton Dohrn in 1872; others exist at Trieste, Villefranche, Cette, and at New Haven and Beaufort in the United States, whilst a large laboratory, on a scale to compare with that at Naples, has this year (1888) been opened at Plymouth by the Marine Biological Association of the United Kingdom.

Expeditions for local study of fauna.

Another result of the stimulus given to zoological research by Darwin's work is the undertaking of voyages to distant lands by skilled anatomists for the purpose of studying on the spot, and with all the advantages of abundant and living material, the structure, and especially the embryology, of rare and exceptionally interesting forms of animal life. In the pre-Darwinian period of this century zoologists who were convinced of the importance of anatomical and embryological study were still content to study specimens immersed in spirit and brought home, often imperfectly preserved, by unskilled collectors, or to confine their attention to such species as could be procured in Europe. Before Cuvier, as we have already pointed out, attention was, with rare exceptions, limited to the dried skeletons and external forms of animals. Now, however, the enterprising zoologist goes to the native land of an interesting animal, there to study it as fully as possible. The most important of these voyages has been that of W. H. Caldwell of Cambridge to Australia (1885-86) for the purpose of studying the embryology of the *Monotrema* and of *Ceratodus*, the fish-like *Dipnoon*, which has resulted in the discovery that the *Monotrema* are oviparous. Similarly Adam Sedgwick proceeded to the Cape in order to study *Peripatus*, Bateson to the coast of Maryland to study *Balanoglossus*, and the brothers Sarassin to Ceylon to investigate the embryology of the *Cœcilia*.

The task of the zoologist has changed and developed in every succeeding period. Pure morphography has long ceased to be a chief line of research; and now even the preoccupation produced by the addition to it of the study of cellular embryology is about to undergo a modification by the demand for knowledge of the facts of heredity and adaptation in greatly extended detail.

Zoo-Mechanics, Zoo-Physics, Zoo-Chemistry.

Study of anatomy and physiology.

The development of that knowledge of the structure of the human body, and of the chemical and physical processes going on in it, which is necessary for the purposes of the medical art forms a distinct history, which has both influenced and been influenced by that of other branches of zoology. The study of the structure and composition of the body of man and of the animals nearest to him was until fifty years ago one with the inquiry into the activities of those parts, and indeed the separation of anatomy and physiology has never been really carried out. For convenience of teaching, the description of the coarser anatomy of the human body has been in modern universities placed in the hands of a special professor, theoretically condemned to occupy himself with the mere formal details of structure, whilst the professor of physiology has usually retained what is called "microscopic anatomy," and necessarily occupies himself with as much structural anatomy as is required for a due description of the functions of organs and the properties of tissues. It would seem that in our medical schools and universities these arrangements should be reconsidered. Anatomy and physiology should be re-united and subdivided as follows,—(1) physiology with anatomy in relation to physiology, (2) anatomy in relation to surgery and medical diagnosis,—the former being a science, the latter a piece of technical training in rule of thumb.

Physiological anatomy or anatomical physiology has its beginnings in Aristotle and other observers of antiquity. The later Græco-Roman and the Arabian physicians carried on the traditional knowledge and added to it. Galen dominated the Middle Ages. The modern development begins with Harvey and with the Italian school in which he studied. Its great names are Fabricius of Acquapendente (1537-1619), Vesalius (1514-1564), Eustachius (*c.* 1500-1574), Riolan (1577-1657), Severino (1580-1656). The history of the discovery of the circulation of the blood and of the controversies connected with it gives an interesting and sufficient presentation of the anatomico-physiological knowledge of the period (see HARVEY). The foundation of the scientific academies and the records of their publications furnish thenceforward a picture of the progress in this study. As an early anatomist Willis (1621-1675), professor of physic in Oxford, deserves notice for his work on the anatomy of the human brain, the plates for which were drawn by young Christopher Wren, the prodigy of Oxford common-rooms, who later built St Paul's Cathedral. The Royal Society, in its early days when Wren was a fellow, met at Gresham College whenever the professor of physic there could obtain a human body for dissection, and amongst its earliest records are the memoirs of Tyson on the anatomy of the Chimpanzee and the experiments on transfusion of blood, extirpation of the spleen, and such like inquiries.

Harvey and the Italian school.

Marcello Malpighi (1628-1694) and Anton van Leeuwenhoek (1632-1723) were the first to introduce the microscope into anatomical research. Malpighi first used the injection of blood-vessels on a large scale, and moreover is to be credited with having first conceived that there is a definite relation of the structure of lower kinds of animals to that of higher and more elaborate kinds, and that this relation is one of gradual transition, so that lower animals are not to be regarded as isolated and arbitrary existences, but are really simpler exhibitions of the same kind of structure and mechanism which occurs in higher animals. It is this conception which later developed into the theory of an actual transmutative development of lower into higher organisms. Leeuwenhoek discovered the red blood corpuscles of Vertebrates, saw the circulation in the capillaries of the Frog's foot, described the fibrillar structure and cross-striping of muscular fibre, the tubular structure of dentine, the scales of the epidermis, the fibres of the lens, and the spermatozoa, these last having been independently discovered at Leyden in 1677 by Ludwig Ham of Stettin. The spermatozoa were regarded by the "animalculists" as the fully formed but minute young which had to be received in the egg, in order to be nourished and increase in size, and were hailed as a decisive blow to Harvey's doctrine of epigenesis and his dictum "omne vivum ex ovo." Albrecht von Haller was the champion of the so-called "evolutionists" in the 18th century, better called "præformationists." Haller wrote, "There is no such thing as development! No part of the animal body is made before another; all are simultaneously created." A corollary of this doctrine was that the germ contains the germs of the next generation, and these of the next, and so *ad infinitum.* It was calculated that Eve at her creation thus contained within her 200,000 millions of human germs. This was the view of the "ovists," who regarded the egg as the true germ, whilst the "animalculists," who regarded the spermatozoon as the essential germ, would have substituted Adam for Eve in the above calculation. These fanciful conceptions—containing as they do a share of important truth—were opposed by Caspar Friedrich Wolff, who in his doctorate dissertation (1759) maintained that the germ is a structureless particle, and acquires its structure by "epigenesis" or gradual development. Wolff has proved to be nearer the truth than Haller; but modern conceptions as to the molecular structure of the egg-protoplasm point to a complexity as great as that imagined by the evolutionists. Later it was maintained that the spermatozoa are parasitic animalcules, and this view prevailed for 150 years, so that in the *Physiology* of Johann Müller (1842) we read, "Whether the spermatozoa are parasitic animalcules or living parts of the animal in which they occur cannot at present be stated with certainty."

Malpighi and Leeuwenhoek.

Ovists *versus* animalculists.

Physiology in the 18th century could only proceed by means of inferences from purely anatomical observation, aided by imaginative conceptions which had no real basis. The explanation of the processes of life in the animal body was waiting for that progress in the knowledge of physics and chemistry which at last arrived, and gave a new impulse to investigation. Albrecht von Haller (1708-1777) was the first to apply experimental methods to the determination of the functions of the various organs made known by anatomists, and from him we may trace a bifurcation in the tendencies of medical men who occupied themselves with the study of the structure and functions of the animal organism. The one class proceeded more and more in the direction of comparative anatomy, the other in the direction of exact analysis and measurement of both the structure and properties of the organs of Vertebrate animals allied to man and of man himself.

Von Haller.

John Hunter (1728-1793) is the most striking figure of this epoch in the relation of medicine to general zoological progress; the preservation of his museum in Lincoln's Inn Fields, London, by the combined action of the state and the Royal College of Surgeons, is an abiding record of the historical progress of biological science. Hunter collected, dissected, and described not only higher but lower animals, with the view of arriving at a knowledge of the function of organs by the most extensive and systematic survey of their modifications in all kinds of animals. His purpose was that of the physiologist and medical man, but he made great contributions to the general knowledge of animal structure. The same class of investigations, when taken up by Cuvier from the point of view of systematic zoology and morphology, led to a reconstruction of classification and laid the foundation of anatomical zoology. Hunter was the younger brother of William Hunter, who also formed an important museum, still preserved in Glasgow. Hunter classified the organs of animals into those which subserve the preservation of the individual, those which subserve the preservation of the species, and those which are the means of relation with the outer world, and he arranged his museum of dissections and preparations on this plan.

The two Hunters.

The great progress of chemistry at the end of the 18th and the beginning of the 19th century was followed by an application of chemical laws and chemical methods to the study of animal life. Curiously enough, as showing how deeply interwoven are the various lines of scientific progress, Priestley in his discovery of oxygen was as much concerned in the study of a chlorophyll-bearing *Protozoon, Euglena viridis,* as in that of the red oxide of mercury; and the interest in "vital spirits" as a physiological factor was an important stimulus to those researches which produced modern chemical knowledge.

Relations of chemistry and zoology.

The purely anatomical side of physiological progress is marked in the beginning of the 19th century by the work

Beginnings of histology.

of Bichat (1771-1802), who distinguished by naked-eye characters the different structural materials of which the organs of man and the higher animals are built, and thus founded in first outline the science of histology. By the end of the first quarter of this century it had become clear to the minds of the anatomico-physiological students of animal life that the animal body was subject to the same physical laws as other matter, although it was still held that some additional and mysterious agent—so-called "vitality"—was at work in living bodies. It had become clear that animal material could be investigated chemically, and that the processes of digestion, assimilation, respiration, and secretion were chemical processes.

Schwann's cell-theory.

To a considerable extent the chemical composition and properties of the tissues, and the chemical nature of the various changes of life and of putrefaction after death, had been investigated, but one step was yet to be taken which brings the study of ultimate structure, chemical activity, form, and the formation of form to a single focus. This was taken by Theodore Schwann (1810-1881), who in 1839 published his epoch-making cell-theory. Schwann was a pupil of Johann Müller, and there can be little doubt that the ideas of the pupil are to be credited in some measure to the master. Schwann took up the thread of microscopic investigation which had been sedulously pursued by a distinct line of students since the days of Hook and Leeuwenhoek, and had resulted in a general doctrine among botanists of the cellular structure of all the parts of plants. Schwann showed not only that plants are uniformly built up by these corpuscular units (of which Robert Browne in 1833 had described the peculiar nucleated structure), but that all animal tissues are also so built up. That, however, was not Schwann's chief point. The cell-theory for which he is famous is this, that the substance of the individual cell is the seat of those chemical processes which seen *en masse* we call life, and that the differences in the properties of the different tissues and organs of animals and plants depend on a difference in the chemical and physical activity of the constituent cells, resulting in a difference in the form of the cells and in a concomitant difference of activity. Schwann thus pointed to the microscopic cell-unit as the thing to be studied in order to arrive at a true knowledge of the processes of life and the significance of form. In founding the study of cell-substance (or protoplasm, as it was subsequently called by Max Schultze in 1861, adopting the name used by botanists for vegetable cell-contents) Schwann united two lines of inquiry, viz., that of minute investigation of structure and development and that of zoo-chemistry and zoo-physics. He spent a large part of the next forty years in an attempt to penetrate further into the structure of cell-substance; he hoped to be able to find in cell-substance ultimate visible molecules, a knowledge of the arrangement and characters of which would explain the varying properties of protoplasm.

Schwann's other discoveries.

It is not a little remarkable that Schwann, who thus brought about the union of physiological and morphological study by his conception of cell-substance, should also have been the initiator of that special kind of experimental investigation of the physical properties of tissues by the exact methods used by physicists which, by the aid of the kymographion, the thermo-electric pile, and the galvanometer, has been so largely pursued during the last thirty years in our physiological laboratories. It is perhaps less surprising that Schwann, who had so vivid a conception of the activity and potentialities of the cell-unit, should have been the discoverer of the immensely important fact that putrefaction and fermentation are not the consequences of death but of life, and that without the presence of living *Bacteria* putrefaction does not occur, whilst he also is the discoverer of the fact that the yeast which causes alcoholic fermentation is a mass of unicellular living organisms.

Development of cell-theory.

From Schwann's time onward the cell became more and more the point of observation and experiment in the progress of both morphography and physiology. It was soon shown, chiefly through Kölliker and Remak, that all cells originate by fission from pre-existing cells,—a fact unknown to Schwann,—and the doctrine "omnis cellula e cellula" was established. It was also demonstrated that the Mammalian egg discovered by Von Baer was a typical nucleated cell, and that all animals, and plants also (this generalization took thirty years to establish), take their origin from an egg, which is in essence and in fact a single nucleated cell. The doctrine of Harvey, "omne vivum ex ovo," thus received its most ample justification. The study of "growth from the egg" became necessarily a study of the multiplication by fission of the egg-cell and its fission-products, their arrangement in layers, and the chemical metamorphosis of their substance and exudations. This study, as well as the allied investigation of the cell-structure of the adult tissues, was immensely facilitated by methods of hardening, staining, section-cutting, and clarifying which grew up after Schwann's time, and have their present highest development in the automatic microtome of Caldwell, which can be worked by a motor, and delivers consecutive sections of animal tissues or embryos $\frac{1}{4000}$th of an inch thick, arranged in the form of ribbons, ready for examination with the microscope, at the rate of one hundred or more per minute. Stricker of Vienna was the first to embed embryos in waxy material for the purpose of cutting thin sections of them, about twenty-five years ago, and R. Leuckart of Leipsic was subsequently the first to employ this method in the study of the structure of small *Invertebrata*.

The knowledge of the anatomical facts of cellular development and cellular structure necessarily gave immensely increased precision to the notion of gradation of structure in the animal series from simple to complex, and rendered Darwin's doctrine the more readily accepted. It was not, however, until after Darwin's date (1859) that the existence of unicellular animals was fully admitted, and the general facts of cellular embryology established throughout the animal kingdom.

Cellular physiology.

Similarly cellular physiology, by establishing the conception of a simple optically homogeneous cell-substance as the seat of the activities which we call "life," rendered it possible to accept the suggestion of a simple "substance of life" which might have been evolved from simpler non-living matter by natural processes depending on physical and chemical laws. It is noteworthy that Darwin himself appears not to have been influenced directly by any such physiological or chemico-physical doctrine as to "protoplasm" or cell-substance. Nevertheless the way was prepared for the reception of Darwin's theory by this state of physiological knowledge.

Protoplasm.

The word "protoplasm" requires a little further notice. Protoplasm was applied by Von Mohl and by Max Schultze to the slimy substance of the cell, including therein both the general thinner material and the nucleus. It is, as Roscoe remarked at Manchester (*Brit. Ass. Address*, 1887), a structure and not a chemical body. Nevertheless gradually physiologists have come to use the word "protoplasm" for *one* of the chemical substances of which Schultze's protoplasm is a structural mixture—namely, that highest point in the chemical elaboration of the molecule which is attained within the protoplasm, and up to which some of the chemical bodies present are tending, whilst others are degradation products resulting from a downward metamorphosis of portions of it. This intangible, unstable, all-pervading element of the protoplasm cannot at present be identified with any visibly separable part of the cell-substance, which consists of a hyaline denser network of excessive tenuity, of a less dense hyaline liquid, and of finest and less fine granules of varying chemical nature. This "critical" substance, sometimes called "true protoplasm," should assuredly be recognized by a distinct name "plasmogen," whilst protoplasm retains its structural connotation.

Plasmology.

The study of the process of fertilization and of the significance in that process of the distinct parts of the sperm-cell and egg-cell—the separate fibrillæ and granules of the nuclei of those cells—at the present moment forms one of the engrossing subjects of zoological investigation.[1] Not less important is the descent, as it were, of physiological investigation in relation to every organ into the arena of the cell: digestion, secretion, muscular contraction, nerve action, all are now questions of plasmology, or the study of cell-substance founded by Schwann.[2]

General Tendency of Zoology since Darwin.

Bionomics.

The serious and broadly-based study of bionomics which was introduced by Darwin, and in his hands gave rise to the doctrine of natural selection, by which the hypothesis of the origin of species by gradual transmutation in the natural process of descent from ancestral forms was established as a scientific doctrine, can hardly be said to have had any history. Buffon (1707-1788) alone among the greater writers of the three past centuries emphasized that view of living things which we call "bionomics." Buffon deliberately opposed himself to the mere exposition of the structural resemblances and differences of animals, and, disregarding classification, devoted his treatise on natural history to a consideration of the habits of animals and their adaptations to their surroundings, whilst a special volume was devoted by him to the subject of reproduction. In special memoirs on this or that animal, and in a subordinate way in systematic works, material is to be found helping to build up a knowledge of bionomics, but Buffon is the only prominent writer who can be accorded historic rank in this study.[3] The special study of man in these relations—such as is concerned with the statistics of population—must be considered as having contributed very importantly to Darwin's wider study of bionomics in general. The work of Malthus *On Population* (1798) exercised the most important influence on Darwin's thought, as he himself tells us, and led him to give attention to the facts of animal population, and so to discover the great moving cause of natural selection—the struggle for existence. Darwin may be said to have founded the science of bionomics, and at the same time to have given new stimulus and new direction to morphography, physiology, and plasmology, by uniting them as contributories to one common biological doctrine—the doctrine of organic evolution—itself but a part of the wider doctrine of universal evolution based on the laws of physics and chemistry.

The full influence of Darwin's work upon the progress and direction of zoological study has not yet been seen. The *immediate* result has been, as pointed out above, a reconstruction of the classification of animals upon a genealogical basis, and an investigation of the individual development of animals in relation to the steps of their gradual building up by cell-division, with a view to obtaining evidence of their genetic relationships. On the other hand, the studies which occupied Darwin himself so largely subsequently to the publication of the *Origin of Species*,

Teleology.

viz., the explanation of animal (and vegetable) mechanism, colouring, habits, &c., as advantageous to the species or to its ancestors—in fact, the new teleology,—has not yet been so vigorously pursued as it must be hereafter. The most important work in this direction has been done by Fritz Müller (*Für Darwin*), by Herman Müller (*Fertilization of Plants by Insects*), and by August Weismann (memoirs translated by Meldola). Here and there observations are from time to time published, but no large progress has yet been made, probably on account of the fact that animals are exceedingly difficult to keep under observation, and that there is no provision in universities and like institutions for the pursuit of these inquiries or even for their academic representation. More has been done with plants than with animals in this way since Darwin, probably owing to the same cause which has, ever since the revival of learning, given botany a real advantage over zoology, namely, the existence of "physick" gardens, now become "botanical" gardens, and the greater ease of management, experiment, and observation in the case of plants than in that of animals. It is true that zoological gardens have existed for the last fifty years in all large European cities, but these have always been conducted with a view to popular exhibition; and, even where scientific influences have been brought to bear on their management, they have been those of the morphographer and systematist rather than of the bionomist. Moreover, zoological gardens have never been part of the equipment of the university professor of zoology, as it may be hoped in future will be the case. The foundation of marine biological laboratories under the control of scientific zoologists offers a prospect of true bionomic observation and experiment on an increased scale in the near future, and, were such laboratories founded in our universities and provided with the necessary appliances for keeping terrestrial and freshwater animals, as well as marine forms, alive and under observation in conditions resembling as nearly as possible those of nature, a step would have been taken towards carrying on the study of bionomics which cannot long be delayed. It seems to be even more important that the academic curriculum of zoology should not, by mere mechanical adhesion to the old lines of morphography, and experimental research on the chemical and physical properties of tissues and organs, confine the attention and training of young students to what are now, comparatively speaking, the less productive lines of research.

Thremmatology.

If we turn to the other branch of bionomics, that concerned with the laws of variation and heredity (thremmatology), we find that since Darwin, and independently of his own work, there has been a more obvious progress than in teleology. In the first place, the continued study of human population has thrown additional light on some of the questions involved, whilst the progress of microscopical research in the hands of Bütschli, Hertwig, Balfour, and August Weismann promises to give us a clear foundation as to the structural facts connected with the origin of the egg-cell and sperm-cell and the process of fertilization. This is not the fitting place in which to give a sketch of the doctrines and hypotheses of thremmatology. They may be gathered from Darwin's writings, more especially the *Origin of Species* and *Animals and Plants under Domestication*.[4] They relate to the causes of variation in animals and plants, the laws of the transmission of parental characters, the share of each parent in the production of the characters of the offspring, atavism, and the relations of young to parents as to number, sex, nourishment, and protection.

An important development of Darwin's conclusions is actually in progress and deserves special notice here, as it

[1] See the memoirs of Weismann on Heredity and F. M. Balfour's *Embryology*.

[2] For a fuller and general history of Physiology, see that article.

[3] The main literary sources made use of by Darwin are the magazines and treatises of horticulturists, farmers, pigeon-fanciers, and the like, in fact what is comprised in the *Field* newspaper.

[4] The reader is also referred to Ribot's *L'Hérédité*, and the writings of Charles Darwin's cousin, Francis Galton.

is the most distinct advance in the department of bionomics since Darwin's own writings, and at the same time touches questions of fundamental interest. The matter strictly relates to the consideration of the "causes of variation," and is as follows.

The fact of variation is a familiar one. No two animals, even of the same brood, are alike: whilst exhibiting a close similarity to their parents, they yet present differences, sometimes very marked differences, from their parents and from one another. Lamarck had put forward the hypothesis that structural alterations acquired by a parent in the course of its life are transmitted to the offspring, and that, as these structural alterations are acquired by an animal or plant in consequence of the direct action of the environment, the offspring inheriting them would as a consequence not unfrequently start with a greater fitness for those conditions than its parents started with. In its turn, being operated upon by the conditions of life, it would acquire a greater development of the same modification, which it would in turn transmit to its offspring. In the course of several generations, Lamarck argued, a structural alteration amounting to such difference as we call "specific" might be thus acquired. The familiar illustration of Lamarck's hypothesis is that of the giraffe, whose long neck might, he suggested, have been acquired by the efforts of a primitively short-necked race of herbivores, who stretched their necks to reach the foliage of trees in a land where grass was deficient, the effort producing a distinct elongation in the neck of each generation, which was then transmitted to the next. This process is known as "direct adaptation;" and there is no doubt that such structural adaptations are acquired by an animal in the course of its life. Whether such acquired characters can be transmitted to the next generation is a separate question. It was not proved by Lamarck that they can be, and, indeed, never has been proved by actual observation. Nevertheless it has been assumed, and also indirectly argued, that such acquired characters *must* be transmitted. Darwin's great merit was that he excluded from his theory of development any *necessary* assumption of the transmission of acquired characters. He pointed to the admitted fact of congenital variation, and he showed that these variations to all intents and purposes have nothing to do with any characters acquired by the parents, but are arbitrary and, so to speak, non-significant. Their causes are extremely difficult to trace in detail, but it appears that they are largely due to a "shaking up" of the living matter which constitutes the fertilized germ or embryo-cell, by the process of mixture in it of the substance of two cells,—the germ-cell and the sperm-cell,—derived from two different individuals. Other mechanical disturbances may assist in this production of congenital variation. Whatever its causes, Darwin showed that it is all-important. In some cases a pair of animals produce ten million offspring, and in such a number a large range of congenital variation is possible. Since on the average only two of the young survive in the struggle for existence to take the place of their two parents, there is a selection out of the ten million young, none of which are exactly alike, and the selection is determined in nature by the survival of the congenital variety which is fittest to the conditions of life. Hence there is no *necessity* for an assumption of the perpetuation of direct adaptations. The selection of the fortuitously (fortuitously, that is to say, so far as the conditions of survival are concerned) produced varieties is sufficient, since it is ascertained that they will tend to transmit those characters with which they themselves were born, although it is *not* ascertained that they could transmit characters *acquired* on the way through life. A simple illustration of the difference is this: a man born with four fingers only on his right hand is ascertained to be likely to transmit this peculiarity to some at least of his offspring; on the other hand, there is not the slightest ground for supposing that a man who has had one finger chopped off, or has even lost his arm at any period of his life, will produce offspring who are defective in the slightest degree in regard to fingers, hand, or arm. Darwin himself, apparently influenced not merely by the consideration of certain classes of facts which seem to favour the Lamarckian hypothesis but also by a respect for the general prejudice in its favour and for Mr Herbert Spencer's authority, was of the opinion that acquired characters are *in some cases* transmitted. It should be observed, however, that Darwin did not attribute an essential part to this Lamarckian hypothesis of the transmission of acquired characters, but expressly assigned to it an entirely subordinate importance.

Causes of congenital variation.

Transmission of acquired and inherited characters.

The new attitude which has been taken since Darwin on this question is to ask for evidence of this asserted transmission of acquired characters. It is held[1] that the Darwinian doctrine of selection of fortuitous congenital variations is sufficient to account for all cases, that the Lamarckian hypothesis of transmission of acquired characters is not supported by experimental evidence, and that the latter should therefore be dismissed. Weismann has also ingeniously argued from the structure of the egg-cell and sperm-cell, and from the way in which, and the period at which, they are derived in the course of the growth of the embryo from the egg—from the fertilized egg-cell—that it is impossible (it would be better to say highly improbable) that an alteration in parental structure *could* produce any exactly representative change in the substance of the germ or sperm-cells.

It does not seem improbable that the doctrine of organic evolution will thus become pure Darwinism and be entirely dissociated from the Lamarckian heresy.

The one fact which the Lamarckians can produce in their favour is the account of experiments by Brown-Séquard, in which he produced epilepsy in guinea-pigs by section of the large nerves or spinal cord, and in the course of which he was led to believe that in a few rare instances the artificially produced epilepsy was transmitted. This instance does not stand the test of criticism. It is not clear whether the guinea-pigs operated upon had or had not already a constitutional tendency to epilepsy, and it is not clear in what proportion of cases the supposed transmission took place, and whether any other disease accompanied it. On the other hand, the vast number of experiments in the cropping of the tails and ears of domestic animals, as well as of similar operations on man, are attended with negative results. No case of the transmission of the results of an injury can be produced. Stories of tailless kittens, puppies, and calves, born from parents one of whom had been thus injured, are abundant, but they have hitherto entirely failed to stand before examination.

Experimental researches on this question are most urgently needed, but they are not provided for either in the morphographical or physiological laboratories of our universities.

Whilst simple evidence of the fact of the transmission of an acquired character is wanting, the *a priori* arguments in its favour break down one after another when discussed. The very cases which are advanced as only to be explained on the Lamarckian assumption are found on examination and experiment to be better explained, or only to be explained, by the Darwinian principle. Thus the occurrence of blind animals in caves and in the deep sea was a fact which Darwin himself regarded as best explained by the atrophy of the organ of vision in successive generations through the absence of light and consequent disuse, and

[1] Weismann, *Vererbung*, &c., 1886.

the transmission (as Lamarck would have supposed) of a more and more weakened and structurally impaired eye to the offspring in successive generations, until the eye finally disappeared. But this instance is really fully explained by the theory of natural selection acting on congenital fortuitous variations. Many animals are thus born with distorted or defective eyes whose parents have not had their eyes submitted to any peculiar conditions. Supposing a number of some species of Arthropod or Fish to be swept into a cavern or to be carried from less to greater depths in the sea,—those individuals with perfect eyes would follow the glimmer of light and eventually escape to the outer air or the shallower depths, leaving behind those with imperfect eyes to breed in the dark place. A natural selection would thus be effected. In every succeeding generation this would be the case, and even those with weak but still seeing eyes would in the course of time escape, until only a pure race of eyeless or blind animals would be left in the cavern or deep sea. Experiments and inquiries with regard to this subject are in progress; amongst those who have occupied themselves with it are August Weismann of Freiburg and E. B. Poulton of Oxford.

Theory of transmission of instincts.

It has been argued that the elaborate structural adaptations of the nervous system which are the corporeal correlatives of complicated instincts must have been slowly built up by the transmission to offspring of acquired experience, that is to say, of acquired brain structure. At first sight it appears difficult to understand how the complicated series of actions which are definitely exhibited as so-called "instincts" by a variety of animals can have been due to the selection of congenital variations, or can be otherwise explained than by the transmission of habits acquired by the parent as the result of experience, and continuously elaborated and added to in successive generations. It is, however, to be noted, in the first place, that the imitation of the parent by the young possibly accounts for some part of these complicated actions, and, secondly, that there are cases in which curiously elaborate actions are performed by animals as a characteristic of the species, and as subserving the general advantage of the race or species, which, nevertheless, can *not* be explained as resulting from the transmission of acquired experience, and must be supposed to be due to the natural selection of a fortuitously developed habit which, like fortuitous colour or form variation, happens to prove beneficial. Mr Poulton has insisted upon the habits of "shamming dead" and the combined posturing and colour peculiarities of certain caterpillars (Lepidopterous larvæ) which cause them to resemble dead twigs or similar surrounding objects. The advantage to the animal of this imitation of surrounding objects is that it escapes the pursuit of (say) a bird which would, were it not deceived by the resemblance, attack and eat the caterpillar. Now it is clear that preceding generations of caterpillars cannot have acquired this habit of posturing by experience. Either the caterpillar postures and escapes, or it does not posture and is eaten; it is not half eaten and allowed to profit by experience. We seem to be justified in assuming that there are many movements of stretching and posturing possible to caterpillars, and that some caterpillars had a congenital fortuitous tendency to one position, some to another, and, finally, that among all the variety of habitual movements thus exhibited one has been selected and perpetuated because it coincided with the necessary conditions of safety, since it happened to give the caterpillar an increased resemblance to a twig.

The view that instinct is the hereditarily fixed result of habit derived from experience has hitherto dominated all inquiry into the subject, but we may now expect to see a renewed and careful study of animal instincts carried out with the view of testing the applicability to each instance of the pure Darwinian theory without the aid of Lamarckism.

The whole of this inquiry has special importance in regard to mankind, since the great questions of influence of race and family as opposed to the influence of education are at issue. If pure Darwinism is to be accepted, then education has no value in directly affecting the mental or physical features of the race, but only in affecting those of the individual. Were acquired characters really and fully transmitted, then every child born would inherit the knowledge of both its parents more or less completely, and from birth onwards would be able to add to its inherited stock, so that the progress of the race in mental acquirements would be prodigiously more rapid than it is. On the other hand, peculiarities of mind and body established in a race or a family acquire increased significance, for they cannot be got rid of by training, but are bound to reappear if the stock which exhibits them is allowed to breed. It seems that the laws of thremmatology may eventually give to mankind the most precise directions, not only as to how to improve the breeds of plants and animals, but as to how to improve the human stock. It is not a little remarkable that the latest development of zoological science should favour that respect to breeding which is becoming less popular than it was, and should tend to modify the current estimate of the results of education.

Relation of zoology to philosophy.

The relation of Darwinism to general philosophy and of the history of zoology to philosophical doctrines is one of the most interesting chapters which might be written on the subject of this article. It belongs, however, rather to the history of philosophy than to that of zoology. Undoubtedly the conceptions of mankind at different periods of history with regard to cosmogony, and the relations of God, nature, and man, have had a very marked influence upon the study of zoology, just as in its turn the study of zoology has reacted upon those conceptions.

Development of the idea of evolution.

In this, as in other phases of mental development, the ancient Greeks stand out in the most striking manner as possessing what is sometimes called the modern spirit. The doctrine of evolution is formulated in unmistakable terms by Heraclitus and other philosophers of antiquity. Not only so, but the direct examination of nature, including the various forms of animal life, was practised by Aristotle and his disciples in a spirit which, though not altogether free from prejudice, was yet far more like that which actuated the founders of the Royal Society less than three hundred years ago than anything which was manifested in the two thousand years intervening between that date and the time of Alexander the Great. The study of zoology in the Middle Ages was simply a fantastic commentary on Aristotle and the records of animals in the various books of the Bible, elaborated as part of a peculiar system of mystic philosophy, which has more analogy with the fetichism and totem worship of savage races than with any Greek or modern conceptions. So far as philosophy affected the study of zoology in the beginning of the modern period, its influence was felt in the general acceptance of what has been called the Miltonic cosmogony,—namely, that interpretation of the Mosaic writings which is set forth by the poet Milton, and of which the characteristic is the conception of the creation of existing things, including living things, nearly or just as they are, by a rapid succession of "fiats" delivered by an anthropomorphic Creator. It was not until the end of the 18th century that Schelling (as quoted above) conceived that unity of nature and general law of development which is now called the doctrine of evolution.

In England Erasmus Darwin (*Zoonomia*, published in 1794-96), in France Lamarck (*Philosophie Zoologique*,

1809) and Geoffroy Saint-Hilaire (*Principes de Philosophie Zoologique*, 1830), and in Germany Oken (*Lehrbuch der Natur-Philosophie*, 1809-11), Goethe (*Zur Natur Wissensch.*, Stuttgart, 1817), and Treviranus (*Biologie*, 1802-5) were the authors of more or less complete systems of a philosophy of nature in which living things were regarded as the outcome of natural law, that is, of the same general processes which had produced the inanimate universe. The "Natur-philosophen," as they were called in Germany, demand the fullest recognition and esteem. But, just in proportion as the "Natur-philosophen" failed to produce an immediate effect on the study of zoology by their theory of natural development, so was the doctrine of evolution itself deprived of completeness and of the most important demonstration of its laws by the long-continued delay in the final introduction of biology into the area of that doctrine.

Darwin by his discovery of the mechanical principle of organic evolution, namely, the survival of the fittest in the struggle for existence, completed the doctrine of evolution, and gave it that unity and authority which was necessary in order that it should reform the whole range of philosophy. The detailed consequences of that new departure in philosophy have yet to be worked out. Its most important initial conception is the derivation of man by natural processes from ape-like ancestors, and the consequent derivation of his mental and moral qualities by the operation of the struggle for existence and natural selection from the mental and moral qualities of animals. Not the least important of the studies thus initiated is that of the evolution of philosophy itself. Zoology thus finally arrives through Darwin at its crowning development: it touches and may even be said to comprise the history of man, sociology, and psychology.

Bibliography.—Engelmann, *Bibliotheca Historico-Naturalis*, vol. i., 1846 (being a list of the separate works and academical memoirs relating to zoology published between 1700 and 1846); Carus and Engelmann, *Bibl. Zoologica*, Leipsic, 1861 (a similar list of works published between 1846 and 1861); J. V. Carus, *Gesch. d. Zoologie*, Munich, 1872; and L. Agassiz, *An Essay on Classification*, London, 1859.

(E. R. L.)

ZOROASTER, one of the great teachers of the East, the founder of what was the national religion of the Perso-Iranian people from the time of the Achæmenidæ to the close of the Sasanian period. The name (Ζωροάστρης) is the Greek form of the old Iranian *Zarathushtra* and the new Persian *Zardusht*; it seems to mean "possessor of old camels."

Zoroaster was already famous in classical antiquity as the founder of the widely renowned wisdom of the Magi. The later Greek writers place him with almost one consent in the east of Iran, and more particularly in Bactria. The name is not mentioned by Herodotus in his sketch of the Medo-Persian religion (i. 131 *sq.*), but it occurs in a fragment (29) of the earlier writer Xanthus. Plato calls Zoroaster the founder of the doctrine of the Magi and a son of Oromazes. According to Hermodorus, one of Plato's disciples, he was a Persian, the first Magian; according to Hermippus, a Bactrian; according to Trogus Pompeius, even king of the Bactrians and founder of the Magian art and knowledge of the stars; according to Diodorus, an Arian, that is, a native of east Iran. A few details as to his life are also given. Thus, according to Pliny, he laughed on the very day of his birth—a statement found also in the *Zardusht-Nâma*—and for thirty years he lived in the wilderness upon cheese. Plutarch speaks of his intercourse with the deity and compares him with Lycurgus and Numa. Dio Chrysostom, Plutarch's contemporary, declares that neither Homer nor Hesiod sang of the chariot and horses of Zeus so worthily as Zoroaster, of whom the Persians tell that out of love to wisdom and righteousness he withdrew himself from men and lived in solitude upon a mountain. The mountain was burnt up, but Zoroaster escaped uninjured and spoke to the multitude. His struggle with Semiramis seems to be an invention of Ctesias. Plutarch, drawing partly on Theopompus, speaks of his religion in his *Isis and Osiris* (cc. 46 and 47).

Ancient writers differ greatly as to Zoroaster's date. Ctesias, as we have seen, makes him a contemporary of Semiramis. Hermippus of Smyrna places him 5000 years before the Trojan War, Xanthus 6000 years before Xerxes. Aristotle assigned him a similar antiquity. Agathias remarks (ii. 24) with perfect truth that it is no longer possible to determine with any certainty when he lived and legislated. "The Persians," he adds, "say that Zoroaster lived under Hystaspes, but do not make it clear whether by this name they mean the father of Darius or another Hystaspes. But, whatever may have been his date, he was their teacher and instructor in the Magian religion." All classical antiquity, however, without a dissentient voice speaks of Zoroaster as an historical person.

He is nowhere mentioned in the cuneiform inscriptions of the Achæmenidæ, although Darius and his successors were without doubt devoted adherents of Zoroastrianism. Very little value can be attached to the fabulous narratives concerning him in the later Persian and Parsee literature, the *Shâh-Nâma* and the *Zardusht-Nâma* (13th century); and the information of the Pahlavi books is very scanty. The Zend-Avesta alone gives abundant details, which, in part at least, may be regarded as authentic.

Before proceeding to compile from these a brief sketch of the life and doctrine of Zoroaster it will be well that we should first look at the question whether we are entitled to regard him as an historical character at all. For Zoroaster too, like his great fellow-teacher Buddha, has fallen under the ban of modern scepticism. According to Darmesteter and Eduard Meyer, the Parsee saint is a mere myth, a divinity invested with human attributes, an incarnation of the storm-god, who with his divine word, the thunder, comes down from heaven and smites the demons. Darmesteter, however, has failed to realize sufficiently the distinction between the Zoroaster of the later Avesta and the Zoroaster of the Gâthâs. It cannot be denied that in the later Avesta, and still more in writings of more recent date, he is presented in a supernatural light and invested with superhuman powers. At his appearing all nature rejoices (*Yasht* 13, 93); he enters into conflict with the demons and rids the earth of their presence (*Yasht* 17, 19); Satan approaches him as tempter to make him renounce his faith (*Vd.*, 19, 6). The *Zardusht-Nâma* is full of miracles and miraculous deliverances wrought by Zoroaster. But it is quite otherwise in the Gâthâs.

The Gâthâs alone within the Avesta make any claim to be the *ipsissima verba* of the prophet; in the rest of that work they are put into Zoroaster's own mouth (*Yasna*, 9, 1) and are expressly called "the Gâthâs of the holy Zoroaster" (*Yasna*, 57, 8). The litanies of the Yasna, and the Yashts, refer to him as a personage belonging to a remote antiquity. The Vendidad also merely gives accounts of the dialogues between Ormuzd and Zoroaster. The Gâthâs alone claim to be authentic utterances of Zoroaster, his genuine expressions in presence of the assembled church.

The person too of the Zoroaster whom we meet with in these hymns differs *toto cœlo* from the Zoroaster of the younger Avesta. He is the exact opposite of the miraculous personage of later legend,—a mere man, standing always on the solid ground of reality, whose only arms are trust in his God and the protection of his powerful allies. And at times his position is precarious enough. He whom we hear in the Gâthâs has had to face, not merely all forms of outward opposition and the unbelief and lukewarmness of adherents, but also the inward misgivings of his own heart as to the truth and final victory of his cause. At one time hope, at another despondency, now assured confidence, now doubt and despair, here a firm faith in the speedy coming of the kingdom of heaven, there the thought of taking refuge by flight,—such is the range of the emotions which find their immediate expression in these hymns. And the whole breathes such a genuine originality, all is psychologically so accurate and just, the earliest beginnings of the new religious movement, the childhood of a new community of faith, are reflected so naturally in them all, that it is impossible for a moment to think of a later period of composition by a priesthood whom we know to have been devoid of any historical sense, and incapable of reconstructing for themselves the spiritual conditions under which Zoroaster lived. As soon as the position has been fully mastered—that in the Gâthâs we have firm historical ground on which Zoroaster and his surroundings may rest, that here we have the beginnings of the Zoroastrian religion—then it becomes impossible to answer otherwise than affirmatively every general question as to the historical character of Zoroaster. On the other hand, we must not expect too much from the Gâthâs in the way of definite detail. They give no historical account of the life and teaching of their prophet, but rather are, so to say, *versus memoriales*, which recapitulate the main points of interest, often again in an allusive way. It must be remembered too that their extent is but limited.

As to the birthplace of Zoroaster the Avesta is silent. In later tradition two places contended for this honour: the older and more widely spread story made him a native of Rai (Rhagæ) in Media, another of Shîz, the capital of Atropatene, also in Media. It is hard to decide whether both traditions rest merely upon priestly pretensions of a later date or whether one of them is not perhaps authentic. According to *Yasna*, 19, 18, the "zarathushtrotema" or supreme head of the Zoroastrian priesthood had at a later (Median or Sasanian?) time his residence in Rhagæ. But there is a passage in even the Gâthâs (*Y.*, 53, 9) which seems to contain a lurking allusion to Rhagæ; unfortunately, however, both text and meaning are uncertain. However this may be, the activity of Zoroaster as a teacher is certainly to be placed in the east of Iran. On this point also the Gâthâs say nothing. The later Avesta names, as the locality of his advent, "Airyanem vaêjô," a quite fabulous country, which, according to *Vd.*, 1, 3 and 7, was not identified with Bactria. He taught under the reign of a ruler named Vîshtâspa (later Gushtâsp, the Greek Hystaspes), with whom and with whose court he stood in close and friendly relations. This Vîshtâspa must be carefully distinguished from Hystaspes the father of Darius. According to the epic legend, Vîshtâspa was king of Bactria. Already in the later Avesta he has become a half mythical figure, the last in the series of heroes of east Iranian legend, in the arrangement of which series priestly influence is unmistakably evident. He stands at the meeting-point between the old world and the new era which begins with Zoroaster. In the Gâthâs he appears as a quite historical personage; it is essentially to his power and good example that the prophet is indebted for his success. In *Yasna*, 53, 2, he is spoken of as a pioneer of the doctrine revealed by Ormuzd. In the relation between Zoroaster and Vîshtâspa already lies the germ of the state church which afterwards became so completely subservient to the interests of the dynasty and sought its protection from it.

Among the grandees of the court of Vîshtâspa mention is made of two brothers Frashaoshtra and Jâmâspa; the latter, according to the later legend, was the minister of Vîshtâspa. Zoroaster was nearly related to both; his wife Hvôvi seems to have been their sister, and the husband of her daughter, Pourucista, was a son of Jâmâspa. Apart from this connexion, the new prophet relies especially upon his own kindred (*hvaêtush*) and their followers (*airyaman*). His first disciple, Maidhyôimâongha, was a relation; his father was, according to the later Avesta, Pourushaspa, his great-grandfather Haêcataspa, and the ancestor of the whole family Spitama, for which reason Zarathushtra usually bears this surname. His sons and daughters are repeatedly spoken of. His death is, for reasons easily intelligible, nowhere mentioned in the Avesta; in the *Shâh-Nâma* he is said to have been murdered at the altar by the Turanians in the storming of Balkh.

We are quite in the dark as to the date of Zoroaster; King Vîshtâspa has no place in any historical chronology, and the Gâthâs give no hint on the subject. But at any rate he must have lived long before Cyrus, by whose time the new religion had already become established in western Iran (Nic. Damasc., fr. 66). Duncker places him about the year 1000 B.C. Merely conjectural also is the opinion once orally expressed by Gutschmid that Zoroaster may have been a contemporary of Moses, thus belonging, according to Gutschmid's view, to about the 14th century B.C.,—a period of great religious activity throughout western Asia.

It was a new religion that Zoroaster taught. This must not, however, be taken as meaning that everything he taught came, so to say, out of his own head. His doctrine was a product of the time, and had its roots in the nature and history of the people to which he belonged. Usually he is spoken of as a reformer of the old Iranian faith. But in order to be sure of this it would be necessary first to know something about the nature of that faith as it existed before he arose. Was it still essentially the same as that of the nearly-allied ancient Hindus, as found in the *Rig-Veda*? To this question no distinct answer is forthcoming; we are ignorant as to how far the way had been prepared for Zoroastrianism or how far it was wholly new. But still there is room for conjecture as to what it was that gave the prophet the first impulse and occasion for his work.

The most striking difference between Zoroaster's doctrine of God and the old religion of India lies in this, that, while in the Avesta the evil spirits are called *daêva* (Modern Persian *dîv*), the Aryans of India, on the other hand, in common with the Italians, Celts, and Letts, gave the name of *dêva* to their good spirits, the spirits of light. An alternative designation for deity in the *Rig-Veda* is *asura*. In the more recent hymns of the *Rig-Veda* and in later India, on the other hand, only *evil* spirits are understood by *asurâs*, while in Iran the corresponding word *ahura* was, and ever has continued to be, the designation of God the Lord, especially of the supreme God, with the epithet of *Mazdâo* (the Wise). Thus *ahura-daêva*, *dêva-asura* in Zoroastrian and in later Brahman theology are in their meanings exactly opposed. This difference no one has as yet satisfactorily accounted for, and yet it supplies the key to the doctrine of Zoroaster.

The difference proceeded from an old distinction between the ideas *deva* and *asura*. An original ideal difference, a different conception of god associated with the two words, grew in the two lands into a sharp antithesis, a formal conflict, but in opposite senses. In India the development still admits of being traced. In the older *Rig-Veda* the difference is latent. Here a god is spoken of as *dêva*, but not every *dêva* is an *asura*. *Asura* is something which is attributed only to certain particular gods as a special attribute, notably to Varuna, though also to others, such as Indra, but only by the so-called "kathenotheism" of the Vedic religion. On the other hand, it is expressly stated that in the case of Indra the dignity of an *asura* was only a conferred one (*Rig-V.*, 6, 10, 2). In *Rig-Veda*, 4, 42 Varuna claims as against Indra the priority in the *asura* dignity. This hymn, like 10, 124, is of importance for the whole question. The contrast there implied between Varuna and Indra, the rivalry between them as to which is the greater, comes to light sometimes more strongly, sometimes less so, throughout the entire *Rig-Veda*. The contrast is really in other terms the old contrast between *asura* and *deva*, between a more spiritualistic and a more materialistic conception of deity. *Asura* is ethically the higher conception, *deva* the lower: *deva* is the vulgar notion of God, *asura* is theosophic. The supersensuous figure of Varuna is the type of an *asura*, the sensuous figure of Indra the type of a *deva*. In the *Rig-Veda*, Varuna, the old king of the gods, is going down, while Indra, the popular national god, is in the ascendant. Along with Varuna, but in a still higher degree, the very conception of *asura* goes down; it becomes unmodern, obsolete, and acquires an undesirable flavour. The *asuras* thus come to form a distinct group of celestial beings mentioned along with the *devas* (*A.-V.*, 10, 10, 26): they become in rank inferior to the *devas* (*A.-V.*, 6, 86, 3) and receive the designation of *asurâ adevâs—asuras* that are no *devas*; and from this it is but a short step to the "*asuras* that are opposed to the gods."

The old contrast between *asura* and *deva* was wrought out and accentuated quite differently on Iranian soil. While in India the entire revolution took place in a bloodless manner wholly within the realm of ideas, the old antithesis led to an open quarrel among the Aryans of Iran. In the background of the picture of Zoroaster's times set before us in the Gâthâs we see the people divided between two opposing and hostile cults, the watchwords of which are *ahura* on the one hand and *daêva* on the other. How it is that matters had come to this pass remains obscure, for we have no source of information to take us further back. The opposing parties are not separated by distance in space or by differing nationality, but occur side by side. "Hard by the believer in *ahura* dwells the worshipper of the *daêvas*," complains Zoroaster. The entire people seems broken up by the religious difference.

It is difficult to focus the scattered references in the Gâthâs so as to obtain a clear picture of the time. Only this much is clear, that in Zoroaster's day not two cults only but two stages of culture are struggling for the mastery. The *ahura* worshippers represent the higher phase; they are breeders of cattle, and the care of the cow is to them a sacred duty. The worshippers of the *daêvas* maltreat the animal and slaughter it in their sacrifices. We perceive that the higher ethical tendency of the old *asura* faith is producing its effects in the higher degree of culture of the believers in Ahura, while the worshippers of the *daêvas* stand on a lower grade.

It is to this period of religious ferment that Zoroaster's appearance on the scene belongs. It is not he who has evoked this religious conflict of parties, as the common assumption is, and just as little is it he who in Ahura with the epithet of Mazdâo offers a new god to his people. He strikes decisively into the existing struggle, mounts to the position of spiritual leader of the *ahura* party and makes the battle a victory. As *zaotâ* (Indian *hotâ*), for so he calls himself, the first in rank of the old Aryan priests, he had all the greater opportunity to make his views known in matters of religion. Mankind had been brought face to face with a critical choice, that of electing between two radically opposed confessions of faith, without having any clearness as to the lasting consequences of the momentous step. He determines to save them, to lead them to a right choice, for he sees further than they, and believes himself to be initiated into the secrets of the godhead and of the life to come. What the other party worship as gods under the name of *daêva* are in reality powers by whom unwitting mankind are led to their destruction,—evil powers, false gods, devils. Such is the position from which all his teaching starts; and thus the change in the conception of *daêva* was a natural development. From the *daêvas* proceeds all the evil in the world. But his speculation does not stop here. The *daêvas* themselves anon become manifest to him as being but the instruments of a higher principle, called by him for the most part *Druj* (falsehood, deception), and more rarely *Angrô Mainyush*, that is the spirit enemy, Ahriman. This Ahriman or evil principle is the most characteristic product of Zoroastrian speculation. From the schism or religious dualism of his time he derived the idea of that dualistic scheme of the universe which has impressed its character upon the whole of the religion called by his name.

Zoroastrian Doctrine.

The fundamental idea of the Zoroastrian creed is dualistic. At the beginning of things there existed two spirits—Ahurô Mazdâo (Ormuzd) and Angrô Mainyush (Ahriman)—who represented good and evil (*Yasna*, 30, 3). The existence of evil in the world is thus presupposed from all eternity. Both spirits possess creative power, which manifests itself in the one positively and in the other negatively. Ormuzd is light and life and all that is pure and good,—in the ethical world law, order, and truth; his antithesis is darkness, filth, death, all that is evil in the world, lawlessness, and lies. When the two are spoken of as *yêma* ("a pair"), this is not to be interpreted as meaning that they are twins:[1] it simply denotes a duality, an opposed couple, a *dvandva*. The two spirits had until then counterbalanced one another. The ultimate triumph of the good spirit is an ethical demand of the religious consciousness and the quintessence of Zoroaster's revelation.

The evil spirit with his wicked hosts appears in the Gâthâs much less endowed with the attributes of personality than does Ahura Mazda. Within the world of the good Ormuzd is Lord and God alone. In this sense Zoroastrianism is often referred to as the faith of Ormuzd or as Mazdaism. Ormuzd in his exalted majesty is the ideal figure of an Oriental king. Of other gods beside him the doctrine of the Gâthâs knows nothing. The natural and symbolical gods of the popular belief have no place in it. Yet Ormuzd is not alone in his doings and conflicts, but has in conjunction with himself a number of genii—for the most part personifications of ethical ideas. These are his creatures, his instruments, servants, and assistants, like the ministers of an autocratic sovereign. They are comprehended under the general name of *ameshâ spentâ* ("immortal holy ones") and are the prototypes of the seven *amshaspands* of a later date. These are—(1) Ashem, afterwards Ashem Vahishtem (Plutarch's ἀλήθεια), corresponding to all that is true, good, and right,—ideas practically identical for Zoroaster, and the embodiment of all that is true, good, and right, upright law and rule; (2) Vohu Manô (εὔνοια), good sense, *i.e.*, the good principle, the idea of the good, the principle that works in man inclining him to what is good; (3) Khshathrem, afterwards Khshathrem Vairîm (εὐνομία), the power and kingdom of Ormuzd, which have subsisted from the first but not in integral completeness, the evil having crept in like the tares among the wheat: the time is yet to come when it shall be fully manifested in all its unclouded majesty; (4) Armaiti (σοφία), or the spirit of docility and obedience, spoken of as daughter of Ormuzd and regarded as having her abode upon the earth; (5) Haurvatât (πλοῦτος), perfection; (6) Ameretatât, immortality. Other ministering angels are Gêush Tashan ("the creator of the cow"), Gêush Urvan ("the genius and defender of animals"), and the holy spirit of Ormuzd, often thought of as having personal existence. Of the elements fire alone ("the son of Ahura Mazda") receives personification and figures as his ally.

As soon as the two at first absolutely separate spirits (comp. *Bundahish*, 1, 4) encounter one another, their creative activity and at the same time their permanent conflict begin. The history of this conflict is the history of the world. A great cleft runs right through the world: all creation divides itself into that which is Ahura's and that which is Ahriman's. Not that the two spirits carry on the struggle in person; they leave it to be fought out by their respective creations and creatures which they send into the field. The field of battle is the present world.

In the centre of battle is man; his soul is the object of the war. Man is a creation of Ormuzd, who therefore has the right to call him to account. But Ormuzd created him free in his determinations and in his actions, wherefore he is accessible to the influences of the evil powers. This freedom of the will is clearly expressed in *Yasna*, 31, 11: "Since thou, O Mazda, didst at the first create our being and our souls in accordance with thy mind, and didst create our understanding and our life together with the body, and works and words in which man according to his own will can frame his confession, the liar and the truth-speaker alike lay hold of the word, the knowing and the ignorant each after his own heart and understanding. Armaiti searches, following thy spirit, where errors are found." Man takes part in this conflict by all his life and activity in the world. By a true confession of faith, by every good deed, by continually keeping pure his body and his soul, he impairs the power of Satan and strengthens the might of goodness, and establishes a claim for reward upon Ormuzd; by a false confession, by every evil deed and defilement, he increases the evil and renders service to Satan.

The life of man falls into two parts,—its earthly portion and that which is lived beyond the grave. The lot assigned to him after death is the result and consequence of his life upon earth. No religion has so clearly grasped the ideas of guilt and of merit. On the works of men here below a strict reckoning will be held in

[1] Later sects sought to rise from the dualism to a higher unity. Thus the Zarvanites represented Ormuzd and Ahriman as twin sons proceeding from the fundamental principle of all, Zrvana Akarana, or limitless time.

heaven (according to later representations by Rashnu and Mithra). All thoughts, words, and deeds of each are entered in the book as separate items (*dâthra*, *Y.*, 31, 14; *Vend.*, 19, 27), all the evil works as debts (*ishudô*). Wicked actions cannot be undone, but in the heavenly account can be counterbalanced by a surplus of good works. It is only in this sense that an evil deed can be atoned for by a good one. Of a remission of sins the doctrine of Zoroaster knows nothing. After death the soul arrives at the *cinvato peretush* or accountant's bridge over which lies the way to heaven. Here the statement of his life account is made out. If he has a balance of good works in his favour, he passes forthwith into paradise (*Garô demâna*) and the blessed life. If his evil works outweigh his good he falls finally under the power of Satan, and the pains of hell are his portion for ever. Should the evil and the good be equally balanced, the soul passes into an intermediate stage of existence (the *Hamêstakâns* of the Pahlavi books) and his final lot is not decided until the last judgment. This court of reckoning, the *judicium particulare*, is called *âka*. The course of inexorable law cannot be turned aside by any sacrifice or offering, nor yet even by the free grace of God.

But man has been smitten with blindness and ignorance: he knows neither the eternal law nor the things which await him after death. He allows himself only too easily to be ensnared by the craft of the evil powers who seek to ruin his future existence. He worships and serves false gods, being unable to distinguish between truth and lies. Therefore it is that Ormuzd in his grace determined to open the eyes of mankind by sending a prophet to lead them by the right way, the way of salvation. According to later legend (*Vd.*, 2, 1), Ormuzd at first wished to entrust this task to Yima (Jemshid), the ideal of an Iranian king. But Yima, the secular man, felt himself unfitted for it and declined it. He contented himself therefore with establishing in his paradise (*vara*) a heavenly kingdom in miniature, to serve at the same time as a pattern for the heavenly kingdom that was to come. Zoroaster at last, as being a spiritual man, was found fit for the mission. Zoroaster experienced within himself the inward call to seek the amelioration of mankind and their deliverance from everlasting ruin, and regarded this inward impulse, intensified as it was by means of dreams and visions, as being the call addressed to him by God Himself. Like Mohammed after him he often speaks of his conversations with God. He calls himself most frequently *manthran* ("prophet"), *ratu* ("spiritual authority"), and *saoshyant* (meaning "he who will deliver," that is to say, when men come to be judged according to their deeds).

The full contents of his dogmatic and ethical teaching we cannot gather from the Gâthâs. He speaks for the most part only in general references of the divine commands and of good and evil works. Among the former those most inculcated are renunciation of Satan, adoration of Ormuzd, purity of soul and body, and care of the cow. We learn little otherwise regarding the practices connected with his doctrines. A ceremonial worship is hardly mentioned. He speaks more in the character of prophet than in that of lawgiver. The contents of the Gâthâs are essentially eschatological. Revelations concerning the last things and the future lot, whether bliss or woe, of human souls, promises for true believers, threatenings for misbelievers, his firm confidence as to the future triumph of the good—such are the themes continually dwelt on with endless variations.

It was not without special reason, Zoroaster believed, that the calling of a prophet should have taken place precisely when it did. It was, he held, the final appeal of Ormuzd to mankind at large. Like John the Baptist and the Apostles of Jesus, Zoroaster also believed that the fulness of time was near, that the kingdom of heaven was at hand. Through the whole of the Gâthâs runs the pious hope that the end of the present world is not far off. He himself hopes along with his followers to live to see the decisive turn of things, the dawn of the new and better æon. Ormuzd will summon together all his powers for a final decisive struggle and break the power of evil for ever; by his help the faithful will achieve the victory over their detested enemies, the *daêva* worshippers, and render them powerless. Thereupon Ormuzd will hold a *judicium universale* (*vîdâiti*) upon all mankind and judge strictly according to justice, punish the wicked, and assign to the good the hoped-for reward. Satan will be cast, along with all those who have been delivered over to him to suffer the pains of hell, into the abyss, where he will thenceforward lie powerless. Forthwith begins the one undivided kingdom of God in heaven and on earth. This is called, sometimes the good kingdom, sometimes simply the kingdom. Here the sun will for ever shine, and all the pious and faithful will live a happy life, that no evil power can disturb, in the fellowship of Ormuzd and his angels for ever.

Zoroaster's teachings show him to have been a man of a highly speculative turn, faithful, however, with all his originality, to the Iranian national character. With zeal for the faith, and boldness and energy, he combined diplomatic skill in his dealings with his exalted protectors. His thinking is consecutive, self-restrained, practical, devoid on the whole of all that might be called fantastic and excessive. His form of expression is tangible and concrete. His system is constructed on a clearly conceived plan.

History and Later Development of Zoroastrianism.—For the great mass of the people Zoroaster's doctrine was too abstract and spiritualistic. Popular faith instinctively and naturally turns to concrete plastic forms of godhead borrowed from surrounding nature, and thus it came to pass that a number of the old Aryan divinities, whom the new teaching had driven into the background, were again restored to their former rank,—especially Mithra, the sun-god. Besides him, in the younger Avesta, Anâhita (Anâitis), the goddess of the waters, Tishtrya (Sirius), and other heavenly bodies are invoked with special preference. The Gâthâs know nothing of a new belief which afterwards arose in the *fravashi*, or guardian angels of the faithful. *Fravashi* properly means "confession of faith," and when personified comes to be regarded as a protecting spirit. Unbelievers have no *fravashi*.

On the basis of the new teaching arose a widely spread priesthood (*âthravanô*) who systematized the doctrines, organized and carried on the worship, and laid down the minutely elaborated laws for the purifying and keeping pure of soul and body which are met with in the Vendidad. To the last-named belong in particular the numerous ablutions, bodily chastisements, love of truth, agriculture, protection of useful animals, as dogs and cattle, the destruction of noxious animals, and the prohibition either to burn or to bury the dead. In the worship the drink prepared from the *haoma* (Indian *soma*) plant had a prominent place. The last things and the end of the world are relegated to the close of a long period of time (3000 years after Zoroaster), when a new Saoshyant is to be born of the seed of Zoroaster, the dead are to come to life, and a new incorruptible world to begin.

The religion of Zoroaster, broadly speaking, never spread beyond the limits of Iran, although some isolated Turanian stems can be reckoned among those who profess it. From the East it doubtless passed in the first instance into Media and thence into Persia proper (comp. PERSIA, vol. xviii. p. 564). In the Persians of Herodotus's time we still see the new proselytes who have indeed accepted the creed, but not yet without reserve all the religious usages which accompany it, and least of all those which run completely counter to sacred and immemorial traditions of their time-honoured customs. According to Herodotus (i. 140), they still refrained from exposing, at least from openly exposing, their dead to dogs and vultures, but continued to bury them. This was practised by the Magi only, that is, by the priesthood, in conformity with the priestly laws. The Persians, however, made so far a concession to their adopted religion that they enveloped their dead bodies in wax, so that the earth might not be defiled.

After the fall of the Achæmenidæ (331 B.C.) Zoroastrianism lost greatly in power and dignity. It was subsequently rehabilitated, however, by the Sasanians, under whom it reached its highest prosperity. Protected by this dynasty, the priesthood developed into a completely organized state church, which was able to employ the power of the state in enforcing strict compliance with the religious law-book hitherto enjoined by their unaided efforts only. The formation of sects was at this period not infrequent (comp. MANICHÆISM). The Mohammedan invasion (636), with the terrible persecutions of the following centuries, was the death-blow of Zoroastrianism. In Persia itself only a few followers of Zoroaster are now found (in Kirman and Yazd). The PARSEES (*q.v.*) in and around Bombay hold by Zoroaster as their prophet and by the ancient religious usages, but their doctrine has reached the stage of a pure monotheism.

Literature.—See under ZEND-AVESTA; also Windischmann, *Zoroastrische Studien*, Berlin, 1863. (K. G.)

ZOSIMUS, a Greek historical writer, held public office (Photius describes him as "comes et exadvocatus fisci") at Constantinople some time in the first half of the 5th century. His *History*, which is mainly a compilation from previous authors (Herennius Dexippus, Eunapius, Olympiodorus), consists of six books: the first sketches very briefly the history of the early emperors from Augustus to Diocletian (305); the second, third, and fourth deal more copiously with the period from the accession of Constantius and Galerius to the death of Theodosius; the fifth and sixth cover the period between 395 and 410. The work is apparently unfinished. The style is characterized by Photius as concise, clear, and pure. The historian's object was to account for the decline of the Roman empire from the pagan point of view, and in this undertaking he has at various points treated the Christians with some unfairness.

A Latin version of the *History* was published by Leunclavius in 1576 (Basel, fol.), and in 1581 H. Stephanus added the Greek text of the first two books to his edition of Herodian. All the six books were published by Sylburgius in vol. iii. of his *Romanæ Historiæ*

Scriptores Græci Minores (Frankfort, 1590). There have been several subsequent editions; that of Reitemeier (Leipsic, 1784) was re-edited by Bekker for Niebuhr's *Corpus Scriptorum Historiæ Byzantinæ* (Bonn, 1837). Zosimus was translated into French by Cousin in 1678; into English, anonymously, in 1684; and into German by Seybold and Heyler in 1804-5.

ZOSIMUS, bishop of Rome from 18th March 417 to 25th December 418, succeeded Innocent I. and was followed by Boniface I. For his attitude in the Pelagian controversy, see PELAGIUS (vol. xviii. p. 472). He took a decided part in the protracted dispute in Gaul as to the jurisdiction of the see of Arles over that of Vienne, giving energetic decisions in favour of the former, but without settling the controversy.

ZOSTEROPS,[1] originally the scientific name of a genus of birds founded by Vigors and Horsfield (*Trans. Linn. Society*, xv. p. 235) on an Australian species called by them *Z. dorsalis*, but subsequently shown to be identical with the *Certhia cærulescens*, and also with the *Sylvia lateralis*, previously described by Latham. Latterly the name has been Anglicized in the same sense, and, whether as a scientific or a vernacular term, applied to a great number of species[2] of little birds which inhabit for the most part the tropical districts of the Old World, from Africa to most of the islands in the Indian and Pacific Oceans, and northwards in Asia through India and China to Amurland and Japan.

The birds of this group are mostly of unpretending appearance, the plumage above being generally either mouse-coloured or greenish olive; but some are sufficiently varied by the white or bright yellow of their throat, breast, or lower parts, and several have the flanks of a more or less lively bay. It is remarkable that several islands are inhabited by two perfectly distinct species, one belonging to the brown and the other to the green section, the former being wholly insular. The greater number of species seem to be confined to single islands, often of very small area, but others have a very wide distribution, and much interest has been excited by the undoubted fact that the type-species, *Z. cærulescens*, has of late years largely extended its range. First described from New South Wales, where it is very plentiful, it had been long known to inhabit all the eastern part of Australia. In 1856 it was noticed by naturalists as occurring in the South Island of New Zealand, when it became known to the Maories by a name signifying "Stranger," and to the English settlers as the "Blight-bird,"[3] from its clearing the fruit-trees of a blight by which they had lately been affected. It soon after appeared in the North Island, where it speedily became common, and it has thence not only spread to the Chatham Islands, but, as Sir Walter Buller states (*Birds N. Zealand*, ed. 2, i. p. 79), it has been met with in considerable numbers 300 miles from land, as though in search of new countries to colonize. Yet this author believes it to be indigenous to the west coast of the South Island, and Sir James Hector joins in that opinion. If they be right, it is, however, pretty certain that until the year before mentioned it must have been confined to an extremely small district, and the only assignable cause of its spreading so rapidly, when it did extend its range, is that of a large surplus population unable to find a living at home. It is known to propagate at a high rate of increase, and at times numbers have been found dead, apparently for want of food. In any case it is obvious that this Zosterops must be a comparatively modern settler in New Zealand.[4]

All the species of Zosterops are sociable, consorting in large flocks, which only separate on the approach of the pairing season. They build nests, described as being variously placed—sometimes suspended from a horizontal fork and sometimes fixed in an upright crotch—and lay (so far as is known) pale blue, spotless eggs, thereby differing wholly from several of the groups of birds to which they have been thought allied. Though mainly insectivorous, the birds of this genus will eat fruits of various kinds and in such quantities as to be at times injurious. The habits of *Z. cærulescens* have been well described by Sir W. Buller (*ut supra*), and those of a species peculiar to Ceylon, *Z. ceylonensis*, by Col. Legge (*B. Ceylon*, p. 586), while those of the widely-ranging Indian *Z. palpebrosa* and of the South-African *Z. capensis* have been succinctly treated by Jerdon (*B. India*, ii. p. 266) and Mr Layard (*B. South Africa*, p. 116) respectively.

It is a remarkable and, if capable of explanation, would doubtless be an instructive fact that the largest known species of the genus, *Z. albigularis*, measuring nearly 6 inches in length, is confined to so small a spot as Norfolk Island, where also another, *Z. tenuirostris*, not much less in size, occurs; while a third, of intermediate stature, *Z. strenua*, inhabits the still smaller Lord Howe's Island. A fourth, *Z. vatensis*, but little inferior in bulk, is found on one of the New Hebrides; but, after these giants of their kind, the rest fall off considerably, being from one-fifth to one-third less in length, and some of the smaller species hardly exceed 3½ inches from end to end.

The affinities of the genus *Zosterops* are by no means clear. Placed by some writers, if not systematists, with the *Paridæ* (*cf.* TITMOUSE), by others among the *Meliphagidæ* (*cf.* HONEY-EATER), and again by others with the *Nectariniidæ* (*cf.* SUNBIRD), the structure of the tongue, as shown by Dr Gadow (*Proc. Zool. Society*, 1883, pp. 63, 68, pl. xvi. fig. 2), entirely removes it from the first and third, and from most of the forms generally included among the second. On the whole it seems safest to regard the genus, at least provisionally, as the type of a distinct Family—*Zosteropidæ*—as Families go among Passerine birds; but, whether the Australian genera *Melithreptus* and *Plectrorhamphus* (otherwise *Plectrorhyncha*) should be included under that heading, as has been done, remains to be proved, and in the meanwhile may be reasonably doubted. (A. N.)

ZOUCH, RICHARD (*c.* 1590-1661), a distinguished writer on civil and international law, was born at Anstey, Wiltshire, about the year 1590. He was educated at Winchester and afterwards at Oxford, where he became a fellow of New College in 1609. In 1613 he published a poem entitled *The Dove, or Passages of Cosmography*, which he dedicated to his relative Edward, Lord Zouch, warden of the Cinque Ports. He was admitted at Doctor's Commons in January 1618, commenced LL.D. in April 1619, and was appointed regius professor of law at Oxford in 1620. In 1625 he became principal of St Alban Hall and chancellor of the diocese of Oxford; in 1641 he was made judge of the High Court of Admiralty. Under the Commonwealth, having submitted to the Parliamentary visitors, he retained his university appointments, though not his judgeship; this last he resumed at the Restoration, dying soon afterwards at his apartments in Doctor's Commons, London, on 1st March 1661.

He published *Elementa jurisprudentiæ* (1629), *Descriptio juris et judicii feudalis, secundum consuetudines Mediolani et Normanniæ, pro introductione ad jurisprudentiam Anglicanam* (1634), *Descriptio juris et judicii temporalis, secundum consuetudines feudales et Normannicas* (1636), *Descriptio juris et judicii ecclesiastici, secundum canones et consuetudines Anglicanas* (1636), *Descriptiones juris et judicii sacri, . . . militaris, . . . maritimi* (1640), *Juris et judicii fecialis sive juris inter gentes . . . explicatio* (1650), and *Solutio quæstionis de legati delinquentis judice competente* (1657). In virtue of the last two he has the distinction of being one of the earliest systematic writers on international law.

ZSCHOKKE, JOHANN HEINRICH DANIEL (1771-1848), German author, was born at Magdeburg on 22d March 1771. He was educated at the cloister school of his native place and at the gymnasium of Altstädt. As a youth he spent some time with a company of strolling players, but afterwards he attended the university of Frankfort-on-the-Oder, where, in 1792, he became a privat-docent. He created much sensation by two extravagant plays, *Abällino, der grosse Bandit* (1794) and *Julius von Sassen* (1796), the success of which shows how urgent was the need for the elevating influence of the dramatic writings of Goethe and Schiller. The Prussian Government having declined

[1] The derivation is ζωστήρ-ηρος and ὤψ, whence the word should be pronounced with all the vowels long. The allusion is to the ring of white feathers round the eyes, which is very conspicuous in many species.

[2] In 1883 Mr Sharpe (*Cat. B. Brit. Museum*, ix. pp. 146-203) admitted 85 species, besides 3 more which he had not been able to examine.

[3] By most English-speaking people in various parts of the world the prevalent species of *Zosterops* is commonly called "White-eye" or "Silver-eye" from the feature before mentioned.

[4] Sir W. Buller says that he and Mr Gould were able to pick out New-Zealand examples from a series otherwise made up of Australian specimens. Hence it would seem as if a slight amount of differentiation had been set up; but the variation would doubtless have been greater had the species been an ancient colonist.

to make him a full professor, Zschokke in 1795, after some time spent in travel, settled in the Grisons, where, in association with the burgomaster Tscharner, he conducted an educational institution in the castle of Reichenau. In recognition of his services the authorities of the Grisons gave him the rights of a citizen, and in 1798 he associated his name permanently with the country by the publication of his *Geschichte des Freistaats der drei Bünde in Rhätien.* The political disturbances of this year compelled him to close his institution; but, being a man of great resource and energy, he was able, during the revolutionary period which now began in Switzerland, to enter upon a new and more important career. He was sent as a deputy to Aarau, where he was made head of the educational department. Afterwards he was sent as Government commissioner to Unterwalden, and his authority was ultimately extended over the cantons of Uri, Schwyz, and Zug. In this high office Zschokke distinguished himself by the vigour of his administration and by the enthusiasm with which he devoted himself to the promotion of the interests of the poorer classes of the community. In 1800 he reorganized the institutions of the Italian cantons, and then he became lieutenant-governor of the canton of Basel. Zschokke retired for a while from public life when the central Government at Bern proposed to re-establish the federal system, but after the changes effected by Bonaparte he entered the service of the canton of Aargau, with which he remained connected. In 1801 he attracted attention by his *Geschichte vom Kampfe und Untergange der schweizerischen Berg- und Wald-Cantone.* Through his *Schweizerbote*, the publication of which began in 1804, he exercised a wholesome influence on public affairs; and the like may be said of his *Miscellen der neuesten Weltkunde*, issued from 1807 to 1813. In 1811 he also started a monthly periodical, the *Erheiterungen.* He wrote various historical works, the most important of which is *Des Schweizerlandes Geschichte für das Schweizervolk*, published in 1822. He was also the author of *Bilder aus der Schweiz*, and of a series of popular tales which greatly extended his reputation,—*Der Creole*, *Alamontade*, *Jonathan Frock*, *Das Goldmacherdorf*, and *Meister Jordan.* In *Stunden der Andacht*, which was widely read, he expounded in a rationalistic spirit what seemed to him the fundamental principles of religion and morality. *Selbstschau* is a kind of autobiography. Zschokke was not a great original writer, but he secured for himself an eminent place in the literature of his time by his enthusiasm for modern ideas in politics and religion, by the sound, practical judgment displayed in his works, and by the energy and lucidity of his style. He died on 27th June 1848.

An edition of his selected works, in forty volumes, was issued in 1824-28. In 1851-54 an edition in thirty-five volumes was published. There are biographies of Zschokke by Münch and by Emil Zschokke.

ZUCCARO, or ZUCCHERO,[1] the name of two Italian painters.

I. TADDEO ZUCCARO (1529-1566), one of the most popular painters of the so-called Roman mannerist school, was the son of an almost unknown painter at St Angelo in Vado, called Ottaviano Zuccaro, where he was born in 1529. While yet a boy Taddeo found his way to Rome; and, though suffering great hardships from poverty and want of friends, he succeeded at an early age in gaining a knowledge of painting and in finding patrons to employ him. His first start in life, while only seventeen years old, was due to a pupil of Correggio, named Daniele da Parma, who engaged him to assist in painting a series of frescos in a chapel at Vitto near Sora, on the borders of the Abruzzi. After that Taddeo returned to Rome in 1548, and began his career as a fresco painter, by executing a series of scenes in monochrome from the life of Furius Camillus on the front of the palace of a wealthy Roman named Jacopo Mattei. From that time his success was assured, and for the rest of his short life he was largely employed by the popes Julius III. and Paul IV., by Della Rovere, duke of Urbino, and by other rich patrons of art in Rome and elsewhere. His best frescos were an historical series painted on the walls of a new palace at Caprarola, built for Cardinal Alessandro Farnese, for which Taddeo also designed a great quantity of rich decorations in stucco relief after the style of Giulio Romano and other pupils of Raphael. Nearly all his paintings were in fresco, very large in scale, and often in *chiaroscuro* or monochrome; they were more remarkable for rapidity of execution and a certain boldness of style than for any higher qualities. The very great estimation in which Taddeo's frescos were held is a striking proof of the very rapid degradation of taste which took place during the second half of the 16th century. His work is mannered in style, artificial and pompous in conception, and lacks any close or accurate knowledge of the human form and its movements. The long chapter which Vasari devotes to this painter and his brother Federigo is only one of many examples of the writer's habit of giving undue prominence to the artists of his own time and school. Taddeo Zuccaro died in Rome in 1566; he is buried in the Pantheon, not far from Raphael.

Taddeo's easel pictures are less common than his decorative frescos. A small painting on copper of the Adoration of the Shepherds, formerly in the collection of James II., is now at Hampton Court; it is a work of very small merit. The Caprarola frescos were engraved and published by Prenner, *Illustri Fatti Farnesiani Coloriti nel Real Palazzo di Caprarola*, Rome, 1748-50.

II. FEDERIGO ZUCCARO (1543-1609), the younger brother and pupil of Taddeo, was born in 1543. In 1550 he was placed under his brother's charge in Rome, and during his lifetime worked as his assistant; he completed the Caprarola frescos, which were unfinished when Taddeo died in 1566. In a short time Federigo attained to an eminence far beyond his very limited merits as a painter, and was perhaps the most popular artist of his generation. Probably no other painter has ever produced so many enormous frescos crowded with figures on the most colossal scale, all executed under the unfortunate delusion, common in his time, that grandeur of effect could be attained merely by great size combined with extravagance of attitude and exaggeration of every kind. Federigo's first work of this sort was the completion of the painting of the dome of the cathedral at Florence, under the patronage of the grand-duke Francesco I.; the work had been begun by the art-historian Vasari, who wrote in the most generous language about his more successful rival. The inner surface of this beautiful cupola was disfigured by Federigo in the most tasteless way. Regardless of the injury to the apparent scale of the interior of the church, he painted about 300 figures, each nearly 50 feet high, sprawling with violent contortions all over the surface. Happily age has so dimmed these pictures that their presence is now almost harmless.

After this achievement Federigo was recalled to Rome by Gregory XIII. to continue in the Pauline chapel of the Vatican the scheme of decoration which had been begun by Michelangelo during his failing years. A quarrel which arose between the painter and some members of the papal court led to his departure from Italy. He first visited Brussels, and there made a series of cartoons for the tapestry-weavers. Thence, in 1574, Federigo passed over to England, where his fame was already known, so that he at once received a large number of commissions to paint the portraits of various distinguished persons, among them Queen Elizabeth, Mary Queen of Scots,[1] Sir Nicholas

[1] So spelt by Vasari.

[1] Engraved by Vertue.

Bacon, Sir Francis Walsingham, Lord High Admiral Howard, and others. A curious full-length portrait of Elizabeth in fancy dress, now at Hampton Court, is attributed to this painter, though very doubtfully. Another picture in the same collection appears to be a *replica* of his painting of the Allegory of Calumny, as suggested by Lucian's description of a celebrated work by Apelles; it was the satire in this directed against some of his courtier enemies which was the immediate cause of the pope's displeasure and Federigo's temporary exile from Rome. His success as a painter of portraits and other works in oil was more reasonable than the admiration expressed for his colossal frescos. A portrait of a Man with Two Dogs in the Pitti Palace at Florence is a work of some real merit, as is also the Dead Christ and Angels in the Borghese Gallery in Rome. After a short exile Federigo was pardoned by the pope and recalled to Rome to finish his work on the vault of the Pauline chapel. In 1585 he was invited by Philip II. of Spain to decorate the new Escorial at a yearly salary of 2000 crowns. He accepted this offer, and worked at the Escorial from January 1586 to the end of 1588, when he returned to Rome. He there founded in 1595, under a charter confirmed by Sixtus V., the Academy of St Luke, of which he was the first president. This is still the chief academy of painters in Italy, and its organization suggested to Sir Joshua Reynolds his scheme for founding the English Royal Academy.

Federigo, like his contemporary Giorgio Vasari, aimed at being an art critic and historian as well as a practical artist, but with very different success. His chief book, *L'Idea de' Pittori, Scultori, ed Architetti* (Turin, 1607), is a senseless mass of the most turgid bombast. Little can be said in praise of his smaller works, consisting of two volumes printed at Bologna in 1608, describing his visit to Parma and a journey through central Italy.

Federigo was raised to the rank of a *cavaliere* not long before his death, which took place at Ancona in 1609.

For both Taddeo and Federigo Zuccaro, see Vasari, pt. iii., and Lanzi, *Storia Pittorica*, Roman School, epoch iii. (J. H. M.)

ZUG,[1] a canton of Switzerland, ranking as eighth in the Confederation. It includes the districts round the Lake of Egeri and on both shores of the northern half of the Lake of Zug, and is the smallest undivided canton both in area and in population. Its total area is 92·3 square miles, 75 of which are classed as productive (forests 12·5), while of the rest 13 are covered with lakes. The highest point in the canton is the Wildspitz (5191 feet), the culminating peak of the Rossberg ridge. The population was 22,994 in 1880, an increase of 2001 on that of 1870, the numbers of men and women being nearly equal. German is the native tongue of 22,592, and 21,734 are Roman Catholics. Till 1814 Zug was in the diocese of Constance, but on the reconstruction of the diocese of Basel in 1828 it was assigned to it. The capital is Zug (4924 inhabitants in 1880); Baar has a population of 3896. The territory of Zug is very fertile and the population mainly agricultural. Cattle and fruit are among the chief articles of export, much cider and "kirschwasser" being manufactured. The town of Zug is connected by railway with Lucerne and Zurich, and a railway is planned to Arth, which will connect Zug directly with the St Gotthard line. On 5th July 1887 a landslip carried the houses of a small portion of the capital, as in 1435, into the lake.

The town of Zug is first mentioned in 1255. In 1273 it was bought by Rudolph of Hapsburg from Anna, the heiress of Kyburg and wife of Eberhard, head of the cadet line of Hapsburg; and in 1278 part of its territory (the valley of Egeri) was pledged by Rudolph as security for a portion of the marriage gift he promised to Joanna, daughter of Edward I. of England, betrothed to Hartmann (Rudolph's son), whose death in 1281 prevented the marriage taking place. The town of Zug was governed by a mayor, appointed by the Hapsburgs, and a council, and was much favoured by that family. Several country districts (Baar, Menzingen, and Egeri) had each its own "landsgemeinde," but were governed by one bailiff, also appointed by the Hapsburgs; these were known as the "Ausser Amt," and were always favourably disposed to the Confederates. Duke Leopold of Austria was defeated on 15th November 1315 by the Confederates at Morgarten Pass, in the territory of Zug (see SWITZERLAND, vol. xxii. p. 783 *sq.*). On 27th January 1352 both the town of Zug and the Ausser Amt entered the Confederation, the latter being received on exactly the same terms as the town (and not, as was usual in the case of country districts, as a subject land); but in September 1352 Zug had to acknowledge its own lords again, and in 1355 to break off its connexion with the League. But about 1364 the town and the Ausser Amt were recovered for the League by the men of Schwyz, and from this time Zug took part as a full member in all the acts of the League. In 1379 the emperor Wenceslaus exempted Zug from all external jurisdictions; in 1389 the Hapsburgs renounced their claims, reserving only (in the treaty of 1394) an annual payment of twenty silver marks, which came to an end in 1415. In 1400 Wenceslaus gave all criminal jurisdiction to the town only. The Ausser Amt then, in 1404, claimed that the banner and seal of Zug should be kept in one of the country districts, and were supported in this claim by Schwyz. The matter was finally settled by arbitration: the banner, &c., was to be kept in the town (access being allowed to the others), whilst the Ausser Amt was fined and Schwyz also. Finally in 1415 the right of electing their landammann was given to Zug by the Confederates, and a share in the criminal jurisdiction was granted to the Ausser Amt by Sigismund. In 1385 Zug joined the league of the Swabian cities against Leopold and shared in the victory of Sempach (9th July 1386), as well as in the various Argovian (1415) and Thurgovian (1460) conquests of the Confederates, and later in those in Italy (1512), having already taken part in the occupation of the Val d'Ossola (1410-14, 1417-22). Between 1379 and 1470 Zug had acquired various districts in her own neighbourhood, which were ruled till 1778 by the town and the Ausser Amt as subject lands.

At the time of the Reformation Zug clung to the old faith and was a member of the "Christliche Vereinigung" of 1529. In 1586 Zug became a member of the Golden League. From 1729 to 1736 the canton was distracted by violent disputes as to the distribution of the French pensions. In 1798 it opposed the French, formed part of the Tellgau, and later one of the districts of the canton of the Waldstätten (of which in 1799 it became the capital) in the Helvetic republic. In 1803 it regained its independence as a separate canton, and by the constitution of 1815 the "landsgemeinde" or assembly of all the citizens (existing for both districts since 1352) became a body of electors to choose a cantonal council. The reform movement of 1830 did not affect the canton, which in 1843 was a member of the Sonderbund and shared in the war of 1847. Both in 1848 and in 1874 it voted against the acceptance of the Federal constitutions. In 1848 the remaining functions of the "landsgemeinde" were abolished by the Liberals. Its present constitution dates from 1873-76, and was amended in 1881. There is a legislature of seventy-three members, fifty-eight (one to every 400 inhabitants) elected in the communes and fifteen by the whole population, both classes holding office for three years; the executive, of seven members, is elected by the communes for three years. By the "facultative or optional referendum," in case of a demand by one-third of the members of the legislative assembly or by 500 citizens any law, and any resolution involving a capital expenditure of 40,000 or an annual one of 10,000 francs, must be submitted to a direct popular vote.

ZULLA, as Salt writes the name, or ZÛLA (Thulla, Dôla), as it is also written, is a village near the head of Annesley Bay on the African coast of the Red Sea. It derives its only interest from ruins in its vicinity which are generally supposed to mark the site of the ancient emporium of Adulis (Ἄδουλις, Ἀδουλεί), the port of Axum and chief outlet in the early centuries of our era for the ivory, hides, slaves, and other exports of the interior. Cosmas Indicopleustes saw here an inscription of Ptolemy Euergetes (247-222 B.C.); and hence, as the earliest mention of Adulis is found in the geographers of the first century after Christ, it is conjectured that the town must have previously existed under another name and may have been the Berenice Panchrysus of the Ptolemies. The ruins in question, which are not very extensive or remarkable, are described by Rüppel, *Reise in Abyssinien*, i. 266 (1838); see also Rohlfs in ***Zeitschr. d. Gesell. f. Erdkunde in Berlin,***

[1] Its name has been rather fancifully derived from "fischzug," meaning a "haul of fish."

iii. . . . (1868), and, for further references to ancient and modern sources, the editions of the *Periplus* by C. Müller (*Geog. Gr. Min.*, i. 259) and Fabricius (1883). An Italian protectorate over the district of Zulla was proclaimed in 1888.

ZULULAND, a territory of South Africa, lying to the north of the colony of Natal, with a coast-line of about 130 miles (see vol. i. pl. II.). It is occupied chiefly by Zulu tribes; but since its conquest by England in 1879 a Boer republic, known as the New Republic, has been carved out of it, which extends into the centre of the country from the Transvaal on its north-west, and comprises an area equal to nearly one-half of the remaining portion of Zululand. This portion is composed of a strip of country adjacent to Natal, lying to the south of the Umhlatuzi river, and the district extending along the coast to the north of that river for a distance inland varying from 50 to 70 miles. The former piece of country has been known since 1882 as the Zulu Reserve. It is bounded on the south-west by the Tugela, Buffalo, and Blood rivers, the last-named being one of the borders of the Transvaal Republic.

Zululand presents very varied physical features: undulating country covered with mimosa "bush," in some parts very densely, alternates with wild and fantastically broken scenery, and thickly-wooded precipices and ravines, and these again with grass-clad hills. Two considerable forests exist in the country,—one, the Ingome Forest, lying in northern Zululand, just within the territory recently ceded to the Boers, the other upon the Natal border. These produce the varieties of timber mentioned under NATAL. The wholesale destruction of woods for domestic purposes, which has robbed that colony of much of its beauty, and is believed to have seriously affected its rainfall, has not proceeded very far at present in Zululand. The mineral resources of the country have yet to be investigated, but gold has been recently found in the Reserve. The rivers, like those in Natal, are rapid streams of small volume, running over rocky beds; the Tugela river is the most considerable. The climate differs but little from that of Natal. The country is very healthy for the most part; but horse sickness prevails in the valleys in the hot season, and the swampy neighbourhood of St Lucia Bay, a lagoon lying at the mouth of the Umfolosi river, is uninhabitable. Like the Natal natives, the Zulus cultivate the ground very superficially, planting maize, gourds of several kinds, and a grain from which a light beer is prepared. Cattle, the sole wealth of the people, were at one time very numerous in the country, and also goats. A few of the chiefs use horses.

Long after big game had become scarce in Natal, Zululand offered excellent opportunities to the sportsman. It still has antelopes of various kinds, including a few koodoo, and, at the mouths of the more northern rivers, hippopotamuses; but the buffalo and rhinoceros are not met with farther south than the densely-wooded hills near the Umfolosi river. The lion is not seen south of the Lebombo Mountains in the north of Zululand, but the leopard and smaller carnivores are plentiful enough in the country. Its natural history is similar to that of Natal; but indications are not wanting in its fauna and flora of its closer proximity to the tropics.

Language.—With the exception of the tongues spoken by the Hottentot-Bushman tribes of the south-west, the languages of Africa from about 5° north of the equator southwards are now recognized as forming one great family, for which the designation Bantu has been adopted, the word *abantu* in Zulu and other members of the group denoting "people" (plural inflex *aba*, root *ntu*). The Zulu tongue, as that of a conquering and superior race, extends beyond the river Zambesi, and is often understood even where another language is the vernacular. In the kingdoms of Lobengula and Umzila it is the language of the ruling classes. Philologists speak highly of the beauty and flexibility of the Bantu languages, and of their grammatical structure. To the student of comparative philology they offer a field of inquiry of the highest importance, both on account of the vast domain occupied by them and of the deep insight they afford into the structure and growth of human speech in general. This great linguistic family occupies about one-half of Africa, extending from near the Niger delta in the north-west, and from Lake Albert Nyanza farther east, to the south-eastern extremity of the continent. It thus comprises such widely separated peoples as the Ba-Farami and Ba-Kwiri of the Cameroons region and the Zulu-Kaffres of the south-east coast on the one hand, and on the other the Wa-Ganda of the Somerset Nile and the Ova-Herero of Damaraland on the south-west coast. But, notwithstanding this widespread range, and although none of the dialects have possessed any written standard till quite recent times, being in fact everywhere spoken by peoples of low culture, the Bantu is distinguished above all other great linguistic families, except perhaps the Semitic, for its astonishing homogeneous character. So close is the resemblance the different branches bear to each other that philologists have been able to describe in broad traits the more salient features of the phonetic system, structure, and syntax common alike to all. They speak unconsciously of the Bantu language, as if it were everywhere essentially one, and this surprising uniformity is reflected in the geographical, and especially the ethnological, terminology of the southern half of the continent. Thus the national or tribal place prefix in its various dialectic forms—*aba, ba, ama, bua, vua, ova, wa, mu, ap*, &c.,—is of constant occurrence throughout the whole of this region.

Their close uniformity is further shown in their common phonetic system, which is at once simple and harmonious, requiring all words to end in a vowel, rejecting all consonantal juxtapositions, except a few characteristic nasal combinations, such as *ng, mb, nd, nt, nw, mf, nk, ns*, throwing the accent as a rule on the first vowel of the stem (*méso*), and lastly repelling all harsh sounds, except the three intruding Hottentot clicks in the Zulu-Kaffre group. Nearly all the consonantal sounds, ranging from about eighteen to twenty, occur in English, while the vowel system everywhere corresponds to that of Italian. But the most marked feature of the Bantu tongues is their so-called *alliterative concord*, which has been compared both to the gender concordance of Aryan and the progressive vowel harmony of Ural-Altaic. But it differs from the former inasmuch as it is initial and not final, and extends to the verb as well as to noun, adjective, participle, and pronoun, as if we should say in Latin, Domina mea pulchra, ama eum. Thus, in the Kongo dialect, *e kintuku kiaku kiavididi ezono kisolokele*= "the coat you lost yesterday it turned up." It differs from the Ural-Altaic system inasmuch as the concordance is regulated, not by the root vowel influencing those of the agglutinated postfixes (see URAL-ALTAIC), but by the prefixed particle, the true nature of which has not yet been determined. But a comparative study of the Bantu tongues shows that in the archaic language whence all descend each noun had a proper prefix of its own, which prefix determined both the class to which the noun belonged and the concordance of all words in the sentence dependent on that noun. That such is the correct view is evident from the fact that, even where the noun has lost its prefix, as sometimes happens, this prefix nevertheless reappears in the dependent adjective, thus revealing its original form. We see, for instance, that *nti*= "tree" was originally in the plural *mi-nti*, because the following adjective still takes *mi*, as in *nti miandwelo* = "small trees." Bleek, the true founder of Bantu philology, has determined in the organic language eighteen such prefixes which still persist to a greater or less extent in the different branches, and have in some even been added to, as *fi*, for instance, in Kongo (W. H. Bentley). The analogy of this alliterative concord with the so-called Aryan grammatical gender is obvious, showing that the Aryan languages themselves were originally non-gender languages and that their present gender agreement is essentially a question of phonetic harmony and not of sex in any intelligible sense of the term. Hence also the extraordinary phenomenon of sex in this system apparently applied to inanimate objects.

Another remarkable feature of Bantu grammar is the wonderful development of verbal inflexion, which is both final and initial. The final, which in some groups yields as many as 300 distinct forms, each conjugated throughout, belongs to the verb itself in its various active, passive, middle, negative, repetitive, reciprocal, causative, and other meanings. The initial expresses mood, tense, person, number, and alliterative concord, and the whole system is immensely complicated by the fact that, as in Basque, the Caucasian, American, and some Ural-Altaic languages, the verb incorporates the direct pronominal object. Thus: *ikuntala*= "I-see-him;" *tukutala*= "we-see-you;" *bekwatala*= "they-see-them;" and so on. Hence the form *kuntonda*= "to-see-her," for instance, will be conjugated throughout, the result being a luxuriant growth of verbal forms fully comparable to that of the richest Ural-Altaic languages.

Bleek has subjected to a comparative study twenty-five members of the family, selected from almost every region that had been explored up to his time (1862). Since then further geographical discovery, especially in the Congo and Ogoway basins, has revealed many more Bantu tongues, of which, however, too little is known to determine their mutual relations with any pretence to accuracy. But, although any attempt at a strictly scientific classification would consequently be premature, the subjoined table, based on geographical distribution, will be found convenient for the purpose of reference.[1]

North-West Group (Cameroons and Ogoway-Gaboon Basins).—Ba-Kisk, Ba-Farami, Ba-Mbuku, Mu-Fundu, Dwalla, Wuri, Ba-Koko, Ba-Kwiri, Ba-Kundu, Mpongwe, Benga, Fernandian, Ba-Kale, Ba-Ngwe, Ivili, Ajuma, Fan (?), A-Shango, Okando, Cabinda, (Ba-Fyot).

Congo Group.—Vua-Nyamezi, Vua-Tuzi, Vua-Hha, Vua-Fipa, Vua-Vinza, Ba-Regga, Ba-Ngala, Wa-Buma, Ba-Bemba, Wa-Biza, Vua-Rua, Ma-Rungu, Ba-Songo, Ka-Lunda, Mboshi, Ba-Mbu, Kioko.

South-West Group (Angola, Damaraland).—Mu-Sorongo, Mu-Shicongo, Kongo proper, (S. Salvador), Bunda, Ba-Nano, Ba-Bwero, Ganguella, Libollo, Mu-Ndombe, Ba-Kwando, Ba-Simba, Ova-Mbo (Ovampo), Ova-Herero.

Zambesi Group.—Amboella, Ba-Lunda, Ba-Viko, Ra-Najoa, Ba-Toana, Ba-Kuba, Ba-Rotse, Ba-Toka, Ba-Shukulompo, Ma-Kalaka, Ma-Shona, Ba-Nyai, Ma-Nyanja.

South Central Group (Bechuana and Basuto Lands).—Ba-Rolong, Ba-Tlapi, Ba-Katla, Ba-Mapela, Ba-Hlokoa, Ba-Soetla, Ba-Suto, Ma-Kololo.

South-eastern Group (Zululand, Natal, Kaffraria).—See under article Kaffraria.

Eastern Group (Gasaland, Mozambique, Zanzibar Coast, Equatorial Lakes).—Chobi, Ma-Kwakwa, Ma-Gwanza, Ma-Longwa, Ba-Hlengwe, Bila-Kulu, Ma-Ndonda, Gwa-Tevi, Ma-Kua, Ma-Ngwangwara, Ma-Tambwe, Wa-Nindi, Ma-Wa, Wa-Hiyao (Yao or Ajawa), Ma-Ganya, Wa-Swaheli, Wa-Segua, Wa-Sambara, Wa-Zaramo, Wa-Kamba, Wa-Nika, Wa-Pokomo.

The pedigree and affinity of the Zulus, that is, the northern branch of the Zulu-Kaffre group, are given under Kaffraria. Here it will suffice to add that since the establishment of the Zulu military ascendency early in the 19th century various Zulu hordes have successively invaded and overrun a great part of south-east Africa, as far as and even beyond the Lake Nyassa district. Throughout these regions they are variously known as Ma-Zitu, Ma-Ravi, Ma-Ngone (Umgone), Matebele (Ama-Ndebeli), Ma-Viti, and Aba-Zanzi. Such is the terror inspired by these fierce warriors that many of the conquered tribes, such as the Wa-Nindi of Mozambique, have adopted the very name of their conquerors or oppressors. Hence the impression that the true Zulus are far more numerous north of the Limpopo than has ever been the case. In most places they have already become extinct or absorbed in the surrounding populations. But they still hold their ground as the ruling element in the region between the Limpopo and the lower Zambesi, which from them takes the name of Matebeleland, and which, like Zululand itself, has recently (1888) become a British protectorate.

Laws and Customs.—The Zulus possess an elaborate system of laws regulating the inheritance of personal property (which consists chiefly of cattle), the complexity arising from the practice of polygamy and the exchange of cattle made upon marriage. The giving of cattle in the latter case is generally referred to as a barter and sale of the bride, from which indeed it is not easily distinguishable. But it is regarded in a different light by the natives themselves. The kraal is under the immediate rule of its headman, who is a patriarch responsible for the good behaviour of all its members. Over the headman, whose authority may extend to more than one kraal, is the tribal chief. The exercise by some of the principal chiefs, during the reigns of mPande and his son, of the power of life and death could not always be controlled by the central authority. Several of the Zulu customs resemble those of the Jews, such as the Feast of First Fruits, held upon the ripening of the maize, when the whole nation gathers at the king's kraal, and the custom of raising up seed to a deceased brother. By the custom of *ukuhlonipa* a woman carefully avoids the utterance of any word which occurs in the names of the principal members of her husband's family: *e.g.*, if she have a brother-in-law named uNkomo, she would not use the Zulu for "cow," *inkomo*, but would invent some other word for it. The employment of "witch doctors" for "smelling out" criminals or *abatagati* (usually translated "wizards," but meaning evildoers of any kind, such as poisoners) is still common in Zululand, as in neighbouring countries, although it was discouraged by Cetshwayo, who established "kraals of refuge" for the reception of persons rescued by him from condemnation as *abatagati*.

Population.—No means exist for estimating the present population of Zululand. The country was at the time of the late war regarded as less densely inhabited than the colony of Natal. The Zulu army was estimated to contain twenty-three regiments, of 40,400 men in all, and, although the enrolment was voluntary, it may be assumed that it comprised nearly all the able-bodied men of the nation. In addition to the heavy mortality sustained by the Zulus in the war many lives have been lost in subsequent conflicts in which they have engaged amongst themselves.

History.—The earliest record of contact between Europeans and the Zulu race is probably the account of the wreck of the "Doddington" in 1756. The survivors met with hospitable treatment at the hands of the natives of Natal, and afterwards proceeded up the coast to St Lucia Bay, where they landed. They describe the natives as "very proud and haughty, and not so accommodating as those lately left." They differed from the other natives in the superior neatness of their method of preparing their food, and were more cleanly in their persons, bathing every morning, apparently as an act of devotion. Their chief pride seemed to be to keep their hair in order. It is added that they watched strictly over their women.

In 1780 the Zulu tribe inhabited the valley of the White Umfolosi river under the chieftainship of Senzangakona. At that time the Zulus numbered some few thousands only, being subject to the paramount chief Dingiswayo, who ruled over the mTetwa tribe, which inhabited the country to the north-east of the Tugela. Dingiswayo is represented as having been very much in advance of other chiefs in those parts in enlightenment and intelligence. He opened up a trade with the Portuguese, bartering ivory and oxen for beads and brass. He was also very warlike, and introduced a strict military organization among his people, by means of which he obtained the ascendency over neighbouring tribes, including that of the Zulus. Upon the death of Senzangakona at the beginning of the 19th century he was succeeded by a son named Tshaka, who had served as an officer in the army of Dingiswayo, whose favour he won through his force of character and talents. Dingiswayo having been killed in battle, the mTetwa tribe sought the protection of Tshaka, who lost no time in further developing the new military organization, and very soon became master of nearly the whole of south-eastern Africa from the Limpopo to Cape Colony, including the settlement of Natal, Basutoland, a large part of the Orange Free State, and the Transvaal Republic. The terror of the Zulu arms was, moreover, carried far into the interior through the revolt of a Zulu chief, Mzilikazi (Moselekatse), who conquered a vast territory towards the north-west.

Tshaka's strict discipline and mode of attack, in which the long missile weapon of the other tribes was replaced by a short stabbing assegai, was such that nothing in the mode of warfare of those opposed to him could withstand him. He overran the district of Natal with his armies in 1820; but crowds of the northern tribes driven before his onslaught passed through the country about 1812.

In 1825 an English naval officer, Lieutenant Farewell, visited Tshaka with the object of obtaining leave to establish a settlement in what is now the district of Natal. He found the king at Umgungindhlovu, "surrounded by a large number of chiefs, and about 8000 or 9000 armed men, observing a state and ceremony in our introduction that we little expected." The king showed his visiter much friendliness, making him a grant of land in that neighbourhood. Lieutenant Farewell took formal possession of the territory he had received, which he described as nearly depopulated and not containing more than 300 or 400 inhabitants, on 27th August 1825. The Zulu monarch, being anxious to open a political connexion with the Cape and English Governments, entrusted in 1828 one of his principal chiefs, Sotobi, and a companion to the care of Lieutenant King, to be conducted on an embassage to Cape Town, Sotobi being commissioned to proceed to the king of England. From causes which are not now certainly known these people were not allowed to proceed beyond Port Elizabeth, and were soon sent back to Zululand. On 23d September 1828 Tshaka was murdered by his brother, Mhlangana, and a few days afterwards Mhlangana was killed by another brother, Dingane. Tshaka's reign had involved an immense sacrifice of human life, but he had set before himself the aim of establishing a great kingdom, and, having succeeded in that, his home rule had been relieved by acts of generosity and statesmanship.

What is recorded of Dingane's reign shows him in the light of a bloodthirsty and cruel monster without a redeeming feature. The attempts made by the emigrant Dutch Boers under Piet Retief to establish friendly relations with him, and obtain a cession of the district of Natal, ended in the massacre of the whole party of seventy of their leading men at the king's kraal (February 1838), and of all members of their families left behind in Natal who could not be collected into fortified camps. Two unsuccessful attempts were made to avenge the deaths of the emigrant Boers. A Dutch command under Pieter Uys invaded the Zulu country, but was compelled to retreat, leaving their leader behind them, while a considerable force, composed of English settlers, Boers, and natives, entered Zululand at the mouth of the Tugela, and was completely annihilated, after inflicting very great loss on the Zulus. A detachment of the Zulu army on this occasion entered Natal and compelled the settlers at the port to take refuge on board a ship. After a further attack by Dingane the emigrant Boers and settlers again invaded Zululand in December 1838, and after a severe

[1] To avoid confusion the names are given with their ethnical instead of their linguistic prefixes. Thus, Ba-Suto, not Se-Suto.

engagement defeated the Zulu army with great slaughter on the banks of the Blood river, which owes its name to the results of the victory. In 1840 the Boers agreed to support Dingane's brother mPande in rebellion against him. The movement was completely successful, several of Dingane's regiments going over to mPande. Dingane passed into Swaziland in advance of his retreating forces, and was there murdered, while mPande was crowned king of Zululand by the Boers, who received in exchange for their services the much-coveted district of Natal. During the next sixteen years of mPande's reign nothing occurred to disturb the peaceful relations between the Zulus and the Natal Government. In 1856 a civil war broke out between two of mPande's sons, Cetshwayo and Umbulazi, who were rival claimants for the succession. A bloody battle was fought between them on the banks of the Tugela in December 1856, in which Umbulazi and many of his followers were slain. The Zulu country continued, however, excited and disturbed, until the Government of Natal in 1861 obtained the formal nomination of a successor to mPande; and Cetshwayo was appointed. mPande died in October 1872, but practically the government of Zululand had been in Cetshwayo's hands since the victory of 1856, owing both to political circumstances and the failing health of his father. In 1873 the Zulu nation appealed to the Natal Government to preside over the installation of Cetshwayo as king; and this request was acceded to. The rule of mPande was in earlier years a severe one, the executions ordered by him being so numerous in 1859 as to evoke remonstrances from Cetshwayo, who warned the king that he would drive all the people over into Natal. In 1856 and for some years afterwards a considerable exodus of refugees did take place into the colony, but by 1871 the tide appeared to be turning the other way. In 1854 the native population in Natal was reckoned at from 100,000 to 120,000. By 1873, owing largely to the influx of refugees from Zululand, it had risen to 282,783; but five years later it had not increased to more than 290,035, some hundreds of heads of families having returned to Zululand.

The encroachments of the Transvaal Boers upon the borders of Zululand having for many years exposed the British Government to urgent appeals on the part of the Zulus for its intervention, a second attempt was made by the Government of Natal, and this time with success, to induce the Boers to submit the boundary disputes between them and their neighbours to arbitration. A commission was appointed, composed of three British officers, who in June 1878 pronounced a decision substantially in favour of the Zulus. But the high commissioner, Sir Bartle Frere, had determined upon measures for re-modelling the Zulu nation with a view to the confederation of the South African colonies and states. The invasion of Zululand took place in January 1879, and the war was ended by the capture of the king at the end of August. Cetshwayo having been conveyed to Cape Town, the Zulu country was portioned out among eleven Zulu chiefs, a white adventurer, and a Basuto chief who had done good service in the war. This arrangement was productive of much bloodshed and disturbance, and in 1882 the British Government determined to restore Cetshwayo again to power. In the meantime, however, the deepest blood feuds had been engendered between the chiefs Zibebu and Hamu on the one side and the neighbouring tribes who supported the ex-king and his family on the other. These people suffered severely at the hands of the two chiefs, who were assisted by a band of white freebooters. Zibebu, having created a formidable force of well-armed and trained warriors, was left in independence on the borders of Cetshwayo's territory, while the latter was restrained by the conditions of his restoration from any military enterprise or defensive measures. A collision very soon took place; but in the conflicts that followed Zibebu's forces were victorious, and on 22d July 1883, led by a troop of mounted whites, he made a sudden descent upon Cetshwayo's kraal at Ulundi, which he destroyed, massacring such of the inmates of both sexes as could not save themselves by flight. The king escaped, though wounded, into the Reserve, which had been placed under British rule; there he died in 1884. He left a son, Dinuzulu, who sought the assistance of some of the Transvaal Boers against Zibebu, whom he defeated and drove into the Reserve. These Boers, not a large number, claimed as a stipulated reward for their services the cession of the greater part, and the more valuable part, of central Zululand. The Government of Natal has recently attempted to mediate on behalf of the Zulus and has accepted on their behalf, in spite of their protests, a line which roughly divides central Zululand into two equal portions. Of these the north-western has been created into the independent Boer state already mentioned. The rest of central Zululand is administered, with the Reserve, as a British protectorate.

See John Chase, *A Reprint of Authentic Documents relating to Natal* (Grahamstown, 1843); Saxe Bannister, *Humane Policy* (London, 1830), and authorities collected in Appendix; Delegorgue, *Voyage de l'Afrique Australe* (Paris, 1847); Allen Francis Gardiner, *Narrative of a Journey to the Zoolu Country* (London, 1836); Leslie, *Among the Zulus* (Edinburgh, 1875); Bishop Colenso, *Extracts from the Blue Books or Digest upon Zulu Affairs* (in the British Museum); Cetshwayo's *Dutchman* (London, 1880); Frances Colenso, *The Ruin of Zululand* (London, 1884); R. N. Cust, *Sketch of the Modern Languages of Africa* (London, 1883). See also authorities cited under NATAL. (F. E. C.-A. H. K.)

ZURBARAN, FRANCISCO (1598-1662), a distinguished Spanish painter, was born at Fuente de Cantos in Estremadura on 7th November 1598. His father was named Luis Zurbaran, a country labourer, his mother Isabel Marquet. The lot apparently marked out for Francisco was that of tilling the ground, like his father; but his natural faculty had decided otherwise. In mere childhood he set about imitating objects with charcoal; and his father was quick-witted and long-headed enough to take him off, still extremely young, to the school of Juan de Roélas in Seville. Francisco soon became the best pupil in the studio of Roélas, surpassing the master himself; and before leaving him he had achieved a solid reputation, full though Seville then was of able painters. He may probably have had here the opportunity of copying some of the paintings of Michelangelo da Caravaggio; at any rate he gained the name of "the Spanish Caravaggio," owing to the very forcible realistic style in which he excelled. He constantly painted direct from nature, following but occasionally improving on his model; and he made great use of the lay-figure in the study of draperies, in which he was peculiarly proficient. He had a special gift for white draperies; and, as a natural consequence, Carthusian monks are abundant in his paintings. To these rigidly faithful methods of work Zurbaran is said to have adhered throughout his career, which was always eminent and prosperous, wholly confined to his native Spain, and varied by few incidents beyond those of his daily laborious and continually productive diligence. His subjects were mostly of a severe and ascetic kind,—religious vigils, the flesh chastised into subjection to the spirit,—the compositions seldom thronged, and often reduced to a single figure. The style is more reserved and chastened than Caravaggio's, the tone of colour often bluish to a morbid excess. Exceptional effects are attained by the precise finish of foregrounds, largely massed out in light and shade. Zurbaran married in Seville Leonor de Jordera, by whom he had several children. Towards 1630 he was appointed painter to Philip IV.; and there is a story that on one occasion the sovereign laid his hand on the artist's shoulder, saying, "Painter to the king, king of painters." It was only late in life that Zurbaran made a prolonged stay in Madrid, Seville being the chief scene of his operations. He died in 1662 in Madrid.

In 1627 he painted the great altarpiece of St Thomas Aquinas, now in the Seville museum; it was executed for the church of the college of that saint in the same city. This is Zurbaran's largest composition, containing figures of Christ and the Madonna, various saints, Charles V. with knights, and Archbishop Deza (founder of the college) with monks and servitors, all the principal personages being beyond the size of life; this work is full of fine portrait-like heads, and it ranks, both in importance and in elevated style, as the painter's masterpiece. It had been preceded by the numerous pictures of the screen of St Peter Nolasco in the cathedral. In the church of Guadalupe he painted various large pictures, eight of which relate to the history of St Jerome, and in the church of St Paul, Seville, a famous figure of the Crucified Saviour, in grisaille, presenting an illusive effect of marble. In 1633 he finished the paintings of the high altar of the Carthusians in Jerez. In the palace of Buenretiro, Madrid, are four large canvases representing the Labours of Hercules, an unusual instance of non-Christian subjects from the hand of Zurbaran. A very fine specimen is in the London National Gallery, a whole-length life-sized figure of a kneeling Franciscan holding a skull (figured in vol. xxi. p. 440, fig. 36).

The principal scholars of this master, whose style has as much affinity to that of Ribera as to Caravaggio's, were Bernabe de Ayala and the brothers Polanco.

ZURICH (Germ. *Zürich*),[1] a canton in Switzerland, ranking as the first in dignity. It is of very irregular shape, consisting simply of the conquests made by the city. It extends from the Lake of Zurich to the Rhine, taking in

[1] The name is derived from the Celtic *dur* (water). The true and accurate Latinized form is *Turicum*, but the false form *Tigurum* was given currency to by Glareanus and held its ground from 1512 to 1748.

the district of Eglisau on the right bank of that river. On the east it is, roughly speaking, limited by the ranges of low hills which separate it from the valley of the Thur, and on the west by those (*e.g.*, the Albis) which divide it from the valleys of the Reuss and the Aar. Its total area is 655·9 square miles, of which 610·6 are classified as fertile (woods covering 186 and vines 21·5). Of 45·2 square miles of non-fertile land 26·2 are covered by the lake. The highest point in the canton is the Schnebelhorn (4250 feet) in the south-east corner. The population in 1880 was 317,576 (an increase of 32,790 since 1870), and in 1887 was estimated to be 339,163. In 1880 there were 313,762 German-speaking and 283,134 Protestant inhabitants. The number of Roman Catholics nearly doubled from 1870 to 1880 (17,942 and 30,298). Besides ZURICH (see below), the capital, the only other town of any size in the canton is WINTERTHUR (*q.v*). The land is very highly cultivated and is held by no less than 36,000 proprietors. The canton is well supplied with railways, the first line of any length in Switzerland being that from Zurich to Baden in Aargau (opened 1847). The line from Zurich to the summit of the Uetliberg (2861 feet) was made in 1875. For the history of the canton, see under the town, below.

ZURICH, chief city of the above canton, and until 1848 practically the capital of the Swiss Confederation, is beautifully situated, at a height of 1506 feet, on the banks of the Limmat where it issues from the Lake of Zurich, and on the river Sihl, which joins the Limmat just above the north end of the lake. That part which lies on the right bank of the Limmat is known as the Large Town, that on the left as the Little Town. The central portion—the "city"—is governed by an executive of seven members and a town council of sixty, both elected by the citizens, and in 1887 had 27,638 inhabitants. The nine outlying townships or "gemeinden" have each a separate organization, distinct from that of the city, and in 1887 had 60,836 inhabitants, of whom 18,527 were in Aussersihl and 10,883 in Riesbach. The total population of the town and its suburbs was thus 88,474 in 1887. These are nearly all Protestants and German-speaking. The number of Roman Catholics has doubled in the last ten years; they are mainly resident in Aussersihl, the workmen's quarter, where also many Italian-speaking persons dwell. There are in Zurich about 7000 Old Catholics.

Of the old buildings the finest and most important is the Gross Münster (or Propstei) on the right bank of the Limmat. This was originally the church of the king's tenants, and in one of the chapels the bodies of Felix, Regula, and Exuperantius, the patron saints of the city, were buried, the town treasury being formerly kept above this chapel. The present building was erected at two periods (1090-1150 and 1225-1300), the high altar having been dedicated in 1278. The towers were first raised above the roof at the end of the 15th century and took their present form in 1779. The chapter consisted of twenty-four secular canons; it was reorganized at the Reformation (1526), and suppressed in 1832. On the site of the canons' houses stands a girls' school (opened 1853), but the fine Romanesque cloisters (12th and 13th centuries) still remain. There is a curious figure of Charlemagne in a niche on one of the towers; to him is attributed the founding or reform of the chapter. On the left bank of the Limmat stands the other great church of Zurich, the Frau Munster (or Abtei), founded for nuns in 853 by Louis the German. The high altar was dedicated in 1170; but the greater part of the buildings are of the 13th and 14th centuries. It was in this church that the relics of the three patron saints of the town were preserved till the Reformation, and it was here that the burgomaster Waldmann was buried in 1489. There were only twelve nuns of noble family, comparatively free from the severer monastic vows; the convent was suppressed in 1524. Of the other old churches may be mentioned St Peter's, the oldest parish church, though the present buildings date from the 13th century only, and formerly the meeting-place of the citizens; the Dominican church (13th century), in the choir of which the cantonal library of 80,000 volumes has been stored since 1873; the church of the Austin friars (14th century), now used by the Old Catholics; and the Wasserkirche. The last-named church is on the site of an old pagan holy place, where the patron saints of the city were martyred; since 1631 it has housed the city library, the largest in Switzerland, which contains 120,000 printed volumes and 4000 MSS. (among these being letters of Zwingli, Bullinger, and Lady Jane Grey), as well as a splendid collection of objects from the lake dwellings of Switzerland. The building itself was erected 1479 to 1484, and near it is a statue of Zwingli, erected in 1885. The existing council house dates from 1698, and the guild houses were mostly rebuilt in the 18th century. Among the modern buildings the polytechnic school, the cantonal school, the reading rooms (museum), the hospital, and the railway station are the most conspicuous. There are some fine old fountains (the oldest dating back to 1568). The quays along the river and the lake are extensive and afford fine views; and there are several good bridges, Roman traces being still seen in the case of the Niederbrücke. The mound of the Lindenhof was formerly crowned by the king's house, which disappeared in the 13th century, and the hillock was planted with limes as early as 1422. Zurich possesses a large number of charitable institutions.

The inhabitants are very industrious and of social habits among themselves, the town being noted for its clubs and societies. It is the intellectual capital of German-speaking Switzerland, and has been called "Athens on the Limmat." Cotton-spinning and the manufacture of machinery are two of the leading industries, but by far the most important of all is the silk trade. This flourished in Zurich in the 12th and 13th centuries, but disappeared about 1420; it was revived by the Protestant exiles from Locarno (1555) and by the Huguenot refugees from France (1682 and 1685). The value of the silk annually exported (mainly to France, the United States, and England) is estimated at £2,916,000 to £3,333,000. The trade employs about 20,000 hand looms and 4500 steam-power looms; but the number of the former is diminishing, while that of the latter is increasing. Poor wine is also made. Zurich is the banking centre of Switzerland. There are a large number of educational establishments, public and private. Besides the excellent primary and secondary schools, there are the cantonal school, including a gymnasium and a technical side (opened 1842), and a high school for girls (opened 1875). The cantonal university and the Federal polytechnic school are housed in the same building, but have no other connexion. The university was founded in 1832-33 (no doubt as a successor to the ancient chapter school at the Gross Münster, said to date back to Charlemagne's time—hence its name the Carolinum—reorganized at the Reformation, and suppressed in 1832); in 1886 it had 51 professors and 481 matriculated students, besides 65 persons attending special courses of lectures. The polytechnic school, founded in 1854, includes six main sections (industrial chemistry, mechanics, engineering, training of scientific and mathematical teachers, architecture, forestry and agriculture), and a general philosophical, mathematical, and literary department. The numbers of students in the first three sections were, in 1885, 122, 97, and 90—in all the six 412, of whom 192 were foreigners; there were about fifty-four professors. The polytechnic school has good collections of botanical specimens and of engravings. Near it is the observatory (1542 feet). There are also in Zurich many institutions for special branches of education—*e.g.*, veterinary surgery, music, industrial art, silk-weaving, &c.

History.—The earliest inhabitants of the future site of Zurich were the lake dwellers. The Celtic Helvetians had a settlement on the Lindenhof when they were succeeded by the Romans, who established a customs station here for goods going to and coming from Italy; during their rule Christianity was introduced early in the 3d century by Felix and Regula, with whom Exuperantius was afterwards associated. The district was later occupied by the Alemanni, who were conquered by the Franks. It is not till the 9th century that we find the beginnings of the Teutonic town of Zurich, which arose from the union of four elements:—(1) the royal house and castle on the Lindenhof, with the king's tenants around, (2) the Gross Münster, (3) the Frau Münster, (4) the community of "free men" (of Alemannian origin) on the Zürichberg. The Frankish kings had special rights over their tenants, were the protectors of the two churches, and had jurisdiction over the free community. In 870 the sovereign placed his powers over all four in the hands of a single official (the Reichsvogt), and the union was still further strengthened by the wall built round the four settlements in the 10th century as a safeguard against Saracen marauders and feudal barons. The Reichsvogtei passed to the counts of Lenzburg (1063-1172), and then to the dukes of Zäringen (extinct 1218). Meanwhile the abbess of the Frau Münster had been acquiring extensive rights and privileges over all the inhabitants, though she never obtained the criminal jurisdiction. The town flourished greatly in the 12th and 13th centuries, the silk trade being introduced from Italy. In 1218 the Reichsvogtei passed back into the hands of the king, who appointed one of the burghers as his deputy, the town thus becoming a free imperial city under the nominal rule of a distant sovereign. The abbess in 1234 became a princess of the empire, but power rapidly passed from her to the council, which she had originally named to look after police, &c., but which (*c.* 1240) came to be elected by the burghers, though the abbess was still "the lady of Zurich." This council was made up of the representatives of certain knightly and rich mercantile families (the "patricians"), who excluded the craftsmen from all share in the government, though it was to these last that the town was largely indebted for its rising wealth and importance.

In October 1291 the town made an alliance with Uri and Schwyz, and in 1292 failed in a desperate attempt to seize the Hapsburg town of Winterthur. After that Zurich began to display strong Austrian leanings, which characterize much of its later history. In 1315 the men of Zurich fought against the Swiss Confederates at Morgarten. The year 1336 marks the admission of the craftsmen to a share in the town government, which was brought about by Rudolph Brun, a patrician. Under the new constitution (the main features of which lasted till 1798) the council was made up of thirteen members from the "constafel" (including the old patricians and the wealthiest burghers) and the thirteen masters of the craft guilds, each of the twenty-six holding office for six months. The office of burgomaster was created and given to Brun for life. Out of this change arose a quarrel with one of the branches of the Hapsburg family, in consequence of which Brun was induced to throw in the lot of Zurich with the Swiss Confederation (1st May 1351). The double position of Zurich as a free imperial city and as a member of the Everlasting League was soon found to be embarrassing to both parties (see SWITZERLAND, vol. xxii. p. 784 *sq.*). Meanwhile the town had been extending its rule far beyond its walls,—a process which began in the 13th century, went on apace in the 14th, and attained its height in the 15th century (1268-1467). This thirst for territorial aggrandizement brought about the first civil war in the Confederation (the "Old Zurich War," 1436-50), in which, at the fight of St Jacob on the Sihl (1443), under the walls of Zurich, the men of Zurich were completely beaten and their burgomaster Stüssi slain. The purchase of the town of Winterthur from the Hapsburgs (1467) marks the culmination of the territorial power of the city. It was to the men of Zurich and their leader Hans Waldmann that the victory of Morat (1476) was due in the Burgundian War; and Zurich took a leading part in the Italian campaign of 1512-15, the burgomaster Schmid naming the new duke of Milan (1512). No doubt her trade connexions with Italy led her to pursue a southern policy, traces of which are seen as early as 1331 in an attack on the Val Leventina and in 1478, when Zurich men were in the van at the fight of Giornico, won by a handful of Confederates over 12,000 Milanese troops.

In 1400 the town received from the emperor the Reichsvogtei, which carried with it complete immunity from the empire and the right of criminal jurisdiction. As early as 1393 the chief power had practically fallen into the hands of the council of 200 (really 212), composed of the former council and a number of other citizens originally elected by it; and in 1498 this change was formally recognized. This transfer of all power to the guilds had been one of the aims of the burgomaster Hans Waldmann (1483-89), who wished to make Zurich a great commercial centre. He also introduced many financial and moral reforms, and subordinated the interests of the country districts to those of the town. He practically ruled the Confederation, and under him Zurich became the real capital of the League. But such great changes excited opposition, and he was overthrown and executed. His main ideas were embodied, however, in the constitution of 1498, by which the patricians became the first of the guilds, and which remained in force till 1798; some special rights were also given to the subjects in country districts. It was, however, the prominent part taken by Zurich in adopting and propagating the principles of the Reformation which finally secured for it the lead of the Confederation; for a detailed account of its policy and the events in which it shared during this period, see SWITZERLAND (vol. xxii. p. 790 *sq.*) and ZWINGLI.

In the 17th and 18th centuries a distinct tendency becomes observable in the city government to limit power to the actual holders. Thus the country districts were consulted for the last time in 1620 and 1640; and a similar breach of the charters of 1489 and 1531 occasioned disturbances in 1777. The council of 200 came to be chosen by a small committee of the members of the guilds actually sitting in the council, and early in the 18th century a determined effort was made to crush by means of heavy duties the flourishing silk trade in Winterthur. In 1655 an attempt was made by Bern and Zurich to set up a central administration in the Confederation, which failed through the jealousy of the other cantons. The first symptoms of active discontent appeared later among the dwellers by the lake, who founded in 1794 a club at Stäfa and claimed the restoration of the liberties of 1489 and 1531, a movement which was put down by force of arms in 1795. The old system of government perished in Zurich, as elsewhere in Switzerland, in 1798, and under the Helvetic constitution the country districts obtained political liberty. But under the cantonal constitution of 1815 the town had 130 representatives in the great council, while the country districts had only 88. A great meeting at Uster on 22d November 1830 demanded that two-thirds of the members in the great council should be chosen by the country districts; and in 1831 a new constitution was drawn up on these lines, though it was not till 1837-38 that the town finally lost the last relics of the privileges which it had so long enjoyed as compared with the country districts. In 1833 Zurich tried hard to secure a revision of the Federal constitution and a strong central Government. The town was the Federal capital for 1839-40, and consequently the victory of the Conservative party there caused a great stir throughout Switzerland. But, when in 1845 the Radicals regained power at Zurich, which was again the Federal capital for 1845-46, that city took the lead in opposing the Sonderbund cantons. In 1869 the cantonal constitution was again thoroughly revised in a very democratic sense; and, with the exception of a few changes made later, it is the existing constitution. There is an executive of seven members and a legislature of 211 (one member to every 1500 inhabitants), each holding office for three years and elected at the same time directly by the vote of the people. The referendum exists in both forms, compulsory and optional: all laws and all money grants of a total sum over 250,000 francs or an annual sum of 20,000 must be submitted to a popular vote, the people meeting for that purpose at least twice in each year, while the executive may submit to a popular vote any other matter, though it fall within its powers as defined by law. One-third of the members of the legislature or 5000 legally qualified voters can force the Government to submit to the people any matter whatsoever (initiative). The constitution provides for the imposition of a graduated and progressive income tax. In 1885 the penalty of death was abolished in the canton. Zurich has sheltered many political refugees of late years, especially Poles and Russians; but its hospitality has been abused by the Socialists, who have given considerable trouble. The Swiss National Agricultural and Industrial Exhibition was held at Zurich in 1883.

For the present state of the town, see *Europäische Wanderbilder* (Nos. 126-129), Zurich, 1887. For the local and architectural history the principal work is S. Vögelin, *Das alte Zürich* (2d ed., 1878), and for general history, J. C. Bluntschli, *Staats- und Rechts-Geschichte der Stadt und Landschaft Zürich* (2d ed., 1856); G. v. Wyss, *Geschichte der Abtei Zürich*, 1851-58 (in vol. viii. of *Mittheil. d. antiquar. Gesellsch. in Z.*); Id., *Die Reichsvogtei Zürich*, 1870 (in vol. xvii. of *Zeitschr. f. Schweiz. Recht*). Many of the recent works on Swiss history, *e.g.*, those of Dändliker, Oechsli, Orelli, Strickler, are by Zurich men and pay special attention to Zurich matters. (W. A. B. C.)

ZUTPHEN, a fortified town of Holland, in the province of Guelderland, 20 miles by rail south from Deventer, stands on the right bank of the Yssel, at its junction with the Berkel. Its most important public building is the church of St Walburga, dating from the 12th century, which contains several interesting monuments of the counts of Zutphen, and good examples of old metal-work and sculpture. The place has an active trade, especially in grain and in the timber floated down from the Black Forest by the Rhine and the Yssel; the industries include tanning, weaving, and oil and paper manufactures. The population in 1887 was 16,357. Some 2½ miles to the north of the town is the agricultural colony of Nederlandsch-Mettray, founded by a private benefactor for the education of poor and friendless boys in 1851, and since that date largely extended.

Zutphen at one time belonged to the Hanseatic League and had an extensive foreign trade. It has been more than once besieged, and it was before Zutphen that Sir Philip Sidney received his mortal wound (22d September 1586).

ZWEIBRÜCKEN. See DEUX PONTS.

ZWICKAU, one of the busiest towns in the industrial district of the kingdom of Saxony to which it gives its name, is situated in a pleasant valley on the left bank of the Zwickauer Mulde, 41 miles south of Leipsic. The river is here crossed by four bridges, two of which are of iron. The town contains six churches, including the fine Late Gothic church of St Mary (1453-1536, restored 1884), with a tower 278 feet high, and the Gothic church of St Catherine (14th to 15th century), of which Thomas Münzer was pastor in 1520-22. Among the secular buildings are the town-house of 1581, the Gothic "Gewandhaus" (now a theatre) of 1522-24, the Government buildings of 1838, the law-courts, the hospital, and the barracks. The railway station, which with its dependencies covers 81 acres, is said to be one of the largest in Germany. The château of Osterstein (1581-91) is now a penitentiary. The manufactures of Zwickau are both extensive and varied: they include machinery, chemicals, porcelain, paper, glass, dye-stuffs, tinware, stockings, and curtains. There are also steam saw-mills, brickfields, iron-foundries, and breweries.

Though no longer so important as when it lay on the chief trade route from Saxony to Bohemia and the Danube, Zwickau still carries on considerable commerce in grain, linen, and coal. The mainstay of the industrial prosperity of the town is the adjacent coalfield, which in 1885 employed 10,000 hands and yielded coal to the value of £854,900. The mines are mentioned as early as 1348; but they have been actively worked only for the last 65 years, during which time the population of the town has increased more than sixfold. In 1885 the population was 39,245; in 1834 it was 6701.

Zwickau is of Slavonic origin, and is mentioned in 1118 as a trading place. From 1290 till 1348 it was a free imperial city, but about the latter date it was forced to accept the protection of the margrave of Meissen. The Anabaptist movement of 1525 began at Zwickau under the inspiration of the "Zwickau prophets." Robert Schumann (1810-1856), the musical composer, was born here. The name is sometimes fancifully derived from the Latin *cygnea*, from a tradition that placed a "swan lake" here which had the property of renewing the youth of those who bathed in it.

ZWINGLI, Huldreich (1484-1531), Swiss Reformer, was born on 1st January 1484 at Wildhaus, at the head of the Toggenburg valley, in the canton of St Gall, Switzerland. His father was a well-to-do peasant proprietor, amman of the township; his mother was Margaret Meili, whose brother was abbot of the cloister of Fischingen in Thurgau. The people of Wildhaus were in Zwingli's time a self-ruled village community. They had also bought from the abbots of St Gall the privilege of electing their own pastor; and the first parish priest chosen by the votes of the parishioners was Bartholomew Zwingli, the uncle of the Reformer, who latterly became dean of Wesen. Zwingli thus came of a free peasant stock, and he carried the marks of his origin all his life. When eight years old he was sent to school at Wesen, where he lived with his uncle, the dean. Two years later he was sent to Basel; and after a three years' sojourn there he became a pupil in the high school of Bern, where his master was Heinrich Wölflin, an accomplished classical scholar, from whom Zwingli acquired that love of classical literature which never left him. From Bern he went to Vienna (in 1500), and after two years' study there he returned to Basel. At Basel the celebrated Thomas Wyttenbach was his master and friend, and taught him those Evangelical truths which he afterwards so signally defended.

It is impossible to avoid contrasting the joyous youth of Zwingli with the sad childhood of Luther. Zwingli was full of love of family, of township, of country, and of Christ. He had none of those dark religious experiences which drove Luther to the convent, and which made him miserable there. He had never to struggle alone in despair of soul, one step at a time, towards the gospel of God's free grace. Wyttenbach was very unlike those nominalist divines from whom Luther learnt mediæval theology. He foresaw many things which a later generation discovered. Zwingli has assured us that Wyttenbach taught him that the death of Christ, and not priests, masses, and pilgrimages, was a sufficient ransom for the sins of the world; that he pointed out the errors of the schoolmen and of Romish theology; and that he asserted that Holy Scripture, and not ecclesiastical tradition, was the sole rule of faith. It cost Zwingli nothing to break with the mediæval church. He had been taught independence from childhood, and shown how to think for himself while a student at Basel.

When twenty-two years of age Zwingli was ordained by the bishop of Constance. He preached his first sermon at Rapperswyl, and said his first mass among his own people at Wildhaus. He was appointed (1506) to the parish of Glarus, where he had leisure for study and began to read extensively and carefully in preparation for future work. At Glarus too he gathered the boys of the district about him (Ægidius Tschudi, the historian of Switzerland, among them) to teach them the classics; and he set himself by a study of the masterpieces of ancient and mediæval rhetoric to learn the art of oratory. He tells us that at this time he foresaw that a man who is called to be a preacher must know many things, two things above all others—God, and how to speak. Meanwhile he tested every doctrine in theology by the Word of God and took his stand firmly upon what it taught him.

The Swiss troops of Zwingli's day were supposed to be the best in Europe, and neighbouring states were glad to have their assistance in war. The Swiss were accustomed to hire out their soldiers for large sums of money to those states who paid best. It was their custom also to send the parish priest of the district from which the troops came as chaplain to the regiment. Zwingli went twice, once in 1512 and again in 1515, with the men of Glarus. He saw the demoralizing tendency of such mercenary warfare and ever afterwards denounced the immoral traffic. In 1521 he persuaded the authorities of the canton of Zurich to renounce it altogether.

In 1516 Zwingli was transferred to Einsiedeln. It was then, and is still, resorted to by thousands of pilgrims yearly, who come to visit the famous image of the Virgin and Child which has been preserved there for at least a thousand years. Zwingli denounced the superstition of pilgrimages. His sermons made a great sensation and attracted attention in Rome. The papal curia had no wish to quarrel with the Swiss, who furnished them with troops, and sought to silence the Reformer by offers of promotion, which he refused. Soon afterwards he was elected, after some opposition, to be preacher in the cathedral at Zurich, and accepted the office (1518), having first obtained a pledge that his liberty to preach the truth should not be interfered with. He began the fight almost on his arrival. Bernhardin Samson, a pardon-seller like Tetzel, had been selling indulgences in the Forest Cantons and proposed to come to Zurich. Zwingli prevailed on the council to send the friar out of the country. In the beginning of 1519 he began a series of discourses on the New Testament Scriptures,—on St Matthew's Gospel, on the Acts of the Apostles, and on the Pauline Epistles. The sermons, preached "in simple Swiss language," had a great effect. The Reformation in Zurich was begun. The council of the canton was on Zwingli's side and protected their preacher. He began to preach against fasting and other Roman practices; some of his followers put his precepts in practice and ate flesh in Lent. The bishop of Constance accused them before the council of Zurich. Zwingli was heard in their defence, and the accusation was abandoned. The victory on the subject of fasting was followed by an attack on the doctrine of the celibacy of the clergy. Pope Adrian VI. interfered, and asked the Zurichers to abandon Zwingli. The Reformer persuaded the council to allow a public disputation, which was held in 1523. Zwingli produced sixty-seven theses,[1] containing a summary of his doctrinal views, and argued in their favour with such power that the council upheld the Reformer and separated the canton from the bishopric of Constance. The Reformation, thus legally established, went forward rapidly. The Latin language was discontinued in the service; the incomes of chapters, convents, and monasteries were applied for education; the celibacy of the clergy was abolished; monks and nuns were freed from their vows; mass and image worship were declared to be idolatrous; and the Eucharist in both kinds was celebrated by a solemn communion of all the Reformed congregations on Maundy Thursday 1525.

[1] *Cf.* Schaff's *Creeds of the Evangelical Protestant Churches*, p. 197.

The progress of the Reformation in Zurich attracted the attention of all Switzerland, and the Confederation became divided into two parties. The Reformers found numerous supporters in the larger towns of Basel, Bern, and Schaffhausen, and in the country districts of Glarus, Appenzell, and the Grisons. The five Forest Cantons—Lucerne, Zug, Schwyz, Uri, and Unterwalden—remained solidly opposed to all reforms. This anti-Reformation party was also strong in the patrician oligarchies which drew papal pensions, and enriched themselves by the nefarious blood traffic denounced by Zwingli. The Zurichers felt it necessary to form a defensive league to prevent their Reformation from being crushed by force. They were especially anxious to gain Bern, and Zwingli challenged the Roman Catholics to a public disputation in that city. No less than 350 ecclesiastics came to Bern from the various cantons to hear the pleadings, which began on 2d January 1528 and lasted nineteen days. Zwingli and his companions undertook to defend against all comers the following ten propositions:—

(1) That the Holy Christian Church, of which Christ is the only Head, is born of the Word of God, abides therein, and does not listen to the voice of a stranger; (2) that this church imposes no laws on the conscience of people without the sanction of the Word of God, and that the laws of the church are binding only in so far as they agree with the Word; (3) that Christ alone is our righteousness and our salvation, and that to trust to any other merit or satisfaction is to deny Him; (4) that it cannot be proved from the Holy Scripture that the body and blood of Christ are corporeally present in the bread and in the wine of the Lord's Supper; (5) that the mass, in which Christ is offered to God the Father for the sins of the living and of the dead, is contrary to Scripture and a gross affront to the sacrifice and death of the Saviour; (6) that we should not pray to dead mediators and intercessors, but to Jesus Christ alone; (7) that there is no trace of purgatory in Scripture; (8) that to set up pictures and to adore them is also contrary to Scripture, and that images and pictures ought to be destroyed where there is danger of giving them adoration; (9) that marriage is lawful to all, to the clergy as well as to the laity; (10) that shameful living is more disgraceful among the clergy than among the laity.

These they defended to such purpose that the Bernese joined heartily in the Reformation, and the enthusiasm of the people was fired by two burning sermons preached by Zwingli from the minster pulpit to overflowing audiences. The two parties henceforward faced each other in Switzerland. The country was in those days a confederacy of republics, and yet was far from being a democracy. Most of the cantons were ruled by aristocratic oligarchies who had pensions from foreign Governments, and Zwingli's appeal had always been from an oligarchy of pope, bishops, and abbots to the congregation with the Bible in hand. He founded his religious Reformation on the congregation, and this of itself suggested that the state was nothing but the people. It so happened that those cantons which remained firmly attached to Roman Catholicism were the least powerful, and yet from historical position and the long custom of the Confederacy had the largest legal influence in the country. The Forest Cantons had been the earliest to free themselves. Isolated towns and districts after successful revolt had claimed the protection of these little republics, and the Forest Cantons governed by means of prefects a large number of places beyond their boundaries. This gave them votes in the diet or federal council far beyond what they were entitled to by their population and actual resources. These cantons felt that, if the Reformation and the political ideas it suggested spread, their supremacy would be overthrown and their rule confined within their own territories. Nor had they in their upland valleys seen the worst abuses of the mediæval church. They dreaded the Reformation. They persecuted inquirers after truth, and imprisoned, beheaded, and burnt the followers of Zwingli when they caught them within their borders. Zwingli, alone among Protestant leaders, saw that the religious and the political questions could not be decided separately, but were for practical statesmanship one and the same problem. His policy was to reorganize the Swiss constitution on the principles of representative democracy, to put an end to the unnatural supremacy of the Forest Cantons by abolishing the prefects and their jurisdiction, and by giving the larger cantons the influence in the diet which was due to their resources and population, and to do this at once, and if necessary by war. His counsels were overruled. Bern was anxious to treat the religious question separately, and to negotiate for religious toleration, leaving the political future to take care of itself. The course of history has fully justified Zwingli. The views of the peace party triumphed, and a religious truce was negotiated under the name of the first peace of Cappel, with guarantees on paper that there was to be toleration in religious matters. But no real securities were given. The provisions of the treaty were never carried out in the Roman Catholic cantons, where authorities were secretly preparing for war. Zwingli in vain proclaimed the danger and urged offensive measures. The Protestant cantons remained heedless to the danger. At length the storm burst. The Forest Cantons advanced (1531) secretly and rapidly on Zurich, with the intention of overcoming the Protestant cantons one by one. The Zurichers met their foes at Cappel, were outnumbered, and were defeated. Zwingli, who had accompanied the troops as field chaplain, and had stood among the fighting men to encourage them, had received two wounds on the thigh when a blow on the head knocked him senseless. After the retreat of the Zurichers, when the victors examined the field, Zwingli was found to be still living. He was not recognized, and was asked if he wished a priest; when he refused, a captain standing near gave him a death-stroke on the neck. Next day his body was recognized. "Then there was a wonderful running to the spot the whole morning, for every man wished to see Zwingli." He had in death the same eager, courageous expression which his hearers were accustomed to see on his face when he preached. A great boulder, roughly squared, standing a little way off the road, marks the place where Zwingli fell. It is inscribed with the words, "'They may kill the body but not the soul': so spoke on this spot Ulrich Zwingli, who for truth and the freedom of the Christian Church died a hero's death, Oct. 11, 1531."

Zwingli's theological views are expressed succinctly in the sixty-seven theses published at Zurich in 1523, and at greater length in the *First Helvetic Confession*, compiled in 1536 by a number of his disciples.[1] They contain the elements of Reformed as distinguished from Lutheran doctrine. As opposed to Luther, Zwingli insisted more firmly on the supreme authority of Scripture, and broke more thoroughly and radically with the mediæval church. Luther was content with changes in one or two fundamental doctrines; Zwingli aimed at a reformation of government and discipline as well as of theology. Zwingli never faltered in his trust in the people, and was earnest to show that no class of men ought to be called *spiritual* simply because they were selected to perform certain functions. He thoroughly believed also that it was the duty of all in authority to rule in Christ's name and to obey His laws. He was led from these ideas to think that there should be no government in the church separate from the civil government which ruled the commonwealth. All rules and regulations about the public worship, doctrines, and discipline of the church were made in Zwingli's time, and with his consent, by the council of Zurich, which was the supreme civil authority in the state. This was the ground of his quarrel with the Swiss Anabaptists, for the main idea in the minds of these greatly maligned men was the modern thought of a free church in a free state. Like all the Reformers, he was strictly Augustinian in theology, but he dwelt chiefly on the positive side of predestination—the election to salvation—and he insisted upon the salvation of infants and of the pious heathen. His most distinctive doctrine is perhaps his theory of the sacrament, which involved him and his followers in a long and, on Luther's part, an acrimonious dispute with the German Protestants. His main idea was that the sacrament of the Lord's Supper

[1] Schaff, *Creeds of the Evangelical Protestant Churches*, p. 211.

was not the *repetition* of the sacrifice of Christ, but the faithful *remembrance* that that sacrifice had been made once for all; and his deeper idea of faith, which included in the act of faith a real union and communion of the faithful soul with Christ, really preserved what was also most valuable in the distinctively Lutheran doctrine. His peculiar theological opinions were set aside in Switzerland for the somewhat profounder views of Calvin. The publication of the Zurich Consensus (*Consensus Tigurinus*) in 1549 marks the adherence of the Swiss to Calvinist theology.

Zwingli's most important writings are—*Von Erkiesen und Fryheit der Spysen* (April 1522); *De Canone Missæ Epichiresis* (September 1523); *Commentarius de Vera et Falsa Religione* (1525); *Vom Touf, vom Wiedertouf, und vom Kindertouf* (1525); *Ein klare Unterrichtung vom Nachtmal Christi* (1526); *De Providentia Dei* (1530); and *Christianæ Fidei Expositio* (1531).

For his theology, compare Seegwart, *Ulrich Zwingli, der Character seiner Theologie*, 1855; especially Hundeshagen, *Beiträge zur Kirchenverfassungsgeschichte u. Kirchenpolitik*, 1864; Usteri, *Ulrich Zwingli, ein Martin Luther ebenbürtiger Zeuge des evangelischen Glaubens*, 1883; and A. Baur, *Zwingli's Theologie, ihr Werden und ihr System*, 1885.

For Zwingli's life, compare Oswald Myconius, *De Huldrichi Zwinglii Fortissimi Herois ac Theologi Doctissimi Vita et Obitu*, 1532; Bullinger, *Reformationsgeschichte*, 1838; Mörikofer, *Ulrich Zwingli*, 1867; and Stähelin, *Huldreich Zwingli und sein Reformationswerk*, 1884. Stähelin is also the author of the remarkably good article on Zwingli in Herzog-Plitt's *Real-Encykl.*, vol. xvii. (T. M. L.)

ZWOLLE, a fortified town of Holland, capital of the province of Overyssel, 55 miles by rail to the north-east of Utrecht, stands on the Zwarte Water, a right-hand tributary of the Yssel, a little above its junction with that river. On the side of the town next the railway station is the Sassen-poort, an old Gothic gateway of brick; but the town has few other historical monuments of interest. The large Gothic church of St Michael in the market place, begun in 1406, contains a fine organ and a richly carved pulpit. The town has a considerable trade by water, and among its more important industries are shipbuilding, cotton manufacture, dyeing and bleaching, tanning, rope-making, and salt-making. The population in 1887 was 25,005.

Zwolle was first fortified in 1223 by the bishop of Utrecht. It afterwards became a free imperial city and a member of the Hanseatic League, and first joined the United Provinces in 1580. Three miles from the town on a gentle eminence stands the monastery of the Agnetenberg, where Thomas a Kempis lived for the greater part of his life. Terburg the painter was a native of Zwolle.

ZYMOTIC DISEASES (ζύμη, ferment), a term in medicine applied by some authorities to the class of acute infectious maladies. As originally employed by Dr Farr of the British registrar-general's department, the term included the diseases which were "epidemic, endemic, and contagious," and owed their origin to the presence of some morbific principle in the system acting in a manner analogous to, although not identical with, the process of fermentation. A very large number of diseases were accordingly included under this designation. The term, however, has come to be restricted in medical nomenclature to the chief fevers and contagious diseases (*e.g.*, typhus and typhoid fevers, smallpox, scarlet fever, measles, erysipelas, cholera, hooping-cough, diphtheria, &c.). Although the name is held by not a few authorities to be objectionable on account of the theory it suggests, it is still made use of in the registrar-general's classification of diseases.

END OF VOLUME TWENTY-FOURTH

Printed by BALLANTYNE, HANSON & CO.
Edinburgh & London

Encyclopædia Britannica.

VOL. XXIV.—(URA–ZYM).

Total number of Articles, 804.

PRINCIPAL CONTENTS.

Z

WAR. Col. J. F. Maurice, R.A., Professor of Military Art and History, Staff College, Farnborough.
Naval Strategy and Tactics. Capt. C. C. Penrose FitzGerald, R.N.
WARBLER. Prof. Alfred Newton.
WARBURTON. Richard Garnett, LL.D.
WARRANT, WARRANTY. James Williams, B.C.L., Barrister-at-Law.
WARSAW. P. A. Kropotkine.
WARTON. Prof. W. Minto.
WARWICK, EARL OF. G. W. Prothero, M.A., Fellow and Tutor of King's College, Cambridge.
WASHINGTON (City). Henry Gannett.
WASHINGTON (Territory). Captain T. W. Symons, U.S. Engineers.
WASHINGTON, GEORGE. Alex. Johnston, Professor of Jurisprudence and Political Economy, Princeton College, N.J.
WASPS. Arthur E. Shipley.
WATCH. The Right Hon. Lord Grimthorpe, LL.D.
WATER. Prof. W. Dittmar.
WATER-SUPPLY. L. F. Vernon-Harcourt, M.A., C.E., Professor of Civil Engineering, University College, London.
WATT. Prof. J. A. Ewing.
WAVE. P. G. Tait, M.A., Professor of Natural Philosophy, University of Edinburgh.
WAVE THEORY. The Right Hon. Lord Rayleigh, D.C.L., F.R.S.
WEALTH. Prof. J. S. Nicholson.
WEAVING. James Paton, Curator, Corporation Galleries of Art, Glasgow.
WEBER. W. S. Rockstro.
WEBER'S LAW. Andrew Seth, M.A., Professor of Logic, University of St. Andrews.
WEBSTER, DANIEL. Prof. Alex. Johnston.
WEBSTER, JOHN. Algernon C. Swinburne.
WEDDERBURN. W. P. Courtney.
WEIGHTS AND MEASURES. W. M. Flinders Petrie, Author of "Inductive Metrology."
WELLINGTON. C. A. Fyffe, M.A., Author of "History of Modern Europe."
WELLS. Prof. J. H. Middleton.
WESTERN AUSTRALIA. James Bonwick, Author of "First Twenty Years of Australia."
WEST INDIES. John Gunn, "Challenger" Expedition Office.
WESTMORLAND. J. G. Goodchild, Geological Survey Office, London.
WEST VIRGINIA. Senator John E. Kenna, Charleston, W.Va.
WHALE. Prof. W. H. Flower.
Whale Fisheries. Robert Gray.
WHATELY. Prof. A. Seth.
WHEAT. M. T. Masters, M.D.
Wheat Pests. Arthur E. Shipley.
WHIRLPOOL. H. R. Mill, D.Sc.
WHIST. Henry Jones ("Cavendish"), Author of "The Laws and Principles of Whist."
WHITEFIELD. Thomas F. Henderson.
WIELAND. James Sime.
WILKES. W. P. Courtney.
WILKIE. J. M. Gray, Curator, Scottish National Portrait Gallery.
WILL. James Williams.
WILLIAM I.-IV. G. W. Prothero.
WILLIAM THE SILENT. James Sime.
WILSON, JOHN. George Saintsbury.
WINCHESTER. Prof. J. H. Middleton.
WINCKELMANN. James Sime.
WINDMILL. W. C. Unwin, B.Sc., F.R.S., Professor of Engineering, Central Institute, City and Guilds of London.
WINDSOR. Prof. J. H. Middleton.
WINE. Prof. W. Dittmar and H. J. Newman.
WISCONSIN. President T. C. Chamberlin and Prof. F. J. Turner, State University, Madison, Wis.
WITCHCRAFT. James Williams.
WÖHLER. Prof. W. Dittmar.
WOLF. Prof. W. H. Flower.
WOLF, FRIEDRICH AUGUST. D. B. Monro, M.A., Provost of Oriel College, Oxford.
WOLFF. Prof. A. Seth.
WOLSEY. T. W. Cameron.
WOMEN, LAW RELATING TO. James Williams.
WOOD, ANTHONY. H. R. Tedder, F.S.A.
WOOD-CARVING. Prof. J. H. Middleton.
WOODCOCK, WOODPECKER. Prof. A. Newton.
WOOL. James Paton.
WORDSWORTH. Prof. W. Minto.
WORM. F. E. Beddard, M.A.
WRECK. James Williams.
WREN. Prof. A. Newton.
WREN, SIR CHRISTOPHER. Prof. J. H. Middleton.
WRESTLING AND BOXING. E. D. Brickwood.
WRIT. James Williams.
WÜRTEMBERG. Findlay Muirhead, M.A.
WURTZ. Alex. Crum Brown, M.D., F.R.S., Professor of Chemistry, University of Edinburgh.
WYCHERLEY. Theodore Watts.
WYCLIFFE. R. Lane Poole, M.A., Ph.D., Lecturer in Modern History, Jesus College, Oxford.
WYOMING. Henry Gannett.
WYTTENBACH. J. S. Reid, Litt.D.
XAVIER. Rev. Dr Littledale.
XENOCRATES, XENOPHANES. Henry Jackson, Litt.D., Fellow and Prælector in Ancient Philosophy, Trinity College, Cambridge.
XENOPHON. Rev. W. J. Brodribb, M.A.
YACHTING. E. D. Brickwood.
YAKUTSK. P. A. Kropotkine.
YARN. James Paton.
YELLOW FEVER. Charles Creighton, M.A., M.D.
YELLOWSTONE PARK. Henry Gannett.
YEMEN. Prof. D. H. Müller, University of Vienna.
YENISEISK. P. A. Kropotkine.
YORK, HOUSE OF. James Gairdner, Public Record Office, London.
YORUBA. Prof. A. H. Keane.
YOUNG, ARTHUR. J. K. Ingram, LL.D., Trinity College, Dublin.
YUCATAN. Prof. A. H. Keane.
Z. John Peile, Litt.D., Master of Christ's College, Cambridge.
ZACHARIAE. John Macdonell, M.A., Author of "The Land Question."
ZAMBESI. Prof. Henry Drummond, M.A., Author of "Tropical Africa."
ZANZIBAR. Prof. A. H. Keane.
ZEBRA. Prof. W. H. Flower.
ZECHARIAH. Julius Wellhausen, D.D., Professor of Semitic Languages and History, University of Marburg.
ZEND-AVESTA. Prof. K. Geldner, Halle.
ZENO. Henry Jackson, Litt.D.
ZEPHANIAH. W. Robertson Smith, LL.D.
ZEUS. Andrew Lang, LL.D., Author of "Myths, Ritual, and Religion."
ZINC. Prof. W. Dittmar.
ZINCKEN. Victor Mabillon, Conservatoire Royal de Musique, Brussels.
ZINZENDORF. Rev. T. M. Lindsay, D.D., Professor of Church History, Free Church College, Glasgow.
ZODIAC. Miss A. M. Clerke, Author of "History of Astronomy."
ZODIACAL LIGHT. Prof. C. Michie Smith, B.Sc., Christian College, Madras.
ZOOLOGY. Prof. E. Ray Lankester.
ZOROASTER. Prof. K. Geldner.
ZOSTEROPS. Prof. Alfred Newton.
ZULULAND. Francis C. Colenso, Barrister-at-Law, and Prof. A. H. Keane.
ZURICH. Rev. W. A. B. Coolidge.
ZWINGLI. Rev. Prof. T. M. Lindsay, D.D.